# PRONUNCIATION KEY

| Vowel Sounds | | Consonant Sounds | |
|---|---|---|---|
| *Symbol* | *Key Words* | *Symbol* | *Key Words* |
| a | at, cap, parrot | b | bed, table, rob |
| ā | ape, play, sail | d | dog, middle, sad |
| ä | cot, father, heart | f | for, phone, cough |
| e | ten, wealth, merry | g | get, wiggle, dog |
| ē | even, feet, money | h | hat, hope, ahead |
| i | is, stick, mirror | hw | which, white |
| ī | ice, high, sky | j | joy, badge, agent |
| ō | go, open, tone | k | kill, cat, quiet |
| ô | all, law, horn | l | let, yellow, ball |
| oo | could, look, pull | m | meet, number, time |
| yoo | cure, furious | n | net, candle, ton |
| o͞o | boot, crew, tune | p | put, sample, escape |
| yo͞o | cute, few, use | r | red, wrong, born |
| oi | boy, oil, royal | s | sit, castle, office |
| ou | cow, out, sour | t | top, letter, cat |
| u | mud, ton, blood, trouble | v | voice, every, love |
| ʉ | her, sir, word | w | wet, always, quart |
| ə | ago, agent, collect, focus | y | yes, canyon, onion |
| 'l | cattle, paddle | z | zoo, misery, rise |
| 'n | sudden, sweeten | ch | chew, nature, punch |
| | | sh | shell, machine, bush |
| | | th | thin, nothing, truth |
| | | *th* | then, other, bathe |
| | | zh | beige, measure, seizure |
| | | ŋ | ring, anger, drink |

Symbols for foreign sounds are explained in the Guide to Pronunciation, pp. xi-xii.

# WEBSTER'S

## NEW COMPACT
## DESK DICTIONARY
### AND
### Style Guide

# WEBSTER'S

## NEW COMPACT
# DESK DICTIONARY

### AND

## Style Guide

Michael Agnes
*Editor in Chief*

Jonathan L. Goldman
*Project Editor*

Katherine Soltis
*Style Guide Editor*

# CONTENTS

Staff. . . . . . . . . . . . . . . . . . . . . . . . . . . . . . . . . . . . . . . . . . . . . . . . . . . . . . . vi

Foreword. . . . . . . . . . . . . . . . . . . . . . . . . . . . . . . . . . . . . . . . . . . . . . . . . . . . vii

Guide to the Use of This Dictionary . . . . . . . . . . . . . . . . . . . . . . . . . . . . . . viii

    I   Guide Words

   II   The Main Entry Word

  III  Part-of-Speech Labels

  IV  Inflected Forms

   V  Etymology

  VI  The Definitions

 VII  Usage Labels

VIII  Run-in Derived Entries

Guide to Pronunciation . . . . . . . . . . . . . . . . . . . . . . . . . . . . . . . . . . . . . . . . . . xi

    I   Pronunciation Style

   II   Pronunciation Key

  III  Foreign Sounds

  IV  Stress Marks

Abbreviations and Symbols Used in This Dictionary . . . . . . . . . . . . . . . . . . . xiii

**The Dictionary** . . . . . . . . . . . . . . . . . . . . . . . . . . . . . . . . . . . . . . . . . . . . 1-562

**Style Guide** . . . . . . . . . . . . . . . . . . . . . . . . . . . . . . . . . . . . . . . . . . . . . 563-676

Weights and Measures . . . . . . . . . . . . . . . . . . . . . . . . . . . . . . . . . . . . . . . . . . 677

International Metric System . . . . . . . . . . . . . . . . . . . . . . . . . . . . . . . . . . . . . . 678

Chemical Elements. . . . . . . . . . . . . . . . . . . . . . . . . . . . . . . . . . . . . . . . . . . . . 679

The United States. . . . . . . . . . . . . . . . . . . . . . . . . . . . . . . . . . . . . . . . . . . . . . 681

Presidents of the United States . . . . . . . . . . . . . . . . . . . . . . . . . . . . . . . . . . . 682

Canada . . . . . . . . . . . . . . . . . . . . . . . . . . . . . . . . . . . . . . . . . . . . . . . . . . . . . . . 683

Nations of the World. . . . . . . . . . . . . . . . . . . . . . . . . . . . . . . . . . . . . . . . . . . . 683

Planets of the Solar System . . . . . . . . . . . . . . . . . . . . . . . . . . . . . . . . . . . . . . 686

Index. . . . . . . . . . . . . . . . . . . . . . . . . . . . . . . . . . . . . . . . . . . . . . . . . . . . . . . . . 687

# FOREWORD

The *Webster's New Compact Desk Dictionary and Style Guide* combines in a single volume a modern dictionary and a comprehensive guide to writing style. It follows in the pioneering footsteps of another landmark publication, *Webster's New Dictionary and Thesaurus*. In an age when information sources compete for limited desk space, we offer this work as a sensible approach to the consolidation of language information in the most efficient and useful package possible.

The database from which the dictionary derives has been the subject of continuous editorial development since 1967. It encompasses the main body of American English, the set of words that a reader may expect to encounter in contemporary life — at home, in school, and in the office. From the outset, the dictionary has been carefully designed and edited to be the most convenient and reliable of its type. Now expanded and updated, it reflects the work of the same staff of experienced, full-time lexicographers that produced *Webster's New College Dictionary*, Fourth Edition. Every entry demonstrates the expertise of professional lexicographers with a combined 150 years of experience in editing dictionaries.

The Style Guide that accompanies the dictionary is designed to meet the needs of those writing in the modern idiom. Its recommendations reflect contemporary yet conservative views on good prose style and will assist writers facing a wide range of grammatical and stylistic challenges. For this second edition the Style Guide has been thoroughly reviewed and revised.

A dictionary and a style guide are two very different types of language resources. A modern dictionary reports on a wide area of language use that exists but that may not necessarily be "recommended." A style guide, on the other hand, is a compendium of recommendations for clear writing. It offers guidelines for clear, effective communication. It is particularly useful to have both works gathered into a single volume, an especially workable combination of information on meaning, spelling, pronunciation, and style. Useful appendixes of other reference material can be found at the end of the book, following the Style Guide.

Users will benefit from a careful reading of the Guide to the Use of This Dictionary, which begins on the following page. It gives a clear explanation of the wealth of information to be found in the dictionary's entries.

Michael Agnes
*Editor in Chief*

# GUIDE TO THE USE OF
# THIS DICTIONARY

## I. GUIDE WORDS

The two GUIDE WORDS at the top of each page indicate the alphabetical range of entries on that page. The first and last main entry words on a page serve as the GUIDE WORDS.

## II. THE MAIN ENTRY WORD

**A. Arrangement of Entries**—All main entries, including single words, hyphenated and unhyphenated compounds, proper names, prefixes, suffixes, combining forms, and abbreviations, are listed in strict alphabetical order and are set in large boldface type.

**a**² (ə; *stressed,* ā) *adj.* ...
**a**³ *abbrev.* **1** about **2** ...
**a-**² *prefix* ...
**aard·vark** (ärd′värk′) *n.* ...
**Aar·on** (er′ən) *n. Bible* ...
**AB**¹ (ā′bē′) *n.* a blood type
**AB**² *abbrev.* **1** Alberta (Canada) **2** ...
**ab-** ⟦L⟧ *prefix* ...
**a·back** (ə bak′) *adv.* [Archaic] backward; back —**taken aback** ...

In biographical entries only the last, or family, name is used in alphabetization; but when two or more persons have the same family name, they appear within the entry block in alphabetical order by first names.

**John·son** (jän′sən) **1 An·drew** ... **2 Lyn·don Baines** ... **3 Samuel** ...

Biographical and geographical names that are spelled the same way are given separate entry blocks.

Idiomatic phrases after a main entry are also listed alphabetically within each group.

**fly**¹ (flī) *vi.* ... —**let fly (at)** ... —**on the fly** ...

**B. Alternative Spellings and Variant Forms**—When different spellings of a word are some distance apart alphabetically, the definition appears with the spelling most frequently used, and the other spellings are cross-referred to this entry. If two commonly used alternative spellings are alphabetically close to each other, they appear as a joint boldface entry, but the order of entry does not necessarily indicate that the form entered first is "more correct" or is preferred.

**the·a·ter** or **the·a·tre** (thē′ə tər) *n.* ...

If an alternative spelling is alphabetically close to the prevailing spelling, it is given at the end of the entry block in small boldface.

**cook·ie** *n.* ...: also **cook′y,** *pl.* **–ies** ...

**C. Cross-references**—When an entry is cross-referred to another term that has the same meaning but is more frequently used, the entry cross-referred to is usually set in small capitals.

**an·aes·the·sia** ... *n.* ANESTHESIA ...

**D. Homographs**—Main entries that are spelled alike but are different in meaning and origin, such as **bat** (a club), **bat** (the animal), and **bat** (to wink), have separate entry blocks and are marked by superscript numbers following the boldface spelling.

**bat**¹ ... *n.* ...
**bat**² ... *n.* ...
**bat**³ ... *vt.* ...

**E. Foreign Terms**—Foreign words and phrases occurring with some frequency in English, but not completely naturalized, are set in boldface italic type. This is a signal to the user of the dictionary to print these terms in italics or underline them in writing.

**bon·jour** (bōn zhōōr′) *interj., n.* ⟦Fr⟧ ...

**F. Prefixes, Suffixes, & Combining Forms**—Prefixes and initial combining forms have a hyphen at the end.

**hemi-** ... *prefix* half ...

Suffixes and terminal combining forms have a hyphen at the beginning.

**-a·ble** ... *suffix* **1** that can or will ...

The abundance of these forms, whose syllabification and pronunciation can be determined from the words containing them, makes it possible for the reader to understand and pronounce many complex terms not entered in the dictionary but formed with affixes and words that are entered.

**G. Word Division**—Boldface entry words are divided into syllables that are separated by either a center dot or a stress mark.

**gen′er·a′tor**
**in′ter·me′di·ar′y**

For information regarding stress marks, see the GUIDE TO PRONUNCIATION.

## III. PART-OF-SPEECH LABELS

This dictionary gives part-of-speech labels, in boldface italic type, for most main entry words that are solid or hyphenated forms. Labels are not given to prefixes, suffixes, combining forms, trademarks and service marks, abbreviations, and biographical and geographical entries.

Here are the part-of-speech labels used in this dictionary:

| | |
|---|---|
| *n.* | noun |
| *pl.n.* | plural noun |
| *sing.n.* | singular noun |
| *fem.n.* | feminine noun |
| *masc.n.* | masculine noun |
| *pron.* | pronoun |

| | |
|---|---|
| *v.* | verb |
| *vt.* | transitive verb |
| *vi.* | intransitive verb |
| *v.aux.* | auxiliary verb |
| *v.impersonal* | impersonal verb |
| *adj.* | adjective |
| *adv.* | adverb |
| *prep.* | preposition |
| *conj.* | conjunction |
| *interj.* | interjection |
| *definite article* | |
| *indefinite article* | |
| *possessive pronominal adj.* | |

When an entry word is used as more than one part of speech, long dashes introduce each separate part-of-speech label.

**round** ... *adj.* ... —*n.* ... —*vt.* ... —*vi.* ... —*adv.* ... —*prep.* ...

Sometimes an entry has two or more part-of-speech labels separated by commas, with a definition or cross-reference that is understood to apply to all parts of speech.

**des·patch** ... *vt., n.* DISPATCH

## IV.  INFLECTED FORMS

This dictionary shows three types of inflected forms: plurals of nouns, principal parts of verbs, and comparative and superlative forms of adjectives and adverbs.

Only inflected forms regarded as irregular or offering difficulty in spelling are entered. They appear in boldface immediately after the part-of-speech label.  They are shortened where possible, and syllabified and pronounced where necessary.

**cit·y** ... *n., pl.* **-ies** ...
**hap·py** ... *adj.* **-pi·er, -pi·est** ...
**an'a·lyze'** ... *vt.* **-lyzed', -lyz'ing** ...

*Plurals:* This dictionary does not show regular plurals:

1) formed by adding -*s* to the singular (**cats**)
2) formed by adding -*es* to a singular that ends with *s, x, z,* and *sh* (**boxes** or **bushes**)
3) formed by adding -*es* to a singular that ends with *ch* when *ch* is pronounced [ch] (**churches**) and by adding -*s* when *ch* is pronounced [k] (**stomachs**)

*Principal Parts:* This dictionary does not show principal parts when:

1) the past tense and past participle are formed by simply adding -*ed* to the infinitive (**search/searched, talk/talked**)
2) the present participle is formed by simply adding -*ing* to the infinitive (**search/searching, talk/talking**)

If only two principal parts are shown, as at **love,** the first is both the past tense and the past participle (**loved**) and the second is the present participle (**loving**).  If three principal parts are shown, as at **go,** the first is the past tense (**went**), the second is the past participle (**gone**), and the third is the present participle (**going**).

*Comparatives & Superlatives:* This dictionary does not show comparatives and superlatives formed by the simple addition of -*er* or -*est* to the base form (**tall/taller/tallest**).

## V.  ETYMOLOGY

The etymology, or word history, appears inside open double brackets immediately before the definitions. The symbols and abbreviations used in the etymologies are found in the list immediately preceding page 1 of the dictionary proper.

**di·shev·el** ... ⟦< OFr *des-,* DIS- + *chevel,* hair⟧ ...

If the parts making up an entry word are obvious to the reader, no etymology appears at that entry.

## VI.  THE DEFINITIONS

**A.  *Order of Senses*—**In general, each entry lists meanings in historical order; the standard, general senses of a word appear first.  Informal, slang, etc. senses come next. Technical senses preceded by field labels, such as *Astron.* or *Chem.,* follow in alphabetical order.

**B.  *Numbering & Grouping of Senses*—** Senses are numbered consecutively within a part of speech in boldface numerals. Where a primary sense of a word is subdivided into several closely related meanings, those meanings are preceded by italicized letters.

**flat**[1] ... *adj.* ... **1** having ... **2** lying ... **10** *Music a*) lower ... *b*) below —*adv.* ... —*n.* **1** anything ... **2** ... **3** *Music a*) a note ... *b*) the symbol ... —*vt.* —*vi.* ...

**C.  *Capitalization*—**If a main entry word is capitalized in all its senses, the entry word itself begins with a capital letter.  If a capitalized main entry word has a sense or senses that are not capitalized, these are marked with the corresponding small-boldface, lowercase letter followed by a short dash and enclosed in brackets.

**Pu·ri·tan** ... *n.* ... **1** ... **2** [p-] ...

If a lowercase main entry word has a meaning or meanings that are capitalized, they are marked with the corresponding small-boldface, uppercase letter followed by a short dash and enclosed in brackets.

**left**[1] ... —*n.* **1** ... **2** [*often* L-] ...

In some of these usage notes, a self-explanatory qualifying word may be added.

**D.  *Plural Forms*—**In a singular noun entry, the designation "[*pl.*]" (or "[*often pl.*]," "[*usually pl.*]," etc.) before a definition indicates that it is (or *often, usually,* etc. is) the plural form of the entry word that has the meaning given in the definition.

**look** ... *vi.* ... —*n.* **1** ... **2** ... **3** [Inf.] *a*) [*usually pl.*] appearance *b*) [*pl.*] personal appearance ...

If a plural is used as a singular with a singular verb, the designation [*with sing. v.*] is added.

**E. Verbs Followed by Prepositions or Objects**—In many cases, one or more specific prepositions follow a particular verb in general use. This dictionary shows this either by including the preposition in the definition, italicized and usually enclosed in parentheses, or by adding a note after the definition giving the particular prepositions associated with that definition of the verb.

In definitions of transitive verbs, the specific or generalized object of the verb, where given, is enclosed in parentheses, since the object is not grammatically part of the definition of the verb.

**F. Illustrative Examples**—Phrases or sentences containing the entry word and showing how it is used in context are enclosed in italic brackets. The word being illustrated is set in italics within its phrase or sentence.

**a·cross** ... ***adv.*** ... ***—prep.*** **1**... **2** ... **3** into contact with by chance [*to come* across *an old friend*]

## VII. USAGE LABELS

People use language in different ways depending on differences in geographic location, age, education, and employment; people's individual language usage varies also according to the situation they are in or their purpose in speaking or writing. The usage labels used in this dictionary are listed below, with an explanation of each.

*Informal:* The word or meaning is widely used in everyday talk, personal letters, etc., but not in formal speaking or writing. Abbreviated *Inf.*

*Slang:* The word or meaning is not generally considered standard usage but is used, even by the best speakers and writers, in very informal situations or for creating special effects. People belonging to a certain group often use their own slang terms.

*Old Informal, Old Slang:* The word or meaning was informal or slang when regularly used in the recent past and is not used much today.

*Obsolete:* The word or meaning is no longer used but occurs in earlier writings. Abbreviated *Obs.*

*Archaic:* The word or meaning is not used in ordinary speech or writing today but occurs in certain special situations such as church ritual and in older books.

*Old-fashioned:* The word or meaning is not yet considered archaic but seems out-of-date.

*Rare:* The word or meaning has never been in general use.

*Now Rare:* The word or meaning is not used much today but was in general use in the past.

*Historical:* The word or meaning refers to something that no longer exists and for which there is not a modern term.

*Old Poetic:* The word or meaning was often used in the past, especially in poetry, but is used today only in certain kinds of traditional or somewhat old-fashioned poetry. Abbreviated *Old Poet.*

*Literary:* The word or meaning is regarded as having an elevated, polished, highly formal quality.

*Dialect:* The word or meaning is used regularly only in certain geographical areas. When a word or meaning is used mainly in some specific area of the U.S., a more specific label, such as *South* or *Northwest*, appears. Abbreviated *Dial.*

*British:* The word or meaning is used mainly in Great Britain and also, usually, in the other English-speaking regions of the world outside the U.S. Abbreviated *Brit.*

*Canadian* (or *Irish,* etc.)*:* The word or meaning is used mainly in Canada (or Ireland, etc.). Abbreviated *Cdn.*, etc.

In addition to the above usage labels, supplementary information often appears in a short note after the definition, indicating that a word or meaning is used in an insulting, familiar, ironic, humorous, or other way.

## VIII. RUN-IN DERIVED ENTRIES

It is possible in English to create an almost infinite number of derived forms simply by adding certain prefixes and suffixes to the base word. The editors have included as many of these common derived words as space permitted, as run-in entries in boldface type—but only when the meaning of such words is immediately clear from the meanings of the base words and the affixes.

Thus, **greatness** and **liveliness** are run in at the end of the entries for **great** and **lively**; the suffix **-ness** is found as a separate entry meaning "state, quality, or instance of being." Many words formed with common suffixes, such as **-able**, **-er**, **-less**, **-like**, **-ly**, and **-tion**, are similarly treated as run-in entries with the base word from which they are derived. All such entries are syllabified and either accented to show stress in pronunciation or, where necessary, pronounced in full or in part.

When a derived word has a meaning or meanings different from those that can be deduced from the sum of its parts, it has been entered separately, pronounced, and fully defined (see **folder**).

# GUIDE TO PRONUNCIATION

## I. PRONUNCIATION STYLE

Pronunciations are provided as needed. Pronunciations are given in parentheses immediately after the boldface entry word:

**mil·len·ni·um** (mi len′ē əm)

Pronunciations have sometimes been shortened so as to cover only a particular part of the entry word, generally the part most likely to cause confusion or difficulty. Hyphens are used to indicate which part of the pronunciation is not shown.

**home′stead′** (-sted′)

More than one pronunciation is sometimes given. Each variant pronunciation may be regarded as having wide currency in American English unless a qualifying note has been added to a particular variant indicating that it is less common. Variants may be also qualified with respect to particular grammatical usage.

**av·o·ca·do** (av′ə kä′dō, ä′və-)

**ex·cuse** (ek skyo͞oz′; *for n.*, -skyo͞os′)

This dictionary does not attempt to cover all pronunciations of a given word and does not indicate differences arising out of various regional dialects.

## II. PRONUNCIATION KEY

The Pronunciation Key lists the pronunciation symbols used in this dictionary along with several Key Words. Key words are short, familiar words that illustrate each of the various sounds represented by the symbols.

### Vowel Sounds

| Symbol | Key Words |
|---|---|
| a | at, cap, parrot |
| ā | ape, play, sail |
| ä | cot, father, heart |
| e | ten, wealth, merry |
| ē | even, feet, money |
| i | is, stick, mirror |
| ī | ice, high, sky |
| ō | go, open, tone |
| ô | all, law, horn |
| o͝o | could, look, pull |
| yo͞o | cure, furious |
| o͞o | boot, crew, tune |
| yo͞o | cute, few, use |
| oi | boy, oil, royal |
| ou | cow, out, sour |
| u | mud, ton, blood, trouble |
| ʉ | her, sir, word |
| ə | ago, agent, collect, focus |
| ′l | cattle, paddle |
| ′n | sudden, sweeten |

### Consonant Sounds

| Symbol | Key Words |
|---|---|
| b | bed, table, rob |
| d | dog, middle, sad |
| f | for, phone, cough |
| g | get, wiggle, dog |
| h | hat, hope, ahead |
| hw | which, white |
| j | joy, badge, agent |
| k | kill, cat, quiet |
| l | let, yellow, ball |
| m | meet, number, time |
| n | net, candle, ton |
| p | put, sample, escape |
| r | red, wrong, born |
| s | sit, castle, office |
| t | top, letter, cat |
| v | voice, every, love |
| w | wet, always, quart |
| y | yes, canyon, onion |
| z | zoo, misery, rise |
| ch | chew, nature, punch |
| sh | shell, machine, bush |
| th | thin, nothing, truth |
| *th* | then, other, bathe |
| zh | beige, measure, seizure |
| ŋ | ring, anger, drink |

## III. FOREIGN SOUNDS

A number of foreign words are entered in the dictionary. An approximation of the native pronunciation—typically French or Spanish in this dictionary—has been provided. Foreign pronunciations use sounds not generally found in English and, therefore, some additional pronunciation symbols are required. Below is a short explanation of these symbols.

à   Used in French; a sound between [a] as in *cat* and [ä] as in *cot*.

ë   Used in French; round the lips as though to say *oh* while pronouncing [e] as in *get*.

ö   Used chiefly in French; round the lips as though to say *oh* while pronouncing the sound [ā] as in *ate*.

ô    Used in French, German, Spanish, etc.; round the lips loosely as though to say *aw* while pronouncing [u] as in *cut*.

ü    Used in French and German; round the lips as though to say *oh* while pronouncing [ē] as in *meet*.

kh    Used in German and Scots English; pronounce [k] while allowing the breath to escape in a stream, as in saying [h].

H    Used in German; pronounce [sh] while keeping the tip of the tongue pointed downward.

*n*    Used chiefly in French; this symbol indicates that the vowel sound preceding it is pronounced with air expelled through both the mouth and the nose.

*r*    Pronounce [r] with a vibrating of the tip of the tongue in Spanish or Italian, or with a trilling of the uvula in French or German.

'    Used in French to indicate that a final consonant is short and unvoiced or that a letter *e* is silent or nearly so.

y'    Used in Russian; pronounce an unvoiced [y] immediately after pronouncing the preceding consonant.

## IV.   STRESS MARKS

Stress marks appear in the pronunciations and in boldface entry words that are not given full pronunciation. A heavy mark ['] after a syllable indicates that the syllable is spoken with the most force. A light mark ['] after a syllable indicates that the syllable is spoken with relatively less force. Syllables with no marking are given the least force.

**dic·tion·ar·y** (dik'shə ner'ē)

# ABBREVIATIONS AND SYMBOLS
# USED IN THIS DICTIONARY

| | | | |
|---|---|---|---|
| abbrev. | abbreviated, abbreviation | Esk | Eskimo |
| adj. | adjective | esp. | especially |
| adv. | adverb | etc. | and the like |
| Afr | African | Ex. | example |
| Afrik | Afrikaans | exc. | except |
| alt. | alternative | F | Fahrenheit |
| Am | American | fem. | feminine |
| AmInd | American Indian | Fl | Flemish |
| AmSp | American Spanish | fol. | following entry |
| Anat. | Anatomy | Fr | French |
| Anglo-Fr | Anglo-French | ft. | foot, feet |
| Ar | Arabic | Gael | Gaelic |
| Aram | Aramaic | Geol. | Geology |
| Archit. | Architecture | Geom. | Geometry |
| Austral. | Australian | Ger | German |
| Biol. | Biology | Gmc | Germanic |
| Bot. | Botany | Gr | Classical Greek |
| Brit | British | Gram. | Grammar |
| C | Celsius | Haw | Hawaiian |
| c. | century | Heb | Hebrew |
| c. | circa | Hung | Hungarian |
| cap. | capital city | IE | Indo-European |
| Cdn | Canadian | i.e. | that is |
| Celt | Celtic | in. | inch(es) |
| cf. | compare | indic. | indicative |
| Ch. | Church | Inf., inf. | informal |
| Chem. | Chemistry | infl. | influenced |
| Chin | Chinese | intens. | intensive |
| compar. | comparative | interj. | interjection |
| Comput. | Computer Science | Ir | Irish |
| conj. | conjunction | It | Italian |
| contr. | contraction (grammar) | Jpn | Japanese |
| Dan | Danish | km | kilometer(s) |
| Dial., dial. | dialectal | L | Classical Latin |
| dim. | diminutive | lb. | pound(s) |
| Du | Dutch | lit. | literally |
| E | eastern, English | LL | Late Latin |
| EC | east central | LowG | Low German |
| Eccles. | Ecclesiastical | m | meter(s) |
| Educ. | Education | masc. | masculine |
| e.g. | for example | Math. | Mathematics |
| Egypt | Egyptian | MDu | Middle Dutch |
| Elec. | Electricity | ME | Middle English |
| Eng | English | Mech. | Mechanics |

| | | | |
|---|---|---|---|
| Med. | Medicine | pres. | present tense |
| met. | metropolitan | prob. | probably |
| Mex | Mexican | pron. | pronoun |
| MHG | Middle High German | Prov | Provençal |
| mi. | mile(s) | prp. | present participle |
| Mil. | Military | pseud. | pseudonym |
| ML | Middle Latin | Psychol. | Psychology |
| ModGr | Modern Greek | pt. | past tense |
| ModL | modern scientific Latin | R.C.Ch. | Roman Catholic Church |
| Myth | Mythology | Rom. | Roman |
| N | northern | Russ | Russian |
| n. | noun | S | southern |
| Naut. | nautical usage | Sans | Sanskrit |
| NC | north central | SC | south central |
| NE | northeastern | Scand | Scandinavian |
| NormFr | Norman French | Scot | Scottish |
| Norw | Norwegian | SE | southeastern |
| NW | northwestern | sing. | singular |
| Obs., obs. | obsolete | sing.n. | singular noun |
| occas. | occasionally | Sp | Spanish |
| OE | Old English | sp. | spelling, spelled |
| OFr | Old French | specif. | specifically |
| OHG | Old High German | sq. | square |
| ON | Old Norse | superl. | superlative |
| orig. | origin, originally | SW | southwestern |
| OS | Old Saxon | Swed | Swedish |
| OSlav | Old Church Slavonic | Theol. | Theology |
| oz. | ounce(s) | transl. | translated, translation |
| pers. | person (grammar) | Turk | Turkish |
| Pers | Persian | ult. | ultimately |
| Photog. | Photography | v. | verb |
| pl. | plural | var. | variant |
| pl.n. | plural noun | v.aux. | auxiliary verb |
| Poet. | Poetic | vi. | intransitive verb |
| Pol | Polish | VL | Vulgar Latin |
| pop. | population | vt. | transitive verb |
| Port | Portuguese | W | western |
| poss. | possessive | WC | west central |
| pp. | past participle | WInd | West Indian |
| prec. | preceding entry | WWI | World War I |
| prep. | preposition | WWII | World War II |

# Symbols

| | | | |
|---|---|---|---|
| < | derived from | & | and |
| ? | uncertain or unknown | ° | degree |
| + | plus | | |

# A

**a**[1] or **A** (ā) *n., pl.* **a's, A's** (āz) the first letter of the English alphabet

**a**[2] (ə; *stressed*, ā) *adj.*, **indefinite article** [[< AN]] **1** one; one sort of **2** each; any one —*prep.* per [*once a day*] Before words beginning with a consonant sound, *a* is used [*a* child, *a* home, *a* uniform] See AN

**a**[3] *abbrev.* **1** about **2** adjective **3** alto **4** answer

**A**[1] (ā) *n.* **1** a blood type **2** a grade indicating excellence **3** *Music* the sixth tone in the scale of C major

**A**[2] *abbrev.* **1** answer **2** April **3** *Baseball, Basketball* assist(s) **4** August

**a-**[1] [[< OE]] *prefix* **1** in, into, on, at, to [*ashore*] **2** in the act or state of [*asleep*]

**a-**[2] *prefix* **1** [[< OE]] up, out [*arise*] **2** [[< OE]] off, of [*akin*] **3** [[< Gr]] not, without [*amoral*]

**AA** *abbrev.* **1** Alcoholics Anonymous **2** Associate in (or of) Arts

**aard·vark** (ärd′värk′) *n.* [[Du, earth pig]] a nocturnal, ant-eating S African mammal

**Aar·on** (er′ən) *n. Bible* the first high priest of the Hebrews

**AB**[1] (ā′bē′) *n.* a blood type

**AB**[2] *abbrev.* **1** Alberta (Canada) **2** Bachelor of Arts: also **A.B.**

**ab-** [[L]] *prefix* away, from, from off, down [*abdicate*]

**ABA** *abbrev.* American Bar Association

**a·back** (ə bak′) *adv.* [Archaic] backward; back — **taken aback** startled and confused; surprised

**ab·a·cus** (ab′ə kəs) *n., pl.* **-cus·es** or **-ci** (-sī′) [[< Gr *abax*]] a frame with sliding beads for doing arithmetic

**a·baft** (ə baft′) *adv.* [[< OE *on*, on + *be*, by + *æftan*, aft]] aft —*prep. Naut.* behind

**ab·a·lo·ne** (ab′ə lō′nē) *n.* [[< AmInd]] an edible sea mollusk with an oval, somewhat spiral shell

ABACUS

**a·ban·don** (ə ban′dən) *vt.* [[< OFr *mettre a bandon*, to put under (another's) ban]] **1** to give up completely **2** to desert —*n.* unrestrained activity; exuberance —**a·ban′don·ment** *n.*

**a·ban′doned** *adj.* **1** deserted **2** shamefully wicked **3** unrestrained

**a·base** (ə bās′) *vt.* **a·based′, a·bas′ing** [[< ML *abassare*, to lower]] to humble —**a·base′ment** *n.*

**a·bash** (ə bash′) *vt.* [[< OFr *es-*, intens. + *baer*, gape]] to make ashamed and uneasy; disconcert — **a·bash′ed·ly** *adv.*

**a·bate** (ə bāt′) *vt., vi.* **a·bat′ed, a·bat′ing** [[< OFr *abattre*, beat down]] **1** to make or become less **2** *Law* to end —**a·bate′ment** *n.*

**ab·at·toir** (ab′ə twär′) *n.* [[Fr: see prec.]] a slaughterhouse

**ab·bé** (a′bā) *n.* [[Fr: see ABBOT]] a French priest's title

**ab·bess** (ab′əs) *n.* [[see ABBOT]] a woman who heads a convent of nuns

**ab·bey** (ab′ē) *n.* **1** a monastery or convent **2** a church belonging to an abbey

**ab·bot** (ab′ət) *n.* [[< Aram *abbā*, father]] a man who heads a monastery

**abbr** or **abbrev** *abbrev.* **1** abbreviated **2** abbreviation

**ab·bre·vi·ate** (ə brē′vē āt′) *vt.* **-at′ed, -at′ing** [[< L *ad-*, to + *brevis*, brief]] to make shorter; esp., to shorten (a word) by omitting letters

**ab·bre·vi·a·tion** (-ā′shən) *n.* **1** a shortening **2** a shortened form of a word or phrase, as *Mr.* for *Mister*

**ABC** (ā′bē′sē′) *n., pl.* **ABC's** [*usually pl.*] **1** the alphabet **2** the basic elements (of a subject)

**ab·di·cate** (ab′di kāt′) *vt., vi.* **-cat′ed, -cat′ing** [[< L *ab-*, off + *dicare*, to proclaim]] **1** to give up formally (a throne, etc.) **2** to surrender (a right, responsibility, etc.) —**ab′di·ca′tion** *n.*

**ab·do·men** (ab′də mən, ab dō′-) *n.* [[L]] the part of the body between the diaphragm and the pelvis; belly —**ab·dom′i·nal** (-däm′ə nəl) *adj.*

**ab·duct** (ab dukt′) *vt.* [[< L *ab-*, away + *ducere*, to lead]] to kidnap —**ab·duc′tion** *n.* —**ab·duc′tor** *n.*

**a·beam** (ə bēm′) *adv., adj.* at right angles to a ship's length or keel

**a·bed** (ə bed′) *adv., adj.* in bed

**A·bel** (ā′bəl) *n. Bible* the second son of Adam and Eve: see CAIN

**a·be·li·a** (ə bēl′yə, ə bē′lē ə) *n.* an evergreen shrub with clusters of fragrant flowers

**ab·er·ra·tion** (ab′ər ā′shən) *n.* [[< L *ab-*, from + *errare*, wander]] **1** a deviation from what is right, true, normal, etc. **2** mental derangement or lapse **3** *Optics* the failure of light rays from one point to converge at a single focus —**ab′er·rant** (-ənt) *adj.* —**ab′er·ra′tion·al** *adj.*

**a·bet** (ə bet′) *vt.* **a·bet′ted, a·bet′ting** [[< OFr *a-*, to + *beter*, to bait]] to urge on or help, esp. in crime — **a·bet′tor** or **a·bet′ter** *n.*

**a·bey·ance** (ə bā′əns) *n.* [[< OFr *a-*, to, at + *bayer*, wait expectantly]] temporary suspension, as of an activity or ruling

**ab·hor** (ab hôr′) *vt.* **-horred′, -hor′ring** [[< L *ab-*, from + *horrere*, to shudder]] to shrink from in disgust, hatred, etc.; detest —**ab·hor′rence** *n.*

**ab·hor′rent** (-ənt) *adj.* causing disgust, hatred, etc.; detestable —**ab·hor′rent·ly** *adv.*

**a·bide** (ə bīd′) *vi.* **a·bode′** or **a·bid′ed, a·bid′ing** [[< OE *ā-*, intens. + *bīdan*, bide]] **1** to remain **2** [Archaic] to reside —*vt.* **1** to await **2** to put up with —**abide by 1** to live up to (a promise, etc.) **2** to submit to and carry out —**a·bid′ance** *n.*

**a·bid′ing** *adj.* enduring; lasting

**a·bil·i·ty** (ə bil′ə tē) *n., pl.* **-ties** [[< L *habilitas*]] **1** a being able; power to do **2** talent or skill

**-a·bil·i·ty** (ə bil′ə tē) [[L *-abilitas*]] *suffix* a (specified) ability, capacity, or tendency

**ab·ject** (ab′jekt′, ab jekt′) *adj.* [[< L *ab-*, from + *jacere*, to throw]] **1** miserable; wretched **2** lacking self-respect; degraded —**ab·ject′ly** *adv.* —**ab·jec′tion** or **ab·ject′ness** *n.*

**ab·jure** (ab joor′, əb-) *vt.* **-jured′, -jur′ing** [[< L *ab-*, away + *jurare*, swear]] **1** to give up (rights, allegiance, etc.) on oath; renounce **2** to recant —**ab·ju·ra·tion** (ab′jə rā′shən) *n.* —**ab·jur′a·to·ry** (-ə tôr′ē) *adj.* —**ab·jur′er** *n.*

**ab·late** (ab lāt′) *vt.* **-lat′ed, -lat′ing** [[see fol.]] **1** to remove, as by surgery **2** to wear away, burn away, or vaporize —*vi.* to be ablated, as a rocket shield in reentry —**ab·la′tion** *n.*

**ab·la·tive** (ab′lə tiv) *n.* [[< L *ab-*, away + *ferre*, to bear]] *Gram.* the case expressing removal, cause, agency, etc., as in Latin

**a·blaze** (ə blāz′) *adj.* **1** burning brightly **2** greatly excited

**a·ble** (ā′bəl) *adj.* **a′bler, a′blest** [[< L *habere*, have]] **1** having enough power, skill, etc. to do something **2** skilled; talented **3** *Law* competent —**a′bly** *adv.*

**-a·ble** (ə bəl) [[< L]] *suffix* **1** that can or will [*perishable*] **2** capable of being __ed [*manageable*] **3** worthy of being __ed [*lovable*] **4** having qualities of [*comfortable*] **5** inclined to [*peaceable*]

**a′ble-bod′ied** *adj.* healthy and strong

**able-bodied seaman** a trained or skilled seaman: also **able seaman**

**a·bloom** (ə blōōm′) *adj.* in bloom

**ab·lu·tion** (ab lōō′shən) *n.* ⟦< L *ab-*, off + *luere*, to wash⟧ [*usually pl.*] a washing of the body, esp. as a religious ceremony

**-a·bly** (ə blē) *suffix* in a way indicating a (specified) ability, tendency, etc.

**ABM** *abbrev.* anti-ballistic missile

**ab·ne·gate** (ab′nə gāt′) *vt.* **-gat′ed, -gat′ing** ⟦< L *ab-*, from + *negare*, deny⟧ to give up (rights, claims, etc.); renounce —**ab′ne·ga′tion** *n.*

**ab·nor·mal** (ab nôr′məl) *adj.* not normal, average, or typical; irregular —**ab·nor′mal·ly** *adv.*

**ab′nor·mal′i·ty** (-mal′ə tē) *n.* **1** an abnormal condition **2** *pl.* **-ties** an abnormal thing

**a·board** (ə bôrd′) *adv., prep.* on or in (a train, ship, etc.)

**a·bode** (ə bōd′) *vi., vt. alt. pt. & pp.* of ABIDE —*n.* a home; residence

**a·bol·ish** (ə bäl′ish) *vt.* ⟦< L *abolere*, destroy⟧ to do away with; void —**a·bol′ish·ment** *n.*

**ab·o·li·tion** (ab′ə lish′ən) *n.* **1** complete destruction; annulment **2** [*occas.* **A-**] the abolishing of slavery in the U.S. —**ab′o·li′tion·ist** *n.*

**a·bom·i·na·ble** (ə bäm′ə nə bəl) *adj.* ⟦see fol.⟧ **1** disgusting; vile **2** very bad —**a·bom′i·na·bly** *adv.*

**a·bom·i·nate′** (-nāt′) *vt.* **-nat′ed, -nat′ing** ⟦< L *abominari*, regard as an ill omen⟧ **1** to hate; loathe **2** to dislike very much —**a·bom′i·na′tion** *n.*

**ab·o·rig·i·nal** (ab′ə rij′ə nəl) *adj.* **1** existing (in a region) from the beginning; first; indigenous **2** of aborigines —*n.* an aborigine

**ab′o·rig′i·ne′** (-nē′) *n., pl.* **-nes′** ⟦L < *ab-*, from + *origine*, origin⟧ **1** any of the first known inhabitants of a region **2** [**A-**] a member of the aboriginal people of Australia

**a·born·ing** (ə bôr′niŋ) *adv.* while being born or created [the plan died *aborning*]

**a·bort** (ə bôrt′) *vi.* ⟦< L *aboriri*, miscarry⟧ to have a miscarriage —*vt.* **1** to cause to have an abortion **2** to cut short (a flight, etc.), as because of an equipment failure

**a·bor·tion** (ə bôr′shən) *n.* any expulsion of a fetus before it is able to survive, esp. if induced on purpose —**a·bor′tion·ist** *n.*

**a·bor·tive** (ə bôrt′iv) *adj.* **1** unsuccessful; fruitless **2** *Biol.* arrested in development

**a·bound** (ə bound′) *vi.* ⟦< L *ab-*, away + *undare*, rise in waves⟧ **1** to be plentiful **2** to be rich (*in*) or teem (*with*)

**a·bout** (ə bout′) *adv.* ⟦< OE *onbūtan*, around⟧ **1** all around **2** near **3** in an opposite direction **4** approximately **5** [Inf.] nearly [*about* ready] —*adj.* **1** astir [he is up and *about*] **2** likely immediately [*about* to leave] —*prep.* **1** on all sides of **2** near to **3** with **4** concerning

**a·bout′-face′** *n.* a reversal of position or opinion —*vi.* **-faced′, -fac′ing** to turn or face in the opposite direction

**a·bove** (ə buv′) *adv.* ⟦OE *abūfan*⟧ **1** in a higher place; up **2** earlier (in a book, etc.) **3** higher in rank, etc. —*prep.* **1** over; on top of **2** better or more than [*above* the average] —*adj.* mentioned earlier —*n.* something that is above —**above all** most of all; mainly

**a·bove′board′** *adv., adj.* without dishonesty or concealment

**a·bove′ground′** *adj., adv.* **1** above or on the surface of the earth **2** not secret(ly); open(ly)

**a·brade** (ə brād′) *vt., vi.* **a·brad′ed, a·brad′ing** ⟦< L *ab-*, away + *radere*, to scrape⟧ to rub off; scrape away

**A·bra·ham** (ā′brə ham′) *Bible* the first patriarch of the Hebrews

**a·bra·sion** (ə brā′zhən) *n.* **1** an abrading **2** an abraded spot

**a·bra′sive** (-siv) *adj.* **1** causing abrasion **2** aggressively annoying; irritating —*n.* a substance, as sandpaper, used for grinding, polishing, etc.

**a·breast** (ə brest′) *adv., adj.* **1** side by side **2** informed (*of*) recent happenings

**a·bridge** (ə brij′) *vt.* **a·bridged′, a·bridg′ing** ⟦< LL *abbreviare*, abbreviate⟧ **1** to shorten, lessen, or curtail **2** to shorten (a piece of writing) while keeping the substance —**a·bridg′ment** or **a·bridge′ment** *n.*

**a·broad** (ə brôd′) *adv.* **1** far and wide **2** in circulation; current **3** outdoors **4** to or in foreign lands —**from abroad** from a foreign land

**ab·ro·gate** (ab′rə gāt′) *vt.* **-gat′ed, -gat′ing** ⟦< L *ab-*, away + *rogare*, ask⟧ to cancel or repeal by authority —**ab′ro·ga′tion** *n.* —**ab′ro·ga′tor** *n.*

**a·brupt** (ə brupt′) *adj.* ⟦< L *ab-*, off + *rumpere*, to break⟧ **1** sudden; unexpected **2** brusque **3** very steep **4** disconnected, as some writing —**a·brupt′ly** *adv.* —**a·brupt′ness** *n.*

**ABS** *abbrev.* anti-lock braking system

**Ab·sa·lom** (ab′sə ləm) *n. Bible* David's son who rebelled against him

**ab·scess** (ab′ses′) *n.* ⟦< L *ab(s)-*, from + *cedere*, go⟧ a swollen area in body tissues, containing pus —*vi.* to form an abscess —**ab′scessed′** *adj.*

**ab·scis·sa** (ab sis′ə) *n., pl.* **-sas** or **-sae** (-ē) ⟦L < *ab-*, from + *scindere*, to cut⟧ *Math.* the horizontal distance of a point from a vertical axis

**ab·scond** (ab skänd′, əb-) *vi.* ⟦< L *ab(s)-*, from + *condere*, hide⟧ to leave hastily and secretly, esp. to escape the law —**ab·scond′er** *n.*

**ab·sence** (ab′səns) *n.* **1** a being absent **2** the time of this **3** a lack

**ab·sent** (ab′sənt; *for v.*, ab sent′) *adj.* ⟦< L *ab-*, away + *esse*, be⟧ **1** not present **2** not existing; lacking **3** not attentive —*vt.* to keep (oneself) away —*prep.* in the absence of [*absent* her testimony, our case is weak] —**ab′sent·ly** *adv.*

**ab·sen·tee** (ab′sən tē′) *n.* one who is absent, as from work —*adj.* designating, of, or from one who is absent —**ab′sen·tee′ism** *n.*

**absentee ballot** a ballot to be marked and sent to a board of elections by a person (**absentee voter**) unable to be at the polls at election time

**ab′sent-mind′ed** or **ab′sent-mind′ed** *adj.* **1** not attentive; preoccupied **2** habitually forgetful —**ab′sent-mind′ed·ly** *adv.* —**ab′sent-mind′ed·ness** *n.*

**absent without leave** *Mil.* absent from duty without official permission

**ab·sinthe** or **ab·sinth** (ab′sinth′) *n.* ⟦< Gr⟧ a green, bitter, toxic liqueur

**ab·so·lute** (ab′sə lōōt′) *adj.* ⟦see ABSOLVE⟧ **1** perfect; complete **2** not mixed; pure **3** not limited [*absolute* power] **4** positive **5** not doubted; real [*absolute* truth] **6** not relative —**ab′so·lute′ly** *adv.*

**absolute value** the value of a real number, disregarding its positive or negative sign [the *absolute value* of -4 or +4 is 4]

**absolute zero** the lower limit on physically obtainable temperatures: equal to -273.16°C or -459.69°F

**ab·so·lu·tion** (ab′sə lōō′shən) *n.* **1** a freeing (*from* guilt) **2** remission (of sin or penalty for it)

**ab·so·lut·ism** (ab′sə lōō tiz′əm) *n.* government by absolute rule; despotism —**ab′so·lut′ist** *n., adj.*

**ab·solve** (ab zälv′, əb-) *vt.* **-solved′, -solv′ing** ⟦< L *ab-*, from + *solvere*, loosen⟧ **1** to free from guilt, a duty, etc. **2** to give religious absolution to

**ab·sorb** (ab sôrb′, -zôrb′; əb-) *vt.* ⟦< L *ab-*, from + *sorbere*, drink in⟧ **1** to suck up **2** to interest greatly; engross **3** to assimilate **4** to pay for (costs, etc.) **5** to take in (a shock, etc.) without recoil **6** to take in and not reflect (light or sound) —**ab·sorb′ing** *adj.*

**ab·sorb′ent** *adj.* capable of absorbing moisture, etc. —*n.* a thing that absorbs —**ab·sorb′en·cy** *n.*

**ab·sorp·tion** (ab sôrp′shən, -zôrp′-; əb-) *n.* **1** an

absorbing or being absorbed **2** great interest —**ab·sorp′tive** *adj.*

**ab·stain** (ab stān′, əb-) *vi.* 〖< L *ab(s)*-, from + *tenere*, to hold〗 to voluntarily do without; refrain *(from)* —**ab·stain′er** *n.* —**ab·sten′tion** (-sten′shən) *n.*

**ab·ste·mi·ous** (ab stē′mē əs, əb-) *adj.* 〖< L *ab(s)*-, from + *temetum*, strong drink〗 moderate in eating and drinking; temperate

**ab·sti·nence** (ab′stə nəns) *n.* an abstaining from some or all food, liquor, etc. —**ab′sti·nent** *adj.*

**ab·stract** (*for adj.* ab strakt′, ab′strakt′; *for n. & vt. 2*, ab′strakt′; *for vt. 1*, ab strakt′) *adj.* 〖< L *ab(s)*-, from + *trahere*, to draw〗 **1** thought of apart from material objects **2** expressing a quality so thought of **3** theoretical **4** *Art* not representing things realistically —*n.* a summary —*vt.* **1** to take away **2** to summarize —**ab·stract′ly** *adv.* —**ab·stract′ness** *n.*

**ab·stract′ed** *adj.* preoccupied

**ab·strac·tion** (ab strak′shən) *n.* **1** an abstracting; removal **2** an abstract idea, thing, etc. **3** mental withdrawal **4** an abstract painting, sculpture, etc.

**ab·struse** (ab strōōs′) *adj.* 〖< L *ab(s)*-, away + *trudere*, to thrust〗 hard to understand —**ab·struse′ly** *adv.* —**ab·struse′ness** *n.*

**ab·surd** (ab surd′, -zurd′; əb-) *adj.* 〖< L *ab*-, intens. + *surdus*, dull, insensible〗 so unreasonable as to be ridiculous —**ab·surd′i·ty** *n.* —**ab·surd′ly** *adv.*

**a·bun·dance** (ə bun′dəns) *n.* 〖see ABOUND〗 a great supply; more than enough —**a·bun′dant** *adj.* —**a·bun′dant·ly** *adv.*

**a·buse** (ə byōōz′; *for n.*, ə byōōs′) *vt.* **a·bused′, a·bus′ing** 〖< L *ab*-, away + *uti*, to use〗 **1** to use wrongly **2** to mistreat, esp. by inflicting physical or sexual harm on **3** to insult; revile —*n.* **1** wrong use **2** mistreatment, esp. by the infliction of physical or sexual harm **3** a corrupt practice **4** insulting language —**a·bu·sive** (ə byōō′siv) *adj.* —**a·bu′sive·ly** *adv.*

**a·but** (ə but′) *vi., vt.* **a·but′ted, a·but′ting** 〖< OFr *a*-, to + *bout*, end〗 to border *(on* or *upon)*

**a·but′ment** *n.* **1** an abutting **2** a part supporting an arch, bridge, etc.

**a·bys·mal** (ə biz′məl) *adj.* **1** of or like an abyss; not measurable **2** very bad; wretched —**a·bys′mal·ly** *adv.*

**a·byss** (ə bis′) *n.* 〖< Gr *a*-, without + *byssos*, bottom〗 **1** a bottomless gulf **2** anything too deep for measurement *[an abyss of shame]*

**Ab·ys·sin·i·a** (ab′ə sin′ē ə) *former name for* ETHIOPIA —**Ab′ys·sin′i·an** *adj., n.*

**ac** *abbrev.* acre(s)

**Ac** *Chem. symbol for* actinium

**AC** *abbrev.* **1** air conditioning **2** alternating current

**-ac** (ak, ək) 〖< Gr〗 *suffix* **1** characteristic of *[elegiac]* **2** relating to *[cardiac]* **3** affected by *[maniac]*

**a·ca·cia** (ə kā′shə) *n.* 〖< Gr *akē*, thorn〗 **1** a tree or shrub with yellow or white flower clusters **2** the locust tree

**ac·a·dem·ic** (ak′ə dem′ik) *adj.* **1** of colleges, universities, etc.; scholastic **2** having to do with the liberal arts rather than technical education **3** formal; pedantic **4** merely theoretical —**ac′a·dem′i·cal·ly** *adv.*

**a·cad·e·mi·cian** (ə kad′ə mish′ən, ak′ə də-) *n.* a member of an ACADEMY (sense 3)

**a·cad·e·my** (ə kad′ə mē) *n., pl.* **-mies** 〖< Gr *akadēmeia*, place where Plato taught〗 **1** a private secondary school **2** a school for special instruction **3** an association of scholars, writers, etc., for advancing an art or science

**a·can·thus** (ə kan′thəs) *n., pl.* **-thus·es** or **-thi** (-thī′, -thē′) 〖< Gr *akē*, a point〗 **1** a plant with lobed, often spiny leaves **2** *Archit.* a representation of these leaves

**a cap·pel·la** (ä′ kə pel′ə) 〖It, in chapel style〗 without instrumental accompaniment: said of vocalists or vocal groups: also sp. **a ca·pel′la**

**A·ca·pul·co** (ä′kə pōōl′kō, ak′ə-) city & seaport in S Mexico, on the Pacific: a winter resort: pop. 593,000

**ac·cede** (ak sēd′) *vi.* **-ced′ed, -ced′ing** 〖< L *ad*-, to + *cedere*, go, yield〗 **1** to enter upon the duties (of an office); attain *(to)* **2** to assent; agree *(to)*

**ac·cel·er·ate** (ak sel′ər āt′, ək-) *vt.* **-at′ed, -at′ing** 〖< L *ad*-, to + *celerare*, hasten〗 **1** to increase the speed of **2** to cause to happen sooner —*vi.* to go faster —**ac·cel′er·a′tion** *n.*

**ac·cel′er·a′tor** *n.* that which accelerates something; esp., the foot throttle of a motor vehicle

**ac·cent** (ak′sent′; *for v., also* ak sent′) *n.* 〖< L *ad*-, to + *canere*, sing〗 **1** emphasis given a spoken syllable or word **2** a mark showing such emphasis or indicating pronunciation **3** a distinguishing manner of pronunciation *[an Irish accent]* **4** special emphasis or attention **5** *Music, Prosody* rhythmic stress —*vt.* **1** to mark with an accent **2** to emphasize; stress

**ac·cen·tu·ate** (ak sen′chōō āt′, ək-) *vt.* **-at′ed, -at′ing** to accent; emphasize —**ac·cen′tu·a′tion** *n.*

**ac·cept** (ak sept′, ək-) *vt.* 〖< L *ad*-, to + *capere*, take〗 **1** to receive, esp. willingly **2** to approve **3** to agree or consent to **4** to believe in **5** to reply "yes" to **6** to agree to pay

**ac·cept′a·ble** *adj.* worth accepting; satisfactory —**ac·cept′a·bil′i·ty** or **ac·cept′a·ble·ness** *n.* —**ac·cept′a·bly** *adv.*

**ac·cept′ance** *n.* **1** an accepting **2** approval **3** belief in; assent **4** a promise to pay

**ac·cept′ed** *adj.* generally regarded as true, proper, etc.; conventional; approved

**ac·cess** (ak′ses′) *n.* 〖see ACCEDE〗 **1** approach or means of approach **2** the right to enter, use, etc. **3** an outburst; fit *[an access of anger]* —*vt.* to get data from, or add data to, a database

**ac·ces·si·ble** (ak ses′ə bəl, ək-) *adj.* **1** that can be approached or entered, esp. easily **2** obtainable **3** easily understood —**ac·ces′si·bil′i·ty** *n.* —**ac·ces′si·bly** *adv.*

**ac·ces·sion** (ak sesh′ən, ək-) *n.* **1** the act of attaining (a throne, power, etc.) **2** assent **3** *a)* increase by addition *b)* an addition

**ac·ces·so·ry** (ak ses′ər ē, ək-) *adj.* 〖see ACCEDE〗 **1** additional; extra **2** helping in an unlawful act —*n., pl.* **-ries 1** something extra or complementary **2** one who, though absent, helps another to break the law

**ac·ci·dent** (ak′sə dənt) *n.* 〖< L *ad*-, to + *cadere*, to fall〗 **1** an unexpected or unintended happening, as one resulting in injury, loss, etc. **2** chance

**ac′ci·den′tal** (-dent′'l) *adj.* happening by chance —**ac′ci·den′tal·ly** *adv.*

**ac′ci·dent-prone′** *adj.* seemingly inclined to become involved in accidents

**ac·claim** (ə klām′) *vt.* 〖< L *ad*-, to + *clamare*, to cry out〗 to greet or announce with loud approval or applause; hail —*n.* loud approval

**ac·cla·ma·tion** (ak′lə mā′shən) *n.* **1** loud applause or approval **2** an approving vote by voice

**ac·cli·mate** (ak′lə māt′, ə klī′mət) *vt., vi.* **-mat·ed, -mat·ing** 〖< L *ad*-, to + Gr *klima*, region〗 to accustom or become accustomed to a new climate or environment —**ac′cli·ma′tion** *n.*

**ac·cli·ma·tize** (ə klī′mə tīz′) *vt., vi.* **-tized′, -tiz′ing** ACCLIMATE —**ac·cli′ma·ti·za′tion** *n.*

**ac·cliv·i·ty** (ə kliv′ə tē) *n., pl.* **-ties** 〖< L *ad*-, up + *clivus*, hill〗 an upward slope

**ac·co·lade** (ak′ə lād′) *n.* 〖< L *ad*, to + *collum*, neck〗 anything done or given to show great respect, appreciation, etc.

**ac·com·mo·date** (ə käm′ə dāt′) *vt.* **-dat′ed, -dat′ing** 〖< L *ad*-, to + *commodare*, to fit〗 **1** to adapt **2** to do a favor for **3** to have space for

**ac·com′mo·dat′ing** *adj.* obliging

**ac·com′mo·da′tion** *n.* **1** adjustment **2** willingness to do favors **3** a help; convenience **4** *[pl.] a)* lodgings *b)* traveling space, as in a train

**ac·com·pa·ni·ment** (ə kum′pə nə mənt, -nē-; *often* ə kump′nə-, -nē-) *n.* anything that accompanies something else, as an instrumental part supporting a solo voice, etc.

**ac·com·pa·ny** (ə kum′pə nē; *often* ə kump′nē) *vt.* **-nied, -ny·ing** ⟦see AD- & COMPANION⟧ **1** to go with **2** to supplement **3** to play or sing an accompaniment for or to —**ac·com′pa·nist** *n.*

**ac·com·plice** (ə käm′plis) *n.* ⟦< ME *a* (the article) + LL *complex*, a confederate⟧ a partner in crime

**ac·com·plish** (ə käm′plish) *vt.* ⟦< L *ad*-, intens. + *complere*, fill up⟧ to succeed in doing; complete

**ac·com′plished** *adj.* **1** done; completed **2** skilled; expert

**ac·com′plish·ment** *n.* **1** completion **2** work completed; an achievement **3** a social art or skill: *usually used in pl.*

**ac·cord** (ə kôrd′) *vt.* ⟦< L *ad*-, to + *cor*, heart⟧ **1** to make agree **2** to grant —*vi.* to agree; harmonize (*with*) —*n.* mutual agreement; harmony —**of one's own accord** willingly —**with one accord** all agreeing

**ac·cord′ance** *n.* agreement; conformity —**ac·cord′ant** *adj.*

**ac·cord′ing** *adj.* in harmony —**according to 1** in agreement with **2** as stated by

**ac·cord′ing·ly** *adv.* **1** in a fitting and proper way **2** therefore

**ac·cor·di·on** (ə kôr′dē ən) *n.* ⟦prob. < It *accordare*, to be in tune⟧ a musical instrument with keys and a bellows, which is pressed to force air through reeds

**ac·cost** (ə kôst′) *vt.* ⟦< L *ad*-, to + *costa*, side⟧ to approach and speak to, esp. in a bold way

**ac·count** (ə kount′) *vt.* ⟦< OFr *a*-, to + *conter*, tell⟧ to judge to be —*vi.* **1** to give a financial reckoning (*to*) **2** to give reasons (*for*) **3** to be the reason (*for*) —*n.* **1** [*often pl.*] a record of business transactions **2** *a*) BANK ACCOUNT *b*) CHARGE ACCOUNT **3** a credit customer or client **4** worth; importance **5** an explanation **6** a report —**on account** as partial payment —**on account of** because of —**on no account** under no circumstances —**take into account** to consider

ACCORDION

**ac·count′a·ble** *adj.* responsible; liable —**ac·count′a·bil′i·ty** *n.*

**ac·count′ant** *n.* one whose work is accounting

**ac·count′ing** *n.* the figuring and recording of financial accounts

**ac·cou·ter** (ə kōōt′ər) *vt.* ⟦prob. < L *consuere*, to sew⟧ to outfit; equip

**ac·cou·ter·ments** or **ac·cou·tre·ments** (ə kōōt′ər mənts, -kōō′trə-) *pl.n.* **1** clothes **2** equipment

**ac·cred·it** (ə kred′it) *vt.* ⟦see CREDIT⟧ **1** to authorize; certify **2** to believe in **3** to attribute —**ac·cred′i·ta′tion** *n.*

**ac·cre·tion** (ə krē′shən) *n.* ⟦< L *ad*-, to + *crescere*, to grow⟧ **1** growth in size, esp. by addition **2** accumulated matter **3** a growing together of parts **4** a part added separately; addition

**ac·crue** (ə krōō′) *vi.* **-crued′, -cru′ing** ⟦see prec.⟧ to come as a natural growth or periodic increase, as interest on money —**ac·cru′al** *n.*

**acct** *abbrev.* account

**ac·cul·tur·ate** (ə kul′chər āt′) *vi., vt.* **-at′ed, -at′ing** to undergo, or change by, acculturation

**ac·cul′tur·a′tion** *n.* **1** adaptation to a culture, esp. a new or different one **2** mutual influence of different cultures

**ac·cu·mu·late** (ə kyōō′myə lāt′) *vt., vi.* **-lat′ed, -lat′ing** ⟦< L *ad*-, to + *cumulare*, to heap⟧ to pile up or collect —**ac·cu·mu·la′tion** *n.* —**ac·cu′mu·la′tive** (-lāt′iv, -lə tiv) *adj.*

**ac·cu·ra·cy** (ak′yoor ə sē, -yər-) *n.* the quality or state of being accurate; precision

**ac′cu·rate** (-it) *adj.* ⟦< L *ad*-, to + *cura*, care⟧ **1** careful and exact **2** free from errors; precise —**ac′cu·rate·ly** *adv.* —**ac′cu·rate·ness** *n.*

**ac·curs·ed** (ə kʉr′sid, -kʉrst′) *adj.* **1** under a curse **2** damnable Also **ac·curst′** —**ac·curs′ed·ness** *n.*

**ac·cu·sa·tion** (ak′yoo zā′shən, -yə-) *n.* **1** an accusing or being accused **2** what one is accused of —**ac·cu·sa·to·ry** (ə kyōō′zə tôr′ē) *adj.*

**ac·cu·sa·tive** (ə kyōō′zə tiv) *n.* ⟦see fol.⟧ *Gram.* the case of the direct object of a verb; also, the objective case in English

**ac·cuse** (ə kyōōz′) *vt.* **-cused′, -cus′ing** ⟦< L *ad*-, to + *causa*, a cause⟧ **1** to blame **2** to bring charges against —**ac·cus′er** *n.*

**ac·cus·tom** (ə kus′təm) *vt.* to make familiar with something by custom, habit, or use; habituate (*to*)

**ac·cus′tomed** *adj.* **1** customary; usual **2** habituated (*to*)

**AC/DC** or **A.C./D.C.** (ā′sē′dē′sē′) *adj.* ⟦< *a*(*lternating*) *c*(*urrent or*) *d*(*irect*) *c*(*urrent*)⟧ [Slang] bisexual

**ace** (ās) *n.* ⟦< L *as*, unit⟧ **1** a playing card, etc. with one spot **2** a point, as in tennis, made by a serve one's opponent cannot return **3** an expert, esp. in combat flying —*adj.* [Inf.] first-rate —*vt.* **aced, ac′ing** [Slang] to defeat completely: often with *out* **2** [Inf.] to earn a grade of A in, on, etc.

**Ace bandage** ⟦< *Ace*, trademark for such a bandage⟧ an elasticized cloth bandage used to provide support, as for a sprain

**ace in the hole** [Slang] any advantage held in reserve

**a·cer·bi·ty** (ə sʉr′bə tē) *n., pl.* **-ties** ⟦< L *acerbus*, bitter⟧ **1** sourness **2** sharpness of temper, words, etc. —**a·cer′bic** *adj.*

**a·cet·a·min·o·phen** (ə sēt′ə min′ə fən, as′ə tə-) *n.* a crystalline powder used to lessen fever and pain

**ac·et·an·i·lide** (as′ət an′ə līd′) *n.* ⟦< ACETIC + ANILINE⟧ a drug used to lessen pain and fever

**ac·e·tate** (as′i tāt′) *n.* **1** a salt or ester of acetic acid **2** something, esp. a fabric, made with an acetate of cellulose

**a·ce·tic** (ə sēt′ik) *adj.* ⟦< L *acetum*, vinegar⟧ of the sharp, sour liquid (**acetic acid**) found in vinegar

**ac·e·tone** (as′i tōn′) *n.* ⟦see prec.⟧ a colorless, flammable liquid used as a solvent, esp. in making rayon —**ac′e·ton′ic** (-tän′ik) *adj.*

**a·cet·y·lene** (ə set′'l ēn′) *n.* a gas used for lighting and, with oxygen, in welding

**a·ce·tyl·sal·i·cyl·ic acid** (ə sēt′'l sal′ə sil′ik) ASPIRIN

**ache** (āk) *vi.* **ached, ach′ing** ⟦< OE *acan*⟧ **1** to have or give dull, steady pain **2** [Inf.] to yearn —*n.* a dull, continuous pain

**a·chene** (ā kēn′, ə-) *n.* ⟦< Gr *a*-, not + *chainein*, to gape⟧ any small, dry fruit with one seed

**a·chieve** (ə chēv′) *vt.* **a·chieved′, a·chiev′ing** ⟦< OFr < *a*-, to + L *caput*, head⟧ **1** to do; accomplish **2** to get by effort —**a·chiev′a·ble** *adj.* —**a·chiev′er** *n.*

**a·chieve′ment** *n.* **1** an achieving **2** a thing achieved; feat

**achievement test** a test for measuring a student's mastery of a given subject or skill

**A·chil·les** (ə kil′ēz′) *n.* a Greek hero killed in the Trojan War

**Achilles' heel** (one's) vulnerable spot

**Achilles tendon** the tendon connecting the heel to the calf muscles

**a·choo** (ä chōō′) *interj.* used to suggest a sneeze

**ach·ro·mat·ic** (ak′rə mat′ik, ā′krə-) *adj.* ⟦< Gr *a*-, without + *chrōma*, color⟧ refracting white light without breaking it up into its component colors

**ach·y** (āk′ē) *adj.* **-i·er, -i·est** having an ache

**ac·id** (as′id) *adj.* ⟦L *acidus*, sour⟧ **1** sour; sharp; tart **2** of an acid —*n.* **1** a sour substance **2**

[Slang] LSD **3** *Chem.* any compound that reacts with a base to form a salt —**a·cid·i·ty** (ə sid′ə tē), *pl.* **-ties,** *n.* —**ac′id·ly** *adv.*

**a·cid·i·fy** (ə sid′ə fī′) *vt., vi.* **-fied′, -fy′ing 1** to make or become sour **2** to change into an acid

**ac·i·do·sis** (as′ə dō′sis) *n.* a condition in which there is an abnormal retention of acid or loss of alkali in the body

**acid rain** rain with a high concentration of acids produced by the gases from burning fossil fuels

**acid test** a crucial, final test

**a·cid·u·lous** (ə sij′oo ləs) *adj.* **1** somewhat acid or sour **2** sarcastic

**-a·cious** (ā′shəs) 〖< L〗 *suffix* inclined to, full of [*tenacious*]

**-ac·i·ty** (as′ə tē) 〖< L〗 *suffix* a (specified) characteristic, quality, or tendency [*tenacity*]

**ac·knowl·edge** (ak näl′ij, ək-) *vt.* **-edged, -edg·ing** 〖see KNOWLEDGE〗 **1** to admit as true **2** to recognize the authority or claims of **3** to respond to **4** to express thanks for **5** to state that one has received (a letter, etc.) —**ac·knowl′edg·ment** or **ac·knowl′edge·ment** *n.*

**ACLU** *abbrev.* American Civil Liberties Union

**ac·me** (ak′mē) *n.* 〖Gr *akmē*, a point, top〗 the highest point; peak

**ac·ne** (ak′nē) *n.* 〖see prec.〗 a skin disorder usually causing pimples on the face, etc.

**ac·o·lyte** (ak′ə līt′) *n.* 〖< Gr *akolouthos*, follower〗 **1** one who helps a priest at services, esp. at Mass **2** an attendant; helper

**ac·o·nite** (ak′ə nīt′) *n.* 〖< Gr〗 a plant with hood-like flowers

**a·corn** (ā′kôrn′) *n.* 〖< OE *æcern*, nut〗 the nut of the oak tree

**acorn squash** a kind of winter squash, acorn-shaped with dark-green skin and yellow flesh

**a·cous·tic** (ə koo̅s′tik) *adj.* 〖< Gr *akouein*, to hear〗 **1** having to do with hearing or acoustics **2** of or using a musical instrument that is not amplified Also **a·cous′ti·cal** —**a·cous′ti·cal·ly** *adv.*

**a·cous′tics** (-tiks) *pl.n.* the qualities of a room, etc. that determine how clearly sounds can be heard in it —*n.* the branch of physics dealing with sound

**ac·quaint** (ə kwānt′) *vt.* 〖< L *ad-*, to + *cognoscere*, know〗 **1** to inform **2** to make familiar (*with*)

**ac·quaint′ance** *n.* **1** knowledge gotten from personal experience **2** a person whom one knows slightly

**ac·qui·esce** (ak′wē es′) *vi.* **-esced′, -esc′ing** 〖< L *ad-*, to + *quiescere*, grow quiet〗 to consent without enthusiasm: often with *in* —**ac′qui·es′cence** *n.* —**ac′qui·es′cent** *adj.*

**ac·quire** (ə kwīr′) *vt.* **-quired′, -quir′ing** 〖< L *ad-*, to + *quaerere*, to seek〗 **1** to gain by one's own efforts **2** to get as one's own —**ac·quire′ment** *n.*

**ac·qui·si·tion** (ak′wə zish′ən) *n.* **1** an acquiring **2** something acquired

**ac·quis·i·tive** (ə kwiz′ə tiv) *adj.* eager to acquire (money, etc.); grasping —**ac·quis′i·tive·ness** *n.*

**ac·quit** (ə kwit′) *vt.* **-quit′ted, -quit′ting** 〖< L *ad-*, to + *quietare*, to quiet〗 **1** to release from an obligation, etc. **2** to clear (a person) of a charge **3** to conduct (oneself); behave —**ac·quit′tal** *n.*

**a·cre** (ā′kər) *n.* 〖OE *æcer*, field〗 a measure of land, 4,840 sq. yards

**a′cre·age** *n.* acres collectively

**ac·rid** (ak′rid) *adj.* 〖< L *acris*, sharp〗 **1** sharp or bitter to the taste or smell **2** sharp in speech, etc. —**a·crid·i·ty** (ə krid′ə tē) *n.* —**ac′rid·ly** *adv.*

**ac·ri·mo·ny** (ak′ri mō′nē) *n., pl.* **-nies** 〖< L *acer*, sharp〗 bitterness or harshness of manner or speech —**ac′ri·mo′ni·ous** *adj.*

**ac·ro·bat** (ak′rə bat′) *n.* 〖< Gr *akrobatos*, walking on tiptoe〗 a performer on the trapeze, tightrope, etc.; gymnast —**ac′ro·bat′ic** *adj.*

**ac′ro·bat′ics** *pl.n.* [*also with sing. v.*] **1** an acrobat's tricks **2** any tricks requiring great skill

**ac·ro·nym** (ak′rə nim′) *n.* 〖< Gr *akros*, at the end + *onyma*, name〗 a word formed from the first (or first few) letters of several words, as *radar*

**ac·ro·pho·bi·a** (ak′rō fō′bē ə) *n.* 〖< Gr *akros*, at the top + PHOBIA〗 an abnormal fear of being in high places

**A·crop·o·lis** (ə kräp′ə lis) 〖< Gr *akros*, at the top + *polis*, city〗 the fortified hill in Athens on which the Parthenon was built

**a·cross** (ə krôs′) *adv.* **1** crosswise **2** from one side to the other —*prep.* **1** from one side to the other of **2** on or to the other side of **3** into contact with by chance [to come *across* an old friend]

**a·cross′-the-board′** *adj.* **1** combining win, place, and show, as a bet **2** including or affecting all classes or groups

**a·cros·tic** (ə krôs′tik) *n.* 〖Gr *akrostichos* < *akros*, at the end + *stichos*, line of verse〗 a poem, etc. in which certain letters in each line, as the first or last, spell out a word, motto, etc.

**a·cryl·ic** (ə kril′ik) *adj.* **1** designating any of a group of synthetic fibers used to make fabrics **2** designating any of a group of clear, synthetic resins used to make paints, plastics, etc.

**act** (akt) *n.* 〖< L *agere*, to do〗 **1** a thing done **2** an action **3** a law **4** a main division of a drama or opera **5** a short performance, as on a variety show **6** something done merely for show —*vt.* to perform in (a play or part) —*vi.* **1** to perform in a play, movie, etc. **2** to behave **3** to function **4** to have an effect (*on*) **5** to appear to be —**act up** [Inf.] to misbehave

**ACTH** 〖*a(dreno)c(ortico)t(ropic) h(ormone)*〗 a pituitary hormone that acts on the adrenal cortex

**act·ing** *adj.* temporarily doing the duties of another —*n.* the art of an actor

**ac·ti·nide series** (ak′tə nīd′) a group of radioactive chemical elements from element 89 (actinium) through element 103 (lawrencium)

**ac·tin·i·um** (ak tin′ē əm) *n.* 〖< Gr *aktis*, ray〗 a white, radioactive, metallic chemical element

**ac·tion** (ak′shən) *n.* **1** the doing of something **2** a thing done **3** [*pl.*] behavior **4** the way of working, as of a machine **5** the moving parts, as of a gun **6** the sequence of events, as in a story **7** a lawsuit **8** military combat **9** [Slang] activity

**ac·ti·vate** (ak′tə vāt′) *vt.* **-vat′ed, -vat′ing 1** to make active **2** to put (a military unit) on active status —**ac′ti·va′tion** *n.* —**ac′ti·va′tor** *n.*

**activated carbon** a form of highly porous carbon that can adsorb gases, vapors, and colloidal particles: also **activated charcoal**

**ac·tive** (ak′tiv) *adj.* **1** acting; working **2** causing motion or change **3** lively; agile **4** *Gram.* indicating the voice of a verb whose subject performs the action —**ac′tive·ly** *adv.*

**ac′tiv·ism′** (-tə viz′əm) *n.* the taking of direct action to achieve a political or social end —**ac′tiv·ist** *adj., n.*

**ac·tiv·i·ty** (ak tiv′ə tē) *n., pl.* **-ties 1** a being active **2** liveliness **3** a specific action or function [student *activities*]

**ac·tor** (ak′tər) *n.* **1** one who does a thing **2** one who acts in plays, movies, etc. —**ac′tress** (-tris) *fem.n.*

**ac·tu·al** (ak′choo əl) *adj.* 〖< L *agere*, to do〗 **1** existing in reality **2** existing at the time —**ac′tu·al·ly** *adv.*

**ac′tu·al′i·ty** (-al′ə tē) *n.* **1** reality **2** *pl.* **-ties** an actual thing; fact

**ac′tu·al·ize′** (-əl īz′) *vt.* **-ized′, -iz′ing 1** to make actual or real **2** to make realistic

**ac·tu·ar·y** (ak′choo er′ē) *n., pl.* **-ies** 〖L *actuarius*, clerk〗 one who figures insurance risks, premiums, etc. —**ac′tu·ar′i·al** *adj.*

**ac·tu·ate** (ak′choo āt′) *vt.* **-at′ed, -at′ing 1** to put into action **2** to cause to take action —**ac′tu·a′tor** *n.*

**a·cu·i·ty** (ə kyoo′ə tē) *n.* 〖< L *acus*, needle〗 keenness of thought or vision

**a·cu·men** (ə kyōō'mən, ak'yə mən) *n.* ⟦< L *acuere*, sharpen⟧ keenness of mind; shrewdness

**ac·u·punc·ture** (ak'yōō puŋk'chər) *n.* ⟦< L *acus*, needle + PUNCTURE⟧ the ancient practice, esp. among the Chinese, of piercing parts of the body with needles to treat disease or relieve pain —**ac'u·punc'tur·ist** *n.*

**a·cute** (ə kyōōt') *adj.* ⟦< L *acuere*, sharpen⟧ **1** sharp-pointed **2** keen of mind **3** sensitive [*acute* hearing] **4** severe, as pain **5** severe but not chronic [an *acute* disease] **6** very serious **7** less than 90° [an *acute* angle] —**a·cute'ly** *adv.* —**a·cute'ness** *n.*

**acute accent** a mark (´) showing primary stress, the quality of a vowel, etc.

**-a·cy** (ə sē) ⟦ult. < Gr⟧ *suffix* quality, condition, etc. [*supremacy*]

**a·cy·clo·vir** (ā sī'klō vir') *n.* a synthetic powder used in the treatment of certain viral infections, as herpes

**ad** (ad) *n.* [Inf.] an advertisement

**AD** or **A.D.** *abbrev.* ⟦L *Anno Domini*, in the year of the Lord⟧ of the Christian era: used with dates

**ad-** ⟦L⟧ *prefix* motion toward, addition to, nearness to: becomes *a-, ac-, af-, ag-, al-, an-,* etc. before certain consonants

**ad·age** (ad'ij) *n.* ⟦< L *ad-*, to + *aio*, I say⟧ an old saying; proverb

**a·da·gio** (ə dä'jō, -zhō) *adv.* ⟦It *ad agio*, at ease⟧ *Music* slowly —*adj.* slow —*n., pl.* **-gios 1** a slow movement in music **2** a slow ballet dance Also written **a·da'gio,** *pl.* **-gios**

**Ad·am** (ad'əm) *n.* ⟦Heb < *adam*, a human being⟧ *Bible* the first man

**ad·a·mant** (ad'ə mənt) *adj.* ⟦< Gr *a-*, not + *daman*, subdue⟧ inflexible; unyielding

**Ad·ams** (ad'əmz) **1** John 1735-1826; 2d president of the U.S. (1797-1801) **2** John Quin·cy (kwin'zē, -sē) 1767-1848; 6th president of the U.S. (1825-29): son of John

**Adam's apple** the projection of cartilage in the front of the throat: seen chiefly in men

**a·dapt** (ə dapt') *vt.* ⟦< L *ad-*, to + *aptare*, to fit⟧ **1** to make suitable, esp. by changing **2** to adjust (oneself) to new circumstances —*vi.* to adjust oneself —**ad·ap·ta·tion** (ad'əp tā'shən) *n.* —**a·dapt'er** or **a·dap'tor** *n.*

**a·dapt'a·ble** *adj.* able to adjust or be adjusted —**a·dapt'a·bil'i·ty** *n.*

ADAM'S APPLE

**add** (ad) *vt.* ⟦< L *ad-*, to + *dare*, to give⟧ **1** to join (*to*) so as to increase **2** to state further **3** to combine (numbers) into a sum —*vi.* **1** to cause an increase (*to*) **2** to find a sum —**add up** to seem reasonable —**add up to** to mean; signify

**ADD** *abbrev.* attention-deficit disorder

**ad·dend** (ad'end') *n.* ⟦< fol.⟧ *Math.* a number or quantity to be added to another

**ad·den·dum** (ə den'dəm) *n., pl.* **-da** (-də) ⟦L⟧ a thing added, as an appendix

**ad·der** (ad'ər) *n.* ⟦< OE *nædre*⟧ **1** a poisonous snake of Europe **2** any of various other snakes, some harmless

**ad·dict** (ə dikt'; *for n.,* ad'ikt) *vt.* ⟦< L *addicere*, give assent⟧ **1** to give (oneself) up *to* a strong habit: usually in the passive voice [*addicted* to heroin] **2** to make an addict of —*n.* one addicted to a habit, as to using drugs —**ad·dic'tion** *n.* —**ad·dic'tive** *adj.*

**Ad·dis A·ba·ba** (ad'is ab'ə bə) capital of Ethiopia: pop. 1,700,000

**ad·di·tion** (ə dish'ən) *n.* **1** an adding of numbers to get a sum **2** a joining of one thing to another **3** a part added —**in addition (to)** besides

**ad·di·tion·al** *adj.* added; more; extra —**ad·di'tion·al·ly** *adv.*

**ad·di·tive** (ad'ə tiv) *adj.* of addition —*n.* a substance added in small quantities

**ad·dle** (ad''l) *vi., vt.* **-dled, -dling** ⟦< OE *adela*, mud⟧ to make or become confused

**ad·dress** (ə dres'; *for n. 2, 3, & 4, also* a'dres') *vt.* ⟦< L *dirigere*, to direct⟧ **1** to direct (words) *to* **2** to speak or write to **3** to write the destination on (a letter, etc.) **4** to apply (oneself) *to* **5** to deal or cope with —*n.* **1** a speech **2** the place where one lives or receives mail **3** the destination indicated on an envelope, etc. **4** *Comput. a*) a code identifying the location of an item of information *b*) a string of characters serving as an e-mail destination or Web location

**ad·dress·ee** (a'dres ē') *n.* the person to whom mail, etc. is addressed

**ad·duce** (ə dōōs') *vt.* **-duced', -duc'ing** ⟦< L *ad-*, to + *ducere*, to lead⟧ to give as a reason or proof

**-ade** (ād) ⟦ult. < L⟧ *suffix* **1** the act of ___ing [*blockade*] **2** participant(s) in an action [*brigade*] **3** ⟦after LEMONADE⟧ drink made from [*limeade*]

**Ad·e·laide** (ad'ə lād') seaport in S Australia: pop. 1,076,000

**A·den** (äd''n, ād''n), **Gulf of** gulf of the Arabian Sea, south of Arabia

**ad·e·nine** (ad'ə nēn') *n.* a purine base contained in the DNA, RNA, and ADP of all tissue

**ad·e·noids** (ad''n oidz', ad'noidz') *pl.n.* ⟦< Gr *adēn*, gland + -OID⟧ lymphoid growths in the throat behind the nose: they can obstruct nasal breathing

**a·dept** (ə dept'; *for n.* ad'ept') *adj.* ⟦< L *ad-*, to + *apisci*, attain⟧ highly skilled —*n.* **ad'ept'** an expert —**a·dept'ly** *adv.* —**a·dept'ness** *n.*

**ad·e·quate** (ad'i kwət) *adj.* ⟦< L *ad-*, to + *aequus*, equal⟧ enough for what is required; sufficient; suitable —**ad'e·qua·cy** (-kwə sē) *n.* —**ad'e·quate·ly** *adv.*

**ad·here** (ad hir', əd-) *vi.* **-hered', -her'ing** ⟦< L *ad-*, to + *haerere*, to stick⟧ **1** to stick fast; stay attached **2** to give allegiance or support (*to*) —**ad·her'ence** *n.*

**ad·her'ent** *n.* a supporter or follower (*of* a person, cause, etc.)

**ad·he·sion** (ad hē'zhən, əd-) *n.* **1** a being stuck together **2** body tissues abnormally joined

**ad·he'sive** (-siv) *adj.* **1** sticking **2** sticky —*n.* an adhesive substance

**ad hoc** (ad häk') ⟦L, to this⟧ for a specific purpose [an *ad hoc* committee]

**a·dieu** (ə dyōō', -dōō'; *Fr* à dyö') *interj., n., pl.* **a·dieus'** or **a·dieux** (ə dyōō', -dōō'; *Fr* à dyö') ⟦Fr⟧ goodbye

**ad in·fi·ni·tum** (ad in'fə nīt'əm) ⟦L⟧ endlessly; without limit

**a·di·os** (a'dē ōs', ä'-; *Sp* ä dyôs') *interj.* ⟦Sp⟧ goodbye

**ad·i·pose** (ad'ə pōs') *adj.* ⟦ult. < Gr *aleipha*, fat⟧ of animal fat; fatty

**Ad·i·ron·dack Mountains** (ad'ə rän'dak') mountain range in NE New York: also **Adirondacks**

**adj** *abbrev.* **1** adjective **2** adjustment

**ad·ja·cent** (ə jā'sənt) *adj.* ⟦< L *ad-*, to + *jacere*, to lie⟧ near or close (*to*); adjoining —**ad·ja'cen·cy** (-sən sē) *n.* —**ad·ja'cent·ly** *adv.*

**ad·jec·tive** (aj'ik tiv) *n.* ⟦< L *adjacere*, lie near⟧ a word used to modify a noun or other substantive —**ad'jec·ti'val** (-tī'vəl) *adj.* —**ad'jec·ti'val·ly** *adv.*

**ad·join** (ə join') *vt.* ⟦< L *ad-*, to + *jungere*, to join⟧ to be next to —*vi.* to be in contact —**ad·join'ing** *adj.*

**ad·journ** (ə jurn') *vt.* ⟦< OFr *a*, at + *jorn*, day⟧ to suspend (a meeting, session, etc.) for a time —*vi.* **1** to close a meeting, etc. for a time **2** [Inf.] to retire (*to* another room, etc.) —**ad·journ'ment** *n.*

**ad·judge** (ə juj') *vt.* **-judged', -judg'ing** ⟦< L *ad-*, to + *judicare*, to judge⟧ **1** to decide by law **2** to declare, order, or award by law

**ad·ju·di·cate** (ə jōō'di kāt') *vt.* **-cat'ed, -cat'ing** to hear and decide (a case) —*vi.* to serve as a judge (*in* or *on*) —**ad·ju′di·ca′tion** *n.* —**ad·ju′di·ca′tor** *n.* —**ad·ju′di·ca·to′ry** (-kə tôr′ē) *adj.*

**ad·junct** (a′juŋkt′) *n.* [see ADJOIN] a secondary or nonessential addition —*adj.* in a temporary or part-time position

**ad·jure** (ə joor′) *vt.* -**jured′, -jur′ing** [< L *ad-,* to + *jurare,* to swear] **1** to charge solemnly under oath **2** to ask earnestly —**ad·ju·ra′tion** (aj′oo rā′shən) *n.*

**ad·just** (ə just′) *vt.* [< OFr *a-,* to + *joster,* to tilt] **1** to change so as to fit **2** to regulate or set (a watch, etc.) **3** to settle rightly **4** to decide the amount to be paid in settling (an insurance claim) —*vi.* to adapt oneself —**ad·just′a·ble** *adj.* —**ad·just′er** or **ad·jus′tor** *n.* —**ad·just′ment** *n.*

**ad·ju·tant** (aj′ə tənt) *n.* [< L *ad-,* to + *juvare,* to help] **1** an assistant **2** a military staff officer who assists the commanding officer

**ad-lib** (ad′lib′) [Inf.] *vt., vi.* -**libbed′, -lib′bing** [< L *ad libitum,* at pleasure] to improvise (words, etc. not in a prepared script, etc.) —*n.* an ad-libbed remark: also **ad lib** —*adj.* spoken or done extemporaneously —*adv.* extemporaneously: also **ad lib**

**adm** or **admin** *abbrev.* **1** administration **2** administrative

**Adm** *abbrev.* admiral

**ad′man** *n., pl.* -**men′** a man whose work is advertising

**ad·min·is·ter** (ad min′is tər, əd-) *vt.* [< L *ad-,* to + *ministrare,* to serve] **1** to manage; direct **2** to give out, as punishment **3** to apply (medicine, etc.) **4** to direct the taking of (an oath, etc.)

**ad·min′is·trate′** (-trāt′) *vt.* -**trat′ed, -trat′ing** to administer; manage

**ad·min·is·tra′tion** (-trā′shən) *n.* **1** management **2** [*often* A-] the executive officials of a government, etc. and their policies **3** their term of office **4** the administering (*of* punishment, medicine, etc.) —**ad·min′is·tra′tive** (-trāt′iv, -trə tiv) *adj.*

**ad·min′is·tra′tor** *n.* **1** one who administers **2** *Law* one appointed to settle an estate

**ad·mi·ra·ble** (ad′mə rə bəl) *adj.* deserving admiration; excellent —**ad′mi·ra·bly** *adv.*

**ad·mi·ral** (ad′mə rəl) *n.* [< Ar ′*amir,* leader + *ālī,* high] **1** the commanding officer of a fleet **2** a naval officer of the highest rank

**ad′mi·ral·ty** *n., pl.* -**ties** [*often* A-] the governmental department in charge of naval affairs, as in England

**ad·mi·ra·tion** (ad′mə rā′shən) *n.* **1** an admiring **2** pleased approval

**ad·mire** (ad mīr′, əd-) *vt.* -**mired′, -mir′ing** [< L *ad-,* at + *mirāri,* to wonder] **1** to regard with wonder and delight **2** to esteem highly —**ad·mir′er** *n.*

**ad·mis·si·ble** (ad mis′ə bəl, əd-) *adj.* that can be accepted or admitted —**ad·mis′si·bil′i·ty** *n.*

**ad·mis·sion** (ad mish′ən, əd-) *n.* **1** an admitting or being admitted **2** an entrance fee **3** a conceding, confessing, etc. **4** a thing conceded, confessed, etc.

**ad·mit** (ad mit′, əd-) *vt.* -**mit′ted, -mit′ting** [< L *ad-,* to + *mittere,* to send] **1** to permit or entitle to enter or use **2** to allow; leave room for **3** to concede or confess —*vi.* **1** to allow: with *of* **2** to concede or confess (*to*) —**ad·mit′tance** *n.*

**ad·mit′ted·ly** *adv.* by admission or general agreement

**ad·mix·ture** (ad miks′chər) *n.* [< L *ad-,* to + *miscere,* to mix] **1** a mixture **2** a thing added in mixing

**ad·mon·ish** (ad män′ish, əd-) *vt.* [< L *ad-,* to + *monere,* to warn] **1** to warn **2** to reprove mildly **3** to exhort —**ad·mo·ni·tion** (ad′mə nish′ən) *n.* —**ad·mon′i·to′ry** (-i tôr′ē) *adj.*

**ad nau·se·am** (ad nô′zē əm) [L] to the point of disgust

**a·do** (ə dōō′) *n.* fuss; trouble

**a·do·be** (ə dō′bē) *n.* [Sp] **1** unburnt, sun-dried

brick **2** clay for making this brick **3** a building of adobe

**ad·o·les·cence** (ad′ə les′əns) *n.* the time of life between puberty and maturity

**ad′o·les′cent** *adj.* [< L *ad-,* to + *alescere,* grow up] of or in adolescence —*n.* a person during adolescence

**A·don·is** (ə dän′is) *n.* **1** *Gr. Myth.* a young man loved by Aphrodite **2** a handsome young man

**a·dopt** (ə däpt′) *vt.* [< L *ad-,* to + *optare,* to choose] **1** to take legally into one's own family and raise as one's own child **2** to take as one's own **3** to choose or accept —**a·dop′tion** *n.*

**a·dop·tive** (ə däp′tiv) *adj.* that has become so by adoption

**a·dor·a·ble** (ə dôr′ə bəl) *adj.* [Inf.] delightful; charming —**a·dor′a·bly** *adv.*

**ad·o·ra·tion** (ad′ə rā′shən) *n.* **1** a worshiping **2** great love or devotion

**a·dore** (ə dôr′) *vt.* -**dored′, -dor′ing** [< L *ad-,* to + *orare,* to speak] **1** to worship as divine **2** to love greatly **3** [Inf.] to like very much

**a·dorn** (ə dôrn′) *vt.* [< L *ad-,* to + *ornare,* fit out] **1** to be an ornament to **2** to put decorations on —**a·dorn′ment** *n.*

**ADP** (ā′dē′pē′) [*a*(*denosine*) *d*(*i*)*p*(*hosphate*)] a basic unit of nucleic acids vital to the energy processes of all living cells

**a·dre·nal** (ə drē′nəl) *adj.* [AD- + RENAL] **1** near the kidneys **2** of two ductless glands (**adrenal glands**) just above the kidneys

**a·dren·a·line** (ə dren′ə lin) *n.* [< *Adrenalin,* a trademark] a hormone secreted by the adrenal glands, which increases endurance, strength, etc.

**A·dri·at·ic** (**Sea**) (ā′drē at′ik) sea between Italy and the Balkan Peninsula

**a·drift** (ə drift′) *adv., adj.* floating without mooring or direction

**a·droit** (ə droit′) *adj.* [< Fr *à,* to + L *dirigere,* lay straight] skillful and clever —**a·droit′ly** *adv.* —**a·droit′ness** *n.*

**ad·sorb** (ad sôrb′, -zôrb′) *vt.* [< AD- + L *sorbere,* drink in] to collect (a gas, etc.) in condensed form on a surface —**ad·sorb′ent** *adj.* —**ad·sorp′tion** (-sôrp′shən, -zôrp′-) *n.*

**ad·u·late** (a′jōō lāt′, -jə-) *vt.* -**lat′ed, -lat′ing** [< L *adulari,* fawn upon] to admire intensely —**ad′u·la′tion** *n.* —**ad′u·la·to′ry** (-lə tôr′ē) *adj.*

**a·dult** (ə dult′, ad′ult′) *adj.* [see ADOLESCENT] **1** grown up; mature **2** for adult people —*n.* a mature person, animal, or plant —**a·dult′hood** *n.*

**a·dul·ter·ate** (ə dul′tər āt′) *vt.* -**at′ed, -at′ing** [< L *ad-,* to + *alter,* other] to make inferior, impure, etc. by adding an improper substance —**a·dul′ter·a′tion** *n.*

**a·dul·ter·y** (ə dul′tər ē) *n., pl.* -**ies** sexual intercourse between a married person and another who is not that person's spouse —**a·dul′ter·er** *n.* —**a·dul′ter·ess** *fem.n.* —**a·dul′ter·ous** *adj.*

**ad·um·brate** (ad um′brāt, ad′əm brāt′) *vt.* -**brat′ed, -brat′ing** [< L *ad-,* to + *umbra,* shade] **1** to outline vaguely **2** to foreshadow —**ad′um·bra′tion** *n.*

**adv** *abbrev.* **1** adverb **2** advertisement

**ad·vance** (ad vans′, əd-) *vt.* -**vanced′, -vanc′ing** [< L *ab-,* from + *ante,* before] **1** to bring forward **2** to promote **3** to suggest **4** to raise the rate of **5** to lend —*vi.* **1** to go forward **2** to improve; progress **3** to rise in rank, price, etc. —*n.* **1** a moving forward **2** an improvement **3** a rise in value **4** [*pl.*] approaches to get favor **5** a payment made before it is due —*adj.* **1** in front [*advance* guard] **2** beforehand —**in advance 1** in front **2** ahead of time —**ad·vance′ment** *n.*

**ad·vanced′** *adj.* **1** in front **2** far on in life; old **3** ahead or higher in progress, price, etc.

**advance man** a person hired to travel in advance of a theatrical company, political candidate, etc. to arrange for publicity, appearances, etc.

**ad·van·tage** (ad vant′ij, əd-) *n.* [< L *ab-* + *ante*:

see ADVANCE] **1** superiority **2** a favorable circumstance, event, etc. **3** gain or benefit —*vt.* **-taged, -tag·ing** to be a benefit or aid to —**take advantage of 1** to use for one's own benefit **2** to impose upon —**ad·van·ta·geous** (ad′van tā′jəs) *adj.*

**Ad·vent** (ad′vent′) *n.* [< L *ad-*, to + *venire*, to come] **1** *Christianity* the period including the four Sundays just before Christmas **2** [a-] a coming or arrival

**ad·ven·ti·tious** (ad′ven tish′əs) *adj.* [see prec.] not inherent; accidental

**ad·ven·ture** (ad ven′chər, əd-) *n.* [see ADVENT] **1** a daring, hazardous undertaking **2** an unusual, stirring, often romantic experience —*vi.* **-tured, -tur·ing** to engage in adventure —**ad·ven′tur·ous** or **ad·ven′ture·some** *adj.* —**ad·ven′tur·ous·ly** *adv.*

**ad·ven·tur·er** *n.* **1** one who has or looks for adventures **2** one who seeks to become rich, etc. by dubious schemes —**ad·ven′tur·ess** *fem.n.*

**ad·verb** (ad′vurb′) *n.* [< L *ad-*, to + *verbum*, word] a word used to modify a verb, an adjective, or another adverb, by expressing time, place, manner, degree, etc. —**ad·ver′bi·al** *adj.* —**ad·ver′bi·al·ly** *adv.*

**ad·ver·sar·i·al** (ad′vər ser′ē əl) *adj.* of or relating to adversaries, as in a lawsuit

**ad′ver·sar′y** *n., pl.* **-ies** [see ADVERT] an opponent; foe

**ad·verse** (ad vurs′, ad′vurs′) *adj.* [see ADVERT] **1** opposed **2** unfavorable —**ad·verse′ly** *adv.*

**ad·ver·si·ty** (ad vur′sə tē) *n.* **1** misfortune; wretched or troubled state **2** *pl.* **-ties** a calamity; disaster

**ad·vert** (ad vurt′) *vi.* [< L *ad*, to + *vertere*, to turn] to call attention (*to*)

**ad·ver·tise** (ad′vər tīz′) *vt.* **-tised′, -tis′ing** [see prec.] to describe or praise publicly, usually so as to promote sales —*vi.* **1** to call public attention to things for sale **2** to ask (*for*) by public notice — **ad′ver·tis′er** *n.* —**ad′ver·tis′ing** *n.*

**ad·ver·tise·ment** (ad′vər tīz′mənt, əd vur′tīz-) *n.* a public notice, usually paid for

**ad·ver·to·ri·al** (ad′vər tôr′ē əl) *n.* [ADVER(TISE) + (EDI)TORIAL] an advertisement, as in a magazine, made to resemble an article or editorial

**ad·vice** (ad vīs′, əd-) *n.* [< L *ad-*, at + *videre*, to look] opinion given as to what to do; counsel

**ad·vis·a·ble** (ad vīz′ə bəl, əd-) *adj.* wise; sensible —**ad·vis′a·bil′i·ty** *n.*

**ad·vise** (ad vīz′, əd-) *vt.* **-vised′, -vis′ing** [< ML *advisum*, advice] **1** to give advice to; counsel **2** to offer as advice **3** to notify; inform —**ad·vi′sor** or **ad·vis′er** *n.*

**ad·vis′ed·ly** (-id lē) *adv.* deliberately

**ad·vise′ment** *n.* careful consideration —**take under advisement** to consider carefully

**ad·vi·so·ry** (ad vī′zə rē, əd-) *adj.* advising or empowered to advise —*n., pl.* **-ries** a report, esp. about weather conditions

**ad·vo·cate** (ad′və kit; *for v.,* -kāt′) *n.* [< L *ad-*, to + *vocare*, to call] one who speaks or writes in support of another or a cause —*vt.* **-cat·ed, -cat·ing** to be an advocate of —**ad′vo·ca·cy** (-kə sē) *n.*

**advt.** *abbrev.* advertisement

**adz** or **adze** (adz) *n.* [< OE *adesa*] an axlike tool for trimming and smoothing wood

**Ae·ge·an (Sea)** (ē jē′ən) sea between Greece and Turkey

**ae·gis** (ē′jis) *n.* [< Gr *aigis*, shield of Zeus] **1** protection **2** sponsorship

**Ae·ne·as** (i nē′əs) *n.* *Gr. & Rom. Myth.* a Trojan whose adventures are told in a poem (the **Ae·ne′id**) by Virgil

**ae·on** (ē′ən, ē′än′) *n. alt. sp.* of EON

**aer·ate** (er′āt′, ā′ər āt′) *vt.* **-at·ed, -at·ing** [AER(O)- + -ATE[1]] **1** to expose to air **2** to charge (liquid) with gas, as to make soda water —**aer·a′tion** *n.* — **aer′a·tor** *n.*

**aer·i·al** (er′ē əl) *adj.* [< Gr *aer,* air + -AL] **1** of, in, or by air **2** unreal; imaginary **3** of aircraft or flying —*n.* a radio or TV antenna

**aer′i·al·ist** *n.* an acrobat on a trapeze, high wire, etc.

**a·er·ie** (ā′ər ē, ē′rē, er′ē, ir′ē) *n.* [prob. < L *ager*, field] **1** the high nest of an eagle or other bird of prey **2** a house or stronghold on a high place

**aero-** [< Gr *aer*, air] *combining form* **1** air **2** aircraft or flying **3** gas, gases Also **aer-** or **aeri-**

**aer·o·bat·ics** (er′ō bat′iks) *pl.n.* [prec. + (ACRO)BATICS] stunts done while flying an aircraft

**aer·o·bic** (er ō′bik) *adj.* [< Gr *aer*, air + *bios*, life] **1** able to live or grow only where free oxygen is present **2** of exercise, as running, that conditions the heart and lungs by increasing efficient intake of oxygen by the body —*n.* [*pl., with sing. or pl. v.*] aerobic exercises

**aer·o·dy·nam·ics** (er′ō dī nam′iks) *n.* the branch of mechanics dealing with forces exerted by air or other gases in motion —*pl.n.* the characteristics of a vehicle's body that affect its efficient movement through the air —**aer′o·dy·nam′ic** *adj.* — **aer′o·dy·nam′i·cal·ly** *adv.*

**aer·o·nau·tics** (er′ə nôt′iks) *n.* the science of making and flying aircraft —**aer′o·nau′ti·cal** *adj.*

**aer·o·sol** (er′ə sôl′, -säl′) *n.* [AERO- + SOL(UTION)] a suspension of insoluble particles in a gas —*adj.* of or from a container in which gas under pressure dispenses liquid spray

**aer·o·space** (er′ō spās′) *n.* the earth's atmosphere and the space outside it —*adj.* of aerospace, or of missiles, etc. for flight in aerospace

**Aes·chy·lus** (es′ki ləs) 525?-456 B.C.; Gr. writer of tragedies

**Ae·sop** (ē′səp, -säp′) Gr. fable writer: supposedly lived 6th c. B.C.

**aes·thete** (es′thēt′) *n.* [Gr *aisthētēs*, one who perceives] a person who is or pretends to be highly sensitive to art and beauty

**aes·thet·ic** (es thet′ik) *adj.* **1** of aesthetics **2** of beauty **3** sensitive to art and beauty

**aes·thet′ics** *n.* the philosophy of art and beauty

**a·far** (ə fär′) *adv.* [Archaic] at or to a distance — **from afar** from a distance

**af·fa·ble** (af′ə bəl) *adj.* [< L *ad-*, to + *fari*, to speak] pleasant; friendly —**af′fa·bil′i·ty** *n.* — **af′fa·bly** *adv.*

**af·fair** (ə fer′) *n.* [< L *ad-*, to + *facere*, to do] **1** any matter, event, etc. **2** [*pl.*] matters of business **3** an event arousing public controversy **4** a social gathering **5** a sexual relationship outside of marriage

**af·fect** (ə fekt′; *for vt.* 3 & 4, *usually* a fekt′; *for n.,* af′ekt′) *vt.* [< L *ad-*, to + *facere*, to do] **1** to have an effect on; influence **2** to stir the emotions of **3** to like to use, wear, etc. **4** to make a pretense of being, feeling, etc. —*n.* an emotion or emotional response

**af·fec·ta·tion** (af′ek tā′shən) *n.* **1** a pretending to like, have, etc. **2** artificial behavior meant to impress others

**af·fect·ed** (ə fekt′id; *for 4 & 5, usually* a-) *adj.* **1** afflicted **2** influenced **3** emotionally moved **4** assumed for effect **5** full of affectation

**af·fect·ing** (ə fekt′iŋ) *adj.* emotionally moving

**af·fec·tion** (ə fek′shən) *n.* fond or tender feeling

**af·fec′tion·ate** *adj.* tender and loving —**af·fec′tion·ate·ly** *adv.*

**af·fect·less** (af′ekt′lis) *adj.* lacking emotion

**af·fer·ent** (af′ər ənt) *adj.* [< L *ad-*, to + *ferre*, to carry] bringing inward to a central part, as nerves

**af·fi·da·vit** (af′ə dā′vit) *n.* [ML, he has made oath] a written statement made under oath

**af·fil·i·ate** (ə fil′ē āt′; *for n., usually,* -it) *vt.* **-at·ed, -at·ing** [< ML *affiliare*, adopt as a son] **1** to take in as a member **2** to associate (oneself) *with* a group, etc. —*vi.* to join —*n.* an affiliated person, club, etc. —**af·fil′i·a′tion** *n.*

**af·fin·i·ty** (ə fin′i tē) *n., pl.* **-ties** ⟦< L *affinis*, adjacent⟧ **1** relationship by marriage **2** close relationship **3** a likeness implying common origin **4** a natural liking or sympathy

**af·firm** (ə furm′) *vt.* ⟦< L *ad-*, to + *firmare*, make firm⟧ **1** to declare positively; assert **2** to confirm; ratify —*vi. Law* to make a formal statement, but not under oath —**af·fir·ma·tion** (af′ər mā′shən) *n.*

**af·firm·a·tive** (ə furm′ə tiv) *adj.* affirming; answering "yes" —*n.* **1** an expression of assent **2** the side upholding the proposition being debated

**affirmative action** a plan to offset past discrimination in employing or educating women, blacks, etc.

**af·fix** (ə fiks′; *for n.* af′iks′) *vt.* ⟦< L *ad-*, to + *figere*, fasten⟧ **1** to fasten; attach **2** to add at the end —*n.* **1** a thing affixed **2** a prefix or suffix

**af·flict** (ə flikt′) *vt.* ⟦< L *ad-*, to + *fligere*, to strike⟧ to cause pain or suffering to; distress greatly

**af·flic·tion** (ə flik′shən) *n.* **1** pain; suffering **2** any cause of suffering

**af·flu·ence** (af′lōō əns) *n.* ⟦< L *ad-*, to + *fluere*, to flow⟧ riches; wealth

**af′flu·ent** *adj.* wealthy; rich —**af′flu·ent·ly** *adv.*

**af·ford** (ə fôrd′) *vt.* ⟦< OE *geforthian*, to advance⟧ **1** to spare (money, time, etc.) without much inconvenience **2** to give; yield *[it affords* pleasure*]* —**af·ford′a·bil′i·ty** *n.* —**af·ford′a·ble** *adj.*

**af·fray** (ə frā′) *n.* ⟦< OFr *esfraer*, frighten⟧ a noisy brawl

**af·front** (ə frunt′) *vt.* ⟦< ML *ad-*, to + *frons*, forehead⟧ to insult openly —*n.* an open insult

**Af·ghan** (af′gan′, -gən) *n.* **1** a native of Afghanistan **2** [a-] a soft blanket or shawl, crocheted or knitted

**Af·ghan·i·stan** (af gan′i stan′) country in SC Asia, east of Iran: 251,773 sq. mi.; pop. 15,551,000

**a·fi·cio·na·do** (ə fish′ə nä′dō) *n.* ⟦Sp⟧ a devotee of some sport, art, etc.

**a·field** (ə fēld′) *adv.* **1** in or to the field **2** away (from home); astray

**a·fire** (ə fīr′) *adv., adj.* on fire

**a·flame** (ə flām′) *adv., adj.* **1** in flames **2** glowing

**AFL-CIO** *abbrev.* American Federation of Labor and Congress of Industrial Organizations

**a·float** (ə flōt′) *adj., adv.* **1** floating **2** at sea **3** flooded **4** current **5** free of debt, etc.

**a·flut·ter** (ə flut′ər) *adv., adj.* in a flutter

**a·foot** (ə foot′) *adv.* **1** on foot **2** in progress

**a·fore·men·tioned** (ə fôr′men′chənd) *adj.* mentioned before

**a·fore′said′** *adj.* spoken of before

**a·fore′thought′** *adj.* thought out beforehand; premeditated

**a·foul** (ə foul′) *adv., adj.* in a collision or a tangle —**run** (or **fall**) **afoul of** to get into trouble with

**a·fraid** (ə frād′) *adj.* ⟦see AFFRAY⟧ feeling frightened: followed by *of, that,* or an infinitive: often used informally to indicate regret *[*I'm *afraid* I must go*]*

**Af·ri·ca** (af′ri kə) second largest continent, south of Europe: *c.* 11,700,000 sq. mi.; pop. *c.* 705,000,000 —**Af′ri·can** *adj., n.*

**Af·ri·can-A·mer′i·can** *n.* a black American of African ancestry —*adj.* of African-Americans, their culture, etc.

**Af·ri·can·ized bee** (af′ri kən īzd′) a hybrid of African and European bees, known for superior honey production; killer bee

**African violet** a tropical African plant with violet, white, or pinkish flowers and hairy leaves, often grown as a houseplant

**Af·ri·kaans** (af′ri käns′, -känz′) *n.* ⟦Afrik < *Afrika,* Africa⟧ an official language of South Africa, based on Dutch

**Af·ro** (af′rō) *n., pl.* **-ros′** a full, bushy hair style, as worn by some African-Americans

**Afro-** ⟦< L *Afer,* an African⟧ *combining form* African, African and

**Af′ro-A·mer′i·can** *n., adj.* AFRICAN-AMERICAN

**aft** (aft) *adv.* ⟦< OE *æftan*⟧ at, near, or toward the stern of a ship or rear of an aircraft

**af·ter** (af′tər) *adv.* ⟦OE *æfter*⟧ **1** behind **2** later —*prep.* **1** behind **2** later than **3** in search of **4** as a result of **5** in spite of *[after* all I've said, he's still going*]* **6** lower in rank or order than **7** in imitation of **8** for *[*named *after* Lincoln*]* —*conj.* following the time when —*adj.* **1** next; later **2** nearer the rear

**af′ter·birth′** *n.* the placenta and membranes expelled after the birth of offspring

**af′ter·burn′er** *n.* a device attached to some engines for burning or utilizing exhaust gases

**af′ter·ef·fect′** *n.* an effect coming later, or as a secondary result

**af′ter·life′** *n.* a life after death

**af′ter·math′** (-math′) *n.* ⟦< AFTER + OE *mæth,* cutting of grass⟧ a result, esp. an unpleasant one

**af·ter·noon** (af′tər nōōn′; *for adj., also* af′tər nōōn′) *n.* the time from noon to evening —*adj.* in the afternoon

**af′ter-tax′** *n.* occurring or remaining after the payment of taxes

**af′ter·thought′** *n.* **1** an idea, explanation, part, etc. coming or added later **2** a thought coming too late to be apt

**af′ter·ward** *adv.* later; subsequently: also **af′ter·wards**

**Ag** ⟦L *argentum*⟧ *Chem. symbol for* silver

**a·gain** (ə gen′) *adv.* ⟦< OE *on-,* up to + *gegn,* direct⟧ **1** back into a former condition **2** once more **3** besides **4** on the other hand —**again and again** often; repeatedly —**as much again** twice as much

**a·gainst** (ə genst′) *prep.* ⟦see prec.⟧ **1** in opposition to **2** toward so as to strike *[*thrown *against* the wall*]* **3** in contact with **4** in preparation for **5** as a charge on

**Ag·a·mem·non** (ag′ə mem′nän′) *n. Gr. Myth.* commander of the Greek army in the Trojan War

**a·gape** (ə gāp′) *adv., adj.* ⟦A-¹ + GAPE⟧ wide open

**a·gar** (ä′gər) *n.* ⟦Malay⟧ a gelatinous product made from seaweed, used in bacterial cultures: also **a′gar-a′gar**

**ag·ate** (ag′it) *n.* ⟦< Gr *achatēs*⟧ a hard, semiprecious stone with striped or clouded coloring

**a·ga·ve** (ə gä′vē) *n.* ⟦< proper name in Gr. myth⟧ a desert plant with thick, fleshy leaves

**agcy** *abbrev.* agency

**age** (āj) *n.* ⟦< L *aetas*⟧ **1** the length of time that a person or thing has existed **2** a stage of life **3** old age **4** a historical or geological period **5** *[often pl.]* [Inf.] a long time —*vi., vt.* **aged, ag′ing** or **age′ing** to grow or make old, ripe, mature, etc. —**of age** having reached the age when one is qualified for full legal rights

**-age** (ij) ⟦< LL *-aticum*⟧ *suffix* **1** act, state, or result of *[usage]* **2** amount or number of *[acreage]* **3** cost of *[postage]* **4** place of *[steerage]*

**a·ged** (ā′jid; *for 2* ājd) *adj.* **1** old **2** of the age of —**the aged** old people

**age·ism** (āj′iz′əm) *n.* ⟦AGE + (RAC)ISM⟧ discrimination against older people

**age′less** *adj.* **1** seemingly not growing older **2** eternal

**a·gen·cy** (ā′jən sē) *n., pl.* **-cies** ⟦< L *agere,* to act⟧ **1** action; power **2** means **3** a firm, etc. empowered to act for another **4** an administrative government division **5** an organization that offers assistance *[*a social *agency]*

**a·gen·da** (ə jen′də) *n., pl.* **-das** ⟦< L *agere,* to do⟧ a list of things to be dealt with, as at a meeting

**a·gent** (ā′jənt) *n.* ⟦< L *agere,* to do⟧ **1** an active force or substance producing an effect **2** a person, firm, etc. empowered to act for another **3** a representative of a government agency

**Agent Orange** ⟦military code name, from *orange*-colored containers⟧ a highly toxic defoliant

**age'-old'** *adj.* ancient

**ag·er·a·tum** (aj'ər ăt'əm) *n.* ⟦< Gr *agēratos*, not growing old⟧ a plant of the composite family with small, thick heads of bluish flowers

**ag·glom·er·ate** (ə glăm'ər āt'; *for adj. & n.*, -it) *vt.*, *vi.* -at'ed, -at'ing ⟦< L *ad*-, to + *glomerare*, form into a ball⟧ to gather into a mass or ball — *adj.* gathered into a mass or ball —*n.* a jumbled heap, mass, etc.

**ag·glu·ti·nate** (ə glo͞ot''n it; *for v.*, -āt') *adj.* ⟦< L *ad*-, to + *gluten*, glue⟧ stuck together —*vt.*, *vi.* -nat'ed, -nat'ing to stick together, as with glue — **ag·glu'ti·na'tion** *n.*

**ag·gran·dize** (ə gran'dīz'; *also,* ag'rən-) *vt.* -dized', -diz'ing ⟦< Fr *a*-, to + *grandir*, to increase⟧ to make greater, more powerful, richer, etc. —**ag·gran·dize·ment** (ə gran'diz mənt, ag'rən dīz'-) *n.*

**ag·gra·vate** (ag'rə vāt') *vt.* -vat'ed, -vat'ing ⟦< L *ad*-, to + *gravis*, heavy⟧ 1 to make worse 2 [Inf.] to annoy; vex —**ag'gra·va'tion** *n.*

**ag'gra·vat'ed** *adj. Law* designating a grave form of a specified offense

**ag·gre·gate** (ag'rə git; *for v.*, -gāt') *adj.* ⟦< L *ad*-, to + *grex*, a herd⟧ total —*n.* a mass of distinct things gathered into a total or whole —*vt.* -gat'ed, -gat'ing 1 to gather into a mass 2 to total — **ag'gre·ga'tion** *n.*

**ag·gres·sion** (ə gresh'ən) *n.* ⟦< L *aggredi*, to attack⟧ 1 an unprovoked attack or warlike act 2 a being aggressive —**ag·gres'sor** *n.*

**ag·gres·sive** (ə gres'iv) *adj.* 1 boldly hostile; quarrelsome 2 bold and active; enterprising — **ag·gres'sive·ly** *adv.* —**ag·gres'sive·ness** *n.*

**ag·grieve** (ə grēv') *vt.* -grieved', -griev'ing ⟦see AGGRAVATE⟧ to cause grief or injury to; offend

**a·ghast** (ə gast') *adj.* ⟦< OE *gast*, ghost⟧ feeling great horror or dismay

**ag·ile** (aj'əl) *adj.* ⟦< L *agere*, to act⟧ quick and easy of movement —**ag'ile·ly** *adv.* —**a·gil·i·ty** (ə jil'ə tē) *n.*

**ag·i·tate** (aj'i tāt') *vt.* -tat'ed, -tat'ing ⟦< L *agere*, to act⟧ 1 to stir up or shake up 2 to excite the feelings of —*vi.* to stir up people so as to produce changes —**ag'i·ta'tion** *n.* —**ag'i·ta'tor** *n.*

**a·gleam** (ə glēm') *adv.*, *adj.* gleaming

**a·glit·ter** (ə glit'ər) *adv.*, *adj.* glittering

**a·glow** (ə glō') *adv.*, *adj.* in a glow (of color or emotion)

**ag·nos·tic** (ag näs'tik) *n.* ⟦< Gr *a*-, not + base of *gignōskein*, know⟧ one who believes it impossible to know if God exists —*adj.* of an agnostic —**ag·nos'ti·cism'** (-ti siz'əm) *n.*

**a·go** (ə gō') *adj.* ⟦< OE *agan*, pass away⟧ gone by; past [years *ago*] —*adv.* in the past [long *ago*]

**a·gog** (ə gäg') *adv.*, *adj.* ⟦< OFr *en*, in + *gogue*, joke⟧ with eager anticipation or excitement

**ag·o·nize** (ag'ə nīz') *vi.* -nized', -niz'ing 1 to struggle 2 to be in agony —*vt.* to torture

**ag·o·ny** (ag'ə nē) *n.*, *pl.* -nies ⟦< Gr *agōn*, a contest⟧ 1 great mental or physical pain 2 death pangs 3 a strong outburst (*of* emotion)

**ag·o·ra·pho·bi·a** (ag'ər ə fō'bē ə) *n.* ⟦< Gr *agora*, marketplace + -PHOBIA⟧ an abnormal fear of being in public places —**ag'o·ra·pho'bic** *adj.*, *n.*

**a·grar·i·an** (ə grer'ē ən) *adj.* ⟦< L *ager*, field⟧ 1 of land or the ownership of land 2 of agriculture

**a·gree** (ə grē') *vi.* -greed', -gree'ing ⟦< L *ad*, to + *gratus*, pleasing⟧ 1 to consent (*to*) 2 to be in accord 3 to be of the same opinion (*with*) 4 to arrive at an understanding (*about* prices, etc.) 5 to be suitable, healthful, etc.: followed by *with* — *vt.* to grant [I agree that it's true]

**a·gree'a·ble** *adj.* 1 pleasing or pleasant 2 willing to consent 3 conformable 4 acceptable —**a·gree'a·bly** *adv.*

**a·gree'ment** *n.* 1 an agreeing 2 an understanding between people, countries, etc. 3 a contract

**agri-** *combining form* agriculture: also **agro-**

**ag·ri·busi·ness** (ag'rə biz'nis) *n.* ⟦see fol. + BUSI-

NESS⟧ farming and associated businesses and industries

**ag·ri·cul·ture** (ag'ri kul'chər) *n.* ⟦< L *ager*, field + *cultura*, cultivation⟧ the work of producing crops and raising livestock; farming —**ag'ri·cul'tur·al** *adj.* —**ag'ri·cul'tur·al·ly** *adv.* —**ag'ri·cul'tur·ist** *n.*

**a·gron·o·my** (ə grän'ə mē) *n.* ⟦< Gr *agros*, field + *nemein*, govern⟧ the science and economics of crop production —**a·gron'o·mist** *n.*

**a·ground** (ə ground') *adv.*, *adj.* on or onto the shore, a reef, etc.

**a·gue** (ā'gyo͞o') *n.* ⟦< ML (*febris*) *acuta*, violent (fever)⟧ a fever, usually malarial, marked by chills

**ah** (ä, ô) *interj.* used to express delight, surprise, pain, etc.

**a·ha** (ä hä') *interj.* used to express triumph, surprise, satisfaction, etc.

**a·head** (ə hed') *adv.*, *adj.* 1 in or to the front 2 forward; onward 3 in advance 4 winning or profiting —**get ahead** to advance financially, etc.

**a·hem** (ə hem') *interj.* used to get someone's attention, etc.

**-a·hol·ic** (ə hôl'ik, -häl'-) *combining form* one preoccupied with (something specified)

**a·hoy** (ə hoi') *interj.* used in hailing [ship *ahoy*!]

**AI** *abbrev.* artificial intelligence

**aid** (ād) *vt.*, *vi.* ⟦< L *ad*-, to + *juvare*, to help⟧ to help; assist —*n.* 1 help or assistance 2 a helper

**aide** (ād) *n.* ⟦Fr⟧ 1 an assistant 2 an aide-de-camp

**aide-de-camp** or **aid-de-camp** (ād'də kamp') *n.*, *pl.* **aides'-** or **aids'-** ⟦Fr⟧ a military officer serving as an assistant to a superior

**AIDS** (ādz) *n.* ⟦A(cquired) I(mmune) D(eficiency) S(yndrome)⟧ a condition of deficiency of certain leukocytes, resulting in infections, cancer, neural degeneration, etc.: see HIV

**ai·grette** or **ai·gret** (ā gret', ā'gret') *n.* ⟦see EGRET⟧ a bunch of the long, white, showy plumes of the egret

**ail** (āl) *vt.* ⟦OE *eglian*, to trouble⟧ to cause pain and trouble to —*vi.* to be in poor health

**ai·le·ron** (ā'lə rän') *n.* ⟦Fr < L *ala*, wing⟧ a pilot-controlled airfoil at the trailing edge of an airplane wing, for controlling rolling

**ail·ment** (āl'mənt) *n.* a mild illness

**aim** (ām) *vi.*, *vt.* ⟦< L *ad*-, to + *aestimare*, to estimate⟧ 1 to direct (a weapon, blow, etc.) so as to hit 2 to direct (one's efforts) 3 to intend —*n.* 1 an aiming 2 the ability to hit a target 3 intention —**take aim** to aim a weapon, etc.

**aim'less** *adj.* having no purpose —**aim'less·ly** *adv.* —**aim'less·ness** *n.*

**ain't** (ānt) ⟦< *amn't*, contr. of *am not*⟧ *contr.* [Inf.] am not: also a dialectal or nonstandard contraction for *is not*, *are not*, *has not*, and *have not*

**ai·o·li** or **aï·o·li** (ī ō'lē) *n.* ⟦ult. < L *allium*, garlic + *oleum*, oil⟧ a mayonnaise containing crushed raw garlic

**air** (er) *n.* ⟦< Gr *aēr*⟧ 1 the invisible mixture of gases surrounding the earth 2 *a*) a breeze; wind *b*) fresh air 3 an outward appearance [an *air* of dignity] 4 general mood 5 [*pl.*] affected, superior manners 6 public expression 7 AIR CONDITIONING 8 a song or tune —*adj.* of or by aircraft —*vt.* 1 to let air into 2 to publicize 3 to broadcast —*vi.* to be broadcast —**in the air** current or prevalent —**on** (or **off**) **the air** that is (or is not) broadcasting —**up in the air** not settled

**air bag** a bag that inflates instantly within an automobile in a collision, to protect riders from being thrown forward

**air base** a base for military aircraft

**air'borne'** *adj.* 1 carried by or through the air 2 aloft or flying

**air brake** a brake operated by the action of compressed air on a piston

**air'brush'** *n.* an atomizer worked by compressed air and used for spraying on paint, etc.: also **air brush** —*vt.* to spray or modify with an airbrush

**air'bus'** *n.* an extremely large passenger airplane, esp. for short trips

**air conditioning** a method of keeping air humidity and temperature at desired levels in buildings, cars, etc. —**air'-con·di'tion** *vt.* —**air conditioner**

**air'-cooled'** *adj.* cooled by having air passed over, into, or through it

**air'craft'** *n.*, *pl.* **-craft'** any machine for traveling through the air

**aircraft carrier** a warship with a large, flat deck, for carrying aircraft

**air'drop'** *n.* the dropping of supplies, troops, etc. from an aircraft in flight —**air'drop'** *vt.*

**Aire·dale** (er'dāl') *n.* ⟦after *Airedale*, valley in England⟧ a large terrier with a wiry coat

**air'fare'** *n.* fare for transportation on a commercial airplane

**air'field'** *n.* a field where aircraft can take off and land

**air'foil'** *n.* a wing, rudder, etc. of an aircraft

**air force** the aviation branch of a country's armed forces

**air'freight'** *n.* cargo transported by air —*vt.* to transport or send by airfreight

**air guitar** the imagined guitar of someone pretending to play music, using movements typical of actual playing

**air gun** a gun or gunlike device operated by compressed air

**air'head'** *n.* [Slang] a silly, ignorant person

**air lane** a route for travel by air; airway

**air'lift'** *n.* a system of transporting troops, supplies, etc. by aircraft —*vt.* to transport by airlift

**air'line'** *n.* a system or company for moving freight and passengers by aircraft —*adj.* of or on an airline

**air'lin'er** *n.* a large airline-operated aircraft for carrying passengers

**air lock** an airtight compartment, with adjustable air pressure, between places of unequal air pressure

**air'mail'** *n.* mail transported by air; esp., in the U.S., mail going overseas by air: also sp. **air mail** —*adj.* of or for mail sent by air —*vt.* to send (mail) by air

**air'man** (-mən) *n.*, *pl.* **-men** (-mən) **1** an aviator **2** an enlisted person in the U.S. Air Force

**air mass** *Meteorol.* a huge, uniform body of air having the properties of its place of origin

**air mattress** a pad filled with air, used as a mattress for camping, etc.

**air'plane'** *n.* a motor-driven or jet-propelled aircraft kept aloft by the forces of air upon its wings

**air'play'** *n.* the playing of a recording over radio or TV

**air pocket** an atmospheric condition that causes an aircraft to make a sudden, short drop while in flight

**air'port'** *n.* a place where aircraft can land and take off, usually with facilities for repair, etc.

**air power** the total capacity of a nation for air war

**air pressure** the pressure of the atmosphere or of compressed air

**air raid** an attack by aircraft, esp. bombers

**air rifle** a rifle operated by compressed air

**air'ship'** *n.* a self-propelled, steerable aircraft that is lighter than air

**air'sick'** *adj.* nauseated because of air travel —**air'sick'ness** *n.*

**air'space'** *n.* the space above a nation over which it can claim jurisdiction

**air'strike'** *n.* an attack made by aircraft

**air'strip'** *n.* a temporary airfield

**air'tight'** *adj.* **1** too tight for air or gas to enter or escape **2** having no weaknesses [an *airtight* alibi]

**air'time'** *n.* *Radio & TV* the period of time during which a program, commercial, etc. may be broadcast: also **air time**

**air'waves'** *pl.n.* the medium through which radio signals are transmitted

**air'way'** *n.* AIR LANE

**air·y** (er'ē) *adj.* **-i·er, -i·est 1** of air **2** open to the air; breezy **3** unsubstantial as air **4** light as air; graceful **5** lighthearted **6** affectedly nonchalant —**air'i·ly** *adv.* —**air'i·ness** *n.*

**aisle** (īl) *n.* ⟦< L *ala*, wing⟧ a passageway, as between sections of seats in rows

**a·jar** (ə jär') *adv.*, *adj.* ⟦OE *cier*, a turn⟧ slightly open, as a door

**AK** Alaska

**aka** (ā'kā'ā') *abbrev.* also known as: used before an alias: also **a.k.a., a k a**

**a·kim·bo** (ə kim'bō) *adv.*, *adj.* ⟦< ON *keng*, bent + *bogi*, a bow⟧ with hands on hips and elbows bent outward [with arms *akimbo*]

**a·kin** (ə kin') *adj.* **1** of one kin; related **2** similar

**Ak·ron** (ak'rən) city in N Ohio: pop. 223,000

**Al** *Chem. symbol for* aluminum

**-al** (əl, 'l) ⟦< L⟧ *suffix* **1** of, like, or suitable for [*theatrical*] **2** the act or process of ___ing [*rehearsal*]

**à la** or **a la** (ä'lə, -lä) ⟦Fr⟧ in the manner or style of

**Al·a·bam·a** (al'ə bam'ə) Southern state of the SE U.S.: 50,750 sq. mi.; pop. 4,041,000; cap. Montgomery: abbrev. **AL** —**Al'a·bam'i·an** or **Al'a·bam'an** *adj.*, *n.*

**al·a·bas·ter** (al'ə bas'tər) *n.* ⟦< Gr *alabastros*, perfume vase⟧ a translucent, whitish variety of gypsum, used for statues, vases, etc.

**a la carte** (ä'lə kärt') ⟦Fr⟧ with a separate price for each item on the menu

**a·lac·ri·ty** (ə lak'rə tē) *n.* ⟦< L *alacer*, lively⟧ eager willingness, often with quick, lively action

**A·lad·din** (ə lad''n) *n.* a boy in *The Arabian Nights* who finds a magic lamp

**à la king** (ä'lə kiŋ') in a cream sauce containing mushrooms, pimentos, etc.

**Al·a·mo** (al'ə mō') Franciscan mission at San Antonio, Texas: scene of a massacre of Texans by Mexican troops (1836)

**a la mode** (al'ə mōd') ⟦< Fr⟧ **1** in fashion **2** served in a certain style, as pie with ice cream Also **à la mode**

**a·lar** (ā'lər) *adj.* ⟦< L *ala*, a wing⟧ **1** of a wing **2** having wings

**a·larm** (ə lärm') *n.* ⟦< It *all'arme*, to arms⟧ **1** [Archaic] a sudden call to arms **2** a warning of danger **3** a mechanism that warns of danger, arouses from sleep, etc. **4** fear caused by danger —*vt.* **1** to warn of danger **2** to frighten

**alarm clock** a clock that can be set to buzz, flash a light, etc. at a given time, as to awaken a person

**a·larm'ing** *adj.* frightening

**a·larm'ist** *n.* one who spreads alarming rumors, exaggerated reports of danger, etc. —*adj.* of an alarmist

**a·las** (ə las') *interj.* an exclamation of sorrow, pity, etc.

**A·las·ka** (ə las'kə) state of the U.S. in NW North America: 570,374 sq. mi.; pop. 550,000; cap. Juneau: abbrev. **AK** —**A·las'kan** *adj.*, *n.*

**alb** (alb) *n.* ⟦< L *albus*, white⟧ a white robe worn by a priest at Mass

**al·ba·core** (al'bə kôr') *n.* ⟦< Ar *al*, the + *buko*, young camel⟧ a tuna with unusually long pectoral fins

**Al·ba·ni·a** (al bā'nē ə) country in the W Balkan Peninsula: 11,101 sq. mi.; pop. 3,185,000 —**Al·ba'ni·an** *adj.*, *n.*

**Al·ba·ny** (ôl'bə nē) capital of New York, on the Hudson: pop. 101,000

**al·ba·tross** (al'bə trôs') *n.* ⟦< Sp < Ar *al qādūs*, a scoop⟧ **1** a large, web-footed sea bird **2** a burden

**al·be·it** (ôl bē'it) *conj.* ⟦ME *al be it*, al(though) it be⟧ although

**Al·ber·ta** (al burt'ə) province of SW Canada:

255,285 sq. mi.; pop. 2,697,000; cap. Edmonton: abbrev. *AB*

**al·bi·no** (al bī′nō) *n.*, *pl.* **-nos** ⟦< L *albus*, white⟧ a person, animal, or plant lacking normal coloration: human albinos have white skin, whitish hair, and pink eyes

**al·bum** (al′bəm) *n.* ⟦< L *albus*, white⟧ **1** a book with blank pages for mounting pictures, stamps, etc. **2** one or more compact discs, LPs, etc. packaged in a holder

**al·bu·men** (al byōō′mən) *n.* ⟦L < *albus*, white⟧ **1** the white of an egg **2** the nutritive protein in seeds, etc. **3** ALBUMIN

**al·bu·min** (al byōō′min) *n.* ⟦see prec.⟧ a water-soluble protein found in milk, egg, blood, vegetable tissues, etc. —**al·bu′mi·nous** *adj.*

**Al·bu·quer·que** (al′bə kur′kē) city in central New Mexico: pop. 385,000

**al·che·my** (al′kə mē) *n.* ⟦< Ar < Gr *chēmeia*; infl. by Gr *cheein*, pour⟧ the chemistry of the Middle Ages, the chief aim of which was to change base metals into gold —**al′che·mist** *n.*

**al·co·hol** (al′kə hôl′) *n.* ⟦< Ar *alkuḥl*, antimony powder⟧ **1** a colorless, volatile, pungent liquid, used in various forms as a fuel, as an intoxicating ingredient in fermented liquors, etc. **2** any such intoxicating liquor

**al′co·hol′ic** *adj.* **1** of alcohol **2** suffering from alcoholism —*n.* one who has chronic alcoholism

**al′co·hol′ism′** *n.* the habitual excessive drinking of alcoholic liquor, or a resulting diseased condition

**al·cove** (al′kōv′) *n.* ⟦< Ar *al*, the + *qubba*, an arch⟧ a recessed section of a room

**al·der** (ôl′dər) *n.* ⟦OE *alor*⟧ a small tree or shrub of the birch family

**al·der·man** (ôl′dər mən) *n.*, *pl.* **-men** (-mən) ⟦< OE *eald*, old + *man*⟧ in some U.S. cities, a municipal officer representing a certain district or ward —**al′der·man′ic** (-man′ik) *adj.*

**ale** (āl) *n.* ⟦OE *ealu*⟧ a fermented drink of malt and hops, like beer

**a·le·a·to·ry** (ā′lē ə tôr′ē) *adj.* ⟦< L *aleatorius*, of gambling < *alea*, chance⟧ depending on chance or luck

**a·lem·bic** (ə lem′bik) *n.* ⟦< Ar *al-anbīq* < Gr *ambix*, a cup⟧ **1** an apparatus formerly used for distilling **2** anything that purifies

**a·lert** (ə lurt′) *adj.* ⟦< L *erigere*, to erect⟧ **1** watchful; vigilant **2** active; nimble —*n.* a warning signal; alarm —*vt.* **1** to warn to be ready, etc. **2** to make aware of *[alert* them to their duties*]* —**on the alert** vigilant —**a·lert′ly** *adv.* —**a·lert′ness** *n.*

**A·leu·tian Islands** (ə lōō′shən) chain of U.S. islands off the SW tip of Alaska —**A·leu′tian** *adj.*, *n.*

**ale·wife** (āl′wīf′) *n.*, *pl.* **-wives′** ⟦< ?⟧ a NW Atlantic fish resembling the herring, used for food and in fertilizers

**Al·ex·an·der the Great** (al′ig zan′dər) 356-323 B.C.; military conqueror: king of Macedonia (336-323)

**Al′ex·an′dri·a** (-drē ə) seaport in N Egypt: pop. 2,319,000

**al·fal·fa** (al fal′fə) *n.* ⟦Sp < Ar *al-fiṣfiṣa*, fodder⟧ a plant of the pea family, used for fodder and pasture and as a cover crop

**Al·fred the Great** (al′frəd) A.D. 849-899; Anglo-Saxon king (871-899)

**al·fres·co** (al fres′kō, äl-) *adv.* ⟦It < *al*, in the + *fresco*, cool⟧ outdoors —*adj.* outdoor Also **al fresco**

**al·gae** (al′jē′) *pl.n.*, *sing.* **al′ga** (-gə) ⟦pl. of L *alga*, seaweed⟧ a group of simple organisms, one-celled or many-celled, containing chlorophyll and found in water or damp places

**al·ge·bra** (al′jə brə) *n.* ⟦< Ar *al*, the + *jabara*, to reunite⟧ a mathematical system using symbols, esp. letters, to generalize certain arithmetical operations and relationships —**al′ge·bra′ic** (-brā′ik) *adj.* —**al′ge·bra′i·cal·ly** *adv.*

**Al·ge·ri·a** (al jir′ē ə) country in N Africa: 919,595 sq. mi.; pop. 22,972,000 —**Al·ge′ri·an** *adj.*, *n.*

**-al·gia** (al′jə) ⟦< Gr *algos*⟧ *combining form* pain *[neuralgia]*

**Al·giers** (al jirz′) seaport & capital of Algeria: pop. 1,688,000

**Al·gon·qui·an** (al gäŋ′kē ən, -kwē-) *adj.* designating or of a widespread family of North American Indian languages —*n.* this family of languages

**al·go·rithm** (al′gə rith′əm) *n.* ⟦ult. < Ar⟧ **1** any systematic method of solving a certain kind of mathematical problem **2** *Comput.* a set of instructions with a limited number of steps for solving a problem

**a·li·as** (ā′lē əs) *n.*, *pl.* **-as·es** ⟦L < *alius*, other⟧ an assumed name —*adv.* otherwise named *[Bell alias Jones]*

**A·li Ba·ba** (ä′lē bä′bə, al′ə bab′ə) in *The Arabian Nights*, a poor man who finds the treasure of forty thieves

**al·i·bi** (al′ə bī′) *n.*, *pl.* **-bis′** ⟦L < *alius ibi*, elsewhere⟧ **1** *Law* the plea or fact that an accused person was elsewhere than at the scene of the crime **2** [Inf.] an excuse —*vi.*, *vt.* **-bied′**, **-bi′ing** [Inf.] to offer an excuse (for)

**al·ien** (āl′yən, āl′ē ən) *adj.* ⟦< L *alius*, other⟧ **1** foreign **2** not natural; strange **3** opposed or repugnant *[beliefs alien to mine]* **4** of aliens —*n.* **1** a foreigner **2** a foreign-born resident who is not naturalized **3** a hypothetical being from outer space

**al′ien·a·ble** (-ə bəl) *adj.* capable of being transferred to a new owner

**al′ien·ate** (-āt′) *vt.* **-at′ed**, **-at′ing** **1** to transfer the ownership of (property) to another **2** to make unfriendly or withdrawn **3** to cause a transference of (affection) —**al′ien·a′tion** *n.*

**a·light**[1] (ə līt′) *vi.* **a·light′ed** or **a·lit′**, **a·light′ing** ⟦ME *alihtan*⟧ **1** to get down or off; dismount **2** to come down after flight

**a·light**[2] (ə līt′) *adj.* lighted up; burning

**a·lign** (ə līn′) *vt.* ⟦< Fr *a-*, to + *ligne*, LINE[1]⟧ **1** to bring into a straight line **2** to bring (components or parts) into adjustment **3** to bring into agreement, etc. —*vi.* to line up —**a·lign′ment** *n.*

**a·like** (ə līk′) *adj.* ⟦< OE *gelic*⟧ like one another —*adv.* **1** similarly **2** equally

**al·i·ment** (al′ə mənt) *n.* ⟦< L *alere*, nourish⟧ nourishment; food

**al′i·men′ta·ry** (-men′tə rē, -men′trē) *adj.* **1** of food or nutrition **2** nourishing

**alimentary canal** (or **tract**) the passage in the body (from the mouth to the anus) that food goes through

**al·i·mo·ny** (al′ə mō′nē) *n.* ⟦< L *alere*, nourish⟧ money a court orders paid to a person by that person's legally separated or divorced spouse

**a·line** (ə līn′) *vt.*, *vi.* **a·lined′**, **a·lin′ing** ALIGN —**a·line′ment** *n.*

**a·lit** (ə lit′) *vi.* alt. pt. & pp. of ALIGHT[1]

**a·live** (ə līv′) *adj.* ⟦< OE *on*, in + *life*, life⟧ **1** having life; living **2** in existence, operation, etc. **3** lively; alert —**alive to** aware of —**alive with** teeming with

**a·li·yah** or **a·li·ya** (ä′lē yä′) *n.* ⟦< Heb, lit., ascent⟧ immigration by Jews to Israel

**al·ka·li** (al′kə lī′) *n.*, *pl.* **-lies′** or **-lis′** ⟦< Ar *al-qili*, the ashes of a certain plant⟧ **1** any base, as soda, that is soluble in water and gives off ions in solution **2** a mineral salt, etc. that can neutralize acids

**al′ka·line** (-lin, -līn′) *adj.* of or like an alkali —**al′ka·lin′i·ty** (-lin′ə tē) *n.*

**al′ka·lize** (-līz′) *vt.* **-lized′**, **-liz′ing** to make alkaline —**al′ka·li·za′tion** *n.*

**al′ka·loid′** (-loid′) *n.* a bitter, alkaline substance, such as caffeine, morphine, etc., containing nitrogen

**al·kyd** (al′kid) *n.* ⟦ult. < ALKALI + (ACI)D⟧ a synthetic resin used in paints, varnishes, etc.: also **alkyd resin**

**all** (ôl) *adj.* ⟦OE *eal*⟧ **1** the whole quantity of [*all* the gold] **2** every one of [*all* men] **3** the greatest possible [in *all* sincerity] **4** any [beyond *all* doubt] **5** alone; only [*all* work and no play] — *pron.* **1** [*with pl. v.*] everyone **2** everything **3** every part or bit —*n.* **1** one's whole property, effort, etc. [gave his *all*] **2** a totality; whole —*adv.* **1** wholly; entirely [*all* worn out] **2** apiece [a score of two *all*] —**after all** nevertheless —**all in** [Inf.] very tired —**all in all 1** considering everything **2** as a whole —**all out** completely —**all the better** (or **worse**) so much the better (or worse) —**all the same 1** nevertheless **2** unimportant —**at all 1** in the least **2** in any way **3** under any considerations —**in all** altogether

**all-** *combining form* **1** wholly, entirely [*all*-American] **2** for every [*all*-purpose] **3** of everything [*all*-inclusive]

**Al·lah** (al′ə, ä′lä) *n.* ⟦< Ar *al*, the + *ilāh*, god⟧ *the Muslim name for* God

**all′-A·mer′i·can** *adj.* representative of the U.S. as a whole, or chosen as the best in the U.S. —*n.* **1** a hypothetical football team, etc. made up of U.S. college players voted the best of the year **2** a player on such a team

**all′-a·round′** *adj.* having many abilities, talents, or uses; versatile

**al·lay** (ə lā′, ə-) *vt.* -layed′, -lay′ing ⟦< OE *a-*, down + *lecgan*, lay⟧ **1** to calm; quiet **2** to relieve (pain, etc.)

**all′-clear′** *n.* a siren or other signal that an air raid or alert is over

**al·le·ga·tion** (al′ə gā′shən) *n.* an assertion, esp. one without proof or to be proved

**al·lege** (ə lej′) *vt.* -leged′, -leg′ing ⟦< L *ex-*, out of + *litigare*, to dispute⟧ **1** to declare or assert, esp. without proof **2** to offer as an excuse

**al·leged** (ə lejd′, ə lej′id) *adj.* **1** declared, but without proof **2** so-called [*alleged* friends] —**al·leg′ed·ly** *adv.*

**Al·le·ghe·ny Mountains** (al′ə gā′nē) mountain range in Pennsylvania, Maryland, West Virginia, & Virginia: also **Al′le·ghe′nies**

**al·le·giance** (ə lē′jəns) *n.* ⟦< OFr *liege*, liege⟧ **1** the duty of being loyal to one's ruler, country, etc. **2** loyalty; devotion, as to a cause

**al·le·go·ry** (al′ə gôr′ē) *n.*, *pl.* -ries ⟦< Gr *allos*, other + *agoreuein*, speak in assembly⟧ a story in which people, things, and events have a symbolic meaning, often instructive —**al′le·gor′i·cal** *adj.* —**al′le·gor′i·cal·ly** *adv.* —**al′le·go′rist** *n.*

**al·le·gret·to** (al′ə gret′ō) *adj.*, *adv.* ⟦It, dim. of *allegro*⟧ *Music* moderately fast: also written *al′le·gret′to*

**al·le·gro** (ə le′grō, -lā′-) *adj.*, *adv.* ⟦It⟧ *Music* fast: also written *al′le·gro′*

**al·lele** (ə lēl′) *n.* ⟦< Gr *allēlōn*, of one another⟧ a gene transferring inherited characteristics

**al·le·lu·ia** (al′ə lōō′yə, ä′lə-) *interj.*, *n.* ⟦LL(Eccles.)⟧ HALLELUJAH

**al·ler·gen** (al′ər jən) *n.* ⟦Ger⟧ a substance inducing an allergic reaction —**al′ler·gen′ic** (-jen′ik) *adj.*

**al·ler·gic** (ə lur′jik) *adj.* **1** of, caused by, or having an allergy **2** [Inf.] averse (*to*)

**al·ler·gist** (al′ər jist) *n.* a doctor who specializes in treating allergies

**al·ler·gy** (al′ər jē) *n.*, *pl.* -gies ⟦Ger < Gr *allos*, other + *ergon*, work⟧ **1** a hypersensitivity to a specific substance (as a food, pollen, dust, etc.) or condition (as heat or cold) **2** an aversion

**al·le·vi·ate** (ə lē′vē āt′) *vt.* -at·ed, -at·ing ⟦< L *ad-*, to + *levis*, light⟧ **1** to lessen or relieve (pain, etc.) **2** to decrease (poverty, etc.) —**al·le′vi·a′tion** *n.*

**al·ley** (al′ē) *n.*, *pl.* -leys ⟦< OFr *aler*, go⟧ **1** a narrow street between or behind buildings **2** a bowling lane

**alley cat** a homeless, mongrel cat

**al′ley·way′** *n.* an alley between buildings

**all′-fired′** *adj.*, *adv.* ⟦< *hell-fired*⟧ [Slang] extreme(ly)

**al·li·ance** (ə lī′əns) *n.* ⟦see ALLY⟧ **1** an allying or close association, as of nations for a common objective, families by marriage, etc. **2** an agreement for this **3** the countries, groups, etc. in such association

**al·lied** (ə līd′, al′īd′) *adj.* **1** united by kinship, treaty, etc. **2** closely related

**al·li·ga·tor** (al′ə gāt′ər) *n.* ⟦< Sp *el*, the + L *lacerta*, lizard⟧ a large reptile of the U.S. and China, like the crocodile but with a shorter, broader snout

**alligator clip** a fastening device with spring-loaded jaws for making an electrical connection

**alligator pear** AVOCADO

**all′-im·por′tant** *adj.* highly important; necessary; essential

**all′-in·clu′sive** *adj.* including everything; comprehensive

ALLIGATOR CLIP

**al·lit·er·a·tion** (ə lit′ər ā′shən) *n.* ⟦< L *ad-*, to + *littera*, letter⟧ repetition of an initial sound in two or more words of a phrase —**al·lit′er·a′tive** (-āt′iv, -ə tiv) *adj.*

**al·lo·cate** (al′ə kāt′) *vt.* -cat·ed, -cat·ing ⟦< L *ad-*, to + *locus*, a place⟧ **1** to set apart for a specific purpose **2** to distribute or allot —**al′lo·ca′tion** *n.*

**al·lot** (ə lät′) *vt.* -lot′ted, -lot′ting ⟦< OFr *a-*, to + *lot*, lot⟧ **1** to distribute in arbitrary shares; apportion **2** to assign as one's share —**al·lot′ment** *n.*

**all′-out′** *adj.* complete or wholehearted

**all′o′ver** *adj.* over the whole surface

**al·low** (ə lou′) *vt.* ⟦see ALLOCATE⟧ **1** to permit; let [I'm not *allowed* to go] **2** to let have [she *allowed* herself no sweets] **3** to acknowledge as valid **4** to provide (a certain amount), as for shrinkage, waste, etc. —**allow for** to leave room, time, etc. for —**al·low′a·ble** *adj.*

**al·low′ance** (-əns) *n.* **1** an allowing **2** something allowed **3** an amount of money, food, etc. given regularly to a child, soldier, etc. **4** a reduction in price, as for a trade-in —**make allowance(s) for** to excuse because of mitigating factors

**al·loy** (al′oi; *also, and for v. usually,* ə loi′) *n.* ⟦< L *ad-*, to + *ligare*, to bind⟧ **1** a substance that is a mixture of two or more metals **2** something that debases another thing when mixed with it —*vt.* to make into an alloy

**all′-pur′pose** *adj.* useful in many ways

**all right 1** satisfactory; adequate **2** unhurt; safe **3** correct **4** yes; very well **5** [Inf.] certainly

**all′-round′** *adj.*, *adv. var. of* ALL-AROUND

**all·spice** (ôl′spīs′) *n.* a spice, that seems to combine the flavors of several spices, made from the berry of a West Indian tree of the myrtle family

**all′-star′** *adj.* **1** made up of outstanding or star performers **2** of or characteristic of an all-star event —*n.* a member of an all-star team

**all′-time′** *adj.* unsurpassed up to the present time

**al·lude** (ə lōōd′) *vi.* -lud′ed, -lud′ing ⟦L *alludere*, to jest⟧ to refer indirectly (*to*)

**al·lure** (ə loor′) *vt.*, *vi.* -lured′, -lur′ing ⟦< OFr *a-*, to + *loirer*, to lure⟧ to tempt with something desirable; attract; entice —*n.* fascination; charm —**al·lure′ment** *n.* —**al·lur′ing** (-loor′iŋ, ə-) *adj.*

**al·lu·sion** (ə lōō′zhən) *n.* **1** an alluding **2** an indirect or casual reference

**al·lu′sive** (-siv) *adj.* **1** containing an allusion **2** full of allusions —**al·lu′sive·ly** *adv.* —**al·lu′sive·ness** *n.*

**al·lu·vi·um** (ə lōō′vē əm) *n.*, *pl.* -vi·ums or -vi·a (-vē ə) ⟦< L *ad-*, to + *luere*, to wash⟧ sand, clay, etc. deposited by moving water —**al·lu′vi·al** *adj.*

**al·ly** (ə lī′; *also, and for n. usually,* al′ī) *vt.*, *vi.* -lied′, -ly′ing ⟦< L *ad-*, to + *ligare*, to bind⟧ **1** to unite or join for a specific purpose **2** to relate by similarity of structure, etc. —*n.*, *pl.* -lies a country or person joined with another for a common purpose

**al·ma ma·ter** (al'mə mät'ər, äl'-) [L, fostering mother] **1** the college or school that one attended **2** its anthem

**al·ma·nac** (ôl'mə nak', al'-) *n.* [< c. 5th-c. Gr *almenichiaka*, calendar] **1** a calendar with astronomical data, weather forecasts, etc. **2** a book published annually, with statistical information

**al·might·y** (ôl mīt'ē) *adj.* all-powerful —**the Almighty** God

**al·mond** (ä'mənd, al'-, ôl'-; am'ənd) *n.* [< Gr *amygdalē*] **1** the edible, nutlike kernel of a peachlike fruit **2** the tree it grows on **3** the light-tan color of its shell —*adj.* shaped like an almond; oval and pointed at one or both ends

**al·most** (ôl'mōst', ôl mōst') *adv.* very nearly; all but

**alms** (ämz) *n., pl.* **alms** [< Gr *eleos*, mercy] money, food, etc. given to poor people —**alms'giv'er** *n.*

**alms'house'** *n.* **1** [Archaic] a poorhouse **2** [Brit.] a privately endowed home for the poor

**al·oe** (al'ō) *n., pl.* **-oes'** [< Gr *aloē*] an African plant of the lily family

**a·loft** (ə lôft') *adv.* [ME < *o*, on+ *loft*, loft] **1** high up **2** in the air; flying **3** high above the deck of a ship

**a·lo·ha** (ä lō'hə, -hä'; ə lō'ə) *n., interj.* [Haw, love] **1** hello **2** goodbye

**a·lone** (ə lōn') *adj., adv.* [ME < *al*, all + *one*, one] **1** apart from anything or anyone else **2** without any other person **3** only **4** without equal —**let alone 1** to refrain from interfering with: also **leave alone 2** not to speak of [we hadn't a dime, *let alone* a dollar]

**a·long** (ə lôŋ') *prep.* [< OE *and-*, over against + *-lang*, long] **1** on or beside the length of **2** in conformity with —*adv.* **1** lengthwise **2** progressively forward **3** together (*with*) **4** with one [take me *along*] **5** advanced [well *along* in years] —**all along** from the beginning —**be along** [Inf.] to come or arrive —**get along 1** to advance **2** to manage **3** to survive **4** to be compatible

**a·long'shore'** *adv.* near or beside the shore

**a·long'side'** *adv.* at or by the side; side by side —*prep.* beside —**alongside of** at the side of

**a·loof** (ə lōōf') *adv.* [< *a-*, on & Du *loef*, windward side] at a distance but in view —*adj.* cool and reserved [an *aloof* manner] —**a·loof'ness** *n.*

**a·loud** (ə loud') *adv.* **1** loudly **2** with the normal voice; not silently

**alp** (alp) *n.* [after ALPS] a high mountain

**al·pac·a** (al pak'ə) *n.* [< AmInd] **1** a South American llama **2** its silky wool, or cloth woven from it

**al·pha** (al'fə) *n.* **1** the first letter of the Greek alphabet (A, α) **2** the beginning of anything —*adj.* of the dominant member of a group

**al'pha·bet'** (-bet') *n.* [< Gr *alpha* & *bēta*, first two letters of the Gr alphabet] the letters used in writing a language, esp. as arranged in their usual order —**al'pha·bet'i·cal** *adj.* —**al'pha·bet'i·cal·ly** *adv.*

**al·pha·bet·ize** (al'fə bə tīz') *vt.* **-ized', -iz'ing** to arrange in the usual order of the alphabet —**al'pha·bet·i·za'tion** *n.*

**al'pha·nu·mer'ic** (-nōō mer'ik) *adj.* having both alphabetical and numerical symbols

**alpha particle** a positively charged particle given off by certain radioactive substances

**alpha ray** a stream of alpha particles

**alpha wave** an electrical brain wave indicating relaxation: also **alpha rhythm**

**Al·pine** (al'pīn') *adj.* **1** of the Alps **2** [a-] of or like high mountains

**Alps** (alps) mountain system in SC Europe

**al·read·y** (ôl red'ē) *adv.* **1** by or before the given or implied time **2** even now or even then

**al·right** (ôl rīt') *adj., adv., interj. disputed sp.* of ALL RIGHT

**Al·sace** (al sās', al'sas') historical region of NE France —**Al·sa'tian** (-sā'shən) *adj., n.*

**al·so** (ôl'sō) *adv.* [< OE *eall*, all + *swa*, so] in addition; likewise; too; besides

**al'so-ran'** *n.* [Inf.] a defeated contestant in a race, election, etc.

**alt** *abbrev.* **1** alternate **2** altitude **3** alto

**al·tar** (ôl'tər) *n.* [< L *altus*, high] **1** a platform where sacrifices are made to a god, etc. **2** a table, etc. for sacred purposes in a place of worship

**altar boy** a boy or man who helps a priest at religious services, esp. at Mass

**al·ter** (ôl'tər) *vt., vi.* [< L *alter*, other] to change; make or become different —**al'ter·a'tion** *n.*

**al·ter·ca·tion** (ôl'tər kā'shən) *n.* [< L *altercari*, to dispute] an angry or heated argument; quarrel

**al'ter e'go** [L, other I] **1** another aspect of oneself **2** a constant companion

**al·ter·nate** (ôl'tər nit; *for v.*, -nāt') *adj.* [< L *alternus*, one after the other] **1** succeeding each other **2** every other **3** ALTERNATIVE (*adj.* 1) —*n.* a substitute —*vt.* **-nat'ed, -nat'ing** to do or use by turns —*vi.* **1** to act, happen, etc. by turns **2** to take turns regularly —**al'ter·nate·ly** *adv.* —**al'ter·na'tion** *n.*

**alternating current** an electric current reversing direction periodically: abbrev. *AC*

**al·ter·na·tive** (ôl tur'nə tiv) *adj.* **1** providing a choice between things **2** of an institution, etc. appealing to unconventional interests [an *alternative* school] —*n.* **1** a choice between things **2** one of the things to be chosen **3** something left to choose

**al·ter·na·tor** (ôl'tər nāt'ər) *n.* an electric generator producing alternating current

**al·though** (ôl thō') *conj.* [ME < *al*, even + THOUGH] in spite of the fact that; though: sometimes sp. **al·tho'**

**al·tim·e·ter** (al tim'ət ər) *n.* [< L *altus*, high + -METER] an instrument for measuring altitude

**al·ti·tude** (al'tə tōōd') *n.* [< L *altus*, high] **1** the height of a thing, esp. above sea level **2** a high place: *usually used in pl.*

**al·to** (al'tō) *n., pl.* **-tos** [It < L *altus*, high] **1** the range of a voice between tenor and mezzo-soprano **2** a voice, singer, or instrument with such a range **3** a part for an alto —*adj.* of or for an alto

**al·to·geth·er** (ôl'tōō geth'ər) *adv.* **1** completely **2** in all **3** on the whole

**al·tru·ism** (al'trōō iz'əm) *n.* [< L *alter*, other] unselfish concern for the welfare of others —**al'tru·ist** *n.* —**al'tru·is'tic** *adj.* —**al'tru·is'ti·cal·ly** *adv.*

**al·um** (al'əm) *n.* [< L *alumen*] any of a group of salts of aluminum, etc., used in manufacturing and medicine

**al·u·min·i·um** (al'yōō min'ē əm) *n.* [Brit.] *var.* of ALUMINUM

**a·lu·mi·num** (ə lōō'mə nəm) *n.* [< L *alumen*, alum] a silvery, lightweight metallic chemical element

**a·lum·nus** (ə lum'nəs) *n., pl.* **-ni** (-nī') [L, foster son] a person, esp. a boy or man, who has attended or is a graduate of a particular school, college, etc. —**a·lum'na** (-nə), *pl.* **-nae** (-nē), *fem.n.*

**al·ways** (ôl'wāz) *adv.* [OE *ealne weg*] **1** at all times **2** all the time **3** at any time **4** in every instance

**Alz·hei·mer's disease** (älts'hī'mərz) [after A. *Alzheimer*, 20th-c. Ger doctor] a degenerative brain disease

**am** (am) *vi.* [OE *eom*] *1st pers. sing., pres. indic., of* BE

**Am** *abbrev.* **1** America **2** American

**AM**[1] (ā'em') *n.* amplitude-modulation broadcasting or sound transmission

**AM**[2] *abbrev.* **1** amplitude modulation **2** [L *ante meridiem*] before noon: used to designate the time from midnight to noon: also **A.M., am,** or

**a.m. 3** ⟦L *Artium Magister*⟧ master of arts: also **A.M.**

**AMA** *abbrev.* American Medical Association

**a·mal·gam** (ə mal′gəm) *n.* ⟦< Gr *malagma*, an emollient⟧ **1** any alloy of mercury with another metal [a dental filling of silver *amalgam*] **2** a mixture; blend

**a·mal·ga·mate′** (-gə māt′) *vt.*, *vi.* -mat′ed, -mat′ing to unite; mix; combine —**a·mal·ga·ma′tion** *n.*

**a·man·dine** (ä′mən dēn′) *adj.* ⟦Fr⟧ prepared with almonds

**a·man·u·en·sis** (ə man′yōō en′sis) *n.*, *pl.* -ses′ (-sēz′) ⟦L < *a-*, from + *manus*, hand + *-ensis*, relating to⟧ a secretary: now a jocular usage

**am·a·ranth** (am′ə ranth′) *n.* ⟦< Gr *amarantos*, unfading⟧ **1** any of a large group of similar plants, some bearing showy flowers **2** [Old Poet.] an imaginary flower that never dies

**am·a·ret·to** (am′ə ret′ō) *n.* ⟦It, rather bitter⟧ [also A-] a liqueur with an almond flavor

**Am·a·ril·lo** (am′ə ril′ō) city in NW Texas: pop. 158,000

**am·a·ryl·lis** (am′ə ril′is) *n.* ⟦< Gr *Amaryllis*, name for a shepherdess⟧ a lilylike plant with white, purple, pink, or red flowers

**a·mass** (ə mas′) *vt.* ⟦< Fr < L *massa*, a lump⟧ to pile up; accumulate

**am·a·teur** (am′ə chər, -tər) *n.* ⟦Fr < L *amare*, to love⟧ **1** one who does something for pleasure, not for money; nonprofessional **2** one who is somewhat unskillful —*adj.* of or done by amateurs — **am′a·teur′ish** (-chŏŏr′-) *adj.* —**am′a·teur·ism′** *n.*

**am·a·to·ry** (am′ə tôr′ē) *adj.* ⟦< L *amare*, to love⟧ of or showing love, esp. sexual love

**a·maze** (ə māz′) *vt.* **a·mazed′**, **a·maz′ing** ⟦OE *āmasian*⟧ to fill with great surprise or wonder; astonish —**a·maze′ment** *n.* —**a·maz′ing** *adj.* —**a·maz′ing·ly** *adv.*

**Am·a·zon**[1] (am′ə zän′, -zən) *n.* **1** *Gr. Myth.* any of a race of female warriors **2** [a-] a tall, strong, aggressive woman

**Am′a·zon′**[2] river in N South America: c. 4,000 mi.

**am·bas·sa·dor** (am bas′ə dər) *n.* ⟦< Prov *ambaissador*⟧ the highest-ranking diplomatic representative of one country to another —**am·bas′sa·do′ri·al** (-dôr′ē əl) *adj.* —**am·bas′sa·dor·ship′** *n.*

**am·ber** (am′bər) *n.* ⟦< Ar *'anbar*, ambergris⟧ **1** a brownish-yellow fossil resin used in jewelry, etc. **2** its color —*adj.* amberlike or amber-colored

**am′ber·gris′** (-grēs′, -gris′) *n.* ⟦< OFr *ambre gris*, gray amber⟧ a grayish, waxy substance in the intestines of sperm whales, used in perfumes

**ambi-** ⟦L⟧ combining form both [*ambidextrous*]

**am·bi·dex·trous** (am′bə deks′trəs) *adj.* ⟦< earlier *ambidexter* + -OUS⟧ using both hands with equal ease —**am′bi·dex·ter′i·ty** (-deks ter′ə tē) *n.*

**am·bi·ence** (am′bē əns, äm′bē äns′) *n.* ⟦Fr: see fol.⟧ an environment or its distinct atmosphere: also sp. **am′bi·ance** (-əns)

**am·bi·ent** (am′bē ənt) *adj.* ⟦< L *ambi-*, around + *ire*, to go⟧ surrounding; on all sides

**am·bi·gu·i·ty** (am′bə gyōō′ə tē) *n.* **1** a being ambiguous **2** *pl.* -ties an ambiguous word, statement, etc.

**am·big·u·ous** (am big′yōō əs) *adj.* ⟦< L *ambi-*, around + *agere*, to do⟧ **1** having two or more meanings **2** not clear; vague —**am·big′u·ous·ly** *adv.*

**am·bi·tion** (am bish′ən) *n.* ⟦< L *ambitio*, a going around (to solicit votes)⟧ **1** a strong desire for fame, power, etc. **2** the thing desired

**am·bi·tious** (-əs) *adj.* **1** full of or showing ambition **2** demanding great effort —**am·bi′tious·ly** *adv.*

**am·biv·a·lence** (am biv′ə ləns) *n.* ⟦AMBI- + VALENCE⟧ simultaneous conflicting feelings —**am·biv′a·lent** *adj.* —**am·biv′a·lent·ly** *adv.*

**am·ble** (am′bəl) *vi.* -bled, -bling ⟦< L *ambulare*, to walk⟧ **1** to move at an easy gait, as a horse **2** to

walk in a leisurely way —*n.* **1** a horse's ambling gait **2** a leisurely walking pace

**am·bro·sia** (am brō′zhə) *n.* ⟦< Gr *a-*, not + *brotos*, mortal⟧ **1** *Gr. & Rom. Myth.* the food of the gods **2** anything that tastes or smells delicious —**am·bro′sial** *adj.*

**am·bu·lance** (am′byə ləns) *n.* ⟦< L *ambulare*, to walk⟧ a vehicle equipped for carrying the sick or wounded

**am·bu·late** (am′byōō lāt′, -byə-) *vi.* -lat′ed, -lat′ing to move about; walk —**am′bu·lant** (-lənt) *adj.* —**am′bu·la′tion** *n.*

**am′bu·la·to′ry** (-lə tôr′ē) *adj.* **1** of or for walking **2** able to walk

**am·bus·cade** (am′bəs kād′) *n.*, *vt.*, *vi.* -cad′ed, -cad′ing AMBUSH

**am·bush** (am′bŏŏsh) *n.* ⟦< ML *in-*, in + *boscus*, woods⟧ **1** a deployment of persons in hiding to make a surprise attack **2** their hiding place **3** a surprise attack —*vt.*, *vi.* to attack from ambush

**a·me·ba** (ə mē′bə) *n.*, *pl.* -bas or -bae (-bē) *alt. sp.* of AMOEBA —**a·me′bic** (-bik) *adj.*

**a·mel·io·rate** (ə mēl′yə rāt′) *vt.*, *vi.* -rat′ed, -rat′ing ⟦< Fr < L *melior*, better⟧ to make or become better; improve —**a·mel′io·ra′tion** *n.*

**a·men** (ā′men′, ä′-) *interj.* ⟦< Heb *amen*, truly⟧ may it be so!: used after a prayer or to express approval

**a·me·na·ble** (ə mē′nə bəl, -men′ə-) *adj.* ⟦< OFr < L *minare*, to drive (animals)⟧ **1** responsible or answerable **2** able to be controlled; submissive — **a·me′na·bil′i·ty** *n.* —**a·me′na·bly** *adv.*

**a·mend** (ə mend′) *vt.* ⟦< L *emendare*⟧ **1** to correct; emend **2** to improve **3** to change or revise (a law, etc.) —*vi.* to improve one's conduct —**a·mend′a·ble** *adj.*

**a·mend′ment** *n.* **1** a correction of errors, faults, etc. **2** improvement **3** a revision or change proposed or made in a bill, law, etc.

**a·mends** (ə mendz′) *pl.n.* ⟦see AMEND⟧ [*sometimes with sing. v.*] payment made or satisfaction given for injury, loss, etc.

**a·men·i·ty** (ə men′ə tē, -mēn′-) *n.*, *pl.* -ties ⟦< L *amoenus*, pleasant⟧ **1** pleasantness **2** an attractive feature or convenience **3** [*pl.*] courteous acts

**am·ent** (am′ənt, ā′mənt) *n.* ⟦< L *amentum*, thong⟧ CATKIN

**Am·er·a·sian** (am′ər ā′zhən) *n.* ⟦AMER(ICAN) + ASIAN⟧ a person of both American and Asian descent —*adj.* both American and Asian [an *Amerasian* child]

**a·merce** (ə murs′) *vt.* **a·merced′**, **a·merc′ing** ⟦< OFr *a merci*, at the mercy of⟧ to punish, esp. by imposing a fine —**a·merce′ment** *n.*

**A·mer·i·ca** (ə mer′i kə) ⟦associated with *Amerigo* VESPUCCI⟧ **1** North America, South America, and the West Indies, considered together: also the **Americas 2** North America **3** the United States of America

**A·mer′i·can** (-kən) *adj.* **1** of or in America **2** of the U.S. or its people —*n.* **1** a person born or living in North or South America **2** a citizen of the U.S.

**A·mer′i·can·a** (ə mer′i kan′ə, -kä′nə) *pl.n.* books, papers, objects, etc. having to do with the U.S., its people, and its history

**American Indian** a member of any of the indigenous peoples of North or South America or the West Indies

**A·mer′i·can·ism′** *n.* **1** a custom or belief of or originating in the U.S. **2** a word or idiom originating in American English **3** devotion to the U.S., its customs, etc.

**A·mer′i·can·ize′** (-īz′) *vt.*, *vi.* -ized′, -iz′ing to make or become American in character, manners, etc. —**A·mer′i·can·i·za′tion** *n.*

**American plan** a system of hotel operation in which the price charged covers room, service, and meals

**American Revolution** the war (1775-83) fought

by the American colonies to gain independence from Great Britain

**American Samoa** group of seven islands in the SW Pacific: an unincorporated territory of the U.S.: 77 sq. mi.; pop. 47,000

**Am·er·in·di·an** (am′ər in′dē ən) *n., adj.* AMERICAN INDIAN —**Am′er·ind′** *n., adj.*

**am·e·thyst** (am′i thist) *n.* 〚< Gr *amethystos*, not drunken: the Greeks thought the amethyst prevented intoxication〛 **1** a purple or violet quartz or corundum, used in jewelry **2** purple or violet

**a·mi·a·ble** (ā′mē ə bəl) *adj.* 〚< L *amicus*, friend〛 good-natured; friendly —**a′mi·a·bil′i·ty** *n.* —**a′mi·a·bly** *adv.*

**am·i·ca·ble** (am′i kə bəl) *adj.* 〚see prec.〛 friendly; peaceable —**am′i·ca·bil′i·ty** *n.* —**am′i·ca·bly** *adv.*

**a·mid** (ə mid′) *prep.* in the middle of; among: also **a·midst** (ə midst′)

**a·mide** (am′īd′) *n.* any of several organic compounds derived from ammonia

**a·mid′ships′** *adv., adj.* in or toward the middle of a ship

**a·mi·go** (ə mē′gō) *n., pl.* **-gos′** (-gōz′) 〚Sp〛 a friend

**a·mi·no acid** (ə mē′nō) 〚< AMMONIA〛 any of the nitrogenous organic acids that form proteins necessary for all life

**Am·ish** (äm′ish, am′-) *pl.n.* 〚after Jacob *Ammann* (or *Amen*), the founder〛 the members of a Christian sect that favors plain living in an agrarian society —*adj.* of this sect

**a·miss** (ə mis′) *adv.* 〚see A-¹ & MISS¹〛 in a wrong way; astray —*adj.* wrong, faulty, improper, etc. [what is *amiss?*]

**am·i·ty** (am′i tē) *n., pl.* **-ties** 〚< L *amicus*, friend〛 peaceful relations

**am·me·ter** (am′mēt′ər) *n.* 〚AM(PERE) + -METER〛 an instrument for measuring an electric current in amperes

**am·mo** (am′ō) *n.* [Slang] ammunition

**am·mo·ni·a** (ə mōn′yə) *n.* 〚prob. from a salt found near Egyptian shrine of Jupiter *Ammon*〛 **1** a colorless, pungent gas, a compound of nitrogen and hydrogen **2** a 10% water solution of this gas

**am·mu·ni·tion** (am′yōō nish′ən) *n.* 〚< L *munire*, fortify〛 **1** bullets, gunpowder, bombs, grenades, rockets, etc. **2** any means of attack or defense

**am·ne·sia** (am nē′zhə) *n.* 〚< Gr *a-*, not + *mnasthai*, to remember〛 partial or total loss of memory

**am·nes·ty** (am′nəs tē) *n., pl.* **-ties** 〚< Gr *amnēstia*, a forgetting〛 a pardon, esp. for political offenses —*vt.* **-tied, -ty·ing** to pardon

**am·ni·o·cen·te·sis** (am′nē ō′sen tē′sis) *n.* 〚< fol. + Gr *kentēsis*, a pricking〛 the surgical procedure of extracting amniotic fluid from a pregnant woman to determine the sex of the fetus, detect disease, etc.

**am·ni·on** (am′nē ən, -än′) *n., pl.* **-ni·ons** or **-ni·a** (-ə) 〚Gr, dim. of *amnos*, lamb〛 the membrane enclosing the embryo of a mammal, reptile, or bird: it is filled with a watery fluid (**amniotic fluid**) —**am′ni·ot′ic** (-ät′ik) *adj.*

**a·moe·ba** (ə mē′bə) *n., pl.* **-bas** or **-bae** (-bē) 〚< Gr *ameibein*, to change〛 a one-celled, microscopic organism reproducing by fission —**a·moe′bic** (-bik) *adj.*

**a·mok** (ə muk′) *adj., adv.* 〚< Malay *amuk*, attacking furiously〛 used chiefly in **run amok**, lose control and behave violently

**a·mong** (ə muŋ′) *prep.* 〚< OE *on*, in + *gemang*, a crowd〛 **1** surrounded by [among friends] **2** in the group of [best *among* books] **3** to or for each or several of [divide it *among* the crowd] **4** by the joint action of Also [Chiefly Brit.] **a·mongst** (ə muŋst′)

**A·mon-Re** (ä′mən rā′) *n.* the ancient Egyptian sun god: also **A′mon-Ra′** (-rä′)

**a·mon·til·la·do** (ə män′tə lä′dō) *n.* 〚< Sp, after *Montilla*, town in Spain〛 a pale, dry sherry

**a·mor·al** (ā môr′əl) *adj.* **1** neither moral nor

immoral **2** without moral sense —**a′mo·ral′i·ty** *n.* —**a·mor′al·ly** *adv.*

**am·o·rous** (am′ə rəs) *adj.* 〚< L *amor*, love〛 **1** fond of making love **2** full of love **3** of sexual love — **am′o·rous·ly** *adv.*

**a·mor·phous** (ə môr′fəs) *adj.* 〚< Gr *a-*, without + *morphē*, form〛 **1** without definite form **2** vague or indefinite **3** *Chem.* not crystalline

**am·or·tize** (am′ər tīz′, ə môr′-) *vt.* **-tized, -tiz′ing** 〚< ME < L *ad*, to + *mors*, death〛 to put money aside at intervals for gradual payment of (a debt, etc.) —**am′or·ti·za′tion** *n.*

**a·mount** (ə mount′) *vi.* 〚< OFr *amont*, upward < L *ad*, to + *mons*, mountain〛 **1** to add up (*to*) **2** to be equal (*to*) in value, etc. —*n.* **1** a sum total **2** the whole value or effect **3** a quantity

**a·mour** (ə moor′) *n.* 〚< L *amor*, love〛 a love affair, esp. an illicit one

**a·mour-pro·pre** (à moŏr prô′pr′) *n.* 〚Fr〛 self-esteem

**amp¹** (amp) *n. short for:* **1** AMPERE **2** AMPLIFIER

**amp²** *abbrev.* **1** amperage **2** ampere(s)

**am·per·age** (am′pər ij) *n.* the strength of an electric current in amperes

**am·pere** (am′pir′) *n.* 〚< A. M. *Ampère*, 19th-c. Fr physicist〛 the standard unit for measuring an electric current, equal to one coulomb per second

**am·per·sand** (am′pər sand′) *n.* 〚< *and per se and*, (the sign) & by itself (is) *and*〛 a sign (&), meaning *and*

**am·phet·a·mine** (am fet′ə mēn′, -min) *n.* a drug used esp. as a stimulant and to lessen appetite

**am·phib·i·an** (am fib′ē ən) *n.* 〚see fol.〛 **1** any amphibious animal, as a frog, or plant **2** any aircraft that can take off from or land on water or land —*adj.* AMPHIBIOUS

**am·phib′i·ous** *adj.* 〚Gr *amphibios*, living a double life < *amphi-*, around + *bios*, life〛 that can live or operate on land and in water

**am·phi·the·a·ter** or **am·phi·the·a·tre** (am′fə thē′ə tər) *n.* 〚< Gr *amphi-*, around + *theatron*, theater〛 a round or oval building with rising rows of seats around an open space

**am·ple** (am′pəl) *adj.* **-pler, -plest** 〚< L *amplus*〛 **1** large in size, scope, etc. **2** more than enough **3** adequate —**am′ply** *adv.*

**am·pli·fi·er** (am′plə fī′ər) *n.* one that amplifies; esp., a device for strengthening electrical signals

**am′pli·fy′** (-fī′) *vt.* **-fied, -fy′ing** 〚< L *amplus*, large + *facere*, to make〛 **1** to make stronger; esp., to strengthen (electrical signals) **2** to develop more fully —**am′pli·fi·ca′tion** *n.*

**am·pli·tude** (am′plə tōōd′) *n.* 〚see AMPLE〛 **1** scope, extent, breadth, etc. **2** abundance **3** range from mean to extreme of a fluctuating quantity, as of an alternating current

**amplitude modulation** the changing of the amplitude of the transmitting radio wave in accordance with the signal being broadcast: abbrev. **AM**

**am·pul** (am′pōōl′) *n.* 〚< L *ampulla*, bottle〛 a small, sealed, glass or plastic container for a single dose of a hypodermic medicine: also **am′pule′** (-pyōōl′) or **am′poule′** (-pōōl′)

**am·pu·tate** (am′pyōō tāt′) *vt., vi.* **-tat′ed, -tat′ing** 〚< L *am-*, AMBI- + *putare*, to prune〛 to cut off (an arm, etc.), esp. by surgery —**am′pu·ta′tion** *n.*

**am·pu·tee′** (-tē′) *n.* one who has had a limb or limbs amputated

**Am·ster·dam** (am′stər dam′) constitutional capital of the Netherlands: pop. 724,000

**amt** *abbrev.* amount

**Am·trak** (am′trak′) *abbrev.* 〚*Am*(*erican*) *tr*(*avel*) (*tr*)*a*(*c*)*k*〛 a national U.S. passenger railroad system

**a·muck** (ə muk′) *n. alt. sp. of* AMOK

**am·u·let** (am′yōō lit) *n.* 〚< L〛 something worn to protect against evil

**a·muse** (ə myōōz′) *vt.* **a·mused′, a·mus′ing** 〚< Fr *à*, at + OFr *muser*, to gaze〛 **1** to keep pleasantly

occupied; entertain **2** to make laugh, smile, etc.
—**a·mus′ed·ly** *adv.*

**a·muse′ment** *n.* **1** a being amused **2** something that amuses; entertainment

**amusement park** an outdoor place with devices for entertainment, as a merry-go-round, roller coaster, etc.

**am·yl·ase** (am′ə lās′) *n.* ⟦< Gr *amylon*, starch⟧ an enzyme that helps change starch into sugar, found in saliva, etc.

**an** (an; *unstressed*, ən, 'n) *adj., indefinite article* ⟦< OE *an*, one⟧ **1** one; one sort of **2** each; any one — *prep.* per ⟦*two an hour*⟧ *An* is used before words beginning with a vowel sound ⟦*an eye, an honor*⟧ See also A²

**-an** (ən, in, 'n) ⟦< L *-anus*⟧ *suffix* **1** (one) belonging to ⟦*diocesan*⟧ **2** (one) born in or living in ⟦*Mexican*⟧ **3** (one) believing in ⟦*Lutheran*⟧

**a·nach·ro·nism** (ə nak′rə niz′əm) *n.* ⟦< Gr *ana-*, against + *chronos*, time⟧ **1** anything out of its proper historical time **2** the representation of this —**a·nach′ro·nis′tic** *adj.*

**an·a·con·da** (an′ə kän′də) *n.* ⟦< Sinhalese *henacandāya*, a snake of Sri Lanka⟧ a long, heavy South American boa living in trees and water

**an·aer·o·bic** (an′ər ō′bik) *adj.* ⟦< Gr *an-*, without + *aēr*, air + *bios*, life⟧ able to live and grow without air or free oxygen, as certain bacteria

**an·aes·the·sia** (an′əs thē′zhə) *n.* ANESTHESIA — **an·aes·thet′ic** (-thet′ik) *adj., n.*

**an·a·gram** (an′ə gram′) *n.* ⟦< Gr *anagrammatizein*, transpose letters⟧ **1** a word, etc. made by rearranging letters (Ex.: *now — won*) **2** [*pl., with sing. v.*] a word game based on this

**An·a·heim** (an′ə hīm′) city in SW California: pop. 266,000

**a·nal** (ā′nəl) *adj.* **1** of or near the anus **2** [Inf.] excessively orderly, stingy, etc.

**an·al·ge·si·a** (an′əl jē′zē ə) *n.* ⟦< Gr *an-*, without + *algēsia*, pain⟧ a fully conscious state in which pain is not felt

**an·al·ge′sic** (-zik) *adj.* of or causing analgesia —*n.* a drug that produces analgesia

**an·a·log** (an′ə lôg′) *adj.* **1** of electronic devices in which the signal corresponds to a physical change **2** using hands, dials, etc. to show numerical amounts, as on a clock: cf. DIGITAL (sense 2) —*n.* ANALOGUE

**a·nal·o·gize** (ə nal′ə jīz′) *vi., vt.* -**gized′**, -**giz′ing** to use, or explain by, analogy

**a·nal′o·gous** (-gəs) *adj.* ⟦see ANALOGY⟧ similar in some way —**a·nal′o·gous·ly** *adv.*

**an·a·logue** (an′ə lôg′) *n.* something analogous

**a·nal·o·gy** (ə nal′ə jē) *n., pl.* -**gies** ⟦< Gr *ana-*, according to + *logos*, word, reckoning⟧ **1** similarity in some ways **2** the inference that certain resemblances imply further similarity

**a·nal·y·sand** (ə nal′ə sand′) *n.* a person undergoing psychoanalysis

**a·nal·y·sis** (-sis) *n., pl.* -**ses′** (-sēz′) ⟦< Gr *ana-*, up + *lysis*, a loosing⟧ **1** *a)* a breaking up of a whole into its parts to find out their nature, etc. *b)* any detailed examination **2** a statement of the results of this **3** PSYCHOANALYSIS **4** *Chem.* an analysis of compounds or mixtures —**an·a·lyt′ic** (an′ə lit′ik) or **an′a·lyt′i·cal** *adj.* —**an′a·lyt′i·cal·ly** *adv.*

**an·a·lyst** (an′ə list) *n.* **1** one who analyzes **2** a psychoanalyst

**an′a·lyze** (-līz′) *vt.* -**lyzed′**, -**lyz′ing** **1** to make an analysis of; examine in detail **2** to psychoanalyze —**an′a·lyz′a·ble** *adj.* —**an′a·lyz′er** *n.*

**an·a·pest** (an′ə pest′) *n.* ⟦< Gr *ana-*, back + *paiein*, to strike⟧ a metrical foot of two unaccented syllables followed by an accented one

**an·ar·chism** (an′ər kiz′əm) *n.* **1** the theory that all forms of government interfere unjustly with individual liberty **2** resistance to all government —**an′ar·chist′** *n.* —**an′ar·chis′tic** *adj.*

**an·ar·chy** (-kē) *n., pl.* -**chies** ⟦< Gr *an-*, without + *archos*, leader⟧ **1** the absence of government **2**

political disorder and violence **3** disorder; confusion —**an·ar·chic** (an är′kik) *adj.* —**an·ar′chi·cal·ly** *adv.*

**a·nath·e·ma** (ə nath′ə mə) *n., pl.* -**mas** ⟦Gr, thing devoted to evil⟧ **1** a thing or person accursed or damned **2** a thing or person greatly detested **3** a formal curse, as in excommunication

**a·nath′e·ma·tize′** (-tīz′) *vt., vi.* -**tized′**, -**tiz′ing** to utter an anathema (against); curse

**a·nat·o·mize** (ə nat′ə mīz′) *vt., vi.* -**mized′**, -**miz′ing** ⟦see ANATOMY⟧ **1** to dissect (an animal or plant) in order to examine the structure **2** to analyze —**a·nat′o·mist** *n.*

**a·nat·o·my** (-mē) *n., pl.* -**mies** ⟦< Gr *ana-*, up + *temnein*, to cut⟧ **1** dissection of an organism to study its structure **2** the science of the structure of animals or plants **3** the structure of an organism **4** any analysis —**an·a·tom·i·cal** (an′ə täm′i kəl) or **an′a·tom′ic** *adj.*

**-ance** (əns) ⟦< L⟧ *suffix* **1** the act or process of ___ing ⟦*discontinuance*⟧ **2** the quality or state of being ⟦*forbearance*⟧ **3** a thing that ___s ⟦*hindrance*⟧ **4** a thing that is ___ed ⟦*utterance*⟧

**an·ces·tor** (an′ses′tər) *n.* ⟦< L *ante-*, before + *cedere*, go⟧ **1** a person from whom one is descended; forebear **2** a precursor or forerunner —**an·ces′tral** (an ses′trəl) *adj.* —**an·ces·tress** (an′ses′trəs) *fem.n.*

**an′ces·try** (-trē) *n., pl.* -**tries** **1** family descent **2** ancestors collectively

STOCK

SHANK

FLUKE

| MUSH-ROOM ANCHOR | STOCKED ANCHOR | STOCK-LESS ANCHOR |

**an·chor** (aŋ′kər) *n.* ⟦< Gr *ankyra*, an anchor, hook⟧ **1** a heavy object, usually an iron weight with flukes, lowered from a vessel, as by cable, to prevent drifting **2** anything giving stability **3** one who anchors a newscast: also **an′chor·per′son** —*vt.* **1** to hold secure as by an anchor **2** to be the final contestant on (a relay team, etc.) **3** to serve as coordinator and chief reporter for (a newscast) —*vi.* **1** to lower an anchor overboard **2** to be or become fixed —**at anchor** kept from drifting by its anchor

**an′chor·age** (-ij) *n.* **1** an anchoring or being anchored **2** a place to anchor

**An·chor·age** (aŋ′kər ij) seaport in S Alaska: pop. 226,000

**an·cho·rite** (aŋ′kə rīt′) *n.* ⟦< Gr *ana-*, back + *chōrein*, retire⟧ a religious recluse; hermit

**an′chor·man′** *n., pl.* -**men′** a person, often, specif., a man, who anchors a newscast —**an′chor·wom′an**, *pl.* -**wom′en**, *fem.n.*

**an·cho·vy** (an′chō′vē) *n., pl.* -**vies** ⟦< Port *anchova*⟧ a herringlike fish, eaten as a relish

**an·cient** (ān′chənt) *adj.* ⟦< L *ante*, before⟧ **1** of times long past **2** very old —*n.* an aged person

**an·cil·la** (an sil′ə) *n.* a handbook or manual

**an·cil·lar·y** (an′sə ler′ē) *adj.* ⟦< L *ancilla*, maidservant⟧ **1** subordinate: often with *to* **2** auxiliary

**-an·cy** (ən sē) *suffix* -ANCE

**and** (and; *unstressed*, ənd, ən) *conj.* ⟦OE⟧ **1** also; in addition **2** plus **3** as a result **4** in contrast; but **5** then; following this **6** [Inf.] to ⟦*try and come today*⟧

**an·dan·te** (än dän′tā) *adj., adv.* ⟦It < *andare*, to

walk⟧ *Music* moderate in tempo: also written **an·dan'te**

**An·der·sen** (an'dər sən), **Hans Christian** (häns, hänz) 1805-75; Dan. writer of fairy tales

**An·des (Mountains)** (an'dēz') mountain system of W South America

**and·i·ron** (and'ī'ərn) *n.* ⟦< OFr *andier*⟧ either of a pair of metal supports for logs in a fireplace

**and/or** (and'ôr') *conj.* either *and* or *or* [personal *and/or* real property]

**An·dor·ra** (an dôr'ə) country in the E Pyrenees: 175 sq. mi.; pop. 63,000

**an·dro·gen** (an'drō jən) *n.* ⟦< Gr *andros*, of man + -GEN⟧ a type of steroid that acts as a male sex hormone —**an'dro·gen'ic** (-jen'ik) *adj.*

**an·drog·y·nous** (an drä'jə nəs) *adj.* ⟦< Gr *andros*, of man + *gynē*, woman⟧ 1 both male and female in one 2 that blends male and female characteristics, roles, etc. 3 not differentiated as to gender [*androgynous* clothing]

**an·droid** (an'droid') *n.* ⟦< Gr *andros*, of man + -OID⟧ in science fiction, a robot made to resemble a human being

**an·ec·dote** (an'ik dōt') *n.* ⟦< Gr *anekdotos*, unpublished⟧ a short, entertaining account of some event —**an'ec·dot'al** *adj.*

**a·ne·mi·a** (ə nē'mē ə) *n.* ⟦< Gr *an*-, without + *haima*, blood⟧ a condition in which the blood is low in red cells or in hemoglobin, resulting in paleness, weakness, etc. —**a·ne'mic** *adj.*

**an·e·mom·e·ter** (an'ə mäm'ət ər) *n.* ⟦< Gr *anemos*, the wind + -METER⟧ a gauge for determining the force or speed of the wind; wind gauge

**a·nem·o·ne** (ə nem'ə nē') *n.* ⟦< Gr *anemos*, the wind⟧ 1 a plant with cup-shaped flowers of white, pink, red, or purple 2 SEA ANEMONE

**a·nent** (ə nent') *prep.* ⟦< OE *on efen*, on even (with)⟧ [Now Rare] concerning; about

**aneroid barometer** (an'ər oid') ⟦< Gr *a*-, without + *nēros*, liquid + -OID⟧ a barometer working by the bending of a thin metal disk instead of by the rise or fall of mercury

**an·es·the·sia** (an'es thē'zhə) *n.* ⟦< Gr *an*-, without + *aisthēsis*, feeling⟧ a partial or total loss of the sense of pain, touch, etc., specif. when induced by an anesthetic

**an·es·the·si·ol·o·gist** (-thē'zē äl'ə jist) *n.* a doctor who specializes in giving anesthetics —**an'es·the·si·ol'o·gy** *n.*

**an·es·thet·ic** (-thet'ik) *adj.* of or producing anesthesia —*n.* a drug, gas, etc. used to produce anesthesia, as before surgery

**an·es·the·tist** (ə nes'thə tist') *n.* one trained to give anesthetics

**an·es·the·tize** (-tīz') *vt.* -tized', -tiz'ing to cause anesthesia in —**an·es'the·ti·za'tion** *n.*

**an·eu·rysm** or **an·eu·rism** (an'yŏŏ riz'əm) *n.* ⟦< Gr *ana*-, up + *eurys*, broad⟧ a sac formed by an enlargement in a weakened wall of an artery, a vein, or the heart

**a·new** (ə nōō') *adv.* 1 once more; again 2 in a new manner or form

**an·gel** (ān'jəl) *n.* ⟦< Gr *angelos*, messenger⟧ 1 *Theol. a*) a messenger of God *b*) a supernatural being with greater than human power, etc. 2 an image of a human figure with wings and a halo 3 a person regarded as beautiful, good, innocent, etc. 4 [Inf.] a financial backer, as for a play —**an·gel·ic** (an jel'ik) or **an·gel'i·cal** *adj.* —**an·gel'i·cal·ly** *adv.*

**angel dust** [Slang] a powerful psychedelic drug

**An·ge·le·no** (an'jə lē'nō) *n., pl.* -**nos** ⟦AmSp⟧ a person born or living in Los Angeles

**an·gel·fish** (ān'jəl fish') *n., pl.* -**fish'** or (for different species) -**fish'es** a bright-colored tropical fish with spiny fins

**angel (food) cake** a light, spongy, white cake made with egg whites

**an·ger** (aŋ'gər) *n.* ⟦< ON *angr*, distress⟧ a feeling of displeasure and hostility that a person has because of being injured, mistreated, opposed, etc. —*vt., vi.* to make or become angry

**an·gi·na** (**pec·to·ris**) (an jī'nə pek'tər is) ⟦L, lit., squeezing of the breast⟧ a condition marked by chest pain, caused by a sudden decrease of blood to the heart

**an·gi·o·gram** (an'jē ō gram') *n.* an X-ray photograph of blood vessels

**an·gi·o·plas·ty** (-plas'tē) *n.* any of various surgical techniques for repairing or replacing damaged blood vessels

**an·gi·o·sperm** (-spurm') *n.* ⟦< Gr *angos*, vessel + *sperma*, seed⟧ any of a large division of plants having seeds produced within a closed pod or ovary

**an·gle**[1] (aŋ'gəl) *n.* ⟦< Gr *ankylos*, bent⟧ 1 the shape or space made by two straight lines or plane surfaces that meet 2 the measure of this space, expressed in degrees, etc. 3 a sharp corner 4 a point of view; aspect 5 [Inf.] a tricky method for achieving a purpose —*vt., vi.* -**gled**, -**gling** 1 to move or bend at an angle 2 [Inf.] to give a specific point of view to (a story, etc.)

**an·gle**[2] (aŋ'gəl) *vi.* -**gled**, -**gling** ⟦< OE *angul*, fishhook⟧ 1 to fish with a hook and line 2 to use tricks to get something [to *angle* for a promotion] —**an'gler** *n.*

**An·gle** (aŋ'gəl) *n.* a member of a Germanic people that settled in E England in the 5th c. A.D.

**angle iron** a piece of iron or steel bent at a right angle, for joining or reinforcing two beams, etc.

**an'gle·worm'** *n.* an earthworm

**An·gli·can** (aŋ'gli kən) *adj.* ⟦< ML *Anglicus*, of the Angles⟧ of or connected with the Church of England —*n.* an Anglican church member

**An'gli·cize'** (-glə sīz') *vt., vi.* -**cized'**, -**ciz'ing** [*also* a-] to change to English idiom, pronunciation, customs, etc. —**An'gli·ci·za'tion** *n.*

**An·glo** (aŋ'glō) *n., pl.* -**glos** ⟦AmSp⟧ [*also* a-] a white inhabitant of the U.S. who is of non-Hispanic descent

**Anglo-** *combining form* 1 English 2 Anglican

**An'glo-A·mer'i·can** (aŋ'glō-) *adj.* English and American —*n.* an American of English birth or ancestry

**An'glo-French'** *adj.* English and French —*n.* the French spoken in England from the Norman Conquest through the Middle Ages

**An'glo-Sax'on** *n.* 1 a member of the Germanic peoples in England at the time of the Norman Conquest 2 the language of these peoples, OLD ENGLISH 3 an Englishman —*adj.* 1 of the Anglo-Saxons 2 of the English

**An·go·la** (aŋ gō'lə, an-) country on the SW coast of Africa: 481,354 sq. mi.; pop. 5,646,000

**An·go·ra** (aŋ gôr'ə, an-) *n.* ⟦former name of ANKARA⟧ 1 a breed of cat, goat, or rabbit with long, silky fur or hair 2 *a*) yarn of Angora rabbit hair *b*) mohair

**an·gry** (aŋ'grē) *adj.* -**gri·er**, -**gri·est** 1 feeling or showing anger 2 wild and stormy —**an'gri·ly** (-grə lē) *adv.*

**ang·strom** (aŋ'strəm) *n.* ⟦after A. J. *Angström*, 19th-c. Swed physicist⟧ one hundred-millionth of a centimeter: a unit used in measuring the length of light waves

**an·guish** (aŋ'gwish) *n.* ⟦< L *angustia*, tightness⟧ great mental or physical pain; agony —*vi., vt.* to feel or cause to feel anguish —**an'guished** *adj.*

**an·gu·lar** (aŋ'gyə lər) *adj.* 1 having or forming an angle or angles; having sharp corners 2 lean; gaunt 3 without ease or grace; stiff —**an'gu·lar'i·ty** (-lar'ə tē), *pl.* -**ties,** *n.*

**an·i·line** (an'ə lin) *n.* ⟦< Ar *an-nīl*, the indigo plant⟧ a colorless, poisonous, oily derivative of benzene, used in making dyes, resins, etc.

**an·i·mad·vert** (an'i məd vurt', -mad'-) *vi.* ⟦L *animadvertere*, lit., to turn the mind⟧ to comment adversely (*on* or *upon*) —**an'i·mad·ver'sion** *n.*

**an·i·mal** (an'i məl) *n.* ⟦L < *anima*, breath, soul⟧ 1 any of a group of living organisms, excluding plants, bacteria, and certain other simple organisms, typically able to move about **2** any such organism other than a human being; esp., any four-footed creature **3** a brutish or inhuman person —*adj.* **1** of or like an animal **2** gross, bestial, etc.

**an·i·mate** (an′i māt′; *for adj.*, -mit) *vt.* -mat′ed, -mat′ing ⟦see prec.⟧ **1** to give life or motion to **2** to make energetic or spirited **3** to inspire —*adj.* living —**an′i·ma′tion** *n.* —**an′i·ma′tor** *n.*

**an′i·mat′ed** *adj.* **1** living or lifelike **2** lively **3** designating or of a movie made by photographing a series of drawings so that the figures in them seem to move

**an·i·mism** (an′i miz′əm) *n.* ⟦< L *anima*, soul⟧ the belief that all life is produced by a spiritual force, or that all natural phenomena have souls —**an′i·mis′tic** *adj.*

**an·i·mos·i·ty** (an′ə mäs′ə tē) *n., pl.* -ties ⟦see fol.⟧ a feeling of strong dislike or hatred; hostility

**an·i·mus** (an′ə məs) *n.* ⟦L, passion⟧ animosity; hostility

**an·i·on** (an′ī′ən) *n.* ⟦< Gr *anion*, thing going up⟧ a negatively charged ion: in electrolysis, anions move toward the anode

**an·ise** (an′is) *n.* ⟦< Gr *anison*⟧ **1** a dicotyledonous plant related to celery and parsley **2** its fragrant seed, used for flavoring: also **an′i·seed′** (-i sēd′)

**an·i·sette** (an′i zet′, -set′) *n.* ⟦Fr⟧ a sweet, anise-flavored liqueur

**An·ka·ra** (aŋ′kər ə, äŋ′-) capital of Turkey: pop. 2,235,000

**ankh** (aŋk) *n.* ⟦Egypt, life, soul⟧ a cross with a loop at the top, an ancient Egyptian symbol of life

**an·kle** (aŋ′kəl) *n.* ⟦OE *ancleow*⟧ **1** the joint that connects the foot and the leg **2** the area of the leg between the foot′ and calf

**an·klet** (aŋk′lit) *n.* **1** an ornament worn around the ankle **2** a short sock

**an·nals** (an′əlz) *pl.n.* ⟦< L *annus*, year⟧ **1** a written account of events year by year **2** historical records; history **3** a journal containing reports of a society, etc. —**an′nal·ist** *n.*

**An·nap·o·lis** (ə nap′ə lis) capital of Maryland: pop. 33,000

**Ann Ar·bor** (an är′bər) city in SE Michigan: pop. 110,000

**an·neal** (ə nēl′) *vt.* ⟦< OE *an-*, on + *æl*, fire⟧ to heat (glass, metals, etc.) and cool to prevent brittleness

**an·ne·lid** (an′ə lid′) *n.* ⟦< L dim. of *anulus*, a ring⟧ any of various wormlike animals, including leeches, having long, segmented bodies

**an·nex** (ə neks′; *for n.*, an′eks′) *vt.* ⟦< L *ad-*, to + *nectere*, to tie⟧ **1** to attach or append, esp. to something larger **2** to incorporate into a country, etc. the territory of (another country, etc.) —*n.* something annexed; esp., an addition to a building —**an·nex·a·tion** (an′eks ā′shən) *n.*

**an·ni·hi·late** (ə nī′ə lāt′) *vt.* -lat′ed, -lat′ing ⟦< L *ad*, to + *nihil*, nothing⟧ to destroy completely —**an·ni′hi·la′tion** *n.* —**an·ni′hi·la′tor** *n.*

**an·ni·ver·sa·ry** (an′ə vur′sə rē) *n., pl.* -ries ⟦< L *annus*, year + *vertere*, to turn⟧ the date on which some event occurred in an earlier year

**an·no·tate** (an′ō tāt′) *vt., vi.* -tat′ed, -tat′ing ⟦< L *ad-*, to + *nota*, a sign⟧ to provide explanatory notes for (a text, etc.) —**an′no·ta′tion** *n.* —**an′no·ta′tor** *n.*

**an·nounce** (ə nouns′) *vt.* -nounced′, -nounc′ing ⟦< L *ad-*, to + *nuntius*, messenger⟧ **1** to declare publicly **2** to make known the arrival of **3** to be an announcer for —*vi.* to serve as announcer —**an·nounce′ment** *n.*

**an·nounc′er** *n.* one who announces; specif., one who introduces radio or TV programs

**an·noy** (ə noi′) *vt.* ⟦< VL *in odio*, in hate⟧ to irritate or bother, as by a repeated action —**an·noy′ance** *n.* —**an·noy′ing** *adj.* —**an·noy′ing·ly** *adv.*

**an·nu·al** (an′yoo əl) *adj.* ⟦< L *annus*, year⟧ **1** of or measured by a year **2** yearly **3** living only one year or season —*n.* **1** a periodical published once

a year **2** a plant living only one year or season —**an′nu·al·ly** *adv.*

**an·nu·i·ty** (ə noo′ə tē) *n., pl.* -ties ⟦see prec.⟧ **1** an investment yielding periodic payments, esp. yearly **2** such a payment —**an·nu′i·tant** *n.*

**an·nul** (ə nul′) *vt.* -nulled′, -nul′ling ⟦< L *ad-*, to + *nullum*, nothing⟧ **1** to do away with **2** to make no longer legally binding; nullify —**an·nul′ment** *n.*

**an·nu·lar** (an′yoo lər) *adj.* ⟦< L *anulus*, a ring⟧ like or forming a ring

**an·nun·ci·a·tion** (ə nun′sē ā′shən) *n.* an announcing —**the Annunciation 1** *Bible* the angel Gabriel's announcement to Mary that she would bear Jesus **2** the church festival commemorating this

**an·ode** (an′ōd) *n.* ⟦< Gr *anodos*, a way up⟧ **1** the positive electrode in an electrolytic cell **2** the principal electrode for collecting electrons in an electron tube **3** the negative electrode in a battery

**an·o·dize** (an′ō dīz′) *vt.* -dized′, -diz′ing to put a protective film on (a metal) by an electrolytic process in which the metal is the anode

**an′o·dyne** (-dīn′) *adj.* ⟦< Gr *an-*, without + *odynē*, pain⟧ **1** soothing **2** bland; insipid —*n.* anything that relieves pain or soothes

**a·noint** (ə noint′) *vt.* ⟦< L *in-*, on + *unguere*, to smear⟧ to put oil on, as in consecrating —**a·noint′ment** *n.*

**a·nom·a·lous** (ə näm′ə ləs) *adj.* ⟦< Gr *an-*, not + *homos*, the same⟧ **1** abnormal **2** inconsistent or odd

**a·nom′a·ly** (-lē) *n., pl.* -lies **1** abnormality **2** anything anomalous

**a·no·mie** or **an·o·my** (an′ə mē) *n.* ⟦Fr < Gr *anomia*, lawlessness⟧ lack of purpose, identity, etc.

**a·non** (ə nän′) *adv.* ⟦< OE *on an*, into one⟧ [Archaic] **1** soon **2** at another time

**Anon** or **anon** *abbrev.* anonymous

**a·non·y·mous** (ə nän′ə məs) *adj.* ⟦< Gr *an-*, without + *onyma*, name⟧ **1** with no name known **2** given, written, etc. by one whose name is withheld or unknown **3** lacking individuality —**an·o·nym·i·ty** (an′ə nim′ə tē) *n.* —**a·non′y·mous·ly** *adv.*

**a·noph·e·les** (ə näf′ə lēz′) *n.* ⟦< Gr *anōphelēs*, harmful⟧ the mosquito that can transmit malaria

**an·o·rex·i·a** (an′ə reks′ē ə) *n.* ⟦< Gr *an-*, without + *orexis*, desire⟧ an eating disorder characterized by obsession with weight loss: in full **anorexia nervo·sa** (nər vō′sə) —**an′o·rex′ic** *adj., n.*

**an·oth·er** (ə nuth′ər) *adj.* **1** one more; an additional **2** a different —*pron.* **1** one additional **2** a different one **3** one of the same kind

**an·swer** (an′sər) *n.* ⟦< OE *and-*, against + *swerian*, swear⟧ **1** a reply to a question, letter, etc. **2** any act in response **3** a solution to a problem —*vi.* **1** to reply **2** to be sufficient **3** to be responsible or liable (*to* a person *for* an action, etc.) **4** to conform (*to*) [he *answers* to the description] —*vt.* **1** to reply or respond to **2** to serve or fulfill [to *answer* the purpose] **3** to defend oneself against (a charge) **4** to conform to [she *answers* the description] —**answer back** [Inf.] to reply forcefully or insolently —**an′swer·a·ble** *adj.*

**an′swer·ing machine** a device for recording telephone messages automatically

**answering service** a business whose function is to answer telephone calls for its clients

**ant** (ant) *n.* ⟦< OE *æmet(t)e*⟧ any of a family of insects, generally wingless, that live in complex colonies

**ant-** *prefix* ANTI-

**-ant** (ənt) ⟦ult. < L⟧ *suffix* **1** that has, shows, or does [*defiant*] **2** one that [*occupant*]

**ant·ac·id** (ant′as′id) *adj.* counteracting acidity, specif. gastric acidity —*n.* an antacid substance

**an·tag·o·nism** (an tag′ə niz′əm) *n.* ⟦see ANTAGO-NIZE⟧ opposition or hostility

**an·tag'o·nist** *n.* an adversary; opponent —**an·tag'o·nis'tic** *adj.* —**an·tag'o·nis'ti·cal·ly** *adv.*

**an·tag'o·nize** (-nīz') *vt.* -**nized', -niz'ing** ⟦< Gr *anti-*, against + *agōn*, a contest⟧ to incur the dislike of or make an enemy of

**ant·arc'tic** (ant ärk'tik, -är'-) *adj.* ⟦see ANTI- & ARCTIC⟧ of or near the South Pole or the region around it —**the Antarctic** the region including Antarctica and the Antarctic Ocean

**Ant·arc'ti·ca** (-ti kə) land area about the South Pole, completely covered by an ice shelf: *c.* 5,400,000 sq. mi.

**Antarctic Circle** [*also* **a- c-**] an imaginary circle parallel to the equator, *c.* 66°34' south of it

**ant bear** a large anteater of Central America and tropical South America

**an·te** (an'tē) *n.* ⟦L, before⟧ *Poker* the stake that each player must put into the pot before receiving cards —*vt., vi.* -**ted** *or* -**teed, -te·ing** *Poker* to put in (one's ante): also **ante up**

**ante-** ⟦see prec.⟧ *prefix* before in time or place

**ant'eat'er** *n.* a mammal with a long snout, that feeds mainly on ants

**an·te·bel'lum** (an'ti bel'əm) *adj.* ⟦L⟧ before the war; specif., before the American Civil War

**an·te·ced'ent** (an'tə sēd''nt) *adj.* ⟦< L *ante-*, before + *cedere*, go⟧ prior; previous —*n.* **1** any thing prior to another **2** [*pl.*] one's ancestry, past life, etc. **3** *Gram.* the word or phrase to which a pronoun refers

**an·te·cham·ber** (an'ti chām'bər) *n.* a room leading into a larger or main room

**an·te·date'** (-dāt') *vt.* -**dat'ed, -dat'ing 1** to put a date on that is earlier than the actual date **2** to come before in time

**an·te·di·lu'vi·an** (-də lōō've ən) *adj.* ⟦< ANTE- + L *diluvium*, a flood + -AN⟧ **1** of the time before the biblical Flood **2** very old or old-fashioned

**an·te·lope** (an'tə lōp') *n.* ⟦< Gr *antholops*, deer⟧ a swift, cud-chewing, horned animal resembling the deer

**an·te me·ri·di·em** (an'tē mə rid'ē əm) ⟦L⟧ before noon

**an·ten·na** (an ten'ə) *n.* ⟦L, sail yard⟧ **1** *pl.* -**nae** (-ē) *or* -**nas** either of a pair of feelers on the head of an insect, crab, etc. **2** *pl.* -**nas** *Radio, TV* an arrangement of wires, rods, etc. used in sending and receiving electromagnetic waves

**an·te·ri·or** (an tir'ē ər) *adj.* ⟦< L *ante*, before⟧ **1** at or toward the front **2** previous; earlier

**an·te·room** (an'tē rōōm') *n.* a room leading to a larger or main room

**an·them** (an'thəm) *n.* ⟦< Gr *anti-*, over against + *phōnē*, voice⟧ **1** a religious choral song **2** a song of praise or devotion, as to a nation

**an·ther** (an'thər) *n.* ⟦< Gr *anthēros*, blooming⟧ the part of a stamen that produces pollen

**ant'hill'** *n.* the soil heaped up by ants around their nest opening

**an·thol·o·gize** (an thäl'ə jīz') *vi.* -**gized', -giz'ing** to make anthologies —*vt.* to include in an anthology —**an·thol'o·gist** (-jist) *or* **an·thol'o·giz'er** *n.*

**an·thol·o·gy** (-jē) *n., pl.* -**gies** ⟦< Gr *anthos*, flower + *legein*, gather⟧ a collection of poems, stories, songs, etc.

**An·tho·ny** (an'thə nē, -tə-), **Mark** *see* ANTONY, Mark

**an·thra·cite** (an'thrə sīt') *n.* ⟦< Gr *anthrax*, coal⟧ hard coal, which gives much heat and little smoke

**an·thrax** (an'thraks') *n.* ⟦< Gr, coal, carbuncle⟧ an infectious disease of cattle, sheep, etc. that can be transmitted to humans

**anthropo-** ⟦< Gr *anthrōpos*, man⟧ *combining form* man, human

**an·thro·po·cen·tric** (an'thrə pō'sen'trik) *adj.* ⟦see ANTHROPO-⟧ centering one's view of everything around humankind

**an·thro·poid** (an'thrə poid') *adj.* ⟦see ANTHROPO- & -OID⟧ **1** resembling a human **2** apelike —*n.*

any of certain highly developed primates, as the chimpanzee and gorilla

**an·thro·pol·o·gy** (an'thrə päl'ə jē) *n.* ⟦ANTHROPO- + -LOGY⟧ the study of the characteristics, customs, etc. of humanity —**an'thro·po·log'i·cal** (-pə läj'i kəl) *adj.* —**an'thro·pol'o·gist** *n.*

**an·thro·po·mor'phism'** (-pō'môr'fiz'əm) *n.* the attributing of human characteristics to gods, objects, etc. —**an'thro·po·mor'phic** *adj.* —**an'thro·po'mor·phi·cal·ly** *adv.* —**an'thro·po·mor'phize'** (-fīz') **-phized', -phiz'ing**, *vt., vi.*

**an·ti** (an'tī, -tē) [Inf.] *n., pl.* -**tis'** ⟦< fol.⟧ a person opposed to something —**prep.** opposed to

**anti-** ⟦< Gr *anti*, against⟧ *prefix* **1** against, hostile to **2** that operates against **3** that prevents, cures, or neutralizes **4** opposite, reverse **5** rivaling

**an·ti·air·craft** (an'tē er'kraft') *adj.* used against hostile aircraft

**an·ti·bal·lis'tic missile** (-bə lis'tik) a missile intended to destroy an enemy ballistic missile in flight

**an·ti·bi·ot'ic** (-bī ät'ik, -bē-) *n.* ⟦< ANTI- + Gr *bios*, life⟧ any of certain substances, as penicillin or streptomycin, produced by various microorganisms and capable of destroying or weakening bacteria, etc. —*adj.* of antibiotics

**an·ti·bod·y** (an'ti bäd'ē) *n., pl.* -**bod'ies** a protein produced in the body to neutralize a toxin or other antigen

**an·tic** (an'tik) *adj.* ⟦< L: see ANTIQUE⟧ odd and funny —*n.* a playful or ludicrous act, trick, etc.: *usually used in pl.*

**An·ti·christ** (an'ti krīst') *n. Bible* the great opponent of Christ: 1 John 2:18

**an·tic·i·pate** (an tis'ə pāt') *vt.* -**pat'ed, -pat'ing** ⟦< L *ante-*, before + *capere*, take⟧ **1** to look forward to **2** to forestall **3** to use or deal with in advance **4** to be ahead of in doing —**an·tic'i·pa'tion** *n.* —**an·tic'i·pa·to·ry** (-pə tôr'ē) *adj.*

**an·ti·cli·max** (an'ti klī'maks') *n.* **1** a sudden drop from the important to the trivial **2** a descent which is in disappointing contrast to a preceding rise —**an'ti·cli·mac'tic** (-klī mak'tik) *adj.*

**an·ti·cline** (an'ti klīn') *n.* ⟦< ANTI- + Gr *klinein*, to lean⟧ *Geol.* a sharply arched fold of stratified rock

**an·ti·co·ag·u·lant** (an'ti kō ag'yōō lənt) *n.* a drug or substance that delays or prevents the clotting of blood

**an·ti·de·pres'sant** (-dē pres'ənt) *adj.* lessening emotional depression —*n.* an antidepressant drug

**an·ti·dote** (an'tə dōt') *n.* ⟦< Gr *anti-*, against + *dotos*, given⟧ **1** a remedy to counteract a poison **2** anything that works against an evil or unwanted condition

**an·ti·freeze** (an'ti frēz') *n.* a substance used, as in the radiator of an automobile, to prevent freezing

**an·ti·gen** (an'tə jən) *n.* ⟦ANTI- + -GEN⟧ any substance to which the body reacts by producing antibodies

**An·ti·gua and Bar·bu·da** (an tē'gwə 'n bär bōō'də) country in the E West Indies, consisting of three small islands: 171 sq. mi.; pop. 66,000

**an·ti·he·ro** (an'tī hir'ō) *n., pl.* -**roes** the protagonist of a novel, etc. who lacks the virtues of a traditional hero

**an·ti·his·ta·mine** (an'ti his'tə mēn', -min) *n.* any of several drugs used to block histamine, as in allergic reactions

**an·ti·in·flam·ma·to·ry** (an'tē in flam'ə tôr'ē) *adj.* reducing inflammation —*n.* an anti-inflammatory medication, as aspirin

**an·ti·knock** (an'tī näk') *n.* a substance added to the fuel of internal-combustion engines to reduce noise resulting from too rapid combustion

**An·til·les** (an til'ēz') group of islands of the West Indies, including Cuba, Jamaica, etc. (**Greater Antilles**) & the Leeward Islands and Windward Islands (**Lesser Antilles**)

**an·ti·lock** (an'tē läk') *adj.* designating an automotive braking system that prevents the wheels from locking during a sudden stop

**an·ti·log·a·rithm** (an'ti lôg'ə rith'əm) *n.* the number resulting when a base is raised to a power by a logarithm

**an·ti·ma·cas·sar** (an'ti mə kas'ər) *n.* ⟦ANTI- + *macassar*, a hair oil⟧ a small cover on the back or arms of a chair, sofa, etc. to prevent soiling

**an·ti·mat·ter** (an'ti mat'ər) *n.* a form of matter in which the electrical charge or other property of each particle is the reverse of that in the usual matter of our universe

**an·ti·mis·sile** (an'tī mis'əl) *adj.* designed as a defense against ballistic missiles

**an·ti·mo·ny** (an'tə mō'nē) *n.* ⟦< ML⟧ a silvery-white, nonmetallic chemical element used in alloys to harden them

**an·ti·pas·to** (an'ti päs'tō, -pas'-) *n.* ⟦It < *anti-*, before + *pasto*, food⟧ an appetizer of meats, cheeses, marinated vegetables, etc.

**an·tip·a·thy** (an tip'ə thē) *n., pl.* **-thies** ⟦< Gr *anti-*, against + *pathein*, to suffer⟧ 1 strong dislike; aversion 2 the object of such dislike

**an·ti·per·son·nel** (an'ti pur'sə nel') *adj.* intended to destroy people rather than objects [*antipersonnel* mines]

**an'ti·per'spi·rant** (-pur'spə rənt) *n.* a substance applied to the skin to reduce perspiration

**an·tiph·o·nal** (an tif'ə nəl) *adj.* ⟦see ANTHEM⟧ sung or chanted in alternation

**an·tip·o·des** (an tip'ə dēz') *pl.n.* ⟦< Gr *anti-*, opposite + *pous*, foot⟧ any two places directly opposite each other on the earth —**an·tip'o·dal** *adj.*

**an·ti·quar·i·an** (an'ti kwer'ē ən) *adj.* 1 of antiques or antiquities 2 of antiquaries 3 dealing in old books —*n.* an antiquary

**an·ti·quar·y** (an'ti kwer'ē) *n., pl.* **-quar·ies** a collector or student of antiquities

**an·ti·quate'** (-kwāt') *vt.* **-quat·ed, -quat·ing** ⟦see fol.⟧ to make old, out-of-date, or obsolete —**an'ti·quat'ed** *adj.* —**an'ti·qua'tion** *n.*

**an·tique** (an tēk') *adj.* ⟦< L *antiquus*, ancient⟧ 1 of ancient times 2 out-of-date 3 of, or in the style of, a former period 4 dealing in antiques —*n.* 1 any ancient relic 2 a piece of furniture, etc. from a former period —*vt.* **-tiqued', -tiqu'ing** to make look antique —*vi.* to shop for antique furniture, etc.

**an·tiq·ui·ty** (an tik'wə tē) *n., pl.* **-ties** ⟦see prec.⟧ 1 the ancient period of history 2 great age 3 [*pl.*] relics, etc. of the distant past

**an·ti·Se·mit·ic** (an'tē sə mit'ik) *adj.* 1 having or showing prejudice against Jews 2 discriminating against or persecuting Jews Also **an'ti·se·mit'ic** —**an'ti·Sem'ite'** (-sem'īt') *n.* —**an'ti·Sem'i·tism'** (-ə tiz'əm) *n.*

**an·ti·sep·sis** (an'tə sep'sis) *n.* ⟦ANTI- + SEPSIS⟧ 1 a being antiseptic 2 the use of antiseptics

**an·ti·sep·tic** (-tik) *adj.* 1 preventing infection, decay, etc. by acting against bacteria, etc. 2 using antiseptics 3 sterile —*n.* any antiseptic substance —**an'ti·sep'ti·cal·ly** *adv.*

**an·ti·se·rum** (an'ti sir'əm) *n., pl.* **-rums** or **-ra** a serum containing antibodies

**an'ti·slav'er·y** (an'tī-) *adj.* against slavery

**an'ti·so'cial** *adj.* 1 not sociable; avoiding others 2 harmful to the welfare of people

**an'ti·tank'** *adj.* for use against tanks in war

**an·tith·e·sis** (an tith'ə sis) *n., pl.* **-ses'** (-sēz') ⟦< Gr *anti-*, against + *tithenai*, to place⟧ 1 a contrast or opposition, as of ideas 2 the exact opposite —**an·ti·thet·i·cal** (an'tə thet'i kəl) *adj.* —**an'ti·thet'i·cal·ly** *adv.*

**an·ti·tox·in** (an'ti täks'in) *n.* 1 a circulating antibody formed by the body to act against a specific toxin 2 a serum containing an antitoxin, injected into a person to prevent a disease

**an·ti·trust'** (an'tī trust') *adj.* opposed to or regulating trusts, or business monopolies

**an·ti·vi·ral** (an'tī vī'rəl) *adj.* capable of checking the growth of a virus

**an'ti·viv'i·sec'tion·ist** (-viv'ə sek'shən ist) *n.* one opposing vivisection

**ant·ler** (ant'lər) *n.* ⟦< OFr *antoillier*⟧ the branched, bony growth on the head of any animal of the deer family —**ant'lered** (-lərd) *adj.*

**An·to·ny** (an'tə nē), **Mark** (or **Marc**) 83?-30 B.C.; Rom. general

**an·to·nym** (an'tə nim') *n.* ⟦< Gr *anti-*, opposite + *onyma*, name⟧ a word meaning the opposite of another

**Ant·werp** (an'twurp') seaport in N Belgium: pop. 459,000

**a·nus** (ā'nəs) *n., pl.* **a'nus·es** or **a'ni'** (-nī') ⟦L⟧ the opening at the lower end of the alimentary canal

**an·vil** (an'vəl) *n.* ⟦< OE *anfilt*⟧ 1 an iron or steel block on which metal objects are hammered into shape 2 one of three small bones in the middle ear

**anx·i·e·ty** (aŋ zī'ə tē) *n., pl.* **-ties** ⟦see fol.⟧ 1 worry or uneasiness about what may happen 2 an eager but uneasy desire [*anxiety* to do well]

**anx·ious** (aŋk'shəs) *adj.* ⟦< L *angere*, to choke⟧ 1 worried 2 causing anxiety 3 eagerly wishing — **anx'ious·ly** *adv.*

**an·y** (en'ē) *adj.* ⟦OE *ænig*⟧ 1 one, no matter which, of more than two [*any* boy may go] 2 some [has he *any* pain?] 3 without limit [*any* number can play] 4 even one or the least amount of [I haven't *any* dimes] 5 every [*any* child can do it] —*pron.* (*sing. & pl.*) any one or ones —*adv.* to any degree or extent; at all [is he *any* better today?]

**an'y·bod'y** (-bäd'ē, -bud'ē) *pron.* any person —*n., pl.* **-bod'ies** a person of some importance

**an'y·how'** *adv.* ANYWAY

**an'y·more'** *adv.* now; nowadays

**an'y·one'** *pron.* any person; anybody

**any one** any single (person or thing)

**an'y·place'** *adv.* [Inf.] in, at, or to any place

**an'y·thing'** *pron.* any object, event, fact, etc. —*n.* a thing, no matter of what kind —*adv.* in any way —**anything but** not at all

**an'y·time'** *adv.* at any time —*conj.* WHENEVER

**an'y·way'** *adv.* 1 in any manner 2 nevertheless; anyhow 3 haphazardly

**an'y·where'** *adv.* 1 in, at, or to any place 2 [Inf.] at all

**A/o** or **a/o** *abbrev.* account of

**A-OK** (ā'ō kā') *adj.* ⟦A(LL) OK⟧ [Inf.] excellent, fine, in working order, etc.: also **A'-O·kay'**

**A one** (ā' wun') [Inf.] first-class: also **A 1** or **A number 1**

**a·or·ta** (ā ôr'tə) *n., pl.* **-tas** or **-tae** (-tē) ⟦< Gr *aeirein*, to raise⟧ the main artery of the body, carrying blood from the heart —**a·or'tic** or **a·or'tal** *adj.*

**AP** *abbrev.* Associated Press

**a·pace** (ə pās') *adv.* at a fast pace

**A·pach·e** (ə pach'ē) *n., pl.* **-es** or **-e** ⟦AmSp⟧ a member of a group of North American Indians of the SW U.S.

**a·part** (ə pärt') *adv.* ⟦< L *ad*, to, at + *pars*, part⟧ 1 aside 2 away in place or time 3 in or to pieces — *adj.* separated —**apart from** other than —**tell apart** to distinguish between or among

**a·part·heid** (ə pär'tāt', -tīt') *n.* ⟦Afrik, separateness⟧ the official policy of racial segregation as practiced in South Africa, *c.* 1950-91

**a·part'ment** *n.* ⟦< It *appartare*, to separate⟧ a room or suite of rooms to live in, esp. one of a number in an **apartment building** (or **house**)

**ap·a·thy** (ap'ə thē) *n., pl.* **-thies** ⟦< Gr *a-*, without + *pathos*, emotion⟧ 1 lack of emotion 2 lack of interest; indifference; listlessness —**ap'a·thet'ic** (-thet'ik) *adj.* —**ap'a·thet'i·cal·ly** *adv.*

**ap·a·tite** (ap'ə tīt') *n.* ⟦< Ger < Gr *apatē*, deceit⟧ a mineral incorporating calcium phosphate and found in rocks, bones, and teeth

**a·pat·o·saur·us** (ə pat'ə sôr'əs) *n.* a huge, plant-eating dinosaur

**APB** (ā'pē'bē') *n.* all-points bulletin

**ape** (āp) *n.* ⟦< OE *apa*⟧ 1 any gibbon or great ape

2 loosely, any monkey 3 a mimic 4 a person who is uncouth, clumsy, etc. —*vt.* **aped, ap′ing** to mimic —**ape′like′** *adj.*

**Ap·en·nines** (ap′ə nīnz′) mountain range of central Italy

**a·pe·ri·tif** (ə per′ə tēf′) *n.* [Fr] an alcoholic drink taken before a meal

**ap·er·ture** (ap′ər chər) *n.* [< L *aperire*, to open] an opening; hole

**a·pex** (ā′peks′) *n., pl.* **a′pex′es** or **ap·i·ces** (ap′ə sēz′) [L] 1 the highest point 2 the pointed end; tip 3 the climax

**a·pha·sia** (ə fā′zhə) *n.* [Gr < *a-*, not + *phanai*, to say] loss of the power to use or understand words —**a·pha′sic** (-zik) *adj.,* n.

**a·phe·li·on** (ə fē′lē ən) *n., pl.* **-li·ons** or **-li·a** (-ə) [< Gr *apo-*, from + *hēlios*, sun] the point farthest from the sun in the orbit of a planet or comet, or of a man-made satellite

**a·phid** (ā′fid, af′id) *n.* [< ModL *aphis*] an insect that lives on plants by sucking their juices

**aph·o·rism** (af′ə riz′əm) *n.* [< Gr *apo-*, from + *horizein*, to bound] a concise statement of a general truth; maxim; adage —**aph′o·ris′tic** *adj.* — **aph′o·ris′ti·cal·ly** *adv.*

**aph·ro·di·si·ac** (af′rə dē′zē ak′) *adj.* [ult. after fol.] arousing or increasing sexual desire —*n.* an aphrodisiac drug, etc.

**Aph·ro·di·te** (af′rə dīt′ē) *n.* the Greek goddess of love and beauty

**a·pi·ar·y** (ā′pē er′ē) *n., pl.* **-ar·ies** [< L *apis*, bee] a place where bees are kept —**a′pi·a·rist** (-ə rist) *n.*

**a·piece** (ə pēs′) *adv.* [ME *a pece*] for each one; each

**a·plen·ty** (ə plen′tē) *adj., adv.* [Inf.] in abundance

**a·plomb** (ə pläm′, -plum′) *n.* [Fr: see PLUMB] self-possession; poise

**a·poc·a·lypse** (ə päk′ə lips′) *n.* [< Gr *apokalyptein*, disclose] 1 a revelation of a violent struggle in which evil will be destroyed 2 a disastrous event, esp. the end of the world 3 [A-] *Bible* the book of Revelation —**a·poc′a·lyp′tic** (-lip′tik) *adj.*

**A·poc·ry·pha** (ə päk′rə fə) *pl.n.* [< Gr *apo-*, away + *kryptein*, to hide] fourteen books of the Septuagint rejected in Judaism and Protestantism: eleven are in the Roman Catholic Bible

**a·poc′ry·phal** (-fəl) *adj.* 1 of doubtful authenticity 2 not genuine; spurious

**ap·o·gee** (ap′ə jē′) *n.* [< Gr *apo-*, from + *gē*, earth] the point farthest from the earth in the orbit of the moon or a satellite

**a·po·lit·i·cal** (ā′pə lit′i kəl) *adj.* not concerned with political matters —**a′po·lit′i·cal·ly** *adv.*

**A·pol·lo** (ə päl′ō) *n.* 1 the Greek and Roman god of music, poetry, prophecy, and medicine 2 *pl.* **-los** a handsome young man

**a·pol·o·get·ic** (ə päl′ə jet′ik) *adj.* showing regret; making an apology —**a·pol′o·get′i·cal·ly** *adv.*

**a·pol·o·gist** (ə päl′ə jist) *n.* one who defends or attempts to justify a doctrine, faith, action, etc.

**a·pol′o·gize** (-jīz′) *vi.* **-gized′, -giz′ing** to make an apology —**a·pol′o·giz′er** *n.*

**a·pol·o·gy** (ə päl′ə jē) *n., pl.* **-gies** [< Gr *apo-*, from + *logos*, speech] 1 a formal defense of some idea, doctrine, etc.: also **a·po·lo·gi·a** (ap′ə lō′jē ə) 2 an expression of regret for a fault, insult, etc.

**ap·o·plex·y** (ap′ə plek′sē) *n.* [< Gr *apo-*, from + *plēssein*, to strike] [Old-fashioned] STROKE (*n.* 3) —**ap′o·plec′tic** (-plek′tik) *adj.*

**a·pos·ta·sy** (ə päs′tə sē) *n., pl.* **-sies** [< Gr *apo-*, away + *stasis*, a standing] an abandoning of what one has believed in, as a faith or cause

**a·pos′tate′** (-tāt′) *n.* a person guilty of apostasy

**a·pos′ta·tize′** (-tə tīz′) *vi.* **-tized′, -tiz′ing** to become an apostate

**a pos·te·ri·o·ri** (ā′ päs tir′ē ôr′ī′) [L] 1 from effect to cause 2 based on observation or experience

**a·pos·tle** (ə päs′əl) *n.* [< Gr *apo-*, from + *stellein*,

send] 1 [*usually* A-] any of the disciples of Jesus, esp. the original twelve 2 the leader of a new movement

**ap·os·tol·ic** (ap′əs täl′ik) *adj.* 1 of the Apostles or their teachings, work, etc. 2 [*often* A-] of the pope; papal

**a·pos·tro·phe** (ə päs′trə fē) *n.* [< Gr *apo-*, from + *strephein*, to turn] 1 a mark (′) indicating: *a)* omission of a letter or letters from a word (Ex.: *it's* for *it is*) *b)* the possessive case (Ex.: *Mary's* dress) *c)* certain plural forms (Ex.: five *6's*, dot the *i's*) 2 an exclamatory address to a person or thing

**a·poth·e·car·y** (ə päth′ə ker′ē) *n., pl.* **-ies** [< Gr *apothēkē*, storehouse] [Old-fashioned] a pharmacist or druggist

**ap·o·thegm** (ap′ə them′) *n.* [< Gr *apo-*, from + *phthengesthai*, to utter] a short, pithy saying

**a·poth·e·o·sis** (ə päth′ē ō′sis, ap′ə thē′ə sis) *n., pl.* **-ses** (-sēz′) [< Gr *apo-*, from + *theos*, god] 1 the deifying of a person 2 the glorification of a person or thing 3 a glorified ideal

**Ap·pa·la·chi·a** (ap′ə lā′chə, -chē ə; -lach′ə) the highland region of the E U.S. extending from SW Pennsylvania through N Alabama

**Ap′pa·la′chi·an Mountains** mountain system extending from S Quebec to N Alabama: also **Appalachians**

**ap·pall** or **ap·pal** (ə pôl′) *vt.* **-palled′, -pal′ling** [ult. < L *ad*, to + *pallere*, to be pale] to horrify, dismay, or shock

**ap·pa·loo·sa** (ap′ə lōō′sə) *n.* [after *Palouse* Indians of NW U.S.] a Western saddle horse with black and white spots on the rump and loins

**ap·pa·ra·tus** (ap′ə rat′əs, -rāt′-) *n., pl.* **-tus** or **-tus·es** [< L *ad-*, to + *parare*, prepare] 1 the instruments, materials, tools, etc. for a specific use 2 any complex device, machine, or system

**ap·par·el** (ə per′əl) *n.* [ult. < L *ad-*, to + *parere*, prepare] clothing; attire —*vt.* **-eled** or **-elled, -eling** or **-el·ling** to clothe; dress

**ap·par·ent** (ə per′ənt) *adj.* [see APPEAR] 1 readily seen; visible 2 evident; obvious 3 appearing real or true —**ap·par′ent·ly** *adv.*

**ap·pa·ri·tion** (ap′ə rish′ən) *n.* [see APPEAR] 1 anything that appears unexpectedly or in a strange way 2 a ghost; phantom

**ap·peal** (ə pēl′) *vt.* [< L *ad-*, to + *pellere*, to drive] to make an appeal of (a case) —*vi.* 1 to appeal a law case to a higher court 2 to make an urgent request (*to* a person *for* help, etc.) 3 to be attractive or interesting —*n.* 1 a call upon some authority for a decision 2 a request for the transference of a case to a higher court for rehearing 3 a request for help, etc. 4 a quality that arouses interest, desire, etc. —**ap·peal′ing** *adj.*

**ap·pear** (ə pir′) *vi.* [< L *ad-*, to + *perere*, be visible] 1 to come into sight 2 to come into being 3 to become understood or obvious 4 to seem; look 5 to present oneself formally in court 6 to come before the public

**ap·pear′ance** *n.* 1 an appearing 2 the look or outward aspect of a person or thing 3 an outward show; pretense —**keep up appearances** to maintain an outward show of being proper, prosperous, etc. —**ap·peal′ing** *adj.*

**ap·pease** (ə pēz′) *vt.* **-peased′, -peas′ing** [ult. < L *ad*, to + *pax*, peace] to pacify, quiet, or satisfy, esp. by giving in to the demands of —**ap·pease′ment** *n.* —**ap·peas′er** *n.*

**ap·pel·lant** (ə pel′ənt) *n.* a person who appeals to a higher court

**ap·pel′late** (-it) *adj. Law* having to do with appeals [*an appellate* court]

**ap·pel·la·tion** (ap′ə lā′shən) *n.* [see APPEAL] 1 a naming 2 a name or title

**ap·pend** (ə pend′) *vt.* [< L *ad-*, to + *pendere*, hang] to attach or affix; add as a supplement or appendix

**ap·pend′age** *n.* 1 anything appended 2 any external organ or part, as a tail

**ap·pen·dec·to·my** (ap′ən dek′tə mē) *n., pl.* **-mies**

[see -ECTOMY] the surgical removal of the appendix

**ap·pen·di·ci·tis** (ə pen'də sīt'is) *n.* [see -ITIS] inflammation of the appendix

**ap·pen·dix** (ə pen'diks) *n.*, *pl.* **-dix·es** or **-di·ces'** (-də sēz') [L, appendage] 1 additional material at the end of a book 2 a small, saclike appendage of the large intestine

**ap·per·tain** (ap'ər tān') *vi.* [< L *ad-*, to + *pertinere*, to reach] to belong as a function, part, etc.; pertain

**ap·pe·ten·cy** (ap'ə tən sē) *n.*, *pl.* **-cies** [see fol.] a craving; appetite

**ap·pe·tite** (ap'ə tīt') *n.* [< L *ad-*, to + *petere*, to desire] 1 a desire for food 2 any strong desire or craving

**ap'pe·tiz'er** (-tī'zər) *n.* a small portion of a tasty food to stimulate the appetite

**ap'pe·tiz'ing** (-tī'ziŋ) *adj.* 1 stimulating the appetite 2 savory; delicious

**ap·plaud** (ə plôd') *vt.*, *vi.* [< L *ad-*, to + *plaudere*, clap hands] 1 to show approval (of) by clapping the hands, etc. 2 to approve —**ap·plaud'er** *n.*

**ap·plause** (ə plôz') *n.* approval, esp. as shown by clapping hands

**ap·ple** (ap'əl) *n.* [< OE *æppel*, fruit, apple] 1 a firm, round, edible fruit 2 the tree it grows on

**apple butter** a thick, sweet spread made from apples stewed with spices

**ap'ple·jack'** *n.* brandy distilled from fermented cider

**ap'ple-pie'** *adj.* [Inf.] 1 neat and tidy [apple-pie order] 2 suggesting wholesomeness

**ap'ple·sauce'** *n.* a dessert or relish of apples cooked to a pulp in water and sweetened

**ap·pli·ance** (ə plī'əns) *n.* a device or machine, esp. one for household use

**ap·pli·ca·ble** (ap'li kə bəl) *adj.* that can be applied; appropriate —**ap'pli·ca·bil'i·ty** (-bil'ə tē) *n.*

**ap'pli·cant** (-kənt) *n.* one who applies, as for employment or help

**ap·pli·ca·tion** (ap'li kā'shən) *n.* 1 an applying 2 anything applied, as a remedy 3 a specific use 4 a request, or a form filled out in making one [an employment *application*] 5 continued effort; diligence 6 relevance or practicality 7 a computer program for performing a specific task

**ap·pli·ca·tor** (ap'li kāt'ər) *n.* any device for applying medicine or paint, polish, etc.

**ap·plied** (ə plīd') *adj.* used in actual practice [applied science]

**ap·pli·qué** (ap'li kā') *n.* [Fr] a decoration made of one material attached to another —*vt.* **-quéd'**, **-qué'ing** to decorate with appliqué

**ap·ply** (ə plī') *vt.* **-plied'**, **-ply'ing** [< L *ad-*, to + *plicare*, to fold] 1 to put or spread on [apply glue] 2 to put to practical or specific use [apply your knowledge] 3 to devote (oneself or one's faculties) diligently —*vi.* 1 to make a formal request 2 to be suitable or relevant —**ap·pli'er** *n.*

**ap·point** (ə point') *vt.* [< L *ad*, to + *punctum*, a point] 1 to set (a date, place, etc.) 2 to name for an office, position, etc. 3 to furnish [well-*appointed*] —**ap·point'ee'** *n.*

**ap·point'ive** *adj.* of or filled by appointment [an appointive office]

**ap·point'ment** *n.* 1 an appointing or being appointed 2 a position filled by appointing 3 an arrangement to meet someone or be somewhere 4 [pl.] furniture; equipment

**Ap·po·mat·tox Court House** (ap'ə mat'əks) former village in central Virginia, where Lee surrendered to Grant (1865)

**ap·por·tion** (ə pôr'shən) *vt.* [see AD- & PORTION] to distribute in shares according to a plan —**ap·por'tion·ment** *n.*

**ap·pose** (ə pōz') *vt.* **-posed'**, **-pos'ing** [< L *ad-*, to + *ponere*, put] to put side by side or opposite

**ap·po·site** (ap'ə zit) *adj.* [see prec.] appropriate; apt —**ap'po·site·ly** *adv.* —**ap'po·site·ness** *n.*

**ap·po·si·tion** (ap'ə zish'ən) *n.* 1 an apposing, or the position resulting from this 2 the placing of a word or phrase beside another in explanation ["my niece" is in *apposition* with "Jill" in "Jill, my niece, is here"] —**ap·pos·i·tive** (ə päz'ə tiv) *adj.*, *n.*

**ap·prais·al** (ə prāz'əl) *n.* 1 an appraising 2 an appraised value

**ap·praise** (ə prāz') *vt.* **-praised'**, **-prais'ing** [< L *ad*, to + *pretium*, price] 1 to set a price for; estimate the value of 2 to judge the quality or worth of —**ap·prais'er** *n.*

**ap·pre·ci·a·ble** (ə prē'shə bəl, -shē ə-) *adj.* [see prec.] enough to be perceived or estimated; noticeable —**ap·pre'ci·a·bly** *adv.*

**ap·pre·ci·ate** (ə prē'shē āt') *vt.* **-at'ed**, **-at'ing** [see APPRAISE] 1 to think well of; esteem 2 to recognize gratefully 3 to estimate the quality of 4 to be fully or sensitively aware of —*vi.* to rise in value —**ap·pre'ci·a'tor** *n.* —**ap·pre'ci·a·to'ry** (-shə tôr'ē, -shē ə-) *adj.*

**ap·pre·ci·a'tion** *n.* 1 grateful recognition, as of a favor 2 sensitive awareness, as of art 3 a rise in value or price

**ap·pre'ci·a·tive** (-shə tiv, -shē ə-) *adj.* feeling or showing appreciation —**ap·pre'ci·a·tive·ly** *adv.*

**ap·pre·hend** (ap'rē hend') *vt.* [< L *ad-*, to + *prehendere*, take] 1 to capture or arrest 2 to perceive; understand 3 to fear; dread

**ap'pre·hen'sion** (-hen'shən) *n.* 1 capture or arrest 2 perception or understanding 3 fear; anxiety

**ap'pre·hen'sive** (-siv) *adj.* anxious; uneasy —**ap'pre·hen'sive·ly** *adv.* —**ap'pre·hen'sive·ness** *n.*

**ap·pren·tice** (ə pren'tis) *n.* [see APPREHEND] 1 a person being taught a craft or trade, now usually as a member of a labor union 2 any beginner —*vt.* **-ticed**, **-tic·ing** to place or accept as an apprentice —**ap·pren'tice·ship'** *n.*

**ap·prise** or **ap·prize** (ə prīz') *vt.* **-prised'** or **-prized'**, **-pris'ing** or **-priz'ing** [see APPREHEND] to inform or notify

**ap·proach** (ə prōch') *vi.* [< L *ad-*, to + *propius*, nearer] to come closer —*vt.* 1 to come nearer to 2 to approximate 3 to make a proposal or request to 4 to begin dealing with —*n.* 1 a coming closer 2 an approximation 3 an overture (to someone): usually used in pl. 4 a means of reaching a person or place; access 5 a means of attaining a goal —**ap·proach'a·ble** *adj.*

**ap·pro·ba·tion** (ap'rə bā'shən) *n.* [see APPROVE] approval

**ap·pro·pri·ate** (ə prō'prē āt'; for adj., -it) *vt.* **-at'ed**, **-at'ing** [< L *ad-*, to + *proprius*, one's own] 1 to take for one's own use, often improperly 2 to set aside (money, etc.) for a specific use —*adj.* suitable; fit; proper —**ap·pro'pri·ate·ly** *adv.* —**ap·pro'pri·ate·ness** *n.* —**ap·pro'pri·a'tor** *n.*

**ap·pro·pri·a'tion** *n.* 1 an appropriating or being appropriated 2 money set aside for a specific use

**ap·prov·al** (ə prōo'vəl) *n.* 1 the act of approving 2 favorable attitude or opinion 3 formal consent —**on approval** for the customer to examine and decide whether to buy or return

**ap·prove** (ə prōov') *vt.* **-proved'**, **-prov'ing** [< L *ad-*, to + *probus*, good] 1 to give one's consent to 2 to consider to be good, satisfactory, etc. —*vi.* to have a favorable opinion (of) —**ap·prov'ing·ly** *adv.*

**ap·prox·i·mate** (ə präk'sə mit; for v., -māt') *adj.* [< L *ad-*, to + *proximus*, nearest] 1 much like; resembling 2 more or less correct or exact —*vt.* **-mat'ed**, **-mat'ing** to come near to; be almost the same as —**ap·prox'i·mate·ly** *adv.*

**ap·prox'i·ma'tion** *n.* an estimate or guess that is approximately correct

**ap·pur·te·nance** (ə purt'n əns) *n.* [see APPERTAIN] 1 anything added to a more important thing 2 [pl.] apparatus or equipment 3 Law an incidental right attached to some thing

**APR** *abbrev.* annual percentage rate

**ap·ri·cot** (ap′ri kät′, ā′pri-) *n.* ⟦Fr *abricot* < L *praecoquum*, early matured (fruit)⟧ **1** a small, yellowish-orange, peachlike fruit **2** the tree it grows on

**A·pril** (ā′prəl) *n.* ⟦< L⟧ the fourth month of the year, having 30 days: abbrev. **Apr**

**a pri·o·ri** (ā′ prī ôr′ī) ⟦L⟧ **1** from cause to effect; deductive or deductively **2** based on theory, logic, etc. instead of experience

**a·pron** (ā′prən) *n.* ⟦< L *mappa*, napkin⟧ **1** a garment worn over the front part of the body to protect one's clothes **2** any extending or protecting part **3** a paved area, as where a driveway broadens to meet the road **4** the part of a stage in front of the proscenium arch

**ap·ro·pos** (ap′rə pō′) *adv.* ⟦Fr *à propos*, to the purpose⟧ at the right time; opportunely —*adj.* relevant; apt —*prep.* with regard to —**apropos of** with regard to

**apse** (aps) *n.* ⟦L *apsis*, an arch⟧ a semicircular or polygonal projection of a church, usually domed or vaulted

**apt**[1] (apt) *adj.* ⟦< L *aptus*⟧ **1** appropriate; fitting [an *apt* remark] **2** tending or inclined; likely [*apt* to rain] **3** quick to learn —**apt′ly** *adv.* —**apt′ness** *n.*

**apt**[2] *abbrev.* apartment

**ap·ti·tude** (ap′tə tōōd′) *n.* ⟦see APT[1]⟧ **1** a natural tendency, ability, or talent **2** quickness to learn

**aq·ua** (ak′wə, äk′-) *n., pl.* **-uas** or **-uae′** (-wē′) ⟦L⟧ water —*adj.* ⟦< AQUAMARINE⟧ bluish-green

**aq′ua·cul′ture** *n.* ⟦prec. + CULTURE⟧ the cultivation of water plants and animals for human use

**aq′ua·ma·rine′** *n.* ⟦L *aqua marina*, sea water⟧ bluish green —*adj.* bluish-green

**aq′ua·naut′** (-nôt′) *n.* ⟦AQUA + (ASTRO)NAUT⟧ one trained to use a watertight underwater chamber as a base for undersea experiments

**aq′ua·plane′** *n.* ⟦AQUA + PLANE[1]⟧ a board on which one rides standing up as it is pulled by a motorboat —*vi.* **-planed′, -plan′ing** to ride on such a board as a sport

**a·quar·i·um** (ə kwer′ē əm) *n., pl.* **-i·ums** or **-i·a** (-ə) ⟦< L *aquarius*, of water⟧ **1** a tank, etc. for keeping live water animals and plants **2** a building where such collections are exhibited

**A·quar′i·us** (-əs) *n.* ⟦L, water carrier⟧ the 11th sign of the zodiac

**a·quat·ic** (ə kwat′ik, -kwät′-) *adj.* **1** growing or living in water **2** done in or upon the water [*aquatic* sports]

**aq·ua·vit** (ak′wə vēt′, äk′-) *n.* ⟦< L *aqua vitae*, water of life⟧ a Scandinavian alcoholic liquor distilled from grain or potatoes and flavored with caraway

**aq·ue·duct** (ak′wə dukt′) *n.* ⟦< L *aqua*, water + *ductus*, a leading⟧ **1** a large pipe or conduit for bringing water from a distant source **2** an elevated structure supporting this

**a·que·ous** (ā′kwē əs, ak′wē-) *adj.* of, like, or formed by water

**aqueous humor** a watery fluid in the space between the cornea and the lens of the eye

**aq·ui·fer** (ak′wə fər, äk′-) *n.* ⟦< L *aqua*, water + *ferre*, carry⟧ an underground layer of porous rock, etc. containing water

**aq·ui·line** (ak′wə līn′, -lin) *adj.* ⟦< L *aquila*, eagle⟧ **1** of or like an eagle **2** curved like an eagle's beak [an *aquiline* nose]

**A·qui·nas** (ə kwī′nəs), Saint **Thom·as** (täm′əs) (1225?-74); It. theologian & philosopher

**Ar** *Chem. symbol for* argon

**AR** Arkansas

**Ar·ab** (ar′əb, er̲′-) *n.* **1** a person born or living in Arabia **2** a member of a Semitic people orig. living in Arabia, now throughout the Middle East

**ar·a·besque** (ar′ə besk′, er′-) *n.* ⟦< It *Arabo*, Arab⟧ an elaborate design of intertwined lines suggesting flowers, foliage, etc.

**A·ra·bi·a** (ə rā′bē ə) peninsula in SW Asia —**A·ra′bi·an** *adj., n.*

**Arabian camel** the one-humped camel ranging from N Africa to India

ARABESQUE

**Arabian Nights, The** a collection of tales from Arabia, India, Persia, etc.

**Arabian Peninsula** ARABIA

**Ar·a·bic** (ar′ə bik, er′-) *adj.* **1** of Arabia **2** of the Arabs or their language or culture —*n.* the Semitic language of the Arabs, spoken in Arabia, Syria, N Africa, etc.

**Arabic numerals** the figures 1, 2, 3, 4, 5, 6, 7, 8, 9, and the 0 (zero)

**ar·a·ble** (ar′ə bəl, er′-) *adj.* ⟦< L *arare*, to plow⟧ suitable for plowing and farming

**a·rach·nid** (ə rak′nid) *n.* ⟦< Gr *arachnē*, spider⟧ any of a class of arthropods with four pairs of legs, including spiders and scorpions

**Ar·a·ma·ic** (ar′ə mā′ik, er′-) *n.* a Semitic language spoken during biblical times

**ar·bi·ter** (är′bət ər) *n.* ⟦L, a witness or judge⟧ an arbitrator; judge

**ar·bi·trage** (är′bə träzh′) *n.* ⟦see prec.⟧ the simultaneous purchase and sale, as of stock, in two financial markets to profit from a price difference

**ar·bit·ra·ment** (är bi′trə mənt) *n.* **1** arbitration **2** an arbitrator's verdict or award

**ar·bi·trar·y** (är′bə trer′ē) *adj.* ⟦see ARBITER⟧ **1** left to one's judgment **2** based on one's preference or whim; capricious **3** absolute; despotic —**ar′bi·trar′i·ly** *adv.*

**ar·bi·trate** (-trāt′) *vt., vi.* **-trat·ed, -trat·ing** ⟦see ARBITER⟧ **1** to submit (a dispute) to an arbitrator **2** to decide (a dispute) as an arbitrator —**ar′bi·tra′tion** *n.*

**ar′bi·tra′tor** *n.* a person selected to judge a dispute, as in collective bargaining

**ar·bor** (är′bər) *n.* ⟦< L *herba*, grass, herb⟧ a place shaded by trees or shrubs or by vines on a latticework; bower

**ar·bo·re·al** (är bôr′ē əl) *adj.* ⟦< L *arbor*, tree⟧ **1** of or like a tree **2** living in trees

**ar·bo·re·tum** (är′bə rēt′əm) *n., pl.* **-tums** or **-ta** (-ə) ⟦L⟧ a place where many kinds of trees and shrubs are grown for exhibition or study

**ar·bor·vi·tae** (är′bər vīt′ē) *n.* ⟦L, tree of life⟧ any of various cypress trees having sprays of scalelike leaves

**ar·bu·tus** (är byōōt′əs) *n.* ⟦L⟧ **1** a tree or shrub with dark-green leaves and strawberrylike fruit **2** a trailing plant with white or pink flower clusters

**arc** (ärk) *n.* ⟦< L *arcus*, a bow, arch⟧ **1** a bowlike curved line or object **2** the band of incandescent light formed when a current leaps a short gap between electrodes **3** any part of a curve, esp. of a circle —*vi.* **arced** or **arcked**, **arc′ing** or **arck′ing** to move in a curved course or form an arc

**ar·cade** (är kād′) *n.* ⟦see prec.⟧ **1** a covered passageway, esp. one lined with shops **2** a line of arches and their supporting columns **3** a penny arcade or a similar place with coin-operated video games

**ar·cane** (är kān′) *adj.* ⟦< L *arcanus*, hidden⟧ secret or esoteric

**arch**[1] (ärch) *n.* ⟦see ARC⟧ **1** a curved structure used as a support over an open space, as in a doorway **2** the form of an arch **3** anything shaped like an arch —*vt.* to span with or as an arch —*vi.* to form an arch

**arch**[2] (ärch) *adj.* ⟦< ARCH-⟧ **1** chief; principal **2** gaily mischievous; pert [an *arch* look]

**Arch** or **arch** *abbrev.* **1** archaic **2** architecture

**arch-** ⟦< Gr *archos*, first, ruler⟧ *prefix* main, principal [*archenemy*]

**-arch** (ärk) [see prec.] *suffix* ruler [*matriarch*]

**ar·chae·ol·o·gy** (är'kē äl'ə jē) *n.* [< Gr *archaios*, ancient + -LOGY] the study of the life of ancient peoples, as by excavation of ancient cities or artifacts: also sp. **ar'che·ol'o·gy** —**ar'chae·o·log'i·cal** (-ə läj'i kəl) *adj.* —**ar'chae·o·log'i·cal·ly** *adv.* —**ar'chae·ol'o·gist** *n.*

**ar·cha·ic** (är kā'ik) *adj.* [< Gr *archaios*, ancient] 1 ancient 2 old-fashioned 3 no longer used except in poetry, church ritual, etc.: said as of the word *thou* —**ar·cha'i·cal·ly** *adv.*

**ar·cha·ism** (är'kā iz'əm) *n.* an archaic word, usage, style, etc. —**ar'cha·is'tic** *adj.*

**arch·an·gel** (ärk'ān'jəl) *n.* an angel of high rank

**arch'bish'op** (ärch'-) *n.* a bishop of the highest rank

**arch'dea'con** *n.* a church official ranking just below a bishop

**arch'di'o·cese** *n.* the diocese of an archbishop —**arch'di·oc'e·san** *adj.*

**arch'duke'** *masc.n.* a sovereign prince, esp. of the former Austrian imperial family —**arch'duch'ess** *fem.n.*

**arch'en'e·my** *n., pl.* -mies a chief enemy —**the archenemy** Satan

**arch·er** (är'chər) *n.* [< L *arcus*, bow] one who shoots with bow and arrow

**arch'er·y** *n.* the sport of shooting with bow and arrow

**ar·che·type** (är'kə tīp') *n.* [< Gr *archos*, first + *typos*, a mark] 1 an original pattern, or model; prototype 2 a perfect example of a type or group —**ar'che·typ'al** (-tīp'əl) or **ar'che·typ'i·cal** (-tip'i kəl) *adj.*

**ar·chi·e·pis·co·pal** (är'kē ē pis'kə pəl) *adj.* of or related to an archbishop

**Ar·chi·me·des** (är'kə mē'dēz') 287?-212 B.C.; Gr. mathematician & inventor

**ar·chi·pel·a·go** (är'kə pel'ə gō') *n., pl.* -goes' or -gos' [< Gr *archi*-, chief + *pelagos*, sea] 1 a sea with many islands 2 a group of many islands

**ar·chi·tect** (är'kə tekt') *n.* [< Gr *archi*-, chief + *tektōn*, carpenter] 1 one who designs buildings and supervises their construction 2 any designer or planner

**ar·chi·tec·ton·ics** (är'kə tek tän'iks) *pl.n.* [*usually with sing. v.*] 1 the science of architecture 2 structural design, as of a symphony —**ar'chi·tec·ton'ic** *adj.*

**ar·chi·tec·ture** (är'kə tek'chər) *n.* 1 the science or profession of designing and constructing buildings 2 a style of construction 3 design and construction —**ar'chi·tec'tur·al** *adj.* —**ar'chi·tec'tur·al·ly** *adv.*

**ar·chi·trave** (är'kə trāv') *n.* [< L *archi*-, first + *trabs*, a beam] in a classical building, the beam resting directly on the tops of the columns

**ar·chive** (är'kīv') *n.* [< Gr *archeion*, town hall] [*usually pl.*] 1 a place for keeping public records, documentary material, etc. 2 the records, material, etc. kept there —*vt.* **-chived', -chiv'ing** to keep in or as in archives —**ar·chi·vist** (är'kə vist, -kī'-) *n.*

**arch·way** (ärch'wā') *n.* a passage under an arch, or the arch itself

**-ar·chy** (är kē) [< Gr *archein*, to rule] *combining form* rule, government [*monarchy*]

**arc·tic** (ärk'tik, är'-) *adj.* [< Gr *arktikos*, northern] 1 of or near the North Pole 2 very cold —**the Arctic** the region around the North Pole

**Arctic Circle** [*also* a- c-] an imaginary circle parallel to the equator, c. 66°34' north of it

**Arctic Ocean** ocean surrounding the North Pole

**-ard** (ərd) [< MHG *hart*, bold] *suffix* one who does something to excess [*drunkard*]

**ar·dent** (är'dənt) *adj.* [< L *ardere*, to burn] 1 passionate 2 zealous 3 glowing or burning —**ar'dent·ly** *adv.*

**ar·dor** (är'dər) *n.* [< L *ardor*, a flame] 1 emotional warmth; passion 2 zeal 3 intense heat Also, Brit. sp., **ar'dour**

**ar·du·ous** (är'jōō əs) *adj.* [L *arduus*, steep] 1 difficult to do; laborious 2 using much energy; strenuous —**ar'du·ous·ly** *adv.*

**are** (är) *vi.* [OE *aron*] *pl. & 2d pers. sing., pres. indic.,* of BE

**ar·e·a** (er'ē ə) *n.* [L, vacant place] 1 a part of the earth's surface; region 2 the measure, in square units, of a surface 3 a location having a specific use or character [*play area*] 4 scope or extent

**area code** a three-digit telephone code assigned to a specific area of the U.S., Canada, etc.

**a·re·na** (ə rē'nə) *n.* [L, sandy place] 1 a place or building for contests, shows, etc. 2 any sphere of struggle [*political arena*]

**arena theater** a theater having a central stage surrounded by seats

**aren't** (ärnt) *contr.* are not

**Ar·es** (er'ēz') *n. Gr. Myth.* the god of war

**ar·gent** (är'jənt) *adj.* [L *argentum*, silver] [Old Poet.] silvery

**Ar·gen·ti·na** (är'jən tē'nə) country in S South America; 1,073,518 sq. mi.; pop. 32,616,000 — **Ar'gen·tine'** (-tēn', -tīn') or **Ar'gen·tin'i·an** (-tin'ē ən) *adj., n.*

**ar·gon** (är'gän') *n.* [Gr, inert] a chemical element, a nonreactive gas found in the air and used in light bulbs, electron tubes, etc.

**Ar·go·naut** (är'gə nôt') *n. Gr. Myth.* any of those who sail with Jason to search for the Golden Fleece

**ar·go·sy** (är'gə sē) *n., pl.* -sies [after *Ragusa*, It name of Dubrovnik in Croatia] [Old Poet.] a large merchant ship or a fleet of such ships

**ar·got** (är'gō, -gət) *n.* [Fr] the specialized vocabulary of a particular group, as of criminals

**ar·gue** (är'gyōō) *vi.* **-gued, -gu·ing** [< L *arguere*, prove] 1 to give reasons (*for* or *against*) 2 to quarrel; dispute —*vt.* 1 to discuss; debate 2 to maintain; contend 3 to persuade by giving reasons —**ar'gu·a·ble** *adj.*

**ar·gu·ment** (är'gyōō mənt) *n.* 1 a reason or reasons offered in arguing 2 an arguing; debate 3 a summary

**ar'gu·men·ta'tion** (-men tā'shən) *n.* the process of arguing; debate

**ar'gu·men'ta·tive** (-men'tə tiv) *adj.* 1 controversial 2 apt to argue; contentious Also **ar'gu·men'tive**

**ar·gyle** (är'gīl') *adj.* [after *Argyll*, Scotland] knitted or woven in a diamond-shaped pattern [*argyle socks*]

**a·ri·a** (ä'rē ə) *n.* [It < L *aer*, air] a song, as in an opera, for solo voice

**-ar·i·an** (er'ē ən) [< L] *suffix* 1 (one) characterized by [*octogenarian*] 2 (one) believing in or associated with [*Unitarian*]

**ar·id** (ar'id) *adj.* [< L *arere*, be dry] 1 dry and barren 2 uninteresting; dull —**a·rid·i·ty** (ə rid'ə tē) *n.*

**Ar·i·es** (er'ēz') *n.* [L, ram (male sheep)] the first sign of the zodiac

**a·right** (ə rīt') *adv.* correctly

**a·rise** (ə rīz') *vi.* **a·rose'** (-rōz'), **a·ris'en** (-riz'ən), **a·ris'ing** [< OE *a*-, out + *risan*, to rise] 1 to get up, as from sleeping 2 to ascend 3 to come into being 4 to result (*from*)

**ar·is·toc·ra·cy** (ar'i stä'krə sē) *n., pl.* -cies [< Gr *aristos*, best + *kratos*, to rule] 1 government by a privileged minority, usually of inherited wealth 2 a country with such government 3 a privileged ruling class

**a·ris·to·crat** (ə ris'tə krat') *n.* 1 a member of the aristocracy 2 one with the tastes, manners, etc. of the upper class —**a·ris'to·crat'ic** *adj.*

**Ar·is·toph·a·nes** (ar'i stäf'ə nēz') 450?-388? B.C.; Gr. writer of comedies

**Ar·is·tot·le** (ar'is tät'l) 384-322 B.C.; Gr. philosopher —**Ar·is·to·te·li·an** (ar'is tə tēl'yən) *adj., n.*

**a·rith·me·tic** (ə rith'mə tik) *n.* [< Gr *arithmos*,

number‖ the science or art of computing by positive, real numbers —**ar·ith·met·ic** (ar'ith met'ik) or **ar·ith·met'i·cal** *adj.* —**ar'ith·me·ti'cian** (-mə tish' ən) *n.*

**arithmetic mean** the average obtained by dividing a sum by the number of its addends

**Ar·i·zo·na** (ar'ə zō'nə) state of the SW U.S.: 113,956 sq. mi.; pop. 3,665,000; cap. Phoenix: abbrev. *AZ* —**Ar'i·zo'nan** or **Ar'i·zo'ni·an** *adj., n.*

**ark** (ärk) *n.* ‖< L *arcere*, enclose‖ **1** ARK OF THE COVENANT **2** an enclosure in a synagogue for the scrolls of the Torah **3** *Bible* the boat in which Noah, his family, and two of every kind of creature survived the Flood

**Ar·kan·sas** (är'kən sô') state of the SC U.S.: 53,187 sq. mi.; pop. 2,351,000; cap. Little Rock: abbrev. *AR* —**Ar·kan'san** (-kan'zən) *adj., n.*

**ark of the covenant** the chest containing the two stone tablets inscribed with the Ten Commandments

**Ar·ling·ton** (är'liŋ tən) city in NE Texas: pop. 262,000

**arm**[1] (ärm) *n.* ‖OE *earm*‖ **1** an upper limb of the human body **2** anything like this in shape, function, position, etc. **3** anything connected to something larger *[arm* of the sea*]* —**with open arms** cordially

**arm**[2] (ärm) *n.* ‖< L *arma*, weapons‖ **1** a weapon: *usually used in pl.* **2** any branch of the military forces —*vt.* to provide with weapons, etc. —*vi.* to prepare for war or any struggle —**under arms** ready for war —**up in arms 1** prepared to fight **2** indignant

**ar·ma·da** (är mä'də) *n.* ‖Sp < L *arma*, weapons‖ **1** a fleet of warships **2** a fleet of military aircraft

**ar·ma·dil·lo** (är'mə dil'ō) *n., pl.* **-los** ‖Sp: see prec.‖ a burrowing mammal of tropical America, covered with bony plates

**Ar·ma·ged·don** (är'mə ged''n) *n.* **1** *Bible* the site of the last, decisive battle between the forces of good and evil **2** any great, decisive battle

**ar·ma·ment** (är'mə mənt) *n.* ‖< L *armare*, to arm‖ **1** *[often pl.]* all the military forces and equipment of a nation **2** all the military equipment of a warship, tank, etc. **3** an arming or being armed for war

**ar·ma·ture** (är'mə chər) *n.* ‖< L *armare*, to arm‖ **1** any protective covering **2** the iron core wound with wire in which electromotive force is produced in a generator or motor

**arm'chair'** *n.* a chair with supports at the sides for one's arms

**armed forces** all the military, naval, and air forces of a country

**Ar·me·ni·a** (är mēn'yə, -mē'nē ə) country in W Asia: 11,490 sq. mi.; pop. 3,305,000 —**Ar·me'ni·an** *adj., n.*

**arm·ful** (ärm'fool) *n., pl.* **-fuls** as much as the arms or one arm can hold

**arm'hole'** *n.* an opening for the arm in a garment

**ar·mi·stice** (är'mə stis) *n.* ‖< L *arma*, weapons + *stare*, to stand‖ a truce preliminary to the signing of a peace treaty

**Armistice Day** Nov. 11, the anniversary of the armistice of WWI in 1918

**arm·let** (ärm'lət) *n.* **1** an ornamental band worn around the upper arm **2** a narrow, deep inlet of the sea

**arm'load'** *n.* an armful

**ar·mor** (är'mər) *n.* ‖< L *armare*, to arm‖ any defensive or protective covering —*vt., vi.* to put armor on —**ar'mored** *adj.*

**armored car** a vehicle covered with armor plate, as a truck for carrying money to or from a bank

**ar·mo·ri·al** (är môr'ē əl) *adj.* of coats of arms

**armor plate** a protective covering of steel plates

**ar·mor·y** (är'mər ē) *n., pl.* **-mor·ies** ‖see ARMOR‖ an arsenal **2** a National Guard unit drill hall

**arm'pit'** *n.* the hollow under the arm at the shoulder

**arm'rest'** *n.* a support for the arm, as on the inside of an automobile door

**ar·my** (är'mē) *n., pl.* **-mies** ‖ult. < L *arma*, weapons‖ **1** a large, organized body of soldiers for waging war, esp. on land **2** a large number of persons, animals, etc. *[an army of ants]*

**Ar·nold** (är'nəld), **Ben·e·dict** (ben'ə dikt') 1741-1801; Am. Revolutionary general who became a traitor

**a·ro·ma** (ə rō'mə) *n.* ‖< Gr *arōma*, spice‖ a pleasant odor; fragrance

**a·ro·ma·ther·a·py** *n.* the therapeutic use of aromatic oils from herbs, etc.

**ar·o·mat·ic** (ar'ə mat'ik) *adj.* of or having an aroma; fragrant or pungent —*n.* an aromatic plant, chemical, etc. —**ar·o·mat'i·cal·ly** *adv.*

**a·rose** (ə rōz') *vi. pt. of* ARISE

**a·round** (ə round') *adv.* ‖ME‖ **1** in a circle **2** in every direction **3** in circumference **4** to the opposite direction **5** [Inf.] nearby *[stay around]* — *prep.* **1** so as to encircle or envelop **2** on the border of **3** in various places in or on **4** about *[around 1890]*

**a·rouse** (ə rouz') *vt.* **a·roused'**, **a·rous'ing 1** to awaken, as from sleep **2** to stir, as to action **3** to evoke *[to arouse pity]* —**a·rous'al** *n.*

**ar·peg·gio** (är pej'ō) *n., pl.* **-gios** ‖It < *arpa*, a harp‖ a chord whose notes are played in quick succession

**ar·raign** (ə rān') *vt.* ‖< L *ad*, to + *ratio*, reason‖ **1** to bring before a law court to answer charges **2** to call to account; accuse —**ar·raign'ment** *n.*

**ar·range** (ə rānj') *vt.* **-ranged'**, **-rang'ing** ‖< OFr *a-*, to + *renger*, to range‖ **1** to put in the correct order **2** to classify **3** to prepare or plan **4** to arrive at an agreement about **5** *Music* to adapt (a composition) to particular instruments or voices —*vi.* *Music* to write arrangements, esp. as a profession —**ar·rang'er** *n.*

**ar·range'ment** *n.* **1** an arranging **2** a result or manner of arranging **3** *[usually pl.]* a plan **4** a settlement **5** *Music a)* an arranging of a composition *b)* the composition as thus arranged

**ar·rant** (ar'ənt) *adj.* ‖var. of ERRANT‖ that is plainly such; out-and-out; notorious

**ar·ras** (ar'əs) *n.* ‖after *Arras*, Fr city‖ a wall hanging, esp. of tapestry

**ar·ray** (ə rā') *vt.* ‖< OFr *areer*‖ **1** to place in order **2** to dress in finery —*n.* **1** an orderly grouping, esp. of troops **2** an impressive display **3** fine clothes

**ar·rears** (ə rirz') *pl.n.* ‖< L *ad*, to + *retro*, behind‖ overdue debts —**in arrears** behind in paying a debt, doing one's work, etc.

**ar·rest** (ə rest') *vt.* ‖< L *ad-*, to + *restare*, to stop‖ **1** to stop or check **2** to seize by authority of the law **3** to catch and keep (one's attention, etc.) — *n.* an arresting or being arrested —**under arrest** in legal custody

**ar·rest'ing** *adj.* attracting attention; interesting

**ar·rhyth·mi·a** (ə rith'mē ə) *n.* ‖< Gr *a-*, without + *rhythmos*, measure‖ an irregularity in the heart's rhythm —**ar·rhyth'mic** or **ar·rhyth'mi·cal** *adj.*

**ar·riv·al** (ə rī'vəl) *n.* **1** an arriving **2** a person or thing that arrives

**ar·rive** (ə rīv') *vi.* **-rived'**, **-riv'ing** ‖< L *ad-*, to + *ripa*, shore‖ **1** to reach one's destination **2** to come *[the time has arrived]* **3** to attain fame, etc. —**arrive at** to reach by thinking, etc.

**ar·ri·ve·der·ci** (är rē've der'chē) *interj.* ‖It‖ goodbye

**ar·ro·gant** (ar'ə gənt) *adj.* ‖< L *arrogare*, to claim‖ full of or due to pride; haughty —**ar'ro·gance** *n.* —**ar'ro·gant·ly** *adv.*

**ar·ro·gate'** (-gāt') *vt.* **-gat'ed**, **-gat'ing** ‖< L *ad-*, for + *rogare*, to ask‖ to claim or seize without right —**ar'ro·ga'tion** *n.*

**ar·row** (ar'ō) *n.* ‖OE *arwe*‖ **1** a pointed shaft for shooting from a bow **2** a sign (←), used to indicate direction

**ar·row·head'** *n.* the separable, pointed tip of an arrow

**ar·row·root'** *n.* ⟦from use as antidote for poisoned arrows⟧ **1** a tropical plant with starchy roots **2** a starch made from its roots

**ar·roy·o** (ə roi′ō) *n., pl.* **-os** ⟦Sp < L *arrugia*, mine shaft⟧ [Southwest] **1** a dry gully **2** a rivulet or stream

**ar·se·nal** (är′sə nəl) *n.* ⟦< Ar *dār aṣṣinā′a*, workshop⟧ **1** a place for making or storing weapons **2** a store or collection

**ar·se·nic** (är′sə nik′; *for adj.* är sen′ik) *n.* ⟦< Gr *arsenikon*⟧ a very poisonous chemical element, compounds of which are used in insecticides, etc. —*adj.* of or containing arsenic: also **ar·sen′i·cal**

**ar·son** (är′sən) *n.* ⟦< L *ardere*, to burn⟧ the crime of purposely setting fire to a building or property —**ar′son·ist** *n.*

**art**[1] (ärt) *n.* ⟦< L *ars*⟧ **1** human creativity **2** skill **3** any specific skill or its application **4** any craft or its principles **5** creative work or its principles **6** any branch of creative work, as painting or sculpture **7** products of this, as paintings or statues **8** *a*) a branch of learning *b*) [*pl.*] LIBERAL ARTS **9** cunning **10** sly trick; wile: *usually used in pl.*

**art**[2] (ärt) *vi. archaic 2d pers. sing., pres. indic.,* of BE: used with *thou*

**art**[3] *abbrev.* **1** article **2** artificial

**art dec·o** (dek′ō) a decorative style of the late 1920s and the 1930s, derived from cubism

**ar·te·ri·al** (är tir′ē əl) *adj.* **1** of or in the arteries **2** of a main road

**ar·te·ri·ole** (är tir′ē ōl′) *n.* ⟦see ARTERY⟧ any of the small blood vessels between the arteries and capillaries

**ar·te·ri·o·scle·ro·sis** (är tir′ē ō′sklə rō′sis) *n.* ⟦< Gr *artēria*, artery + SCLEROSIS⟧ an abnormal thickening and hardening of the walls of the arteries

**ar·ter·y** (ärt′ər ē) *n., pl.* **-ter·ies** ⟦< Gr *aeirein*, to lift⟧ **1** any of the blood vessels that carry blood away from the heart **2** a main route

**ar·te·sian well** (är te′zhən) ⟦Fr *artésien*, of Artois (in France)⟧ a deep well in which water is forced up by pressure of underground water draining from higher ground

**art film** a film characterized by artistic sophistication, realism, etc.

**art·ful** (ärt′fəl) *adj.* **1** skillful or clever **2** cunning; crafty —**art′ful·ly** *adv.* —**art′ful·ness** *n.*

**art house** a theater that shows art films, etc.

**ar·thri·tis** (är thrīt′is) *n.* ⟦Gr < *arthron*, joint + -ITIS⟧ inflammation of a joint or joints —**ar·thrit·ic** (är thrit′ik) *adj.*

**arthro-** ⟦< Gr *arthron*, joint⟧ *combining form* joint, joints

**ar·thro·pod** (är′thrə päd′) *n.* ⟦prec. + -POD⟧ any of a phylum of invertebrates with jointed legs and a segmented body

**ar′thro·scope′** (-skōp′) *n.* ⟦ARTHRO- + -SCOPE⟧ an endoscope used inside a joint —**ar′thro·scop′ic** (-skäp′ik) *adj.*

**Ar·thur**[1] (är′thər) *n.* legendary 6th-c. king of Britain —**Ar·thu·ri·an** (är thoor′ē ən) *adj.*

**Ar·thur**[2] (är′thər), Ches·ter A(lan) (ches′tər) 1829-86; 21st president of the U.S. (1881-85)

**ar·ti·choke** (ärt′ə chōk′) *n.* ⟦ult. < Ar *al-ḥarshaf*⟧ **1** a thistlelike plant **2** its edible flower head

**ar·ti·cle** (ärt′i kəl) *n.* ⟦< L *artus*, joint⟧ **1** one of the sections of a document **2** a complete piece of writing, as in a newspaper, magazine, etc. **3** a separate item [an *article* of luggage] **4** *Gram.* any one of the words *a, an,* or *the,* used as adjectives

**ar·tic·u·late** (är tik′yōō lit; *for v.,* -lāt′) *adj.* ⟦< L prec.⟧ **1** jointed: usually **ar·tic′u·lat′ed 2** made up of distinct sounds, as speech **3** able to speak **4** expressing oneself clearly —*vt.* **-lat′ed, -lat′ing 1** to connect by joints **2** to arrange in connected

sequence **3** to utter distinctly **4** to express clearly —*vi.* **1** to speak distinctly **2** to be jointed or connected —**ar·tic′u·late·ly** *adv.* —**ar·tic′u·la′tion** *n.*

**ar·ti·fact** (ärt′ə fakt′) *n.* any object made by human work

**ar·ti·fice** (ärt′ə fis) *n.* ⟦< L *ars,* art + *facere,* make⟧ **1** skill or ingenuity **2** trickery **3** an artful trick

**ar·tif·i·cer** (är tif′ə sər) *n.* **1** a skilled craftsman **2** an inventor

**ar·ti·fi·cial** (ärt′ə fish′əl) *adj.* ⟦see ARTIFICE⟧ **1** made by human work; not natural **2** simulated [*artificial* teeth] **3** affected [an *artificial* smile] —**ar·ti·fi·ci·al′i·ty** (-fish′ē al′ə tē), *pl.* **-ties,** *n.* —**ar·ti·fi′cial·ly** *adv.*

**artificial intelligence 1** the capability of computers to mimic human thought processes **2** the science dealing with this

**artificial respiration** the maintenance of breathing by artificial means, as by forcing air into the mouth

**ar·til·ler·y** (är til′ər ē) *n.* ⟦< OFr *atillier,* equip⟧ **1** mounted guns, as cannon or missile launchers **2** gunnery —**the artillery** the branch of an army using heavy mounted guns —**ar·til′ler·y·man** (-mən), *pl.* **-men** (-mən), *n.*

**ar·ti·san** (ärt′ə zən) *n.* ⟦ult. < L *ars,* art⟧ a skilled craftsman

**art·ist** (ärt′ist) *n.* **1** one who is skilled in any of the fine arts **2** one who does anything very well **3** a professional in any of the performing arts

**ar·tis·tic** (är tis′tik) *adj.* **1** of art or artists **2** done skillfully and tastefully **3** sensitive to beauty —**ar·tis′ti·cal·ly** *adv.*

**art·ist·ry** (ärt′is trē) *n.* artistic quality, ability, or work

**art·less** (ärt′lis) *adj.* **1** lacking skill or art **2** simple; natural **3** without guile; ingenuous; innocent —**art′less·ly** *adv.*

**Arts and Crafts** a 19th-c. movement that promoted handwork and craftsmanship

**art·y** (ärt′ē) *adj.* **art′i·er, art′i·est** [Inf.] affectedly artistic —**art′i·ness** *n.*

**ar·um** (er′əm) *n.* ⟦L⟧ any of a family of plants with flowers enveloped within a hoodlike leaf

**Ar·y·an** (er′ē ən) *n.* ⟦< Sans *āzya-,* noble⟧ **1** [Obs.] the hypothetical parent language of the Indo-European family **2** a person supposed to be a descendant of the prehistoric peoples that spoke this language: *Aryan* is not a valid ethnological term

**as** (az) *adv.* ⟦< ALSO⟧ **1** equally [just *as* happy at home] **2** for instance [a card game, *as* bridge] **3** when related in a specified way [my view *as* contrasted with yours] —*conj.* **1** to the same amount or degree that [straight *as* an arrow] **2** in the same manner that [do *as* you are told] **3** while [she wept *as* she spoke] **4** because [*as* you object, we won't go] **5** that the consequence is [so obvious *as* to need no reply] **6** though [tall *as* he was, he couldn't reach it] —*pron.* **1** a fact that [we are tired, *as* you can see] **2** that: preceded by *such* or *the same* [such books *as* I own] —*prep.* in the role or function of [he poses *as* a friend] —**as for** (or **to**) concerning — **as if** (or **though**) as it (or one) would if —**as is** [Inf.] just as it is —**as it were** as if it were so

**As** *Chem. symbol for* arsenic

**ASAP** *abbrev.* as soon as possible

**as·bes·tos** (as bes′təs, az-) *n.* ⟦< Gr *a-,* not + *sbennynai,* extinguish⟧ a nonconducting, fireproof mineral used, esp. formerly, in electrical insulation, roofing, etc.

**as·cend** (ə send′) *vi.* ⟦< L *ad-,* to + *scandere,* to climb⟧ to move upward; rise —*vt.* **1** to move upward along; mount **2** to succeed to (a throne)

**as·cend·an·cy** or **as·cend·en·cy** (ə sen′dən sē) *n.* a position of control; domination

**as·cend′ant** or **as·cend′ent** (-dənt) *adj.* **1** rising

**2** in control; dominant —**in the ascendant** at or approaching the height of power, fame, etc.

**as·cen'sion** (-shən) *n.* **1** an ascending **2** [A-] the 40th day after Easter, celebrating the Ascension —**the Ascension** *Bible* the bodily ascent of Jesus into heaven

**as·cent** (ə sent′) *n.* **1** an ascending **2** an upward slope

**as·cer·tain** (as′ər tān′) *vt.* [[see AD- & CERTAIN]] to find out with certainty

**as·cet·ic** (ə set′ik) *adj.* [[< Gr *askein*, to train the body]] self-denying; austere —*n.* [[< Gr *awkētēs*, monk]] one who leads a life of strict self-denial, esp. for religious purposes —**as·cet′i·cism′** (-ə siz′əm) *n.*

**ASCII** (as′kē) *n.* a code that facilitates information exchange among various computers

**a·scor·bic acid** (ə skôr′bik) [A-² + SCORB(UTIC) + -IC]] vitamin C

**as·cot** (as′kət, -kät′) *n.* a necktie with very broad ends hanging from the knot

**as·cribe** (ə skrīb′) *vt.* -cribed′, -crib′ing [[< L *ad-*, to + *scribere*, write]] **1** to assign (something) *to* a supposed cause **2** to regard (something) as belonging *to* or coming from someone — **as·crip·tion** (ə skrip′shən) *n.*

**a·sep·tic** (ā sep′tik, ə-) *adj.* free from disease-producing bacteria, etc.

**a·sex·u·al** (ā sek′shoŏ əl) *adj.* **1** having no sex or sexual organs **2** without the union of male and female germ cells **3** having little or no sexual activity, desire, character, etc. —**a·sex′u·al·ly** *adv.*

ASCOT

**ash¹** (ash) *n.* [[< OE *æsce*]] **1** the grayish powder left after something has burned **2** fine, volcanic lava **3** the gray color of wood ash  See also ASHES

**ash²** (ash) *n.* [[< OE *æsc*]] **1** a shade tree of the olive family **2** its wood

**a·shamed** (ə shāmd′) *adj.* **1** feeling shame **2** reluctant because fearing shame beforehand —**a·sham·ed·ly** (ə shām′id lē) *adv.*

**ash·en** (ash′ən) *adj.* **1** of ashes **2** like ashes, esp. in color; pale

**ash·es** (ash′iz) *pl.n.* **1** the grayish powder and small particles left after a thing has burned **2** human remains, esp. the part left after cremation

**a·shore** (ə shôr′) *adv., adj.* **1** to or on the shore **2** to or on land

**ash·ram** (äsh′rəm) *n.* [[< Sans *ā*, toward + *śrama*, penance]] **1** a secluded place for a Hindu religious community **2** such a community

**ash′tray′** *n.* a container for smokers' tobacco ashes, etc.: also **ash tray**

**Ash Wednesday** the first day of Lent: from the putting of ashes on the forehead in penitence

**ash′y** *adj.* -i·er, -i·est **1** of or covered with ashes **2** ashen; pale

**A·sia** (ā′zhə) largest continent, in the Eastern Hemisphere: *c.* 17,400,000 sq. mi.; pop. *c.* 3,451,000,000 —**A′sian** or less preferred **A·si·at·ic** (ā′zhē at′ik) *adj., n.*

**Asia Minor** large peninsula in W Asia, between the Black Sea and the Mediterranean

**a·side** (ə sīd′) *adv.* **1** on or to one side **2** in reserve [put one *aside* for me] **3** apart; notwithstanding [joking *aside*] —*n.* words spoken by an actor but supposedly not heard by the other actors —**aside from 1** with the exception of **2** apart from

**as·i·nine** (as′ə nīn′) *adj.* [[< L *asinus*, ass]] like an ass; stupid; silly —**as′i·nine′ly** *adv.* —**as′i·nin′i·ty** (-nin′ə tē) *n.*

**ask** (ask) *vt.* [[OE *āscian*]] **1** to use words in seeking the answer to (a question) **2** to inquire of (a person) **3** to request or demand **4** to invite —*vi.*

**1** to make a request (*for*) **2** to inquire (*about* or *after*) —**ask′er** *n.*

**a·skance** (ə skans′) *adv.* [[ME]] **1** with a sideways glance **2** with suspicion, disapproval, etc.

**a·skew** (ə skyoŏ′) *adv.* to one side; awry —*adj.* on one side; awry

**asking price** the price asked by a seller, esp. as a basis for bargaining

**a·slant** (ə slant′) *adv.* on a slant —*prep.* on a slant across —*adj.* slanting

**a·sleep** (ə slēp′) *adj.* **1** sleeping **2** inactive; dull **3** numb **4** dead —*adv.* into a sleeping condition

**a·so·cial** (ā sō′shəl) *adj.* **1** avoiding contact with others **2** selfish

**asp** (asp) *n.* [[< Gr *aspis*]] a poisonous snake of Africa, Arabia, etc.

**as·par·a·gus** (ə spar′ə gəs, -sper′-) *n.* [[< Gr *asparagos*]] **1** a plant of the lily family, with edible shoots **2** these shoots

**as·par·tame** (as′pər tām′) *n.* an artificial, low-calorie sweetener, used in soft drinks, candy, etc.

**as·pect** (as′pekt′) *n.* [[< L *ad-*, to + *specere*, to look]] **1** the way one appears **2** the appearance of something from a specific position or viewpoint **3** a side facing in a given direction

**as·pen** (as′pən) *n.* [[OE *æspe*]] a poplar tree whose leaves flutter in the least breeze

**as·per·i·ty** (ə sper′ə tē) *n., pl.* -ties [[< L *asper*, rough]] **1** roughness or harshness **2** sharpness of temper

**as·per·sion** (ə spur′zhən) *n.* a damaging or disparaging remark; slander

**as·phalt** (as′fôlt′) *n.* [[< Gr *asphaltos*]] a brown or black tarlike substance mixed with sand or gravel and used for paving, roofing, etc. —*vt.* to pave, roof, etc. with asphalt

**as·pho·del** (as′fə del′) *n.* [[< Gr *asphodelos*]] a plant of the lily family, having white or yellow flowers

**as·phyx·i·ate** (as fik′sē āt′) *vt.*, *vi.* -at·ed, -at·ing [[< Gr *a-*, not + *sphyzein*, to throb]] **1** to make or become unconscious from lack of oxygen in the blood **2** to suffocate —**as·phyx′i·a′tion** *n.*

**as·pic** (as′pik′) *n.* [[< OFr *aspe*, asp]] a cold jelly of meat juice, tomato juice, etc., served as a garnish or in a mold

**as·pi·rant** (as′pə rənt, ə spī′-) *adj.* aspiring —*n.* one who aspires

**as·pi·rate** (as′pə rāt′; *for n.,* -pər it) *vt.* -rat·ed, -rat·ing **1** to begin (a word) with the sound of English (h) **2** to follow (a consonant) with an audible puff of breath **3** to suck in or draw in **4** *Med.* to remove (fluid, etc.) by suction —*n.* an aspirated sound

**as·pi·ra·tion** (as′pə rā′shən) *n.* **1** *a*) strong desire or ambition, as for advancement *b*) the thing so desired **2** a drawing in by breathing or suction **3** *Med.* removal of fluid, etc. by suction

**as′pi·ra′tor** *n.* an apparatus using suction to remove air, fluids, etc.

**as·pire** (ə spīr′) *vi.* -pired′, -pir′ing [[< L *ad-*, to + *spirare*, breathe]] to be ambitious (*to* get or do something); seek (*after*)

**as·pi·rin** (as′pə rin′, -prin′) *n.* [[Ger]] **1** a white, crystalline powder used for reducing fever, relieving pain, etc. **2** a tablet of this

**ass** (as) *n.* [[< L *asinus*]] **1** a horselike animal having long ears and a short mane **2** a stupid or silly person

**as·sail** (ə sāl′) *vt.* [[< L *ad-*, to + *salire*, to leap]] **1** to attack physically and violently **2** to attack with arguments, etc. —**as·sail′a·ble** *adj.*

**as·sail′ant** (-ənt) *n.* an attacker

**as·sas·sin** (ə sas′ən) *n.* [[< Ar *hashshāshīn*, hashish users]] a murderer who strikes suddenly; now, esp., the murderer of a politically important or prominent person

**as·sas′si·nate** (-āt′) *vt.* -nat·ed, -nat·ing to murder as an assassin does —**as·sas′si·na′tion** *n.*

**as·sault** (ə sôlt′) *n.* [[< L *ad-*, to + *salire*, to leap]] **1** a violent attack **2** *euphemism for* RAPE¹ **3** *Law* an unlawful threat or attempt to harm another physically —*vt.*, *vi.* to make an assault (upon)

**assault and battery** *Law* the carrying out of threatened physical harm

**as·say** (as'ā, a sā'; *for v.* a sā') *n.* ⟦< OFr *essai*, trial⟧ **1** a testing **2** an analysis of the ingredients of an ore, drug, etc. —*vt.* **1** to make an assay of; test **2** to try; attempt —*vi.* to be shown by assay to have a specified proportion of something —**as·say'er** *n.*

**as·sem·blage** (ə sem'blij; *for 3, also* ä'sem bläzh') *n.* **1** an assembling **2** a group of persons or things gathered together **3** *Art* things assembled in a sculptured collage

**as·sem·ble** (ə sem'bəl) *vt.*, *vi.* **-bled, -bling** ⟦< L *ad-*, to + *simul*, together⟧ **1** to gather into a group; collect **2** to fit or put together the parts of —**as·sem'bler** *n.*

**as·sem·bly** (-blē) *n.*, *pl.* **-blies 1** an assembling **2** a group of persons gathered together **3** *a)* a legislative body *b)* [A-] the lower house of some state legislatures **4** a fitting together of parts to make a whole

**assembly line** in many factories, a method whereby each worker performs a specific task in assembling the work as it is passed along

**as·sem·bly·man** (-mən) *n.*, *pl.* **-men** a member of a legislative assembly —**as·sem'bly·wom'an**, *pl.* **-wom'en**, *fem.n.*

**as·sent** (ə sent') *vi.* ⟦< L *ad-*, to + *sentire*, to feel⟧ to express acceptance; agree (*to*) —*n.* consent or agreement

**as·sert** (ə surt') *vt.* ⟦< L *ad-*, to + *serere*, join⟧ **1** to declare; affirm **2** to maintain or defend (rights, etc.) —**assert oneself** to insist on one's rights, or on being recognized —**as·sert'er** or **as·ser'tor** *n.*

**as·ser·tion** (ə sur'shən) *n.* **1** an asserting **2** a positive statement

**as·ser·tive** (ə surt'iv) *adj.* persistently, forcefully, or boldly positive or confident —**as·ser'tive·ly** *adv.* —**as·ser'tive·ness** *n.*

**as·sess** (ə ses') *vt.* ⟦< L *ad-*, to + *sedere*, sit⟧ **1** to set an estimated value on (property, etc.) for taxation **2** to set the amount of (a tax, fine, etc.) **3** to impose a tax, etc. on **4** to judge the worth or importance of —**as·sess'ment** *n.* —**as·ses'sor** *n.*

**as·set** (as'et) *n.* ⟦< L *ad*, to + *satis*, enough⟧ **1** anything owned that has value **2** a desirable thing [charm is an *asset*] **3** [*pl.*] the accounting entries showing the resources of a person or business **4** [*pl.*] *Law* property available to pay debts

**as·sev·er·ate** (ə sev'ə rāt') *vt.* **-at'ed, -at'ing** ⟦< L *ad-*, to + *severus*, earnest⟧ to state positively; assert —**as·sev'er·a'tion** *n.*

**as·sid·u·ous** (ə sij'ō̃ əs) *adj.* ⟦< L *assidere*, to assist⟧ diligent; persevering; careful —**as·si·du·i·ty** (as'ə dyō̃'ə tē), *pl.* **-ties**, *n.* —**as·sid'u·ous·ly** *adv.* —**as·sid'u·ous·ness** *n.*

**as·sign** (ə sīn') *vt.* ⟦< L *ad-*, to + *signare*, to sign⟧ **1** to set apart or mark for a specific purpose; designate **2** to appoint, as to a duty **3** to give out as a task; allot **4** to ascribe; attribute **5** *Law* to transfer (a right, etc.) —**as·sign'a·ble** *adj.* —**as·sign'er** or *Law* **as·sign·or** (ə sīn'ôr') *n.*

**as·sig·na·tion** (as'ig nā'shən) *n.* an appointment to meet, esp. one made secretly by lovers, or the meeting itself

**as·sign·ment** (ə sīn'mənt) *n.* **1** an assigning or being assigned **2** anything assigned

**as·sim·i·late** (ə sim'ə lāt') *vt.* **-lat'ed, -lat'ing** ⟦< L *ad-*, to + *similare*, make similar⟧ **1** to absorb and incorporate **2** to make like or alike: with *to* —*vi.* **1** to become like or alike **2** to become absorbed and incorporated —**as·sim'i·la'tion** *n.*

**as·sist** (ə sist') *vt.*, *vi.* ⟦< L *ad-*, to + *sistere*, make stand⟧ to help; aid —*n.* an instance or act of helping —**assist at** to be present at; attend

**as·sist·ance** (ə sis'təns) *n.* help; aid

**as·sist'ant** (-tənt) *adj.* assisting; helping —*n.* one who assists; helper; aid

**assisted living** a living arrangement providing assistance to elderly or disabled persons

**as·siz·es** (ə sīz'iz) *pl.n.* ⟦see ASSESS⟧ **1** court sessions held periodically in each county of England **2** the time or place of these

**assn** *abbrev.* association

**assoc** *abbrev.* **1** associate(s) **2** association

**as·so·ci·ate** (ə sō'shē āt', -sē-; *for n. & adj.*, -it) *vt.* **-at'ed, -at'ing** ⟦< L *ad-*, to + *socius*, companion⟧ **1** to connect; combine; join **2** to bring into relationship as partner, etc. **3** to connect in the mind —*vi.* to join (*with*) as a partner, friend, etc. —*n.* **1** a friend, partner, co-worker, etc. **2** a degree granted by a junior college —*adj.* **1** joined with others in work, etc. **2** having less than full status

**as·so·ci·a·tion** *n.* **1** an associating or being associated **2** fellowship; partnership **3** an organization, society, etc. **4** a mental connection between ideas, etc.

**association football** soccer

**as·so·ci·a·tive** (-shē āt'iv, -sē-; -shə tiv) *adj.* **1** of, by, or causing association **2** *Math.* producing the same result regardless of how the elements are grouped

**as·so·nance** (as'ə nəns) *n.* ⟦< L *ad-*, to + *sonare*, to sound⟧ **1** likeness of sound **2** a partial rhyme made by repetition of a vowel sound —**as'so·nant** *adj.*, *n.*

**as·sort** (ə sôrt') *vt.* ⟦ult. < L *ad-*, to + *sors*, lot, fate⟧ to sort or classify

**as·sort'ed** *adj.* **1** various; miscellaneous **2** sorted; classified

**as·sort'ment** *n.* **1** an assorting **2** a miscellaneous collection; variety

**asst** *abbrev.* assistant

**as·suage** (ə swāj') *vt.* **-suaged', -suag'ing** ⟦< L *ad-*, to + *suavis*, sweet⟧ **1** to lessen (pain, distress, etc.) **2** to calm (anger, etc.) **3** to satisfy or slake (thirst, etc.)

**as·sume** (ə sōōm') *vt.* **-sumed', -sum'ing** ⟦< L *ad-*, to + *sumere*, to take⟧ **1** to take on (the appearance, role, etc. of) **2** to seize; usurp **3** to undertake **4** to take for granted; suppose **5** to pretend to have; feign —**as·sum'a·ble** *adj.*

**as·sumed'** *adj.* **1** pretended; fictitious **2** taken for granted

**as·sump·tion** (ə sump'shən) *n.* **1** [A-] *R.C.Ch. a)* the ascent of the Virgin Mary into heaven *b)* a feast on Aug. 15 celebrating this **2** an assuming **3** a supposition —**as·sump'tive** *adj.*

**as·sur·ance** (ə shoor'əns) *n.* **1** an assuring or being assured **2** a promise, guarantee, etc. **3** self-confidence **4** [Chiefly Brit.] insurance

**as·sure** (ə shoor') *vt.* **-sured', -sur'ing** ⟦< L *ad-*, to + *securus*, secure⟧ **1** to make (a person) sure of something **2** to give confidence to; reassure **3** to tell or promise confidently **4** to guarantee **5** [Chiefly Brit.] to insure against loss

**as·sured'** *adj.* **1** made sure; certain **2** confident; sure of oneself —**as·sur·ed·ly** (ə shoor'id lē) *adv.*

**As·syr·i·a** (ə sir'ē ə) ancient empire in SW Asia —**As·syr'i·an** *adj.*, *n.*

**as·ter** (as'tər) *n.* ⟦< Gr *astēr*, star⟧ any of several plants of the composite family with variously colored daisylike flowers

**as·ter·isk** (as'tər isk') *n.* ⟦< Gr dim. of *astēr*, star⟧ a starlike sign (*) used in printing to mark footnotes, etc.

**a·stern** (ə sturn') *adv.* **1** behind a ship or aircraft **2** AFT **3** backward

**as·ter·oid** (as'tər oid') *n.* ⟦see ASTER & -OID⟧ any of the small planets in orbits mainly between Mars and Jupiter

**asth·ma** (az'mə) *n.* ⟦Gr⟧ a chronic disorder characterized by wheezing, coughing, difficulty in breathing, etc. —**asth·mat·ic** (az mat'ik) *adj.*, *n.*

**a·stig·ma·tism** (ə stig'mə tiz'əm) *n.* ⟦< Gr *a-*, without + *stigma*, a mark + -ISM⟧ an irregularity in the lens of the eye, that prevents proper focusing of light rays, causing distortion, poor eyesight, etc. —**as·tig·mat·ic** (as'tig mat'ik) *adj.*

**a·stil·be** (ə stil'bē) *n.* a plant having spikes of white, pink, or red flowers

**a·stir** (ə stʉr') *adv., adj.* **1** in motion **2** out of bed

**as·ton·ish** (ə stän'ish) *vt.* ⟦< L *ex-*, intens. + *tonare*, to thunder⟧ to fill with sudden wonder; amaze —**as·ton'ish·ing** *adj.* —**as·ton'ish·ing·ly** *adv.* —**as·ton'ish·ment** *n.*

**as·tound** (ə stound') *vt.* ⟦see prec.⟧ to astonish greatly —**as·tound'ing** *adj.* —**as·tound'ing·ly** *adv.*

**a·strad·dle** (ə strad''l) *adv.* in a straddling position

**as·tra·khan** (as'trə kən) *n.* ⟦after *Astrakhan*, Russ city⟧ loosely curled fur from young lamb pelts, or a wool fabric resembling this

**as·tral** (as'trəl) *adj.* ⟦< Gr *astron*, star⟧ of, from, or like the stars

**a·stray** (ə strā') *adv., adj.* ⟦ME < pp. of OFr *estraier*, stray⟧ **1** off the right path **2** in error

**a·stride** (ə strīd') *adv.* with a leg on either side —*prep.* **1** with a leg on either side of **2** extending over or across

**as·trin·gent** (ə strin'jənt) *adj.* ⟦< L *ad-*, to + *stringere*, to draw tight⟧ **1** that contracts body tissue and stops secretions **2** harsh; biting —*n.* an astringent substance —**as·trin'gen·cy** *n.*

**astro-** ⟦< Gr *astron*, star⟧ *combining form* star or stars [*astrophysics*]

**as·tro·bi·ol·o·gy** (as'trō bī äl'ə jē) *n.* the branch of biology that investigates the existence of living organisms on planets other than earth

**as·tro·dy·nam'ics** *n.* the branch of dynamics dealing with the motion and gravitation of objects in space

**as·trol·o·gy** (ə sträl'ə jē) *n.* ⟦< Gr *astron*, star + -*logia*, -LOGY⟧ a method or theory based on the assumption that the positions of the moon, sun, and stars affect human affairs and can be used to foretell the future —**as·trol'o·ger** *n.* —**as·tro·log·i·cal** (as'trə läj'i kəl) *adj.*

**as·tro·naut** (as'trə nôt') *n.* ⟦< Fr < Gr *astron*, star + *nautēs*, sailor⟧ one trained to make flights into outer space —**as'tro·nau'tics** *n.*

**as·tro·nom·i·cal** (as'trə näm'i kəl) *adj.* **1** of astronomy **2** extremely large: said as of numbers Also **as'tro·nom'ic** —**as'tro·nom'i·cal·ly** *adv.*

**astronomical unit** a unit of length based on the mean distance of the earth from the sun, *c.* 149.6 million km (*c.* 93 million mi.)

**as·tron·o·my** (ə strän'ə mē) *n.* ⟦< Gr *astron*, star + *nomos*, law⟧ the science that studies the origin, size, motion, etc. of stars, planets, etc. —**as·tron'o·mer** *n.*

**as·tro·phys·ics** (as'trō fiz'iks) *n.* the branch of astronomy dealing with the physical properties of the universe —**as'tro·phys'i·cist** (-ə sist) *n.*

**As'tro·Turf'** (-tʉrf') *trademark for* a grasslike synthetic carpet used in stadiums, etc.

**as·tute** (ə stōōt') *adj.* ⟦< L *astus*, craft, cunning⟧ clever or shrewd; keen —**as·tute'ly** *adv.* —**as·tute'ness** *n.*

**a·sun·der** (ə sun'dər) *adv.* ⟦< OE *on sundran*⟧ **1** into pieces **2** apart in direction or position

**a·sy·lum** (ə sī'ləm) *n.* ⟦< Gr *a-*, without + *sylon*, right of seizure⟧ **1** a place of safety; refuge **2** an institution for the care of mentally ill, aged, or poor people: a term now rarely used

**a·sym·me·try** (ā sim'ə trē) *n.* lack of symmetry —**a·sym·met·ri·cal** (ā'sə me'tri kəl) *adj.* —**a'sym·met'ri·cal·ly** *adv.*

**a·symp·to·mat·ic** (ā'simp tə ma'tik) *adj.* without symptoms

**at** (at) *prep.* ⟦< OE *æt*⟧ **1** on; in; near; by [*at* the office] **2** to or toward [look *at* her] **3** from [visible *at* one mile] **4** attending [*at* a party] **5** busy with [*at* work] **6** in the state or manner of [*at* war, *at* a trot] **7** because of [sad *at* his death] **8** with reference to [good *at* tennis] **9** in the amount, etc. of [*at* five cents each] **10** on or near the time or age of [*at* noon, *at* twenty-one] **11** attacking, etc. [they're *at* him again]

**at·a·vism** (at'ə viz'əm) *n.* ⟦< L *at-*, beyond + *avus*, grandfather⟧ resemblance or reversion to a characteristic of a remote ancestor —**at'a·vis'tic** *adj.*

**a·tax·i·a** (ə tak'sē ə) *n.* ⟦< Gr *a-*, not + *tassein*, arrange⟧ an inability to coordinate one's movements, as in walking —**a·tax'ic** *adj., n.*

**ate** (āt; *Brit, or U.S. dial.*, et) *vt., vi. pt. of* EAT

**-ate¹** (āt; *for 2*, it) *suffix* **1** to become, cause to become, form, provide with [*maturate, ulcerate*] **2** of or characteristic of, characterized by, having [*passionate*]

**-ate²** (āt, it) *suffix* an office, function, agent, or official [*directorate*]

**at·el·ier** (at''l yā') *n.* ⟦Fr⟧ a studio or workshop, esp. of an artist

**Ath·a·bas·kan** or **Ath·a·bas·can** (ath'ə bas'kən) *n.* a family of North American Indian languages, including Navajo —*adj.* designating or of these languages or the peoples that speak them

**a·the·ism** (ā'thē iz'əm) *n.* ⟦< Gr *a-*, without + *theos*, god⟧ the belief that there is no God —**a'the·ist** *n.* —**a'the·is'tic** *adj.*

**A·the·na** (ə thē'nə) *n.* the Greek goddess of wisdom, skills, and warfare

**Ath·ens** (ath'ənz) capital of Greece, in the SE part: pop. 772,000 —**A·the·ni·an** (ə thē'nē ən) *adj., n.*

**ath·er·o·scle·ro·sis** (ath'ər ō'sklə rō'sis) *n.* ⟦< Gr *athērōma*, grainy tumor + SCLEROSIS⟧ formation of fatty nodules on hardening artery walls

**a·thirst** (ə thʉrst') *adj.* **1** [Archaic] thirsty **2** eager; longing (*for*)

**ath·lete** (ath'lēt') *n.* ⟦< Gr *athlon*, a prize⟧ a person trained in exercises or games requiring strength, skill, stamina, etc.

**athlete's foot** ringworm of the feet

**ath·let·ic** (ath let'ik) *adj.* **1** of or like athletes or athletics **2** physically strong, active, fit, etc. —**ath·let'i·cal·ly** *adv.* —**ath·let'i·cism'** (-ə siz'əm) *n.*

**ath·let'ics** *pl.n.* [*sometimes with sing. v.*] athletic sports, games, etc.

**-a·thon** (ə thän') ⟦< (MAR)ATHON⟧ *suffix* an event marked by length or endurance [*walkathon*]

**a·thwart** (ə thwôrt') *prep.* **1** across **2** against —*adv.* crosswise

**a·tilt** (ə tilt') *adj., adv.* tilted

**-a·tion** (ā'shən) ⟦< Fr or L⟧ *suffix* the act, condition, or result of [*alteration*]

**-a·tive** (ə tiv, āt'iv) ⟦< Fr or L⟧ *suffix* of or relating to, serving to [*informative*]

**At·lan·ta** (at lan'tə) capital of Georgia: pop. 394,000

**At·lan·tic** (at lan'tik) ocean touching the Americas to the west and Europe and Africa to the east

**Atlantic City** city in SE New Jersey: an ocean resort: pop. 38,000

**At·lan·tis** (at lan'tis) *n.* ⟦< Gr⟧ legendary sunken continent in the Atlantic

**At·las** (at'ləs) *n.* **1** *Gr. Myth.* a giant who supports the heavens on his shoulders **2** [a-] a book of maps

**ATM** (ā'tē em') *n.* ⟦*a*(*utomated*) *t*(*eller*) *m*(*achine*)⟧ a computer terminal that allows a bank customer to deposit, withdraw, or transfer funds automatically

**at·mos·phere** (at'məs fir') *n.* ⟦< Gr *atmos*, vapor + *sphaira*, sphere⟧ **1** the air surrounding the earth **2** a pervading mood or spirit **3** the general tone or effect **4** a unit of pressure equal to 101,325 newtons per sq. m —**at'mos·pher'ic** (-fer'ik, -fir'-) *adj.* —**at'mos·pher'i·cal·ly** *adv.*

**at·oll** (a'tôl') *n.* ⟦< Malayalam *atolu*⟧ a ring-shaped coral island surrounding a lagoon

**at·om** (at'əm) *n.* ⟦< Gr *a-*, not + *temnein*, to cut⟧ **1** a tiny particle; jot **2** *Chem., Physics* any of the smallest particles of an element that combine with similar particles of other elements to form molecules —**the atom** nuclear energy

**atom bomb** ATOMIC BOMB

**a·tom·ic** (ə täm'ik) *adj.* **1** of an atom or atoms **2**

of or using atomic energy or atomic bombs **3** tiny —**a·tom′i·cal·ly** *adv.*

**atomic bomb** an extremely destructive bomb whose power results from a chain reaction of nuclear fission

**atomic energy** NUCLEAR ENERGY

**atomic number** *Chem.* a number indicating the number of protons in the nucleus of an atom of an element

**atomic weight** *Chem.* the weight of one atom of an element based upon the average weight of the element's isotopes

**at·om·iz·er** (at′əm ī zər) *n.* a device used to shoot out a fine spray, as of medicine or perfume

**a·to·nal·i·ty** (ā′tō nal′ə tē) *n. Music* the organization of tones without relation to a key —**a·ton·al** (ā tōn′əl) *adj.* —**a·ton′al·ly** *adv.*

**a·tone** (ə tōn′) *vi.* **a·toned′, a·ton′ing** [< ME *at one*, in accord] to make amends (*for* wrongdoing, etc.)

**a·tone′ment** *n.* **1** an atoning **2** amends —**the Atonement** *Theol.* the redeeming of humanity by the death of Jesus

**a·top** (ə täp′) *adv.* on or at the top —*prep.* on the top of

**a·top·ic** (ā täp′ik) *adj.* of allergic reactions, as a type of dermatitis, thought to be inherited

**-a·to·ry** (ə tôr′ē) [< L] *suffix* -ORY

**ATP** (ā′tē′pē′) *n.* [*a(denosine) t(ri)p(hosphate)*] an organic compound present in, and vital to, all living cells

**a·tri·um** (ā′trē əm) *n., pl.* **a′tri·a** (-ə) or **a′tri·ums** [L] **1** the central court or main room of an ancient Roman house **2** a court or entrance hall, usually of more than one story **3** either of the heart's upper chambers

**a·tro·cious** (ə trō′shəs) *adj.* [< L *atrox*, fierce] **1** very cruel, evil, etc. **2** very bad or unpleasant; offensive —**a·tro′cious·ly** *adv.* —**a·tro′cious·ness** *n.*

**a·troc·i·ty** (ə träs′ə tē) *n., pl.* **-ties 1** atrocious behavior **2** an atrocious act **3** [Inf.] a very displeasing thing

**at·ro·phy** (a′trə fē) *n.* [< Gr *a-*, not + *trephein*, to feed] a wasting away or failure to grow, esp. of body tissue, an organ, etc. —*vi.* **-phied, -phy·ing** to undergo atrophy —*vt.* to cause atrophy in

**at·ro·pine** (at′rə pēn′, -pin′) *n.* [< Gr *Atropos*, one of the Fates + -INE³] an alkaloid obtained from belladonna, used to relieve spasms, etc.

**at·tach** (ə tach′) *vt.* [< OFr *estache*, a post, stake] **1** to fasten by sticking, tying, etc. **2** to join: often used reflexively **3** to connect by ties of affection, etc. **4** to add (a signature, etc.) **5** to ascribe **6** *Law* to take (property) by writ —**at·tach′a·ble** *adj.*

**at·ta·ché** (at′ə shā′; *chiefly Brit* ə tash′ā) *n.* [Fr: see prec.] a member of an ambassador's diplomatic staff

**attaché case** a briefcase

**at·tach′ment** *n.* **1** an attaching or being attached **2** anything that attaches; fastening **3** devotion **4** anything attached **5** an accessory for an electrical appliance, etc. **6** *Law* a taking of property into custody

**at·tack** (ə tak′) *vt.* [< It *attaccare*] **1** to use force against in order to harm **2** to speak or write against **3** to undertake vigorously **4** to begin acting upon harmfully —*vi.* to make an assault —*n.* **1** an attacking **2** any hostile action, esp. with troops **3** the onset of a disease **4** a beginning of a task, undertaking, etc. —**at·tack′er** *n.*

**at·tain** (ə tān′) *vt.* [< L *ad-*, to + *tangere*, to touch] **1** to gain; accomplish; achieve **2** to reach; arrive at —**at·tain′a·bil′i·ty** *n.* —**at·tain′a·ble** *adj.*

**at·tain′der** (-dər) *n.* [see prec.] loss of civil rights and property of one sentenced to death or outlawed

**at·tar** (at′ər) *n.* [< Ar *'iṭr*, perfume] a perfume made from flower petals, esp. of roses (**attar of roses**)

**at·tempt** (ə tempt′) *vt.* [< L *ad-*, to + *temptare*, to

try] to try to do, get, etc. —*n.* **1** a try; endeavor **2** an attack, as on a person's life

**at·tend** (ə tend′) *vt.* [< L *ad-*, to + *tendere*, to stretch] **1** [Now Rare] to take care of **2** to go with **3** to accompany as a result **4** to be present at —*vi.* **1** to pay attention **2** to wait (*on* or *upon*) **3** to apply oneself (*to*) **4** to give the required care (*to*)

**at·tend′ance** *n.* **1** an attending **2** the number of persons attending

**at·tend′ant** *adj.* **1** attending or serving **2** being present **3** accompanying —*n.* one who attends or serves

**at·ten·tion** (ə ten′shən) *n.* [see ATTEND] **1** mental concentration or readiness **2** notice or observation **3** care or consideration **4** an act of courtesy or devotion: *usually used in pl.* **5** the erect posture of soldiers ready for a command

**attention-deficit hyperactivity disorder** a mental disorder marked by inability to concentrate, impulsiveness, etc.

**at·ten′tive** (-tiv) *adj.* **1** paying attention **2** courteous, devoted, etc. —**at·ten′tive·ly** *adv.* —**at·ten′tive·ness** *n.*

**at·ten·u·ate** (ə ten′yoo āt′) *vt.* **-at·ed, -at·ing** [< L *ad-*, to + *tenuis*, thin] **1** to make thin **2** to dilute **3** to lessen or weaken —*vi.* to become thin, weak, etc. —**at·ten′u·a′tion** *n.* —**at·ten′u·a′tor** *n.*

**at·test** (ə test′) *vt.* [< L *ad-*, to + *testari*, to bear witness] **1** to declare to be true or genuine **2** to certify, as by oath **3** to serve as proof of —*vi.* to bear witness (*to*) —**at·tes·ta·tion** (at′əs tā′shən) *n.*

**at·tic** (at′ik) *n.* [< Gr *Attikos*, of Attica (ancient Gr state): with reference to architectural style] the room or space just below the roof; garret

**At·ti·la** (at′′l ə, ə til′ə) A.D. 406?-453; king of the Huns: called *Attila the Hun*

**at·tire** (ə tīr′) *vt.* **-tired′, -tir′ing** [< OFr *a*, to + *tire*, order, row] to dress, esp. in fine garments; clothe —*n.* clothes, esp. fine or rich apparel

**at·ti·tude** (at′ə tood′) *n.* [ult. < L *aptus*, apt] **1** a bodily posture showing mood, action, etc. **2** a manner showing one's feelings or thoughts **3** one's disposition, opinion, etc. **4** [Slang] a quarrelsome or haughty temperament or manner

**at·ti·tu·di·nize** (at′ə tood′′n īz′) *vi.* **-nized′, -niz′ing** to pose for effect

**Attn** or **attn** *abbrev.* attention

**at·tor·ney** (ə tur′nē) *n., pl.* **-neys** [< OFr *a-*, to + *torner*, to turn] any person legally empowered to act for another; esp., a lawyer

**attorney at law** a lawyer

**attorney general** *pl.* **attorneys general** or **attorney generals** the chief law officer of a government

**at·tract** (ə trakt′) *vt.* [< L *ad-*, to + *trahere*, to draw] **1** to draw to itself or oneself **2** to get the admiration, attention, etc. of; allure —*vi.* to be attractive —**at·tract′a·ble** *adj.*

**at·trac·tion** (ə trak′shən) *n.* **1** an attracting or being attracted **2** power to attract; esp., charm **3** anything that attracts **4** *Physics* the mutual tendency of bodies to draw together

**at·trac′tive** (-tiv) *adj.* that attracts; esp., pleasing, charming, pretty, etc. —**at·trac′tive·ly** *adv.* —**at·trac′tive·ness** *n.*

**at·trib·ute** (ə trib′yoot; *for n.* a′trə byoot′) *vt.* **-ut·ed, -ut·ing** [< L *ad-*, to + *tribuere*, assign] to think of as belonging *to* a certain person or thing —*n.* a characteristic or quality of a person or thing —**at·trib′ut·a·ble** *adj.* —**at·tri·bu·tion** (a′trə byoo′shən) *n.*

**at·trib·u·tive** (ə trib′yoo tiv) *adj.* **1** attributing **2** preceding the noun it modifies: said of an adjective —**at·trib′u·tive·ly** *adv.*

**at·tri·tion** (ə trish′ən) *n.* [< L *ad-*, to + *terere*, to rub] **1** a wearing away by or as by friction **2** a normal loss of personnel, as by retirement

**at·tune** (ə toon′) *vt.* **-tuned′, -tun′ing 1** to tune **2** to bring into harmony

**atty** *abbrev.* attorney

**ATV** (ā′tē′vē′) *n., pl.* **ATVs** ⟦*A*(*ll*-)*T*(*errain*) *V*(*ehi-cle*)⟧ a small motor vehicle for traveling over rough ground, snow and ice, etc.

**a·twit·ter** (ə twit′ər) *adv., adj.* twittering

**a·typ·i·cal** (ā tip′i kəl) *adj.* not typical; abnormal —a·typ′i·cal·ly *adv.*

**Au** ⟦L *aurum*⟧ *Chem. symbol for* gold

**au·burn** (ô′bərn) *adj., n.* ⟦< L *albus*, white: infl. by ME *brun*, brown⟧ reddish brown

**Auck·land** (ôk′lənd) seaport in N New Zealand: pop. 910,000

**auc·tion** (ôk′shən) *n.* ⟦< L *augere*, to increase⟧ a public sale of items, one by one, to the highest bidder for each item —*vt.* to sell at auction — **auction off** to sell at auction —**auc′tion·eer′** *n.*

**au·da·cious** (ô dā′shəs) *adj.* ⟦< L *audax*, bold⟧ 1 bold; daring 2 too bold; brazen; insolent —au·da′cious·ly *adv.* —au·da′cious·ness *n.*

**au·dac·i·ty** (ô das′ə tē) *n.* 1 bold courage 2 insolence; impudence 3 *pl.* **-ties** an audacious act or remark

**au·di·ble** (ô′də bəl) *adj.* ⟦< L *audire*, hear⟧ loud enough to be heard —**au′di·bil′i·ty** (-bil′ə tē) *n.* — au′di·bly *adv.*

**au·di·ence** (ô′dē əns) *n.* ⟦< L *audire*, hear⟧ 1 those assembled to hear and see something 2 all those reached by a TV or radio program, book, etc. 3 a hearing, esp. a formal interview

**au·di·o** (ô′dē ō′) *adj.* ⟦< L *audire*, hear⟧ 1 of frequencies corresponding to audible sound waves 2 of sound reproduction, as of the sound phase of television

**au′di·o·book′** *n.* a recording of a reading of a book, as by the author

**au·di·ol·o·gy** (ô′dē äl′ə jē) *n.* evaluation and treatment of hearing defects —**au′di·ol′o·gist** *n.*

**au·di·om′e·ter** (-äm′ət ər) *n.* an instrument for measuring the sharpness and range of hearing — au′di·o·met′ric (-ō me′trik) *adj.*

**au·di·o·phile** (ô′dē ō fīl′) *n.* a devotee of high-fidelity sound reproduction, as from recordings

**au·di·o·vis·u·al** (ô′dē ō vizh′ōō əl) *adj.* 1 involving both hearing and sight 2 of teaching aids such as films and recordings

**au·dit** (ôd′it) *n.* ⟦< L *auditus*, a hearing⟧ a formal checking of financial records —*vt., vi.* 1 to check (accounts, etc.) 2 to attend (a college class) as a listener receiving no credit

**au·di·tion** (ô dish′ən) *n.* ⟦< L *audire*, hear⟧ a hearing to try out an actor, singer, etc. —*vt., vi.* to try out in an audition

**au·di·tor** (ô′dit ər) *n.* 1 a listener 2 one who audits accounts 3 one who audits classes

**au·di·to·ri·um** (ô′də tôr′ē əm) *n.* 1 a room where an audience sits 2 a building or hall for speeches, concerts, etc.

**au·di·to·ry** (ô′də tôr′ē) *adj.* of hearing or the sense of hearing

**auf Wie·der·seh·en** (ouf vē′dər zā′ən) ⟦Ger⟧ goodbye

**au·ger** (ô′gər) *n.* ⟦< OE *nafu*, hub (of a wheel) + *gar*, a spear⟧ a tool for boring holes in wood

**aught** (ôt) *n.* ⟦< OE *a*, ever + *wiht*, creature⟧ 1 anything whatever 2 ⟦< (N)AUGHT⟧ a zero

**aug·ment** (ôg ment′) *vt., vi.* ⟦< L *augere*, to increase⟧ to make or become greater —**aug′men·ta′tion** *n.* —aug·ment′er *n.*

**au gra·tin** (ō grat′′n, -grät′-) ⟦Fr⟧ with a crust of bread crumbs and grated cheese

**au·gur** (ô′gər) *n.* ⟦L, priest at fertility rites⟧ a prophet; soothsayer —*vt., vi.* 1 to prophesy 2 to be an omen (of) —**augur ill** (or **well**) to be a bad (or good) omen

**au·gu·ry** (ô′gyōō rē) *n.* 1 the practice of divination 2 *pl.* **-ries** an omen; portent

**au·gust** (ô gust′) *adj.* ⟦L *augustus*⟧ inspiring awe; imposing —**au·gust′ly** *adv.* —au·gust′ness *n.*

**Au·gust** (ô′gəst) *n.* ⟦< L *Augustus*⟧ the eighth month of the year, having 31 days: abbrev. **Aug**

**Au·gus·ta** (ô gus′tə) capital of Maine: pop. 21,000

**Au·gus·tine** (ô′gəs tēn′, ə gus′tin), Saint (A.D. 354-430); early Christian church father

**Au·gus·tus** (ô gus′təs) 63 B.C.-A.D. 14; 1st Rom. emperor (27 B.C.-A.D. 14)

**au jus** (ō zhōō′, ō jōōs′) ⟦Fr⟧ served in its natural juices: said of meat

**auk** (ôk) *n.* ⟦< ON *alka*⟧ a diving bird of northern seas, with webbed feet and short wings used as paddles

**auld lang syne** (ôld′ laŋ′ zīn′) ⟦Scot, lit., old long since⟧ the good old days

**aunt** (ant, änt) *n.* ⟦< L *amita*⟧ 1 a sister of one's mother or father 2 the wife of one's uncle

**au poivre** (ō pwäv′rə) ⟦Fr⟧ with crushed black peppercorns and a sauce

**au·ra** (ô′rə) *n., pl.* **-ras** or **-rae** (-rē) ⟦< Gr⟧ 1 an invisible emanation 2 a particular quality surrounding a person or thing

**au·ral** (ô′rəl) *adj.* ⟦< L *auris*, ear⟧ of the ear or the sense of hearing

**au·re·ole** (ô′rē ōl′) *n.* ⟦< L *aurum*, gold⟧ 1 a halo 2 a corona around the sun

**Au·re·o·my·cin** (ô′rē ō mī′sin) *trademark* for an antibiotic used to treat infections and viruses

**au re·voir** (ō′rə vwär′) ⟦Fr⟧ goodbye

**au·ri·cle** (ô′ri kəl) *n.* ⟦< L dim. of *auris*, ear⟧ the outer part of the ear

**Au·ro·ra**[1] (ô rôr′ə) *n., pl.* for 2 & 3 **-ras** or **-rae** (-ē) 1 the Rom. goddess of dawn 2 [a-] the dawn 3 [a-] a luminous band in the night sky

**Au·ro·ra**[2] (ô rôr′ə) city in central Colorado: pop. 222,000

**aurora aus·tra·lis** (ô strä′lis) the aurora in the sky of the S Hemisphere

**aurora bo·re·al·is** (bôr′ē al′is) the aurora in the sky of the N Hemisphere

**aus·cul·ta·tion** (ôs′kəl tā′shən) *n.* ⟦L *auscultare*, to listen⟧ a listening, often with a stethoscope, to sounds in the chest, abdomen, etc. so as to determine the condition of the heart, lungs, etc. — aus′cul·tate′, -tat·ed, -tat·ing, *vt., vi.*

**aus·pice** (ôs′pis) *n., pl.* **-pi·ces** (-pə siz, -sēz′) ⟦< L *auspicium*, omen⟧ 1 an omen 2 a favorable omen or sign 3 [*pl.*] sponsorship; patronage

**aus·pi·cious** (ôs pish′əs) *adj.* 1 favorable; propitious 2 successful —**aus·pi′cious·ly** *adv.* —aus·pi′cious·ness *n.*

**Aus·sie** (ôs′ē) *adj., n.* [Inf.] Australian

**Aus·ten** (ôs′tən), Jane 1775-1817; Eng. novelist

**aus·tere** (ô stir′) *adj.* ⟦< Gr *austēros*, dry⟧ 1 stern; severe 2 showing strict self-control; ascetic 3 very plain; lacking ornament —**aus·tere′ly** *adv.*

**aus·ter·i·ty** (ô ster′ə tē) *n., pl.* **-ties** 1 sternness 2 an austere practice, act, or manner 3 tightened economy

**Aus·tin** (ôs′tən) capital of Texas, in the central part: pop. 466,000

**aus·tral** (ôs′trəl) *adj.* ⟦< L *auster*, the south⟧ southern

**Aus·tral·ia** (ô strāl′yə) 1 island continent between the S Pacific and Indian oceans 2 country comprising this continent & Tasmania: 2,966,150 sq. mi.; pop. 16,849,000 —**Aus·tral′ian** *adj., n.*

**Aus·tri·a** (ôs′trē ə) country in central Europe: 32,378 sq. mi.; pop. 7,796,000 —**Aus′tri·an** *adj., n.*

**au·then·tic** (ô then′tik) *adj.* ⟦< Gr *authentikos*, genuine⟧ 1 credible, reliable, etc.: said as of a news report 2 genuine; real —**au·then′ti·cal·ly** *adv.* —au·then·tic·i·ty (ô′thən tis′ə tē) *n.*

**au·then′ti·cate′** (-ti kāt′) *vt.* **-cat·ed, -cat·ing** 1 to make authentic or valid 2 to verify 3 to prove to be genuine —**au·then′ti·ca′tion** *n.*

**au·thor** (ô′thər) *n.* ⟦< L *augere*, to increase⟧ 1 one who makes or creates something 2 a writer of books, etc. —*vt.* to be the author of

**au·thor·i·tar·i·an** (ə thôr′ə ter′ē ən) *adj.* believing in or characterized by absolute obedience to authority —*n.* an advocate or enforcer of such obedience —**au·thor′i·tar′i·an·ism′** *n.*

**au·thor'i·ta·tive** (-tāt'iv) *adj.* **1** having authority; official **2** based on competent authority; reliable —**au·thor'i·ta·tive·ly** *adv.* —**au·thor'i·ta·tive·ness** *n.*

**au·thor'i·ty** (-tē) *n.*, *pl.* **-ties** ⟦see AUTHOR⟧ **1** the power or right to command, act, etc. **2** [*pl.*] officials with this power **3** power or influence resulting from knowledge, prestige, etc. **4** a person, writing, etc. cited to support an opinion **5** an expert

**au·thor·ize** (ô'thər īz') *vt.* **-ized'**, **-iz'ing 1** to give official approval to **2** to give power or authority to **3** to justify —**au'thor·i·za'tion** *n.* —**au'thor·iz'er** *n.*

**Authorized Version** the revised English translation of the Bible published in England in 1611 with the authorization of King James I

**au'thor·ship'** *n.* origin or source with regard to author or originator

**au·tism** (ô'tiz'əm) *n.* ⟦AUT(O)- + -ISM⟧ a developmental disorder marked by impaired social interaction, communication difficulties, etc. —**au·tis'tic** (-tis'tik) *adj.*

**au·to** (ôt'ō) *n.*, *pl.* **-tos** an automobile

**auto-** ⟦< Gr *autos*, self⟧ *combining form* **1** self **2** by oneself or itself **3** automatic

**au·to·bi·og·ra·phy** (ôt'ō bī ä'grə fē) *n.*, *pl.* **-phies** the story of one's own life written by oneself —**au'to·bi'o·graph'i·cal** (-bī'ə graf'i kəl) *adj.* —**au'to·bi'o·graph'i·cal·ly** *adv.*

**au·toc·ra·cy** (ô tä'krə sē) *n.* ⟦see fol.⟧ **1** government in which one person has absolute power **2** *pl.* **-cies** a country with such government

**au·to·crat** (ôt'ə krat') *n.* ⟦< Gr *autos*, self + *kratos*, power⟧ **1** a ruler with absolute power **2** any domineering person —**au'to·crat'ic** *adj.* —**au'to·crat'i·cal·ly** *adv.*

**au·to·di·dact** (ôt'ō dī'dakt') *n.* ⟦see AUTO- & DIDACTIC⟧ a person who is self-taught

**au·to·graph** (ôt'ə graf') *n.* ⟦< Gr *autos*, self + *graphein*, write⟧ a person's own signature or handwriting —*vt.* to write one's signature on or in

**au'to·mate** (-māt') *vt.* **-mat'ed**, **-mat'ing** ⟦< AUTO-MATION⟧ to convert to automation or use automation in

**au·to·mat·ic** (ôt'ə mat'ik) *adj.* ⟦Gr *automatos*, self-moving⟧ **1** done unthinkingly, as from habit or by reflex **2** working by itself **3** using automatic equipment **4** capable of firing continuously until the trigger is released —*n.* **1** an automatic firearm **2** a motor vehicle with a transmission that shifts gears automatically —**au'to·mat'i·cal·ly** *adv.*

**automatic pilot** a gyroscopic instrument that automatically keeps an aircraft, missile, etc. to a predetermined course and position

**au'to·ma'tion** (-mā'shən) *n.* ⟦AUTOMA(TIC) + -TION⟧ a manufacturing system in which many or all of the processes are automatically performed or controlled, as by electronic devices

**au·tom·a·tism** (ô täm'ə tiz'əm) *n.* automatic quality, condition, or action —**au·tom'a·tize** (-tīz'), **-tized'**, **-tiz'ing**, *vt.*

**au·tom'a·ton'** (-tän', -tən) *n.*, *pl.* **-tons'** or **-ta** (-tə) ⟦see AUTOMATIC⟧ **1** any automatic device, esp. a robot **2** a person acting like a robot

**au·to·mo·bile** (ôt'ə mə bēl') *n.* ⟦Fr: see AUTO- & MOBILE⟧ a four-wheeled passenger car with a built-in engine

**au'to·mo'tive** (-mōt'iv) *adj.* ⟦AUTO- + -MOTIVE⟧ **1** self-moving **2** having to do with automobiles, trucks, etc.

**au·to·nom'ic** (-näm'ik) *adj.* of or controlled by the part of the nervous system regulating motor functions of the heart, lungs, etc.

**au·ton·o·mous** (ô tän'ə məs) *adj.* ⟦< Gr *autos*, self + *nomos*, law⟧ **1** having self-government **2** existing or functioning independently —**au·ton'o·mous·ly** *adv.* —**au·ton'o·my** (-mē) *n.*

**au·top·sy** (ô'täp'sē) *n.*, *pl.* **-sies** ⟦< Gr *autos*, self + *opsis*, a sight⟧ examination of a dead body to discover the cause of death

**au·tumn** (ôt'əm) *n.* ⟦< L *autumnus*⟧ the season

between summer and winter; fall —**au·tum·nal** (ô tum'nəl) *adj.*

**aux·il·ia·ry** (ôg zil'yə rē, -ə rē) *adj.* ⟦< L *augere*, to increase⟧ **1** helping **2** subsidiary **3** supplementary —*n.*, *pl.* **-ries** an auxiliary person or thing

**auxiliary verb** *Gram.* a verb that helps form tenses, moods, voices, etc. of other verbs, as *have, be, do, will, must*

**aux·in** (ôk'sin) *n.* ⟦< Gr *auxein*, to increase⟧ a plant hormone that promotes and controls growth

**av** *abbrev.* **1** average **2** avoirdupois

**Av** *abbrev.* **1** Avenue **2** avoirdupois

**a·vail** (ə vāl') *vi.*, *vt.* ⟦< L *ad*, to + *valere*, be strong⟧ to be of use, help, or worth (to) —*n.* use or help; advantage *[to no avail]* —**avail oneself of** to take advantage of; utilize

**a·vail'a·ble** *adj.* **1** that can be used **2** that can be gotten or had; handy —**a·vail'a·bil'i·ty** *n.*

**av·a·lanche** (av'ə lanch') *n.* ⟦Fr⟧ **1** a large mass of loosened snow, earth, etc. sliding down a mountain **2** an overwhelming amount coming suddenly

**a·vant-garde** (ə vänt'gärd', ä'-) *n.* ⟦Fr⟧ the leaders in new movements, esp. in the arts; vanguard —*adj.* of such movements

**av·a·rice** (av'ə ris) *n.* ⟦< L *avere*, to desire⟧ greed for money —**av·a·ri·cious** (av'ə rish'əs) *adj.* —**av'a·ri'cious·ly** *adv.*

**a·vast** (ə vast') *interj.* ⟦< Du *houd vast*, hold fast⟧ *Naut.* stop! cease!

**av·a·tar** (av'ə tär') *n.* ⟦Sans *avatāra*, descent⟧ **1** *Hinduism* a god's coming to earth in bodily form **2** an embodiment, as of a quality in a person

**a·vaunt** (ə vônt') *interj.* ⟦< L *ab*, from + *ante*, before⟧ [Archaic] go away!

**avdp** *abbrev.* avoirdupois

**Ave** *abbrev.* Avenue

**A·ve Ma·ri·a** (ä'vā mə rē'ə) ⟦L⟧ *R.C.Ch.* the prayer beginning with the words "Hail, Mary"

**a·venge** (ə venj') *vt.* **a·venged'**, **a·veng'ing** ⟦< L *ad*, to + *vindicare*, to claim⟧ **1** to get revenge for (an injury, etc.) **2** to take vengeance on behalf of —**a·veng'er** *n.*

**av·e·nue** (av'ə nōō') *n.* ⟦< L *ad-*, to + *venire*, come⟧ **1** a street, drive, etc., esp. when broad **2** a way of approach

**a·ver** (ə vur') *vt.* **a·verred'**, **a·ver'ring** ⟦< L *ad-*, to + *verus*, true⟧ to declare to be; affirm; assert

**av·er·age** (av'ər ij, av'rij) *n.* ⟦< OFr *avarie*, damage to ship or goods; hence, idea of shared losses⟧ **1** the result of dividing the sum of two or more quantities by the number of quantities **2** the usual kind, amount, etc. —*adj.* **1** constituting an average **2** ordinary; normal —*vt.* **-aged**, **-ag·ing 1** to figure out the average of **2** to do, take, etc. on average *[to average six sales a day]* **3** to divide proportionally —**average out** to arrive at an average eventually —**on (the) average** as an average amount, rate, etc.

**a·verse** (ə vurs') *adj.* ⟦see AVERT⟧ unwilling; opposed (*to*)

**a·ver·sion** (ə vur'zhən) *n.* **1** an intense dislike **2** the object arousing this

**a·vert** (ə vurt') *vt.* ⟦< L *a-*, from + *vertere*, to turn⟧ **1** to turn (the eyes, etc.) away **2** to ward off; prevent

**avg** *abbrev.* average

**a·vi·an** (ā'vē ən) *adj.* ⟦< L *avis*, bird + -AN⟧ of or having to do with birds

**a·vi·ar·y** (ā'vē er'ē) *n.*, *pl.* **-ar'ies** ⟦< L *avis*, bird⟧ a large cage or building for keeping many birds

**a·vi·a·tion** (ā'vē ā'shən) *n.* ⟦see prec.⟧ **1** the art or science of flying airplanes **2** the field of aircraft design, construction, etc.

**a'vi·a'tor** *n.* ⟦Fr *aviateur*⟧ an airplane pilot —**a'vi·a'trix** (-triks), *pl.* **-trix·es** or **-tri·ces'** (-tri sēz'), *fem.n.*

**av·id** (av'id) *adj.* ⟦< L *avere*, to desire⟧ very eager or greedy —**a·vid·i·ty** (ə vid'ə tē) *n.* —**av'id·ly** *adv.*

**a·vi·on·ics** (ā′vē än′iks) *n.* ⟦AVI(ATION) + (ELEC-TR)ONICS⟧ electronics as applied in aviation and astronautics

**av·o·ca·do** (av′ə kä′dō, ä′və-) *n.*, *pl.* **-dos** ⟦< AmInd⟧ **1** a thick-skinned, pear-shaped tropical fruit with yellow, buttery flesh **2** the tree it grows on **3** a yellowish-green color

**av·o·ca·tion** (av′ə kā′shən) *n.* ⟦< L *a-*, away + *vocare*, to call⟧ something done in addition to one's regular work; hobby —**av′o·ca′tion·al** *adj.*

**a·void** (ə void′) *vt.* ⟦ME < OFr *esvuidier*, to empty⟧ **1** to keep away from; evade; shun **2** to prevent — **a·void′a·ble** *adj.* —**a·void′a·bly** *adv.* —**a·void′ance** *n.*

**av·oir·du·pois** (av′ər də poiz′) *n.* ⟦< OFr *aveir de peis*, goods of weight⟧ **1** a system of weights in which 16 oz. = 1 lb.: also **avoirdupois weight 2** [Inf.] weight, esp. of a person

**a·vouch** (ə vouch′) *vt.* ⟦see ADVOCATE⟧ **1** to vouch for **2** to affirm **3** to avow

**a·vow** (ə vou′) *vt.* ⟦see ADVOCATE⟧ to declare or acknowledge openly —**a·vow′al** *n.* —**a·vowed′** *adj.* —**a·vow′ed·ly** *adv.*

**a·vun·cu·lar** (ə vuŋ′kyōō lər) *adj.* ⟦< L *avunculus*⟧ of or like an uncle

**aw** (ô) *interj.* a sound of protest, sympathy, etc.

**a·wait** (ə wāt′) *vt.*, *vi.* **1** to wait for or expect **2** to be in store for

**a·wake** (ə wāk′) *vt.*, *vi.* **a·woke′** or **a·waked′**, **a·waked′** or **a·wok′en**, **a·wak′ing** ⟦< OE⟧ **1** to rouse from sleep **2** to rouse from inactivity —*adj.* **1** not asleep **2** active or alert

**a·wak·en** (ə wā′kən) *vt.*, *vi.* to awake; wake up — **a·wak′en·ing** *n.*, *adj.*

**a·ward** (ə wôrd′) *vt.* ⟦< ME < Anglo-Fr *eswarder*⟧ **1** to give, as by legal decision **2** to give (a prize, etc.); grant —*n.* **1** *Law* a decision, as by a judge **2** something awarded; prize

**a·ware** (ə wer′) *adj.* ⟦< OE *wær*, cautious⟧ knowing; realizing; conscious —**a·ware′ness** *n.*

**a·wash** (ə wôsh′) *adv.*, *adj.* **1** at a level where the water washes over the surface **2** flooded

**a·way** (ə wā′) *adv.* ⟦< OE *on weg*⟧ **1** from a place [run *away*] **2** *a*) in another place or direction [*away* from here] *b*) in the proper place [put your tools *away*] **3** off; aside [turn *away*] **4** far [*away* behind] **5** from one's possession [give it *away*] **6** at once [fire *away*] **7** continuously [working *away* all night] —*adj.* **1** absent **2** at a distance [a mile *away*] —*interj.* begone! —**away with** go, come, or take away —**do away with** get rid of or kill

**awe** (ô) *n.* ⟦< ON *agi*⟧ a mixed feeling of reverence, fear, and wonder —*vt.* **awed, aw′ing** to fill with awe —**stand** (or **be**) **in awe of** to respect and fear

**a·weigh** (ə wā′) *adj.* just clear of the bottom: said of an anchor

**awe·some** (ô′səm) *adj.* **1** inspiring awe **2** [Slang] wonderful; impressive —**awe′some·ly** *adv.* —**awe′some·ness** *n.*

**awe-struck** (ô′struk′) *adj.* filled with awe: also **awe′strick·en** (-strik′ən)

**aw·ful** (ô′fəl) *adj.* **1** inspiring awe **2** terrifying **3** very bad —*adv.* [Inf.] very —**aw′ful·ness** *n.*

**aw·ful·ly** (ô′fə lē, ô′flē) *adv.* **1** in an awful way **2** [Inf.] very

**a·while** (ə wīl′, -hwīl′) *adv.* for a short time

**awk·ward** (ôk′wərd) *adj.* ⟦< ON *ǫfugr*, turned backward⟧ **1** clumsy; bungling **2** hard to handle; unwieldy **3** uncomfortable [an *awkward* pose] **4** embarrassed or embarrassing —**awk′ward·ly** *adv.* —**awk′ward·ness** *n.*

**awl** (ôl) *n.* ⟦< OE *æl*⟧ a small, pointed tool for making holes in wood, leather, etc.

**awn** (ôn) *n.* ⟦< ON *ǫgn*⟧ the bristly fibers on a head of barley, oats, etc.

**awn·ing** (ôn′iŋ) *n.* ⟦< ? MFr *auvent*, a sloping roof⟧ a structure, as of canvas, extended before a window, door, etc. as a protection from the sun or rain

**a·woke** (ə wōk′) *vt.*, *vi. pt. of* AWAKE

**a·wok′en** *vt.*, *vi. alt. pp. of* AWAKE

**A·WOL** or **a·wol** (ā′wôl′) *adj.*, *adv. Mil.* absent without leave

**a·wry** (ə rī′) *adv.*, *adj.* ⟦see A-¹ & WRY⟧ **1** with a twist to a side; askew **2** wrong; amiss [our plans went *awry*]

**ax** or **axe** (aks) *n.*, *pl.* **ax′es** ⟦< OE *æx*⟧ a tool with a long handle and a head with a blade, for chopping wood, etc. —*vt.* **axed, ax′ing 1** to trim, split, etc. with an ax **2** to get rid of —**give** (or **get**) **the ax** [Inf.] to discharge (or be discharged) from a job —**have an ax to grind** [Inf.] to have an object of one's own to gain or promote

**ax·el** (ak′səl) *n.* ⟦after *Axel* Paulsen (1865-1938), Norw skater⟧ a jump in which a skater turns in the air and lands facing in the opposite direction

**ax·i·al** (ak′sē əl) *adj.* **1** of, like, or forming an axis **2** around, on, or along an axis —**ax′i·al·ly** *adv.*

**ax·i·om** (ak′sē əm) *n.* ⟦< Gr *axios*, worthy⟧ **1** *a*) a statement universally accepted as true; maxim *b*) a self-evident truth **2** an established principle, scientific law, etc. —**ax′i·o·mat′ic** (-ə mat′ik) *adj.*

**ax·is** (ak′sis) *n.*, *pl.* **ax′es** (-sēz′) ⟦L⟧ **1** a real or imaginary straight line on which an object rotates **2** a central line around which the parts of a thing, system, etc. are evenly arranged —**the Axis** Germany, Italy, and Japan in WWII

**ax·le** (ak′səl) *n.* ⟦< ON *ǫxull*⟧ **1** a rod on or with which a wheel turns **2** *a*) a bar connecting two opposite wheels, as of an automobile *b*) the spindle at either end of such a bar

**Ax·min·ster** (aks′min′stər) *n.* ⟦< English town where first made⟧ varicolored, patterned carpet with a cut pile

**ax·o·lotl** (ak′sə lät′'l) *n.* ⟦< AmInd⟧ a dark salamander of Mexico and the W U.S.

**ax·on** (ak′sän′) *n.* ⟦< Gr *axōn*, axis⟧ that part of a nerve cell through which impulses travel away from the cell body

**a·ya·tol·lah** (ī′yə tō′lə) *n.* ⟦< Ar *āyat*, sign + *Allah*, Allah⟧ a leader of a Muslim sect, serving as teacher, judge, etc.

**aye¹** (ā) *adv.* ⟦< ON *ei*⟧ [Old Poet.] always; ever: also **ay**

**aye²** (ī) *adv.* ⟦prob. < *I*, pers. pron.⟧ yes —*n.* an affirmative vote or voter Also **ay**

**AZ** Arizona

**a·za·lea** (ə zāl′yə) *n.* ⟦< Gr *azaleos*, dry: it thrives in dry soil⟧ **1** a shrub of the heath family, with flowers of various colors **2** the flower

**Az·er·bai·jan** (äz′ər bī jän′, az′-) country in W Asia: formerly a republic of the U.S.S.R.: 33,430 sq. mi.; pop. 7,021,000

**az·i·muth** (az′ə məth) *n.* ⟦< Ar *al*, the + *samt*, way⟧ *Astronomy, Surveying* distance clockwise in degrees from the north point or, in the Southern Hemisphere, south point

**A·zores** (ā′zôrz′, ə zôrz′) group of Portuguese islands in the N Atlantic, west of Portugal

**AZT** (ā′zē′tē′) *n.* ⟦*az*(*ido*)*t*(*hymidine*)⟧ an antiviral drug used to treat AIDS

**Az·tec** (az′tek′) *n.* **1** a member of an Amerindian people that had an advanced civilization in Mexico before the Spanish conquest in 1519 **2** the language of this people —*adj.* of the Aztecs, their language, etc.: also **Az′tec·an**

**az·ure** (azh′ər) *adj.* ⟦< Pers *lāzhuward*, lapis lazuli⟧ sky-blue —*n.* **1** sky blue or any similar blue color **2** [Old Poet.] the blue sky

# B

**b¹** or **B** (bē) *n., pl.* **b's, B's** the second letter of the English alphabet

**b²** *abbrev.* born

**B¹** (bē) *n.* **1** a blood type **2** a grade indicating above-average but not outstanding work **3** *Music* the seventh tone in the scale of C major —*adj.* inferior to the best [a *B* movie]

**B²** *abbrev.* **1** bachelor **2** *Baseball a)* base *b)* baseman **3** *Music* bass Also **b**

**B³** *Chem. symbol for* boron

**Ba** *Chem. symbol for* barium

**BA** or **B.A.** *abbrev.* Bachelor of Arts

**baa** (bä) *vi., n.* [echoic] bleat

**Ba·al** (bā′əl) *n.* [< Heb] an ancient fertility god

**bab·ble** (bab′əl) *vi.* **-bled, -bling** [echoic] **1** to talk like a small child; prattle **2** to talk foolishly or too much **3** to murmur, as a brook does when flowing over stones —*vt.* to say incoherently or foolishly —*n.* **1** incoherent vocal sounds **2** foolish talk **3** a murmuring sound —**bab′bler** *n.*

**babe** (bāb) *n.* **1** a baby **2** a naive person: also **babe in the woods 3** [Slang] a girl or young woman, esp. an attractive one

**Ba·bel** (bā′bəl, bab′əl) *n.* **1** *Bible* a city thwarted in building a tower to heaven when God created a confusion of tongues **2** [*also* **b-**] a confusion of voices, sounds, etc. or the scene of this

**ba·boon** (ba bōōn′, bə-) *n.* [< OFr *babuin,* ape, fool] a large, fierce, dog-faced, short-tailed monkey of Africa and Arabia

**ba·bush·ka** (bə bōōsh′kə) *n.* [Russ, grandmother] a woman's scarf worn on the head and tied under the chin

**ba·by** (bā′bē) *n., pl.* **-bies** [ME *babi*] **1** a very young child; infant **2** one who acts like an infant **3** a very young animal **4** the youngest or smallest in a group **5** [Slang] darling; honey **6** [Slang] any person or thing —*adj.* **1** of or for an infant **2** very young **3** small of its kind **4** childish —*vt.* **-bied, -by·ing** to pamper; coddle —**ba′by·hood′** *n.* —**ba′by·ish** *adj.*

**baby beef** meat from a prime heifer or steer that is one to two years old

**baby boom′er** a person born during the birthrate increase (the **baby boom**) after 1945

**baby carriage** a small vehicle, pushed by hand, for wheeling a baby about: also **baby buggy**

**baby grand** a small grand piano

**Bab·y·lon** (bab′ə län′) capital of Babylonia: noted for luxury and wickedness

**Bab·y·lo·ni·a** (bab′ə lō′nē ə) ancient empire in SW Asia —**Bab′y·lo′ni·an** *adj., n.*

**baby's breath** a plant with small, delicate, white or pink flowers

**baby sitter** a person hired to take care of a child or children, as when the parents are away for the evening —**ba′by-sit′, -sat′, -sit′ting,** *vi., vt.*

**baby talk** playful talk for amusing a baby or in imitating a baby

**bac·ca·lau·re·ate** (bak′ə lôr′ē it) *n.* [< ML *baccalaris,* young nobleman seeking knighthood] **1** the degree of Bachelor of Arts, Bachelor of Science, etc. **2** a commencement address

**bac·cha·nal** (bak′ə nal′) *n.* a drunken orgy —**bac′cha·na′li·an** (-nā′lē ən) *adj., n.*

**Bac·chus** (bak′əs) *n.* the Greek and Roman god of wine and revelry

**Bach** (bäkh), **Jo·hann Se·bas·ti·an** (yō′hän′ zā bäs′tē än′) 1685-1750; Ger. organist & composer

**bach·e·lor** (bach′ə lər, bach′lər) *n.* [< ML *baccalaris:* see BACCALAUREATE] an unmarried man —**bach′e·lor·hood′** *n.*

**Bachelor of Arts** (or **Science,** etc.) **1** a degree given by a college or university to one who has completed a four-year course in the humanities (or in science, etc.): also **bachelor's degree 2** one who holds this degree

**bachelor's button** any of several plants with white, pink, or blue flowers, as the cornflower

**ba·cil·lus** (bə sil′əs) *n., pl.* **-cil′li′** (-ī′) [< L *bacillum,* little stick] **1** any of a genus of rod-shaped bacteria **2** loosely, any of the bacteria —**bac·il·lar·y** (bas′ə ler′ē, bə sil′ər ē) *adj.*

**back** (bak) *n.* [< OE *baec*] **1** the rear (or, in some animals, the top) part of the body from the nape of the neck to the end of the spine **2** the backbone **3** a part that supports or fits the back **4** the rear part or reverse of anything **5** *Sports* a player or position behind the front line —*adj.* **1** at the rear **2** remote **3** of or for the past [*back* pay] **4** backward —*adv.* **1** at, to, or toward the rear **2** to or toward a former condition, time, etc. **3** in reserve or concealment **4** in return or requital [pay him *back*] —*vt.* **1** to move backward **2** to support **3** to bet on **4** to provide or be a back for —*vi.* to go backward —**back and forth** backward and forward —**back down** to withdraw from a position or claim —(**in**) **back of** behind —**back off 1** to move back **2** [Inf.] BACK DOWN —**back out (of) 1** to withdraw from an enterprise **2** to evade keeping a promise, etc. —**back up 1** to support **2** to move backward: also **back away 3** to accumulate because of restricted movement [traffic *backed up*] **4** *Comput.* to make a standby copy of (data, etc.) —**go back on** [Inf.] **1** to be disloyal to; betray **2** to fail to keep (one's word, etc.) —**turn one's back on 1** to turn away from, as in contempt **2** to abandon

**back′ache′** *n.* an ache or pain in the back

**back′bite′** *vt., vi.* **-bit′, -bit′ten** or **-bit′, -bit′ing** to slander (someone absent) —**back′bit′er** *n.*

**back′board′** *n.* **1** a board at or forming the back of something **2** *Basketball* the board behind the basket

**back′bone′** *n.* **1** the spine **2** a main support **3** willpower, courage, etc.

**back′break′ing** *adj.* very tiring

**back′coun′try** *n.* a remote, thinly populated area

**back′drop′** *n.* **1** a curtain, often scenic, at the back of a stage **2** background or setting

**back′er** *n.* **1** a patron; sponsor **2** one who bets on a contestant

**back′field′** *n.* *Football* the players behind the line

**back′fire′** *n.* **1** the burning out of a small area, as in a forest, to check the spread of a big fire **2** premature ignition or an explosion of gases in an internal-combustion engine **3** reverse explosion in a gun —*vi.* **-fired′, -fir′ing 1** to explode as a backfire **2** to go awry or boomerang

**back′gam′mon** (-gam′ən) *n.* [BACK + ME *gammen,* game] a game for two, with dice governing moves of pieces on a special board

**back′ground′** *n.* **1** the distant part of a scene **2** surroundings, sounds, etc. behind or subordinate to something **3** one's training and experience **4** events leading up to something

**back′ground′er** *n.* a press briefing at which background information is provided

**back′hand′** *n.* **1** handwriting that slants up to the left **2** a backhand catch, stroke, etc. —*adj.* **1** done with the back of the hand; specif., done with the back of the hand turned inward, as for a baseball catch, or forward, as for a tennis stroke, and with the arm across the body **2** written in backhand —*adv.* with a backhand —*vt.* to hit, catch, swing, etc. backhand

**back′hand′ed** *adj.* **1** BACKHAND **2** indirect or sarcastic —*adv.* with a backhand

**back'hoe'** (-hō') *n.* an excavating vehicle with a hinged bucket at the end of a long arm

**back'ing** *n.* 1 something forming a back for support 2 support given to a person or cause 3 supporters; backers

**back'lash'** *n.* sharp reaction or recoil

**back'log'** *n.* an accumulation or reserve —*vi.*, *vt.* -logged', -log'ging to accumulate as a backlog

**back order** an order not yet filled

**back'pack'** *n.* a knapsack, specif. one attached to a frame and worn as by hikers —*vi.*, *vt.* to hike with, or carry in, a backpack —**back'pack'er** *n.*

**back'ped'al** *vi.* -ped'aled or -ped'alled, -ped'al-ing or -ped'al-ling 1 to pedal backward, as in braking a bicycle 2 to move backward; retreat 3 to retract an earlier opinion

**back'rest'** *n.* a support for or at the back

**back'-scratch'ing** *n.* [Inf.] a reciprocal exchange of favors, etc.

**back'side'** *n.* 1 the back part 2 the rump

**back'slap'per** (-slap'ər) *n.* [Inf.] an effusively friendly person

**back'slash'** *n.* a short diagonal line (\): a character found esp. on computer keyboards

**back'slide'** *vi.* -slid', -slid' or -slid'den, -slid'ing to regress in morals, etc. —**back'slid'er** *n.*

**back'space'** *vi.* -spaced', -spac'ing to move a typewriter carriage, cursor, etc. one or more spaces back along the line

**back'spin'** *n.* a backward spin given to a ball, etc., making it reverse direction upon hitting a surface

**back'splash'** *n.* a washable surface behind a sink, etc. to protect a wall from splashes

**back'stage'** *adv.*, *adj.* behind and off the stage, as in the wings or dressing rooms

**back'stairs'** *adj.* involving intrigue or scandal; secret: also **back'stair'**

**back'stop'** *n.* a fence, screen, etc. to keep balls from going too far, as behind the catcher in baseball

**back'stretch'** *n.* the part of a racetrack opposite the homestretch

**back'stroke'** *n.* a swimming stroke made while lying face upward

**back'swing'** *n.* that part of a player's swing in which the golf club, tennis racket, etc. is swung backward before being swung forward

**back talk** [Inf.] insolent replies

**back'-to-back'** *adj.* [Inf.] one right after another

**back'track'** *vi.* 1 to return by the same path 2 to retreat or reverse

**back'up'** or **back'-up'** *adj.* 1 standing by as an alternate or auxiliary 2 supporting —*n.* a backing up; specif., *a)* an accumulation *b)* a support or help

**back'ward** *adv.* 1 toward the back 2 with the back foremost 3 in reverse order 4 in a way opposite to usual 5 into the past Also **back'wards** —*adj.* 1 turned toward the rear or in the opposite way 2 shy 3 slow or retarded — **back'ward-ness** *n.*

**back'wash'** *n.* 1 water or air moved backward, as by a ship, propeller, etc. 2 a reaction caused by some event

**back'wa'ter** *n.* 1 water moved or held back by a dam, tide, etc. 2 stagnant water in an inlet, etc. 3 a backward place or condition

**back'woods'** *pl.n.* [*occas. with sing. v.*] 1 heavily wooded areas far from centers of population 2 any remote, thinly populated area —*adj.* of or like the backwoods —**back'woods'man** (-mən), *pl.* -men (-mən), *n.*

**ba·con** (bā'kən) *n.* [< OS *baco*, side of bacon] salted and smoked meat from the back or sides of a hog

**Ba·con** (bā'kən), **Fran·cis** (fran'sis) 1561-1626; Eng. philosopher & writer

**bac·te·ri·a** (bak tir'ē ə) *pl.n.*, *sing.* -ri·um (-əm) or -ri·a [< Gr *baktērion*, small staff] microorganisms which have no chlorophyll and multiply by simple division: some bacteria cause diseases, but others are necessary for fermentation, etc. —**bac·te'ri·al** *adj.*

**bac·te'ri·cide'** (-tir'ə sīd') *n.* an agent that destroys bacteria —**bac·te'ri·cid'al** *adj.*

**bac·te'ri·ol'o·gy** (-tir'ē äl'ə jē) *n.* the science that deals with bacteria —**bac·te'ri·o·log'i·cal** (-ə läj'ə kəl) *adj.* —**bac·te'ri·ol'o·gist** *n.*

**bad**[1] (bad) *adj.* **worse, worst** ⟦ME⟧ 1 not good; not as it should be 2 inadequate or unfit 3 unfavorable *[bad* news*]* 4 rotten or spoiled 5 incorrect or faulty 6 *a)* wicked; immoral *b)* misbehaving; mischievous 7 harmful 8 severe 9 ill 10 sorry; distressed *[he feels bad* about it*]* 11 offensive —*adv.* [Inf.] badly —*n.* anything bad —**not bad** [Inf.] fairly good —**bad'ness** *n.*

**bad**[2] (bad) *vt.*, *vi.* archaic pt. of BID

**bad blood** (mutual) ill will

**bade** (bad) *vt.*, *vi.* alt. pt. of BID

**bad egg** [Slang] a mean or dishonest person: also **bad actor, bad apple,** or **bad lot**

**bad faith** insincerity; dishonesty

**badge** (baj) *n.* ⟦ME *bage*⟧ 1 an emblem worn to show rank, membership, etc. 2 any distinctive sign, etc.

**badg·er** (baj'ər) *n.* [< ?] 1 a burrowing animal with a broad back and thick, short legs 2 its fur —*vt.* to nag or torment

**bad·i·nage** (bad'n äzh') *n.* ⟦Fr⟧ playful talk; banter

**bad·lands** (bad'landz') *pl.n.* 1 an area of barren land with dry soil and soft rocks eroded into odd shapes 2 [B-] any of several such W U.S. areas

**bad'ly** *adv.* **worse, worst** 1 in a bad manner 2 [Inf.] very much; greatly

**bad'man'** (-man') *n.*, *pl.* -men (-men') a cattle thief or desperado of the old West

**bad·min·ton** (bad'mint'n) *n.* ⟦after *Badminton,* Eng estate⟧ a game in which a shuttlecock is batted back and forth with rackets across a net

**bad'-mouth'** *vt.* [Slang] to find fault with; disparage

**bad'-tem'pered** *adj.* irritable

**Bae·de·ker** (bā'də kər) *n.* 1 any of a series of guidebooks to foreign countries, first published in Germany 2 loosely, any guidebook

**baf·fle** (baf'əl) *vt.* -fled, -fling [< ?] 1 to perplex completely; bewilder 2 to impede; check —*n.* a wall or screen to deflect air, sound, etc. —**baf'fle-ment** *n.* —**baf'fler** *n.* —**baf'fling** *adj.*

**bag** (bag) *n.* ⟦< ON *baggi*⟧ 1 a nonrigid container of paper, plastic, etc., with an open top 2 a satchel; suitcase, etc. 3 a purse 4 game taken in hunting 5 a baglike shape or part 6 a bagful 7 [Slang] an unattractive woman 8 [Slang] one's special interest 9 *Baseball* a base —*vt.* **bagged, bag'ging** 1 to put into a bag 2 to capture 3 to kill in hunting 4 [Slang] to obtain —*vi.* 1 to swell; bulge 2 to hang loosely —**in the bag** [Slang] having its success assured

**bag·a·telle** (bag'ə tel') *n.* ⟦Fr < L *baca*, berry⟧ a trifle

**ba·gel** (bā'gəl) *n.* ⟦Yiddish⟧ a chewy bread roll shaped like a small doughnut

**bag'ful'** *n.*, *pl.* -fuls' as much as a bag will hold

**bag·gage** (bag'ij) *n.* ⟦< ML *bagga*, chest, bag⟧ 1 the bags, etc. of a traveler; luggage 2 burdensome beliefs, practices, etc.

**bag·gie** (bag'ē) *n.* ⟦< *Baggies,* a trademark for such bags⟧ a small, clear plastic bag for storing food, etc.

**bag·gy** (bag'ē) *adj.* -gi·er, -gi·est puffed out or hanging loosely —**bag'gi·ly** *adv.* —**bag'gi·ness** *n.*

**Bagh·dad** (bag'dad) capital of Iraq: pop. 1,900,000: also sp. **Bag·dad**

**bag lady** [Slang] a homeless, poor woman who wanders city streets carrying her belongings in shopping bags

**bag'pipe'** *n.* [*often pl.*] a wind instrument, now chiefly Scottish, played by forcing air from a bag

into reed pipes and fingering the stops

**bah** (bä, ba) *interj.* used to express contempt, scorn, or disgust

**Ba·ha·mas** (bə hä′məz) country on a group of islands (**Bahama Islands**) in the West Indies: 5,353 sq. mi.; pop. 264,000

**Bah·rain** (bä rān′) country on a group of islands in the Persian Gulf: 266 sq. mi.; pop. 518,000: also sp. **Bah·rein**

BAGPIPE

**bail**¹ (bāl) *n.* ⟦< L *bajulare*, bear a burden⟧ **1** money deposited with the court to get a prisoner temporarily released **2** such a release —*vt.* **1** to have (a prisoner) set free by giving bail **2** to help out of financial or other difficulty Often with *out* —**bail′a·ble** *adj.*

**bail**² (bāl) *n.* ⟦ME *baille*, bucket⟧ a bucket for dipping up water from a boat —*vi., vt.* to dip out (water) from (a boat): usually with *out* —**bail out 1** to parachute from an aircraft **2** [Inf.] to flee a difficult situation

**bail**³ (bāl) *n.* ⟦ME *beil*⟧ a hoop-shaped handle for a bucket, etc.

**bail·iff** (bā′lif) *n.* ⟦ME *bailif*⟧ **1** a deputy sheriff **2** a court officer who guards the jurors, keeps order in the court, etc. **3** in England, a district official **4** [Chiefly Brit.] a steward of an estate

**bail·i·wick** (bā′lə wik′) *n.* ⟦ME < *baili*, bailiff + *wik*, village⟧ **1** a bailiff's district **2** one's particular area of activity, authority, interest, etc.

**bails·man** (bālz′mən) *n., pl.* **-men** (-mən) a person who gives bail for another

**bairn** (bern) *n.* [Scot.] a child

**bait** (bāt) *vt.* ⟦< ON *beita*⟧ **1** to set dogs on for sport [to *bait* bears] **2** to torment or harass, esp. by verbal attacks **3** to goad or provoke **4** to put food on (a hook or trap) as a lure for game **5** to lure; entice; tempt —*n.* **1** food, etc. put on a hook or trap as a lure **2** anything used as a lure

**bait′-and-switch′** *adj.* of or using an unethical sales technique in which a seller lures customers by advertising an often nonexistent bargain item and then tries to switch their attention to more expensive items

**baize** (bāz) *n.* ⟦< L *badius,* brown⟧ a coarse, felt-like woolen cloth

**Ba·ja Ca·li·for·nia** (bä′hä kä′lē fôr′nyä) state of NW Mexico, south of California: 27,071 sq. mi.; pop. 1,661,000

**Baja California Sur** state of NW Mexico, south of Baja California: 28,447 sq. mi.; pop. 318,000

**bake** (bāk) *vt.* **baked, bak′ing** ⟦< OE *bacan*⟧ **1** to cook (food) by dry heat, esp. in an oven **2** to dry and harden (pottery, etc.) by heat; fire —*vi.* **1** to bake bread, etc. **2** to become baked —*n.* **1** a baking **2** a social affair at which baked food is served

**baked beans** navy beans baked with salt pork, molasses or brown sugar, etc.

**bak·er** (bā′kər) *n.* one whose work or business is baking bread, etc.

**baker's dozen** thirteen

**Bak·ers·field** (bā′kərz fēld′) city in SC California: pop. 175,000

**bak′er·y** *n.* **1** *pl.* **-er·ies** a place where bread, etc. is baked or sold **2** [Dial.] baked goods

**baking powder** a leavening agent containing baking soda and an acid-forming substance

**baking soda** sodium bicarbonate, used as a leavening agent and as an antacid

**bal·a·lai·ka** (bal′ə līk′ə) *n.* ⟦Russ⟧ a Russian stringed instrument somewhat like a guitar

**bal·ance** (bal′əns) *n.* ⟦< LL *bilanx,* having two scales⟧ **1** an instrument for weighing, esp. one with two matched hanging scales **2** a state of equilibrium in weight, value, etc. **3** bodily equilibrium **4** mental or emotional stability **5** harmonious proportion of elements in a design, etc. **6** a weight, value, etc. that counteracts another **7** equality of debits and credits, or the difference between them **8** a remainder —*vt.* **-anced, -anc·ing 1** to weigh in or as in a balance **2** to compare as to relative value, etc. **3** to counteract; offset **4** to bring into proportion, harmony, etc. **5** to make or be equal to in weight, value, etc. **6** to find the difference between, or to equalize, the debits and credits of (an account) —*vi.* **1** to be in equilibrium **2** to be equal in weight, value, etc. **3** to have the credits and debits equal —**in the balance** not yet settled

**balance sheet** a statement showing the financial status of a business

**bal·co·ny** (bal′kə nē) *n., pl.* **-nies** ⟦< It *balcone*⟧ **1** a platform projecting from an upper story and enclosed by a railing **2** an upper floor of seats in a theater, etc., often projecting over the main floor

**bald** (bôld) *adj.* ⟦< ME⟧ **1** having a head with white fur, etc. growing on it **2** lacking hair on the head **3** not covered by natural growth **4** having the tread worn off **5** plain or blunt [bald truth] —**bald′ly** *adv.* —**bald′ness** *n.*

**bald eagle** a large eagle of North America, with a white-feathered head

**bal·der·dash** (bôl′dər dash′) *n.* ⟦orig. (17th c.), an odd mixture⟧ nonsense

**bald·faced** (bôld′fāst′) *adj.* brazen; shameless [a *baldfaced* lie]

**bald′ing** *adj.* becoming bald

**bal·dric** (bôl′drik′) *n.* ⟦ult. < L *balteus,* belt⟧ a belt worn over one shoulder to support a sword, etc.

**bale** (bāl) *n.* ⟦< OHG *balla,* ball⟧ a large bundle, esp. a standardized quantity of goods, as raw cotton, compressed and bound —*vt.* **baled, bal′ing** to make into bales —**bal′er** *n.*

**ba·leen** (bə lēn′) *n.* ⟦ult. < Gr *phallaina,* whale⟧ the horny, elastic material hanging from the upper jaw of some whales (**baleen whales**)

**bale·ful** (bāl′fəl) *adj.* ⟦< OE *bealu,* evil⟧ deadly; harmful; ominous

**Ba·li** (bä′lē, bal′ē) island of Indonesia —**Ba′li·nese′**, *pl.* **-nese′, *adj., n.***

**balk** (bôk) *n.* ⟦OE *balca,* ridge⟧ **1** an obstruction, hindrance, etc. **2** *Baseball* an illegal motion by the pitcher entitling base runners to advance one base —*vt.* to obstruct; foil —*vi.* **1** to stop and refuse to move or act **2** to hesitate or recoil (*at*)

**Balkan Peninsula** peninsula in SE Europe, east of Italy

**Bal·kans** (bôl′kənz) countries of Yugoslavia, Slovenia, Croatia, Bosnia and Herzegovina, Macedonia, Romania, Bulgaria, Albania, Greece, & European Turkey, in SE Europe —**Bal′kan** *adj.*

**balk·y** (bôk′ē) *adj.* **-i·er, -i·est** stubbornly resisting

**ball**¹ (bôl) *n.* ⟦ME *bal*⟧ **1** any round object; sphere; globe **2** *a*) a round or egg-shaped object used in various games *b*) any of several such games, esp. baseball **3** a throw or pitch of a ball [a fast *ball*] **4** a missile for a cannon, rifle, etc. **5** a rounded part of the body **6** *Baseball* a pitched ball that is not hit and is not a strike —*vi., vt.* to form into a ball —**ball up** [Slang] to muddle or confuse —**be on the ball** [Slang] to be alert; be efficient

**ball**² (bôl) *n.* ⟦< Fr < Gr *ballizein,* to dance⟧ **1** a formal social dance **2** [Slang] a good time

**bal·lad** (bal′əd) *n.* ⟦< OFr *ballade,* dancing song⟧ **1** a sentimental song with the same melody for each stanza **2** a narrative song or poem, usually anonymous, with simple words, short stanzas, and a refrain **3** a popular love song —**bal′lad·eer′** *n.* —**bal′lad·ry** *n.*

**ball′-and-sock′et joint** a joint, as of the hip, formed by a ball in a socket

**bal·last** (bal′əst) *n.* ⟦< MDu *bal,* bad⟧ **1** anything heavy carried in a ship or vehicle to give stability

**2** crushed rock or gravel, used in railroad beds, etc. —*vt.* to furnish with ballast

**ball bearing 1** a bearing in which the parts turn on freely rolling metal balls **2** one of these balls

**bal·le·ri·na** (bal′ə rē′nə) *n.* ⟦It⟧ a girl or woman ballet dancer

**bal·let** (ba lā′, bal′ā) *n.* ⟦Fr⟧ **1** an artistic dance form of graceful, precise gestures and movements **2** a play, etc. performed by ballet dancers, or the music for this **3** ballet dancers

**ball′game′** *n.* **1** a game played with a ball **2** [Inf.] a set of circumstances [a different *ballgame*]

BALL BEARING

**ballistic missile** a long-range guided missile designed to fall free as it approaches its target

**bal·lis·tics** (bə lis′tiks) *n.* the science dealing with the motion and impact of projectiles —**bal·lis′tic** *adj.*

**ball joint** a ball-and-socket joint used in automotive vehicles to connect the tie rods to the turning wheels

**bal·loon** (bə lōōn′) *n.* ⟦< Fr < It *palla*, ball⟧ **1** a large, airtight bag that rises when filled with hot air or a gas lighter than air **2** an airship with such a bag **3** an inflatable rubber bag, used as a toy **4** the large final payment on certain loans —*vt.* to inflate —*vi.* to swell; expand —*adj.* like a balloon —**bal·loon′ist** *n.*

**bal·lot** (bal′ət) *n.* ⟦< It *palla*, ball⟧ **1** a ticket, card, form, etc. by which a vote is registered **2** act or right of voting, as by ballots **3** the total number of votes cast —*vi.* to vote

**ball′park′** *n.* a baseball stadium

**ball′-peen′ hammer** a hammer with one end of the head rounded and the other end flat

**ball′play′er** *n.* a baseball player

**ball′point′** (**pen**) a writing pen with a small ball bearing instead of a point: also **ball′-point′** *n.*

**ball′room′** *n.* a large hall for dancing

**bal·lute** (bal lōōt′) *n.* ⟦BALL(OON) + (PARACH)UTE⟧ a balloonlike device used to slow down a spacecraft reentering the atmosphere

**bal·ly·hoo** (bal′ē hōō′) *n.* ⟦< ?⟧ noisy talk, sensational advertising, etc. —*vt., vi.* **-hooed′, -hoo′ing** [Inf.] to promote with ballyhoo

**balm** (bäm) *n.* ⟦< Gr *balsamon*⟧ **1** a fragrant, healing ointment or oil **2** anything healing or soothing

**balm′y** *adj.* **-i·er, -i·est 1** soothing, mild, etc. **2** [Slang, Chiefly Brit.] crazy

**ba·lo·ney** (bə lō′nē) *n.* ⟦< *bologna*⟧ **1** bologna **2** [Slang] nonsense

**bal·sa** (bôl′sə) *n.* ⟦Sp⟧ **1** the wood, very light in weight, of a tropical American tree **2** the tree

**bal·sam** (bôl′səm) *n.* ⟦see BALM⟧ **1** an aromatic resin obtained from certain trees **2** any of various aromatic, resinous oils or fluids **3** balm **4** any of various trees yielding balsam

**bal·sam·ic vinegar** (bôl sam′ik) aromatic, dark-brown vinegar used in salad dressings, etc.

**Bal·tic Sea** (bôl′tik) sea in N Europe, west of Latvia, Lithuania, & Estonia

**Bal·ti·more** (bôl′tə môr′) seaport in N Maryland: pop. 736,000

**bal·us·ter** (bal′əs tər) *n.* ⟦< Gr *balaustion*, wild pomegranate flower: from the shape⟧ any of the small posts of a railing, as on a staircase

**bal·us·trade** (bal′əs trād′) *n.* a railing having an upper rail supported by balusters

**Bal·zac** (bál zäk′; *E* bôl′zak), **Ho·no·ré de** (ô nô rā′ də) 1799-1850; Fr. novelist

**bam·boo** (bam bōō′) *n.* ⟦Malay *bambu*⟧ a treelike tropical grass with woody, jointed, often hollow stems used for furniture, canes, etc.

**bam·boo·zle** (bam bōō′zəl) *vt.* **-zled, -zling** ⟦< ?⟧ **1** to trick; cheat; dupe **2** to confuse; puzzle

**ban** (ban) *vt.* **banned, ban′ning** ⟦< OE *bannan*, summon⟧ to prohibit or forbid, esp. officially —*n.* **1** a condemnation by church authorities **2** a curse **3** an official prohibition **4** strong public condemnation

**ba·nal** (bā′nəl, bə nal′) *adj.* ⟦Fr: see prec.⟧ trite; hackneyed —**ba·nal′i·ty,** *pl.* **-ties,** *n.* —**ba′nal·ly** *adv.*

**ba·nan·a** (bə nan′ə) *n.* ⟦Sp & Port⟧ **1** a tropical plant with large clusters of edible fruit **2** the narrow, curved fruit, having soft pulp and thick, usually yellow skin

**band**[1] (band) *n.* ⟦ON⟧ **1** something that binds, ties, or encircles, as a strip or ring of wood, rubber, metal, etc. **2** a strip of color or of material **3** a division of an LP phonograph record **4** a range of wavelengths —*vt.* to put a band on or around

**band**[2] (band) *n.* ⟦< Gothic *bandwa*, a sign⟧ **1** a group of people united for some purpose **2** a group of musicians playing together, esp. upon wind and percussion instruments —*vi., vt.* to unite for some purpose

**band·age** (ban′dij) *n.* ⟦Fr < *bande*, a strip⟧ a strip of cloth, etc. used to bind or cover an injury —*vt.* **-aged, -ag·ing** to put a bandage on

**Band-Aid** (band′ād′) ⟦prec. + AID⟧ *trademark for* a small bandage of gauze and adhesive tape —*n.* [*also* **band-aid**] such a bandage: also **band′aid′**

**ban·dan·na** *or* **ban·dan·a** (ban dan′ə) *n.* ⟦Hindi *bāndhnū*, a method of dyeing⟧ a large, colored handkerchief

**band′box′** *n.* a light, round box to hold hats, etc.

**ban·deau** (ban dō′) *n., pl.* **-deaux′** (-dōz′) ⟦Fr⟧ **1** a narrow ribbon **2** a band of material covering the breasts, as a strapless bikini top

**ban·dit** (ban′dit) *n.* ⟦< It⟧ **1** a robber; brigand **2** one who steals, defrauds, etc. —**ban′dit·ry** *n.*

**ban·do·leer** *or* **ban·do·lier** (ban′də lir′) *n.* ⟦< Fr⟧ a broad belt with pockets for bullets, etc., worn over one shoulder and across the chest

**band saw** an endless toothed steel belt on pulleys, powered for sawing

**bands·man** (bandz′mən) *n., pl.* **-men** (-mən) a member of a band of musicians

**band′stand′** *n.* a platform for a band, esp. one for outdoor concerts

**band′wag′on** *n.* a wagon for a band to ride on, as in a parade —**on the bandwagon** [Inf.] on the popular or apparently winning side

**band′width′** *n.* the transmission rate of information along electronic communications lines

**ban·dy**[1] (ban′dē) *vt.* **-died, -dy·ing** ⟦Fr *bander*, bandy at tennis⟧ **1** to toss or hit back and forth **2** to pass (rumors, etc.) freely **3** to exchange (words), esp. angrily

**ban·dy**[2] (ban′dē) *adj.* ⟦Fr *bandé*, bent⟧ curved outward; bowed

**ban′dy·leg′ged** (-leg′id, -legd′) *adj.* bowlegged

**bane** (bān) *n.* ⟦OE *bana*⟧ **1** ruin, death, harm, or their cause **2** [Obs.] poison —**bane′ful** *adj.*

**bang**[1] (baŋ) *vt.* ⟦ON *banga*, to pound⟧ to hit, shut, etc. hard and noisily —*vi.* **1** to make a loud noise **2** to hit noisily or sharply —*n.* **1** a hard, noisy blow or impact **2** a loud, sudden noise **3** [Inf.] a burst of vigor **4** [Slang] a thrill —*adv.* **1** hard and noisily **2** abruptly —**bang up** to damage

**bang**[2] (baŋ) *n.* ⟦< prec.: see *adv.*, 2⟧ [*usually pl.*] hair cut to hang straight across the forehead

**Bang·kok** (baŋ′käk′) seaport & capital of Thailand: pop. 4,697,000

**Ban·gla·desh** (bäŋ′glə desh′, baŋ′-) country in S Asia, on the Bay of Bengal: 57,295 sq. mi.; pop. 109,887,000

**ban·gle** (baŋ′gəl) *n.* ⟦Hindi *bangrī*⟧ a decorative bracelet or anklet

**bang-up** (baŋ′up′) *adj.* [Inf.] very good; excellent

**ban·ish** (ban′ish) *vt.* ⟦< OFr *banir*⟧ **1** to exile **2** to get rid of —**ban′ish·ment** *n.*

**ban·is·ter** (ban′is tər) *n.* ⟦< BALUSTER⟧ a handrail, specif. one with balusters

**ban·jo** (ban′jō′) *n., pl.* **-jos′** *or* **-joes′** ⟦of Afr orig.⟧ a musical instrument with a long neck, circular body, and strings that are plucked —**ban'jo·ist** *n.*

**bank**[1] (baŋk) *n.* ⟦ult. < OHG *bank*, bench⟧ **1** an establishment for receiving or lending money **2** a reserve supply; pool —*vi.* to do business with a bank —*vt.* to deposit (money) in a bank —**bank on** [Inf.] to rely on —**bank'a·ble** *adj.*

**bank**[2] (baŋk) *n.* ⟦< ON *bakki*⟧ **1** a long mound or heap **2** a steep slope **3** a rise of land along a river, etc. **4** a shallow place, as in a sea **5** the lateral, slanting turn of an aircraft —*vt.* **1** to cover (a fire) with ashes and fuel so that it will burn slowly **2** to pile up so as to form a bank **3** to slope (a curve in a road, etc.) **4** to make (an aircraft) slant laterally on a turn **5** to make (a billiard ball) recoil from a cushion

**bank**[3] (baŋk) *n.* ⟦< OFr *banc*, bench⟧ **1** a row of oars **2** a row or tier, as of keys in a keyboard —*vt.* to arrange in a row or tier

**bank account** money deposited in a bank and credited to the depositor

**bank'book'** *n.* a book recording a bank depositor's deposits and withdrawals; passbook

**bank card** an encoded plastic card issued by a bank as for use at an ATM

**bank'er** *n.* a person who owns or manages a bank

**bank'ing** *n.* the business of a bank

**bank note** a promissory note issued by a bank: a form of paper money

**bank'roll'** *n.* a supply of money —*vt.* [Inf.] to supply with money; finance

**bank·rupt** (baŋk'rupt') *n.* ⟦< Fr < It *banca*, bench + *rotta*, broken⟧ a person legally declared unable to pay debts —*adj.* **1** that is a bankrupt; insolvent **2** lacking in some quality [morally *bankrupt*] —*vt.* to make bankrupt —**bank'rupt·cy**, *pl.* **-cies**, *n.*

**ban·ner** (ban'ər) *n.* ⟦ME *banere* < OFr *baniere*⟧ **1** a flag **2** a headline running across a newspaper page —*adj.* foremost

**banns** (banz) *pl.n.* ⟦see BAN⟧ the proclamation made in church of an intended marriage

**ban·quet** (baŋ'kwət) *n.* ⟦ult. < OHG *bank*, bench⟧ **1** a feast **2** a formal dinner —*vt.* to honor with a banquet

**ban·quette** (baŋ ket') *n.* ⟦Fr⟧ **1** a gunners' platform inside a trench, etc. **2** an upholstered bench

**ban·shee** or **ban·shie** (ban'shē) *n.* ⟦< Ir *bean*, woman + *sith*, fairy⟧ *Celt. Folklore* a female spirit whose wailing warns of impending death

**ban·tam** (ban'təm) *n.* ⟦after *Bantam*, former province in Java⟧ **1** any of various small, domestic fowls **2** a small but aggressive person —*adj.* like a bantam

**ban'tam·weight'** *n.* a boxer weighing 113 to 118 lb.

**ban·ter** (ban'tər) *vt.* ⟦17th-c. slang⟧ to tease playfully —*vi.* to exchange banter (with someone) —*n.* playful teasing —**ban'ter·ing·ly** *adv.*

**Ban·tu** (ban'tōō') *n.* ⟦Bantu *ba-ntu*, the men⟧ **1** a large group of languages of S Africa, including Swahili and Zulu **2** *pl.* **-tus'** or **-tu'** a member of a Bantu-speaking people

**ban·yan** (ban'yən) *n.* ⟦ult. < Sans⟧ an Indian fig tree whose branches grow shoots that take root and become new trunks over a wide area

**ba·o·bab** (bā'ō bab', bä'-) *n.* ⟦< Ethiopian native name⟧ a thick-trunked tree of Africa, with edible, gourdlike fruit

**bap·tism** (bap'tiz'əm) *n.* ⟦see BAPTIZE⟧ **1** the sacrament of admitting a person into a Christian church by immersing the individual in water or by sprinkling water on the individual **2** an initiating experience —**bap·tis'mal** (-tiz'məl) *adj.*

**Bap'tist** (-tist) *n.* a member of a Protestant denomination practicing baptism of believers by immersion

**bap'tis·ter·y** (-tis tər ē, -tis trē) *n.*, *pl.* **-ies** a place, esp. in a church, used for baptizing: also **bap'tis·try**, *pl.* **-tries**

**bap·tize** (bap tīz', bap'tīz) *vt.* **-tized', -tiz'ing** ⟦< Gr *baptizein*, to immerse⟧ **1** to administer baptism to **2** to initiate **3** to christen

**bar** (bär) *n.* ⟦< ML *barra*⟧ **1** any long, narrow piece of wood, metal, etc., often used as a barrier, lever, etc. **2** an oblong piece, as of soap **3** anything that obstructs or hinders **4** a band or strip **5** a law court, esp. that part, enclosed by a railing, where the lawyers sit **6** lawyers collectively **7** the legal profession **8** a counter, as for serving alcoholic drinks **9** a place with such a counter **10** *Music a)* a vertical line dividing a staff into measures *b)* a measure —*vt.* **barred, bar'ring 1** to fasten with a bar **2** to obstruct; close **3** to oppose **4** to exclude —*prep.* excluding [the best, *bar* none] —**cross the bar** to die

**barb** (bärb) *n.* ⟦< L *barba*, beard⟧ **1** a beardlike growth **2** a sharp point projecting backward from the main point of a fishhook, etc. **3** a cutting remark —*vt.* to provide with a barb —**barbed** *adj.*

**Bar·ba·dos** (bär bā'dōs, -dōz) country on an island in the West Indies: 166 sq. mi.; pop. 263,000

**bar·bar·i·an** (bär ber'ē ən) *n.* ⟦see BARBAROUS⟧ **1** a member of a people considered primitive, savage, etc. **2** a cruel person —*adj.* uncivilized, cruel, etc. —**bar·bar'i·an·ism'** *n.*

**bar·bar·ic** (-ber'ik) *adj.* **1** uncivilized; primitive **2** wild, crude, etc.

**bar·ba·rism** (bär'bə riz'əm) *n.* **1** a nonstandard word or expression **2** the state of being primitive or uncivilized **3** a barbarous act or custom

**bar·bar·i·ty** (bär ber'ə tē) *n.*, *pl.* **-ties 1** cruelty; brutality **2** a barbaric taste, manner, etc.

**bar·ba·rize** (bär'bə rīz') *vt.* **-rized', -riz'ing** to make or become barbarous —**bar'ba·ri·za'tion** *n.*

**bar·ba·rous** (bär'bə rəs) *adj.* ⟦< Gr *barbaros*, foreign⟧ **1** uncivilized; primitive **2** crude, coarse, etc. **3** cruel; brutal —**bar'ba·rous·ly** *adv.*

**bar·be·cue** (bär'bə kyōō') *n.* ⟦AmSp *barbacoa*⟧ **1** *a)* a hog, steer, etc. roasted whole over an open fire *b)* any meat broiled over an open fire **2** a party, picnic, etc. featuring this —*vt.* **-cued', -cu'ing** to roast or broil over an open fire, often with a highly seasoned sauce (**barbecue sauce**)

**barbed wire** wire with barbs at close intervals

**bar·bel** (bär'bəl) *n.* ⟦< L *barba*, beard⟧ a threadlike growth from the lips or jaws of certain fishes

BARBELL

**bar·bell** (bär'bel') *n.* ⟦BAR + (DUMB)BELL⟧ a metal bar with weights attached at each end, used for weight lifting: also **bar bell**

**bar·ber** (bär'bər) *n.* ⟦see BARB⟧ one whose work is cutting hair, shaving beards, etc. —*vt.* to cut the hair of, shave, etc. —*vi.* to work as a barber

**bar·ber·ry** (bär'ber'ē, -bə rē) *n.*, *pl.* **-ries** ⟦< ML *barberis*⟧ **1** a spiny shrub with sour, red berries **2** the berry

**bar·bi·tu·rate** (bär bich'ər it, -bich'ə wit) *n.* ⟦< Ger⟧ a salt or ester of a crystalline acid (**bar'bi·tu'ric acid**), used as a sedative

**barb'wire'** *n.* BARBED WIRE

**bar·ca·role** or **bar·ca·rolle** (bär'kə rōl') *n.* ⟦< Fr < It⟧ a Venetian gondolier song, or music like this

**Bar·ce·lo·na** (bär'sə lō'nə) seaport in NE Spain: pop. 1,753,000

**bar code** UNIVERSAL PRODUCT CODE

**bard** (bärd) *n.* ⟦Gael & Ir⟧ **1** an ancient Celtic poet **2** a poet

**bare** (ber) *adj.* **bar'er, bar'est** ⟦OE *bær*⟧ **1** not covered or clothed; naked **2** without furnishings; empty **3** simple; plain **4** mere *[bare needs]* —*vt.* **bared, bar'ing** to make bare; uncover —**lay bare** to uncover; expose —**bare'ness** *n.*

**bare'back'** *adv., adj.* on a horse with no saddle

**bare'-bones'** *adj.* simple; basic

**bare'faced'** *adj.* **1** with the face uncovered **2** open; shameless

**bare'foot** *adj., adv.* without shoes and stockings: also **bare'foot'ed**

**bare'hand'ed** *adj., adv.* **1** with hands uncovered or unprotected **2** without weapons, etc.

**bare'head'ed** *adj., adv.* wearing no hat or other covering on the head

**bare'leg'ged** (-leg'id, -legd') *adj., adv.* with the legs bare

**bare·ly** (ber'lē) *adv.* **1** plainly **2** only just; scarcely **3** scantily

**bar·gain** (bär'gən) *n.* ⟦< OFr *bargaignier,* haggle⟧ **1** a mutual agreement or contract **2** such an agreement with regard to worth *[a bad bargain]* **3** something sold at a price favorable to the buyer —*vi.* **1** to haggle **2** to make a bargain —**bargain for** (or **on**) to expect; count on —**into** (or **in**) **the bargain** besides —**bar'gain·er** *n.*

**bargain counter** a store counter for displaying goods at reduced prices

**barge** (bärj) *n.* ⟦< ML *barga*⟧ **1** a large, flat-bottomed boat for freight on rivers, etc. **2** a large pleasure boat —*vi.* **barged, barg'ing** **1** to move slowly and clumsily **2** to come or go (*in* or *into*) rudely or abruptly

**bar graph** a graph in which the lengths of parallel bars are used to compare quantities, etc.

**Bar Harbor** resort town on an island off E Maine: pop. 4,400

**bar·i·tone** (bar'ə tōn') *n.* ⟦< Gr *barys,* deep + *tonos,* tone⟧ **1** the range of a male voice between 'tenor and bass **2** a voice, singer, or instrument with such a range

**bar·i·um** (ber'ē əm) *n.* ⟦< Gr *barys,* heavy⟧ a metallic chemical element

**bark**[1] (bärk) *n.* ⟦< ON *bǫrkr*⟧ the outside covering of trees and woody plants —*vt.* **1** to remove bark from **2** [Inf.] to scrape; skin (the knees, etc.)

**bark**[2] (bärk) *vi.* ⟦OE *beorcan*⟧ **1** to make the sharp, abrupt cry of a dog or a similar sound **2** to speak sharply; snap —*n.* the characteristic cry of a dog, or any noise like this —**bark up the wrong tree** to misdirect one's attack, energies, etc.

**bark**[3] (bärk) *n.* ⟦< LL *barca*⟧ **1** [Old Poet.] a boat **2** a sailing vessel with two square-rigged masts forward and a fore-and-aft mast aft

**bar'keep'er** *n.* **1** an owner of a barroom **2** a bartender Also **bar'keep'**

**bark'er** *n.* one who talks loud to attract customers to a sideshow, etc.

**bar·ley** (bär'lē) *n.* ⟦OE *bærlic*⟧ **1** a cereal grass **2** its grain, used in making malt, in soups, etc.

**bar'maid'** *n.* a waitress who serves alcoholic drinks in a bar

**bar mitz·vah** (bär mits'və) ⟦< Yiddish < Aram *bar,* son of + Heb *mitsva,* commandment⟧ *[also* **B-M-**] **1** a Jewish boy who has arrived at the age of religious responsibility, thirteen years **2** the ceremony celebrating this event

**barn** (bärn) *n.* ⟦OE *bern*⟧ a farm building for sheltering harvested crops, livestock, machines, etc.

**bar·na·cle** (bär'nə kəl) *n.* ⟦ME *bernacle*⟧ a saltwater shellfish that attaches itself to rocks, ship bottoms, etc.

**barn'burn'er** *n.* [Slang] something dramatic and exciting, as a close contest

**barn'storm'** *vi., vt.* to tour (the country, esp. rural areas) giving speeches or lectures, performing exhibitions, etc. —**barn'storm'er** *n.*

**barn'yard'** *n.* the ground near a barn —*adj.* of, like, or fit for a barnyard; specif., earthy or crude

**ba·rom·e·ter** (bə räm'ət ər) *n.* ⟦< Gr *baros,* weight + -METER⟧ **1** an instrument for measuring atmospheric pressure and thus forecasting weather **2** anything that marks change —**bar·o·met·ric** (bar'ə me'trik) *adj.*

**bar·on** (bar'ən) *n.* ⟦ME⟧ **1** a member of the lowest rank of British nobility **2** a magnate — **bar'on·age** *n.* —**bar'on·ess** *fem.n.* —**ba·ro·ni·al** (bə rō'nē əl) *adj.*

**bar'on·et** (-ət) *n.* a man holding the lowest hereditary British title, below a baron —**bar'on·et·cy,** *pl.* **-cies,** *n.*

**ba·roque** (bə rōk') *adj.* ⟦Fr < Port *barroco,* imperfect pearl⟧ **1** [*often* **B-**] *a*) very ornate and full of curved lines, as much art and architecture of about 1600-1750 *b*) full of highly embellished melodies, fugues, etc., as much music of that time **2** gaudily ornate

**bar·racks** (bar'əks) *pl.n.* ⟦< Sp *barro,* clay⟧ [*often with sing. v.*] a building or group of buildings for housing soldiers, etc.

**bar·ra·cu·da** (bar'ə kōō'də) *n., pl.* **-da** or **-das** ⟦AmSp⟧ a fierce, pikelike fish of tropical seas

**bar·rage** (bə räzh', -räj') *n.* ⟦Fr < *barrer,* to stop⟧ **1** artillery fire that holds down the enemy while one's army attacks **2** any prolonged attack —*vi., vt.* **-raged', -rag'ing** to subject to a barrage

**barred** (bärd) *adj.* **1** having bars or stripes **2** closed off with bars **3** not allowed

**bar·rel** (bar'əl) *n.* ⟦< ML *barillus*⟧ **1** a large, cylindrical container with slightly bulging sides and flat ends **2** a similar cylindrical container **3** the capacity of a standard barrel, used as a measure **4** the straight tube of a gun —*vt.* **-reled** or **-relled, -rel·ing** or **-rel·ling** to put in barrels —*vi.* [Slang] to go at high speed

**bar'rel·ful'** (-fool') *n.* **1** as much as a barrel will hold **2** [Inf.] a great amount

**bar'rel·head'** *n.* the flat end of a barrel —**on the barrelhead** when delivered *[to pay cash on the barrelhead]*

**barrel organ** a mechanical musical instrument played by turning a crank

**bar·ren** (bar'ən) *adj.* ⟦< OFr⟧ **1** that cannot bear offspring; sterile **2** without vegetation **3** unproductive **4** boring; dull **5** devoid (*of*) —**bar'ren·ness** *n.*

**bar·rette** (bə ret') *n.* ⟦Fr⟧ a bar or clasp for holding a woman's hair in place

**bar·ri·cade** (bar'i kād'; *also, esp. for v.,* bar'ə kād') *n.* ⟦Fr < It *barricare,* fortify⟧ a barrier, esp. one put up hastily for defense —*vt.* **-cad'ed, -cad'ing** to block with a barricade

**bar·ri·er** (bar'ē ər) *n.* ⟦< ML *barra*⟧ **1** an obstruction, as a fence **2** anything that blocks or hinders

**bar·ring** (bär'iŋ) *prep.* excepting

**bar·ris·ter** (bar'is tər) *n.* ⟦< *bar* (law court)⟧ in England, a lawyer who pleads cases in court

**bar'room'** *n.* a room with a bar where alcoholic drinks are sold

**bar·row**[1] (bar'ō) *n.* ⟦< OE *beran,* to bear⟧ a handbarrow or wheelbarrow

**bar·row**[2] (bar'ō) *n.* ⟦< OE *beorg,* hill⟧ a heap of earth or rocks covering a grave

**bar'tend'er** *n.* one who serves alcoholic drinks at a bar

**bar·ter** (bärt'ər) *vi., vt.* ⟦< OFr *barater*⟧ to trade by exchanging (goods) without money —*n.* **1** a bartering **2** anything bartered —**bar'ter·er** *n.*

**Bar·tók** (bär'tôk'), **Bé·la** (bā'lä) 1881-1945; Hung. composer

**bar·y·on** (bar'ē än') *n.* ⟦< Gr *barys,* heavy + (ELEC-TR)ON⟧ any of certain subatomic particles including the proton and neutron

**ba·sal** (bā'səl) *adj.* **1** of or at the base **2** basic; fundamental

**basal metabolism** the minimum quantity of energy used by an organism at rest to sustain its life

**ba·salt** (bə sôlt′, bā′sôlt′) *n.* ⟦L *basaltes*⟧ a hard, dark volcanic rock

**base**[1] (bās) *n.* ⟦< Gr *basis*⟧ **1** the thing or part on which something rests **2** the most important element or principal ingredient **3** the part of a word to which affixes are attached **4** a basis **5** any of the four markers a baseball player must consecutively touch to score a run **6** a headquarters or a source of supply **7** *Chem.* a substance that forms a salt when it reacts with an acid —*adj.* forming a base —*vt.* **based, bas′ing 1** to make a base for **2** to establish

**base**[2] (bās) *adj.* **bas′er, bas′est** ⟦< VL *bassus*, low⟧ **1** mean; ignoble **2** menial **3** poor in quality **4** of comparatively low worth [*base* metal] —**base′ly** *adv.* —**base′ness** *n.*

**base′ball′** *n.* **1** a game played with a ball and bat by two opposing teams on a field with four bases forming a diamond **2** the ball used in this game

**base′board′** *n.* a board or molding at the base of a wall

**base hit** *Baseball* a play in which the batter hits a fair ball and gets on base without an error or without forcing out a teammate

**base′less** *adj.* having no basis in fact; unfounded —**base′less·ness** *n.*

**base line 1** a line serving as a base **2** *Baseball* the lane between any two consecutive bases **3** *Basketball, Tennis* the line at either end of the court Also **base′line′**

**base′man** (-mən) *n., pl.* **-men** (-mən) *Baseball* an infielder stationed at first, second, or third base

**base′ment** *n.* the story below the main floor

**base on balls** *Baseball* WALK

**base pay** the basic rate of pay not counting overtime pay, etc.

**base runner** *Baseball* a player who is on base or is trying to reach a base

**bash** (bash) *vt.* ⟦echoic⟧ [Inf.] to hit hard —*n.* [Slang] a party

**bash′ful** (-fəl) *adj.* ⟦(A)BASH + -FUL⟧ easily embarrassed; shy —**bash′ful·ly** *adv.* —**bash′ful·ness** *n.*

**bas·ic** (bā′sik) *adj.* **1** fundamental **2** *Chem.* alkaline —*n.* a basic principle, factor, etc. —**bas′i·cal·ly** *adv.*

**BASIC** (bā′sik) *n.* ⟦*B*(*eginner's*) *A*(*ll-purpose*) *S*(*ymbolic*) *I*(*nstruction*) *C*(*ode*)⟧ a simple computer language that uses common words and algebra

**bas·il** (bā′zəl, baz′əl) *n.* ⟦< Gr *basilikon*⟧ a fragrant herb of the mint family, used in cooking

**ba·sil·i·ca** (bə sil′i kə) *n.* ⟦< Gr *basilikē* (*stoa*), royal (portico)⟧ **1** a church with a broad nave, side aisles, and an apse **2** *R.C.Ch.* a church with certain ceremonial rights

**ba·sin** (bā′sin) *n.* ⟦< VL *bacca*, water vessel⟧ **1** a wide, shallow container for liquid **2** its contents **3** a sink **4** any shallow, rounded hollow, often containing water **5** RIVER BASIN

**ba·sis** (bā′sis) *n., pl.* **-ses** (-sēz′) ⟦< Gr, a base⟧ **1** a base or foundation **2** a principal constituent **3** a fundamental principle or theory

**bask** (bask) *vi.* ⟦ME *basken*, to wallow⟧ **1** to warm oneself pleasantly **2** to enjoy a warm feeling from being in a certain situation

**bas·ket** (bas′kit) *n.* ⟦ME⟧ **1** a container made of interwoven cane, wood strips, etc. **2** its contents **3** *Basketball a)* the goal, a round, open, hanging net *b)* a goal made by shooting the ball through this net

**bas′ket·ball′** *n.* ⟦invented & named (1891) by James A. Naismith (1861-1939)⟧ **1** a team game played with a bouncy, round ball on a court having a raised basket at each end **2** this ball

**basket weave** a weave of fabrics resembling the weave used in making baskets

**bas′ket·work′** *n.* work that is woven like a basket; wickerwork

**bas mitz·vah** (bäs mits′və) BAT MITZVAH

**Basque** (bask) *n.* **1** a member of a people living in the W Pyrenees **2** the language of this people —*adj.* of the Basques

**bas-re·lief** (bä′ri lēf′, bas′-) *n.* ⟦Fr < It: see BASS[1] & RELIEF⟧ sculpture in which figures project slightly from a flat background

**bass**[1] (bās) *n.* ⟦< VL *bassus*, low⟧ **1** the range of the lowest male voice **2** a voice, singer, or instrument with such a range; specif., a double bass **3** a part for a bass **4** a low, deep sound —*adj.* of or for a bass

**bass**[2] (bas) *n., pl.* **bass** or **bass′es** ⟦OE *baers*⟧ a spiny-finned food and game fish of fresh or salt water

**bas·set** (bas′it) *n.* ⟦< OFr *bas*, low⟧ a hunting hound with a long body, short forelegs, and long, drooping ears

**bas·si·net** (bas′ə net′) *n.* ⟦< Fr dim. of *berceau*, a cradle⟧ a basketlike bed for an infant, often hooded and on wheels

**bas·so** (bas′ō, bäs′-) *n., pl.* **-sos** or **-si** (-sē) ⟦< VL *bassus*, low⟧ a bass voice or singer

**bas·soon** (ba sōōn′, bə-) *n.* ⟦< VL *bassus*, low⟧ a double-reed bass woodwind instrument

**bast** (bast) *n.* ⟦OE *bæst*⟧ plant fiber used in ropes, mats, etc.

**bas·tard** (bas′tərd) *n.* ⟦< OFr⟧ an illegitimate child —*adj.* **1** of illegitimate birth **2** inferior, sham, etc. —**bas′tar·dy** (-tər dē) *n.*

**bas·tard·ize** (bas′tər dīz′) *vt.* **-ized′, -iz′ing 1** to make, declare, or show to be a bastard **2** to make corrupt; debase —**bas′tard·i·za′tion** *n.*

BASSOON

**baste**[1] (bāst) *vt.* **bast′ed, bast′ing** ⟦< Gmc *bastjan*, make with bast⟧ to sew temporarily with long, loose stitches until properly sewed

**baste**[2] (bāst) *vt.* **bast′ed, bast′ing** ⟦< OFr *bassin*, basin⟧ to moisten (meat) with melted butter, drippings, etc. while roasting —**bast′er** *n.*

**baste**[3] (bāst) *vt.* **bast′ed, bast′ing** ⟦ON *beysta*⟧ **1** to beat soundly **2** to attack with words

**bas·tille** or **bas·tile** (bas tēl′) *n.* ⟦< OFr *bastir*, to build⟧ a prison —**the Bastille** a state prison in Paris destroyed (1789) in the French Revolution

**bas·tion** (bas′chən, -tē ən) *n.* ⟦see BASTILLE⟧ **1** a projection from a fortification **2** any strong defense

**bat**[1] (bat) *n.* ⟦OE *batt*⟧ **1** a stout club **2** a club to hit the ball in baseball, etc. **3** a turn at batting **4** [Inf.] a blow —*vt.* **bat′ted, bat′ting** to hit, as with a bat —*vi.* to take a turn at batting

**bat**[2] (bat) *n.* ⟦< Scand⟧ a furry, nocturnal flying mammal with membranous wings

**bat**[3] (bat) *vt.* **bat′ted, bat′ting** ⟦< OFr *battre*, to batter⟧ [Inf.] to wink —**not bat an eye** [Inf.] not show surprise

**batch** (bach) *n.* ⟦OE *bacan*, to bake⟧ **1** the amount (of bread, etc.) in one baking **2** one set, lot, group, etc. **3** an amount of work for processing by a computer in a single run

**bate** (bāt) *vt.* **bat′ed, bat′ing** ⟦< OFr *abattre*, beat down⟧ to abate or lessen —**with bated breath** holding the breath, as in fear

**bath** (bath) *n., pl.* **baths** (ba*th*z, baths) ⟦OE *bæth*⟧ **1** a washing, esp. of the body, in water **2** water, etc. for bathing or for soaking or treating something **3** a bathtub **4** a bathroom **5** a BATHHOUSE (sense 1)

**bathe** (bā*th*) *vt.* **bathed, bath′ing** ⟦OE *bæth*⟧ **1** to put into a liquid **2** to give a bath to **3** to cover as with liquid —*vi.* **1** to take a bath **2** to soak oneself in something —**bath·er** (bā′*th*ər) *n.*

**bath′house′** *n.* **1** a public building for taking baths **2** a building used by bathers for changing clothes

**bathing suit** a swimsuit

**bath′mat′** *n.* a mat used in or next to a bathtub

**ba·thos** (bā′thäs′) *n.* 〚< Gr *bathys*, deep〛 **1** ANTI-CLIMAX (sense 1) **2** excessive sentimentality **3** triteness —**ba·thet·ic** (bə thet′ik) *adj.*

**bath′robe′** *n.* a loose robe worn to and from the bath, etc.

**bath′room′** *n.* **1** a room with a bathtub, toilet, etc. **2** a lavatory

**bath′tub′** *n.* a tub to bathe in

**bath·y·scaph** (bath′ə skaf′) *n.* 〚< Gr *bathys*, deep + *skaphē*, boat〛 a deep-sea diving apparatus for reaching great depths without a cable: also **bath′y·scaphe′** (-skaf′, -skāf′)

**ba·tik** (bə tēk′) *n.* 〚Malay〛 cloth with a design made by dyeing only the parts not coated with wax

**ba·tiste** (bə tēst′, ba-) *n.* 〚Fr: after supposed orig. maker, *Baptiste*〛 a fine, thin cloth of cotton, rayon, etc.

**bat mitz·vah** (bät mits′və) [*also* B- M-] **1** a Jewish girl who has arrived at the age of religious responsibility, 13 years **2** the ceremony celebrating this event

**ba·ton** (bə tän′, ba-) *n.* 〚Fr〛 **1** a staff serving as a symbol of office **2** a slender stick used in directing music **3** a metal rod twirled by a drum major **4** a short, light rod used in relay races

**Bat·on Rouge** (bat′'n rōōzh′) capital of Louisiana: pop. 220,000

**bat·tal·ion** (bə tal′yən) *n.* 〚< VL *battalia*, battle〛 a tactical military unit forming part of a division

**bat·ten**[1] (bat′'n) *n.* 〚var. of *baton*〛 **1** a sawed strip of wood **2** a strip of wood put over a seam between boards as a fastening or covering —*vt.* to fasten or supply with battens

**bat·ten**[2] (bat′'n) *vi., vt.* 〚ON *batna*, improve〛 to fatten; thrive

**bat·ten**[3] (bat′'n) *n.* 〚< OFr *battre*, to batter〛 in a loom, the movable frame that presses into place the threads of a woof

**bat·ter**[1] (bat′ər) *vt.* 〚< L *battuere*, to beat〛 **1** to strike with blow after blow **2** to injure by pounding, hard wear, or use —*vi.* to pound noisily and repeatedly

**bat·ter**[2] (bat′ər) *n. Baseball, Cricket* the player at bat

**bat·ter**[3] (bat′ər) *n.* 〚OFr *bature*〛 a flowing mixture of flour, milk, etc. for making pancakes, etc.

**battering ram** a heavy beam, etc. for battering down gates, etc.

**bat·ter·y** (bat′ər ē) *n., pl.* **-ies** 〚< OFr *battre*, to batter〛 **1** a battering **2** a set of things used together **3** *Baseball* the pitcher and the catcher **4** *Elec.* a cell or group of cells storing an electrical charge and able to furnish a current **5** *Law* any illegal beating of another person: see ASSAULT AND BATTERY **6** *Mil.* a set of heavy guns, rockets, etc.

**bat·ting** (bat′'n, -iŋ) *n.* 〚OE *batt*, BAT[1]〛 cotton, wool, or synthetic fiber wadded into sheets

**bat·tle** (bat′'l) *n.* 〚< L *battuere*, to beat〛 **1** a large-scale fight between armed forces **2** armed fighting **3** any fight or conflict —*vt., vi.* **-tled, -tling** to fight —**give** (or **do**) **battle** to fight

**bat′tle-ax′** or **bat′tle-axe′** *n.* **1** a heavy ax formerly used as a weapon **2** [Slang] a harsh, domineering woman

**bat′tle·field′** *n.* the site of a battle: also **bat′tle·ground′**

**bat′tle·ment** (-mənt) *n.* 〚< OFr *batailler*, fortify〛 a parapet with spaces for shooting, built atop a tower, etc.

**battle royal** *pl.* **battles royal** **1** a free-for-all **2** a heated dispute

**bat′tle·ship′** *n.* a large warship with big guns and very heavy armor

**bat·ty** (bat′ē) *adj.* **-ti·er, -ti·est** 〚< BAT[2]〛 [Slang] crazy or eccentric

**bau·ble** (bô′bəl) *n.* 〚< L *bellus*, pretty〛 a showy trifle; trinket

**baud** (bôd) *n.* 〚after J. M. E. *Baudot* (1845-1903), Fr inventor〛 the number of bits per second transmitted in a computer system

**baux·ite** (bôks′īt′) *n.* 〚Fr, after (*Les*) *Baux*, town in S France〛 a claylike sedimentary rock, the chief ore of aluminum

**Ba·var·i·a** (bə ver′ē ə) state of SW Germany —**Ba·var′i·an** *adj., n.*

**bawd** (bôd) *n.* 〚< ? OFr *baud*, licentious〛 [Literary] a person, esp. a woman, who keeps a brothel

**bawd·y** (bô′dē) *adj.* **-i·er, -i·est** indecent; lewd —**bawd′i·ness** *n.*

**bawl** (bôl) *vi., vt.* 〚< ML *baulare*, to bark〛 **1** to shout **2** to weep loudly —*n.* **1** an outcry **2** a noisy weeping —**bawl out** [Slang] to scold angrily

**bay**[1] (bā) *n.* 〚< ML *baia*〛 a wide inlet of a sea or lake, along the shoreline

**bay**[2] (bā) *n.* 〚< VL *batare*, to gape〛 **1** an alcove or recess **2** BAY WINDOW

**bay**[3] (bā) *vi.* 〚< OFr *baiier*〛 to bark or howl in long, deep tones —*n.* **1** the sound of baying **2** the situation of a hunted animal forced to turn and fight —**at bay 1** cornered **2** held off —**bring to bay** to corner

**bay**[4] (bā) *n.* 〚< L *baca*, berry〛 **1** LAUREL (*n.* 1) **2** [*pl.*] a laurel wreath

**bay**[5] (bā) *adj.* 〚< L *badius*〛 reddish-brown —*n.* **1** a reddish-brown horse, etc. **2** reddish brown

**bay′ber′ry** *n., pl.* **-ries 1** a shrub with small, wax-coated, berrylike fruit **2** the fruit

**bay leaf** the dried, aromatic leaf of certain laurel plants, used as a seasoning

**bay·o·net** (bā′ə net′, bā′ə nət) *n.* 〚< Fr: after *Bayonne*, city in France〛 a detachable blade put on a rifle muzzle, for stabbing —*vt., vi.* **-net′ed** or **-net′ted, -net′ing** or **-net′ting** to stab with a bayonet

**bay·ou** (bī′ōō′) *n.* 〚< AmInd *bayuk*, small stream〛 in S U.S., a marshy inlet or outlet of a lake, river, etc.

**bay window 1** a window or set of windows jutting out from a wall **2** [Slang] a large protruding belly

**ba·zaar** (bə zär′) *n.* 〚Pers *bāzār*〛 **1** a marketplace, esp. in the Middle East **2** a benefit sale for a church, etc.

**ba·zoo·ka** (bə zōō′kə) *n.* 〚< name of a comic horn〛 a portable weapon for launching armor-piercing rockets

**BB** (bē′bē′) *n., pl.* **BB′s** 〚designation of size〛 a pellet of shot (diameter, .18 in.) fired from an air rifle (**BB gun**) or shotgun

**bbl** *abbrev.* barrel

**BC** *abbrev.* **1** before Christ: also **B.C. 2** British Columbia

**B cell** any of the lymphatic leukocytes not derived from the thymus, that build antibodies: cf. T CELL

**be** (bē) *vi.* **was** or **were, been, being** 〚OE *beon*〛 **1** to exist; live **2** to happen; occur **3** to remain or continue *Note: be* is used to link its subject to a predicate complement /she *is* nice/ or as an auxiliary: (1) with a past participle: *a*) to form the passive voice /he will *be* sued/ *b*) [Archaic] to form the perfect tense /Christ *is* risen/ (2) with a present participle to express continuation /he *is* running/ (3) with a present participle or infinitive to express futurity, possibility, obligation, intention, etc. /she *is* going soon, he *is* to cut it/ *Be* is conjugated in the present indicative: (I) *am*, (he, she, it) *is*, (we, you, they) *are*; in the past indicative: (I, he, she, it) *was*, (we, you, they) *were*

**Be** *Chem. symbol for* beryllium

**be-** 〚< OE *bi-, be-,* at〛 *prefix* **1** around /beset/ **2** completely /bedeck/ **3** away /betake/ **4** about /bemoan/ **5** to make /besot/ **6** to furnish with, affect by /becloud/

**beach** (bēch) *n.* 〚E dial., pebbles〛 a sandy shore —*vt., vi.* to ground (a boat) on a beach

**beach′comb′er** (-kōm′ər) *n.* **1** COMBER (sense 2)

**2** one who lives on items found on beaches —**beach′comb′ing** *n.*

**beach′head′** *n.* a position gained, specif. by invading an enemy shore

**beach′wear′** *n.* garments worn at the beach, as swimsuits

**bea·con** (bē′kən) *n.* ⟦< OE *beacen,* a signal⟧ **1** a light for warning or guiding **2** a radio transmitter sending guiding signals for aircraft

**bead** (bēd) *n.* ⟦< OE *bed,* prayer bead⟧ **1** a small ball of glass, etc., pierced for stringing **2** [*pl.*] a rosary **3** [*pl.*] a string of beads **4** any small, round object, as the front sight of a rifle **5** a drop or bubble **6** the rim edge of a rubber tire —*vt.* to decorate with beads —**draw a bead on** to take careful aim at —**say one's beads** to pray with a rosary —**bead′y,** *-i·er,* *-i·est, adj.*

**bea·dle** (bēd′'l) *n.* ⟦ME *bidel*⟧ [Historical] a minor officer in the Church of England, who kept order in church

**bea·gle** (bē′gəl) *n.* ⟦< ? Fr *bee gueule,* wide throat⟧ a small hound with short legs and drooping ears

**beak** (bēk) *n.* ⟦< L *beccus*⟧ **1** a bird's bill **2** a beaklike part, as the snout of various insects

**beak·er** (bēk′ər) *n.* ⟦< ? Gr *bikos,* vessel with handles⟧ **1** a goblet **2** *Chem.* a glass or metal container with a beaklike lip for pouring

**beam** (bēm) *n.* ⟦ME⟧ **1** a long, thick piece of wood, metal, etc. **2** the crossbar of a balance **3** a ship's breadth at its widest point **4** a shaft of light, etc. **5** a radiant look, smile, etc. **6** a steady radio or radar signal for guiding aircraft or ships —*vt.* **1** to give out (shafts of light) **2** to direct (a radio signal, etc.) —*vi.* **1** to shine brightly **2** to smile warmly —**on the beam** [Inf.] working well

**bean** (bēn) *n.* ⟦OE *bean*⟧ **1** a plant of the pea family, bearing kidney-shaped seeds **2** the edible, smooth seed of this plant **3** any beanlike seed [coffee *bean*] **4** [Slang] the head or brain —*vt.* [Slang] to hit on the head —**full of beans** [Slang] lively —**spill the beans** [Inf.] to tell a secret

**bear**[1] (ber) *vt.* **bore, borne** or **born, bear′ing** ⟦OE *beran*⟧ **1** to carry **2** to have or show **3** to give birth to **4** to produce or yield **5** to support or sustain **6** to withstand or endure **7** to need [this *bears* watching] **8** to carry or conduct (oneself) **9** to give [to *bear* witness] —*vi.* **1** to be productive **2** to lie, point, or move in a given direction **3** to have bearing (*on*) **4** to tolerate —**bear down (on)** **1** to exert pressure or effort (on) **2** to approach —**bear out** to confirm —**bear up** to endure —**bear′a·ble** *adj.* —**bear′er** *n.*

**bear**[2] (ber) *n., pl.* **bears** or **bear** ⟦OE *bera*⟧ **1** a large, heavy mammal with shaggy fur and a short tail **2** one who is clumsy, rude, etc. **3** one who sells stocks, etc., hoping to buy them back later at a lower price **4** [Slang] a difficult task —*adj.* falling in price —**bear′like′** *adj.*

**beard** (bird) *n.* ⟦OE⟧ **1** the hair on the chin and cheeks of a man **2** any beardlike part **3** an awn —*vt.* **1** to defy **2** to provide with a beard —**beard′ed** *adj.* —**beard′less** *adj.*

**bear·ing** (ber′iŋ) *n.* **1** way of carrying and conducting oneself **2** a supporting part **3** a producing or ability to produce **4** endurance **5** [*often pl.*] relative direction or position **6** [*pl.*] awareness of one's situation **7** relevance; relation **8** a part of a machine on which another part revolves, slides, etc.

**bear′ish** *adj.* **1** bearlike; rude, rough, etc. **2** falling, or causing, expecting, etc. a fall, in prices on the stock exchange —**bear′ish·ly** *adv.*

**bé·ar·naise sauce** (bā′är nāz′) a creamy sauce, esp. for meat or fish

**bear′skin′** *n.* the fur or hide of a bear **2** a rug, coat, etc. made from this

**beast** (bēst) *n.* ⟦< L *bestia*⟧ **1** any large, four-footed animal **2** one who is gross, brutal, etc.

**beast′ly** *adj.* **-li·er, -li·est 1** of or like a beast; brutal, etc. **2** [Inf.] disagreeable; unpleasant —**beast′li·ness** *n.*

**beast of burden** any animal used for carrying things

**beast of prey** any animal that hunts and kills other animals for food

**beat** (bēt) *vt.* **beat, beat′en, beat′ing** ⟦OE *beatan*⟧ **1** to hit repeatedly; pound **2** to punish by so hitting; whip, spank, etc. **3** to dash repeatedly against **4** *a*) to form (a path, etc.) by repeated treading or riding *b*) to keep walking on **5** to mix (eggs, etc.) by hard stirring **6** to move (esp. wings) up and down **7** to search through (a forest, etc.) **8** to defeat or outdo **9** to mark (time or rhythm) by tapping, etc. **10** [Inf.] to baffle **11** [Inf.] to cheat or trick **12** [Slang] to escape the penalties of (an indictment, rap, etc.) —*vi.* **1** to hit or dash repeatedly **2** to throb, vibrate, etc. —*n.* **1** a beating, as of the heart **2** any of a series of movements, blows, etc. **3** a throb **4** a habitual route **5** the unit of musical rhythm **6** BEATNIK —*adj.* **1** [Inf.] tired out **2** of a group of young persons, esp. of the 1950s, expressing social disillusionment by unconventional dress, actions, etc. —**beat down** to put or force down —**beat it!** [Slang] go away! —**beat off** to drive back —**beat up (on)** [Slang] to give a beating to —**beat′er** *n.*

**beat′en** *adj.* **1** shaped by hammering **2** much traveled [a *beaten* path] **3** crushed in spirit; defeated **4** tired out

**be·a·tif·ic** (bē′ə tif′ik) *adj.* **1** making blessed **2** showing happiness or delight

**be·at·i·fy** (bē at′ə fī′) *vt.* **-fied′, -fy′ing** ⟦< L *beatus,* happy + *facere,* to make⟧ **1** to make blissfully happy **2** *R.C.Ch.* to declare (a deceased person) to be in heaven —**be·at′i·fi·ca′tion** *n.*

**beat′ing** *n.* **1** the act of one that beats **2** a whipping **3** a throbbing **4** a defeat

**be·at·i·tude** (bē at′ə tōōd′) *n.* ⟦< L *beatus,* happy⟧ perfect blessedness or happiness —**the Beatitudes** the pronouncements in the Sermon on the Mount

**beat·nik** (bēt′nik) *n.* a member of the beat group

**beat′-up′** *adj.* [Slang] worn-out, dilapidated, etc.

**beau** (bō) *n., pl.* **beaus** or **beaux** (bōz) ⟦Fr < L *bellus,* pretty⟧ [Old-fashioned] a woman's sweetheart

**beau·te·ous** (byōōt′ē əs) *adj.* ⟦ME⟧ beautiful —**beau′te·ous·ly** *adv.*

**beau·ti·cian** (byōō tish′ən) *n.* one who works in a beauty shop

**beau·ti·ful** (byōōt′ə fəl) *adj.* having beauty —**beau′ti·ful·ly** *adv.*

**beau·ti·fy** (-fī′) *vt., vi.* **-fied′, -fy′ing** to make or become beautiful —**beau′ti·fi·ca′tion** *n.* —**beau′ti·fi′er** *n.*

**beau·ty** (byōōt′ē) *n., pl.* **-ties** ⟦< L *bellus,* pretty⟧ **1** the quality of being very pleasing, as in form, color, etc. **2** a thing with this quality **3** good looks **4** a very attractive person, feature, etc.

**beauty salon** (or **shop, parlor,** etc.) a place where people, esp. women, go for hair styling, manicuring, etc.

**bea·ver** (bē′vər) *n.* ⟦< OE *beofor*⟧ **1** a large amphibious rodent with soft, brown fur, webbed hind feet, and a flat, broad tail **2** its fur

**be·calm** (bē käm′, bi-) *vt.* **1** to make calm **2** to make (a ship) motionless from lack of wind

**be·cause** (bē kôz′, -kuz′; bi-) *conj.* ⟦ME *bi,* by + *cause*⟧ for the reason or cause that —**because of** by reason of

**beck** (bek) *n.* a beckoning gesture —**at the beck and call of** at the service of

**beck·on** (bek′'n) *vi., vt.* ⟦OE *beacnian*⟧ **1** to summon by a gesture **2** to lure; entice

**be·cloud** (bē kloud′, bi-) *vt.* **1** to cloud over **2** to confuse; muddle

**be·come** (bē kum′, bi kum′) *vi.* **-came′, -come′, -com′ing** ⟦OE *becuman*⟧ to come or grow to be —*vt.* to befit; suit [modesty *becomes* her] —**become of** to happen to

**be·com′ing** *adj.* **1** appropriate; fit **2** suitable to the wearer

**bed** (bed) *n.* ⟦OE⟧ **1** a piece of furniture for sleeping or resting on **2** a plot of soil where plants are raised **3** the bottom of a river, lake, etc. **4** any flat surface used as a foundation **5** a geologic layer; stratum **6** the flat surface of a truck —*vt.* **bed′ded, bed′ding 1** to put to bed **2** to provide with a sleeping place **3** to embed **4** to plant in a bed of earth **5** to arrange in layers —*vi.* **1** to go to bed; rest; sleep **2** to stratify

**bed′-and-break′fast** *adj., n.* (of) a hotel, etc. that provides breakfast as part of the price: also **bed and breakfast**

**be·daz·zle** (bē daz′əl, bi-) *vt.* **-zled, -zling** to dazzle thoroughly; bewilder

**bed′bug′** *n.* a small, wingless, biting insect that infests beds, etc.

**bed′clothes′** *pl.n.* sheets, blankets, etc. for a bed

**bed′cov′er** *n.* a cover for a bed; bedspread

**bed′ding** *n.* **1** mattresses and bedclothes **2** a bottom layer; base **3** straw, etc. for animals to sleep on

**be·deck** (bē dek′, bi-) *vt.* to adorn

**be·dev·il** (bē dev′əl, bi-) *vt.* **-iled** or **-illed, -il·ing** or **-il·ling** to plague or bewilder —**be·dev′il·ment** *n.*

**bed′fel′low** *n.* **1** a person who shares one's bed **2** an associate, ally, etc.

**be·dim** (bē dim′, bi-) *vt.* **-dimmed′, -dim′ming** to make (the eyes or the vision) dim

**bed·lam** (bed′ləm) *n.* ⟦after (the old London mental hospital of St. Mary of) *Bethlehem*⟧ any place or condition of noise and confusion

**bed of roses** [Inf.] a situation or position of ease and luxury

**Bed·ou·in** (bed′oo in′) *n., pl.* **-ins** or **-in** ⟦< Ar *badāwīn*, desert dwellers⟧ [*also* **b**-] an Arab of the desert tribes of Arabia, Syria, or N Africa

**bed′pan′** *n.* a shallow pan for use as a toilet by one confined to bed

**be·drag·gle** (bē drag′əl, bi-) *vt.* **-gled, -gling** to make wet, limp, and dirty, as by dragging through mire

**bed′rid′den** (-rid′'n) *adj.* confined to bed by illness, infirmity, etc.

**bed′rock′** *n.* **1** solid rock beneath the soil, etc. **2** a foundation or bottom

**bed′roll′** *n.* a portable roll of bedding, as for sleeping outdoors

**bed′room′** *n.* a room for sleeping

**bed′side′** *n.* the space beside a bed —*adj.* near a bed

**bed′sore′** *n.* a sore on the body of a bedridden person, caused by chafing

**bed′spread′** *n.* an ornamental spread covering the blanket on a bed

**bed′stead′** (-sted′) *n.* a framework for supporting the mattress, etc. of a bed

**bed′time′** *n.* one's usual time for going to bed

**bee**[1] (bē) *n.* ⟦OE *beo*⟧ a broad-bodied, four-winged, hairy insect that gathers pollen and nectar and that can sting

**bee**[2] (bē) *n.* ⟦OE *ben*, compulsory service⟧ a meeting of people to work together or to compete [a spelling *bee*]

**beech** (bēch) *n.* ⟦OE *bece*⟧ **1** a tree with smooth, gray bark, hard wood, and edible nuts **2** its wood

**beech′nut′** *n.* the small, three-cornered, edible nut of the beech tree

**beef** (bēf) *n., pl.* for 1 & 5, **beefs**; for 1, also **beeves** ⟦< L *bos*, ox⟧ **1** a full-grown ox, cow, bull, or steer, esp. one bred for meat **2** such animals collectively **3** their meat **4** [Inf.] *a*) human flesh *b*) strength **5** [Slang] a complaint —*vi.* [Slang] to complain —**beef up** [Inf.] to reinforce

**beef′cake′** *n.* ⟦BEEF (*n.* 4*a*) + (CHEESE)CAKE⟧ [Inf.] display of the figure of a nude or partly nude, muscular man, as in a photograph

**beef′steak′** *n.* a thick slice of beef for broiling or frying

**beef′y** *adj.* **-i·er, -i·est** brawny —**beef′i·ness** *n.*

**bee′hive′** *n.* **1** a shelter for a colony of bees **2** a place of great activity

**bee′keep′er** *n.* one who keeps bees for producing honey —**bee′keep′ing** *n.*

**bee′line′** *n.* a straight line or direct route

**Be·el·ze·bub** (bē el′zə bub′) *n. Bible* the chief devil; Satan

**been** (bin; *often* ben) *vi. pp. of* BE

**beep** (bēp) *n.* ⟦echoic⟧ the brief, high-pitched sound of a horn or electronic signal —*vi., vt.* to make or cause to make this sound

**beer** (bir) *n.* ⟦OE *beor*⟧ **1** an alcoholic, fermented drink made from malt and hops **2** a soft drink made from extracts of roots, etc. [root *beer*]

**bees′wax′** *n.* wax secreted by honeybees, used to make their honeycombs: it is used in candles, etc.

**beet** (bēt) *n.* ⟦< L *beta*⟧ **1** a plant with edible leaves and a thick, fleshy, white or red root **2** the edible root, also a source of sugar

**Bee·tho·ven** (bā′tō′vən), **Lud·wig van** (loot′viH vän) 1770-1827; Ger. composer

**bee·tle**[1] (bēt′'l) *n.* ⟦OE *bītan*, to bite⟧ an insect with hard front wings that cover the membranous hind wings when these are folded

**bee·tle**[2] (bēt′'l) *vi.* **-tled, -tling** ⟦prob. < fol.⟧ to overhang —*adj.* overhanging: also **bee′tling**

**bee′tle-browed′** (-broud′) *adj.* ⟦< ME < ? *bitel*, sharp + *brouwe*, brow⟧ **1** having overhanging or bushy eyebrows **2** frowning

**be·fall** (bē fôl′, bi-) *vi., vt.* **-fell′, -fall′en, -fall′ing** ⟦< OE *be*-, BE- + *feallan*, to fall⟧ to happen or occur (to)

**be·fit** (bē fit′, bi-) *vt.* **-fit′ted, -fit′ting** to be suitable or proper for; be suited to —**be·fit′ting** *adj.*

**be·fog** (bē fôg′, -fäg′; bi-) *vt.* **-fogged′, -fog′ging 1** to envelop in fog; make foggy **2** to obscure; confuse

**be·fore** (bē fôr′, bi-) *adv.* ⟦OE *be*-, by + *foran*, fore⟧ **1** ahead; in front **2** previously **3** earlier; sooner —*prep.* **1** ahead of in time, space, order, etc. **2** located in front of **3** in or into the sight, presence, etc. of **4** earlier than; prior to **5** in preference to **6** being considered, judged, or decided by [a case *before* the court] —*conj.* **1** earlier than the time that [call *before* you go] **2** rather than [I'd die *before* I'd tell]

**be·fore′hand′** *adv., adj.* ahead of time; in anticipation

**be·foul** (bē foul′, bi-) *vt.* **1** to make filthy **2** to slander

**be·friend** (bē frend′, bi-) *vt.* to act as a friend to

**be·fud·dle** (bē fud′'l, bi-) *vt.* **-dled, -dling** to confuse or stupefy

**beg** (beg) *vt., vi.* **begged, beg′ging** ⟦< Du *beggaert*, religious mendicant⟧ **1** to ask for (alms) **2** to ask earnestly; entreat —**beg off** to ask to be released from —**go begging** to be available but unwanted

**be·gan** (bē gan′, bi-) *vi., vt. pt. of* BEGIN

**be·get** (bē get′, bi-) *vt.* **-got′** or [Archaic] **-gat′** (-gat′), **-got′ten** or **-got′, -get′ting** ⟦< OE *begietan*, acquire⟧ **1** to be the father of **2** to produce; cause

**beg·gar** (beg′ər) *n.* **1** one who begs **2** a pauper —*vt.* **1** to make poor **2** to make (a description, etc.) seem inadequate —**beg′gar·y,** *pl.* **-ies,** *n.*

**beg′gar·ly** *adj.* very poor, worthless, inadequate, etc.

**be·gin** (bē gin′, bi-) *vi., vt.* **-gan′, -gun′, -gin′ning** ⟦< OE *beginnan*⟧ **1** to start doing, acting, etc. **2** to originate **3** to have a first part or be the first part of

**be·gin′ner** *n.* one just beginning to do or learn something; novice

**be·gin′ning** *n.* **1** a starting **2** the time or place of starting; origin **3** the first part **4** [*usually pl.*] an early stage or example

**be·gone** (bē gôn′, bi-) *interj., vi.* (to) be gone; go away; get out

**be·gon·ia** (bi gōn′yə) *n.* 〖after M. *Bégon* (1638-1710), Fr patron of science〗 a tropical plant with showy flowers and ornamental leaves

**be·got** (bē gät′, bi-) *vt. pt. & alt. pp. of* BEGET

**be·got′ten** *vt. alt. pp. of* BEGET

**be·grime** (bē grīm′, bi-) *vt.* **-grimed′, -grim′ing** to cover with grime; soil

**be·grudge** (bē gruj′, bi gruj′) *vt.* **-grudged′, -grudg′ing** **1** to resent another's possession of (something) **2** to give with reluctance —**be·grudg′ing·ly** *adv.*

**be·guile** (bē gīl′, bi-) *vt.* **-guiled′, -guil′ing** **1** to mislead by tricking, etc.; deceive **2** to deprive *of* or cheat *out of* by deceit **3** to pass (time) pleasantly **4** to charm or delight —**be·guile′ment** *n.* —**be·guil′er** *n.*

**be·gun** (bē gun′, bi-) *vi., vt. pp. of* BEGIN

**be·half** (bē haf′, bi-) *n.* 〖OE *be*, by + *healf*, side〗 support —**in** (or **on**) **behalf of** in the interest of; for

**be·have** (bē hāv′, bi-) *vt., vi.* **-haved′, -hav′ing** 〖see BE- & HAVE〗 **1** to conduct (oneself) in a specified way; act **2** to conduct (oneself) properly

**be·hav′ior** (-yər) *n.* way of behaving; conduct or action —**be·hav′ior·al** *adj.*

**behavioral science** any of the sciences, as sociology, that study human behavior

**be·head** (bē hed′, bi-) *vt.* to cut off the head of

**be·held** (bē held′, bi-) *vt. pt. & pp. of* BEHOLD

**be·he·moth** (bə hē′məth) *n.* 〖< Heb *behema*, beast〗 **1** *Bible* some huge animal **2** any huge or powerful animal or thing

**be·hest** (bē hest′, bi-) *n.* 〖< OE *behæs*, a vow〗 an order, command, or request

**be·hind** (bē hīnd′, bi-) *adv.* 〖< OE *behindan*〗 **1** in or to the rear **2** in a former time, place, etc. **3** in or into arrears **4** slow; late —*prep.* **1** remaining after **2** in or to the rear of **3** inferior to in position, achievement, etc. **4** later than *[behind schedule]* **5** beyond **6** gone by or ended for *[school was behind him now]* **7** supporting *[behind their team]* **8** prompting or instigating *[behind the plot]* **9** hidden by *[what's behind this news]* —*n.* [Inf.] the buttocks

**be·hind′hand′** *adv., adj.* behind in payment, time, or progress

**be·hold** (bē hōld′, bi-) *vt.* **-held′, -hold′ing** 〖< OE *bihealdan*〗 to look at; see —*interj.* look! see! —**be·hold′er** *n.*

**be·hold′en** *adj.* obliged to feel grateful; indebted

**be·hoove** (bē hōōv′, bi-) *vt.* **-hooved′, -hoov′ing** 〖< OE *behofian*, to need〗 to be incumbent upon or proper for *[it behooves* you to drive carefully*]*

**beige** (bāzh) *n., adj.* 〖Fr〗 grayish tan

**Bei·jing** (bā′jiŋ′, -zhiŋ′) capital of China, in the NE part: pop. 5,531,000

**be·ing** (bē′iŋ) *n.* 〖see BE〗 **1** existence; life **2** fundamental nature **3** one that lives or exists **4** personality —**being as** (or **that**) [Inf. or Dial.] since; because —**for the time being** for now

**Bei·rut** (bā rōōt′) seaport & capital of Lebanon: pop. c. 1,500,000

**be·jew·el** (bē jōō′əl, bi-) *vt.* **-eled** or **-elled, -el·ing** or **-el·ling** to decorate with or as with jewels

**be·la·bor** (bē lā′bər, bi-) *vt.* **1** to beat severely **2** to scold **3** to spend too much time on

**Bel·a·rus** (bel′ə rōōs′) country in central Europe: formerly part of the U.S.S.R.: 80,134 sq. mi.; pop. 10,152,000

**be·lat·ed** (bē lāt′id, bi-) *adj.* late or too late —**be·lat′ed·ly** *adv.*

**be·lay** (bi lā′) *vt., vi.* **-layed′, -lay′ing** 〖< OE *belecgan*, make fast〗 **1** to make (a rope) secure by winding around a cleat, etc. **2** [Inf.] *Naut.* to hold; stop **3** to secure by a rope

**bel can·to** (bel′kän′tō) 〖It〗 a style of singing with brilliant vocal display

**belch** (belch) *vi., vt.* 〖OE *bealcian*〗 **1** to expel (gas) through the mouth from the stomach **2** to throw forth (its contents) violently —*n.* a belching

**be·lea·guer** (bē lē′gər, bi-) *vt.* 〖< Du < *be-*, around

+ *leger*, a camp〗 **1** to besiege by encircling **2** to beset or harass

**Bel·fast** (bel′fast) seaport & capital of Northern Ireland: pop. 284,000

**bel·fry** (bel′frē) *n., pl.* **-fries** 〖ult. < OHG〗 **1** a bell tower **2** the part of a tower that holds the bells

**Belg** Belgium

**Bel·gium** (bel′jəm) kingdom in W Europe: 11,778 sq. mi.; pop. 9,979,000 —**Bel′gian** *adj., n.*

**Bel·grade** (bel′grād, -grād′) capital of Yugoslavia: pop. 1,470,000

**be·lie** (bē lī′, bi-) *vt.* **-lied′, -ly′ing** **1** to disguise or misrepresent **2** to leave unfulfilled; disappoint **3** to prove false

**be·lief** (bə lēf′, bē-) *n.* 〖< OE *geleafa*〗 **1** conviction that certain things are true **2** religious faith **3** trust or confidence **4** creed or doctrine **5** an opinion; expectation; judgment

**be·lieve** (bə lēv′, bē-) *vt.* **-lieved′, -liev′ing** 〖< OE *geliefan*〗 **1** to take as true, real, etc. **2** to trust a statement or promise (of a person) **3** to suppose or think —*vi.* to have trust, faith, or confidence (*in*) —**be·liev′a·ble** *adj.* —**be·liev′er** *n.*

**be·lit·tle** (bē lit″l, bi-) *vt.* **-tled, -tling** to make seem little, less important, etc. —**be·lit′tle·ment** *n.*

**Be·lize** (bə lēz′) country in Central America, on the Caribbean: 8,866 sq. mi.; pop. 184,000

**bell** (bel) *n.* 〖OE *belle*〗 **1** a hollow, cuplike object, as of metal, which rings when struck **2** the sound of a bell **3** anything shaped like a bell **4** *Naut.* a bell rung to mark the periods of the watch —*vt.* to attach a bell to —*vi.* to flare out like a bell

**Bell** (bel), **Al·ex·an·der Gra·ham** (al′ig zan′dər grā′əm) 1847-1922; U.S. inventor of the telephone, born in Scotland

**bel·la·don·na** (bel′ə dän′ə) *n.* 〖< It, beautiful lady〗 **1** a poisonous plant with purplish flowers and black berries **2** ATROPINE

**bell′-bot′tom** *adj.* flared at the ankles, as trousers or slacks: also **bell′-bot′tomed** —*n.* [*pl.*] bell-bottom trousers

**bell′boy′** *n.* BELLHOP

**belle** (bel) *n.* 〖Fr, fem. of *beau*〗 a pretty woman or girl

**belles-let·tres** (bel le′tr′, -trə) *pl.n.* 〖Fr〗 literature as distinguished from technical writings

**bell′hop′** *n.* one employed by a hotel, club, etc. to carry luggage and do errands

**bel·li·cose** (bel′i kōs′) *adj.* 〖< L *bellicus*, of war〗 quarrelsome; warlike —**bel′li·cos′i·ty** (-käs′ə tē) *n.*

**bel·lig·er·ent** (bə lij′ər ənt) *adj.* 〖< L *bellum*, war + *gerere*, carry on〗 **1** at war **2** of war **3** warlike **4** ready to fight or quarrel —*n.* a belligerent person, group, or nation —**bel·lig′er·ence** *n.* —**bel·lig′er·en·cy** *n.* —**bel·lig′er·ent·ly** *adv.*

**bell jar** a bell-shaped container made of glass, used to keep air, moisture, etc. in or out: also **bell glass**

**bel·low** (bel′ō) *vi.* 〖< OE *bylgan*〗 **1** to roar with a reverberating sound, as a bull **2** to cry out loudly, as in anger —*vt.* to utter loudly or powerfully —*n.* a bellowing sound

**bel·lows** (bel′ōz′) *n.* 〖< ME *beli*, belly〗 [*with sing. or pl. v.*] **1** a device that forces air out when its sides are pressed together: used in pipe organs, for blowing fires, etc. **2** anything like a bellows

**bell pepper** a large, sweet red pepper

**Bell's palsy** 〖after C. *Bell* (1774-1842), Scot anatomist〗 a sudden, usually temporary paralysis of the muscles on one side of the face

BELLOWS

**bell·weth·er** (bel′weth′ər) *n.* 〖ME〗 **1** a male

sheep, usually wearing a bell, that leads the flock 2 a leader

**bel·ly** (bel′ē) *n.*, *pl.* **-lies** [< OE *belg*, leather bag] 1 the part of the body between the chest and thighs; abdomen 2 the underside of an animal's body 3 the stomach 4 the deep interior, as of a ship —*vt.*, *vi.* **-lied, -ly·ing** to swell out

**bel′ly·ache′** *n.* pain in the abdomen —*vi.* **-ached′, -ach′ing** [Slang] to complain

**bel′ly·but′ton** *n.* [Inf.] the navel

**bel′ly·ful′** (-fool′) *n.* 1 enough or more than enough to eat 2 [Slang] all that one can bear

**belly laugh** [Inf.] a hearty laugh

**be·long** (bē lôŋ′, bi-) *vi.* [< ME] 1 to have a proper place [it *belongs* here] 2 to be related (*to*) 3 to be a member: with *to* 4 to be owned: with *to*

**be·long′ings** *pl.n.* possessions

**be·lov·ed** (bi luv′id, -luvd′) *adj.* [ME *biloven*] dearly loved —*n.* a dearly loved person

**be·low** (bi lō′) *adv.*, *adj.* [see BE- & LOW¹] 1 in or to a lower place; beneath 2 later (in a book, etc.) 3 in or to hell 4 on earth 5 under in rank, amount, etc. —*prep.* 1 lower than 2 unworthy of

**Bel·shaz·zar** (bel shaz′ər) *n. Bible* the last king of Babylon

**belt** (belt) *n.* [ult. < L *balteus*] 1 a band of leather, etc. worn around the waist 2 any encircling thing like this 3 an endless band for transferring motion, as with pulleys, or conveying things 4 a distinctive area [the Corn *Belt*] 5 [Inf.] a hard blow; punch 6 [Slang] *a*) a gulp, esp. of liquor *b*) a thrill —*vt.* 1 to encircle or fasten with a belt 2 [Inf.] to hit hard 3 [Inf.] to sing loudly: usually with *out* 4 [Slang] to gulp (liquor): often with *down* —**below the belt** unfair(ly) — **tighten one's belt** to live more thriftily —**under one's belt** [Inf.] as part of one's experience

**belt′-tight′en·ing** *n.* an economizing —*adj.* involving the cutting of expenses

**belt′way′** *n.* an expressway passing around an urban area

**be·moan** (bē mōn′, bi-) *vt.*, *vi.* to lament

**be·muse** (bē myōōz′, bi-) *vt.* **-mused′, -mus′ing** [BE- + MUSE] 1 to confuse or stupefy 2 to preoccupy —**be·muse′ment** *n.*

**bench** (bench) *n.* [OE *benc*] 1 a long, hard seat 2 the place where judges sit in a court 3 [*sometimes* B-] *a*) the status of a judge *b*) judges collectively *c*) a law court 4 WORKBENCH 5 a seat on which members of a sports team sit when they are not playing —*vt. Sports* to take (a player) out of a game —**on the bench** 1 serving as a judge 2 *Sports* not playing

**bench mark** a standard in measuring, judging quality, etc.: also **bench′mark′** *n.*

**bench press** a weight-lifting exercise, done while one is lying on a bench with the feet on the floor, in which a barbell is pushed upward from the chest —**bench′-press′** *vt.*

**bench warrant** an order issued by a judge or court for the arrest of a person

**bend¹** (bend) *vt.* **bent, bend′ing** [< OE *bendan*, confine with a string] 1 to make curved or crooked 2 to turn, esp. from a straight line 3 to make submit —*vi.* 1 to turn, esp. from a straight line 2 to yield by curving, as from pressure 3 to curve the body; stoop (*over* or *down*) 4 to give in; yield —*n.* 1 a bending or being bent 2 a bent part —**bend′a·ble** *adj.*

**bend²** (bend) *n.* [ME < prec.] any of various knots for tying rope

**be·neath** (bē nēth′, bi-) *adv.*, *adj.* [OE *beneothan*] in a lower place; underneath —*prep.* 1 below 2 under; underneath 3 unworthy of [it is *beneath* him to cheat]

**ben·e·dic·tion** (ben′ə dik′shən) *n.* [< L *bene*, well + *dicere*, speak] 1 a blessing 2 an invocation of blessing, esp. at the end of a religious service

**ben·e·fac·tion** (ben′ə fak′shen) *n.* [< L *bene*, well

+ *facere*, do] 1 the act of helping, esp. by charitable gifts 2 the money or help given

**ben·e·fac·tor** (ben′ə fak′tər) *n.* one who has given help, esp. financially; patron —**ben′e·fac′tress** (-tris) *fem.n.*

**ben·e·fice** (ben′ə fis) *n.* [< L *beneficium*, a kindness] an endowed church office providing a living for a vicar, rector, etc.

**be·nef·i·cence** (bə nef′ə səns) *n.* [see BENEFACTION] 1 a being kind 2 a charitable act or gift

**be·nef·i·cent** (-sənt) *adj.* showing beneficence; doing or resulting in good —**be·nef′i·cent·ly** *adv.*

**ben·e·fi·cial** (ben′ə fish′əl) *adj.* producing benefits; advantageous; favorable —**ben′e·fi′cial·ly** *adv.*

**ben·e·fi·ci·ar·y** (-fish′ē er′ē, -fish′ər ē) *n.*, *pl.* **-ar′ies** anyone receiving or to receive benefits, as funds from a will or insurance policy

**ben·e·fit** (ben′ə fit) *n.* [see BENEFACTION] 1 anything contributing to improvement; advantage 2 [*often pl.*] payments made by an insurance company, public agency, etc. as during sickness or retirement, or for death 3 a public performance, bazaar, etc. the proceeds of which are to help some person or cause —*vt.* **-fit·ed, -fit·ing** to help; aid —*vi.* to receive advantage; profit

**be·nev·o·lence** (bə nev′ə ləns) *n.* [< L *bene*, well + *volens*, wishing] 1 an inclination to do good; kindliness 2 a kindly, charitable act —**be·nev′o·lent** *adj.* —**be·nev′o·lent·ly** *adv.*

**Ben·gal** (ben gôl′), **Bay of** part of the Indian Ocean, east of India

**be·night·ed** (bē nīt′id, bi-) *adj.* 1 surrounded by darkness 2 not enlightened; ignorant

**be·nign** (bi nīn′) *adj.* [< L *benignus*, good, lit., well-born] 1 good-natured; kindly 2 favorable; beneficial 3 *Med.* not malignant; specif., not cancerous —**be·nign′ly** *adv.*

**be·nig·nant** (bi nig′nənt) *adj.* [< prec.] 1 kindly or gracious 2 BENIGN (senses 2 & 3)

**be·nig·ni·ty** (-nə tē) *n.* 1 kindliness 2 *pl.* **-ties** a kind act

**Be·nin** (be nēn′) country in WC Africa: 43,484 sq. mi.; pop. 4,855,000

**ben·i·son** (ben′ə zən, -sən) *n.* [OFr < L: see BENEDICTION] [Archaic] a blessing

**bent¹** (bent) *vt.*, *vi. pt.* & *pp.* of BEND¹ —*adj.* 1 curved or crooked 2 strongly determined: with *on* 3 [Slang] *a*) dishonest *b*) eccentric; odd —*n.* a natural leaning; propensity

**bent²** (bent) *n.* [OE *beonot*] a dense, low-growing grass that spreads by runners, used for lawns: also **bent′grass′**

**bent′wood′** *adj.* of furniture made of wood permanently bent into various forms

**be·numb** (bē num′, bi-) *vt.* 1 to make numb 2 to deaden the mind, will, etc. of

**ben·zene** (ben′zēn, ben zēn′) *n.* [ult. < Ar *lubān jāwi*, incense of Java] a clear, flammable, poisonous, aromatic liquid used as a solvent, in plastics, etc.

**ben·zo·caine** (ben′zō kān′, -zə-) *n.* [< BENZENE & COCAINE] a white, odorless powder used in ointments as a local anesthetic and for protection against sunburn

**be·queath** (bē kwēth′, -kwēth′; bi-) *vt.* [< OE *be-*, BE- + *cwethan*, say] 1 to leave (property) to another by one's will 2 to hand down; pass on

**be·quest′** (-kwest′) *n.* 1 a bequeathing 2 anything bequeathed

**be·rate** (bē rāt′, bi-) *vt.* **-rat′ed, -rat′ing** [BE- + RATE²] to scold severely

**Ber·ber** (bur′bər) *n.* 1 a member of a Muslim people of N Africa 2 the language of this people — *adj.* of the Berbers

**be·reave** (bē rēv′, bi-) *vt.* **-reaved′** or **-reft′** (-reft′), **-reav′ing** [< OE *be-*, BE- + *reafian*, rob] 1 to deprive: now usually in the pp. *bereft* [*bereft* of hope] 2 to leave forlorn, as by death —**be·reave′ment** *n.*

**be·ret** (bə rā′) *n.* [< Fr < L *birrus*, a hood] a flat, round cap of felt, wool, etc.

**berg** (bʉrg) *n.* ICEBERG

**ber·i·ber·i** (ber'ē ber'ē) *n.* ⟦Sinhalese, intens. of *beri*, weakness⟧ a disease caused by lack of vitamin B₁ and characterized by nerve disorders, etc.

**Ber·ing Sea** (ber'iŋ) part of the N Pacific, between Siberia & Alaska

**Bering Strait** strait joining the Bering Sea with the Arctic Ocean

**Berke·ley** (bʉrk'lē) city in California, near San Francisco: pop. 103,000

**Ber·lin** (bər lin') city & state of E Germany; capital of Germany (1871-1945; 1990- ): formerly divided into four sectors of occupation, the eastern sector (*East Berlin*), capital of East Germany, and three western sectors (*West Berlin*), a state of West Germany: pop. 3,305,000

**berm** (bʉrm) *n.* ⟦< MDu *baerm*⟧ **1** a ledge **2** [Dial.] a shoulder, as along the edge of a paved road

**Ber·mu·da** (bər myoo'də) group of British islands in the W Atlantic

**Bermuda shorts** knee-length pants: also **bermu'das** *pl.n.*

**Bern** or **Berne** (bʉrn) capital of Switzerland: pop. 134,000

**ber·ry** (ber'ē) *n., pl.* **-ries** ⟦OE *berie*⟧ **1** any small, juicy, fleshy fruit, as a strawberry **2** the dry seed of various plants, as a coffee bean —*vi.* **-ried, -ry·ing 1** to produce berries **2** to pick berries — **ber'ry·like'** *adj.*

**ber·serk** (bər sʉrk', -zʉrk'; bə-) *adj., adv.* ⟦ON *berserkr*, warrior⟧ in or into a violent rage or frenzy

**berth** (bʉrth) *n.* ⟦< BEAR¹ + -TH¹⟧ **1** a place where a ship anchors or moors **2** a position, job, etc. **3** a built-in bed, as on a ship or train —*vt.* to put into or furnish with a berth —*vi.* to occupy a berth — **give (a) wide berth to** to keep well clear of

**ber·yl** (ber'əl) *n.* ⟦< Gr *bēryllos*⟧ a very hard mineral of which emerald and aquamarine are two varieties

**be·ryl·li·um** (bə ril'ē əm) *n.* ⟦< L *beryllus*, beryl⟧ a hard, silver-white, metallic chemical element used in forming alloys

**be·seech** (bē sēch', bi-) *vt.* **-sought'** or **-seeched'**, **-seech'ing** ⟦< OE *be- + secan*, seek⟧ **1** to ask (someone) earnestly; entreat **2** to beg for —**be·seech'ing·ly** *adv.*

**be·seem** (bē sēm', bi-) *vi.* [Archaic] to be suitable or appropriate (to)

**be·set** (bē set', bi-) *vt.* **-set', -set'ting** ⟦< OE *be- + settan*, set⟧ **1** to attack from all sides; harass **2** to surround or hem in

**be·set'ting** *adj.* constantly harassing

**be·side** (bē sīd', bi-) *prep.* ⟦OE *bi sidan*⟧ **1** at the side of; near **2** in comparison with [*beside* yours my share seems small] **3** in addition to **4** other than **5** not relevant to [that's *beside* the point] — **beside oneself** wild or upset, as with fear or rage

**be·sides** (-sīdz') *adv.* **1** in addition **2** except for that mentioned **3** moreover —*prep.* **1** in addition to **2** other than

**be·siege** (bē sēj', bi-) *vt.* **-sieged', -sieg'ing 1** to hem in with armed forces **2** to crowd around **3** to overwhelm, harass, etc. [she was besieged with queries]

**be·smear** (bē smir', bi-) *vt.* ⟦OE *bismerian*⟧ to smear over; soil

**be·smirch** (bē smʉrch', bi-) *vt.* to soil

**be·som** (bē'zəm) *n.* ⟦OE *besma*⟧ a broom, esp. one made of twigs tied to a handle

**be·sot** (bē sät', bi-) *vt.* **-sot'ted, -sot'ting** to stupefy, as with liquor —**be·sot'ted** *adj.*

**be·sought** (bē sôt', bi-) *vt.* alt. pt. & alt. pp. of BESEECH

**be·span·gle** (bē spaŋ'gəl, bi-) *vt.* **-gled, -gling** to cover with or as with spangles

**be·spat·ter** (bē spat'ər, bi-) *vt.* to spatter, as with mud or slander

**be·speak** (bē spēk', bi-) *vt.* **-spoke'** (-spōk'), **-spo'ken** or **-spoke', -speak'ing 1** to speak for in advance; reserve **2** to be indicative of; show

**best** (best) *adj.* ⟦OE *betst*⟧ **1** *superl. of* GOOD **2** most excellent **3** most suitable, desirable, etc. **4** largest [the *best* part of a day] —*adv.* **1** *superl. of* WELL² **2** in the most excellent manner **3** in the highest degree —*n.* **1** the most excellent person, thing, etc. **2** the utmost [she did her *best*] —*vt.* to defeat or outdo —**all for the best** turning out to be good after all —**at best** under the most favorable conditions —**get the best of 1** to defeat **2** to outwit —**make the best of** to do as well as one can with

**bes·tial** (bes'chəl, -tyəl; *often* bēs'-) *adj.* ⟦< L *bestia*, beast⟧ like a beast; savage, brutal, etc. — **bes·ti·al·i·ty** (bes'chē al'ə tē, -tē-; *often* bēs'-), *pl.* **-ties,** *n.*

**bes·tial·ize** (bes'chəl īz', -tyəl-; *often* bēs'-) *vt.* **-ized', -iz'ing** to make bestial

**bes·ti·ar·y** (bes'tē er'ē) *n., pl.* **-ies** ⟦< L *bestia*, beast⟧ a medieval book with fables about real or mythical animals

**be·stir** (bē stʉr', bi-) *vt.* **-stirred', -stir'ring** to stir to action; busy (oneself)

**best man** the principal attendant of the bridegroom at a wedding

**be·stow** (bē stō', bi-) *vt.* ⟦see BE- & STOW⟧ to present as a gift: often with *on* or *upon* —**be·stow'al** *n.*

**be·strew** (bē strōō', bi-) *vt.* **-strewed', -strewed'** or **-strewn', -strew'ing 1** to cover (a surface) *with* something **2** to strew or scatter about a surface

**be·stride** (bē strīd', bi-) *vt.* **-strode'** (-strōd'), **-strid'den** (-strid'ʼn), **-strid'ing** to sit on, mount, or stand over with a leg on each side

**bet** (bet) *n.* ⟦prob. < ABET⟧ **1** an agreement in which the person proved wrong about the outcome of something will do or pay what is stipulated **2** the thing or sum thus staked **3** a person or thing with regard to its likelihood of bringing about some result [a good *bet* to win the election] —*vt., vi.* **bet** or **bet'ted, bet'ting 1** to declare as in a bet **2** to stake (money, etc.) in a bet with (someone)

**be·ta** (bāt'ə) *n.* the second letter of the Greek alphabet (B, β)

**beta blocker** a drug used to control heartbeat, treat hypertension, etc.

**beta car·o·tene** (kar'ə tēn') a hydrocarbon found in butter, carrots, etc. and converted by the liver into vitamin A

**be·take** (bē tāk', bi-) *vt.* **-took'** (-took'), **-tak'en, -tak'ing** ⟦ME *bitaken*⟧ to go (used reflexively) [he *betook* himself to his castle]

**beta particle** an electron or positron ejected from the nucleus of an atom during radioactive disintegration

**beta ray** a stream of beta particles

**be·tel nut** (bēt'ʼl) ⟦Port < Malayalam *veṭṭilai*⟧ the fruit of a palm (**betel palm**), chewed together with lime and the leaves of a pepper plant (**betel pepper**) by some Asians as a mild stimulant

**be·think** (bē thiŋk', bi-) [Archaic] *vt.* **-thought'** (-thôt'), **-think'ing** ⟦OE *bethencan*⟧ to remind (oneself)

**Beth·le·hem** (beth'lə hem') ancient town in Judea: traditionally regarded as Jesus' birthplace

**be·tide** (bē tīd', bi-) *vi., vt.* **-tid'ed, -tid'ing** ⟦< ME *be-*, BE- + *tiden*, happen⟧ to happen (to); befall

**be·times** (bē tīmz', bi-) *adv.* [Archaic] **1** early or early enough **2** promptly

**be·to·ken** (bē tō'kən, bi-) *vt.* ⟦ME *betocnen*⟧ **1** to be a token or sign of **2** to show beforehand; presage

**be·tray** (bē trā', bi-) *vt.* ⟦< L *tradere*, hand over⟧ **1** to help the enemy of (one's country, etc.) **2** to expose treacherously **3** to fail to uphold [to *betray* a trust] **4** to deceive; specif., to seduce and then desert **5** to reveal unknowingly **6** to disclose (secrets, etc.) —**be·tray'al** *n.* —**be·tray'er** *n.*

**be·troth** (bē trō*th*'; -trôth', bi-) *vt.* [< ME: see BE- & TRUTH] to promise in marriage —**be·troth'al** *n.*

**be·trothed'** (-trō*th*d', -trôtht') *adj.* engaged to be married —*n.* the person to whom one is engaged

**bet·ta** (bet'ə) *n.* [ModL] a brightly colored gourami of SE Asia: often an aquarium fish

**bet·ter** (bet'ər) *adj.* [OE *betera*] 1 *compar. of* GOOD 2 more excellent 3 more suitable, desirable, etc. 4 larger [the *better* part of a day] 5 improved in health —*adv.* 1 *compar. of* WELL² 2 in a more excellent manner 3 in a higher degree 4 more —*n.* 1 a person superior in authority, etc. 2 a more excellent thing, condition, etc. —*vt.* 1 to outdo; surpass 2 to improve —**better off** in a better situation —**get** (or **have**) **the better of** 1 to outdo 2 to outwit —**had better** ought to

**bet'ter·ment** (-mənt) *n.* a bettering; improvement

**bet'tor** (bet'ər) *n.* one who bets: also **bet'ter**

**be·tween** (bē twēn', bi-) *prep.* [OE *betweonum*] 1 in the space, time, etc. that separates (two things) 2 connecting [a bond *between* friends] 3 by the joint action of 4 possessed jointly by 5 from one or the other of [choose *between* us] 6 involving *Between* is sometimes used of more than two if each part is seen as individually related to each of the others [peace *between* nations] —*adv.* in an intermediate space, time, etc. —**between ourselves** as a secret: also **between you and me**

**be·twixt** (bē twikst', bi-) *prep., adv.* [< OE *be*, by + *twegen*, twain] between: archaic except in **betwixt and between**, in an intermediate position

**BeV** or **bev** (bev) *abbrev.* one billion (10⁹) electron-volts

**bev·el** (bev'əl) *n.* [< ?] 1 a tool for measuring or marking angles, etc. 2 an angle other than a right angle 3 sloping part or surface —*adj.* beveled —*vt.* -eled or -elled, -el·ing or -el·ling to cut to an angle other than a right angle —*vi.* to slope at an angle; slant

**bevel gear** a gearwheel meshed with another at an angle

**bev·er·age** (bev'ər ij', bev'rij) *n.* [< L *bibere*, to drink] any liquid for drinking, esp. one other than water

**bev·y** (bev'ē) *n., pl.* -ies [ME *bevey*] 1 a group, esp. of girls or women 2 a flock: now used chiefly of quail

**be·wail** (bē wāl', bi-) *vt.* to wail over; lament; mourn

**be·ware** (bē wer', bi-) *vi., vt.* -wared', -war'ing [prob. < OE *bewarian*, keep watch] to be wary or careful (of)

**be·wigged** (bē wigd', bi-) *adj.* wearing a wig

**be·wil·der** (bē wil'dər, bi-) *vt.* [ult. < OE *wilde*, wild] to confuse hopelessly; puzzle —**be·wil'der·ing·ly** *adv.* —**be·wil'der·ment** *n.*

**be·witch** (bē wich', bi-) *vt.* [< OE *wicca*, sorcerer] 1 to cast a spell over 2 to attract and delight greatly —**be·witch'ing** *adj.*

**bey** (bā) *n.* [Turk] a Turkish title of respect and former title of rank

**be·yond** (bē änd') *prep.* [< OE *be*, by + *geond*, yonder] 1 farther on than; past 2 later than 3 outside the reach of [*beyond* help] 4 more than —*adv.* farther away —**the** (**great**) **beyond** whatever follows death

**bez·el** (bez'əl) *n.* [< ?] 1 a sloping surface, as the cutting edge of a chisel 2 the slanting faces of the upper part of a cut gem 3 the groove and flange holding a gem, watch crystal, etc. in place

**Bhu·tan** (bōō tän') kingdom in the Himalayas, SC Asia: 18,000 sq. mi.; pop. 600,000

**Bi** *Chem.* symbol *for* bismuth

**bi-** [L] *prefix* 1 having two 2 doubly 3 happening every two (specified periods) 4 happening twice during every (specified period) 5 using two or both 6 joining or involving two

**bi·an·nu·al** (bī an'yōō əl) *adj.* coming twice a year; semiannual —**bi·an'nu·al·ly** *adv.*

**bi·as** (bī'əs) *n., pl.* -as·es [MFr *biais*, a slant] 1 a slanting or diagonal line, cut or sewn in cloth 2 partiality; prejudice —*adj.* slanting; diagonal —*adv.* diagonally —*vt.* -ased or -assed, -as·ing or -as·sing to prejudice —**on the bias** diagonally

**bi·ath·lon** (bī ath'län') *n.* [BI- + Gr *athlon*, contest] a winter sports event combining cross-country skiing and rifle marksmanship

**bib** (bib) *n.* [< L *bibere*, to drink] 1 a cloth or plastic cover tied under a child's chin at meals 2 the upper front part of an apron

**Bib** *abbrev.* 1 Bible 2 Biblical

**bibb lettuce** (bib) [after J. *Bibb* (1789-1884), who developed it] a type of lettuce with loose heads of crisp, dark-green leaves

**Bi·ble** (bī'bəl) *n.* [< Gr *biblos*, papyrus < *Byblos*, Phoenician city that exported papyrus] 1 the sacred book of Christianity; Old Testament and New Testament 2 the Holy Scriptures of Judaism; Old Testament 3 [b-] any book regarded as authoritative or official —**bib·li·cal** or **Bib·li·cal** (bib'li kəl) *adj.*

**biblio-** [< Gr *biblion*, book] *combining form* book, books [*bibliophile*]

**bib·li·og·ra·phy** (bib'lē äg'rə fē) *n., pl.* -phies a list of writings on a given subject or by a given author, or of those used by the author of a given work —**bib'li·og'ra·pher** *n.* —**bib'li·o·graph'ic** (-ə graf'ik) *adj.*

**bib'li·o·phile'** (-ə fīl') *n.* a person who loves or collects books

**bib·u·lous** (bib'yōō ləs) *adj.* [< L *bibere*, to drink] addicted to or fond of alcoholic beverages

**bi·cam·er·al** (bī kam'ər əl) *adj.* [< BI- + L *camera*, chamber] having two legislative chambers

**bi·car·bon·ate of soda** (bī kär'bən it) SODIUM BICARBONATE

**bi·cen·ten·ni·al** (bī'sen ten'ē əl) *adj.* happening once in every 200 years —*n.* a 200th anniversary

**bi·ceps** (bī'seps') *n., pl.* -ceps or -ceps'es [< L < *bis*, two + *caput*, head] a muscle with two points of origin; esp., the large muscle in the front of the upper arm

**bick·er** (bik'ər) *vi.* [ME *bikeren*] to squabble; quarrel —**bick'er·er** *n.*

**bi·con·cave** (bī kän'kāv') *adj.* concave on both surfaces [a *biconcave* lens]

**bi·con·vex** (-veks') *adj.* convex on both surfaces [a *biconvex* lens]

**bi·cus·pid** (bī kus'pid) *adj.* [< BI- + L *cuspis*, pointed end] having two points —*n.* any of eight adult teeth with two-pointed crowns

**bi·cy·cle** (bī'sik'əl, -si kəl) *n.* [Fr: see BI- & CYCLE] a vehicle consisting of a metal frame on two large wheels, with handlebars, foot pedals, and a seat —*vi.* -cled, -cling to ride or travel on a bicycle —*vt.* 1 to carry on or as on a bicycle 2 to travel over by bicycle —**bi'cy'clist** *n.*

**bid** (bid) *vt.* **bade** or **bid**, **bid'den** or **bid**, **bid'ding** [< OE *biddan*, to urge & *beodan*, to command] 1 to command, ask, or tell 2 to state (an amount) as the price one will pay or accept 3 to express [to *bid* farewell] 4 *Card Games* to state (a number of tricks) and declare (trump) —*vi.* to make a bid —*n.* 1 a bidding 2 an amount bid 3 a chance to bid 4 an attempt or try (*for*) 5 [Inf.] an invitation —**bid fair** to seem likely —**bid'der** *n.*

**bid·dy** (bid'ē) *n., pl.* -dies [< ?] 1 a hen 2 [Inf.] an elderly woman regarded as annoying, gossipy, etc.: usually **old biddy**

**bide** (bīd) *vi.* **bode** or **bid'ed**, **bid'ed**, **bid'ing** [OE *bidan*] [Now Chiefly Dial.] 1 to stay; continue 2 to dwell 3 to wait —*vt.* [Now Chiefly Dial.] to endure or tolerate —**bide one's time** to wait patiently for an opportunity [she *bided* her time]

**bi·det** (bē dā') *n.* [Fr] a low, bowl-shaped bathroom fixture, with running water, for bathing the crotch

**bi·en·ni·al** (bī en'ē əl) *adj.* [< L *bi-*, BI- + *annus*, year] 1 happening every two years 2 lasting for

two years —*n.* **1** a biennial event **2** *Bot.* a plant that lasts two years —**bi·en′ni·al·ly** *adv.*

**bier** (bir) *n.* ⟦OE *bær*⟧ a portable framework on which a coffin is placed

**bi·fo·cals** (bī′fō′kəlz) *pl.n.* eyeglasses with lenses having one part ground for close focus and the other for distant focus

**bi·fur·cate** (bī′fər kāt′) *vt.*, *vi.* **-cat·ed, -cat·ing** ⟦< L *bi-*, BI- + *furca*, a fork⟧ to divide into two parts or branches —**bi·fur·ca′tion** *n.*

**big** (big) *adj.* **big′ger, big′gest** ⟦ME⟧ **1** of great size; large **2** great in amount or force **3** full-grown **4** elder *[his big sister]* **5** noticeably pregnant (*with*) **6** loud **7** important *[big plans]* **8** famous **9** extravagant *[big talk]* **10** noble *[a big heart]* —*adv.* [Inf.] **1** boastfully **2** impressively —**big′ness** *n.*

**big·a·my** (big′ə mē) *n.* ⟦< L *bi-*, BI- + Gr *gamos*, marriage⟧ the crime of marrying a second time when one is already legally married —**big′a·mist** *n.* —**big′a·mous** *adj.* —**big′a·mous·ly** *adv.*

**big′-bang′ theory** a theory that the expansion of the universe began with a gigantic explosion (**big bang**) between 12 and 20 billion years ago

**Big Dipper, the** a dipper-shaped group of bright stars in the northern sky

**big game 1** large wild animals hunted for sport, as lions, tigers, moose, etc. **2** the object of any important or dangerous undertaking

**big′heart′ed** (-här′tid) *adj.* quick to give or forgive; generous —**big′heart′ed·ly** *adv.*

**big′horn′** *n.*, *pl.* **-horns′** or **-horn′** a Rocky Mountain wild sheep with large horns

**bight** (bīt) *n.* ⟦OE *byht*, a bend⟧ **1** a slack part in a rope **2** a curve in a coastline **3** a bay formed by such a curve

**big′mouth′** *n.* [Slang] a person who talks too much, esp. in an opinionated way

**big·ot** (big′ət) *n.* ⟦Fr < ?⟧ **1** one who holds blindly and intolerantly to a particular creed, opinion, etc. **2** a prejudiced person —**big′ot·ed** *adj.* —**big′ot·ry** *n.*

**big shot** [Slang] an important or influential person: also **big wheel**

**big′-time′** *adj.*, *adv.* [Slang] at, of, or to a very great degree, extent, etc.

**bike** (bīk) *n.* [Inf.] **1** a bicycle **2** a motorcycle —**bik′er** *n.*

**bi·ki·ni** (bi kē′nē) *n.* ⟦Fr after *Bikini*, Pacific atoll⟧ **1** a very brief two-piece swimsuit for women **2** very brief, legless underpants or swimming trunks

**bi·lat·er·al** (bī lat′ər əl) *adj.* **1** of, having, or involving two sides, factions, etc. **2** affecting both sides equally; reciprocal *[a bilateral pact]* —**bi·lat′er·al·ly** *adv.*

**bile** (bīl) *n.* ⟦Fr < *bilis*⟧ **1** the bitter, greenish fluid secreted by the liver: it aids digestion **2** bad temper; anger

**bilge** (bilj) *n.* ⟦var. of BULGE⟧ **1** the rounded lower part of a ship's hold **2** stagnant water that collects there: also **bilge water 3** [Slang] nonsense

**bi·lin·gual** (bī liŋ′gwəl) *adj.* ⟦< L *bi-*, BI- + *lingua*, tongue⟧ of, in, or able to use two languages —**bi·lin′gual·ism′** *n.*

**bil·ious** (bil′yəs) *adj.* ⟦< L *bilis*, bile⟧ **1** having or appearing to have some ailment of the bile or liver **2** bad-tempered

**bilk** (bilk) *vt.* ⟦? < BALK⟧ to cheat or swindle; defraud —**bilk′er** *n.*

**bill¹** (bil) *n.* ⟦< ML *bulla*, sealed document⟧ **1** a statement of charges for goods or services; invoice **2** a list, as a menu or theater program **3** a poster or handbill **4** a draft of a proposed law **5** a bill of exchange **6** a piece of paper money **7** *Law* a written declaration of charges or complaints filed —*vt.* **1** to make out a bill of (items) **2** to present a statement of charges to **3** *a*) to advertise by bills *b*) to book (a performer) —**fill the bill** [Inf.] to meet the requirements —**bill′a·ble** *adj.*

**bill²** (bil) *n.* ⟦OE *bile*⟧ **1** the projecting jaws of a bird, usually pointed; beak **2** a beaklike part of

the mouth, as that of a turtle —*vi.* to touch bills together —**bill and coo** to kiss, talk softly, etc. in a loving way

**bill′board′** *n.* a signboard, usually outdoors, for advertising posters

**bil·let** (bil′it) *n.* [see BILL¹] **1** *a*) a written order to provide lodging for military personnel *b*) the lodging **2** a position, job, or situation —*vt.* to assign to lodging by billet

**bil·let-doux** (bē′yä dōō′) *n.*, *pl.* **bil·lets-doux** (bē′yä dōō′) ⟦Fr, sweet letter⟧ a love letter

**bill′fold′** (bil′fōld′) *n.* a wallet

**bil·liard** (bil′yərd) *adj.* of or for billiards

**bil′liards** (-yərdz) *n.* ⟦< Fr *billard*, orig., a cue⟧ a game played with a cue and three hard balls on a table with raised, cushioned edges

**bill·ing** (bil′iŋ) *n.* **1** the listing of actors' names on a theater marquee, etc. **2** the order in which the names are listed

**bil·lings·gate** (bil′iŋz gāt′) *n.* ⟦after a London fish market⟧ foul, vulgar, abusive talk

**bil·lion** (bil′yən) *n.* ⟦Fr < *bi-*, two + (*mi*)*llion*⟧ **1** a thousand millions (1,000,000,000) **2** *former Brit. term for* TRILLION (a million millions) —**bil′lionth** *adj.*, *n.*

**bil′lion·aire′** (-yə ner′) *n.* a person whose wealth comes to at least a billion dollars, pounds, francs, etc.

**bill of exchange** a written order to pay a certain sum of money to the person named

**bill of fare** a menu

**bill of lading** a receipt issued to a shipper by a carrier, describing the goods to be shipped

**Bill of Rights** the first ten amendments to the U.S. Constitution, which guarantee civil liberties

**bill of sale** a written statement transferring ownership of something by sale

**bil·low** (bil′ō) *n.* ⟦ON *bylgja*⟧ **1** a large wave **2** any large swelling mass or surge, as of smoke —*vi.* to surge or swell in a billow —**bil′low·y, -i·er, -i·est**, *adj.*

**bil·ly** (bil′ē) *n.*, *pl.* **-lies** [ult. < OFr *bille*, tree trunk] a club, esp. a policeman's heavy stick: in full **billy club**

**billy goat** a male goat

**Bi·lox·i** (bə luk′sē, -läk′sē) city in SE Mississippi, on the Gulf of Mexico: pop. 46,000

**bi·me·tal·lic** (bī′mə tal′ik) *adj.* ⟦< Fr *bi-*, BI- + *métallique*, metallic⟧ **1** of, containing, or using two metals **2** of or based on bimetallism

**bi·met·al·lism** (bī met′'l iz′əm) *n.* the use of two metals, esp. gold and silver, as the monetary standard, with fixed values in relation to each other

**bi·month·ly** (bī munth′lē) *adj.*, *adv.* **1** once every two months **2** [Now Rare] twice a month

**bin** (bin) *n.* ⟦OE, crib⟧ a box or enclosed space used for storage

**bi·na·ry** (bī′nə rē) *adj.* ⟦< L *bis*, double⟧ **1** made up of two parts; double **2** designating or of a number system in which the base used is two, each number being expressed by using only two digits, specif. 0 and 1 —*n.*, *pl.* **-ries** something with two parts

**bi·na·tion·al** (bī nash′ə nəl) *adj.* involving two nations or two nationalities

**bin·au·ral** (bī nôr′əl) *adj.* **1** of or involving both ears **2** of or using two sources of sound

**bind** (bīnd) *vt.* **bound, bind′ing** ⟦< OE *bindan*⟧ **1** to tie together, as with rope **2** to hold or restrain **3** to encircle with a belt, etc. **4** to bandage: often with *up* **5** to constipate **6** to reinforce or ornament the edges of by a band, as of tape **7** to fasten together the pages of (a book) and enclose in a cover **8** to obligate by duty, love, etc. **9** to compel, as by oath, legal restraint, or contract —*vi.* **1** to do the act of binding **2** to be or become tight or stiff **3** to stick together **4** to be obligatory or binding in force —*n.* **1** anything that binds **2** [Inf.] a difficult or restrictive situation

**bind′er** *n.* **1** one that binds **2** a substance that binds, as tar **3** a cover for holding sheets of paper together

**bind′er·y** *n.,* *pl.* **-er·ies** a place where books are bound

**bind′ing** *n.* a thing that binds, as a band, a tape, the covers and backing of a book, or a cohesive substance —*adj.* that binds, obligates, etc.

**binge** (binj) [Inf.] *n.* unrestrained activity; spree —*vi.* **binged, binge′ing** to indulge without restraint

**bin·go** (biŋ′gō) *n.* a game played with cards having rows of numbered squares: the first player with an entire row drawn by lot wins —*interj.* used to signify sudden success, etc.

**bin·na·cle** (bin′ə kəl) *n.* [ult. < L *habitaculum,* dwelling place] the case holding a ship's compass

**bin·oc·u·lar** (bī näk′yə lər; *for n.,* bi-) *adj.* [< L *bini,* double + *oculus,* eye] using, or for, both eyes —*n.* [*pl.*] field glasses

**bi·no·mi·al** (bī nō′mē əl) *n.* [< L *bi-,* BI- + Gr *nomos,* law] **1** *Math.* an expression consisting of two terms connected by a plus or minus sign **2** a two-word scientific name of a plant or animal, indicating the genus and species

**bi·o** (bī′ō) *n., pl.* **bios** [Inf.] a biography

**bio-** [Gr < *bios,* life] *combining form* life, of living things

**bi·o·chem·is·try** (bī′ō kem′is trē) *n.* the study of the chemistry of life processes in plants and animals —**bi′o·chem′ist** *n.*

**bi·o·cide** (bī′ō sīd′) *n.* [BIO- + -CIDE] a substance that kills microorganisms

**bi·o·de·grad·a·ble** (bī′ō di grā′də bəl) *adj.* [BIO- + *degrad(e),* decompose + -ABLE] capable of being readily decomposed by the action of microbes, as some detergents

**bi·o·di·ver·si·ty** *n.* variety in the living things of a particular area

**bi·o·feed′back′** *n.* a technique of seeking to control certain emotional states by training oneself, using electronic devices, to modify autonomic body functions, such as heartbeat

**biog** *abbrev.* **1** biographical **2** biography

**bi·og·ra·phy** (bī äg′rə fē) *n., pl.* **-phies** [Gr: see BIO- & -GRAPHY] a person's life story written by another —**bi·og′ra·pher** *n.* —**bi·o·graph·i·cal** (bī′ə graf′i kəl) *adj.*

**biol** *abbrev.* **1** biological **2** biology

**biological warfare** the use of toxic microorganisms, etc. in war

**bi·ol·o·gy** (bī äl′ə jē) *n.* [see BIO- & -LOGY] the science that deals with the origin, history, characteristics, etc. of plants and animals —**bi·o·log·i·cal** (bī′ə läj′i kəl) *adj.* —**bi′o·log′i·cal·ly** *adv.* —**bi·ol′o·gist** *n.*

**bi·on·ic** (bī än′ik) *adj.* [see fol.] **1** of bionics **2** having an artificial body part or parts, as in science fiction, so as to enhance strength, etc.

**bi·on′ics** *n.* [BI(O)- + (ELECTR)ONICS] the science of designing instruments or systems modeled after living organisms

**bi·o·phys·ics** (bī′ō fiz′iks) *n.* the study of biological phenomena in relation to physics —**bi′o·phys′i·cal** *adj.* —**bi′o·phys′i·cist** *n.*

**bi·o·pic** (bī′ō pik′) *n.* [Inf.] a film dramatizing the life of a famous person

**bi·op·sy** (bī′äp′sē) *n., pl.* **-sies** [BI(O)- + Gr *opsis,* a sight] *Med.* the removal of bits of living tissue for diagnosis

**bi·o·rhythm** (bī′ō rith′əm) *n.* any biological cycle that involves periodic changes in blood pressure, body temperature, etc.

**bi·o·tin** (bī′ə tin) *n.* [< Gr *bios,* life] a factor of the vitamin B group

**bi·par·ti·san** (bī pär′tə zən) *adj.* of, representing, or supported by two parties —**bi·par′ti·san·ship′** *n.*

**bi·par·tite** (bī pär′tīt′) *adj.* [< L *bi-,* BI- + *partire,* to divide] **1** having two parts **2** involving two

**bi·ped** (bī′ped′) *n.* [< L *bi-,* BI- + *pes,* foot] any two-footed animal —**bi·ped′al** *adj.*

**bi·plane** (bī′plān′) *n.* an airplane with two sets of wings, one above the other

**bi·po·lar** (bī pō′lər) *adj.* **1** of or involving poles or polarity **2** having alternating periods of mania and mental depression

**bi·ra·cial** (bī rā′shəl) *adj.* consisting of or involving two races

**birch** (bʉrch) *n.* [OE *beorc*] **1** a tree having smooth bark in thin layers, and hard, close-grained wood **2** its wood **3** a bunch of birch twigs used for whipping —*vt.* to flog

**bird** (bʉrd) *n.* [< OE *bridd,* young bird] a warm-blooded vertebrate with feathers and wings —*vi.* to observe wild birds in their habitat —**birds of a feather** people with the same traits or tastes —**for the birds** [Slang] ridiculous, foolish, etc.

**bird′er** *n.* a bird-watcher

**bird′ie** *n. Golf* a score of one stroke under par for a hole

**bird′ing** *n.* bird-watching

**bird's′-eye** *adj.* having marks resembling birds' eyes [*bird's-eye* maple]

**bird's-eye view 1** a view from high above **2** an overall, but cursory, view

**bird′-watch′ing** *n.* a hobby involving observation of wild birds in their habitat —**bird′-watch′er** *n.*

**bi·ret·ta** (bə ret′ə) *n.* [< LL *birrettum,* small cloak] a square ceremonial hat with three or four vertical projections, worn by Roman Catholic clergy

**Bir·ming·ham** (bʉr′miŋ əm; *for 2,* -ham′) **1** city in central England: county district pop. 961,000 **2** city in N Alabama: pop. 265,000

**birth** (bʉrth) *n.* [< ON *byrth*] **1** the act of bringing forth offspring **2** a being born **3** origin or descent **4** the beginning of anything —*vi., vt.* to give birth (to) —**give birth (to) 1** to bring forth (offspring) **2** to create

**birth′day′** *n.* the anniversary of the day of a person's birth

**birth′ing** *adj., n.* (of or for) giving birth

**birth′mark′** *n.* a skin blemish or mark present at birth

**birth′place′** *n.* the place of one's birth or of a thing's origin

**birth′rate′** *n.* the number of births per year per thousand people in a given area, group, etc.: also **birth rate**

**birth′right′** *n.* any right that a person has by birth

**birth′stone′** *n.* a gem symbolizing the month of a person's birth

**bis·cot·ti** (bi skät′ē) *pl.n., sing.* **-to** or **-ti** [It, cognate with fol.] hard, bar-shaped cookie made with almonds, etc.

**bis·cuit** (bis′kit) *n., pl.* **-cuits** or **-cuit** [< L *bis,* twice + *coquere,* to cook] **1** [Chiefly Brit.] a cracker or cookie **2** *a)* a quick bread baked in small pieces *b)* any of these pieces

**bi·sect** (bī sekt′) *vt.* [< L *bi-,* BI- + *secare,* to cut] **1** to cut in two **2** *Geom.* to divide into two equal parts —*vi.* to divide; fork —**bi·sec′tor** (-sekt′ər) *n.*

**bi·sex·u·al** (bī sek′shoo əl) *adj.* of, or sexually attracted to, both sexes —*n.* one who is bisexual

**bish·op** (bish′əp) *n.* [< Gr *episkopos,* overseer] **1** a high-ranking member of the Christian clergy, governing a diocese or church district **2** a chess piece that can move in a diagonal direction only

**bish·op·ric** (bish′əp rik) *n.* the district, office, or rank of a bishop

**Bis·marck**[1] (biz′märk′), Prince **Ot·to von** (ät′ō vän) 1815-98; Prussian chancellor (1871-90) who unified Germany

**Bis·marck**[2] (biz′märk′) capital of North Dakota: pop. 49,000

**bis·muth** (biz′məth) *n.* [< Ger *wismut*] a brittle, grayish-white metallic chemical element used in alloys of low melting point

**bi·son** (bī′sən) *n., pl.* **bi′son** [< L, wild ox] a bovine ruminant having a shaggy mane and a humped back, as the American buffalo

**bisque** (bisk) *n.* ⟦Fr⟧ a thick, creamy soup made as from shellfish or vegetables

**bis·tro** (bē′strō′) *n.* ⟦Fr⟧ a small cafe

**bit**[1] (bit) *n.* ⟦< OE *bite*, a bite⟧ **1** the part of a bridle in the horse's mouth, used as a control **2** anything that curbs or controls **3** a drilling or boring tool for use in a brace, drill press, etc.

**bit**[2] (bit) *n.* ⟦< OE *bita*, a piece⟧ **1** *a*) a small piece or quantity *b*) small extent [a *bit* bored] *c*) a short time **2** [Inf.] 12½ cents: now usually in *two bits* —*adj.* very small [a *bit* role] —**bit by bit** gradually —**do one's bit** to do one's share

**bit**[3] (bit) *n.* ⟦*b(inary) (dig)it*⟧ **1** a single digit in a binary number system **2** a unit of information

**bitch** (bich) *n.* ⟦OE *bicce*⟧ **1** the female of the dog, fox, etc. **2** a woman regarded as bad-tempered, malicious, etc. **3** [Slang] anything especially difficult —*vi.* [Slang] to complain

**bitch·y** *adj.* -i·er, -i·est [Slang] bad-tempered or malicious: used esp. of a woman

**bite** (bīt) *vt.* **bit** (bit), **bit·ten** (bit′'n) or **bit**, **bit′ing** ⟦OE *bītan*⟧ **1** to seize or pierce with or as with the teeth **2** to cut into, as with a sharp weapon **3** to sting, as an insect **4** to cause to smart **5** to eat into; corrode —*vi.* **1** to press or snap the teeth (*into, at*, etc.) **2** to cause a biting sensation **3** to grip **4** to seize a bait **5** to be caught, as by a trick —*n.* **1** a biting **2** biting quality; sting **3** a wound or sting from biting **4** *a*) a mouthful *b*) a snack **5** [Inf.] a sum deducted, as by a tax —**bite the bullet** to confront a painful situation bravely: from the patient's biting a bullet during battlefield surgery without an anesthetic

**bit·ing** (bīt′iŋ) *adj.* **1** cutting; sharp **2** sarcastic —**bit′ing·ly** *adv.*

**bit·ter** (bit′ər) *adj.* ⟦OE *biter*, akin to *bītan*, to bite⟧ **1** having a sharp, often unpleasant taste **2** causing or showing sorrow, pain, etc. **3** sharp and disagreeable; harsh [a *bitter* wind] **4** resentful or cynical —**bit′ter·ly** *adv.* —**bit′ter·ness** *n.*

**bit·tern** (bit′ərn) *n.* ⟦< OFr *butor*⟧ a wading bird with a thumping cry

**bit′ters** *pl.n.* a liquor containing bitter herbs, etc. and usually alcohol, used as in some cocktails

**bit′ter·sweet′** *n.* **1** a woody vine bearing small orange fruits with bright-red fleshy seeds **2** a poisonous vine with purple flowers and red berries **3** pleasure mixed with sadness —*adj.* **1** both bitter and sweet **2** pleasant and sad

**bi·tu·men** (bi tōō′mən) *n.* ⟦L < Celt⟧ any of various black mixtures of hydrocarbons obtained in the distillation of petroleum, used for paints, roofing, etc. —**bi·tu′mi·nous** (-mə nəs) *adj.*

**bituminous coal** coal that yields pitch or tar when it burns; soft coal

**bi·va·lent** (bī vā′lənt) *adj. Chem.* DIVALENT

**bi·valve** (bī′valv′) *n.* any mollusk having a shell made of two valves hinged together, as a clam

**biv·ou·ac** (biv′wak′) *n.* ⟦Fr < OHG *bi-*, by + *wahta*, watchman⟧ a temporary encampment (esp. of soldiers) in the open —*vi.* **-acked′, -ack′ing** to encamp in the open

**bi·week·ly** (bī wēk′lē) *adj., adv.* **1** once every two weeks **2** [Now Rare] semiweekly

**bi·zarre** (bi zär′) *adj.* ⟦Fr < Basque *bizar*, beard⟧ **1** odd; grotesque **2** unexpected; fantastic

**bk** *abbrev.* **1** bank **2** book

**bl** *abbrev.* **1** bale(s) **2** barrel(s)

**B/L** or **b/l** *abbrev.* bill of lading

**blab** (blab) *vt., vi.* **blabbed, blab′bing** ⟦ME *blabben*⟧ **1** to reveal (a secret) **2** to chatter; prattle Also **blab′ber** —*n.* gossip

**blab′ber·mouth′** *n.* [Inf.] one who blabs

**black** (blak) *adj.* ⟦OE *blæc*⟧ **1** opposite to white; of the color of coal **2** [*sometimes* B-] of or for the dark-skinned peoples of Africa, etc. or their descendants elsewhere, specif. African-Americans in the U.S. [*black* studies] **3** without light; dark **4** dirty **5** evil; wicked **6** sad; dismal **7** sul-

len —*n.* **1** black color or pigment **2** black clothes, esp. when worn in mourning **3** [*sometimes* B-] a member of a black people **4** darkness —*vt., vi.* to blacken —**black out** to lose consciousness —**in the black** operating at a profit —**black′ish** *adj.* —**black′ly** *adv.* —**black′ness** *n.*

**black′-and-blue′** *adj.* discolored, as by a bruise

**black′ball′** *n.* a vote against —*vt.* **1** to vote against **2** to ostracize

**black belt** a black belt or sash awarded to an expert of the highest skill in judo or karate

**black′ber′ry** (-ber′ē, -bər ē) *n., pl.* **-ries 1** the fleshy, purple or black, edible fruit of various brambles of the rose family **2** a bush or vine bearing this fruit

**black′bird′** *n.* any of various birds the male of which is almost entirely black

**black′board′** *n.* a smooth, usually dark surface on which to write with chalk

**black′en** (-ən) *vi.* to become black or dark —*vt.* **1** to make black; darken **2** to slander; defame

**black eye 1** a discoloration of the skin around an eye, resulting from a blow or contusion **2** [Inf.] dishonor, or its cause

**black′-eyed′ Su′san** (-sōō′zən) a yellow, daisylike wildflower with a dark center

**black·guard** (blag′ərd) *n.* a scoundrel; villain

**black′head′** *n.* a dark plug of dried fatty matter in a pore of the skin

**black hole 1** an object or region in space with intense gravitation from which light, etc. cannot escape **2** *a*) an emptiness or void *b*) anything endlessly devouring resources, etc.

**black′jack′** *n.* **1** a small, leather-covered bludgeon with a flexible handle **2** a gambling card game in which a player getting closer to 21 points than the dealer, without exceeding it, wins —*vt.* to hit with a blackjack

**black light** ultraviolet or infrared radiation used for fluorescent effects

**black′list′** *n.* a list of those who are censured, refused employment, etc. —*vt.* to put on a blacklist

**black lung (disease)** a disease of the lungs caused by the inhalation of coal dust

**black magic** sorcery

**black′mail′** *n.* ⟦lit., black rent < ME *male*, rent⟧ **1** payment extorted to prevent disclosure of information that could bring disgrace **2** extortion of such payment —*vt.* to get or try to get blackmail from —**black′mail′er** *n.*

**black mark** an unfavorable item in one's record

**black market** a system for selling goods illegally —**black marketeer** (or **marketer**)

**black′out′** *n.* **1** an extinguishing of stage lights to end a scene **2** a concealing of lights that might be visible to enemy aircraft at night **3** a temporary loss of electric power **4** temporary unconsciousness **5** suppression, as of news by censorship

**black power** political and economic power as sought by black Americans in the struggle for civil rights

**Black Sea** sea between Asia & SE Europe, north of Turkey

**black sheep** a family or group member regarded as not so respectable as the others

**black′smith′** *n.* a smith who works in iron and makes and fits horseshoes

**black′thorn′** *n.* a thorny shrub with purple or black, plumlike fruit; sloe

**black′top′** *n.* a bituminous mixture, usually asphalt, used as a surface for roads, etc. —*vt.* **-topped′, -top′ping** to cover with blacktop

**black widow** a black spider with a red mark underneath: the female has a poisonous bite and sometimes eats its mate

**blad·der** (blad′ər) *n.* ⟦OE *blæddre*⟧ **1** a sac that fills with fluid or gas, esp. one that holds urine flowing from the kidneys **2** a thing like this

**blade** (blād) *n.* ⟦OE *blæd*, leaf⟧ **1** *a*) the leaf of a plant, esp. of grass *b*) the flat part of a leaf **2** a broad, flat surface or part, as of an oar or snowplow **3** the cutting part of a tool, knife, etc. **4** a sword or swordsman

**Blair** (bler), **To·ny** (tō′nē) 1953- ; Brit. prime minister (1997- )

**blam·a·ble** or **blame·a·ble** (blām′ə bəl) *adj.* that deserves blame —**blam′a·bly** *adv.*

**blame** (blām) *vt.* **blamed, blam′ing** ⟦see BLASPHEME⟧ **1** to accuse of being at fault; condemn (*for*) **2** to put the responsibility of (an error, etc.) *on* —*n.* **1** a blaming **2** responsibility for a fault —**be to blame** to be at fault —**blame′less** *adj.* — **blame′less·ly** *adv.* —**blame′less·ness** *n.*

**blame′wor′thy** *adj.* deserving to be blamed

**blanch** (blanch) *vt.* ⟦< OFr *blanc*, white⟧ **1** to whiten or bleach **2** to make pale **3** to scald (vegetables, almonds, etc.) —*vi.* to turn pale

**bland** (bland) *adj.* ⟦L *blandus*, mild⟧ **1** gently agreeable **2** mild; not harsh **3** insipid —**bland′ly** *adv.* —**bland′ness** *n.*

**blan·dish** (blan′dish) *vt., vi.* ⟦< L *blandiri*, to flatter⟧ to flatter; coax; cajole —**blan′dish·ment** *n.*

**blank** (blaŋk) *adj.* ⟦< OFr *blanc*, white⟧ **1** not written on **2** empty; vacant; plain **3** dazed or vacant *[a blank look]* **4** utter; complete *[a blank denial]* —*n.* **1** an empty space, esp. one to be filled out in a printed form **2** such a printed form **3** an empty place or time **4** a powder-filled cartridge without a bullet —*vt.* to hold (an opponent) scoreless —**blank out** to conceal by covering over —**draw a blank** [Inf.] **1** to be unsuccessful **2** to be unable to remember a particular thing — **blank′ly** *adv.* —**blank′ness** *n.*

**blank check 1** a bank check not yet filled in **2** a signed check with no amount filled in **3** permission to use an unlimited amount of money, authority, etc.

**blan·ket** (blaŋk′it) *n.* ⟦< OFr dim. of *blanc*, white⟧ **1** a large piece of cloth used for warmth, esp. as a bed cover **2** any covering like this *[a blanket of leaves]* —*adj.* including many or all items *[blanket insurance]* —*vt.* **1** to cover; overlie **2** to obscure

**blank verse** unrhymed verse having five iambic feet per line

**blan·quette** (blän ket′) *n.* ⟦Fr⟧ a stew, as of chicken or veal, in cream sauce

**blare** (bler) *vt., vi.* **blared, blar′ing** ⟦ME *bleren*, to wail⟧ to sound or exclaim loudly —*n.* a loud, harsh sound

**blar·ney** (blär′nē) *n.* ⟦< *Blarney* stone in Ireland, traditionally kissed to gain skill in flattery⟧ smooth or flattering talk

**bla·sé** (blä zā′) *adj.* ⟦Fr⟧ unexcited or jaded

**blas·pheme** (blas fēm′) *vt.* **-phemed′, -phem′ing** ⟦< Gr *blasphēmein*, to speak evil of⟧ **1** to speak profanely of or to (God or sacred things) **2** to curse —*vi.* to utter blasphemy —**blas·phem′er** *n.*

**blas′phe·my** (-fə mē) *n., pl.* **-mies** profane speech, writing, or action concerning God or sacred things —**blas′phe·mous** *adj.*

**blast** (blast) *n.* ⟦OE *blæst*, puff of wind⟧ **1** a strong rush of air or gas **2** the sound of a sudden rush of air, as through a horn **3** a blight **4** an explosion, as of dynamite **5** an outburst, as of criticism **6** [Slang] an exciting, enjoyable experience —*vi.* **1** to make a loud, harsh sound **2** to set off explosives, etc. —*vt.* **1** to wither; ruin **2** to blow up; explode **3** to criticize sharply —**blast off** to take off: said of a rocket, etc. —**(at) full blast** at full speed or capacity

**blast furnace** a smelting furnace in which a blast of air forced in from below produces the intense heat

**blast′off′** or **blast′-off′** *n.* the launching of a rocket, spacecraft, etc.

**bla·tant** (blāt′′nt) *adj.* ⟦prob. < L *blaterare*, to bab-

ble⟧ **1** disagreeably loud; noisy **2** boldly conspicuous or obtrusive —**bla′tan·cy** *n.*

**blaze**[1] (blāz) *n.* ⟦OE *blæse*⟧ **1** a bright burst of flame; fire **2** a very bright light **3** a spectacular outburst or display —*vi.* **blazed, blaz′ing 1** to burn rapidly or shine brightly **2** to be excited, as with anger

**blaze**[2] (blāz) *n.* ⟦< ON *blesi*⟧ **1** a light-colored spot on an animal's face **2** a mark made on a tree by cutting off bark —*vt.* **blazed, blaz′ing** to mark (a tree or trail) with blazes

**blaze**[3] (blāz) *vt.* **blazed, blaz′ing** ⟦ME *blasen*, to blow < OE or ON⟧ to proclaim

**blaz·er** (blā′zər) *n.* a light sport coat usually in a solid color and with metal buttons

**bla·zon** (blā′zən) *n.* ⟦OFr *blason*, a shield⟧ a coat of arms —*vt.* **1** to proclaim **2** to adorn

**bldg** *abbrev.* building

**bleach** (blēch) *vt., vi.* ⟦OE *blæcan*⟧ to make or become white or colorless —*n.* a substance for bleaching

**bleach′ers** *pl.n.* benches in tiers, for spectators as at sporting events

**bleak** (blēk) *adj.* ⟦ON *bleikr*, pale⟧ **1** exposed to wind and cold; bare **2** cold; harsh **3** gloomy **4** not hopeful —**bleak′ly** *adv.* —**bleak′ness** *n.*

**blear·y** (blir′ē) *adj.* **-i·er, -i·est** ⟦< ME *blere*⟧ dim or blurred, as the eyes by tears, fatigue, etc.: also **blear**

**bleat** (blēt) *vi.* ⟦OE *blætan*⟧ to make the cry of a sheep, goat, or calf —*n.* a bleating cry or sound

**bleed** (blēd) *vi.* **bled** (bled), **bleed′ing** ⟦< OE *blod*, blood⟧ **1** to emit or lose blood **2** to feel pain, grief, or sympathy **3** to ooze sap, juice, etc. **4** to show through or run together: said of dyes, stains, etc. —*vt.* **1** to draw blood from **2** to ooze (sap, juice, etc.) **3** to draw off (liquid, etc.) slowly —**bleed′er** *n.*

**bleep** (blēp) *n., vi.* ⟦echoic⟧ beep —*vt.* to censor (something said) in a telecast, etc., as with a beep

**blem·ish** (blem′ish) *vt.* ⟦< OFr *blesmir*, injure⟧ to mar; spoil —*n.* a flaw, defect, etc., as a spot or scar

**blench** (blench) *vt., vi.* to blanch

**blend** (blend) *vt.* **blend′ed** or **blent, blend′ing** ⟦OE *blendan*⟧ **1** to mix or mingle (varieties of tea, etc.) **2** to mix thoroughly —*vi.* **1** to mix or merge **2** to pass gradually into each other, as colors **3** to harmonize —*n.* **1** a blending **2** a mixture of varieties

**blend′er** *n.* an electrical appliance that can chop, whip, mix, or liquefy foods

**bless** (bles) *vt.* **blessed** or **blest, bless′ing** ⟦< OE *bletsian*, consecrate with blood⟧ **1** to make holy **2** to ask divine favor for **3** to endow (*with*) **4** to make happy **5** to glorify **6** to make the sign of the cross over

**bless·ed** (bles′id, blest) *adj.* **1** holy; sacred **2** blissful **3** beatified **4** bringing comfort or joy — **bless′ed·ly** *adv.* —**bless′ed·ness** *n.*

**bless′ing** *n.* **1** an invocation or benediction **2** a grace said before or after eating **3** good wishes or approval **4** anything that gives happiness

**blew** (blōō) *vi., vt. pt. of* BLOW[1] & BLOW[3]

**blight** (blīt) *n.* ⟦? < ON *blikja*, turn pale⟧ **1** any insect, disease, etc. that destroys plants **2** anything that destroys, frustrates, etc. —*vt.* **1** to wither **2** to destroy

**blimp** (blimp) *n.* [Inf.] a nonrigid or semirigid airship

**blind** (blīnd) *adj.* ⟦OE⟧ **1** without the power of sight **2** of or for sightless persons **3** lacking insight **4** hard to see; hidden **5** closed at one end *[a blind alley]* **6** not controlled by intelligence *[blind destiny]* **7** guided only by instruments *[a blind landing]* —*vt.* **1** to make sightless **2** to dazzle **3** to deprive of insight —*n.* **1** anything that obscures sight or keeps out light, as a window shade **2** a place of concealment **3** a decoy — *adv.* **1** blindly **2** guided only by instruments *[to fly blind]* —**blind′ly** *adv.* —**blind′ness** *n.*

**blind date** [Inf.] **1** a date with a stranger,

arranged by a third person **2** either person involved

**blind'ers** *pl.n.* bridle flaps for preventing a horse from seeing to the side

**blind'fold'** *vt.* [< ME *blindfeld*, struck blind] to cover the eyes of, as with a cloth —*n.* a cloth used to cover the eyes —*adj., adv.* **1** with the eyes covered **2** reckless(ly)

**blind'side'** *vt.* -sid'ed, -sid'ing to attack (someone) from an unexpected direction

**blink** (bliŋk) *vi.* [ME *blenken*] **1** to wink one or more times **2** to flash on and off **3** to ignore (with *at*) —*vt.* **1** to cause (eyes, light, etc.) to blink **2** to evade or avoid —*n.* **1** a blinking **2** a glimmer — **on the blink** [Slang] not working right

**blink'er** *n.* a flashing warning light

**blintz** (blints) *n.* [Yiddish *blintze* < Russ *blin*, pancake] a thin pancake rolled with a filling of cottage cheese, fruit, etc.

**blip** (blip) *n.* [echoic of a brief sound] a luminous image on an oscilloscope

**bliss** (blis) *n.* [< OE *blithe*, blithe] **1** great happiness **2** spiritual joy —**bliss'ful** *adj.* —**bliss'ful·ly** *adv.* —**bliss'ful·ness** *n.*

**blis·ter** (blis'tər) *n.* [< ?] **1** a raised patch of skin, filled with watery matter and caused as by a burn **2** anything like a blister —*vt.* **1** to raise blisters on **2** to lash with words —*vi.* to form blisters

**blis'ter·ing** *adj.* very hot, intense, etc.

**blithe** (bli*th*, blīth) *adj.* [OE] cheerful; carefree; lighthearted: also **blithe'some** (-səm) —**blithe'ly** *adv.* —**blithe'ness** *n.*

**blitz** (blits) *n.* [< Ger *blitz*, lightning] a sudden destructive or overwhelming attack —*vt.* to subject to a blitz

**bliz·zard** (bliz'ərd) *n.* [? < dial. *bliz*, violent blow] a violent snowstorm with very cold winds

**bloat** (blōt) *vt., vi.* [< ON *blautr*, soft] **1** to swell, as with water or air **2** to puff up, as with pride

**blob** (bläb) *n.* [echoic] **1** a drop or a small lump or spot **2** something of indefinite shape —*vt.* **blobbed, blob'bing** to splash, as with blobs

**bloc** (bläk) *n.* [Fr < MDu *block*, log] an alliance of persons, nations, etc.

**block** (bläk) *n.* [< OFr *bloc* & MDu *block*] **1** a large, solid piece of wood, stone, metal, etc. **2** a heavy stand on which chopping, etc. is done **3** an auctioneer's platform **4** an obstruction or hindrance **5** a pulley in a frame **6** [Now Brit.] a group or row of buildings **7** an area with streets or buildings on four sides **8** a number of things regarded as a unit **9** a toy brick, typically a cube of wood, etc. **10** *Printing* a piece of wood, etc. engraved with a design —*vt.* **1** to obstruct; hinder **2** to mount or mold on a block **3** to sketch roughly: often with *out* —**block'er** *n.*

**block·ade** (blä kād') *n.* [prec. + -ADE] **1** a shutting off of a place by troops or ships to prevent passage **2** any strategic barrier —*vt.* -ad'ed, -ad'ing to subject to a blockade

**block and tackle** an arrangement of pulley blocks and ropes, used for lifting heavy objects

**block'bust'er** *n.* a particularly effective person or thing; specif., an expensive film, etc. generating widespread appeal

**block'bust'ing** *n.* [Inf.] the inducing of owners to sell their homes out of fear that a minority group may move into the neighborhood

**block grant** a grant of federal funds to a state or local government to fund a block of programs

**block'head'** *n.* a stupid person

**block'house'** *n.* **1** [Historical] a wooden, two-story fortified building **2** a reinforced structure for observers, as of missile launchings

**blond** (bländ) *adj.* [OFr < ? Gmc] **1** having light-colored hair and, often, fair skin **2** light in color Also **blonde** —*n.* a blond person —**blonde** *fem.n.* —**blond'ness** *n.*

**blood** (blud) *n.* [OE *blod*] **1** the red fluid circulating in the arteries and veins of animals **2** bloodshed **3** the essence of life; life **4** the sap of a

---

plant **5** passion, temperament, etc. **6** parental heritage; lineage **7** kinship **8** people, esp. youthful people [new *blood* in a group] —**bad blood** anger; hatred —**in cold blood 1** with cruelty **2** deliberately

**blood bank** a supply of blood stored for future use in transfusion

**blood count** the number of red or white cells in a given volume of blood

**blood'cur'dling** (-kʉrd'liŋ) *adj.* frightening; terrifying

**blood'ed** *adj.* **1** having (a specified kind of) blood [hot-*blooded*] **2** of fine breed

**blood'hound'** *n.* any of a breed of large tracking dogs with a keen sense of smell

**blood'less** *adj.* **1** without bloodshed **2** anemic or pale **3** having little energy —**blood'less·ly** *adv.* —**blood'less·ness** *n.*

**blood'line'** *n.* line of descent

**blood'mo·bile'** (-mō bēl') *n.* a traveling unit for collecting blood from donors for blood banks

**blood poisoning** *nontechnical term for* SEPTICEMIA

**blood pressure** the pressure of the blood against the blood-vessel walls

**blood relation** (or **relative**) a person related by birth

**blood'shed'** *n.* the shedding of blood; killing

**blood'shot'** *adj.* tinged with red because small blood vessels are broken: said of eyes

**blood'suck'er** *n.* an animal that sucks blood, esp. a leech

**blood'thirst'y** *adj.* murderous; very cruel —**blood'thirst'i·ness** *n.*

**blood vessel** an artery, vein, or capillary

**blood'y** *adj.* -i·er, -i·est **1** of, like, containing, or covered with blood **2** involving bloodshed **3** bloodthirsty **4** [Brit. Slang] cursed; damned —*adv.* [Brit. Slang] very —*vt.* -ied, -y·ing to stain with blood —**blood'i·ly** *adv.* —**blood'i·ness** *n.*

**bloody mar·y** (mer'ē) *pl.* **bloody mar'ys** a drink made of vodka and tomato juice

**bloom** (blōōm) *n.* [< ON *blomi*, flowers] **1** a flower; blossom **2** the state or time of flowering **3** a period of greatest health, vigor, etc. **4** a youthful, healthy glow **5** the powdery coating on some fruits and leaves —*vi.* **1** to blossom **2** to be in one's prime **3** to glow with health, etc.

**bloom'ers** *pl.n.* [after Amelia *Bloomer* (1818-94), U.S. feminist] baggy trousers gathered at the knee, once worn by women for athletics

**bloom'ing** *adj.* **1** blossoming **2** flourishing **3** [Inf.] complete [a *blooming* idiot]

**bloop·er** (blōōp'ər) *n.* [*bloop*, echoic + -ER] **1** a stupid mistake **2** *Baseball* a fly that falls just beyond the infield for a hit

**blos·som** (bläs'əm) *n.* [OE *blostma*] **1** a flower, esp. of a fruit-bearing plant **2** a state or time of flowering —*vi.* **1** to have or open into blossoms **2** to begin to flourish —**blos'som·y** *adj.*

**blot** (blät) *n.* [ME < ?] **1** a spot or stain, esp. of ink **2** anything that spoils or mars **3** disgrace —*vt.* **blot'ted, blot'ting 1** to spot; stain **2** to disgrace **3** to erase, obscure, or get rid of: often with *out* **4** to dry, as with blotting paper —*vi.* **1** to make blots **2** to become blotted **3** to be absorbent

**blotch** (bläch) *n.* [? < prec.] **1** a discoloration on the skin **2** any large blot or stain —*vt.* to mark with blotches —**blotch'y**, -i·er, -i·est, *adj.*

**blot·ter** (blät'ər) *n.* **1** a piece of blotting paper **2** a book for recording events as they occur [a police *blotter*]

**blotting paper** a thick, soft, absorbent paper used to dry a surface freshly written on in ink

**blouse** (blous) *n.* [Fr, workman's smock] **1** a garment like a shirt, worn by women and girls **2** a uniform coat worn by soldiers, etc. —*vi., vt.* **bloused, blous'ing** to gather in and drape over loosely

**blow**[1] (blō) *vi.* **blew, blown, blow'ing** [[OE *blawan*]] **1** to move with some force, as the wind **2** to send forth air, as with the mouth **3** to pant **4** to give sound by blowing or being blown **5** to spout water and air, as whales do **6** to be carried by the wind **7** to be stormy **8** to burst suddenly: often with *out* **9** [Slang] to leave —*vt.* **1** to force air from, into, onto, or through **2** to drive or expel by blowing **3** to sound by blowing **4** to form by blown air or gas **5** to burst by an explosion: often with *up* **6** to melt (a fuse, etc.) **7** [Inf.] to spend (money) freely **8** [Slang] to leave **9** [Slang] to bungle **10** [Slang] to reveal [to *blow* one's cover] —*n.* **1** a blowing **2** a blast of air or a gale —**blow over** to pass over or by —**blow up 1** to enlarge or exaggerate **2** [Inf.] to lose one's temper —**blow'er** *n.*

**blow**[2] (blō) *n.* [[ME *blowe*]] **1** a hard hit, as with the fist **2** a sudden attack **3** a sudden calamity; shock —**come to blows** to begin fighting one another

**blow**[3] (blō) *vi.* **blew, blown, blow'ing** [[OE *blowan*]] [Archaic] to bloom

**blow'-by-blow'** *adj.* told in great detail

**blow'-dry'** *vt.* **-dried', -dry'ing** to dry (wet hair) with hot air blown from an electric device (**blow'-dry'er**)

**blow'fly'** *n., pl.* **-flies'** a fly that lays its eggs on meat, in wounds, etc.

**blow'gun'** *n.* a long tube through which darts, etc. are blown

**blow'hard'** *n.* [Slang] a loudly boastful person

**blow'out'** *n.* **1** the bursting of a tire **2** [Slang] a party, banquet, etc.

**blow'torch'** *n.* a small torch that shoots out a hot flame

**blow'up'** *n.* **1** an explosion **2** an enlarged photograph **3** [Inf.] an angry outburst

**blow'y** *adj.* **-i·er, -i·est** windy

**blowz·y** (blou'zē) *adj.* **-i·er, -i·est** [[< obs. *blouze,* wench]] slovenly: also **blows'y**

**BLT** (bē'el'tē') *n.* a bacon, lettuce, and tomato sandwich

**blub·ber**[1] (blub'ər) *n.* [[ME *blober,* a bubble]] the fat of the whale —**blub'ber·y** *adj.*

**blub·ber**[2] (blub'ər) *vi.* [[ME *bloberen,* to bubble]] to weep loudly, like a child

**bludg·eon** (bluj'ən) *n.* [[? < earlier Fr *bouge,* club]] a short club with a heavy end —*vt., vi.* **1** to strike with a bludgeon **2** to bully or coerce

**blue** (blōo) *adj.* [[< ?]] **1** of the color of the clear sky **2** livid: said of the skin **3** sad and gloomy **4** puritanical **5** [Inf.] indecent; risqué —*n.* **1** the color of the clear sky **2** any blue pigment —**out of the blue** unexpectedly —**the blue 1** the sky **2** the sea

**blue baby** a baby born with bluish skin, esp. because of a heart defect

**blue'bell'** *n.* any of various plants with blue, bell-shaped flowers

**blue'ber'ry** (-ber'ē, -bər ē) *n., pl.* **-ries 1** a shrub bearing small, edible, blue-black berries **2** any of the berries

**blue'bird'** *n.* a small North American songbird with a bluish back

**blue blood** an aristocrat: also **blue'blood'** *n.* —**blue'-blood'ed** *adj.*

**blue cheese** a strong cheese containing bluish mold

**blue'-chip'** *adj.* [[< high-value *blue chips* of poker]] **1** of any high-priced stock with good earnings and a stable price **2** [Inf.] valuable

**blue'-col'lar** *adj.* [[< color of work shirts]] designating or of industrial workers

**blue flu** [[< *blue* police uniforms]] a sickout, esp. by police officers

**blue'gill'** *n.* a freshwater sunfish of a bluish color

**blue'grass'** *n.* **1** a type of grass with bluish-green horizontal stems **2** fast, bluesy country music

**blue'jack'et** *n.* an enlisted person in the navy

**blue jay** a common crested bird with a blue upper body and head: sometimes **blue'jay'** *n.*

**blue'jeans'** (-jēnz') *pl.n.* jeans made of blue denim: also **blue jeans**

**blue law** a puritanical law, esp. one prohibiting certain activities on Sunday

**blue'nose'** *n.* [Inf.] a puritanical person

**blue'-pen'cil** *vt.* **-ciled** or **-cilled, -cil·ing** or **-cil·ling** to edit or correct with or as with a blue pencil

**blue'-plate' special** an inexpensive restaurant meal served at a fixed price

**blue'point'** *n.* [[after *Blue Point,* Long Island, New York]] a small oyster, usually eaten raw

**blue'print'** *n.* **1** a photographic reproduction in white on a blue background, as of architectural plans **2** any detailed plan or outline —*vt.* to make a blueprint of

**blues** (blōoz) *pl.n.* [with *sing.* or *pl. v.*] **1** [Inf.] a depressed feeling: with *the* **2** black folk music having, usually, slow tempo, melancholy words, etc.: often with *the* —**blues'y, -i·er, -i·est,** *adj.*

**blue'stock'ing** *n.* a learned or bookish woman

**blu·et** (blōo'it) *n.* [[< Fr dim. of *bleu,* blue]] a small plant having little, pale-blue flowers

**blue whale** a baleen whale with a blue-gray back: the largest animal

**bluff**[1] (bluf) *vt., vi.* [[prob. < Du *bluffen,* to brag, or *verbluffen,* to baffle]] to mislead (a person) by a false, bold front —*n.* **1** a bluffing **2** one who bluffs: also **bluff'er**

**bluff**[2] (bluf) *adj.* [[? < Du *blaf,* flat]] **1** having a flat, steep front **2** having a rough, frank manner —*n.* a high, steep bank or cliff

**blu·ing** (blōo'iŋ) *n.* a blue rinse used on white fabrics to prevent yellowing

**blu'ish** (-ish) *adj.* somewhat blue: also **blue'ish**

**blun·der** (blun'dər) *vi.* [[< ON *blunda,* shut the eyes]] **1** to move clumsily **2** to make a foolish mistake —*n.* a foolish mistake —**blun'der·er** *n.*

**blun'der·buss'** (-bus') *n.* [[< Du *donderbus,* thunder box]] [Historical] a short gun with a broad muzzle

**blunt** (blunt) *adj.* [[< ?]] **1** having a dull edge, etc. **2** plain-spoken —*vt., vi.* to make or become dull —**blunt'ly** *adv.* —**blunt'ness** *n.*

**blur** (blur) *vt., vi.* **blurred, blur'ring** [[< ?]] **1** to smear or smudge **2** to make or become indistinct in shape, etc. **3** to dim —*n.* anything indistinct or hazy —**blur'ry, -ri·er, -ri·est,** *adj.* —**blur'ri·ness** *n.*

**blurb** (blurb) *n.* [a coinage] an advertisement, as on a book jacket, esp. a laudatory one

**blurt** (blurt) *vt.* [prob. echoic] to say impulsively: often with *out*

**blush** (blush) *vi.* [[< OE *blyscan,* to shine]] **1** to become red in the face, as from embarrassment **2** to be ashamed: usually with *at* or *for* **3** to become rosy —*n.* **1** a reddening of the face, as from shame **2** a rosy color **3** BLUSHER (sense 2) —*adj.* rosy —**at first blush** at first sight

**blush'er** *n.* **1** one who blushes readily **2** a red or reddish cosmetic powder, cream, etc. for the cheeks

**blush wine** a dry, pale-pink wine

**blus·ter** (blus'tər) *vi.* [? < LowG *blüstern*] **1** to blow stormily: said of wind **2** to speak in a noisy, swaggering manner —*n.* **1** stormy blowing or noisy commotion **2** noisy or swaggering talk —**blus'ter·er** *n.* —**blus'ter·y** *adj.*

**Blvd** *abbrev.* Boulevard

**BM** *abbrev.* [Inf.] bowel movement

**BO** *abbrev.* body odor

**bo·a** (bō'ə) *n.* [[L]] **1** a tropical snake that suffocates its prey in its coils, as the anaconda **2** a woman's long scarf, as of fur or feathers

**boar** (bôr) *n., pl.* **boars** or **boar** [[OE *bar*]] **1** a mature, uncastrated male pig **2** a wild hog

**board** (bôrd) *n.* [[OE *bord,* plank]] **1** a long, flat piece of sawed wood **2** a flat piece of wood, etc. for some special use [bulletin *board*] **3** pasteboard **4** meals, esp. as provided regularly for pay

**5** a group of administrators; council **6** [*also* B-] [*pl.*] *Educ.* a qualifying examination for admission to an academic program —*vt.* **1** to cover (*up*) with boards **2** to provide with meals, or room and meals, regularly for pay **3** to get on (a ship, train, etc.) —*vi.* to receive meals, or room and meals, regularly for pay —**on board 1** on a ship, aircraft, etc. **2** in a group as a member, etc. —**the boards** the stage (of a theater) —**board'er** *n.*

**board'ing·house'** *n.* a house where meals, or room and meals, can be had for pay: also **boarding house**

**board'walk'** *n.* a walk made of thick boards, esp. one along a beach

**boast** (bōst) *vi.* ⟦< Anglo-Fr⟧ to talk, esp. about oneself, with too much pride; brag —*vt.* **1** to brag about **2** glory in having or doing (something) —*n.* **1** a boasting **2** anything boasted of —**boast'er** *n.* —**boast'ful** *adj.* —**boast'ful·ly** *adv.*

**boat** (bōt) *n.* ⟦OE *bat*⟧ **1** a small, open vehicle for traveling on water **2** loosely, a ship **3** a boat-shaped dish —**in the same boat** in the same unfavorable situation —**rock the boat** [Inf.] to disturb the status quo —**boat'man** (-mən), *pl.* **-men** (-mən), *n.*

**boat'er** *n.* a stiff straw hat with a flat crown and brim

**boat'ing** *n.* rowing, sailing, etc.

**boat·swain** (bō'sən) *n.* a ship's petty officer in charge of the deck crew, the rigging, anchors, boats, etc.

**bob** (bäb) *n.* ⟦ME *bobbe*, hanging cluster; 3 & 4 < the *v.*⟧ **1** any knoblike hanging weight **2** a woman's or child's short haircut **3** a quick, jerky motion **4** a float on a fishing line —*vt.* **bobbed**, **bob'bing** ⟦ME *bobben*, knock against⟧ **1** to make move with a jerky motion **2** to cut (hair, etc.) short —*vi.* to move with a jerky motion —**bob up** to appear suddenly

**bob·bin** (bäb'in) *n.* ⟦Fr *bobine* < ?⟧ a spool for thread or yarn, used in spinning, machine sewing, etc.

**bob·ble** (bäb'əl) *n.* [Inf.] *Sports* an awkward fumbling of the ball —*vt.* **-bled**, **-bling** [Inf.] to make a bobble with (a ball)

**bob·by** (bäb'ē) *n.*, *pl.* **-bies** ⟦after Sir Robert (*Bobby*) Peel (1788-1850), who reorganized the London police force⟧ [Inf., Chiefly Brit.] a British policeman

**bobby pin** ⟦from use with *bobbed* hair⟧ a small metal hairpin with the sides pressing close together

**bobby socks** (or **sox**) ⟦< BOB (*vt.* 2)⟧ [Inf.] esp. in the 1940s and 1950s, girls' ankle-length socks

**bob'by·sox'er** or **bob'by·sox'er** (-säks'ər) *n.* [Inf.] esp. in the 1940s, a girl in her early teens

**bob'cat'** *n.* a small North American lynx

**bob'sled'** *n.* a long racing sled with a protective shell —*vi.* **-sled'ded**, **-sled'ding** to ride or race on a bobsled

**Boc·cac·ci·o** (bō käch'ē ō; *It* bô kä'chô), **Gio·van·ni** (jô vän'nē) 1313-75; It. writer

**boc·cie**, **boc·ce**, or **boc·ci** (bäch'ē) *n.* ⟦It *bocce*, (wooden) balls⟧ an Italian game similar to lawn bowling

**bode**[1] (bōd) *vt.* **bod'ed**, **bod'ing** ⟦< OE *boda*, messenger⟧ to be an omen of —**bode ill** (or **well**) to be a bad (or good) omen

**bode**[2] (bōd) *vi. alt. pt. of* BIDE

**bod·ice** (bäd'is) *n.* ⟦altered < *bodies*, pl. of *body*⟧ the upper part of a dress

**bod·i·ly** (bäd'l ē) *adj.* **1** physical **2** of, in, by, or to the body —*adv.* **1** in person **2** as a single group

**bod·kin** (bäd'kin) *n.* ⟦ME *bodekin* < ?⟧ [Obs.] a dagger

**bod·y** (bäd'ē) *n.*, *pl.* **-ies** ⟦OE *bodig*, cask⟧ **1** the whole physical substance of a human being, animal, or plant **2** the trunk of a human being or animal **3** a corpse **4** [Inf.] a person **5** a distinct group of people or things **6** the main part **7** a distinct mass [a *body* of water] **8** density or consistency, as of paint or fabric **9** richness of flavor

**bod'y·guard'** *n.* a person or persons assigned to guard someone

**body language** gestures, unconscious bodily movements, etc. that serve as nonverbal communication

**body politic** the people who collectively constitute a political unit under a government

**body stocking** a tightfitting garment, usually of one piece, that covers the torso and, sometimes, the legs

**bod'y·suit'** *n.* a one-piece, tightfitting garment that covers the torso, usually worn with slacks, a skirt, etc.: also **body shirt**

**Boer** (bôr, boor, bō'ər) *n.* ⟦Du *boer*, peasant⟧ a South African of Dutch descent

**bog** (bäg, bôg) *n.* ⟦< Gael & Ir *bog*, soft, moist⟧ wet, spongy ground; a small marsh —*vt.*, *vi.* **bogged**, **bog'ging** to sink in or as in a bog: often with *down* —**bog'gy** *adj.*

**bo·gey** (bō'gē; *for 1, usually* boog'ē) *n.* **1** BOGY **2** ⟦after an imaginary Col. *Bogey*⟧ *Golf* one stroke more than par on a hole: also **bogy**

**bog·gle** (bäg'əl) *vi.* **-gled**, **-gling** ⟦< Scot *bogle*, specter⟧ **1** to be startled (*at*) **2** to hesitate (*at*) —*vt.* to confuse (the mind, imagination, etc.)

**Bo·go·tá** (bō'gə tä') capital of Colombia: pop. 3,975,000

**bo·gus** (bō'gəs) *adj.* ⟦< ?⟧ not genuine; false

**bo·gy** (boog'ē, bō'gē) *n.*, *pl.* **-gies** ⟦< Scot *bogle*, specter⟧ an imaginary evil spirit; goblin: also **bo'gie**

**bo·gy·man** or **bo·gey·man** (boog'ē man', bō'gē-) *n.*, *pl.* **-men** (-men') BOOGEYMAN

**Bo·he·mi·a** (bō hē'mē ə) region of Czech Republic: a former kingdom

**Bo·he'mi·an** (-ən) *n.* **1** CZECH (*n.* 2) **2** a person born or living in Bohemia **3** [*usually* b-] one who lives unconventionally —*adj.* **1** of Bohemia or its people, etc. **2** [*usually* b-] like a bohemian —**Bo·he'mi·an·ism'** *n.*

**bo·ho** (bō'hō') [Slang] *n.* BOHEMIAN (*n.* 3) —*adj.* BOHEMIAN (*adj.* 2)

**boil**[1] (boil) *vi.* ⟦< L *bulla*, a bubble⟧ **1** to bubble up and vaporize over direct heat **2** to seethe like a boiling liquid **3** to be agitated, as with rage **4** to cook in boiling liquid —*vt.* **1** to heat to the boiling point **2** to cook in boiling liquid —*n.* the act or state of boiling —**boil down 1** to lessen in quantity by boiling **2** to condense

**boil**[2] (boil) *n.* ⟦OE *byle*⟧ an inflamed, painful, pus-filled swelling on the skin

**boil'er** *n.* **1** a container in which things are boiled or heated **2** a tank in which water is turned to steam **3** a tank for heating water and storing it

**boiling point 1** the temperature at which a specified liquid boils **2** the point at which one loses one's temper

**Boi·se** (boi'zē, -sē) capital of Idaho: pop. 126,000: also **Boise City**

**bois·ter·ous** (bois'tər əs) *adj.* ⟦ME *boistreous*, crude⟧ **1** rough and stormy; turbulent **2** loud and exuberant; rowdy —**bois'ter·ous·ly** *adv.*

**bok choy** (bäk' choi') ⟦Chin⟧ a variety of Chinese cabbage

**bo·la** (bō'lə) *n.* ⟦< Sp, a ball⟧ a set of cords with heavy balls at the ends, thrown to entangle cattle

**bold** (bōld) *adj.* ⟦OE *beald*⟧ **1** daring; fearless **2** too free in manner; impudent **3** steep **4** prominent and clear —**bold'ly** *adv.* —**bold'ness** *n.*

**bold'face'** *n.* a heavy, dark printing type

**bold'faced'** *adj.* impudent

**bole** (bōl) *n.* ⟦ON *bolr*⟧ a tree trunk

**bo·le·ro** (bō ler'ō) *n.*, *pl.* **-ros** ⟦Sp < L *bulla*, a bubble⟧ **1** a lively Spanish dance, or the music for it **2** a short, open vest

**Bol·í·var** (bäl'ə vər), **Si·món** (sī'mən) 1783-1830; South American revolutionary leader

**Bo·liv·i·a** (bə liv'ē ə) inland country in WC South

America: 424,165 sq. mi.; pop. 7,610,000 —**Bo·liv'i·an** *adj., n.*

**boll** (bōl) *n.* [ME *bolle,* BOWL¹] the roundish seed pod of a plant, esp. of cotton or flax

**boll weevil** a small weevil whose larvae destroy cotton bolls

**bo·lo·gna** (bə lō'nē) *n.* [after *Bologna,* It city] a large smoked sausage of beef, pork, or veal

**Bol·she·vik** (bōl'shə vik') *n., pl.* **-viks'** or **-vi'ki** (-vē'kē) [Russ < *ból'she,* larger] [*also* **b-**] **1** a member of a faction that seized power in Russia in 1917 **2** a Communist, esp. of the Soviet Union —**Bol'she·vism'** *n.* —**Bol'she·vist** *n., adj.*

**bol·ster** (bōl'stər) *n.* [OE] **1** a long, narrow pillow **2** any bolsterlike object or support —*vt.* to prop up as with a bolster: often with *up*

**bolt¹** (bōlt) *n.* [OE] **1** a short, blunt arrow shot from a crossbow **2** a flash of lightning **3** a sudden dash **4** a sliding bar for locking a door, etc. **5** a threaded metal rod used with a nut for joining parts **6** a roll (*of* cloth, paper, etc.) —*vt.* **1** to say suddenly; blurt (*out*) **2** to swallow (food) hurriedly **3** to fasten as with a bolt **4** to abandon (a party, group, etc.) —*vi.* **1** to start suddenly; spring away **2** to withdraw support from one's party, etc. —**bolt upright** erect or erectly

**bolt²** (bōlt) *vt.* [< OFr *buleter*] to sift (flour, grain, etc.)

**bo·lus** (bō'ləs) *n.* [< Gr *bōlos*] **1** a small, round lump **2** a mass injected into a blood vessel, as a radioactive tracer **3** a large pill

**bomb** (bäm) *n.* [prob. < Gr *bombos,* hollow sound] **1** a container filled as with an explosive or incendiary chemical, for dropping, hurling, etc. **2** a small container with compressed gas in it [an aerosol *bomb*] **3** [Inf.] a complete failure —*vt.* to attack with bombs —*vi.* [Inf.] to be a complete failure

**bom·bard** (bäm bärd') *vt.* [< Fr *bombarde,* mortar] **1** to attack with artillery or bombs **2** to attack with questions, etc. **3** to direct a stream of particles at (atomic nuclei) —**bom·bard'ment** *n.*

**bom·bar·dier'** (-bər dir') *n.* one who releases the bombs in a bomber

**bom·bast** (bäm'bast') *n.* [< Pers *pambak,* cotton] grand, pompous language with little real meaning —**bom·bas'tic** *adj.* —**bom·bas'ti·cal·ly** *adv.*

**Bom·bay** (bäm'bā') seaport in W India: pop. 8,243,000: now officially *Mumbai*

**bomb·er** (bäm'ər) *n.* **1** an airplane for dropping bombs **2** one who bombs

**bomb·shell'** *n.* **1** a bomb **2** any sudden, shocking surprise

**bo·na fi·de** (bō'nə fīd', bō'nə fī'dē) [L] **1** in good faith; without fraud [a *bona fide* offer] **2** genuine; real [a *bona fide* movie star]

**bo·nan·za** (bə nan'zə) *n.* [Sp, prosperity] **1** a rich vein of ore **2** any source of wealth

**Bo·na·parte** (bō'nə pärt'), **Na·po·le·on** (nə pō'lē ən) 1769-1821; Fr. military leader & emperor (1804-15)

**bon·bon** (bän'bän'; *Fr* bōn bōn') *n.* [< Fr *bon,* good] a small piece of candy

**bond** (bänd) *n.* [ult. < Gothic *bindan,* bind] **1** anything that binds, fastens, or unites **2** [*pl.*] shackles **3** a binding agreement **4** an obligation imposed by a contract, promise, etc. **5** the status of goods kept in a warehouse until taxes or duties are paid **6** an interest-bearing certificate issued by a government or business, redeemable on a specified date **7** surety provided against theft, embezzlement, etc. **8** an amount paid for bail, etc. —*vt.* **1** to join; bind **2** to furnish surety for (someone) **3** to place or hold (goods) in bond

**bond·age** (bän'dij) *n.* [ult. < ON *bua,* inhabit] **1** serfdom or slavery **2** subjection to some force, influence, etc.

**bond'ing** *n.* the development of a close relationship, esp. between family members

**bond'man** (-mən) *n., pl.* **-men** (-mən) **1** a serf **2** a slave —**bond'wom'an,** *pl.* **-wom'en,** *fem.n.*

**bond paper** [orig. used for bonds, etc.] high-quality writing paper

**bonds·man** (bändz'mən) *n., pl.* **-men** (-mən) **1** BONDMAN **2** one who furnishes bail, etc.

**bone** (bōn) *n.* [< OE *ban*] **1** any of the parts of hard tissue forming the skeleton of most vertebrates **2** this hard tissue **3** a bonelike substance or thing —*vt.* **boned, bon'ing** to remove the bones from —*vi.* [Slang] to study hard: usually with *up* —**have a bone to pick** [Inf.] to have cause to quarrel —**make no bones about** [Inf.] admit freely —**boneless** *adj.*

**bone china** translucent china made of white clay to which the ash of burned bones has been added

**bone'-dry'** *adj.* [Inf.] very dry

**bone meal** crushed or ground bones, used as feed, fertilizer, or a nutritional supplement

**bon·er** (bōn'ər) *n.* [Slang] a blunder

**bon·fire** (bän'fīr') *n.* [ME *banefyre,* bone fire, pyre] an outdoor fire

**bong** (bôŋ, bäŋ) *n.* [echoic] a deep ringing sound, as of a large bell —*vi.* to make this sound

**bon·go** (bäŋ'gō) *n., pl.* **-gos** [AmSp < ?] either of a pair of small drums of different pitch struck with the fingers: in full **bongo drum**

BONGOS

**bo·ni·to** (bō nēt'ō, bə-) *n., pl.* **-tos** or **-toes** [Sp] a saltwater food fish similar to a tuna

**bon·jour** (bōn zhōōr') *interj., n.* [Fr] good day; hello

**bonk·ers** (bäŋ'kərz) *adj.* [Slang] crazy

**bon mot** (bōn' mō'; *Fr* bōn mō') *pl.* **bons mots** (bōn' mōz'; *Fr,* -mō') [Fr, lit., good word] a clever or witty remark

**Bonn** (bän) city in W Germany: capital of West Germany (1949-90): pop. 298,000

**bon·net** (bän'it) *n.* [< OFr *bonet*] [Inf.] any hat worn by a woman or girl

**bon·ny** or **bon·nie** (bän'ē) *adj.* **-ni·er, -ni·est** [< L *bonus,* good] [Now Chiefly Brit.] **1** handsome or pretty, with a healthy glow **2** pleasant

**bo·no·bo** (bə nō'bō) *n., pl.* **-bos** a kind of chimpanzee, small with long limbs

**bon·sai** (bän'sī') *n., pl.* **-sai'** [Jpn] a tree or shrub grown in a pot and dwarfed by pruning, etc.

**bo·nus** (bō'nəs) *n., pl.* **-nus·es** [L, good] anything given in addition to the customary or required amount

**bon voy·age** (bän' voi äzh') [Fr] pleasant journey

**bon·y** (bō'nē) *adj.* **-i·er, -i·est** **1** of, like, or having bones **2** thin; emaciated

**bony fish** any fish with an air bladder, covered gills, and a bony skeleton

**boo** (bōō) *interj., n., pl.* **boos** a sound made to express disapproval, etc., or to startle someone —*vi., vt.* **booed, boo'ing** to shout "boo" (at)

**boo-boo** or **boo·boo** (bōō'bōō) *n., pl.* **-boos'** [Slang] a stupid mistake

**boob tube** [Slang] TV or a TV set

**boo·by** (bōō'bē) *n., pl.* **-bies** [prob. < Sp *bobo*] a fool; nitwit: also **boob** (bōōb)

**booby trap** any scheme or device for tricking a person unexpectedly

**boo·dle** (bōōd''l) *n.* [< Du *boedel,* property] [Old Slang] **1** something given as a bribe; graft **2** the loot taken in a robbery

**boo·gey·man** (boog'ē man', bō'gē-) *n., pl.* **-men'** (-men') a frightening imaginary being

**book** (book) *n.* [OE *boc*] **1** a printed work on sheets of paper bound together, usually between protective covers **2** a main division of a literary work **3** [*usually pl.*] the records or accounts of a business **4** [*pl.*] studies; lessons **5** *a*) a libretto *b)* the script of a play  **6** a booklike package, as of matches —*vt.* **1** to record in a book; list **2** to engage (rooms, etc.) ahead of time  **3** to record charges against on a police record —**by the book** according to the rules —**the (Good) Book** the Bible

**book′bind′ing** *n.* the art, trade, or business of binding books —**book′bind′er** *n.*

**book′case′** *n.* a set of shelves or a cabinet for holding books

**book′end′** *n.* a support, usually one of a pair, used to keep a row of books upright

**book′ie** (-ē) *n.* [Slang] a bookmaker

**book′ing** *n.* an engagement, as for a concert

**book′ish** (-ish) *adj.* **1** inclined to read and study **2** pedantic

**book′keep′ing** *n.* the work of keeping a record of business transactions —**book′keep′er** *n.*

**book′let** (-lit) *n.* a small book

**book′mak′er** *n.* a person in the business of taking bets, as on horses

**book′mark′** *n.* a thing put between the pages of a book to mark a place

**book matches** safety matches made of paper and fastened into a cardboard holder

**book′mo·bile′** (-mō bēl′) *n.* a lending library in a van that visits rural schools, etc.

**book′plate′** *n.* a label pasted in a book to identify its owner

**book′shelf** *n.*, *pl.* **-shelves′** a shelf on which books are kept

**book′store′** *n.* a store where books are sold: also **book′shop′**

**book′worm′** *n.* **1** an insect larva that feeds on the binding, paste, etc. of books **2** one who reads or studies frequently

**boom**[1] (bōōm) *vi.*, *vt.* [echoic] to make, or say with, a deep, hollow, resonant sound —*n.* this sound

**boom**[2] (bōōm) *n.* [Du, a beam] **1** a spar extending from a mast to hold the bottom of a sail outstretched **2** a long beam extending as from an upright for supporting and guiding anything lifted *[the boom of a derrick]*  **3** a barrier, as of logs, to prevent floating logs from dispersing —*vi.* to go rapidly along

**boom**[3] (bōōm) *vi.* [< ? prec. *vi.*] to increase or grow rapidly —*n.* a period of prosperity

**boom′box′** *n.* [Slang] a large portable radio and tape player

**boom′er** *n. short for* BABY BOOMER

**boom·er·ang** (bōōm′ər aŋ′) *n.* [< Australian native name] **1** a flat, curved stick that can be thrown so that it returns to the thrower **2** a scheme gone awry, to the schemer's harm —*vi.* to act as a boomerang

**boom′town′** *n.* a town that has grown very rapidly: also **boom town**

**boon**[1] (bōōn) *n.* [ON *bon,* a petition] a welcome benefit; blessing

**boon**[2] (bōōn) *adj.* [< L *bonus,* good] merry; convivial: now only in **boon companion,** a close friend

**boon·docks** (bōōn′däks′) *pl.n.* [< native Philippine name] [Inf.] **1** a jungle or wilderness **2** any remote rural region  Used with *the*

**boon·dog·gle** (bōōn′dôg′əl, -däg′-) *n.* a trifling, pointless project —*vi.* **-gled, -gling** to engage in a boondoggle —**boon′dog′gler** *n.*

**boor** (boor) *n.* [Du *boer,* a peasant] a rude, awkward, or ill-mannered person —**boor′ish** *adj.* —**boor′ish·ly** *adv.*

**boost** (bōōst) *vt.* [< ?] **1** to raise as by a push from below **2** to urge others to support **3** to increase —*n.* **1** a push upward or forward **2** an increase —**boost′er** *n.*

**booster shot** a later injection of a vaccine, for maintaining immunity

**boot**[1] (bōōt) *n.* [OFr *bote*] **1** a covering of leather, rubber, etc. for the foot and part of the leg  **2** a kick —*vt.* **1** to put boots on **2** to kick **3** [Inf.] to dismiss (a person) **4** to start (a computer): often

with *up* —*vi.* to start a computer: usually with *up* —**the boot** [Slang] dismissal

**boot**[2] (bōōt) *n.*, *vt.*, *vi.* [OE *bot,* advantage] [Archaic] profit —**to boot** besides; in addition

**boot′black′** *n.* one whose work is shining shoes or boots

**boot·ee** *or* **boot·ie** (bōō tē′; *for* 2 bōōt′ē) *n.* **1** a short boot for women or children **2** a baby's knitted or cloth shoe

**booth** (bōōth) *n.*, *pl.* **booths** (bōōths, bōō*th*z) [< ON *bua,* dwell] **1** a stall for selling goods **2** a small enclosure for voting **3** a small structure to house a public telephone, etc.  **4** an eating area in a restaurant with a table and benchlike seats

**boot′leg′** *vt.*, *vi.* **-legged′, -leg′ging** [< hiding liquor in a boot] to make or sell (liquor, etc.) illegally —*adj.* bootlegged; illegal —*n.* bootlegged liquor, etc. —**boot′leg′ger** *n.*

**boot′less** *adj.* [BOOT[2] + -LESS] useless

**boo·ty** (bōōt′ē) *n.*, *pl.* **-ties** [LowG *bute*] **1** spoils of war **2** plunder

**booze** (bōōz) *vi.* **boozed, booz′ing** [< MDu *busen*] [Inf.] to drink too much liquor —*n.* [Inf.] liquor —[Slang] **booz′er** *n.*

**bop**[1] (bäp) *vt.* **bopped, bop′ping** [Inf.] to hit; punch

**bop**[2] (bäp) *n.* a style of jazz (c. 1945-55) marked by complex rhythms, harmonic experimentation, etc. —*vi.* **bopped, bop′ping** [Slang] to walk, esp. in an easy, strutting way

**bo·rax** (bôr′aks′) *n.* [< Pers *būrah*] a white crystalline salt used in the manufacture of glass, soaps, etc.

**Bor·deaux** (bôr dō′) *n.* [after *Bordeaux,* city and region in SW France] [*also* b-] **1** a red or white wine from the Bordeaux region **2** a similar wine made elsewhere

**bor·der** (bôr′dər) *n.* [< OFr *border,* to border] **1** an edge or part near an edge; margin **2** a dividing line between two countries, etc. **3** a narrow strip along an edge —*vt.* **1** to provide with a border **2** to extend along the edge of —*adj.* of or near a border —**border on** (or **upon**) **1** to be next to **2** to be like; almost be

**bor′der·land′** *n.* **1** land near a border **2** a vague condition

**bor′der·line′** *n.* a boundary —*adj.* **1** on a boundary **2** indefinite

**bore**[1] (bôr) *vt.* **bored, bor′ing** [< OE *bor,* auger] **1** to make a hole in with a drill, etc. **2** to make (a well, etc.) as by drilling **3** to weary by being dull —*vi.* to bore a hole or passage —*n.* **1** a hole made as by boring **2** *a)* the hollow part of a tube or gun barrel *b)* its inside diameter **3** a tiresome, dull person or thing

**bore**[2] (bôr) *vt.*, *vi. pt. of* BEAR[1]

**bore·dom** (bôr′dəm) *n.* the condition of being bored or uninterested

**bo·ric acid** (bôr′ik) a white crystalline compound, used as an antiseptic, in making glass, etc.

**born** (bôrn) *vt.*, *vi. alt. pp. of* BEAR[1] —*adj.* **1** brought into life **2** natural, as if from birth *[a born athlete]*

**born-a·gain** (bôrn′ə gen′) *adj.* having a new, strong faith or belief

**borne** (bôrn) *vt.*, *vi. alt. pp. of* BEAR[1]

**Bor·ne·o** (bôr′nē ō′) large island in the Malay Archipelago

**bo·ron** (bôr′än′) *n.* [< BORAX] a nonmetallic chemical element

**bor·ough** (bur′ō) *n.* [OE *burg,* town] **1** a self-governing, incorporated town **2** any of the five administrative units of New York City

**bor·row** (bär′ō, bôr′-) *vt.*, *vi.* [OE *borgian*] **1** to take or receive (something) with the intention of returning it **2** to adopt (an idea, etc.) as one's own —**bor′row·er** *n.*

**borscht** *or* **borsch** (bôrsh) *n.* [Russ *borshch*] a beet soup, served usually with sour cream

**bor·zoi** (bôr′zoi′) *n.* ⟦Russ *borzój*, swift⟧ a large dog with a narrow head, long legs, and silky coat

**bosh** (bäsh) *n., interj.* ⟦Turk, empty⟧ [Inf.] nonsense

**Bos·ni·a and Her·ze·go·vi·na** (bäz′nē ə and hert′sə gō vē′nə) country in SE Europe: 19,741 sq. mi.; pop. 4,366,000 —**Bos′ni·an** *adj., n.*

**bos·om** (booz′əm; *also* boo̅′zəm) *n.* ⟦OE *bosm*⟧ 1 the human breast 2 the breast regarded as the source of feelings 3 the inside; midst ⟦in the *bosom* of one's family⟧ 4 the part of a garment that covers the breast —*adj.* close; intimate ⟦a *bosom* friend⟧

**bos′om·y** *adj.* having large breasts

**bos·on** (bō′sän) *n.* ⟦after S. N. *Bose* (1894-1974), Indian physicist + -ON⟧ any of certain subatomic particles, including photons and mesons

**boss**[1] (bôs, bäs) *n.* ⟦Du *baas*, a master⟧ 1 an employer or manager 2 one who controls a political organization —*vt.* 1 to act as boss of 2 [Inf.] to order (a person) about —*adj.* [Slang] excellent

**boss**[2] (bôs, bäs) *n.* ⟦OFr *boce*, a swelling⟧ a protruding ornament or projecting knob

**boss′y** *adj.* **-i·er, -i·est** [Inf.] domineering —**boss′i·ness** *n.*

**Bos·ton** (bôs′tən, bäs′-) seaport & capital of Massachusetts: pop. 574,000 —**Bos·to′ni·an** (-tō′nē ən) *adj., n.*

**bo·sun** (bō′sən) *n. phonetic sp. of* BOATSWAIN

**bot·a·ny** (bät′'n ē) *n.* ⟦< Gr *botanē*, a plant⟧ the science that deals with plants and plant life —**bo·tan·i·cal** (bə tan′i kəl) *or* **bo·tan′ic** *adj.* —**bot′a·nist** *n.*

**botch** (bäch) *vt.* ⟦ME *bocchen*, to repair < ?⟧ to bungle —*n.* a bungled piece of work —**botch′er** *n.*

**bot·fly** (bät′flī′) *n., pl.* **-flies**′ a fly resembling a small bumblebee

**both** (bōth) *adj., pron.* ⟦OE *ba tha*, both these⟧ the two ⟦*both* birds sang loudly⟧ —*conj., adv.* together; equally ⟦*both* tired and hungry⟧

**both·er** (bäth′ər) *vt., vi.* ⟦prob. < *pother*⟧ 1 to worry; harass 2 to concern (oneself) —*n.* 1 worry; trouble 2 one who gives trouble —**both′er·some** (-səm) *adj.*

**Bot·swa·na** (bät swä′nə) country in S Africa: 224,607 sq. mi.; pop. 1,327,000

**Bot·ti·cel·li** (bät′ə chel′ē; *It* bôt′tē chel′ē), **San·dro** (sän′drō) 1445?-1510; It. painter

**bot·tle** (bät′'l) *n.* ⟦< LL *buttis*, a cask⟧ 1 a narrow-necked container for liquids, usually of glass 2 its contents —*vt.* **-tled, -tling** to put into a bottle —**bottle up** to restrain —**hit the bottle** [Slang] to drink much alcoholic liquor —**bot′tler** *n.*

**bot·tle·neck**′ *n.* 1 a narrow passage or road where traffic is slowed or stopped 2 any similar hindrance to movement or progress

**bot·tom** (bät′əm) *n.* ⟦OE *botm*, ground⟧ 1 the lowest part or place 2 the part on which something rests 3 the side underneath 4 the seat of a chair 5 the ground beneath a body of water 6 basis; cause; source 7 [Inf.] the buttocks —*adj.* lowest; last; basic —**at bottom** fundamentally —**bot′tom·less** *adj.*

**bottom line** 1 [Inf.] profits or losses, as of a business 2 [Slang] *a)* the basic factor, etc. *b)* the final statement, decision, etc.

**bot·u·lism** (bäch′ə liz′əm) *n.* ⟦< L *botulus*, sausage⟧ poisoning, often fatal, by the toxin produced by a bacterium sometimes found in foods improperly canned or preserved

**bou·doir** (boo̅ dwär′, boo̅′dwär′) *n.* ⟦< Fr, lit., pouting room⟧ a woman's private room

**bouf·fant** (boo̅ fänt′) *adj.* ⟦< Fr *bouffer*, puff out⟧ puffed out; full

**bou·gain·vil·le·a** *or* **bou·gain·vil·lae·a** (boo̅′gən vil′ē ə, -vil′yə, -vē′yə) *n.* ⟦ModL⟧ a woody tropical vine having large, showy purple or red bracts

**bough** (bou) *n.* ⟦OE *bog*, shoulder or arm⟧ a main branch of a tree

**bought** (bôt) *vt. pt. & pp. of* BUY

**bouil·lon** (bool′yän′, -yən) *n.* ⟦< Fr *bouillir*, to boil⟧ a clear broth

**boul·der** (bōl′dər) *n.* ⟦< ME *bulderston*, noisy stone⟧ a large rock worn by weather and water

**bou·le·vard** (bool′ə värd′) *n.* ⟦Fr < MDu *bolwerc*, bulwark⟧ a broad street lined with trees, etc.

**bounce** (bouns) *vi.* **bounced, bounc′ing** ⟦ME *bounsen*, to thump⟧ 1 to spring back, as upon impact; rebound 2 to spring; leap 3 [Slang] to be returned: said of a worthless check —*vt.* 1 to cause (a ball, etc.) to bounce 2 [Slang] to put (a person) out by force 3 [Slang] to fire from a job —*n.* 1 *a)* a bouncing; rebound *b)* a leap or jump 2 capacity for bouncing 3 [Inf.] energy, zest, etc. —**the bounce** [Slang] dismissal —**bounc′y** *adj.*

**bounc′er** *n.* [Slang] a person hired to remove disorderly people from a nightclub, restaurant, etc.

**bounc′ing** *adj.* big, healthy, etc.

**bound**[1] (bound) *vi.* ⟦< OFr *bondir*, to leap⟧ 1 to move with a leap or leaps 2 to bounce; rebound —*vt.* to cause to bound or bounce —*n.* 1 a jump; leap 2 a bounce; rebound

**bound**[2] (bound) *vt., vi. pt. & pp. of* BIND —*adj.* 1 tied 2 closely connected 3 certain; sure ⟦*bound* to lose⟧ 4 obliged 5 having a binding: said as of a book 6 [Inf.] determined; resolved

**bound**[3] (bound) *adj.* ⟦< ON *bua*, prepare⟧ going; headed ⟦*bound* for home⟧

**bound**[4] (bound) *n.* ⟦< ML *butina*, boundary⟧ 1 a boundary 2 [*pl.*] an area near a boundary —*vt.* 1 to limit 2 to be a limit or boundary to 3 to name the boundaries of —**out of bounds** 1 beyond the boundaries 2 forbidden

**bound·a·ry** (boun′drē, -də rē) *n., pl.* **-ries** anything marking a limit; bound

**bound′en** *adj.* ⟦old pp. of BIND⟧ 1 [Archaic] obligated; indebted 2 obligatory ⟦one's *bounden* duty⟧

**bound′er** *n.* ⟦< BOUND[1]⟧ [Inf., Chiefly Brit.] a cad

**bound′less** *adj.* unlimited; vast

**boun·te·ous** (boun′tē əs) *adj.* ⟦see BOUNTY⟧ 1 generous 2 plentiful —**boun′te·ous·ly** *adv.*

**boun′ti·ful** (-tə fəl) *adj.* BOUNTEOUS

**boun′ty** (-tē) *n., pl.* **-ties** ⟦< L *bonus*, good⟧ 1 generosity 2 a generous gift 3 a reward or premium

**bou·quet** (bō kā′; *for 2, usually* boo̅-) *n.* ⟦Fr⟧ 1 a bunch of flowers 2 aroma, as of wine

**bour·bon** (bur′bən) *n.* ⟦after *Bourbon* County, KY⟧ [*sometimes* B-] a whiskey distilled from corn mash

**bour·geois** (boor zhwä′) *n., pl.* **-geois**′ ⟦Fr < OFr *borc*, town⟧ a member of the bourgeoisie —*adj.* of the bourgeoisie: used variously to mean conventional, smug, materialistic, etc.

**bour·geoi·sie** (boor′zhwä zē′) *n.* ⟦*with sing. or pl. v.*⟧ the social class between the very wealthy and the working class; middle class

**bout** (bout) *n.* ⟦ME *bught*⟧ 1 a struggle or contest 2 a period of some activity, as a spell of illness

**bou·tique** (boo̅ tēk′; *occas.,* bō-) *n.* ⟦Fr < L *apotheca*, storehouse⟧ a small shop where fashionable articles are sold

**bou·ton·niere** *or* **bou·ton·nière** (boo̅′tə nir′, -tən yer′) *n.* ⟦Fr, buttonhole⟧ a flower worn in a buttonhole

**bo·vine** (bō′vīn′, -vēn′) *adj.* ⟦< L *bos*, ox⟧ 1 of an ox, cow, etc. 2 slow, dull, stupid, etc.

**bow**[1] (bou) *vi.* ⟦< OE *bugan*, to bend⟧ 1 to bend down the head or body in respect, agreement, etc. 2 to give in —*vt.* 1 to bend (the head or body) down in respect, etc. 2 to weigh (*down*) —*n.* a bending down of the head or body, as in respect or greeting —**take a bow** to acknowledge applause, etc.

**bow**[2] (bō) *n.* ⟦OE *boga*⟧ 1 anything curved ⟦a *rainbow*⟧ 2 a curve; bend 3 a flexible, curved strip of wood with a cord connecting the two ends, for shooting arrows 4 a slender stick strung with horsehairs, as for playing a violin 5 a decorative knot, as a bowknot —*adj.* curved —*vt., vi.* 1 to bend; curve 2 to play (a violin, etc.) with a bow

**bow³** (bou) *n.* 〖< LowG *bug*〗 the front part of a ship, etc.

**bowd·ler·ize** (boud'lər īz') *vt.* **-ized', -iz'ing** 〖after T. *Bowdler* (1754-1825), Eng editor〗 to expurgate —**bowd'ler·ism'** *n.* —**bowd'ler·i·za'tion** *n.*

**bow·el** (bou'əl) *n.* 〖< L *botulus*, sausage〗 **1** an intestine, esp. of a human being **2** [*pl.*] the inner part —**move one's bowels** to defecate

**bow·er** (bou'ər) *n.* 〖< OE *bur*, dwelling〗 a place enclosed by boughs or vines; arbor

**bow·ie knife** (bōō'ē, bō'-) 〖after Col. J. *Bowie* (1799?-1836)〗 a long single-edged hunting knife

**bow·knot** (bō'nät') *n.* a decorative knot, usually with two loops and two ends

**bowl¹** (bōl) *n.* 〖OE *bolla*〗 **1** a deep, rounded dish **2** the contents of a bowl **3** a bowl-like thing or part **4** an amphitheater or stadium — **bowl'like'** *adj.*

**bowl²** (bōl) *n.* 〖< L *bulla*, bubble〗 **1** the wooden ball used in the game of lawn bowling **2** a roll of the ball in bowling —*vi.* **1** to roll a ball or participate in bowling **2** to move swiftly and smoothly —**bowl over 1** to knock over **2** [Inf.] to astonish —**bowl'er** *n.*

**bowl·der** (bōl'dər) *n.* *alt. sp. of* BOULDER

**bow·leg** (bō'leg') *n.* a leg with outward curvature —**bow'leg'ged** (-leg'id, -legd') *adj.*

**bowl·ing** *n.* **1** a game in which a heavy ball is rolled along a wooden lane (**bowling alley**) at ten wooden pins **2** LAWN BOWLING

**bowling green** a lawn for lawn bowling

**bowls** (bōlz) *n.* LAWN BOWLING

**bow·man** (bō'mən) *n.*, *pl.* **-men** (-mən) an archer

**bow·sprit** (bou'sprit', bō'-) *n.* 〖prob. < Du〗 a tapered spar extending forward from the bow of a sailing ship

**bow tie** (bō) a necktie tied in a bow

**box¹** (bäks) *n.* 〖< Gr *pyxos*, BOX³〗 **1** a container, usually rectangular and lidded; case **2** the contents of a box **3** a boxlike thing or space [*a jury box*] **4** a small, enclosed group of seats, as in a theater **5** a booth [*a sentry box*] **6** *Baseball* an area designated for the batter, catcher, etc. —*vt.* to put into a box —**box in** (or **up**) to shut in or keep in; surround or confine —**in a box** [Inf.] in difficulty —**box'like'** *adj.* —**box'y, -i·er, -i·est,** *adj.*

**box²** (bäks) *n.* 〖< ?〗 a blow struck with the hand — *vt.* **1** to strike with such a blow **2** to engage in boxing with —*vi.* to fight with the fists

**box³** (bäks) *n.* 〖< Gr *pyxos*〗 an evergreen shrub with small leathery leaves: also **box'wood'**

**box'car'** *n.* a fully enclosed railroad freight car

**box'er** *n.* **1** one who boxes; prizefighter **2** a medium-sized dog with a sturdy body and a smooth coat

**box'ing** *n.* the skill or sport of fighting with the fists, esp. in padded leather mittens (**boxing gloves**)

**box office 1** a place where admission tickets are sold, as in a theater **2** [Inf.] the power of a show or performer to attract a paying audience

**box wrench** a wrench with an enclosed head

**boy** (boi) *n.* 〖ME *boie*〗 **1** a male child **2** any man: familiar term **3** a male servant: a patronizing term —*interj.* [Slang] used to express pleasure, surprise, etc.: often **oh, boy!** —**boy'hood'** *n.* — **boy'ish** *adj.*

**boy·cott** (boi'kät') *vt.* 〖after Capt. *Boycott*, Irish land agent so treated in 1880〗 to join together in refusing to deal with, buy, etc. so as to punish or coerce —*n.* a boycotting

**boy'friend'** *n.* [Inf.] **1** a sweetheart or escort of a girl or woman **2** a boy who is someone's friend

**Boy Scout** a member of the **Boy Scouts**, a boys' organization that stresses outdoor life and service to others

**boy·sen·ber·ry** (boi'zən ber'ē) *n.*, *pl.* **-ries** 〖after R. *Boysen*, U.S. horticulturist, developer (*c.* 1935)〗 a berry that is a cross of the raspberry, loganberry, and blackberry

**Br¹** *abbrev.* **1** Branch **2** British **3** Brother

**Br²** *Chem. symbol for* bromine

**bra** (brä) *n.* 〖< BRASSIERE〗 a woman's undergarment for supporting the breasts

**brace** (brās) *vt.* **braced, brac'ing** 〖< Gr *brachiōn*, arm〗 **1** to bind **2** to strengthen by supporting the weight of, etc. **3** to make ready for an impact, shock, etc. **4** to stimulate; invigorate —*n.* **1** a couple; pair **2** a thing that clasps or connects **3** [*pl.*] [Brit.] suspenders **4** a device for setting up or maintaining tension **5** either of the signs { }, used to connect words, lines, etc. **6** any propping device **7** *a*) a device for supporting a weak part of the body *b*) [*often pl.*] a device worn for straightening teeth **8** a tool for holding a drilling bit — **brace up** to call forth one's courage, etc.

**brace and bit** a tool for boring, consisting of a removable drill (*bit*) in a rotating handle (*brace*)

**brace·let** (brās'lit) *n.* 〖< Gr *brachiōn*, arm〗 an ornamental band or chain worn around the wrist or arm —**brace'let·ed** *adj.*

**brack·en** (brak'ən) *n.* 〖ME *braken*〗 a large, weedy fern found in meadows, woods, etc.

**brack·et** (brak'it) *n.* 〖< Fr *brague*, knee pants〗 **1** a support projecting from a wall, etc. **2** any angle-shaped support **3** either of the signs [ ], used to enclose a word, etc. **4** the part of a classified grouping within certain limits [*high income bracket*] —*vt.* **1** to support with brackets **2** to enclose within brackets **3** to classify together

**brack·ish** (brak'ish) *adj.* 〖< MDu *brak*〗 **1** salty **2** nauseating —**brack'ish·ness** *n.*

**bract** (brakt) *n.* 〖L *bractea*, thin metal plate〗 a modified leaf growing at the base of a flower or on its stalk

**brad** (brad) *n.* 〖ON *broddr*, arrow〗 a thin wire nail with a small head

**brae** (brā, brē) *n.* 〖ON *bra*, brow〗 [Scot.] a sloping bank; hillside

**brag** (brag) *vt., vi.* **bragged, brag'ging** 〖ME *braggen* < ?〗 to boast —*n.* boastful talk —**brag'ger** *n.*

**brag'gart** (-ərt) *n.* an offensively boastful person —*adj.* boastful

**Brah·ma** (brä'mə) *n.* Hindu god regarded as the creator of the universe

**Brah·man** (brä'mən) *n.*, *pl.* **-mans** 〖Hindi < Sans, worship〗 **1** a member of the Hindu priestly caste **2** a breed of domestic cattle developed from the zebu of India and having a large hump

**Brahms** (brämz), **Jo·han·nes** (yō hän'əs) 1833-97; Ger. composer

**braid** (brād) *vt.* 〖< OE *bregdan*, to move quickly〗 **1** to interweave three or more strands of (hair, straw, etc.) **2** to make by such interweaving —*n.* **1** a length of hair, etc. formed by braiding **2** a woven band of cloth, etc., used to bind or decorate clothing

**Braille** (brāl) *n.* 〖after L. *Braille* (1809-52), its Fr inventor〗 [*also* **b-**] a system of printing for the blind, using raised dots felt with the fingers

**brain** (brān) *n.* 〖OE *brægen*〗 **1** the mass of nerve tissue in the cranium of vertebrates **2** [*often pl.*] intelligence **3** [Inf.] an intelligent person —*vt.* [Slang] to hit hard on the head

**brain'child'** *n.* [Inf.] an idea, plan, etc. produced by a person's own mental labor

**brain drain** [Inf.] an exhausting of the intellectual or professional resources of a country, region, etc., esp. through emigration

**brain'less** *adj.* foolish or stupid

**brain'storm'** *n.* [Inf.] a sudden inspiration, idea, or plan —*vi.* to engage in brainstorming

**brain'storm'ing** *n.* the unrestrained offering of ideas by all members of a group to seek solutions to problems

**brain'wash'** *vt.* [Inf.] to indoctrinate so thoroughly as to effect a radical change of beliefs and attitudes

**brain wave** a series of rhythmic electric impulses from the nerve centers in the brain

**brain·y** *adj.* **-i·er, -i·est** [Inf.] having a good mind; intelligent

**braise** (brāz) *vt.* **braised, brais'ing** [< Fr *braise,* live coals] to brown (meat, etc.) and then simmer slowly

**brake** (brāk) *n.* [< ODu *breken,* to break] any device for slowing or stopping a vehicle or machine, as by causing a block, band, etc. (**brake shoe**) to press against a moving part —*vt., vi.* **braked, brak'ing** to slow down or stop with or as with a brake —**brake'less** *adj.*

**brake'man** (-mən) *n., pl.* **-men** (-mən) a railroad worker who operated the brakes on a train, but is now chiefly an assistant to the conductor

**bram·ble** (bram'bəl) *n.* [< OE *brom,* broom (the plant)] a prickly shrub of the rose family, as the raspberry or blackberry —**bram'bly** *adj.*

**Bramp·ton** (bramp'tən) city in SE Ontario, Canada: pop. 268,000

**bran** (bran) *n.* [OFr *bren*] the husk of grains of wheat, rye, etc. separated from the flour

**branch** (branch) *n.* [< LL *branca,* a claw] 1 any woody extension from a tree or shrub; limb 2 a tributary stream 3 any part or extension of a main body or system, as a division of a family or a separately located unit of a business, library, etc. —*vi.* 1 to put forth branches 2 to come out (*from* the main part) as a branch —**branch off** 1 to separate into branches 2 to diverge —**branch out** to extend one's interests, activities, etc. — **branched** (brancht) *adj.* —**branch'like** *adj.*

**brand** (brand) *n.* [OE < *biernan,* to burn] 1 a burning or partially burned stick 2 a mark burned on the skin, formerly used to punish criminals, now used on cattle to show ownership 3 the iron used in branding 4 a stigma 5 *a)* an identifying mark or label on a company's products *b)* the make of a commodity [a *brand* of coffee] *c)* a special kind —*vt.* 1 to mark with a brand 2 to put a stigma on —**brand'er** *n.*

**brand'ing** *n.* the marketing of products by connecting them with a popular brand name

**bran·dish** (bran'dish) *vt.* [< OFr *brandir*] to wave menacingly or as a challenge; flourish

**brand name** the name by which a certain brand or make of commodity is known —**brand'-name'** *adj.*

**brand'-new'** *adj.* [orig., fresh from the fire: see BRAND] entirely new

**bran·dy** (bran'dē) *n., pl.* **-dies** [< Du *brandewijn,* distilled wine] an alcoholic liquor distilled from wine or from fermented fruit juice —*vt.* **-died, -dy·ing** to flavor or preserve with brandy

**brant** (brant) *n.* [< ?] a wild goose of Europe and North America

**brash** (brash) *adj.* [orig. Brit dial.; < ?] 1 hasty and reckless 2 insolent; impudent

**Bra·sí·lia** (brä zē'lyä; E brə zil'yə) capital of Brazil, in the central part: pop. 1,596,000

**brass** (bras) *n., pl.* **brass'es** [OE *bræs*] 1 a yellowish metal, an alloy of copper and zinc 2 [often with pl. v.] musical instruments made of brass 3 [Inf.] bold impudence 4 [often with pl. v.] [Slang] officers or officials of high rank —*adj.* of brass — **brass'y, -i·er, -i·est,** *adj.*

**bras·siere** or **bras·sière** (brə zir') *n.* [Fr < *bras,* an arm] a bra

**brass tacks** [Inf.] basic facts: used chiefly in **get** (or **come**) **down to brass tacks**

**brat** (brat) *n.* [< Gael *bratt,* cloth, rag, ? child's bib] a child, esp. an impudent, unruly child: scornful or playful term

**Bra·ti·sla·va** (brä'ti slä'və) capital of Slovakia, on the Danube: pop. 448,000

**brat·wurst** (brät'wurst') *n.* [Ger < OHG, *brato,*

lean meat + *wurst,* sausage] highly seasoned, fresh sausage of veal and pork

**braun·schwei·ger** (broun'shwī'gər) *n.* [after *Braunschweig,* Germany, where orig. made] smoked liver sausage

**bra·va·do** (brə vä'dō) *n.* [< Sp < *bravo,* brave] pretended courage or feigned defiant confidence

**brave** (brāv) *adj.* **brav'er, brav'est** [Fr < It *bravo*] 1 not afraid; having courage 2 having a fine appearance —*n.* 1 any brave man 2 a North American Indian warrior —*vt.* **braved, brav'ing** 1 to face with courage 2 to defy; dare —**brave'ly** *adv.* —**brave'ness** *n.*

**brav·er·y** (brāv'ər ē) *n.* courage; valor

**bra·vo** (brä'vō) *interj.* [It] well done! excellent! — *n., pl.* **-vos** a shout of "bravo!"

**bra·vu·ra** (brə vyoor'ə) *n.* [It < *bravo,* brave] 1 bold daring; dash 2 a brilliant musical passage or brilliant technique

**brawl** (brôl) *vi.* [ME *braulen,* to cry out] to quarrel or fight noisily —*n.* a noisy quarrel or fight

**brawn** (brôn) *n.* [< OFr *braon,* muscle] 1 strong, well-developed muscles 2 muscular strength — **brawn'y, -i·er, -i·est,** *adj.* —**brawn'i·ness** *n.*

**bray** (brā) *vi.* [< OFr *braire*] to make the loud, harsh cry of a donkey —*n.* the harsh cry of a donkey, or a sound like this

**braze** (brāz) *vt.* **brazed, braz'ing** [Fr *braser*] to solder with a metal having a high melting point

**bra·zen** (brā'zən) *adj.* [< OE *bræsen,* brass] 1 of brass 2 like brass in color, etc. 3 shameless; bold; impudent 4 harsh and piercing —**brazen it out** to act in a bold, unashamed way —**bra'zen·ly** *adv.* —**bra'zen·ness** *n.*

**bra·zier**[1] (brā'zhər) *n.* [see BRAISE] a metal container to hold burning coals

**bra·zier**[2] (brā'zhər) *n.* [see BRASS] a person who works in brass

**Bra·zil** (brə zil') country in South America, on the Atlantic: 3,286,485 sq. mi.; pop. 146,155,000 — **Bra·zil'ian** *adj., n.*

**Brazil nut** the edible, three-sided seed of a tree of South America

**breach** (brēch) *n.* [< OE *brecan,* to break] 1 a failure to observe a law, promise, etc. 2 an opening made by a breakthrough 3 a break in friendly relations —*vt.* 1 to make a breach in 2 to violate (a contract, etc.) —**breach of promise** a breaking of a promise, esp. to marry

**bread** (bred) *n.* [OE, crumb] 1 a baked food made of flour or meal mixed with water, etc. 2 livelihood [to earn one's *bread*] —*vt.* to coat with bread crumbs before cooking —**break bread** to eat

**breadth** (bredth) *n.* [< OE *brad,* broad] 1 width 2 scope; extent 3 lack of restriction

**bread·win·ner** (bred'win'ər) *n.* one who supports dependents by his or her earnings

**break** (brāk) *vt.* **broke, bro'ken, break'ing** [OE *brecan*] 1 to split or crack into pieces; smash 2 to cut open the surface of (soil, the skin, etc.) 3 to make unusable by cracking, disrupting, etc. 4 to tame as with force 5 to get rid of (a habit) 6 to demote 7 to make poor, ill, bankrupt, etc. 8 to surpass (a record) 9 to violate (a law, promise, etc.) 10 to disrupt the order of [break ranks] 11 to interrupt (a journey, electric circuit, etc.) 12 to reduce the force of by interrupting (a fall, etc.) 13 to bring to an end suddenly or by force 14 to penetrate (silence, darkness, etc.) 15 to disclose 16 to decipher or solve [break a code] —*vi.* 1 to split into pieces; come apart 2 to force one's way (through obstacles, etc.) 3 to stop associating (with) 4 to become unusable 5 to change suddenly [his voice broke] 6 to begin suddenly [to break into song] 7 to come suddenly into being, notice, etc. [the story broke] 8 to stop activity temporarily 9 to suffer a collapse as of spirit —*n.* 1 a breaking 2 a broken place 3 a beginning or appearance [the break of day] 4 an interruption of regularity 5 a gap, interval, or rest 6 a sudden change 7 an escape 8 a chance piece of luck —**break down** 1 to go out of working order 2 to have a physical or nervous collapse **3** to analyze —**break in 1** to enter forcibly **2** to interrupt **3** to train (a beginner) **4** to prepare (something new) by use or wear —**break off** to stop abruptly —**break out 1** to become covered with pimples, etc. **2** to escape suddenly —**break up 1** to separate; disperse **2** to stop **3** [Inf.] to laugh or make laugh —**give someone a break** [Inf.] to stop treating someone harshly, critically, etc. —**break′a·ble** *adj., n.*

**break′age** *n.* **1** a breaking **2** things broken **3** loss due to breaking or the sum allowed for it

**break′down′** *n.* **1** a breaking down **2** a failure of health **3** an analysis

**break′er** *n.* **1** a person or thing that breaks **2** a wave that breaks into foam

**break·fast** (brek′fəst) *n.* the first meal of the day —*vi.* to eat breakfast

**break·front** (brāk′frunt′) *adj.* having a projecting center section in front —*n.* a breakfront cabinet

**break′-in′** *n.* the act of forcibly entering a building, esp. in order to rob

**break′neck′** *adj.* very fast, reckless, or dangerous *[breakneck speed]*

**break′through′** *n.* **1** the act of forcing a way through against resistance, as in warfare **2** a very important advance or discovery

**break′up′** *n.* **1** a dispersion **2** a disintegration **3** a collapse

**break′wa′ter** *n.* a barrier to break the impact of waves, as before a harbor

**breast** (brest) *n.* ⟦OE *breost*⟧ **1** either of two milk-secreting glands on a woman's body **2** the upper front part of the body **3** the part of a garment, etc. over the breast **4** the breast regarded as the center of emotions —*vt.* to face firmly; oppose

**breast′bone′** *n.* STERNUM

**breast′-feed′** *vt.* **-fed′, -feed′ing** to feed (a baby) milk from the breast

**breast′plate′** *n.* a piece of armor for the breast

**breast stroke** a swimming stroke in which both arms are brought out sideways from the chest

**breast′work′** *n.* a low wall put up quickly as a defense in battle

**breath** (breth) *n.* ⟦< OE *bræth*, odor⟧ **1** air taken into the lungs and then let out **2** respiration **3** the power to breathe easily **4** life; spirit **5** a fragrant odor **6** a slight breeze **7** a whisper; murmur —**catch one's breath 1** to gasp **2** [Inf.] to rest or pause —**in the same breath** almost simultaneously —**out of breath** breathless, as from exertion —**take someone's breath away** to thrill someone —**under** (or **below**) **one's breath** in a whisper

**breathe** (brēth) *vi., vt.* **breathed, breath′ing 1** to take (air) into the lungs and let it out again; inhale and exhale **2** to live **3** to rest —**breathe again** to have a feeling of relief —**breath′a·ble** *adj.*

**breath·er** (brē′thər) *n.* **1** one who breathes **2** [Inf.] a pause for rest

**breath·less** (breth′lis) *adj.* **1** without breath **2** panting; gasping **3** unable to breathe easily because of emotion —**breath′less·ly** *adv.*

**breath′tak′ing** *adj.* very exciting

**breath′y** *adj.* **-i·er, -i·est** marked by an audible emission of breath

**bred** (bred) *vt., vi. pt. & pp. of* BREED

**breech** (brēch) *n.* ⟦OE *brec*⟧ **1** the buttocks **2** the part of a gun behind the barrel

**breech′cloth′** *n.* LOINCLOTH

**breech·es** (brich′iz) *pl.n.* ⟦see BREECH⟧ **1** trousers reaching to the knees **2** [Inf.] any trousers

**breed** (brēd) *vt.* **bred, breed′ing** ⟦< OE *brod*, fetus⟧ **1** to bring forth (offspring) **2** to be the source of; produce **3** to raise (animals) **4** to rear; train —*vi.* **1** to be produced; originate **2** to reproduce —*n.* **1** a stock; strain **2** a sort; type —**breed′er** *n.*

**breed′ing** *n.* **1** the producing of young **2** good upbringing **3** the producing of plants and animals, esp. for improving the stock

**breeze** (brēz) *n.* ⟦16th-c. nautical term *brise*, prob. < Du⟧ **1** a gentle wind **2** [Inf.] a thing easy to do —*vi.* **breezed, breez′ing** [Inf.] to move or go quickly

**breeze′way′** *n.* a covered passageway, as between a house and garage

**breez′y** *adj.* **-i·er, -i·est 1** slightly windy **2** light and lively —**breez′i·ly** *adv.* —**breez′i·ness** *n.*

**Bre·men** (brem′ən) seaport in NW Germany: pop. 553,000

**breth·ren** (breth′rən) *pl.n.* ⟦ME *bretheren*⟧ brothers: now chiefly religious

**bre·vet** (brə vet′) *n.* ⟦< L *brevis*, brief⟧ [Historical] *Mil.* a commission of higher honorary rank without extra pay —*vt.* **-vet′ted** or **-vet′ed, -vet′ting** or **-vet′ing** to give a brevet to

**bre·vi·ar·y** (brē′vē er′ē) *n., pl.* **-ar·ies** ⟦< L *brevis*, brief⟧ a book of Psalms, prayers, etc. to be recited daily by priests, nuns, etc.

**brev·i·ty** (brev′ə tē) *n.* ⟦< L *brevis*, brief⟧ **1** briefness **2** conciseness

**brew** (brōō) *vt.* ⟦OE *breowan*⟧ **1** to make (beer, etc.) from malt and hops by boiling and fermenting **2** to steep (tea, etc.) **3** to plot —*vi.* to begin to form —*n.* a brewed beverage —**brew′er** *n.*

**brew·er·y** (brōō′ər ē) *n., pl.* **-er·ies** a place where beer, etc. is brewed

**bri·ar**[1] (brī′ər) *n.* BRIER[1]

**bri·ar**[2] (brī′ər) *n.* a tobacco pipe made from the root of the BRIER[2]

**bribe** (brīb) *n.* ⟦< OFr *briber*, to beg⟧ anything given or promised as an inducement, esp. to do something illegal or wrong —*vt.* **bribed, brib′ing** to offer or give a bribe to —**brib′er·y** *n.*

**bric-a-brac** (brik′ə brak′) *n.* ⟦< Fr *de bric et de brac*, by hook or by crook⟧ **1** small artistic objects used to ornament a room **2** knickknacks

**brick** (brik) *n.* ⟦MDu < *breken*, piece of baked clay⟧ **1** an oblong block of baked clay, used in building, etc. **2** anything shaped like a brick **3** bricks collectively —*adj.* built or paved with brick —*vt.* to build or cover with brick

**brick′bat′** *n.* **1** a piece of brick used as a missile **2** an unfavorable remark

**brick′lay′er** *n.* one whose work is building with bricks —**brick′lay′ing** *n.*

**brid·al** (brīd′l) *adj.* ⟦< OE *bryd ealu*, marriage feast⟧ **1** of a bride **2** of a wedding

**bride** (brīd) *n.* ⟦OE *bryd*⟧ a woman just married or about to be married

**bride′groom′** *n.* ⟦< OE *bryd*, bride + *guma*, man⟧ a man just married or about to be married

**brides·maid** (brīdz′mād′) *n.* one of the women who attend the bride at a wedding

**bridge**[1] (brij) *n.* ⟦OE *brycge*⟧ **1** a structure built over a river, etc. to provide a way across **2** a thing that provides connection, contact, etc. **3** the bony upper part of the nose **4** a raised platform on a ship **5** a mounting for false teeth **6** *Music* a connecting passage —*vt.* **bridged, bridg′ing** to build or be a bridge over —**burn one's bridges (behind one)** to follow a course from which there is no retreat —**bridge′a·ble** *adj.*

**bridge**[2] (brij) *n.* ⟦< ? Russ⟧ a card game, for two pairs of players, in which they bid for the right to name the trump suit or declare no-trump

**bridge′head′** *n.* a fortified position established by an attacking force on the enemy's side of a bridge, river, etc.

**Bridge·port** (brij′pôrt′) seaport in SW Connecticut: pop. 142,000

**bridge′work′** *n.* a dental bridge or bridges

**bri·dle** (brīd′l) *n.* ⟦< OE *bregdan*, move quickly⟧ **1** a head harness for guiding a horse: it has a bit for the mouth to which the reins are fastened **2**

anything that controls or restrains —*vt.* **bri′dled, bri′dling 1** to put a bridle on **2** to curb or control —*vi.* **1** to pull one's head back quickly as an expression of anger, scorn, etc. **2** to take offense (*at*)

BIT    REINS

BRIDLE

**bridle path** a path for horseback riding

**brief** (brēf) *adj.* ⟦< L *brevis*⟧ **1** short **2** concise —*n.* **1** a summary, specif. of the main points of a law case **2** [*pl.*] legless undershorts —*vt.* **1** to summarize **2** to supply with all pertinent information —**brief′ly** *adv.* —**brief′ness** *n.*

**brief′case′** *n.* a flat, flexible case for carrying papers, books, etc.

**brief′ing** *n.* a supplying of pertinent information

**bri·er¹** (brī′ər) *n.* ⟦OE *brer*⟧ any thorny bush, as a bramble

**bri·er²** (brī′ər) *n.* ⟦Fr *bruyère*⟧ a variety of heath, whose root is used for making tobacco pipes

**brig¹** (brig) *n.* ⟦< BRIGANTINE⟧ a two-masted ship with square sails

**brig²** *n.* ⟦< ?⟧ a prison, as on a warship

**bri·gade** (bri gād′) *n.* ⟦< OIt *briga,* strife⟧ **1** a military unit composed of two or more battalions with service and administrative units **2** a group of people organized to function as a unit in some work [a fire *brigade*]

**brig·a·dier general** (brig′ə dir′) *U.S. Mil.* a military officer ranking just above a colonel

**brig·and** (brig′ənd) *n.* ⟦see BRIGADE⟧ a bandit, esp. one of a roving band

**brig′and·age** *n.* plundering by brigands

**brig·an·tine** (brig′ən tēn′) *n.* ⟦< OIt *brigantino,* pirate vessel⟧ a ship with a square-rigged foremast and a square-rigged topsail on the mainmast

**bright** (brīt) *adj.* ⟦OE *bryht*⟧ **1** shining with light **2** brilliant in color or sound; vivid **3** lively; cheerful **4** mentally quick; smart **5** favorable or hopeful **6** illustrious —**bright′ly** *adv.* —**bright′ness** *n.*

**bright′en** *vt., vi.* to make or become bright or brighter

**Brigh·ton** (brīt′'n) resort city in S England: county district pop. 144,000

**bril·liant** (bril′yənt) *adj.* ⟦< Fr < It *brillare,* to sparkle⟧ **1** shining brightly **2** vivid; intense **3** very splendid **4** very intelligent, talented, etc. — **bril′liance** or **bril′lian·cy** *n.* —**bril′liant·ly** *adv.*

**bril·lian·tine** (bril′yən tēn′) *n.* ⟦< Fr⟧ an oily substance for grooming the hair

**brim** (brim) *n.* ⟦ME *brimme*⟧ **1** the topmost edge of a cup, glass, etc. **2** a projecting rim, as of a hat —*vt., vi.* **brimmed, brim′ming** to fill or be full to the brim —**brim′less** *adj.*

**brim′ful′** (-fool′) *adj.* full to the brim

**brim′stone′** *n.* ⟦< OE *bærnan,* to kindle + *stan,* stone⟧ sulfur

**brin·dle** (brin′dəl) *adj.* BRINDLED —*n.* **1** a brindled color **2** a brindled animal

**brin′dled** (-dəld) *adj.* ⟦prob. < ME *brennen,* to burn⟧ having a gray or tawny coat streaked or spotted with a darker color

**brine** (brīn) *n.* ⟦OE⟧ **1** water full of salt **2** the ocean —**brin′y, -i·er, -i·est,** *adj.*

**bring** (briŋ) *vt.* **brought, bring′ing** ⟦OE *bringan*⟧ **1** to carry or lead "here" or to a place where the speaker will be **2** to cause to be, happen, appear, have, etc. **3** to lead to an action or belief **4** to sell for —**bring about** to cause —**bring forth** to give birth to; produce —**bring off** to accomplish —**bring out 1** to reveal **2** to offer (a play, book, etc.) to the public —**bring up 1** to rear (children) **2** to introduce, as into discussion

**brink** (briŋk) *n.* ⟦< MLowG or Dan, shore⟧ the edge, esp. at the top of a steep place; verge

**brink′man·ship′** (-mən ship′) *n.* the policy of pursuing a risky course of action to the brink of disaster: also **brinks′man·ship′**

**bri·oche** (brē ōsh′) *n.* ⟦Fr⟧ a light, rich roll made with flour, butter, eggs, and yeast

**bri·quette** or **bri·quet** (bri ket′) *n.* ⟦Fr < *brique,* brick⟧ a small block of charcoal, coal dust, etc., used for fuel or kindling

**Bris·bane** (briz′bān′, -bən) seaport in E Australia: pop. 1,455,000

**brisk** (brisk) *adj.* ⟦< ? Fr *brusque,* brusque⟧ **1** quick in manner; energetic **2** keen, bracing, etc. —**brisk′ly** *adv.* —**brisk′ness** *n.*

**bris·ket** (bris′kit) *n.* ⟦ME *brusket*⟧ meat cut from the breast of an animal

**bris·ling** (bris′liŋ) *n.* ⟦< Dan *bretling*⟧ SPRAT

**bris·tle** (bris′əl) *n.* ⟦< OE *byrst*⟧ **1** any short, stiff hair **2** such a hair, or a piece like it, in a brush — *vi.* **-tled, -tling 1** to be stiff and erect **2** to have the bristles become erect **3** to stiffen with anger **4** to be thickly covered (*with*) —**bris′tly** (-lē), **-tli·er, -tli·est,** *adj.*

**bris′tle·cone′ pine** a Rocky Mountain pine tree of the W U.S.

**Bris·tol** (bris′təl) seaport in SW England: county district pop. 376,000

**Brit** *abbrev.* British

**Brit·ain** (brit′'n) GREAT BRITAIN

**britch·es** (brich′iz) *pl.n.* [Inf.] BREECHES (sense 2)

**Brit·i·cism** (brit′ə siz′əm) *n.* a word or idiom peculiar to British English

**Brit·ish** (brit′ish) *adj.* of Great Britain or its people, language, etc. —**the British** the people of Great Britain

**British Columbia** province of SW Canada: 367,671 sq. mi.; pop. 3,725,000; cap. Victoria: abbrev. *BC*

**British Commonwealth (of Nations)** *former name for* THE COMMONWEALTH

**British Isles** group of islands including Great Britain, Ireland, etc.

**British thermal unit** a unit of heat equal to about 252 calories

**Brit·on** (brit′'n) *n.* **1** a member of an early Celtic people of S Britain **2** a person born or living in Great Britain, esp. in England

**brit·tle** (brit′l) *adj.* ⟦< OE *breotan,* to break⟧ easily broken or shattered —*n.* a brittle, crunchy candy with nuts in it —**brit′tle·ness** *n.*

**broach** (brōch) *n.* ⟦< ML *brocca,* a spike⟧ a tapering bit for boring holes —*vt.* **1** to make a hole in so as to let out liquid **2** to ream with a broach **3** to start a discussion of

**broad** (brôd) *adj.* ⟦OE *brad*⟧ **1** of large extent from side to side; wide **2** extending about; full [*broad* daylight] **3** obvious [a *broad* hint] **4** tolerant; liberal [a *broad* view] **5** wide in range [a *broad* variety] **6** not detailed; general [in *broad* outline] —**broad′ly** *adv.* —**broad′ness** *n.*

**broad′band′** *adj.* designating cable, communication devices, etc. allowing the transmission of much data at high speeds

**broad′-based′** *adj.* comprehensive or extensive

**broad′cast′** (-kast′) *vt., vi.* **-cast′** or **-cast′ed, -cast′ing 1** to scatter or spread widely **2** to transmit by radio or TV —*adj.* of or for radio or TV broadcasting —*n.* a radio or TV program —*adv.* far and wide —**broad′cast′er** *n.*

**broad′cloth′** *n.* a fine, smooth woolen, cotton, or silk cloth

**broad′en** *vt., vi.* to widen

**broad jump** *former name for* LONG JUMP

**broad′loom′** *adj.* woven on a wide loom

**broad′-mind′ed** *adj.* tolerant of unconventional opinions and behavior; liberal —**broad′-mind′ed·ly** *adv.* —**broad′-mind′ed·ness** *n.*

**broad′side′** *n.* **1** the firing of all guns on one side of a warship **2** a vigorous attack in words —*adv.*

**1** with the side facing **2** in the side [hit *broadside*] **3** indiscriminately

**broad'-spec'trum** *adj.* effective against a wide range of germs

**broad'sword'** *n.* a broad-bladed sword for slashing

**Broad·way** (brôd'wā') street in New York City, with many theaters, etc.

**bro·cade** (brō kād') *n.* [< Sp < It *broccare*, embroider] a rich cloth with a raised design woven into it —*vt.* **-cad'ed, -cad'ing** to weave a raised design into (cloth)

**broc·co·li** (bräk'ə lē) *n.* [It < ML *brocca*, a spike] a plant related to the cauliflower but bearing tender shoots with greenish buds

**bro·chette** (brō shet') *n.* [Fr] a skewer for broiling chunks of meat, etc.

**bro·chure** (brō shoor') *n.* [Fr < *brocher*, to stitch] a pamphlet

**bro·gan** (brō'gən) *n.* [Ir] a heavy work shoe, fitting high on the ankle

**brogue**[1] (brōg) *n.* [< ?] a dialectal pronunciation, esp. that of English by the Irish

**brogue**[2] (brōg) *n.* [< Ir *brōg*, a shoe] a man's heavy oxford shoe

**broil** (broil) *vt., vi.* [< OFr *bruillir*] to cook by exposure to direct heat

**broil'er** *n.* **1** a pan, grill, etc. for broiling **2** a chicken suitable for broiling

**broke** (brōk) *vt., vi. pt. of* BREAK —*adj.* [Inf.] without money; bankrupt

**bro·ken** (brō'kən) *vt., vi. pp. of* BREAK —*adj.* **1** splintered, fractured, etc. **2** not in working order **3** violated [a *broken* promise] **4** ruined **5** interrupted; discontinuous **6** imperfectly spoken **7** tamed —**bro'ken·ly** *adv.* —**bro'ken·ness** *n.*

**bro'ken-down'** *adj.* **1** sick or worn out **2** out of order; useless

**bro'ken·heart'ed** *adj.* crushed by sorrow, grief, etc.

**bro·ker** (brō'kər) *n.* [< OFr *brokier*, to tap; orig. sense "wine dealer"] **1** a person hired as an agent in negotiating contracts, buying and selling, etc. **2** STOCKBROKER —*vt., vi.* **1** to act as a broker (for) **2** to negotiate

**bro'ker·age** *n.* **1** the business or office of a broker **2** a broker's fee

**bro·mide** (brō'mīd') *n.* **1** a compound of bromine with another element or a radical **2** potassium bromide, used as a sedative **3** a trite saying

**bro·mid'ic** (-mid'ik) *adj.* trite or dull

**bro·mine** (brō'mēn') *n.* [< Gr *brōmos*, stench] a chemical element, a reddish-brown, corrosive liquid

**bron·chi** (brän'kī) *pl.n., sing.* **-chus** (-kəs) [< Gr *bronchos*, windpipe] the two main branches of the windpipe —**bron'chi·al** (-kē əl) *adj.*

**bron·chi'tis** (-kīt'is) *n.* an inflammation of the bronchial tubes

**bron·co** (brän'kō) *n., pl.* **-cos** [Sp, rough] a wild or only partly tamed horse or pony of the W U.S.: also **bron'cho** *n., pl.* **-chos**

**bron'co·bust'er** *n.* [Inf.] a tamer of broncos — **bron'co·bust'ing** *n.*

**Bron·të** (brän'tē) **1 Char·lotte** (shär'lət) 1816-55; Eng. novelist **2 Em·i·ly** (em'ə lē) 1818-48; Eng. novelist: sister of Charlotte

**bron·to·saur** (brän'tō sôr', -tə-) *n.* [< Gr *brontē*, thunder + *sauros,* lizard] APATOSAURUS: also **bron'to·saur'us**

**Bronx** (bräŋks) borough of New York City: pop. 1,204,000: used with *the*

**bronze** (bränz) *n.* [Fr, prob. ult. < Pers *biriṇ̃*, copper] **1** an alloy of copper and tin **2** a reddish-brown color —*adj.* of or like bronze —*vt.* **bronzed, bronz'ing** [Fr *bronzer* < the *n.*] to make bronze in color

**brooch** (brōch, brōōch) *n.* [see BROACH] a large ornamental pin with a clasp

**brood** (brōōd) *n.* [OE *brod*] **1** a group of birds hatched at one time **2** the children in a family — *vi.* **1** to sit on and hatch eggs **2** to worry: often with *on, over,* or *about*

**brood'er** *n.* **1** one that broods **2** a heated shelter for raising fowl

**brood'mare'** *n.* a mare kept for breeding

**brook**[1] (brook) *n.* [< OE *broc*] a small stream

**brook**[2] (brook) *vt.* [OE *brucan*, to use] to put up with; endure

**Brook·lyn** (brook'lən) borough of New York City: pop. 2,301,000

**broom** (brōōm, broom) *n.* [OE *brom*, brushwood] **1** a flowering shrub of the pea family **2** a bundle of fibers or straws fastened to a long handle (**broom'stick**), used for sweeping

**Bros** or **bros** *abbrev.* brothers

**broth** (brôth) *n.* [OE] a thin soup made by boiling meat, etc. in water

**broth·el** (bräth'əl) *n.* [< OE *broethan,* go to ruin] a house of prostitution

**broth·er** (bruth'ər) *n., pl.* **-ers** or **breth'ren** [OE *brothor*] **1** a male related to one by having the same parents **2** a friend who is like a brother **3** a fellow member of the same race, church, profession, etc. **4** [*often* B-] a lay member of a men's religious order

**broth'er·hood'** *n.* **1** the state of being brothers **2** an association of men united in some interest, work, etc. **3** a feeling of unity among all people

**broth'er-in-law'** *n., pl.* **broth'ers-in-law'** **1** the brother of one's spouse **2** the husband of one's sister **3** the husband of the sister of one's spouse

**broth'er·ly** *adj.* **1** of or like a brother **2** friendly, kind, loyal, etc.

**brought** (brôt) *vt. pt. & pp. of* BRING

**brou·ha·ha** (brōō'hä hä') *n.* [Fr] an uproar or commotion

**brow** (brou) *n.* [OE *bru*] **1** the eyebrow **2** the forehead **3** the edge of a cliff

**brow'beat'** *vt.* **-beat', -beat'en, -beat'ing** to intimidate with harsh, stern looks and talk; bully

**brown** (broun) *adj.* [OE *brun*] **1** having the color of chocolate, a mixture of red, black, and yellow **2** tanned; dark-skinned —*n.* brown color —*vt., vi.* to make or become brown —**brown'ish** *adj.*

**brown'-bag'** *vt., vi.* **-bagged', -bag'ging** to carry (one's lunch) to work or school, as in a brown paper bag

**brown·ie** (broun'ē) *n.* **1** a small, helpful elf **2** a small square cut from a flat chocolate cake

**Brown·ing** (broun'iŋ), **Rob·ert** (räb'ərt) 1812-89; Eng. poet

**brown'out'** *n.* a dimming of lights in a city, as during an electric power shortage

**brown rice** rice that has not had its brown outer coating removed

**brown'stone'** *n.* a reddish-brown sandstone, used for building

**brown study** deep thought; reverie

**brown sugar** sugar whose crystals retain a brown coating of syrup

**browse** (brouz) *n.* [< OS *brustian*, to sprout] leaves, shoots, etc. which animals feed on —*vi.* **browsed, brows'ing 1** to nibble at (leaves, shoots, etc.) **2** to examine (a book, articles for sale, etc.) in a casual way

**brows'er** *n.* **1** one that browses **2** software for gaining access to the World Wide Web

**bru·in** (brōō'in) *n.* [Du, brown] a bear

**bruise** (brōōz) *vt.* **bruised, bruis'ing** [< OE *brysan*, crush] **1** to injure and discolor (body tissue) without breaking the skin **2** to injure the surface of, causing spoilage, denting, etc. **3** to hurt (the feelings, spirit, etc.) —*vi.* to be or become bruised —*n.* a bruised area, as of tissue

**bruis'er** *n.* [Inf.] a strong, pugnacious man

**bruit** (brōōt) *vt.* [< OFr, noise, rumor] to spread (*about*) by rumor

**brunch** (brunch) *n.* a combined breakfast and lunch —*vi.* to eat brunch

**Bru·nei** (brōō nī′) country on the N coast of Borneo: 2,226 sq. mi.; pop. 261,000

**bru·net** (brōō net′) *adj.* [< OFr, dim. of *brun*, brown] having black or dark-brown hair, often with dark eyes and complexion —*n.* a brunet person

**bru·nette′** (-net′) *adj.* BRUNET —*n.* a brunette woman or girl

**Bruns·wick** (brunz′wik) city in NC Germany: pop. 258,000

**brunt** (brunt) *n.* [ME *bront*] 1 the shock (of an attack) or impact (of a blow) 2 the hardest part

**brush**[1] (brush) *n.* [< OFr *broce*, bush] 1 BRUSHWOOD 2 sparsely settled country 3 a device for cleaning, painting, etc., having bristles, wires, etc. fastened into a back 4 a brushing 5 a light, grazing stroke 6 a bushy tail, as of a fox —*vt.* 1 to clean, paint, etc. with a brush 2 to apply, remove, etc. as with a brush 3 to touch or graze in passing —*vi.* to graze past something —**brush up** to refresh one's memory

**brush**[2] (brush) *n.* [< ME *bruschen*, to rush] a short, quick fight

**brush′off′** *n.* [Slang] a curt dismissal, esp. in the phrase **give** (or **get**) **the brushoff**

**brush′wood′** *n.* 1 chopped-off tree branches 2 underbrush

**brusque** (brusk) *adj.* [Fr < ML *bruscus*, brushwood] rough and abrupt in manner or speech; curt: also **brusk** —**brusque′ly** *adv.* —**brusque′ness** *n.*

**Brus·sels** (brus′əlz) capital of Belgium: pop. 952,000

**Brussels sprout** 1 *often* **Brussels sprouts** a plant that bears small cabbagelike heads on an erect stem 2 one of its edible heads

**bru·tal** (brōōt′'l) *adj.* 1 like a brute; very savage, cruel, etc. 2 very harsh —**bru′tal·ly** *adv.*

**bru·tal·i·ty** (brōō tal′ə tē) *n.* 1 a being brutal 2 *pl.* **-ties** a brutal act

**bru·tal·ize** (brōōt′'l īz′) *vt.* **-ized′, -iz′ing** 1 to make brutal 2 to treat in a brutal way —**bru′tal·i·za′tion** *n.*

**brute** (brōōt) *adj.* [< L *brutus*, irrational] of or like an animal; specif., savage, stupid, etc. —*n.* 1 an animal 2 a brutal person —**brut′ish** *adj.* —**brut′ish·ly** *adv.*

**bs** *abbrev.* bill of sale

**BS** *abbrev.* Bachelor of Science: also **B.S.**

**Btu** *abbrev.* British thermal unit(s): also **BTU** or **btu**

**bu** *abbrev.* bushel(s)

**bub·ble** (bub′əl) *n.* [echoic] 1 a film of liquid forming a ball around air or gas 2 a tiny ball of air or gas in a liquid or solid 3 a transparent dome 4 a plausible scheme that proves worthless —*vi.* **-bled, -bling** 1 to rise in bubbles; boil 2 to make a gurgling sound —**on the bubble** with the outcome uncertain but already being determined —**bub′bly, -bli·er, -bli·est,** *adj.*

**bubble gum** a kind of chewing gum that can be blown into large bubbles

**bub′ble·head′** *n.* a person who is silly, ignorant, etc.

**Bubble Wrap** *trademark for* plastic packaging material with air bubbles —[b- w-] such packaging material

**bu·bo** (byōō′bō′) *n., pl.* **-boes′** [< Gr *boubōn*, groin] an inflamed swelling of a lymph node, esp. in the armpit or groin

**bu·bon′ic plague** (-bän′ik) a contagious disease characterized by buboes, fever, and delirium

BRUSSELS SPROUT

**buc·ca·neer** (buk′ə nir′) *n.* [< Fr *boucanier*] a pirate

**Bu·chan·an** (byōō kan′ən), **James** (jāmz) 1791-1868; 15th president of the U.S. (1857-61)

**Bu·cha·rest** (bōō′kə rest′) capital of Romania: pop. 1,990,000

**buck**[1] (buk) *n.* [OE *bucca*, male goat] 1 a male deer, goat, etc.: see DOE 2 the act of bucking 3 BUCKSKIN 4 [Inf.] a bold, vigorous young man —*vi.* 1 to rear upward quickly, as to throw off a rider: said of a horse 2 [Inf.] to resist something as if plunging against it —*vt.* 1 to dislodge or throw by bucking 2 [Inf.] to resist stubbornly —**buck for** [Slang] to work eagerly for (a promotion, etc.) —**buck up** [Inf.] to cheer up

**buck**[2] (buk) *n.* [< ?] [Slang] a dollar —**pass the buck** [Inf.] to try to shift blame or responsibility onto another person

**buck′board′** *n.* [BUCK[1], *vi.* + BOARD] an open carriage whose floorboards rest directly on the axles

**buck·et** (buk′it) *n.* [< OE *buc*, pitcher] 1 a cylindrical container with a curved handle, for carrying water, etc.; pail 2 the amount held by a bucket: also **buck′et·ful′,** *pl.* **-fuls′** 3 a thing like a bucket, as a scoop on a steam shovel —**kick the bucket** [Slang] to die

**bucket seat** a single contoured seat with a movable back, as in sports cars

**buck·eye** (buk′ī′) *n.* [BUCK[1] + EYE < the appearance of the seed] 1 a horse chestnut with large capsules enclosing shiny brown seeds 2 the seed

**buck·le**[1] (buk′əl) *n.* [< L *buccula*, cheek strap of a helmet] a clasp for fastening a strap, belt, etc. —*vt., vi.* **-led, -ling** to fasten with a buckle —**buckle down** to apply oneself energetically

**buck·le**[2] (buk′əl) *vt., vi.* **-led, -ling** [prob. infl. by OFr *bocler*, to bulge: see prec.] to bend or crumple —*n.* a bend, bulge, etc.

**buck·ler** (buk′lər) *n.* [< OFr *bocler*] a small, round shield

**buck′-pass′er** *n.* [Inf.] one who regularly tries to shift blame or responsibility to someone else —**buck′-pass′ing** *n.*

**buck·ram** (buk′rəm) *n.* [? < *Bukhara*, city in central Asia] a coarse, stiff cloth used in bookbinding, etc.

**buck′saw′** *n.* a wood-cutting saw set in a frame

**buck′shot′** *n.* a large lead shot for shooting deer and other large game

**buck′skin′** *n.* 1 a soft leather made from the skins of deer or sheep 2 [*pl.*] clothes made of buckskin

**buck′tooth′** *n., pl.* **-teeth′** a projecting front tooth —**buck′toothed′** *adj.*

**buck′wheat′** *n.* [< OE *boc-*, beech + WHEAT] 1 a plant with beechnut-shaped seeds 2 a dark flour made from the seeds

**bu·col·ic** (byōō käl′ik) *adj.* [< Gr *boukolos*, herdsman] 1 of shepherds; pastoral 2 of country life; rustic —**bu·col′i·cal·ly** *adv.*

**bud** (bud) *n.* [ME *budde*] 1 a small swelling on a plant, from which a shoot, leaf, or flower develops 2 an early stage of development —*vi.* **bud′ded, bud′ding** 1 to put forth buds 2 to begin to develop —**in** (**the**) **bud** 1 in a budding condition 2 in an early stage —**bud′like′** *adj.*

**Bu·da·pest** (bōō′də pest′) capital of Hungary: pop. 2,104,000

**Bud·dha** (bōō′də) religious leader who lived in India 563?-483? B.C.: founder of Buddhism

**Bud·dhism** (bōō′diz′əm) *n.* a religion of Asia teaching that by right thinking and self-denial one achieves nirvana, a state of blessedness —**Bud′dhist** *n., adj.*

**bud·dy** (bud′ē) *n., pl.* **-dies** [< ?] [Inf.] a close friend; comrade

**budge** (buj) *vt., vi.* **budged, budg′ing** [< OFr *bouger*, to move] to move even a little

**budg·er·i·gar** (buj′ər i gär′) *n.* [native name] a greenish-yellow Australian parakeet: also [Inf.] **budg′ie**

**budg·et** (buj'it) *n.* ⟦< L *bulga*, bag⟧ **1** a plan adjusting expenses to income **2** estimated cost of living, operating, etc. **3** amount allotted for a specific use —*vt.* **1** to put on a budget **2** to plan *[budget your time]* —**budg'et·ar·y** *adj.*

**Bue·nos Ai·res** (bwā'nəs er'ēz) seaport & capital of Argentina: pop. 2,908,000

**buff** (buf) *n.* ⟦< Fr < It *bufalo*, buffalo⟧ **1** a soft, brownish-yellow leather **2** a dull brownish yellow **3** [Inf.] a devotee; fan —*adj.* of the color buff —*vt.* to polish or shine, as with soft leather —**in the buff** naked

**buf·fa·lo** (buf'ə lō') *n., pl.* **-loes'**, **-lo'**, or **-los'** ⟦It *bufalo* < Gr *bous*, ox⟧ **1** any of various wild oxen, as the water buffalo of India **2** popularly, the American bison —*vt.* **-loed'**, **-lo'ing** [Slang] to baffle, bluff, etc.

**Buf·fa·lo** (buf'ə lō') city in W New York, on Lake Erie: pop. 328,000

**Buffalo wings** [after prec.] [*also* b- w-] spicy fried segments of chicken wings

**buff·er**[1] (buf'ər) *n.* ⟦BUFF, *v.* + -ER⟧ **1** one who buffs **2** something used for buffing

**buff·er**[2] (buf'ər) *n.* ⟦< OFr *buffe*, a blow⟧ **1** anything that lessens shock, as of collision **2** a temporary storage area in a computer, for data being transferred to another device

**buf·fet**[1] (buf'it) *n.* ⟦OFr < *buffe*, a blow⟧ a blow or shock —*vt.* **1** to punch; hit **2** to thrust about

**buf·fet**[2] (bə fā', boo-) *n.* ⟦Fr⟧ **1** a sideboard **2** a counter or table at which guests, etc. serve themselves food **3** a meal served on such a table, etc.

**buf·foon** (bə foon') *n.* ⟦< Fr < It *buffare*, to jest⟧ one who is always clowning and trying to be funny; clown —**buf·foon'er·y** *n.* —**buf·foon'ish** *adj.*

**bug** (bug) *n.* ⟦prob. < ME *bugge*: see fol.⟧ **1** an insect with sucking mouthparts **2** any small arthropod, as a cockroach **3** a defect, as in a machine **4** [Inf.] a germ or virus **5** [Inf.] a hidden microphone —*vt.* **bugged**, **bug'ging** **1** [Inf.] to hide a microphone in (a room, etc.) **2** [Slang] to annoy, anger, etc.

**bug'bear'** *n.* ⟦ME *bugge*, a hobgoblin + BEAR[2]⟧ **1** an imaginary evil being **2** a cause of needless fear Also **bug'a·boo'** (-ə boo') *n., pl.* **-boos'**

**bug'-eyed'** *adj.* [Slang] with bulging eyes

**bug·gy**[1] (bug'ē) *n., pl.* **-gies** ⟦< ?⟧ **1** a light one-horse carriage with one seat **2** BABY CARRIAGE

**bug·gy**[2] (bug'ē) *adj.* **-gi·er**, **-gi·est** infested with bugs

**bu·gle** (byoo'gəl) *n.* ⟦< L *buculus*, young ox⟧ a brass instrument like a small trumpet, usually without valves —*vi., vt.* **-gled**, **-gling** to signal by blowing a bugle —**bu'gler** *n.*

**build** (bild) *vt.* **built**, **build'ing** ⟦< OE *bold*, house⟧ **1** to make by putting together materials, parts, etc.; construct **2** to establish; base *[build a theory on facts]* **3** to create or develop: often with *up* —*vi.* **1** to put up buildings **2** to grow or intensify: often with *up* —*n.* the way a thing is built or shaped *[a stocky build]* —**build up** to make more attractive, healthy, etc. —**build'er** *n.*

**build'ing** *n.* **1** anything that is built; structure **2** the work or business of making houses, etc.

**build'up'** or **build'-up'** *n.* [Inf.] **1** praise or favorable publicity **2** a gradual increase or expansion

**built** (bilt) *vt., vi. pt. & pp. of* BUILD

**built'-in'** *adj.* **1** made as part of the structure **2** inherent

**built'-up'** *adj.* **1** made higher, stronger, etc. with added parts **2** having many buildings on it

**bulb** (bulb) *n.* ⟦< Gr *bolbos*⟧ **1** an underground bud with roots and a short, scaly stem, as in a lily or onion **2** a tuber or tuberous root resembling a bulb, as in a crocus **3** anything shaped like a bulb *[an electric light bulb]* —**bul'bous** *adj.*

**Bul·gar·i·a** (bəl ger'ē ə, bool-) country in SE Europe: 42,855 sq. mi.; pop. 8,473,000 —**Bul·gar'i·an** *adj., n.*

**bulge** (bulj) *n.* ⟦< L *bulga*, leather bag⟧ an out-ward swelling; protuberance —*vi., vt.* **bulged**, **bulg'ing** to swell or bend outward —**bulg'y**, **-i·er**, **-i·est**, *adj.*

**bu·lim·i·a** (byoo lē'mē ə) *n.* ⟦< Gr *bous*, ox + *limos*, hunger⟧ **1** *Med.* a continuous, abnormal hunger **2** a disorder characterized by eating large quantities of food followed by self-induced vomiting, etc.: also **bulimia nervosa** —**bu·lim'ic** *adj.*

**bulk** (bulk) *n.* ⟦< ON *bulki*, a heap⟧ **1** size, mass, or volume, esp. if great **2** the main mass; largest part —*vi.* to have, or to increase in, size or importance —*adj.* **1** total; aggregate **2** not put up in individual packages —**bulk'y**, **-i·er**, **-i·est**, *adj.*

**bulk·head** (bulk'hed') *n.* ⟦< ON *balkr*, partition + HEAD⟧ **1** an upright partition, as in a ship, that is watertight, fireproof, etc. **2** a retaining wall **3** a boxlike structure over an opening

**bull**[1] (bool) *n.* ⟦< OE *bula*, a steer⟧ **1** the adult male of any bovine animal, as the ox, or of certain other large animals, as the elephant or whale **2** a speculator who buys stocks expecting their prices to rise, or who seeks to bring about such a rise **3** [Slang] insincere talk; nonsense —*adj.* **1** male **2** rising in price

**bull**[2] (bool) *n.* ⟦< LL *bulla*, a seal⟧ an official document from the pope

**bull'dog'** *n.* a short-haired, heavily built dog with a strong stubborn grip —*adj.* like a bulldog; stubborn —*vt.* **-dogged'**, **-dog'ging** to throw (a steer) by holding its horns and twisting its neck

**bull'doze'** (-dōz') *vt.* **-dozed'**, **-doz'ing** ⟦< *bull*, a flogging + DOSE⟧ **1** [Inf.] to force or frighten by threatening; bully **2** to move, make level, etc. with a bulldozer

**bull'doz'er** *n.* a tractor with a large, shovel-like blade, for pushing earth, debris, etc.

**bul·let** (bool'it) *n.* ⟦< L *bulla*, a knob⟧ a small, shaped piece of lead, steel, etc., to be shot from a firearm

**bul·le·tin** (bool'ə tin) *n.* ⟦< LL *bulla*, a seal⟧ **1** a brief statement of the latest news **2** a regular publication, as of an organization

**bulletin board** a board or wall area on which bulletins, notices, etc. are put up

**bul'let·proof'** *adj.* that bullets cannot pierce —*vt.* to make bulletproof

**bull'fight'** *n.* a spectacle in which a bull is first provoked in various ways and then killed with the thrust of a sword by a matador —**bull'fight'er** *n.* —**bull'fight'ing** *n.*

**bull'frog'** *n.* a large North American frog with a deep, loud croak

**bull'head'ed** *adj.* blindly stubborn; headstrong —**bull'head·ed·ness** *n.*

**bull'horn'** *n.* a portable electronic voice amplifier

**bul·lion** (bool'yən) *n.* ⟦< OFr *billon*, small coin⟧ ingots, bars, etc. of gold or silver

**bull·ish** (bool'ish) *adj.* **1** of or like a bull **2** rising, or causing a rise, in prices on the stock exchange **3** optimistic

**bull'ock** (-ək) *n.* ⟦< OE dim. of *bula*, steer⟧ a castrated bull; steer

**bull'pen'** *n.* **1** [Inf.] a temporary detention room in a jail **2** *Baseball a)* a practice area for relief pitchers *b)* the relief pitchers of one team

**bull's'-eye'** *n.* **1** the central mark of a target **2** a direct hit

**bul·ly** (bool'ē) *n., pl.* **-lies** ⟦< MHG *buole*, lover; later infl. by BULL[1]⟧ a person who hurts or browbeats those who are weaker —*vt.* **-lied**, **-ly·ing** to behave as a bully toward —*adj., interj.* [Inf.] fine; good

**bul·rush** (bool'rush) *n.* ⟦< ME *bol*, stem + *rusche*, a rush⟧ a tall plant of the sedge family, found in wet places

**bul·wark** (bool'wərk) *n.* ⟦MDu *bolwerc*⟧ **1** a defensive wall; rampart **2** a defense; protection **3** [*usually pl.*] a ship's side above the deck

**bum** (bum) *n.* ⟦prob. < Ger *bummeln*, go slowly⟧ [Inf.] **1** a vagrant **2** a loafer **3** a devotee, as of golf or skiing —*vi.* **bummed, bum'ming** [Inf.] to live as a bum or by begging —*vt.* [Slang] to get by begging *[to bum a cigarette]* —*adj.* **bum'mer, bum'mest** [Slang] **1** poor in quality **2** false **3** lame —**bum someone out** [Slang] to annoy, depress, bore, etc. someone —**on the bum** [Inf.] **1** living as a vagrant **2** out of repair

**bum·ble** (bum'bəl) *vi.* **-bled, -bling** to blunder — *vt.* to bungle or botch —**bum'bler** *n.*

**bum'ble·bee'** *n.* [< ME *bomben,* to buzz] a large, hairy, yellow-and-black bee

**bummed** *adj.* [< BUM] [Slang] depressed, upset, annoyed, etc.: usually with *out*

**bum·mer** (bum'ər) *n.* [Slang] an unpleasant experience

**bump** (bump) *vt., vi.* [echoic] to collide (with) or hit (against) with a jolt —*n.* **1** a knock; light jolt **2** a swelling, esp. one caused by a blow —**bump into** [Inf.] to meet unexpectedly —**bump off** [Slang] to murder —**bump'y, -i·er, -i·est,** *adj.*

**bump'er**[1] *n.* a device to absorb the shock of a collision; esp., either of the bars at the front and rear of a motor vehicle

**bump'er**[2] *adj.* [prob. < obs. *bombard,* liquor jug] unusually abundant *[a bumper crop]*

**bumper sticker** a gummed paper with a printed slogan, witticism, etc., for sticking on a vehicle's bumper

**bump·kin** (bump'kin) *n.* [prob. < MDu *bommekijn,* small cask] an awkward or simple person from the country

**bump'tious** (-shəs) *adj.* [prob. < BUMP] disagreeably conceited or forward —**bump'tious·ly** *adv.* — **bump'tious·ness** *n.*

**bun** (bun) *n.* [prob. < OFr *buigne,* a swelling] **1** a small roll made of bread dough, sometimes sweetened **2** hair worn in a roll or knot

**bunch** (bunch) *n.* [< Fl *boudje,* little bundle] **1** a cluster of similar things growing or grouped together **2** [Inf.] a group of people —*vt., vi.* to collect into a bunch —**bunch'y, -i·er, -i·est,** *adj.*

**bun·combe** (buŋ'kəm) *n.* [after *Buncombe* county, NC] [Inf.] BUNKUM

**bun·dle** (bun'dəl) *n.* [MDu *bondel*] **1** a number of things bound together **2** a package **3** a bunch; collection —*vt.* **-dled, -dling 1** to make into a bundle **2** to hustle *(away, off, out,* or *into)* —**bundle up** to dress warmly

**Bundt** (bunt, boont) *trademark for* a deep cake pan with a tube in the center and grooved sides — *adj.* [*often* **b-**] designating or baked in such a pan

**bung** (buŋ) *n.* [< MDu *bonge*] a stopper for a bunghole

**bun·ga·low** (buŋ'gə lō') *n.* [< Hindi *bānglā,* thatched house] a small house or cottage, usually of one story and an attic

**bun·gee cord** (bun'jē) elasticized cord used as to secure luggage or to hold persons leaping for sport from great heights

**bung·hole** (buŋ'hōl') *n.* a hole in a barrel or keg for pouring in or drawing out liquid

**bun·gle** (buŋ'gəl) *vt., vi.* **-gled, -gling** [< ?] to do or make (something) badly or clumsily —*n.* **1** a bungling **2** a bungled piece of work —**bun'gler** *n.* —**bung'ling·ly** *adv.*

**bun·ion** (bun'yən) *n.* [< OFr: see BUN] an inflamed swelling at the base of the big toe

**bunk**[1] (buŋk) *n.* [prob. < Scand cognate of BENCH] **1** a shelflike bed built against a wall, as in a ship **2** [Inf.] any sleeping place —*vi.* to sleep in a bunk —*vt.* to provide a sleeping place for

**bunk**[2] (buŋk) *n.* [Slang] *short for* BUNKUM

**bunk'er** *n.* [Scot < ?] **1** a large bin, as for a ship's fuel **2** an underground fortification **3** a sand trap or other area serving as a hazard on a golf course

**bunk'house'** *n.* a barracks for ranch hands

**bun·kum** (buŋ'kəm) *n.* [respelling of BUNCOMBE] [Inf.] empty, insincere talk

**bun·ny** (bun'ē) *n., pl.* **-nies** [dim. of dial. *bun*] a rabbit: a child's term

**buns** (bunz) *pl.n.* [Slang] the human buttocks

**Bun·sen burner** (bun'sən) [after R. W. *Bunsen,* 19th-c. Ger chemist] a small tubular gas burner that produces a hot, blue flame

**bunt** (bunt) *vt., vi.* [< ? ME *bounten,* to return] *Baseball* to bat (a pitch) lightly without swinging so that it rolls within the infield —*n.* a bunted ball

**bun·ting**[1] (bun'tiŋ) *n.* [< ? ME *bonten,* sift] **1** a thin cloth for making flags, etc. **2** decorative flags

**bun·ting**[2] (bun'tiŋ) *n.* [ME] a small, brightly colored, short-billed bird

**buoy** (boo'ē, boi) *n.* [< L *boia,* fetter] **1** a floating object anchored in water to warn of a hazard, etc. **2** a ring-shaped life preserver —*vt.* [< Sp *boyar,* to float] **1** to mark with a buoy **2** to keep afloat **3** to lift up in spirits

**buoy·ant** (boi'ənt; *also* boo'yənt) *adj.* [< ? Sp *boyar,* to float] **1** having the ability or tendency to float **2** cheerful —**buoy'an·cy** *n.*

**bur** (bur) *n.* [< Scand] **1** a rough, prickly seed capsule of certain plants **2** a plant with burs **3** BURR[1] & BURR[2]

**Bur** *abbrev.* Bureau

**bur·den**[1] (burd'n) *n.* [< OE *byrthen*] **1** anything that is carried; load **2** heavy load, as of work, care, or duty **3** the carrying capacity of a ship — *vt.* to put a burden on; oppress —**bur'den·some** *adj.*

**bur·den**[2] (burd'n) *n.* [< OFr *bourdon,* a humming] **1** a chorus or refrain of a song **2** a repeated, central idea; theme

**bur·dock** (bur'däk') *n.* [BUR + DOCK[3]] a plant with large leaves and purple-flowered heads with prickles

**bu·reau** (byoor'ō) *n., pl.* **-reaus** or **-reaux** (-ōz) [Fr, desk] **1** a chest of drawers, as for clothing **2** an agency **3** a government department

**bu·reauc·ra·cy** (byoo rä'krə sē) *n., pl.* **-cies 1** government by departmental officials following an inflexible routine **2** the officials collectively **3** inflexible governmental routine **4** the concentration of authority in administrative bureaus —**bu·reau·crat** (byoor'ə krat') *n.* —**bu'reau·crat'ic** *adj.* —**bu'reau·crat'i·cal·ly** *adv.*

**bu·reauc'ra·tize'** (-tīz') *vt., vi.* **-tized', -tiz'ing** to develop into a bureaucracy —**bu·reauc'ra·ti·za'tion** *n.*

**burg** (burg) *n.* [Inf.] a quiet or dull town

**bur·geon** (bur'jən) *vi.* [< OFr *burjon,* a bud] **1** to put forth buds, etc. **2** to grow or develop rapidly

**bur·ger** (bur'gər) *n.* [Inf.] a hamburger, cheeseburger, etc.

**-bur·ger** (bur'gər) *combining form* sandwich of ground meat, etc. *[hamburger]*

**burgh** (burg; *Scot* bu'rə) *n.* [Scot var. of BOROUGH] **1** [Brit.] a borough **2** in Scotland, a chartered town

**burgh·er** (bur'gər) *n.* a citizen of a town

**bur·glar** (bur'glər) *n.* [< OFr *burgeor*] one who commits burglary

**bur'glar·ize'** *vt.* **-ized', -iz'ing** to commit burglary in

**bur'gla·ry** (-glə rē) *n., pl.* **-ries** the act of breaking into a building to commit a felony, as theft, or a misdemeanor

**bur·gle** (bur'gəl) *vt., vi.* **-gled, -gling** [Inf.] to burglarize or commit burglary

**bur·go·mas·ter** (bur'gō mas'tər, -gə-) *n.* [< MDu *burg,* town + *meester,* master] the mayor of a town in the Netherlands, Flanders, Austria, or Germany

**Bur·gun·dy** (bur'gən dē) *n., pl.* **-dies** [*often* **b-**] a red or white wine, typically dry, orig. made in Burgundy, a region in E France —**Bur·gun·di·an** (bər gun'dē ən) *adj., n.*

**bur·i·al** (ber'ē əl) *n.* the burying of a dead body in a grave, tomb, etc.

**Bur·ki·na Fa·so** (boor kē′nə fä′sō) country in W Africa: 105,839 sq. mi.; pop. 7,967,000

**burl** (burl) *n.* ⟦< OFr *bourle,* ends of threads⟧ 1 a knot in thread or yarn that makes cloth look nubby 2 a knot on some tree trunks 3 veneer from wood with burls —**burled** *adj.*

**bur·lap** (bur′lap′) *n.* ⟦< ? ME *borel*⟧ a coarse cloth of jute or hemp

**bur·lesque** (bər lesk′) *n.* ⟦Fr < It *burla,* a jest⟧ 1 any broadly comic or satirical imitation; parody 2 a sort of vaudeville with low comedy, striptease acts, etc. —*vt., vi.* -**lesqued′, -lesqu′ing** to imitate comically

**bur·ley** (bur′lē) *n.* ⟦< ?⟧ [*also* B-] a thin-leaved, light-colored tobacco grown in Kentucky, etc.

**bur·ly** (bur′lē) *adj.* -**li·er, -li·est** ⟦ME *borlich,* excellent⟧ 1 big and strong 2 hearty in manner

**Bur·ma** (bur′mə) *former name for* MYANMAR — **Bur·mese** (bər mēz′), *pl.* -**mese′,** *adj., n.*

**burn** (burn) *vt.* **burned** *or* **burnt, burn′ing** ⟦< OE *beornan,* to be on fire⟧ 1 to set on fire, as in order to produce heat, light, or power 2 to destroy by fire 3 to injure or damage by fire, acid, etc. 4 to consume as fuel 5 to sunburn 6 to cause (a hole, etc.) as by fire 7 to cause a sensation of heat in 8 to transform (body fat, etc.) into energy 9 [Slang] to cheat or trick ⟦I got *burned* in that deal⟧ —*vi.* 1 to be on fire 2 to give out light or heat 3 to be destroyed or injured by fire or heat 4 to feel hot 5 to be excited —*n.* 1 an injury or damage caused by fire, heat, etc. 2 the process or result of burning —**burn down** to burn to the ground —**burn out** to exhaust or become exhausted from overwork, etc. —**burn up** [Slang] to make or become angry —**burn′a·ble** *adj., n.*

**burn′er** *n.* the part of a stove, furnace, etc. from which the flame comes

**bur·nish** (bur′nish) *vt., vi.* ⟦< OFr *brunir,* make brown⟧ to make or become shiny by rubbing —*n.* a gloss or polish —**bur′nish·er** *n.*

**bur·noose** (bər n̅o̅o̅s′) *n.* ⟦< Ar *burnus*⟧ a hooded cloak worn by Arabs

**burn·out** (burn′out′) *n.* 1 the point at which a rocket's fuel is burned up and the rocket enters free flight or is jettisoned 2 a state of emotional exhaustion from mental stress

**Burns** (burnz), **Rob·ert** (rä′bərt) 1759-96; Scot. poet

**burnt** (burnt) *vt., vi. alt. pt. & pp. of* BURN

**burp** (burp) *n., vi.* ⟦echoic⟧ belch —*vt.* to cause (a baby) to belch

**burr**[1] (bur) *n.* ⟦var. of BUR⟧ 1 a bur 2 a rough edge left on metal, etc. by cutting or drilling —*vt.* to form a rough edge on

**burr**[2] (bur) *n.* ⟦prob. echoic⟧ 1 the trilling of *r,* as in Scottish speech 2 a whir

**bur·ri·to** (bə rē′tō) *n., pl.* -**tos** ⟦MexSp < Sp, little burro⟧ a Mexican dish consisting of a flour tortilla wrapped around a filling of meat, cheese, fried beans, etc.

**bur·ro** (bur′ō) *n., pl.* -**ros** ⟦Sp < LL *burricus,* small horse⟧ a donkey

**bur·row** (bur′ō) *n.* ⟦see BOROUGH⟧ 1 a hole dug in the ground by an animal 2 any similar hole —*vi.* 1 to make a burrow 2 to live or hide in a burrow 3 to search, as if by digging —*vt.* 1 to make burrows in 2 to make by burrowing

**bur·sa** (bur′sə) *n., pl.* -**sae** (-sē) *or* -**sas** ⟦< Gr *byrsa,* a hide⟧ *Anat.* a sac or cavity with a lubricating fluid, as between a tendon and bone

**bur·sar** (bur′sər) *n.* ⟦< ML *bursa,* a purse⟧ a treasurer, as of a college

**bur·si·tis** (bər sīt′is) *n.* ⟦< BURSA + -ITIS⟧ inflammation of a bursa

**burst** (burst) *vi.* **burst, burst′ing** ⟦OE *berstan*⟧ 1 to come apart suddenly and violently; explode 2 to give sudden vent; break (*into* tears, etc.) 3 to appear, start, etc. suddenly 4 *a)* to be as full or crowded as possible *b)* to be filled (*with* pride, etc.) —*vt.* to cause to burst —*n.* 1 a bursting 2 a break or rupture 3 a sudden action or effort; spurt 4 a volley of shots

**Bu·run·di** (boo roon′dē, -run′-) country in EC Africa, east of Democratic Republic of the Congo: 10,759 sq. mi.; pop. 5,293,000

**bur·y** (ber′ē) *vt.* -**ied, -y·ing** ⟦OE *byrgan*⟧ 1 to put (a dead body) into the earth, a tomb, etc. 2 to hide or cover 3 to put away 4 to immerse [to *bury* oneself in work]

**bus** (bus) *n., pl.* **bus′es** *or* **bus′ses** ⟦< (OMNI)BUS⟧ a large motor coach for many passengers, usually following a regular route —*vt.* **bused** *or* **bussed, bus′ing** *or* **bus′sing** 1 to transport by bus 2 to clear dirty dishes from —*vi.* 1 to go by bus 2 to do the work of a busboy

**bus′boy′** *n.* a restaurant worker who clears tables, brings water, etc.

**bus·by** (buz′bē) *n., pl.* -**bies** ⟦prob. < name *Busby*⟧ a tall fur hat worn with a full-dress uniform

**bush** (boosh) *n.* ⟦OE *busc*⟧ 1 a low woody plant with spreading branches; shrub 2 anything like a bush 3 uncleared land —*vi.* to grow thickly — **beat around the bush** to talk around a subject without getting to the point

**Bush** (boosh) 1 **George (Herbert Walker)** 1924- ; 41st president of the U.S. (1989-93) 2 **George W(alker)** 1946- ; 43d president of the U.S. (2001- ): son of George

**bushed** (boosht) *adj.* [Inf.] very tired; exhausted

**bush·el** (boosh′əl) *n.* ⟦< OFr *boisse,* grain measure⟧ a dry measure equal to 4 pecks or 32 quarts

**bush·ing** (boosh′iŋ) *n.* ⟦< MDu *busse,* box⟧ a removable metal lining for reducing friction on moving parts

**bush league** [Slang] a small or second-rate minor league, etc. —**bush′-league′** *adj.* —**bush leaguer**

**bush′man** (-mən) *n., pl.* -**men** (-mən) one who lives in the Australian bush

**bush′mas′ter** *n.* a large poisonous snake of Central and South America

**bush′whack′** *vt., vi.* to ambush —**bush′whack′er** *n.*

**bush·y** *adj.* -**i·er, -i·est** thick and spreading out like a bush

**bush′y-tailed′** *adj.* used mainly in **bright-eyed and bushy-tailed,** alert, eager, etc.

**bus·i·ly** (biz′ə lē) *adv.* in a busy manner

**busi·ness** (biz′nis) *n.* ⟦OE *bisignes:* see BUSY⟧ 1 one's work; occupation 2 a special task, duty, etc. 3 rightful concern [no one's *business* but his own] 4 a matter or activity 5 commerce; trade 6 a commercial or industrial establishment —*adj.* of or for business —**mean business** [Inf.] to be in earnest

**business administration** college studies covering finance, management, etc. to prepare for a business career

**business agent** a representative of a labor union local

**business card** a small card identifying one's business connection, given to clients, etc.

**business college** a school of typing, bookkeeping, etc.

**busi′ness·like′** *adj.* efficient, methodical, systematic, etc.

**busi′ness·man′** *n., pl.* -**men′** (-men′) a man in business, esp. as an owner —**busi′ness·wom′an,** *pl.* -**wom′en, fem.n.**

**business school** a school offering graduate courses in business administration

**bus·ing** *or* **bus·sing** (bus′iŋ) *n.* the transporting of children by bus to a school outside of their neighborhood, esp. so as to desegregate the school

**bus·kin** (bus′kin) *n.* ⟦? < MDu *brosekin,* small boot⟧ 1 a high, laced boot worn in ancient tragedy 2 tragic drama

**buss** (bus) *n., vt., vi.* ⟦prob. of echoic orig.⟧ [Now Chiefly Dial.] kiss

**bust**[1] (bust) *n.* ⟦< It *busto*⟧ 1 a sculpture of a person's head and shoulders 2 a woman's bosom

**bust**[2] (bust) [Inf.] *vt., vi.* ⟦< BURST⟧ 1 to burst or break **2** to make or become bankrupt or demoted **3** to hit **4** to arrest —*n.* **1** a failure **2** financial collapse **3** a punch **4** a spree **5** an arrest —**bust′ed** *adj.*

**bus·tle**[1] (bus′əl) *vi., vt.* **-tled, -tling** [< ME *busken*, prepare] to hurry busily —*n.* busy and noisy activity

**bus·tle**[2] (bus′əl) *n.* [< ?] a padding formerly worn to fill out the upper back of a woman's skirt

**bus·y** (biz′ē) *adj.* **-i·er, -i·est** [OE *bisig*] **1** active; at work **2** full of activity **3** in use, as a telephone **4** too detailed —*vt.* **bus′ied, bus′y·ing** to make or keep busy —**bus′y·ness** *n.*

**bus′y·bod′y** *n., pl.* **-ies** a meddler in the affairs of others

**but** (but) *prep.* [OE *butan*, without] except; save [nobody went *but* me] —*conj.* **1** yet; still [it's good, *but* not great] **2** on the contrary [I am old, *but* you are young] **3** unless [it never rains *but* it pours] **4** that [I don't doubt *but* you're right] **5** that . . . not [I never gamble *but* I lose] —*adv.* **1** only [if I had *but* known] **2** merely [he is *but* a child] —*pron.* who . . . not; which . . . not [not a man *but* felt it] —**but for** if it were not for

**bu·tane** (byoo′tān′) *n.* [ult. < L *butyrum*, butter] a hydrocarbon used as a fuel, etc.

**butch** (booch) *adj.* [< ? fol.] [Slang] masculine: sometimes said of a lesbian —*n.* [Inf.] BUZZ CUT

**butch·er** (booch′ər) *n.* [< OFr *bouc*, he-goat] **1** one whose work is killing and dressing animals for meat **2** one who cuts meat for sale **3** a brutal killer —*vt.* **1** to kill or dress (animals) for meat **2** to kill brutally or senselessly **3** to botch —**butch′er·y,** *pl.* **-ies,** *n.*

**but·ler** (but′lər) *n.* [< OFr *bouteille*, bottle] a manservant, usually the head servant of a household

**butt**[1] (but) *n.* [< ?] **1** the thick end of anything **2** a stub or stump, as of a cigar **3** a target **4** an object of ridicule **5** [Slang] a cigarette —*vt., vi.* to join end to end

**butt**[2] (but) *vt., vi.* [< OFr *buter*, thrust against] **1** to ram with the head **2** to project —*n.* a butting —**butt in** (or **into**) [Inf.] to mix into (another's business, etc.)

**butt**[3] (but) *n.* [< LL *buttis*, cask] a large cask for wine or beer

**butte** (byoot) *n.* [Fr, mound] a steep hill with a flat top, surrounded by a plain

**but·ter** (but′ər) *n.* [< Gr *bous*, cow + *tyros*, cheese] **1** the solid, yellowish, edible fat that results from churning cream **2** any substance somewhat like butter —*vt.* **1** to spread with butter **2** [Inf.] to flatter: often with *up* —**but′ter·y** *adj.*

**butter bean** a light-colored bean, as a lima bean or wax bean

**but′ter·cup′** *n.* a plant with yellow, cup-shaped flowers

**but′ter·fat′** *n.* the fatty part of milk, from which butter is made

**but′ter·fin′gers** *n.* [Inf.] one who often fumbles and drops things

**but′ter·fly′** *n., pl.* **-flies′** [OE *buttorfleoge*] an insect with a slender body and four broad, usually brightly colored wings

**but′ter·milk′** *n.* **1** the liquid left after churning butter from milk **2** a drink made from skim milk

**but′ter·nut′** *n.* **1** a walnut tree of E North America **2** its edible, oily nut

**but′ter·scotch′** *n.* **1** a hard, sticky candy made with brown sugar, butter, etc. **2** the flavor of this candy **3** a syrup with this flavor

**but·tock** (but′ək) *n.* [< OE *buttuc*, end] **1** either of the fleshy, rounded parts behind the hips **2** [*pl.*] the rump

**but·ton** (but′'n) *n.* [< OFr *boton*] **1** any small disk or knob used as a fastening, ornament, etc., as on a garment **2** anything small and shaped like a button —*vt., vi.* to fasten with a button or buttons

**but′ton-down′** *adj.* **1** designating a collar, as on

a shirt, fastened down by small buttons **2** conservative, unimaginative, etc.

**but′ton·hole′** *n.* a slit or loop through which a button is inserted —*vt.* **-holed′, -hol′ing 1** to make buttonholes in **2** to detain and talk to

**but·tress** (bu′tris) *n.* [see BUTT[2]] **1** a structure built against a wall to support or reinforce it **2** a support or prop —*vt.* to prop up; bolster

**bux·om** (buk′səm) *adj.* [ME, humble] having a shapely, full-bosomed figure: said of a woman

**buy** (bī) *vt.* **bought, buy′ing** [OE *bycgan*] **1** to get by paying money; purchase **2** to get by an exchange [*buy* victory with human lives] **3** to bribe **4** [Slang] to accept as true [I can't *buy* this excuse] —*n.* **1** anything bought **2** [Inf.] something worth its price —**buy in** [Slang] to pay money so as to participate —**buy into** [Slang] BUY (*vt.* 4) —**buy off** to bribe —**buy out** to buy all the stock, rights, etc. of —**buy up** to buy all that is available of

**buy′back′** *n. Finance* the buying by a corporation of its own stock to reduce the outstanding shares

**buy′er** *n.* **1** one who buys; consumer **2** one whose work is to buy merchandise for a retail store

**buy′out′** *n.* the outright purchase of a business, as by the employees or management

**buzz** (buz) *vi.* [echoic] **1** to hum like a bee **2** to gossip **3** to be filled with noisy activity or talk —*vt.* **1** to fly an airplane low over (a building, etc.) **2** to signal with a buzzer —*n.* **1** a sound like a bee's hum **2** [Inf.] BUZZ CUT

**buz·zard** (buz′ərd) *n.* [< L *buteo*, kind of hawk] **1** a kind of hawk that is slow and heavy in flight **2** TURKEY VULTURE

**buzz cut** [Inf.] a man's very short haircut

**buzz′er** *n.* an electrical device that makes a buzzing sound as a signal

**buzz saw** a saw with teeth around the edge of a large disk fixed on a motor-driven shaft

**bx** *abbrev.* box

**by** (bī) *prep.* [OE *be, bi*] **1** near; at [sit *by* the fire] **2** *a*) in or during [to travel *by* day] *b*) not later than [be back *by* noon] **3** *a*) through; via [to Boston *by* Route 6] *b*) past; beyond [he walked right *by* me] **4** toward [east *by* northeast] **5** within a distance of [missed *by* a foot] **6** in behalf of [she did well *by* me] **7** through the agency of [gained *by* fraud] **8** according to [to go *by* the book] **9** at the rate of [getting dark *by* degrees] **10** following in series [marching two *by* two] **11** *a*) in or to the amount of [apples *by* the peck] *b*) and in another dimension [two *by* four] *c*) using (the given number) as multiplier or divisor —*adv.* **1** close at hand [stand *by*] **2** away; aside [to put money *by*] **3** past [she sped *by*] **4** at the place specified [stop *by* on your way] —**by and by** soon or eventually —**by and large** considering everything —**by the by** incidentally

**by-** *prefix* **1** near **2** secondary [*byproduct*]

**by-and-by** (bī′ən bī′) *n.* a future time

**bye** (bī) *n.* [var. of BY] the privilege, granted a contestant in a tournament with an uneven number of participants, of not being paired with another contestant in the first round

**bye-bye** (bī′bī′) *n., interj.* [Inf.] goodbye

**by·gone** (bī′gôn′) *adj.* past; former —*n.* anything gone or past

**by′law′** *n.* [< ME *bi*, village + *laue*, law] any of a set of rules adopted by an organization or assembly for its own meetings or affairs

**by′line′** *n.* a line identifying the writer of a newspaper or magazine article

**by′pass′** *n.* **1** a way, pipe, channel, etc. between two points that avoids or is auxiliary to the main way **2** a surgical operation to allow fluid to pass around a diseased or blocked part or organ —*vt.* **1** to detour **2** to furnish with a bypass **3** to ignore

**by′path′** or **by′-path′** *n.* a byway

**by′play′** *n.* action, gestures, etc. going on aside from the main action or conversation

**by'prod'uct** or **by'-prod'uct** *n.* anything produced in the course of making another thing

**By·ron** (bī'rən), George Gor·don (jôrj gôrd''n) 1788-1824; Eng. poet

**by'stand'er** *n.* a person who stands near but does not participate

**byte** (bīt) *n.* ⟦arbitrary formation⟧ a string of binary digits (*bits*), usually eight, operated on as a basic unit by a digital computer

**by'way'** *n.* a secondary road or path, esp. one not much used

**by'word'** *n.* **1** a proverb **2** one well-known for some quality **3** an object of scorn or ridicule **4** a favorite word or phrase

**Byz·an·tine Empire** (biz'ən tēn', -tīn'; bi zan'tin) empire (A.D. 395-1453) in SE Europe & SW Asia

# C

**c** or **C** (sē) *n.,* *pl.* **c's, C's** the third letter of the English alphabet

**C¹** (sē) *n.* **1** a Roman numeral for 100 **2** *Educ.* a grade for average work **3** *Music* the first tone in the scale of C major

**C²** *abbrev.* **1** carat(s) **2** *Baseball* catcher **3** Catholic **4** Celsius (or centigrade) **5** cent(s) **6** *Sports* center **7** centimeter(s) **8** Central **9** century **10** chapter **11** circa: also **ca** **12** College **13** copyright **14** cup(s) **15** cycle(s) Also, except 3, 4, 8, & 12, **c**

**C³** *Chem. symbol for* carbon

**Ca** *Chem. symbol for* calcium

**CA** California

**cab** (kab) *n.* ⟦< Fr *cabriole,* a leap⟧ **1** a carriage, esp. one for public hire **2** TAXICAB **3** the place in a truck, crane, etc. where the operator sits —*vi.* **cabbed, cab'bing** [Inf.] to take or drive a taxicab

**ca·bal** (kə bäl') *n.* ⟦Fr, intrigue⟧ **1** a small group joined in a secret intrigue **2** an intrigue; plot

**cab·a·la** (kab'ə lə, kə bä'lə) *n.* ⟦< Heb *kabala,* tradition⟧ **1** a Jewish mystical movement **2** any esoteric or secret doctrine

**ca·bal·le·ro** (kab'ə ler'ō, -əl yer'ō) *n., pl.* **-ros** ⟦Sp⟧ **1** a Spanish gentleman **2** [Southwest] *a)* a horseman *b)* a lady's escort

**ca·ban·a** (kə ban'ə, -bä'nə) *n.* ⟦Sp < LL *capanna*⟧ **1** a cabin or hut **2** a small bathhouse

**cab·a·ret** (kab'ə rā') *n.* ⟦Fr, tavern⟧ a cafe with musical entertainment

**cab·bage** (kab'ij) *n.* ⟦OFr *caboche* < ?⟧ a vegetable with thick leaves formed into a round head

**cab·by** or **cab·bie** (kab'ē) *n., pl.* **-bies** [Inf.] one who drives a cab

**ca·ber·net** (kab'ər nā') *n.* [also C-] a dry red wine; esp., CABERNET SAUVIGNON

**cabernet sau·vi·gnon** (sō vē nyōn') [also C- S-] a fragrant, dry red wine

**cab·in** (kab'in) *n.* ⟦< LL *capanna,* hut⟧ **1** a small, crudely or simply built house; hut **2** a room on a ship or boat **3** the space for passengers, crew, or cargo in an aircraft

**cab·i·net** (kab'ə nit) *n.* ⟦Fr, prob. ult. < L *cavea,* cage⟧ **1** a case with drawers or shelves **2** a case holding a TV, radio, etc. **3** [often C-] a body of official advisors to a chief executive

**cab'i·net·mak'er** *n.* a maker of fine furniture

**cab'i·net·work'** *n.* articles made by a cabinetmaker: also **cab'i·net·ry**

**cabin fever** a condition of increased anxiety caused by being confined or isolated

**ca·ble** (kā'bəl) *n.* ⟦< L *capere,* to take hold⟧ **1** a thick, heavy rope, often of wire strands **2** a bundle of insulated wires to carry an electric current **3** a cablegram **4** CABLE TV —*vt.* **-bled, -bling** **1** to fasten with a cable **2** to send a cablegram to — *vi.* to send a cablegram

**cable car** a car drawn by a moving cable, as up a steep incline

**ca'ble·cast'** *vt.* **-cast', -cast'ing** to transmit to receivers by coaxial cable —*n.* a program that is cablecast

**ca'ble·gram'** *n.* a message sent by undersea cable

**cable TV** a TV system in which various antennas receive local and distant signals and transmit them by cable to subscribers' receivers

**cab·o·chon** (kab'ə shän') *n.* ⟦Fr < *caboche,* head⟧ any precious stone cut in convex shape

**ca·bood·le** (kə bōōd''l) *n.* ⟦< BOODLE⟧ [Inf.] lot; group /the whole *caboodle]*

**ca·boose** (kə bōōs') *n.* ⟦MDu *kambuis,* cabin house⟧ the car at the rear of a freight train, used by the crew when eating, sleeping, etc.

**ca·ca·o** (kə kā'ō, -kä'-) *n., pl.* **-os** ⟦Sp < AmInd (Mexico)⟧ **1** the seed of a tropical American tree from which cocoa and chocolate are made: also **cacao bean** **2** this tree

**cache** (kash) *n.* ⟦Fr < L *cogere,* to collect⟧ **1** a safe place in which stores of food, supplies, etc. are hidden **2** anything so hidden —*vt.* **cached, cach'ing** to place in a cache

**cache·pot** (kash'pät, -pō') *n.* ⟦Fr < *cacher,* to hide⟧ a decorative jar for holding potted plants: also **cache pot**

**ca·chet** (ka shā') *n.* ⟦Fr⟧ **1** a stamp or official seal, as on a document **2** any sign of official approval, authenticity, superior quality, etc. **3** distinction; prestige

**cack·le** (kak'əl) *vi.* **-led, -ling** ⟦echoic⟧ **1** to make the shrill, broken vocal sounds of a hen **2** to laugh or chatter with similar sounds —*n.* a cackling

**ca·coph·o·ny** (kə käf'ə nē) *n., pl.* **-nies** ⟦< Gr *kakos,* bad + *phōnē,* voice⟧ harsh, jarring sound; discord —**ca·coph'o·nous** *adj.*

**cac·tus** (kak'təs) *n., pl.* **-tus·es** or **-ti'** (-tī') ⟦< Gr *kaktos,* kind of thistle⟧ any of various desert plants with fleshy stems and spinelike leaves

**cad** (kad) *n.* ⟦< CADET⟧ a man whose behavior is not gentlemanly —**cad'dish** *adj.* —**cad'dish·ly** *adv.* —**cad'dish·ness** *n.*

**ca·dav·er** (kə dav'ər) *n.* ⟦L, prob. < *cadere,* to fall⟧ a corpse, as for dissection

**ca·dav'er·ous** *adj.* ⟦< L⟧ of or like a cadaver; esp., pale, ghastly, etc.

**CAD/CAM** (kad'kam') *n.* ⟦*C(omputer-)A(ided) D(esign)/C(omputer-)A(ided) M(anufacturing)*⟧ design and manufacturing by means of a computer system, as for complex wiring diagrams

**cad·die** (kad'ē) *n.* ⟦Scot form of Fr *cadet:* see CADET⟧ one who attends a golfer, carrying the clubs, etc. —*vi.* **-died, -dy·ing** to act as a caddie

**cad·dy¹** (kad'ē) *n., pl.* **-dies** ⟦< Malay *kātī,* unit of weight⟧ a small container for holding or storing

**cad·dy²** (kad'ē) *n., vi.* CADDIE

**-cade** (kād) ⟦< (CAVAL)CADE⟧ *suffix* procession, parade *[motorcade]*

**ca·dence** (kād'ns) *n.* ⟦< L *cadere,* to fall⟧ **1** fall of the voice in speaking **2** any rhythmic flow of sound **3** measured movement, as in marching

**ca·den·za** (kə den'zə) *n.* ⟦It: see prec.⟧ an elaborate passage for the solo instrument in a concerto

**ca·det** (kə det') *n.* ⟦Fr < L dim. of *caput,* head⟧ **1** a student in training at an armed forces academy **2** any trainee, as a practice teacher

**cadge** (kaj) *vt., vi.* **cadged, cadg'ing** ⟦< ?⟧ to beg or get by begging; sponge —**cadg'er** *n.*

**cad·mi·um** (kad'mē əm) *n.* ⟦< L *cadmia,* zinc ore

(with which it occurs)] a silver-white, metallic chemical element used in alloys, pigments, etc.

**ca·dre** (ka′drē, -drā; kä′-) *n.* [< Fr < L *quadrum*, a square] a nucleus around which an expanded organization, as a military unit, can be built

**ca·du·ce·us** (kə dōō′sē əs) *n., pl.* **-ce·i′** (-sē ī′) [L] the winged staff of Mercury: now a symbol of the medical profession

**Cae·sar**[1] (sē′zər) *n.* [after fol.] **1** the title of the Roman emperors from 27 B.C. to A.D. 138 **2** [*often* **c-**] any emperor or dictator

**Cae·sar**[2] (sē′zər), **Jul·ius** (jōōl′yəs) 100?-44 B.C.; Rom. general & dictator (49-44)

**Cae·sar·e·an section** (sə zer′ē ən) CESAREAN (SECTION)

**cae·su·ra** (si zyoor′ə, -zhoor′ə) *n., pl.* **-ras** or **-rae** (-ē) [L < *caedere*, to cut down] a break or pause in a line of verse, usually in the middle

CADUCEUS

**ca·fe** or **ca·fé** (kə fā′, ka-) *n.* [Fr, coffeehouse] a small restaurant or a barroom, nightclub, etc.

**caf·e·te·ri·a** (kaf′ə tir′ē ə) *n.* [AmSp, coffee store] a self-service restaurant

**caf·feine** or **caf·fein** (ka fēn′, kaf′ēn′) *n.* [Ger *kaffein*] the alkaloid present in coffee, tea, cola nuts, etc.: it is a stimulant

**caf·tan** (kaf′tən, -tan′) *n.* [Turk *qaftān*] **1** a long-sleeved robe, worn in eastern Mediterranean countries **2** a long, loose dress with wide sleeves

**cage** (kāj) *n.* [< L *cavea*, hollow place] **1** a structure of wires, bars, etc., for confining animals **2** any openwork structure or frame —*vt.* **caged**, **cag′ing** to put or confine, as in a cage

**cag·er** (kāj′ər) *n.* [Slang] a basketball player

**ca·gey** or **ca·gy** (kā′jē) *adj.* **-gi·er**, **-gi·est** [< ?] [Inf.] **1** sly; tricky; cunning **2** cautious —**ca′gi·ly** *adv.* —**ca′gi·ness** *n.*

**ca·hoots** (kə hōōts′) *pl.n.* [< ?] [Slang] used chiefly in **in cahoots** (**with**), in league (with): usually applied to questionable dealing, etc.

**Cain** (kān) *n. Bible* oldest son of Adam and Eve: he killed his brother Abel —**raise Cain** [Slang] to create a great commotion, cause trouble, etc.

**cairn** (kern) *n.* [Scot] a conical heap of stones built as a monument

**Cai·ro** (kī′rō) capital of Egypt: pop. 5,084,000

**cais·son** (kā′sən) *n.* [Fr < L *capsa*, box] **1** a two-wheeled wagon with a chest for ammunition **2** a watertight box for underwater construction work

**cai·tiff** (kāt′if) *n.* [< L *captivus*, CAPTIVE] a mean or cowardly person —*adj.* mean or cowardly

**ca·jole** (kə jōl′) *vt., vi.* **-joled′**, **-jol′ing** [< Fr] to coax with flattery and insincere talk —**ca·jol′er** *n.* —**ca·jol′er·y** *n.*

**Ca·jun** or **Ca·jan** (kā′jən) *n.* **1** a native of Louisiana of Canadian French ancestry **2** the dialect of Cajuns —*adj.* of spicy cooking

**cake** (kāk) *n.* [< ON] **1** a small, flat mass of baked or fried dough, batter, hashed food, etc. **2** a mixture of flour, eggs, sugar, etc. baked as in a loaf and often covered with icing **3** a shaped, solid mass, as of soap —*vt., vi.* **caked**, **cak′ing** to form into a hard mass or crust —**take the cake** [Inf.] to be the prime example of something: usually used ironically —**cak′y** or **cak′ey**, **-i·er**, **-i·est**, *adj.*

**cal** *abbrev.* **1** caliber **2** calorie(s)

**cal·a·bash** (kal′ə bash′) *n.* [< Sp *calabaza*] **1** the gourdlike fruit of a tropical American tree **2** *a*) the bottle-shaped, gourdlike fruit of a tropical vine *b*) a large smoking pipe made from it **3** a gourd

**cal·a·boose** (kal′ə bōōs′) *n.* [Sp *calabozo*] [Dial. or Old Slang] a prison; jail

**ca·la·ma·ri** (kä′lə mä′rē) *n.* squid cooked as food, esp. as an Italian dish

**cal·a·mine** (kal′ə mīn′) *n.* [Fr < L *cadmia*, zinc ore] a zinc oxide powder used in skin lotions

**ca·lam·i·ty** (kə lam′ə tē) *n., pl.* **-ties** [< L *calamitas*] a great misfortune; disaster —**ca·lam′i·tous** *adj.*

**cal·car·e·ous** (kal ker′ē əs) *adj.* [< L *calx*, lime] of or like limestone, calcium, or lime

**cal·ci·fy** (kal′sə fī′) *vt., vi.* **-fied′**, **-fy′ing** [< L *calx*, lime + -FY] to change into a hard, stony substance by the deposit of lime or calcium salts —**cal′ci·fi·ca′tion** *n.*

**cal′ci·mine′** (-mīn′) *n.* [< L *calx*, lime] a white liquid, used as a wash for plastered surfaces —*vt.* **-mined′**, **-min′ing** to coat with calcimine

**cal·cine** (kal′sīn′) *vt., vi.* **-cined′**, **-cin′ing** [< L *calx*, lime] to change to an ashy powder by heat

**cal·cite** (kal′sīt′) *n.* CALCIUM CARBONATE

**cal·ci·um** (kal′sē əm) *n.* [< L *calx*, lime] a soft, silver-white, metallic chemical element found combined in limestone, chalk, etc.

**calcium carbonate** a white powder or crystalline compound found in limestone, chalk, marble, bones, shells, etc.

**cal·cu·late** (kal′kyə lāt′) *vt.* **-lat·ed**, **-lat·ing** [< L *calculare*, reckon] **1** to determine by using mathematics; compute **2** to determine by reasoning; estimate **3** to plan or intend for a purpose —*vi.* **1** to compute **2** to rely (*on*) —**cal′cu·la·ble** (-lə bəl) *adj.*

**cal·cu·lat·ed** *adj.* deliberately planned or carefully considered —**cal′cu·lat·ed·ly** *adv.*

**cal·cu·lat·ing** *adj.* shrewd or scheming

**cal·cu·la·tion** *n.* **1** a calculating **2** something deduced by calculating **3** careful planning or forethought —**cal′cu·la·tive** *adj.*

**cal·cu·la·tor** *n.* **1** one who calculates **2** a device for the automatic performance of mathematical operations

**cal·cu·lus** (-ləs) *n., pl.* **-li′** (-lī′) or **-lus·es** [L, pebble used in counting] **1** an abnormal stony mass in the body **2** *Math.* a system of calculation or analysis using special symbolic notation

**Cal·cut·ta** (kal kut′ə) seaport in NE India: pop. 9,194,000

**cal·de·ra** (kal der′ə) *n.* [Sp < L *caldarium*, room for hot baths] a broad, craterlike basin of a volcano

**cal·dron** (kôl′drən) *n.* [< L *calidus*, warm, hot] **1** a large kettle or boiler **2** a state of violent agitation

**cal·en·dar** (kal′ən dər) *n.* [< L *kalendarium*, account book] **1** a system of determining the length and divisions of a year **2** a table that shows the days, weeks, and months of a given year **3** a schedule, as of programs

**cal·en·der** (kal′ən dər) *n.* [< Gr *kylindros*, cylinder] a machine with rollers for giving paper, cloth, etc. a smooth or glossy finish

**calf**[1] (kaf) *n., pl.* **calves** [< OE *cealf*] **1** a young cow or bull **2** the young of some other large animals, as the elephant or seal **3** CALFSKIN

**calf**[2] (kaf) *n., pl.* **calves** [ON *kalfi*] the fleshy back part of the leg below the knee

**calf′skin′** *n.* soft leather made from the skin of a calf

**Cal·ga·ry** (kal′gə rē) city in S Alberta, Canada: pop. 768,000

**cal·i·ber** (kal′ə bər) *n.* [Fr & Sp, ult. < Gr *kalopodion*, shoemaker's last] **1** the diameter of a cylindrical body, esp. of a bullet or shell **2** the diameter of the bore of a gun **3** quality or ability Also, esp. Brit., **cal′i·bre**

**cal·i·brate** (kal′ə brāt′) *vt.* **-brat·ed**, **-brat·ing** **1** to determine the caliber of **2** to fix or correct the graduations of (a measuring instrument) —**cal′i·bra′tion** *n.* —**cal′i·bra′tor** *n.*

**cal·i·co** (kal′i kō′) *n., pl.* **-coes′** or **-cos′** [after Cali-

**cut**, city in India‖ a printed cotton fabric —*adj.* spotted like calico /a *calico* cat/

**Cal·i·for·nia** (kal′ə fôr′nyə) state of the SW U.S., on the Pacific: 155,973 sq. mi.; pop. 29,760,000; cap. Sacramento: abbrev. *CA* —**Cal′i·for′nian** *adj.*, *n.*

**cal·i·per** (kal′ə pər) *n.* ‖var. of CALIBER‖ **1** [*usually pl.*] an instrument consisting of a pair of hinged legs, for measuring thickness or diameter **2** a part of a braking system on a bicycle or motor vehicle

**ca·liph** (kā′lif; *also*, kal′if) *n.* ‖Ar *khalīfa*‖ supreme ruler: the title taken by Mohammed's successors as heads of Islam —**ca′liph·ate** (-ət, -āt′) *n.*

**cal·is·then·ics** (kal′is then′iks) *pl.n.* ‖< Gr *kallos*, beauty + *sthenos*, strength‖ athletic exercises — **cal′is·then′ic** *adj.*

**calk** (kôk) *vt.* CAULK —**calk′er** *n.*

**call** (kôl) *vt.* ‖< ON *kalla*‖ **1** to say in a loud tone; shout **2** to summon **3** to give or apply a name to **4** to describe as specified **5** to awaken **6** to telephone **7** to give orders for (a strike, etc.) **8** to stop (a game, etc.) **9** to demand payment of (a loan, etc.) **10** to expose (someone's bluff) by challenging it **11** *Poker* to equal (the preceding bet) or to equal the bet of (the last previous bettor) —*vi.* **1** to shout **2** to visit for a short while: often with *on* **3** to telephone —*n.* **1** a calling **2** a loud utterance **3** the distinctive cry of an animal or bird **4** a summons; invitation **5** an act of telephoning **6** CALLING (sense 3) **7** an economic demand, as for a product **8** need /no *call* for tears/ **9** a demand for payment **10** a brief visit **11** an option to buy a stock, commodity, etc. at a specified price and time **12** a referee's decision —**call down** [Inf.] to scold —**call for 1** to demand **2** to come and get — **call off** to cancel (a scheduled event) —**call up 1** to recall **2** to summon for duty **3** to telephone — **on call** available when summoned —**call′er** *n.*

**cal·la** (kal′ə) *n.* ‖< L, a plant (of uncert. kind)‖ a plant with a large, white leaf around a yellow flower spike: also **calla lily**

**call forwarding** a telephone service that allows incoming calls to be transferred automatically to another number

**call girl** a prostitute who is called by telephone to assignations

**cal·lig·ra·phy** (kə lig′rə fē) *n.* ‖< Gr *kallos*, beauty + *graphein*, write‖ artistic handwriting —**cal·lig′ra·pher** *n.* —**cal·li·graph·ic** (kal′ə graf′ik) *adj.*

**call′-in′** *adj.* of a radio or TV program whose audience members telephone to comment, ask questions, etc.

**call′ing** *n.* **1** the act of one that calls **2** one's work or profession **3** an inner urging toward some vocation

**calling card 1** a small card with one's name and address on it **2** a credit card for long-distance telephone calls

**cal·li·o·pe** (kə lī′ə pē′, kal′ē ōp′) *n.* ‖< Gr *kallos*, beauty + *ops*, voice‖ a keyboard instrument like an organ, having a series of steam whistles

**call letters** the letters, and sometimes numbers, that identify a radio or TV station

**cal·lous** (kal′əs) *adj.* ‖< L *callum*, hard skin‖ **1** hardened: usually **cal′loused 2** unfeeling —**cal·los·i·ty** (kə läs′ə tē) *n.* —**cal′lous·ly** *adv.* —**cal′lous·ness** *n.*

**cal·low** (kal′ō) *adj.* ‖OE *calu*, bare‖ immature; inexperienced —**cal′low·ness** *n.*

**cal·lus** (kal′əs) *n., pl.* **-lus·es** ‖L, var. of *callum*, hard skin‖ a hardened, thickened place on the skin

**call waiting** a telephone service that signals an incoming call to a person already talking and allows that person to take that call by putting the first call on hold

**calm** (käm) *n.* ‖< Gr *kauma*, heat‖ **1** lack of motion; stillness **2** lack of excitement; tranquillity —*adj.* **1** still; quiet **2** not excited; tranquil —

*vt., vi.* to make or become calm: often with *down* —**calm′ly** *adv.* —**calm′ness** *n.*

**ca·lor·ic** (kə lôr′ik) *adj.* of calories —**ca·lor′i·cal·ly** *adv.*

**cal·o·rie** (kal′ə rē) *n.* ‖Fr < L *calor*, heat‖ a unit for measuring heat, esp. for measuring the energy produced by food when oxidized in the body

**cal·o·rif·ic** (kal′ə rif′ik) *adj.* ‖< L *calor*, heat + *facere*, make‖ producing heat

**cal·u·met** (kal′yə met′) *n.* ‖CdnFr < L *calamus*, reed‖ a long-stemmed ceremonial pipe, smoked by North American Indians as a token of peace

**ca·lum·ni·ate** (kə lum′nē āt′) *vt., vi.* **-at′ed, -at′ing** ‖see fol.‖ to slander

**cal·um·ny** (kal′əm nē) *n., pl.* **-nies** ‖< L *calumnia*, slander‖ a false and malicious statement; slander

**Cal·va·ry** (kal′və rē) *n. Bible* the place where Jesus was crucified

**calve** (kav) *vi., vt.* **calved, calv′ing** to give birth to (a calf)

**calves** (kavz) *n. pl. of* CALF[1] & CALF[2]

**Cal·vin** (kal′vin), **John** 1509-64; Fr. Protestant reformer

**Cal′vin·ism′** *n.* the Christian doctrines of John Calvin and his followers, esp. predestination — **Cal′vin·ist** *n., adj.* —**Cal′vin·is′tic** *adj.*

**ca·lyp·so** (kə lip′sō) *n.* ‖< ?‖ a kind of lively, topical folk song that originated in Trinidad

**ca·lyx** (kā′liks′; *also* kal′iks′) *n., pl.* **-lyx′es** or **-ly·ces′** ‖L, pod‖ the outer whorl of protective leaves, or sepals, of a flower

**cam** (kam) *n.* ‖Du *cam*, orig., a comb‖ a wheel, projection on a wheel, etc. that gives irregular motion, as to a wheel or shaft, or receives such motion from it

**ca·ma·ra·de·rie** (kam′ə räd′ə rē, käm′-) *n.* ‖Fr‖ loyalty and warm, friendly feeling among comrades

**cam·ber** (kam′bər) *n.* ‖OFr < L *camur*, arched‖ a slight convex curve of a surface, as of a road —*vt., vi.* to arch slightly

**cam·bi·um** (kam′bē əm) *n.* ‖< LL *cambiare*, to change‖ a layer of cells between the wood and bark in woody plants, which will eventually become more wood and bark —**cam′bi·al** *adj.*

**Cam·bo·di·a** (kam bō′dē ə) country in S Indochina: 69,898 sq. mi.; pop. 5,756,000; cap. Phnom Penh —**Cam·bo′di·an** *adj., n.*

**cam·bric** (kām′brik) *n.* ‖after *Cambrai*, Fr city‖ a fine linen or cotton cloth

**Cam·bridge** (kām′brij′) **1** city in EC England: county district pop. 92,000 **2** city in E Massachusetts: pop. 96,000

**cam·cord·er** (kam′kôrd′ər) *n.* a small, portable videotape recorder and TV camera

**came** (kām) *vi. pt. of* COME

**cam·el** (kam′əl) *n.* ‖ult. < Heb *gāmāl*‖ a large, domesticated mammal with a humped back and long neck: because it can store water in its body, it is used in Asian and African deserts

**ca·mel·lia** (kə mēl′yə, -mē′lē ə) *n.* ‖after G. J. *Kamel* (1661-1706), missionary to the Far East‖ **1** an Asiatic evergreen tree or shrub with glossy leaves and roselike flowers **2** the flower

**Cam·em·bert (cheese)** (kam′əm ber′, -bərt) ‖after *Camembert*, Fr village‖ a soft, rich, creamy cheese

**cam·e·o** (kam′ē ō′) *n., pl.* **-os′** ‖< It < ML *camaeus*‖ **1** a gem carved with a figure raised in relief **2** a choice minor role, esp. one played by a notable actor

**cam·er·a** (kam′ər ə, kam′rə) *n.* ‖L, vault‖ **1** a device for taking photographs: a closed box containing a sensitized plate or film on which an image is formed when light enters through a lens **2** *TV* the device that receives the image and transforms it into a flow of electrical impulses for transmission —**in camera** in privacy or secrecy

**cam·er·a·man** (-man') *n., pl.* **-men** (-men') an operator of a film or TV camera

**Cam·e·roon** (kam'ə roon') country in WC Africa, on the Atlantic: 183,569 sq. mi.; pop. 10,494,000 —**Cam'e·roon'i·an** *adj., n.*

**cam·i·sole** (kam'i sōl') *n.* [Fr < LL *camisia*, shirt] a woman's sleeveless undergarment for the upper body

**cam·o·mile** (kam'ə mīl', -mēl') *n.* [< Gr *chamaimēlon*, earth apple] a plant whose dried, daisylike flower heads are used in a medicinal tea

**cam·ou·flage** (kam'ə fläzh', -fläj') *n.* [Fr < *camoufler*, to disguise] 1 a disguising, as of ships or guns, to conceal them from the enemy 2 a disguise; deception —*vt., vi.* **-flaged', -flag'ing** to disguise (a thing or person) for concealment — **cam'ou·flag'er** *n.*

**camp** (kamp) *n.* [< L *campus*, field] 1 *a*) a place where temporary tents, huts, etc. are put up, as for soldiers *b*) a group of such tents, etc. 2 the supporters of a particular cause 3 a recreational place in the country for vacationers, esp. children 4 the people living in a camp 5 [Slang] banality, artifice, etc. so extreme as to amuse or have a perversely sophisticated appeal —*vi.* 1 to set up a camp 2 to live or stay in a camp: often with *out* —**break camp** to dismantle a camp and depart

**cam·paign** (kam pān') *n.* [Fr < L *campus*, field] 1 a series of military operations with a particular objective 2 a series of planned actions, as to elect a candidate —*vi.* to participate in a campaign — **cam·paign'er** *n.*

**cam·pa·ni·le** (kam'pə nē'lē) *n., pl.* **-les** or **-li** (-lē) [It < LL *campana*, a bell] a bell tower

**camp·er** (kam'pər) *n.* 1 a vacationer at a camp 2 a motor vehicle or trailer equipped for camping out

**camp'fire'** *n.* 1 an outdoor fire at a camp 2 a social gathering around such a fire

**cam·phor** (kam'fər) *n.* [< Sans *karpuraḥ*, camphor tree] a crystalline substance with a strong odor, derived from the wood of an E Asian evergreen tree (**camphor tree**): used to repel moths, in medicine as a stimulant, etc. —**cam'phor·at'ed** *adj.*

**camp meeting** a religious meeting held outdoors or in a tent, etc.

**camp'site'** *n.* 1 any site for a camp 2 an area in a park set aside for camping

**cam·pus** (kam'pəs) *n., pl.* **-pus·es** [L, a field] the grounds, and sometimes buildings, of a school or college —*adj.* of a school or college [*campus* politics]

**camp'y** *adj.* **-i·er, -i·est** [Slang] characterized by CAMP (*n.* 5)

**cam'shaft'** *n.* a shaft having a cam, or to which a cam is fastened

**can**[1] (kan; *unstressed* kən) *vi., v.aux. pt.* **could** [< OE *cunnan*, to know] 1 know(s) how (to) 2 am, are, or is able (to) 3 am, are, or is likely (to) [*can* that be true?] 4 have or has the right (to) 5 [Inf.] am, are, or is permitted (to); may —**can but** can only

**can**[2] (kan) *n.* [OE *canne*, a cup] 1 a container, usually metal, with a separate cover [a garbage *can*] 2 a tinned metal container in which foods, etc. are sealed for preservation 3 the amount a can holds —*vt.* **canned, can'ning** 1 to put up in cans or jars for preservation 2 [Slang] to dismiss

**Ca·naan** (kā'nən) ancient region at the SE end of the Mediterranean: the Biblical Promised Land

**Can·a·da** (kan'ə də) country in N North America: 3,849,671 sq. mi.; pop. 28,847,000; cap. Ottawa — **Ca·na·di·an** (kə nā'dē ən) *adj., n.*

**Canadian bacon** cured, smoked pork taken from the loin

**Canadian English** English as spoken and written in Canada

**Ca·na'di·an·ism'** *n.* 1 a custom or belief originat-

ing in Canada 2 a word or phrase originating in Canadian English

**ca·nal** (kə nal') *n.* [< L *canalis*, channel] 1 an artificial waterway for transportation or irrigation 2 *Anat.* a tubular passage or duct

**Canal Zone** former name for a strip of land on either side of the Panama Canal: leased by the U.S. (1904-79)

**ca·na·pé** (kan'ə pā', kan'ə pē) *n.* [Fr] a small piece of bread or a cracker, spread with spiced meat, cheese, etc., served as an appetizer

**ca·nard** (kə närd') *n.* [Fr, a duck] a false, esp. malicious, report

**ca·nar·y** (kə ner'ē) *n., pl.* **-ies** [after *Canary* Islands] 1 a small, yellow finch 2 a light yellow

**Canary Islands** group of Spanish islands off NW Africa

**ca·nas·ta** (kə nas'tə) *n.* [Sp, basket] a card game using a double deck

**Can·ber·ra** (kan'ber'ə, -bə rə) capital of Australia: pop. 328,000

**can·can** (kan'kan') *n.* [Fr] a lively dance with much high kicking

**can·cel** (kan'səl) *vt.* **-celed** or **-celled, -cel·ing** or **-cel·ling** [< L *cancellus*, lattice] 1 to mark over with lines, etc., as in deleting written matter or marking a postage stamp, check, etc. as used 2 to make invalid 3 to do away with; abolish 4 to neutralize or balance: often with *out* 5 *Math.* to remove (a common factor, equivalents, etc.) — **can'cel·la'tion** *n.*

**can·cer** (kan'sər) *n.* [L, crab] 1 [C-] the fourth sign of the zodiac 2 a malignant tumor that can spread 3 anything bad or harmful that spreads —**can'cer·ous** *adj.*

**can·de·la·brum** (kan'də lä'brəm, -lä'-) *n., pl.* **-bra** (-brə) or **-brums** [L: see CHANDELIER] a large branched candlestick: also **can'de·la'bra**, *pl.* **-bras**

**can·did** (kan'did) *adj.* [L *candidus*, white, pure, sincere] 1 very honest or frank 2 unposed and informal [a *candid* photo] —**can'did·ly** *adv.*

**can·di·date** (kan'də dāt', -dət) *n.* [L *candidatus*, white-robed, as were Roman office seekers] 1 one seeking an office, award, etc. 2 one seemingly destined to come to a certain end

**can·died** (kan'dēd') *adj.* cooked in sugar or syrup until glazed or encrusted

**can·dle** (kan'dəl) *n.* [< L *candela*] a cylinder of tallow or wax with a wick through it, which gives light when burned —*vt.* **-dled, -dling** to examine (eggs) for freshness by placing in front of a light —**can'dler** *n.*

**can'dle·stick'** *n.* a cupped or spiked holder for a candle or candles

**can'-do'** *adj.* [Inf.] confident of one's ability to accomplish something

**can·dor** (kan'dər) *n.* [L, openness] unreserved honesty or frankness in expressing oneself: Brit. sp. **can'dour**

**can·dy** (kan'dē) *n., pl.* **-dies** [< Pers *qand*, cane sugar] a solid confection of sugar or syrup with flavoring, fruit, nuts, etc. —*vt.* **-died, -dy·ing** 1 to cook in sugar, esp. so as to preserve 2 to crystallize into sugar

**cane** (kān) *n.* [< Gr *kanna*] 1 the slender, jointed stem of certain plants, as bamboo 2 a plant with such a stem, as sugar cane 3 WALKING STICK 4 split rattan —*vt.* **caned, can'ing** 1 to flog with a cane 2 to make (chair seats, etc.) with cane — **can'er** *n.*

**cane·brake** (kān'brāk') *n.* a dense growth of cane plants

**ca·nine** (kā'nīn') *adj.* [< L *canis*, dog] 1 of or like a dog 2 of the family of carnivores that includes dogs, wolves, and foxes —*n.* 1 a dog or other canine animal 2 any of the sharp-pointed teeth next to the incisors: in full **canine tooth**

**can·is·ter** (kan'is tər) *n.* [< Gr *kanastron*, wicker basket] a small box or can for coffee, tea, etc.

**can·ker** (kaŋ'kər) *n.* [< L *cancer*, a crab] an ulcerlike sore, esp. in the mouth —**can'ker·ous** *adj.*

**can·na·bis** (kan′ə bis) *n.* ⟦L, hemp⟧ **1** HEMP **2** marijuana or any other substance made from the flowering tops of the hemp

**canned** (kand) *adj.* **1** preserved, as in cans **2** [Slang] recorded for reproduction, as on radio or TV

**can·nel** (**coal**) (kan′əl) a dense bituminous coal that burns with a steady, bright flame

**can·ner·y** (kan′ər ē) *n., pl.* **-ies** a factory where foods are canned

**can·ni·bal** (kan′ə bəl) *n.* ⟦Sp *canibal*⟧ **1** a person who eats human flesh **2** an animal that eats its own kind —*adj.* of or like cannibals —**can′ni·bal·ism′** *n.* —**can′ni·bal·is′tic** *adj.*

**can′ni·bal·ize′** (-īz′) *vt., vi.* **-ized′, -iz′ing** to strip (old or worn equipment) of parts for use in other units

**can·non** (kan′ən) *n., pl.* **-nons** or **-non** ⟦< L *canna*, cane⟧ **1** a large, mounted piece of artillery **2** an automatic gun on an aircraft

**can′non·ade′** (-ād′) *n.* a continuous firing of artillery —*vt., vi.* **-ad′ed, -ad′ing** to fire artillery (at)

**can·not** (kan′ät, kə nät′) can not —**cannot but** have or has no choice but to

**can·ny** (kan′ē) *adj.* **-ni·er, -ni·est** ⟦< CAN¹⟧ cautious and shrewd —**can′ni·ly** *adv.* —**can′ni·ness** *n.*

**ca·noe** (kə nōō′) *n.* ⟦< Sp *canoa* < WInd⟧ a light, narrow boat moved by paddles —*vi.* **-noed′, -noe′ing** to paddle, or go in, a canoe —**ca·noe′ist** *n.*

**ca·no·la** (**oil**) (kə nō′lə) an oil from the seed of the rape plant, used in cooking

**can·on** (kan′ən) *n.* ⟦OE, a rule < L⟧ **1** a law or body of laws of a church **2** *a*) a basic rule or principle *b*) a criterion **3** an official list, as of books of the Bible **4** the complete works, as of an author **5** *Music* a round **6** a clergyman serving in a cathedral

**ca·ñon** (kan′yən) *n. alt. sp. of* CANYON

**ca·non·i·cal** (kə nän′i kəl) *adj.* **1** of or according to church law **2** of or belonging to a canon

**can·on·ize** (kan′ən īz′) *vt.* **-ized′, -iz′ing 1** to declare (a deceased person) a saint **2** to glorify —**can′on·i·za′tion** *n.*

**can·o·py** (kan′ə pē) *n., pl.* **-pies** ⟦< Gr *kōnōpeion*, couch with mosquito nets⟧ **1** a drapery, etc. fastened above a bed, throne, etc., or held over a person **2** a rooflike projection —*vt.* **-pied, -py·ing** to place or form a canopy over; cover

**cant**¹ (kant) *n.* ⟦< L *cantus*, song⟧ **1** the secret slang of beggars, thieves, etc.; argot **2** the special vocabulary of those in a certain occupation; jargon **3** insincere talk, esp. when pious —*vi.* to use cant

**cant**² (kant) *n.* ⟦L *cantus*, tire of a wheel⟧ **1** an outside angle **2** a beveled edge **3** a tilt, turn, slant, etc. —*vt., vi.* to slant; tilt

**can't** (kant, känt) *contr.* cannot

**can·ta·loupe** or **can·ta·loup** (kant′ə lōp′) *n.* ⟦Fr < It *Cantalupo*, estate near Rome, where first grown in Europe⟧ a muskmelon with a rough rind and juicy, orange flesh

**can·tan·ker·ous** (kan taŋ′kər əs) *adj.* ⟦prob. < ME *contakour*, troublemaker⟧ bad-tempered; quarrelsome —**can·tan′ker·ous·ly** *adv.* —**can·tan′ker·ous·ness** *n.*

**can·ta·ta** (kän tät′ə, kən-) *n.* ⟦It < *cantare*, to sing⟧ a choral composition that sets to music the words of a story to be sung but not acted

**can·teen** (kan tēn′) *n.* ⟦< Fr < It *cantina*, wine cellar⟧ **1** a recreation center for military personnel, teenagers, etc. **2** a place where food is dispensed, as in a disaster area **3** a small flask for carrying water

**can·ter** (kant′ər) *n.* ⟦< *Canterbury gallop*, a riding pace⟧ a moderate gallop —*vi., vt.* to ride at a canter

**can·ti·cle** (kan′ti kəl) *n.* ⟦< L *cantus*, song⟧ a hymn with words taken from the Bible

**can·ti·le·ver** (kant″l ē′vər, -ev′ər) *n.* ⟦< ?⟧ a bracket or block projecting as a support; esp., a

projecting structure anchored at one end to a pier or wall —*vt.* to support by means of cantilevers —**can′ti·le′vered** *adj.*

**can·to** (kan′tō) *n., pl.* **-tos** ⟦It < L *cantus*, song⟧ any of the main divisions of certain long poems

**can·ton** (kan′tən, -tän′) *n.* ⟦Fr < LL *cantus*, corner⟧ any of the states in the Swiss Republic

**Can·ton** (kan tän′) *a former transliteration of* GUANGZHOU

**Can·ton·ese** (kan′tə nēz′) *n.* **1** *pl.* **-ese′** a person born or living in Canton, China **2** the variety of Chinese spoken in Canton —*adj.* of Canton

**can·ton·ment** (kan tän′mənt, -tōn′-) *n.* ⟦Fr: see CANTON⟧ temporary quarters for troops

**can·tor** (kan′tər) *n.* ⟦L, singer⟧ a singer of liturgical solos in a synagogue

**can·vas** (kan′vəs) *n.* ⟦< L *cannabis*, hemp⟧ **1** a coarse cloth of hemp, cotton, etc., used for tents, sails, etc. **2** a sail, tent, etc. **3** an oil painting on canvas

**can′vas·back′** *n.* a North American wild duck with a grayish back

**can·vass** (kan′vəs) *vt., vi.* ⟦< *canvas* < ?⟧ use of canvas for sifting⟧ **1** to go through (places) or among (people) asking for (votes, opinions, orders, etc.) —*n.* a canvassing —**can′vass·er** *n.*

**can·yon** (kan′yən) *n.* ⟦Sp *cañon*, tube < L *canna*, a reed⟧ a long, narrow valley between high cliffs

**cap**¹ (kap) *n.* ⟦< LL *cappa*, hooded cloak⟧ **1** any closefitting head covering, with or without a visor or brim **2** a caplike part or thing; cover or top —*vt.* **capped, cap′ping 1** to put a cap on **2** to cover the top or end of **3** to equal or excel

**cap**² *abbrev.* **1** capacity **2** capital

**ca·pa·ble** (kā′pə bəl) *adj.* ⟦< L *capere*, to take⟧ having ability; skilled; competent —**capable of 1** having the qualities necessary for **2** able or ready to —**ca′pa·bil′i·ty,** *pl.* **-ties,** *n.* —**ca′pa·bly** *adv.*

**ca·pa·cious** (kə pā′shəs) *adj.* ⟦< L *capere*, to take⟧ roomy; spacious —**ca·pa′cious·ly** *adv.* —**ca·pa′cious·ness** *n.*

**ca·pac·i·tor** (kə pas′ə tər) *n.* a device for storing an electric charge

**ca·pac·i·ty** (-tē) *n., pl.* **-ties** ⟦< L *capere*, take⟧ **1** the ability to contain, absorb, or receive **2** all that can be contained; volume **3** ability **4** maximum output **5** position; function

**ca·par·i·son** (kə par′i sən, -zən) *n.* ⟦< LL *cappa*, cloak⟧ trappings for a horse —*vt.* to cover (a horse) with trappings

**cape**¹ (kāp) *n.* ⟦see prec.⟧ a sleeveless garment fastened at the neck and hanging over the back and shoulders

**cape**² (kāp) *n.* ⟦< L *caput*, head⟧ a piece of land projecting into a body of water

**ca·per**¹ (kā′pər) *vi.* ⟦? < Fr *capriole*, a leap⟧ to skip about in a playful manner —*n.* **1** a playful leap **2** a prank **3** [Slang] a criminal act, esp. a robbery —**cut a caper** (or **cut capers**) to caper

**ca·per**² (kā′pər) *n.* ⟦< Gr *kapparis*⟧ the green flower bud of a Mediterranean bush, pickled and used as a seasoning

**cape′skin′** *n.* ⟦orig. made from the skin of goats from the *Cape* of Good Hope⟧ fine leather made from sheepskin

**Cape Town** seaport in South Africa: seat of the legislature: pop. 855,000

**Cape Verde** (vʉrd) country on a group of islands in the Atlantic, west of Senegal: 1,557 sq. mi.; pop. 337,000

**cap·il·lar·y** (kap′ə ler′ē) *adj.* ⟦< L *capillus*, hair⟧ very slender —*n., pl.* **-ies 1** a tube with a very small bore: also **capillary tube 2** any of the tiny blood vessels connecting the arteries with the veins

**capillary attraction** the action by which liquids in contact with solids, as in a capillary tube, rise or fall: also **capillary action**

**cap·i·tal** (kap′ət ′l) *adj.* ⟦< L *caput*, head⟧ **1** punishable by death **2** principal; chief **3** of, or being, the seat of government **4** of capital, or wealth **5** excellent —**n. 1** CAPITAL LETTER **2** a city that is the seat of government of a state or nation **3** money or property owned or used in business **4** [*often* **C-**] capitalists collectively **5** the top part of a column

**capital gain** profit resulting from the sale of capital investments such as stocks

**cap′i·tal·ism′** *n.* an economic system in which the means of production and distribution are privately owned and operated for profit

**cap′i·tal·ist** *n.* **1** an owner of wealth used in business **2** an upholder of capitalism **3** a wealthy person —**cap′i·tal·is′tic** *adj.*

**cap′i·tal·ize′** (-īz′) *vt.* **-ized′, -iz′ing 1** to use as or convert into capital **2** to supply capital to or for **3** to begin (a word) with a capital letter —**capitalize on something** to use something to one's advantage —**cap′i·tal·i·za′tion** *n.*

**capital letter** the form of an alphabetical letter used to begin a sentence or proper name, as *A, B,* or *C*

**cap′i·tal·ly** *adv.* very well

**capital punishment** the penalty of death for a crime

**Cap·i·tol** (kap′ət ′l) *n.* [< L *Capitolium,* temple of Jupiter in Rome] **1** the building in which the U.S. Congress meets in Washington, DC **2** [*usually* **c-**] the building in which a state legislature meets

**ca·pit·u·late** (kə pich′yoo lāt′, -pich′ə lāt′) *vi.* **-lat′ed, -lat′ing** [< LL *capitulare,* arrange conditions] **1** to give up (*to* an enemy) on prearranged conditions **2** to stop resisting —**ca·pit′u·la′tion** *n.*

**cap·let** (kap′lit) *n.* a solid, elongated medicine tablet, coated for easy swallowing

**ca·pon** (kā′pän′, -pən) *n.* [< L *capo*] a castrated rooster fattened for eating

**cap·puc·ci·no** (kä′pə chē′nō, kap′ə-) *n.* [It] espresso coffee mixed with steamed milk and topped with cinnamon, etc.

**ca·price** (kə prēs′) *n.* [Fr < It] **1** a sudden, impulsive change in thinking or acting **2** a capricious quality

**ca·pri·cious** (kə prish′əs) *adj.* subject to caprices; erratic —**ca·pri′cious·ly** *adv.* —**ca·pri′cious·ness** *n.*

**Cap·ri·corn** (kap′ri kôrn′) *n.* [< L *caper,* goat + *cornu,* horn] the tenth sign of the zodiac

**cap·size** (kap′sīz′, kap sīz′) *vt., vi.* **-sized′, -siz′ing** [< ?] to overturn or upset: said esp. of a boat

**cap·stan** (kap′stən) *n.* [? < L *capere,* take] an upright cylinder, as on ships, around which cables are wound for hoisting anchors, etc.

**cap·sule** (kap′səl, -syool′) *n.* [Fr < L *capsa,* box] **1** a soluble gelatin container enclosing a dose of medicine **2** a detachable compartment to hold people, instruments, etc. in a rocket: in full **space capsule 3** *Bot.* a seed vessel —*adj.* in a concise form —**cap′su·lar** *adj.*

**cap′sul·ize′** (-īz′) *vt.* **-ized′, -iz′ing 1** to enclose in a capsule **2** to condense

**Capt** *abbrev.* Captain

**cap·tain** (kap′tən) *n.* [< L *caput,* head] **1** a chief; leader **2** *U.S. Mil.* an officer ranking just above first lieutenant **3** *U.S. Navy* an officer ranking just above commander **4** *a*) the person in command of a ship *b*) the pilot of an airplane **5** the leader of a team, as in sports —*vt.* to be captain of —**cap′tain·cy,** *pl.* **-cies,** *n.*

**cap·tion** (kap′shən) *n.* [< L *capere,* to take] **1** a heading or title, as of a newspaper article or illustration **2** *Film, TV* a subtitle —*vt.* to supply a caption for

**cap′tious** (-shəs) *adj.* [see prec.] **1** made only for the sake of argument or faultfinding [a *captious* remark] **2** quick to find fault —**cap′tious·ly** *adv.* —**cap′tious·ness** *n.*

**cap·ti·vate** (kap′tə vāt′) *vt.* **-vat′ed, -vat′ing** to capture the attention or affection of —**cap′ti·vat′ing·ly** *adv.* —**cap′ti·va′tion** *n.* —**cap′ti·va′tor** *n.*

**cap·tive** (kap′tiv) *n.* [< L *capere,* to take] a prisoner —*adj.* **1** taken or held prisoner **2** obliged to listen [a *captive* audience] —**cap·tiv′i·ty,** *pl.* **-ties,** *n.*

**cap′tor** (-tər) *n.* one who captures

**cap′ture** (-chər) *vt.* **-tured, -tur·ing** [< L *capere,* to take] **1** to take or seize by force, surprise, etc. **2** to represent in a more permanent form [to *capture* her charm on canvas] —*n.* a capturing or being captured

**car** (kär) *n.* [< L *carrus,* chariot] **1** any vehicle on wheels **2** a vehicle that moves on rails, as a streetcar **3** an automobile **4** an elevator cage

**Ca·ra·cas** (kə räk′əs, -rak′-) capital of Venezuela: pop. 1,825,000

**car·a·cul** (kar′ə kul′, -kəl) *n. alt. sp. of* KARAKUL (esp. sense 2)

**ca·rafe** (kə raf′, -räf′) *n.* [Fr] a glass bottle for serving wine, water, or coffee

**car·a·mel** (kär′məl, kar′ə məl) *n.* [Fr] **1** burnt sugar used to color or flavor food **2** a chewy candy made from sugar, milk, etc.

**car′a·mel·ize′** (-īz′) *vt., vi.* **-ized′, -iz′ing** to turn into CARAMEL (sense 1)

**car·a·pace** (kar′ə pās′) *n.* [Fr < Sp] the upper shell of the turtle, crab, etc.

**car·at** (kar′ət) *n.* [Fr < Gr *keration,* little horn] **1** a unit of weight for precious stones, equal to 200 milligrams **2** KARAT

**car·a·van** (kar′ə van′) *n.* [< Pers *kārwān*] **1** a company of people traveling together for safety, as through a desert **2** VAN²

**car·a·van·sa·ry** (kar′ə van′sə rē) *n., pl.* **-ries** [< Pers *kārwān,* caravan + *sarāī,* palace] in the Middle East, an inn for caravans

**car·a·way** (kar′ə wā′) *n.* [< Ar *al-karawiyā′*] the spicy seeds of an herb, used to flavor bread, etc.

**car·bide** (kär′bīd′) *n.* a solid compound of a metal with carbon

**car·bine** (kär′bīn′, -bēn′) *n.* [< Fr *scarabée,* beetle] **1** a short-barreled rifle **2** a light, semiautomatic or automatic rifle of relatively limited range

**carbo-** *combining form* carbon: also **carb-**

**car·bo·hy·drate** (kär′bō hī′drāt, -bə-) *n.* [prec. + HYDRATE] an organic compound composed of carbon, hydrogen, and oxygen, as a sugar or starch

**car·bol·ic acid** (kär bäl′ik) *see* PHENOL

**car·bon** (kär′bən) *n.* [< L *carbo,* coal] **1** a nonmetallic chemical element found esp. in all organic compounds: diamond and graphite are pure carbon: a radioactive isotope of carbon (**carbon-14**) is used in dating fossils, etc. **2** CARBON PAPER **3** a copy made with carbon paper —*adj.* of or like carbon

**car′bon·ate** (-bə nit; *also, and for v. always,* -nāt′) *n.* a salt or ester of carbonic acid —*vt.* **-at′ed, -at′ing** to charge with carbon dioxide —**car′bon·a′tion** *n.*

**carbon black** carbon produced by the incomplete burning of oil or gas

**carbon copy 1** a copy made with carbon paper **2** anything very much like another

**carbon dating** a method of establishing the approximate age of fossils, etc. by measuring the amount of carbon-14 in them —**car′bon-date′, -dat′ed, -dat′ing,** *vt.*

**carbon di·ox·ide** (dī äks′īd′) a heavy, colorless, odorless gas: it passes out of the lungs in respiration

**car·bon·ic acid** (kär bän′ik) a weak acid formed by carbon dioxide in water

**car·bon·if·er·ous** (kär′bə nif′ər əs) *adj.* containing carbon or coal

**carbon mon·ox·ide** (mə näks′īd′) a colorless, odorless, highly poisonous gas

**carbon paper** thin paper coated on one side, as with a carbon preparation, used to make copies of letters, etc.

**carbon tet·ra·chlo·ride** (te′trə klôr′īd′) a nonflammable liquid, used as a solvent for fats and oils, etc.

**Car·bo·run·dum** (kär'bə run'dəm) ⟦CARB(ON) + (c)*orundum*⟧ *trademark for* a hard abrasive, esp. of carbon and silicon —*n.* [**c-**] such a substance

**car·boy** (kär'boi') *n.* ⟦< Pers *qarābah*⟧ a large bottle enclosed in a protective container, for holding corrosive liquids

**car·bun·cle** (kär'buŋ'kəl) *n.* ⟦< L dim. of *carbo*, coal⟧ a painful bacterial infection deep beneath the skin —**car·bun'cu·lar** (-kyōo lər) *adj.*

**car·bu·ret·or** (kär'bə rāt'ər) *n.* a device for mixing air with gasoline spray to make an explosive mixture in an internal-combustion engine

**car·cass** (kär'kəs) *n.* ⟦< Fr *carcasse*⟧ **1** the dead body of an animal **2** a framework or shell

**car·cin·o·gen** (kär sin'ə jən) *n.* ⟦< fol. + -GEN⟧ any substance that produces cancer —**car·ci·no·gen·ic** (kär'sə nō jen'ik) *adj.*

**car·ci·no·ma** (kär'sə nō'mə) *n., pl.* **-mas** or **-ma·ta** (-mə tə) ⟦L < Gr *karkinos*, crab⟧ any of several kinds of epithelial cancer

**car coat** a short overcoat

**card**¹ (kärd) *n.* ⟦< Gr *chartēs*, layer of papyrus⟧ **1** a flat, stiff piece of paper or pasteboard; specif., *a*) any of a pack of playing cards *b*) a card identifying a person, esp. as a member, agent, etc. *c*) a postcard *d*) an illustrated, usually folded card bearing a greeting *e*) any of a series of cards on which information is recorded **2** a small, plug-in circuit board **3** [Inf.] a witty or clowning person —**put** (or **lay**) **one's cards on the table** to reveal something frankly

**card**² (kärd) *n.* ⟦< L *carrere*, to card⟧ a metal comb or a machine with wire teeth for combing fibers of wool, cotton, etc. —*vt.* to use a card on

**card'board'** *n.* stiff, thick paper or pasteboard, used for cards, boxes, etc.

**car·di·ac** (kär'dē ak') *adj.* ⟦< Gr *kardia*, heart⟧ of or near the heart

**cardiac arrest** the complete failure of the heart to pump blood

**car·di·gan** (kär'di gən) *n.* ⟦after 7th Earl of *Cardigan*⟧ a sweater or jacket, usually knitted and collarless, that opens down the front

**car·di·nal** (kärd''n əl) *adj.* ⟦< L *cardo*, pivot⟧ **1** principal; chief **2** bright-red —*n.* **1** an official appointed by the pope to his council **2** a bright-red American songbird **3** CARDINAL NUMBER

**cardinal number** any number used in counting or in showing how many (e.g., two, 40, 627, etc.)

**cardio-** ⟦< Gr *kardia*, heart⟧ *combining form of* the heart

**car·di·o·gram** (kär'dē ō gram', -dē ə-) *n.* ELECTRO-CARDIOGRAM

**car'di·o·graph'** (-graf') *n.* ELECTROCARDIOGRAPH

**car'di·ol'o·gy** (-äl'ə jē) *n.* the branch of medicine dealing with the heart —**car'di·ol'o·gist** *n.*

**car·di·o·pul·mo·nar·y** (kär'dē ō pool' mə ner'ē) *adj.* of or involving the heart and lungs

**car'di·o·vas'cu·lar** (-vas'kyə lər) *adj.* of the heart and the blood vessels as a unified body system

**cards** *pl.n.* any game played with a deck of playing cards, as poker

**card'sharp'** *n.* [Inf.] a professional cheater at cards: also **card shark**

**care** (ker) *n.* ⟦< OE *caru*, sorrow⟧ **1** *a*) a troubled state of mind; worry *b*) a cause of such a mental state **2** close attention; heed **3** a liking or regard (*for*) **4** custody; protection **5** a responsibility —*vi.* **cared**, **car'ing 1** to feel concern **2** to feel love or a liking (*for*) **3** to look after; provide (*for*) **4** to wish (*for*); want —*vt.* **1** to feel concern about or interest in **2** to wish —(**in**) **care of** at the address of —**take care of 1** to attend to **2** to provide for

**ca·reen** (kə rēn') *vt., vi.* ⟦< L *carina*, keel⟧ to lean or cause to lean sideways; tip; tilt; lurch

**ca·reer** (kə rir') *n.* ⟦< L *carrus*, car⟧ **1** [Archaic] a swift course **2** one's progress through life **3** a profession or occupation —*vi.* to rush wildly

**care'free'** *adj.* free from worry

**care'ful** *adj.* **1** cautious; wary **2** accurate; thor-

---

ough; painstaking —**care'ful·ly** *adv.* —**care'ful·ness** *n.*

**care'giv'er** *n.* one who takes care of a child, invalid, etc.

**care'less** *adj.* **1** carefree; untroubled **2** not paying enough heed; neglectful **3** done or made without enough attention, precision, etc. —**care'less·ly** *adv.* —**care'less·ness** *n.*

**ca·ress** (kə res') *vt.* ⟦ult. < L *carus*, dear⟧ to touch lovingly or gently —*n.* an affectionate touch

**car·et** (kar'it, ker'-) *n.* ⟦L, there is lacking⟧ a mark (∧) used to show where something is to be inserted in a written or printed line

**care'tak'er** *n.* **1** a person hired to take care of something or someone **2** one acting as temporary replacement

**care'worn'** *adj.* worn out by, or showing the effects of, troubles and worry; haggard

**car·fare** (kär'fer') *n.* the price of a ride on a subway, bus, etc.

**car·go** (kär'gō) *n., pl.* **-goes** or **-gos** ⟦< Sp *cargar*, to load⟧ the load carried by a ship, truck, etc.; freight

**car'hop'** *n.* ⟦CAR + (BELL)HOP⟧ one who serves food at a drive-in restaurant

**Car·ib·be·an (Sea)** (kar'ə bē'ən, kə rib'ē ən) part of the Atlantic, bounded by the West Indies, Central America, and N South America

**car·i·bou** (kar'ə bōō') *n.* ⟦CdnFr⟧ a large North American reindeer

**car·i·ca·ture** (kar'i kə chər) *n.* ⟦Fr < It *caricare*, exaggerate⟧ **1** the exaggerated imitation of a person, literary style, etc. for satirical effect **2** a picture, etc. in which this is done —*vt.* **-tured**, **-tur·ing** to depict as in a caricature —**car'i·ca·tur·ist** *n.*

**car·ies** (ker'ēz') *n.* ⟦L, decay⟧ decay of bones or, esp., of teeth

**car·il·lon** (kar'ə län') *n.* ⟦Fr, chime of four bells < L *quattuor*, four⟧ a set of bells tuned to the chromatic scale

**ca·ri·tas** (kär'ē täs') *n.* love for all people

**car·jack·ing** (kär'jak'iŋ) *n.* the taking of a car and its passengers by force —**car'jack'** *vt.* —**car'jack'er** *n.*

**car·mine** (kär'min, -mīn') *n.* ⟦ult. < Ar *qirmiz*, crimson⟧ a red or purplish-red color —*adj.* red or purplish-red

**car·nage** (kär'nij) *n.* ⟦Fr < L *caro*, flesh⟧ extensive slaughter, esp. in battle

**car·nal** (-nəl) *adj.* ⟦< L *caro*, flesh⟧ **1** of the flesh; material; worldly **2** sensual or sexual —**car·nal'i·ty** (-nal'i tē) *n., pl.* **-ties**, *n.* —**car'nal·ly** *adv.*

**car·na·tion** (kär nā'shən) *n.* ⟦< L *caro*, flesh⟧ **1** a plant of the pink family, widely cultivated for its white, pink, or red flowers **2** its flower

**car·nel·ian** (kär nēl'yən) *n.* ⟦< L *carnis*, of flesh (color)⟧ a red variety of chalcedony, used in jewelry

**car·ni·val** (kär'nə vəl) *n.* ⟦< Fr *carnaval* (or It *carnevale*)⟧ **1** the period of feasting and revelry just before Lent **2** a reveling; festivity **3** an entertainment with sideshows, rides, etc.

**car·ni·vore** (kär'nə vôr') *n.* a carnivorous animal or plant

**car·niv·o·rous** (kär niv'ə rəs) *adj.* ⟦< L *caro*, flesh + *vorare*, to devour⟧ **1** flesh-eating **2** of the carnivores —**car·niv'o·rous·ness** *n.*

**car·ob** (kar'əb) *n.* a tree of the E Mediterranean region with sweet pods used in making candy, etc.

**car·ol** (kar'əl) *n.* ⟦< OFr *carole*, kind of dance⟧ a song of joy or praise; esp., a Christmas song —*vi.*, *vt.* **-oled** or **-olled**, **-ol·ing** or **-ol·ling** to sing; esp., to sing Christmas carols —**car'ol·er** or **car'ol·ler** *n.*

**car·om** (kar'əm) *n.* ⟦< Sp *carambola*⟧ **1** *Billiards* a shot in which the cue ball successively hits two balls **2** a hitting and rebounding —*vi.* **1** to make a carom **2** to hit and rebound

**ca·rot·id** (kə rät'id) *adj.* ⟦Gr *karōtis*⟧ designating or of either of the two main arteries, one on each

side of the neck, which convey blood to the head
—*n.* a carotid artery

**ca·rouse** (kə rouz') *vi.* **-roused'**, **-rous'ing** [< Ger
*gar austrinken*, to drink] to engage in a noisy
drinking party —*n.* a noisy drinking party

**car·ou·sel** (kar'ə sel') *n.* [Fr < It dial. (Naples)
*carusiello*, kind of tournament] **1** a merry-go-
round **2** a circular baggage conveyor in an airport

**carp**[1] (kärp) *n.*, *pl.* **carp** or **carps** [< VL *carpa*] an
edible freshwater fish widely cultivated for food

**carp**[2] (kärp) *vi.* [< ON *karpa*, to brag] to find fault
in a petty or nagging way —**carp'er** *n.*

**car·pal** (kär'pəl) *adj.* of the carpus —*n.* a bone of
the carpus

**carpal tunnel syndrome** a condition of a
pinched nerve in the wrist, often caused by
repetitive movement

**car·pel** (kär'pəl) *n.* [< Gr *karpos*, fruit] a simple
pistil, regarded as a modified leaflike structure

**car·pen·ter** (kär'pən tər) *n.* [< L *carpentum*, a
cart] one who builds and repairs wooden things,
esp. buildings, ships, etc. —**car'pen·try** (-trē) *n.*

**carpenter ant** a large ant that gnaws holes in
trees, wooden buildings, etc. for its nest

**car·pet** (kär'pət) *n.* [< L *carpere*, to card] **1** a
heavy fabric for covering a floor **2** anything that
covers like a carpet —*vt.* to cover as with a carpet
—**on the carpet** being reprimanded

**car'pet·bag'** *n.* an old-fashioned traveling bag,
made of carpeting

**car'pet·bag'ger** *n.* a politician, promoter, etc.
from the outside whose influence is resented

**car'pet·ing** *n.* carpets or carpet fabric

**car pool** a plan by a group to rotate the use of
their cars, as for going to work —**car'pool'** *vi.*, *vt.*

**car·port** (kär'pôrt') *n.* an automobile shelter built
as a roof extending from the side of a building

**car·pus** (kär'pəs) *n.*, *pl.* **-pi'** (-pī') [< Gr *karpos*,
wrist] *Anat.* the wrist, or the wrist bones

**car·rel** or **car·rell** (kar'əl) *n.* [< ML *carula*] a
small enclosure in a library, for privacy in studying or reading

**car·riage** (kar'ij) *n.* [ult. < L *carrus*, chariot] **1** a
carrying; transportation **2** the manner of carrying oneself; bearing **3** *a*) a horse-drawn passenger vehicle, esp. one with four wheels *b*) a baby
carriage **4** a moving part, as on a typewriter, that
supports and shifts something

**car·ri·er** (kar'ē ər) *n.* **1** one that carries **2** one in
the business of transporting **3** one that transmits
disease germs **4** AIRCRAFT CARRIER **5** *a*) a tele-
phone-service company *b*) an insurance company

**carrier pigeon** *former name for* HOMING PIGEON

**car·ri·on** (kar'ē ən) *n.* [< L *caro*, flesh] the
decaying flesh of a dead body

**Car·roll** (kar'əl), **Lew·is** (lōō'is) (pseud. of *C. L.
Dodgson*) 1832-98; Eng. writer

**car·rot** (kar'ət) *n.* [< Gr *karōton*] **1** a plant with
an edible, fleshy, orange-red root **2** the root

**car·rou·sel** (kar'ə sel') *n.* *alt. sp. of* CAROUSEL

**car·ry** (kar'ē) *vt.* **-ried**, **-ry·ing** [< L *carrus*, chariot]
**1** to hold or support **2** to take from one place to
another **3** to keep with one [*to carry* an ID] **4** to
transmit [*air carries* sounds] **5** to transfer or
extend **6** to have as a quality, consequence, etc.
[*to carry* a guarantee] **7** to bear (oneself) in a
specified way **8** to win (an election, argument,
etc.) **9** *a*) to keep in stock *b*) to keep on one's
account books, etc. **10** to publish or broadcast [*to
carry* a syndicated column, a TV show, etc.] —*vi.*
to cover a range or distance: said of a voice, missile, etc. —*n.*, *pl.* **-ries** the distance covered by a
gun, ball, etc. —**be** (or **get**) **carried away** to
become very emotional or enthusiastic —**carry on
1** to engage in **2** to go on (*with*) **3** [Inf.] to behave
wildly or childishly —**carry out** (or **through**) **1** to
put (plans, etc.) into practice **2** to accomplish —
**carry over** to postpone

**carrying charge** interest paid on the balance
owed in installment buying

**car'ry-on'** *adj.* small enough to fit under an airplane seat or in an overhead compartment —*n.* a
piece of carry-on luggage

**car'ry-out'** *adj.* designating or of prepared food
sold as by a restaurant to be consumed elsewhere

**car'ry-o'ver** *n.* something carried over or left over

**car seat** a seat in an automobile, specif., a portable seat for securing a small child

**car'sick'** *adj.* nauseated from riding in an automobile, bus, etc.

**Car·son City** (kär'sən) capital of Nevada, in the
W part: pop. 40,000

**cart** (kärt) *n.* [< ON *kartr*] **1** a small wagon, carriage, etc. **2** a handcart —*vt.*, *vi.* to carry as in a
cart, truck, etc.; transport

**cart·age** (kärt'ij) *n.* **1** the work of carting **2** the
charge for this

**carte blanche** (kärt' blänsh') [Fr, lit., white
card] full authority or freedom

**car·tel** (kär tel') *n.* [< Ger < Fr] an association of
businesses in an international monopoly; trust

**Car·ter** (kärt'ər), **Jim·my** (jim'ē) (legal name
*James Earl Carter, Jr.*) 1924- ; 39th president of
the U.S. (1977-81)

**car·ti·lage** (kärt'l ij) *n.* [< L *cartilago*] tough,
elastic tissue forming parts of the skeleton;
gristle —**car'ti·lag'i·nous** (-aj'ə nəs) *adj.*

**car·tog·ra·phy** (kär täg'rə fē) *n.* [see CARD[1] &
-GRAPHY] the art of making maps or charts —**car·
tog'ra·pher** *n.*

**car·ton** (kärt'n) *n.* [Fr < It *carta*, card] a cardboard box or container

**car·toon** (kär tōōn') *n.* [< Fr: see prec.] **1** a drawing caricaturing a person or event **2** *a*) COMIC
STRIP *b*) an animated cartoon —*vi.* to draw a cartoon —**car·toon'ist** *n.*

**car·tridge** (kärt'rij) *n.* [< Fr < It *carta*, card] **1** a
cylindrical case containing the charge and
primer, and usually the projectile, for a firearm **2**
a small container, as for camera film or ink for a
pen

**cart'wheel'** *n.* a handspring performed sideways

**carve** (kärv) *vt.* **carved**, **carv'ing** [OE *ceorfan*] **1**
to make or shape by or as by cutting **2** to deco-
rate the surface of with cut designs **3** to divide by
cutting; slice —*vi.* **1** to carve statues or designs
**2** to carve meat —**carv'er** *n.* —**carv'ing** *n.*

**car'wash'** *n.* an establishment at which automobiles are washed

**car·y·at·id** (kar'ē at'id) *n.*, *pl.* **-ids** or **-i·des'** (-ə
dēz') [< Gr *karyatides*, priestesses at Karyai, in
ancient Greece] a supporting column having the
form of a draped female figure

**ca·sa·ba** (kə sä'bə) *n.* [after *Kasaba*, town in Asia
Minor] a kind of cultivated melon with a hard,
yellow rind

**Ca·sa·blan·ca** (kas'ə blaŋ'kə, kä'sə blän'kə) seaport in NW Morocco: pop. 1,506,000

**Ca·sa·no·va** (kaz'ə nō'və, kas'ə-) *n.* [after G.
*Casanova* (1725-98), It adventurer] a man who
has many love affairs

**cas·cade** (kas kād') *n.* [Fr < L *cadere*, to fall] **1** a
small, steep waterfall **2** anything resembling
this, as a shower of sparks —*vt.*, *vi.* **-cad'ed**,
**-cad'ing** to fall or drop in a cascade

**cas·car·a** (kas ker'ə) *n.* [Sp *cáscara*, bark] a
thorny tree growing on the Pacific coast of the
U.S.

**case**[1] (kās) *n.* [< L *casus*, a chance < *cadere*, to
fall] **1** an example or instance [*a case* of flu] **2** a
person being helped, as by a doctor **3** any matter
requiring study or investigation **4** *a*) the argument of one side, as in a law court *b*) convincing
arguments [he has no *case*] **5** a lawsuit **6** *Gram.*
the syntactic function of a noun or pronoun
[nominative, objective, or possessive *case*] —*vt.*
**cased**, **cas'ing** [Slang] to look over carefully —**in
any case** anyhow —**in case** in the event that; if —
**in case of** in the event of —**in no case** never

**case**² (kās) *n.* [[< L *capsa*, box]] **1** a container, as a box **2** a protective cover [a watch *case*] **3** a full box or its contents [a *case* of beer] **4** a frame, as for a window —*vt.* **cased, cas′ing 1** to put in a container **2** to enclose; encase

**case′hard′en** (-härd′n) *vt. Metallurgy* to form a hard surface on (an iron alloy)

**ca·se·in** (kā′sē in, -sēn′) *n.* [[< L *caseus*, cheese]] a protein that is one of the chief constituents of milk

**case′load′** *n.* the number of cases handled by a court, social agency, etc.

**case′ment** (-mənt) *n.* [[ult. < OFr *enchassement*]] a window frame that opens on hinges along the side

**case′work′** *n.* social work in which guidance is given in cases of personal or family maladjustment —**case′work′er** *n.*

**cash** (kash) *n.* [[< L *capsa*, box]] **1** money that a person actually has; esp., ready money **2** bills and coins **3** money, a check, etc. paid at the time of purchase —*vt.* to give or get cash for —*adj.* of or for cash —**cash in** to exchange for cash

**cash·ew** (kash′ōō; *also*, kə shōō′) *n.* [[< AmInd (Brazil) *acajú*]] **1** a tropical tree bearing kidney-shaped nuts **2** the nut

**cash·ier**¹ (ka shir′) *n.* [[Fr]] a person handling the cash transactions of a bank or store

**cash·ier**² (ka shir′) *vt.* [[< LL *cassare*, destroy]] to dismiss in dishonor

**cash·mere** (kash′mir′, kazh′-) *n.* [[after *Kashmir*, region in India]] **1** a fine carded wool from goats of N India and Tibet **2** a soft, twilled cloth as of this wool

**cash register** a device, usually with a money drawer, used for registering visibly the amount of a sale

**cas·ing** (kās′iŋ) *n.* **1** the skin of a sausage **2** the outer covering of a pneumatic tire **3** a frame, as for a door

**ca·si·no** (kə sē′nō) *n., pl.* **-nos** [[It < *casa*, house]] **1** a room or building for dancing, gambling, etc. **2** a card game for two to four players

**cask** (kask) *n.* [[ult. < L *quassare*, shatter]] **1** a barrel of any size, esp. one for liquids **2** its contents

**cas·ket** (kas′kit) *n.* [[< NormFr *casse*, box]] **1** a small box or chest, as for valuables **2** a coffin

**Cas·pi·an (Sea)** (kas′pē ən) inland salt sea between Asia and extreme SE Europe

**Cas·san·dra** (kə san′drə) *n. Gr. Myth.* a Trojan prophetess of doom whose prophecies are never believed

**cas·sa·va** (kə sä′və) *n.* [[< Fr < WInd *casávi*]] **1** a tropical American plant with starchy roots **2** a starch made from these roots, used in tapioca

**cas·se·role** (kas′ə rōl′) *n.* [[Fr < Gr *kyathos*, a bowl]] **1** a baking dish in which food can be cooked and served **2** the food baked in such a dish

**cas·sette** (kə set′, ka-) *n.* [[< NormFr *casse*, box]] a case with magnetic tape or film in it, for loading a tape recorder, VCR, camera, etc. quickly

**cas·sia** (kash′ə, kas′ē ə) *n.* [[ult. < Heb *qeṣī′āh*, lit., something scraped off]] **1** *a)* the bark of a tree of SE Asia: a source of cinnamon *b)* the tree **2** any of various tropical plants whose leaves yield senna

**cas·si·no** (kə sē′nō) *n. alt. sp. of* CASINO

**cas·sock** (kas′ək) *n.* [[prob. < Turk *qazaq*, nomad]] a long, closefitting vestment worn by clergymen, etc.

**cast** (kast) *vt.* **cast, cast′ing** [[< ON *kasta*]] **1** to throw with force; hurl **2** to deposit (a ballot or vote) **3** to direct [to *cast* one's eyes] **4** to project [to *cast* light] **5** to throw off or shed (a skin) **6** to shape (molten metal, etc.) by pouring into a mold **7** to select (an actor) for (a role or play) **8** to calculate —*vi.* to throw —*n.* **1** a casting; throw **2** *a)* something formed in a mold *b)* a mold or impression **3** a plaster form for immobilizing a broken limb **4** the set of actors in a play, movie, etc. **5** an appearance, as of features **6** a kind;

---

quality **7** a tinge; shade —**cast about** to look (*for*) —**cast aside** (or **away** or **off**) to discard

**cas·ta·nets** (kas′tə nets′) *pl.n.* [[< Sp < L *castanea*, chestnut: from the shape]] a pair of small, hollowed pieces of hard wood or ivory, clicked together in the hand in time to music

CASTANETS

**cast′a·way′** *n.* a shipwrecked person —*adj.* **1** discarded **2** shipwrecked

**caste** (kast) *n.* [[Fr < L *castus*, pure]] **1** any of the hereditary Hindu social classes of a formerly segregated system of India **2** any exclusive group **3** rigid class distinction based on birth, wealth, etc. —**lose caste** to lose social status

**cast′er** *n.* **1** a container for vinegar, oil, etc. at the table **2** any of a set of small wheels for supporting and moving furniture

**cas·ti·gate** (kas′ti gāt′) *vt.* **-gat′ed, -gat′ing** [[< L *castigare*]] to rebuke severely, esp. by public criticism —**cas′ti·ga′tion** *n.* —**cas′ti·ga′tor** *n.*

**cast′ing** *n.* a thing, esp. of metal, cast in a mold

**cast iron** a hard, brittle alloy of iron used for casting —**cast′-i′ron** *adj.*

**cas·tle** (kas′əl) *n.* [[< L *castrum*, fort]] **1** a large, fortified building or group of buildings **2** any massive dwelling like this **3** *Chess* ROOK²

**cast′off′** *adj.* discarded; abandoned —*n.* a person or thing cast off

**cas·tor-oil plant** (kas′tər oil′) a tropical plant with large seeds that yield an oil (**castor oil**) used as a cathartic

**cas·trate** (kas′trāt′) *vt.* **-trat′ed, -trat′ing** [[< L *castrare*]] to remove the testicles of; emasculate —**cas·tra′tion** *n.*

**cas·u·al** (kazh′ōō əl) *adj.* [[< L *casus*, chance]] **1** happening by chance; not planned; incidental **2** occasional **3** careless or cursory **4** nonchalant **5** *a)* informal *b)* for informal use —**cas′u·al·ly** *adv.* —**cas′u·al·ness** *n.*

**cas·u·al·ty** (kazh′ōō əl tē) *n., pl.* **-ties 1** an accident, esp. a fatal one **2** a member of the armed forces killed, wounded, captured, etc. **3** anyone hurt or killed in an accident **4** anything lost, destroyed, etc.

**cas·u·ist·ry** (kazh′ōō is trē) *n., pl.* **-ries** [[< L *casus*, CASE¹]] subtle but false reasoning, esp. about moral issues; sophistry —**cas′u·ist** *n.*

**cat** (kat) *n.* [[OE]] **1** a small, soft-furred animal, often kept as a pet or for killing mice **2** any flesh-eating mammal related to this, as the lion, tiger, leopard, etc. **3** a spiteful woman —**let the cat out of the bag** to let a secret be found out

**cat·a·clysm** (kat′ə kliz′əm) *n.* [[< Gr *kata-*, down + *klyzein*, to wash]] any sudden, violent change, as in war —**cat′a·clys′mic** (-kliz′mik) *adj.*

**cat·a·comb** (kat′ə kōm′) *n.* [[< ? L *cata*, by + *tumba*, tomb]] a gallery in an underground burial place: *usually used in pl.*

**cat′a·falque′** (-falk′, -fôlk′) *n.* [[Fr < It *catafalco*, funeral canopy]] a wooden framework on which a body in a coffin lies in state

**cat′a·lep′sy** (-lep′sē) *n.* [[< Gr *katalēpsis*, a seizing]] a condition of muscle rigidity and sudden, temporary loss of consciousness, as in epilepsy —**cat′a·lep′tic** *adj., n.*

**cat·a·log** or **cat·a·logue** (kat′ə lôg′) *n.* [[< Gr *kata-*, down + *legein*, to count]] a complete list, as a card file of the books in a library, a list of articles for sale, etc. —*vt., vi.* **-loged′** or **-logued′**, **-log′ing** or **-logu′ing** to arrange (an item or items) in a catalog —**cat′a·log′er** or **cat′a·logu′er** *n.*

**ca·tal·pa** (kə tal′pə) *n.* [[< AmInd]] a tree with heart-shaped leaves and slender, beanlike pods

**ca·tal·y·sis** (kə tal'ə sis) *n., pl.* **-ses'** (-sēz') ⟦< Gr *katalysis*, dissolution⟧ the speeding up or, sometimes, slowing down of a chemical reaction by adding a substance which itself is not changed thereby

**cat·a·lyst** (kat'ə list) *n.* **1** a substance serving as the agent in catalysis **2** anything bringing about or hastening a result —**cat'a·lyt'ic** (-lit'ik) *adj.*

**catalytic converter** a chemical filter connected to the exhaust system of an automotive vehicle, to reduce air pollution

**cat·a·ma·ran** (kat'ə mə ran') *n.* ⟦Tamil *kaṭṭumaram*⟧ **1** a narrow log raft propelled by sails or paddles **2** a boat like this with two parallel hulls

**cat·a·mount** (kat'ə mount') *n.* a wildcat, esp. a cougar or lynx

**cat·a·pult** (kat'ə pult) *n.* ⟦< Gr *kata-*, down + *pallein*, to hurl⟧ **1** an ancient military contrivance for throwing large stones, etc. **2** a device for launching an airplane, missile, etc. as from a deck or ramp —*vt.* to shoot or launch as from a catapult —*vi.* to leap

**cat·a·ract** (kat'ə rakt') *n.* ⟦< Gr *kata-*, down + *rhassein*, to strike or ? *arassein*, to smite⟧ **1** a large waterfall **2** *a)* an eye disease in which the lens becomes opaque, causing partial or total blindness *b)* the opaque area

**ca·tas·tro·phe** (kə tas'trə fē) *n.* ⟦< Gr *kata-*, down + *strephein*, to turn⟧ any great and sudden disaster —**cat·a·stroph·ic** (kat'ə sträf'ik) *adj.*

**cat·a·ton·ic** (kat'ə tän'ik) *adj.* ⟦< Gr *kata-*, down + *tonos*, tension⟧ of or having a psychiatric condition involving catalepsy —*n.* a catatonic person

**cat'bird'** *n.* a slate-gray North American songbird with a call like a cat's

**cat'boat'** *n.* a sailboat with a single sail on a mast set well forward

**cat'call'** *n.* a shrill shout or whistle expressing derision, etc. —*vi.* to make catcalls

**catch** (kach, kech) *vt.* **caught, catch'ing** ⟦< L *capere*, to take hold⟧ **1** to seize and hold; capture **2** to take by a trap **3** to deceive **4** to surprise in some act **5** *a)* to get to in time [to *catch* a train] *b)* to overtake **6** to lay hold of; grab [to *catch* a ball] **7** to become infected with [he *caught* a cold] **8** to understand **9** to cause to be entangled or snagged **10** [Inf.] to see, hear, etc. —*vi.* **1** to become held, fastened, etc. **2** to take hold, as fire **3** to keep hold, as a lock —*n.* **1** a catching **2** a thing that catches **3** something caught **4** one worth catching, esp. as a spouse **5** a break in the voice **6** [Inf.] a tricky qualification or condition —**catch at** to seize desperately —**catch on 1** to understand **2** to become popular —**catch up 1** to seize; snatch **2** to overtake

**catch'all'** *n.* a container or place for holding all sorts of things

**catch'er** *n. Baseball* the player behind home plate, who catches pitched balls

**catch'ing** *adj.* **1** contagious; infectious **2** attractive

**catch'phrase'** *n.* a phrase that has become popular

**catch'up'** (-up') *n.* KETCHUP

**catch'y** *adj.* **-i·er, -i·est 1** attracting attention and easily remembered [a *catchy* tune] **2** tricky

**cat·e·chism** (kat'ə kiz'əm) *n.* ⟦< Gr *kata-*, thoroughly + *ēchein*, to sound⟧ **1** a handbook of questions and answers for teaching the principles of a religion **2** a close questioning

**cat·e·gor·i·cal** (kat'ə gôr'i kəl) *adj.* **1** positive; explicit: said of a statement, etc. **2** of, as, or in a category —**cat'e·gor'i·cal·ly** *adv.*

**cat·e·go·rize** (kat'ə gə rīz') *vt.* **-rized', -riz'ing** to place in a category; classify

**cat'e·go'ry** (-gôr'ē) *n., pl.* **-ries** ⟦< Gr *katēgorein*, to assert⟧ a division in a scheme of classification

**ca·ter** (kāt'ər) *vi.* ⟦< L *ad-*, to + *capere*, take hold⟧

**1** to provide food and service, as for parties **2** to seek to gratify another's needs or desires: with *to* —*vt.* to serve as caterer for (a banquet, etc.) — **ca'ter·er** *n.*

**cat·er-cor·nered** (kat'ə kôr'nərd, kat'ē-) *adj.* ⟦< OFr *catre*, four + CORNERED⟧ diagonal —*adv.* diagonally Also **cat'er-cor'ner**

**cat·er·pil·lar** (kat'ər pil'ər, kat'ə-) *n.* ⟦< L *catta pilosus*, hairy cat⟧ the wormlike larva of a butterfly, moth, etc. —[C-] *trademark for* a kind of tractor for rough or muddy ground

**cat·er·waul** (kat'ər wôl') *vi.* ⟦prob. echoic⟧ to make a shrill sound like that of a cat; wail —*n.* such a sound

**cat'fight'** *n.* [Inf.] a fight between two women

**cat'fish'** *n., pl.* **-fish'** or (for different species) **-fish'es** a fish with long, whiskerlike feelers about the mouth

**cat'gut'** *n.* a tough thread made from dried intestines, as of sheep, and used for surgical sutures, etc.

**ca·thar·sis** (kə thär'sis) *n.* ⟦< Gr *katharos*, pure⟧ a relieving of emotional tensions, as through the arts or psychotherapy

**ca·thar'tic** (-tik) *adj.* purging —*n.* a medicine for purging the bowels; purgative

**ca·the·dral** (kə thē'drəl) *n.* ⟦< Gr *kata-*, down + *hedra*, a seat⟧ **1** the main church of a bishop's see **2** any large, imposing church

**cath·e·ter** (kath'ət ər) *n.* ⟦< Gr *kata-*, down + *hienai*, to send⟧ a slender tube inserted into a body passage, as into the bladder for drawing off urine —**cath'e·ter·ize'** (-īz') **-ized', -iz'ing,** *vt.* —**cath'e·ter·i·za'tion** *n.*

**cath·ode** (kath'ōd') *n.* ⟦< Gr < *kata-*, down + -ODE⟧ **1** the negative electrode in an electrolytic cell **2** the electron emitter in an electron tube **3** the positive terminal of a battery

**cathode rays** streams of electrons projected from a cathode: they produce X-rays when they strike solids

**cath'ode-ray' tube** a vacuum tube in which a stream of electrons can be focused on a fluorescent screen: such tubes are used as picture tubes, etc.

**cath·o·lic** (kath'ə lik, kath'lik) *adj.* ⟦< Gr *kata-*, completely + *holos*, whole⟧ **1** all-inclusive; universal **2** broad in sympathies, tastes, etc. **3** [C-] ROMAN CATHOLIC —*n.* [C-] ROMAN CATHOLIC —**Ca·thol·i·cism** (kə thäl'ə siz'əm) *n.* —**cath·o·lic·i·ty** (kath'ə lis'i tē) *n.*

**cat·i·on** (kat'ī'ən) *n.* ⟦< Gr *kata*, down + *ienai*, to go⟧ a positively charged ion: in electrolysis, cations move toward the cathode

**cat·kin** (kat'kin) *n.* ⟦< Du *katte*, cat⟧ a drooping, scaly spike of small flowers without petals, as on poplars, walnuts, etc.

**cat'nap'** *n.* a short nap; doze —*vi.* **-napped', -nap'ping** to doze briefly

**cat'nip'** *n.* ⟦CAT + dial. *nep*, catnip⟧ an herb of the mint family: cats like its odor

**cat-o'-nine-tails** (kat'ə nīn'tālz') *n., pl.* **-tails'** a whip made of nine knotted cords attached to a handle

**CAT scan** (kat) ⟦*c(omputerized) a(xial) t(omography)*⟧ CT SCAN —**CAT scanner** —**CAT scanning**

**cat's cradle** a game in which a string looped over the fingers is transferred back and forth on the hands of the players so as to form designs

**Cats·kill Mountains** (kats'kil') mountain range in SE New York: also **Cats'kills'**

**cat's-paw** (kats'pô') *n.* a person used to do distasteful or unlawful work

**cat·sup** (kat'səp) *n.* KETCHUP

**cat'tail'** *n.* a tall marsh plant with long, brown, fuzzy spikes

**cat·tle** (kat''l) *pl.n.* ⟦ult. < L *caput*, head⟧ **1** [Archaic] farm animals **2** cows, bulls, steers, or oxen —**cat'tle·man** (-mən), *pl.* **-men** (-mən), *n.*

**cat·ty** (kat'ē) *adj.* **-ti·er, -ti·est 1** of or like a cat **2** spiteful, mean, malicious, etc. —**cat'ti·ness** *n.*

**cat'ty-cor'nered** *adj.*, *adv.* CATER-CORNERED: also **cat'ty-cor'ner**

**cat'walk'** *n.* a narrow, elevated walk

**Cau·ca·sian** (kô kā'zhən) *adj.* **1** of the Caucasus or its people, etc. **2** CAUCASOID —*n.* **1** a person born or living in the Caucasus **2** CAUCASOID

**Cau·ca·soid** (kô'kə soid') *adj.* designating or of one of the major geographical varieties of human beings, loosely called the *white race* —*n.* a member of the Caucasoid population

**Cau·ca·sus** (kô'kə səs) **1** border region between SE Europe & W Asia, between the Black and Caspian seas: often called **the Caucasus 2** mountain range in this region

**cau·cus** (kô'kəs) *n.* [[< ?]] **1** a meeting of a party or faction to decide on policy, pick candidates, etc. **2** the group attending such a meeting **3** a faction of politicians —*vi.* **-cused** or **-cussed, -cus·ing** or **-cus·sing** to hold a caucus

**cau·dal** (kôd'l) *adj.* [[< L *cauda*, tail + -AL]] of, like, at, or near the tail

**caught** (kôt) *vt.*, *vi.* *pt. & pp. of* CATCH

**caul** (kôl) *n.* the membrane enveloping the head of a child at birth

**caul·dron** (kôl'drən) *n. alt. sp. of* CALDRON

**cau·li·flow·er** (kô'lə flou'ər) *n.* [[< It *cavolo*, cabbage + *fiore*, flower]] **1** a variety of cabbage with a dense white head of fleshy flower stalks **2** the head, eaten as a vegetable

**caulk** (kôk) *vt.* [[< L *calx*, a heel]] to stop up (cracks, etc.) of (a boat, etc.) as with a puttylike sealant or oakum —*n.* a soft, puttylike compound used in caulking: also **caulking compound** —**caulk'er** *n.*

**caus·al** (kôz'əl) *adj.* **1** of, being, or expressing a cause **2** relating to cause and effect —**cau·sal·i·ty** (kô zal'i tē), *pl.* **-ties,** *n.* —**caus'al·ly** *adv.*

**cau·sa·tion** (kô zā'shən) *n.* **1** a causing **2** a causal agency; anything producing an effect

**cause** (kôz) *n.* [[< L *causa*]] **1** anything producing an effect or result **2** a reason or motive for producing an effect **3** any objective or movement that people are interested in and support **4** *Law* a case to be resolved by a court —*vt.* **caused, caus'ing** to be the cause of; bring about —**caus'a·tive** *adj.* —**cause'less** *adj.* —**caus'er** *n.*

**cau·se·rie** (kô'zə rē') *n.* [[Fr]] **1** a chat **2** a short, informal piece of writing

**cause·way** (kôz'wā') *n.* [[ult. < L *calx*, lime + WAY]] a raised path or road, as across wet ground or shallow water

**caus·tic** (kôs'tik) *adj.* [[< Gr *kaiein*, to burn]] **1** that can burn tissue by chemical action; corrosive **2** sarcastic; biting —*n.* a caustic substance —**caus'ti·cal·ly** *adv.* —**caus·tic'i·ty** (-tis'i tē) *n.*

**cau·ter·ize** (kôt'ər īz') *vt.* **-ized', -iz'ing** [[see prec.]] to burn with a hot needle, a laser, a caustic substance, etc. so as to destroy dead tissue, etc. —**cau'ter·i·za'tion** *n.*

**cau·tion** (kô'shən) *n.* [[< L *cautio*]] **1** a warning **2** wariness; prudence —*vt.* to warn —**cau'tion·ar'y** *adj.*

**cau·tious** (kô'shəs) *adj.* full of caution; careful to avoid danger —**cau'tious·ly** *adv.* —**cau'tious·ness** *n.*

**cav·al·cade** (kav'əl kād', kav'əl kād') *n.* [[Fr < L *caballus*, horse]] a procession, as of horsemen, carriages, etc.

**cav·a·lier** (kav'ə lir') *n.* [[Fr: see prec.]] **1** an armed horseman; knight **2** a gallant gentleman, esp. a lady's escort —*adj.* **1** casual or indifferent toward important matters **2** arrogant —**cav'a·lier'ly** *adv.*

**cav·al·ry** (kav'əl rē) *n.*, *pl.* **-ries** [[< Fr: see CAVALCADE]] combat troops mounted originally on horses but now often riding in motorized armored vehicles —**cav'al·ry·man** (-mən), *pl.* **-men** (-mən), *n.*

**cave** (kāv) *n.* [[< L *cavus*, hollow]] a hollow place inside the earth; cavern —*vi.* **caved, cav'ing** to cave in —**cave in 1** to collapse **2** [Inf.] to give in; yield

**ca·ve·at emp·tor** (kā'vē at' emp'tôr') [[L]] let the buyer beware

**79**

**cave'-in'** *n.* **1** a caving in **2** a place where the ground, etc. has caved in

**cave man** a prehistoric human being of the Stone Age who lived in caves

**cav·ern** (kav'ərn) *n.* a cave, esp. a large cave —**cav'ern·ous** *adj.*

**cav·i·ar** or **cav·i·are** (kav'ē är') *n.* [[Fr < Pers *khāya*, egg + *-dār*, bearing]] the salted eggs of sturgeon, etc. eaten as an appetizer

**cav·il** (kav'əl) *vi.* **-iled** or **-illed, -il·ing** or **-il·ling** [[< L *cavilla*, jeering]] to object unnecessarily; quibble —*n.* a trivial objection; quibble —**cav'il·er** or **cav'il·ler** *n.*

**cav·i·ty** (kav'i tē) *n., pl.* **-ties** [[see CAVE]] **1** a natural hollow place within the body **2** a hollow place, as one caused by decay in a tooth

**ca·vort** (kə vôrt') *vi.* [[< ?]] **1** to prance or caper **2** to romp; frolic

**caw** (kô) *n.* [[echoic]] the harsh cry of a crow —*vi.* to make this sound

**cay·enne (pepper)** (kī en', kā-) [[< AmInd (Brazil) *kynnha*]] very hot red pepper made from the dried fruit of a pepper plant

**cay·use** (kī'yōos, kī yōos') *n., pl.* **-us'es** or **-use'** [[< AmInd tribal name]] a small Western horse used by cowboys

**CB** (sē'bē') *adj.* [[c(*itizens'*) b(*and*)]] designating or of shortwave radio frequencies set aside by the FCC for local use by private persons or businesses

**cc** *abbrev.* **1** carbon copy **2** cubic centimeter(s)

**CD** (sē'dē') *n.* a compact disc

**Cd** *Chem. symbol for* cadmium

**CDC** *abbrev.* Centers for Disease Control and Prevention

**Cdn** *abbrev.* Canadian

**CD-ROM** (sē'dē'räm') *n.* a compact disc on which stored data can be accessed

**cease** (sēs) *vt.*, *vi.* **ceased, ceas'ing** [[see CEDE]] to end; stop

**cease'-fire'** *n.* a temporary cessation of warfare; truce

**cease'less** *adj.* unceasing; continual

**ce·cum** (sē'kəm) *n., pl.* **-ca** (-kə) [[< L *caecus*, blind]] the pouch at the beginning of the large intestine

**ce·dar** (sē'dər) *n.* [[< Gr *kedros*]] **1** a pine tree having fragrant, durable wood **2** its wood —*adj.* of cedar

**cede** (sēd) *vt.* **ced'ed, ced'ing** [[< L *cedere*, to yield]] **1** to surrender formally **2** to transfer the title of

**ce·dil·la** (sə dil'ə) *n.* [[Sp dim. of *zeda*, a zeta or *z*]] a hooklike mark put under *c*, as in some French words (Ex.: *façade*) to show that it has an *s* sound

**ceil·ing** (sēl'iŋ) *n.* [[< L *caelum*, heaven]] **1** the inside top part of a room, opposite the floor **2** an upper limit [a price *ceiling*] **3** *Aeronautics* cloud cover affecting visibility, or the height of this —**hit the ceiling** [Slang] to lose one's temper

**cel·an·dine** (sel'ən dīn', -dēn') *n.* **1** a plant related to the poppy, with yellow flowers **2** a plant of the buttercup family, with yellow flowers

**cel·e·brate** (sel'ə brāt') *vt.* **-brat'ed, -brat'ing** [[< L *celebrare*, to honor]] **1** to perform (a ritual, etc.) **2** to commemorate (an anniversary, holiday, etc.) with festivity **3** to honor publicly —*vi.* to mark a happy occasion with festive activities —**cel'e·brant** (-brənt) *n.* —**cel'e·bra'tion** *n.* —**cel'e·bra'tor** *n.*

**cel·e·brat·ed** *adj.* famous; renowned

**ce·leb·ri·ty** (sə leb'rə tē) *n.* **1** fame **2** *pl.* **-ties** a famous person

**ce·ler·i·ty** (sə ler'i tē) *n.* [[< L *celer*, swift]] swiftness; speed

**cel·er·y** (sel'ər ē, sel'rē) *n.* [[< Gr *selinon*, parsley]] a plant whose crisp leafstalks are eaten as a vegetable

**ce·les·tial** (sə les'chəl) *adj.* [[< L *caelum*, heaven]] **1** of or in the sky or universe **2** of heaven; divine **3** of the finest kind

**cel·i·ba·cy** (sel′ə bə sē) *n.* **1** the state of being unmarried **2** sexual abstinence

**cel·i·bate** (sel′ə bət) *n.* ⟦< L *caelebs*⟧ **1** an unmarried person **2** one who abstains from sexual intercourse —*adj.* of or in a state of celibacy

**cell** (sel) *n.* ⟦< L *cella*⟧ **1** a small room, as in a prison **2** a small hollow, as in a honeycomb **3** a small unit of protoplasm: all plants and animals are made up of one or more cells **4** a container holding an electrolyte, used to generate electricity **5** a small unit of an organization —**celled** *adj.*

**cel·lar** (sel′ər) *n.* ⟦see prec.⟧ a room or rooms below ground and usually under a building

**cel·lo** (chel′ō) *n., pl.* **-los** or **-li** (-ē) ⟦< VIOLONCELLO⟧ an instrument of the violin family, between the viola and double bass in size and pitch —**cel′list** *n.*

**cel·lo·phane** (sel′ə fān′) *n.* ⟦< CELLULOSE⟧ a thin, clear material made from cellulose, used as a wrapping

**cell′phone′** *n. short for* CELLULAR PHONE

**cel·lu·lar** (sel′yōō lər) *adj.* of, like, or containing a cell or cells

**cellular phone** a mobile radio phone used in a communications system of geographically distributed transmitters: also **cellular telephone**

CELLO

**cel·lu·lite** (sel′yōō līt′) *n.* ⟦Fr⟧ fatty deposits on the hips and thighs: a nonmedical term

**cel·lu·loid** (sel′yōō loid′) *n.* ⟦fol. + -OID⟧ a tough, flammable plastic substance used, esp. formerly, for making various articles, photographic film, etc.

**cel·lu·lose** (sel′yōō lōs′) *n.* ⟦Fr < L *cella*, cell + -OSE[1]⟧ the chief substance in the cell walls of plants, used in making paper, textiles, etc.

**cellulose acetate** any of several nonflammable thermoplastics, used in making lacquers, etc.

**ce·lo·sia** (sə lō′shə, -sē ə) *n.* an annual garden plant with large clusters of tiny, brilliant red or yellow flowers

**Cel·si·us** (sel′sē əs) *adj.* ⟦after A. *Celsius* (1701-44), Swed astronomer, the inventor⟧ designating or of a thermometer on which 0° is the freezing point and 100° is the boiling point of water

**Celt** (kelt; *also* selt) *n.* ⟦< L⟧ a Celtic-speaking person

**Celt′ic** *adj.* of the Celts, their languages, etc. —*n.* a subfamily of languages including Gaelic and Welsh

**ce·ment** (sə ment′) *n.* ⟦< L *caementum*, rough stone⟧ **1** a powdered substance of lime and clay, mixed with water and sand to make mortar or with water, sand, and gravel to make concrete: it hardens upon drying **2** CONCRETE **3** anything that bonds —*vt.* **1** to unite as with cement **2** to cover with cement

**cem·e·ter·y** (sem′ə ter′ē) *n., pl.* **-ies** ⟦< Gr < *koiman*, to put to sleep⟧ a place for the burial of the dead

**cen·o·bite** (sen′ə bīt′) *n.* ⟦< Gr < *koinos*, common + *bios*, life⟧ a member of a religious order living in a monastery or convent

**cen·o·taph** (sen′ə taf′) *n.* ⟦< Gr *kenos*, empty + *taphos*, tomb⟧ a monument honoring a dead person whose remains are elsewhere

**Ce·no·zo·ic** (sē′nə zō′ik, sen′ə-) *adj.* ⟦*ceno-* (< Gr *kainos*, recent) + ZO(O)- + -IC⟧ designating the geologic era that includes the present, during which the various mammals have developed

**cen·ser** (sen′sər) *n.* a container in which incense is burned

**cen·sor** (sen′sər) *n.* ⟦L < *censere*, to judge⟧ an official with the power to examine literature, mail,

etc. and remove or prohibit anything considered obscene, objectionable, etc. —*vt.* to subject (a book, etc.) to a censor's examination —**cen′sor·ship′** *n.*

**cen·so·ri·ous** (sen sôr′ē əs) *adj.* inclined to find fault; harshly critical

**cen·sure** (sen′shər) *n.* ⟦< L *censor*, censor⟧ strong disapproval; condemnation —*vt.* **-sured, -sur·ing** to condemn as wrong —**cen′sur·a·ble** *adj.*

**cen·sus** (sen′səs) *n.* ⟦L < *censere*, enroll⟧ an official count of population and gathering of demographic data

**cent**[1] (sent) *n.* ⟦< L *centum*, hundred⟧ a 100th part of a dollar, or a coin of this value; penny

**cent**[2] *abbrev.* century; centuries

**cen·taur** (sen′tôr′) *n.* ⟦< Gr *Kentauros*⟧ *Gr. Myth.* a monster with a man's head, trunk, and arms, and a horse's body and legs

**cen·ta·vo** (sen tä′vō) *n., pl.* **-vos** ⟦Sp, a hundredth < L *centum*, hundred⟧ a 100th part of the monetary unit of various countries

**cen·te·nar·i·an** (sen′tə ner′ē ən) *n.* ⟦< fol.⟧ a person at least 100 years old

**cen·te·nar·y** (sen′tə ner′ē, sen ten′ər ē) *adj.* ⟦< L *centum*, hundred⟧ **1** of a century **2** of a centennial —*n., pl.* **-ies** CENTENNIAL

**cen·ten·ni·al** (sen ten′ē əl) *adj.* ⟦< L *centum*, hundred + *annus*, year + -AL⟧ of or lasting 100 years —*n.* a 100th anniversary or its commemoration

**cen·ter** (sen′tər) *n.* ⟦< Gr *kentron*, sharp point⟧ **1** a point equally distant from all points on the circumference of a circle or surface of a sphere **2** a pivot **3** the approximate middle point or part of anything **4** a focal point of activity **5** [*often* C-] a group or position between the left (liberals) and right (conservatives) **6** *Sports* a player whose position is at the center of the line or playing area —*vt.* **1** to place in or near the center **2** to gather to one place —*vi.* to be focused

**cen′ter·board′** *n.* a movable board or plate that, when lowered through a slot in the floor of a sailboat, functions like a keel

**cen′ter·fold′** *n.* the center facing pages of a magazine, often with an extra fold, showing a photograph, as of a nude woman or man

**center of gravity** that point in a body or system around which its weight is evenly balanced

**cen′ter·piece′** *n.* an ornament for the center of a table

**centi-** ⟦L⟧ *combining form* **1** one hundred **2** a 100th part of

**cen·ti·grade** (sen′tə grād′) *adj.* ⟦Fr: see prec. & GRADE⟧ CELSIUS

**cen·time** (sän′tēm′; *Fr* sän tēm′) *n.* ⟦Fr⟧ a 100th part of a franc

**cen·ti·me·ter** (sen′tə mēt′ər) *n.* ⟦Fr: see CENTI- & METER[1]⟧ a unit of measure, 1/100 meter: Brit. sp. **cen′ti·me′tre**

**cen·ti·pede** (sen′tə pēd′) *n.* ⟦Fr < L *centi*-, CENTI- + *pes*, FOOT⟧ an elongated arthropod with a pair of legs for each body segment

**cen·tral** (sen′trəl) *adj.* ⟦L *centralis*⟧ **1** in, near, or of the center **2** equally accessible from various points **3** main; basic **4** of a controlling source in a system —**cen·tral′i·ty** (-tral′i tē) *n.* —**cen′tral·ly** *adv.*

**Central African Republic** country in central Africa: 240,324 sq. mi.; pop. 2,568,000

**Central America** part of North America between Mexico and South America —**Central American**

**central city** the crowded, industrial, central area of a large city

**cen′tral·ize′** (-īz′) *vt.* **-ized′, -iz′ing** **1** to make central; bring to a center **2** to organize under one control —*vi.* to become centralized —**cen′tral·i·za′tion** *n.* —**cen′tral·iz′er** *n.*

**cen·tre** (sen′tər) *n., vt., vi.* **-tred, -tring** *Brit. sp.* of CENTER

**centri-** *combining form* CENTRO-

**cen·trif·u·gal** (sen trif′ə gəl) *adj.* ⟦< prec. + *fugere*, to flee + -AL⟧ using or acted on by a force (**centrifugal force**) that tends to make rotating bodies move away from the center of rotation

**cen·tri·fuge** (sen′trə fyo͞oj′) *n.* a machine using centrifugal force to separate particles of varying density

**cen·trip·e·tal** (sen trip′ət′l) *adj.* 〚< CENTRI- + L *petere*, rush at〛 using or acted on by a force (**centripetal force**) that tends to make rotating bodies move toward the center of rotation

**cen·trist** (sen′trist) *n.* a person with moderate political opinions —**cen′trism′** *n.*

**centro-** 〚< L *centrum*, center〛 *combining form* center

**cen·tu·ri·on** (sen to͝or′ē ən) *n.* [see fol.〛 the commanding officer of an ancient Roman military unit, originally of 100 men

**cen·tu·ry** (sen′chə rē) *n., pl.* **-ries** 〚L < *centum*, hundred〛 a period of 100 years, esp. as reckoned from A.D.1

**CEO** *abbrev.* chief executive officer

**ce·phal·ic** (sə fal′ik) *adj.* 〚< Gr < *kephalē*, head〛 **1** of the head or skull **2** in, on, near, or toward the head

**cephalo-** [see prec.〛 *combining form* the head, skull, or brain

**ce·ram·ic** (sə ram′ik) *adj.* 〚Gr < *keramos*, potter's clay〛 **1** of pottery, porcelain, etc. **2** of ceramics —*n.* **1** [*pl., with sing v.*] the art or work of making pottery, etc. of baked clay **2** an object made of baked clay: *often used in pl.*

**ce·ram·ist** (ser′ə mist, sə ram′ist) *n.* one who works in ceramics; ceramic artist: also **ce·ram·i·cist** (sə ram′ə sist)

**ce·re·al** (sir′ē əl) *adj.* 〚< L *Cerealis*, of Ceres, Rom goddess of agriculture〛 of grain —*n.* **1** any grain used for food, as wheat, rice, etc. **2** any grass producing such grain **3** food made from grain, as oatmeal

**cer·e·bel·lum** (ser′ə bel′əm) *n., pl.* **-lums** or **-la** (-ə) 〚L, dim. of *cerebrum*〛 the section of the brain behind and below the cerebrum

**cer·e·bral** (ser′ə brəl, sə rē′-) *adj.* **1** of the brain or cerebrum **2** of, by, or for the intellect

**cerebral palsy** a muscular disorder resulting from damage to the nervous system, esp. at birth

**cer·e·brate** (ser′ə brāt′) *vi.* **-brat·ed, -brat·ing** 〚< L *cerebrum*, the brain + -ATE¹〛 to think —**cer′e·bra′tion** *n.*

**cer·e·brum** (ser′ə brəm, sə rē′brəm) *n., pl.* **-brums** or **-bra** (-brə) 〚L〛 the upper, main part of the brain of vertebrates

**cer·e·ment** (ser′ə mənt, sir′mənt) *n.* 〚< Gr *kēros*, wax〛 [*usually pl.*] a shroud for a dead person

**cer·e·mo·ni·al** (ser′ə mō′nē əl) *adj.* of or consisting of ceremony; formal —*n.* **1** a system of rites **2** a rite or ceremony —**cer′e·mo′ni·al·ly** *adv.*

**cer′e·mo′ni·ous** (-nē əs) *adj.* **1** full of ceremony **2** very polite or formal —**cer′e·mo′ni·ous·ly** *adv.*

**cer·e·mo·ny** (ser′ə mō′nē) *n., pl.* **-nies** 〚< L *caerimonia*〛 **1** a set of formal acts proper to a special occasion, as a religious rite **2** behavior that follows rigid etiquette **3** *a)* formality *b)* empty or meaningless formality —**stand on ceremony** to insist on formality

**ce·rise** (sə rēz′, -rēs′) *n., adj.* 〚< OFr *cerise*, cherry〛 cherry red

**cer·met** (sur′met′) *n.* 〚CER(AMIC) + MET(AL)〛 a bonded mixture of ceramic material and a metal

**cert** *abbrev.* **1** certificate **2** certified

**cer·tain** (surt′'n) *adj.* 〚< L *certus*, determined〛 **1** fixed; settled **2** inevitable **3** reliable; dependable **4** sure; positive **5** definite, but unnamed [*a certain* person] **6** some [*to a certain* extent] —**for certain** without doubt

**cer′tain·ly** *adv.* undoubtedly; surely

**cer′tain·ty** *n.* **1** the state or fact of being certain **2** *pl.* **-ties** anything certain

**cer·tif·i·cate** (sər tif′i kit; *for v.*, -kāt′) *n.* 〚see CERTIFY〛 a document attesting to a fact, qualification, etc. —*vt.* **-cat·ed, -cat·ing** to issue a certificate to

**certificate of deposit** a bank certificate issued for a specified deposit of money that draws interest and requires written notice for withdrawal

**certified public accountant** a public accountant certified as having passed a state examination

**cer·ti·fy** (surt′ə fī′) *vt.* **-fied′, -fy′ing** 〚< L *certus*, certain + -FY〛 **1** to declare (a thing) true, accurate, etc. by formal statement **2** to declare officially insane **3** to guarantee (a check, document, etc.) **4** to issue a certificate or license to —**cer′ti·fi′a·ble** *adj.* —**cer′ti·fi·ca′tion** *n.*

**cer·ti·tude** (surt′ə to͞od′) *n.* sureness; inevitability

**ce·ru·le·an** (sə ro͞o′lē ən) *adj.* 〚< L < *caelum*, heaven〛 sky-blue; azure

**Cer·van·tes** (sər van′tēz′, -vän′-), **Mi·guel de** (mē gel′ *the*) 1547-1616; Sp. writer

**cer·vix** (sur′viks) *n., pl.* **cer·vi·ces** (sər vī′sēz′, sur′və-) or **-vix·es** 〚L, neck〛 a necklike part, esp. of the uterus —**cer′vi·cal** (-vi kəl) *adj.*

**ce·sar·e·an** (**section**) (sə zer′ē ən) [from the ancient story that Julius CAESAR was born this way] surgery to deliver a baby by cutting through the mother's abdominal and uterine walls

**ce·si·um** (sē′zē əm) *n.* 〚ult. < L *caesius*, bluish-gray〛 a metallic chemical element, used in photoelectric cells, radiation therapy, etc.

**ces·sa·tion** (se sā′shən) *n.* 〚< L *cessare*, cease〛 a ceasing or stopping

**ces·sion** (sesh′ən) *n.* 〚< L *cedere*, to yield〛 a ceding (of rights, property, etc.) to another

**cess·pool** (ses′po͞ol′) *n.* 〚< ? It *cesso*, privy〛 a deep hole in the ground to receive drainage or sewage from the sinks, toilets, etc. of a house

**ce·ta·cean** (sə tā′shən) *n.* 〚< L *cetus*, whale〛 any of certain fishlike water mammals, including whales, porpoises, etc. —*adj.* of the cetaceans

**Cey·lon** (sə län′, sā-, sē-) *former name for* SRI LANKA —**Cey·lo·nese** (sel′ə nēz′, sā′lə-), *pl.* **-nese′**, *adj., n.*

**Cé·zanne** (sā zán′), **Paul** 1839-1906; Fr. painter

**cf** 〚L *confer*〛 *abbrev.* compare

**CFO** *abbrev.* chief financial officer

**cg** or **cgm** *abbrev.* centigram(s)

**Ch** or **ch** *abbrev.* **1** chapter **2** church

**Cha·blis** (sha blē′) *n.* [*occas.* **c-**] a dry white Burgundy wine, orig. from Chablis, France

**Chad** (chad) country in NC Africa: 495,755 sq. mi.; pop. 6,288,000

**chafe** (chāf) *vt.* **chafed, chaf′ing** 〚< L *calefacere*, make warm〛 **1** to rub so as to make warm **2** to wear away or make sore by rubbing **3** to annoy; irritate —*vi.* **1** to rub (*on* or *against*) **2** to be annoyed or impatient

**chaff** (chaf) *n.* 〚OE *ceaf*〛 **1** threshed or winnowed husks of grain **2** anything worthless **3** teasing; banter —*vt., vi.* to tease in a good-natured way

**chaf·ing dish** (chāf′iŋ) a pan with a heating apparatus beneath it, as to cook food at the table

**cha·grin** (shə grin′) *n.* 〚Fr〛 embarrassment and annoyance due to failure, disappointment, etc. —*vt.* **-grined′, -grin′ing** to cause to feel chagrin

**chain** (chān) *n.* 〚< L *catena*〛 **1** a flexible series of joined links **2** [*pl.*] *a)* bonds; shackles *b)* captivity **3** a chainlike measuring instrument, as for surveying **4** a series of things connected causally, logically, physically, etc. **5** a number of stores, etc. owned by one company —*vt.* **1** to fasten with chains **2** to restrain, etc.

**chain gang** a gang of prisoners chained together, as when working

**chain reaction 1** a self-sustaining series of chemical or nuclear reactions in which the reaction products keep the process going **2** a series of events, each of which results in the following one

**chain saw** a portable power saw with an endless chain that carries the cutting teeth

**chair** (cher) *n.* 〚< L *cathedra*: see CATHEDRAL〛 **1** a piece of furniture with a back, for one person to sit on **2** an important or official position **3** a chairman —*vt.* to preside over as chairman

**chair'lift'** *n.* seats suspended from a power-driven endless cable, used to carry skiers up a slope

**chair'man** (-mən) *n., pl.* **-men** (-mən) a person in charge of a meeting, etc.: also **chair'per'son** — **chair'man·ship'** *n.* —**chair'wom'an,** *pl.* **-wom'en,** *fem.n.*

**chaise** (shāz) *n.* ⟦Fr⟧ a lightweight carriage, having two or four wheels

**chaise longue** (lôŋ; *also* louŋj) ⟦Fr, lit., long chair⟧ a couchlike chair with a long seat: also **chaise lounge** (louŋj)

CHAISE LONGUE

**chal·ced·o·ny** (kal sed' 'n ē) *n.* quartz having a waxy luster and, often, colored bands

**cha·let** (shal ā', shal'ā) *n.* ⟦Swiss-Fr⟧ **1** a Swiss house with overhanging eaves **2** any similar building

**chal·ice** (chal'is) *n.* ⟦< L *calix,* cup⟧ **1** a cup; goblet **2** the cup for Communion wine

**chalk** (chôk) *n.* ⟦< L *calx,* limestone⟧ **1** a soft, whitish limestone **2** a piece of chalk or chalklike substance used for writing on a blackboard —*adj.* made with chalk —*vt.* to mark or rub with chalk —**chalk up 1** to score, get, or achieve **2** to ascribe —**chalk'i·ness** *n.* —**chalk'y, -i·er, -i·est,** *adj.*

**chalk'board'** *n.* BLACKBOARD

**chal·lenge** (chal'ənj) *n.* ⟦< L *calumnia,* calumny⟧ **1** a demand for identification **2** a calling into question **3** a call to a duel, contest, etc. **4** anything that calls for special effort —*vt.* **-lenged, -leng·ing** to subject to a challenge —*vi.* to make a challenge —**chal'leng·er** *n.*

**chal'lenged** *adj.* disabled or handicapped

**chal·lis** (shal'ē) *n.* ⟦< ?⟧ a soft, lightweight fabric of wool, etc.

**cham·ber** (chām'bər) *n.* ⟦< LL *camera,* a chamber, room⟧ **1** a room, esp. a bedroom **2** [*pl.*] a judge's office near the courtroom **3** an assembly hall **4** a legislative or judicial body **5** a council [*chamber* of commerce] **6** an enclosed space; compartment; specif. the part of a gun holding a cartridge — **cham'bered** *adj.*

**cham'ber·lain** (-lin) *n.* ⟦< OHG *chamarlinc*⟧ **1** an officer in charge of the household of a ruler or lord; steward **2** [Brit.] a treasurer

**cham'ber·maid'** *n.* a woman whose work is taking care of bedrooms, as in a hotel

**chamber music** music for performance by a small group, as a string quartet

**chamber of commerce** an association established to further the business interests of its community

**cham·bray** (sham'brā') *n.* ⟦var. of *cambric*⟧ a smooth fabric of cotton, etc. with white threads woven across a colored warp

**cha·me·le·on** (kə mē'lē ən, -mēl'yən) *n.* ⟦< Gr *chamai,* on the ground + *leōn,* LION⟧ any of various lizards that can change the color of their skin

**cham·ois** (sham'ē) *n., pl.* **-ois** ⟦Fr⟧ **1** a small, goatlike antelope of the mountains of Europe and the Caucasus **2** a soft leather made from the skin of chamois, sheep, deer, etc.: also **cham·my** (sham' ē), *pl.* **-mies**

**cham·o·mile** (kam'ə mīl', -mēl') *n. alt. sp. of* CAMOMILE

**champ**[1] (champ) *vt.* ⟦prob. echoic⟧ to chew hard and noisily; munch —**champ at the bit** to be impatient when held back

**champ**[2] (champ) *n.* [Inf.] CHAMPION (sense 2)

**cham·pagne** (sham pān') *n.* an effervescent white wine, orig. from Champagne, region in NE France

**cham·paign** (sham pān') *n.* ⟦< L *campus,* field⟧ flat, open country

**cham·pi·on** (cham'pē ən) *n.* ⟦< LL *campio,* gladiator⟧ **1** one who fights for another or for a cause; defender **2** a winner of first place in a competition —*adj.* excelling all others —*vt.* to fight for; defend; support —**cham'pi·on·ship'** *n.*

**chance** (chans) *n.* ⟦< L *cadere,* to fall⟧ **1** the happening of events without apparent cause; luck **2** an unpredictable event **3** a risk or gamble **4** a ticket in a lottery **5** an opportunity **6** [*often pl.*] a possibility or probability —*adj.* accidental —*vi.* chanced, chanc'ing to have the fortune, good or bad —*vt.* to risk —**by chance** accidentally — **chance on** (or **upon**) to find or meet by chance — **(the) chances are** the likelihood is —**on the (off) chance** relying on the (remote) possibility

**chan·cel** (chan'səl) *n.* ⟦< L *cancelli,* lattices⟧ the part of a church around the altar, for the clergy and the choir

**chan'cel·ler·y** (-sə lər ē) *n., pl.* **-ies** ⟦< ML *cancellaria*⟧ the rank or position of a chancellor

**chan'cel·lor** (-sə lər) *n.* ⟦< LL *cancellarius,* secretary⟧ **1** a high government official, as, in certain countries, a prime minister **2** in some universities, the president or other executive officer

**chan·cer·y** (chan'sər ē) *n., pl.* **-ies** ⟦< ML *cancellaria*⟧ **1** a court of equity **2** an office of public archives **3** *R.C.Ch.* the diocesan office performing secretarial services for the bishop

**chan·cre** (shaŋ'kər) *n.* ⟦Fr: see CANCER⟧ a sore or ulcer of syphilis

**chanc·y** (chan'sē) *adj.* **-i·er, -i·est** risky; uncertain —**chanc'i·ness** *n.*

**chan·de·lier** (shan'də lir') *n.* ⟦Fr < L *candela,* candle⟧ a lighting fixture hung from a ceiling, with branches for candles, light bulbs, etc.

**chan·dler** (chand'lər) *n.* ⟦< L *candela,* candle⟧ **1** a maker of candles **2** a retailer of supplies, as for ships

**Chang** (chäŋ) river in central China, flowing into the East China Sea: former transliteration YANGTZE

**change** (chānj) *vt.* changed, chang'ing ⟦< L *cambire,* to barter⟧ **1** to put or take (a thing) in place of something else [to *change* jobs] **2** to exchange [to *change* seats] **3** to make different; alter —*vi.* **1** to alter; vary **2** to leave one train, plane, etc. and board another **3** to put on other clothes —*n.* **1** a substitution, alteration, or variation **2** variety **3** another set of clothes **4** *a)* money returned as the difference between the price and the greater sum presented *b)* coins or bills that together equal a single larger coin or bill *c)* small coins —**change off** to take turns —**ring the changes** to ring a set of bells with all possible variations —**change'a·ble** *adj.* —**change'less** *adj.*

**change'ling** (-liŋ) *n.* a child secretly put in the place of another, as, in folk tales, by fairies

**change of life** MENOPAUSE: also [Inf.] **the change**

**change'o'ver** *n.* a complete change, as in goods produced

**chan·nel** (chan'əl) *n.* ⟦see CANAL⟧ **1** the bed or deeper part of a river, harbor, etc. **2** a body of water joining two larger ones **3** any means of passage **4** [*pl.*] the official course of transmission of communications **5** a groove or furrow **6** a frequency band assigned to a radio or television station —*vt.* **-neled** or **-nelled, -nel·ing** or **-nel·ling 1** to make a channel in **2** to send through a channel

**Channel Islands** group of British islands in the English Channel

**chan'nel·ize'** (-īz') *vt.* **-ized', -iz'ing** to provide a channel for

**chan·son** (shän sôn') *n., pl.* **-sons'** (-sôn') ⟦Fr⟧ a song

**chant** (chant) *n.* ⟦< L *cantare,* to sing⟧ **1** a song; esp., a liturgical song with a series of syllables or words sung to each tone **2** a singsong way of speaking —*vi., vt.* to sing or say in a chant — **chant'er** *n.*

**chan·teuse** (shän tœz') *n.* ⟦Fr⟧ a woman singer, esp. of popular ballads

**chan·tey** (shan'tē, chan'tē) *n., pl.* **-teys** a song formerly sung by sailors while working: also **chan'ty**, pl. **-ties**

**chan·ti·cleer** (chan'ti klir') *n.* [< OFr *chante-cler*, lit., sing loud] a rooster

**Cha·nu·kah** (khä'noo kä') *n.* HANUKKAH

**cha·os** (kā'äs') *n.* [< Gr, space] extreme confusion or disorder —**cha·ot·ic** (kā ät'ik) *adj.*

**chap**[1] (chap) *n.* [< Brit *chapman*, peddler] [Inf.] a man; fellow

**chap**[2] (chap) *vt.*, *vi.* **chapped** or **chapt, chap'ping** [ME *chappen*, cut] to crack open; split; roughen, as skin —*n.* a chapped place in the skin

**chap**[3] *abbrev.* **1** chaplain **2** chapter

**chap·ar·ral** (shap'ə ral', chap'-) *n.* [Sp < *chaparro*, evergreen oak] [Southwest] a thicket of shrubs, etc.

**cha·peau** (sha pō') *n.*, *pl.* **-peaus'** or **-peaux'** (-pōz') [Fr] a hat

**chap·el** (chap'əl) *n.* [< ML *cappella*, dim. of *cappa*, cape] **1** a small church **2** a private place of worship, as in a hospital **3** a religious service

**chap·er·on** or **chap·er·one** (shap'ər ōn', shap'ər ōn') *n.* [< OFr, hood] one who accompanies young, unmarried people to supervise their behavior, as at dances —*vt.*, *vi.* **-oned', -on'ing** to act as chaperon (to)

**chap·lain** (chap'lən) *n.* [see CHAPEL] **1** a clergyman attached to a chapel **2** a clergyman serving in a religious capacity with the armed forces, or in a prison, hospital, etc.

**chap·let** (chap'lit) *n.* [< LL *cappa*, cape] **1** a garland for the head **2** a string of beads, esp. prayer beads

**chaps** (chaps, shaps) *pl.n.* [< MexSp *chaparreras*] leather trousers without a seat, worn over ordinary trousers by cowboys to protect their legs

**chap·ter** (chap'tər) *n.* [< L *caput*, head] **1** a main division, as of a book **2** a local branch of an organization

**chapter book** a book divided into chapters, intended for very young readers

**char** (chär) *vt.*, *vi.* **charred, char'ring** [< CHARCOAL] **1** to reduce to charcoal by burning **2** to burn slightly; scorch

**char·ac·ter** (kar'ik tər) *n.* [< Gr *charassein*, engrave] **1** any letter, figure, or symbol used in writing and printing **2** a distinctive trait, quality, etc.; characteristic **3** kind or sort **4** behavior typical of a person or group **5** moral strength **6** reputation **7** status; position **8** a person in a play, novel, etc. **9** [Inf.] an eccentric person

**char·ac·ter·is·tic** (-is'tik) *adj.* typical; distinctive —*n.* a distinguishing trait or quality —**char'ac·ter·is'ti·cal·ly** *adv.*

**char'ac·ter·ize'** (-īz') *vt.* **-ized', -iz'ing 1** to describe the particular traits of **2** to be a characteristic of —**char'ac·ter·i·za'tion** *n.*

**cha·rade** (shə rād') *n.* [Fr < Prov *charrar*, to gossip] **1** [pl.] a game in which words to be guessed are pantomimed, often syllable by syllable **2** an obvious pretense or fiction

**char·broil** or **char-broil** (chär'broil') *vt.* to broil over a charcoal fire

**char·coal** (chär'kōl') *n.* [ME *char cole*] **1** a dark, porous form of carbon made by partially burning wood or other organic matter in an airless kiln or retort: used for fuel, etc. **2** a very dark gray or brown

**chard** (chärd) *n.* [< L *carduus*, thistle] a kind of beet with edible leaves and stalks

**char·don·nay** (shär'də nā') *n.* [also C-] a dry white wine

**charge** (chärj) *vt.* **charged, charg'ing** [ult. < L *carrus*, wagon] **1** to load or fill (*with* something) **2** to add an electrical charge to (a battery, etc.) **3** to give as a duty, command, etc. to **4** to accuse **5** to make liable for (an error, etc.) **6** to ask as a price **7** to record as a debt **8** to pay for by using a credit card **9** to attack vigorously —*vi.* **1** to ask payment (*for*) **2** to attack vigorously —*n.* **1** a load or burden **2** the necessary quantity, as of fuel, for a container or device **3** the amount of chemical

energy stored in a battery **4** a cartridge or shell, or the amount of gunpowder needed to discharge a gun, etc. **5** responsibility or care (*of*) **6** a person or thing entrusted to someone's care **7** instruction; command **8** accusation; indictment **9** cost **10** a debt, debit, or expense **11** an onslaught **12** the signal for an attack **13** [Slang] a thrill —**in charge** (**of**) having the responsibility, control, or supervision (of) —**charge'a·ble** *adj.*

**charge account** an arrangement by which a customer may pay for purchases within a specified future period

**charge card** a thin, flat, plastic card embossed with the owner's name, account number, etc., used when charging purchases

**charg'er** *n.* **1** a person or thing that charges **2** a horse ridden in battle **3** a device used to charge storage batteries

**char·grill** (chär'gril') *vt.* to grill (meat) over a charcoal fire, etc.

**char·i·ly** (cher'ə lē, char'-) *adv.* cautiously —**char'i·ness** *n.*

**char·i·ot** (char'ē ət) *n.* [see CAR] a horse-drawn, two-wheeled cart used in ancient times for war, racing, etc. —**char'i·ot·eer'** (-ə tir') *n.*

**cha·ris·ma** (kə riz'mə) *n.* [< Gr, favor, grace] a special quality in one that inspires devotion or fascination

**char·is·mat·ic** (kar'iz mat'ik) *adj.* **1** of or having charisma **2** designating or of a religious group that stresses direct divine inspiration, manifested as in glossolalia, etc. —*n.* a member of a charismatic group

**char·i·ta·ble** (char'i tə bəl) *adj.* **1** generous to the needy **2** of or for charity **3** kind and forgiving; lenient —**char'i·ta·bly** *adv.*

**char·i·ty** (char'i tē) *n.*, *pl.* **-ties** [< L *caritas*, affection] **1** *Christian Theol.* love for one's fellow human beings **2** leniency in judging others **3** *a*) generosity toward the needy *b*) help so given **4** a welfare institution, fund, etc.

**char·la·tan** (shär'lə tən) *n.* [ult. < VL *cerretanus*, seller of papal indulgences] a fraud; quack

**Char·le·magne** (shär'lə mān') A.D. 742-814; king of the Franks (768-814): emperor of the Holy Roman Empire (800-814)

**Charles·ton**[1] (chärls'tən) *n.* [< name of the seaport] a lively dance of the 1920s, in 4/4 time

**Charles·ton**[2] (chärls'tən) capital of West Virginia, in the W part: pop. 57,000

**char·ley horse** (chär'lē) [Inf.] a cramp in a muscle, esp. a thigh muscle

**Char·lotte** (shär'lət) city in S North Carolina: pop. 396,000

**Char·lotte·town** (shär'lət toun') capital of Prince Edward Island, Canada: pop. 33,000

**charm** (chärm) *n.* [< L *carmen*] **1** an action, object, or words assumed to have magic power **2** a trinket worn on a bracelet, etc. **3** a quality that attracts or delights **4** *Particle Physics* a property of certain quarks —*vt.*, *vi.* **1** to act on as if by magic **2** to fascinate; delight —**charm'er** *n.* —**charm'ing** *adj.* —**charm'ing·ly** *adv.*

**char·meuse** (shär mōōz', -mōōs') *n.* [Fr < *charmer*, to bewitch] a smooth fabric of silk or polyester

**char·nel** (**house**) (chär'nəl) [< LL *carnale*, graveyard] a building or place where corpses or bones are deposited

**Cha·ron** (ker'ən) *n.* *Gr. Myth.* the ferryman on the river Styx

**chart** (chärt) *n.* [< Gr *chartēs*, layer of papyrus] **1** a map, esp. for use in navigation **2** an information sheet with tables, graphs, etc. **3** a table, graph, etc. —*vt.* **1** to make a chart of **2** to plan (a course of action)

**char·ter** (chärt'ər) *n.* [see prec.] **1** a franchise granted by a government **2** a written statement of basic laws or principles; constitution **3** written permission to form a local chapter or lodge of a society **4** the hire or lease of an airplane, bus, etc. —*vt.* **1** to grant a charter to **2** to hire for exclusive use

**charter member** a founder or original member

**charter school** a publicly-funded alternative school founded on a charter with the government

**char·treuse** (shär trōōz′, -trōōs′) *n.* ⟦Fr⟧ pale, yellowish green

**char·wom·an** (chär′wŏŏm′ən) *n., pl.* **-wom′en** ⟦see CHORE⟧ a cleaning woman

**char·y** (cher′ē, char′ē) *adj.* **-i·er, -i·est** ⟦< OE *cearig*, sorrowful⟧ **1** careful; cautious **2** sparing

**chase**¹ (chās) *vt.* **chased, chas′ing** ⟦ult. < L *capere*, to take⟧ **1** to follow so as to catch **2** to run after; pursue **3** to drive away **4** to hunt —*vi.* **1** to go in pursuit **2** [Inf.] to rush —*n.* **1** a chasing; pursuit **2** the hunting of game —**give chase** to pursue

**chase**² (chās) *vt.* **chased, chas′ing** ⟦< OFr *enchasser*⟧ to ornament (metal) as by engraving

**chas′er** *n.* **1** one that chases or hunts; pursuer **2** a mild drink, as water, taken after whiskey, etc.

**chasm** (kaz′əm) *n.* ⟦< Gr *chasma*⟧ **1** a deep crack in the earth's surface; abyss **2** any break or gap

**chas·sis** (chas′ē, shas′ē) *n., pl.* **-sis′** (-ēz′) ⟦Fr⟧ **1** the frame, wheels, engine, etc. of a motor vehicle, but not the body **2** *a)* a frame, as for the parts of a TV set *b)* the assembled frame and parts

**chaste** (chāst) *adj.* ⟦< L *castus*, pure⟧ **1** not indulging in unlawful sexual activity; virtuous **2** decent; modest **3** simple in style; not ornate —**chaste′ly** *adv.*

**chas·ten** (chās′ən) *vt.* ⟦< L *castigare*, punish⟧ **1** to punish so as to correct **2** to restrain or subdue

**chas·tise** (chas tīz′, chas′tīz′) *vt.* **-tised′, -tis′ing** ⟦see prec.⟧ **1** to punish, esp. by beating **2** to scold sharply —**chas·tise′ment** *n.* —**chas·tis′er** *n.*

**chas·ti·ty** (chas′tə tē) *n.* a being chaste; specif., *a)* virtuousness *b)* sexual abstinence; celibacy *c)* decency or modesty

**chas·u·ble** (chaz′ə bəl, chas′-) *n.* ⟦< ML *casula*⟧ a sleeveless outer vestment worn by priests at Mass

**chat** (chat) *vi.* **chat′ted, chat′ting** ⟦< CHATTER⟧ **1** to talk in a light, informal manner **2** to hold an electronic conversation by exchanging typed messages on computers —*n.* light, informal talk

**châ·teau** (sha tō′) *n., pl.* **-teaux′** (-tōz′, -tō′) or **-teaus′** ⟦Fr < L *castellum*, castle⟧ **1** a French feudal castle **2** a large country house and estate, esp. in France Also **cha·teau′**

**chat·e·laine** (shat″l ān′) *n.* ⟦Fr⟧ **1** the mistress of a château **2** a woman's ornamental chain or clasp

**Chat·ta·noo·ga** (chat′ə nōō′gə) city in SE Tennessee: pop. 152,000

**chat·tel** (chat″l) *n.* ⟦see CATTLE⟧ a movable item of personal property, as furniture

**chat·ter** (chat′ər) *vi.* ⟦echoic⟧ **1** to make short, rapid, indistinct sounds, as squirrels do **2** to talk much and foolishly **3** to click together rapidly, as teeth do from cold —*n.* **1** a chattering **2** foolish talk —**chat′ter·er** *n.*

**chat′ter·box′** *n.* an incessant talker

**chat·ty** (chat′ē) *adj.* **-ti·er, -ti·est** fond of chatting —**chat′ti·ness** *n.*

**Chau·cer** (chô′sər), **Geof·frey** (jef′rē) 1340?-1400; Eng. poet

**chauf·feur** (shō′fər, shō fur′) *n.* ⟦Fr, lit., stoker⟧ one hired to drive a private automobile for someone else —*vt.* to act as chauffeur to

**chau·vin·ism** (shō′vin iz′əm) *n.* ⟦after N. *Chauvin*, fanatical Fr patriot⟧ **1** militant and boastful patriotism; jingoism **2** unreasoning and boastful devotion to one's race, sex, etc. —**chau′vin·ist** *n., adj.* —**chau′vin·is′tic** *adj.* —**chau′vin·is′ti·cal·ly** *adv.*

**cheap** (chēp) *adj.* ⟦ult. < L *caupo*, tradesman⟧ **1** low in price **2** worth more than the price **3** easily gotten [a *cheap* victory] **4** of little value **5** contemptible **6** [Inf.] stingy —*adv.* at a low cost —**cheap′ly** *adv.* —**cheap′ness** *n.*

**cheap′en** *vt., vi.* to make or become cheap or cheaper

**cheap shot** [Slang] an unnecessarily rough or mean action or remark

**cheap′skate′** *n.* [Slang] a stingy person

**cheat** (chēt) *n.* ⟦< L *ex-*, out + *cadere*, to fall⟧ **1** a fraud; swindle **2** a swindler —*vt.* **1** to defraud; swindle **2** to foil, deprive, or elude [to *cheat* death] —*vi.* **1** to be dishonest or deceitful **2** [Slang] to be sexually unfaithful: often with *on* —**cheat′er** *n.*

**check** (chek) *n.* ⟦< OFr *eschec*, a check in chess⟧ **1** a sudden stop **2** any restraint **3** one that restrains **4** a supervision or test of accuracy, etc. **5** a mark (✓) to show verification **6** an identification ticket, token, etc. [a *hat check*] **7** one's bill at a restaurant or bar **8** a written order to a bank to pay a sum of money **9** a pattern of squares, or one of the squares **10** *Chess* the state of a king that is in danger **11** *Hockey* a bumping of an opponent —*interj.* [Inf.] agreed! right! —*vt.* **1** to stop suddenly **2** to restrain; curb; block **3** to test, verify, etc. by examination or comparison: often with *out* **4** to mark with a check (✓): often with *off* **5** to mark with a pattern of squares **6** to deposit temporarily, as in a checkroom **7** to clear (esp. luggage) for shipment **8** *Chess* to place (the opponent's king) in check **9** *Hockey* to bump (an opponent) —*vi.* **1** to agree with one another, item for item: often with *out* **2** to investigate or verify: often with *on, up on* —**check in 1** to register at a hotel, etc. **2** [Inf.] to present oneself, as at work —**check out 1** to pay and leave a hotel, etc. **2** to add up the prices of (items selected) for payment **3** to prove to be accurate, in good condition, etc. — **in check** under control —**check′er** *n.*

**check′book′** *n.* a book of detachable forms for writing bank checks

**checked** (chekt) *adj.* having a pattern of squares

**check′er·board′** *n.* a square board with 64 squares of two alternating colors, used in checkers and chess

**check·ered** (chek′ərd) *adj.* **1** having a pattern of squares **2** varied [a *checkered* career]

**check′ers** (-ərz) *n.* **1** a game for two played with flat disks on a checkerboard **2** the disks

**checking account** a bank account against which the depositor can draw checks

**check′list′** *n.* a list of things, names, etc. to be referred to: also **check list**

**check′mate′** *n.* ⟦ult. < Pers *šāh māt*, the king is dead⟧ **1** *Chess a)* the move that wins the game by checking the opponent's king so that it cannot be protected *b)* the condition of the king after this move **2** total defeat, frustration, etc. —*vt.* **-mat′ed, -mat′ing 1** *Chess* to place in checkmate **2** to defeat; thwart

**check′off′** *n.* the withholding of members' dues for the union by the employer

**check′out′** *n.* **1** the act or place of checking out purchases **2** the time by which one must check out of a hotel, etc.

**check′point′** *n.* a place on a road, etc. where traffic is inspected

**check′room′** *n.* a room in which hats, coats, etc. may be left until called for

**check′up′** *n.* an examination, esp. a medical one

**ched·dar** (**cheese**) (ched′ər) ⟦after *Cheddar*, England⟧ [*often* C-] a hard, smooth cheese

**cheek** (chēk) *n.* ⟦OE *ceoke*, jaw⟧ **1** either side of the face below the eye **2** either of two sides of anything **3** [Inf.] sauciness; impudence

**cheek′bone′** *n.* the bone across the upper cheek, just below the eye

**cheek′y** *adj.* **-i·er, -i·est** [Inf.] saucy; impudent — **cheek′i·ness** *n.*

**cheep** (chēp) *n.* ⟦echoic⟧ the short, shrill sound made by a young bird —*vt., vi.* to make, or utter with, this sound —**cheep′er** *n.*

**cheer** (chir) *n.* ⟦< Gr *kara*, the head⟧ **1** state of mind or of feeling; spirit [be of good *cheer*] **2** gladness; joy **3** festive entertainment **4** encouragement **5** *a*) a glad, excited shout to urge on, greet, etc. *b*) a rallying cry, etc. —*vt.* **1** to gladden; comfort: often with *up* **2** to urge on, greet, or applaud with cheers —*vi.* **1** to become cheerful: usually with *up* **2** to shout cheers

**cheer′ful** *adj.* **1** full of cheer; joyful **2** bright and attractive **3** willing; ready *[a cheerful helper]* — **cheer′ful·ly** *adv.* —**cheer′ful·ness** *n.*

**cheer·i·o′** (-ē ō′) *interj.* [Brit. Inf.] **1** goodbye **2** good health: used as a toast

**cheer′lead′** (-lēd′) *vi., vt.* to act as a cheerleader (for) —**cheer′lead′ing** *n.*

**cheer′lead′er** *n.* a leader of cheers, as at football games

**cheer′less** *adj.* not cheerful; dismal; dreary — **cheer′less·ly** *adv.* —**cheer′less·ness** *n.*

**cheers** (chirz) *interj.* good health: used as a toast

**cheer′y** *adj.* -i·er, -i·est cheerful; lively; bright — **cheer′i·ly** *adv.* —**cheer′i·ness** *n.*

**cheese** (chēz) *n.* [OE *cyse*] a solid food made from milk curds

**cheese′burg′er** *n.* a hamburger topped with melted cheese

**cheese′cake′** *n.* **1** a cake made with cottage cheese or cream cheese **2** [Inf.] photographic display of the figure, esp. the legs, of a pretty woman

**cheese′cloth′** *n.* [from its use for wrapping cheese] a thin cotton cloth with a very loose weave

**chees′y** *adj.* -i·er, -i·est **1** like cheese **2** [Slang] inferior; poor

**chee·tah** (chēt′ə) *n.* [Hindi < Sans *chitraka*, spotted] a swift cat of Africa and S Asia, with long legs and a spotted coat

**chef** (shef) *n.* [Fr, head, chief] **1** a head cook **2** any cook

**Che·khov** (chek′ôf), **An·ton** (än tôn′) 1860-1904; Russ. writer

**chem** *abbrev.* **1** chemical(s) **2** chemistry

**chem·i·cal** (kem′i kal) *adj.* **1** of, made by, or used in chemistry **2** made with or operated by chemicals **3** of or involving a drug, alcohol, etc. *[chemical dependency]* —*n.* **1** any substance used in or obtained by a chemical process **2** [Slang] a drug, alcoholic beverage, etc. —**chem′i·cal·ly** *adv.*

**chemical abuse** the habitual use of a mood-altering drug, alcohol, etc. —**chemical abuser**

**chemical engineering** the science or profession of applying chemistry to industrial uses

**chemical warfare** warfare by means of poisonous gases, etc.

**che·mise** (shə mēz′) *n.* [< LL *camisia*, tunic] **1** a woman's loose, short slip **2** a straight, loose dress

**chem·ist** (kem′ist) *n.* [ult. < Ar < ? Gr *cheein*, to pour] **1** a specialist in chemistry **2** [Brit.] a pharmacist, or druggist

**chem·is·try** (kem′is trē) *n.* [< prec.] **1** the science dealing with the composition and properties of substances, and with the reactions by which substances are produced from or converted into other substances **2** [Inf.] rapport

**che·mo** (kē′mō) *n.* [Inf.] *short for* CHEMOTHERAPY

**chemo-** *combining form* of, with, or by chemicals: also, before a vowel, **chem-**

**che′mo·ther′a·py** (kē′mō-) *n.* the use of drugs to prevent or treat a disease

**chem·ur·gy** (kem′ər jē) *n.* chemistry dealing with the use of organic, esp. farm, products in industrial manufacture

**che·nille** (shə nēl′) *n.* [Fr, lit., caterpillar] **1** a tufted, velvety yarn **2** a fabric filled or woven with this

**cheque** (chek) *n.* Brit. sp. of CHECK (*n.* 8)

**cher·ish** (cher′ish) *vt.* [< L *carus*, dear] **1** to feel or show love for **2** to protect; foster **3** to cling to the idea or feeling of

**Cher·o·kee** (cher′ə kē′) *n., pl.* -kees′ or -kee′ a member of a North American Indian people now chiefly of Oklahoma and North Carolina

**che·root** (shə rōōt′) *n.* [< Tamil] a cigar with both ends cut square

**cher·ry** (cher′ē) *n., pl.* -ries [< Gr *kerasion*] **1** a small, fleshy fruit with a smooth, hard pit **2** the tree that bears this fruit **3** the wood of this tree **4** a bright red color —*adj.* bright-red

**chert** (churt) *n.* a very dense type of quartz, including jasper and flint

**cher·ub** (cher′əb) *n., pl.* -ubs; for 1 usually -u·bim′ (-yōō bim′, -ə bim′) *or* -u·bims [< Heb *kerūbh*] **1** any of a kind of angel, often represented as a chubby, rosy-faced child with wings **2** a child, etc. having a sweet, innocent face —**che·ru·bic** (chə rōō′bik) *adj.* —**che·ru′bi·cal·ly** *adv.*

**cher·vil** (chur′vəl) *n.* [< Gr *chairephyllon*] an herb like parsley, with leaves used to flavor salads, soups, etc.

**Ches·a·peake Bay** (ches′ə pēk′) arm of the Atlantic, extending into Virginia and Maryland

**chess** (ches) *n.* [< OFr *eschec*, a check in chess] a game played on a chessboard by two players, using a variety of pieces (**chess′men**)

**chess′board′** *n.* a checkerboard used for chess

**chest** (chest) *n.* [< Gr *kistē*, a box] **1** a box with a lid **2** a cabinet with drawers, as for clothes **3** a cabinet with shelves, as for medicines **4** the part of the body enclosed by the ribs, breastbone, and diaphragm

**ches·ter·field** (ches′tər fēld′) *n.* [after a 19th-c. Earl of *Chesterfield*] a single-breasted topcoat, usually with a velvet collar

**chest·nut** (ches′nut′) *n.* [< Gr *kastaneia*] **1** the edible nut of various trees of the beech family **2** such a tree, or its wood **3** reddish brown **4** a reddish-brown horse **5** [Inf.] an old, stale joke, story, etc. —*adj.* reddish-brown

**chev·i·ot** (shev′ē ət; *also* chev′ē ət) *n.* [after *Cheviot* Hills, on the Scottish-English border] *[sometimes* **C-**] a rough, twilled wool fabric

**chèvre** or **che·vre** (shev′rə) *n.* a soft cheese made from goat's milk

**chev·ron** (shev′rən) *n.* [< OFr, rafter] a V-shaped bar on the sleeve of a uniform, showing rank

**chew** (chōō) *vt., vi.* [OE *ceowan*] to bite and crush with the teeth —*n.* **1** a chewing **2** something chewed or for chewing —**chew′er** *n.* —**chew′y**, -i· er, -i·est, *adj.*

**chew′ing gum** a gummy substance, as chicle, flavored for chewing

**Chey·enne¹** (shī an′, -en′) *n., pl.* -ennes′ or -enne′ a member of a North American Indian people now chiefly of Oklahoma

**Chey·enne²** (shī an′, -en′) capital of Wyoming, in the SE part: pop. 50,000

**chg(d)** *abbrev.* charge(d)

**chi** (kī, kē) *n.* the 22d letter of the Greek alphabet (X, χ)

**Chi·an·ti** (kē än′tē, -an′-) *n.* [It] *[also* **c-**] a dry red wine

**chi·a·ro·scu·ro** (kē är′ə skoor′ō) *n., pl.* -ros [It < L *clarus*, clear + *obscurus*, dark] **1** light and shade in a painting, etc. treated to suggest depth or for effect **2** a style of painting, etc. emphasizing this **3** a painting in which this is used

**chic** (shēk) *n.* [Fr < medieval LowG *schick*, skill] smart elegance of style —*adj.* pleasingly stylish

**Chi·ca·go** (shə kä′gō, -kô′-) city and port in NE Illinois: pop. 2,784,000 (met. area, 6,070,000)

**chi·can·er·y** (shi kān′ər ē) *n., pl.* -ies [< Fr] **1** trickery **2** a trick

**Chi·ca·no** (chi kä′nō) *n., pl.* -nos [< AmSp] a U.S. citizen or inhabitant of Mexican descent —*adj.* of Chicanos —**Chi·ca′na** (-nə), *pl.* -nas, *fem.n.*

**chi·chi** or **chi·chi** (shē′shē) *adj.* [Fr] extremely chic, specif. in a showy way

**chick** (chik) *n.* [ME *chike*] **1** a young chicken or bird **2** [Slang] a young woman

**chick·a·dee** (chik′ə dē′) *n.* [echoic] any of various titmice

**chick·en** (chik′ən) *n.* [< OE *cycen*] **1** a common farm bird raised for its edible eggs or flesh; hen or rooster, esp. a young one **2** its flesh **3** [Slang] a cowardly person —*adj.* [Slang] cowardly —*vi.* [Slang] to quit from fear: usually with *out*

**chicken feed** [Slang] a small sum of money

**chick′en-fried′** *adj.* coated with seasoned flour or batter and fried

**chick′en-heart′ed** *adj.* cowardly; timid: also **chick′en-liv′ered**

**chick′en-pox′** *n.* an acute, contagious viral disease, esp. of children, characterized by skin eruptions

**chicken wire** light, pliable wire fencing

**chick′pea′** *n.* **1** a bushy annual plant with short, hairy pods **2** its edible seed

**chick′weed′** *n.* a low-growing plant often found as a weed in lawns, etc.

**chic·le** (chik′əl) *n.* [AmSp] a gumlike substance from a tropical American tree, used in chewing gum

**chic·ly** (shek′lē) *adv.* in a chic way —**chic′ness** *n.*

**chic·o·ry** (chik′ə rē) *n., pl.* **-ries** [< Gr *kichora*] **1** a plant usually with blue flowers: the leaves are used for salad **2** its root, ground for mixing with coffee or for use as a coffee substitute

**chide** (chīd) *vt., vi.* **chid′ed** or **chid** (chid), **chid′ed** or **chid** or **chid·den** (chid″n), **chid′ing** [OE *cidan*] to reprove mildly —**chid′ing·ly** *adv.*

**chief** (chēf) *n.* [< L *caput*, head] a leader; head —*adj.* main; principal

**chief′ly** *adv.* **1** most of all **2** mainly —*adj.* of or like a chief

**chief′tain** (-tən) *n.* [< L *caput*, head] a chief, esp. of a clan or tribe

**chif·fon** (shi fän′) *n.* [Fr] a sheer, silky fabric —*adj.* **1** of chiffon **2** made fluffy as with beaten egg whites *[lemon chiffon pie]*

**chif·fo·nier** or **chif·fon·nier** (shif′ə nir′) *n.* [Fr] a narrow, high chest of drawers, often with a mirror

**chig·ger** (chig′ər) *n.* [of Afr orig.] the tiny, red larva of certain mites, whose bite causes severe itching

**chi·gnon** (shēn′yän) *n.* [Fr < L *catena*, chain] a coil of hair worn at the back of the neck

**Chi·hua·hua**[1] (chi wä′wä) *n.* [after fol.] a Mexican breed of very small dog with large, pointed ears

**Chi·hua·hua**[2] (chi wä′wä) state of N Mexico, on the U.S. border: 95,401 sq. mi.; pop. 2,442,000

**chil·blain** (chil′blān′) *n.* [CHIL(L) + *blain* < OE *blegen*, a sore] a painful swelling or sore, esp. on the fingers or toes, caused by exposure to cold

**child** (chīld) *n., pl.* **chil′dren** [OE *cild*] **1** an infant **2** a boy or girl before puberty **3** a son or daughter; offspring —**with child** pregnant —**child′hood′** *n.* —**child′less** *adj.*

**child′birth′** *n.* the act of giving birth to a child

**child′ish** *adj.* of or like a child; specif., immature, silly, etc. —**child′ish·ly** *adv.* —**child′ish·ness** *n.*

**child′like′** *adj.* of or like a child; specif., innocent, trusting etc.

**chil·dren** (chil′drən) *n. pl. of* CHILD

**child′s play** any very simple task

**Chi·le** (chil′ē) country on the SW coast of South America: 284,520 sq. mi.; pop. 13,232,000 —**Chil·e·an** (chi lā′ən, chil′ē ən) *adj., n.*

**chi·le re·lle·no** (chē′le re yā′nō) *pl.* **chi·les re·lle·nos** (chē′les re yā′nōs) a hot, green pepper stuffed with cheese, meat, etc. and fried

**chil·i** (chil′ē) *n., pl.* **-ies** or **-is** [MexSp] **1** the very hot, dried pod of red pepper, often ground as a seasoning (**chili powder**) **2** any of certain other peppers used in Mexican cooking **3** a highly spiced dish of beef, chilies or chili powder, and often beans and tomatoes: in full **chil′i con car′ne** (-kän kär′nē) Also **chil′e**

**chili dog** a hot dog served with chili con carne

**chili sauce** a spiced sauce of chopped tomatoes, sweet peppers, onions, etc.

**chill** (chil) *n.* [< OE *ciele*] **1** coldness or coolness causing shivers **2** a moderate coldness **3** a sudden fear, etc. **4** unfriendliness —*adj.* CHILLY —*vi.* **1** to become cold **2** to shake or shiver **3** [Slang] to relax or calm down: usually with *out* —*vt.* **1** to make cool or cold **2** to cause a chill in **3** to check (enthusiasm, etc.)

**chill factor** WINDCHILL FACTOR

**chill′y** *adj.* **-i·er**, **-i·est 1** moderately cold **2** unfriendly —**chill′i·ness** *n.*

**chime** (chīm) *n.* [< Gr *kymbalon*, cymbal] **1** [*usually pl.*] *a*) a set of tuned bells or metal tubes *b*) the musical sounds made by these **2** a single bell, as in a clock —*vi.* **chimed**, **chim′ing 1** to sound as a chime or bells **2** to agree —*vt.* to give (the time) by chiming —**chime in 1** to join in **2** to agree —**chim′er** *n.*

**Chi·me·ra** (kī mir′ə, ki-) *n.* [< Gr *chimaira*, orig., she-goat] **1** *Gr. Myth.* a monster, with a lion's head, goat's body, and serpent's tail **2** [c-] an impossible fancy

**chi·mer′i·cal** (-mer′i kəl) *adj.* **1** imaginary; unreal **2** fanciful

**chim·ney** (chim′nē) *n., pl.* **-neys** [ult. < Gr *kaminos*, oven] **1** the passage or structure through which smoke escapes from a fire, usually extending above the roof **2** a glass tube around the flame of a lamp **3** a narrow column of rock

**chim·pan·zee** (chim′pan zē′, chim pan′zē) *n.* [< Bantu] a medium-sized great ape of Africa: also [Inf.] **chimp** (chimp)

**chin** (chin) *n.* [OE *cin*] the part of the face below the lower lip —*vt.* **chinned**, **chin′ning** to pull (oneself) up, while hanging by the hands from a bar, until the chin is just above the bar

**Chin** *abbrev.* Chinese

**chi·na** (chī′nə) *n.* [orig. made in China] **1** porcelain or any ceramic ware like porcelain **2** dishes, etc. made of china **3** any earthenware Also **chi′na·ware′**

**Chi·na** (chī′nə) country in E Asia: 3,696,100 sq. mi.; pop. 1,130,511,000

**chin·chil·la** (chin chil′ə) *n.* [prob. dim. of Sp *chinche*, a small bug] **1** a small rodent of South America **2** its soft, gray fur

**chine** (chīn) *n.* [< OFr *eschine*, spine] a cut of meat from the backbone

**Chi·nese** (chī nēz′, -nēs′) *n.* **1** *pl.* **-nese′** a person born or living in China **2** the standard language of China, any related language of China, or the group consisting of these languages —*adj.* of China or its people, language, etc.

**Chinese checkers** a game in which marbles are moved as checkers, on a board with holes arranged in the shape of a six-pointed star

**Chinese lantern** a paper lantern that can be folded up

**chink**[1] (chiŋk) *n.* [OE *chine*] a crack —*vt.* to close up the chinks in

**chink**[2] (chiŋk) *n.* [echoic] a sharp, clinking sound —*vi., vt.* to make or cause to make this sound

**chi·no** (chē′nō, shē′-) *n., pl.* **-nos** [< ?] **1** a strong, twilled cotton, khaki cloth **2** [*pl.*] pants of chino for casual wear

**Chi·nook** (shə nook′, -nōōk′; chə-) *n., pl.* **-nooks′** or **-nook′** [< AmInd name] a member of a North American Indian people of Washington and Oregon

**chintz** (chints) *n.* [< Hindi *chhīnt*] a cotton cloth printed in colored designs and usually glazed

**chintz′y** (-ē) *adj.* **-i·er**, **-i·est** [prec. + -Y³] **1** like chintz **2** [Inf.] cheap, stingy, etc.

**chin-up** *n.* PULL-UP

**chip** (chip) *vt.* **chipped**, **chip′ping** [< OE] to break or cut off small pieces from —*vi.* **1** to break off in small pieces **2** *Golf* to make a short, lofted shot (**chip shot**) —*n.* **1** a small piece of wood, etc. cut or broken off **2** a place where a small piece has been chipped off **3** a small disk used in gambling games as a counter **4** a thin slice of food *[a potato chip]* **5** INTEGRATED CIRCUIT —**chip in** [Inf.] to contribute (money, etc.) —**chip on one's shoulder** [Inf.] an inclination to fight or quarrel

**chip·munk** (-muŋk′) *n.* ⟦< AmInd⟧ a small, striped North American squirrel

**chipped beef** dried or smoked beef sliced into shavings

**chip·per** (chip′ər) *adj.* ⟦< N Brit Dial.⟧ [Inf.] sprightly; in good spirits

**chiro-** ⟦< Gr *cheir*, hand⟧ *combining form* hand

**chi·rog·ra·phy** (kī räg′rə fē) *n.* ⟦prec. + -GRAPHY⟧ handwriting

**chi·rop·o·dy** (kī räp′ə dē) *n.* ⟦CHIRO- + -POD + -Y⁴⟧ PODIATRY —**chi·rop′o·dist** *n.*

**chi·ro·prac·tic** (kī′rō prak′tik) *n.* ⟦< CHIRO- + Gr *praktikos*, practical⟧ a method of treating disease by manipulation of the body joints, esp. of the spine —**chi′ro·prac′tor** *n.*

**chirp** (churp) *vi., vt.* ⟦echoic⟧ to make, or utter in, short, shrill tones, as some birds do —*n.* this sound

**chir·rup** (chir′əp) *vi.* ⟦< prec.⟧ to chirp repeatedly —*n.* a chirruping sound

**chis·el** (chiz′əl) *n.* ⟦< L *caedere*, to cut⟧ a sharp-edged hand tool for cutting or shaping wood, stone, etc. —*vi., vt.* -eled or -elled, -el·ing or -el·ling 1 to cut or shape with a chisel 2 [Inf.] to swindle or get by swindling —**chis′el·er** or **chis′el·ler** *n.*

**chit** (chit) *n.* ⟦< Hindi⟧ a voucher of a small sum owed for food, etc.

**chit·chat** (chit′chat′) *n.* ⟦< CHAT⟧ 1 light, informal talk 2 gossip

**chi·tin** (kī′tin) *n.* ⟦< Gr *chitōn*, tunic⟧ the tough, horny outer covering of insects, crustaceans, etc.

**chi·ton** (kī′tən) *n.* ⟦Gr *chitōn*, tunic⟧ a small marine mollusk with a dorsal shell of eight plates

**chit·ter·lings, chit·lins,** or **chit·lings** (chit′linz) *pl.n.* ⟦< Gmc base⟧ small intestines of pigs, used for food

**chiv·al·rous** (shiv′əl rəs) *adj.* 1 gallant, courteous, etc. like an ideal knight 2 of chivalry Also **chiv·al′ric** (-rik′, shi val′rik) —**chiv′al·rous·ly** *adv.*

**chiv·al·ry** (-rē) *n.* ⟦< OFr *chevaler*, knight < *cheval*, horse⟧ 1 medieval knighthood 2 the qualities of an ideal knight, as courage, honor, etc.

**chives** (chīvz) *pl.n.* ⟦< L *cepa*, onion⟧ [*sometimes with sing. v.*] an herb with slender, hollow leaves and a mild onion odor, used for flavoring

**chla·myd·i·a** (klə mid′ē ə) *n.* a widespread venereal disease

**chlo·ral (hydrate)** (klôr′əl) a colorless, crystal-line compound used as a sedative

**chlo·ride** (-īd′) *n.* a compound of chlorine with another element or radical

**chlo·ri·nate** (-ə nāt′) *vt.* -nat·ed, -nat·ing to combine (a substance) with chlorine; esp., to treat (water or sewage) with chlorine for purification —**chlo′ri·na′tion** *n.*

**chlo·rine** (-ēn′) *n.* ⟦< Gr *chlōros*, pale green⟧ a greenish-yellow, poisonous, gaseous chemical element with a disagreeable odor, used in bleaching, water purification, etc.

**chloro-** ⟦< Gr *chlōros*, pale green⟧ *combining form* 1 green 2 having chlorine in the molecule

**chlo·ro·form** (klôr′ə fôrm′) *n.* ⟦< Fr: see prec. & FORMIC⟧ a colorless, volatile liquid used as a solvent and, formerly, as an anesthetic —*vt.* to anesthetize or kill with chloroform

**chlo·ro·phyll′** or **chlo′ro·phyl′** (-fil′) *n.* ⟦< Fr, ult. < Gr *chlōros*, green + *phyllon*, leaf⟧ the green pigment found in plant cells, essential to photosynthesis

**chock** (chäk) *n.* ⟦NormFr *choque*, a block⟧ a block or wedge placed under a wheel, etc. to prevent motion —*vt.* to wedge fast as with a chock —*adv.* as close or tight as can be

**chock′-full′** *adj.* as full as possible

**choc·o·late** (chôk′lət, chäk′-; chôk′ə lət, chäk′ə-) *n.* ⟦ult. < AmInd (Mexico)⟧ 1 a substance made from roasted and ground cacao seeds 2 a drink or candy made with chocolate 3 reddish brown —

87 ◄ **chopsticks**

*adj.* 1 made of or flavored with chocolate 2 reddish-brown —**choc′o·lat·y** or **choc′o·lat·ey** *adj.*

**choice** (chois) *n.* ⟦< OFr < Gothic *kausjan*, to test⟧ 1 a choosing; selection 2 the right or power to choose 3 a person or thing chosen 4 the best part 5 a variety from which to choose 6 an alternative —*adj.* **choic′er, choic′est** 1 of special excellence 2 carefully chosen —**of choice** that is preferred

**choir** (kwīr) *n.* ⟦< L < Gr *choros*⟧ 1 a group of singers, esp. in a church 2 the part of a church they occupy

**choke** (chōk) *vt.* **choked, chok′ing** ⟦< OE *aceocian*⟧ 1 to prevent from breathing by blocking the windpipe; strangle; suffocate 2 to obstruct by clogging 3 to hinder the growth or action of 4 to cut off some air from the carburetor of (a gasoline engine) so as to make a richer gasoline mixture —*vi.* 1 to be suffocated 2 [Inf.] to be unable to perform because of fear, tension, etc. —*n.* 1 a choking 2 a sound of choking 3 the valve that chokes a carburetor —**choke back** to hold back (feelings, sobs, etc.) —**choke down** to swallow with difficulty —**choke off** to bring to an end

**choke collar** a training collar for a dog, that tightens when the dog strains at the leash: also **choke chain**

**choke′hold′** *n.* 1 a locking one's arms around another's neck 2 absolute control

**chok′er** *n.* a closefitting necklace

**chol·er** (käl′ər) *n.* ⟦< L *cholera*: see fol.⟧ [Now Rare] anger or ill humor

**chol·er·a** (käl′ər ə) *n.* ⟦< Gr *cholē*, bile⟧ any of several severe intestinal diseases

**chol·er·ic** *adj.* easily angered

**cho·les·ter·ol** (kə les′tər ôl′, -ōl′) *n.* ⟦< Gr *cholē*, bile + *stereos*, solid⟧ a crystalline alcohol found esp. in animal fats, blood, nerve tissue, and bile

**chomp** (chämp) *vt., vi.* ⟦var. of CHAMP¹⟧ 1 to chew hard and noisily 2 to bite down (*on*) repeatedly —**chomp at the bit** to be impatient when held back

**Chong·qing** (choon′chin′) city in SC China: pop. 2,673,000

**choose** (choōz) *vt., vi.* **chose, cho′sen, choos′ing** ⟦OE *ceosan*⟧ 1 to take as a choice; select 2 to decide or prefer [to choose to go] —**cannot choose but** cannot do otherwise than —**choos′er** *n.*

**choos′y** or **choos′ey** *adj.* **-i·er, -i·est** [Inf.] careful or fussy in choosing

**chop** (chäp) *vt.* **chopped, chop′ping** ⟦ME *choppen*⟧ 1 to cut by blows with a sharp tool 2 to cut into small bits; mince —*vi.* to make quick, cutting strokes —*n.* 1 a short, sharp stroke 2 a cut of meat and bone from the rib, loin, or shoulder 3 a short, broken movement of waves

**Cho·pin** (shō′pan; *Fr* shô pan′), **Fré·dé·ric** (fred′rik; *Fr* frā dā rēk′) 1810-49; Pol. composer, in France after 1831

**chop·per** (chäp′ər) *n.* 1 one that chops 2 [*pl.*] [Slang] teeth 3 [Inf.] a helicopter

**chop′py** *adj.* **-pi·er, -pi·est** 1 rough with short, broken waves, as the sea 2 making abrupt starts and stops —**chop′pi·ness** *n.*

**chops** (chäps) *pl.n.* 1 the jaws 2 the mouth and lower cheeks

CHOPSTICKS

**chop′sticks′** *pl.n.* ⟦Pidgin English⟧ two small sticks held together in one hand and used, mainly in parts of Asia, as an eating utensil

**chop su·ey** (chäp′ sōō′ē) [< Chin *tsa-sui*, various pieces] a Chinese-American dish of meat, bean sprouts, etc., served with rice

**cho·ral** (kôr′əl) *adj.* of, for, or sung by a choir or chorus —**cho′ral·ly** *adv.*

**cho·rale** or **cho·ral** (kə ral′, -räl′) *n.* 1 a hymn tune 2 a choir or chorus

**chord**[1] (kôrd) *n.* [altered (infl. by L *chorda*) < CORD] 1 [Archaic] the string of a musical instrument 2 *Geom.* a straight line joining any two points on an arc

**chord**[2] (kôrd) *n.* [< ME *accord*, accord] *Music* a combination of three or more tones sounded together in harmony

**chor·date** (kôr′dāt′) *n.* [L *chorda*, CORD + -ATE[1]] any of a phylum of animals having a dorsal nerve cord, including the vertebrates

**chore** (chôr) *n.* [< OE *cierr*, job] 1 a routine task 2 a hard task

**chor·e·o·graph** (kôr′ē ə graf′) *vt.*, *vi.* [< fol.] 1 to design or plan the movements of (a dance) 2 to plan (something) in careful detail —**chor′e·og′ra·pher** (-äg′rə fər) *n.*

**chor·e·og·ra·phy** (kôr′ē äg′rə fē) *n.* [Gr *choreia*, dance + -GRAPHY] 1 dancing, esp. ballet dancing 2 the devising of dances, esp. ballets —**chor′e·o·graph′ic** (-ə graf′ik) *adj.*

**chor·is·ter** (kôr′is tər) *n.* [see CHORUS] a member of a choir

**cho·roid** (kôr′oid′) *n.* [Gr < *chorion*, fetal membrane + *-eidēs*, -OID] the dark, middle membrane of the eye

**chor·tle** (chôrt′l) *vi.* -tled, -tling [prob. < CHUCKLE + SNORT] to make a gleeful chuckling or snorting sound —*n.* such a sound —**chor′tler** *n.*

**cho·rus** (kôr′əs) *n.* [< Gr *choros*] 1 a group of dancers and singers performing together 2 the part of a drama, song, etc. performed by a chorus 3 a group singing or speaking something together 4 music written for group singing 5 the refrain of a song —*vt.*, *vi.* to sing, speak, or say in unison —**in chorus** in unison

**chose** (chōz) *vt.*, *vi. pt. & obs. pp. of* CHOOSE

**cho·sen** (chō′zən) *vt.*, *vi. pp. of* CHOOSE —*adj.* selected

**Chou En-lai** (jō′en′lī′) 1898-1976; Chin. premier (1949-76): Pinyin *Zhou En-lai*

**chow** (chou) *n.* [< Chin] 1 any of a breed of medium-sized dog, originally from China: also **chow chow** 2 [Slang] food

**chow·der** (chou′dər) *n.* [Fr *chaudière*, a pot] a thick soup usually of onions and potatoes and, often, clams and milk

**chow′hound′** *n.* [Slang] a glutton

**chow mein** (chou′ mān′) [Chin *ch'ao*, fry + *mien*, flour] a Chinese-American dish of meat, bean sprouts, etc., served with fried noodles

**Chré·tien** (krā tyan′), **Jean** (zhän) 1934- ; prime minister of Canada (1993- )

**chrism** (kriz′əm) *n.* [< Gr *chrisma*, oil] holy oil used as in baptism

**Christ** (krīst) [< Gr *christos*, the anointed] Jesus of Nazareth, regarded by Christians as the prophesied Messiah

**chris·ten** (kris′ən) *vt.* 1 to baptize 2 to give a name to, as at baptism 3 [Inf.] to use for the first time —**chris′ten·ing** *n.*

**Chris·ten·dom** (-dəm) *n.* 1 Christians collectively 2 those parts of the world where most of the inhabitants profess Christianity

**Chris·tian** (kris′chən) *n.* a believer in Jesus as the prophesied Messiah, or in the religion based on the teachings of Jesus —*adj.* 1 of Jesus Christ 2 of or professing the religion based on his teachings 3 having the qualities taught by Jesus Christ, as love, kindness, humility, etc. 4 of Christians or Christianity

**Chris·ti·an·i·ty** (kris′chē an′ə tē) *n.* 1 Christians collectively 2 the Christian religion 3 the state of being a Christian

**Chris·tian·ize** (kris′chən īz′) *vt.* -ized′, -iz′ing to make Christian

**Christian name** the baptismal name or given name, as distinguished from the surname or family name

**Christian Science** a religion and system of healing: official name **Church of Christ, Scientist**

**Chris·tie** (kris′tē) *n.*, *pl.* -ties [after *Christiania*, former name of Oslo, Norway] *Skiing* a high-speed turn with the skis parallel

**Christ·mas** (kris′məs) *n.* [see CHRIST & MASS] a holiday on Dec. 25 celebrating the birth of Jesus Christ

**chro·mat·ic** (krō mat′ik) *adj.* [< Gr *chrōma*, color] 1 of or having color or colors 2 *Music* progressing by semitones —**chro·mat′i·cal·ly** *adv.*

**chro·ma·tin** (krō′mə tin) *n.* [< Gr *chrōma*, color] a substance in cell nuclei containing the genes: it readily absorbs a coloring agent, as for observation under a microscope

**chrome** (krōm) *n.* [Fr: see CHROMIUM] chromium or chromium alloy —*adj.* designating any of various pigments (**chrome red**, **chrome yellow**) made from chromium compounds —*vt.* **chromed**, **chrom′ing** to plate with chromium

**-chrome** (krōm) [< Gr *chrōma*, color] *combining form* 1 color or coloring agent 2 chromium

**chro·mi·um** (krō′mē əm) *n.* [< Gr *chrōma*, color] a hard, metallic chemical element resistant to corrosion

**chromo-** [< Gr *chrōma*, color] *combining form* color or pigment [*chromosome*] Also **chrom-**

**chro·mo·some** (krō′mə sōm′) *n.* [< prec.] any of the microscopic rod-shaped bodies carrying the genes

**chron·ic** (krän′ik) *adj.* [< Gr *chronos*, time] 1 lasting a long time or recurring: said of a disease 2 having had an ailment for a long time 3 habitual —**chron′i·cal·ly** *adv.*

**chron·i·cle** (krän′i kəl) *n.* [< Gr *chronika*, annals] a historical record of events in the order in which they happened —*vt.* -cled, -cling to tell the history of; recount; record —**chron′i·cler** *n.*

**chrono-** [< Gr *chronos*, time] *combining form* time: also **chron-**

**chro·nol·o·gy** (krə näl′ə jē) *n.*, *pl.* -gies [prec. + -LOGY] 1 the science of measuring time and of dating events 2 the arrangement of events in the order of occurrence —**chron·o·log·i·cal** (krän′ə läj′i kəl) *adj.* —**chron′o·log′i·cal·ly** *adv.*

**chro·nom·e·ter** (-näm′ət ər) *n.* [CHRONO- + -METER] a highly accurate kind of clock or watch

**chrys·a·lis** (kris′ə lis) *n.*, *pl.* **chry·sal·i·des** (kri sal′ə dēz′) or **chrys′a·lis·es** [< Gr *chrysallis*] 1 the pupa of a butterfly, encased in a cocoon 2 the cocoon

**chrys·an·the·mum** (kri san′thə məm) *n.* [< Gr *chrysos*, gold + *anthemon*, flower] 1 a late-blooming plant of the composite family, with showy flowers 2 the flower

**chub** (chub) *n.*, *pl.* **chub** or **chubs** a small freshwater fish often used as bait

**chub·by** (chub′ē) *adj.* -bi·er, -bi·est round and plump —**chub′bi·ness** *n.*

**chuck**[1] (chuk) *vt.* [< ? Fr *choquer*, strike against] 1 to tap playfully, esp. under the chin 2 to throw; toss 3 [Slang] to get rid of —*n.* a chucking

**chuck**[2] (chuk) *n.* [prob. var. of CHOCK] 1 a cut of beef from around the neck and shoulder blade 2 a clamplike holding device, as on a lathe

**chuck′-full′** *adj. var. of* CHOCK-FULL

**chuck′hole′** *n.* [see CHOCK & HOLE] a rough hole in pavement

**chuck·le** (chuk′əl) *vi.* -led, -ling [? < var. of CLUCK] to laugh softly in a low tone —*n.* a soft, low-toned laugh

**chuck wagon** a wagon equipped as a kitchen for feeding cowboys, etc.

**chuck·wal·la** (chuk′wäl′ə) *n.* [< AmInd (Mexico)] a large, edible iguana of Mexico and SW U.S.

**chug** (chug) *n.* [echoic] any of a series of puffing or

**chugged, chug′ging** to make, or move with, such sounds —*vt.* [Slang] to drink in gulps

**chuk·ka** (**boot**) (chuk′ə) an ankle-high bootlike shoe

**chum** (chum) [Inf.] *n.* ⟦prob. < *chamber* (*mate*)⟧ a close friend —*vi.* **chummed, chum′ming** to be close friends —**chum′my, -mi·er, -mi·est,** *adj.* — **chum′mi·ness** *n.*

**chump** (chump) *n.* ⟦akin to MHG *kumpf,* dull⟧ [Inf.] a fool or dupe

**Chung·king** (choon′kin′) *a former transliteration of* CHONGQING

**chunk** (chunk) *n.* ⟦< ? CHUCK[2]⟧ a short, thick piece

**chunk′y** *adj.* **-i·er, -i·est 1** short and thick **2** stocky **3** containing chunks —**chunk′i·ness** *n.*

**church** (church) *n.* ⟦< Gr *kyriakē* (*oikia*), Lord's (house)⟧ **1** a building for public worship, esp. Christian worship **2** religious service **3** [*usually* C-] *a*) all Christians *b*) a particular Christian denomination **4** a religious congregation **5** ecclesiastical, as opposed to secular, government

**church′go′er** (-gō′ər) *n.* a person who attends church, esp. regularly

**Church·ill** (chur′chil), Sir **Win·ston** (win′stən) 1874-1965; Brit. prime minister (1940-45; 1951-55)

**church′man** (-mən) *n., pl.* **-men** (-mən) **1** a clergyman **2** a church member

**Church of England** the episcopal church of England; Anglican Church: it is an established church headed by the sovereign

**church′war′den** (-wôrd′'n) *n.* a lay officer handling certain secular matters in a church

**church′yard′** *n.* the ground adjoining a church, often used as a cemetery

**churl** (churl) *n.* ⟦OE *ceorl,* peasant⟧ **1** a peasant **2** a surly person; boor —**churl′ish** *adj.* —**churl′ish·ness** *n.*

**churn** (churn) *n.* ⟦OE *cyrne*⟧ a container in which milk or cream is stirred or shaken to form butter —*vt., vi.* **1** to stir or shake (milk or cream) in a churn **2** to make (butter) thus **3** to stir up or move vigorously —**churn out** to produce in abundance

**chute**[1] (shoot) *n.* ⟦Fr, a fall⟧ an inclined or vertical trough or passage down which things slide or drop

**chute**[2] (shoot) *n.* [Inf.] *short for* PARACHUTE

**chut·ney** (chut′nē) *n., pl.* **-neys** ⟦Hindi *chatnī*⟧ a relish of fruits, spices, herbs, and vinegar

**chutz·pah** or **chutz·pa** (hoots′pə, khoots′-) *n.* ⟦Yiddish < Heb⟧ [Inf.] impudence; brass

**chyme** (kīm) *n.* ⟦< Gr *chymos,* juice⟧ the semifluid mass formed as the stomach digests food: it passes into the small intestine

**CIA** *abbrev.* Central Intelligence Agency

**ci·ca·da** (si kā′də) *n., pl.* **-das** or **-dae** (-dē) ⟦L⟧ a large, flylike insect with transparent wings: the male makes a loud, shrill sound

**cic·a·trix** (sik′ə triks′) *n., pl.* **cic·a·tri·ces** (sik′ə trī′sēz′) or **cic′a·trix′es** ⟦L⟧ a scar

**Cic·e·ro** (sis′ə rō′) 106-43 B.C.; Rom. statesman & orator

**-cide** (sīd) ⟦< L *caedere,* to kill⟧ *suffix* **1** a killer **2** a killing

**ci·der** (sī′dər) *n.* ⟦< Gr *sikera,* an intoxicant⟧ juice pressed from apples, used as a drink or for making vinegar

**ci·gar** (si gär′) *n.* ⟦Sp *cigarro*⟧ a roll of cut tobacco wrapped in a tobacco leaf for smoking

**cig·a·rette** or **cig·a·ret** (sig′ə ret′, sig′ə ret′) *n.* ⟦Fr⟧ a small roll of finely cut tobacco wrapped in thin paper for smoking

**cig·a·ril·lo** (sig′ə ril′ō) *n., pl.* **-los** ⟦Sp, dim. of *cigarro,* cigar⟧ a small, thin cigar

**ci·lan·tro** (si lan′trō, -län′-) *n.* coriander leaves used as an herb

**cil·i·a** (sil′ē ə) *pl.n., sing.* **-i·um** (-ē əm) ⟦< L⟧ small hairlike projections, as those extending from certain plant cells or from around protozoa

**ci·met·i·dine** (sə met′ə dēn′) *n.* a drug that reduces gastric secretion: used to treat peptic ulcers

**cinch** (sinch) *n.* ⟦< Sp < L *cingulum,* girdle⟧ **1** a saddle or pack girth **2** [Slang] a thing easy to do —*vt.* **1** to fasten (a saddle) on (a horse, etc.) with a cinch **2** [Slang] to make sure of

**cin·cho·na** (sin kō′nə) *n.* ⟦after 17th-c. Peruvian Countess del *Chinchón*⟧ **1** a tropical tree with a bitter bark from which quinine is made **2** this bark

**Cin·cin·nat·i** (sin′sə nat′ē, -ə) city in SW Ohio: pop. 364,000

**cinc·ture** (sink′chər) *n.* ⟦L *cinctura*⟧ a belt or girdle

**cin·der** (sin′dər) *n.* ⟦OE *sinder,* slag⟧ **1** a tiny piece of partly burned coal, wood, etc. **2** [*pl.*] ashes from coal or wood

**Cin·der·el·la** (sin′dər el′ə) *n.* in a fairy tale, a household drudge who eventually marries a prince

**cin·e·ma** (sin′ə mə) *n.* ⟦< Gr *kinēma,* motion⟧ [Chiefly Brit.] a film theater —**the cinema 1** the making of films **2** films collectively —**cin′e·mat′ic** *adj.*

**cin·e·ma·tog·ra·phy** (sin′ə mə täg′rə fē) *n.* the art, science, and work of photography in making films —**cin′e·ma·tog′ra·pher** *n.* —**cin′e·mat′o·graph′ic** (-mat′ə graf′ik) *adj.*

**cin·na·bar** (sin′ə bär′) *n.* ⟦< Gr *kinnabari*⟧ mercuric sulfide, a heavy, bright-red mineral

**cin·na·mon** (sin′ə mən) *n.* ⟦< Heb *qinnāmōn*⟧ **1** the yellowish-brown spice made from the dried inner bark of a laurel tree of the East Indies **2** this bark

**ci·pher** (sī′fər) *n.* ⟦< Ar *ṣifr*⟧ **1** the symbol 0; zero **2** a nonentity **3** secret writing based on a key; code **4** the key to such a code

**cir·ca** (sur′kə) *prep.* ⟦L⟧ about: used before an approximate date or figure: also written *cir′ca*

**cir·ca·di·an** (sər kā′dē ən) *adj.* ⟦coined < L *circa,* about + *dies,* day⟧ of the behavioral or physiological rhythms associated with the 24-hour cycle of the earth's rotation

**Cir·ce** (sur′sē) *n.* in the *Odyssey,* an enchantress who turns men into swine

**cir·cle** (sur′kəl) *n.* ⟦< Gr *kirkos*⟧ **1** a plane figure bounded by a single curved line every point of which is equally distant from the center **2** this curved line **3** anything like a circle, as a ring **4** a complete or recurring series; cycle **5** a group of people with common interests **6** extent, as of influence; scope —*vt.* **-cled, -cling 1** to form a circle around **2** to move around, as in a circle —*vi.* to go around in a circle —**cir′cler** *n.*

**cir′clet** (-klit) *n.* **1** a small circle **2** a circular ornament, as for the head

**cir·cuit** (sur′kit) *n.* ⟦< L *circum,* around + *ire,* go⟧ **1** a boundary line or its length **2** a going around something **3** the regular journey through a district of a person at work, as a preacher **4** the district of a U.S. Court of Appeals **5** a chain or association, as of theaters or resorts **6** the path or line of an electric current —*vi.* to go in a circuit —*vt.* to make a circuit about —**cir′cuit·al** *adj.*

**circuit breaker** a device that automatically interrupts the flow of an electric current

**circuit court** a court that holds sessions in various places within its district

**cir·cu·i·tous** (sər kyōō′ət əs) *adj.* roundabout; indirect —**cir·cu′i·tous·ly** *adv.* —**cir·cu′i·tous·ness** *n.*

**cir·cuit·ry** (sur′kə trē) *n.* the system or the elements of an electric circuit

**cir·cu·lar** (sur′kyə lər) *adj.* **1** in the shape of a circle; round **2** moving in a circle **3** circuitous — *n.* an advertisement, etc., intended for many readers —**cir′cu·lar′i·ty** (-ler′ə tē) *n.*

**cir′cu·lar·ize′** (-īz′) *vt.* **-ized′, -iz′ing 1** to make circular **2** to send circulars to **3** to canvass —**cir′cu·lar·i·za′tion** *n.* —**cir′cu·lar·iz′er** *n.*

**cir·cu·late** (sʉr′kyə lāt′) *vi.* **-lat′ed, -lat′ing** ⟦< L *circulari*, form a circle⟧ **1** to move in a circle or circuit and return, as the blood **2** to go from person to person or from place to place —*vt.* to make circulate —**cir′cu·lat′or** *n.* —**cir′cu·la·to′ry** (-lə tôr′ē) *adj.*

**cir·cu·la·tion** (sʉr′kyə lā′shən) *n.* **1** a circulating **2** the movement of blood through the arteries and veins **3** the distribution of newspapers, magazines, etc. **4** the average number of copies of a periodical sold in a given period

**circum-** ⟦< L *circum*⟧ *prefix* around, about, surrounding

**cir·cum·cise** (sʉr′kəm sīz′) *vt.* **-cised′, -cis′ing** ⟦< *circum*, around + *caedere*, to cut⟧ to cut off all or part of the foreskin of —**cir′cum·ci′sion** (-sizh′ən) *n.*

**cir·cum·fer·ence** (sər kum′fər əns, -frəns) *n.* ⟦< L *circum*, around + *ferre*, to carry⟧ **1** the line bounding a circle, ball, etc. **2** the length of this line

**cir·cum·flex** (sʉr′kəm fleks′) *n.* ⟦< L *circum*, around + *flectere*, to bend⟧ a mark (^ or ~) used over a vowel to indicate pronunciation

**cir′cum·lo·cu′tion** (-lō kyōō′shən) *n.* ⟦< L: see CIRCUM- & LOCUTION⟧ a roundabout way of saying something

**cir′cum·nav′i·gate′** (-nav′ə-) *vt.* **-gat′ed, -gat′ing** ⟦< L: see CIRCUM- & NAVIGATE⟧ to sail or fly around (the earth, etc.) —**cir′cum·nav′i·ga′tion** *n.*

**cir′cum·scribe′** (-skrīb′) *vt.* **-scribed′, -scrib′ing** ⟦< L: see CIRCUM- & SCRIBE⟧ **1** to trace a line around; encircle **2** to limit; confine —**cir′cum·scrip′tion** (-skrip′shən) *n.*

**cir′cum·spect′** (-spekt′) *adj.* ⟦< L *circumspicere*, look about⟧ cautious; discreet —**cir′cum·spec′tion** *n.* —**cir′cum·spect′ly** *adv.*

**cir′cum·stance′** (-stans′) *n.* ⟦< L *circum*, around + *stare*, to stand⟧ **1** a fact or event, specif. one accompanying another **2** [*pl.*] conditions affecting a person, esp. financial conditions **3** chance; luck **4** ceremony; show —*vt.* **-stanced′, -stanc′ing** to place in certain circumstances —**under no circumstances** never —**cir′cum·stanced′** *adj.*

**cir′cum·stan′tial** (-stan′shəl) *adj.* **1** having to do with, or depending on, circumstances **2** incidental **3** complete in detail —**cir′cum·stan′tial·ly** *adv.*

**circumstantial evidence** *Law* indirect evidence of a fact at issue, based on attendant circumstances

**cir′cum·vent′** (-vent′) *vt.* ⟦< L *circum*, around + *venire*, come⟧ to get the better of or prevent by craft or ingenuity —**cir′cum·ven′tion** *n.*

**cir·cus** (sʉr′kəs) *n.* ⟦L, a circle⟧ **1** in ancient Rome, an amphitheater **2** a traveling show of acrobats, trained animals, clowns, etc. **3** [Inf.] a place or event regarded as being frenzied, wildly entertaining, etc.

**ci·ré** (sē rā′) *adj.* ⟦< Fr *cire*, wax⟧ having a smooth, glossy finish

**cir·rho·sis** (sə rō′sis) *n.* ⟦< Gr *kirrhos*, tawny + -OSIS⟧ a degenerative disease, esp. of the liver, marked by excess formation of connective tissue —**cir·rhot′ic** (-rät′ik) *adj.*

**cir·rus** (sir′əs) *n.*, *pl.* **cir′rus** ⟦L, a curl⟧ the type of cloud resembling a wispy filament and found at high altitudes

**CIS** *abbrev.* Commonwealth of Independent States

**cis-** ⟦< L *cis*, on this side⟧ *prefix* on this side of

**cis·tern** (sis′tərn) *n.* ⟦< L *cista*, chest⟧ a large tank for storing water, esp. rainwater

**cit·a·del** (sit′ə del′) *n.* ⟦< L *civitas*, city⟧ a fortress

**cite** (sīt) *vt.* **cit′ed, cit′ing** ⟦< L *citare*, summon⟧ **1** to summon before a court of law **2** to quote **3** to mention by way of example, proof, etc. **4** to mention in an official report as meritorious —**ci·ta′tion** *n.*

**cit·i·fied** (sit′i fīd′) *adj.* having the manners, dress, etc. of city people

**cit·i·zen** (sit′ə zən) *n.* ⟦< L *civis*, townsman⟧ a member of a state or nation who owes allegiance to it by birth or naturalization and is entitled to full civil rights —**cit′i·zen·ship′** *n.*

**cit′i·zen·ry** *n.* citizens as a group

**cit·ric** (si′trik) *adj.* designating or of an acid obtained from citrus fruits

**cit′ron** (-trən) *n.* ⟦< Fr, lemon⟧ **1** a yellow, thick-skinned, lemonlike fruit **2** its candied rind

**cit·ron·el·la** (si′trə nel′ə) *n.* ⟦see prec.⟧ a sharp-smelling oil used in soap, insect repellents, etc.

**cit′rus** (-trəs) *n.* ⟦L⟧ **1** any of the trees that bear oranges, lemons, limes, etc. **2** any such fruit —*adj.* of these trees: also **cit′rous**

**cit·y** (sit′ē) *n.*, *pl.* **-ies** ⟦< L *civis*, townsman⟧ **1** a population center larger or more important than a town **2** in the U.S., an incorporated municipality with boundaries and powers defined by state charter **3** the people of a city —*adj.* of, in, or for a city —**cit′y·wide′** *adj.*

**city hall** (a building that houses) a municipal government

**civ·et** (siv′it) *n.* ⟦< Ar *zabād*⟧ **1** the musky secretion of a catlike carnivore (**civet cat**) of Africa and S Asia: used in some perfumes **2** the animal, or its fur

**civ·ic** (siv′ik) *adj.* ⟦< L *civis*, townsman⟧ of a city, citizens, or citizenship

**civ′ic-mind′ed** *adj.* having or showing concern for the welfare of one's community

**civ′ics** (-iks) *n.* the study of civic affairs and the duties and rights of citizenship

**civ·il** (siv′əl) *adj.* ⟦see CIVIC⟧ **1** of a citizen or citizens **2** polite **3** of citizens in matters not military or religious **4** having to do with the private rights of individuals —**civ′il·ly** *adv.*

**civil disobedience** nonviolent opposition to a law through refusal to comply with it, on grounds of conscience

**civil engineering** engineering dealing with the construction of highways, bridges, harbors, etc. —**civil engineer**

**ci·vil·ian** (sə vil′yən) *n.* ⟦see CIVIC⟧ a person not in military or naval service —*adj.* of or for civilians; nonmilitary

**ci·vil·i·ty** (-ə tē) *n.* **1** politeness **2** *pl.* **-ties** a civil, or polite, act

**civ·i·li·za·tion** (siv′ə lə zā′shən) *n.* **1** a civilizing or being civilized **2** the total culture of a people, period, etc. **3** the peoples considered to have attained a high social development

**civ′i·lize′** (-līz′) *vt.* **-lized′, -liz′ing** ⟦see CIVIC⟧ **1** to bring out of a primitive or savage condition to a higher level of social organization and of cultural and technological development **2** to make refined, sophisticated, etc. —**civ′i·lized′** *adj.*

**civil law** the body of law having to do with private rights

**civil liberties** liberties guaranteed to all individuals by law, custom, court decisions, etc.; rights, as of speaking or acting as one likes, granted without hindrance except in the interests of the public welfare

**civil rights** those rights guaranteed to all individuals by the 13th, 14th, 15th, and 19th Amendments to the U.S. Constitution, as the right to vote and the right to equal treatment under the law

**civil servant** a civil service employee

**civil service** all those employed in government administration, esp. through competitive public examination

**civil war** war between different factions of the same nation —**the Civil War** the war between the North (the Union) and the South (the Confederacy) in the U.S. (1861-65)

**civ·vies** (siv′ēz) *pl.n.* [Inf.] civilian clothes: also **civ′ies**

**ck** *abbrev.* check

**cl** *abbrev.* centiliter(s)

**Cl** *Chem. symbol for* chlorine

**clack** (klak) *vi., vt.* ⟦prob. echoic < ON⟧ to make or

cause to make a sudden, sharp sound —*n.* this
sound

**clad** (klad) *vt. alt. pt. & pp. of* CLOTHE —*adj.* **1**
clothed; dressed **2** having a bonded outer layer of
another metal or an alloy *[clad* steel]

**clad′ding** *n.* a layer of some metal or alloy bonded
to another metal

**claim** (klām) *vt.* ⟦< L *clamare,* cry out⟧ **1** to
demand as rightfully belonging to one **2** to
require; deserve *[to claim* attention] **3** to assert
—*n.* **1** a claiming **2** a right to something **3**
something claimed **4** an assertion —**claim′a·ble**
*adj.* —**claim′ant** or **claim′er** *n.*

**clair·voy·ance** (kler voi′əns) *n.* ⟦Fr < *clair,* clear +
*voyant,* seeing⟧ the supposed ability to perceive
things that are not in sight —**clair·voy′ant** *n., adj.*

**clam** (klam) *n.* ⟦< obs. *clam,* a clamp⟧ any of various hard-shelled, usually edible, bivalve mollusks
—*vi.* **clammed, clam′ming** to dig for clams —**clam
up** [Inf.] to keep silent —**clam′mer** *n.*

**clam′bake′** *n.* **1** a picnic at which steamed or
baked clams are served **2** [Inf.] any large, noisy
party

**clam·ber** (klam′bər) *vi.* ⟦ME *clambren*⟧ to climb
clumsily, esp. by using both the hands and the
feet

**clam·my** (klam′ē) *adj.* **-mi·er, -mi·est** ⟦ME, prob. <
OE *clam,* mud⟧ unpleasantly moist, cold, and
sticky —**clam′mi·ly** *adv.* —**clam′mi·ness** *n.*

**clam·or** (klam′ər) *n.* ⟦< L *clamare,* cry out⟧ **1** a
loud outcry; uproar **2** a loud demand or complaint, as by the public —*vi.* to make a clamor —
**clam′or·ous** *adj.*

**clamp** (klamp) *n.* ⟦< MDu *klampe*⟧ a device for
clasping or fastening things together —*vt.* to fasten or brace, as with a clamp —**clamp down (on)**
to become more strict (with)

**clan** (klan) *n.* ⟦< Gael < L *planta,* offshoot⟧ **1** a
group of families claiming descent from a common ancestor **2** a group of people with interests
in common —**clans·man** (klanz′mən), *pl.* **-men**
(-mən), *n.*

**clan·des·tine** (klan des′tin) *adj.* ⟦< L *clam,*
secret⟧ secret or hidden; furtive —**clan·des′tine·ly**
*adv.*

**clang** (klaŋ) *vi., vt.* ⟦echoic⟧ to make or cause to
make a loud, ringing sound, as by striking metal
—*n.* this sound

**clang′or** (-ər) *n.* ⟦L < *clangere,* to sound⟧ a continuous clanging sound

**clank** (klaŋk) *n.* ⟦echoic⟧ a sharp, metallic sound
—*vi., vt.* to make or cause to make this sound

**clan·nish** (klan′ish) *adj.* **1** of a clan **2** tending to
associate closely with one's own group only —
**clan′nish·ly** *adv.* —**clan′nish·ness** *n.*

**clap** (klap) *vi.* **clapped, clap′ping** ⟦OE *clæppan,* to
beat⟧ **1** to make a sudden, explosive sound, as of
two flat surfaces struck together **2** to strike the
hands together, as in applauding —*vt.* **1** to strike
together briskly **2** to strike with an open hand **3**
to put, move, etc. swiftly *[he was clapped* into jail]
—*n.* **1** the sound or act of clapping **2** a sharp
slap

**clap·board** (klab′ərd) *n.* ⟦transl. of MDu *klapholt*
< *klappen,* to fit + *holt,* wood⟧ a thin board with
one thicker edge, used as siding —*vt.* to cover
with clapboards

**clap′per** *n.* **1** a person who claps **2** the moving
part of a bell, that strikes the side of the bell

**clap′trap′** *n.* ⟦CLAP + TRAP¹⟧ insincere, empty talk
intended to get applause

**claque** (klak) *n.* ⟦Fr < *claquer,* to clap⟧ **1** a group
of people paid to applaud at a play, etc. **2** a group
of fawning admirers

**clar·et** (klar′it) *n.* ⟦< OFr (*vin*) *claret,* clear (wine)⟧
a dry red wine

**clar·i·fy** (klar′ə fī′) *vt., vi.* **-fied′, -fy′ing** ⟦< L
*clarus,* clear + *facere,* to make⟧ to make or become
clear —**clar′i·fi·ca′tion** *n.*

**clar·i·net** (klar′ə net′) *n.* ⟦< Fr < L *clarus,* clear⟧ a
single-reed woodwind instrument played by

means of holes and keys —**clar′i·net′ist** or **clar′i·
net′tist** *n.*

**clar·i·on** (klar′ē ən) *adj.* ⟦< L *clarus,* clear⟧ clear,
sharp, and ringing *[a clarion* call]

**clar·i·ty** (klar′ə tē) *n.* ⟦< L *clarus,* clear⟧ the quality of being clear; clearness

**clash** (klash) *vi.* ⟦echoic⟧ **1** to collide with a loud,
harsh, metallic noise **2** to conflict; disagree —*vt.*
to strike with a clashing noise —*n.* **1** the sound of
clashing **2** conflict

**clasp** (klasp) *n.* ⟦ME *claspe*⟧ **1** a fastening, as a
hook, to hold things together **2** a holding or
grasping; embrace **3** a grip of the hand —*vt.* **1** to
fasten with a clasp **2** to hold or embrace tightly
**3** to grip with the hand

**class** (klas) *n.* ⟦< L *classis*⟧ **1** a number of people
or things grouped together because of certain
likenesses; kind; sort **2** a social or economic rank
*[the working class]* **3** *a)* a group of students
taught together *b)* a meeting of such a group *c)*
a group graduating together **4** grade or quality **5**
[Inf.] excellence, as of style or appearance —*vt.* to
classify —**class′less** *adj.*

**class action (suit)** a legal action brought by one
or more persons on behalf of themselves and a
much larger group

**clas·sic** (klas′ik) *adj.* ⟦< L *classis,* class⟧ **1** being
an excellent model of its kind **2** CLASSICAL
(senses 2 & 3) **3** balanced, formal, regular, simple, etc. **4** famous as traditional or typical —*n.* **1**
a literary or artistic work of the highest excellence **2** a creator of such a work **3** *[pl.]* the works
of outstanding ancient Greek and Roman
authors: usually with *the* **4** a famous traditional
or typical event

**clas·si·cal** (klas′i kəl) *adj.* **1** CLASSIC (*adj.* 1 & 3)
**2** of the art, literature, etc. of the ancient Greeks
and Romans **3** typical of or derived from the
artistic standards of the ancient Greeks and
Romans **4** well versed in Greek and Roman culture **5** standard and traditional *[classical* eco-
nomics] **6** designating, of, or like music conforming to certain standards of form, complexity, etc.
—**clas′si·cal·ly** *adv.* —**class′i·cal′i·ty** (-kal′ə tē) *n.*

**clas′si·cism′** (-ə siz′əm) *n.* **1** the aesthetic principles of ancient Greece and Rome **2** adherence to
these principles **3** knowledge of classical literature and art —**clas′si·cist** *n.*

**class·i·fied** (klas′ə fīd′) *adj.* **1** confidential and
available only to authorized persons **2** of classified advertising —*n.* [*pl.*] a section of classified
advertisements

**classified advertising** advertising arranged
according to subject, under such listings as *help
wanted* —**classified advertisement**

**clas·si·fy** (klas′ə fī′) *vt.* **-fied′, -fy′ing** **1** to arrange
in classes according to a system **2** to designate
(government documents) to be secret or restricted
to use by authorized persons only —**clas′si·fi′a·ble**
*adj.* —**clas′si·fi·ca′tion** *n.* —**clas′si·fi′er** *n.*

**class′mate′** *n.* a member of the same class at a
school or college

**class′room′** *n.* a room in a school or college in
which classes are taught

**class′y** *adj.* **-i·er, -i·est** [Inf.] first-class, esp. in
style; elegant —**class′i·ness** *n.*

**clat·ter** (klat′ər) *vi., vt.* ⟦ME *clateren*⟧ to make or
cause to make a clatter —*n.* **1** a rapid succession
of loud, sharp noises **2** a tumult; hubbub

**clause** (klôz) *n.* ⟦< L *claudere,* to close⟧ **1** a group
of words containing a subject and a finite verb:
see DEPENDENT CLAUSE, INDEPENDENT CLAUSE **2**
a provision in a document —**claus′al** *adj.*

**claus·tro·pho·bi·a** (klôs′trə fō′bē ə) *n.* ⟦< L *claus-
trum,* enclosed place + -PHOBIA⟧ an abnormal fear
of being in an enclosed or confined place —
**claus′tro·pho′bic** *adj.*

**clav·i·chord** (klav′i kôrd′) *n.* ⟦< L *clavis,* key +
*chorda,* string⟧ a stringed musical instrument
with a keyboard, predecessor of the piano

**clav·i·cle** (klav′i kəl) *n.* ⟦< L *clavis,* key⟧ a bone connecting the breastbone with the shoulder blade

**cla·vier** (klə vir′; *for 1, also* klā′vē ər) *n.* ⟦Fr < L *clavis,* key⟧ 1 the keyboard of an organ, piano, etc. 2 any stringed keyboard instrument

**claw** (klô) *n.* ⟦OE *clawu*⟧ 1 a sharp, hooked nail on an animal's or bird's foot 2 the pincers of a lobster, etc. —*vt., vi.* to scratch, clutch, tear, etc. with or as with claws

**clay** (klā) *n.* ⟦OE *clæg*⟧ 1 a firm, plastic earth, used in making bricks, etc. 2 *a)* earth *b)* the human body —**clay′ey, clay′i·er, clay′i·est,** *adj.*

**clean** (klēn) *adj.* ⟦OE *clæne*⟧ 1 *a)* free from dirt and impurities; unsoiled *b)* free from disease, radioactivity, pollutants, etc. 2 morally pure 3 fair; sportsmanlike 4 neat and tidy 5 well-formed 6 clear 7 thorough —*adv.* [Inf.] completely —*vt., vi.* to make or be made clean —**clean up** 1 to make neat 2 [Inf.] to finish 3 [Slang] to make much profit —**come clean** [Slang] to confess —**clean′ly** *adv.* —**clean′ness** *n.*

**clean′-cut′** *adj.* 1 with a sharp edge or outline 2 well-formed 3 trim, neat, etc.

**clean′er** *n.* a person or thing that cleans; specif., one who dry-cleans clothing

**clean·ly** (klen′lē) *adj.* -li·er, -li·est 1 keeping oneself or one's surroundings clean 2 always kept clean —**clean′li·ness** *n.*

**clean room** a room designed to be nearly 100% free of dust, pollen, etc.

**cleanse** (klenz) *vt.* **cleansed, cleans′ing** ⟦OE *clænsian*⟧ to make clean, pure, etc. —**cleans′er** *n.*

**clean′up′** *n.* 1 a cleaning up 2 elimination of crime

**clear** (klir) *adj.* ⟦< L *clarus*⟧ 1 free from clouds; bright 2 transparent 3 easily seen or heard; distinct 4 keen or logical *[a clear* mind*]* 5 not obscure; obvious 6 certain; positive 7 free from guilt 8 free from deductions; net 9 free from debt 10 free from obstruction; open —*adv.* 1 in a clear way 2 completely —*vt.* 1 to make clear 2 to free from impurities, blemishes, etc. 3 to make lucid; clarify 4 to open *[to clear* a path*]* 5 to get rid of 6 to prove the innocence of 7 to pass or leap over, by, etc., esp. without touching 8 to be passed or approved by 9 to make as profit 10 *Banking* to pass (a check, etc.) through a clearinghouse —*vi.* 1 to become clear 2 *Banking* to pass through a clearinghouse: said as of a check —**clear away** (or **off**) to remove so as to leave a cleared space —**clear out** [Inf.] to depart —**clear up** to make or become clear —**in the clear** 1 free from obstructions 2 [Inf.] guiltless —**clear′ly** *adv.* —**clear′ness** *n.*

**clear′ance** (-əns) *n.* the clear space between a moving object and that which it is passing

**clear′-cut′** *adj.* 1 clearly outlined 2 distinct; definite 3 with all its trees cut down

**clear′ing** *n.* an area of land cleared of trees

**clear′ing·house′** *n.* 1 an office maintained by several banks for exchanging checks, balancing accounts, etc. 2 a central office, as for exchanging information

**cleat** (klēt) *n.* ⟦ME *clete*⟧ a piece of wood or metal fastened to something to strengthen it or give secure footing

**cleav·age** (klēv′ij) *n.* 1 a cleaving; dividing 2 a cleft; fissure; division

**cleave**[1] (klēv) *vt., vi.* **cleaved** or **cleft** or **clove, cleaved** or **cleft** or **clo′ven, cleav′ing** ⟦OE *cleofan*⟧ to divide by a blow; split; sever —**cleav′a·ble** *adj.*

**cleave**[2] (klēv) *vi.* **cleaved, cleav′ing** ⟦OE *cleofan*⟧ 1 to adhere; cling *(to)* 2 to be faithful *(to)*

**cleav·er** (klēv′ər) *n.* a heavy cutting tool with a broad blade, used by butchers

**clef** (klef) *n.* ⟦Fr < L *clavis,* key⟧ a symbol used at the beginning of a musical staff to indicate the pitch of the notes

**cleft**[1] (kleft) *n.* ⟦< OE *cleofan:* see CLEAVE[1]⟧ an opening or hollow made by or as if by cleaving; crack; crevice

**cleft**[2] (kleft) *vt., vi. alt. pt. & pp. of* CLEAVE[1] —*adj.* split; divided

**cleft lip** a vertical cleft in the upper lip, often accompanying a CLEFT PALATE

**cleft palate** a cleft from front to back along the middle of the roof of the mouth, due to incomplete prenatal development

**clem·a·tis** (klem′ə tis) *n.* ⟦< Gr *klēma,* vine⟧ a vine of the buttercup family, with bright-colored flowers

**clem·en·cy** (klem′ən sē) *n.* mercy; forbearance

**Clem·ens** (klem′ənz), **Sam·u·el Lang·horne** (sam′ yōō əl laŋ′hôrn) (pseud. *Mark Twain*) 1835-1910; U.S. writer & humorist

**clem′ent** (-ənt) *adj.* ⟦L *clemens*⟧ 1 lenient 2 mild: said as of weather

**clench** (klench) *vt.* ⟦< OE *(be)clencan,* to make cling⟧ 1 to close (the teeth or fist) firmly 2 to grip tightly —*n.* a firm grip

**Cle·o·pa·tra** (klē′ō pa′trə, klē′ ə-) 69?-30 B.C.; queen of Egypt (51-49; 48-30)

**clere·sto·ry** (klir′stôr′ē) *n., pl.* **-ries** ⟦< ME *cler,* clear + *storie,* story (of a building)⟧ the upper part of a wall, as of a church, having windows for lighting the central space

**cler·gy** (klur′jē) *n., pl.* **-gies** ⟦see CLERK⟧ ministers, priests, rabbis, etc., collectively

**cler′gy·man** (-mən) *n., pl.* **-men** (-mən) a member of the clergy; minister, priest, rabbi, etc. —**cler′gy·wom′an,** *pl.* **-wom′en,** *fem.n.*

**cler·ic** (kler′ik) *n.* a member of the clergy

**cler·i·cal** (kler′i kəl) *adj.* 1 of the clergy or one of its members 2 of office clerks or their work

**cler′i·cal·ism′** (-iz′əm) *n.* political power of the clergy —**cler′i·cal·ist** *n.*

**clerk** (klurk) *n.* ⟦< Gr *klērikos,* a cleric⟧ 1 a lay member of a church with minor duties 2 an office worker who types, files, etc. 3 an official who keeps the records of a court, town, etc. 4 a salesclerk —*vi.* to work as a salesclerk

**Cleve·land**[1] (klēv′lənd), **(Stephen) Gro·ver** (grō′ vər) 1837-1908; 22d and 24th president of the U.S. (1885-89; 1893-97)

**Cleve·land**[2] (klēv′lənd) city and port in NE Ohio: pop. 506,000

**clev·er** (klev′ər) *adj.* ⟦? < Norw *klöver*⟧ 1 skillful; adroit 2 intelligent; ingenious; smart —**clev′er·ly** *adv.* —**clev′er·ness** *n.*

**clev·is** (klev′is) *n.* ⟦see CLEAVE[2]⟧ a U-shaped piece of iron with holes for a pin, for attaching one thing to another

**clew** (klōō) *n.* ⟦OE *cliwen*⟧ 1 a ball of thread or yarn 2 *archaic sp. of* CLUE

**cli·ché** (klē shā′) *n.* ⟦Fr < pp. of *clicher,* to stereotype⟧ a trite expression or idea

**cli·chéd** (klē shād′) *adj.* trite; stereotyped

**click** (klik) *n.* ⟦echoic⟧ a slight, sharp sound like that of a door latch snapping into place —*vi., vt.* to make or cause to make a click

**cli·ent** (klī′ənt) *n.* ⟦< L *cliens,* follower⟧ 1 a person or company for whom a lawyer, accountant, etc. is acting 2 a customer

**cli·en·tele** (klī′ən tel′) *n.* ⟦< Fr < L *clientela,* patronage⟧ all one's clients or customers, collectively

**cliff** (klif) *n.* ⟦OE *clif*⟧ a high, steep face of rock

**cliff′hang′er** or **cliff′-hang′er** *n.* a suspenseful film, story, situation, etc.

**cli·mac·ter·ic** (klī mak′tər ik, klī′mak ter′ik) *n.* ⟦< Gr *klimax,* ladder⟧ a crucial period in life; esp., menopause —*adj.* crucial

**cli·mate** (klī′mət) *n.* ⟦< Gr *klima,* region⟧ 1 the prevailing weather conditions of a place 2 a region with reference to its prevailing weather —**cli·mat′ic** (-mat′ik) *adj.*

**cli·max** (klī′maks′) *n.* ⟦L < Gr *klimax,* ladder⟧ 1 the final, culminating element in a series; highest point of interest, excitement, etc. 2 the turning point of action in a drama, etc. 3 an orgasm —*vi.,*

**vt.** to reach, or bring to, a climax —**cli·mac'tic** (-mak'tik) *adj.*

**climb** (klīm) *vi., vt.* **climbed, climb'ing** ⟦OE *climban*⟧ **1** to move up by using the feet and, often, the hands **2** to ascend gradually **3** to move (*down, over, along,* etc.) using the hands and feet **4** to grow upward on (a wall, etc.) —*n.* **1** a climbing **2** a thing or place to be climbed —**climb'a·ble** *adj.* —**climb'er** *n.*

**clime** (klīm) *n.* ⟦see CLIMATE⟧ [Old Poet.] a region, esp. with regard to climate

**clinch** (klinch) *vt.* ⟦var. of CLENCH⟧ **1** to fasten (a driven nail, etc.) by bending the projecting end **2** to settle (an argument, bargain, etc.) definitely — *vi.* **1** *Boxing* to grip the opponent with the arms so as to hinder punching effectiveness **2** [Slang] to embrace —*n.* a clinching

**clinch'er** *n.* **1** one that clinches **2** a decisive point, argument, act, etc.

**cling** (kliŋ) *vi.* **clung, cling'ing** ⟦OE *clingan*⟧ **1** to adhere; hold fast, as by embracing **2** to be or stay near **3** to be emotionally attached —**cling'er** *n.* — **cling'y, -i·er, -i·est,** *adj.*

**clin·ic** (klin'ik) *n.* ⟦< Gr *klinē,* bed⟧ **1** the teaching of medicine by treatment of patients in the presence of students **2** a place where medical specialists practice as a group **3** an outpatient department, as in a hospital **4** an intensive session of group instruction, as in a certain skill

**clin'i·cal** (-i kəl) *adj.* **1** of or connected with a clinic or sickbed **2** having to do with the treatment and observation of patients, as distinguished from theoretical study **3** purely scientific —**clin'i·cal·ly** *adv.*

**cli·ni·cian** (kli nish'ən) *n.* one who practices clinical medicine, psychology, etc.

**clink** (kliŋk) *vi., vt.* ⟦echoic⟧ to make or cause to make a slight, sharp sound, as of glasses striking together —*n.* **1** such a sound **2** [Inf.] a jail

**clink·er** (kliŋ'kər) *n.* ⟦Du *klinker*⟧ **1** a hard mass of fused stony matter, formed as from burned coal **2** [Slang] a mistake

**Clin·ton** (klint'ʼn), **Bill** (bil) (legal name *William Jefferson Clinton;* born *William Jefferson Blythe IV*) 1946- ; 42d president of the U.S. (1993-2001)

**clip**[1] (klip) *vt.* **clipped, clip'ping** ⟦< ON *klippa*⟧ **1** to cut, as with shears **2** to cut short **3** to cut the hair of **4** [Inf.] to hit sharply **5** [Slang] to swindle —*vi.* to move rapidly —*n.* **1** a clipping **2** an excerpt from a film, videotape, etc. **3** a rapid pace **4** [Inf.] a quick, sharp blow

**clip**[2] (klip) *vi., vt.* **clipped, clip'ping** ⟦OE *clyppan,* to embrace⟧ to grip tightly; fasten —*n.* any of various devices that clip, fasten, hold, etc.

**clip'board'** *n.* a writing board with a hinged clip at the top to hold papers

**clip joint** [Slang] a nightclub, store, etc. that charges excessive prices

**clipped form** a shortened form of a word, as *pike* (for *turnpike*) or *fan* (for *fanatic*)

**clip·per** (klip'ər) *n.* **1** [*usually pl.*] a tool for cutting or trimming **2** a sailing ship built for great speed

**clip'ping** *n.* a piece cut out or off, as an item clipped from a newspaper

**clique** (klik, klēk) *n.* ⟦Fr < OFr *cliquer,* make a noise⟧ a small, exclusive circle of people; coterie —**cliqu'ish** *adj.* —**cliqu'ish·ly** *adv.*

**clit·o·ris** (klit'ər is) *n., pl.* **clit'o·ris·es** (-is iz) or **cli·tor·i·des** (kli tôr'i dēz') ⟦< Gr⟧ a small, sensitive, erectile organ of the vulva

**clo·a·ca** (klō ā'kə) *n., pl.* **-cae** (-sē', -kē') or **-cas** ⟦L < *cluere,* to cleanse⟧ a cavity, as in reptiles and birds, into which both the intestinal and the genitourinary tracts empty

**cloak** (klōk) *n.* ⟦< ML *clocca,* bell: from its shape⟧ **1** a loose, usually sleeveless outer garment **2** something that covers or conceals; disguise —*vt.* **1** to cover with a cloak **2** to conceal

**clob·ber** (kläb'ər) *vt.* ⟦< ?⟧ [Slang] **1** to beat or hit repeatedly **2** to defeat decisively

**cloche** (klōsh) *n.* ⟦Fr, a bell⟧ a woman's closefitting, bell-shaped hat

**clock**[1] (kläk) *n.* ⟦ME *clokke,* orig., clock with bells < ML *clocca,* bell⟧ a device for measuring and indicating time, usually by means of pointers moving over a dial: clocks are not meant to be worn or carried about —*vt.* to record the time of (a race, etc.) with a stopwatch

**clock**[2] (kläk) *n.* ⟦< ? prec., because of original bell shape⟧ a woven or embroidered ornament on a sock, going up from the ankle

**clock radio** a radio with a built-in clock that can turn it on or off

**clock'wise'** *adv., adj.* in the direction in which the hands of a clock rotate

**clock'work'** *n.* **1** the mechanism of a clock **2** any similar mechanism, with springs and gears —**like clockwork** very regularly

**clod** (kläd) *n.* ⟦OE⟧ **1** a lump, esp. of earth or clay **2** a dull, stupid person —**clod'dish** *adj.*

**clod'hop·per** *n.* ⟦prec. + HOPPER⟧ **1** a plowman **2** a clumsy, stupid person **3** a coarse, heavy shoe

**clog** (kläg) *n.* ⟦ME *clogge,* lump of wood⟧ **1** anything that hinders or obstructs; hindrance **2** a shoe with a thick, usually wooden, sole —*vt.* **clogged, clog'ging 1** to hinder **2** to obstruct (a passage); jam —*vi.* to become clogged

**cloi·son·né** (kloi'zə nā') *adj.* ⟦Fr, lit., partitioned⟧ designating enamel work in which the surface decoration is set in hollows formed by thin strips of wire

**clois·ter** (klois'tər) *n.* ⟦< L *claudere,* to close⟧ **1** a monastery or convent **2** monastic life **3** a covered walk along a courtyard wall in a monastery, etc., with an open colonnade —*vt.* to confine as in a cloister —**clois'tered** *adj.*

**clomp** (klämp) *vi.* to walk heavily or noisily

**clone** (klōn) *n.* ⟦< Gr *klōn,* a twig⟧ **1** all the descendants derived asexually from a single organism **2** a genetically identical duplicate of an organism, produced by replacing the nucleus of an unfertilized ovum with the nucleus of a body cell from the organism **3** [Inf.] a person or thing very much like another —*vt.* **cloned, clon'ing** to produce a clone of —**clon'al** *adj.*

**clop** (kläp) *n.* ⟦echoic⟧ a clattering sound, like hoofbeats —*vi.* **clopped, clop'ping** to make, or move with, such a sound

**close**[1] (klōs) *adj.* **clos'er, clos'est** ⟦see fol.⟧ **1** confined or confining [*close* quarters] **2** secretive; reserved **3** miserly; stingy **4** warm and stuffy **5** with little space between; near together **6** compact; dense [*close* weave] **7** near to the surface [a *close* shave] **8** intimate; familiar [a *close* friend] **9** strict; careful [*close* attention] **10** nearly alike [a *close* resemblance] **11** nearly equal or even [a *close* contest] —*adv.* in a close manner —**close'ly** *adv.* —**close'ness** *n.*

**close**[2] (klōz) *vt.* **closed, clos'ing** ⟦< L *claudere,* to close⟧ **1** to shut **2** to fill up or stop (an opening) **3** to finish —*vi.* **1** to undergo shutting **2** to come to an end **3** to come close or together —*n.* an end or conclusion —**close down** (or **up**) to shut or stop entirely —**close in** to draw near from all directions —**close out** to dispose of (goods) by sale

**close call** (klōs) [Inf.] a narrow escape from danger: also **close shave**

**close-cropped** (klōs'kräpt') *adj.* clipped very short [*close-cropped* hair]

**closed circuit** a system for telecasting by cable, etc. only to receivers connected in the circuit — **closed'-cir'cuit** *adj.*

**close·fist·ed** (klōs'fis'tid) *adj.* stingy

**close'fit·ting** (-fit'iŋ) *adj.* fitting tightly

**close'-knit'** (-nit') *adj.* closely united or joined

**close·mouthed** (klōz'mou⁀thd', -mou⁀th') *adj.* not talking much; taciturn

**close'out'** (-out') *n.* a discounted sale of goods no longer carried, or of those of a business being closed down through liquidation

**clos·er** (klō′zər) *n.* a person adept at completing a deal, an assignment, etc. successfully

**clos·et** (kläz′it) *n.* [< L *claudere*, to close] 1 a small room or cupboard for clothes, supplies, etc. 2 a small, private room 3 a state of secrecy —*vt.* to shut up in a private room for confidential talk

**close-up** (klōs′up′) *n.* a photograph, etc. taken at very close range

**clo·sure** (klō′zhər) *n.* [< L *claudere*, to close] 1 a closing or being closed 2 a finish; end 3 anything that closes 4 CLOTURE

**clot** (klät) *n.* [OE] a soft lump or thickened mass [a blood *clot*] —*vt.*, *vi.* **clot′ted, clot′ting** to form into a clot or clots; coagulate

**cloth** (klôth) *n.*, *pl.* **cloths** (klôthz, klôths) [OE *clath*] 1 a woven, knitted, or pressed fabric of fibrous material, as cotton, wool, silk, or synthetic fibers 2 a tablecloth, washcloth, etc. —*adj.* made of cloth —**the cloth** the clergy collectively

**clothe** (klōth) *vt.* **clothed** or **clad, cloth′ing** [see prec.] 1 to provide with or dress in clothes 2 to cover

**clothes** (klōthz, klōz) *pl.n.* [OE *clathas*] articles, usually of cloth, for covering, protecting, or adorning the body

**clothes′pin′** *n.* a small clip for fastening clothes on a line, as for drying

**cloth·ier** (klōth′yər) *n.* a dealer in clothes or cloth

**cloth·ing** (klō′thiŋ) *n.* 1 clothes; garments 2 a covering

**clo·ture** (klō′chər) *n.* [see CLOSURE] the ending of legislative debate by having the bill put to an immediate vote

**cloud** (kloud) *n.* [OE *clud*, mass of rock] 1 a visible mass of condensed water droplets or ice crystals in the sky 2 a mass of smoke, dust, etc. 3 a crowd; swarm [a *cloud* of locusts] 4 anything that darkens, obscures, etc. —*vt.* 1 to darken or obscure as with clouds 2 to make gloomy 3 to sully (a reputation, etc.) —*vi.* to become cloudy, gloomy, etc. —**under a cloud** under suspicion — **cloud′less** *adj.* —**cloud′y, -i·er, -i·est,** *adj.* — **cloud′i·ness** *n.*

**cloud′burst′** *n.* a sudden, heavy rain

**clout** (klout) *n.* [< OE *clut*, a patch] 1 a blow, as with the hand 2 [Inf.] power, esp. political power —*vt.* 1 [Inf.] to strike, as with the hand 2 to hit (a ball) hard

**clove**[1] (klōv) *n.* [< L *clavus*, nail: from its shape] 1 the dried flower bud of a tropical evergreen tree, used as a spice 2 the tree

**clove**[2] (klōv) *n.* [OE *clufu*] a segment of a bulb, as of garlic

**clove**[3] (klōv) *vt.*, *vi. alt. pt. of* CLEAVE[1]

**clo·ven** (klō′vən) *vt.*, *vi. alt. pp. of* CLEAVE[1] —*adj.* divided; split [a *cloven* foot]

**clo·ver** (klō′vər) *n.* [OE *clafre*] any of various low-growing plants of the pea family, with leaves of three leaflets and small flowers in dense heads

**clo′ver·leaf′** *n.*, *pl.* **-leafs′** a highway interchange with an overpass and curving ramps, allowing traffic to move unhindered in any of four directions

**clown** (kloun) *n.* [< ? Scand] 1 a clumsy or boorish person 2 one who entertains, as in a circus, by antics, jokes, etc. 3 a buffoon —*vi.* to act as a clown does —**clown′ish** *adj.*

**cloy** (kloi) *vt.* [< OFr *encloyer*, nail up < L *clavus*, nail] to surfeit with too much of something that is sweet, rich, etc.

**cloy′ing** *adj.* 1 displeasing because of excess [*cloying* sweetness] 2 overly sweet or sentimental

**club** (klub) *n.* [< ON *klubba*, cudgel] 1 a heavy stick used as a weapon 2 an implement used to hit the ball in golf 3 *a*) a group of people united for a common purpose *b*) its meeting place 4 *a*) any of a suit of playing cards marked with black figures shaped like leaves of clover (♣) *b*) [*pl.*] this suit —*vt.* **clubbed, club′bing** to strike as with a club —*vi.* to unite for a common purpose

**club′foot′** *n.*, *pl.* **-feet′** a congenitally misshapen, often clublike, foot

**club′house′** *n.* 1 a building used by a club 2 a locker room used by an athletic team

**club soda** SODA WATER

**cluck** (kluk) *vi.* [echoic] to make a low, sharp, clicking sound, as of a hen calling her chicks —*n.* this sound

**clue** (klōō) *n.* a fact, object, etc. that helps to solve a problem or mystery —*vt.* **clued, clu′ing** [Inf.] to provide with clues or needed facts: often with *in*

**clue′less** *adj.* [Inf.] 1 stupid 2 uninformed, esp. about a given situation

**clump** (klump) *n.* [< LowG *klump*] 1 a lump; mass 2 a cluster, as of trees 3 the sound of heavy footsteps —*vi.* 1 to walk heavily 2 to form clumps —**clump′y, -i·er, -i·est,** *adj.*

**clum·sy** (klum′zē) *adj.* **-si·er, -si·est** [ME *clumsid*, numb with cold] 1 lacking grace or skill; awkward 2 awkwardly shaped or made —**clum′si·ly** *adv.* —**clum′si·ness** *n.*

**clung** (kluŋ) *vi. pt. & pp. of* CLING

**clunk** (kluŋk) *n.* [echoic] a dull, heavy, hollow sound —*vi.* to move with a clunk or clunks

**clunk′er** *n.* [Slang] an old machine or automobile in poor repair

**clus·ter** (klus′tər) *n.* [OE *clyster*] a number of persons or things grouped together —*vi.*, *vt.* to gather or grow in a cluster

**cluster bomb** a bomb that explodes in midair and scatters smaller bombs widely

**clutch**[1] (kluch) *vt.* [OE *clyccan*, to clench] to grasp or hold eagerly or tightly —*vi.* to snatch or seize (*at*) —*n.* 1 [*usually pl.*] power; control 2 a grasp; grip 3 a device for engaging and disengaging a motor or engine 4 a woman's small purse

**clutch**[2] (kluch) *n.* [< ON *klekja*, to hatch] 1 a nest of eggs 2 a brood of chicks 3 a cluster

**clut·ter** (klut′ər) *n.* [< CLOT] a number of things scattered in disorder; jumble —*vt.* to put into disorder; jumble: often with *up*

**cm** *abbrev.* centimeter(s)

**Cmdr** *abbrev.* Commander

**cni·dar·i·an** (ni der′ē ən) *n.* any of a phylum of invertebrates, as jellyfishes, having stinging cells and a saclike body with only one opening

**Co**[1] or **co** *abbrev.* 1 company 2 county

**Co**[2] *Chem. symbol for* cobalt

**CO** 1 Colorado 2 Commanding Officer

**co-** [var. of COM-] *prefix* 1 together 2 equally [*coextensive*] 3 joint or jointly [*copilot*]

**C/O** or **c/o** *abbrev.* care of

**coach** (kōch) *n.* [after *Kócs*, village in Hungary] 1 a large, covered, four-wheeled carriage 2 a railroad passenger car 3 the lowest-priced class of airline accommodations 4 a bus 5 an instructor or trainer, as of athletes, actors, or singers —*vt.*, *vi.* to instruct and train (athletes, actors, etc.)

**coach′man** (-mən) *n.*, *pl.* **-men** (-mən) the driver of a coach, or carriage

**co·ad·ju·tor** (kō aj′ə tər) *n.* [< L *co-*, together + *adjuvare*, to help] an assistant, esp. to a bishop

**co·ag·u·late** (kō ag′yōō lāt′) *vt.* **-lat′ed, -lat′ing** [< L *co-*, together + *agere*, to drive] to cause (a liquid) to become somewhat firm; clot —*vi.* to become coagulated —**co·ag′u·lant** (-lənt) *n.* —**co·ag′u·la′tion** *n.*

**coal** (kōl) *n.* [OE *col*] 1 a black, combustible mineral solid used as fuel 2 a piece (or pieces) of this 3 an ember —*vt.*, *vi.* to supply or be supplied with coal —**haul** (or **rake, drag,** or **call**) **over the coals** to criticize sharply

**co·a·lesce** (kō′ə les′) *vi.* **-lesced′, -lesc′ing** [< L *co-*, together + *alescere*, grow up] to unite into a single body or group —**co′a·les′cence** (-əns) *n.*

**co·a·li·tion** (-lish′ən) *n.* [see prec.] a combination or alliance, as of factions, esp. a temporary one

**coal oil** 1 kerosene 2 oil produced from coal, used as a lamp fuel

**coal tar** a thick, black liquid obtained from the

distillation of bituminous coal: used in dyes, medicines, etc.

**co·an·chor** (kō'aŋ'kər) *n.* one of the usually two anchors of a TV or radio newscast

**coarse** (kôrs) *adj.* **coars'er, coars'est** [[< COURSE in the sense "ordinary or usual order"]] **1** of poor quality; common **2** consisting of rather large particles [*coarse* sand] **3** rough; harsh **4** unrefined; vulgar; crude —**coarse'ly** *adv.* —**coarse'ness** *n.*

**coars·en** (kôr'sən) *vt., vi.* to make or become coarse

**coast** (kōst) *n.* [< L *costa*, rib, side]] **1** land alongside the sea; seashore **2** a slide down an incline, as on a sled —*vi.* **1** to sail near or along a coast **2** to go down an incline, as on a sled **3** to continue in motion on momentum —**coast·al** (kōs'təl) *adj.*

**coast'er** *n.* **1** a person or thing that coasts **2** a small mat, disk, etc. placed under a glass to protect a table

**coaster brake** a brake on a bicycle operated by reverse pressure on the pedals

**coast guard** **1** a governmental force employed to defend a nation's coasts, aid vessels in distress, etc. **2** [C- G-] such a branch of the U.S. armed forces

**coast'line'** *n.* the outline of a coast

**coat** (kōt) *n.* [[OFr *cote*, a coat]] **1** a sleeved outer garment opening down the front **2** the natural covering of an animal or plant **3** a layer of some substance, as paint, over a surface —*vt.* to cover with a coat or layer

**coat'ing** *n.* a surface coat or layer

**coat of arms** *pl.* **coats of arms** a group of heraldic emblems, as on a shield, used as the insignia of a family or group

**coat'tail'** *n.* either half of the divided lower back part of a coat

**co·au·thor** (kō'ô'thər) *n.* a joint author; collaborator

**coax** (kōks) *vt., vi.* [< obs. slang *cokes*, a fool]] to urge with or use soft words, flattery, etc. — **coax'er** *n.* —**coax'ing·ly** *adv.*

**co·ax·i·al** (kō ak'sē əl) *adj.* **1** having a common axis **2** designating a double-conductor high-frequency transmission line, as for television

**cob** (käb) *n.* [[prob. < LowG]] **1** a corncob **2** a short-legged, thickset horse

**co·balt** (kō'bôlt) *n.* [< Ger *kobold*, lit., goblin]] a hard, steel-gray, metallic chemical element

**cob·ble** (käb'əl) *vt.* **-bled, -bling** [[ME < *cobelere*, cobbler]] **1** to mend (shoes, etc.) **2** to put together clumsily: often with *up*

**cob·bler**[1] (käb'lər) *n.* [< ?]] a kind of deep-dish fruit pie

**cob·bler**[2] (käb'lər) *n.* [[ME *cobelere* < ?]] one who makes or mends shoes

**cob'ble·stone'** *n.* a rounded stone formerly much used for paving streets

**CO·BOL** (kō'bôl) *n.* [[*co(mmon) b(usiness) o(riented) l(anguage)*]] a computer language using English words, for business applications

**co·bra** (kō'brə) *n.* [< Port]] a very poisonous snake of Asia and Africa

**cob·web** (käb'web') *n.* [[ME *coppe*, spider + WEB]] **1** a web spun by a spider **2** anything flimsy, gauzy, or ensnaring like this —**cob'web'by** *adj.*

**co·caine** (kō kān') *n.* [< *coca*, tropical shrub from whose leaves it is extracted] a crystalline alkaloid that is habit-forming when used as a stimulant

**coc·cus** (käk'əs) *n., pl.* **coc'ci'** (-sī') [< Gr *kokkos*, kernel]] a spherical bacterium

**coc·cyx** (käk'siks) *n., pl.* **coc·cy·ges** (käk sī'jēz') [< Gr *kokkyx*, cuckoo: it is shaped like a cuckoo's beak]] a small bone at the base of the spine

**co-chair** (kō cher', kō'cher') *n.* one who presides over a meeting, etc. jointly with another —*vt.* to preside over as co-chair

**coch·le·a** (käk'lē ə) *n., pl.* **-ae'** (-ē') or **-as** [< Gr *kochlias*, snail]] the spiral-shaped part of the inner ear —**coch'le·ar** *adj.*

**cock**[1] (käk) *n.* [[OE *coc*]] **1** a rooster or other male

bird **2** a faucet or valve **3** *a)* the hammer of a gun *b)* its firing position **4** a jaunty tilt, as of a hat —*vt.* **1** to tilt jauntily **2** to raise erectly **3** to turn toward **4** to set (a gun) to fire

**cock**[2] (käk) *n.* [[ME *cokke*]] a small, cone-shaped pile, as of hay

**cock·ade** (käk ād') *n.* [< OFr *coq*, COCK[1] (*n.* 1)] a rosette, knot of ribbon, etc. worn on the hat as a badge

**cock·a·ma·mie** (käk'ə mā'mē) *adj.* [< *decalcomania*: see DECAL]] [Slang] **1** inferior **2** ridiculous

**cock'-and-bull' story** an absurd, improbable story

**cock·a·too** (käk'ə tōō') *n., pl.* **-toos'** [< Malay *kakatua*] a crested parrot of Australia and the East Indies

**cock·a·trice'** (-tris') *n.* [< L *calcare*, to tread]] a mythical serpent supposedly able to kill by a look

**cocked hat** a three-cornered hat with a turned-up brim

**cock·er** (käk'ər) *n.* [Slang] an old man

**cock'er·el** (-əl) *n.* a young rooster, less than a year old

**cocker spaniel** [< use in hunting woodcock]] a small spaniel with long, silky hair and drooping ears

**cock'eyed'** *adj.* [< COCK[1], *v.* + EYE]] **1** cross-eyed **2** [Slang] *a)* awry *b)* silly; foolish *c)* drunk

**cock'fight'** *n.* a fight between gamecocks, usually wearing metal spurs —**cock'fight'ing** *n.*

**cock·le** (käk'əl) *n.* [< Gr *konchē*, mussel]] an edible mollusk having two heart-shaped shells —**warm the cockles of someone's heart** to make someone pleased or cheerful

**cock·ney** (käk'nē) *n., pl.* **-neys** [[ME *cokenei*, spoiled child, milksop]] [*often* C-] **1** one born in the East End of London, England, speaking a characteristic dialect **2** this dialect

**cock'pit'** *n.* **1** an enclosed area for cockfights **2** the space in a small airplane for the crew and passengers, or in a large one for the crew

**cock'roach'** *n.* [[Sp *cucaracha*]] an insect with long feelers and a flat, soft body: a household pest

**cocks·comb** (käks'kōm') *n.* the red, fleshy growth on a rooster's head

**cock'sure'** *adj.* [COCK[1] + SURE]] absolutely sure or self-confident, esp. stubbornly or overbearingly

**cock'tail'** *n.* [< ?]] **1** a mixed alcoholic drink, usually iced **2** an appetizer, as of shrimp or juice

**cock'y** *adj.* **-i·er, -i·est** [< COCK[1] + -Y[2]] [Inf.] jauntily conceited; aggressively self-confident —**cock'i·ly** *adv.* —**cock'i·ness** *n.*

**co·co** (kō'kō) *n., pl.* **-cos'** [Sp < Gr *kokkos*, berry]] **1** the coconut palm tree **2** its fruit; coconut

**co·coa** (kō'kō) *n.* [var. of CACAO] **1** powder made from roasted cacao seeds **2** a drink made of this and sugar, hot milk, etc. **3** a reddish-yellow brown

**cocoa butter** a yellowish-white fat prepared from cacao seeds

**co·co·nut** or **co·coa·nut** (kō'kə nut') *n.* the oval fruit of a tropical tree (**coconut palm**), with a hard, brown husk, edible white meat, and a sweet, milky fluid (**coconut milk**) inside

**co·coon** (kə kōōn') *n.* [< Fr < ML *coco*, shell]] the silky or fibrous case which the larva of certain insects spins about itself for shelter during the pupa stage

**cod** (käd) *n., pl.* **cod** or **cods** [[ME]] a food fish of northern seas

**Cod** (käd), **Cape** hook-shaped peninsula in E Massachusetts: 64 mi. long

**COD** or **cod** *abbrev.* cash, or collect, on delivery

**co·da** (kō'də) *n.* [[It < L *cauda*, tail]] an added concluding passage, as in music

**cod·dle** (käd'l) *vt.* **-dled, -dling** [< ?]] **1** to cook (esp. eggs in shells) in water not quite boiling **2** to pamper

**code** (kōd) *n.* [< L *codex*, wooden tablet]] **1** a sys-

**tematized** body of laws **2** a set of principles, as of ethics **3** a set of signals for sending messages **4** a system of symbols for secret writing, etc. —*vt.* **cod′ed, cod′ing** to put into code —**cod′er** *n.*

**co·deine** (kō′dēn′) *n.* ⟦< Gr *kōdeia*, poppy head⟧ an alkaloid derived from opium: used for pain relief and in cough medicines: also **co′dein′**

**co·de·pend·ent** or **co-de·pend·ent** (kō′dē pen′dənt) *adj.* psychologically influenced by or needing another who is addicted to alcohol, etc. —*n.* one who is codependent —**co′de·pend′ence** or **co′-de·pend′ence** *n.* —**co′de·pend′en·cy** or **co′-de·pend′en·cy,** *pl.* **-cies,** *n.*

**co·dex** (kō′deks′) *n.,* *pl.* **co·di·ces** (kō′də sēz′, kăd′ə-) ⟦L: see CODE⟧ a manuscript volume, esp. of the Scriptures or of a classic text

**cod′fish′** *n.,* *pl.* **-fish′** or (for different species) **-fish′es** a cod

**codg·er** (kăj′ər) *n.* ⟦prob. var. of CADGER⟧ [Inf.] an elderly fellow, sometimes one who is eccentric

**cod·i·cil** (kăd′i səl) *n.* ⟦see CODE⟧ an addition to a will

**cod·i·fy** (kăd′ə fī′) *vt.* **-fied′, -fy′ing** to arrange (laws, rules, etc.) systematically —**cod′i·fi·ca′tion** *n.* —**cod′i·fi′er** *n.*

**cod′-liv′er oil** oil from the liver of the cod: it is rich in vitamins A & D

**co·ed** or **co-ed** (kō′ed′) [Inf.] *n.* a young woman attending a coeducational college —*adj.* **1** coeducational **2** of a coed

**co·ed·u·ca·tion** (kō′ej′ə kā′shən) *n.* an educational system in which students of both sexes attend classes together —**co′ed′u·ca′tion·al** *adj.*

**co·ef·fi·cient** (kō′ə fish′ənt) *n.* ⟦CO- + EFFICIENT⟧ **1** a factor that contributes to a result **2** a multiplier of a variable or unknown quantity (Ex.: *6* in *6ab*) **3** a number used as a multiplier in measuring some property

**coe·len·ter·ate** (si len′tər it) *n.* ⟦< Gr *koilos,* hollow + *enteron,* intestine⟧ CNIDARIAN

**co·e·qual** (kō ē′kwəl) *adj., n.* equal —**co′e·qual′i·ty** (-ē kwäl′ə tē) *n.* —**co·e′qual·ly** *adv.*

**co·erce** (kō urs′) *vt.* **-erced′, -erc′ing** ⟦< L *co-,* together + *arcere,* confine⟧ **1** to restrain by force **2** to compel **3** to enforce —**co·er′cion** (-ur′shən) *n.* —**co·er′cive** (-siv) *adj.*

**co·e·val** (kō ē′vəl) *adj., n.* ⟦< L *co-,* together + *aevum,* age⟧ contemporary

**co′ex·ist′** (-ig zist′) *vi.* **1** to exist together at the same time or in the same place **2** to live together peacefully, despite differences —**co′ex·ist′ence** *n.* —**co′ex·ist′ent** *adj.*

**co′ex·ten′sive** (-ik sten′siv) *adj.* extending equally in time or space

**C of E** *abbrev.* Church of England

**cof·fee** (kôf′ē) *n.* ⟦< Ar *qahwa*⟧ **1** a drink made from the roasted, ground, beanlike seeds of a tall tropical shrub of the madder family **2** the seeds, whole or ground, or the shrub **3** light brown

**coffee break** a brief respite from work when coffee, etc. is taken

**cof′fee·cake′** *n.* a kind of cake or roll to be eaten as with coffee

**cof′fee·house′** *n.* a place where coffee is served and people gather for talk, entertainment, etc.

**cof′fee·pot′** *n.* a container with a spout, for making or serving coffee

**coffee shop** a small, informal restaurant serving coffee and light refreshments or meals

**coffee table** a low table, usually in front of a sofa

**cof·fer** (kôf′ər) *n.* ⟦see fol.⟧ **1** a chest for holding money or valuables **2** [*pl.*] a treasury; funds

**cof·fin** (kôf′in) *n.* ⟦< Gr *kophinos,* basket⟧ the case or box in which a dead body is buried

**cog** (käg) *n.* ⟦ME⟧ **1** one of the teeth on the rim of a cogwheel **2** a cogwheel

**co·gent** (kō′jənt) *adj.* ⟦< L *co-,* together + *agere,* to drive⟧ convincingly to the point —**co′gen·cy** *n.*

**cog·i·tate** (käj′ə tāt′) *vi., vt.* **-tat′ed, -tat′ing** ⟦< L⟧

to think deeply (about); ponder —**cog′i·ta′tion** *n.* —**cog′i·ta′tive** *adj.*

**co·gnac** (kōn′yak′, kôn′-) *n.* ⟦Fr⟧ **1** a brandy from Cognac, France **2** loosely, any brandy

**cog·nate** (käg′nāt′) *adj.* ⟦< L *co-,* together + *gnasci,* to be born⟧ **1** related by family **2** from a common original form, as two words **3** related or similar —*n.* a cognate person or thing

**cog·ni·tion** (käg nish′ən) *n.* ⟦< L *co-,* together + *gnoscere,* know⟧ **1** the process of knowing, perceiving, etc. **2** an idea, perception, etc. —**cog′ni·tive** (-nə tiv) *adj.*

**cognitive science** the study of cognition

**cog·ni·za·ble** (käg′ni zə bəl) *adj.* **1** that can be known or perceived **2** *Law* within the jurisdiction of a court

**cog′ni·zance** (-zəns) *n.* **1** perception or knowledge **2** notice; heed —**cog′ni·zant** *adj.*

**cog·no·men** (käg nō′mən) *n.* ⟦< L *co-,* with + *nomen,* name⟧ **1** surname **2** any name; esp., a nickname

**cog′wheel′** *n.* a wheel rimmed with teeth that mesh with those of another wheel, etc., to transmit or receive motion

**co·hab·it** (kō hab′it) *vi.* ⟦< L *co-,* together + *habitare,* dwell⟧ to live together, esp. as if legally married —**co·hab′i·ta′tion** *n.*

**co·heir** (kō′er′, kō er′) *n.* one who inherits jointly with another or others

**co·here** (kō hir′) *vi.* **-hered′, -her′ing** ⟦< L *co-,* together + *haerere,* to stick⟧ **1** to stick together **2** to be connected naturally or logically

**co·her·ent** (-hir′ənt, -her′-) *adj.* **1** sticking together; cohering **2** logically connected and intelligible **3** capable of logical, intelligible speech, thought, etc. —**co·her′ence** *n.* —**co·her′ent·ly** *adv.*

**co·he·sion** (-hē′zhən) *n.* a cohering; tendency to stick together —**co·he′sive** (-hēs′iv) *adj.*

**co·ho** (kō′hō′) *n., pl.* **-ho** or **-hos′** a small Pacific salmon now fished in N U.S. waters

**co·hort** (kō′hôrt′) *n.* ⟦< L *cohors,* enclosure⟧ **1** a band of soldiers **2** any group or band **3** an associate

**coif** (koif; *for 2 usually* kwäf) *n.* **1** ⟦< LL *cofea,* a cap⟧ a closefitting cap **2** ⟦< fol.⟧ a hairstyle

**coif·fure** (kwä fyoor′) *n.* ⟦Fr⟧ **1** a headdress **2** a hairstyle

**coil** (koil) *vt., vi.* ⟦< L *com-,* together + *legere,* gather⟧ to wind into circular or spiral form —*n.* **1** a series of rings or a spiral, or anything in this form **2** a single turn of a coil **3** *Elec.* a spiral of wire

**coin** (koin) *n.* ⟦< L *cuneus,* a wedge⟧ **1** a piece of stamped metal, issued by a government as money **2** such pieces collectively —*vt.* **1** to make (coins) by stamping metal **2** to invent (a new word, phrase, etc.) —**coin′age** *n.*

**co·in·cide** (kō′in sīd′) *vi.* **-cid′ed, -cid′ing** ⟦< L *co-,* together + *incidere,* fall upon⟧ **1** to take up the same place in space **2** to occur at the same time **3** to agree exactly

**co·in·ci·dence** (kō in′sə dəns) *n.* **1** a coinciding **2** an accidental, but seemingly planned, occurrence of events, ideas, etc. at the same time —**co·in′ci·dent** or **co·in′ci·den′tal** *adj.* —**co·in′ci·den′tal·ly** *adv.*

**co·i·tus** (kō′it əs) *n.* ⟦< L < *co-,* together + *ire,* go⟧ sexual intercourse: also **co·i′tion** (kō ish′ən)

**coke**[1] (kōk) *n.* ⟦< ME *colke,* core⟧ coal from which most of the gases have been removed by heating: used as an industrial fuel

**coke**[2] (kōk) *n.* [Slang] COCAINE

**col** *abbrev.* column

**COL** *abbrev.* **1** Colonel **2** cost of living

**col-** *prefix* COM-: used before *l*

**co·la** (kō′lə) *n.* ⟦< Afr name⟧ **1** an African tree with nuts that yield an extract used in soft drinks and medicine **2** a carbonated soft drink flavored with this extract

**col·an·der** (kul′ən dər, käl′-) *n.* ⟦prob. ult. < L

*colum*, strainer‖ a perforated pan for draining off liquids

**cold** (kōld) *adj.* ⟦OE *cald*⟧ **1** of a temperature much lower than normal, expected, or comfortable **2** not warmed or warmed up **3** unfriendly, indifferent, or depressing **4** devoid of feeling; emotionless **5** *a*) not fresh (said of a hunting scent) *b*) off the track **6** [Inf.] unconscious [knocked *cold*] **7** [Inf.] unlucky or ineffective [a *cold* streak in shooting a basketball] —*adv.* [Inf.] **1** completely [she was stopped *cold*] **2** without preparation —*n.* **1** lack of heat or warmth **2** cold weather **3** a viral infection of the respiratory tract, causing sneezing, coughing, etc. —**catch (or take) cold** to become ill with a cold —**have (or get) cold feet** [Inf.] to be (or become) timid —**in the cold** neglected —**cold'ly** *adv.* —**cold'ness** *n.*

**cold'blood'ed** *adj.* **1** having a body temperature that varies with the surrounding air, water, etc., as fish and reptiles **2** cruel or callous

**cold cream** a creamy preparation for softening and cleansing the skin

**cold cuts** sliced cold meats and, usually, cheeses

**cold front** the forward edge of a cold air mass advancing under a warmer mass

**cold shoulder** [Inf.] a slight; rebuff; snub —**cold'-shoul'der** *vt.*

**cold sore** a sore, caused by a viral infection, consisting of little blisters in or around the mouth during a cold or fever; herpes simplex

**cold turkey** [Slang] **1** totally and abruptly: said of withdrawal from drugs or tobacco by an addict or user **2** without preparation

**cold war** an extended period of conflict between nations that does not include direct warfare

**cole** (kōl) *n.* ⟦< L *caulis*, cabbage⟧ any of various plants related to the cabbage; esp., rape

**cole'slaw'** (-slô') *n.* ⟦< Du: see prec. & SLAW⟧ a salad of shredded raw cabbage: also **cole slaw**

**co·le·us** (kō'lē əs) *n.* ⟦< Gr *koleos*, a sheath⟧ any of various plants of the mint family with bright-colored leaves

**col·ic** (käl'ik) *n.* ⟦< Gr *kōlon*, colon⟧ **1** acute abdominal pain **2** a condition of infants with frequent crying from discomfort —**col'ick·y** *adj.*

**col·i·se·um** (käl'ə sē'əm) *n.* ⟦< L *colosseum*⟧ a large stadium

**co·li·tis** (kō lit'is) *n.* ⟦< COLON² + -ITIS⟧ inflammation of the large intestine

**coll** *abbrev.* **1** collect **2** college

**col·lab·o·rate** (kə lab'ə rāt') *vi.* -rat'ed, -rat'ing ⟦< L *com-*, with + *laborare*, to work⟧ **1** to work together, esp. in some literary or scientific undertaking **2** to cooperate with the enemy —**col·lab'o·ra'tion** *n.* —**col·lab'o·ra'tor** *n.*

**col·lage** (kə läzh') *n.* ⟦Fr, a pasting⟧ an art form in which bits of objects are pasted together on a surface

**col·la·gen** (käl'ə jən) *n.* a fibrous protein in bone and cartilage

**col·lapse** (kə laps') *vi.* -lapsed', -laps'ing ⟦< L *com-*, together + *labi*, to fall⟧ **1** to fall down or cave in **2** to break down suddenly **3** to fail suddenly in health **4** to fold together compactly —*vt.* to make collapse —*n.* a collapsing —**col·laps'i·ble** *adj.*

**col·lar** (käl'ər) *n.* ⟦< L *collum*, neck⟧ **1** the part of a garment that encircles the neck **2** a band of leather, etc. for an animal's neck **3** anything like a collar —*vt.* **1** to put a collar on **2** [Inf.] to seize, as by the collar

**col'lar·bone'** *n.* CLAVICLE

**col'lard** (käl'ərd) *n.* ⟦< ME⟧ a kind of kale with coarse leaves

**col·late** (kō'lāt', kä'-) *vt.* -lat'ed, -lat'ing ⟦< L *com-*, together + *latus*, brought⟧ **1** to compare (texts, etc.) carefully **2** to put (pages) in proper order —**col·la'tor** *n.*

**col·lat·er·al** (kə lat'ər əl) *adj.* ⟦< L *com-*, together + *lateralis*, lateral⟧ **1** parallel or corresponding **2** accompanying or supporting [*collateral* evidence] **3** having the same ancestors but in a different

line **4** designating or of security given as a pledge for the repayment of a loan, etc. —*n.* **1** a collateral relative **2** collateral security

**col·la·tion** (kə lā'shən) *n.* **1** the act or result of collating **2** a light meal

**col·league** (käl'ēg') *n.* ⟦< Fr < L *com-*, with + *legare*, appoint as deputy⟧ a fellow worker in the same profession

**col·lect** (kə lekt') *vt.* ⟦< L *com-*, together + *legere*, gather⟧ **1** to gather together **2** to gather (stamps, etc.) as a hobby **3** to call for and receive (money) for (bills, etc.) **4** to regain control of (oneself) —*vi.* to assemble or accumulate —*adj., adv.* with payment to be made by the receiver [to telephone someone *collect*] —**col·lect'i·ble** or **col·lect'a·ble** *adj., n.* —**col·lec'tor** *n.*

**col·lect'ed** *adj.* **1** gathered together **2** in control of oneself; calm

**col·lec'tion** *n.* **1** a collecting **2** things collected **3** a mass or pile; accumulation **4** money collected

**col·lec'tive** *adj.* **1** formed by collecting **2** of, as, or by a group [*collective* effort] **3** designating a singular noun, as *tribe*, denoting a collection of individuals —*n.* **1** any collective enterprise; specif., a collective farm **2** the people who work together in it **3** a collective noun —**col·lec'tive·ly** *adv.*

**collective bargaining** negotiation between organized workers and their employer concerning wages, hours, etc.

**col·lec'tiv·ism'** *n.* collective ownership and control —**col·lec'tiv·ist** *n., adj.* —**col·lec'tiv·ize', -ized', -iz'ing**, *vt.* —**col·lec'ti·vi·za'tion** *n.*

**col·leen** (kä lēn') *n.* ⟦< Ir *caile*, girl⟧ [Irish] a girl

**col·lege** (käl'ij) *n.* ⟦see COLLEAGUE⟧ **1** a group of individuals with certain powers and duties [the electoral *college*] **2** an institution of higher education that grants degrees **3** any of the schools of a university **4** a school offering specialized instruction [a business *college*] **5** the building or buildings of a college

**col·le·gial** (kə lē'jəl) *adj.* **1** collegiate **2** characterized by consideration and respect among colleagues —**col·le'gi·al'i·ty** (-jē al'ə tē) *n.*

**col·le·gian** (kə lē'jən) *n.* a college student

**col·le'giate** (-jit) *adj.* of or like a college or college students

**col·lide** (kə līd') *vi.* -lid'ed, -lid'ing ⟦< L *com-*, together + *laedere*, to strike⟧ **1** to come into violent contact; crash **2** to conflict; clash

**col·lid'er** *n.* a research device for directing beams of subatomic particles at each other

**col·lie** (käl'ē) *n.* ⟦< ?⟧ a large, long-haired dog, orig. bred as a sheepdog

**col·lier** (käl'yər) *n.* ⟦< ME: see COAL & -IER⟧ [Chiefly Brit.] **1** a coal miner **2** a coal freighter

**col'lier·y** *n., pl.* -ies [Chiefly Brit.] a coal mine and its buildings, etc.

**col·li·sion** (kə lizh'ən) *n.* **1** a colliding **2** a clash or conflict

**col·lo·cate** (käl'ə kāt') *vt.* -cat'ed, -cat'ing ⟦< L *com-*, together + *locare*, to place⟧ to arrange; esp., to set side by side —**col'lo·ca'tion** *n.*

**col·lo·di·on** (kə lō'dē ən) *n.* a nitrocellulose solution that dries into a tough, elastic film

**col·loid** (käl'oid') *n.* ⟦< Gr *kolla*, glue + -OID⟧ a substance made up of tiny particles that remain suspended in a medium of different matter —**col·loi'dal** *adj.*

**col·lo·qui·al** (kə lō'kwē əl) *adj.* ⟦see COLLOQUY⟧ **1** conversational **2** INFORMAL (sense *d*) —**col·lo'qui·al·ism'** *n.* —**col·lo'qui·al·ly** *adv.*

**col·lo'qui·um** (-əm) *n., pl.* -qui·a (-ə) or -qui·ums ⟦L: see fol.⟧ an organized conference or seminar on some subject

**col·lo·quy** (käl'ə kwē) *n., pl.* -quies ⟦< L *com-*, together + *loqui*, speak⟧ a conversation or conference

**col·lude** (kə lōōd') *vi.* -lud'ed, -lud'ing to act in collusion; conspire

**col·lu·sion** (kə lōō′zhən) *n.* ⟦< L *com-*, with + *ludere*, to play⟧ a secret agreement for fraudulent or illegal purpose; conspiracy —**col·lu′sive** (-siv) *adj.* —**col·lu′sive·ly** *adv.*

**co·logne** (kə lōn′) *n.* ⟦< Fr *eau de cologne*, lit., water of Cologne, city in Germany⟧ a perfumed toilet water made of alcohol and aromatic oils

**Co·logne** (kə lōn′) city in W Germany, on the Rhine: pop. 962,000

**Co·lom·bi·a** (kə lum′bē ə) country in NW South America: 440,829 sq. mi.; pop. 29,482,000 —**Co·lom′bi·an** *adj., n.*

**co·lon**[1] (kō′lən) *n.* ⟦< Gr *kōlon*, verse part⟧ a mark of punctuation (:) used before a long quotation, explanation, example, series, etc. and after the salutation of a formal letter

**co·lon**[2] (kō′lən) *n., pl.* **-lons** or **-la** (-lə) ⟦< Gr *kolon*⟧ that part of the large intestine extending from the cecum to the rectum

**colo·nel** (kur′nəl) *n.* ⟦< It *colonna*, (military) column⟧ a military officer ranking just above a lieutenant colonel

**co·lo·ni·al** (kə lō′nē əl) *adj.* **1** of, in, or having a colony **2** [*often* C-] of the thirteen British colonies that became the U.S. —*n.* an inhabitant of a colony

**co·lo′ni·al·ism**′ *n.* the system by which a country maintains foreign colonies, esp. for economic exploitation —**co·lo′ni·al·ist** *n., adj.*

**col·o·nist** (käl′ə nist) *n.* a settler or inhabitant of a colony

**col′o·nize**′ (-nīz′) *vt., vi.* **-nized**′, **-niz′ing** **1** to found a colony (in) **2** to settle in a colony —**col′o·ni·za′tion** *n.* —**col′o·niz′er** *n.*

**col·on·nade** (käl′ə nād′) *n.* ⟦< L *columna*, column⟧ *Archit.* a row of columns, as along the side of a building

**co·lon·os·co·py** (kō′lən äs′kə pē) *n.* an examination of the inside of the colon using a fiber-optic device

**col·o·ny** (käl′ə nē) *n., pl.* **-nies** ⟦< L *colere*, cultivate⟧ **1** *a*) a group of settlers in a distant land, under the jurisdiction of their native land *b*) the region settled **2** any territory ruled over by a distant state **3** a community of the same nationality or pursuits, as within a city **4** *Biol.* a group living or growing together

**col·o·phon** (käl′ə fən, -fän′) *n.* ⟦LL < Gr *kolophōn*, top⟧ a publisher's emblem

**col·or** (kul′ər) *n.* ⟦L⟧ **1** the property of reflecting light of a particular visible wavelength: the *colors* of the spectrum are red, orange, yellow, green, blue, indigo, and violet **2** any coloring matter; dye; pigment **3** color of the face or skin **4** [*pl.*] a colored badge, etc. to identify the wearer **5** [*pl.*] a flag **6** outward appearance **7** vivid quality —*vt.* **1** to give color to; paint, dye, etc. **2** to change the color of **3** to alter, as by distorting [to *color* a story] —*vi.* **1** to become colored **2** to change color **3** to blush or flush **4** to draw or color pictures with wax crayons —**show one's (true) colors** to reveal one's true self

**Col·o·rad·o** (käl′ə rad′ō, -rä′dō) Mountain State of the W U.S.: 103,729 sq. mi.; pop. 3,294,000; cap. Denver: abbrev. *CO* —**Col′o·rad′an** *adj., n.*

**Colorado Springs** city in central Colorado: site of the U.S. Air Force Academy: pop. 280,000

**col·or·ant** (kul′ər ənt) *n.* a coloring agent

**col·or·a′tion** (-ā′shən) *n.* a coloring

**col·o·ra·tu·ra** (kul′ə rə toor′ə) *n.* ⟦It⟧ **1** brilliant runs, trills, etc., used to display a singer's skill **2** a soprano capable of singing such music: also **coloratura soprano**

**col′or·blind**′ *adj.* **1** unable to distinguish certain colors or any colors **2** not influenced by considerations of race —**col′or·blind′ness** *n.*

**co·lo·rec·tal** (kō′lə rek′təl) *adj.* of the colon and rectum

**col·ored** (kul′ərd) *adj.* **1** having color **2** *a*) non-Caucasoid *b*) [Old-fashioned] BLACK (*adj.* 2)

**col′or·fast**′ *adj.* with color not subject to fading or running

**col′or·ful** *adj.* **1** full of color **2** picturesque, vivid, etc. —**col′or·ful·ly** *adv.* —**col′or·ful·ness** *n.*

**col′or·ing** *n.* **1** anything applied to impart color; pigment, etc. **2** the way a thing is colored **3** false appearance

**col′or·less** *adj.* **1** without color **2** lacking interest; dull —**col′or·less·ly** *adv.* —**col′or·less·ness** *n.*

**color line** the barrier of social, political, and economic restrictions imposed on blacks or other nonwhites: also **color bar**

**co·los·sal** (kə läs′əl) *adj.* enormous in size, degree, etc.; astonishingly great —**co·los′sal·ly** *adv.*

**co·los·sus** (kə läs′əs) *n., pl.* **-si**′ (-ī′) or **-sus·es** ⟦< Gr⟧ **1** a gigantic statue **2** anything huge or important

**co·los·to·my** (kə läs′tə mē) *n., pl.* **-mies** a surgical construction of an artificial anal opening from the colon

**co·los·trum** (kə läs′trəm) *n.* ⟦L⟧ fluid secreted by the mammary glands just after a birth

**col·our** (kul′ər) *n., vt., vi. Brit. sp. of* COLOR

**colt** (kōlt) *n.* ⟦OE⟧ a young male horse, etc.

**colt′ish** *adj.* of or like a colt; esp., frisky, frolicsome, etc. —**colt′ish·ly** *adv.*

**Co·lum·bi·a** (kə lum′bē ə, -byə) **1** capital of South Carolina: pop. 98,000 **2** river flowing from Canada through Washington, & along the Washington-Oregon border into the Pacific

**col·um·bine** (käl′əm bīn′) *n.* ⟦< L *columbinus*, dovelike⟧ a plant of the buttercup family, having dainty, spurred flowers of various colors

**Co·lum·bus**[1] (kə lum′bəs), **Chris·to·pher** (kris′tə fər) 1451?-1506; It. explorer: discovered America (1492)

**Columbus**[2] **1** capital of Ohio, in the central part: pop. 633,000 **2** city in W Georgia: pop. 179,000

**col·umn** (käl′əm) *n.* ⟦< L *columna*⟧ **1** a slender upright structure, usually a supporting member in a building **2** anything like a column [the spinal *column*] **3** a file formation of troops, etc. **4** any of the vertical sections of printed matter on a page **5** a feature article appearing regularly in a newspaper, etc. —**co·lum·nar** (kə lum′nər) *adj.*

**col·um·nist** (käl′əm nist′) *n.* a writer of a COLUMN (sense 5)

**Com** *abbrev.* **1** Commissioner **2** Committee

**com-** ⟦< L *com-*, with⟧ *prefix* with, together: also used as an intensive

**co·ma** (kō′mə) *n.* ⟦< Gr *kōma*, deep sleep⟧ a period of deep, prolonged unconsciousness caused by injury or disease

**co·ma·tose** (kō′mə tōs′, käm′ə-) *adj.* **1** of, like, or in a coma **2** lethargic

**comb** (kōm) *n.* ⟦< OE *camb*⟧ **1** a thin strip of hard rubber, plastic, etc., with teeth, used to arrange or clean the hair **2** any similar tool, as for cleaning and straightening wool, flax, etc. **3** a red, fleshy outgrowth on the head, as of a rooster **4** a honeycomb —*vt.* **1** to arrange, etc. with a comb **2** to search thoroughly

**com·bat** (kəm bat′; *for n. & adj.,* käm′bat′) *vi.* **-bat′ed** or **-bat′ted**, **-bat′ing** or **-bat′ting** ⟦< Fr < L *com-*, with + *battuere*, to fight⟧ to fight, contend, or struggle —*vt.* to fight or actively oppose —*n.* **1** armed fighting; battle **2** any struggle or conflict —*adj.* of or for military combat —**com·bat′ant** *adj., n.*

**combat fatigue** a psychiatric condition involving anxiety, depression, etc., as after prolonged combat in warfare

**com·bat′ive** *adj.* ready or eager to fight

**comb′er** *n.* **1** one that combs **2** a large wave that breaks on a beach, etc.

**com·bi·na·tion** (käm′bə nā′shən) *n.* **1** a combining or being combined **2** a thing formed by combining **3** an association of persons, firms, etc. for a common purpose **4** the series of numbers to which a dial is turned on a lock (**combination lock**) to open it

**com·bine** (kəm bīn′; *for n.* käm′bīn′) *vt.*, *vi.*
**-bined′, -bin′ing** [[< L *com-*, together + *bini*, two by
two]] to join into one, as by blending; unite —*n.* **1**
a machine for harvesting and threshing grain **2**
an association of persons, corporations, etc. for
commercial or political purposes —**com·bin′er** *n.*

**comb′ings** *pl.n.* loose hair, wool, etc. removed in
combing

**combining form** a word form occurring only in
compounds and derivatives (Ex.: *cardio-* in *car-
diograph*)

**com·bo** (käm′bō′) *n.*, *pl.* **-bos′** **1** [Inf.] a combination **2** a small jazz ensemble

**com·bust** (kəm bust′) *vi.* to burn

**com·bus·ti·ble** (kəm bus′tə bəl) *adj.* that can
burn; flammable —**com·bus′ti·bil′i·ty** *n.* —**com·
bus′ti·bly** *adv.*

**com·bus′tion** (-chən) *n.* [[< L *com-*, intens. +
*urere*, to burn]] the act or process of burning

**come** (kum) *vi.* **came, come, com′ing** [[< OE
*cuman*]] **1** to move from "there" to "here" **2** to
arrive or appear **3** to extend; reach **4** to happen
**5** to occur mentally [the answer *came* to me] **6** to
occur in a certain order [after 8 *comes* 9] **7** to be
derived or descended **8** to be a native or resident:
with *from* [to *come* from Ohio] **9** to be caused;
result **10** to proceed or progress (*along*) **11** to
become [to *come* loose] **12** to be available [it
*comes* in four sizes] **13** to amount (*to*) —*interj.*
used to express irritation, impatience, etc. —
**come about 1** to happen **2** to turn about —**come
across** (or **upon**) to meet or find by chance —**come
along 1** to appear or arrive **2** to proceed or succeed —**come around** (or **round**) **1** to recover **2** to
yield —**come by** to get; gain —**come down with**
to contract (a flu, etc.) —**come into 1** to enter into
**2** to inherit —**come off 1** to become detached **2**
to end up **3** [Inf.] to prove effective, etc. —**come
out 1** to be disclosed **2** to make a debut **3** to end
up **4** to reveal that one is homosexual —**come
out for** to announce endorsement of —**come
through 1** to complete something successfully **2**
[Inf.] to do or give what is wanted —**come to** to
recover consciousness —**come up** to arise, as a
point in a discussion —**how come?** [Inf.] why?

**come′back′** *n.* **1** a return to a previous state or
position, as of power **2** a witty answer; retort

**co·me·di·an** (kə mē′dē ən) *n.* **1** an actor who
plays comic parts **2** an entertainer who tells
jokes —**co·me′di·enne′** (-en′) *fem.n.*

**co·me′dic** (-dik) *adj.* having to do with comedy

**come′down′** *n.* a loss of status

**com·e·dy** (käm′ə dē) *n.*, *pl.* **-dies** [[< Gr *kōmos*,
revel + *aeidein*, sing]] **1** a humorous play, etc.
with a nontragic ending **2** an amusing event

**come·ly** (kum′lē) *adj.* **-li·er, -li·est** [[< OE *cymlic*]]
attractive; fair —**come′li·ness** *n.*

**come′-on′** *n.* [Slang] an inducement

**co·mes·ti·ble** (kə mes′tə bəl) *n.* [[< L *com-*, intens.
+ *edere*, to eat]] [*usually pl.*] food

**com·et** (käm′it) *n.* [[< Gr *komē*, hair]] a small, frozen mass of dust and gas revolving around the
sun: as it nears the sun it vaporizes, usually
forming a long, luminous tail

**come·up·pance** (kum′up′əns) *n.* [Inf.] deserved
punishment

**com·fit** (kum′fit, käm′-) *n.* [[< L *com-*, with +
*facere*, do]] a candied fruit, nut, etc.

**com·fort** (kum′fərt) *vt.* [[< L *com-*, intens. + *fortis,*
strong]] to soothe in distress or sorrow; console —
*n.* **1** relief from distress, etc. **2** one that comforts
**3** a state of, or thing that provides, ease and quiet
enjoyment —**com′fort·ing** *adj.* —**com′fort·less**
*adj.*

**com·fort·a·ble** (kumf′tər bəl, kum′fərt ə bəl) *adj.*
**1** providing comfort **2** at ease in body or mind **3**
[Inf.] sufficient to satisfy [a *comfortable* salary] —
com′fort·a·bly *adv.*

**com′fort·er** *n.* **1** one that comforts **2** a quilted
bed covering

**comfort station** a public toilet or restroom

**com·fy** (kum′fē) *adj.* **-fi·er, -fi·est** [Inf.] comfortable

**com·ic** (käm′ik) *adj.* **1** of comedy **2** amusing;
funny —*n.* **1** a comedian **2** the humorous
element in art or life **3** *a)* COMIC STRIP *b)* [*pl.*] a
section of comic strips *c)* a comic book

**com′i·cal** (-i kəl) *adj.* causing amusement; humorous; funny —**com′i·cal′i·ty** (-kal′ə tē) *n.* —**com′i·
cal·ly** *adv.*

**comic strip** a series of cartoons telling a humorous or adventurous story, as in a newspaper or in
a booklet (**comic book**)

**com·ing** (kum′iŋ) *adj.* **1** approaching; next **2**
showing promise of being successful, etc. —*n.*
arrival or approach

**com·i·ty** (käm′ə tē) *n.* [[< L *comis*, polite]] civility

**comm** *abbrev.* **1** commission **2** committee

**com·ma** (käm′ə) *n.* [[< Gr *komma*, clause]] a mark
of punctuation (,) used to indicate a slight separation of sentence elements

**com·mand** (kə mand′) *vt.* [[< L *com-*, intens. +
*mandare*, entrust]] **1** to give an order to; direct **2**
to have authority over; control **3** to have for use
[*to command* a fortune] **4** to deserve and get [to
*command* respect] **5** to control (a position); overlook —*vi.* to have authority —*n.* **1** an order;
direction **2** controlling power or position **3** mastery **4** military or naval force, or district, under a
specified authority

**com·man·dant** (käm′ən dant′, -dänt′) *n.* a commanding officer, as of a fort

**com′man·deer′** (-dir′) *vt.* [[see COMMAND]] **1** to
seize (property) for military or government use **2**
[Inf.] to take forcibly

**com·mand′er** *n.* **1** one who commands **2** *U.S.
Navy* an officer ranking just above a lieutenant
commander

**commander in chief** *pl.* **commanders in chief**
the supreme commander of the armed forces of a
nation

**com·mand′ing** *adj.* **1** having authority **2**
impressive **3** very large

**com·mand′ment** *n.* a command; specif., any of
the TEN COMMANDMENTS

**com·man·do** (kə man′dō) *n.*, *pl.* **-dos** or **-does**
[[Afrik < Port]] a member of a small military force
trained to operate within enemy territory

**command post** the field headquarters of a military unit, from which operations are directed

**com·mem·o·rate** (kə mem′ə rāt′) *vt.* **-rat′ed,
-rat′ing** [[< L *com-*, intens. + *memorare*, remind]]
**1** to honor the memory of, as by a ceremony **2** to
serve as a memorial to —**com·mem′o·ra′tion** *n.* —
**com·mem′o·ra′tor** *n.*

**com·mem′o·ra·tive** (-rə tiv, -rāt′iv) *adj.* commemorating —*n.* a stamp or coin marking an
event, honoring a person, etc.

**com·mence** (kə mens′) *vi.*, *vt.* **-menced′,
-menc′ing** [[< L *com-*, together + *initiare*, begin]] to
begin; start

**com·mence′ment** *n.* **1** a beginning; start **2** the
ceremony of conferring degrees or diplomas at a
school

**com·mend** (kə mend′) *vt.* [[see COMMAND]] **1** to
put in the care of another; entrust **2** to recommend **3** to praise —**com·mend′a·ble** *adj.* —**com·
mend′a·bly** *adv.* —**com·men·da·tion** (käm′ən dā′
shən) *n.*

**com·mend·a·to·ry** (kə men′də tôr′ē) *adj.* praising
or recommending

**com·men·su·ra·ble** (kə men′shoor ə bəl, -sər-)
*adj.* [[< L *com-*, together + *mensura*, measure-
ment]] measurable by the same standard or measure

**com·men·su·rate** (-shoor it, -sər-) *adj.* [[see prec.]]
**1** equal in measure or size; coextensive **2** propor-
tionate **3** commensurable

**com·ment** (käm′ent′) *n.* [[< L *com-*, intens. +
*meminisse*, remember]] **1** an explanatory or criti-

cal note **2** a remark or observation **3** talk; gossip —*vi.* to make a comment or comments

**com·men·tar·y** (käm′ən ter′ē) *n., pl.* **-ies** a series of explanatory notes or remarks

**com′men·tate′** (-tāt′) *vi.* **-tat′ed, -tat′ing** to perform as a commentator

**com′men·ta′tor** (-tāt′ər) *n.* one who reports and analyzes events, trends, etc., as on television

**com·merce** (käm′ərs) *n.* [< L *com-,* together + *merx,* merchandise] trade on a large scale, as between countries

**com·mer·cial** (kə mur′shəl) *adj.* **1** of commerce or business **2** made or done for profit —*n. Radio, TV* a paid advertisement —**com·mer′cial·ism′** *n.* —**com·mer′cial·ly** *adv.*

**com·mer′cial·ize′** (-īz′) *vt.* **-ized′, -iz′ing** to make use of mainly for profit —**com·mer·cial·i·za′tion** *n.*

**com·min·gle** (kə miŋ′gəl) *vt., vi.* **-gled, -gling** to mingle together

**com·mis·er·ate** (kə miz′ər āt′) *vi.* **-at′ed, -at′ing** [< L *com-,* intens. + *miserari,* to pity] to sympathize (*with*) —**com·mis′er·a′tion** *n.*

**com·mis·sar** (käm′ə sär′) *n.* [Russ *komissar*] the head of any former U.S.S.R. COMMISSARIAT (sense 2): now called *minister*

**com·mis·sar′i·at** (-ser′ē ət) *n.* [Fr < L: see COMMIT] **1** an army branch providing food and supplies **2** a government department in the U.S.S.R.: now called *ministry*

**com′mis·sar′y** (-ser′ē) *n., pl.* **-ies** [see COMMIT] **1** a store, as in an army camp, where food and supplies are sold **2** a restaurant in a movie or TV studio

**com·mis·sion** (kə mish′ən) *n.* [see COMMIT] **1** *a)* an authorization to perform certain duties or tasks *b)* a document giving such authorization *c)* the authority so granted **2** that which one is authorized to do **3** a group of people appointed to perform specified duties **4** a committing; doing **5** a percentage of money from sales, allotted to an agent, etc. **6** *Mil. a)* an official certificate conferring rank *b)* the rank conferred —*vt.* **1** to give a commission to **2** to authorize **3** to put (a ship or boat) into service —**in** (or **out of**) **commission** in (or not in) working order

**commissioned officer** an officer in the armed forces holding a commission

**com·mis′sion·er** *n.* **1** a person authorized to do certain things by a commission or warrant **2** a member of a COMMISSION (*n.* 3) **3** an official in charge of a government bureau, etc. **4** a person selected to regulate and control a professional sport, an amateur league, etc.

**com·mit** (kə mit′) *vt.* **-mit′ted, -mit′ting** [< L *com-,* together + *mittere,* send] **1** to deliver for safekeeping; entrust; consign **2** to put in custody or confinement [*committed* to prison] **3** to do or perpetrate (a crime) **4** to bind, as by a promise; pledge —*vi.* [Inf.] to make a pledge: often with *to* —**com·mit′ment** *n.* —**com·mit′tal** *n.*

**com·mit·tee** (kə mit′ē) *n.* [see prec.] a group of people chosen to report or act upon a certain matter —**com·mit′tee·man** (-mən), *pl.* **-men,** *n.* —**com·mit′tee·wom′an,** *pl.* **-wom′en,** *fem.n.*

**com·mode** (kə mōd′) *n.* [Fr < L: see COM- & MODE] **1** a chest of drawers **2** a toilet

**com·mod·i·fy** (kə mäd′ə fī′) *vt.* **-fied′, -fy′ing** to treat like or make into a mere commodity —**com·mod′i·fi·ca′tion** *n.*

**com·mo·di·ous** (kə mō′dē əs) *adj.* [see COMMODE] spacious; roomy

**com·mod·i·ty** (kə mäd′ə tē) *n., pl.* **-ties** [see COMMODE] **1** any useful thing **2** anything bought and sold **3** [*pl.*] basic products, as of agriculture

**com·mo·dore** (käm′ə dôr′) *n.* [see COMMAND] *U.S. Navy* [Historical] an officer ranking just above a captain

**com·mon** (käm′ən) *adj.* [< L *communis*] **1** belonging to or shared by each or all **2** general; widespread **3** familiar; usual **4** not of the upper

classes [the *common* people] **5** vulgar; coarse **6** designating a noun (as *book*) that refers to any of a group —*n.* [*sometimes pl.*] land owned or used by all the inhabitants of a place —**in common** shared by each or all —**com′mon·ly** *adv.*

**com′mon·al·ty** (-əl tē) *n.* the common people; public: also **com′mon·al′i·ty** (-al′ə tē)

**common carrier** a person or company that transports people or goods for a fee

**common denominator 1** a common multiple of the denominators of two or more fractions **2** a characteristic, etc. held in common

**com′mon·er** *n.* a person not of the nobility; one of the common people

**common law** the law based on custom, usage, and judicial decisions

**com′mon-law′ marriage** *Law* a marriage not solemnized by religious or civil ceremony

**common market** an association of countries for closer economic union

**common multiple** *Math.* a multiple of each of two or more quantities

**com′mon·place′** *n.* **1** a platitude **2** anything common or ordinary —*adj.* trite or ordinary

**common pleas** *Law* in some States, a court having jurisdiction over civil and criminal trials

**com′mons** *pl.n.* **1** the common people **2** [C-] HOUSE OF COMMONS **3** [*often with sing. v.*] a room, building, etc. for dining, as at a college

**common sense** good sense or practical judgment —**com′mon-sense′** *adj.*

**common stock** stock in a company without the privileges of preferred stock, but usually giving its owner a vote

**com′mon·weal′** (-wēl′) *n.* the public good; general welfare

**com′mon·wealth′** (-welth′) *n.* **1** the people of a nation or state **2** a democracy or republic **3** a federation of states —**the Commonwealth** association of independent nations united under the British crown for purposes of consultation and mutual assistance

**Commonwealth of Independent States** a loose confederation of countries that were part of the U.S.S.R.

**com·mo·tion** (kə mō′shən) *n.* [< L *com-,* together + *movere,* to move] **1** violent motion **2** confusion; bustle

**com·mu·nal** (kə myōon′əl, käm′yə nəl) *adj.* **1** of a commune **2** of the community; public **3** marked by common ownership of property —**com·mu′nal·ize′, -ized′, -iz′ing,** *vt.* —**com·mu′nal·ly** *adv.*

**com·mune¹** (kə myōon′) *vi.* **-muned′, -mun′ing** [< OFr *comuner,* to share] **1** to talk together intimately **2** to be in close rapport

**com·mune²** (käm′yōon′) *n.* [< L *communis,* common] **1** the smallest administrative district of local government in some European countries **2** a small group of people living communally

**com·mu·ni·ca·ble** (kə myōo′ni kə bəl) *adj.* that can be communicated, as an idea, or transmitted, as a disease —**com·mu′ni·ca·bil′i·ty** *n.*

**com·mu′ni·cant** (-kənt) *n.* one who receives Holy Communion

**com·mu·ni·cate** (kə myōo′ni kāt′) *vt.* **-cat′ed, -cat′ing** [< L *communicare*] **1** to impart; transmit **2** to give (information, etc.) —*vi.* **1** to give or exchange information **2** to have a meaningful relationship **3** to be connected, as rooms —**com·mu′ni·ca′tor** *n.*

**com·mu′ni·ca′tion** *n.* **1** a transmitting **2** *a)* a giving or exchanging of information, etc. *b)* a message, letter, etc. **3** a means of communicating —**com·mu′ni·ca′tive** (-kāt′iv, -kə tiv) *adj.*

**com·mun·ion** (kə myōon′yən) *n.* [see COMMON] **1** possession in common **2** a communing **3** a Christian denomination **4** [C-] HOLY COMMUNION

**com·mu·ni·qué** (kə myōo′ni kā′, kə myōo′ni kā′) *n.* [Fr] an official communication

**com·mu·nism** (käm′yōo niz′əm, -yə-) *n.* [see COMMON] **1** any theory or system of common ownership of property **2** [*often* **C-**] *a*) socialism as formulated by Marx, Lenin, etc. *b*) any government or political movement supporting this

**com′mu·nist** (-nist) *n.* **1** an advocate or supporter of communism **2** [**C-**] a member of a Communist Party —*adj.* of, like, or supporting communism or communists —**com′mu·nis′tic** *adj.*

**com·mu·ni·ty** (kə myōō′nə tē) *n., pl.* **-ties** [see COMMON] **1** *a*) any group living in the same area or having interests, work, etc. in common *b*) such an area **2** the general public **3** a sharing in common

**community college** a junior college serving a certain community

**community service** unpaid work for the community

**com·mu·ta·tive** (kə myōōt′ə tiv, käm′yə tāt′iv) *adj.* **1** involving exchange or replacement **2** *Math.* of an operation in which the order of the elements does not affect the result, as, in addition, $3 + 2 = 2 + 3$

**com·mute** (kə myōōt′) *vt.* **-mut′ed, -mut′ing** [< L *com-,* intens. + *mutare,* to change] **1** to exchange; substitute **2** to change (an obligation, punishment, etc.) to a less severe one —*vi.* to travel as a commuter —*n.* [Inf.] the trip of a commuter —**com·mu·ta·tion** (käm′yə tā′shən) *n.*

**com·mut′er** *n.* a person who travels regularly by train, bus, etc. between two locations that are some distance apart

**Com·o·ros** (käm′ə rōz′) country on a group of islands in the W Indian Ocean: 719 sq. mi.; pop. 347,000

**comp** *abbrev.* **1** comparative **2** compound

**com·pact** (kəm pakt′, käm′pakt; *for n.* käm′pakt) *adj.* [< L *com-,* with, together + *pangere,* to fix] **1** closely and firmly packed **2** taking little space **3** terse; concise —*vt.* **1** to pack or join firmly together **2** to make by putting together —*n.* **1** a small cosmetic case, usually containing face powder and a mirror **2** a relatively small car **3** an agreement; covenant —**com·pact′ly** *adv.* —**com·pact′ness** *n.*

**compact disc** (or **disk**) a digital disc on which music, data, etc. has been encoded for playing on a device using a laser beam to read the encoded matter

**com·pac·tor** (kəm pak′tər, käm′pak′tər) *n.* a device that compresses trash into small bundles

**com·pan·ion** (kəm pan′yən) *n.* [< L *com-,* with + *panis,* bread] **1** an associate; comrade **2** a person paid to live or travel with another **3** one of a pair or set —**com·pan′ion·a·ble** *adj.* —**com·pan′ion·ship′** *n.*

**com·pan′ion·way′** *n.* a stairway leading from one deck of a ship to another

**com·pa·ny** (kum′pə nē) *n., pl.* **-nies** [see COMPANION] **1** companionship; society **2** a group of people gathered or associated for some purpose **3** a guest or guests **4** a body of troops **5** a ship's crew —**keep company 1** to associate (*with*) **2** to go together, as a couple intending to marry —**part company** to stop associating (*with*)

**com·pa·ra·ble** (käm′pə rə bəl, kəm par′ə bəl) *adj.* **1** that can be compared **2** worthy of comparison —**com′pa·ra·bly** *adv.*

**com·par·a·tive** (kəm par′ə tiv) *adj.* **1** involving comparison **2** not absolute; relative **3** *Gram.* designating the second degree of comparison of adjectives and adverbs —*n. Gram.* the comparative degree ["finer" is the *comparative* of "fine"] —**com·par′a·tive·ly** *adv.*

**com·pare** (kəm per′) *vt.* **-pared′, -par′ing** [< L *com-,* with + *parare,* make equal] **1** to liken (*to*) **2** to examine for similarities or differences **3** *Gram.* to form the degrees of comparison of —*vi.* **1** to be worth comparing (*with*) **2** to make comparisons —**beyond** (or **past** or **without**) **compare** incomparably good, bad, great, etc.

**com·par·i·son** (kəm par′ə sən) *n.* **1** a comparing or being compared **2** likeness; similarity **3** *Gram.* change in an adjective or adverb to show

the positive, comparative, and superlative degrees —**in comparison with** compared with

**com·part·ment** (kəm pärt′mənt) *n.* [< L *com-,* intens. + *partire,* divide] **1** any of the divisions into which a space is partitioned off **2** a separate section or category —**com·part·men·tal·ize** (käm′pärt ment′'l īz′), **-ized′, -iz′ing,** *vt.*

**com·pass** (kum′pəs; *also* käm′-) *vt.* [< L *com-,* together + *passus,* a step] **1** [Archaic] to go around **2** to surround **3** to understand **4** to achieve or contrive —*n.* **1** [*often pl.*] an instrument with two adjustable legs, for drawing circles, for measuring, etc. **2** a boundary **3** an enclosed area **4** range; scope **5** an instrument for showing direction, esp. one with a swinging magnetic needle pointing north

**com·pas·sion** (kəm pash′ən) *n.* [< L *com-,* together + *pati,* suffer] deep sympathy; pity —**com·pas′sion·ate** *adj.* —**com·pas′sion·ate·ly** *adv.*

**com·pat·i·ble** (kəm pat′ə bəl) *adj.* [see prec.] **1** getting along or going well together **2** that can be mixed, used, etc. together effectively —**com·pat′i·bil′i·ty** *n.* —**com·pat′i·bly** *adv.*

**com·pa·tri·ot** (kəm pā′trē ət) *n.* [see COM- & PATRIOT] a person of one's own country

**com·peer** (käm′pir′, käm pir′) *n.* [see COM- & PAR] **1** an equal; peer **2** a comrade

**com·pel** (kəm pel′) *vt.* **-pelled′, -pel′ling** [< L *com-,* together + *pellere,* to drive] to force or get by force —**com·pel′ling·ly** *adv.*

**com·pen·di·um** (kəm pen′dē əm) *n., pl.* **-ums** or **-a** (-ə) [< L *com-,* together + *pendere,* weigh] a concise but comprehensive summary

**com·pen·sate** (käm′pən sāt′) *vt.* **-sat′ed, -sat′ing** [< L *com-,* with + *pendere,* weigh] **1** [Now Rare] to make up for; counterbalance **2** to make suitable payment to —*vi.* to make or serve as amends (*for*) —**com′pen·sa′tion** *n.* —**com·pen·sa·to·ry** (kəm pen′sə tôr′ē) *adj.*

**com·pete** (kəm pēt′) *vi.* **-pet′ed, -pet′ing** [< L *com-,* together + *petere,* to desire] to be in rivalry; contend; vie (*in* a contest, etc.)

**com·pe·tence** (käm′pə təns) *n.* **1** sufficient means for one's needs **2** ability; fitness **3** legal power, jurisdiction, etc. Also **com′pe·ten·cy** (-tən sē)

**com′pe·tent** (-tənt) *adj.* [see COMPETE] **1** capable; fit **2** sufficient; adequate **3** having legal competence —**com′pe·tent·ly** *adv.*

**com·pe·ti·tion** (käm′pə tish′ən) *n.* [L *competitio*] **1** a competing; rivalry **2** a contest; match **3** rivalry in business **4** those against whom one competes —**com·pet·i·tive** (kəm pet′ə tiv) *adj.*

**com·pet·i·tor** (kəm pet′ət ər) *n.* [LL] one who competes, as a business rival

**com·pile** (kəm pīl′) *vt.* **-piled′, -pil′ing** [< L *com-,* together + *pilare,* to compress] **1** to collect and assemble (statistics, facts, etc.) **2** to compose (a book, etc.) of materials from various sources —**com·pi·la·tion** (käm′pə lā′shən) *n.*

**com·pla·cen·cy** (kəm plā′sən sē) *n.* [< L *com-,* intens. + *placere,* to please] contentment; often, specif., self-satisfaction, or smugness: also **com·pla′cence** —**com·pla′cent** *adj.*

**com·plain** (kəm plān′) *vi.* [< L *com-,* intens. + *plangere,* to strike] **1** to express pain, displeasure, etc. **2** to find fault **3** to make an accusation —**com·plain′er** *n.*

**com·plain′ant** (-ənt) *n. Law* a plaintiff

**com·plaint′** (-plānt′) *n.* **1** a complaining **2** a cause for complaining **3** an ailment **4** *Law* a formal charge or accusation

**com·plai·sant** (kəm plā′zənt, -sənt) *adj.* [see COMPLACENCY] willing to please; obliging —**com·plai′sant·ly** *adv.* —**com·plai′sance** *n.*

**com·plect′ed** (-plek′tid) *adj.* COMPLEXIONED

**com·ple·ment** (käm′plə mənt; *for v.,* -ment′) *n.* [see fol.] **1** that which completes or perfects **2** the amount needed to fill or complete **3** *Math.* the number of degrees that must be added to a given angle to make it equal 90 degrees —*vt.* to make complete —**com·ple·men·ta·ry** (-men'tə rē) *adj.*

**com·plete** (kəm plēt') *adj.* [< L *com-*, intens. + *plere*, fill] **1** whole; entire **2** finished **3** thorough; absolute —*vt.* **-plet'ed, -plet'ing 1** to finish **2** to make whole or perfect **3** to successfully execute —**com·plete'ly** *adv.* —**com·plete'ness** *n.* —**com·ple'tion** (-plē'shən) *n.*

**com·plex** (käm pleks', käm'pleks' *for n.* käm'pleks') *adj.* [< L *com-*, with + *plectere*, to weave] **1** consisting of two or more related parts **2** complicated —*n.* **1** a complex whole **2** an assemblage of units, as buildings **3** *Psychoanalysis a)* a group of mainly unconscious impulses, etc. strongly influencing behavior *b)* popularly, an exaggerated dislike or fear —**com·plex'i·ty** *n.*

**complex fraction** a fraction with a fraction in its numerator or denominator, or in both

**com·plex·ion** (kəm plek'shən) *n.* [see COMPLEX] **1** the color, texture, etc. of the skin, esp. of the face **2** nature; character; aspect

**com·plex'ioned** *adj.* having a (specified) complexion [light-*complexioned*]

**complex sentence** a sentence consisting of an independent clause and one or more dependent clauses

**com·pli·ance** (kəm plī'əns) *n.* **1** a complying; acquiescence **2** a tendency to give in readily to others Also **com·pli'an·cy** —**com·pli'ant** *adj.*

**com·pli·cate** (käm'pli kāt') *vt., vi.* **-cat'ed, -cat'ing** [< L *com-*, together + *plicare*, to fold] to make or become intricate, difficult, or involved —**com'pli·ca'tion** *n.*

**com'pli·cat'ed** *adj.* intricately involved; hard to solve, analyze, etc.

**com·plic·i·tous** (kəm plis'ə təs) *adj.* having complicity; implicated: also **com·plic'it** (-it)

**com·plic'i·ty** (-tē) *n., pl.* **-ties** [see COMPLICATE] partnership in wrongdoing

**com·pli·ment** (käm'plə mənt; *for v.,* -ment') *n.* [Fr < L: see COMPLETE] **1** a formal act of courtesy **2** something said in praise **3** [*pl.*] respects —*vt.* to pay a compliment to

**com'pli·men'ta·ry** (-men'tə rē) *adj.* **1** paying or containing a compliment **2** given free as a courtesy

**com·ply** (kəm plī') *vi.* **-plied', -ply'ing** [see COMPLETE] to act in accordance (*with* a request, order, etc.)

**com·po·nent** (kəm pō'nənt) *adj.* [see COMPOSITE] serving as one of the parts of a whole —*n.* a part, element, or ingredient

**com·port** (kəm pôrt') *vt.* [< L *com-*, together + *portare*, carry] to behave (oneself) in a specified manner —*vi.* to accord (*with*) —**com·port'ment** *n.*

**com·pose** (kəm pōz') *vt.* **-posed', -pos'ing** [< OFr *com-*, with + *poser*, to place] **1** to make up; constitute **2** to put in proper form **3** to create (a musical or literary work) **4** to make calm **5** *a)* to set (type) *b)* to produce (printed matter) as by computer, etc. —*vi.* to create musical works, etc. —**com·pos'er** *n.*

**com·posed'** *adj.* calm; self-possessed

**com·pos·ite** (kəm päz'it) *adj.* [< L *com-*, together + *ponere*, to place] **1** compound **2** *Bot.* designating a large family of plants with flower heads composed of dense clusters of small flowers, including the daisy and the chrysanthemum —*n.* a thing of distinct parts —**com·pos'ite·ly** *adv.*

**com·po·si·tion** (käm'pə zish'ən) *n.* **1** a composing, esp. of literary or musical works **2** the makeup of a person or thing **3** something composed

**com·pos·i·tor** (kəm päz'ət ər) *n.* one who sets matter for printing, esp. a typesetter

**com·post** (käm'pōst') *n.* [see COMPOSITE] a mixture of decomposing vegetable refuse for fertilizing soil —*vt.* to convert (vegetable matter) into compost

**com·po·sure** (kəm pō'zhər) *n.* [see COMPOSE] calmness; self-possession

**com·pote** (käm'pōt') *n.* [Fr: see COMPOSITE] **1** a dish of stewed fruits **2** a long-stemmed dish, as for candy

**com·pound**[1] (käm pound', käm'pound'; *for adj. usually & for n. always,* käm'pound') *vt.* [see COMPOSITE] **1** to mix or combine **2** to make by combining parts **3** to compute (compound interest) **4** to increase or intensify by adding something new —*adj.* made up of two or more parts —*n.* a thing formed by combining parts **2** a substance containing two or more elements chemically combined —**compound a felony** (or **crime**) to agree, for payment, not to inform about or prosecute a felony (or crime)

**com·pound**[2] (käm'pound') *n.* [Malay *kampong*] an enclosed area with a building or buildings in it

**compound eye** an eye made up of numerous simple eyes functioning collectively, as in insects

**compound fracture** a fracture in which the broken bone pierces the skin

**compound interest** interest paid on both the principal and the accumulated unpaid interest

**compound sentence** a sentence consisting of two or more independent, coordinate clauses

**com·pre·hend** (käm'prē hend', -pri-) *vt.* [< L *com-*, with + *prehendere*, seize] **1** to grasp mentally; understand **2** to include; take in; comprise —**com'pre·hen'si·ble** (-hen'sə bəl) *adj.* —**com'pre·hen'sion** *n.*

**com'pre·hen'sive** (-hen'siv) *adj.* wide in scope; inclusive —**com'pre·hen'sive·ly** *adv.* —**com'pre·hen'sive·ness** *n.*

**com·press** (kəm pres'; *for n.* käm'pres') *vt.* [< L *com-*, together + *premere*, to press] to press together and make more compact —*n.* a pad of folded cloth, often wet or medicated, applied to the skin —**com·pressed'** *adj.* —**com·pres'sion** *n.*

**com·pres'sor** (-pres'ər) *n.* a machine, esp. a pump, for compressing air, gas, etc.

**com·prise** (-prīz') *vt.* **-prised', -pris'ing** [see COMPREHEND] **1** to consist of **2** to make up; form

**com·pro·mise** (käm'prə mīz') *n.* [< L *com-*, together + *promittere*, to promise] **1** a settlement in which each side makes concessions **2** something midway —*vt., vi.* **-mised', -mis'ing 1** to adjust by compromise **2** to lay open to suspicion, disrepute, etc. **3** to weaken

**comp·trol·ler** (kən trō'lər) *n.* [altered (infl. by Fr *compte,* an account) < CONTROLLER] CONTROLLER (sense 1, esp. in government usage)

**com·pul·sion** (kəm pul'shən) *n.* **1** a compelling or being compelled **2** a driving force —**com·pul'sive** (-siv) *adj.* —**com·pul'sive·ly** *adv.*

**com·pul'so·ry** (-sə rē) *adj.* **1** obligatory; required **2** compelling

**com·punc·tion** (kəm puŋk'shən) *n.* [< L *com-*, intens. + *pungere*, to prick] an uneasy feeling prompted by guilt; remorse

**com·pute** (kəm pyōōt') *vt.* **-put'ed, -put'ing** [< L *com-*, with + *putare*, reckon] to calculate (an amount, etc.) —*vi.* **1** to calculate an amount, etc. **2** [Inf.] to make sense —**com·pu·ta·tion** (käm'pyōō tā'shən) *n.*

**com·put'er** *n.* an electronic machine that performs rapid, complex calculations or compiles and correlates data —**com·put'er·ize', -ized', -iz'ing,** *vt.* —**com·put'er·i·za'tion** *n.*

**com·rade** (käm'rad', -rəd) *n.* [< Sp *camarada*, chamber mate < L *camera*, room] **1** a friend; close companion **2** an associate —**com'rade·ship'** *n.*

**con**[1] (kän) *adv.* [< L *contra*] against —*n.* an opposing reason, vote, etc.

**con**[2] (kän) *vt.* **conned, con'ning** [< OE *cunnan*, know] to study carefully

**con**[3] (kän) *adj.* [Slang] CONFIDENCE [a con man] —*vt.* **conned, con'ning** [Slang] to swindle or trick

**con**[4] (kän) *n.* [Slang] *short for* CONVICT

**con-** *prefix* COM-: used before *c, d, g, j, n, q, s, t, v,* and sometimes *f*

**con·cat·e·na·tion** (kən kat′'n ā′shən, kän-) *n.* [< L *com-*, together + *catena*, a chain] a connected series, as of events

**con·cave** (kän kāv′, kän′kāv′) *adj.* [< L *com-*, intens. + *cavus*, hollow] hollow and curved like the inside half of a bowl —**con·cav′i·ty** (-kav′ə tē), *pl.* **-ties**, *n.*

**con·ceal** (kən sēl′) *vt.* [< L *com-*, together + *celare*, to hide] **1** to hide **2** to keep secret —**con·ceal′ment** *n.*

**con·cede** (kən sēd′) *vt.* **-ced′ed, -ced′ing** [< L *com-*, with + *cedere*, cede] **1** to admit as true, valid, certain, etc. **2** to grant as a right

**con·ceit** (kən sēt′) *n.* [see CONCEIVE] **1** an exaggerated opinion of oneself, one's merits, etc.; vanity **2** a fanciful expression or notion

**con·ceit′ed** *adj.* vain

**con·ceiv·a·ble** (kən sēv′ə bəl) *adj.* that can be understood, imagined, or believed —**con·ceiv′a·bil′i·ty** *n.* —**con·ceiv′a·bly** *adv.*

**con·ceive** (kən sēv′) *vt.* **-ceived′, -ceiv′ing** [< L *com-*, together + *capere*, take] **1** to become pregnant with **2** to form in the mind; imagine **3** to understand —*vi.* **1** to become pregnant **2** to form an idea (*of*)

**con·cen·trate** (kän′sən trāt′) *vt.* **-trat′ed, -trat′ing** [< L *com-*, together + *centrum*, center + -ATE¹] **1** to focus (one's thoughts, efforts, etc.) **2** to increase the strength, density, etc. of —*vi.* to fix one's attention (*on* or *upon*) —*n.* a concentrated substance —**con′cen·tra′tion** *n.*

**concentration camp** a prison camp for political dissidents, ethnic minorities, etc.

**con·cen·tric** (kən sen′trik) *adj.* [< L *com-*, together + *centrum*, center] having a common center: said of circles —**con·cen′tri·cal·ly** *adv.*

**con·cept** (kän′sept′) *n.* [see CONCEIVE] an idea or thought; abstract notion

**con·cep·tion** (kən sep′shən) *n.* **1** a conceiving or being conceived in the womb **2** the beginning, as of a process **3** the formulation of ideas **4** a concept **5** an original idea or design

**con·cep·tu·al** (-chōō əl) *adj.* of conception or concepts —**con·cep′tu·al·ly** *adv.*

**con·cep·tu·al·ize** (-īz′) *vt.* **-ized′, -iz′ing** to form a concept of —**con·cep′tu·al·i·za′tion** *n.*

**con·cern** (kən surn′) *vt.* [< L *com-*, with + *cernere*, sift] **1** to have a relation to **2** to engage or involve **3** to cause to feel uneasy —*n.* **1** a matter of interest to one **2** interest in or regard for a person or thing **3** worry; anxiety **4** a business firm —**as concerns** in regard to —**concern oneself 1** to busy oneself **2** to be worried

**con·cerned′** *adj.* **1** involved or interested (*in*) **2** uneasy or anxious

**con·cern′ing** *prep.* relating to; about

**con·cert** (kän′sərt) *n.* [< L *com-*, with + *certare*, strive] **1** mutual agreement; concord **2** a performance of music —**in concert** in unison

**con·cert·ed** (kən surt′id) *adj.* mutually arranged or agreed upon; combined —**con·cert′ed·ly** *adv.*

**con·cer·ti·na** (kän′sər tē′nə) *n.* [< CONCERT] a small accordion

**con·cert·ize** (kän′sər tīz′) *vi.* **-ized′, -iz′ing** to perform as a soloist in concerts, esp. while touring

**con′cert·mas′ter** *n.* the leader of the first violin section of a symphony orchestra, and often the assistant to the conductor

**con·cer·to** (kən cher′tō) *n., pl.* **-tos** or **-ti** (-tē) [It] a musical composition for one or more solo instruments and an orchestra

**con·ces·sion** (kən sesh′ən) *n.* **1** a conceding **2** a thing conceded; acknowledgment **3** a privilege granted by a government, company, etc., as the right to sell food at a park

**con·ces′sion·aire′** (-ə ner′) *n.* [< Fr] the holder of a CONCESSION (sense 3)

**conch** (käŋk, känch) *n., pl.* **conchs** (käŋks) or **conch·es** (kän′chiz) [< Gr *konchē*] the spiral, one-piece shell of various sea mollusks

**con·ci·erge** (kän′sē erzh′; *Fr* kôn syerzh′) *n.* [Fr <

L *conservus*, fellow slave] a custodian or head porter, as of an apartment house or hotel

**con·cil·i·ar** (kən sil′ē ər) *adj.* of, from, or by means of a council

**con·cil·i·ate′** (-āt′) *vt.* **-at′ed, -at′ing** [see COUNCIL] to win over; make friendly; placate —**con·cil′i·a′tion** *n.* —**con·cil′i·a′tor** *n.* —**con·cil′i·a·to′ry** (-ə tôr′ē) *adj.*

**con·cise** (kən sīs′) *adj.* [< L *com-*, intens. + *caedere*, to cut] brief and to the point; short and clear —**con·cise′ly** *adv.* —**con·cise′ness** *n.* —**con·ci′sion** (-sizh′ən) *n.*

**con·clave** (kän′klāv′) *n.* [< L *com-*, with + *clavis*, a key] **1** a private meeting; specif., one held by cardinals to elect a pope **2** any large convention

**con·clude** (kən klōōd′) *vt., vi.* **-clud′ed, -clud′ing** [< L *com-*, together + *claudere*, to shut] **1** to end; finish **2** to deduce **3** to decide; determine **4** to arrange (a treaty, etc.)

**con·clu·sion** (-klōō′zhən) *n.* **1** the end **2** a judgment or opinion formed after thought **3** an outcome **4** a concluding (*of* a treaty, etc.) —**in conclusion** lastly; in closing

**con·clu·sive** (-siv) *adj.* final; decisive —**con·clu′sive·ly** *adv.* —**con·clu′sive·ness** *n.*

**con·coct** (kən käkt′) *vt.* [< L *com-*, together + *coquere*, to cook] **1** to make by combining ingredients **2** to devise; plan —**con·coc′tion** *n.*

**con·com′i·tant** (-käm′ə tənt) *adj.* [< L *com-*, together + *comes*, companion] accompanying; attendant —*n.* a concomitant thing —**con·com′i·tant·ly** *adv.*

**con·cord** (kän′kôrd′, käŋ′-) *n.* [< L *com-*, together + *cor*, heart] **1** agreement; harmony **2** peaceful relations, as between nations

**Con·cord** (kän′kôrd; *for 2* kän′kərd) **1** city in W California: pop. 111,000 **2** capital of New Hampshire: pop. 36,000

**con·cord·ance** (kən kôrd′ns) *n.* **1** agreement **2** an alphabetical list of the words used in a book, with references to the passages in which they occur

**con·cord′ant** *adj.* agreeing

**con·cor·dat** (kən kôr′dat′) *n.* [Fr < L: see CONCORD] a formal agreement

**Con·cord (grape)** (käŋ′kərd) a large, dark-blue grape used esp. for juice and jelly

**con·course** (kän′kôrs′) *n.* [see CONCUR] **1** a crowd; throng **2** an open space for crowds, as in a park **3** a broad thoroughfare

**con·crete** (kän′krēt′, kän krēt′) *adj.* [< L *com-*, together + *crescere*, grow] **1** having a material existence; real; actual **2** specific, not general **3** made of concrete —*n.* **1** anything concrete **2** a hard building material made of sand and gravel, bonded together with cement —*vt., vi.* **-cret′ed, -cret′ing 1** to solidify **2** to cover with concrete —**con·crete′ly** *adv.* —**con·crete′ness** *n.*

**con·cre·tion** (kən krē′shən) *n.* **1** a solidifying **2** a solidified mass

**con·cu·bine** (kän′kyōō bīn′, käŋ′-) *n.* [< L *com-*, with + *cubare*, lie down] in some societies, a secondary wife, of inferior social and legal status

**con·cu·pis·cence** (kən kyōōp′ə səns) *n.* [< L *com-*, intens. + *cupiscere*, to desire] strong desire, esp. sexual desire; lust —**con·cu′pis·cent** *adj.*

**con·cur** (kən kur′) *vi.* **-curred′, -cur′ring** [< L *com-*, together + *currere*, to run] **1** to occur at the same time **2** to act together **3** to agree (*with*) —**con·cur′rence** *n.*

**con·cur′rent** *adj.* **1** occurring at the same time **2** acting together **3** *Law* having equal authority —**con·cur′rent·ly** *adv.*

**con·cus·sion** (kən kush′ən) *n.* [< L *com-*, together + *quatere*, to shake] **1** a violent shaking; shock, as from impact **2** a condition of impaired functioning, esp. of the brain, caused by a violent blow —**con·cus′sive** (-kus′iv) *adj.*

**con·demn** (kən dem′) *vt.* [< L *com-*, intens. + *damnare*, to harm] **1** to disapprove of strongly **2**

to declare guilty **3** to inflict a penalty upon **4** to doom **5** to appropriate (property) for public use **6** to declare unfit for use —**con·dem·na·tion** (kän′dem nā′shən) *n.* —**con·dem·na·to·ry** (kən dem′nə tôr′ē) *adj.* —**con·demn′er** *n.*

**con·dense** (kən dens′) *vt.* **-densed′, -dens′ing** ⟦< L *com-,* intens. + *densus,* dense⟧ **1** to make more dense or compact **2** to express in fewer words **3** to change to a denser form, as from gas to liquid —*vi.* to become condensed —**con·den·sa·tion** (kän′dən sā′shən) *n.*

**condensed milk** milk made very thick by evaporation, sweetened with sugar, and then canned

**con·dens′er** *n.* one that condenses; specif., *a*) an apparatus for liquefying gases *b*) a lens for concentrating light rays *c*) *Elec.* CAPACITOR

**con·de·scend** (kän′di send′) *vi.* ⟦< L *com-,* together + *descendere,* descend⟧ **1** to be gracious about doing a thing regarded as beneath one's dignity **2** to deal with others in a proud or haughty way —**con′de·scend′ing·ly** *adv.* —**con′de·scen′sion** (-sen′shən) *n.*

**con·dign** (kən dīn′, kän′dīn′) *adj.* ⟦< L *com-,* intens. + *dignus,* worthy⟧ deserved; suitable: said esp. of punishment

**con·di·ment** (kän′də mənt) *n.* ⟦< L *condire,* to pickle⟧ a seasoning or relish, as pepper, mustard, or a sauce

**con·di·tion** (kən dish′ən) *n.* ⟦< L *com-,* together + *dicere,* to speak⟧ **1** anything required for the performance, completion, or existence of something else; provision or prerequisite **2** *a*) state of being *b*) an illness *c*) a healthy state **3** social position; rank —*vt.* **1** to stipulate **2** to impose a condition on **3** to bring into fit condition **4** to make accustomed (*to*) —**on condition that** provided that; if —**con·di′tion·er** *n.*

**con·di′tion·al** *adj.* containing, expressing, or dependent on a condition; qualified —*n. Gram.* a word, clause, tense, etc. expressing a condition —**con·di′tion·al·ly** *adv.*

**con·di′tioned** *adj.* **1** subject to conditions **2** in a desired condition **3** affected by conditioning **4** accustomed (*to*)

**con·do** (kän′dō) *n., pl.* **-dos** or **-does** *short for* CONDOMINIUM (sense 3)

**con·dole** (kən dōl′) *vi.* **-doled′, -dol′ing** ⟦< L *com-,* with + *dolere,* grieve⟧ to express sympathy; commiserate —**con·do′lence** *n.*

**con·dom** (kän′dəm, kun′-) *n.* ⟦< It *guanto,* a glove⟧ a thin, latex sheath for the penis, used as a prophylactic or contraceptive

**con·do·min·i·um** (kän′də min′ē əm) *n.* ⟦ult. < L *com-,* with + *dominium,* ownership⟧ **1** joint rule by two or more states **2** the territory ruled **3** one of the units in a multiunit dwelling, each separately owned; also, the dwelling as a whole

**con·done** (kən dōn′) *vt.* **-doned′, -don′ing** ⟦< L *com-,* intens. + *donare,* give⟧ to forgive or overlook (an offense) —**con·don′a·ble** *adj.*

**con·dor** (kän′dər, -dôr) *n.* ⟦< Sp < AmInd (Peru)⟧ **1** a large vulture of the South American Andes, with a bare head and neck **2** a similar vulture of S California

**con·duce** (kən dōōs′) *vi.* **-duced′, -duc′ing** ⟦< L *com-,* together + *ducere,* to lead⟧ to tend or lead (*to* an effect) —**con·du′cive** *adj.*

**con·duct** (kän′dukt′; *for v.* kən dukt′) *n.* ⟦< L *com-,* together + *ducere,* to lead⟧ **1** management **2** behavior —*vt.* **1** to lead **2** to manage **3** to direct (an orchestra, etc.) **4** to behave (oneself) **5** to transmit or convey —**con·duc′tion** (-duk′shən) *n.* —**con·duc′tive** *adj.* —**con′duc·tiv′i·ty** (-duk tiv′ə tē) *n.*

**con·duct·ance** (kən duk′təns) *n.* the ability to conduct electricity

**con·duc′tor** *n.* **1** the leader of an orchestra, etc. **2** one in charge of the passengers on a train **3** a thing that conducts electricity, heat, etc.

**con·du·it** (kän′dōō it) *n.* ⟦see CONDUCE⟧ **1** a channel for conveying fluids **2** a tube for electric wires

**cone** (kōn) *n.* ⟦< Gr *kōnos*⟧ **1** a solid with a circle for its base and a curved surface tapering to a point **2** any cone-shaped object **3** the scaly fruit of evergreen trees **4** a light-sensitive cell in the retina

**Co·ney Island** (kō′nē) beach & amusement park in Brooklyn, New York

**con·fab** (kän′fab′) *n.* ⟦ult. < L *com-,* together + *fabulari,* to converse⟧ [Inf.] a chat

**con·fec·tion** (kən fek′shən) *n.* ⟦< L *com-,* with + *facere,* make⟧ a candy or other sweet, as ice cream

**con·fec′tion·er** *n.* one who makes or sells candy and other confections

**con·fec′tion·er·y** (-er′ē) *n., pl.* **-ies** a confectioner's shop; candy store

**con·fed·er·a·cy** (kən fed′ər ə sē) *n., pl.* **-cies** a league or alliance —**the Confederacy** the 11 Southern states that seceded from the U.S. in 1860 & 1861: official name, **Confederate States of America**

**con·fed′er·ate** (-it; *for v.,* -āt′) *adj.* ⟦< L *com-,* together + *foedus,* a league⟧ **1** united in an alliance **2** [-C-] of the Confederacy —*n.* **1** an ally; associate **2** an accomplice **3** [C-] a Southern supporter of the Confederacy —*vt., vi.* **-at′ed, -at′ing** to unite in a confederacy; ally

**con·fed′er·a′tion** *n.* a league or federation

**con·fer** (kən fur′) *vt.* **-ferred′, -fer′ring** ⟦< L *com-,* together + *ferre,* to bear⟧ to give or bestow —*vi.* to have a conference —**con·fer·ee** (kän′fər ē′) *n.* —**con·fer′rer** *n.*

**con·fer·ence** (kän′fər əns) *n.* **1** a formal meeting for discussion **2** an association of schools, churches, etc.

**con·fer·ral** (kən fur′əl) *n.* the bestowing of an honor, degree, or favor: also **con·fer′ment** *n.*

**con·fess** (kən fes′) *vt., vi.* ⟦< L *com-,* together + *fateri,* acknowledge⟧ **1** to admit or acknowledge (a fault, crime, belief, etc.) **2** *a*) to tell (one's sins) to God or a priest *b*) to hear the confession of (a person) (said of a priest) —**confess to** to acknowledge

**con·fess′ed·ly** (-id lē) *adv.* admittedly

**con·fes·sion** (kən fesh′ən) *n.* **1** a confessing **2** something confessed **3** *a*) a creed *b*) a church having a creed

**con·fes′sion·al** *n.* an enclosure in a church, where a priest hears confessions

**con·fes′sor** *n.* **1** one who confesses **2** a priest who hears confessions

**con·fet·ti** (kən fet′ē) *n.* ⟦< It, sweetmeats⟧ bits of colored paper scattered about at celebrations

**con·fi·dant** (kän′fə dant′, -dänt′) *n.* a close, trusted friend —**con′fi·dante′** (-dant′, -dänt′) *fem.n.*

**con·fide** (kən fīd′) *vi.* **-fid′ed, -fid′ing** ⟦< L *com-,* intens. + *fidere,* to trust⟧ to trust (*in* someone), esp. by sharing secrets —*vt.* **1** to tell about as a secret **2** to entrust

**con·fi·dence** (kän′fə dəns) *n.* **1** trust; reliance **2** assurance **3** belief in one's own abilities **4** the belief that another will keep a secret **5** something told as a secret —*adj.* swindling or used so as to swindle

**confidence game** a swindle effected by one (**confidence man**) who first gains the confidence of the victim

**con′fi·dent** (-dənt) *adj.* full of confidence; specif., *a*) certain *b*) sure of oneself —**con′fi·dent·ly** *adv.*

**con′fi·den′tial** (-den′shəl) *adj.* **1** secret **2** of or showing trust **3** entrusted with private matters —**con′fi·den′ti·al′i·ty** (-shē al′ə tē) *n.* —**con′fi·den′tial·ly** *adv.*

**con·fig·u·ra·tion** (kən fig′yə rā′shən) *n.* ⟦< L *com-,* together + *figurare,* to form⟧ **1** arrangement of parts **2** contour; outline

**con·fig′ure** (-yər) *vt.* **-ured, -ur·ing** to arrange in a certain way

**con·fine** (kän′fīn′; *for v.* kən fīn′) *n.* ⟦< L *com-,* with + *finis,* an end] [*usually pl.*] a boundary or bounded region —*vt.* -fined', -fin'ing **1** to keep within limits; restrict **2** to keep shut up, as in prison or a sickbed —con·fine'ment *n.*

con·firm (kən furm') *vt.* [< L *com-,* intens. + *firmare,* strengthen] **1** to make firm **2** to give formal approval to **3** to prove the truth of **4** to cause to undergo religious confirmation

con·fir·ma·tion (kän'fər mā'shən) *n.* 1 a confirming **2** something that confirms **3** a Christian ceremony admitting a person to full church membership, etc. **4** a Jewish ceremony reaffirming basic beliefs

con·firmed' *adj.* **1** firmly established; habitual **2** corroborated

con·fis·cate (kän'fis kāt') *vt.* -cat'ed, -cat'ing [< L *com-,* together + *fiscus,* treasury] **1** to seize (private property) for the public treasury as a penalty **2** to seize by or as by authority; appropriate — con'fis·ca'tion *n.* —con'fis·ca'tor *n.*

con·fis·ca·to·ry (kən fis'kə tôr'ē) *adj.* of or effecting confiscation

con·fla·gra·tion (kän'flə grā'shən) *n.* [< L *com-,* intens. + *flagrare,* to burn] a big, destructive fire

con·flict (kən flikt'; *for n.* kän'flikt') *vi.* [< L *com-,* together + *fligere,* to strike] to be antagonistic, incompatible, etc. —*n.* **1** a fight or war **2** sharp disagreement, as of interests or ideas **3** emotional disturbance due to conflicting impulses, ideas, etc.

con·flict'ed *adj.* in emotional conflict

conflict of interest a conflict between one's obligation to the public, as that of a public officeholder, and one's self-interest

con·flic·tu·al (kən flik'choo əl) *adj.* characterized by or having to do with conflict

con·flu·ence (kän'floo əns) *n.* [< L *com-,* together + *fluere,* to flow] **1** a flowing together, esp. of streams **2** the place of this **3** a crowd —con'flu·ent *adj.*

con·form (kən fôrm') *vt.* [< L *com-,* together + *formare,* to form] **1** to make similar **2** to bring into agreement —*vi.* **1** to be or become similar **2** to be in agreement **3** to act in accordance with accepted rules, customs, etc. —con·form'ism' *n.* —con·form'ist *n.*

con·for·ma·tion (kän'fôr mā'shən) *n.* **1** a symmetrical arrangement of the parts of a thing **2** the shape or outline, as of an animal

con·form·i·ty (kən fôr'mə tē) *n., pl.* -ties **1** agreement; correspondence; similarity **2** conventional behavior

con·found (kən found'; *for 2* kän'-) *vt.* [< L *com-,* together + *fundere,* pour] **1** to confuse or bewilder **2** to damn: a mild oath —con·found'ed *adj.*

con·fra·ter·ni·ty (kän'frə tur'nə tē) *n., pl.* -ties [see CON- & FRATERNAL] **1** brotherhood **2** a religious society, usually of laymen

con·frere (kän'frer', kän frer') *n.* [OFr] a colleague or associate

con·front (kən frunt') *vt.* [< L *com-,* together + *frons,* forehead] **1** to face, esp. boldly or defiantly **2** to bring face to face (*with*) —con·fron·ta·tion (kän'frən tā'shən) *n.* —con'fron·ta'tion·al *adj.*

Con·fu·cius (kən fyoo'shəs) 551?-479? B.C.; Chin. philosopher —Con·fu'cian (-shən) *adj., n.*

con·fuse (kən fyooz') *vt.* -fused', -fus'ing [see CONFOUND] **1** to put into disorder **2** to bewilder or embarrass **3** to mistake the identity of —con·fus'ed·ly *adv.*

con·fu'sion (-fyoo'zhən) *n.* a confusing or being confused; specif., disorder, bewilderment, etc.

con·fute (kən fyoot') *vt.* -fut'ed, -fut'ing [L *confutare*] to prove to be in error or false —con·fu·ta·tion (kän'fyoo tā'shən) *n.*

Cong abbrev. **1** Congregational **2** Congress

con·geal (kən jēl') *vt., vi.* [< L *com-,* together + *gelare,* freeze] **1** to freeze **2** to thicken; coagulate; jell —con·geal'ment *n.*

con·ge·nial (kən jēn'yəl) *adj.* [see CON- & GENIAL] **1** kindred; compatible **2** like-minded; friendly **3** suited to one's needs; agreeable —con·ge'ni·al'i·ty (-jē'nē al'ə tē) *n.* —con·ge'nial·ly *adv.*

con·gen·i·tal (kən jen'ə təl) *adj.* [< L *congenitus,* born together with] existing as such at birth — con·gen'i·tal·ly *adv.*

con·ger (eel) (käŋ'gər) [< Gr *gongros*] a large, edible saltwater eel

con·ge·ries (kän'jə rēz') *n., pl.* -ries' [L: see fol.] a heap or pile of things

con·gest (kən jest') *vt.* [< L *com-,* together + *gerere,* carry] **1** to cause too much blood, mucus, etc. to accumulate in (a part of the body) **2** to fill to excess; overcrowd —con·ges'tion *n.* —con·ges'tive *adj.*

con·glom·er·ate (kən gläm'ər āt'; *for adj. & n.,* -it) *vt., vi.* -at'ed, -at'ing [< L *com-,* together + *glomus,* ball] to form into a rounded mass —*adj.* **1** formed into a rounded mass **2** formed of substances collected into a single mass, esp. of rock fragments or pebbles cemented together by clay, silica, etc. —*n.* **1** a conglomerate mass **2** a large corporation formed by merging many diverse companies **3** a conglomerate rock —con·glom'er·a'tion *n.*

Con·go (käŋ'gō) **1** river in central Africa, flowing into the Atlantic **2** Democratic Republic of the Congo country in central Africa: 905,365 sq. mi.; pop. 29,671,000: formerly *Belgian Congo* (1908-60), *Zaire* (1971-97) **3** Republic of the Congo country in WC Africa, west of Democratic Republic of the Congo: 131,978 sq. mi.; pop. 1,909,000: formerly *People's Republic of the Congo* —Con·go·lese (käŋ'gə lēz') *adj., n.*

con·grat·u·late (kən grach'ə lāt') *vt.* -lat'ed, -lat'ing [< L *com-,* together + *gratulari,* to wish joy] to express to (another) one's pleasure at that person's good fortune, etc.; felicitate [*congratulate* the winner] —con·grat'u·la·to'ry (-lə tôr'ē) *adj.*

con·grat·u·la'tion (-lā'shən) *n.* **1** a congratulating **2** [*pl.*] expressions of pleasure in another's good fortune, etc.

con·gre·gate (käŋ'grə gāt') *vt., vi.* -gat'ed, -gat'ing [< L *com-,* together + *grex,* a flock] to gather into a crowd; assemble

con·gre·ga'tion (-gā'shən) *n.* **1** a gathering; assemblage **2** an assembly of people for religious worship **3** its members

con·gre·ga'tion·al *adj.* **1** of or like a congregation **2** [C-] of a Protestant denomination in which each member church is self-governing

con·gress (käŋ'grəs) *n.* [< L *com-,* together + *gradi,* to walk] **1** an association or society **2** an assembly or conference **3** a legislature, esp. of a republic **4** [C-] the legislature of the U.S.; the Senate and the House of Representatives —con·gres·sion·al (kən gresh'ə nəl) *adj.* —con·gres'sion·al·ly *adv.*

con'gress·man (-mən) *n., pl.* -men (-mən) [*often* C-] a member of Congress, esp. of the House of Representatives: also con'gress·per'son (-pur'sən) —con'gress·wom'an, *pl.* -wom'en, *fem.n.*

con·gru·ent (käŋ'groo ənt, kən groo'ənt) *adj.* [< L *congruere,* agree] **1** corresponding; harmonious **2** of geometric figures of the same shape and size —con'gru·ence *n.*

con·gru·ous (käŋ'groo əs) *adj.* **1** congruent **2** fitting; suitable; appropriate —con·gru·i·ty (kän groo'ə tē) *n., pl.* -ties, *n.* —con'gru·ous·ly *adv.* — con'gru·ous·ness *n.*

con·i·cal (kän'i kəl) *adj.* **1** of a cone **2** shaped like a cone Also con'ic —con'i·cal·ly *adv.*

con·i·fer (kän'ə fər, kō'nə-) *n.* [L < *conus,* cone + *ferre,* to bear] any of a class of cone-bearing trees and shrubs, mostly evergreens —co·nif·er·ous (kō nif'ər əs, kə-) *adj.*

conj abbrev. **1** conjugation **2** conjunction

con·jec·ture (kən jek'chər) *n.* [< L *com-,* together + *jacere,* to throw] **1** an inferring, theorizing, or predicting from incomplete evidence; guesswork

**2** a guess —*vt., vi.* **-tured, -tur·ing** to guess —**con·jec'tur·al** *adj.* —**con·jec'tur·al·ly** *adv.*

**con·join** (kən join') *vt., vi.* ⟦< L *com-*, together + *jungere*, join⟧ to join together —**con·joint'** *adj.*

**con·ju·gal** (kän'jə gəl) *adj.* ⟦< L *conjunx*, spouse⟧ of marriage or the relation between husband and wife —**con'ju·gal·ly** *adv.*

**con·ju·gate** (kän'jə gət; *also, and for v. always,* -gāt') *adj.* ⟦< L *com-*, together + *jugare*, join⟧ joined together; coupled —*vt.* **-gat'ed, -gat'ing** *Gram.* to give in order the inflectional forms of (a verb) —**con'ju·ga'tion** *n.*

**con·junc·tion** (kən juŋk'shən) *n.* ⟦see CONJOIN⟧ **1** a joining together; union; combination **2** coincidence **3** a word used to connect words, phrases, or clauses (Ex.: *and, but, or, if*) —**con·junc'tive** *adj.*

**con·junc·ti·va** (kän'jəŋk tī'və) *n., pl.* **-vas** or **-vae** (-vē) ⟦see CONJOIN⟧ the mucous membrane covering the inner eyelids and the front of the eyeball

**con·junc·ti·vi·tis** (kən juŋk'tə vīt'is) *n.* inflammation of the conjunctiva

**con·junc·ture** (kən juŋk'chər) *n.* ⟦see CONJOIN⟧ a combination of events creating a crisis

**con·jure** (kun'jər, kän'-; *for vt.* kən joor') *vi.* **-jured, -jur·ing** ⟦< L *com-*, together + *jurare*, swear⟧ **1** to summon a demon or spirit by magic **2** to practice magic —*vt.* to entreat solemnly — **conjure up** to cause to appear as by magic — **con'ju·ra'tion** (-jə rā'shən) *n.* —**con'jur·er** or **con'ju·ror** *n.*

**conk** (käŋk, kôŋk) *n., vt.* ⟦< CONCH⟧ [Slang] hit on the head —**conk out** [Slang] **1** to fail suddenly: said as of a motor **2** to fall asleep from fatigue

**con man** [Slang] a confidence man; swindler

**con·nect** (kə nekt') *vt.* ⟦< L *com-*, together + *nectere*, fasten⟧ **1** to join (two things together, or one thing *with* or *to* another) **2** to show or think of as related —*vi.* to join —**con·nec'tor** or **con·nect'er** *n.*

**Con·nect·i·cut** (kə net'ə kət) New England state of the U.S.: 4,844 sq. mi.; pop. 3,287,000; cap. Hartford: abbrev. *CT*

**con·nec·tion** (kə nek'shən) *n.* **1** a connecting or being connected **2** a thing that connects **3** a relationship; association **4** *a)* a relative, as by marriage *b)* an influential associate, etc.: *usually used in pl.* **5** [*often pl.*] a transferring from one bus, plane, etc. to another

**con·nec'tive** (-tiv) *adj.* connecting —*n.* that which connects, esp. a connecting word, as a conjunction

**connective tissue** body tissue, as cartilage, serving to connect and support other tissues

**con·nip·tion** (kə nip'shən) *n.* ⟦pseudo-L⟧ [*often pl.*] [Inf.] a fit of anger, hysteria, etc.; tantrum: also **conniption fit**

**con·nive** (kə nīv') *vi.* **-nived', -niv'ing** ⟦< L *conivere*, to wink, connive⟧ **1** to pretend not to look (*at* crime, etc.), thus giving tacit consent **2** to cooperate secretly (*with* someone), esp. in wrongdoing; scheme —**con·niv'ance** *n.* —**con·niv'er** *n.*

**con·nois·seur** (kän'ə sur') *n.* ⟦< Fr < L *cognoscere*, know⟧ one who has expert knowledge and keen discrimination, esp. in the fine arts — **con'nois·seur'ship** *n.*

**con·note** (kə nōt') *vt.* **-not'ed, -not'ing** ⟦< L *com-*, together + *notare*, to mark⟧ to suggest or convey (associations, etc.) in addition to the explicit, or denoted, meaning —**con·no·ta·tion** (kän'ə tā'shən) *n.* —**con'no·ta'tive** or **con'no·ta'tion·al** *adj.*

**con·nu·bi·al** (kə nōō'bē əl) *adj.* ⟦< L *com-*, together + *nubere*, marry⟧ of marriage; conjugal —**con·nu'bi·al·ly** *adv.*

**con·quer** (käŋ'kər) *vt.* ⟦< L *com-*, intens. + *quaerere*, seek⟧ **1** to get control of as by winning a war **2** to overcome; defeat —*vi.* to win —**con'quer·a·ble** *adj.* —**con'quer·or** *n.*

**con·quest** (kän'kwest') *n.* **1** a conquering **2** something conquered **3** a winning of someone's affection

**con·quis·ta·dor** (kän kwis'tə dôr', -kēs'-) *n., pl.* **-dors** or **con·quis'ta·do'res** (-dôr'ēz') ⟦Sp, conqueror⟧ any of the 16th-cent. Spanish conquerors of Mexico, Peru, etc.

**con·san·guin·e·ous** (kän'saŋ gwin'ē əs) *adj.* ⟦see CON- & SANGUINE⟧ having the same ancestor — **con'san·guin'i·ty** *n.*

**con·science** (kän'shəns) *n.* ⟦< L *com-*, with + *scire*, know⟧ a sense of right and wrong, with an urge to do right —**con'science·less** *adj.*

**con·sci·en·tious** (kän'shē en'shəs) *adj.* ⟦see prec. & -OUS⟧ **1** governed by one's conscience; scrupulous **2** painstaking —**con'sci·en'tious·ly** *adv.* — **con'sci·en'tious·ness** *n.*

**conscientious objector** one who for reasons of conscience refuses to take part in warfare

**con·scious** (kän'shəs) *adj.* ⟦< L: see CONSCIENCE⟧ **1** having an awareness (*of* or *that*) **2** able to feel and think; awake **3** aware of oneself as a thinking being **4** intentional [*conscious* humor] **5** known to oneself —**con'scious·ly** *adv.*

**con'scious·ness** *n.* **1** the state of being conscious; awareness **2** the totality of one's thoughts and feelings

**con·script** (kən skript'; *for n.* kän'skript') *vt.* ⟦ult. < L *com-*, with + *scribere*, write⟧ to enroll for compulsory service in the armed forces; draft —*n.* a draftee —**con·scrip'tion** *n.*

**con·se·crate** (kän'si krāt') *vt.* **-crat'ed, -crat'ing** ⟦< L *com-*, together + *sacrare*, make holy⟧ **1** to set apart as holy **2** to devote to sacred or serious use —**con'se·cra'tion** *n.*

**con·sec·u·tive** (kən sek'yōō tiv) *adj.* ⟦see CONSEQUENCE⟧ following in order, without interruption; successive —**con·sec'u·tive·ly** *adv.* —**con·sec'u·tive·ness** *n.*

**con·sen·sus** (kən sen'səs) *n.* ⟦see fol.⟧ **1** an opinion held by all or most **2** general agreement, esp. in opinion

**con·sent** (kən sent') *vi.* ⟦< L *com-*, with + *sentire*, feel⟧ to agree, permit, or assent —*n.* **1** permission; approval **2** agreement [by common *consent*] —**con·sen'su·al** (-sen'shōō əl) *adj.*

**con·se·quence** (kän'si kwens', -kwəns) *n.* ⟦< L *com-*, with + *sequi*, follow⟧ **1** a result; effect **2** importance —**take the consequences** to accept the results of one's actions

**con'se·quent'** (-kwent', -kwənt) *adj.* following as a result; resulting —**con'se·quent'ly** *adv.*

**con'se·quen'tial** (-kwen'shəl) *adj.* **1** consequent **2** important

**con·ser·va·tion** (kän'sər vā'shən) *n.* **1** a conserving; preservation **2** the official care or management of natural resources —**con'ser·va'tion·ist** *n.*

**con·serv·a·tive** (kən sur'və tiv) *adj.* **1** tending to conserve **2** tending to preserve established institutions, etc.; opposed to change **3** moderate; cautious —*n.* a conservative person —**con·serv'a·tism'** *n.* —**con·serv'a·tive·ly** *adv.*

**con·serv·a·to·ry** (-tôr'ē) *n., pl.* **-ries 1** a greenhouse **2** a music school

**con·serve** (kən surv'; *for n., usually* kän'surv') *vt.* **-served', -serv'ing** ⟦< L *com-*, with + *servare*, keep⟧ to keep from being damaged, lost, or wasted; save —*n.* [*often pl.*] a jam made of two or more fruits

**con·sid·er** (kən sid'ər) *vt.* ⟦< L *considerare*, observe⟧ **1** to think about in order to understand or decide **2** to keep in mind **3** to be thoughtful of (others) **4** to regard as

**con·sid'er·a·ble** *adj.* **1** worth considering; important **2** much or large —**con·sid'er·a·bly** *adv.*

**con·sid'er·ate** (-it) *adj.* having regard for others and their feelings —**con·sid'er·ate·ly** *adv.* —**con·sid'er·ate·ness** *n.*

**con·sid·er·a·tion** (-ā'shən) *n.* **1** the act of considering; deliberation **2** thoughtful regard for others **3** something considered in making a decision **4** a recompense; fee **5** something given, as to make a binding contract —**take into consideration** to keep in mind —**under consideration** being thought over or discussed

**con·sid′ered** *adj.* arrived at after careful thought

**con·sid′er·ing** *prep.* in view of; taking into account

**con·sign** (kən sīn′) *vt.* ⟦< L *consignare*, to seal⟧ 1 to hand over; deliver 2 to entrust 3 to assign to an inferior place 4 to send (goods to be sold)

**con·sign′ment** *n.* 1 a consigning or being consigned 2 a shipment of goods sent to a dealer for sale —**on consignment** with payment due after sale of the consignment

**con·sist** (kən sist′) *vi.* ⟦< L *com-*, together + *sistere*, to stand⟧ 1 to be formed or composed (*of*) 2 to be contained or inherent (*in*)

**con·sis′ten·cy** (-sis′tən sē) *n., pl.* -**cies** 1 firmness or thickness, as of a liquid 2 agreement; harmony 3 conformity with previous practice

**con·sis′tent** (-tənt) *adj.* 1 in agreement or harmony; compatible 2 holding to the same principles or practice —**con·sis′tent·ly** *adv.*

**con·sis′to·ry** (-tə rē) *n., pl.* -**ries** ⟦see CONSIST⟧ 1 a church council or court 2 its session

**con·so·la·tion** (kän′sə lā′shən) *n.* 1 comfort; solace 2 one that consoles

**con·sole**[1] (kən sōl′) *vt.* -**soled**′, -**sol′ing** ⟦< L *com-*, with + *solari*, to comfort, solace⟧ to make feel less sad or disappointed; comfort —**con·sol′a·ble** *adj.* —**con·sol′ing·ly** *adv.*

**con·sole**[2] (kän′sōl) *n.* ⟦Fr⟧ 1 the desklike frame containing the keys, stops, etc. of an organ 2 a radio, television, or phonograph cabinet designed to stand on the floor 3 a control panel for operating aircraft, computers, electronic systems, etc. 4 a raised portion between automobile bucket seats

**con·sol·i·date** (kən säl′ə dāt′) *vt., vi.* -**dat′ed**, -**dat′ing** ⟦< L *com-*, together + *solidus*, solid⟧ 1 to combine into a single whole; unite 2 to make or become strong or stable [to consolidate one's power] —**con·sol′i·da′tion** *n.* —**con·sol′i·da′tor** *n.*

**con·som·mé** (kän′sə mā′) *n.* ⟦Fr⟧ a clear, strained meat soup

**con·so·nance** (kän′sə nəns) *n.* ⟦< L *com-*, with + *sonus*, sound⟧ 1 harmony of parts or elements 2 musical harmony 3 repetition of consonants

**con′so·nant** (-nənt) *adj.* in harmony or accord — *n.* 1 a speech sound made by obstructing the air stream 2 a letter representing such a sound, as *p, t, l,* or *f*

**con·sort** (kän′sôrt′; *for v.* kən sôrt′) *n.* ⟦< L *com-*, with + *sors*, a share⟧ a wife or husband, esp. of a reigning king or queen —*vt., vi.* to associate

**con·sor·ti·um** (kən sôrt′ē əm, -sôr′shē əm) *n., pl.* -**ti·a** (-ə) ⟦see prec.⟧ an international alliance, as of business firms or banks

**con·spec·tus** (kən spek′təs) *n.* ⟦L: see fol.⟧ 1 a general view 2 a summary; digest

**con·spic·u·ous** (kən spik′yo͞o əs) *adj.* ⟦< L *com-*, intens. + *specere*, see⟧ 1 easy to see 2 outstanding; striking —**con·spic′u·ous·ly** *adv.* —**con·spic′u·ous·ness** *n.*

**con·spir·a·cy** (kən spir′ə sē) *n., pl.* -**cies** 1 a conspiring 2 an unlawful plot 3 a conspiring group

**con·spire** (kən spīr′) *vi.* -**spired**′, -**spir′ing** ⟦< L *com-*, together + *spirare*, breathe⟧ 1 to plan together secretly, esp. to commit a crime 2 to work together for any purpose or effect —**con·spir′a·tor** (-spir′ət ər) *n.* —**con·spir′a·to′ri·al** (-spir′ə tôr′ē əl) *adj.*

**con·sta·ble** (kän′stə bəl) *n.* ⟦< LL *comes stabuli*, lit., count of the stable⟧ 1 a peace officer in a small town 2 [Chiefly Brit.] a police officer

**con·stab·u·lar·y** (kən stab′yə ler′ē) *n., pl.* -**ies** 1 constables, collectively 2 militarized police

**con·stant** (kän′stənt) *adj.* ⟦< L *com-*, together + *stare*, to stand⟧ 1 not changing; faithful, regular, stable, etc. 2 continual; persistent —*n.* anything that does not change or vary —**con′stan·cy** *n.* —**con′stant·ly** *adv.*

**Con·stan·tine I** (kän′stən tēn′, -tīn′) A.D. 280?-337; first Christian emperor of Rome (306-337)

**Con·stan·ti·no·ple** (kän′stan tə nō′pəl) *former name* (A.D. 330-1930) *for* ISTANBUL

**con·stel·la·tion** (kän′stə lā′shən) *n.* ⟦< L *com-*, with + *stella*, star⟧ 1 a visible grouping of stars in the sky, usually named for some object, animal, etc. suggested by its outline 2 any brilliant group or gathering

**con·ster·na·tion** (kän′stər nā′shən) *n.* ⟦< L *consternare*, terrify⟧ great fear or shock

**con·sti·pate** (kän′stə pāt′) *vt.* -**pat′ed**, -**pat′ing** ⟦< L *com-*, together + *stipare*, cram⟧ to cause constipation in

**con′sti·pa′tion** (-pā′shən) *n.* infrequent and difficult movement of the bowels

**con·stit·u·en·cy** (kən stich′o͞o ən sē) *n., pl.* -**cies** the voters in a district

**con·stit′u·ent** (-ənt) *adj.* ⟦see fol.⟧ 1 necessary to the whole; component [a *constituent* part] 2 that elects —*n.* 1 a voter in a district 2 a component

**con·sti·tute** (kän′stə to͞ot′) *vt.* -**tut′ed**, -**tut′ing** ⟦< L *com-*, together + *statuere*, to set⟧ 1 to establish (a law, government, etc.) 2 to set up (an assembly, etc.) in a legal form 3 to appoint 4 to make up; form —**con′sti·tu′tive** *adj.*

**con′sti·tu′tion** (-to͞o′shən) *n.* 1 a constituting 2 structure; organization 3 *a*) the system of basic laws and principles of a government, society, etc. *b*) a document stating these laws and principles *c*) [C-] such a document of the U.S.

**con′sti·tu′tion·al** (-shə nəl) *adj.* 1 of or in one's constitution or structure; basic 2 of or in accordance with the constitution of a government, society, etc. —*n.* a walk taken for one's health —**con′sti·tu′tion·al′i·ty** (-shə nal′ə tē) *n.* —**con′sti·tu′tion·al·ly** *adv.*

**con·strain** (kən strān′) *vt.* ⟦< L *com-*, together + *stringere*, draw tight⟧ 1 to confine 2 to restrain 3 to compel

**con·straint′** (-strānt′) *n.* 1 confinement or restriction 2 force; compulsion 3 forced, unnatural manner 4 something that constrains

**con·strict** (kən strikt′) *vt.* ⟦see CONSTRAIN⟧ to make smaller or narrower by squeezing, etc. —**con·stric′tion** *n.*

**con·stric′tor** (-strik′tər) *n.* a snake that kills its prey by squeezing

**con·struct** (kən strukt′; *for n.* kän′strukt′) *vt.* ⟦< L *com-*, together + *struere*, pile up⟧ to build, devise, etc. —*n.* 1 something put together systematically 2 a concept or theory —**con·struc′tor** *n.*

**con·struc′tion** (-struk′shən) *n.* 1 a constructing or manner of being constructed 2 a structure 3 an interpretation, as of a statement 4 the arrangement of words in a sentence

**construction paper** sturdy, colored paper for children's art projects, etc.

**con·struc′tive** *adj.* leading to improvement; positive

**con·strue** (kən stro͞o′) *vt., vi.* -**strued**′, -**stru′ing** ⟦see CONSTRUCT⟧ 1 to analyze the construction of (a sentence) 2 to explain; interpret

**con·sul** (kän′səl) *n.* ⟦< L *consulere*, to deliberate⟧ 1 a chief magistrate of ancient Rome 2 a government official appointed to live in a foreign city and look after his or her country's citizens and business there —**con′sul·ar** (-ər) *adj.*

**con′sul·ate** (-it) *n.* 1 the position, powers, etc. of a consul 2 the office or residence of a consul

**con·sult** (kən sult′) *vi.* ⟦< L *consulere*, consider⟧ to talk things over; confer —*vt.* 1 to seek advice or information from 2 to consider —**con·sul·ta·tion** (kän′səl tā′shən) *n.*

**con·sult′ant** *n.* an expert who gives professional or technical advice —**con·sult′an·cy**, *pl.* -**cies**, *n.*

**con·sume′** (-so͞om′) *vt.* -**sumed**′, -**sum′ing** ⟦< L *com-*, together + *sumere*, to take⟧ 1 to destroy, as by fire 2 to use up or waste (time, money, etc.) 3 to eat or drink up; devour 4 to engross

**con·sum′er** *n.* one that consumes; specif., one who buys goods or services for personal needs only rather than to produce other goods

**con·sum′er·ism′** *n.* a movement for protecting

the consumer against defective products, misleading business practices, etc.

**con·sum·mate** (kän′sə mit, kən sum′it; *for v.* kän′sə māt′) *adj.* ⟦< L *com-*, together + *summa*, a sum⟧ perfect; supreme —*vt.* **-mat′ed, -mat′ing 1** to complete **2** to complete (a marriage) by sexual intercourse —**con′sum·mate·ly** *adv.* —**con·sum·ma′tion** (kän′sə mā′shən) *n.*

**con·sump·tion** (kən sump′shən) *n.* **1** a consuming or being consumed **2** the using up of goods or services **3** the amount consumed **4** [Old-fashioned] tuberculosis of the lungs

**cont** *abbrev.* continued

**con·tact** (kän′takt′) *n.* ⟦< L *com-*, together + *tangere*, to touch⟧ **1** a touching or meeting **2** the state of being in association (*with*) **3** a connection **4** an influential acquaintance **5** *short for* CONTACT LENS —*vt.* **1** to come into contact with **2** to get in touch with —*vi.* to come into contact

**contact lens** a tiny, thin correctional lens worn directly over the cornea of the eye

**con·ta·gion** (kən tā′jən) *n.* ⟦see CONTACT⟧ **1** the spreading of disease by contact **2** a contagious disease **3** the spreading of an emotion, idea, etc.

**con·ta′gious** (-jəs) *adj.* **1** spread by contact: said of diseases **2** carrying the causative agent of a contagious disease **3** spreading from person to person —**con·ta′gious·ness** *n.*

**con·tain** (kən tān′) *vt.* ⟦< L *com-*, together + *tenere*, to hold⟧ **1** to have in it; hold **2** to have the capacity for holding **3** to hold back or restrain within fixed limits —**con·tain′ment** *n.*

**con·tain′er** *n.* a thing for containing something; box, can, etc.

**con·tain′er·ize′** *vt.* **-ized′, -iz′ing** to pack (cargo) into huge, standardized containers for shipment

**con·tam·i·nant** (kən tam′ə nənt) *n.* a contaminating substance

**con·tam′i·nate′** (-nāt′) *vt.* **-nat′ed, -nat′ing** ⟦< L *com-*, together + *tangere*, to touch⟧ to make impure, corrupt, etc. by contact; pollute; taint —**con·tam′i·na′tion** *n.*

**contd** *abbrev.* continued

**con·tem·plate** (kän′təm plāt′) *vt.* **-plat′ed, -plat′ing** ⟦< L *contemplari*, observe⟧ **1** to look at or think about intently **2** to expect or intend —*vi.* to muse —**con′tem·pla′tion** (-plā′shən) *n.* —**con·tem·pla·tive** (kən tem′plə tiv, kän′təm plāt′iv) *adj.*

**con·tem·po·ra·ne·ous** (kən tem′pə rā′nē əs) *adj.* ⟦see fol.⟧ happening in the same period —**con·tem′po·ra·ne′i·ty** (-rə nē′ə tē; -nā′-) *n.* —**con·tem′po·ra′ne·ous·ly** *adv.*

**con·tem′po·rar′y** (-rer′ē) *adj.* ⟦< L *com-*, with + *tempus*, time⟧ **1** living or happening in the same period **2** of about the same age **3** of the present time; modern —*n., pl.* **-ies** one living in the same period as another or others

**con·tempt** (kən tempt′) *n.* ⟦< L *com-*, intens. + *temnere*, to scorn⟧ **1** the feeling one has toward somebody or something one considers low, worthless, etc. **2** the condition of being despised **3** a showing disrespect for the dignity of a court (or legislature)

**con·tempt′i·ble** *adj.* deserving of contempt or scorn; despicable —**con·tempt′i·bly** *adv.*

**con·temp·tu·ous** (kən temp′chōō əs) *adj.* full of contempt; scornful —**con·temp′tu·ous·ly** *adv.* —**con·temp′tu·ous·ness** *n.*

**con·tend** (kən tend′) *vi.* ⟦< L *com-*, together + *tendere*, to stretch⟧ **1** to fight or argue **2** to compete —*vt.* to assert —**con·tend′er** *n.*

**con·tent**[1] (kən tent′) *adj.* ⟦see CONTAIN⟧ happy with one's lot; satisfied —*vt.* to satisfy —*n.* contentment

**con·tent**[2] (kän′tent′) *n.* ⟦see CONTAIN⟧ **1** [*usually pl.*] *a)* what is in a container *b)* what is dealt with in a book, speech, etc. **2** substance or meaning **3** amount contained

**con·tent′ed** *adj.* satisfied —**con·tent′ed·ly** *adv.* —**con·tent′ed·ness** *n.*

**con·ten·tion** (kən ten′shən) *n.* ⟦see CONTEND⟧ **1** strife, dispute, etc. **2** a point argued for —**in** (or **out of**) **contention** having a (or no) chance to win —**con·ten′tious** *adj.* —**con·ten′tious·ly** *adv.* —**con·ten′tious·ness** *n.*

**con·tent′ment** *n.* the state or fact of being contented

**con·ter·mi·nous** (kən tʉr′mə nəs) *adj.* ⟦< L *com-*, together + *terminus*, an end⟧ **1** having a common boundary **2** contained within the same boundaries —**con·ter′mi·nous·ly** *adv.*

**con·test** (kən test′; *for n.* kän′test′) *vt.* ⟦< L *com-*, together + *testis*, a witness⟧ **1** to dispute (a point, etc.) **2** to fight for (a position, etc.) —*vi.* to struggle (*with* or *against*) —*n.* **1** a fight; struggle **2** a competitive game, race, etc. —**con·test′a·ble** *adj.*

**con·test′ant** *n.* ⟦Fr⟧ a competitor in a game, etc.

**con·text** (kän′tekst′) *n.* ⟦< L *com-*, together + *texere*, to weave⟧ **1** the parts just before and after a passage, that determine its meaning **2** the whole background or environment, as of an event —**con·tex·tu·al** (kən teks′chōō əl) *adj.*

**con·tex·tu·al·ize** (kən teks′chōō əl īz′) *vt.* **-ized′, -iz·ing** to put in a context, as for analysis

**con·tig·u·ous** (kən tig′yōō əs) *adj.* ⟦see CONTACT⟧ **1** in contact; touching **2** near or next —**con·ti·gu·i·ty** (kän′tə gyōō′ə tē) *n.*

**con·ti·nence** (känt′′n əns) *n.* ⟦see CONTAIN⟧ self-restraint; specif., a refraining from all sexual activity

**con′ti·nent** (-ənt) *adj.* ⟦see CONTAIN⟧ characterized by continence —*n.* any of the main large areas of the earth

**con′ti·nen′tal** (-ent′′l) *adj.* **1** of a continent **2** [*sometimes* C-] European **3** [C-] of the American colonies at the time of the American Revolution

**continental breakfast** a light breakfast, as of rolls and coffee

**continental drift** the theory that continents slowly shift position

**continental shelf** submerged land sloping out gradually from the edge of a continent

**con·tin·gen·cy** (kən tin′jən sē) *n., pl.* **-cies 1** dependence on chance **2** a possible or chance event

**con·tin′gent** *adj.* ⟦see CONTACT⟧ **1** possible **2** accidental **3** dependent (*on* or *upon* an uncertainty) —*n.* **1** a quota, as of troops **2** a part of a larger group

**con·tin·u·al** (kən tin′yōō əl) *adj.* **1** repeated often **2** continuous —**con·tin′u·al·ly** *adv.*

**con·tin′u·ance** *n.* **1** a continuing **2** duration **3** *Law* postponement or adjournment

**con·tin′u·a′tion** (-ā′shən) *n.* **1** a continuing **2** a beginning again; resumption **3** a part added; sequel

**con·tin·ue** (kən tin′yōō) *vi.* **-ued, -u·ing** ⟦< L *continuare*, join⟧ **1** to last; endure **2** to go on in a specified course of action or condition **3** to extend **4** to stay **5** to go on again after an interruption —*vt.* **1** to go on with **2** to extend **3** to cause to remain, as in office **4** *Law* to postpone

**con·ti·nu·i·ty** (kän′tə nōō′ə tē, -nyōō′-) *n., pl.* **-ties** ⟦OFr < L *continuitas*⟧ **1** a continuous state or quality **2** an unbroken, coherent whole **3** the script for a film, radio or TV program, etc.

**con·tin·u·ous** (kən tin′yōō əs) *adj.* going on without interruption; unbroken —**con·tin′u·ous·ly** *adv.*

**con·tin′u·um** (-yōō əm) *n., pl.* **-u·a** (-yōō ə) or **-u·ums** ⟦L⟧ a continuous whole, quantity, or series

**con·tort** (kən tôrt′) *vt., vi.* ⟦< L *com-*, together + *torquere*, to twist⟧ to twist or wrench out of shape; distort —**con·tor′tion** *n.*

**con·tor′tion·ist** *n.* one who can contort his or her body into unnatural positions

**con·tour** (kän′toor′) *n.* ⟦Fr < L *com-*, intens. + *tornare*, to turn⟧ the outline of a figure, land, etc. —*vt.* to shape to the contour of something —*adj.* conforming to the shape or contour of something

**con·tra** (kän′trə) *prep.* against

**contra-** [< L *contra*] *prefix* against, opposite, opposed to

**con·tra·band** (kän′trə band′) *n.* [< Sp < It] smuggled goods —*adj.* illegal to import or export

**con·tra·cep·tion** (kän′trə sep′shən) *n.* [CONTRA- + (CON)CEPTION] prevention of the fertilization of an ovum, as by special devices or drugs —**con′tra·cep′tive** *adj., n.*

**con·tract** (kän′trakt′ *for n. & usually for vt. 1 & vi. 1*; kən trakt′ *for v. generally*) *n.* [< L *com-*, together + *trahere*, draw] an agreement between two or more people, esp. a written one enforceable by law —*vt.* **1** to undertake by contract **2** to get or incur (a disease, debt, etc.) **3** to reduce in size; shrink —*vi.* **1** to make a contract **2** to become smaller

**con·trac·tile** (kən trak′til) *adj.* having the power of contracting

**con·trac·tion** (kən trak′shən) *n.* **1** a contracting or being contracted **2** the shortening of a muscle of the uterus during labor **3** the shortened form of a word or phrase (Ex.: *aren't* for *are not*)

**con·trac·tor** (kän′trak′tər) *n.* a builder, etc. who contracts to do work or supply materials

**con·trac·tu·al** (kən trak′chōō əl) *adj.* of, or having the nature of, a contract —**con·trac′tu·al·ly** *adv.*

**con·tra·dict** (kän′trə dikt′) *vt.* [< L *contra-*, against + *dicere*, speak] **1** to assert the opposite of (something said) **2** to deny the statement of (someone) **3** to be contrary to —**con′tra·dic′tion** *n.* —**con′tra·dic′to·ry** *adj.*

**con·tra·dis·tinc·tion** (-dis tiŋk′shən) *n.* distinction by contrast

**con·trail** (kän′trāl′) *n.* [CON(DENSATION) + TRAIL] a white trail of water vapor in an aircraft's wake

**con·tra·in·di·cate** (kän′trə in′di kāt′) *vt.* -cat′ed, -cat′ing to make (as an indicated medical treatment) inadvisable

**con·tral·to** (kən tral′tō) *n., pl.* -tos [It: see CONTRA- & ALTO] **1** the range of the lowest female voice; alto **2** a voice or singer with such a range

**con·trap·tion** (kən trap′shən) *n.* [< ?] a contrivance or gadget

**con·tra·pun·tal** (kän′trə punt′'l) *adj.* [< It *contrappunto*, counterpoint] of or characterized by counterpoint

**con·trar·i·an** (kän trer′ē ən) *n., adj.* (one) characterized by thought or action that is contrary to accepted opinion

**con·trar·i·wise** (kän′trer′ē wīz′) *adv.* **1** on the contrary **2** in the opposite way, order, etc.

**con·trar·y** (kän′trer′ē; *for adj. 4, often* kən trer′ē) *adj.* [< L *contra*, against] **1** opposed **2** opposite in nature, order, etc.; altogether different **3** unfavorable **4** always resisting or disagreeing —*n., pl.* **-ies** the opposite —**on the contrary** as opposed to what has been said —**to the contrary** to the opposite effect —**con′tra·ri′e·ty** (-trə rī′ə tē) *n.* —**con′trar′i·ly** *adv.* —**con′trar′i·ness** *n.*

**con·trast** (kən trast′; *for n.* kän′trast′) *vt.* [< L *contra*, against + *stare*, to stand] to compare so as to point out the differences —*vi.* to show differences when compared —*n.* **1** a contrasting or being contrasted **2** a striking difference between things being compared **3** a person or thing showing differences when compared with another

**con·tra·vene** (kän′trə vēn′) *vt.* -vened′, -ven′ing [< L *contra*, against + *venire*, come] **1** to go against; violate **2** to contradict —**con′tra·ven′tion** (-ven′shən) *n.*

**con·tre·temps** (kän′trə tän′) *n., pl.* -temps (-tän′) [Fr] a confusing, embarrassing, or awkward occurrence

**con·trib·ute** (kən trib′yōōt) *vt., vi.* -ut·ed, -ut·ing [< L: see CON- & TRIBUTE] **1** to give jointly with others **2** to write (an article, etc.) as for a magazine **3** to furnish (ideas, etc.) —**contribute to** to be partly responsible for (a result) —**con·trib′u·tor** *n.* —**con·trib′u·to′ry** *adj.*

**con·tri·bu·tion** (kän′trə byōō′shən) *n.* **1** a contributing **2** something contributed, as money

**con·trite** (kən trīt′) *adj.* [< L *com-*, together + *terere*, to rub] having or showing deep sorrow for having done wrong; repentant —**con·trite′ly** *adv.* —**con·trite′ness** *n.* —**con·tri′tion** (-trish′ən) *n.*

**con·triv·ance** (kən trī′vəns) *n.* **1** the act, way, or power of contriving **2** something contrived; device, invention, etc.

**con·trive** (kən trīv′) *vt.* -trived′, -triv′ing [ult. < VL *contropare*, compare] **1** to think up; devise **2** to make inventively **3** to bring about; manage —**con·triv′er** *n.*

**con·trol** (kən trōl′) *vt.* -trolled′, -trol′ling [< ML *contrarotulus*, a register] **1** to regulate **2** to verify (an experiment) by comparison **3** to exercise authority over; direct **4** to restrain —*n.* **1** power to direct or regulate **2** a means of controlling; check **3** an apparatus to regulate a mechanism: *usually used in pl.* —**con·trol′la·ble** *adj.*

**control group** the group, in an experiment, that is not given the drug, etc. being tested

**controlled substance** a drug whose sale is regulated by law

**con·trol′ler** *n.* **1** the person in charge of auditing accounts, as in a business **2** a person or device that controls

**control tower** an airport tower from which air traffic is directed

**con·tro·ver·sial** (kän′trə vur′shəl) *adj.* subject to or stirring up controversy

**con·tro·ver·sy** (-sē) *n., pl.* -sies [< L *contra*, against + *vertere*, to turn] a conflict of opinion; dispute

**con·tro·vert** (kän′trə vurt′, kän′trə vurt′) *vt.* **1** to argue against; dispute **2** to argue about; debate —**con′tro·vert′i·ble** *adj.*

**con·tu·ma·cy** (kän′tyōō mə sē) *n., pl.* -cies [< L *com-*, intens. + *tumere*, swell up] stubborn resistance to authority —**con′tu·ma′cious** (-mā′shəs) *adj.*

**con·tu·me·ly** (kän′tōō mə lē, -tōōm lē; kən tōō′mə lē) *n., pl.* -lies [< L *contumelia*, abuse] **1** humiliating treatment **2** a scornful insult —**con′tu·me′li·ous** (-mē′lē əs) *adj.*

**con·tu·sion** (kən tyōō′zhən, -tōō′-) *n.* [< L *com-*, intens. + *tundere*, to beat] a bruise

**co·nun·drum** (kə nun′drəm) *n.* [pseudo-L] **1** a riddle whose answer contains a pun **2** any puzzling problem

**con·ur·ba·tion** (kän′ər bā′shən) *n.* [< CON- + L *urbs*, city + -ATION] a vast urban area around and including a large city

**con·va·lesce** (kän′və les′) *vi.* -lesced′, -lesc′ing [< L *com-*, intens. + *valere*, be strong] to regain strength and health —**con′va·les′cence** *n.* —**con′va·les′cent** *adj., n.*

**con·vec·tion** (kən vek′shən) *n.* [< L *com-*, together + *vehere*, carry] **1** a transmitting **2** *a)* movement of parts of a fluid within the fluid because of differences in heat, etc. *b)* heat transference by such movement —**con·vec′tion·al** *adj.* —**con·vec′tive** *adj.*

**con·vene** (kən vēn′) *vi., vt.* -vened′, -ven′ing [< L *com-*, together + *venire*, come] to assemble for a meeting —**con·ven′er** *n.*

**con·ven·ience** (kən vēn′yəns) *n.* [see prec.] **1** the quality of being convenient **2** comfort **3** anything that adds to one's comfort or saves work —**at someone's convenience** at a time or place suitable to someone

**con·ven′ient** (-yənt) *adj.* easy to do, use, or get to; handy —**con·ven′ient·ly** *adv.*

**con·vent** (kän′vənt, -vent′) *n.* [see CONVENE] **1** the residence of a religious community, esp. of women **2** the community itself

**con·ven·ti·cle** (kən ven′ti kəl) *n.* [see CONVENE] a religious assembly held illegally and secretly

**con·ven·tion** (kən ven′shən) *n.* [see CONVENE] **1** *a)* an assembly, often periodical, of members or delegates *b)* such members or delegates **2** an agreement, as between nations **3** a customary practice **4** customary practices collectively —**con·ven′tion·eer′** n.

**con·ven·tion·al** adj. **1** having to do with a convention **2** sanctioned by or following custom or usage; customary **3** formal **4** nonnuclear [conventional weapons] —**con·ven′tion·al′i·ty** (-nal′ə tē) n. —**con·ven′tion·al·ly** adv.

**con·ven′tion·al·ize′** vt. -ized′, -iz′ing to make conventional

**con·verge** (kən vʉrj′) vi. -verged′, -verg′ing ⟦< L com-, together + vergere, to bend⟧ to come together at a point —**con·ver′gence** n. —**con·ver′gent** adj.

**con·ver·sant** (kən vʉr′sənt, kän′vər-) adj. familiar or acquainted (with)

**con·ver·sa·tion** (kän′vər sā′shən) n. a conversing; informal talk —**con′ver·sa′tion·al** adj. —**con′ver·sa′tion·al·ist** n. —**con′ver·sa′tion·al·ly** adv.

**conversation piece** something, as an unusual article of furniture, that invites comment

**con·verse¹** (kən vʉrs′; for n. kän′vʉrs′) vi. -versed′, -vers′ing ⟦< L conversari, live with⟧ to hold a conversation; talk —n. conversation

**con·verse²** (kän′vʉrs′; also, for adj., kən vʉrs′) adj. ⟦see CONVERT⟧ reversed in position, order, etc.; opposite; contrary —n. a thing related in a converse way; the opposite —**con·verse′ly** adv.

**con·ver·sion** (kən vʉr′zhən) n. a converting or being converted

**con·vert** (kən vʉrt′; for n. kän′vʉrt) vt. ⟦< L com-, together + vertere, to turn⟧ **1** to change; transform **2** to change from one religion, doctrine, etc. to another **3** to exchange for something equal in value —vi. to be converted —n. a person converted, as to a religion —**con·vert′er** n.

**con·vert·i·ble** (kən vʉrt′ə bəl) adj. that can be converted —n. an automobile with a folding or removable top

**con·vex** (kän veks′, kän′veks′) adj. ⟦< L com-, together + vehere, bring⟧ curving outward like the surface of a sphere —**con·vex′i·ty** n.

**con·vey** (kən vā′) vt. ⟦< L com-, together + via, way⟧ **1** to take from one place to another; transport; carry **2** to transmit **3** Law to transfer (property, etc.) —**con·vey′a·ble** adj.

CONVEX LENSES

**con·vey′ance** n. **1** a conveying **2** a means of conveying; esp., a vehicle

**con·vey′or** (**belt**) a device, consisting of a continuous moving belt, for conveying things: also **con·vey′er** (**belt**)

**con·vict** (kən vikt′; for n. kän′vikt) vt. ⟦see CONVINCE⟧ to prove or find (a person) guilty —n. a convicted person serving a prison sentence

**con·vic·tion** (kən vik′shən) n. **1** a convicting or being convinced **2** a being convinced; strong belief

**con·vince** (kən vins′) vt. -vinced′, -vinc′ing ⟦< L com-, intens. + vincere, conquer⟧ to persuade by argument or evidence; make feel sure —**con·vinc′ing** adj. —**con·vinc′ing·ly** adv.

**con·viv·i·al** (kən viv′ē əl) adj. ⟦< L com-, together + vivere, to live⟧ **1** festive **2** fond of eating, drinking, and good company; sociable —**con·viv′i·al′i·ty** (-al′ə tē) n.

**con·vo·ca·tion** (kän′vō kā′shən) n. **1** a convoking **2** an ecclesiastical or academic assembly

**con·voke** (kən vōk′) vt. -voked′, -vok′ing ⟦< L com-, together + vocare, to call⟧ to call together; convene

**con·vo·lut·ed** (kän′və lōōt′id) adj. **1** having convolutions; coiled **2** involved; complicated

**con·vo·lu·tion** (-lōō′shən) n. ⟦< L com-, together + volvere, to roll⟧ **1** a twisting, coiling, or winding together **2** a fold, twist, or coil

**con·voy** (kän′voi′) vt. ⟦see CONVEY⟧ to escort in order to protect —n. **1** a convoying **2** a protecting escort **3** a group of ships, vehicles, etc. traveling together

**con·vulse** (kən vuls′) vt. -vulsed′, -vuls′ing ⟦< L com-, together + vellere, to pluck⟧ **1** to shake violently; agitate **2** to cause to shake with laughter, rage, etc. —**con·vul′sive** adj. —**con·vul′sive·ly** adv.

**con·vul·sion** (-vul′shən) n. **1** a violent, involuntary spasm of the muscles: often used in pl. **2** a fit of laughter **3** a violent disturbance

**coo** (kōō) vi. ⟦echoic⟧ to make the soft, murmuring sound of pigeons or doves —n. this sound

**COO** abbrev. chief operating officer

**cook** (kook) n. ⟦< L coquere, to cook⟧ one who prepares food —vt. to prepare (food) by boiling, baking, frying, etc. —vi. **1** to be a cook **2** to undergo cooking —**cook up** [Inf.] to devise; invent —**cook′er** n.

**cook′book′** n. a book containing recipes and other food-preparation information

**cook′er·y** n. [Chiefly Brit.] the art or practice of cooking

**cook′ie** n. ⟦prob. < Du koek, cake⟧ a small, sweet cake, usually flat and either crisp or chewy: also **cook′y**, pl. -ies

**cook′out′** n. a meal cooked and eaten outdoors

**cook′top′** n. a stove top, with burners, or such a unit installed as on a kitchen counter

**cool** (kōōl) adj. ⟦OE col⟧ **1** moderately cold **2** tending to reduce the effects of heat [cool clothes] **3** not excited; composed **4** showing dislike or indifference **5** calmly bold **6** [Inf.] without exaggeration [a cool $1,000] **7** [Slang] very good —n. **1** a cool place, time, etc. [the cool of the evening] **2** [Slang] cool, dispassionate manner —vt., vi. to make or become cool or colder —**cool′ly** adv. —**cool′ness** n.

**cool′ant** n. a fluid or other substance for cooling engines, etc.

**cool′er** n. **1** a container or room for keeping things cool **2** a cold, refreshing drink **3** [Slang] jail: with the

**Coo·lidge** (kōō′lij), (**John**) **Calvin** 1872-1933; 30th president of the U.S. (1923-29)

**coo·lie** (kōō′lē) n. ⟦Hindi qulī, servant⟧ an unskilled native laborer, esp. formerly, in India, China, etc.

**coon** (kōōn) n. short for RACCOON

**coon′skin′** n. the skin of a raccoon, used as a fur

**coop** (kōōp) n. ⟦< L cupa, cask⟧ a small pen as for poultry —vt. to confine as in a coop: usually with up

**co-op** (kō′äp′) n. [Inf.] a cooperative

**coop·er** (kōōp′ər) n. ⟦see COOP⟧ one whose work is making or repairing barrels and casks

**co·op·er·ate** or **co-op·er·ate** (kō äp′ər āt′) vi. -at′ed, -at′ing ⟦< L co-, with + opus, work⟧ to act or work together with another or others —**co·op′er·a′tion** or **co-op′er·a′tion** n.

**co·op′er·a·tive** or **co-op′er·a·tive** (-ər ə tiv, -ər āt′iv) adj. **1** cooperating **2** owned collectively by members who share in its benefits —n. a cooperative store, etc.

**co-opt** (kō äpt′, kō′äpt′) vt. ⟦< L < co-, with + optare, choose⟧ **1** to get (an opponent) to join one's side **2** to take over for one's own purposes

**co·or·di·nate** or **co-or·di·nate** (kō ôrd′'n it; for v., -āt′) adj. ⟦< L co-, with + ordo, order⟧ **1** of the same order, importance, etc. [coordinate clauses in a sentence] **2** of coordination or coordinates —n. **1** a coordinate person or thing **2** [pl.] items of clothing, luggage, etc. that form a pleasing ensemble —vt. -nat′ed, -nat′ing **1** to make coordinate **2** to bring into proper order or relation; adjust —**co·or′di·na′tor** or **co-or′di·na′tor** n.

**coordinating conjunction** a conjunction connecting coordinate words, clauses, etc. (Ex.: and, but, nor)

**co·or·di·na·tion** or **co-or·di·na·tion** n. **1** a coordinating or being coordinated **2** harmonious action, as of muscles

**coot** (kōōt) n. ⟦ME cote⟧ **1** a ducklike water bird **2** [Inf.] an eccentric old man

**coot·ie** (kōōt′ē) *n.* [Slang] a louse

**cop** (käp) *vt.* **copped, cop′ping** [prob. < L *capere,* take] [Slang] to seize, steal, etc. —*n.* [Slang] a policeman —**cop out** [Slang] **1** to renege **2** to give up; quit

**co·part·ner** (kō pärt′nər, kō′pärt′-) *n.* an associate

**co·pay·ment** (kō′pā′mənt) *n.* the part of a medical bill, often a fixed fee, not covered by insurance

**cope**[1] (kōp) *vi.* **coped, cop′ing** [< OFr *coper,* to strike] **1** to fight or contend (*with*) successfully **2** to deal with problems, etc.

**cope**[2] (kōp) *n.* [< LL *cappa*] **1** a large, capelike vestment worn by priests **2** any cover like this

**Co·pen·ha·gen** (kō′pən hā′gən, -hä′-) capital of Denmark: pop. 626,000

**Co·per·ni·cus** (kō pʉr′ni kəs), **Nic·o·la·us** (nik′ə lā′ əs) 1473-1543; Pol. astronomer —**Co·per′ni·can** *adj.*

**cop·i·er** (käp′ē ər) *n.* **1** one who copies **2** a duplicating machine

**co·pi·lot** (kō′pī′lət) *n.* the assistant pilot of an airplane

**cop·ing** (kō′piŋ) *n.* [< COPE[2]] the top layer of a masonry wall

**co·pi·ous** (kō′pē əs) *adj.* [< L *copia,* abundance] plentiful; abundant —**co′pi·ous·ly** *adv.* —**co′pi·ous·ness** *n.*

**cop′-out′** *n.* [Slang] a copping out, as by reneging or quitting

**cop·per** (käp′ər) *n.* [< LL *cuprum*] **1** a reddish-brown, ductile, metallic chemical element **2** a reddish brown —*adj.* **1** of copper **2** reddish-brown —**cop′per·y** *adj.*

**cop′per·head′** *n.* a poisonous North American snake

**co·pra** (kä′prə, kō′-) *n.* [Port < Hindi *khoprā*] dried coconut meat, the source of coconut oil

**copse** (käps) *n.* [< OFr *coper,* to strike] a thicket of small trees or shrubs: also **cop·pice** (käp′is)

**cop·ter** (käp′tər) *n. short for* HELICOPTER

**cop·u·la** (käp′yōō lə) *n., pl.* **-las** [L, a link] LINKING VERB —**cop′u·la′tive** (-lāt′iv) *adj.*

**cop·u·late** (käp′yōō lāt′) *vi.* **-lat′ed, -lat′ing** [< L *co-,* together + *apere,* to join] to have sexual intercourse —**cop′u·la′tion** *n.*

**cop·y** (käp′ē) *n., pl.* **-ies** [< L *copia,* plenty] **1** a thing made just like another; imitation or reproduction **2** any of a number of books, magazines, etc. having the same contents **3** matter to be typeset **4** the words of an advertisement —*vt., vi.* **cop′ied, cop′y·ing** **1** to make a copy of **2** to imitate **3** [Inf.] to provide (with) a copy —**cop′y·ist** *n.*

**cop′y·cat′** *n.* an imitator: chiefly a child's term —*adj.* done in imitation [a *copycat* crime]

**cop′y·right′** *n.* the exclusive right to the publication, sale, etc. of a literary or artistic work —*vt.* to protect (a book, etc.) by copyright

**cop′y·writ′er** *n.* a writer of copy, esp. for advertisements

**co·quette** (kō ket′) *n.* [Fr] a girl or woman who flirts —**co·quet′tish** *adj.*

**cor-** *prefix* COM-: used before *r*

**cor·al** (kôr′əl) *n.* [< Gr *korallion*] **1** the hard skeleton secreted by certain marine polyps: reefs and atolls of coral occur in tropical seas **2** a piece of coral **3** a yellowish red —*adj.* of coral

**coral snake** a small, poisonous snake marked with coral, yellow, and black bands

**cor·bel** (kôr′bəl) *n.* [< L *corvus,* raven] a piece of stone, wood, etc. projecting from a wall and supporting a cornice, arch, etc.

**cord** (kôrd) *n.* [< Gr *chordē*] **1** a thick string **2** a measure of wood cut for fuel (128 cubic feet) **3** a rib on the surface of a fabric **4** ribbed cloth **5** [*pl.*] corduroy trousers **6** *Anat.* any part like a cord **7** *Elec.* a slender cable

**cord′age** *n.* cords and ropes

**cor·dial** (kôr′jəl) *adj.* [< L *cor,* heart] warm; hearty; sincere —*n.* a liqueur —**cor′di·al′i·ty** (-jē al′ə tē) *n.* —**cor′dial·ly** *adv.*

**cor·dil·le·ra** (kôr′dil yer′ə, -də ler′ə) *n.* [Sp < L *chorda,* a cord] a system or chain of mountains

**cord·ite** (kôr′dīt′) *n.* [< CORD: it is stringy] a smokeless explosive made of nitroglycerin, etc.

**cord·less** (kôrd′lis) *adj.* operated by batteries, as an electric shaver

**cor·don** (kôr′dən) *n.* [see CORD] a line or circle of police, troops, etc. guarding an area —*vt.* to encircle with a cordon

**cor·do·van** (kôr′də vən) *n.* [after *Córdoba,* Spain] a soft, colored leather

**cor·du·roy** (kôr′də roi′) *n.* [prob. < CORD + obs. *duroy,* a coarse fabric] a heavy, ribbed cotton fabric

**core** (kôr) *n.* [prob. < L *cor,* heart] **1** the central part of an apple, pear, etc. **2** the central part of anything **3** the most important part —*vt.* **cored, cor′ing** to remove the core of

**co·re·spond·ent** (kō′ri spän′dənt) *n.* [CO- + RESPONDENT] *Law* a person charged with having committed adultery with the wife or husband from whom a divorce is being sought

**co·ri·an·der** (kôr′ē an′dər) *n.* [< Gr *koriandron*] an annual herb with strong-smelling, seedlike fruit used as a flavoring

**cork** (kôrk) *n.* [ult. < L *quercus,* oak] **1** the light, thick, elastic outer bark of an oak tree (**cork oak**) **2** a stopper made of cork, for a bottle, etc. **3** any stopper —*adj.* of cork —*vt.* to stop with a cork

**cork′board′** *n.* a bulletin board made of granulated cork

**cork′screw′** *n.* a spiral-shaped device for pulling corks out of bottles —*adj.* spiral —*vi., vt.* to move in a spiral; twist

**corm** (kôrm) *n.* [< Gr *kormos,* a log] a fleshy, underground stem, as that of the gladiolus

**cor·mo·rant** (kôr′mə rənt) *n.* [< L *corvus,* raven + *marinus,* marine] a large, voracious sea bird

**corn**[1] (kôrn) *n.* [OE] **1** a small, hard seed, esp. of a cereal grass; kernel **2** *a*) an American cereal plant with kernels growing in rows along a woody husk-enclosed core (**corncob**) *b*) the kernels **3** [Brit.] grain, esp. wheat **4** the leading cereal crop in a place **5** [Inf.] ideas, humor, etc. regarded as old-fashioned, trite, etc. —*vt.* to pickle (meat, etc.) in brine

**corn**[2] (kôrn) *n.* [< L *cornu,* horn] a hard, thick, painful growth of skin, esp. on a toe

**corn′ball′** *adj.* [CORN[1], *n.* 5 + (SCREW)BALL] [Slang] corny

**corn bread** bread made with cornmeal

**cor·ne·a** (kôr′nē ə) *n.* [< L *cornu,* horn] the transparent outer coat of the eyeball —**cor′ne·al** *adj.*

**cor·ner** (kôr′nər) *n.* [< L *cornu,* horn] **1** the point or place where lines or surfaces join and form an angle **2** the angle formed **3** any of the angles formed at a street intersection **4** a remote, secluded place **5** a region; quarter **6** a position hard to escape from **7** a monopoly acquired on a stock or commodity so as to raise the price —*vt.* **1** to force into a CORNER (*n.*6) **2** to get a monopoly on (a stock, etc.) —*vi.* to turn corners: said of a vehicle —*adj.* at, on, or for a corner —**cut corners** to cut down expenses, time, etc. —**cor′nered** *adj.*

**cor′ner·back′** *n. Football* either of two defensive backs positioned outside the linebackers

**cor′ner·stone′** *n.* **1** a stone laid at a corner of a building, esp. at a ceremony for the beginning of construction **2** the basic part; foundation

**cor·net** (kôr net′) *n.* [< L *cornu,* horn] a brass instrument similar to the trumpet but more compact

**corn′flow′er** *n.* an annual plant with tiny, white, pink, or blue flowers that form a round head

**cor·nice** (kôr′nis) *n.* [< Gr *korōnis,* wreath] **1** a horizontal molding projecting along the top of a wall, etc. **2** a decorative cover for a curtain rod

**corn′meal′** *n.* meal made from corn

**corn′starch′** *n.* a powdery starch made from corn, used in cooking

**corn syrup** a syrup made from cornstarch

**cor·nu·co·pi·a** (kôr′nə kō′pē ə) *n.* ⟦L *cornu copiae*, horn of plenty⟧ 1 a horn-shaped container overflowing with fruits, flowers, etc. 2 an abundance

**corn·y** (kôr′nē) *adj.* -i·er, -i·est [Inf.] trite, sentimental, etc.

**co·rol·la** (kə rōl′ə, -räl′ə) *n.* ⟦< L, dim. of *corona*, crown⟧ the petals of a flower

**cor·ol·lar·y** (kôr′ə ler′ē) *n., pl.* -ies ⟦see prec.⟧ 1 a proposition that follows from one already proved 2 a normal result

**co·ro·na** (kə rō′nə) *n., pl.* -nas or -nae (-nē) ⟦L⟧ 1 the layer of ionized gas surrounding the sun 2 a ring of colored light seen around a luminous body, as the sun or moon

**cor·o·nar·y** (kôr′ə ner′ē) *adj.* 1 of or like a crown 2 of the arteries supplying blood to the heart muscle —*n., pl.* -ies a thrombosis in a coronary artery: in full **coronary thrombosis**

**cor·o·na·tion** (kôr′ə nā′shən) *n.* the crowning of a sovereign

**cor·o·ner** (kôr′ə nər) *n.* ⟦ME, officer of the crown⟧ a public officer who must determine the cause of any death not obviously due to natural causes

**cor·o·net** (kôr′ə net′, kôr′ə net′) *n.* ⟦< OFr *corone*, crown⟧ 1 a small crown worn by nobility 2 a band of jewels, flowers, etc. for the head

**Corp** *abbrev.* 1 Corporal 2 Corporation: also **corp**

**cor·po·ral**[1] (kôr′pə rəl, -prəl) *n.* ⟦< L *caput*, head⟧ the lowest-ranking noncommissioned officer, just below a sergeant

**cor·po·ral**[2] (kôr′pə rəl, -prəl) *adj.* ⟦< L *corpus*, body⟧ of the body; bodily

**corporal punishment** bodily punishment, as flogging

**cor·po·rate** (kôr′pə rit, -prit) *adj.* ⟦< L *corpus*, body⟧ 1 of, like, or being a corporation 2 shared; joint

**cor·po·ra·tion** (-pə rā′shən) *n.* a legal entity, usually a group of people, that has a charter granting it certain legal powers generally given to individuals, as to buy and sell property or to enter into contracts

**cor·po·re·al** (kôr pôr′ē əl) *adj.* ⟦< L *corpus*, body⟧ 1 of or for the body; physical 2 of a material nature; tangible

**corps** (kôr) *n., pl.* **corps** (kôrz) ⟦< L *corpus*, body⟧ 1 a body of people associated under common direction 2 *Mil. a)* a specialized branch of the armed forces *b)* a tactical subdivision of an army

**corpse** (kôrps) *n.* ⟦var. of prec.⟧ a dead body, esp. of a person

**cor·pu·lence** (kôr′pyōō ləns, -pyə-) *n.* ⟦< L *corpus*, body⟧ fatness; obesity —**cor′pu·lent** *adj.*

**cor·pus** (kôr′pəs) *n., pl.* **cor′po·ra** (-pə rə) ⟦L⟧ 1 a body, esp. a dead one 2 a complete collection, as of laws

**Cor·pus Chris·ti** (kôr′pəs kris′tē) city in SE Texas: pop. 257,000

**cor·pus·cle** (kôr′pus′əl) *n.* ⟦< L dim. of *corpus*, body⟧ an unattached body cell, esp. a red or white blood cell —**cor·pus′cu·lar** (-kyōō lər) *adj.*

**corpus de·lic·ti** (də lik′tī′) ⟦ModL, lit., body of the crime⟧ 1 the facts constituting a crime 2 loosely, the body of a murder victim

**cor·ral** (kə ral′) *n.* ⟦Sp < L *currere*, to run⟧ an enclosure for horses, cattle, etc.; pen —*vt.* -ralled′, -ral′ling 1 to drive into or confine in a corral 2 to surround or capture

**cor·rect** (kə rekt′) *vt.* ⟦< L *com-*, together + *regere*, to rule⟧ 1 to make right 2 to point out or mark the errors of 3 to scold or punish 4 to cure or remove (a fault, etc.) —*adj.* 1 conforming to an established standard 2 true; accurate; right —**cor·rect′a·ble** *adj.* —**cor·rec′tive** *adj., n.* —**cor·rect′ly** *adv.* —**cor·rect′ness** *n.*

**cor·rec′tion** (-rek′shən) *n.* 1 a correcting or being corrected 2 a change that corrects a mistake 3 punishment to correct faults 4 *Finance* a tempo-

rary reversal in rising stock prices, etc. —**cor·rec′tion·al** *adj.*

**cor·re·late** (kôr′ə lāt′) *vi.*, *vt.* -lat′ed, -lat′ing ⟦COM- & RELATE⟧ to be in or bring into mutual relation —**cor′re·la′tion** *n.*

**cor·rel·a·tive** (kə rel′ə tiv) *adj.* 1 having a mutual relationship 2 *Gram.* expressing mutual relation and used in pairs, as the conjunctions *neither* and *nor* —*n.* a correlative word, etc.

**cor·re·spond** (kôr′ə spänd′) *vi.* ⟦< L *com-*, together + *respondere*, respond⟧ 1 to be in agreement (*with* something) 2 to be similar or equal (*to* something) 3 to communicate by letters —**cor′re·spond′ing·ly** *adv.*

**cor′re·spond′ence** *n.* 1 agreement; conformity 2 similarity 3 *a)* communication by letters *b)* the letters

**cor′re·spond′ent** *adj.* corresponding; agreeing; analogous —*n.* 1 a thing that corresponds 2 one who exchanges letters with another 3 one hired by a newspaper, radio network, etc. to furnish news, etc. from a distant place

**cor·ri·dor** (kôr′ri dər, -dôr′) *n.* ⟦Fr < L *currere*, to run⟧ a long hall

**cor·rob·o·rate** (kə räb′ə rāt′) *vt.* -rat′ed, -rat′ing ⟦< L *com-*, intens. + *robur*, strength⟧ to confirm; support —**cor·rob′o·ra′tion** *n.* —**cor·rob′o·ra′tive** (-ə rāt′iv, -ər ə tiv) *adj.* —**cor·rob′o·ra′tor** *n.*

**cor·rode** (kə rōd′) *vt., vi.* -rod′ed, -rod′ing ⟦< L *com-*, intens. + *rodere*, gnaw⟧ to eat into or wear away gradually, as by rusting or the action of chemicals —**cor·ro′sion** (-rō′zhən) *n.* —**cor·ro′sive** (-rō′siv) *adj., n.* —**cor·ro′sive·ly** *adv.*

**cor·ru·gate** (kôr′ə gāt′) *vt., vi.* -gat′ed, -gat′ing ⟦< L *com-*, intens. + *rugare*, to wrinkle⟧ to shape into parallel grooves and ridges —**cor′ru·ga′tion** *n.*

**cor·rupt** (kə rupt′) *adj.* ⟦< L *com-*, together + *rumpere*, to break⟧ 1 evil; depraved 2 taking bribes 3 containing alterations, errors, etc. —*vt., vi.* to make or become corrupt —**cor·rupt′i·ble** *adj.* —**cor·rup′tion** *n.* —**cor·rupt′ly** *adv.*

**cor·sage** (kôr säzh′) *n.* ⟦see CORPS & -AGE⟧ a small bouquet for a woman to wear, as at the waist or shoulder

**cor·sair** (kôr′ser′) *n.* ⟦< Fr < L *cursus*, course⟧ a pirate or a pirate ship

**cor·set** (kôr′sit) *n.* ⟦see CORPS⟧ a closefitting undergarment worn, chiefly by women, to give support to or shape the body

**cor·tege** or **cor·tège** (kôr tezh′, -tāzh′) *n.* ⟦Fr < L *cohors*⟧ 1 a retinue 2 a ceremonial procession

**cor·tex** (kôr′teks) *n., pl.* -ti·ces′ (-tə sēz′) ⟦L, bark of a tree⟧ 1 the outer part of an internal organ; esp., the outer layer of gray matter over most of the brain 2 an outer layer of plant tissue —**cor′ti·cal** (-ti kəl) *adj.*

**cor·ti·sone** (kôrt′ə sōn′, -zōn′) *n.* ⟦so named by E. C. Kendall (1886-1972), U.S. physician⟧ a hormone used to treat adrenal insufficiency, inflammatory diseases, etc.

**co·run·dum** (kə run′dəm) *n.* ⟦< Sans *kuruvinda*, ruby⟧ a very hard mineral used for grinding and polishing

**cor·us·cate** (kôr′ə skāt′) *vi.* -cat′ed, -cat′ing ⟦< L *coruscus*, vibrating⟧ to glitter; sparkle —**cor′us·ca′tion** *n.*

**cor·vette** (kôr vet′) *n.* ⟦Fr⟧ a fast warship smaller than a destroyer and used chiefly for convoy duty

**Co·sa Nos·tra** (kō′sə nō′strə) *name for* MAFIA, esp. in U.S.

**co·sign** (kō′sīn′) *vt., vi.* 1 to sign (a promissory note) in addition to the maker, thus becoming responsible if the maker defaults 2 to sign jointly —**co′sign′er** *n.*

**co·sig·na·to·ry** (-sig′nə tôr′ē) *n., pl.* -ries one of two or more joint signers, as of a treaty

**cos·met·ic** (käz met′ik) *adj.* ⟦< Gr *kosmos*, order⟧ beautifying, or correcting faults in, the face, hair, etc. —*n.* a cosmetic preparation, as lipstick —**cos·met′i·cal·ly** *adv.*

**cos′me·tol′o·gy** (-mə täl′ə jē) *n.* the work of a beautician —**cos′me·tol′o·gist** *n.*

**cos·mic** (käz′mik) *adj.* [< Gr *kosmos*, universe] 1 of the cosmos 2 vast

**cosmic rays** streams of high-energy charged particles from outer space

**cos·mog·o·ny** (käz mäg′ə nē) *n.* [< Gr *kosmos*, universe + *-gonos*, generation] 1 the study of the origin of the universe 2 *pl.* **-nies** a theory of this

**cos·mol′o·gy** (-mäl′ə jē) *n.* [< ML] 1 the scientific study of the form, evolution, etc. of the universe 2 the branch of metaphysics dealing with the origin and structure of the universe —**cos′mo·log′i·cal** (-mə läj′ə kəl) *adj.*

**cos·mo·naut** (käz′mə nôt′) *n.* [Russ *kosmonavt*] a Soviet or Russian astronaut

**cos·mo·pol·i·tan** (käz′mə päl′ə tən) *adj.* [< Gr *kosmos*, universe + *polis*, city-state] 1 common to or representative of all or many parts of the world 2 not bound by local or national habits or prejudices; at home in all places —*n.* a cosmopolitan person or thing: also **cos·mop′o·lite′** (-mäp′ə līt′)

**cos·mos** (käz′məs, -mōs′) *n.* [< Gr *kosmos*, universe] 1 the universe considered as an orderly system 2 any complete and orderly system

**co·spon·sor** (kō′spän′sər) *n.* a joint sponsor, as of a proposed piece of legislation —*vt.* to be a cosponsor of —**co′spon′sor·ship′** *n.*

**Cos·sack** (käs′ak′, -ək) *n.* a member of any of several groups of peasants that lived in autonomous communal settlements, esp. in the Ukraine, until the late 19th c.

**cost** (kôst) *vt.* **cost, cost′ing** [< L *com-*, together + *stare*, to stand] 1 to be obtained for (a certain price) 2 to require the expenditure, loss, etc. of —*n.* 1 the amount of money, etc. asked or paid for a thing; price 2 the time, effort, etc. needed to do something 3 loss; sacrifice —**at all costs** by any means required

**co·star** (kō′stär′; *for v., usually* kō′stär′) *n.* any featured actor or actress given equal billing with another in a movie, play, etc. —*vt., vi.* **-starred′, -star′ring** to present as or be a costar

**Cos·ta Ri·ca** (käs′tə rē′kə, kôs′-, kōs′-) country in Central America: 19,730 sq. mi.; pop. 2,417,000 —**Cos′ta Ri′can**

**cost-ef·fec·tive** (kôst′ə fek′tiv) *adj.* producing good results for the amount of money spent; efficient or economical —**cost′-ef·fec′tive·ness** *n.*

**cos·tive** (käs′tiv, kôs′-) *adj.* [< L *constipare*, to press together] constipated or constipating

**cost·ly** *adj.* **-li·er, -li·est** [ME] 1 costing much; expensive 2 magnificent —**cost′li·ness** *n.*

**cost of living** the average cost of the necessities of life, as food, shelter, and clothes

**cos·tume** (käs′tōōm′, -tyōōm′) *n.* [< L *consuetudo*, custom] 1 *a)* the style of dress typical of a certain country, period, etc. *b)* a set of such clothes, as worn in a play 2 a set of outer clothes —*vt.* **-tumed′, -tum′ing** to provide with a costume

**co·sy** (kō′zē) *adj.* **-si·er, -si·est**, *n.*, *pl.* **-sies** *chiefly Brit. sp. of* COZY —**co′si·ly** *adv.* —**co′si·ness** *n.*

**cot**[1] (kät) *n.* [< Sans *khátvā*] a narrow, collapsible bed, as one made of canvas on a folding frame

**cot**[2] (kät) *n.* [OE] a small shelter

**cote** (kōt) *n.* [ME] a small shelter for doves, sheep, etc.

**co·te·rie** (kōt′ər ē) *n.* [Fr] a close circle of friends; clique

**co·ter·mi·nous** (kō tur′mə nəs) *adj.* CONTERMINOUS

**co·til·lion** (kō til′yən) *n.* [< OFr *cote*, coat] 1 an intricate, formal group dance 2 a formal ball Also sp. **co·til′lon**

**cot·tage** (kät′ij) *n.* [ME] 1 a small house 2 a house used for vacations —**cot′tag·er** *n.*

**cottage cheese** a soft, white cheese made from the curds of sour milk

**cot·ter pin** (kät′ər) a pin with two stems that can be spread apart to fasten the pin in place

**cot·ton** (kät′′n) *n.* [< Ar *quṭun*] 1 the soft, white hairs around the seeds of certain plants of the

mallow family 2 such a plant or plants 3 thread or cloth made of cotton —**cotton to** [Inf.] to take a liking to —**cot′ton·y** *adj.*

**cotton gin** [see GIN[2]] a machine for separating cotton from the seeds

**cot′ton·mouth′** *n.* WATER MOCCASIN

**cot′ton·seed′** *n.* the seed of the cotton plant, yielding an oil (**cottonseed oil**) used in margarine, cooking oil, soap, etc.

**cot′ton·tail′** *n.* a common American rabbit with a short, fluffy tail

**cot′ton·wood′** *n.* a poplar that has seeds thickly covered with cottony or silky hairs

**cot·y·le·don** (kät′ə lēd′′n) *n.* [< Gr *kotylē*, cavity] the first leaf or one of the first pair of leaves produced by the embryo of a flowering plant

**couch** (kouch) *n.* [< OFr *coucher*, lie down] an article of furniture on which one may sit or lie down; sofa —*vt.* 1 to place as on a couch 2 to word in a certain way; phrase; express

**cou·gar** (kōō′gər) *n.* [< AmInd (Brazil)] a large, powerful, tawny cat; mountain lion; puma

**cough** (kôf) *vi.* [ME *coughen*] to expel air suddenly and noisily from the lungs —*vt.* to expel by coughing —*n.* 1 the act of coughing 2 a condition causing frequent coughing —**cough up** [Slang] to hand over (money, etc.)

**cough drop** a small medicated tablet for the relief of coughs, etc.

**could** (kood) *v.aux.* 1 *pt. of* CAN[1] 2 an auxiliary verb generally equivalent to CAN[1], expressing esp. a shade of doubt [it *could* be so]

**cou·lomb** (kōō′läm′, -lōm′) *n.* [after C. A. de *Coulomb* (1736-1806), Fr physicist] a unit of electric charge equal to the charge of $6.281 \times 10^{18}$ electrons

**coun·cil** (koun′səl) *n.* [< L *com-*, together + *calere*, to call] 1 a group of people called together for discussion, advice, etc. 2 an administrative, advisory, or legislative body —**coun′cil·man** (-mən), *pl.* **-men** (-mən), *n.* —**coun′cil·per·son** *n.* —**coun′cil·wom·an**, *pl.* **-wom·en**, *fem.n.*

**coun′ci·lor** (-sə lər) *n.* a member of a council

**coun·sel** (koun′səl) *n.* [< L *consilium*] 1 advice 2 a lawyer or group of lawyers 3 a consultant —*vt.* **-seled** or **-selled, -sel·ing** or **-sel·ling** 1 to give advice to 2 to recommend (an action, etc.)

**coun′se·lor** or **coun′sel·lor** (-sə lər) *n.* 1 an advisor 2 a lawyer 3 one in charge of children at a camp

**count**[1] (kount) *vt.* [< L *computare*, compute] 1 to name or add up, unit by unit, to get a total 2 to take account of; include 3 to believe to be; consider —*vi.* 1 to name numbers or add up items in order 2 to be taken into account; have importance 3 to have a specified value: often with *for* 4 to rely or depend (*on* or *upon*) —*n.* 1 a counting 2 the total number 3 a reckoning 4 *Law* any of the charges in an indictment

**count**[2] (kount) *n.* [< L *comes*, companion] a European nobleman with a rank equal to that of an English earl

**count′down′** *n.* 1 the schedule of operations just before the firing of a rocket, etc. 2 the counting off, in reverse order, of time units in this schedule

**coun·te·nance** (koun′tə nəns, kount′′n əns) *n.* [< L *continentia*, bearing] 1 facial expression 2 the face 3 approval; support —*vt.* **-nanced, -nanc·ing** to approve or tolerate

**count·er**[1] (kount′ər) *n.* 1 a person, device, etc. that counts something 2 a small disk for keeping count in games 3 an imitation coin or token 4 a long table, cabinet top, etc. for the displaying of goods, serving of food, etc. —**under the counter** in a secret manner: said of sales, etc. made illegally

**coun·ter**[2] (kount′ər) *adv.* [< L *contra*, against] in opposition; opposite —*adj.* contrary; opposed —*n.* the opposite; contrary —*vt., vi.* to act, do, etc. counter to; oppose

**counter-** [< L *contra-*, against] *combining form* 1

contrary to [*counterclockwise*] **2** in retaliation [*counterattack*] **3** complementary [*counterpart*]

**coun'ter·act'** *vt.* to act against; neutralize — **coun'ter·ac'tion** *n.*

**coun'ter·at·tack'** *n.* an attack made in opposition to another attack —*vt.*, *vi.* to attack so as to offset the enemy's attack

**coun'ter·bal'ance** *n.* a weight, force, etc. that balances another —*vt.* **-anced**, **-anc·ing** to be a counterbalance to; offset

**coun'ter·claim'** *n.* an opposing claim —*vt.*, *vi.* to present as, or make, a counterclaim

**coun'ter·clock'wise'** *adj.*, *adv.* in a direction opposite to that in which the hands of a clock move

**coun'ter·cul'ture** *n.* a culture with a lifestyle that is opposed to the prevailing culture

**coun·ter·es'pi·o·nage'** *n.* actions to prevent or thwart enemy espionage

**coun'ter·feit'** (-fit') *adj.* [< OFr *contre-*, counter- + *faire*, to make] **1** made in imitation of something genuine so as to deceive; forged **2** sham; pretended —*n.* an imitation made to deceive; forgery —*vt.*, *vi.* **1** to make an imitation of (money, etc.), usually to deceive **2** to pretend —**coun'ter·feit'er** *n.*

**count'er·man'** (-man') *n.*, *pl.* **-men'** (-men') a man who serves customers at a counter, as of a lunchroom

**coun'ter·mand'** (-mand') *vt.* [< L *contra*, against + *mandare*, to command] to cancel or revoke by a contrary order

**coun'ter·mel'o·dy** *n.* a melody distinct from the principal melody

**coun'ter·pane'** (-pān') *n.* [ult. < L *culcita puncta*, embroidered quilt] a bedspread

**coun'ter·part'** *n.* **1** one that closely resembles another **2** a copy or duplicate

**coun'ter·point'** *n.* [< It: see COUNTER- & POINT] **1** the technique of combining two or more distinct lines of music that sound simultaneously **2** any melody played or sung against a basic melody **3** a thing set up in contrast with another

**coun'ter·poise'** *n.* [see COUNTER² & POISE] **1** a counterbalance **2** equilibrium —*vt.* **-poised'**, **-pois'ing** to counterbalance

**coun'ter·pro·duc'tive** *adj.* having results contrary to those intended

**coun'ter·rev'o·lu'tion** *n.* a political movement against a government set up by a previous revolution —**coun'ter·rev'o·lu'tion·ar'y**, *pl.* **-ies**, *n.*, *adj.*

**coun'ter·sign'** *n.* **1** a signature added to a previously signed document, as for confirmation **2** a secret signal to another, as a password —*vt.* to confirm with one's own signature

**coun'ter·sink'** *vt.* **-sunk'**, **-sink'ing** **1** to enlarge the top part of (a hole) so that the head of a bolt, etc. will fit flush with the surface **2** to sink (a bolt, etc.) into such a hole

**coun'ter·ten'or** *n.* **1** the range of the highest male voice, above tenor **2** a voice or singer with such a range

**count'er·top'** *n.* the upper surface of a COUNTER¹ (sense 4)

**coun'ter·weight'** *n.* a counterbalance

**count·ess** (kount'is) *n.* **1** the wife or widow of a count or earl **2** a woman of nobility with a rank equal to that of a count or earl

**count·less** (kount'lis) *adj.* too many to count; innumerable; myriad

**coun·try** (kun'trē) *n.*, *pl.* **-tries** [< L *contra*, against] **1** an area of land; region **2** the whole land, or the people, of a nation **3** the land of one's birth or citizenship **4** land with farms and small towns **5** *short for* COUNTRY MUSIC

**country club** a social club with a clubhouse, golf course, etc.

**coun'try·man** (-mən) *n.*, *pl.* **-men** (-mən) a person of one's own country

**country music** popular music that derives from the rural folk music of the S U.S.

**coun'try·side'** *n.* a rural region

**coun'try·wide'** *adj.*, *adv.* throughout the entire nation

**coun·ty** (kount'ē) *n.*, *pl.* **-ties** [< ML *comitatus*, jurisdiction of a count] a small administrative district of a country, U.S. state, etc.

**coup** (kōō) *n.*, *pl.* **coups** (kōōz) [Fr < L *colaphus*, a blow] **1** a sudden, successful action **2** COUP D'ÉTAT

**coup de grâce** (kōō' də gräs') [Fr, stroke of mercy] **1** the blow, shot, etc. that brings death to a sufferer **2** a finishing stroke

**coup d'é·tat** (kōō' dā tä') [Fr, stroke of state] the sudden, forcible overthrow as of a ruler or government

**coupe** (kōōp) *n.* [< Fr *couper*, to cut] a closed, two-door automobile

**cou·ple** (kup'əl) *n.* [< L *copula*] **1** a link **2** a pair of things or persons, as a man and woman who are engaged, married, etc. **3** [Inf.] a few —*vt.*, *vi.* **-pled**, **-pling** to link or unite

**cou·plet** (kup'lit) *n.* two successive lines of poetry, esp. two that rhyme

**cou·pling** (kup'liŋ) *n.* **1** a joining together **2** a mechanical device for joining parts together

**cou·pon** (kōō'pän', kyōō'-) *n.* [Fr < *couper*, to cut] **1** a detachable printed statement on a bond, specifying the interest due at a given time **2** a certificate entitling one to a specified right, as a discount or gift

**cour·age** (kur'ij) *n.* [< L *cor*, heart] the quality of being brave; valor

**cou·ra·geous** (kə rā'jəs) *adj.* having or showing courage; brave —**cou·ra'geous·ly** *adv.*

**cou·ri·er** (koor'ē ər, kur'-) *n.* [< L *currere*, to run] a messenger

**course** (kôrs) *n.* [< L *currere*, to run] **1** an onward movement; progress **2** a way, path, or channel **3** the direction taken **4** a regular manner of procedure or conduct [our wisest *course*] **5** a series of like things in order **6** a part of a meal served at one time **7** *Educ. a*) a complete series of studies, as for a degree *b*) any of the separate units of such a series —*vi.* **coursed**, **cours'ing** to run or race —**in due course** in the usual sequence (of events) —**in the course of** during —**of course 1** naturally **2** certainly

**cours·er** (kôr'sər) *n.* a graceful, spirited, or swift horse

**court** (kôrt) *n.* [< L *cohors*, enclosure] **1** a courtyard **2** a short street **3** a space for playing a game, as basketball **4** *a*) the palace, or the family, etc., of a sovereign *b*) a sovereign and councilors, etc. as a governing body *c*) a formal gathering held by a sovereign **5** attention paid to someone in order to get something **6** *Law a*) a judge or judges *b*) a place where trials are held — *vt.* **1** to pay attention to (a person) so as to get something **2** to seek as a mate; woo **3** to try to get [to *court* favor] —*vi.* to carry on a courtship

**cour·te·ous** (kurt'ē əs) *adj.* [see prec. & -EOUS] polite and gracious —**cour'te·ous·ly** *adv.*

**cour·te·san** (kôrt'ə zən) *n.* [see COURT] a prostitute: also **cour'te·zan**

**cour·te·sy** (kurt'ə sē) *n.*, *pl.* **-sies 1** courteous behavior **2** a polite or considerate act or remark —*adj.* provided free; complimentary

**court'house'** *n.* **1** a building housing law courts **2** a building housing offices of a county government

**cour·ti·er** (kôrt'ē ər, -yər) *n.* an attendant at a royal court

**court'ly** *adj.* **-li·er**, **-li·est** suitable for a king's court; dignified; elegant —**court'li·ness** *n.*

**court'-mar'tial** *n.*, *pl.* **courts'-mar'tial**; for 2, now often **court'-mar'tials 1** a court in the armed forces for the trial of persons accused of breaking military law **2** a trial by a court-martial **3** a conviction by a court-martial —*vt.* **-tialed** or **-tialled**,

**-tial·ing** or **-tial·ling** to try or convict by a court-martial

**court reporter** one who records exactly what is said in a courtroom during a trial

**court'room'** *n. Law* a room in which trials are held

**court'ship'** *n.* the act, process, or period of wooing

**court'side'** *n. Sports* the area immediately around a basketball court, tennis court, etc.

**court'yard'** *n.* a space enclosed by walls, adjoining or within a large building

**cous·cous** (kōōs′kōōs′) *n.* ⟦Fr < Ar *kaskasa*, to grind⟧ a N African dish made with crushed grain, served as with lamb in a spicy sauce

**cous·in** (kuz′ən) *n.* ⟦ult. < L *com-*, with + *soror*, sister⟧ **1** the son or daughter of one's uncle or aunt **2** loosely, any relative by blood or marriage

**cous'in·age** (-ij) *n.* **1** the relationship between cousins **2** a group of cousins or relatives

**cou·tu·ri·er** (kōō′toor ē ā′) *n.* ⟦Fr⟧ a designer of women's fashions —**cou'tu·ri·ère'** (-ē er′) *fem.n.*

**cove** (kōv) *n.* ⟦OE *cofa*, cave⟧ a small bay or inlet

**cov·en** (kuv′ən) *n.* ⟦see CONVENE⟧ a gathering or meeting, esp. of witches

**cov·e·nant** (kuv′ə nant) *n.* ⟦see CONVENE⟧ an agreement; compact —*vt.* to promise by a covenant —*vi.* to make a covenant

**cov·er** (kuv′ər) *vt.* ⟦< L *co-*, intens. + *operire*, to hide⟧ **1** to place something on or over **2** to extend over **3** to clothe **4** to conceal; hide **5** to shield, protect, or watch (someone or something) **6** to include; deal with [to *cover* a subject] **7** to protect financially [to *cover* a loss] **8** to accept (a bet) **9** to travel over **10** to point a firearm at **11** *Journalism* to gather the details of (a news story) —*vi.* **1** to spread over a surface, as a liquid does **2** to provide an alibi (*for*) —*n.* **1** anything that covers, as a lid, top, etc. **2** a shelter for protection **3** a tablecloth and setting **4** COVER CHARGE **5** something used to hide one's real actions, etc. — **cover up** to keep blunders, crimes, etc. from being known —**take cover** to seek shelter —**under cover** in secrecy or concealment

**cov'er·age** (-ij) *n.* **1** the amount, extent, etc. covered by something **2** *Insurance* the risks covered by a policy

**cov'er·all'** *n.* [*usually pl.*] a one-piece outer garment, often worn over regular clothing while working, etc.

**cover charge** a fixed charge in addition to the cost of food and drink, as at a nightclub or restaurant

**cover crop** a crop, as clover, grown to prevent erosion and restore soil fertility

**covered wagon** a large wagon with an arched cover of canvas

**cov'er·ing** *n.* anything that covers

**cov'er·let** (-lit) *n.* ⟦< OFr *covrir*, to cover + *lit*, bed⟧ a bedspread

**cover letter** an explanatory letter sent with an enclosure or package: also **covering letter**

**cover story** the article in a magazine that deals with the subject depicted on the cover

**cov·ert** (kō′vərt, kuv′ərt) *adj.* ⟦see COVER⟧ hidden or disguised —*n.* a protected place, as for game — **cov'ert·ly** *adv.*

**cov'er·up'** *n.* an attempt to hide blunders, crimes, etc.

**cov·et** (kuv′it) *vt., vi.* ⟦< L *cupiditas*, cupidity⟧ to want intensely (esp., something that another person has)

**cov'et·ous** *adj.* tending to covet; greedy —**cov'et·ous·ly** *adv.* —**cov'et·ous·ness** *n.*

**cov·ey** (kuv′ē) *n., pl.* **-eys** ⟦< OFr *cover*, to hatch⟧ a small flock of birds, esp. partridges or quail

**cow**[1] (kou) *n.* ⟦OE *cu*⟧ **1** the mature female of domestic cattle, valued for its milk **2** the mature female of certain other mammals, as the whale

**cow**[2] (kou) *vt.* ⟦< ON *kūga*, subdue⟧ to make timid; intimidate

**cow·ard** (kou′ərd) *n.* ⟦ult. < L *cauda*, tail⟧ a per-

son who lacks courage, esp. one who is shamefully afraid

**cow'ard·ice'** (-ər dis′) *n.* lack of courage

**cow'ard·ly** *adj.* of or like a coward —*adv.* in the manner of a coward —**cow'ard·li·ness** *n.*

**cow'boy'** *n.* a ranch worker who herds cattle: also **cow'hand'** —**cow'girl'** *fem.n.*

**cow·er** (kou′ər) *vi.* ⟦ME *couren*⟧ to crouch or huddle up, as from fear or cold; shrink; cringe

**cow'hide'** *n.* **1** the hide of a cow **2** leather from it

**cowl** (koul) *n.* ⟦< L *cucullus*, hood⟧ **1** a monk's hood or a monk's cloak with a hood **2** a hood-shaped part or structure

**cow·lick** (kou′lik′) *n.* ⟦< its looking as if licked by a cow⟧ a tuft of hair that cannot easily be combed flat

**cowl·ing** (koul′iŋ) *n.* ⟦see COWL⟧ a metal covering for an airplane engine, etc.

**co-work·er** (kō′wur′kər) *n.* a fellow worker

**cow'poke'** *n.* [Inf.] COWBOY

**cow pony** a horse for herding cattle

**cow'pox'** *n.* a disease of cows: a vaccine with its virus gives temporary immunity to smallpox

**cox·comb** (käks′kōm′) *n.* ⟦for *cock's comb*⟧ a silly, vain fellow; dandy

**cox·swain** (käk′sən, -swān′) *n.* ⟦< *cock*, small boat + SWAIN⟧ one who steers a boat or racing shell

**coy** (koi) *adj.* ⟦ME, quiet⟧ **1** bashful; shy **2** pretending to be shy —**coy'ly** *adv.* —**coy'ness** *n.*

**coy·o·te** (kī ōt′ē, kī′ōt′) *n.* ⟦< AmInd (Mex)⟧ a small, wolflike animal of North America

**coz·en** (kuz′ən) *vt., vi.* ⟦< ME *cosin*, fraud⟧ to cheat; deceive —**coz'en·age** *n.*

**co·zy** (kō′zē) *adj.* **-zi·er**, **-zi·est** ⟦Scot⟧ warm and comfortable; snug —*n., pl.* **-zies** a padded cover for a teapot, to keep the tea hot —**cozy up to** [Inf.] to try to ingratiate oneself with —**co'zi·ly** *adv.* —**co'zi·ness** *n.*

**CPA** *abbrev.* Certified Public Accountant

**CPI** *abbrev.* consumer price index

**CPO** *abbrev.* Chief Petty Officer

**CPR** *abbrev.* cardiopulmonary resuscitation

**CPU** (sē′pē′yōō′) *n.* central processing unit: also **cpu**

**Cr** *Chem. symbol for* chromium

**crab** (krab) *n.* ⟦OE *crabba*⟧ **1** a crustacean with four pairs of legs and a pair of pincers **2** a peevish person —*vi.* **crabbed**, **crab'bing** [Inf.] to complain

BLUE CRAB

**crab apple 1** a small, very sour apple **2** a tree bearing crab apples: also **crab tree**

**crab·bed** (krab′id) *adj.* ⟦< CRAB (APPLE)⟧ **1** peevish **2** hard to read or understand, as handwriting —**crab'bed·ness** *n.*

**crab'by** *adj.* **-bi·er**, **-bi·est** ⟦see prec.⟧ cross and complaining —**crab'bi·ly** *adv.* —**crab'bi·ness** *n.*

**crab grass** a weedy grass, with freely rooting stems, that spreads rapidly

**crack**[1] (krak) *vi.* ⟦< OE *cracian*, resound⟧ **1** to make a sudden, sharp noise, as in breaking **2** to break or split, usually without separation of parts **3** to rasp or shift erratically in register: said of the voice **4** [Inf.] to break down as from strain — *vt.* **1** to cause to make a sharp, sudden noise **2** to cause to break or split **3** to break down (petroleum) into the lighter hydrocarbons of gasoline, etc. **4** to hit hard **5** to solve **6** [Inf.] to break into or force open **7** [Slang] to make (a joke) —*n.* **1** a sudden, sharp noise **2** a partial break; fracture **3** a chink; crevice **4** a cracking of the voice **5** a sudden, sharp blow **6** [Inf.] an attempt or try **7** [Slang] a joke or gibe —*adj.* [Inf.] excellent; first-rate —**crack down (on)** to become strict (with) —

**cracked up to be** [Inf.] believed to be —**crack up 1** to crash **2** [Inf.] *a*) to break down physically or mentally *b*) to laugh or cry

**crack²** (krak) *n.* [Slang] a highly potent and purified form of cocaine for smoking

**crack'down'** *n.* a resorting to strict or stricter discipline or punishment

**cracked** *adj.* **1** having a crack or cracks **2** sounding harsh or strident **3** [Inf.] crazy

**crack'er** *n.* **1** a firecracker **2** a thin, crisp wafer

**crack'er·jack'** *adj.* [Slang] outstanding; excellent —*n.* [Slang] an excellent person or thing

**crack'head'** *n.* [Slang] a habitual user of CRACK²

**crack·le** (krak'əl) *vi.* **-led, -ling** [ME *crakelen,* to crack] to make a series of slight, sharp, popping sounds —*n.* **1** a series of such sounds **2** the fine, irregular surface cracks on some pottery, etc.

**crack'pot'** *n.* [Inf.] a crazy or eccentric person — *adj.* [Inf.] crazy or eccentric

**crack'up'** *n.* **1** a crash **2** [Inf.] a physical or mental breakdown

**-cra·cy** (krə sē) [< Gr *kratos,* rule] *combining form* a (specified) type of government; rule by *[autocracy]*

**cra·dle** (krād''l) *n.* [OE *cradol*] **1** a baby's small bed, usually on rockers **2** infancy **3** the place of a thing's beginning **4** anything like a cradle —*vt.* **-dled, -dling 1** to place, rock, or hold in or as in a cradle **2** to take care of in infancy

**cra'dle·song'** *n.* a lullaby

**craft** (kraft) *n.* [OE *cræft,* power] **1** a special skill or art **2** an occupation requiring special skill **3** the members of a skilled trade **4** guile; slyness **5** *pl.* **craft** a boat, ship, or aircraft

**crafts·man** (krafts'mən) *n., pl.* **-men** (-mən) a skilled worker; artisan —**crafts'man·ship'** *n.*

**craft'y** *adj.* **-i·er, -i·est** [ME *crafti,* sly] subtly deceitful; sly —**craft'i·ly** *adv.* —**craft'i·ness** *n.*

**crag** (krag) *n.* [< Celt] a steep, rugged rock rising from a rock mass —**crag'gy, -gi·er, -gi·est,** *adj.*

**cram** (kram) *vt.* **crammed, cram'ming** [OE *crammian*] **1** to pack full or too full **2** to stuff; force **3** to feed to excess —*vi.* **1** to eat too much or too quickly **2** to study a subject in a hurried, intensive way, as for an examination

**cramp** (kramp) *n.* [< OFr *crampe,* bent] **1** a sudden, painful, involuntary contraction of a muscle from chill, strain, etc. **2** [*usually pl.*] abdominal or uterine spasms and pain —*vt.* **1** to cause a cramp or cramps in **2** [< MDu *krampe,* bent in] to hamper; restrain

**cramped** *adj.* **1** confined or restricted **2** irregular and crowded, as some handwriting

**cran·ber·ry** (kran'ber'ē, -bər ē) *n., pl.* **-ries** [< Du *kranebere*] **1** a firm, sour, edible, red berry, the fruit of an evergreen shrub **2** the shrub

**crane** (krān) *n.* [OE *cran*] **1** a large wading bird with very long legs and neck **2** a machine for lifting or moving heavy weights, using a movable projecting arm or a horizontal traveling beam — *vt., vi.* **craned, cran'ing** to stretch (the neck)

**cra·ni·um** (krā'nē əm) *n., pl.* **-ni·ums** or **-ni·a** (-ə) [< Gr *kranion*] the skull, esp. the part containing the brain —**cra'ni·al** *adj.*

**crank** (kraŋk) *n.* [OE *cranc-,* something twisted] **1** a handle or arm bent at right angles and connected to a machine shaft to transmit motion **2** [Inf.] an eccentric or irritable person —*vt.* to start or operate by a crank —**crank out** [Inf.] to produce steadily and prolifically

**crank'case'** *n.* the metal casing that encloses the crankshaft of an internal-combustion engine

**crank'shaft'** *n.* a shaft with one or more cranks for transmitting motion

**crank'y** *adj.* **-i·er, -i·est 1** apt to operate poorly **2** irritable **3** eccentric —**crank'i·ly** *adv.* —**crank'i·ness** *n.*

**cran·ny** (kran'ē) *n., pl.* **-nies** [< VL *crena,* a notch] a crevice; crack

**crap** (krap) *n.* [< ML *crappa,* chaff] [Slang] **1** nonsense **2** junk; trash **3** excrement: somewhat vulgar —**crap'py, -pi·er, -pi·est,** *adj.*

**crape** (krāp) *n.* **1** CREPE (sense 1) **2** a piece of black crepe as a sign of mourning

**crap·pie** (krap'ē) *n.* a small North American sunfish

**craps** (kraps) *n.* [Fr *crabs*] a gambling game played with two dice

**crap'shoot'** *n.* [Inf.] a very risky undertaking

**crap·shoot·er** (krap'shōōt'ər) *n.* a gambler at craps

**crash** (krash) *vi.* [ME] **1** to fall, collide, or break with a loud noise **2** to collapse; fail **3** [Slang] to sleep or get a temporary place to sleep —*vt.* **1** to cause (a car, airplane, etc.) to crash **2** to force with or as with a crashing noise: with *in, out, through,* etc. **3** [Inf.] to get into (a party, etc.) without an invitation, etc. —*n.* **1** a loud, sudden noise **2** a crashing **3** a sudden collapse, as of business —*adj.* [Inf.] using all possible resources, effort, and speed *[a crash program to build roads]*

**crash'-land'** *vt., vi.* to bring (an airplane) down in a forced landing, esp. without use of the landing gear —**crash landing**

**crash pad** [Slang] a place to live or sleep temporarily

**crass** (kras) *adj.* [L *crassus,* thick] **1** tasteless, insensitive, etc. **2** materialistic —**crass'ly** *adv.* — **crass'ness** *n.*

**-crat** (krat) [< Gr *kratos,* rule] *combining form* member or supporter of (a specified kind of) government

**crate** (krāt) *n.* [L *cratis,* wickerwork] a packing case made of slats of wood —*vt.* **crat'ed, crat'ing** to pack in a crate

**cra·ter** (krāt'ər) *n.* [< Gr *kratēr,* mixing bowl] **1** a bowl-shaped cavity, as at the mouth of a volcano **2** a pit made by an exploding bomb, etc. —*vt.* to make craters in —*vi.* to form craters

**cra·vat** (krə vat') *n.* [< Fr] a necktie

**crave** (krāv) *vt.* **craved, crav'ing** [OE *crafian*] **1** to ask for earnestly; beg **2** to desire strongly

**cra·ven** (krā'vən) *adj.* [< L *crepare,* to rattle] cowardly —*n.* a coward —**cra'ven·ly** *adv.* —**cra'ven·ness** *n.*

**crav'ing** *n.* an intense and prolonged desire, as for affection or for a food or drug

**craw** (krô) *n.* [ME *craue*] **1** the crop of a bird **2** the stomach

**craw·fish** (krô'fish') *n., pl.* **-fish'** or (for different species) **-fish'es** crayfish

**crawl** (krôl) *vi.* [< ON *krafla*] **1** to move slowly by dragging the body along the ground **2** to go on hands and knees; creep **3** to move slowly **4** to move or act in a servile manner **5** to swarm (*with* crawling things) —*n.* **1** a slow movement **2** an overarm swimming stroke

**crawl space** an unfinished space, as under a floor, allowing access to wiring, plumbing, etc.

**crawl'y** *adj.* **-i·er, -i·est** CREEPY

**cray·fish** (krā'fish') *n., pl.* **-fish'** or (for different species) **-fish'es** [< OHG *krebiz*] a freshwater crustacean somewhat like a little lobster

**cray·on** (krā'ən, -än') *n.* [Fr, pencil < L *creta,* chalk] **1** a small stick of chalk, charcoal, or colored wax, used for drawing, coloring, or writing **2** a drawing made with crayons —*vt.* to draw or color with crayons

**craze** (krāz) *vt., vi.* **crazed, craz'ing** [ME *crasen,* to crack] to make or become insane —*n.* a fad

**cra·zy** (krā'zē) *adj.* **-zi·er, -zi·est** [< prec.] **1** unsound of mind; insane **2** [Inf.] foolish; not sensible **3** [Inf.] very enthusiastic or eager —*n., pl.* **-zies** [Slang] a crazy person —**like crazy** [Inf.] with great energy, intensity, etc. —**cra'zi·ly** *adv.* —**cra'zi·ness** *n.*

**crazy bone** FUNNY BONE

**crazy quilt 1** a patchwork quilt with no regular design **2** a hodgepodge

**creak** (krēk) *vi., vt.* [echoic] to make, cause to

make, or move with a harsh, squeaking sound —
**n.** such a sound —**creak'y, -i·er, -i·est,** *adj.* —
**creak'i·ly** *adv.* —**creak'i·ness** *n.*

**cream** (krēm) **n.** ⟦< OFr⟧ **1** the oily, yellowish
part of milk **2** a cosmetic, emulsion, or food with
a creamy consistency **3** the best part **4** yellowish
white —*adj.* made of or with cream —*vt.* **1** to add
cream to **2** to beat into a creamy consistency **3**
[Slang] *a)* to beat or defeat soundly *b)* to hurt,
damage, etc., as by striking with great force —
**cream of** creamed purée of —**cream'y, -i·er, -i·est,**
*adj.* —**cream'i·ness** *n.*

**cream cheese** a soft, white cheese made of cream
or of milk and cream

**cream'er** *n.* **1** a pitcher for cream **2** a nondairy
substance used in place of cream

**cream'·er·y** *n., pl.* **-ies** a place where dairy products are processed or sold

**cream of tartar** a white substance used in baking powder, etc.

**crease** (krēs) **n.** ⟦< ME *creste*, crest⟧ **1** a line made
by folding and pressing **2** a fold or wrinkle —*vt.*
**creased, creas'ing 1** to make a crease in **2** to
wrinkle —*vi.* to become creased

**cre·ate** (krē āt') *vt.* **-at'ed, -at'ing** ⟦< L *creare*⟧ **1**
to cause to come into existence; make; originate **2**
to bring about; give rise to; cause

**cre·a'tion** (-ā'shən) *n.* **1** a creating or being created **2** the universe **3** anything created —**the
Creation** God's creating of the world

**cre·a'tive** (-āt'iv) *adj.* **1** creating or able to create
**2** inventive **3** stimulating the imagination —**cre-
a'tive·ly** *adv.* —**cre·a'tive·ness** *n.* —**cre'a·tiv'i·ty**
(-ā tiv'ə tē) *n.*

**cre·a'tor** (-āt'ər) *n.* ⟦L⟧ one who creates —**the
Creator** God

**crea·ture** (krē'chər) *n.* ⟦< L *creatura*⟧ a living
being, animal or human

**crèche** (kresh, krāsh) *n.* ⟦Fr⟧ a display of the stable scene of Jesus' birth

**cre·dence** (krēd'ns) *n.* ⟦< L *credere*, believe⟧
belief, esp. in the reports or testimony of another

**cre·den·tial** (kri den'shəl) *n.* ⟦see prec.⟧ [*usually
pl.*] a letter or certificate showing one's right to a
certain position or authority

**cre·den·za** (kri den'zə) *n.* ⟦It⟧ **1** a type of buffet
or sideboard **2** a low office cabinet

**credibility gap 1** a disparity between what is
said and the facts **2** the inability to have one's
truthfulness or honesty accepted

**cred·i·ble** (kred'ə bəl) *adj.* ⟦< L *credere*, believe⟧
that can be believed; reliable —**cred'i·bil'i·ty** *n.* —
**cred'i·bly** *adv.*

**cred·it** (kred'it) *n.* ⟦< L *credere*, believe⟧ **1** belief;
confidence **2** favorable reputation **3** praise or
approval **4** a person or thing bringing approval
or honor **5** *a)* acknowledgment of work done *b)*
[*pl.*] a list of such acknowledgments in a film,
book, etc. **6** a sum available to one, as in a bank
account **7** the entry, in an account, of payment
on a debt **8** trust in one's ability to meet payments when due **9** the time allowed for payment
**10** a completed unit of study in a school —*vt.* **1** to
believe; trust **2** to give credit to or commendation
for **3** to give credit in a bank account, etc. —**do
credit to** to bring honor to —**on credit** with an
agreement to pay later

**cred'it·a·ble** *adj.* deserving some credit or praise
—**cred'it·a·bly** *adv.*

**credit card** a card entitling one to charge
purchases, etc. at certain businesses

**cred'i·tor** (-it ər) *n.* one to whom money is owed

**credit union** a cooperative association for pooling
savings of members and making low-interest
loans to them

**cred'it·wor'thy** *adj.* sufficiently sound financially
to be granted credit —**cred'it·wor'thi·ness** *n.*

**cre·do** (krē'dō, krā'-) *n., pl.* **-dos'** ⟦L, I believe⟧ a
creed

**cred·u·lous** (krej'oo ləs, -ə ləs) *adj.* ⟦< L *credere*,
believe⟧ tending to believe too readily —**cre·du·li·
ty** (krə dōō'lə tē, -dyōō-) *n.* —**cred'u·lous·ly** *adv.*

**creed** (krēd) *n.* ⟦< L *credo*, I believe⟧ **1** a brief
statement of religious belief, esp. one accepted as
authoritative by a church **2** any statement of
belief, principles, etc.

**creek** (krēk, krik) *n.* ⟦< ON *kriki*, a bend, winding⟧
a small stream —**up the creek** [Slang] in trouble

**creel** (krēl) *n.* ⟦< L *cratis*, wickerwork⟧ a wicker
basket for holding fish

**creep** (krēp) *vi.* **crept, creep'ing** ⟦OE *creopan*⟧ **1**
to move with the body close to the ground, as on
hands and knees **2** to move slowly or stealthily **3**
to grow along the ground or a wall, as ivy —*n.* **1**
the act of creeping **2** [Slang] an annoying or disgusting person —**make one's flesh creep** to give
one a feeling of fear, disgust, etc. —**the creeps**
[Inf.] a feeling of fear, disgust, etc. —**creep'er** *n.*

**creep'y** *adj.* **-i·er, -i·est** having or causing a feeling
of fear or disgust —**creep'i·ly** *adv.* —**creep'i·ness**
*n.*

**cre·mains** (krē mānz') *pl.n.* the ashes remaining
after cremation

**cre·mate** (krē'māt', kri māt') *vt.* **-mat'ed, -mat'ing**
⟦< L *cremare*⟧ to burn (a dead body) to ashes —
**cre·ma'tion** *n.*

**cre·ma·to·ry** (krē'mə tôr'ē, krem'ə-) *n., pl.* **-ries** a
furnace for cremating: also **cre'ma·to'ri·um** (-ē
əm), *pl.* **-ri·ums, -ri·a** (-ē ə), or **-ries** —*adj.* of or for
cremation

**crème de menthe** (krem' də mänt', menth',
mint') ⟦Fr, cream of mint⟧ a sweet, mint-flavored
liqueur

**crème fraîche** (krem' fresh') ⟦Fr, fresh cream⟧
slightly fermented high-fat cream, used in
sauces, desserts, etc.

**cren·el·ate** or **cren·el·late** (kren'əl āt') *vt.* **-el·
at'ed** or **-el·lat'ed, -el·at'ing** or **-el·lat'ing** ⟦< VL
*crena*, a notch⟧ to furnish with battlements or
with squared notches —**cren'el·a'tion** or **cren'el·
la'tion** *n.*

**Cre·ole** (krē'ōl') *n.* ⟦< Fr < Port *crioulo*, native⟧ **1**
a person descended from the original French settlers of Louisiana **2** a person of mixed Creole and
black descent **3** [**c-**] a language that develops
when different languages remain in contact with
each other —*adj.* [*usually* **c-**] prepared with sau-
téed tomatoes, green peppers, onions, spices, etc.

**cre·o·sote** (krē'ə sōt') *n.* ⟦< Gr *kreas*, flesh +
*sōzein*, to save⟧ an oily liquid distilled from tar
and used as a wood preservative, etc.

**crepe** or **crêpe** (krāp; *for 5, also* krep) *n.* ⟦< Fr < L
*crispus*, curly⟧ **1** a thin, crinkled cloth of silk,
rayon, wool, etc. **2** CRAPE (sense 2) **3** wrinkled
soft rubber used for shoe soles: also **crepe rubber
4** thin, crinkled paper: also **crepe paper 5** a thin
pancake, rolled and filled

**crêpes su·zette** (krāp' sōō zet') ⟦Fr⟧ crêpes rolled
in a hot, orange-flavored sauce and served in
flaming brandy

**crept** (krept) *vi. pt. & pp. of* CREEP

**cre·scen·do** (kri shen'dō') *adj., adv.* ⟦It < L
*crescere*, grow⟧ *Music* with a gradual increase in
loudness: also written **cre·scen'do** —*n., pl.* **-dos'** a
gradual increase in loudness, force, etc.

**cres·cent** (kres'ənt) *n.* ⟦< L *crescere*, grow⟧ **1** a
phase of a planet or a moon, when it appears to
have one concave edge and one convex edge **2**
anything shaped like this —*adj.* shaped like a
crescent

**crescent wrench** ⟦< *Crescent*, a trademark⟧ a
wrench with a crescent-shaped head and an
adjustable jaw

**cress** (kres) *n.* ⟦OE *cressa*⟧ a plant with pungent
leaves, as watercress, used in salads, etc.

**crest** (krest) *n.* ⟦< L *crista*⟧ **1** any growth on the
head of an animal, as a comb or tuft **2** a heraldic
device placed on seals, silverware, etc. **3** the top
line or surface; summit **4** the highest point, level,
degree, etc. —*vi.* to form or reach a crest —
**crest'ed** *adj.*

**crest'fall'en** *adj.* dejected, disheartened, etc.

**Cre·ta·ceous** (kri tā′shəs, krē-) *adj.* ⟦< L *creta*, chalk⟧ of the latest period of the Mesozoic Era, marked by the dying out of dinosaurs, the rise of mammals and flowering plants, and the formation of oil deposits

**Crete** (krēt) Greek island in the E Mediterranean —**Cre·tan** (krēt′n) *adj.*, *n.*

**cre·tonne** (krē tän′, krē′tän′) *n.* ⟦Fr, after *Creton*, village in Normandy⟧ a heavy, printed cotton or linen cloth, used for curtains, slipcovers, etc.

**cre·vasse** (krə vas′) *n.* ⟦Fr⟧ a deep crack, esp. in a glacier

**crev·ice** (krev′is) *n.* ⟦< L *crepare*, to rattle⟧ a narrow opening caused by a crack or split; fissure

**crew**¹ (krōō) *n.* ⟦< L *crescere*, grow⟧ 1 a group of people working together [a road *crew*] 2 a ship's personnel, excluding the officers —**crew′man**, *pl.* **-men** (-mən), *n.*

**crew**² (krōō) *vi.* [Chiefly Brit.] *alt. pt. of* CROW² (sense 1)

**crew cut** a man's haircut in which the hair is cropped close to the head

**crew·el** (krōō′əl) *n.* ⟦ME *crule*⟧ a loosely twisted, worsted yarn —**crew′el·work**′ *n.*

**crib** (krib) *n.* ⟦OE, ox stall⟧ 1 a rack or box for fodder 2 a small bed with high sides, for a baby 3 an enclosure for storing grain 4 an underwater structure serving as a pier, water intake, etc. 5 [Inf.] a translation or other aid used dishonestly in doing schoolwork —*vt.* **cribbed, crib′bing** 1 to confine 2 to furnish with a crib 3 [Inf.] to plagiarize —*vi.* [Inf.] to do schoolwork dishonestly

**crib·bage** (krib′ij) *n.* a card game in which the object is to form combinations for points

**crib death** SUDDEN INFANT DEATH SYNDROME

**crick**¹ (krik) *n.* ⟦< ON *kriki*, bend⟧ a painful cramp in the neck, back, etc.

**crick**² (krik) *n.* [Dial.] CREEK

**crick·et**¹ (krik′it) *n.* ⟦< OFr *criquer*, to creak⟧ a leaping insect similar to a grasshopper

**crick·et**² (krik′it) *n.* ⟦OFr *criquet*, a bat⟧ an outdoor game played by two teams of eleven players each, using a ball, bats, and wickets

**cried** (krīd) *vi.*, *vt. pt. & pp. of* CRY

**cri·er** (krī′ər) *n.* 1 one who cries 2 one who shouts out announcements, news, etc.

**crime** (krīm) *n.* ⟦< L *crimen*, offense⟧ 1 an act in violation of a law; specif., a serious violation, as a felony 2 a sin

**Cri·me·a** (krī mē′ə) peninsula in SW Ukraine, extending into the Black Sea —**Cri·me′an** *adj.*

**crim·i·nal** (krim′ə nəl) *adj.* 1 having the nature of crime 2 relating to or guilty of crime —*n.* a person guilty of a crime —**crim′i·nal′i·ty** (-nal′ə tə) *n.* —**crim′i·nal·ly** *adv.*

**crim·i·nal·ist** (-nəl ist) *n.* an expert in the scientific analysis of criminal evidence

**crim·i·nol·o·gy** (-näl′ə jē) *n.* the scientific study of crime and criminals —**crim′i·nol′o·gist** *n.*

**crimp** (krimp) *vt.* ⟦< MDu *crimpen*, to wrinkle⟧ 1 to press into narrow folds; pleat 2 to curl (hair) 3 to pinch together —*n.* 1 a crimping 2 anything crimped —**put a crimp in** [Inf.] to hinder

**crim·son** (krim′zən, -sən) *n.* ⟦< Ar *qirmiz*⟧ deep red —*adj.* deep-red —*vt.*, *vi.* to make or become crimson

**cringe** (krinj) *vi.* **cringed, cring′ing** ⟦< OE *cringan*, to fall (in battle)⟧ 1 to draw back, crouch, etc., as when afraid; cower 2 to act timidly servile

**crin·kle** (kriŋ′kəl) *vi.*, *vt.* **-kled, -kling** ⟦see prec.⟧ 1 to wrinkle 2 to rustle or crackle, as crushed paper —**crin′kly, -kli·er, -kli·est,** *adj.*

**crin·o·line** (krin′ə lin) *n.* ⟦Fr < It < *crino*, horsehair + *lino*, linen⟧ 1 a coarse, stiff cloth used as a lining in garments 2 HOOP SKIRT

**crip·ple** (krip′əl) *n.* ⟦< OE *creopan*, to creep⟧ a disabled person: now somewhat offensive —*vt.* **-pled, -pling** 1 to lame 2 to disable; impair

**cri·sis** (krī′sis) *n.*, *pl.* **-ses**′ (-sēz′) ⟦L < Gr *krinein*, to separate⟧ 1 the turning point of a disease for better or worse 2 a decisive or crucial time, etc. 3 a time of great danger, etc.

**crisp** (krisp) *adj.* ⟦< L *crispus*, curly⟧ 1 easily crumbled 2 fresh and firm 3 sharp and clear 4 fresh and invigorating 5 curled and wiry Also **crisp′y, -i·er, -i·est** —**crisp′ly** *adv.* —**crisp′ness** *n.*

**criss·cross** (kris′krôs′) *n.* ⟦ME *Christcros*, Christ's cross⟧ a mark or pattern made of crossed lines —*adj.* marked by crossing lines —*vt.* to mark with crossing lines —*vi.* to move to and fro —*adv.* 1 crosswise 2 awry

**cri·te·ri·on** (krī tir′ē ən) *n.*, *pl.* **-ri·a** (-ē ə) or **-ri·ons** ⟦< Gr *kritēs*, judge⟧ a standard, test, etc. by which a thing can be judged

**crit·ic** (krit′ik) *n.* ⟦< Gr *krinein*, discern⟧ 1 one who judges books, music, plays, etc., as for a newspaper 2 one who finds fault

**crit·i·cal** (-i kəl) *adj.* 1 tending to find fault 2 of critics or criticism 3 of or forming a crisis; decisive or dangerous —**crit′i·cal·ly** *adv.*

**crit·i·cism**′ (-ə siz′əm) *n.* 1 the act of making judgments, esp. of literary or artistic work 2 a review, article, etc. expressing such judgment 3 censure 4 the principles or methods of critics

**crit·i·cize**′ (-ə sīz′) *vi.*, *vt.* **-cized, -ciz′ing** 1 to analyze and judge as a critic 2 to find fault (with) —**crit′i·ciz′a·ble** *adj.* —**crit′i·ciz′er** *n.*

**cri·tique** (kri tēk′) *n.* ⟦Fr⟧ a critical analysis or review —*vt.*, *vi.* **-tiqued′, -tiqu′ing** to criticize (a subject, art work, etc.)

**crit·ter** (krit′ər) *n. dial. var. of* CREATURE

**croak** (krōk) *vi.* ⟦echoic⟧ 1 to make a deep, hoarse sound, as a frog does 2 [Slang] to die —*vt.* to utter in deep, hoarse tones —*n.* a croaking sound

**Cro·at** (krō′at′, -ət) *n.* a person born or living in Croatia

**Cro·a·tia** (krō ā′shə) country in SE Europe: 21,829 sq. mi.; pop. 4,784,000 —**Cro·a′tian** *adj.*, *n.*

**cro·chet** (krō shā′) *n.* ⟦Fr, small hook⟧ needlework done with one hooked needle —*vi.*, *vt.* **-cheted**′ (-shād′), **-chet′ing** to do, or make by, crochet —**cro·chet′er** *n.*

**crock** (kräk) *n.* ⟦OE *crocca*⟧ an earthenware pot or jar —**crock′er·y** *n.*

**crocked** (kräkt) *adj.* ⟦< *crock*, to disable⟧ [Slang] drunk

**croc·o·dile** (kräk′ə dīl′) *n.* ⟦< Gr *krokodilos*, lizard⟧ a large, lizardlike reptile of tropical streams, having a long, narrow head with massive jaws

**cro·cus** (krō′kəs) *n.*, *pl.* **-cus·es** or **-ci**′ (-sī′) ⟦< Gr *krokos*, saffron⟧ a spring-blooming plant of the iris family, with a yellow, purple, or white flower

**Croe·sus** (krē′səs) flourished 6th c. B.C.; king noted for his great wealth

**crois·sant** (krə sänt′; *Fr* krwä sän′) *n.* ⟦Fr, crescent⟧ a crescent-shaped, flaky bread roll

**Cro-Mag·non** (krō mag′nən) *adj.* ⟦after *Cro-Magnon* cave in France⟧ of a Stone Age type of tall human of the European continent

**Crom·well** (kräm′wel), **Ol·i·ver** (äl′ə vər) 1599-1658; Eng. revolutionary leader & head (Lord Protector) of England (1653-58)

**crone** (krōn) *n.* ⟦< MDu *kronje*, old ewe⟧ an ugly, withered old woman

**cro·ny** (krō′nē) *n.*, *pl.* **-nies** ⟦< Gr *chronos*, time⟧ a close companion

**crook** (krook) *n.* ⟦< ON *krōkr*, hook⟧ 1 a hooked or curved staff, etc.; hook 2 a bend or curve 3 [Inf.] a swindler or thief —*vt.*, *vi.* **crooked** (krookt), **crook′ing** to bend or curve

**crook·ed** (krookt; *for 2 & 3* krook′id) *adj.* 1 having a crook 2 not straight; bent 3 dishonest —**crook′ed·ly** *adv.* —**crook′ed·ness** *n.*

**crook′neck**′ *n.* a squash with a long, curved neck

**croon** (krōōn) *vi.*, *vt.* ⟦ME *cronen*⟧ 1 to sing or hum in a low, gentle tone 2 to sing (popular songs) softly and sentimentally —*n.* a low, gentle singing or humming —**croon′er** *n.*

**crop** (kräp) *n.* ⟦OE *croppa*, a cluster⟧ 1 a saclike part of a bird's gullet, in which food is stored

**before** digestion **2** any agricultural product, growing or harvested **3** the yield of any product in one season or place **4** a group **5** the handle of a whip **6** a riding whip **7** hair cut close to the head —*vt.* **cropped, crop′ping 1** to cut or bite off the tops or ends of **2** to cut (the hair, etc.) short —**crop out** (or **up**) to appear unexpectedly

**crop′-dust′ing** *n.* the spraying of crops with pesticides from an airplane —**crop′-dust′** *vi.*, *vt.*

**crop′per** *n.* **1** one that crops **2** a sharecropper — **come a cropper** [Inf.] to come to ruin; fail

**cro·quet** (krō kā′) *n.* [Fr, dial. form of *crochet*, small hook] an outdoor game in which the players use mallets to drive a ball through hoops in the ground

**cro·quette** (krō ket′) *n.* [Fr < *croquer*, to crunch] a small mass of meat, fish, etc. fried in deep fat

**cro·sier** (krō′zhər) *n.* [< OFr *croce*] the staff carried by a bishop or abbot

**cross** (krôs) *n.* [< L *crux*] **1** an upright post with a bar across it, on which the ancient Romans executed people **2** a representation of this as a symbol of the crucifixion of Jesus, hence of Christianity **3** any trouble or affliction **4** any design or mark made by two intersecting lines, bars, etc. **5** a crossing of varieties or breeds —*vt.*, *vi.* **1** to make the sign of the cross (upon) **2** to place or lie across or crosswise **3** to intersect **4** to draw a line or lines across **5** to go or extend across **6** to meet and pass (each other) **7** to oppose **8** to interbreed (animals or plants) —*adj.* **1** lying or passing across **2** contrary; opposed **3** cranky; irritable **4** of mixed variety or breed —**cross off** (or **out**) to cancel as by drawing lines across — **cross someone's mind** to come suddenly to someone's mind —**cross someone's path** to meet someone —**cross′ly** *adv.*

**cross′bar′** *n.* a bar, line, or stripe placed crosswise

**cross′beam′** *n.* any transverse beam in a structure

**cross′bones′** *n.* a representation of two bones placed across each other, under that of a skull, used to symbolize death or danger

**cross′bow′** (-bō′) *n.* a weapon consisting of a bow set transversely on a grooved wooden stock — **cross′bow′man** (-mən), *pl.* **-men** (-mən), *n.*

**cross′breed′** *vt.*, *vi.* **-bred′**, **-breed′ing** HYBRIDIZE —*n.* HYBRID (sense 1)

**cross′-coun′try** *adj.*, *adv.* across open country or fields [a *cross-country* race]

**cross′cut′ saw** a saw designed to cut across the grain of wood

**cross′-dress′ing** *n.* the wearing of clothing worn by the opposite sex

**cross′-ex·am′ine** *vt.*, *vi.* **-ined**, **-in·ing** *Law* to question (a witness called by the opposing side) in order to challenge the witness's previous testimony —**cross′-ex·am′i·na′tion** *n.*

**cross′-eye′** *n.* an abnormal condition in which the eyes are turned toward each other —**cross′-eyed′** *adj.*

**cross′fire′** *n.* **1** lines of fire from two or more positions that cross **2** an energetic exchange, as by opposing forces or of opposing opinions

**cross′hatch′** (-hach′) *vt.*, *vi.* to shade (a drawing) with two sets of parallel lines that cross each other

**cross′ing** *n.* **1** the act of passing across, interbreeding, etc. **2** an intersection, as of streets **3** a place where a street, etc. may be crossed

**cross′piece′** *n.* a piece lying across another

**cross′-pol′li·nate** *vt.*, *vi.* **-nat′ed**, **-nat′ing** to transfer pollen from the anther of (a flower) to the stigma of (a genetically different flower) — **cross′-pol′li·na′tion** *n.*

**cross′-pur′pose** *n.* a contrary purpose —**at cross-purposes** having a misunderstanding as to each other's purposes

**cross′-ref′er·ence** *n.* a reference from one part of a book, etc. to another —*vt.* **-enced**, **-enc·ing** to provide (an index, etc.) with cross-references — **cross′-re·fer′** *vt.*, *vi.*

**cross′road′** *n.* **1** a road that crosses another **2** [*usually pl.*, often with *sing. v.*] *a*) the place where roads intersect *b*) any center of activity, etc. *c*) a time of important changes or major decisions

**cross section 1** *a*) a cutting through something *b*) a piece so cut off *c*) a representation of this **2** a representative part of a whole —**cross′-sec′tion** *vt.*

**cross′town′** *adj.* **1** going across a city [a *crosstown* bus] **2** on the other side of a city [a *crosstown* rival]

**cross′walk′** *n.* a lane marked off for pedestrians to use in crossing a street

**cross′wise′** *adv.* so as to cross: also **cross′ways′**

**cross′word′ puzzle** an arrangement of numbered squares to be filled in with the letters of words, arranged vertically and horizontally, whose synonyms and definitions are given as clues

**crotch** (kräch) *n.* [ME *crucche*, crutch] **1** a forked place, as on a tree **2** the place where the legs fork from the human body or from the upper part of a pair of trousers

**crotch·et** (kräch′it) *n.* [ult. < OFr *croc*, a hook] a peculiar whim or stubborn notion —**crotch′et·y** *adj.*

**crouch** (krouch) *vi.* [< OFr *croc*, a hook] to stoop low with legs bent —*n.* a crouching position

**croup** (krōōp) *n.* [< obs. or dial. *croup*, speak hoarsely] an inflammation of the respiratory passages, with labored breathing, hoarse coughing, etc.

**crou·pi·er** (krōō′pē ā′, -ər) *n.* [Fr] one in charge of a gambling table

**crou·ton** (krōō′tän′, krōō tän′) *n.* [Fr < *croûte*, a crust] a small, crisp piece of toasted bread served in soup or salads

**crow**[1] (krō) *n.* [OE *crawa*] a large, glossy-black bird with a harsh call —**as the crow flies** in a straight, direct line —**eat crow** [Inf.] to admit an error

**crow**[2] (krō) *vi.* **crowed** or, for 1, [Chiefly Brit.] **crew** (krōō), **crowed, crow′ing** [OE *crawan*] **1** to make the shrill cry of a rooster **2** to boast in triumph **3** to make a sound of pleasure —*n.* a crowing sound

**crow′bar′** *n.* a long metal bar used as a lever for prying, etc.

**crowd** (kroud) *vi.* [< OE *crudan*] **1** to push one's way (into) **2** to throng —*vt.* **1** to press or push **2** to fill too full; cram —*n.* **1** a large number of people or things grouped closely **2** the common people; the masses **3** [Inf.] a set; clique — **crowd′ed** *adj.*

CROWBAR

**crow′foot′** *n.*, *pl.* **-foots′** or **-feet′** a plant of the buttercup family, with leaves resembling a crow's foot

**crown** (kroun) *n.* [< Gr *korōnē*, wreath] **1** a wreath worn on the head in victory **2** a reward; honor **3** a monarch's headdress **4** [*often* C-] *a*) the power of a monarch *b*) the monarch **5** a British coin equal to 25 (new) pence: no longer minted **6** the top part, as of the head **7** the highest quality, state, etc. of anything **8** *a*) the part of a tooth outside the gum *b*) an artificial substitute for this —*vt.* **1** to put a crown on **2** to make (a person) a monarch **3** to honor **4** to be the highest part of **5** to complete successfully

**crown prince** the male heir apparent to a throne —**crown princess**

**crow′s-foot** (krōz′foot′) *n.*, *pl.* **-feet′** any of the wrinkles that often develop at the outer corners of the eyes of adults

**crow′s′-nest** (-nest′) *n.* a lookout's platform high on a ship's mast

**cro·zier** (krō′zhər) *n.* CROSIER

**CRT** (sē′är′tē′) *n.* a cathode-ray tube

**cru·cial** (krōō′shəl) *adj.* [< L *crux,* a cross] deci- sive; critical —**cru′cial·ly** *adv.*

**cru·ci·ble** (krōō′sə bəl) *n.* [ML *crucibulum,* lamp] 1 a heat-resistant container for melting ores, met- als, etc. 2 a severe trial

**cru·ci·fix** (krōō′sə fiks′) *n.* [see CRUCIFY] a cross with the figure of the crucified Jesus Christ on it

**cru·ci·fix′ion** (-fik′shən) *n.* 1 a crucifying 2 [C-] the crucifying of Jesus, or a representation of this

**cru′ci·form′** (-fôrm′) *adj.* cross-shaped

**cru·ci·fy** (-fī′) *vt.* **-fied′, -fy′ing** [< L *crux,* a cross + *figere,* fasten] 1 to execute by nailing or binding to a cross and leaving to die 2 to be very cruel to; torment

**crude** (krōōd) *adj.* **crud′er, crud′est** [< L *crudus,* raw] 1 in a raw or natural condition 2 lacking grace, tact, taste, etc. 3 roughly made —**crude′ly** *adv.* —**crude′ness** *n.* —**cru·di·ty** (krōō′də tē) *n.*

**cru·di·tés** (krōō′də tā′) *pl.n.* [Fr, raw things] raw vegetables cut up and served as hors d'oeuvres, usually with a dip or sauce

**cru·el** (krōō′əl) *adj.* [see CRUDE] causing pain and suffering; pitiless —**cru′el·ly** *adv.* —**cru′el·ness** *n.* —**cru′el·ty,** *pl.* **-ties,** *n.*

**cru·et** (krōō′it) *n.* [< OFr *crue,* earthen pot] a small glass bottle, as for holding vinegar or oil for the table

**cruise** (krōōz) *vi.* **cruised, cruis′ing** [< Du *kruisen,* to cross] 1 to sail or ride about from place to place, as for pleasure or in search of something 2 to move at the most efficient speed for sustained travel 3 to operate at a predetermined speed by use of a regulating mechanism (**cruise control**) — *vt.* to sail or journey over or about —*n.* a cruising voyage

**cruise missile** a long-range, jet-propelled winged missile that can be launched from an airplane, submarine, ship, etc. and guided to its target by remote control

**cruis′er** *n.* 1 anything that cruises, as a police car 2 a fast warship smaller than a battleship

**crul·ler** (krul′ər) *n.* [Du < *krullen,* to curl] a kind of twisted doughnut

**crumb** (krum) *n.* [< OE *cruma,* a bit scraped from bread crust] 1 a small piece broken off, as of bread 2 any bit or scrap *[crumbs* of knowledge] —**crumb·y** (krum′ē), **-i·er, -i·est,** *adj.*

**crum·ble** (krum′bəl) *vt.,* **-bled, -bling** [< prec.] to break into crumbs —*vi.* to fall to pieces; disinte- grate —**crum′bly** (-blē), **-bli·er, -bli·est,** *adj.*

**crum·my** (krum′ē) *adj.* **-mi·er, -mi·est** [Slang] 1 dirty, cheap, etc. 2 inferior, worthless, etc.

**crum·pet** (krum′pit) *n.* [< OE *crump,* twisted] an unsweetened batter cake baked on a griddle

**crum·ple** (krum′pəl) *vt.,* **-pled, -pling** [ult. < MDu *crimpen,* to wrinkle] to crush together into wrin- kles

**crunch** (krunch) *vi., vt.* [echoic] 1 to chew, press, grind, etc. with a noisy, crackling sound 2 [Inf.] to process (a large quantity of data) rapidly *[crunching* numbers on a computer] —*n.* 1 the act or sound of crunching 2 [Slang] a showdown or tight situation —**crunch′y, -i·er, -i·est,** *adj.*

**crunch′time′** *n.* [Slang] the tense, crucial phase of some activity

**crup·per** (krup′ər, kroop′-) *n.* [< OFr *crope,* rump] a leather strap attached to a saddle or harness and passed under a horse's tail

**cru·sade** (krōō sād′) *n.* [ult. < L *crux,* a cross] 1 *[sometimes* C-] any of the Christian military expeditions (11th-13th c.) to recover the Holy Land from the Muslims 2 a vigorous, concerted action for some cause, or against some abuse —*vi.* **-sad′ed, -sad′ing** to engage in a crusade —**cru· sad′er** *n.*

**cruse** (krōōs, krōōz) *n.* [OE] a small container for water, oil, etc.

**crush** (krush) *vt.* [< OFr *croisir,* to crash, break] 1 to press with force so as to break or put out of shape 2 to grind or pound into small bits 3 to subdue; overwhelm —*vi.* to become crushed —*n.* 1 a crushing; severe pressure 2 a crowded mass of people 3 [Inf.] an infatuation —**crush′er** *n.*

**crush′ing** *adj.* 1 overwhelming 2 hurtful

**crust** (krust) *n.* [< L *crusta*] 1 the hard, outer part of bread 2 any dry, hard piece of bread 3 the pastry shell of a pie 4 any hard surface layer 5 [Slang] insolence 6 *Geol.* the solid outer layer of the earth —*vt., vi.* to cover or become covered with a crust —**crust′y, -i·er, -i·est,** *adj.*

**crus·ta·cean** (krus tā′shən) *n.* [see prec.] any of a class of arthropods, including shrimps, crabs, and lobsters, that have a hard outer shell

**crutch** (kruch) *n.* [< OE *crycce,* staff] 1 a device used by lame people as an aid in walking, typi- cally a staff with a crosspiece on top that fits under the armpit 2 any prop or support

**crux** (kruks) *n., pl.* **crux′es** or **cru·ces** (krōō′sēz′) [L, a cross] 1 a difficult problem 2 the essential or deciding point

**cry** (krī) *vi.* **cried, cry′ing** [< L *quiritare,* to wail] 1 to utter a loud sound, as in pain or fright 2 to sob and shed tears; weep 3 to plead or clamor *(for)* 4 to show a great need *(for)* 5 to utter its character- istic call: said of an animal —*vt.* to utter loudly; shout —*n., pl.* **cries** 1 a shout 2 a plea 3 a fit of weeping 4 the characteristic call of an animal — **a far cry** a great distance or difference

**cry′ba·by** *n., pl.* **-bies** one who complains when failing to get his or her own way

**cry·o·gen·ics** (krī′ō jen′iks, -ə-) *n.* [< Gr *kryos,* cold + -GEN- + -ICS] the science that deals with the production of very low temperatures and their effect on the properties of matter —**cry′o·gen′ic** *adj.*

**cry′o·sur′ger·y** *n.* [< Gr *kryos,* cold + SURGERY] surgery that destroys tissues by freezing them

**crypt** (kript) *n.* [< Gr *kryptein,* to hide] an under- ground vault, esp. one under a church, used for burial

**cryp·tic** (krip′tik) *adj.* 1 hidden or mysterious; baffling 2 obscure and curt in expression — **cryp′ti·cal·ly** *adv.*

**crypto-** [see CRYPT] *combining form* 1 secret or hidden *[cryptogram]* 2 being such secretly and not publicly *[a crypto-*Fascist*]*

**cryp·to·gram** (krip′tō gram′, -tə-) *n.* [prec. + -GRAM] a message in code or cipher

**cryp·tog·ra·phy** (krip tä′grə fē) *n.* [CRYPTO- + -GRAPHY] the art of writing or deciphering messages in code —**cryp·tog′ra·pher** *n.*

**crys·tal** (kris′təl) *n.* [< Gr *krystallos,* crystal, ice < *kryos,* frost] 1 pure quartz 2 *a)* a very clear, bril- liant glass *b)* articles of such glass, as goblets 3 anything clear like crystal, as the cover on a watch face 4 a solidified form of a substance hav- ing plane faces arranged in a symmetrical, three- dimensional pattern —*adj.* 1 of or made of crys- tal 2 like crystal; clear

**crys′tal·line** (-tə lin) *adj.* 1 made of crystal 2 like crystal; clear and transparent

**crys′tal·lize′** (-tə līz′) *vi., vt.* **-lized′, -liz′ing** 1 to become or cause to become crystalline 2 to take on or cause to take on a definite form —**crys′tal·li· za′tion** *n.*

**cs** *abbrev.* case(s)

**Cs** *Chem. symbol for* cesium

**C-sec·tion** (sē′sek′shən) *n.* [Inf.] CESAREAN (SEC- TION)

**CST** *abbrev.* Central Standard Time

**ct** *abbrev.* 1 cent 2 court

**CT** *abbrev.* 1 Central Time 2 Connecticut

**CT scan** [*c(omputerized) t(omography)*] 1 a diag- nostic X-raying of soft tissues, using many single- plane X-rays *(tomograms)* to form the image 2 such an image —**CT scanner** —**CT scanning**

**cu** *abbrev.* cubic

**Cu** [L *cuprum*] *Chem. symbol for* copper

**cub** (kub) *n.* [< ? Old Ir *cuib,* a whelp] 1 a young

fox, bear, lion, whale, etc. **2** an inexperienced or immature person

**Cu·ba** (kyōō′bə) country on an island in the West Indies, south of Florida: 42,803 sq. mi.; pop. 9,724,000 —**Cu′ban** *adj., n.*

**cub·by·hole** (kub′ē hōl′) *n.* ⟦< Brit dial. *cub*, little shed + HOLE⟧ a small, enclosed space: also **cub′by**

**cube** (kyōōb) *n.* ⟦< Gr *kybos*⟧ **1** a solid with six equal, square sides **2** the product obtained by multiplying a given number by its square ⟦the *cube* of 3 is 27⟧ —*vt.* **cubed, cub′ing 1** to obtain the cube of (a number) **2** to cut or shape into cubes —**cub′er** *n.*

**cube root** the number of which a given number is the cube ⟦the *cube root* of 8 is 2⟧

**cu·bic** (kyōō′bik) *adj.* **1** having the shape of a cube: also **cu′bi·cal** (-bi kəl) **2** having the volume of a cube whose length, width, and depth each measure the given unit ⟦a *cubic* foot⟧

**cu·bi·cle** (kyōō′bi kəl) *n.* ⟦< L *cubare*, lie down⟧ a small compartment

**cub·ism** (kyōōb′iz′əm) *n.* a school of modern art characterized by the use of cubes and other geometric forms in abstract arrangements —**cub′ist** *n., adj.* —**cu·bis′tic** *adj.*

**cu·bit** (kyōō′bit) *n.* ⟦< L *cubitum*, elbow⟧ an ancient measure of length, about 18 to 22 inches

**cuck·old** (kuk′əld) *n.* ⟦see fol.⟧ a man whose wife has committed adultery —*vt.* to make a cuckold of —**cuck′old·ry** (-rē) *n.*

**cuck·oo** (kōō′kōō′) *n.* ⟦< OFr *cucu*, echoic⟧ **1** a gray-brown bird with a long, slender body: many species lay eggs in the nests of other birds **2** its call —*adj.* [Slang] crazy; foolish

**cu·cum·ber** (kyōō′kum′bər) *n.* ⟦< L *cucumis*⟧ a long, green-skinned fruit with firm, white flesh, used in salads or preserved as pickles

**cud** (kud) *n.* ⟦OE *cudu*⟧ a mouthful of swallowed food regurgitated from the first two parts of the stomach of cattle and other ruminants and chewed again

**cud·dle** (kud′l) *vt.* **-dled, -dling** [early Modern Eng, make comfortable] to hold lovingly in one's arms —*vi.* to lie close and snug; nestle —*n.* an embrace; hug

**cud′dly** (-lē) *adj.* **-dli·er, -dli·est** that invites cuddling: also **cud′dle·some**

**cudg·el** (kuj′əl) *n.* ⟦< OE *cycgel*⟧ a short, thick stick or club —*vt.* **-eled** or **-elled, -el·ing** or **-el·ling** to beat with a cudgel

**cue**[1] (kyōō) *n.* ⟦< *q, Q* (? for L *quando*, when) found in 16th-c. plays⟧ **1** a signal in dialogue, etc. for an actor's entrance or speech **2** any signal to do something **3** a hint —*vt.* **cued, cu′ing** or **cue′ing** to give a cue to

**cue**[2] (kyōō) *n.* ⟦var. of QUEUE⟧ a long, tapering rod used in billiards and pool to strike the white ball (**cue ball**)

**Cuer·na·va·ca** (kwer′nə vä′kə) city in SC Mexico: pop. 281,000

**cuff** (kuf) *n.* ⟦< ME *cuffe*, glove⟧ **1** a band or fold at the end of a sleeve **2** a turned-up fold at the bottom of a trouser leg **3** a slap —*vt.* to slap —**off the cuff** [Slang] in an offhand manner; extemporaneously —**on the cuff** [Slang] on credit

**cuff link** a pair of linked buttons or any similar small device for fastening a shirt cuff

**cui·sine** (kwi zēn′, kwē-) *n.* ⟦Fr < L *coquere*, to cook⟧ **1** a style of cooking or preparing food **2** the food prepared, as at a restaurant

**cuke** (kyōōk) *n.* [Inf.] *short for* CUCUMBER

**cul-de-sac** (kul′də sak′) *n., pl.* **-sacs′** ⟦Fr, bottom of a sack⟧ a dead-end street

**cu·li·nar·y** (kyōō′lə ner′ē, kul′ə-) *adj.* ⟦< L *culina*, kitchen⟧ of cooking

**cull** (kul) *vt.* ⟦< L *colligere*, collect⟧ **1** to pick out and discard **2** to select and gather —*n.* something rejected as not being up to standard

**cul·mi·nate** (kul′mə nāt′) *vi.* **-nat′ed, -nat′ing** ⟦< L

---

*culmen*, peak⟧ to reach its highest point or climax —**cul′mi·na′tion** *n.*

**cu·lotte** (kōō lät′) *n.* ⟦Fr < L *culus*, posterior⟧ [*often pl.*] a woman's garment consisting of trousers made full in the legs to resemble a skirt

**cul·pa·ble** (kul′pə bəl) *adj.* ⟦< L *culpa*, fault⟧ deserving blame —**cul′pa·bil′i·ty** *n.* —**cul′pa·bly** *adv.*

**cul·prit** (kul′prit) *n.* ⟦< Anglo-Fr *culpable*, guilty + *prit*, ready (to prove)⟧ a person guilty of a crime or offense

**cult** (kult) *n.* ⟦< L *cultus*, care, cultivation⟧ **1** a system of religious worship or ritual **2** devoted attachment to a person, principle, etc. **3** a sect —**cult′ism′** *n.* —**cult′ist** *n.*

**cul·ti·vate** (kul′tə vāt′) *vt.* **-vat′ed, -vat′ing** ⟦< L *colere*, to till⟧ **1** to prepare (land) for growing crops; till **2** to loosen the soil and kill weeds around (plants) **3** to grow (plants) **4** to develop or improve ⟦*cultivate* your mind⟧ **5** to seek to become familiar with —**cul′ti·va·ble** (-və bəl) or **cul′ti·vat′a·ble** *adj.* —**cul′ti·va′tor** *n.*

**cul′ti·va′tion** *n.* **1** the act of cultivating **2** refinement, or culture

**cul·ture** (kul′chər) *n.* ⟦see CULT⟧ **1** cultivation of the soil **2** a growth of bacteria, etc. in a prepared substance **3** improvement of the mind, manners, etc. **4** development by special training or care **5** the skills, arts, etc. of a given people in a given period; civilization —*vt.* **-tured, -tur·ing** to cultivate —**cul′tur·al** *adj.* —**cul′tur·al·ly** *adv.*

**culture shock** the alienation, confusion, etc. that may be experienced by someone encountering new surroundings, a different culture, etc.

**cul·vert** (kul′vərt) *n.* ⟦< ?⟧ a drain or conduit under a road or embankment

**cum** (kum, koom) *prep.* ⟦L⟧ with

**cum·ber** (kum′bər) *vt.* ⟦< OFr *combre*, a barrier⟧ to hinder; hamper

**cum′ber·some** *adj.* burdensome; unwieldy: also **cum′brous** (-brəs)

**cum·in** (kum′in, kōō′min) *n.* ⟦< Gr *kyminon*⟧ **1** an herb related to parsley and celery **2** its aromatic fruits, used as a seasoning

**cum·mer·bund** (kum′ər bund′) *n.* ⟦< Ar-Pers *kamar*, loins + Pers *band*, band⟧ a wide sash worn as a waistband, esp. with men's formal dress

**cu·mu·la·tive** (kyōō′myə lə tiv′, -lāt′iv) *adj.* ⟦< L *cumulus*, a heap⟧ increasing in effect, size, etc. by successive additions

**cu·mu·lus** (kyōō′myə ləs) *n., pl.* **-li′** (-lī′) ⟦L, a heap⟧ a bright, billowy type of cloud with a dark, flat base

**cu·ne·i·form** (kyōō nē′ə fôrm′) *adj.* ⟦< L *cuneus*, a wedge + -FORM⟧ **1** wedge-shaped **2** designating the characters in ancient Assyrian and Babylonian inscriptions —*n.* cuneiform writing

**cun·ning** (kun′iŋ) *adj.* ⟦< ME *cunnen*, know⟧ **1** sly; crafty **2** made with skill **3** pretty and delicate; cute —*n.* slyness; craftiness —**cun′ning·ly** *adv.*

**cup** (kup) *n.* ⟦< L *cupa*, tub⟧ **1** a small, open container for beverages, usually bowl-shaped and with a handle **2** a cup and its contents **3** a cupful **4** anything shaped like a cup —*vt.* **cupped, cup′ping** to shape like a cup

**cup·board** (kub′ərd) *n.* a closet or cabinet with shelves for cups, plates, food, etc.

**cup′cake′** *n.* a small, round cake, often iced

**cup′ful′** *n., pl.* **-fuls′** as much as a cup will hold; specif., eight ounces

**Cu·pid** (kyōō′pid) *n.* **1** Rom. Myth. the god of love **2** [c-] a representation of Cupid as a naked, winged boy with bow and arrow

**cu·pid·i·ty** (kyōō pid′ə tē) *n.* ⟦< L *cupere*, to desire⟧ strong desire for wealth; avarice

**cu·po·la** (kyo͞o′pə lə) *n.* ⟦It < L *cupa*, a tub⟧ a small dome, etc. on a roof

**cu·pro·nick·el** (kyo͞o′prō nik′əl) *n.* an alloy of copper and nickel, used as in coins

**cur** (kur) *n.* ⟦prob. < ON *kurra*, to growl⟧ 1 a dog of mixed breed; mongrel 2 a contemptible person

**cu·rate** (kyoor′it) *n.* ⟦< L *cura*, care⟧ a member of the clergy who assists a vicar or rector —**cu′ra·cy** (-ə sē), *pl.* -cies

**cu·ra·tive** (kyoor′ət iv) *adj.* having the power to cure — *n.* a remedy

CUPOLA

**cu·ra·tor** (kyo͞o rāt′ər, kyoor′āt′ər) *n.* ⟦< L *curare*, take care of⟧ a person in charge of a department or collection in a museum, etc. —**cu·ra·to·ri·al** (kyoor′ə tôr′ē əl) *adj.* —**cu·ra′tor·ship** *n.*

**curb** (kurb) *n.* ⟦< L *curvus*, bent⟧ 1 a chain or strap attached to a horse's bit, used to check the horse 2 anything that checks or restrains 3 a stone or concrete edging along a street —*vt.* to restrain; control

**curb service** service offered to customers in parked cars, as at some restaurants

**curb′side′** *adj.* at the curb or on the sidewalk adjacent to the street

**curb′stone′** *n.* any of the stones or a row of stones, making up a curb

**curd** (kurd) *n.* ⟦< ME *crud*, coagulated substance⟧ [*often pl.*] the coagulated part of soured milk, from which cheese is made

**cur·dle** (kurd′'l) *vt., vi.* -dled, -dling to form into curd; coagulate

**cure** (kyoor) *n.* ⟦< L *cura*, care⟧ 1 a healing or being healed 2 a remedy 3 a method of medical treatment —*vt.* cured, cur′ing 1 to restore to health 2 to get rid of (an ailment, evil, etc.) 3 *a*) to preserve (meat), as by salting or smoking *b*) to process (tobacco, leather, etc.), as by drying or aging —**cur′a·ble** *adj.* —**cur′er** *n.*

**cu·ré** (kyo͞o rā′) *n.* ⟦Fr < L *cura*, care⟧ in France, a parish priest

**cure′-all′** *n.* something supposed to cure all ailments or evils

**cu·ret·tage** (kyo͞o ret′ij, kyo͞o′rə täzh′) *n.* ⟦Fr⟧ the process of cleaning or scraping the walls of a body cavity with a spoonlike instrument

**cur·few** (kur′fyo͞o) *n.* ⟦< OFr *covrefeu*, lit., cover fire: orig. a nightly signal to cover fires and retire⟧ a time in the evening beyond which children, etc. may not appear on the streets or in public places

**Cu·ri·a** (kyoor′ē ə) *n., pl.* -ri·ae (-ē′) ⟦L⟧ the official body governing the Roman Catholic Church under the authority of the pope

**Cu·rie** (kyo͞o rē′, kyoor′ē), **Ma·rie** (mə rē′) 1867-1934; Pol. chemist in France

**cu·ri·o** (kyoor′ē ō′) *n., pl.* -os′ ⟦contr. of fol.⟧ an unusual or rare article

**cu·ri·os·i·ty** (kyoor′ē äs′ə tē) *n., pl.* -ties 1 a desire to learn or know 2 inquisitiveness 3 anything curious, rare, etc.

**cu·ri·ous** (kyoor′ē əs) *adj.* ⟦< L *curiosus*, careful⟧ 1 eager to learn or know 2 prying or inquisitive 3 unusual; strange —**cu′ri·ous·ly** *adv.*

**curl** (kurl) *vt.* ⟦< ME *crul*, curly⟧ 1 to twist (esp. hair) into ringlets 2 to cause to bend around —*vi.* 1 to form curls 2 to form a spiral or curve —*n.* 1 a ringlet of hair 2 anything with a curled shape —**curl′er** *n.* —**curl′y,** -i·er, -i·est, *adj.* —**curl′i·ness** *n.*

**cur·lew** (kur′lo͞o′, kurl′yo͞o′) *n.* ⟦echoic⟧ a large, brownish wading bird with long legs

**curl·i·cue** (kur′li kyo͞o′) *n.* ⟦< CURLY + CUE²⟧ a fancy curve, flourish, etc.

**curl·ing** (kur′liŋ) *n.* a game played on ice by two teams, in which a heavy disk of stone or iron is slid toward a target

**cur·rant** (kur′ənt) *n.* ⟦ult. < *Corinth*, ancient Gr city⟧ 1 a small, seedless raisin from the Mediterranean region 2 *a*) the sour berry of several species of hardy shrubs, made into jelly or jam *b*) any such shrub

**cur·ren·cy** (kur′ən sē) *n., pl.* -cies [see fol.] 1 circulation 2 the money in circulation in any country; often, specif., paper money 3 general use or acceptance

**cur·rent** (kur′ənt) *adj.* ⟦< L *currere*, to run⟧ 1 now going on; of the present time 2 circulating 3 commonly accepted; prevalent —*n.* 1 a flow of water or air in a definite direction 2 a general tendency or drift, as of opinion 3 the flow or rate of flow of electricity in a conductor —**cur′rent·ly** *adv.*

**cur·ric·u·lum** (kə rik′yo͞o ləm, -yə-) *n., pl.* -la (-lə) or -lums ⟦L, course for racing⟧ a course of study in a school —**cur·ric′u·lar** *adj.*

**cur·ry¹** (kur′ē) *vt.* -ried, -ry·ing ⟦< OFr *correier*, to put in order⟧ 1 to use a currycomb on 2 to prepare (tanned leather) —**curry favor** to try to win favor as by flattery

**cur·ry²** (kur′ē) *n., pl.* -ries ⟦Tamil *kari*, sauce⟧ 1 a powder prepared from various spices, or a sauce made with this 2 a stew made with curry —*vt.* -ried, -ry·ing to prepare with curry

**cur′ry·comb′** *n.* a circular comb with teeth or ridges, for rubbing down and cleaning a horse's coat —*vt.* to use a currycomb on

**curse** (kurs) *n.* ⟦OE *curs*⟧ 1 a calling on God or the gods to bring evil on some person or thing 2 a profane or obscene oath 3 evil or injury that seems to come in answer to a curse —*vt.* cursed, curs′ing 1 to call evil down on 2 to swear at 3 to afflict —*vi.* to swear; blaspheme —**be cursed with** to suffer from

**curs·ed** (kur′sid, kurst) *adj.* 1 under a curse 2 deserving to be cursed; evil; hateful

**cur·sive** (kur′siv) *adj.* ⟦ult. < L *currere*, to run⟧ designating writing in which the letters are joined

**cur·sor** (kur′sər) *n.* ⟦L, runner⟧ a movable indicator light on a computer video screen, marking the current position at which a character may be entered, changed, etc.

**cur·so·ry** (kur′sə rē) *adj.* ⟦ult. < L *currere*, to run⟧ hastily, often superficially, done —**cur′so·ri·ly** *adv.* —**cur′so·ri·ness** *n.*

**curt** (kurt) *adj.* ⟦L *curtus*, short⟧ brief, esp. to the point of rudeness —**curt′ly** *adv.* —**curt′ness** *n.*

**cur·tail** (kər tāl′) *vt.* ⟦< L *curtus*, short⟧ to cut short; reduce —**cur·tail′ment** *n.*

**cur·tain** (kurt′'n) *n.* ⟦< LL *cortina*⟧ a piece of cloth, etc. hung at a window, in front of a stage, etc. to decorate or conceal —*vt.* to provide with or shut off as with a curtain

**curtain call** 1 a call, usually by applause, for performers to return to the stage 2 such a return

**curt·sy** (kurt′sē) *n., pl.* -sies ⟦var. of COURTESY⟧ a woman's gesture of greeting, respect, etc. made by bending the knees and lowering the body slightly —*vi.* -sied, -sy·ing to make a curtsy Also sp. **curt′sey**

**cur·va·ceous** (kər vā′shəs) *adj.* ⟦< CURVE⟧ having a full, shapely figure: said of a woman

**cur·va·ture** (kur′və chər) *n.* 1 a curving or being curved 2 a curve

**curve** (kurv) *n.* ⟦< L *curvus*, bent⟧ 1 a line having no straight part; bend with no angles 2 something shaped like, or moving in, a curve —*vt., vi.* curved, curv′ing 1 to form a curve by bending 2 to move in a curve —**curv′y,** -i·er, -i·est, *adj.*

**cush·ion** (koosh′ən) *n.* ⟦< ML *coxinum*⟧ 1 a pillow or pad 2 a thing like this in shape or use 3 anything that absorbs shock —*vt.* to provide with a cushion

**cush·y** (koosh′ē) *adj.* -i·er, -i·est ⟦< Pers *khūsh*, pleasant⟧ [Slang] easy; comfortable

**cusp** (kusp) *n.* ⟦L *cuspis*⟧ a point or pointed end, as on the chewing surface of a tooth —**on the cusp** at a time of transition

**cus·pid** (kus′pid) *n.* ⟦see prec.⟧ a tooth with one cusp; canine tooth

**cus·pi·dor** (kus′pə dôr′) *n.* ⟦< Port *cuspir*, to spit⟧ a spittoon

**cuss** (kus) *n.*, *vt.*, *vi.* [Inf.] CURSE

**cus·tard** (kus′tərd) *n.* ⟦< L *crusta*, crust⟧ a mixture of eggs, milk, sugar, etc., boiled or baked

**cus·to·di·an** (kəs tō′dē ən) *n.* ⟦< fol.⟧ **1** one who is responsible for the custody or care of something; caretaker **2** a person responsible for the maintenance of a building

**cus·to·dy** (kus′tə dē) *n.*, *pl.* **-dies** ⟦< L *custos*, a guard⟧ a guarding or keeping safe; care; guardianship —**in custody** under arrest —**cus·to′di·al** (-tō′dē əl) *adj.*

**cus·tom** (kus′təm) *n.* ⟦< L *com-*, intens. + *suere*, be accustomed⟧ **1** a usual practice; habit **2** *a*) a social practice carried on by tradition *b*) such practices collectively **3** [*pl.*] duties or taxes imposed on imported goods **4** the regular patronage of a business —*adj.* **1** made or done to order **2** making things to order

**cus′tom·ar′y** *adj.* in keeping with custom; usual; habitual —**cus′tom·ar′i·ly** *adv.*

**cus′tom-built′** *adj.* built to order, to the customer's specifications

**cus′tom·er** *n.* a person who buys, esp. one who buys regularly

**cus′tom·house′** *n.* an office where customs or duties are paid

**cus′tom·ize′** *vt.* **-ized′**, **-iz′ing** to make according to individual specifications

**cus′tom-made′** *adj.* made to order, to the customer's specifications

**cut** (kut) *vt.* **cut**, **cut′ting** ⟦ME *cutten*⟧ **1** to make an opening in with a sharp-edged instrument; gash **2** to pierce sharply so as to hurt **3** to have (a new tooth) grow through the gum **4** to divide into parts with a sharp-edged instrument; sever **5** to intersect; divide **6** to hew **7** to mow or reap **8** to reduce; curtail **9** to trim; pare **10** to divide (a pack of cards) **11** to make or do as by cutting **12** to hit (a ball) so that it spins **13** [Inf.] to pretend not to recognize (a person) **14** [Inf.] to stay away from (a school class, etc.) without being excused **15** [Slang] to stop —*vi.* **1** to pierce, sever, gash, etc. **2** to take cutting [pine *cuts* easily] **3** to go (*across* or *through*) **4** to change direction suddenly **5** to make a sudden shift, as from one scene to another in a film **6** [Inf.] to swing a bat, etc. at a ball —*adj.* **1** that has been cut **2** made or formed by cutting —*n.* **1** a cutting or being cut **2** a stroke or opening made by a sharp-edged instrument **3** a piece cut off, as of meat **4** a reduction **5** a passage or channel cut out **6** the style in which a thing is cut **7** an act, remark, etc. that hurts one's feelings **8** a block or plate engraved for printing, or the impression from this **9** [Inf.] an unauthorized absence from school, etc. **10** [Inf.] a share, as of profits —**cut and dried 1** arranged beforehand **2** lifeless; dull —**cut down** to reduce; lessen —**cut it out** [Inf.] to stop doing what one is doing —**cut off 1** to sever **2** to stop abruptly; shut off —**cut out** [Inf.] fit or suited — **cut up 1** to cut into pieces **2** [Slang] to clown, joke, etc.

**cu·ta·ne·ous** (kyōō tā′nē əs) *adj.* ⟦< L *cutis*, skin⟧ of or on the skin

**cut′a·way′** *n.* a man's formal coat cut so as to curve back to the tails

**cut′back′** *n.* a reduction or discontinuance, as of production

**cute** (kyōōt) *adj.* **cut′er**, **cut′est** ⟦< ACUTE⟧ [Inf.] **1** clever; shrewd **2** pretty or attractive, esp. in a dainty way —**cute′ly** *adv.* —**cute′ness** *n.*

**cute·sy** or **cute·sie** (kyōōt′sē) *adj.* **-si·er**, **-si·est** [Inf.] cute in an affected way

**cut·i·cle** (kyōōt′i kəl) *n.* ⟦< L *cutis*, skin⟧ **1** the outer layer of the skin **2** hardened skin, as at the base and sides of a fingernail

**cut·lass** (kut′ləs) *n.* ⟦< L *culter*, plowshare⟧ a short, thick, curved sword

**cut·ler·y** (kut′lər ē) *n.* ⟦< L *culter*, plowshare⟧ **1** cutting implements, as knives and scissors **2** implements used in preparing and eating food

**cut·let** (kut′lit) *n.* ⟦< L *costa*, rib⟧ **1** a small slice of meat from the ribs or leg **2** a small, flat croquette of chopped meat or fish

**cut′off′** *n.* a road, etc. that is a shortcut

**cut′-rate′** *adj.* selling at a lower price

**cut·ter** (kut′ər) *n.* **1** a person or thing that cuts **2** a small, swift boat or ship

**cut′throat′** *n.* a murderer —*adj.* **1** murderous **2** merciless; ruthless

**cut·ting** (kut′iŋ) *n.* a shoot cut away from a plant for rooting or grafting —*adj.* **1** that cuts; sharp **2** chilling or piercing **3** sarcastic; wounding — **cut′ting·ly** *adv.*

**cutting edge** the leading or most advanced position; vanguard

**cut·tle·fish** (kut′'l fish′) *n.*, *pl.* **-fish′** or (for different species) **-fish′es** ⟦OE *cudele*⟧ a sea mollusk with eight arms and two tentacles and a hard internal shell (**cut′tle·bone′**)

**cwt** *abbrev.* hundredweight

**-cy** (sē) ⟦< Gr *-kia*⟧ *suffix* **1** quality, condition, or fact of being [*idiocy*] **2** position, rank, or office of [*captaincy*]

**cy·a·nide** (sī′ə nīd′) *n.* a white, crystalline compound that is extremely poisonous

**cy·ber·net·ics** (sī′bər net′iks) *n.* ⟦< Gr *kybernan*, to steer + -ICS⟧ the comparative study of human control systems, as the brain, and complex electronic systems —**cy′ber·net′ic** *adj.*

**cy·ber·punk** (sī′bər puŋk′) *n.* ⟦*cyber-* (see prec.) + PUNK² (*n.* 2)⟧ science fiction describing a future filled with violence, computers, and drugs

**cy′ber·space′** (-spās′) *n.* the electronic system of linked computer networks, etc., thought of as an unlimited environment for accessing information, communicating, etc.

**cy·cla·men** (sī′klə mən) *n.* ⟦< Gr⟧ a plant of the primrose family with heart-shaped leaves

**cy·cle** (sī′kəl) *n.* ⟦< Gr *kyklos*, a circle⟧ **1** *a*) a period within which a round of regularly recurring events is completed *b*) a complete set of such events **2** a series of poems or songs on one theme **3** a bicycle, motorcycle, etc. **4** *Elec.* one complete period of the reversal of an alternating current from positive to negative and back again —*vi.* **-cled**, **-cling** to ride a bicycle, etc.

**cy·cli·cal** (sik′li kəl) *adj.* of, or having the nature of, a cycle; occurring in cycles

**cy·clist** (sīk′list, sī′kə list) *n.* one who rides a bicycle, motorcycle, etc.

**cyclo-** ⟦< Gr *kyklos*, a circle⟧ *combining form* of a circle or wheel; circular

**cy·clom·e·ter** (sī kläm′ət ər) *n.* ⟦prec. + -METER⟧ an instrument that records the revolutions of a wheel for measuring distance traveled

**cy·clone** (sī′klōn′) *n.* ⟦< Gr *kyklōma*, wheel⟧ a storm with strong winds rotating about a center of low pressure

**cyclone fence** a heavy-duty fence of interwoven steel links

**Cy·clops** (sī′kläps′) *n.*, *pl.* **Cy·clo·pes** (sī klō′pēz′) *Gr. Myth.* any of a race of one-eyed giants

**cy·clo·tron** (sī′klō trän′, -klə-) *n.* a circular apparatus for giving high energy to positive ions, as protons, used in atomic research

**cyg·net** (sig′net, -nit) *n.* ⟦< Gr *kyknos*, swan⟧ a young swan

**cyl·in·der** (sil′ən dər) *n.* ⟦< Gr *kylindein*, to roll⟧ **1** a solid, tubular figure consisting of two equal, parallel, circular bases joined by a smooth, continuous surface **2** anything with this shape; specif., *a*) the turning part of a revolver *b*) the piston chamber of an engine —**cy·lin·dri·cal** (sə lin′dri kəl) *adj.*

**cym·bal** (sim′bəl) *n.* 〖< Gr *kymbē*, hollow of a vessel〗 *Music* a circular brass plate that makes a sharp, ringing sound when hit —**cym′bal·ist** *n.*

**cyn·ic** (sin′ik) *n.* 〖< Gr *kynikos*, doglike〗 a cynical person

**cyn′i·cal** (-i kəl) *adj.* **1** denying the sincerity of people's motives and actions **2** sarcastic, sneering, etc. —**cyn′i·cal·ly** *adv.*

**cyn′i·cism′** (-ə siz′əm) *n.* **1** the attitude or beliefs of a cynic **2** a cynical remark, idea, etc.

CYMBALS

**cy·no·sure** (sī′nə shoor′, sin′ə-) *n.* 〖< Gr *kynosoura*, dog's tail〗 a center of attention or interest

**cy·pher** (sī′fər) *n.*, *vi. Brit. sp. of* CIPHER

**cy·press** (sī′prəs) *n.* 〖< Gr *kyparissos*〗 **1** an evergreen tree with cones and dark foliage **2** its wood

**Cy·prus** (sī′prəs) country on an island at the E end of the Mediterranean: 3,572 sq. mi.; pop. 714,000 —**Cyp·ri·ot** (sip′rē ət) *adj., n.*

**cyst** (sist) *n.* 〖< Gr *kystis*, sac〗 a saclike structure in plants or animals, esp. one filled with diseased matter —**cyst′ic** *adj.*

**cystic fibrosis** a children's disease marked by fibrosis of the pancreas and by frequent respiratory infections

**cy·tol·o·gy** (sī täl′ə jē) *n.* 〖< Gr *kytos*, a hollow + -LOGY〗 the branch of biology dealing with cells —**cy·tol′o·gist** *n.*

**cy·to·plasm** (sīt′ō plaz′əm) *n.* 〖< Gr *kytos*, a hollow + *plasma*, something molded〗 the protoplasm of a cell, outside the nucleus

**cy·to·sine** (sīt′ō sēn′) *n.* 〖Ger *zytosin*〗 one of the four bases that combine to form DNA

**czar** (zär) *n.* 〖Russ < L *Caesar*〗 **1** the title of any of the former emperors of Russia **2** a person with wide-ranging power —**cza·ri·na** (zä rē′nə) *fem.n.*

**Czech** (chek) *n.* **1** a member of a Slavic people of central Europe **2** the West Slavic language of the Czechs **3** loosely, a person born or living in Czechoslovakia **4** a person born or living in the Czech Republic —*adj.* of the Czech Republic, its people, or their language

**Czech·o·slo·va·ki·a** (chek′ə slō vä′kē ə) former country in central Europe: divided (1993) into Czech Republic and Slovakia —**Czech′o·slo′vak** or **Czech′o·slo·vak′i·an** *adj., n.*

**Czech Republic** country in central Europe: formerly the W republic of Czechoslovakia: 30,450 sq. mi.; pop. 10,324,000

# D

**d¹** or **D** (dē) *n., pl.* **d's, D's** the fourth letter of the English alphabet

**d²** *abbrev.* **1** day(s) **2** degree **3** diameter **4** died **5** 〖L *denarii*〗 penny; pence

**D¹** (dē) *n.* **1** a Roman numeral for 500 **2** a grade for below-average work **3** *Music* the second tone in the scale of C major

**D²** *abbrev.* **1** December **2** Democrat

**-'d** *contr.* **1** had or would: a shortened form used in contractions [*I'd* seen; *they'd* see] **2** old sp. of -ED [*foster'd*]

**DA** or **D.A.** *abbrev.* District Attorney

**dab** (dab) *vt., vi.* **dabbed, dab′bing** 〖ME *dabben*, to strike〗 **1** to touch lightly and quickly; pat **2** to put on (paint, etc.) with light, quick strokes —*n.* **1** a tap; pat **2** a soft or moist bit of something

**dab·ble** (dab′əl) *vi.* **-bled, -bling** 〖Du *dabbelen*, freq. of MDu *dabben*, to strike, dab〗 **1** to play, dip, or paddle in water **2** to do something superficially: with *in* or *at*

**Dac·ca** (dä′kä) former sp. of DHAKA

**dace** (dās) *n., pl.* **dace** or **daces** a small freshwater fish related to the carp

**dachs·hund** (däks′hoont′) *n.* 〖Ger < *dachs*, badger + *hund*, dog〗 a small dog with a long body, short legs, and drooping ears

**Da·cron** (dā′krän′, dak′rän′) *trademark for* a synthetic wrinkle-resistant fabric —*n.* [*also* **d-**] this fabric

DACHSHUND

**dac·tyl** (dak′təl) *n.* 〖< Gr *daktylos*, finger〗 a metrical foot consisting of one accented syllable followed by two unaccented ones —**dac·tyl′ic** (-til′ik) *adj.*

**dad** (dad) *n.* 〖< child's cry *dada*〗 [Inf.] father: also **dad·dy** (dad′ē), *pl.* **-dies**

**daddy long′legs′** an arachnid with long legs

**da·do** (dā′dō) *n., pl.* **-does** 〖< L *datum*, a die〗 **1** the part of a pedestal between the cap and the base **2** the lower part of a wall if decorated differently from the upper part **3** a rectangular groove cut in a board, used in forming a joint

**daf·fo·dil** (daf′ə dil′) *n.* 〖< Gr *asphodelos*〗 a narcissus with long leaves and yellow flowers

**daf·fy** (daf′ē) *adj.* **-fi·er, -fi·est** 〖< ME *dafte*, daft〗 [Inf.] crazy; silly —**daf′fi·ness** *n.*

**daft** (daft) *adj.* 〖< OE (*ge*)*dæfte*, mild〗 **1** silly **2** insane

**dag·ger** (dag′ər) *n.* 〖< Prov *daga*〗 **1** a weapon with a short, pointed blade, used for stabbing **2** *Printing* a reference mark (†)

**da·guerre·o·type** (də ger′ō tīp′) *n.* 〖after L. J. M. *Daguerre*, 19th-c. Fr inventor〗 an early kind of photograph made on a chemically treated plate —*vt.* **-typed′, -typ′ing** to photograph by this method

**dahl·ia** (dal′yə, däl′-) *n.* 〖after A. *Dahl*, 18th-c. Swed botanist〗 a perennial plant with large, showy flowers

**dai·li·ness** (dā′lē nəs) *n.* the ordinary, routine aspects of a way of life

**dai·ly** (dā′lē) *adj.* done, happening, or published every (week)day —*n., pl.* **-lies** a daily newspaper —*adv.* every day

**daily double** a bet or betting procedure in which winning depends on choosing both winners in two specified races

**dain·ty** (dān′tē) *n., pl.* **-ties** 〖< OFr *deinté*〗 a delicacy —*adj.* **-ti·er, -ti·est 1** delicious and choice **2** delicately pretty **3** *a*) of refined taste; fastidious *b*) squeamish —**dain′ti·ly** *adv.* —**dain′ti·ness** *n.*

**dai·qui·ri** (dak′ər ē) *n.* 〖after *Daiquirí*, Cuban village〗 a cocktail made of rum, sugar, and lime or lemon juice

**dair·y** (der′ē) *n., pl.* **-ies** 〖ME *daie*, dairymaid〗 **1** a building or room where milk and cream are made into butter and cheese, etc. **2** a farm that produces, or a store that sells, milk and milk products —*adj.* of milk and milk products —**dair′y·man** (-mən), *pl.* **-men,** *n.*

**dair′y·ing** *n.* the business of producing or selling dairy products

**da·is** (dā′is) *n., pl.* **da′is·es** 〖< ML *discus*, table〗 a raised platform, as for a speaker

**dai·sy** (dā′zē) *n., pl.* **-sies** 〖< OE *dæges eage*, day's eye] a plant of the composite family, bearing flowers with white rays around a yellow disk

**Da·lai La·ma** (dä′lī lä′mə) the high priest of Lamaism

**dale** (dāl) *n.* [OE *dæl*] a valley

**Dal·las** (dal′əs) city in NE Texas: pop. 1,008,000

**dal·ly** (dal′ē) *vi.* **-lied, -ly·ing** [< OFr *dalier*, to trifle] **1** to flirt **2** to deal carelessly (*with*); toy **3** to waste time; loiter **—dal·liance** (dal′yəns, -ē əns) *n.*

**Dal·ma·tian** (dal mā′shən) *n.* a large, short-haired dog with dark spots on a white coat

DALMATIAN

**dam**[1] (dam) *n.* [ME] a barrier built to hold back flowing water — *vt.* **dammed, dam′ming 1** to build a dam in **2** to keep back or confine

**dam**[2] (dam) *n.* [see DAME] the female parent of any four-legged animal

**dam·age** (dam′ij) *n.* [< L *damnum*] **1** injury or harm resulting in a loss **2** [*pl.*] *Law* money compensating for injury, loss, etc. **—vt. -aged, -ag·ing** to do damage to **—dam′age·a·ble** *adj.*

**Da·mas·cus** (də mas′kəs) capital of Syria: pop. 1,497,000

**dam·ask** (dam′əsk) *n.* [after prec.] **1** a reversible fabric in figured weave, used for table linen, etc. **2** deep pink or rose **—adj. 1** of or like damask **2** deep-pink or rose

**dame** (dām) *n.* [< L *domina*, lady] **1** [D-] in Great Britain, a woman's title of honor **2** [Slang] any woman

**damn** (dam) *vt.* **damned, damn′ing** [< L *damnare*, condemn] **1** to condemn to an unhappy fate **2** *Theol.* to condemn to hell **3** to condemn as bad, inferior, etc. **4** to swear at by saying "damn" **—n.** the saying of "damn" as a curse **—adj., adv.** [Inf.] *short for* DAMNED **—interj.** used to express anger, etc.

**dam·na·ble** (dam′nə bəl) *adj.* **1** deserving damnation **2** deserving to be sworn at **—dam′na·bly** *adv.*

**dam·na′tion** (-nā′shən) *n.* a damning or being damned **—interj.** used to express anger, etc.

**damned** (damd) *adj.* **1** condemned, as to hell **2** [Inf.] deserving cursing; outrageous **—adv.** [Inf.] very

**Dam·o·cles** (dam′ə klēz′) *n. Classical Legend* a man whose king seated him under a sword hanging by a hair to show him the perils of a ruler's life

**damp** (damp) *n.* [MDu, vapor] a slight wetness — *adj.* somewhat moist or wet; humid **—vt. 1** to bank (a fire): usually with *down* **2** to check or reduce **—damp′ness** *n.*

**damp′-dry′** *vt.* **-dried′, -dry′ing** to dry (laundry) so that some moisture is retained **—adj.** designating or of laundry so treated

**damp·en** (dam′pən) *vt.* **1** to make damp; moisten **2** to deaden, depress, or reduce **—damp′en·er** *n.*

**damp·er** (dam′pər) *n.* [see DAMP] **1** anything that deadens or depresses **2** a valve in a flue to control the draft **3** a device to check vibration in piano strings

**dam·sel** (dam′zəl) *n.* [see DAME] [Old-fashioned] a girl; maiden

**dam′sel·fly′** *n., pl.* **-flies′** a slow-flying, brightly colored dragonfly

**dam·son** (dam′zən) *n.* [ult. < *Damascenus*, of DAMASCUS] a small, purple plum

**Dan** *abbrev.* Danish

**dance** (dans) *vi.* **danced, danc′ing** [< OFr *danser*] **1** to move the body and feet in rhythm, ordinarily to music **2** to move lightly, rapidly, gaily, etc. — *vt.* **1** to perform (a dance) **2** to cause to dance —

*n.* **1** rhythmic movement, ordinarily to music **2** a particular kind of dance **3** the art of dancing **4** a party for dancing **5** a piece of music for dancing **6** rapid movement **—danc′er** *n.*

**D and C** dilation (of the cervix) and curettage (of the uterus)

**dan·de·li·on** (dan′də lī′ən) *n.* [< OFr *dent*, tooth + *de*, of + *lion*, lion] a common weed with yellow flowers

**dan·der** (dan′dər) *n.* [< ?] **1** tiny, allergenic particles from fur, etc. **2** [Inf.] anger or temper

**dan·dle** (dan′dəl) *vt.* **-dled, -dling** [< ?] to move (a child) up and down on the knee or in the arms

**dan·druff** (dan′drəf) *n.* [< earlier *dandro* + dial. *hurf*, scab] little scales of dead skin on the scalp

**dan·dy** (dan′dē) *n., pl.* **-dies** [< ?] **1** a man overly attentive to his clothes and appearance **2** [Inf.] something very good **—adj. -di·er, -di·est** [Inf.] very good; fine

**Dane** (dān) *n.* a person born or living in Denmark

**dan·ger** (dān′jər) *n.* [ult. < L *dominus*, a master] **1** liability to injury, damage, loss, etc.; peril **2** a thing that may cause injury, pain, etc.

**dan′ger·ous** *adj.* full of danger; unsafe; perilous **—dan′ger·ous·ly** *adv.*

**dan·gle** (daŋ′gəl) *vi.* **-gled, -gling** [< Scand] to hang loosely so as to swing back and forth **—vt.** to cause to dangle **—dan′gler** *n.*

**Dan·iel** (dan′yəl) *n. Bible* a Hebrew prophet whose faith saved him in the lions' den

**Dan·ish** (dān′ish) *adj.* of Denmark or its people, language, etc. **—n. 1** the language of the Danes **2** [*also* d-] (a) rich, flaky pastry filled with fruit, cheese, etc.: in full **Danish pastry**

**dank** (daŋk) *adj.* [ME] disagreeably damp **—dank′ly** *adv.* **—dank′ness** *n.*

**dan·seuse** (dän sooz′) *fem.n.* [Fr] a female ballet dancer **—dan·seur′** (-sur′) *masc.n.*

**Dan·te (Alighieri)** (dän′tā, dan′tē) 1265-1321; It. poet

**Dan·ube** (dan′yoob) river in S Europe, flowing from S Germany into the Black Sea

**dap·per** (dap′ər) *adj.* [MDu, nimble] **1** small and active **2** trim, neat, or dressed stylishly

**dap·ple** (dap′əl) *adj.* [< ON *depill*, a spot] marked with spots; mottled: also **dap′pled** **—vt. -pled, -pling** to cover with spots

**Dar·da·nelles** (där′də nelz′) strait separating the Balkan Peninsula from Asia Minor

**dare** (der) *vt., vi.* **dared, dar′ing** [OE *durran*] **1** to have enough courage for (some act) **2** to challenge (someone) to do something **—n.** a challenge **—dare say** to think probable **—dar′er** *n.*

**dare′dev′il** (-dev′əl) *adj.* bold and reckless **—n. 1** a bold, reckless person **2** one who performs dangerous stunts

**dar′ing** *adj.* fearless; bold **—n.** bold courage **—dar′ing·ly** *adv.*

**dark** (därk) *adj.* [< OE *deorc*] **1** entirely or partly without light **2** *a*) almost black *b*) not light in color **3** hidden; secret **4** gloomy **5** evil; sinister **6** ignorant **—n. 1** the state of being dark **2** night or nightfall **—in the dark** uninformed; ignorant **—dark′ly** *adv.* **—dark′ness** *n.*

**Dark Ages** the Middle Ages, esp. the earlier part

**dark·en** (där′kən) *vt., vi.* to make or become dark or darker **—dark′en·er** *n.*

**dark horse** a little-known contestant thought unlikely to win

**dark′room′** *n.* a darkened room for developing photographs

**dar·ling** (där′liŋ) *n.* [OE *deorling*] a person much loved by another **—adj. 1** very dear; beloved **2** [Inf.] cute or attractive

**darn**[1] (därn) *vt., vi.* [< Fr dial. *darner*] to mend (cloth) by sewing a network of stitches across the gap **—n.** a darned place in fabric

**darn**[2] (därn) *vt., n., adj., adv., interj.* [Inf.] damn: a euphemism **—darned** *adj., adv.*

**dart** (därt) *n.* [< OFr] **1** a small, pointed missile for throwing or shooting **2** a sudden movement **3** a short, tapered seam **4** [*pl., with sing. v.*] a game in which darts (see sense 1) are thrown at a target (**dart′board′**) —*vt., vi.* to send out or move suddenly and fast

**Dar·von** (där′vän′) *trademark for* an analgesic drug containing a narcotic painkiller

**Dar·win** (där′win), **Charles** (**Robert**) (chärlz) 1809-82; Eng. naturalist: originated theory of evolution —**Dar·win′i·an** *adj., n.* —**Dar′win·ism′** *n.*

**dash** (dash) *vt.* [< Scand] **1** to throw so as to break; smash **2** to throw or thrust (*away, down,* etc.) **3** to splash **4** to destroy, frustrate —*vi.* **1** to strike violently (*against*) **2** to rush —*n.* **1** a splash **2** a bit of something added [*a dash* of salt] **3** a rush **4** a short, fast race **5** spirit; vigor **6** the mark of punctuation (— or –) used to indicate a break, omission, etc. —**dash off** to do, write, etc. hastily —**dash′er** *n.*

**dash′board′** *n.* a panel with controls and gauges, as in an automobile

**da·shi·ki** (dä shē′kē) *n.* a loosefitting, brightly colored robe or tunic, modeled after an African tribal garment

**dash′ing** *adj.* **1** full of dash or spirit; lively **2** showy; striking; stylish —**dash′ing·ly** *adv.*

**das·tard·ly** (das′tərd lē) *adj.* [< ME *dastard,* a craven] mean, cowardly, etc.

**dat** *abbrev.* dative

**da·ta** (dāt′ə, dat′ə) *pl.n.* [*now usually with sing. v.*] **1** facts or figures from which conclusions can be drawn **2** information in a form suitable for computer storage, etc.

**da′ta·base′** *n.* a mass of data, as in a computer, arranged for rapid expansion, updating, and retrieval: also **data base**

**data processing** the handling of large amounts of information, esp. by a computer —**data processor**

**date**[1] (dāt) *n.* [< L *dare,* give] **1** the time at which a thing happens, was made, etc. **2** the day of the month **3** [*pl.*] a person's birth and death dates **4** *a)* an appointment *b)* a romantic social engagement with a person *c)* this person —*vt.* **dat′ed, dat′ing 1** to mark (a letter, etc.) with a date **2** to find out or give the date of **3** to make seem old-fashioned **4** to have romantic social engagements with —*vi.* **1** to belong to a definite period in the past: usually with *from* **2** to have romantic social engagements —**to date** up to now —**dat′er** *n.*

**date**[2] (dāt) *n.* [< Gr *daktylos,* a date] the sweet, fleshy fruit of a desert palm tree (**date palm**)

**date′book′** *n.* a notebook for entering appointments, etc.

**date′line′** *n.* the date and place of writing or issue, as given in a line in a newspaper story, etc.

**da·tive** (dāt′iv) *n.* [< L *dativus,* relating to giving] *Gram.* the case of the indirect object of a verb

**da·tum** (dāt′əm, dat′-) *n.* [L, what is given] *sing. of* DATA

**daub** (dôb) *vt., vi.* [< L *de-,* intens. + *albus,* white] **1** to cover or smear with sticky, soft matter **2** to paint badly —*n.* **1** anything daubed on **2** a daubing stroke —**daub′er** *n.*

**daugh·ter** (dôt′ər) *n.* [< OE *dohtor*] **1** a girl or woman as she is related to either or both parents **2** a female descendant —**daugh′ter·ly** *adj.*

**daugh′ter-in-law′** *n., pl.* **daugh′ters-in-law′** the wife of one's son

**Dau·mier** (dō myā′), **Ho·no·ré** (ô nô rā′) 1808-79; Fr. painter

**daunt** (dônt) *vt.* [< L *domare,* to tame] to intimidate or dishearten

**daunt′less** *adj.* that cannot be daunted; fearless —**daunt′less·ly** *adv.* —**daunt′less·ness** *n.*

**dau·phin** (dô′fin) *n.* [Fr, dolphin] the eldest son of the king of France: a title used from 1349 to 1830

**dav·en·port** (dav′ən pôrt′) *n.* [< ?] a large couch or sofa

**Da·vid** (dā′vid) *n. Bible* the second king of Israel and Judah

**da Vin·ci** (də vin′chē), **Le·o·nar·do** (lē′ə när′dō) 1452-1519; It. painter, sculptor, architect, & scientist

**Da·vis** (dā′vis), **Jefferson** 1808-89; president of the Confederacy (1861-65)

**da·vit** (dā′vit, dav′it) *n.* [OFr dim. of *David*] either of a pair of uprights on a ship for lowering or raising a small boat

**daw·dle** (dôd′'l) *vi., vt.* **-dled, -dling** [< ?] to waste (time) in trifling or by being slow —**daw′dler** *n.*

**dawn** (dôn) *vi.* [< OE *dagian*] **1** to begin to be day **2** to begin to appear, develop, etc. **3** to begin to be understood or felt —*n.* **1** daybreak **2** the beginning (*of* something)

**day** (dā) *n.* [OE *dæg*] **1** the period of light between sunrise and sunset **2** the time (24 hours) that it takes the earth to rotate once on its axis **3** [*also pl.*] a period; era **4** a time of power, glory, etc. **5** daily work period [an 8-hour *day*] —**day after day** every day: also **day in, day out**

**day′bed′** *n.* a couch that can also be used as a bed

**day′break′** *n.* the time in the morning when light first appears

**day care** daytime care given to children, as at a day-care center, or to the elderly, as at a social agency —**day′-care′** *adj.*

**day′dream′** *n.* **1** a pleasant, dreamy series of thoughts **2** a visionary scheme —*vi.* to have daydreams

**day′light′** *n.* **1** the light of day **2** dawn **3** understanding

**daylight saving time** [*often* D- S- T-] time that is one hour later than standard time: also **daylight savings time**

**Day of Atonement** Yom Kippur

**day′time′** *n.* the time between dawn and sunset

**day′-to-day′** *adj.* daily; routine

**Day·ton** (dāt′'n) city in SW Ohio: pop. 182,000

**Day·to·na Beach** (dā tō′nə) resort city in NE Florida, on the Atlantic: pop. 62,000

**day trading** rapid buying and selling of stocks on the Internet —**day trader**

**daze** (dāz) *vt.* **dazed, daz′ing** [< ON *dasi,* tired] to stun or bewilder —*n.* a dazed condition —**daz′ed·ly** *adv.*

**daz·zle** (daz′əl) *vt., vi.* **-zled, -zling** [freq. of DAZE] **1** to overpower or be overpowered by bright light **2** to surprise or arouse admiration with brilliant qualities, display, etc. —*n.* a dazzling —**daz′zler** *n.*

**db** or **dB** *abbrev.* decibel(s)

**DC** *abbrev.* **1** direct current: also **dc 2** District of Columbia

**DD** or **D.D.** *abbrev.* Doctor of Divinity

**DDS** or **D.D.S.** *abbrev.* Doctor of Dental Surgery

**DDT** (dē′dē′tē′) *n.* [< its chemical name] a powerful insecticide

**de-** [< Fr *dé-* or L *de*] *prefix* **1** away from, off [*derail*] **2** down [*degrade*] **3** entirely [*defunct*] **4** reverse the action of [*decode*]

**DE** Delaware

**DEA** *abbrev.* Drug Enforcement Administration

**dea·con** (dē′kən) *n.* [< Gr *diakonos,* servant] **1** a cleric ranking just below a priest **2** a church officer who helps the minister —**dea′con·ess** *fem.n.*

**de·ac·ti·vate** (dē ak′tə vāt′) *vt.* **-vat′ed, -vat′ing 1** to make (an explosive, chemical, etc.) inactive **2** *Mil.* to demobilize

**dead** (ded) *adj.* [OE] **1** no longer living **2** without life **3** deathlike **4** lacking warmth, interest, brightness, etc. **5** without feeling, motion, or power **6** extinguished or extinct **7** no longer used; obsolete **8** unerring [a *dead* shot] **9** complete [a *dead* stop] **10** precise [*dead* center] **11** [Inf.] very tired —*n.* the time of most darkness, most cold, etc. [the *dead* of night] —*adv.* **1** completely **2** directly [*dead* ahead] —**the dead** those who have died

**dead'beat'** *n.* [Slang] one who tries to evade paying debts

**dead'bolt'** *n.* a lock for a door, with a bolt that can be moved only by turning the key

**dead·en** (ded′'n) *vt.* **1** to lessen the vigor or intensity of; dull **2** to numb

**dead end 1** a street, alley, etc. closed at one end **2** an impasse —**dead'-end'** *adj.*

**dead heat** a race in which two or more contestants finish even; tie

**dead letter 1** a rule, law, etc. no longer enforced **2** an unclaimed postal letter

**dead'line'** *n.* the latest time by which something must be done

**dead'lock'** *n.* a standstill resulting from the action of equal and opposed forces —*vt.*, *vi.* to bring or come to a deadlock

**dead'ly** *adj.* **-li·er, -li·est 1** causing or likely to cause death **2** implacable [*deadly* enemies] **3** typical of death [*deadly* pallor] **4** extreme **5** very boring **6** very accurate [*deadly* aim] —*adv.* extremely —**dead'li·ness** *n.*

**dead'-on'** *adj.* [Inf.] completely accurate

**dead'pan'** *adj.*, *adv.* without expression; blank(ly)

**Dead Sea** inland body of salt water on the Israeli-Jordanian border

**dead'wood'** *n.* anything useless or burdensome

**deaf** (def) *adj.* [OE] **1** unable to hear **2** unwilling to respond, as to a plea —**deaf'ness** *n.*

**deaf'en** (-ən) *vt.* **1** to make deaf **2** to overwhelm with noise —**deaf'en·ing** *adj.*

**deaf'-mute'** *n.* a person who is deaf and therefore has not learned to speak

**deal**[1] (dēl) *vt.* **dealt** (delt), **deal'ing** [< OE *dǣlan*] **1** to portion out or distribute **2** to give; administer (a blow, etc.) **3** [Slang] to sell (illegal drugs) —*vi.* **1** to have to do (*with*) [science *deals* with facts] **2** to conduct oneself [*deal* fairly with others] **3** to do business (*with* or *in*) **4** to distribute playing cards to the players —*n.* **1** the distributing of playing cards **2** a business transaction **3** a bargain or agreement, esp. when secret **4** [Inf.] treatment [a fair *deal*] —**deal'er** *n.*

**deal**[2] (dēl) *n.* [OE *dǣl*, a part] an indefinite amount —**a good** (or **great**) **deal 1** a large amount **2** very much

**deal'er·ship'** *n.* a franchise to sell a product in a specified area

**deal'ing** *n.* **1** way of acting **2** [usually pl.] transactions or relations

**dean** (dēn) *n.* [< LL *decanus*, chief of ten (monks, etc.)] **1** the presiding official of a cathedral **2** a college official in charge of students or faculty **3** the senior or preeminent member of a group

**dean's list** a list of students at a college who have earned high grades

**dear** (dir) *adj.* [OE *deore*] **1** much loved **2** esteemed: a polite form of address [*Dear* Sir] **3** high-priced; costly **4** earnest [our *dearest* wish] —*n.* a loved person; darling —**dear'ly** *adv.* —**dear'ness** *n.*

**Dear John** (**letter**) [Inf.] a letter, as to a fiancé, breaking off a close relationship

**dearth** (durth) *n.* [ME *derth*] scarcity or lack

**death** (deth) *n.* [OE] **1** the act or fact of dying **2** the state of being dead **3** end or destruction **4** the cause of death —**death'like'** *adj.*

**death'bed'** *n.* used chiefly in the phrase **on one's deathbed**, during the last hours of one's life

**death'blow'** *n.* **1** a blow that kills **2** a thing fatal (*to* something)

**death'less** *adj.* that cannot die; immortal —**death'less·ly** *adv.*

**death'ly** *adj.* like or characteristic of death —*adv.* extremely [*deathly* ill]

**death'trap'** *n.* an unsafe building, vehicle, etc.

**Death Valley** dry, hot desert basin in E California & S Nevada

**deb** (deb) *n.* [Inf.] short for DEBUTANTE

**de·ba·cle** (di bä′kəl) *n.* [Fr *débâcler*, break up] **1** a crushing defeat **2** a ruinous collapse

**de·bar** (dē bär′) *vt.* **-barred', -bar'ring** [< Anglo-Fr: see DE- & BAR] to keep (a person) *from* some right, etc. —**de·bar'ment** *n.*

**de·bark** (dē bärk′) *vt.*, *vi.* [< Fr: see DE- & BARK[3]] to unload from or leave a ship or aircraft —**de·bar·ka·tion** (dē′bär kā′shən) *n.*

**de·base** (dē bās′) *vt.* **-based', -bas'ing** [DE- + BASE[2]] to make lower in value, dignity, etc. —**de·base'ment** *n.*

**de·bate** (dē bāt′) *vi.*, *vt.* **-bat'ed, -bat'ing** [< OFr: see DE- & BATTER[1]] **1** to discuss reasons for and against (something) **2** to take part in a debate with (a person) or about (a question) —*n.* **1** a discussion of opposing reasons **2** a formal contest of skill in reasoned argument —**de·bat'a·ble** *adj.* —**de·bat'er** *n.*

**de·bauch** (dē bôch′) *vt.* [< OFr *desbaucher*, seduce] to lead astray morally; corrupt —*n.* an orgy —**de·bauch'er·y**, *pl.* **-ies**, *n.*

**deb·au·chee** (deb′ô shē′, di bôch′ē′) *n.* a dissipated person

**de·ben·ture** (di ben′chər) *n.* [< L: see DEBT] **1** a voucher acknowledging a debt **2** an interest-bearing bond issued without specified security

**de·bil·i·tate** (dē bil′ə tāt′) *vt.* **-tat'ed, -tat'ing** [< L *debilis*, weak] to make weak

**de·bil·i·ty** (də bil′ə tē) *n.*, *pl.* **-ties** [see prec.] weakness; feebleness

**deb·it** (deb′it) *n.* [< L *debere*, owe] **1** an entry in an account of money owed **2** the total of such entries —*vt.* to enter as a debit

**debit card** a bank card that allows the cost of purchases to be deducted from a bank account

**deb·o·nair** (deb′ə ner′) *adj.* [< OFr *de bon aire*, lit., of good breed] **1** carefree; jaunty **2** urbane Also sp. **deb'o·naire'** —**deb'o·nair'ly** *adv.*

**de·brief** (dē brēf′) *vt.* [DE- + BRIEF] to receive information from (a pilot, emissary, etc.) about a recent mission

**de·bris** or **dé·bris** (də brē′) *n.* [Fr < OFr *desbrisier*, break apart] bits and pieces of stone, rubbish, etc.

**debt** (det) *n.* [< L *debere*, owe] **1** something owed to another **2** the condition of owing [to be in *debt*]

**debt'or** (-ər) *n.* one who owes a debt

**de·bug** (dē bug′) *vt.* **-bugged', -bug'ging** [DE- + BUG] **1** to correct defects in **2** [Inf.] to find and remove hidden electronic listening devices from

**de·bunk** (dē buŋk′) *vt.* [DE- + BUNK[2]] to expose the exaggerated or false claims, etc. of

**De·bus·sy** (də bü sē′; *E* deb′yoo sē′), **Claude** (klōd; *E* klôd) 1862-1918; Fr. composer

**de·but** or **dé·but** (dā byoō′, dā′byoō) *n.* [Fr < *débuter*, to lead off] **1** a first public appearance **2** the formal introduction of a young woman into society —*vi.* to make a debut

**deb·u·tante** (deb′yoō tänt′) *n.* [Fr] a young woman making a debut into society

**dec** *abbrev.* deceased

**Dec** *abbrev.* December

**deca-** [< Gr *deka*, ten] *combining form* ten: also **dec-**

**dec·ade** (dek′ād) *n.* [< Gr *deka*, ten] a period of ten years

**dec·a·dence** (dek′ə dəns, di kād′'ns) *n.* [< L *de-*, from + *cadere*, to fall] a decline, as in morals, art, etc.; deterioration —**dec'a·dent** *adj.*, *n.*

**de·caf** (dē′kaf′) *n.* [Inf.] decaffeinated coffee

**de·caf·fein·at·ed** (dē kaf′ə nāt′id) *adj.* with caffeine removed

**de·cal** (dē′kal, di kal′) *n.* [< *decalcomania* < Fr < L *calcare*, to tread + Gr *mania*, madness] a picture or design transferred from prepared paper to glass, wood, etc.

**Dec·a·logue** or **Dec·a·log** (dek′ə lôg′) *n.* [see DECA- & -LOGUE] [*sometimes* d-] TEN COMMANDMENTS

**de·camp** (dē kamp′) *vi.* [< Fr] **1** to break camp **2** to go away suddenly and secretly

**de·cant** (dē kant′) *vt.* [< Fr < L *de-*, from + *can-thus*, tire of a wheel] to pour gently from one container into another

**de·cant′er** *n.* a decorative glass bottle for serving wine, etc.

**de·cap·i·tate** (dē kap′ə tāt′) *vt.* -tat′ed, -tat′ing [< L *de-*, off + *caput*, head] to behead —**de·cap′i·ta′tion** *n.*

**de·cath·lon** (di kath′län′) *n.* [DEC(A)- + Gr *athlon*, a prize] an athletic contest in which each contestant takes part in ten TRACK (sense 6*b*) events

**de·cay** (dē kā′) *vi.* [see DECADENCE] 1 to lose strength, prosperity, etc. gradually; deteriorate 2 to rot 3 to undergo radioactive disintegration —*vt.* to cause to decay —*n.* 1 deterioration 2 a rotting or rottenness

**de·cease** (dē sēs′) *n.* [< L *de-*, from + *cedere*, go] death

**de·ceased** (dē sēst′) *adj.* dead —**the deceased** the dead person or persons

**de·ce·dent** (dē sēd′'nt) *n.* [see DECEASE] *Law* a deceased person

**de·ceit** (dē sēt′) *n.* 1 a deceiving or lying 2 a dishonest action 3 deceitful quality

**de·ceit′ful** *adj.* 1 apt to lie or cheat 2 deceptive; false —**de·ceit′ful·ly** *adv.*

**de·ceive** (dē sēv′) *vt.*, *vi.* -ceived′, -ceiv′ing [< L *de-*, from + *capere*, take] to make (a person) believe what is not true; mislead —**de·ceiv′er** *n.* —**de·ceiv′ing·ly** *adv.*

**de·cel·er·ate** (dē sel′ər āt′) *vt.*, *vi.* -at′ed, -at′ing [DE- + (AC)CELERATE] to reduce the speed (of); slow down —**de·cel′er·a′tion** *n.*

**De·cem·ber** (dē sem′bər) *n.* [< L *decem*, ten: tenth month in Roman calendar] the twelfth and last month of the year, having 31 days

**de·cen·cy** (dē′sən sē) *n.*, *pl.* -cies a being decent; propriety, courtesy, etc.

**de·cen·ni·al** (dē sen′ē əl) *adj.* [< L *decem*, ten + *annus*, year] 1 happening every ten years 2 lasting ten years

**de·cent** (dē′sənt) *adj.* [< L *decere*, befit] 1 proper and fitting 2 not obscene 3 respectable 4 adequate *[decent* wages] 5 fair and kind —**de′cent·ly** *adv.*

**de·cen·tral·ize** (dē sen′trə līz′) *vt.* -ized′, -iz′ing to break up a concentration of (governmental authority, industry, etc.) and distribute more widely —**de·cen′tral·i·za′tion** *n.*

**de·cep·tion** (dē sep′shən) *n.* 1 a deceiving or being deceived 2 an illusion or fraud —**de·cep′tive** *adj.*

**deci-** [< L *decem*, ten] *combining form* one tenth part of

**dec·i·bel** (des′ə bəl) *n.* [prec. + *bel*, after BELL] a unit for measuring relative loudness of a sound

**de·cide** (dē sīd′) *vt.* -cid′ed, -cid′ing [< L *de-*, off + *caedere*, to cut] 1 to end (a contest, dispute, etc.) by giving one side the victory 2 to reach a decision about; resolve —*vi.* to reach a decision —**de·cid′a·ble** *adj.*

**de·cid·ed** *adj.* 1 definite; clear-cut 2 determined —**de·cid′ed·ly** *adv.*

**de·cid·u·ous** (dē sij′o͞o əs) *adj.* [< L *de-*, off, down + *cadere*, to fall] 1 falling off or out at a certain season or stage of growth, as some leaves or antlers do 2 shedding leaves annually

**dec·i·mal** (des′ə məl) *adj.* [< L *decem*, ten] of or based on the number 10 —*n.* a fraction with a denominator of 10 or some power of 10, shown by a point (**decimal point**) before the numerator (Ex.: .5 = $\frac{5}{10}$)

**dec·i·mate** (des′ə māt′) *vt.* -mat′ed, -mat′ing [< L *decem*, ten] to destroy or kill a large part of (lit., a tenth part of) —**dec′i·ma′tion** *n.*

**de·ci·pher** (dē sī′fər) *vt.* [DE- + CIPHER] 1 DECODE 2 to make out the meaning of (illegible writing, etc.)

**de·ci·sion** (dē sizh′ən) *n.* 1 the act of deciding or settling a dispute or question 2 the act of making

up one's mind 3 a judgment or conclusion 4 determination; firmness of mind

**de·ci·sive** (dē sī′siv) *adj.* 1 that settles a dispute, question, etc.; conclusive 2 critically important; crucial 3 showing firmness —**de·ci′sive·ly** *adv.*

**deck**[1] (dek) *n.* [prob. < earlier LowG *verdeck*] 1 a floor of a ship 2 any platform, floor, etc., like a ship's deck 3 a pack of playing cards 4 TAPE DECK

**deck**[2] (dek) *vt.* [MDu *decken*, to cover] to array or adorn: often with *out*

**de·claim** (dē klām′) *vi.*, *vt.* [< L *de-*, intens. + *clamare*, to cry] to recite or speak in a studied, dramatic, or impassioned way —**dec·la·ma·tion** (dek′lə mā′shən) *n.* —**de·clam·a·to·ry** (dē klam′ə tôr′ē) *adj.*

**dec·la·ra·tion** (dek′lə rā′shən) *n.* 1 a declaring; announcement 2 a formal statement

**de·clar·a·tive** (dē kler′ə tiv) *adj.* making a statement or assertion

**de·clare** (dē kler′) *vt.* -clared′, -clar′ing [< L *de-*, intens. + *clarus*, clear] 1 to announce openly or formally 2 to show or reveal 3 to say emphatically —**de·clar′er** *n.*

**de·clas·si·fy** (dē klas′ə fī′) *vt.* -fied′, -fy′ing to make (secret documents, etc.) available to the public —**de·clas′si·fi·ca′tion** *n.*

**de·clen·sion** (dē klen′shən) *n.* [see fol.] 1 a descent 2 a decline 3 *Gram.* the inflection of nouns, pronouns, or adjectives

**de·cline** (dē klīn′) *vi.* -clined′, -clin′ing [< L *de-*, from + *clinare*, to bend] 1 to bend or slope downward 2 to deteriorate; decay 3 to refuse something —*vt.* 1 to cause to bend or slope downward 2 to refuse politely 3 *Gram.* to give the inflected forms of (a noun, pronoun, or adjective) —*n.* 1 a declining; dropping, failing, decay, etc. 2 a period of decline 3 a downward slope —**dec·li·na·tion** (dek′lə nā′shən) *n.*

**de·cliv·i·ty** (dē kliv′ə tē) *n.*, *pl.* -ties [< L *de-*, down + *clivus*, a slope] a downward slope

**de·code** (dē kōd′) *vt.* -cod′ed, -cod′ing to decipher (a coded message)

**dé·col·le·té** (dā käl′ə tā′) *adj.* [Fr < L *de*, from + *collum*, neck] cut low so as to bare the neck and shoulders

**de·col·o·ni·za·tion** (dē käl′ə nə zā′shən) *n.* a freeing or being freed from colonial status —**de·col′o·nize′** (-ə nīz′), -nized′, -niz′ing, *vt.*, *vi.*

**de·com·pose** (dē′kəm pōz′) *vt.*, *vi.* -posed′, -pos′ing [< Fr: see DE- & COMPOSE] 1 to break up into basic parts 2 to rot —**de·com·po·si·tion** (dē käm pə zish′ən) *n.*

**de·com·press** (dē′kəm pres′) *vt.* to free from pressure, esp. from air pressure —**de′com·pres′sion** *n.*

**de·con·gest·ant** (dē′kən jes′tənt) *n.* a medication that relieves congestion, as in the nasal passages

**de·con·struct** (dē′kən strukt′) *vt.* [Fr] 1 to analyze rigorously 2 to take apart; disassemble —**de′con·struc′tion** *n.*

**de·con·tam·i·nate** (dē′kən tam′ə nāt′) *vt.* -nat′ed, -nat′ing to rid of a harmful substance, as radioactive material

**dé·cor** or **de·cor** (dā kôr′) *n.* [Fr] a decorative scheme, as of a room

**dec·o·rate** (dek′ə rāt′) *vt.* -rat′ed, -rat′ing [< L *decus*, an ornament] 1 to adorn; ornament 2 to paint or wallpaper 3 to give a medal or similar honor to —**dec′o·ra·tive** (dek′ə rə tiv, -ə rāt′iv) *adj.* —**dec′o·ra′tor** *n.*

**dec′o·ra′tion** *n.* 1 a decorating 2 an ornament 3 a medal, etc.

**Decoration Day** MEMORIAL DAY

**dec·o·rous** (dek′ə rəs, di kôr′əs) *adj.* having or showing decorum, good taste, etc. —**dec′o·rous·ly** *adv.*

**de·co·rum** (di kôr′əm) *n.* [< L *decorus*, proper] propriety and good taste in behavior, speech, etc.

**dé·cou·page** or **dé·cou·page** (dā′ko͞o päzh′) *n.* [< Fr *dé-*, DE- + *couper*, to cut] the art of decorating a surface with varnished paper cutouts

**de·coy** (dē koi'; *for n., usually* dē'koi') *n.* [< Du *de kooi*, the cage] **1** an artificial or trained bird, etc. used to lure game within gun range **2** a thing or person used to lure into danger —*vt.* to lure into danger

**de·crease** (dē krēs'; *for n., usually* dē'krēs') *vi., vt.* -creased', -creas'ing [< L *de-*, from + *crescere*, grow] to become or make less, smaller, etc.; diminish —*n.* **1** a decreasing **2** amount of decreasing

**de·cree** (dē krē') *n.* [< L *de-*, from + *cernere*, to judge] an official order or decision —*vt.* -creed', -cree'ing to order or decide by decree

**de·crep·it** (dē krep'it) *adj.* [< L *de-*, intens. + *crepare*, to creak] broken down or worn out by old age or long use —**de·crep'i·tude'** (-ə tood') *n.*

**de·cre·scen·do** (dā'krə shen'dō, dē'-) [*also in italics*] *Music adj., adv.* [It < L, DECREASE] gradually decreasing in loudness —*n., pl.* -dos a gradual decrease in loudness

**de·crim·i·nal·ize** (dē krim'ə nəl īz') *vt.* -ized', -iz'ing to eliminate or reduce the penalties for (a crime)

**de·cry** (dē krī') *vt.* -cried', -cry'ing [< Fr: see DE- & CRY] to speak out against openly; denounce

**ded·i·cate** (ded'i kāt') *vt.* -cat'ed, -cat'ing [< L *de-*, intens. + *dicare*, proclaim] **1** to set apart for, or devote to, a special purpose **2** to address (a book, etc.) to someone as a sign of honor —**ded'i·ca'tion** *n.*

**ded'i·cat'ed** *adj.* **1** devoted; faithful **2** designating a device, etc. to be used only for a particular purpose

**de·duce** (dē doos') *vt.* -duced', -duc'ing [< L *de-*, down + *ducere*, to lead] to infer or decide by reasoning —**de·duc'i·ble** *adj.*

**de·duct** (dē dukt') *vt.* [see prec.] to take away or subtract (a quantity)

**de·duct·i·ble** (-duk'tə bəl) *adj.* that can be deducted —*n.* an amount stipulated in an insurance policy to be paid by the person insured in the event of a loss, etc., with the insurer paying the remainder

**de·duc'tion** (-duk'shən) *n.* **1** a deducting; subtraction **2** an amount deducted **3** *a*) reasoning from the general to the specific *b*) a conclusion reached by such reasoning —**de·duc'tive** *adj.*

**deed** (dēd) *n.* [< OE *dēd*] **1** a thing done; act **2** a feat of courage, skill, etc. **3** a legal document which transfers a property —*vt.* to transfer (property) by deed

**deem** (dēm) *vt., vi.* [< OE *deman*, to judge] to think, believe, or judge

**de·em·pha·size** (dē em'fə sīz') *vt.* -sized', -siz'ing to lessen the importance of —**de·em'pha·sis** (-sis) *n.*

**deep** (dēp) *adj.* [OE *deop*] **1** extending far downward, inward, backward, etc. **2** hard to understand; abstruse **3** serious; profound **4** dark and rich [a *deep* red] **5** absorbed by: with *in* [*deep* in thought] **6** great in degree; intense **7** of low pitch [a *deep* voice] **8** large; big —*n.* a deep place —*adv.* far down, far back, etc. —**the deep** [Old Poet.] the ocean —**deep'ly** *adv.* —**deep'ness** *n.*

**deep'en** *vt., vi.* to make or become deep or deeper

**deep'freeze'** *n.* a condition of suspended activity, etc. —*vt.* -froze', -fro'zen, -freez'ing to subject (foods) to sudden freezing so as to preserve and store

**deep'-fry'** *vt.* -fried', -fry'ing to fry in a deep pan of boiling fat or oil

**deep'-root'ed** *adj.* **1** having deep roots **2** firmly fixed

**deep'-seat'ed** *adj.* **1** buried deep **2** firmly fixed

**deep'-six'** *vt.* [< six fathoms] [Slang] to get rid of, as by throwing overboard

**deep space** OUTER SPACE

**deer** (dir) *n., pl.* **deer** or **deers** [OE *deor*, wild animal] any of various ruminants, including the elk, moose, and reindeer, the male of which grows and sheds antlers annually

**de·es·ca·late** (dē es'kə lāt') *vi., vt.* -lat'ed, -lat'ing

to reduce in scope, magnitude, etc. —**de·es'ca·la'tion** *n.*

**de·face** (dē fās') *vt.* -faced', -fac'ing [see DE- & FACE] to spoil the look of; mar —**de·face'ment** *n.*

**de fac·to** (dē fak'tō) [L] actually existing but not officially approved

**de·fal·cate** (dē fal'kāt) *vi.* -cat'ed, -cat'ing [< L *de-*, from + *falx*, a sickle] to steal or misuse funds entrusted to one's care; embezzle —**de'fal·ca'tion** *n.*

**de·fame** (dē fām') *vt.* -famed', -fam'ing [< L *dis-*, from + *fama*, fame] to attack the reputation of; slander or libel —**def·a·ma·tion** (def'ə mā'shən) *n.* —**de·fam·a·to·ry** (dē fam'ə tôr'ē) *adj.* —**de·fam'er** *n.*

**de·fang** (dē faŋ') *vt.* **1** to remove the fangs of **2** to make harmless —**de·fanged'** *adj.*

**de·fault** (dē fôlt') *n.* [< L *de-*, away + *fallere*, fail] failure to do or appear as required; specif., failure to pay money due —*vi.* **1** to fail to do or pay when required **2** to lose (a contest) by default —**de·fault'er** *n.*

**de·feat** (dē fēt') *vt.* [< L *dis-*, from + *facere*, do] **1** to win victory over **2** to bring to nothing; frustrate —*n.* a defeating or being defeated

**de·feat'ist** *n.* one who too readily accepts or expects defeat —**de·feat'ism'** *n.*

**def·e·cate** (def'i kāt') *vi.* -cat'ed, -cat'ing [< L *de-*, from + *faex*, dregs] to excrete waste matter from the bowels —**def'e·ca'tion** *n.*

**de·fect** (dē'fekt'; *for v.* dē fekt') *n.* [< L *de-*, from + *facere*, do] **1** lack of something necessary for completeness **2** an imperfection or weakness; fault —*vi.* to forsake a party, cause, etc., esp. so as to join the opposition —**de·fec'tion** *n.* —**de·fec'tor** *n.*

**de·fec·tive** (dē fek'tiv) *adj.* having defects; imperfect; faulty

**de·fend** (dē fend') *vt.* [< L *de-*, away + *fendere*, to strike] **1** to guard from attack; protect **2** to support or justify **3** *Law a*) to oppose (an action) *b*) to act as lawyer for (an accused) —**de·fend'er** *n.*

**de·fend·ant** (dē fen'dənt, -dant') *n. Law* the person sued or accused

**de·fense** (dē fens', dē'fens') *n.* **1** a defending against attack **2** something that defends **3** justification by speech or writing **4** *a*) the arguments of a defendant *b*) the defendant and his or her counsel Brit. sp. **defence** —**de·fense'less** *adj.* —**de·fen'si·ble** *adj.*

**defense mechanism** any thought process used unconsciously to protect oneself against painful feelings

**de·fen'sive** *adj.* **1** defending **2** of or for defense —*n.* a position of defense —**de·fen'sive·ly** *adv.*

**de·fer¹** (dē fur') *vt., vi.* -ferred', -fer'ring [see DIFFER] **1** to postpone; delay **2** to postpone the induction of (a person) into compulsory military service —**de·fer'ment** or **de·fer'ral** *n.*

**de·fer²** (dē fur') *vi.* -ferred', -fer'ring [< L *de-*, down + *ferre*, to BEAR¹] to yield with courtesy (*to*)

**def·er·ence** (def'ər əns) *n.* **1** a yielding in opinion, judgment, etc. **2** courteous respect

**def·er·en·tial** (-en'shəl) *adj.* showing deference; very respectful

**de·fi·ance** (dē fī'əns) *n.* a defying; open, bold resistance to authority —**de·fi'ant** *adj.* —**de·fi'ant·ly** *adv.*

**de·fi·cien·cy** (dē fish'ən sē) *n.* [< L *de-*, from + *facere*, do] **1** a being deficient **2** *pl.* -cies a shortage

**deficiency disease** a disease caused by a lack of vitamins, minerals, etc. in the diet

**de·fi·cient** (dē fish'ənt) *adj.* [see DEFICIENCY] **1** lacking in some essential; incomplete **2** inadequate in amount

**def·i·cit** (def'ə sit) *n.* [L < *deficere*, to lack] the amount by which a sum of money is less than the required amount, as when there are more expenditures than income

**de·file**[1] (dē fīl′) *vt.* **-filed′, -fil′ing** [< OFr *defouler*, tread underfoot] **1** to make filthy **2** to profane; sully —**de·file′ment** *n.* —**de·fil′er** *n.*

**de·file**[2] (dē fīl′, dē′fīl′) *vi.* **-filed′, -fil′ing** [< Fr *dé-*, from + *fil*, thread] to march in single file —*n.* a narrow passage, valley, etc.

**de·fine** (dē fīn′) *vt.* **-fined′, -fin′ing** [< L *de-*, from + *finis*, boundary] **1** to determine the limits or nature of; describe exactly **2** to state the meaning of (a word, etc.) —**de·fin′er** *n.*

**def·i·nite** (def′ə nit) *adj.* [see prec.] **1** having exact limits **2** precise in meaning; explicit **3** certain; positive **4** *Gram.* limiting or specifying [“the” is the *definite* article] —**def′i·nite·ly** *adv.* —**def′i·nite·ness** *n.*

**def·i·ni′tion** (-nish′ən) *n.* **1** a defining or being defined **2** a statement of the meaning of a word **3** clarity of outline, sound, etc.

**de·fin·i·tive** (dē fin′ə tiv) *adj.* **1** conclusive; final **2** most nearly complete **3** serving to define

**de·flate** (dē flāt′) *vt., vi.* **-flat′ed, -flat′ing** [DE- + (IN)FLATE] **1** to collapse by letting out air or gas **2** to lessen in size, importance, etc. **3** to cause deflation of (currency, etc.)

**de·fla′tion** *n.* **1** a deflating **2** a reduction in prices resulting from severe economic decline

**de·flect** (dē flekt′) *vt., vi.* [< L *de-*, from + *flectere*, to bend] to turn or make go to one side —**de·flec′tion** *n.* —**de·flec′tive** *adj.* —**de·flec′tor** *n.*

**De·foe** (di fō′), **Daniel** 1660-1731; Eng. writer

**de·fog·ger** (dē fôg′ər) *n.* an apparatus for clearing condensed moisture, as from a car window

**de·fo·li·ant** (dē fō′lē ənt) *n.* a chemical substance that causes leaves to fall from growing plants

**de·fo·li·ate** (-āt′) *vt.* **-at′ed, -at′ing** [< L *de-*, from + *folium*, leaf] to strip (trees, etc.) of leaves —**de·fo′li·a′tion** *n.*

**de·form** (dē fôrm′) *vt.* [< L *de-*, from + *forma*, form] to impair the form of **2** to make ugly —**de·for·ma·tion** (dē′fôr mā′shən, def′ər-) *n.*

**de·formed′** *adj.* misshapen

**de·form′i·ty** *n., pl.* **-ties** **1** a deformed part, as of the body **2** ugliness or depravity

**de·fraud** (dē frôd′) *vt.* to take property, rights, etc. from by fraud; cheat —**de·fraud′er** *n.*

**de·fray** (dē frā′) *vt.* [Fr *défrayer*] to pay (the cost or expenses) —**de·fray′a·ble** *adj.* —**de·fray′al** *n.*

**de·frost** (dē frôst′) *vt., vi.* to rid or get rid of frost or ice —**de·frost′er** *n.*

**deft** (deft) *adj.* [see DAFT] skillful; dexterous —**deft′ly** *adv.*

**de·funct** (dē fuŋkt′) *adj.* [< L *defungi*, to finish] no longer existing; dead or extinct

**de·fuse** (dē fyōoz′) *vt.* **-fused′, -fus′ing** **1** to remove the fuse from (a bomb, etc.) **2** to make harmless, less tense, etc.

**de·fy** (dē fī′) *vt.* **-fied′, -fy′ing** [< LL *dis-*, from + *fidus*, faithful] **1** to resist or oppose boldly or openly **2** to dare to do or prove something

**de·gen·er·ate** (dē jen′ər it; *for v.*, -āt′) *adj.* [< L *de-*, from + *genus*, race] **1** having sunk below a former or normal condition, etc.; deteriorated **2** depraved —*n.* a degenerate person —*vi.* **-at′ed, -at′ing** to lose former normal or higher qualities —**de·gen′er·a·cy** (-ə sē) *n.* —**de·gen′er·a′tion** *n.* —**de·gen′er·a·tive** (-ə tiv, -āt′iv) *adj.*

**de·grad·a·ble** (dē grād′ə bəl) *adj.* capable of being degraded, esp. of being readily decomposed by chemicals, as some plastics

**de·grade** (dē grād′) *vt.* **-grad′ed, -grad′ing** [< L *de-*, down + *gradus*, a step] **1** to demote **2** to lower in quality, moral character, dignity, etc.; debase, dishonor, etc. —**deg·ra·da·tion** (deg′rə dā′shən) *n.*

**de·gree** (di grē′) *n.* [see prec.] **1** any of the successive steps in a process **2** social or official rank **3** extent, amount, or intensity **4** a rank given by a college or university to one who has completed a course of study, or to a distinguished person as an honor **5** a grade of comparison of adjectives and adverbs [the superlative *degree*] **6** *Law* the seriousness of a crime [murder in the first *degree*] **7** *Math.* a unit of measure for angles or arcs, one 360th of the circumference of a circle **8** *Physics* a unit of measure for temperature —**to a degree** somewhat

**de·greed′** (-grēd′) *adj.* having a college or university degree

**de·hu·man·ize** (dē hyōo′mə nīz′) *vt.* **-ized′, -iz′ing** to deprive of human qualities; make machinelike —**de·hu′man·i·za′tion** *n.*

**de·hu·mid·i·fy** (dē′hyōo mid′ə fī′) *vt.* **-fied′, -fy′ing** to remove moisture from (air, etc.) —**de′hu·mid′i·fi′er** *n.*

**de·hy·drate** (dē hī′drāt′) *vt.* **-drat′ed, -drat′ing** to remove water from (a substance, etc.); dry —*vi.* to lose water —**de′hy·dra′tion** *n.* —**de·hy′dra′tor** *n.*

**de-ice** (dē īs′) *vt.* **-iced′, -ic′ing** to melt ice from —**de-ic′er** *n.*

**de·i·fy** (dē′ə fī′) *vt.* **-fied′, -fy′ing** [< L *deus*, god + *facere*, make] **1** to make a god of **2** to look upon as a god —**de′i·fi·ca′tion** (-fi kā′shən) *n.*

**deign** (dān) *vi., vt.* [< L *dignus*, worthy] to condescend (to do or give)

**de·ism** (dē′iz′əm) *n.* [< L *deus*, god] the belief that God exists and created the world but takes no part in its functioning —**de′ist** *n.*

**de·i·ty** (dē′ə tē) *n.* [< L *deus*, god] **1** the state of being a god **2** *pl.* **-ties** a god or goddess —**the Deity** God

**dé·jà vu** (dā′zhə vōo′) [Fr, already seen] a feeling of having been in a place or experienced something before

**de·ject** (dē jekt′) *vt.* [< L *de-*, down + *jacere*, throw] to dishearten; depress —**de·ject′ed** *adj.* —**de·jec′tion** *n.*

**Del·a·ware** (del′ə wer′, -war′) state of the E U.S.: 1,955 sq. mi.; pop. 666,000; cap. Dover: abbrev. *DE* —**Del′a·war′e·an** *adj.*

**de·lay** (dē lā′) *vt.* [< OFr *de-*, intens. + *laier*, to leave] **1** to put off; postpone **2** to make late; detain —*vi.* to linger —*n.* **1** a delaying or being delayed **2** the time one is delayed

**de·lec·ta·ble** (dē lek′tə bəl) *adj.* [see DELIGHT] delightful or delicious

**de·lec·ta·tion** (dē′lek tā′shən) *n.* [see DELIGHT] delight; enjoyment

**del·e·gate** (del′ə git; *for v.*, -gāt′) *n.* [< L *de-*, from + *legare*, send] a person authorized to act for others; representative —*vt.* **-gat′ed, -gat′ing** **1** to appoint as a delegate **2** to entrust (authority, etc.) to another

**del·e·ga′tion** (-gā′shən) *n.* **1** a delegating or being delegated **2** a body of delegates

**de·lete** (dē lēt′) *vt.* **-let′ed, -let′ing** [< L *delere*, destroy] to take out (a word, etc.); cross out —**de·le′tion** *n.*

**del·e·te·ri·ous** (del′ə tir′ē əs) *adj.* [< Gr *dēleis-thai*, injure] harmful to health or well-being

**delft·ware** (delft′wer′) *n.* [after *Delft*, city in the Netherlands] glazed earthenware, usually blue and white: also **delft**

**Del·hi** (del′ē) city in N India: pop. 4,884,000: see also NEW DELHI

**del·i** (del′ē) *n. short for* DELICATESSEN

**de·lib·er·ate** (di lib′ər it; *for v.*, -āt′) *adj.* [< L *de-*, intens. + *librare*, weigh] **1** carefully thought out; premeditated **2** not rash or hasty **3** unhurried —*vi., vt.* **-at′ed, -at′ing** to consider carefully —**de·lib′er·ate·ly** *adv.* —**de·lib′er·a′tive** (-āt′iv, -ə tiv) *adj.*

**de·lib·er·a′tion** (-ā′shən) *n.* **1** a deliberating **2** [*often pl.*] consideration of alternatives **3** carefulness; slowness

**del·i·ca·cy** (del′i kə sē) *n., pl.* **-cies** **1** the quality of being delicate; fineness, weakness, sensitivity, etc. **2** a choice food

**del·i·cate** (-kit) *adj.* [< L *delicatus*, delightful] **1** pleasing in its lightness, mildness, etc. **2** beautifully fine in texture, workmanship, etc. **3** slight and subtle **4** easily damaged **5** frail in health **6**

*a*) needing careful handling *b*) showing tact, consideration, etc. **7** finely sensitive —**del'i·cate·ly** *adv.* —**del'i·cate·ness** *n.*

**del·i·ca·tes·sen** (del'i kə tes'ən) *n.* ⟦< Ger pl. < Fr *délicatesse*, delicacy⟧ **1** prepared cooked meats, fish, cheeses, salads, etc., collectively **2** a shop where such foods are sold

**de·li·cious** (di lish'əs) *adj.* ⟦see fol.⟧ **1** delightful **2** very pleasing to taste or smell —**de·li'cious·ly** *adv.* —**de·li'cious·ness** *n.*

**de·light** (di līt') *vt.* ⟦< L *de-*, from + *lacere*, entice⟧ to give great pleasure to —*vi.* **1** to give great pleasure **2** to be highly pleased; rejoice —*n.* **1** great pleasure **2** something giving great pleasure —**de·light'ed** *adj.*

**de·light'ful** *adj.* giving delight; very pleasing —**de·light'ful·ly** *adv.*

**De·li·lah** (di lī'lə) *n.* *Bible* the mistress and betrayer of Samson

**de·lim·it** (dē lim'it) *vt.* to fix the limits of —**de·lim'i·ta'tion** *n.*

**de·lin·e·ate** (di lin'ē āt') *vt.* **-at'ed, -at'ing** ⟦< L *de-*, from + *linea*, a line⟧ **1** to draw; sketch **2** to depict in words —**de·lin'e·a'tion** *n.*

**de·lin·quent** (di liŋ'kwənt) *adj.* ⟦< L *de-*, from + *linquere*, leave⟧ **1** failing to do what duty or law requires **2** overdue, as taxes —*n.* a delinquent person; esp., a juvenile delinquent —**de·lin'quen·cy,** *pl.* **-cies,** *n.* —**de·lin'quent·ly** *adv.*

**del·i·quesce** (del'i kwes') *vi.* **-quesced', -quesc'ing** ⟦< L < *de-*, from + *liquere*, be liquid⟧ to become liquid by absorbing moisture from the air —**del'i·ques'cent** *adj.*

**de·lir·i·ous** (di lir'ē əs) *adj.* **1** in a state of delirium **2** of or caused by delirium **3** wildly excited —**de·lir'i·ous·ly** *adv.* —**de·lir'i·ous·ness** *n.*

**de·lir·i·um** (-əm) *n.* ⟦< L *de-*, from + *lira*, a line⟧ **1** a temporary mental disturbance, as during a fever, marked by confused speech and hallucinations **2** uncontrollably wild excitement

**de·liv·er** (di liv'ər) *vt.* ⟦< L *de-*, intens. + *liber*, free⟧ **1** to set free or rescue **2** to assist at the birth of **3** to make (a speech, etc.) **4** to hand over **5** to distribute (mail, etc.) **6** to strike (a blow) **7** to throw (a ball, etc.) —*vi.* **1** to make deliveries **2** to produce, etc. something promised

**de·liv'er·ance** *n.* a freeing or being freed; rescue

**de·liv'er·y** *n.,* *pl.* **-ies 1** a handing over **2** a distributing, as of mail **3** a giving birth **4** any giving forth **5** the act or manner of delivering a speech, ball, etc. **6** something delivered

**dell** (del) *n.* ⟦OE *dell*⟧ a small, secluded valley or glen, usually wooded

**del·phin·i·um** (del fin'ē əm) *n.* ⟦< Gr *delphin*, dolphin⟧ a tall plant bearing spikes of flowers, usually blue

**del·ta** (del'tə) *n.* **1** the fourth letter of the Greek alphabet (Δ, δ) **2** a deposit of soil, usually triangular, formed at the mouth of a large river

**de·lude** (di lōōd') *vt.* **-lud'ed, -lud'ing** ⟦< L *de-*, from + *ludere*, to play⟧ to mislead; deceive

**del·uge** (del'yōōj') *n.* ⟦< L *dis*, off + *luere*, to wash⟧ **1** a great flood **2** a heavy rainfall **3** an overwhelming rush of anything —*vt.* **-uged', -ug'ing 1** to flood **2** to overwhelm

**de·lu·sion** (di lōō'zhən) *n.* **1** a deluding or being deluded **2** a false belief, specif. one that persists psychotically —**de·lu'sive** or **de·lu'sion·al** *adj.*

**de·luxe** (di luks', -lōōks') *adj.* ⟦Fr, of luxury⟧ of extra fine quality —*adv.* in a deluxe manner

**delve** (delv) *vi.* **delved, delv'ing** ⟦OE *delfan*⟧ **1** [Now Dial., Chiefly Brit.] to dig **2** to search (*into*) —**delv'er** *n.*

**Dem** *abbrev.* **1** Democrat **2** Democratic

**de·mag·net·ize** (dē mag'nə tīz') *vt.* **-ized', -iz'ing** to remove magnetism or magnetic properties from —**de·mag'net·i·za'tion** *n.*

**dem·a·gogue** or **dem·a·gog** (dem'ə gäg') *n.* ⟦< Gr *dēmos*, the people + *agōgos*, leader⟧ one who tries to stir up people's emotions in order to win them over and so gain power —**dem'a·gog'y** (-gä'jē, -gäg'ē) or **dem'a·gogu'er·y** (-gäg'ər ē) *n.*

**de·mand** (di mand') *vt.* ⟦L *de-*, from + *mandare*, entrust⟧ **1** to ask for boldly or urgently **2** to ask for as a right **3** to require; need —*vi.* to make a demand —*n.* **1** a demanding **2** a thing demanded **3** a strong request **4** an urgent requirement **5** *Economics* the desire for a commodity together with ability to pay for it; also, the amount people are ready to buy at a certain price —**in demand** wanted or sought —**on demand** when presented for payment

**de·mand'ing** *adj.* making difficult demands on one's patience, energy, etc.

**de·mar·ca·tion** (dē'mär kā'shən) *n.* ⟦< Sp *de-*, from + *marcar*, to mark⟧ **1** the act of setting and marking limits or boundaries **2** a limit or boundary

**de·mean**[1] (dē mēn') *vt.* ⟦DE- + MEAN[2]⟧ to degrade; humble

**de·mean**[2] (dē mēn') *vt.* ⟦see fol.⟧ to behave or conduct (oneself)

**de·mean·or** (di mēn'ər) *n.* ⟦< OFr *demener*, to lead⟧ outward behavior; conduct; deportment: Brit. sp. **demeanour**

**de·ment·ed** (dē ment'id) *adj.* ⟦see fol.⟧ mentally deranged; insane

**de·men·tia** (di men'shə) *n.* ⟦< L *de-*, out from + *mens*, the mind⟧ a disorder of the mind impairing perception, memory, etc.

**de·mer·it** (dē mer'it) *n.* ⟦< L *de-*, intens. + *merere*, to deserve, with *de-* taken as negative⟧ **1** a fault; defect **2** a mark recorded against a student, etc. for poor conduct or work

**de·mesne** (di mān', -mēn') *n.* ⟦see DOMAIN⟧ a region or domain

**De·me·ter** (di mēt'ər) *n.* *Gr. Myth.* the goddess of agriculture

**demi-** ⟦< L *dimidius*, half⟧ *prefix* **1** half **2** less than usual in size, power, etc. [*demigod*]

**dem·i·god** (dem'i gäd') *n.* **1** a minor deity **2** a godlike person

**dem'i·john'** (-jän') *n.* ⟦Fr *dame-jeanne*⟧ a large bottle of glass or earthenware in a wicker casing

**de·mil·i·ta·rize** (dē mil'ə tə rīz') *vt.* **-rized', -riz'ing** to free from organized military control

**dem·i·monde** (dem'i mänd') *n.* ⟦Fr < *demi-* + *monde*, world⟧ the class of women who have lost social standing because of sexual promiscuity

**de·mise** (dē mīz') *n.* ⟦< L *de-*, down + *mittere*, send⟧ **1** *Law* a transfer of an estate by lease **2** death —*vt.* **-mised', -mis'ing** to transfer (an estate) by lease

**dem·i·tasse** (dem'i täs', -tas') *n.* ⟦Fr < *demi-* + *tasse*, cup⟧ a small cup of or for after-dinner coffee

**dem·o** (dem'ō) *n.,* *pl.* **-os 1** a recording made to demonstrate a song, the talent of a performer, etc. **2** a product used in demonstrations

**de·mo·bi·lize** (dē mō'bə līz') *vt.* **-lized', -liz'ing** to disband (troops) —**de·mo'bi·li·za'tion** *n.*

**de·moc·ra·cy** (di mäk'rə sē) *n.,* *pl.* **-cies** ⟦< Gr *dēmos*, the people + *kratein*, to rule⟧ **1** government by the people, directly or through representatives **2** a country, etc. with such government **3** equality of rights, opportunity, and treatment

**dem·o·crat** (dem'ə krat') *n.* **1** one who supports or practices democracy **2** [D-] a Democratic Party member

**dem'o·crat'ic** *adj.* **1** of or for democracy **2** of or for all the people **3** not snobbish **4** [D-] of the Democratic Party —**dem'o·crat'i·cal·ly** *adv.*

**Democratic Party** one of the two major political parties in the U.S.

**de·mod·u·la·tion** (dē mä'jə lā'shən) *n.* *Radio* the recovery, at the receiver, of a signal that has been modulated on a carrier wave

**dem·o·graph·ics** (dem'ə graf'iks) *pl.n.* demographic characteristics of a population, as age, sex, or income, used for research, etc.

**de·mog·ra·phy** (di mä'grə fē) *n.* ⟦< Gr *dēmos*, people + -GRAPHY⟧ the statistical study of human populations —**de·mog′ra·pher** *n.* —**dem·o·graph·ic** (dem′ə graf′ik) *adj.* —**dem′o·graph′i·cal·ly** *adv.*

**de·mol·ish** (di mäl′ish) *vt.* ⟦< L *de*-, down + *moliri*, build⟧ **1** to pull down or smash **2** to destroy; ruin —**dem·o·li·tion** (dem′ə lish′ən) *n.*

**de·mon** (dē′mən) *n.* ⟦< L *daemon*⟧ **1** a devil; evil spirit **2** one regarded as evil, cruel, etc. **3** one with great energy, skill, etc. —**de·mon·ic** (di män′ik) *adj.* —**de·mon′i·cal·ly** *adv.*

**de·mon·e·tize** (dē män′ə tīz′) *vt.* -**tized′**, -**tiz′ing** to deprive (esp. currency) of its standard value

**de·mon·ize** (dē′mən īz′) *vt.* -**ized′**, -**iz′ing 1** to make into a demon **2** to characterize as evil, cruel, etc. —**de′mon·i·za′tion** *n.*

**de·mon·stra·ble** (di män′strə bəl) *adj.* that can be demonstrated, or proved —**de·mon′stra·bly** *adv.*

**dem·on·strate** (dem′ən strāt′) *vt.* -**strat′ed**, -**strat′ing** ⟦< L *de*-, from + *monstrare*, to show⟧ **1** to show by reasoning; prove **2** to explain by using examples, etc. **3** to show how something works — *vi.* to show feelings or views publicly by meetings, etc. —**dem′on·stra′tion** *n.* —**dem′on·stra′tor** *n.*

**de·mon·stra·tive** (di män′strə tiv) *adj.* **1** illustrative **2** giving proof (*of*) **3** showing feelings openly **4** *Gram.* pointing out [“this” is a *demonstrative* pronoun] —*n. Gram.* a demonstrative pronoun or adjective —**de·mon′stra·tive·ly** *adv.*

**de·mor·al·ize** (dē môr′ə līz′) *vt.* -**ized′**, -**iz′ing 1** to lower the morale of **2** to throw into confusion — **de·mor′al·i·za′tion** *n.*

**De·mos·the·nes** (di mäs′thə nēz′) 384-322 B.C.; Athenian orator

**de·mote** (dē mōt′) *vt.* -**mot′ed**, -**mot′ing** ⟦DE- + (PRO)MOTE⟧ to reduce to a lower rank —**de·mo′tion** *n.*

**de·mul·cent** (dē mul′sənt) *adj.* ⟦< L *de*-, down + *mulcere*, to stroke⟧ soothing —*n.* a soothing ointment

**de·mur** (dē mur′, di-) *vi.* -**murred′**, -**mur′ring** ⟦< L *de*-, from + *mora*, a delay⟧ to hesitate, as because of doubts; have scruples; object —*n.* a demurring: also **de·mur′ral**

**de·mure** (di myoor′) *adj.* ⟦< ME *de*- (prob. intens.) + OFr *mëur*, mature⟧ **1** modest or reserved **2** affectedly modest; coy —**de·mure′ly** *adv.*

**de·mur·rage** (di mur′ij) *n.* **1** the compensation payable for delaying a vehicle or vessel carrying freight, as by failure to load or unload **2** the delay itself

**de·mur·rer** (di mur′ər) *n.* ⟦see DEMUR⟧ **1** a plea for dismissal of a lawsuit because statements supporting a claim are defective **2** an objection

**den** (den) *n.* ⟦OE *denn*⟧ **1** the lair of a wild animal **2** a haunt, as of thieves **3** a small, cozy room where a person can be alone to read, work, etc.

**de·na·ture** (dē nā′chər) *vt.* -**tured**, -**tur·ing 1** to change the nature of **2** to make (alcohol) unfit to drink

**den·drite** (den′drīt′) *n.* ⟦< Gr *dendron*, tree⟧ the part of a nerve cell that carries impulses toward the cell body

**Deng Xiao·ping** (duŋ′ shou′piŋ′) 1904-97; Chin. Communist leader; held various official titles (1967-89); China’s de facto ruler (c. 1981-97)

**de·ni·al** (dē nī′əl) *n.* **1** a denying; saying “no” (to a request, etc.) **2** a contradiction **3** a refusal to believe or accept (a doctrine, etc.) **4** SELF-DENIAL

**de·nier**[1] (den′yər) *n.* ⟦< L *deni*, by tens⟧ a unit of weight for measuring the fineness of threads of silk, nylon, etc.

**de·ni·er**[2] (dē nī′ər) *n.* one who denies

**den·i·grate** (den′ə grāt′) *vt.* -**grat′ed**, -**grat′ing** ⟦< L < *de*-, entirely + *nigrare*, blacken⟧ to belittle the character of; defame —**den′i·gra′tion** *n.*

**den·im** (den′im) *n.* ⟦< Fr (*serge*) *de Nîmes*, (serge) of Nîmes, town in France⟧ a coarse, twilled cotton cloth

**den·i·zen** (den′ə zən) *n.* ⟦< L *de intus*, from within⟧ an inhabitant or frequenter of a particular place

**Den·mark** (den′märk′) country in Europe, on a peninsula & several islands in the North & Baltic seas: 16,631 sq. mi.; pop. 4,938,000

**de·nom·i·nate** (dē näm′ə nāt′) *vt.* -**nat′ed**, -**nat′ing** ⟦< L *de*-, intens. + *nominare*, to name⟧ to name; call

**de·nom′i·na′tion** (-nā′shən) *n.* **1** the act of naming **2** a name **3** a class or kind, as of coins, having a specific name or value **4** a particular religious body

**de·nom′i·na′tion·al** *adj.* of, or under the control of, a religious denomination

**de·nom′i·na′tor** (-nāt′ər) *n.* **1** a shared characteristic **2** *Math.* the term below the line in a fraction

**de·note** (dē nōt′) *vt.* -**not′ed**, -**not′ing** ⟦< L *de*-, down + *notare*, to mark⟧ **1** to indicate **2** to signify; mean —**de·no·ta·tion** (dē′nō tā′shən) *n.*

**de·noue·ment** or **dé·noue·ment** (dā′nōō män′) *n.* ⟦Fr⟧ the outcome or unraveling of a plot in a drama, story, etc.

**de·nounce** (dē nouns′) *vt.* -**nounced′**, -**nounc′ing** ⟦see DENUNCIATION⟧ **1** to accuse publicly; inform against **2** to condemn strongly and usually publicly —**de·nounce′ment** *n.*

**dense** (dens) *adj.* **dens′er**, **dens′est** ⟦< L *densus*, compact⟧ **1** packed tightly together **2** difficult to get through, penetrate, etc. **3** stupid —**dense′ly** *adv.* —**dense′ness** *n.*

**den·si·ty** (den′sə tē) *n., pl.* -**ties 1** a dense condition **2** stupidity **3** number per unit, as of area [population *density*] **4** ratio of the mass of an object to its volume

**dent** (dent) *n.* ⟦ME, var. of DINT⟧ **1** a slight hollow made in a surface by a blow **2** a noticeable effect —*vt., vi.* to make or receive a dent (in)

**den·tal** (dent′l) *adj.* ⟦< L *dens*, tooth⟧ of or for the teeth or dentistry

**dental floss** thread for removing food particles from between the teeth

**den·ti·frice** (den′tə fris) *n.* ⟦< L *dens*, tooth + *fricare*, rub⟧ any preparation for cleaning teeth

**den·tin** (den′tin) *n.* ⟦see DENTAL⟧ the hard tissue under the enamel of a tooth: also **den′tine′** (-tēn′, -tin)

**den·tist** (den′tist) *n.* one whose profession is the care and repair of teeth —**den′tist·ry** *n.*

**den·ti·tion** (den tish′ən) *n.* the arrangement of teeth in the mouth

**den·ture** (den′chər) *n.* ⟦see DENTAL⟧ [*often pl.*] a set of artificial teeth

**de·nu·cle·ar·ize** (dē nōō′klē ər īz′) *vt.* -**ized′**, -**iz′ing** to prohibit the possession of nuclear weapons in

**de·nude** (dē nōōd′) *vt.* -**nud′ed**, -**nud′ing** ⟦< L *de*-, off + *nudare*, to strip⟧ to make bare or naked; strip

**de·nun·ci·a·tion** (dē nun′sē ā′shən) *n.* ⟦< L *de*-, intens. + *nuntiare*, announce⟧ the act of denouncing

**Den·ver** (den′vər) capital of Colorado: pop. 468,000

**de·ny** (dē nī′) *vt.* -**nied′**, -**ny′ing** ⟦< L *de*-, intens. + *negare*, to deny⟧ **1** to declare (a statement) untrue **2** to refuse to accept as true or right **3** to repudiate **4** to refuse to grant or give **5** to refuse the request of

**de·o·dor·ant** (dē ō′dər ənt) *adj.* that can counteract undesired odors —*n.* any deodorant preparation, esp. one for use on the body

**de·o′dor·ize** (-dər īz′) *vt.* -**ized′**, -**iz′ing** to counteract the odor of —**de·o′dor·iz′er** *n.*

**de·part** (dē pärt′) *vi.* ⟦< L *dis*-, apart + *partire*, divide⟧ **1** to go away; leave or set out **2** to die **3** to deviate (*from*) —*vt.* to leave

**de·part′ed** *adj.* **1** gone away **2** dead —**the departed** the dead

**de·part·ment** (dē pärt′mənt) *n.* **1** a separate

part or division, as of a business **2** a field of activity —**de'part·men'tal** (-ment′'l) *adj.*

**de·part·men·tal·ize** (-men′t'l īz′) *vt.* **-ized′, -iz′ing** to organize into departments —**de·part·men'tal·i·za'tion** *n.*

**department store** a large retail store for the sale of many kinds of goods arranged in departments

**de·par·ture** (dē pär′chər) *n.* **1** a departing **2** a starting out, as on a trip **3** a deviation (*from*)

**de·pend** (dē pend′) *vi.* ⟦< L *de-*, down + *pendere*, to hang⟧ **1** to be determined by something else; be contingent (*on*) **2** to have trust; rely (*on*) **3** to rely (*on*) for support or aid

**de·pend'a·ble** *adj.* trustworthy; reliable —**de·pend'a·bil'i·ty** *n.* —**de·pend'a·bly** *adv.*

**de·pend'ence** *n.* **1** a being dependent **2** reliance (*on*) for support or aid **3** reliance; trust **4** DEPENDENCY (sense 4)

**de·pend'en·cy** *n.*, *pl.* **-cies 1** dependence **2** something dependent **3** a territory, as a possession, subordinate to its governing country **4** addiction to alcohol or drugs

**de·pend'ent** *adj.* **1** hanging down **2** determined by something else **3** relying (*on*) for support, etc. **4** subordinate **5** addicted —*n.* one relying on another for support, etc. Also **de·pend'ant** —**de·pend'ent·ly** *adv.*

**dependent clause** *Gram.* a clause that cannot function as a complete sentence by itself

**de·pict** (dē pikt′) *vt.* ⟦< L *de-*, intens. + *pingere*, to paint⟧ **1** to represent by drawing, painting, etc. **2** to describe —**de·pic'tion** *n.*

**de·pil·a·to·ry** (di pil′ə tôr′ē) *adj.* ⟦< L *de-*, from + *pilus*, hair⟧ serving to remove unwanted hair —*n.*, *pl.* **-ries** a depilatory substance or device

**de·plane** (dē plān′) *vi.* **-planed′, -plan'ing** to get out of an airplane after it lands

**de·plete** (dē plēt′) *vt.* **-plet'ed, -plet'ing** ⟦< L *de-*, from + *plere*, fill⟧ **1** to use up (funds, etc.) **2** to use up the resources, etc. of —**de·ple'tion** *n.*

**de·plor·a·ble** (dē plôr′ə bəl) *adj.* regrettable, very bad, wretched, etc.

**de·plore** (dē plôr′) *vt.* **-plored′, -plor'ing** ⟦< L *de-*, intens. + *plorare*, weep⟧ **1** to be sorry about **2** to disapprove of

**de·ploy** (dē ploi′) *vt.* ⟦< L *dis-*, apart + *plicare*, to fold⟧ to spread out or position (troops, equipment, etc.) according to a plan —*vi.* to be deployed —**de·ploy'ment** *n.*

**de·po·lar·ize** (dē pō′lər īz′) *vt.* **-ized′, -iz'ing** to destroy or counteract the polarization of —**de·po'lar·i·za'tion** *n.*

**de·po·lit·i·cize** (dē pō′lit′ə sīz′) *vt.* **-cized′, -ciz'ing** to remove from political influence

**de·po·nent** (dē pōn′ənt) *n.* ⟦< L *de-*, down + *ponere*, put⟧ *Law* one who makes a deposition

**de·pop·u·late** (dē päp′yə lāt′) *vt.* **-lat'ed, -lat'ing** to reduce the population of —**de·pop'u·la'tion** *n.*

**de·port** (dē pôrt′) *vt.* ⟦< L *de-*, from + *portare*, carry⟧ **1** to conduct (oneself) in a specified way **2** to expel (an alien) —**de·por·ta'tion** *n.*

**de·port'ment** *n.* conduct; behavior

**de·pose** (dē pōz′) *vt.* **-posed′, -pos'ing** ⟦< OFr *de-*, from + *poser*, cease⟧ **1** to remove from office **2** *Law* to take the deposition of

**de·pos·it** (dē päz′it) *vt.* ⟦< L *de-*, down + *ponere*, put⟧ **1** to place (money, etc.) for safekeeping, as in a bank **2** to give as a pledge or partial payment **3** to put or set down **4** to cause (sediment, etc.) to settle —*n.* **1** something placed for safekeeping, as money in a bank **2** a pledge or partial payment **3** a natural accumulation, as of minerals —**de·pos'i·tor** *n.*

**dep·o·si·tion** (dep′ə zish′ən) *n.* **1** a deposing or being deposed, as from office **2** something deposited **3** *Law* testimony made under oath that is written down for later use

**de·pos·i·to·ry** (dē päz′ə tôr′ē) *n.*, *pl.* **-ries** a place where things are put for safekeeping

**de·pot** (dē′pō; *military & Brit* dep′ō) *n.* ⟦< Fr: see

DEPOSIT⟧ **1** a warehouse **2** a railroad or bus station **3** a storage place for military supplies

**de·prave** (dē prāv′) *vt.* **-praved′, -prav'ing** ⟦< L *de-*, intens. + *pravus*, crooked⟧ to make morally bad; corrupt —**de·praved'** *adj.* —**de·prav'i·ty** (-prav′ə tē), *pl.* **-ties,** *n.*

**dep·re·cate** (dep′rə kāt′) *vt.* **-cat'ed, -cat'ing** ⟦< L *de-*, off + *precari*, pray⟧ **1** to express disapproval of **2** to belittle —**dep're·ca'tion** *n.* —**dep're·ca·to'ry** (-kə tôr′ē) *adj.*

**de·pre·ci·ate** (dē prē′shē āt′) *vt.*, *vi.* **-at'ed, -at'ing** ⟦< L *de-*, from + *pretium*, price⟧ **1** to lessen in value or price **2** to belittle —**de·pre'ci·a'tion** *n.*

**dep·re·da·tion** (dep′rə dā′shən) *n.* ⟦< L *de-*, intens. + *praedari*, to plunder⟧ a robbing or plundering

**de·press** (dē pres′) *vt.* ⟦< L *de-*, down + *premere*, to press⟧ **1** to press down **2** to sadden or discourage **3** to weaken or make less active **4** to lower in value, price, etc. —**de·pressed'** *adj.*

**de·pres'sant** *n.* a medicine, drug, etc. that lessens nervous activity

**de·pres·sion** (dē presh′ən) *n.* **1** a depressing or being depressed **2** a hollow or low place **3** low spirits; dejection **4** a condition marked by hopelessness, self-doubt, lethargy, etc. **5** a decrease in force, activity, etc. **6** a period of reduced business, much unemployment, etc.

**de·pres·sive** (dē pres′iv) *adj.* **1** tending to depress **2** characterized by psychological depression —*n.* one suffering from psychological depression

**de·pres·sur·ize** (dē presh′ər īz′) *vt.* **-ized′, -iz'ing** to reduce pressure in

**de·prive** (dē prīv′) *vt.* **-prived′, -priv'ing** ⟦< L *de-*, intens. + *privare*, to separate⟧ **1** to take away from forcibly **2** to keep from having, etc. —**dep·ri·va·tion** (dep′rə vā′shən) *n.*

**de·pro·gram** (dē prō′gram′, -grəm) *vt.* **-grammed′** or **-gramed′, -gram'ming** or **-gram'ing** to cause to abandon rigidly held beliefs, etc. by undoing the effects of indoctrination

**dept** *abbrev.* **1** department **2** deputy

**depth** (depth) *n.* ⟦< ME *dep*, deep + -TH¹⟧ **1** the distance from the top downward, or from front to back **2** deepness **3** intensity **4** profundity of thought **5** [*usually pl.*] the deepest or inmost part —**in depth** comprehensively

**dep·u·ta·tion** (dep′yōō tā′shən) *n.* **1** a deputing **2** a delegation

**de·pute** (dē pyōōt′) *vt.* **-put'ed, -put'ing** ⟦< L *de-*, from + *putare*, cleanse⟧ **1** to give (authority, etc.) to a deputy **2** to appoint as one's substitute, etc.

**dep·u·tize** (dep′yōō tīz′) *vt.* **-tized′, -tiz'ing** to appoint as deputy

**dep·u·ty** (dep′yōō tē) *n.*, *pl.* **-ties** a person appointed to act as a substitute or assistant

**de·rail** (dē rāl′) *vt.*, *vi.* to run off the rails, as a train —**de·rail'ment** *n.*

**de·rail·leur** (də rāl′ər) *n.* [Fr] a gear-shifting mechanism on a bicycle for shifting the sprocket chain from one size of sprocket wheel to another

**de·range** (dē rānj′) *vt.* **-ranged′, -rang'ing** ⟦< OFr *des-*, apart + *rengier*, to range⟧ **1** to upset or disturb **2** to make insane —**de·range'ment** *n.*

**Der·by** (dur′bē; *Brit* där′-) *n.*, *pl.* **-bies 1** ⟦after an Earl of *Derby*, who founded the race held in England⟧ any of various horse races, as ones held annually in England, Kentucky, etc. **2** [d-] any of various contests or races, open to anyone **3** [d-] a stiff felt hat with a round crown

**de·reg·u·late** (dē reg′yə lāt′) *vt.* **-lat'ed, -lat'ing** to remove regulations governing —**de·reg'u·la'tion** *n.*

**der·e·lict** (der′ə likt′) *adj.* ⟦< L *de-*, intens. + *relinquere*: see RELINQUISH⟧ **1** deserted by the owner; abandoned **2** negligent —*n.* **1** an abandoned ship on the open sea **2** a destitute and rejected person

**der·e·lic·tion** (-lik'shən) *n.* **1** a forsaking or being forsaken **2** a neglect of, or failure in, duty

**de·ride** (di rīd') *vt.* -rid'ed, -rid'ing ⟦< L *de-*, down + *ridere*, to laugh⟧ to laugh at in scorn; ridicule — **de·ri·sion** (-rizh'ən) *n.* —**de·ri·sive** (-rī'siv) *adj.* — **de·ri·sive·ly** *adv.*

**der·i·va·tion** (der'ə vā'shən) *n.* **1** a deriving or being derived **2** the source or origin of something, specif. of a word

**de·riv·a·tive** (də riv'ə tiv) *adj.* derived; specif., not original or novel —*n.* something derived

**de·rive** (di rīv') *vt.* -rived', -riv'ing ⟦< L *de-*, from + *rivus*, a stream⟧ **1** to get or receive (something) *from* a source **2** to deduce or infer **3** to trace from or to a source —*vi.* to come (*from*)

**der·ma·bra·sion** (dur'mə brā'zhən) *n.* ⟦DERM(IS) + ABRASION⟧ the surgical procedure of scraping off upper layers of the skin with an abrasive device, to remove acne scars, blemishes, etc.

**der·ma·ti·tis** (dur'mə tīt'is) *n.* ⟦< Gr *derma*, skin + -ITIS⟧ inflammation of the skin

**der·ma·tol·o·gy** (dur'mə täl'ə jē) *n.* ⟦< Gr *derma*, skin + -LOGY⟧ the branch of medicine dealing with the skin —**der'ma·tol'o·gist** *n.*

**der·mis** (dur'mis) *n.* ⟦see EPIDERMIS⟧ the layer of skin just below the epidermis

**der·o·gate** (der'ə gāt') *vi.*, *vt.* -gat'ed, -gat'ing ⟦< L *de-*, from + *rogare*, ask⟧ to detract (*from*) or disparage —**der'o·ga'tion** *n.*

**de·rog·a·to·ry** (di räg'ə tôr'ē) *adj.* ⟦see prec.⟧ disparaging; belittling —**de·rog'a·to'ri·ly** *adv.*

**der·rick** (der'ik) *n.* ⟦after Thos. *Derrick*, London hangman of the early 17th c.: orig. applied to a gallows⟧ **1** a pivoted beam for lifting and moving heavy objects **2** a tall framework, as over an oil well, to support drilling machinery, etc.

**der·ri·ère** (der'ē er') *n.* ⟦Fr, back part⟧ the buttocks

**der·rin·ger** (der'in jər) *n.* ⟦after H. *Deringer*, 19th-c. U.S. gunsmith⟧ a small, short-barreled pistol

**der·vish** (dur'vish) *n.* ⟦< Pers *darvēsh*, beggar⟧ a member of any of various Muslim ascetic religious groups

DERRICK (sense 2)

**de·sal·i·na·tion** (dē'sal'ə nā'shən) *n.* ⟦DE- + SALIN(E) + -ATION⟧ the removal of salt, esp. from sea water to make it drinkable —**de·sal'i·nate'**, -nat'ed, -nat'ing, *vt.*

**Des·cartes** (dā kärt'), **Re·né** (rə nā') 1596-1650; Fr. philosopher

**de·scend** (dē send') *vi.* ⟦< L *de-*, down + *scandere*, climb⟧ **1** to move down to a lower place **2** to pass from an earlier to a later time, from greater to less, etc. **3** to slope downward **4** to come down (*from* a source) **5** to lower oneself or stoop (*to*) **6** to make a sudden raid (*on* or *upon*) —*vt.* to move down along

**de·scend·ant** (-sen'dənt) *n.* an offspring of a certain ancestor, family, group, etc.

**de·scent'** (-sent') *n.* **1** a coming down or going down **2** ancestry **3** a downward slope **4** a way down **5** a sudden attack (*on* or *upon*) —*vt.* to move down along

**de·scribe** (di skrīb') *vt.* -scribed', -scrib'ing ⟦< L *de-*, from + *scribere*, write⟧ **1** to tell or write about **2** to trace the outline of —**de·scrib'er** *n.*

**de·scrip·tion** (di skrip'shən) *n.* **1** the act or technique of describing **2** a statement or passage that describes **3** sort; kind ⟦books of every *description*⟧ **4** a tracing or outlining —**de·scrip'tive** *adj.*

**de·scry** (di skrī') *vt.* -scried', -scry'ing ⟦< OFr *descrier*, proclaim⟧ **1** to catch sight of; discern **2** to detect

**des·e·crate** (des'i krāt') *vt.* -crat'ed, -crat'ing ⟦DE- (sense 4) + (CON)SECRATE⟧ to violate the sacredness of; profane —**des'e·cra'tion** *n.*

**de·seg·re·gate** (dē seg'rə gāt') *vt.*, *vi.* -gat'ed, -gat'ing to abolish racial segregation in (public schools, etc.) —**de·seg're·ga'tion** *n.*

**de·sen·si·tize** (dē sen'sə tīz') *vt.* -tized', -tiz'ing to make less sensitive, as to an allergen

**de·sert¹** (di zurt') *vt.*, *vi.* ⟦< L *de-*, from + *serere*, join⟧ **1** to abandon; forsake **2** to leave (one's military post, etc.) without permission and with no intent to return —**de·sert'er** *n.* —**de·ser'tion** (-zur'shən) *n.*

**des·ert²** (dez'ərt) *n.* ⟦see prec.⟧ **1** an uninhabited region; wilderness **2** a dry, barren, sandy region, often one that is hot —*adj.* wild and uninhabited ⟦a *desert* island⟧

**de·sert³** (di zurt') *n.* ⟦see fol.⟧ [often *pl.*] deserved reward or punishment ⟦one's just *deserts*⟧

**de·serve** (di zurv') *vt.*, *vi.* -served', -serv'ing ⟦< L *de-*, intens. + *servire*, serve⟧ to be worthy (of); merit —**de·served'·ly** (-zur'vid lē) *adv.*

**des·ic·cate** (des'i kāt') *vt.*, *vi.* -cat'ed, -cat'ing ⟦< L *de-*, intens. + *siccus*, dry⟧ to dry out completely — **des'ic·ca'tion** *n.*

**de·sid·er·a·tum** (di sid'ə rät'əm) *n.*, *pl.* -ta (-ə) ⟦see DESIRE⟧ something needed and wanted

**de·sign** (di zīn') *vt.* ⟦< L *de-*, out + *signum*, a mark⟧ **1** to sketch an outline for; plan **2** to contrive **3** to intend —*vi.* to make original plans, etc. —*n.* **1** a plan; scheme **2** purpose; aim **3** a working plan; pattern **4** arrangement of parts, form, color, etc. —**by design** purposely —**de·sign'er** *n.*

**des·ig·nate** (dez'ig nāt') *vt.* -nat'ed, -nat'ing ⟦see prec.⟧ **1** to point out; specify **2** to name **3** to appoint —**des'ig·na'tion** *n.*

**designated driver** the one in a group who refrains from drinking alcoholic beverages so as to be able to safely transport the others in a motor vehicle

**de·sign·ing** *adj.* scheming; crafty —*n.* the art of creating designs, etc.

**de·sir·a·ble** (di zir'ə bəl) *adj.* **1** worth having **2** arousing desire —**de·sir·a·bil'i·ty** *n.* —**de·sir'a·bly** *adv.*

**de·sire** (di zīr') *vt.* -sired', -sir'ing ⟦< L *desiderare*⟧ **1** to long for; crave **2** to ask for —*vi.* to have a desire —*n.* **1** a wish; craving **2** sexual appetite **3** a request **4** a thing desired —**de·sir'ous** *adj.*

**de·sist** (di zist', -sist') *vi.* ⟦< L *de-*, from + *stare*, stand⟧ to cease; stop

**desk** (desk) *n.* ⟦< ML *desca*, table⟧ a piece of furniture with a flat surface for writing, etc. —*adj.* of, for, or at a desk ⟦a *desk* job⟧

**desk'top'** *n.*, *adj.* (equipment, as a microcomputer) for use on a desk or table

**desk·top publishing** the production of printed matter by means of a microcomputer and special software for laying out text and illustrations

**Des Moines** (də moin') capital of Iowa: pop. 193,000

**des·o·late** (des'ə lit; *for v.*, -lāt') *adj.* ⟦< L *de-*, intens. + *solus*, alone⟧ **1** lonely; solitary **2** uninhabited **3** laid waste **4** forlorn —*vt.* -lat'ed, -lat'ing **1** to rid of inhabitants **2** to lay waste **3** to make forlorn

**des·o·la·tion** *n.* **1** a making desolate **2** a desolate condition or place **3** misery **4** loneliness

**de·spair** (di sper') *vi.* ⟦< L *de-*, without + *sperare*, to hope⟧ to lose hope —*n.* **1** loss of hope **2** a person or thing causing despair

**des·patch** (di spach') *vt.*, *n.* DISPATCH

**des·per·a·do** (des'pər ä'dō, -ä'-) *n.*, *pl.* -does or -dos ⟦< 17th-c. Sp < L *desperare*: see DESPAIR⟧ a dangerous criminal; bold outlaw

**des·per·ate** (des'pər it) *adj.* **1** rash or violent because of despair **2** having a very great need **3** very serious, dangerous, etc. **4** drastic —**des'per·ate·ly** *adv.*

**des·per·a·tion** (des'pər ä'shən) *n.* **1** the state of being desperate **2** recklessness resulting from despair

**des·pi·ca·ble** (di spik'ə bəl) *adj.* deserving scorn; contemptible

**de·spise** (di spīz′) *vt.* -**spised′, -spis′ing** ⟦< L *de-*, down + *specere*, look at⟧ 1 to scorn 2 to loathe

**de·spite** (di spīt′) *prep.* ⟦see prec.⟧ in spite of; notwithstanding

**de·spoil** (dē spoil′) *vt.* ⟦< L *de-*, intens. + *spoliare*, to strip⟧ to rob; plunder —**de·spo·li·a·tion** (di spō′ lē ā′shən) *n.*

**de·spond·en·cy** (di spän′dən sē) *n.* ⟦< L *de-*, from + *spondere*, to promise⟧ loss of hope; dejection: also **de·spond′ence** —**de·spond′ent** *adj.*

**des·pot** (des′pət) *n.* ⟦< Gr *despotēs*, a master⟧ 1 an absolute ruler 2 anyone like a tyrant —**des·pot′ic** (-pät′ik) *adj.* —**des′pot·ism′** (-pə tiz′əm) *n.*

**des·sert** (di zurt′) *n.* ⟦< L *de*, from + *servire*, serve⟧ the final course of a meal, typically cake, pie, etc.

**des·ti·na·tion** (des′tə nā′shən) *n.* the place toward which one is going or sent

**des·tine** (des′tin) *vt.* -**tined, -tin·ing** ⟦< L *de-*, intens. + *stare*, to stand⟧ 1 to predetermine, as by fate 2 to intend —**destined for** 1 headed for 2 intended for

**des·ti·ny** (des′tə nē) *n.*, *pl.* -**nies** 1 the seemingly inevitable succession of events 2 (one's) fate

**des·ti·tute** (des′tə tōōt′) *adj.* ⟦< L *de-*, down + *statuere*, to set⟧ 1 lacking: with *of* 2 totally impoverished —**des′ti·tu′tion** *n.*

**de·stroy** (di stroi′) *vt.* ⟦< L *de-*, down + *struere*, to build⟧ 1 to tear down; demolish 2 to ruin 3 to do away with 4 to kill

**de·stroy′er** *n.* 1 one that destroys 2 a small, fast warship

**de·struct** (di strukt′, dē′strukt′) *vi.* ⟦< fol.⟧ to be automatically destroyed

**de·struc·tion** (di struk′shən) *n.* 1 a destroying or being destroyed 2 the cause or means of destroying —**de·struc′tive** *adj.* —**de·struc′tive·ly** *adv.* —**de·struc′tive·ness** *n.*

**des·ue·tude** (des′wi tōōd′) *n.* ⟦< L *de-*, from + *suescere*, be accustomed⟧ disuse

**des·ul·to·ry** (des′əl tôr′ē) *adj.* ⟦< L *de-*, from + *salire*, to leap⟧ 1 aimless; disconnected 2 random

**de·tach** (dē tach′) *vt.* ⟦< Fr: see DE- & ATTACH⟧ 1 to unfasten and remove; disconnect; disengage 2 to send (troops, etc.) on a special mission —**de·tach′a·ble** *adj.*

**de·tached′** *adj.* 1 not connected 2 aloof; disinterested; impartial

**de·tach′ment** *n.* 1 a detaching 2 a unit of troops, etc. on a special mission 3 impartiality or aloofness

**de·tail** (di tāl′, dē′tāl′) *n.* ⟦< Fr < *dé-*, from + *tailler*, to cut⟧ 1 a dealing with things item by item 2 a minute account *[to go into detail]* 3 a small part; item 4 *a)* one or more soldiers, etc. on special duty *b)* the duty —*vt.* 1 to tell, item by item 2 to assign to special duty —**in detail** with particulars

**de·tain** (dē tān′) *vt.* ⟦< L *de-*, off + *tenere*, to hold⟧ 1 to keep in custody; confine 2 to keep from going on —**de·tain′ee′** (-ē′) *n.* —**de·tain′ment** *n.*

**de·tect** (dē tekt′) *vt.* ⟦< L *de-*, from + *tegere*, to cover⟧ to discover (something hidden, not clear, etc.) —**de·tect′a·ble** or **de·tect′i·ble** *adj.* —**de·tec′tion** *n.* —**de·tec′tor** *n.*

**de·tec′tive** (-tek′tiv) *n.* one whose work is to investigate crimes, uncover evidence, etc.

**dé·tente** or **de·tente** (dā tänt′) *n.* ⟦Fr⟧ a lessening of tension, esp. between nations

**de·ten·tion** (dē ten′shən) *n.* 1 a detaining or being detained 2 the punishment of having to stay after school

**detention home** a place where juvenile offenders are held in custody

**de·ter** (dē tur′) *vt.* -**terred′, -ter′ring** ⟦< L *de-*, from + *terrere*, frighten⟧ to keep or discourage (a person or group) from doing something through fear, doubt, etc. —**de·ter′ment** *n.* —**de·ter′rence** *n.*

**de·ter·gent** (dē tur′jənt) *adj.* ⟦< L *de-*, off +

*tergere*, wipe⟧ cleansing —*n.* cleansing substance that emulsifies dirt and oil

**de·te·ri·o·rate** (dē tir′ē ə rāt′) *vt.*, *vi.* -**rat′ed, -rat′ing** ⟦< L *deterior*, worse⟧ to make or become worse —**de·te′ri·o·ra′tion** *n.*

**de·ter·mi·nant** (dē tur′mi nənt) *n.* a thing or factor that determines

**de·ter′mi·nate** (-nit) *adj.* clearly determined; fixed; settled

**de·ter′mi·na′tion** (-nā′shən) *n.* 1 a determining or being determined 2 a firm intention 3 firmness of purpose

**de·ter′mine** (-mən) *vt.* -**mined, -min·ing** ⟦< L *de-*, from + *terminus*, a limit⟧ 1 to set limits to 2 to settle conclusively 3 to decide or decide upon 4 to affect the nature or quality of 5 to find out exactly —*vi.* to decide —**de·ter′mi·na·ble** *adj.*

**de·ter′mined** (-mənd) *adj.* 1 having one's mind made up 2 resolute; firm

**de·ter′rent** *adj.* deterring —*n.* something that deters

**de·test** (dē test′) *vt.* ⟦< L *detestari*, to curse by the gods⟧ to dislike intensely; hate —**de·test′a·ble** *adj.* —**de·tes·ta′tion** (-tes tā′shən) *n.*

**de·thatch** (dē thach′) *vt.* to remove the thatch from (a lawn)

**de·throne** (dē thrōn′) *vt.* -**throned′, -thron′ing** to depose (a monarch)

**det·o·nate** (det′′n āt′) *vi.*, *vt.* -**nat′ed, -nat′ing** ⟦< L *de-*, intens. + *tonare*, to thunder⟧ to explode violently —**det′o·na′tion** *n.* —**det′o·na′tor** *n.*

**de·tour** (dē′toor′) *n.* ⟦< Fr: see DE- & TURN⟧ 1 a roundabout way 2 a substitute route —*vi.*, *vt.* to go or route on a detour

**de·tox** (dē täks′; *for n.* dē′täks′) [Inf.] *vt. short for* DETOXIFY —*n. short for* DETOXIFICATION

**de·tox·i·fy** (dē täk′si fī′) *vt.* -**fied′, -fy′ing** ⟦DE- + TOXI(N) + -FY⟧ 1 to remove a poison or poisonous effect from 2 to treat for drug or alcohol addiction —**de·tox′i·fi·ca′tion** *n.*

**de·tract** (dē trakt′) *vt.* ⟦< L *de-*, from + *trahere*, to draw⟧ to take away —*vi.* to take something desirable (*from*) —**de·trac′tion** *n.*

**de·trac′tor** (-trak′tər) *n.* one who disparages

**det·ri·ment** (de′trə mənt) *n.* ⟦< L *de-*, off + *terere*, to rub⟧ 1 damage; injury 2 anything that causes this —**det′ri·men′tal** (-men′təl) *adj.*

**de·tri·tus** (dē trīt′əs) *n.* ⟦L, a rubbing away: see prec.⟧ debris, specif. rock fragments

**De·troit** (di troit′) city & port in SE Michigan: pop. 1,028,000

**deuce** (dōōs) *n.* ⟦< L *duo*, two⟧ 1 a playing card or side of a die with two spots 2 *Tennis, Badminton, etc.* a tie score after which one side must score twice in a row to win

**deu·te·ri·um** (dōō tir′ē əm) *n.* ⟦< Gr *deuteros*, second⟧ a hydrogen isotope used in nuclear reactors

**Deu·ter·on·o·my** (dōōt′ər än′ə mē) *n.* ⟦< Gr *deuteros*, second + *nomos*, law⟧ the fifth book of the Pentateuch

**deutsche mark** (doich′ märk′) the monetary unit of Germany

**de·val·ue** (dē val′yōō) *vt.* -**ued, -u·ing** 1 to lessen the value of 2 to lower the exchange value of (a currency) —**de·val′u·a′tion** *n.*

**dev·as·tate** (dev′ə stāt′) *vt.* -**tat′ed, -tat′ing** ⟦< L *de-*, intens. + *vastus*, empty⟧ 1 to lay waste; ravage; destroy 2 to make helpless; overwhelm —**dev′as·ta′tion** *n.* —**dev′as·ta′tor** *n.*

**de·vel·op** (di vel′əp) *vt.* ⟦< OFr *des-*, apart + *voloper*, to wrap⟧ 1 to make fuller, bigger, better, etc. 2 to show or work out by degrees 3 to enlarge upon 4 *Photog.* to put (film, etc.) into chemicals to make the picture visible —*vi.* 1 to come into being or activity; occur 2 to become developed —**de·vel′op·er** *n.* —**de·vel′op·ment** *n.* —**de·vel′op·men′tal** (-ment′′l) *adj.*

**de·vi·ant** (dē′vē ənt) *adj.* deviating, esp. from what is considered normal —*n.* one whose behavior is deviant —**de′vi·ance** or **de′vi·an·cy** *n.*

**de·vi·ate** (dē′vē āt′; *for adj. & n.,* -it) *vi.* -at′ed, -at′ing ⟦< L *de*-, from + *via,* road⟧ to turn aside (*from* a course, standard, etc.); diverge —*adj.* DEVIANT —*n.* a deviant, esp. in sexual behavior — **de·vi·a′tion** *n.* —**de′vi·a′tor** *n.*

**de·vice** (di vīs′) *n.* ⟦see DEVISE⟧ 1 a thing devised; plan, scheme, or trick 2 a mechanical contrivance 3 an ornamental figure or design 4 an emblem, as on a coat of arms —**leave to one's own devices** to allow to do as one wishes

**dev·il** (dev′əl) *n.* ⟦ult. < Gr *diabolos,* slanderous⟧ 1 *Theol.* a) [*often* D-] the chief evil spirit; Satan (with *the*) b) any evil spirit; demon 2 a very wicked person 3 a person who is mischievous, reckless, unlucky, etc. 4 anything hard to operate, control, etc. —*vt.* -iled or -illed, -il·ing or -il·ling 1 to prepare (food) with hot seasoning 2 to annoy; tease —**dev′il·ish** *adj.*

**dev′il·fish** *n., pl.* -fish′ or (for different species) -fish′es MANTA

**dev′il-may-care′** *adj.* careless or reckless

**dev′il·ment** *n.* mischievous action

**devil's advocate** a person upholding the wrong side for argument's sake

**dev′il's-food′ cake** a rich chocolate cake

**dev′il·try** (-trē) *n., pl.* -tries reckless mischief

**de·vi·ous** (dē′vē əs) *adj.* ⟦< L *de*-, from + *via,* road⟧ 1 not direct; roundabout or deviating 2 not straightforward; dishonest —**de′vi·ous·ness** *n.*

**de·vise** (di vīz′) *vt., vi.* -vised′, -vis′ing ⟦< L *dividere,* to divide⟧ 1 to work out or create (a plan, device, etc.) 2 *Law* to bequeath (real property) by a will —*n. Law* a bequest of property

**de·vi·tal·ize** (dē vīt′'l īz′) *vt.* -ized′, -iz′ing to deprive of vitality

**de·void** (di void′) *adj.* ⟦see DE- & VOID⟧ completely without; empty (*of*)

**de·volve** (di välv′, -vôlv′) *vt., vi.* -volved′, -volv′ing ⟦< L *de*-, down + *volvere,* to roll⟧ 1 to pass (*on*) to another: said of duties, responsibilities, etc. 2 to degenerate —**dev·o·lu·tion** (dev′ə lōō′shən) *n.*

**de·vote** (di vōt′) *vt.* -vot′ed, -vot′ing ⟦< L *de*-, from + *vovere,* to vow⟧ to set apart for or give up to some purpose, activity, or person; dedicate

**de·vot′ed** (-id) *adj.* very loving, loyal, or faithful —**de·vot′ed·ly** *adv.*

**dev·o·tee** (dev′ə tē′, -tā′) *n.* one who is strongly devoted to something

**de·vo·tion** (di vō′shən) *n.* 1 a devoting or being devoted 2 piety 3 religious worship 4 [*often pl.*] one or more prayers, etc. 5 loyalty or deep affection —**de·vo′tion·al** *adj.*

**de·vour** (di vour′) *vt.* ⟦< L *de*-, intens. + *vorare,* swallow whole⟧ 1 to eat hungrily 2 to swallow up 3 to take in greedily, as with the eyes

**de·vout** (di vout′) *adj.* ⟦see DEVOTE⟧ 1 very religious; pious 2 earnest; sincere —**de·vout′ly** *adv.*

**dew** (dōō) *n.* ⟦OE *deaw*⟧ 1 atmospheric moisture condensed in drops on cool surfaces at night 2 anything refreshing, pure, etc., like dew —**dew′y,** -i·er, -i·est, *adj.*

**dew′ber′ry** *n., pl.* -ries 1 a trailing blackberry plant 2 its fruit

**dew′drop′** *n.* a drop of dew

**dew′lap′** *n.* ⟦see DEW & LAP¹⟧ loose skin under the throat of cattle, etc.

**dew point** the temperature at which water vapor in the air starts to condense into liquid

**dex·ter·i·ty** (deks ter′ə tē) *n.* ⟦see fol.⟧ skill in using one's hands, body, or mind

**dex·ter·ous** (deks′tər əs, -trəs) *adj.* ⟦< L *dexter,* right⟧ having or showing dexterity: also **dex′trous**

**dex·trose** (deks′trōs′) *n.* a glucose found in plants and animals

**Dhak·a** (däk′ə, dak′ə) capital of Bangladesh: pop. 3,459,000

**dho·ti** (dō′tē) *n.* ⟦Hindi *dhotī*⟧ a loincloth worn by Hindu men

**dhur·rie** or **dur·rie** (dur′ē, du′rē) *n.* a coarse rug woven in India

**di-**¹ ⟦Gr *di-* < *dis-,* twice⟧ *prefix* twice, double, twofold

**di-**² *prefix* DIS-

**di·a·be·tes** (dī′ə bēt′ēz′, -is) *n.* ⟦< Gr *diabainein,* to pass through⟧ a disease caused by an insulin deficiency and characterized by excess sugar in the blood and urine: also **sugar diabetes** —**di′a·bet′ic** (-bet′ik) *adj., n.*

**di·a·bol·ic** (dī′ə bäl′ik) *adj.* ⟦see DEVIL⟧ very wicked or cruel; fiendish: also **di′a·bol′i·cal**

**di·a·crit·i·cal mark** (dī′ə krit′i kəl) ⟦< Gr *dia-,* across + *krinein,* discern⟧ a mark, as a macron, put on a letter or symbol to show pronunciation, etc.: also **di′a·crit′ic** *n.*

**di·a·dem** (dī′ə dem′) *n.* ⟦< Gr *diadēma,* a band, fillet⟧ 1 a crown 2 an ornamental headband

**di·ag·nose** (dī′əg nōs′) *vt., vi.* -nosed′, -nos′ing to make a diagnosis (of)

**di′ag·no′sis** (-nō′sis) *n., pl.* -ses′ (-sēz′) ⟦< Gr *dia-,* through + *gignoskein,* to know⟧ 1 the act of deciding the nature of a disease, situation, problem, etc. by examination and analysis 2 the resulting decision —**di′ag·nos′tic** (-näs′tik) *adj.* —**di′ag·nos·ti′cian** (-tish′ən) *n.*

**di·ag·o·nal** (dī ag′ə nəl, -ag′nəl) *adj.* ⟦< Gr *dia-,* through + *gōnia,* an angle⟧ 1 extending slantingly between opposite corners 2 slanting; oblique —*n.* a diagonal line, plane, course, part, etc. —**di·ag′o·nal·ly** *adv.*

**di·a·gram** (dī′ə gram′) *n.* ⟦< Gr *dia-,* across + *graphein,* write⟧ a sketch, plan, graph, etc. that explains something, as by outlining its parts —*vt.* -gramed′ or -grammed′, -gram′ing or -gram′ming to make a diagram of

**di·al**¹ (dī′əl) *n.* ⟦< L *dies,* day⟧ 1 the face of a clock, etc. 2 the face of a meter, etc., for indicating, as by a pointer, an amount, direction, etc. 3 a graduated disk, strip, knob, etc., as on a radio or TV for tuning in stations, etc. 4 a rotating disk, or set of numbered push buttons, on a telephone, used to make automatic connections —*vt., vi.* -aled or -alled, -al·ing or -al·ling 1 to tune in (a radio station, etc.) 2 to call by using a telephone dial

**dial**² *abbrev.* 1 dialect(al) 2 dialectic(al)

**di·a·lect** (dī′ə lekt′) *n.* ⟦< Gr *dia,* between + *legein,* to talk⟧ the form of a spoken language peculiar to a region, social group, etc. —**di′a·lec′tal** *adj.*

**di·a·lec·tic** (dī′ə lek′tik) *n.* 1 [*often pl.*] the practice of examining ideas logically 2 logical argumentation —*adj.* DIALECTICAL

**di′a·lec′ti·cal** (-ti kəl) *adj.* 1 of or using dialectic 2 of a dialect

**di·a·logue** (dī′ə lôg′, -läg′) *n.* ⟦see DIALECT⟧ 1 interchange of ideas by open discussion 2 the passages of talk in a play, story, etc. Also sp. **di′a·log′**

**di·al·y·sis** (dī al′ə sis) *n., pl.* -ses′ (-sēz′) ⟦< Gr *dia-,* apart + *lyein,* dissolve⟧ the separation of smaller dissolved molecules from the larger molecules in a solution by diffusion through a membrane: used in purifying the blood of those with impaired kidney function

**di·am·e·ter** (dī am′ət ər) *n.* ⟦< Gr *dia-,* through + *metron,* a measure⟧ 1 a line segment passing through the center of a circle, sphere, etc. from one side to the other 2 its length

**di·a·met·ri·cal** (dī′ə me′tri kəl) *adj.* designating an opposite, a difference, etc. that is wholly so; complete

**di·a·mond** (dī′mənd, dī′ə mənd) *n.* ⟦< Gr *adamas*⟧ 1 nearly pure, colorless, crystalline carbon, the hardest mineral known, used for gems or cutting tools 2 a gem or other piece cut from this 3 *a*) a conventionalized figure of a diamond (◇) *b*) any of a suit of playing cards marked with such figures in red 4 *Baseball* the infield or the whole field —*adj.* 1 of a diamond 2 marking the 60th, or sometimes 75th, year

**di·a·mond·back'** *n.* a large, poisonous rattle-snake of the S U.S.

**Di·an·a** (dī an'ə) *n. Rom. Myth.* the goddess of the moon and of hunting

**di·a·pa·son** (dī'ə pā'zən) *n.* [[< Gr *dia*, through + *pas*, all]] an organ stop covering the instrument's entire range

**di·a·per** (dī'pər, dī'ə pər) *n.* [[< ML *diasprum*, flowered cloth]] a soft, absorbent cloth folded and arranged between the legs and around the waist of a baby —*vt.* to put a diaper on (a baby)

**di·aph·a·nous** (dī af'ə nəs) *adj.* [[< Gr *dia-*, through + *phainein*, to show]] transparent or translucent

**di·a·phragm** (dī'ə fram') *n.* [[< Gr *dia-*, through + *phragma*, fence]] 1 the muscular partition between the chest cavity and abdominal cavity 2 a vibrating disk producing sound waves 3 a vaginal contraceptive device

**di·ar·rhe·a** (dī'ə rē'ə) *n.* [[< Gr *dia-*, through + *rhein*, to flow]] too frequent and loose bowel movements: chiefly Brit. sp. **di·ar·rhoe'a**

**di·a·ry** (dī'ə rē) *n., pl.* **-ries** [[< L *dies*, day]] a daily written record of the writer's experiences, etc. — **di'a·rist** *n.*

**di·a·stase** (dī'ə stās') *n.* [[< Gr *dia*, apart + *histanai*, stand]] an enzyme in the seed of grains and malt capable of changing starches into dextrose

**di·as·to·le** (dī as'tə lē') *n.* [[< Gr *dia-*, apart + *stellein*, put]] the usual rhythmic expansion of the heart —**di·a·stol·ic** (dī'ə stäl'ik) *adj.*

**di·a·ther·my** (dī'ə thur'mē) *n.* [[< Gr *dia-*, through + *thermē*, heat]] medical treatment by means of heat produced under the skin, as by radiation

**di·a·tom** (dī'ə täm') *n.* [[< Gr *diatomos*, cut in two]] any of various microscopic algae that are an important source of food for marine life

**di·a·tom·ic** (dī'ə täm'ik) *adj.* [[DI-¹ + ATOMIC]] having two atoms or radicals in the molecule

**di·a·ton·ic** (dī'ə tän'ik) *adj.* [[< Gr *dia-*, through + *teinein*, to stretch]] *Music* designating or of a scale of eight tones that is either a MAJOR SCALE or a MINOR SCALE

**di·a·tribe** (dī'ə trīb') *n.* [[< Gr *dia-*, through + *tribein*, to rub]] a bitter, abusive denunciation

**dib·ble** (dib'əl) *n.* [[ME *dibbel*]] a pointed tool used for making holes in the soil for seeds, bulbs, etc.

**dice** (dīs) *pl.n., sing.* **die** or **dice** [[see DIE²]] small cubes marked on each side with a different number of spots (from one to six), used in games of chance —*vi.* **diced, dic'ing** to play or gamble with dice —*vt.* to cut (vegetables, etc.) into small cubes —**no dice** [Inf.] 1 no: used in refusing a request 2 no luck

**di·chot·o·my** (dī kät'ə mē) *n., pl.* **-mies** [[< Gr *dicha*, in two + *temnein*, to cut]] division into two parts or groups

**dick** (dik) *n.* [Slang] a detective

**Dick·ens** (dik'ənz), **Charles** (chärlz) (pseud. *Boz*) 1812-70; Eng. novelist

**dick·er** (dik'ər) *vi.* [[ult. < L *decem*, ten]] to bargain or haggle

**dick·ey** (dik'ē) *n., pl.* **-eys** [[< nickname *Dick*]] 1 a detachable shirt front 2 a small bird: also **dickey bird** Also **dick'y,** *pl.* **-ies**

**Dick·in·son** (dik'in sən), **Em·i·ly** (em'ə lē) 1830-86; U.S. poet

**di·cot·y·le·don** (dī'kät'ə lēd''n) *n.* a plant with two seed leaves (*cotyledons*): also **di'cot'** — **di'cot'y·le'don·ous** *adj.*

**Dic·ta·phone** (dik'tə fōn') [[fol. + -PHONE]] *trademark for* a machine that records and plays back speech for typed transcripts, etc. —*n.* [*sometimes* **d-**] any such machine

**dic·tate** (dik'tāt') *vt., vi.* **-tat·ed, -tat·ing** [[< L *dicere*, speak]] 1 to speak (something) aloud for someone else to write down 2 to command forcefully 3 to give (orders) with authority —*n.* an authoritative order —**dic·ta'tion** *n.*

**dic·ta·tor** *n.* one who dictates; esp., a ruler or

tyrant with absolute power —**dic'ta·to'ri·al** (-tə tôr'ē əl) *adj.* —**dic·ta'tor·ship'** *n.*

**dic·tion** (dik'shən) *n.* [[< L *dicere*, say]] 1 manner of expression in words; wording 2 enunciation

**dic·tion·ar·y** (dik'shə ner'ē) *n., pl.* **-ar·ies** [see prec.] a book of alphabetically listed words in a language, with definitions, pronunciations, etc.

**dic·tum** (dik'təm) *n., pl.* **-tums** or **-ta** (-tə) [[< L *dicere*, say]] a formal statement of opinion; pronouncement

**did** (did) *vt., vi. pt. of* DO¹

**di·dac·tic** (dī dak'tik) *adj.* [[< Gr *didaskein*, teach]] 1 intended for instruction 2 morally instructive

**did·dle** (did''l) *vt., vi.* **-dled, -dling** [[< ?]] [Inf.] 1 to cheat 2 to waste (time) in trifling —**did'dler** *n.*

**di·do** (dī'dō) *n., pl.* **-does** or **-dos** [[< ?]] [Inf.] a mischievous or foolish action

**die¹** (dī) *vi.* **died, dy'ing** [[< ON *deyja*]] 1 to stop living 2 to stop functioning; end 3 to lose force or activity 4 [Inf.] to wish very much [*I'm dying* to go] —**die away** (or **down**) to cease gradually — **die off** to die one by one until all are gone —**die out** to stop existing

**die²** (dī) *n., pl.* for 2, **dies** (dīz) [[< L *dare*, give]] 1 *sing. of* DICE 2 a tool for shaping, punching, etc. metal or other material

**die'-hard'** or **die'hard'** *n.* a person stubbornly resistant to new ideas, reform, etc.

**di·e·lec·tric** (dī'i lek'trik) *n.* [[< *dia-*, across + ELECTRIC]] a material that does not conduct electricity

**di·er·e·sis** (dī er'ə sis) *n., pl.* **-ses** (-sēz') [[< Gr *dia-*, apart + *hairein*, to take]] a mark ( ¨ ) placed over the second of two consecutive vowels to show that it is pronounced separately

**die·sel** (dē'zəl, -səl) *n.* [after R. *Diesel* (1858-1913), Ger inventor] [*often* **D-**] an internal-combustion engine that burns oil ignited by heat from air compression: also **diesel engine** (or **motor**) — *vi.* to continue to run after the ignition is turned off: said of an internal-combustion engine

**di·et¹** (dī'ət) *n.* [[< Gr *diaita*, way of life]] 1 what a person or animal usually eats or drinks 2 a special or limited selection of food and drink, chosen or prescribed as to bring about weight loss —*vi.*, *vt.* to adhere to or place on a diet —**di'et·er** *n.* — **di'e·tar'y** (-ə ter'ē) *adj.*

**di·et²** (dī'ət) *n.* [[< ML *dieta*]] 1 a formal assembly 2 in some countries, a legislative assembly

**di·e·tet·ic** (-ə tet'ik) *adj.* of or for a particular diet of food and drink

**di·e·tet·ics** (-iks) *n.* the study of the kinds and quantities of food needed for health

**di·e·ti·tian** (dī'ə tish'ən) *n.* an expert in dietetics

**dif-** *prefix* DIS-: used before *f*

**dif·fer** (dif'ər) *vi.* [[< L *dis-*, apart + *ferre*, to bring]] 1 to be unlike or not the same 2 to be of opposite or unlike opinions; disagree

**dif·fer·ence** (dif'ər əns, dif'rəns) *n.* 1 a being different 2 the way in which people or things are different 3 a differing in opinion; disagreement 4 a dispute 5 *Math.* the amount by which one quantity is less than another

**dif·fer·ent** *adj.* 1 not alike 2 not the same 3 various 4 unusual —**dif'fer·ent·ly** *adv.*

**dif·fer·en·tial** (dif'ər en'shəl) *adj.* of, showing, or constituting a difference —*n.* 1 a differentiating amount, degree, etc. 2 a differential gear

**differential gear** (or **gearing**) a gear arrangement allowing one axle of an automobile to turn faster than the other

**dif·fer·en·ti·ate'** (-shē āt') *vt.* **-at·ed, -at·ing** 1 to constitute a difference in or between 2 to make unlike 3 to distinguish between —*vi.* 1 to become different or differentiated 2 to note a difference —**dif·fer·en'ti·a'tion** *n.*

**dif·fi·cult** (dif'i kult', -kəlt) *adj.* 1 hard to do, understand, etc. 2 hard to satisfy, deal with, etc.

**dif·fi·cul·ty** *n., pl.* **-ties** [[< L *dis-*, not + *facilis*, easy‖ **1** a being difficult **2** something difficult, as a problem, obstacle, or objection **3** trouble

**dif·fi·dent** (-dənt) *adj.* ‖< L *dis-*, not + *fidere*, to trust‖ lacking self-confidence; shy —**dif′fi·dence** *n.*

**dif·frac·tion** (di frak′shən) *n.* ‖< L *dis-*, apart + *frangere*, to break‖ **1** the breaking up of light waves as into the colors of the spectrum **2** a similar breaking up as of sound waves

**dif·fuse** (di fyo͞os′; *for v.*, -fyo͞oz′) *adj.* ‖< L *dis-*, apart + *fundere*, to pour‖ **1** spread out; not concentrated **2** using more words than are needed — *vt.*, *vi.* -**fused′**, -**fus′ing** to pour in every direction; spread widely —**dif·fuse′ly** *adv.* —**dif·fuse′ness** *n.* —**dif·fu′sion** *n.* —**dif·fu′sive** *adj.*

**dig** (dig) *vt.* **dug**, **dig′ging** ‖< OFr < Du *dijk*, dike‖ **1** to turn up or remove (ground, etc.) with a spade, the hands, etc. **2** to make (a hole, etc.) by digging **3** to get out by digging **4** to find out, as by careful study **5** to jab **6** [Slang] *a*) to understand *b*) to like —*vi.* **1** to dig the ground **2** to make a way by digging —*n.* **1** [Inf.] *a*) a poke, nudge, etc. *b*) a taunt **2** an archaeological excavation —**dig′ger** *n.*

**di·gest** (dī′jest′; *for v.* di jest′, dī-) *n.* ‖< L *di-*, apart + *gerere*, to carry‖ an organized collection of condensed information; summary —*vt.* **1** to summarize **2** to change (food taken into the body) into an absorbable form **3** to absorb mentally —*vi.* to undergo digestion —**di·gest′i·ble** *adj.*

**di·ges′tion** *n.* a digesting or being digested **2** the ability to digest —**di·ges′tive** *adj.*

**dig·it** (dij′it) *n.* ‖< L *digitus*, a finger‖ **1** a finger or toe **2** any number from 0 to 9

**dig·i·tal** (dij′i təl, -it′l) *adj.* **1** of or like a digit **2** using a row of digits, rather than numbers on a dial /a *digital* watch/ **3** designating, of, or used by a computer that processes data represented by groups of electronic bits **4** designating a recording technique in which sounds or images are converted into electronic bits: the bits are read electronically, as by a laser beam, for reproduction

**dig·i·tal·is** (dij′i tal′is) *n.* ‖ModL, foxglove: see DIGIT‖ **1** a plant with long spikes of thimblelike flowers; foxglove **2** a medicine made from the leaves of the purple foxglove, used as a heart stimulant

**dig·i·tize** (dij′i tīz′) *vt.* -**tized′**, -**tiz′ing** to translate (analog data) into digital data

**dig·ni·fied** (dig′nə fīd′) *adj.* having or showing dignity

**dig·ni·fy** (dig′nə fī′) *vt.* -**fied′**, -**fy′ing** ‖< L *dignus*, worthy + *facere*, make‖ to give dignity to; exalt

**dig′ni·tar′y** (-ter′ē) *n.*, *pl.* -**tar′ies** ‖< L *dignitas*, dignity‖ a person holding a high position or office

**dig·ni·ty** (-tē) *n.*, *pl.* -**ties** ‖< L *dignus*, worthy‖ **1** honorable quality; worthiness **2** high repute or honor, or the degree of this **3** a high position, rank, or title **4** stately appearance or manner **5** self-respect

**di·graph** (dī′graf′) *n.* a combination of two letters to represent one sound (Ex.: *read*, gra*ph*ic)

**di·gress** (di gres′, dī-) *vi.* ‖< L *dis-*, apart + *gradi*, to go‖ to wander temporarily from the subject, in talking or writing —**di·gres′sion** (-gresh′ən) *n.* — **di·gres′sive** *adj.*

**Di·jon mustard** (dē zhän′, dē′zhän′) ‖after *Dijon*, city in France‖ a mild mustard paste blended with white wine

**dike** (dīk) *n.* ‖OE *dic*, ditch‖ an embankment or dam made to prevent flooding as by the sea

**di·lap·i·dat·ed** (də lap′ə dāt′id) *adj.* ‖< L *dis-*, apart + *lapidare*, throw stones at‖ falling to pieces; broken down —**di·lap·i·da′tion** *n.*

**di·late** (dī′lāt′, dī lāt′) *vt.* -**lat′ed**, -**lat′ing** ‖< L *dis-*, apart + *latus*, wide‖ to make wider or larger —*vi.* **1** to become wider or larger **2** to speak or write in detail (*on* or *upon* a subject) —**di·la′tion** or **dil·a·ta·tion** (dil′ə tā′shən) *n.*

**dil·a·to·ry** (dil′ə tôr′ē) *adj.* ‖see prec.‖ **1** causing delay **2** inclined to delay; slow; tardy —**dil′a·to·ri·ness** *n.*

**di·lem·ma** (di lem′ə) *n.* ‖< LGr *di-*, two + *lēmma*, proposition‖ **1** any situation requiring a choice between unpleasant alternatives **2** any serious problem

**dil·et·tante** (dil′ə tänt′, dil′ə tänt′) *n.*, *pl.* -**tantes′** or -**tan′ti′** (-tē′, -tē) ‖It < L *delectare*, to delight‖ one who dabbles in an art, science, etc. in a superficial way —**dil′et·tant′ish** *adj.* —**dil′et·tant′ism′** *n.*

**dil·i·gent** (dil′ə jənt) *adj.* ‖< L *di-*, apart + *legere*, choose‖ **1** persevering and careful in work; hardworking **2** done carefully —**dil′i·gence** *n.* —**dil′i·gent·ly** *adv.*

**dill** (dil) *n.* ‖OE *dile*‖ an herb related to parsley, with bitter seeds and aromatic leaves, used to flavor pickles, soups, etc.

**dil·ly** (dil′ē) *n.*, *pl.* -**lies** ‖? < DEL(IGHTFUL) + -Y²‖ [Slang] a remarkable person or thing

**dil·ly·dal·ly** (dil′ē dal′ē) *vi.* -**lied**, -**ly·ing** ‖< DALLY‖ to waste time by hesitating; loiter or dawdle

**di·lute** (di lo͞ot′, dī-) *vt.* -**lut′ed**, -**lut′ing** ‖< L *dis-*, off + *lavare*, to wash‖ to thin down or weaken as by mixing with water —*adj.* diluted —**di·lu′tion** *n.*

**dim¹** (dim) *adj.* **dim′mer**, **dim′mest** ‖OE‖ **1** not bright, clear, or distinct; dull, obscure, etc. **2** not seeing, hearing, or understanding clearly **3** [Inf.] stupid —*vt.*, *vi.* **dimmed**, **dim′ming** to make or grow dim —**dim′ly** *adv.* —**dim′ness** *n.*

**dim²** *abbrev.* diminutive

**dime** (dīm) *n.* ‖< L *decem*, ten‖ a U.S. or Canadian 10-cent coin

**di·men·sion** (də men′shən) *n.* ‖< L *dis-*, off, from + *metiri*, to measure‖ **1** any measurable extent, as length, width, or depth **2** [*pl.*] measurements in length, width, and often depth **3** [*often pl.*] extent; scope —**di·men′sion·al** *adj.*

**dime store** FIVE-AND-TEN-CENT STORE

**di·min·ish** (də min′ish) *vt.*, *vi.* ‖< L *diminuere*, reduce‖ to make or become smaller in size, degree, importance, etc.; lessen —**dim·i·nu·tion** (dim′ə no͞o′shən, -nyo͞o′-) *n.*

**di·min·u·en·do** (də min′yo͞o en′dō) *adj.*, *adv.* ‖It: see prec.‖ *Music* with gradually diminishing volume: also written **di·min′u·en′do**

**di·min·u·tive** (də min′yo͞o tiv) *adj.* ‖see DIMINISH‖ very small; tiny —*n.* a word having a suffix that expresses smallness, endearment, etc. (Ex.: *piglet*)

**dim·i·ty** (dim′ə tē) *n.*, *pl.* -**ties** ‖< Gr *dis-*, two + *mitos*, a thread‖ a thin, corded or patterned cotton cloth

**dim′mer** *n.* a device, as a rheostat, for dimming electric lights

**dim·ple** (dim′pəl) *n.* ‖ME *dimpel*‖ a small, natural hollow, as on the cheek or chin —*vi.*, *vt.* -**pled**, -**pling** to form dimples (in) —**dim′ply** (-plē) *adj.*

**dim sum** (dim′ sum′, -so͞om′) ‖Chin‖ small dumplings filled with meat, vegetables, etc.; also, a light meal of these together with other foods

**dim′wit′** *n.* [Slang] a stupid person; simpleton — **dim′wit′ted** *adj.*

**din** (din) *n.* ‖OE *dyne*‖ a loud, continuous noise; confused uproar —*vt.* **dinned**, **din′ning** to repeat insistently or noisily —*vi.* to make a din

**din-din** (din′din′) *n.* [Inf.] dinner

**dine** (dīn) *vi.* **dined**, **din′ing** ‖ult. < L *dis-*, away + *jejunus*, hungry‖ to eat dinner —*vt.* to provide a dinner for

**din·er** (dīn′ər) *n.* **1** a person eating dinner **2** a railroad car equipped to serve meals **3** a small restaurant built to look like such a car

**di·nette** (dī net′) *n.* an alcove or small space used as a dining room

**ding** (diŋ) *n.* ‖< Scand‖ the sound of a bell: also **ding′-dong′** (-dôŋ′)

**din·ghy** (diŋ′gē) *n.*, *pl.* -**ghies** ‖Hindi *ḍīṅgī*‖ any of various small boats, as one carried on a ship

**din·gle** (diŋ′gəl) *n.* ‖ME *dingel*, abyss‖ a small, deep, wooded valley

**din·go** (diŋ′gō) *n.*, *pl.* **-goes** ⟦native name⟧ the Australian wild dog, usually tawny in color

**ding·us** (diŋ′əs) *n.* ⟦< Du *ding*, thing⟧ [Inf.] any device; gadget

**din·gy** (din′jē) *adj.* **-gi·er, -gi·est** ⟦orig. dial. var. < DUNG⟧ **1** not bright or clean; grimy **2** dismal; shabby —**din′gi·ness** *n.*

**dining room** a room where meals are eaten

**dink·y** (diŋ′kē) *adj.* **-i·er, -i·est** ⟦< Scot *dink*, trim⟧ [Inf.] small and unimportant

**din·ner** (din′ər) *n.* ⟦see DINE⟧ **1** the main meal of the day **2** a banquet in honor of a person or event

**dinner jacket** a tuxedo jacket

**din′ner·ware′** *n.* plates, cups, saucers, etc., collectively

**di·no·saur** (dī′nə sôr′) *n.* ⟦< Gr *deinos*, terrible + *sauros*, lizard⟧ an extinct prehistoric reptile, often huge

**dint** (dint) *n.* ⟦OE *dynt*⟧ force; exertion: now chiefly in **by dint of**

**di·o·cese** (dī′ə sis, -sēz′) *n.* ⟦< Gr *dioikein*, to keep house⟧ the district under a bishop's jurisdiction —**di·oc′e·san** (-äs′ə sən) *adj.*

**di·ode** (dī′ōd′) *n.* ⟦DI-¹ + -ODE⟧ an electron tube used esp. to convert alternating current into direct current

**Di·og·e·nes** (dī äj′ə nēz′) 412?-323? B.C.; Gr. philosopher

**Di·o·ny·sus** or **Di·o·ny·sos** (dī′ə nī′səs) *n.* Gr. Myth. the god of wine and revelry

**di·o·ram·a** (dī′ə ram′ə) *n.* ⟦< Gr *dia-*, through + *horama*, a view⟧ a scenic display, as of three-dimensional figures against a painted background

**di·ox·in** (dī äk′sin) *n.* a highly toxic chemical contaminant found in some herbicides

**dip** (dip) *vt.* **dipped, dip′ping** ⟦OE *dyppan*⟧ **1** to immerse briefly **2** to scoop (liquid) up or out **3** to lower (a flag, etc.) and immediately raise again — *vi.* **1** to plunge into a liquid and quickly come out **2** to sink suddenly **3** to decline slightly **4** to slope down **5** to lower a container, the hand, etc. as into water **6** to read or inquire superficially: with *into* —*n.* **1** a dipping or being dipped **2** a brief plunge into water, etc. **3** a liquid, sauce, etc. into which something is dipped **4** a portion removed by dipping **5** a downward slope or plunge

**diph·the·ri·a** (dif thir′ē ə, dip-) *n.* ⟦< Gr *diphthera*, leather⟧ an acute infectious disease marked by high fever and difficult breathing

**diph·thong** (dif′thôŋ; *often* dip′-) *n.* ⟦< Gr *di-*, two + *phthongos*, a sound⟧ a sound made by gliding from one vowel to another within one syllable, as the sound (oi) in *oil*

**di·plo·ma** (də plō′mə) *n.* ⟦< Gr *diplōma*, folded letter⟧ a certificate issued by a school, college, etc. indicating graduation or the conferring of a degree

**di·plo·ma·cy** (-sē) *n.* **1** the conducting of relations between nations **2** tact

**dip·lo·mat** (dip′lə mat′) *n.* **1** a representative of a government who conducts relations with another government **2** a tactful person

**dip·lo·mat′ic** *adj.* **1** of diplomacy **2** tactful — **dip′lo·mat′i·cal·ly** *adv.*

**di·pole** (dī′pōl′) *n.* a kind of radio or TV antenna with a single line separated at the center for connection to the receiver

**dip·per** (dip′ər) *n.* a long-handled cup, etc. for dipping

**dip·so·ma·ni·a** (dip′sə mā′nē ə) *n.* ⟦< Gr *dipsa*, thirst + *mania*, madness⟧ an abnormal craving for alcoholic drink —**dip′so·ma′ni·ac′** (-ak′) *n.*

**dip′stick′** *n.* a graduated rod for measuring quantity or depth

**dir** *abbrev.* director

**dire** (dīr) *adj.* **dir′er, dir′est** ⟦L *dirus*⟧ **1** dreadful; terrible: also **dire′ful 2** urgent [a *dire* need]

**di·rect** (də rekt′; *also* dī-) *adj.* ⟦< L *di-*, apart + *regere*, to rule⟧ **1** not roundabout or interrupted; straight **2** honest; frank [a *direct* answer] **3** with

139                                            ◄ **disagreeable**

nothing between; immediate **4** in an unbroken line of descent; lineal **5** exact; complete [the *direct* opposite] **6** in the exact words [a *direct* quote] —*vt.* **1** to manage; guide **2** to order; command **3** to turn or point; aim; head **4** to tell (a person) the way to a place **5** to address (a letter, etc.) **6** *a*) to plan and supervise the action and effects of (a play, film, etc.) *b*) to conduct the performance of (a choir, band, etc.) —*adv.* directly — **di·rect′ness** *n.*

**direct current** an electric current flowing in one direction

**di·rec·tion** (də rek′shən; *also* dī-) *n.* **1** a directing **2** [*usually pl.*] instructions for doing, using, etc. **3** a command **4** the point toward which something faces or the line along which it moves or lies —**di·rec′tion·al** *adj.*

**di·rec′tive** (-rek′tiv) *adj.* directing —*n.* a general order issued authoritatively

**di·rect′ly** *adv.* **1** in a direct way or line; straight **2** with nothing or no one between [*directly* responsible] **3** exactly [*directly* opposite] **4** instantly; right away

**direct object** *Gram.* the word or words denoting the receiver of the action of a transitive verb (Ex.: *me* in "he saw me")

**di·rec′tor** (-rek′tər) *n.* one who directs a school, corporation, etc. or a play, choir, etc. —**di·rec′tor·ship′** *n.*

**di·rec′tor·ate** (-it) *n.* **1** the position of director **2** a board of directors

**di·rec′to·ry** (-tə rē) *n.*, *pl.* **-ries** a book listing the names, addresses, etc. of a specific group of persons

**dirge** (durj) *n.* ⟦< L *dirige* (direct), first word of a prayer⟧ a song, poem, etc. of grief or mourning

**dir·i·gi·ble** (dir′ə jə bəl, də rij′ə-) *n.* ⟦see DIRECT & -IBLE⟧ AIRSHIP

**dirk** (durk) *n.* ⟦< ?⟧ a long dagger

**dirn·dl** (durn′dəl) *n.* ⟦< Ger *dirne*, girl⟧ a full skirt gathered at the waist

**dirt** (durt) *n.* ⟦< ON *drita*, excrement⟧ **1** any unclean matter, as mud or trash; filth **2** earth; soil **3** dirtiness, corruption, etc. **4** obscenity **5** malicious gossip

**dirt′-cheap′** *adj.*, *adv.* [Inf.] very inexpensive(ly)

**dirt′-poor′** *adj.* extremely poor

**dirt′y** *adj.* **-i·er, -i·est 1** not clean **2** obscene **3** contemptible or nasty **4** unfair; dishonest **5** showing anger [a *dirty* look] **6** rough [*dirty* weather] —*vt.*, *vi.* **dirt′ied, dirt′y·ing** to make or become dirty —**dirt′i·ly** *adv.* —**dirt′i·ness** *n.*

**dis** (dis) *vt.* **dissed, dis′sing** [Slang] to insult

**dis-** ⟦< L⟧ *prefix* separation, negation, reversal [*disbar, disable, disintegrate*]

**dis·a·bil·i·ty** (dis′ə bil′ə tē) *n.*, *pl.* **-ties 1** a disabled condition **2** that which disables, as an illness or physical limitation

**dis·a·ble** (dis ā′bəl) *vt.* **-bled, -bling** to make unable or unfit; cripple; incapacitate

**dis·a′bled** *adj.* having a physical or mental disability

**dis·a·buse** (dis′ə byōōz′) *vt.* **-bused′, -bus′ing** to rid of false ideas

**dis·ad·van·tage** (dis′əd vant′ij) *n.* **1** an unfavorable situation or circumstance **2** detriment — **dis′ad·van·ta′geous** (-ad′van tā′jəs) *adj.*

**dis′ad·van′taged** *adj.* underprivileged

**dis·af·fect** (dis′ə fekt′) *vt.* to make unfriendly, discontented, or disloyal —**dis′af·fect′ed** *adj.* — **dis′af·fec′tion** *n.*

**dis·af·fil·i·ate** (-ə fil′ē āt′) *vt.*, *vi.* **-at′ed, -at′ing** to end an affiliation (with) —**dis′af·fil′i·a′tion** *n.*

**dis·a·gree′** (-ə grē′) *vi.* **-greed′, -gree′ing 1** to fail to agree; differ **2** to differ in opinion **3** to give distress: with *with* [plums *disagree* with me] — **dis′a·gree′ment** *n.*

**dis′a·gree′a·ble** *adj.* **1** unpleasant; offensive **2** quarrelsome —**dis′a·gree′a·bly** *adv.*

**dis·al·low** (dis'ə lou') *vt.* to refuse to allow (a claim, etc.); reject

**dis·ap·pear'** (-ə pir') *vi.* 1 to cease to be seen; vanish 2 to cease existing —**dis'ap·pear'ance** *n.*

**dis·ap·point'** (-ə point') *vt.* to fail to satisfy the hopes or expectations of —**dis·ap·point'ment** *n.*

**dis·ap·pro·ba·tion** (dis'ap'rə bā'shən) *n.* disapproval

**dis·ap·prove** (dis'ə pr⁻o⁻ov'), *vt., vi.* -proved', -prov'ing 1 to have or express an unfavorable opinion (of) 2 to refuse to approve —**dis'ap·prov'al** *n.* —**dis'ap·prov'ing·ly** *adv.*

**dis·arm** (dis ärm') *vt.* 1 to take away weapons from 2 to make harmless 3 to make friendly — *vi.* to reduce armed forces and armaments —**dis·ar'ma·ment** (-är'mə mənt) *n.*

**dis·ar·range** (dis'ə ränj') *vt.* -ranged', -rang'ing to undo the order of; make less neat

**dis'ar·ray'** (-ə rā') *n.* disorder

**dis·as·sem'ble** (-ə sem'bəl) *vt.* -bled, -bling to take apart

**dis·as·so'ci·ate'** (-ə sō'shē āt', -sē-) *vt.* -at'ed, -at'ing to disconnect or separate; dissociate

**dis·as·ter** (di zas'tər) *n.* [< L *dis*-, away + *astrum*, a star] any happening that causes great harm or damage; calamity —**dis·as'trous** (-trəs) *adj.*

**dis·a·vow** (dis'ə vou') *vt.* to deny any knowledge of or responsibility for; disclaim —**dis'a·vow'al** *n.*

**dis·band** (dis band') *vt., vi.* to break up: said of an organization or its members

**dis·bar'** (-bär') *vt.* -barred', -bar'ring to deprive (a lawyer) of the right to practice law —**dis·bar'ment** *n.*

**dis·be·lieve** (dis'bə lēv') *vt., vi.* -lieved', -liev'ing to refuse to believe —**dis'be·lief'** (-lēf') *n.*

**dis·burse** (dis bʉrs') *vt.* -bursed', -burs'ing [< OFr *desbourser*] to pay out; expend —**dis·burse'ment** *n.* —**dis·burs'er** *n.*

**disc** (disk) *n.* 1 DISK 2 a phonograph record

**dis·card** (dis kärd'; *for n.* dis'kärd') *vt.* [< OFr: see DIS- & CARD[1]] 1 *Card Games* to remove (a card or cards) from one's hand 2 to get rid of as no longer useful —*n.* 1 a discarding or being discarded 2 something discarded

**disc brake** a brake, as on a car, with two friction pads that press on a disc rotating with the wheel

**dis·cern** (di sʉrn', -zʉrn') *vt.* [< L *dis*-, apart + *cernere*, to separate] to perceive or recognize clearly —**dis·cern'i·ble** *adj.* —**dis·cern'ment** *n.*

**dis·cern'ing** *adj.* having good judgment; astute

**dis·charge** (dis chärj'; *also, and for n. usually,* dis' chärj') *vt.* -charged', -charg'ing [< L *dis*-, from + *carrus*, wagon] 1 to release or dismiss 2 to unload (a cargo) 3 to shoot (a gun or projectile) 4 to emit [*to discharge* pus] 5 to pay (a debt) or perform (a duty) 6 *Elec.* to remove stored energy from (a battery, etc.) —*vi.* 1 to get rid of a load, etc. 2 to go off, as a gun —*n.* 1 a discharging or being discharged 2 that which discharges or is discharged

**dis·ci·ple** (di sī'pəl) *n.* [< L *dis*-, apart + *capere*, to hold] 1 a pupil or follower of any teacher or school 2 an early follower of Jesus, esp. one of the Apostles —**dis·ci'ple·ship'** *n.*

**dis·ci·pli·nar·i·an** (dis'ə pli ner'ē ən) *n.* a person who believes in or enforces strict discipline

**dis·ci·pline** (dis'ə plin') *n.* [see DISCIPLE] 1 a branch of learning 2 training that develops self-control, efficiency, etc. 3 strict control to enforce obedience 4 self-control 5 a system of rules, as for a church 6 treatment that corrects or punishes —*vt.* -plined', -plin'ing 1 to train; control 2 to punish —**dis'ci·pli·nar'y** (-pli ner'ē) *adj.*

**disc jockey** one who conducts a radio program of recorded music

**dis·claim** (dis klām') *vt.* 1 to give up any claim to 2 to repudiate; deny

**dis·claim'er** *n.* a denial or renunciation, as of responsibility

**dis·close** (dis klōz') *vt.* -closed', -clos'ing to reveal —**dis·clo'sure** (-klō'zhər) *n.*

**dis·co** (dis'kō) *n. pl.* -cos a place for dancing to recorded music 2 a kind of popular dance music with a strong beat

**dis·col·or** (dis kul'ər) *vt., vi.* to change in color as by fading, streaking, or staining: Brit. sp. **dis·col'our** —**dis'col·or·a'tion** *n.*

**dis·com·fit** (dis kum'fit) *vt.* [< L *dis*-, away + *conficere*, prepare] to frustrate or disconcert —**dis·com'fi·ture** (-fi chər) *n.*

**dis·com·fort** (dis kum'fərt) *n.* 1 lack of comfort; uneasiness 2 anything causing this —*vt.* to cause discomfort to

**dis·com·mode** (dis'kə mōd') *vt.* -mod'ed, -mod'ing [< DIS- + L *commodare*, to make suitable] to cause bother to; inconvenience

**dis'com·pose'** (-kəm pōz') *vt.* -posed', -pos'ing to disturb; fluster —**dis'com·po'sure** (-pō'zhər) *n.*

**dis'con·cert'** (-kən sʉrt') *vt.* to upset; embarrass

**dis'con·nect'** (-kə nekt') *vt.* to break the connection of; separate —**dis'con·nec'tion** *n.*

**dis'con·nect'ed** *adj.* 1 separated 2 incoherent

**dis·con·so·late** (dis kän'sə lit) *adj.* [see DIS- & CONSOLE[1]] inconsolable; dejected —**dis·con'so·late·ly** *adv.*

**dis·con·tent** (dis'kən tent') *adj.* [ME] DISCONTENTED —*n.* dissatisfaction with one's situation: also **dis'con·tent'ment** —*vt.* to make discontented

**dis'con·tent'ed** *adj.* not contented; wanting something more or different

**dis·con·tin·ue** (dis'kən tin'y⁻o⁻o) *vt., vi.* -ued, -u·ing to stop; cease; give up —**dis'con·tin'u·ance** or **dis'con·tin'u·a'tion** *n.*

**dis'con·tin'u·ous** (-y⁻o⁻o əs) *adj.* not continuous; having interruptions or gaps

**dis·cord** (dis'kôrd') *n.* [< L *dis*-, apart + *cor*, heart] 1 disagreement 2 harsh noise 3 a lack of musical harmony —**dis·cord'ant** *adj.*

**dis·co·thèque** (dis'kə tek') *n.* [Fr] DISCO (sense 1)

**dis·count** (dis'kount'; *for v., also* dis kount') *n.* [see DIS- & COMPUTE] 1 a reduction from a usual or list price 2 the rate of interest charged on a discounted bill, note, etc.: also called **discount rate** —*vt.* 1 to pay or receive the value of (a bill, promissory note, etc.), minus a deduction for interest 2 to deduct an amount from (a bill, price, etc.) 3 to sell at less than the regular price 4 *a*) to allow for exaggeration, bias, etc. in (a story, etc.) *b*) to disregard 5 to lessen the effect of by anticipating

**dis·coun·te·nance** (dis kount''n əns) *vt.* -nanced, -nanc·ing 1 to make ashamed or embarrassed 2 to refuse approval or support

**discount house** (or **store**) a retail store that sells goods for less than regular prices

**dis·cour·age** (di skʉr'ij) *vt.* -aged, -ag·ing 1 to deprive of courage or confidence 2 to persuade (a person) to refrain 3 to try to prevent by disapproving —**dis·cour'age·ment** *n.*

**dis·course** (dis'kôrs'; *also, and for v. usually,* dis kôrs') *n.* [< L *dis*-, from + *currere*, to run] 1 talk; conversation 2 a formal treatment of a subject, in speech or writing —*vi.* -coursed', -cours'ing to talk; confer

**dis·cour·te·ous** (dis kʉr'tē əs) *adj.* impolite; rude; ill-mannered

**dis·cour·te·sy** (-kʉrt'ə sē) *n.* 1 lack of courtesy 2 *pl.* -sies a rude or impolite act or remark

**dis·cov·er** (di skuv'ər) *vt.* [see DIS- & COVER] 1 to be the first to find out, see, etc. 2 to learn of the existence of —**dis·cov'er·er** *n.*

**dis·cov·er·y** (di skuv'ər ē) *n., pl.* -er·ies 1 a discovering 2 anything discovered

**dis·cred·it** (dis kred'it) *vt.* 1 to disbelieve 2 to cast doubt on 3 to disgrace —*n.* 1 loss of belief; doubt 2 disgrace —**dis·cred'it·a·ble** *adj.*

**dis·creet** (di skrēt') *adj.* [see DISCERN] careful about what one says or does; prudent —**dis·creet'ly** *adv.*

**dis·crep·an·cy** (di skrep'ən sē) *n., pl.* -cies [< L

*dis-*, from + *crepare*, to rattle‖ (a) lack of agreement; inconsistency

**dis·crete** (di skrēt′) *adj.* ‖see DISCERN‖ separate and distinct; unrelated

**dis·cre·tion** (di skresh′ən) *n.* 1 the freedom to make decisions 2 the quality of being discreet; prudence —**dis·cre′tion·ar′y** *adj.*

**dis·crim·i·nate** (di skrim′i nāt′) *vi.* -nat′ed, -nat′ing ‖see DISCERN‖ 1 to distinguish 2 to make distinctions in treatment; show partiality or prejudice —**dis·crim′i·nat′ing** *adj.* —**dis·crim′i·na′tion** *n.*

**dis·crim′i·na·to′ry** (-nə tôr′ē) *adj.* showing discrimination or bias

**dis·cur·sive** (di skʉr′siv) *adj.* ‖see DISCOURSE‖ wandering from one topic to another; rambling

**dis·cus** (dis′kəs) *n.* ‖< Gr *diskos*‖ a heavy disk, usually of metal and wood, thrown for distance at a track meet

**dis·cuss** (di skus′) *vt.* ‖< L *dis-*, apart + *quatere*, to shake‖ to talk or write about; consider the pros and cons of —**dis·cus′sion** (-skush′ən) *n.*

DISCUS

**dis·cus′sant** (-ənt) *n.* a participant in an organized discussion

**dis·dain** (dis dān′) *vt.* ‖< L *dis-*, DIS- + *dignari*, deign‖ to regard as beneath one's dignity; scorn —*n.* aloof contempt —**dis·dain′ful** *adj.*

**dis·ease** (di zēz′) *n.* ‖< OFr *des-*, DIS- + *aise*, ease‖ 1 illness in general 2 a particular destructive process in an organism; specif., an illness 3 any harmful condition, as of society —**dis·eased′** *adj.*

**dis·em·bark** (dis′im bärk′) *vi.*, *vt.* to leave, or unload from, a ship, aircraft, etc. —**dis′em·bar·ka′tion** *n.*

**dis·em·bod·y** (-im bäd′ē) *vt.* -bod′ied, -bod′y·ing to free from bodily existence —**dis′em·bod′i·ment** *n.*

**dis·em·bow·el** (-im bou′əl) *vt.* -eled or -elled, -el·ing or -el·ling to take out the entrails of

**dis·en·chant′** (-in chant′) *vt.* 1 to free from an enchantment or illusion 2 DISILLUSION (sense 2) —**dis′en·chant′ment** *n.*

**dis·en·cum·ber** (-in kum′bər) *vt.* to relieve of a burden

**dis·en·fran·chise** (dis′in fran′chīz) *vt.* -chised′, -chis′ing to deprive of a right, privilege, etc., esp. the right to vote

**dis·en·gage′** (-in gāj′) *vt.*, *vi.* -gaged′, -gag′ing to release or get loose from something that engages, holds, entangles, etc.; unfasten —**dis′en·gage′ment** *n.*

**dis·en·tan·gle** (-in taŋ′gəl) *vt.* -gled, -gling to free from something that entangles, confuses, etc.; extricate; untangle

**dis·es·teem′** (-i stēm′) *n.* lack of esteem; disfavor

**dis·fa·vor** (dis fā′vər) *n.* 1 an unfavorable opinion; dislike; disapproval 2 the state of being disliked, etc.

**dis·fig·ure** (-fig′yər) *vt.* -ured, -ur·ing to hurt the appearance of; deface —**dis·fig′ure·ment** *n.*

**dis·gorge** (-gôrj′) *vt.*, *vi.* -gorged′, -gorg′ing ‖< OFr: see DIS- & GORGE‖ 1 to vomit 2 to pour forth (its contents); empty (itself)

**dis·grace** (-grās′) *n.* ‖< It *dis-*, not + *grazia*, favor‖ 1 loss of favor or respect; shame; disrepute 2 a person or thing bringing shame —*vt.* -graced′, -grac′ing to bring shame or dishonor upon —**dis·grace′ful** *adj.*

**dis·grun·tle** (-grunt′′l) *vt.* -tled, -tling ‖ult. < DIS- + GRUNT‖ to make peevishly discontented; make sullen

**dis·guise** (-gīz′) *vt.* -guised′, -guis′ing ‖< OFr: see DIS- & GUISE‖ 1 to make appear, sound, etc. so different as to be unrecognizable 2 to hide the

141   ◀ **dislocate**

real nature of —*n.* 1 anything that disguises 2 a being disguised

**dis·gust′** (-gust′) *n.* ‖< DIS- + L *gustus*, a taste‖ a sickening dislike —*vt.* to cause to feel disgust —**dis·gust′ed** *adj.* —**dis·gust′ing** *adj.*

**dish** (dish) *n.* ‖see DISCUS‖ 1 a container, generally shallow and concave, for holding food 2 as much as a dish holds 3 a particular kind of food 4 any dishlike object —*vt.* to serve in a dish: with *up* or *out* —**dish it out** [Slang] to subject others to criticism, etc.

**dis·ha·bille** (dis′ə bēl′) *n.* ‖< Fr *dés-*, DIS- + *habiller*, to dress‖ the state of being dressed only partially or in night clothes

**dish antenna** a radio or TV antenna with a dish-shaped reflector

**dis·har·mo·ny** (dis här′mə nē) *n.* absence of harmony; discord —**dis′har·mo′ni·ous** (-mō′nē əs) *adj.*

**dish′cloth′** *n.* a cloth for washing dishes, etc.

**dis·heart·en** (dis härt′′n) *vt.* to discourage; depress —**dis·heart′en·ing** *adj.*

**di·shev·el** (di shev′əl) *vt.* -eled or -elled, -el·ing or -el·ling ‖< OFr *des-*, DIS- + *chevel*, hair‖ to cause (hair, clothing, etc.) to become disarranged; rumple —**di·shev′el·ment** *n.*

**dis·hon·est** (dis än′ist) *adj.* not honest; lying, cheating, etc. —**dis·hon′est·ly** *adv.*

**dis·hon·es·ty** *n.* 1 a being dishonest 2 *pl.* -ties a dishonest act

**dis·hon·or** (dis än′ər) *n.* 1 loss of honor or respect; shame; disgrace 2 a cause of dishonor —*vt.* 1 to insult or disgrace 2 to refuse to pay (a check, etc.) —**dis·hon′or·a·ble** *adj.*

**dish′pan′** *n.* a pan in which dishes, cups, etc. are washed

**dish′rag′** *n.* DISHCLOTH

**dish′wash′er** *n.* a person or machine that washes dishes, cups, etc.

**dis·il·lu·sion** (dis′i lōō′zhən) *vt.* 1 to free from illusion 2 to take away the idealism of and make bitter, etc. —**dis′il·lu′sion·ment** *n.*

**dis·in·clined** (dis′in klīnd′) *adj.* unwilling; reluctant

**dis·in·fect** (dis′in fekt′) *vt.* to destroy the harmful bacteria, viruses, etc. in —**dis′in·fect′ant** *n.*

**dis·in·for·ma·tion** (-in′fər mā′shən) *n.* deliberately false information leaked so as to confuse another nation's intelligence operations

**dis·in·gen·u·ous** (dis′in jen′yōō əs) *adj.* not candid or frank; insincere

**dis·in·her·it** (dis′in her′it) *vt.* to deprive of an inheritance

**dis·in·te·grate** (dis in′tə grāt′) *vt.*, *vi.* -grat′ed, -grat′ing 1 to separate into parts or fragments; break up 2 to undergo nuclear transformation —**dis·in′te·gra′tion** *n.*

**dis·in·ter** (dis′in tʉr′) *vt.* -terred′, -ter′ring to remove from a grave, etc.; exhume

**dis·in·ter·est·ed** (dis in′trəs tid, -int′ər əs tid) *adj.* 1 impartial; unbiased 2 uninterested; indifferent

**dis′in′ter·me·di·a′tion** (-in′tər mē′dē ā′shən) *n.* the withdrawal of funds from banks to invest them at higher rates of interest, as in government securities

**dis·joint′** (-joint′) *vt.* 1 to put out of joint; dislocate 2 to dismember 3 to destroy the unity, connections, etc. of —**dis·joint′ed** *adj.*

**disk** (disk) *n.* ‖L *discus*: see DISCUS‖ 1 any thin, flat, circular thing 2 DISC 3 a thin, flat, circular plate coated with magnetic particles, for storing computer data 4 a layer of fibrous cartilage between adjacent vertebrae

**disk·ette** (di sket′) *n.* FLOPPY DISK

**dis·like** (dis līk′) *vt.* -liked′, -lik′ing to have a feeling of not liking —*n.* a feeling of not liking

**dis·lo·cate** (dis′lō kāt′) *vt.* -cat′ed, -cat′ing 1 to displace (a bone) from its proper position 2 to disarrange; disrupt —**dis·lo·ca′tion** *n.*

**dis·lodge** (dis läj′) *vt.* **-lodged′, -lodg′ing** to force from a place

**dis·loy·al** (-loi′əl) *adj.* not loyal or faithful —**dis·loy′al·ty** *n.*

**dis·mal** (diz′məl) *adj.* ⟦< ML *dies mali*, evil days⟧ **1** causing gloom or misery **2** dark and gloomy

**dis·man·tle** (dis mant′'l) *vt.* **-tled, -tling** ⟦see DIS- & MANTLE⟧ **1** to strip (a ship, etc.), as of equipment **2** to take apart —**dis·man′tle·ment** *n.*

**dis·may′** (-mā′) *vt.* ⟦< Anglo-Fr⟧ to make startled and discouraged by some problem, etc. difficult to resolve —*n.* upset and discouragement caused by a problem, etc. difficult to resolve

**dis·mem′ber** (-mem′bər) *vt.* ⟦see DIS- & MEMBER⟧ **1** to cut or tear the limbs from **2** to pull or cut to pieces —**dis·mem′ber·ment** *n.*

**dis·miss′** (-mis′) *vt.* ⟦< L *dis-*, from + *mittere*, send⟧ **1** to cause or allow to leave **2** to discharge from employment, etc. **3** to put aside mentally **4** *Law* to reject (a claim, etc.) —**dis·miss′al** *n.*

**dis·mis′sive** (-mis′iv) *adj.* condescending in dismissing from consideration

**dis·mount′** (-mount′) *vi.* to get off, as from a horse —*vt.* **1** to remove (a thing) from its mounting **2** to take apart; dismantle

**dis·o·be·di·ence** (dis′ō bē′dē əns) *n.* refusal to obey; insubordination —**dis′o·be′di·ent** *adj.*

**dis·o·bey′** (-ō bā′) *vt., vi.* to refuse to obey

**dis·o·blige′** (-ə blīj′) *vt.* **-bliged′, -blig′ing** **1** to refuse to oblige **2** to offend

**dis·or·der** (-ôr′dər) *n.* **1** a lack of order; confusion **2** a breach of public peace; riot **3** an ailment —*vt.* **1** to throw into disorder **2** to upset the normal functions of

**dis·or·der·ly** *adj.* **1** untidy **2** violating public peace, safety, etc. —**dis·or′der·li·ness** *n.*

**dis·or·gan·ize** (dis ôr′gə nīz′) *vt.* **-ized′, -iz′ing** to break up the order or system of; throw into confusion —**dis·or′gan·i·za′tion** *n.*

**dis·o′ri·ent′** (-ôr′ē ent′) *vt.* ⟦see DIS- & ORIENT, *v.*⟧ **1** to cause to lose one's bearings **2** to confuse mentally —**dis·o′ri·en·ta′tion** *n.*

**dis·own′** (-ōn′) *vt.* to refuse to acknowledge as one's own; repudiate

**dis·par·age** (di spar′ij) *vt.* **-aged, -ag·ing** ⟦< OFr *des-* (see DIS-) + *parage*, rank⟧ **1** to discredit **2** to belittle —**dis·par′age·ment** *n.*

**dis·pa·rate** (dis′pə rət) *adj.* ⟦< L *dis-*, not + *par*, equal⟧ distinct or different in kind; unequal —**dis·par′i·ty** (di spar′ə tē), *pl.* **-ties,** *n.*

**dis·pas·sion·ate** (dis pash′ə nət) *adj.* free from passion or bias; impartial —**dis·pas′sion·ate·ly** *adv.*

**dis·patch** (di spach′; *for n., also* dis′pach′) *vt.* ⟦< L *dis-*, away + *pes*, foot⟧ **1** to send promptly, as on an errand **2** to kill **3** to finish quickly —*n.* **1** a sending off **2** a killing **3** speed; promptness **4** a message **5** a news story sent by a reporter —**dis·patch′er** *n.*

**dis·pel** (di spel′) *vt.* **-pelled′, -pel′ling** ⟦< L *dis-*, apart + *pellere*, to drive⟧ to scatter and drive away

**dis·pen·sa·ble** (di spen′sə bəl) *adj.* **1** that can be dealt out **2** that can be dispensed with; not important

**dis·pen′sa·ry** (-sə rē) *n., pl.* **-ries** a room or place where medicines and first-aid treatment are available

**dis·pen·sa·tion** (dis′pən sā′shən) *n.* **1** a dispensing **2** something dispensed **3** an administrative system **4** a release from an obligation **5** *Theol.* the ordering of events under divine authority

**dis·pense** (di spens′) *vt.* **-pensed′, -pens′ing** ⟦< L *dis-*, out + *pendere*, weigh⟧ **1** to give out; distribute **2** to prepare and give out (medicines) **3** to administer (the law or justice) —**dispense with 1** to get rid of **2** to do without —**dis·pens′er** *n.*

**dis·perse′** (-spurs′) *vt.* **-persed′, -pers′ing** ⟦< L *dis-*, out + *spargere*, scatter⟧ **1** to break up and

scatter **2** to dispel (mist, etc.) —*vi.* to scatter —**dis·per′sal** *n.* —**dis·per′sion** *n.*

**dis·pir·it** (di spir′it) *vt.* to depress; discourage —**dis·pir′it·ed** *adj.*

**dis·place** (dis plās′) *vt.* **-placed′, -plac′ing** **1** to move from its usual place **2** to remove from office; discharge **3** to replace

**displaced person** one forced from one's country, esp. as a result of war

**dis·place′ment** *n.* **1** a displacing or being displaced **2** the weight or volume of air, water, or other fluid displaced by a floating object

**dis·play** (di splā′) *vt.* ⟦< L *dis-*, apart + *plicare*, to fold⟧ **1** [Obs.] to spread out; unfold **2** to exhibit —*n.* **1** an exhibition **2** anything displayed

**dis·please** (dis plēz′) *vt., vi.* **-pleased′, -pleas′ing** to fail to please; offend

**dis·pleas·ure** (-plezh′ər) *n.* a being displeased

**dis·port** (di spôrt′) *vi.* ⟦< OFr *des-* (see DIS-) + *porter*, carry⟧ to play; frolic —*vt.* to amuse (oneself)

**dis·pos·al** (di spō′zəl) *n.* **1** a disposing **2** a device in the drain of a kitchen sink to grind up garbage

**dis·pose′** (-spōz′) *vt.* **-posed′, -pos′ing** ⟦see DIS- & POSITION⟧ **1** to arrange **2** to settle (affairs) **3** to make willing; incline —**dispose of 1** to settle **2** to give away or sell **3** to get rid of —**dis·pos′a·ble** *adj.*

**dis·po·si·tion** (dis′pə zish′ən) *n.* **1** arrangement **2** management of affairs **3** a selling or giving away **4** the authority to settle, etc.; control **5** a tendency **6** one's temperament

**dis′pos·sess′** (-pə zes′) *vt.* to deprive of the possession of land, a house, etc.; oust

**dis·praise′** (-prāz′) *vt.* **-praised′, -prais′ing** ⟦< OFr *despreisier*⟧ to blame; censure —*n.* blame

**dis′pro·por′tion** (-prə pôr′shən) *n.* a lack of proportion —**dis′pro·por′tion·al** or **dis′pro·por′tion·ate** *adj.*

**dis·prove′** (-prōōv′) *vt.* **-proved′, -proved′** or **-prov′en, -prov′ing** to prove to be false

**dis·pu·ta·tion** (dis′pyōō tā′shən) *n.* **1** a disputing **2** debate

**dis′pu·ta′tious** (-pyōō tā′shəs) *adj.* inclined to dispute; contentious —**dis′pu·ta′tious·ly** *adv.*

**dis·pute** (di spyōōt′) *vi.* **-put′ed, -put′ing** ⟦< L *dis-*, apart + *putare*, to think⟧ **1** to argue; debate **2** to quarrel —*vt.* **1** to argue (a question) **2** to doubt **3** to oppose in any way —*n.* **1** a disputing; debate **2** a quarrel —**in dispute** not settled —**dis·put′a·ble** *adj.* —**dis·pu′tant** *adj., n.*

**dis·qual·i·fy** (dis kwôl′ə fī′) *vt.* **-fied′, -fy′ing** to make or declare unqualified, unfit, or ineligible —**dis·qual′i·fi·ca′tion** *n.*

**dis·qui·et** (dis kwī′ət) *vt.* to make uneasy; disturb —*n.* restlessness: also **dis·qui′e·tude** (-ə tōōd′)

**dis·qui·si·tion** (dis′kwi zish′ən) *n.* ⟦< L *dis-*, apart + *quaerere*, to seek⟧ a formal discussion; treatise

**dis·re·gard** (dis′ri gärd′) *vt.* **1** to pay little or no attention to **2** to treat without due respect —*n.* **1** lack of attention **2** lack of due regard or respect

**dis′re·pair′** (-ri per′) *n.* the condition of needing repairs; state of neglect

**dis·rep′u·ta·ble** (-rep′yōō tə bəl) *adj.* **1** not reputable **2** not fit to be seen

**dis′re·pute′** (-ri pyōōt′) *n.* lack or loss of repute; bad reputation; disgrace

**dis′re·spect′** (-ri spekt′) *n.* lack of respect; discourtesy —**dis′re·spect′ful** *adj.*

**dis·robe** (dis rōb′) *vt., vi.* **-robed′, -rob′ing** to undress

**dis·rupt** (dis rupt′) *vt., vi.* ⟦< L *dis-*, apart + *rumpere*, to break⟧ **1** to break apart **2** to disturb or interrupt —**dis·rup′tion** *n.* —**dis·rup′tive** *adj.*

**dis·sat·is·fy′** (-sat′is fī′) *vt.* **-fied′, -fy′ing** to fail to satisfy; displease —**dis·sat·is·fac′tion** *n.*

**dis·sect** (di sekt′) *vt.* ⟦< L *dis-*, apart + *secare*, to cut⟧ **1** to cut apart piece by piece, as a body for purposes of study **2** to examine or analyze closely —**dis·sec′tion** *n.* —**dis·sec′tor** *n.*

**dis·sem·ble** (di sem′bəl) *vt., vi.* **-bled, -bling** ⟦<

OFr *dessembler*] to conceal (the truth, one's feelings, motives, etc.) under a false appearance — **dis·sem'blance** *n.* —**dis·sem'bler** *n.*

**dis·sem·i·nate** (di sem'ə nāt') *vt.* **-nat'ed, -nat'ing** [< L *dis-*, apart + *seminare*, to sow] to scatter about; spread widely —**dis·sem'i·na'tion** *n.*

**dis·sen·sion** (di sen'shən) *n.* a dissenting; disagreement or quarreling

**dis·sent** (di sent') *vi.* [< L *dis-*, apart + *sentire*, feel] **1** to disagree **2** to reject doctrines of an established church —*n.* a dissenting —**dis·sent'er** *n.*

**dis·ser·ta·tion** (dis'ər tā'shən) *n.* [< L *dis-*, apart + *serere*, join] a formal discourse or treatise, esp. one written to fulfill the requirements for a doctorate from a university

**dis·serv·ice** (dis sur'vis) *n.* harm

**dis·sev·er** (di sev'ər) *vt.* **1** to sever; separate **2** to divide into parts —*vi.* to separate; disunite

**dis·si·dence** (dis'ə dəns) *n.* [< L *dis-*, apart + *sidere*, sit] disagreement; dissent —**dis'si·dent** (-dənt) *adj., n.*

**dis·sim·i·lar** (dis sim'ə lər) *adj.* not similar; different —**dis'sim'i·lar'i·ty** (-lar'ə tē), *pl.* **-ties,** *n.*

**dis·si·mil·i·tude** (dis'si mil'ə tōōd') *n.* difference

**dis·sim·u·late** (di sim'yōō lāt') *vt., vi.* **-lat'ed, -lat'ing** [see DIS- & SIMULATE] to dissemble —**dis·sim'u·la'tion** *n.* —**dis·sim'u·la'tor** *n.*

**dis·si·pate** (dis'ə pāt') *vt.* **-pat'ed, -pat'ing** [< L *dis-*, apart + *supare*, to throw] **1** to scatter; disperse **2** to make disappear **3** to waste or squander —*vi.* **1** to vanish **2** to indulge in pleasure to the point of harming oneself —**dis·si·pa'tion** *n.*

**dis·so·ci·ate** (di sō'shē āt') *vt.* **-at'ed, -at'ing** [< L *dis-*, apart + *sociare*, join] to break the connection between; disunite —**dis·so'ci·a'tion** *n.*

**dis·so·lute** (dis'ə lōōt') *adj.* [see DISSOLVE] dissipated and immoral; profligate —**dis'so·lute'ly** *adv.* —**dis'so·lute'ness** *n.*

**dis·so·lu·tion** (dis'ə lōō'shən) *n.* a dissolving or being dissolved; specif., *a)* a breaking up or into parts *b)* a termination *c)* death

**dis·solve** (di zälv', -zôlv') *vt., vi.* **-solved', -solv'ing** [< L *dis-*, apart + *solvere*, loosen] **1** to make or become liquid; melt **2** to pass or make pass into solution **3** to break up **4** to end as by breaking up; terminate **5** to disappear or make disappear

**dis·so·nance** (dis'ə nəns) *n.* [< L *dis-*, apart + *sonus*, a sound] **1** an inharmonious combination of sounds; discord **2** any lack of harmony or agreement —**dis'so·nant** *adj.*

**dis·suade** (di swād') *vt.* **-suad'ed, -suad'ing** [< L *dis-*, away + *suadere*, to persuade] to turn (a person) aside (*from* a course, etc.) by persuasion or advice —**dis·sua'sion** (-swā'zhən) *n.*

**dist** *abbrev.* **1** distance **2** district

**dis·taff** (dis'taf') *n.* [< OE *dis-*, flax + *stæf*, staff] a staff on which flax, wool, etc. is wound for use in spinning —*adj.* female; specif., of the maternal side of a family

**dis·tal** (dis'təl) *adj.* [DIST(ANT) + -AL] *Anat.* farthest from the point of attachment or origin; terminal —**dis'tal·ly** *adv.*

**dis·tance** (dis'təns) *n.* [< L *dis-*, apart + *stare*, to stand] **1** a being separated in space or time; remoteness **2** a gap, space, or interval between two points in space or time **3** a remoteness in behavior; reserve **4** a faraway place —*vt.* **-tanced, -tanc·ing** to place at an emotional distance (*from*)

**dis·tant** (-tənt) *adj.* **1** far away in space or time **2** away [100 miles *distant*] **3** far apart in relationship **4** aloof; reserved **5** from or at a distance —**dis'tant·ly** *adv.*

**dis·taste** (dis tāst') *n.* dislike —**dis·taste'ful** *adj.*

**dis·tem·per** (dis tem'pər) *n.* [< ML *distemperare*, to disorder] an infectious viral disease of young dogs, horses, etc.

**dis·tend** (di stend') *vt., vi.* [< L *dis-*, apart + *tendere*, to stretch] **1** to stretch out **2** to expand, as by pressure from within; make or become swollen —**dis·ten'tion** or **dis·ten'sion** *n.*

**dis·till** or **dis·til** (di stil') *vi., vt.* **-tilled', -till'ing** [< L *de-*, down + *stillare*, to drop] **1** to fall or let fall in drops **2** to undergo, subject to, or produce by distillation —**dis·till'er** *n.*

**dis·til·late** (dis'tə lāt', -lit) *n.* a liquid obtained by distilling

**dis·til·la·tion** (dis'tə lā'shən) *n.* **1** the process of heating a mixture and condensing the resulting vapor to produce a more nearly pure substance **2** anything distilled; distillate

**dis·till·er·y** (di stil'ər ē) *n., pl.* **-ies** a place where alcoholic liquors are distilled

**dis·tinct** (di stiŋkt') *adj.* [see DISTINGUISH] **1** not alike **2** separate **3** clearly perceived or marked off **4** unmistakable; definite —**dis·tinct'ly** *adv.*

**dis·tinc·tion** (-stiŋk'shən) *n.* **1** the act of making or keeping distinct **2** difference **3** a quality or feature that differentiates **4** fame; eminence **5** the quality that makes one seem superior **6** a mark of special recognition or honor

**dis·tinc'tive** *adj.* making distinct; characteristic —**dis·tinc'tive·ly** *adv.* —**dis·tinc'tive·ness** *n.*

**dis·tin·guish** (di stiŋ'gwish) *vt.* [< L *dis-*, apart + *-stinguere*, to prick] **1** to perceive or show the difference in **2** to characterize **3** to perceive clearly **4** to classify **5** to make famous —*vi.* to make a distinction (*between* or *among*) —**dis·tin'guish·a·ble** *adj.*

**dis·tin'guished** *adj.* celebrated; famous

**dis·tort** (di stôrt') *vt.* [< L *dis-*, intens. + *torquere*, to twist] **1** to twist out of shape **2** to misrepresent (facts, etc.) **3** to modify so as to reproduce unfaithfully —**dis·tor'tion** *n.*

**dis·tract** (di strakt') *vt.* [< L *dis-*, apart + *trahere*, draw] **1** to draw (the mind, etc.) away in another direction; divert **2** to confuse; bewilder —**dis·tract'ed** *adj.* —**dis·tract'ing** *adj.*

**dis·trac·tion** *n.* **1** a distracting or being distracted **2** anything that distracts confusingly or amusingly; diversion **3** great mental distress

**dis·trait** (di strā') *adj.* [see DISTRACT] absent-minded; inattentive

**dis·traught'** (-strôt') *adj.* [var. of prec.] **1** mentally confused; distracted **2** driven mad; crazed

**dis·tress** (di stres') *vt.* [ult. < L *dis-*, apart + *stringere*, to stretch] to cause misery or suffering to —*n.* **1** pain, suffering, etc. **2** an affliction **3** a state of danger or trouble —**dis·tressed'** *adj.*

**dis·trib·ute** (di strib'yōōt) *vt.* **-ut·ed, -ut·ing** [< L *dis-*, apart + *tribuere*, allot] **1** to give out in shares **2** to spread out **3** to classify **4** to put (things) in various distinct places —**dis'tri·bu'tion** *n.*

**dis·trib'u·tor** *n.* one that distributes; specif., *a)* a dealer who distributes goods to consumers *b)* a device for distributing electric current to the spark plugs of a gasoline engine

**dis·trict** (dis'trikt) *n.* [< L *dis-*, apart + *stringere*, to stretch] **1** a division of a state, city, etc. made for a specific purpose **2** any region

**district attorney** the prosecuting attorney for the state or the federal government in a specified district

**District of Columbia** federal district of the U.S., on the Potomac: 61 sq. mi.; pop. 607,000; coextensive with the city of Washington: abbrev. *DC*

**dis·trust** (dis trust') *n.* a lack of trust; doubt —*vt.* to have no trust in; doubt —**dis·trust'ful** *adj.*

**dis·turb** (dis sturb') *vt.* [< L *dis-*, intens. + *turbare*, to disorder] **1** to break up the quiet or settled order of **2** to make uneasy; upset **3** to interrupt —**dis·turb'er** *n.*

**dis·turb'ance** *n.* **1** a disturbing or being disturbed **2** anything that disturbs **3** commotion; disorder

**dis·u·nite** (dis'yōō nīt') *vt., vi.* **-nit'ed, -nit'ing** to divide or separate into parts, factions, etc. —**dis·u'ni·ty** *n.*

**dis·use'** (-yōōs') *n.* lack of use

**ditch** (dich) *n.* [OE *dic*] a long, narrow channel

dug into the earth, as for drainage —*vt.* **1** to make a ditch in **2** [Slang] to get rid of

**dith·er** (dith′ər) *vi.* [ME *dideren*] **1** to be nervously excited or confused **2** to be indecisive —*n.* a nervously excited or confused state

**dit·sy** (dit′sē) *adj.* **-si·er, -si·est** [? < DIZZY] [Slang] silly, flighty, eccentric, etc.: also sp. **dit′zy**

**dit·to** (dit′ō) *n.,* pl. **-tos** [It < L *dicere*, to say] **1** the same (as above or before) **2** DITTO MARK

**ditto mark** a mark (″) used in lists or tables to show that the item above is to be repeated

**dit·ty** (dit′ē) *n.,* pl. **-ties** [< L *dicere*, to say] a short, simple song

**di·u·ret·ic** (dī′yoo ret′ik) *adj.* [< Gr *dia-*, through + *ourein*, urinate] increasing the flow of urine —*n.* a diuretic drug or substance

**di·ur·nal** (dī ur′nəl) *adj.* [< L *dies*, day] **1** daily **2** of the daytime —**di·ur′nal·ly** *adv.*

**div** *abbrev.* **1** dividend **2** division

**di·va** (dē′və) *n.,* pl. **-vas** or **-ve** (-ve) [It < L, goddess] a leading woman singer

**di·va·lent** (dī′vā′lənt, dī vā′-) *adj. Chem.* having two valences or a valence of two

**di·van** (di van′, dī′van′) *n.* [< Pers *dīwān*] a large, low couch or sofa

**dive** (dīv) *vi.* **dived** or **dove, dived, div′ing** [OE *dyfan*] **1** to plunge headfirst into water **2** to submerge **3** to plunge suddenly into something **4** to make a steep descent, as an airplane —*n.* **1** a diving **2** any sudden plunge **3** a sharp descent **4** [Inf.] a cheap, disreputable saloon, etc. —**div′er** *n.*

**di·verge** (dī vurj′, di-) *vi.* **-verged′, -verg′ing** [< L *dis-*, apart + *vergere*, to turn] **1** to go or move in different directions; branch off **2** to differ, as in opinion —**di·ver′gence** *n.* —**di·ver′gent** *adj.*

**di·vers** (dī′vərz) *adj.* [see fol.] various

**di·verse** (də vurs′, dī-) *adj.* [< L *dis-*, apart + *vertere*, to turn] **1** different **2** varied —**di·verse′ly** *adv.*

**di·ver·si·fy** (də vur′sə fī′) *vt.* **-fied′, -fy′ing 1** to make diverse; vary **2** to divide up (investments, etc.) among different companies, etc. —*vi.* to expand product lines, etc. —**di·ver′si·fi·ca′tion** *n.*

**di·ver·sion** (də vur′zhən, dī-) *n.* **1** a diverting or turning aside **2** distraction of attention **3** a pastime

**di·ver′sion·ar′y** *adj.* serving to divert or distract [*diversionary* tactics]

**di·ver·si·ty** (də vur′sə tē, dī-) *n.,* pl. **-ties 1** difference **2** variety

**di·vert** (də vurt′, dī-) *vt.* [see DIVERSE] **1** to turn (a person or thing) aside from a course, etc. **2** to distract **3** to amuse

**di·ver·tic·u·li·tis** (dī′vər tik′yoo līt′is) *n.* [< L *de-*, from + *vertere*, to turn + -ITIS] inflammation of a sac (**di′ver·tic′u·lum**) opening out from a tubular organ or main cavity

**di·vest** (də vest′, dī-) *vt.* [< L *dis-*, from + *vestire*, to dress] **1** to strip *of* clothing, etc. **2** to deprive *of* rank, rights, etc. **3** to rid *of* something unwanted

**di·vide** (də vīd′) *vt.* **-vid′ed, -vid′ing** [< L *dividere*] **1** to separate into parts; sever **2** to classify **3** to make or keep separate **4** to apportion **5** to cause to disagree **6** *Math.* to separate into equal parts by a divisor —*vi.* **1** to be or become separate **2** to disagree **3** to share **4** *Math.* to do division —*n.* a boundary; specif., a ridge that divides two drainage areas —**di·vid′er** *n.*

**div·i·dend** (div′ə dend′) *n.* **1** the number or quantity to be divided **2** *a)* a sum to be divided among stockholders, etc. *b)* a single share of this **3** a bonus

**div·i·na·tion** (div′ə nā′shən) *n.* [see fol.] **1** the practice of trying to foretell the future **2** a prophecy

**di·vine** (də vīn′) *adj.* [< L *divus*, god] **1** of, like, or from God or a god; holy **2** devoted to God; religious **3** [Inf.] very pleasing, etc. —*n.* a member of the clergy —*vt.* **-vined′, -vin′ing 1** to prophesy **2**

to guess **3** to find out by intuition —**di·vine′ly** *adv.*

**divining rod** a forked stick believed to dip downward when held over an underground supply of water, etc.

**di·vin·i·ty** (də vin′ə tē) *n.* **1** a being divine **2** pl. **-ties** a god **3** theology —**the Divinity** God

**di·vis·i·ble** (də viz′ə bəl) *adj.* that can be divided, esp. without leaving a remainder —**di·vis′i·bil′i·ty** *n.*

**di·vi·sion** (də vizh′ən) *n.* **1** a dividing or being divided **2** an apportioning **3** a difference of opinion **4** anything that divides **5** a segment, section, department, class, etc. **6** the process of finding how many times a number (the *divisor*) is contained in another (the *dividend*) **7** a major military unit

**di·vi·sive** (də vī′siv) *adj.* causing disagreement or dissension —**di·vi′sive·ly** *adv.* —**di·vi′sive·ness** *n.*

**di·vi·sor** (də vī′zər) *n.* the number by which the dividend is divided

**di·vorce** (də vôrs′) *n.* [< L *dis-*, apart + *vertere*, to turn] **1** legal dissolution of a marriage **2** any complete separation —*vt.* **-vorced′, -vorc′ing 1** to dissolve legally a marriage between **2** to dissolve the marriage with (one's spouse) **3** to separate —**di·vorce′ment** *n.*

**di·vor·cée** or **di·vor·cee** (di vôr′sā′, -sē′) *fem.n.* [Fr] a divorced woman —**di·vor′cé′** (-sā′, -sē′) *masc.n.*

**div·ot** (div′ət) *n.* [Scot] *Golf* a lump of turf dislodged in making a stroke

**di·vulge** (də vulj′) *vt.* **-vulged′, -vulg′ing** [< L *dis-*, apart + *vulgare*, make public] to make known; reveal

**div·vy** (div′ē) *vt., vi.* **-vied, -vy·ing** [Slang] to share; divide (*up*)

**Dix·ie** (dik′sē) [< *Dixie*, the minstrel song] the Southern states of the U.S.

**Dix′ie·land′** *adj.* in, of, or like a style of jazz with a ragtime tempo

**DIY** (dē′ī′wī′) *n.* DO-IT-YOURSELF

**diz·zy** (diz′ē) *adj.* **-zi·er, -zi·est** [OE *dysig*, foolish] **1** feeling giddy or unsteady **2** causing giddiness **3** confused **4** [Inf.] silly; harebrained —**diz′zi·ly** *adv.* —**diz′zi·ness** *n.*

**DJ** (dē′jā′) *abbrev. n.* DISC JOCKEY

**djel·la·ba** or **djel·la·bah** (jə lä′bə) *n.* [< Ar] a long, loose outer garment worn in Arabic countries

**Dji·bou·ti** (ji boōt′ē) country in E Africa: 8,958 sq. mi.; pop. 695,000

**DMZ** *abbrev.* demilitarized zone

**DNA** (dē′en·ā′) *n.* [< *d(eoxyribo)n(ucleic) a(cid)*] the basic chromosome material, containing and transmitting the hereditary pattern

**Dne·pr** (nē′pər) river in W Russia, Belarus, & Ukraine, flowing into the Black Sea

**do**¹ (doō) *vt.* **did, done, do′ing** [OE *don*] **1** to perform (an action, etc.) **2** to complete; finish **3** to cause [it *does* no harm] **4** to exert [*do* your best] **5** to deal with as is required [*do* the ironing] **6** to have as one's occupation; work at **7** to move at a speed of [to *do* 65 mph] **8** [Inf.] to serve (a jail term) **9** [Slang] to ingest [to *do* drugs] —*vi.* **1** to behave or perform [*do* as you please] **2** to be active [up and *doing*] **3** to get along; fare [he is *doing* well after surgery] **4** to be adequate [casual dress will *do*] **5** to take place [anything *doing* tonight?] —*v.aux.* **1** used to give emphasis [*do* stay a while] **2** used to ask a question [*did* you go?] **3** used as a substitute verb [act as I *do* (act)] **4** used in a negative construction [*do* not go] —**do in 1** [Slang] to kill **2** [Inf.] to tire out —**do over** [Inf.] to redecorate —**do up** to wrap up —**do with** to make use of —**do without** to get along without —**have to do with** to be related to

**do**² (dō) *n.* [It] *Music* the first or last tone of the diatonic scale

**DOA** *abbrev.* dead on arrival

**do·a·ble** (doō′ə bəl) *adj.* that can be done

**Do·ber·man** (**pin·scher**) (dō′bər mən pin′chər) ⟦< Ger after L. *Dobermann*, 19th-c. breeder + *pin-scher*, terrier⟧ a large dog with a short, dark coat

**doc** (däk) *n.* [Slang] doctor

**do·cent** (dō′sənt) *n.* ⟦< L *docere*, to teach⟧ a lecturer or tour guide, as at a museum

**doc·ile** (däs′əl) *adj.* ⟦see prec.⟧ easy to discipline; submissive —**do·cil·i·ty** (dō sil′ə tē, dä-) *n.*

**dock**[1] (däk) *n.* ⟦< It *doccia*, canal⟧ **1** an excavated basin for receiving ships **2** a wharf; pier **3** the water between two piers **4** a platform for loading and unloading trucks, etc. —*vt., vi.* to bring or come to or into a dock: said of a ship

**dock**[2] (däk) *n.* ⟦< Fl *dok*, a cage⟧ the place where the accused stands or sits in court

**dock**[3] (däk) *n.* ⟦OE *docce*⟧ a tall, coarse weed of the buckwheat family

**dock**[4] (däk) *vt.* ⟦ME *dok*, tail⟧ **1** to cut off the end of (a tail, etc.); bob **2** to deduct from (wages, etc.)

**dock·et** (däk′it) *n.* ⟦< ?⟧ **1** a list of cases to be tried by a law court **2** an agenda —*vt.* to enter in a docket

**dock′yard**′ *n.* SHIPYARD

**doc·tor** (däk′tər) *n.* ⟦< L, teacher⟧ **1** one who holds a doctorate **2** a physician or surgeon **3** one licensed to practice any of the healing arts —*vt.* [Inf.] **1** to try to heal **2** to tamper with

**doc′tor·ate** (-it) *n.* the highest degree awarded by universities —**doc′tor·al** *adj.*

**Doctor of Philosophy** the highest doctorate awarded for original research

**doc·tri·naire** (däk′tri ner′) *adj.* ⟦Fr⟧ adhering to a doctrine dogmatically —**doc′tri·nair′ism**′ *n.*

**doc·trine** (däk′trin) *n.* ⟦see DOCTOR⟧ something taught, esp. as the principles of a religion, political party, etc.; tenet or tenets; dogma —**doc′tri·nal** (-tri nəl) *adj.*

**doc·u·dra·ma** (däk′yo͞o drä′mə) *n.* a TV dramatization of real events

**doc·u·ment** (däk′yo͞o mənt, -yə-; *for v.*, -ment′) *n.* ⟦< L *documentum*, proof⟧ anything printed, written, etc. that contains information or is relied upon to record or prove something —*vt.* to provide with or support by documents

**doc′u·men′ta·ry** (-ment′ə rē) *adj.* **1** of or supported by documents **2** depicting news events, social conditions, etc. in nonfictional but dramatic form —*n., pl.* **-ries** a documentary film, etc.

**doc′u·men·ta′tion** (-mən tā′shən, -men-) *n.* **1** the supplying of documents **2** the documents thus supplied **3** instructions for using computer hardware or software

**dod·der** (däd′ər) *vi.* ⟦ME *daderen*⟧ **1** to shake or tremble, as from old age **2** to totter —**dod′der·ing** *adj.*

**dodge** (däj) *vi., vt.* **dodged, dodg′ing** ⟦< ?⟧ **1** to move quickly aside, or avoid by so moving **2** to use tricks or evasions, or evade by so doing —*n.* **1** a dodging **2** a trick used in evading or cheating —**dodg′er** *n.*

**do·do** (dō′dō) *n., pl.* **-dos** or **-does** ⟦Port *doudo*, lit., stupid⟧ **1** a large, flightless bird, now extinct **2** [Slang] a stupid person

**doe** (dō) *n.* ⟦OE *da*⟧ the female deer, antelope, rabbit, etc.

**do·er** (do͞o′ər) *n.* **1** one who does something **2** one who gets things done

**does** (duz) *vt., vi.* 3d pers. sing., pres. indic., of DO[1]

**doe′skin**′ *n.* **1** leather from the skin of a female deer **2** a soft woolen cloth

**doff** (däf, dôf) *vt.* ⟦see DO[1] & OFF⟧ to take off (one's hat, clothes, etc.)

**dog** (dôg) *n.* ⟦OE *docga*⟧ **1** any of various canines, esp. one of a domesticated breed kept as a pet, for hunting, etc. **2** a mean, contemptible fellow **3** [*pl.*] [Slang] feet **4** [Slang] an unattractive person or unsatisfactory thing **5** *Mech.* a device for holding or grappling —*vt.* **dogged, dog′ging** to follow or hunt doggedly —**go to the dogs** [Inf.] to deteriorate

**dog days** the hot, uncomfortable days in July and August

**dog′-ear**′ *n.* a turned-down corner of a page —**dog′-eared**′ *adj.*

**dog′fight**′ *n.* a violent fight; specif., combat between fighter planes

**dog′fish**′ *n., pl.* **-fish**′ or (for different species) **-fish′es** any of various small sharks

**dog·ged** (dôg′id) *adj.* persistent; stubborn —**dog′ged·ly** *adv.*

**dog·ger·el** (dôg′ər əl) *n.* ⟦ME *dogerel*⟧ trivial poetry with a monotonous rhythm

**dog·gie bag** (dôg′ē) a bag supplied by a restaurant for carrying leftovers, as for one's dog

**dog′gone**′ *interj.* damn! darn! —*adj.* [Inf.] damned

**dog′house**′ *n.* a structure for sheltering a dog —**in the doghouse** [Slang] in disfavor

**do·gie** (dō′gē) *n.* ⟦< ?⟧ [West] a stray calf

**dog·ma** (dôg′mə) *n.* ⟦< Gr, opinion⟧ a doctrine; tenet, esp. a theological doctrine strictly adhered to

**dog·mat′ic** (-mat′ik) *adj.* **1** of or like dogma **2** asserted without proof **3** stating opinion positively or arrogantly —**dog·mat′i·cal·ly** *adv.*

**dog′ma·tism**′ (-mə tiz′əm) *n.* dogmatic assertion of opinion —**dog′ma·tist** *n.*

**do′-good′er** *n.* [Inf.] an idealistic, but impractical person who seeks to correct social ills

**dog′-tired**′ *adj.* very tired; exhausted

**dog′trot**′ *n.* a slow, easy trot

**dog′wood**′ *n.* a small, flowering tree of the E U.S.

**doi·ly** (doi′lē) *n., pl.* **-lies** ⟦after a 17th-c. London draper⟧ a small mat, as of lace, put under a vase, etc. as a decoration or to protect a surface

**do·ings** (do͞o′iŋz) *pl.n.* actions or events

**do′-it-your·self**′ *n.* the practice of making or repairing things oneself, instead of hiring another —**do′-it-your·self′er** *n.*

**Dol·by** (dōl′bē) ⟦after R. *Dolby*, U.S. recording engineer⟧ *trademark for* an electronic system used to reduce unwanted noise

**dol·drums** (dōl′drəmz, däl′-) *pl.n.* ⟦< ? DULL⟧ **1** *a*) low spirits *b*) sluggishness **2** equatorial ocean regions having little wind

**dole** (dōl) *n.* ⟦OE *dal*, a share⟧ **1** money or food given in charity **2** money paid by a government to the unemployed —*vt.* **doled, dol′ing** to give (*out*) sparingly or as a dole

**dole′ful** (-fəl) *adj.* ⟦< L *dolere*, suffer⟧ sad; mournful —**dole′ful·ly** *adv.*

**doll** (däl) *n.* ⟦< nickname for *Dorothy*⟧ **1** a child's toy made to resemble a human being **2** [Slang] any attractive or lovable person —*vt., vi.* [Inf.] to dress stylishly or showily: with *up*

**dol·lar** (däl′ər) *n.* ⟦< Ger *thaler*, a coin⟧ **1** the monetary unit of the U.S., equal to 100 cents **2** the monetary unit of various other countries, as of Canada **3** a piece of money worth one dollar

**dol·lop** (däl′əp) *n.* ⟦< ?⟧ **1** a soft mass **2** a quantity, often a small one

**dol·ly** (däl′ē) *n., pl.* **-lies** **1** a doll: child's word **2** a low, flat, wheeled frame for moving heavy objects

**dol·men** (dōl′mən, däl′-) *n.* ⟦Fr⟧ a prehistoric monument consisting of a large, flat stone laid across upright stones

**do·lo·mite** (dō′lə mīt′, däl′ə-) *n.* ⟦after D. *Dolomieu*, 18th-c. Fr geologist⟧ **1** a mineral used in making cement, etc. **2** a sedimentary rock used as a building stone

**do·lor·ous** (dō′lər əs, däl′ər-) *adj.* ⟦< L *dolere*, suffer⟧ sorrowful; sad —**do′lor·ous·ly** *adv.*

**dol·phin** (däl′fin, dôl′-) *n.* ⟦< Gr *delphis*⟧ a highly intelligent toothed whale with a beaklike snout

**dolt** (dōlt) *n.* ⟦prob. < ME *dolte*⟧ a stupid person —**dolt′ish** *adj.*

**-dom** (dəm) ⟦OE *dom*, state⟧ *suffix* **1** rank or

domain of [*kingdom*] **2** fact or state of being [*martyrdom*] **3** all who are [*officialdom*]

**do·main** (dō mān′) *n.* ⟦< L *dominus*, a lord⟧ **1** territory under one government or ruler **2** field of activity or influence

**dome** (dōm) *n.* ⟦< Gr *dōma*, housetop⟧ **1** a rounded roof or ceiling **2** any dome-shaped structure or object; specif., a sports stadium covered with a dome

**do·mes·tic** (dō mes′tik, də-) *adj.* ⟦< L *domus*, house⟧ **1** of the home or family **2** of or made in one's country **3** tame: said of animals **4** enjoying family life —*n.* a maid, cook, etc. in the home — **do·mes′ti·cal·ly** *adv.*

**do·mes·ti·cate** (-ti kāt′) *vt.* **-cat′ed, -cat′ing 1** to accustom to home life **2** to tame or cultivate for human use —**do·mes′ti·ca′tion** *n.*

**do·mes·tic·i·ty** (dō′mes tis′ə tē) *n.* home life or devotion to it

**dom·i·cile** (däm′ə sīl′, -sil; *also* dō′mə-) *n.* ⟦< L *domus*, home⟧ a home; residence —*vt.* **-ciled′, -cil′ing** to establish in a domicile

**dom·i·nant** (däm′ə nənt) *adj.* dominating; ruling; prevailing —**dom′i·nance** *n.* —**dom′i·nant·ly** *adv.*

**dom·i·nate** (-nāt′) *vt., vi.* **-nat′ed, -nat′ing** ⟦< L *dominus*, a master⟧ **1** to rule or control by superior power **2** to rise above (the surroundings) — **dom′i·na′tion** *n.*

**dom·i·neer** (däm′ə nir′) *vi., vt.* ⟦< Du: see prec.⟧ to rule (*over*) in a harsh or arrogant way; tyrannize

**dom′i·neer′ing** *adj.* overbearing

**Do·min·i·can Republic** (dō min′i kən, də-) country in the E part of Hispaniola, in the West Indies: 18,700 sq. mi.; pop. 5,648,000 —**Do·min′i·can** *adj., n.*

**do·min·ion** (də min′yən) *n.* ⟦see DOMINATE⟧ **1** rule or power to rule **2** a governed territory or country **3** [D-] [Historical] a self-governing nation of the Commonwealth

**dom·i·no** (däm′ə nō′) *n., pl.* **-noes′** or **-nos′** ⟦Fr & It⟧ **1** a hooded cloak and a mask, worn at masquerades **2** a small mask that covers the area around the eyes **3** *a*) a small, oblong tile marked with dots *b*) [*pl., with sing. v.*] a game played with such tiles

**don**[1] (dän) *n.* ⟦Sp < L *dominus*, master⟧ **1** [D-] Sir; Mr.: a Spanish title of respect **2** a Spanish gentleman **3** [Chiefly Brit.] a teacher at a British university **4** a Mafia leader

**don**[2] (dän) *vt.* **donned, don′ning** ⟦contr. of *do on*⟧ to put on (clothes)

**Don** (dän) river in SC European Russia, flowing into the Black Sea

**Do·ña** (dô′nyä) *n.* ⟦Sp⟧ Lady; Madam: a Spanish title of respect

**do·nate** (dō′nāt′) *vt., vi.* **-nat′ed, -nat′ing** ⟦< L *donum*, gift⟧ to give or contribute —**do·na′tion** *n.* —**do′nat′or** (-ər) *n.*

**done** (dun) *vt., vi. pp. of* DO[1] —*adj.* **1** completed **2** cooked —**done** (**for**) [Inf.] dead, ruined, etc.

**Don Juan** (dän′ wän′) *Sp. Legend* a dissolute nobleman and seducer of women

**don·key** (däŋ′kē, dôŋ′-, duŋ′-) *n., pl.* **-keys** ⟦< ?⟧ **1** a domesticated ass **2** a stupid or foolish person

**don·ny·brook** (dän′ē brook′) *n.* ⟦after a fair formerly held near Dublin⟧ [Inf.] a rowdy fight or free-for-all

**do·nor** (dō′nər, -nôr) *n.* one who donates

**Don Qui·xo·te** (dän′kē hōt′ē, dän′ kwik′sət) **1** a satirical novel by Cervantes **2** its chivalrous but unrealistic hero

**don't** (dōnt) *contr.* do not

**do·nut** (dō′nut) *n. inf. sp. of* DOUGHNUT

**doo·dle** (dōōd′'l) *vi.* **-dled, -dling** ⟦Ger *dudeln*, to trifle⟧ to scribble aimlessly —*n.* a mark made in doodling —**doo′dler** *n.*

**doo-doo** (dōō′dōō′) *n.* **1** [Inf.] excrement **2** [Slang] trouble

---

**doom** (dōōm) *n.* ⟦OE *dom*⟧ **1** a judgment; sentence **2** fate **3** ruin or death —*vt.* **1** to pass judgment on; condemn **2** to destine to a tragic fate

**dooms′day′** *n.* Judgment Day

**doom′y** *adj.* filled with a sense of doom or disaster

**door** (dôr) *n.* ⟦OE *duru*⟧ **1** a movable structure for opening or closing an entrance **2** a doorway **3** a means of access —**out of doors** outdoors

**door′bell′** *n.* a bell, etc. at the entrance of a building or room, sounded to alert the occupants of a visitor

**door′man′** (-man′, -mən) *n., pl.* **-men′** (-men′, -mən) one whose work is opening the door of a building, hailing taxicabs, etc.

**door′mat′** *n.* a mat to wipe the shoes on before entering a house, etc.

**door′step′** *n.* a step that leads from an outer door to a path, lawn, etc.

**door′-to-door′** *adj., adv.* from one home to the next, calling on each in turn

**door′way′** *n.* **1** an opening in a wall that can be closed by a door **2** any means of access

**door′yard′** *n.* a yard onto which a door of a house opens

**do·pa** (dō′pə) *n.* ⟦< chemical name⟧ an amino acid that is converted by an enzyme in the blood into certain biological chemicals: one isomer (*L-dopa*) is used in treating Parkinson's disease

**dope** (dōp) *n.* ⟦Du *doop*, sauce⟧ **1** any thick liquid used as a lubricant, varnish, filler, etc. **2** [Inf.] a drug or narcotic **3** [Inf.] a stupid person **4** [Slang] information —*vt.* **doped, dop′ing** to drug

**dop′er** *n.* [Slang] a drug addict

**dop·ey** or **dop·y** (dō′pē) *adj.* **-i·er, -i·est** [Inf.] **1** lethargic **2** stupid

**Dor·ic** (dôr′ik) *adj.* designating or of a classical style of architecture marked by fluted columns with plain capitals

**dorm** (dôrm) *n.* [Inf.] DORMITORY

**dor·mant** (dôr′mənt) *adj.* ⟦< L *dormire*, to sleep⟧ **1** inactive **2** *Biol.* in a resting or torpid state — **dor′man·cy** *n.*

**dor·mer** (dôr′mər) *n.* ⟦see prec.⟧ **1** a window set upright in a structure projecting from a sloping roof: also **dormer window 2** such a structure

**dor·mi·to·ry** (dôr′mə tôr′ē) *n., pl.* **-ries** ⟦see DORMANT⟧ **1** a room with beds for a number of people **2** a building with rooms for many people to sleep and live in, as at a college

**dor·mouse** (dôr′mous′) *n., pl.* **-mice′** (-mīs′) ⟦ME *dormous*⟧ a small, furry-tailed Old World rodent

DORMER

**dor·sal** (dôr′səl) *adj.* ⟦< L *dorsum*, the back⟧ of, on, or near the back

**do·ry** (dôr′ē) *n., pl.* **-ries** ⟦< ? AmInd (Central America) *dori*, dugout⟧ a flat-bottomed fishing boat with high sides

**dose** (dōs) *n.* ⟦< Gr *dosis*, a giving⟧ an amount of a medicine to be taken at one time —*vt.* **dosed, dos′ing** to give doses to —**dos′age** *n.*

**do·sim·e·ter** (dō sim′ət ər) *n.* a device for measuring exposure to ionizing radiation

**dos·si·er** (däs′ē ā′) *n.* ⟦Fr⟧ a collection of documents about some person or matter

**dost** (dust) *vt., vi. archaic 2d pers. sing., pres. indic., of* DO[1]: used with *thou*

**Dos·to·ev·ski** or **Dos·to·yev·sky** (dôs′tô yef′skē), **Feo·dor** (fyô′dôr′) 1821-81; Russ. novelist

**dot** (dät) *n.* ⟦OE *dott*, head of boil⟧ **1** a tiny speck or mark **2** a small, round spot —*vt.* **dot′ted,**

**dot'ting** to mark with or as with a dot or dots — **on the dot** [Inf.] at the exact time

**dot·age** (dōt′ij) *n.* ⟦ME < *doten*, DOTE⟧ childish state due to old age

**dot'ard** (-ərd) *n.* one in his or her dotage

**dot.com** (dät′käm′) *adj.* [Inf.] designating or of a company doing business mostly on the Web: also **dot-com**

**dote** (dōt) *vi.* **dot'ed, dot'ing** ⟦ME *doten*⟧ to be excessively fond: with *on* or *upon*

**doth** (duth) *vt., vi. archaic* 3d *pers. sing., pres. indic., of* DO¹

**dot'ing** (dōt′iŋ) *adj.* foolishly or excessively fond —**dot'ing·ly** *adv.*

**dot'-ma'trix** *adj.* of or by printing in which characters are formed of closely spaced dots

**Dou·ay Bible** (dōō ā′) an English version of the Bible for Roman Catholics: after Douai, France, where the Old Testament was published

**dou·ble** (dub′əl) *adj.* ⟦< L *duplus*⟧ **1** twofold **2** having two layers **3** paired or repeated [*a double consonant*] **4** being of two kinds [*a double standard*] **5** twice as much, as many, etc. **6** made for two —*adv.* **1** twofold or twice **2** two together — *n.* **1** anything twice as much, as many, etc. as normal **2** a duplicate; counterpart **3** a fold **4** [*pl.*] a game of tennis, etc. with two players on each side **5** *Baseball* a hit on which the batter reaches second base **6** *Bridge* the doubling of an opponent's bid —*vt.* **-bled, -bling 1** to make twice as much or as many **2** to fold **3** to repeat or duplicate **4** *Bridge* to increase the point value or penalty of (an opponent's bid) —*vi.* **1** to become double **2** to turn sharply backward **3** to serve as a double **4** to serve an additional purpose **5** *Baseball* to hit a double —**double back** to turn back in the direction from which one came — **double up 1** to clench (one's fist) **2** to bend over, as in pain **3** to share a room, etc. with someone —**on the double** [Inf.] quickly

**double agent** a spy employed by two rival espionage organizations

**dou'ble-bar'reled** *adj.* **1** having two barrels, as a kind of shotgun **2** having a double purpose or meaning

**double bass** (bās) the largest, deepest-toned instrument of the violin family

**dou'ble-blind'** *adj.* designating or of a test of the effects of a drug, treatment, etc. in which neither the subjects nor the researchers know who is receiving the drug, treatment, etc.

**double boiler** a cooking utensil in which one pan, for food, fits over another, for boiling water

**dou'ble-breast'ed** *adj.* overlapping across the breast, as a coat

**dou'ble-cross'** *vt.* [Inf.] to betray —**dou'ble-cross'er** *n.*

**double date** [Inf.] a social engagement shared by two couples —**dou'ble-date', -dat'ed, -dat'ing,** *vi., vt.*

**dou'ble-deal'ing** *n.* duplicity

**dou'ble-deck'er** *n.* **1** any structure or vehicle with an upper deck **2** [Inf.] a sandwich with two layers of filling and three slices of bread

**dou'ble-dig'it** *adj.* amounting to ten percent or more [*double-digit* inflation]

**double dipping** an unethical receiving of pay from two or more sources

**dou·ble-en·ten·dre** (dub′əl än tän′drə, dōō′blôn tôn′drə) *n.* ⟦< Fr⟧ a term with two meanings, esp. when one is risqué

**dou'ble-head'er** *n.* two games played in succession on the same day

**dou'ble-joint'ed** *adj.* having joints that permit limbs, fingers, etc. to bend at other than the usual angles

**dou'ble-knit'** *adj.* knit with a double stitch that makes the fabric extra thick

**double play** *Baseball* a play in which two players are put out

**dou'ble-reed'** *adj.* designating or of a woodwind

instrument, as the oboe, having two reeds separated by a narrow opening

**double standard** a system, code, etc. applied unequally; specif., a moral code stricter for women than for men

**dou·blet** (dub′lit) *n.* ⟦< OFr *double*, orig., something folded⟧ **1** a man's closefitting jacket of the 14th-16th c. **2** a pair, or one of a pair

**double take** a delayed reaction, as a second glance, following unthinking acceptance

**double talk 1** ambiguous and deceptive talk **2** meaningless syllables made to sound like talk

**dou·bloon** (də blōōn′) *n.* ⟦< Fr < Sp < L *duplus*, double⟧ an obsolete Spanish gold coin

**dou·bly** (dub′lē) *adv.* **1** twice **2** two at a time

**doubt** (dout) *vi.* ⟦< L *dubius*, uncertain⟧ to be uncertain or undecided —*vt.* **1** to be uncertain about **2** to tend to disbelieve —*n.* **1** *a)* a wavering of opinion or belief *b)* lack of trust **2** a condition of uncertainty —**beyond** (or **without**) **doubt** certainly —**no doubt 1** certainly **2** probably — **doubt'er** *n.* —**doubt'ing·ly** *adv.*

**doubt'ful** *adj.* **1** uncertain **2** causing doubt or suspicion **3** feeling doubt —**doubt'ful·ly** *adv.*

**doubt'less** *adv.* **1** without doubt; certainly **2** probably —**doubt'less·ly** *adv.*

**douche** (dōōsh) *n.* ⟦Fr < It *doccia*⟧ **1** a jet of liquid applied externally or internally to the body **2** a device for douching —*vt., vi.* **douched, douch'ing** to apply a douche (to)

**dough** (dō) *n.* ⟦OE *dag*⟧ **1** a mixture of flour, liquid, etc. worked into a soft mass for baking **2** [Slang] money

**dough'nut'** *n.* a small, usually ring-shaped cake, fried in deep fat

**dough·ty** (dout′ē) *adj.* **-ti·er, -ti·est** ⟦OE *dohtig*⟧ [Now Rare] valiant; brave

**dough·y** (dō′ē) *adj.* **-i·er, -i·est** of or like dough; soft, pasty, etc.

**Doug·las fir** (dug′ləs) ⟦after D. *Douglas*, 19th-c. Scot botanist in U.S.⟧ a giant North American evergreen tree valued for its wood

**dour** (door, dour) *adj.* ⟦< L *durus*, hard⟧ **1** [Scot.] stern; severe **2** sullen; gloomy

**douse** (dous) *vt.* **doused, dous'ing** ⟦< ?⟧ **1** to thrust suddenly into liquid **2** to drench **3** [Inf.] to put out (a light or fire) quickly

**dove**¹ (duv) *n.* ⟦ME *douve*⟧ **1** any of the smaller species of pigeon: often used as a symbol of peace **2** an advocate of measures which avoid or end wars

**dove**² (dōv) *vi. alt. pt. of* DIVE

**dove'cote'** *n.* a cote with compartments for nesting pigeons

**Do·ver** (dō′vər) capital of Delaware: pop. 28,000

**dove·tail** (duv′tāl′) *n.* a projecting part that fits into a corresponding cut-out space to form a joint —*vt.* to fasten or piece together, as by means of dovetails —*vi.* to fit together closely or logically

**dow·a·ger** (dou′ə jər) *n.* ⟦< L *dotare*, endow⟧ **1** a widow with a title or property derived from her dead husband **2** an elderly, wealthy woman

**dow·dy** (dou′dē) *adj.* **-di·er, -di·est** ⟦< ME *doude*, plain woman⟧ not neat or smart in dress —**dow'di·ness** *n.*

DOVETAIL

**dow·el** (dou′əl) *n.* ⟦ME *doule*⟧ a peg of wood, etc., usually fitted into corresponding holes in two pieces to fasten them together —*vt.* **-eled** or **-elled, -el·ing** or **-el·ling** to fasten with dowels

**dow·er** (dou′ər) *n.* ⟦< L *dare*, give⟧ that part of a man's property which his widow inherits for life

**down**[1] (doun) *adv.* 〖OE *adune*, from the hill〗 1 to, in, or on a lower place or level 2 in or to a low or lower condition, amount, etc. 3 southward *[down* to Mexico*]* 4 from an earlier to a later period 5 out of one's hands *[put it down]* 6 in a serious manner *[get down* to work*]* 7 completely *[loaded down]* 8 when purchased *[$5 down* and $5 a week*]* 9 in writing *[take down* notes*]* —*adj.* 1 descending 2 in a lower place 3 gone, brought, etc. down 4 dejected; discouraged 5 ill 6 finished *[four down,* six to go*]* 7 inoperative *[the computer is down]* —*prep.* down toward, along, through, into, or upon —*vt.* 1 to put or throw down 2 to swallow quickly —*n.* 1 a misfortune *[ups and downs]* 2 *Football* one of a series of plays in which a team tries to advance the ball —**down and out** penniless, ill, etc. —**down on** [Inf.] angry or annoyed with —**down with!** do away with!

**down**[2] (doun) *n.* 〖< ON *dūnn*〗 1 soft, fine feathers 2 soft, fine hair

**down**[3] (doun) *n.* 〖OE *dun,* hill〗 an expanse of open, high, grassy land: *usually used in pl.*

**down'-and-dirt'y** *adj.* [Slang] 1 coarse; vulgar 2 unscrupulous 3 fiercely competitive

**down'beat'** *n. Music* the first beat of each measure

**down'cast'** *adj.* 1 directed downward 2 unhappy; dejected

**Down East** [*also* d- e-] [Inf.] in or into New England, esp. Maine

**down'er** *n.* [Slang] any depressant or sedative

**down'fall'** *n.* 1 a sudden fall, as from power 2 the cause of this

**down'grade'** *n.* a downward slope —*vt.* -grad'ed, -grad'ing 1 to demote 2 to belittle

**down'heart'ed** *adj.* discouraged

**down'hill'** *adv.* toward the bottom of a hill —*adj.* 1 going downward 2 without difficulty

**Down·ing Street** (doun'iŋ) street in London, location of some of the principal government offices of the United Kingdom

**down'load'** *vt., vi.* to transfer (information) as from a network or main computer to another computer

**down payment** a partial payment at the time of purchase

**down'play'** *vt.* to play down; minimize

**down'pour'** *n.* a heavy rain

**down'right'** *adv.* utterly —*adj.* 1 absolute; utter 2 plain; frank

**down'scale'** *adj.* of or for people who are unstylish, not affluent, etc. —*vt., vi.* -scaled', -scal'ing to make smaller, less, cheaper, etc.

**down'size'** *vt., vi.* -sized', -siz'ing to make or become smaller, as by eliminating employees

**down'stage'** *adj., adv.* of or toward the front of the stage

**down'stairs'** *adv.* 1 down the stairs 2 on or to a lower floor —*adj.* on a lower floor —*n.* a lower floor

**down'state'** *adj., adv.* in, to, or from the southerly part of a U.S. state

**down'stream'** *adv., adj.* in the direction of the current of a stream

**down'swing'** *n.* 1 a downward swing, as of a golf club 2 a downward trend: also **down'turn'**

**Down** (or **Down's**) **syndrome** 〖after J. *Down,* 19th-c. Brit physician〗 a congenital condition characterized by mental deficiency, a broad face, etc.

**down'time'** *n.* the time a machine, factory, etc. is not working or functioning

**down'-to-earth'** *adj.* 1 realistic .or practical 2 without affectation

**down'town'** *adj., adv.* in or toward the main business section of a city —*n.* the downtown section of a city

**down'trod'den** *adj.* oppressed

**down'ward** (-wərd) *adv., adj.* toward a lower place, position, etc.: also **down'wards** *adv.*

**down'y** *adj.* -i·er, -i·est 1 covered with soft, fine feathers or hair 2 soft and fluffy, like down

**dow·ry** (dou'rē) *n., pl.* -ries 〖see DOWER〗 property a woman brings to her husband at marriage

**dowse** (douz) *vi.* dowsed, dows'ing 〖< ?〗 to use a divining rod —**dows'er** *n.*

**dox·ol·o·gy** (däks äl'ə jē) *n., pl.* -gies 〖< Gr *doxa,* praise + *-logia,* -LOGY〗 a hymn of praise to God

**doz** *abbrev.* dozen(s)

**doze** (dōz) *vi.* dozed, doz'ing 〖prob. < Scand〗 to sleep lightly; nap —*n.* a light sleep —**doz'er** *n.*

**doz·en** (duz'ən) *n., pl.* -ens or -en 〖< L *duo,* two + *decem,* ten〗 a set of twelve —**doz'enth** *adj.*

**dpt** *abbrev.* 1 department 2 deponent

**Dr** or **Dr.** *abbrev.* 1 Doctor 2 Drive

**drab** (drab) *n.* 〖< VL *drappus,* cloth〗 a dull yellowish brown —*adj.* drab'ber, drab'best 1 dull yellowish-brown 2 dull; dreary —**drab'ness** *n.*

**drach·ma** (drak'mə) *n.* 〖< Gr *drachmē*〗 1 an ancient Greek coin 2 the monetary unit of modern Greece

**Drac·u·la** (drak'yə lə) *n.* the title character in a novel (1897): a Romanian VAMPIRE (sense 1)

**draft** (draft) *n.* 〖OE *dragan,* to draw〗 1 a drawing or pulling, as of a vehicle or load 2 *a)* a drawing in of a fish net *b)* the amount of fish caught in one draw 3 *a)* a drinking or the amount taken at one drink *b)* [Inf.] a portion of beer, etc. drawn from a cask 4 an inhalation 5 a preliminary or tentative piece of writing 6 a plan or drawing of a work to be done 7 a current of air 8 a device for regulating the current of air in a heating system 9 a written order for payment of money; check 10 *a)* the choosing or taking of persons, esp. for compulsory military service *b)* those so taken 11 the depth of water that a ship needs in order to float —*vt.* 1 to take, as for military service, by drawing from a group 2 to make a sketch of or plans for —*adj.* 1 used for pulling loads 2 drawn from a cask *[draft* beer*]* —**draft'er** *n.*

**draft·ee** (draf tē') *n.* a person drafted, esp. for military service

**drafts·man** (drafts'mən) *n., pl.* -men (-mən) 1 one who draws plans, as of machinery 2 an artist skillful in drawing —**drafts'man·ship** *n.*

**draft'y** *adj.* -i·er, -i·est open to drafts of air

**drag** (drag) *vt., vi.* dragged, drag'ging 〖see DRAW〗 1 to pull or be pulled with effort, esp. along the ground 2 to search (a lake bottom, etc.) with a dragnet or the like 3 to draw (something) out over a period of time; move or pass too slowly: often with *on* or *out* —*n.* 1 a dragging 2 a dragnet, grapnel, etc. 3 anything that hinders 4 [Slang] influence 5 [Slang] clothing of the opposite sex, esp. as worn by a male homosexual 6 [Slang] a puff of a cigarette, etc. 7 [Slang] street *[the main drag]* 8 [Slang] a dull person, situation, etc.

**drag'gy** (-ē) *adj.* -gi·er, -gi·est dragging; slow-moving, dull, etc.

**drag'net'** *n.* 1 a net dragged along a lake bottom, etc., as for catching fish 2 an organized system or network for catching criminals, etc.

**drag·on** (drag'ən) *n.* 〖< Gr *drakōn*〗 a mythical monster, usually shown as a large, winged reptile breathing out fire

**drag'on·fly'** *n., pl.* -flies' a large, long-bodied insect with transparent, net-veined wings

**dra·goon** (drə gōōn') *n.* 〖< Fr *dragon,* DRAGON〗 a heavily armed cavalryman —*vt.* to force *into* doing something; coerce

**drag race** a race between cars accelerating from a standstill on a short, straight course (**drag strip**) —**drag'-race', -raced', -rac'ing,** *vi.*

**drain** (drān) *vt.* 〖OE *dryge,* dry〗 1 to draw off (liquid) gradually 2 to draw liquid from gradually 3 to drink all the liquid from (a cup, etc.) 4 to exhaust (strength, resources, etc.) gradually —*vi.* 1 to flow off or trickle through gradually 2 to become dry by draining 3 to disappear gradually;

fade —*n.* **1** a channel or pipe for draining **2** a draining **3** that which gradually exhausts strength, etc. —**drain'er** *n.*

**drain'age** *n.* **1** a draining **2** a system of drains **3** that which is drained off **4** an area drained

**drain'pipe'** *n.* a pipe used to carry off water, sewage, etc.

**drake** (drāk) *n.* ⟦ME⟧ a male duck

**dram** (dram) *n.* ⟦< Gr *drachmē*, handful⟧ **1** a unit of apothecaries' weight equal to 3.89 grams **2** a unit of avoirdupois weight equal to 1.77 grams **3** a small drink of alcoholic liquor

**dra·ma** (drä'mə, dram'ə) *n.* ⟦< Gr⟧ **1** a literary composition to be performed by actors; play, esp. one that is not a comedy **2** the art of writing, acting, or producing plays **3** a series of events suggestive of those of a play **4** dramatic quality

**Dram·a·mine** (dram'ə mēn') *trademark for* a drug to relieve motion sickness

**dra·mat·ic** (drə mat'ik) *adj.* **1** of drama **2** like a play **3** vivid, striking, etc. —**dra·mat'i·cal·ly** *adv.*

**dra·mat·ics** *pl.n.* **1** [*usually with sing. v.*] the performing or producing of plays **2** exaggerated emotionalism

**dram·a·tist** (dram'ə tist, drä'mə-) *n.* a playwright

**dram·a·tize** ('-tīz') *vt.* **-tized', -tiz'ing** **1** to make into a drama **2** to regard or show in a dramatic manner —**dram'a·ti·za'tion** *n.*

**drank** (draŋk) *vt., vi. pt. of* DRINK

**drape** (drāp) *vt.* **draped, drap'ing** ⟦< VL *drappus*, cloth⟧ **1** to cover or hang as with cloth in loose folds **2** to arrange (a garment, etc.) in folds or hangings —*n.* **1** cloth hanging in loose folds **2** a heavy curtain hanging in loose folds

**drap·er** (drā'pər) *n.* [Brit.] a dealer in cloth and dry goods

**drap·er·y** *n., pl.* **-er·ies** **1** [Brit.] DRY GOODS **2** hangings or clothing arranged in loose folds **3** [*pl.*] curtains of heavy material

**dras·tic** (dras'tik) *adj.* ⟦Gr *drastikos*, active⟧ having a strong effect; extreme —**dras'ti·cal·ly** *adv.*

**draught** (draft) *n., vt., adj. now chiefly Brit. sp. of* DRAFT

**draughts** (drafts) *n.* [Brit.] the game of checkers

**draw** (drô) *vt.* **drew, drawn, draw'ing** ⟦OE *dragan*⟧ **1** to make move toward one; pull **2** to pull up, down, back, in, or out **3** to need (a specified depth of water) to float in: said of a ship **4** to attract **5** to breathe in **6** to elicit (a reply, etc.) **7** to bring on; provoke **8** to receive [to *draw* a salary] **9** to withdraw (money) held in an account **10** to write (a check or draft) **11** to reach (a conclusion, etc.); deduce **12** to take or get (a playing card, etc.) **13** to stretch **14** to make (lines, pictures, etc.), as with a pencil **15** to make (comparisons, etc.) **16** to cause to flow —*vi.* **1** to draw something **2** to be drawn **3** to come; move **4** to shrink **5** to allow a draft of air, smoke, etc. to move through **6** to make a demand (*on*) —*n.* **1** a drawing or being drawn **2** the result of drawing **3** a thing drawn **4** a tie; stalemate **5** a thing that attracts **6** a shallow ravine —**draw out 1** to extend **2** to take out; extract **3** to get (a person) to talk —**draw up 1** to arrange in order **2** to draft (a document) **3** to stop

**draw'back'** *n.* anything that prevents or lessens satisfaction; shortcoming

**draw'bridge'** *n.* a bridge that can be raised or drawn aside, as to permit passage of ships

**draw·er** (drô'ər; *for 2* drôr) *n.* **1** one that draws **2** a sliding box in a table, chest, etc.

**drawers** (drôrz) *pl.n.* UNDERPANTS

**draw'ing** *n.* **1** the act of one that draws; specif., the art of making pictures, etc., as with a pencil **2** a picture, etc. thus made **3** a lottery

**drawing board** a flat board to hold paper, etc. for making drawings —**back to the drawing board** [Inf.] back to the beginning, as to see where went wrong

**drawing card** an entertainer, show, etc. that draws a large audience

**drawing room** ⟦< *withdrawing room*: guests withdrew there after dinner⟧ a room where guests are received or entertained; living room

**drawl** (drôl) *vt., vi.* ⟦prob. < DRAW, *v.*⟧ to speak slowly, prolonging the vowels —*n.* such a way of speaking

**drawn** (drôn) *vt., vi. pp. of* DRAW —*adj.* **1** pulled out **2** disemboweled **3** tense; haggard

**drawn butter** melted butter

**draw'string'** *n.* a string drawn through a hem, as to tighten a garment

**dray** (drā) *n.* ⟦OE *dragan*, to draw⟧ a low cart for carrying heavy loads

**dread** (dred) *vt.* ⟦OE *ondrædan*⟧ to anticipate with fear or distaste —*n.* **1** intense fear **2** fear mixed with awe **3** reluctance and uneasiness —*adj.* inspiring dread

**dread'ful** (-fəl) *adj.* **1** awesome or terrible **2** [Inf.] very bad, offensive, etc. —**dread'ful·ly** *adv.*

**dread'locks'** *pl.n.* hair worn in long, thin braids or uncombed, twisted locks

**dread'nought'** or **dread'naught'** (-nôt') *n.* a large, heavily armored battleship

**dream** (drēm) *n.* ⟦OE, joy, music⟧ **1** a sequence of images, etc. passing through a sleeping person's mind **2** a daydream; reverie **3** a fond hope **4** anything dreamlike —*vi., vt.* **dreamed** or **dreamt** (dremt), **dream'ing** to have a dream or remote idea (*of*) —**dream up** [Inf.] to devise (a fanciful plan, etc.) —**dream'er** *n.* —**dream'less** *adj.* —**dream'like'** *adj.*

**dream'land'** *n.* **1** any lovely but imaginary place **2** sleep

**dream world 1** DREAMLAND **2** the realm of fantasy

**dream'y** *adj.* **-i·er, -i·est** **1** filled with dreams **2** fond of daydreaming **3** like something in a dream **4** soothing **5** [Slang] wonderful —**dream'i·ly** *adv.*

**drear·y** (drir'ē) *adj.* **-i·er, -i·est** ⟦OE *dreorig*, sad⟧ dismal: also [Old Poet.] **drear** —**drear'i·ly** *adv.* —**drear'i·ness** *n.*

**dredge**[1] (drej) *n.* ⟦prob. < MDu⟧ an apparatus for scooping up mud, etc., as in deepening channels —*vt., vi.* **dredged, dredg'ing** **1** to search for or gather (*up*) as with a dredge **2** to enlarge or clean out with a dredge

**dredge**[2] (drej) *vt.* **dredged, dredg'ing** ⟦ME *dragge*, sweetmeat⟧ to coat (food) with flour, etc.

**dregs** (dregz) *pl.n.* ⟦< ON *dregg*⟧ **1** particles settling at the bottom in a liquid **2** the most worthless part

**Drei·ser** (drī'sər, -zər), **The·o·dore** (**Herman Albert**) (thē'ə dôr') 1871-1945; U.S. novelist

**drench** (drench) *vt.* ⟦OE *drincan*, to drink⟧ to make wet all over; soak

**Dres·den** (drez'dən) city in E Germany: pop. 481,000

**dress** (dres) *vt.* **dressed** or **drest, dress'ing** ⟦< L *dirigere*, lay straight⟧ **1** to put clothes on; clothe **2** to trim; adorn **3** to arrange (the hair) in a certain way **4** to align (troops) **5** to apply medicines and bandages to (a wound, etc.) **6** to prepare for use, esp. for cooking [to *dress* a fowl] **7** to smooth or finish (stone, wood, etc.) —*vi.* **1** to put on clothes **2** to dress formally **3** to line up in rank —*n.* **1** clothing **2** the usual outer garment of women, generally of one piece with a skirt —*adj.* **1** of or for dresses **2** for formal wear —**dress down 1** to scold **2** to wear casual clothes to work, etc. —**dress up** to dress formally, elegantly, etc.

**dres·sage** (dre säzh') *n.* ⟦Fr, training⟧ horsemanship using slight movements to control the horse

**dress circle** a semicircle of seats in a theater, etc., usually behind and above the orchestra seats

**dress code** a set of rules governing clothing to be worn, as in a given school or business

**dress'er** *n.* **1** one who dresses (in various senses)

**2** a chest of drawers for clothes, usually with a mirror

**dress'ing** *n.* **1** the act of one that dresses **2** bandages, etc. applied to wounds **3** a sauce for salads, etc. **4** a stuffing for roast fowl, etc.

**dress'ing-down'** *n.* a sound scolding

**dressing gown** a loose robe for one not fully clothed, as when lounging

**dress'mak·er** *n.* one who makes dresses, etc. — **dress'mak'ing** *n.*

**dress rehearsal** a final rehearsal, as of a play, with costumes, etc.

**dress'y** *adj.* **-i·er, -i·est 1** showy or elaborate in dress or appearance **2** stylish, elegant, etc. — **dress'i·ness** *n.*

**drew** (drōo) *vt., vi. pt. of* DRAW

**drib·ble** (drib'əl) *vi., vt.* **-bled, -bling** [[< DRIP]] **1** to flow, or let flow, in drops **2** to drool **3** *Sports* to move (a ball or puck) along by repeated bouncing, kicking, or tapping —*n.* **1** a dribbling **2** a tiny amount: also **drib'let** (-lit) — **drib'bler** *n.*

**dried** (drīd) *vt., vi. pt. & pp. of* DRY

**dri·er** (drī'ər) *n.* **1** a substance added to paint, etc. to make it dry fast **2** DRYER —*adj. compar. of* DRY

**dri'est** (-ist) *adj. superl. of* DRY

**drift** (drift) *n.* [[OE *drifan*, to drive]] **1** *a)* a being carried along, as by a current *b)* the course of this **2** a trend; tendency **3** general meaning; intent **4** a heap of snow, sand, etc. piled up by wind —*vi.* **1** to be carried along, as by a current **2** to go along aimlessly **3** to pile up in drifts —*vt.* to cause to drift —**drift'er** *n.*

**drift'wood'** *n.* wood drifting in the water or washed ashore

**drill**[1] (dril) *n.* [[< Du *drillen*, to bore]] **1** a tool for boring holes **2** *a)* systematic military or physical training *b)* the method or practice of teaching by repeated exercises —*vt., vi.* **1** to bore with a drill (the tool) **2** to train in, or teach by means of, a drill —**drill'er** *n.*

**drill**[2] (dril) *n.* [[< ?]] a planting machine for making holes or furrows and dropping seeds into them

**drill**[3] (dril) *n.* [[< L *trilix*, three-threaded]] a coarse, twilled cotton cloth, used for uniforms, etc.

**drill'mas·ter** *n.* **1** an instructor in military drill **2** one who teaches by drilling

**drill press** a power-driven machine for drilling holes in metal, etc.

**dri·ly** (drī'lē) *adv.* DRYLY

**drink** (driŋk) *vt.* **drank, drunk, drink'ing** [[OE *drincan*]] **1** to swallow (liquid) **2** to absorb (liquid) **3** to swallow the contents of —*vi.* **1** to swallow liquid **2** to drink alcoholic liquor, esp. to excess —*n.* **1** any liquid for drinking **2** alcoholic liquor —**drink in** to take in eagerly with the senses or mind —**drink to** to drink a toast to — **drink'a·ble** *adj.* —**drink'er** *n.*

**drip** (drip) *vi., vt.* **dripped** or **dript, drip'ping** [[OE *dryppan*]] to fall, or let fall, in drops —*n.* **1** a dripping **2** the sound of falling drops of a liquid **3** [Slang] a dull person —**drip'per** *n.*

**drip'-dry'** *adj.* designating garments that dry quickly when hung wet and require little or no ironing

**drive** (drīv) *vt.* **drove, driv·en** (driv'ən), **driv'ing** [[OE *drifan*]] **1** to force to go; push forward **2** to force into or from a state or act **3** to force to work, esp. to excess **4** to hit (a ball, etc.) hard **5** to make penetrate **6** *a)* to control the movement of; operate (a car, bus, etc.) *b)* to transport in a car, etc. **7** to push (a bargain, deal, etc.) **8** to motivate, influence, etc. —*vi.* **1** to advance violently **2** to try hard, as to reach a goal **3** to drive a blow, ball, etc. **4** to be driven: said of a car, bus, etc. **5** to operate, or go in, a car, etc. —*n.* **1** a driving **2** a trip in a car, etc. **3** *a)* a road for cars, etc. *b)* a driveway **4** a rounding up of animals **5** an organized effort to gain an objective **6** energy and initiative **7** a strong impulse or urge **8** the propelling mechanism of a machine, etc. **9** a com-

puter device that reads and writes data —**drive at** to mean; intend —**drive in 1** to force in, as by a blow **2** *Baseball* to cause (a runner) to score or (a run) to be scored

**drive'-by'** *n., pl.* **-bys'** a shooting in which the shots are fired from a passing car, etc.

**drive'-in'** *n.* a restaurant, movie theater, bank, etc. designed to serve people seated in their cars

**driv·el** (driv'əl) *vi., vt.* **-eled** or **-elled, -el·ing** or **-el·ling** [[OE *dreflian*]] **1** to let (saliva) drool **2** to speak or say in a silly, stupid way —*n.* silly, stupid talk —**driv'el·er** or **driv'el·ler** *n.*

**driv'en** (-ən) *adj.* acting because of urgency or compulsion

**driv·er** (drī'vər) *n.* a person or thing that drives, as *a)* one who drives a car, etc. *b)* one who herds cattle *c)* a golf club for hitting from the tee

**drive shaft** a shaft that transmits motion, as to the rear axle of a car

**drive'-through'** *n.* a restaurant, bank, etc. that provides service through a window to a person in a car, etc.: also sp. **drive'-thru'**

**drive'train'** *n.* the system that transmits an engine's power to wheels, a propeller, etc.

**drive'way'** *n.* a path for cars, from a street to a garage, house, etc.

**driz·zle** (driz'əl) *vi., vt.* **-zled, -zling** [[prob. < ME]] to rain in fine, misty drops —*n.* a fine, misty rain —**driz'zly** *adj.*

**drogue** (drōg) *n.* [[prob. < Scot *drug*, drag]] a funnel-shaped device towed behind an aircraft, etc., as for its drag effect or as a target

**droll** (drōl) *adj.* [[< Fr < MDu *drol*, stout fellow]] amusing in an odd or wry way —**droll'er·y** (-ər ē), *pl.* **-ies,** *n.* —**droll'ness** *n.* —**drol'ly** *adv.*

**drom·e·dar·y** (dräm'ə der'ē) *n., pl.* **-ies** [[< LL *dromedarius* (*camelus*), running (camel)]] an Arabian camel, esp. one for riding

**drone**[1] (drōn) *n.* [[OE *dran*]] **1** a male bee or ant that does no work **2** an idler; loafer **3** a drudge **4** a pilotless airplane

**drone**[2] (drōn) *vi.* **droned, dron'ing** [[< prec.]] **1** to make a continuous humming sound **2** to talk in a monotonous way —*vt.* to utter in a monotonous tone —*n.* a droning sound

**drool** (drōol) *vi.* [[< DRIVEL]] **1** to let saliva flow from one's mouth **2** to flow from the mouth, as saliva —*n.* saliva running from the mouth

**droop** (drōop) *vi.* [[< ON *drūpa*]] **1** to sink, hang, or bend down **2** to lose strength or vitality **3** to become dejected —*vt.* to let hang down —*n.* a drooping —**droop'y, -i·er, -i·est,** *adj.* —**droop'i·ness** *n.*

**drop** (dräp) *n.* [[OE *dropa*]] **1** a bit of liquid rounded in shape by falling, etc. **2** anything like this in shape, etc. **3** a very small quantity **4** a sudden fall, descent, slump, etc. **5** something that drops, as a curtain or trapdoor **6** the distance between a higher and lower level —*vi.* **dropped, drop'ping 1** to fall in drops **2** to fall; come down **3** to fall exhausted, wounded, or dead **4** to pass into a specified state [to *drop* off to sleep] **5** to come to an end [let the matter *drop*] **6** to become lower —*vt.* **1** to let or make fall **2** to utter (a hint, etc.) casually **3** to send (a letter) **4** to stop, end, or dismiss **5** to lower or lessen **6** [Inf.] to leave at a specified place: often with *off* **7** to omit or remove **8** [Slang] to lose (money, etc.) —**drop in** (or **over** or **by**) to pay a casual visit — **drop off** [Inf.] to fall asleep —**drop out** to stop participating —**drop'let** (-lit) *n.*

**drop'-dead'** [Slang] *adj.* spectacular; striking — *adv.* extremely [*drop-dead* handsome]

**drop kick** *Rugby, etc.* a kick of a dropped ball just as it hits the ground —**drop'-kick'** *vt., vi.* —**drop'-kick'er** *n.*

**drop'-off'** *n.* **1** a very steep drop **2** a decline, as in sales or prices

**drop'out'** *n.* one who withdraws from school before graduating

**drop'per** *n.* a small tube with a hollow rubber

bulb at one end, used to measure out a liquid in drops

**drop·sy** (dräp′sē) *n.* ⟦< Gr *hydrōps* < *hydōr*, water⟧ *former term for* EDEMA

**dross** (drôs) *n.* ⟦OE *dros*⟧ **1** scum on molten metal **2** refuse; rubbish

**drought** (drout) *n.* ⟦< OE *drugoth*, dryness⟧ **1** prolonged dry weather **2** a prolonged shortage

**drove**[1] (drōv) *n.* ⟦OE *draf*⟧ **1** a number of cattle, sheep, etc. driven or moving along as a group; flock; herd **2** a moving crowd of people: *usually used in pl.*

**drove**[2] (drōv) *vt., vi. pt. of* DRIVE

**dro·ver** (drō′vər) *n.* one who herds droves of animals, esp. to market

**drown** (droun) *vi.* ⟦ME *drounen*⟧ to die by suffocation in water —*vt.* **1** to kill by such suffocation **2** to flood **3** to be so loud as to overcome (another sound): usually with *out*

**drowse** (drouz) *vi.* **drowsed, drows′ing** ⟦< OE *drusian*, become sluggish⟧ to be half asleep; doze —*n.* a doze

**drows·y** (drou′zē) *adj.* **-i·er, -i·est** being or making sleepy or half asleep —**drows′i·ly** *adv.* —**drows′i·ness** *n.*

**drub** (drub) *vt.* **drubbed, drub′bing** ⟦< Ar *daraba*, to cudgel⟧ **1** to beat as with a stick **2** to defeat soundly —**drub′ber** *n.* —**drub′bing** *n.*

**drudge** (druj) *n.* ⟦ME *druggen*⟧ one who does hard or tedious work —*vi.* **drudged, drudg′ing** to do such work —**drudg′er·y,** *pl.* **-ies,** *n.*

**drug** (drug) *n.* ⟦< OFr *drogue*⟧ **1** any substance used as or in a medicine **2** a narcotic, hallucinogen, etc. —*vt.* **drugged, drug′ging 1** to put a harmful drug in (a drink, etc.) **2** to stupefy as with a drug —**drug on the market** a thing in plentiful supply for which there is little or no demand

**drug′gie** (-ē) *n.* [Slang] a habitual user of drugs: also **drug′gy,** *pl.* **-gies**

**drug·gist** (-ist) *n.* **1** a dealer in drugs, medical supplies, etc. **2** a pharmacist **3** a drugstore owner or manager

**drug′store′** *n.* a store where drugs, medical supplies, and various items are sold and prescriptions are filled

**dru·id** (drōō′id) *n.* ⟦< Celt⟧ [*often* D-] a member of a Celtic religious order in ancient Britain, Ireland, and France —**dru′id·ism′** *n.*

**drum** (drum) *n.* ⟦< Du *trom*⟧ **1** a percussion instrument consisting of a hollow cylinder with a membrane stretched over the end or ends **2** the sound produced by beating a drum **3** any drumlike cylindrical object **4** the eardrum —*vi.* **drummed, drum′ming 1** to beat a drum **2** to tap continually —*vt.* **1** to play (a rhythm, etc.) as on a drum **2** to instill (ideas, facts, etc.) *into* by continued repetition —**drum out** to expel from in disgrace —**drum up** to get (business, etc.) by soliciting

**drum·lin** (drum′lin) *n.* ⟦< Ir⟧ a low, flattened, oval mound or hill formed by a glacier

**drum major** one who leads a marching band, keeping time with a baton —**drum ma′jor·ette′** (-et′) *fem.*

**drum′mer** *n.* **1** a drum player **2** [Old Inf.] a traveling salesman

**drum′stick′** *n.* **1** a stick for beating a drum **2** the lower half of the leg of a cooked fowl

**drunk** (druŋk) *vt., vi. pp. of* DRINK —*adj.* **1** overcome by alcoholic liquor; intoxicated **2** overcome by any powerful emotion **3** [Inf.] DRUNKEN (sense 2) Usually used in the predicate —*n.* **1** [Inf.] a drunken person **2** [Slang] a drinking spree

**drunk′ard** *n.* a person who often gets drunk

**drunk′en** *adj.* **1** intoxicated **2** caused by or occurring during intoxication Used before a noun —**drunk′en·ly** *adv.* —**drunk′en·ness** *n.*

**drupe** (drōōp) *n.* ⟦< Gr *druppa* (elaa), olive⟧ any fleshy fruit with an inner stone, as a peach

**dry** (drī) *adj.* **dri′er, dri′est** ⟦OE *dryge*⟧ **1** not

**151**                                    ◄ **ductile**

under water [*dry land*] **2** not wet or damp **3** lacking rain or water; arid **4** thirsty **5** not yielding milk **6** solid; not liquid **7** not sweet [*dry wine*] **8** prohibiting alcoholic beverages [*a dry town*] **9** funny in a quiet but sharp way [*dry wit*] **10** unproductive **11** boring; dull —*n., pl.* **drys** [Inf.] a prohibitionist —*vt., vi.* **dried, dry′ing** to make or become dry —**dry up 1** to make or become thoroughly dry **2** to make or become unproductive **3** [Slang] to stop talking —**dry′ly** *adv.* —**dry′ness** *n.*

**dry·ad** (drī′ad) *n.* ⟦< Gr *drys*, tree⟧ [*also* D-] *Gr. & Rom. Myth.* a tree nymph

**dry cell** a voltaic cell containing a moist, pastelike electrolyte which cannot spill

**dry′-clean′** *vt.* to clean (garments, etc.) with a solvent other than water, as naphtha —**dry cleaner**

**dry dock** a dock from which the water can be emptied, used for building and repairing ships

**dry′er** *n.* **1** one that dries; specif., an appliance for drying clothes with heat **2** DRIER

**dry farming** farming without irrigation, by conserving the soil's moisture, etc.

**dry goods** cloth, cloth products, etc.

**dry ice** solidified carbon dioxide: used as a refrigerant

**dry run** [Inf.] a simulated or practice performance; rehearsal

**dry′wall′** *n.* PLASTERBOARD —*vt., vi.* to cover (a wall, etc.) with plasterboard

**DSL** *abbrev.* digital subscriber line

**DST** *abbrev.* daylight saving time

**Du** *abbrev.* Dutch

**du·al** (dōō′əl) *adj.* ⟦< L *duo*, two⟧ **1** of two **2** double; twofold —**du′al·ism′** *n.* —**du·al′i·ty** (-al′ə tē) *n.*

**dub**[1] (dub) *vt.* **dubbed, dub′bing** ⟦< OE *dubbian*, to strike⟧ **1** *a)* to confer a title or rank upon *b)* to name or nickname **2** to smooth by hammering, scraping, etc. —**dub′ber** *n.*

**dub**[2] (dub) *vt.* **dubbed, dub′bing** ⟦< DOUBLE⟧ to provide with a soundtrack, esp. one with dialogue in another language —**dub in** to insert (dialogue, music, etc.) in the soundtrack —**dub′ber** *n.*

**dub·bin** (dub′in) *n.* ⟦< DUB[1]⟧ a greasy preparation for waterproofing leather

**du·bi·e·ty** (dōō bī′ə tē) *n.* **1** a being dubious **2** *pl.* **-ties** a doubtful thing

**du·bi·ous** (dōō′bē əs) *adj.* ⟦< L *dubius*, uncertain⟧ **1** causing doubt **2** skeptical **3** questionable —**du′bi·ous·ly** *adv.*

**Dub·lin** (dub′lən) capital of Ireland: pop. 478,000

**du·cal** (dōō′kəl) *adj.* ⟦< LL *ducalis*, of a leader⟧ of a duke or dukedom

**duc·at** (duk′ət) *n.* ⟦see DUCHY⟧ any of several former European coins

**duch·ess** (duch′is) *n.* **1** a duke's wife or widow **2** a woman ruling a duchy

**duch′y** (-ē) *n., pl.* **-ies** ⟦< L *dux*, leader⟧ the territory ruled by a duke or duchess

**duck**[1] (duk) *n.* ⟦< OE *duce*, diver⟧ **1** a small waterfowl with a flat bill, a short neck, and webbed feet **2** the flesh of a duck as food

**duck**[2] (duk) *vt., vi.* ⟦ME *douken*⟧ **1** to plunge or dip under water for a moment **2** to lower or bend (the head, body, etc.) suddenly, as to avoid a blow **3** [Inf.] to avoid (an issue, etc.) —*n.* a ducking

**duck**[3] (duk) *n.* ⟦Du *doek*⟧ a cotton or linen cloth like canvas but lighter in weight

**duck′bill′** *n.* PLATYPUS

**duck′ling** *n.* a young duck

**duck′pins′** *n.* a game like bowling, played with smaller pins and balls

**duck′y** *adj.* **-i·er, -i·est** [Old Slang] pleasing, delightful, etc.

**duct** (dukt) *n.* ⟦< L *ducere*, to lead⟧ a tube, channel, or pipe, as for passage of a liquid —**duct′less** *adj.*

**duc·tile** (duk′til) *adj.* ⟦see prec.⟧ **1** that can be

drawn or hammered thin without breaking: said of metals **2** easily led; tractable —**duc·til′i·ty** (-til′ ə tē) *n.*

**ductless gland** an endocrine gland

**duct tape** a very strong, waterproof tape, used to seal ducts, hoses, etc.

**duct′work′** *n.* a system of ducts used to circulate air for heating, cooling, etc.

**dud** (dud) *n.* ⟦prob. < Du *dood,* dead⟧ [Inf.] **1** a bomb, etc. that fails to explode **2** a failure

**dude** (dōōd) *n.* ⟦< ?⟧ **1** a dandy; fop **2** [West Slang] a tourist at a ranch **3** [Slang] any man or boy —*vt., vi.* **dud′ed, dud′ing** [Slang] to dress up, esp. in showy clothes: usually with *up*

**dude ranch** a vacation resort on a ranch, with horseback riding, etc.

**dud·geon** (duj′ən) *n.* now chiefly in **in high dudgeon,** very angry, offended, etc.

**due** (dōō, dyōō) *adj.* ⟦< L *debere,* owe⟧ **1** owed or owing as a debt; payable **2** suitable; proper **3** enough [*due care*] **4** expected or scheduled to arrive —*adv.* exactly; directly [*due west*] —*n.* **1** deserved recognition **2** [*pl.*] fees or other charges [union *dues*] —**due to 1** caused by **2** [Inf.] because of —**pay one's dues** [Slang] to earn a right, etc., as by having suffered in struggle

**due bill** a receipt for money paid, exchangeable for goods or services only

**du·el** (dōō′əl) *n.* ⟦< medieval L *duellum*⟧ **1** a prearranged fight between two persons armed with deadly weapons **2** any contest like this —*vi., vt.* **-eled** or **-elled, -el·ing** or **-el·ling** to fight a duel with —**du′el·ist** or **du′el·list, du′el·er** or **du′el·ler** *n.*

**due process (of law)** legal proceedings established to protect individual rights and liberties

**du·et** (dōō et′) *n.* ⟦< L *duo,* two⟧ **1** a composition for two voices or instruments **2** the two performers of this

**duf·fel** (or **duf·fle**) **bag** (duf′əl) ⟦after *Duffel,* town in Belgium⟧ a large cloth bag for carrying clothing, etc.

**duff·er** (duf′ər) *n.* ⟦< thieves' slang *duff,* to fake⟧ [Inf.] **1** a slow-witted or dawdling elderly person **2** a relatively unskilled golfer

**dug** (dug) *vt., vi. pt. & pp. of* DIG

**dug·out′** *n.* **1** a boat hollowed out of a log **2** a shelter, as in warfare, dug in the ground **3** *Baseball* a covered shelter, one for each team

**DUI** (dē′yōō ī′) *n.* a citation for driving while under the influence of alcohol, drugs, etc.

**du jour** (dōō zhoor′) offered on this day [soup *du jour*]

**duke**[1] (dōōk) *n.* ⟦< L *dux,* leader⟧ **1** a prince ruling an independent duchy **2** a nobleman next in rank to a prince —**duke′dom** *n.*

**duke**[2] (dōōk) *n.* [*pl.*] [Slang] the fists or hands — **duke it out** to fight, esp. with the fists

**dul·cet** (dul′sit) *adj.* ⟦< L *dulcis,* sweet⟧ soothing or pleasant to hear

**dul·ci·mer** (dul′sə mər) *n.* ⟦< L *dulce,* sweet + *melos,* song⟧ a musical instrument with metal strings, which are struck with two small hammers or plucked with a plectrum or quill

**dull** (dul) *adj.* ⟦OE *dol*⟧ **1** mentally slow; stupid **2** physically slow; sluggish **3** boring; tedious **4** not sharp; blunt **5** not feeling or felt keenly **6** not vivid or bright [a *dull* color] **7** not distinct; muffled [a *dull* thud] —*vt., vi.* to make or become dull —**dull′ness** *n.* —**dull′ly** *adv.*

**dull′ard** (-ərd) *n.* a stupid person

**Du·luth** (də lōōth′) city & port in NE Minnesota, on Lake Superior: pop. 85,000

**du·ly** (dōō′lē) *adv.* in due manner; in the proper way, at the right time, etc.

**Du·mas** (dōō mä′), **Alexandre** 1802-70; Fr. novelist & playwright

**dumb** (dum) *adj.* ⟦OE⟧ **1** lacking the power of speech; mute **2** silent **3** ⟦Ger *dumm*⟧ [Inf.] stupid —**dumb down** [Inf.] to make or become less intellectually demanding —**dumb′ly** *adv.* —**dumb′ness** *n.*

**dumb′bell′** *n.* **1** a device consisting of round weights joined by a short bar, lifted for muscular exercise **2** [Slang] a stupid person

**dumb′found′** or **dum′found′** *vt.* ⟦DUMB + (CON)FOUND⟧ to make speechless by shocking; amaze

**dumb′wait′er** *n.* a small elevator for sending food, etc. between floors

**dum·dum (bullet)** (dum′dum′) ⟦after *Dumdum,* arsenal in India⟧ a soft-nosed bullet that expands when it hits, causing a large wound

**dum·my** (dum′ē) *n., pl.* **-mies 1** a figure made in human form, as for displaying clothing **2** an imitation; sham **3** [Slang] a stupid person **4** *Bridge* the declarer's partner, whose hand is exposed on the table and played by the declarer —*adj.* sham

**dump** (dump) *vt.* ⟦prob. < ON⟧ **1** to unload in a heap or mass **2** to throw away (rubbish, etc.) **3** to sell (a commodity) in a large quantity at a low price **4** *Comput. a*) to transfer (data) to another section of storage *b*) to make a printout of (data) —*n.* **1** a place for dumping rubbish, etc. **2** *Mil.* a temporary storage center in the field **3** an ugly, run-down place —**(down) in the dumps** [Inf.] in low spirits —**dump on** [Slang] to treat with contempt

**dump′er** *n.* [Slang] a container for refuse

**dump·ling** (dump′liŋ) *n.* ⟦< ?⟧ **1** a small piece of steamed or boiled dough served with meat or soup **2** a crust of baked dough filled with fruit

**Dump·ster** (dump′stər) *trademark for* a large metal trash bin, often one emptied by a special truck —*n.* [*usually* d-] such a trash bin

**dump′y** *adj.* **-i·er, -i·est 1** short and thick; squat **2** [Inf.] ugly, run-down, etc.

**dun**[1] (dun) *adj., n.* ⟦OE⟧ dull grayish-brown

**dun**[2] (dun) *vt., vi.* dunned, dun′ning ⟦? dial. var. of DIN⟧ to ask (a debtor) repeatedly for payment —*n.* an insistent demand for payment

**dunce** (duns) *n.* ⟦after John *Duns* Scotus, 13th-c. Scot scholar⟧ a dull, ignorant person

**dune** (dōōn) *n.* ⟦Fr < MDu⟧ a rounded hill or ridge of drifted sand

**dung** (duŋ) *n.* ⟦OE⟧ animal excrement; manure

**dun·ga·ree** (duŋ′gə rē′) *n.* ⟦Hindi *dungrī*⟧ **1** a coarse cotton cloth **2** [*pl.*] work trousers or overalls made of this

**dun·geon** (dun′jən) *n.* ⟦< OFr *donjon*⟧ a dark underground cell or prison

**dung′hill′** *n.* a heap of dung

**dunk** (duŋk) *vt.* ⟦Ger *tunken*⟧ **1** to dip (bread, etc.) into coffee, etc. before eating it **2** to immerse briefly

**Dun·kirk** (dun′kurk′) seaport in N France: scene of the evacuation of Allied troops under fire (1940)

**du·o** (dōō′ō) *n., pl.* **du′os** ⟦It⟧ **1** DUET (esp. sense 2) **2** a pair; couple

**du·o·de·num** (dōō′ō dē′nəm, dōō äd′'n əm) *n., pl.* **-na** (-nə) or **-nums** ⟦< L *duodeni,* twelve each: its length is about twelve fingers' breadth⟧ the first section of the small intestine, below the stomach —**du′o·de′nal** *adj.*

**dup** *abbrev.* duplicate

**dupe** (dōōp) *n.* ⟦< L *upupa,* stupid bird⟧ a person easily tricked —*vt.* duped, dup′ing to deceive; fool; trick —**dup′er** *n.*

**du·plex** (dōō′pleks′) *adj.* ⟦L < *duo,* TWO + *-plex,* -fold⟧ double —*n.* **1** an apartment with rooms on two floors **2** a house consisting of two separate family units

**du·pli·cate** (dōō′pli kit; *for v.,* -kāt′) *adj.* ⟦< L *duplicare,* to double⟧ **1** double **2** corresponding exactly —*n.* an exact copy —*vt.* **-cat′ed, -cat′ing 1** to make an exact copy of **2** to make or do again — **du′pli·ca′tion** *n.*

**duplicating machine** a machine for making copies of a letter, drawing, etc.

**du·plic·i·ty** (dōō plis′ə tē) *n.*, *pl.* **-ties** 〖< LL *duplicitas*〗 hypocritical cunning or deception

**du·ra·ble** (door′ə bəl) *adj.* 〖< L *durare*, to last〗 **1** lasting in spite of hard wear or frequent use **2** stable —**du′ra·bil′i·ty** *n.* —**du′ra·bly** *adv.*

**du·ra ma·ter** (door′ə māt′ər) 〖< ML, lit., hard mother, transl. of Ar term〗 the tough, outermost membrane covering the brain and spinal cord

**dur·ance** (door′əns) *n.* 〖see DURABLE〗 long imprisonment: mainly in **in durance vile**

**du·ra·tion** (dōō rā′shən) *n.* 〖see DURABLE〗 the time that a thing continues or lasts

**du·ress** (dōō res′) *n.* 〖< L *durus*, hard〗 coercion

**Dur·ham** (dʉr′əm) city in NC North Carolina: pop. 137,000

**dur·ing** (door′iŋ) *prep.* 〖see DURABLE〗 **1** throughout the entire time of **2** in the course of

**durst** (dʉrst) *vt.*, *vi. now chiefly dial. pt. of* DARE

**du·rum** (door′əm) *n.* 〖< L *durus*, hard〗 a hard wheat that yields flour for macaroni, spaghetti, etc.

**dusk** (dusk) *n.* 〖< OE *dox*, dark-colored〗 **1** the dim part of twilight **2** dusky quality —**dusk′y, -i·er, -i·est,** *adj.*

**dust** (dust) *n.* 〖OE〗 **1** powdery earth or any finely powdered matter **2** earth **3** disintegrated mortal remains **4** anything worthless —*vt.* **1** to sprinkle with dust, powder, etc. **2** to rid of dust, as by wiping: often with *off* —*vi.* to remove dust, as from furniture —**bite the dust** [Inf.] to die, esp. in battle —**dust′less** *adj.*

**dust bowl** an arid region with eroded topsoil easily blown off by winds

**dust′er** *n.* **1** a person or thing that dusts **2** a lightweight housecoat

**dust′pan′** *n.* a shovel-like pan into which floor dust is swept

**dust′y** *adj.* **-i·er, -i·est 1** covered with or full of dust **2** powdery **3** muted with gray: said of a color —**dust′i·ness** *n.*

**Dutch** (duch) *n.* the language of the Netherlands —*adj.* of the Netherlands or its people, language, or culture —**go Dutch** [Inf.] to have each pay his or her own expenses —**in Dutch** [Inf.] in trouble or disfavor —**the Dutch** Dutch people

**Dutch door** a door with upper and lower halves that can be opened separately

**Dutch oven** a heavy pot with an arched lid, for pot roasts, etc.

**Dutch treat** [Inf.] any date, etc. on which each pays his or her own expenses

**Dutch uncle** [Inf.] one who bluntly and sternly lectures another, often with benevolent intent

**du·te·ous** (dōōt′ē əs) *adj.* dutiful; obedient —**du′te·ous·ly** *adv.*

**du·ti·a·ble** (dōōt′ē ə bəl) *adj.* necessitating payment of a duty or tax

**du·ti·ful** (dōōt′i fəl) *adj.* showing, or resulting from, a sense of duty; obedient —**du′ti·ful·ly** *adv.*

**du·ty** (dōōt′ē) *n.*, *pl.* **-ties** 〖see DUE & -TY〗 **1** obedience or respect to be shown to one's parents, elders, etc. **2** any action required by one's position or by moral or legal considerations, etc. **3** service, esp. military service *[overseas duty]* **4** a tax, as on imports —**on** (or **off**) **duty** at (or temporarily relieved from) one's work

**du·vet** (dōō vā′, dyōō-) *n.* a comforter, often downfilled, within a slipcover

**DVD** *n.* 〖< *d(igital) v(ideo) d(isc)*〗 a digital optical disc for recording images, sounds, or data for reproduction, specif. one on which a film has been recorded

**dwarf** (dwôrf) *n.*, *pl.* **dwarfs** or **dwarves** (dwôrvz) 〖< OE *dweorg*〗 **1** any abnormally small person, animal, or plant **2** *Folklore* a little being in human form, with magic powers —*vt.* **1** to stunt the growth of **2** to make seem small in comparison —*vi.* to become dwarfed —*adj.* undersized —**dwarf′ish** *adj.* —**dwarf′ism′** *n.*

**dweeb** (dwēb) *n.* [Slang] a person regarded as dull, awkward, unsophisticated, etc.

**dwell** (dwel) *vi.* **dwelt** or **dwelled, dwell′ing** 〖< OE *dwellan*, to hinder〗 to make one's home; reside —**dwell on** (or **upon**) to think or talk about at length —**dwell′er** *n.*

**dwell′ing** (**place**) 〖ME: see prec.〗 a residence; abode

**DWI** (dē′dub′əl yōō′ī′) *n.* a citation for driving while intoxicated

**dwin·dle** (dwin′dəl) *vi.* **-dled, -dling** 〖< OE *dwīnan*, waste away〗 to keep on becoming smaller or less; diminish; shrink

**dyb·buk** (dib′ək) *n.* 〖Heb *dibbûq*〗 *Jewish Folklore* the spirit of a dead person that enters the body of a living person

**dye** (dī) *n.* 〖< OE *deag*〗 a substance or solution for coloring fabric, hair, etc.; also, the color produced —*vt.* **dyed, dye′ing** to color with dye —**dy′er** *n.*

**dyed′-in-the-wool′** *adj.* not changing, as in beliefs

**dye′stuff′** *n.* any substance constituting or yielding a dye

**dy·ing** (dī′iŋ) *vi. prp. of* DIE[1] —*adj.* **1** about to die or end **2** at death —*n.* death

**dy·nam·ic** (dī nam′ik) *adj.* 〖< Gr *dynasthai*, be able〗 **1** relating to bodies in motion **2** energetic; vigorous —**dy·nam′i·cal·ly** *adv.*

**dy·nam′ics** *n.* the science dealing with motions produced by given forces —*pl.n.* the forces operative in any field

**dy·na·mite** (dī′nə mīt′) *n.* 〖see DYNAMIC〗 a powerful explosive made with nitroglycerin —*vt.* **-mit′ed, -mit′ing** to blow up with dynamite

**dy·na·mo** (dī′nə mō′) *n.*, *pl.* **-mos** 〖see DYNAMIC〗 **1** *former term for* GENERATOR **2** a dynamic person

**dy·nas·ty** (dī′nəs tē) *n.*, *pl.* **-ties** 〖< Gr *dynasteia*, rule〗 a succession of rulers who are members of the same family —**dy·nas′tic** (-nas′tik) *adj.*

**dys-** 〖Gr〗 *prefix* bad, ill, difficult, etc.

**dys·en·ter·y** (dis′ən ter′ē) *n.* 〖< Gr *dys*-, bad + *entera*, bowels〗 an intestinal inflammation characterized by abdominal pain and bloody diarrhea

**dys·func·tion** (dis funk′shən) *n.* abnormal or impaired functioning —**dys·func′tion·al** *adj.*

**dys·lex·i·a** (dis lek′sē ə) *n.* 〖< DYS- + L *lexis*, speech〗 impairment of the ability to read —**dys·lex′ic** or **dys·lec′tic** *adj.*, *n.*

**dys·pep·si·a** (dis pep′sē ə, -shə) *n.* 〖< Gr *dys*-, bad + *pepsis*, digestion〗 indigestion —**dys·pep′tic** *adj.*, *n.*

**dz** *abbrev.* dozen(s)

# E

**e** or **E** (ē) *n., pl.* **e's, E's** the fifth letter of the English alphabet

**E**[1] (ē) *n.* **1** *Educ.* a grade for below-average work or, sometimes, excellence **2** *Music* the third tone in the scale of C major

**E**[2] *abbrev.* **1** east(ern) **2** *Baseball* error(s) **3** *Physics* energy

**e-** *prefix* EX-

**E-** or **e-** *prefix* done, etc. electronically on the Internet *[E-commerce]*

**each** (ēch) *adj., pron.* ⟦OE *ælc*⟧ every one of two or more considered separately —*adv.* apiece Abbrev. **ea.** —**each other** each one the other or others; one another

**ea·ger** (ē'gər) *adj.* ⟦< L *acer*⟧ keenly desiring; impatient or anxious —**ea'ger·ly** *adv.* —**ea'ger·ness** *n.*

**ea·gle** (ē'gəl) *n.* ⟦< L *aquila*⟧ **1** a large bird of prey, with sharp vision and powerful wings **2** a representation of the eagle, as the U.S. emblem **3** *Golf* a score of two under par on a hole

**ea'gle-eyed'** *adj.* having keen vision

**ea·glet** (ē'glit) *n.* a young eagle

**ear**[1] (ir) *n.* ⟦OE *ēare*⟧ **1** the part of the body that perceives sound **2** the visible, external part of the ear **3** one's sense of hearing or hearing ability **4** anything like an ear —**be all ears** to listen attentively —**give** (or **lend**) **ear** to give attention; heed —**play by ear** to play (music) without using notation —**play it by ear** [Inf.] to improvise

**ear**[2] (ir) *n.* ⟦< OE *ēar*⟧ the grain-bearing spike of a cereal plant, esp. of corn —*vi.* to sprout ears

**ear'ache'** *n.* an ache in the ear

**ear'drum'** *n.* TYMPANIC MEMBRANE

**earl** (url) *n.* ⟦< OE *eorl*, warrior⟧ a British nobleman ranking above a viscount —**earl'dom** *n.*

**ear'lobe'** *n.* the fleshy lower part of the external ear

**ear·ly** (ur'lē) *adv., adj.* **-li·er, -li·est** ⟦< OE *ær*, before + -*lice*, -ly⟧ **1** near the beginning **2** before the expected or usual time **3** in the distant past **4** in the near future —**early on** at an early stage —**ear'li·ness** *n.*

**ear'mark'** *n.* **1** a mark put on the ear of livestock **2** an identifying mark or feature —*vt.* **1** to put such a mark on **2** to reserve for a special purpose

**ear'muffs'** (-mufs') *pl.n.* coverings worn over the ears in cold weather

**earn** (urn) *vt.* ⟦OE *earnian*⟧ **1** to receive (wages, etc.) for one's work **2** to get as deserved **3** to receive (interest, etc.) as from a bank account —**earn'er** *n.*

**ear·nest**[1] (ur'nist) *adj.* ⟦OE *eornoste*⟧ serious and intense; not joking —**in earnest 1** serious **2** in a determined manner —**ear'nest·ly** *adv.* —**ear'nest·ness** *n.*

**ear·nest**[2] (ur'nist) *n.* ⟦ult. < Heb *eravon*⟧ money, etc. given as a pledge in binding a bargain

**earn'ings** *pl.n.* **1** wages or other recompense **2** profits, interest, etc.

**ear'phone'** *n.* a receiver for radio, etc., held to, or put into, the ear

**ear'ring'** *n.* a ring or other small ornament for the lobe of the ear

**ear'shot'** *n.* the distance within which a sound can be heard

**ear'split'ting** *adj.* so loud as to hurt the ears; deafening

**earth** (urth) *n.* ⟦OE *eorthe*⟧ **1** [*often* E-] the planet we live on, the third planet from the sun: see PLANET **2** this world, as distinguished from heaven and hell **3** land, as distinguished from sea or sky **4** soil; ground —**down to earth 1** practical; realistic **2** sincere; without affectation

**Earth Day** April 22, a day on which environmentalist concerns are acknowledged

**earth'en** *adj.* made of earth or clay

**earth'en·ware'** *n.* clay pottery

**earth'ling** *n.* a human being: now mainly in science fiction

**earth'ly** *adj.* **1** *a*) terrestrial *b*) worldly **2** conceivable *[no earthly reason]*

**earth'quake'** *n.* a trembling of the earth's crust, caused by underground volcanic forces or shifting of rock

**earth'ward** *adv., adj.* toward the earth: also **earth'wards** *adv.*

**earth'work'** *n.* an embankment made by piling up earth, esp. as a fortification

**earth'worm'** *n.* a round, segmented worm that burrows in the soil

**earth'y** *adj.* **-i·er, -i·est 1** of or like earth **2** *a*) coarse; unrefined *b*) simple and natural

**ease** (ēz) *n.* ⟦< L *adjacens*, lying nearby⟧ **1** freedom from pain or trouble; comfort **2** natural manner; poise **3** freedom from difficulty; facility **4** affluence —*vt.* **eased, eas'ing 1** to free from pain or trouble; comfort **2** to lessen (pain, anxiety, etc.) **3** to facilitate **4** to reduce the strain or pressure of **5** to move by careful shifting, etc. —*vi.* to become less tense, severe, etc.

**ea·sel** (ē'zəl) *n.* ⟦ult. < L *asinus*, ass⟧ an upright frame or tripod to hold an artist's canvas, etc.

**ease·ment** (ēz'mənt) *n. Law* a right that one may have in another's land, as the right to pass through

**eas·i·ly** (ē'zə lē) *adv.* **1** with ease **2** certainly **3** very likely

**east** (ēst) *n.* ⟦OE⟧ **1** the direction in which sunrise occurs (90° on the compass) **2** a region in or toward this direction —*adj.* **1** in, of, toward, or facing the east **2** from the east *[an east wind]* —*adv.* in or toward the east —**the East 1** the eastern part of the U.S. **2** Asia and the nearby islands

**East Asia** countries of E Asia, including China, Japan, North & South Korea, and Mongolia —**East Asian**

**East Berlin** *see* BERLIN

**East China Sea** part of the Pacific Ocean, between China & Japan

**Eas·ter** (ēs'tər) *n.* ⟦< OE *Eastre*, dawn goddess⟧ an annual Christian festival in the spring, celebrating the resurrection of Jesus

**east'er·ly** *adj., adv.* **1** in or toward the east **2** from the east

**east'ern** *adj.* **1** in, of, or toward the east **2** from the east **3** [E-] of the East

**east'ern·er** *n.* a person born or living in the east

**Eastern Hemisphere** that half of the earth which includes Europe, Africa, Asia, and Australia

**Eastern Orthodox Church** the Christian church dominant in E Europe, W Asia, and N Africa

**East Germany** *see* GERMANY

**East In·dies** (in'dēz') Malay Archipelago; esp., the islands of Indonesia —**East Indian**

**east'ward** *adv., adj.* toward the east *[moving slowly eastward]*: also **east'wards** *adv.*

**eas·y** (ē'zē) *adj.* **-i·er, -i·est** ⟦see EASE⟧ **1** not difficult **2** free from anxiety, pain, etc. **3** comfortable; restful **4** free from constraint; not stiff **5** not strict or severe **6** *a*) unhurried *b*) gradual —*adv.* [Inf.] easily —**take it easy** [Inf.] **1** to refrain from anger, haste, etc. **2** to relax; rest —**eas'i·ness** *n.*

**easy chair** a stuffed armchair

**eas·y·go·ing** *adj.* **1** acting in a relaxed manner **2** not strict; lenient

**eat** (ēt) *vt.* **ate, eat'en, eat'ing** ⟦OE *etan*⟧ **1** to chew and swallow (food) **2** to consume or ravage: with *away* or *up* **3** to destroy, as acid does; corrode **4** to make by or as by eating [acid *eats* holes in cloth] **5** [Slang] to worry or bother —*vi.* to eat food; have a meal —**eat'a·ble** *adj.* —**eat'er** *n.*

**eat·er·y** (ēt'ər ē) *n., pl.* **-ies** [Inf.] a restaurant

**eats** *pl.n.* [Inf.] food

**eaves** (ēvz) *pl.n., sing.* **eave** ⟦< OE *efes*, edge⟧ the projecting lower edge or edges of a roof

**eaves'drop'** *vi.* **-dropped', -drop'ping** ⟦prob. < *eavesdropper*, one who stands under eaves to listen⟧ to listen secretly to a private conversation — **eaves'drop'per** *n.*

**ebb** (eb) *n.* ⟦OE *ebba*⟧ **1** the flow of the tide back toward the sea **2** a lessening —*vi.* **1** to recede, as the tide **2** to lessen; decline

**eb·on·y** (eb'ə nē) *n., pl.* **-ies** ⟦< Gr *ebenos*⟧ the hard, heavy, dark wood of certain tropical trees — *adj.* **1** of ebony **2** like ebony; specif., dark or black

**e·bul·lient** (i bool'yənt, -bul'-) *adj.* ⟦< L *e-*, out + *bullire*, to boil⟧ **1** bubbling; boiling **2** enthusiastic; exuberant —**e·bul'lience** *n.*

**EC** European Community

**ec·cen·tric** (ək sen'trik) *adj.* ⟦< Gr *ek-*, out of + *kentron*, center⟧ **1** not concentric: said of two circles, one inside the other **2** with its axis off center [an *eccentric* wheel] **3** not exactly circular **4** odd, as in conduct; unconventional —*n.* **1** a disk set off center on a shaft, for converting circular motion into back-and-forth motion **2** an eccentric person —**ec·cen'tri·cal·ly** *adv.* —**ec·cen·tric·i·ty** (ek'sen tris'ə tē), *pl.* **-ties,** *n.*

**Ec·cle·si·as·tes** (e klē'zē as'tēz') *n.* ⟦< Gr *ek-*, out + *kalein*, to call⟧ a book of the Old Testament

**ec·cle·si·as·tic** (-tik) *adj.* ⟦see prec.⟧ ECCLESIASTICAL —*n.* a member of the clergy

**ec·cle·si·as·ti·cal** (-ti kəl) *adj.* of the church or the clergy

**ech·e·lon** (esh'ə län') *n.* ⟦< Fr < L *scala*, ladder⟧ **1** a steplike formation of ships, troops, or aircraft **2** a subdivision of a military force **3** any of the levels of responsibility in an organization

**e·chi·no·derm** (ē kī'nō dʉrm') *n.* ⟦< ModL⟧ a marine animal with a hard, spiny skeleton and radial body, as the starfish

**ech·o** (ek'ō) *n., pl.* **-oes** ⟦< Gr *ēchō*⟧ **1** the repetition of a sound by reflection of sound waves from a surface **2** a sound so produced **3** any repetition or imitation of the words, ideas, etc. of another — *vi.* **-oed, -o·ing 1** to reverberate **2** to make an echo —*vt.* to repeat (another's words, ideas, etc.)

**e·cho·ic** (e kō'ik) *adj.* imitative in sound, as the word *tinkle*

**é·clair** (ā kler', i-, ē-) *n.* ⟦Fr, lit., lightning⟧ an oblong pastry shell filled with custard, etc.

**é·clat** (ā klä', i-, ē-) *n.* ⟦Fr < *éclater*, burst (out)⟧ **1** brilliant success **2** striking effect **3** acclaim; fame

**ec·lec·tic** (ek lek'tik) *adj.* ⟦< Gr *ek-*, out + *legein*, choose⟧ selecting or selected from various sources —*n.* one who uses eclectic methods —**ec·lec'ti·cal·ly** *adv.* —**ec·lec'ti·cism'** (-tə siz'əm) *n.*

**e·clipse** (i klips', ē-) *n.* ⟦< Gr *ek-*, out + *leipein*, leave⟧ **1** the obscuring of the sun when the moon comes between it and the earth (**solar eclipse**), or of the moon when the earth's shadow is cast upon it (**lunar eclipse**) **2** any obscuring of light, or of fame, glory, etc. —*vt.* **e·clipsed', e·clips'ing 1** to cause an eclipse of **2** to surpass

**e·clip·tic** (i klip'tik) *n.* the sun's apparent annual path, as seen from the orbiting earth

**ec·logue** (ek'lôg') *n.* ⟦see ECLECTIC⟧ a short pastoral poem

**eco-** ⟦< Gr *oikos*, house⟧ *combining form* **1** environment or habitat **2** ecology

**ec·o·cide** (ē'kō sīd') *n.* ⟦prec. + -CIDE⟧ the destruction of the environment, as by pollutants

**e·col·o·gy** (ē käl'ə jē) *n.* ⟦< Gr *oikos*, house + *-logia*, -LOGY⟧ the branch of biology that deals with the relations between living organisms and their environment —**ec'o·log'i·cal** *adj.* —**ec'o·log'i·cal·ly** *adv.* —**e·col'o·gist** *n.*

**econ** *abbrev.* economic(s)

**ec·o·nom·ic** (ek'ə näm'ik, ē'kə-) *adj.* **1** of the management of income, expenditures, etc. **2** of economics **3** of the satisfaction of the material needs of people

**ec'o·nom'i·cal** *adj.* **1** not wasting money, time, etc.; thrifty **2** that uses no more of something than is necessary —**ec'o·nom'i·cal·ly** *adv.*

**ec'o·nom'ics** *n.* **1** the science that deals with the production, distribution, and consumption of wealth **2** economic factors

**e·con·o·mist** (i kän'ə mist, ē-) *n.* a specialist in economics

**e·con'o·mize'** (-mīz') *vi.* **-mized', -miz'ing** to reduce waste or expenses —**e·con'o·miz'er** *n.*

**e·con'o·my** (-mē) *n., pl.* **-mies** ⟦< Gr *oikos*, house + *nomos*, law⟧ **1** the management of the income, expenditures, etc. of a household, government, etc. **2** careful management of wealth, etc.; thrift **3** efficient use of one's materials **4** an instance of thrift **5** a system of producing and distributing wealth —*adj.* costing less or less per unit than the standard kind

**ec·o·sys·tem** (ē'kō sis'təm) *n.* ⟦< Gr *oikos*, house + SYSTEM⟧ a community of animals and plants, together with its environment

**ec·sta·sy** (ek'stə sē) *n., pl.* **-sies** ⟦< Gr *ek-*, out + *histanai*, to set⟧ a state or feeling of overpowering joy; rapture —**ec·stat·ic** (ek stat'ik) *adj.* —**ec·stat'i·cal·ly** *adv.*

**-ec·to·my** (ek'tə mē) ⟦< Gr *ek-*, out + *temnein*, to cut⟧ *combining form* a surgical excision of

**Ec·ua·dor** (ek'wə dôr') country on the NW coast of South America: 104,506 sq. mi.; pop. 9,648,000 — **Ec'ua·do're·an, Ec'ua·do'ri·an,** or **Ec'ua·dor'an** *adj., n.*

**ec·u·men·i·cal** (ek'yoo men'i kəl) *adj.* ⟦< Gr *oikoumenē* (*gē*), the inhabited (world)⟧ **1** general, or universal; esp., of the Christian church as a whole **2** furthering religious unity, esp. among Christian churches —**ec'u·men'i·cal·ly** *adv.*

**ec·u·men·ism** (ek'yoo mə niz'əm, e kyoo'-) *n.* the ecumenical movement, esp. among Christian churches —**ec'u·men·ist** *n.*

**ec·ze·ma** (ek'zə mə, eg'zə-) *n.* ⟦< Gr *ek-*, out + *zein*, to boil⟧ a skin disorder characterized by inflammation, itching, and scaliness

**ed** *abbrev.* **1** edited (by) **2** *a*) edition *b*) editor *c*) education

**-ed** ⟦OE⟧ *suffix* **1** forming the past tense or past participle of certain verbs **2** forming adjectives from nouns or verbs [*cultured, bearded*]

**E·dam (cheese)** (ē'dam, -dam') ⟦after *Edam*, Netherlands⟧ a mild, yellow cheese

**ed·dy** (ed'ē) *n., pl.* **-dies** ⟦prob. < ON *itha*⟧ a little whirlpool or whirlwind —*vi.* **-died, -dy·ing** to move in an eddy

**e·del·weiss** (ā'dəl vīs') *n.* ⟦Ger < *edel*, noble + *weiss*, white⟧ a small, flowering plant, esp. of the Alps, with white and woolly leaves

**e·de·ma** (ē dē'mə) *n., pl.* **-mas** or **-ma·ta** (-mə tə) ⟦< Gr *oidēma*, swelling⟧ an abnormal accumulation of fluid in body tissues or cavities

**E·den** (ēd''n) *n.* **1** *Bible* the garden where Adam and Eve first lived; Paradise **2** any delightful place —**E·den'ic** or **e·den·ic** (ē den'ik) *adj.*

**edge** (ej) *n.* ⟦OE *ecg*⟧ **1** the sharp, cutting part of a blade **2** sharpness; keenness **3** the projecting ledge of a cliff, etc.; brink **4** the part farthest from the middle; border; margin **5** [Inf.] advantage [he has the *edge* on me] —*vt., vi.* **edged, edg'ing 1** to form an edge (on) **2** to make (one's way) sideways **3** to move gradually —**on edge 1** very tense; irritable **2** impatient —**edg'er** *n.*

**edge′ways′** (-wāz′) *adv.* with the edge foremost: also **edge′wise′** (-wīz′)

**edg′ing** *n.* a fringe, trimming, etc. for a border

**edg·y** (ej′ē) *adj.* **-i·er, -i·est 1** irritable; on edge **2** [Inf.] innovative, daring, etc. —**edg′i·ness** *n.*

**ed·i·ble** (ed′ə bəl) *adj.* [< L *edere*, eat] fit to be eaten —*n.* anything fit to be eaten: *usually used in pl.* —**ed′i·bil′i·ty** (-bil′ə tē) *n.*

**e·dict** (ē′dikt′) *n.* [< L *e*-, out + *dicere*, speak] a public order; decree

**ed·i·fice** (ed′i fis) *n.* [see fol.] a building, esp. a large, imposing one

**ed·i·fy** (ed′i fī′) *vt.* **-fied′, -fy′ing** [< L *aedificare*, build] to instruct so as to improve or uplift morally —**ed′i·fi·ca′tion** *n.* —**ed′i·fi′er** *n.*

**Ed·in·burgh** (ed′'n bur′ə, -ō) capital of Scotland: district pop. 419,000

**Ed·i·son** (ed′i sən), **Thom·as Alva** (täm′əs al′və) 1847-1931; U.S. inventor

**ed·it¹** (ed′it) *vt.* [< EDITOR] **1** to prepare (a manuscript) for publication by arranging, revising, etc. **2** to control the policy and publication of (a newspaper, etc.) **3** to prepare (a film, tape, etc.) for presentation by cutting, dubbing, etc. **4** to make changes in (a computer file)

**edit²** *abbrev.* **1** edited (by) **2** edition **3** editor

**e·di·tion** (i dish′ən) *n.* [see fol.] **1** the size or form in which a book is published **2** the total number of copies of a book, etc. published at one time **3** any particular issue of a newspaper

**ed·i·tor** (ed′it ər) *n.* [L < *e*-, out + *dare*, give] **1** one that edits **2** a department head of a newspaper, etc.

**ed·i·to·ri·al** (ed′i tôr′ē əl) *adj.* of or by an editor —*n.* a statement of opinion in a newspaper, etc., as by an editor, publisher, or owner —**ed′i·to′ri·al·ly** *adv.*

**ed′i·to′ri·al·ize′** (-īz′) *vi.* **-ized′, -iz′ing** to express editorial opinions

**editor in chief** *pl.* **editors in chief** the editor who heads the editorial staff of a publication

**Ed·mon·ton** (ed′mən tən) capital of Alberta, Canada: pop. 616,000

**educ** *abbrev.* **1** education **2** educational

**ed·u·ca·ble** (ej′ŏŏ kə bəl, ej′ə-) *adj.* that can be educated or trained —**ed′u·ca·bil′i·ty** *n.*

**ed′u·cate′** (-kāt′) *vt.* **-cat′ed, -cat′ing** [< L *e*-, out + *ducere*, to lead] **1** to develop the knowledge, skill, or character of, esp. by formal schooling; teach **2** to pay for the schooling of —**ed′u·ca′tor** *n.*

**ed′u·cat′ed** *adj.* **1** having much education **2** based on experience

**ed′u·ca′tion** (-kā′shən) *n.* **1** the process of educating; teaching **2** knowledge, etc. thus developed **3** formal schooling —**ed′u·ca′tion·al** *adj.*

**e·duce** (ē dŏŏs′) *vt.* **e·duced′, e·duc′ing** [see EDUCATE] **1** to draw out; elicit **2** to deduce

**-ee** (ē) [< Anglo-Fr pp. ending] *suffix* **1** the recipient of a (specified) action [*appointee*] **2** one in a (specified) condition [*absentee*]

**EEG** *abbrev.* electroencephalogram

**eel** (ēl) *n.* [OE *æl*] a long, slippery, snakelike fish

**EEOC** *abbrev.* Equal Employment Opportunity Commission

**e′er** (er, ar) *adv.* [Old Poet.] EVER

**-eer** (ir) [< L *-arius*] *suffix* **1** *a*) one having to do with [*auctioneer*] *b*) one who writes, makes, etc. [*profiteer*] **2** to have to do with [*electioneer*]

EEL

**ee·rie** or **ee·ry** (ir′ē) *adj.* **-ri·er, -ri·est** [< OE *earg*, timid] mysterious, uncanny, or weird —**ee′ri·ly** *adv.* —**ee′ri·ness** *n.*

**ef-** *prefix* EX-: used before *f* [*efface*]

**ef·face** (ə fās′, i-) *vt.* **-faced′, -fac′ing** [< L *ex*-, out

+ *facies*, face] **1** to rub out; erase **2** to make (oneself) inconspicuous —**ef·face′ment** *n.*

**ef·fect** (e fekt′, i-) *n.* [< L *ex*-, out + *facere*, do] **1** anything brought about by a cause; result **2** the power to cause results **3** influence **4** meaning [spoke to this *effect*] **5** an impression made on the mind, or its cause **6** a being operative or in force **7** [pl.] belongings; property —*vt.* to bring about; accomplish —**in effect 1** actually **2** virtually **3** in operation —**take effect** to become operative

**ef·fec′tive** *adj.* **1** producing a desired effect; efficient **2** in effect; operative **3** impressive —**ef·fec′tive·ly** *adv.* —**ef·fec′tive·ness** *n.*

**ef·fec·tu·al** (e fek′chŏŏ əl, i-) *adj.* **1** producing, or able to produce, the desired effect **2** having legal force; valid —**ef·fec′tu·al·ly** *adv.*

**ef·fec′tu·ate′** (-āt′) *vt.* **-at′ed, -at′ing** to bring about; effect

**ef·fem·i·nate** (e fem′ə nit, i-) *adj.* [< L *ex*-, out + *femina*, woman] having qualities attributed to women, as weakness, delicacy, etc.; unmanly —**ef·fem′i·na·cy** *n.*

**ef·fer·ent** (ef′ər ənt) *adj.* [< L *ex*-, out + *ferre*, to bear] carrying away from a central part, as nerves

**ef·fer·vesce** (ef′ər ves′) *vi.* **-vesced′, -vesc′ing** [< L *ex*-, out + *fervere*, to boil] **1** to give off gas bubbles; bubble **2** to be lively —**ef′fer·ves′cence** *n.* —**ef′fer·ves′cent** *adj.*

**ef·fete** (e fēt′, i-) *adj.* [< L *ex*-, out + *fetus*, productive] **1** no longer able to produce; sterile **2** decadent, soft, too refined, etc. —**ef·fete′ly** *adv.* —**ef·fete′ness** *n.*

**ef·fi·ca·cious** (ef′i kā′shəs) *adj.* [see EFFECT] that produces the desired effect —**ef′fi·ca′cious·ly** *adv.* —**ef′fi·ca·cy** (-kə sē) *n.*

**ef·fi′cien·cy** *n.* **1** a being efficient **2** a small, usually one-room, apartment: in full **efficiency apartment**

**ef·fi′cient** (e fish′ənt, i-) *adj.* [see EFFECT] producing the desired result with a minimum of effort, expense, or waste —**ef·fi′cient·ly** *adv.*

**ef·fi·gy** (ef′i jē) *n., pl.* **-gies** [< L *ex*-, out + *fingere*, to form] a statue or other image; often, a crude representation of a despised person that is hanged or burned to show protest

**ef·flu·ent** (ef′lŏŏ ənt) *adj.* [< L *effluere*, flow out] flowing out —*n.* the outflow of a sewer, septic tank, etc. —**ef′flu·ence** *n.*

**ef·flu·vi·um** (e flŏŏ′vē əm) *n., pl.* **-vi·a** (-ə) or **-vi·ums** [see prec.] a disagreeable vapor or odor

**ef·fort** (ef′ərt) *n.* [< L *ex*-, intens. + *fortis*, strong] **1** the use of energy to do something **2** a try; attempt **3** a result of working or trying —**ef′fort·less** *adj.* —**ef′fort·less·ly** *adv.*

**ef·fron·ter·y** (e frunt′ər ē, i-) *n.* [< L *ex*-, from + *frons*, forehead] impudence; audacity

**ef·ful·gence** (e ful′jəns, i-) *n.* [< L *ex*-, forth + *fulgere*, shine] radiance; brilliance —**ef·ful′gent** *adj.*

**ef·fuse** (e fyŏŏz′, i-) *vt., vi.* **-fused′, -fus′ing** [< L *ex*-, out + *fundere*, pour] **1** to pour out or forth **2** to spread out; diffuse

**ef·fu·sion** (-fyŏŏ′zhən) *n.* **1** a pouring forth **2** unrestrained expression in speaking or writing —**ef·fu′sive** *adj.* —**ef·fu′sive·ly** *adv.* —**ef·fu′sive·ness** *n.*

**e.g.** *abbrev.* [L *exempli gratia*] for example

**e·gad** (ē gad′) *interj.* [prob. < *oh God*] [Archaic] used as a softened oath

**e·gal·i·tar·i·an** (ē gal′ə ter′ē ən) *adj.* [< Fr *égalité*, equality] advocating full political, social, and economic equality for all people —*n.* a person advocating this

**egg¹** (eg) *n.* [ON] **1** the oval or round body laid by a female bird, fish, etc., containing the germ of a new individual **2** a reproductive cell produced by a female; ovum **3** a hen's egg, raw or cooked

**egg²** (eg) *vt.* [< ON *eggja*, give edge to] to urge or incite: with *on*

**egg′beat′er** *n.* a kitchen utensil for beating eggs, whipping cream, etc.

**egg foo yong** (or **young** or **yung**) (eg'foo yuŋ') a Chinese-American dish of beaten eggs cooked with bean sprouts, onions, minced pork or shrimp, etc.

**egg'head'** *n.* [Slang] an intellectual

**egg'nog'** (-näg') *n.* ⟦EGG¹ + *nog*, strong ale⟧ a drink made of beaten eggs, milk, sugar, nutmeg, and, often, whiskey or rum

**egg'plant'** *n.* **1** a plant with a large, ovoid, purple-skinned fruit eaten as a vegetable **2** the fruit

**egg roll** a Chinese-American dish, a thin egg pancake wrapped around minced vegetables, meat, etc. and deep-fried

**eg·lan·tine** (eg'lən tīn', -tēn') *n.* ⟦< L *aculeus*, a sting⟧ a European rose with sweet-scented leaves and pink flowers

**e·go** (ē'gō) *n.*, *pl.* **-gos** ⟦L, I²⟧ **1** the self; the individual as self-aware **2** egotism **3** *Psychoanalysis* the part of the psyche that organizes thoughts rationally and governs action

**e'go·cen'tric** (-sen'trik) *adj.* viewing everything in relation to oneself —**e'go·cen'tri·cal·ly** *adv.* —**e'go·cen'trism'** *n.*

**e'go·ism'** *n.* **1** selfishness; self-interest **2** egotism; conceit —**e'go·ist** *n.* —**e'go·is'tic** or **e'go·is'ti·cal** *adj.*

**e'go·tism'** *n.* **1** excessive reference to oneself in speaking or writing **2** conceit; vanity —**e'go·tist** *n.* —**e'go·tis'tic** or **e'go·tis'ti·cal** *adj.* —**e'go·tis'ti·cal·ly** *adv.*

**ego trip** [Slang] an experience that gratifies or indulges the ego

**e·gre·gious** (ē grē'jəs, i-) *adj.* ⟦< L *e-*, out + *grex*, a herd⟧ remarkably bad; flagrant —**e·gre'gious·ly** *adv.* —**e·gre'gious·ness** *n.*

**e·gress** (ē'gres') *n.* ⟦< L *e-*, out + *gradi*, go⟧ a way out; exit

**e·gret** (ē'gret', -grit) *n.* ⟦< OFr *aigrette*⟧ **1** a kind of heron with long, white plumes **2** AIGRETTE

**E·gypt** (ē'jipt) country in NE Africa, on the Mediterranean: 386,662 sq. mi.; pop. 48,205,000

**E·gyp·tian** (ē jip'shən, i-) *n.* **1** the language of the ancient Egyptians **2** a person born or living in Egypt —*adj.* of Egypt or its people, language, etc.

**eh** (ā, e) *interj.* **1** used to express doubt or surprise **2** used to make an inquiry

**ei·der** (ī'dər) *n.* ⟦ult. < ON *æthr*⟧ **1** a large sea duck of northern regions **2** EIDERDOWN

**ei'der·down'** *n.* the fine, soft down of the eider, used as a stuffing for quilts, pillows, etc.

**eight** (āt) *adj.*, *n.* ⟦< OE *eahta*⟧ one more than seven; 8; VIII —**eighth** (ātth) *adj.*, *n.*

**eight ball** a black ball with the number eight on it, used in playing pool —**behind the eight ball** [Slang] in a very unfavorable position

**eight·een** (ā'tēn') *adj.*, *n.* eight more than ten; 18; XVIII —**eight'eenth'** *adj.*, *n.*

**eight'y** *adj.*, *n.*, *pl.* **-ies** eight times ten; 80; LXXX —**the eighties** the numbers or years, as of a century, from 80 through 89 —**eight'i·eth** *adj.*, *n.*

**Ein·stein** (īn'stīn') **Al·bert** (al'bərt) 1879-1955; U.S. physicist, born in Germany: formulated theory of relativity

**Eir·e** (er'ə) *Ir. name for* IRELAND

**Ei·sen·how·er** (ī'zen hou'ər), **Dwight David** (dwīt) 1890-1969; U.S. general & 34th president of the U.S. (1953-61)

**ei·ther** (ē'thər, ī'-) *adj.* ⟦OE *æghwæther*⟧ **1** one or the other (of two) **2** each (of two) —*pron.* one or the other (of two) —*conj.* a correlative used with *or* to imply a choice of alternatives [*either* go or stay] —*adv.* any more than the other; also [if you don't go, I won't *either*]

**e·jac·u·late** (ē jak'yōō lāt', i-) *vt.*, *vi.* **-lat'ed**, **-lat'ing** ⟦see fol.⟧ **1** to eject (esp. semen) **2** to utter suddenly; exclaim —**e·jac'u·la'tion** *n.*

**e·ject** (ē jekt', i-) *vt.* ⟦< L *e-*, out + *jacere*, to throw⟧ to throw or force out; expel —**e·jec'tion** *n.*

**eke** (ēk) *vt.* **eked**, **ek'ing** ⟦< OE *eacan*, to increase⟧ to manage to make (a living) with difficulty: with *out*

**EKG** *abbrev.* electrocardiogram

**e·lab·o·rate** (ē lab'ə rit, i-; *for v.*, -rāt') *adj.* ⟦< L *e-*, out + *labor*, work⟧ developed in great detail; complicated —*vt.* **-rat'ed**, **-rat'ing** to work out in great detail —*vi.* to add more details: usually with *on* or *upon* —**e·lab'o·rate·ly** *adv.* —**e·lab'o·rate·ness** *n.* —**e·lab'o·ra'tion** *n.*

**é·lan** (ā län', -län') *n.* ⟦Fr < *élancer*, to dart⟧ spirited self-assurance; dash

**e·lapse** (ē laps', i-) *vi.* **e·lapsed'**, **e·laps'ing** ⟦< L *e-*, out + *labi*, to glide⟧ to slip by; pass: said of time

**e·las·tic** (ē las'tik, i-) *adj.* ⟦< Gr *elaunein*, set in motion⟧ **1** able to spring back to its original size, shape, etc. after being stretched, squeezed, etc.; flexible **2** able to recover easily, as from dejection; buoyant **3** adaptable —*n.* an elastic band or fabric —**e·las·tic'i·ty** (-tis'ə tē) *n.*

**e·las'ti·cize'** (-tə sīz') *vt.* **-cized'**, **-ciz'ing** to make (fabric) elastic

**e·late** (ē lāt', i-) *vt.* **-lat'ed**, **-lat'ing** ⟦< L *ex-*, out + *ferre*, to bear⟧ to raise the spirits of; make very proud, happy, etc. —**e·la'tion** *n.*

**el·bow** (el'bō') *n.* ⟦see ELL² & BOW²⟧ **1** the joint between the upper and lower arm; esp., the outer angle made by a bent arm **2** anything bent like an elbow —*vt.*, *vi.* to shove as with the elbows

**elbow grease** [Inf.] vigorous physical effort

**el'bow·room'** *n.* ample space or room

**eld·er¹** (el'dər) *adj.* ⟦< OE *eald*, old⟧ older —*n.* **1** an older or aged person **2** an older person with some authority, as in a tribe **3** any of certain church officers

**el·der²** (el'dər) *n.* ⟦OE *ellern*⟧ a shrub or tree of the honeysuckle family, with red or purple berries

**el'der·ber'ry** (-ber'ē) *n.*, *pl.* **-ries 1** ELDER² **2** its berry, used for making wine, jelly, etc.

**eld'er·ly** *adj.* **1** somewhat old **2** in old age; aged

**eld·est** (el'dist) *adj.* oldest; esp., firstborn

**El Do·ra·do** or **El·do·ra·do** (el'də rä'dō) *n.*, *pl.* **-dos** ⟦Sp, the gilded⟧ any place supposed to be rich in gold, opportunity, etc.

**e·lect** (ē lekt', i-) *adj.* ⟦< L *e-*, out + *legere*, choose⟧ **1** chosen **2** elected but not yet installed in office: usually used in combination [mayor-*elect*] —*vt.*, *vi.* **1** to select for an office by voting **2** to choose; select —**e·lect'a·ble** *adj.* —**e·lect·a·bil'i·ty** *n.*

**e·lec·tion** (ē lek'shən, i-) *n.* **1** a choosing or choice **2** a choosing or being chosen by vote

**e·lec'tion·eer'** *vi.* to canvass votes in an election

**e·lec'tive** (-tiv) *adj.* **1** *a)* filled by election [an *elective* office] *b)* chosen by election **2** having the power to choose **3** optional —*n.* an optional course or subject in a school curriculum

**e·lec·tor** (-tər) *n.* **1** one who elects; specif., a qualified voter **2** a member of the electoral college —**e·lec'tor·al** *adj.*

**electoral college** an assembly elected by the voters to perform the formal duty of electing the president and vice president of the U.S.

**e·lec'tor·ate** (-it) *n.* all those qualified to vote in an election

**E·lec·tra** (ē lek'trə, i-) *n.* *Gr. Myth.* a daughter of Agamemnon: she plots the death of her mother

**e·lec·tric** (ē lek'trik, i-) *adj.* ⟦< Gr *ēlektron*, amber: from the effect of friction upon amber⟧ **1** of, charged with, or conducting electricity **2** producing, or produced by, electricity **3** operated by electricity **4** using electronic amplification [an *electric* guitar] **5** very tense or exciting Also **e·lec'tri·cal** —**e·lec'tri·cal·ly** *adv.*

**electric chair** a chair equipped for use in electrocuting persons sentenced to death

**e·lec·tri·cian** (ē'lek trish'ən, ē lek'-) *n.* one whose work is the construction and repair of electric apparatus

**e·lec·tric'i·ty** (-tris'i tē) *n.* **1** a property of certain fundamental particles of all matter, as electrons (negative charges) and protons or positrons (positive charges): electrical charge is generated by friction, induction, or chemical change **2** an electric current **3** electric current as a public utility for lighting, heating, etc.

**e·lec·tri·fy** (ē lek′trə fī′, i-) *vt.* **-fied′, -fy′ing 1** to charge with electricity **2** to excite; thrill **3** to equip for the use of electricity —**e·lec′tri·fi·ca′tion** *n.* —**e·lec′tri·fi′er** *n.*

**electro-** *combining form* electric, electricity

**e·lec·tro·car·di·o·gram** (ē lek′trō kär′dē ə gram′, i-) *n.* a tracing showing the variations in electric force which trigger heart contractions

**e·lec′tro·car′di·o·graph** (-graf′) *n.* an instrument for making electrocardiograms

**e·lec′tro·cute′** (-trə kyo͞ot′) *vt.* **-cut′ed, -cut′ing** ⟦ELECTRO- + (EXE)CUTE⟧ to kill or execute with electricity —**e·lec′tro·cu′tion** *n.*

**e·lec′trode′** (-trōd′) *n.* ⟦ELECTR(O)- + -ODE⟧ any terminal by which electricity enters or leaves a battery, etc.

**e·lec′tro·en·ceph′a·lo·gram′** (-trō en sef′ə lō gram′) *n.* ⟦see ENCEPHALITIS & -GRAM⟧ a tracing of the variations in electric force in the brain

**e·lec′tro·en·ceph′a·lo·graph′** (-graf′) *n.* an instrument for making electroencephalograms

**e·lec′trol′y·sis** (-i sis) *n.* ⟦ELECTRO- + -LYSIS⟧ **1** the decomposition of an electrolyte by the action of an electric current passing through it **2** the eradication of unwanted hair with an electrified needle

**e·lec′tro·lyte** (ē lek′trō līt′, i-) *n.* ⟦ELECTRO- + -LYTE⟧ any chemical compound that ionizes when molten or in solution and becomes capable of conducting electricity —**e·lec′tro·lyt′ic** (-lit′ik) *adj.*

**e·lec′tro·mag′net** (-mag′nit) *n.* a soft iron core that becomes a magnet when an electric current flows through a surrounding coil —**e·lec′tro·mag·net′ic** (-net′ik) *adj.*

**electromagnetic wave** a wave generated by an oscillating electric charge

**e·lec′tro·mo′tive** (-mōt′iv) *adj.* producing an electric current through differences in potential

**e·lec·tron** (ē lek′trän′, i-) *n.* ⟦see ELECTRIC⟧ a stable, negatively charged elementary particle that forms a part of all atoms

**e·lec·tron·ic** (ē′lek trän′ik) *adj.* **1** of electrons **2** operating, produced, or done by the action of electrons —**e·lec·tron′i·cal·ly** *adv.*

**electronic mail** E-MAIL

**electronic music** music in which the sounds are originated or altered by electronic devices

**e·lec·tron′ics** *n.* the science dealing with the action of electrons, and with the use of electron tubes, transistors, etc.

**electron microscope** a device that focuses a beam of electrons on a fluorescent screen, etc. to form a greatly enlarged image of an object

**electron tube** a sealed glass tube with gas or a vacuum inside, used to control the flow of electrons

**e·lec·tro·plate** (ē lek′trō plāt′, i-) *vt.* **-plat′ed, -plat′ing** to deposit a coating of metal on by electrolysis

**e·lec′tro·scope′** (-skōp′) *n.* a device for detecting very small charges of electricity or radiation —**e·lec′tro·scop′ic** (-skäp′ik) *adj.*

**e·lec′tro·shock′ therapy** shock therapy using electricity

**e·lec′tro·type′** *n. Printing* a plate made by electroplating a wax or plastic impression of the surface to be reproduced

**el·ee·mos·y·nar·y** (el′i mäs′ə ner′ē, el′ē ə-) *adj.* ⟦< Gr *eleēmosynē*, pity⟧ of, for, or supported by charity

**el·e·gant** (el′ə gənt) *adj.* ⟦< L *e-*, out + *legere*, choose⟧ **1** having dignified richness and grace, as of manner, design, or dress; tastefully luxurious **2** cleverly apt and simple [an *elegant* solution] **3** [Inf.] excellent —**el′e·gance** *n.* —**el′e·gant·ly** *adv.*

**el·e·gi·ac** (el ē′jē ak′, el′ə jī′ak′) *adj.* **1** of, like, or fit for an elegy **2** sad; mournful

**el·e·gy** (el′ə jē) *n., pl.* **-gies** ⟦< Gr *elegos*, a lament⟧ a mournful poem, esp. of lament and praise for the dead

**el·e·ment** (el′ə mənt) *n.* ⟦< L *elementum*⟧ **1** the natural or suitable environment for a person or thing **2** a component part or quality, often one that is basic or essential **3** *Chem.* any substance that cannot be separated into different substances by ordinary chemical methods, but only by radioactive decay or by nuclear reactions: all matter is composed of such substances —**the elements 1** the first principles; rudiments **2** wind, rain, etc.; forces of the atmosphere

**el·e·men·tal** (el′ə ment′'l) *adj.* **1** of or like basic, natural forces; primal **2** ELEMENTARY (sense 2*a*) **3** being an essential part or parts

**el′e·men′ta·ry** (-ə rē) *adj.* **1** ELEMENTAL **2** *a*) of first principles or fundamentals; basic; simple *b*) of the formal instruction of children in basic subjects

**elementary particle** a subatomic particle that cannot be divided

**elementary school** a school of the first six (sometimes eight) grades, where basic subjects are taught

**el·e·phant** (el′ə fənt) *n.* ⟦< Gr *elephas*⟧ a huge, thick-skinned mammal with a long, flexible snout, or trunk, and, usually, two ivory tusks

AFRICAN

**el·e·phan·ti·a·sis** (el′ə fən tī′ə sis) *n.* a chronic disease causing the enlargement of certain body parts and hardening of the surrounding skin

**el·e·phan·tine** (el′ə fan′tēn′) *adj.* like an elephant; huge; clumsy, etc.

ASIATIC

**el·e·vate** (el′ə vāt′) *vt.* **-vat′ed, -vat′ing** ⟦< L *e-*, out + *levare*, to lift⟧ **1** to lift up; raise **2** to raise in rank **3** to raise to a higher intellectual or moral level **4** to elate; exhilarate

ELEPHANTS

**el′e·va′tion** (-vā′shən) *n.* **1** an elevating or being elevated **2** a high place or position **3** height above the surface of the earth or above sea level

**el′e·va′tor** (-vāt′ər) *n.* **1** one that elevates, or lifts up **2** a suspended cage for hoisting or lowering people or things **3** a tall warehouse for storing and discharging grain: in full **grain elevator**

**e·lev·en** (ē lev′ən, i-) *adj., n.* ⟦OE *endleofan*⟧ one more than ten; 11; XI —**e·lev′enth** (-ənth) *adj., n.*

**elf** (elf) *n., pl.* **elves** (elvz) ⟦OE *ælf*⟧ *Folklore* a tiny, often mischievous fairy —**elf′in** or **elf′ish** *adj.*

**El Gre·co** (el grek′ō) 1541?-1614?; painter in Italy & Spain, born in Crete

**e·lic·it** (ē lis′it, i-) *vt.* ⟦< L *e-*, out + *lacere*, entice⟧ to draw forth; evoke (a response, etc.) —**e·lic′i·ta′tion** *n.*

**e·lide** (ē līd′, i-) *vt.* **e·lid′ed, e·lid′ing** ⟦< L *e-*, out + *laedere*, to hurt⟧ to leave out; esp., to slur over (a vowel, etc.) in pronunciation —**e·li′sion** (-lizh′ən) *n.*

**el·i·gi·ble** (el′i jə bəl) *adj.* ⟦see ELECT⟧ fit to be chosen; qualified —**el′i·gi·bil′i·ty** *n.*

**E·li·jah** (ē lī′jə, i-) *n. Bible* a prophet of Israel in the 9th c. B.C.

**e·lim·i·nate** (ē lim′ə nāt′, i-) *vt.* **-nat′ed, -nat′ing** ⟦< L *e-*, out + *limen*, threshold⟧ **1** to remove; get rid of **2** to leave out of consideration; omit **3** to excrete —**e·lim′i·na′tion** *n.*

**El·i·ot** (el′ē ət) **1 George** (pseud. of *Mary Ann Evans*) 1819-80; Eng. novelist **2 T(homas) S(tearns)** 1885-1965; Brit. poet, born in the U.S.

**e·lite** (i lēt′, ā-) *n.* ⟦Fr < L: see ELECT⟧ [*also with pl. v.*] the group or part of a group regarded as the best, most powerful, etc.

**e·lit′ism′** *n.* government or control by an elite —**e·lit′ist** *adj., n.*

**e·lix·ir** (i liks′ir) *n.* ⟦< Ar *al-iksīr*⟧ **1** a hypothetical substance sought by medieval alchemists to change base metals into gold or (in full **elixir of life**) to prolong life indefinitely **2** *Pharmacy* a sweetened solution used for medicines, etc.

**E·liz·a·beth** (ē liz′ə bəth, i-) **1 Elizabeth I** 1533-1603; queen of England (1558-1603) **2 Elizabeth II** 1926- ; queen of Great Britain & Northern Ireland (1952- )

**E·liz·a·be·than** (ē liz′ə bē′thən) *adj.* of or characteristic of the time of Elizabeth I's reign —*n.* an English person, esp. a writer, of that time

**elk** (elk) *n.* ⟦< OE *eolh*⟧ **1** MOOSE: the common term in Europe **2** WAPITI

**ell**[1] (el) *n.* **1** an extension or wing at right angles to the main structure **2** an L-shaped pipe, etc.

**ell**[2] (el) *n.* ⟦< OE *eln*⟧ a former English unit of measure, equal to 45 inches

**el·lipse** (e lips′, i-) *n., pl.* **-lip′ses** (-sēz′) ⟦< Gr *elleipein*, fall short⟧ *Geom.* a closed curve in the form of a symmetrical oval

**el·lip′sis** (-lip′sis) *n., pl.* **-ses** (-sēz′) ⟦see prec.⟧ **1** *Gram.* the omission of a word or words understood in the context (Ex.: "if possible" for "if it is possible") **2** a mark (. . .) indicating an omission of words: in full **ellipsis points**

ELLIPSES

**el·lip′ti·cal** (-ti kəl) *adj.* **1** of, or having the form of, an ellipse **2** of or characterized by ellipsis Also **el·lip′tic** —**el·lip′ti·cal·ly** *adv.*

**elm** (elm) *n.* ⟦OE⟧ **1** a tall, deciduous shade tree **2** its hard, heavy wood

**El Ni·ño** (el nēn′yō) a warm inshore current annually flowing south along the coast of Ecuador

**el·o·cu·tion** (el′ə kyōō′shən) *n.* ⟦see ELOQUENT⟧ the art of public speaking —**el′o·cu′tion·ar′y** *adj.* —**el′o·cu′tion·ist** *n.*

**e·lo·de·a** (ē lō′dē ə, el′ə dē′ə) *n.* ⟦< Gr *helōdēs*, swampy⟧ a submerged water plant with whorls of short, grasslike leaves

**e·lon·gate** (ē lôŋ′gāt, i-) *vt., vi.* **-gat′ed, -gat′ing** ⟦< L *e-*, out + *longus*, long⟧ to make or become longer; stretch —**e′lon·ga′tion** *n.*

**e·lope** (ē lōp′, i-) *vi.* **e·loped′, e·lop′ing** ⟦prob. < OE *a-*, away + *hleapan*, to run⟧ to run away secretly, esp. in order to get married —**e·lope′ment** *n.*

**el·o·quent** (el′ə kwənt) *adj.* ⟦< L *e-*, out + *loqui*, speak⟧ vivid, forceful, fluent, etc. in speech or writing —**el′o·quence** *n.* —**el′o·quent·ly** *adv.*

**El Pas·o** (el pas′ō) city in westernmost Texas.: pop. 515,000

**El Sal·va·dor** (el sal′və dôr′) country in Central America, on the Pacific: 8,124 sq. mi.; pop. 5,048,000

**else** (els) *adj.* ⟦OE *elles*⟧ **1** different; other [*somebody else*] **2** in addition [is there anything *else*?] —*adv.* **1** differently; otherwise [where *else* can I go?] **2** if not [study, (or) *else* you will fail] **else′where′** *adv.* in or to some other place; somewhere else

**e·lu·ci·date** (ə lōō′sə dāt′) *vt., vi.* **-dat′ed, -dat′ing** ⟦< L *e-*, out + *lucidus*, clear⟧ to make (something) clear; explain —**e·lu′ci·da′tion** *n.*

**e·lude** (ē lōōd′, i-) *vt.* **e·lud′ed, e·lud′ing** ⟦< L *e-*, out + *ludere*, to play⟧ **1** to avoid or escape from by quickness, cunning, etc.; evade **2** to escape the mental grasp of [his name *eludes* me]

**e·lu′sive** (-lōō′siv) *adj.* tending to elude; evasive — **e·lu′sive·ly** *adv.* —**e·lu′sive·ness** *n.*

**elves** (elvz) *n. pl. of* ELF

**E·ly·si·um** (ē lizh′əm, -liz′ē əm; i-) *n.* **1** *Gr. Myth.* the dwelling place of virtuous people after death

**2** any state of ideal bliss; paradise —**E·ly′si·an** (-lizh′ən, -liz′ē ən) *adj.*

**em** (em) *n.* ⟦< the letter *M*⟧ *Printing* a unit of measure, as of column width

**'em** (əm) *pron.* [Inf.] them

**em-** *prefix* EN-: used before *b, m,* or *p*

**e·ma·ci·ate** (ē mā′shē āt′, -sē-; i-) *vt.* **-at′ed, -at′ing** ⟦< L *e-*, out + *macies*, leanness⟧ to cause to become abnormally lean —**e·ma′ci·a′tion** *n.*

**e-mail** (ē′māl′) *n.* [*also* E-] messages sent from one computer terminal to another, as by telephone line

**em·a·nate** (em′ə nāt′) *vi.* **-nat′ed, -nat′ing** ⟦< L *e-*, out + *manare*, to flow⟧ to come forth; issue, as from a source —**em′a·na′tion** *n.*

**e·man·ci·pate** (ē man′sə pāt′, i-) *vt.* **-pat′ed, -pat′ing** ⟦< L *e-*, out + *manus*, the hand + *capere*, to take⟧ **1** to set free (a slave, etc.) **2** to free from restraint —**e·man′ci·pa′tion** *n.* —**e·man′ci·pa′tor** *n.*

**e·mas·cu·late** (ē mas′kyōō lāt′) *vt.* **-lat′ed, -lat′ing** ⟦< L *e-*, out + *masculus*, male⟧ **1** to castrate **2** to weaken —**e·mas′cu·la′tion** *n.*

**em·balm** (em bäm′, im-) *vt.* ⟦see EN- & BALM⟧ to preserve (a dead body) with various chemicals — **em·balm′er** *n.*

**em·bank** (em baŋk′, im-) *vt.* to protect, support, or enclose with a bank of earth, etc. —**em·bank′ment** *n.*

**em·bar·go** (em bär′gō, im-) *n., pl.* **-goes** ⟦Sp < L *in-*, in + ML *barra*, a bar⟧ **1** a government order prohibiting the entry or departure of commercial ships at its ports **2** any legal restriction of commerce —*vt.* **-goed, -go·ing** to put an embargo upon

**em·bark** (em bärk′, im-) *vt.* ⟦ult. < L *in-*, in + *barca*, small boat⟧ to put or take (passengers or goods) aboard a ship, aircraft, etc. —*vi.* **1** to go aboard a ship, aircraft, etc. **2** to begin; start — **em′bar·ka′tion** (-bär kā′shən) *n.*

**em·bar·rass** (em bar′əs, im-) *vt.* ⟦< It *in-*, in + ML *barra*, a bar⟧ **1** to cause to feel self-conscious **2** to hinder **3** to cause to be in debt —**em·bar′rass·ing** *adj.* —**em·bar′rass·ment** *n.*

**em·bas·sy** (em′bə sē) *n., pl.* **-sies** ⟦see AMBASSADOR⟧ **1** the residence or offices of an ambassador **2** an ambassador and his or her staff **3** a group sent on an official mission

**em·bat·tled** (em bat′'ld) *adj.* ⟦< OFr⟧ engaged in battle or conflict

**em·bed** (em bed′, im-) *vt.* **-bed′ded, -bed′ding** to set or fix firmly in earth, in the mind or memory, etc. —**em·bed′ment** *n.*

**em·bel·lish** (em bel′ish, im-) *vt.* ⟦< OFr *em-*, in + *bel*, beautiful⟧ **1** to adorn **2** to improve (a story, etc.) by adding details, often fictitious —**em·bel′lish·ment** *n.*

**em·ber** (em′bər) *n.* ⟦OE *æmerge*⟧ **1** a glowing piece of coal, wood, etc. **2** [*pl.*] the smoldering remains of a fire

**em·bez·zle** (em bez′əl, im-) *vt.* **-zled, -zling** ⟦< OFr *en-*, in + *besillier*, destroy⟧ to steal (money, etc. entrusted to one) —**em·bez′zle·ment** *n.* —**em·bez′zler** *n.*

**em·bit·ter** (-bit′ər) *vt.* to make bitter —**em·bit′ter·ment** *n.*

**em·bla·zon** (-blā′zən) *vt.* ⟦EM- (see EN-) + BLAZON⟧ **1** to decorate (*with* coats of arms, etc.) **2** to display brilliantly **3** to extol —**em·bla′zon·ment** *n.*

**em·blem** (em′bləm) *n.* ⟦< Gr *en-*, in + *ballein*, throw⟧ a visible symbol of a thing, idea, etc.; sign; badge —**em′blem·at′ic** (-blə mat′ik) *adj.*

**em·bod·y** (em bäd′ē, im-) *vt.* **-ied, -y·ing** **1** to give bodily form to **2** to give definite form to **3** to bring together into an organized whole; incorporate —**em·bod′i·ment** *n.*

**em·bold′en** (-bōl′dən) *vt.* to give courage to

**em·bo·lism** (em′bə liz′əm) *n.* ⟦< Gr *en-*, in + *bal-*

*lein*, to throw] the obstruction of a blood vessel as by a blood clot or air bubble

**em·boss** (em bôs´, -bäs´; im-) *vt.* [see EN- & BOSS²] 1 to decorate with raised designs, patterns, etc. 2 to raise (a design, etc.) in relief —**em·boss´er** *n.*

**em·bou·chure** (äm´boo shoor´) *n.* [Fr < L *in*, in + *bucca*, cheek] the method of applying the lips and tongue to the mouthpiece of a wind instrument

**em·brace** (em brās´, im-) *vt.* **-braced´, -brac´ing** [< L *im-*, in + *brachium*, an arm] 1 to clasp in the arms lovingly; hug 2 to accept readily 3 to take up or adopt 4 to encircle 5 to include —*vi.* to clasp each other in the arms —*n.* an embracing; hug —**em·brace´a·ble** *adj.*

**em·bra·sure** (em brā´zhər, im-) *n.* [Fr < obs. *embraser*, widen an opening] 1 an opening (for a door, window, etc.) wider on the inside than on the outside 2 an opening in a wall or parapet for a gun, with the sides slanting outward

**em·broi·der** (em broi´dər, im-) *vt., vi.* [< OFr *en-*, on + *brosder*, embroider] 1 to make (a design, etc.) on (fabric) with needlework 2 to embellish (a story); exaggerate

**em·broi´der·y** *n., pl.* **-ies** 1 the art of embroidering 2 embroidered work or fabric 3 embellishment

**em·broil** (em broil´, im-) *vt.* [< OFr *en-*, in + *brouillier*, to dirty] 1 to confuse; muddle 2 to involve in conflict or trouble —**em·broil´ment** *n.*

**em·bry·o** (em´brē ō´) *n., pl.* **-os´** [< Gr *en-*, in + *bryein*, to swell] 1 an animal in the earliest stages of its development in the uterus or egg 2 the rudimentary plant contained in a seed 3 an early stage of something —**em´bry·on´ic** (-än´ik) *adj.*

**em´bry·ol´o·gy** (-äl´ə jē) *n.* [prec. + -LOGY] the branch of biology dealing with the formation and development of embryos —**em´bry·ol´o·gist** *n.*

**em·cee** (em´sē´) *vi., vt.* **-ceed´, -cee´ing** [< MC, sense 1] [Inf.] to act as master of ceremonies (for) —*n.* [Inf.] a master of ceremonies

**e·mend** (ē mend´, i-) *vt.* [< L *emendare*, to correct] to make scholarly corrections in (a text) —**e·men·da·tion** (ē´men dā´shən, em´ən-) *n.*

**em·er·ald** (em´ər əld) *n.* [< Gr *smaragdos*] 1 a transparent, bright-green precious stone 2 bright green

**e·merge** (ē murj´, i-) *vi.* **e·merged´, e·merg´ing** [< L *e-*, out + *mergere*, to dip] 1 to rise as from a fluid 2 to become visible or apparent 3 to evolve —**e·mer´gence** *n.* —**e·mer´gent** *adj.*

**e·mer·gen·cy** (ē mur´jən sē, i-) *n., pl.* **-cies** [orig. sense, emergence] a sudden, generally unexpected occurrence demanding immediate action —*adj.* for use in an emergency

**emergency room** a hospital unit for accident victims and others needing immediate treatment

**e·mer·i·tus** (ē mer´i təs, i-) *adj.* [< L *e-*, out + *mereri*, to serve] retired from active service, usually for age, but retaining one's title *[professor emeritus]*

**Em·er·son** (em´ər sən), **Ralph Wal·do** (ralf wôl´dō) 1803-82; U.S. writer & philosopher

**em·er·y** (em´ər ē) *n.* [< Gr *smyris*] a dark, coarse variety of corundum used for grinding, polishing, etc.

**emery board** a small, flat stick coated with powdered emery, used to shape the fingernails

**e·met·ic** (ē met´ik, i-) *adj.* [< Gr *emein*, to vomit] causing vomiting —*n.* an emetic substance

**-e·mi·a** (ē´mē ə) [< Gr *haima*, blood] *combining form* a (specified) condition of the blood *[leukemia]*

**em·i·grate** (em´i grāt´) *vi.* **-grat´ed, -grat´ing** [< L *e-*, out + *migrare*, to move] to leave one country or region to settle in another —**em´i·grant** (-grənt) *adj., n.* —**em´i·gra´tion** *n.*

**é·mi·gré** or **e·mi·gré** (em´i grā´) *n.* [Fr] 1 one who emigrates 2 one forced to flee his or her country for political reasons

**em·i·nence** (em´i nəns) *n.* [< L *eminere*, stand out] 1 a high place, thing, etc. 2 superiority in rank, position, etc. 3 [E-] a title of a cardinal: preceded by *Your* or *His*

**em´i·nent** (-nənt) *adj.* [< L *eminens*] 1 high; lofty 2 projecting; prominent 3 renowned; distinguished 4 outstanding —**em´i·nent·ly** *adv.*

**eminent domain** the right of a government to take or purchase private property for public use, with just compensation to the owner

**e·mir** (e mir´, ə-) *n.* [< Ar *amara*, to command] in Muslim countries, a ruler or prince

**em·is·sar·y** (em´i ser´ē) *n., pl.* **-ies** [see EMIT] a person or agent sent on a specific mission

**e·mis·sion** (ē mish´ən, i-) *n.* 1 an emitting 2 something emitted; discharge

**e·mit** (ē mit´, i-) *vt.* **e·mit´ted, e·mit´ting** [< L *e-*, out + *mittere*, send] 1 to send out; give forth; discharge 2 to utter (words, etc.) —**e·mit´ter** *n.*

**e·mol·li·ent** (ē mäl´yənt, i-) *adj.* [< L *e-*, out + *mollire*, soften] softening; soothing —*n.* something that softens or soothes, as a preparation applied to the skin

**e·mol·u·ment** (-yoo mənt) *n.* [< L *e-*, out + *molere*, to grind] payment received for work; salary, fees, etc.

**e·mote** (ē mōt´, i-) *vi.* **e·mot´ed, e·mot´ing** [Inf.] to act in an emotional or theatrical manner

**e·mo·tion** (ē mō´shən, i-) *n.* [< L *e-*, out + *movere*, to move] 1 strong feeling 2 any specific feeling, as love, hate, fear, or anger

**e·mo·tion·al** *adj.* 1 of or showing emotion 2 easily aroused to emotion 3 appealing to the emotions; moving —**e·mo·tion·al·ism´** *n.* —**e·mo´tion·al·ly** *adv.*

**e·mo·tion·al·ize** *vt.* **-ized´, -iz´ing** to treat in an emotional way

**em·pa·thet·ic** (em´pə thet´ik) *adj.* of or showing empathy: also **em·path´ic** (-path´ik)

**em·pa·thize** (em´pə thīz´) *vt.* **-thized´, -thiz´ing** to feel empathy (*with*)

**em·pa·thy** (-thē) *n.* [< Gr *en-*, in + *pathos*, feeling] the ability to share in another's emotions, thoughts, or feelings

**em·per·or** (em´pər ər) *n.* [< L *in-*, in + *parare*, to set in order] the supreme ruler of an empire

**em·pha·sis** (em´fə sis) *n., pl.* **-ses´** (-sēz´) [< Gr *en-*, in + *phainein*, to show] 1 force of expression, action, etc. 2 special stress given to a word or phrase in speaking 3 importance; stress

**em´pha·size´** (-sīz´) *vt.* **-sized´, -siz´ing** to give emphasis to; stress

**em·phat·ic** (em fat´ik, im-) *adj.* 1 felt or done with emphasis 2 using emphasis in speaking, etc. 3 forcible; striking —**em·phat´i·cal·ly** *adv.*

**em·phy·se·ma** (em´fə sē´mə, -zē´-) *n.* [< Gr *en-*, in + *physaein*, to blow] a condition of the lungs in which the air sacs become distended and lose elasticity

**em·pire** (em´pīr´) *n.* [see EMPEROR] 1 supreme rule 2 government by an emperor or empress 3 a group of states or territories under one ruler 4 an extensive organization under the control of a single person, corporation, etc.

**em·pir·i·cal** (em pir´i kəl) *adj.* [< Gr *en-*, in + *peira*, trial] relying or based on experiment or experience —**em·pir´i·cal·ly** *adv.* —**em·pir´i·cism´** (-siz´əm) *n.*

**em·place·ment** (em plās´ mənt, im-) *n.* the prepared position from which a heavy gun or guns are fired

**em·ploy** (em ploi´, im-) *vt.* [< L *in-*, in + *plicare*, to fold] 1 to use 2 to keep busy or occupied 3 to engage the services of; hire —*n.* employment

**em·ploy´a·ble** *adj.* that can be employed; specif., physically or mentally fit to be hired for work

**em·ploy·ee** or **em·ploy´e** (-ē) *n.* one hired by another for wages or salary

**em·ploy´er** *n.* one who employs others for wages or salary

**em·ploy´ment** *n.* 1 an employing or being

employed **2** work; occupation **3** the number or percentage of persons gainfully employed

**em·po·ri·um** (em pôr′ē əm) *n.*, *pl.* **-ri·ums** or **-ri·a** (-ə) 〖< Gr *en-*, in + *poros*, way〗 a large store with a wide variety of things for sale

**em·pow·er** (em pou′ər, im-) *vt.* **1** to give power to; authorize **2** to enable —**em·pow′er·ment** *n.*

**em·press** (em′pris) *n.* **1** an emperor's wife **2** a woman ruler of an empire

**emp·ty** (emp′tē) *adj.* **-ti·er, -ti·est** 〖OE *æmettig*〗 **1** having nothing or no one in it; unoccupied **2** worthless *[empty pleasure]* **3** insincere *[empty promises]* —*vt.* **-tied, -ty·ing 1** to make empty **2** to remove (the contents) of something —*vi.* **1** to become empty **2** to pour out; discharge —*n.*, *pl.* **-ties** an empty truck, bottle, etc. —**emp′ti·ly** *adv.* —**emp′ti·ness** *n.*

**emp·ty-hand·ed** *adj.* bringing or carrying away nothing

**em·py·re·an** (em pir′ē ən, em′pī rē′ən) *n.* 〖< Gr *en-*, in + *pyr*, fire〗 **1** the highest heaven **2** the sky; firmament

**EMT** *abbrev.* emergency medical technician

**e·mu** (ē′myōō′) *n.* 〖< Port *ema*, a crane〗 a large, flightless Australian bird, somewhat like the ostrich but smaller

**em·u·late** (em′yōō lāt′, -yə-) *vt.* **-lat·ed, -lat·ing** 〖< L *aemulus*, trying to equal or excel〗 **1** to try to equal or surpass **2** to imitate (a person or thing admired) **3** to rival successfully —**em′u·la′tion** *n.* —**em′u·la′tive** *adj.* —**em′u·la′tor** *n.*

**e·mul·si·fy** (ē mul′sə fī′, i-) *vt.*, *vi.* **-fied′, -fy′ing** to form into an emulsion —**e·mul′si·fi·ca′tion** *n.*

**e·mul′sion** (-shən) *n.* 〖< L *e-*, out + *mulgere*, to milk〗 a colloidal suspension of one liquid in another, as photographic film coatings, some medications, etc.

**en-** 〖< L *in-*, in〗 *prefix* **1** to put or get into or on *[enthrone]* **2** to make, cause to be *[endanger]* **3** in or into *[encase]*

**-en** (ən, 'n) 〖OE〗 *suffix* **1** *a*) to become or cause to be *[darken]* *b*) to cause to have *[heighten]* **2** made of *[wooden]* **3** forming plurals *[children]*

**en·a·ble** (en ā′bəl, in-) *vt.* **-bled, -bling 1** to make able; provide with means, power, etc. (*to* do something) **2** to support the dysfunctional behavior of, as by compensating for it —**en·a′bler** *n.*

**en·act** (en akt′, in-) *vt.* **1** to pass (a bill, law, etc.) **2** to represent as in a play —**en·act′ment** *n.*

**en·am·el** (e nam′əl, i-) *n.* 〖< OFr *esmail*〗 **1** a glassy, opaque substance fused to metal, pottery, etc. as an ornamental or protective coating **2** the hard, white coating of teeth **3** paint that dries to a smooth, glossy surface —*vt.* **-eled** or **-elled, -el·ing** or **-el·ling** to coat with enamel —**en·am′el·er** or **en·am′el·ler** *n.*

**en·am·or** (en am′ər, in-) *vt.* 〖ult. < L *in-*, in + *amor*, love〗 to fill with love; charm: now mainly in the passive voice, with *of [enamored* of her*]*

**en bloc** (en bläk′) 〖Fr, lit., in a block〗 in a mass; all together

**en bro·chette** (än brô shet′) 〖Fr〗 broiled on small skewers

**en·camp** (en kamp′, in-) *vi.*, *vt.* to set up, or put in, a camp —**en·camp′ment** *n.*

**en·cap·su·late** (en kap′sə lāt′) *vt.* **-lat·ed, -lat·ing 1** to enclose in a capsule **2** to make concise; condense Also **en·cap′sule** (-səl, -syōōl′), **-suled, -sul·ing** —**en·cap′su·la′tion** *n.*

**en·case** (en kās′, in-) *vt.* **-cased′, -cas′ing** to enclose, as in a case

**en cas·se·role** (en kas′ə rōl′) 〖Fr〗 (baked and served) in a casserole

**-ence** (əns, 'ns) 〖< L〗 *suffix* act, state, or result *[conference]*

**en·ceph·a·li·tis** (en sef′ə līt′is) *n.* 〖< Gr *en-*, in + *kephalē*, the head + -ITIS〗 inflammation of the brain

**en·chain** (en chān′) *vt.* to bind with chains; fetter

**en·chant** (en chant′, in-) *vt.* 〖< L *in-*, intens. + *cantare*, sing〗 **1** to cast a spell over **2** to charm

greatly; delight —**en·chant′er** *n.* —**en·chant′ing** *adj.* —**en·chant′ment** *n.*

**en·chi·la·da** (en′chi lä′də) *n.* 〖AmSp〗 a tortilla rolled with meat inside, served with a chili-flavored sauce

**en·cir·cle** (en sur′kəl, in-) *vt.* **-cled, -cling 1** to surround **2** to move in a circle around —**en·cir′cle·ment** *n.*

**encl** *abbrev.* enclosure

**en·clave** (en′klāv′, än′-) *n.* 〖< L *in*, in + *clavis*, a key〗 a territory surrounded by another country's territory

**en·close** (en klōz′, in-) *vt.* **-closed′, -clos′ing 1** to shut in all around; surround **2** to insert in an envelope, etc., often along with something else

**en·clo′sure** (-klō′zhər) *n.* **1** an enclosing or being enclosed **2** something that encloses, as a fence **3** something enclosed, as in an envelope or by a wall

**en·code** (en kōd′, in-) *vt.* **-cod′ed, -cod′ing** to put (a message, etc.) into code

**en·co·mi·um** (en kō′mē əm) *n.*, *pl.* **-ums** or **-a** (-ə) 〖< Gr *en-*, in + *kōmos*, a revel〗 high praise; eulogy

**en·com·pass** (en kum′pəs, in-) *vt.* **1** to surround **2** to contain; include

**en·core** (än′kôr′) *interj.* 〖Fr〗 again; once more — *n.* a further performance, etc. in answer to an audience's applause

**en·coun·ter** (en koun′tər, in-) *vt.* 〖< L *in*, in + *contra*, against〗 **1** to meet unexpectedly **2** to meet in conflict **3** to meet with (difficulties, etc.) —*n.* **1** a direct meeting, as in battle **2** a meeting, esp. when unexpected

**en·cour·age** (en kur′ij, in-) *vt.* **-aged, -ag·ing 1** to give courage, hope, or confidence to **2** to give support to; help —**en·cour′age·ment** *n.*

**en·croach** (en krōch′, in-) *vi.* 〖< OFr *en-*, in + *croc*, a hook〗 to trespass or intrude (*on* or *upon*) —**en·croach′ment** *n.*

**en croûte** (än krōōt′) 〖Fr〗 wrapped in pastry and baked: said esp. of meats

**en·crust** (en krust′) *vt.* to cover as with a crust — *vi.* to form a crust —**en′crus·ta′tion** (-krus tā′shən) *n.*

**en·cum·ber** (en kum′bər, in-) *vt.* 〖see EN- & CUMBER〗 **1** to hold back the motion or action of; hinder **2** to burden —**en·cum′brance** *n.*

**-en·cy** (ən sē) 〖L *-entia*〗 *suffix* -ENCE *[dependency]*

**en·cyc·li·cal** (en sik′li kəl, in-) *n.* 〖< Gr *en-*, in + *kyklos*, a circle〗 a papal document addressed to the bishops

**en·cy·clo·pe·di·a** or **en·cy·clo·pae·di·a** (en sī′ klə pē′dē ə) *n.* 〖< Gr *enkyklios*, general + *paideia*, education〗 a book or set of books with alphabetically arranged articles on all branches, or on one field, of knowledge —**en·cy′clo·pe′dic** or **en·cy′clo·pae′dic** *adj.*

**en·cyst** (en sist′) *vt.*, *vi.* to enclose or become enclosed in a cyst, sac, etc. —**en·cyst′ment** *n.*

**end** (end) *n.* 〖OE *ende*〗 **1** a limit; boundary **2** the last part of anything; finish; conclusion **3** a ceasing to exist; death or destruction **4** the part at or near an extremity; tip **5** an object; purpose **6** an outcome; result **7** *Football* a player at either end of the line —*vt.*, *vi.* to bring or come to an end; finish; stop —*adj.* at the end; final —**make (both) ends meet** to manage to keep one's expenses within one's income —**put an end to 1** to stop **2** to do away with

**en·dan·ger** (en dān′jər, in-) *vt.* to expose to danger, harm, etc.; imperil —**en·dan′ger·ment** *n.*

**endangered species** a species of animal or plant in danger of becoming extinct

**en·dear** (en dir′, in-) *vt.* to make dear or beloved —**en·dear′ing** *adj.*

**en·dear′ment** *n.* **1** an endearing **2** a word or act expressing affection

**en·deav·or** (en dev′ər, in-) *vi.* 〖< EN- + OFr *deveir*, duty〗 to make an earnest attempt; try: usually with an infinitive —*n.* an earnest attempt or effort Brit. sp. **en·deav′our**

**en·dem·ic** (en dem′ik) *adj.* [< Gr *en-*, in + *dēmos*, people] native to or constantly present in, a particular place, as a plant or disease —**en·dem′i·cal·ly** *adv.*

**end′ing** *n.* 1 the last part; finish 2 death

**en·dive** (en′dīv′, än′dēv′) *n.* [< Gr *entybon*] a cultivated plant with curled, narrow leaves used in salads

**end′less** *adj.* 1 having no end; eternal; infinite 2 lasting too long [an *endless* speech] 3 continual [*endless* problems] 4 with the ends joined to form a closed unit [an *endless* chain] —**end′less·ly** *adv.* —**end′less·ness** *n.*

**end′most′** *adj.* at the end; farthest

**endo-** [< Gr *endon*] *combining form* within, inner

**en·do·crine** (en′dō krin′, -krīn′; -də-) *adj.* [prec. + Gr *krinein*, to separate] designating or of any gland producing a hormone

**en·dorse** (en dôrs′, in-) *vt.* -**dorsed′**, -**dors′ing** [< L *in*, on + *dorsum*, the back] 1 to write on the back of (a title, check, etc.) to transfer ownership, make a deposit, etc. 2 to sanction, approve, or support 3 to recommend (an advertised product) for a fee —**en·dorse′ment** *n.* —**en·dors′er** *n.*

**en·do·scope** (en′dō skōp′, -də-) *n.* an instrument for examining visually the inside of a hollow organ or cavity of the body, as the rectum

**en·dow** (en dou′, in-) *vt.* [< OFr *en-*, in + *dotare*, to endow] 1 to provide with some talent, quality, etc. [*endowed* with courage] 2 to give money or property to (a college, etc.) —**en·dow′ment** *n.*

**end′point′** *n.* a point of completion or furthest progress

**end product** the final result of a series of changes, processes, etc.

**end table** a small table placed at the end of a sofa, etc.

**en·due** (en dōō′, in-) *vt.* -**dued′**, -**du′ing** [< L *in-*, in + *ducere*, to lead] to provide (*with* qualities)

**en·dur·ance** (en door′əns, in-) *n.* the ability to last, stand pain, etc.

**en·dure** (en door′, in-) *vt.* -**dured′**, -**dur′ing** [< L *durus*, hard] 1 to hold up under (pain, etc.) 2 to tolerate —*vi.* 1 to continue; last 2 to bear pain, etc. without flinching —**en·dur′a·ble** *adj.*

**end′ways′** (-wāz′) *adv.* 1 upright 2 with the end foremost 3 lengthwise Also **end′wise′** (-wīz′)

**-ene** (ēn) [after Gr *-enos*, adj. suffix] *Chem. suffix* a certain type of hydrocarbon [*benzene*]

**en·e·ma** (en′ə mə) *n.* [< Gr *en-*, in + *hienai*, send] the forcing of a liquid, as a purgative, medicine, etc., into the colon through the anus

**en·e·my** (en′ə mē) *n.*, *pl.* -**mies** [< L *in-*, not + *amicus*, friend] 1 one who hates and wishes to injure another 2 *a*) a nation or force hostile to another *b*) troops, ship, etc. of a hostile nation 3 one hostile to an idea, cause, etc. 4 anything injurious or harmful

**en·er·get·ic** (en′ər jet′ik) *adj.* having or showing energy; vigorous —**en·er·get′i·cal·ly** *adv.*

**en·er·gize** (en′ər jīz′) *vt.* -**gized′**, -**giz′ing** to give energy to; activate —**en′er·giz′er** *n.*

**en·er·gy** (en′ər jē) *n.*, *pl.* -**gies** [< Gr *en-*, in + *ergon*, work] 1 force of expression 2 *a*) inherent power; capacity for action *b*) [often *pl.*] such power, esp. in action 3 a resource, as oil or gas, from which usable energy can be produced 4 *Physics* the capacity for doing work

**en·er·vate** (en′ər vāt′) *vt.* -**vat′ed**, -**vat′ing** [< L *e-*, out + *nervus*, nerve] to deprive of strength, force, vigor, etc.; devitalize —**en′er·va′tion** *n.*

**en·fee·ble** (en fē′bəl, in-) *vt.* -**bled**, -**bling** to make feeble

**en·fi·lade** (en′fə lād′, en′fə lād′) *n.* [Fr] gunfire directed along a line of troops

**en·fold** (en fōld′, in-) *vt.* 1 to wrap in folds; wrap up 2 to embrace

**en·force** (en fôrs′, in-) *vt.* -**forced′**, -**forc′ing** 1 to impose by force [to *enforce* one's will] 2 to compel

observance of (a law, etc.) —**en·force′a·ble** *adj.* —**en·force′ment** *n.* —**en·forc′er** *n.*

**en·fran·chise** (en fran′chīz, in-) *vt.* -**chised′**, -**chis′ing** 1 to free from slavery 2 to give the right to vote —**en·fran′chise·ment** (-chiz mənt) *n.*

**Eng** *abbrev.* 1 England 2 English

**en·gage** (en gāj′, in-) *vt.* -**gaged′**, -**gag′ing** [see EN- & GAGE[1]] 1 to pledge (oneself) 2 to bind by a promise of marriage 3 to hire 4 to involve or occupy 5 to attract and hold (the attention, etc.) 6 to enter into conflict with (the enemy) 7 to mesh (gears, etc.) —*vi.* 1 to pledge oneself 2 to occupy or involve oneself [to *engage* in dramatics] 3 to enter into conflict 4 to mesh

**en·gaged′** *adj.* 1 betrothed 2 occupied; employed 3 involved in combat, as troops 4 in gear; meshed

**en·gage′ment** *n.* an engaging or being engaged; specif., *a*) a betrothal *b*) an appointment *c*) employment *d*) a conflict; battle

**en·gag′ing** *adj.* attractive; pleasant; charming —**en·gag′ing·ly** *adv.*

**en·gen·der** (en jen′dər, in-) *vt.* [< L *in-*, in + *generare*, beget] to bring into being; cause; produce

**en·gine** (en′jən) *n.* [< L *in-*, in + base of *gignere*, beget] 1 any machine that uses energy to develop mechanical power 2 a railroad locomotive 3 any machine

**en·gi·neer** (en′jə nir′) *n.* 1 one skilled in some branch of engineering 2 one who operates or supervises the operation of engines or technical equipment [a locomotive *engineer*] —*vt.* 1 to plan, construct, etc. as an engineer 2 to manage skillfully

**en·gi·neer′ing** *n.* 1 the science concerned with putting scientific knowledge to practical uses 2 the planning, designing, construction, or management of machinery, roads, bridges, etc.

**Eng·land** (iŋ′glənd) division of the United Kingdom in S Great Britain: 50,357 sq. mi.; pop. 46,382,000

**Eng·lish** (iŋ′glish) *adj.* 1 of England, its people, etc. 2 of the language of England and the U.S. —*n.* 1 the Germanic language of England and the U.S., also spoken in the Commonwealth, etc. 2 [*sometimes* e-] a spinning motion given to a ball —**the English** the people of England

**English Channel** arm of the Atlantic, between England & France

**English horn** a double-reed woodwind instrument

**Eng′lish·man** (-mən) *n.*, *pl.* -**men** (-mən) a person born or living in England —**Eng′lish·wom′an**, *pl.* -**wom′en**, *fem.n.*

**en·gorge** (en gôrj′, in-) *vt.* -**gorged′**, -**gorg′ing** [< OFr *en-*, in + *gorge*, gorge] 1 to devour greedily 2 *Med.* to congest (tissue, etc.) with fluid, as blood

**en·grave** (en grāv′, in-) *vt.* -**graved′**, -**grav′ing** [< Fr *en-*, in + *graver*, to incise] 1 to cut or etch letters, designs, etc. in or on (a metal plate, etc.) 2 to print with such a plate 3 to impress deeply —**en·grav′er** *n.*

**en·grav′ing** *n.* 1 the act or art of one who engraves 2 an engraved plate, drawing, etc. 3 a print made from an engraved surface

**en·gross** (en grōs′, in-) *vt.* [< OFr *engroissier*, become thick] to take the entire attention of; occupy wholly —**en·gross′ing** *adj.*

**en·gulf** (en gulf′, in-) *vt.* to swallow up

**en·hance** (en hans′, in-) *vt.* -**hanced′**, -**hanc′ing** [< L *in-*, in + *altus*, high] to make greater, better, etc.; heighten —**en·hance′ment** *n.*

**e·nig·ma** (i nig′mə, e-) *n.* [< Gr *ainos*, story] 1 a riddle 2 a perplexing or baffling matter, person, etc. —**en·ig·mat·ic** (en′ig mat′ik) *adj.*

**en·jamb·ment** or **en·jambe·ment** (en jam′mənt) *n.* [< Fr *enjamber*, to encroach] in poetry, the movement from one line to the next without a pause

**en·join** (en join′, in-) *vt.* [< L *in-*, in + *jungere*,

**join**] **1** to command; order; impose **2** to prohibit, esp. by legal injunction

**en·joy** (en joi′, in-) *vt.* [< OFr *en-*, in + *joir*, rejoice] **1** to get pleasure from; relish **2** to have the use or benefit of —**enjoy oneself** to have a good time — **en·joy′a·ble** *adj.* —**en·joy′ment** *n.*

**en·large** (en lärj′, in-) *vt.* **-larged′**, **-larg′ing** to make larger; expand —*vi.* **1** to become larger; expand **2** to speak or write at greater length: with *on* or *upon* —**en·large′ment** *n.*

**en·light·en** (en līt′'n, in-) *vt.* **1** to free from ignorance, prejudice, etc. **2** to inform —**en·light′en·ment** *n.*

**en·list** (en list′, in-) *vt., vi.* **1** to enroll in some branch of the armed forces **2** to engage in support of a cause or movement —**en·list′ment** *n.*

**en·list′ed** *adj.* of a person in the armed forces who is not a commissioned officer or warrant officer

**en·liv·en** (en li′vən, in-) *vt.* to make active, cheerful, etc.; liven up

**en masse** (en mas′) [Fr, lit., in mass] in a group; as a whole

**en·mesh** (en mesh′, in-) *vt.* to catch as in the meshes of a net; entangle

**en·mi·ty** (en′mə tē) *n., pl.* **-ties** [see ENEMY] the bitter attitude or feelings of an enemy or enemies; hostility

**en·no·ble** (e nō′bəl, i-) *vt.* **-bled**, **-bling** to give a noble quality to; dignify —**en·no′ble·ment** *n.*

**en·nui** (än′wē) *n.* [Fr] weariness and dissatisfaction from lack of interest; boredom

**e·nor·mi·ty** (ē nôr′mə tē, i-) *n., pl.* **-ties** [< L *enormis*, immense] **1** great wickedness **2** an outrageous act **3** enormous size or extent

**e·nor·mous** (ē nôr′məs, i-) *adj.* [see prec.] of great size, number, etc.; huge; vast; immense —**e·nor′mous·ly** *adv.*

**e·nough** (ē nuf′, i-) *adj.* [OE *genoh*] as much or as many as necessary; sufficient —*n.* the amount needed —*adv.* **1** sufficiently **2** fully; quite [oddly *enough*] **3** tolerably

**e·now** (ē nou′, i-) *adj., n., adv.* [Archaic] enough

**en·plane** (en plān′, in-) *vi.* **-planed′**, **-plan′ing** to board an airplane

**en·quire** (en kwīr′, in-) *vt., vi.* **-quired′**, **-quir′ing** INQUIRE —**en·quir′y** (-ē), *pl.* **-ies**, *n.*

**en·rage** (en rāj′, in-) *vt.* **-raged′**, **-rag′ing** to put into a rage; infuriate

**en·rap·ture** (en rap′chər, in-) *vt.* **-tured**, **-tur·ing** to fill with delight

**en·rich** (en rich′, in-) *vt.* to make rich or richer; give greater value, better quality, etc. to —**en·rich′ment** *n.*

**en·roll** or **en·rol** (en rōl′, in-) *vt., vi.* **-rolled′**, **-roll′ing** **1** to record or be recorded in a roll or list **2** to enlist **3** to make or become a member —**en·roll′ment** or **en·rol′ment** *n.*

**en route** (än rōōt′, en-) [Fr] on the way

**en·sconce** (en skäns′, in-) *vt.* **-sconced′**, **-sconc′ing** [< Du *schans*, small fort] to place or settle snugly or securely

**en·sem·ble** (än säm′bəl) *n.* [Fr < L *in-*, in + *simul*, at the same time] **1** total effect **2** a whole costume of matching parts **3** *a)* a small group of musicians, actors, etc. *b)* the performance of such a group

**en·shrine** (en shrīn′, in-) *vt.* **-shrined′**, **-shrin′ing** **1** to enclose in a shrine **2** to hold as sacred; cherish —**en·shrine′ment** *n.*

**en·shroud** (en shroud′, in-) *vt.* to cover as if with a shroud; hide; obscure

**en·sign** (en′sīn′; *also, & for 2 always*, -sən) *n.* [see INSIGNIA] **1** a flag or banner **2** *U.S. Navy* a commissioned officer of the lowest rank

**en·si·lage** (en′sə lij) *n.* [ult. < L *in-*, in + Gr *siros*, silo] the preserving of green fodder in a silo

**en·slave** (en slāv′, in-) *vt.* **-slaved′**, **-slav′ing** **1** to make a slave of **2** to subjugate —**en·slave′ment** *n.*

**en·snare** (en sner′, in-) *vt.* **-snared′**, **-snar′ing** to catch in or as in a snare

**en·sue** (en sōō′, in-) *vi.* **-sued′**, **-su′ing** [< L *in-*, in + *sequi*, follow] **1** to come afterward **2** to result

**en·sure** (en shoor′, in-) *vt.* **-sured′**, **-sur′ing** **1** to make sure **2** to protect

**-ent** (ənt) [< OFr *-ent*, L *-ens*, prp. ending] *suffix* **1** that has, shows, or does [*insistent*] **2** a person or thing that [*superintendent, solvent*]

**en·tail** (en tāl′, in-) *vt.* [< OFr *taillier*, to cut] **1** *Law* to limit the inheritance of (real property) to a specific line of heirs **2** to make necessary; require

**en·tan·gle** (en taŋ′gəl, in-) *vt.* **-gled**, **-gling** **1** to involve in a tangle **2** to involve in difficulty **3** to confuse **4** to complicate —**en·tan′gle·ment** *n.*

**en·tente** (än tänt′) *n.* [Fr < OFr *entendre*, understand] **1** an understanding or agreement, as between nations **2** the parties to this

**en·ter** (ent′ər) *vt.* [< L *intra*, within] **1** to come or go into **2** to penetrate **3** to insert **4** to write down in a list, etc. **5** to become a member of or participant in **6** to get (a person, etc.) admitted **7** to begin **8** to put on record, formally or before a law court **9** to input (data, etc.) into a computer —*vi.* **1** to come or go into some place **2** to penetrate —**enter into 1** to take part in **2** to form a part of —**enter on** (or **upon**) to begin; start

**en·ter·i·tis** (en′tər īt′is) *n.* [< Gr *enteron*, intestine + -ITIS] inflammation of the intestine

**en·ter·prise** (ent′ər prīz′) *n.* [ult. < L *inter*, in + *prehendere*, take] **1** an undertaking, esp. a big, bold, or difficult one **2** energy and initiative

**en′ter·pris′ing** *adj.* showing enterprise; full of energy and initiative

**en·ter·tain** (ent′ər tān′) *vt.* [ult. < L *inter*, between + *tenere*, to hold] **1** to amuse; divert **2** to have as a guest **3** to have in mind; consider — *vi.* to give hospitality to guests

**en′ter·tain′er** *n.* one who entertains; esp., a popular singer, comedian, etc.

**en′ter·tain′ing** *adj.* interesting and pleasurable; amusing

**en′ter·tain′ment** *n.* **1** an entertaining or being entertained **2** something that entertains; esp., a show or performance

**en·thrall** or **en·thral** (en thrôl′, in-) *vt.* **-thralled′**, **-thrall′ing** [[see EN- & THRALL]] to captivate; fascinate

**en·throne** (en thrōn′, in-) *vt.* **-throned′**, **-thron′ing** **1** to place on a throne **2** to exalt

**en·thuse** (en thōōz′, in-) [Inf.] *vi.* **-thused′**, **-thus′ing** to express enthusiasm —*vt.* to make enthusiastic

**en·thu·si·asm** (en thōō′zē az′əm, in-) *n.* [< Gr *en-*, in + *theos*, god] intense or eager interest; zeal —**en·thu′si·ast′** (-ast′, -əst) *n.* —**en·thu′si·as′tic** *adj.* —**en·thu′si·as′ti·cal·ly** *adv.*

**en·tice** (en tīs′, in-) *vt.* **-ticed′**, **-tic′ing** [< L *in*, in + *titio*, a burning brand] to tempt with hope of reward or pleasure —**en·tice′ment** *n.*

**en·tire** (en tīr′, in-) *adj.* [< L *integer*, whole] not lacking any parts; whole; complete; intact —**en·tire′ly** *adv.*

**en·tire·ty** (-tē) *n., pl.* **-ties** **1** the state or fact of being entire; wholeness **2** an entire thing; whole

**en·ti·tle** (en tīt′'l, in-) *vt.* **-tled**, **-tling** **1** to give a title or name to **2** to give a right or claim to

**en·ti·tle·ment** *n.* something to which one is entitled, esp. a benefit, as Medicare, provided by certain government programs

**en·ti·ty** (en′tə tē) *n., pl.* **-ties** [ult. < L *esse*, to be] **1** existence **2** a thing that has definite existence

**en·tomb** (en tōōm′, in-) *vt.* to place in a tomb; bury —**en·tomb′ment** *n.*

**en·to·mol·o·gy** (en′tə mäl′ə jē) *n.* [< Gr *entomon*, insect + -LOGY] the branch of zoology that deals with insects —**en′to·mo·log′i·cal** (-mə läj′i kəl) *adj.* —**en′to·mol′o·gist** *n.*

**en·tou·rage** (än′tōō räzh′) *n.* [Fr < *entourer*, surround] a group of accompanying attendants, etc.; retinue

**en·trails** (en′trālz, -trəlz) *pl.n.* ⟦< L *interaneus*, internal⟧ the inner organs; specif., the intestines

**en·trance**[1] (en′trəns) *n.* **1** the act of entering **2** a place for entering; door, etc. **3** permission or right to enter; admission

**en·trance**[2] (en trans′, in-) *vt.* **-tranced′, -tranc′ing** ⟦see EN- & TRANCE⟧ to fill with delight; enchant

**en·trant** (en′trənt) *n.* one who enters

**en·trap** (en trap′, in-) *vt.* **-trapped′, -trap′ping** to catch in or as in a trap —**en·trap′ment** *n.*

**en·treat** (en trēt′, in-) *vt., vi.* ⟦< OFr *en-*, in + *traiter*, to treat⟧ to ask earnestly; beg; implore

**en·treat′y** *n., pl.* **-ies** an earnest request; prayer

**en·tree** or **en·trée** (än′trā) *n.* ⟦Fr < OFr *entrer*, enter⟧ **1** right to enter, use, etc.; access **2** the main course of a meal

**en·trench** (en trench′, in-) *vt.* **1** to surround or fortify with trenches **2** to establish securely

**en·tre·pre·neur** (än′trə prə nur′) *n.* ⟦Fr: see ENTERPRISE⟧ one who organizes a business undertaking, assuming the risk for the sake of the profit —**en′tre·pre·neur′i·al** *adj.*

**en·tro·py** (en′trə pē) *n.* ⟦< Gr *entropē*, a turning toward⟧ **1** a thermodynamic measure of the energy unavailable for useful work in a changing system **2** a process of degeneration with increasing uncertainty, chaos, etc., specif., when regarded as the final stage of a social system

**en·trust** (en trust′, in-) *vt.* **1** to charge with a trust or duty **2** to turn over for safekeeping

**en·try** (en′trē) *n., pl.* **-tries** ⟦< OFr: see ENTER⟧ **1** an entering; entrance **2** a way by which to enter **3** an item or note in a list, journal, etc. **4** one entered in a race, etc.

**en·try-lev·el** *adj.* **1** designating a job with low pay but possible advancement **2** basic; introductory

**en·twine** (en twīn′, in-) *vt., vi.* **-twined′, -twin′ing** to twine together or around

**e·nu·mer·ate** (ē nōō′mər āt′, i-) *vt.* **-at·ed, -at·ing** ⟦< L *e-*, out + *numerare*, to count⟧ **1** to count **2** to name one by one —**e·nu′mer·a′tion** *n.*

**e·nun·ci·ate** (ē nun′sē āt′, i-) *vt., vi.* **-at·ed, -at·ing** ⟦< L *e-*, out + *nuntiare*, announce⟧ **1** to state definitely **2** to announce **3** to pronounce (words), esp. clearly —**e·nun′ci·a′tion** *n.*

**en·u·re·sis** (en′yōō rē′sis) *n.* ⟦ult. < L *in*, in + Gr *ouron*, urine⟧ inability to control urination

**en·vel·op** (en vel′əp, in-) *vt.* ⟦< OFr: see EN- & DEVELOP⟧ **1** to wrap up; cover completely **2** to surround **3** to conceal; hide —**en·vel′op·ment** *n.*

**en·ve·lope** (än′və lōp′, en′-) *n.* **1** a thing that envelops; covering **2** a folded paper container for a letter, etc., usually with a gummed flap

**en·ven·om** (en ven′əm, in-) *vt.* **1** to put venom into **2** to fill with hate

**en·vi·a·ble** (en′vē ə bəl) *adj.* good enough to be envied or desired —**en′vi·a·bly** *adv.*

**en·vi·ous** (en′vē əs) *adj.* feeling or showing envy —**en′vi·ous·ly** *adv.*

**en·vi·ron·ment** (en vī′rən mənt, in-) *n.* ⟦see ENVIRONS⟧ **1** surroundings **2** all the conditions, etc. surrounding, and affecting the development of, an organism, food chain, etc. —**en·vi′ron·men′tal** *adj.*

**en·vi·ron·men·tal·ist** *n.* one working to solve environmental problems, as air and water pollution

**en·vi·rons** (en vī′rənz, in-) *pl.n.* ⟦< OFr *en-*, in + *viron*, a circuit⟧ **1** the districts surrounding a city; suburbs **2** surrounding area; vicinity

**en·vis·age** (en viz′ij, in-) *vt.* **-aged, -ag·ing** ⟦see EN- & VISAGE⟧ to form an image of in the mind; visualize

**en·vi·sion** (en vizh′ən, in-) *vt.* ⟦EN- + VISION⟧ to imagine (something not yet in existence)

**en·voy** (än′voi, en′-) *n.* ⟦< Fr < L *in*, in + *via*, way⟧ **1** a messenger **2** a diplomatic agent just below an ambassador

**en·vy** (en′vē) *n., pl.* **-vies** ⟦< L *in-*, in + *videre*, to look⟧ **1** discontent and ill will over another's advantages, possessions, etc. **2** desire for something that another has **3** an object of such feeling —*vt.* **-vied, -vy·ing** to feel envy toward or because of —**en′vy·ing·ly** *adv.*

**en·zyme** (en′zīm′) *n.* ⟦< Gr *en-*, in + *zymē*, leaven⟧ a protein, formed in plant and animal cells or made synthetically, acting as a catalyst in chemical reactions

**e·on** (ē′ən, ē′än′) *n.* ⟦< Gr *aiōn*, an age⟧ an extremely long, indefinite period of time

**-e·ous** (ē əs) ⟦< L *-eus* + -OUS⟧ *suffix var. of* -OUS [*gaseous*]

**EPA** *abbrev.* Environmental Protection Agency

**ep·au·let** or **ep·au·lette** (ep′ə let′, ep′ə let′) *n.* ⟦< Fr dim. of *épaule*, shoulder⟧ a shoulder ornament, esp. on military uniforms

**e·pee** or **é·pée** (ā pā′) *n.* ⟦Fr⟧ a fencing sword like a foil, but heavier and more rigid

EPAULETS

**e·phed·rine** (e fe′drin) *n.* ⟦< L *ephedra*, the plant horsetail⟧ an alkaloid used to relieve nasal congestion and asthma

**e·phem·er·al** (e fem′ər əl, i-) *adj.* ⟦< Gr *epi-*, upon + *hēmera*, day⟧ **1** lasting one day **2** short-lived; transitory

**epi-** ⟦< Gr *epi*, at, on⟧ *prefix* on, upon, over, among [*epiglottis*]

**ep·ic** (ep′ik) *n.* ⟦< Gr *epos*, a word, song, epic⟧ a long narrative poem in a dignified style about the deeds of a hero or heroes —*adj.* of or like an epic; heroic; grand

**ep·i·cen·ter** (ep′i sent′ər) *n.* **1** the area of the earth's surface directly above the place of origin of an earthquake **2** a focal or central point

**ep·i·cure** (ep′i kyoor′) *n.* ⟦after *Epicurus*, ancient Gr philosopher⟧ one who enjoys and has a discriminating taste for fine foods and drinks

**ep·i·cu·re·an** (ep′i kyōō rē′ən, ep′i kyoor′ē ən) *adj.* fond of sensuous pleasure, esp. that of eating and drinking —*n.* an epicure

**ep·i·dem·ic** (ep′ə dem′ik) *adj.* ⟦< Fr < Gr *epi-*, among + *dēmos*, people⟧ spreading rapidly among many people in a community, as a disease —*n.* **1** an epidemic disease **2** the spreading of such a disease **3** a rapid, widespread growth —**ep′i·dem′i·cal·ly** *adv.*

**ep·i·de·mi·ol·o·gy** (ep′ə dē′mē äl′ə jē) *n.* ⟦prec. + -LOGY⟧ the branch of medicine that studies epidemics

**ep·i·der·mis** (ep′ə dur′mis) *n.* ⟦< Gr *epi-*, upon + *derma*, the skin⟧ the outermost layer of the skin —**ep′i·der′mal** or **ep′i·der′mic** *adj.*

**ep·i·du·ral** (ep′ə door′əl) *adj.* on or outside the dura mater —*n.* local anesthesia of the lower body by epidural injection

**ep·i·glot·tis** (ep′ə glät′is) *n.* ⟦see EPI- & GLOTTIS⟧ the thin, lidlike piece of cartilage that covers the windpipe during swallowing

**ep·i·gram** (ep′ə gram′) *n.* ⟦< Gr *epi-*, upon + *graphein*, write⟧ a terse, witty, pointed statement —**ep′i·gram·mat′ic** (-gram mat′ik) *adj.*

**e·pig·ra·phy** (ē pig′rə fē, i-) *n.* the study of inscriptions, esp. ancient ones

**ep·i·lep·sy** (ep′ə lep′sē) *n.* ⟦< Gr *epi-*, upon + *lambanein*, seize⟧ a recurrent disorder of the nervous system, characterized by seizures that cause convulsions, unconsciousness, etc.

**ep′i·lep′tic** (-tik) *adj.* of or having epilepsy —*n.* one who has epilepsy

**ep·i·logue** or **ep·i·log** (ep′ə lôg′) *n.* ⟦< Gr *epi-*, upon + *legein*, speak⟧ a closing section added to a novel, play, etc., providing further comment, as a speech by an actor to the audience

**E·piph·a·ny** (ē pif′ə nē, i-) *n., pl.* **-nies** ⟦< Gr *epiphainein*, show forth⟧ **1** a Christian feast day (Jan. 6) commemorating the revealing of Jesus as the Christ to the Gentiles **2** [e-] *a)* a flash of insight *b)* an experience that brings this about

**e·pis·co·pa·cy** (ē pis′kə pə sē, i-) *n., pl.* **-cies** [< Gr *epi-*, upon + *skopein*, to look] **1** church government by bishops **2** EPISCOPATE

**e·pis′co·pal** (-pəl) *adj.* **1** of or governed by bishops **2** [E-] designating or of any of various churches governed by bishops

**E·pis′co·pa′lian** (-pāl′yən) *adj.* Episcopal —*n.* a member of the Protestant Episcopal Church

**e·pis′co·pate** (-pit, -pāt′) *n.* **1** the position, rank, etc. of a bishop **2** bishops collectively

**ep·i·sode** (ep′ə sōd′) *n.* [< Gr *epi-*, upon + *eisodos*, entrance] **1** any part of a novel, poem, etc. that is complete in itself **2** an event or series of events complete in itself —**ep′i·sod′ic** (-säd′ik) *adj.* — **ep′i·sod′i·cal·ly** *adv.*

**e·pis·tle** (ē pis′əl) *n.* [< Gr *epi-*, to + *stellein*, send] **1** a letter **2** [E-] any of the letters in the New Testament —**e·pis′to·lar′y** (-tə ler′ē) *adj.*

**ep·i·taph** (ep′ə taf′) *n.* [< Gr *epi-*, upon + *taphos*, tomb] an inscription on a tomb, etc. in memory of a dead person

**ep·i·the·li·um** (ep′i thē′lē əm) *n., pl.* **-li·ums** or **-li·a** (-ə) [< Gr *epi-*, upon + *thēlē*, nipple] cellular tissue covering external body surfaces or lining internal surfaces —**ep′i·the′li·al** (-əl) *adj.*

**ep·i·thet** (ep′ə thet′) *n.* [< Gr *epi-*, on + *tithenai*, put] a word or phrase characterizing some person or thing

**e·pit·o·me** (ē pit′ə mē′, i-) *n., pl.* **-mes** (-mēz′) [< Gr *epi-*, upon + *temnein*, to cut] **1** an abstract; summary **2** a person or thing that shows the typical qualities of something

**e·pit′o·mize′** (-mīz′) *vt.* **-mized′, -miz′ing** to make or be an epitome of

**e plu·ri·bus u·num** (ē′ ploor′ē boos′ ōō′noom) [L] out of many, one: a motto of the U.S.

**ep·och** (ep′ək) *n.* [< Gr *epi-*, upon + *echein*, to hold] **1** the start of a new period in the history of anything **2** a period of time in terms of noteworthy events, persons, etc. —**ep′och·al** *adj.*

**ep·ox·y** (e päk′sē, i-) *adj.* [EP(I)- + OXY(GEN)] designating a resin used in strong, resistant glues, enamels, etc. —*n., pl.* **-ies** an epoxy resin

**ep·si·lon** (ep′sə län′) *n.* [Gr *e psilon*, plain *e*] the fifth letter of the Greek alphabet (E, ε)

**Ep·som salts** (or **salt**) (ep′sem) [after *Epsom*, town in England] a white, crystalline salt, magnesium sulfate, used as a cathartic

**Ep·stein-Barr virus** (ep′stīn bär′) a herpes-like virus that causes infectious mononucleosis and may cause various forms of cancer

**eq·ua·ble** (ek′wə bəl) *adj.* [see fol.] steady; uniform; even; tranquil —**eq′ua·bil′i·ty** *n.* —**eq′ua·bly** *adv.*

**e·qual** (ē′kwəl) *adj.* [< L *aequus*, even] **1** of the same quantity, size, value, etc. **2** having the same rights, ability, rank, etc. **3** evenly proportioned **4** having the necessary ability, strength, etc.: with *to* —*n.* any person or thing that is equal —*vt.* **e′qualed** or **e′qualled, e′qual·ing** or **e′qual·ling 1** to be equal to **2** to do or make something equal to —**e·qual·i·ty** (ē kwôl′ə tē, -kwäl′-), *pl.* **-ties,** *n.* —**e′qual·ly** *adv.*

**e·qual·ize** (ē′kwəl īz′) *vt.* **-ized′, -iz′ing** to make equal or uniform —**e′qual·i·za′tion** *n.* —**e′qual·iz′er** *n.*

**e′qual-op′por·tu′ni·ty** *adj.* treating all employees and job applicants equally, without regard to race, sex, etc.

**equal sign** the sign (=), indicating that the terms on either side of it are equal or equivalent

**e·qua·nim·i·ty** (ek′wə nim′ə tē, ē′kwə-) *n.* [< L *aequus*, even + *animus*, mind] evenness of temper; composure

**e·quate** (ē kwāt′, i-) *vt.* **e·quat′ed, e·quat′ing 1** to make equal **2** to treat, regard, or express as equal —**e·quat′a·ble** *adj.*

**e·qua·tion** (ē kwā′zhən, i-) *n.* **1** an equating or being equated **2** a statement of equality between two quantities, as shown by the equal sign (=)

---

165 ◄ **eraser**

**e·qua·tor** (ē kwāt′ər, i-) *n.* an imaginary circle around the earth, equally distant from the North Pole and the South Pole —**e·qua·to·ri·al** (ē′kwə tôr′ē əl, ek′wə-) *adj.*

**Equatorial Guinea** country in WC Africa: 10,831 sq. mi.; pop. 304,000

**eq·uer·ry** (ek′wər ē, ē kwer′ē) *n., pl.* **-ries** [< Fr] **1** [Historical] an officer in charge of royal horses **2** an officer who attends a person of royalty

**e·ques·tri·an** (ē kwes′trē ən, i-) *adj.* [< L *equus*, horse] **1** of horses or horsemanship **2** on horseback —*n.* a rider or circus performer on horseback —**e·ques′tri·enne′** (-trē en′) *fem.n.*

**equi-** *combining form* equal, equally [*equidistant*]

**e·qui·dis·tant** (ē′kwi dis′tənt) *adj.* equally distant

**e′qui·lat′er·al** (-lat′ər əl) *adj.* [< L *aequus*, even + *latus*, side] having all sides equal

**e′qui·lib′ri·um** (-lib′rē əm) *n., pl.* **-ri·ums** or **-ri·a** (-ə) [< L *aequus*, even + *libra*, a balance] a state of balance between opposing forces

**e·quine** (ē′kwīn′) *adj.* [< L *equus*, horse] of or like a horse

**e·qui·nox** (ē′kwi näks′, ek′wə näks′) *n.* [< L *aequus*, even + *nox*, night] the time when the sun crosses the equator, making night and day of equal length in all parts of the earth —**e′qui·noc′tial** (-näk′shəl) *adj.*

**e·quip** (ē kwip′, i-) *vt.* **e·quipped′, e·quip′ping** [< OFr *esquiper*, embark] to provide with what is needed

**eq·ui·page** (ek′wi pij) *n.* a carriage with horses and liveried servants

**e·quip·ment** (ē kwip′mənt, i-) *n.* **1** an equipping or being equipped **2** whatever one is equipped with; supplies, furnishings, etc.

**eq·ui·poise** (ek′wi poiz′, ē′kwi-) *n.* [EQUI- + POISE] **1** state of equilibrium **2** a counterbalance

**eq·ui·ta·ble** (ek′wit ə bəl) *adj.* [see EQUITY] fair; just —**eq′ui·ta·bly** *adv.*

**eq·ui·ta·tion** (ek′wi tā′shən) *n.* [< L *equitare*, to ride] the art of riding on horseback

**eq·ui·ty** (ek′wit ē) *n., pl.* **-ties** [< L *aequus*, even] **1** fairness; impartiality; justice **2** the value of property beyond the amount owed on it **3** *Finance a)* assets minus liabilities; net worth *b)* [*pl.*] shares of stock **4** *Law* a system of doctrines supplementing common and statute law

**e·quiv·a·lent** (ē kwiv′ə lənt, i-) *adj.* [< L *aequus*, equal + *valere*, be worth] equal in quantity, value, force, meaning, etc. —*n.* an equivalent thing —**e·quiv′a·lence** *n.*

**e·quiv·o·cal** (ē kwiv′ə kəl, i-) *adj.* [< L *aequus*, even + *vox*, voice] **1** having two or more meanings; purposely ambiguous **2** uncertain; doubtful **3** suspicious [*equivocal conduct*] —**e·quiv′o·cal·ly** *adv.* —**e·quiv′o·cal·ness** *n.*

**e·quiv′o·cate′** (-kāt′) *vi.* **-cat′ed, -cat′ing** to use equivocal terms in order to deceive, hedge, etc. — **e·quiv′o·ca′tion** *n.* —**e·quiv′o·ca′tor** *n.*

**ER** *abbrev.* emergency room

**-er** (ər) [ME] *suffix* **1** *a)* a person or thing having to do with [*hatter*] *b)* a person living in [*New Yorker*] *c)* one that ___s [*roller*] **2** forming the comparative degree [*later*] **3** repeatedly: added to verbs [*flicker*]

**e·ra** (ir′ə, er′ə) *n.* [LL *aera*] **1** a period of time measured from some important event **2** a period of time having some special characteristic

**ERA** *abbrev.* **1** *Baseball* earned run average: also **era 2** Equal Rights Amendment

**e·rad·i·cate** (ē rad′i kāt′, i-) *vt.* **-cat′ed, -cat′ing** [< L *e-*, out + *radix*, root] to uproot; wipe out; destroy —**e·rad′i·ca′tion** *n.* —**e·rad′i·ca′tor** *n.*

**e·rase** (ē rās′, i-) *vt.* **e·rased′, e·ras′ing** [< L *e-*, out + *radere*, scrape] **1** to rub, scrape, or wipe out (esp. writing) **2** to remove (something recorded) from (magnetic tape) **3** to obliterate, as from the mind —**e·ras′a·ble** *adj.*

**e·ras′er** *n.* a thing that erases; specif., a rubber

device for erasing ink or pencil marks, or a pad for removing chalk marks from a blackboard

**E·ras·mus** (i raz′məs), **Des·i·der·i·us** (des′ə dir′ē əs) 1466?-1536; Du. humanist & theologian

**e·ra·sure** (ē rā′shər, i-) *n.* **1** an erasing **2** an erased word, mark, etc.

**ere** (er) [Old Poet.] *prep.* ⟦OE ær⟧ before (in time) —*conj.* **1** before **2** rather than

**e·rect** (ē rekt′, i-) *adj.* ⟦< L e-, up + regere, make straight⟧ upright —*vt.* **1** to construct (a building, etc.) **2** to set in an upright position; raise **3** to set up; assemble —**e·rec′tion** *n.* —**e·rect′ly** *adv.* —**e·rect′ness** *n.* —**e·rec′tor** *n.*

**e·rec·tile** (ē rek′til, i-) *adj.* that can become erect: used esp. of tissue that becomes rigid when filled with blood

**erg** (ʉrg) *n.* ⟦< Gr ergon, work⟧ *Physics* a unit of work or energy

**er·go** (er′gō) *adv.* ⟦L⟧ therefore

**er·go·nom·ics** (ʉr′gō näm′iks) *n.* ⟦ult. < Gr ergon, work + (EC)ONOMICS⟧ the science of adapting working conditions to the needs of the worker

**Er·ie** (ir′ē), **Lake** one of the Great Lakes, between Lake Huron & Lake Ontario

**Er·in** (er′in) old poet. name for IRELAND

**Er·i·tre·a** (er′ə trē′ə) country in E Africa: 36,171 sq. mi.; pop. 3,525,000 —**Er′i·tre′an** *adj., n.*

**er·mine** (ʉr′min) *n.* ⟦prob. < OHG harmo, weasel⟧ **1** a weasel whose fur is white in winter **2** its white fur

**e·rode** (ē rōd′, i-) *vt.* **e·rod′ed, e·rod′ing** ⟦< L e-, out + rodere, gnaw⟧ **1** to wear away **2** to form by wearing away gradually —*vi.* to become eroded

**e·rog·e·nous** (ē räj′ə nəs, i-) *adj.* ⟦< Gr erōs, love + -GEN + -OUS⟧ sensitive to sexual stimulation: also **e·ro·to·gen·ic** (er′ə tō′jen′ik)

**E·ros** (er′äs′, ir′-) *n.* **1** *Gr. Myth.* the god of love **2** [e-] sexual love or desire

**e·ro·sion** (ē rō′zhən, i-) *n.* an eroding or being eroded —**e·ro′sive** (-siv) *adj.*

**e·rot·ic** (ē rät′ik, i-) *adj.* ⟦< Gr erōs, love⟧ of or arousing sexual feelings or desires; amatory —**e·rot′i·cal·ly** *adv.*

**e·rot′i·ca** (-i kə) *pl.n.* [often with sing. v.] erotic books, pictures, etc.

**err** (ʉr, er) *vi.* ⟦< L errare, wander⟧ **1** to be wrong or mistaken **2** to deviate from the established moral code

**er·rand** (er′ənd) *n.* ⟦OE ærende, mission⟧ **1** a trip to do a thing, often esp. for someone else **2** the thing to be done

**er·rant** (er′ənt) *adj.* ⟦see ERR⟧ **1** roving or wandering, esp. in search of adventure [a medieval knight-*errant*] **2** erring **3** shifting about [an *errant* wind]

**er·rat·ic** (i rat′ik) *adj.* ⟦< L errare, wander⟧ **1** irregular; random **2** eccentric; queer —**er·rat′i·cal·ly** *adv.*

**er·ra·tum** (e rät′əm, -rāt′-) *n., pl.* **-ta** (-ə) ⟦see ERR⟧ an error in a work already printed

**er·ro·ne·ous** (e rō′nē əs) *adj.* containing error; mistaken; wrong —**er·ro′ne·ous·ly** *adv.*

**er·ror** (er′ər) *n.* ⟦see ERR⟧ **1** the state of believing what is untrue **2** a wrong belief **3** something incorrectly done; mistake **4** a transgression **5** *Baseball* any misplay in fielding

**er·satz** (er′zäts′, er zäts′) *n., adj.* ⟦Ger⟧ substitute or synthetic, and usually inferior

**Erse** (ʉrs) *adj., n.* ⟦ME Erish, var. of Irisc, Irish⟧ (of) GAELIC and, sometimes, IRISH (*n.* 1)

**erst·while** (ʉrst′hwīl′) *adv.* [Archaic] formerly —*adj.* former

**e·ruct** (ē rukt′) *vt., vi.* ⟦< L e-, out + ructare, to belch⟧ to belch —**e·ruc·ta′tion** *n.*

**er·u·dite** (er′yo͞o dīt′, -o͞o-) *adj.* ⟦< L e-, out + rudis, rude⟧ learned; scholarly —**er′u·dite′ly** *adv.*

**er·u·di·tion** (er′yo͞o dish′ən) *n.* learning acquired by reading and study

**e·rupt** (ē rupt′, i-) *vi.* ⟦< L e-, out + rumpere, to break⟧ **1** to burst forth or out [lava *erupting*] **2** to throw forth lava, water, etc. **3** to break out in a rash —*vt.* to cause to burst forth

**e·rup·tion** (ē rup′shən, i-) *n.* **1** a bursting forth or out **2** *a*) a breaking out in a rash *b*) a rash

**-er·y** (ər ē, er′ē) ⟦< LL -aria⟧ *suffix* **1** a place to [*tannery*] **2** a place for [*nunnery*] **3** the practice or act of [*midwifery*] **4** the product of [*pottery*] **5** a collection of [*greenery*] **6** the condition of [*drudgery*]

**er·y·sip·e·las** (er′i sip′ə ləs) *n.* ⟦ult. < Gr erythros, red + -pelas, skin⟧ a bacterial infection of the skin or mucous membranes

**e·ryth·ro·cyte** (e rith′rō sīt′) *n.* ⟦< Gr erythros, red + kytos, a hollow⟧ a mature red blood cell that contains hemoglobin, which carries oxygen to the body tissues

**-es** (iz, əz, z) ⟦< OE⟧ *suffix* **1** forming plurals [*glasses*] **2** forming the 3d person sing., pres. indic., of verbs [he *kisses*]

**E·sau** (ē′sô′) *n. Bible* Isaac's son who sold his birthright to his brother, Jacob

**es·ca·late** (es′kə lāt′) *vi.* **-lat·ed, -lat·ing** **1** to rise as on an escalator **2** to expand step by step **3** to increase rapidly —**es′ca·la′tion** *n.*

**es′ca·la·tor** (-ər) *n.* ⟦ult. < L scala, ladder⟧ a moving stairway on an endless belt

**es·ca·pade** (es′kə pād′) *n.* ⟦Fr: see fol.⟧ a reckless adventure or prank

**es·cape** (e skāp′, i-) *vi.* **-caped′, -cap′ing** ⟦< L ex-, out of + LL cappa, cloak⟧ **1** to get free **2** to avoid an illness, accident, etc. **3** to leak away —*vt.* **1** to get away from **2** to avoid [to *escape* death] **3** to come from involuntarily [a scream *escaped* her lips] **4** to be missed or forgotten by —*n.* **1** an escaping **2** a means of escape **3** a leakage **4** a temporary mental release from reality —*adj.* providing an escape

**es·cap·ee** (e skāp′ē′, es′kā pē′) *n.* one who has escaped, as from prison

**es·cape′ment** *n.* a notched wheel with a detaining catch that controls the action of a mechanical clock or watch

**escape velocity** the minimum speed required for a particle, space vehicle, etc. to escape permanently from the gravitational field of a planet, star, etc.

**es·cap·ism′** *n.* a tendency to escape from reality, responsibilities, etc. through the imagination —**es·cap′ist** *adj., n.*

**es·car·got** (es′kär gō′) *n.* ⟦Fr⟧ an edible snail

**es·ca·role** (es′kə rōl′) *n.* ⟦Fr⟧ ENDIVE

**es·carp·ment** (e skärp′mənt) *n.* ⟦< Fr⟧ a steep slope or cliff

**-es·cence** (es′əns) ⟦see fol.⟧ *suffix* the process of becoming [*obsolescence*]

**-es·cent** (es′ənt) ⟦L -escens⟧ *suffix* **1** starting to be, being, or becoming [*obsolescent*] **2** giving off light (as specified) [*phosphorescent*]

**es·chew** (es cho͞o′) *vt.* ⟦< OHG sciuhan, to fear⟧ to shun; avoid —**es·chew′al** *n.*

**es·cort** (es′kôrt′; for v. i skôrt′) *n.* ⟦< L ex-, out + corrigere, set right⟧ **1** one or more persons, cars, etc. accompanying another or others to give protection or show honor **2** a man accompanying a woman —*vt.* to go with as an escort

**es·cri·toire** (es′kri twär′) *n.* ⟦OFr < L scribere, write⟧ a writing desk

**es·crow** (es′krō′) *n.* ⟦see SCROLL⟧ used chiefly in **in escrow**, put in the care of a third party until certain conditions are fulfilled

**es·cutch·eon** (e skuch′ən, i-) *n.* ⟦< L scutum, shield⟧ a shield on which a coat of arms is displayed

**-ese** (ēz, ēs) ⟦< L -ensis⟧ *suffix* **1** of a country or place [*Javanese*] **2** (in) the language of [*Cantonese*] **3** a person born or living in [*Portuguese*]

**Es·ki·mo** (es′kə mō′) *n.* ⟦prob. < Fr < AmInd⟧ **1** *pl.* **-mos′** or **-mo′** a member of a group of North American peoples in Greenland, N Canada, and

Alaska **2** any of the languages of the Eskimos — *adj.* of the Eskimos or their languages, etc.

**Eskimo dog** any of several large, strong dogs used by the Eskimos to pull sleds

**ESL** *abbrev.* English as a second language

**e·soph·a·gus** (i säf′ə gəs) *n., pl.* **-gi′** (-jī′) ⟦< Gr *oisophagos*⟧ the tube through which food passes from the pharynx to the stomach

**es·o·ter·ic** (es′ə ter′ik) *adj.* ⟦< Gr *esōteros*, inner⟧ intended for or understood by only a chosen few

**ESP** (ē′es′pē′) *n.* extrasensory perception

**esp.** *abbrev.* especially

**es·pa·drille** (es′pə dril′) *n.* ⟦Fr < Sp *esparto*, coarse grass⟧ a casual shoe with a canvas upper and a sole of twisted rope

**es·pal·ier** (es pal′yər) *n.* ⟦Fr < It *spalla*, shoulder⟧ **1** a lattice on which trees or shrubs are trained to grow flat **2** a plant trained in this way —*vt.* to provide with an espalier

**es·pe·cial** (e spesh′əl, i-) *adj.* special; particular — **es·pe′cial·ly** *adv.*

**Es·pe·ran·to** (es′pə rän′tō, -ran′-) *n.* an invented international language based on European word roots

**es·pi·o·nage** (es′pē ə näzh′) *n.* ⟦< Fr < It *spia*, spy⟧ the act or practice of spying

**es·pla·nade** (es′plə näd′, -näd′) *n.* ⟦< Fr < It < L *explanare*, to level⟧ a level, open stretch of ground, esp. one serving as a public walk

**es·pous·al** (e spou′zəl, i-) *n.* an espousing (of some cause, idea, etc.); advocacy

**es·pouse** (e spouz′, i-) *vt.* **-poused′, -pous′ing** ⟦see SPOUSE⟧ **1** to marry **2** to advocate (some cause, idea, etc.)

**es·pres·so** (e spres′ō) *n., pl.* **-sos** ⟦It⟧ coffee made by forcing steam through finely ground coffee beans

**es·prit de corps** (e sprē′ də kôr′) ⟦Fr⟧ group spirit; pride, etc. shared by those in the same group

**es·py** (e spī′, i-) *vt.* **-pied′, -py′ing** ⟦see SPY⟧ to catch sight of; spy

**-esque** (esk) ⟦Fr < It *-esco*⟧ *suffix* **1** in the manner or style of *[Romanesque]* **2** like *[statuesque]*

**es·quire** (es′kwīr′) *n.* ⟦< L *scutum*, a shield⟧ **1** [Historical] a candidate for knighthood; squire **2** in England, a member of the gentry ranking just below a knight **3** [E-] a title of courtesy: in the U.S., now specif. used by lawyers: usually abbrev. **Esq** or **Esqr**

**-ess** (es, is, əs) ⟦< LL *-issa*⟧ *suffix* female *[lioness]*

**es·say** (e sā′; *for n.* **1** usually, & *for n.* **2** always, es′ā) *vt.* ⟦< LL *ex-*, out of + *agere*, to do⟧ to try; attempt —*n.* **1** a trying or testing **2** a short literary composition in which the author analyzes or interprets something in a personal way —**es·say′er** *n.* —**es′say·ist** *n.*

**es·sence** (es′əns) *n.* ⟦< L *esse*, to be⟧ **1** the basic nature (of something) **2** *a)* a concentrated substance that keeps the flavor, etc. of that from which it is extracted *b)* perfume

**Es·sene** (es′ēn′, e sēn′) *n.* a member of an ancient Jewish ascetic sect that existed to the middle of the 1st c. A.D.

**es·sen·tial** (ə sen′shəl, i-) *adj.* **1** of or constituting the essence of something; basic **2** absolutely necessary; indispensable —*n.* something necessary or fundamental —**es·sen′tial·ly** *adv.*

**est** *abbrev.* **1** established: also **estab 2** estimate **3** estimated

**EST** *abbrev.* Eastern Standard Time

**-est** (est, ist, əst) ⟦OE⟧ *suffix* forming the superlative degree *[greatest]*

**es·tab·lish** (ə stab′lish, i-) *vt.* ⟦< L *stabilis*, stable⟧ **1** to order, ordain, or enact (a law, etc.) permanently **2** to set up (a nation, business, etc.) **3** to cause to be; bring about **4** to set up in a business, etc. **5** to cause to be accepted **6** to prove; demonstrate

**es·tab·lish·ment** *n.* **1** an establishing or being established **2** a thing established, as a business

—**the Establishment** an inner circle thought of as holding decisive power in a nation, institution, etc.

**es·tate** (ə stāt′, i-) *n.* ⟦< OFr *estat*⟧ **1** a condition or stage of life **2** property; possessions **3** a large, individually owned piece of land containing a residence

**es·teem** (ə stēm′, i-) *vt.* ⟦< L *aestimare*, to value⟧ **1** to value highly; respect **2** to consider —*n.* favorable opinion

**es·ter** (es′tər) *n.* ⟦Ger < *essig*, vinegar + *äther*, ether⟧ an organic compound formed by the reaction of an acid and an alcohol

**Es·ther** (es′tər) *n. Bible* the Jewish wife of a Persian king: she saved her people from slaughter

**es·thete** (es′thēt′) *n.* AESTHETE —**es·thet′ics** (-thet′iks) *pl.n.*

**es·ti·ma·ble** (es′tə mə bəl) *adj.* worthy of esteem

**es·ti·mate** (es′tə māt′; *for n.*, -mit) *vt.* **-mat·ed, -mat′ing** ⟦see ESTEEM⟧ **1** to form an opinion about **2** to calculate approximately (size, cost, etc.) —*n.* **1** a general calculation; esp., an approximate computation of probable cost **2** an opinion or judgment —**es′ti·ma′tor** *n.*

**es·ti·ma′tion** *n.* **1** an estimate or judgment **2** esteem; regard

**Es·to·ni·a** (e stō′nē ə, -stōn′yə) country in N Europe: formerly a republic of the U.S.S.R.: 17,413 sq. mi.; pop. 1,566,000 —**Es·to′ni·an** *adj., n.*

**es·trange** (e strānj′, i-) *vt.* **-tranged′, -trang′ing** ⟦< L *extraneus*, strange⟧ to turn (a person) from an affectionate attitude to an indifferent or unfriendly one —**es·trange′ment** *n.*

**es·tro·gen** (es′trə jən) *n.* ⟦< Gr *oistros*, frenzy + -GEN⟧ any of several female sex hormones or synthetic compounds

**es·trous cycle** (es′trəs) the regular female reproductive cycle of most placental mammals

**es·tu·ar·y** (es′tyōō er′ē, -chōō-) *n., pl.* **-ies** ⟦< L *aestus*, the tide⟧ the wide mouth of a river into which the tide flows from the sea

**ET** *abbrev.* Eastern Time

**-et** (et, it, ət) ⟦< LL *-itus*⟧ *suffix* little *[islet]*

**e·ta** (āt′ə, ēt′ə) *n.* the seventh letter of the Greek alphabet (H, η)

**ETA** *abbrev.* estimated time of arrival

**é·ta·gère** (ā′tä zher′) *n.* ⟦Fr⟧ a stand with open shelves, for displaying art objects, ornaments, etc.

**et al.** *abbrev.* ⟦L *et alii*⟧ and others

**et cet·er·a** (et set′ər ə, se′trə) ⟦L⟧ and others; and the like: abbrev. **etc.**

**etch** (ech) *vt.* ⟦< MHG *ezzen*, eat⟧ to make (a drawing, design, etc.) on metal, glass, etc. by the action of an acid —**etch′er** *n.*

**etch′ing** *n.* **1** the art of an etcher **2** a print made from an etched plate

**e·ter·nal** (ē tur′nəl, i-) *adj.* ⟦< L *aeturnus*⟧ **1** without beginning or end; everlasting **2** always the same; unchanging **3** seeming never to stop —**e·ter′nal·ly** *adv.* —**e·ter′nal·ness** *n.*

**e·ter·ni·ty** (ē tur′nə tē, i-) *n., pl.* **-ties 1** the state or fact of being eternal **2** infinite or endless time **3** a long period of time that seems endless **4** the endless time after death

**eth·ane** (eth′ān′) *n.* ⟦< fol.⟧ an odorless, colorless, gaseous hydrocarbon, found in natural gas and used as a fuel

**e·ther** (ē′thər) *n.* ⟦< Gr *aithein*, to burn⟧ **1** an imaginary substance once thought to pervade space **2** the upper regions of space **3** a volatile, colorless, highly flammable liquid used as an anesthetic and a solvent

**e·the·re·al** (ē thir′ē əl, i-) *adj.* **1** very light; airy; delicate **2** not earthly; heavenly; celestial —**e·the′re·al·ly** *adv.*

**eth·ic** (eth′ik) *n.* ⟦see fol.⟧ a system of moral standards

**eth·i·cal** (eth′i kəl) *adj.* ⟦< Gr *ēthos*, character⟧ **1**

having to do with ethics; of or conforming to moral standards **2** conforming to professional standards of conduct —**eth′i·cal·ly** *adv.*

**eth·ics** (eth′iks) *n.* **1** the study of standards of conduct and moral judgment **2** [*with sing. or pl. verb*] the system of morals of a particular person, religion, group, etc.

**E·thi·o·pi·a** (ē′thē ō′pē ə) country in E Africa: 423,940 sq. mi.; pop. 42,019,000 —**E′thi·o′pi·an** *adj., n.*

**eth·nic** (eth′nik) *adj.* [< Gr *ethnos*, nation] designating or of a group of people having common customs, characteristics, language, etc. —*n.* a member of an ethnic group, esp. a minority or nationality group —**eth′ni·cal·ly** *adv.*

**eth·nic·i·ty** (eth nis′ə tē) *n.* ethnic classification or affiliation

**eth·nol·o·gy** (eth näl′ə jē) *n.* [< Gr *ethnos*, nation + -LOGY] the branch of anthropology that studies comparatively the cultures of contemporary, or recent, societies or language groups —**eth′no·log′i·cal** (-nə läj′i kəl) *adj.* —**eth·nol′o·gist** *n.*

**e·thos** (ē′thäs′) *n.* [Gr *ēthos*, character] the characteristic attitudes, habits, etc. of an individual or group

**eth·yl** (eth′əl) *n.* [< ETHER] the hydrocarbon radical that forms the base of ethyl alcohol, ether, etc.

**ethyl alcohol** ALCOHOL (sense 1)

**eth·yl·ene** (eth′əl ēn′) *n.* [ETHYL + -ENE] a colorless, flammable, gaseous hydrocarbon used to synthesize organic chemicals, esp. polyethylene

**ethylene gly·col** (glī′kôl′) a colorless, viscous liquid used as an antifreeze, solvent, etc.

**e·ti·ol·o·gy** (ēt′ē äl′ə jē) *n., pl.* -**gies** [< Gr *aitia*, cause + *logia*, description] **1** the cause assigned, as for a disease **2** the science of causes or origins —**e′ti·o·log′ic** (-ə läj′ik) *adj.*

**et·i·quette** (et′i kit) *n.* [Fr *étiquette*, lit., ticket] the forms, manners, etc. conventionally acceptable or required in society, a profession, etc.

**Et·na** (et′nə), **Mount** volcanic mountain in E Sicily

**E·to·bi·coke** (i tō′bi kō′) city within metropolitan Toronto, Canada: pop. 329,000

**E·trus·can** (i trus′kən) *adj.* of an ancient country (*Etruria*) in what is now central Italy

**et seq.** *abbrev.* [L *et sequens*] and the following

**-ette** (et) [Fr: see -ET] *suffix* **1** little [*statuette*] **2** female [*majorette*]

**é·tude** (ā′to͞od′) *n.* [Fr, a study] a musical composition for a solo instrument, designed to give practice in some point of technique

**et·y·mol·o·gy** (et′ə mäl′ə jē) *n., pl.* -**gies** [< Gr *etymos*, true + *logos*, word] **1** the origin and development of a word **2** the linguistic study of word origins —**et′y·mo·log′i·cal** (-mə läj′i kəl) *adj.* —**et′y·mol′o·gist** *n.*

**EU** *abbrev.* European Union

**eu-** [Fr < Gr] *prefix* good, well [*eulogy, euphony*]

**eu·ca·lyp·tus** (yo͞o′kə lip′təs) *n., pl.* -**tus·es** or -**ti** (-tī′) [< Gr *eu-*, well + *kalyptos*, covered] a tall, aromatic, chiefly Australian evergreen tree of the myrtle family

**Eu·cha·rist** (yo͞o′kə rist) *n.* [< Gr *eucharistia*, gratitude] **1** HOLY COMMUNION **2** the consecrated bread and wine used in this —**Eu′cha·ris′tic** *adj.*

**eu·chre** (yo͞o′kər) *n.* [< ?] a card game played with thirty-two cards

**Eu·clid** (yo͞o′klid) flourished 4th c. B.C.; Gr. mathematician: author of a basic work in geometry —**Eu·clid′e·an** (-ē ən) or **Eu·clid′i·an** *adj.*

**Eu·gene** (yo͞o jēn′, yo͞o′jēn) city in W Oregon: pop. 113,000

**eu·gen·ics** (yo͞o jen′iks) *n.* [see EU- & GENESIS] the movement devoted to improving the human species by controlling heredity —**eu·gen′ic** *adj.* —**eu·gen′i·cal·ly** *adv.* —**eu·gen′i·cist** (-ə sist) *n.*

**eu·lo·gize** (yo͞o′lə jīz′) *vt.* -**gized′**, -**giz′ing** [see fol.] to praise highly —**eu′lo·gist** or **eu′lo·giz′er** *n.*

**eu·lo·gy** (-jē) *n., pl.* -**gies** [< Gr *eulegein*, speak well of] **1** speech or writing praising a person or thing; esp., a funeral oration **2** high praise —**eu′lo·gis′tic** (-jis′tik) *adj.*

**eu·nuch** (yo͞o′nək) *n.* [< Gr *eunouchos*, guardian of the bed] a castrated man

**eu·phe·mism** (yo͞o′fə miz′əm) *n.* [< Gr *eu-*, good + *phēmē*, speech] **1** the use of a less direct word or phrase for one considered offensive **2** a word or phrase so substituted —**eu′phe·mis′tic** *adj.* —**eu′phe·mis′ti·cal·ly** *adv.*

**eu·pho·ni·ous** (yo͞o fō′nē əs) *adj.* having a pleasant sound; harmonious —**eu·pho′ni·ous·ly** *adv.*

**eu·pho·ny** (yo͞o′fə nē) *n., pl.* -**nies** [< Gr *eu-*, good + *phōnē*, voice] a pleasant combination of agreeable sounds, as in speech

**eu·pho·ri·a** (yo͞o fôr′ē ə) *n.* [< Gr *eu-*, well + *pherein*, to bear] a feeling of well-being —**eu·phor′ic** *adj.*

**Eu·phra·tes** (yo͞o frāt′ēz) river flowing from EC Turkey through Syria & Iraq into the Persian Gulf: cf. TIGRIS

**Eur·a·sia** (yoor ā′zhə) land mass made up of Europe & Asia

**Eur·a′sian** (-zhən) *adj.* **1** of Eurasia **2** of mixed European and Asian descent —*n.* a person of Eurasian descent

**eu·re·ka** (yoo rē′kə) *interj.* [< Gr *heurēka*, I have found] used to express triumphant achievement

**Eu·rip·i·des** (yoo rip′ə dēz′) 480-406 B.C.; Gr. writer of tragedies

**eu·ro** (yoor′ō) *n.* the basic monetary unit of the European Union: introduced for business use beginning in 1999

**Eu·rope** (yoor′əp) continent between Asia & the Atlantic: *c.* 3,800,000 sq. mi.; pop. *c.* 710,000,000 —**Eu·ro·pe·an** (yoor′ə pē′ən) *adj., n.*

**European Community** an organization of European countries established in 1967 to bring about the political and economic unification of W Europe

**European plan** a system of hotel operation in which guests are charged for rooms and pay for meals separately

**European Union** a union of European nations created in 1993 to bring about the gradual unification of Europe

**eu·ryth·mics** (yo͞o rith′miks) *n.* [< Gr *eu-*, good + *rhythmos*, rhythm] the art of performing bodily movements in rhythm, usually to music

**eu·sta·chian tube** (yo͞o stā′shən) [after B. *Eustachio*, 16th-c. It anatomist] [*also* E- **t**-] a slender tube between the middle ear and the pharynx

**eu·tha·na·si·a** (yo͞o′thə nā′zhə) *n.* [< Gr *eu-*, good + *thanatos*, death] the act of causing death painlessly, so as to end suffering

**eu·tha·nize** (yo͞o′thə nīz′) *vt.* -**nized′**, -**niz′ing** to put to death by euthanasia

**e·vac·u·ate** (ē vak′yo͞o āt′) *vt.* -**at′ed**, -**at′ing** [< L *e-*, out + *vacuus*, empty] **1** to make empty **2** to discharge (bodily waste, esp. feces) **3** to withdraw from —*vi.* to withdraw —**e·vac′u·a′tion** *n.* —**e·vac′u·ee′** (-ē′) *n.*

**e·vade** (ē vād′, i-) *vi., vt.* **e·vad′ed**, **e·vad′ing** [< L *e-*, out, from + *vadere*, go] **1** to avoid or escape (from) by deceit or cleverness **2** to avoid doing or answering directly —**e·vad′er** *n.*

**e·val·u·ate** (ē val′yo͞o āt′, i-) *vt.* -**at′ed**, -**at′ing** [ult. < L *valere*, be well] **1** to find the value or amount of **2** to judge the worth of —**e·val′u·a′tion** *n.*

**ev·a·nes·cent** (ev′ə nes′ənt) *adj.* [< L *e-*, out + *vanescere*, vanish] tending to fade from sight; fleeting; ephemeral —**ev′a·nes′cence** *n.*

**e·van·gel·i·cal** (ē′van jel′i kəl, ev′ən-) *adj.* [< Gr *euangelos*, bringing good news] **1** of or according to the Gospels or the New Testament **2** of those Protestant churches that emphasize salvation by faith in Jesus

**e·van·ge·list** (ē van′jə list) *n.* **1** [E-] any of the four writers of the Gospels: Matthew, Mark, Luke, or John **2** a revivalist or a preacher who holds large public services in various cities, now often televised —e·van'ge·lism' n.

e·van'ge·lize' (-līz') vt. -lized', -liz'ing to convert to Christianity —vi. to preach the gospel

e·vap·o·rate (ē vap'ə rāt') vt. -rat·ed, -rat'ing 〚< L e-, out, from + vaporare, emit vapor〛 1 to change (a liquid or solid) into vapor 2 to remove moisture from (milk, etc.), as by heating, so as to get a concentrated product —vi. 1 to become vapor 2 to give off vapor 3 to disappear like vapor; vanish —e·vap'o·ra'tion n. —e·vap'o·ra'tor n.

e·va'sion (ē vā'zhən, i-) n. 1 an evading; specif., an avoiding of a duty, question, etc. by deceit or cleverness 2 a way of doing this; subterfuge

e·va'sive (-siv) adj. 1 tending or seeking to evade 2 elusive —e·va'sive·ly adv. —e·va'sive·ness n.

eve (ēv) n. 〚< OE æfen, evening〛 1 [Old Poet.] evening 2 [often E-] the evening or day before a holiday 3 the period just prior to some event

Eve (ēv) n. Bible the first woman, Adam's wife

e·ven (ē'vən) adj. 〚OE efne〛 1 flat; level; smooth 2 not varying; constant [an even tempo] 3 calm; tranquil [an even temper] 4 in the same plane or line [even with the rim] 5 owing and being owed nothing 6 equal in number, quantity, etc. 7 exactly divisible by two 8 exact [an even mile] 9 revenged for a wrong, etc. —adv. 1 however improbable; indeed 2 exactly; just [it happened even as I expected] 3 still; yet [he's even better] —vt., vi. to make or become even —even if though —e'ven·ly adv. —e'ven·ness n.

e'ven·hand'ed adj. impartial; fair

eve·ning (ēv'niŋ) n. 〚< OE æfnung〛 1 the last part of the day and early part of night 2 [Dial.] afternoon

even money equal stakes in betting, with no odds

e·vent (ē vent') n. 〚< L e-, out + venire, come〛 1 an occurrence, esp. when important 2 a particular contest in a program of sports 3 any organized activity, celebration, etc. —in any event no matter what happens; anyway —in the event of in case of —in the event that if it should happen that

e'ven-tem'pered adj. not quickly angered; calm

e·vent'ful adj. 1 full of outstanding events 2 having an important outcome —e·vent'ful·ly adv.

e·ven·tide (ē'vən tīd') n. [Archaic] evening

e·ven·tu·al (ē ven'chōō əl) adj. ultimate; final —e·ven'tu·al·ly adv.

e·ven'tu·al'i·ty (-al'ə tē) n., pl. -ties a possible event or outcome

e·ven'tu·ate' (-āt') vi. -at·ed, -at'ing to happen in the end; result

ev·er (ev'ər) adv. 〚< OE æfre〛 1 always [ever the same] 2 at any time [do you ever see her?] 3 at all; by any chance [how can I ever repay you?] —ever so [Inf.] very

Ev·er·est (ev'ər ist, ev'rist), Mount peak of the Himalayas: highest known mountain in the world: 29,035 ft.

ev'er·glade' n. marshy land

ev'er·green' adj. having green leaves all year long, as most conifers —n. an evergreen plant or tree

ev'er·last'ing adj. lasting forever; eternal —n. eternity

ev'er·more' adv. [Archaic] forever; constantly

ev·er·y (ev'rē) adj. 〚OE æfre ælc, lit., ever each〛 1 each, individually and separately 2 the greatest possible [to make every effort] 3 each interval [take a pill every three hours] —every now and then occasionally: also [Inf.] every so often — every other each alternate, as the first, third, fifth, etc. —every which way [Inf.] in complete disorder

ev'er·y·bod'y (-bäd'ē, -bud'ē) pron. every person; everyone

ev'er·y·day' adj. 1 daily 2 suitable for ordinary days [everyday shoes] 3 usual; common

ev'er·y·one' pron. every person

every one every person or thing of those named [every one of the boys]

ev'er·y·thing' pron. every thing; all

ev'er·y·where' adv. in or to every place

e·vict (ē vikt') vt. 〚< L e-, intens. + vincere, conquer〛 to remove (a tenant) by legal procedure —e·vic'tion n.

ev·i·dence (ev'ə dəns) n. 1 something that makes another thing evident; sign 2 a statement of a witness, an object, etc. bearing on or establishing the point in question in a court of law —vt. -denced, -denc·ing to make evident —in evidence plainly seen

ev·i·dent (ev'ə dənt) adj. 〚< L e-, from + videre, see〛 easy to see or perceive; clear —ev'i·dent·ly adv.

e·vil (ē'vəl) adj. 〚OE yfel〛 1 morally bad or wrong; wicked 2 harmful; injurious 3 unlucky; disastrous —n. 1 wickedness; sin 2 anything that causes harm, pain, etc. —e'vil·ly adv.

e'vil·do'er n. one who does evil —e'vil·do'ing n.

e·vince (ē vins') vt. e·vinced', e·vinc'ing 〚< L e-, intens. + vincere, conquer〛 to show plainly; make clear

e·vis·cer·ate (ē vis'ər āt') vt. -at·ed, -at'ing 〚< L e-, out + viscera, viscera〛 1 to remove the entrails from 2 to deprive of an essential part —e·vis'cer·a'tion n.

e·voke (ē vōk') vt. e·voked', e·vok'ing 〚< L e-, out, from + vox, voice〛 1 to call forth 2 to elicit (a reaction, etc.) —ev'o·ca·tion (ev'ə kā'shən, ē'vō-) n.

ev·o·lu·tion (ev'ə lōō'shən) n. 〚see fol.〛 1 an unfolding; process of development or change 2 a thing evolved 3 a movement that is part of a series 4 Biol. a) the development of a species, organism, etc. from its original to its present state b) the theory that all species developed from earlier forms —ev'o·lu'tion·ar'y adj. —ev'o·lu'tion·ist n.

e·volve (ē välv', -vôlv') vt., vi. e·volved', e·volv'ing 〚< L e-, out + volvere, to roll〛 1 to develop gradually 2 to develop by evolution

ewe (yōō) n. 〚OE eowu〛 a female sheep

ew·er (yōō'ər) n. 〚< L aqua, water〛 a large, wide-mouthed water pitcher

ex abbrev. 1 example 2 exchange

ex- 〚< OFr or L〛 prefix 1 a) from, out [expel] b) beyond c) thoroughly d) upward 2 former, previous [ex-president]

ex·ac·er·bate (eg zas'ər bāt') vt. -bat·ed, -bat'ing 〚< L ex-, intens. + acerbus, bitter〛 1 to aggravate (pain, annoyance, etc.) 2 to exasperate; annoy; irritate —ex·ac'er·ba'tion n.

ex·act (eg zakt') adj. 〚< L ex-, out + agere, to do〛 1 characterized by or requiring accuracy; methodical; correct 2 without variation; precise —vt. 1 to extort 2 to demand; require —ex·act'ly adv. —ex·act'ness n.

ex·act'ing adj. 1 making severe demands; strict 2 demanding great care, effort, etc.; arduous —ex·act'ing·ly adv.

ex·ac·tion (eg zak'shən) n. 1 an exacting 2 an extortion 3 an exacted fee, tax, etc.

ex·ac'ti·tude' (-tə tōōd') n. 〚Fr〛 the quality of being exact; accuracy

ex·ag·ger·ate (eg zaj'ər āt') vt., vi. -at·ed, -at'ing 〚< L ex-, out + agger, a heap〛 to think or tell of (something) as greater than it is; overstate —ex·ag'ger·a'tion n. —ex·ag'ger·a'tive adj. —ex·ag'ger·a'tor n.

ex·alt (eg zôlt') vt. 〚< L ex-, up + altus, high〛 1 to raise in status, dignity, etc. 2 to praise; glorify 3 to fill with joy, pride, etc.; elate —ex·al·ta·tion (eg'zôl tā'shən) n.

ex·am·i·na·tion (eg zam'ə nā'shən) n. 1 an examining or being examined 2 a set of questions asked in testing: also ex·am'

ex·am·ine (eg zam'ən) vt. -ined, -in·ing 〚< L examinare, weigh〛 1 to look at critically or methodically; investigate; inspect **2** to test by questioning —**ex·am′in·er** *n.*

**ex·am·ple** (eg zam′pəl) *n.* 〚< L *eximere*, take out〛 **1** something selected to show the character of the rest; sample **2** a case that serves as a warning **3** a model; pattern **4** an instance that illustrates a principle

**ex·as·per·ate** (eg zas′pər āt′) *vt.* **-at′ed, -at′ing** 〚< L *ex-*, out + *asper*, rough〛 to irritate; anger; vex —**ex·as′per·a′tion** *n.*

**ex·ca·vate** (eks′kə vāt′) *vt.* **-vat′ed, -vat′ing** 〚< L *ex-*, out + *cavus*, hollow〛 **1** to make a hole or cavity in **2** to form (a tunnel, etc.) by hollowing out **3** to unearth **4** to dig out (earth, soil, etc.) —**ex′ca·va′tion** *n.* —**ex′ca·va′tor** *n.*

**ex·ceed** (ek sēd′) *vt.* 〚< L *ex-*, out + *cedere*, to go〛 **1** to go or be beyond (a limit, etc.) **2** to surpass

**ex·ceed′ing** *adj.* surpassing; extreme —**ex·ceed′ing·ly** *adv.*

**ex·cel** (ek sel′) *vi., vt.* **-celled′, -cel′ling** 〚< L *ex-*, out of + *-cellere*, to rise〛 to be better or greater than (another or others)

**ex·cel·lence** (ek′sə ləns) *n.* **1** the fact or state of excelling; superiority **2** a particular virtue

**ex′cel·len·cy** (-lən sē) *n., pl.* **-cies 1** [E-] a title of honor for certain dignitaries **2** EXCELLENCE

**ex·cel·lent** (ek′sə lənt) *adj.* 〚see EXCEL〛 outstandingly good of its kind; of exceptional merit —**ex′cel·lent·ly** *adv.*

**ex·cel·si·or** (eks sel′sē ôr′; *for n.* ek sel′sē ər) *interj.* 〚see EXCEL〛 always upward! —*n.* long, thin wood shavings used for packing

**ex·cept** (ek sept′) *vt.* 〚< L *ex-*, out + *capere*, to take〛 to leave out or take out; exclude —*prep.* leaving out; but —*conj.* [Inf.] were it not that; only —**except for** if it were not for

**ex·cept′ing** *prep., conj.* EXCEPT

**ex·cep′tion** *n.* **1** an excepting **2** *a)* a case to which a rule does not apply *b)* a person or thing different from others of the same class **3** an objection —**take exception 1** to object **2** feel offended

**ex·cep′tion·a·ble** *adj.* liable to exception; open to objection

**ex·cep′tion·al** *adj.* **1** unusual; esp., unusually good **2** needing special education, as because mentally gifted or mentally handicapped —**ex·cep′tion·al·ly** *adv.*

**ex·cerpt** (ek surpt′; *for n.* ek′surpt) *vt.* 〚< L *ex-*, out + *carpere*, to pick〛 to select or quote (passages from a book, etc.); extract —*n.* a passage selected or quoted; extract

**ex·cess** (ek ses′; *also, esp. for adj.,* ek′ses′) *n.* 〚see EXCEED〛 **1** action that goes beyond a reasonable limit **2** an amount greater than is necessary **3** the amount by which one thing exceeds another —*adj.* extra; surplus —**in excess of** more than

**ex·ces′sive** *adj.* being too much; immoderate —**ex·ces′sive·ly** *adv.*

**ex·change** (eks chānj′) *vt., vi.* **-changed′, -chang′ing** 〚see EX- & CHANGE〛 **1** to give or receive (something) *for* another thing; barter; trade **2** to interchange (similar things) —*n.* **1** an exchanging; interchange **2** a thing exchanged **3** a place for exchanging [a stock *exchange*] **4** a central office providing telephone service **5** the value of one currency in terms of another —**ex·change′a·ble** *adj.*

**exchange rate** the rate at which one currency can be exchanged for another

**ex·cheq·uer** (eks chek′ər) *n.* 〚ME *escheker*, lit., chessboard < OFr *eschekier*: accounts of revenue were kept on a squared board〛 **1** a national treasury **2** funds; finances

**ex·cise**[1] (ek′sīz′) *n.* 〚ult. < L *assidere*, assist (in office)〛 a tax on various commodities, as liquor or tobacco, within a country: also **excise tax**

**ex·cise**[2] (ek sīz′) *vt.* **-cised′, -cis′ing** 〚< L *ex-*, out + *caedere*, to cut〛 to remove by cutting out —**ex·ci′sion** (-sizh′ən) *n.*

**ex·cit·a·ble** (ek sīt′ə bəl) *adj.* easily excited —**ex·cit′a·bil′i·ty** *n.*

**ex·cite** (ek sīt′) *vt.* **-cit′ed, -cit′ing** 〚< L *ex-*, out + *ciere*, to call〛 **1** to make active; stir up **2** to arouse; provoke **3** to arouse the feelings of —**ex·ci·ta·tion** (ek′sī tā′shən) *n.* —**ex·cit′ed·ly** *adv.* —**ex·cit′er** *n.*

**ex·cite′ment** *n.* **1** an exciting or being excited; agitation **2** that which excites

**ex·cit′ing** *adj.* causing excitement; stirring, thrilling, etc.

**ex·claim** (ek sklām′) *vi., vt.* 〚< L *ex-*, out + *clamare*, to shout〛 to cry out; say suddenly and vehemently

**ex·cla·ma·tion** (ek′sklə mā′shən) *n.* **1** an exclaiming **2** something exclaimed; interjection —**ex·clam·a·to·ry** (ek sklam′ə tôr′ē) *adj.*

**exclamation point** (or **mark**) a mark (!) used in punctuating to show surprise, strong emotion, etc.

**ex·clude** (eks klo͞od′) *vt.* **-clud′ed, -clud′ing** 〚< L *ex-*, out + *claudere*, to close〛 **1** to refuse to admit, consider, etc.; reject **2** to put or force out —**ex·clu′sion** (-klo͞o′zhən) *n.*

**ex·clu·sive** (-klo͞o′siv) *adj.* **1** excluding all others **2** not shared or divided; sole [an *exclusive* right] **3** excluding certain people, as for social or economic reasons —*n.* something exclusive; specif., a news item distributed by only one news organization —**exclusive of** not including —**ex·clu′sive·ly** *adv.* —**ex·clu′sive·ness** *n.*

**ex·com·mu·ni·cate** (eks′kə myo͞o′ni kāt′) *vt.* **-cat′ed, -cat′ing** to exclude from the rights, privileges, etc. of a church —**ex′com·mu′ni·ca′tion** *n.*

**ex·co·ri·ate** (eks kôr′ē āt′) *vt.* **-at′ed, -at′ing** 〚< L *ex-*, off + *corium*, the skin〛 to denounce harshly —**ex·co′ri·a′tion** *n.*

**ex·cre·ment** (eks′krə mənt) *n.* waste matter excreted from the bowels

**ex·cres·cence** (eks kres′əns) *n.* 〚< L *ex-*, out + *crescere*, grow〛 an abnormal outgrowth or addition

**ex·cre·ta** (eks krēt′ə) *pl.n.* waste matter excreted from the body

**ex·crete** (eks krēt′) *vt., vi.* **-cret′ed, -cret′ing** 〚< L *ex-*, out of + *cernere*, sift〛 to eliminate (waste matter) from the body —**ex·cre′tion** *n.* —**ex·cre·to·ry** (eks′krə tôr′ē) *adj.*

**ex·cru·ci·at·ing** (eks kro͞o′shē āt′iŋ) *adj.* **1** intensely painful; agonizing **2** intense or extreme

**ex·cul·pate** (eks′kəl pāt′) *vt.* **-pat′ed, -pat′ing** 〚< L *ex*, out + *culpa*, fault〛 to free from blame; prove guiltless —**ex′cul·pa′tion** *n.* —**ex·cul′pa·to′ry** *adj.*

**ex·cur·sion** (eks kur′zhən) *n.* 〚< L *ex-*, out + *currere*, to run〛 **1** a short trip; jaunt **2** a round trip at reduced rates —*adj.* for an excursion

**ex·cur·sive** (eks kur′siv) *adj.* rambling; digressive —**ex·cur′sive·ly** *adv.* —**ex·cur′sive·ness** *n.*

**ex·cuse** (ek skyo͞oz′; *for n.,* -skyo͞os′) *vt.* **-cused′, -cus′ing** 〚< L *ex-*, from + *causa*, a charge〛 **1** to apologize or give reasons for **2** to overlook (an offense or fault) **3** to release from an obligation, etc. **4** to permit to leave **5** to justify —*n.* **1** a defense of some action; apology **2** something that excuses **3** a pretext —**excuse oneself 1** to apologize **2** to ask for permission to leave —**ex·cus′a·ble** *adj.*

**exec** *abbrev.* **1** executive **2** executor

**ex·e·cra·ble** (ek′si krə bəl) *adj.* 〚see fol.〛 **1** detestable **2** very inferior

**ex′e·crate′** (-krāt′) *vt.* **-crat′ed, -crat′ing** 〚< L *execrare*, to curse〛 **1** to denounce scathingly **2** to loathe; abhor —**ex′e·cra′tion** *n.*

**ex·e·cute** (ek′si kyo͞ot′) *vt.* **-cut′ed, -cut′ing** 〚see EXECUTOR〛 **1** to carry out; do **2** to administer (laws, etc.) **3** to put to death by a legal sentence **4** to create in accordance with a plan, etc. **5** to make valid (a deed, will, etc.)

**ex′e·cu′tion** *n.* **1** an executing; specif., *a)* a carrying out, performing, etc. *b)* a putting to death by a legal sentence **2** the manner of performing

**ex·e·cu'tion·er** *n.* one who carries out a court-imposed death penalty

**ex·ec·u·tive** (eg zek'yōō tiv) *adj.* ⟦see fol.⟧ **1** of or capable of carrying out duties, functions, etc. **2** empowered to administer (laws, government affairs, etc.) —*n.* **1** the branch of government administering the laws and matters of business of a nation **2** one who administers or manages matters of business of a corporation, etc.

**ex·ec·u·tor** (eg zek'yōō tər) *n.* ⟦< L *ex-*, intens. + *sequi*, to follow⟧ a person appointed to carry out the provisions of a will

**ex·e·ge·sis** (ek'sə jē'sis) *n., pl.* **-ses'** (-sēz') ⟦< Gr *ex-*, out + *hēgeisthai*, to lead⟧ interpretation of a word, passage, etc., esp. in the Bible

**ex·em·plar** (eg zem'plər, -plär') *n.* ⟦< L *exemplum*, a pattern⟧ **1** a model; pattern **2** a typical specimen

**ex·em·pla·ry** (eg zem'plə rē) *adj.* ⟦< L *exemplum*, a pattern⟧ serving as a model or example *[an exemplary life]*

**ex·em·pli·fy** (eg zem'plə fī') *vt.* **-fied'**, **-fy'ing** ⟦< L *exemplum*, example + *facere*, to make⟧ to show by example —**ex·em'pli·fi·ca'tion** *n.*

**ex·empt** (eg zempt') *vt.* ⟦< L *ex-*, out + *emere*, to buy⟧ to free from a rule or obligation which applies to others —*adj.* freed from a usual rule, duty, etc. —**ex·emp'tion** *n.*

**ex·er·cise** (ek'sər sīz') *n.* ⟦< L *exercere*, put to work⟧ **1** active use or operation **2** performance (of duties, etc.) **3** activity for developing the body or mind **4** a task to be practiced for developing some skill **5** [*pl.*] a program of speeches, etc. —*vt.* **-cised'**, **-cis'ing 1** to put into action; use **2** to carry out (duties, etc.); perform **3** to put into use so as to develop or train **4** to exert (influence, etc.) **5** to engage so as to worry, harass, etc. —*vi.* to do exercises

**ex·ert** (eg zʉrt') *vt.* ⟦< L *exserere*, stretch out⟧ **1** to put into action **2** to apply (oneself) with great effort

**ex·er'tion** *n.* **1** active use of strength, power, etc. **2** effort

**ex·hale** (eks hāl') *vt., vi.* **-haled'**, **-hal'ing** ⟦< L *ex-*, out + *halare*, breathe⟧ **1** to breathe out (air) **2** to give off (vapor, etc.) —**ex·ha·la·tion** (eks'hə lā'shən) *n.*

**ex·haust** (eg zôst') *vt.* ⟦< L *ex-*, out + *haurire*, to draw⟧ **1** to use up **2** to empty completely; drain **3** to tire out **4** to deal with thoroughly —*n.* **1** the discharge of used steam, gas, etc. from an engine **2** the pipes through which it is released **3** fumes, etc. given off —**ex·haust'i·ble** *adj.*

**ex·haus·tion** (eg zôs'chən) *n.* **1** an exhausting **2** great fatigue

**ex·haus·tive** *adj.* leaving nothing out —**ex·haus'tive·ly** *adv.*

**ex·hib·it** (eg zib'it) *vt.* ⟦< L *ex-*, out + *habere*, to hold⟧ **1** to show; display **2** to present to public view —*vi.* to put art objects, etc. on public display —*n.* **1** a display **2** a thing exhibited **3** *Law* an object produced as evidence in a court —**ex·hib'i·tor** *n.*

**ex·hi·bi·tion** (ek'sə bish'ən) *n.* **1** an exhibiting **2** that which is exhibited **3** a public showing, as of art

**ex'hi·bi'tion·ism'** *n.* **1** a tendency to call attention to oneself or show off **2** a tendency to expose oneself sexually —**ex'hi·bi'tion·ist** *n.*

**ex·hil·a·rate** (eg zil'ə rāt') *vt.* **-rat'ed**, **-rat'ing** ⟦< L *ex-*, intens. + *hilaris*, glad⟧ **1** to make cheerful or lively **2** to stimulate —**ex·hil'a·ra'tion** *n.* —**ex·hil'a·ra'tive** *adj.*

**ex·hort** (eg zôrt') *vt., vi.* ⟦< L *ex-*, out + *hortari*, to urge⟧ to urge earnestly; advise strongly —**ex'hor·ta'tion** *n.*

**ex·hume** (eks hyōōm', eg zyōōm') *vt.* **-humed'**, **-hum'ing** ⟦< L *ex-*, out + *humus*, the ground⟧ **1** to dig out of the earth; disinter **2** to bring to light; reveal —**ex'hu·ma'tion** *n.*

**ex·i·gen·cy** (eks'ə jən sē) *n., pl.* **-cies** ⟦< L *exigere*, drive out⟧ **1** urgency **2** a situation calling for

immediate attention **3** [*pl.*] pressing needs —**ex'i·gent** *adj.*

**ex·ig·u·ous** (eg zig'yōō əs) *adj.* ⟦see prec.⟧ scanty; meager

**ex·ile** (ek'sīl', eg'zīl') *n.* ⟦< L *exul*, an exile⟧ **1** a prolonged living away from one's country, usually enforced **2** a person in exile —*vt.* **-iled'**, **-il'ing** to force (a person) into exile; banish

**ex·ist** (eg zist') *vi.* ⟦< L *ex-*, out + *sistere*, to set, place⟧ **1** to have reality or being; be **2** to occur or be present **3** to continue being; live

**ex·ist'ence** *n.* **1** the act or fact of being **2** life; living **3** occurrence —**ex·ist'ent** *adj.*

**ex·is·ten·tial** (eg'zis ten'shəl) *adj.* **1** of existence **2** of existentialism

**ex'is·ten'tial·ism'** *n.* a philosophical movement stressing individual existence and holding that human beings are totally free and responsible for their acts —**ex'is·ten'tial·ist** *adj., n.*

**ex·it** (ek'sit, eg'zit) *n.* ⟦< L *ex-*, out + *ire*, to go⟧ **1** an actor's departure from the stage **2** a going out; departure **3** a way out **4** a road leading from an expressway —*vi.* to leave a place —*vt.* to leave (a building, expressway, etc.)

**exo-** ⟦< Gr *exō*⟧ *prefix* outside, outer, outer part

**ex·o·bi·ol·o·gy** (eks'ō bī äl'ə jē) *n.* the branch of biology investigating the possibility of extraterrestrial life

**ex·o·dus** (eks'ə dəs) *n.* ⟦< Gr *ex-*, out + *hodos*, way⟧ **1** [E-] the departure of the Israelites from Egypt: with *the* **2** [E-] the second book of the Bible, describing this **3** a going out or forth

**ex of·fi·ci·o** (eks' ə fish'ē ō') ⟦L, lit., from office⟧ by virtue of one's position

**ex·on·er·ate** (eg zän'ər āt') *vt.* **-at'ed**, **-at'ing** ⟦< L *ex-*, out + *onerare*, to load⟧ to declare or prove blameless —**ex·on'er·a'tion** *n.*

**ex·or·bi·tant** (eg zôr'bi tənt) *adj.* ⟦< L *ex-*, out + *orbita*, a track⟧ going beyond what is reasonable, just, etc.; excessive —**ex·or'bi·tance** *n.*

**ex·or·cise** or **ex·or·cize** (eks'ôr sīz') *vt.* **-cised'** or **-cized'**, **-cis'ing** or **-ciz'ing** ⟦< Gr *ex-*, out + *horkos*, an oath⟧ **1** to drive (an evil spirit) out or away by ritual prayers, etc. **2** to free from such a spirit —**ex'or·cism'** (-siz'əm) *n.* —**ex'or·cist** *n.*

**ex·o·skel·e·ton** (eks'ō skel'ə tən) *n.* any hard, external supporting structure, as the shell of an oyster

**ex'o·ther'mic** (-thʉr'mik) *adj.* designating or of a chemical change in which heat is liberated

**ex·ot·ic** (eg zät'ik) *adj.* ⟦< Gr *exō*, outside⟧ **1** foreign **2** strangely beautiful, enticing, etc. —**ex·ot'i·cal·ly** *adv.*

**exp** *abbrev.* experience(d)

**ex·pand** (ek spand') *vt., vi.* ⟦< L *ex-*, out + *pandere*, to spread⟧ **1** to spread out; unfold **2** to increase in size, scope, etc.; enlarge; develop

**ex·panse** (ek spans') *n.* a large area or unbroken surface; wide extent

**ex·pan·si·ble** *adj.* that can be expanded: also **ex·pand'a·ble**

**ex·pan'sion** *n.* **1** an expanding or being expanded; enlargement **2** an expanded thing or part **3** the degree or extent of expansion

**expansion bolt** a bolt with an attachment that expands as the bolt is turned

**ex·pan'sive** *adj.* **1** that can expand **2** broad; extensive **3** effusive; demonstrative —**ex·pan'sive·ly** *adv.*

**ex·pa·ti·ate** (eks pā'shē āt') *vi.* **-at'ed**, **-at'ing** ⟦< L *ex(s)patiari*, wander⟧ to speak or write at length (*on* or *upon*) —**ex·pa'ti·a'tion** *n.*

**ex·pa·tri·ate** (eks pā'trē āt'; *for n.*; -it) *vt., vi.* **-at'ed**, **-at'ing** ⟦< L *ex*, out of + *patria*, fatherland⟧ to exile (a person or oneself) —*n.* an expatriated person —**ex·pa'tri·a'tion** *n.*

**ex·pect** (ek spekt') *vt.* ⟦< L *ex-*, out + *spectare*, to look⟧ **1** to look for as likely to occur or appear **2** to look for as proper or necessary **3** [Inf.] to suppose; guess —**be expecting** [Inf.] to be pregnant

**ex·pect·an·cy** *n.*, *pl.* **-cies** **1** EXPECTATION **2** that which is expected, esp. on a statistical basis

**ex·pect·ant** *adj.* that expects; expecting —**ex·pect'ant·ly** *adv.*

**ex·pec·ta·tion** (ek'spek tā'shən) *n.* **1** an expecting; anticipation **2** a thing looked forward to **3** [*also pl.*] a reason for expecting something

**ex·pec·to·rant** (ek spek'tə rənt) *n.* [see fol.] a medicine that helps to bring up phlegm

**ex·pec'to·rate'** (-tə rāt') *vt.*, *vi.* **-rat'ed, -rat'ing** [< L *ex-*, out + *pectus*, breast] to spit —**ex·pec'to·ra'tion** *n.*

**ex·pe·di·en·cy** (ek spē'dē ən sē) *n.*, *pl.* **-cies** **1** a being expedient; suitability for a given purpose **2** the doing of what is selfish rather than of what is right or just; self-interest **3** an expedient Also **ex·pe'di·ence**

**ex·pe'di·ent** *adj.* [see fol.] **1** useful for effecting a desired result; convenient **2** based on or guided by self-interest —*n.* an expedient thing; means to an end

**ex·pe·dite** (eks'pə dīt') *vt.* **-dit'ed, -dit'ing** [< L *expedire*, lit., to free the foot] **1** to speed up the progress of; facilitate **2** to do quickly

**ex'pe·dit'er** *n.* one employed to expedite urgent or involved projects: also sp. **ex'pe·di'tor**

**ex·pe·di·tion** (eks'pə dish'ən) *n.* [see EXPEDITE] **1** *a*) a voyage, march, etc., as for exploration or battle *b*) those on such a journey **2** efficient speed —**ex'pe·di'tion·ar·y** *adj.*

**ex'pe·di'tious** (-dish'əs) *adj.* efficient and speedy; prompt —**ex'pe·di'tious·ly** *adv.*

**ex·pel** (ek spel') *vt.* **-pelled', -pel'ling** [< L *ex-*, out + *pellere*, to thrust] **1** to drive out by force **2** to dismiss by authority *[expelled* from college*]* —**ex·pel'la·ble** *adj.* —**ex·pel'ler** *n.*

**ex·pend** (ek spend') *vt.* [< L *ex-*, out + *pendere*, to weigh] **1** to spend **2** to use up

**ex·pend'a·ble** *adj.* **1** that can be expended **2** *Mil.* designating equipment (or personnel) expected to be used up (or sacrificed) in service

**ex·pend·i·ture** (ek spen'di chər) *n.* **1** an expending of money, time, etc. **2** the amount of money, time, etc. expended

**ex·pense** (ek spens') *n.* [see EXPEND] **1** financial cost; charge **2** any cost or sacrifice **3** [*pl.*] charges met with in doing one's work, etc.

**ex·pen'sive** *adj.* costly; high-priced

**ex·pe·ri·ence** (ek spir'ē əns) *n.* [< L *experiri*, to try] **1** the act of living through an event **2** anything or everything observed or lived through **3** *a*) training and personal participation *b*) knowledge, skill, etc. resulting from this —*vt.* **-enced, -enc·ing** to have experience of; undergo

**ex·pe'ri·enced** *adj.* having had or having learned from experience

**ex·per·i·ment** (ek sper'ə mənt; *also, and for v. usually,* -ment') *n.* [< L *experimentum*, a trial] a test, trial, action, etc. undertaken to discover or demonstrate something —*vi.* to make, perform, conduct, etc. experiments —**ex·per'i·men·ta'tion** (-mən tā'shən) *n.* —**ex·per'i·ment'er** *n.*

**ex·per'i·men'tal** *adj.* **1** based on or used for experiments **2** designed to test **3** tentative —**ex·per'i·men'tal·ly** *adv.*

**ex·pert** (eks'pərt) *adj.* [see EXPERIENCE] very skillful —*n.* one who is very skillful or well-informed in some special field —**ex'pert·ly** *adv.* —**ex'pert·ness** *n.*

**ex·per·tise** (ek'spər tēz') *n.* [Fr] the skill or knowledge of an expert

**ex·pi·ate** (eks'pē āt') *vt.* **-at'ed, -at'ing** [< L *ex-*, out + *piare*, to appease] to make amends for (wrongdoing or guilt); atone for —**ex'pi·a'tion** *n.* —**ex'pi·a·to'ry** (-ə tôr'ē) *adj.*

**ex·pire** (ek spīr') *vi.* **-pired', -pir'ing** [< L *ex-*, out + *spirare*, breathe] **1** to exhale **2** to die **3** to come to an end —**ex·pi·ra·tion** (ek'spə rā'shən) *n.*

**ex·plain** (ek splān') *vt.* [< L *ex-*, out + *planus*, level] **1** to make plain or understandable **2** to

give the meaning of; expound **3** to account for —*vi.* to give an explanation —**ex·plain'a·ble** *adj.*

**ex·pla·na·tion** (eks'plə nā'shən) *n.* **1** an explaining **2** something that explains; interpretation, meaning, etc.

**ex·plan·a·to·ry** (ek splan'ə tôr'ē) *adj.* explaining or intended to explain

**ex·ple·tive** (eks'plə tiv) *n.* [< L *ex-*, out, up + *plere*, to fill] an oath or exclamation

**ex·pli·ca·ble** (eks'pli kə bəl, ik splik'ə bəl) *adj.* that can be explained

**ex·pli·cate** (eks'pli kāt') *vt.* **-cat'ed, -cat'ing** [< L *ex-*, out + *plicare*, to fold] to make clear; explain fully

**ex·plic·it** (eks plis'it) *adj.* [see prec.] **1** clearly stated or shown; definite **2** outspoken —**ex·plic'it·ly** *adv.*

**ex·plode** (ek splōd') *vt.* **-plod'ed, -plod'ing** [orig., to drive off the stage < L *ex-*, off + *plaudere*, applaud] **1** to expose as false **2** to make burst with a loud noise **3** to cause to change suddenly and violently, as from a solid to an expanding gas —*vi.* to burst forth noisily —**ex·plod'a·ble** *adj.*

**ex·ploit** (eks'ploit'; *also, and for v. usually,* ek sploit') *n.* [see EXPLICATE] a daring act; bold deed —*vt.* **1** to make use of **2** to make unethical use of for one's own profit —**ex'ploi·ta'tion** *n.* —**ex·ploit'a·tive** *adj.* —**ex·ploit'er** *n.*

**ex·plore** (ek splôr') *vt.*, *vi.* **-plored', -plor'ing** [< L *ex-*, out + *plorare*, cry out] **1** to examine (something) carefully; investigate **2** to travel in (a little-known region) to learn about it —**ex·plo·ra·tion** (eks'plə rā'shən) *n.* —**ex·plor'a·to'ry** (-ə tôr'ē) *adj.* —**ex·plor'er** *n.*

**ex·plo·sion** (ek splō'zhən) *n.* **1** an exploding **2** the noise made by exploding **3** a noisy outburst **4** a sudden, widespread increase

**ex·plo'sive** (-siv) *adj.* **1** of, causing, or like an explosion **2** tending to explode —*n.* a substance that can explode, as gunpowder —**ex·plo'sive·ly** *adv.* —**ex·plo'sive·ness** *n.*

**ex·po·nent** (ek spōn'ənt; *also, esp. for 3,* eks'pōn'-) *n.* [see EXPOUND] **1** one who expounds or promotes (principles, etc.) **2** a person or thing that is an example or symbol (*of* something) **3** *Algebra* a symbol placed at the upper right of another to show how many times the latter is to be multiplied by itself (Ex.: $b^2 = b \times b$)

**ex·po·nen·tial** (eks'pō nen'shəl) *adj.* **1** *Math.* of an exponent **2** of or increasing by very large amounts, etc.

**ex·port** (ek spôrt'; *also, and for n. always,* eks'pôrt') *vt.* [< L *ex-*, out + *portare*, to carry] **1** to send (goods) to another country, esp. for sale **2** to send (ideas, culture, etc.) from one place to another —*n.* **1** something exported **2** an exporting —**ex'por·ta'tion** *n.* —**ex·port'er** *n.*

**ex·pose** (ek spōz') *vt.* **-posed', -pos'ing** [see EXPOUND] **1** to lay open (*to* danger, attack, etc.) **2** to reveal; exhibit **3** to make (a crime, etc.) known **4** *Photog.* to subject (a sensitized film or plate) to light, etc.

**ex·po·sé** (eks'pō zā') *n.* [Fr] a public disclosure of a scandal, crime, etc.

**ex·po·si·tion** (eks'pə zish'ən) *n.* [see EXPOUND] **1** a detailed explanation **2** writing or speaking that explains **3** a large public exhibition or show

**ex·pos·i·tor** (ek späz'ət ər) *n.* one who expounds or explains

**ex·pos'i·to'ry** (-ə tôr'ē) *adj.* of or containing exposition; explanatory

**ex post fac·to** (eks' pōst fak'tō) [L, from (the thing) done afterward] done afterward, but retroactive

**ex·pos·tu·late** (ek späs'chə lāt') *vi.* **-lat'ed, -lat'ing** [< L *ex-*, intens. + *postulare*, to demand] to reason with a person earnestly, objecting to that person's actions —**ex·pos'tu·la'tion** *n.*

**ex·po·sure** (ek spō'zhər) *n.* **1** an exposing or being exposed **2** a location, as of a house, in relation to the sun, etc. *[an eastern exposure]* **3** frequent appearance before the public **4** *Photog.* a)

the subjection of a sensitized film or plate to light,
X-rays, etc. *b*) a section of a film for one picture
*c*) the time during which such a section is exposed

**ex·pound** (ek spound′) *vt.* 〚< L *ex-*, out + *ponere*,
to put〛 **1** to set forth; state in detail **2** to explain

**ex·press** (ek spres′) *vt.* 〚< L *ex-*, out + *premere*, to
press〛 **1** to squeeze out (juice, etc.) **2** to put into
words; state **3** to reveal; show **4** to symbolize;
signify **5** to send by express —*adj.* **1** expressed;
stated; explicit **2** specific **3** fast, direct, and making few stops [an *express* bus] **4** marked by speed
[an *express* highway] **5** having to do with an
express train, bus, service, etc. —*adv.* by express
—*n.* **1** an express train, bus, etc. **2** *a*) a service
for transporting things rapidly *b*) the things sent
by express

**ex·pres·sion** (ek spresh′ən) *n.* **1** a putting into
words; stating **2** a manner of expressing, esp.
with eloquence **3** a particular word or phrase **4** a
showing of feeling, character, etc. **5** a look, into-
nation, etc. that conveys meaning **6** a mathematical symbol or set of symbols —**ex·pres′sion·
less** *adj.*

**ex·pres′sion·ism′** *n.* [*often* E-] a 20th-c. movement in art, literature, etc. seeking to give symbolic, objective expression to inner experience —
**ex·pres′sion·ist** *adj., n.* —**ex·pres′sion·is′tic** *adj.*

**ex·pres′sive** *adj.* **1** that expresses **2** full of
meaning or feeling —**ex·pres′sive·ly** *adv.* —**ex·
pres′sive·ness** *n.*

**ex·press′ly** *adv.* **1** plainly; definitely **2** especially; particularly

**ex·press′way′** *n.* a divided highway for high-
speed, through traffic, with grade separations at
intersections

**ex·pro·pri·ate** (eks prō′prē āt′) *vt.* -at′ed, -at′ing
〚< L *ex-*, out + *proprius*, one's own〛 to take (land,
etc.) from its owner, esp. for public use —**ex·
pro′pri·a′tion** *n.*

**ex·pul·sion** (ek spul′shən) *n.* an expelling or being
expelled

**ex·punge** (ek spunj′) *vt.* -punged′, -pung′ing 〚< L
*ex-*, out + *pungere*, to prick〛 to blot or strike out;
erase

**ex·pur·gate** (eks′pər gāt′) *vt.* -gat′ed, -gat′ing 〚<
L *ex-*, out + *purgare*, cleanse〛 to remove (passages
considered obscene, etc.) from (a book, etc.) —
**ex′pur·ga′tion** *n.*

**ex·qui·site** (eks′kwi zit, ek skwiz′it) *adj.* 〚< L *ex-*,
out + *quaerere*, to ask〛 **1** carefully or elaborately
done **2** very beautiful, delicate, etc. **3** of highest
quality **4** very intense; keen

**ext** *abbrev.* extension

**ex·tant** (eks′tənt, ek stant′) *adj.* 〚< L *ex-*, out +
*stare*, to stand〛 still existing; not extinct

**ex·tem·po·ra·ne·ous** (eks′tem′pə rā′nē əs) *adj.*
[see fol.] done or spoken with little preparation;
offhand —**ex′tem′po·ra′ne·ous·ly** *adv.*

**ex·tem·po·re** (ek stem′pə rē) *adv., adj.* 〚< L *ex-*,
out + *tempus*, time〛 with little preparation;
offhand

**ex·tem′po·rize′** (-rīz′) *vi., vt.* -rized′, -riz′ing to
speak, perform, etc. extempore; improvise

**ex·tend** (ek stend′) *vt.* 〚< L *ex-*, out + *tendere*, to
stretch〛 **1** to make longer; stretch out; prolong **2**
to enlarge in area, scope, etc.; expand **3** to stretch
forth **4** to offer; grant **5** to make (oneself) work
very hard —*vi.* to be extended —**ex·tend′ed** *adj.*
—**ex·tend′er** *n.* —**ex·ten′si·ble** (-sten′sə bəl) or **ex·
tend′i·ble** *adj.*

**extended care** nursing care for a limited time
after hospitalization

**extended family** a nuclear family together with
other relatives living with them or nearby

**ex·ten·sion** (-sten′shən) *n.* **1** an extending or
being extended **2** range; extent **3** a part forming
a continuation or addition **4** an extra telephone
connected to the main line

**ex·ten·sive** (-siv) *adj.* having great extent; vast;
far-reaching; comprehensive —**ex·ten′sive·ly** *adv.*
—**ex·ten′sive·ness** *n.*

**ex·tent** (ek stent′) *n.* **1** the space, amount, or

degree to which a thing extends; size **2** scope;
limits **3** an extended space; vast area

**ex·ten·u·ate** (ek sten′yōō āt′) *vt.* -at′ed, -at′ing 〚<
L *ex-*, out + *tenuis*, thin〛 to make (an offense, etc.)
seem less serious —**ex·ten′u·a′tion** *n.*

**ex·te·ri·or** (ek stir′ē ər) *adj.* 〚see EXTERNAL〛 **1** *a*)
on the outside; outer *b*) to be used on the outside
[*exterior* paint] **2** coming from without —*n.* an
outside or outside surface

**ex·ter·mi·nate** (ek stur′mə nāt′) *vt.* -nat′ed,
-nat′ing 〚< L *ex-*, out + *terminus*, boundary〛 to
destroy entirely; wipe out —**ex·ter′mi·na′tion** *n.*

**ex·ter′mi·na′tor** (-nāt′ər) *n.* one that extermi-
nates; specif., one whose work is exterminating
vermin

**ex·ter·nal** (ek stur′nəl) *adj.* 〚< L *externus*〛 **1** on
or of the outside **2** existing apart from the mind;
material **3** coming from without **4** superficial **5**
foreign —*n.* an outside surface or part —**ex·
ter′nal·ly** *adv.*

**ex·tinct** (ek stiŋkt′) *adj.* 〚see EXTINGUISH〛 **1** having died down; extinguished **2** no longer in existence

**ex·tinc′tion** *n.* **1** an extinguishing **2** a destroying or being destroyed **3** a dying out: said as of a
species

**ex·tin·guish** (ek stiŋ′gwish) *vt.* 〚< L *ex-*, out +
*stinguere*, extinguish〛 **1** to put out (a fire, etc.) **2**
to destroy —**ex·tin′guish·er** *n.*

**ex·tir·pate** (eks′tər pāt′) *vt.* -pat′ed, -pat′ing 〚< L
*ex-*, out + *stirps*, root〛 to destroy completely —
**ex′tir·pa′tion** *n.*

**ex·tol** or **ex·toll** (ek stōl′) *vt.* -tolled′, -tol′ling 〚<
L *ex-*, up + *tollere*, to raise〛 to praise highly; laud

**ex·tort** (ek stôrt′) *vt.* 〚< L *ex-*, out + *torquere*, to
twist〛 to get (money, etc.) from someone by force
or threats

**ex·tor′tion** *n.* **1** an extorting **2** something
extorted —**ex·tor′tion·ate** *adj.* —**ex·tor′tion·ist** or
**ex·tor′tion·er** *n.*

**ex·tra** (eks′trə) *adj.* 〚< L *extra*, more than〛 more
or better than normal, expected, etc.; additional
or superior —*n.* an extra person or thing; specif.,
*a*) a special edition of a newspaper *b*) an extra
benefit *c*) an actor hired by the day to play a
minor part —*adv.* more than usually; esp., exceptionally

**extra-** 〚see EXTERNAL〛 *prefix* outside, beyond,
besides

**ex·tract** (ek strakt′; *for n.* eks′trakt) *vt.* 〚< L *ex-*,
out + *trahere*, to draw〛 **1** to draw out by effort **2**
to obtain by pressing, distilling, etc. **3** to deduce,
derive, or elicit **4** to select or quote (a passage,
etc.) —*n.* something extracted; specif., *a*) a concentrate [beef *extract*] *b*) an excerpt

**ex·trac′tion** *n.* **1** the act or process of extracting
**2** origin; descent

**ex·tra·cur·ric·u·lar** (eks′trə kə rik′yōō lər) *adj.* not
part of the required curriculum

**ex·tra·dite** (eks′trə dīt′) *vt.* -dit′ed, -dit′ing 〚< L
*ex-*, out + *traditio*, a surrender〛 to turn over (an
alleged criminal, etc.) to the jurisdiction of
another country, U.S. state, etc. —**ex′tra·di′tion**
(-dish′ən) *n.*

**ex·tra·le·gal** (eks′trə lē′gəl) *adj.* outside of legal
control

**ex·tra·mar·i·tal** (-mar′ət′l) *adj.* having to do with
sexual intercourse with someone other that one's
spouse

**ex·tra·ne·ous** (ek strā′nē əs) *adj.* 〚L *extraneus*,
foreign〛 **1** coming from without; foreign **2** not
pertinent; irrelevant —**ex·tra′ne·ous·ly** *adv.*

**ex·tra·or·di·nar·y** (ek strôrd′'n er′ē) *adj.* 〚< L
*extra ordinem*, out of order〛 **1** not ordinary **2**
going far beyond the ordinary; unusual; remarkable

**ex·trap·o·late** (ek strap′ə lāt′) *vt., vi.* -lat′ed,
-lat′ing 〚see EXTRA- & INTERPOLATE〛 to estimate
(something unknown) on the basis of known facts
—**ex·trap′o·la′tion** *n.*

**ex·tra·sen·so·ry** (eks′trə sen′sə rē) *adj.* apart from, or in addition to, normal sense perception

**ex′tra·ter·res′tri·al** (-tə res′trē əl) *adj.* being, of, or from outside the earth's limits —*n.* an extraterrestrial being, as in science fiction

**ex·trav·a·gant** (ek strav′ə gənt) *adj.* ⟦< L *extra*, beyond + *vagari*, to wander⟧ 1 going beyond reasonable limits; excessive 2 costing or spending too much; wasteful —**ex·trav′a·gance** *n.*

**ex·trav·a·gan·za** (ek strav′ə gan′zə) *n.* ⟦< It *estravaganza*, extravagance⟧ a spectacular theatrical production

**ex·treme** (ek strēm′) *adj.* ⟦< L *exterus*, outer⟧ 1 farthest away; utmost 2 *a)* very great *b)* excessive 3 unconventional or radical, as in politics 4 harsh; drastic —*n.* 1 either of two things that are as different or far as possible from each other 2 an extreme act, state, etc. 3 *Math.* the first or last term of a proportion —**ex·treme′ly** *adv.* —**ex·treme′ness** *n.*

**ex·trem′ism′** *n.* a going to extremes, esp. in politics —**ex·trem′ist** *adj., n.*

**ex·trem·i·ty** (ek strem′ə tē) *n., pl.* **-ties** 1 the outermost part; end 2 the greatest degree 3 great need, danger, etc. 4 an extreme measure: *usually used in pl.* 5 [*pl.*] the hands and feet

**ex·tri·cate** (eks′tri kāt′) *vt.* **-cat·ed, -cat·ing** ⟦< L *ex-*, out + *tricae*, vexations⟧ to set free (*from* a net, difficulty, etc.) —**ex′tri·ca′tion** *n.*

**ex·trin·sic** (eks trin′sik, -zik) *adj.* ⟦< L *exter*, without + *secus*, otherwise⟧ not inherent —**ex·trin′si·cal·ly** *adv.*

**ex·tro·vert** (eks′trə vurt′) *n.* ⟦< L *extra-*, outside + *vertere*, to turn⟧ one who is active and expressive rather than introspective —**ex′tro·ver′sion** (-vur′zhən) *n.* —**ex′tro·vert′ed** *adj.*

**ex·trude** (ek strōōd′) *vt.* **-trud·ed, -trud·ing** ⟦< L *ex-*, out + *trudere*, to thrust⟧ to force out, as through a small opening —*vi.* to be extruded —**ex·tru′sion** *n.*

**ex·u·ber·ant** (eg zōō′bər ənt) *adj.* ⟦< L *ex-*, intens. + *uberare*, bear abundantly⟧ 1 growing profusely; luxuriant 2 characterized by good health and high spirits —**ex·u′ber·ance** *n.* —**ex·u′ber·ant·ly** *adv.*

**ex·ude** (eg zōōd′) *vt., vi.* **-ud·ed, -ud·ing** ⟦< L *ex-*, out + *sudare*, to sweat⟧ 1 to ooze 2 to seem to radiate [*to exude* joy] —**ex·u·da·tion** (eks′yōō dā′shən, egz′-) *n.*

**ex·ult** (eg zult′) *vi.* ⟦< L *ex-*, intens. + *saltare*, to leap⟧ to rejoice greatly; glory —**ex·ult′ant** *adj.* —**ex·ul·ta·tion** (eg′zəl tā′shən, eks′əl-) *n.*

**ex·ur·bi·a** (eks ur′bē ə) *n.* ⟦EX- + (SUB)URBIA⟧ the semirural communities beyond the suburbs, typically lived in by upper-income families —**ex·ur′ban** *adj.* —**ex·ur′ban·ite′** *adj., n.*

**eye** (ī) *n.* ⟦OE *ēage*⟧ 1 the organ of sight in humans and animals 2 *a)* the eyeball *b)* the iris [brown *eyes*] 3 the area around the eye [a black *eye*] 4 [*often pl.*] sight; vision 5 a look; glance 6 attention; observation 7 the power of judging, etc. by eyesight [a good *eye* for detail] 8 [*often pl.*] judgment; opinion [in the *eyes* of the law] 9 a thing like an eye in appearance or function —*vt.* **eyed, eye′ing** or **ey′ing** to look at; observe —**have an eye for** to have a keen appreciation of —**keep an eye on** to look after —**lay** (or **set** or **clap**) **eyes on** to look at —**make eyes at** to look at amorously —**see eye to eye** to agree completely —**with an eye to** paying attention to; considering

**eye′ball′** *n.* the ball-shaped part of the eye —*vt.* [Inf.] to examine or measure visually

**eye′brow′** *n.* the bony arch over each eye, or the hair growing on this

**eye′-catch′er** *n.* something that especially attracts one's attention —**eye′-catch′ing** *adj.*

**eye′drops′** *pl.n.* liquid medicine for the eyes, applied as with a dropper

**eye′ful′** (-fool′) *n.* [Slang] a person or thing that looks striking or unusual

**eye′glass′** *n.* 1 a lens to help faulty vision 2 [*pl.*] a pair of such lenses in a frame; glasses

**eye′lash′** *n.* any of the hairs on the edge of the eyelid

**eye′let** (-lit) *n.* 1 a small hole for receiving a cord, hook, etc. 2 a metal ring for reinforcing such a hole 3 a small hole edged by stitching in embroidery

**eye′lid′** *n.* either of the two folds of flesh that cover and uncover the eyeball

**eye′-o′pen·er** (-ō′pə nər) *n.* a surprising piece of news, sudden realization, etc. —**eye′-o′pen·ing** *adj.*

**eye′piece′** *n.* in a telescope, microscope, etc., the lens or lenses nearest the viewer's eye

**eye′sight′** *n.* 1 the power of seeing; sight 2 the range of vision

**eye′sore′** *n.* an unpleasant sight

**eye′strain′** *n.* a tired or strained condition of the eye muscles

**eye′tooth′** *n., pl.* **-teeth′** a canine tooth of the upper jaw

**eye′wear′** *n.* eyeglasses, sunglasses, etc.

**eye′wit′ness** *n.* one who sees or has seen something happen, as an accident, etc.

**ey·rie** or **ey·ry** (er′ē, ir′ē) *n., pl.* **-ries** AERIE

# F

**f¹** or **F** (ef) *n., pl.* **f's, F's** the sixth letter of the English alphabet
**f²** *abbrev.* ⟦It⟧ *Music* FORTE²
**F¹** (ef) *n.* 1 *Educ.* a grade for failing work or, sometimes, fair or average work 2 *Music* the fourth tone in the scale of C major
**F²** *abbrev.* 1 Fahrenheit 2 female or feminine 3 folio(s) 4 following 5 franc(s) 6 Friday
**F³** *Chem. symbol for* fluorine
**fa** (fä) *n.* ⟦< ML⟧ *Music* the fourth tone of the diatonic scale
**FAA** *abbrev.* Federal Aviation Administration
**fa·ble** (fā′bəl) *n.* ⟦< L *fabula*, a story⟧ 1 a fictitious story, usually about animals, meant to teach a moral lesson 2 a myth or legend 3 a falsehood
**fa′bled** *adj.* 1 mythical; legendary 2 unreal; fictitious
**fab·ric** (fab′rik) *n.* ⟦< L *fabrica*, workshop⟧ 1 a framework; structure 2 a material, as cloth, made from fibers, etc. by weaving, felting, etc.

**fab·ri·cate** (fab′ri kāt′) *vt.* **-cat·ed, -cat·ing** ⟦see prec.⟧ 1 to make, build, construct, etc.; manufacture 2 to make up (a story, lie, etc.); invent —**fab′ri·ca′tion** *n.* —**fab′ri·ca′tor** *n.*

**fab·u·lous** (fab′yōō ləs) *adj.* ⟦see FABLE⟧ 1 of or like a fable; fictitious 2 incredible; astounding 3 [Inf.] wonderful —**fab′u·lous·ly** *adv.*

**fa·cade** or **fa·çade** (fə säd′) *n.* ⟦Fr: see fol.⟧ 1 the front or main face of a building 2 an imposing appearance concealing something inferior

**face** (fās) *n.* ⟦< L *facies*⟧ 1 the front of the head 2 the expression of the countenance 3 the main or front surface 4 the surface that is marked, as of a clock, etc., or that is finished, as of fabric, etc. 5 the appearance; outward aspect 6 dignity; self-respect: usually in **lose** (or **save**) **face** —*vt.* **faced, fac′ing** 1 to turn, or have the face turned, toward 2 to confront with boldness, etc. 3 to cover with a new surface —*vi.* to turn, or have the face turned, in a specified direction —**face to face** 1 confronting each other 2 very near to: with *with* —

**face up to** to face with courage —**in the face of 1** in the presence of **2** in spite of —**make a face** to grimace —**on the face of it** apparently

**-faced** (fāst) *combining form* having a (specified kind of) face [round-*faced*]

**face'less** *adj.* without individuality; anonymous

**face'-lift'** *n.* **1** plastic surgery to remove wrinkles, etc. from the face **2** an altering, cleaning, etc., as of a building's exterior Also **face lift** —*vt.* to perform a face-lift on

**face'-off'** *n.* **1** *Hockey* the start or resumption of play when the referee drops the puck between two opposing players **2** [Inf.] a confrontation

**face'-sav'ing** *adj.* preserving one's dignity or self-respect

**fac·et** (fas'it) *n.* ⟦see FACE⟧ **1** any of the polished plane surfaces of a cut gem **2** any of a number of sides or aspects, as of a personality —*vt.* **-et·ed** or **-et·ted**, **-et·ing** or **-et·ting** to cut or make facets on

**fa·ce·tious** (fə sē'shəs) *adj.* ⟦< L *facetus*, witty⟧ joking, esp. at an inappropriate time —**fa·ce'tious·ly** *adv.*

FACETS OF A GEM

**face value 1** the value printed on a bill, bond, etc. **2** the seeming value

**fa·cial** (fā'shəl) *adj.* of or for the face —*n.* a cosmetic treatment, massage, etc. for the skin of the face

**facial tissue** a sheet of soft tissue paper used as a handkerchief, etc.

**fac·ile** (fas'il) *adj.* ⟦Fr < L *facere*, do⟧ **1** not hard to do **2** working or done easily **3** superficial

**fa·cil·i·tate** (fə sil'ə tāt') *vt.* **-tat·ed**, **-tat·ing** ⟦see prec.⟧ to make easy or easier —**fa·cil'i·ta'tion** *n.* —**fa·cil'i·ta'tor** *n.*

**fa·cil·i·ty** (-tē) *n., pl.* **-ties 1** ease of doing **2** skill; dexterity **3** [*usually pl.*] the means by which something can be done **4** a building, room, etc. for some activity

**fac·ing** (fās'iŋ) *n.* **1** a lining on the edge of a garment **2** a covering of contrasting material on a building

**fac·sim·i·le** (fak sim'ə lē) *n.* ⟦< L *facere*, make + *simile*, like⟧ an exact reproduction or copy

**fact** (fakt) *n.* ⟦< L *facere*, do⟧ **1** a deed, esp. a criminal deed [an accessory before (or after) the *fact*] **2** a thing that has actually happened or is really true **3** reality; truth **4** something stated to be true —**as a matter of fact** in reality: also **in fact**

**fac·tion** (fak'shən) *n.* ⟦see prec.⟧ **1** a group of people in an organization working in a common cause against the main body **2** dissension —**fac'tion·al** *adj.* —**fac'tion·al·ism'** *n.*

**fac'tious** (-shəs) *adj.* causing dissension or faction

**fac·ti·tious** (fak tish'əs) *adj.* ⟦see FACT⟧ forced or artificial

**fac·toid** (fak'toid) *n.* ⟦FACT + -OID⟧ a trivial or useless fact or statistic

**fac·tor** (fak'tər) *n.* ⟦< L *facere*, do⟧ **1** one who transacts business for another **2** any of the conditions, etc. that bring about a result **3** *Math.* any of the quantities which form a product when multiplied together —*vt. Math.* to resolve into factors —**factor in** (or **into**) to include as a factor

**fac·to·ry** (fak'tə rē; *often* fak'trē) *n., pl.* **-ries** ⟦see prec.⟧ a building or buildings in which things are manufactured

**fac·to·tum** (fak tōt'əm) *n.* ⟦< L *facere*, do + *totum*, all⟧ a handyman

**fac·tu·al** (fak'chōō əl) *adj.* **1** of or containing facts **2** real; actual

**fac·ul·ty** (fak'əl tē) *n., pl.* **-ties** ⟦see FACILE⟧ **1** any natural or specialized power of a living organism **2** special aptitude or skill **3** all the teachers of a school or of one of its departments

**fad** (fad) *n.* ⟦< Brit dial.⟧ a style, etc. that interests many people for a short time; passing fashion —**fad'dish** *adj.*

**fade** (fād) *vi.* **fad'ed**, **fad'ing** ⟦< OFr *fade*, pale⟧ **1** to lose color, brilliance, etc. **2** to lose freshness or strength **3** to disappear slowly; die out —*vt.* to cause to fade —**fade in** (or **out**) *Film, Radio, TV* to appear (or disappear) gradually

**fa·er·ie** or **fa·er·y** (fā'ər ē, fer'ē) *n.* [Archaic] **1** fairyland **2** *pl.* **-ies** a fairy

**fag** (fag) *vi., vt.* **fagged**, **fag'ging** ⟦< ?⟧ to make or become very tired by hard work

**fag·ot** or **fag·got** (fag'ət) *n.* ⟦ult. < Gr *phakelos*, a bundle⟧ a bundle of sticks or twigs, esp. for use as fuel

**fag·ot·ing** or **fag·got·ing** (fag'ət iŋ) *n.* **1** a hemstitch with wide spaces **2** openwork with crisscross or barlike stitches across the open seam

**Fahr·en·heit** (fer'ən hīt') *adj.* ⟦after G. D. *Fahrenheit* (1686-1736), Ger physicist⟧ designating or of a thermometer on which 32° is the freezing point and 212° is the boiling point of water

**fail** (fāl) *vi.* ⟦< L *fallere*, deceive⟧ **1** to be insufficient; fall short **2** to weaken; die away **3** to stop operating **4** to be negligent in a duty, expectation, etc. **5** to be unsuccessful **6** to become bankrupt **7** *Educ.* to get a grade of failure —*vt.* **1** to be of no help to; disappoint **2** to leave; abandon **3** to neglect: used with an infinitive **4** *Educ.* to give a grade of failure to or get such a grade in —**without fail** without failing (to occur, do, etc.)

**fail'ing** *n.* **1** a failure **2** a fault —*prep.* without; lacking

**faille** (fīl, fāl) *n.* ⟦Fr⟧ a soft, ribbed fabric of silk or rayon

**fail'-safe'** *adj.* of an intricate procedure for preventing a malfunction or accidental operation, as of nuclear weapons

**fail·ure** (fāl'yər) *n.* **1** *a)* a falling short *b)* a weakening *c)* a breakdown in operation *d)* neglect *e)* a not succeeding *f)* a becoming bankrupt **2** one that does not succeed **3** *Educ.* a failing to pass, or a grade showing this

**fain** (fān) *adj., adv.* ⟦< OE *fægen*, glad⟧ [Archaic] glad(ly); willing(ly)

**faint** (fānt) *adj.* ⟦see FEIGN⟧ **1** weak; feeble **2** timid **3** feeling weak and dizzy **4** dim; indistinct —*n.* a state of temporary unconsciousness —*vi.* to fall into a faint —**faint'ly** *adv.* —**faint'ness** *n.*

**fair**[1] (fer) *adj.* ⟦< OE *fæger*⟧ **1** attractive; beautiful **2** unblemished; clean **3** blond [*fair* hair] **4** clear and sunny **5** easy to read [a *fair* hand] **6** just and honest **7** according to the rules **8** moderately large **9** average [in *fair* condition] **10** *Baseball* that is not foul —*adv.* in a fair manner —**fair'ness** *n.*

**fair**[2] (fer) *n.* ⟦< L *feriae*, festivals⟧ **1** [Historical] a regular gathering for barter and sale of goods **2** a carnival or bazaar, often for charity **3** a competitive exhibition of farm, household, and manufactured products, with various amusements and educational displays **4** a show or convention with exhibits, vendors, etc. [a science *fair*]

**Fair·banks** (fer'baŋks') city in EC Alaska: pop. 31,000

**fair game** a legitimate object of attack or pursuit

**fair'-haired'** *adj.* **1** having blond hair **2** [Inf.] favorite

**fair'ly** *adv.* **1** justly; honestly **2** somewhat; moderately

**fair shake** [Inf.] fair or just treatment

**fair'way'** *n.* the mowed part of a golf course between a tee and a green

**fair·y** (fer'ē) *n., pl.* **-ies** ⟦< OFr *fee*⟧ a tiny, graceful imaginary being in human form, with magic powers —*adj.* **1** of fairies **2** graceful; delicate

**fair'y·land'** *n.* **1** the imaginary land where the fairies live **2** a lovely, enchanting place

**fairy tale 1** a story about fairies, magic deeds, etc. **2** an unbelievable or untrue story

**fait ac·com·pli** (fe tà kôn plē'; *E* fāt'ə käm'plē') ⟦Fr⟧ something done or in effect, making opposition useless

**faith** (fāth) *n.* [< L *fidere*, to trust] **1** unquestioning belief, specif. in God, a religion, etc. **2** a particular religion **3** complete trust or confidence **4** loyalty

**faith′ful** (-fəl) *adj.* **1** loyal **2** conscientious **3** accurate; reliable —**faith′ful·ly** *adv.* —**faith′ful·ness** *n.*

**faith′less** (-lis) *adj.* **1** dishonest or disloyal **2** unreliable —**faith′less·ly** *adv.* —**faith′less·ness** *n.*

**fa·ji·ta** (fä hē′tä) *n.* [AmSp] a dish of grilled strips of beef or chicken, often wrapped in a soft tortilla

**fake** (fāk) *vt., vi.* **faked, fak′ing** [< ?] to make (something) seem real, etc. by deception —*n.* a fraud; counterfeit —*adj.* **1** sham; false **2** artificial —**fak′er·n.** —**fak′er·y** *n.*

**fa·kir** (fə kir′) *n.* [Ar *faqīr*, lit., poor] a Muslim or Hindu itinerant beggar, often one reputed to perform marvels

**fa·la·fel** (fə läf′əl) *n.* [< Ar] a deep-fried patty of ground chickpeas

**fal·con** (fal′kən, fôl′-, fäl′-) *n.* [ult. < L *falx*, sickle] any bird of prey trained to hunt small game —**fal′con·er** *n.* —**fal′con·ry** *n.*

**fall** (fôl) *vi.* **fell, fall′en, fall′ing** [OE *feallan*] **1** to come down by gravity; drop; descend **2** to come down suddenly from an upright position; tumble or collapse **3** to be wounded or killed in battle **4** to take a downward direction **5** to become lower, less, weaker, etc. **6** to lose power, status, etc. **7** to do wrong; sin **8** to be captured **9** to take on a sad look [my face *fell*] **10** to take place; occur **11** to come by lot, inheritance, etc. **12** to pass into a specified condition [to *fall* ill] **13** to be directed by chance **14** to be divided (*into*) —*n.* **1** a dropping; descending **2** a coming down suddenly from an upright position **3** a downward direction or slope **4** a becoming lower or less **5** an overthrow; ruin **6** a loss of status, reputation, etc. **7** a yielding to temptation **8** autumn **9** the amount of what has fallen [a six-inch *fall* of snow] **10** the distance that something falls **11** [*usually pl., often with sing. v.*] water falling over a cliff, etc. **12** a long tress of hair, added to a woman's hairdo —*adj.* of, in, for, or like autumn —**fall back** to withdraw; retreat —**fall for** [Inf.] **1** to fall in love with **2** to be tricked by —**fall in** to line up in formation —**fall off** to become smaller, worse, etc. —**fall on** (or **upon**) to attack —**fall out 1** to quarrel **2** to leave one's place in a formation —**fall short** to fail to reach, suffice, etc. —**fall through** to fail —**fall to 1** to begin **2** to start eating

**fal·la·cious** (fə lā′shəs) *adj.* [see fol.] **1** erroneous **2** misleading or deceptive —**fal·la′cious·ly** *adv.*

**fal·la·cy** (fal′ə sē) *n., pl.* **-cies** [< L *fallere*, deceive] **1** a mistaken idea; error **2** a flaw in reasoning

**fall·en** (fôl′ən) *adj.* that fell; dropped, prostrate, ruined, dead, etc.

**fall guy** [Slang] one put in a position to take the blame, etc. for a scheme that has miscarried

**fal·li·ble** (fal′ə bəl) *adj.* [< L *fallere*, deceive] liable to be mistaken, deceived, or erroneous —**fal′li·bil′i·ty** or **fal′li·ble·ness** *n.* —**fal′li·bly** *adv.*

**fall′ing-out′** *n.* a quarrel

**falling star** METEOR (sense 1)

**fall′off′** *n.* a decline

**fal·lo·pi·an tube** (fə lō′pē ən) [after G. *Fallopius*, 16th-c. It anatomist] [*also* F- t-] either of two tubes that carry ova to the uterus

**fall′out′** *n.* **1** the descent to earth of radioactive particles, as after a nuclear explosion **2** these particles **3** an incidental consequence

**fal·low** (fal′ō) *adj.* [< OE *fealh*] **1** left unplanted **2** inactive

**false** (fôls) *adj.* **fals′er, fals′est** [< L *fallere*, deceive] **1** not true; incorrect; wrong **2** untruthful; lying **3** unfaithful **4** misleading **5** not real; artificial —*adv.* in a false manner —**false′ly** *adv.* —**false′ness** *n.*

**false′hood′** *n.* **1** falsity **2** a lie

**fal·set·to** (fôl set′ō) *n., pl.* **-tos** [It, dim. of *falso*, false] an artificial way of singing in which the voice is much higher pitched than normal

**fal·si·fy** (fôl′sə fī′) *vt.* **-fied′, -fy′ing 1** to misrepresent **2** to alter (a record, etc.) fraudulently —**fal′si·fi·ca′tion** *n.* —**fal′si·fi′er** *n.*

**fal·si·ty** (-tē) *n.* **1** the quality of being false **2** *pl.* **-ties** a lie

**Fal·staff** (fôl′staf′), Sir **John** in Shakespeare's plays, a fat, witty, boastful knight

**fal·ter** (fôl′tər) *vi.* [prob. < ON] **1** to move unsteadily; stumble **2** to stammer **3** to act hesitantly; waver —**fal′ter·ing·ly** *adv.*

**fame** (fām) *n.* [< L *fama*] **1** reputation, esp. for good **2** the state of being well known —**famed** *adj.*

**fa·mil·ial** (fə mil′yəl) *adj.* of or common to a family

**fa·mil·iar** (fə mil′yər) *adj.* [see FAMILY] **1** friendly or intimate **2** too friendly; unduly intimate **3** closely acquainted (*with*) **4** common; ordinary —**fa·mil′iar·ly** *adv.*

**fa·mil·i·ar·i·ty** (-ē er′ə tē) *n., pl.* **-ties 1** intimacy **2** informal behavior **3** undue intimacy **4** close acquaintance (*with* something)

**fa·mil·iar·ize′** (-yər īz′) *vt.* **-ized′, -iz′ing 1** to make commonly known **2** to make (another or oneself) fully acquainted —**fa·mil′iar·i·za′tion** *n.*

**fam·i·ly** (fam′ə lē, fam′lē) *n., pl.* **-lies** [< L *familia*] **1** parents and their children **2** relatives **3** all those descended from a common ancestor; lineage **4** a group of similar or related things —*adj.* suitable for a family; specif., wholesome

**family planning** the regulation, as by birth control methods, of the size, etc. of a family

**family practitioner** a doctor specializing in the general medical needs of the family

**family room** a room in a home set apart for relaxation and recreation

**family tree** a genealogical chart for a given family

**fam·ine** (fam′in) *n.* [< L *fames*, hunger] **1** an acute and general shortage of food **2** any acute shortage

**fam′ish** (-ish) *vt., vi.* [see prec.] to make or be very hungry

**fa·mous** (fā′məs) *adj.* **1** having fame; renowned **2** [Inf.] excellent; very good

**fa′mous·ly** *adv.* **1** in a way, statement, etc. that has become famous **2** very well

**fan¹** (fan) *n.* [< L *vannus*, basket for winnowing grain] any device used to set up a current of air for ventilating or cooling —*vt.* **fanned, fan′ning 1** to move (air) as with a fan **2** to direct air toward as with a fan **3** to stir up; excite **4** to strike (a batter) out —*vi.* Baseball to strike out —**fan out** to spread out

**fan²** (fan) *n.* [< FAN(ATIC)] a person enthusiastic about a specified sport, performer, etc.

**fa·nat·ic** (fə nat′ik) *n.* [< L *fanum*, temple] a fanatic person —*adj.* fanatical —**fa·nat′i·cism′** *n.*

**fa·nat′i·cal** *adj.* unreasonably enthusiastic; overly zealous —**fa·nat′i·cal·ly** *adv.*

**fan·ci·er** (fan′sē ər) *n.* a person with a special interest in something, specif. in plant or animal breeding

**fan·ci·ful** (fan′sə fəl) *adj.* **1** full of fancy; imaginative **2** imaginary; not real —**fan·ci·ful·ly** *adv.*

**fan·cy** (fan′sē) *n., pl.* **-cies** [contr. < ME *fantasie*, fantasy] **1** imagination when light, playful, etc. **2** a mental image **3** a notion; caprice; whim **4** a liking or fondness —*adj.* **-ci·er, -ci·est 1** extravagant [a *fancy* price] **2** ornamental; elaborate [a *fancy* necktie] **3** of superior skill or quality —*vt.* **-cied, -cy·ing 1** to imagine **2** to be fond of **3** to suppose —**fan′ci·ly** *adv.* —**fan′ci·ness** *n.*

**fan′cy-free′** *adj.* carefree

**fan′cy·work′** *n.* embroidery, crocheting, and other ornamental needlework

**fan·dom** (fan′dəm) *n.* fans collectively, as of a sport or entertainer

**fan·fare** (fan′fer′) [Fr, prob. < *fanfaron*, braggart]

**n. 1** a loud flourish of trumpets **2** noisy or showy display

**fang** (faŋ) *n.* ⟦OE < *fon*, seize⟧ **1** one of the long, pointed teeth of meat-eating mammals **2** one of the long, hollow teeth through which poisonous snakes inject venom

**fan·ta·sia** (fan tā′zhə) *n.* a musical composition having no fixed form

FANGS

**fan·ta·size** (fant′ə sīz′) *vt.*, *vi.* **-sized′**, **-siz′ing** to indulge in fantasies or have daydreams (about)

**fan·tas·tic** (fan tas′tik) *adj.* ⟦see fol.⟧ **1** imaginary; unreal **2** grotesque; odd **3** extravagant **4** incredible **—fan·tas′ti·cal·ly** *adv.*

**fan·ta·sy** (fant′ə sē) *n.*, *pl.* **-sies** ⟦< Gr *phainein*, to show⟧ **1** imagination or fancy **2** an illusion or reverie **3** fiction portraying highly IMAGINATIVE (sense 2) characters or settings

**fan′ta·sy·land′** *n.* any imaginary or unreal place

**far** (fär) *adj.* **far′ther**, **far′thest** ⟦OE *feorr*⟧ **1** distant in space or time **2** more distant /the *far* side/ **3** very different in quality or nature /*far* from poor/ **—adv. 1** very distant in space, time, or degree **2** to or from a distance in time or position **3** very much /*far* better/ **—as far as** to the distance or degree that **—by far** very much; considerably: also **far and away —(in) so far as** to the extent that **—so far** up to this place, time, or degree

**far′a·way′** *adj.* **1** distant in time, place, etc. **2** dreamy

**farce** (färs) *n.* ⟦Fr < L *farcire*, to stuff⟧ **1** (an) exaggerated comedy based on broadly humorous situations **2** an absurd or ridiculous action, pretense, etc. **—far′ci·cal** (fär′si kəl) *adj.*

**fare** (fer) *vi.* **fared**, **far′ing** ⟦< OE *faran*, go⟧ **1** to happen; result **2** to be in a specified condition /to *fare* well/ **—n. 1** money paid for transportation **2** a passenger who pays a fare **3** food

**Far East** EAST ASIA

**fare·well** (fer wel′; *for adj.* fer′wel′) *interj.* goodbye **—n.** good wishes at parting **—adj.** parting; final /a *farewell* gesture/

**far-fetched** (fär′fecht′) *adj.* barely believable; strained; unlikely

**far′-flung′** (-fluŋ′) *adj.* extending over a wide area

**fa·ri·na** (fə rē′nə) *n.* ⟦< L, meal⟧ flour or meal made from cereal grains, potatoes, etc. and eaten as a cooked cereal

**far·i·na·ceous** (far′ə nā′shəs) *adj.* ⟦see prec.⟧ **1** consisting of or made from flour or meal **2** like meal

**farm** (färm) *n.* ⟦< ML *firma*, fixed payment⟧ **1** a piece of land (with house, barns, etc.) on which crops or animals are raised: orig., such land let out to tenants **2** any place where certain things are raised /a fish *farm*/ **—vt.** to cultivate (land) **—vi.** to work on or operate a farm **—farm out** to send (work) from an office, etc. to workers outside the office

**farm′er** *n.* a person who manages or operates a farm

**farm′hand′** *n.* a hired farm worker

**farm′house′** *n.* a house on a farm

**farm′ing** *n.* the business of operating a farm; agriculture

**farm′yard′** *n.* the yard surrounding or enclosed by farm buildings

**far·o** (fer′ō) *n.* ⟦Fr *pharaon*, pharaoh: from the picture of a Pharaoh on early French faro cards⟧ a gambling game played with cards

**far′-off′** *adj.* distant; remote

**far′-out′** *adj.* [Inf.] nonconformist; esp., avant-garde

**far·ra·go** (fə rā′gō, -rä′-) *n.*, *pl.* **-goes** ⟦< L *far*, kind of grain⟧ a jumble

**far′-reach′ing** *adj.* having a wide range, extent, influence, or effect

**far·ri·er** (far′ē ər) *n.* ⟦< L *ferrum*, iron⟧ [Chiefly Brit.] a blacksmith

**far·row** (far′ō) *n.* ⟦< OE *fearh*, young pig⟧ a litter of pigs **—vt.**, *vi.* to give birth to (a litter of pigs)

**far·sight·ed** (fär′sīt′id; *for 2*, -sīt′əd) *adj.* **1** planning ahead; provident: also **far′see′ing 2** seeing distant objects more clearly than near ones **—far′sight′ed·ness** *n.*

**far·ther** (fär′thər) *adj.* **1** *compar. of* FAR **2** more distant **3** additional; further **—adv. 1** *compar. of* FAR **2** at or to a greater distance **3** to a greater degree; further Cf. FURTHER

**far·thest** (fär′thist) *adj.* **1** *superl. of* FAR **2** most distant **—adv. 1** *superl. of* FAR **2** at or to the greatest distance or degree

**far·thing** (fär′thiŋ) *n.* ⟦OE *feorthing*⟧ a former British coin worth ¼ penny

**fas·ci·nate** (fas′ə nāt′) *vt.* **-nat′ed**, **-nat′ing** ⟦< L *fascinum*, a charm⟧ to hold the attention of, as by being very interesting or delightful; charm; captivate **—fas′ci·na′tion** *n.*

**fas·cism** (fash′iz′əm) *n.* ⟦< It < L *fasces*, rods bound about an ax, ancient Roman symbol of authority⟧ [*sometimes* F-] a system of government characterized by dictatorship, belligerent nationalism and racism, militarism, etc. **—fas′cist** *n.*, *adj.*

**fash·ion** (fash′ən) *n.* ⟦< L *factio*, a making⟧ **1** the form or shape of a thing **2** way; manner **3** the current style of dress, conduct, etc. **—vt. 1** to make; form **2** to fit; accommodate (*to*) **—after** (or **in**) **a fashion** to some extent **—fash′ion·er** *n.*

**fash′ion·a·ble** *adj.* **1** stylish **2** of or used by people who follow fashion **—fash′ion·a·bly** *adv.*

**fast**[1] (fast) *adj.* ⟦OE *fæst*⟧ **1** firm; firmly fastened **2** loyal; devoted **3** nonfading /*fast* colors/ **4** swift; quick **5** ahead of time /a *fast* watch/ **6** wild, promiscuous, or reckless **7** [Inf.] glib **8** *Photog.* allowing very short exposure time **—adv. 1** firmly; fixedly **2** thoroughly /*fast* asleep/ **3** rapidly

**fast**[2] (fast) *vi.* ⟦OE *fæstan*⟧ to abstain from all or certain foods **—n. 1** a fasting **2** a period of fasting

**fas·ten** (fas′ən) *vt.* ⟦see FAST[1]⟧ **1** to attach; connect **2** to make secure, as by locking, buttoning, etc. **3** to fix (the attention, etc.) *on* something **—vi.** to become fastened **—fas′ten·er** *n.*

**fas′ten·ing** *n.* anything used to fasten; bolt, clasp, hook, etc.

**fast′-food′** *adj.* designating a business that offers food, as hamburgers, prepared and served quickly

**fast forward 1** the setting on a VCR, etc. that allows the user to advance the tape or disc rapidly **2** the act or condition of speeding up and advancing **—fast′-for′ward** *vi.*, *vt.*

**fas·tid·i·ous** (fa stid′ē əs) *adj.* ⟦< L *fastus*, disdain⟧ **1** not easy to please **2** daintily refined; oversensitive **—fas·tid′i·ous·ly** *adv.* **—fas·tid′i·ous·ness** *n.*

**fast′ness** *n.* **1** a being fast **2** a stronghold

**fast′-talk′** *vt.* [Inf.] to persuade with smooth, but often deceitful talk

**fat** (fat) *adj.* **fat′ter**, **fat′test** ⟦< OE *fætt*⟧ **1** containing fat; oily **2** *a*) fleshy; plump *b*) too plump **3** thick; broad **4** fertile /*fat* land/ **5** profitable /a *fat* job/ **6** plentiful **—n. 1** an oily or greasy material found in animal tissue and plant seeds **2** the richest part of anything **3** superfluous part **—chew the fat** [Slang] to chat **—fat′ly** *adv.* **—fat′ness** *n.*

**fa·tal** (fāt′l) *adj.* **1** fateful; decisive **2** resulting in death **3** destructive; disastrous **—fa′tal·ly** *adv.*

**fa′tal·ism′** *n.* the belief that all events are determined by fate and are hence inevitable **—fa′tal·ist** *n.* **—fa′tal·is′tic** *adj.* **—fa′tal·is′ti·cal·ly** *adv.*

**fa·tal·i·ty** (fā tal′ə tē, fə-) *n.*, *pl.* **-ties 1** a deadly effect; deadliness **2** a death caused by a disaster or accident

**fat′back′** *n.* fat from a hog's back, usually dried and salted in strips

**fat cat** [Slang] a wealthy, influential donor, esp. to a political campaign

**fate** (fāt) *n.* ⟦< L *fatum*, oracle⟧ **1** the power supposed to determine the outcome of events; destiny **2** one's lot or fortune **3** final outcome **4** death; destruction

**fat·ed** (fāt′id) *adj.* **1** destined **2** doomed

**fate′ful** (-fəl) *adj.* **1** prophetic **2** significant; decisive **3** controlled as if by fate —**fate′ful·ly** *adv.*

**Fates** (fāts) *pl.n. Gr. & Rom. Myth.* the three goddesses who control human destiny and life

**fa·ther** (fä′thər) *n.* ⟦OE *fæder*⟧ **1** a male parent **2** an ancestor **3** an originator, founder, or inventor **4** [*often* F-] a Christian priest: used esp. as a title **5** [F-] God —*vt.* to be the father of —**fa′ther·hood′** *n.* —**fa′ther·less** *adj.*

**fa·ther-in-law′** *n., pl.* **fa′thers-in-law′** the father of one's spouse

**fa′ther·land′** *n.* one's native land

**fa′ther·ly** *adj.* of or like a father; kind, protective, etc. —**fa′ther·li·ness** *n.*

**fath·om** (fath′əm) *n.* ⟦< OE *fæthm*, the two arms outstretched⟧ a length of 6 feet, used as a nautical unit of depth or length —*vt.* **1** to measure the depth of **2** to understand thoroughly —**fath′om·a·ble** *adj.* —**fath′om·less** *adj.*

**fa·tigue** (fə tēg′) *n.* ⟦Fr < L *fatigare*, to weary⟧ **1** exhaustion; weariness **2** [*pl.*] soldiers' work clothing **3** the tendency of a metal, etc. to crack under continued stress —*vt., vi.* **-tigued′, -tigu′ing** to tire out

**fat·so** (fat′sō) *n., pl.* **-sos** or **-soes** [Slang] a fat person

**fat·ten** (fat′n) *vt., vi.* to make or become fat (in various senses)

**fat′ty** *adj.* **-ti·er, -ti·est 1** of or containing fat **2** like fat; greasy

**fatty acid** any of a group of organic acids in animal or vegetable fats and oils

**fat·u·ous** (fach′ōō əs) *adj.* ⟦L *fatuus*⟧ complacently stupid; foolish —**fa·tu·i·ty** (fə tōō′ə tē) *n.* —**fat′u·ous·ly** *adv.* —**fat′u·ous·ness** *n.*

**fau·cet** (fô′sit) *n.* ⟦prob. < OFr *faulser*, to breach⟧ a device with a valve for regulating the flow of a liquid from a pipe, etc.; tap

**Faulk·ner** (fôk′nər), **Wil·liam** (wil′yəm) 1897-1962; U.S. novelist

**fault** (fôlt) *n.* ⟦< L *fallere*, deceive⟧ **1** something that mars; defect or failing **2** a misdeed or mistake **3** blame for something wrong **4** a fracture in rock strata **5** *Tennis, etc.* an improper serve — **at fault** deserving blame —**find fault (with)** to criticize

**fault′find′ing** *n., adj.* criticizing

**fault′less** *adj.* perfect

**fault′y** *adj.* **fault′i·er, fault′i·est** having a fault or faults; defective —**fault′i·ly** *adv.* —**fault′i·ness** *n.*

**faun** (fôn) *n.* ⟦< L *faunus*⟧ any of a class of minor Roman deities, half man and half goat

**fau·na** (fô′nə) *n.* ⟦< LL *Fauna*, Roman goddess⟧ the animals of a specified region or time

**Faust** (foust) *n.* a man in legend and literature who sells his soul to the devil for knowledge and power —**Faus′ti·an** *adj.*

**faux pas** (fō pä′) *pl.* **faux pas** (fō päz′) ⟦Fr, lit., false step⟧ a social blunder

**fa·vor** (fā′vər) *n.* ⟦< L *favere*, to favor⟧ **1** friendly regard; approval **2** partiality **3** a kind or obliging act **4** a small gift or token —*vt.* **1** to approve or like **2** to be partial to **3** to support; advocate **4** to make easier; help **5** to do a kindness for **6** to resemble [to *favor* one's mother] **7** to use gently [to *favor* a sore leg] Brit. sp. **fa′vour** —**in favor of 1** approving **2** to the advantage of —**fa′vor·er** *n.*

**fa′vor·a·ble** *adj.* **1** approving **2** helpful **3** pleasing —**fa′vor·a·bly** *adv.*

**fa·vor·ite** (fā′vər it) *n.* **1** a person or thing regarded with special liking **2** a contestant regarded as most likely to win —*adj.* highly regarded; preferred

**fa′vor·it·ism′** *n.* partiality; bias

**fawn**[1] (fôn) *vi.* ⟦< OE *fægen*, glad⟧ **1** to show friendliness by licking hands, etc.: said of a dog **2** to try to gain favor by acting humble, flattering, etc. —**fawn′er** *n.* —**fawn′ing·ly** *adv.*

**fawn**[2] (fôn) *n.* ⟦< L *fetus*, progeny⟧ **1** a deer less than one year old **2** a pale, yellowish brown — *adj.* of this color

**fax** (faks) *n.* ⟦< FACSIMILE⟧ **1** the electronic sending (as over a telephone line) and reproduction of pictures, print, etc. **2** a reproduction made in this way —*vt.* to send by fax

**fay** (fā) *n.* ⟦see FATE⟧ a fairy

**faze** (fāz) *vt.* **fazed, faz′ing** ⟦< OE *fesian*, to drive⟧ to disturb; disconcert

**FBI** *abbrev.* Federal Bureau of Investigation

**FCC** *abbrev.* Federal Communications Commission

**FDA** *abbrev.* Food and Drug Administration

**FDIC** *abbrev.* Federal Deposit Insurance Corporation

**Fe** ⟦L *ferrum*⟧ *Chem. symbol for* iron

**fe·al·ty** (fē′əl tē) *n., pl.* **-ties** ⟦< L *fidelitas*, fidelity⟧ loyalty, esp. as owed to a feudal lord

**fear** (fir) *n.* ⟦< OE *fær*, sudden attack⟧ **1** anxiety caused by real or possible danger, pain, etc.; fright **2** awe; reverence **3** apprehension; concern **4** a cause for fear —*vt., vi.* **1** to be afraid (of) **2** to be in awe (of) **3** to expect with misgiving [I *fear* it will rain] —**fear′less** *adj.* —**fear′less·ly** *adv.*

**fear′ful** (-fəl) *adj.* **1** causing, feeling, or showing fear **2** [Inf.] very bad, great, etc. —**fear′ful·ly** *adv.* —**fear′ful·ness** *n.*

**fear′some** *adj.* causing fear; frightful

**fea·si·ble** (fē′zə bəl) *adj.* ⟦< OFr *faire*, to do⟧ **1** capable of being done; possible **2** likely; probable **3** suitable —**fea′si·bil′i·ty** *n.* —**fea′si·bly** *adv.*

**feast** (fēst) *n.* ⟦< L *festus*, festal⟧ **1** a religious festival **2** a rich and elaborate meal; banquet — *vi.* to have a feast —*vt.* **1** to entertain at a feast **2** to delight [to *feast* one's eyes on a sight]

**feat** (fēt) *n.* ⟦< L *factum*, a deed⟧ a deed of unusual daring or skill; exploit

**feath·er** (feth′ər) *n.* ⟦OE *fether*⟧ any of the soft, light growths covering the body of a bird —*vt.* **1** to provide or adorn with feathers **2** to turn (an oar or propeller blade) so that the edge is foremost —**feather in one's cap** a distinctive achievement —**feath′er·y** *adj.*

**feath′er·bed′ding** *n.* the practice of limiting output or requiring extra, standby workers

**feath′er·weight′** *n.* **1** a boxer with a maximum weight of 126 pounds **2** any person or thing of light weight or small size

**fea·ture** (fē′chər) *n.* ⟦< L *facere*, to make⟧ **1** *a*) [*pl.*] facial form or appearance *b*) any of the parts of the face **2** a distinct or outstanding part or quality of something **3** a special attraction, sale item, newspaper article, etc. **4** a film running more than 34 minutes —*vt.* **-tured, -tur·ing** to make a feature of —*vi.* to have a prominent part —**fea′ture·less** *adj.*

**fe·brile** (fē′brəl, feb′rəl) *adj.* ⟦< L *febris*, FEVER⟧ feverish

**Feb·ru·ar·y** (feb′rōō er′ē, feb′yōō-) *n., pl.* **-ies** or **-ys** ⟦< L *Februarius* (*mensis*), orig. month of expiation⟧ the second month of the year, having 28 days (or 29 days in leap years): abbrev. **Feb.**

**fe·ces** (fē′sēz′) *pl.n.* ⟦< L *faeces*, dregs⟧ excrement —**fe′cal** (-kəl) *adj.*

**feck·less** (fek′lis) *adj.* ⟦Scot < *feck*, effect + -LESS⟧ **1** weak; ineffective **2** irresponsible —**feck′less·ly** *adv.*

**fe·cund** (fē′kənd, fek′ənd) *adj.* ⟦< L *fecundus*⟧ fertile; productive —**fe·cun·di·ty** (fē kun′də tē) *n.*

**fe·cun·date** (fē′kən dāt′, fek′ən-) *vt.* **-dat′ed, -dat′ing 1** to make fecund **2** to fertilize

**fed** (fed) *vt., vi. pt. & pp. of* FEED —**fed up** [Inf.]

having had enough to become disgusted, bored, etc.

**Fed** *abbrev.* **1** Federal **2** Federation

**fed·a·yeen** (fed′ä yēn′) *pl.n.* [[Ar *fidā′īyīn*, sacrificers]] Arab guerrillas

**fed·er·al** (fed′ər əl) *adj.* [[< L *foedus*, a league]] **1** designating or of a union of states, etc. in which each member subordinates its power to a central authority **2** *a*) designating or of a central government in such a union *b*) [*often* F-] designating or of the central government of the U.S. **3** [F-] of or supporting a former U.S. political party (**Federalist Party**) which favored a strong centralized government **4** [F-] of or supporting the Union in the Civil War —*n.* [F-] a supporter or soldier of the Union in the Civil War —**fed′er·al·ism′** *n.* — **fed′er·al·ist** *adj., n.* —**fed′er·al·ly** *adv.*

**fed′er·al·ize′** (-īz′) *vt.* **-ized′, -iz′ing** **1** to unite (states, etc.) in a federal union **2** to put under federal authority —**fed′er·al·i·za′tion** *n.*

**fed·er·ate** (fed′ər āt′) *vt., vi.* **-at′ed, -at′ing** to unite in a federation

**fed·er·a·tion** (fed′ər ā′shən) *n.* [[see FEDERAL]] **1** a union of states, groups, etc. in which each subordinates its power to that of the central authority **2** a federated organization

**fe·do·ra** (fə dôr′ə) *n.* [[Fr]] a soft felt hat worn by men

**fee** (fē) *n.* [[ult < Gmc]] a charge for professional services, licenses, etc.

**fee·ble** (fē′bəl) *adj.* **-bler, -blest** [[< L *flere*, weep]] **1** weak; infirm [a *feeble* old man] **2** without force or effectiveness [a *feeble* attempt] —**fee′ble·ness** *n.* —**fee′bly** *adv.*

**feed** (fēd) *vt.* **fed, feed′ing** [[< OE *foda*, food]] **1** to give food to **2** to provide something necessary for the growth, operation, etc. of **3** to gratify [to *feed* one's vanity] —*vi.* to eat: said esp. of animals —*n.* **1** food for animals; fodder **2** *a*) the material fed into a machine *b*) the part of the machine supplying this material **3** *Radio, TV* a transmission sent by a network, etc. to individual stations for broadcast —**feed′er** *n.*

**feed′back′** *n.* **1** the transfer of part of the output back to the input, as of electricity or information **2** a response

**feed′stock′** *n.* raw material for industrial processing

**feel** (fēl) *vt.* **felt, feel′ing** [[OE *felan*]] **1** to touch; examine by handling **2** to be aware of through physical sensation **3** to experience (an emotion or condition); be affected by **4** to be aware of **5** to think or believe —*vi.* **1** to have physical sensation **2** to appear to be to the senses [it *feels* warm] **3** to grope **4** to be aware of being [I *feel* sad] **5** to be moved to sympathy, pity, etc. (*for*) —*n.* **1** the act of feeling **2** the sense of touch **3** the nature of a thing as perceived through touch **4** an instinctive ability or appreciation [a *feel* for politics] —**feel like** [Inf.] to have a desire for —**feel one's way** to advance cautiously —**feel out** to try cautiously to find out the opinions of (someone) — **feel up to** [Inf.] to feel capable of

**feel′er** *n.* **1** a specialized organ of touch in an animal or insect, as an antenna **2** a cautious remark, offer, etc. made to learn more about something

**feel′ing** *n.* **1** the sense of touch **2** the ability to experience physical sensation **3** an awareness; sensation **4** an emotion **5** [*pl.*] sensibilities [hurt *feelings*] **6** sympathy; pity **7** an opinion or sentiment

**fee simple** absolute and unrestricted ownership of real property

**feet** (fēt) *n. pl. of* FOOT

**feign** (fān) *vt., vi.* [[< L *fingere*, to shape]] **1** to make up (an excuse, etc.) **2** to pretend; dissemble

**feint** (fānt) *n.* [[see prec.]] a pretended attack intended to take the opponent off guard, as in boxing —*vi., vt.* to deliver (such an attack)

**feist·y** (fīs′tē) *adj.* **-i·er, -i·est** [[< Norw *fisa*, to puff + -Y²]] [Inf. or Dial.] full of spirit; specif., quarrel-

some, lively, spunky, etc. —**feist′i·ly** *adv.* —**feist′i·ness** *n.*

**feld·spar** (feld′spär′) *n.* [[< Ger *feld*, field + *spath*, a mineral]] any of several hard, glassy minerals

**fe·lic·i·tate** (fə lis′i tāt′) *vt.* **-tat′ed, -tat′ing** [[< L *felix*, happy]] to wish happiness to; congratulate —**fe·lic′i·ta′tor** *n.*

**fe·lic′i·tous** (-təs) *adj.* [[< fol.]] used or expressed in a way suitable to the occasion; appropriate

**fe·lic′i·ty** (-tē) *n., pl.* **-ties** [[< L *felix*, happy]] **1** happiness; bliss **2** anything producing happiness **3** apt and pleasing expression in writing, etc.

**fe·line** (fē′līn) *adj.* [[< L *feles*, cat]] **1** of a cat or the cat family **2** catlike; sly —*n.* any animal of the cat family

**fell¹** (fel) *vi., vt. pt. of* FALL

**fell²** (fel) *vt.* [[OE *fellan*]] **1** to knock down **2** to cut down (a tree)

**fell³** (fel) *adj.* [[< ML *fello*]] fierce; cruel

**fel·low** (fel′ō, -ə) *n.* [[Late OE *feolaga*, partner]] **1** an associate **2** one of the same rank; equal **3** one of a pair; mate **4** one holding a fellowship in a college, etc. **5** a member of a learned society **6** [Inf.] a man or boy —*adj.* **1** having the same position, work, etc. **2** associated [*fellow* workers]

**fel′low·ship′** *n.* **1** companionship **2** a mutual sharing **3** a group of people with the same interests **4** an endowment for the support of a student or scholar doing advanced work

**fellow traveler** a nonmember who supports the cause of a party

**fel·on¹** (fel′ən) *n.* [[< ML *felo*, villain]] a person guilty of a felony; criminal

**fel·on²** (fel′ən) *n.* [[ME]] a painful infection at the end of a finger or toe

**fel·o·ny** (fel′ə nē) *n., pl.* **-nies** [[< ML *felonia*, treachery]] a major crime, as murder, arson, etc. —**fe·lo·ni·ous** (fə lō′nē əs) *adj.*

**felt¹** (felt) *n.* [[< OE]] a fabric of wool, often mixed with fur, hair, cotton, etc., worked together by pressure, etc. —*adj.* made of felt —*vt.* to make into felt

**felt²** (felt) *vt., vi. pt. and pp. of* FEEL

**fem** *abbrev.* **1** female **2** feminine

**fe·male** (fē′māl′) *adj.* [[< L *femina*, woman]] **1** designating or of the sex that bears offspring **2** of, like, or suitable to women or girls; feminine **3** consisting of women or girls **4** having a hollow part for receiving an inserted part (called *male*): said of electric sockets, etc. —*n.* a female person, animal, or plant

**fem·i·nine** (fem′ə nin) *adj.* [[< L *femina*, woman]] **1** of women or girls **2** having qualities characteristic of or suitable to women; gentle, delicate, etc. **3** *Gram.* designating or of the gender of words referring to females or other words with no distinction of sex —**fem′i·nin′i·ty** *n.*

**fem′i·nism′** (-niz′əm) *n.* the movement to win political, economic, and social equality for women —**fem′i·nist** *n., adj.* —**fem′i·nis′tic** *adj.*

**fe·mur** (fē′mər) *n., pl.* **fe′murs** or **fem·o·ra** (fem′ə rə) [[< L, thigh]] the bone extending from the hip to the knee —**fem′o·ral** *adj.*

**fen** (fen) *n.* [[OE]] an area of low, flat, marshy land; swamp; bog

**fence** (fens) *n.* [[< ME *defens*, defense]] **1** a protective or confining barrier of posts, wire mesh, etc. **2** one who deals in stolen goods —*vt.* **fenced, fenc′ing** **1** to enclose, as with a fence: with *in, off*, etc. **2** to keep (*out*) as by a fence **3** to sell (stolen property) to a fence —*vi.* **1** to practice the art of fencing **2** to avoid giving a direct reply —**on the fence** uncommitted or undecided —**fenc′er** *n.*

**fenc′ing** *n.* **1** the art of fighting with a foil or other sword **2** material for making fences **3** a system of fences

**fend** (fend) *vt.* [[ME *fenden*, defend]] to turn aside; ward (*off*) —*vi.* —**fend for oneself** to manage by oneself

**fend′er** *n.* anything that fends off or protects

something else, as the part of an automobile body over the wheel

**fen·nel** (fen′əl) *n.* 〚< L *fenum,* hay〛 a tall herb with aromatic seeds used to flavor foods and medicines

**fe·ral** (fir′əl, fer′-) *adj.* 〚< L *ferus,* wild〛 **1** untamed; wild **2** savage; fierce

**fer·ment** (fʉr′ment′; *for v.* fər ment′) *n.* 〚< L *fervere,* to boil〛 **1** a substance causing fermentation, as yeast **2** excitement or agitation —*vt.* **1** to cause fermentation in **2** to excite; agitate —*vi.* **1** to be in the process of fermentation **2** to be excited or agitated; seethe

**fer·men·ta·tion** (fʉr′mən tā′shən) *n.* **1** the breakdown of complex molecules in organic compounds, caused by the influence of a ferment /bacteria cause milk to curdle by *fermentation*/ **2** excitement; agitation

**fer·mi·on** (fer′mē än′, fʉr′-) *n.* 〚after E. *Fermi,* 20th-c. U.S. nuclear physicist〛 any of a major subdivision of subatomic particles, including leptons and baryons

**fern** (fʉrn) *n.* 〚< OE *fearn*〛 any of a large group of nonflowering plants having roots, stems, and fronds, and reproducing by spores

**fe·ro·cious** (fə rō′shəs) *adj.* 〚< L *ferus,* wild〛 **1** fierce; savage; violently cruel **2** [Inf.] very great /a *ferocious* appetite/ —**fe·ro′cious·ly** *adv.* —**fe·roc·i·ty** (fə räs′ə tē) *n.*

**-fer·ous** (fər əs) 〚< L *ferre,* to bear〛 *suffix* bearing, yielding

FERN

**fer·ret** (fer′ət) *n.* 〚< L *fur,* thief〛 a small European polecat, easily tamed for hunting rats, etc. —*vt.* **1** to force out of hiding with or as if with a ferret **2** to find out by investigation: with *out*

**fer·ric** (fer′ik) *adj.* 〚< L *ferrum,* iron〛 of, containing, or derived from iron

**Fer·ris wheel** (fer′is) 〚after G. *Ferris* (1859-96), U.S. engineer〛 a large, upright wheel revolving on a fixed axle and having suspended seats: used as an amusement ride

**ferro-** 〚< L *ferrum,* iron〛 *combining form* **1** iron **2** iron and

**fer·rous** (fer′əs) *adj.* 〚< L *ferrum,* iron〛 of, containing, or derived from iron

**fer·rule** (fer′əl, -ool′) *n.* 〚< L *viriae,* bracelets〛 a metal ring or cap put around the end of a cane, tool handle, etc. to give added strength

**fer·ry** (fer′ē) *vt.* **-ried, -ry·ing** 〚OE *ferian*〛 **1** to take (people, cars, etc.) across a river, etc. **2** to deliver (airplanes) by flying them **3** to transport by airplane —*n., pl.* **-ries 1** a system for carrying people, goods, etc. across a river, etc. by boat **2** a boat used for this: also **fer′ry·boat′**

**fer·tile** (fʉrt′'l) *adj.* 〚< L *ferre,* to bear〛 **1** producing abundantly; fruitful; prolific **2** able to produce young, seeds, fruit, pollen, spores, etc. **3** fertilized /a *fertile* egg/ —**fer·til·i·ty** (fər til′ə tē) *n.*

**fer·til·ize′** (-īz′) *vt.* **-ized, -iz′ing 1** to make fertile **2** to spread fertilizer on **3** to make (the female cell or female) fruitful by pollinating, or impregnating, with the male gamete —**fer′til·iz′a·ble** *adj.* —**fer′til·i·za′tion** *n.*

**fer′til·iz′er** *n.* manure, chemicals, etc., used to enrich the soil

**fer·ule** (fer′əl, -ool′) *n.* 〚< L *ferula,* a whip, rod〛 a flat stick or ruler used for punishing children

**fer·vent** (fʉr′vənt) *adj.* 〚< L *fervere,* to glow〛 showing great warmth of feeling; intensely

devoted or earnest —**fer′ven·cy** *n.* —**fer′vent·ly** *adv.*

**fer·vid** (fʉr′vid) *adj.* 〚see prec.〛 impassioned; fervent —**fer′vid·ly** *adv.*

**fer·vor** (fʉr′vər) *n.* 〚see FERVENT〛 great warmth of emotion; ardor; zeal

**-fest** (fest) 〚< Ger *fest,* a feast〛 *combining form* an occasion of much or many /songfest/

**fes·tal** (fes′təl) *adj.* 〚< L *festum,* feast〛 of or like a joyous celebration; festive

**fes·ter** (fes′tər) *n.* 〚< L *fistula,* ulcer〛 a small sore filled with pus —*vi.* **1** to form pus **2** to grow more bitter, virulent, etc.

**fes·ti·val** (fes′tə vəl) *n.* 〚see fol.〛 **1** a time or day of feasting or celebration **2** a celebration or series of performances

**fes·tive** (fes′tiv) *adj.* 〚< L *festum,* feast〛 **1** of or for a feast or festival **2** merry; joyous —**fes′tive·ly** *adv.* —**fes′tive·ness** *n.*

**fes·tiv·i·ty** (fes tiv′ə tē) *n., pl.* **-ties 1** merrymaking; gaiety **2** a festival **3** [*pl.*] things done in celebration

**fes·toon** (fes toon′) *n.* 〚< It *festa,* feast〛 a wreath or garland of flowers, etc. hanging in a loop or curve —*vt.* to adorn with festoons

**fet·a (cheese)** (fet′ə) 〚< ModGr < It *fetta,* a slice〛 a soft, white cheese, first made in Greece

**fe·tal** (fēt′'l) *adj.* of a fetus

**fetch** (fech) *vt.* 〚OE *feccan*〛 **1** to go after and bring back; get **2** to cause to come **3** to sell for

**fetch′ing** *adj.* attractive; charming

**fete** or **fête** (fāt, fet) *n.* 〚Fr *fête:* see FEAST〛 a festival; entertainment, esp. outdoors —*vt.* **fet′ed** or **fêt′ed, fet′ing** or **fêt′ing** to honor with a fete

**fet·id** (fet′id) *adj.* 〚< L *foetere,* to stink〛 having a bad smell; stinking; putrid —**fet′id·ness** *n.*

**fet·ish** (fet′ish) *n.* 〚< Port *feitiço*〛 **1** any object believed to have magic power **2** anything to which one is irrationally devoted **3** any nonsexual object that abnormally excites erotic feelings Also **fet′ich** —**fet′ish·ism′** *n.* —**fet′ish·ist** *n.*

**fet·lock** (fet′läk′) *n.* 〚< ME *fet,* feet〛 **1** a tuft of hair on the back of a horse's leg above the hoof **2** the joint bearing this tuft

**fe·to·scope** (fē′tə skōp′) *n.* **1** an endoscope used to examine a fetus in the womb **2** a special stethoscope used to listen to the fetal heartbeat

**fet·ter** (fet′ər) *n.* 〚< OE *fot,* foot〛 **1** a shackle or chain for the feet **2** any check or restraint —*vt.* **1** to bind with fetters **2** to restrain

**fet·tle** (fet′'l) *n.* 〚ME *fetlen,* make ready〛 condition; state /in fine *fettle*/

**fe·tus** (fēt′əs) *n., pl.* **-tus·es** 〚L, a bringing forth〛 the unborn young of an animal, esp. in its later stages and specif., in humans, from about the eighth week after conception until birth

**feud** (fyood) *n.* 〚< OFr *faide*〛 a deadly quarrel, esp. between clans or families —*vi.* to carry on a feud; quarrel

**feu·dal** (fyood′'l) *adj.* 〚ML *feudalis*〛 of or like feudalism

**feu·dal·ism′** *n.* the economic, political, and social system in medieval Europe, in which land, worked by serfs, was held by vassals in exchange for military and other services they give to overlords —**feu′dal·is′tic** *adj.*

**fe·ver** (fē′vər) *n.* 〚< L *febris*〛 **1** an abnormally increased body temperature **2** any disease marked by a high fever **3** a restless excitement —**fe′ver·ish** *adj.* —**fe′ver·ish·ly** *adv.*

**fever blister** (or **sore**) COLD SORE

**few** (fyoo) *adj.* 〚OE *feawe*〛 not many; a small number of —*pron.* not many; a small number — **few and far between** scarce; rare —**the few** the minority

**fey** (fā) *adj.* 〚OE *fæge,* fated〛 strange or unusual; specif., eccentric, whimsical, etc. —**fey′ness** *n.*

**fez** (fez) *n., pl.* **fez′zes** 〚after *Fez,* city in Morocco〛 a red, brimless felt hat, shaped like a truncated cone, worn formerly by Turkish men

**ff** *abbrev.* **1** folios **2** following (pages, etc.)

**fi·an·cé** (fē'än sā') *n.* 〚Fr < OFr *fiance*, a promise〛 a man who is engaged to be married

**fi·an·cée** (fē'än sā') *n.* 〚Fr: see prec.〛 a woman who is engaged to be married

**fi·as·co** (fē as'kō) *n., pl.* **-coes** or **-cos** 〚Fr < It〛 a complete, ridiculous failure

**fi·at** (fē'ät, fī'at') *n.* 〚L, let it be done〛 **1** a decree; order **2** a sanction; authorization **3** any arbitrary order

**fib** (fib) *n.* 〚< ? FABLE〛 a small or trivial lie —*vi.* **fibbed, fib'bing** to tell such a lie —**fib'ber** *n.*

**fi·ber** (fī'bər) *n.* 〚< L *fibra*〛 **1** a threadlike structure that combines with others to form animal or vegetable tissue **2** any substance that can be separated into threadlike parts for weaving, etc. **3** texture **4** character or nature **5** ROUGHAGE —**fi'brous** (-brəs) *adj.*

**fi'ber·board'** *n.* a building material consisting of fibers of wood, etc. pressed into stiff sheets

**Fi'ber·glas'** (-glas') *trademark for* finespun filaments of glass made into textiles, insulating material, or molded plastic —*n.* this substance

**fi'ber·glass'** (-glas') *n.* finespun filaments of glass like Fiberglas

**fiber optics 1** the science of transmitting light and images, as around curves, through transparent fibers **2** such fibers —**fi'ber-op'tic** or **fiber optic** *adj.*

**fi·bril·la·tion** (fib'ri lā'shən) *n.* 〚< L *fibra*, fiber + -ATION〛 very rapid contractions of part of the heart muscle, causing irregular heartbeats

**fi·brin** (fī'brin) *n.* a fibrous, insoluble blood protein formed in blood clots

**fi·brin·o·gen** (fī brin'ə jən) *n.* 〚prec. + -GEN〛 a protein in the blood from which fibrin is formed

**fi·broid** (fī'broid') *adj.* like or composed of fibrous tissue: said as of a tumor

**fi·bro·sis** (fī brō'sis) *n.* an excessive growth of fibrous connective tissue in an organ, part, etc.

**fib·u·la** (fib'yōō lə) *n., pl.* **-lae** (-lē') or **-las** 〚L, a clasp〛 the long, thin outer bone of the lower leg —**fib'u·lar** *adj.*

**-fic** (fik) 〚< L *facere*, make〛 *suffix* making [*terrific*]

**FICA** (fī'kə) *abbrev.* Federal Insurance Contributions Act

**-fi·ca·tion** (fi kā'shən) 〚see -FIC〛 *suffix* a making [*glorification*]

**fich·u** (fish'ōō) *n.* 〚Fr〛 a triangular lace or muslin cape for women, worn tied in front

**fick·le** (fik'əl) *adj.* 〚< OE *ficol*, tricky〛 changeable or unstable; capricious

**fic·tion** (fik'shən) *n.* 〚< L *fingere*, to form〛 **1** an imaginary statement, story, etc. **2** *a)* literary narratives, collectively, with imaginary characters or events, specif. novels and short stories *b)* a narrative of this kind —**fic'tion·al** *adj.*

**fic'tion·al·ize'** (-shə nəl īz') *vt.* **-ized', -iz'ing** to deal with (historical events) in fictional form —**fic'tion·al·i·za'tion** *n.*

**fic·ti·tious** (fik tish'əs) *adj.* **1** of or like fiction; imaginary **2** false **3** assumed for disguise [a *fictitious* name]

**fic·tive** (fik'tiv) *adj.* **1** of fiction **2** imaginary —**fic'tive·ly** *adv.*

**fi·cus** (fī'kəs) *n., pl.* **fi'cus** 〚< L, fig tree〛 any of a genus of tropical shrubs, trees, etc. with glossy, leathery leaves

**fid·dle** (fid'l) [Inf.] *n.* 〚OE *fithele*〛 a violin —*vi.* **-dled, -dling 1** to play a fiddle **2** to tinker (*with*) nervously —**fid'dler** *n.*

**fid'dle·sticks'** *interj.* nonsense!

**fi·del·i·ty** (fə del'ə tē) *n., pl.* **-ties** 〚< L *fides*, faith〛 **1** faithful devotion to duty; loyalty **2** accuracy of description, sound reproduction, etc.

**fidg·et** (fij'it) *n.* 〚< ME < ?〛 a restless or nervous state: esp. in phrase **the fidgets** —*vi.* to move about restlessly or nervously —**fidg'et·y** *adj.*

**fi·du·ci·ar·y** (fi dōō'shē er'ē) *adj.* 〚< L *fiducia*, trust〛 holding or held in trust —*n., pl.* **-ies** TRUSTEE (sense 1)

**fie** (fī) *interj.* [Archaic] for shame!

**fief** (fēf) *n.* 〚Fr: see FEE〛 in feudalism, heritable land held by a vassal

**fief'dom** (-dəm) *n.* **1** FIEF **2** anything under a person's complete control

**field** (fēld) *n.* 〚OE *feld*〛 **1** a stretch of open land **2** a piece of cleared land for crops or pasture **3** a piece of land used for a particular purpose [a landing *field*] **4** any wide, unbroken expanse [a *field* of ice] **5** *a)* a battlefield *b)* a battle **6** a realm of knowledge or work **7** the background, as on a flag **8** *a)* an area for athletics or games *b)* all the entrants in a contest **9** *Physics* a physical quantity specified at points throughout a region of space —*vt.* **1** to stop or catch and throw (a baseball, etc.) **2** to put (a player or team) into active play **3** [Inf.] to answer (a question) extemporaneously —**play the field** to not confine one's activities to one object —**field'er** *n.*

**field day** an occasion of extraordinary opportunity or highly successful activity

**field glasses** a small, portable binocular telescope

**field goal 1** *Basketball* a shot, made from play, scoring two points or, if from a certain distance, three points **2** *Football* a goal kicked from the field, scoring three points

**field guide** a handbook for identifying plants, etc., as while hiking

**field hand** a hired farm laborer

**field hockey** HOCKEY (sense 2)

**field marshal** in some armies, an officer of the highest rank

**field'-test'** *vt.* to test (a device, method, etc.) under operating conditions

**fiend** (fēnd) *n.* 〚OE *feond*, the one hating〛 **1** an evil spirit; devil **2** an inhumanly wicked person **3** [Inf.] an addict [a dope *fiend*] —**fiend'ish** *adj.*

**fierce** (firs) *adj.* **fierc'er, fierc'est** 〚< L *ferus*, wild〛 **1** savage **2** violent **3** intense [a *fierce* embrace] —**fierce'ly** *adv.* —**fierce'ness** *n.*

**fi·er·y** (fī'ər ē) *adj.* **-er·i·er, -er·i·est 1** like fire; glaring, hot, etc. **2** ardent; spirited **3** excitable **4** inflamed

**fi·es·ta** (fē es'tə) *n.* 〚Sp < L *festus*, festal〛 **1** a religious festival **2** any gala celebration; holiday

**fife** (fīf) *n.* 〚Ger *pfeife*〛 a small flute used mainly with drums in playing marches

**fif·teen** (fif'tēn') *adj., n.* 〚OE *fiftene*〛 five more than ten; 15; XV —**fif'teenth'** (-tēnth') *adj., n., adv.*

**fifth** (fifth) *adj.* 〚< OE *fif*, five〛 preceded by four others in a series; 5th —*n.* **1** the one following the fourth **2** any of the five equal parts of something; ⅕ **3** a fifth of a gallon —*adv.* in the fifth place, rank, etc.

**Fifth Amendment** an amendment to the U.S. Constitution mainly guaranteeing certain protections in criminal cases; specif., the clause protecting persons from being compelled to testify against themselves

**fifth column** a group of people aiding an enemy from within their own country

**fifth wheel** a superfluous person or thing

**fif·ty** (fif'tē) *adj., n., pl.* **-ties** 〚OE *fiftig*〛 five times ten; 50; L —**the fifties** the numbers or years, as of a century, from 50 through 59 —**fif'ti·eth** (-ith) *adj., n.*

**fif'ty-fif'ty** [Inf.] *adj.* equal; even —*adv.* equally

**fig**[1] (fig) *n.* 〚< L *ficus*〛 **1** *a)* a small, sweet, pear-shaped fruit that grows on a tree related to the mulberry *b)* the tree **2** a trifle [not worth a *fig*]

**fig**[2] *abbrev.* **1** figurative(ly) **2** figure(s)

**fight** (fīt) *n.* **fought, fight'ing** 〚OE *feohtan*〛 to take part in a struggle, contest, etc., esp. against a foe or for a cause —*vt.* **1** to oppose physically or in battle **2** to struggle against **3** to engage in (a war, etc.) **4** to gain (one's way) by struggle —*n.* **1** any struggle, contest, or quarrel **2** power or readiness to fight

**fight′er** *n.* **1** one that fights **2** a prizefighter **3** a fast, highly maneuverable combat airplane

**fig·ment** (fig′mənt) *n.* ⟦< L *fingere*, to form⟧ something merely imagined

**fig·ur·a·tive** (fig′yoor ə tiv′) *adj.* **1** representing by means of a figure or symbol **2** not in its literal sense; metaphorical **3** using figures of speech — **fig′ur·a·tive·ly** *adv.*

**fig·ure** (fig′yər) *n.* ⟦< L *fingere*, to form⟧ **1** an outline or shape; form **2** the human form **3** a person thought of in a specified way [a historical *figure*] **4** a likeness of a person or thing **5** an illustration; diagram **6** a design; pattern **7** the symbol for a number **8** [*pl.*] arithmetic **9** a sum of money **10** *Geom.* a surface or space bounded by lines or planes — *vt.* **-ured, -ur·ing 1** to represent in definite form **2** to imagine **3** to ornament with a design **4** to compute with figures **5** [Inf.] to believe; consider — *vi.* **1** to appear prominently **2** to do arithmetic — **figure in** to include — **figure on** to rely on — **figure out 1** to solve **2** to understand — **figure up** to add; total

**fig′ure·head′** *n.* **1** a carved figure on the bow of a ship **2** one put in a position of leadership, but having no real power or authority

**figure of speech** an expression, as a metaphor or simile, using words in a nonliteral sense or unusual way

**figure skating** ice skating with emphasis on tracing patterns on the ice or, now, performing leaps and spins — **figure skater**

**fig·u·rine** (fig′yoō rēn′) *n.* ⟦Fr⟧ a small sculptured or molded figure

**Fi·ji** (fē′jē) country on a group of islands (**Fiji Islands**) in the SW Pacific: 7,078 sq. mi.; pop. 715,000

**fil·a·ment** (fil′ə mənt) *n.* ⟦< L *filum*, thread⟧ a very slender thread or threadlike part; specif., the fine wire in a light bulb or electron tube

**fil·bert** (fil′bərt) *n.* ⟦ME *filberde*⟧ the edible nut of a hazel tree

**filch** (filch) *vt.* ⟦ME *filchen*⟧ to steal (usually something small or petty)

**file**[1] (fīl) *vt.* **filed, fil′ing** ⟦< L *filum*, thread⟧ **1** to put (papers, etc.) in order for future reference **2** to dispatch or register (a news story, application, etc.) **3** to put on public record — *vi.* **1** to move in a line **2** to make application (*for* divorce, etc.) — *n.* **1** a container for keeping papers in order **2** an orderly arrangement of papers, etc. **3** a line of persons or things **4** *Comput.* a collection of data stored as a single unit — **file′a·ble** *adj.* — **fil′er** *n.*

**file**[2] (fīl) *n.* ⟦OE *feol*⟧ a steel tool with a rough, ridged surface for smoothing or grinding — *vt.* **filed, fil′ing** to smooth or grind, as with a file

**fi·let** (fi lā′, fil′ā′) *n.* ⟦< OFr: see FILLET⟧ FILLET (*n.* 2) — *vt.* FILLET

**fi·let mi·gnon** (fi lā′min yōn′, -yän′) ⟦Fr, lit., tiny fillet⟧ a thick, round cut of lean beef tenderloin

**fil·i·al** (fil′ē əl, fil′yəl) *adj.* ⟦< L *filius*, son⟧ of, suitable to, or due from a son or daughter

**fil·i·bus·ter** (fil′i bus′tər) *n.* ⟦< Sp < MDu *vrijbuiter*, freebooter⟧ **1** the making of long speeches, etc. to obstruct a bill's passage in the Senate **2** a Senator who does this — *vt.*, *vi.* to obstruct (a bill) by a filibuster

**fil·i·gree** (fil′i grē′) *n.* ⟦< L *filum*, thread + *granum*, grain⟧ lacelike ornamental work of intertwined wire of gold, silver, etc. — *vt.* **-greed′, -gree′ing** to ornament with filigree

**fil·ing** (fīl′iŋ) *n.* a small piece scraped off with a file: *usually used in pl.*

**Fil·i·pi·no** (fil′i pē′nō) *n.*, *pl.* **-nos** ⟦Sp⟧ a person born or living in the Philippines — *adj.* of the Philippines or its people, etc. — **Fil′i·pi′na** (-nə), *pl.* **-nas**, *fem.n.*, *adj.*

**fill** (fil) *vt.* ⟦OE *fyllan*⟧ **1** to put as much as possible into **2** to occupy wholly **3** to put a person into or to occupy (a position, etc.) **4** to supply the things called for in (an order, etc.) **5** to close or

plug (holes, etc.) — *vi.* to become full — *n.* **1** enough to make full or to satisfy **2** anything that fills — **fill in 1** to complete by supplying something **2** to supply for completion **3** to be a substitute — **fill out 1** to make or become larger, etc. **2** to make (a document, etc.) complete by supplying information — **fill up** to make or become completely full — **fill′er** *n.*

**fil·let** (fil′it; *for n. 2 & vt., usually* fi lā′, fil′ā′) *n.* ⟦OFr *filet* < L *filum*, thread⟧ **1** a thin strip or band **2** a lean, boneless piece of meat or fish — *vt.* to bone and slice (meat or fish)

**fill′-in′** *n.* one that fills a vacancy or gap, often temporarily

**fill′ing** *n.* a substance used to fill something, as gold in a tooth cavity

**filling station** SERVICE STATION

**fil·lip** (fil′ip) *n.* ⟦< FLIP[1]⟧ **1** an outward snap of a finger from the thumb **2** something that stimulates — *vt.* to strike or toss with a fillip

**Fill·more** (fil′môr), **Mill·ard** (mil′ərd) 1800-74; 13th president of the U.S. (1850-53)

**fil·ly** (fil′ē) *n.*, *pl.* **-lies** ⟦< ON *fylja*⟧ a young female horse

**film** (film) *n.* ⟦OE *filmen*⟧ **1** a fine, thin skin, coating, etc. **2** a flexible cellulose material coated with an emulsion sensitive to light and used in photography **3** a haze or blur **4** a series of still pictures projected on a screen in such rapid succession as to create the illusion of moving persons and objects **5** a play, story, etc. in this form — *vt.*, *vi.* **1** to cover or be covered as with a film **2** to photograph or make a film (of)

**film′strip′** *n.* a length of film with still photographs, often of illustrations, charts, etc., for projection separately

**film′y** *adj.* **-i·er, -i·est 1** gauzy; sheer; thin **2** blurred; hazy — **film′i·ness** *n.*

**fil·ter** (fil′tər) *n.* ⟦< ML *filtrum*, FELT[1]⟧ **1** a device for straining out solid particles, impurities, etc. from a liquid or gas **2** a device or substance for screening out electric oscillations, light waves, etc. of certain frequencies — *vt.*, *vi.* **1** to pass through or as through a filter **2** to remove with a filter — **fil′ter·a·ble** or **fil′tra·ble** (-trə bəl) *adj.*

**filter tip 1** a cigarette tip of cellulose, charcoal, etc. for filtering the smoke **2** a cigarette with such a tip

**filth** (filth) *n.* ⟦OE *fylthe*⟧ **1** foul dirt **2** obscenity — **filth′y, -i·er, -i·est**, *adj.* — **filth′i·ness** *n.*

**fil·trate** (fil′trāt′) *vt.* **-trat′ed, -trat′ing** to filter — *n.* a filtered liquid — **fil·tra′tion** *n.*

**fin** (fin) *n.* ⟦OE *finn*⟧ **1** any of several winglike organs on the body of a fish, dolphin, etc., used in swimming **2** anything like a fin in shape or use

**fi·na·gle** (fə nā′gəl) *vt.*, *vi.* **-gled, -gling** ⟦< ?⟧ [Inf.] to get by, or use, craftiness, trickery, etc. — **fi·na′gler** *n.*

**fi·nal** (fī′nəl) *adj.* ⟦< L *finis*, end⟧ **1** of or coming at the end; last **2** deciding; conclusive — *n.* **1** anything final **2** [*pl.*] the last of a series of contests **3** a final examination — **fi·nal′i·ty** (-nal′ə tē) *n.* — **fi′nal·ly** *adv.*

**fi·na·le** (fə nal′ē) *n.* ⟦It⟧ the concluding part of a musical work, etc.

**fi′nal·ist** *n.* a contestant in the final, deciding contest of a series

**fi′nal·ize′** *vt.* **-ized′, -iz′ing** ⟦FINAL + -IZE⟧ to make final; complete — **fi′nal·i·za′tion** *n.*

**fi·nance** (fī′nans′, fə nans′) *n.* ⟦< L *finis*, end⟧ **1** [*pl.*] money resources, income, etc. **2** the science of managing money — *vt.* **-nanced′, -nanc′ing** to supply or get money for — **fi·nan′cial** (-nan′shəl) *adj.* — **fi·nan′cial·ly** *adv.*

**fin·an·cier** (fin′ən sir′, fī′nən-) *n.* ⟦Fr⟧ one skilled in finance

**finch** (finch) *n.* ⟦OE *finc*⟧ any of various small, seed-eating birds, including canaries, goldfinches, etc.

**find** (fīnd) *vt.* **found, find′ing** ⟦OE *findan*⟧ **1** to discover by chance; come upon **2** to get by searching **3** to perceive; learn **4** to recover (something lost) **5** to reach; attain **6** to decide and declare to be —*vi.* to reach a decision /the jury *found* for the accused/ —*n.* **1** a finding **2** something found — **find out** to discover; learn —**find′er** *n.*

**find′ing** *n.* **1** discovery **2** something found **3** [*often pl.*] the verdict of a judge, scholar, etc.

**fine**[1] (fīn) *adj.* [< L *finis*, end] **1** very good; excellent **2** with no impurities; refined **3** in good health **4** clear and bright /*fine* weather/ **5** not heavy or coarse /*fine* sand/ **6** very thin or small /*fine* print/ **7** sharp /a *fine* edge/ **8** subtle; delicate /a *fine* distinction/ **9** elegant —*adv.* in a fine manner —**fine′ly** *adv.* —**fine′ness** *n.*

**fine**[2] (fīn) *n.* [see prec.] a sum of money paid as a penalty —*vt.* **fined, fin′ing** to order to pay a fine

**fine art** any of the art forms that include drawing, painting, sculpture, etc.: *usually used in pl.*

**fin·er·y** (fīn′ər ē) *n., pl.* **-ies** elaborate clothes, jewelry, etc.

**fines herbes** (fēn zerb′) [Fr] a seasoning of chopped herbs, traditionally parsley, chives, tarragon, and chervil

**fi·nesse** (fə nes′) *n.* [see FINE[1]] **1** adroitness; skill **2** the ability to handle difficult situations diplomatically **3** cunning; artfulness —*vt.* **-nessed′, -ness′ing 1** to manage or bring about by finesse **2** to evade (a problem, etc.)

**fin·ger** (fiŋ′gər) *n.* [OE] **1** any of the five jointed parts extending from the palm of the hand, esp. any one other than the thumb **2** anything like a finger in shape or use —*vt.* **1** to touch with the fingers; handle **2** *Music* to play by using the fingers in a certain way —**have (or keep) one's fingers crossed** to hope for or against something — **put one's finger on** to ascertain exactly

**fin′ger·board′** *n.* the part of a stringed instrument against which the strings are pressed to produce the desired tones

**fin′ger·ling** (-liŋ) *n.* a small fish

**fin′ger·nail′** *n.* the horny substance at the upper end of a finger

**finger painting** a painting done by using the fingers, hand, or arm to spread, on wet paper, paints (**finger paints**) made of starch, glycerin, and pigments —**fin′ger-paint′** *vi., vt.*

**fin′ger-point′ing** *n.* the act of assigning blame to others, often so as to deflect blame from oneself

**fin′ger·print′** *n.* an impression of the lines and whorls on a finger tip, used to identify a person — *vt.* to take the fingerprints of

**fin′ger·tip′** *n.* the tip of a finger —**have at one's fingertips** to have available for instant use

**fin·i·al** (fin′ē əl) *n.* [ult. < L *finis*, end] a decorative terminal part at the tip of a spire, lamp, etc.

**fin·ick·y** (fin′ik ē) *adj.* [< FINE[1]] too particular; fussy: also **fin′i·cal** (-i kəl) or **fin′ick·ing**

**fin·is** (fin′is; *also, as if Fr,* fē nē′) *n., pl.* **-nis·es** the end; finish

**fin·ish** (fin′ish) *vt.* [< L *finis*, an end] **1** *a)* to bring to an end *b)* to come to the end of **2** to consume all of **3** to give final touches to; perfect **4** to give (wood, etc.) a desired surface effect —*vi.* to come to an end —*n.* **1** the last part; end **2** *a)* anything used to finish a surface *b)* the finished effect **3** means or manner of completing or perfecting **4** polished manners, speech, etc. —**finish off 1** to end **2** to kill or ruin —**finish with** to bring to an end —**fin′ished** *adj.* —**fin′ish·er** *n.*

**fi·nite** (fī′nīt′) *adj.* [< L *finis*, end] having definable limits; not infinite

**fink** (fiŋk) *n.* [Ger, lit., finch] [Slang] **1** an informer **2** a strikebreaker —*vi.* [Slang] to inform (*on*)

**Fin·land** (fin′lənd) country in N Europe: 130,937 sq. mi.; pop. 5,078,000

**Finn** (fin) *n.* a person born or living in Finland

**fin·nan had·die** (fin′ən had′ē) [prob. < *Findhorn* (Scotland) *haddock*] smoked haddock

**Finn·ish** (fin′ish) *n.* the language spoken in Finland —*adj.* of Finland or its people, language, etc.

**fin·ny** (fin′ē) *adj.* **1** having fins **2** like a fin **3** of or being fish

**fiord** (fyôrd) *n.* [Norw < ON *fjörthr*] a narrow inlet of the sea bordered by steep cliffs

**fir** (fur) *n.* [OE *fyrh*] **1** a cone-bearing evergreen tree of the pine family **2** its wood

**fire** (fīr) *n.* [OE *fyr*] **1** the flame, heat, and light of combustion **2** something burning **3** a destructive burning /a forest *fire*/ **4** strong feeling **5** a discharge of firearms —*vt., vi.* **fired, fir′ing 1** to start burning; ignite **2** to supply with fuel **3** to bake (bricks, etc.) in a kiln **4** to excite or become excited **5** to shoot (a gun, bullet, etc.) **6** to hurl or direct with force **7** to dismiss from a position; discharge —**catch (on) fire** to ignite —**on fire 1** burning **2** greatly excited —**under fire** under attack —**fir′er** *n.*

**fire′arm′** *n.* any hand weapon from which a shot is fired by explosive force, as a rifle or pistol

**fire′base′** *n.* a military base in a combat zone, from which artillery, rockets, etc. are fired

**fire′bomb′** *n.* an incendiary bomb —*vt.* to attack or damage with a firebomb

**fire′brand′** *n.* **1** a piece of burning wood **2** one who stirs up others to rebellion or strife

**fire′break′** *n.* a strip of forest or prairie land cleared or plowed to stop the spread of fire

**fire·brick** (fīr′brik′) *n.* a highly heat-resistant brick for lining fireplaces, furnaces, etc.

**fire′bug′** *n.* [Inf.] one who deliberately starts destructive fires; pyromaniac

**fire′crack′er** *n.* a roll of paper containing an explosive, set off as a noisemaker at celebrations, etc.

**fire′damp′** *n.* an explosive gas, largely methane, formed in coal mines

**fire engine** a motor truck with equipment for fighting fires

**fire escape** an outside stairway for escaping from a burning building

**fire′fight′** *n.* a short, intense exchange of gunfire between small units of soldiers

**fire′fight′er** *n.* a person whose work is putting out fires —**fire′fight′ing** *n.*

**fire′fly′** *n., pl.* **-flies′** a winged beetle whose abdomen glows with a luminescent light

**fire′man** (-mən) *n., pl.* **-men** (-mən) **1** FIREFIGHTER **2** a person who tends a fire in a furnace, etc.

**fire′place′** *n.* a place for a fire, esp. an open place built in a wall under a chimney

**fire′plug′** *n.* a street hydrant supplying water for fighting fires

**fire′proof′** *adj.* not easily destroyed by fire —*vt.* to make fireproof

**fire′side′** *n.* **1** the space around a fireplace **2** home or home life

**fire′storm′** *n.* **1** an intense fire over a large area, as one caused by an atomic explosion with its high winds **2** a strong, often violent, outburst or upheaval

**fire tower** a tower used as a lookout for forest fires

**fire′trap′** *n.* a building easily set on fire or hard to get out of if on fire

**fire′truck′** *n.* FIRE ENGINE

**fire′wa′ter** *n.* alcoholic beverage: now humorous

**fire′wood′** *n.* wood used as fuel

**fire′works′** *pl.n.* **1** firecrackers, rockets, etc., for noisy effects or brilliant displays: *sometimes used in sing.* **2** a noisy quarrel or display of anger

**firing line 1** the line from which gunfire is directed at the enemy **2** the forefront in any kind of activity

**firm**[1] (furm) *adj.* [< L *firmus*] **1** solid; hard **2** not moved easily; fixed **3** unchanging; steady **4** resolute; constant **5** showing determination; strong **6** definite /a *firm* contract/ —*vt., vi.* to make or become firm —**firm′ly** *adv.* —**firm′ness** *n.*

**firm**[2] (furm) *n.* [< It < L *firmus*: see prec.] a business company

**fir·ma·ment** (fur′mə mənt) *n.* [< L *firmare*, strengthen] the sky, viewed poetically as a solid arch or vault

**first** (furst) *adj.* [OE *fyrst*] 1 before all others in a series; 1st 2 earliest 3 foremost, as in rank or quality —*adv.* 1 before any other person or thing 2 for the first time 3 sooner; preferably —*n.* 1 any person or thing that is first 2 the beginning 3 a first happening or thing of its kind 4 the winning place, as in a race 5 the slowest forward gear ratio of a motor vehicle transmission

**first aid** emergency treatment for injury or sudden illness, before regular medical care is available —**first′-aid′** *adj.*

**first′born′** *adj.* born first in a family; oldest —*n.* the firstborn child

**first′-class′** *adj.* 1 of the highest class, quality, etc. 2 designating the most expensive accommodations 3 designating or of the most expensive class of ordinary mail —*adv.* 1 with first-class accommodations 2 as or by first-class mail

**first family** [*often* F- F-] the family of the U.S. president

**first′hand′** *adj., adv.* from the original producer or source; direct

**first lady** [*often* F- L-] the wife of the U.S. president

**first lieutenant** a military officer ranking just above a second lieutenant

**first′ly** *adv.* in the first place; first

**first person** the form of a pronoun or verb that refers to the speaker or writer

**first′-rate′** *adj.* highest in rank, quality, etc. —*adv.* [Inf.] very well

**first′-string′** *adj.* [Inf.] *Sports* that is the first choice for regular play at a specified position

**firth** (furth) *n.* [< ON *fjörthr*] a narrow inlet or arm of the sea

**fis·cal** (fis′kəl) *adj.* [< L *fiscus*, public chest] 1 relating to the public treasury or revenues 2 financial 3 designating or of government policies of spending and taxation —**fis′cal·ly** *adv.*

**fish** (fish) *n., pl.* **fish** or (for different species) **fish′es** [OE *fisc*] 1 any of a large group of cold-blooded vertebrate animals living in water and having fins, gills for breathing, and, usually, scales 2 the flesh of a fish used as food —*vi.* 1 to catch or try to catch fish 2 to try to get something indirectly: often with *for* —*vt.* to grope for, find, and bring to view: often with *out*

**fish′er** *n.* 1 the largest marten, having very dark fur 2 this fur

**fish′er·man** (-mən) *n., pl.* **-men** (-mən) 1 a person who fishes for sport or for a living 2 a commercial fishing vessel

**fish′er·y** *n., pl.* **-ies** 1 the business of catching, selling, etc. fish 2 a place where fish, etc. are caught or bred

**fish′hook′** *n.* a hook, usually barbed, for catching fish

**fish′ing** *n.* the catching of fish for sport or for a living

**fish meal** ground, dried fish, used as fertilizer or fodder

**fish′wife′** *n., pl.* **-wives′** a coarse, scolding woman

**fish′y** *adj.* **-i·er, -i·est** 1 like a fish in odor, taste, etc. 2 dull or expressionless [*fishy* eyes] 3 [Inf.] questionable; odd —**fish′i·ly** *adv.* —**fish′i·ness** *n.*

**fis·sion** (fish′ən, fizh′-) *n.* [< L *findere*, to split] 1 a splitting apart; cleavage 2 NUCLEAR FISSION —**fis′sion·a·ble** *adj.*

**fis·sure** (fish′ər) *n.* [see prec.] a cleft or crack

**fist** (fist) *n.* [OE *fyst*] a hand with the fingers closed tightly into the palm

**fist·i·cuffs** (fis′ti kufs′) *pl.n.* [Old-fashioned] a fight with the fists

**fis·tu·la** (fis′tyoo lə, -chə lə) *n., pl.* **-las** or **-lae′** (-lē′) [L, a pipe, ulcer] an abnormal passage, as from an abscess to the skin

**fit**[1] (fit) *vt.* **fit′ted** or **fit, fit′ting** [ME *fitten*] 1 to be suitable to 2 to be the proper size, shape, etc. for 3 to adjust so as to fit 4 to equip; outfit —*vi.* 1 [Archaic] to be suitable or proper 2 to have the proper size or shape —*adj.* **fit′ter, fit′test** 1 suited to some purpose, function, etc. 2 proper; right 3 healthy 4 [Inf.] inclined [she was *fit* to scream] —*n.* the manner of fitting [a tight *fit*] —**fit′ly** *adv.* —**fit′ness** *n.* —**fit′ter** *n.*

**fit**[2] (fit) *n.* [OE *fitt*, conflict] 1 any sudden, uncontrollable attack, as of coughing 2 an outburst, as of anger 3 a seizure involving convulsions, loss of consciousness, etc. —**by fits (and starts)** in an irregular way —**have (or throw) a fit** [Inf.] to become very angry or upset

**fit′ful** (-fəl) *adj.* characterized by intermittent activity; spasmodic —**fit′ful·ly** *adv.* —**fit′ful·ness** *n.*

**fit′ting** *adj.* suitable; proper —*n.* 1 an adjustment or trying on of clothes, etc. 2 a small part used to join or adjust other parts 3 [*pl.*] fixtures

**five** (fīv) *adj., n.* [OE *fif*] one more than four; 5; V

**five′-and-ten′-cent′ store** a store that sells a wide variety of inexpensive merchandise: also **five′-and-ten′**

**five′-star′** *adj.* having the highest rating, based on a given set of criteria for excellence

**fix** (fiks) *vt.* **fixed, fix′ing** [< L *figere*, fasten] 1 to fasten firmly 2 to set firmly in the mind 3 to direct (one's eyes) steadily at something 4 to make rigid 5 to make permanent 6 to establish (a date, etc.) definitely 7 to set in order; adjust 8 to repair 9 to prepare (food or meals) 10 [Inf.] to influence the result or action of (a race, jury, etc.), as by bribery 11 [Inf.] to punish —*vi.* 1 to become fixed 2 [Inf. or Dial.] to prepare or intend —*n.* 1 the position of a ship, etc. determined from the bearings of two known positions 2 [Inf.] a predicament 3 [Slang] a contest, etc. that has been fixed 4 [Slang] an injection of a narcotic by an addict —**fix up** [Inf.] 1 to repair 2 to arrange; set in order —**fix′a·ble** *adj.* —**fix′er** *n.*

**fix·a·tion** (fik sā′shən) *n.* 1 a fixing or being fixed 2 an obsession 3 a remaining at an early stage of psychosexual development

**fix·a·tive** (fik′sə tiv) *adj.* that is able or tends to make permanent, prevent fading, etc. —*n.* a fixative substance

**fixed** (fikst) *adj.* 1 firmly in place 2 established; settled 3 resolute; unchanging 4 persistent [a *fixed* idea] —**fix·ed·ly** (fiks′id lē) *adv.*

**fix·ings** (fik′sinz′) *pl.n.* [Inf.] accessories or trimmings [turkey and all the *fixings*]

**fix·i·ty** (fik′si tē) *n.* the quality or state of being fixed or steady

**fix·ture** (fiks′chər) *n.* [see FIX] 1 anything firmly in place 2 any attached piece of equipment in a house, etc. 3 a person long established in a job, etc.

**fizz** (fiz) *n.* [? akin to fol.] 1 a hissing, sputtering sound 2 an effervescent drink —*vi.* 1 to make a hissing sound 2 to effervesce

**fiz·zle** (fiz′əl) *vi.* **-zled, -zling** [< ME] 1 FIZZ (*vi.* 1) 2 [Inf.] to fail, esp. after a good start —*n.* 1 a hissing sound 2 [Inf.] a failure

**fl** *abbrev.* 1 floor 2 [L *floruit*] (he or she) flourished 3 fluid

**FL** *abbrev.* Florida

**flab** (flab) *n.* [< FLABBY] [Inf.] sagging flesh

**flab·ber·gast** (flab′ər gast′) *vt.* [18th-c. slang < ?] to dumbfound

**flab·by** (flab′ē) *adj.* **-bi·er, -bi·est** [< FLAP] 1 limp and soft 2 weak —**flab′bi·ly** *adv.* —**flab′bi·ness** *n.*

**flac·cid** (flak′sid, flas′id) *adj.* [< L *flaccus*] soft or limp; flabby

**flack** (flak) *n.* [< ?] [Slang] PRESS AGENT —**flack′er·y** *n.*

**fla·con** (flak′ən; *Fr* flȧ kôn′) *n., pl.* **-cons** (-enz; -kôn′) [Fr] a small flask with a stopper, as for perfume

**flag**¹ (flag) *n.* [< FLAG⁴, in obs. sense "to flutter"] a cloth with colors, patterns, etc., used as a symbol of a nation, state, etc., or as a signal —*vt.* **flagged, flag′ging** 1 to signal with or as with a flag; esp., to signal to stop: often with *down* 2 to mark with a symbol

**flag**² (flag) *n.* [< ON *flaga,* slab of stone] FLAG-STONE

**flag**³ (flag) *n.* [ME *flagge*] any of various irises, or a flower or leaf of one

**flag**⁴ (flag) *vi.* **flagged, flag′ging** [prob. < ON *flogra,* to flutter] 1 to become limp; droop 2 to grow weak or tired

**flag·el·late** (flaj′ə lāt′) *vt.* **-lat′ed, -lat′ing** [< L *flagellum,* a whip] to whip; flog —**flag′el·la′tion** *n.*

**fla·gel·lum** (flə jel′əm) *n., pl.* **-la** (-ə) or **-lums** [L, a whip] a whiplike part of some cells, as of bacteria or protozoans, used as for moving about

**flag·on** (flag′ən) *n.* [< LL *flasco*] a container for liquids, with a handle, a narrow neck, a spout, and, often, a lid

**flag′pole′** *n.* a pole on which a flag is raised and flown: also **flag′staff′**

**fla·grant** (flā′grənt) *adj.* [< L *flagrare,* to blaze] glaringly bad; outrageous —**fla′gran·cy** (-grən sē) or **fla′grance** *n.* —**fla′grant·ly** *adv.*

**flag′ship′** *n.* 1 the ship that carries the commander of a fleet or other large naval unit 2 the largest or most important member or part, as of a group

**flag′stone′** *n.* a flat paving stone

**flail** (flāl) *n.* [< L *flagellum,* a whip] a farm tool for threshing grain by hand —*vt., vi.* 1 to thresh with a flail 2 to beat 3 to move (one's arms) like flails

**flair** (fler) *n.* [< L *fragrare,* to smell] 1 a natural talent; aptitude 2 a sense of style; dash

**flak** (flak) *n.* [Ger acronym] 1 the fire of antiaircraft guns 2 [Inf.] strong criticism Also sp. **flack**

**flake** (flāk) *n.* [< Scand] 1 a small, thin mass 2 a piece split off; chip —*vt., vi.* **flaked, flak′ing** 1 to form into flakes 2 to peel off in flakes

**flak′y** *adj.* **-i·er, -i·est** 1 of or producing flakes 2 [Slang] eccentric

**flam·bé** (fläm bā′) *adj.* [Fr] served with a sauce of flaming brandy, rum, etc. —*n.* a dessert so served

**flam·boy·ant** (flam boi′ənt) *adj.* [Fr < L *flamma,* a flame] 1 flamelike or brilliant 2 too showy or ornate —**flam·boy′ance** or **flam·boy′an·cy** *n.* —**flam·boy′ant·ly** *adv.*

**flame** (flām) *n.* [< L *flamma*] 1 the burning gas of a fire, appearing as a tongue of light 2 the state of burning with a blaze 3 a thing like a flame 4 an intense emotion 5 a sweetheart —*vi.* **flamed, flam′ing** 1 to burst into flame 2 to grow red or hot 3 to become excited —*vt.* [Inf.] to attack, as by e-mail

**fla·men·co** (flə meŋ′kō) *n.* [Sp] a Spanish gypsy style of dance or music

**flame′out′** *n.* 1 a failure of combustion in a jet's engine during flight 2 a sudden and complete failure

**flame′throw′er** *n.* a weapon that shoots flaming oil, napalm, etc.

**fla·min·go** (flə miŋ′gō) *n., pl.* **-gos′** or **-goes′** [Port] a tropical wading bird with long legs and pink or red feathers

**flam·ma·ble** (flam′ə bəl) *adj.* easily set on fire; that will burn readily or quickly —**flam′ma·bil′i·ty** *n.*

**Flan·ders** (flan′dərz) region in NW Europe, in France & Belgium

**flange** (flanj) *n.* [< ? ME] a projecting rim on a

wheel, etc., that serves to hold it in place, give it strength, etc.

**flank** (flaŋk) *n.* [< OFr *flanc*] 1 the side of an animal between the ribs and the hip 2 the side of anything 3 *Mil.* the right or left side of a formation or force —*vt.* 1 to be at the side of 2 *Mil.* to attack, or pass around, the side of (enemy troops)

FLANGE

**flan·nel** (flan′əl) *n.* [prob. < Welsh *gwlan,* wool] 1 a loosely woven cloth of wool or cotton 2 [*pl.*] trousers, etc. made of this

**flan·nel·ette** or **flan·nel·et** (flan′əl et′) *n.* a soft, napped cotton cloth

**flap** (flap) *n.* [ME *flappe*] 1 anything flat and broad hanging loose at one end 2 the motion or sound of a swinging flap 3 [Inf.] a commotion; stir —*vt.* **flapped, flap′ping** 1 to slap 2 to move back and forth or up and down

**flap′jack′** *n.* a pancake

**flap′per** *n.* [Inf.] in the 1920s, a bold, unconventional young woman

**flare** (fler) *vi.* **flared, flar′ing** [ME *fleare* < ?] 1 *a*) to blaze brightly *b*) to burn unsteadily 2 to burst out suddenly, as in anger: often with *up* or *out* 3 to curve outward, as a bell's rim —*n.* 1 a bright, unsteady blaze 2 a brightly flaming light for signaling, etc. 3 an outburst, as of emotion 4 a curving outward

**flare′-up′** *n.* a sudden outburst of flame or of anger, trouble, etc.

**flash** (flash) *vi.* [ME *flashen,* to splash] 1 to send out a sudden, brief light 2 to sparkle 3 to come or pass suddenly —*vt.* 1 to cause to flash 2 to send (news, etc.) swiftly 3 [Inf.] to display or expose briefly —*n.* 1 a sudden, brief light 2 a brief moment 3 a sudden, brief display 4 a brief item of late news 5 a gaudy display —*adj.* happening swiftly or suddenly —**flash′er** *n.*

**flash′back′** *n.* 1 an interruption in the continuity of a story, etc. by the telling or showing of an earlier episode 2 a sudden, vivid recollection of a past event

**flash′bulb′** *n.* a bulb giving a brief, bright light, for taking photographs

**flash′cube′** *n.* a rotating cube with flashbulbs in four sides

**flash′-for′ward** *n.* an interruption in the continuity of a story, etc. by the telling or showing of a future episode

**flash′ing** *n.* sheets of metal used to weatherproof roof joints or edges

**flash′light′** *n.* a portable electric light

**flash point** the lowest temperature at which vapor, as of an oil, will ignite with a flash

**flash′y** *adj.* **-i·er, -i·est** 1 dazzling 2 gaudy; showy —**flash′i·ness** *n.*

**flask** (flask) *n.* [< L *flasca,* bottle] 1 any bottle-shaped container used in laboratories, etc. 2 a small, flat container for liquor, etc., to be carried in the pocket

**flat**¹ (flat) *adj.* **flat′ter, flat′test** [< ON *flatr*] 1 having a smooth, level surface 2 lying spread out 3 broad, even, and thin 4 absolute [a *flat* denial] 5 not fluctuating [a *flat* rate] 6 tasteless; insipid 7 not interesting 8 emptied of air [a *flat* tire] 9 without gloss [*flat* paint] 10 *Music a*) lower in pitch by a half step *b*) below true pitch —*adv.* 1 in a flat manner or position 2 exactly 3 *Music* below true pitch —*n.* 1 anything flat, esp. a surface, part, or expanse 2 a deflated tire 3 *Music a*) a note one half step below another *b*) the symbol (♭) for this —*vt.* **flat′ted, flat′ting** *Music* to make flat —*vi.* to sing or play below true pitch —**fall flat** to fail in the desired effect —**flat′ly** *adv.* —**flat′ness** *n.* —**flat′tish** *adj.*

**flat²** (flat) *n.* [< Scot dial. *flet*, floor] [Chiefly Brit.] an apartment or suite of rooms

**flat'bed'** *n.* a truck, trailer, etc. having a bed or platform without sides or stakes

**flat'boat'** *n.* a flat-bottomed boat for carrying freight in shallow bodies of water or on rivers

**flat'car'** *n.* a railroad freight car without sides or a roof

**flat'fish'** *n.*, *pl.* **-fish'** or (for different species) **-fish'es** a fish having both eyes and mouth on the upper side of a very flat body

**flat'foot'** *n.* **1** a condition of the foot in which the instep arch is flattened **2** *pl.* **-foots'** or **-feet'** [Slang] a policeman —**flat'-foot'ed** *adj.*

**flat'i'ron** *n.* an iron for clothes

**flat'-out'** *adj.* [Inf.] **1** at full speed, with maximum effort, etc. **2** absolute; thorough

**flat·ten** (flat''n) *vt.*, *vi.* to make or become flat or flatter

**flat·ter** (flat'ər) *vt.* [< OFr *flater*, to smooth] **1** to praise insincerely **2** to try to please, as by praise **3** to make seem more attractive than is so **4** to gratify the vanity of —**flat'ter·er** *n.* —**flat'ter·ing·ly** *adv.* —**flat'ter·y** *n.*

**flat'top'** *n.* [Slang] **1** an aircraft carrier **2** a haircut in which the hair on top of the head is cut so as to form a flat surface

**flat·u·lent** (flach'ə lənt) *adj.* [see fol.] **1** having or producing gas in the stomach or intestines **2** pompous —**flat'u·lence** *n.*

**fla·tus** (flāt'əs) *n.* [L < *flare*, to blow] intestinal gas

**flat'ware'** *n.* knives, forks, and spoons

**flat'worm'** *n.* any of various worms with flat bodies, as the tapeworm

**Flau·bert** (flō ber'), **Gus·tave** (güs tàv') 1821-80; Fr. novelist

**flaunt** (flônt) *vi.* [? < dial. *flant*, to strut] to make a gaudy or defiant display —*vt.* **1** to show off proudly or defiantly **2** FLOUT: usage objected to by many —**flaunt'ing·ly** *adv.*

**flau·tist** (flôt'ist, flout'-) *n.* [< It] *var.* of FLUTIST

**fla·vor** (flā'vər) *n.* [ult. < L *flare*, to blow] **1** that quality of a substance that is a mixing of its characteristic taste and smell **2** flavoring **3** characteristic quality —*vt.* to give flavor to   Brit. sp. **fla'vour** —**fla'vor·ful** *adj.* —**fla'vor·less** *adj.*

**fla'vor·ing** *n.* an essence, extract, etc. that adds flavor to food or drink

**flaw** (flô) *n.* [ME, a flake, splinter] **1** a crack, etc. as in a gem **2** a fault, as in reasoning —**flaw'less** *adj.* —**flaw'less·ly** *adv.* —**flaw'less·ness** *n.*

**flax** (flaks) *n.* [< OE *fleax*] **1** a slender, erect plant with delicate blue flowers: its seed (**flax'seed'**) is used to make linseed oil **2** the fibers of this plant, which are spun into linen thread

**flax·en** (flak'sən) *adj.* **1** of or made of flax **2** paleyellow

**flay** (flā) *vt.* [OE *flean*] **1** to strip off the skin of, as by whipping **2** to criticize harshly

**flea** (flē) *n.* [OE *fleah*] a small, wingless jumping insect that is a bloodsucking parasite as an adult

**flea market** an outdoor bazaar dealing mainly in cheap, secondhand goods

**fleck** (flek) *n.* [ON *flekkr*] a spot, speck, or flake —*vt.* to spot; speckle

**fled** (fled) *vi.*, *vt.* *pt. & pp. of* FLEE

**fledg·ling** (flej'liŋ) *n.* [< ME *flegge*, ready to fly] **1** a young bird just able to fly **2** a young, inexperienced person   Also, chiefly Brit., **fledge'ling**

**flee** (flē) *vi.* **fled**, **flee'ing** [OE *fleon*] **1** to go swiftly or escape, as from danger **2** to pass away swiftly —*vt.* to run away or try to escape from

**fleece** (flēs) *n.* [OE *fleos*] **1** the wool covering a sheep or similar animal **2** a soft, warm, napped fabric —*vt.* **fleeced**, **fleec'ing** **1** to shear the fleece from **2** to swindle —**fleec'er** *n.*

**fleec·y** (flēs'ē) *adj.* **-i·er**, **-i·est** of or like fleece; soft and light —**fleec'i·ness** *n.*

**fleet¹** (flēt) *n.* [OE *fleot*] **1** a number of warships under one command **2** any group of ships, trucks, etc. under one control

**fleet²** (flēt) *adj.* [< OE *fleotan*, to float] swift; rapid —**fleet'ness** *n.*

**fleet'ing** *adj.* passing swiftly —**fleet'ing·ly** *adv.* —**fleet'ing·ness** *n.*

**Flem·ish** (flem'ish) *adj.* of Flanders or its people, language, etc. —*n.* the West Germanic language of Flanders

**flesh** (flesh) *n.* [OE *flæsc*] **1** the soft substance of the body; esp., the muscular tissue **2** meat **3** the pulpy part of fruits and vegetables **4** the body as distinct from the soul **5** all humankind **6** yellowish pink —**in the flesh 1** alive **2** in person — **one's (own) flesh and blood** one's close relatives —**flesh'y**, **-i·er**, **-i·est**, *adj.*

**flesh'-and-blood'** *adj.* **1** alive **2** actual **3** present; in person

**flesh'ly** *adj.* **-li·er**, **-li·est** **1** of the body; corporeal **2** sensual

**fleur-de-lis** (flur'də lē') *n.*, *pl.* **fleurs-de-lis** (flur'də lē', -lēz') [< OFr *flor de lis*, lit., flower of the lily] a lilylike emblem: the coat of arms of the former French royal family

**flew** (flo͞o) *vi.*, *vt. pt. of* FLY¹

**flex** (fleks) *vt.*, *vi.* [< L *flectere*, to bend] **1** to bend (an arm, knee, etc.) **2** to shorten and thicken (a muscle) in action

**flex·i·ble** (flek'sə bəl) *adj.* **1** able to bend without breaking; pliant **2** easily influenced **3** adjustable to change — **flex'i·bil'i·ty** *n.*

FLEUR-DE-LIS

**flex'time'** *n.* a system allowing individual employees some flexibility in choosing when they work

**flib·ber·ti·gib·bet** (flib'ər tē jib'it) *n.* [< ?] a frivolous, flighty person

**flick¹** (flik) *n.* [echoic] a light, quick stroke —*vt.* to strike, remove, etc. with a light, quick stroke

**flick²** (flik) *n.* [< fol.] [Slang] a film —**the flicks** [Slang] a showing of a film

**flick·er** (flik'ər) *vi.* [OE *flicorian*] **1** to move with a quick, light, wavering motion **2** to burn or shine unsteadily —*n.* **1** a flickering **2** a dart of flame or light

**fli·er** (flī'ər) *n.* **1** a thing that flies **2** an aviator **3** a bus, train, etc. with a fast schedule **4** a widely distributed handbill **5** [Inf.] a reckless gamble

**flight¹** (flīt) *n.* [OE *flyht*] **1** the act, manner, or power of flying **2** the distance flown **3** a group of things flying together **4** an airplane scheduled to fly a certain trip **5** a trip by airplane **6** a soaring above the ordinary [a *flight* of fancy] **7** a set of stairs, as between landings

**flight²** (flīt) *n.* [< OE *fleon*, flee] a fleeing from or as from danger

**flight attendant** an airplane attendant who sees to passengers' comfort and safety

**flight'less** *adj.* not able to fly

**flight'y** *adj.* **-i·er**, **-i·est** **1** given to sudden whims; frivolous **2** easily excited, upset, etc. —**flight'i·ness** *n.*

**flim·sy** (flim'zē) *adj.* **-si·er**, **-si·est** [< ?] **1** easily broken or damaged; frail **2** ineffectual [a *flimsy* excuse] —**flim'si·ly** *adv.* —**flim'si·ness** *n.*

**flinch** (flinch) *vi.* [< OFr *flenchir*] to draw back from a blow or anything difficult or painful —*n.* a flinching

**fling** (fliŋ) *vt.* **flung**, **fling'ing** [< ON *flengja*, to whip] **1** to throw, esp. with force; hurl **2** to put abruptly or violently **3** to move (one's limbs, head, etc.) suddenly —*n.* **1** a flinging **2** a brief time of wild pleasures **3** a spirited dance **4** [Inf.] a try **5** [Inf.] a brief love affair

**flint** (flint) *n.* ⟦OE⟧ a very hard, siliceous rock, usually gray, that produces sparks when struck against steel —**flint′y, -i·er, -i·est,** *adj.*

**flip**[1] (flip) *vt.* **flipped, flip′ping** ⟦echoic⟧ **1** to toss with a quick jerk; flick **2** to snap (a coin) into the air with the thumb **3** to turn or turn over —*vi.* **1** to move jerkily **2** [Slang] to lose self-control —*n.* a flipping —**flip one's lid** (or **wig**) [Slang] to go berserk

**flip**[2] (flip) *adj.* **flip′per, flip′pest** [Inf.] flippant

**flip chart** a series of large paper sheets containing information, charts, etc., fastened loosely for sequential display

**flip′pant** (-ənt) *adj.* ⟦prob. < FLIP[1]⟧ frivolous and disrespectful; saucy —**flip′pan·cy,** *pl.* **-cies,** *n.* — **flip′pant·ly** *adv.*

**flip′per** (-ər) *n.* ⟦< FLIP[1]⟧ **1** a broad, flat limb adapted for swimming, as in seals **2** a paddlelike rubber device worn on each foot by skin divers, etc.

**flirt** (flurt) *vt.* ⟦< ?⟧ to move jerkily *[the bird flirted its tail]* —*vi.* **1** to pay amorous attention to someone, without serious intentions **2** to trifle or toy *[to flirt with an idea]* —*n.* **1** a quick, jerky movement **2** one who flirts with others

**flir·ta·tion** (flər tā′shən) *n.* a frivolous love affair —**flir·ta′tious** *adj.*

**flit** (flit) *vi.* **flit′ted, flit′ting** ⟦< ON *flytja*⟧ to pass or fly lightly and rapidly

**float** (flōt) *n.* ⟦< OE *flota,* a ship⟧ **1** anything that stays on the surface of a liquid, as a raftlike platform for swimmers, a cork on a fishing line, etc. **2** a floating ball, etc. that regulates a valve, as in a water tank **3** a low, flat vehicle decorated for exhibit in a parade **4** a beverage with ice cream floating in it —*vi.* **1** to stay on the surface of a liquid **2** to drift easily on water, in air, etc. **3** to move about aimlessly **4** to fluctuate freely: said of exchange rates —*vt.* **1** to cause to float **2** to put into circulation *[to float a bond issue]* **3** to arrange for (a loan) —**float′er** *n.*

**flock** (fläk) *n.* ⟦OE *flocc*⟧ **1** a group of certain animals, as sheep, birds, etc., living or feeding together **2** any group, esp. a large one —*vi.* to assemble or travel in a flock or crowd

**flock·ing** (fläk′iŋ) *n.* ⟦< L *floccus,* tuft of wool⟧ **1** tiny fibers of wool, rayon, etc. applied to a fabric, wallpaper, etc. as a velvetlike surface: also **flock 2** such a fabric, etc.

**floe** (flō) *n.* ⟦? < Norw *flo,* layer⟧ ICE FLOE

**flog** (fläg, flôg) *vt.* **flogged, flog′ging** ⟦? < L *flagellare,* to whip⟧ to beat with a stick, whip, etc. — **flog′ger** *n.*

**flood** (flud) *n.* ⟦OE *flod*⟧ **1** an overflowing of water on an area normally dry **2** the rising of the tide **3** a great outpouring, as of words —*vt.* **1** to cover or fill, as with a flood **2** to put too much water, fuel, etc. on or in —*vi.* **1** to gush out in a flood **2** to become flooded —**the Flood** *Bible* the great flood in Noah's time

**flood′light′** *n.* **1** a lamp that casts a broad beam of bright light **2** such a beam of light —*vt.* **-light′ed** or **-lit′, -light′ing** to illuminate by a floodlight

**flood tide** the rising tide

**floor** (flôr) *n.* ⟦OE *flor*⟧ **1** the inside bottom surface of a room **2** the bottom surface of anything *[the ocean floor]* **3** a story in a building **4** the right to speak in an assembly —*vt.* **1** to furnish with a floor **2** to knock down **3** [Inf.] *a)* to defeat *b)* to flabbergast; astound

**floor′board′** *n.* **1** a board in a floor **2** the floor of an automobile, etc.

**floor exercise** any gymnastic exercise done without apparatus

**floor′ing** *n.* **1** a floor or floors **2** material for making a floor

**floor show** a show presenting singers, dancers, etc., as in a nightclub

**flop** (fläp) *vt.* **flopped, flop′ping** ⟦var. of FLAP⟧ to flap or throw noisily and clumsily —*vi.* **1** to move, drop, or flap around loosely or clumsily **2**

---

[Inf.] to fail —*n.* **1** the act or sound of flopping **2** [Inf.] a failure —**flop′py, -pi·er, -pi·est,** *adj.*

**flop′house′** *n.* [Inf.] a cheap hotel for indigents

**floppy disk** a small, flexible computer disk for storing data

**flo·ra** (flôr′ə) *n.* ⟦L < *flos,* a flower⟧ the plants of a specified region or time

**flo′ral** (-əl) *adj.* of or like flowers

**Flor·ence** (flôr′əns) city in central Italy: pop. 403,000 —**Flor′en·tine′** (-ən tēn′) *adj., n.*

**flo·res·cence** (flô res′əns) *n.* ⟦< L *flos,* a flower⟧ blooming or flowering —**flo·res′cent** *adj.*

**flor·id** (flôr′id) *adj.* ⟦< L *flos,* a flower⟧ **1** ruddy: said of the complexion **2** gaudy; showy; ornate

**Flor·i·da** (flôr′ə də, flär′-) Southern state of the SE U.S.: 53,937 sq. mi.; pop. 12,938,000; cap. Tallahassee: abbrev. *FL* —**Flo·rid·i·an** (flô rid′ē ən) or **Flor′i·dan** *adj., n.*

**flor·in** (flôr′in) *n.* ⟦< L *flos,* a flower⟧ any of various European or South African silver or gold coins

**flo·rist** (flôr′ist) *n.* ⟦< L *flos,* a flower⟧ one who grows or sells flowers

**floss** (flôs, fläs) *n.* ⟦ult. < L *floccus,* tuft of wool⟧ **1** the short, downy waste fibers of silk **2** a soft, loosely twisted thread or yarn, as of silk, for embroidery **3** a substance like this **4** DENTAL FLOSS —*vt., vi.* to clean (the teeth) with dental floss —**floss′y, -i·er, -i·est,** *adj.*

**flo·ta·tion** (flō tā′shən) *n.* the act or condition of floating

**flo·til·la** (flō til′ə) *n.* ⟦Sp, dim. of *flota,* a fleet⟧ **1** a small fleet **2** a fleet of boats or small ships

**flot·sam** (flät′səm) *n.* ⟦< MDu *vloten,* to float⟧ the wreckage of a ship or its cargo floating at sea: used in the phrase **flotsam and jetsam**

**flounce**[1] (flouns) *vi.* **flounced, flounc′ing** ⟦< ? Scand⟧ to move with quick, flinging motions of the body, as in anger —*n.* a flouncing

**flounce**[2] (flouns) *n.* ⟦< OFr *froncir,* to wrinkle⟧ a wide ruffle sewn to a skirt, sleeve, etc. —**flounc′y, -i·er, -i·est,** *adj.*

**floun·der**[1] (floun′dər) *vi.* ⟦< ? FOUNDER⟧ **1** to struggle awkwardly, as in deep mud **2** to speak or act in an awkward, confused manner

**floun·der**[2] (floun′dər) *n.* ⟦< Scand⟧ any of various flatfishes caught for food, as the halibut

**flour** (flour) *n.* ⟦orig., flower (i.e., best) of meal⟧ **1** a fine, powdery substance produced by grinding and sifting grain, esp. wheat **2** any finely powdered substance —**flour′y** *adj.*

**flour·ish** (flur′ish) *vi.* ⟦< L *flos,* a flower⟧ **1** to grow vigorously; thrive **2** to be at the peak of development, etc. —*vt.* to brandish (a sword, etc.) —*n.* **1** anything done in a showy way **2** a brandishing **3** decorative lines in handwriting **4** a musical fanfare

**flout** (flout) *vt., vi.* ⟦< ? ME *flouten,* play the flute⟧ to mock or scoff —*n.* a scornful act or remark — **flout′er** *n.*

**flow** (flō) *vi.* ⟦OE *flowan*⟧ **1** to move as a liquid does **2** to move gently and smoothly **3** to pour out **4** to issue; proceed **5** to hang loose *[flowing hair]* **6** to be plentiful —*n.* **1** a flowing **2** the rate of flow **3** anything that flows **4** the rising of the tide

**flow′chart′** *n.* a diagram showing steps in a sequence of operations, as in manufacturing

**flow·er** (flou′ər) *n.* ⟦< L *flos*⟧ **1** the seed-producing structure of a flowering plant; blossom **2** a plant cultivated for its blossoms **3** the best or finest part —*vi.* **1** to produce blossoms **2** to reach the best stage —**in flower** flowering

**flow′er·pot′** *n.* a container in which to grow plants

**flow′er·y** *adj.* **-i·er, -i·est 1** covered or decorated with flowers **2** full of ornate expressions and fine words —**flow′er·i·ness** *n.*

**flown** (flōn) *vi., vt. pp. of* FLY[1]

**flu** (flōō) *n.* **1** *short for* INFLUENZA **2** a respiratory or intestinal infection caused by a virus

**flub** (flub) [Inf.] *vt., vi.* **flubbed, flub′bing** ⟦< ? FL(OP) + (D)UB[1]⟧ to bungle (a job, stroke, etc.) —*n.* a blunder

**fluc·tu·ate** (fluk′chōō āt′) *vi.* **-at′ed, -at′ing** ⟦< L *fluctus*, a wave⟧ to be continually varying in an irregular way —**fluc′tu·a′tion** *n.*

**flue** (flōō) *n.* ⟦< ? OFr *fluie*, a flowing⟧ a tube or shaft for the passage of smoke, hot air, etc., esp. in a chimney

**flu·ent** (flōō′ənt) *adj.* ⟦< L *fluere*, to flow⟧ **1** flowing or moving smoothly **2** able to write or speak easily, expressively, etc. —**flu′en·cy** *n.* —**flu′ent·ly** *adv.*

**fluff** (fluf) *n.* ⟦? blend of *flue*, soft mass + PUFF⟧ **1** soft, light down **2** a loose, soft mass, as of hair **3** something trivial —*vt.* **1** to shake or pat until loose or fluffy **2** to bungle (one's lines), as in acting

**fluff′y** *adj.* **-i·er, -i·est** soft and light like fluff; feathery

**flu·id** (flōō′id) *adj.* ⟦< L *fluere*, to flow⟧ **1** that can flow as a liquid or gas does **2** that can change rapidly or easily **3** available for investment or as cash —*n.* a liquid or gas —**flu·id′i·ty** *n.* —**flu′id·ly** *adv.*

**fluke**[1] (flōōk) *n.* ⟦OE *floc*, a flatfish⟧ TREMATODE

**fluke**[2] (flōōk) *n.* ⟦< ?⟧ **1** a pointed end of an anchor, which catches in the ground **2** a barb of a harpoon, etc. **3** a lobe of a whale's tail **4** [Inf.] a stroke of luck

**flung** (fluŋ) *vt. pt. & pp. of* FLING

**flunk** (fluŋk) *vt., vi.* ⟦< ?⟧ [Inf.] to fail, as in a school assignment

**flunk·y** (fluŋ′kē) *n., pl.* **-ies** ⟦orig. Scot⟧ **1** a toady **2** a person with menial tasks Also **flunk′ey**

**fluo·resce** (flô res′) *vi.* **-resced′, -resc′ing** to produce, show, or undergo fluorescence

**fluo·res′cence** (-res′əns) *n.* ⟦ult. < L *fluor*, flux⟧ **1** the property of producing light when acted upon by radiant energy **2** the production of such light **3** light so produced —**fluo·res′cent** *adj.*

**fluorescent lamp** (or **tube**) a glass tube coated on the inside with a fluorescent substance that gives off light (**fluorescent light**) when mercury vapor in the tube is acted upon by a stream of electrons

**fluo·ri·date** (flôr′ə dāt′, floor′-) *vt.* **-dat′ed, -dat′ing** to add fluorides to (a supply of drinking water) in order to reduce tooth decay —**fluo′ri·da′tion** *n.*

**fluo·ride** (flôr′īd′, floor′īd′) *n.* any of various compounds of fluorine, esp. one put in toothpaste, etc. to prevent tooth decay

**fluo·rine′** (-ēn′) *n.* ⟦< L *fluor*, flux⟧ a greenish-yellow, gaseous chemical element

**fluo·rite′** (-īt′) *n.* ⟦< L *fluor*, flux⟧ calcium fluoride, a transparent, crystalline mineral: the principal source of fluorine

**fluo·ro·car·bon** (-kär′bən) *n.* any of certain compounds containing carbon, fluorine, and, sometimes, hydrogen

**fluo·ro·scope′** (-skōp′) *n.* a machine for examining internal structures by viewing the shadows cast on a fluorescent screen by objects through which X-rays are directed

**flur·ry** (flur′ē) *n., pl.* **-ries** ⟦< ?⟧ **1** a sudden gust of wind, rain, or snow **2** a sudden commotion —*vt.* **-ried, -ry·ing** to confuse; agitate

**flush**[1] (flush) *vi.* ⟦blend of FLASH & ME *flusshen*, fly up suddenly⟧ **1** to flow rapidly **2** to blush or glow **3** to be washed out with a sudden flow of water **4** to start up from cover: said of birds —*vt.* **1** to wash out with a sudden flow of water **2** to make blush or glow **3** to excite [*flushed* with victory] **4** to drive (birds) from cover —*n.* **1** a rapid flow, as of water **2** a sudden, vigorous growth **3** sudden excitement **4** a blush; glow **5** a sudden feeling of heat, as in a fever —*adj.* **1** well sup-

plied, esp. with money **2** abundant **3** level or even (*with*) **4** direct; full —*adv.* **1** so as to be level **2** directly

**flush**[2] (flush) *n.* ⟦< L *fluere*, to flow⟧ a hand of cards all in the same suit

**flus·ter** (flus′tər) *vt., vi.* ⟦prob. < Scand⟧ to make or become confused —*n.* a being flustered

**flute** (flōōt) *n.* ⟦< Prov *fläut*⟧ **1** a high-pitched wind instrument consisting of a long, slender tube with finger holes and keys **2** a groove in the shaft of a column, etc. —**flut′ed** *adj.* —**flut′ing** *n.* —**flut′ist** *n.*

**flut·ter** (flut′ər) *vi.* ⟦< OE *fleotan*, to float⟧ **1** to flap the wings rapidly, without flying **2** to wave, move, or beat rapidly and irregularly —*vt.* to cause to flutter —*n.* **1** a fluttering movement **2** an excited or confused state —**flut′ter·y** *adj.*

**flux** (fluks) *n.* ⟦< L *fluere*, to flow⟧ **1** a flowing **2** a continual change **3** a substance used to help metals fuse together, as in soldering

**fly**[1] (flī) *vi.* **flew, flown, fly′ing** ⟦OE *fleogan*⟧ **1** to move through the air in an aircraft or by using wings, as a bird does **2** to wave or float in the air **3** to move or pass swiftly **4** to flee **5** flied, fly′ing *Baseball* to hit a fly —*vt.* **1** to cause to float in the air **2** to operate (an aircraft) **3** to flee from —*n., pl.* **flies 1** a flap that conceals the zipper, etc. in a garment **2** a flap serving as the door of a tent **3** *Baseball* a ball batted high in the air **4** [*pl.*] *Theater* the space above a stage —**let fly (at) 1** to throw (at) **2** to direct a verbal attack (at) —**on the fly** [Inf.] while in a hurry

**fly**[2] (flī) *n., pl.* **flies** ⟦OE *fleoge*⟧ **1** any of a large group of insects with two or four wings **2** an artificial fly used as a lure in fishing

**fly′a·ble** *adj.* suitable for flying

**fly′by′** or **fly′-by′** *n., pl.* **-bys′** a flight past a designated point or place by an aircraft or spacecraft

**fly′-by-night′** *adj.* financially irresponsible —*n.* an absconding debtor

**fly′-by-wire′** *adj.* of a system for controlling an airplane or spacecraft electronically, as by computer

**fly′-cast′** *vt.* **-cast′, -cast′ing** to fish by casting artificial flies

**fly′catch′er** *n.* a small bird that catches insects in flight

**fly′er** *n. alt. sp. of* FLIER

**flying buttress** a buttress connected with a wall by an arch, serving to resist outward pressure

**flying colors** used in **with flying colors**, with notable success

**fly′ing·fish′** *n., pl.* **-fish′** or (for different species) **-fish′es** a fish with winglike fins used in gliding through the air: also **flying fish**

**flying saucer** a UFO

**fly′leaf′** *n., pl.* **-leaves′** a blank leaf at the beginning or end of a book

**fly′pa′per** *n.* a sticky or poisonous paper set out to catch flies

**fly′speck′** *n.* **1** a speck of fly excrement **2** any tiny spot or petty flaw

**fly′way′** *n.* a route taken regularly by birds migrating to and from breeding grounds

FLYING BUTTRESS

**fly′weight′** *n.* a boxer who weighs 112 pounds or less

**fly′wheel′** *n.* a heavy wheel on a machine, for regulating its speed

**FM**[1] (ef′em′) *n.* frequency-modulation broadcasting or sound transmission

**FM**[2] *abbrev.* frequency modulation

**f-num·ber** (ef′num′bər) *n. Photog.* a number indicating the relative aperture of a lens: a higher number means a smaller opening

**foal** (fōl) *n.* ⟦OE *fola*⟧ a young horse, mule, etc.; colt or filly —*vt., vi.* to give birth to (a foal)

**foam** (fōm) *n.* ⟦OE *fam*⟧ **1** the whitish mass of

bubbles formed on or in liquids by agitation, fermentation, etc. **2** something like foam, as frothy saliva **3** a rigid or spongy cellular mass, made from liquid rubber, plastic, etc. —*vi.* to produce foam —**foam′y, -i·er, -i·est,** *adj.*

**fob** (fäb) *n.* [prob. < dial. Ger *fuppe,* a pocket] **1** a short ribbon or chain attached to a pocket watch **2** any ornament worn on such a chain, etc.

**fo·cal** (fō′kəl) *adj.* of or at a focus

**focal length** the distance from the optical center of a lens to the point where the light rays converge

**fo′c′sle** or **fo′c′s′le** (fōk′səl) *contr. n. phonetic sp.* of FORECASTLE

**fo·cus** (fō′kəs) *n., pl.* **-cus·es** or **-ci′** (-sī′) [L, hearth] **1** the point where rays of light, heat, etc. come together; specif., the point where rays of reflected or refracted light meet **2** a FOCAL LENGTH **3** an adjustment of this to make a clear image [bring a lens into *focus*] **4** any center of activity, attention, etc. —*vt.* **-cused** or **-cussed, -cus·ing** or **-cus·sing** **1** to bring into focus **2** to adjust the focal length of (the eye, a lens, etc.) so as to produce a clear image **3** to concentrate —**in focus** clear and sharp —**out of focus** blurred

**fod·der** (fäd′ər) *n.* [OE *fodor*] coarse food for cattle, horses, etc., as hay

**foe** (fō) *n.* [OE *fah,* hostile] an enemy

**foe·tus** (fēt′əs) *n. alt. sp. of* FETUS

**fog** (fôg, fäg) *n.* [prob. < Scand] **1** a large mass of water vapor condensed to fine particles, at or just above the earth's surface **2** a state of mental confusion —*vt., vi.* **fogged, fog′ging** to make or become foggy

**fog′gy** *adj.* **-gi·er, -gi·est** **1** full of fog **2** dim; blurred **3** confused —**fog′gi·ness** *n.*

**fog′horn′** *n.* a horn blown to warn ships in a fog

**fo·gy** (fō′gē) *n., pl.* **-gies** [< ?] one who is old-fashioned: usually with *old:* also **fo′gey,** *pl.* **-geys**

**foi·ble** (foi′bəl) *n.* [< Fr *faible,* feeble] a small weakness in character

**foil¹** (foil) *vt.* [< OFr *fuler,* trample] to keep from being successful; thwart

**foil²** (foil) *n.* [< L *folium,* leaf] **1** a very thin sheet of metal **2** a person or thing that sets off another by contrast **3** [< ?] a long, thin, blunted fencing sword

**foist** (foist) *vt.* [prob. < dial. Du *vuisten,* to hide in the hand] to get (a thing) accepted, sold, etc. by fraud, deception, etc.; palm off: with *on* or *upon*

**fol** *abbrev.* **1** folio(s) **2** following

**fold¹** (fōld) *vt.* [OE *faldan*] **1** to double (material) up on itself **2** to draw together and intertwine [to *fold* the arms] **3** to embrace **4** to wrap up; envelop —*vi.* **1** to be or become folded **2** [Inf.] *a)* to fail, as a business, play, etc. *b)* to fail suddenly; collapse —*n.* a folded part

**fold²** (fōld) *n.* [OE *fald*] **1** a pen for sheep **2** a flock of sheep **3** a group sharing a common faith, goal, etc.

**-fold** (fōld) [< OE *-feald*] *suffix* **1** having (a specified number of) parts **2** (a specified number of) times as many or as much [to *fold* tenfold]

**fold′a·way′** *adj.* that can be folded together for easy storage

**fold′er** *n.* **1** a sheet of heavy paper folded for holding loose papers **2** a pamphlet or circular of one or more folded, unstitched sheets

**fo·li·age** (fō′lē ij) *n.* [< L *folia*] leaves, as of a plant or tree

**fo·lic acid** (fō′lik) [< L *folium,* leaf] a substance belonging to the vitamin B complex, used in treating anemia

**fo·li·o** (fō′lē ō′) *n., pl.* **-os′** [< L *folium,* leaf] **1** a large sheet of paper folded once **2** a large size of book, about 12 by 15 inches, made of sheets so folded **3** the number of a page in a book

**folk** (fōk) *n., pl.* **folks** or **folk** [OE *folc*] **1** a people or nation **2** [*pl.*] people; persons —*adj.* of or originating among the common people —**one's** (or **the**)

**folks** [Inf.] one's family, esp. one's parents

**folk′lore′** *n.* [prec. + LORE] the traditional beliefs, legends, etc. of a culture

**folk song** **1** a song made and handed down among the common people **2** a song composed in imitation of this —**folk singer**

**folk′sy** (-sē) *adj.* **-si·er, -si·est** [Inf.] friendly or sociable

**fol·li·cle** (fäl′i kəl) *n.* [< L *follis,* bellows] any small sac, cavity, or gland for excretion or secretion [a hair *follicle*]

**fol·low** (fäl′ō) *vt.* [< OE *folgian*] **1** to come or go after **2** to pursue **3** to go along [follow the road] **4** to take up (a trade, etc.) **5** to result from **6** to take as a model; imitate **7** to obey **8** to watch or listen to closely **9** to be interested in developments in [to *follow* local politics] **10** to understand —*vi.* **1** to come or go after something else in place, time, etc. **2** to result —**follow out** (or **up**) to carry out fully —**follow through** to continue and complete a stroke or action

**fol′low·er** *n.* one that follows; specif., *a)* one who follows another's teachings; disciple *b)* an attendant

**fol′low·ing** *adj.* that follows; next after —*n.* a group of followers —*prep.* after [following dinner they left]

**fol′low-up′** *n.* a letter, visit, etc. that follows as a review, addition, etc.

**fol·ly** (fäl′ē) *n., pl.* **-lies** [see FOOL] **1** a lack of sense; foolishness **2** a foolish action or belief **3** a foolish and useless but expensive undertaking

**fo·ment** (fō ment′) *vt.* [< L *fovere,* keep warm] to stir up (trouble); incite —**fo′men·ta′tion** *n.*

**fond** (fänd) *adj.* [< ME *fonnen,* be foolish] **1** tender and affectionate; loving or doting **2** cherished [a fond hope] —**fond of** having a liking for —**fond′ly** *adv.* —**fond′ness** *n.*

**fon·dle** (fän′dəl) *vt.* **-dled, -dling** [< prec.] to caress or handle lovingly

**fon·due** or **fon·du** (fän dōō′, fän′dōō′) *n.* [Fr < *fondre,* melt] melted cheese, etc. used as a dip for cubes of bread

**font¹** (fänt) *n.* [< L *fons,* spring] **1** a basin to hold baptismal water **2** a container for holy water **3** a source

**font²** (fänt) *n.* [see FOUND²] *Printing* a complete assortment of type in one size and style

**fon·ta·nel** or **fon·ta·nelle** (fänt′n el′) *n.* [ME *fontinel,* a hollow] a soft, boneless area in the skull of a baby or young animal, that gradually closes up as bone is formed

**food** (fōōd) *n.* [OE *foda*] **1** any substance, esp. a solid, taken in by a plant or animal to enable it to live and grow **2** anything that nourishes

**food chain** *Ecology* a sequence (as grass, rabbit, fox) of organisms in a community in which each member feeds on the one below it

**food poisoning** sickness caused by contaminants, as bacteria, in food, or by naturally poisonous foods

**food processor** an electrical appliance that can blend, purée, slice, grate, chop, etc. foods rapidly

**food stamp** any of the federal coupons given to qualifying low-income persons for use in buying food

**food′stuff′** *n.* any substance used as food

**fool** (fōōl) *n.* [< L *follis,* windbag] **1** a silly or stupid person **2** a jester **3** a victim of a trick, etc.; dupe —*vi.* **1** to act like a fool **2** to joke **3** [Inf.] to meddle (*with*) —*vt.* to trick; deceive —**fool around** [Inf.] to trifle —**fool′er·y** *n.*

**fool′har·dy** *adj.* **-di·er, -di·est** foolishly daring; reckless —**fool′har′di·ly** *adv.* —**fool′har′di·ness** *n.*

**fool′ish** *adj.* **1** silly; unwise **2** ridiculous **3** embarrassed —**fool′ish·ly** *adv.* —**fool′ish·ness** *n.*

**fool′proof′** *adj.* so simple, well-designed, etc. as not to be mishandled, damaged, misunderstood, etc. even by a fool

**fools·cap** (fōōlz′kap′) *n.* [from a watermark of a

jester's cap‖ a size of writing paper, 13 by 16 in. in the U.S.

**foot** (foot) *n., pl.* **feet** ⟦OE *fot*⟧ **1** the end part of the leg, on which one stands **2** the base or bottom [the *foot* of a page] **3** the muscular part of a mollusk used in burrowing, moving, etc. **4** a measure of length equal to 12 inches: symbol ′ **5** [*with pl. v.*] [Brit.] infantry **6** a group of syllables serving as a unit of meter in verse —*vt.* **1** to add (a column of figures): often with *up* **2** [Inf.] to pay (costs, etc.) —**foot it** [Inf.] to dance, walk, etc. —**on foot** walking —**under foot** in the way

**foot′age** (-ij) *n.* **1** measurement in feet, as of film **2** a length of film that has been shot

**foot′-and-mouth′ disease** a contagious disease of cloven-footed animals, causing blisters in the mouth and around the hoofs

**foot′ball′** *n.* **1** a game played on a rectangular field with an inflated, oval leather ball by two teams that try to score touchdowns **2** [Brit.] *a)* soccer *b)* rugby **3** the ball used in any of these games

**foot′bridge′** *n.* a bridge for pedestrians

**foot′-can′dle** *n.* a unit for measuring illumination

**foot′ed** *adj.* having feet of a specified number or kind [four-*footed*]

**foot′fall′** *n.* the sound of a footstep

**foot′hill′** *n.* a low hill at or near the foot of a mountain or mountain range

**foot′hold′** *n.* **1** a secure place for a foot, as in climbing **2** a secure position

**foot′ing** *n.* **1** a secure placing of the feet **2** the condition of a surface, as for walking **3** a foothold **4** a secure position **5** a basis for relationship

**foot′less** (-lis) *adj.* **1** without a foot or feet **2** without basis **3** [Inf.] clumsy; inept

**foot′lights′** *pl.n.* a row of lights along the front of a stage floor —**the footlights** the theater or the profession of acting

**foot′lock′er** *n.* a small trunk, usually kept at the foot of a bed

**foot′loose′** *adj.* free to go wherever, or do whatever, one likes

**foot′man** (-mən) *n., pl.* **-men** (-mən) a male servant who assists the butler

**foot′note′** *n.* **1** a note of comment or reference at the bottom of a page **2** such a note at the end of a chapter or a book **3** an additional comment, etc. —*vt.* **-not′ed, -not′ing** to add a footnote or footnotes to

**foot′path′** *n.* a narrow path for use by pedestrians only

**foot′-pound′** *n.* a unit of energy or work, the amount required to raise one pound a distance of one foot

**foot′print′** *n.* **1** a mark made by a foot **2** an area, or its shape, which something affects, occupies, etc.

**foot′sore′** *adj.* having sore or tender feet, as from much walking

**foot′step′** *n.* **1** the distance covered in a step **2** the sound of a step **3** FOOTPRINT (sense 1) —**follow in someone's footsteps** to follow someone's example, etc.

**foot′stool′** *n.* a low stool for supporting the feet of a seated person

**foot′wear′** *n.* shoes, boots, etc.

**foot′work′** *n.* the act or manner of using the feet, as in boxing or dancing

**fop** (fäp) *n.* ⟦ME *foppe*, a fool⟧ DANDY (*n.* 1) —**fop′per·y,** *pl.* **-ies,** *n.* —**fop′pish** *adj.* —**fop′pish·ly** *adv.*

**for** (fôr, fur) *prep.* ⟦OE⟧ **1** in place of [use a rope *for* a belt] **2** in the interest of [to act *for* another] **3** in favor of [vote *for* the levy] **4** in honor of [a party *for* her] **5** in order to be, get, have, keep, find, etc. [walk *for* exercise, start *for* home] **6** meant to be received by [flowers *for* a friend] **7** suitable to [a room *for* sleeping] **8** with regard to; concerning [an ear *for* music] **9** as being [to know *for* a fact] **10** considering the nature of [cool *for* July] **11** because of [a cry *for* pain] **12** at the price of [sold *for* $20,000] **13** to the length, amount, or duration of —*conj.* because; since —**for all** in spite of

**for-** ⟦OE⟧ *prefix* away, apart, off [*forbid, forgo*]

**for·age** (fôr′ij, fär′-) *n.* [< OFr *forre,* fodder⟧ **1** food for domestic animals **2** a search for food —*vi.* **-aged, -ag·ing 1** to search for food **2** to search for something one wants —*vt.* to take food from; raid —**for′ag·er** *n.*

**for·ay** (fôr′ā) *vt., vi.* ⟦< OFr *forrer,* to forage⟧ to plunder —*n.* a raid in order to seize things

**for·bear**[1] (fôr ber′) *vt.* **-bore′, -borne′, -bear′ing** ⟦see FOR- & BEAR[1]⟧ to refrain from (doing, saying, etc.) —*vi.* **1** to refrain **2** to control oneself under provocation

**for′bear′**[2] *n. alt. sp. of* FOREBEAR

**for·bear′ance** *n.* **1** the act of forbearing **2** self-restraint

**for·bid** (fər bid′, fôr-) *vt.* **-bade′** (-bad′) **or -bad′, -bid′den, -bid′ding** ⟦see FOR- & BID⟧ **1** to order (a person) not to do (something); prohibit **2** to prevent

**for·bid′ding** *adj.* looking dangerous or disagreeable; repellent —**for·bid′ding·ly** *adv.*

**force** (fôrs) *n.* ⟦< L *fortis,* strong⟧ **1** strength; power **2** physical coercion against a person or thing **3** the power to control, persuade, etc.; effectiveness **4** military power **5** any group of people organized for some activity [a sales *force*] **6** energy that causes or alters motion [*Law* binding power; validity —*vt.* **forced, forc′ing 1** to make do something by force; compel **2** to break open, into, or through by force **3** to take by force; extort **4** to impose by force: with *on* or *upon* **5** to produce as by force [to *force* a smile] **6** to cause (plants, etc.) to develop faster by artificial means —**in force 1** in full strength **2** in effect; valid —**force′less** *adj.*

**forced** (fôrst) *adj.* **1** compulsory [*forced* labor] **2** not natural; strained [a *forced* smile] **3** due to necessity [a *forced* landing] **4** at a faster pace [a *forced* march] —**forc·ed·ly** (fôrs′id lē) *adv.*

**force′-feed′** *vt.* **-fed′, -feed′ing** to feed as by a tube through the throat to the stomach

**force′ful** (-fəl) *adj.* full of force; powerful, vigorous, effective, etc. —**force′ful·ly** *adv.* —**force′ful·ness** *n.*

**for·ceps** (fôr′seps′) *n., pl.* **-ceps′** ⟦L < *formus,* warm + *capere,* to take⟧ small tongs or pincers for grasping, pulling, etc.

**for·ci·ble** (fôr′sə bəl) *adj.* **1** done by force **2** having force —**for′ci·bly** *adv.*

**ford** (fôrd) *n.* ⟦OE⟧ a shallow place in a stream, etc. where one can cross by wading —*vt.* to cross at a ford —**ford′a·ble** *adj.*

**Ford** (fôrd) **1** Ger·ald R(udolph), Jr. (jer′əld) 1913- ; 38th president of the U.S. (1974-77) **2** Henry 1863-1947; U.S. automobile manufacturer

**fore** (fôr) *adv., adj.* ⟦OE⟧ at, in, or toward the front part, as of a ship —*n.* the front —*interj. Golf* a shout warning that one is about to hit the ball

**fore-** ⟦OE⟧ *prefix* **1** before in time, place, etc. [*forenoon*] **2** the front part of [*forehead*]

**fore-and-aft** (fôr′ən aft′) *adj. Naut.* from the bow to the stern; set lengthwise, as sails

**fore′arm′**[1] *n.* the part of the arm between the elbow and the wrist

**fore·arm′**[2] *vt.* to arm in advance

**fore′bear′** (-ber′) *n.* ⟦< FORE + BE + -ER⟧ an ancestor

**fore·bode′** (-bōd′) *vt., vi.* **-bod′ed, -bod′ing** ⟦< OE⟧ **1** to foretell; predict **2** to have a presentiment of (something bad) —**fore·bod′ing** *n.*

**fore′cast′** *vt.* **-cast′ or -cast′ed, -cast′ing 1** to predict **2** to serve as a prediction of —*n.* a prediction —**fore′cast′er** *n.*

**fore·cas·tle** (fōk′səl, fôr′kas′əl) *n.* **1** the upper deck of a ship in front of the foremast **2** the front part of a merchant ship, where the crew's quarters are located

**fore·close** (fôr klōz′) *vt., vi.* **-closed′, -clos′ing** ⟦< OFr *fors,* outside + *clore,* CLOSE²⟧ to take away the right to redeem (a mortgage) —**fore·clo′sure** (-klō′zhər) *n.*

**fore·doom′** *vt.* to doom in advance

**fore′fa′ther** *n.* an ancestor

**fore′fin′ger** *n.* the finger nearest the thumb

**fore′foot′** *n., pl.* **-feet′** either of the front feet of an animal

**fore′front′** *n.* **1** the extreme front **2** the position of most importance, activity, etc.

**fore·go′**[1] *vt., vi.* **-went′, -gone′, -go′ing** to go before in place, time, etc.; precede

**fore·go′**[2] *vt. alt. sp. of* FORGO

**fore′go′ing** *adj.* previously said, written, etc.; preceding

**fore·gone′** *adj.* **1** previous **2** previously determined; inevitable

**fore′ground′** *n.* **1** the part of a scene, etc. nearest to the viewer **2** the most noticeable position —*vt.* to place in the foreground; emphasize

**fore′hand′** *n.* a stroke, as in tennis, made with the palm of the hand turned forward —*adj.* done as with a forehand

**fore·head** (fôr′ed′, -hed′; fär′-) *n.* the part of the face between the eyebrows and the line where the hair normally begins

**for·eign** (fôr′in, fär′-) *adj.* ⟦< L *foras,* out-of-doors⟧ **1** situated outside one's own country, locality, etc. **2** of, from, or having to do with other countries **3** not belonging; not characteristic

**for′eign-born′** *adj.* born in some other country; not native

**for′eign·er** *n.* a person from another country; alien

**foreign minister** a member of a governmental cabinet in charge of foreign affairs for the country

**fore·know** (fôr nō′) *vt.* **-knew′, -known′, -know′ing** to have knowledge of beforehand — **fore·knowl′edge** (-näl′ij) *n.*

**fore′leg′** *n.* either of the front legs of an animal

**fore′lock′** *n.* a lock of hair growing just above the forehead

**fore′man** (-mən) *n., pl.* **-men** (-mən) **1** the chairman of a jury **2** the head of a group of workers

**fore′mast′** *n.* the mast nearest the bow of a ship

**fore′most′** *adj.* first in place, time, etc. —*adv.* first

**fore′noon′** *n.* the time from sunrise to noon; morning

**fo·ren·sic** (fə ren′sik, -zik) *adj.* ⟦< L *forum,* marketplace⟧ **1** of or suitable for public debate **2** involving the application of scientific, esp. medical, knowledge to legal matters —*n.* [*pl.*] debate or formal argumentation —**fo·ren′si·cal·ly** *adv.*

**forensic medicine** MEDICAL JURISPRUDENCE

**fore′or·dain′** *vt.* to ordain beforehand; predestine —**fore′or′di·na′tion** *n.*

**fore′run′ner** *n.* **1** a herald **2** a sign that tells or warns of something to follow **3** a predecessor; ancestor

**fore′sail′** (-sāl′, -səl) *n.* the lowest sail on the foremast of a square-rigged ship or a schooner

**fore·see′** *vt.* **-saw′, -seen′, -see′ing** to see or know beforehand —**fore·see′a·ble** *adj.* —**fore·se′er** *n.*

**fore·shad′ow** *vt.* to indicate or suggest beforehand; prefigure

**fore·short′en** *vt.* in drawing, etc., to shorten

some lines of (an object) to give the illusion of proper relative size

**fore′sight′** *n.* **1** *a*) the act of foreseeing *b*) the power to foresee **2** prudent regard or provision for the future

**fore′skin′** *n.* the fold of skin that covers the end of the penis

**for·est** (fôr′ist) *n.* ⟦< L *foris,* out-of-doors⟧ a thick growth of trees, etc. covering a large tract of land —*vt.* to plant with trees

**fore·stall′** *vt.* ⟦< OE *foresteall,* ambush⟧ **1** to prevent by doing something ahead of time **2** to act in advance of; anticipate

FORESHORTENED ARM

**for·est·a·tion** (fôr′is tā′shən, fär′-) *n.* the planting or care of forests

**for′est·ed** *adj.* covered with trees and underbrush

**for′est·er** *n.* one trained in forestry

**for′est·ry** *n.* the science of planting and taking care of forests

**fore·taste** (fôr′tāst′) *n.* a taste or sample of what can be expected

**fore·tell′** *vt.* **-told′, -tell′ing** to tell or indicate beforehand; predict

**fore′thought′** *n.* **1** a thinking or planning beforehand **2** foresight

**for·ev·er** (fôr ev′ər, fər-) *adv.* **1** for always; endlessly **2** at all times; always Also **for·ev′er·more′**

**fore·warn** (fôr wôrn′) *vt.* to warn beforehand

**fore′wom′an** *n., pl.* **-wom′en** a woman serving as a foreman

**fore′word** *n.* an introductory statement in a book

**for·feit** (fôr′fit) *n.* ⟦< OFr *forfaire,* transgress⟧ **1** a fine or penalty for some crime, fault, or neglect **2** the act of forfeiting —*adj.* lost or taken away as a forfeit —*vt.* to lose or be deprived of as a forfeit

**for′fei·ture** (-fə chər) *n.* **1** the act of forfeiting **2** anything forfeited

**for·gath·er** (fôr gath′ər) *vi.* to come together; meet; assemble

**for·gave** (fər gāv′, fôr-) *vt., vi. pt. of* FORGIVE

**forge**[1] (fôrj) *n.* ⟦< L *faber,* workman⟧ **1** a furnace for heating metal to be wrought **2** a place where metal is heated and wrought; smithy —*vt.* **forged, forg′ing 1** to form or shape (metal) by heating and hammering **2** to form; shape **3** to imitate (a signature) fraudulently, counterfeit (a check), etc. —*vi.* **1** to work at a forge **2** to commit forgery —**forg′er** *n.*

**forge**[2] (fôrj) *vi.* **forged, forg′ing** ⟦prob. < FORCE⟧ to move forward steadily: often with *ahead*

**for′ger·y** *n., pl.* **-ies 1** the act or crime of imitating or counterfeiting documents, signatures, etc. to deceive **2** anything forged

**for·get** (fər get′, fôr-) *vt., vi.* **-got′, -got′ten** or **-got′, -get′ting** ⟦OE *forgietan*⟧ **1** to be unable to remember **2** to overlook or neglect (something) — **forget oneself** to act in an improper manner — **for·get′ta·ble** *adj.*

**for·get′ful** *adj.* **1** apt to forget **2** heedless or negligent —**for·get′ful·ly** *adv.* —**for·get′ful·ness** *n.*

**for·get′-me-not′** *n.* a marsh plant with small blue, white, or pink flowers

**for·give** (fər giv′, fôr-) *vt., vi.* **-gave′, -giv′en, -giv′ing** ⟦OE *forgiefan*⟧ **1** to give up resentment against or the desire to punish; pardon (an offense or offender) **2** to cancel (a debt) —**for·giv′a·ble** *adj.* —**for·give′ness** *n.* —**for·giv′er** *n.*

**for·giv′ing** *adj.* inclined to forgive —**for·giv′ing·ly** *adv.*

**for·go** (fôr gō′) *vt.* **-went′, -gone′, -go′ing** ⟦OE *forgan*⟧ to do without; abstain from; give up — **for·go′er** *n.*

**for·got** (fər gät′) *vt., vi. pt. & alt. pp. of* FORGET

**for·got′ten** *vt., vi. alt. pp. of* FORGET

**fork** (fôrk) *n.* ⟦< L *furca*⟧ **1** an instrument of varying size with prongs at one end, as for eating food, pitching hay, etc. **2** something like a fork in shape, etc. **3** the place where a road, etc. divides into branches **4** any of these branches —*vi.* to divide into branches —*vt.* to pick up or pitch with a fork —**fork over** (or **out** or **up**) [Inf.] to pay out; hand over —**fork′ful′**, *pl.* -**fuls′,** *n.*

**fork′lift′** *n.* **1** a device for lifting heavy objects by means of projecting prongs that are slid under the load **2** a small truck with such a device

**for·lorn** (fôr lôrn′) *adj.* ⟦< OE *forleosan*, lose utterly⟧ **1** abandoned **2** wretched; miserable **3** without hope —**for·lorn′ly** *adv.*

**form** (fôrm) *n.* ⟦< L *forma*⟧ **1** shape; general structure **2** the figure of a person or animal **3** a mold **4** a particular mode, kind, type, etc. /ice is a *form* of water, the *forms* of poetry/ **5** arrangement; style **6** a way of doing something requiring skill **7** a customary or conventional way of acting; ceremony; ritual **8** a printed document with blanks to be filled in **9** condition of mind or body **10** RACING FORM **11** a changed appearance of a word to show inflection, etc. **12** type, etc. locked in a frame for printing **13** what is expected, based on past performances /according to *form*/ —*vt.* **1** to shape; fashion **2** to train; instruct **3** to develop (habits) **4** to make up; constitute **5** to organize into /to *form* a club/ —*vi.* to be formed

**-form** (fôrm) ⟦< L⟧ *combining form* having the form of /cuneiform/

**for·mal** (fôr′məl) *adj.* ⟦< L *formalis*⟧ **1** according to fixed customs, rules, etc. **2** stiff in manner **3** *a*) designed for wear at ceremonies, etc. *b*) requiring clothes of this kind **4** done or made in explicit, definite form /a *formal* contract/ **5** designating language usage characterized by expanded vocabulary, complex syntax, etc. **6** designating education in schools, etc. —*n.* **1** a formal dance **2** a woman's evening dress —**for′mal·ly** *adv.*

**form·al·de·hyde** (fôr mal′də hīd′) *n.* ⟦FORM(IC) + *aldehyde*⟧ a pungent gas used in solution as a disinfectant and preservative

**for·mal·ism′** *n.* strict attention to outward forms and traditions

**for·mal·i·ty** (fôr mal′ə tē) *n., pl.* -**ties 1** *a*) an observing of customs, rules, etc.; propriety *b*) excessive attention to convention; stiffness **2** a formal act; ceremony

**for·mal·ize** (fôr′mə līz′) *vt.* -**ized′, -iz′ing 1** to shape **2** to make formal —**for′mal·i·za′tion** *n.*

**for′mal·wear′** *n.* formal clothes, as tuxedos

**for·mat** (fôr′mat′) *n.* ⟦< L *formatus*, formed⟧ **1** the shape, size, and arrangement of a book, etc. **2** the arrangement or plan, as of a TV program **3** a specific way in which computer data is stored, processed, etc. **4** a particular type of audio or video recording and playback system —*vt.* -**mat′ted, -mat′ting** to arrange according to a format

**for·ma·tion** (fôr mā′shən) *n.* **1** a forming or being formed **2** a thing formed **3** the way in which something is formed; structure **4** an arrangement or positioning, as of troops

**form·a·tive** (fôr′mə tiv) *adj.* helping or involving formation or development

**for·mer** (fôr′mər) *adj.* ⟦ME *formere*⟧ **1** earlier; past /in *former* times/ **2** being the first mentioned of two

**for′mer·ly** *adv.* in the past

**form′-fit′ting** *adj.* fitting the body closely: also **form′fit′ting**

**for·mic** (fôr′mik) *adj.* ⟦< L *formica*, ant⟧ designating a colorless acid found in ants, spiders, etc.

**For·mi·ca** (fôr mī′kə) *trademark for* a laminated, heat-resistant plastic used for counter tops, etc.

**for·mi·da·ble** (fôr′mə də bəl, fôr mid′ə bəl) *adj.* ⟦<

L *formidare*, to dread⟧ **1** causing fear, dread, or awe **2** hard to handle

**form′less** *adj.* shapeless; amorphous

**form letter** a standardized letter, usually one of many, with the date, address, etc. added separately

**for·mu·la** (fôr′myōō lə, -myə-) *n., pl.* -**las** or -**lae′** (-lē′, -lī′) ⟦L < *forma*, form⟧ **1** a fixed form of words, esp. a conventional expression **2** a conventional rule for doing something **3** a prescription or recipe **4** fortified milk for a baby **5** a set of symbols expressing a mathematical rule, fact, etc. **6** *Chem.* an expression of the composition, as of a compound, using symbols and figures

**for·mu·late′** (-lāt′) *vt.* -**lat′ed, -lat′ing 1** to express in a formula **2** to express in a definite way **3** to work out in one's mind; devise —**for′mu·la′tion** *n.* —**for′mu·la′tor** *n.*

**for·ni·cate** (fôr′ni kāt′) *vi.* -**cat′ed, -cat′ing** ⟦< L *fornix*, a brothel⟧ to commit fornication —**for′ni·ca′tor** *n.*

**for·ni·ca′tion** *n.* sexual intercourse between unmarried persons

**for·sake** (fôr sāk′) *vt.* -**sook′** (-sook′), -**sak′en, -sak′ing** ⟦< OE *for-*, for- + *sacan*, to strive⟧ **1** to give up (a habit, etc.) **2** to leave; abandon

**for·sooth** (fôr sooth′) *adv.* ⟦ME *forsoth*⟧ [Archaic] indeed

**for·swear** (fôr swer′) *vt.* -**swore′, -sworn′, -swear′ing** to deny or renounce on oath —*vi.* to commit perjury

**for·syth·i·a** (fôr sith′ē ə, fər-) *n.* ⟦after W. *Forsyth* (1737-1804), Eng botanist⟧ a shrub with yellow, bell-shaped flowers that bloom in early spring

**fort** (fôrt) *n.* ⟦< L *fortis*, strong⟧ **1** a fortified place for military defense **2** a permanent army post

**forte**[1] (fôrt; *often* fôr′tā′) *n.* ⟦< OFr: see prec.⟧ that which one does particularly well

**for·te**[2] (fôr′tā′) *adj., adv.* ⟦It < L *fortis*, strong⟧ [*also in italics*] *Music* loud

**forth** (fôrth) *adv.* ⟦OE⟧ **1** forward; onward **2** out into view

**Forth** (fôrth), **Firth of** long estuary of the Forth River in SE Scotland

**forth′com′ing** *adj.* **1** about to appear; approaching **2** ready when needed **3** friendly, outgoing, etc. **4** open; frank

**forth′right′** *adj.* direct and frank

**forth′with′** (-with′, -with′) *adv.* at once

**for·ti·fy** (fôr′tə fī′) *vt.* -**fied′, -fy′ing** ⟦< L *fortis*, strong + *facere*, to make⟧ **1** to strengthen physically, emotionally, etc. **2** to strengthen against attack, as with forts **3** to support **4** to add alcohol to (wine, etc.) **5** to add vitamins, etc. to (milk, etc.) —**for′ti·fi·ca′tion** *n.* —**for′ti·fi′er** *n.*

**for·tis·si·mo** (fôr tis′ə mō′) *adj., adv.* ⟦It, superl. of *forte*, strong⟧ [*also in italics*] *Music* very loud

**for·ti·tude** (fôr′tə tōōd′) *n.* ⟦< L *fortis*, strong⟧ patient endurance of trouble, pain, etc.; courage

**Fort Knox** (näks) military reservation in N Kentucky: site of U.S. gold bullion depository

**Fort Lau·der·dale** (lô′dər dāl′) city on the SE coast of Florida: pop. 149,000

**fort·night** (fôrt′nīt′) *n.* ⟦< OE *feowertyn niht*, lit., fourteen nights⟧ [Chiefly Brit.] a period of two weeks —**fort′night′ly** *adj., adv.*

**for·tress** (fôr′tris) *n.* ⟦< L *fortis*, strong⟧ a fortified place; fort

**for·tu·i·tous** (fôr tōō′ə təs) *adj.* ⟦< L *fors*, luck⟧ **1** happening by chance **2** lucky —**for·tu′i·tous·ly** *adv.*

**for·tu·nate** (fôr′chə nət) *adj.* **1** having good luck **2** coming by good luck; favorable —**for′tu·nate·ly** *adv.*

**for·tune** (fôr′chən) *n.* ⟦< L *fors*, luck⟧ **1** luck; chance; fate **2** [*also pl.*] one's future lot, good or bad **3** good luck; success **4** wealth; riches

**for′tune·tell′er** *n.* one who professes to foretell the future of others —**for′tune·tell′ing** *n., adj.*

**Fort Wayne** (wān) city in NE Indiana: pop. 173,000

**for·ty** (fôr′ē) *adj., n., pl.* **-ties** ⟦OE *feowertig*⟧ four times ten; 40; XL —**the forties** the numbers or years, as of a century, from 40 through 49 — **for′ti·eth** (-ith) *adj.*

**fo·rum** (fôr′əm) *n.* ⟦L⟧ 1 the public square of an ancient Roman city 2 an assembly, program, etc. for the discussion of public matters

**for·ward** (fôr′wərd) *adj.* ⟦OE *foreweard*⟧ 1 at, toward, or of the front 2 advanced 3 onward; advancing 4 prompt; ready 5 bold; presumptuous 6 of or for the future —*adv.* toward the front; ahead —*n. Basketball, Hockey, etc.* a player positioned ahead of the rest of the team, esp. when on the offense —*vt.* 1 to promote 2 to send on

**for′wards** *adv.* FORWARD

**fos·sil** (fäs′əl) *n.* ⟦< L *fossilis*, dug up⟧ 1 any hardened remains of a plant or animal of a previous geologic period, preserved in the earth's crust 2 a person with outmoded ideas or ways —*adj.* 1 of or like a fossil 2 dug from the earth [coal is a *fossil* fuel] 3 antiquated

**fos′sil·ize** (-īz′) *vt., vi.* **-ized**, **-iz′ing** 1 to change into a fossil 2 to make or become out of date, rigid, etc. —**fos′sil·i·za′tion** *n.*

**fos·ter** (fôs′tər) *vt.* ⟦OE *fostrian*, to nourish⟧ 1 to bring up; rear 2 to help to develop; promote — *adj.* having a specified standing in a family but not by birth or adoption [a *foster* brother]

**fought** (fôt) *vi., vt. pt. & pp.* of FIGHT

**foul** (foul) *adj.* ⟦OE *ful*⟧ 1 stinking; loathsome 2 extremely dirty 3 indecent; profane 4 wicked; abominable 5 stormy [*foul* weather] 6 tangled [a *foul* rope] 7 not within the limits or rules set 8 designating lines setting limits on a playing area 9 dishonest 10 [Inf.] unpleasant, disagreeable, etc. —*adv.* in a foul manner —*n. Sports* a hit, blow, move, etc. that is FOUL (*adj.* 7) —*vt.* 1 to make filthy 2 to dishonor 3 to obstruct [grease *fouls* drains] 4 to entangle (a rope, etc.) 5 to make a foul against, as in a game 6 *Baseball* to bat (the ball) foul —*vi.* to be or become fouled — **foul up** [Inf.] to bungle —**foul′ly** *adv.* —**foul′ness** *n.*

**fou·lard** (foo lärd′) *n.* ⟦Fr⟧ a lightweight printed fabric of silk, etc.

**foul′-up′** *n.* [Inf.] a mix-up; botch

**found¹** (found) ⟦OE *funden*⟧ *vt., vi. pp. & pt.* of FIND

**found²** (found) *vt.* ⟦< L *fundus*, bottom⟧ 1 to set for support; base 2 to bring into being; set up; establish —**found′er** *n.*

**found³** (found) *vt.* ⟦< L *fundere*, pour⟧ 1 to melt and pour (metal) into a mold 2 to make by founding metal

**foun·da·tion** (foun dā′shən) *n.* 1 a founding or being founded; establishment 2 *a)* an endowment for an institution *b)* such an institution 3 basis 4 the base of a wall, house, etc. 5 cosmetic over which other makeup is applied

**foun·der** (foun′dər) *vi.* ⟦< L *fundus*, bottom⟧ 1 to stumble, fall, or go lame 2 to fill with water and sink: said of a ship 3 to break down

**found·ling** (found′liŋ) *n.* an infant of unknown parents, found abandoned

**found·ry** (foun′drē) *n., pl.* **-ries** a place where metal is cast

**fount** (fount) *n.* ⟦< L *fons*⟧ 1 [Old Poet.] a fountain or spring 2 a source

**foun·tain** (fount′'n) *n.* ⟦< L *fons*⟧ 1 a natural spring of water 2 a source 3 *a)* an artificial jet or flow of water [a drinking *fountain*] *b)* the basin where this flows 4 a reservoir, as for ink

**foun′tain·head′** *n.* the source, as of a stream

**fountain pen** a pen which is fed ink from its own reservoir or cartridge

**four** (fôr) *adj., n.* ⟦OE *feower*⟧ one more than three; 4; IV

**four′-flush′er** (-flush′ər) *n.* ⟦< FLUSH²⟧ [Inf.] one who bluffs in an effort to deceive

**four′-in-hand′** *n.* a necktie tied in a slipknot with the ends left hanging

**four′score′** *adj., n.* four times twenty; eighty

**four′some** (-səm) *n.* four people

**four·square** (fôr′skwer′) *adj.* 1 square 2 unyielding; firm 3 frank; forthright —*adv.* in a square form or manner

**four·teen** (fôr′tēn′) *adj., n.* ⟦OE *feowertyne*⟧ four more than ten; 14; XIV —**four′teenth′** *adj., n.*

**fourth** (fôrth) *adj.* ⟦OE *feortha*⟧ preceded by three others in a series; 4th —*n.* 1 the one following the third 2 any of the four equal parts of something; ¼ 3 the fourth forward gear

**fourth′-class′** *adj., adv.* of or in a class of mail consisting of merchandise, printed matter, etc. not included in first-class, second-class, or third-class; parcel post

**fourth dimension** in the theory of relativity, time added as a dimension to those of length, width, and depth

**fourth estate** [often F- E-] journalism or journalists

**Fourth of July** see INDEPENDENCE DAY

**4WD** *abbrev.* four-wheel-drive (vehicle)

**four′-wheel′** *adj.* 1 having four wheels 2 affecting four wheels [a *four-wheel* drive]

**fowl** (foul) *n.* ⟦OE *fugol*⟧ 1 any bird 2 any of the domestic birds used as food, as the chicken, duck, etc. 3 the flesh of these birds used for food

**fox** (fäks) *n.* ⟦OE⟧ 1 a small, wild animal of the dog family, considered sly and crafty 2 its fur 3 a sly, crafty person —*vt.* to trick by slyness

**fox′glove′** *n.* DIGITALIS

**fox′hole′** *n.* a hole dug in the ground as a protection against enemy gunfire

**fox′hound′** *n.* a sturdy breed of hound that is trained to hunt foxes

**fox terrier** a small terrier with a smooth or wiry coat, formerly trained to drive foxes from hiding

**fox trot** a dance for couples in 4/4 time, or music for it —**fox′-trot′**, **-trot′ted**, **-trot′ting**, *vi.*

**fox′y** *adj.* **-i·er**, **-i·est** foxlike; crafty; sly 2 [Slang] attractive or sexy: used esp. of women

**foy·er** (foi′ər; *also* foi′ā′, -yā′) *n.* ⟦Fr < L *focus*, hearth⟧ an entrance hall or lobby, as in a theater or hotel

**Fr** *abbrev.* 1 Father 2 French

**frab·jous** (frab′jəs) *adj.* ⟦coined by Lewis CARROLL⟧ [Inf.] splendid; fine

**fra·cas** (frā′kəs) *n.* ⟦Fr < It *fracassare*, to smash⟧ a noisy fight; brawl

**frac·tion** (frak′shən) *n.* ⟦< L *frangere*, to break⟧ 1 a small part, amount, etc. 2 *Math. a)* a quotient of two whole numbers, as $\frac{4}{4}$, $\frac{2}{3}$ *b)* any quantity expressed in terms of a numerator and denominator —**frac′tion·al** *adj.* —**frac′tion·al·ly** *adv.*

**frac·tious** (frak′shəs) *adj.* ⟦< ?⟧ 1 hard to manage; unruly; rebellious 2 peevish; irritable; cross —**frac′tious·ly** *adv.* —**frac′tious·ness** *n.*

**frac·ture** (frak′chər) *n.* ⟦< L *frangere*, to break⟧ a breaking or break, esp. in a bone —*vt., vi.* **-tured**, **-tur·ing** to break, crack, or split

**frag·ile** (fraj′əl) *adj.* ⟦< L *frangere*, to break⟧ easily broken or damaged; delicate —**fra·gil·i·ty** (frə jil′ə tē) *n.*

**frag·ment** (frag′mənt; *for v., also,* -ment′) *n.* ⟦< L *frangere*, to break⟧ 1 a part broken away 2 an incomplete part, as of a novel —*vt., vi.* to break up —**frag′men·ta′tion** (-mən tā′shən) *n.*

**frag′men·tar′y** (-mən ter′ē) *adj.* consisting of fragments; not complete

**fra·grant** (frā′grənt) *adj.* ⟦< L *fragrare*, to emit a (sweet) smell⟧ having a pleasant odor; sweet-smelling —**fra′grance** *n.* —**fra′grant·ly** *adv.*

**frail** (frāl) *adj.* ⟦see FRAGILE⟧ 1 easily broken; delicate 2 not robust; weak 3 easily tempted; morally weak —**frail′ly** *adv.*

**frail′ty** (-tē) *n.* 1 a being frail; esp., moral weak-

ness **2** *pl.* **-ties** a fault arising from such weakness

**frame** (frām) *vt.* **framed, fram'ing** ⟦prob. < ON
*frami*, profit or benefit⟧ **1** to form according to a
pattern; design *[to frame* laws*]* **2** to construct **3**
to put into words *[to frame* an excuse*]* **4** to
enclose (a picture, etc.) in a border **5** [Inf.] to
falsify evidence in order to make (an innocent
person) appear guilty —*n.* **1** body structure **2**
the framework, as of a house **3** the structural
case enclosing a window, door, etc. **4** an ornamental border, as around a picture **5** the way
anything is put together; form **6** condition; state
*[a good frame* of mind*]* **7** one exposure in a strip
of film **8** *Bowling, etc.* a division of a game —*adj.*
having a wooden framework *[a frame* house*]* —
**fram'er** *n.*

**frame'-up'** *n.* [Inf.] a secret, deceitful scheme, as
a falsifying of evidence to make a person seem
guilty

**frame'work'** *n.* **1** a structure to hold together or
support something **2** the basic structure, system,
etc.

**franc** (fraŋk) *n.* ⟦Fr < L *Francorum rex*, king of the
French, phrase on the coin in 1360⟧ the monetary
unit of Belgium, France, Switzerland, Chad, etc.

**France** (frans, fräns) country in W Europe:
210,033 sq. mi.; pop. 56,615,000

**fran·chise** (fran'chīz') *n.* ⟦< OFr *franc*, free⟧ **1**
any special right or privilege granted by a government **2** the right to vote; suffrage **3** the right to
sell a product or service —*vt.* **-chised', -chis'ing** to
grant a franchise to

**Franco-** *combining form* French, French and

**fran·gi·ble** (fran'jə bəl) *adj.* ⟦< L *frangere*, to
break⟧ breakable; fragile

**frank** (fraŋk) *adj.* ⟦< OFr *franc*, free⟧ free in
expressing oneself; candid —*vt.* to send (mail)
free of postage —*n.* **1** the right to send mail free
**2** a mark indicating this right —**frank'ly** *adv.* —
**frank'ness** *n.*

**Frank** (fraŋk) *n.* a member of the Germanic peoples whose 9th-c. empire extended over what is
now France, Germany, and Italy

**Frank·en·stein** (fraŋ'kən stīn') *n.* **1** the title
character in a novel (1818), creator of a monster
that destroys him **2** popularly, the monster **3**
anything that becomes dangerous to its creator

**Frank·fort** (fraŋk'fərt) capital of Kentucky: pop.
26,000

**Frank·furt** (fraŋk'fərt; *Ger* fräŋk'foort) city in W
Germany: pop. 656,000

**frank·furt·er** (fraŋk'fər tər) *n.* ⟦Ger: after prec.⟧ a
smoked sausage of beef, beef and pork, etc.; wiener: also [Inf.] **frank**

**frank·in·cense** (fraŋ'kin sens') *n.* ⟦see FRANK &
INCENSE[1]⟧ a gum resin burned as incense

**Frank·ish** (fraŋ'kish) *n.* the West Germanic language of the Franks —*adj.* of the Franks or their
language, etc.

**Frank·lin** (fraŋk'lin), **Ben·ja·min** (ben'jə mən)
1706-90; Am. statesman, scientist, inventor, &
writer

**fran·tic** (fran'tik) *adj.* ⟦< Gr *phrenitis*, delirium⟧
wild with anger, pain, worry, etc. —**fran'ti·cal·ly**
*adv.*

**frap·pé** (fra pā') *n.* ⟦Fr < *frapper*, to strike⟧ **1** a
dessert made of partly frozen fruit juices, etc. **2** a
beverage poured over shaved ice **3** [New Eng-
land] a milkshake Also, esp. for 3, **frappe** (frap)

**fra·ter·nal** (frə tur'nəl) *adj.* ⟦< L *frater*, brother⟧
**1** of brothers; brotherly **2** designating or of a
society organized for fellowship **3** designating
twins developed from separate ova and thus not
identical —**fra·ter'nal·ly** *adv.*

**fra·ter·ni·ty** (frə tur'nə tē) *n., pl.* **-ties** **1** brotherliness **2** a group of men joined together for fellowship, etc., as in college **3** a group of people
with the same beliefs, work, etc.

**frat·er·nize** (frat'ər nīz') *vi.* **-nized', -niz'ing** to
associate in a friendly way —**frat'er·ni·za'tion** *n.*

**frat·ri·cide** (fra'trə sīd') *n.* ⟦< L *frater*, brother +
*caedere*, to kill⟧ **1** the killing of one's own brother
or sister **2** one who commits fratricide —**frat'ri·
ci'dal** *adj.*

**Frau** (frou) *n., pl.* **Frau'en** (-ən) ⟦Ger⟧ **1** Mrs.;
Madam: a German title of respect, used to
address a married woman and now also a single
woman **2** a wife

**fraud** (frôd) *n.* ⟦< L *fraus*⟧ **1** deceit; trickery **2**
*Law* intentional deception **3** a trick **4** an impostor or cheat

**fraud·u·lent** (frô'jə lənt) *adj.* **1** based on or using
fraud **2** done or obtained by fraud —**fraud'u·
lence** *n.* —**fraud'u·lent·ly** *adv.*

**fraught** (frôt) *adj.* ⟦< MDu *vracht*, a load⟧ **1** filled
or loaded (*with*) *[a life fraught* with hardship*]* **2**
tense, anxious, etc.

**Fräu·lein** (froi'līn'; *E* froi'-) *n., pl.* **-lein** or Eng.
**-leins'** ⟦Ger⟧ **1** Miss: a German title of respect **2**
an unmarried woman: see note at FRAU

**fray**[1] (frā) *n.* ⟦< AFFRAY⟧ a noisy quarrel or fight;
brawl

**fray**[2] (frā) *vt., vi.* ⟦< L *fricare*, to rub⟧ **1** to make
or become worn or ragged **2** to make or become
weakened or strained

**fraz·zle** (fraz'əl) [Inf.] *vt., vi.* **-zled, -zling** ⟦< dial.
*fazle*⟧ **1** to wear to tatters; fray **2** to make or
become exhausted —*n.* the state of being frazzled

**freak** (frēk) *n.* ⟦< ?⟧ **1** an odd notion; whim **2** an
unusual happening **3** any abnormal animal, person, or plant **4** [Slang] *a*) a user of a specified
drug *b*) a devotee; buff *[a chess freak]* —*adj.*
oddly different; abnormal —**freak out** [Slang] **1**
to have hallucinations, etc., as from a psychedelic
drug **2** to make or become very excited, distressed, etc. —**freak'ish** or **freak'y, -i·er, -i·est,** *adj.*
—**freak'ish·ly** *adv.*

**freak'out'** *n.* [Slang] the act or an instance of
freaking out

**freck·le** (frek'əl) *n.* ⟦< Scand⟧ a small, brownish
spot on the skin —*vt., vi.* **-led, -ling** to make or
become spotted with freckles —**freck'led** *adj.*

**Fred·er·ick the Great** (fred'rik, -ər ik) 1712-86;
king of Prussia (1740-86)

**Fred·er·ic·ton** (fred'ə rik tən) capital of New
Brunswick, Canada: pop. 47,000

**free** (frē) *adj.* **fre'er, fre'est** ⟦< OE *freo*⟧ **1** not
under the control or power of another; having liberty; independent **2** having civil and political liberty **3** able to move in any direction; loose **4** not
burdened by obligations, debts, discomforts, etc.
**5** not confined to the usual rules *[free* verse*]* **6** not
exact *[a free* translation*]* **7** generous; profuse *[a
free* spender*]* **8** frank **9** with no charge or cost
**10** exempt from taxes, duties, etc. **11** clear of
obstructions *[a free* road ahead*]* **12** not fastened
*[a rope's free* end*]* —*adv.* **1** without cost **2** in a
free manner —*vt.* **freed, free'ing** to make free;
specif., *a*) to release from bondage or arbitrary
power, obligation, etc. *b*) to clear of obstruction,
etc. —**free from** (or **of**) without —**free up** to make
available for use *[he freed up* funds*]* —**make free
with** to use freely —**free'ly** *adv.* —**free'ness** *n.*

**-free** (frē) *combining form* free of or from, exempt
from, without

**free'base'** *n.* a concentrated form of cocaine for
smoking —*vt., vi.* **-based', -bas'ing** to prepare or
use such a form of (cocaine)

**free·bie** or **free·bee** (frē'bē) *n.* [Slang] something given or gotten free of charge, as a theater
ticket

**free'boot'er** (-boot'ər) *n.* ⟦< Du *vrij*, free + *buit*,
plunder⟧ a pirate

**freed·man** (frēd'mən) *n., pl.* **-men** (-mən) a man
legally freed from slavery

**free·dom** (frē'dəm) *n.* **1** a being free; esp., *a*)
independence *b*) civil or political liberty *c*)
exemption from an obligation, discomfort, etc. *d*)
a being able to act, use, etc. freely *e*) ease of
movement *f*) frankness **2** a right or privilege

**free fall** any unchecked fall, as of a parachutist before the parachute opens

**free flight** any flight or part of a flight, as of a rocket, occurring without propulsion —**free'-flight'** *adj.*

**free'-for-all'** *n.* a disorganized, general fight; brawl —*adj.* open to anyone

**free'-form'** *adj.* 1 irregular in shape 2 spontaneous, unrestrained, etc.

**free'hand'** *adj.* drawn by hand without the use of instruments, etc.

**free'hold'** *n.* an estate in land held for life or with the right to pass it on to heirs —**free'hold'er** *n.*

**free·lance** or **free-lance** (frē'lans') *n.* a writer, artist, etc. who sells his or her services to individual buyers: also **free'lanc'er** or **free'-lanc'er** —*adj.* of or working as a freelance —*vi.* **-lanced'**, **-lanc'ing** to work as a freelance

**free'load'er** (-lōd'ər) *n.* [Inf.] a person who habitually imposes on others for free food, etc. —**free'load'** *vi.*

**free·man** (frē'mən) *n., pl.* **-men** (-mən) 1 a person not in slavery 2 a citizen

**Free·ma·son** (frē'mā'sən) *n.* a member of an international secret society based on brotherliness and mutual aid —**Free'ma'son·ry** *n.*

**free on board** delivered (by the seller) aboard the train, ship, etc. at no extra charge to the buyer

**free'stone'** *n.* a peach, etc. in which the pit does not cling to the pulp

**free'think'er** *n.* one who forms opinions about religion, morals, etc. independently

**Free'town'** seaport & capital of Sierra Leone: pop. 470,000

**free trade** trade carried on without protective tariffs, quotas, etc.

**free verse** poetry without regular meter, rhyme, etc.

**free'way'** *n.* a multiple-lane divided highway with fully controlled access

**free'will'** *adj.* voluntary

**freeze** (frēz) *vi.* **froze, fro'zen, freez'ing** [OE *freosan*] 1 to be formed into, or become covered with, ice; be solidified by cold 2 to become very cold 3 to be damaged or killed by cold 4 to become motionless 5 to be made speechless by strong emotion 6 to become formal or unfriendly —*vt.* 1 to form into, or cover with, ice; solidify by cold 2 to make very cold 3 to preserve (food) by rapid refrigeration 4 to kill or damage by cold 5 to make motionless 6 to make formal or unfriendly 7 *a*) to fix (prices, etc.) at a given level by authority *b*) to make (funds, etc.) unavailable to the owners —*n.* 1 a freezing or being frozen 2 a period of freezing weather —**freeze out** 1 to die out through freezing, as plants do 2 [Inf.] to keep out by a cold manner, competition, etc. —**freeze over** to become covered with ice —**freez'a·ble** *adj.*

**freeze'-dry'** *vt.* **-dried', -dry'ing** to quick-freeze (food, etc.) and then dry under high vacuum

**freez'er** *n.* 1 a refrigerator, compartment, etc. for freezing and storing perishable foods 2 a machine for making ice cream

**freezing point** the temperature at which a liquid freezes: the freezing point of water is 32°F or 0°C

**freight** (frāt) *n.* [< MDu *vracht*, a load] 1 the transporting of goods by water, land, or air 2 the cost for this 3 the goods transported 4 a railroad train for transporting goods: in full **freight train** —*vt.* 1 to load; burden 2 to send by freight

**freight'er** *n.* a ship for freight

**Fre·mont** (frē'mänt) city in W California, on San Francisco Bay: pop. 173,000

**French** (french) *adj.* of France or its people, language, etc. —*n.* the language of France —**the French** the people of France —**French'man** (-mən), *pl.* **-men** (-mən), *n.*

**French bread** bread with a crisp crust made with white flour in a long, slender loaf

**French cuff** a shirt-sleeve cuff turned back on itself and fastened with a cuff link

**French doors** a pair of doors hinged at the sides to open in the middle

**French dressing** a creamy, orange-colored salad dressing

**French fries** [*often* f- f-] strips of potato that have been French fried

**French fry** [*often* f- f-] to fry in hot deep fat

**French Gui·a·na** (gē an'ə, -ä'nə) French administrative division in NE South America

**French horn** a mellow-toned brass instrument with a long, spiral tube and a flaring bell: in classical music, now usually *horn*

**French leave** an unauthorized departure

**French toast** sliced bread dipped in a batter of egg and milk and then fried

**fre·net·ic** (frə net'ik) *adj.* [see PHRENETIC] frantic; frenzied —**fre·net'i·cal·ly** *adv.*

**fren·zy** (fren'zē) *n., pl.* **-zies** [< Gr *phrenitis*, madness] wild excitement; delirium

**Fre·on** (frē'än') *trademark for* any of a series of gaseous compounds of fluorine, carbon, etc.: used as refrigerants, aerosol propellants, etc.

**fre·quen·cy** (frē'kwən sē) *n., pl.* **-cies** 1 frequent occurrence 2 the number of times any event recurs in a given period 3 *Physics* the number of oscillations or cycles per unit of time

**frequency modulation** the variation of the frequency of a carrier wave in accordance with the signal being broadcast: abbrev. *FM*

**fre·quent** (frē'kwənt; *for v.* frē kwent') *adj.* [< L *frequens*, crowded] 1 occurring often 2 constant; habitual —*vt.* to go to or be at often —**fre'quent·ly** *adv.*

**fres·co** (fres'kō) *n., pl.* **-coes** or **-cos** [It, fresh] a painting made with watercolors on wet plaster

**fresh**[1] (fresh) *adj.* [OE *fersc*] 1 recently made, grown, etc. [*fresh* coffee] 2 not salted, pickled, frozen, etc. 3 not spoiled 4 not tired; lively 5 not worn, soiled, faded, etc. 6 new; recent 7 inexperienced 8 cool and refreshing [a *fresh* spring day] 9 brisk: said of wind 10 not salt: said of water —**fresh'ly** *adv.* —**fresh'ness** *n.*

**fresh**[2] (fresh) *adj.* [< Ger *frech*, bold] [Slang] bold; saucy; impertinent

**fresh'en** *vt., vi.* to make or become fresh —**freshen up** to bathe, change into fresh clothes, etc. —**fresh'en·er** *n.*

**fresh'man** (-mən) *n., pl.* **-men** (-mən) [FRESH[1] + MAN] 1 a beginner 2 a person in his or her first year in college, Congress, etc.

**fresh'wa'ter** *adj.* 1 of or living in water that is not salty 2 sailing only on inland waters

**Fres·no** (frez'nō) city in central California: pop. 354,000

**fret**[1] (fret) *vt., vi.* **fret'ted, fret'ting** [OE *fretan*, to devour] 1 to gnaw, wear away, rub, etc. 2 to make or become rough or disturbed [wind *fretting* the water] 3 to irritate or be irritated; worry —*n.* irritation; worry —**fret'ter** *n.*

**fret**[2] (fret) *n.* [ME *frette*] a running design of interlacing small bars

**fret**[3] (fret) *n.* [OFr *frette*, a band] any of the ridges on the fingerboard of a banjo, guitar, etc.

**fret'ful** (-fəl) *adj.* irritable; peevish —**fret'ful·ly** *adv.* —**fret'ful·ness** *n.*

**fret'work'** *n.* decorative carving or openwork, as of interlacing lines

**Freud** (froid), **Sig·mund** (sig'mənd) 1856-1939; Austrian physician: founder of psychoanalysis —**Freud'i·an** *adj., n.*

**Freudian slip** a mistake made in speaking that, it is thought, inadvertently reveals unconscious motives, desires, etc.

**Fri** *abbrev.* Friday

**fri·a·ble** (frī'ə bəl) *adj.* [Fr < L *friare*, to rub] easily crumbled

**fri·ar** (frī′ər) *n.* ⟦< L *frater*, brother⟧ *R.C.Ch.* a member of certain religious orders

**fric·as·see** (frik′ə sē′, frik′ə sē′) *n.* ⟦< Fr *fricasser*, cut up and fry⟧ a dish consisting of meat cut into pieces, stewed or fried, and served in a sauce of its own gravy —*vt.* -seed′, -see′ing to prepare in this way

**fric·tion** (frik′shən) *n.* ⟦< L *fricare*, to rub⟧ 1 a rubbing of one object against another 2 conflict, as because of differing opinions 3 *Mech.* the resistance to motion of moving surfaces that touch —**fric′tion·al** *adj.* —**fric′tion·less** *adj.*

**Fri·day** (frī′dā) *n.* ⟦after *Frigg*, Germanic goddess⟧ 1 the sixth day of the week 2 ⟦after the devoted servant of ROBINSON CRUSOE⟧ a faithful helper: usually **man** (or **girl**) **Friday**

**fridge** (frij) *n.* [Inf.] a refrigerator

**fried** (frīd) *vt., vi. pt. & pp. of* FRY¹

**fried′cake′** *n.* a small cake fried in deep fat; doughnut or cruller

**friend** (frend) *n.* ⟦OE *freond*⟧ 1 a person whom one knows well and is fond of 2 an ally, supporter, or sympathizer 3 [F-] a member of the Society of Friends; Quaker —**make** (or **be**) **friends with** to become (or be) a friend of —**friend′less** *adj.*

**friend′ly** *adj.* -li·er, -li·est 1 of or like a friend; kindly 2 not hostile; amicable 3 supporting; helping —**friend′li·ly** *adv.* —**friend′li·ness** *n.*

**friend′ship′** *n.* 1 the state of being friends 2 friendly feeling

**fries** (frīz) *pl.n.* [Inf.] *short for* FRENCH FRIES

**frieze** (frēz) *n.* ⟦< ML *frisium*⟧ an ornamental band with designs or carvings, positioned along a wall, around a room, etc.

**frig·ate** (frig′it) *n.* ⟦< It *fregata*⟧ a fast, medium-sized sailing warship of the 18th and early 19th c.

**fright** (frīt) *n.* ⟦OE *fyrhto*⟧ 1 sudden fear; alarm 2 an ugly, startling, etc. person or thing

**fright′en** *vt.* 1 to make suddenly afraid; scare 2 to force (*away, out,* or *off*) by scaring —**fright′en·ing·ly** *adv.*

**fright′ful** (-fəl) *adj.* 1 causing fright; alarming 2 shocking; terrible 3 [Inf.] *a*) unpleasant; annoying *b*) great [in a *frightful* hurry] —**fright′ful·ly** *adv.* —**fright′ful·ness** *n.*

**frig·id** (frij′id) *adj.* ⟦< L *frigus*, coldness⟧ 1 extremely cold 2 not warm or friendly 3 sexually unresponsive: said of a woman —**fri·gid·i·ty** (fri jid′ə tē) *n.* —**frig′id·ly** *adv.*

**Frigid Zone** either of two zones (**North Frigid Zone** or **South Frigid Zone**) between the polar circles and the poles

**frill** (fril) *n.* ⟦< ?⟧ 1 any unnecessary ornament 2 a ruffle —**frill′y**, -i·er, -i·est, *adj.*

**fringe** (frinj) *n.* ⟦< LL *fimbria*⟧ 1 a border of threads, etc. hanging loose or tied in bunches 2 an outer edge; border 3 a marginal or minor part —*vt.* fringed, fring′ing to be or make a fringe for —*adj.* 1 at the outer edge 2 additional 3 minor

**fringe benefit** any form of employee compensation other than wages, as insurance or a pension

**frip·per·y** (frip′ər ē) *n., pl.* -ies ⟦< OFr *frepe*, a rag⟧ 1 cheap, gaudy clothes 2 showy display in dress, manners, etc.

**Fris·bee** (friz′bē) ⟦< "Mother *Frisbie's*" pie tins⟧ *trademark for* a saucer-shaped plastic disk sailed back and forth in a simple game —*n.* [*also* f-] 1 such a disk 2 the game

**fri·sé** (frē zā′, fri-) *n.* ⟦Fr < *friser*, to curl⟧ an upholstery fabric with a thick pile in loops

**Fri·sian** (frizh′ən) *n.* the West Germanic language of an island chain, the Frisian Islands, along the coast of N Netherlands, Germany, & Denmark

**frisk** (frisk) *vi.* ⟦< OHG *frisc*, lively⟧ to move about in a lively way; frolic —*vt.* [Slang] to search (a person) for weapons, etc. by passing the hands quickly over the person's clothing

**frisk·y** (fris′kē) *adj.* -i·er, -i·est lively; frolicsome —**frisk′i·ly** *adv.* —**frisk′i·ness** *n.*

**frit·ter**¹ (frit′ər) *vt.* ⟦< L *frangere*, to break⟧ to waste (money, time, etc.) bit by bit: usually with *away*

**frit·ter**² (frit′ər) *n.* ⟦< L *frigere*, to fry⟧ a small cake of fried batter, usually containing corn, fruit, etc.

**friv·o·lous** (friv′ə ləs) *adj.* ⟦< L *frivolus*, silly⟧ 1 of little value; trivial 2 silly and light-minded; giddy —**fri·vol·i·ty** (fri väl′ə tē), *pl.* -ties, *n.* —**friv′o·lous·ly** *adv.*

**frizz** or **friz** (friz) *vt., vi.* frizzed, friz′zing ⟦Fr *friser*⟧ to form into small, tight curls —**friz′zy**, -zi·er, -zi·est, *adj.*

**friz·zle**¹ (friz′əl) *vi., vt.* -zled, -zling ⟦< FRY¹⟧ to sizzle, as in frying

**friz·zle**² (friz′əl) *n., vt., vi.* -zled, -zling FRIZZ —**friz′zly** *adj.*

**fro** (frō) *adv.* ⟦< ON *frā*⟧ backward; back: now only in TO AND FRO (at TO)

**frock** (fräk) *n.* ⟦< OFr *froc*⟧ 1 a robe worn by friars, monks, etc. 2 a dress

**frog** (frôg, fräg) *n.* ⟦OE *frogga*⟧ 1 a tailless, leaping amphibian with long hind legs and webbed feet 2 a fancy loop of braid used to fasten clothing —**frog in one's throat** temporary hoarseness

**frog′man′** *n., pl.* -men (-′men) a person trained and equipped for underwater demolition, exploration, etc.

**frol·ic** (fräl′ik) *n.* ⟦< MDu *vrō*, merry⟧ 1 a lively party or game 2 merriment; fun —*vi.* -icked, -ick·ing 1 to make merry; have fun 2 to romp about; gambol —**frol′ick·er** *n.*

**frol′ic·some** (-səm) *adj.* playful; merry

**from** (frum) *prep.* ⟦OE⟧ 1 beginning at; starting with [*from* noon to midnight] 2 out of [*from* her purse] 3 originating in [a letter *from* me] 4 out of the possibility of or use of [kept *from* going] 5 as not being like [to know good *from* evil] 6 because of [to tremble *from* fear]

**frond** (fränd) *n.* ⟦< L *frons*, leafy branch⟧ the leaf of a fern or palm

**front** (frunt) *n.* ⟦< L *frons*, forehead⟧ 1 *a*) outward behavior [a bold *front*] *b*) [Inf.] an appearance of social standing, wealth, etc. 2 the part facing forward 3 the first part; beginning 4 a forward or leading position 5 the land bordering a lake, street, etc. 6 the advanced battle area in warfare 7 an area of activity [the home *front*] 8 a person or group used to hide another's activity 9 *Meteorol.* the boundary between two differing air masses —*adj.* at, to, in, on, or of the front —*vt., vi.* 1 to face 2 to serve as a front (*for*) —**in front of** before —**fron′tal** *adj.*

**front·age** (frunt′ij) *n.* 1 the front part of a building 2 the front boundary line of a lot or the length of this line 3 land bordering a street, lake, etc.

**fron·tier** (frun tir′) *n.* ⟦see FRONT⟧ 1 the border between two countries 2 the part of a country which borders an unexplored region 3 any new field of learning, etc. or any part of a field that is not fully investigated —*adj.* of, on, or near a frontier —**fron·tiers′man** (-tirz′mən), *pl.* -men (-mən), *n.*

**fron·tis·piece** (frunt′is pēs′) *n.* ⟦ult. < L *frons*, front + *specere*, to look⟧ an illustration facing the title page of a book

**front office** the management or administration, as of a company

**front′-run′ner** *n.* a leading contestant

**front′-wheel′ drive** an automotive design in which only the front wheels receive driving power

**frost** (frôst, fräst) *n.* ⟦OE < *freosan*, to freeze⟧ 1 a temperature low enough to cause freezing 2 frozen dew or vapor; rime —*vt.* 1 to cover with frost 2 to cover with frosting 3 to give a frostlike, opaque surface to (glass) —**frost′y**, -i·er, -i·est, *adj.*

**Frost** (frôst, fräst), **Robert** (**Lee**) (rä′bərt) 1874-1963; U.S. poet

**frost′bite′** *vt.* -bit′, -bit′ten, -bit′ing to injure the tissues of (a body part) by exposing to intense cold —*n.* injury caused by such exposure

**frost'ing** *n.* **1** a mixture of sugar, butter, flavoring, etc. for covering a cake; icing **2** a dull finish on glass, metal, etc.

**frost line** the limit of penetration of soil by frost

**froth** (frôth, fräth) *n.* [< ON *frotha*] **1** foam **2** foaming saliva **3** light, trifling talk, ideas, etc. — *vi.* to foam —**froth'y, -i·er, -i·est,** *adj.*

**frou·frou** (frōō′frōō′) *n.* [Fr] [Inf.] excessive ornateness

**fro·ward** (frō′wərd, -ərd) *adj.* [see FRO & -WARD] not easily controlled; willful; contrary —**fro′ward·ness** *n.*

**frown** (froun) *vi.* [< OFr *froigne*, sullen face] **1** to contract the brows, as in displeasure **2** to show disapproval: with *on* or *upon* —*n.* a frowning

**frow·zy** (frou′zē) *adj.* **-zi·er, -zi·est** [< ?] dirty and untidy; slovenly —**frow′zi·ly** *adv.* —**frow′zi·ness** *n.*

**froze** (frōz) *vi., vt. pt. of* FREEZE

**fro·zen** (frō′zən) *vi., vt. pp. of* FREEZE —*adj.* **1** turned into or covered with ice; solidified by cold **2** damaged or killed by freezing **3** preserved by freezing: said as of food **4** made motionless **5** kept at a fixed level **6** not readily convertible into cash *[frozen* assets*]*

**frozen custard** a food resembling ice cream, but softer and with less butterfat

**fruc·ti·fy** (fruk′tə fī′) *vi., vt.* **-fied′, -fy′ing** [< L *fructificare*] to bear or cause to bear fruit

**fruc·tose** (fruk′tōs′, frook′-) *n.* [< L *fructus*, fruit + -OSE[1]] a sugar found in sweet fruits and in honey

**fru·gal** (frōō′gəl) *adj.* [< L *frugi*, fit for food] **1** not wasteful; thrifty **2** inexpensive or meager —**fru·gal′i·ty** (-gal′ə tē), *pl.* **-ties,** *n.* —**fru′gal·ly** *adv.*

**fruit** (frōōt) *n.* [< L *fructus*] **1** any plant product, as grain or vegetables: *usually used in pl.* **2** *a*) an edible plant structure, often sweet, containing the seeds inside a juicy pulp: many true fruits that are not sweet, as tomatoes, are popularly called *vegetables b) Bot.* the mature seed-bearing part of a flowering plant **3** the result or product of any action

**fruit'cake'** *n.* a rich cake containing nuts, preserved fruit, citron, spices, etc.

**fruit fly** any of various small flies whose larvae feed on fruits and vegetables

**fruit'ful** (-fəl) *adj.* **1** bearing much fruit **2** productive; prolific **3** profitable

**fru·i·tion** (frōō ish′ən) *n.* **1** the bearing of fruit **2** a coming to fulfillment; realization

**fruit'less** (-lis) *adj.* **1** without results; unsuccessful **2** bearing no fruit; sterile; barren —**fruit'less·ly** *adv.* —**fruit'less·ness** *n.*

**frump** (frump) *n.* [prob. < Du *rompelen,* rumple] a dowdy woman —**frump'ish** *adj.* —**frump'y, -i·er, -i·est,** *adj.*

**frus·trate** (frus′trāt′) *vt.* **-trat'ed, -trat'ing** [< L *frustra*, in vain] **1** to cause to have no effect **2** to prevent from achieving a goal or gratifying a desire —**frus·tra'tion** *n.*

**fry**[1] (frī) *vt., vi.* **fried, fry'ing** [< L *frigere*, to fry] to cook in a pan over direct heat, usually in hot fat —*n., pl.* **fries 1** [pl.] fried potatoes **2** a social gathering at which food is fried and eaten *[a fish fry]*

**fry**[2] (frī) *pl.n., sing.* **fry** [< OFr *freier,* to rub, spawn] young fish

**fry'er** *n.* **1** a utensil for deep-frying **2** a chicken for frying

**FSLIC** *abbrev.* Federal Savings and Loan Insurance Corporation

**ft** *abbrev.* foot; feet

**Ft** *abbrev.* Fort

**FTC** *abbrev.* Federal Trade Commission

**fuch·sia** (fyōō′shə) *n.* [after L. *Fuchs* (1501-66), Ger botanist] **1** a shrubby plant with pink, red, or purple flowers **2** purplish red

**fud·dle** (fud′'l) *vt.* **-dled, -dling** [< ?] to confuse or

stupefy as with alcoholic liquor —*n.* a fuddled state

**fud·dy-dud·dy** (fud′ē dud′ē) *n., pl.* **-dies** [Inf.] a fussy or old-fashioned person

**fudge** (fuj) *n.* [< ?] a soft candy made of butter, milk, sugar, chocolate or other flavoring, etc. —*vi.* **fudged, fudg'ing 1** to refuse to commit oneself; hedge **2** to be dishonest; cheat

**fu·el** (fyōō′əl, fyōol) *n.* [< L *focus*, fireplace] **1** coal, oil, gas, wood, etc., burned to supply heat or power **2** material from which nuclear energy can be obtained **3** anything that intensifies strong feeling —*vt., vi.* **fu'eled** or **fu'elled, fu'el·ing** or **fu'el·ling** to supply with or get fuel

**fuel injection** a system for injecting a fine spray of fuel into the combustion chambers of an engine

**fu·gi·tive** (fyōō′ji tiv) *adj.* [< L *fugere*, to flee] **1** fleeing, as from danger or justice **2** fleeting —*n.* one who is fleeing from justice, etc. —**fu'gi·tive·ly** *adv.*

**fugue** (fyōōg) *n.* [< L *fugere*, to flee] a musical work in which a theme is taken up successively and developed by the various parts or voices in counterpoint

**-ful** (fəl; *for 2, usually* fool) [< FULL[1]] *suffix* **1** *a*) full of, having *[joyful] b*) having the qualities of or tendency to *[helpful]* **2** the quantity that will fill *[handful]*

**ful·crum** (fool′krəm, ful′-) *n., pl.* **-crums** or **-cra** (-krə) [L, a support] the support on which a lever turns in raising something

**ful·fill** (fool fil′) *vt.* **-filled′, -fill′ing** [OE *fullfyllan*] **1** to carry out (a promise, etc.) **2** to do (a duty, etc.); obey **3** to satisfy (a condition) Brit. sp. **ful·fil′, -filled′, -fill′ing** —**ful·fill′ment** or **ful·fil′ment** *n.*

**full**[1] (fool) *adj.* [OE] **1** having in it all there is space for; filled **2** having eaten all that one wants **3** having a great deal or number (*of*) **4** complete *[a full* dozen*]* **5** having reached the greatest size, extent, etc. *[a full* moon*]* **6** plump; round *[a full* face*]* **7** with wide folds; flowing *[a full* skirt*]* —*n.* the greatest amount, extent, etc. —*adv.* **1** to the greatest degree; completely **2** directly; exactly — **full'ness** or **ful'ness** *n.*

**full**[2] (fool) *vt., vi.* [< L *fullo*, cloth fuller] to shrink and thicken (wool cloth) —**full'er** *n.*

**full'back'** *n. Football* one of the running backs, used typically for blocking an opponent

**full'-blood'ed** *adj.* **1** of unmixed breed or race **2** vigorous

**full'-blown'** *adj.* **1** in full bloom **2** fully developed; matured

**full'-bore'** *adv.* to the greatest degree or extent — *adj.* all-out

**full'-fledged'** *adj.* completely developed or trained; of full status

**full moon** the moon when it reflects light as a full disk

**full'-scale'** *adj.* **1** according to the original or standard scale **2** to the utmost degree; all-out

**full'-size'** *adj.* **1** of the usual or standard size **2** of a large size Also **full'-sized'**

**full'-throat'ed** *adj.* **1** having or producing deep, rich sound **2** complete and unmitigated

**full'-time'** *adj.* of or engaged in work, study, etc. that takes all of one's regular working hours

**full'y** *adv.* **1** completely; thoroughly **2** at least

**ful·mi·nate** (ful′mə nāt′) *vi.* **-nat'ed, -nat'ing** [< L *fulmen*, lightning] to express strong disapproval —**ful'mi·na'tion** *n.*

**ful·some** (fool′səm) *adj.* [see FULL[1] & -SOME[1], but infl. by ME *ful*, foul] disgusting, esp. because excessive

**fum·ble** (fum′bəl) *vi., vt.* **-bled, -bling** [prob. < ON *famla*] **1** to grope (*for*) or handle (a thing) clumsily **2** to lose one's grasp on (a football, etc.) —*n.* a fumbling —**fum'bler** *n.*

**fume** (fyōōm) *n.* [< L *fumus*] [*often pl.*] a gas, smoke, or vapor, esp. if offensive or suffocating —

*vi.* **fumed, fum'ing 1** to give off fumes **2** to show anger

**fu·mi·gate** (fyōō'mə gāt') *vt.* **-gat'ed, -gat'ing** ⟦< L *fumus,* smoke + *agere,* do⟧ to expose to fumes, esp. so as to disinfect or kill the vermin in — **fu'mi·ga'tion** *n.* —**fu'mi·ga'tor** *n.*

**fum·y** (fyōōm'ē) *adj.* **-i·er, -i·est** full of or producing fumes; vaporous

**fun** (fun) *n.* ⟦< ME *fonne,* foolish⟧ **1** *a)* lively, joyous play or playfulness *b)* pleasure **2** a source of amusement —*adj.* [Inf.] intended for pleasure or amusement —**make fun of** to ridicule

**func·tion** (funk'shən) *n.* ⟦< L *fungi,* to perform⟧ **1** the normal or characteristic action of anything **2** a special duty required in work **3** a formal ceremony or social occasion **4** a thing that depends on and varies with something else —*vi.* to act in a required manner; work; be used —**func'tion·less** *adj.*

**func'tion·al** *adj.* **1** of a function **2** performing a function **3** *Med.* affecting a function of some organ without apparent organic changes

**functional illiterate** a person who cannot read well enough to carry out everyday activities

**func'tion·ar'y** (-shə ner'ē) *n., pl.* **-ies** an official performing some function

**function word** a word, as an article or conjunction, serving mainly to show grammatical relationship

**fund** (fund) *n.* ⟦L *fundus,* bottom⟧ **1** a supply that can be drawn upon; stock **2** *a)* a sum of money set aside for a purpose *b)* [*pl.*] ready money —*vt.* **1** to put or convert into a long-term debt that bears interest **2** to provide funds for (a project, retirement of a debt, etc.)

**fun·da·men·tal** (fun'də ment''l) *adj.* ⟦see prec.⟧ of or forming a foundation or basis; basic; essential —*n.* a principle, theory, law, etc. serving as a basis —**fun'da·men'tal·ly** *adv.*

**fun·da·men'tal·ism'** *n.* [*sometimes* F-] religious beliefs based on a literal interpretation of the Bible —**fun'da·men'tal·ist** *n., adj.*

**fund'rais'er** (-rā'zər) *n.* **1** one soliciting money for a charity, political party, etc. **2** an event held to obtain such money —**fund'rais'ing** *n.*

**fu·ner·al** (fyōō'nər əl) *n.* ⟦< L *funus*⟧ the ceremonies connected with burial or cremation of a dead person

**funeral director** one who manages a funeral home

**funeral home** (or **parlor**) an establishment where the bodies of the dead are prepared for burial or cremation and where funeral services can be held

**fu·ne·re·al** (fyōō nir'ē əl) *adj.* suitable for a funeral; sad and solemn; dismal —**fu·ne're·al·ly** *adv.*

**fun·gi·cide** (fun'jə sīd') *n.* ⟦see -CIDE⟧ any substance that kills fungi

**fun·gus** (fun'gəs) *n., pl.* **fun·gi** (fun'jī') or **fun'gus·es** ⟦< L⟧ any of various plants or plantlike organisms, as molds, mildews, mushrooms, etc., that lack chlorophyll, stems, and leaves and reproduce by spores —**fun'gal** or **fun'gous** *adj.*

**fu·nic·u·lar** (fyōō nik'yōō lər) *n.* ⟦< L *funiculus,* little rope⟧ a mountain railway with counterbalanced cable cars on parallel sets of rails: also **funicular railway**

**funk** (funk) *n.* ⟦< ? Fl *fonck,* dismay⟧ **1** [Inf.] a state of great fear; panic **2** [Inf.] a depressed mood **3** popular music derived from rhythm and blues

**funk·y** (fun'kē) *adj.* **-i·er, -i·est** ⟦orig., earthy⟧ **1** *Jazz* having an earthy style derived from early blues **2** [Slang] unconventional, eccentric, offbeat, etc.

**fun·nel** (fun'əl) *n.* ⟦ult. < L *fundere,* to pour⟧ **1** a tapering tube with a cone-shaped mouth, for pouring things into small-mouthed containers **2** the smokestack of a steamship —*vi., vt.* **-neled** or

**-nelled, -nel·ing** or **-nel·ling** to move or pour as through a funnel

**fun·nies** (fun'ēz) *pl.n.* [Inf.] comic strips

**fun·ny** (fun'ē) *adj.* **-ni·er, -ni·est 1** causing laughter; humorous **2** [Inf.] *a)* strange *b)* tricky — **fun'ni·ly** *adv.* —**fun'ni·ness** *n.*

**funny bone** a place on the elbow where a sharp impact on a nerve causes a tingling sensation

**funny farm** [Slang] an institution for the mentally ill

FUNNEL

**fur** (fur) *n.* ⟦< OFr *fuerre,* sheath⟧ **1** the soft, thick hair covering certain animals **2** a processed skin bearing such hair —*adj.* of fur —**furred** *adj.*

**fur·be·low** (fur'bə lō') *n.* ⟦ult. < Fr *falbala*⟧ **1** a flounce or ruffle **2** a showy, useless decorative addition

**fur·bish** (fur'bish) *vt.* ⟦< OFr *forbir*⟧ **1** to polish; burnish **2** to renovate

**Fu·ries** (fyoor'ēz) *pl.n. Gr. & Rom. Myth.* the three terrible female spirits who punish the perpetrators of unavenged crimes

**fu·ri·ous** (fyoor'ē əs) *adj.* **1** full of fury; very angry **2** very great, intense, wild, etc. —**fu'ri·ous·ly** *adv.*

**furl** (furl) *vt.* ⟦< L *firmus,* FIRM[1] + *ligare,* to tie⟧ to roll up (a sail, flag, etc.) tightly and make secure

**fur·long** (fur'lôn') *n.* ⟦< OE *furh,* a furrow + *lang,* LONG[1]⟧ a measure of distance equal to ⅛ of a mile

**fur·lough** (fur'lō) *n.* ⟦< Du *verlof*⟧ a leave of absence, esp. for military personnel —*vt.* to grant a furlough to

**fur·nace** (fur'nəs) *n.* ⟦< L *fornax,* furnace⟧ an enclosed structure in which heat is produced, as by burning fuel

**fur·nish** (fur'nish) *vt.* ⟦< OFr *furnir*⟧ **1** to supply with furniture, etc.; equip **2** to supply; provide

**fur'nish·ings** *pl.n.* **1** the furniture, carpets, etc. as for a house **2** things to wear [*men's furnishings*]

**fur·ni·ture** (fur'ni chər) *n.* ⟦Fr *fourniture*⟧ **1** the things in a room, etc. which equip it for living, as chairs, beds, etc. **2** necessary equipment

**fu·ror** (fyoor'ôr') *n.* ⟦< L⟧ **1** fury; frenzy **2** *a)* a widespread enthusiasm; craze *b)* a commotion or uproar Also [Chiefly Brit.] **fu'rore'**

**fur·ri·er** (fur'ē ər) *n.* one who processes furs or deals in fur garments

**fur·ring** (fur'in) *n.* thin strips of wood fixed on a wall, floor, etc. before adding boards or plaster

**fur·row** (fur'ō) *n.* ⟦< OE *furh*⟧ **1** a narrow groove made in the ground by a plow **2** anything like this, as a deep wrinkle —*vt.* to make furrows in —*vi.* to become wrinkled

**fur·ry** (fur'ē) *adj.* **-ri·er, -ri·est 1** of or like fur **2** covered with fur —**fur'ri·ness** *n.*

**fur·ther** (fur'thər) *adj.* ⟦OE *furthor*⟧ **1** *alt. compar.* of FAR **2** additional **3** more distant; farther —*adv.* **1** *alt. compar.* of FAR **2** to a greater degree or extent **3** in addition **4** at or to a greater distance; farther —*vt.* to give aid to; promote In sense 3 of the *adj.* and sense 4 of the *adv.*, FARTHER is more commonly used —**fur'ther·ance** *n.*

**fur'ther·more'** *adv.* in addition; besides; moreover

**fur·thest** (fur'thist) *adj.* **1** *alt. superl.* of FAR **2** most distant; farthest: also **fur'ther·most'** —*adv.* **1** *alt. superl.* of FAR **2** at or to the greatest distance or degree

**fur·tive** (fur'tiv) *adj.* ⟦< L *fur,* a thief⟧ done or acting in a stealthy manner; sneaky —**fur'tive·ly** *adv.* —**fur'tive·ness** *n.*

**fu·ry** (fyoor'ē) *n., pl.* **-ries** ⟦< L *furere,* to rage⟧ **1** violent anger; wild rage **2** violence; vehemence

**furze** (furz) *n.* ⟦OE *fyrs*⟧ a prickly evergreen shrub native to Europe

**fuse**[1] (fyōōz) *vt., vi.* **fused, fus'ing** ⟦< L *fundere*, to shed⟧ **1** to melt **2** to unite as if by melting together

**fuse**[2] (fyōōz) *n.* ⟦< L *fusus*, spindle⟧ **1** a tube or wick filled with combustible material, for setting off an explosive charge **2** *Elec.* a strip of easily melted metal placed in a circuit: it melts and breaks the circuit if the current becomes too strong

**fu·see** (fyōō zē′) *n.* ⟦Fr *fusée*, a rocket⟧ a colored flare used as a signal by railroad workers, truck drivers, etc.

**fu·se·lage** (fyōō′sə läzh′, -läj′) *n.* ⟦Fr⟧ the body of an airplane, exclusive of the wings, tail assembly, and engines

**fu·si·ble** (fyōō′zə bəl) *adj.* that can be fused or easily melted

**fu·si·lier** or **fu·sil·eer** (fyōō′zə lir′) *n.* ⟦Fr⟧ [Historical] a soldier armed with a flintlock musket

**fu·sil·lade** (fyōō′sə läd′, -läd′) *n.* ⟦Fr < *fusiller*, to shoot⟧ a simultaneous or rapid and continuous discharge of many firearms

**fu·sion** (fyōō′zhən) *n.* ⟦L *fusio*⟧ **1** a fusing or melting together **2** a blending; coalition **3** NUCLEAR FUSION **4** a style of popular music blending elements of jazz, rock, etc.

**fuss** (fus) *n.* ⟦prob. echoic⟧ **1** nervous, excited activity; bustle **2** a nervous state **3** a quarrel **4** a showy display of approval, etc. —*vi.* **1** to bustle about or worry over trifles **2** to whine, as a baby

**fuss'budg'et** (-buj′it) *n.* ⟦prec. + BUDGET⟧ [Inf.] a fussy person: also [Inf., Chiefly Brit.] **fuss'pot'** (-pät′)

**fuss'y** *adj.* **-i·er, -i·est** **1** *a)* worrying over trifles *b)* hard to please *c)* whining, as a baby **2** full of unnecessary details —**fuss'i·ly** *adv.* —**fuss'i·ness** *n.*

**fus·tian** (fus′chən) *n.* ⟦< L *fustis*, wooden stick⟧ pompous, pretentious talk or writing; bombast

**fus·ty** (fus′tē) *adj.* **-ti·er, -ti·est** ⟦< OFr *fust*, a cask⟧ **1** musty; moldy **2** old-fashioned —**fus'ti·ly** *adv.* —**fus'ti·ness** *n.*

**fut** *abbrev.* future

**fu·tile** (fyōōt′'l) *adj.* ⟦< L *futilis*, lit., that easily pours out⟧ useless; vain —**fu'tile·ly** *adv.* —**fu·til·i·ty** (fyōō til′ə tē) *n., pl.* **-ties, n.**

**fu·ton** (fōō′tän′) *n.* ⟦Sino-Jpn⟧ a thin mattress like a quilt, placed as on the floor or a platform frame for use as a bed

**fu·ture** (fyōō′chər) *adj.* ⟦< L *futurus*, about to be⟧ **1** that is to be or come **2** indicating time to come [the *future* tense] —*n.* **1** the time that is to come **2** what is going to be **3** the chance to succeed, etc. **4** [*usually pl.*] a contract for a commodity bought or sold for delivery at a later date —**fu'tur·is'tic** *adj.*

**fu·tu·ri·ty** (fyōō toor′ə tē, -tyoor′-) *n., pl.* **-ties 1** the future **2** a future condition or event **3** a race for two-year-old horses in which the entries are selected before birth: in full **futurity race**

**fu·tur·ol·o·gy** (fyōō′chər äl′ə jē) *n.* ⟦FUTUR(E) + -OLOGY⟧ the study of probable or presumed future conditions as extrapolated from known facts —**fu'tur·ol'o·gist** *n.*

**futz** (futs) *vi.* ⟦? < Yiddish⟧ [Slang] to trifle or fool (*around*)

**fuzz** (fuz) *n.* ⟦< ?⟧ **1** loose, light particles of down, wool, etc.; fine hairs or fibers —**the fuzz** [Slang] a policeman or the police —**fuzz'y, -i·er, -i·est, adj.**

**fuzzy logic** ⟦< *fuzzy* (set), coined (1965) by L. A. Zadeh, U.S. scientist⟧ a type of logic used in computers for processing imprecise or variable data

**-fy** (fī) ⟦< L *facere*, do⟧ *suffix* **1** to make [*liquefy*] **2** to cause to have [*glorify*] **3** to become [*putrefy*]

**FYI** *abbrev.* for your information

# G

**g** or **G** (jē) *n., pl.* **g's, G's** the seventh letter of the English alphabet

**G**[1] (jē) *n. Music* the fifth tone in the scale of C major

**G**[2] *trademark for* a film rating indicating content suitable for persons of all ages

**G**[3] *abbrev.* **1** game(s) **2** German **3** goal(s) **4** gram(s) **5** guard **6** gulf Also, except for 2 & 6, **g**

**Ga** *Chem. symbol for* gallium

**GA** Georgia

**gab** (gab) *n., vt.* **gabbed, gab'bing** ⟦ON *gabba*, to mock⟧ [Inf.] chatter

**gab·ar·dine** (gab′ər dēn′) *n.* ⟦< OFr *gaverdine*, kind of cloak⟧ a twilled cloth of wool, cotton, etc., with a fine, diagonal weave: Brit. sp. **gab'er·dine'**

**gab·ble** (gab′əl) *vi., vt.* **-bled, -bling** ⟦< GAB⟧ to talk or utter rapidly or incoherently —*n.* such talk

**gab·by** (gab′ē) *adj.* **-bi·er, -bi·est** [Inf.] talkative —**gab'bi·ness** *n.*

**gab'fest'** (-fest′) *n.* [Inf.] an informal gathering of people to talk with one another

**ga·ble** (gā′bəl) *n.* ⟦< Gmc⟧ a triangular part of a wall enclosed by the sloping sides of a peaked roof —**ga'bled** *adj.*

**Ga·bon** (ga bōn′) country on the W coast of Africa: 103,347 sq. mi.; pop. 1,012,000

**Ga·bri·el** (gā′brē əl) *n. Bible* one of the archangels, the herald of good news

**gad** (gad) *vi.* **gad'ded, gad'ding** ⟦ME *gadden*, to hurry⟧ to wander about in an idle or restless way —**gad'der** *n.*

**gad'a·bout'** *n.* one who gads about, looking for fun, etc.

**gad'fly'** *n., pl.* **-flies'** ⟦see GOAD & FLY[2]⟧ **1** a large fly that bites livestock **2** one who annoys others, esp. by rousing them from complacency

**gadg·et** (gaj′it) *n.* ⟦< ?⟧ any small mechanical contrivance or device

**Gael·ic** (gā′lik) *adj.* of the Celtic people of Ireland, Scotland, or the Isle of Man —*n.* **1** the Celtic language of Scotland **2** the language group that includes GAELIC (*n.* 1), IRISH (*n.* 1), etc.

**gaff** (gaf) *n.* ⟦< OProv *gaf* or Sp *gafa*⟧ **1** a large hook on a pole for landing fish **2** a spar supporting a fore-and-aft sail

**gaffe** (gaf) *n.* ⟦Fr⟧ a blunder

**gaf·fer** (gaf′ər) *n.* a person in charge of lighting on the set of a film

**gag** (gag) *vt.* **gagged, gag'ging** ⟦echoic⟧ **1** to cause to retch **2** to keep from speaking, as by stopping up the mouth of —*vi.* to retch —*n.* **1** something put into or over the mouth to prevent talking, etc. **2** any restraint of free speech **3** a joke

**gage**[1] (gāj) *n.* ⟦< OFr, a pledge⟧ a glove, etc. thrown down as by a knight as a challenge to fight

**gage**[2] (gāj) *n., vt.* **gaged, gag'ing** *alt. sp. of* GAUGE

**gag·gle** (gag′əl) *n.* ⟦echoic⟧ **1** a flock of geese **2** any group or cluster

**gai·e·ty** (gā′ə tē) *n., pl.* **-ties 1** the quality of being GAY (*adj.* 1); cheerfulness **2** merrymaking

**gai·ly** (gā′lē) *adv.* in a gay manner; specif., *a)* merrily *b)* brightly

**gain** (gān) *n.* ⟦< OFr *gaaigne*⟧ **1** an increase; specif., *a)* [*often pl.*] profit *b)* an increase in advantage **2** acquisition —*vt.* **1** to earn **2** to win **3** to attract **4** to get as an addition, profit, or advantage **5** to make an increase in **6** to get to; reach —*vi.* **1** to make progress **2** to increase in weight —**gain on** to draw nearer to (an opponent in a race, etc.)

**gain·er** *n.* **1** a person or thing that gains **2** a fancy dive forward, but with a backward somersault

**gain·ful** *adj.* producing gain; profitable —**gain·ful·ly** *adv.*

**gain·say** (gān′sā′) *vt.* -**said**′ (-sed′), -**say′ing** ⟦< OE *gegn*, against + *secgan*, to say⟧ **1** to deny **2** to contradict —**gain′say′er** *n.*

**gait** (gāt) *n.* ⟦< ON *gata*, path⟧ **1** manner of walking or running **2** any of the various foot movements of a horse, as a trot, pace, canter, etc.

**gai·ter** (gāt′ər) *n.* ⟦< Fr *guêtre*⟧ a cloth or leather covering for the instep, ankle, and lower leg

**gal**[1] (gal) *n.* [Slang] a girl or woman

**gal**[2] *abbrev.* gallon(s)

**ga·la** (gā′lə, gal′ə) *n.* ⟦ult. < It *gala*⟧ a celebration —*adj.* festive

**gal·a·bi·a** or **gal·a·bi·ya** (gal′ə bē′ə, gə lä′bē ə) *n.* ⟦< Ar⟧ *var. of* DJELLABA

**Gal·a·had** (gal′ə had′) *n. Arthurian Legend* the knight who, because of his purity, finds the Holy Grail

**gal·ax·y** (gal′ək sē) *n., pl.* -**ies** ⟦< Gr *gala*, milk⟧ **1** [*often* G-] MILKY WAY **2** a large, independent system of stars **3** a group of illustrious people —**ga·lac·tic** (gə lak′tik) *adj.*

**gale** (gāl) *n.* ⟦< ?⟧ **1** a strong wind **2** an outburst [*a gale* of laughter]

**ga·le·na** (gə lē′nə) *n.* ⟦L, lead ore⟧ native lead sulfide, a soft, lead-gray mineral with a metallic luster

**Gal·i·lee** (gal′ə lē′), **Sea of** lake in NE Israel

**Gal·i·le·o** (gal′ə lē′ō, -lā′-) 1564-1642; It. astronomer & physicist

**gall**[1] (gôl) *n.* ⟦OE *galla*⟧ **1** BILE (sense 1) **2** something bitter or distasteful **3** bitter feeling **4** impudence

**gall**[2] (gôl) *n.* [see fol.] a sore on the skin caused by chafing —*vt.* **1** to make sore by rubbing **2** to annoy; vex

**gall**[3] (gôl) *n.* ⟦< L *galla*⟧ a tumor on plant tissue caused by stimulation by fungi, insects, etc.

**gal·lant** (gal′ənt; *for adj.* 3 & *n., usually* gə lant′, -länt′) *adj.* ⟦< OFr *galer*, to make merry⟧ **1** stately; imposing **2** brave and noble **3** polite and attentive to women —*n.* **1** [Now Rare] a high-spirited, stylish man **2** a man attentive and polite to women

**gal·lant·ry** (gal′ən trē) *n., pl.* -**ries 1** heroic courage **2** the behavior of a gallant **3** a courteous act or remark

**gall·blad·der** (gôl′blad′ər) *n.* a membranous sac closely attached to the liver, in which excess gall, or bile, is stored

**gal·le·on** (gal′ē ən) *n.* ⟦ult. < Gr *galeos*, shark⟧ a large sailing ship of the 15th and 16th c.

**gal·le·ri·a** (gal′ə rē′ə) *n.* a large arcade or court, sometimes with a glass roof

**gal·ler·y** (gal′ər ē) *n., pl.* -**ies** ⟦< ML *galeria*⟧ **1** a covered walk or porch open at one side or having the roof supported by pillars **2** a long, narrow, outside balcony **3** *a)* a balcony in a theater, etc.; esp., the highest balcony with the cheapest seats *b)* the people in these seats **4** the spectators at a sports event, etc. **5** a place for exhibiting or selling works of art; specif., a display room in a museum

**gal·ley** (gal′ē) *n., pl.* -**leys** ⟦< Gr *galeos*, shark⟧ **1** a long, low ship of ancient times, propelled by oars and sails **2** a ship's kitchen **3** *Printing a)* a shallow tray for holding composed type *b)* proof

printed from such type (in full, **galley proof**)

**Gal·lic** (gal′ik) *adj.* **1** of ancient Gaul or its people **2** French

**Gal·li·cism** (gal′i siz′əm) *n.* ⟦< prec.⟧ [*also* **g**-] a French idiom, custom, etc.

**gal·li·um** (gal′ē əm) *n.* ⟦named after L *Gallia*, France⟧ a bluish-white, metallic chemical element with a low melting point, used in semiconductors, lasers, etc.

GALLEY

**gal·li·vant** (gal′ə vant′) *vi.* ⟦arbitrary elaboration of GALLANT⟧ to go about in search of amusement

**gal·lon** (gal′ən) *n.* ⟦< OFr *jalon*⟧ a liquid measure equal to 4 quarts

**gal·lop** (gal′əp) *vi., vt.* ⟦< OFr *galoper*⟧ to go, or cause to go, at a gallop —*n.* the fastest gait of a horse, etc., a succession of leaping strides

**gal·lows** (gal′ōz) *n., pl.* -**lows** or -**lows·es** ⟦OE *galga*⟧ an upright frame with a crossbeam and a rope, for hanging condemned persons

**gall·stone** (gôl′stōn′) *n.* a small, solid mass sometimes formed in the gallbladder or bile duct

**ga·lore** (gə lôr′) *adj.* ⟦Ir *go leōr*, enough⟧ in abundance; plentifully [*to attract crowds galore*]

**ga·losh** or **ga·loshe** (gə läsh′) *n.* ⟦< OFr *galoche*⟧ a high, warmly lined overshoe of rubber and fabric

**gal·van·ic** (gal van′ik) *adj.* ⟦after L. *Galvani* (1737-98), It physicist⟧ **1** of or producing direct current from a chemical reaction, as in a battery **2** startling

**gal·va·nize** (gal′və nīz′) *vt.* -**nized**′, -**niz′ing 1** to stimulate as if by electric shock; rouse; stir **2** to plate (metal) with zinc

**gal′va·nom′e·ter** (-näm′ət ər) *n.* an instrument for detecting and measuring a small electric current

**Gam·bi·a** (gam′bē ə) country on the W coast of Africa: 4,361 sq. mi.; pop. 1,026,000

**gam·bit** (gam′bit) *n.* ⟦< Sp *gambito*, a tripping⟧ **1** *Chess* an opening in which a pawn, etc. is sacrificed to get an advantage in position **2** an action intended to gain an advantage

**gam·ble** (gam′bəl) *vi.* -**bled**, -**bling** ⟦ME *gamen*, to play⟧ **1** to play games of chance for money, etc. **2** to take a risk for some advantage —*vt.* to risk in gambling; bet —*n.* an undertaking involving risk —**gam′bler** *n.*

**gam·bol** (gam′bəl) *n.* ⟦< It *gamba*, leg⟧ a gamboling; frolic —*vi.* -**boled** or -**bolled**, -**bol·ing** or -**bol·ling** to jump and skip about in play; frolic

**gam·brel (roof)** (gam′brəl) a roof with two slopes on each of its two sides

**game**[1] (gām) *n.* ⟦OE *gamen*⟧ **1** any form of play; amusement **2** *a)* any specific game or sport involving competition under rules *b)* a single contest in such a competition **3** the number of points required for winning **4** a scheme; plan **5** wild birds or animals hunted for sport or food **6** [Inf.] a business or job, esp. one involving risk —*vi.* **gamed, gam′ing** to play cards, etc. for stakes; gamble —*adj.* **1** designating or of wild birds or animals hunted for sport or food **2** *a)* plucky; courageous *b)* enthusiastic; ready (*for* something) —**the game is up** failure is certain —**game′ly** *adv.* —**game′ness** *n.*

**game**[2] (gām) *adj.* ⟦< ?⟧ lame or injured [*a game leg*]

**game′cock**′ *n.* a specially bred rooster trained for cockfighting

**game′keep′er** *n.* a person who takes care of game birds and animals, as on an estate

**game plan 1** the strategy planned before a game **2** any long-range strategy

**game point 1** the situation when the next point scored could win a game **2** the winning point

**games·man·ship** (gāmz′mən ship′) *n.* skill in using ploys to gain an advantage

**game·ster** (gām′stər) *n.* a gambler

**gam·ete** (gam′ēt, gə mēt′) *n.* ⟦< Gr *gamos*, marriage⟧ a reproductive cell that unites with another to form the cell that develops into a new individual

**gam·in** (gam′in) *n.* ⟦Fr⟧ **1** a neglected child who roams the streets **2** a girl with saucy charm: also **ga·mine** (ga mēn′)

**gam·ma** (gam′ə) *n.* the third letter of the Greek alphabet (Γ, γ)

**gamma glob·u·lin** (gläb′yōō lin) that fraction of blood serum which contains most antibodies

**gamma ray** an electromagnetic radiation with a very short wavelength, produced as by the reactions of nuclei

**gam·ut** (gam′ət) *n.* ⟦< Gr letter *gamma*, for the lowest note of the medieval scale⟧ **1** any complete musical scale **2** the entire range or extent, as of emotions

**gam·y** (gām′ē) *adj.* **-i·er, -i·est** **1** having the strong flavor of cooked game **2** slightly tainted **3** risqué **4** coarse or crude —**gam′i·ness** *n.*

**gan·der** (gan′dər) *n.* ⟦OE *gan(d)ra*⟧ **1** a male goose **2** [Slang] a look: chiefly in **take a gander**

**Gan·dhi** (gän′dē), **Mo·han·das** (mō hän′dəs) 1869-1948; Hindu nationalist leader: called *Mahatma Gandhi*

**gang** (gaŋ) *n.* ⟦< OE *gangan*, to go⟧ a group of people working or acting together; specif., a group of criminals or juvenile delinquents —**gang up on** [Inf.] to attack as a group

**Gan·ges** (gan′jēz) river in N India & Bangladesh

**gan·gling** (gaŋ′gliŋ) *adj.* ⟦< ?⟧ thin, tall, and awkward: also **gan′gly**

**gan·gli·on** (gaŋ′glē ən) *n., pl.* **-gli·a** (-ə) or **-gli·ons** ⟦ult. < Gr, tumor⟧ a mass of nerve cells from which nerve impulses are transmitted

**gang′plank′** *n.* a movable ramp by which to board or leave a ship

**gan·grene** (gaŋ′grēn′, gaŋ grēn′) *n.* ⟦< Gr *gran*, gnaw⟧ decay of body tissue when the blood supply is obstructed —**gan′gre·nous** (-grə nəs) *adj.*

**gang·ster** (gaŋ′stər) *n.* a member of a gang of criminals —**gang′ster·ism′** *n.*

**gang′way′** *n.* ⟦OE *gangweg*⟧ **1** a passageway **2** *a)* an opening in a ship's bulwarks for loading, etc. *b)* GANGPLANK —*interj.* clear the way!

**gant·let** (gônt′lit, gänt′-, gant′-) *n.* ⟦< Swed *gata*, lane + *lopp*, a run⟧ **1** a former punishment in which the offender ran between two rows of men who struck him **2** a series of troubles Now sp. equally *gauntlet*

**gan·try** (gan′trē) *n., pl.* **-tries** ⟦< L *canterius*, beast of burden⟧ **1** a framework, often on wheels, for a traveling crane **2** a wheeled framework with a crane, platforms, etc., for readying a rocket to be launched

**GAO** *abbrev.* General Accounting Office

**gaol** (jāl) *n. Brit. sp. of* JAIL

**gap** (gap) *n.* ⟦< ON *gapa*, to gape⟧ **1** an opening made by breaking or parting **2** a mountain pass or ravine **3** a blank space; lacuna **4** a lag or disparity

**gape** (gāp) *vi.* **gaped, gap′ing** ⟦< ON *gapa*⟧ **1** to open the mouth wide, as in yawning **2** to stare with the mouth open **3** to open wide —*n.* **1** a gaping **2** a wide opening —**gap′ing·ly** *adv.*

**gar** (gär) *n., pl.* **gar** or **gars** ⟦< OE *gar*, a spear⟧ a freshwater fish with a long, beaklike snout: also **gar′fish′**

**ga·rage** (gə räzh′, -räj′) *n.* ⟦Fr < *garer*, to protect⟧ **1** a shelter for motor vehicles **2** a business place where motor vehicles are stored, repaired, etc.

**garage sale** a sale of used or unwanted household articles, etc.

**garb** (gärb) *n.* ⟦< It *garbo*, elegance⟧ clothing; style of dress [clerical *garb*] —*vt.* to clothe

**gar·bage** (gär′bij) *n.* ⟦ME, entrails of fowls⟧ **1** spoiled or waste food **2** any worthless, offensive, etc. matter

**gar·ble** (gär′bəl) *vt.* **-bled, -bling** ⟦< Ar *gharbāl*, a sieve⟧ to distort or confuse (a story, etc.)

**gar·çon** (gär sōn′) *n., pl.* **-çons′** (-sōn′) ⟦Fr⟧ a waiter

**gar·den** (gärd′'n) *n.* ⟦< Frankish⟧ **1** a piece of ground for growing vegetables, flowers, etc. **2** an area of fertile land: also **garden spot** **3** [*often pl.*] a public, parklike place, sometimes having displays of animals or plants —*vi.* to take care of a garden —*adj.* of, for, or grown in a garden —**gar′den·er** *n.*

**gar·de·ni·a** (gär dēn′yə) *n.* ⟦after A. *Garden* (1730-91), Am botanist⟧ a plant with fragrant, waxy flowers

**gar′den-va·ri′e·ty** *adj.* ordinary; commonplace

**Gar·field** (gär′fēld), **James A·bram** (jāmz ā′brəm) 1831-81; 20th president of the U.S. (1881): assassinated

**Gar·gan·tu·a** (gär gan′chōō ə) *n.* a giant king in a satire by Rabelais —**gar·gan′tu·an** *adj.*

**gar·gle** (gär′gəl) *vt., vi.* **-gled, -gling** ⟦< Fr *gargouille*, throat⟧ to rinse (the throat) with a liquid kept in motion by the expulsion of air from the lungs —*n.* a liquid for gargling

**gar·goyle** (gär′goil′) *n.* ⟦see prec.⟧ a waterspout formed like a fantastic creature, projecting from a building

**Gar·i·bal·di** (gar′ə bôl′dē), **Giu·sep·pe** (jōō zep′pe) 1807-82; It. patriot & general

**gar·ish** (gar′ish, ger′-) *adj.* ⟦prob. < ME *gauren*, to stare⟧ too bright or gaudy; showy —**gar′ish·ly** *adv.* —**gar′ish·ness** *n.*

**gar·land** (gär′lənd) *n.* ⟦< OFr *garlande*⟧ a wreath of flowers, leaves, etc. —*vt.* to decorate with garlands

**Gar·land** (gär′lənd) city in NE Texas: pop. 181,000

**gar·lic** (gär′lik) *n.* ⟦< OE *gar*, a spear + *leac*, leek⟧ **1** an herb of the lily family **2** its strong-smelling bulb, used as seasoning —**gar′lick·y** *adj.*

**gar·ment** (gär′mənt) *n.* ⟦see GARNISH⟧ any article of clothing

**gar·ner** (gär′nər) *vt.* ⟦< L *granum*, grain⟧ **1** to gather and store **2** to get or earn

**gar·net** (gär′nit) *n.* ⟦< ML *granatum*⟧ a hard, glasslike mineral: red varieties are often used as gems

**gar·nish** (gär′nish) *vt.* ⟦< OFr *garnir*, furnish⟧ **1** to decorate **2** to decorate (food) with something that adds color or flavor **3** *Law* to attach (a debtor's property, wages, etc.) so that it can be used to pay the debt —*n.* **1** a decoration **2** something used to garnish food, as parsley

**gar·nish·ee** (gär′ni shē′) *vt.* **-eed′, -ee′ing** ⟦< prec.⟧ GARNISH (*vt.* 3): now rare in legal usage

**gar′nish·ment** *n. Law* a proceeding by which a creditor seeks to attach a debtor's wages, etc.

**gar·ret** (gar′it) *n.* ⟦< OFr *garite*, watchtower⟧ an attic

**gar·ri·son** (gar′ə sən) *n.* ⟦< OFr *garir*, to watch⟧ **1** troops stationed in a fort or fortified place **2** a military post or station —*vt.* to station (troops) in (a fortified place) for its defense

**gar·rote** (gə rät′, -rōt′) *n.* ⟦Sp⟧ **1** a cord, thong, etc. used in strangling a person in a surprise attack **2** a strangling in this way —*vt.* **-rot′ed** or **-rot′ted, -rot′ing** or **-rot′ting** to execute or attack by such strangling Also **ga·rotte′** or **gar·rotte′** —**gar·rot′er** *n.*

**gar·ru·lous** (gar′ə ləs) *adj.* ⟦< L *garrire*, to chatter⟧ talking much, esp. about unimportant things —**gar·ru·li·ty** (gə rōō′lə tē) or **gar′ru·lous·ness** *n.* —**gar′ru·lous·ly** *adv.*

**gar·ter** (gärt′ər) *n.* ⟦< OFr *garet*, the back of the knee⟧ an elastic band or strap for holding a stocking in place

**garter belt** a belt of elastic fabric with hanging garters, worn by women

**garter snake** a small, harmless snake common in North America

**Gar·y** (ger′ē) city in NW Indiana: pop. 117,000

**gas** (gas) *n.*, *pl.* **gas′es** or **gas′ses** ⟦coined < Gr *chaos*, space⟧ **1** the fluid form of a substance in which it can expand indefinitely; vapor **2** any mixture of flammable gases used for lighting or heating **3** any gas used as an anesthetic **4** any poisonous substance dispersed in the air, as in war **5** [Inf.] GASOLINE —*vt.* **gassed**, **gas′sing** to injure or kill by gas —**gas up** [Inf.] to supply (a vehicle) with gasoline —**gas′e·ous** (-ē əs) *adj.*

**gas chamber** a room in which people are put to be killed with poison gas

**gash** (gash) *vt.* ⟦< Gr *charassein*, to cut⟧ to make a long, deep cut in; slash —*n.* a long, deep cut

**gas·ket** (gas′kit) *n.* ⟦prob. < OFr *garcete*, small cord⟧ a piece or ring of rubber, metal, etc. used to make a joint leakproof

**gas mask** a filtering mask worn to prevent the breathing in of poisonous gases

**gas·o·hol** (gas′ə hôl′) *n.* a motor fuel mixture of gasoline and alcohol

**gas·o·line** (gas′ə lēn′, gas′ə lēn′) *n.* ⟦< *gas* + L *oleum*, oil⟧ a volatile, flammable liquid distilled from petroleum, used chiefly as a fuel in internal-combustion engines: also **gas′o·lene′**

**gasp** (gasp) *vi.* ⟦< ON *geispa*, to yawn⟧ to inhale suddenly, as in surprise, or breathe with effort — *vt.* to say with gasps —*n.* a gasping

**gas station** SERVICE STATION

**gas′sy** *adj.* **-si·er**, **-si·est 1** full of gas; esp., flatulent **2** like gas

**gas·tric** (gas′trik) *adj.* ⟦GASTR(O)- + -IC⟧ of, in, or near the stomach

**gastric juice** the clear, acid digestive fluid produced by glands in the stomach lining

**gas·tri·tis** (gas trīt′is) *n.* ⟦fol. + -ITIS⟧ inflammation of the stomach

**gastro-** ⟦< Gr *gastēr*⟧ *combining form* stomach (and)

**gas·tron·o·my** (gas trän′ə mē) *n.* ⟦< Gr *gastēr*, stomach + *nomos*, a rule⟧ the art or science of good eating —**gas′tro·nom′ic** (-trə näm′ik) or **gas′tro·nom′i·cal** *adj.*

**gas·tro·pod** (gas′trō päd′) *n.* ⟦GASTRO- + -POD⟧ a mollusk of the class including snails, slugs, etc.

**gate** (gāt) *n.* ⟦OE⟧ **1** a movable structure controlling passage through an opening in a fence or wall **2** a gateway **3** a movable barrier **4** a structure controlling the flow of water, as in a canal **5** the total amount or number of paid admissions to a performance —**give** (or **get**) **the gate** [Slang] to subject (or be subjected) to dismissal

**-gate** (gāt) ⟦< (*Water*)*gate*, political scandal, after the *Watergate*, building in Washington, D.C., site of 1972 burglary⟧ *combining form* a scandal marked by charges of corruption on the part of public officials, etc.

**gate′-crash′er** *n.* [Inf.] one who attends a social affair without an invitation or attends a performance without paying

**gate′fold′** *n.* an oversize page, as in a magazine, bound so it can be unfolded and opened out

**gate′way′** *n.* **1** an entrance as in a wall, fitted with a gate **2** a means of access

**gath·er** (gath′ər) *vt.* ⟦OE *gad(e)rian*⟧ **1** to bring together in one place or group **2** to get gradually; accumulate **3** to collect by picking; harvest **4** to infer; conclude **5** to draw (cloth) into folds or puckers —*vi.* **1** to assemble **2** to increase —*n.* a pucker or fold —**gath′er·er** *n.*

**gath′er·ing** *n.* **1** a meeting; crowd **2** a gather in cloth

**ga·tor** or **'ga·tor** (gā′tər) *n. short for* ALLIGATOR

**gauche** (gōsh) *adj.* ⟦Fr < MFr *gauchir*, become warped⟧ lacking social grace; awkward; tactless

**gau·che·rie** (gō′shə rē) *n.* gauche behavior or a gauche act

**gau·cho** (gou′chō) *n.*, *pl.* **-chos** ⟦AmSp⟧ a South American cowboy

**gaud·y** (gô′dē) *adj.* **-i·er**, **-i·est** ⟦< ME *gaude*, trinket⟧ bright and showy, but lacking in good taste —**gaud′i·ly** *adv.* —**gaud′i·ness** *n.*

**gauge** (gāj) *n.* ⟦NormFr⟧ **1** a standard measure or criterion **2** any device for measuring **3** the distance between the rails of a railroad **4** the size of the bore of a shotgun **5** the thickness of sheet metal, wire, etc. —*vt.* **gauged**, **gaug′ing 1** to measure the size, amount, etc. of **2** to judge

**Gaul**[1] (gôl) *n.* a member of the people of ancient Gaul

**Gaul**[2] (gôl) ancient division of the Roman Empire, in W Europe

**Gaul′ish** *n.* the Celtic language of ancient Gaul

**gaunt** (gônt) *adj.* ⟦ME *gawnte*⟧ **1** thin and bony; haggard, as from great hunger **2** looking grim and forbidding —**gaunt′ness** *n.*

**gaunt·let**[1] (gônt′lit, gänt′-) *n.* ⟦< OFr *gant*, glove⟧ **1** a knight's armored glove **2** a long glove with a flaring cuff —**throw down the gauntlet** to challenge, as to combat

**gaunt·let**[2] (gônt′lit, gänt′-) *n. see* GANTLET

**gauze** (gôz) *n.* ⟦< Fr *gaze* < Ar *ḳazz*, silk⟧ any very thin, transparent, loosely woven material, as of cotton or silk —**gauz′y**, **-i·er**, **-i·est**, *adj.*

**gave** (gāv) *vt.*, *vi. pt. of* GIVE

**gav·el** (gav′əl) *n.* ⟦? < Scot *gable*, fork⟧ a small mallet rapped on the table, as by a presiding officer, to call for attention, etc.

**ga·votte** (gə vät′) *n.* ⟦Fr⟧ a 17th-c. dance like the minuet, but livelier

**gawk** (gôk) *vi.* ⟦prob. < *gowk*, stupid person⟧ to stare stupidly

**gawk·y** (gô′kē) *adj.* **-i·er**, **-i·est** ⟦see prec.⟧ clumsy; ungainly —**gawk′i·ly** *adv.* —**gawk′i·ness** *n.*

**gay** (gā) *adj.* ⟦OFr *gai*⟧ **1** joyous and lively; merry **2** bright; brilliant [*gay* colors] **3** homosexual —*n.* a homosexual; esp., a homosexual man

**gay·e·ty** (gā′ə tē) *n.*, *pl.* **-ties** *alt. sp. of* GAIETY

**gay·ly** (gā′lē) *adv. alt. sp. of* GAILY

**gaze** (gāz) *vi.* **gazed**, **gaz′ing** ⟦< Scand⟧ to look steadily; stare —*n.* a steady look

**ga·ze·bo** (gə zē′bō, -zā′-) *n.*, *pl.* **-bos** or **-boes** ⟦< prec.⟧ a summerhouse, windowed balcony, etc. from which one can gaze at the scenery around it

**ga·zelle** (gə zel′) *n.* ⟦< Ar *ghazāl*⟧ a small, swift antelope of Africa and Asia, with large, lustrous eyes

**ga·zette** (gə zet′) *n.* ⟦Fr < It dial. *gazeta*, a small coin, price of the newspaper⟧ **1** a newspaper: now mainly in newspaper titles **2** in England, an official publication —*vt.* **-zet′ted**, **-zet′ting** [Brit.] to publish or announce in a gazette

**gaz·et·teer** (gaz′ə tir′) *n.* a dictionary or index of geographical names

**ga·zil·lion** (gə zil′yən) *n.* [Slang] a very large, indefinite number

**gaz·pa·cho** (gäs pä′chō, gäz-) *n.* ⟦Sp⟧ a cold Spanish soup of chopped raw tomatoes, cucumbers, onions, and peppers, mixed with oil, vinegar, etc.

**GB** *abbrev.* **1** gigabyte(s) **2** Great Britain

**Ge** *Chem. symbol for* germanium

**gear** (gir) *n.* ⟦prob. < ON *gervi*, preparation⟧ **1** clothing **2** equipment, esp. for some task **3** *a*) a toothed wheel designed to mesh with another *b*) [*often pl.*] a system of such gears meshed together to pass motion along *c*) a specific adjustment of such a system *d*) a part of a mechanism with a specific function [the steering *gear*] —*vt.* **1** to connect by or furnish with gears **2** to adapt (one thing) to conform with another [to *gear* supply to demand] —**in** (or **out of**) **gear 1** (not) connected to the motor **2** (not) in proper working order

**gear′shift′** *n.* the lever for engaging or disengaging any of several sets of transmission gears to a motor, etc.

**gear'wheel'** *n.* a toothed wheel in a system of gears; cogwheel

**geck·o** (gek'ō) *n., pl.* **-os** or **-oes** [[prob. < Malay]] a tropical lizard with suction pads on its feet

**GED**[1] *trademark for* General Educational Development

**GED**[2] *abbrev.* general equivalency diploma

**gee** (jē) *interj.* [[< JE(SUS)]] [Slang] used to express surprise, wonder, etc.

**geek** (gēk) *n.* [Slang] a person considered to be different from others in a negative way, as in being socially awkward —**geek'y, -i·er, -i·est,** *adj.*

**geese** (gēs) *n. pl. of* GOOSE

**gee whiz** an exclamation used to express surprise, enthusiasm, protest, etc.

**gee·zer** (gē'zər) *n.* [< GUISE] [Slang] an old man

**ge·fil·te fish** (gə fil'tə) [[E Yiddish]] chopped, seasoned fish, boiled and served in balls or cakes

**Gei·ger counter** (gī'gər) [[after H. *Geiger* (1882-1945), Ger physicist]] an instrument for detecting and counting ionizing particles, as from radioactive ores

**gei·sha** (gā'shə) *n., pl.* **-sha** or **-shas** [[Sino-Jpn *gei*, art + *sha*, person]] a Japanese woman trained in singing, conversation, etc. to serve as a hired companion to men

**gel** (jel) *n.* [< fol.] **1** a jellylike substance formed from a colloidal solution **2** any of various jellylike preparations for setting hair, brushing teeth, etc. —*vi.* **gelled, gel'ling** to form a gel

**gel·a·tin** (jel'ə tin) *n.* [< L *gelare*, freeze]] a tasteless, odorless substance extracted by boiling bones, horns, etc., or a similar vegetable substance: dissolved and cooled, it forms a jellylike substance used in foods, photographic film, etc.: also **gel'a·tine** (-tēn, -tin) —**ge·lat·i·nous** (jə lat'n əs) *adj.*

**geld** (geld) *vt.* **geld'ed** or **gelt, geld'ing** [< ON *geldr*, barren]] to castrate (esp. a horse)

**geld'ing** *n.* a castrated horse

**gel·id** (jel'id) *adj.* [< L *gelu*, frost]] extremely cold; frozen

**gem** (jem) *n.* [< L *gemma*, a bud]] **1** a cut and polished gemstone or a pearl **2** someone or something very precious or valuable

**Gem·i·ni** (jem'ə nī', -nē') *n.* [L, twins]] the third sign of the zodiac

**gem'stone'** *n.* any mineral that can be used in a piece of jewelry when cut and polished

**ge·müt·lich** (gə müt'liH) *adj.* [Ger]] agreeable, cheerful, cozy, etc.

**gen** *abbrev.* general

**Gen** *abbrev.* **1** General **2** *Bible* Genesis

**-gen** (jən, jen) [< Gr *-genēs*, born]] *suffix* **1** something that produces [*hydrogen*] **2** something produced (in a specified way)

**gen·darme** (zhän därm') *n.* [Fr < *gens d'armes*, men-at-arms]] a French police officer

**gen·der** (jen'dər) *n.* [< L *genus*, origin]] **1** *Gram.* the classification by which words are grouped as masculine, feminine, or neuter **2** the fact of being a male or female human being, esp. as it affects a person's self-image, social relationships, etc.

**gen'dered** *adj.* affected by issues of GENDER (*n.* 2)

**gene** (jēn) *n.* [see -GEN]] any of the units in the chromosomes by which hereditary characteristics are transmitted

**ge·ne·al·o·gy** (jē'nē äl'ə jē) *n., pl.* **-gies** [< Gr *genea*, race + *-logia*, -LOGY]] **1** a recorded history of a person's ancestry **2** the study of family descent **3** lineage —**ge'ne·a·log'i·cal** (-ə läj'i kəl) *adj.* —**ge'ne·al'o·gist** *n.*

**gen·er·a** (jen'ər ə) *n. pl. of* GENUS

**gen·er·al** (jen'ər əl) *adj.* [< L *genus*, class]] **1** of, for, or from all; not local, special, or specialized **2** of or for a whole genus, kind, etc. **3** widespread [*general* unrest] **4** most common; usual **5** not specific or precise [in *general* terms] **6** highest in rank [attorney *general*] —*n.* a military officer ranking above a colonel, specif. one ranking above

---

a lieutenant general —**in general 1** usually **2** without specific details —**gen'er·al·ship'** *n.*

**general assembly** [often G- A-] **1** the legislative assembly in some U.S. states **2** the deliberative assembly of the United Nations

**general delivery** delivery of mail at the post office to addressees who call for it

**gen·er·al·is·si·mo** (jen'ər ə lis'i mō') *n., pl.* **-mos'** [[It]] in some countries, the commander in chief of the armed forces

**gen·er·al·i·ty** (jen'ər al'ə tē) *n., pl.* **-ties 1** the quality of being general **2** a general or vague statement, idea, etc. **3** the main body

**gen·er·al·ize** (jen'ər əl īz') *vt.* **-ized', -iz'ing 1** to state in terms of a general law **2** to infer or derive (a general law) from (particular instances) —*vi.* **1** to formulate general principles **2** to talk in generalities

**gen'er·al·ly** *adv.* **1** widely; popularly **2** usually **3** not specifically

**general practitioner** a practicing physician who does not specialize in a particular field of medicine

**gen·er·ate** (jen'ər āt') *vt.* **-at'ed, -at'ing** [< L *genus*, race]] **1** to produce (offspring); beget **2** to bring into being —**gen'er·a'tive** (-āt'iv, -ə tiv) *adj.*

**gen·er·a'tion** *n.* **1** the producing of offspring **2** production **3** a single stage in the succession of descent **4** the average period (*c.* 30 years) between human generations **5** all the people born and living at about the same time —**gen'er·a'tion·al** *adj.*

**generation gap** the differences in attitudes, experiences, etc. between contemporary older and younger generations

**Generation X** (eks) the generation of persons born in the 1960s and 1970s

**gen·er·a'tor** *n.* a machine for changing mechanical energy into electrical energy; dynamo

**ge·ner·ic** (jə ner'ik) *adj.* [< L *genus*, race, kind]] **1** of a whole kind, class, or group; inclusive **2** without a brand name —*n.* a product, as a drug, without a brand name: *often used in pl.* —**ge·ner'i·cal·ly** *adv.*

**gen·er·ous** (jen'ər əs) *adj.* [< L *generosus*, noble]] **1** noble-minded; magnanimous **2** willing to give or share; unselfish **3** large; ample —**gen·er·os·i·ty** (jen'ər äs'ə tē) *n.* —**gen'er·ous·ly** *adv.*

**gen·e·sis** (jen'ə sis) *n.* [Gr]] **1** the beginning; origin **2** [G-] the first book of the Bible

**gene therapy** the experimental treatment of diseases with new chemicals or organisms created by the recombining of units of DNA

**genetic code** the arrangement of chemical substances in DNA or RNA that determines the characteristics of an organism

**ge·net·ics** (jə net'iks) *n.* [ult. < GENESIS]] the branch of biology dealing with heredity and variation in animal and plant species —**ge·net'ic** *adj.* —**ge·net'i·cal·ly** *adv.* —**ge·net'i·cist** (-ə sist) *n.*

**Ge·ne·va** (jə nē'və) city in SW Switzerland: pop. 174,000

**Gen·ghis Khan** (geŋ'gis kän', jeŋ'-) 1162?-1227; Mongol conqueror

**gen·ial** (jēn'yəl) *adj.* [see GENIUS]] **1** good for life and growth [a *genial* climate] **2** cheerful and friendly; amiable —**ge·ni·al·i·ty** (jē'nē al'ə tē) *n.* —**gen'ial·ly** *adv.*

**ge·nie** (jē'nē) *n.* [< Fr < Ar *jinnī*] JINNI

**gen·i·tal** (jen'i təl) *adj.* [< L *genere*, beget]] of reproduction or the sexual organs

**gen'i·tals** *pl.n.* [see prec.]] the reproductive organs; esp., the external sex organs: also **gen'i·ta'li·a** (-tā'lē ə, -tāl'yə)

**gen·i·tive** (jen'i tiv) *n.* [< Gr *genos*, genus]] *Gram.* a case expressing possession, source, etc., or referring to a part of a whole

**gen·i·to·u·ri·nar·y** (jen'i tō yoor'ə ner'ē) *adj.* of the genital and urinary organs

**gen·i·us** (jēn'yəs) *n.* [L, guardian spirit]] **1** par-

ticular spirit or nature of a nation, place, age, etc.
**2** natural ability; strong inclination (*for*) **3** great
mental capacity and inventive ability **4** one having such capacity or ability

**Gen·o·a** (jen′ə wə) seaport in NW Italy: pop.
679,000

**gen·o·cide** (jen′ə sīd′) *n.* [< Gr *genos*, race +
-CIDE] the systematic killing of a whole people or
nation —**gen·o·ci′dal** *adj.*

**gen·re** (zhän′rə) *n.* [Fr < L *genus*, a kind] **1** a
kind, or type, as of works of literature, art, or
popular fiction **2** painting in which everyday subjects are treated realistically

**gent** (jent) *n.* [Inf.] a gentleman

**gen·teel** (jen tēl′) *adj.* [< Fr *gentil*] polite or well-
bred; now, esp., affectedly refined, polite, etc. —
**gen·teel′ly** *adv.*

**gen·tian** (jen′shən) *n.* [< L *gentiana*] a plant typically having fringed, blue flowers

**gen·tile** (jen′tīl′) [*also* G-] *n.* [< L *gentilis*, of the
same clan] any person not a Jew —*adj.* not Jew-
ish

**gen·til·i·ty** (jen til′i tē) *n.* [see fol.] the quality of
being genteel

**gen·tle** (jent′′l) *adj.* -tler, -tlest [< L *gentilis*, of the
same clan] **1** of the upper classes **2** generous;
kind **3** tame [*a gentle dog*] **4** kindly; patient **5**
not harsh or rough [*a gentle tap*] **6** gradual [*a
gentle slope*] —**gen′tle·ness** *n.* —**gen′tly** *adv.*

**gen·tle·folk** *pl.n.* people of high social standing:
*also* **gen′tle·folks′**

**gen·tle·man** (-mən) *n.*, *pl.* -men (-mən) **1** [Obs.] a
man of good family and high social standing **2** a
courteous, gracious, and honorable man **3** any
man: a polite term, esp. as (in *pl.*) a form of
address —**gen′tle·man·ly** *adj.* —**gen′tle·wom′an**,
*pl.* -wom′en, *fem.n.*

**gen·tri·fy** (jen′tri fī′) *vt.* -fied′, -fy′ing [< fol. +
-FY] **1** to convert (an aging neighborhood) into a
more affluent one, as by remodeling homes **2** to
raise to a higher status —**gen′tri·fi·ca′tion** *n.*

**gen·try** (jen′trē) *n.* [see GENTLE] people of high
social standing

**gen·u·flect** (jen′yə flekt′) *vi.* [< L *genu*, knee +
*flectere*, to bend] to bend the knee, as in worship
—**gen′u·flec′tion** *n.*

**gen·u·ine** (jen′yo̅o̅ in) *adj.* [L *genuinus*, inborn] **1**
not counterfeit or artificial; real; true **2** sincere
—**gen′u·ine·ly** *adv.* —**gen′u·ine·ness** *n.*

**ge·nus** (jē′nəs) *n.*, *pl.* **gen·er·a** (jen′ər ə) *or* **ge′nus·
es** [L, race, kind] **1** a class; kind; sort **2** a category used in classifying plants or animals that
are similar in structure

**geo-** [< Gr *gē*] *combining form* earth, of the earth

**ge·o·cen·tric** (jē′ō sen′trik) *adj.* **1** viewed as from
the center of the earth **2** having the earth as a
center —**ge′o·cen′tri·cal·ly** *adv.*

**ge·ode** (jē′ōd′) *n.* [< Gr *geōdēs*, earthlike] a
globular stone with a cavity lined with crystals or
silica

**ge·o·des·ic** (jē′ə des′ik) *adj.* **1** GEODETIC (sense 1)
**2** *a*) designating the shortest line between two
points on a curved surface *b*) of the geometry of
such lines **3** having a surface formed of straight
bars in a grid of polygons [*geodesic* dome]

**ge·o·det·ic** (jē′ə det′ik) *adj.* **1** of or concerned
with the measurement of the earth and its surface **2** GEODESIC (sense 2)

**ge·og·ra·phy** (jē äg′rə fē) *n.* [< Gr *gē*, earth +
*graphein*, write] **1** the science dealing with the
earth's surface, continents, climates, plants, animals, resources, etc. **2** the physical features of a
region —**ge·og′ra·pher** *n.* —**ge′o·graph′i·cal** (-ə
graf′i kəl) *or* **ge′o·graph′ic** *adj.* —**ge′o·graph′i·cal·
ly** *adv.*

**ge·ol·o·gy** (jē äl′ə jē) *n.* [see GEO- & -LOGY] the
science dealing with the development of the
earth's crust, its rocks and fossils, etc. —**ge′o·
log′ic** (-ə läj′ik) *or* **ge′o·log′i·cal** *adj.* —**ge′o·log′i·
cal·ly** *adv.* —**ge·ol′o·gist** *n.*

**ge·o·mag·net·ic** (jē′ō mag net′ik) *adj.* of the magnetic properties of the earth —**ge′o·mag′ne·tism′**
*n.*

**ge·om·e·try** (jē äm′ə trē) *n.* [< Gr *gē*, earth +
*metrein*, to measure] the branch of mathematics
dealing with the properties, measurement, and
relationships of points, lines, planes, and solids —
**ge′o·met′ric** (-ə me′trik) *or* **ge′o·met′ri·cal** *adj.* —
**ge′o·met′ri·cal·ly** *adv.*

**ge·o·phys·ics** (jē′ō fiz′iks) *n.* the science dealing
with the effects of weather, winds, tides, earthquakes, etc. on the earth —**ge′o·phys′i·cal** *adj.* —
**ge′o·phys′i·cist** *n.*

**George III** (jôrj) 1738-1820; king of Great Britain
& Ireland (1760-1820)

**George′town′** section of Washington, DC

**Geor·gia** (jôr′jə) **1** Southern state of the SE U.S.:
57,910 sq. mi.; pop. 6,478,000; cap. Atlanta:
abbrev *GA* **2** country in W Asia: formerly part of
the U.S.S.R.: 26,900 sq. mi.; pop. 5,456,000 —
**Geor·gian** (jôr′jən) *adj.*, *n.*

**ge·o·sta·tion·ar·y** (jē′ō stā′shə ner′ē) *adj.* designating or of a satellite orbiting the earth at a
speed which keeps it always above the same point
on the earth's surface: *also* **ge′o·syn′chro·nous**
(-siŋ′krə nəs)

**ge·o·syn′cline′** (-sin′klīn′) *n.* a very large depression in the earth's surface

**ge·o·ther′mal** (-thur′məl) *adj.* [GEO- + Gr *thermē*,
heat] of the heat inside the earth: sometimes
**ge′o·ther′mic** (-thur′mik)

**Ger** *abbrev.* **1** German **2** Germany

**ge·ra·ni·um** (jə rā′nē əm) *n.* [< Gr *geranos*, a
crane] **1** a common garden plant with showy red,
white, etc. flowers **2** a related wildflower

**ger·bil** (jur′bəl) *n.* [ult. < Ar] a small rodent with
long hind legs, often kept as a pet

**ger·i·at·rics** (jer′ē a′triks) *n.* [< Gr *gēras*, old age +
-IATRICS] the branch of medicine dealing with the
diseases of old age —**ger·i·at′ric** *adj.*

**germ** (jurm) *n.* [< L *germen*] **1** the rudimentary
form from which a new organism is developed;
seed; bud **2** any microscopic disease-bearing
organism; esp., one of the bacteria **3** an origin
[*the germ* of an idea]

**Ger·man** (jur′mən) *n.* **1** a person born or living in
Germany **2** the language of Germany, Austria,
etc. —*adj.* of Germany or its people, language,
etc.

**ger·mane** (jər mān′) *adj.* [see GERM] truly relevant; pertinent

**Ger·man·ic** (jər man′ik) *adj.* designating or of
GERMANIC (*n.* 2) —*n.* **1** [Obs.] the original language of the German people **2** the group of languages descended from it, including English

**ger·ma·ni·um** (jər mā′nē əm) *n.* [< L *Germania*,
Germany] a nonmetallic chemical element used
in making transistors, etc.

**German measles** RUBELLA

**German shepherd** a large dog with a bushy tail
and erect ears, originally used to herd sheep, now
often used as a guard dog

**Ger·ma·ny** (jur′mə nē) country in NC Europe: formerly partitioned (1949-90) into the **Federal
Republic of Germany**, also called *West Germany*,
and the **German Democratic Republic**, also called
*East Germany*: 137,822 sq. mi.; pop. 80,975,000

**germ cell** an ovum or sperm cell

**ger·mi·cide** (jur′mə sīd′) *n.* [< GERM + -CIDE] any
antiseptic, etc. used to destroy germs —**ger′mi·
ci′dal** *adj.*

**ger·mi·nal** (jur′mə nəl) *adj.* **1** of or like germ cells
**2** in the first stage of growth

**ger·mi·nate** (-nāt′) *vi.*, *vt.* -nat′ed, -nat′ing [< L
*germen*, a sprout] **1** to sprout or cause to sprout,
as from a seed **2** to start developing —**ger′mi·
na′tion** *n.*

**germ′y** *adj.* -i·er, -i·est full of germs

**ger·on·tol·o·gy** (jer′ən täl′ə jē) *n.* [< Gr *gerōn*, old
man + -LOGY] the study of aging and the

problems of the aged —**ger·on·to·log'i·cal** (-tə läj'i kəl) *adj.* —**ger'on·tol'o·gist** *n.*

**ger·ry·man·der** (jer'ē man'dər) *vt., vi.* ⟦after Elbridge *Gerry*, governor of MA (1812) + (SALA)MANDER (from the shape of the county redistricted then)⟧ to divide (a voting area) unfairly, so as to give one political party an advantage

**ger·und** (jer'ənd) *n.* ⟦< L *gerere*, carry out⟧ *Gram.* an English verbal noun ending in *-ing*

**Ge·sta·po** (gə stä'pō) *n.* ⟦< Ger *Ge(heime) Sta(ats)po(lizei)*, secret state police⟧ the terrorist secret police force of Nazi Germany

**ges·ta·tion** (jes tā'shən) *n.* ⟦< L *gerere*, to bear⟧ the act or period of carrying young in the uterus; pregnancy —**ges'tate'**, **-tat·ed**, **-tat·ing**, *vt.*

**ges·tic·u·late** (jes tik'yōō lāt') *vi.* **-lat·ed**, **-lat·ing** ⟦see fol.⟧ to make gestures, esp. with the hands —**ges·tic·u·la'tion** *n.*

**ges·ture** (jes'chər) *n.* ⟦< L *gerere*, to bear⟧ **1** a movement of part of the body to express or emphasize ideas, emotions, etc. **2** any act or remark conveying a state of mind, intention, etc., often made merely for effect —*vi.* **-tured**, **-tur·ing** to make gestures

**get** (get) *vt.* **got**, **got'ten** or **got**, **get'ting** ⟦< ON *geta*⟧ **1** to come into the state of having; receive, obtain, acquire, etc. **2** to arrive at [*get* home early] **3** to go and bring [*get* your books] **4** to catch **5** to persuade [*get* him to leave] **6** to cause to be [*get* the jar open] **7** to prepare [to *get* lunch] **8** to manage or contrive [to *get* to do something] **9** [Inf.] *a*) to be obliged (with *have* or *has*) [he's *got* to pass] *b*) to possess (with *have* or *has*) [he's *got* red hair] *c*) to strike, kill, baffle, defeat, etc. *d*) to understand **10** [Slang] to cause an emotional response in [her singing *gets* me] —*vi.* **1** to come, go, or arrive [when I *get* to work] **2** to come to be [to *get* caught] *Get* is used as an auxiliary for emphasis in passive constructions [to *get* praised] —*n.* the young of an animal —**get anywhere** to have any success —**get around 1** to move from place to place; circulate: also **get about 2** to circumvent **3** to influence as by flattery —**get away 1** to go away **2** to escape —**get away with** [Inf.] to do without being discovered or punished —**get by** [Inf.] to survive; manage —**get it** [Inf.] **1** to understand **2** to be punished —**get off 1** to come off, down, or out of **2** to leave or start **3** to escape or help to escape —**get on 1** to go on or into **2** to put on **3** to proceed **4** to grow older **5** to succeed —**get out 1** to go out or away **2** to take out **3** to be disclosed **4** to publish —**get over 1** to recover from **2** to forget —**get through 1** to finish **2** to manage to survive —**get together 1** to assemble **2** [Inf.] to reach an agreement —**get up 1** to rise (from sleep, etc.) **2** to organize

**get'a·way'** *n.* **1** the act of starting, as in a race **2** the act of escaping

**get'-go'** *n.* [Inf.] beginning: used chiefly in **from the get-go**

**get'-to·geth'er** *n.* an informal social gathering or meeting

**Get·tys·burg** (get'iz burg') town in S Pennsylvania: site of a crucial Civil War battle (July, 1863)

**get'-up'** *n.* [Inf.] costume; dress

**GeV** *abbrev.* one billion electron-volts

**gew·gaw** (gyōō'gô) *n.* ⟦ME⟧ a trinket

**gey·ser** (gī'zər) *n.* ⟦< ON *gjosa*, to gush⟧ a spring from which columns of boiling water and steam gush into the air at intervals

**Gha·na** (gä'nə) country on the W coast of Africa: 92,099 sq. mi.; pop. 12,296,000

**ghast·ly** (gast'lē) *adj.* **-li·er**, **-li·est** ⟦< OE *gast*, spirit⟧ **1** horrible; frightful **2** ghostlike; pale **3** [Inf.] very bad —**ghast'li·ness** *n.*

**gher·kin** (gur'kin) *n.* ⟦< Pers *angārah*, watermelon⟧ a small pickled cucumber

**ghet·to** (get'ō) *n., pl.* **-tos** or **-toes** ⟦It⟧ **1** a section of some European cities to which Jews were once restricted **2** any section of a city in which many

members of a minority group live, or to which they are restricted as by social discrimination

**ghet'to·ize'** (-īz') *vt.* **-ized'**, **-iz'ing 1** to restrict to a ghetto **2** to make into a ghetto

**ghost** (gōst) *n.* ⟦< OE *gast*⟧ **1** *Folklore* the disembodied spirit of a dead person, appearing as a pale, shadowy apparition **2** a slight trace; shadow [not a *ghost* of a chance] —**give up the ghost** to die —**ghost'ly** *adj.*

**ghost'writ'er** *n.* one who writes books, articles, etc. for another who professes to be the author —**ghost'write'**, **-wrote'**, **-writ'ten**, **-writ'ing**, *vt., vi.*

**ghoul** (gōōl) *n.* ⟦< Ar *ghāla*, to seize⟧ *Muslim Folklore* an evil spirit that robs graves and feeds on the dead —**ghoul'ish** *adj.* —**ghoul'ish·ness** *n.* —**ghoul'ish·ly** *adv.*

**GHQ** *abbrev.* General Headquarters

**GI** (jē'ī') *adj.* **1** government issue: designating clothing, etc. issued to military personnel **2** [Inf.] of or characteristic of the U.S. armed forces [a *GI* haircut] —*n., pl.* **GI's** or **GIs** [Inf.] a U.S. enlisted soldier

**gi·ant** (jī'ənt) *n.* ⟦< Gr *gigas*⟧ **1** any imaginary being of superhuman size **2** a person or thing of great size, strength, intellect, etc. —*adj.* like a giant —**gi'ant·ess** *fem.n.*

**gib·ber** (jib'ər) *vi., vt.* ⟦echoic⟧ to speak rapidly and incoherently

**gib'ber·ish** *n.* unintelligible chatter

**gib·bet** (jib'it) *n.* ⟦< OFr *gibet*⟧ **1** a gallows **2** a structure from which bodies of executed criminals were hung and exposed to public scorn —*vt.* to hang on a gibbet

**gib·bon** (gib'ən) *n.* ⟦Fr⟧ a small, slender, long-armed ape of India, S China, and the East Indies

**Gib·bon** (gib'ən), **Ed·ward** (ed'wərd) 1737-94; Eng. historian

**gibe** (jīb) *vi., vt.* **gibed**, **gib'ing** ⟦< ?⟧ to jeer or taunt —*n.* a jeer or taunt

**gib·let** (jib'lit) *n.* ⟦< OFr *gibelet*, stew made of game⟧ any of the edible internal parts of a fowl, as the gizzard or heart

**Gi·bral·tar** (ji brôl'tər) British colony occupying a peninsula consisting mostly of a rocky hill (**Rock of Gibraltar**) at the S tip of Spain

**gid·dy** (gid'ē) *adj.* **-di·er**, **-di·est** ⟦< OE *gydig*, insane⟧ **1** having or causing a whirling, unsteady sensation; dizzy **2** frivolous —**gid'di·ly** *adv.* —**gid'di·ness** *n.*

**Gid·e·on** (gid'ē ən) *n. Bible* a judge of Israel and a victorious leader in battle

**gift** (gift) *n.* ⟦< OE *giefan*, give⟧ **1** something given; present **2** the act of giving **3** a natural ability —*vt.* **1** to present a gift to **2** to present as a gift

**gift'ed** *adj.* **1** having a natural ability; talented **2** of superior intelligence

**gig**[1] (gig) *n.* ⟦ME *gigge*, whirligig⟧ **1** a light, two-wheeled open carriage **2** a long, light ship's boat

**gig**[2] (gig) *n.* ⟦< ?⟧ [Slang] a job, esp. one performing jazz or rock

**gi·ga·byte** (gig'ə bīt') *n.* $2^{30}$ bytes, or, loosely, one billion bytes

**gi·gan·tic** (jī gan'tik) *adj.* ⟦see GIANT⟧ huge; enormous; immense

**gig·gle** (gig'əl) *vi.* **-gled**, **-gling** ⟦< Du *giggelen*⟧ to laugh with high, quick sounds in a silly or nervous way —*n.* such a sound —**gig'gly**, **-gli·er**, **-gli·est**, *adj.*

**gig·o·lo** (jig'ə lō') *n., pl.* **-los'** ⟦Fr⟧ a man paid to be a woman's escort

**Gi·la monster** (hē'lə) ⟦after the *Gila* River, AZ⟧ a stout, poisonous lizard of SW U.S. deserts

**gild** (gild) *vt.* **gild'ed** or **gilt**, **gild'ing** ⟦< OE *gyldan*⟧ **1** to coat with gold leaf or a gold color **2** to make seem more attractive or valuable than it is —**gild'er** *n.* —**gild'ing** *n.*

**gill**[1] (gil) *n.* ⟦ME *gile*⟧ the breathing organ of most water animals, as fish

**gill**[2] (jil) *n.* [< LL *gillo*, cooling vessel] a unit of liquid measure equal to ¼ pint

**gilt** (gilt) *vt. alt. pt. & pp.* of GILD —*n.* gold leaf or color —*adj.* coated with gilt

**gilt'-edged'** *adj.* of the highest quality [*gilt-edged* securities]: also **gilt'-edge'**

**gim·bal** (gim'bəl, jim'-) *n.* [< L *gemellus*, twin] [*often pl.*] a device consisting of a pivoted ring or rings mounted on a fixed frame, used as to keep a ship's compass level

**gim·crack** (jim'krak') *adj.* [< ME *gibbecrak*, an ornament] showy but cheap and useless —*n.* a gimcrack thing —**gim'crack'er·y** *n.*

**gim·let** (gim'lit) *n.* [< MDu *wimmel*] a small tool for making holes

**gim·mick** (gim'ik) *n.* [< ?] [Inf.] **1** a tricky device **2** an attention-getting device or feature, as for promoting a product —**gim'mick·y** *adj.*

**gimp·y** (gim'pē) *adj.* [prob. < Norw dial. *gimpa*, to rock] [Inf.] lame; limping

**gin**[1] (jin) *n.* [ult. < L *juniperus*, juniper] a distilled alcoholic liquor typically flavored with juniper berries

GIMLET

**gin**[2] (jin) *n.* [< OFr *engin*, engine] **1** a snare, as for game **2** COTTON GIN —*vt.* ginned, gin'ning to remove seeds from (cotton) with a gin

**gin**[3] (jin) *n.* GIN RUMMY

**gin·ger** (jin'jər) *n.* [< Gr *zingiberi*] **1** a tropical herb with rhizomes used esp. as a spice **2** this spice **3** [Inf.] vigor; spirit —**gin'ger·y** *adj.*

**ginger ale** a carbonated soft drink flavored with ginger

**gin'ger·bread'** *n.* **1** a cake flavored with ginger and molasses **2** showy ornamentation

**gin'ger·ly** *adv.* very carefully —*adj.* very careful; cautious

**gin'ger·snap'** *n.* a crisp cookie flavored with ginger and molasses

**ging·ham** (giŋ'əm) *n.* [< Malay *ginggang*] a cotton cloth, usually woven in stripes, checks, or plaids

**gin·gi·vi·tis** (jin'jə vīt'is) *n.* [< L *gingiva*, the gum + -ITIS] inflammation of the gums

**gink·go** (giŋ'kō) *n., pl.* -goes [Jpn *ginkyo*] an Asian tree with fan-shaped leaves: also **ging'ko**

**gin rummy** (jin) a variety of the card game rummy

**gip** (jip) *n., vt., vi. alt. sp.* of GYP

**Gip·sy** (jip'sē) *n.* GYPSY

**gi·raffe** (jə raf') *n.* [< Ar *zarāfa*] a large African ruminant with a very long neck and long legs

**gird** (gurd) *vt.* gird'ed or girt, gird'ing [OE *gyrdan*] **1** to encircle or fasten with a belt **2** to surround **3** to prepare (oneself) for action

**gird·er** (gur'dər) *n.* a large wooden or steel beam for supporting joists, the framework of a building, etc.

**gir·dle** (gur'd'l) *n.* [OE *gyrdel*] **1** [Archaic] a belt for the waist **2** anything that encircles **3** a woman's elasticized undergarment for supporting the waist and hips —*vt.* -dled, -dling to encircle or bind, as with a girdle

**girl** (gurl) *n.* [ME *girle*, youngster] **1** a female child **2** a young, unmarried woman **3** a female servant **4** [Inf.] a woman of any age **5** [Inf.] a sweetheart —**girl'hood'** *n.* —**girl'ish** *adj.*

**girl'friend'** *n.* [Inf.] **1** a sweetheart of a boy or man **2** a girl who is someone's friend **3** a woman friend of a woman

**Girl Scout** a member of the **Girl Scouts of the United States of America**, a girls' organization providing healthful, character-building activities

**girt**[1] (gurt) *vt. alt. pt. & pp.* of GIRD

**girt**[2] (gurt) *vt.* to fasten with a girth

**girth** (gurth) *n.* [< ON *gyrtha*, encircle] **1** a band put around the belly of a horse, etc. to hold a saddle or pack **2** the circumference, as of a tree trunk

**gist** (jist) *n.* [< OFr *giste*, point at issue] the essence or main point, as of an article or argument

**give** (giv) *vt.* gave, giv'en, giv'ing [OE *giefan*] **1** to make a gift of **2** to hand over [to *give* the porter a bag] **3** to hand over in or for payment **4** to pass (regards, etc.) along **5** to cause to have [to *give* pleasure] **6** to act as host or sponsor of **7** to produce; supply [cows *give* milk] **8** to devote or sacrifice **9** to concede; yield **10** to offer [to *give* advice] **11** to perform [to *give* a concert] **12** to utter [to *give* a reply] **13** to inflict (punishment, etc.) —*vi.* **1** to bend, move, yield, etc. from force or pressure **2** to make gifts, donations, etc. —*n.* a bending, moving, etc. under pressure —**give away 1** to make a gift of **2** to present (the bride) to the bridegroom **3** [Inf.] to reveal or betray —**give forth** (or **off**) to emit —**give in** to yield —**give it to** [Inf.] to beat or scold —**give or take** plus or minus —**give out 1** to emit **2** to make public **3** to distribute **4** to become worn out, etc. —**give up 1** to hand over **2** to cease **3** to stop trying **4** to despair of **5** to sacrifice —**giv'er** *n.*

**give'-and-take'** *n.* **1** mutual concession **2** repartee or banter

**give'a·way'** *n.* **1** an unintentional revelation **2** something given free or sold cheap **3** an instance of giving something away free **4** a radio or television program giving prizes

**give'back'** *n.* a previously negotiated workers' benefit relinquished to management, as for some concession

**giv·en** (giv'ən) *vt., vi. pp.* of GIVE —*adj.* **1** accustomed (*to*) by habit, etc.; prone (*to*) **2** specified; stated **3** assumed; granted —*n.* something assumed or accepted as fact

**given name** a person's first name

**giz·mo** (giz'mō) *n., pl.* -mos [< ?] [Slang] a gadget: also sp. **gis'mo**

**giz·zard** (giz'ərd) *n.* [< L *gigeria*, cooked entrails of poultry] the muscular second stomach of a bird

**Gk** *abbrev.* Greek

**gla·cé** (gla sā') *adj.* [< L *glacies*, ice] **1** glossy, as silk **2** candied, as fruits —*vt.* -céed', -cé'ing to glaze (fruits, etc.)

**gla·cial** (glā'shəl) *adj.* of or like ice or glaciers —**gla'cial·ly** *adv.*

**gla·cier** (glā'shər) *n.* [< L *glacies*, ice] a large mass of ice and snow moving slowly down a mountain or valley

**glad** (glad) *adj.* glad'der, glad'dest [OE *glæd*] **1** happy **2** causing joy **3** very willing **4** bright —**glad'ly** *adv.* —**glad'ness** *n.*

**glad·den** (glad'n) *vt.* to make glad

**glade** (glād) *n.* [ME] an open space in a forest

**glad hand** [Inf.] a cordial or effusive welcome —**glad'-hand'er** *n.*

**glad·i·a·tor** (glad'ē āt'ər) *n.* [L < *gladius*, sword] **1** in ancient Rome, a man, often a slave, who fought in an arena as a public show **2** any person taking part in a fight —**glad'i·a·to'ri·al** (-ə tôr'ē əl) *adj.*

**glad·i·o·lus** (glad'ē ō'ləs) *n., pl.* -lus·es or -li' (-lī') [L, small sword] a plant of the iris family with swordlike leaves and tall spikes of funnel-shaped flowers: also **glad'i·o'la** (-lə), *pl.* -las

**glad·some** (glad'səm) *adj.* joyful or cheerful —**glad'some·ly** *adv.*

**glam·or·ize** (glam'ər īz') *vt.* -ized', -iz'ing to make glamorous: also sp. **glam'our·ize'** —**glam'or·i·za'tion** *n.*

**glam·our** (glam'ər) *n.* [Scot var. of *grammar*, magic] **1** seemingly mysterious allure; bewitching charm **2** elegance, luxury, etc. Also sp. **glam'or** —**glam'or·ous** or **glam'our·ous** *adj.*

**glance** (glans) *vi.* glanced, glanc'ing [ME *glansen*] **1** to strike a surface obliquely and go off at an angle: with *off* **2** to flash **3** to take a quick look —*n.* **1** a glancing off **2** a flash **3** a quick look

**gland** (gland) *n.* [< L *glans*, acorn] any organ or group of cells that produces secretions, as insulin, or excretions, as urine —**glan·du·lar** (glan'jə lər) *adj.*

**glans** (glanz) *n.* [L, lit., acorn] 1 the head of the penis 2 the tip of the clitoris

**glare** (gler) *vi.* **glared, glar'ing** [ME *glaren*] 1 to shine with a steady, dazzling light 2 to stare fiercely —*n.* 1 a steady, dazzling light 2 a fierce stare 3 a bright, glassy surface, as of ice

**glar'ing** *adj.* 1 dazzlingly bright 2 too showy 3 staring fiercely 4 flagrant [a *glaring* error] —**glar'ing·ly** *adv.*

**Glas·gow** (glas'kō, glaz'gō) seaport in SC Scotland: district pop. 663,000

**glas·nost** (gläs'nôst) *n.* [Russ, lit., openness] Soviet official policy after 1985 of publicly acknowledging internal problems

**glass** (glas) *n.* [OE *glæs*] 1 a hard, brittle substance, usually transparent, made by fusing silicates with soda, lime, etc. 2 GLASSWARE 3 *a*) a glass article, as a drinking container *b*) [*pl.*] eyeglasses or binoculars 4 the amount held by a drinking glass —*vt.* to equip with glass panes; glaze —*adj.* of or made of glass —**glass'ful'** *n.*

**glass ceiling** an unofficial policy that prevents women or minorities from advancing within a company, organization, etc.

**glass'ware'** *n.* articles made of glass

**glass'y** *adj.* **-i·er, -i·est** 1 like glass, as in smoothness 2 expressionless [a *glassy* stare] —**glass'i·ly** *adv.* —**glass'i·ness** *n.*

**glau·co·ma** (glô kō'mə) *n.* [< Gr *glaukos*, gleaming] any of various eye disorders marked by increased pressure within the eye causing impaired vision, etc.

**glaze** (glāz) *vt.* **glazed, glaz'ing** [ME *glasen*] 1 to fit (windows, etc.) with glass 2 to give a hard, glossy finish to (pottery, etc.) 3 to cover (foods) with a coating of sugar syrup, etc. —*vi.* to become glassy or glossy —*n.* 1 a glassy finish or coating 2 a thin coating of ice

**gla·zier** (glā'zhər) *n.* one whose work is fitting glass in windows, etc.

**gleam** (glēm) *n.* [OE *glæm*] 1 a flash or beam of light 2 a faint light 3 a reflected brightness, as from a polished surface 4 a faint manifestation, as of hope, understanding, etc. —*vi.* 1 to shine with a gleam 2 to appear suddenly —**gleam'y** *adj.*

**glean** (glēn) *vt., vi.* [< Celt] 1 to collect (grain left by reapers) 2 to collect (facts, etc.) gradually —**glean'ings** *pl.n.*

**glee** (glē) *n.* [OE *gleo*] lively joy; merriment —**glee'ful** *adj.*

**glee club** a group that sings part songs, etc.

**glen** (glen) *n.* [medieval Scot] a narrow, secluded valley

**Glen·dale** (glen'dāl) city in SW California: pop. 180,000

**glen plaid** [*also* G- p-] a plaid pattern with thin crossbarred stripes

**glib** (glib) *adj.* **glib'ber, glib'best** [< or akin to Du *glibberig*, slippery] speaking or spoken smoothly, often too smoothly to be convincing —**glib'ly** *adv.* —**glib'ness** *n.*

**glide** (glīd) *vi.* **glid'ed, glid'ing** [OE *glidan*] 1 to move smoothly and easily 2 *Aeronautics* to descend with little or no engine power —*vt.* to cause to glide —*n.* 1 a gliding 2 a disk or ball, as of nylon, under a furniture leg to allow easy sliding

**glid·er** (glīd'ər) *n.* 1 an engineless aircraft carried

along by air currents 2 a porch swing suspended in a frame

**glim·mer** (glim'ər) *vi.* [< OE *glæm*, gleam] 1 to give a faint, flickering light 2 to appear faintly —*n.* a faint, flickering light 2 a faint manifestation —**glim'mer·ing** *n.*

**glimpse** (glimps) *vt.* **glimpsed, glimps'ing** [< OE *glæm*, gleam] to catch a brief, quick view of —*vi.* to look quickly (*at*) —*n.* a brief, quick view

GLIDER

**glint** (glint) *vi.* [ME *glenten*] to gleam or glitter —*n.* a gleam, flash, etc.

**glis·san·do** (gli sän'dō) *n., pl.* **-di** (-dē) *or* **-dos** [as if It < Fr *glisser*, to slide] *Music* a sliding effect achieved by a rapid sounding of tones

**glis·ten** (glis'ən) *vi.* [OE *glisnian*] to shine with reflected light, as a wet surface

**glitch** (glich) *n.* [< Ger *glitsche*, a slip] [Slang] a mishap, error, etc.

**glit·ter** (glit'ər) *vi.* [prob. < ON *glitra*] 1 to shine brightly; sparkle 2 to be brilliant or showy —*n.* 1 a bright, sparkling light 2 striking or showy brilliance 3 bits of glittering material —**glit'ter·y** *adj.*

**glitz** (glits) *n.* [< ?] [Inf.] gaudy or glittery showiness —**glitz'y, -i·er, -i·est,** *adj.*

**gloam·ing** (glōm'iŋ) *n.* [< OE *glom*] evening dusk; twilight

**gloat** (glōt) *vi.* [prob. < ON *glotta*, grin scornfully] to gaze or think with malicious pleasure: often with *over*

**glob** (gläb) *n.* [prob. < GLOBULE] a rounded mass or lump, as of jelly

**glob·al** (glō'bəl) *adj.* 1 worldwide 2 complete or comprehensive —**glob'al·ly** *adv.*

**glob'al·ism'** (-iz'əm) *n.* a policy, outlook, etc. that is worldwide in scope

**global warming** a slight, continuing rise in atmospheric temperature, usually attributed to an intensifying of the greenhouse effect

**globe** (glōb) *n.* [< L *globus*, a ball] 1 anything spherical or somewhat spherical 2 the earth, or a model of the earth

**globe'-trot'ter** *n.* one who travels widely about the world —**globe'-trot'ting** *n., adj.*

**glob·u·lar** (gläb'yə lər) *adj.* 1 spherical 2 made up of globules

**glob'ule'** (-yōōl') *n.* [< L *globulus*] 1 a tiny ball or globe 2 a drop of liquid

**glock·en·spiel** (gläk'ən spēl') *n.* [Ger *glocke*, bell + *spiel*, to play] a percussion instrument with tuned metal bars in a frame, played with small hammers

**gloom** (glōom) *n.* [prob. < Scand] 1 darkness; dimness 2 deep sadness; dejection —**gloom'y, -i·er, -i·est,** *adj.*

**glop** (gläp) *n.* [< ? GL(UE) + (SL)OP] [Inf.] any soft, gluey substance —**glop'py** *adj.*

**glo·ri·fy** (glôr'ə fī') *vt.* **-fied', -fy'ing** [< L *gloria*, glory + *facere*, to make] 1 to give glory to 2 to exalt (God), as in worship 3 to honor; extol 4 to make seem better, greater, etc. than is so —**glo'ri·fi·ca'tion** *n.*

**glo·ri·ous** (-ē əs) *adj.* 1 having, giving, or deserving glory 2 splendid 3 [Inf.] very delightful or enjoyable —**glo'ri·ous·ly** *adv.*

**glo·ry** (glôr'ē) *n., pl.* **-ries** [< L *gloria*] 1 great honor or fame, or its source 2 adoration 3 great splendor, prosperity, etc. 4 heavenly bliss —*vi.* **-ried, -ry·ing** to exult (*in*)

**gloss**[1] (glôs, gläs) *n.* [< ? Scand] 1 the shine of a polished surface 2 a deceptive outward show —*vt.* 1 to give a shiny surface to 2 to hide (an error, etc.) or make seem right or trivial: often with *over* —**gloss'y, -i·er, -i·est,** *adj.*

**gloss**[2] (glôs, gläs) *n.* [< Gr *glōssa*, tongue] a note of comment or explanation, as in a footnote —*vt.* to provide glosses for

**glos·sa·ry** (glôs′ə rē, gläs′-) *n., pl.* **-ries** ⟦see prec.⟧ a list of difficult terms with explanations, as for a book

**glos·so·la·li·a** (gläs′ō lā′lē ə, glôs′-) *n.* ⟦< Gr *glōssa*, tongue + *lalein*, to speak⟧ an uttering of unintelligible sounds, as in a religious ecstasy

**glot·tis** (glät′is) *n.* ⟦ModL < Gr *glōssa*, tongue⟧ the opening between the vocal cords in the larynx — **glot′tal** *adj.*

**glove** (gluv) *n.* ⟦OE *glof*⟧ **1** a covering for the hand, with separate sheaths for the fingers and thumb **2** a baseball player's mitt **3** a padded mitten worn by boxers —*vt.* **gloved, glov′ing** to cover with a glove

**glow** (glō) *vi.* ⟦OE *glowan*⟧ **1** to give off a bright light as a result of great heat **2** to give out a steady light **3** to give out heat **4** to be elated **5** to be bright with color **6** to be ruddy, flushed, etc., as from enthusiasm —*n.* **1** a light given off, as a result of great heat **2** steady, even light **3** brightness, warmth, ardor, etc. —**glow′ing** *adj.* — **glow′ing·ly** *adv.*

**glow·er** (glou′ər) *vi.* ⟦prob. < ON⟧ to stare with sullen anger; scowl —**glow′er·ing** *adj.*

**glow′worm′** (glō′-) *n.* a wingless, luminescent female or larva of the firefly

**glu·cose** (glōō′kōs′) *n.* ⟦Fr < Gr *gleúkos*, sweetness⟧ **1** a crystalline sugar occurring naturally in fruits, honey, etc. **2** a sweet syrup prepared by the hydrolysis of starch

**glue** (glōō) *n.* ⟦< LL *glus*⟧ **1** a sticky, viscous liquid made from animal gelatin, used as an adhesive **2** any similar substance —*vt.* **glued, glu′ing** to make stick as with glue —**glu′ey, -i·er, -i·est,** *adj.*

**glum** (glum) *adj.* **glum′mer, glum′mest** ⟦prob. < ME *glomen*, look morose⟧ gloomy; sullen — **glum′ly** *adv.* —**glum′ness** *n.*

**glut** (glut) *vi.* **glut′ted, glut′ting** ⟦< L *gluttire*, to swallow⟧ to eat to excess —*vt.* **1** to feed, fill, etc. to excess **2** to supply (the market) beyond demand —*n.* **1** a glutting or being glutted **2** a supply greater than the demand

**glu·ten** (glōōt′'n) *n.* ⟦L, glue⟧ a gray, sticky, nutritious mixture of proteins found in wheat, etc. — **glu′ten·ous** *adj.*

**glu·ti·nous** (glōōt′'n əs) *adj.* ⟦see prec.⟧ gluey; sticky —**glu′ti·nous·ly** *adv.*

**glut·ton** (glut′'n) *n.* ⟦see GLUT⟧ **1** one who eats to excess **2** one with a great capacity for something —**glut′ton·ous** *adj.* —**glut′ton·ous·ly** *adv.*

**glut·ton·y** *n., pl.* **-ies** the habit or act of eating too much

**glyc·er·in** (glis′ər in) *n.* ⟦< Gr *glykeros*, sweet⟧ *nontechnical term for* GLYCEROL: also **glyc′er·ine**

**glyc·er·ol** (glis′ər ôl′, -ōl′) *n.* ⟦< prec.⟧ a colorless, syrupy liquid made from fats and oils: used in skin lotions, in making explosives, etc.

**gly·co·gen** (glī′kə jən) *n.* ⟦< Gr *glykys*, sweet + -GEN⟧ a substance in animal tissues that is changed into glucose as the body needs it

**GM** *abbrev.* General Manager

**Gmc** *abbrev.* Germanic

**gnarl** (närl) *n.* ⟦< ME *knorre*⟧ a knot on a tree trunk or branch —*vt.* to make knotted; twist

**gnarled** *adj.* **1** knotty and twisted **2** roughened, hardened, etc.: said as of hands Also **gnarl′y, -i·er, -i·est**

**gnash** (nash) *vt., vi.* ⟦prob. < ON⟧ to grind (the teeth) together, as in anger —*n.* a gnashing

**gnat** (nat) *n.* ⟦OE *gnæt*⟧ any of various small, two-winged insects, which often bite

**gnaw** (nô) *vt.* ⟦OE *gnagen*⟧ **1** to bite away bit by bit; consume **2** to harass or vex —*vi.* **1** to bite repeatedly: with *on, away,* etc. **2** to produce a corroding, tormenting, etc. effect: with *on, at,* etc. —**gnaw′ing** *n.*

**gneiss** (nīs) *n.* ⟦< OHG *gneisto*, a spark⟧ a granite-like rock formed of layers of quartz, mica, etc.

**gnome** (nōm) *n.* ⟦< Gr *gnōmē*, thought⟧ *Folklore* a dwarf who dwells in the earth and guards its treasures —**gnom′ish** *adj.*

**GNP** *abbrev.* gross national product

**gnu** (nōō) *n.* ⟦< the native name⟧ a large African antelope with an oxlike head and a horselike tail

**go** (gō) *vi.* **went, gone, go′ing** ⟦< OE *gan*⟧ **1** to move along; travel; proceed **2** to work properly; operate /the clock is *going*/ **3** to act, sound, etc. as specified /the balloon *went* "pop"/ **4** to turn out; result /the war *went* badly/ **5** to pass: said of time **6** to pass from person to person **7** to become /to *go* mad/ **8** to be expressed, sung, etc. /as the saying *goes*/ **9** to harmonize; agree /blue *goes* with gold/ **10** to be accepted, valid, etc. **11** to leave; depart **12** to come to an end; fail /his eyesight is *going*/ **13** to be allotted (*to*) or sold (*for*) **14** to extend, reach, etc. **15** to be able to pass (*through*), fit (*into*), etc. **16** to belong /socks *go* in that drawer/ —*vt.* **1** to travel along /to *go* the wrong way/ **2** [Inf.] to furnish (bail) for an arrested person **3** [Inf.] to say /he *goes* "Wow!"/ —*n., pl.* **goes 1** a success /to make a *go* of marriage/ **2** [Inf.] animation; energy **3** [Inf.] a try; attempt —**go back on** [Inf.] **1** to betray **2** to break (a promise, etc.) —**go for 1** to try to get **2** [Inf.] to attack **3** [Inf.] to be attracted by —**go in for** [Inf.] to engage or indulge in —**go into** to be contained in /5 *goes into* 10 twice/ —**go off 1** to depart **2** to explode —**go on 1** to proceed; continue **2** to happen **3** [Inf.] to chatter —**go out 1** to be extinguished, become outdated, etc. **2** to attend social affairs, etc. —**go over 1** to examine thoroughly **2** to do again **3** [Inf.] to be successful —**go through 1** to endure; experience **2** to look through —**go through with** to pursue to the end —**go together 1** to match; harmonize **2** [Inf.] to date only each other —**go under** to fail, as in business —**let go 1** to let escape **2** to release one's hold **3** to dismiss from a job; fire —**let one-self go** to be unrestrained —**on the go** [Inf.] in constant motion or action —**to go** [Inf.] **1** to be taken out: said of food in a restaurant **2** still to be done, etc.

**goad** (gōd) *n.* ⟦OE *gad*⟧ **1** a sharp-pointed stick used in driving oxen **2** any driving impulse; spur —*vt.* to drive as with a goad; urge on

**go′-a·head′** *n.* permission or a signal to proceed: usually with *the*

**goal** (gōl) *n.* ⟦ME *gol*, boundary⟧ **1** the place at which a race, trip, etc. is ended **2** an end that one strives to attain **3** in some games, *a*) the line or net over or into which the ball or puck must go to score *b*) the score made

**goal′keep′er** *n.* in some games, a player stationed at a goal to prevent the ball or puck from entering it: also **goal′ie** or **goal′tend′er**

**goat** (gōt) *n.* ⟦OE *gat*⟧ **1** a cud-chewing mammal with hollow horns, closely related to sheep, antelopes, etc. **2** a lecherous man **3** [Inf.] a scapegoat —**get someone's goat** [Inf.] to annoy someone

**goat·ee** (gō tē′) *n.* a small, pointed beard on a man's chin

**goat′herd′** *n.* one who herds goats

**goat′skin′** *n.* the skin of a goat, or leather made from this skin

**gob**[1] (gäb) *n.* ⟦< OFr *gobe*, mouthful⟧ **1** a soft lump or mass **2** [*pl.*] [Inf.] a large quantity

**gob**[2] (gäb) *n.* ⟦< ?⟧ [Slang] a sailor in the U.S. Navy

**gob·ble**[1] (gäb′əl) *n.* ⟦echoic⟧ the throaty sound made by a male turkey —*vi.* **-bled, -bling** to make this sound

**gob·ble**[2] (gäb′əl) *vt., vi.* **-bled, -bling** ⟦< OFr *gobet*, mouthful⟧ **1** to eat quickly and greedily **2** to seize eagerly; snatch (*up*)

**gob′ble·dy·gook′** (-dē gook′) *n.* ⟦? echoic of turkey cries⟧ [Slang] pompous, wordy talk or writing that is meaningless

**gob·bler** (gäb′lər) *n.* a male turkey

**go'·be·tween'** *n.* one who makes arrangements between each of two sides; intermediary

**Go·bi** (gō'bē) large desert plateau in E Asia, chiefly in Mongolia

**gob·let** (gäb'lit) *n.* ⟦< OFr *gobel*⟧ a drinking glass with a base and stem

**gob·lin** (gäb'lin) *n.* ⟦< ML *gobelinus*⟧ *Folklore* an evil or mischievous spirit

**go'·by'** *n.* [Inf.] an intentional disregard or slight

**god** (gäd, gôd) *n.* ⟦OE⟧ **1** any of various beings conceived of as supernatural and immortal; esp., a male deity **2** an idol **3** a person or thing deified **4** [G-] in monotheistic religions, the creator and ruler of the universe; Supreme Being —**god'like'** *adj.*

**god'child'** *n., pl.* **-chil'dren** the person a godparent sponsors

**god'daugh'ter** *n.* a female godchild

**god·dess** (gäd'is) *n.* **1** a female god **2** a woman of great beauty, charm, etc.

**god'fa'ther** *n.* **1** a male godparent **2** [*often* G-] *a*) [Inf.] the head of a Mafia crime syndicate *b*) [Slang] a very influential or authoritative person

**god'head'** *n.* **1** godhood **2** [G-] God: usually with *the*

**god'hood'** *n.* the state of being a god; divinity

**Go·di·va** (gə dī'və) *n. Eng. Legend* an 11th-c. noblewoman who rode naked through the streets so that her husband would abolish a heavy tax

**god'less** *adj.* **1** irreligious; atheistic **2** wicked — **god'less·ness** *n.*

**god'ly** *adj.* **-li·er, -li·est** devoted to God; devout — **god'li·ness** *n.*

**god'moth'er** *n.* a female godparent

**god'par'ent** *n.* a person who sponsors a child, as at baptism, taking responsibility for its faith

**god'send'** *n.* anything unexpected and needed or desired that comes at the opportune moment, as if sent by God

**god'son'** *n.* a male godchild

**God·win Aus·ten** (gäd'win ôs'tən) mountain in the Himalayas: 2d highest mountain in the world: 28,250 ft.: commonly called *K2*

**Goe·the** (gö'tə; *E* gur'tə), **Jo·hann Wolf·gang von** (yō'hän vôlf'gäŋk fôn) 1749-1832; Ger. poet & dramatist

**go·fer** or **go-fer** (gō'fər) *n.* ⟦from being asked to *go for* something⟧ [Slang] an employee who performs menial tasks, as running errands

**go-get·ter** (gō'get'ər) *n.* [Inf.] an enterprising and aggressive person who usually achieves ambitions, goals, etc.

**gog·gle** (gäg'əl) *vi.* **-gled, -gling** ⟦ME *gogelen*⟧ to stare with bulging eyes —*n.* [*pl.*] large spectacles to protect the eyes against dust, wind, sparks, etc. —*adj.* bulging or rolling: said of the eyes

**go'-go'** *adj.* ⟦short for *à gogo* < Fr, in plenty⟧ **1** of dancing to rock music, as in discothèques **2** of a dancer performing erotic movements to rock music, as in a bar

**go·ing** (gō'iŋ) *n.* **1** a departure **2** the condition of the ground or land as it affects traveling, walking, etc. **3** [Slang] current situation [tough *going* in the trial] —*adj.* **1** moving; working **2** conducting its business successfully [a *going* concern] **3** available **4** commonly accepted; current [the *going* rate] —**be going to** will or shall

**go'ing-o'ver** *n.* [Inf.] **1** a thorough inspection **2** a severe scolding or beating

**go'ings-on'** *pl.n.* [Inf.] actions or events, esp. when disapproved of

**goi·ter** (goit'ər) *n.* ⟦< L *guttur*, throat⟧ an enlargement of the thyroid gland, often visible as a swelling in the front of the neck: also [Chiefly Brit.] **goi'tre**

**gold** (gōld) *n.* ⟦OE⟧ **1** a heavy, yellow, metallic, highly malleable chemical element: it is a precious metal **2** money; wealth **3** bright yellow

**gold'brick'** *n.* [Mil. Slang] one who avoids work: also **gold'brick'er** —*vi.* [Mil. Slang] to shirk a duty or avoid work

**gol·den** (gōl'dən) *adj.* **1** made of or containing gold **2** bright-yellow **3** very valuable; excellent **4** flourishing **5** marking the 50th year [*golden* anniversary] **6** favorable [a *golden* opportunity]

**golden ag·er** (ā'jər) [*also* G- A-] [Inf.] an elderly person, specif. one 65 or older and retired

**Golden Fleece** *Gr. Myth.* the fleece of gold captured by Jason

**Golden Gate** strait between San Francisco Bay & the Pacific

**gold'en·rod'** *n.* a North American plant with long, branching stalks bearing clusters of small, yellow flowers

**golden rule** the precept that one should act toward others as one would want them to act toward oneself

**gold'-filled'** *adj.* made of a base metal overlaid with gold

**gold'finch'** *n.* ⟦OE *goldfinc*⟧ any of various yellow-and-black finches

**gold'fish'** *n., pl.* **-fish'** a small, golden-yellow or orange fish, often kept in ponds or aquariums

**gold leaf** gold beaten into very thin sheets, used for gilding

**gold'smith'** *n.* an artisan who makes and repairs articles of gold

**gold standard** a monetary standard in which the basic currency unit equals a specified quantity of gold

**golf** (gôlf, gälf) *n.* ⟦? < Du *kolf*, a club⟧ an outdoor game played with a small, hard ball and a set of clubs, the object being to hit the ball into each of a series of 9 or 18 holes with the fewest possible strokes —*vi.* to play golf —**golf'er** *n.*

**golf course** (or **links**) a tract of land for playing golf

**Go·li·ath** (gə lī'əth) *n. Bible* the Philistine giant killed by David

**gol·ly** (gäl'ē) *interj.* used to express surprise, wonder, etc.: orig. a euphemism for *God*

**Go·mor'rah** *n.* see SODOM AND GOMORRAH

**-gon** (gän, gən) ⟦< Gr *gōnia*, an angle⟧ *combining form* a figure having (a specified number of) angles

**go·nad** (gō'nad) *n.* ⟦< Gr *gonē*, a seed⟧ an animal organ or gland that produces reproductive cells; esp., an ovary or testis

**gon·do·la** (gän'də lə, gän dō'lə) *n.* ⟦It⟧ **1** a narrow boat used on the canals of Venice **2** a railroad freight car with no top and, often, with low sides **3** a cabin suspended under an airship or balloon

**gon·do·lier'** (-lir') *n.* a man who propels a gondola

**gone** (gôn, gän) *vi., vt. pp. of* GO —*adj.* ⟦ME *gon* < OE *gan*⟧ **1** departed **2** ruined **3** lost **4** dead **5** used up; consumed **6** ago; past

**gon·er** (gôn'ər) *n.* a person or thing certain to die, be ruined, etc.

**gong** (gôŋ, gäŋ) *n.* ⟦Malay *guṅ*⟧ a slightly convex metallic disk that gives a loud, resonant tone when struck

**gon·or·rhe·a** or **gon·or·rhoe·a** (gän'ə rē'ə) *n.* ⟦< Gr *gonos*, semen + *rheein*, to flow⟧ a venereal disease with inflammation of the genital organs

**goo** (gōō) *n.* [Inf.] **1** anything sticky, or sticky and sweet **2** excessive sentimentality —**goo'ey, -i·er, -i·est,** *adj.*

**goo·ber** (gōō'bər) *n.* ⟦< Afr *nguba*⟧ [Chiefly South] a peanut

**good** (good) *adj.* **bet'ter, best** ⟦OE *gōd*⟧ **1** effective; efficient **2** beneficial **3** valid; real [*good* money] **4** healthy or sound [*good* eyesight, *good* investments] **5** honorable [one's *good* name] **6** enjoyable, pleasant, etc. **7** reliable **8** thorough **9** excellent **10** virtuous, devout, kind, dutiful, etc. **11** proper; correct **12** skilled **13** considerable [a *good* many] **14** at least [waiting a *good* six hours] —*n.* something good; worth, benefit, etc. —*adv.* [Inf. or Dial.] well; fully —**as good as** virtually; nearly —**for good (and all)** permanently —**good**

and [Inf.] very or altogether —**good for 1** able to endure or be used for (a period of time) **2** worth **3** able to pay or give —**no good** useless; worthless

**good'bye'** or **good'-bye'** (-bī′) *interj., n., pl.* **-byes'** [[contr. of *God be with ye*]] farewell: also sp. **good'by', good'-by'**

**good faith** good intentions; sincerity

**Good Friday** the Friday before Easter, commemorating the Crucifixion

**good'-heart'ed** *adj.* kind and generous —**good'-heart'ed·ly** *adv.* —**good'-heart'ed·ness** *n.*

**Good Hope, Cape of** cape at the SW tip of Africa

**good humor** a cheerful, agreeable mood — **good'-hu'mored** *adj.* —**good'-hu'mored·ly** *adv.*

**good'-look'ing** *adj.* handsome or beautiful

**good'ly** *adj.* **-li·er, -li·est 1** of good appearance or quality **2** ample

**good'-na'tured** *adj.* agreeable; affable —**good'-na'tured·ly** *adv.*

**good'ness** *n.* the state or quality of being good; virtue, kindness, etc. —*interj.* used to express surprise or wonder: orig. a euphemism for *God*

**goods** (goodz) *pl.n.* **1** movable personal property **2** merchandise; wares **3** fabric; cloth —**get** (or **have**) **the goods on** [Slang] to discover (or know) something incriminating about

**good Sa·mar·i·tan** (sə mer′ə tən) one who helps another or others unselfishly: see Luke 10:30-37

**good'-sized'** *adj.* ample; fairly big

**good'-tem'pered** *adj.* amiable

**good turn** a friendly, helpful act; favor

**good'will'** *n.* **1** benevolence **2** willingness **3** the value of a business as a result of patronage, reputation, etc., beyond its tangible assets Also **good will**

**good'y** *n., pl.* **-ies** [Inf.] something good to eat, as a piece of candy —*interj.* used to express approval or delight: mainly a child's term

**good'y-good'y** [Inf.] *adj.* affectedly moral or pious —*n.* a goody-goody person

**goof** (goof) [Inf.] *n.* **1** a stupid or silly person **2** a mistake; blunder —*vi.* **1** to err or blunder **2** to waste time, shirk duties, etc.: with *off* or *around* —**goof'y, -i·er, -i·est,** *adj.*

**gook** (gook, gook) *n.* [[GOO + (GUN)K]] [Slang] any sticky or slimy substance

**goon** (goon) *n.* [Slang] **1** a ruffian or thug **2** a grotesque or stupid person

**goop** (goop) *n.* [[GOO + (SOU)P]] [Slang] any sticky, semiliquid substance

**goose** (goos) *n., pl.* **geese** [[< OE *gos*]] **1** a long-necked, web-footed waterfowl like a duck but larger **2** its flesh as food **3** a silly person —**cook someone's goose** [Inf.] to spoil someone's chances

**goose'ber'ry** *n., pl.* **-ries 1** a small, sour berry **2** the shrub it grows on

**goose bumps** a momentary roughened condition of the skin, induced by cold, fear, etc.: also **goose flesh** (or **pimples**)

**GOP** (jē′ō′pē′) *n.* [[G(rand) O(ld) P(arty)]] *name for* REPUBLICAN PARTY

**go·pher** (gō′fər) *n.* [[< ? Fr *gaufre*, honeycomb: from its burrowing]] **1** a burrowing rodent with wide cheek pouches **2** a striped ground squirrel of the prairies of North America

**gore**¹ (gôr) *n.* [[OE *gor*, filth]] blood from a wound, esp. when clotted

**gore**² (gôr) *vt.* **gored, gor'ing** [[< OE *gar*, a spear]] **1** to pierce with or as with a horn or tusk **2** to insert gores in —*n.* a tapering piece of cloth inserted in a skirt, sail, etc. to give it fullness

**gorge** (gôrj) *n.* [[< L *gurges*, whirlpool]] **1** the throat or gullet **2** the contents of the stomach **3** resentment, disgust, etc. **4** a deep, narrow pass between steep heights —*vi., vt.* **gorged, gorg'ing** to eat greedily or swallow gluttonously

**gor·geous** (gôr′jəs) *adj.* [[< OFr *gorgias*]] **1** bril-

liantly showy; magnificent **2** [Inf.] beautiful, delightful, etc. —**gor'geous·ly** *adv.*

**go·ril·la** (gə ril′ə) *n.* [[ult. < name in an ancient W Afr language]] the largest, and most powerful, of the great apes, native to Africa

**Gor·ki** or **Gor'ky** (gôr′kē) *name* (1932-90) *for* NIZHNY NOVGOROD

**gor·mand·ize** (gôr′mən dīz′) *vi., vt.* **-ized', -iz'ing** [[< Fr *gourmandise*, gluttony]] to eat like a glutton

**go'-round'** *n.* one of a series of actions, encounters, etc., often involving conflict

**gorp** (gôrp) *n.* a mixture of raisins, nuts, etc. eaten as by hikers for quick energy

**gorse** (gôrs) *n.* [[OE *gorst*]] FURZE

**gor·y** (gôr′ē) *adj.* **-i·er, -i·est 1** covered with gore; bloody **2** with much bloodshed —**gor'i·ness** *n.*

**gosh** (gäsh, gôsh) *interj.* used to express surprise, wonder, etc.: a euphemism for *God*

**gos·ling** (gäz′liŋ) *n.* a young goose

**gos·pel** (gäs′pəl) *n.* [[< OE *godspel*, good news]] **1** [*often* G-] the teachings of Jesus and the Apostles **2** [G-] any of the first four books of the New Testament **3** anything proclaimed or accepted as the absolute truth: also **gospel truth**

**gos·sa·mer** (gäs′ə mər) *n.* [[ME *gosesomer*, lit., goose summer]] **1** a filmy cobweb **2** a very thin, filmy cloth —*adj.* light, thin, and filmy

**gos·sip** (gäs′əp) *n.* [[< Late OE *godsibbe*, godparent]] **1** one who chatters idly about others **2** such talk —*vi.* to be a gossip —**gos'sip·y** *adj.*

**got** (gät) *vt., vi. pt. & alt. pp. of* GET

**Goth** (gäth, gôth) *n.* a member of a Germanic people that conquered most of the Roman Empire in the 3d, 4th, and 5th c. A.D.

**Goth·ic** (gäth′ik) *adj.* **1** of the Goths or their language **2** designating or of a style of architecture developed in W Europe between the 12th and 16th c., with pointed arches, steep roofs, etc. **3** [*sometimes* g-] uncivilized **4** [*sometimes* g-] of a type of fiction that uses remote, gloomy settings and a sinister atmosphere to suggest mystery — *n.* **1** the East Germanic language of the Goths **2** Gothic style, esp. in architecture

**got·ten** (gät′'n) *vt., vi. alt. pp. of* GET

**Gou·da (cheese)** (goo′də, gou′-) [[after *Gouda*, Netherlands]] a mild cheese sometimes coated with red wax

**gouge** (gouj) *n.* [[< LL *gulbia*]] **1** a chisel for cutting grooves or holes in wood **2** such a groove or hole —*vt.* **gouged, goug'ing 1** to make a groove, etc. in (something) as with a gouge **2** to scoop out **3** [Inf.] to cheat out of money —**goug'er** *n.*

**gou·lash** (goo′läsh′) *n.* [[< Hung *gulyás*]] a beef or veal stew seasoned with paprika

**gou·ra·mi** (goo rä′mē, goor′ə mē) *n., pl.* **-mies** or **-mi** [[Malay *gurami*]] any of various freshwater tropical fishes; esp., a food fish of SE Asia

**gourd** (gôrd, goord) *n.* [[< L *cucurbita*]] **1** any trailing or climbing plant of a family that includes the squash, melon, etc. **2** the fruit of one inedible species or its dried, hollowed-out shell, used as a cup, dipper, etc.

**gour·mand** (goor mänd′) *n.* [[OFr]] one who indulges in good food and drink excessively

**gour·met** (goor′mā, gôr-) *n.* [[Fr < OFr, *gormet*, wine taster]] one who likes and is an excellent judge of fine food and drink

**gout** (gout) *n.* [[< L *gutta*, a drop]] a form of arthritis characterized by painful swelling of the joints, esp. in the big toe —**gout'y, -i·er, -i·est,** *adj.*

**gov** or **Gov** *abbrev.* **1** government **2** governor

**gov·ern** (guv′ərn) *vt., vi.* [[< Gr *kybernan*, to steer]] **1** to exercise authority over; rule, control, etc. **2** to influence the action of; guide **3** to determine — **gov'ern·a·ble** *adj.*

**gov'ern·ance** (-ər nəns) *n.* the action, function, or power of government

**gov'ern·ess** (-ər nis) *n.* a woman employed in a private home to train and teach the children

**gov·ern·ment** (guv′ərn mənt, -ər mənt) *n.* **1** the exercise of authority over a state, organization, etc.; control; rule **2** a system of ruling, political administration, etc. **3** those who conduct the affairs of a state, etc.; administration —**gov′ern·men′tal** *adj.*

**gov·er·nor** (guv′ə nər, -ər nər) *n.* **1** one who governs; esp., *a)* one appointed to govern a province, etc. *b)* the elected head of any state of the U.S. **2** a mechanical device for automatically controlling the speed of an engine —**gov′er·nor·ship′** *n.*

**governor general** *pl.* **governors general** or **governor generals** a governor who has subordinate or deputy governors

**govt** or **Govt** *abbrev.* government

**gown** (goun) *n.* ⟦< LL *gunna*⟧ **1** a long, loose outer garment; specif., *a)* a nightgown *b)* a long, flowing robe worn by judges, clergymen, scholars, etc. **2** a woman's formal dress

**GP** or **gp** *abbrev.* general practitioner

**gr** *abbrev.* **1** grain(s) **2** gross

**Gr** *abbrev.* **1** Greece **2** Greek

**grab** (grab) *vt.* **grabbed**, **grab′bing** ⟦prob. < MDu *grabben*⟧ **1** to snatch suddenly **2** to get by unscrupulous methods **3** [Slang] to impress greatly —*n.* a grabbing —**grab′ber** *n.*

**grab′by** *adj.* **-bi·er**, **-bi·est** [Inf.] greedy; avaricious

**grace** (grās) *n.* ⟦< L *gratus*, pleasing⟧ **1** beauty or charm of form, movement, or expression **2** goodwill; favor **3** a delay granted for payment of an obligation **4** a short prayer of thanks for a meal **5** [G-] a title of an archbishop, duke, or duchess **6** the love and favor of God toward human beings —*vt.* **graced**, **grac′ing 1** to decorate **2** to dignify —**in the good** (or **bad**) **graces of** in favor (or disfavor) with

**grace′ful** *adj.* having beauty of form, movement, etc. —**grace′ful·ly** *adv.* —**grace′ful·ness** *n.*

**grace′less** *adj.* **1** lacking any sense of what is proper **2** clumsy or inelegant —**grace′less·ly** *adv.* —**grace′less·ness** *n.*

**gra·cious** (grā′shəs) *adj.* ⟦see GRACE⟧ **1** having or showing kindness, courtesy, charm, etc. **2** compassionate **3** polite to supposed inferiors **4** marked by luxury, ease, etc. *[gracious* living] —**gra′cious·ly** *adv.* —**gra′cious·ness** *n.*

**grack·le** (grak′əl) *n.* ⟦L *graculus*, jackdaw⟧ any of several blackbirds somewhat smaller than a crow

**grad¹** (grad) *n.* [Inf.] a graduate

**grad²** *abbrev.* **1** graduate **2** graduated

**gra·da·tion** (grā dā′shən) *n.* **1** an arranging in grades, or stages **2** a gradual change by stages **3** a step or degree in a graded series

**grade** (grād) *n.* ⟦< L *gradus*⟧ **1** a stage or step in a progression **2** *a)* a degree in a scale of quality, rank, etc. *b)* a group of people of the same rank, merit, etc. **3** *a)* the degree of rise or descent of a sloping surface *b)* such a surface **4** any of the divisions of a school curriculum, usually by years **5** a mark or rating on an examination, etc. —*vt.* **grad′ed**, **grad′ing 1** to classify by grades; sort **2** to give a GRADE (*n.* 5) to **3** to make (ground) level or evenly sloped, as for a road —**make the grade** to succeed

**grade crossing** the place where a railroad intersects another railroad or a roadway on the same level

**grade school** ELEMENTARY SCHOOL

**grade separation** a crossing with an overpass or underpass

**gra·di·ent** (grā′dē ənt) *n.* ⟦< L *gradi*, to step⟧ **1** a slope, as of a road **2** the degree of such slope

**grad·u·al** (gra′jōō əl) *adj.* ⟦< L *gradus*, a step⟧ taking place by degrees; developing little by little —**grad′u·al·ly** *adv.* —**grad′u·al·ness** *n.*

**grad′u·al·ism′** *n.* the principle of promoting gradual rather than rapid change

**grad·u·ate** (gra′jōō it; *for v.*, -āt′) *n.* ⟦< L *gradus*, a step⟧ one who has completed a course of study at a school or college —*vt.* **-at′ed**, **-at′ing 1** to give a degree or diploma to upon completion of a course of study **2** [Inf.] to become a graduate of *[to graduate* college] **3** to mark with degrees for measuring **4** to classify into grades according to

---

amount, size, etc. —*vi.* to become a graduate of a school, etc. —*adj.* **1** having been graduated from a school, etc. **2** of or for degrees above the bachelor's —**grad′u·a′tor** *n.*

**grad·u·a′tion** *n.* **1** a graduating from a school or college **2** the ceremony connected with this

**graf·fi·ti** (grə fēt′ē) *pl.n., sing.* **-to** (-ō) ⟦It < L: see fol.⟧ [*now usually with sing. v.*] inscriptions or drawings on a wall or other public surface

**graft** (graft) *n.* ⟦ult. < Gr *grapheion*, stylus⟧ **1** *a)* a shoot or bud of one plant or tree inserted into another, where it grows permanently *b)* the inserting of such a shoot **2** the transplanting of skin, bone, etc. **3** *a)* the dishonest use of one's position to gain money, etc., as in politics *b)* anything so gained —*vt., vi.* to insert (a graft) —**graft′er** *n.*

**gra·ham** (grā′əm, gram) *adj.* ⟦after S. *Graham*, 19th-c. U.S. dietary reformer⟧ designating or made of whole-wheat flour *[graham* crackers*]*

**Grail** (grāl) *n.* ⟦< ML *gradalis*, cup⟧ *Medieval Legend* the cup used by Jesus at the Last Supper: also **Holy Grail**

**grain** (grān) *n.* ⟦< L *granum*⟧ **1** the small, hard seed of any cereal plant, as wheat or corn **2** cereal plants **3** a tiny, solid particle, as of salt or sand **4** a tiny bit **5** the smallest unit in the system of weights used in the U.S. **6** *a)* the arrangement or direction of fibers, layers, etc. of wood, leather, etc. *b)* the markings or texture due to this **7** disposition; nature

**grain′y** *adj.* **-i·er**, **-i·est 1** having a clearly defined grain: said as of wood **2** coarsely textured; granular —**grain′i·ness** *n.*

**gram¹** (gram) *n.* ⟦< Gr *gramma*, small weight⟧ the basic unit of mass in the metric system, equal to 0.03527 ounce

**gram²** *abbrev.* grammar

**-gram** (gram) ⟦< Gr *gramma*, writing⟧ *combining form* something written *[telegram]*

**gram·mar** (gram′ər) *n.* ⟦< Gr *gramma*, writing⟧ **1** language study dealing with the forms of words and with their arrangement in sentences **2** a system of rules for speaking and writing a given language **3** one's manner of speaking or writing as judged by such rules —**gram·mar·i·an** (grə mer′ē ən) *n.* —**gram·mat′i·cal** (-mat′i kəl) *adj.* —**gram·mat′i·cal·ly** *adv.*

**grammar school** [Now Rare] ELEMENTARY SCHOOL

**gran·a·ry** (gran′ə rē, grān′-) *n., pl.* **-ries** ⟦< L *granum*, grain⟧ a building for storing threshed grain

**grand** (grand) *adj.* ⟦< L *grandis*, large⟧ **1** higher in rank than others *[a grand* duke*]* **2** most important; main *[the grand* ballroom*]* **3** imposing in size, beauty, and extent **4** distinguished; illustrious **5** complete; overall *[the grand* total*]* **6** [Inf.] excellent; delightful —*n., pl.* **grand** [Slang] a thousand dollars —**grand′ly** *adv.*

**grand-** *combining form* of the generation older (or younger) than *[grandmother, grandson]*

**grand′child′** *n., pl.* **-chil′dren** a child of one's son or daughter

**grand′daugh′ter** *n.* a daughter of one's son or daughter

**grande dame** (gränd däm′) ⟦Fr⟧ a woman, esp. an older one, of great dignity

**gran·dee** (gran dē′) *n.* ⟦Sp & Port *grande*: see GRAND⟧ a man of high rank

**gran·deur** (gran′jər, -jŏŏr′; -dyŏŏr′) *n.* ⟦see GRAND⟧ **1** splendor; magnificence **2** moral or intellectual greatness

**grand′fa′ther** *n.* **1** the father of one's father or mother **2** a forefather —*vt.* [Inf.] to exempt (a practice, person, etc.) from a new law or regulation

**grandfather** (or **grandfather's**) **clock** a large clock with a pendulum, in a tall, narrow case

**gran·dil·o·quent** (gran dil′ə kwənt) *adj.* ⟦< L

*grandis*, grand + *loqui*, speak⟧ using pompous, bombastic words —**gran·dil′o·quence** *n.* —**gran·dil′o·quent·ly** *adv.*

**gran·di·ose** (gran′dē ōs′) *adj.* ⟦< L *grandis*, great⟧ **1** having grandeur; imposing **2** pompous and showy —**gran·di·os′i·ty** (-äs′ə tē) *n.*

**grand jury** a jury that investigates accusations and indicts persons for trial if there is sufficient evidence

**grand′ma′** *n.* [Inf.] GRANDMOTHER

**grand′mas′ter** *n.* a chess player of the highest rating

**grand′moth′er** *n.* **1** the mother of one's father or mother **2** a female ancestor

**grand opera** opera in which the whole text is set to music

**grand′pa′** *n.* [Inf.] GRANDFATHER

**grand′par′ent** *n.* a grandfather or grandmother

**grand piano** a large piano with strings set horizontally in a wing-shaped case

**Grand Rapids** city in SW Michigan: pop. 189,000

**grand slam 1** *Baseball* a home run hit when there is a runner on each base **2** *Bridge* the winning of all the tricks in a deal

**grand′son′** *n.* a son of one's son or daughter

**grand′stand′** *n.* the main seating structure for spectators at a sporting event

**grange** (grānj) *n.* ⟦< L *granum*, grain⟧ a farm —**the Grange** a fraternal organization, originally of farmers, in the U.S.

**gran·ite** (gran′it) *n.* ⟦< L *granum*, grain⟧ a hard, grainy igneous rock consisting mainly of feldspar and quartz —**gra·nit·ic** (grə nit′ik) *adj.*

**gran·ny** or **gran·nie** (gran′ē) *n., pl.* **-nies** [Inf.] **1** a grandmother **2** an old woman —*adj.* of a style like that formerly worn by elderly women [*granny glasses*]

**gran·o·la** (grə nō′lə) *n.* ⟦< ? L *granum*, grain⟧ a breakfast cereal of rolled oats, wheat germ, sesame seeds, brown sugar or honey, dried fruit or nuts, etc.

**grant** (grant) *vt.* ⟦ult. < L *credere*, believe⟧ **1** to give (what is requested, as permission) **2** to give or transfer by legal procedure **3** to admit as true; concede —*n.* **1** a granting **2** something granted, as property or a right —**take for granted** to consider as true, already settled, etc. —**grant′er** *n.*

**Grant** (grant), **Ulysses S(impson)** 1822-85; 18th president of the U.S. (1869-77): Union commander in the Civil War

**grant′-in-aid′** *n., pl.* **grants′-in-aid′** a grant of funds, as by the federal government to a state or by a foundation to a scientist, artist, etc., to support a specific project

**grants′man·ship′** *n.* skill in acquiring grants-in-aid

**gran·u·lar** (gran′yə lər) *adj.* **1** containing or consisting of grains **2** like grains or granules —**gran′u·lar′i·ty** (-ler′ə tē) *n.*

**gran′u·late′** (-lāt′) *vt., vi.* **-lat′ed, -lat′ing** to form into grains or granules —**gran′u·la′tion** *n.*

**gran·ule** (gran′yool) *n.* ⟦< L *granum*, grain⟧ a small grain or particle

**grape** (grāp) *n.* ⟦< OFr *graper*, to gather with a hook⟧ **1** a small, round, juicy berry, growing in clusters on a woody vine **2** a grapevine **3** a dark purplish red

**grape′fruit′** *n.* a large, round, sour citrus fruit with a yellow rind

**grape hyacinth** a small plant of the lily family, with spikes of small, bell-shaped flowers of blue or white

**grape′shot′** *n.* a cluster of small iron balls, formerly fired from a cannon

**grape′vine′** *n.* **1** a woody vine bearing grapes **2** a secret means of spreading information **3** a rumor

**graph** (graf) *n.* ⟦< *graph*(*ic formula*)⟧ a diagram representing quantitative information and rela-

tionships, such as successive changes in a variable quantity —*vt.* to represent by a graph

**-graph** (graf) ⟦< Gr *graphein*, to write⟧ *combining form* **1** something that writes or records [*telegraph*] **2** something written, etc. [*monograph*]

**graph·ic** (graf′ik) *adj.* ⟦< Gr *graphein*, to write⟧ **1** described in realistic detail; vivid **2** of those arts (**graphic arts**) that include any form of visual artistic representation, esp. painting, drawing, etching, etc. Also **graph′i·cal** —**graph′i·cal·ly** *adv.*

**graph′ics** *n.* **1** design as employed in the graphic arts **2** the graphic arts

**graph·ite** (graf′īt′) *n.* ⟦< Gr *graphein*, to write⟧ a soft, black form of carbon used in pencils, electrodes, etc.

**graph·ol·o·gy** (graf äl′ə jē) *n.* ⟦< Fr: see GRAPHIC & -LOGY⟧ the study of handwriting, esp. as a clue to character —**graph·ol′o·gist** *n.*

**-gra·phy** (grə fē) ⟦< Gr *graphein*, to write⟧ *combining form* **1** a process or method of writing or graphically representing [*calligraphy*] **2** a descriptive science [*geography*]

**grap·nel** (grap′nəl) *n.* ⟦< Prov *grapa*, a hook⟧ a small anchor with several curved, pointed arms

**grap·ple** (grap′əl) *n.* ⟦OFr *grapil*⟧ **1** GRAPNEL **2** a hand-to-hand fight —*vt.* **-pled, -pling** to grip and hold —*vi.* **1** to use a GRAPNEL **2** to wrestle **3** to try to cope (*with*)

**grappling iron** (or **hook**) GRAPNEL

**grasp** (grasp) *vt.* ⟦ME *graspen*⟧ **1** to grip, as with the hand **2** to take hold of eagerly; seize **3** to comprehend —*vi.* **1** to try to seize: with *at* **2** to accept eagerly: with *at* —*n.* **1** a grasping; grip **2** control; possession **3** the power to hold or seize **4** comprehension —**grasp′a·ble** *adj.*

**grasp′ing** *adj.* avaricious; greedy

**grass** (gras, gräs) *n.* ⟦OE *græs*⟧ **1** a plant with long, narrow leaves, jointed stems, and seedlike fruit, as wheat or rye **2** any of various green plants with narrow leaves, growing densely in meadows, lawns, etc. **3** pasture or lawn **4** [Slang] marijuana —**grass′y, -i·er, -i·est,** *adj.*

**grass′hop′per** *n.* any of various winged, planteating insects with powerful hind legs for jumping

**grass roots** [Inf.] **1** the common people **2** the basic source or support, as of a movement —**grass′-roots′** *adj.*

**grass widow** a woman divorced or separated from her husband

GRASSHOPPER

**grate**[1] (grāt) *vt.* **grat′ed, grat′ing** ⟦< OFr *grater*⟧ **1** to grind into particles by scraping **2** to rub against (an object) or grind (the teeth) together with a harsh sound **3** to irritate; annoy; fret —*vi.* **1** to rub with or make a rasping sound **2** to be irritating —**grat′er** *n.*

**grate**[2] (grāt) *n.* ⟦< L *cratis*, a hurdle⟧ **1** GRATING[1] **2** a frame of metal bars for holding fuel in a fireplace, etc. **3** a fireplace

**grate·ful** (grāt′fəl) *adj.* ⟦obs. *grate*, pleasing (< L *gratus*)⟧ **1** thankful **2** welcome —**grate′ful·ly** *adv.* —**grate′ful·ness** *n.*

**grat·i·fy** (grat′i fī′) *vt.* **-fied′, -fy′ing** ⟦< L *gratus*, pleasing + *-ficare*, -FY⟧ **1** to please or satisfy **2** to indulge; humor —**grat′i·fi·ca′tion** *n.* —**grat′i·fy′ing** *adj.*

**grat·ing**[1] (grāt′iŋ) *n.* a framework of bars set in a window, door, etc.

**grat′ing**[2] *adj.* **1** rasping **2** irritating

**gra·tis** (grat′is, grät′-) *adv., adj.* [L < *gratia*, a favor] free of charge

**grat·i·tude** (grat′i tōōd′) *n.* [< L *gratus*, pleasing] thankful appreciation for favors or benefits received

**gra·tu·i·tous** (grə tōō′i təs, -tyōō′-) *adj.* [< L *gratus*, pleasing] 1 given free of charge 2 uncalled-for —**gra·tu′i·tous·ly** *adv.*

**gra·tu′i·ty** (-tē) *n., pl.* **-ties** a gift of money for a service; tip

**gra·va·men** (grə vā′mən) *n., pl.* **-mens** or **gra·vam′i·na** (-vam′i nə) [LL, a burden] *Law* the essential part of a complaint or accusation

**grave**[1] (grāv) *adj.* **grav′er, grav′est** [< L *gravis*, heavy] 1 important 2 serious [a *grave* illness] 3 solemn or sedate 4 somber; dull —**grave′ly** *adv.* —**grave′ness** *n.*

**grave**[2] (grāv) *n.* [< OE *grafan*, to dig] 1 *a)* a hole in the ground in which to bury a dead body *b)* any burial place; tomb 2 death —*vt.* **graved, grav′en** or **graved, grav′ing** 1 [Archaic] to sculpture or engrave 2 to impress sharply

**grave accent** (grāv, gräv) a mark ( ` ) showing stress, the quality of a vowel, etc.

**grav·el** (grav′əl) *n.* [< OFr *grave*, coarse sand] a loose mixture of pebbles and rock fragments coarser than sand

**grav′el·ly** (-ē) *adj.* 1 full of or like gravel 2 harsh or rasping [a *gravelly* voice]

**grav·en** (grāv′ən) *vt. alt. pp. of* GRAVE[2]

**grave′stone′** *n.* a tombstone

**grave′yard′** *n.* a cemetery

**graveyard shift** [Inf.] work shift at night, esp. one starting at midnight

**grav·id** (grav′id) *adj.* [< L *gravis*, heavy] pregnant

**gra·vim·e·ter** (grə vim′ət ər) *n.* [< L *gravis*, heavy + Fr *-mètre*, -METER] 1 a device for determining specific gravity 2 an instrument for measuring the earth's gravitational pull

**grav·i·tate** (grav′i tāt′) *vi.* **-tat′ed, -tat′ing** 1 to move or tend to move in accordance with the force of gravity 2 to be attracted (*toward*)

**grav·i·ta′tion** *n.* 1 a gravitating 2 *Physics* the force by which every mass attracts and is attracted by every other mass —**grav′i·ta′tion·al** *adj.*

**grav·i·ty** (grav′i tē) *n., pl.* **-ties** [< L *gravis*, heavy] 1 graveness; seriousness 2 weight [specific *gravity*] 3 *Physics* gravitation; esp., the pull on all bodies in the earth's sphere toward the earth's center

**gra·vy** (grā′vē) *n., pl.* **-vies** [< ?] 1 the juice given off by meat in cooking 2 a sauce made from this juice 3 [Slang] any benefit beyond what is expected

**gray** (grā) *n.* [< OE *græg*] a color that is a blend of black and white —*adj.* 1 of this color 2 having hair this color 3 *a)* darkish; dull *b)* dreary; dismal 4 designating a vague, intermediate area —*vt., vi.* to make or become gray —**gray′ish** *adj.* —**gray′ness** *n.*

**gray′beard′** *n.* an old man

**gray matter** 1 grayish nerve tissue of the brain and spinal cord 2 [Inf.] intellectual capacity; brains

**graze**[1] (grāz) *vt.* **grazed, graz′ing** [< OE *græs*, grass] 1 to put livestock to feed on (growing grass, etc.) 2 to tend (feeding livestock) —*vi.* to feed on growing grass, etc.

**graze**[2] (grāz) *vt., vi.* **grazed, graz′ing** [prob. < prec.] to scrape or rub lightly in passing —*n.* a grazing

**Gr Brit** or **Gr Br** Great Britain

**grease** (grēs; *for v., also* grēz) *n.* [< L *crassus*, fat] 1 melted animal fat 2 any thick, oily substance or lubricant —*vt.* **greased, greas′ing** to smear or lubricate with grease

**grease′paint′** *n.* greasy coloring matter used in making up for the stage

**greas·y** (grē′sē, -zē) *adj.* **-i·er, -i·est** 1 soiled with

grease 2 containing much grease 3 oily —**greas′i·ness** *n.*

**great** (grāt) *adj.* [OE] 1 of much more than ordinary size, extent, etc. [the *Great* Lakes] 2 much above the average; esp., *a)* intense [*great* pain] *b)* eminent [a *great* writer] 3 most important; main 4 [Inf.] skillful: often with *at* 5 [Inf.] excellent; fine —*n.* a distinguished person —**great′ly** *adv.* —**great′ness** *n.*

**great-** *combining form* older (or younger) by one generation [*great*-aunt, *great-great*-grandson]

**great ape** any of a family of primates consisting of the gorilla, chimpanzee, and orangutan

**Great Britain** principal island of the United Kingdom, including England, Scotland, & Wales

**Great Dane** a very large, muscular dog with a short, smooth coat

**great′-grand′child′** *n., pl.* **-chil′dren** a child of any of one's grandchildren

**great′-grand′par′ent** *n.* a parent of any of one's grandparents

**great′heart′ed** *adj.* 1 brave; fearless 2 generous; unselfish

**Great Lakes** chain of five freshwater lakes in EC North America

**Great Salt Lake** shallow saltwater lake in NW Utah

**grebe** (grēb) *n.* [Fr *grèbe*] a diving and swimming bird with broadly lobed webbed feet

**Gre·cian** (grē′shən) *adj., n.* GREEK

**Greco-** [< L *Graecus*] *combining form* Greek, Greek and [*Greco*-Roman]

**Greece** (grēs) country in the S Balkan Peninsula, on the Mediterranean: 50,949 sq. mi.; pop. 10,260,000

**greed** (grēd) *n.* [< fol.] excessive desire, esp. for wealth; avarice

**greed·y** (grēd′ē) *adj.* **-i·er, -i·est** [OE *grædig*] 1 desiring more than one needs or deserves 2 having too strong a desire for food and drink; gluttonous —**greed′i·ly** *adv.* —**greed′i·ness** *n.*

**Greek** (grēk) *n.* 1 a person born or living in Greece 2 the language, ancient or modern, of the Greeks —*adj.* of Greece or its people, language, etc.

**green** (grēn) *adj.* [OE *grene*] 1 of the color of growing grass 2 overspread with green plants or foliage 3 sickly or bilious 4 unripe 5 inexperienced or naive 6 not dried or seasoned 7 [Inf.] jealous —*n.* 1 the color of growing grass 2 [*pl.*] green leafy vegetables, as spinach 3 an area of smooth turf [a putting *green*] —**green′ish** *adj.* —**green′ly** *adv.* —**green′ness** *n.*

**green′back′** *n.* any piece of U.S. paper money printed in green ink on the back

**Green Bay** city & port in Wisconsin: pop 96,000

**green bean** the edible, immature green pod of the kidney bean

**green′belt′** *n.* a beltlike area around a city, reserved for park land or farms

**green′er·y** *n.* green vegetation; verdure

**green′-eyed′** *adj.* very jealous

**green′gro′cer** *n.* [Brit.] a retail dealer in fresh vegetables and fruit

**green′horn′** *n.* 1 an inexperienced person 2 a person easily deceived

**green′house′** *n.* a heated building, mainly of glass, for growing plants

**greenhouse effect** the warming of the earth and its lower atmosphere, caused by trapped solar radiation

**Green·land** (grēn′lənd) self-governing Danish island northeast of North America

**green light** [Inf.] permission to proceed with some undertaking —**green′light′, -light′ed** or **-lit′, -light′ing,** *vt.*

**green manure** a crop, as of clover, plowed under to fertilize the soil

**green onion** an immature onion with green leaves, often eaten raw; scallion

**green pepper** the green immature fruit of a red pepper, esp. the bell pepper

**green power** money as the source of economic power

**Greens·bor·o** (grēnz′bur′ō) city in NC North Carolina: pop. 184,000

**green′sward′** *n.* green, grassy turf

**green thumb** a talent for growing plants

**Green·wich** (gren′ich; *chiefly Brit,* grin′ij) borough of London, on the prime meridian: pop. 208,000

**Green·wich Village** (gren′ich) section of New York City: noted as a center for artists, writers, etc.

**green′wood′** *n.* a forest in leaf

**greet** (grēt) *vt.* ⟦OE *gretan*⟧ **1** to address with friendliness **2** to meet or receive (a person, event, etc.) in a specified way **3** to come or appear to; meet —**greet′er** *n.*

**greet′ing** *n.* **1** the act or words of one who greets **2** [*often pl.*] a message of regards

**greeting card** CARD¹ (*n.* 1*d*)

**gre·gar·i·ous** (grə ger′ē əs) *adj.* ⟦< L *grex,* herd⟧ **1** living in herds **2** fond of the company of others; sociable —**gre·gar′i·ous·ly** *adv.* —**gre·gar′i·ous·ness** *n.*

**Gre·go·ri·an calendar** (grə gôr′ē ən) the calendar now widely used, introduced by Pope Gregory XIII in 1582

**Gregorian chant** ⟦after Pope Gregory I⟧ a kind of plainsong formerly widely used in the Roman Catholic Church

**grem·lin** (grem′lin) *n.* ⟦prob. < Dan *gram,* a devil⟧ a small imaginary creature humorously blamed for malfunctions or disruptions

**Gre·na·da** (grə nā′də) country on an island group in the West Indies: 133 sq. mi.; pop. 95,000

**gre·nade** (grə nād′) *n.* ⟦Fr < OFr, pomegranate⟧ a small bomb detonated by a fuse and usually thrown by hand

**gren·a·dier** (gren′ə dir′) *n.* **1** [Archaic] a soldier who threw grenades **2** a member of a special regiment or corps

**gren·a·dine** (gren′ə dēn′) *n.* ⟦Fr⟧ a red syrup made from pomegranate juice

**grew** (grōō) *vi., vt. pt. of* GROW

**grey** (grā) *n., adj., vt., vi. chiefly Brit. sp. of* GRAY

**grey′hound′** *n.* a tall, slender, swift dog with a narrow head

**grid** (grid) *n.* ⟦short for GRIDIRON⟧ **1** a framework of parallel bars; grating **2** a metallic plate in a storage battery **3** an electrode, in spiral or grid-like shape, for controlling the flow of electrons in an electron tube

**grid·dle** (grid′'l) *n.* ⟦< L *craticula,* gridiron⟧ a flat, heavy metal pan for cooking pancakes, etc.

**grid′dle·cake′** *n.* a pancake

**grid·i·ron** (grid′ī′ərn) *n.* ⟦see GRIDDLE⟧ **1** GRILL (*n.* 1) **2** a football field

**grid′lock′** *n.* a traffic jam in which no vehicle can move in any direction

**grief** (grēf) *n.* ⟦see GRIEVE⟧ **1** intense emotional suffering caused as by a loss **2** a cause of such suffering —**come to grief** to fail or be ruined

**griev·ance** (grēv′əns) *n.* **1** a circumstance thought to be unjust and ground for complaint **2** complaint against a real or imagined wrong

**grieve** (grēv) *vi., vt.* **grieved, griev′ing** ⟦< L *gravis,* heavy⟧ to feel or cause to feel grief

**griev·ous** (grēv′əs) *adj.* **1** causing grief **2** showing or full of grief **3** severe **4** deplorable; atrocious —**griev′ous·ly** *adv.*

**grif·fin** (grif′in) *n.* ⟦< Gr *gryps*⟧ a mythical monster, part lion and part eagle

**grill** (gril) *n.* ⟦see GRIDDLE⟧ **1** a unit for broiling meat, etc., consisting of a framework of metal bars or wires **2** a large griddle **3** grilled food **4** a restaurant that specializes in grilled foods —*vt.* **1** to broil **2** to question relentlessly

GRIFFIN

**grille** (gril) *n.* ⟦see GRIDDLE⟧ an open grating forming a screen

**grim** (grim) *adj.* **grim′mer, grim′mest** ⟦OE *grimm*⟧ **1** hard and unyielding; stern **2** appearing forbidding, harsh, etc. **3** repellent; ghastly —**grim′ly** *adv.* —**grim′ness** *n.*

**gri·mace** (gri mās′, grim′is) *n.* ⟦Fr⟧ a distortion of the face, as in expressing pain, disgust, etc. —*vi.* **-maced′, -mac′ing** to make grimaces

**grime** (grīm) *n.* ⟦prob. < Fl *grijm*⟧ dirt rubbed into or covering a surface, as of the skin —**grim′y, -i·er, -i·est,** *adj.* —**grim′i·ness** *n.*

**Grimm** (grim) **1 Ja·kob** (Ludwig Karl) (yä′kôp) 1785-1863; Ger. philologist **2 Wil·helm** (Karl) (vil′helm) 1786-1859; Ger. philologist: brother of Jakob, with whom he collected fairy tales

**grin** (grin) *vi.* **grinned, grin′ning** ⟦< OE *grennian,* bare the teeth⟧ **1** to smile broadly as in amusement **2** to show the teeth in pain, scorn, etc. —*n.* the act or look of grinning

**grind** (grīnd) *vt.* **ground, grind′ing** ⟦OE *grindan*⟧ **1** to crush or chop into fine particles; pulverize **2** to oppress **3** to sharpen or smooth by friction **4** to rub (the teeth, etc.) together gratingly **5** to operate by turning the crank of —*n.* **1** a grinding **2** long, difficult work or study **3** [Inf.] a student who studies hard —**grind out** to produce by steady or laborious effort

**grind·er** (grīn′dər) *n.* **1** a person or thing that grinds **2** [*pl.*] [Inf.] the teeth **3** *chiefly New England var. of* HERO SANDWICH

**grind′stone′** *n.* a revolving stone disk for sharpening tools or polishing things —**keep one's nose to the grindstone** to work hard and steadily

**grip** (grip) *n.* ⟦< OE *grīpan,* seize⟧ **1** a secure grasp; firm hold **2** the manner of holding a club, bat, etc. **3** the power of grasping firmly **4** mental grasp **5** firm control **6** a handle **7** a small traveling bag —*vt.* **gripped** or **gript, grip′ping 1** to take firmly and hold fast **2** to get and hold the attention of —*vi.* to get a grip —**come to grips** to struggle (*with*) —**grip′per** *n.*

**gripe** (grīp) *vt.* **griped, grip′ing** ⟦OE *grīpan,* seize⟧ **1** to cause sharp pain in the bowels of **2** [Slang] to annoy —*vi.* [Slang] to complain —*n.* **1** a sharp pain in the bowels: *usually used in pl.* **2** [Slang] a complaint —**grip′er** *n.*

**grippe** (grip) *n.* ⟦Fr⟧ *former term for* INFLUENZA

**gris-gris** (grē′grē′) *n., pl.* **gris′-gris′** ⟦of Afr orig.⟧ an amulet, charm, or spell of African origin

**gris·ly** (griz′lē) *adj.* **-li·er, -li·est** ⟦OE *grislic*⟧ terrifying; ghastly —**gris′li·ness** *n.*

**grist** (grist) *n.* ⟦OE⟧ grain that is to be or has been ground

**gris·tle** (gris′əl) *n.* ⟦OE⟧ cartilage, esp. as found in meat —**gris′tly (-lē)** *adj.*

**grist′mill′** *n.* a mill for grinding grain

**grit** (grit) *n.* ⟦< OE *greot*⟧ **1** rough particles, as of sand **2** coarse sandstone **3** stubborn courage; pluck —*vt.* **grit′ted, grit′ting** to clench or grind (the teeth) as in determination —*vi.* to make a grating sound —**grit′ty, -ti·er, -ti·est,** *adj.*

**grits** (grits) *pl.n.* ⟦OE *grytte*⟧ [*often with sing. v.*] coarsely ground grain; esp., hominy

**griz·zled** (griz′əld) *adj.* ⟦< OFr *gris,* gray⟧ **1** gray or streaked with gray **2** having gray hair

**griz′zly (-lē)** *adj.* **-zli·er, -zli·est** grayish; grizzled

**grizzly** (**bear**) a large, brown bear of W North America

**groan** (grōn) *vi.*, *vt.* [< OE *granian*] to utter (with) a deep sound expressing pain, distress, etc. —*n.* such a sound

**gro·cer** (grō'sər) *n.* [< OFr *grossier*] a dealer in food and household supplies

**gro·cer·y** *n.*, *pl.* **-ies** 1 a grocer's store 2 [*pl.*] the food and supplies sold by a grocer

**grog** (gräg) *n.* [after Old *Grog*, nickname of an 18th-c. Brit admiral] 1 rum diluted with water 2 any alcoholic liquor

**grog·gy** *adj.* **-gi·er**, **-gi·est** [< prec. + -Y²] 1 [Archaic] intoxicated 2 dizzy 3 sluggish or dull —**grog'gi·ly** *adv.* —**grog'gi·ness** *n.*

**groin** (groin) *n.* [prob. < OE *grynde*, abyss] 1 the fold where the abdomen joins either thigh 2 *Archit.* the sharp, curved edge at the junction of two vaults

**grom·met** (gräm'it) *n.* [< obs. Fr *gromette*, a curb] 1 a ring of rope 2 a metal eyelet in cloth, etc.

**groom** (grōōm) *n.* [ME *grom*, boy] 1 one whose work is tending horses 2 a bridegroom —*vt.* 1 to clean and curry (a horse, etc.) 2 to make neat and tidy 3 to train for a particular purpose

**groove** (grōōv) *n.* [< ON *grof*, a pit] 1 a long, narrow furrow cut with a tool 2 any channel or rut 3 a settled routine —*vt.* **grooved**, **groov'ing** to make a groove in

**groov·y** *adj.* **-i·er**, **-i·est** [Slang] very pleasing or attractive

**grope** (grōp) *vi.* **groped**, **grop'ing** [< OE *grapian*, to touch] to feel or search about blindly or uncertainly —*vt.* 1 to seek or find (one's way) by groping 2 [Slang] to fondle sexually —**grop'er** *n.* —**grop'ing·ly** *adv.*

**gros·beak** (grōs'bēk') *n.* [Fr: see GROSS & BEAK] a songbird with a thick, strong, conical bill

**gros·grain** (grō'grān') *n.* [Fr, lit., coarse grain] a ribbed silk or rayon fabric for ribbons, etc.

**gross** (grōs) *adj.* [< LL *grossus*, thick] 1 fat and coarse-looking 2 flagrant; very bad 3 lacking in refinement 4 vulgar; coarse 5 with no deductions; total 6 [Slang] disgusting —*n.* 1 *pl.* **gross'es** overall total 2 *pl.* **gross** twelve dozen —*vt.*, *vi.* to earn (a specified total amount) before expenses are deducted —**gross out** [Slang] to disgust —**gross'ly** *adv.*

**gross national product** the total value of a nation's annual output of goods and services

**gro·tesque** (grō tesk') *adj.* [< It *grotta*, grotto: from designs found in caves] 1 distorted or fantastic in appearance, shape, etc. 2 ridiculous; absurd —**gro·tesque'ly** *adv.*

**grot·to** (grät'ō) *n.*, *pl.* **-toes** or **-tos** [< It < L *crypta*, crypt] 1 a cave 2 a cavelike summerhouse, shrine, etc.

**grouch** (grouch) *vi.* [< ME *grucchen*] to grumble or complain sulkily —*n.* 1 one who grouches 2 a sulky mood —**grouch'y**, **-i·er**, **-i·est**, *adj.* —**grouch'i·ly** *adv.* —**grouch'i·ness** *n.*

**ground¹** (ground) *n.* [OE *grund*, bottom] 1 the solid surface of the earth 2 soil; earth 3 [*often pl.*] a tract of land [*grounds* of an estate] 4 area, as of discussion 5 [*often pl.*] basis; foundation 6 valid reason or motive: *often used in pl.* 7 the background, as in a design 8 [*pl.*] sediment [*coffee grounds*] 9 the connection of an electrical conductor with a ground —*adj.* of, on, or near the ground —*vt.* 1 to set on the ground 2 to cause to run aground 3 to base; found; establish 4 to instruct in the first principles of 5 *a*) to keep (an aircraft or pilot) from flying *b*) [Inf.] to punish (a teenager) by not permitting him or her to leave home for dates, etc. 6 *Elec.* to connect (a conductor) to a ground —*vi.* 1 to run ashore 2 *Baseball* to be put out on a grounder: usually with *out* —**break ground** 1 to dig; excavate 2 to plow 3 to start building —**gain** (**or lose**) **ground** to gain (or lose) in achievement, popularity, etc. —**give**

ground to retreat; yield —**hold** (or **stand**) one's ground to remain firm, not yielding

**ground²** (ground) *vt.*, *vi. pt. & pp.* of GRIND

**ground control** personnel and equipment on the ground, for guiding airplanes and spacecraft in takeoff, landing, etc.

**ground cover** low, dense-growing plants used for covering bare ground

**ground crew** a group of workers who maintain and repair aircraft

**ground'er** *n. Baseball* a batted ball that travels along the ground: also **ground ball**

**ground floor** that floor of a building approximately level with the ground; first floor —**in on the ground floor** [Inf.] in at the start (of a business, etc.)

**ground glass** nontransparent glass with a surface that has been ground to diffuse light

**ground'hog'** *n.* WOODCHUCK: also **ground hog**

**ground'less** *adj.* without reason or cause

**ground rule** 1 *Baseball* a rule adapted to playing conditions in a specific ballpark 2 any basic rule

**ground'swell'** *n.* 1 a violent rolling of the ocean 2 a wave of popular feeling

**ground'wa'ter** *n.* water found underground

**ground'work'** *n.* a foundation; basis

**group** (grōōp) *n.* [< It *gruppo*] a number of persons or things gathered or classified together —*vt.*, *vi.* to form into a group or groups

**grou·per** (grōō'pər) *n.* [Port *garupa*] a large sea bass found in warm seas

**group·ie** (grōō'pē) *n.* [Inf.] 1 a female fan of rock groups or other popular personalities, who follows them about 2 a fan; devotee

**group therapy** (or **psychotherapy**) a form of treatment for a group of patients with similar emotional problems, as by group discussions

**grouse¹** (grous) *n.*, *pl.* **grouse** [< ?] a game bird with a plump body and mottled feathers

**grouse²** (grous) *vi.* **groused**, **grous'ing** [< ?] [Inf.] to complain

**grout** (grout) *n.* [ME] a thin mortar used as between tiles

**grove** (grōv) *n.* [< OE *graf*] a group of trees, without undergrowth

**grov·el** (gräv'əl, gruv'-) *vi.* **-eled** or **-elled**, **-el·ing** or **-el·ling** [< ME *grufelinge*, down on one's face] 1 to lie or crawl in a prostrate position, esp. abjectly 2 to behave abjectly —**grov'el·er** or **grov'el·ler** *n.*

**grow** (grō) *vi.* **grew**, **grown**, **grow'ing** [< OE *growan*] 1 to come into being or be produced naturally 2 to develop or thrive, as a living thing 3 to increase in size, quantity, etc. 4 to become [*to grow* weary] —*vt.* to cause to or let grow; raise; cultivate —**grow on** [Inf.] to come gradually to seem more likable, attractive, etc. to —**grow up** to mature —**grow'er** *n.*

**growl** (groul) *n.* [ME *groulen*] a rumbling, menacing sound such as an angry dog makes —*vi.*, *vt.* to make, or express by, such a sound

**grown** (grōn) *vi.*, *vt. pp.* of GROW —*adj.* having completed its growth; mature

**grown'-up'** *adj.*, *n.* adult: also, for *n.*, **grown'up'**

**growth** (grōth) *n.* 1 a growing or developing 2 *a*) increase in size, etc. *b*) the full extent of this 3 something that grows or has grown 4 a tumor or other abnormal mass of tissue

**grub** (grub) *vi.* **grubbed**, **grub'bing** [ME *grubben*] 1 to dig in the ground 2 to work hard —*vt.* 1 to clear (ground) of roots 2 to uproot —*n.* 1 a wormlike larva, esp. of a beetle 2 [Slang] food

**grub'by** *adj.* **-bi·er**, **-bi·est** dirty; untidy —**grub'bi·ness** *n.*

**grub'stake'** *n.* [GRUB, *n.* 2 + STAKE] [Inf.] 1 money or supplies advanced, as to a prospector 2 money advanced for any enterprise

**grudge** (gruj) *vt.* **grudged**, **grudg'ing** [< OFr

*grouchier*‖ **1** BEGRUDGE **2** to give with reluctance —*n.* a feeling of resentment or ill will over some grievance —**grudg'ing·ly** *adv.*

**gru·el** (grōō′əl) *n.* ‖< ML *grutum*, meal‖ thin porridge made by cooking meal in water or milk

**gru·el·ing** or **gru·el·ling** *adj.* ‖prp. of obs. v. *gruel*, punish‖ very trying; exhausting

**grue·some** (grōō′səm) *adj.* ‖< dial. *grue*, to shudder + -SOME¹‖ causing horror or disgust; grisly

**gruff** (gruf) *adj.* ‖< Du *grof*‖ **1** rough or surly; brusquely rude **2** harsh and throaty; hoarse —**gruff'ly** *adv.* —**gruff'ness** *n.*

**grum·ble** (grum′bəl) *vi.* **-bled, -bling** ‖prob. < Du *grommelen*‖ **1** to growl **2** to mutter in discontent **3** to rumble —*vt.* to express by grumbling —*n.* a grumbling —**grum'bler** *n.*

**grump·y** (grum′pē) *adj.* **-i·er, -i·est** ‖prob. echoic‖ grouchy; peevish

**grunge** (grunj) *n.* [Slang] garbage or dirt

**grun·gy** (grun′jē) *adj.* **-gi·er, -gi·est** [Slang] dirty, messy, etc.

**grun·ion** (grun′yən) *n.* ‖prob. < Sp *gruñón*, grumbler‖ a fish of the California coast: it spawns on sandy beaches

**grunt** (grunt) *vi., vt.* ‖< OE *grunian*‖ to utter (with) the deep, hoarse sound of a hog —*n.* **1** this sound **2** [Slang] one whose job involves routine tasks, strenuous labor, etc.; specif., a U.S. infantryman

**Gru·yère** (**cheese**) (grōō yer′, grē-) ‖after *Gruyère*, Switzerland‖ [*often* **g- c-**] a light-yellow Swiss cheese, rich in butterfat

**Gua·da·la·ja·ra** (gwäd′l ə här′ə) city in W Mexico: capital of Jalisco: pop. 1,626,000

**Guam** (gwäm) island in the W Pacific: an unincorporated territory of the U.S.: 209 sq. mi.; pop. 133,000

**Guang·zhou** (gwäŋ′jō) seaport in SE China: pop. 3,182,000

**gua·nine** (gwä′nēn) *n.* ‖< fol. + -INE³‖ a crystalline base contained in the nucleic acids of all tissue

**gua·no** (gwä′nō) *n., pl.* **-nos** ‖Sp < AmInd (Peru)‖ manure of seabirds, used as fertilizer

**guar** *abbrev.* guaranteed

**guar·an·tee** (gar′ən tē′) *n.* **1** GUARANTY (sense 1) **2** *a*) a pledge to replace something if it is not as represented *b*) an assurance that something will be done as specified **3** a guarantor —*vt.* **-teed′, -tee'ing 1** to give a guarantee for **2** to promise

**guar·an·tor** (gar′ən tôr′) *n.* one who gives a guaranty or guarantee

**guar'an·ty** (-tē) *n., pl.* **-ties** ‖< OFr *garant*, a warrant‖ **1** a pledge or security for another's debt or obligation **2** an agreement that secures the existence or maintenance of something —*vt.* **-tied, -ty·ing** GUARANTEE

**guard** (gärd) *vt.* ‖< OFr *garder*‖ **1** to watch over and protect; defend **2** to keep from escaping or from trouble **3** to control or restrain —*vi.* **1** to keep watch (*against*) **2** to act as a guard —*n.* **1** defense; protection **2** a posture of readiness for defense **3** any device to protect against injury or loss **4** a person or group that guards **5** *Basketball* either of two players who are the main ball handlers **6** *Football* either of two players next to the center —**on** (**one's**) **guard** vigilant

**guard'ed** *adj.* **1** kept safe **2** cautious [a *guarded* reply] —**guard'ed·ly** *adv.*

**guard'house'** *n. Mil.* **1** a building used by a guard when not walking a post **2** a jail for temporary confinement

**guard'i·an** (-ē ən) *n.* **1** one who guards or protects; custodian **2** a person legally in charge of the affairs of a minor or of a person of unsound mind —*adj.* protecting —**guard'i·an·ship'** *n.*

**guard'rail'** *n.* a protective railing

**Gua·te·ma·la** (gwät′ə mä′lə) country in Central America: 42,042 sq. mi.; pop. 6,054,000

**gua·va** (gwä′və) *n.* ‖< native name‖ a yellow, pear-shaped tropical American fruit

**gua·ya·be·ra** (gwä′yä ber′ä) *n.* ‖AmSp‖ a kind of loosefitting shirt worn with the shirttail outside the trousers

**gu·ber·na·to·ri·al** (gōō′bər nə tôr′ē əl) *adj.* ‖L *gubernator*, governor‖ of a governor or the office of governor

**Guern·sey** (gurn′zē) *n., pl.* **-seys** ‖after *Guernsey*, one of the Channel Islands‖ a breed of dairy cattle, usually fawn-colored with white markings

**guer·ril·la** (gə ril′ə) *n.* ‖Sp, dim. of *guerra*, war‖ a member of a small defensive force of irregular soldiers, making surprise raids: also sp. **gue·ril'la**

**guess** (ges) *vt., vi.* ‖ME *gessen*‖ **1** to form a judgment or estimate of (something) without actual knowledge; surmise **2** to judge correctly by doing this **3** to think or suppose —*n.* **1** a guessing **2** something guessed; conjecture —**guess'er** *n.*

**guess'work'** *n.* **1** a guessing **2** a judgment, result, etc. arrived at by guessing

**guest** (gest) *n.* ‖< ON *gestr*‖ **1** a person entertained at the home, club, etc. of another **2** any paying customer of a hotel, restaurant, etc. —*adj.* **1** for guests **2** performing by special invitation [a *guest* artist]

**guff** (guf) *n.* ‖echoic‖ [Slang] **1** nonsense **2** brash or insolent talk

**guf·faw** (gə fô′) *n.* ‖echoic‖ a loud, coarse burst of laughter —*vi.* to laugh in this way

**guid·ance** (gīd′ns) *n.* **1** a guiding; leadership **2** advice or assistance

**guide** (gīd) *vt.* **guid'ed, guid'ing** ‖< OFr *guider*‖ **1** to point out the way for; lead **2** to direct the course of; control —*n.* **1** one whose work is conducting tours, etc. **2** a controlling device **3** a book of basic instruction

**guide'book'** *n.* a book containing directions and information for tourists

**guided missile** a military missile whose course is controlled as by electronic signals

**guide'line'** *n.* a principle by which to determine a course of action

**guild** (gild) *n.* ‖< OE *gieldan*, to pay‖ an association for mutual aid and the promotion of common interests

**guil·der** (gil′dər) *n.* ‖< MDu *gulden*, golden‖ the monetary unit of the Netherlands

**guile** (gīl) *n.* ‖< OFr‖ slyness and cunning in dealing with others —**guile'ful** *adj.* —**guile'less** *adj.*

**guil·lo·tine** (gil′ə tēn′, gē′ə-; *for v., usually* gil′ə tēn′, gē′ə-) *n.* ‖Fr: after J. *Guillotin* (1738-1814), Fr physician who advocated its use‖ an instrument for beheading, having a heavy blade dropped between two grooved uprights —*vt.* **-tined′, -tin'ing** to behead with a guillotine

**guilt** (gilt) *n.* ‖OE *gylt*, a sin‖ **1** the state of having done a wrong or committed an offense **2** a feeling of self-reproach from believing that one has done a wrong —**guilt'less** *adj.*

**guilt'y** *adj.* **-i·er, -i·est 1** having guilt **2** legally judged an offender **3** of or showing guilt [a *guilty* look] —**guilt'i·ly** *adv.* —**guilt'i·ness** *n.*

**guin·ea** (gin′ē) *n.* ‖first coined of gold from *Guinea*‖ a former English gold coin equal to 21 shillings

**Guin·ea** (gin′ē) country on the W coast of Africa: 94,926 sq. mi.; pop. 7,300,000

**Guin'ea-Bis·sau'** (-bi sou′) country on the W coast of Africa: 13,948 sq. mi.; pop. 777,000

**guinea fowl** (or **hen**) ‖orig. imported from *Guinea*‖ a domestic fowl with a rounded body and speckled feathers

**guinea pig** ‖prob. orig. brought to England by ships plying between *Guinea*, *Guinea*, and South America‖ **1** a small, plump rodent, often used in biological experiments **2** any subject used in an experiment

**guise** (gīz) *n.* ‖< OHG *wisa*, manner‖ **1** manner of dress; garb **2** outward appearance **3** a false appearance; pretense

**gui·tar** (gi tär′) *n.* ⟦ult. < Gr *kithara*, lyre⟧ a musical instrument with usually six strings plucked with the fingers or a plectrum —**gui·tar′ist** *n.*

**gulch** (gulch) *n.* ⟦prob. < dial., to swallow greedily⟧ a deep, narrow ravine

**gulf** (gulf) *n.* ⟦ult. < Gr *kolpos*, bosom⟧ **1** a large area of ocean reaching into land **2** a wide, deep chasm **3** a wide gap or separation

**Gulf Stream** warm ocean current flowing from the Gulf of Mexico northward and then eastward toward Europe

**gull**[1] (gul) *n.* ⟦< Celt⟧ a white and gray water bird with webbed feet

**gull**[2] (gul) *n.* ⟦ME, lit., unfledged bird⟧ a person easily tricked; dupe —*vt.* to cheat or trick

**gul·let** (gul′ət) *n.* ⟦< L *gula*, throat⟧ **1** the esophagus **2** the throat

**gul·li·ble** (gul′ə bəl) *adj.* easily gulled; credulous —**gul′li·bil′i·ty** *n.*

**gul·ly** (gul′ē) *n., pl.* **-lies** ⟦see GULLET⟧ a small, narrow ravine

**gulp** (gulp) *vt.* ⟦prob. < Du *gulpen*⟧ to swallow hastily or greedily —*vi.* to catch the breath as in swallowing —*n.* a gulping or swallowing

**gum**[1] (gum) *n.* ⟦< LL *gumma*⟧ **1** a sticky substance found in certain trees and plants **2** an adhesive **3** CHEWING GUM —*vt.* **gummed, gum′ming** to coat or unite with gum —**gum up** [Slang] to cause to go awry —**gum′my, -mi·er, -mi·est,** *adj.*

**gum**[2] (gum) *n.* ⟦OE *goma*⟧ [often *pl.*] the firm flesh surrounding the base of the teeth —*vt.* **gummed, gum′ming** to chew with toothless gums

**gum arabic** a gum from certain acacias, used in medicine, candy, etc.

**gum·bo** (gum′bō) *n.* ⟦< Bantu name for okra⟧ a soup thickened with okra

**gum′drop′** *n.* a small, firm candy made of sweetened gelatin, etc.

**gump·tion** (gump′shən) *n.* ⟦< Scot⟧ [Inf.] courage and initiative

**gun** (gun) *n.* ⟦< ME *gonnilde*, cannon < ON⟧ **1** any weapon with a metal tube from which a projectile is discharged by the force of an explosive **2** any similar device not discharged by an explosive [an air *gun*] **3** anything like a gun in shape or use —*vi.* **gunned, gun′ning** to shoot or hunt with a gun —*vt.* **1** [Inf.] to shoot (a person) **2** [Slang] to advance the throttle of (an engine) —**gun for** [Slang] to try to get —**jump the gun** [Inf.] to begin before the proper time —**stick to one's guns** [Inf.] to be resolute —**under the gun** [Inf.] in a tense situation, often one involving a deadline

**gun′boat′** *n.* a small armed ship

**gun′fight′** *n.* a fight between persons using pistols or revolvers —**gun′fight′er** *n.*

**gun′fire′** *n.* the firing of guns

**gung-ho** (guŋ′hō′) *adj.* ⟦Chin *kung-ho*, lit., work together⟧ [Inf.] enthusiastic

**gunk** (guŋk) *n.* ⟦< ?⟧ [Slang] any viscous or thick, messy substance

**gun′man** (-mən) *n., pl.* **-men** (-mən) an armed gangster or hired killer

**gun′met′al** *n.* **1** a bronze with a dark tarnish **2** its dark-gray color

**gun′ner** *n.* **1** a soldier, etc. who helps fire artillery **2** a naval warrant officer in charge of guns, missiles, etc.

**gun′ner·y** *n.* the science of making and using heavy guns and projectiles

**gun·ny** (gun′ē) *n., pl.* **-nies** ⟦< Sans *gōnī*, a sack⟧ a coarse fabric of jute or hemp

**gun′ny·sack′** *n.* a sack made of gunny

**gun′play′** *n.* an exchange of gunshots, as between gunmen and police

**gun′point′** *n.* used chiefly in **at gunpoint,** under threat of being shot with a gun at close range

**gun′pow′der** *n.* an explosive powder used in guns, for blasting, etc.

**gun′ship′** *n.* a heavily armed helicopter used to assault enemy ground forces

**gun′shot′** *n.* the shooting of a gun

**gun′-shy′** *adj.* **1** easily frightened at the firing of a gun [a *gun-shy* dog] **2** wary, mistrustful, etc., as because of a previous experience

**gun′smith′** *n.* one who makes or repairs small guns

**gun·wale** (gun′əl) *n.* ⟦< bulwarks supporting a ship's guns⟧ the upper edge of the side of a ship or boat

**gup·py** (gup′ē) *n., pl.* **-pies** ⟦after R. J. L. *Guppy*, of Trinidad⟧ a very small freshwater fish of the West Indies, etc.

**gur·gle** (gur′gəl) *vi.* **-gled, -gling** ⟦< L *gurgulio*, gullet⟧ to make a bubbling sound —*n.* such a sound

**gur·ney** (gur′nē) *n., pl.* **-neys** ⟦< ?⟧ a hospital stretcher on wheels

**gu·ru** (gōō′rōō′; *also* gōō rōō′) *n.* ⟦< Sans *guruh*, venerable⟧ in Hinduism, one's personal spiritual advisor or teacher

**gush** (gush) *vi.* ⟦ME *guschen*⟧ **1** to flow out plentifully **2** to have a sudden flow **3** to talk or write effusively —*vt.* to cause to gush —*n.* a gushing —**gush′y, -i·er, -i·est,** *adj.*

**gush′er** *n.* **1** one who gushes **2** an oil well from which oil spouts forth

**gus·set** (gus′it) *n.* ⟦< OFr *gousset*⟧ a triangular piece inserted in a garment, etc. to make it stronger or roomier

**gus·sy** or **gus·sie** (gus′ē) *vt., vi.* **-sied, -sy·ing** ⟦nickname for *Augusta*, a feminine name⟧ [Slang] to dress (*up*) in a fine or showy way

**gust** (gust) *n.* ⟦< ON *gjosa*, to gush⟧ **1** a sudden, strong rush of air **2** a sudden outburst of rain, laughter, etc. —**gust′y, -i·er, -i·est,** *adj.*

**gus·ta·to·ry** (gus′tə tôr′ē) *adj.* ⟦< L *gustus*, taste⟧ of the sense of taste

**gus·to** (gus′tō) *n.* ⟦see prec.⟧ **1** zest; relish **2** great vigor or liveliness

**gut** (gut) *n.* ⟦< OE *geotan*, to pour⟧ **1** [*pl.*] the entrails **2** the stomach or belly **3** the intestine **4** tough cord made from animal intestines **5** [*pl.*] [Inf.] daring; courage —*vt.* **gut′ted, gut′ting 1** to remove the intestines from **2** to destroy the interior of —*adj.* [Slang] **1** basic **2** easy

**gut′less** *adj.* [Inf.] lacking courage

**guts·y** (gut′sē) *adj.* **-i·er, -i·est** [Inf.] courageous, forceful, etc.

**gut·ter** (gut′ər) *n.* ⟦< L *gutta*, a drop⟧ **1** a channel to carry off water, as along the eaves of a roof or the side of a street **2** a place or condition characterized by squalor —*vi.* to flow in a stream

**gut·tur·al** (gut′ər əl) *adj.* ⟦L *guttur*, throat⟧ harsh; rasping: said of vocal sounds

**guv** (guv) *n. slang var. of* GOVERNOR

**guy**[1] (gī) *n.* ⟦< OFr *guier*, to guide⟧ a rope, chain, etc. used to steady or guide something —*vt.* to guide or steady with a guy

**guy**[2] (gī) [Inf.] *n.* ⟦after *Guy* Fawkes, Eng conspirator⟧ **1** a man or boy **2** any person —*vt.* to make fun of; ridicule

**Guy·a·na** (gī an′ə) country in NE South America: 83,000 sq. mi.; pop. 730,000

**guz·zle** (guz′əl) *vi., vt.* **-zled, -zling** ⟦< ? OFr *gosier*, throat⟧ to drink greedily or continually

**gym** (jim) *n.* [Inf.] **1** *short for* GYMNASIUM **2** PHYSICAL EDUCATION

**gym·na·si·um** (jim nā′zē əm) *n., pl.* **-si·ums** or **-si·a** (-ə) ⟦< Gr *gymnos*, naked⟧ a room or building equipped for physical training and sports

**gym·nas·tics** (jim nas′tiks) *n.* a sport combining tumbling and acrobatic feats —**gym′nast′** *n.* —**gym·nas′tic** *adj.* —**gym·nas′ti·cal·ly** *adv.*

**gym·no·sperm** (jim′nō spurm′, -nə-) *n.* ⟦< Gr *gymnos*, naked + *sperma*, seed⟧ any of a large division of seed plants, as seed ferns, conifers, etc., having the ovules not enclosed within an ovary

**GYN** *abbrev.* **1** gynecologic(al) **2** gynecologist **3** gynecology

**gy·ne·col·o·gy** (gī′nə käl′ə jē) *n.* ⟦< Gr *gynē*, woman + -LOGY⟧ the branch of medicine dealing with women's diseases, etc. —**gy′ne·co·log′ic** (-kə läj′ik) or **gy′ne·co·log′i·cal** *adj.* —**gy′ne·col′o·gist** *n.*

**gyp** (jip) [Inf.] *n.* ⟦prob. < GYPSY⟧ **1** a swindle **2** a swindler: also **gyp′per** or **gyp′ster** —*vt.*, *vi.* **gypped, gyp′ping** to swindle; cheat

**gyp·sum** (jip′səm) *n.* ⟦< Gr *gypsos*⟧ a sulfate of calcium used to make plaster of Paris and cement

**Gyp·sy** (jip′sē) *n.*, *pl.* **-sies** ⟦< *Egipcien*, Egyptian: orig. thought to be from Egypt⟧ **1** [*also* **g-**] a member of a wandering Caucasoid people, perhaps orig. from India, with dark skin and black hair **2** the language of this people; Romany **3** [**g-**] one who looks or lives like a Gypsy

**gypsy moth** a moth in the E U.S.: its larvae feed on leaves, damaging trees

**gy·rate** (jī′rāt′) *vi.* **-rat′ed, -rat′ing** ⟦< Gr *gyros*, a circle⟧ to move in a circular or spiral path; whirl —**gy·ra′tion** *n.* —**gy′ra·tor** *n.*

**gy·ro** (yir′ō, jī′rō′) *n.*, *pl.* **-ros** ⟦see prec.⟧ **1** layers of lamb and beef roasted and sliced **2** a pita sandwich of this Also **gy·ros** (yir′ôs)

**gyro-** ⟦see GYRATE⟧ *combining form* gyrating [*gyroscope*]

**gy·ro·scope** (jī′rō skōp′, -rə-) *n.* ⟦prec. + -SCOPE⟧ a wheel mounted in a set of rings so that its axis is free to turn in any direction: when the wheel is spun rapidly, it will keep its original plane of rotation

GYROSCOPE

# H

**h** or **H** (āch) *n.*, *pl.* **h's, H's** the eighth letter of the English alphabet

**H¹** or **h** *abbrev.* **1** height **2** high **3** *Baseball* hit(s) **4** hour(s) **5** hundred(s) **6** husband

**H²** *Chem. symbol for* hydrogen

**ha** (hä) *interj.* ⟦echoic⟧ used to express surprise, wonder, anger, triumph, etc.

**ha·be·as cor·pus** (hā′bē əs kôr′pəs) ⟦L, (that) you have the body⟧ *Law* a writ requiring that a detained person be brought before a court to decide the legality of the detention

**hab·er·dash·er** (hab′ər dash′ər) *n.* ⟦< ME⟧ a dealer in men's hats, shirts, neckties, etc. —**hab′er·dash′er·y** *n.*

**ha·bil·i·ment** (hə bil′ə mənt) *n.* ⟦< MFr *habiller*, to clothe⟧ **1** [*usually pl.*] clothing; attire **2** [*pl.*] equipment; trappings

**hab·it** (hab′it) *n.* ⟦< L *habere*, to have⟧ **1** a distinctive costume, as of a nun **2** a thing done often and, hence, easily **3** a usual way of doing **4** an addiction, esp. to narcotics

**hab·it·a·ble** *adj.* fit to be lived in

**hab·i·tat** (hab′i tat′) *n.* ⟦L, it inhabits⟧ **1** the region where a plant or animal naturally lives **2** the place where a person is ordinarily found

**hab·i·ta·tion** (hab′i tā′shən) *n.* **1** an inhabiting **2** a dwelling; home

**hab·it-form′ing** *adj.* resulting in the formation of a habit or in addiction

**ha·bit·u·al** (hə bich′ōō əl) *adj.* **1** done or acquired by habit **2** steady; inveterate [a *habitual* smoker] **3** much seen, done, or used; usual —**ha·bit′u·al·ly** *adv.* —**ha·bit′u·al·ness** *n.*

**ha·bit·u·ate′** (-āt′) *vt.* **-at′ed, -at′ing** to accustom (*to*) —**ha·bit′u·a′tion** *n.*

**ha·bit′u·é′** (-ā′) *n.* ⟦Fr⟧ one who frequents a certain place

**ha·ci·en·da** (hä′sē en′də) *n.* ⟦Sp < L *facere*, do⟧ in Spanish America, a large estate or ranch, or its main house

**hack¹** (hak) *vt.* ⟦OE *haccian*⟧ to chop or cut crudely, roughly, etc. —*vi.* **1** to make rough cuts **2** to give harsh, dry coughs —*n.* **1** a gash **2** a harsh, dry cough

**hack²** (hak) *n.* ⟦< HACKNEY⟧ **1** a horse for hire **2** an old, worn-out horse **3** one hired to do routine or dull writing **4** a coach for hire **5** [Inf.] a taxicab —*adj.* **1** employed as, or done by, a hack [*hack* writer] **2** trite; hackneyed

**hack′er** *n.* **1** an unskilled golfer, etc. **2** a talented amateur user of computers

**hack·le** (hak′əl) *n.* ⟦ME *hechele*⟧ **1** the neck feathers of a rooster, pigeon, etc. **2** [*pl.*] the hairs on a dog's neck and back that bristle

**hack·ney** (hak′nē) *n.*, *pl.* **-neys** ⟦after *Hackney*, England⟧ **1** a horse for driving or riding **2** a carriage for hire

**hack′neyed′** (-nēd′) *adj.* made trite by overuse

**hack′saw′** *n.* a fine-toothed saw for cutting metal: also **hack saw**

**had** (had) *vt. pt. & pp. of* HAVE

**had·dock** (had′ək) *n.*, *pl.* **-dock** or **-docks** ⟦ME *hadok*⟧ an Atlantic food fish, related to the cod

**Ha·des** (hā′dēz′) *n.* ⟦Gr *Haidēs*⟧ **1** *Gr. Myth.* the home of the dead **2** [*often* **h-**] hell

**haft** (haft) *n.* ⟦OE *hæft*⟧ the handle or hilt of a knife, ax, etc.

**hag** (hag) *n.* ⟦< OE *hægtes*⟧ **1** a witch **2** an ugly, often vicious old woman —**hag′gish** *adj.*

**hag·gard** (hag′ərd) *adj.* ⟦MFr *hagard*, untamed (hawk)⟧ having a wild, wasted, worn look; gaunt

**hag·gle** (hag′əl) *vi.* **-gled, -gling** ⟦< Scot *hag*, to hack⟧ to argue about terms, price, etc. —*n.* a haggling —**hag′gler** *n.*

**Hague** (hāg), **The** political capital of the Netherlands (cf. AMSTERDAM): pop. 445,000

**hah** (hä) *interj.*, *n.* HA

**hai·ku** (hī′kōō′) *n.* ⟦Jpn⟧ **1** a Japanese verse form of three unrhymed lines of 5, 7, and 5 syllables, respectively **2** *pl.* **-ku** a poem in this form

**hail¹** (hāl) *vt.* ⟦< ON *heill*, whole, sound⟧ **1** to greet with cheers; acclaim **2** to call out to [to *hail* a cab] —*n.* a greeting —*interj.* used to signify tribute, greeting, etc. —**hail from** to be from

**hail²** (hāl) *n.* ⟦OE *hægel*⟧ **1** frozen raindrops falling during thunderstorms **2** a shower of or like hail —*vt.*, *vi.* to pour down like hail

**hail′stone′** *n.* a pellet of hail

**hail′storm′** *n.* a storm with hail

**hair** (her, har) *n.* ⟦OE *hær*⟧ **1** any of the threadlike outgrowths from the skin **2** a growth of these, as on the human head **3** a very small space, degree, etc. **4** a threadlike growth on a plant —**get in someone's hair** [Slang] to annoy someone —**split hairs** to quibble —**hair′less** *adj.* —**hair′like′** *adj.*

**hair′ball′** *n.* a ball of hair that may form in the stomach of a cow, cat, or other animal that licks its coat

**hair′breadth′** (-bredth′) *n.* an extremely small space or amount —*adj.* very narrow; close Also **hairs′breadth′** or **hair′s-breadth′**

**hair′cut′** *n.* the act of, or a style of, cutting the hair

**hair'do'** (-dōō') *n.*, *pl.* **-dos'** the style in which hair is arranged; coiffure

**hair'dress'er** *n.* one whose work is dressing, or arranging, hair

**-haired** (herd) having (a specified kind of) hair [*short-haired*]

**hair'line'** *n.* **1** a very thin line **2** the outline of the hair on the head

**hair'piece'** *n.* a toupee or wig

**hair'pin'** *n.* a small, bent piece of wire, etc., for keeping the hair in place —*adj.* U-shaped [a *hairpin* turn in the road]

**hair'-rais'ing** *adj.* terrifying or shocking

**hair'split'ting** *adj.*, *n.* making petty distinctions

**hair'spring'** *n.* a slender, hairlike coil spring, as in a watch

**hair'y** *adj.* **-i·er**, **-i·est** covered with hair —**hair'i·ness** *n.*

**Hai·ti** (hāt'ē) country occupying the W portion of the island of Hispaniola, West Indies: 10,700 sq. mi.; pop. 5,054,000 —**Hai·tian** (hā'shən) *adj.*, *n.*

**hake** (hāk) *n.* [prob. < ON] a marine food fish related to the cod

**hal·berd** (hal'bərd) *n.* [ult. < MHG *helmbarte*] a combined spear and battle-ax of the 15th-16th c.

**hal·cy·on** (hal'sē ən) *adj.* [< Gr *alkyōn*, kingfisher (fabled calmer of the sea)] tranquil, happy, idyllic, etc. [*halcyon* days]

**hale**[1] (hāl) *adj.* **hal'er**, **hal'est** [OE *hal*] vigorous and healthy

**hale**[2] (hāl) *vt.* **haled**, **hal'ing** [< OFr *haler*] to force (a person) to go [*haled* him into court]

**half** (haf, häf) *n.*, *pl.* **halves** [OE *healf*] **1** either of the two equal parts of something **2** either of the two equal parts of some games —*adj.* **1** being a half **2** incomplete; partial —*adv.* **1** to the extent of a half **2** partly [*half* done] **3** at all: used with *not* [not *half* bad]

**half-** *combining form* **1** one half [*half*-life] **2** partly [*half*-baked]

**half'-and-half'** *n.* something that is half of one thing and half of another, as a mixture of milk and cream —*adj.* combining two things equally —*adv.* in two equal parts

**half'back'** *n.* *Football* one of the running backs, typically smaller and faster than a fullback

**half'-breed'** *n.* one whose parents are of different ethnic types: an offensive term

**half brother** a brother through one parent only

**half dollar** a coin of the U.S. or Canada, worth 50 cents

**half'heart'ed** *adj.* with little enthusiasm, determination, interest, etc. —**half'heart'ed·ly** *adv.*

**half'-life'** *n.* the constant time period required for the disintegration of half of the atoms in a sample of a radioactive substance: also **half life**

**half'-mast'** *n.* the position of a flag halfway down its staff, esp. as a sign of mourning

**half note** *Music* a note having one half the duration of a whole note

**half·pen·ny** (hāp'nē, hā'pən ē) *n.*, *pl.* **-pence** (hā'pəns) or **-pen·nies** a former British coin equal to half a penny

**half sister** a sister through one parent only

**half sole** a sole (of a shoe or boot) from the arch to the toe

**half'track'** *n.* an army truck, armored vehicle, etc. with tractor treads instead of rear wheels

**half'way'** *adj.* **1** midway between two points, etc. **2** partial [*halfway* measures] —*adv.* **1** to the midway point **2** partially —**meet halfway** to be willing to compromise (with)

**halfway house** a place for helping people adjust to society after being imprisoned, hospitalized, etc.

**half'-wit'** *n.* a stupid or silly person; fool —**half'-wit'ted** *adj.*

**hal·i·but** (hal'ə bət) *n.*, *pl.* **-but** or **-buts** [ME *hali*, holy + *butt*, a flounder (so called because eaten on holidays)] a large, edible flounder found in northern seas

**Hal·i·fax** (hal'ə faks') capital of Nova Scotia, Canada: pop. 114,000

**hal·ite** (hal'īt, hā'līt) *n.* rock salt

**hal·i·to·sis** (hal'i tō'sis) *n.* [< L *halitus*, breath] bad-smelling breath

**hall** (hôl) *n.* [OE *heall*] **1** the main dwelling on an estate **2** a public building with offices, etc. **3** a large room for gatherings, exhibits, etc. **4** a college building **5** a vestibule at the entrance of a building **6** an area onto which rooms open

**hal·le·lu·jah** or **hal·le·lu·iah** (hal'ə lōō'yə) *interj.* [< Heb < *hallelū*, praise (imper.) + *yāh*, Jehovah] used to express praise, thanks, etc., esp. in a hymn or prayer —*n.* a hymn of praise to God

**hall·mark** (hôl'märk') *n.* [< the mark stamped on gold and silver articles at Goldsmith's Hall] a mark or symbol of genuineness or high quality

**hal·loo** (hə lōō') *n.*, *interj.* (a shout or call) used esp. to attract attention —*vi.*, *vt.* **-looed'**, **-loo'ing** to call out (to)

**hal·low** (hal'ō) *vt.* [OE *halgian*] to make or regard as holy

**hal'lowed** (-ōd) *adj.* holy or sacred

**Hal·low·een** or **Hal·low·e'en** (hal'ə wēn', häl'-) *n.* [contr. < *all hallow even*] the evening of Oct. 31, followed by All Saints' Day: now celebrated with masquerading, etc.

**hal·lu·ci·nate** (hə lōō'si nāt') *vi.*, *vt.* **-nat'ed**, **-nat'ing** [see fol.] to have or cause to have hallucinations

**hal·lu·ci·na·tion** (hə lōō'si nā'shən) *n.* [< L *hallucinari*, to wander mentally] **1** the apparent perception of sights, sounds, etc. that are not actually present **2** the thing perceived —**hal·lu·ci·na·to·ry** (-nə tôr'ē) *adj.*

**hal·lu·ci·no·gen** (hə lōō'si nə jən) *n.* a drug or other substance that produces hallucinations —**hal·lu·ci·no·gen'ic** *adj.*

**hall'way'** *n.* a passageway; corridor

**ha·lo** (hā'lō) *n.*, *pl.* **-los** or **-loes** [< Gr *halōs*, circular threshing floor] **1** a ring of light, as around the sun **2** a symbolic ring of light around the head of a saint, etc., as in pictures

**hal·o·gen** (hal'ə jən) *n.* [< Gr *hals*, salt] any of the five nonmetallic chemical elements fluorine, chlorine, bromine, astatine, and iodine

**halt**[1] (hôlt) *n.*, *vi.*, *vt.* [< Ger *halt machen*] stop

**halt**[2] (hôlt) *vi.* [< OE *healt*] **1** [Archaic] to limp **2** to hesitate —*adj.* lame —**the halt** those who are lame

**hal·ter** (hôl'tər) *n.* [OE *hælftre*] **1** a rope or strap for tying or leading an animal **2** a hangman's noose **3** a woman's upper garment, held up by a loop around the neck

**halve** (hav, häv) *vt.* **halved**, **halv'ing** **1** to divide into two equal parts **2** to reduce to half

**halves** (havz, hävz) *n.* *pl.* of HALF —**by halves** halfway; imperfectly —**go halves** to share expenses equally

HALTER

**hal·yard** (hal'yərd) *n.* [< ME *halier*: see HALE[2]] a rope or tackle for raising or lowering a flag, sail, etc.

**ham** (ham) *n.* [OE *hamm*] **1** the back of the thigh **2** the upper part of a hog's hind leg, salted, smoked, etc. **3** [Inf.] an amateur radio operator **4** [Slang] an actor who overacts —**ham'my**, **-mi·er**, **-mi·est**, *adj.*

**Ham·burg** (ham'bərg) seaport in N Germany: pop. 1,603,000

**ham·burg·er** (ham'bur'gər) *n.* [after *Hamburg*, Germany] **1** ground beef **2** a cooked patty of such meat, often in a sandwich Also **ham'burg** (-bərg)

**Ham·il·ton**[1] (ham'əl tən), **Alexander** 1755?-1804; Am. statesman

**Ham·il·ton**[2] (ham′əl tən) city & port in SE Ontario, Canada: pop. 322,000

**ham·let** (ham′lit) *n.* 〖< OFr *hamelete* < LowG *hamm*, enclosed area〗 a very small village

**Ham·let** (ham′lit) *n.* the title hero of a tragedy by Shakespeare

**ham·mer** (ham′ər) *n.* 〖OE *hamor*〗 1 a tool for pounding, having a metal head and a handle 2 a thing like this in shape or use, as the part of a gun that strikes the firing pin 3 one of the three small bones in the middle ear —*vt., vi.* 1 to strike repeatedly, as with a hammer 2 to drive, force, or shape, as with hammer blows —**hammer (away)** at to keep emphasizing —**ham′mer·er** *n.*

**hammer and sickle** the emblem of Communist parties in some countries

**ham′mer·head′** *n.* 1 the head of a hammer 2 a shark with a mallet-shaped head having an eye at each end

**ham′mer·toe′** *n.* a toe that is deformed, with its first joint bent downward

**ham·mock** (ham′ək) *n.* 〖Sp *hamaca*, of WInd orig.〗 a kind of bed of canvas, etc. swung from ropes at both ends

**ham·per**[1] (ham′pər) *vt.* 〖ME *hampren*〗 to hinder; impede; encumber

**ham·per**[2] (ham′pər) *n.* 〖< OFr *hanap*, a cup〗 a large basket, usually covered

**ham·ster** (ham′stər) *n.* 〖< OHG *hamustro*〗 a rodent of Europe and Asia, used in scientific experiments or kept as a pet

**ham·string** (ham′striŋ′) *n.* a tendon at the back of the knee —*vt.* **-strung′, -string′ing** 1 to disable by cutting a hamstring 2 to lessen the power of

**hand** (hand) *n.* 〖OE〗 1 the body part attached to the wrist, used for grasping 2 a side or direction [at my right *hand*] 3 [*pl.*] possession or care [the land is in my *hands*] 4 control [to strengthen one's *hand*] 5 an active part [take a *hand* in the work] 6 a promise to marry 7 skill 8 one having a special skill 9 manner of doing something 10 handwriting 11 applause 12 help [to lend a *hand*] 13 a hired worker [a farm *hand*] 14 a source [to get news at first *hand*] 15 anything like a hand, as a pointer on a clock 16 the breadth of a hand 17 *Card Games a)* the cards held by a player at one time *b)* a round of play — *adj.* of, for, or controlled by the hand —*vt.* 1 to give as with the hand 2 to help or conduct with the hand —**at hand** near —**hand in hand** together —**hand it to** [Slang] to give credit to —**hand over fist** [Inf.] easily and in large amounts —**hands down** easily —**on hand** 1 near 2 available 3 present —**on the one** (or **other**) **hand** from one (or the opposed) point of view

**hand′bag′** *n.* a woman's purse

**hand′ball′** *n.* a game in which players bat a small rubber ball against a wall with their hands

**hand′bar′row** *n.* a frame carried by two people holding handles at the ends

**hand′bill′** *n.* a small printed notice to be passed out by hand

**hand′book′** *n.* a compact reference book; manual

**hand′breadth′** *n.* the breadth of the human palm, about 4 inches

**hand′car′** *n.* a small, open car, originally hand-powered, used on railroads

**hand′cart′** *n.* a small cart moved by hand

**hand′clasp′** *n.* HANDSHAKE

**hand′craft′** *n.* HANDICRAFT —*vt.* to make skillfully by hand —**hand′craft′ed** *adj.*

**hand′cuff′** *n.* either of a pair of connected rings for shackling the wrists of a prisoner: *usually used in pl.* —*vt.* to put handcuffs on; manacle

**-hand·ed** (han′did) *combining form* having or involving (a specified kind or number of) hands [right-*handed*, two-*handed*]

**Han·del** (han′dəl), **George Fri·der·ic** (frē′dər ik, -drik) 1685-1759; Eng. composer, born in Germany

**hand′ful′** *n., pl.* **-fuls′** 1 as much or as many as the hand will hold 2 a few; not many 3 [Inf.] someone or something that is hard to manage

**hand′gun′** *n.* any firearm that is held and fired with one hand, as a pistol

**hand′-held′** *adj.* small enough to be held in the hand while being used

**hand·i·cap** (hand′dē kap′) *n.* 〖< *hand in cap*, former kind of lottery〗 1 a competition in which difficulties are imposed on, or advantages given to, the various contestants to equalize their chances 2 such a difficulty or advantage 3 *a)* any hindrance *b)* a physical disability —*vt.* **-capped′, -cap′ping** 1 to give a handicap to 2 to hinder — **the handicapped** those who are physically disabled or mentally retarded

**hand′i·capped′** *adj.* physically disabled

**hand′i·cap′per** *n.* a person, as a sportswriter, who tries to predict the winners in horse races

**hand·i·craft** (han′dē kraft′) *n.* skill with the hands, or work calling for it

**hand′i·work′** *n.* 1 HANDWORK 2 anything made or done by a particular person

**hand·ker·chief** (haŋ′kər chif′) *n.* 〖HAND + KERCHIEF〗 a small cloth used for wiping the nose, face, etc., or worn for ornament

**han·dle** (han′dəl) *n.* 〖OE < *hand*〗 that part of a tool, etc. by which it is held, lifted, etc. —*vt.* **-dled, -dling** 1 to touch, lift, operate, etc. with the hand 2 to manage; control 3 to deal with; treat 4 to sell or deal in —*vi.* to respond to control [the car *handles* well] —**han′dler** *n.*

**han′dle·bar′** *n.* [*often pl.*] a curved metal bar with handles on the ends, for steering a bicycle, etc.

**hand′made′** *adj.* made by hand, not by machine

**hand′maid′en** *n.* [Archaic] a woman or girl servant: also **hand′maid′**

**hand′-me-down′** *n.* [Inf.] a used garment, etc. passed on to another person

**hand′out′** *n.* 1 a gift of food, clothing, etc., as to a beggar 2 a leaflet handed out 3 a news release

**hand′pick′** *vt.* 1 to pick by hand 2 to choose with care or for a purpose

**hand′rail′** *n.* a rail serving as a guard or support, as along a staircase

**hand′set′** *n.* a telephone mouthpiece and receiver in a single unit

**hand′shake′** *n.* a gripping of each other's hand in greeting, agreement, etc.

**hands′-off′** *adj.* designating or of a policy, etc. of not interfering or intervening

**hand·some** (han′səm, hand′-) *adj.* 〖orig., easily handled〗 1 large; considerable 2 generous; gracious 3 good-looking, esp. in a manly or impressive way —**hand′some·ness** *n.*

**hand′spring′** *n.* an acrobatic feat in which one turns over in midair with one or both hands touching the ground

**hand′-to-hand′** *adj.* at close quarters: said of fighting

**hand′-to-mouth′** *adj.* needing to consume all that is obtained

**hand′work′** *n.* work done or made by hand

**hand′wring′ing** or **hand′wring′ing** *n.* expression of distress or anxiety

**hand′writ′ing** *n.* 1 writing done by hand, with a pen, a pencil, etc. 2 a style of such writing — **hand′writ′ten** *adj.*

**hand′y** *adj.* **-i·er, -i·est** 1 close at hand; easily reached 2 easily used; convenient 3 clever with the hands; deft —**hand′i·ly** *adv.* —**hand′i·ness** *n.*

**hand′y·man′** (-man′) *n., pl.* **-men′** (-men′) a man who does odd jobs

**hang** (haŋ) *vt.* **hung, hang′ing**; for *vt.* 3 & *vi.* 5, **hanged** is preferred pt. & pp. 〖OE *hangian*〗 1 to attach from above with no support from below; suspend 2 to attach (a door, etc.) so as to permit free motion at the point of attachment 3 to kill by suspending from a rope about the neck 4 to attach (wallpaper, etc.) to walls 5 to let (one's head) droop downward 6 to deadlock (a jury) —

*vi.* **1** to be attached above with no support from below **2** to hover in the air **3** to swing freely **4** to fall or drape: said as of cloth **5** to die by hanging **6** to droop; bend —*n.* the way that a thing hangs —**get** (or **have**) **the hang of** **1** to learn (or have) the knack of **2** to understand the meaning or idea of —**hang around** (or **about**) [Inf.] to loiter around —**hang back** (or **off**) to be reluctant, as from shyness —**hang in** (**there**) [Inf.] to persevere —**hang loose** [Slang] to be relaxed, easygoing, etc. —**hang on** **1** to go on; persevere **2** to depend on **3** to listen attentively to —**hang out** [Slang] to spend much time —**hang up** **1** to put on a hanger, hook, etc. **2** to end a telephone call by replacing the receiver **3** to delay

**hang·ar** (haŋ′ər) *n.* [Fr] a repair shed or shelter for aircraft

**hang′dog′** *adj.* abject or ashamed

**hang′er** *n.* **1** one who hangs things **2** a thing on which something is hung

**hang gliding** the sport of gliding through the air while hanging suspended by a harness from a large type of kite (**hang glider**)

**hang′ing** *adj.* that hangs —*n.* **1** a killing by hanging **2** something hung on a wall, etc.

**hang′man** (-mən) *n.*, *pl.* **-men** (-mən) one who hangs convicted criminals

**hang′nail′** *n.* [OE *angnægl*, a corn (on the toe)] a bit of torn skin hanging next to a fingernail

**hang′o′ver** *n.* headache, nausea, etc. as an after-effect of drinking much alcoholic liquor

**hang′-up′** *n.* [Slang] an emotional or psychological problem, difficulty, etc.

**hank** (haŋk) *n.* [prob. < Scand] a skein of yarn or thread

**han·ker** (haŋ′kər) *vi.* [prob. < Du] to long or yearn: used with *for* — **han′ker·ing** *n.*

**han·ky-pan·ky** (haŋ′kē paŋ′kē) *n.* [Inf.] trickery or deception, as with illicit sex

**Ha·noi** (ha noi′) capital of Vietnam, in the N part: pop. 2,571,000

HANSOM CAB

**han·som** (**cab**) (han′səm) [after J. A. *Hansom* (1803-82), Eng inventor] a two-wheeled covered carriage pulled by one horse, with the driver's seat above and behind

**Ha·nuk·kah** (khä′noo kä′, -kə; hä′-) *n.* [< Heb *chanuka*, lit., dedication] an 8-day Jewish festival commemorating the rededication of the Temple: also **Ha′nu·ka′**

**hap** (hap) *n.* [< ON *happ*] luck

**hap·haz·ard** (hap′haz′ərd) *adj.* not planned; random —*adv.* by chance

**hap·less** (hap′lis) *adj.* unlucky

**hap·loid** (hap′loid′) *adj. Biol.* having the full number of chromosomes normally occurring in the mature germ cell, or half the number of the usual somatic cell —*n.* a haploid cell or gamete

**hap′ly** *adv.* [Archaic] by chance; perhaps

**hap·pen** (hap′ən) *vi.* [ME *happen*] **1** to take place; occur **2** to be, occur, or come by chance **3** to have the luck or occasion [I *happened* to see it] —**happen on** (or **upon**) to meet or find by chance

**hap′pen·ing** *n.* occurrence; event

**hap′pen·stance′** (-stans′) *n.* [Inf.] a chance or accidental happening

**hap·py** (hap′ē) *adj.* **-pi·er**, **-pi·est** [< HAP] **1** lucky; fortunate **2** having, showing, or causing great pleasure or joy **3** suitable and clever; apt — **hap′pi·ly** *adv.* —**hap′pi·ness** *n.*

**hap′py-go-luck′y** *adj.* easygoing

**happy hour** a time, as in the late afternoon, when a bar features drinks at reduced prices

**har·a-kir·i** (här′ə kir′ē) *n.* [Jpn < *hara*, belly + *kiri*, a cutting] ritual suicide by cutting the abdomen

**ha·rangue** (hə raŋ′) *n.* [< OIt *aringo*, site for public assemblies] a long, blustering speech; tirade —*vi.*, *vt.* **-rangued′**, **-rangu′ing** to speak or address in a harangue

**har·ass** (har′əs, hə ras′) *vt.* [< OFr *harer*, to set a dog on] **1** to worry or torment **2** to trouble by repeated raids or attacks —**har′ass·ment** *n.*

**Har·bin** (här′bin′) city in NE China: pop. 2,519,000

**har·bin·ger** (här′bin jər) *n.* [< OFr *herberge*, a shelter] a forerunner; herald

**har·bor** (här′bər) *n.* [< OE *here*, army + *beorg*, shelter] **1** a shelter **2** a protected inlet for anchoring ships; port —*vt.* **1** to shelter or house **2** to hold in the mind [to *harbor* envy] —*vi.* to take shelter Brit. sp. **har′bour**

**hard** (härd) *adj.* [OE *heard*] **1** firm and unyielding to the touch; solid and compact **2** powerful [a *hard* blow] **3** difficult to do, understand, or deal with **4** *a*) unfeeling [a *hard* heart] *b*) unfriendly [*hard* feelings] **5** harsh; severe **6** having mineral salts that interfere with lathering **7** energetic [a *hard* worker] **8** containing much alcohol [*hard* liquor] **9** addictive and harmful [heroin is a *hard* drug] **10** *a*) of currency, not credit (said of money) *b*) readily accepted as foreign exchange [a *hard* currency] —*adv.* **1** energetically [work *hard*] **2** with strength [hit *hard*] **3** with difficulty [*hard*-earned] **4** close; near [we live *hard* by] **5** so as to be solid [frozen *hard*] **6** fully [turn *hard* right] —**hard and fast** invariable; strict —**hard of hearing** partially deaf —**hard up** [Inf.] in great need of money —**hard′ness** *n.*

**hard′back′** *n.* a hardcover book

**hard′ball′** *n.* BASEBALL

**hard′-bit′ten** *adj.* tough; dogged

**hard′-boiled′** *adj.* **1** boiled until solid: said of an egg **2** [Inf.] unfeeling; tough; callous

**hard copy** a computer printout, often supplied along with or instead of a video screen display

**hard′-core′** *adj.* absolute; unqualified

**hard′cov′er** *adj.*, *n.* (designating) any book bound in a stiff cover

**hard disk** a computer disk with a rigid metal base

**hard drive** a computer drive for hard disks

**hard·en** (härd′n) *vt.*, *vi.* to make or become hard —**hard′en·er** *n.*

**hard hat** **1** a protective helmet worn by construction workers, miners, etc. **2** [Slang] such a worker

**hard′head′ed** *adj.* **1** shrewd and unsentimental; practical **2** stubborn; dogged

**hard′heart′ed** *adj.* unfeeling; cruel

**har·di·hood** (här′dē hood′) *n.* boldness

**Har·ding** (här′diŋ), **War·ren G(amaliel)** (wôr′ən, wär′-) 1865-1923; 29th president of the U.S. (1921-23)

**hard′line′** *adj.* aggressive; unyielding, as in politics, etc.

**hard′-lin′er** (-ər) *n.* one who takes a hard-line position

**hard·ly** (härd′lē) *adv.* **1** only just; scarcely **2** probably not; not likely

**hard′-nosed′** *adj.* [Inf.] tough and stubborn or shrewd

**hard′-pressed′** *adj.* confronted with a difficulty

**hard·scrab·ble** (härd′skrab′əl) *adj.* producing or earning only a very small amount; barren [a *hardscrabble* farm, life, etc.]

**hard sell** high-pressure salesmanship

**hard′ship′** *n.* a thing hard to bear, as poverty

**hard′stand′** *n.* a paved area for parking aircraft or other vehicles

**hard′tack′** *n.* unleavened bread made in large, hard wafers

**hard′top′** *n.* a motor vehicle having a rigid top

**hard′ware′** *n.* **1** articles made of metal, as tools,

nails, or fittings **2** the mechanical, magnetic, and electronic devices of a computer

**hard'wood'** *n.* **1** any tough, heavy timber with a compact texture **2** the wood of any tree with broad, flat leaves, as the oak or maple

**har·dy** (här'dē) *adj.* **-di·er, -di·est** ⟦< OFr *hardir*, to make bold⟧ **1** bold and resolute **2** robust; vigorous **—har'di·ly** *adv.* **—har'di·ness** *n.*

**hare** (her, har) *n.* ⟦OE *hara*⟧ a mammal related to and resembling the rabbit

**hare'brained'** *adj.* having or showing little sense, flighty, etc.

**Ha·re Krishna** (hä'rē) ⟦< Hindi⟧ a member of a cult stressing devotion to Krishna

**hare'lip'** *n.* CLEFT LIP

**ha·rem** (her'əm, har'-) *n.* ⟦Ar *harīm*, lit., prohibited (place)⟧ **1** the part of a Muslim household in which the women live **2** the women in a harem

**hark** (härk) *vi.* ⟦ME *herkien*⟧ to listen carefully: usually in the imperative **—hark back** to go back in thought or speech

**hark·en** (här'kən) *vi.* HEARKEN

**Har·le·quin** (här'li kwin, -kin) *n.* **1** a comic character in pantomime, who wears a mask and diamond-patterned tights of many colors **2** [h-] a clown

**har·lot** (här'lət) *n.* ⟦< OFr, rogue⟧ PROSTITUTE **—har'lot·ry** (-lə trē) *n.*

**harm** (härm) *n.* ⟦OE *hearm*⟧ hurt; injury; damage **—vt.** to do harm to

**harm'ful** *adj.* causing harm; hurtful **—harm'ful·ly** *adv.* **—harm'ful·ness** *n.*

**harm'less** *adj.* causing no harm **—harm'less·ly** *adv.* **—harm'less·ness** *n.*

**har·mon·ic** (här män'ik) *adj.* of or in harmony **—** *n. Music* a pure tone making up a composite tone **—har·mon'i·cal·ly** *adv.*

**har·mon'i·ca** (-i kə) *n.* a small wind instrument with metal reeds that vibrate and produce tones when air is blown or sucked across them

**har·mo·ni·ous** (här mō'nē əs) *adj.* **1** having parts arranged in an orderly or pleasing way **2** having similar ideas, interests, etc. **3** having musical tones combined to give a pleasing effect **—har·mo'ni·ous·ly** *adv.*

**har·mo·nize** (här'mə nīz') *vi.* **-nized', -niz'ing 1** to be in harmony **2** to sing in harmony **—vt.** to make harmonious **—har'mo·ni·za'tion** *n.* **—har'mo·niz'er** *n.*

**har·mo·ny** (här'mə nē) *n.*, *pl.* **-nies** ⟦< Gr *harmos*, a fitting⟧ **1** pleasing arrangement of parts in color, size, etc. **2** agreement in action, ideas, etc.; friendly relations **3** the sounding of two or more tones together in a chord, esp. when satisfying

**har·ness** (här'nis) *n.* ⟦< OFr *harneis*, armor⟧ **1** the combination of leather straps and metal pieces by which a horse, etc. is fastened to a vehicle, etc. **2** anything like this **—vt. 1** to put a harness on **2** to control so as to use the power of

**harp** (härp) *n.* ⟦OE *hearpe*⟧ a musical instrument having strings stretched vertically in an open, triangular frame and played by plucking **—vi. 1** to play a harp **2** to persist in talking or writing tediously (*on* or *upon* something) **—harp'ist** *n.*

**Har·pers Ferry** (här'pərz) town in West Virginia: site of an antislavery raid (1859): pop. 300

**har·poon** (här pōōn') *n.* ⟦< ON *harpa*, to squeeze⟧ a barbed spear with a line attached to it, used for spearing whales, etc. **—vt.** to strike or catch with a harpoon

**harp·si·chord** (härp'si kôrd') *n.* ⟦< It *arpa*, harp + *corda*, CORD⟧ a pianolike keyboard instrument whose strings are plucked rather than struck **—harp'si·chord'ist** *n.*

**Har·py** (här'pē) *n.*, *pl.* **-pies** ⟦< Gr *harpazein*, to snatch⟧ **1** *Gr. Myth.* any of several monsters, part woman and part bird **2** [h-] *a*) a greedy person *b*) a shrewish woman

**har·ri·dan** (har'i dən) *n.* ⟦prob. < Fr *haridelle*,

worn-out horse⟧ a nasty, bad-tempered old woman

**har·ri·er** (har'ē ər) *n.* ⟦< HARE + -IER⟧ **1** a small hound used for hunting hares **2** a cross-country runner

**Har·ris·burg** (har'is burg') capital of Pennsylvania, in the S part: pop. 52,000

**Har·ri·son** (har'ə sən) **1** Ben·ja·min (ben'jə mən) 1833-1901; 23d president of the U.S. (1889-93): grandson of William Henry **2** William Henry 1773-1841; 9th president of the U.S. (1841)

**har·row** (har'ō) *n.* ⟦prob. < ON⟧ a heavy frame with spikes or disks, used for breaking up and leveling plowed ground, etc. **—vt. 1** to draw a harrow over (land) **2** to cause mental distress to **—har'row·ing** *adj.*

**har·ry** (har'ē) *vt.* **-ried, -ry·ing** ⟦< OE *here*, army⟧ **1** to raid and ravage or rob **2** to torment or worry

**harsh** (härsh) *adj.* ⟦ME *harsk*⟧ **1** unpleasantly rough or sharp to the eye, ear, taste, or touch **2** offensive to the mind or feelings **3** cruel or severe **—harsh'ly** *adv.* **—harsh'ness** *n.*

**hart** (härt) *n.* ⟦OE *heorot*⟧ a full-grown, male European red deer

**har·te·beest** (här'tə bēst', härt'bēst') *n.* ⟦obs. Afrik < *harte*, hart + *beest*, beast⟧ a large African antelope with long horns curved backward

**Hart·ford** (härt'fərd) capital of Connecticut, in the central part: pop. 140,000

**har·um-scar·um** (her'əm sker'əm) *adj.* ⟦< ?⟧ reckless or irresponsible **—adv.** in a harumscarum way

**har·vest** (här'vist) *n.* ⟦OE *hærfest*⟧ **1** the time of the year when grain, fruit, etc. are gathered in **2** a season's crop **3** the gathering in of a crop **4** the outcome of any effort **—vt., vi.** to gather in (a crop, etc.) **—har'vest·er** *n.*

**has** (haz; *before "to"* has) *vt.* 3d pers. sing., pres. indic., of HAVE

**has'-been'** *n.* [Inf.] a person or thing whose popularity is past

**hash** (hash) *vt.* ⟦< Fr *hacher*, to chop⟧ to chop up (meat or vegetables) for cooking **—n. 1** a chopped mixture of cooked meat and vegetables, usually baked **2** a mixture **3** a muddle; mess **4** [Slang] hashish **—hash out** [Inf.] to settle by long discussion **—hash over** [Inf.] to discuss at length

**hash·ish** (hash'ēsh', ha shēsh') *n.* ⟦Ar *hashīsh*, dried hemp⟧ a narcotic and intoxicant made from hemp

**hasp** (hasp, häsp) *n.* ⟦OE *hæsp*⟧ a hinged fastening for a door, etc.; esp., a metal piece fitted over a staple and held in place by a pin or padlock

**has·sle** (has'əl) *n.* ⟦< ?⟧ [Inf.] **1** a heated argument; squabble **2** a troublesome situation **—vi. -sled, -sling** [Inf.] to have a hassle **—vt.** [Slang] to annoy, harass, etc.

HASP

**has·sock** (has'ək) *n.* ⟦OE *hassuc*, (clump of) coarse grass⟧ a firm cushion used as a footstool or seat

**hast** (hast) *vt.* archaic 2d pers. sing., pres. indic., of HAVE: used with *thou*

**haste** (hāst) *n.* ⟦OFr⟧ **1** quickness of motion; rapidity **2** careless or reckless hurrying **—make haste** to hurry

**has·ten** (hās'ən) *vt.* to cause to be or come faster; speed up **—vi.** to move or act swiftly; hurry

**hast·y** (hās'tē) *adj.* **-i·er, -i·est 1** done with haste; hurried **2** done, made, or acting rashly or too quickly **—hast'i·ly** *adv.* **—hast'i·ness** *n.*

**hat** (hat) *n.* ⟦OE *hætt*⟧ a head covering, usually with a brim and a crown **—pass the hat** to take up a collection **—talk through one's hat** [Inf.] to talk nonsense **—throw one's hat into the ring** to enter a contest, esp. one for political office **—under one's hat** [Inf.] strictly confidential

**hatch**[1] (hach) *vt.* ⟦ME *hacchen*⟧ **1** to bring forth (young) from (an egg or eggs) **2** to contrive (a plan, plot, etc.) —*vi.* **1** to bring forth young: said of eggs **2** to emerge from the egg

**hatch**[2] (hach) *n.* ⟦OE *hæcc*, grating⟧ **1** HATCHWAY **2** a lid for a hatchway

**hatch'back'** *n.* ⟦prec. + BACK⟧ an automobile with a rear section that swings up, giving wide entry to a storage area

**hat'check'** *adj.* of or working in a checkroom for hats, coats, etc.

**hatch·er·y** *n., pl.* **-ies** a place for hatching eggs, esp. of fish or poultry

**hatch·et** (hach'it) *n.* ⟦< OFr *hache*, an ax⟧ a small ax with a short handle —**bury the hatchet** to make peace

**hatchet job** [Inf.] a biased, malicious attack on another's character

**hatch'way'** *n.* an opening in a ship's deck, or in a floor or roof

**hate** (hāt) *vt.* **hat'ed, hat'ing** ⟦OE *hatian*⟧ **1** to have strong dislike or ill will for **2** to wish to avoid *[to hate fights]* —*vi.* to feel hatred —*n.* **1** a strong feeling of dislike or ill will; hatred **2** a person or thing hated —**hat'er** *n.*

**hate'ful** *adj.* **1** causing or deserving hate; loathsome **2** nasty, unpleasant, etc. —**hate'ful·ly** *adv.* —**hate'ful·ness** *n.*

**hath** (hath) *vt.* archaic 3d pers. sing., pres. indic., of HAVE

**ha·tred** (hā'trid) *n.* strong dislike or ill will; hate

**hat·ter** (hat'ər) *n.* one who makes, sells, or cleans hats, esp. men's hats

**hau·berk** (hô'bərk) *n.* ⟦< Frankish *hals*, neck + *bergan*, to protect⟧ a medieval coat of armor, usually of chain mail

**haugh·ty** (hôt'ē) *adj.* **-ti·er, -ti·est** ⟦< OFr *haut*, high⟧ having or showing great pride in oneself and contempt for others; arrogant —**haugh'ti·ly** *adv.* —**haugh'ti·ness** *n.*

**haul** (hôl) *vt.* ⟦< OFr *haler*⟧ **1** to move by pulling; drag **2** to transport by wagon, truck, etc. —*n.* **1** the act of hauling; pull **2** [Inf.] the amount gained, earned, etc. at one time **3** the distance over which something is transported —**haul off** [Inf.] to draw the arm back before hitting —**in (or over) the long haul** over a long period of time

**haunch** (hônch, hänch) *n.* ⟦< OFr *hanche* < Gmc⟧ **1** the hip, buttock, and upper thigh together **2** an animal's loin and leg together

**haunt** (hônt) *vt.* ⟦< OFr *hanter*, to frequent⟧ **1** to visit often or continually **2** to recur repeatedly to *[haunted* by memories*]* —*n.* a place often visited

**haunt'ed** *adj.* supposedly frequented by ghosts

**haunt'ing** *adj.* not easily forgotten

**haute cou·ture** (ōt'kōō tōor') [Fr, high sewing] high fashion for women

**haute cui·sine** (ōt'kwē zēn') ⟦Fr, high kitchen⟧ **1** the preparation of fine food by skilled chefs **2** food prepared in this way

**hau·teur** (hō tʉr') *n.* ⟦Fr < *haut*, high⟧ disdainful pride; haughtiness

**Ha·van·a**[1] (hə van'ə) *n.* a cigar made of Cuban tobacco

**Havana**[2] capital of Cuba: pop. 2,078,000

**have** (hav; *before* "to" haf) *vt.* **had, hav'ing** ⟦OE *habban*⟧ **1** to hold; own; possess *[to have money, a week has 7 days]* **2** to experience *[have a good time]* **3** to hold mentally *[to have an idea]* **4** to state *[so rumor has it]* **5** to get, take, consume, etc. *[have a drink]* **6** to bear or beget (offspring) **7** to engage in *[to have a fight]* **8** to cause to or cause to be *[have her sing]* **9** to permit; tolerate *[I won't have this noise]* **10** [Inf.] *a)* to hold at a disadvantage *b)* to deceive; cheat *Have* is used as an auxiliary to express completed action (Ex.: I *had* left) and with infinitives to express obligation or necessity (Ex.: we *have* to go). *Have got* often replaces *have. Have* is conjugated in the present indicative: (I) *have*, (he, she, it) *has*, (we, you, they) *have* —*n.* a wealthy person or nation —**have**

**it out** to settle an issue by fighting or discussion —**have on** to be wearing

**ha·ven** (hā'vən) *n.* ⟦OE *hæfen*⟧ **1** a port **2** any sheltered place; refuge

**have-not** (hav'nät') *n.* a person or nation with little or no wealth

**hav·er·sack** (hav'ər sak') *n.* ⟦< Ger *habersack*, lit., sack of oats⟧ a canvas bag for rations, etc., worn over one shoulder

**hav·oc** (hav'ək, -äk') *n.* ⟦< OFr *havot*⟧ great destruction and devastation —**play havoc with** to devastate; ruin

**haw**[1] (hô) *n.* ⟦OE *haga*⟧ **1** the berry of the hawthorn **2** HAWTHORN

**haw**[2] (hô) *vi.* ⟦echoic⟧ *see* HEM AND HAW *under* HEM[2]

**Ha·wai·i** (hə wä'ē, -wī'ē) **1** state of the U.S., consisting of a group of islands (**Hawaiian Islands**) in the N Pacific: 6,423 sq. mi.; pop. 1,108,000; cap. Honolulu: abbrev. *HI* **2** the largest of these islands —**Ha·wai'ian** (-yən) *adj., n.*

**hawk**[1] (hôk) *n.* ⟦OE *hafoc*⟧ **1** a bird of prey with short, rounded wings, a long tail, and a hooked beak and claws **2** an advocate of war

**hawk**[2] (hôk) *vt.* ⟦< HAWKER⟧ to advertise or peddle (goods) in the streets by shouting

**hawk**[3] (hôk) *vi., vt.* ⟦echoic⟧ to clear the throat (of) audibly

**hawk'er** *n.* ⟦< Old LowG *hoker*⟧ a peddler or huckster

**hawk'-eyed'** (-īd') *adj.* keen-sighted

**haw·ser** (hô'zər) *n.* ⟦< OFr *haucier* < L *altus*, high⟧ a large rope used as for mooring a ship

**haw·thorn** (hô'thôrn') *n.* ⟦< OE *haga*, hedge + THORN⟧ a thorny shrub or small tree of the rose family, with flowers and small, red fruits

**Haw·thorne** (hô'thôrn'), **Na·than·iel** (nə than'yəl) 1804-64; U.S. writer

**hay** (hā) *n.* ⟦< OE *hieg*⟧ grass, clover, etc. cut and dried for fodder —*vi.* to mow and dry grass, etc. for hay —**hit the hay** [Slang] to go to bed to sleep

**hay'cock'** *n.* a small, conical heap of hay drying in a field

**Hay·dn** (hīd''n), (**Franz**) **Jo·seph** (yō'zef) 1732-1809; Austrian composer

**Hayes** (hāz), **Ruth·er·ford B**(irchard) (ruth'ər fərd) 1822-93; 19th president of the U.S. (1877-81)

**hay fever** an allergy to pollen, causing inflammation of the eyes and respiratory tract

**hay'loft'** *n.* a loft, or upper story, in a barn or stable, for storing hay

**hay'mow'** (-mou') *n.* **1** a pile of hay in a barn **2** HAYLOFT

**hay'stack'** *n.* a large heap of hay piled up outdoors

**hay'wire'** *adj.* [Inf.] **1** out of order; disorganized **2** crazy —**go haywire** [Inf.] **1** to behave erratically **2** to become crazy

**haz·ard** (haz'ərd) *n.* ⟦< OFr *hasard*, game of dice⟧ **1** risk; danger **2** an obstacle on a golf course —*vt.* to risk

**haz'ard·ous** *adj.* risky; dangerous

**haze**[1] (hāz) *n.* ⟦prob. < HAZY⟧ **1** a thin cloud of fog, smoke, etc. in the air **2** a slight vagueness of mind —*vi., vt.* **hazed, haz'ing** to make or become hazy: often with *over*

**haze**[2] (hāz) *vt.* **hazed, haz'ing** ⟦< ?⟧ to initiate or discipline by forcing to do ridiculous or painful things

**ha·zel** (hā'zəl) *n.* ⟦OE *hæsel*⟧ **1** a shrub or tree of the birch family, with edible nuts **2** a reddish brown —*adj.* **1** light reddish-brown **2** greenish-gray or greenish-brown: said of eyes

**ha'zel·nut'** *n.* FILBERT

**ha·zy** (hā'zē) *adj.* **-zi·er, -zi·est** ⟦prob. < OE *hasu*, dusky⟧ **1** somewhat foggy or smoky **2** somewhat vague —**ha'zi·ly** *adv.* —**ha'zi·ness** *n.*

**H-bomb** (āch'bäm') *n.* HYDROGEN BOMB

**hdqrs** *abbrev.* headquarters

**HDTV** *abbrev.* high-definition television

**he** (hē) *pron., pl. see* THEY ⟦OE⟧ **1** the man, boy, or male animal previously mentioned **2** anyone *[he who laughs last laughs best]* —*n.* a male

**He** *Chem. symbol for* helium

**head** (hed) *n.* ⟦OE *heafod*⟧ **1** the part of the body containing the brain, jaws, eyes, ears, nose, mouth, etc. **2** the mind; intelligence **3** *pl.* **head** a unit of counting *[ten head of cattle]* **4** the main side of a coin: often **heads 5** the uppermost part or thing; top **6** the topic or title of a section, chapter, etc. **7** the foremost or projecting part; front **8** the part designed for holding, striking, etc. *[the head of a nail]* **9** the part of a tape recorder that records or plays back the magnetic signals on the tape **10** the membrane across the end of a drum, etc. **11** the source of a river, etc. **12** froth, as on beer **13** a position of leadership or honor **14** a leader, ruler, etc. **15** *Bot.* a dense cluster of small flowers **16** [Slang] a person dedicated to, addicted to, etc. some interest, activity, etc. —*adj.* **1** most important; principal **2** at the top or front **3** striking against the front *[head winds]* —*vt.* **1** to be the chief of; command **2** to lead; precede **3** to cause to go in a specified direction —*vi.* to set out; travel —**come to a head 1** to be about to suppurate, as a boil **2** to culminate, or reach a crisis —**go to someone's head 1** to confuse or intoxicate someone **2** to make someone vain —**head off** to get ahead of and intercept —**head over heels** deeply; completely —**heads up!** [Inf.] look out! —**keep** (or **lose**) **one's head** to keep (or lose) one's poise, self-control, etc. —**on** (or **upon**) **someone's head** as someone's responsibility or misfortune —**over someone's head 1** too difficult for someone to understand **2** to a higher authority —**turn one's head** to make one vain —**head′less** *adj.*

**head′ache′** *n.* **1** a continuous pain in the head **2** [Inf.] a cause of worry, annoyance, or trouble

**head′board′** *n.* a board that forms the head of a bed, etc.

**head cold** a common cold with congestion of the nasal passages

**head′dress′** *n.* a decorative head covering

**-head·ed** (hed′id) *combining form* having a (specified kind or number of) head or heads *[light-headed, two-headed]*

**head′er** *n.* **1** a pipe, etc. that brings other pipes together, as in an exhaust system **2** in word processing, text repeated at the top of each page **3** [Inf.] a headlong fall or dive

**head′first′** *adv.* **1** with the head in front; headlong **2** recklessly; rashly —*adj.* with the head first

**head′gear′** *n.* a hat, cap, etc.

**head′ing** *n.* **1** something forming the head, top, or front **2** the title, topic, etc., as of a chapter **3** the direction in which a ship, plane, etc. is moving

**head′land** (-lənd) *n.* a cape or point of land reaching out into the water; promontory

**head′light′** *n.* a light with a reflector and lens, at the front of a vehicle

**head′line′** *n.* printed lines at the top of a newspaper article, giving the topic —*vt.* **-lined′, -lin′ing 1** to give (a performer, etc.) featured billing or publicity **2** to be the featured performer, etc. in

**head′long′** (-lôŋ′) *adv., adj.* ⟦ME *hedelinge(s)*⟧ **1** with the head first **2** with uncontrolled speed or force **3** reckless(ly); rash(ly)

**head′mas′ter** *n.* the male principal of a private school —**head′mis′tress** *fem.n.*

**head′-on′** *adj., adv.* **1** with the head or front foremost *[a head-on collision]* **2** directly *[to meet a problem head-on]*

**head′phone′** *n.* [*usually pl.*] a listening device for a radio, stereo, etc. worn over the head to position its speakers over the ears

**head′quar′ters** *pl.n.* [*with sing. or pl. v.*] **1** the main office, or center of operations, of one in command, as in an army **2** the main office in any organization

**head′rest′** *n.* a support for the head

**head′room′** *n.* space overhead, as in a doorway, tunnel, etc.

**head start** an early start or other competitive advantage

**head′stone′** *n.* a stone marker placed at the head of a grave

**head′strong′** *adj.* determined to do as one pleases

**head′wa′ters** *pl.n.* the small streams that are the sources of a river

**head′way′** *n.* **1** forward motion **2** progress or success

**head′y** *adj.* **-i·er, -i·est 1** intoxicating **2** having, using, etc. good judgment or intelligence

**heal** (hēl) *vt., vi.* ⟦OE *hælan*⟧ **1** to make or become well or healthy again **2** to cure (a disease) or mend, as a wound —**heal′er** *n.*

**health** (helth) *n.* ⟦OE *hælth*⟧ **1** physical and mental well-being; freedom from disease, etc. **2** condition of body or mind *[poor health]* **3** a wish for one's health and happiness, as in a toast **4** soundness, as of a society or culture

**health′care′** *n.* the prevention and treatment of illness or injury on an ongoing basis

**health food** food thought to be especially healthful; specif., food grown with natural fertilizers and free of chemical additives

**health′ful** *adj.* helping to produce or maintain health; wholesome

**health′y** *adj.* **-i·er, -i·est 1** having good health **2** showing or resulting from good health *[a healthy color]* **3** HEALTHFUL —**health′i·ness** *n.*

**heap** (hēp) *n.* ⟦< OE *heap*, a troop⟧ **1** a pile or mass of jumbled things **2** [*often pl.*] [Inf.] a large amount —*vt.* **1** to make a heap of **2** to give in large amounts **3** to fill (a plate, etc.) full or to overflowing —*vi.* to rise in a heap

**hear** (hir) *vt.* **heard** (hurd), **hear′ing** ⟦OE *hieran*⟧ **1** to be aware of (sounds) by the ear **2** to listen to **3** to conduct a hearing of (a law case, etc.) **4** to be informed of; learn —*vi.* **1** to be able to hear sounds **2** to be told (*of* or *about*) —**hear from** to get a letter, etc. from —**not hear of** to refuse to consider —**hear′er** *n.*

**hear′ing** *n.* **1** the act or process of perceiving sounds **2** the ability to hear **3** an opportunity to be heard **4** an appearance before a judge, investigative committee, etc. **5** the distance a sound will carry *[within hearing]*

**hark·en** (härk′ən) *vi.* ⟦OE *heorknian*⟧ [Now Literary] to listen carefully; pay heed: with *to*

**hear·say** (hir′sā′) *n.* rumor; gossip

**hearse** (hurs) *n.* ⟦< L *hirpex*, a harrow⟧ a vehicle used in a funeral for carrying the corpse

**heart** (härt) *n.* ⟦OE *heorte*⟧ **1** the hollow, muscular organ that circulates the blood by alternate dilation and contraction **2** the central, vital, or main part; core **3** the human heart considered as the center of emotions, personality attributes, etc.; specif., *a)* inmost thought and feeling *b)* love, sympathy, etc. *c)* spirit or courage **4** a conventionalized design of a heart (♥) **5** any of a suit of playing cards marked with such symbols in red —**after someone's own heart** that pleases someone perfectly —**at heart** in one's innermost nature —**by heart** by or from memorization —**set one's heart on** to have a fixed desire for —**take to heart 1** to consider seriously **2** to be troubled by

**heart′ache′** *n.* sorrow or grief

**heart attack** any sudden instance of heart failure; esp., a coronary

**heart′beat′** *n.* **1** one full contraction and dilation of the heart **2** a moment; instant

**heart′break′** *n.* overwhelming sorrow, grief, etc. —**heart′bro′ken** *adj.* —**heart′break′ing** *adj.*

**heart′break′er** *n.* one that causes heartbreak

**heart′burn′** *n.* a burning, acid sensation beneath the breastbone

**-heart·ed** (härt'id) 〖ME〗 *combining form* having a (specified kind of) heart [*stouthearted*]

**heart·en** (härt'n) *vt.* to encourage

**heart failure** the inability of the heart to pump enough blood to supply the body tissues adequately

**heart'felt'** *adj.* sincere; genuine

**hearth** (härth) *n.* 〖OE *heorth*〗 **1** the stone or brick floor of a fireplace **2** *a*) the fireside *b*) family life; home

**heart'land'** *n.* a geographically central area having crucial importance

**heart'less** *adj.* unkind; unfeeling —**heart'less·ly** *adv.* —**heart'less·ness** *n.*

**heart'-rend'ing** *adj.* causing much grief or mental anguish

**heart'sick'** *adj.* sick at heart; extremely unhappy or despondent

**heart'strings'** *pl.n.* deepest feelings or affections

**heart'-to-heart'** *adj.* intimate and candid

**heart'warm'ing** *adj.* causing genial feelings

**heart'y** *adj.* **-i·er, -i·est** **1** warm and friendly; cordial **2** strongly felt; unrestrained [*hearty* laughter] **3** strong and healthy **4** nourishing and plentiful [a *hearty* meal] —**heart'i·ly** *adv.* —**heart'i·ness** *n.*

**heat** (hēt) *n.* 〖OE *hætu*〗 **1** the quality of being hot; hotness, or the perception of this **2** much hotness **3** hot weather or climate **4** the warming of a house, etc. **5** *a*) strong feeling; ardor, anger, etc. *b*) the period of this **6** a single bout, round, or trial **7** the period of sexual excitement in animals, esp. females **8** [Slang] coercion —*vt., vi.* **1** to make or become warm or hot **2** to make or become excited

**heat'ed** *adj.* **1** hot **2** vehement or angry —**heat'ed·ly** *adv.*

**heat'er** *n.* an apparatus for giving heat; stove, furnace, radiator, etc.

**heath** (hēth) *n.* 〖OE *hæth*〗 **1** a tract of open wasteland, esp. in the British Isles **2** any of various shrubs that grow on heaths, as heather

**hea·then** (hē'thən) *n., pl.* **-thens** or **-then** 〖OE *hæthen*〗 **1** anyone not a Jew, Christian, or Muslim **2** a person regarded as irreligious, uncivilized, etc. —*adj.* **1** pagan **2** irreligious, uncivilized, etc. —**hea'then·ish** *adj.*

**heath·er** (heth'ər) *n.* 〖ME *haddyr*〗 a plant of the heath family, esp. common in the British Isles, with small, bell-shaped, purplish-pink flowers

**heating pad** a pad consisting of an electric heating element covered with fabric, for applying heat to the body

**heat lightning** lightning without thunder, seen on hot evenings

**heat'stroke'** *n.* a condition of high fever, collapse, etc. resulting from exposure to intense heat

**heat wave** **1** unusually hot weather **2** a period of such weather

**heave** (hēv) *vt.* **heaved** or (esp. *Naut.*) **hove, heav'ing** 〖OE *hebban*〗 **1** to lift, esp. with effort **2** to lift in this way and throw **3** to utter (a sigh, etc.) with effort —*vi.* **1** to swell up **2** to rise and fall rhythmically **3** *a*) to vomit *b*) to pant; gasp —*n.* the act or effort of heaving —**heave to** *Naut.* to stop

**heave'-ho'** (-hō') *n.* [Inf.] dismissal, as from a job: chiefly in **give** (or **get**) **the** (**old**) **heave-ho**

**heav·en** (hev'ən) *n.* 〖OE *heofon*〗 **1** [*usually pl.*] the visible sky; firmament **2** [*often* H-] *Theol. a*) a state or place of complete happiness, etc. attained by the good after death *b*) the abode of God, his angels, and the blessed *c*) God **3** any place of great beauty or state of great happiness —**heav'en·ly** *adj.*

**heav'en·ward** *adv., adj.* toward heaven: also **heav'en·wards** *adv.*

**heav·y** (hev'ē) *adj.* **-i·er, -i·est** 〖OE *hefig*〗 **1** hard to lift because of great weight **2** of more than the usual, expected, or defined weight **3** larger, greater, or more intense than usual [a *heavy*

blow, a *heavy* vote] **4** to an unusual extent [a *heavy* drinker] **5** hard to do [*heavy* work] **6** sorrowful [a *heavy* heart] **7** burdened with sleep [*heavy* eyelids] **8** hard to digest [a *heavy* meal] **9** clinging; penetrating [a *heavy* odor] **10** cloudy; gloomy [a *heavy* sky] **11** designating any large, basic industry that uses massive machinery **12** [Slang] serious and, often, depressing —*adv.* in a heavy manner —*n., pl.* **-ies** **1** *Theater* a villain **2** [Slang] an important person —**heav'i·ly** *adv.* —**heav'i·ness** *n.*

**heav'y-du'ty** *adj.* made to withstand great strain, bad weather, etc.

**heav'y-hand'ed** *adj.* **1** clumsy or tactless **2** oppressive or tyrannical

**heav'y-heart'ed** *adj.* sad; depressed

**heav'y·set'** *adj.* having a stout or stocky build

**heav'y·weight'** *n.* **1** one weighing more than average; esp., a boxer in the heaviest weight class **2** [Inf.] a very influential or important person

**He·bra·ic** (hē brā'ik, hi-) *adj.* of or characteristic of the Hebrews, their language, or culture; Hebrew

**He·brew** (hē'brōō') *n.* **1** *a*) a member of an ancient Semitic people; Israelite *b*) a Jew **2** *a*) the ancient Semitic language of the Israelites *b*) its modern form, the language of Israel —*adj.* **1** of Hebrew or the Hebrews **2** JEWISH

**Heb·ri·des** (heb'rə dēz') group of islands off the W coast of Scotland

**heck** (hek) *interj., n.* [Inf.] *euphemism for* HELL

**heck·le** (hek'əl) *vt.* **-led, -ling** 〖ME *hechele*〗 to harass (a speaker) by interrupting with questions or taunts —**heck'ler** *n.*

**hec·tare** (hek'ter') *n.* 〖Fr〗 a metric unit of area, 10,000 square meters

**hec·tic** (hek'tik) *adj.* 〖< Gr *hektikos*, habitual〗 **1** feverish; flushed **2** confused, rushed, excited, etc. —**hec'ti·cal·ly** *adv.*

**Hec·tor** (hek'tər) *n.* in Homer's *Iliad*, a Trojan hero, killed by Achilles —*vt., vi.* [h-] to browbeat; bully

**hedge** (hej) *n.* 〖OE *hecg*〗 **1** a dense row of shrubs, etc. forming a boundary **2** any fence or barrier **3** a hedging —*vt.* **hedged, hedg'ing** **1** to put a hedge around **2** to hinder or guard as with a barrier: often with *in* **3** to try to avoid loss in (a bet, etc.) by making counterbalancing bets, etc. —*vi.* to avoid giving a direct answer

**hedge fund** a partnership of investors who pool large sums for speculating in securities

**hedge'hog'** *n.* **1** a small, insect-eating mammal of the Old World, with sharp spines on the back **2** the American porcupine

**he·don·ism** (hēd''n iz'əm) *n.* 〖< Gr *hēdonē*, pleasure + -ISM〗 the self-indulgent pursuit of pleasure as a way of life —**he'don·ist** *n.* —**he'do·nis'tic** *adj.*

**-he·dron** (hē'drən) 〖< Gr〗 *combining form* a geometric figure or crystal having (a specified number of) surfaces

**heed** (hēd) *vt., vi.* 〖OE *hedan*〗 to pay close attention (to) —*n.* close attention —**heed'ful** *adj.* —**heed'less** *adj.* —**heed'less·ly** *adv.* —**heed'less·ness** *n.*

**hee·haw** (hē'hô') *n., vi.* 〖echoic〗 bray

**heel**[1] (hēl) *n.* 〖OE *hela*〗 **1** the back part of the foot, under the ankle **2** that part of a stocking, shoe, etc. at the heel **3** anything like a heel in location, shape, crushing power, etc. **4** [Inf.] a despicable person —*vt.* **1** to furnish with a heel **2** to follow closely **3** [Inf.] to provide (a person) with money, etc. —*vi.* to follow along at the heels of someone —**down at** (**the**) **heel** (or **heels**) shabby; seedy —**kick up one's heels** have fun —**on** (or **upon**) **the heels of** close behind

**heel**[2] (hēl) *vi.* 〖OE *hieldan*〗 to lean to one side: said esp. of a ship —*vt.* to cause (a ship) to heel

**heft** (heft) [Inf.] *n.* 〖< base of HEAVE〗 **1** weight; heaviness **2** importance; influence —*vt.* to try to judge the weight of by lifting

**heft·y** *adj.* **-i·er, -i·est** [Inf.] **1** heavy **2** large and powerful **3** big —**heft′i·ness** *n.*

**he·gem·o·ny** (hi jem′ə nē) *n., pl.* **-nies** ⟦< Gr *hēgeisthai,* to lead⟧ leadership or dominance, esp. that of one state or nation over others

**he·gi·ra** (hi ji′rə) *n.* ⟦< Ar *hijrah,* flight⟧ **1** [*often* H-] Mohammed's flight from Mecca in A.D. 622 **2** a journey, esp. one made to escape

**Hei·del·berg** (hīd′'l burg′) city in SW Germany: site of a famous university: pop. 140,000

**heif·er** (hef′ər) *n.* ⟦OE *heahfore*⟧ a young cow that has not borne a calf

**height** (hīt) *n.* ⟦< OE *heah,* high⟧ **1** the topmost point **2** the highest limit; extreme **3** the distance from the bottom to the top **4** elevation above a given level; altitude **5** a relatively great distance above a given level **6** [*often pl.*] an elevation; hill

**height′en** (-'n) *vt., vi.* **1** to bring or come to a higher position **2** to make or become larger, greater, etc.

**Heim·lich maneuver** (hīm′lik) ⟦after H. J. *Heimlich,* 20th-c. U.S. surgeon⟧ an emergency technique for dislodging an object stuck in the windpipe, using air forced up the windpipe by applying sharp pressure to the abdomen

**hei·nous** (hā′nəs) *adj.* ⟦< OFr *hair,* to hate⟧ outrageously evil —**hei′nous·ly** *adv.* —**hei′nous·ness** *n.*

**heir** (er) *n.* ⟦< L *heres*⟧ one who inherits or is entitled to inherit another's property, title, etc.

**heir apparent** *pl.* **heirs apparent** the heir whose right to inherit cannot be denied if the heir outlives the ancestor and the ancestor dies intestate

**heir′ess** (-is) *n.* a female heir, esp. to great wealth

**heir′loom′** *n.* ⟦see HEIR & LOOM[1]⟧ any treasured possession handed down from generation to generation

**heist** (hīst) [Slang] *n.* ⟦< HOIST⟧ a robbery —*vt.* to rob or steal

**held** (held) *vt., vi. pt. & pp. of* HOLD[1]

**Hel·e·na** (hel′ə nə) capital of Montana: pop. 25,000

**Helen of Troy** *Gr. Legend* the beautiful wife of the king of Sparta: the Trojan War was started because of her abduction by Paris to Troy

**hel·i·cal** (hel′i kəl) *adj.* ⟦< Gr *helix,* spiral⟧ shaped like a helix; spiral

**hel·i·cop·ter** (hel′i käp′tər) *n.* ⟦< Gr *helix,* spiral + *pteron,* wing⟧ a vertical-lift aircraft, capable of hovering or moving in any direction, having a motor-driven, horizontal rotor —*vi., vt.* to travel or convey by helicopter

**he·li·o·cen·tric** (hē′lē ō sen′trik) *adj.* ⟦< Gr *hēlios,* the sun + *kentron,* a point⟧ having or regarding the sun as the center

**he·li·o·trope** (hē′lē ə trōp′) *n.* ⟦< Gr *hēlios,* the sun + *trepein,* to turn⟧ **1** a plant with fragrant clusters of small, white or reddish-purple flowers **2** reddish purple —*adj.* reddish-purple

**hel·i·port** (hel′i pôrt′) *n.* ⟦HELI(COPTER) + (AIR)PORT⟧ an airport for helicopters: also **hel′i·pad′** (-pad′)

**he·li·um** (hē′lē əm) *n.* ⟦< Gr *hēlios,* the sun⟧ a chemical element, a colorless, odorless, very light, nonreactive gas having the lowest known boiling and melting points

**he·lix** (hē′liks) *n., pl.* **-lix·es** or **hel·i·ces** (hel′i sēz′) ⟦L & Gr⟧ a spiral

**hell** (hel) *n.* ⟦< OE *helan,* to hide⟧ **1** [*often* H-] *Theol.* the state or place of total and final separation from God and so of eternal misery and suffering, arrived at by those who die unrepentant in grave sin **2** any place or condition of evil, pain, etc. —**catch** (or **get**) **hell** [Slang] to receive a severe scolding, punishment, etc.

**hell′bent′** or **hell′-bent′** *adj.* [Slang] **1** recklessly determined **2** moving fast or recklessly

**hell′cat′** *n.* an evil, spiteful woman

**hel·le·bore** (hel′ə bôr′) *n.* ⟦< Gr *helleboros*⟧ a plant with buttercuplike flowers, whose rhizomes were once used in medicine

**Hel·len·ic** (hə len′ik) *adj.* **1** Greek **2** of the history, language, or culture of the ancient Greeks —**Hel·len·ism** (hel′ən iz′əm) *n.* —**Hel′len·is′tic** *adj.*

**hell·gram·mite** or **hell·gra·mite** (hel′grəm īt′) *n.* ⟦< ?⟧ a dark-brown, aquatic fly larva, often used as fish bait

**hel·lion** (hel′yən) *n.* ⟦< Scot dial. *hallion,* a low fellow⟧ [Inf.] a person fond of deviltry; troublemaker

**hell′ish** *adj.* **1** devilish; fiendish **2** [Inf.] very unpleasant —**hell′ish·ly** *adv.* —**hell′ish·ness** *n.*

**hel·lo** (he lō′, hel′ō′) *interj.* used to express greeting

**helm** (helm) *n.* ⟦OE *helma*⟧ **1** the wheel or tiller by which a ship is steered **2** the control or leadership of an organization, government, etc.

**hel·met** (hel′mət) *n.* ⟦< OFr *helme*⟧ a protective, rigid head covering for use in combat, certain sports, etc.

**helms·man** (helmz′mən) *n., pl.* **-men** (-mən) one who steers a ship

**hel·ot** (hel′ət) *n.* ⟦after *Helos,* ancient Greek town⟧ a serf or slave

**help** (help) *vt.* ⟦OE *helpan*⟧ **1** to make things easier or better for; aid; assist **2** to relieve [*to help* a cough] **3** to keep from; avoid [can't help crying] **4** to serve or wait on (a customer, etc.) —*vi.* to give aid; be useful —*n.* **1** a helping; aid; assistance **2** relief **3** one that helps; esp., a hired person or persons; servant(s), farmhand(s), etc. —*interj.* used to summon assistance, esp. urgently —**help oneself to** to take without asking —**help out** to help in getting or doing something —**help′er** *n.*

**help′ful** *adj.* giving help; useful —**help′ful·ly** *adv.* —**help′ful·ness** *n.*

**help′ing** *n.* a portion of food served to one person

**help′less** *adj.* **1** not able to help oneself; weak **2** lacking help or protection **3** incompetent or ineffective —**help′less·ly** *adv.* —**help′less·ness** *n.*

**help′mate′** *n.* ⟦< fol.⟧ a helpful companion; specif., a wife or husband

**help′meet′** *n.* ⟦misreading of "an *help meet* for him" (Genesis 2:18)⟧ HELPMATE

**Hel·sin·ki** (hel′siŋ kē) capital of Finland: pop. 516,000

**hel·ter-skel·ter** (hel′tər skel′tər) *adv.* in haste and confusion —*adj.* disorderly

**helve** (helv) *n.* ⟦OE *helfe*⟧ the handle of a tool, esp. of an ax

**Hel·ve·tian** (hel vē′shən) *adj., n.* Swiss

**hem**[1] (hem) *n.* ⟦OE⟧ the border on a garment, etc. made by folding the edge and sewing it down —*vt.* **hemmed, hem′ming** to fold back the edge of and sew down —**hem in 1** to encircle **2** to confine

**hem**[2] (hem) *interj., n.* the sound made in clearing the throat —*vi.* **hemmed, hem′ming 1** to make this sound, as in trying to get attention **2** to grope about in speech for the right words: usually used in the phrase **hem and haw**

**he·ma-** *combining form* HEMO-

**he′-man′** *n.* [Inf.] a strong, virile man

**hem·a·tite** (hem′ə tīt′, hē′mə-) *n.* ⟦< Gr *haimatītēs,* bloodlike⟧ native ferric oxide, an important iron ore

**he·ma·tol·o·gy** (hē′mə täl′ə jē) *n.* ⟦< Gr *haima,* blood + -LOGY⟧ the study of blood and blood diseases —**he′ma·tol′o·gist** *n.*

**he′ma·to′ma** (-tō′mə) *n., pl.* **-mas** or **-ma·ta** (-mə tə) ⟦< Gr *haima,* blood + -ōma, a mass⟧ a tumorlike collection of blood outside a blood vessel

**heme** (hēm) *n.* ⟦ult. < Gr *haima,* blood⟧ the iron-containing pigment in hemoglobin

**hemi-** ⟦Gr *hēmi-*⟧ *prefix* half [hemisphere]

**Hem·ing·way** (hem′iŋ wā′), **Er·nest** (ur′nist) 1899-1961; U.S. writer

**hem·i·sphere** (hem′i sfir′) *n.* ⟦< Gr *hēmisphairion*⟧ **1** half of a sphere, globe, celestial body, etc. **2** any of the halves (northern, southern, eastern, or western) of the earth —**hem′i·spher′i·cal** (-sfer′i kəl) or **hem′i·spher′ic** *adj.*

**hem·line'** *n.* the bottom edge of a dress, skirt, coat, etc.

**hem·lock** (hem'läk') *n.* 〖OE *hemlic*〗 **1** *a*) a poisonous European plant related to parsley *b*) a poison made from this plant **2** *a*) an evergreen tree of the pine family *b*) the wood of this tree

**hemo-** 〖< Gr *haima*〗 *combining form* blood

**he·mo·glo·bin** (hē'mə glō'bin) *n.* 〖< prec. + GLOBULE〗 the red coloring matter of the red blood corpuscles

**he·mo·phil·i·a** (hē'mə fil'ē ə) *n.* 〖< HEMO- + -PHILE〗 a hereditary disorder in which the blood fails to clot normally, causing prolonged bleeding from even minor cuts —**he'mo·phil'i·ac'** (-ak') *n.*

**hem·or·rhage** (hem'ər ij', hem'rij') *n.* 〖< Gr *haima*, blood + *rhēgnynai*, to break〗 the escape of large quantities of blood from a blood vessel; heavy bleeding —*vi.* **-rhaged'**, **-rhag'ing** (-ij'iŋ) to have a hemorrhage —**hem'or·rhag'ic** (-aj'ik) *adj.*

**hem·or·rhoid** (hem'ər oid', hem'roid') *n.* 〖< Gr *haima*, blood + *rheein*, to flow〗 a painful swelling of a vein in the region of the anus, often with bleeding: *usually used in pl.* —**hem'or·rhoi'dal** *adj.*

**he·mo·stat** (hē'mō stat') *n.* 〖see HEMO- & STATIC〗 anything used to stop bleeding, as a surgical clamp

**hemp** (hemp) *n.* 〖OE *hænep*〗 **1** a tall Asiatic plant having tough fiber **2** the fiber, used to make rope, sailcloth, etc. **3** a substance, as marijuana, made from its leaves and flowers

**hem'stitch'** *n.* an ornamental stitch, used esp. at a hem, made by pulling out several parallel threads and tying the cross threads into small bunches —*vt.* to put hemstitches on

**hen** (hen) *n.* 〖OE *henn*〗 **1** the female of the domesticated chicken **2** the female of various other birds

**hence** (hens) *adv.* 〖< OE *heonan*, from here〗 **1** from this place; away *[go hence]* **2** from this time *[a year hence]* **3** as a result; therefore

**hence·forth'** *adv.* from this time on; after this: also **hence'for'ward**

**hench·man** (hench'mən) *n., pl.* **-men** (-mən) 〖< OE *hengest*, stallion + *-man*〗 a trusted helper or follower

**hen·na** (hen'ə) *n.* 〖Ar *ḥinnā'*〗 **1** an Old World plant with tiny, white or red flowers **2** a dye extracted from its leaves, used to tint the hair auburn **3** reddish brown —*adj.* reddish-brown —*vt.* **-naed**, **-na·ing** to tint with henna

**hen·peck** (hen'pek') *vt.* to nag and domineer over (one's husband) —**hen'pecked'** *adj.*

**Hen·ry VIII** (hen'rē) 1491-1547; king of England (1509-47)

**hep** (hep) *adj.* [Slang] *var. of* HIP²

**hep·a·rin** (hep'ə rin) *n.* 〖< Gr *hēpar*, liver〗 a substance found in the liver, that slows the clotting of blood

**he·pat·ic** (hi pat'ik) *adj.* 〖< Gr *hēpar*, liver〗 of or like the liver

**hep·a·ti·tis** (hep'ə tīt'is) *n.* 〖< Gr *hēpar*, liver + -ITIS〗 inflammation of the liver

**her** (hur) *pron.* 〖OE *hire*〗 *objective form of* SHE —*poss. pronominal adj.* of, belonging to, or done by her

**He·ra** (hir'ə, her'ə) *n. Gr. Myth.* the wife of Zeus and queen of the gods

**her·ald** (her'əld) *n.* 〖< OFr *heralt*〗 **1** [Historical] an official who made proclamations, carried state messages, etc. **2** one who announces significant news, etc. **3** a forerunner; harbinger —*vt.* to announce, foretell, etc.

**he·ral·dic** (hə ral'dik) *adj.* of heraldry or heralds

**her'ald·ry** *n.* **1** the study of coats of arms, genealogies, etc. **2** ceremony or pomp

**herb** (urb, hurb) *n.* 〖< L *herba*〗 **1** any seed plant whose stem withers away annually **2** any plant used as a medicine, seasoning, or flavoring —**her·ba·ceous** (hər bā'shəs, ər-) *adj.* —**herb'al** *adj.*

---

**herb·al·ist** (hur'bəl ist, ur'-) *n.* one who grows or deals in herbs

**her·bi·cide** (hur'bə sīd', ur'-) *n.* any chemical substance used to destroy plants, esp. weeds —**her'bi·ci'dal** *adj.*

**her·bi·vore** (hur'bə vôr') *n.* 〖Fr〗 a herbivorous animal

**her·biv·o·rous** (hər biv'ər əs) *adj.* 〖< L *herba*, herb + *vorare*, devour〗 feeding chiefly on grass or other plants

**her·cu·le·an** (hər kyoo'lē ən, hur'kyoo lē'ən) *adj.* [*sometimes* H-] **1** having the great size or strength of Hercules **2** calling for great strength, size, or courage

**Her·cu·les** (hur'kyoo lēz') *n.* **1** *Gr. & Rom. Myth.* a hero famous for feats of strength **2** [h-] a very large, strong man

**herd** (hurd) *n.* 〖OE *heord*〗 **1** a number of cattle or other animals feeding or living together **2** *a*) a crowd *b*) the common people; masses (a contemptuous term) —*vt., vi.* to gather or move as a herd

**herds·man** (hurdz'mən) *n., pl.* **-men** (-mən) one who keeps or tends a herd

**here** (hir) *adv.* 〖OE *her*〗 **1** at or in this place: often used as an intensive *[John here is an actor]* **2** to or into this place *[come here]* **3** at this point; now **4** in earthly life —*n.* this place —**neither here nor there** irrelevant

**here'a·bout'** *adv.* in this general vicinity: also **here'a·bouts'**

**here·af'ter** *adv.* **1** from now on; in the future **2** following this —*n.* **1** the future **2** the state after death

**here·by'** *adv.* by this means

**he·red·i·tar·y** (hə red'i ter'ē) *adj.* **1** *a*) of, or passed down by, inheritance from an ancestor *b*) having title, etc. by inheritance **2** of, or passed down by, heredity

**he·red·i·ty** (hə red'i tē) *n., pl.* **-ties** 〖< L *heres*, heir〗 the transmission of characteristics from parent to offspring by means of genes

**here·in'** *adv.* **1** in here **2** in this writing

**here·of'** *adv.* of or concerning this

**here's** (hirz) *contr.* here is

**her·e·sy** (her'ə sē) *n., pl.* **-sies** 〖< Gr *hairesis*, selection, sect〗 **1** a religious belief opposed to the orthodox doctrines of a church **2** any opinion opposed to official or established views

**her·e·tic** (-tik) *n.* one who professes a heresy; esp., a church member who holds beliefs opposed to church dogma —**he·ret·i·cal** (hə ret'i kəl) *adj.* —**he·ret'i·cal·ly** *adv.*

**here'to·fore'** *adv.* up until now

**here·up·on'** *adv.* **1** immediately following this; at once **2** concerning this subject, etc.

**here·with'** *adv.* **1** along with this **2** by this method or means

**her·it·a·ble** (her'it ə bəl) *adj.* that can be inherited

**her·it·age** (her'i tij) *n.* **1** property that is or can be inherited **2** tradition, etc. handed down from one's ancestors or the past

**her·maph·ro·dite** (hər maf'rə dīt') *n.* 〖after *Hermaphroditos*, son of Hermes and Aphrodite, who became united in a single body with a nymph〗 a person, animal, or plant with the sexual organs of both the male and the female —**her·maph'ro·dit'ic** (-dit'ik) *adj.*

**Her·mes** (hur'mēz') *n. Gr. Myth.* the god who is the messenger of the other gods

**her·met·ic** (hər met'ik) *adj.* 〖after prec. (reputed founder of alchemy)〗 airtight: also **her·met'i·cal** —**her·met'i·cal·ly** *adv.*

**her·mit** (hur'mit) *n.* 〖< Gr *erēmos*, desolate〗 one who lives alone in a secluded spot; recluse

**her'mit·age** (-mə tij) *n.* a secluded retreat, as the place where a hermit lives

**hermit crab** a soft-bodied crab that lives in an empty mollusk shell

**her·ni·a** (hur′nē ə) *n.*, *pl.* **-as** or **-ae** (-ē′, -ī′) [L] the protrusion of all or part of an organ, esp. the intestine, through a tear in the wall of the surrounding structure; rupture —**her′ni·al** *adj.*

**her·ni·ate** (-āt′) *vi.* **-at·ed, -at′ing** to protrude so as to form a hernia —**her′ni·a′tion** *n.*

**he·ro** (hir′ō, hē′rō′) *n.*, *pl.* **-roes** [< Gr *hērōs*] 1 any person, esp. a man, admired for courage, nobility, etc. 2 the central male character in a novel, play, etc.

**He·rod·o·tus** (hə räd′ə təs) 484?-425? B.C.; Gr. historian

**he·ro·ic** (hi rō′ik) *adj.* 1 of or like a hero 2 of or about a hero and his deeds 3 daring and risky — *n.* [pl.] heroic behavior, talk, or deeds —**he·ro′i·cal·ly** *adv.*

**her·o·in** (her′ō in) *n.* [Ger, orig. a trademark] a habit-forming narcotic derived from morphine

**her·o·ine** (her′ō in) *n.* a female hero in life or literature

**her′o·ism** *n.* the qualities and actions of a hero or heroine

**her·on** (her′ən) *n.* [< OFr *hairon*] a wading bird with a long neck, long legs, and a long, tapered bill

**hero sandwich** a long roll sliced and filled with meats, cheeses, vegetables, etc.

**her·pes** (hur′pēz) *n.* [L < Gr *herpein*, to creep] a viral disease causing small blisters on the skin and mucous membranes

**herpes sim·plex** (sim′pleks′) a recurrent, incurable form of herpes usually affecting the mouth, lips, face, or genitals

GREAT BLUE HERON

**herpes zos·ter** (zäs′tər) [< HERPES + Gr *zōstēr*, a girdle] a viral infection of certain sensory nerves, causing pain and an eruption of blisters; shingles

**her·pe·tol·o·gy** (hur′pə täl′ə jē) *n.* [< Gr *herpeton*, reptile] the branch of zoology having to do with the study of reptiles and amphibians —**her′pe·tol′o·gist** *n.*

**Herr** (her) *n.*, *pl.* **Her′ren** (-ən) [Ger] 1 Mr.; Sir: a German title of respect 2 a man; gentleman

**her·ring** (her′iŋ) *n.* [OE *hæring*] a small, silvery food fish of the North Atlantic

**her′ring·bone′** *n.* 1 the spine of a herring, having numerous thin, parallel bony extensions on each side 2 a pattern with such a design, or anything having such a pattern, as a twill weave

**hers** (hurz) *pron.* that or those belonging to her: poss. form of SHE [hers are better]

**her·self′** (hər-) *pron.* a form of SHE, used as an intensive [she went *herself*], as a reflexive [she hurt *herself*], or with the meaning "her true self" [she is not *herself* today]

**hertz** (hurts) *n.*, *pl.* **hertz** [after H. R. *Hertz*, 19th-c. Ger physicist] the international unit of frequency, equal to one cycle per second

**Hertz·i·an waves** (hert′sē ən, hurt′-) [see prec.] [*sometimes* h- w-] radio waves or other electromagnetic radiation resulting from the oscillations of electricity in a conductor

**he's** (hēz) *contr.* 1 he is 2 he has

**hes·i·tant** (hez′i tənt) *adj.* hesitating or undecided; doubtful —**hes′i·tan·cy** *n.* —**hes′i·tant·ly** *adv.*

**hes′i·tate′** (-tāt′) *vi.* **-tat′ed, -tat′ing** [< L *haerere*, to stick] 1 to stop because of indecision 2 to pause 3 to be reluctant [I *hesitate* to ask] 4 to pause continually in speaking —**hes′i·tat′ing·ly** *adv.* —**hes′i·ta′tion** *n.*

**hetero-** [Gr *hetero-*] *combining form* other, another, different: also **heter-**

**het·er·o·dox** (het′ər ə däks′) *adj.* [< prec. + Gr *doxa*, opinion] opposed to the usual beliefs, esp. in religion; unorthodox —**het′er·o·dox′y**, *pl.* **-ies**, *n.*

**het·er·o·ge·ne·ous** (het′ər ə jē′nē əs) *adj.* [< HETERO- + Gr *genos*, a kind] 1 differing in structure, quality, etc.; dissimilar 2 composed of unlike parts

**het·er·o·sex·u·al** (-sek′shoo əl) *adj.* 1 of or characterized by sexual desire for those of the opposite sex 2 *Biol.* of different sexes —*n.* a heterosexual individual —**het′er·o·sex·u·al′i·ty** *n.*

**heu·ris·tic** (hyoo ris′tik) *adj.* [< Gr *heuriskein*, invent] helping to learn, as by a method of education based on following rules to find answers

**hew** (hyoo) *vt.* **hewed, hewed** or **hewn, hew′ing** [OE *heawan*] 1 to chop or cut with an ax, knife, etc.; hack 2 to make or shape in this way —*vi.* to conform (*to* a line, rule, principle, etc.)

**hex** (heks) *n.* [Pennsylvania Ger *hexe*, witch] a sign, spell, etc. believed to bring bad luck —*vt.* to cause to have bad luck

**hexa-** [< Gr *hex*, six] *combining form* six: also **hex-**

**hex·a·gon** (heks′ə gän′) *n.* [< Gr *hex*, six + *gōnia*, an angle] a plane figure with six angles and six sides —**hex·ag·o·nal** (hek sag′ə nəl) *adj.*

**hex·am·e·ter** (hek sam′ə tər) *n.* [see HEXA- & METER¹] a line of verse containing six metrical feet

**hey** (hā) *interj.* used to attract attention, express surprise, etc.

**hey·day** (hā′dā′) *n.* the time of greatest health, vigor, etc.; prime

HEXAGONS

**Hg** [L *hydrargyrum*] *Chem. symbol for* mercury

**hgt** *abbrev.* height

**HHS** *abbrev.* (Department of) Health and Human Services

**hi** (hī) *interj.* [Inf.] hello

**HI** Hawaii

**Hi·a·le·ah** (hī′ə lē′ə) city in SE Florida.: pop. 188,000

**hi·a·tus** (hī āt′əs) *n.*, *pl.* **-tus·es** or **-tus** [L < *hiare*, to gape] 1 a gap or break, as where a part is missing 2 any gap or interruption, as in time

**hi·ba·chi** (hi bä′chē) *n.*, *pl.* **-chis** [Jpn < *hi*, fire + *bachi*, bowl] a small charcoal-burning grill

**hi·ber·nate** (hī′bər nāt′) *vi.* **-nat′ed, -nat′ing** [< L *hibernus*, wintry] to spend the winter in a dormant state —**hi′ber·na′tion** *n.*

**hi·bis·cus** (hī bis′kəs, hi-) *n.* [< L] a plant of the mallow family, with large, colorful flowers

**hic·cup** (hik′up′, -əp) *n.* [echoic] a sudden contraction of the diaphragm that causes the glottis to close, producing an abrupt sound —*vi.* **-cuped′** or **-cupped′, -cup′ing** or **-cup′ping** to make a hiccup Also sp. **hic′cough′**

**hick** (hik) *n.* [altered < *Richard*] [Inf.] an awkward, unsophisticated person regarded as typical of rural areas: a contemptuous term

**hick·ey** (hik′ē) *n.*, *pl.* **-eys** or **-ies** [Inf.] any device or gadget

**hick·o·ry** (hik′ə rē, hik′rē) *n.*, *pl.* **-ries** [< AmInd *pawcohiccora*] 1 a North American tree of the walnut family 2 its hard, tough wood 3 its hard, edible nut: usually **hickory nut**

**hid·den** (hid′'n) *vt.*, *vi.* [OE *gehydd*] *alt. pp. of* HIDE¹ —*adj.* concealed; secret

**hide¹** (hīd) *vt.* **hid** (hid), **hid′den** or **hid, hid′ing** [OE *hydan*] 1 to put or keep out of sight; conceal 2 to keep secret 3 to keep from sight by obscuring, etc. —*vi.* to conceal oneself

**hide²** (hīd) *n.* [OE *hid*] an animal skin or pelt, either raw or tanned

**hide′a·way′** *n.* [Inf.] a place where one can hide, be secluded, etc.

**hide′bound′** *adj.* obstinately conservative and narrow-minded

**hid·e·ous** (hid′ē əs) *adj.* [< OFr *hide*, fright] horrible; very ugly; dreadful —**hide'e·ous·ly** *adv.* —**hide'e·ous·ness** *n.*

**hide'-out'** *n.* [Inf.] a hiding place

**hie** (hī) *vi., vt.* **hied, hie'ing** or **hy'ing** [OE *higian*] to hasten: usually used reflexively

**hi·er·ar·chy** (hī'ər är'kē) *n., pl.* **-chies** [< Gr *hieros*, sacred + *archos*, ruler] **1** church government by clergy in graded ranks **2** the highest officials in such a system **3** a group of persons or things arranged in order of rank, grade, etc. —**hi'er·ar'chi·cal** (-ki kəl) *adj.*

**hi·er·o·glyph·ic** (hī'ər ō glif'ik, hī'rō-) *n.* [< Gr *hieros*, sacred + *glyphein*, to carve] **1** a picture or symbol representing a word, syllable, or sound, used by the ancient Egyptians and others **2** [*usually pl.*] picture writing **3** a symbol, etc. that is hard to understand —*adj.* of or like hieroglyphics

**hi·er·o·phant** (hī'ər ō fant') *n.* [< Gr *hieros*, sacred + *phainein*, to show] in ancient Greece, a priest of a mystery cult

**hi-fi** (hī'fī') *n.* a radio, phonograph, etc. having high fidelity —*adj.* of or having high fidelity of sound reproduction

**high** (hī) *adj.* [OE *heah*] **1** lofty; tall **2** extending upward a (specified) distance **3** reaching to, situated at, or done from a height **4** above others in rank, position, etc.; superior **5** grave [*high* treason] **6** greater in size, amount, degree, etc. than usual [*high* prices] **7** luxurious [*high* living] **8** raised in pitch [a *high* note] **9** slightly tainted: said of meat, esp. game **10** excited [*high* spirits] **11** [Slang] *a*) drunk *b*) under the influence of a drug —*adv.* in or to a high level, place, degree, etc. —*n.* **1** a high level, place, etc. **2** an area of high barometric pressure **3** the gear of a motor vehicle, etc. producing the greatest speed **4** [Slang] a condition of euphoria induced as by drugs —**high and low** everywhere —**high on** [Inf.] enthusiastic about —**on high** in heaven

**high'ball'** *n.* whiskey or brandy mixed with water, soda water, ginger ale, etc.

**high'born'** *adj.* of noble birth

**high'boy'** *n.* a high chest of drawers mounted on legs

**high'brow'** *n.* one having or affecting highly cultivated tastes; intellectual —*adj.* of or for a highbrow

**high'chair'** *n.* a baby's chair with long legs and, usually, a tray for food

**high'-def·i·ni'tion** *adj.* designating TV transmission with greater clarity of image and sound than that of standard television

**high'-end'** *adj.* [Inf.] expensive and of very high quality

**high'er-up'** *n.* [Inf.] a person of higher rank or position

**high'fa·lu'tin** (-fə lōōt''n) *adj.* [Inf.] pretentious or pompous: also sp. **high'fa·lu'ting**

**high fidelity** in radio, sound recording, etc., nearly exact reproduction of sound

**high'-five'** *n.* [Inf.] a slapping of the upraised open hand of another person, as in celebration

**high'-flown'** *adj.* **1** extravagantly ambitious **2** bombastic

**high frequency** any radio frequency between 3 and 30 megahertz

**High German** the group of West Germanic dialects spoken in central and S Germany

**high'hand'ed** *adj.* overbearing —**high'hand'ed·ly** *adv.* —**high'hand'ed·ness** *n.*

**high'-hat'** (-hat'; *for v., usually*, -hat') *adj.* [Slang] snobbish —*vt.* **-hat'ted, -hat'ting** [Slang] to snub

**high'land** (-lənd) *n.* a region with many hills or mountains —**the Highlands** mountainous region occupying most of N Scotland —**High'land·er** *n.*

**high'-lev'el** *adj.* **1** of or by persons of high office or rank **2** in a high office

**high'light'** *n.* **1** a part on which light is brightest: also **high light 2** the most important or interesting part, scene, etc. —*vt.* **1** to give highlights to **2** to give prominence to; emphasize

**high'light'er** *n.* a pen with a broad felt tip for marking passages as in a textbook

**high'ly** *adv.* **1** very much **2** favorably **3** at a high level, wage, etc.

**high'-mind'ed** *adj.* having high ideals, principles, etc. —**high'-mind'ed·ly** *adv.*

**high'ness** *n.* **1** height **2** [H-] a title used in speaking to or of a member of a royal family

**high'-pres'sure** *adj.* **1** having or withstanding high pressure **2** using forcefully persuasive or insistent methods —*vt.* **-sured, -sur·ing** [Inf.] to urge with such methods

**high'-pro'file** *adj.* well-known, highly publicized, etc.

**high'-rise'** *adj.* tall and having many stories —*n.* a high-rise building

**high road 1** [Chiefly Brit.] a highway **2** an easy or direct way Also **high'road'** *n.*

**high roller 1** a person who gambles for high stakes **2** a person who spends money freely

**high school** a secondary school that includes grades 10, 11, 12, and sometimes 9

**high seas** open ocean waters outside the territorial limits of any nation

**high sign** a secret signal, given as in warning

**high'-spir'it·ed** (-spir'i tid) *adj.* **1** courageous **2** spirited; fiery **3** lively; merry

**high'-strung'** *adj.* highly sensitive or nervous and tense

**high tech** (tek) **1** of specialized, complex technology: in full **high technology 2** furnishings, fashions, etc. whose design or look suggests industrial use —**high'-tech'** *adj.*

**high'-ten'sion** *adj.* having or carrying a high voltage

**high tide** the highest level to which the tide rises

**high time** time beyond the proper time but before it is too late

**high'way'** *n.* **1** a public road **2** a main road; thoroughfare

**high'way·man** (-mən) *n., pl.* **-men** (-mən) a man who formerly robbed travelers on a highway

**high wire** a cable stretched high above the ground, on which aerialists perform

**hi·jack** (hī'jak') *vt.* **1** to steal (goods in transit, etc.) by force **2** to seize control forcibly of (an aircraft, etc.), esp. in order to go to a nonscheduled destination —**hi'jack'er** *n.*

**hike** (hīk) *vi.* **hiked, hik'ing** [< dial. *heik*] to take a long walk —*vt.* [Inf.] **1** to pull up; hoist **2** to raise (prices, etc.) —*n.* **1** a long walk **2** [Inf.] a rise —**hik'er** *n.*

**hi·lar·i·ous** (hi ler'ē əs) *adj.* [< Gr *hilaros*, cheerful] **1** noisily merry **2** very funny —**hi·lar'i·ous·ly** *adv.* —**hi·lar'i·ty** (-i tē) *n.*

**hill** (hil) *n.* [OE *hyll*] **1** a natural raised part of the earth's surface, smaller than a mountain **2** a small pile, heap, or mound

**hill'bil'ly** *n., pl.* **-lies** [prec. + *Billy*] [Inf.] one who lives in or comes from the mountains or backwoods of the South, specif. Appalachia: sometimes a contemptuous term

**hill'side'** *n.* the side of a hill

**hill'top'** *n.* the top of a hill

**hill'y** *adj.* **-i·er, -i·est** full of hills —**hill'i·ness** *n.*

**hilt** (hilt) *n.* [OE] the handle of a sword, dagger, tool, etc.

**him** (him) *pron.* [OE] *objective form of* HE

**Hi·ma·la·yas** (him'ə lā'əz) mountain system of SC Asia, mostly in India & China —**Hi'ma·la'yan** *adj.*

**him·self'** *pron.* a form of HE, used as an intensive [he went *himself*], as a reflexive [he hurt *himself*], or with the meaning "his true self" [he is not *himself* today]

**hind¹** (hīnd) *adj.* [see HINDER²] back; rear

**hind²** (hīnd) *n.* [OE] the female of the red deer

**Hind** *abbrev.* **1** Hindi **2** Hindu

**hin·der¹** (hin'dər) *vt.* [OE *hindrian*] **1** to keep back; stop **2** to impede; thwart

**hind·er**[2] (hīn′dər) *adj.* ⟦OE⟧ [Now Rare] rear

**Hin·di** (hin′dē) *n.* the main (and official) language of India

**hind′most′** *adj.* farthest back; last

**hind′quar′ter** *n.* either of the two hind legs and the adjoining part of a carcass of veal, beef, etc.

**hin·drance** (hin′drəns) *n.* **1** the act of hindering **2** an obstacle

**hind′sight′** *n.* ability to see, after the event, what should have been done

**Hin·du** (hin′dōō′) *n.* a follower of Hinduism —*adj.* designating or of the Hindus or Hinduism

**Hin′du·ism′** *n.* the principal religion of India

**Hin·du·stan** (hin′dōō stan′) **1** region in N India **2** the entire Indian subcontinent **3** the republic of India

**hinge** (hinj) *n.* ⟦< ME *hengen*, to hang⟧ **1** a joint on which a door, lid, etc. swings **2** a natural joint, as of the shell of a clam —*vt.* **hinged, hing′ing** to attach by a hinge —*vi.* to hang as on a hinge; depend

**hint** (hint) *n.* ⟦prob. < OE *hentan*, to grasp⟧ a slight indication; indirect suggestion —*vt., vi.* to give a hint (of)

**hin·ter·land** (hin′tər land′) *n.* ⟦Ger⟧ **1** the land behind that bordering a coast or river **2** a remote area

**hip**[1] (hip) *n.* ⟦OE *hype*⟧ the part of the body around the joint formed by each thighbone and the pelvis

BUTT HINGE

T-HINGE

STRAP HINGE

KINDS OF HINGES

**hip**[2] (hip) *adj.* **hip′per, hip′pest** ⟦< ? HEP⟧ [Slang] **1** sophisticated; aware; fashionable **2** of hippies

**hip′-hop′** *n.* a style of music and dance that originated among inner-city African-American youths in the 1980s

**hip·pie** (hip′ē) *n.* [Slang] a young person of the 1960s and 1970s who, in a state of alienation from conventional society, turned variously to mysticism, psychedelic drugs, etc.

**hip·po** (hip′ō) *n., pl.* **-pos** [Inf.] HIPPOPOTAMUS

**Hip·poc·ra·tes** (hi päk′rə tēz′) 460?-377? B.C.; Gr. physician

**Hip·po·crat·ic oath** (hip′ə krat′ik) the oath, attributed to Hippocrates, generally taken by medical school graduates: it sets forth their ethical code

**hip·po·drome** (hip′ə drōm′) *n.* ⟦< Gr *hippos*, horse + *dromos*, course⟧ an arena for circuses, games, etc.

**hip·po·pot·a·mus** (hip′ə pät′ə məs) *n., pl.* **-a·mus·es, -a·mi′** (-mī′), or **-a·mus** ⟦< Gr *hippos*, a horse + *potamos*, river⟧ a large, plant-eating mammal with a heavy, thick-skinned body and short legs: it lives chiefly in or near African rivers

**hip·py** (hip′ē) *n., pl.* **-pies** *alt. sp. of* HIPPIE

**hire** (hīr) *n.* ⟦< OE *hyr*, wages⟧ **1** the amount paid in hiring **2** a hiring —*vt.* **hired, hir′ing** to pay for the services of (a person) or the use of (a thing) — **hire out** to work for pay

**hire′ling** (-liŋ) *n.* one who will follow anyone's orders for pay; mercenary

**Hi·ro·shi·ma** (hir′ə shē′mə, hi rō′shi mə) seaport in SW Honshu, Japan: largely destroyed (Aug. 6, 1945) by a U.S. atomic bomb, the first ever used in warfare: pop. 1,077,000

**hir·sute** (hur′sōōt′, hər sōōt′) *adj.* ⟦L *hirsutus*⟧ hairy; shaggy

**his** (hiz) *pron.* ⟦OE⟧ that or those belonging to

him: poss. form of HE [*his* are better] —*poss. pronominal adj.* of, belonging to, or done by him

**His·pan·ic** (hi span′ik) *adj.* **1** Spanish or Spanish-and-Portuguese **2** of or relating to Hispanics —*n.* a Spanish-speaking person of Latin American origin who lives in the U.S. For *adj.* 2 and the *n., Latino* and *Latina* are now often preferred

**His·pan·io·la** (his′pən yō′lə) island in the West Indies, between Cuba & Puerto Rico

**hiss** (his) *vi.* ⟦echoic⟧ **1** to make a sound like that of a prolonged *s* **2** to show disapproval by hissing —*vt.* to say or indicate by hissing —*n.* the act or sound of hissing

**his·sy fit** (his′ē) [Dial.] a fit of anger: usually in **have** (or **throw**) **a hissy fit**: also **his′sy** *n., pl.* **-sies**

**hist**[1] (st) *interj.* [Inf.] used to attract attention

**hist**[2] *abbrev.* history

**his·ta·mine** (his′tə mēn′, -min′) *n.* ⟦< Gr *histos*, web + AMMONIA⟧ an ammonia derivative in all organic matter: it is released in allergic reactions, lowers the blood pressure, etc.

**his·tol·o·gy** (his täl′ə jē) *n.* ⟦< Gr *histos*, web + -LOGY⟧ *Biol.* the microscopic study of tissue structure —**his·tol′o·gist** *n.*

**his·to·ri·an** (his tôr′ē ən) *n.* a writer of, or authority on, history

**his·tor·ic** (-ik) *adj.* having, or likely to have, lasting importance

**his·tor′i·cal** (-i kəl) *adj.* **1** of or concerned with history **2** based on people or events of the past **3** established by history; factual —**his·tor′i·cal·ly** *adv.*

**historical present** the present tense used for the narration of past events

**his·to·ric·i·ty** (his′tə ris′ə tē) *n.* historical authenticity

**his·to·ri·og·ra·phy** (his tôr′ē äg′rə fē) *n.* the study of the techniques of historical research

**his·to·ry** (his′tə rē, -trē) *n., pl.* **-ries** ⟦< Gr *histōr*, knowing⟧ **1** an account of what has happened, esp. in the life of a people, country, etc. **2** all recorded past events **3** the branch of knowledge that deals systematically with the past **4** a known or recorded past [the odd *history* of his coat]

**his·tri·on·ic** (his′trē än′ik) *adj.* ⟦< L *histrio*, actor⟧ **1** of acting or actors **2** overacted or overacting; affected

**his′tri·on′ics** *pl.n.* [*sometimes with sing. v.*] **1** dramatics **2** an artificial manner, display of emotion, etc.

**hit** (hit) *vt., vi.* **hit, hit′ting** ⟦< ON *hitta*, meet with⟧ **1** to come against (something) with force; knock **2** to give a blow (to); strike **3** to strike with a missile **4** to affect strongly [a town hard *hit* by floods] **5** to come (upon) by accident or after search **6** to arrive at [stocks *hit* a new high] **7** *Baseball* to get (a hit) —*n.* **1** a blow that strikes its mark **2** a collision **3** a successful and popular song, book, etc. **4** an instance of finding particular data in a computer search **5** [Slang] a murder **6** [Slang] a dose of a drug, a drink of liquor, etc. **7** *Baseball* BASE HIT —**hit it off** to get along well together —**hit′ter** *n.*

**hit-and-run** (hit′n run′) *adj.* hitting a person, car, etc. with a moving vehicle and fleeing the scene immediately: also **hit′-skip′**

**hitch** (hich) *vi.* ⟦ME *hicchen*⟧ **1** to move jerkily **2** to become fastened or caught **3** [Slang] to hitchhike —*vt.* **1** to move, pull, etc. with jerks **2** to fasten with a hook, knot, etc. —*n.* **1** a tug; jerk **2** a limp **3** a hindrance; obstacle **4** a fastening or catch **5** [Slang] a period of time served **6** a kind of knot

**hitch′hike′** *vi.* **-hiked′, -hik′ing** to travel by asking for rides from passing drivers —**hitch′hik′er** *n.*

**hith·er** (hith′ər) *adv.* ⟦< OE *hider*⟧ to this place; here

**hith′er·to′** *adv.* until this time

**Hit·ler** (hit′lər), **Ad·olf** (ad′ôlf′, ä′dôlf′) 1889-1945; Nazi dictator of Germany (1933-45), born in Austria —**Hit·ler′i·an** (-lir′ē ən) *adj.*

**hit man** [Inf.] a hired murderer

**hit'-or-miss'** *adj.* haphazard; random

**HIV** *n.* a retrovirus that infects human T cells and causes AIDS

**hive** (hīv) *n.* ⟦< OE *hyfe*⟧ **1** a shelter for a colony of bees; beehive **2** a colony of bees; swarm **3** a crowd of busy people **4** a place of great activity — *vt.* **hived, hiv'ing** to gather (bees) into a hive —*vi.* to enter a hive

**hives** (hīvz) *pl.n.* ⟦orig. Scot dial.⟧ [*with sing. or pl. v.*] an allergic skin condition characterized by itching, burning, and the formation of smooth patches

**HMO** *n., pl.* **HMO's** ⟦*h(ealth) m(aintenance) o(rganization)*⟧ a healthcare system in which an organization hires medical professionals to provide services for its subscribers

**HMS** *abbrev.* **1** Her (or His) Majesty's Service **2** Her (or His) Majesty's Ship

**hoa·gie** or **hoa·gy** (hō'gē) *n., pl.* **-gies** HERO SANDWICH

**hoard** (hôrd) *n.* ⟦OE *hord*⟧ a supply stored up and hidden —*vi., vt.* to accumulate and store away (money, goods, etc.) —**hoard'er** *n.* —**hoard'ing** *n.*

**hoar·frost** (hôr'frôst') *n.* FROST (sense 2)

**hoarse** (hôrs) *adj.* **hoars'er, hoars'est** ⟦OE *has*⟧ **1** harsh and grating in sound **2** having a rough, husky voice —**hoarse'ly** *adv.* —**hoarse'ness** *n.*

**hoar·y** (hôr'ē) *adj.* **-i·er, -i·est** ⟦< OE *har*⟧ **1** white or gray **2** having white or gray hair from old age **3** very old Also **hoar** —**hoar'i·ness** *n.*

**hoax** (hōks) *n.* ⟦< ? HOCUS-POCUS⟧ a trick or fraud; esp., a practical joke —*vt.* to deceive with a hoax

**hob·ble** (häb'əl) *vi.* **-bled, -bling** ⟦ME *hobelen*⟧ to go unsteadily; limp —*vt.* **1** to cause to limp **2** to hamper (a horse, etc.) by tying two feet together **3** to hinder —*n.* **1** a limp **2** a rope, etc. used to hobble a horse

**hob·by** (häb'ē) *n., pl.* **-bies** ⟦ME *hobi*⟧ **1** HOBBY-HORSE **2** something that one likes to do in one's spare time —**hob'by·ist** *n.*

**hob'by·horse'** *n.* **1** a child's toy consisting of a stick with a horse's head **2** ROCKING HORSE **3** an idea with which one is preoccupied

**hob·gob·lin** (häb'gäb'lin) *n.* ⟦*hob*, elf or goblin + GOBLIN⟧ **1** an elf **2** a bugbear

**hob'nail'** *n.* ⟦*hob*, a peg + NAIL⟧ a short nail with a broad head, put on the soles of heavy shoes to prevent wear or slipping —*vt.* to put hobnails on

**hob'nob'** (-näb') *vi.* **-nobbed', -nob'bing** ⟦< ME *habben*, have + *nabben*, not to have⟧ to be on close terms (*with*)

**ho·bo** (hō'bō) *n., pl.* **-bos** or **-boes** **1** a migratory worker **2** a tramp

**Ho Chi Minh City** (hō'chē'min') seaport in S Vietnam: formerly (as *Saigon*) capital of South Vietnam (1954-76): pop. 3,420,000

**hock**[1] (häk) *n.* ⟦< OE *hoh*, heel⟧ the joint bending backward in the hind leg of a horse, ox, etc.

**hock**[2] (häk) *vt., n.* ⟦< Du *hok*, prison⟧ [Slang] PAWN[1] —**in** (or **out of**) **hock** [Slang] in (or out of) debt

**hock·ey** (häk'ē) *n.* ⟦prob. < OFr *hoquet*, bent stick⟧ **1** a team game played on ice skates, with curved sticks and a hard rubber disk (*puck*) **2** a similar game played on foot on a field, with a small ball; field hockey

**hock'shop'** *n.* [Slang] PAWNSHOP

**ho·cus-po·cus** (hō'kəs pō'kəs) *n.* ⟦imitation L⟧ **1** meaningless words used as a formula by conjurers **2** a magician's trick or tricks **3** trickery

**hod** (häd) *n.* ⟦prob. < MDu *hodde*⟧ **1** a V-shaped device with a long handle, used for carrying bricks, mortar, etc. on the shoulder **2** a coal scuttle

**hodge·podge** (häj'päj') *n.* ⟦< OFr *hochepot*, a stew⟧ a jumbled mixture

**Hodg·kin's disease** (häj'kinz) ⟦after T. *Hodgkin*, 19th-c. Eng physician⟧ a chronic disease of unknown cause characterized by progressive enlargement of the lymph nodes

**hoe** (hō) *n.* ⟦< OHG *houwan*, to cut⟧ a tool with a thin blade set across the end of a long handle, for weeding, loosening soil, etc. —*vt., vi.* **hoed, hoe'ing** to weed, cultivate, etc. with a hoe

**hoe'cake'** *n.* a thin bread made of cornmeal

**hoe'down'** *n.* **1** a lively, rollicking dance **2** a party with such dances

GARDEN HOE

**hog** (hôg, häg) *n.* ⟦OE *hogg*⟧ **1** any swine, esp. a domesticated adult ready for market **2** [Inf.] a selfish, greedy, gluttonous, or filthy person —*vt.* **hogged, hog'ging** [Slang] to take all of or an unfair share of —**go (the) whole hog** [Slang] to go all the way —**high on** (or **off**) **the hog** [Inf.] in a luxurious or costly way —**hog'gish** *adj.* —**hog'gish·ly** *adv.*

**ho·gan** (hō'gôn', -gən) *n.* ⟦< AmInd⟧ a Navajo Indian dwelling, built of earth walls supported by timbers

**hogs·head** (hôgz'hed') *n.* **1** a large barrel or cask holding from 63 to 140 gallons **2** a liquid measure, esp. one equal to 63 gallons

**hog'tie'** *vt.* **-tied', -ty'ing** or **-tie'ing 1** to tie the four feet or the hands and feet of **2** [Inf.] to make incapable of effective action

**hog'wash'** *n.* **1** refuse fed to hogs; swill **2** insincere talk, writing, etc.

**ho-hum** (hō'hum') *interj.* used to show boredom: an utterance suggesting a yawn —*adj.* [Inf.] boring or tiresome

**hoi pol·loi** (hoi'pə loi') ⟦Gr, the many⟧ the common people; the masses

**hoist** (hoist) *vt.* ⟦< Du *hijschen*⟧ to raise aloft; lift, esp. with a pulley, crane, etc. —*n.* **1** a hoisting **2** an apparatus for lifting; elevator; tackle

**hoke** (hōk) *vt.* **hoked, hok'ing** ⟦< fol.⟧ [Slang] to treat in a sentimental or crudely comic way: usually with *up* —**hok'ey** *adj.*

**ho·kum** (hō'kəm) *n.* ⟦< HOCUS(-POCUS)⟧ [Slang] **1** trite sentiment, crude humor, etc. **2** nonsense or humbug

**hold**[1] (hōld) *vt.* **held, hold'ing** ⟦OE *haldan*⟧ **1** to keep in the hands, arms, etc.; grasp **2** to keep in a certain position or condition **3** to restrain or control; keep back **4** to possess; occupy [to hold an office] **5** to guard; defend [hold the fort] **6** to carry on (a meeting, etc.) **7** to contain [the jar holds a pint] **8** to regard; consider [I hold the story to be true] **9** *Law* to decide; decree —*vi.* **1** to go on being firm, loyal, etc. **2** to remain unbroken or unyielding [the rope held] **3** to be true or valid [this rule holds for any case] **4** to continue [the wind held steady] —*n.* **1** a grasping or seizing; grip **2** a thing to hold on by **3** a dominating force [she has a hold over him] —**catch (get, lay, or take) hold of** to take, seize, acquire, etc. —**hold forth** to preach; lecture —**hold on** [Inf.] stop! wait! —**hold out 1** to last; endure **2** to stand firm **3** to offer **4** [Inf.] to refuse to give (what is to be given) —**hold over 1** to postpone **2** to keep for an additional period —**hold up 1** to prop up **2** to show **3** to last; endure **4** to stop; delay **5** to stop forcibly and rob —**hold'er** *n.*

**hold**[2] (hōld) *n.* ⟦< HOLE or < MDu *hol*⟧ **1** the interior of a ship below decks, where the cargo is carried **2** the compartment for cargo in an aircraft

**hold'ing** *n.* **1** land, esp. a farm, rented from another **2** [*pl.*] property owned, as stocks and bonds

**hold'o'ver** *n.* [Inf.] one staying on from a previous period

**hold'up'** *n.* **1** a delay **2** the act of stopping forcibly and robbing

**hole** (hōl) *n.* ⟦OE *hol*⟧ **1** a hollow place; cavity **2**

an animal's burrow; den **3** a small, dingy, squalid place **4** an opening in anything; break; gap; tear **5** *Golf a)* a small cup sunk into a green, into which the ball is to be hit  *b)* a section of a course including the tee, fairway, and green —**hole up** [Inf.] **1** to hibernate  **2** to shut oneself in  **3** to hide out —**in the hole** [Inf.] financially embarrassed or behind

**-hol·ic** (häl'ik) *combining form* -AHOLIC

**hol·i·day** (häl'ə dā') *n.* **1** a religious festival; holy day  **2** a day of freedom from labor, often one set aside by law  **3** *[often pl.]* [Chiefly Brit.] a vacation —*adj.* of or for a holiday; joyous; gay

**ho·li·er-than-thou** (hō'lē ər *th*ən *th*ou') *adj.* annoyingly self-righteous

**ho·li·ness** (hō'lē nis) *n.* **1** a being holy  **2** [H-] a title of the pope

**ho·lis·tic** (hō lis'tik) *adj.* of or dealing with wholes or integrated systems rather than with their parts —**ho·lis'ti·cal·ly** *adv.*

**Hol·land** (häl'ənd) NETHERLANDS —**Hol'land·er** *n.*

**hol·lan·daise sauce** (häl'ən dāz') [Fr, of Holland] a creamy sauce made of butter, egg yolks, lemon juice, etc.

**hol·ler** (häl'ər) *vi., vt., n.* [Inf.] shout or yell

**hol·low** (häl'ō') *adj.* [OE *holh*] **1** having a cavity inside; not solid  **2** shaped like a bowl; concave  **3** sunken *[hollow* cheeks*]* **4** empty or worthless *[hollow* praise*]* **5** hungry  **6** deep-toned and muffled —*n.* **1** a hollow place; cavity  **2** a valley —*vt., vi.* to make or become hollow —**hol'low·ness** *n.*

**hol·ly** (häl'ē) *n., pl.* **-lies** [OE *holegn*] an evergreen shrub or tree with stiff, glossy, sharp-pointed leaves and bright-red berries

**hol'ly·hock'** (-häk') *n.* [< OE *halig*, holy + *hoc*, mallow] a tall plant of the mallow family, with large, showy flowers

**Hol·ly·wood** (häl'ē wood') section of Los Angeles, California, once the site of many U.S. film studios

**Holmes** (hōmz, hōlmz), **Ol·i·ver Wen·dell** (äl'ə vər wen'dəl) 1841-1935; associate justice, U.S. Supreme Court (1902-32)

**hol·o·caust** (häl'ə kôst', hō'lə-) *n.* [< Gr *holos*, whole + *kaustos*, burnt] a great destruction of life, esp. by fire —**the Holocaust** [*also* **the h-**] the systematic killing of millions of European Jews by the Nazis

**Hol·o·cene** (häl'ō sēn', hō'lə-) *adj.* [< Gr *holos*, whole + *kainos*, recent] designating the present epoch of geologic time

**hol·o·gram** (häl'ə gram', hō'lə-) *n.* a photographic image produced by holography

**hol'o·graph'** (-graf') *n.* [< Gr *holos*, whole + *graphein*, to write] a document, letter, etc. in the handwriting of the person under whose name it appears

**hol'o·graph'ic** (-graf'ik) *adj.* **1** of or in the form of a holograph  **2** of holography

**ho·log·ra·phy** (hō läg'rə fē) *n.* [< Gr *holos*, whole + -GRAPHY] a method of making three-dimensional photographs using a laser beam

**Hol·stein** (hōl'stēn', -stīn') *n.* [after the region of Schleswig-*Holstein*, Germany] a breed of large, black-and-white dairy cattle

**hol·ster** (hōl'stər) *n.* [Du] a pistol case attached to a belt, saddle, etc.

**ho·ly** (hō'lē) *adj.* **-li·er** or **-li·est** [OE *halig*] *[often* H-] **1** dedicated to religious use; sacred  **2** spiritually pure; sinless  **3** deserving deep respect, awe, etc.

**Holy Communion** a Christian rite in which bread and wine are consecrated and received as the body and blood of Jesus or as symbols of them

**Holy Land** PALESTINE

**Holy Roman Empire** empire of WC Europe, from A.D. 962 until 1806

**Holy Spirit** (or **Ghost**) the third person of the Trinity; spirit of God

**hom·age** (häm'ij, äm'-) *n.* [< L *homo*, man] anything given or done to show reverence, honor, etc.

**hom·burg** (häm'bərg) *n.* [after *Homburg*, Prussia] a man's felt hat with a crown dented front to back and a stiff, curved brim

**home** (hōm) *n.* [OE *hām*] **1** the place where one lives  **2** the place where one was born or reared  **3** a place thought of as home  **4** a household and its affairs  **5** an institution for orphans, the aged, etc.  **6** the natural environment of an animal, plant, etc.  **7** HOME PLATE —*adj.* **1** of one's home or country; domestic  **2** central *[home* office*]* —*adv.* **1** at, to, or in the direction of home  **2** to the point aimed at *[to* drive a nail *home]* —**at home 1** in one's home  **2** at ease —**bring home to** to impress upon —**home'less** *adj.* —**home'like'** *adj.*

**home'boy'** *masc.n.* [Slang] **1** a boy or man from one's neighborhood, town, etc.  **2** a close male friend —**home'girl'** *fem.n.*

**home'-care'** *adj.* of medical care, etc. provided in a person's home

**home economics** the science and art of homemaking, nutrition, etc.

**home'land'** *n.* the country in which one was born or makes one's home

**home'ly** *adj.* **-li·er, -li·est 1** suitable for home life; everyday  **2** crude  **3** plain or unattractive —**home'li·ness** *n.*

**home'made'** *adj.* made, or as if made, at home

**home'mak'er** *n.* one who manages a household

**ho·me·op·a·thy** (hō'mē äp'ə thē) *n.* the treatment of a disease using, in small doses, drugs that produce symptoms like those of the disease —**ho'me·o·path'ic** (-ə path'ik) *adj.*

**home page** a website or the initial page of a website

**home plate** *Baseball* the base that the batter stands beside: it is the last base touched in scoring a run

**Ho·mer** (hō'mər) semilegendary Gr. epic poet of *c.* 8th c. B.C. —**Ho·mer·ic** (hō mer'ik) *adj.*

**home run** *Baseball* a hit that allows the batter to touch all bases and score a run: also [Inf.] **hom'er** *n.*

**home'sick'** *adj.* unhappy at being away from home —**home'sick'ness** *n.*

**home'spun'** *n.* coarse loosely-woven cloth —*adj.* **1** spun at home  **2** plain; homely

**home'stead'** (-sted') *n.* **1** a place where a family makes its home  **2** a tract of land granted by the U.S. government to a settler —**home'stead'er** *n.*

**home'stretch'** *n.* **1** the part of a racetrack between the last turn and the finish line  **2** the final part of any undertaking

**home'ward** *adv., adj.* toward home *[homeward* bound*]*: also **home'wards** *adv.*

**home'work'** *n.* **1** work, esp. piecework, done at home  **2** lessons to be done outside the classroom  **3** preparation for some project: usually in **do one's homework**

**home'y** *adj.* **hom'i·er, hom'i·est** familiar, cozy, etc. —**home'y·ness** *n.*

**hom·i·cide** (häm'ə sīd') *n.* [< L *homo*, a man + *caedere*, to kill] **1** the killing of one person by another  **2** a person who kills another —**hom'i·ci'dal** *adj.*

**hom·i·let·ics** (häm'ə let'iks) *pl.n.* [see fol.] the art of preparing and delivering sermons

**hom·i·ly** (häm'ə lē) *n., pl.* **-lies** [< Gr *homilos*, assembly] **1** a sermon  **2** a solemn, moralizing talk or writing

**homing pigeon** a pigeon trained to find its way home from distant places

**hom·i·nid** (häm'ə nid) *n.* [< L *homo*, a man] a human, extinct or living

**hom·i·ny** (häm'ə nē) *n.* [< AmInd] dry corn hulled and coarsely ground (**hominy grits**): it is boiled for food

**homo-** [< Gr *homos*] *combining form* same, equal, like

**ho·mo·ge·ne·ous** (hō'mō jē'nē əs, häm'ō-) *adj.* [see prec. & GENUS] **1** the same in structure, quality, etc.; similar **2** composed of similar parts —**ho'mo·ge·ne'i·ty** (-jə nē'ə tē, -nā'-) *n.*

**ho·mog·e·nize** (hə mäj'ə nīz') *vt.* **-nized', -niz'ing** to make homogeneous, or more uniform throughout; specif., to process (milk) so that fat particles are so finely emulsified that the cream does not separate

**hom·o·graph** (häm'ə graf', hō'mə-) *n.* ⟦HOMO- + -GRAPH⟧ a word with the same spelling as another but with a different meaning and origin

**ho·mol·o·gous** (hō mäl'ə gəs) *adj.* ⟦Gr *homologos*, agreeing⟧ matching in structure, position, etc.

**hom·o·nym** (häm'ə nim') *n.* ⟦< Gr *homos*, same + *onyma*, name⟧ a word with the same pronunciation as another but with a different meaning, origin, and, usually, spelling

**ho·mo·pho·bi·a** (hō'mə fō'bē ə) *n.* ⟦HOMO(SEX-UAL) + -PHOBIA⟧ irrational hatred or fear of homosexuals or homosexuality —**ho'mo·pho'bic** (-fō'bik) *adj.*

**Ho·mo sa·pi·ens** (hō'mō sā'pē enz') ⟦ModL *homo*, man + *sapiens*, prp. of *sapere*, to know⟧ mankind; human being

**ho·mo·sex·u·al** (hō'mō sek'shōō əl, -mə-) *adj.* of or having sexual desire for those of the same sex —*n.* a homosexual person —**ho'mo·sex'u·al'i·ty** (-al'ə tē) *n.*

**Hon** *abbrev.* honorable

**Hon·du·ras** (hän door'əs) country in Central America: 43,277 sq. mi.; pop. 4,444,000

**hone** (hōn) *n.* ⟦OE *han*, a stone⟧ a hard stone used to sharpen cutting tools —*vt.* **honed, hon'ing** to sharpen, as with a hone

**hon·est** (än'ist) *adj.* ⟦< L *honor*, honor⟧ **1** truthful; trustworthy **2** *a)* sincere or fair *[honest effort] b)* gained by fair means *[an honest living]* **3** being what it seems **4** frank and open *[an honest face]* —**hon'est·ly** *adv.* —**hon'es·ty** *n.*

**hon·ey** (hun'ē) *n., pl.* **-eys** ⟦OE *hunig*⟧ **1** a sweet, syrupy substance that bees make as food from the nectar of flowers **2** sweetness **3** darling

**hon'ey·comb'** *n.* the structure of six-sided wax cells made by bees to hold their honey or eggs —*vt.* to cause to have holes like a honeycomb —*adj.* of or like a honeycomb: also **hon'ey·combed'**

**hon'ey·dew' melon** a variety of melon with a smooth, whitish rind and sweet, greenish flesh

**hon'ey·lo'cust** *n.* a North American tree having featherlike foliage and large, twisted pods

**hon'ey·moon'** *n.* the vacation spent together by a newly married couple —*vi.* to have or spend a honeymoon —**hon'ey·moon'er** *n.*

**hon'ey·suck'le** (-suk'əl) *n.* a plant with small, fragrant flowers of red, yellow, or white

**Hong Kong** or **Hong·kong** (häŋ'käŋ', hôŋ'kôŋ') administrative region of China, on the South China Sea: formerly a British colony

**honk** (hôŋk, häŋk) *n.* ⟦echoic⟧ **1** the call of a wild goose **2** a similar sound, as of an automobile horn —*vi., vt.* to make or cause to make such a sound

**hon·ky-tonk** (hôŋ'kē tôŋk') *n.* **1** [Old Slang] a cheap, noisy nightclub **2** [Slang] a bar, esp. one where country music if played —*adj.* designating music played on a piano with a tinkling sound

**Hon·o·lu·lu** (hän'ə lōō'lōō) capital of Hawaii: seaport on Oahu: pop. 365,000

**hon·or** (än'ər) *n.* ⟦L⟧ **1** high regard or respect; esp., *a)* glory; fame *b)* good reputation **2** adherence to principles considered right; integrity **3** chastity **4** high rank; distinction **5** [H-] a title of certain officials, as judges **6** something done or given as a token of respect **7** a source of respect and fame —*vt.* **1** to respect greatly **2** to show high regard for **3** to do or give something in honor of **4** to accept and pay *[to honor a check]* Brit. sp. **hon'our** —**do the honors** to act as host

**hon'or·a·ble** *adj.* **1** worthy of being honored **2** honest; upright **3** bringing honor —**hon'or·a·bly** *adv.*

**hon·o·ra·ri·um** (än'ə rer'ē əm) *n., pl.* **-ri·ums** or

-**ri·a** (-ə) ⟦L⟧ a payment as to a professional person for services on which no fee is set

**hon·or·ar·y** (än'ə rer 'ē) *adj.* **1** given as an honor **2** designating or in an office held as an honor, without service or pay —**hon'or·ar·i·ly** *adv.*

**hon·or·if·ic** (-ə rif'ik) *adj.* ⟦< L *honor* + *facere*, to make⟧ conferring honor; showing respect

**Hon·shu** (hän'shōō') largest of the islands forming Japan

**hood** (hood) *n.* ⟦OE *hod*⟧ **1** a covering for the head and neck, often part of a coat, etc. **2** anything resembling a hood, as the metal cover over an automobile engine —*vt.* to cover as with a hood —**hood'ed** *adj.*

**-hood** (hood) ⟦OE *had*⟧ *suffix* **1** state or quality *[childhood]* **2** the whole group of *[priesthood]*

**hood·lum** (hood'ləm, hōōd'-) *n.* ⟦prob. < Ger dial. *hudilump*, wretch⟧ a lawless person, as a member of a gang of criminals

**hoo·doo** (hōō'dōō') *n., pl.* **-doos'** ⟦var. of VOODOO⟧ **1** VOODOO **2** [Inf.] bad luck or its cause

**hood'wink'** *vt.* ⟦HOOD + WINK⟧ to mislead by trickery; dupe

**hoo·ey** (hōō'ē) *interj., n.* ⟦echoic⟧ [Slang] nonsense

**hoof** (hoof, hoof) *n., pl.* **hoofs** or **hooves** (hoovz, hoovz) ⟦OE *hof*⟧ the horny covering on the feet of cattle, horses, etc., or the entire foot —*vt., vi.* [Inf.] to walk: often with *it* —**hoofed** *adj.*

**hook** (hook) *n.* ⟦OE *hoc*⟧ **1** a bent piece of metal, etc. used to catch, hold, or pull something **2** a fishhook **3** something shaped like a hook **4** something moving in a hooklike path, as a punch delivered with the elbow bent —*vt.* to catch, fasten, throw, etc. with a hook —*vi.* **1** to curve as a hook does **2** to be fastened or caught by a hook — **by hook or by crook** by any means, honest or dishonest —**hook up** to connect (a radio, etc.) — **off the hook** [Inf.] out of trouble

**hook·ah** or **hook·a** (hook'ə, hōō'kə) *n.* ⟦Ar *huqqa*⟧ a tobacco pipe with a tube for drawing the smoke through a vessel of water to cool it

**hooked** (hookt) *adj.* **1** like a hook **2** made with a hook *[hooked* rug] **3** [Slang] *a)* obsessed with or addicted to (often with *on) b)* married

**hook'er** *n.* [Slang] a prostitute

**hook'up'** *n.* the arrangement and connection of parts, circuits, etc., as in a radio

**hook'worm'** *n.* a small, parasitic, intestinal roundworm with hooks around the mouth

**hook'y** *n.* [Inf.] used only in **play hooky**, be a truant

**hoo·li·gan** (hōō'li gən) *n.* ⟦< ? *Hooligan*, a family name⟧ [Slang] a hoodlum

**hoop** (hoop) *n.* ⟦OE *hop*⟧ **1** a circular band for holding together the staves of a barrel, etc. **2** anything like this, as a metal basketball rim —*vt.* to bind or fasten as with a hoop

**hoop·la** (hoop'lä') *n.* ⟦< ?⟧ [Inf.] **1** great excitement **2** showy publicity

**hoop skirt** a skirt worn over a framework of hoops

**hoo·ray** (hoo rā', hə-; hōō-) *interj., n., vi., vt. var. of* HURRAY

**hoose·gow** (hōōs'gou') *n.* ⟦< Sp *juzgado*, court of justice⟧ [Slang] a jail

**Hoo·sier** (hōō'zhər) *n.* [Inf.] a person born or living in Indiana

**hoot** (hōōt) *n.* ⟦echoic⟧ **1** the sound that an owl makes **2** any sound like this, as a shout of scorn **3** [Inf.] an amusing person, thing, etc. —*vi.* to utter a hoot —*vt.* to express (scorn) of (someone) by hooting —**hoot'er** *n.*

**hoot·en·an·ny** (hōōt''n an'ē) *n., pl.* **-nies** a meeting of folk singers, as for public entertainment

**Hoo·ver** (hōō'vər), **Her·bert** (**Clark**) (hur'bərt) 1874-1964; 31st president of the U.S. (1929-33)

**hop**[1] (häp) *vi.* **hopped, hop'ping** ⟦OE *hoppian*⟧ **1** to make a short leap or leaps on one foot **2** to leap with both, or all, feet at once, as a frog **3** [Inf.] *a)* to go briskly *b)* to take a short trip —*vt.* **1** to jump over **2** to get aboard —*n.* **1** a hopping **2** [Inf.] *a)* a dance *b)* a short flight in an airplane

**hop**[2] (häp) *n.* ⟦< MDu *hoppe*⟧ **1** a twining vine with flowers borne in small cones **2** [*pl.*] the dried ripe cones, used for flavoring beer, ale, etc. —**hop up** to stimulate, as by a drug

**hope** (hōp) *n.* ⟦OE *hopa*⟧ **1** a feeling that what is wanted will happen; desire accompanied by expectation **2** the object of this **3** a person or thing on which one may base some hope —*vt.* **hoped, hop′ing** to want and expect —*vi.* to have hope (*for*) —**hope′ful** *adj.* —**hope′ful·ly** *adv.* — **hope′less** *adj.* —**hope′less·ly** *adv.*

**hop′head′** *n.* [Slang] a drug addict

**hop·per** (häp′ər) *n.* **1** one that hops **2** any hopping insect **3** a box, tank, etc. from which the contents can be emptied slowly and evenly

**hop·sack·ing** (häp′sak′iŋ) *n.* a sturdy fabric resembling coarse material used for bags, that is made into coats, suits, etc. Also **hop′sack′**

**hop·scotch** (häp′skäch′) *n.* a children's game in which a player hops from section to section of a figure drawn on the ground

**Hor·ace** (hôr′is, här′-) 65-8 B.C.; Rom. poet

**horde** (hôrd) *n.* ⟦ult. < Tatar *urdu*, a camp⟧ a crowd or throng; swarm —*vi.* **hord′ed, hord′ing** to form or gather in a horde

**hore·hound** (hôr′hound′) *n.* ⟦OE *harhune*⟧ **1** a bitter plant of the mint family **2** medicine or candy made from its juice

**ho·ri·zon** (hə rī′zən) *n.* ⟦< Gr *horos*, boundary⟧ **1** the line where the sky seems to meet the earth **2** [*usually pl.*] the limit of one's experience, interest, etc.

**hor·i·zon·tal** (hôr′i zänt′'l) *adj.* **1** parallel to the plane of the horizon; not vertical **2** flat and even; level —**hor′i·zon′tal·ly** *adv.*

**hor·mone** (hôr′mōn′) *n.* ⟦< Gr *hormē*, impulse⟧ a substance formed in some organ of the body and carried to another part, where it takes effect — **hor·mo′nal** *adj.*

**horn** (hôrn) *n.* ⟦OE⟧ **1** a hard, bonelike projection growing on the head of a cow, goat, etc. **2** the substance horns are made of **3** anything like a horn in position, shape, etc. **4** any brass instrument; specif., FRENCH HORN **5** a device sounded to give a warning —*adj.* made of horn —**horn in** (**on**) to intrude or meddle (in) —**horned** *adj.* — **horn′less** *adj.* —**horn′like′** *adj.*

**Horn, Cape** southernmost point of South America, on an island of Chile

**horn·blende** (hôrn′blend′) *n.* ⟦Ger⟧ a hard, heavy, dark-colored mineral

**horned toad** a small, scaly, insect-eating lizard with hornlike spines: also **horned lizard**

**hor·net** (hôr′nit) *n.* ⟦OE *hyrnet*⟧ a large, yellow and black wasp

**horn of plenty** CORNUCOPIA

**horn′pipe′** *n.* ⟦ME⟧ a lively dance formerly popular with sailors

**horn·y** (hôr′nē) *adj.* **-i·er, -i·est 1** made of horn **2** toughened and calloused [*horny* hands] **3** [Slang] easily aroused sexually

**ho·rol·o·gy** (hō räl′ə jē) *n.* ⟦< Gr *hōra*, hour + -LOGY⟧ the science of measuring time or making timepieces

**hor·o·scope** (hôr′ə skōp′) *n.* ⟦< Gr *hōra*, hour + *skopos*, watcher⟧ a chart of the zodiacal signs and positions of planets, etc., esp. at the time of a person's birth, used by an astrologer to make a forecast

**hor·ren·dous** (hô ren′dəs) *adj.* ⟦see HORRID⟧ horrible; frightful

**hor·ri·ble** (hôr′ə bəl) *adj.* ⟦see fol.⟧ **1** causing horror; terrible; dreadful **2** [Inf.] very bad, ugly, unpleasant, etc. —**hor′ri·bly** *adv.*

**hor·rid** (hôr′id) *adj.* ⟦< L *horrere*, to bristle, shake, be afraid⟧ **1** causing horror; terrible **2** very bad, ugly, unpleasant, etc. —**hor′rid·ly** *adv.*

**hor·rif·ic** (hô rif′ik, hə-) *adj.* horrifying

**hor·ri·fy** (hôr′ə fī′) *vt.* **-fied′, -fy′ing 1** to cause to feel horror **2** [Inf.] to shock or disgust

**hor·ror** (hôr′ər) *n.* ⟦see HORRID⟧ **1** the strong feeling caused by something frightful or shocking **2** strong dislike **3** something that causes horror

***hors de com·bat*** (ôr də kōn bä′) ⟦Fr, out of combat⟧ disabled

**hors d'oeuvre** (ôr′durv′) *pl.* **hors′ d'oeuvres′** ⟦Fr, lit., outside of work⟧ an appetizer, as canapés, served before a meal

**horse** (hôrs) *n.* ⟦OE *hors*⟧ **1** a large, four-legged, solid-hoofed animal with flowing mane and tail, domesticated for drawing loads, carrying riders, etc. **2** a frame with legs to support something — *adj.* of or on horses —**hold one's horses** [Slang] to curb one's impatience —**horse around** [Slang] to engage in horseplay

**horse′back′** *n.* the back of a horse —*adv.* on horseback

**horse chestnut 1** a flowering tree with large leaves and glossy brown seeds **2** its seed

**horse′feath′ers** *n., interj.* [Slang] nonsense

**horse′fly′** *n., pl.* **-flies′** a large fly that sucks the blood of horses, etc.

**horse′hair′** *n.* **1** hair from the mane or tail of a horse **2** a stiff fabric made from this hair

**horse′hide′** *n.* **1** the hide of a horse **2** leather made from this

**horse′laugh′** *n.* a loud, boisterous, usually derisive laugh; guffaw

**horse′man** (-mən) *n., pl.* **-men** (-mən) a man skilled in the riding, managing, or care of horses —**horse′man·ship′** *n.* —**horse′wom′an,** *pl.* **-wom′en, fem.n.**

**horse opera** [Slang] WESTERN (*n.*)

**horse′play′** *n.* rough, boisterous fun

**horse′pow′er** *n., pl.* **-pow′er** a unit for measuring the power of engines, etc., equal to 746 watts or 33,000 foot-pounds per minute

**horse′rad′ish** *n.* **1** a plant with a pungent, white, fleshy root **2** a relish made of the grated root

**horse sense** [Inf.] common sense

**horse′shoe′** *n.* **1** a flat, U-shaped metal plate nailed to a horse's hoof to protect it **2** anything shaped like this **3** [*pl.*, *with sing. v.*] a game in which players toss horseshoes at two stakes

**horseshoe crab** a sea arthropod shaped like the base of a horse's foot, with a long, spinelike tail

**horse′tail′** *n.* a common rushlike plant found in moist areas

**horse′whip′** *n.* a whip for driving horses —*vt.* **-whipped′, -whip′ping** to lash with a horsewhip

**hors·y** (hôr′sē) *adj.* **-i·er, -i·est 1** of, like, or suggesting a horse **2** of or like people who are fond of horses, fox-hunting, horse racing, etc. Also **hors′ey**

**hor·ta·to·ry** (hôr′tə tôr′ē) *adj.* ⟦< L *hortari*, incite⟧ exhorting; advising

**hor·ti·cul·ture** (hôr′tə kul′chər) *n.* ⟦< L *hortus*, garden + *cultura*, cultivation⟧ the art or science of growing flowers, fruits, and vegetables —**hor′ti·cul′tur·al** *adj.*

**ho·san·na** (hō zan′ə, -zä′nə) *n., interj.* ⟦< Heb *hōshī′āh nnā*, lit., save, we pray⟧ an exclamation of praise to God

**hose** (hōz) *n., pl.* **hose** or, for 2, **hos′es** ⟦OE *hosa*⟧ **1** [*pl.*] stockings or socks **2** a flexible tube used to convey fluids —*vt.* **hosed, hos′ing** to water with a hose: often with *down*

**ho·sier·y** (hō′zhər ē) *n.* stockings

**hos·pice** (häs′pis) *n.* ⟦< L *hospes*, host, guest⟧ **1** a shelter for travelers **2** a homelike facility for the care of terminally ill patients

**hos·pi·ta·ble** (häs′pit ə bəl, häs pit′-) *adj.* ⟦see prec.⟧ friendly and solicitous toward guests, new arrivals, etc. —**hos′pi·ta·bly** *adv.*

**hos·pi·tal** (häs′pit′'l) *n.* ⟦< L *hospes*, host, guest⟧

an institution providing medical treatment for people who are ill, injured, pregnant, etc.

**hos·pi·tal·i·ty** (häs′pi tal′ə tē) *n., pl.* **-ties** the act, practice, or quality of being hospitable

**hos·pi·tal·ize** (häs′pit′l iz′) *vt.* **-ized′, -iz′ing** to put in, or admit to, a hospital —**hos′pi·tal·i·za′tion** *n.*

**host**¹ (hōst) *n.* ⟦< ML *hostia*⟧ a wafer of the bread used in the Eucharist

**host**² (hōst) *n.* ⟦< L *hospes*, host, guest⟧ **1** one who entertains guests, esp. at home **2** a person who keeps an inn or hotel **3** any organism on or in which a parasitic organism lives —*vi., vt.* to act as host (to)

**host**³ (hōst) *n.* ⟦< ML *hostis*, army⟧ **1** an army **2** a great number

**hos·tage** (häs′tij) *n.* ⟦< OFr⟧ a person kept or given as a pledge until certain conditions are met

**hos·tel** (häs′təl) *n.* ⟦< L *hospes*, host, guest⟧ an inn: also **hos′tel·ry** (-rē), *pl.* **-ries**

**hos′tel·er** *n.* a traveler who stops at hostels

**host·ess** (hōs′tis) *n.* **1** a woman who entertains guests, esp. at home; sometimes, the host's wife **2** a woman employed in a restaurant to supervise serving, seating, etc.

**hos·tile** (häs′təl) *adj.* ⟦< L *hostis*, enemy⟧ **1** of or characteristic of an enemy **2** unfriendly; antagonistic —**hos′tile·ly** *adv.*

**hos·til·i·ty** (häs til′ə tē) *n., pl.* **-ties 1** a feeling of enmity, ill will, etc. **2** *a)* an expression of enmity, ill will, etc. *b)* [*pl.*] warfare

**hos·tler** (häs′lər, äs′-) *n.* ⟦contr. of HOSTELER⟧ one who takes care of horses at an inn, stable, etc.

**hot** (hät) *adj.* **hot′ter, hot′test** ⟦OE *hat*⟧ **1** *a)* having a temperature higher than that of the human body *b)* having a relatively high temperature **2** producing a burning sensation [*hot* pepper] **3** characterized by strong feeling or intense activity, etc.; specif., *a)* impetuous [a *hot* temper] *b)* violent [a *hot* battle] *c)* lustful *d)* very controversial **4** following closely [in *hot* pursuit] **5** electrically charged [a *hot* wire] **6** [Inf.] recent; fresh [*hot* news] **7** [Slang] *a)* recently stolen or smuggled *b)* excellent; good —**make it hot for** [Inf.] to make things uncomfortable for —**hot′ly** *adv.* —**hot′ness** *n.*

**hot air** [Slang] empty talk

**hot′bed′** *n.* **1** a bed of earth covered with glass and heated, as by manure, for forcing plants **2** a place of rapid growth or extensive activity

**hot′blood′ed** *adj.* easily excited; excitable

**hot′box′** *n.* an overheated bearing on an axle or shaft

**hot cake** a pancake —**sell like hot cakes** [Inf.] to be sold rapidly and in large quantities

**hot dog** [Inf.] a wiener, esp. one served hot in a long, soft roll

**ho·tel** (hō tel′) *n.* ⟦< OFr *hostel*, hostel⟧ an establishment providing lodging and, usually, meals for travelers, etc.

**ho·tel·ier** (hō tel′yər) *n.* ⟦Fr *hôtelier*⟧ an owner or manager of a hotel

**hot flash** the sensation of a wave of heat passing over the body, often experienced by women during menopause

**hot′foot′** *vi.* [Inf.] to hurry; hasten: with *it*

**hot′head′ed** *adj.* **1** quick-tempered **2** impetuous —**hot′head′** *n.*

**hot′house′** *n.* GREENHOUSE

**hot line** an emergency telephone line between government leaders or to a social agency

**hot plate** a small portable stove for cooking food

**hot potato** [Inf.] a troubling problem that no one wants to handle

**hot rod** [Slang] an automobile, often an old one, rebuilt for great speed —**hot rod′der**

**hot seat** [Slang] **1** ELECTRIC CHAIR **2** a difficult situation

**hot′shot′** *n.* [Slang] one seen as an expert or as very aggressive: often used ironically

**hot′-tem′pered** *adj.* having a fiery temper

**Hot·ten·tot** (hät′'n tät′) *n.* **1** a member of a nomadic people of SW Africa **2** the language of this people

**hot tub** a large wooden tub in which several people can soak in hot water together

**hound** (hound) *n.* ⟦OE *hund*, dog⟧ **1** any of several breeds of hunting dog **2** any dog —*vt.* **1** to hunt or chase with or as with hounds **2** to urge on

**hounds·tooth check** (houndz′tooth′) a pattern of irregular broken checks, used in woven material

**hour** (our) *n.* ⟦< Gr *hōra*⟧ **1** one of the twenty-four parts of a day; sixty minutes **2** the time for a particular activity [lunch *hour*] **3** [*pl.*] a period fixed for work, etc. [office *hours*] **4** the time of day [the *hour* is 2:30] **5** *Educ.* a credit, equal to one hour spent in class per week —**after hours** after the regular hours for business, school, etc. —**hour after hour** every hour

**hour′glass′** *n.* an instrument for measuring time by the trickling of sand, etc. from one glass bulb to another

**hour hand** the short hand of a clock or watch, which indicates the hours

HOURGLASS

**hou·ri** (hoo′rē, hou′-) *n., pl.* **-ris** ⟦< Ar *ḥūrīyah*, black-eyed woman⟧ a beautiful nymph of the Muslim Paradise

**hour′ly** *adj.* **1** happening every hour **2** done during an hour **3** frequent —*adv.* **1** once an hour **2** often

**house** (hous; *for v.* houz) *n., pl.* **hous·es** (hou′ziz) ⟦OE *hus*⟧ **1** a building to live in; specif., a building occupied by one family or person **2** the people who live in a house; household **3** [*often* H-] a family as including kin, ancestors, and descendants, esp. a royal family **4** shelter, living or storage space, etc. **5** *a)* a theater *b)* the audience in a theater **6** a business firm **7** [*often* H-] a legislative assembly —*adj.* of a salad dressing, wine, etc. at a particular restaurant —*vt.* **housed, hous′ing 1** to provide a house or lodgings for **2** to cover, shelter, etc. —**keep house** to take care of a home —**on the house** at the expense of the establishment

**house′boat′** *n.* a large, flat-bottomed boat used as a residence

**house′bound′** *adj.* confined to one's home, as by illness

**house′break′ing** *n.* the act of breaking into and entering another's house to commit theft or another felony

**house′bro′ken** *adj.* trained to live in a house (i.e., to urinate, etc. in a special place or outside): said of a dog, cat, etc.

**house′fly′** *n., pl.* **-flies′** a two-winged fly found in and around houses

**house′guest′** *n.* a person who stays overnight in another's home

**house′hold′** *n.* **1** all those living in one house **2** the home and its affairs —**house′hold′er** *n.*

**household word** a common saying or thing, familiar to nearly everyone

**house′hus′band** *n.* a married man whose job is keeping house and taking care of domestic affairs

**house′keep′er** *n.* one who runs a home, esp. a woman hired to do this

**house′maid′** *n.* a maid who does housework

**House of Commons** the lower house of the legislature of Great Britain or Canada

**House of Lords** the upper house of the legislature of Great Britain

**House of Representatives** the lower house of the legislature of the U.S. and most of the states of the U.S.

**house′plant′** *n.* a plant grown indoors, mainly for decoration

**house′wares′** (-werz′) *pl.n.* articles for household use, esp. in the kitchen

**house′warm′ing** *n.* a party to celebrate moving into a new home

**house′wife′** *n., pl.* **-wives′** a married woman whose job is keeping house and taking care of domestic affairs

**house′work′** *n.* the work involved in keeping house; cleaning, cooking, etc.

**hous·ing** (hou′zin) *n.* **1** the providing of shelter or lodging **2** shelter or lodging **3** houses collectively **4** *Mech.* a frame, box, etc. for containing some part, mechanism, etc.

**Hous·ton** (hyōōs′tən) city & port in SE Texas: pop. 1,630,000

**hove** (hōv) *vt., vi. alt. pt. & pp. of* HEAVE

**hov·el** (huv′əl, häv′-) *n.* ⟦ME⟧ any small, miserable dwelling; hut

**hov·er** (huv′ər, häv′-) *vi.* ⟦< ME *hoven*, to stay (suspended)⟧ **1** to flutter in the air near one place **2** to linger close by **3** to waver (*between*)

**how** (hou) *adv.* ⟦OE *hu*⟧ **1** in what manner or way **2** in what state or condition **3** for what reason **4** to what extent, degree, etc. *How* is also used as an intensive —**how about something** (or **someone**)? [Inf.] what is your opinion, etc. concerning something (or someone)?

**how·be·it** (hou bē′it) *adv.* [Archaic] however it may be; nevertheless

**how·dah** (hou′də) *n.* ⟦< Hindi *hauda*⟧ a seat for riding on the back of an elephant or camel

**how·ev·er** *adv.* **1** in whatever manner **2** to whatever degree **3** nevertheless

**how·itz·er** (hou′it sər) *n.* ⟦< Czech *houfnice*, orig., a sling⟧ a short cannon, firing shells in a high trajectory

**howl** (houl) *vi.* ⟦ME *hulen*⟧ **1** to utter the long, wailing cry of wolves, dogs, etc. **2** to utter a similar cry of pain, anger, etc. **3** to shout or laugh in scorn, mirth, etc. —*vt.* **1** to utter with a howl **2** to drive by howling —*n.* **1** the wailing cry of a wolf, dog, etc. **2** any similar sound **3** [Inf.] a joke

**howl′er** *n.* **1** one that howls **2** [Inf., Chiefly Brit.] a ludicrous blunder

**how·so·ev·er** (hou′sō ev′ər) *adv.* **1** to whatever degree or extent **2** by whatever means

**hoy·den** (hoid′'n) *n.* ⟦< ? Du⟧ a bold, boisterous girl; tomboy

**Hoyle** (hoil) *n.* a book of rules for card games, orig. compiled by E. Hoyle (1672-1769) —**according to Hoyle** according to the rules

**HP** *abbrev.* horsepower: usually written **hp**

**HQ** or **hq** *abbrev.* headquarters

**hr** *abbrev.* hour

**HR** *abbrev.* **1** *Baseball* home run(s) **2** House of Representatives

**HRH** *abbrev.* Her (or His) Royal Highness

**HS** *abbrev.* high school

**ht** *abbrev.* height

**HTML** *abbrev.* Hypertext Markup Language

**Huang He** (hwän′ hu′) river in N China, flowing into the Yellow Sea

**hua·ra·ches** (wə rä′chēz, hə-) *pl.n.* ⟦MexSp⟧ flat sandals with uppers made of straps or woven leather strips

**hub** (hub) *n.* ⟦< ?⟧ **1** the center part of a wheel **2** a center of activity

**hub·bub** (hub′bub′) *n.* ⟦prob. < Gael exclamation⟧ an uproar; tumult

**hub′cap′** *n.* a tight cap over the hub of a wheel, esp. on an automobile

**hu·bris** (hyōō′bris) *n.* ⟦Gr *hybris*⟧ arrogance caused by excessive pride

**huck·le·ber·ry** (huk′əl ber′ē) *n., pl.* **-ries** ⟦prob. ult. < ME *hurtilberye*⟧ **1** a shrub with blue berries **2** this berry

**huck·ster** (huk′stər) *n.* ⟦< MDu *hoeken*, peddle⟧ **1** a peddler **2** [Inf.] one engaged in advertising — *vt.* to peddle

**HUD** *abbrev.* (Department of) Housing and Urban Development

**hud·dle** (hud′'l) *vi.,* *vt.* **-dled, -dling** ⟦< ?⟧ **1** to crowd close together **2** to draw (oneself) up —*n.* **1** a confused crowd or heap **2** [Inf.] a private conference **3** *Football* a grouping of a team to get signals before a play

**Hud·son** (hud′sən) river in E New York

**Hudson Bay** inland sea in NE Canada; arm of the Atlantic

**hue**[1] (hyōō) *n.* ⟦< OE *heow*⟧ **1** color **2** a particular shade or tint of a color

**hue**[2] (hyōō) *n.* ⟦< OFr *hu*, outcry⟧ a shouting: now only in **hue and cry**

**huff** (huf) *vi.* to blow; puff —*n.* a state of smoldering anger or resentment —**huff′y, -i·er, -i·est,** *adj.*

**hug** (hug) *vt.* **hugged, hug′ging** ⟦prob. < ON *hugga*, to comfort⟧ **1** to clasp closely and fondly in the arms; embrace **2** to cling to (a belief, etc.) **3** to keep close to —*vi.* to embrace each other —*n.* a close embrace

**huge** (hyōōj) *adj.* **hug′er, hug′est** ⟦< OFr *ahuge*⟧ very large; gigantic; immense —**huge′ly** *adv.*

**Hu·go** (hyōō′gō), **Vic·tor (Marie)** (vik′tər) 1802-85; Fr. poet, novelist, & playwright

**Hu·gue·not** (hyōō′gə nät′) *n.* a French Protestant of the 16th or 17th c.

**huh** (hu, hun) *interj.* [Inf.] used to express contempt, surprise, etc., or to ask a question

**hu·la** (hōō′lə) *n.* ⟦Haw⟧ a native Hawaiian dance: also **hu′la-hu′la**

**hulk** (hulk) *n.* ⟦< Gr *holkas*, towed ship⟧ **1** the hull of an old, dismantled ship **2** a big, clumsy person or thing

**hulk′ing** *adj.* bulky and clumsy

**hull** (hul) *n.* ⟦OE *hulu*⟧ **1** the outer covering of a seed or fruit, as the husk of grain or shell of a nut **2** the frame or main body of a ship, airship, etc. **3** any outer covering —*vt.* to take the hulls off (nuts, etc.) —**hull′er** *n.*

**hul·la·ba·loo** (hul′ə bə lōō′) *n.* ⟦echoic⟧ noise and confusion; hubbub

**hum** (hum) *vi.* **hummed, hum′ming** ⟦echoic⟧ **1** to make a low, continuous, murmuring sound **2** to sing with closed lips **3** [Inf.] to be full of activity —*vt.* to sing (a tune) with closed lips —*n.* a continuous murmur

**hu·man** (hyōō′mən) *adj.* ⟦< L *humanus*⟧ of, characteristic of, or having the qualities typical of people, or human beings —*n.* a person: also **human being** —**hu′man·ness** *n.*

**hu·mane** (hyōō mān′) *adj.* ⟦var. of prec.⟧ **1** kind, tender, merciful, etc. **2** civilizing; refining —**hu·mane′ly** *adv.* —**hu·mane′ness** *n.*

**hu·man·ism** (hyōō′mə niz′əm) *n.* **1** any system of thought based on the interests and ideals of humanity **2** [H-] the intellectual movement that stemmed from the study of the Greek and Latin classics during the Middle Ages —**hu′man·ist** *n., adj.* —**hu′man·is′tic·al·ly** *adv.*

**hu·man·i·tar·i·an** (hyōō man′ə ter′ē ən) *n.* a person devoted to promoting the welfare of humanity; philanthropist —*adj.* helping humanity —**hu·man′i·tar′i·an·ism′** *n.*

**hu·man·i·ty** (hyōō man′ə tē) *n., pl.* **-ties 1** the fact or quality of being human or humane **2** people — **the humanities** literature, philosophy, history, etc., as distinguished from the sciences

**hu·man·ize** (hyōō′mə nīz′) *vt.* **-ized′, -iz′ing** to make or become human or humane —**hu′man·i·za′tion** *n.* —**hu′man·iz′er** *n.*

**hu′man·kind′** *n.* mankind; people

**hu′man·ly** *adv.* **1** in a human manner **2** within human ability or knowledge

**hu′man·oid′** (-mə noid′) *adj.* nearly human —*n.* a nearly human creature

**hum·ble** (hum′bəl) *adj.* **-bler, -blest** ⟦< L *humilis*, low⟧ **1** having or showing a consciousness of one's shortcomings; modest **2** lowly; unpretentious —*vt.* **-bled, -bling 1** to lower in condition or rank; abase **2** to lower in pride; make modest —**hum′ble·ness** n. —**hum′bly** adv.

**hum·bug** (hum′bug′) n. ⟦< ?⟧ **1** fraud; sham; hoax **2** an impostor —vt. **-bugged′, -bug′ging** to dupe; deceive —interj. nonsense!

**hum·drum** (hum′drum′) adj. ⟦echoic⟧ dull

**hu·mer·us** (hyōō′mər əs) n., pl. **-mer·i′** (-ī′) ⟦L⟧ the bone of the upper arm or forelimb —**hu′mer·al** adj.

**hu·mid** (hyōō′mid) adj. ⟦< L umere, be moist⟧ damp; moist

**hu·mid·i·fy** (hyōō mid′ə fī′) vt. **-fied′, -fy′ing** to make humid; dampen —**hu·mid′i·fi·er** n.

**hu·mid′i·ty** (-ə tē) n. **1** moistness; dampness **2** the amount of moisture in the air

**hu·mi·dor** (hyōō′mə dôr′) n. a case or jar for keeping tobacco moist

**hu·mil·i·ate** (hyōō mil′ē āt′) vt. **-at′ed, -at′ing** ⟦< L humilis, humble⟧ to hurt the pride or dignity of; mortify —**hu·mil′i·a′tion** n.

**hu·mil′i·ty** (-ə tē) n. the state or quality of being humble

**hum·ming·bird** (hum′iŋ burd′) n. a very small, brightly colored bird with narrow wings that vibrate rapidly, often with a humming sound

**hum·mock** (hum′ək) n. ⟦< ?⟧ a low, rounded hill; knoll —**hum′mock·y** adj.

**hum·mus** (hum′əs) n. ⟦Turk humus⟧ a Middle Eastern puree of chickpeas, garlic, etc.

**hu·mon·gous** (hyōō mäŋ′gəs, -muŋ′-) adj. ⟦? a blend of HUGE + MONSTROUS⟧ [Slang] enormous

**hu·mor** (hyōō′mər) n. ⟦< L humor, fluid: after former belief in four body fluids (humors) held responsible for one's disposition⟧ **1** mood; state of mind **2** whim; caprice **3** a comical quality **4** a) the ability to appreciate or express what is funny, amusing, etc. b) the expression of this —vt. to comply with the mood or whim of; indulge Brit. sp. **hu′mour** —**out of humor** not in a good mood —**hu′mor·ist** n. —**hu′mor·less** adj.

**hu′mor·ous** adj. funny; amusing; comical —**hu′mor·ous·ly** adv.

**hump** (hump) n. ⟦prob. < LowG⟧ a rounded, protruding lump, as on a camel's back —vt. to hunch; arch —**over the hump** [Inf.] past the worst or most difficult part

**hump′back′** n. **1** a humped, deformed back **2** HUNCHBACK (sense 2) **3** a large whale with long flippers and a raised back —**hump′backed′** adj.

**hu·mus** (hyōō′məs) n. ⟦L, earth⟧ the dark part of the soil, from partially decayed leaves, etc.

**Hun** (hun) n. a member of a warlike Asiatic people that invaded Europe in the 4th and 5th c. A.D.

**hunch** (hunch) vt. ⟦< ?⟧ to arch into a hump —vi. to move forward jerkily —n. **1** a hump **2** a feeling not based on known facts; premonition

**hunch·back** (hunch′bak′) n. **1** HUMPBACK (sense 1) **2** a person having a back with a hump —**hunch′backed′** adj.

**hun·dred** (hun′drəd) n., adj. ⟦OE⟧ ten times ten; 100; C —**hun′dredth** (-drədth) adj., n.

**hun′dred·fold′** adj., adv. (having) a hundred times as much or as many

**hun′dred·weight′** n. a unit of weight equal to 100 pounds in the U.S. and 112 pounds in Great Britain

**hung** (huŋ) vt., vi. pt. & pp. of HANG —**hung over** [Slang] having a hangover —**hung up (on)** [Slang] disturbed, frustrated, or obsessed (by)

**Hung** abbrev. **1** Hungarian **2** Hungary

**Hun·gar·i·an** (huŋ ger′ē ən) n. **1** the language of Hungary **2** a person born or living in Hungary —adj. of Hungary or its people, language, etc.

**Hun·ga·ry** (huŋ′gə rē) country in SC Europe: 35,911 sq. mi.; pop. 10,375,000

**hun·ger** (huŋ′gər) n. ⟦OE hungor⟧ **1** discomfort caused by a need for food **2** starvation **3** a desire for food **4** any strong desire —vi. **1** to be hungry **2** to desire —**hun′gry, -gri·er, -gri·est,** adj. —**hun′gri·ly** adv.

**hunger strike** the refusal of a prisoner, demonstrator, etc. to eat until certain demands are met

**hung jury** a jury unable to reach a verdict

**hunk** (huŋk) n. ⟦Fl hunke⟧ [Inf.] a large piece

**hun·ker** (huŋ′kər) vi. ⟦< dial.⟧ to squat or crouch: often with down —n. [pl.] haunches or buttocks

**hunt** (hunt) vt., vi. ⟦OE huntian⟧ **1** to kill or catch (game) for food or sport **2** to try to find; search (for) **3** to chase —n. **1** a hunting **2** a group of people who hunt together **3** a search —**hunt′er** or **hunts′man** (-mən), pl. **-men** (-mən), n. —**hunt′ress** fem.n.

**Hun·ting·ton Beach** (hun′tiŋ tən) city in SW California: pop. 182,000

**Hunts·ville** (hunts′vil) city in N Alabama: pop. 160,000

**hur·dle** (hurd′l) n. ⟦OE hyrdel⟧ **1** a framelike barrier over which horses or runners must leap in a race **2** an obstacle —vt. **-dled, -dling 1** to jump over **2** to overcome (an obstacle) —**hur′dler** n.

**hur·dy-gur·dy** (hur′dē gur′dē) n., pl. **-dies** ⟦? echoic⟧ popularly, a barrel organ

**hurl** (hurl) vt. ⟦prob. < ON⟧ **1** to throw with force or violence **2** to cast down **3** to utter vehemently —vi. [Inf.] Baseball to pitch —**hurl′er** n.

JUMPING A HURDLE

**hurl·y-burl·y** (hur′lē bur′lē) n., pl. **-burl′ies** a turmoil; uproar

**Hu·ron** (hyōōr′än), **Lake** second largest of the Great Lakes, between Michigan & Canada

**hur·rah** (hə rä′, -rô′) n., interj., vi., vt. HURRAY

**hur·ray** (hə rä′) n., interj. ⟦echoic⟧ (exclamation) used to express joy, approval, etc. —vi., vt. to shout "hurray" (for); cheer

**hur·ri·cane** (hur′i kān′) n. ⟦< WInd huracan⟧ a violent tropical cyclone

**hurricane lamp 1** an oil lamp or candlestick with a glass chimney to protect the flame **2** an electric lamp like this

**hur·ry** (hur′ē) vt. **-ried, -ry·ing** ⟦prob. akin to HURL⟧ **1** to move or send with haste **2** to cause to occur or be done more rapidly or too rapidly **3** to urge to act soon or too soon —vi. to move or act with haste —n. **1** rush; urgency **2** eagerness to do, go, etc. quickly —**hur′ried·ly** adv.

**hurt** (hurt) vt. hurt, hurt′ing ⟦< OFr hurter, to hit⟧ **1** to cause pain or injury to **2** to harm **3** to offend —vi. **1** to cause injury, pain, etc. **2** to have pain; be sore —n. **1** a pain or injury **2** harm; damage —adj. injured; damaged

**hurt′ful** adj. causing hurt; harmful

**hur·tle** (hurt′l) vi., vt. **-tled, -tling** ⟦ME hurtlen⟧ to move or throw with great speed or much force

**hus·band** (huz′bənd) n. ⟦< ON hūs, house + bondi, freeholder⟧ a married man —vt. to manage economically; conserve

**hus′band·ry** n. **1** thrift **2** farming

**hush** (hush) vt. ⟦< ME huscht, quiet (adj.)⟧ **1** to make quiet or silent **2** to soothe; lull —vi. to become quiet or silent —n. quiet; silence —interj. used to call for silence

**hush′-hush′** adj. [Inf.] very secret

**hush puppy** a small ball of fried cornmeal dough

**husk** (husk) n. ⟦prob. < MDu huus, house⟧ **1** the dry outer covering of various fruits or seeds, as of an ear of corn **2** any dry, rough, or useless covering —vt. to remove the husk from

**hus·ky**[1] (hus′kē) n., pl. **-kies** ⟦< a var. of ESKIMO⟧ [also H-] a dog of any of several breeds for pulling sleds in the Arctic

**husk·y**[2] (hus′kē) adj. **-i·er, -i·est 1** hoarse; rough **2** ⟦< toughness of a husk⟧ big and strong

**hus·sar** (hoo zär′) *n.* [< Serb *husar*] a European light-armed cavalryman, usually with a brilliant dress uniform

**hus·sy** (huz′ē, hus′-) *n.*, *pl.* **-sies** [< ME *huswife*, housewife] **1** a woman of low morals **2** a bold, saucy girl

**hus·tings** (hus′tiŋz) *pl.n.* [< ON *hūsthing*, house council] [*usually with sing. v.*] the process of, or a place for, political campaigning

**hus·tle** (hus′əl) *vt.* **-tled**, **-tling** [Du *husselen*, shake up] **1** to push about; jostle **2** to force in a rough, hurried manner —*vi.* **1** to move hurriedly **2** [Inf.] to work energetically **3** [Slang] to obtain money aggressively or dishonestly —*n.* **1** a hustling **2** [Inf.] energetic action; drive —**hus′tler** *n.*

**hut** (hut) *n.* [< OHG *hutta*] a very plain or crude little house or cabin

**hutch** (huch) *n.* [< ML *hutica*, chest] **1** a chest or cupboard **2** a pen or coop for small animals **3** a hut

**hutz·pah** (hoots′pə) *n.* CHUTZPAH

**huz·zah** or **huz·za** (hə zä′) *n.*, *interj.*, *vi.*, *vt.* *archaic var. of* HURRAH (see HURRAY)

**HVAC** *abbrev.* heating, ventilating, and air conditioning

**hwy** *abbrev.* highway

**hy·a·cinth** (hī′ə sinth′) *n.* [< Gr *hyakinthos*] a plant of the lily family, with spikes of bell-shaped flowers

**hy·brid** (hī′brid) *n.* [L *hybrida*] **1** the offspring of two animals or plants of different varieties, species, etc. **2** anything of mixed origin —*adj.* of or like a hybrid —**hy′brid·ism′** *n.*

**hy·brid·ize** (hī′bri dīz′) *vi.*, *vt.* **-ized′**, **-iz′ing** to produce or cause to produce hybrids; crossbreed

**Hy·der·a·bad** (hī′dər ə bad′, -bäd′) city in SC India: pop. 2,546,000

**hy·dra** (hī′drə) *n.*, *pl.* **-dras** or **-drae** (-drē′) [< Gr, water serpent] a small, freshwater polyp with a soft, tubelike body

**hy·dran·ge·a** (hī drān′jə, -dran′-; -jē ə) *n.* [< HYDR(O)- + Gr *angeion*, vessel] a shrub with large, showy clusters of white, blue, or pink flowers

**hy·drant** (hī′drənt) *n.* [< Gr *hydōr*, water] a large pipe with a valve for drawing water from a water main; fireplug

**hy·drate** (hī′drāt′) *n.* [HYDR(O)- + -ATE[1]] a chemical compound of water and some other substance

**hy·drau·lic** (hī drô′lik) *adj.* [ult. < Gr *hydōr*, water + *aulos*, tube] **1** of hydraulics **2** operated by the movement and force of liquid [*hydraulic* brakes] —**hy·drau′li·cal·ly** *adv.*

**hy·drau′lics** *n.* the science dealing with the mechanical properties of liquids, as water, in motion and their application in engineering

**hydro-** [< Gr *hydōr*, WATER] *combining form* **1** water [*hydrometer*] **2** hydrogen

**hy·dro·car·bon** (hī′drə kär′bən) *n.* any compound containing only hydrogen and carbon

**hy·dro·chlo·ric acid** (hī′drə klôr′ik) a strong, highly corrosive acid that is a water solution of the gas hydrogen chloride

**hy·dro·e·lec·tric** (hī′drō ē lek′trik) *adj.* producing, or relating to the production of, electricity by water power —**hy′dro·e′lec′tric′i·ty** *n.*

**hy·dro·foil** (hī′drə foil′) *n.* [HYDRO- + (AIR)FOIL] **1** a winglike structure that lifts and carries a watercraft just above the water at high speed **2** such a watercraft

**hy·dro·gen** (hī′drə jən) *n.* [see HYDRO- & -GEN] a flammable, colorless, odorless, gaseous chemical element: the lightest known substance

**hy·dro·gen·ate** (hī drä′jə nāt′) *vt.* **-nat′ed**, **-nat′ing** to combine with or treat with hydrogen [vegetable oil is *hydrogenated* to make a solid fat]

**hydrogen bomb** an extremely destructive nuclear bomb in which an atomic bomb explosion starts a nuclear fusion explosion of heavy hydrogen atoms

**hydrogen peroxide** a colorless liquid used as a bleach or disinfectant

**hy·drol·o·gy** (hī dräl′ə jē) *n.* [see HYDRO- & -LOGY] the study of the earth's waters, their distribution, and the cycle involving evaporation, precipitation, flow, etc.

**hy·drol·y·sis** (-ə sis) *n.*, *pl.* **-ses′** (-sēz′) [HYDRO- + -LYSIS] a chemical reaction in which a substance reacts with water so as to be changed into one or more other substances

**hy·drom·e·ter** (hī dräm′ət ər) *n.* [HYDRO- + -METER] an instrument for measuring the specific gravity of liquids —**hy·drom′e·try** *n.*

**hy·dro·pho·bi·a** (hī′drə fō′bē ə) *n.* [see HYDRO- & -PHOBIA] **1** an abnormal fear of water **2** [from symptomatic inability to swallow liquids] RABIES

**hy·dro·phone** (hī′drə fōn′) *n.* [HYDRO- + -PHONE] an instrument for registering the distance and direction of sound transmitted through water

**hy′dro·plane′** (-plān′) *n.* **1** a small, high-speed motorboat with hydrofoils or a flat bottom **2** SEAPLANE

**hy′dro·pon′ics** (-pän′iks) *n.* [< HYDRO- & Gr *ponos*, labor] the science of growing plants in nutrient-rich solutions —**hy′dro·pon′ic** *adj.*

**hy′dro·sphere′** (-sfir′) *n.* [HYDRO- + -sphere, a layer of the earth's atmosphere] all the water on the surface of the earth, including oceans, etc.

**hy′dro·ther′a·py** *n.* the treatment of disease, etc. by the use of water

**hy·drous** (hī′drəs) *adj.* [HYDR(O)- + -OUS] containing water, esp. in chemical combination

**hy·drox·ide** (hī dräk′sīd′) *n.* [HYDR(O)- + OXIDE] a compound consisting of an element or radical combined with the radical OH

**hy·e·na** (hī ē′nə) *n.* [< Gr *hyaina*] a wolflike, flesh-eating animal of Africa and Asia, with a shrill cry

**hy·giene** (hī′jēn′) *n.* [< Gr *hygiēs*, healthy] **1** the science of maintaining health **2** cleanliness

**hy·gi·en·ic** (hī jen′ik) *adj.* **1** of hygiene or health **2** sanitary —**hy′gi·en′i·cal·ly** *adv.*

**hy·grom·e·ter** (hī gräm′ət ər) *n.* [< Gr *hygros*, wet + *metron*, a measure] an instrument for measuring humidity

**hy·men** (hī′mən) *n.* [Gr *hymēn*, membrane] the thin mucous membrane that closes part or sometimes all of the opening of the vagina

**hy·me·ne·al** (hī′mə nē′əl) *adj.* [< Gr *Hymēn*, god of marriage] of marriage

**hymn** (him) *n.* [< Gr *hymnos*] a song of praise, esp. in honor of God

**hym·nal** (him′nəl) *n.* a collection of hymns: also **hymn′book′**

**hype**[1] (hīp) *vt.* **hyped**, **hyp′ing** [Slang] to stimulate, excite, etc. by or as by a drug injection: usually with *up*

**hype**[2] (hīp) [Inf.] *n.* [? < HYPERBOLE] **1** deception **2** excessive promotion —*vt.* **hyped**, **hyp′ing** to promote in a sensational way

**hy·per** (hī′pər) *adj.* [Inf.] high-strung; keyed up

**hyper-** [< Gr *hyper*] *prefix* over, above, excessive

**hy·per·ac·tive** (hī′pər ac′tiv) *adj.* abnormally active —**hy′per·ac·tiv′i·ty** *n.*

**hy·per·bo·la** (hī pur′bə lə) *n.*, *pl.* **-las** or **-lae** (-lē′) [< Gr *hyperbolē*, a throwing beyond, excess] *Geom.* a curve formed by the intersection of a cone with a plane more steeply inclined than its side

**hy·per·bo·le** (hī pur′bə lē) *n.* [see prec.] exaggeration for effect, not meant to be taken literally —**hy·per·bol·ic** (hī′pər bäl′ik) *adj.*

**hy′per·crit·i·cal** (hī′pər krit′i kəl) *adj.* too critical

**hy′per·ex·tend′** (-ek stend′) *vt.* to injure (a knee, etc.) by bending it beyond its normal straightened position

**hy′per·gly·ce′mi·a** (-glī sē′mē ə) *n.* [< HYPER- + Gr *glykys*, sweet + -EMIA] an abnormally high amount of sugar in the blood

**hy′per·sen′si·tive** (-sen′sə tiv) *adj.* excessively sensitive —**hy′per·sen′si·tiv′i·ty** *n.*

**hy·per·ten·sion** (-ten′shən) *n.* abnormally high blood pressure

**hy′per·text′** (-tekst′) *n.* computer data organized so that related items can be accessed easily

**hy′per·thy′roid·ism′** (-thī′roid iz′əm) *n.* excessive activity of the thyroid gland, causing nervousness, rapid pulse, etc. —**hy′per·thy′roid′** *adj., n.*

**hy′per·ven′ti·la′tion** (-vent′′l ā′shən) *n.* extremely rapid or deep breathing that may cause dizziness, fainting, etc. —**hy′per·ven′ti·late′, -lat′ed, -lat′ing,** *vi., vt.*

**hy·phen** (hī′fən) *n.* ⟦< Gr *hypo-*, under + *hen*, one⟧ a mark (-) used between the parts of a compound word or the syllables of a divided word

**hy·phen·ate** (hī′fə nāt′) *vt.* **-at′ed, -at′ing** to connect or write with a hyphen —**hy′phen·a′tion** *n.*

**hyp·no·sis** (hip nō′sis) *n., pl.* **-ses′** (-sēz′) ⟦< Gr *hypnos*, sleep + -OSIS⟧ a trancelike condition usually induced by another person, in which the subject responds to suggestions made by that person

**hyp·not′ic** (-nät′ik) *adj.* **1** causing sleep; soporific **2** of, like, or inducing hypnosis —*n.* any agent causing sleep —**hyp·not′i·cal·ly** *adv.*

**hyp′no·tism′** (-nə tiz′əm) *n.* the act or practice of inducing hypnosis —**hyp′no·tist** *n.*

**hyp′no·tize′** (-tīz′) *vt.* **-tized′, -tiz′ing** to induce hypnosis in

**hy·po** (hī′pō) *n., pl.* **-pos** *short for* HYPODERMIC

**hypo-** ⟦Gr < *hypo*, under⟧ *prefix* **1** under, beneath [*hypodermic*] **2** less than

**hy·po·chon·dri·a** (hī′pə kän′drē ə) *n.* ⟦LL, pl., abdomen (supposed seat of the condition)⟧ abnormal anxiety over one's health, often with imaginary illnesses —**hy′po·chon′dri·ac′** (-ak′) *adj., n.*

**hy·poc·ri·sy** (hi päk′rə sē) *n., pl.* **-sies** ⟦< Gr *hypokrisis*, acting a part⟧ a pretending to be what one is not, or to feel what one does not feel; esp., a pretense of virtue, piety, etc.

**hyp·o·crite** (hip′ə krit′) *n.* ⟦see prec.⟧ one who pretends to be pious, virtuous, etc. without really being so —**hyp′o·crit′i·cal** *adj.*

**hy·po·der·mic** (hī′pə dur′mik) *adj.* ⟦< HYPO- + Gr

*derma*, skin⟧ injected under the skin —*n.* a hypodermic syringe or injection

**hypodermic syringe** a syringe attached to a hollow needle (**hypodermic needle**) and used for the injection of a medicine or drug under the skin

**hy·po·gly·ce·mi·a** (hī′pō glī sē′mē ə) *n.* ⟦< HYPO- + Gr *glykys*, sweet + -EMIA⟧ an abnormally low amount of sugar in the blood

**hy·pot·e·nuse** (hī pät′′n ōōs′) *n.* ⟦< Gr *hypo-*, under + *teinein*, to stretch⟧ the side of a right-angled triangle located opposite the right angle

**hy·po·thal·a·mus** (hī′pō thal′ə məs) *n., pl.* **-mi′** (-mī′) ⟦see HYPO- & THALAMUS⟧ the part of the brain that regulates many basic body functions, as temperature

**hy′po·ther′mi·a** (-thur′mē ə) *n.* ⟦< HYPO- + Gr *thermē*, heat⟧ a subnormal body temperature —**hy′po·ther′mal** *adj.*

**hy·poth·e·sis** (hī päth′ə sis) *n., pl.* **-ses′** (-sēz′) ⟦< Gr *hypo-*, under + *tithenai*, to place⟧ an unproved theory, etc. tentatively accepted to explain certain facts —**hy·poth′e·size′** (-sīz′), **-sized′, -siz′ing,** *vi., vt.*

**hy·po·thet·i·cal** (hī′pə thet′i kəl) *adj.* based on a hypothesis; assumed; supposed —**hy′po·thet′i·cal·ly** *adv.*

**hy·po·thy·roid·ism** (hī′pō thī′roid iz′əm) *n.* deficient activity of the thyroid gland, causing sluggishness, puffiness, etc. —**hy′po·thy′roid** *adj., n.*

**hys·sop** (his′əp) *n.* ⟦< Heb *ēzōbh*⟧ a fragrant, blue-flowered herb of the mint family

**hys·ter·ec·to·my** (his′tər ek′tə mē) *n., pl.* **-mies** ⟦< Gr *hystera*, uterus + -ECTOMY⟧ surgical removal of all or part of the uterus

**hys·te·ri·a** (hi ster′ē ə) *n.* ⟦< Gr *hystera*, uterus: orig. thought to occur more often in women than in men⟧ **1** a psychiatric condition characterized by excitability, anxiety, the simulation of organic disorders, etc. **2** any outbreak of wild, uncontrolled feeling: also **hys·ter′ics** —**hys·ter′i·cal** or **hys·ter′ic** *adj.* —**hys·ter′i·cal·ly** *adv.*

**Hz** *abbrev.* hertz

# I

**i** or **I** (ī) *n., pl.* **i′s, I′s** the ninth letter of the English alphabet

**I¹** (ī) *n.* a Roman numeral for 1

**I²** (ī) *pron.* ⟦OE *ic*⟧ the person speaking or writing

**I³** *abbrev.* **1** island(s) **2** isle(s)

**I⁴** *Chem. symbol for* iodine

**IA** *abbrev.* Iowa

**-i·al** (ē əl, yəl) ⟦L *-ialis*⟧ *suffix* -AL

**i·amb** (ī′amb′, -am′) *n.* ⟦< Gr *iambos*⟧ a metrical foot of one unaccented syllable followed by one accented one

**i·am·bic** (ī am′bik) *adj.* ⟦< Gr *iambikos*⟧ of or made up of iambs —*n.* an iamb

**-i·at·rics** (ē a′triks′) ⟦< Gr *iatros*, physician⟧ *combining form* treatment of disease [*pediatrics*]

**-i·a·try** (ī′ə trē) ⟦< Gr *iatreia*, healing⟧ *combining form* medical treatment [*psychiatry*]

**I·be·ri·a** (ī bir′ē ə) peninsula in SW Europe, comprising Spain & Portugal: also **Iberian Peninsula** —**I·be′ri·an** *adj., n.*

**i·bex** (ī′beks′) *n., pl.* **i′bex·es** or **i·bi·ces** (ī′bə sēz′) ⟦L⟧ a wild goat of the Old World, with large, backward-curved horns

**ibid.** *abbrev.* ⟦L *ibidem*⟧ in the same place, i.e., the book, page, etc. just cited: also **ib.**

**-i·bil·i·ty** (ə bil′ə tē) ⟦L *-ibilitas*⟧ *suffix* -ABILITY

**i·bis** (ī′bis) *n.* ⟦Egypt *hb*⟧ a large wading bird found chiefly in tropical regions

**-i·ble** (i bəl, ə bəl) ⟦L *-ibilis*⟧ *suffix* -ABLE

**Ib·sen** (ib′sən), **Hen·rik** (hen′rik) 1828-1906; Norw. playwright

**i·bu·pro·fen** (ī′byōō prō′fən) *n.* a drug used to reduce fever and relieve pain, esp. arthritic pain

**-ic** (ik) ⟦< Gr *-ikos*⟧ *suffix* **1** *a*) of, having to do with [*volcanic*] *b*) like [*angelic*] *c*) produced by [*anaerobic*] *d*) consisting of, containing [*dactylic*] *e*) having, showing [*lethargic*] **2** a person or thing: *a*) having [*paraplegic*] *b*) supporting [*heretic*] *c*) producing [*hypnotic*] Also **-i·cal** (i kəl, ə kəl)

**ICBM** *n.* an intercontinental ballistic missile

**ICC** *abbrev.* Interstate Commerce Commission

**ice** (īs) *n.* ⟦OE *īs*⟧ **1** water frozen solid by cold **2** a frozen dessert of fruit juice, sugar, etc. **3** [Slang] diamonds —*vt.* **iced, ic′ing 1** to change into ice; freeze **2** to cool with ice **3** to cover with icing —*vi.* to freeze: often with *up* or *over* —**break the ice** to make a start, as in getting acquainted —**cut no ice** [Inf.] to have no influence —**on thin ice** [Inf.] in danger

**Ice** *abbrev.* **1** Iceland **2** Icelandic

**ice′berg′** (-burg′) *n.* ⟦prob. < Du *ijsberg*, ice mountain⟧ a great mass of ice broken off from a glacier and floating in the sea

**ice′bound′** *adj.* held fast or shut in by ice

**ice′box′** *n.* a refrigerator, esp. one using ice

**ice′break′er** *n.* a sturdy boat for cutting channels through ice

**ice′cap′** *n.* a mass of glacial ice that spreads slowly from a center

**ice cream** ⟦orig., *iced cream*⟧ a sweet, frozen food of flavored cream or milk —**ice′-cream′** *adj.*

**ice floe** a piece of floating sea ice

**ice hockey** *see* HOCKEY (sense 1)

**Ice·land** (īs′lənd) country on an island in the North Atlantic, southeast of Greenland: 39,758 sq. mi.; pop. 229,000 —**Ice′land·er** *n.*

**Ice·lan·dic** (īs lan′dik) *n.* the Germanic language of Iceland —*adj.* of Iceland or its people, language, etc.

**ice·man** (īs′man′, -mən) *n.*, *pl.* -**men′** (-men′, -mən) one who sells or delivers ice

**ice milk** a frozen dessert like ice cream, but with less butterfat

**ice skate** *see* SKATE¹ (*n.* 1) —**ice′-skate′, -skat′ed, -skat′ing,** *vi.*

**ich·thy·ol·o·gy** (ik′thē äl′ə jē) *n.* ⟦< Gr *ichthys,* a fish + -LOGY⟧ the branch of zoology dealing with fish —**ich′thy·ol′o·gist** *n.*

**i·ci·cle** (ī′sik′əl, -sə kəl) *n.* ⟦< OE īs, ice + *gicel,* piece of ice⟧ a hanging piece of ice, formed by the freezing of dripping water

**ic·ing** (īs′iŋ) *n.* a mixture variously of sugar, butter, flavoring, egg whites, etc. for covering a cake; frosting

**ick·y** (ik′ē) *adj.* -**i·er, -i·est** ⟦< STICKY⟧ [Slang] **1** unpleasantly sticky or sweet **2** disgusting

**i·con** (ī′kän′) *n.* ⟦< Gr *eikōn,* image⟧ **1** *a)* an image; figure *b)* a stylized figure on a computer screen, representing a function **2** *Eastern Orthodox Ch.* a sacred image or picture of Jesus, Mary, etc. **3** one that is revered or that represents an era, etc. —**i·con′ic** *adj.*

**i·con·o·clast** (ī kän′ə klast′) *n.* ⟦< c. 6th-c. Gr *eikōn,* image + *klaein,* to break⟧ one who attacks widely accepted ideas, beliefs, etc. —**i·con′o·clasm′** *n.* —**i·con′o·clas′tic** *adj.*

**-ics** (iks) ⟦-IC + -S (pl.)⟧ *suffix* [*usually with sing. v.*] art, science, study [*mathematics*]

**ICU** *abbrev.* intensive care unit

**i·cy** (ī′sē) *adj.* **i′ci·er, i′ci·est 1** full of or covered with ice **2** of or like ice; specif., *a)* slippery *b)* very cold **3** cold in manner; unfriendly —**i′ci·ly** *adv.* —**i′ci·ness** *n.*

**id** (id) *n.* ⟦L, it⟧ *Psychoanalysis* that part of the psyche which is the source of psychic energy

**ID¹** (ī′dē′) *n.*, *pl.* **ID's** or **IDs** [Inf.] a document, as a license to drive a car, serving as identification

**ID²** *abbrev.* identification

**id.** *abbrev.* ⟦L *idem*⟧ the same

**I·da·ho** (ī′də hō′) Mountain State of the NW U.S.: 82,751 sq. mi.; pop. 1,007,000; cap. Boise: abbrev. **ID** —**I′da·ho′an** *adj., n.*

**i·de·a** (ī dē′ə) *n.* ⟦L < Gr, appearance of a thing⟧ **1** a thought; mental conception or image **2** an opinion or belief **3** a plan; scheme **4** meaning or significance

**i·de·al** (ī dē′əl, -dēl′) *adj.* ⟦see prec.⟧ **1** existing as an idea, model, etc. **2** thought of as perfect **3** imaginary —*n.* **1** a conception of something in its most excellent form **2** a perfect model **3** a noble goal or principle

**i·de·al·ism′** *n.* **1** behavior or thought based on a conception of things as one thinks they should be **2** a striving to achieve one's ideals —**i·de′al·ist** *n.* —**i·de′al·is′tic** *adj.*

**i·de·al·ize** (ī dē′əl īz′) *vt.* -**ized′, -iz′ing** to regard or show as perfect or more nearly perfect than is true —**i·de′al·i·za′tion** *n.* —**i·de′al·iz′er** *n.*

**i·de′al·ly** *adv.* **1** in an ideal manner; perfectly **2** in theory

**i·den·ti·cal** (ī den′ti kəl) *adj.* ⟦< L *idem,* the same⟧ **1** the very same **2** exactly alike —**i·den′ti·cal·ly** *adv.*

**i·den·ti·fi·ca·tion** (ī den′tə fi kā′shən) *n.* **1** an identifying or being identified **2** anything by which one can be identified

**i·den·ti·fy** (ī den′tə fī′) *vt.* -**fied′, -fy′ing 1** to make identical; treat as the same **2** to fix the identity of [*to identify* a biological specimen] **3** to connect or associate closely

**i·den·ti·ty** (ī den′tə tē) *n.*, *pl.* -**ties 1** the state or fact of being the same **2** *a)* the state or fact of being a specific person or thing; individuality *b)* the state of being as described

**identity crisis** the state of being uncertain about oneself regarding character, goals, etc., esp. in adolescence

**id·e·o·gram** (id′ē ō gram′, ī′dē-) *n.* ⟦see IDEA & -GRAM⟧ a symbol representing an object or idea without expressing the word for it: also **id′e·o·graph′** (-graf′)

**i·de·ol·o·gy** (ī′dē äl′ə jē, id′ē-) *n.*, *pl.* -**gies** ⟦see IDEA & -LOGY⟧ the doctrines, etc. on which a particular political or social system is based —**i·de′o·log′i·cal** *adj.* —**i·de·ol′o·gist** *n.*

**ides** (īdz) *pl.n.* ⟦< L *idus*⟧ [*often with sing. v.*] in the ancient Roman calendar, the 15th day of March, May, July, or October, or the 13th of the other months

**id·i·o·cy** (id′ē ə sē) *n.* **1** great foolishness or stupidity **2** *pl.* -**cies** an idiotic act or remark

**id·i·om** (id′ē əm) *n.* ⟦< Gr *idios,* one's own⟧ **1** the language or dialect of a people, region, class, etc. **2** the usual way that the words of a language are joined to express thought **3** a phrase or expression with an unusual syntactic pattern or with a meaning differing from the literal meaning of its parts **4** a characteristic style, as in art or music —**id′i·o·mat′ic** (-ə mat′ik) *adj.*

**id·i·o·path·ic** (id′ē ə′path′ik) *adj.* ⟦< Gr *idiopatheia,* feeling for oneself alone⟧ of a disease whose cause is unknown

**id·i·o·syn·cra·sy** (id′ē ō siŋ′krə sē) *n.*, *pl.* -**sies** ⟦< Gr *idio-,* one's own + *synkrasis,* a mixing⟧ any personal peculiarity, mannerism, etc. —**id′i·o·syn·crat′ic** (-sin krat′ik) *adj.*

**id·i·ot** (id′ē ət) *n.* ⟦< Gr *idiōtēs,* ignorant person⟧ **1** [Obs.] a person mentally inferior to a child two years old **2** a very foolish or stupid person —**id′i·ot′ic** (-ät′ik) *adj.* —**id′i·ot′i·cal·ly** *adv.*

**i·dle** (īd′'l) *adj.* **i′dler, i′dlest** ⟦OE *idel,* empty⟧ **1** useless; futile [an *idle* wish] **2** unfounded [*idle* rumors] **3** *a)* unemployed; not busy *b)* inactive; not in use **4** lazy —*vi.* **i′dled, i′dling 1** to move slowly or aimlessly **2** to be unemployed or inactive **3** to operate without transmitting power [the motor *idled*] —*vt.* **1** to waste: usually with *away* **2** to cause (a motor, etc.) to idle —**i′dle·ness** *n.* — **i′dler** *n.* —**i′dly** *adv.*

**i·dol** (īd′'l) *n.* ⟦< Gr *eidōlon,* image⟧ **1** an image of a god, used as an object of worship **2** any object of ardent or excessive devotion

**i·dol·a·try** (ī däl′ə trē) *n.*, *pl.* -**tries 1** worship of idols **2** excessive reverence for or devotion to a person or thing —**i·dol′a·ter** *n.* —**i·dol′a·trous** *adj.*

**i·dol·ize** (īd′'l īz′) *vt.* -**ized′, -iz′ing 1** to make an idol of **2** to love or admire excessively

**i·dyll** or **i·dyl** (īd′'l; Brit īd′'l) *n.* ⟦< Gr *eidos,* a form⟧ **1** a short poem, etc. describing a simple, peaceful scene of rural life **2** a scene or incident suitable for this —**i·dyl·lic** (ī dil′ik) *adj.*

**IE** *abbrev.* Indo-European

**-ie** (ē) ⟦earlier form of -Y¹⟧ *suffix* **1** small or little (one, as specified) [*lassie*] **2** *a)* one that is as specified [*softie*] *b)* one connected with [*groupie*]

**i.e.** *abbrev.* ⟦L *id est*⟧ that is (to say)

**-i·er** (ē′ər, yər, ir, ər) ⟦< L *-arius*⟧ *suffix* a person concerned with (a specified action or thing) [*bombardier*]

**if** (if) *conj.* ⟦OE *gif*⟧ **1** on condition that; in case that [*if* I were you, I would quit] **2** allowing that [*if* she was there, I didn't see her] **3** whether [ask him *if* he knows her]

**if·fy** (if′ē) *adj.* -**fi·er, -fi·est** [Inf.] not definite; containing doubtful elements

**ig·loo** (ig′lōō′) *n.*, *pl.* -**loos′** ⟦Esk *igdlu,* snow house]] an Eskimo hut, usually dome-shaped and built of blocks of packed snow

**ig·ne·ous** (ig'nē əs) *adj.* [[< L *ignis*, a fire]] **1** of fire **2** produced by volcanic action or intense heat *[igneous rock]*

IGLOO

**ig·nite** (ig nīt') *vt.* **-nit'ed, -nit'ing** [[see prec.]] to set fire to —*vi.* to catch on fire; start burning —**ig·nit'a·ble** or **ig·nit'i·ble** *adj.*

**ig·ni·tion** (ig nish'ən) *n.* **1** an igniting or being ignited **2** the key-operated switch or system for igniting the explosive mixture in the cylinder of an internal-combustion engine

**ig·no·ble** (ig nō'bəl) *adj.* [[< L *in-*, not + *nobilis* (< earlier *gnobilis*, known]] not noble; base; mean — **ig·no'bly** *adv.*

**ig·no·min·y** (ig'nə min'ē) *n.* [[< L *in-*, no, not + *nomen*, name]] loss of reputation; shame; disgrace —**ig'no·min'i·ous** *adj.* —**ig'no·min'i·ous·ly** *adv.*

**ig·no·ra·mus** (ig'nə rā'məs, -ram'əs) *n., pl.* **-mus·es** an ignorant person

**ig·no·rant** (ig'nə rənt) *adj.* [[see fol.]] **1** lacking knowledge or experience **2** caused by or showing lack of knowledge **3** unaware (*of*) —**ig'no·rance** *n.* —**ig'no·rant·ly** *adv.*

**ig·nore** (ig nôr') *vt.* **-nored', -nor'ing** [[< L *in-*, not + *gnarus*, knowing]] to disregard; pay no attention to

**i·gua·na** (i gwä'nə) *n.* [[Sp < WInd]] a large tropical American lizard

**IL** Illinois

**il-** *prefix* **1** IN-[1] **2** IN-[2] Used before *l*

**-ile** (il, əl, 'l, īl) *suffix* of or like

**Il·i·ad** (il'ē əd) *n.* [[< Gr *Ilios*, Troy]] a Greek epic poem, ascribed to Homer, about the Trojan War

**ilk** (ilk) *n.* [[< OE *ilca*, same]] kind; sort; class: only in **of that** (or **his, her,** etc.) **ilk**

**ill** (il) *adj.* **worse, worst** [[< ON *illr*]] **1** bad *[ill* repute, *ill* will, *ill* omen*]* **2** not well; sick —*n.* an evil or a disease —*adv.* **worse, worst 1** badly **2** scarcely *[I can ill* afford it*]* —**ill at ease** uneasy; uncomfortable

**ill-ad·vised** (il'əd vīzd') *adj.* showing or resulting from poor advice; unwise

**ill'-bred'** *adj.* rude; impolite

**il·le·gal** (i lē'gəl) *adj.* prohibited by law; against the law —**il·le·gal·i·ty** (il'ē gal'i tē), *pl.* **-ties,** *n.* —**il·le'gal·ly** *adv.*

**il·leg·i·ble** (i lej'ə bəl) *adj.* hard or impossible to read because badly written or printed —**il·leg'i·bly** *adv.*

**il·le·git·i·mate** (il'ə jit'ə mət) *adj.* **1** born of parents not married to each other **2** not legal or logical —**il·le·git'i·ma·cy** (-mə sē), *pl.* **-cies,** *n.*

**ill-fat·ed** (il'fāt'id) *adj.* **1** certain to have an evil fate or unlucky end **2** unlucky

**ill'-fa'vored** *adj.* ugly or unpleasant

**ill'-got'ten** *adj.* obtained unlawfully or dishonestly

**il·lib·er·al** (i lib'ər əl) *adj.* **1** narrow-minded **2** not generous

**il·lic·it** (i lis'it) *adj.* [[< L *illicitus*, not allowed]] unlawful; improper —**il·lic'it·ly** *adv.* —**il·lic'it·ness** *n.*

**il·lim·it·a·ble** (i lim'i tə bəl) *adj.* without limit; immeasurable

**Il·li·nois** (il'ə noi') Midwestern state of the U.S.: 55,646 sq. mi.; pop. 11,431,000; cap. Springfield: abbrev. IL —**Il'li·nois'an** *adj., n.*

**il·liq·uid** (i lik'wid) *adj.* not readily convertible into cash

**il·lit·er·a·cy** (i lit'ər ə sē) *n.* **1** a being illiterate **2** *pl.* **-cies** a mistake in grammar suggesting this

**il·lit·er·ate** (i lit'ər it) *adj.* uneducated; esp., not knowing how to read or write —*n.* an illiterate person

**ill-man·nered** (il'man'ərd) *adj.* having bad manners; rude; impolite

**ill nature** a disagreeable or mean disposition — **ill'-na'tured** *adj.*

**ill'ness** *n.* the condition of being in poor health; sickness; disease

**il·log·i·cal** (i läj'i kəl) *adj.* not logical or reasonable —**il·log'i·cal·ly** *adv.*

**ill-starred** (il'stärd') *adj.* unlucky

**ill'-suit'ed** *adj.* not suited or appropriate

**ill'-tem'pered** *adj.* sullen; irritable

**ill'-timed'** *adj.* inopportune

**ill'-treat'** *vt.* to treat unkindly, unfairly, etc. —**ill'-treat'ment** *n.*

**il·lu·mi·nate** (i lōō'mə nāt') *vt.* **-nat'ed, -nat'ing** [[< L *in-*, in + *luminare*, to light]] **1** to give light to; light up **2** *a)* to make clear; explain *b)* to inform **3** to decorate with lights **4** to decorate (a page border, etc.) by hand —**il·lu'mi·na·ble** (-nə bəl) *adj.*

**il·lu·mi·na·tion** *n.* **1** an illuminating **2** the intensity of light per unit of area

**il·lu'mine** (-mən) *vt.* **-mined, -min·ing** to light up

**illus** *abbrev.* **1** illustrated **2** illustration **3** illustrator

**ill-us·age** (il'yōō'sij) *n.* unkind or cruel treatment; abuse: also **ill usage**

**ill'-use'** (-yōōz'; *for n.,* -yōōs') *vt.* **-used', -us'ing** to treat unkindly; abuse —*n.* ILL-USAGE

**il·lu·sion** (i lōō'zhən) *n.* [[< L *illudere,* to mock]] **1** a false idea or conception **2** an unreal or misleading appearance or image —**il·lu'so·ry** (-sə rē) or **il·lu'sive** (-siv) *adj.*

**il·lus·trate** (il'ə strāt') *vt.* **-trat'ed, -trat'ing** [[< L *in-*, in + *lustrare,* illuminate]] **1** to explain; make clear, as by examples **2** to furnish (books, etc.) with explanatory or decorative pictures, etc. — **il'lus·tra'tor** *n.*

**il·lus·tra·tion** (-strā'shən) *n.* **1** an illustrating **2** an example, etc. used to help explain **3** a picture, diagram, etc. used to decorate or explain

**il·lus·tra·tive** (i lus'trə tiv, il'ə strāt'iv) *adj.* serving as an illustration or example

**il·lus·tri·ous** (i lus'trē əs) *adj.* [[< L *illustris,* clear]] distinguished; famous; outstanding —**il·lus'tri·ous·ly** *adv.* —**il·lus'tri·ous·ness** *n.*

**ill will** hostility; hate; dislike

**I'm** (īm) *contr.* I am

**im-** *prefix* **1** IN-[1] **2** IN-[2] Used before *b, m,* or *p*

**im·age** (im'ij) *n.* [[< L *imago*]] **1** a representation of a person or thing; esp., a statue **2** the visual impression of something in a mirror, through a lens, etc. **3** a copy **4** *a)* a mental picture; idea *b)* the concept of a person, product, etc. held by the general public **5** a metaphor or simile —*vt.* **-aged, -ag·ing 1** to make a representation of **2** to reflect **3** to imagine

**im·age·ry** (im'ij rē) *n.* **1** mental images **2** figurative language

**i·mag·i·na·ble** (i maj'i nə bəl) *adj.* that can be imagined

**i·mag'i·nar'y** (-ner'ē) *adj.* existing only in the imagination; unreal

**i·mag'i·na'tion** (-nā'shən) *n.* **1** *a)* the act or power of forming mental images of what is not present *b)* the act or power of creating new ideas by combining previous experiences **2** the ability to understand the imaginative creations of others **3** resourcefulness

**i·mag'i·na·tive** (-nə tiv) *adj.* **1** having, using, or showing imagination **2** of or resulting from imagination —**i·mag'i·na·tive·ly** *adv.*

**i·mag·ine** (i maj'in) *vt.,* *vi.* **-ined, -in·ing** [[< L *imago,* image]] **1** to make a mental image (of); conceive in the mind **2** to suppose; think

**im'ag·ing** *n.* the production of images, esp. by electronic means as in a CAT scan, ultrasound, etc.

**i·mam** (i mäm') *n.* [*often* I-] a Muslim leader, as of prayer, or ruler: often used as a title

**im·bal·ance** (im bal'əns) *n.* lack of balance, as in proportion or force

**im·be·cile** (im'bə sil) *n.* ⟦< L *imbecilis*, feeble⟧ **1** [Obs.] a retarded person mentally equal to a child between three and eight years old **2** a foolish or stupid person —*adj.* foolish or stupid: also **im'be·cil'ic** (-sil'ik) —**im·be·cil'i·ty** *n.*

**im·bed** (im bed') *vt. var. of* EMBED

**im·bibe** (im bīb') *vt.* **-bibed'**, **-bib'ing** ⟦< L *in-*, in + *bibere*, to drink⟧ **1** to drink (esp. alcoholic liquor) **2** to take in with the senses or mind —*vi.* to drink, esp. alcoholic liquor

**im·bro·glio** (im brōl'yō) *n., pl.* **-glios** ⟦It < *imbrogliare*, embroil⟧ **1** an involved and confusing situation **2** a confused misunderstanding

**im·bue** (im byōō') *vt.* **-bued'**, **-bu'ing** ⟦< L *imbuere*, to wet⟧ **1** to dye **2** to permeate (*with* ideas, emotions, etc.)

**im·i·tate** (im'i tāt') *vt.* **-tat'ed**, **-tat'ing** ⟦< L *imitari*⟧ **1** to seek to follow the example of **2** to mimic **3** to reproduce in form, color, etc. **4** to resemble —**im'i·ta'tor** *n.*

**im·i·ta·tion** (-tā'shən) *n.* **1** an imitating **2** the result of imitating; copy —*adj.* not real; sham *[imitation* leather*/* —**im'i·ta'tive** *adj.*

**im·mac·u·late** (i mak'yə lit) *adj.* ⟦< L *in-*, not + *macula*, a spot⟧ **1** perfectly clean **2** without a flaw or error **3** pure; innocent; sinless —**im·mac'u·late·ly** *adv.* —**im·mac'u·late·ness** *n.*

**im·ma·nent** (im'ə nənt) *adj.* ⟦< L *in-*, in + *manere*, remain⟧ **1** operating within; inherent **2** present throughout the universe: said of God —**im'ma·nence** *n.* —**im'ma·nent·ly** *adv.*

**im·ma·te·ri·al** (im'ə tir'ē əl) *adj.* **1** not consisting of matter **2** not pertinent; unimportant

**im·ma·ture** (im'ə toor', -choor') *adj.* **1** not mature; not completely developed **2** not finished or perfected —**im'ma·tu'ri·ty** *n.*

**im·meas·ur·a·ble** (i mezh'ər ə bəl) *adj.* that cannot be measured; boundless; vast —**im·meas'ur·a·bly** *adv.*

**im·me·di·a·cy** (i mē'dē ə sē) *n.* a being immediate; esp., direct relevance to the present time, purpose, etc.

**im·me·di·ate** (i mē'dē it) *adj.* ⟦see IN-² & MEDI-ATE⟧ **1** not separated in space; closest **2** without delay; instant **3** next in order or relation **4** direct; firsthand —**im·me'di·ate·ly** *adv.*

**im·me·mo·ri·al** (im'ə môr'ē əl) *adj.* extending back beyond memory or record; ancient

**im·mense** (i mens') *adj.* ⟦< L *in-*, not + *metiri*, to measure⟧ very large; vast; huge —**im·mense'ly** *adv.* —**im·men'si·ty** *n.*

**im·merse** (i murs') *vt.* **-mersed'**, **-mers'ing** ⟦< L *immergere*⟧ **1** to plunge into or as if into a liquid **2** to baptize by submerging in water **3** to absorb deeply; engross *[immersed* in study*]* —**im·mer'sion** (-mur'zhən, -shən) *n.*

**immersion heater** an electric coil or rod immersed in water to heat it

**im·mi·grant** (im'ə grənt) *n.* one who immigrates —*adj.* immigrating

**im'mi·grate'** (-grāt') *vi.* **-grat'ed**, **-grat'ing** ⟦see IN-¹ & MIGRATE⟧ to come into a new country, etc., esp. to settle there —**im'mi·gra'tion** *n.*

**im·mi·nent** (im'ə nənt) *adj.* ⟦< L *in-*, on + *minere*, to project⟧ likely to happen without delay; impending

**im·mo·bile** (i mō'bəl) *adj.* **1** firmly placed; stable **2** motionless —**im'mo·bil'i·ty** *n.* —**im·mo'bi·lize'** (-bə līz'), **-lized'**, **-liz'ing**, *vt.*

**im·mod·er·ate** (i mäd'ər it) *adj.* without restraint; unreasonable; excessive

**im·mod·est** (i mäd'ist) *adj.* **1** indecent **2** not shy; forward —**im·mod'est·ly** *adv.* —**im·mod'es·ty** *n.*

**im·mo·late** (im'ə lāt') *vt.* **-lat'ed**, **-lat'ing** ⟦< L *immolare*, sprinkle with sacrificial meal⟧ to kill as a sacrifice —**im'mo·la'tion** *n.*

**im·mor·al** (i môr'əl) *adj.* **1** not moral **2** lewd —**im·mor'al·ly** *adv.*

**im·mo·ral·i·ty** (im'ôr al'i tē) *n.* **1** a being immoral **2** *pl.* **-ties** an immoral act or practice; vice

**im·mor·tal** (i môrt''l) *adj.* **1** not mortal; living forever **2** enduring **3** having lasting fame —*n.* an immortal being —**im·mor·tal·i·ty** (im'môr tal'i tē) *n.*

**im·mor'tal·ize'** (-īz') *vt.* **-ized'**, **-iz'ing** to make immortal, as in fame

**im·mov·a·ble** (i mōōv'ə bəl) *adj.* **1** firmly fixed **2** unyielding; steadfast

**im·mune** (i myōōn') *adj.* ⟦< L *in-*, without + *munia*, duties⟧ **1** exempt from or protected against something disagreeable or harmful **2** not susceptible to some specified disease

**im·mu·ni·ty** (i myōōn'ə tē) *n., pl.* **-ties** **1** exemption from something burdensome, as a legal obligation **2** resistance to infection or a specified disease

**im·mu·nize** (im'yōō nīz') *vt.* **-nized'**, **-niz'ing** to make immune, as by inoculation —**im'mu·ni·za'tion** *n.*

**im·mu·nol·o·gy** (im'yōō näl'ə jē) *n.* the branch of science dealing with immunity, as to infection or a disease, and with the body mechanisms producing it —**im'mu·nol'o·gist** *n.*

**im·mure** (i myoor') *vt.* **-mured'**, **-mur'ing** ⟦< L *in-*, in + *murus*, wall⟧ to shut up within walls; confine

**im·mu·ta·ble** (i myōōt'ə bəl) *adj.* unchangeable —**im·mu'ta·bly** *adv.*

**imp** (imp) *n.* ⟦< Gr *em-*, in + *phyton*, growth⟧ **1** a young demon **2** a mischievous child —**imp'ish** *adj.*

**im·pact** (im pakt'; *for n.* im'pakt') *vt.* ⟦< L *impingere*, press firmly together⟧ **1** to force tightly together **2** to affect —*vi.* **1** to hit with force **2** to have an effect (*on*) —*n.* **1** a violent contact **2** the power to move feelings, influence thinking, etc.

**im·pact'ed** *adj.* lodged in the jaw: said of a tooth

**im·pair** (im per') *vt.* ⟦< L *in-*, intens. + *pejor*, worse⟧ to make worse, less, etc. —**im·pair'ment** *n.*

**im·pa·la** (im pä'lə) *n., pl.* **-la** or **-las** a reddish antelope of central and S Africa

**im·pale** (im pāl') *vt.* **-paled'**, **-pal'ing** ⟦< L *in-*, on + *palus*, a pole⟧ to pierce through with, or fix on, something pointed —**im·pale'ment** *n.*

**im·pal·pa·ble** (im pal'pə bəl) *adj.* **1** not perceptible to the touch **2** too subtle to be easily understood

**im·pan·el** (im pan'əl) *vt.* **-eled** or **-elled**, **-el·ing** or **-el·ling** to choose (a jury) in a law case —**im·pan'el·ment** *n.*

**im·part** (im pärt') *vt.* ⟦see IN-¹ & PART⟧ **1** to give a part of **2** to make known; reveal

**im·par·tial** (im pär'shəl) *adj.* without bias; fair —**im·par'ti·al'i·ty** (-shē al'i tē) *n.* —**im·par'tial·ly** *adv.*

**im·pass·a·ble** (im pas'ə bəl) *adj.* that cannot be passed or traveled over

**im·passe** (im'pas', im pas') *n.* ⟦Fr⟧ a situation offering no escape or resolution, as a deadlocked argument

**im·pas·sioned** (im pash'ənd) *adj.* passionate; fiery; ardent

**im·pas·sive** (im pas'iv) *adj.* not feeling or showing emotion; calm —**im·pas·siv·i·ty** (im'pa siv'i tē) *n.*

**im·pas·to** (im päs'tō) *n.* ⟦It⟧ painting in which the paint is laid thickly on the canvas

**im·pa·tient** (im pā'shənt) *adj.* lacking patience; specif., *a)* annoyed because of delay, opposition, etc. *b)* restlessly eager to do something, etc. —**im·pa'tience** *n.*

**im·peach** (im pēch') *vt.* ⟦< L *in-*, in + *pedica*, a fetter⟧ **1** to discredit (a person's honor, etc.) **2** to charge (a public official) with wrongdoing —**im·peach'a·ble** *adj.* —**im·peach'ment** *n.*

**im·pec·ca·ble** (im pek'ə bəl) *adj.* ⟦< L *in-*, not + *peccare*, to sin⟧ without defect or error; flawless —**im·pec'ca·bil'i·ty** *n.* —**im·pec'ca·bly** *adv.*

**im·pe·cu·ni·ous** (im'pi kyōō'nē əs) *adj.* ⟦< L *in-*, not + *pecunia*, money⟧ having no money; poor

**im·ped·ance** (im pēd''ns) *n.* ⟦< fol. + -ANCE⟧ the

resistance in an electric circuit to a flow of alternating current

**im·pede** (im pēd′) *vt.* **-ped′ed, -ped′ing** ⟦< L *in*-, in + *pes*, foot⟧ to hinder the progress of; obstruct

**im·ped·i·ment** (im ped′ə mənt) *n.* anything that impedes; specif., a speech defect

**im·ped′i·men′ta** (-men′tə) *pl.n.* encumbrances, as baggage or supplies

**im·pel** (im pel′) *vt.* **-pelled′, -pel′ling** ⟦< L *in*-, in + *pellere*, to drive⟧ **1** to drive or move forward **2** to force, compel, or urge —**im·pel′ler** *n.*

**im·pend** (im pend′) *vi.* ⟦< L *in*-, in + *pendere*, hang⟧ to be about to happen; be imminent [*impending* disaster] —**im·pend′ing** *adj.*

**im·pen·e·tra·ble** (im pen′i trə bəl) *adj.* **1** that cannot be penetrated **2** that cannot be solved or understood

**im·pen·i·tent** (im pen′ə tənt) *adj.* without regret, shame, or remorse

**im·per·a·tive** (im per′ə tiv) *adj.* ⟦< L *imperare*, to command⟧ **1** indicating authority or command **2** necessary; urgent **3** designating or of the mood of a verb that expresses a command, etc. —*n.* a command

**im·per·cep·ti·ble** (im′pər sep′tə bəl) *adj.* not easily perceived by the senses or the mind; very slight, subtle, etc. —**im′per·cep′ti·bly** *adv.*

**im·per·cep′tive** (-tiv) *adj.* not perceiving — **im′per·cep′tive·ness** *n.*

**im·per·fect** (im pur′fikt) *adj.* **1** not complete **2** not perfect **3** designating a verb tense that indicates a past action or state as uncompleted or continuous —**im·per′fect·ly** *adv.*

**im·per·fec·tion** (im′pər fek′shən) *n.* **1** a being imperfect **2** a defect; fault

**im·pe·ri·al** (im pir′ē əl) *adj.* ⟦< L *imperium*, empire⟧ **1** of an empire, emperor, or empress **2** having supreme authority **3** majestic; august **4** of great size or superior quality —*n.* a small, pointed chin beard

**imperial gallon** the standard British gallon, equal to 4.546 liters (about 1¼ U.S. gallons)

**im·pe′ri·al·ism′** *n.* **1** imperial state or authority **2** the policy of forming and maintaining an empire, as by establishing colonies **3** the policy of seeking to dominate the affairs of weaker countries —**im·pe′ri·al·ist** *n., adj.* —**im·pe′ri·al·is′tic** *adj.*

**im·per·il** (im per′əl) *vt.* **-iled** or **-illed, -il·ing** or **-il·ling** to put in peril; endanger

**im·pe·ri·ous** (im pir′ē əs) *adj.* ⟦< L *imperium*, empire⟧ **1** overbearing, arrogant, etc. **2** urgent; imperative —**im·pe′ri·ous·ly** *adv.*

**im·per·ish·a·ble** (im per′ish ə bəl) *adj.* not perishable; indestructible

**im·per·ma·nent** (im pur′mə nənt) *adj.* not permanent; temporary —**im·per′ma·nent·ly** *adv.*

**im·per·son·al** (im pur′sə nəl) *adj.* **1** without reference to any particular person **2** not existing as a person [an *impersonal* force] **3** designating or of a verb occurring only in the third person singular, usually with *it* as subject —**im·per′son·al·ly** *adv.*

**im·per·son·ate** (im pur′sə nāt′) *vt.* **-at′ed, -at′ing** to assume the role of or pretend to be, for purposes of entertainment or fraud —**im·per′son·a′tion** *n.* —**im·per′son·a′tor** *n.*

**im·per·ti·nent** (im purt′'n ənt) *adj.* **1** not pertinent **2** insolent; impudent —**im·per′ti·nence** *n.*

**im·per·turb·a·ble** (im′pər tur′bə bəl) *adj.* that cannot be disconcerted, disturbed, or excited

**im·per·vi·ous** (im pur′vē əs) *adj.* **1** incapable of being penetrated, as by moisture **2** not affected by: with *to*

**im·pe·ti·go** (im′pə tī′gō) *n.* ⟦see IMPETUS⟧ a contagious skin disease characterized by pustules

**im·pet·u·ous** (im pech′o͞o əs) *adj.* ⟦see fol.⟧ acting or done suddenly with little thought; rash —**im·pet′u·os′i·ty** (-äs′i tē) *n.* —**im·pet′u·ous·ly** *adv.*

**im·pe·tus** (im′pə təs) *n., pl.* **-tus·es** ⟦< L *in*-, in + *petere*, rush at⟧ **1** the force with which a body

---

moves against resistance **2** driving force or motive; incentive

**im·pi·e·ty** (im pī′ə tē) *n.* **1** lack of reverence for God **2** *pl.* **-ties** an impious act or remark

**im·pinge** (im pinj′) *vi.* **-pinged′, -ping′ing** ⟦< L *in*-, in + *pangere*, to strike⟧ **1** to strike, hit, etc. (*on* or *upon*) **2** to encroach (*on* or *upon*) —**im·pinge′ment** *n.*

**im·pi·ous** (im′pē əs) *adj.* not pious; specif., lacking reverence for God

**im·plac·a·ble** (im plak′ə bəl, -plā′kə-) *adj.* not to be placated or appeased; relentless —**im·plac′a·bly** *adv.*

**im·plant** (im plant′; *for n.* im′plant′) *vt.* **1** to plant firmly **2** to fix firmly in the mind **3** to insert surgically —*n.* an implanted organ, etc.

**im·plau·si·ble** (im plô′zə bəl) *adj.* not plausible — **im·plau′si·bly** *adv.*

**im·ple·ment** (im′plə mənt; *for v.*, -ment′) *n.* ⟦< L *in*-, in + *plere*, to fill⟧ something used in a given activity; tool, instrument, etc. —*vt.* to carry into effect; accomplish —**im′ple·men·ta′tion** (-mən tā′shən) *n.*

**im·pli·cate** (im′pli kāt′) *vt.* **-cat′ed, -cat′ing** ⟦see IMPLY⟧ to show to be party to a crime, etc. — **im′pli·ca′tive** *adj.*

**im′pli·ca′tion** (-kā′shən) *n.* **1** an implicating or being implicated **2** an implying or being implied **3** something implied

**im·plic·it** (im plis′it) *adj.* ⟦see IMPLY⟧ **1** suggested though not plainly expressed; implied **2** necessarily involved though not apparent; inherent **3** without reservation or doubt —**im·plic′it·ly** *adv.*

**im·plode** (im plōd′) *vt., vi.* **-plod′ed, -plod′ing** ⟦< IN-¹ + (EX)PLODE⟧ to burst or cause to burst inward —**im·plo′sion** (-plō′zhən) *n.* —**im·plo′sive** (-plō′siv) *adj.*

**im·plore** (im plôr′) *vt.* **-plored′, -plor′ing** ⟦< L *in*-, intens. + *plorare*, cry out⟧ **1** to ask earnestly for **2** to beg (a person) to do something —**im·plor′ing·ly** *adv.*

**im·ply** (im plī′) *vt.* **-plied′, -ply′ing** ⟦< L *in*-, in + *plicare*, to fold⟧ **1** to have as a necessary part, condition, etc. **2** to indicate indirectly; hint; suggest

**im·po·lite** (im′pə līt′) *adj.* not polite; discourteous —**im′po·lite′ly** *adv.*

**im·pol·i·tic** (im päl′ə tik′) *adj.* not politic; unwise

**im·pon·der·a·ble** (im pän′dər ə bəl) *adj.* that cannot be weighed, measured, explained, etc. —*n.* anything imponderable

**im·port** (im pôrt′, *also, and for n. always* im′pôrt′) *vt.* ⟦< L *in*-, in + *portare*, carry⟧ **1** to bring in (goods) from another country, especially for sale **2** to mean; signify —*n.* **1** something imported **2** meaning; signification **3** importance —**im′por·ta′tion** *n.* —**im·port′er** *n.*

**im·por·tant** (im pôrt′'nt) *adj.* ⟦see prec.⟧ **1** meaning a great deal; having much significance or value **2** having, or acting as if having, power, authority, etc. —**im·por′tance** *n.* —**im·por′tant·ly** *adv.*

**im·por·tu·nate** (im pôr′chə nət) *adj.* persistent in asking or demanding

**im·por·tune** (im′pôr to͞on′) *vt., vi.* **-tuned′, -tun′ing** ⟦< L *importunus*, troublesome⟧ to urge or entreat persistently or repeatedly —**im′por·tu′ni·ty**, *pl.* **-ties,** *n.*

**im·pose** (im pōz′) *vt.* **-posed′, -pos′ing** ⟦< L *in*-, on + *ponere*, to place⟧ **1** to place (a burden, tax, etc. *on* or *upon*) **2** to force (oneself) on others — **impose on** (or **upon**) **1** to take advantage of **2** to cheat or defraud —**im′po·si′tion** (-pə zish′ən) *n.*

**im·pos·ing** *adj.* impressive because of great size, strength, dignity, etc. —**im·pos′ing·ly** *adv.*

**im·pos·si·ble** (im päs′ə bəl) *adj.* **1** not capable of being, being done, or happening **2** not capable of being endured, used, etc. because disagreeable or unsuitable —**im·pos′si·bil′i·ty**, *pl.* **-ties,** *n.* —**im·pos′si·bly** *adv.*

**im·post** (im′pōst′) *n.* ⟦see IMPOSE⟧ a tax; esp., a duty on imported goods

**im·pos·tor** or **im·post′er** (im päs′tər) *n.* ⟦see IMPOSE⟧ one who deceives or cheats others by pretending to be what he or she is not

**im·pos′ture** (-chər) *n.* the act or practice of an impostor; fraud

**im·po·tent** (im′pə tənt) *adj.* **1** lacking physical strength **2** ineffective; powerless **3** unable to engage in sexual intercourse: said of males — **im′po·tence** or **im′po·ten·cy** *n.* —**im′po·tent·ly** *adv.*

**im·pound** (im pound′) *vt.* **1** to shut up (an animal) in a pound **2** to take and hold in legal custody **3** to gather and enclose (water), as for irrigation

**im·pov·er·ish** (im päv′ər ish) *vt.* ⟦< L *in-*, in + *pauper*, poor⟧ **1** to make poor **2** to deprive of strength, resources, etc. —**im·pov′er·ish·ment** *n.*

**im·prac·ti·ca·ble** (im prak′ti kə bəl) *adj.* not capable of being carried out in practice

**im·prac·ti·cal** (im prak′ti kəl) *adj.* not practical

**im·pre·ca·tion** (im′prə kā′shən) *n.* ⟦< L *in-*, on + *precari*, pray⟧ a curse

**im·pre·cise** (im′pri sīs′) *adj.* not precise; vague — **im′pre·cise′ly** *adv.* —**im′pre·ci′sion** (-sizh′ən) *n.*

**im·preg·na·ble** (im preg′nə bəl) *adj.* **1** that cannot be captured or entered by force **2** unyielding —**im·preg′na·bil′i·ty** *n.* —**im·preg′na·bly** *adv.*

**im·preg·nate** (im preg′nāt′) *vt.* **-nat′ed, -nat′ing 1** to make pregnant; fertilize **2** to saturate **3** to imbue (*with* ideas, etc.) —**im′preg·na′tion** *n.*

**im·pre·sa·ri·o** (im′prə sä′rē ō′) *n.*, *pl.* **-os** ⟦It⟧ one who manages an opera, organizes concert series, etc.

**im·press**[1] (im pres′) *vt.* ⟦< IN-[1] + PRESS[2]⟧ **1** to force (a person) into military service **2** to seize for public use

**im·press**[2] (im pres′; *for n.* im′pres′) *vt.* ⟦see IMPRINT⟧ **1** to stamp; imprint **2** to affect strongly the mind or emotions of **3** to fix in the memory: with *on* or *upon* —*n.* **1** an impressing **2** an imprint

**im·press′i·ble** (-ə bəl) *adj.* that can be impressed —**im·press′i·bil′i·ty** *n.*

**im·pres·sion** (im presh′ən) *n.* **1** an impressing *a)* a mark, imprint, etc. *b)* an effect produced on the mind **3** a vague notion **4** an amusing impersonation; mimicking

**im·pres′sion·a·ble** *adj.* easily impressed or influenced; sensitive

**im·pres′sion·ism′** *n.* a theory of art, music, etc. whose aim is to capture a brief, immediate impression —**im·pres′sion·ist** *n.* —**im·pres′sion·is′tic** *adj.*

**im·pres·sive** (im pres′iv) *adj.* tending to impress the mind or emotions; eliciting wonder or admiration —**im·pres′sive·ly** *adv.*

**im·pri·ma·tur** (im′pri mät′ər) *n.* ⟦ModL, lit., let it be printed⟧ **1** permission to publish a book, etc., as granted by a Catholic bishop **2** any sanction or approval

**im·print** (im print′; *for n.* im′print′) *vt.* ⟦< L *in-*, on + *premere*, to press⟧ to mark or fix as by pressing or stamping —*n.* **1** a mark made by imprinting **2** a lasting effect **3** a note in a book giving facts of its publication

**im·pris·on** (im priz′ən) *vt.* to put in or as in prison —**im·pris′on·ment** *n.*

**im·prob·a·ble** (im präb′ə bəl) *adj.* not probable; unlikely —**im·prob·a·bil′i·ty**, *pl.* **-ties**, *n.* —**im·prob′a·bly** *adv.*

**im·promp·tu** (im prämp′tōō′) *adj., adv.* ⟦< L *in promptu*, in readiness⟧ without preparation; offhand

**im·prop·er** (im präp′ər) *adj.* **1** not suitable; unfit **2** incorrect **3** not in good taste —**im·prop′er·ly** *adv.*

**im·pro·pri·e·ty** (im′prō prī′ə tē) *n., pl.* **-ties 1** a being improper **2** an improper act, word usage, etc.

**im·prove** (im prōōv′) *vt.* **-proved′, -prov′ing** ⟦< Anglo-Fr *en-*, in + *prou*, gain⟧ **1** to make better **2** to make (real estate) more valuable by cultivation, construction, etc. —*vi.* to become better — **improve on** (or **upon**) to do or make better than —**im·prov′a·ble** *adj.*

**im·prove′ment** *n.* **1** an improving or being improved **2** an addition or change that improves something

**im·prov·i·dent** (im präv′ə dənt) *adj.* lacking foresight or thrift —**im·prov′i·dence** *n.* —**im·prov′i·dent·ly** *adv.*

**im·pro·vise** (im′prə vīz′) *vt., vi.* **-vised′, -vis′ing** ⟦< L *in-*, not + *providere*, foresee⟧ **1** to compose and perform without preparation **2** to make or do with whatever is at hand —**im·prov′i·sa′tion** (-präv′i zā′shən) *n.* —**im·prov′i·sa′tion·al** *adj.*

**im·pru·dent** (im prōōd′′nt) *adj.* not prudent; rash —**im·pru′dence** *n.*

**im·pu·dent** (im′pyōō dənt) *adj.* ⟦< L *in-*, not + *pudere*, feel shame⟧ shamelessly bold; insolent — **im′pu·dence** *n.* —**im′pu·dent·ly** *adv.*

**im·pugn** (im pyōōn′) *vt.* ⟦< L *in-*, against + *pugnare*, to fight⟧ to challenge as false or questionable

**im·pulse** (im′puls′) *n.* ⟦see IMPEL⟧ **1** *a)* an impelling force; impetus *b)* the motion or effect caused by such a force **2** *a)* incitement to action by a stimulus *b)* a sudden inclination to act **3** a brief surge in an electric current

**im·pul·sion** (im pul′shən) *n.* **1** an impelling or being impelled **2** IMPULSE (sense 1*a*) **3** IMPULSE (sense 2)

**im·pul·sive** (im pul′siv) *adj.* **1** driving forward **2** likely to act on impulse —**im·pul′sive·ly** *adv.*

**im·pu·ni·ty** (im pyōō′ni tē) *n.* ⟦< L *in-*, without + *poena*, punishment⟧ exemption from punishment, harm, etc.

**im·pure** (im pyoor′) *adj.* **1** unclean; dirty **2** immoral; obscene **3** mixed with foreign matter; adulterated —**im·pure′ly** *adv.* —**im·pure′ness** *n.*

**im·pu·ri·ty** (-pyoor′ə tē) *n.* **1** a being impure **2** *pl.* **-ties** an impure thing or part

**im·pute** (im pyōōt′) *vt.* **-put′ed, -put′ing** ⟦< L *in-*, in, to + *putare*, to think⟧ to attribute (esp. a fault or misconduct) to another —**im′pu·ta′tion** (-pyōō tā′shən) *n.*

**in**[1] (in) *prep.* ⟦OE⟧ **1** contained by [*in* the room] **2** wearing [dressed *in* furs] **3** during [done *in* a day] **4** at the end of [due *in* an hour] **5** not beyond [*in* sight] **6** employed, enrolled, etc. at [*in* college] **7** out of a group of [one *in* ten] **8** amidst [*in* a storm] **9** affected by [*in* trouble] **10** with regard to [to vary *in* size] **11** using [speak *in* English] **12** because of; for [to cry *in* pain] **13** into [come *in* the house] **14** living or located at [*in* Rome] —*adv.* **1** to the inside [he went *in*] **2** to or at a certain place **3** so as to be contained by a certain space, condition, etc. **4** inside one's home, etc. (to stay *in*) —*adj.* **1** that is in power [the *in* group] **2** inner; inside **3** gathered, counted, etc. **4** [Inf.] currently smart, popular, etc. —**in** one that is in power: *usually used in pl.* **2** [Inf.] special influence; pull —**have it in for** [Inf.] to hold a grudge against —**ins and outs** all the details and intricacies —**in that** because; since —**in with** associated with

**in**[2] *abbrev.* inch(es)

**IN** Indiana

**in-**[1] ⟦< the prep. IN[1] or L *in*, in⟧ *prefix* in, into, within, on, toward [*in*breed]

**in-**[2] ⟦L⟧ *prefix* no, not, without, NON- The following list includes some common compounds formed with *in-*, with no special meanings; they will be understood if "not" or "lack of" is used with the meaning of the base word:

| | |
|---|---|
| inability | inaction |
| inaccessible | inactive |
| inaccuracy | inadequacy |
| inaccurate | inadequate |

inadmissible
inadvisable
inanimate
inapplicable
inappropriate
inapt
inaudible
inauspicious
incapable
incautious
incivility
incombustible
incommensurate
incommunicable
incomprehensible
inconceivable
inconclusive
inconsistency
inconsistent
incorrect
incurable
indecorous
indefinable
indiscernible
indisputable
indistinct
indistinguishable

indivisible
inedible
ineffective
ineffectual
inefficacious
inelastic
ineligible
inequality
inequitable
inequity
inexact
inexcusable
inexpensive
infertile
inharmonious
inhospitable
inhumane
injudicious
inopportune
inseparable
insignificance
insignificant
insolvable
insufficient
insurmountable
insusceptible
invariable

**-in** (in) *combining form* a mass action or gathering of a (specified) type [*pray-in*, *be-in*]

**in ab·sen·ti·a** (in ab sen′shə, -shē ə) [[L]] although not present [*to receive an award in absentia*]

**in·ac·ti·vate** (in ak′tə vāt′) *vt.* **-vat′ed, -vat′ing** to make inactive —**in·ac′ti·va′tion** *n.*

**in·ad·vert·ent** (in′ad vʉrt″nt, -əd-) *adj.* not on purpose; accidental —**in′ad·vert′ence** *n.* —**in′ad·vert′ent·ly** *adv.*

**in·al·ien·a·ble** (in āl′yən ə bəl) *adj.* [see ALIEN] that may not be taken away or transferred —**in·al′ien·a·bly** *adv.*

**in·am·o·ra·ta** (in am′ə rät′ə) *n.* [[It]] a sweetheart or lover: said of a woman

**in·ane** (in ān′) *adj.* [[L *inanis*, empty]] lacking sense; silly —**in·an′i·ty** (-an′i tē) *n.*

**in·ar·tic·u·late** (in′är tik′yoo lit, -yə-) *adj.* **1** without the articulation of normal speech [*an inarticulate cry*] **2** not able to speak; mute **3** unable to speak clearly or coherently **4** unexpressed or unexpressible

**in·as·much as** (in′əz much′ az′) **1** since; because **2** to the extent that

**in·at·ten·tion** (in′ə ten′shən) *n.* failure to pay attention; negligence —**in′at·ten′tive** *adj.*

**in·au·gu·ral** (in ô′gyə rəl) *adj.* [[Fr]] **1** of an inauguration **2** first in a series —*n.* **1** a speech made at an inauguration **2** an inauguration

**in·au′gu·rate′** (-rāt′) *vt.* **-rat′ed, -rat′ing** [[< L *inaugurare*, to practice augury]] **1** to induct into office with a formal ceremony **2** to make a formal beginning of **3** to dedicate formally —**in·au′gu·ra′tion** *n.*

**in·au·then·tic** (in′ô then′tik) *adj.* not authentic

**in·board** (in′bôrd′) *adv., adj.* **1** inside the hull of a ship or boat **2** close to the fuselage of an aircraft —*n.* a boat with an inboard motor

**in·born** (in′bôrn′) *adj.* present in the organism at birth; innate

**in·bound** (in′bound′) *adj.* traveling or going inward —*vt., vi. Basketball* to put (the ball) in play from out of bounds

**in·bred** (in′bred′) *adj.* **1** innate; inborn **2** resulting from inbreeding

**in·breed** (in′brēd′) *vt.* **-bred′, -breed′ing** to breed by continual mating of individuals of the same or closely related stocks —*vi.* **1** to engage in such breeding **2** to become too refined, effete, etc. —**in′breed′ing** *n.*

**inc** *abbrev.* **1** incorporated: also **Inc. 2** increase

**In·ca** (iŋ′kə) *n.* a member of the highly civilized Indian people that dominated ancient Peru until the Spanish conquest —**In′can** *adj.*

**in·cal·cu·la·ble** (in kal′kyoo lə bəl) *adj.* **1** that cannot be calculated; too great or too many to be counted **2** unpredictable —**in·cal′cu·la·bly** *adv.*

**in·can·des·cent** (in′kən des′ənt) *adj.* [[< L *in-*, in + *candere*, to shine]] **1** glowing with intense heat **2** very bright —**in′can·des′cence** *n.*

**incandescent lamp** a lamp with a filament in a vacuum heated to incandescence by an electric current

**in·can·ta·tion** (in′kan tā′shən) *n.* [[< L *in-*, intens. + *cantare*, to sing]] words chanted in magic spells or rites

**in·ca·pac·i·tate** (in′kə pas′ə tāt′) *vt.* **-tat′ed, -tat′ing** to make unable or unfit

**in′ca·pac′i·ty** *n.* lack of capacity, power, or fitness

**in·car·cer·ate** (in kär′sər āt′) *vt.* **-at′ed, -at′ing** [[< L *in-*, in + *carcer*, prison]] to imprison —**in·car′cer·a′tion** *n.*

**in·car·na·dine** (in kär′nə dīn′) *vt.* **-dined′, -din′ing** to make red

**in·car·nate** (in kär′nit; *also, and for v. always,* -nāt′) *adj.* [[< L *in-*, in + *caro*, flesh]] endowed with a human body; personified —*vt.* **-nat′ed, -nat′ing 1** to give bodily form to **2** to be the type or embodiment of —**in′car·na′tion** *n.*

**in·cen·di·ar·y** (in sen′dē er′ē) *adj.* [[< L *incendium*, a fire]] **1** having to do with the willful destruction of property by fire **2** designed to cause fires, as certain bombs **3** willfully stirring up strife, riot, etc. —*n., pl.* **-ar′ies 1** one who willfully stirs up strife, riot, etc. **2** an incendiary bomb, etc.

**in·cense**[1] (in′sens′) *n.* [[< L *in-*, in + *candere*, to burn]] **1** any substance burned to produce a pleasant odor **2** the odor from this

**in·cense**[2] (in sens′) *vt.* **-censed′, -cens′ing** [[see prec.]] to make very angry

**in·cen·tive** (in sent′iv) *n.* [[< L *in-*, in, on + *canere*, sing]] a stimulus; motive

**in·cep·tion** (in sep′shən) *n.* [[see INCIPIENT]] the beginning of something; start

**in·cer·ti·tude** (in sʉrt′ə tood′) *n.* **1** doubt **2** insecurity

**in·ces·sant** (in ses′ənt) *adj.* [[< L *in-*, not + *cessare*, cease]] never ceasing; continuing without stopping; constant —**in·ces′sant·ly** *adv.*

**in·cest** (in′sest′) *n.* [[< L *in-*, not + *castus*, chaste]] sexual intercourse between persons too closely related to marry legally —**in·ces·tu·ous** (in ses′tyoo əs, -choo-) *adj.* —**in·ces′tu·ous·ly** *adv.* —**in·ces′tu·ous·ness** *n.*

**inch** (inch) *n.* [[< L *uncia*, twelfth part]] a measure of length equal to $\frac{1}{12}$ foot: symbol, ″ —*vt., vi.* to move very slowly, or by degrees —**every inch** in all respects —**inch by inch** gradually: also **by inches** —**within an inch of** very close to

**in·cho·ate** (in kō′it) *adj.* [[< L *inchoare*, begin]] **1** just begun; rudimentary **2** not yet clearly formed

**in·ci·dence** (in′sə dəns) *n.* **1** the degree or range of occurrence or effect **2** [Inf.] an instance

**in·ci·dent** (-dənt) *adj.* [[< L *in-*, on + *cadere*, to fall]] **1** likely to happen as a result **2** falling upon or affecting [*incident* rays] —*n.* **1** an event, esp. a minor one **2** a minor conflict

**in·ci·den·tal** (-dent″l) *adj.* **1** happening in connection with something more important; casual **2** secondary or minor —*n.* **1** something incidental **2** [pl.] miscellaneous items

**in′ci·den′tal·ly** *adv.* **1** in an incidental manner **2** by the way

**in·cin·er·ate** (in sin′ər āt′) *vt., vi.* **-at′ed, -at′ing** [[< L *in-*, in + *cinis*, ashes]] to burn to ashes; burn up —**in·cin′er·a′tion** *n.*

**in·cin′er·a′tor** *n.* a furnace for burning trash

**in·cip·i·ent** (in sip′ē ənt) *adj.* [[< L *in-*, in + *capere*, to take]] just beginning to exist or appear —**in·cip′i·ence** *n.*

**in·cise** (in sīz′) *vt.* **-cised′, -cis′ing** [[< L *in-*, into + *caedere*, to cut]] to cut into with a sharp tool; specif., to engrave or carve

**in·ci·sion** (in sizh′ən) *n.* **1** an incising **2** a cut; specif., one made surgically

**in·ci·sive** (in sī′siv) *adj.* **1** cutting into **2** sharp; penetrating —**in·ci′sive·ly** *adv.* —**in·ci′sive·ness** *n.*

**in·ci·sor** (in sī′zər) *n.* any of the front cutting teeth between the canines

**in·cite** (in sīt′) *vt.* **-cit′ed, -cit′ing** ⟦< L *in-*, on + *citare*, to urge⟧ to urge to action; rouse —**in·cite′ment** *n.*

**incl** *abbrev.* **1** including **2** inclusive

**in·clem·ent** (in klem′ənt) *adj.* ⟦< L *in-*, on + *clemens*, lenient⟧ **1** rough; stormy **2** lacking mercy; harsh —**in·clem′en·cy**, *pl.* **-cies**, *n.*

**in·cli·na·tion** (in′klə nā′shən) *n.* **1** a bending, leaning, or sloping **2** an inclined surface; slope **3** *a)* a bias; tendency *b)* a preference

**in·cline** (in klīn′; *for n., usually* in′klīn′) *vi.* **-clined′, -clin′ing** ⟦< L *in-*, on + *clinare*, to lean⟧ **1** to lean; slope **2** to have a tendency **3** to have a preference or liking —*vt.* **1** to cause to lean, slope, etc. **2** to make willing; influence —*n.* a slope; grade

INCLINED PLANE

**inclined plane** a sloping plane surface, esp. one sloping slightly

**in·close** (in klōz′) *vt.* **-closed′, -clos′ing** ENCLOSE —**in·clo′sure** (-klō′zhər) *n.*

**in·clude** (in klōōd′) *vt.* **-clud′ed, -clud′ing** ⟦< L *in-*, in + *claudere*, to close⟧ **1** to have as part of a whole; contain **2** to make part of a whole **3** to take into account —**in·clu′sion** (-klōō′zhən) *n.*

**in·clu·sive** (-klōō′siv) *adj.* **1** taking everything into account **2** including the terms or limits mentioned *[the third to the fifth inclusive]* —**inclusive of** including —**in·clu′sive·ly** *adv.*

**in·cog·ni·to** (in′käg nē′tō′, in käg′ni tō′) *adj., adv.* ⟦It < L *in-*, not + *cognitus*, known⟧ with true identity unrevealed or disguised

**in·co·her·ent** (in′kō hir′ənt, -her′-) *adj.* **1** not logically connected; disjointed **2** characterized by speech, etc. like this —**in′co·her′ence** *n.* —**in′co·her′ent·ly** *adv.*

**in·come** (in′kum′) *n.* money, etc. received in a given period, as wages, rent, interest, etc.

**in·com·mu·ni·ca·do** (in′kə myōō′ni kä′dō) *adj., adv.* ⟦Sp⟧ not allowed or willing to communicate with others

**in·com·pa·ra·ble** (in käm′pə rə bəl) *adj.* **1** having no basis of comparison **2** beyond comparison; matchless

**in·com·pat·i·ble** (in′kəm pat′ə bəl) *adj.* not compatible; specif., unable to live together harmoniously —**in′com·pat′i·bil′i·ty**, *pl.* **-ties**, *n.*

**in·com·pe·tent** (in käm′pə tənt) *adj.* without adequate ability, knowledge, fitness, etc. —*n.* an incompetent person —**in·com′pe·tence** *n.* —**in·com′pe·tent·ly** *adv.*

**in·com·plete** (in′kəm plēt′) *adj.* **1** lacking a part or parts **2** unfinished —*n. Educ.* a grade, etc. indicating assigned work is not complete

**in·con·gru·ous** (in käŋ′grōō əs) *adj.* **1** lacking harmony or agreement of parts, etc. **2** inappropriate —**in′con·gru′i·ty** (-kän grōō′i tē) *n.*

**in·con·se·quen·tial** (in kän′si kwen′shəl) *adj.* unimportant; trivial

**in·con·sid·er·a·ble** (in′kən sid′ər ə bəl) *adj.* trivial; small

**in′con·sid′er·ate** (-it) *adj.* without thought or consideration for others; thoughtless —**in′con·sid′er·ate·ly** *adv.* —**in′con·sid′er·ate·ness** or **in′con·sid′er·a′tion** (-ər ā′shən) *n.*

**in·con·sol·a·ble** (in′kən sōl′ə bəl) *adj.* that cannot be consoled

**in·con·spic·u·ous** (in′kən spik′yōō əs) *adj.* attracting little attention

**in·con·stant** (in kän′stənt) *adj.* not constant; changeable, irregular, etc. —**in·con′stan·cy** *n.*

**in·con·test·a·ble** (in′kən tes′tə bəl) *adj.* unquestionable; indisputable —**in′con·test′a·bil′i·ty** *n.* —**in′con·test′a·bly** *adv.*

**in·con·ti·nent** (in känt′′n ənt) *adj.* **1** without self-restraint, esp. in sexual activity **2** unable to restrain a natural discharge, as of urine —**in·con′ti·nence** *n.*

**in·con·ven·ience** (in′kən vēn′yəns) *n.* **1** lack of comfort, ease, etc. **2** anything inconvenient —*vt.* **-ienced, -ienc·ing** to cause inconvenience to

**in′con·ven′ient** (-yənt) *adj.* not favorable to one's comfort; causing bother, etc.

**in·cor·po·rate** (in kôr′pə rāt′) *vt.* **-rat·ed, -rat·ing** ⟦see IN-[1] & CORPORATE⟧ **1** to combine; include; embody **2** to bring together into a single whole; merge **3** to form into a corporation —*vi.* **1** to combine into a single whole **2** to form a corporation —**in·cor′po·ra′tion** *n.*

**in·cor·ri·gi·ble** (in kôr′ə jə bəl) *adj.* ⟦< LL *incorrigibilis*⟧ that cannot be corrected or reformed, esp. because set in bad habits —**in·cor′ri·gi·bil′i·ty** *n.* —**in·cor′ri·gi·bly** *adv.*

**in·cor·rupt·i·ble** (in′kə rup′tə bəl) *adj.* that cannot be corrupted, esp. morally

**in·crease** (in krēs′, in′krēs′) *vi.* **-creased′, -creas′ing** ⟦< L *in-*, in + *crescere*, grow⟧ to become greater in size, amount, degree, etc. —*vt.* to make greater in size, etc. —*n.* **1** an increasing or becoming increased **2** the result or amount of an increasing —**on the increase** increasing

**in·creas′ing·ly** *adv.* more and more

**in·cred·i·ble** (in kred′ə bəl) *adj.* **1** not credible **2** seeming too unusual to be possible —**in·cred′i·bly** *adv.*

**in·cred·u·lous** (in krej′ōō ləs) *adj.* **1** unwilling to believe **2** showing doubt or disbelief —**in·cre·du·li·ty** (in′krə dōō′lə tē) *n.*

**in·cre·ment** (in′krə mənt, iŋ′-) *n.* ⟦< L *incrementum*⟧ **1** an increase **2** amount of increase

**in·crim·i·nate** (in krim′i nāt′) *vt.* **-nat·ed, -nat·ing** ⟦< L *in-*, in + *crimen*, offense⟧ **1** to accuse of a crime **2** to involve in, or make appear guilty of, a crime or fault —**in·crim′i·na′tion** *n.*

**in·crust** (in krust′) *vt., vi.* ENCRUST —**in·crus·ta·tion** (in′krus tā′shən) *n.*

**in·cu·bate** (in′kyōō bāt′, iŋ′-) *vt.* **-bat·ed, -bat·ing** ⟦< L *in-*, on + *cubare*, to lie⟧ **1** to sit on and hatch (eggs) **2** to heat, etc. so as to hatch or grow, as in an incubator **3** to develop, as by planning —*vi.* to undergo incubation —**in′cu·ba′tion** *n.*

**in′cu·ba′tor** *n.* **1** a heated container for hatching eggs **2** any similar device, as for protecting premature babies, growing cell cultures, etc.

**in·cu·bus** (in′kyə bəs, iŋ′-) *n.* ⟦LL⟧ **1** a nightmare **2** an oppressive burden

**in·cul·cate** (in kul′kāt′, in′kul-) *vt.* **-cat·ed, -cat·ing** ⟦< L *in-*, in + *calcare*, trample underfoot⟧ to impress upon the mind, as by persistent urging —**in′cul·ca′tion** *n.*

**in·cul·pate** (in kul′pāt′, in′kul-) *vt.* **-pat·ed, -pat·ing** ⟦< L *in*, on + *culpa*, blame⟧ INCRIMINATE

**in·cum·ben·cy** (in kum′bən sē) *n., pl.* **-cies** tenure of office

**in·cum′bent** (-bənt) *adj.* ⟦< L *in-*, on + *cubare*, lie down⟧ currently in office —*n.* one currently in office —**incumbent on** (or **upon**) resting upon as a duty or obligation

**in·cum′ber** (-bər) *vt.* ENCUMBER —**in·cum′brance** (-brəns) *n.*

**in·cu·nab·u·la** (in′kyōō nab′yōō lə) *pl.n., sing.* **-u·lum** (-ləm) ⟦< L *in-*, in + *cunabula*, pl., a cradle⟧ books printed before 1500

**in·cur** (in kur′) *vt.* **-curred′, -cur′ring** ⟦< L *in-*, in + *currere*, to run⟧ **1** to acquire (something undesirable) **2** to bring upon oneself

**in·cu·ri·ous** (in kyoor′ē əs) *adj.* not curious; uninterested

**in·cur·sion** (in kur′zhən) *n.* ⟦see INCUR⟧ an invasion or raid

**ind** *abbrev.* **1** independent **2** index

**Ind** *abbrev.* **1** India **2** Indian

**in·debt·ed** (in det'id) *adj.* **1** in debt **2** owing gratitude, as for a favor

**in·debt'ed·ness** *n.* **1** a being indebted **2** the amount owed

**in·de·cent** (in dē'sənt) *adj.* not decent; specif., *a)* improper *b)* morally offensive; obscene —**in·de'cen·cy** *n.* —**in·de'cent·ly** *adv.*

**in·de·ci·pher·a·ble** (in'dē sī'fər ə bəl) *adj.* that cannot be deciphered

**in·de·ci·sion** (in'dē sizh'ən) *n.* inability to decide; vacillation

**in·de·ci·sive** (-sī'siv) *adj.* **1** not conclusive or final **2** showing indecision —**in·de·ci'sive·ly** *adv.* —**in·de·ci'sive·ness** *n.*

**in·deed** (in dēd') *adv.* certainly; truly —**interj.** used to express surprise, doubt, sarcasm, etc.

**in·de·fat·i·ga·ble** (in'di fat'i gə bəl) *adj.* [< L in-, not + *defatigare*, tire out] that cannot be tired out

**in·de·fen·si·ble** (in'dē fen'sə bəl) *adj.* **1** that cannot be defended **2** that cannot be justified

**in·def·i·nite** (in def'ə nit) *adj.* not definite; specif., *a)* having no exact limits *b)* not precise in meaning; vague *c)* blurred; indistinct *d)* uncertain *e) Gram.* not limiting or specifying ["a" and "an" are *indefinite* articles] —**in·def'i·nite·ly** *adv.*

**in·del·i·ble** (in del'ə bəl) *adj.* [< L in-, not + *delere*, destroy] **1** that cannot be erased, blotted out, etc. **2** leaving an indelible mark

**in·del·i·cate** (in del'i kit) *adj.* lacking propriety or modesty; coarse —**in·del'i·ca·cy**, *pl.* -**cies**, *n.*

**in·dem·ni·fy** (in dem'ni fī') *vt.* -**fied**, -**fy'ing** [< L *indemnis*, unhurt + -FY] **1** to insure against loss, damage, etc. **2** to repay for (loss or damage) —**in·dem'ni·fi·ca'tion** *n.*

**in·dem'ni·ty** (-tē) *n., pl.* -**ties** **1** insurance against loss, damage, etc. **2** repayment for loss, damage, etc.

**in·dent**[1] (in dent') *vt.* [< L in, in + *dens*, tooth] **1** to notch **2** to space (a line, paragraph, etc.) in from the margin of a page

**in·dent**[2] (in dent') *vt.* [IN-[1] + DENT] to make a dent in

**in·den·ta·tion** (in'den tā'shən) *n.* **1** a being indented **2** a notch, cut, inlet, etc. **3** a dent **4** a spacing in from a margin, or a blank space so made

**in·den·ture** (in den'chər) *n.* **1** a written contract **2** [often *pl.*] a contract binding a person to work for another —*vt.* -**tured**, -**tur·ing** to bind by indenture

**in·de·pend·ence** (in'dē pen'dəns) *n.* a being independent; freedom from the influence or control of others

**In·de·pend·ence** (in'dē pen'dəns) city in W Missouri: pop. 112,000

**Independence Day** the anniversary of the adoption of the Declaration of Independence on July 4, 1776

**in'de·pend'ent** (-dənt) *adj.* **1** free from the influence or control of others; specif., *a)* self-governing *b)* self-reliant *c)* not adhering to any political party *d)* not connected with others [an *independent* grocer] **2** not depending on another for financial support —*n.* one who is independent in thinking, action, etc. —**in'de·pend'ent·ly** *adv.*

**independent clause** a clause that can function as a complete sentence

**in'-depth'** *adj.* detailed; thorough

**in·de·scrib·a·ble** (in'di skrīb'ə bəl) *adj.* beyond the power of description —**in'de·scrib'a·bly** *adv.*

**in·de·struct·i·ble** (in'di struk'tə bəl) *adj.* that cannot be destroyed —**in'de·struct'i·bil'i·ty** *n.*

**in·de·ter·mi·nate** (in'dē tur'mi nit, -di-) *adj.* **1** indefinite; vague **2** doubtful or inconclusive —**in'de·ter'mi·na·cy** (-nə sē) *n.*

**in·dex** (in'deks') *n., pl.* -**dex·es** or -**di·ces'** (-di sēz') [L, indicator] **1** forefinger: in full **index finger 2** a pointer or indicator **3** an indication [an *index* of ability] **4** an alphabetical list of names, subjects, etc. indicating pages where found, as in a book **5**

a number used to measure change in prices, wages, etc. —*vt.* to make or be an index of or for

**index fund** a mutual fund tied to a particular stock-market index

**In·di·a** (in'dē ə) **1** region in S Asia, south of the Himalayas **2** republic in the central & S part of this region: 1,222,243 sq. mi.; pop. 846,303,000

**India ink** a black liquid ink

**In'di·an** *n.* **1** a person born or living in India or the East Indies **2** AMERICAN INDIAN —*adj.* **1** of India, or the East Indies, their people, etc. **2** of the American Indians, their culture, etc.

**In·di·an·a** (in'dē an'ə) Midwestern state of the U.S.: 35,870 sq. mi.; pop. 5,544,000; cap. Indianapolis: abbrev. *IN* —**In'di·an'an** or **In'di·an'i·an** (-an'ē ən) *adj., n.*

**In·di·an·ap·o·lis** (in'dē ə nap'ə lis) capital of Indiana, in the central part: pop. 742,000

**Indian corn** CORN[1] (sense 2)

**Indian file** SINGLE FILE

**Indian Ocean** ocean south of Asia, between Africa & Australia

**Indian summer** mild, warm weather following the first frosts of late autumn

**India paper 1** a thin, absorbent paper for taking proofs from engraved plates **2** a thin, opaque printing paper, as for Bibles

**in·di·cate** (in'di kāt') *vt.* -**cat'ed**, -**cat'ing** [< L in-, in + *dicare*, declare] **1** to direct attention to; point out **2** to be a sign of; signify **3** to show the need for **4** to express briefly or generally —**in'di·ca'tion** *n.*

**in·dic·a·tive** (in dik'ə tiv) *adj.* **1** giving an indication **2** designating or of the mood of a verb used to express an act, state, etc. as actual, or to ask a question of fact —*n.* the indicative mood

**in·di·ca·tor** (in'di kāt'ər) *n.* one that indicates; specif., a gauge, dial, etc. that measures

**in·dict** (in dīt') *vt.* [ult. < L in, against + *dicere*, speak] to charge with a crime —**in·dict'ment** *n.*

**in·dif·fer·ent** (in dif'ər ənt, -dif'rənt) *adj.* **1** neutral **2** unconcerned; apathetic **3** of no importance **4** average —**in·dif'fer·ence** *n.* —**in·dif'fer·ent·ly** *adv.*

**in·dig·e·nous** (in dij'ə nəs) *adj.* [< L *indegena*, a native] existing or growing naturally in a region or country; native

**in·di·gent** (in'di jənt) *adj.* [< L *indegere*, to be in need] poor; needy —*n.* an indigent person —**in'di·gence** *n.* —**in'di·gent·ly** *adv.*

**in·di·gest·i·ble** (in'di jes'tə bəl) *adj.* not easily digested

**in'di·ges'tion** (-jes'chən) *n.* **1** difficulty in digesting food **2** discomfort caused by this

**in·dig·nant** (in dig'nənt) *adj.* [< L in-, not + *dignus*, worthy] feeling or expressing anger, esp. at unjust or mean action —**in·dig'nant·ly** *adv.*

**in·dig·na·tion** (in'dig nā'shən) *n.* righteous anger

**in·dig·ni·ty** (in dig'nə tē) *n., pl.* -**ties** an insult or affront to one's dignity or self-respect

**in·di·go** (in'di gō') *n., pl.* -**gos'** or -**goes'** [Sp < Gr *Indikos*, Indian] **1** a blue dye obtained from certain plants or made synthetically **2** a deep violet blue —*adj.* of this color

**in·di·rect** (in'də rekt') *adj.* **1** not straight **2** not straight to the point **3** dishonest [indirect dealing] **4** not immediate; secondary [an *indirect* result] —**in'di·rect'ly** *adv.* —**in'di·rect'ness** *n.*

**indirect object** *Gram.* the word or words denoting the person or thing indirectly affected by the action of the verb (Ex.: *him* in "give *him* the ball")

**in·dis·creet** (in'di skrēt') *adj.* not prudent, as in speech or action; unwise

**in'dis·cre'tion** (-skresh'ən) *n.* **1** lack of discretion; imprudence **2** an indiscreet act or remark

**in·dis·crim·i·nate** (in'di skrim'i nit) *adj.* **1** mixed or random **2** not making careful distinctions —**in'dis·crim'i·nate·ly** *adv.*

**in·dis·pen·sa·ble** (in′di spen′sə bəl) *adj.* absolutely necessary

**in·dis·posed** (in′di spōzd′) *adj.* **1** slightly ill **2** unwilling; disinclined —**in·dis·po·si·tion** (in′dis pə zish′ən) *n.*

**in·dis·sol·u·ble** (in′di säl′yōō bəl) *adj.* that cannot be dissolved or destroyed; lasting

**in·dite** (in dīt′) *vt.* -dit′ed, -dit′ing 〖see INDICT〗 to compose and write

**in·di·vid·u·al** (in′də vij′ əl) *adj.* 〖< L < *in*-, not + *dividere*, to divide〗 **1** existing as a separate thing or being; single **2** of, for, by, or relating to a single person or thing —*n.* **1** a single thing or being **2** a person

**in′di·vid′u·al·ism′** *n.* **1** individuality **2** the doctrine that the state exists for the individual **3** the leading of one's life in one's own way —**in′di·vid′u·al·ist** *n.*, *adj.* —**in′di·vid′u·al·is′tic** *adj.*

**in′di·vid′u·al′i·ty** (-al′ə tē) *n.*, *pl.* -ties **1** the sum of the characteristics that set one person or thing apart **2** the condition of being different from others

**in′di·vid′u·al·ize′** (-īz′) *vt.* -ized′, -iz′ing **1** to make individual **2** to treat as an individual — **in′di·vid′u·al·i·za′tion** *n.*

**in′di·vid′u·al·ly** *adv.* **1** as individuals; separately **2** distinctively

**In·do·chi·na** (in′dō chī′nə) **1** large peninsula south of China, including Myanmar, Thailand, etc. **2** E part of this peninsula, consisting of Laos, Cambodia, & Vietnam

**in·doc·tri·nate** (in däk′trə nāt′) *vt.* -nat′ed, -nat′ing to instruct in, or imbue with, doctrines, theories, etc. —**in·doc′tri·na′tion** *n.*

**In·do-Eu·ro·pe·an** (in′dō yoor′ə pē′ən) *adj.* designating a family of languages including most of those of Europe and many of those of Asia

**in·do·lent** (in′də lənt) *adj.* 〖< L *in*-, not + *dolere*, feel pain〗 idle; lazy —**in′do·lence** *n.* —**in′do·lent·ly** *adv.*

**in·dom·i·ta·ble** (in däm′i tə bəl) *adj.* 〖< L *in*-, not + *domitare*, to tame〗 not easily discouraged or defeated

**In·do·ne·sia** (in′də nē′zhə) republic in the Malay Archipelago, consisting of Java, Sumatra, & most of Borneo: 741,098 sq. mi.; pop. 179,379,000

**In′do·ne′sian** *n.* **1** a person born or living in Indonesia **2** the official Malay language of Indonesia —*adj.* of Indonesia, its people, language, etc.

**in′door′** *adj.* living, belonging, etc. in a building

**in′doors′** *adv.* in or into a building

**in·dorse** (in dôrs′) *vt.* -dorsed′, -dors′ing ENDORSE

**in·du·bi·ta·ble** (in dōō′bi tə bəl) *adj.* that cannot be doubted; certain —**in·du′bi·ta·bly** *adv.*

**in·duce** (in dōōs′) *vt.* -duced′, -duc′ing 〖< L *in*-, in + *ducere*, to lead〗 **1** to persuade **2** to bring on or about; cause **3** to draw (a conclusion) from particular facts **4** to bring about (an electric or magnetic effect) in a body by placing it within a field of force —**in·duc′er** *n.*

**in·duce′ment** *n.* **1** an inducing or being induced **2** a motive; incentive

**in·duct** (in dukt′) *vt.* 〖see INDUCE〗 **1** to place formally in an office, a society, etc. **2** to enroll (esp. a draftee) in the armed forces

**in·duct′ance** *n.* the property of an electric circuit by which a varying current in it produces a magnetic field that induces voltages in the same or a nearby circuit

**in·duct·ee** (in′duk tē′) *n.* a person inducted, esp. into the armed forces

**in·duc·tion** (in duk′shən) *n.* **1** an inducting or being inducted **2** reasoning from particular facts to a general conclusion **3** the inducing of an electric or magnetic effect by a field of force —**in·duc′tive** *adj.*

**in·dulge** (in dulj′) *vt.* -dulged′, -dulg′ing 〖L *indulgere*, be kind to〗 **1** to satisfy (a desire) **2** to gratify the wishes of; humor —*vi.* to give way to one's own desires —**in·dulg′er** *n.*

**in·dul·gence** (in dul′jəns) *n.* **1** an indulging or being indulgent **2** a thing indulged in **3** a favor or privilege **4** *R.C.Ch.* remission of punishment still due for a sin committed but forgiven

**in·dul′gent** (-jənt) *adj.* indulging or inclined to indulge; kind or lenient, often to excess —**in·dul′gent·ly** *adv.*

**in·dus·tri·al** (in dus′trē əl) *adj.* **1** having to do with industry, its workers, etc. **2** made as for industrial use —**in·dus′tri·al·ly** *adv.*

**industrial arts** the mechanical and technical skills used in industry

**in·dus′tri·al·ism′** *n.* social and economic structure characterized by large industries, machine production, etc.

**in·dus′tri·al·ist** *n.* one who owns or controls an industrial enterprise

**in·dus′tri·al·ize′** (-īz′) *vt.*, *vi.* -ized′, -iz′ing **1** to establish or develop industrialism (in) **2** to organize as an industry —**in·dus′tri·al·i·za′tion** *n.*

**industrial park** a planned area for industrial use, usually on the outskirts of a city

**Industrial Revolution** [*often* i- r-] the societal change resulting from the introduction of machinery and large-scale production; esp., this change in England from *c.* 1760

**in·dus·tri·ous** (in dus′trē əs) *adj.* diligent; hardworking —**in·dus′tri·ous·ly** *adv.* —**in·dus′tri·ous·ness** *n.*

**in·dus·try** (in′dəs trē) *n.*, *pl.* -tries 〖< L *industrius*, active〗 **1** earnest, steady effort **2** *a*) any particular branch of productive, esp. manufacturing, enterprise *b*) manufacturing enterprises collectively **3** any large-scale business activity [the tourist *industry*] **4** the owners and managers of industry

**-ine**[1] (īn, in, ēn, ən) 〖< L *-inus*〗 *suffix* of, having the nature of, like [*aquiline, crystalline*]

**-ine**[2] (in, ən) 〖< L *-ina*〗 *suffix* forming abstract nouns [*discipline, doctrine*]

**-ine**[3] (ēn, in, īn, ən) 〖< L *-inus*〗 *suffix* forming chemical names, as of *a*) halogens [*iodine*] *b*) alkaloids or nitrogenous bases [*morphine*]

**in·e·bri·ate** (in ē′brē āt′; *for n.,* -it′) *vt.* -at′ed, -at′ing 〖< L *in*-, intens. + *ebrius*, drunk〗 to make drunk —*n.* a drunkard —**in·e′bri·a′tion** *n.*

**in·ed·u·ca·ble** (in ej′ōō kə bəl, -ej′ə-) *adj.* thought to be incapable of being educated

**in·ef·fa·ble** (in ef′ə bəl) *adj.* 〖< L *in*-, not + *effabilis*, utterable〗 **1** inexpressible **2** too sacred to be spoken

**in·ef·fi·cient** (in′ə fish′ənt) *adj.* not producing the desired effect with minimum energy, time, etc. —**in′ef·fi′cien·cy** *n.* —**in′ef·fi′cient·ly** *adv.*

**in·el·e·gant** (in el′ə gənt) *adj.* not elegant; crude —**in·el′e·gant·ly** *adv.*

**in·e·luc·ta·ble** (in′i luk′tə bəl) *adj.* 〖< L *in*-, not + *eluctari*, to struggle〗 not to be avoided or escaped; inevitable —**in′e·luc′ta·bly** *adv.*

**in·ept** (in ept′) *adj.* 〖< L *in*-, not + *aptus*, apt〗 **1** unsuitable; unfit **2** foolish **3** awkward; clumsy —**in·ep′ti·tude** (-ep′tə tōōd′) *n.* —**in·ept′ness** *n.*

**in·ert** (in urt′) *adj.* 〖< L *in*-, not + *ars*, skill〗 **1** without power to move or to resist **2** inactive; dull; slow **3** exhibiting little or no chemical activity [an *inert* gas]

**in·er·tia** (in ur′shə) *n.* 〖see prec.〗 **1** *Physics* the tendency of matter to remain at rest or to continue in a fixed direction unless affected by some outside force **2** a disinclination to move or act —**in·er′tial** *adj.*

**in·es·cap·a·ble** (in′e skāp′ə bəl) *adj.* that cannot be escaped or avoided

**in·es·ti·ma·ble** (in es′tə mə bəl) *adj.* too great to be properly measured

**in·ev·i·ta·ble** (in ev′i tə bəl) *adj.* 〖< L *in*-, not + *evitabilis*, avoidable〗 certain to happen; unavoidable —**in·ev′i·ta·bil′i·ty** *n.* —**in·ev′i·ta·bly** *adv.*

**in·ex·haust·i·ble** (in'eg zôs'tə bəl) *adj.* **1** that cannot be used up or emptied **2** tireless

**in·ex·o·ra·ble** (in eks'ə rə bəl) *adj.* ⟦< L *in-*, not + *exorare*, move by entreaty⟧ **1** that cannot be influenced by persuasion or entreaty; unrelenting **2** that cannot be altered, checked, etc. —**in·ex'o·ra·bly** *adv.*

**in·ex·pe·ri·ence** (in'ek spir'ē əns) *n.* lack of experience or of the knowledge or skill resulting from experience —**in'ex·pe'ri·enced** *adj.*

**in·ex·pert** (in ek'spərt, in'ek spurt') *adj.* not expert; unskillful

**in·ex·pli·ca·ble** (in eks'pli kə bəl) *adj.* that cannot be explained or understood

**in·ex·press·i·ble** (in'eks pres'ə bəl) *adj.* that cannot be expressed; indescribable

**in·ex·tin·guish·a·ble** (in'ek stiŋ'gwish ə bəl) *adj.* that cannot be put out or stopped

**in tre·mis** (in' eks trē'mis) ⟦L, in extremity⟧ at the point of death

**in·ex·tri·ca·ble** (in eks'tri kə bəl) *adj.* **1** that one cannot extricate oneself from **2** that cannot be untied **3** so complicated as to be unsolvable

**in·fal·li·ble** (in fal'ə bəl) *adj.* ⟦see IN-² & FAL-LIBLE⟧ **1** incapable of error **2** dependable; reliable —**in·fal'li·bil'i·ty** *n.* —**in·fal'li·bly** *adv.*

**in·fa·mous** (in'fə məs) *adj.* **1** having a very bad reputation; notorious **2** causing a bad reputation; scandalous

**in'fa·my** (-mē) *n., pl.* -**mies 1** very bad reputation; disgrace **2** great wickedness **3** an infamous act

**in·fan·cy** (in'fən sē) *n., pl.* -**cies 1** the state or period of being an infant **2** the earliest stage of anything

**in·fant** (in'fənt) *n.* ⟦< L *in-*, not + *fari*, speak⟧ a very young child; baby —*adj.* **1** of or for infants **2** in a very early stage

**in·fan·ti·cide** (in fan'tə sīd') *n.* **1** the murder of a baby **2** a person guilty of this

**in·fan·tile** (in'fən tīl') *adj.* **1** of infants **2** like an infant; babyish

**in·fan·try** (in'fən trē) *n., pl.* -**tries** ⟦< L *infans*, child⟧ **1** that branch of an army consisting of soldiers trained to fight on foot **2** such soldiers collectively —**in'fan·try·man** (-mən), *pl.* -**men,** *n.*

**in·farct** (in färkt') *n.* ⟦< L *in-*, in + *farcire*, to stuff⟧ an area of dying or dead tissue resulting from inadequate blood flow to that area: also **in·farc'tion** (-färk'shən)

**in·fat·u·at·ed** (in fach'oo āt'id) *adj.* ⟦< L *in-*, intens. + *fatuus*, foolish⟧ completely carried away by foolish love or affection

**in·fat'u·a'tion** *n.* a being infatuated

**in·fect** (in fekt') *vt.* ⟦< L *inficere*, to stain⟧ **1** to contaminate or cause to become diseased by contact with a disease-producing organism or matter **2** to imbue with one's feelings, beliefs, etc.

**in·fec·tion** (in fek'shən) *n.* **1** an infecting or being infected **2** an infectious disease

**in·fec'tious** (-shəs) *adj.* **1** likely to cause infection **2** designating a disease that can be communicated by certain bacteria, viruses, etc. **3** tending to affect others, as a laugh —**in·fec'tious·ly** *adv.* —**in·fec'tious·ness** *n.*

**in·fe·lic·i·tous** (in'fə lis'ə təs) *adj.* not felicitous; unfortunate or unsuitable —**in'fe·lic'i·ty,** *pl.* -**ties,** *n.*

**in·fer** (in fur') *vt.* -**ferred'**, -**fer'ring** ⟦< L *in-*, in + *ferre*, to carry⟧ **1** to conclude by reasoning from something known or assumed **2** to imply: still sometimes regarded as a loose usage —**in·fer·ence** (in'fər əns) *n.*

**in·fer·en·tial** (in'fər en'shəl) *adj.* based on or having to do with inference

**in·fe·ri·or** (in fir'ē ər) *adj.* ⟦< L *inferus*, low⟧ **1** located below or lower down **2** lower in order, status, etc. **3** lower in quality than: with *to* **4** poor in quality —*n.* an inferior person or thing —**in·fe'ri·or'i·ty** (-ôr'ə tē) *n.*

**in·fer·nal** (in fur'nəl) *adj.* ⟦< L *inferus*, below⟧ **1** of hell or Hades **2** hellish; fiendish

**in·fer·no** (in fur'nō) *n., pl.* -**nos** ⟦see prec.⟧ **1** HELL **2** any place characterized by flames or great heat

**in·fest** (in fest') *vt.* ⟦< L *infestus*, hostile⟧ **1** to overrun in large numbers, usually so as to be harmful **2** to be parasitic in or on —**in'fes·ta'tion** *n.* —**in·fest'er** *n.*

**in·fi·del** (in'fə del') *n.* ⟦< L *in-*, not + *fidelis*, faithful⟧ **1** one who does not believe in a particular religion **2** one who has no religion

**in·fi·del·i·ty** (in'fə del'ə tē) *n.* **1** unfaithfulness, esp. in marriage **2** *pl.* -**ties** an unfaithful act

**in·field** (in'fēld') *n.* **1** the diamond-shaped area enclosed by the four base lines on a baseball field **2** the players (**in'field'ers**) whose field positions are there

**in·fight·ing** (in'fīt'iŋ) *n.* **1** fighting, esp. boxing, at close range **2** personal conflict within a group —**in'fight'er** *n.*

**in·fil·trate** (in fil'trāt', in'fil trāt') *vi., vt.* -**trat·ed**, -**trat'ing 1** to filter or pass gradually through or into **2** to penetrate (enemy lines, a region, etc.) gradually or stealthily, so as to attack or to seize control from within —**in'fil·tra'tion** *n.* —**in'fil·tra'tor** *n.*

**in·fi·nite** (in'fə nit) *adj.* ⟦see IN-² & FINITE⟧ **1** lacking limits or bounds; endless **2** very great; vast —*n.* something infinite —**in'fi·nite·ly** *adv.*

**in·fin·i·tes·i·mal** (in'fin i tes'i məl) *adj.* ⟦< L *infinitus*, infinite⟧ too small to be measured —**in'fin·i·tes'i·mal·ly** *adv.*

**in·fin·i·tive** (in fin'i tiv) *n.* ⟦see INFINITE⟧ the form of a verb without reference to person, number, or tense: typically with *to*, as in "I want *to go*" —**in·fin'i·ti'val** (-tī'vəl) *adj.*

**in·fin'i·tude'** (-tood', -tyood') *n.* ⟦< L *infinitus*, INFINITE, prob. infl. by MAGNITUDE⟧ **1** a being infinite **2** an infinite quantity

**in·fin'i·ty** (-tē) *n., pl.* -**ties** ⟦< L *infinitas*⟧ **1** the quality of being infinite **2** unlimited space, time, etc. **3** an indefinitely large quantity

**in·firm** (in furm') *adj.* **1** weak; feeble, as from old age **2** not firm; unstable; frail; shaky —**in·firm'ly** *adv.* —**in·firm'ness** *n.*

**in·fir·ma·ry** (in fur'mə rē) *n., pl.* -**ries** a school dispensary

**in·fir'mi·ty** (-mə tē) *n., pl.* -**ties** (a) physical weakness or defect

**in·flame** (in flame') *vt., vi.* -**flamed'**, -**flam'ing** ⟦see IN-¹ & FLAME⟧ **1** to arouse, excite, etc. or become aroused, excited, etc. **2** to undergo or cause to undergo inflammation

**in·flam·ma·ble** (in flam'ə bəl) *adj.* **1** FLAMMABLE **2** easily excited —**in·flam'ma·bil'i·ty** *n.*

**in·flam·ma·tion** (in'flə mā'shən) *n.* **1** an inflaming or being inflamed **2** redness, pain, heat, and swelling in the body, due to injury, disease, etc.

**in·flam·ma·to·ry** (in flam'ə tôr'ē) *adj.* **1** rousing excitement, anger, etc. **2** *Med.* of or caused by inflammation

**in·flate** (in flāt') *vt.* -**flat'ed**, -**flat'ing** ⟦< L *in-*, in + *flare*, to blow⟧ **1** to blow full as with air or gas **2** to puff up with pride **3** to increase beyond what is normal; specif., to cause inflation of (money, credit, etc.) —*vi.* to become inflated —**in·flat'a·ble** *adj.*

**in·fla'tion** *n.* **1** an inflating or being inflated **2** *a)* an increase in the amount of money and credit in relation to the supply of goods and services *b)* an excessive or persistent increase in the general price level as a result of this, causing a decline in purchasing power —**in·fla'tion·ar'y** *adj.*

**in·flect** (in flekt') *vt.* ⟦< L *in-*, in + *flectere*, to bend⟧ **1** to vary the tone of (the voice) **2** *Gram.* to change the form of (a word) by inflection

**in·flec·tion** (in flek'shən) *n.* **1** a change in the tone of the voice **2** the change of form in a word to indicate number, case, tense, etc. Brit. sp. **in·flex'ion** —**in·flec'tion·al** *adj.*

**in·flex·i·ble** (in flek′sə bəl) *adj.* not flexible; stiff, rigid, fixed, unyielding, etc. —**in·flex′i·bil′i·ty** *n.*

**in·flict** (in flikt′) *vt.* ⟦< L *in-*, on + *fligere*, to strike⟧ 1 to cause (pain, wounds, etc.) as by striking 2 to impose (a punishment, etc.) *on* or *upon* —**in·flic′tion** *n.* —**in·flic′tive** *adj.*

**in-flight** (in′flīt′) *adj.* done, shown, etc. while an aircraft is in flight *[in-flight* movies*]*

**in·flo·res·cence** (in′flō res′əns, -flô-) *n. Bot.* 1 the producing of blossoms 2 the arrangement of flowers on a stem 3 a flower cluster 4 flowers collectively

**in·flu·ence** (in′flōō əns) *n.* ⟦< L *in-*, in + *fluere*, to flow⟧ 1 power to affect others 2 power to produce effects because of wealth, high position, etc. 3 one that has influence —*vt.* **-enced, -enc·ing** to have influence or an effect on

**in′flu·en′tial** (-en′shəl) *adj.* exerting influence, esp. great influence

**in·flu·en·za** (in′flōō en′zə) *n.* ⟦It, an influence⟧ an acute, contagious viral disease, characterized by inflammation of the respiratory tract, fever, and muscular pain

**in·flux** (in′fluks′) *n.* ⟦see INFLUENCE⟧ a flowing in or streaming in

**in·fo** (in′fō) *n.* [Slang] *short for* INFORMATION (sense 2)

**in·fold** (in fōld′) *vt. var. of* ENFOLD

**in·fo·mer·cial** (in′fō mur′shəl) *n.* ⟦INFO(RMATION) + (COM)MERCIAL⟧ a long TV commercial made to resemble a talk show, interview, etc.

**in·form** (in fôrm′) *vt.* ⟦see IN-¹ & FORM⟧ to give knowledge of something to —*vi.* to give information, esp. in accusing another

**in·for·mal** (in fôr′məl) *adj.* not formal; specif., *a)* not according to fixed customs, rules, etc. *b)* casual, relaxed, etc. *c)* not requiring formal dress *d)* designating or of the words, phrases, etc. characteristic of speech or writing that is casual, ordinary, etc. —**in′for·mal′i·ty** (-mal′ə tē), *pl.* **-ties,** *n.* —**in·for′mal·ly** *adv.*

**in·form·ant** (in fôr′mənt) *n.* a person who gives information; specif., an informer

**in·for·ma·tion** (in′fər mā′shən) *n.* 1 a being informed 2 something told or facts learned; news or knowledge 3 data stored in or retrieved from a computer

**information science** the science dealing with the collection, storage, and retrieval of information

**in·form·a·tive** (in fôr′mə tiv) *adj.* giving information; instructive

**in·formed′** *adj.* having or based on knowledge or education

**in·form′er** *n.* one who secretly gives evidence against another

**in·fo·tain·ment** (in′fō tān′mənt) *n.* ⟦INFO(RMATION) + (ENTER)TAINMENT⟧ TV programming of information, as about celebrities, in a dramatic or sensational style

**in·fra-** ⟦< L⟧ *prefix* below, beneath

**in·frac·tion** (in frak′shən) *n.* ⟦see INFRINGE⟧ a violation of a law, pact, etc.

**in·fra·red** (in′frə red′) *adj.* designating or of those invisible rays just beyond the red of the visible spectrum: they have a penetrating heating effect

**in′fra·son′ic** (-sän′ik) *adj.* of a frequency of sound below the range audible to the human ear

**in′fra·struc′ture** (-struk′chər) *n.* basic installations and facilities, as roads, power plants, transportation and communication systems, etc.

**in·fre·quent** (in frē′kwənt) *adj.* not frequent; happening seldom; rare; uncommon —**in·fre′quen·cy** or **in·fre′quence** *n.* —**in·fre′quent·ly** *adv.*

**in·fringe** (in frinj′) *vt.* **-fringed′, -fring′ing** ⟦< L *in-*, in + *frangere*, to break⟧ to break (a law or pact) —**infringe on** (or **upon**) to encroach on (the rights, etc. of others) —**in·fringe′ment** *n.*

**in·fu·ri·ate** (in fyoor′ē āt′) *vt.* **-at′ed, -at′ing** ⟦< L *in-*, in + *furia*, rage⟧ to make very angry; enrage

**in·fuse** (in fyōōz′) *vt.* **-fused′, -fus′ing** ⟦< L *in-*, in + *fundere*, pour⟧ 1 to instill or impart (qualities, etc.) 2 to fill; inspire 3 to steep (tea leaves, etc.) to extract the essence —**in·fus′er** *n.* —**in·fu′sion** *n.*

**-ing** (iŋ) ⟦< OE⟧ *suffix* used to form the present participle or verbal nouns *[talking, painting]*

**in·gath·er·ing** (in′gath′ər iŋ) *n.* a gathering together

**in·gen·ious** (in jēn′yəs) *adj.* ⟦< L *in-*, in + *gignere*, to produce⟧ 1 clever, resourceful, etc. 2 made or done in a clever or original way —**in·gen′ious·ly** *adv.*

**in·gé·nue** (an′zhə nōō′, än′-) *n.* ⟦Fr, ingenuous⟧ *Theater* the role of an inexperienced young woman, or an actress in this role

**in·ge·nu·i·ty** (in′jə nōō′ə tē, -nyōō′-) *n.* the quality of being ingenious; cleverness

**in·gen·u·ous** (in jen′yōō əs) *adj.* ⟦< L *in-*, in + *gignere*, to produce⟧ 1 frank; open 2 simple; naive —**in·gen′u·ous·ly** *adv.* —**in·gen′u·ous·ness** *n.*

**in·gest** (in jest′) *vt.* ⟦< L *in-*, into + *gerere*, carry⟧ to take (food, etc.) into the body, as by swallowing, inhaling, or absorbing —**in·ges′tion** *n.*

**in·glo·ri·ous** (in glôr′ē əs) *adj.* shameful; disgraceful

**in·got** (iŋ′gət) *n.* ⟦prob. < OFr *lingo*, tongue⟧ a mass of metal cast into a bar or other convenient shape

**in·grained** (in′grānd′) *adj.* 1 firmly established, as habits 2 inveterate *[an ingrained* liar*]*

**in·grate** (in′grāt′) *n.* ⟦< L *in-*, not + *gratus*, grateful⟧ an ungrateful person

**in·gra·ti·ate** (in grā′shē āt′) *vt.* **-at′ed, -at′ing** ⟦< L *in-*, in + *gratia*, favor⟧ to bring (oneself) into another's favor —**in·gra′ti·a′tion** *n.*

**in·grat·i·tude** (in grat′i tōōd′) *n.* lack of gratitude; ungratefulness

**in·gre·di·ent** (in grē′dē ənt) *n.* ⟦see fol.⟧ 1 any of the things that a mixture is made of 2 a component

**in·gress** (in′gres′) *n.* ⟦< L *in-*, into + *gradi*, to go⟧ entrance

**in·grown** (in′grōn′) *adj.* grown inward, esp. into the flesh, as a toenail

**in·gui·nal** (iŋ′gwi nəl) *adj.* ⟦< L *inguen*, groin⟧ of or near the groin

**in·hab·it** (in hab′it) *vt.* ⟦< L *in-*, in + *habitare*, dwell⟧ to live in —**in·hab′it·a·ble** *adj.*

**in·hab′it·ant** (-i tənt) *n.* a person or animal inhabiting a specified place

**in·hal·ant** (in hāl′ənt) *n.* a medicine, etc. to be inhaled

**in·ha·la·tor** (in′hə lāt′ər) *n.* 1 INHALER (*n.* 3) 2 RESPIRATOR (sense 2)

**in·hale** (in hāl′) *vt., vi.* **-haled′, -hal′ing** ⟦< L *in-*, in + *halare*, breathe⟧ to breathe in (air, vapor, etc.) —**in·ha·la·tion** (in′hə lā′shən) *n.*

**in·hal·er** (in hāl′ər) *n.* 1 one who inhales 2 RESPIRATOR (sense 1) 3 a device used in inhaling medicinal vapors

**in·here** (in hir′) *vi.* **-hered′, -her′ing** ⟦< L *in-*, in + *haerere*, to stick⟧ to be inherent

**in·her·ent** (in hir′ənt, -her′-) *adj.* existing in someone or something as a natural and inseparable quality —**in·her′ent·ly** *adv.*

**in·her·it** (in her′it) *vt., vi.* ⟦< L *in*, in + *heres*, heir⟧ 1 to receive (property, etc.) as an heir 2 to have (certain characteristics) as by heredity —**in·her′i·tor** *n.*

**in·her·it·ance** (in her′i təns) *n.* 1 the action of inheriting 2 something inherited

**in·hib·it** (in hib′it) *vt.* ⟦< L *in-*, in, on + *habere*, to hold⟧ to check or repress

**in·hi·bi·tion** (in′hi bish′ən, in′i-) *n.* 1 an inhibiting or being inhibited 2 a mental process that restrains an action, emotion, or thought

**in′-house′** *adj., adv.* (done) within an organization, company, etc. rather than outside it

**in·hu·man** (in hyōō′mən) *adj.* not having worthy human characteristics; heartless, cruel, brutal, etc. —**in′hu·man′i·ty** (-man′ə tē) *n.*

**in·im·i·cal** (i nim′i kəl) *adj.* 〚< L *in-*, not + *amicus*, friend〛 1 hostile; unfriendly 2 in opposition; adverse

**in·im·i·ta·ble** (i nim′i tə bəl) *adj.* that cannot be imitated or matched

**in·iq·ui·ty** (i nik′wi tē) *n.* 〚< L *in-*, not + *aequus*, equal〛 1 wickedness 2 *pl.* -**ties** a wicked or unjust act —**in·iq′ui·tous** *adj.*

**in·i·tial** (i nish′əl) *adj.* 〚< L *in-*, into, in + *ire*, go〛 of or at the beginning; first —*n.* the first letter of a name —*vt.* -**tialed** or -**tialled**, -**tial·ing** or -**tial·ling** to mark with initials —**in·i′tial·ly** *adv.*

**in·i·ti·ate** (i nish′ē āt′) *vt.* -**at·ed**, -**at·ing** 〚see prec.〛 1 to bring into practice or use 2 to teach the fundamentals of a subject to 3 to admit as a member into a fraternity, club, etc., esp. with a special or secret ceremony —**in·i′ti·a′tion** *n.* —**in·i′ti·a·to′ry** (-ə tôr′ē) *adj.*

**in·i·ti·a·tive** (i nish′ə tiv, -ē ə tiv) *n.* 1 the action of taking the first step or move 2 ability in originating new ideas or methods 3 the introduction of proposed legislation, as by voters' petitions

**in·ject** (in jekt′) *vt.* 〚< L *in-*, in + *jacere*, to throw〛 1 to force (a fluid) into a cavity or chamber; esp., to introduce (a liquid) into a vein, tissue, etc. with a syringe 2 to introduce (a remark, quality, etc.) —**in·jec′tion** *n.* —**in·jec′tor** *n.*

**in·junc·tion** (in juŋk′shən) *n.* 〚< L *in-*, in + *jungere*, join〛 1 a command; order 2 a court order prohibiting or ordering a given action

**in·jure** (in′jər) *vt.* -**jured**, -**jur·ing** 〚see INJURY〛 1 to do harm or damage to; hurt 2 to wrong or offend

**in·ju·ri·ous** (in joor′ē əs) *adj.* injuring or likely to injure; harmful

**in·ju·ry** (in′jə rē) *n., pl.* -**ries** 〚< L *in-*, not + *jus*, right〛 1 harm or damage 2 an injurious act

**in·jus·tice** (in jus′tis) *n.* 1 a being unjust 2 an unjust act; wrong

**ink** (iŋk) *n.* 〚< Gr *en-*, in + *kaiein*, to burn〛 1 a colored liquid used for writing, printing, etc. 2 a dark, liquid secretion ejected by cuttlefish, squid, etc. —*vt.* to cover, mark, or color with ink

**ink′blot′** *n.* any of the patterns made by blots of ink that are used in the RORSCHACH TEST

**ink·ling** (iŋk′liŋ) *n.* 〚ME *ingkiling*〛 1 a hint 2 a vague notion

**ink′well′** *n.* a container for ink

**ink′y** *adj.* -**i·er**, -**i·est** 1 like ink in color; dark; black 2 covered with ink —**ink′i·ness** *n.*

**in·laid** (in′lād′, in lād′) *adj.* set into a surface or formed, decorated, etc. by inlaying

**in·land** (in′lənd; *for n. & adv.*, -land′, -lənd) *adj.* of or in the interior of a region —*n.* an inland region —*adv.* into or toward this region

**in·law** (in′lô) *n.* 〚< *mother-* (or *father-*, etc.) *in-law*〛 [Inf.] a relative by marriage

**in·lay** (in′lā′, in lā′; *for n.* in′lā′) *vt.* -**laid**, -**lay·ing** 1 to set (pieces of wood, etc.) into a surface, specif. for decoration 2 to decorate thus —*n., pl.* -**lays** 1 inlaid decoration or material 2 a shaped filling, as of gold, cemented into the cavity of a tooth

**in·let** (in′let′) *n.* a narrow strip of water extending into a body of land

**in′-line′ skate** a kind of roller skate with its wheels in a line from toe to heel

**in·mate** (in′māt′) *n.* a person confined with others in a prison or mental institution

**in·most** (in′mōst′) *adj.* INNERMOST

**inn** (in) *n.* 〚OE〛 1 a hotel or motel 2 a restaurant or tavern: now usually only in the names of such places

**in·nards** (in′ərdz) *pl.n.* 〚< INWARDS〛 [Inf. or Dial.] the inner organs or parts

**in·nate** (i nāt′, in′āt) *adj.* 〚< L *in-*, in + *nasci*, be born〛 inborn; natural

**in·ner** (in′ər) *adj.* 1 farther within 2 of the mind or spirit *[inner peace]* 3 more secret

**inner circle** the small, exclusive, most influential part of a group

**inner city** the central sections of a large city, esp. when crowded or run-down

**inner ear** the part of the ear consisting of the semicircular canals, vestibule, and cochlea

**in′ner·most′** *adj.* 1 farthest within 2 most secret

**in′ner·sole′** *n.* INSOLE

**in′ner·spring′ mattress** a mattress with built-in coil springs

**in·ning** (in′iŋ) *n.* 〚< OE *innung*, getting in〛 *[pl. for Cricket]* Baseball, Cricket 1 a team's turn at bat 2 a numbered round of play in which both teams have a turn at bat

**inn′keep′er** *n.* the owner of an inn

**in·no·cent** (in′ə sənt) *adj.* 〚< L *in-*, not + *nocere*, to harm〛 1 free from sin, evil, etc.; specif., not guilty of a specific crime 2 harmless 3 knowing no evil 4 without guile —*n.* an innocent person, as a child —**in′no·cence** *n.* —**in′no·cent·ly** *adv.*

**in·noc·u·ous** (i näk′yōō əs) *adj.* 〚see prec.〛 1 harmless 2 not controversial or offensive —**in·noc′u·ous·ly** *adv.* —**in·noc′u·ous·ness** *n.*

**in·no·va·tion** (in′ə vā′shən) *n.* 〚< L *in-*, in + *novus*, new〛 1 the process of introducing new methods, devices, etc. 2 a new method, custom, device, etc. —**in′no·vate′**, -**vat·ed**, -**vat·ing**, *vi., vt.* —**in′no·va′tive** *adj.* —**in′no·va′tor** *n.*

**in·nu·en·do** (in′yōō en′dō) *n., pl.* -**does** or -**dos** 〚< L *in-*, in + *-nuere*, to nod〛 a hint or sly remark, usually derogatory; insinuation

**in·nu·mer·a·ble** (i nōō′mer ə bəl) *adj.* too numerous to be counted

**in·oc·u·late** (i näk′yə lāt′) *vt.* -**lat·ed**, -**lat·ing** 〚< L *in-*, in + *oculus*, eye〛 to inject a serum, vaccine, etc. into, esp. in order to create immunity —**in·oc′u·la′tion** *n.*

**in·of·fen·sive** (in′ə fen′siv) *adj.* causing no harm or annoyance; not objectionable —**in′of·fen′sive·ly** *adv.*

**in·op·er·a·ble** (in äp′ər ə bəl) *adj.* not operable; specif., incapable of being treated by surgery

**in·op·er·a·tive** (in äp′ər ə tiv, -ər āt′iv) *adj.* not working or functioning

**in·or·di·nate** (in ôrd′'n it) *adj.* 〚ult. < L *in-*, not + *ordo*, order〛 excessive; immoderate —**in·or′di·nate·ly** *adv.*

**in·or·gan·ic** (in′ôr gan′ik) *adj.* not organic; specif., designating or of matter not animal or vegetable; not living

**in·pa·tient** (in′pā′shənt) *n.* a patient who stays in a hospital, etc. while receiving treatment

**in·put** (in′poot′) *n.* 1 what is put in; specif., *a)* power put into a machine, etc. *b)* data or programs entered into a computer 2 opinion; advice —*vt.* -**put′**, -**put′ting** to enter (data) into a computer —**in′put′ter** *n.*

**in·quest** (in′kwest′) *n.* 〚see INQUIRE〛 a judicial inquiry, esp. before a jury, as a coroner's investigation of a death

**in·qui·e·tude** (in kwī′ə tood′) *n.* restlessness; uneasiness

**in·quire** (in kwīr′) *vi.* -**quired′**, -**quir′ing** 〚< L *in-*, into + *quaerere*, seek〛 1 to ask a question or questions 2 to investigate: usually with *into* —*vt.* to seek information about —**in·quir′er** *n.*

**in·quir·y** (in′kwər ē, in kwīr′ē) *n., pl.* -**ies** 1 an inquiring; investigation 2 a question

**in·qui·si·tion** (in′kwə zish′ən) *n.* 1 an investigation or inquest 2 [I-] *R.C.Ch.* the tribunal established in the 13th c. for suppressing heresy and heretics 3 any relentless questioning or harsh suppression —**in·quis′i·tor** (in kwiz′ə tər) *n.*

**in·quis·i·tive** (in kwiz′ə tiv) *adj.* 1 inclined to ask many questions 2 unnecessarily curious; prying —**in·quis′i·tive·ness** *n.*

**in re** (in rē′, -rā′) 〚L〛 in the matter (of)

**-in-res′i·dence** *combining form* appointed to

work at, and usually residing at, an institution, as a college, for a certain period

**in·road** (in′rōd′) *n.* an encroachment: usually used in plural

**ins** *abbrev.* insurance

**in·sane** (in sān′) *adj.* 1 not sane; mentally ill or deranged 2 of or for insane people 3 very foolish, extravagant, etc. —**in·sane′ly** *adv.* —**in·san′i·ty** (-san′ə tē) *n.*

**in·sa·ti·a·ble** (in sā′shə bəl, -shē ə bəl) *adj.* ⟦see IN-² & SATIATE⟧ that cannot be satisfied —**in·sa′ti·a·bil′i·ty** *n.* —**in·sa′ti·a·bly** *adv.*

**in·scribe** (in skrīb′) *vt.* -scribed′, -scrib′ing ⟦< L *in-*, in + *scribere*, write⟧ 1 to mark or engrave (words, etc.) on (a surface) 2 *a*) to dedicate (a book, etc.) to someone *b*) to autograph 3 to fix in the mind —**in·scrip′tion** (-skrip′shən) *n.*

**in·scru·ta·ble** (in skrōot′ə bəl) *adj.* ⟦< L *in-*, not + *scrutari*, examine⟧ not easily understood; enigmatic —**in·scru′ta·bly** *adv.*

**in·seam** (in′sēm′) *n.* an inner seam; specif., the seam from the crotch to the bottom of a trouser leg

**in·sect** (in′sekt′) *n.* ⟦< L *insectum*, lit., notched⟧ any of a large class of small, usually winged, invertebrates, as beetles, flies, or wasps, having three pairs of legs

**in·sec·ti·cide** (in sek′tə sīd′) *n.* any substance used to kill insects —**in·sec′ti·ci′dal** *adj.*

**in·sec·ti·vore** (in sek′tə vôr′) *n.* ⟦see fol.⟧ any of various small mammals, as moles and shrews, that are active mainly at night and that feed principally on insects

**in·sec·tiv·o·rous** (in′sek tiv′ə rəs) *adj.* ⟦< INSECT + L *vorare*, devour⟧ feeding chiefly on insects

**in·se·cure** (in′si kyoor′) *adj.* 1 not safe from danger 2 feeling anxiety 3 not firm or dependable —**in′se·cu′ri·ty** *adv.* —**in′se·cu′ri·ty**, *pl.* -**ties**, *n.*

**in·sem·i·nate** (in sem′ə nāt′) *vt.* -nat′ed, -nat′ing ⟦< L *in-*, in + *semen*, seed⟧ 1 to sow seeds in; esp., to impregnate 2 to imbue (with ideas, etc.) —**in·sem′i·na′tion** *n.*

**in·sen·sate** (in sen′sāt′, -sit) *adj.* 1 not feeling sensation 2 foolish 3 cold; insensitive

**in·sen·si·ble** (in sen′sə bəl) *adj.* 1 unable to perceive with the senses 2 unconscious 3 unaware; indifferent 4 so small as to be virtually imperceptible —**in·sen′si·bil′i·ty** *n.*

**in·sen·si·tive** (-sə tiv) *adj.* 1 not sensitive; not responsive 2 tactless —**in·sen′si·tive·ly** *adv.* —**in·sen′si·tiv′i·ty** *n.*

**in·sen·tient** (in sen′shənt, -shē ənt) *adj.* not sentient; not having life, consciousness, or feeling —**in·sen′tience** *n.*

**in·sert** (in surt′; *for n.* in′surt′) *vt.* ⟦< L *in-*, in + *serere*, join⟧ to put or fit (something) into something else —*n.* anything inserted or for insertion —**in·ser′tion** *n.*

**in·set** (in set′; *for n.* in′set′) *vt.* -set′, -set′ting to set in; insert —*n.* something inserted

**in·shore** (in′shôr′, in shôr′) *adv.*, *adj.* in, near, or toward the shore

**in·side** (in′sīd′, in′sīd′, in sīd′) *n.* 1 the inner side, surface, or part 2 [*pl.*] [Inf.] the internal organs of the body —*adj.* 1 internal 2 known only to insiders; secret —*adv.* 1 on or to the inside; within 2 indoors —*prep.* in or within —**inside of** within the space or time of —**inside out** 1 reversed 2 [Inf.] thoroughly

**in·sid·er** (in′sīd′ər, in sīd′ər) *n.* 1 one inside a given place or group 2 one having secret or confidential information

**in·sid·i·ous** (in sid′ē əs) *adj.* ⟦< L *insidiae*, an ambush⟧ 1 characterized by treachery or slyness 2 more dangerous than seems evident

**in·sight** (in′sīt′) *n.* 1 the ability to see and understand clearly the inner nature of things, esp. by intuition 2 an instance of such understanding

**in·sig·ni·a** (in sig′nē ə) *pl.n.*, *sing.* **in·sig′ne** (-nē) ⟦ult. < L *in-*, in + *signum*, a mark⟧ badges,

emblems, or distinguishing marks, as of rank or membership —*sing.n.*, *pl.* **in·sig′ni·as** such a badge, etc.

**in·sin·cere** (in′sin sir′) *adj.* not sincere; deceptive or hypocritical —**in′sin·cere′ly** *adv.* —**in′sin·cer′i·ty** (-ser′ə tē), *pl.* -**ties**, *n.*

**in·sin·u·ate** (in sin′yōō āt′) *vt.* -at′ed, -at′ing ⟦< L *in-*, in + *sinus*, a curve⟧ 1 to introduce or work into gradually, indirectly, etc. 2 to hint or suggest indirectly; imply —**in·sin′u·a′tion** *n.* —**in·sin′u·a′tive** *adj.* —**in·sin′u·a′tor** *n.*

**in·sip·id** (in sip′id) *adj.* ⟦< L *in-*, not + *sapidus*, savory⟧ 1 without flavor; tasteless 2 not exciting or interesting; dull

**in·sist** (in sist′) *vi.* ⟦< L *in-*, in, on + *sistere*, to stand⟧ to take and maintain a stand: often with *on* or *upon* —*vt.* 1 to demand strongly 2 to declare firmly —**in·sist′ing·ly** *adv.*

**in·sist′ent** *adj.* insisting; persistent —**in·sist′ence** *n.* —**in·sist′ent·ly** *adv.*

**in si·tu** (in sī′tōō′) ⟦L⟧ in position; in its original place

**in·so·far** (in′sō fär′) *adv.* to such a degree or extent: usually with *as*

**in·sole** (in′sōl′) *n.* 1 the inside sole of a shoe 2 a removable inside sole put in for comfort

**in·so·lent** (in′sə lənt) *adj.* ⟦< L *in-*, not + *solere*, be accustomed⟧ boldly disrespectful; impudent —**in′so·lence** *n.*

**in·sol·u·ble** (in säl′yə bəl) *adj.* 1 that cannot be solved 2 that cannot be dissolved —**in·sol′u·bil′i·ty** *n.*

**in·sol·vent** (in säl′vənt) *adj.* not solvent; unable to pay debts; bankrupt —**in·sol′ven·cy** *n.*

**in·som·ni·a** (in säm′nē ə) *n.* ⟦< L *in-*, without + *somnus*, sleep⟧ abnormal inability to sleep —**in·som′ni·ac′** (-ak′) *n.*, *adj.*

**in·so·much** (in′sō much′) *adv.* 1 to such a degree or extent; so: with *that* 2 inasmuch (*as*)

**in·sou·ci·ant** (in sōō′sē ənt) *adj.* ⟦Fr < *in-*, not + *soucier*, to care⟧ calm and untroubled; carefree

**in·spect** (in spekt′) *vt.* ⟦< L *in-*, at + *specere*, look at⟧ 1 to look at carefully 2 to examine or review officially —**in·spec′tion** *n.*

**in·spec′tor** *n.* 1 one who inspects 2 an officer on a police force, ranking next below a superintendent or police chief

**in·spi·ra·tion** (in′spə rā′shən) *n.* 1 an inspiring or being inspired mentally or emotionally 2 *a*) any stimulus to creative thought or action *b*) an inspired idea, action, etc. —**in′spi·ra′tion·al** *adj.*

**in·spire** (in spir′) *vt.* -spired′, -spir′ing ⟦< L *in-*, in, on + *spirare*, breathe⟧ 1 to inhale 2 to stimulate or impel, as to some creative effort 3 to motivate as by divine influence 4 to arouse (a thought or feeling) in (someone) 5 to occasion or cause —*vi.* 1 to inhale 2 to give inspiration

**in·spir·it** (in spir′it) *vt.* to put spirit into; cheer; hearten

**inst** *abbrev.* 1 institute 2 institution

**in·sta·bil·i·ty** (in′stə bil′ə tē) *n.* lack of firmness, determination, etc.

**in·stall** or **in·stal** (in stôl′) *vt.* -stalled′, -stall′ing ⟦< ML *in-*, in + *stallum*, a place⟧ 1 to place in an office, rank, etc., with ceremony 2 to establish in a place 3 to fix in position for use [to *install* new fixtures] —**in·stal·la·tion** (in′stə lā′shən) *n.* —**in·stall′er** *n.*

**in·stall′ment** or **in·stal′ment** *n.* 1 an installing or being installed 2 any of the parts of a sum of money to be paid at regular specified times 3 any of several parts, as of a serial

**installment plan** a credit system by which debts, as for purchased articles, are paid in installments

**in·stance** (in′stəns) *n.* ⟦see fol.⟧ 1 an example; case 2 a step in proceeding; occasion [in the first *instance*] —*vt.* -stanced, -stanc·ing to give as an example; cite —**at the instance of** at the suggestion or instigation of

**in·stant** (in′stənt) *adj.* ⟦< L *in-*, in, upon + *stare*, to stand⟧ 1 immediate 2 soluble, concentrated, or precooked for quick preparation: said of a food or beverage —*n.* **1** a moment **2** a particular moment —**the instant** as soon as

**in·stan·ta·ne·ous** (in'stən tā'nē əs) *adj.* done or happening in an instant —**in'stan·ta'ne·ous·ly** *adv.*

**in·stan·ter** (in stan'tər) *adv.* ⟦L⟧ *Law* immediately

**in'stant·ly** *adv.* immediately

**in·state** (in stāt') *vt.* -stat'ed, -stat'ing ⟦IN-¹ + STATE⟧ to put in a particular position, rank, etc.; install

**in·stead** (in sted') *adv.* ⟦IN¹ + STEAD⟧ in place of the one mentioned —**instead of** in place of

**in·step** (in'step') *n.* the top surface of the foot, between the ankle and the toes

**in·sti·gate** (in'stə gāt') *vt.* -gat'ed, -gat'ing ⟦< L *in-*, on + *-stigare*, to prick⟧ **1** to urge on to some action **2** to foment (rebellion, etc.) —**in'sti·ga'tion** *n.* —**in'sti·ga'tor** *n.*

**in·still** or **in·stil** (in stil') *vt.* -stilled', -still'ing ⟦< L *in-*, in + *stilla*, a drop⟧ **1** to put in drop by drop **2** to put (an idea, etc.) *in* or *into* gradually

**in·stinct** (in'stiŋkt) *n.* ⟦< L *instinguere*, to impell⟧ **1** (an) inborn tendency to behave in a way characteristic of a species **2** a natural or acquired tendency; knack —**in·stinc'tive** *adj.* —**in·stinc'tu·al** *adj.*

**in·sti·tute** (in'stə tōōt') *vt.* -tut'ed, -tut'ing ⟦< L *in-*, in, on + *statuere*, to cause to set up⟧ **1** to set up; establish **2** to start; initiate —*n.* something instituted; specif., *a)* an organization for the promotion of art, science, etc. *b)* a school or college specializing in some field —**in'sti·tut'er** or **in'sti·tu'tor** *n.*

**in·sti·tu·tion** (in'stə tōō'shən) *n.* **1** an instituting or being instituted **2** an established law, custom, etc. **3** *a)* an organization having a public character, as a school, church, bank, or hospital *b)* the building housing it **4** a person or thing long established in a place —**in'sti·tu'tion·al** *adj.*

**in·sti·tu'tion·al·ize'** (-īz') *vt.* -ized', -iz'ing **1** to make into an institution **2** to place in an institution, as for treatment —**in'sti·tu'tion·al·i·za'tion** *n.*

**in·struct** (in strukt') *vt.* ⟦< L *in-*, in + *struere*, pile up⟧ **1** to teach; educate **2** to inform **3** to order or direct

**in·struc'tion** (-struk'shən) *n.* **1** an instructing; education **2** something taught **3** any of the steps to be followed, as in operating something: *usually used in pl.* —**in·struc'tion·al** *adj.*

**in·struc'tive** *adj.* giving knowledge

**in·struc'tor** *n.* **1** a teacher **2** a college teacher of the lowest rank

**in·stru·ment** (in'strə mənt) *n.* ⟦see INSTRUCT⟧ **1** a thing by means of which something is done **2** a tool or implement **3** any of various devices for indicating, measuring, controlling, etc. **4** any of various devices producing musical sound **5** *Law* a formal document

**in'stru·men'tal** (-mənt'l) *adj.* **1** serving as a means; helpful **2** of, performed on, or written for a musical instrument or instruments

**in'stru·men'tal·ist** *n.* a person who performs on a musical instrument

**in'stru·men'tal'i·ty** (-men'tal'ə tē) *n.*, *pl.* -ties a means; agency

**in'stru·men'ta'tion** (-tā'shən) *n.* **1** the writing or scoring of music for instruments **2** the use of or an equipping with instruments

**instrument flying** the flying of an aircraft by the use of instruments only

**in·sub·or·di·nate** (in'sə bôrd''n it) *adj.* not submitting to authority; disobedient —**in'sub·or'di·na'tion** *n.*

**in·sub·stan·tial** (in'səb stan'shəl) *adj.* not substantial; specif., *a)* not real; imaginary *b)* weak or flimsy

**in·suf·fer·a·ble** (in suf'ər ə bəl) *adj.* intolerable; unbearable

**in·su·lar** (in'sə lər) *adj.* ⟦< L *insula*, island⟧ **1** of

---

253 ◄ **integument**

or like an island or islanders **2** narrow-minded; illiberal

**in·su·late'** (-lāt') *vt.* -lat'ed, -lat'ing ⟦< L *insula*, island⟧ **1** to set apart; isolate **2** to cover with a nonconducting material in order to prevent the escape of electricity, heat, sound, etc.

**in·su·la'tion** *n.* **1** an insulating or being insulated **2** material for this

**in·su·lin** (in'sə lin) *n.* ⟦< L *insula*, island⟧ **1** a hormone vital to carbohydrate metabolism, secreted by the islets of Langerhans **2** an extract from the pancreas of sheep, oxen, etc., used in the treatment of diabetes

**insulin shock** the abnormal condition caused by an excess of insulin: it is characterized by tremors, cold sweat, convulsions, and coma

**in·sult** (in sult'; *for n.* in'sult') *vt.* ⟦< L *in-*, on + *salire*, to leap⟧ to subject to an act, remark, etc. meant to hurt the feelings or pride —*n.* an insulting act, remark, etc.

**in·su·per·a·ble** (in sōō'pər ə bəl) *adj.* ⟦< L *insuperabilis*⟧ that cannot be overcome

**in·sup·port·a·ble** (in'sə pôrt'ə bəl) *adj.* **1** intolerable; unbearable **2** incapable of being upheld, proved, etc.

**in·sur·ance** (in shoor'əns) *n.* **1** an insuring or being insured against loss **2** a contract (**insurance policy**) purchased to guarantee compensation for a specified loss by fire, death, etc. **3** the amount for which something is insured **4** the business of insuring against loss

**in·sure** (in shoor') *vt.* -sured', -sur'ing ⟦ME *ensuren*: see ENSURE⟧ **1** to take out or issue insurance on **2** ENSURE —**in·sur'a·ble** *adj.*

**in·sured'** *n.* a person whose life, property, etc. is insured against loss

**in·sur'er** *n.* a person or company that insures others against loss

**in·sur'gence** (-jəns) *n.* a rising in revolt; uprising: also **in·sur'gen·cy**, *pl.* -cies

**in·sur'gent** (in sur'jənt) *adj.* ⟦< L *in-*, upon + *surgere*, rise⟧ rising up against established authority —*n.* an insurgent person

**in·sur·rec·tion** (in'sə rek'shən) *n.* ⟦see prec.⟧ a rising up against established authority; rebellion —**in'sur·rec'tion·ist** *n.*

**int** *abbrev.* **1** interest **2** interjection **3** international

**in·tact** (in takt') *adj.* ⟦< L *in-*, not + *tactus*, touched⟧ unimpaired or uninjured; kept or left whole

**in·ta·glio** (in tal'yō') *n.*, *pl.* -glios' ⟦It < *in-*, in + *tagliare*, to cut⟧ a design carved or engraved below the surface

**in·take** (in'tāk') *n.* **1** a taking in **2** the amount taken in **3** the place in a pipe, etc. where a fluid is taken in

**in·tan·gi·ble** (in tan'jə bəl) *adj.* **1** that cannot be touched; incorporeal **2** of certain business assets, esp. goodwill, having monetary value but no material being **3** that cannot be easily defined; vague —*n.* something intangible

**in·te·ger** (in'tə jər) *n.* ⟦L, whole⟧ a whole number (e.g., 5, -10) or zero

**in·te·gral** (in'tə grəl; *often* in teg'rəl) *adj.* ⟦see prec.⟧ **1** necessary for completeness; essential **2** made up of parts forming a whole

**in'te·grate'** (-grāt') *vt.*, *vi.* -grat'ed, -grat'ing ⟦< L *integer*, whole⟧ **1** to make or become whole or complete **2** to bring (parts) together into a whole **3** *a)* to remove barriers imposing segregation upon (racial groups) *b)* to abolish segregation in —**in'te·gra'tion** *n.* —**in'te·gra'tive** *adj.*

**integrated circuit** an electronic circuit with many interconnected circuit elements formed on a single body, or chip, of semiconductor material

**in·teg·ri·ty** (in teg'rə tē) *n.* ⟦see INTEGER⟧ **1** completeness **2** unimpaired condition; soundness **3** honesty, sincerity, etc.

**in·teg·u·ment** (in teg'yōō mənt) *n.* ⟦< L *in-*, upon

+ *tegere*, to cover] an outer covering; skin, shell, rind, etc.

**in·tel·lect** (in′tə lekt′) *n.* [< L *inter-*, between + *legere*, choose] **1** the ability to reason or understand **2** high intelligence **3** a very intelligent person

**in·tel·lec·tu·al** (in′tə lek′chōō əl) *adj.* **1** of, involving, or appealing to the intellect **2** requiring intelligence **3** having intellectual interests or tastes **4** showing high intelligence —*n.* one with intellectual interests or tastes —**in′tel·lec′tu·al·ly** *adv.* —**in′tel·lec′tu·al′i·ty** *n.*

**in·tel·lec′tu·al·ize′** (-īz′) *vt.* **-ized′, -iz′ing** to examine or interpret rationally, often without regard for emotional considerations

**intellectual property** something produced by the mind, the rights to which may be protected by a copyright, patent, etc.

**in·tel·li·gence** (in tel′ə jəns) *n.* [see INTELLECT] **1** *a)* the ability to learn or understand *b)* the ability to cope with a new situation **2** news or information **3** those engaged in gathering secret, esp. military, information

**intelligence quotient** *see* IQ

**in·tel·li·gent** (-jənt) *adj.* having or showing intelligence; clever, wise, etc. —**in·tel′li·gent·ly** *adv.*

**in·tel·li·gent′si·a** (-jent′sē ə) *pl.n.* [< Russ] [*also with sing. v.*] intellectuals collectively

**in·tel·li·gi·ble** (in tel′i jə bəl) *adj.* that can be understood; clear —**in·tel′li·gi·bil′i·ty** *n.* —**in·tel′li·gi·bly** *adv.*

**in·tem·per·ate** (in tem′pər it, -prit) *adj.* **1** not temperate or moderate; excessive **2** drinking too much alcoholic liquor —**in·tem′per·ance** *n.*

**in·tend** (in tend′) *vt.* [< L *in-*, at + *tendere*, to stretch] **1** to plan; have in mind as a purpose **2** to mean (something) to be or be used (*for*) **3** to mean; signify

**in·tend′ed** *n.* [Inf.] one's prospective spouse; fiancé(e)

**in·tense** (in tens′) *adj.* [see INTEND] **1** very strong [an *intense* light] **2** strenuous; earnest [*intense* thought] **3** characterized by much action, strong emotion, etc. —**in·tense′ly** *adv.*

**in·ten·si·fy** (in ten′sə fī′) *vt., vi.* **-fied′, -fy′ing** to make or become intense or more intense —**in·ten′si·fi·ca′tion** *n.*

**in·ten′si·ty** *n., pl.* **-ties 1** a being intense **2** great energy or vehemence, as of emotion **3** the amount of force or energy of heat, light, sound, etc.

**in·ten′sive** *adj.* **1** of or characterized by intensity; thorough **2** designating very attentive care given to critically ill patients **3** *Gram.* giving force or emphasis ["very" is an *intensive* adverb] —*n. Gram.* an intensive word, prefix, etc. —**in·ten′sive·ly** *adv.* —**in·ten′sive·ness** *n.*

**-in·ten′sive** *combining form* intensively using or requiring large amounts of (a specified thing) [*energy-intensive*]

**in·tent** (in tent′) *adj.* [see INTEND] **1** firmly directed; earnest **2** having one's attention or purpose firmly fixed [*intent* on going] —*n.* **1** an intending **2** something intended; purpose or meaning —**to all intents and purposes** in almost every respect; practically; virtually —**in·tent′ly** *adv.* —**in·tent′ness** *n.*

**in·ten·tion** (in ten′shən) *n.* **1** determination to act in a specified way **2** anything intended; purpose

**in·ten′tion·al** *adj.* done purposely —**in·ten′tion·al·ly** *adv.*

**in·ter** (in tur′) *vt.* **-terred′, -ter′ring** [< L *in*, in + *terra*, earth] to put (a dead body) into a grave or tomb; bury

**inter-** [L] *prefix* **1** between or among: the second element of the compound is singular in form [*interstate*] **2** with or on each other (or one another) [*interact*]

**in·ter·act** (in′tər akt′) *vi.* to act on one another —**in′ter·ac′tion** *n.*

**in·ter·ac′tive** (-ak′tiv) *adj.* **1** acting on one another **2** designating or of programming or electronic equipment, as for TV, which allows viewers to participate, as by making a response **3** of or involving the continual exchange of information between the computer and the user at a video screen

**in·ter·breed** (in′tər brēd′, in′tər brēd′) *vt., vi.* **-bred′, -breed′ing** HYBRIDIZE

**in·ter·cede′** (-sēd′) *vi.* **-ced′ed, -ced′ing** [< L *inter-*, between + *cedere*, go] **1** to plead or make a request in behalf of another **2** to mediate; intervene

**in·ter·cept′** (-sept′) *vt.* [< L *inter-*, between + *capere*, take] **1** to seize or stop in its course [to *intercept* a message] **2** *Math.* to cut off or mark off between two points, lines, etc. —**in′ter·cep′tion** *n.*

**in·ter·ces′sion** (-sesh′ən) *n.* an interceding; mediation or prayer in behalf of another —**in′ter·ces′sor** (-ses′ər) *n.* —**in′ter·ces′so·ry** *adj.*

**in·ter·change** (in′tər chānj′; *for n.* in′tər chānj′) *vt.* **-changed′, -chang′ing 1** to give and take mutually; exchange **2** to put (each of two things) in the other's place **3** to alternate —*n.* **1** an interchanging **2** a junction which allows movement of traffic between highways on different levels, as a cloverleaf —**in′ter·change′a·ble** *adj.*

**in·ter·col·le·gi·ate** (-kə lē′jit) *adj.* between or among colleges and universities

**in·ter·com** (in′tər käm′) *n.* a radio or telephone intercommunication system, as between rooms

**in′ter·com·mu′ni·cate′** (-kə myōō′ni kāt′) *vt., vi.* **-cat′ed, -cat′ing** to communicate with or to one another —**in′ter·com·mu′ni·ca′tion** *n.*

**in′ter·con·nect′** (-kə nekt′) *vt., vi.* to connect or be connected with one another —**in′ter·con·nec′tion** *n.*

**in′ter·con·ti·nen′tal** (-känt′'n ent′'l) *adj.* **1** between or among continents **2** able to travel from one continent to another: said as of a missile

**in·ter·cos′tal** (-käs′təl, -kôs′-) *adj.* between the ribs —*n.* an intercostal muscle, etc.

**in·ter·course** (in′tər kôrs′) *n.* [see INTER- & COURSE] **1** communication or dealings between or among people, countries, etc. **2** SEXUAL INTERCOURSE

**in′ter·de·nom′i·na′tion·al** (-dē näm′ə nā′shən əl) *adj.* between or among religious denominations

**in′ter·de·part·men′tal** (-dē′pärt ment′'l) *adj.* between or among departments

**in′ter·de·pend′ence** (-dē pen′dəns) *n.* mutual dependence —**in′ter·de·pend′ent** *adj.*

**in·ter·dict** (in′tər dikt′; *for n.* in′tər dikt′) *vt.* [< L *inter-*, between + *dicere*, speak] **1** to prohibit (an action) **2** to restrain from doing or using something —*n.* an official prohibition —**in′ter·dic′tion** *n.*

**in′ter·dis′ci·pli·nar′y** (-dis′ə pli ner′ē) *adj.* involving two or more disciplines, or branches of learning

**in·ter·est** (in′trist; *for v., also,* -tə rest′) *n.* [< L *inter-*, between + *esse*, be] **1** a right to, or a share in, something **2** anything in which one has a share **3** [*often pl.*] advantage; benefit **4** [*usually pl.*] those having a common concern or power in some industry, cause, etc. [the steel *interests*] **5** *a)* a feeling of concern, curiosity, etc. about something *b)* the power of causing this feeling *c)* something causing this feeling **6** *a)* money paid for the use of money *b)* the rate of such payment —*vt.* **1** to involve or excite the interest or attention of **2** to cause to have an interest or take part in —**in the interest(s) of** for the sake of

**in′ter·est·ed** *adj.* **1** having an interest or share **2** influenced by personal interest; biased **3** feeling or showing interest

**in′ter·est·ing** *adj.* exciting curiosity or attention; of interest

**in·ter·face** (in'tər fās') *n.* **1** a plane forming the common boundary between two parts of matter or space **2** a point or means of interaction between two systems, groups, etc. —*vt., vi.* -faced', -fac'ing to interact with (another system, group, etc.)

**in'ter·faith'** (-fāth') *adj.* between or involving persons adhering to different religions

**in·ter·fere** (in'tər fir') *vi.* -fered', -fer'ing ⟦ult. < L *inter-*, between + *ferire*, to strike⟧ **1** to clash; collide **2** *a*) to come in or between; intervene *b*) to meddle **3** to hinder an opposing player in any of various illegal ways —**interfere with** to hinder — **in'ter·fer'ence** *n.*

**in·ter·fer·on** (in'tər fir'än') *n.* ⟦INTERFER(E) + -*on*, arbitrary suffix⟧ a cellular protein produced in response to infection by a virus and acting to inhibit viral growth

**in·ter·gen'er·a'tion·al** (-jen'ə rā'shə nəl) *adj.* of or involving persons of different generations

**in·ter·im** (in'tər im) *n.* ⟦< L *inter*, between⟧ the period of time between; meantime —*adj.* temporary

**in·te·ri·or** (in tir'ē ər) *adj.* ⟦< L *inter*, between⟧ **1** situated within; inner **2** inland **3** private —*n.* **1** the interior part, as of a building or country **2** the internal, or domestic, affairs of a country

**interior decoration** the art or business of decorating and furnishing the interiors of houses, offices, etc. —**interior decorator**

**in·te'ri·or·ize'** (-īz') *vt.* -ized', -iz'ing to make (a concept, value, etc.) part of one's inner nature

**interj** *abbrev.* interjection

**in·ter·ject** (in'tər jekt') *vt.* ⟦< L *inter-*, between + *jacere*, to throw⟧ to throw in between; interrupt with; insert

**in'ter·jec'tion** (-jek'shən) *n.* **1** an interjecting **2** something interjected **3** *Gram.* an exclamation or other word(s) inserted into an utterance without grammatical connection to it

**in'ter·lace'** (-lās') *vt., vi.* -laced', -lac'ing to lace or weave together

**in'ter·lard'** (-lärd') *vt.* ⟦see INTER- & LARD⟧ to intersperse; diversify [to *interlard* a talk with quotations]

**in·ter·leu·kin** (in'tər lōō'kin) *n.* any of several proteins derived from many cell types and affecting the activity of other cells, as in stimulating the growth of T cells

**in'ter·line'** (-līn') *vt.* -lined', -lin'ing to put an inner lining under the ordinary lining of (a garment)

**in'ter·lock'** (-läk') *vt., vi.* to lock together; join with one another

**in·ter·loc·u·to·ry** (in'tər läk'yōō tôr'ē, -yə-) *adj.* *Law* not final [an *interlocutory* divorce decree]

**in·ter·lop·er** (in'tər lō'pər) *n.* ⟦INTER- + -*loper* < Du *lopen*, to run⟧ one who meddles

**in·ter·lude** (in'tər lōōd') *n.* ⟦< L *inter*, between + *ludus*, a play⟧ **1** anything that fills time between two events, as music between acts of a play **2** intervening time

**in'ter·mar'ry** (-mar'ē) *vi.* -ried, -ry·ing **1** to become connected by marriage: said of different clans, races, etc. **2** to marry: said of closely related persons —**in'ter·mar'riage** *n.*

**in'ter·me'di·ar'y** (-mē'dē er'ē) *adj.* **1** acting as a go-between or mediator **2** intermediate —*n., pl.* -ar'ies a go-between; mediator

**in'ter·me'di·ate** (-mē'dē it) *adj.* ⟦< L *inter-*, between + *medius*, middle⟧ **1** in the middle; in between **2** of an automobile larger than a compact but smaller than the standard size —*n.* an intermediate automobile

**in·ter·ment** (in tur'mənt) *n.* the act of interring; burial

**in·ter·mez·zo** (in'tər met'sō) *n., pl.* -zos' or -zi' (-sē') ⟦It < L: see INTERMEDIATE⟧ a short piece of music, as between parts of a composition

**in·ter·mi·na·ble** (in tur'mi nə bəl) *adj.* lasting, or seeming to last, forever; endless —**in·ter'mi·na·bly** *adv.*

**in·ter·min·gle** (in'tər miŋ'gəl) *vt., vi.* -gled, -gling to mix together; mingle

**in·ter·mis·sion** (in'tər mish'ən) *n.* ⟦< L *inter-*, between + *mittere*, send⟧ an interval of time between periods of activity, as between acts of a play

**in'ter·mit'tent** (-mit'nt) *adj.* ⟦see prec.⟧ stopping and starting at intervals; periodic

**in·tern** (in'turn'; *for vt.* in turn', in'turn') *n.* ⟦< L *internus*, inward⟧ **1** a doctor serving as assistant resident in a hospital generally just after graduation from medical school **2** a student, etc. doing supervised temporary work in a field to gain experience —*vi.* to serve as an intern —*vt.* to detain or confine (foreign persons, etc.), as during a war —**in·tern'ment** *n.* —**in'tern'ship'** *n.*

**in·ter·nal** (in tur'nəl) *adj.* ⟦< L *internus*⟧ **1** of or on the inside; inner **2** to be taken inside the body [*internal* remedies] **3** intrinsic [*internal* evidence] **4** domestic [*internal* revenue] —**in·ter'nal·ly** *adv.*

**in·ter'nal-com·bus'tion engine** an engine, as in an automobile, powered by the explosion of a fuel-and-air mixture within the cylinders

**in·ter'nal·ize'** (-īz') *vt.* -ized', -iz'ing to make (others' ideas, etc.) a part of one's thinking —**in·ter'nal·i·za'tion** *n.*

**internal medicine** the branch of medicine that deals with the diagnosis and nonsurgical treatment of diseases

**internal revenue** governmental income from taxes on income, profits, etc.

**in·ter·na·tion·al** (in'tər nash'ə nəl) *adj.* **1** between or among nations **2** concerned with the relations between nations **3** for the use of all nations **4** of or for people in various nations — **in'ter·na'tion·al·ize'**, -ized', -iz'ing, *vt.* —**in'ter·na'tion·al·ly** *adv.*

**International Phonetic Alphabet** a set of phonetic symbols for international use: each symbol represents a single human speech sound

**in·ter·ne·cine** (in'tər nē'sin) *adj.* ⟦< L *inter-*, between + *necare*, kill⟧ deadly or harmful to both sides of a group in a conflict

**In·ter·net** (in'tər net') *n.* an extensive computer network linking thousands of smaller networks: also with *the*

**in·tern·ist** (in'turn'ist, in turn'ist) *n.* a doctor who specializes in INTERNAL MEDICINE

**in·ter·of·fice** (in'tər ôf'is) *adj.* between or among the offices of an organization

**in·ter·per'son·al** (-pur'sə nəl) *adj.* between persons [*interpersonal* relationships]

**in'ter·plan'e·tar'y** (-plan'ə ter'ē) *adj.* between planets

**in'ter·play'** (-plā') *n.* action, effect, or influence on each other or one another

**in·ter·po·late** (in tur'pə lāt') *vt.* -lat'ed, -lat'ing ⟦< L *inter-*, between + *polire*, to polish⟧ **1** to change (a text, etc.) by inserting new material **2** to insert between or among others —**in·ter'po·la'tion** *n.*

**in·ter·pose** (in'tər pōz') *vt., vi.* -posed', -pos'ing **1** to place or come between **2** to intervene (with) **3** to interrupt (with) —**in'ter·po·si'tion** (-pə zish'ən) *n.*

**in·ter·pret** (in tur'prət) *vt.* ⟦< L *interpres*, agent, broker⟧ **1** to explain or translate **2** to construe [to *interpret* a silence as contempt] **3** to give one's own conception of (a work of art), as in performance or criticism —*vi.* to explain or translate —**in·ter'pre·ta'tion** *n.* —**in·ter'pret·er** *n.*

**in·ter'pre·tive** (-prə tiv) *adj.* that interprets; explanatory: also **in·ter'pre·ta'tive** (-tāt'iv)

**in·ter·ra·cial** (in'tər rā'shəl) *adj.* between, among, or for members of different races: also **in'ter·race'**

**in'ter·re·late'** (-rē lāt') *vt., vi.* -lat'ed, -lat'ing to make or be mutually related —**in'ter·re·lat'ed** *adj.*

**in·ter·ro·gate** (in tur'ə gāt') *vi., vt.* -gat'ed, -gat'ing ⟦< L *inter-*, between + *rogare*, ask⟧ to ask questions (of), esp. formally —**in·ter'ro·ga'tion** *n.* —**in·ter'ro·ga'tor** *n.*

**in·ter·rog·a·tive** (in'tə räg'ə tiv) *adj.* asking a question: also **in'ter·rog'a·to'ry** (-ə tôr'ē)

**in·ter·rupt** (in'tə rupt') *vt.* [< L *inter-*, between + *rumpere*, to break] **1** to break into (a discussion, etc.) or to break in upon (a speaker, worker, etc.) **2** to make a break in the continuity of —*vi.* to interrupt an action, talk, etc. —**in'ter·rup'tion** *n.*

**in·ter·scho·las·tic** (in'tər skə las'tik) *adj.* between or among schools

**in·ter·sect** (in'tər sekt') *vt.* [< L *inter-*, between + *secare*, to cut] to divide into two parts by passing through or across —*vi.* to cross each other

**in'ter·sec'tion** (-sek'shən) *n.* **1** an intersecting **2** the place where two lines, roads, etc. meet

**in'ter·serv'ice** (-sur'vis) *adj.* between or among branches of the armed forces

**in'ter·ses'sion** (-sesh'ən) *n.* a short session between regular sessions of a college year, for concentrating on specialized projects

**in·ter·sperse** (in'tər spurs') *vt.* **-spersed'**, **-spers'ing** [< L *inter-*, among + *spargere*, scatter] **1** to put here and there; scatter **2** to vary with things scattered here and there

**in'ter·state'** (-stāt') *adj.* between or among states, esp. of the U.S. —*n.* one of a network of U.S. highways

**in'ter·stel'lar** (-stel'ər) *adj.* between or among the stars

**in·ter·stice** (in tur'stis) *n.*, *pl.* **-sti·ces'** (-stə siz', -sēz') [< L *inter-*, between + *sistere*, to set] a crack; crevice

**in'ter·twine'** (-twīn') *vt.*, *vi.* **-twined'**, **-twin'ing** to twine together

**in'ter·ur·ban** (-ur'bən) *adj.* between cities or towns —*n.* an interurban railway, etc.

**in·ter·val** (in'tər vəl) *n.* [< L *inter-*, between + *vallum*, wall] **1** a space between things; gap **2** the time between events **3** the difference in pitch between two tones —**at intervals 1** once in a while **2** here and there

**in·ter·vene** (in'tər vēn') *vi.* **-vened'**, **-ven'ing** [< L *inter-*, between + *venire*, come] **1** to come or be between **2** to occur between two events, etc. **3** to come between to modify, settle, or hinder some action, etc.

**in'ter·ven'tion** (-ven'shən) *n.* **1** an intervening **2** interference, esp. of one country in the affairs of another

**in·ter·view** (-vyōō') *n.* **1** a meeting of people face to face to confer **2** *a)* a meeting in which a person is asked about personal views, etc., as by a reporter *b)* a published, taped, or filmed account of this —*vt.* to have an interview with —**in'ter·view·ee'** *n.* —**in'ter·view'er** *n.*

**in'ter·weave'** (-wēv') *vt.*, *vi.* **-wove'**, **-wo'ven**, **-weav'ing 1** to weave together **2** to connect closely

**in·tes·ta·cy** (in tes'tə sē) *n.* the fact or state of dying intestate

**in·tes·tate** (in tes'tāt', -tit) *adj.* [< L *in-*, not + *testari*, make a will] having made no will

HUMAN INTESTINES

Labels: LIVER, DUODENUM, TRANSVERSE COLON, ASCENDING COLON, JEJUNUM, CECUM, ILEUM, APPENDIX, STOMACH, PANCREAS, LARGE INTESTINE, DESCENDING COLON, SMALL INTESTINE, SIGMOID FLEXURE, RECTUM

**in·tes·tine** (in tes'tən) *n.* [< L *intus*, within] [*usu-*

*ally pl.*] the lower part of the alimentary canal, extending from the stomach to the anus and consisting of the SMALL INTESTINE and the LARGE INTESTINE; bowels —**in·tes'tin·al** *adj.*

**in·ti·mate** (in'tə mət; *for vt.*, -māt') *adj.* [< L *intus*, within] **1** most private or personal **2** very close or familiar **3** deep and thorough —*n.* an intimate friend —*vt.* **-mat'ed**, **-mat'ing** to hint or imply —**in'ti·ma·cy** (-mə sē), *pl.* **-cies**, *n.* —**in'ti·mate·ly** *adv.* —**in'ti·ma'tion** *n.*

**in·tim·i·date** (in tim'ə dāt') *vt.* **-dat'ed**, **-dat'ing** [< L *in-*, in + *timidus*, afraid] to make afraid, as with threats —**in·tim'i·da'tion** *n.*

**intl** *abbrev.* international: also **intnl**

**in·to** (in'tōō) *prep.* [OE] **1** from the outside to the inside of [*into* a room] **2** continuing to the midst of [to talk *into* the night] **3** to the form, substance, or condition of [divided *into* parts] **4** so as to strike [to run *into* a wall] **5** [Inf.] involved or interested in [she's *into* jazz now]

**in·tol·er·a·ble** (in täl'ər ə bəl) *adj.* unbearable; too severe, painful, etc. to be endured —**in·tol'er·a·bly** *adv.*

**in·tol'er·ant** (-ənt) *adj.* unwilling to tolerate others' beliefs, etc. —**intolerant of** not able or willing to tolerate —**in·tol'er·ance** *n.*

**in·to·na·tion** (in'tō nā'shən, -tə-) *n.* **1** an intoning **2** the quality of producing tones in or out of tune with regard to a given standard of pitch **3** variations in pitch within an utterance

**in·tone** (in tōn') *vt.*, *vi.* **-toned'**, **-ton'ing** to speak or recite in a singing tone; chant —**in·ton'er** *n.*

**in to·to** (in tō'tō) [L] as a whole

**in·tox·i·cate** (in täk'si kāt') *vt.* **-cat'ed**, **-cat'ing** [< L *in-*, in + *toxicum*, poison] **1** to make drunk **2** to excite greatly —**in·tox'i·cant** *n.* —**in·tox'i·ca'tion** *n.*

**intra-** [L, within] *prefix* within, inside

**in·tra·cit·y** (in'trə sit'ē) *adj.* of or within a large municipality, often, specif. the inner city

**in·trac·ta·ble** (in trak'tə bəl) *adj.* hard to manage; unruly or stubborn

**in·tra·der·mal** (in'trə dur'məl) *adj.* within the skin or between the layers of the skin

**in'tra·mu'ral** (-myoor'əl) *adj.* [INTRA- + MURAL] between or among members of the same school, college, etc. [*intramural* athletics]

**in·tra·net** (in'trə net') *n.* a private Internet computer network for one organization, company, etc.

**in·tran·si·gent** (in tran'sə jənt, -zə-) *adj.* [< L *in-*, not + *transigere*, to settle] refusing to compromise —**in·tran'si·gence** *n.*

**in·tran·si·tive** (in tran'sə tiv, -zə-) *adj.* not transitive; designating a verb that does not require a direct object —**in·tran'si·tive·ly** *adv.*

**in·tra·u·ter·ine (contraceptive) device** (in'trə yōōt'ər in) any of various devices, as a plastic loop, inserted in the uterus as a contraceptive

**in'tra·ve'nous** (-vē'nəs) *adj.* [INTRA- + VENOUS] directly into a vein —**in'tra·ve'nous·ly** *adv.*

**in·trench** (in trench') *vt.* ENTRENCH

**in·trep·id** (in trep'id) *adj.* [< L *in-*, not + *trepidus*, alarmed] bold; fearless; brave —**in·trep'id·ly** *adv.*

**in·tri·cate** (in'tri kit) *adj.* [< L *in-*, in + *tricae*, vexations] **1** hard to follow or understand because full of puzzling parts, details, etc. **2** full of elaborate detail —**in'tri·ca·cy** (-kə sē), *pl.* **-cies**, *n.* —**in'tri·cate·ly** *adv.*

**in·trigue** (in trēg'; *for n., also* in'trēg') *vi.* **-trigued'**, **-trigu'ing** [see prec.] to plot secretly or underhandedly —*vt.* to excite the interest or curiosity of —*n.* **1** a secret or underhanded plotting **2** a secret or underhanded plot or scheme **3** a secret love affair —**in·trigu'er** *n.* —**in·trigu'ing** *adj.* —**in·trigu'ing·ly** *adv.*

**in·trin·sic** (in trin'sik, -zik) *adj.* [< L *intra-*, within + *secus*, following] belonging to the real nature of a thing; inherent —**in·trin'si·cal·ly** *adv.*

**intro-** [L] *prefix* into, within, inward

**in·tro·duce** (in'trə dōōs') *vt.* **-duced'**, **-duc'ing** [< L *intro-*, in + *ducere*, to lead] **1** to put in; insert **2**

to bring in as a new feature **3** to bring into use or fashion **4** *a*) to make acquainted; present *[intro-duce* me to her*] b*) to give experience of *[they introduced* him to music*]* **5** to bring forward **6** to start; begin *[to introduce* a talk with a joke*]*

**in·tro·duc'tion** (-duk′shən) *n.* **1** an introducing or being introduced **2** the preliminary section of a book, speech, etc.; preface

**in·tro·duc'to·ry** (-duk′tə rē) *adj.* serving to introduce; preliminary

**in·tro·it** (in trō′it, in′troit) *n.* ⟦< L *intro-*, in + *ire*, to go⟧ **1** a psalm or hymn at the opening of a Christian worship service **2** [I-] *R.C.Ch.* the first variable part of the Mass

**in·tro·spec·tion** (in′trə spek′shən) *n.* ⟦< L *intro-*, within + *specere*, to look⟧ a looking into one's own mind, feelings, etc. —**in′tro·spec′tive** *adj.*

**in·tro·vert** (in′trə vurt′) *n.* ⟦< L *intro-*, within + *vertere*, to turn⟧ one who is introspective rather than being interested in others —**in′tro·ver′sion** (-vur′zhən) *n.* —**in′tro·vert′ed** *adj.*

**in·trude** (in trood′) *vt., vi.* -**trud′ed**, -**trud′ing** ⟦< L *in-*, in + *trudere*, to push⟧ to force (oneself) upon others unasked —**in·trud′er** *n.*

**in·tru·sion** (in troo′zhən) *n.* an intruding —**in·tru′sive** (-siv) *adj.* —**in·tru′sive·ly** *adv.* —**in·tru′sive·ness** *n.*

**in·trust** (in trust′) *vt.* ENTRUST

**in·tu·bate** (in′too bāt′) *vt.* -**bat′ed**, -**bat′ing** to insert a tube into (an orifice or hollow organ) to admit air, etc.

**in·tu·i·tion** (in′too ish′ən) *n.* ⟦< L *in-*, in + *tueri* to view⟧ the direct knowing of something without the conscious use of reasoning —**in·tu·i·tive** (in too′i tiv) *adj.*

**In·u·it** (in′oo it) *n.* ⟦Esk⟧ ESKIMO: now the preferred term, esp. in Canada

**in·un·date** (in′ən dāt′) *vt.* -**dat′ed**, -**dat′ing** ⟦< L *in-*, in + *unda*, a wave⟧ to cover with or as with a flood; deluge —**in′un·da′tion** *n.*

**in·ure** (in yoor′) *vt.* -**ured′**, -**ur′ing** ⟦ME *in ure*, in practice⟧ to accustom to pain, trouble, etc.

**in u·ter·o** (in yōōt′ər ō) ⟦L⟧ in the uterus

**in·vade** (in vād′) *vt.* -**vad′ed**, -**vad′ing** ⟦< L *in-*, in + *vadere*, to come, go⟧ **1** to enter forcibly or hostilely **2** to intrude upon; violate —**in·vad′er** *n.*

**in·va·lid**[1] (in′və lid) *adj.* ⟦< L *in-*, not + *validus*, strong⟧ **1** weak and sickly **2** of or for invalids —*n.* one who is ill or disabled

**in·val·id**[2] (in val′id) *adj.* not valid

**in·val·i·date′** (-ə dāt′) *vt.* -**dat′ed**, -**dat′ing** to make invalid; deprive of legal force —**in·val′i·da′tion** *n.*

**in·val·u·a·ble** (in val′yoo ə bəl) *adj.* too valuable to be measured; priceless —**in·val′u·a·bly** *adv.*

**in·va·sion** (in vā′zhən) *n.* an invading or being invaded, as by an army

**in·va′sive** (-siv) *adj.* **1** having to do with (an) invasion **2** penetrating into the body

**in·vec·tive** (in vek′tiv) *n.* ⟦see fol.⟧ a violent verbal attack; vituperation

**in·veigh** (in vā′) *vi.* ⟦< L *in-*, in + *vehere*, carry⟧ to make a violent verbal attack; rail (*against*)

**in·vei·gle** (in vā′gəl) *vt.* -**gled**, -**gling** ⟦< MFr *aveugler*, to blind⟧ to entice or trick into doing or giving something —**in·vei′gler** *n.*

**in·vent** (in vent′) *vt.* ⟦< L *in-*, in + *venire*, come⟧ **1** to think up *[to invent* excuses*]* **2** to think out or produce (a new device, process, etc.); originate —**in·ven′tor** *n.*

**in·ven′tion** (-ven′shən) *n.* **1** an inventing **2** the power of inventing **3** something invented

**in·ven′tive** (-tiv) *adj.* **1** of invention **2** skilled in inventing —**in·ven′tive·ly** *adv.* —**in·ven′tive·ness** *n.*

**in·ven·to·ry** (in′vən tôr′ē) *n.*, *pl.* -**ries** ⟦see INVENT⟧ **1** an itemized list of goods, property, etc., as of a business **2** the store of goods, etc. for such listing; stock —*vt.* -**ried**, -**ry·ing** to make an inventory of

**in·verse** (in vurs′, in′vurs′) *adj.* inverted; directly opposite —*n.* any inverse thing —**in·verse′ly** *adv.*

**in·ver·sion** (in vur′zhən) *n.* **1** an inverting or being inverted **2** something inverted; reversal **3** *Meteorol.* a temperature reversal in which a layer of warm air traps cooler air near the surface of the earth

**in·vert** (in vurt′) *vt.* ⟦< L *in-*, to + *vertere*, to turn⟧ **1** to turn upside down **2** to reverse the order, position, direction, etc. of

**in·ver·te·brate** (in vur′tə brit, -brāt′) *adj.* not vertebrate; having no backbone —*n.* any invertebrate animal

**in·vest** (in vest′) *vt.* ⟦< L *in-*, in + *vestis*, clothing⟧ **1** to clothe **2** to install in office with ceremony **3** to furnish with power, authority, etc. **4** to put (money) into business, stocks, etc. in order to get a profit —*vi.* to invest money —**in·ves′tor** *n.*

**in·ves·ti·gate** (in ves′tə gāt′) *vi., vt.* -**gat′ed**, -**gat′ing** ⟦< L *in-*, in + *vestigare*, to track⟧ to search (into); inquire —**in·ves′ti·ga′tor** *n.*

**in·ves·ti·ga·tion** (-gā′shən) *n.* an investigating; careful search; systematic inquiry

**in·ves·ti·ture** (-chər) *n.* a formal investing, as with an office

**in·vest·ment** (in vest′mənt) *n.* **1** an investing or being invested **2** *a*) money invested *b*) anything in which money is or may be invested

**in·vet·er·ate** (in vet′ər it) *adj.* ⟦< pp. of L *inveterare*, to age⟧ **1** firmly established **2** habitual —**in·vet′er·a·cy** *n.*

**in·vid·i·ous** (in vid′ē əs) *adj.* ⟦< L *invidia*, envy⟧ such as to excite ill will; giving offense, as by discriminating unfairly —**in·vid′i·ous·ly** *adv.* —**in·vid′i·ous·ness** *n.*

**in·vig·or·ate** (in vig′ər āt′) *vt.* -**at′ed**, -**at′ing** to give vigor to; fill with energy —**in·vig′or·a′tion** *n.*

**in·vin·ci·ble** (in vin′sə bəl) *adj.* ⟦< L *invincibilis*, not easily overcome⟧ that cannot be overcome; unconquerable —**in·vin′ci·bil′i·ty** *n.*

**in·vi·o·la·ble** (in vī′ə lə bəl) *adj.* **1** not to be violated; not to be profaned or injured; sacred **2** indestructible —**in·vi′o·la·bil′i·ty** *n.*

**in·vi′o·late** (-lit) *adj.* not violated; kept sacred or unbroken

**in·vis·i·ble** (in viz′ə bəl) *adj.* **1** not visible; that cannot be seen **2** out of sight **3** imperceptible —**in·vis′i·bil′i·ty** *n.* —**in·vis′i·bly** *adv.*

**in·vi·ta·tion** (in′və tā′shən) *n.* **1** an inviting **2** a message used in inviting

**in′vi·ta′tion·al** *adj.* only for those invited to take part: said as of an art show

**in·vite** (in vīt′; *for n.* in′vīt′) *vt.* -**vit′ed**, -**vit′ing** ⟦< L *invitare*⟧ **1** to ask to come somewhere or do something **2** to ask for **3** to give occasion for *[action that invites* scandal*]* **4** to tempt; entice —*n.* [Inf.] an invitation —**in′vit·ee′** *n.*

**in·vit′ing** *adj.* tempting; enticing

**in vi·tro** (in vē′trō) ⟦L, in glass⟧ isolated from the living organism and artificially maintained, as in a test tube

**in·vo·ca·tion** (in′və kā′shən) *n.* an invoking of God, the Muses, etc.

**in·voice** (in′vois′) *n.* ⟦prob. < ME *envoie*, message⟧ a list of goods shipped or services rendered, stating prices, etc.; bill —*vt.* -**voiced′**, -**voic′ing** to present an invoice for or to

**in·voke** (in vōk′) *vt.* -**voked′**, -**vok′ing** ⟦< L *in-*, in, on + *vocare*, to call⟧ **1** to call on (God, the Muses, etc.) for blessing, help, etc. **2** to resort to (a law, ruling, etc.) as pertinent **3** to conjure **4** to beg for; implore

**in·vol·un·tar·y** (in väl′ən ter′ē) *adj.* **1** not done by choice **2** not consciously controlled —**in·vol′un·tar′i·ly** *adv.* —**in·vol′un·tar′i·ness** *n.*

**in·vo·lu·tion** (in′və loo′shən) *n.* **1** an involving or being involved **2** a complication; intricacy

**in·volve** (in välv′, -vôlv′) *vt.* -**volved′**, -**volv′ing** ⟦< L *in-*, in + *volvere*, to roll⟧ **1** to make intricate or complicated **2** to entangle in difficulty, danger, etc.; implicate **3** to affect or include *[the riot involved* thousands*]* **4** to require *[saving involves* thrift/ **5** to make busy; occupy [*involved* the class in research/ —**in·volved'** *adj.* —**in·volve'ment** *n.*

**in·vul·ner·a·ble** (in vul′nər ə bəl) *adj.* **1** that cannot be wounded or injured **2** proof against attack —**in·vul′ner·a·bil′i·ty** *n.*

**in·ward** (in′wərd) *adj.* **1** situated within; internal **2** mental or spiritual **3** directed toward the inside **4** sensitive, subtle, reticent, etc. —*adv.* **1** toward the inside **2** into the mind or soul Also **in′wards** *adv.*

**in′ward·ly** *adv.* **1** in or on the inside **2** in the mind or spirit **3** toward the inside

**in′-your′-face′** *adj.* [Slang] done in a direct, often aggressive way; assertive; daring

**I/O** *abbrev.* input/output

**i·o·dine** (ī′ə dīn′, -din) *n.* [< Gr *iōdēs*, violetlike] **1** a nonmetallic chemical element, used in medicine, etc. **2** a tincture of iodine, used as an antiseptic

**i′o·dize′** (-dīz′) *vt.* **-dize′, -diz′ing** to treat with iodine

**i·on** (ī′ən, -än′) *n.* [ult. < Gr *ienai*, to go] an electrically charged atom or group of atoms

**-ion** (ən) [< L *-io*] *suffix* **1** the act or condition of **2** the result of

**I·on·ic** (ī än′ik) *adj.* designating or of a Greek or Roman style of architecture, distinguished by ornamental scrolls on the capitals

**i·on·ize** (ī′ən īz′) *vt., vi.* **-ized′, -iz′ing** to dissociate into ions, as a salt dissolved in water, or become electrically charged, as a gas under radiation — **i′on·i·za′tion** *n.* —**i′on·iz′er** *n.*

**i·on·o·sphere** (ī än′ə sfir′) *n.* the outer layers of the earth's atmosphere, with some electron and ion content

**i·o·ta** (ī ōt′ə) *n.* **1** the ninth letter of the Greek alphabet (I, ι) **2** a very small quantity; jot

**IOU** (ī′ō′yōō′) *n., pl.* **IOU's** [for *I owe you*] a signed paper bearing the letters *IOU*, acknowledging a specified debt

**-i·ous** (ē əs, yəs, əs) [see -OUS] *suffix* characterized by [*furious*]

**I·o·wa** (ī′ə wə) Midwestern state of the U.S.: 55,875 sq. mi.; pop. 2,777,000; cap. Des Moines: abbrev. *IA* —**I′o·wan** *adj., n.*

**ip·e·cac** (ip′i kak′) *n.* [< AmInd (Brazil) name] an emetic made as from the dried roots of a South American plant

**IPO** *abbrev.* initial public offering

**ip·so fac·to** (ip′sō fak′tō) [L] by that very fact

**IQ** *n., pl.* **IQ's** [I(NTELLIGENCE) Q(UOTIENT)] a number intended to indicate a person's intelligence, based on a test

**I·qa·lu·it** (ē kä′lōō ēt′) capital of Nunavut, Canada: pop. 4,200

**Ir**[1] *abbrev.* **1** Ireland **2** Irish

**Ir**[2] *Chem. symbol for* iridium

**ir-** *prefix* **1** IN-[1] **2** IN-[2] Used before *r*

**IRA** (är′ā′; ī′rə) *n., pl.* **IRA's** [I(ndividual) R(etirement) A(ccount)] a personal retirement plan with taxes on the earnings deferred until funds are withdrawn

**I·ran** (i ran′, -rän′) country in SW Asia: 634,293 sq. mi.; pop. 49,445,000: former name PERSIA —**I·ra·ni·an** (i rä′nē ən, ī-; -rä′-) *adj., n.*

**I·raq** (i räk′, -rak′) country in SW Asia, at the head of the Persian Gulf: 169,235 sq. mi.; pop. 16,335,000 —**I·ra·qi** (i rä′kē, -rak′ē), *pl.* **-qis,** *n., adj.*

**i·ras·ci·ble** (i ras′ə bəl) *adj.* [see fol.] easily angered; hot-tempered

**i·rate** (ī rāt′, ī′rāt′) *adj.* [< L *ira*, anger] angry; wrathful; incensed —**i·rate′ly** *adv.* —**i·rate′ness** *n.*

**ire** (īr) *n.* [< L *ira*] anger; wrath

**Ire·land** (īr′lənd) **1** one of the British Isles, west of Great Britain **2** republic comprising most of this island: 27,137 sq. mi.; pop. 3,560,000

**i·ren·ic** (ī ren′ik) *adj.* [< Gr *eirēnē*, peace] promoting peace

(ir′i des′ənt) *adj.* [< Gr *iris*, rainbow] having or showing an interplay of rainbowlike colors —**ir′i·des′cence** *n.*

**i·rid·i·um** (ī rid′ē əm) *n.* [see fol.] a white metallic chemical element

**i·ris** (ī′ris) *n., pl.* **i′ris·es** [Gr, rainbow] **1** the round, pigmented membrane surrounding the pupil of the eye **2** a plant with sword-shaped leaves and a showy flower

**I·rish** (ī′rish) *adj.* of Ireland or its people, language, etc. —*n.* **1** the Celtic language of Ireland **2** the English dialect of Ireland —**the Irish** the people of Ireland —**I′rish·man** (-mən), *pl.* **-men** (-mən), *n.* —**I′rish·wom′an,** *pl.* **-wom′en,** *fem.n.*

**Irish coffee** brewed coffee with Irish whiskey, topped with whipped cream

**Irish Sea** arm of the Atlantic between Ireland & Great Britain

**irk** (urk) *vt.* [ME *irken*, be weary of] to annoy, irritate, tire out, etc.

**irk′some** (-səm) *adj.* that tends to irk; tiresome or annoying

**i·ron** (ī′ərn) *n.* [OE *iren*] **1** a metallic chemical element, the most common of all metals **2** any device of iron; esp., such a device with a flat undersurface, heated for pressing cloth **3** [*pl.*] iron shackles **4** firm strength; power **5** any of certain golf clubs with angled metal heads —*adj.* **1** of iron **2** like iron; strong; firm —*vt., vi.* to press with a hot iron —**iron out** to smooth out; eliminate

**i′ron·clad′** *adj.* **1** covered or protected with iron **2** difficult to change or break [*an ironclad lease*]

**iron curtain 1** [*often* I- C-] a barrier of secrecy and censorship seen as isolating the U.S.S.R., etc.: often with *the* **2** any similar barrier

**i′ron·fist′ed** (-fis′tid) *adj.* despotic and brutal

**i·ron·ic** (ī rän′ik) *adj.* **1** meaning the contrary of what is expressed **2** using irony **3** opposite to what is or might be expected Also **i·ron′i·cal** —**i·ron′i·cal·ly** *adv.*

**i·ron·man** (ī′ərn man′) *n., pl.* **-men** (-men′) [*often* I-] a man of great physical strength

**i′ron·ware′** *n.* things made of iron

**i·ro·ny** (ī′rə nē, ī′ər nē) *n., pl.* **-nies** [< Gr *eirōn*, dissembler in speech] **1** expression in which the intended meaning of the words is the direct opposite of their usual sense **2** an event or result that is the opposite of what is expected

**Iro·quois** (ir′ə kwoi′) *n., pl.* **-quois′** (-kwoi′, -kwoiz′) a member of a confederation of North American Indian peoples that lived in upstate New York —*adj.* of the Iroquois —**Ir′o·quoi′an** *n., adj.*

**ir·ra·di·ate** (i rā′dē āt′) *vt.* **-at′ed, -at′ing 1** to shine upon; light up **2** to enlighten **3** to radiate **4** to expose to X-rays or other radiant energy —*vi.* to emit rays; shine —**ir·ra′di·a′tion** *n.*

**ir·ra·tion·al** (i rash′ə nəl) *adj.* **1** lacking the power to reason **2** senseless; unreasonable; absurd —**ir·ra′tion·al′i·ty** (-ə nal′ə tē), *pl.* **-ties,** *n.* —**ir·ra′tion·al·ly** *adv.*

**ir·re·claim·a·ble** (ir′i klām′ə bəl) *adj.* that cannot be reclaimed

**ir·rec·on·cil·a·ble** (i rek′ən sīl′ə bəl) *adj.* that cannot be brought into agreement; incompatible

**ir·re·cov·er·a·ble** (ir′i kuv′ər ə bəl) *adj.* that cannot be recovered, rectified, or remedied

**ir·re·deem·a·ble** (ir′i dēm′ə bəl) *adj.* **1** that cannot be bought back **2** that cannot be converted into coin: said as of certain paper money **3** that cannot be changed or reformed

**ir·ref·u·ta·ble** (i ref′yōō tə bəl, ir′i fyōōt′ə bəl) *adj.* indisputable —**ir·ref′u·ta·bly** *adv.*

**ir·re·gard·less** (ir′i gärd′lis) *adj., adv.* REGARD-LESS: a nonstandard or humorous usage

**ir·reg·u·lar** (i reg′yə lər) *adj.* **1** not conforming to an established rule, standard, etc. **2** not straight, even, or uniform **3** *Gram.* not inflected in the usual way —**ir·reg′u·lar′i·ty,** *pl.* **-ties,** *n.*

**ir·rel·e·vant** (i rel′ə vənt) *adj.* not pertinent; not

to the point —**ir·rel′e·vance** *n.* —**ir·rel′e·vant·ly**
*adv.*

**ir·re·li·gious** (ir′i lij′əs) *adj.* **1** not religious **2**
indifferent or hostile to religion **3** profane; impious —**ir′re·li′gious·ly** *adv.*

**ir·re·me·di·a·ble** (ir′i mē′dē ə bəl) *adj.* that cannot be remedied or corrected —**ir′re·me′di·a·bly**
*adv.*

**ir·rep·a·ra·ble** (i rep′ə rə bəl) *adj.* that cannot be repaired, mended, etc.

**ir·re·place·a·ble** (ir′i plās′ə bəl) *adj.* that cannot be replaced

**ir′re·press′i·ble** (-pres′ə bəl) *adj.* that cannot be repressed

**ir′re·proach′a·ble** (-prō′chə bəl) *adj.* blameless; faultless

**ir′re·sist′i·ble** (-zis′tə bəl) *adj.* that cannot be resisted; too strong, fascinating, etc. to be withstood —**ir′re·sist′i·bly** *adv.*

**ir·res·o·lute** (i rez′ə lōōt′) *adj.* not resolute; wavering; indecisive —**ir·res′o·lu′tion** (-lōō′shən) *n.*

**ir·re·spec·tive** (ir′i spek′tiv) *adj.* regardless (*of*)

**ir′re·spon′si·ble** (-spän′sə bəl) *adj.* **1** not responsible for actions **2** lacking a sense of responsibility —**ir′re·spon′si·bil′i·ty** *n.*

**ir′re·triev′a·ble** (-trēv′ə bəl) *adj.* that cannot be retrieved —**ir′re·triev′a·bly** *adv.*

**ir·rev·er·ence** (i rev′ər əns) *n.* lack of reverence; disrespect —**ir·rev′er·ent** *adj.*

**ir·re·vers·i·ble** (ir′i vur′sə bəl) *adj.* that cannot be reversed; esp., that cannot be annulled or turned back

**ir·rev·o·ca·ble** (i rev′ə kə bəl) *adj.* that cannot be revoked or undone —**ir·rev′o·ca·bly** *adv.*

**ir·ri·ga·ble** (ir′i gə bəl) *adj.* that can be irrigated

**ir·ri·gate** (ir′ə gāt′) *vt.* **-gat·ed, -gat·ing** [< L *in-*, in + *rigare*, to water] **1** to supply (land) with water, as by means of artificial ditches **2** *Med.* to wash out (a cavity, wound, etc.) —**ir′ri·ga′tion** *n.*

**ir·ri·ta·ble** (ir′i tə bəl) *adj.* **1** easily annoyed or provoked **2** *Med.* excessively sensitive to a stimulus —**ir′ri·ta·bil′i·ty** *n.* —**ir′ri·ta·bly** *adv.*

**ir′ri·tant** (-tənt) *adj.* causing irritation —*n.* a thing that irritates

**ir′ri·tate′** (-tāt′) *vt.* **-tat·ed, -tat·ing** [< L *irritare*, excite] **1** to provoke to anger; annoy **2** to make inflamed or sore —**ir′ri·ta′tion** *n.*

**ir·rupt** (i rupt′) *vi.* [< L *in-*, in + *rumpere*, to break] to burst suddenly or violently (*into*) —**ir·rup′tion**
*n.* —**ir·rup′tive** *adj.*

**IRS** *abbrev.* Internal Revenue Service

**Ir·ving** (ʉr′viŋ) city in NW Texas: pop. 155,000

**is**[1] (iz) *vi.* [OE] *3d pers. sing., pres. indic., of* BE

**is**[2] *abbrev.* **1** island(s) **2** islet(s)

**I·saac** (ī′zək) *n. Bible* one of the patriarchs, son of Abraham, and father of Jacob and Esau

**I·sa·iah** (ī zā′ə) *n. Bible* **1** a Hebrew prophet of the 8th c. B.C. **2** the book containing his teachings

**-ise** (īz) *suffix* chiefly Brit. sp. of -IZE

**-ish** (ish) [< OE *-isc*] *suffix* **1** of (a specified people) [*Irish*] **2** somewhat [*tallish*] **3** [Inf.] approximately [*thirtyish*] **4** like or characteristic of

**Ish·tar** (ish′tär′) *n.* the Babylonian and Assyrian goddess of fertility

**i·sin·glass** (ī′zin glas′, -ziŋ-) *n.* [prob. < MDu *huizen*, sturgeon + *blas*, bladder] mica, esp. in thin sheets

**I·sis** (ī′sis) *n.* the Egyptian goddess of fertility

**isl** *abbrev.* **1** island **2** isle

**Is·lam** (is′läm′, iz′-) *n.* [Ar *islām*, lit., submission (to God's will)] **1** the Muslim religion, a monotheistic religion founded by Mohammed **2** Muslims collectively or the lands in which they predominate —**Is·lam′ic** (-läm′ik) *adj.*

**Is·lam·a·bad** (is läm′ə bäd′) capital of Pakistan, in the NE part: pop. 201,000

**is·land** (ī′lənd) *n.* [< OE *igland*, lit., island land: sp. after *isle*] **1** a land mass smaller than a continent and surrounded by water **2** anything like this in position or isolation

259

◀ **it**

**is′land·er** *n.* a person born or living on an island

**isle** (īl) *n.* [< L *insula*] an island, esp. a small island

**is·let** (ī′lit) *n.* a very small island

**islets (or islands) of Lang·er·hans** (läŋ′ər häns′) [after P. *Langerhans* (1847-88), Ger histologist] endocrine cells in the pancreas that produce the hormone insulin

**ism** (iz′əm) *n.* a doctrine, theory, system, etc. whose name ends in *-ism*

**-ism** (iz′əm) [< Gr *-ismos*] *suffix* **1** act or result of [*terrorism*] **2** condition, conduct, or qualities of [*patriotism*] **3** theory of [*socialism*] **4** devotion to [*nationalism*] **5** an instance of [*witticism*]

**is·n't** (iz′ənt) *contr.* is not

**ISO** *abbrev.* International Standards Organization

**iso-** [< Gr *isos*] *combining form* equal, similar, identical [*isomorph*]

**i·so·bar** (ī′sō bär′) *n.* [< prec. + Gr *baros*, weight] a line on a map connecting points of equal barometric pressure

**i·so·late** (ī′sə lāt′; *for n., usually,* -lit) *vt.* **-lat·ed, -lat·ing** [< It *isola* (< L *insula*), island] to set apart from others; place alone —*n.* a person or thing that is isolated —**i′so·lat′ed** *adj.* —**i′so·la′tion** *n.* —**i′so·la′tor** *n.*

**i′so·la′tion·ist** *n.* one who opposes the involvement of a country in international alliances, etc. —*adj.* of isolationists —**i′so·la′tion·ism′** *n.*

**i·so·mer** (ī′sə mər) *n.* [< Gr *isos*, equal + *meros*, a part] any of two or more chemical compounds whose molecules contain the same atoms but in different arrangements —**i′so·mer′ic** (-mer′ik) *adj.*

**i′so·met′ric** (-met′rik) *adj.* [< Gr *isos*, equal + *metron*, measure] **1** equal in measure **2** of isometrics —*n.* [*pl.*] exercise in which muscles are briefly tensed in opposition to other muscles or to an immovable object —**i′so·met′ri·cal·ly** *adv.*

**i·sos·ce·les** (ī säs′ə lēz′) *adj.* [< Gr *isos*, equal + *skelos*, leg] designating a triangle with two equal sides

**i·so·tope** (ī′sə tōp′) *n.* [< ISO- + Gr *topos*, place] any of two or more forms of an element having the same atomic number but different atomic weights

**ISP** *n., pl.* **ISPs** [I(*nternet*) s(*ervice*) p(*rovider*)] a company that provides access to the Internet

**Is·ra·el**[1] (iz′rē əl) *n. Bible* Jacob

**Is·ra·el**[2] (iz′rē əl) **1** ancient land of the Hebrews at the SE end of the Mediterranean **2** kingdom in the N part of this land **3** country between the Mediterranean Sea & Jordan: 8,463 sq. mi.; pop. 4,038,000

**Is·rae·li** (iz rā′lē) *n.* a person born or living in modern Israel —*adj.* of modern Israel or its people

**Is·ra·el·ite** (iz′rē ə līt′) *n.* any of the people of ancient Israel; Hebrew

**is·su·ance** (ish′ōō əns) *n.* an issuing; issue

**is·sue** (ish′ōō) *n.* [< L *ex-*, out + *ire*, go] **1** an outgoing; outflow **2** a result; consequence **3** offspring **4** a point under dispute **5** a sending or giving out **6** all that is put forth at one time [an *issue* of bonds, a periodical, etc.] —*vi.* **-sued, -su·ing 1** to go or flow out; emerge **2** to result (*from*) or end (*in*) —*vt.* **1** to give or deal out [to *issue* supplies] **2** to publish —**at issue** in dispute — **take issue** to disagree —**is′su·er** *n.*

**-ist** (ist, əst) [< Gr *-istēs*] *suffix* **1** one who does, makes, or practices [*satirist*] **2** one skilled in or occupied with [*druggist, violinist*] **3** an adherent of [*anarchist*]

**Is·tan·bul** (is′tan bool′, -tän-) seaport in NW Turkey: pop. 5,476,000

**isth·mus** (is′məs) *n., pl.* **-mus·es** or **-mi′** (-mī′) [< Gr *isthmos*, a neck] a narrow strip of land having water at each side and connecting two larger bodies of land

**it** (it) *pron., pl. see* THEY [< OE *hit*] **1** the animal or thing previously mentioned **2** *it* is also used as: *a*) the subject of an impersonal verb [*it is snowing*] *b*) a subject or object of indefinite sense in various idiomatic constructions [*it's* all right, he lords *it* over us] —*n.* the player, as in tag, who must try to catch another —**with it** [Slang] alert, informed, or hip

**It** or **Ital** *abbrev.* **1** Italian **2** Italy

**IT** *abbrev.* information technology

**I·tal·ian** (i tal′yən) *adj.* of Italy or its people, language, etc. —*n.* **1** a person born or living in Italy **2** the Romance language of Italy

**i·tal·ic** (i tal′ik, ī-) *adj.* [< its early use in *Italy*] designating a type in which the characters slant upward to the right (Ex.: *this is italic type*) —*n.* [*usually pl., sometimes with sing. v.*] italic type or print: abbrev. **ital**

**i·tal·i·cize** (i tal′ə sīz′, ī-) *vt.* **-cized′, -ciz′ing** to print in italics

**It·a·ly** (it′′l ē) country in S Europe: 116,333 sq. mi.; pop. 56,778,000

**itch** (ich) *vi.* [OE *giccan*] **1** to feel a tingling of the skin, with the desire to scratch **2** to have a restless desire —*vt.* [Inf.] SCRATCH —*n.* **1** an itching **2** a restless desire —**itch′y,** **-i·er, -i·est,** *adj.*

**-ite** (īt) [< Gr *itēs*] *suffix* **1** an inhabitant of [*Akronite*] **2** an adherent of [*laborite*] **3** a manufactured product [*dynamite*]

**i·tem** (īt′əm) *n.* [< L *ita,* so, thus] **1** an article; unit; separate thing **2** a bit of news or information

**i′tem·ize′** (-īz′) *vt.* **-ized′, -iz′ing** to specify the items of; set down by items —**i′tem·i·za′tion** *n.*

**it·er·ate** (it′ər āt′) *vt.* **-at′ed, -at′ing** [< L *iterum,* again] to utter or do again —**it′er·a′tion** *n.*

**i·tin·er·ant** (ī tin′ər ənt) *adj.* [< L *iter,* a walk] traveling from place to place —*n.* a traveler

**i·tin′er·ar′y** (-er′ē) *n., pl.* **-ar′ies** **1** a route **2** a record of a journey **3** a detailed plan for a journey

**-i·tis** (īt′is) [< Gr *-itis*] *suffix* inflammation of (a specified part or organ) [*neuritis*]

**its** (its) *pron.* that or those belonging to it —*poss. pronominal adj.* of, belonging to, or done by it

**it's** (its) *contr.* **1** it is **2** it has

**it·self** (it self′) *pron.* a form of IT, used as an intensive [*the work itself* is easy], as a reflexive [*the dog bit itself*], or with the meaning "its true self" [*the bird is not itself* today]

**it·ty-bit·ty** (it′ē bit′ē) *adj.* [baby talk < *little bit*] [Inf.] very small; tiny: also **it·sy-bit·sy** (it′sē bit′sē)

**-i·ty** (ə tē, i-) [< L *-itas*] *suffix* state, quality, or instance [*chastity*]

**IUD** *n.* intrauterine (contraceptive) device

**IV¹** *n., pl.* **IVs** [< I(NTRA)V(ENOUS)] *Med.* **1** a procedure in which a hypodermic needle is inserted into a vein to supply blood, nutrients, etc. **2** the apparatus used for this, including the bag of fluid, tubing, and needle

**IV²** *abbrev.* intravenous(ly)

**-ive** (iv) [< L *-ivus*] *suffix* **1** of or having the nature of [*sportive*] **2** tending to [*retrospective*]

**i·vied** (ī′vēd) *adj.* covered or overgrown with ivy

**i·vo·ry** (ī′vər ē, īv′rē) *n., pl.* **-ries** [ult. < Egypt 3*bw*] **1** the hard, white substance forming the tusks of elephants, walruses, etc. **2** any substance like ivory **3** creamy white —*adj.* **1** of or like ivory **2** creamy-white

**Ivory Coast** country on the W coast of Africa: 123,855 sq. mi.; pop. 10,813,000

**ivory tower** a retreat away from reality or action

**i·vy** (ī′vē) *n., pl.* **i′vies** [OE *ifig*] **1** a climbing vine with a woody stem and evergreen leaves **2** any of various similar climbing plants

**-ize** (īz) [< Gr *-izein*] *suffix* **1** to cause to be [*sterilize*] **2** to become (like) [*crystallize*] **3** to combine with [*oxidize*] **4** to engage in [*soliloquize*]

# J

**j** or **J** (jā) *n., pl.* **j's, J's** the tenth letter of the English alphabet

**jab** (jab) *vt., vi.* **jabbed, jab′bing** [< ME *jobben,* to peck] **1** to poke, as with a sharp instrument **2** to punch with short, straight blows —*n.* a quick thrust or blow

**jab·ber** (jab′ər) *vi., vt.* [prob. echoic] to speak or say quickly, incoherently, or foolishly; chatter —*n.* chatter —**jab′ber·er** *n.*

**ja·bot** (zha bō′) *n.* [Fr, bird's crop] a ruffle or frill down the front of a blouse, etc.

**jack** (jak) *n.* [< the name *Jack*] **1** [*often* J-] a man or boy **2** any of various machines used to lift something heavy a short distance [an automobile *jack*] **3** a playing card with a picture of a royal male servant or soldier **4** a small flag flown on a ship's bow to show nationality **5** any of the small, 6-pronged metal pieces tossed and picked up in a game (**jacks**) **6** *Elec.* a plug-in receptacle used to make electrical contact —*vt.* to raise by means of a jack: usually with *up* —**jack up** [Inf.] to raise (prices, wages, etc.)

**jack-** [see prec.] *combining form* **1** male [*jackass*] **2** large or strong [*jackknife*] **3** boy; fellow [*jack-in-the-box*]

**jack·al** (jak′əl) *n.* [< Sans] a wild dog of Asia and N Africa

**jack·ass** (jak′as′) *n.* [JACK- + ASS] **1** a male donkey **2** a fool

**jack′boot′** (-bōōt′) *n.* [JACK- + BOOT¹] a long, heavy military boot that covers the knee

**jack′daw′** (-dô′) *n.* [JACK- + ME *dawe,* jackdaw] a small European crow

**jack·et** (jak′it) *n.* [< Ar *shakk*] **1** a short coat **2** an outer covering, as the removable paper cover on a book, the metal casing of a bullet, etc.

**Jack Frost** frost or cold weather personified

**jack′ham′mer** *n.* a portable type of pneumatic hammer, used for breaking up concrete, rock, etc.

**jack′-in-the-box′** *n., pl.* **-box′es** a toy consisting of a box from which a figure on a spring jumps up when the lid is lifted: also **jack′-in-a-box′**

**jack′-in-the-pul′pit** (-pool′pit) *n., pl.* **-pits** a plant with a flower spike partly arched over by a hoodlike covering

JACK-IN-THE-PULPIT

**jack′knife′** *n., pl.* **-knives′** **1** a large pocketknife **2** a dive in which the diver keeps knees unbent, touches the feet, and then straightens out —*vi., vt.* **-knifed′, -knif′ing** to bend or fold at the middle or at a connection

**jack′-of-all-trades′** *n., pl.* **jacks′-** [*often* J-] one who can do many kinds of work acceptably

**jack-o′-lan·tern** (jak′ə lant′ərn) *n., pl.* **-terns** a hollow pumpkin cut to look like a face and used esp. as a decoration at Halloween

**jack′pot′** *n.* [*jack,* playing card + *pot*] **1** cumulative stakes, as in poker **2** any large prize, etc.

**jack rabbit** a large hare of W North America, with long ears and strong hind legs

**Jack·son¹** (jak′sən), **An·drew** (an′drōō′) 1767-1845; 7th president of the U.S. (1829-37)

**Jack·son**[2] (jak'sən) capital of Mississippi, in the SW part: pop. 197,000

**Jack·son·ville** (jak'sən vil') port in NE Florida: pop. 673,000

**Ja·cob** (jā'kəb) *n. Bible* a son of Isaac

**jac·quard** (jak'ärd, jə kärd') *n.* ⟦after J. M. *Jacquard* (1752-1834), Fr inventor⟧ [*sometimes* J-] a fabric with a figured weave

**Ja·cuz·zi** (jə kōō'zē) ⟦< *Jacuzzi,* U.S. developers⟧ *trademark for* a kind of whirlpool bath

**jade** (jād) *n.* ⟦< Sp (*piedra de*) *ijada,* (stone of) the side: supposed to cure pains in the side⟧ **1** a hard, greenish, ornamental gemstone **2** a medium green color

**jad·ed** (jād'id) *adj.* **1** tired; worn-out **2** dulled or satiated —**jad'ed·ly** *adv.* —**jad'ed·ness** *n.*

**jade plant** a thick-leaved plant native to S Africa and Asia

**jag**[1] (jag) *n.* ⟦ME *jagge*⟧ a sharp, toothlike projection

**jag**[2] (jag) *n.* ⟦< ?⟧ [Slang] a drunken spree

**jag·ged** (jag'id) *adj.* having sharp projecting points; notched or ragged —**jag'ged·ly** *adv.* —**jag'ged·ness** *n.*

**jag·uar** (jag'wär') *n.* ⟦Port < AmInd (Brazil)⟧ a large, leopardlike cat found from SW U.S. to Argentina

**jai a·lai** (hī'lī', hī'ə lī') ⟦< Basque *jai,* celebration + *alai,* merry⟧ a game like handball, played with a basketlike racket

**jail** (jāl) *n.* ⟦ult. < L *cavea,* cage⟧ a prison, esp. for minor offenders or persons awaiting trial —*vt.* to put or keep in jail

**jail'break'** *n.* a breaking out of jail

**jail'er** or **jail'or** *n.* a person in charge of a jail or of prisoners

**Ja·kar·ta** (jə kär'tə) capital of Indonesia, on Java island: pop. *c.* 6,503,000

**ja·la·pe·ño** (hä'lə pän'yō) *n.* ⟦Mex⟧ a kind of hot pepper, orig. from Mexico

**Ja·lis·co** (hä lēs'kô) state of W Mexico, on the Pacific: 30,941 sq. mi.; pop. 5,303,000

**ja·lop·y** (jə läp'ē) *n., pl.* **-lop'ies** ⟦< ?⟧ [Slang] an old, ramshackle car

**jal·ou·sie** (jal'ə sē') *n.* ⟦Fr < It *gelosia,* jealousy⟧ a window, shade, or door formed of adjustable horizontal slats of wood, metal, or glass

**jam**[1] (jam) *vt.* **jammed, jam'ming** ⟦< ?⟧ **1** to squeeze into a confined space **2** to crush **3** to crowd **4** to crowd into or block (a passageway, etc.) **5** to make stick so that it cannot move or work **6** to make (radio broadcasts, etc.) unintelligible, as by sending out other signals on the same wavelength —*vi.* **1** *a)* to become stuck fast *b)* to become unworkable because of jammed parts **2** to become squeezed into a confined space **3** [Inf.] *Jazz* to improvise, as in a gathering of musicians (**jam session**) —*n.* **1** a jamming or being jammed [a traffic *jam*] **2** [Inf.] a difficult situation

**jam**[2] (jam) *n.* ⟦< ? prec.⟧ fruit boiled with sugar to a thick mixture

**Ja·mai·ca** (jə mā'kə) country on an island in the West Indies, south of Cuba: 4,411 sq. mi.; pop. 2,374,000 —**Ja·mai'can** *adj., n.*

**jamb** (jam) *n.* ⟦< LL *gamba,* hoof⟧ a side post of a doorway, window, etc.

**jam·bo·ree** (jam'bə rē') *n.* ⟦< ?⟧ **1** a noisy party, gathering, etc. **2** large assembly of Boy Scouts from many places

**James** (jāmz), **Henry** 1843-1916; U.S. novelist, in England

**James·town** (jāmz'toun') former village in Virginia: the 1st permanent English colonial settlement in America (1607)

**jam·packed** (jam'pakt') *adj.* [Inf.] tightly packed

**jan·gle** (jaŋ'gəl) *vi.* **-gled, -gling** ⟦< OFr *jangler*⟧ to make a harsh, usually metallic sound —*vt.* **1** to cause to jangle **2** to irritate [to *jangle* someone's nerves] —*n.* a jangling —**jan'gler** *n.*

**jan·i·tor** (jan'i tər) *n.* ⟦L, doorkeeper⟧ one who

takes care of a building, doing routine repairs, etc. —**jan'i·to'ri·al** (-i tôr'ē əl) *adj.*

**Jan·u·ar·y** (jan'yōō er'ē) *n., pl.* **-ar'ies** ⟦< L < *Janus,* Roman god who was a patron of beginnings and endings⟧ the first month of the year, having 31 days: abbrev. *abbrev.* **Jan.**

**ja·pan** (jə pan') *n.* ⟦orig. made in Japan⟧ a lacquer giving a hard, glossy finish

**Ja·pan** (jə pan') **1** island country in the Pacific, off the E coast of Asia: 145,841 sq. mi.; pop. 123,612,000 **2 Sea of** arm of the Pacific, between Japan & E Asia

**Jap·a·nese** (jap'ə nēz') *adj.* of Japan or its people, language, etc. —*n.* **1** *pl.* **-nese'** a person born or living in Japan **2** the language of Japan

**Japanese beetle** a shiny, green-and-brown beetle, orig. from Japan, damaging to crops

**jape** (jāp) *vi.* **japed, jap'ing** ⟦< OFr *japer,* to howl⟧ **1** to joke **2** to play tricks —*n.* **1** a joke **2** a trick

**jar**[1] (jär) *vi.* **jarred, jar'ring** ⟦ult. echoic⟧ **1** to make a harsh sound; grate **2** to have an irritating effect (*on* one) **3** to vibrate from an impact **4** to clash; conflict —*vt.* to jolt —*n.* **1** a grating sound **2** a vibration due to impact **3** a jolt

**jar**[2] (jär) *n.* ⟦< Ar *jarrah,* earthen container⟧ **1** a container made of glass, earthenware, etc., with a large opening **2** as much as a jar will hold: also **jar'ful'**

**jar·di·niere** (jär'də nir') *n.* ⟦< Fr < *jardin,* a garden⟧ an ornamental pot or stand for flowers or plants

**jar·gon** (jär'gən) *n.* ⟦< MFr, a chattering⟧ **1** unintelligible talk **2** the specialized vocabulary of those in the same work, way of life, etc.

**jas·mine** (jaz'min, jas'-) *n.* ⟦< Pers *yāsamīn*⟧ any of certain plants of warm regions, with fragrant flowers of yellow, red, or white

**Ja·son** (jā'sən) *n. Gr. Myth.* the leader of the Argonauts: cf. ARGONAUT

**jas·per** (jas'pər) *n.* ⟦< Gr *iaspis*⟧ an opaque variety of colored quartz, usually reddish

**jaun·dice** (jôn'dis) *n.* ⟦< L *galbus,* yellow⟧ a diseased condition in which the eyeballs, skin, and urine become abnormally yellowish as a result of increased bile in the blood —*vt.* **-diced, -dic·ing 1** to cause to have jaundice **2** to make bitter through envy, etc.

**jaunt** (jônt) *vi.* ⟦< ?⟧ to take a short pleasure trip —*n.* such a trip

**jaun·ty** (jôn'tē) *adj.* **-ti·er, -ti·est** ⟦< Fr *gentil,* genteel⟧ showing an easy confidence; sprightly or perky —**jaun'ti·ly** *adv.* —**jaun'ti·ness** *n.*

**Ja·va**[1] (jä'və, jav'ə) *n.* **1** a coffee grown on Java **2** [*often* j-] [Slang] any coffee

**Java**[2] (jä'və, jav'ə) large island of Indonesia —**Jav·a·nese** (jä'və nēz'), *pl.* **-nese'**, *adj., n.*

**jav·e·lin** (jav'lin, jav'ə lin) *n.* ⟦MFr *javeline*⟧ a light spear, esp. one thrown for distance in an athletic contest

**jaw** (jô) *n.* ⟦< OFr *joue,* cheek⟧ **1** either of the two bony parts that hold the teeth and frame the mouth **2** either of two movable parts that grasp or crush something, as in a vise —*vi.* [Slang] to talk

**jaw'bone'** *n.* a bone of a jaw, esp. of the lower jaw —*vt., vi.* **-boned', -bon'ing** to try to persuade by using the influence of one's office or position

**jaw'break'er** *n.* **1** a hard, usually round candy **2** [Slang] a word hard to pronounce

**jaw'less fish** a jawless fish with an eel-like body and a circular sucking mouth, as the lamprey

**jay** (jā) *n.* ⟦< LL *gaius,* jay⟧ any of several birds, usually strikingly colored, as the blue jay

**jay'walk'** *vi.* to walk across a street without obeying traffic rules and signals —**jay'walk'er** *n.*

**jazz** (jaz) *n.* ⟦< ?⟧ **1** a kind of syncopated, highly rhythmic music originated by Southern blacks in the late 19th c. **2** [Slang] talk, acts, etc. regarded disparagingly —*vt.* [Slang] to enliven or embellish: usually with *up*

**jazz·y** *adj.* **-i·er, -i·est 1** of or like jazz **2** [Slang] lively, flashy, etc.

**JD** *abbrev.* **1** ⟦L *Jurum Doctor*⟧ Doctor of Laws: also **J.D. 2** juvenile delinquent: also **jd**

**jeal·ous** (jel′əs) *adj.* ⟦see ZEAL⟧ **1** watchful in guarding [*jealous* of one's rights] **2** *a*) resentfully suspicious of rivalry [a *jealous* lover] *b*) resentfully envious *c*) resulting from such feelings [a *jealous* rage] —**jeal′ous·ly** *adv.*

**jeal′ous·y** *n.* **1** the quality or condition of being jealous **2** *pl.* **-ous·ies** a jealous feeling

**jean** (jēn) *n.* ⟦< L *Genua*, Genoa, city in Italy⟧ **1** a durable, twilled cotton cloth **2** [*pl.*] trousers of this or of denim

**jeep** (jēp) *n.* ⟦< creature in comic strip by E. C. Segar (1894-1938)⟧ a small, rugged military vehicle of WWII —[**J-**] *trademark for* a similar vehicle for civilian use

**jeer** (jir) *vt., vi.* ⟦< ? CHEER⟧ to make fun of (a person or thing) in a rude, sarcastic manner; scoff (at) —*n.* a jeering remark

**Jef·fer·son** (jef′ər sən), **Thom·as** (täm′əs) 1743-1826; 3d president of the U.S. (1801-09)

**Jefferson City** capital of Missouri: pop. 35,000

**Je·ho·vah** (ji hō′və) *n.* ⟦< Heb⟧ God

**je·june** (ji jōōn′) *adj.* ⟦L *jejunus*, empty⟧ **1** not interesting or satisfying **2** not mature; childish

**je·ju·num** (jē jōō′nəm) *n., pl.* **-na** (-nə) ⟦< L *jejunus*, empty⟧ the middle part of the small intestine

**jell** (jel) *vi., vt.* ⟦< L *gelare*, freeze⟧ **1** to become, or make into, jelly **2** [Inf.] to crystallize [plans haven't *jelled* yet]

**jell·o** (jel′ō) *n.* ⟦< *Jell-O*, a trademark⟧ a flavored gelatin used as a dessert, etc.

**jel·ly** (jel′ē) *n., pl.* **-lies** ⟦< L *gelare*, freeze⟧ **1** a soft, gelatinous food made from cooked fruit syrup or meat juice **2** any substance like this —*vi., vt.* **-lied, -ly·ing** JELL (sense 1)

**jelly bean** a small, bean-shaped, gelatinous candy: also **jel′ly·bean′** *n.*

**jel·ly·fish′** *n., pl.* **-fish′** or (for different species) **-fish′es 1** a sea animal with an umbrella-shaped, jellylike body and long tentacles **2** [Inf.] a weak-willed person

**jel·ly·roll′** *n.* a thin sheet of sponge cake spread with jelly and rolled up

**jeop·ard·ize** (jep′ər dīz′) *vt.* **-ized′, -iz′ing** to put in jeopardy

**jeop′ard·y** (-dē) *n.* ⟦< OFr *jeu parti*, lit., a game with even chances⟧ great danger or risk

**jer·e·mi·ad** (jer′ə mī′ad′, -əd) *n.* a long lamentation or complaint: in allusion to the *Lamentations of Jeremiah*

JELLYFISH

**Jer·e·mi·ah** (-ə) *n. Bible* a Hebrew prophet of the 7th and 6th c. B.C.

**Jer·i·cho** (jer′i kō′) city in W Jordan: site of an ancient city in Canaan

**jerk** (jurk) *n.* ⟦< ?⟧ **1** a sharp, abrupt pull, twist, etc. **2** a sudden muscular contraction **3** [Slang] a person regarded as disagreeable, contemptible, etc. —*vi., vt.* **1** to move with a jerk; pull sharply **2** to twitch

**jer·kin** (jur′kin) *n.* ⟦< ?⟧ a short, closefitting jacket, often sleeveless

**jerk′wa′ter** *adj.* [Inf.] small, unimportant, etc. [a *jerkwater* town]

**jerk·y** (jur′kē) *adj.* **jerk′i·er, jerk′i·est 1** moving by jerks; spasmodic **2** [Slang] foolish, mean, etc. —**jerk′i·ly** *adv.*

**jer·ky²** (jur′kē) *n.* ⟦< Sp *charqui*⟧ meat preserved by being sliced into strips and dried in the sun

**jer·ry-built** (jer′ē bilt′) *adj.* built poorly, of cheap materials

**jer·sey** (jur′zē) *n., pl.* **-seys** ⟦after *Jersey*, one of the Channel Islands⟧ **1** [**J-**] any of a breed of reddish-brown dairy cattle, orig. from Jersey **2** a soft, knitted cloth **3** a closefitting, knitted upper garment

**Jer·sey City** (jur′zē) city in NE New Jersey, across the Hudson from New York City: pop. 229,000

**Je·ru·sa·lem** (jə rōōz′ə ləm) capital of Israel (the country): pop. 591,000

**jest** (jest) *n.* ⟦< L *gerere*, perform⟧ **1** a mocking remark; taunt **2** a joke **3** fun; joking **4** something to be laughed at —*vi.* **1** to jeer **2** to joke

**jest′er** *n.* one who jests; esp., a man employed to amuse a medieval ruler

**Jes·u·it** (jezh′ōō it, jez′-) *n.* a member of the Society of Jesus, a Roman Catholic religious order for men, founded in 1534

**Je·sus** (jē′zəs, -zəs) *c.* 8-4 B.C.-A.D. 29?; founder of the Christian religion: also **Jesus Christ**

**jet¹** (jet) *vt., vi.* **jet′ted, jet′ting** ⟦< L *jacere*, to throw⟧ **1** to gush out in a stream **2** to travel or convey by jet airplane —*n.* **1** a stream of liquid or gas suddenly emitted **2** a spout or nozzle for emitting a jet **3** a jet-propelled airplane: in full **jet** (air)**plane** —*adj.* driven by jet propulsion

**jet²** (jet) *n.* ⟦after *Gagas*, town in Asia Minor⟧ **1** a hard, black mineral like coal, polished and used in jewelry **2** a lustrous black —*adj.* black like jet

**jet lag** a disruption of the daily body rhythms, associated with high-speed travel by jet airplane to distant time zones —**jet′-lagged′** *adj.*

**jet′port′** *n.* a large airport with long runways, for use by jetliners

**jet propulsion** propulsion of airplanes, boats, etc. by the forcing of compressed outside air and hot exhaust gases through a jet nozzle —**jet′-propelled′** (-prə peld′) *adj.*

**jet·sam** (jet′səm) *n.* ⟦var. of JETTISON⟧ cargo thrown overboard to lighten a ship in danger

**jet set** fashionable people who frequently travel, often by jet, as for pleasure —**jet′-set′ter** *n.*

**Jet Ski** *trademark for* a motorcyclelike watercraft propelled by a jet of water —[**j- s-**] any such watercraft

**jet stream** high-velocity winds moving from west to east, high above the earth

**jet·ti·son** (jet′ə sən) *vt.* ⟦< L *jactare*, to throw⟧ **1** to throw (goods) overboard so as to lighten a ship in danger **2** to discard

**jet·ty** (jet′ē) *n., pl.* **-ties** ⟦see JET¹⟧ **1** a wall built out into the water to restrain currents, protect a harbor, etc. **2** a landing pier

**Jew** (jōō) *n.* ⟦< Heb *yehūdī*, citizen of Judah⟧ **1** a person descended, or regarded as descended, from the ancient Hebrews **2** a person whose religion is Judaism

**jew·el** (jōō′əl) *n.* ⟦ult. < L *jocus*, a joke⟧ **1** a valuable ring, necklace, etc., esp. one set with gems **2** a precious stone; gem **3** any person or thing that is very precious or valuable **4** a small gem used as a bearing in a watch —*vt.* **-eled** or **-elled, -eling** or **-el·ling** to decorate or set with jewels

**jewel box** a thin plastic case used to hold a compact disk

**jew′el·er** or **jew′el·ler** (-ər) *n.* ⟦ME *jueler* < OFr *joieleor* < *joel*: see JEWEL⟧ one who makes, repairs, or deals in jewelry, watches, etc.

**jew′el·ry** *n.* ornaments such as rings, bracelets, etc., collectively

**Jew·ish** (jōō′ish) *adj.* of or having to do with Jews or Judaism —*n.* loosely, Yiddish —**Jew′ish·ness** *n.*

**Jew·ry** (jōō′rē) *n.* the Jewish people

**jew's-harp** or **jews'-harp** (jōōz′härp′) *n.* ⟦< Du *jeugdtromp*, child's trumpet⟧ a small, metal musical instrument held between the teeth and plucked to produce twanging tones

**Jez·e·bel** (jez′ə bel′) *n. Bible* a wicked queen of Israel

**Ji·ang Ze·min** (jē äŋ′ zə min′) 1926- ; president of China (1993- )

**jib** (jib) *n.* ⟦Dan *gib*⟧ a triangular sail secured forward of the mast or foremast

**jibe**¹ (jīb) *vi.* **jibed, jib'ing** ⟦< Du *gijpen*⟧ **1** to shift from one side of a ship to the other, as a fore-and-aft sail **2** to change the course of a ship so that the sails jibe **3** [Inf.] to be in agreement or accord: often with *with*

**jibe**² (jīb) *vi., vt.,* **jibed, jib'ing,** *n.* GIBE

**jif·fy** (jif'ē) *n., pl.* **-fies** ⟦< ?⟧ [Inf.] a very short time: also **jiff**

**jig** (jig) *n.* ⟦prob. < MFr *giguer,* to dance⟧ **1** a fast, springy dance in triple time, or music for this **2** a device used to guide a tool —*vi., vt.* **jigged, jig'ging** to dance (a jig) —**in jig time** [Inf.] very quickly —**the jig is up** [Slang] no chance is left

**jig·ger** (jig'ər) *n.* **1** a small glass, usually of 1½ ounces, used to measure liquor **2** the contents of a jigger

**jig·gle** (jig'əl) *vt., vi.* **-gled, -gling** ⟦< JIG⟧ to move in quick, slight jerks —*n.* a jiggling

**jig·saw** (jig'sô') *n.* a saw with a narrow blade set in a frame, for cutting curves, etc.

**jigsaw puzzle** a puzzle consisting of a picture cut up into irregularly shaped pieces, which must be put together again

**jilt** (jilt) *vt.* ⟦< *Jill,* sweetheart⟧ to reject or cast off (a previously accepted lover, etc.)

**Jim Crow** ⟦name of an early black minstrel song⟧ [*also* **j- c-**] [Inf.] discrimination against or segregation of blacks —**Jim'-Crow'** *vt., adj.*

**jim·my** (jim'ē) *n., pl.* **-mies** ⟦< *James*⟧ a short crowbar, used as by burglars to pry open windows, etc. —*vt.* **-mied, -my·ing** to pry open with or as with a jimmy

**jim·son weed** (jim'sən) ⟦< *Jamestown weed*⟧ a poisonous weed with white or purplish, trumpet-shaped flowers

**jin·gle** (jin'gəl) *vi.* **-gled, -gling** ⟦echoic⟧ to make light, ringing sounds, as small bells —*vt.* to cause to jingle —*n.* **1** a jingling sound **2** a catchy verse or song with easy rhythm, simple rhymes, etc.

**jin·go·ism** (jiŋ'gō iz'əm) *n.* ⟦< phrase *by jingo* in patriotic Brit song⟧ chauvinistic advocacy of an aggressive, warlike foreign policy —**jin'go·ist** *n.* —**jin'go·is'tic** *adj.*

**jin·ni** (ji nē', jin'ē) *n., pl.* **jinn** ⟦Ar⟧ *Muslim Folklore* a supernatural being that can influence human affairs

**jin·rik·i·sha** (jin rik'shô') *n.* ⟦Jpn < *jin,* a man + *riki,* power + *sha,* carriage⟧ a small, two-wheeled carriage, pulled by a man, esp. formerly in East Asia: also sp. **jin·rick'sha'** or **jin·rik'sha'**

**jinx** (jiŋks) [Inf.] *n.* ⟦< Gr *iynx,* the wryneck (bird used in black magic)⟧ a person or thing supposed to bring bad luck —*vt.* to be a jinx to

**jit·ney** (jit'nē) *n., pl.* **-neys** ⟦< ? Fr *jeton,* a token⟧ a small bus or a car carrying passengers for a low fare

**jit·ter·bug** (jit'ər bug') *n.* a fast, acrobatic dance for couples, esp. in the 1940s —*vi.* **-bugged', -bug'ging** to do this dance

**jit·ters** (jit'ərz) *pl.n.* [Inf.] an uneasy, nervous feeling; fidgets: with *the* —**jit'ter·y** *adj.*

**jive** (jīv) [Slang] *n.* ⟦< JIBE²⟧ foolish, exaggerated, or insincere talk —*adj.* insincere, fraudulent, etc.

**Joan of Arc** (jōn əv ärk), Saint (1412-31); Fr. military heroine: burned at the stake for witchcraft

**job** (jäb) *n.* ⟦< ?⟧ **1** a piece of work done for pay **2** a task; duty **3** the thing or material being worked on **4** employment; work —*adj.* hired or done by the job —*vt., vi.* **jobbed, job'bing 1** to deal in (goods) as a jobber **2** to let or sublet (work, contracts, etc.) —**job'hold'er** *n.* —**job'less** *adj.*

**Job** (jōb) *n. Bible* a man who suffered much but kept his faith in God

**job action** a refusal by a group of employees (esp. a group forbidden by law to strike) to perform their duties in an effort to win certain demands

**job·ber** (jäb'ər) *n.* **1** one who buys goods in quantity and sells them to dealers; wholesaler **2** one who works by the job or does piecework

**job lot** an assortment of goods for sale as one quantity

**jock** (jäk) *n.* **1** *short for:* **a**) JOCKEY **b**) JOCKSTRAP **2** [Slang] a male athlete

**jock·ey** (jäk'ē) *n., pl.* **-eys** ⟦< Scot dim. of JACK⟧ one whose work is riding horses in races —*vt., vi.* **-eyed, -ey·ing 1** to cheat; swindle **2** to maneuver for position or advantage

**jock·strap** (jäk'strap') *n.* ⟦slang *jock,* penis + STRAP⟧ an elastic belt with a pouch for supporting the genitals, worn by male athletes

**jo·cose** (jō kōs') *adj.* ⟦< L *jocus,* a joke⟧ joking or playful —**jo·cose'ly** *adv.* —**jo·cos'i·ty** (-käs'ə tē), *pl.* **-ties,** or **jo·cose'ness** *n.*

**joc·u·lar** (jäk'yə lər) *adj.* ⟦< L *jocus,* a joke⟧ joking; full of fun —**joc'u·lar'i·ty** (-lar'ə tē), *pl.* **-ties,** *n.*

**joc·und** (jäk'ənd) *adj.* ⟦< L *jucundus,* pleasant⟧ cheerful; genial —**joc'und·ly** *adv.*

**jodh·purs** (jäd'pərz) *pl.n.* ⟦after *Jodhpur,* former state in India⟧ riding breeches made loose and full above the knees and closefitting below

**jog**¹ (jäg) *vt.* **jogged, jog'ging** ⟦ME *joggen,* to spur (a horse)⟧ **1** to give a little shake to; nudge **2** to rouse (the memory) —*vi.* to move along at a slow, steady, jolting pace or trot; specif., to engage in jogging as a form of exercise —*n.* **1** a little shake or nudge **2** a slow, steady, jolting motion or trot **3** a jogging —**jog'ger** *n.*

**jog**² (jäg) *n.* ⟦var. of JAG¹⟧ **1** a projecting or notched part in a surface or line **2** a sharp change of direction

**jog'ging** *n.* trotting slowly and steadily as a form of exercise

**jog·gle** (jäg'əl) *vt., vi.* **-gled, -gling** ⟦< JOG¹⟧ to shake or jolt slightly —*n.* a slight jolt

**Jo·han·nes·burg** (jō han'is burg') city in NE South Africa: pop. 713,000

**john** (jän) *n.* [Slang] **1** a toilet **2** [*also* J-] a prostitute's customer

**John** (jän) *n. Bible* **1** a Christian apostle, the reputed author of the fourth Gospel **2** this book

**John Bull** *personification of* England or an Englishman

**John Doe** (dō) a fictitious name used in legal papers for an unknown person

**John·son** (jän'sən) **1 An·drew** (an'drōō') 1808-75; 17th president of the U.S. (1865-69) **2 Lyn·don Baines** (lin'dən bānz') 1908-73; 36th president of the U.S. (1963-69) **3 Samuel** 1709-84; Eng. lexicographer & writer

**John the Baptist** *Bible* the forerunner and baptizer of Jesus

**join** (join) *vt., vi.* ⟦< L *jungere*⟧ **1** to bring or come together (with); connect; unite **2** to become a part or member of (a club, etc.) **3** to participate (*in* a conversation, etc.)

**join·er** *n.* a carpenter who finishes interior woodwork

**joint** (joint) *n.* ⟦< L *jungere*⟧ **1** a place where, or way in which, two things are joined **2** any of the parts of a jointed whole **3** a large cut of meat with the bone still in it **4** [Slang] a cheap bar, restaurant, etc., or any house, building, etc. **5** [Slang] a marijuana cigarette —*adj.* **1** common to two or more [*joint* property] **2** sharing with another [a *joint* owner] —*vt.* **1** to connect by or provide with a joint or joints **2** to cut (meat) into joints —**out of joint 1** dislocated **2** disordered

**joint'ly** *adv.* in common

**joist** (joist) *n.* ⟦< OFr *giste,* a bed⟧ any of the parallel beams that hold up the planks of a floor or the laths of a ceiling

**joke** (jōk) *n.* ⟦L *jocus*⟧ **1** anything said or done to arouse laughter, as a funny anecdote **2** a thing done or said merely in fun **3** a person or thing to be laughed at —*vi.* **joked, jok'ing** to make jokes —**jok'ing·ly** *adv.*

**jok·er** *n.* **1** one who jokes: also **joke'ster 2** a cunningly worded provision, as in a legal document, intended to deceive **3** a playing card with the image of a jester on it **4** [Slang] a contemptibly foolish or inept person

**jok′ey** *adj.* comical or lighthearted: also **jok′y** — **jok′i·ness** *n.*

**jol·li·ty** (jäl′ə tē) *n.* a being jolly

**jol·ly** (jäl′ē) *adj.* **-li·er, -li·est** ⟦OFr *joli*⟧ **1** full of high spirits and good humor; merry **2** [Inf.] enjoyable —*vt., vi.* **-lied, -ly·ing** [Inf.] to try to make (a person) feel good, as by coaxing: often with *along* —**jol′li·ly** *adv.* —**jol′li·ness** *n.*

**jolt** (jōlt) *vt.* ⟦< earlier *jot*⟧ **1** to shake up, as with a bumpy ride **2** to shock or surprise —*vi.* to move along in a bumpy manner —*n.* **1** a sudden jerk, bump, etc. **2** a shock or surprise

**Jo·nah** (jō′nə) *n.* **1** *Bible* a Hebrew prophet: cast overboard and swallowed by a big fish, he was later cast up unharmed **2** one who brings bad luck

**Jones** (jōnz), **John Paul** 1747-92; Am. naval officer in the Revolutionary War, born in Scotland

**jon·quil** (jän′kwil, jän′-) *n.* ⟦< L *juncus*, a rush⟧ a species of narcissus with small, yellow flowers

**Jon·son** (jän′sən), **Ben** (ben) 1572?-1637; Eng. dramatist & poet

**Jor·dan** (jôrd′'n) **1** river in the Near East, flowing into the Dead Sea **2** country east of Israel: 37,738 sq. mi.; pop. 2,133,000 —**Jor·da·ni·an** (jôr dā′nē ən) *adj., n.*

**Jo·seph** (jō′zəf, -səf) *n. Bible* **1** one of Jacob's sons, who became a high official in Egypt **2** the husband of Mary, mother of Jesus

**josh** (jäsh) *vt., vi.* ⟦< ?⟧ [Inf.] to tease; banter

**Josh·u·a** (jäsh′yōō ə, -ōō-) *n. Bible* Moses' successor, who led the Israelites into the Promised Land

**jos·tle** (jäs′əl) *vt., vi.* **-tled, -tling** ⟦see JOUST⟧ to push, as in a crowd; shove roughly —*n.* a jostling

**jot** (jät) *n.* ⟦< Gr *iōta*, the smallest letter⟧ a very small amount —*vt.* **jot′ted, jot′ting** to make a brief note of: usually with *down* —**jot′ter** *n.*

**joule** (jōōl) *n.* ⟦after J. P. *Joule*, 19th-c. Eng physicist⟧ *Physics* a unit of work or energy

**jounce** (jouns) *vt., vi.* **jounced, jounc′ing** ⟦< ?⟧ to jolt or bounce —*n.* a jolt —**jounc′y** *adj.*

**jour·nal** (jur′nəl) *n.* ⟦< L *diurnalis*, daily⟧ **1** a daily record of happenings, as a diary **2** a newspaper or periodical **3** *Bookkeeping* a book for recording transactions in the order in which they occur **4** ⟦orig. Scot⟧ the part of an axle or shaft that turns in a bearing

**jour·nal·ese′** (-ēz′) *n.* a facile style of writing found in many newspapers, magazines, etc.

**jour·nal·ism′** *n.* the work of gathering news for, or producing, a newspaper, etc. —**jour′nal·ist** *n.* — **jour′nal·is′tic** *adj.*

**jour·ney** (jur′nē) *n., pl.* **-neys** ⟦< OFr *journee*; ult. < L *dies*, day⟧ a traveling from one place to another; trip —*vi.* **-neyed, -ney·ing** to travel — **jour′ney·er** *n.*

**jour′ney·man** (-mən) *n., pl.* **-men** (-mən) ⟦ME < *journee*, day's work + *man*⟧ **1** a worker qualified to work at a specified trade **2** any sound, experienced, but not brilliant performer

**joust** (joust) *n.* ⟦ult. < L *juxta*, close to⟧ a combat with lances between two knights on horseback — *vi.* to engage in a joust

**jo·vi·al** (jō′vē əl) *adj.* ⟦< LL *Jovialis*, of Jupiter: from astrological notion of planet's influence⟧ full of playful good humor —**jo′vi·al′i·ty** (-al′ə tē) *n.* — **jo′vi·al·ly** *adv.*

**jowl**[1] (joul) *n.* ⟦OE *ceafl*, jaw⟧ **1** the lower jaw **2** the cheek, esp. of a hog

**jowl**[2] (joul) *n.* ⟦OE *ceole*, throat⟧ [*usually pl.*] the fleshy hanging part under the jaw —**jowl′y** *adj.*

**joy** (joi) *n.* ⟦ult. < L *gaudium*, joy⟧ **1** a very glad feeling; happiness; delight **2** anything causing this

**Joyce** (jois), **James** 1882-1941; Ir. novelist

**joy′ful** *adj.* feeling, expressing, or causing joy; glad —**joy′ful·ly** *adv.*

**joy′ous** *adj.* joyful; happy —**joy′ous·ly** *adv.*

**joy ride** [Inf.] an automobile ride, often at a reckless speed, taken for pleasure, sometimes, specif., in a stolen car —**joy rider** —**joy riding**

**joy′stick′** *n.* **1** [Slang] the control stick of an airplane **2** a device with a lever for controlling a cursor, etc. as in a video game

**JP** *abbrev.* Justice of the Peace

**Jpn** *abbrev.* **1** Japan **2** Japanese

**Jr** *abbrev.* junior: also **jr**

**ju·bi·lant** (jōō′bə lənt) *adj.* ⟦< L *jubilum*, wild shout⟧ joyful and triumphant; elated; rejoicing

**ju·bi·la·tion** (jōō′bə lā′shən) *n.* **1** a rejoicing **2** a happy celebration

**ju·bi·lee** (jōō′bə lē′) *n.* ⟦< Heb *yōbēl*, a ram's horn (trumpet)⟧ **1** a 50th or 25th anniversary **2** a time of rejoicing **3** jubilation

**Ju·dah**[1] (jōō′də) *n. Bible* one of Jacob's sons

**Ju·dah**[2] (jōō′də) ancient kingdom in the S part of Palestine

**Ju·da·ism** (jōō′dā iz′əm, -dē-, -də-) *n.* the Jewish religion —**Ju·da′ic** (-dā′ik) *adj.*

**Judas** (jōō′dəs) *n.* **1** *Bible* the disciple who betrayed Jesus for money: in full **Judas Is·car·i·ot** (is ker′ē ət) **2** a traitor or betrayer

**Ju·de·a** (jōō dē′ə) ancient region of S Palestine

**Judeo-** *combining form* Jewish

**judge** (juj) *n.* ⟦< L *jus*, law + *dicere*, say⟧ **1** a public official with authority to hear and decide cases in a court of law **2** a person designated to determine the winner, settle a controversy, etc. **3** a person qualified to decide on the relative worth of anything **4** a governing leader of the Israelites before the time of the kings —*vt., vi.* **judged, judg′ing 1** to hear and pass judgment on in a court of law **2** to determine the winner of (a contest) or settle (a controversy) **3** to form an opinion about **4** to criticize or censure **5** to think or suppose —**judge′ship′** *n.*

**judg·ment** (juj′mənt) *n.* **1** a judging; deciding **2** a legal decision; order given by a judge, etc. **3** an opinion **4** the ability to come to an opinion **5** [J-] *short for* LAST JUDGMENT Also **judge′ment**

**judg·men′tal** (-ment′'l) *adj.* making judgments as to value, etc., often, specif., judgments considered to be lacking in tolerance, objectivity, etc.

**Judgment Day** *Theol.* the time of God's final judgment of all people

**ju·di·ca·to·ry** (jōō′di kə tôr′ē) *adj.* ⟦see JUDGE⟧ having to do with administering justice —*n., pl.* **-ries** a law court, or law courts collectively

**ju′di·ca·ture** (-chər) *n.* **1** the administering of justice **2** jurisdiction **3** judges or courts collectively

**ju·di·cial** (jōō dish′əl) *adj.* **1** of judges, courts, or their functions **2** allowed, enforced, etc. by a court **3** befitting a judge **4** fair; impartial

**ju·di·ci·ar·y** (jōō dish′ē er′ē) *adj.* of judges or courts —*n., pl.* **-ar′ies 1** the part of government that administers justice **2** judges collectively

**ju·di·cious** (-dish′əs) *adj.* having or showing sound judgment —**ju·di′cious·ly** *adv.*

**ju·do** (jōō′dō) *n.* ⟦Jpn < *jū*, soft + *dō*, way⟧ a form of jujitsu

**jug** (jug) *n.* ⟦a pet form of *Judith* or *Joan*⟧ **1** a large container for liquids, with a small opening and a handle **2** [Slang] a jail

**jug·ger·naut** (jug′ər nôt′) *n.* ⟦< Sans *Jagannātha*, lord of the world⟧ a relentless, irresistible force

**jug·gle** (jug′əl) *vt.* **-gled, -gling** ⟦< L *jocus*, a joke⟧ **1** to perform skillful tricks of sleight of hand with (balls, etc.) **2** to catch or hold awkwardly **3** to manipulate so as to deceive —*vi.* to toss up balls, etc. and keep them in the air —**jug′gler** *n.*

**jug·u·lar** (jug′yoō lər) *adj.* ⟦< L *jugum*, a yoke⟧ of the neck or throat —*n.* JUGULAR VEIN

**jugular vein** either of two large veins in the neck carrying blood from the head

**juice** (jōōs) *n.* ⟦< L *jus*, broth, juice⟧ **1** the liquid part of a plant, fruit, etc. **2** a liquid in or from animal tissue **3** [Inf.] vitality **4** [Slang] *a*) electricity *b*) alcoholic liquor *c*) power or influence — *vt.* **juiced, juic′ing** to extract juice from —*vi.* [Slang] to drink alcoholic beverages to excess

**juiced** (jōōst) *adj.* [Slang] drunk; intoxicated

**juic·er** (jōō′sər) *n.* **1** a device for extracting juice from fruit **2** [Slang] a drunkard

**juic·y** (jōō′sē) *adj.* **-i·er, -i·est 1** full of juice **2** [Inf.] *a*) full of interest [*juicy* gossip] *b*) highly profitable —**juic′i·ness** *n.*

**ju·jit·su** (jōō jit′sōō′) *n.* [< Jpn *jū*, soft, pliant + *jutsu*, art] a Japanese system of wrestling in which an opponent's strength and weight are used against him or her

**ju·ju·be** (jōō′jōō bē′) *n.* [< Gr *zizyphon*, name of a fruit] a fruit-flavored, jellylike lozenge

**ju·jut·su** (jōō jit′sōō′, -jut′-) *n.* JUJITSU

**juke·box** (jōōk′bäks′) *n.* [< Am black *juke*, wicked] a coin-operated player for records, CD's, etc. as in a bar

**ju·lep** (jōō′ləp) *n.* [< Pers *gul*, rose + *āb*, water] MINT JULEP

**ju·li·enne** (jōō′lē en′) *adj.* [Fr] cut into strips: said of vegetables, etc.: also **ju′li·enned′** (-end′)

**Ju·li·et** (jōō′lē et′, jōō′lē et′) *n.* the heroine of Shakespeare's tragedy *Romeo and Juliet*

**Ju·ly** (joo lī′) *n.* [< L < *Julius* Caesar] the seventh month of the year, having 31 days: abbrev. *abbrev.* **Jul**

**jum·ble** (jum′bəl) *vt., vi.* **-bled, -bling** [? blend of JUMP + TUMBLE] to mix or be mixed in a confused heap —*n.* a confused mixture or heap

**jum·bo** (jum′bō) *n., pl.* **-bos** [< Am black *jamba*, elephant] a large person, animal, or thing —*adj.* very large

**jump** (jump) *vi.* [< ?] **1** to spring or leap from the ground, a height, etc. **2** to jerk; bob **3** to move or act eagerly: often with *at* **4** to pass suddenly, as to a new topic **5** to rise suddenly, as prices **6** [Slang] to be lively —*vt.* **1** *a*) to leap over *b*) to pass over **2** to cause to leap **3** to leap upon **4** to cause (prices, etc.) to rise **5** [Inf.] *a*) to attack suddenly *b*) to react to prematurely **6** [Slang] to leave suddenly [to *jump* town] —*n.* **1** a jumping **2** a distance jumped **3** a sudden transition **4** a sudden rise, as in prices **5** a sudden, nervous start —**get** (or **have**) **the jump on** [Slang] to get (or have) an advantage over —**jump bail** to forfeit bail by running away

**jump·er**[1] (jum′pər) *n.* **1** one that jumps **2** a short wire to make a temporary electrical connection

**jump·er**[2] (jum′pər) *n.* [< dial. *jump*, short coat] **1** a loose jacket **2** a sleeveless dress for wearing over a blouse, etc.

**jumper cables** a pair of thick, insulated electrical wires with clamplike terminals, used to jump-start a motor vehicle with a dead battery

**jump′-start′** *vt.* **1** to start (a motor-vehicle engine) with jumper cables **2** [Inf.] to energize, revive, etc. —*n.* a starting in such a way

**jump′suit′** *n.* **1** a coverall worn by paratroops, etc. **2** a lounging outfit like this

**jump·y** (jum′pē) *adj.* **-i·er, -i·est 1** moving in jumps or jerks **2** easily startled **3** nervous — **jump′i·ly** *adv.* —**jump′i·ness** *n.*

**jun·co** (juŋ′kō′) *n., pl.* **-cos** [< Sp] a small bird with a gray or black head

**junc·tion** (juŋk′shən) *n.* [< L *jungere*, join] **1** a joining or being joined **2** a place of joining, as of roads —**junc′tion·al** *adj.*

**junc·ture** (juŋk′chər) *n.* **1** a junction **2** a point of time **3** a crisis

**June** (jōōn) *n.* [< L *Junius*, of *Juno*] the sixth month of the year, having 30 days: abbrev. *abbrev.* **Jun**

**Ju·neau** (jōō′nō′) capital of Alaska: seaport on the SE coast: pop. 27,000

**jun·gle** (juŋ′gəl) *n.* [< Sans *jaṅgala*, wasteland] **1** land densely covered with trees, vines, etc., as in the tropics **2** [Slang] a situation in which people struggle fiercely for survival

**jun·ior** (jōōn′yər) *adj.* [L < *juvenis*, young] **1** the

younger: written *Jr.* after a son's name if it is the same as his father's **2** of more recent position or lower status [a *junior* partner] **3** of juniors —*n.* **1** one who is younger, of lower rank, etc. **2** a student in the next-to-last year, as of college

**junior college** a school offering courses two years beyond high school

**junior high school** a school usually including grades 7, 8, and 9

**ju·ni·per** (jōō′ni pər) *n.* [L *juniperus*] an ever-green shrub or tree with berrylike cones

**junk**[1] (juŋk) *n.* [< ?] **1** old metal, paper, rags, etc. that might be reusable in some way **2** [Inf.] worthless stuff; trash **3** [Slang] heroin —*vt.* [Inf.] to scrap; discard —**junk′y, -i·er, -i·est,** *adj.*

**junk**[2] (juŋk) *n.* [< Malay *adjong*] a Chinese or Japanese flat-bottomed ship

**junk bond** [Inf.] a speculative BOND (*n.* 6), often issued to finance the takeover of a corporation

**junk·er** (juŋ′kər) *n.* [Slang] an old, dilapidated car or truck

**Jun·ker** (yooŋ′kər) *n.* [Ger] [Historical] a Prussian of the mili-taristic landowning class

JUNK

**jun·ket** (juŋ′kit) *n.* [ME *joncate*, cream cheese] **1** milk sweetened, flavored, and thick-ened into curd **2** a picnic **3** an excursion, esp. one by an official at public expense —*vi.* to go on a junket —**jun′ket·eer′** (-ki tir′) or **jun′ket·er** *n.*

**junk food** snack food with chemical additives and little food value

**junk·ie** or **junk·y** (juŋ′kē) *n., pl.* **-ies** [< JUNK[1], *n.* 3] [Slang] **1** a narcotics addict **2** one who is addicted to a specified activity, food, etc.

**junk mail** advertisements, solicitations, etc. mailed in large quantities

**Ju·no** (jōō′nō) *n. Gr. Myth.* the wife of Jupiter and queen of the gods

**jun·ta** (hoon′tə, jun′-) *n.* [Sp < L *jungere*, join] a group of political intriguers, esp. military men, in power after a coup d'état

**Ju·pi·ter** (jōō′pit ər) *n.* **1** the chief Roman god **2** the largest planet of the solar system: see PLANET

**Ju·ras·sic** (jōō ras′ik) *adj.* [< Fr, after *Jura* Moun-tains, between France and Switzerland] of the geologic period characterized by the dominance of dinosaurs

**ju·rid·i·cal** (jōō rid′i kəl, joo-) *adj.* [< L *jus*, law + *dicere*, declare] of judicial proceedings or law

**ju·ried** (joor′ēd) *adj.* of a competition in which the winners are selected by a jury

**ju·ris·dic·tion** (joor′is dik′shən) *n.* [see JURIDICAL] **1** legal authority **2** the range of authority

**ju·ris·pru·dence** (joor′is prōōd′'ns) *n.* [< L *jus*, law + *prudentia*, a foreseeing] **1** the science or philosophy of law **2** a division of law [medical *jurisprudence*]

**ju·rist** (joor′ist) *n.* [< L *jus*, law] **1** an expert in law or writer on law **2** JUDGE (*n.* 1)

**ju·ror** (joor′ər, -ôr′) *n.* a member of a jury

**ju·ry** (joor′ē) *n., pl.* **-ries** [L *jurare*, to swear] **1** a group of people sworn to hear evidence in a law case and to give a decision **2** a committee that decides winners in a contest

**just** (just) *adj.* [< L *jus*, law] **1** right or fair [a *just* decision] **2** righteous [a *just* man] **3** deserved [*just* praise] **4** lawful **5** proper **6** correct or true **7** accurate; exact —*adv.* **1** exactly [*just* one o'clock] **2** nearly **3** only [*just* a taste] **4** barely [*just* missed him] **5** a very short time ago [she's *just* left] **6** immediately [*just* east of here] **7**

[Inf.] really *[just* beautiful*]* —**just the same** [Inf.] nevertheless —**just'ly** *adv.* —**just'ness** *n.*

**jus·tice** (jus'tis) *n.* **1** a being righteous **2** fairness **3** rightfulness **4** reward or penalty as deserved **5** the use of authority to uphold what is just **6** the administration of law **7** *a)* JUDGE (*n.* 1) *b)* JUSTICE OF THE PEACE —**do justice to** to treat fairly

**justice of the peace** a local magistrate who decides minor cases, performs marriages, etc.

**jus·ti·fy** (jus'tə fī') *vt.* -**fied'**, -**fy'ing** [< L *justus,* just + *facere,* to do] **1** to show to be just, right, etc. **2** *Theol.* to free from blame or guilt **3** to supply grounds for —**jus'ti·fi·a·ble** *adj.* —**jus'ti·fi·ca'tion** (-fi kā'shən) *n.*

**Jus·tin·i·an I** (jus tin'ē ən) A.D. 483-565; ruler of Byzantine Empire (527-565): codified Roman law

**jut** (jut) *vi., vt.* **jut'ted, jut'ting** [prob. var. of JET¹] to stick out; project —*n.* a part that juts

**jute** (jōōt) *n.* [< Sans *jūta,* matted hair] **1** a strong fiber used for making burlap, rope, etc. **2** a S Asian plant yielding this fiber

**ju·ve·nile** (jōō'və nīl', -nəl) *adj.* [< L *juvenis,* young] **1** young; immature **2** of or for young persons —*n.* **1** a young person **2** an actor who plays youthful roles **3** a book for children —**ju've·nil'i·ty** (-nil'i tē), *pl.* -**ties,** *n.*

**juvenile delinquency** antisocial or illegal behavior by minors, usually 18 years of age or younger —**juvenile delinquent**

**jux·ta·pose** (juks'tə pōz') *vt.* -**posed'**, -**pos'ing** [< Fr < L *juxta,* beside + POSE] to put side by side —**jux'ta·po·si'tion** *n.*

**JV** *abbrev.* junior varsity

# K

**k** or **K** (kā) *n., pl.* **k's, K's** the eleventh letter of the English alphabet

**K¹** *n.* **1** *Comput.* KILOBYTE **2** [Inf.] a thousand dollars

**K²** *abbrev.* **1** karat (carat) **2** kilometer **3** kindergarten **4** *Baseball* strikeout **5** *Comput.* the number 1,024, or 2¹⁰ Also, for 1 & 2, **k**

**K³** [ModL *kalium*] *Chem. symbol for* potassium

**Ka·bu·ki** (kä bōō'kē) *n.* [*also* k-] a form of Japanese drama, chiefly in formalized pantomime

**kad·dish** (käd'ish) *n.* [Aram *kadish,* lit., holy] *Judaism* a hymn in praise of God, recited at the daily service or as a mourner's prayer

**kaf·fee·klatsch** (kä'fä kläch', kô'fē klach') *n.* [Ger < *kaffee,* coffee + *klatsch,* gossip] [*also* **K-**] an informal gathering to drink coffee and chat

**Kai·ser** (kī'zər) *n.* [ME *caiser,* emperor < L *Caesar*] the title of the former rulers of Austria and Germany

**kaiser roll** [Ger *kaisersemmel,* kaiser bun] a large, round roll with a hard crust

**kale** (kāl) *n.* [var. of COLE] a hardy cabbage with spreading leaves

**ka·lei·do·scope** (kə lī'də skōp') *n.* [< Gr *kalos,* beautiful + *eidos,* form + -SCOPE] **1** a small tube containing bits of colored glass reflected by mirrors so that symmetrical patterns appear when the tube is rotated **2** anything that constantly changes —**ka·lei'do·scop'ic** (-skäp'ik) *adj.*

**ka·mi·ka·ze** (kä'mə kä'zē) *adj.* [Jpn, divine wind] of a suicidal attack by a WWII Japanese airplane pilot

**kan·ga·roo** (kaŋ'gə rōō') *n.* [< ?] a leaping marsupial of Australia and nearby islands, with short forelegs and strong, large hind legs

**kangaroo court** [Inf.] an irregular court, usually disregarding normal legal procedure

**Kan·sas** (kan'zəs) Midwestern state of the U.S.: 81,823 sq. mi.; pop. 2,478,000; cap. Topeka: abbrev. *KS* —**Kan'san** *adj., n.*

**Kansas City 1** city in W Missouri, on the Missouri River: pop. 435,000 **2** city opposite this, in NE Kansas: pop. 150,000

**Kant** (känt), **Im·man·u·el** (i man'yōō el') 1724-1804; Ger. philosopher

**ka·o·lin** (kā'ə lin) *n.* [Fr < Chin name of hill where found] a white clay used in porcelain, etc.

**ka·pok** (kā'päk') *n.* [Malay] the silky fibers around the seeds of certain tropical trees, used for stuffing mattresses, etc.

**kap·pa** (kap'ə) *n.* the tenth letter of the Greek alphabet (Κ, κ)

**ka·put** (kə pŏŏt', -pōōt') *adj.* [Ger *kaputt*] [Slang] ruined, destroyed, etc.

**Ka·ra·chi** (kə rä'chē) seaport in S Pakistan: former capital: pop. 5,076,000

**kar·a·kul** (kar'ə kul', -kəl) *n.* [ult. < Turkic *qara köl,* dark lake] **1** a sheep native to central Asia **2** the curly black fur from the fleece of its lambs: usually sp. *caracul*

**ka·ra·o·ke** (kar'ē ō'kē) *n.* a form of entertainment in which bar patrons, etc. take turns singing while a special device plays prerecorded music

**kar·at** (kar'ət) *n.* [var. of CARAT] one 24th part (of pure gold)

**ka·ra·te** (kə rät'ē) *n.* [Jpn] a Japanese system of self-defense by sharp, quick blows with the hands and feet

**kar·ma** (kär'mə) *n.* [Sans, act] **1** *Buddhism, Hinduism* the totality of one's acts in each state of one's existence **2** loosely, fate

**kart** (kärt) *n.* [< CART] a small, flat, motorized vehicle, used in racing (**kart'ing**)

**ka·ty·did** (kāt'ē did') *n.* [echoic of the male's shrill sound] a large, green tree insect

**kay·ak** (kī'ak') *n.* [Esk] a canoe, originally used by Eskimos, with only a small opening in its shell for the paddler —*vi.* to go in a kayak —**kay'ak'er** *n.*

**kay·o** (kā'ō') [Slang] *vt.* -**oed'**, -**o'ing** [< KO] *Boxing* to knock out —*n. Boxing* a knockout

**Ka·zakh·stan** (kä'zäk stän') country in W Asia: formerly a republic of the U.S.S.R.: 1,049,155 sq. mi.; pop. 16,464,000

**ka·zoo** (kə zōō') *n.* [echoic] a toy musical instrument that makes buzzing tones when hummed into

**KB** *abbrev.* kilobyte(s)

**kc** *abbrev.* kilocycle(s)

**Keats** (kēts), **John** 1795-1821; Eng. poet

**ke·bab** or **ke·bob** (kə bäb') *n.* [Ar *kabāb*] any of the small pieces of marinated meat used in making shish kebab

**keel** (kēl) *n.* [< ON *kjǫlr*] the chief timber or piece extending along the length of the bottom of a boat or ship —**keel over 1** to capsize **2** to fall over suddenly —**on an even keel** upright or steady

**keen¹** (kēn) *adj.* [OE *cene,* wise] **1** having a sharp edge or point *[a keen knife]* **2** cutting *[a keen wind]* **3** very perceptive *[keen eyes]* **4** shrewd **5** eager **6** intense —**keen'ly** *adv.* —**keen'ness** *n.*

**keen²** (kēn) *vt., vi.* [< Ir *caoinim,* I wail] to make a mournful, wailing sound

**keep** (kēp) *vt.* **kept, keep'ing** [OE *cœpan,* behold] **1** to celebrate; observe *[to keep the Sabbath]* **2** to fulfill (a promise, etc.) **3** to protect; guard; take care of; tend **4** to preserve **5** to provide for; support **6** to make regular entries in *[to keep a diary]* **7** to maintain in a specified state, position, etc. *[to keep prices down]* **8** to hold for the future; retain **9** to hold and not let go; detain, withhold, restrain, etc. **10** to stay in or on (a course, place, etc.) —*vi.* **1** to stay in a specified state, position, etc. **2** to continue; go on **3** to refrain *[to keep* from eating] **4** to stay fresh; not spoil —*n.* **1** food and shelter; support **2** the inner stronghold of a castle —**for keeps** [Inf.] **1** with the winner keeping what he wins **2** permanently —**keep to oneself 1** to avoid others **2** to refrain from telling —**keep up 1** to maintain in good condition **2** to continue **3** to maintain the pace **4** to remain informed about: with *on* or *with*

**keep'er** *n.* **1** one that keeps; specif., *a*) a guard *b*) a guardian *c*) a custodian **2** [Inf.] something worth keeping

**keep'ing** *n.* **1** observance (of a rule, holiday, etc.) **2** care; charge —**in keeping with** in conformity or accord with

**keep'sake′** *n.* something kept, or to be kept, in memory of the giver

**keg** (keg) *n.* [< ON *kaggi,* keg] **1** a small barrel **2** a unit of weight for nails, equal to 100 lb.

**kelp** (kelp) *n.* [ME *culp*] a large, coarse, brown seaweed, rich in iodine

**Kel·vin** (kel′vin) *adj.* [after 1st Baron *Kelvin,* 19th-c. Brit physicist] designating or of a scale of temperature measured from absolute zero (-273.16°C)

**ken** (ken) *vt.* **kenned, ken′ning** [OE *cennan,* cause to know] [Scot.] to know —*n.* range of knowledge

**Ken·ne·dy** (ken′ə dē), **John Fitz·ger·ald** (fits jer′əld) 1917-63; 35th president of the U.S. (1961-63): assassinated

**ken·nel** (ken′əl) *n.* [< L *canis,* dog] **1** a doghouse **2** [*often pl.*] a place where dogs are bred or kept — *vt.* **-neled** or **-nelled, -nel·ing** or **-nel·ling** to keep in a kennel

**Ken·tuck·y** (kən tuk′ē) EC state of the U.S.: 39,732 sq. mi.; pop. 3,685,000; cap. Frankfort: abbrev. *KY* —**Ken·tuck′i·an** *adj., n.*

**Ken·ya** (ken′yə, kēn′-) country on the E coast of Africa: 224,961 sq. mi.; pop. 29,295,000

**kept** (kept) *vt., vi. pt. & pp. of* KEEP —*adj.* maintained so as to be a sexual partner [a *kept* woman]

**ker·a·tin** (ker′ə tin) *n.* [< Gr *keras,* horn] a tough, fibrous protein, the basic substance of hair, nails, etc.

**kerb** (kurb) *n.* Brit. sp. of CURB (*n.* 3)

**ker·chief** (kur′chif) *n.* [< OFr *covrir,* to cover + *chef,* head] **1** a piece of cloth worn over the head or around the neck **2** a handkerchief

**ker·nel** (kur′nəl) *n.* [< OE *cyrnel*] **1** a grain or seed, as of corn **2** the inner, softer part of a nut, etc. **3** the central, most important part; essence

**ker·o·sene** (ker′ə sēn′) *n.* [Gr *kēros,* wax] a thin oil distilled from petroleum, used as a fuel, solvent, etc.: also **ker′o·sine′**

**kes·trel** (kes′trəl) *n.* [echoic of its cry] a small European falcon

**ketch** (kech) *n.* [ME *cache*] a small sailing vessel rigged fore-and-aft

**ketch·up** (kech′əp) *n.* [? Malay *kēchap,* sauce] a sauce for meat, fish, etc.; esp., a thick sauce (**tomato ketchup**) of tomatoes, onions, spices, etc.

**ket·tle** (ket′'l) *n.* [< L *catinus,* container for food] **1** a metal container for boiling or cooking things **2** a teakettle

**ket′tle·drum′** *n.* a hemispheric percussion instrument of copper with a parchment top that can be tightened or loosened to change the pitch

**Kev·lar** (kev′lär′) *trademark* for a tough, light, synthetic fiber used in bulletproof vests, boat hulls, etc.

**key¹** (kē) *n., pl.* **keys** [OE *cæge*] **1** a device for moving the bolt of a lock and thus locking or unlocking something **2** any of the buttons, levers, etc. pressed in operating a piano, typewriter, etc. **3** a thing that explains or solves something else, as a code, the legend of a map,

KETTLEDRUM

etc. **4** an essential person or thing **5** tone or style of expression **6** *Music* a system of related tones based on a keynote and forming a given scale — *adj.* essential; important —*vt.* **keyed, key′ing 1** to furnish with a key **2** to regulate the tone or pitch of **3** to bring into harmony —**key in** to input (data) by means of a keyboard —**key up** to make tense or excited

**key²** (kē) *n., pl.* **keys** [Sp *cayo*] a reef or low island

**key′board′** *n.* **1** the row or rows of keys of a piano, typewriter, computer terminal, etc. **2** a musical instrument with a keyboard —*vt., vi.* to write (text) or input (data) by means of a keyboard —**key′board′er** *n.*

**key′hole′** *n.* an opening (in a lock) into which a key is inserted

**key′note′** *n.* **1** the lowest, basic note or tone of a musical scale **2** the basic idea or ruling principle —*vt.* **-not′ed, -not′ing 1** to give the keynote of **2** to give the keynote speech at —**key′not′er** *n.*

**keynote speech** (or **address**) a speech, as at a convention, setting forth the main line of policy

**key′pad′** *n.* the keys or push buttons on a computer keyboard, telephone, etc.

**key′stone′** *n.* **1** the central, topmost stone of an arch **2** the main part or principle

**key′stroke′** *n.* any of the strokes made in operating a keyboard

**Key West** island off S Florida, in the Gulf of Mexico

**kg** *abbrev.* kilogram(s)

**kha·ki** (kak′ē, kä′kē) *adj.* [< Pers *khāk,* dust] **1** dull yellowish-brown **2** made of khaki (cloth) — *n., pl.* **-kis 1** a dull yellowish brown **2** strong, twilled cloth of this color **3** [*often pl.*] a khaki uniform or pants

**khan** (kän, kan) *n.* [< Mongolian *qan,* lord] **1** a title of Tatar or Mongol rulers in the Middle Ages **2** a title of various dignitaries in Iran, Afghanistan, etc.

**Khar·kov** (kär′kôf′) city in NE Ukraine: pop. 1,611,000

**Khar·toum** (kär tōōm′) capital of Sudan, on the Nile: pop. 476,000

**kHz** *abbrev.* kilohertz

**kib·butz** (ki bōōts′, -bōōts′) *n., pl.* **kib·but·zim** (kē′bōō tsēm′) [ModHeb] an Israeli collective settlement, esp. a collective farm

**kib·itz·er** (kib′it sər) *n.* [Yiddish < Ger *kiebitz*] [Inf.] **1** an onlooker at a card game, etc., esp. one who volunteers advice **2** a giver of unwanted advice or meddler in others′ affairs —**kib′itz** *vi.*

**ki·bosh** (kī′bäsh′, ki bäsh′) *n.* [< ?] used chiefly in **put the kibosh on,** to check, squelch, etc.

**kick** (kik) *vi.* [ME *kiken*] **1** to strike out with the foot **2** to recoil, as a gun **3** [Inf.] to complain **4** *Football* to kick the ball —*vt.* **1** to strike with the foot **2** to drive, force, etc., as by kicking **3** to score (a goal, etc.) by kicking **4** [Slang] to get rid of (a habit) —*n.* **1** an act or method of kicking **2** a sudden recoil **3** a complaint **4** [Inf.] an intoxicating effect **5** [*often pl.*] [Inf.] pleasure —**kick in** [Slang] to pay (one′s share) —**kick over** to start up, as an automobile engine —**kick′er** *n.*

**kick′back′** *n.* [Slang] **1** a giving back of part of money received as payment, often because of coercion or a previous agreement **2** the money so returned

**kick′off′** *n.* **1** *Football* a kick that puts the ball into play **2** a beginning, as of a campaign

**kick′stand′** *n.* a pivoted metal bar that can be kicked down to support a bicycle, etc. in an upright position

**kick′-start′** *vt.* **1** to start (a motorcycle, etc.) with a lever attached to a pedal that one kicks downward **2** [Inf.] to start, energize, revive, etc.

**kick′y** *adj.* **-i·er, -i·est** [Slang] **1** fashionable **2** exciting

**kid** (kid) *n.* [ME *kide*] **1** a young goat **2** leather from the skin of young goats **3** [Inf.] a child —

**adj.** [Inf.] younger [my *kid* sister] —**vt.**, **vi.**
**kid′ded**, **kid′ding** [Inf.] to tease or fool playfully
**kid′die** or **kid′dy** (-ē) *n.*, *pl.* **-dies** [dim. of prec., *n.*
3] [Inf.] a child
**kid·nap** (kid′nap′) **vt.** **-napped′** or **-naped′**,
**-nap′ping** or **-nap′ing** [KID, *n.* 3 + dial. *nap*, to
snatch] to seize and hold (a person) by force or
fraud, as in order to get a ransom —**kid′nap′per**
or **kid′nap′er** *n.*
**kid·ney** (kid′nē) *n.*, *pl.* **-neys** [< ?] 1 either of a
pair of glandular organs that separate water and
waste products from the blood and excrete them
as urine 2 an animal's kidney, used as food 3 *a*)
disposition *b*) class; kind
**kidney bean** the kidney-shaped seed of the common garden bean
**kidney stone** a hard mineral deposit sometimes
formed in the kidney
**kid′skin′** *n.* leather from the skin of young goats
**kiel·ba·sa** (kēl bä′sə, kil-) *n.*, *pl.* **-si** (-sē) or **-sas**
[Pol] a Polish smoked sausage
**Ki·ev** (kē′ef′, -ev′) capital of Ukraine, on the
Dnepr: pop. 2,587,000
**kill** (kil) **vt.** [< ? OE *cwellan*] 1 to cause the death
of; slay 2 to destroy; put an end to 3 to defeat or
veto (legislation) 4 to spend (time) on trivial matters 5 to turn off (an engine, etc.) 6 to stop publication of —*n.* 1 the act of killing 2 an animal or
animals killed —**kill′er** *n.*
**killer bee** AFRICANIZED BEE
**killer whale** a large dolphin that hunts in packs
and preys on large fish, seals, etc.
**kill′ing** *adj.* 1 causing death; deadly 2 exhausting; fatiguing —*n.* 1 slaughter; murder 2 [Inf.] a
sudden great profit
**kill′joy′** *n.* one who destroys or lessens other people's enjoyment: also **kill′-joy′**
**kiln** (kil, kiln) *n.* [< L *culina*, cookstove] a furnace
or oven for drying, burning, or baking bricks, pottery, etc.
**ki·lo** (kē′lō, kil′ō) *n.*, *pl.* **-los** [Fr] 1 KILOGRAM 2
KILOMETER
**kilo-** [< Gr *chilioi*] *combining form* one thousand
**kil·o·byte** (kil′ə bīt′) *n.* 1,024 bytes, or, loosely,
1,000 bytes
**kil′o·cy′cle** (-sī′kəl) *n. former term for* KILOHERTZ
**kil′o·gram′** (-gram′) *n.* 1,000 grams
**kil′o·hertz′** (-herts′, -hurts′) *n.*, *pl.* **-hertz′** 1,000
hertz
**kil′o·li·ter** (-lēt′ər) *n.* 1,000 liters, or one cubic
meter
**kil·o·me·ter** (kə läm′ət ər, kil′ə mēt′ər) *n.* 1,000
meters
**kil·o·ton** (kil′ə tun′) *n.* the explosive force of 1,000
tons of TNT
**kil′o·watt′** (-wät′) *n.* 1,000 watts
**kilt** (kilt) *n.* [prob. < ON] a knee-length, pleated
tartan skirt worn sometimes by men of the Scottish Highlands
**kil·ter** (kil′tər) *n.* [< ?] [Inf.] good condition;
proper order: now chiefly in **out of kilter**
**ki·mo·no** (kə mō′nə) *n.*, *pl.* **-nos** [Jpn] 1 a robe
with wide sleeves and a sash,
part of the traditional Japanese
costume 2 a woman's dressing
gown
**kin** (kin) *n.* [OE *cynn*] relatives;
family
**-kin** (kin) [< MDu *-ken*] *suffix* little [*lambkin*]
**kind** (kīnd) *n.* [OE *cynd*] 1 a
natural group or division 2
essential character 3 sort; variety; class —*adj.* sympathetic,
gentle, benevolent, etc. —**in kind**
in the same way —**kind of** [Inf.]
somewhat; rather —**of a kind**
alike

KIMONO

**kin·der·gar·ten** (kin′dər gärt′'n) *n.* [Ger < *kinder*,

child + *garten*, garden] a school or class for young
children, usually four to six years old, that develops basic skills and social behavior by games,
music, handicrafts, etc. —**kin′der·gart′ner** or
**kin′der·gar′ten·er** (-gärt′nər) *n.*
**kind′heart′ed** *adj.* kind
**kin·dle** (kin′dəl) **vt.** **-dled**, **-dling** [< ON *kynda*] 1
to set on fire; ignite 2 to excite (interest, feelings,
etc.) —**vi.** 1 to catch fire 2 to become excited
**kin·dling** (kind′liŋ) *n.* material, as bits of dry
wood, for starting a fire
**kind·ly** (kīnd′lē) *adj.* **-li·er**, **-li·est** 1 kind; gracious
2 agreeable; pleasant —*adv.* 1 in a kind, gracious
manner 2 agreeably; favorably 3 please [*kindly*
shut the door] —**kind′li·ness** *n.*
**kind′ness** *n.* 1 the state, quality, or habit of
being kind 2 a kind act
**kin·dred** (kin′drid) *n.* [< OE *cynn*, kin + *ræden*,
condition] relatives or family —*adj.* of like
nature; similar [*kindred* spirits]
**kine** (kīn) *pl.n.* [< OE *cy*, cows] [Archaic] cows;
cattle
**ki·net·ic** (ki net′ik) *adj.* [< Gr *kinein*, to move] of
or resulting from motion
**kin·folk** (kin′fōk′) *pl.n.* family; relatives; kin: also
**kin′folks′**
**king** (kiŋ) *n.* [< OE *cyning*] 1 a male ruler of a
nation 2 a man who is supreme in some field 3
something supreme in its class 4 a playing card
with a picture of a king on it 5 *Chess* the chief
piece —*adj.* chief (in size, importance, etc.) —
**king′ly** *adj.*
**King** (kiŋ), **Mar·tin Luther, Jr.** (märt′'n) 1929-68;
U.S. clergyman & leader in the civil rights movement: assassinated
**king′dom** (-dəm) *n.* 1 a country headed by a king
or queen; monarchy 2 a realm; domain [the *kingdom* of poetry] 3 any of three divisions into
which all natural objects have been classified [the
animal, vegetable, and mineral *kingdoms*]
**king′fish′er** *n.* a short-tailed diving bird that
feeds chiefly on fish
**King James Version** AUTHORIZED VERSION
**King Lear** (lir) the title character of a tragedy by
Shakespeare
**king′pin′** *n.* 1 the pin at the front of a triangle of
bowling pins 2 [Inf.] the essential person or
thing
**king′-size′** *adj.* larger than the regular kind: also
**king′-sized′**
**kink** (kiŋk) *n.* [< Scand] 1 a short twist, curl, or
bend in a rope, wire, hair, etc. 2 a painful cramp
in the neck, back, etc. 3 a mental twist; eccentric-
ity —*vi.*, *vt.* to form or cause to form a kink or
kinks
**kink′y** *adj.* **-i·er**, **-i·est** 1 tightly curled 2 [Slang]
weird, eccentric, etc.; specif., sexually abnormal
**kin·ship** (kin′ship′) *n.* 1 family relationship 2
close connection
**kins·man** (kinz′mən) *n.*, *pl.* **-men** (-mən) a relative; esp., a male relative —**kins′wom′an**, *pl.*
**-wom′en**, *n.*
**ki·osk** (kē′äsk′) *n.* [< Pers *kūshk*, palace] a small,
open structure used as a newsstand, etc.
**kip·per** (kip′ər) **vt.** [< ?] to cure (herring, salmon,
etc.) by salting and drying or smoking —*n.* a kip-
pered herring, etc.
**Kir·i·bati** (kir′ə bas′) country on a group of islands
in the WC Pacific, on the equator: 277 sq. mi.;
pop. 72,000
**kirk** (kurk) *n.* [Scot. or North Eng.] a church
**kis·met** (kiz′met) *n.* [< Ar *qasama*, to divide] fate;
destiny
**kiss** (kis) **vt.**, **vi.** [OE *cyssan*] 1 to touch or caress
with the lips as an act of affection, greeting, etc.
2 to touch lightly or gently —*n.* 1 an act of kiss-
ing 2 a light, gentle touch 3 any of various candies —**kiss′a·ble** *adj.*
**kit** (kit) *n.* [ME *kyt*, tub] 1 *a*) personal equipment,
esp. as packed for travel *b*) a set of tools *c*)
equipment for some particular activity, etc. *d*)

set of parts to be assembled **2** a box, bag, etc. for carrying such parts, equipment, or tools —**the whole kit and caboodle** [Inf.] the whole lot

**kitch·en** (kich′ən) *n.* ⟦ult. < L *coquere,* to cook⟧ a room or place for the preparation and cooking of food

**Kitch·e·ner** (kich′ə nər) city in SE Ontario, Canada: pop. 178,000

**kitch′en·ette′** or **kitch′en·et′** (-et′) *n.* a small, compact kitchen

**kitch′en·ware′** (-wer′) *n.* kitchen utensils

**kite** (kīt) *n.* ⟦< OE *cyta*⟧ **1** any of several long-winged birds of prey **2** a light wooden frame covered with paper or cloth, to be flown in the wind at the end of a string

**kith** (kith) *n.* ⟦< OE *cyth*⟧ friends: now only in **kith and kin** *a)* friends and relatives *b)* relatives

**kitsch** (kich) *n.* ⟦Ger, gaudy trash⟧ pretentious but shallow art or writing —**kitsch′y** *adj.*

**kit·ten** (kit′'n) *n.* ⟦< OFr dim. of *chat,* cat⟧ a young cat —**kit′ten·ish** *adj.*

**kit·ty**[1] (kit′ē) *n., pl.* **-ties 1** a kitten **2** *a pet name for* a cat

**kit·ty**[2] (kit′ē) *n., pl.* **-ties** ⟦prob. < KIT⟧ **1** the stakes in a poker game **2** money pooled for some purpose

**kit·ty-cor·nered** (kit′ē kôr′nərd) *adj., adv.* CATER-CORNERED: also **kit′ty-cor′ner**

**ki·wi** (kē′wē) *n., pl.* **-wis** ⟦echoic of its cry⟧ **1** a flightless bird of New Zealand **2** [*also* K-] a hairy, egg-sized fruit with sweet, green pulp

**KKK** *abbrev.* Ku Klux Klan

**Klee·nex** (klē′neks′) *trademark for* soft tissue paper used as a handkerchief, etc. —*n.* [*occas.* k-] a piece of such paper

**klep·to·ma·ni·a** (klep′tō mā′nē ə) *n.* ⟦< Gr *kleptēs,* thief + -MANIA⟧ a persistent, abnormal impulse to steal —**klep′to·ma′ni·ac′** *n., adj.*

**klieg light** (klēg) ⟦after A. & J. *Kliegl,* who developed it in 1911⟧ a very bright arc light used on motion picture sets

**Klon·dike** (klän′dīk′) gold-mining region in W Yukon Territory, Canada

**klutz** (kluts) *n.* ⟦< Yiddish *klots,* lit., wooden block⟧ [Slang] a clumsy or stupid person

**km** *abbrev.* kilometer(s)

**knack** (nak) *n.* ⟦ME *knak,* sharp blow⟧ **1** a clever expedient **2** ability to do something easily

**knack·wurst** (näk′wurst′) *n.* ⟦Ger < *knacken,* burst + *wurst,* sausage⟧ a thick, highly seasoned sausage

**knap·sack** (nap′sak′) *n.* ⟦< Du *knappen,* eat + *zak,* a sack⟧ a bag of leather, canvas, or nylon for carrying equipment or supplies on the back

**knave** (nāv) *n.* ⟦< OE *cnafa,* boy⟧ **1** a dishonest, deceitful person; rogue **2** JACK (*n.* 3) —**knav′ish** *adj.*

**knav·er·y** (nāv′ər ē) *n., pl.* **-ies** rascality; dishonesty

**knead** (nēd) *vt.* ⟦< OE *cnedan*⟧ **1** to work (dough, clay, etc.) into a pliable mass by folding, pressing, and squeezing **2** to massage —**knead′er** *n.*

**knee** (nē) *n.* ⟦< OE *cneow*⟧ **1** the joint between the thigh and the lower leg **2** anything shaped like a bent knee —*vt.* **kneed, knee′ing** to hit or touch with the knee

**knee′cap′** *n.* PATELLA

**knee′-deep′** *adj.* **1** up to the knees [*knee-deep mud*] **2** very much involved

**knee′-jerk′** *adj.* ⟦< the reflex when the knee is tapped⟧ [Inf.] characterized by or reacting with an automatic, predictable response

**kneel** (nēl) *vi.* **knelt** or **kneeled, kneel′ing** ⟦< OE *cneow,* knee⟧ to bend or rest on a knee or the knees

**kneel′er** *n.* a cushion, stool, etc. to kneel on in a church pew

**knell** (nel) *vi.* ⟦< OE *cnyllan*⟧ **1** to ring slowly; toll **2** to sound ominously —*vt.* to call or announce by or as by a knell —*n.* **1** the sound of a bell rung

slowly, as at a funeral **2** an omen of death, failure, etc.

**knelt** (nelt) *vi. alt. pt. and pp. of* KNEEL

**knew** (nōō) *vt., vi. pt. of* KNOW

**knick·ers** (nik′ərz) *pl.n.* ⟦after D. *Knickerbocker,* fictitious Du author of W. Irving's *History of New York*⟧ loose breeches gathered just below the knees: also **knick′er·bock′ers** (-ər bäk′ərz)

**knick·knack** (nik′nak′) *n.* ⟦< KNACK⟧ a small ornamental article

**knife** (nīf) *n., pl.* **knives** ⟦< OE *cnif*⟧ **1** a cutting instrument with a sharp-edged blade set in a handle **2** a cutting blade, as in a machine —*vt.* **knifed, knif′ing 1** to cut or stab with a knife **2** [Inf.] to injure or defeat by treachery —**under the knife** [Inf.] undergoing surgery

**knight** (nīt) *n.* ⟦< OE *cniht,* boy⟧ **1** in medieval times, a man formally raised to special military rank and pledged to chivalrous conduct **2** in Great Britain, a man who for some achievement is given honorary rank entitling him to use *Sir* before his given name **3** a chess piece shaped like a horse's head —*vt.* to make (a man) a knight

**knight′-er·rant** (-er′ənt) *n., pl.* **knights′-er′rant 1** a medieval knight wandering in search of adventure **2** a chivalrous or quixotic person

**knight′hood′** *n.* **1** the rank, status, or vocation of a knight **2** knights collectively

**knight′ly** *adj.* of, like, or befitting a knight; chivalrous, brave, etc.

**knit** (nit) *vt., vi.* **knit′ted** or **knit, knit′ting** ⟦< OE *cnotta,* a knot⟧ **1** to make (a fabric) by looping yarn or thread together with special needles **2** to join or grow together closely and firmly: said as of a broken bone **3** to draw or become drawn together in wrinkles: said of the brows —**knit′ter** *n.*

**knit′wear′** *n.* knitted clothing

**knob** (näb) *n.* ⟦ME *knobbe*⟧ **1** a rounded lump or protuberance **2** *a)* a handle, usually round, of a door, drawer, etc. *b)* a similar device used to control a radio, TV, etc.

**knob′by** *adj.* **-bi·er, -bi·est 1** covered with knobs **2** like a knob

**knock** (näk) *vi.* ⟦< OE *cnocian*⟧ **1** to strike a blow **2** to rap on a door **3** to bump; collide **4** to make a thumping noise: said of an engine, etc. —*vt.* **1** to hit; strike **2** to make by hitting [*to knock* a hole in a wall*] **3** [Inf.] to find fault with —*n.* **1** a knocking **2** a hit; rap **3** a thumping noise in an engine, etc., as because of faulty combustion **4** [Inf.] an adverse criticism —**knock about** (or **around**) [Inf.] to wander about —**knock down 1** to hit so as to cause to fall **2** to take apart **3** to indicate the sale of (an article) at an auction —**knock off 1** [Inf.] to stop working **2** [Inf.] to deduct **3** [Slang] to kill, overcome, etc. —**knock out** to make unconscious or exhausted —**knock together** to make or compose hastily

**knock′er** *n.* one that knocks; esp., a small ring, knob, etc. on a door for use in knocking

**knock′-kneed′** (-nēd′) *adj.* having legs that bend inward at the knees

**knock′out′** *n.* **1** a knocking out or being knocked out **2** [Slang] a very attractive person or thing **3** *Boxing* a victory won when the opponent is unable to continue to fight, as because of having been knocked unconscious

**knock·wurst** (näk′wurst′) *n. alt. sp. of* KNACK-WURST

**knoll** (nōl) *n.* ⟦OE *cnoll*⟧ a small hill; mound

**knot** (nät) *n.* ⟦< OE *cnotta*⟧ **1** a lump in a thread, etc., formed by a tightened loop or a tangle **2** a fastening made by tying together pieces of string, rope, etc. **3** an ornamental bow of ribbon, etc. **4** a small group or cluster **5** something that ties closely; esp., the bond of marriage **6** a problem; difficulty **7** a hard lump on a tree where a branch grows out, or a cross section of such a lump in a board **8** *Naut.* a unit of speed of one nautical

mile (6,076.12 feet) an hour —*vt., vi.* **knot'ted,
knot'ting 1** to make or form a knot (in) **2** to entangle or become entangled —**tie the knot** [Inf.] to get married

**knot'hole'** *n.* a hole in a board, etc. where a knot has fallen out

**knot'ty** *adj.* **-ti·er, -ti·est** [ME] **1** full of knots [*knotty* pine] **2** hard to solve; puzzling [a *knotty* problem]

**know** (nō) *vt.* **knew, known, know'ing** [< OE *cnawan*] **1** to be well informed about **2** to be aware of [to *know* that one is loved] **3** to be acquainted with **4** to recognize or distinguish [to *know* right from wrong] —*vi.* **1** to have knowledge **2** to be sure or aware —**in the know** [Inf.] having confidential information

**know'-how'** *n.* [Inf.] technical skill

**know'ing** *adj.* **1** having knowledge **2** shrewd; clever **3** implying shrewd or secret understanding [a *knowing* look] —**know'ing·ly** *adv.*

**know'-it-all'** *n.* [Inf.] one claiming to know much about almost everything

**knowl·edge** (näl'ij) *n.* **1** the fact or state of knowing **2** range of information or understanding **3** what is known; learning **4** the body of facts, etc. accumulated by humanity —**to** (**the best of**) **one's knowledge** as far as one knows

**knowl'edge·a·ble** *adj.* having knowledge or intelligence —**knowl'edge·a·bly** *adv.*

**known** (nōn) *vt., vi. pp. of* KNOW —*adj.* **1** familiar **2** recognized, proven, etc. [a *known* expert]

**Knox·ville** (näks'vil') city in E Tennessee: pop. 165,000

**knuck·le** (nuk'əl) *n.* [< or akin to MDu & LowG *knokel,* dim. of *knoke,* bone] **1** a joint of the finger; esp., the joint connecting a finger to the rest of the hand **2** the knee or hock joint of an animal, used as food —**knuckle down** to work hard —**knuckle under** to yield; give in

**knuck'le·head'** *n.* [Inf.] a stupid person

**knurl** (nʉrl) *n.* [prob. < *knur,* a knot + GNARL] **1** a knot, knob, etc. **2** any of a series of small beads or ridges, as along the edge of a coin —*vt.* to make knurls on

**KO** (kā'ō') [Slang] *vt.* **KO'd, KO'ing** *Boxing* to knock out —*n., pl.* **KO's** *Boxing* a knockout Also **K.O.** or **k.o.**

**ko·a·la** (kō ä'lə) *n.* [< native name] a tree-dwelling Australian marsupial with thick, gray fur

**Ko·di·ak** (kō'dē ak') island off the SW coast of Alaska

**kohl·ra·bi** (kōl rä'bē) *n., pl.* **-bies** [< It *cavolo rapa*] a vegetable related to the cabbage, with an edible, turniplike stem

**ko·la** (kō'lə) *n.* COLA (sense 1)

**kook** (kook) *n.* [prob. < CUCKOO] [Slang] a person regarded as silly, eccentric, etc. —**kook'y** or **kook'ie, -i·er, -i·est,** *adj.*

**kook·a·bur·ra** (kook'ə bʉr'ə) *n.* [< native name] an Australian kingfisher with a harsh cry like loud laughter

**ko·peck** or **ko·pek** (kō'pek') *n.* [Russ < *kopye,* a lance] a 100th part of a ruble

**Ko·ran** (kə ran', kôr'an') *n.* [< Ar *qur'ān,* book] the sacred book of Islam

**Ko·re·a** (kə rē'ə) peninsula & country northeast of China: divided (1948) into *a*) **Korean People's Democratic Republic** (**North Korea**): 47,399 sq. mi.; pop. 23,030,000 *b*) **Republic of Korea** (**South Korea**): 38,326 sq. mi.; pop. 43,412,000 —**Ko·re'an** *adj., n.*

**ko·sher** (kō'shər) *adj.* [< Heb *kāshēr,* proper] *Judaism* clean or fit to eat according to the dietary laws

**kow·tow** (kou'tou') *vi.* [Chin *k'o-t'ou,* lit., bump head] to show great deference, respect, etc. (*to*)

**KP** *abbrev.* kitchen police: a detail to assist the cooks in an army kitchen

**kraal** (kräl) *n.* [Afrik] **1** a village of South African native people **2** in South Africa, an enclosure for cattle or sheep

**Krem·lin** (krem'lin) *n.* [< Russ *kryeml'*] **1** the citadel of Moscow, housing many Russian, or, formerly, Soviet, government offices **2** the Russian, or, formerly, Soviet, government

**Krish·na** (krish'nə) *n.* a Hindu god, an incarnation of Vishnu

**kro·na** (krō'nə) *n., pl.* **-nor** (-nôr') [ult. < L *corona,* crown] the monetary unit of Sweden

**kró·na** (krō'nə) *n., pl.* **-nur** (-nər) [see prec.] the monetary unit of Iceland

**kro·ne** (krō'nə) *n., pl.* **-ner** (-nər) [see KRONA] the monetary unit of Denmark and Norway

**KS** Kansas

**K2** GODWIN AUSTEN

**ku·chen** (kōō'kən) *n.* [Ger, cake] a coffeecake made of yeast dough, often with raisins, nuts, etc.

**ku·dos** (kyōō'däs', kōō'-) *n.* [Gr *kydos*] credit for an achievement; glory; fame: often wrongly taken to be the plural (*pron.* -dōz) of an assumed word "*kudo*"

**kud·zu** (kood'zōō') *n.* [Jpn] a fast-growing perennial vine with large, three-part leaves

**Ku Klux Klan** (kōō' kluks' klan') [< Gr *kyklos,* circle] a U.S. secret society that is anti-black, anti-Semitic, anti-Catholic, etc., and uses terrorist methods

**kum·quat** (kum'kwät') *n.* [< Mandarin *chin-chü,* lit., golden orange] a small, orange-colored, oval fruit with a sour pulp and a sweet rind

**kung fu** (kooŋ' fōō', gooŋ'-) [< Chin] a Chinese system of self-defense, like karate but with circular movements

**Ku·wait** (kōō wāt') independent Arab state in E Arabia: 6,880 sq. mi.; pop. 1,697,000 —**Ku·wai'ti** (-wāt'ē) *adj., n.*

**kvetch** (kə vech') *vi.* [< Yiddish] [Slang] to complain in a nagging way

**kW** or **kw** *abbrev.* kilowatt(s)

**Kwang·chow** (kwäŋ'chō') *a former transliteration of* GUANGZHOU

**Kwan·zaa** (kwän'zä) *n.* [ult. < Swahili] an African-American cultural festival, Dec. 26 through Jan. 1

**KY** Kentucky

**Kyo·to** (kē ōt'ō) city in S Honshu, Japan: pop. 1,473,000

**Kyr·gyz·stan** (kir'gi stan') country in south-central Asia: formerly a republic of the U.S.S.R.: 77,180 sq. mi.; pop. 4,463,000

# L

**l** or **L** (el) *n., pl.* **l's, L's** the 12th letter of the English alphabet

**L** (el) *n., pl.* **L's 1** an extension forming an L with the main structure **2** a Roman numeral for 50

**l** *abbrev.* **1** latitude **2** left **3** length **4** line **5** liter(s) **6** long **7** loss(es)

**L** *abbrev.* **1** Lake **2** large **3** Latin **4** left **5** length **6** liter(s) **7** longitude **8** [L *libra, pl. librae*] pound(s): now usually £

**la** (lä) *n.* [< L] *Music* the sixth tone of the diatonic scale

**LA 1** Los Angeles **2** Louisiana

**lab** (lab) *n.* [Inf.] a laboratory

**la·bel** (lā'bəl) *n.* [OFr, a rag] **1** a card, paper, etc.

marked and attached to an object to indicate its contents, owner, destination, etc. **2** a term of generalized classification —*vt.* **-beled** or **-belled**, **-bel·ing** or **-bel·ling 1** to attach a label to **2** to classify as

**la·bi·al** (lā′bē əl) *adj.* ⟦< L *labium*, lip⟧ **1** of the lips **2** *Phonetics* articulated with one or both lips: said as of (f), (b), and (ü)

**la′bi·um** (-əm) *n., pl.* **-bi·a** (-ə) ⟦L, lip⟧ a lip or liplike organ

**la·bor** (lā′bər) *n.* ⟦< L⟧ **1** physical or mental exertion; work **2** a specific task **3** all wage-earning workers **4** labor unions collectively **5** the process of childbirth —*vi.* **1** to work **2** to work hard **3** to move slowly and with difficulty **4** to be burdened with a liability or limitation (with *under*) **5** to be in childbirth —*vt.* to develop in too great detail; belabor

**lab·o·ra·to·ry** (lab′rə tôr′ē) *n., pl.* **-ries** ⟦see prec.⟧ a room, building, etc. for scientific experimentation or research

**Labor Day** the first Monday in September, a legal holiday honoring working people

**la·bored** (lā′bərd) *adj.* made or done with great effort; strained

**la′bor·er** *n.* one who labors; esp., a wage-earning worker whose work is largely hard physical labor

**la·bo·ri·ous** (lə bôr′ē əs) *adj.* **1** involving much hard work; difficult **2** LABORED —**la·bo′ri·ous·ly** *adv.*

**labor union** an association of workers to promote and protect the welfare, rights, etc. of its members

**la·bour** (lā′bər) *n., vi., vt. Brit. sp.* of LABOR

**Lab·ra·dor** (lab′rə dôr′) **1** region along the Atlantic in NE Canada: the mainland part of Newfoundland **2** large peninsula between the Atlantic & Hudson Bay, containing this region & Quebec

**Labrador retriever** a retriever with a short, dense, black, yellow, or brown coat

**la·bur·num** (lə bur′nəm) *n.* ⟦< L⟧ a small tree or shrub of the pea family, with drooping yellow flowers

**lab·y·rinth** (lab′ə rinth′) *n.* ⟦< Gr *labyrinthos*⟧ a structure containing winding passages hard to follow without losing one's way; maze

**lac** (lak) *n.* ⟦< Sans *lākṣā*⟧ a resinous substance secreted on certain trees in India, etc. by a certain kind of insect: source of shellac

**lace** (lās) *n.* ⟦< L *laqueus*, noose⟧ **1** a string, etc. used to draw together and fasten the parts of a shoe, corset, etc. **2** a fine netting of cotton, silk, etc., woven in ornamental designs —*vt.* **laced, lac′ing 1** to fasten with a lace **2** to weave together; intertwine **3** to hit hard **4** to add a dash of alcoholic liquor to (a drink)

**lac·er·ate** (las′ər āt′) *vt.* **-at′ed, -at′ing** ⟦< L *lacer*, lacerated⟧ to tear jaggedly; mangle (flesh, etc.) — **lac′er·a′tion** *n.*

**lace′work′** *n.* lace, or any openwork decoration like lace

**lach·ry·mal** (lak′ri məl) *adj.* ⟦< L *lacrima*, TEAR²⟧ **1** of or producing tears **2** LACRIMAL (sense 1)

**lach′ry·mose′** (-mōs′) *adj.* ⟦see prec.⟧ shedding, or causing to shed, tears; tearful or sad

**lack** (lak) *n.* ⟦< or akin to medieval LowG *lak*⟧ **1** the fact or state of not having enough or not having any **2** the thing that is needed —*vt., vi.* to be deficient in or entirely without (something)

**lack·a·dai·si·cal** (lak′ə dā′zi kəl) *adj.* ⟦< archaic *lackaday*, an exclamation of regret, etc.⟧ showing lack of interest or spirit; listless

**lack·ey** (lak′ē) *n., pl.* **-eys** ⟦< Sp *lacayo*⟧ **1** a male servant of low rank, usually in some sort of livery or uniform **2** a servile follower; toady

**lack·lus·ter** (lak′lus′tər) *adj.* **1** lacking brightness; dull **2** lacking vitality; boring Also [Chiefly Brit.] **lack′lus′tre**

**la·con·ic** (lə kän′ik) *adj.* ⟦< Gr *Lakōn*, a Spartan⟧ terse in expression; concise —**la·con′i·cal·ly** *adv.*

**lac·quer** (lak′ər) *n.* ⟦< Fr < Port *laca*, lac⟧ **1** a coating substance made of shellac, gum resins, etc. dissolved in ethyl alcohol or other solvent that evaporates rapidly **2** a resinous varnish obtained from certain E Asian trees —*vt.* to coat with lacquer

**lac·ri·mal** (lak′ri məl) *adj.* **1** of or near the glands that secrete tears **2** LACHRYMAL (sense 1)

**la·crosse** (lə krôs′) *n.* ⟦CdnFr, lit., the crutch⟧ a ballgame played by two teams using long-handled, pouched rackets

**lac·tate** (lak′tāt′) *vi.* **-tat·ed, -tat·ing** to secrete milk

**lac·ta·tion** (lak tā′shən) *n.* ⟦< L *lac*, milk⟧ **1** the secretion of milk by a mammary gland **2** the period during which milk is secreted

**lac·te·al** (lak′tē əl) *adj.* ⟦< L *lac*, milk⟧ of or like milk; milky

**lac·tic** (lak′tik) *adj.* ⟦< L *lac*, milk⟧ of or obtained from milk

**lactic acid** a clear, syrupy acid formed when milk sours

LACROSSE PLAYER

**lac·tose** (lak′tōs′) *n.* ⟦< L *lac*, milk⟧ a sugar found in milk: used in foods

**la·cu·na** (lə kyōō′nə) *n., pl.* **-nas** or **-nae** (-nē) ⟦L, a ditch⟧ a blank space; esp., a missing portion in a text, etc.

**lac·y** (lās′ē) *adj.* **-i·er, -i·est** of or like lace —**lac′i·ness** *n.*

**lad** (lad) *n.* ⟦ME *ladde*⟧ a boy; youth

**lad·der** (lad′ər) *n.* ⟦OE *hlæder*⟧ **1** a framework consisting of two sidepieces connected by a series of rungs, for use in climbing up or down **2** any means of climbing

**lad·die** (lad′ē) *n.* [Chiefly Scot.] a young lad

**lad·en** (lād′'n) *adj.* ⟦< OE⟧ **1** loaded **2** burdened

**la·di·da** (lä′dē dä′) *adj.* [imitative] [Inf.] affectedly refined

**lad·ing** (lād′iŋ) *n.* a load; cargo; freight

**la·dle** (lād′'l) *n.* ⟦OE *hlædel*⟧ a long-handled, cuplike spoon —*vt.* **-dled, -dling** to dip out with a ladle

**la·dy** (lād′ē) *n., pl.* **-dies** ⟦< OE *hlaf*, loaf + *dæge*, kneader⟧ **1** *a)* a woman of high social position *b)* a woman who is polite, refined, etc. **2** any woman: used (in pl.) to address a group **3** [L-] a British title given to women of certain ranks — *adj.* [Inf.] female

**la′dy·bug′** *n.* a small, roundish beetle with a spotted back: also **la′dy·bird′**

**la′dy·fin′ger** *n.* a small spongecake shaped somewhat like a finger

**la′dy-in-wait′ing** *n., pl.* **la′dies-in-wait′ing** a woman waiting upon a queen or princess

**la′dy·like′** *adj.* like or suitable for a lady; refined; well-bred

**la′dy·love′** *n.* a female sweetheart

**la′dy·ship′** *n.* **1** the rank or position of a lady **2** [*usually* L-] a title used in speaking to or of a woman holding the rank of lady

**la′dy-slip′per** *n.* an orchid with flowers that somewhat resemble slippers: also **la′dy's-slip′per**

**la·e·trile** (lā′ə tril′) *n.* any of several compounds obtained chiefly from apricot kernels, claimed by some to be effective in treating cancer

**La·fa·yette** (lä′fē et′, -fä-), Marquis **de** 1757-1834; Fr. general: served (1777-81) in the American Revolutionary army

**lag** (lag) *vi.* **lagged, lag′ging** ⟦< ?⟧ **1** to fall behind or move slowly; loiter **2** to become less intense — *n.* **1** a falling behind **2** the amount of this

**la·ger (beer)** (lä′gər) ⟦Ger *lagerbier*, storehouse beer⟧ a beer aged at a low temperature

**lag·gard** (lag′ərd) *n.* ⟦< LAG + -ARD⟧ a slow person, esp. one who falls behind —*adj.* slow; falling behind

**la·gniappe** or **la·gnappe** (lan yap′, lan′yap′) *n.* ⟦Creole < Fr & Sp⟧ a gratuity

**la·goon** (lə gōōn′) *n.* ⟦< L *lacuna*, pool⟧ 1 a shallow lake or pond, esp. one connected with a larger body of water 2 the water enclosed by a circular coral reef 3 an area of shallow salt water separated from the sea by sand dunes

**La·hore** (lə hôr′) city in NE Pakistan: pop. 2,953,000

**laid** (lād) *vt., vi. pt. & pp.* of LAY[1]

**laid′-back′** *adj.* [Slang] relaxed, easygoing, etc.; not frenetic or hurried

**lain** (lān) *vi. pp.* of LIE[1]

**lair** (ler) *n.* ⟦OE *leger*⟧ a resting place of a wild animal; den

**lais·sez faire** (les′ā fer′) ⟦Fr, allow to do⟧ noninterference; specif., absence of government control over industry and business

**la·i·ty** (lā′i tē) *n., pl.* -ties ⟦< LAY[3]⟧ laymen collectively

**lake** (lāk) *n.* ⟦< L *lacus*⟧ 1 a large inland body of usually fresh water 2 a pool of oil or other liquid

**lake′front′** *n.* the land along the shore of a lake —*adj.* near, at, or of the lakefront

**lal·ly·gag** (lä′lē gag′) *vi.* -gagged′, -gag′ging [Inf.] LOLLYGAG

**lam** (lam) [Slang] *n.* ⟦< ?⟧ headlong flight —*vi.* lammed, lam′ming to flee; escape —**on the lam** in flight, as from the police

**la·ma** (lä′mə) *n.* ⟦Tibetan *blama*⟧ a priest or monk in Lamaism

**La·ma·ism** (lä′mə iz′əm) *n.* a form of Buddhism in Tibet and Mongolia

**la·ma·ser·y** (lä′mə ser′ē) *n., pl.* -ies a monastery of lamas

**La·maze** (lə mäz′) *n.* ⟦after F. *Lamaze*, 20th-c. Fr physician⟧ a training program in natural childbirth, involving the help of the father

**lamb** (lam) *n.* ⟦OE⟧ 1 a young sheep 2 its flesh, used as food 3 a gentle, innocent, or gullible person

**lam·baste** (lam bāst′, -bast′) *vt.* -bast′ed, -bast′ing ⟦< *lam*, to beat + *baste*, to flog⟧ [Inf.] 1 to beat soundly 2 to scold or denounce severely

**lamb·da** (lam′də) *n.* the 11th letter of the Greek alphabet (Λ, λ)

**lam·bent** (lam′bənt) *adj.* ⟦< L *lambere*, to lick⟧ 1 playing lightly over a surface: said of a flame, etc. 2 glowing softly 3 light and graceful [*lambent wit*] —**lam′ben·cy** *n.*

**lamb′kin** *n.* a little lamb: sometimes applied to a child, etc. as a term of affection

**lame** (lām) *adj.* ⟦OE *lama*⟧ 1 crippled; esp., having an injury that makes one limp 2 stiff and painful 3 poor; ineffectual [a *lame* excuse] —*vt.* lamed, lam′ing to make lame —**lame′ly** *adv.* — **lame′ness** *n.*

**la·mé** (la mā′, lä-) *n.* ⟦< Fr *lame*, metal plate⟧ a cloth interwoven with metal threads, as of gold

**lame duck** an elected official whose term ends after someone else has been elected to the office

**la·mel·la** (lə mel′ə) *n., pl.* -lae (-ē) or -las ⟦L⟧ a thin plate, scale, or layer

**la·ment** (lə ment′) *vi., vt.* ⟦< L *lamentum*, a wailing⟧ to feel or express deep sorrow (for); mourn — *n.* 1 a lamenting 2 an elegy, dirge, etc. mourning some loss or death —**lam·en·ta·ble** (lam′ən tə bəl, lə men′-) *adj.* —**lam·en·ta·tion** (lam′ən tā′shən) *n.*

**lam·i·na** (lam′i nə) *n., pl.* -nae′ (-nē′) or -nas ⟦L⟧ a thin scale or layer, as of metal, tissue, etc.

**lam·i·nate** (lam′i nāt′; *for adj. usually*, -nit) *vt.* -nat′ed, -nat′ing ⟦see prec.⟧ 1 to cover with one or more thin layers 2 to make by building up in layers —*adj.* LAMINATED —**lam′i·na′tion** *n.*

**lam′i·nat′ed** *adj.* 1 built in thin sheets or layers

2 covered with a thin protective layer, as of clear plastic

**lamp** (lamp) *n.* ⟦< Gr *lampein*, to shine⟧ 1 a container with a wick for burning oil, etc. to produce light or heat 2 any device for producing light or heat, as an electric light bulb 3 a holder or base for such a device

**lamp′black′** *n.* fine soot used as a black pigment

**lam·poon** (lam pōōn′) *n.* ⟦< Fr *lampons*, let us drink: used as a refrain⟧ a satirical writing attacking someone —*vt.* to attack in a lampoon

**lamp·post** (lamp′pōst′) *n.* a post supporting a street lamp

**lam·prey** (lam′prē) *n., pl.* -preys ⟦< ML *lampreda*⟧ an eel-like fish with a jawless, sucking mouth

**la·na·i** (lə nä′ē, -nī′) *n.* ⟦Haw⟧ a veranda or open-sided living room

**lance** (lans) *n.* ⟦< L *lancea*⟧ 1 a long, wooden spear with a sharp metal head 2 *a)* LANCER *b)* LANCET 3 any instrument like a lance —*vt.* lanced, lanc′ing 1 to pierce with a lance 2 to cut open (a boil, etc.) with a lancet

**Lan·ce·lot** (län′sə lət, -lät′) *n.* the most celebrated of the Knights of the Round Table

**lanc·er** (lans′ər) *n.* a cavalry soldier armed with a lance

**lan·cet** (lan′sit) *n.* ⟦< OFr dim. of *lance*, lance⟧ a small, pointed surgical knife, usually two-edged

**land** (land) *n.* ⟦OE⟧ 1 the solid part of the earth's surface 2 a country or nation 3 ground or soil 4 real estate —*vt.* 1 to put on shore from a ship 2 to bring to a particular place or condition [it *landed* him in jail] 3 to set (an aircraft) down on land or water 4 to catch [to *land* a fish] 5 [Inf.] to get or secure [to *land* a job] 6 [Inf.] to deliver (a blow) —*vi.* 1 to leave a ship and go on shore 2 to come to a port, etc.: said of a ship 3 to arrive at a specified place 4 to come to rest

**land contract** a real estate contract in which a buyer makes payments over a specified period until the full price is paid, after which the seller transfers his interest to the buyer

**land′ed** *adj.* owning land [*landed* gentry]

**land′fall′** *n.* 1 a sighting of land from a ship at sea 2 the land sighted

**land′fill′** *n.* 1 a place used to dispose of garbage, rubbish, etc. by burying it in the ground 2 garbage, etc. so disposed of

**land grant** a grant of land by the government for a railroad, state college, etc.

**land′hold′er** *n.* an owner of land —**land′hold′ing** *adj., n.*

**land′ing** *n.* 1 the act of coming to shore 2 a place where a ship or boat is loaded or unloaded 3 a platform at the end of a flight of stairs 4 the act of alighting, as after a flight or jump

**landing gear** the system of parts on an aircraft or spacecraft used for support or mobility on land or water

**land′locked′** *adj.* 1 surrounded by land, as a country 2 cut off from the sea and confined to fresh water [*landlocked* salmon]

**land′lord′** *n.* 1 a person who leases land, houses, etc. to others 2 a man who keeps a rooming house, inn, etc. —**land′la′dy**, *pl.* -dies, *fem.n.*

**land′lub′ber** (-lub′ər) *n.* one who has had little experience at sea

**land′mark′** *n.* 1 an object that marks the boundary of a piece of land 2 any prominent feature of the landscape, distinguishing a locality 3 an important event or turning point

**land′mass′** *n.* a very large area of land; esp., a continent

**land office** a government office that handles the sales of public lands

**land′-of′fice business** [Inf.] a booming business

**land′scape′** (-skāp′) *n.* ⟦< Du *land*, land + -*schap*, -ship⟧ 1 a picture of natural, inland scenery 2 an expanse of natural scenery —*vt.* -scaped′, -scap′ing to make (a plot of ground) more attractive, as by adding a lawn, trees, bushes, etc. —**land′scap′er** n.

**land′slide′** n. **1** the sliding of a mass of earth or rocks down a slope **2** the mass sliding down **3** an overwhelming victory, esp. in an election

**land′ward** (-wərd) adv., adj. toward the land: also **land′wards** adv.

**lane** (lān) n. ⟦OE lanu⟧ **1** a narrow way, path, road, etc. **2** a path or route designated, for reasons of safety, for ships, aircraft, automobiles, etc. **3** Bowling a long, narrow strip of polished wood, along which the balls are rolled

**lan·guage** (laŋ′gwij) n. ⟦< L lingua, tongue⟧ **1** human speech or the written symbols for speech **2** a) any means of communicating b) a special set of symbols used in a computer **3** the speech of a particular nation, etc. [the French language] **4** the particular style of verbal expression characteristic of a person, group, profession, etc.

**lan·guid** (laŋ′gwid) adj. ⟦< L languere, be weary⟧ **1** without vigor or vitality; weak **2** listless; indifferent **3** slow; dull —**lan′guid·ly** adv.

**lan′guish** (-gwish) vi. ⟦see prec.⟧ **1** to become weak; droop **2** to live under distressing conditions [to languish in poverty] **3** to long; pine **4** to put on an air of sentimental tenderness

**lan·guor** (laŋ′gər) n. ⟦see LANGUID⟧ lack of vigor or vitality; weakness; listlessness —**lan′guor·ous** adj.

**lank** (laŋk) adj. ⟦OE hlanc⟧ **1** long and slender **2** straight and limp: said of hair

**lank·y** (laŋ′kē) adj. -i·er, -i·est awkwardly tall and lean

**lan·o·lin** (lan′ə lin′) n. ⟦< L lana, wool + oleum, oil⟧ a fatty substance obtained from wool and used in ointments, cosmetics, etc.

**Lan·sing** (lan′siŋ) capital of Michigan, in the SC part: pop. 127,000

**lan·tern** (lan′tərn) n. ⟦ult. < Gr lampein, to shine⟧ a transparent case for holding and shielding a light

**lan′tern-jawed′** adj. having long, thin jaws and sunken cheeks

**lan·yard** (lan′yərd) n. ⟦< OFr lasne, noose⟧ a short rope used on board ship for holding or fastening something

**La·os** (lä′ōs′) country in the NW part of Indochina: 91,400 sq. mi.; pop. 3,722,000 —**La·o·tian** (lā ō′shən) adj., n.

**lap**[1] (lap) n. ⟦OE læppa⟧ **1** the front part, from the waist to the knees, of a sitting person **2** the part of the clothing covering this **3** that in which a person or thing is cared for **4** a) an overlapping b) a part that overlaps **5** one complete circuit of a racetrack —vt. **lapped, lap′ping 1** to fold (over or on) **2** to wrap; enfold **3** to overlap **4** to get a lap ahead of (an opponent) in a race —vi. **1** to overlap **2** to extend beyond something in space or time: with over

**lap**[2] (lap) vi., vt. **lapped, lap′ping** ⟦OE lapian⟧ **1** to drink (a liquid) by dipping it up with the tongue as a dog does **2** to strike gently with a light splash: said of waves —n. **1** a lapping **2** the sound of lapping

**La Paz** (lə päz′) city & seat of government of Bolivia: pop. 711,000

**lap′board′** n. a board placed on the lap for use as a table or desk

**lap dog** any pet dog small enough to be held in the lap: also written **lap′dog′** n.

**la·pel** (lə pel′) n. ⟦dim. of LAP[1]⟧ the front part of a coat folded back and forming a continuation of the collar

**lap·i·dar·y** (lap′ə der′ē) n., pl. -dar′ies ⟦< L lapis, a stone⟧ one who cuts and polishes precious stones —adj. **1** of the art of a lapidary **2** precise and elegant [lapidary prose]

**lap·in** (lap′in) n. ⟦Fr, rabbit⟧ rabbit fur, often dyed to resemble other skins

**lap·is laz·u·li** (lap′is laz′yōō lī′, -lazh′-; -lē′) ⟦< L lapis, a stone + ML lazulus, azure⟧ an azure, opaque, semiprecious stone

**Lap·land** (lap′land′) region of N Europe, including the N parts of Norway, Sweden, & Finland

**Lapp** (lap) n. ⟦Swed⟧ a member of a people living in Lapland: also **Lapp′land·er**

**lap·pet** (lap′it) n. ⟦dim. of LAP[1]⟧ a loose flap or fold of a garment or head covering

**lapse** (laps) n. ⟦< L labi, to slip⟧ **1** a small error **2** a) a moral slip b) a falling into a lower condition **3** a passing, as of time **4** the termination as of a privilege through failure to meet requirements —vi. **lapsed, laps′ing 1** to fall into a specified state [he lapsed into silence] **2** to backslide **3** to elapse **4** to come to an end; stop **5** to become void because of failure to meet requirements

**lap′top′** n. a small, light, portable microcomputer having, in a single unit, a CPU, keyboard, screen, etc., and, usually, a rechargeable battery

**lar·board** (lär′bərd) adj., n. ⟦< OE hladan, lade + bord, side⟧ (of) the port side of a ship

**lar·ce·ny** (lär′sə nē) n., pl. -nies ⟦ult. < L latro, robber⟧ the unlawful taking of another's property; theft —**lar′ce·nist** n. —**lar′ce·nous** adj.

**larch** (lärch) n. ⟦< L larix⟧ **1** a tree of the pine family that sheds its needles annually **2** its tough wood

**lard** (lärd) n. ⟦< L lardum⟧ a white, soft solid made by melting the fat of hogs —vt. **1** to put strips of fat pork, bacon, etc. on (meat, etc.) before cooking **2** to embellish [a talk larded with jokes]

**lard′er** n. **1** a place where food supplies are kept; pantry **2** food supplies; provisions

**large** (lärj) adj. **larg′er, larg′est** ⟦< L largus⟧ **1** of great extent or amount; big, bulky, spacious, etc. **2** bigger than others of its kind **3** operating on a big scale [a large producer] —adv. in a large way [write large] —**at large 1** free; not confined **2** taken altogether **3** representing no particular district [a congressman at large] —**large′ness** n. —**larg′ish** adj.

**large′heart′ed** adj. generous; kindly

**large intestine** the relatively large section of the intestines of vertebrates, including the cecum, colon, and rectum

**large′ly** adv. for the most part; mainly

**large′-scale′** adj. **1** drawn to a large scale **2** of wide scope; extensive

**lar·gess** or **lar·gesse** (lär jes′, lär′jis) n. ⟦see LARGE⟧ **1** generous giving **2** a gift or gifts generously given

**lar·go** (lär′gō) adj., adv. ⟦It, slow⟧ Music slow and stately: also written **largo**

**lar·i·at** (lar′ē ət) n. ⟦Sp la reata, the rope⟧ **1** a rope used for tethering grazing horses, etc. **2** LASSO

**lark**[1] (lärk) n. ⟦< OE læwerce⟧ any of a large family of chiefly Old World birds, esp. the skylark

**lark**[2] (lärk) vi. ⟦? < ON leika⟧ to play or frolic —n. a frolic or spree

**lark·spur** (lärk′spur′) n. DELPHINIUM

**lar·va** (lär′və) n., pl. -vae′ (-vē′) or -vas ⟦L, ghost⟧ the early form of any animal that changes structurally when it becomes an adult [the tadpole is the larva of the frog] —**lar′val** adj.

**lar·yn·gi·tis** (lar′in jīt′is) n. an inflammation of the larynx, often with a temporary loss of voice

**lar·ynx** (lar′iŋks) n., pl. **lar′ynx·es** or **la·ryn·ges** (lə rin′jēz′) ⟦< Gr⟧ the structure at the upper end of the trachea, containing the vocal cords

**la·sa·gna** (lə zän′yə) n. ⟦It⟧ a dish of wide noodles baked in layers with tomato sauce, ground meat, and cheese

**las·civ·i·ous** (lə siv′ē əs) adj. ⟦< L lascivus, wanton⟧ **1** characterized by or expressing lust **2** exciting lust

**la·ser** (lā′zər) n. ⟦l(ight) a(mplification by) s(timulated) e(mission of) r(adiation)⟧ a device containing a substance whose atoms or molecules can be raised to a higher energy state, so that it emits light in an intense, narrow beam

**la′ser·disc′** n. a videodisc for recording audio and

video data to be read by a laser beam: also **la'ser·disk'**, **laser disc**, or **laser disk**

**lash**[1] (lash) *n.* [< ?] **1** the flexible striking part of a whip **2** a stroke as with a whip **3** an eyelash — *vt.* **1** to strike or drive as with a lash **2** to jerk or swing sharply [the cat *lashed* her tail] **3** to censure or rebuke —*vi.* to make strokes as with a whip —**lash out 1** to strike out violently **2** to speak angrily

**lash**[2] (lash) *vt.* [see LACE] to fasten or tie with a rope, etc.

**lass** (las) *n.* [prob. < ON *lǫskr*, weak] a young woman

**las·sie** (las'ē) *n.* [Scot.] a young woman

**las·si·tude** (las'i tōōd') *n.* [< L *lassus*, faint] weariness; languor

**las·so** (las'ō) *n., pl.* **-sos** or **-soes** [< Sp < L *laqueus*, noose] a rope with a sliding noose used to catch cattle, etc. —*vt.* **-soed**, **-so·ing** to catch with a lasso

**last**[1] (last) *adj.* **1** *alt. superl.* of LATE **2** being or coming after all others in place or time; final **3** only remaining **4** most recent [*last* month] **5** least likely [the *last* person to suspect] **6** conclusive [the *last* word] —*adv.* **1** after all others **2** most recently **3** finally; in conclusion —*n.* the one coming last —**at (long) last** after a long time; finally

**last**[2] (last) *vi.* [OE *læstan*] to remain in existence, use, etc.; endure —*vt.* **1** to continue during **2** to be enough for

**last**[3] (last) *n.* [< OE *last*, footstep] a form shaped like the foot, used in making or repairing shoes

**last hurrah** a final attempt or appearance

**last'ing** *adj.* that lasts a long time —**last'ing·ly** *adv.*

**Last Judgment** *Theol.* the final judgment at the end of the world

**last'ly** *adv.* in conclusion; finally

**last straw** [< the straw that broke the camel's back] a final trouble that results in a defeat, loss of patience, etc.: with *the*

**Las Ve·gas** (läs vā'gəs) city in SE Nevada: pop. 258,000

**lat** *abbrev.* latitude

**Lat** *abbrev.* Latin

**latch** (lach) *n.* [< OE *læccan*] a fastening for a door, gate, or window; esp., a bar that fits into a notch —*vt., vi.* to fasten with a latch —**latch onto** [Inf.] to get or obtain

**late** (lāt) *adj.* **lat'er** or **lat'ter**, **lat'est** or **last** [OE *læt*] **1** happening, coming, etc. after the usual or expected time, or at a time far advanced in a period [*late* to class, *late* Victorian] **2** recent **3** having recently died —*adv.* **lat'er**, **lat'est** or **last 1** after the expected time **2** at or until an advanced time of the day, year, etc. **3** toward the end of a period **4** recently —**of late** recently — **late'ness** *n.*

**late'ly** *adv.* recently; not long ago

**la·tent** (lāt''nt) *adj.* [< L *latere*, lurk] lying hidden and undeveloped in a person or thing —**la'ten·cy** *n.*

**lat·er·al** (lat'ər əl) *adj.* [< L *latus*, a side] of, at, from, or toward the side; sideways —**lat'er·al·ly** *adv.*

**la·tex** (lā'teks') *n.* [L, a fluid] **1** a milky liquid in certain plants and trees: used esp. as the basis of rubber **2** a suspension in water of particles of rubber or plastic: used in adhesives, paints, etc.

**lath** (lath) *n., pl.* **laths** (lath*z*, laths) [< ME] **1** any of the thin, narrow strips of wood used as a foundation for plaster, etc. **2** any foundation for plaster

**lathe** (lāth) *n.* [prob. < MDu *lade*] a machine for shaping wood, metal, etc. by holding and turning it rapidly against the edge of a cutting tool —*vt.* **lathed**, **lath'ing** to shape on a lathe

**lath·er** (lath'ər) *n.* [OE *leathor*, soap] **1** the foam formed by soap and water **2** foamy sweat, as on a

racehorse **3** [Slang] an excited state —*vt., vi.* to cover with or form lather —**lath'er·y** *adj.*

**Lat·in** (lat''n) *adj.* [< *Latium*, ancient country in central Italy] **1** of ancient Rome or its people, language, etc. **2** designating or of the languages derived from Latin, the peoples that speak them, their countries, etc. —*n.* **1** a person born or living in ancient Rome **2** the language of ancient Rome **3** a person whose language is derived from Latin, as a Spaniard, Italian, or Latin American

**Latin America** that part of the Western Hemisphere south of the U.S. where Spanish, Portuguese, & French are the official languages —**Latin American**

**La·ti·no** (la tē'nō) *n., pl.* **-nos** [< L *Latinus*, LATIN] a Latin American, esp. one who lives in the U.S. —*adj.* of or relating to Latinos Now often preferred to *Hispanic* —**La·ti'na** (-nə) *fem.n.*

**lat·ish** (lāt'ish) *adj., adv.* somewhat late

**lat·i·tude** (lat'ə tōōd') *n.* [< L *latus*, wide] **1** freedom from narrow restrictions **2** *a)* distance, measured in degrees, north or south from the equator *b)* a region with reference to this distance

**la·trine** (lə trēn') *n.* [< L *lavare*, to wash] a toilet for the use of a large number of people, as in an army camp

**lat·te** (lä'tā) *n.* [It] espresso coffee mixed with steamed milk

**lat·ter** (lat'ər) *adj.* [orig. compar. of LATE] **1** *alt. compar.* of LATE **2** *a)* later; more recent *b)* nearer the end or close **3** being the last mentioned of two

**lat·tice** (lat'is) *n.* [< OHG *latta*, lath] an openwork structure of crossed strips of wood, metal, etc. used as a screen, support, etc.

**lat'tice·work'** *n.* **1** a lattice **2** lattices collectively

**Lat·vi·a** (lat'vē ə) country in N Europe: formerly a republic of the U.S.S.R.: 24,595 sq. mi.; pop. 2,606,000 —**Lat'vi·an** *adj., n.*

**laud** (lôd) *vt.* [< L *laus*, glory] to praise; extol

**laud'a·ble** *adj.* praiseworthy; commendable

**lau·da·num** (lôd''n əm) *n.* [< L *ladanum*, a dark resin] **1** [Archaic] any of various opium preparations **2** a solution of opium in alcohol

**laud·a·to·ry** (lôd'ə tôr'ē) *adj.* expressing praise; commendatory

**laugh** (laf) *vi.* [< OE *hleahhan*] to make the sounds and facial movements that express mirth, ridicule, etc. —*n.* **1** the act or sound of laughing **2** a cause of laughter **3** [*pl.*] [Inf.] mere diversion or pleasure —**laugh at 1** to be amused by **2** to make fun of

**laugh'a·ble** *adj.* amusing or ridiculous —**laugh'a·bly** *adv.*

**laugh'ing·stock'** *n.* an object of ridicule

**laugh'ter** *n.* the action or sound of laughing

**launch**[1] (lônch) *vt.* [< L *lancea*, a lance] **1** to hurl or send forth with some force [to *launch* a rocket] **2** to slide (a new vessel) into the water **3** to set in operation or on some course; start [to *launch* an attack] —*vi.* **1** to start something new: often with *out* or *forth* **2** to plunge (*into*) —*n.* a launching — *adj.* designating or of vehicles, sites, etc. used in launching spacecraft or missiles

**launch**[2] (lônch) *n.* [Sp or Port *lancha*] an open, or partly enclosed, motorboat

**launch'pad'** or **launch pad** *n.* the platform from which a rocket, guided missile, etc. is launched: also **launching pad**

**laun·der** (lôn'dər) *vt.* [< L *lavare*, to wash] **1** to wash, or wash and iron (clothes, etc.) **2** to exchange or invest (illegally gotten money) so as to conceal its source —**laun'der·er** *n.* —**laun'dress** (-dris) *fem.n.*

**laun·dro·mat** (lôn'drə mat') *n.* [< *Laundromat*, a former service mark] a self-service laundry: also **laun·der·mat** (lôn'dər mat')

**laun·dry** (lôn'drē) *n., pl.* **-dries 1** a place for laundering **2** clothes, etc. laundered or to be laundered

**laun'dry·man'** (-man', -mən) *n., pl.* **-men'** (-man', -mən) a man who works in or for a laundry, esp. one who collects and delivers laundry

**lau·re·ate** (lôr'ē it) *adj.* ⟦< L *laurus*, laurel⟧ honored, as with a crown of laurel —*n.* POET LAUREATE

**lau·rel** (lôr'əl) *n.* ⟦< L *laurus*⟧ **1** an evergreen tree or shrub of S Europe, with large, glossy leaves **2** its foliage, esp. as woven into wreaths once used to crown the victors in contests **3** [*pl.*] fame; honor **4** any of various trees and shrubs resembling the true laurel

**la·va** (lä'və, lav'ə) *n.* ⟦It < L *labi*, to slide⟧ **1** melted rock issuing from a volcano **2** such rock when solidified by cooling

**La·val** (lə val') city in SW Quebec, Canada, near Montreal: pop. 330,000

**lav·a·liere** or **lav·a·lier** (lav'ə lir', lävə-) *n.* ⟦< Fr⟧ an ornament on a chain, worn around the neck

**lav·a·to·ry** (lav'ə tôr'ē) *n., pl.* **-ries** ⟦< L *lavare*, to wash⟧ a room with a washbowl and a toilet

**lave** (lāv) *vt., vi.* **laved, lav'ing** ⟦< L *lavare*⟧ [Old Poet.] to wash or bathe

**lav·en·der** (lav'ən dər) *n.* ⟦< ML *lavandria*⟧ **1** a fragrant European plant of the mint family with spikes of pale-purplish flowers **2** its dried flowers and leaves, used to perfume clothes, etc. **3** a pale purple —*adj.* pale-purple

**lav·ish** (lav'ish) *adj.* ⟦< OFr *lavasse*, downpour⟧ **1** very generous; prodigal **2** very abundant —*vt.* to give or spend generously —**lav'ish·ly** *adv.*

**law** (lô) *n.* ⟦OE *lagu*⟧ **1** *a*) all the rules of conduct established by the authority or custom of a nation, etc. *b*) any one of such rules **2** obedience to such rules **3** the study of such rules; jurisprudence **4** the seeking of justice in courts under such rules **5** the profession of lawyers, judges, etc. **6** *a*) a sequence of natural events occurring with unvarying uniformity under the same conditions *b*) the stating of such a sequence **7** any rule expected to be observed [the *laws* of health] —**the Law 1** the Mosaic law, or the part of the Jewish Scriptures containing it **2** [**the l-**] [Inf.] a policeman or the police

**law'-a·bid'ing** *adj.* obeying the law

**law'break'er** *n.* a person who violates the law —**law'break'ing** *adj., n.*

**law'ful** *adj.* **1** in conformity with the law **2** recognized by law [*lawful* debts] —**law'ful·ly** *adv.*

**law'giv'er** *n.* a lawmaker; legislator

**law'less** *adj.* **1** not regulated by the authority of law **2** not in conformity with law; illegal **3** not obeying the law; unruly —**law'less·ness** *n.*

**law'mak'er** *n.* one who makes or helps to make laws; esp., a legislator

**lawn**[1] (lôn) *n.* ⟦< OFr *launde*, heath⟧ land covered with grass kept closely mowed, esp. around a house

**lawn**[2] (lôn) *n.* ⟦after *Laon*, city in France⟧ a fine, sheer cloth of linen or cotton

**lawn bowling** a bowling game played on a smooth lawn with wooden balls

**lawn mower** a machine for cutting the grass of a lawn

**Law·rence** (lôr'əns), **D(avid) H(erbert)** 1885-1930; Eng. novelist & poet

**law'suit'** *n.* a suit between private parties in a law court

**law·yer** (lô'yər) *n.* one whose profession is advising others in matters of law or representing them in lawsuits

**lax** (laks) *adj.* ⟦< L *laxus*⟧ **1** loose; slack; not tight **2** not strict or exact —**lax'ly** *adv.*

**lax·a·tive** (lak'sə tiv) *adj.* [see prec.] making the bowels loose and relieving constipation —*n.* any laxative medicine

**lax·i·ty** (lak'si tē) *n.* lax quality or condition

**lay**[1] (lā) *vt.* **laid, lay'ing** ⟦< OE *lecgan*⟧ **1** to cause to fall with force; knock down **2** to place or put in a resting position: often with *on* or *in* **3** to put down (bricks, carpeting, etc.) in the correct posi-

tion or way **4** to place; put; set [to *lay* emphasis on accuracy] **5** to produce (an egg) **6** to allay, suppress, etc. **7** to bet (a specified sum, etc.) **8** to devise [to *lay* plans] **9** to present or assert [to *lay* claim to property] —*n.* the way or position in which something is situated [the *lay* of the land] —**lay aside** to put away for future use; save: also **lay away** or **lay by** —**lay in** to get and store away —**lay into** [Slang] to attack with blows or words —**lay off 1** to discharge (an employee), esp. temporarily **2** [Slang] to cease —**lay open 1** to cut open **2** to expose —**lay out 1** to spend **2** to arrange according to a plan **3** to spread out (clothes, etc.) ready for wear, etc. —**lay over** to stop a while in a place before going on —**lay up 1** to store for future use **2** to confine to a sickbed

**lay**[2] (lā) *vi. pt. of* LIE[1]

**lay**[3] (lā) *adj.* ⟦< Gr *laos*, the people⟧ **1** of a layman **2** not belonging to a given profession

**lay**[4] (lā) *n.* ⟦ME & OFr *lai*⟧ **1** a short poem, esp. a narrative poem, orig. for singing **2** [Obs.] a song

**lay'a·way'** *n.* a method of buying by making a deposit on something which is delivered only after full payment

**lay'er** *n.* **1** a person or thing that lays **2** a single thickness, fold, etc.

**lay·ette** (lā et') *n.* ⟦< MDu *lade*, chest⟧ a complete outfit of clothes, bedding, etc. for a newborn baby

**lay·man** (lā'mən) *n., pl.* **-men** (-mən) a person not a clergyman or one not belonging to a given profession: also **lay'per'son** —**lay'wom'an,** *pl.* **-wom'en, fem.n.**

**lay'off'** *n.* temporary unemployment, or the period of this

**lay'out'** *n.* **1** the manner in which anything is laid out; specif., the makeup of a newspaper, advertisement, etc. **2** the thing laid out

**lay'o'ver** *n.* a stop during a journey

**Laz·a·rus** (laz'ə rəs) *n.* Bible a man raised from the dead by Jesus

**laze** (lāz) *vi., vt.* **lazed, laz'ing** to idle or loaf

**la·zy** (lā'zē) *adj.* **-zi·er, -zi·est** ⟦prob. < medieval LowG or MDu⟧ **1** not eager or willing to work or exert oneself **2** sluggish —*vi., vt.* **-zied, -zy·ing** LAZE —**la'zi·ly** *adv.* —**la'zi·ness** *n.*

**la'zy·bones'** *n.* [Inf.] a lazy person

**Lazy Su·san** (sō̄'zən) a rotating tray for food

**lb** *symbol* ⟦abbrev. for LIBRA⟧ pound; pounds: also, for the plural, **lbs**

**l.c.** *abbrev.* ⟦L *loco citato*⟧ in the place cited

**LCD** *n.* ⟦l(iquid-)c(rystal) d(isplay)⟧ a device for alphanumeric displays, as on digital watches, using a crystalline liquid

**LD** *abbrev.* **1** learning disability **2** learning-disabled

**lea** (lē) *n.* ⟦OE *leah*⟧ [Old Poet.] a meadow

**leach** (lēch) *vt.* ⟦prob. < OE *leccan*, to water⟧ **1** to wash (some material) with a filtering liquid **2** to extract (a soluble substance) from some material —*vi.* to dissolve and be washed away

**lead**[1] (lēd) *vt.* **led, lead'ing** ⟦OE *lædan*⟧ **1** to direct, as by going before or along with, by physical contact, pulling a rope, etc.; guide **2** to guide by influence **3** to be the head of (an expedition, orchestra, etc.) **4** to be at the head of [to *lead* one's class] **5** to be ahead of in a contest **6** to live; spend [to *lead* a hard life] —*vi.* **1** to show the way, as by going before **2** to tend in a certain direction: with *to, from*, etc. **3** to bring as a result: with *to* [hate *led* to war] **4** to be or go first —*n.* **1** the role or example of a leader **2** first or front place **3** the amount or distance ahead [to hold a safe *lead*] **4** anything that leads, as a clue **5** the leading role in a play, etc. **6** the right of playing first in cards or the card played **7** the most important news story, as in a newspaper or telecast —**lead off** to begin —**lead on** to lure —**lead up to** to prepare the way for

**lead**[2] (led) *n.* ⟦OE⟧ **1** a heavy, soft, bluish-gray metallic chemical element **2** a weight for measuring depth at sea **3** bullets **4** a stick of graphite, used in pencils —*adj.* of or containing lead —*vt.* to cover, line, or weight with lead

**lead·ed** (led′əd) *adj.* containing a lead compound: said of gasoline

**lead·en** (led′'n) *adj.* **1** of lead **2** heavy **3** sluggish **4** gloomy **5** gray

**lead·er** (lēd′ər) *n.* one that leads; guiding head —**lead′er·ship′** *n.*

**lead·ing** (lēd′iŋ) *adj.* **1** that leads; guiding **2** principal; chief

**leading question** a question put in such a way as to suggest the answer sought

**lead time** (lēd) the period of time between the decision to make a product and the start of production

**leaf** (lēf) *n., pl.* **leaves** ⟦OE⟧ **1** any of the flat, thin parts, usually green, growing from the stem of a plant **2** a sheet of paper **3** a very thin sheet of metal **4** a hinged or removable section of a table top —*vi.* **1** to bear leaves **2** to turn the pages of a book: with *through* —**leaf′less** *adj.*

**leaf′let** (-lit) *n.* **1** a small or young leaf **2** a separate sheet of printed matter, often folded

**leaf′stalk′** *n.* the part of a leaf supporting the blade and attached to the stem

**leaf′y** *adj.* **-i·er, -i·est** having many or broad leaves *[a leafy vegetable]*

**league**[1] (lēg) *n.* ⟦< L *ligare*, bind⟧ **1** an association of nations, groups, etc. for promoting common interests **2** *Sports* a group of teams organized to play one another —*vt., vi.* **leagued, leagu′ing** to form into a league

**league**[2] (lēg) *n.* ⟦ult. < OE *leowe*, mile⟧ a measure of distance, about three miles

**leak** (lēk) *vi.* ⟦< ON *leka*, to drip⟧ **1** to let a fluid out or in accidentally **2** to pass in or out of a container thus **3** to become known gradually, by accident, etc. —*vt.* to allow to leak —*n.* **1** an accidental crack, etc. that lets something out or in **2** any accidental means of escape **3** leakage **4** a disclosure of confidential information —**leak′y, -i·er, -i·est,** *adj.*

**leak′age** *n.* **1** a leaking **2** that which leaks or the amount that leaks

**lean**[1] (lēn) *vi.* **leaned** or [Chiefly Brit.] **leant** (lent), **lean′ing** ⟦OE *hlinian*⟧ **1** to bend or slant from an upright position **2** to bend the body so as to rest part of one's weight on something **3** to rely (*on* or *upon*) **4** to tend (*toward* or *to*) —*vt.* to cause to lean —**lean′er** *n.*

**lean**[2] (lēn) *adj.* ⟦OE *hlæne*⟧ **1** with little flesh or fat; thin; spare **2** meager —**lean′ness** *n.*

**lean′ing** *n.* a tendency; inclination

**lean′-to′** *n., pl.* **-tos′** a structure whose sloping roof abuts another building, a wall, etc.

**leap** (lēp) *vi.* **leapt** (lept, lēpt) or **lept** or **leaped, leap′ing** ⟦OE *hleapan*⟧ **1** to jump; spring; bound **2** to accept eagerly something offered: with *at* —*vt.* **1** to pass over by a jump **2** to cause to leap —*n.* **1** a jump; spring **2** the distance covered in a jump **3** a sudden transition —**leap′er** *n.*

**leap′frog′** *n.* a game in which each player in turn leaps over the bent backs of the other players —*vt., vi.* **-frogged′, -frog′ging** to leap or jump in or as in this way; skip (*over*)

**leap year** every fourth year, containing an extra day in February

**learn** (lurn) *vt., vi.* **learned** (lurnd) or [Chiefly Brit.] **learnt** (lurnt), **learn′ing** ⟦OE *leornian*⟧ **1** to get knowledge of (a subject) or skill in (an art, trade, etc.) by study, experience, etc. **2** to come to

know; hear (*of* or *about*) **3** to memorize —**learn′er** *n.*

**learn·ed** (lurn′id; *for 2* lurnd) *adj.* **1** having or showing much learning **2** acquired by study, experience, etc.

**learn′ing** *n.* **1** the acquiring of knowledge or skill **2** acquired knowledge or skill

**learning disability** any of several conditions, believed to involve the nervous system, that interfere with mastering a skill such as reading or writing —**learn′ing-dis·a′bled** *adj.*

**lease** (lēs) *n.* ⟦< L *laxus*, loose⟧ a contract by which a landlord rents lands, buildings, etc. to a tenant for a specified time —*vt.* **leased, leas′ing** to give or get by a lease —**leas′er** *n.*

**lease′hold′** *n.* **1** the act of holding by lease **2** land, buildings, etc. held by lease

**leash** (lēsh) *n.* ⟦< L *laxus*, loose⟧ a cord, strap, etc. by which a dog or the like is held in check —*vt.* to check or control as by a leash

**least** (lēst) *adj.* ⟦OE *læst*⟧ **1** *alt. superl. of* LITTLE **2** smallest or slightest in size, degree, etc. —*adv.* **1** *superl. of* LITTLE **2** in the smallest degree —*n.* the smallest in amount, importance, etc. —**at (the) least 1** at the lowest **2** at any rate —**not in the least** not at all

**least′wise′** *adv.* [Inf.] at least; anyway: also [Chiefly Dial.] **least′ways′**

**leath·er** (leth′ər) *n.* ⟦< OE *lether-*⟧ animal skin prepared for use by removing the hair and tanning —*adj.* of leather

**leath′er·neck′** *n.* ⟦< former leather-lined uniform collar⟧ [Slang] a U.S. Marine

**leath′er·y** *adj.* like leather; tough and flexible —**leath′er·i·ness** *n.*

**leave**[1] (lēv) *vt.* **left, leav′ing** ⟦OE *læfan*, let remain⟧ **1** to allow to remain *[leave it open]* **2** to have remaining behind or after one **3** to bequeath **4** to go away from **5** to abandon **6** [Chiefly Dial.] to let *[leave us go]* —*vi.* to go away or set out —**leave off** to stop —**leave out** to omit —**leav′er** *n.*

**leave**[2] (lēv) *n.* ⟦OE *leaf*⟧ **1** permission **2** *a)* permission to be absent from duty *b)* the period for which this is granted —**take leave of** to say goodbye to —**take one's leave** to depart

**leave**[3] (lēv) *vi.* **leaved, leav′ing** to bear leaves; leaf

**leav·en** (lev′ən) *n.* ⟦< L *levare*, raise⟧ **1** LEAVENING (sense 1) **2** LEAVENING (sense 2) —*vt.* **1** to make (dough) rise **2** to spread through, causing gradual change

**leav′en·ing** *n.* **1** a substance, as baking powder or yeast, used to make dough rise **2** a tempering or modifying quality or thing **3** a causing to be leavened

**Leav·en·worth** (lev′ən wurth′) city in NE Kansas: pop 38,000: site of a federal prison

**leave of absence** permission to be absent from work or duty, esp. for a long time; also, the period for which this is granted

**leaves** (lēvz) *n. pl. of* LEAF

**leave′-tak′ing** *n.* a parting; farewell

**leav·ings** (lēv′iŋz) *pl.n.* leftovers, remnants, refuse, etc.

**Leb·a·non** (leb′ə nän′) country in SW Asia, on the Mediterranean: 4,036 sq. mi.; pop. 2,760,000 —**Leb′a·nese′** (-nēz′), *pl.* **-nese′,** *adj., n.*

**lech·er** (lech′ər) *n.* ⟦OFr *lechier*, live debauchedly⟧ a lewd, grossly sensual man —**lech′er·ous** *adj.* **lech′er·y** *n.*

**lec·i·thin** (les′i thin) *n.* ⟦< Gr *lekithos*, egg yolk⟧ a nitrogenous, fatty compound found in animal and plant cells: used in medicine, foods, etc.

**lec·tern** (lek′tərn) *n.* 〚< L *legere*, to read〛 a reading stand

**lec·ture** (lek′chər) *n.* 〚< L *legere*, read〛 **1** an informative talk to a class, etc. **2** a lengthy scolding —*vt.*, *vi.* **-tured, -tur·ing 1** to give a lecture (to) **2** to scold —**lec′tur·er** *n.*

**led** (led) *vt.*, *vi. pt. & pp. of* LEAD[1]

**LED** (el′ē′dē′) *n.* 〚*l(ight-)e(mit-ting) d(iode)*〛 a semiconductor diode that emits light when voltage is applied: used in lamps and digital watches

**ledge** (lej) *n.* 〚ME *legge*〛 **1** a shelf or shelflike projection **2** a projecting ridge of rocks

**ledg·er** (lej′ər) *n.* 〚ME *legger*〛 a book of final entry, in which a record of debits and credits is kept

**lee** (lē) *n.* 〚OE *hleo*, shelter〛 **1** shelter **2** *Naut.* the side or direction away from the wind —*adj.* of or on the side away from the wind

**Lee** (lē), **Rob·ert E(dward)** (räb′ərt) 1807-70; commander in chief of the Confederate army

**leech** (lēch) *n.* 〚OE *læce*〛 **1** a bloodsucking worm living in water and used, esp. formerly, to bleed patients **2** one who clings to another for personal advantage —*vi.* to cling (*onto*) thus

**leek** (lēk) *n.* 〚OE *leac*〛 a vegetable that resembles a thick green onion

**leer** (lir) *n.* 〚OE *hleor*〛 a sly, sidelong look showing lust, malicious triumph, etc. —*vi.* to look with a leer —**leer′ing·ly** *adv.*

**leer′y** *adj.* **-i·er, -i·est** wary; suspicious

**lees** (lēz) *pl.n.* 〚< ML *lia*〛 dregs or sediment, as of wine

**lee·ward** (lē′wərd′; *naut.* lōō′ərd) *adj.* away from the wind —*n.* the side or direction away from the wind —*adv.* toward the lee

**Lee·ward Islands** (lē′wərd) N group of islands in the Lesser Antilles of the West Indies

**lee·way** (lē′wā′) *n.* **1** the leeward drift of a ship or aircraft from its course **2** [Inf.] *a*) margin of time, money, etc. *b*) room for freedom of action

**left**[1] (left) *adj.* 〚< OE *lyft*, weak〛 **1** of or on the side that is toward the west when one faces north **2** closer to the left side of one who is facing the thing mentioned —*n.* **1** the left side **2** [*often* L-] *Politics* a liberal or radical position, party, etc.: often with *the* —*adv.* on or toward the left hand or side

**left**[2] (left) *vt.*, *vi. pt. & pp. of* LEAVE[1]

**left′-hand** *adj.* **1** on or toward the left **2** of, for, or with the left hand

**left′-hand′ed** *adj.* **1** using the left hand more skillfully than the right **2** done with or made for use with the left hand **3** ambiguous or backhanded [*a left-handed* compliment] —*adv.* **1** with the left hand [to write *left-handed*] **2** in such a way that the bat, club, etc. swings rightward

**left′ist** *n.*, *adj.* liberal or radical

**left′o·ver** *n.* **1** something remaining unused, etc. **2** [*usually pl.*] food left from a previous meal —*adj.* remaining unused, eaten, etc.

**left wing** the more liberal or radical section of a political party, group, etc. —**left′-wing′** *adj.* —**left′-wing′er** *n.*

**left′y** *n.*, *pl.* **-ies** [Slang] a left-handed person

**leg** (leg) *n.* 〚ON *leggr*〛 **1** one of the parts of the body by means of which humans and animals stand and walk **2** the part of a garment covering the leg **3** anything like a leg in shape or use **4** a stage, as of a trip —*vi.* **legged, leg′ging** [Inf.] to walk or run: chiefly in the phrase **leg it**

**leg·a·cy** (leg′ə sē) *n.*, *pl.* **-cies** 〚ult. < L *lex*, law〛 **1** money or property left to someone by a will **2** anything handed down as from an ancestor

**le·gal** (lē′gəl) *adj.* 〚< L *lex*, law〛 **1** of or based

upon law **2** permitted by law **3** of or for lawyers —**le′gal·ly** *adv.*

**le·gal·ese** (-ēz′) *n.* the special language of legal forms, etc., often considered incomprehensible

**legal holiday** a holiday set by law

**le·gal·ism′** *n.* strict or too strict adherence to the law —**le′gal·is′tic** *adj.*

**le·gal·i·ty** (li gal′i tē) *n.*, *pl.* **-ties** quality, condition, or instance of being legal or lawful

**le·gal·ize** (lē′gəl īz′) *vt.* **-ized′, -iz′ing** to make legal or lawful —**le′gal·i·za′tion** *n.*

**legal pad** a pad of lined writing paper, 8 ½ by 13 or 14 inches

**legal tender** money acceptable by law in payment of an obligation

**leg·ate** (leg′it) *n.* 〚< L *lex*, law〛 an envoy or ambassador

**leg·a·tee** (leg′ə tē′) *n.* one to whom a legacy is bequeathed

**le·ga·tion** (li gā′shən) *n.* **1** a diplomatic minister and staff collectively **2** the headquarters of such a group

**le·ga·to** (li gät′ō) *adj.*, *adv.* 〚< L *ligare*, to tie〛 *Music* in a smooth, even style, with no breaks between notes: also written *legato*

**leg·end** (lej′ənd) *n.* 〚< L *legere*, read〛 **1** a story or body of stories handed down for generations and popularly believed to have a historical basis **2** a notable person or the stories told about his or her exploits **3** an inscription on a coin, etc. **4** a title, key, etc. accompanying an illustration or map

**leg·end·ar·y** (lej′ən der′ē) *adj.* **1** of, based on, or presented in legends **2** famous or remarkable

**leg·er·de·main** (lej′ər di mān′) *n.* 〚< Fr *leger de main*, light of hand〛 **1** sleight of hand **2** trickery

**-leg·ged** (leg′id, legd) *combining form* having (a specified number or kind of) legs [*short-legged*]

**leg·ging** (leg′in, -in) *n.* **1** a covering for the lower leg **2** [*pl.*] a child's outer garment with legs **3** [*pl.*] a garment like tights but without feet

**leg·gy** (leg′ē) *adj.* **-gi·er, -gi·est 1** having long legs **2** [Inf.] having long, spindly stems

**leg·horn** (leg′hôrn′, -ərn) *n.* 〚after *Leghorn*, It seaport〛 [*sometimes* L-] any of a breed of small chicken

**leg·i·ble** (lej′ə bəl) *adj.* 〚< L *legere*, read〛 that can be read —**leg′i·bil′i·ty** *n.* —**leg′i·bly** *adv.*

**le·gion** (lē′jən) *n.* 〚< L *legere*, choose〛 **1** a large group of soldiers; army **2** a large number; multitude —**le′gion·naire′** (-jə ner′) *n.*

**leg·is·late** (lej′is lāt′) *vi.* **-lat′ed, -lat′ing** 〚see fol.〛 to make or pass a law or laws —*vt.* to cause to be, go, etc. by making laws —**leg′is·la′tor** *n.*

**leg·is·la·tion** *n.* 〚< L *lex*, law + *latio*, a bringing〛 **1** the making of laws **2** the law or laws made

**leg·is·la·tive** *adj.* **1** of legislation or a legislature **2** having the power to make laws

**leg·is·la·ture** (-chər) *n.* a body of persons given the power to make laws

**le·git·i·mate** (lə jit′ə mət; *for v.*, -māt′) *adj.* 〚< L *lex*, law〛 **1** born of parents married to each other **2** lawful **3** *a*) reasonable *b*) justifiable **4** conforming to accepted rules, standards, etc. **5** of stage plays, as distinguished from films, vaudeville, etc. —*vt.* **-mat′ed, -mat′ing** LEGITIMIZE —**le·git′i·ma·cy** (-mə sē) *n.* —**le·git′i·mate·ly** *adv.*

**le·git·i·ma·tize′** (-mə tīz′) *vt.* **-tized′, -tiz′ing** LEGITIMIZE

**le·git′i·mize′** (-mīz′) *vt.* **-mized′, -miz′ing** to make or declare legitimate —**le·git′i·mi·za′tion** *n.*

**leg·man** (leg′man′) *n.*, *pl.* **-men′** (-mən′) **1** a news reporter who transmits information from the scene **2** an assistant who does routine tasks outside the office

**leg′room′** *n.* adequate space for the legs while seated, as in a car

**leg·ume** (leg′yōōm′, li gyōōm′) *n.* 〚< L *legere*, gather〛 **1** any of an order of plants having seeds growing in pods, including peas, beans, etc. **2** the

LECTERN

pod or seed of such a plant —**le·gu·mi·nous** (lə gyōō′mə nəs) *adj.*

**leg′work′** *n.* [Inf.] necessary, routine work, typically involving walking, as part of a job

**lei** (lā, lā′ē) *n., pl.* **leis** ⟦Haw⟧ in Hawaii, a garland of flowers, generally worn about the neck

**Leip·zig** (līp′sig) city in E Germany: pop. 494,000

**lei·sure** (lē′zhər, lezh′ər) *n.* ⟦< L *licere*, be permitted⟧ free time during which one may indulge in rest, recreation, etc. —*adj.* **1** free and unoccupied **2** done or used during one's leisure

**lei′sure·ly** *adj.* without haste; slow —*adv.* in an unhurried manner

**leit·mo·tif** or **leit·mo·tiv** (līt′mō tēf′) *n.* ⟦Ger *leitmotiv* < *leiten*, to guide + *motiv*, motive⟧ a dominant theme, as in a musical composition

**lem·ming** (lem′iŋ) *n.* ⟦< ON *læmingi*⟧ a small arctic rodent with a short tail

**lem·on** (lem′ən) *n.* ⟦< Pers *līmūn*⟧ **1** a small, sour, yellow citrus fruit **2** the spiny, semitropical tree that it grows on **3** [Slang] something that is defective —*adj.* yellow

**lem′on·ade′** (-ād′) *n.* a drink made of lemon juice, sugar, and water

**le·mur** (lē′mər) *n.* ⟦< L *lemures*, ghosts⟧ a small, tree-dwelling primate with large eyes

**lend** (lend) *vt.* lent, lend′ing ⟦< OE *læn*, a loan⟧ **1** to let another use or have (a thing) temporarily **2** to let out (money) at interest **3** to give; impart —*vi.* to make loans —**lend itself** (or **oneself**) **to** to be useful for or adapted to —**lend′er** *n.*

**length** (leŋkth) *n.* ⟦< OE *lang*, long⟧ **1** the distance from end to end of a thing **2** extent in space or time **3** a long stretch or extent **4** a piece of a certain length —**at length 1** finally **2** for a long time or in great detail

**length′en** *vt., vi.* to make or become longer

**length′wise′** *adv., adj.* in the direction of the length: also **length′ways′**

**length′y** *adj.* -i·er, -i·est long; esp., too long — **length′i·ly** *adv.*

**le·ni·ent** (lēn′yənt, lē′nē ənt) *adj.* ⟦< L *lenis*, soft⟧ not harsh or severe; merciful —**le′ni·en·cy** or **le′ni·ence** *n.* —**le′ni·ent·ly** *adv.*

**Len·in** (len′in), V(ladimir) I(lyich) 1870-1924; Russ. leader of the Communist revolution of 1917

**Len′in·grad′** (-grad′) *name* (1924-91) *for* ST. PETERSBURG (Russia)

**len·i·tive** (len′ə tiv) *adj.* ⟦< L *lenire*, to soften⟧ lessening pain or distress

**lens** (lenz) *n.* ⟦L, lentil: < its shape⟧ **1** a curved piece of glass, plastic, etc. for bringing together or spreading rays of light passing through it: used in optical instruments to form an image **2** a similar transparent part of the eye: it focuses light rays upon the retina **3** any device used to focus microwaves, sound waves, etc.

**lent** (lent) *vt., vi. pt. & pp. of* LEND

**Lent** (lent) *n.* ⟦OE *lengten*, the spring⟧ *Christianity* the forty weekdays of fasting and penitence from Ash Wednesday to Easter —**Lent′en** or **lent′en** *adj.*

**len·til** (lent′'l) *n.* ⟦< L *lens*⟧ **1** a kind of legume, with small, edible seeds **2** this seed

**Le·o** (lē′ō) *n.* ⟦L, lion⟧ the fifth sign of the zodiac

**le·o·nine** (lē′ə nīn′) *adj.* ⟦< L *leo*, lion⟧ of or like a lion

**leop·ard** (lep′ərd) *n.* ⟦< Gr *leōn*, lion + *pardos*, panther⟧ any of various large, ferocious cats, including the jaguar; esp., one with a black-spotted, tawny coat, found in Africa and Asia

**le·o·tard** (lē′ə tärd′) *n.* ⟦after J. *Léotard*, 19th-c. Fr aerial performer⟧ a tightfitting garment for acrobats, dancers, etc.

**lep·er** (lep′ər) *n.* ⟦< Gr *lepros*, scaly⟧ a person having leprosy

**lep·re·chaun** (lep′rə kôn′, -kän′) *n.* ⟦< Old Ir *lu*, little + *corp*, body⟧ *Ir. Folklore* a fairy who can reveal hidden treasure

**lep·ro·sy** (lep′rə sē) *n.* ⟦see LEPER⟧ a progressive infectious disease of the skin, flesh, nerves, etc., characterized by ulcers, white scaly scabs, deformities, etc. —**lep′rous** *adj.*

**lept** (lept) *vi., vt. alt. pt. of* LEAP

**lep·ton** (lep′tän′) *n.* ⟦< Gr *leptos*, thin⟧ any of certain atomic particles, as the electron or neutrino

**les·bi·an** (lez′bē ən) *n.* ⟦after *Lesbos*, Gr. island home of the poetess Sappho⟧ a homosexual woman —**les′bi·an·ism′** *n.*

**lèse-ma·jest·é** (lez′ma′zhes tā′, -maj′is tē) *n.* ⟦Fr < L *laesa majestas*, injured majesty⟧ **1** a crime or offense against the sovereign **2** any lack of proper respect as toward one in authority

**le·sion** (lē′zhən) *n.* ⟦< L *laedere*, to harm⟧ an injury of an organ or tissue resulting in impairment of function

**Le·so·tho** (le sōō′tōō) country in SE Africa, surrounded by South Africa: 11,720 sq. mi.; pop. 1,578,000

**less** (les) *adj.* ⟦OE *læs(sa)*⟧ **1** *alt. compar. of* LITTLE **2** not so much **3** fewer —*adv.* **1** *compar. of* LITTLE **2** to a smaller extent —*n.* a smaller amount —*prep.* minus —**less and less** decreasingly

**-less** (lis, ləs) ⟦OE *leas*, free⟧ *suffix* **1** without **2** not able to **3** not able to be ___ed

**les·see** (les ē′) *n.* ⟦see LEASE⟧ one to whom a lease is given; tenant

**less′en** *vt., vi.* to make or become less; decrease

**less′er** *adj.* **1** *alt. compar. of* LITTLE **2** smaller, less, or less important

**les·son** (les′ən) *n.* ⟦< L *legere*, to read⟧ **1** an exercise for a student to learn **2** something learned for one's safety, etc. **3** [*pl.*] course of instruction **4** a selection from the Bible read as part of a religious service

**les·sor** (les′ôr′) *n.* ⟦see LEASE⟧ one who gives a lease; landlord

**lest** (lest) *conj.* ⟦< OE *thy læs the*, lit., by the less that⟧ for fear that

**let**[1] (let) *vt.* let, let′ting ⟦OE *lætan*, leave behind⟧ **1** to leave: now only in **let alone**, **let be 2** *a*) to rent *b*) to assign (a contract) **3** to cause to escape [to *let* blood] **4** to allow; permit Also used as an auxiliary in commands or suggestions [*let* us go] —*vi.* to be rented [a house to *let*] —**let down 1** to lower **2** to slow up **3** to disappoint —**let off 1** to give forth **2** to deal leniently with —**let on** [Inf.] **1** to indicate one's awareness **2** to pretend —**let out 1** to release **2** to rent out **3** to make a garment larger —**let up 1** to relax **2** to cease

**let**[2] (let) *n.* ⟦< OE *lettan*, make late⟧ *Law* an obstacle: in **without let or hindrance**

**-let** (lit, lət) ⟦Fr *-el* + *-et*, dim. suffixes⟧ *suffix* small [*piglet*]

**let′down′** *n.* **1** a slowing up **2** a disappointment

**le·thal** (lē′thəl) *adj.* ⟦< L *letum*, death⟧ causing death; fatal

**leth·ar·gy** (leth′ər jē) *n., pl.* -gies ⟦< Gr *lēthē*, oblivion + *argos*, idle⟧ **1** an abnormal drowsiness **2** sluggishness, apathy, etc. —**le·thar·gic** (li thär′jik) *adj.* —**le·thar′gi·cal·ly** *adv.*

**let's** (lets) *contr.* let us

**let·ter** (let′ər) *n.* ⟦< L *littera*⟧ **1** any character in an alphabet **2** a written or printed message, usually sent by mail **3** [*pl.*] *a*) literature *b*) learning; knowledge **4** the literal meaning —*vt.* to mark with letters —**let′ter·er** *n.*

**letter carrier** a postal employee who delivers mail

**let′ter·head′** *n.* the name, address, etc. as a heading on stationery

**let′ter·ing** *n.* the act of making or inscribing letters, or such letters

**let′ter·per′fect** *adj.* entirely correct

**let·tuce** (let′əs) *n.* ⟦< L *lac*, milk⟧ **1** a plant with crisp, green leaves **2** the leaves, much used for salads

**let·up** (let′up′) *n.* [Inf.] **1** a slackening **2** a stop or pause

**leu·ke·mi·a** (lōō kē′mē ə) *n.* ⟦see fol. & -EMIA⟧ a

disease characterized by an abnormal increase in the number of leukocytes: also sp. **leu·kae′mi·a**

**leu·ko·cyte** (lōō′kō sīt′, -kə-) *n.* [< Gr *leukos*, white + *kytos*, hollow] a colorless cell in the blood, etc. that destroys disease-causing organisms; white blood cell

**lev·ee** (lev′ē) *n.* [ult. < L *levare*, to raise] an embankment to prevent a river from flooding bordering land

**lev·el** (lev′əl) *n.* [< L *libra*, a balance] 1 an instrument for determining an even horizontal plane 2 a horizontal plane or line [sea *level*] 3 a horizontal area 4 normal position with reference to height [water seeks its *level*] 5 position in a scale of values [income *level*] —*adj.* 1 perfectly flat and even 2 not sloping 3 even in height (*with*) 4 equal in importance, advancement, quality, etc. 5 calm or steady —*vt.*, *vi.* **-eled** or **-elled**, **-el·ing** or **-el·ling** 1 to make or become level 2 to demolish 3 to aim (a gun, etc.) —**level with** [Slang] to be honest with —**lev′el·er** or **lev′el·ler** *n.*

**lev·el·head·ed** *adj.* having an even temper and sound judgment

**lev·er** (lev′ər, lē′vər) *n.* [< L *levare*, to raise] 1 a bar used as a pry 2 a means to an end 3 a device consisting of a bar turning about a fixed point, using force at a second point to lift a weight at a third

LEVER

**lev′er·age** (-ij) *n.* 1 the action or mechanical power of a lever 2 means of accomplishing something —*vt.* **-aged**, **-ag·ing** *Finance* to speculate in (a business venture) with borrowed funds

**le·vi·a·than** (lə vī′ə thən) *n.* [< Heb *liwyāthān*] 1 *Bible* a sea monster 2 anything huge

**Le·vi's** (lē′vīz) [after *Levi* Strauss, U.S. manufacturer] *trademark for* trousers of heavy denim — *pl.n.* such trousers: also written **Le′vis** or **le′vis**

**lev·i·ta·tion** (lev′ə tā′shən) *n.* [< L *levis*, light] the illusion of raising a body in the air with no support —**lev′i·tate′**, **-tat′ed**, **-tat′ing**, *vt.*, *vi.*

**Le·vit·i·cus** (lə vit′i kəs) *n.* the third book of the Pentateuch

**Lev·it·town** (lev′it toun′) city in SE New York: post-WWII planned community of mass-produced houses: pop. 53,000

**lev·i·ty** (lev′i tē) *n.*, *pl.* **-ties** [< L *levis*, light] gaiety, esp. improper gaiety; frivolity

**lev·y** (lev′ē) *n.*, *pl.* **lev′ies** [< L *levare*, to raise] 1 an imposing and collecting of a tax, fine, etc. 2 the amount imposed 3 compulsory enlistment for military service 4 a group so enlisted —*vt.* **-ied**, **-y·ing** 1 to impose (a tax, fine, etc.) 2 to enlist (troops) 3 to wage (war)

**lewd** (lōōd) *adj.* [OE *lǣwede*, unlearned] indecent; lustful; obscene —**lewd′ly** *adv.* —**lewd′ness** *n.*

**lex·i·cog·ra·phy** (lek′sə käg′rə fē) *n.* [see fol. & -GRAPHY] the act, art, or work of writing a dictionary —**lex′i·cog′ra·pher** *n.*

**lex·i·con** (lek′si kän′) *n.* [< Gr *lexis*, word] 1 a dictionary 2 a special vocabulary —**lex′i·cal** *adj.*

**Lex·ing·ton** (lek′siŋ tən) city in NC Kentucky: with the county in which it is located, pop. 225,000

**lg** *abbrev.* large

**Li** *Chem. symbol for* lithium

**li·a·bil·i·ty** (lī′ə bil′ə tē) *n.*, *pl.* **-ties** 1 the state of being liable 2 anything for which a person is liable 3 a debt of a person or business 4 something that works to one's disadvantage

**li·a·ble** (lī′ə bəl) *adj.* [< L *ligare*, bind] 1 legally bound or responsible 2 subject to [*liable* to heart attacks] 3 likely *to* [*liable* to get hurt]

**li·ai·son** (lē ā′zän′, -zən) *n.* [< L *ligare*, bind] 1 a linking up, as of units of a military force 2 an illicit love affair

**li·ar** (lī′ər) *n.* one who tells lies

**lib** (lib) *n.* [Inf.] *short for* LIBERATION

**li·ba·tion** (lī bā′shən) *n.* [< L *libare*, pour out] 1

the ritual of pouring out wine or oil in honor of a god 2 this liquid 3 an alcoholic drink

**li·bel** (lī′bəl) *n.* [< L *liber*, book] 1 any written or printed matter tending to injure a person's reputation unjustly 2 the act or crime of publishing such a thing —*vt.* **-beled** or **-belled**, **-bel·ing** or **-bel·ling** to make a libel against —**li′bel·er** or **li′bel·ler** *n.* —**li′bel·ous** or **li′bel·lous** *adj.*

**lib·er·al** (lib′ər əl) *adj.* [< L *liber*, free] 1 generous 2 ample; abundant 3 not literal or strict 4 tolerant; broad-minded 5 favoring reform or progress —*n.* one who favors reform or progress —**lib′er·al·ism′** *n.* —**lib′er·al·ly** *adv.* —**lib′er·al·ness** *n.*

**liberal arts** literature, languages, history, etc. as courses or a course of study

**lib′er·al′i·ty** (-al′i tē) *n.*, *pl.* **-ties** 1 generosity 2 broad-mindedness

**lib′er·al·ize** (-əl īz′) *vt.*, *vi.* **-ized′**, **-iz′ing** to make or become liberal —**lib′er·al·i·za′tion** *n.*

**lib·er·ate** (lib′ər āt′) *vt.* **-at′ed**, **-at′ing** [< L *liber*, free] to release from slavery, oppression, enemy occupation, etc. —**lib′er·a′tion** *n.* —**lib′er·a′tor** *n.*

**Li·be·ri·a** (lī bir′ē ə) country on the W coast of Africa: founded (1821) as settlement for freed U.S. slaves: 38,250 sq. mi.; pop. 2,102,000 —**Li·ber′i·an** *adj.*, *n.*

**lib·er·tar·i·an** (lib′ər ter′ē ən) *n.* an advocate of full individual freedom of thought and action

**lib·er·tine** (lib′ər tēn′) *n.* [< L *liber*, free] one who is sexually promiscuous —*adj.* licentious

**lib·er·ty** (lib′ər tē) *n.*, *pl.* **-ties** [< L *liber*, free] 1 freedom from slavery, captivity, etc. 2 a particular right, freedom, etc. 3 a too free or impertinent action or attitude 4 permission given to a sailor to go ashore See also CIVIL LIBERTIES —**at liberty** 1 not confined 2 permitted (to do or say something) 3 not busy or in use —**take liberties** 1 to be too familiar or impertinent 2 to deal inaccurately (*with* facts, data, etc.)

**li·bid·i·nous** (li bid′'n əs) *adj.* [see fol.] lustful; lascivious

**li·bi·do** (li bē′dō) *n.* [< L, pleasure] 1 the sexual urge 2 *Psychoanalysis* psychic energy; specif., that comprising the positive, loving instincts

**Li·bra** (lē′brə) *n.* [L, balance, scales] the seventh sign of the zodiac

**li·brar·i·an** (lī brer′ē ən) *n.* one in charge of a library or trained in library science

**li·brar·y** (lī′brer′ē) *n.*, *pl.* **-ies** [< L *liber*, book] 1 a collection of books, etc. 2 a room or building for, or an institution in charge of, such a collection

**li·bret·to** (li bret′ō) *n.*, *pl.* **-tos** or **-ti** (-ē) [It < L *liber*, book] the words, or text, of an opera, oratorio, etc. —**li·bret′tist** *n.*

**Lib·y·a** (lib′ē ə) country in N Africa, on the Mediterranean: 679,358 sq. mi.; pop. 3,637,000 —**Lib′y·an** *adj.*, *n.*

**lice** (līs) *n. pl. of* LOUSE

**li·cense** (lī′səns) *n.* [< L *licere*, be permitted] 1 formal or legal permission to do something specified 2 a document, etc. indicating such permission 3 freedom to deviate from rule, practice, etc. [poetic *license*] 4 excessive freedom, constituting an abuse of liberty Brit. sp. **li′cence** —*vt.* **-censed**, **-cens·ing** to permit formally

**li·cen·see** (lī′səns ē′) *n.* a person to whom a license is granted

**li·cen·ti·ate** (lī sen′shē it, -āt′) *n.* a person having a professional license

**li·cen·tious** (lī sen′shəs) *adj.* [see LICENSE] sexually unrestrained; lascivious —**li·cen′tious·ness** *n.*

**li·chen** (lī′kən) *n.* [< Gr *leichein*, to lick] a plant resembling moss but actually a combination of fungus and algae, growing in patches on rock, wood, soil, etc.

**lic·it** (lis′it) *adj.* [< L *licitus*, permitted] lawful —**lic′it·ly** *adv.*

**lick** (lik) *vt.* [OE *liccian*] 1 to pass the tongue over 2 to pass lightly over like a tongue 3 [Inf.] *a*) to thrash *b*) to vanquish —*vi.* to move lightly, as a

**flame** —*n.* **1** a licking with the tongue **2** a small quantity **3** *short for* SALT LICK **4** [Inf.] a sharp blow —**lick up** to consume as by licking

**lic·o·rice** (lik′ə rish) *n.* [< Gr *glykys*, sweet + *rhiza*, root] **1** a black flavoring extract made from the root of a European plant **2** candy flavored with this extract or in imitation of it

**lid** (lid) *n.* [OE *hlid*] **1** a movable cover, as for a box, pot, etc. **2** *short for* EYELID **3** [Inf.] a restraint

**lid·ded** (lid′id) *adj.* **1** having a lid **2** having (a specified kind of) eyelids [heavy-*lidded*]

**lie**[1] (lī) *vi.* **lay, lain, ly′ing** [OE *licgan*] **1** to be or put oneself in a reclining or horizontal position **2** to rest on a support in a horizontal position **3** to be in a specified condition **4** to be situated [Canada *lies* to the north] **5** to extend **6** to be or be found —*n.* the way in which something is situated; lay

**lie**[2] (lī) *vi.* **lied, ly′ing** [OE *leogan*] to make a statement that one knows is false —*vt.* to bring, put, accomplish, etc. by lying [to *lie* his way into office] —*n.* a false statement made with intent to deceive

**Lieb·frau·milch** (lēb′frou milk′) *n.* [Ger] a white wine

**Liech·ten·stein** (lik′tən stīn′) country between Switzerland & Austria: 62 sq. mi.; pop. 29,000

**lie detector** a polygraph used on persons suspected of lying

**lief** (lēf) *adv.* [< OE *leof*, dear] willingly; gladly: only in **would** (or **had**) **as lief**

**liege** (lēj) *adj.* [OFr] loyal; faithful —*n. Feudal Law* **1** a lord or sovereign **2** a subject or vassal

**li·en** (lēn, lē′ən) *n.* [Fr < L *ligare*, to bind] a legal claim on another's property as security for the payment of a debt

**lieu** (lōō) *n.* [< L *locus*] place: chiefly in **in lieu of**, instead of

**Lieut** *abbrev.* Lieutenant

**lieu·ten·ant** (lōō ten′ənt) *n.* [< Fr *lieu*, place + *tenant*, holding] **1** one who acts for a superior **2** *U.S. Mil.* an officer ranking below a captain: see FIRST LIEUTENANT, SECOND LIEUTENANT **3** *U.S. Navy* an officer ranking just above a lieutenant junior grade —**lieu·ten′an·cy** *n.*

**lieutenant colonel** *U.S. Mil.* an officer ranking just above a major

**lieutenant commander** *U.S. Navy* an officer ranking just above a lieutenant

**lieutenant general** *U.S. Mil.* an officer ranking just above a major general

**lieutenant governor** an elected official of a U.S. state who ranks below and substitutes for the governor

**lieutenant junior grade** *U.S. Navy* an officer ranking just above an ensign

**life** (līf) *n., pl.* **lives** [OE *lif*] **1** that property of plants and animals (ending at death) which makes it possible for them to take in food, get energy from it, grow, etc. **2** the state of having this property **3** a human being [100 *lives* were lost] **4** living things collectively [plant *life*] **5** the time a person or thing is alive or exists **6** one's manner of living [a *life* of ease] **7** the people and activities of a given time, place, etc. [military *life*] **8** *a)* one's animate existence *b)* a biography **9** the source of liveliness [the *life* of the party] **10** vigor; liveliness

**life belt** a life preserver in belt form

**life′blood′** *n.* **1** the blood necessary to life **2** a vital element

**life′boat′** *n.* one of the small boats carried by a ship for use in an emergency

**life′-form′** *n.* a particular type of organism, often one that is unusual or newly found

**life′guard′** *n.* a swimmer employed as at a beach to prevent drownings

**life insurance** insurance in which a stipulated sum is paid at the death of the insured

**life jacket** (or **vest**) a life preserver like a sleeveless jacket or vest

**life′less** *adj.* **1** without life; specif., *a)* inanimate *b)* dead **2** dull

**life′like′** *adj.* resembling real life or a real person or thing

**life′line′** *n.* **1** a rope or line for saving life, as one thrown to a person in the water **2** a very important commercial route

**life′long′** *adj.* lasting or not changing during one's whole life

LIFE JACKET

**life net** a strong net used as by firefighters to catch people jumping from a burning building

**life preserver** a buoyant device for saving a person from drowning by keeping the body afloat

**lif′er** *n.* [Slang] a person sentenced to prison for life

**life raft** a small, inflatable raft for emergency use at sea

**life′sav′er** *n.* **1** a lifeguard **2** [Inf.] a help in time of need

**life′-size′** *adj.* as big as the person or thing represented [a *life-size* portrait]: also **life′-sized′**

**life′style′** *n.* an individual's way of living

**life′-sup·port′** *adj. Med.* for providing support needed to maintain life [a *life-support* system]

**life′time′** *n.* **1** the period of time that someone lives or that a thing lasts **2** a very long time

**life′work′** *n.* the work to which a person's life is devoted

**lift** (lift) *vt.* [< ON *lopt*, air] **1** to bring up to a higher position; raise **2** to raise in rank, condition, etc.; exalt **3** to pay off (a mortgage, debt, etc.) **4** to end (a blockade, etc.) **5** [Slang] to steal —*vi.* **1** to exert strength in raising something **2** to rise; go up —*n.* **1** a lifting or rising **2** the distance something is lifted **3** lifting power or influence **4** elevation of mood **5** a ride in the direction one is going **6** help of any kind **7** *a)* [Brit.] ELEVATOR *b)* SKI LIFT

**lift′off′** *n.* **1** the initial vertical takeoff of a rocket, helicopter, etc. **2** the time this occurs

**lig·a·ment** (lig′ə mənt) *n.* [< L *ligare*, bind] a band of tissue connecting bones or holding organs in place

**lig·a·ture** (lig′ə chər) *n.* [< L *ligare*, bind] **1** a tying or binding together **2** a tie, bond, etc. **3** two or more letters united, as æ, th **4** *Surgery* a thread used to tie up an artery, etc.

**light**[1] (līt) *n.* [OE *leoht*] **1** *a)* the form of radiant energy acting on the retina of the eye to make sight possible *b)* ultraviolet or infrared radiation **2** brightness; illumination **3** h source of light, as the sun, a lamp, etc. **4** daylight **5** a thing used to ignite something **6** a window or windowpane **7** knowledge; enlightenment **8** public view [to bring new facts to *light*] **9** aspect [viewed in another *light*] —*adj.* **1** having light; bright **2** pale in color; fair —*adv.* palely [a *light* blue color] —*vt.* **light′ed** or **lit, light′ing 1** to ignite [to *light* a bonfire] **2** to cause to give off light **3** to furnish with light **4** to brighten; animate —*vi.* **1** to catch fire **2** to be lighted: usually with *up* —**in the light of** considering —**see the light** (**of day**) **1** to come into existence **2** to come to public view **3** to understand

**light**[2] (līt) *adj.* [OE *leoht*] **1** having little weight; not heavy, esp. for its size **2** less than usual in weight, amount, force, etc. [a *light* blow] **3** not serious or profound **4** easy to bear [a *light* tax] **5** easy to do [*light* work] **6** merry; happy **7** dizzy; giddy **8** containing fewer calories **9** moderate [a *light* meal] **10** moving with ease [*light* on one's feet] **11** producing small products [*light* industry] —*adv.* LIGHTLY —*vi.* **light′ed** or **lit, light′ing 1** to come to rest after traveling through the air **2** to come or happen (*on* or *upon*) —**light into** [Inf.]

to attack —**light out** [Inf.] to depart suddenly — **make light of** to treat as unimportant

**light·en**[1] *vt., vi.* **1** to make or become light or brighter **2** to shine; flash

**light·en**[2] *vt., vi.* **1** to make or become lighter in weight **2** to make or become more cheerful

**light·er**[1] *n.* a person or thing that starts something burning

**light·er**[2] *n.* [< MDu *licht*, LIGHT[2]] a large barge used to load or unload ships anchored in a harbor

**light'-fin·gered** *adj.* **1** skillful at stealing **2** likely to steal

**light'-foot·ed** *adj.* stepping lightly and gracefully

**light'head·ed** *adj.* **1** giddy; dizzy **2** flighty; frivolous

**light'heart·ed** *adj.* free from care; cheerful — **light'heart·ed·ly** *adv.* —**light'heart·ed·ness** *n.*

**light heavyweight** a boxer with a maximum weight of 175 lb.

**light'house'** *n.* a tower with a very bright light to guide ships at night

**light·ing** *n.* the act or manner of giving light, or illuminating

**light·ly** *adv.* **1** with little weight or pressure; gently **2** to a small degree or amount **3** nimbly; deftly **4** cheerfully **5** with indifference

**light meter** an instrument to measure intensity of light, used in photography

**light'-mind·ed** *adj.* silly; frivolous

**light'ness**[1] *n.* **1** the amount of light; brightness **2** paleness in color

**light'ness**[2] *n.* **1** a being light, not heavy **2** mildness, nimbleness, cheerfulness, etc.

**light'ning** (-niŋ) *n.* a flash of light in the sky caused by the discharge of atmospheric electricity

**lightning bug** FIREFLY

**lightning rod** a metal rod placed high on a building and grounded to divert lightning from the structure

**light opera** OPERETTA

**light'weight'** *n.* a boxer with a maximum weight of 135 lb. —*adj.* light in weight

**light'-year'** *n.* a unit of distance equal to the distance light travels in one year, *c.* 6 trillion miles

**lig·nite** (lig'nīt') *n.* [< L *lignum*, wood] a soft coal, brownish-black in color and retaining the texture of the original wood

**lik·a·ble** (līk'ə bəl) *adj.* pleasant, genial, etc.: also **like'a·ble** —**lik'a·ble·ness** or **lik·a·bil'i·ty** *n.*

**like**[1] (līk) *adj.* [OE *gelic*] having the same characteristics; similar; equal —*adv.* [Inf.] likely *[like* as not, he'll go*]* —*prep.* **1** similar to **2** similarly to *[to sing like* a bird*]* **3** characteristic of *[not like* her to cry*]* **4** in the mood for *[to feel like* sleeping*]* **5** indicative of *[it looks like* rain*]* **6** as for example *[fruit, like* pears and plums*]* —*conj.* [Inf.] **1** as *[it's just like* he said*]* **2** as if *[it looks like* he's late*]* —*n.* an equal or counterpart *[I've never met her like]* —**nothing like** not at all like —**something like** almost like —**the like** others of the same kind —**the like (or likes) of** [Inf.] any person or thing like

**like**[2] (līk) *vi.* **liked, lik'ing** [OE *lician*] to be inclined *[do* as you *like]* —*vt.* **1** to be pleased with; enjoy **2** to wish *[I'd like* to go*]* —*n.* [*pl.*] preferences or tastes —**lik'er** *n.*

**-like** (līk) *suffix* like, characteristic of *[homelike, bull-like]*

**like·li·hood** (līk'lē hood') *n.* a being likely to happen; probability

**like·ly** (līk'lē) *adj.* **-li·er, -li·est** [OE *geliclic*] **1** credible *[a likely* cause*]* **2** reasonably to be expected *[likely* to rain*]* **3** suitable *[a likely* place to swim*]* —*adv.* probably *[she'll likely* go*]*

**like'-mind·ed** *adj.* having the same ideas, plans, tastes, etc. —**like'-mind·ed·ness** *n.*

**lik·en** (līk'ən) *vt.* to compare

**like'ness** *n.* **1** a being like **2** (the same) form **3** a copy, portrait, etc.

**like'wise'** *adv.* [< *in like wise*] **1** in the same manner **2** also; too

**lik·ing** (līk'iŋ) *n.* **1** fondness; affection **2** preference; taste; pleasure

**li·lac** (lī'lək, -läk', -lak') *n.* [ult. < Pers *līlak*, bluish] **1** a shrub with large clusters of tiny, fragrant flowers **2** pale purple —*adj.* pale-purple

**Lil·li·pu·tian** (lil'ə pyōō'shən) *adj.* [after *Lilliput*, place in J. Swift's *Gulliver's Travels*] **1** tiny **2** petty

**lilt** (lilt) *n.* [ME *lilten*, to sound] a light, swingy rhythm or tune —**lilt'ing** *adj.*

**lil·y** (lil'ē) *n., pl.* **lil'ies** [< L *lilium*] **1** a plant grown from a bulb and having typically trumpet-shaped flowers **2** its flower **3** any similar plant, as the waterlily —*adj.* like a lily, as in whiteness, purity, etc.

**lil'y-liv'ered** *adj.* cowardly; timid

**lily of the valley** *pl.* **lilies of the valley** a low plant with a spike of white, bell-shaped flowers

**Li·ma** (lē'mə) capital of Peru: pop. 5,706,000

**li·ma bean** (lī'mə) [after *Lima*, Peru] **1** a bean with broad pods **2** its broad, flat, edible seed

**limb** (lim) *n.* [OE *lim*] **1** an arm, leg, or wing **2** a large branch of a tree —**out on a limb** [Inf.] in a precarious position —**limb'less** *adj.*

**lim·ber** (lim'bər) *adj.* [< ? prec.] **1** easily bent; flexible **2** able to bend the body easily; supple — *vt., vi.* to make or become limber

**lim·bo** (lim'bō) *n., pl.* **-bos** [< L *(in) limbo*, (on) the border] **1** [*usually* L-] in some Christian theologies, the abode after death of unbaptized infants, etc. **2** an indefinite state **3** a condition of neglect, oblivion, etc.

**Lim·burg·er (cheese)** (lim'burg'ər) a semisoft cheese with a strong odor, originally from Limburg, Belgium

**lime**[1] (līm) *n.* [OE *lim*] a white substance, calcium oxide, obtained from limestone, etc. and used in mortar and cement and to neutralize acid soil — *vt.* **limed, lim'ing** to treat with lime

**lime**[2] (līm) *n.* [< Ar *līmaħ*] a small, lemon-shaped, greenish-yellow citrus fruit with a juicy, sour pulp

**lime'ade'** (-ād') *n.* a drink made of lime juice, sugar, and water

**lime'light'** *n.* **1** a brilliant light created by the incandescence of lime, formerly used in theaters **2** a prominent position before the public

**lim·er·ick** (lim'ər ik) *n.* [prob. after *Limerick*, Ir county] a rhymed nonsense poem of five lines

**lime'stone'** *n.* rock consisting mainly of calcium carbonate

**lim·i·nal** (lim'i nəl) *adj.* at a boundary or transitional point between two conditions, stages, etc.

**lim·it** (lim'it) *n.* [< L *limes*] **1** the point, line, etc. where something ends; boundary **2** [*pl.*] bounds **3** the greatest amount allowed —*vt.* to set a limit to; restrict —**lim'i·ta'tion** *n.* —**lim'it·er** *n.* —**lim'it·less** *adj.*

**lim'it·ed** *adj.* **1** *a)* restricted *b)* narrow in scope *c)* brief **2** making a restricted number of stops: said of a train, bus, etc.

**limn** (lim) *vt.* **limned, limn·ing** (lim'iŋ, -niŋ) [< L *illuminare*, to illuminate] **1** to paint or draw **2** to describe

**lim·nol·o·gy** (lim näl'ə jē) *n.* [< Gr *limnē*, marsh + -LOGY] the science that deals with the physical, etc. properties and features of fresh waters, esp. lakes, etc.

**lim·o** (lim'ō) *n., pl.* **-os** [Inf.] LIMOUSINE

**lim·ou·sine** (lim'ə zēn') *n.* [Fr, lit., cloak] a large, luxurious sedan, esp. one driven by a chauffeur

**limp** (limp) *vi.* [< OE *limpan*] to walk with or as with a lame leg —*n.* a lameness in walking —*adj.* lacking firmness; wilted, flexible, etc. —**limp'ly** *adv.* —**limp'ness** *n.*

**lim·pet** (lim'pit) *n.* [< ML *lempreda*] a mollusk that clings to rocks, etc.

**lim·pid** (lim'pid) *adj.* [< L *limpidus*] perfectly clear; transparent —**lim·pid'i·ty** *n.*

**lim·y** (līm′ē) *adj.* **-i·er, -i·est** of, like, or containing lime

**lin·age** (līn′ij) *n.* the number of written or printed lines, as on a page

**linch·pin** (linch′pin′) *n.* ⟦OE *lynis*, linchpin⟧ **1** a pin in an axle to keep the wheel from coming off **2** anything holding together the parts of a whole

**Lin·coln**[1] (liŋ′kən), **Abraham** 1809-65; 16th president of the U.S. (1861-65): assassinated

**Lin·coln**[2] (liŋ′kən) capital of Nebraska, in the SE part: pop. 192,000

**lin·den** (lin′dən) *n.* ⟦OE⟧ a tree with heart-shaped leaves

**line**[1] (līn) *n.* ⟦< L *linea*, lit., linen thread⟧ **1** a cord, rope, wire, etc. **2** any wire, pipe, etc., or system of these, conducting fluid, electricity, etc. **3** a thin, threadlike mark **4** a border or boundary **5** a limit **6** outline; contour **7** a row of persons or things, as of printed letters across a page **8** a succession of persons or things **9** lineage **10** a transportation system of buses, ships, etc. **11** the course a moving thing takes **12** a course of conduct, action, explanation, etc. **13** a person's trade or occupation **14** a stock of goods **15** a short letter, note, etc. **16** [*pl.*] all the speeches of a character in a play **17** *Football* the forward combat position in warfare **18** *Football* the players in the forward row **19** *Math.* the path of a moving point —*vt.* **lined, lin′ing 1** to mark with lines **2** to form a line along —**bring (or come) into line** to bring (or come) into alignment or conformity —**draw the (or a) line** to set a limit —**hold the line** to stand firm —**in line for** being considered for —**line up** to form, or bring into, a line

**line**[2] (līn) *vt.* **lined, lin′ing** ⟦< L *linum*, flax⟧ to put, or serve as, a lining in

**lin·e·age** (lin′ē ij) *n.* ⟦see LINE[1]⟧ **1** direct descent from an ancestor **2** ancestry; family

**lin·e·al** (lin′ē əl) *adj.* **1** in the direct line of descent from an ancestor **2** hereditary **3** of lines; linear

**lin·e·a·ment** (lin′ē ə mənt) *n.* ⟦< L *linea*, line⟧ a distinctive feature, esp. of the face: *usually used in pl.*

**lin·e·ar** (lin′ē ər) *adj.* **1** of, made of, or using a line or lines **2** logical and not complex **3** in relation to length only

**line·back·er** (līn′bak′ər) *n. Football* a defensive player directly behind the line

**line drive** a baseball hit in a straight line parallel to the ground

**line′man** (-mən) *n., pl.* **-men** (-mən) **1** one who sets up and repairs telephone lines, electric power lines, etc. **2** *Football* a player in the line

**lin·en** (lin′ən) *n.* ⟦< OE *lin*, flax: see LINE[2]⟧ **1** thread or cloth made of flax **2** [*often pl.*] sheets, cloths, etc. of linen, or of cotton, etc.

**lin·er** (līn′ər) *n.* **1** a steamship, airplane, etc. in regular service for a specific line **2** LINE DRIVE **3** a cosmetic applied in a fine line, as along the eyelid

**lines·man** (līnz′mən) *n., pl.* **-men** (-mən) **1** *Football* an official who marks the yardage gained or lost **2** *Tennis* an official who decides whether the ball is inside or outside the lines

**line′up′** *n.* an arrangement of persons or things in or as in a line

**-ling** (liŋ) ⟦OE⟧ *suffix* **1** small [*duckling*] **2** unimportant or contemptible [*hireling*]

**lin·ger** (liŋ′gər) *vi.* ⟦OE *lengan*, to delay⟧ **1** to continue to stay, esp. through reluctance to leave **2** to loiter —**lin′ger·er** *n.* —**lin′ger·ing** *adj.*

**lin·ge·rie** (län′zhə rā′) *n.* ⟦Fr⟧ women's underwear and nightclothes of silk, nylon, etc.

**lin·go** (liŋ′gō) *n., pl.* **-goes** ⟦< L *lingua*, tongue⟧ [Inf.] a dialect, jargon, etc. that one is not familiar with

**lin·gua fran·ca** (liŋ′gwə fraŋ′kə) a hybrid language used for communication by speakers of different languages

**lin·gual** (liŋ′gwəl) *adj.* ⟦see LANGUAGE⟧ of, or pronounced with, the tongue

**lin·gui·ne** (liŋ gwē′nē) *n.* ⟦< It *lingua*, tongue⟧ pasta in thin, flat, narrow strips: also sp. **lin·gui′ni**

**lin·guist** (liŋ′gwist) *n.* ⟦< L *lingua*, tongue⟧ a specialist in linguistics

**lin·guis′tics** (-gwis′tiks) *n.* **1** the science of language **2** the study of the structure, development, etc. of a particular language —**lin·guis′tic** *adj.*

**lin·i·ment** (lin′ə mənt) *n.* ⟦< L *linere*, to smear⟧ a soothing medicated liquid for the skin

**lin·ing** (līn′iŋ) *n.* the material covering an inner surface

**link** (liŋk) *n.* ⟦< Scand⟧ **1** any of the loops making up a chain **2** *a)* a section of something like a chain [a *link* of sausage] *b)* an element in a series [a weak *link* in the evidence] **3** anything that connects [a *link* with the past] —*vt., vi.* to join; connect

**link′age** *n.* **1** a linking **2** a series or system of links

**linking verb** a verb that functions chiefly as a connection between a subject and a predicate (Ex.: *be, seem, become*)

**links** (liŋks) *pl.n.* ⟦OE *hlinc*, a slope⟧ GOLF COURSE

**link′up′** *n.* a linking together

**Lin·nae·us** (li nē′əs), **Car·o·lus** (kar′ə ləs) 1707-78; Swed. botanist

**lin·net** (lin′it) *n.* ⟦< L *linum*, flax: it feeds on flaxseed⟧ a small finch of either an Old World or New World species

**li·no·le·um** (li nō′lē əm) *n.* ⟦< L *linum*, flax + *oleum*, oil⟧ **1** a smooth, washable floor covering, formerly much used, esp. in kitchens **2** any floor covering like linoleum

**lin·seed** (lin′sēd′) *n.* ⟦OE *linsæd*⟧ the seed of flax; flaxseed

**linseed oil** a yellowish oil extracted from flaxseed, used in oil paints, etc.

**lint** (lint) *n.* ⟦< L *linum*, flax⟧ bits of thread, fluff, etc. from cloth or yarn —**lint′y, -i·er, -i·est,** *adj.*

**lin·tel** (lin′təl) *n.* ⟦ult. < L *limen*, threshold⟧ the horizontal crosspiece over a door, window, etc.

**li·on** (lī′ən) *n.* ⟦< Gr *leōn*⟧ **1** a large, powerful cat, found in Africa and SW Asia **2** a person of great courage or strength **3** a celebrity —**li′on·ess** *fem.n.*

**li′on·heart′ed** *adj.* very brave

**li·on·ize** (lī′ə nīz′) *vt.* **-ized′, -iz′ing** to treat as a celebrity

**lip** (lip) *n.* ⟦OE *lippa*⟧ **1** either of the two fleshy folds forming the edges of the mouth **2** anything like a lip, as the rim of a pitcher **3** [Slang] insolent talk —*adj.* spoken, but insincere [*lip* worship] —**keep a stiff upper lip** [Inf.] to bear pain or distress bravely

**lip·id** (lip′id) *n.* ⟦< Gr *lipos*, fat⟧ any of a group of organic compounds consisting of the fats and other similar substances: also **lip·ide** (lip′īd′, -id)

**lip·o·suc·tion** (lip′ō suk′shən) *n.* ⟦< LIPID + SUCTION⟧ surgical removal of fatty tissue under the skin by means of suction

**lip·py** (lip′ē) *adj.* **-pi·er, -pi·est** [Slang] impudent; insolent —**lip′pi·ness** *n.*

**lip reading** the act or skill of recognizing words by watching a speaker's lips: it is taught esp. to the deaf —**lip′-read′** *vt., vi.* —**lip reader**

**lip service** insincere words of support, etc.

**lip′stick′** *n.* a small stick of cosmetic paste for coloring the lips

**lip′-sync′** or **lip′-synch′** (-siŋk′) *vt., vi.* ⟦< lip sync(hronization)⟧ to move the lips silently so as to seem to be speaking or singing (something recorded)

**liq·ue·fy** (lik′wi fī′) *vt., vi.* **-fied′, -fy′ing** ⟦< L *liquere*, be liquid + *facere*, make⟧ to change into a liquid —**liq′ue·fac′tion** (-fak′shən) *n.*

**li·queur** (li kur′, -koor′) *n.* ⟦Fr⟧ a sweet, syrupy, flavored alcoholic liquor

**liq·uid** (lik′wid) *adj.* ⟦< L *liquidus*⟧ **1** readily flowing; fluid **2** clear; limpid **3** flowing smoothly and musically, as verse **4** readily convertible into cash —*n.* a substance that, unlike a solid, flows readily but, unlike a gas, does not expand indefinitely —**liq·uid′i·ty** *n.*

**liq·ui·date** (lik′wi dāt′) *vt.* **-dat′ed, -dat′ing** ⟦see prec.⟧ **1** to settle the accounts of (a business) by apportioning assets and debts **2** to pay (a debt) **3** to convert into cash **4** to get rid of, as by killing —**liq′ui·da′tion** *n.* —**liq′ui·da′tor** *n.*

**liq′uid·ize′** (-wid īz′) *vt.* **-ized′, -iz′ing** to cause to become liquid

**liq·ui·fy** (lik′wi fī′) *vt., vi.* **-fied′, -fy′ing** *alt. sp. of* LIQUEFY

**liq·uor** (lik′ər) *n.* ⟦L⟧ **1** any liquid **2** an alcoholic drink, esp. a distilled drink, as whiskey or rum

**li·ra** (lir′ə) *n., pl.* **li′re** (-ā) or **li′ras** ⟦< L *libra,* a pound⟧ the monetary unit of Italy

**Lis·bon** (liz′bən) capital of Portugal: pop. 817,000

**lisle** (līl) *n.* ⟦after *Lisle* (now *Lille*), city in France⟧ **1** a fine, hard, extra-strong cotton thread **2** a fabric woven of lisle

**lisp** (lisp) *vi.* ⟦< OE *wlisp,* a lisping⟧ **1** to substitute the sounds (th) and (*th*) for the sounds of *s* and *z,* respectively **2** to speak imperfectly —*vt.* to utter with a lisp —*n.* the act or sound of lisping

**lis·some** or **lis·som** (lis′əm) *adj.* ⟦< *lithesome*⟧ lithe, supple, limber, agile, etc.

**list**[1] (list) *n.* ⟦< OE *liste,* border⟧ a series of names, numbers, etc. set forth in order —*vt.* to enter in a list, directory, etc.

**list**[2] (list) *vi.* ⟦prob. ult. < OE *lust,* desire⟧ to tilt to one side: said of a ship, etc. —*n.* such a tilting

**lis·ten** (lis′ən) *vi.* ⟦< OE *hlysnan*⟧ **1** to make a conscious effort to hear **2** to give heed; take advice —**lis′ten·er** *n.*

**list′ing** *n.* **1** the making of a list **2** an entry in a list

**list′less** (-lis) *adj.* ⟦< OE *lust,* desire + -LESS⟧ indifferent because of illness, dejection, etc.; languid —**list′less·ly** *adv.* —**list′less·ness** *n.*

**list price** retail price as given in a list or catalog

**lists** (lists) *pl.n.* ⟦< ME *liste,* border⟧ a fenced area in which knights jousted

**Liszt** (list), **Franz** (fränts) 1811-86; Hung. composer & pianist

**lit**[1] (lit) *vt., vi. alt. pt. & pp. of* LIGHT[1]

**lit**[2] *abbrev.* **1** liter(s) **2** literally **3** literary **4** literature

**lit·a·ny** (lit′'n ē) *n., pl.* **-nies** ⟦< Gr *litē,* a request⟧ a series of fixed invocations and responses, used as a prayer

**li·tchi** (lē′chē′) *n.* ⟦< Chin⟧ the raisinlike fruit of a Chinese evergreen tree, enclosed in a papery shell

**lite** (līt) *adj. informal sp. of* LIGHT[2] (*adj.* 8)

**li·ter** (lēt′ər) *n.* ⟦< Gr *litra,* a pound⟧ the basic metric unit of volume, equal to 1 cubic decimeter or 61.0237 cubic inches: Brit. sp. **li′tre**

**lit·er·a·cy** (lit′ər ə sē) *n.* the ability to read and write

**lit·er·al** (lit′ər əl) *adj.* ⟦< L *littera,* a letter⟧ **1** following exactly the wording of the original *[a literal translation]* **2** in a basic or strict sense *[the literal meaning]* **3** prosaic; matter-of-fact *[a literal mind]* **4** restricted to the facts *[the literal truth]* —**lit′er·al·ly** *adv.*

**lit·er·ar·y** (lit′ər er′ē) *adj.* **1** of or having to do with literature or books **2** familiar with or versed in literature

**lit·er·ate** (lit′ər it) *adj.* ⟦< L *littera,* a letter⟧ **1** able to read and write **2** well-educated —*n.* a literate person

**lit·er·a·ti** (lit′ə rät′ē) *pl.n.* ⟦It < L *litterati:* see prec.⟧ writers, scholars, etc.

**lit·er·a·ture** (lit′ər ə chər′) *n.* ⟦< L *littera,* a letter⟧ **1** *a)* all writings in prose or verse of an imaginative character *b)* all such writings having permanent value, excellence of form, etc. *c)* all the writings of a particular time, country, etc. *d)* all the writings on a particular subject **2** any printed matter

**lithe** (līth) *adj.* **lith′er, lith′est** ⟦OE *lithe,* soft⟧ bending easily; flexible; supple: also **lithe′some** (-səm)

**lith·i·um** (lith′ē əm) *n.* ⟦< Gr *lithos,* stone⟧ a soft, silver-white, chemical element

**lithium carbonate** a white, powdery salt, used in making glass, dyes, etc. and in treating manic-depressive disorders

**lith·o·graph** (lith′ə graf′) *n.* a print made by lithography —*vi., vt.* to make (prints or copies) by this process —**li·thog·ra·pher** (li thäg′rə fər) *n.*

**li·thog·ra·phy** (li thäg′rə fē) *n.* ⟦< Gr *lithos,* stone + -GRAPHY⟧ printing from a flat stone or metal plate, parts of which have been treated to repel ink —**lith·o·graph·ic** (lith′ə graf′ik) *adj.*

**lith·o·sphere** (lith′ō sfir′) *n.* ⟦< Gr *lithos,* stone + *sphaira,* sphere⟧ the solid, rocky part of the earth; earth's crust

**Lith·u·a·ni·a** (lith′ōō ā′nē ə) country in N Europe: formerly a republic of the U.S.S.R.: 25,170 sq. mi.; pop. 3,675,000 —**Lith′u·a′ni·an** *adj., n.*

**lit·i·gant** (lit′i gənt) *n.* ⟦see fol.⟧ a party to a lawsuit

**lit′i·gate′** (-gāt′) *vt., vi.* **-gat′ed, -gat′ing** ⟦< L *lis,* dispute + *agere,* do⟧ to contest in a lawsuit —**lit′i·ga′tion** *n.* —**lit′i·ga′tor** *n.*

**li·ti·gious** (li tij′əs) *adj.* ⟦see prec.⟧ **1** *a)* given to carrying on lawsuits *b)* quarrelsome **2** of lawsuits —**li·ti′gious·ness** *n.*

**lit·mus** (lit′məs) *n.* ⟦< ON *litr,* color + *mosi,* moss⟧ a purple coloring matter obtained from various lichens: paper treated with it (**litmus paper**) turns blue in bases and red in acids

**litmus test** a test in which a single factor determines the finding

**LittD** or **Litt.D.** *abbrev.* Doctor of Letters

**lit·ter** (lit′ər) *n.* ⟦< L *lectus,* a couch⟧ **1** a framework enclosing a couch on which a person can be carried **2** a stretcher for carrying the sick or wounded **3** straw, hay, etc. used as bedding for animals **4** granular clay used in an indoor receptacle (**litter box**) to absorb cat waste **5** the young borne at one time by a dog, cat, etc. **6** things lying about in disorder, esp. bits of rubbish —*vt.* **1** to make untidy **2** to scatter about carelessly

**lit′ter·bug′** (-bug′) *n.* [Inf.] one who litters public places with rubbish, etc.

**lit·tle** (lit′'l) *adj.* **lit′tler** or **less** or **less′er, lit′tlest** or **least** ⟦OE *lytel*⟧ **1** small in size, amount, degree, etc. **2** short in duration; brief **3** small in importance or power *[the rights of the little man]* **4** narrow-minded *[a little mind]* —*adv.* **less, least 1** slightly; not much **2** not in the least —*n.* a small amount, degree, etc. —**little by little** gradually —**make** (or **think**) **little of** to consider as not very important —**lit′tle·ness** *n.*

**Little Dipper, the** a dipper-shaped group of stars containing the North Star

**Little Rock** capital of Arkansas: pop. 176,000

**lit·to·ral** (lit′ə rəl) *adj.* ⟦< L *litus,* seashore⟧ of or along the shore

**lit·ur·gy** (lit′ər jē) *n., pl.* **-gies** ⟦ult. < Gr *leōs, laos,* people + *ergon,* work⟧ prescribed ritual for public worship —**li·tur·gi·cal** (lə tur′ji kəl) *adj.*

**liv·a·ble** (liv′ə bəl) *adj.* **1** fit or pleasant to live in *[a livable house]* **2** endurable: said as of a way of life Also **live′a·ble**

**live**[1] (liv) *vi.* **lived, liv′ing** ⟦OE *libban*⟧ **1** to have life **2** *a)* to remain alive *b)* to endure **3** to pass one's life in a specified manner **4** to enjoy life *[to know how to live]* **5** to feed *[to live on fruit]* **6** to reside —*vt.* **1** to carry out in one's life *[to live one's faith]* **2** to spend; pass *[to live a useful life]* —**live down** to live so as to wipe out the shame of (a misdeed, etc.) —**live up to** to live or act in accordance with (one's ideals, etc.)

**live**[2] (līv) *adj.* ⟦< ALIVE⟧ **1** having life **2** of present interest *[a live issue]* **3** still burning *[a live spark]* **4** unexploded *[a live shell]* **5** carrying electrical current *[a live wire]* **6** *a)* in person *b)* broadcast, recorded, etc. during the actual performance **7** *Sports* in play /a *live* ball/

**live·bear·er** (līv′ber′ər) *n.* any of various small, tropical, American, freshwater fishes, as the guppy and molly

**-lived** (līvd, livd) *combining form* having (a specified kind of) life /long-*lived*/

**live′-in′** *adj.* living in someone's residence as a domestic, lover, etc.

**live·li·hood** (līv′lē hood′) *n.* [< OE *lif*, life + *-lad*, course] means of living or of supporting life

**live·long** (liv′lôŋ′) *adj.* [ME *lefe longe*, lit., lief long: *lief* is merely intens.] long in passing; whole /the *livelong* day/

**live·ly** (līv′lē) *adj.* **-li·er, -li·est** [OE *liflic*] **1** full of life; vigorous **2** full of spirit; exciting **3** animated, cheerful, vivacious, etc. **4** vivid; keen **5** bounding back with great resilience /a *lively* ball/ —**live′li·ness** *n.*

**liv·en** (līv′ən) *vt.*, *vi.* to make or become lively; cheer: often with *up*

**liv·er** (liv′ər) *n.* [OE *lifer*] **1** the largest glandular organ in vertebrate animals: it secretes bile and is important in metabolism **2** the liver of cattle, fowl, etc., used as food

**Liv·er·pool** (liv′ər pōōl′) seaport in NW England: county district pop. 452,000

**liv·er·wurst** (liv′ər wurst′) *n.* [< Ger *leber*, liver + *wurst*, sausage] a sausage containing ground liver

**liv·er·y** (liv′ər ē) *n.*, *pl.* **-er·ies** [ME, gift of clothes to a servant] **1** an identifying uniform as of a servant **2** *a*) the care and feeding of horses for a fee *b*) the keeping of horses or vehicles for hire *c*) a stable for this (usually **livery stable**) **3** a place where boats can be rented

**lives** (līvz) *n. pl. of* LIFE

**live·stock** (līv′stäk′) *n.* domestic animals raised for use and sale

**liv·id** (liv′id) *adj.* [< L *lividus*] **1** discolored by a bruise; black-and-blue **2** grayish-blue: sometimes taken to mean pale or red /*livid* with rage/ **3** enraged

**liv·ing** (liv′iŋ) *adj.* **1** alive; having life **2** in active operation or use /a *living* institution/ **3** of persons alive /within *living* memory/ **4** true; lifelike **5** of life /*living* conditions/ —*n.* **1** a being alive **2** livelihood **3** manner of existence —**the living** those that are still alive

**living room** a room in a home, with sofas, chairs, etc., used for social activities, entertaining guests, etc.

**living wage** a wage sufficient to maintain a reasonable level of comfort

**living will** a document directing that the signer's life not be artificially supported during a terminal illness

**liz·ard** (liz′ərd) *n.* [< L *lacerta*] any of various slender, scaly reptiles with four legs and a tail, as the chameleon and iguana

**ll** *abbrev.* lines

**LL** *abbrev.* Late Latin

**-'ll** (əl) *suffix* will or shall: used in contractions /*she'll* sing/

**lla·ma** (lä′mə) *n.* [Sp < AmInd (Peru)] a South American beast of burden related to the camel but smaller

**lla·no** (lä′nō) *n.*, *pl.* **-nos** [Sp < L *planus*, plain] any of the level, grassy plains of Spanish America

**LLB** or **LL.B.** *abbrev.* Bachelor of Laws

**LLD** or **LL.D.** *abbrev.* Doctor of Laws

**lo** (lō) *interj.* [OE *la*] look! see!

**load** (lōd) *n.* [< OE *lad*, a course, journey] **1** an amount carried at one time **2** something borne with difficulty; burden **3** [*often pl.*] [Inf.] a great amount or number **4** *Finance* an amount added to the price of mutual fund shares to cover costs, etc. —*vt.* **1** to put (a load) into or upon (a carrier) **2** to burden; oppress **3** to supply in large quan-

tities **4** to put a charge of ammunition into (a firearm) **5** *Comput.* to transfer (a program or data) into main memory from a disk, etc. —**load′er** *n.* —**load′ing** *n.*

**load·star** (lōd′stär′) *n.* LODESTAR

**load·stone** (lōd′stōn′) *n.* LODESTONE

**loaf¹** (lōf) *n.*, *pl.* **loaves** (lōvz) [OE *hlaf*] **1** a portion of bread baked in one piece **2** any food baked in this shape

**loaf²** (lōf) *vi.* [prob. < fol.] to spend time idly; idle, dawdle, etc.

**loaf′er** *n.* [prob. < Ger *landläufer*, a vagabond] one who loafs; idler

**Loaf′er** *trademark for* a casual shoe like a moccasin —*n.* [l-] a shoe similar to this

**loam** (lōm) *n.* [OE *lam*] a rich soil, esp. one composed of clay, sand, and some organic matter — **loam′y, -i·er, -i·est,** *adj.*

**loan** (lōn) *n.* [< ON *lān*] **1** the act of lending **2** something lent, esp. money at interest —*vt.*, *vi.* to lend

**loan′er** *n.* **1** one who loans something **2** an automobile, TV, etc. lent in place of one left for repair

**loan shark** [Inf.] one who lends money at illegal rates of interest

**loan′word′** *n.* a word of one language taken into and used in another

**loath** (lōth) *adj.* [< OE *lath*, hostile] reluctant /to be *loath* to depart/

**loathe** (lōth) *vt.* **loathed, loath′ing** [< OE *lathian*, be hateful] to feel intense dislike or disgust for; abhor

**loath′ing** *n.* intense dislike, disgust, or hatred; abhorrence

**loath′some** *adj.* causing loathing; disgusting

**loaves** (lōvz) *n. pl. of* LOAF¹

**lob** (läb) *vt.*, *vi.* **lobbed, lob′bing** [< ME *lobbe*, heavy] to toss or hit (a ball) in a high curve —**lob′ber** *n.*

**lob·by** (läb′ē) *n.*, *pl.* **-bies** [LL *lobia*] **1** an entrance hall, as of a hotel or theater **2** a group of lobbyists representing the same interest —*vi.* **-bied, -by·ing** to act as a lobbyist

**lob′by·ist** *n.* a person, acting on behalf of a group, who tries to get legislators to support certain measures

**lobe** (lōb) *n.* [< Gr *lobos*] a rounded projecting part, as the lower part of the ear or any of the divisions of the lung

**lo·bot·o·my** (lō bät′ə mē) *n.*, *pl.* **-mies** [< prec. + -TOMY] a surgical incision into a lobe of the brain: now rarely used as a treatment

**lob·ster** (läb′stər) *n.* [< OE *loppe*, spider + *-estre*, -ster] an edible sea crustacean usually with four pairs of legs and a pair of large pincers

**lobster tail** the tail of any of various crustaceans, prepared as food

LOBSTER

**lo·cal** (lō′kəl) *adj.* [< L *locus*, a place] **1** of, characteristic of, or confined to a particular place **2** of or for a particular part of the body /*local* anesthesia/ **3** making all stops along its run /a *local* bus/ —*n.* **1** a local train, bus, etc. **2** a branch, as of a labor union —**lo′cal·ly** *adv.*

**lo·cale** (lō kal′) *n.* [OFr *local*] a place or locality, esp. with reference to events, etc. associated with it

**lo·cal·i·ty** (lō kal′ə tē) *n.*, *pl.* **-ties** a place; district; neighborhood

**lo·cal·ize** (lō′kəl īz′) *vt.* **-ized′, -iz′ing** to limit, confine, or trace to a particular place —**lo′cal·i·za′tion** *n.*

**lo·cate** (lō′kāt′, lō kāt′) *vt.* **-cat′ed, -cat′ing** [< L *locus*, a place‖ **1** to establish in a certain place [offices *located* downtown] **2** to discover the position of **3** to show the position of [to *locate* Guam on a map] —*vi.* [Inf.] to settle [she *located* in Ohio]

**lo·ca'tion** *n.* **1** a locating or being located **2** position; place —**on location** *Film* in an outdoor setting, away from the studio

**loc. cit.** *abbrev.* ‖L *loco citato*‖ in the place cited

**loch** (läk, läkh) *n.* ‖< Gael & Old Ir‖ [Scot.] **1** a lake **2** an arm of the sea

**lock**[1] (läk) *n.* ‖< OE *loc*, a bolt‖ **1** a mechanical device for fastening a door, strongbox, etc. as with a key or combination **2** an enclosed part of a canal, etc. equipped with gates for changing the water level to raise or lower boats **3** the mechanism of a firearm that explodes the charge —*vt.* **1** to fasten with a lock **2** to shut (*up, in,* or *out*) by means of a lock **3** to link [to *lock* arms] **4** to jam together so as to make immovable —*vi.* **1** to become locked **2** to interlock

**lock**[2] (läk) *n.* ‖OE *loc*‖ a curl of hair

**lock'er** *n.* **1** a chest, closet, etc. which can be locked **2** a large compartment for freezing and storing foods

**lock·et** (läk'it) *n.* ‖< OFr *loc*, a latch, lock‖ a small, hinged case of gold, etc. for holding a picture, lock of hair, etc.: usually worn on a necklace

**lock'jaw'** *n.* a form of tetanus, in which the jaws become firmly closed

**lock'out'** *n.* the shutdown of a plant to bring the workers to an agreement

**lock'smith'** *n.* one whose work is making or repairing locks and making keys

**lock'up'** *n.* a jail

**lo·co** (lō'kō) *adj.* ‖Sp, mad‖ [Slang] crazy; demented

**loco disease** a nervous disease of horses, cattle, etc. caused by locoweed poison

**lo·co·mo·tion** (lō'kə mō'shən) *n.* ‖< L *locus*, a place + MOTION‖ motion, or the power of moving, from one place to another

**lo'co·mo'tive** (-mōt'iv) *adj.* of locomotion —*n.* an electric, steam, or diesel engine on wheels, designed to push or pull a railroad train

**lo·co·weed** (lō'kō wēd') *n.* a plant of W North America that causes the loco disease of cattle, horses, etc.

**lo·cus** (lō'kəs) *n., pl.* **lo'ci** (-sī') ‖L‖ **1** a place **2** *Math.* a line, plane, etc. every point of which satisfies a given condition

**lo·cust** (lō'kəst) *n.* ‖< L *locusta*‖ **1** a large grasshopper often traveling in swarms and destroying vegetation **2** SEVENTEEN-YEAR LOCUST **3** a tree of the E or Central U.S., with clusters of fragrant, white flowers

**lo·cu·tion** (lō kyōō'shən) *n.* ‖< L *loqui*, speak‖ a word, phrase, or expression

**lode** (lōd) *n.* ‖< OE *lad*, course‖ a vein, stratum, etc. of metallic ore

**lode'star'** *n.* a star by which one directs one's course; esp., the North Star

**lode'stone'** *n.* a strongly magnetic variety of iron ore

**lodge** (läj) *n.* ‖< OFr *loge*, arbor‖ **1** *a*) a small house for some special use [a hunting *lodge*] *b*) a resort hotel or motel **2** the local chapter or hall of a fraternal society —*vt.* **lodged, lodg'ing 1** to house temporarily **2** to shoot, thrust, etc. firmly (*in*) **3** to bring (a complaint, etc.) before legal authorities **4** to confer (powers) upon: with *in* — *vi.* **1** to live (*with* or *in*) as a paying guest **2** to come to rest and stick firmly (*in*)

**lodg'er** *n.* one who lives in a rented room in another's home

**lodg'ing** *n.* **1** a place to live in, esp. temporarily **2** [*pl.*] a room or rooms rented in a private home

**loft** (lôft, läft) *n.* ‖< ON *lopt*, upper room, air‖ **1** the space just below the roof of a house, barn, etc. **2** an upper story of a warehouse or factory; specif., a dwelling space, artist's studio, etc. in

such an upper story **3** a gallery [a choir *loft*] **4** height given to a ball hit or thrown —*vt.* to send (a ball) into a high curve

**loft bed** a bed on a platform or balcony allowing the use of the floor area below as part of a living room, etc.

**loft'y** *adj.* **-i·er, -i·est 1** very high **2** elevated; noble **3** haughty; arrogant —**loft'i·ness** *n.*

**log**[1] (lôg, läg) *n.* ‖ME *logge*‖ **1** a section of the trunk or of a large branch of a felled tree **2** a device for measuring the speed of a ship **3** a record of progress, speed, etc., specif. one kept on a ship's voyage or aircraft's flight —*vt.* **logged, log'ging 1** to saw (trees) into logs **2** to record in a log **3** to sail or fly (a specified distance) —*vi.* to cut down trees and remove the logs —**log on** (or **off**) to enter the necessary information to begin (or end) a session on a computer terminal

**log**[2] (lôg, läg) *n. short for* LOGARITHM

**-log** (lôg, läg) *combining form* -LOGUE

**lo·gan·ber·ry** (lō'gən be'rē) *n., pl.* **-ries** ‖after J. H. *Logan*, who developed it (1881)‖ **1** a hybrid bramble developed from the blackberry and the red raspberry **2** its purplish-red fruit

**log·a·rithm** (lôg'ə rith əm, läg'-) *n.* ‖< Gr *logos*, ratio + *arithmos*, number‖ *Math.* the exponent expressing the power to which a fixed number must be raised to produce a given number — **log'a·rith'mic** *adj.*

**loge** (lōzh) *n.* ‖OFr: see LODGE‖ **1** a theater box or mezzanine section **2** a luxury suite in a stadium or arena

**log'ger** *n.* a person whose work is felling trees for use as lumber, etc.

**log'ger·head'** *n.* ‖dial. *logger*, block of wood + HEAD‖ used chiefly in **at loggerheads**, in sharp disagreement

**log·ic** (läj'ik) *n.* ‖ult. < Gr *logos*, word‖ **1** correct reasoning, or the science of this **2** way of reasoning [bad *logic*] **3** what is expected by the working of cause and effect **4** *Comput.* the system of switching functions, circuits, or devices —**lo·gi·cian** (lō jish'ən) *n.*

**log'i·cal** (-i kəl) *adj.* ‖ML *logicalis*‖ **1** based on or using logic **2** expected because of what has gone before —**log'i·cal·ly** *adv.*

**lo·gis·tics** (lō jis'tiks) *n.* ‖< Fr *loger*, to quarter, lodge‖ the military science of procuring, maintaining, and transporting materiel and personnel —**lo·gis'tic** or **lo·gis'ti·cal** *adj.* —**lo·gis'ti·cal·ly** *adv.*

**log'jam'** *n.* **1** an obstacle formed by logs jamming together in a stream **2** piled-up work, etc. that obstructs progress **3** a deadlock

**log·o** (lō'gō) *n.* ‖< Gr *logos*, a word‖ a distinctive company signature, trademark, etc.: also **log·o·type** (lôg'ə tip', läg'-)

**log'roll'ing** *n.* **1** mutual exchange of favors, esp. among legislators **2** the sport of balancing oneself on a floating log while rotating it with one's feet

**-logue** (lôg, läg) ‖see LOGIC‖ *combining form* a (specified kind of) speaking or writing [*Decalogue*]

**lo·gy** (lō'gē) *adj.* **-gi·er, -gi·est** ‖< ? Du *log*, dull‖ [Inf.] dull or sluggish

**-lo·gy** (lə jē) ‖see LOGIC‖ *combining form* **1** a (specified kind of) speaking [*eulogy*] **2** the science, doctrine, or theory of [*biology*]

**loin** (loin) *n.* ‖< L *lumbus*‖ **1** [*usually pl.*] the lower part of the back between the hipbones and the ribs **2** the front part of the hindquarters of beef, lamb, etc. **3** [*pl.*] the hips and the lower abdomen regarded as the region of strength, etc.

**loin'cloth'** *n.* a cloth worn about the loins, as by some peoples in warm climates

**loi·ter** (loit'ər) *vi.* ‖< MDu *loteren*‖ **1** to spend time idly; linger **2** to move slowly and idly —**loi'ter·er** *n.*

**loll** (läl) *vi.* ‖< MDu *lollen*, mumble, doze‖ **1** to lean or lounge about lazily **2** to hang loosely;

droop /the camel's tongue *lolled* out/ —*vt.* to let hang loosely

**lol·li·pop** or **lol·ly·pop** (läl′ē päp′) *n.* [prob. < dial. *lolly*, the tongue + *pop*] a piece of hard candy on the end of a stick

**lol·ly·gag** (läl′ē gag′) *vi.* -gagged′, -gag′ging [var. of *lallygag* < ?] [Inf.] to waste time in trifling or aimless activity

**Lon·don** (lun′dən) **1** capital of England, the United Kingdom, & the Commonwealth: pop. 7,567,000 **2** city in SE Ontario, Canada: pop. 326,000

**lone** (lōn) *adj.* [< *alone*] **1** by oneself; solitary **2** isolated

**lone·ly** *adj.* -li·er, -li·est **1** solitary or isolated **2** unhappy at being alone —**lone′li·ness** *n.*

**lon·er** (lōn′ər) *n.* [Inf.] one who prefers to be independent of others, as by living or working alone

**lone·some** *adj.* **1** having or causing a lonely feeling **2** unfrequented

**long**[1] (lôŋ) *adj.* [< OE] **1** measuring much in space or time **2** in length /six feet *long*/ **3** of greater than usual length, quantity, etc. /a *long* list/ **4** tedious; slow **5** far-reaching /a *long* view of the matter/ **6** well-supplied /*long* on excuses/ —*adv.* **1** for a long time **2** from start to finish /all day *long*/ **3** at a remote time /*long* ago/ —**as** (or **so**) **long as 1** during the time that **2** seeing that; since **3** provided that —**before long** soon

**long**[2] (lôŋ) *vi.* [< OE *langian*] to feel a strong yearning; wish earnestly

**long**[3] *abbrev.* longitude

**Long Beach** seaport in SW California, on the Pacific: pop. 429,000

**long distance** a telephone service for calls to and from distant places —**long′-dis′tance** *adj.*, *adv.*

**lon·gev·i·ty** (län jev′ə tē, lôn-) *n.* [< L *longus*, long + *aevum*, age] long life

**long′-faced′** *adj.* glum

**long′hair′** *adj.* [Inf.] of intellectuals or intellectual tastes

**long′hand′** *n.* ordinary handwriting, as distinguished from shorthand or typed characters

**long·ing** *n.* strong desire; yearning —*adj.* feeling or showing a yearning

**Long Island** island in SE New York, in the Atlantic south of Connecticut

**lon·gi·tude** (län′jə tōōd′) *n.* [< L *longus*, long] distance east or west of the prime meridian, expressed in degrees or by the difference in time

**lon′gi·tu′di·nal** (-tōōd′'n əl) *adj.* **1** of or in length **2** running or placed lengthwise **3** of longitude

**long jump** *Sports* a jump for distance made with a running start

**long′-lived′** (-līvd′, -livd′) *adj.* having or tending to have a long life span

**long′-range′** *adj.* **1** having a range of a great distance **2** taking the future into consideration

**long·shore·man** (lôŋ′shôr′mən) *n.*, *pl.* -men (-mən) [< *alongshore* + MAN] a person who works on a waterfront loading and unloading ships; stevedore

**long shot** [Inf.] **1** in betting, a choice that is little favored and, hence, carries great odds **2** a venture with only a slight chance of success, but offering great rewards

**long′-stand′ing** *adj.* having continued for a long time

**long′-suf′fer·ing** *adj.* bearing trouble, etc. patiently for a long time

**long′-term′** *adj.* for or extending over a long time

**long ton** TON (sense 2)

**Lon·gueuil** (lôn gāl′) city in S Quebec: suburb of Montreal: pop. 128,000

**long′-wind′ed** (-win′did) *adj.* **1** speaking or writing at great length **2** tiresomely long

**look** (look) *vi.* [< OE *locian*] **1** to direct one's eyes in order to see **2** to search **3** to appear; seem **4** to be facing in a specified direction —*vt.* **1** to direct one's eyes on **2** to have an appearance befitting /to *look* the part/ —*n.* **1** a looking; glance **2** appearance; aspect **3** [Inf.] *a*) [*usually pl.*] personal appearance *b*) [*pl.*] personal appearance —*interj.* **1** see! **2** pay attention! —**look after** to take care of —**look down on** (or **upon**) to regard with contempt —**look for** to expect —**look forward to** to anticipate —**look in** (**on**) to pay a brief visit (to) —**look into** to investigate —**look out** to be careful —**look over** to examine —**look to 1** to take care of **2** to rely on —**look up 1** to search for as in a reference book **2** [Inf.] to call on —**look up to** to admire —**look′er** *n.*

**look′er-on′** *n.*, *pl.* **look′ers-on′** an observer or spectator; onlooker

**looking glass** a (glass) mirror

**look′out′** *n.* **1** a careful watching **2** a place for keeping watch **3** a person detailed to watch **4** [Inf.] concern

**look′-see′** *n.* [Inf.] a quick look

**loom**[1] (lōōm) *n.* [< OE *(ge)loma*, tool] a machine for weaving thread or yarn into cloth

**loom**[2] (lōōm) *vi.* [< ?] to come into sight indistinctly, esp. threateningly

**loon**[1] (lōōn) *n.* [< ON *lomr*] a fish-eating, diving bird, similar to a duck

**loon**[2] (lōōn) *n.* [< ?] a stupid or crazy person

**loon′ie** *n.* [< LOON[1], depicted on the reverse] [Cdn.] the Canadian one-dollar coin

**loon′y** *adj.* -i·er, -i·est [< LUNATIC] [Slang] crazy; demented

**loop** (lōōp) *n.* [ME *loup*] **1** the figure made by a line, thread, etc. that curves back to cross itself **2** anything forming this figure **3** an intrauterine contraceptive device **4** a segment of movie film or magnetic tape joined end to end —*vt.* **1** to make a loop in or of **2** to fasten with a loop —*vi.* to form a loop or loops

**loop′hole′** *n.* [prob. < MDu *lupen*, to peer + HOLE] **1** a hole in a wall for looking or shooting through **2** a means of evading an obligation, etc.

**loop′y** *adj.* -i·er, -i·est [Slang] **1** slightly crazy **2** confused

**loose** (lōōs) *adj.* **loos′er, loos′est** [< ON *lauss*] **1** not confined or restrained; free **2** not firmly fastened **3** not tight or compact **4** not precise; inexact **5** sexually immoral **6** [Inf.] relaxed —*adv.* loosely —*vt.* **loosed, loos′ing 1** to set free; unbind **2** to make less tight, compact, etc. **3** to relax **4** to release (an arrow, etc.) —**on the loose** not confined; free —**loose′ly** *adv.* —**loose′ness** *n.*

**loose ends** unsettled details —**at loose ends** unsettled, idle, etc.

**loose′-leaf′** *adj.* having leaves, or sheets, that can be removed or replaced easily

**loos·en** (lōōs′ən) *vt.*, *vi.* to make or become loose or looser

**loos·ey-goos·ey** (lōō′sē gōō′sē) [Slang] *adj.* relaxed; easy —*adv.* in a loose, relaxed way

**loot** (lōōt) *n.* [Hindi *lūt*] **1** goods stolen or taken by force; plunder **2** [Slang] money, gifts, etc. —*vt.*, *vi.* to plunder

**lop**[1] (läp) *vt.* **lopped, lop′ping** [< OE *loppian*] **1** to trim (a tree, etc.) by cutting off branches, etc. **2** to remove by or as by cutting off: usually with *off*

**lop**[2] (läp) *vi.* **lopped, lop′ping** [prob. akin to LOB] to hang down loosely

**lope** (lōp) *vi.* **loped, lop′ing** [< ON *hlaupa*, to leap] to move with a long, swinging stride —*n.* such a stride

**lop·sid·ed** (läp′sīd′id) *adj.* noticeably heavier, bigger, or lower on one side

**lo·qua·cious** (lō kwā′shəs) *adj.* [< L *loqui*, speak] very talkative —**lo·qua′cious·ness** *n.* —**lo·quac′i·ty** (-kwas′ə tē) *n.*

**lord** (lôrd) *n.* [< OE *hlaf*, loaf + *weard*, keeper] **1** a ruler; master **2** the head of a feudal estate **3** [L-] *a*) God *b*) Jesus Christ **4** in Great Britain, a titled nobleman —**lord it over** to be overbearing toward

**lord'ly** *adj.* **-li·er, -li·est 1** noble; grand **2** haughty —*adv.* in the manner of a lord —**lord'li·ness** *n.*

**Lord's Day** [*sometimes* **L- d-**] Sunday: with *the*

**lord'ship'** *n.* **1** the rank or authority of a lord **2** rule; dominion **3** the territory of a lord **4** [*often* **L-**] a title used in speaking to or of a lord

**Lord's Prayer** the prayer beginning *Our Father*: Matt. 6:9-13

**lore** (lôr) *n.* [< OE *lar*] knowledge; learning, esp. of a traditional nature

**lor·gnette** (lôr nyet') *n.* [Fr < OFr *lorgne*, squinting] eyeglasses, or opera glasses, attached to a handle

**lo·ris** (lô'ris, lôr'is) *n.* [ult. < Du *loer*, a clown] a small, slow-moving, large-eyed Asiatic lemur that lives in trees and is active at night

**lor·ry** (lôr'ē) *n., pl.* **-ries** [prob. < dial. *lurry*, to pull] [Brit.] a motor truck

**Los Al·a·mos** (lôs al'ə mōs') town in NC New Mexico: site of nuclear energy facility where the atomic bomb was developed: pop. 11,000

**Los An·ge·les** (lôs an'jə ləs) city & seaport on the SW coast of California: pop. 3,486,000 (met. area, incl. Long Beach, 8,863,000)

**lose** (lōōz) *vt.* **lost, los'ing** [OE *losian*] **1** to become unable to find [to *lose* one's keys] **2** to have taken from one by accident, death, removal, etc. **3** to fail to keep [to *lose* one's temper] **4** to fail to see, hear, or understand **5** to fail to have, get, etc. [to *lose* one's chance] **6** to fail to win **7** to cause the loss of **8** to wander from (one's way, etc.) **9** to squander —*vt.* to suffer (a) loss —**lose oneself** to become absorbed —**los'er** *n.*

**loss** (lôs, läs) *n.* [ME *los*] **1** a losing or being lost **2** the damage, trouble, etc. caused by losing **3** the person, thing, or amount lost —**at a loss to** uncertain how to

**lost** (lôst, läst) *vt., vi. pt. & pp. of* LOSE —*adj.* **1** ruined; destroyed **2** not to be found; missing **3** no longer held, seen, heard, etc. **4** not gained or won **5** having wandered astray **6** wasted

**lot** (lät) *n.* [< OE *hlot*] **1** the deciding of a matter by chance, as by drawing counters **2** the decision thus arrived at **3** one's share by lot **4** fortune [her unhappy *lot*] **5** a plot of ground **6** a group of persons or things **7** [*often pl.*] [Inf.] a great number or amount [a *lot* of cars, *lots* of fun] **8** [Inf.] sort [he's a bad *lot*] —**a (whole) lot** a great deal; very much: somewhat informal —**draw (or cast) lots** to decide by lot

**Lo·thar·i·o** (lō ther'ē ō') *n., pl.* **-i·os** [after the rake in the play *The Fair Penitent* (1703)] [*often* **l-**] a seducer of women; rake

**lo·tion** (lō'shən) *n.* [< L *lavare*, to wash] a liquid preparation used, as on the skin, for cleansing, healing, etc.

**lots** *adv.* a great deal; very much: somewhat informal

**lot·ter·y** (lät'ər ē) *n., pl.* **-ies** [< MDu *lot*, lot] **1** a game of chance in which people buy numbered tickets on prizes, winners being chosen by lot **2** a drawing, event, etc. based on chance

**lot·to** (lät'ō) *n.* [It < MDu: see LOT] a game resembling bingo

**lo·tus** (lōt'əs) *n.* [< Gr *lōtos*] **1** *Gr. Legend* a plant whose fruit induced forgetfulness **2** any of several tropical waterlilies

**lotus position** in yoga, an erect sitting position with the legs crossed close to the body

**loud** (loud) *adj.* [< OE *hlud*] **1** strongly audible: said of sound **2** making a loud sound **3** noisy **4** emphatic [loud denials] **5** [Inf.] flashy —*adv.* in a loud manner —**loud'ly** *adv.* —**loud'ness** *n.*

**loud'mouthed'** (-mouthd', -moutht') *adj.* talking in a loud, irritating voice

**loud'speak'er** *n.* SPEAKER (*n.* 2)

**Lou·is** (lōō'ē; *Fr* lwē) **1** Louis XIV 1638-1715; king of France (1643-1715) **2** Louis XV 1710-74; king of France (1715-74) **3** Louis XVI 1754-93; king of France (1774-92): guillotined

**Lou·i·si·an·a** (lōō ē'zē an'ə) Southern state of the U.S.: 43,566 sq. mi.; pop. 4,220,000; cap. Baton

Rouge: abbrev. *LA* —**Lou·i·si·an'i·an** or **Lou·i'si·an' an** *adj., n.*

**Lou·is·ville** (lōō'ə vəl) city in N Kentucky: pop. 270,000

**lounge** (lounj) *vi.* **lounged, loung'ing** [Scot dial. < ? *lungis*, a laggard] **1** to move, sit, lie, etc. in a relaxed way **2** to spend time in idleness —*n.* **1** a room with comfortable furniture for lounging **2** a couch or sofa

**lounge'wear'** *n.* loose-fitting clothing for casual wear, esp. at home

**louse** (lous) *n., pl.* **lice** [< OE *lus*] **1** a small, wingless insect parasitic on humans and other animals **2** any similar insect parasitic on plants **3** *pl.* **lous'es** [Slang] a mean, contemptible person —**louse up** [Slang] to spoil; botch

**lous·y** (lou'zē) *adj.* **-i·er, -i·est 1** infested with lice **2** [Slang] *a*) disgusting *b*) poor; inferior **3** well supplied (*with*) —**lous'i·ness** *n.*

**lout** (lout) *n.* [prob. < or akin to ME *lutien*, to lurk] a clumsy, stupid fellow —**lout'ish** *adj.*

**lou·ver** (lōō'vər) *n.* [< MDu *love*, gallery] **1** an opening, window, etc. fitted with a series of sloping slats arranged so as to admit light and air but shed rain **2** any of these slats

**love** (luv) *n.* [< OE *lufu*] **1** strong affection or liking for someone or something **2** a passionate affection of one person for another **3** the object of such affection; a sweetheart or lover **4** *Tennis* a score of zero —*vt., vi.* to feel love (for) —**fall in love (with)** to begin to feel love (for) —**in love** feeling love —**make love 1** to woo, embrace, etc. **2** to have sexual intercourse —**lov'a·ble** or **love'a·ble** *adj.* —**love'less** *adj.*

**love'bird'** *n.* any of various small Old World parrots often kept as cage birds

**love'lorn'** (-lôrn') *adj.* [LOVE + obs. *lorn*, lost] sad because not loved in return

**love'ly** *adj.* **-li·er, -li·est 1** beautiful **2** [Inf.] highly enjoyable —**love'li·ness** *n.*

**lov·er** (luv'ər) *n.* **1** a person who greatly enjoys something **2** one who loves; specif., either partner in a sexual relationship, often an illicit one **3** [*pl.*] a couple in love with, or in a sexual relationship with, each other

**love seat** a small sofa for two people

**lov'ing** *adj.* feeling or expressing love —**lov'ing·ly** *adv.*

**loving cup** a large drinking cup with two handles, often given as a trophy

**low**[1] (lō) *adj.* [< ON *lagr*] **1** not high or tall **2** below the normal level [*low* ground] **3** shallow **4** less in size, degree, etc. than usual [*low* speed] **5** deep in pitch **6** depressed in spirits **7** not of high rank; humble **8** vulgar; coarse **9** poor; inferior **10** not loud —*adv.* in or to a low level, degree, etc. —*n.* **1** a low level, degree, etc. **2** an arrangement of gears giving the lowest speed and greatest power **3** *Meteorol.* an area of low barometric pressure —**lay low** to overcome or kill —**lie low** to keep oneself hidden —**low'ness** *n.*

**low**[2] (lō) *n., vi.* [< OE *hlowan*] MOO

**low'born'** *adj.* of humble birth

**low'boy'** *n.* a chest of drawers mounted on short legs

**low'brow'** *n.* one considered to lack cultivated tastes —*adj.* of or for a lowbrow

**Low Countries** the Netherlands, Belgium, & Luxembourg

**low'down'** (lō'doun'; *for adj.,* -doun') *n.* [Slang] the true, pertinent facts: with *the* —*adj.* [Inf.] mean; contemptible

**low'-end'** *adj.* [Inf.] **1** inexpensive and low in quality **2** having only the basic features

**low·er**[1] (lō'ər) *adj.* [compar. of LOW[1]] **1** below in place, rank, etc. **2** less in amount, degree, etc. **3** farther south —*vt.* **1** to let or put down [*lower* the window] **2** to reduce in height, amount, etc. **3** to bring down in respect, etc. —*vi.* to become lower

**low·er**[2] (lou′ər) *vi.* ⟦ME *louren*⟧ **1** to scowl or frown **2** to appear dark and threatening: said as of the sky —**low′er·ing** *adj.* —**low′er·ing·ly** *adv.*

**low·er·case** (lō′ər kās′) *n.* small-letter type used in printing, as distinguished from capital letters —*adj.* of or in lowercase

**low′er·class′man** (-klas′mən) *n., pl.* **-men** (-mən) a student in the freshman or sophomore class of a high school or college

**low frequency** any radio frequency between 30 and 300 kilohertz

**Low German 1** the group of dialects of N Germany **2** the branch of Germanic languages including English, Dutch, Flemish, etc.

**low′-grade′** *adj.* of low quality, degree, etc.

**low′-key′** *adj.* of low intensity, tone, etc.; subdued: also **low′-keyed′**

**low′land** (-lənd, -land′) *n.* land below the level of the surrounding land —*adj.* of, in, or from such a region —**the Lowlands** lowland region of SC Scotland

**low′life′** *n., pl.* **-lifes′** a vulgar or undignified person

**low′ly** *adj.* **-li·er, -li·est 1** of low position or rank **2** humble; meek —**low′li·ness** *n.*

**low′-mind′ed** *adj.* having or showing a coarse, vulgar mind

**low′-spir′it·ed** *adj.* sad; depressed

**low tide** the lowest level reached by the ebbing tide

**lox**[1] (läks) *n.* ⟦< Yiddish < Ger *lachs*, salmon⟧ a kind of smoked salmon

**lox**[2] (läks) *n.* ⟦*l(iquid) ox(ygen)*⟧ liquid oxygen, esp. when used in rockets: also **LOX**

**loy·al** (loi′əl) *adj.* ⟦see LEGAL⟧ **1** faithful to one's country, friends, ideals, etc. **2** showing such faithfulness —**loy′al·ly** *adv.* —**loy′al·ty,** *pl.* **-ties,** *n.*

**loy′al·ist** *n.* one who supports the government during a revolt

**loz·enge** (läz′ənj) *n.* ⟦< OFr *losenge*⟧ a cough drop, candy, etc., orig. diamond-shaped

**LP** *n.* ⟦*L(ong) P(laying)*⟧ a phonograph record having microgrooves, for playing at 33⅓ revolutions per minute

**LPN** *n., pl.* **LPNs** licensed practical nurse

**Lr** *Chem. symbol for* lawrencium

**LSD** *n.* ⟦*l(y)s(ergic acid) d(iethylamide)*⟧ a chemical compound used in the study of mental disorders and as a psychedelic drug

**Lt** *abbrev.* Lieutenant

**Ltd** or **ltd** *abbrev.* limited

**lu·au** (lōo′ou′) *n.* a Hawaiian feast

**Lub·bock** (lub′ək) city in NW Texas: pop. 186,000

**lube** (lōob) *n.* **1** a lubricating oil for machinery: also **lube oil 2** [Inf.] a lubrication

**lu·bri·cant** (lōo′bri kənt) *adj.* reducing friction by providing a smooth film over parts coming into contact —*n.* a lubricant oil, etc.

**lu′bri·cate′** (-kāt′) *vt.* **-cat·ed, -cat·ing** ⟦< L *lubricus*, smooth⟧ **1** to make slippery or smooth **2** to apply a lubricant to (machinery, etc.) —*vi.* to serve as a lubricant —**lu′bri·ca′tion** *n.* —**lu′bri·ca′tor** *n.*

**lu·cid** (lōo′sid) *adj.* ⟦< L *lucere,* to shine⟧ **1** [Old Poet.] shining **2** transparent **3** sane **4** clear; readily understood —**lu·cid′i·ty** *n.* —**lu′cid·ly** *adv.*

**Lu·ci·fer** (lōo′sə fər) *n.* Satan

**Lu·cite** (lōo′sīt′) ⟦< L *lux,* light⟧ *trademark for* an acrylic resin that is molded into transparent or translucent sheets, rods, etc.

**luck** (luk) *n.* ⟦prob. < MDu *gelucke*⟧ **1** the seemingly chance happening of events that affect someone; fortune; lot **2** good fortune —**luck out** [Inf.] to be lucky —**luck′less** *adj.*

**luck′y** *adj.* **-i·er, -i·est 1** having good luck **2** resulting fortunately **3** believed to bring good luck —**luck′i·ly** *adv.* —**luck′i·ness** *n.*

**lu·cra·tive** (lōo′krə tiv) *adj.* ⟦< L *lucrum,* riches⟧ producing wealth or profit; profitable

**lu·cre** (lōo′kər) *n.* ⟦< L *lucrum,* riches⟧ riches; money: chiefly humorously derogatory

**lu·cu·brate** (lōo′kə brāt′, -kyōo-) *vi.* **-brat·ed, -brat·ing** ⟦< L *lucubrare,* to work by candlelight⟧ to work, study, or write laboriously, esp. late at night —**lu′cu·bra′tion** *n.*

**lu·di·crous** (lōo′di krəs) *adj.* ⟦< L *ludus,* a game⟧ causing laughter because absurd or ridiculous —**lu′di·crous·ly** *adv.* —**lu′di·crous·ness** *n.*

**luff** (luf) *vi.* ⟦< ME *lof*⟧ to turn the bow of a ship toward the wind

**lug** (lug) *vt.* **lugged, lug′ging** ⟦prob. < Scand⟧ to carry or drag (something heavy) —*n.* **1** an earlike projection by which a thing is held or supported **2** a heavy bolt, used, with a nut (**lug nut**), to secure a wheel to an axle

**lug·gage** (lug′ij) *n.* ⟦< prec.⟧ suitcases, trunks, etc.; baggage

**lu·gu·bri·ous** (lə gōo′brē əs) *adj.* ⟦< L *lugere,* mourn⟧ very sad or mournful, esp. in an exaggerated way —**lu·gu′bri·ous·ly** *adv.* —**lu·gu′bri·ous·ness** *n.*

**Luke** (lōok) *n. Bible* **1** an early Christian, the reputed author of the third Gospel **2** this Gospel

**luke·warm** (lōok′wôrm′) *adj.* ⟦< ME *luke,* tepid + *warm,* warm⟧ **1** slightly warm **2** lacking enthusiasm —**luke′warm′ly** *adv.* —**luke′warm′ness** *n.*

**lull** (lul) *vt.* ⟦ME *lullen*⟧ **1** to calm by gentle sound or motion **2** to bring into a specified condition by soothing and reassuring —*vi.* to become calm —*n.* a short period of calm

**lull′a·by′** (-ə bī′) *n., pl.* **-bies′** ⟦< ME, echoic⟧ a song for lulling a baby to sleep

**lum·ba·go** (lum bā′gō) *n.* ⟦L < *lumbus,* loin⟧ pain in the lower back

**lum·bar** (lum′bär) *adj.* ⟦< L *lumbus,* loin⟧ of or near the loins

**lum·ber**[1] (lum′bər) *n.* ⟦< ? pawnbrokers of *Lombardy,* Italy; hence, stored articles⟧ timber sawed into boards, etc. —*vt.* to cut down timber and saw it into lumber —**lum′ber·er** *n.* —**lum′ber·ing** *n.*

**lum·ber**[2] (lum′bər) *vi.* ⟦< ? Scand⟧ to move heavily and noisily —**lum′ber·ing** *adj.*

**lum′ber·jack′** (-jak′) *n.* LOGGER

**lum′ber·man** (-mən) *n., pl.* **-men** (-mən) one who deals in lumber

**lu·mi·nar·y** (lōo′mə ner′ē) *n., pl.* **-nar·ies** ⟦< L *lumen,* a light⟧ **1** a body that gives off light, such as the sun **2** a famous or notable person

**lu·mi·nes·cence** (lōo′mə nes′əns) *n.* ⟦< L *lumen,* a light + -ESCENCE⟧ the giving off of light without heat, as in fluorescence or phosphorescence —**lu′mi·nes′cent** *adj.*

**lu·mi·nous** (lōo′mə nəs) *adj.* ⟦< L *lumen,* a light⟧ **1** giving off light; bright **2** clear; readily understood —**lu′mi·nos′i·ty** (-näs′ə tē) *n.*

**lum·mox** (lum′əks) *n.* ⟦< ?⟧ [Inf.] a clumsy, stupid person

**lump**[1] (lump) *n.* ⟦ME *lompe*⟧ **1** an indefinitely shaped mass of something **2** a swelling **3** [*pl.*] [Inf.] hard blows, criticism, etc. —*adj.* in a lump or lumps —*vt.* **1** to put together in a lump or lumps **2** to treat or deal with in a mass —*vi.* to become lumpy —**lump′i·ness** *n.* —**lump′y, -i·er, -i·est,** *adj.*

**lump**[2] (lump) *vt.* ⟦< ?⟧ [Inf.] to have to put up with (something disagreeable) /like it or *lump* it/

**lump sum** a gross, or total, sum paid at one time

**lu·na·cy** (lōo′nə sē) *n.* ⟦< LUNATIC⟧ **1** insanity **2** great folly or a foolish act

**lu·nar** (lōo′nər) *adj.* ⟦< L *luna,* the moon⟧ of or like the moon

**lu·na·tic** (lōo′nə tik) *adj.* ⟦< L *luna,* the moon⟧ **1** insane or for insane persons **2** utterly foolish —*n.* an insane person

**lunch** (lunch) *n.* ⟦< ? Sp *lonja,* slice of ham⟧ a light meal; esp., the midday meal between breakfast and dinner —*vi.* to eat lunch

**lunch·eon** (lun′chən) *n.* a lunch; esp., a formal lunch

**lunch·eon·ette** (lun′chən et′) *n.* a place where light lunches are served

**luncheon meat** meat processed in the form of loaves, sausages, etc. and ready to eat: also [Inf.] **lunch′meat′** *n.*

**lung** (luŋ) *n.* [OE *lungen*] either of the two spongelike breathing organs in the thorax of vertebrates

**lunge** (lunj) *n.* [< Fr *allonger*, lengthen] 1 a sudden thrust as with a sword 2 a sudden plunge forward —*vi.*, *vt.* **lunged**, **lung′ing** to move, or cause to move, with a lunge

**lung·fish** (luŋ′fish′) *n.*, *pl.* **-fish′** or (for different species) **-fish′es** any of various fishes having lungs as well as gills

**lunk·head** (luŋk′hed′) *n.* [prob. echoic alteration of LUMP[1] + HEAD] [Inf.] a stupid person: also **lunk**

**lu·pine** (lōō′pīn′; *for n.*, -pin) *adj.* [< L *lupus*, wolf] of or like a wolf —*n.* a plant with long spikes of white, rose, yellow, or blue flowers

**lu·pus** (lōō′pəs) *n.* [< L, a wolf] any of various diseases with skin lesions

**lurch**[1] (lurch) *vi.* [< ?] 1 to pitch or sway suddenly to one side 2 to stagger —*n.* a lurching movement

**lurch**[2] (lurch) *n.* [prob. < OFr *lourche*, duped] a difficult situation: only in **leave someone in the lurch**

**lure** (loor) *n.* [< OFr *loirre*] 1 anything that tempts or entices 2 a bait used in fishing —*vt.* **lured**, **lur′ing** to attract; tempt; entice

**lu·rid** (loor′id) *adj.* [L *luridus*, ghastly] 1 glowing through a haze: said as of flames enveloped by smoke 2 shocking; sensational —**lu′rid·ly** *adv.* —**lu′rid·ness** *n.*

**lurk** (lurk) *vi.* [ME *lurken*] to stay hidden, ready to attack, spring out, etc.

**lus·cious** (lush′əs) *adj.* [ME *lucius*] 1 highly gratifying to taste or smell; delicious 2 delighting any of the senses —**lus′cious·ness** *n.*

**lush**[1] (lush) *adj.* [< ? OFr *lasche*, lax] 1 of or showing luxuriant growth 2 rich, abundant, extravagant, etc. —**lush′ness** *n.*

**lush**[2] (lush) *n.* [Slang] an alcoholic

**lust** (lust) *n.* [OE, pleasure] 1 bodily appetite; esp., excessive sexual desire 2 overwhelming desire [a *lust* for power] —*vi.* to feel an intense desire —**lust′ful** *adj.* —**lust′ful·ly** *adv.* —**lust′ful·ness** *n.*

**lus·ter** (lus′tər) *n.* [< L *lustrare*, illumine] 1 gloss; sheen 2 brightness; radiance 3 brilliant beauty or fame; glory Also [Chiefly Brit.] **lus′tre**

**lus′trous** (-trəs) *adj.* having luster; shining

**lust·y** (lus′tē) *adj.* **-i·er**, **-i·est** full of vigor; robust —**lust′i·ly** *adv.* —**lust′i·ness** *n.*

**lute** (lōōt) *n.* [ult. < Ar *al′ūd*, the wood] an old stringed instrument like the guitar, with a rounded body

**lu·te·nist** (lōōt′'n ist) *n.* a lute player: also **lu′ta·nist**

**Lu·ther** (lōō′thər), **Mar·tin** (märt′'n) 1483-1546; Ger. Reformation leader

**Lu′ther·an** *adj.* of the Protestant denomination founded by Luther —*n.* a member of a Lutheran Church —**Lu′ther·an·ism′** *n.*

**lut·ist** (lōōt′ist) *n.* LUTENIST

**Lux·em·bourg** (luk′səm burg′) grand duchy in W Europe, north of France: 999 sq. mi.; pop. 401,000

**lux·u·ri·ant** (lug zhoor′ē ənt) *adj.* [see LUXURY] 1 growing with vigor and in abundance 2 having rich ornamentation, etc. —**lux·u′ri·ance** *n.*

**lux·u′ri·ate′** (-āt′) *vi.* **-at′ed**, **-at′ing** 1 to live in great luxury 2 to revel (*in*) —**lux·u′ri·a′tion** *n.*

**lux·u′ri·ous** (-əs) *adj.* 1 fond of or indulging in luxury 2 constituting luxury; rich, comfortable, etc. —**lux·u′ri·ous·ly** *adv.*

**lux·u·ry** (luk′shə rē, lug′zhə rē) *n.*, *pl.* **-ries** [< L *luxus*] 1 the use and enjoyment of the best and

most costly things 2 anything contributing to such enjoyment, usually something not necessary —*adj.* characterized by luxury

**Lu·zon** (lōō zän′) main island of the Philippines

**-ly**[1] (lē) [< OE *-lic*] *suffix* 1 like or characteristic of [*manly*] 2 happening (once) every (specified period of time) [*monthly, hourly*]

**-ly**[2] (lē) [< OE *-lice*] *suffix* 1 in a (specified) manner or direction, to a (specified) extent, in or at a (specified) time or place [*harshly, inwardly, hourly*] 2 in the (specified) order [*thirdly*]

**ly·ce·um** (lī sē′əm) *n.* [< Gr *Lykeion*, grove at Athens where Aristotle taught] 1 a lecture hall 2 an organization presenting lectures, etc.

**Ly·cra** (lī′krə) *trademark for* a spandex fabric used in underwear, athletic apparel, etc.

**lye** (lī) *n.* [OE *leag*] any strongly alkaline substance, used in cleaning, making soap, etc.

**ly·ing**[1] (lī′iŋ) *vi. prp. of* LIE[1]

**ly·ing**[2] (lī′iŋ) *vt.*, *vi. prp. of* LIE[2] —*adj.* false; not truthful —*n.* the telling of a lie or lies

**ly′ing-in′** *n.* confinement in childbirth —*adj.* of or for childbirth

**lymph** (limf) *n.* [L *lympha*, spring water] a clear, yellowish body fluid resembling blood plasma, found in the spaces between cells and in the lymphatic vessels

**lym·phat·ic** (lim fat′ik) *adj.* containing lymph

**lymph node** any of the small, compact structures lying in groups along the course of the lymphatic vessels

**lym·pho·cyte** (lim′fō sīt′) *n.* a leukocyte formed in lymphatic tissue, important in the synthesis of antibodies

**lymph·oid** (lim′foid) *adj.* of or like lymph or the tissue of the lymph nodes

**lym·pho·ma** (lim fō′mə) *n.* any of a group of diseases resulting from the proliferation of malignant lymphoid cells

**lynch** (linch) *vt.* [after W. *Lynch*, vigilante in VA in 1780] to murder (an accused person) by mob action and without lawful trial, as by hanging —**lynch′ing** *n.*

**lynx** (liŋks) *n.* [< Gr *lynx*] a wildcat found throughout the Northern Hemisphere, having a short tail and tufted ears

**lynx′-eyed′** (-īd′) *adj.* keen-sighted

**Lyon** (lyōn) city in EC France: pop. 415,000

**ly·on·naise** (lī′ə nāz′) *adj.* [Fr] prepared with sliced onions

**lyre** (līr) *n.* [< Gr *lyra*] a small stringed instrument of the harp family, used by the ancient Greeks

**lyr·ic** (lir′ik) *adj.* [< Gr *lyrikos*] 1 suitable for singing; specif., designating or of poetry expressing the poet's personal emotion 2 or having a high voice with a light, flexible quality [a *lyric* tenor] —*n.* 1 a lyric poem 2 [*usually pl.*] the words of a song

LYRE

**lyr′i·cal** (-i kəl) *adj.* 1 LYRIC 2 expressing rapture or great enthusiasm

**lyr′i·cism′** (-ə siz′əm) *n.* lyric quality or style

**lyr′i·cist** (-ə sist) *n.* a writer of lyrics, esp. lyrics for popular songs

**ly·ser·gic acid** (lī sur′jik) *see* LSD

**-ly·sis** (lə sis, li-) [< Gr *lysis*, a loosening] *combining form* a loosening, dissolution, dissolving, destruction [*catalysis, electrolysis*]

**-lyte** (līt) [< Gr *lyein*, dissolve] *combining form* a substance undergoing decomposition [*electrolyte*]

# M

**m**[1] or **M** (em) *n.*, *pl.* **m's, M's** the 13th letter of the English alphabet

**m**[2] *abbrev.* **1** married **2** masculine **3** medium **4** meter(s) **5** mile(s) **6** minute(s)

**M**[1] (em) *n.* a Roman numeral for 1,000

**M**[2] *abbrev.* **1** male **2** married **3** medium **4** Monday **5** Monsieur

**ma** (mä) *n.* [Inf.] MOTHER (*n.* 1)

**MA** *abbrev.* **1** Massachusetts **2** [L *Magister Artium*] Master of Arts: also **M.A.**

**ma'am** (mam, mäm) *contr. n.* [Inf.] madam: used in direct address

**ma·ca·bre** (mə käb′rə, mə käb′) *adj.* [< OFr (*danse*) *Macabré*, (dance) of death] grim and horrible; gruesome

**mac·ad·am** (mə kad′əm) *n.* [after J. L. *McAdam* (1756-1836), Scot engineer] small broken stones used in making roads, esp. such stones mixed with tar or asphalt

**Ma·cao** (mə kou′) administrative zone of China, near Hong Kong: formerly under Portuguese administration

**mac·a·ro·ni** (mak′ə rō′nē) *n.* [It *maccaroni*, ult. < Gr *makar*, blessed] pasta in the form of tubes, etc.

**mac·a·roon** (mak′ə rōōn′) *n.* [see prec.] a small, chewy cookie made with crushed almonds or coconut

**ma·caw** (mə kô′) *n.* [prob. < AmInd (Brazil)] a large, bright-colored parrot of Central and South America

**Mac·beth** (mək beth′) *n.* the title character of a tragedy by Shakespeare

**Mac·ca·bees** (mak′ə bēz′) *n.* a family of Jewish patriots who headed a successful revolt against the Syrians (175-164 B.C.)

**mace**[1] (mās) *n.* [OFr *masse*] **1** a heavy, spiked war club, used in the Middle Ages **2** a staff used as a symbol of authority by certain officials

**mace**[2] (mās) *n.* [< ML *macis*] a spice made from the husk of the nutmeg

**Mace** (mās) [< MACE[1]] *trademark for* a gas, sold in aerosol containers, that temporarily stuns its victims —*n.* [often m-] such a substance, or a container of it —*vt.* **Maced, Mac′ing** [often m-] to spray with Mace

**Mac·e·do·ni·a** (mas′ə dō′nē ə) **1** ancient kingdom in SE Europe **2** country in the Balkan Peninsula: 9,928 sq. mi.; pop. 1,937,000 —**Mac′e·do′ni·an** *adj.*, *n.*

**mac·er·ate** (mas′ər āt′) *vt.* **-at′ed, -at′ing** [< L *macerare*, soften] **1** to soften and separate into parts by soaking in liquid **2** to steep (fruit or vegetables), as in wine **3** loosely, to tear, chop, etc. into bits —**mac′er·a′tion** *n.*

**ma·che·te** (mə shet′ē, -chet′ē) *n.* [Sp < L *marcus*, hammer] a large knife used for cutting sugar cane, underbrush, etc., esp. in Central and South America

**Mach·i·a·vel·li·an** (mak′ē ə vel′ē ən, mäk′-) *adj.* [after N. *Machiavelli* (1469-1527), It statesman] crafty; deceitful

**mach·i·na·tion** (mak′ə nā′shən) *n.* [< L *machinari*, to plot] a plot or scheme, esp. one with evil intent: *usually used in pl.*

**ma·chine** (mə shēn′) *n.* [< Gr *mēchos*, contrivance] **1** a structure consisting of a framework with various moving parts, for doing some kind of work **2** an organization functioning like a machine **3** the controlling group in a political party **4** *Mech.* a device, as the lever, that transmits, or changes the application of, energy —*adj.* **1** of machines **2** done by machinery —*vt.*

**-chined′, -chin′ing** to make, shape, etc. by machinery

**machine gun** an automatic gun, firing a rapid stream of bullets

**machine language** a language entirely in binary digits, used directly by a computer

**ma·chin·er·y** (mə shēn′ər ē, -shēn′rē) *n.*, *pl.* **-ies** **1** machines collectively **2** the working parts of a machine **3** the means for keeping something going

**ma·chin·ist** *n.* one who makes, repairs, or operates machinery

**ma·chis·mo** (mä chēz′mō) *n.* [Sp < *macho*, masculine + *-ismo*, -ISM] overly assertive or exaggerated masculinity

**Mach number** (mäk) [after E. *Mach* (1838-1916), Austrian physicist] [*also* m- n-] a number indicating the ratio of an object's speed to the speed of sound in the surrounding medium

**ma·cho** (mä′chō) *adj.* [Sp, masculine] exhibiting or characterized by machismo

**mack·er·el** (mak′ər əl) *n.*, *pl.* **-el** or **-els** [< OFr *maquerel*] an edible fish of the North Atlantic

**Mack·i·naw (coat)** (mak′ə nô′) [after *Mackinac* Island in N Lake Huron] [*also* m-] a short, heavy, double-breasted woolen coat, usually plaid

**mack·in·tosh** (mak′in täsh′) *n.* [after C. *Macintosh*, 19th-c. Scot inventor] a raincoat, orig., one made of rubberized cloth

**Ma·con** (mā′kən) city in central Georgia: pop. 107,000

**mac·ra·mé** (mak′rə mā′) *n.* [Fr, ult. < Ar *miqramah*, a veil] a coarse fringe or lace made as of cord knotted in designs

**macro-** [< Gr *makros*, long] *combining form* long, large, enlarged

**mac·ro·bi·ot·ics** (mak′rō bī ät′iks) *pl.n.* [< prec. + Gr *bios*, life] [*with sing. v.*] the study of prolonging life, as by special diets —**mac′ro·bi·ot′ic** *adj.*

**mac′ro·cosm′** (-käz′əm) *n.* [see MACRO- & COSMOS] **1** the universe **2** any large, complex entity

**ma·cron** (mā′krən) *n.* [< Gr *makros*, long] a mark (‾) placed over a vowel to indicate its pronunciation

**mad** (mad) *adj.* **mad′der, mad′dest** [< OE (*ge*)*mædan*, make mad] **1** insane **2** frantic [*mad* with fear] **3** foolish and rash **4** infatuated [he's *mad* about her] **5** wildly amusing **6** having rabies [*a mad dog*] **7** angry: often with *at* — **mad′ly** *adv.* —**mad′ness** *n.*

**Mad·a·gas·car** (mad′ə gas′kər) island country off the SE coast of Africa: 226,658 sq. mi.; pop. 13,469,000

**mad·am** (mad′əm) *n.*, *pl.* **mad′ams**; for 1, usually **mes·dames** (mā däm′, -dam′) [Fr *madame*, orig. *ma dame*, my lady] **1** a woman; lady: a polite term of address **2** a woman in charge of a brothel

**ma·dame** (mə däm′, -dam′; mad′əm; *Fr* mà dàm′) *n.*, *pl.* **mes·dames** (mā däm′, -dam′; *Fr* mā dàm′) [Fr: see prec.] **1** a married woman: French title equivalent to *Mrs.* **2** a distinguished woman: used in English as a title of respect

**mad·cap** (mad′kap′) *n.* [MAD + CAP[1], figurative for head] a reckless, impulsive person —*adj.* reckless and impulsive

**mad·den** (mad′n) *vt.*, *vi.* to make or become insane, angry, or wildly excited —**mad′den·ing** *adj.* —**mad′den·ing·ly** *adv.*

**mad·der** (mad′ər) *n.* [OE *mædere*] **1** any of various related plants, esp. a vine with yellow flowers and a red root **2** a red dye made from this root

**made** (mād) *vt.*, *vi. pt. & pp. of* MAKE

**ma·de·moi·selle** (mad′ə mə zel′; *Fr* mād mwà zel′) *n.*, *pl.* **-selles′**; Fr. **mes·de·moi·selles** (mād mwä zel′) [Fr < *ma*, my + *demoiselle,* young lady] an unmarried woman or girl: French title equivalent to *Miss*

**made′-to-or′der** *adj.* made to conform to the customer's specifications

**made′-up′** *adj.* **1** put together **2** invented; false *[a made-up story]* **3** with cosmetics applied

**mad′house′** *n.* **1** an insane asylum **2** any place of turmoil, noise, etc.

**Mad·i·son**[1] (mad′ə sən), **James** 1751-1836; 4th president of the U.S. (1809-17)

**Mad·i·son**[2] (mad′ə sən) capital of Wisconsin: pop. 191,000

**mad′man′** (-man′, -mən) *n., pl.* **-men′** (-men′, -mən) an insane person —**mad′wom′an,** *pl.* **-wom′en,** *fem.n.*

**Ma·don·na** (mə dän′ə) *n.* [It < *ma*, my + *donna,* lady] **1** Mary, mother of Jesus **2** a picture or statue of Mary

**ma·dras** (ma′drəs, mə dras′) *n.* [after fol.] a fine, firm cotton cloth, usually striped or plaid

**Ma·dras** (mə dras′, -dräs′) seaport on the SE coast of India: pop. 4,289,000: now officially *Chennai*

**Ma·drid** (mə drid′) capital of Spain, in the central part: pop. 3,159,000

**mad·ri·gal** (ma′dri gəl) *n.* [< It] a part song, without accompaniment, popular in the 15th to 17th c.

**mael·strom** (māl′strəm) *n.* [< Du *malen,* to grind + *stroom,* a stream] **1** a large or violent whirlpool **2** an agitated state of mind, affairs, etc.

**ma·es·tro** (mīs′trō) *n., pl.* **-tros** or **-tri** (-trē) [It < L *magister,* master] a master in any art; esp., a great composer or conductor of music

**Ma·fi·a** (mä′fē ə) *n.* [It *maffia*] a secret society engaged in illegal activities

**Ma·fi·o·so** (mä′fē ō′sō) *n., pl.* **-si** (-sē) [*also* **m-**] a member of the Mafia

**mag·a·zine** (mag′ə zēn′) *n.* [< Ar *makhzan,* storehouse] **1** a military supply depot **2** a space in which explosives are stored, as in a fort **3** a supply chamber, as in a rifle or camera **4** a periodical publication containing stories, articles, etc.

**Ma·gel·lan** (mə jel′ən), **Fer·di·nand** (furd′n and′) 1480?-1521; Port. navigator in the service of Spain

**ma·gen·ta** (mə jen′tə) *n.* [after *Magenta,* town in Italy] **1** a purplish-red dye **2** purplish red —*adj.* purplish-red

**mag·got** (mag′ət) *n.* [ME *magotte*] a wormlike insect larva, as of the housefly —**mag′got·y** *adj.*

**Ma·gi** (mā′jī′) *pl.n., sing.* **-gus** (-gəs) [< Old Pers *magus,* magician] the wise men who came bearing gifts to the infant Jesus

**mag·ic** (maj′ik) *n.* [< Gr *magikos,* of the Magi, ancient Persian priests] **1** the use of charms, spells, etc. in seeking or pretending to control events **2** any mysterious power *[the magic of love]* **3** the art of producing illusions by sleight of hand, etc. —*adj.* **1** of, produced by, or using magic **2** producing extraordinary results, as if by magic —**mag′i·cal** *adj.* —**mag′i·cal·ly** *adv.*

**magic bullet** an invention, discovery, etc. that solves a particular problem; esp., a medicine that can cure a disease

**ma·gi·cian** (mə jish′ən) *n.* [< OFr *magicien*] an expert in magic

**mag·is·te·ri·al** (maj′is tir′ē əl) *adj.* **1** of or suitable for a magistrate or master **2** authoritative —**mag′is·te′ri·al·ly** *adv.*

**mag·is·trate** (maj′is trāt′) *n.* [< L *magister,* master] **1** a civil officer empowered to administer the law **2** a minor official, as a justice of the peace

**mag·ma** (mag′mə) *n.* [< Gr *massein,* knead] liquid or molten rock in the earth, which solidifies to produce igneous rock

**Mag·na Car·ta** or **Mag·na Char·ta** (mag′nə kär′tə) [ML, great charter] the charter, granted in 1215, that guarantees certain civil and political liberties to the English people

**mag·nan·i·mous** (mag nan′ə məs) *adj.* [< L *magnus,* great + *animus,* soul] generous in over-

looking injury or insult; rising above pettiness; noble —**mag′na·nim′i·ty** (-nə nim′ə tē) *n.* —**mag·nan′i·mous·ly** *adv.*

**mag·nate** (mag′nāt) *n.* [< L *magnus,* great] a very influential person, esp. in business

**mag·ne·sia** (mag nē′zhə, -shə) *n.* [ModL, ult. < Gr *Magnēsia,* ancient Gr city] magnesium oxide, a white powder, used as a mild laxative and antacid

**mag·ne′si·um** (-zē əm) *n.* [ModL: see prec.] a lightweight, metallic chemical element

**mag·net** (mag′nit) *n.* [see MAGNESIA] **1** any piece of iron or certain other materials that has the property of attracting similar material **2** one that attracts

**mag·net·ic** (mag net′ik) *adj.* **1** having the properties of a magnet **2** of, producing, or caused by magnetism **3** of the earth's magnetism **4** that can be magnetized **5** powerfully attractive —**mag·net′i·cal·ly** *adv.*

MAGNET

**magnetic field** a physical field arising from an electric charge in motion, producing a force on a moving electric charge

**magnetic tape** a thin plastic ribbon with a magnetized coating for recording sounds, digital computer data, etc.

**mag·net·ism** (mag′nə tiz′əm) *n.* **1** the property, quality, or condition of being magnetic **2** the force to which this is due **3** personal charm

**mag′net·ite′** (-tīt′) *n.* [< Ger] black iron oxide, an important iron ore

**mag′net·ize′** (-tīz′) *vt.* **-ized′, -iz′ing 1** to give magnetic properties to (steel, iron, etc.) **2** to charm (a person) —**mag′net·i·za′tion** *n.*

**mag·ne·to** (mag nēt′ō) *n., pl.* **-tos** an electric generator, often a small one, in which one or more permanent magnets produce the magnetic field

**mag·ne·tom·e·ter** (mag′nə täm′ət ər) *n.* **1** an instrument for measuring magnetic forces **2** such an instrument used as to detect concealed metal weapons at airports, etc.

**magnet school** a public school offering new and special courses to attract students from a broad urban area so as to bring about desegregation

**mag·nif·i·cent** (mag nif′ə sənt) *adj.* [< L *magnus,* great + *facere,* do] **1** splendid, stately, or sumptuous, as in form **2** exalted: said of ideas, etc. **3** [Inf.] excellent —**mag·nif′i·cence** *n.* —**mag·nif′i·cent·ly** *adv.*

**mag·ni·fy** (mag′nə fī′) *vt.* **-fied′, -fy′ing** [see prec.] **1** to exaggerate **2** to increase the apparent size of, esp. with a lens **3** [Archaic] to praise —*vi.* to have the power of increasing the apparent size of an object —**mag′ni·fi·ca′tion** *n.* —**mag′ni·fi′er** *n.*

**mag′ni·tude′** (-tōōd′) *n.* [< L *magnus,* great] **1** greatness of size, extent, etc. **2** *a*) size *b*) loudness (of sound) *c*) importance **3** the degree of brightness of a star, etc.

**mag·no·li·a** (mag nō′lē ə, -nōl′yə) *n.* [after P. *Magnol* (1638-1715), Fr botanist] a tree with large, fragrant flowers of white, pink, or purple

**mag·num** (mag′nəm) *n.* [< L *magnus,* great] **1** a wine bottle holding 1.5 liters **2** [*usually* **M-**] a firearm, esp. a revolver, that fires magnum cartridges —*adj.* of or pertaining to a cartridge having great explosive force for its size

**mag·num o·pus** (mag′nəm ō′pəs) [L] a great work; masterpiece

**mag·pie** (mag′pī′) *n.* [< *Mag,* dim. of *Margaret* + *pie,* magpie] **1** a noisy, black-and-white bird related to the jay **2** a person who chatters

**Mag·yar** (mag′yär′) *n.* **1** a member of the main ethnic group of Hungary **2** the language of this people

**ma·ha·ra·jah** or **ma·ha·ra·ja** (mä′hə rä′jə) *n.* [< Sans *mahā,* great + *rājā,* king] [Historical] in India, a prince, specif. the ruler of a native state —**ma′ha·ra′ni** or **ma′ha·ra′nee** (-nē) *fem.n.*

**ma·ha·ri·shi** (mä′hə rish′ē) *n.* 〚Hindi < *mahā,* great + *r̥shi,* sage〛 a Hindu teacher of mysticism

**ma·hat·ma** (mə hat′mə, -hät′-) *n.* 〚< Sans *mahā,* great + *ātman,* soul〛 in India, any of a class of wise and holy persons held in special regard

**mah-jongg** or **mah·jong** (mä′jôŋ′, -zhôŋ′) *n.* 〚< Chin *ma-ch′iao,* sparrow, a figure on one of the tiles〛 a game of Chinese origin played with small pieces called *tiles*

**Mah·ler** (mä′lər), **Gus·tav** (gōōs′täf′) 1860-1911; Austrian composer & conductor

**ma·hog·a·ny** (mə häg′ə nē, -hôg′-) *n., pl.* -nies 〚< ?〛 1 *a)* a tropical American tree *b)* the reddish-brown wood of this tree 2 reddish brown

**Ma·hom·et** (mə häm′it) *var. of* MOHAMMED

**ma·hout** (mə hout′) *n.* 〚< Hindi〛 in India, an elephant driver or keeper

**maid** (mād) *n.* 1 [Now Chiefly Literary] a girl or young unmarried woman 2 a female servant

**maid·en** (mād′′n) *n.* 〚OE *mægden*〛 [Now Rare] a girl or young unmarried woman —*adj.* 1 of or for a maiden 2 unmarried or virgin 3 untried 4 first *[a maiden* voyage*]* —**maid′en·hood′** *n.* — **maid′en·ly** *adj.*

**maid′en·hair′** (**fern**) a delicate fern

**maid′en·head′** (-hed′) *n.* the hymen

**maiden name** the surname that a married woman had when not yet married

**maid of honor** an unmarried woman acting as chief attendant to a bride

**maid′ser′vant** *n.* a female servant

**mail**[1] (māl) *n.* 〚< OHG *malaha,* wallet〛 1 letters, packages, etc. transported and delivered by the post office 2 a postal system —*adj.* of mail —*vt.* to send by mail —**mail′er** *n.*

**mail**[2] (māl) *n.* 〚< L *macula,* mesh of a net〛 flexible body armor made of small metal rings, scales, etc.

**mail′box′** *n.* 1 a box into which mail is put when delivered 2 a box into which mail is put for collection Also **mail box**

**mail carrier** a person who carries and delivers mail

**mail′man′** (-man′, -mən) *n., pl.* -men′ (-men′, -mən) a man who is a mail carrier

**mail order** an order for goods to be sent by mail —**mail′-or′der** *adj.*

**maim** (mām) *vt.* 〚OFr *mahaigner*〛 to disable; mutilate

SUIT OF MAIL

**main** (mān) *n.* 〚OE *mægen,* strength〛 1 a principal pipe in a distribution system for water, gas, etc. 2 [Old Poet.] the ocean —*adj.* chief in size, importance, etc.; principal —**by main force (or strength)** by sheer force (or strength) —**in the main** mostly; chiefly —**with might and main** with all one's strength

**main clause** *Gram.* INDEPENDENT CLAUSE

**main drag** [Slang] the principal street of a city or town

**Maine** (mān) New England state of the U.S.: 30,865 sq. mi.; pop. 1,228,000; cap. Augusta: abbrev. *ME* —**Main·er** (mā′nər) *n.*

**main·frame** (mān′frām′) *n.* 1 the central processing unit of a large computer 2 a very large computer, to which several terminals may be connected

**main·land′** (-land′, -lənd) *n.* the principal land mass of a continent, as distinguished from nearby islands —**main′land′er** *n.*

**main′line′** *n.* the principal road, course, etc. —*vt.* -lined′, -lin′ing [Slang] to inject (a narcotic drug) directly into a large vein

**main′ly** *adv.* chiefly; principally

**main′mast′** (-mast′; *naut.,* -məst) *n.* the principal mast of a vessel

**main′sail′** (-sāl′; *naut.,* -səl) *n.* the principal sail of a vessel, set from the mainmast

**main′spring′** *n.* 1 the principal spring in a clock, watch, etc. 2 the chief motive or cause

**main′stay′** *n.* 1 the supporting line extending forward from the mainmast 2 a chief support

**main′stream′** *n.* a major trend or line of thought, action, etc. —*vt.* to cause to undergo mainstreaming

**main′stream′ing** *n.* the placement of disabled people into regular school classes, workplaces, etc.

**main·tain** (mān tān′) *vt.* 〚< L *manu tenere,* hold in the hand〛 1 to keep or keep up; carry on 2 to keep in continuance or in a certain state, as of repair 3 to affirm or assert 4 to support by providing what is needed —**main·tain′a·ble** *adj.*

**main·te·nance** (mānt′′n əns) *n.* a maintaining or being maintained

**mai tai** (mī′ tī′) 〚Tahitian, lit., good〛 [*often* M- T-] a cocktail of rum, fruit juices, etc.

**mai·tre d′** (māt′ər dē′) 〚< fol.〛 [Inf.] MAÎTRE D′HÔTEL

**maî·tre d′hô·tel** (me tr′ dô tel′) 〚Fr, master of the house〛 a supervisor of waiters and waitresses

**maize** (māz) *n.* 〚< WInd *mahiz*〛 1 *chiefly Brit.* name for CORN[1] (*n.* 2) 2 yellow

**Maj** *abbrev.* Major

**ma·jes·tic** (mə jes′tik) *adj.* grand; stately —**ma·jes′ti·cal·ly** *adv.*

**maj·es·ty** (maj′is tē) *n., pl.* -ties 〚< L *magnus,* great〛 1 [M-] a title used in speaking to or of a sovereign 2 grandeur

**ma·jol·i·ca** (mə jäl′i kə) *n.* 〚It〛 Italian glazed pottery

**ma·jor** (mā′jər) *adj.* 〚L, compar. of *magnus,* great〛 1 greater in size, amount, importance, etc. 2 *Music* designating an interval greater than the corresponding minor by a half tone —*vi. Educ.* to specialize (*in* a field of study) —*n.* 1 *U.S. Mil.* an officer ranking just above a captain 2 a field of study in which a student specializes

**ma′jor-do′mo** (-dō′mō) *n., pl.* -mos 〚< L *major,* greater + *domus,* house〛 a man in charge of a great household

**ma′jor·ette′** (-et′) *n.* a girl or woman with a baton, who leads or accompanies a marching band; drum majorette

**major general** *pl.* **major generals** *U.S. Mil.* an officer ranking just above a brigadier general

**ma·jor·i·ty** (mə jôr′ə tē) *n., pl.* -ties 〚see MAJOR〛 1 [*also with pl. v.*] the greater number; more than half of a total 2 the number by which the votes cast for the candidate who receives more than half the votes, exceed the remaining votes 3 full legal age 4 the military rank of a major

**major scale** a musical scale with semitones between the third and fourth and the seventh and eighth tones, and whole tones in all other positions

**make** (māk) *vt.* **made, mak′ing** 〚OE *macian*〛 1 to bring into being; build, create, produce, etc. 2 to cause to be or become *[made* king, *made* sad*]* 3 to prepare for use *[make* the beds*]* 4 to amount to *[two pints make* a quart*]* 5 to have the qualities of *[to make* a fine leader*]* 6 to acquire; earn 7 to cause the success of *[that* venture *made* her*]* 8 to regard as the meaning (*of*) *[what* do you *make* of that?*]* 9 to execute, do, etc. *[to make* a speech*]* 10 to cause or force: with an infinitive without *to [make* him behave*]* 11 to arrive at; reach *[the* ship *made* port*]* 12 [Inf.] to get on or in *[to make* the team*]* —*vi.* 1 to behave as specified *[make* bold*]* 2 to cause something to be as specified *[make* ready*]* —*n.* 1 the way in which something is made; style 2 a type or brand —**make away with** to steal —**make believe** to pretend —**make someone's day** [Slang] to give pleasure that will be the high point of someone's day —**make do** to manage with what is available —**make for** 1 to go toward **2** to help effect —**make good 1** to repay or replace **2** to fulfill **3** to succeed —**make it** [Inf.] to achieve a certain thing —**make off with** to steal —**make out 1** to see with difficulty **2** to understand **3** to fill out (a blank form, etc.) **4** to (try to) show or prove to be **5** to succeed; get along **6** [Slang] *a*) to kiss and caress as lovers *b*) to have sexual intercourse —**make over 1** to change; renovate **2** to transfer the ownership of —**make something of 1** to treat as of great importance **2** [Inf.] to make an issue of —**make up 1** to put together **2** to form; constitute **3** to invent **4** to complete by providing what is lacking **5** to compensate (*for*) **6** to become friendly again after a quarrel **7** to put on cosmetics, etc. —**make up one's mind** to come to a decision —**make up** to try to win over, as by flattering —**mak'er** *n.*

**make'-be·lieve'** *n.* pretense; feigning —*adj.* pretended; feigned

**make'o'ver** *n.* **1** a renovation **2** a change in someone's appearance made by altering makeup, hairstyle, etc.

**make'shift'** *n.* a temporary substitute or expedient —*adj.* that will do as a temporary substitute

**make'up'** or **make'-up'** *n.* **1** the way something is put together; composition **2** nature; disposition **3** the cosmetics, etc. used by an actor **4** cosmetics generally

**make'-work'** *adj.* that serves no other purpose than to give an idle or unemployed person something to do [*a make-work project*]

**mal-** [< L *malus,* bad] *prefix* bad or badly, wrong, ill

**mal·ad·just·ed** (mal'ə jus'tid) *adj.* poorly adjusted; specif., unable to adjust to the stresses of daily life —**mal'ad·just'ment** *n.*

**mal·a·droit** (mal'ə droit') *adj.* [Fr: see MAL- & ADROIT] awkward; clumsy; bungling —**mal'a·droit'ly** *adv.*

**mal·a·dy** (mal'ə dē) *n., pl.* **-dies** [< VL *male habitus,* badly kept] a disease; illness

**ma·laise** (ma lāz') *n.* [Fr < *mal,* bad + *aise,* ease] a vague feeling of illness

**mal·a·mute** (mal'ə myōōt') *n.* [< *Malemute,* an Eskimo tribe] a strong dog developed as a sled dog by Alaskan Eskimos

**mal·a·prop·ism** (mal'ə präp'iz'əm) *n.* [after Mrs. *Malaprop* in Sheridan's *The Rivals* (1775)] a ludicrous misuse of words that sound alike

**ma·lar·i·a** (mə ler'ē ə) *n.* [It < *mala aria,* bad air] an infectious disease transmitted by the anopheles mosquito, characterized by severe chills and fever —**ma·lar'i·al** *adj.*

**ma·lar·key** or **ma·lar·ky** (mə lär'kē) *n.* [< ?] [Slang] nonsensical talk

**mal·a·thi·on** (mal'ə thī'än') *n.* [< chemical names] an organic insecticide

**Ma·la·wi** (mä'lä wē') country in SE Africa: 45,747 sq. mi.; pop. 7,983,000

**Ma·lay** (mā'lā', mə lā') *n.* **1** the language of a large group of indigenous peoples of the Malay Peninsula and the Malay Archipelago, now the official language of Malaysia and Indonesia **2** a member of any of these peoples —*adj.* of these peoples or their language or culture

**Mal·a·ya·lam** (mal'ə yä'ləm) *n.* a language of the SW coast of India

**Malay Archipelago** large group of islands between SE Asia & Australia

**Malay Peninsula** peninsula in SE Asia

**Ma·lay·sia** (mə lā'zhə) **1** MALAY ARCHIPELAGO **2** country in SE Asia, mostly on the Malay Peninsula: 127,317 sq. mi.; pop. 17,567,000 —**Ma·lay'sian** *adj., n.*

**mal·con·tent** (mal'kən tent') *adj.* [OFr: see MAL- & CONTENT[1]] dissatisfied or rebellious —*n.* a malcontent person

**Mal·dives** (mal'dīvz) country on a group of islands (**Mal'dive Islands**) in the Indian Ocean: 115 sq. mi.; pop. 213,000

**male** (māl) *adj.* [< L *mas,* a male] **1** designating or of the sex that fertilizes the ovum **2** of, like, or

suitable for men or boys; masculine **3** having a part shaped to fit into a corresponding hollow part (called *female*): said of electric plugs, etc. —*n.* a male person, animal, or plant

**mal·e·dic·tion** (mal'ə dik'shən) *n.* [see MAL- & DICTION] a curse

**mal'e·fac'tor** (-fak'tər) *n.* [< L *male,* evil + *facere,* do] an evildoer or criminal —**mal'e·fac'tion** *n.*

**ma·lef·i·cent** (mə lef'ə sənt) *adj.* [< L: see prec.] harmful; evil —**ma·lef'i·cence** *n.*

**ma·lev·o·lent** (mə lev'ə lənt) *adj.* [< L *male,* evil + *velle,* to wish] wishing evil or harm to others; malicious —**ma·lev'o·lence** *n.*

**mal·fea·sance** (mal fē'zəns) *n.* [< Fr *mal,* evil + *faire,* do] wrongdoing, esp. by a public official

**mal·for·ma·tion** (mal'fôr mā'shən) *n.* faulty or abnormal formation of a body or part —**mal·formed'** *adj.*

**mal·func·tion** (mal funk'shən) *vi.* to fail to function as it should —*n.* an instance of malfunctioning

**Ma·li** (mä'lē) country in W Africa: 478,841 sq. mi.; pop. 9,820,000

**mal·ice** (mal'is) *n.* [< L *malus,* bad] **1** active ill will; desire to harm another **2** *Law* evil intent

**ma·li·cious** (mə lish'əs) *adj.* having, showing, or caused by malice; spiteful —**ma·li'cious·ly** *adv.*

**ma·lign** (mə līn') *vt.* [< L *male,* ill + *genus,* born] to speak evil of; slander —*adj.* **1** malicious **2** evil; baleful **3** very harmful

**ma·lig'nan·cy** (-nən sē) *n.* **1** malignant quality **2** *pl.* **-cies** a malignant tumor

**ma·lig·nant** (mə lig'nənt) *adj.* [see MALIGN] **1** having an evil influence **2** wishing evil **3** very harmful **4** causing or likely to cause death; specif., cancerous —**ma·lig'ni·ty** (-nə tē), *pl.* **-ties,** *n.*

**ma·lin·ger** (mə liŋ'gər) *vi.* [< Fr *malingre,* sickly] to feign illness so as to escape duty —**ma·lin'ger·er** *n.*

**mall** (môl) *n.* [< *maul,* mallet: from use in a game on outdoor lanes] **1** a shaded walk or public promenade **2** *a*) a shop-lined street for pedestrians only *b*) an enclosed shopping center

**mal·lard** (mal'ərd) *n.* [< OFr *malart*] the common wild duck

**mal·le·a·ble** (mal'ē ə bəl) *adj.* [< L *malleus,* a hammer] **1** that can be hammered, pounded, or pressed into various shapes without breaking **2** adaptable —**mal'le·a·bil'i·ty** *n.*

**mal·let** (mal'ət) *n.* [< L *malleus,* a hammer] **1** a short-handled hammer with a wooden head, for driving a chisel, etc. **2** any similar, long-handled hammer, as for use in croquet or polo **3** a small hammer for playing a xylophone, etc.

**mal·low** (mal'ō) *n.* [< L *malva*] any of a family of plants, including the hollyhock, cotton, and okra, with large, showy flowers

**mal·nour·ished** (mal nur'isht) *adj.* improperly nourished

**mal·nu·tri·tion** (mal'nōō trish'ən) *n.* faulty or inadequate nutrition or nourishment

**mal·oc·clu·sion** (-ə klōō'zhən) *n.* improper meeting of the upper and lower teeth

**mal·o·dor·ous** (-ō'dər əs) *adj.* having a bad odor; stinking

**mal·prac·tice** (-prak'tis) *n.* professional misconduct or improper practice, esp. by a physician

**malt** (môlt) *n.* [OE *mealt*] barley or other grain soaked until it sprouts, then dried in a kiln: used in brewing and distilling —*adj.* made with malt

**Mal·ta** (môl'tə) country on a group of islands in the Mediterranean, south of Sicily: 122 sq. mi.; pop. 376,000

**malt'ed** (**milk**) a drink made by mixing a preparation of powdered malt and dried milk, with milk, ice cream, etc.

**Mal·tese** (môl tēz') *n.* **1** the language of Malta, closely related to Arabic **2** *pl.* **Mal·tese'** a person born or living in Malta —*adj.* of Malta or its people, language, etc.

**malt liquor** beer, ale, or the like made from malt by fermentation

**mal·treat** (mal trēt′) *vt.* ⟦see MAL- & TREAT⟧ to treat roughly, unkindly, or brutally; abuse —**mal·treat′ment** *n.*

**ma·ma** or **mam′ma** (mä′mə, mə mä′) *n. child's term for* MOTHER

**mam·mal** (mam′əl) *n.* ⟦< L *mamma*, breast⟧ any of a large group of warmblooded vertebrates the females of which have milk-secreting glands (**mam′ma·ry glands**) for feeding their offspring — **mam·ma·li·an** (mə mā′lē ən) *adj., n.*

**mam·mo·gram** (mam′ə gram′) *n.* an X-ray obtained by mammography

**mam·mog·ra·phy** (mə mäg′rə fē) *n.* ⟦< L *mamma*, breast + -GRAPHY⟧ an X-ray technique for detecting breast tumors before they can be seen or felt

**mam·mon** (mam′ən) *n.* ⟦< Aram⟧ [*often* M-] riches regarded as an object of worship and greedy pursuit

**mam·moth** (mam′əth) *n.* ⟦< Russ *mamont*⟧ an extinct elephant with long tusks and hairy skin —*adj.* huge; enormous

**man** (man) *n., pl.* **men** (men) ⟦OE *mann*⟧ **1** a human being; person **2** the human race; mankind **3** an adult male person **4** an adult male servant, employee, etc. **5** a husband or male lover **6** any of the pieces used in chess, checkers, etc. —*vt.* **manned**, **man′ning 1** to furnish with a labor force for work, defense, etc. **2** to take one's station in or at **3** to strengthen; brace [*to man* oneself for an ordeal] —**as a** (or **one**) **man** in unison; unanimously —**to a man** with no exception

MAMMOTH

**Man** (man), **Isle of** one of the British Isles, between Northern Ireland & England

**-man** (mən, man) *combining form* man or person of a (specified) kind, in a (specified) activity, etc.: now often replaced by -PERSON or -WOMAN

**man·a·cle** (man′ə kəl) *n.* ⟦< L *manus*, hand⟧ a handcuff: *usually used in pl.* —*vt.* **-cled, -cling 1** to put handcuffs on **2** to restrain

**man·age** (man′ij) *vt.* **-aged, -ag·ing** ⟦< L *manus*, hand⟧ **1** to control the movement or behavior of **2** to have charge of; direct [*to manage* a hotel] **3** to succeed in accomplishing —*vi.* **1** to carry on business **2** to contrive to get along —**man′age·a·ble** *adj.*

**managed care** a plan or system for providing medical services at reduced costs to patients who agree to use specified doctors and hospitals

**man′age·ment** *n.* **1** a managing or being managed **2** the persons managing a business, institution, etc.

**man′ag·er** *n.* one who manages; esp., one who manages a business, etc.

**man·a·ge·ri·al** (man′ə jir′ē əl) *adj.* of a manager or management

**ma·ña·na** (mä nyä′nä) *n., adv.* ⟦Sp⟧ tomorrow or (at) an indefinite future time

**Ma·nas·sas** (mə nas′əs) city in NE Virginia: site of two Civil War battles: pop. 28,000

**man·a·tee** (man′ə tē′) *n.* ⟦< WInd native name⟧ a large aquatic mammal of tropical waters

**Man·ches·ter** (man′ches′tər) city & port in NW England: county district pop. 405,000

**Man·chu** (man chōō′, man′chōō) *n.* **1** *pl.* **-chus′** or **-chu** a member of a Mongolian people of Manchuria that ruled China from 1644 to 1912 **2** the language of this people —*adj.* of the Manchus, their language, etc.

**Man·chu·ri·a** (man choor′ē ə) region in NE China —**Man·chu′ri·an** *adj., n.*

**man·da·rin** (man′də rin) *n.* ⟦< Sans *mantrin*, counselor⟧ **1** a high official in the Chinese empire **2** [M-] the main dialect of Chinese

**man·date** (man′dāt′) *n.* ⟦< L *mandare*, to command⟧ **1** an order or command **2** [Historical] *a*) a League of Nations commission to a country to administer some region *b*) this region **3** the will of voters as expressed in an election —*vt.* **-dat′ed, -dat′ing** to require as by law

**man·da·to·ry** (man′də tôr′ē) *adj.* authoritatively commanded; obligatory

**man·di·ble** (man′də bəl) *n.* ⟦< L *mandere*, chew⟧ the jaw; specif., *a*) the lower jaw of a vertebrate *b*) either jaw of a beaked animal

**man·do·lin** (man′də lin′) *n.* ⟦< Gr *pandoura*, kind of lute⟧ a lute-like musical instrument with four to six pairs of strings

**man·drake** (man′drāk′) *n.* ⟦< Gr *mandragoras*⟧ a poisonous plant of the nightshade family

**man·drill** (man′dril) *n.* ⟦MAN + *drill*, kind of monkey⟧ a baboon of W Africa: the male has blue and scarlet patches on the face and rump

**mane** (mān) *n.* ⟦OE *manu*⟧ the long hair growing on the neck of the horse, lion, etc. —**maned** *adj.*

**man′-eat′er** *n.* an animal that eats human flesh —**man′-eat′ing** *adj.*

**ma·neu·ver** (mə nōō′vər) *n.* ⟦< L *manu operare*, to work by hand⟧ **1** a planned and controlled movement of troops, warships, etc. **2** a skillful change of direction **3** a skillful or shrewd move; stratagem —*vi., vt.* **1** to perform or cause to perform a maneuver or maneuvers **2** to manage or plan skillfully **3** to move, get, make, etc. by some scheme —**ma·neu′ver·a·ble** *adj.*

**man·ful** (man′fəl) *adj.* manly; brave, resolute, etc. —**man′ful·ly** *adv.*

**man·ga·nese** (maŋ′gə nēs′, -nēz′) *n.* ⟦ult. < ML *magnesia*: see MAGNESIA⟧ a grayish-white, metallic chemical element, used in alloys

**mange** (mānj) *n.* ⟦< OFr *mangeue*, an itch⟧ a skin disease of mammals, causing itching, hair loss, etc.

**man·ger** (mān′jər) *n.* ⟦< L *mandere*, chew⟧ a box or trough to hold fodder for horses or cattle to eat

**man·gle**[1] (maŋ′gəl) *vt.* **-gled, -gling** ⟦prob. < OFr *mehaigner, maim*⟧ **1** to mutilate by roughly cutting, tearing, crushing, etc. **2** to spoil; botch; mar

**man·gle**[2] (maŋ′gəl) *n.* ⟦< Gr *manganon*, war machine⟧ a machine for pressing and smoothing sheets, etc. between rollers

**man·go** (maŋ′gō) *n., pl.* **-goes** or **-gos** ⟦< Tamil *mān-kāy*⟧ **1** the yellow-red, somewhat acid fruit of a tropical tree **2** this tree

**man·grove** (maŋ′grōv) *n.* ⟦< WInd name⟧ a tropical tree of swampy areas, usually with roots that rise out of the water

**man·gy** (mān′jē) *adj.* **-gi·er, -gi·est 1** having mange **2** filthy, low, etc. —**man′gi·ness** *n.*

**man·han·dle** (man′han′dəl) *vt.* **-dled, -dling** to handle roughly

**Man·hat·tan**[1] (man hat′'n) *n.* [after fol.] [*often* m-] a cocktail made of whiskey and sweet vermouth

**Man·hat·tan**[2] (man hat′'n) island in SE New York: borough of New York City: pop. 1,488,000

**man′hole′** *n.* a hole through which one can enter a sewer, conduit, etc.

**man′hood′** *n.* **1** the state or time of being a man **2** manly qualities; manliness **3** men collectively

**man′-hour′** *n.* a time unit equal to one hour of work done by one person

**man′hunt′** *n.* a hunt for a fugitive

**ma·ni·a** (mā′nē ə) *n.* ⟦Gr, madness⟧ **1** wild or violent mental disorder **2** an excessive enthusiasm

**-ma·ni·a** (mā′nē ə) ⟦see prec.⟧ *combining form* **1** a (specified) type of mental disorder **2** an intense enthusiasm for

**ma·ni·ac** (mā′nē ak′) *adj.* wildly insane —*n.* a violently insane person —**ma·ni·a·cal** (mə nī′ə kəl) *adj.*

**man·ic** (man′ik) *adj.* **1** having, characterized by, or like mania **2** [Inf.] very excited, elated, etc. —**man′ic·al·ly** *adv.*

**man·ic-de·pres′sive** (-dē pres′iv) *adj.* BIPOLAR (sense 2)

**man·i·cure** (man′i kyoor′) *n.* [[< L *manus,* a hand + *cura,* care]] a trimming, polishing, etc. of the fingernails —*vt.* **-cured′, -cur′ing 1** to trim, polish, etc. (fingernails) **2** [Inf.] to trim, clip, etc. meticulously —**man′i·cur′ist** *n.*

**man·i·fest** (man′ə fest′) *adj.* [[< L *manifestus,* lit., struck by the hand]] apparent to the senses or the mind; obvious —*vt.* to show plainly; reveal —*n.* an itemized list of a craft's cargo or passengers —**man′i·fest′ly** *adv.*

**man·i·fes·ta′tion** (-fes tā′shən) *n.* **1** a manifesting or being manifested **2** something that manifests or is manifested

**man·i·fes′to** (-fes′tō) *n., pl.* **-toes** or **-tos** [[It < *manifestare,* to manifest]] a public declaration of intention by an important person or group

**man·i·fold** (man′ə fōld′) *adj.* [[see MANY & -FOLD]] **1** having many forms, parts, etc. **2** of many sorts —*n.* a pipe with several outlets, as for conducting cylinder exhaust from an engine

**man·i·kin** (man′i kin) *n.* [[Du *manneken* < *man,* man + *-ken,* -KIN]] **1** a little man; dwarf **2** an anatomical model of the human body, used as in art classes **3** MANNEQUIN

**Ma·nil·a** (mə nil′ə) capital & seaport of the Philippines, in SW Luzon: pop. 1,630,000 (met. area, 7,929,000)

**Manila hemp** [[after prec.]] [*often* m- h-] a strong fiber from the leafstalks of a Philippine plant, used for making rope, paper, etc.

**Manila paper** [*often* m- p-] a strong, buff-colored paper, orig. made of Manila hemp

**man in the street** the average person

**ma·nip·u·late** (mə nip′yōō lāt′, -yə-) *vt.* **-lat′ed, -lat′ing** [[ult. < L *manus,* a hand + *plere,* to fill]] **1** to handle skillfully **2** to manage artfully or shrewdly, often in an unfair way **3** to falsify (figures, etc.) for one's own purposes —**ma·nip′u·la′tion** *n.*

**Man·i·to·ba** (man′ə tō′bə) province of SC Canada: 250,946 sq. mi.; pop. 1,114,000; cap. Winnipeg: abbrev. *MB* —**Man′i·to′ban** *adj., n.*

**man·kind** (man′kind′) *n.* **1** the human race **2** all human males

**man·ly** (man′lē) *adj.* **-li·er, -li·est** having the qualities regarded as suitable for a man; virile, brave, etc. —**man′li·ness** *n.*

**man′-made′** *adj.* artificial or synthetic

**Mann** (tō′mäs), **Thom·as** 1875-1955; Ger. novelist, in the U.S. 1938-52

**man·na** (man′ə) *n.* [[< Heb *mān*]] **1** *Bible* food miraculously provided for the Israelites in the wilderness **2** anything badly needed that comes unexpectedly

**man·ne·quin** (man′ə kin) *n.* [[see MANIKIN]] **1** a model of the human body, used as by tailors **2** a woman who models clothes in stores, etc.

**man·ner** (man′ər) *n.* [[< L *manus,* a hand]] **1** a way in which something is done or happens **2** a way, esp. a usual way, of acting **3** [*pl.*] *a)* ways of social behavior [*bad manners*] *b)* polite ways of social behavior [*to learn manners*] **4** kind; sort

**man′nered** (-ərd) *adj.* **1** having manners of a specified sort [*ill-mannered*] **2** artificial, stylized, etc.

**man′ner·ism′** *n.* **1** excessive use of some distinctive manner or style in art, literature, etc. **2** a peculiarity of manner in behavior, speech, etc.

**man′ner·ly** *adj.* polite

**man·ni·kin** (man′ə kin) *n. alt. sp. of* MANIKIN

**man·nish** (man′ish) *adj.* like a man or man's: used in referring to a woman having characteristics generally attributed to men

**ma·noeu·vre** (mə nōō′vər) *n., vi., vt.* **-vred, -vring** *chiefly Brit. sp. of* MANEUVER

**man of letters** a writer, scholar, editor, etc., esp. in the field of literature

**man′-of-war′** *n., pl.* **men′-of-war′** an armed naval vessel; warship

**ma·nom·e·ter** (mə näm′ət ər) *n.* [[Fr < Gr *manos,* rare (as in "thin, sparse") + Fr *-mètre,* -METER]] an instrument for measuring the pressure of gases or liquids

**man on the street** *var. of* MAN IN THE STREET

**man·or** (man′ər) *n.* [[< L *manere,* remain, dwell]] **1** in England, an estate **2** the main house on an estate —**ma·no·ri·al** (mə nôr′ē əl) *adj.*

**man′pow′er** *n.* **1** power furnished by human strength **2** the collective strength or availability for work of the people of an area, nation, etc.

**man·qué** (män kā′) *adj.* [[Fr < *manquer,* be lacking]] unfulfilled; would-be [*a poet manqué*]

**man·sard** (**roof**) (man′särd) [[after F. *Mansard,* 17th-c. Fr architect]] a roof with two slopes on each of four sides, the lower steeper than the upper

MANSARD ROOF

**manse** (mans) *n.* [[see MANOR]] the residence of a minister; parsonage

**man′ser′vant** *n., pl.* **men′ser′vants** a male servant: also **man servant**

**-man·ship** (mən ship) *combining form* talent or skill (esp. in gaining advantage) in connection with [*grantsmanship*]

**man·sion** (man′shən) *n.* [[< L *manere,* remain, dwell]] a large, imposing house

**man′-sized′** *adj.* [Inf.] of a size fit for a man; big: also **man′-size′**

**man′slaugh′ter** (-slôt′ər) *n.* the killing of a human being by another, esp. when unlawful but without malice

**man·ta** (man′tə) *n.* [[Sp < LL *mantum,* a cloak]] a giant ray, with winglike pectoral fins: also **manta ray**

**man·tel** (man′təl) *n.* [[var. of MANTLE]] **1** the facing of stone, etc. about a fireplace, including a projecting shelf **2** this shelf Also **man′tel·piece′**

**man·til·la** (man til′ə, -tē′ə) *n.* [[Sp: see MANTA]] a woman's scarf, as of lace, worn over the hair and shoulders

**man·tis** (man′tis) *n., pl.* **-tis·es** or **-tes′** (-tēz′) [[< Gr, prophet]] an insect with forelegs often held up together as if praying

**man·tis·sa** (man tis′ə) *n.* [[L, (useless) addition]] the decimal part of a logarithm

**man·tle** (man′təl) *n.* [[< L *mantellum*]] **1** a loose, sleeveless cloak: sometimes used figuratively to connote authority **2** anything that envelops or conceals **3** a small hood which when placed over a flame gives off incandescent light —*vt.* **-tled, -tling** to cover as with a mantle —*vi.* to blush

**man′-to-man′** *adj.* frank; candid

**man·tra** (man′trə, män′-) *n.* [[Sans]] a chant or a Vedic hymn, text, etc.

**man·u·al** (man′yōō əl) *adj.* [[< L *manus,* a hand]] **1** of the hands **2** made, done, or worked by hand **3** involving skill or hard work with the hands —*n.* **1** a handy book of facts, etc. for use as a guide, reference, etc. **2** prescribed drill in the handling of a weapon —**man′u·al·ly** *adv.*

**man·u·fac·ture** (man′yōō fak′chər, -yə-) *n.* [[< L *manus,* a hand + *facere,* make]] **1** the making of goods, esp. by machinery and on a large scale **2** the making of something in any way, esp. when regarded as merely mechanical —*vt.* **-tured, -tur·ing 1** to make, esp. by machinery **2** to make up (excuses, etc.); fabricate —**man′u·fac′tur·er** *n.*

**man·u·mit** (man′yoo mit′) *vt.* **-mit′ted, -mit′ting** [< L *manus,* a hand + *mittere,* send] to free from slavery —**man′u·mis′sion** *n.*

**ma·nure** (mə noor′) *vt.* **-nured′, -nur′ing** [< OFr *manouvrer,* work with the hands] to put manure on or into —*n.* animal excrement, etc. used to fertilize soil

**man·u·script** (man′yoo skript′, -yə-) *adj.* [< L *manus,* hand + *scriptus,* written] written by hand or typewritten —*n.* **1** a written or typewritten document, book, etc., esp. one submitted to a publisher **2** writing as opposed to print

**Manx** (maŋks) *n.* the Celtic language of the Isle of Man, now nearly extinct —*adj.* of the Isle of Man or its people, etc.

**man·y** (men′ē) *adj.* **more, most** [OE *manig*] numerous —*pl.n.* a large number (of persons or things) —*pron.* many persons or things

**Ma·o·ri** (mä′ō rē, mou′rē) *n.* **1** *pl.* **-ris** or **-ri** a member of a Polynesian people native to New Zealand **2** the language of this people —*adj.* of the Maoris or their language, etc.

**Mao Tse-tung** (mou′ dzu′dooŋ′) 1893-1976; Chinese Communist leader: Pinyin *Mao Zedong* — **Mao′ism′** *n.* —**Mao′ist** *adj., n.*

**map** (map) *n.* [< L *mappa,* napkin, cloth] **1** a representation of all or part of the earth's surface, showing countries, bodies of water, cities, etc. **2** a representation of the sky, showing the stars, etc. —*vt.* **mapped, map′ping 1** to make a map of **2** to plan

**ma·ple** (mā′pəl) *n.* [OE *mapel*] **1** any of a large group of trees with two-winged fruits, grown for wood, sap, or shade **2** the hard, light-colored wood **3** the flavor of the syrup or sugar made from the sap

**mar** (mär) *vt.* **marred, mar′ring** [OE *mierran,* hinder] to injure or damage so as to make imperfect, etc.; spoil

**mar·a·bou** (mar′ə boo′) *n.* [Fr < Ar *murābit,* hermit] a large-billed African stork

**ma·ra·ca** (mə rä′kə) *n.* [Port *maracá* < native name in Brazil] a percussion instrument that is a dried gourd or a gourd-shaped rattle with pebbles, etc. in it

**mar·a·schi·no** (mar′ə shē′nō, -skē′-) *n.* [It < *marasca,* kind of cherry] a liqueur made from a sour cherry

**maraschino cherries** cherries in a syrup flavored with maraschino or imitation maraschino

**mar·a·thon** (mar′ə thän′) *n.* [after *Marathon,* plain in ancient Greece] **1** a race on foot, 26 miles and 385 yards in length **2** any contest or endeavor testing endurance —**mar′a·thon′er** *n.*

**ma·raud** (mə rôd′) *vi., vt.* [< Fr *maraud,* vagabond] to raid and plunder —**ma·raud′er** *n.*

**mar·ble** (mär′bəl) *n.* [< Gr *marmaros,* white stone] **1** a hard limestone, white, colored, or mottled, which takes a high polish **2** a piece of this stone, used in sculpture, etc. **3** anything like marble in hardness, coldness, coloration, etc. **4** *a*) a little ball of stone, glass, etc. *b*) [*pl., with sing. v.*] a children's game played with such balls **5** [*pl.*] [Slang] mental soundness; wits —*adj.* of or like marble —*vt.* **-bled, -bling** to make (book edges) look mottled like marble

**mar′bled** *adj.* **1** mottled or streaked **2** streaked with fat: said of meat

**mar′ble·ize′** (-īz′) *vt.* **-ized′, -iz′ing** to make look like marble

**mar′bling** *n.* a streaked or mottled appearance like that of marble

**march**[1] (märch) *vi.* [Fr *marcher*] **1** to walk with regular steps, as in military formation **2** to advance steadily —*vt.* to cause to march —*n.* **1** a marching **2** a steady advance; progress **3** a regular, steady step **4** the distance covered in marching **5** a piece of music with a beat suitable for marching —**on the march** marching or advancing

—**steal a march on** to get an advantage over secretly —**march′er** *n.*

**march**[2] (märch) *n.* [< OFr] a border or frontier

**March** (märch) *n.* [< L *Mars,* the god Mars] the third month of the year, having 31 days: abbrev. **Mar.**

**March hare** a hare in breeding time, proverbially an example of madness

**marching orders 1** orders to march, go, or leave **2** notice of dismissal

**mar·chion·ess** (mär′shən is) *n.* **1** the wife or widow of a marquess **2** a lady of the rank of a marquess

**Mar·co·ni** (mär kō′nē), **Gu·gliel·mo** (goo lyel′mō) 1874-1937; It. physicist: developed wireless telegraphy

**Mar·di Gras** (mär′dē grä′) [Fr, fat Tuesday] [*sometimes* **M- g-**] the last day before Lent: a day of carnival in New Orleans, etc.

**mare**[1] (mer) *n.* [< OE *mere*] a mature female horse, mule, donkey, etc.

**ma·re**[2] (mä′rā′) *n., pl.* **ma·ri·a** (mä′rē ə) [L, sea] a large, dark area on the moon

**mare's-nest** (merz′nest′) *n.* **1** a hoax **2** a jumble; mess

**mar·ga·rine** (mär′jə rin) *n.* [Fr] a spread or cooking fat of vegetable oils processed, often with milk or whey, to the consistency of butter

**mar·gin** (mär′jən) *n.* [< L *margo*] **1** a border; edge **2** the blank border of a printed or written page **3** an amount beyond what is needed **4** provision for increase, error, etc. **5** the amount or degree by which things differ **6** the difference between the cost and the selling price of goods **7** collateral deposited with a broker, either to meet legal requirements or to insure against loss on contracts, as for buying stocks

**mar′gin·al** *adj.* **1** of, in, or near the margin **2** limited or minimal

**mar·gi·na·li·a** (mär′jə nā′lē ə) *pl.n.* notes written or printed in the margin

**mar′gin·al·ize′** *vt.* **-ized′, -iz′ing** to exclude or ignore

**ma·ri·a·chi** (mär′ē ä′chē) *n., pl.* **-chis** [MexSp < Fr *mariage,* marriage: from playing at wedding celebrations] **1** a member of a strolling band of musicians in Mexico **2** such a band **3** its music

**Mar·i·an** (mer′ē ən, mar′-) *adj.* of the Virgin Mary

**Ma·rie An·toi·nette** (mə rē′ an′twə net′) 1755-93; wife of Louis XVI: queen of France (1774-92): guillotined

**mar·i·gold** (mar′ə gōld′) *n.* [< *Marie* (prob. the Virgin Mary) + GOLD] a plant of the composite family, with red, yellow, or orange flowers

**mar·i·jua·na** or **mar·i·hua·na** (mar′ə wä′nə) *n.* [AmSp] **1** HEMP (*n.* 1) **2** its dried leaves and flowers, smoked for euphoric effects

**ma·rim·ba** (mə rim′bə) *n.* [< native name in Africa] a kind of xylophone with a resonant tube beneath each bar

**ma·ri·na** (mə rē′nə) *n.* [< L *mare,* sea] a small harbor with docks, services, etc. for pleasure craft

**mar·i·nade** (mar′ə nād′) *n.* [Fr < Sp *marinar,* to pickle] a spiced pickling solution for steeping meat, fish, etc., often before cooking —*vt.* **-nad′ed, -nad′ing** MARINATE

**mar·i·nate** (mar′ə nāt′) *vt.* **-nat′ed, -nat′ing** [< It *marinare,* to pickle] to steep in a marinade

**ma·rine** (mə rēn′) *adj.* [< L *mare,* sea] **1** of or found in the sea **2** *a*) maritime; nautical *b*) naval —*n.* **1** a member of a military force trained for service at sea **2** [*often* **M-**] a member of the MARINE CORPS

**Marine Corps** a branch of the United States armed forces trained for land, sea, and aerial combat

**mar·i·ner** (mar′ə nər) *n.* a sailor

**mar·i·o·nette** (mar′ē ə net′, mer′-) *n.* [Fr < *Marie,* Mary] a jointed puppet moved by strings or wires

**mar·i·tal** (mar′ət'l) *adj.* [< L *maritus,* a husband] of marriage; matrimonial —**mar′i·tal·ly** *adv.*

**mar·i·time** (mar′ə tīm′) *adj.* [< L *mare*, sea] **1** on, near, or living near the sea **2** of sea navigation, shipping, etc.

**mar·jo·ram** (mär′jə rəm) *n.* [prob. ult. < Gr *amarakos*] a fragrant herb of the mint family, used in cooking

**mark**[1] (märk) *n.* [OE *mearc*, boundary] **1** a line, dot, spot, scratch, etc. on a surface **2** a printed or written symbol [*punctuation marks*] **3** a brand or label on an article showing the maker, etc. **4** an indication of some quality **5** a grade [a *mark* of B in Latin] **6** a standard of quality **7** impression; influence **8** an object of known position, serving as a guide **9** a line, dot, etc. indicating position, as on a graduated scale **10** an object aimed at; target **11** a goal; end; aim —*vt.* **1** to put or make a mark or marks on **2** to identify as by a mark **3** to indicate by a mark **4** to show plainly [her smile *marked* her joy] **5** to set off; characterize **6** to listen to [*mark* my words] **7** to grade; rate — **make one's mark** to achieve fame —**mark down** (or **up**) to mark for sale at a reduced (or an increased) price —**mark time 1** to keep time while at a halt by lifting the feet as if marching **2** to suspend progress for a time —**mark′er** *n.*

**mark**[2] (märk) *n.* [< ON *mǫrk*] DEUTSCHE MARK

**Mark** (märk) *n. Bible* **1** one of the four Evangelists, the reputed author of the second Gospel **2** this Gospel

**mark′down′** *n.* **1** a selling at a reduced price **2** the amount of reduction in price

**marked** (märkt) *adj.* **1** having a mark or marks **2** noticeable; obvious —**mark·ed·ly** (märk′id lē) *adv.*

**mar·ket** (mär′kit) *n.* [ult. < L *merx*, merchandise] **1** a gathering of people for buying and selling things **2** an open space or a building where goods are shown for sale: also **mar′ket·place′ 3** a shop for the sale of provisions [a meat *market*] **4** a region in which goods can be bought and sold [the European *market*] **5** trade; buying and selling **6** demand [for goods, etc.] [a good *market* for tea] — *vt.* **1** to offer for sale **2** to sell —*vi.* to buy provisions —**mar′ket·a·ble** *adj.* —**mar′ket·eer′** (-kə tir′) *n.* —**mar′ket·er** *n.*

**mar·ket·ing** *n.* **1** a buying or selling in a market **2** the total of activities involved in the moving of goods from the producer to the consumer, including selling, advertising, etc.

**market share** a company's percentage of the total sales of some commodity

**Mark·ham** (mär′kəm) city in SE Ontario, Canada: pop. 173,000

**mark′ing** *n.* **1** a mark or marks **2** the characteristic arrangement of marks, as of an animal

**marks·man** (märks′mən) *n., pl.* **-men** (-mən) a person who shoots, esp. one who shoots well — **marks′man·ship′** *n.*

**mark′up′** *n.* **1** a selling at an increased price **2** the amount of increase in price

**mar·lin** (mär′lin) *n., pl.* **-lin** or **-lins** [< fol.: from the shape] a large, slender deep-sea fish

**mar·line·spike** (mär′lin spīk′) *n.* [< Du *marlijn*, small cord + SPIKE[1]] a pointed metal tool for separating the strands of a rope in splicing

**mar·ma·lade** (mär′mə lād′) *n.* [ult. < Gr *meli*, honey + *mēlon*, apple] a jamlike preserve of oranges, etc.

**mar·mo·set** (mär′mə zet′, -set′) *n.* [< OFr *marmouset*, grotesque figure] a small monkey of South and Central America

**mar·mot** (mär′mət) *n.* [prob. < L *mus montanus*, mountain mouse] any of a group of thick-bodied rodents, as the woodchuck

**ma·roon**[1] (mə rōōn′) *n., adj.* [Fr *marron*, chestnut] dark brownish red

**ma·roon**[2] (mə rōōn′) *vt.* [< AmSp *cimarrón*, wild] **1** to put (a person) ashore in a lonely place and abandon that person **2** to leave abandoned, helpless, etc.

**marque** (märk) *n.* [Fr, a sign] a distinctive emblem on an automobile

**mar·quee** (mär kē′) *n.* [< Fr *marquise*, awning] a rooflike projection over an entrance, as to a theater

**mar·quess** (mär′kwis) *n.* [var. of MARQUIS] **1** a British nobleman ranking above an earl **2** MARQUIS

**mar·que·try** (mär′kə trē) *n.* [Fr, ult. < *marque*, a mark] decorative inlaid work, as in furniture

**mar·quis** (mär′kwis) *n.* [< ML *marchisus*, prefect] in some European countries, a nobleman ranking above an earl or count

**mar·quise** (mär kēz′) *n.* **1** the wife or widow of a marquis **2** a lady of the rank of a marquis

**mar·qui·sette** (mär′ki zet′, -kwi-) *n.* [see MARQUEE] a thin, meshlike fabric used for curtains, etc.

**mar·riage** (mar′ij) *n.* **1** the state of being married **2** the act of marrying; wedding **3** a close union — **mar′riage·a·ble** *adj.*

**mar·ried** (mar′ēd) *adj.* **1** being husband and wife **2** having a husband or wife **3** of marriage —*n.* a married person

**mar·row** (mar′ō) *n.* [OE *mearg*] the soft, fatty tissue that fills the cavities of most bones

**mar·ry** (mar′ē) *vt.* **-ried, -ry·ing** [< L *maritus*, husband] **1** to join as husband and wife **2** to take as husband or wife **3** to unite —*vi.* to get married — **marry off** to give in marriage

**Mars** (märz) *n.* **1** the Roman god of war **2** a planet of the solar system: see PLANET

**Mar·seille** (mär sā′) seaport in SE France: pop. 801,000 Eng. sp. **Mar·seilles′**

**marsh** (märsh) *n.* [OE *merisc*] a tract of low, wet, soft land; swamp; bog —**marsh′y, -i·er, -i·est,** *adj.*

**mar·shal** (mär′shəl) *n.* [< OHG *marah*, horse + *scalh*, servant] **1** in various foreign armies, a general officer of the highest rank **2** an official in charge of ceremonies, parades, etc. **3** in the U.S., *a*) a federal officer appointed to a judicial district with duties like those of a sheriff *b*) the head of some police or fire departments —*vt.* **-shaled** or **-shalled, -shal·ing** or **-shal·ling 1** to arrange (troops, ideas, etc.) in order **2** to guide

**Mar·shall** (mär′shəl), **John** 1755-1835; U.S. chief justice (1801-35)

**Marshall Islands** country on a group of islands in the W Pacific: formerly part of a U.S. territory: 70 sq. mi.; pop. 43,000

**marsh·mal·low** (märsh′mel′ō) *n.* [orig. made of the root of a mallow found in marshes] a soft, spongy confection of sugar, gelatin, etc.

**mar·su·pi·al** (mär sōō′pē əl) *adj.* [< Gr *marsypos*, pouch] of a group of mammals that carry their incompletely developed young in an external abdominal pouch on the mother —*n.* such an animal, as a kangaroo or opossum

**mart** (märt) *n.* [MDu *markt*] a market

**mar·ten** (märt′n) *n.* [< OFr *martre*] **1** a small mammal like a weasel, with soft, thick fur **2** the fur

**mar·tial** (mär′shəl) *adj.* [< L *martialis*, of Mars] **1** of or suitable for war **2** warlike; bold **3** military —**mar′tial·ly** *adv.*

**martial arts** systems of self-defense originating in E Asia, such as karate or kung fu, also engaged in for sport

**martial law** temporary rule by military authorities over civilians, as during a war

**Mar·tian** (mär′shən) *adj.* of Mars —*n.* a being from or living on Mars, as in science fiction

**mar·tin** (märt′n) *n.* [Fr] any of several birds of the swallow family

**mar·ti·net** (märt′n et′) *n.* [after *Martinet*, 17th-c. Fr general] a very strict disciplinarian

**mar·ti·ni** (mär tē′nē) *n., pl.* **-nis** [< ?] a cocktail made of gin (or vodka) and dry vermouth

**mar·tyr** (märt′ər) *n.* [< Gr *martyr*, a witness] **1** one who chooses to suffer or die for one's faith or principles **2** one who suffers great pain or misery for a long time —*vt.* to kill or persecute for a belief —**mar·tyr·dom** *n.*

**mar·vel** (mär′vəl) *n.* ⟦< L *mirari*, wonder at⟧ a wonderful thing —*vi.* **-veled** or **-velled, -vel·ing** or **-vel·ling** to be filled with wonder —*vt.* to wonder at or about: followed by a clause

**mar′vel·ous** (-və ləs) *adj.* **1** causing wonder; extraordinary, etc. **2** fine; splendid Also [Chiefly Brit.] **mar′vel·lous** —**mar′vel·ous·ly** *adv.*

**Marx** (märks), **Karl** (kärl) 1818-83; Ger. founder of modern socialism

**Marx′ism** *n.* the system of thought developed by Karl Marx and Friedrich Engels (1820-95, Ger. socialist leader & writer), serving as a basis for socialism and communism —**Marx′ist** or **Marx′i·an** *adj., n.*

**Mar·y** (mer′ē) *n. Bible* mother of Jesus

**Mar·y·land** (mer′ə lənd) state of the E U.S.: 9,775 sq. mi.; pop. 4,781,000; cap. Annapolis: abbrev. *MD* —**Mar′y·land·er** (-lən dər, -lan′-) *n.*

**Mary Mag·da·lene** (mag′də lən) *Bible* a repentant woman whom Jesus forgave

**mar·zi·pan** (mär′zi pan′) *n.* ⟦Ger < It *marzapane*⟧ a confection that is a paste of ground almonds, sugar, and egg white, variously shaped

**masc** or **mas** *abbrev.* masculine

**mas·car·a** (mas kar′ə) *n.* ⟦< It *maschera*, mask⟧ a cosmetic for darkening the eyelashes —*vt.* **-car′aed, -car′a·ing** to put mascara on

**mas·cot** (mas′kät′) *n.* ⟦< Prov *masco*, sorcerer⟧ **1** any person, animal, or thing supposed to bring good luck **2** any person, animal, or thing adopted, as by a sports team, as a symbol

**mas·cu·line** (mas′kyə lin) *adj.* ⟦< L *mas*, male⟧ **1** male; of men or boys **2** suitable to or having qualities regarded as typical of men; strong, vigorous, manly, etc. **3** mannish: said of women **4** *Gram.* designating or of the gender of words referring to males as well as to other words to which no sex is attributed —**mas′cu·lin′i·ty** *n.*

**mash** (mash) *n.* ⟦< OE *mascwyrt*⟧ **1** crushed malt or meal soaked in hot water for making wort **2** a mixture of watered bran, meal, etc. for feeding horses, etc. **3** any soft mass —*vt.* **1** to change into a soft mass by beating, crushing, etc. **2** to crush and injure

**mask** (mask) *n.* ⟦< Fr < It *maschera*⟧ **1** a covering to conceal or protect the face **2** anything that conceals or disguises **3** *a)* a molded likeness of the face *b)* a grotesque representation of a face, worn to amuse or frighten —*vt.* to conceal or cover with or as with a mask —**masked** *adj.*

**mas·o·chism** (mas′ə kiz′əm) *n.* ⟦after L. von Sacher-*Masoch* (1835-95), Austrian writer⟧ the getting of pleasure, often sexual pleasure, from being hurt or humiliated —**mas′o·chist** *n.* —**mas′o·chis′tic** *adj.* —**mas′o·chis′ti·cal·ly** *adv.*

**ma·son** (mā′sən) *n.* ⟦< ML *macio*⟧ **1** one whose work is building with stone, brick, etc. **2** [M-] FREEMASON

**Ma·son-Dix·on line** (mā′sən dik′sən) ⟦after C. *Mason* & J. *Dixon*, who surveyed it, 1763-67⟧ boundary line between Pennsylvania & Maryland, regarded as separating the North from the South

**Ma·son·ic** (mə sän′ik) *adj.* [*also* m-] of Freemasons or Freemasonry

**ma·son·ry** (mā′sən rē) *n.* **1** a mason's trade **2** *pl.* **-ries** something built, as by a mason, of stone, brick, etc. **3** [*usually* M-] FREEMASONRY

**masque** (mask) *n.* ⟦see MASK⟧ **1** MASQUERADE (*n.* 1) **2** a former kind of dramatic entertainment, with lavish costumes, music, etc. —**masqu′er** *n.*

**mas·quer·ade** (mas′kə rād′) *n.* ⟦see MASK⟧ **1** a ball or party at which masks and fancy costumes are worn **2** *a)* a disguise *b)* an acting under false pretenses —*vi.* **-ad′ed, -ad′ing** **1** to take part in a masquerade **2** to act under false pretenses

**mass** (mas) *n.* ⟦< Gr *maza*, barley cake⟧ **1** a quantity of matter of indefinite shape and size; lump

**2** a large quantity or number [a *mass* of bruises] **3** bulk; size **4** the main part **5** *Physics* the quantity of matter in a body as measured by its inertia —*adj.* of or for the masses or for a large number —*vt., vi.* to gather or form into a mass —**the masses** the common people

**Mass** (mas) *n.* ⟦< L *missa* in the words said by the priest: *ite, missa est* (*contio*), go, (the meeting) is dismissed⟧ [*also* m-] *R.C.Ch.* the service that includes the Eucharist

**Mas·sa·chu·setts** (mas′ə chōō′sits) New England state of the U.S.: 7,838 sq. mi.; pop. 6,016,000; cap. Boston: abbrev. *MA*

**mas·sa·cre** (mas′ə kər) *n.* ⟦< OFr *maçacre*, butchery⟧ the indiscriminate, merciless killing of many people or animals —*vt.* **-cred, -cring** (-kər iŋ, -kriŋ) to kill in large numbers

**mas·sage** (mə säzh′) *n.* ⟦Fr < Ar *massa*, to touch⟧ a rubbing, kneading, etc. of part of the body, as to stimulate circulation or relieve tension —*vt.* **-saged′, -sag′ing** to give a massage to

**mas·seur** (mə sur′, -sōōr′) *n.* ⟦Fr⟧ a man whose work is giving massages —**mas·seuse** (mə sōōz′, -sōōs′) *fem.n.*

**mas·sive** (mas′iv) *adj.* **1** forming or consisting of a large mass; big and solid **2** large and imposing —**mas′sive·ly** *adv.* —**mas′sive·ness** *n.*

**mass media** those means of communication that reach and influence large numbers of people, as newspapers, radio, and TV

**mass noun** a noun denoting an abstraction or something that cannot be counted (Ex.: *love, water, news*)

**mass number** the number of neutrons and protons in the nucleus of an atom

**mass production** quantity production of goods, esp. by machinery and division of labor —**mass′-pro·duce′, -duced′, -duc′ing,** *vt.*

**mast** (mast) *n.* ⟦OE *mæst*⟧ **1** a tall vertical spar used to support the sails, yards, radar, etc. on a ship **2** a vertical pole

**mas·tec·to·my** (mas tek′tə mē) *n., pl.* **-mies** the surgical removal of all or part of a breast

**mas·ter** (mas′tər) *n.* ⟦< L *magister*⟧ **1** a man who rules others or has control over something; specif., *a)* one who is head of a household *b)* an employer *c)* one who owns a slave or an animal *d)* the captain of a merchant ship **2** *a)* a person very skilled and able in some work, profession, science, etc.; expert *b)* an artist regarded as great **3** [M-] a title applied to a boy too young to be addressed as *Mr.* —*adj.* **1** being a master **2** of a master **3** chief; main; controlling —*vt.* **1** to become master of **2** to become an expert in (an art, science, etc.)

**mas′ter·ful** *adj.* **1** acting the part of a master; domineering **2** expert; skillful —**mas′ter·ful·ly** *adv.*

**master key** a key that will open every one of a set of locks

**mas′ter·ly** *adj.* expert; skillful

**mas′ter·mind′** *n.* a very clever person, esp. one who plans or runs a project —*vt.* to be the mastermind of

**Master of Arts** (or **Science,** etc.) a degree given by a college or university to one who has completed a prescribed course at the first level of graduate study: also **master's** (**degree**)

**master of ceremonies** one who supervises or presides over a ceremony, program, etc.

**mas′ter·piece′** *n.* ⟦< Ger *meisterstück*⟧ **1** a thing made or done with masterly skill **2** the greatest work of a person or group

**master sergeant** *U.S. Mil.* a noncommissioned officer of high rank

**mas′ter·stroke′** *n.* a masterly action, move, or achievement

**mas′ter·work′** *n.* MASTERPIECE

**mas′ter·y** *n., pl.* **-ies** **1** rule; control **2** ascendancy or victory **3** expert skill or knowledge

**mast′head′** *n.* **1** the top part of a ship's mast **2** a box or section in a newspaper or magazine, giving the owner, editors, etc.

**mas·ti·cate** (mas′ti kāt′) *vt.* -cat′ed, -cat′ing ⟦ult. < Gr *mastax*, mouth⟧ to chew —**mas′ti·ca′tion** *n.*

**mas·tiff** (mas′tif) *n.* ⟦< L *mansuetus*, tame⟧ a large, powerful dog with a short, thick coat

**mas·to·don** (mas′tə dän′) *n.* ⟦< Gr *mastos*, breast + *odous*, tooth: from the nipplelike processes on its molar⟧ a large, extinct mammal resembling the elephant but larger

**mas·toid** (mas′toid′) *adj.* ⟦< Gr *mastos*, breast + -*eidēs*, -OID⟧ designating, of, or near a projection of the temporal bone behind the ear —*n.* the mastoid projection

**mas·tur·bate** (mas′tər bāt′) *vi.* -bat′ed, -bat′ing ⟦< L *masturbari*⟧ to manipulate the genitals for sexual gratification —**mas′tur·ba′tion** *n.*

**mat**[1] (mat) *n.* ⟦< LL *matta*⟧ **1** a flat piece of cloth, rubber, woven straw, etc. used for protection, as on a floor or under a vase **2** a thickly padded floor covering, esp. one used for wrestling, etc. **3** anything densely interwoven or growing in a thick tangle —*vt.*, *vi.* mat′ted, mat′ting **1** to cover as with a mat **2** to form into a thick tangle —**go to the mat** [Inf.] to engage in a struggle or dispute

**mat**[2] (mat) *n.* ⟦< OFr⟧ **1** MATTE **2** a border, as of cardboard, put around a picture —*vt.* mat′ted, mat′ting to frame with a mat

**mat**[3] (mat) *n.* [Inf.] *Printing* a matrix

**mat·a·dor** (mat′ə dôr′) *n.* ⟦< Sp *matar*, to kill⟧ a bullfighter whose specialty is killing the bull

**match**[1] (mach) *n.* ⟦< OFr *mesche*⟧ a slender piece of wood, cardboard, etc. tipped with a substance that catches fire by friction

**match**[2] (mach) *n.* ⟦OE (*ge*)*mæcca*, mate⟧ **1** any person or thing equal or similar to another **2** two persons or things that go well together **3** a contest or game **4** a marriage or mating —*vt.* **1** to put in opposition (*with*); pit (*against*) **2** to be equal or similar to **3** to make or get a counterpart or equivalent to **4** to fit (one thing) to another —*vi.* to be equal, similar, suitable, etc.

**match′book′** *n.* a folder of book matches

**match′less** *adj.* having no equal

**match′mak′ing** *n.* the arranging of marriages, or of boxing matches, etc. —**match′mak′er** *n.*

**match′stick′** *n.* a thin strip of wood, cardboard, etc., as or like that of a match

**mate** (māt) *n.* ⟦< MDu⟧ **1** a companion or fellow worker **2** one of a matched pair **3** *a*) a husband or wife *b*) the male or female of paired animals **4** an officer of a merchant ship, ranking below the captain —*vt.*, *vi.* mat′ed, mat′ing **1** to join as a pair **2** to couple in marriage or sexual union

**ma·te·ri·al** (mə tir′ē əl) *adj.* ⟦< L *materia*, matter⟧ **1** of matter; physical [a *material* object] **2** of the body or bodily needs, comfort, etc.; not spiritual **3** important, pertinent, etc. —*n.* **1** what a thing is, or may be, made of; elements or parts **2** cloth; fabric **3** [*pl.*] tools, articles, etc. needed to make or do something

**ma·te·ri·al·ism′** *n.* **1** the doctrine that everything in the world, including thought, can be explained in terms of matter alone **2** the tendency to be more concerned with material than with spiritual or intellectual values —**ma·te′ri·al·ist** *n.*, *adj.* —**ma·te′ri·al·is′tic** *adj.*

**ma·te′ri·al·ize′** (-īz′) *vt.* -ized′, -iz′ing to give material form to —*vi.* **1** to become fact; be realized **2** to take on bodily form: said of spirits, etc. —**ma·te′ri·al·i·za′tion** *n.*

**ma·te′ri·al·ly** *adv.* **1** physically **2** to a great extent; substantially

**ma·te·ri·el** or **ma·té·ri·el** (mə tir′ē el′) *n.* ⟦Fr⟧ the necessary materials and tools; specif., military weapons, equipment, etc.

**ma·ter·nal** (mə tur′nəl) *adj.* ⟦< L *mater*, mother⟧ **1** of, like, or from a mother **2** related through the mother's side of the family —**ma·ter′nal·ly** *adv.*

**ma·ter′ni·ty** (-nə tē) *n.* the state of being a mother; motherhood —*adj.* **1** for pregnant

women **2** for the care of mothers and their newborn babies

**math**[1] (math) *n.* [Inf.] mathematics

**math**[2] *abbrev.* mathematics

**math·e·mat·i·cal** (math′ə mat′i kəl) *adj.* ⟦< Gr *manthanein*, learn⟧ **1** of, like, or concerned with mathematics **2** very precise, accurate, etc. —**math′e·mat′i·cal·ly** *adv.*

**math·e·mat·ics** (math′ə mat′iks) *n.* ⟦see prec. & -ICS⟧ the science dealing with quantities, forms, etc. and their relationships, by the use of numbers and symbols —**math′e·ma·ti′cian** (-mə tish′ən) *n.*

**mat·i·nee** or **mat·i·née** (mat′'n ā′) *n.* ⟦< Fr *matin*, morning⟧ an afternoon performance of a play, etc.

**mat·ins** (mat′'nz) *pl.n.* ⟦< L *matutinus*, of the morning⟧ [*often* M-] [*usually with sing. v.*] a church service of morning prayer

**Ma·tisse** (mä tēs′), **Hen·ri** (än re′) 1869-1954; Fr. painter

**matri-** ⟦< L *mater*⟧ *combining form* mother: also **matr-**

**ma·tri·arch** (mā′trē ärk′) *n.* ⟦prec. + -ARCH⟧ **1** a woman who rules a family, tribe, etc. **2** a highly respected elderly woman —**ma′tri·ar′chal** (-är′kəl) *adj.* —**ma′tri·arch′y**, *pl.* -ies, *n.*

**mat·ri·cide** (ma′trə sīd′) *n.* **1** the murdering of one's mother **2** a person who does this —**mat′ri·ci′dal** *adj.*

**ma·tric·u·late** (mə trik′yōō lāt′, -yə-) *vt.*, *vi.* -lat′ed, -lat′ing ⟦< LL: see MATRIX⟧ to enroll, esp. as a student in a college —**ma·tric′u·la′tion** *n.*

**mat·ri·mo·ny** (ma′trə mō′nē) *n.*, *pl.* -nies ⟦< L *mater*, mother⟧ **1** the act or rite of marriage **2** married life —**mat′ri·mo′ni·al** *adj.*

**ma·trix** (mā′triks′) *n.*, *pl.* **ma·tri·ces** (mā′trə sēz′, ma′trə-) or **ma′trix′es** ⟦< L *mater*, mother⟧ that within which something originates or develops

**ma·tron** (mā′trən) *n.* ⟦< L *mater*, mother⟧ **1** a wife or widow, esp. one with a mature appearance and manner **2** a woman manager of the domestic arrangements of a hospital, prison, etc. —**ma′tron·ly** *adj.*

**matron of honor** a married woman acting as chief attendant to a bride

**matte** (mat) *n.* ⟦var. of MAT[2]⟧ a dull surface or finish —*adj.* not shiny Also **matt**

**mat·ted** (mat′id) *adj.* closely tangled in a dense mass [*matted* hair]

**mat·ter** (mat′ər) *n.* ⟦< L *materia*⟧ **1** what a thing is made of; material **2** whatever occupies space and is perceptible to the senses **3** any specified substance [coloring *matter*] **4** material of thought or expression **5** an amount or quantity [a *matter* of a few days] **6** *a*) a thing or affair *b*) cause or occasion [no laughing *matter*] **7** importance [it's of no *matter*] **8** trouble; difficulty: with *the* [what's the *matter*?] **9** mail —*vi.* to be of importance —**as a matter of fact** see this phrase at FACT —**no matter 1** it is not important **2** regardless of

**mat′ter-of-fact′** *adj.* sticking to facts; literal, unimaginative, etc.

**Mat·thew** (math′yōō′) *n. Bible* **1** a Christian apostle, reputed author of the first Gospel **2** this Gospel: abbrev. **Matt.**

**mat·ting** (mat′iŋ) *n.* **1** a woven fabric of fiber, as straw, for mats, etc. **2** mats collectively

**mat·tock** (mat′ək) *n.* ⟦OE *mattuc*⟧ a tool like a pickax, for loosening the soil, digging roots, etc.

**mat·tress** (ma′trəs) *n.* ⟦< Ar *matrah*, cushion⟧ a casing of strong cloth filled with cotton, foam rubber, coiled springs, etc., used on a bed

**ma·ture** (mə toor′, -choor′) *adj.* ⟦< L *maturus*, ripe⟧ **1** full-grown; ripe **2** fully developed, perfected, etc. **3** due: said of a note, bond, etc. —*vt.*, *vi.* -tured′, -tur′ing to make or become mature —**mat·u·ra·tion** (mach′ə rā′shən) *n.* —**ma·ture′ly** *adv.* —**ma·tu′ri·ty** *n.*

**mat·zo** (mät′sə, -sō) *n.*, *pl.* **mat′zot**, **mat′zoth**

(-sōt), or **mat'zos** [Heb *matstsāh*, unleavened] **1** thin, crisp unleavened bread eaten during the Passover **2** a piece of this

**maud·lin** (môd'lin) *adj.* [< ME *Maudeleyne*, (Mary) Magdalene (often represented as weeping)] foolishly, often tearfully, sentimental

**maul** (môl) *n.* [< L *malleus*, a hammer] a heavy hammer for driving stakes, etc. —*vt.* **1** to bruise or lacerate **2** to handle roughly; manhandle

**maun·der** (môn'dər) *vi.* [< earlier *mander*, to grumble] to talk or move in a confused way

**Mau·ri·ta·ni·a** (môr'ə tā'nē ə) country in NW Africa, on the Atlantic: 398,000 sq. mi.; pop. 1,864,000

**Mau·ri·ti·us** (mô rish'ē əs, -rish'əs) island country in the Indian Ocean: 788 sq. mi.; pop. 1,059,000

**mau·so·le·um** (mô'sə lē'əm, mä'-; -zə-) *n., pl.* **-le'ums** or **-le'a** (-ə) [after the tomb of King *Mausolus*, in ancient Asia Minor] **1** a large, imposing tomb **2** a building with spaces for entombing a number of bodies

**mauve** (mōv, môv) *n.* [Fr, mallow] any of several shades of pale purple —*adj.* of such a color

**mav·er·ick** (mav'ər ik) *n.* [after S. *Maverick*, 19th-c. Texan whose cattle had no brand] **1** an unbranded animal, esp. a lost calf **2** [Inf.] one who takes an independent stand, as in politics

**maw** (mô) *n.* [OE *maga*] **1** [Archaic] the stomach **2** the throat, jaws, or mouth of a voracious animal

**mawk·ish** (mô'kish) *adj.* [< ON *mathkr*, maggot] sentimental in a weak, insipid way —**mawk'ish·ly** *adv.*

**max**[1] (maks) [Slang] *n., adj.* maximum —**to the max** to the possible degree

**max**[2] *abbrev.* maximum

**maxi-** [< MAXI(MUM)] *combining form* maximum, very large, very long

**max·il·la** (mak sil'ə) *n., pl.* **-lae** (-ē) [L] the upper jawbone —**max'il·lar'y** (-sə ler'ē) *adj.*

**max·im** (mak'sim) *n.* [< LL *maxima* (*propositio*), the greatest (premise)] a concise rule of conduct

**max·i·mize** (mak'sə mīz') *vt.* **-mized'**, **-miz'ing** to increase to the maximum

**max·i·mum** (mak'sə məm) *n., pl.* **-mums** or **-ma** (-mə) [< L superl. of *magnus*, great] **1** the greatest quantity, number, etc. possible or permissible **2** the highest degree or point reached —*adj.* greatest possible, permissible, or reached —**max'i·mal** (-məl) *adj.*

**may** (mā) *v.aux. pt.* **might** [OE *mæg*] used to express *a*) possibility [it *may* rain] *b*) permission [you *may* go] (see also CAN[1]) *c*) contingency [they died that we *may* be free] *d*) a wish or hope [*may* he live]

**May** (mā) *n.* [< L *Maius*] the fifth month of the year, having 31 days

**Ma·ya** (mä'yə, mī'ə) *n.* [Sp < native name] **1** *pl.* **-ya** or **-yas** a member of an American Indian people of Central America that had a highly developed civilization **2** the language of this people — **Ma'yan** *adj., n.*

**may·be** (mā'bē) *adv.* [ME (for *it may be*)] perhaps

**May Day** May 1: a traditional spring festival, now also a labor holiday in many countries

**may'flow'er** *n.* **1** an early spring flower, as the trailing arbutus **2** [M-] the ship on which the Pilgrims came to America (1620)

**may'fly'** *n., pl.* **-flies'** [thought to be prevalent in May] a delicate insect with gauzy wings

**may·hem** (mā'hem, -əm) *n.* [see MAIM] **1** *Law* the offense of maiming a person **2** any deliberate destruction

**may·o** (mā'ō) *n.* [Inf.] short for MAYONNAISE

**may·on·naise** (mā'ə nāz') *n.* [after *Mahón*, port on a Sp island] a creamy sauce of egg yolks, oil, vinegar, etc. beaten together

**may·or** (mā'ər) *n.* [< L *major*, greater] the chief administrative official of a city, town, etc. —**may'or·al** (mā'ər əl, mā ôr'əl) *adj.*

**may'or·al·ty** *n., pl.* **-ties** the office or term of office of a mayor

**may·pole** (mā'pōl') *n.* [*often* M-] a high pole with flowers, streamers, etc., for dancing around on May Day

**Ma·za·tlán** (mä'sät län') seaport & resort on the Pacific coast of Mexico: pop. 314,000

**maze** (māz) *n.* [< OE *amasian*, to amaze] **1** a confusing, intricate network of pathways **2** a confused state

**maz·el tov** (mä'zəl tōv', -tôf') [Heb, good luck] used to express congratulations: also **maz'el·tov'** *interj.*

**ma·zur·ka** or **ma·zour·ka** (mə zur'kə) *n.* [Pol] a lively Polish folk dance in 3/4 or 3/8 time

MAZE

**MB** *abbrev.* **1** Manitoba **2** megabyte(s): also **mb**

**MBA** or **M.B.A.** *abbrev.* Master of Business Administration

**MC** *abbrev.* **1** Master of Ceremonies **2** Member of Congress

**Mc·Kin·ley**[1] (mə kin'lē), **William** 1843-1901; 25th president of the U.S. (1897-1901): assassinated

**Mc·Kin·ley**[2] (mə kin'lē), **Mount** mountain in Alaska: highest peak in North America: 20,320 ft.: popularly called *Denali*

**MD** *abbrev.* **1** [L *Medicinae Doctor*] Doctor of Medicine: also **M.D. 2** Maryland

**mdse** *abbrev.* merchandise

**me** (mē) *pron.* [OE] objective form of I[2]

**ME** Maine

**mead**[1] (mēd) *n.* [OE *meodu*] an alcoholic liquor made of fermented honey and water

**mead**[2] (mēd) *n.* [Old Poet.] *var. of* MEADOW

**mead·ow** (med'ō) *n.* [< OE *mæd*] **1** a grassland where the grass is grown for hay **2** low, level grassland

**mea·ger** (mē'gər) *adj.* [< L *macer*, lean] **1** thin; lean **2** poor; not full or rich; inadequate Brit. sp. **mea'gre** —**mea'ger·ly** *adv.* —**mea'ger·ness** *n.*

**meal**[1] (mēl) *n.* [OE *mæl*] **1** any of the times for eating, as lunch or dinner **2** the food served at such a time

**meal**[2] (mēl) *n.* [OE *melu*] **1** any edible grain, coarsely ground [*cornmeal*] **2** any substance similarly ground —**meal'y, -i·er, -i·est,** *adj.*

**meal·y-mouthed** (mēl'ē mouthd') *adj.* not outspoken or blunt; euphemistic

**mean**[1] (mēn) *vt.* **meant** (ment), **mean'ing** [OE *mænan*] **1** to have in mind; intend [he *means* to go] **2** to intend to express [say what you *mean*] **3** to signify; denote [the German word "*ja*" *means* "yes"] —*vi.* to have a (specified) degree of importance, effect, etc. [honors *mean* little to him] — **mean well** to have good intentions

**mean**[2] (mēn) *adj.* [OE (ge)mæne] **1** low in quality or value; paltry **2** poor in appearance; shabby **3** petty **4** stingy **5** pettily bad-tempered, disagreeable, etc. **6** [Slang] *a*) hard to cope with *b*) skillful —**mean'ly** *adv.* —**mean'ness** *n.*

**mean**[3] (mēn) *adj.* [< L *medius*, middle] **1** halfway between extremes **2** average —*n.* **1** what is between extremes **2** *Math.* a number between the smallest and largest values of a set of quantities; esp., an average

**me·an·der** (mē an'dər) *vi.* [< Gr *Maiandros*, a winding river in Asia Minor] **1** to take a winding course: said of a stream **2** to wander idly —*n.* an aimless wandering

**mean·ie** or **mean·y** (mē'nē) *n., pl.* **-ies** [Inf.] one who is mean, selfish, etc.

**mean'ing** *n.* what is meant; what is intended to be signified, understood, indicated, etc.; import; sense [the *meaning* of a word] —**mean'ing·ful** *adj.* —**mean'ing·less** *adj.*

**means** (mēnz) *pl.n.* [< MEAN[3], *n.*] **1** [*with sing.* or

**pl. v.]** that by which something is done or obtained; agency *[a means of travel]* **2** resources; wealth —**by all means 1** without fail **2** certainly —**by means of** by using —**by no means** not at all

**means test** an investigation of a person's financial resources, to determine that person's eligibility for welfare payments, etc.

**meant** (ment) *vt., vi. pt. & pp. of* MEAN[1]

**mean'time'** *adv.* **1** in or during the intervening time **2** at the same time —*n.* the intervening time Also **mean'while'**

**mea·sles** (mē′zəlz) *n.* ⟦ME *maseles*⟧ **1** an acute, infectious, communicable viral disease, usually of children, characterized by small, red spots on the skin, high fever, etc. **2** a similar but milder disease; esp., rubella (*German measles*)

**mea·sly** (mēz′lē) *adj.* -sli·er, -sli·est [Inf.] contemptibly slight or worthless

**meas·ure** (mezh′ər) *n.* ⟦< L *metiri*, to measure⟧ **1** the extent, dimensions, capacity, etc. of anything **2** a determining of this; measurement **3** *a)* a unit of measurement *b)* any standard of valuation **4** a system of measurement **5** an instrument for measuring **6** a definite quantity measured out **7** a course of action *[reform measures]* **8** a statute; law **9** a rhythmical pattern or unit; specif., the notes and rests between two bars on a musical staff —*vt.* -ured, -ur·ing **1** to find out or estimate the extent, dimensions, etc. of, esp. by a standard **2** to mark off by measuring: often with *off* or *out* **3** to be a measure of —*vi.* **1** to take measurements **2** to be of a specified dimension, etc. — **beyond measure** exceedingly —**for good measure** as a bonus or something extra —**measure up to** to reach (a standard, etc.) —**meas'ur·a·ble** *adj.* —**meas'ur·a·bly** *adv.* —**meas'ure·less** *adj.*

**meas'ured** *adj.* **1** determined or marked off by a standard **2** regular or steady *[measured steps]* **3** careful and guarded: said of speech, etc.

**meas'ure·ment** *n.* **1** a measuring or being measured **2** extent or quantity determined by measuring **3** a system of measuring or of measures

**meat** (mēt) *n.* ⟦OE *mete*⟧ **1** food: now archaic except in **meat and drink 2** the flesh of animals, esp. of mammals, used as food **3** the edible, inner part *[the meat of a nut]* **4** the substance or essence —**meat′y,** -i·er, -i·est, *adj.*

**meat'-and-po·ta'toes** *adj.* [Inf.] **1** basic; fundamental **2** ordinary; everyday

**meat'pack'ing** *n.* the process or industry of preparing the meat of animals for market

**Mec·ca**[1] (mek′ə) *n.* ⟦after fol.⟧ *[often* m-] any place many people feel drawn to *[a tourist mecca]*

**Mecca**[2] (mek′ə) city in W Saudi Arabia: birthplace of Mohammed & hence a holy city of Islam: pop. 618,000

**me·chan·ic** (mə kan′ik) *n.* ⟦< Gr *mēchanē*, machine⟧ a worker skilled in using tools, repairing machines, etc.

**me·chan'i·cal** *adj.* **1** having to do with machinery or tools **2** produced or operated by machinery or a mechanism **3** of the science of mechanics **4** machinelike; lacking warmth, spontaneity, etc. — **me·chan'i·cal·ly** *adv.*

**me·chan'ics** *n.* **1** the science of motion and of the action of forces on bodies **2** knowledge of machinery —*pl.n.* [*sometimes with sing. v.*] the technical part *[the mechanics of writing]*

**mech·a·nism** (mek′ə niz′əm) *n.* ⟦< Gr *mēchanē*, machine⟧ **1** the working parts of a machine **2** any system of interrelated parts **3** any physical or mental process by which a result is produced — **mech'a·nis'tic** *adj.*

**mech'a·nize'** (-nīz′) *vt.* -nized′, -niz'ing **1** to make mechanical **2** to equip (an industry) with machinery or (an army, etc.) with motor vehicles, tanks, etc. —**mech'a·ni·za'tion** *n.*

**med** *abbrev.* **1** medical **2** medicine **3** medium

**med·al** (med′'l) *n.* ⟦< LL *medialis*, medial⟧ **1** a small, flat piece of inscribed metal commemorating some event or awarded for some distin-

guished action, merit, etc. **2** a similar piece of metal bearing a religious figure or symbol

**med·al·ist** *n.* one awarded a medal

**me·dal·lion** (mə dal′yən) *n.* ⟦Fr *médaillon*⟧ **1** a large medal **2** a design, portrait, etc. resembling a medal

**med·dle** (med′'l) *vi.* -dled, -dling ⟦< L *miscere*, to mix⟧ to interfere in another's affairs —**med'dler** *n.* —**med'dle·some** (-səm) *adj.*

**me·di·a** (mē′dē ət) *n. alt. pl. of* MEDIUM: see MEDIUM (*n.* 3) —**the media** [*usually with sing. v.*] all the means of communication such as newspapers, radio, and TV

**me·di·al** (mē′dē əl) *adj.* ⟦< L *medius*⟧ **1** of or in the middle **2** average

**me·di·an** (mē′dē ən) *adj.* **1** middle; intermediate **2** designating the middle number in a series —*n.* **1** a median number, point, line, etc. **2** the strip of land separating the lanes of opposing traffic of a divided highway: in full **median strip**

**me·di·ate** (mē′dē āt′) *vi.* -at·ed, -at·ing ⟦< L *medius*, middle⟧ to be an intermediary —*vt.* to settle (differences) between persons, nations, etc. by friendly or diplomatic intervention —**me·di·a'tion** *n.* —**me'di·a'tor** *n.*

**med·ic** (med′ik) *n.* [Inf.] **1** a physician or surgeon **2** a medical officer who gives first aid in combat

**Med'ic·aid'** (-i kād′) *n.* ⟦MEDIC(AL) + AID⟧ [*also* m-] a state and federal health program for paying certain medical expenses of persons of low income

**med'i·cal** (-i kəl) *adj.* of or connected with the practice or study of medicine —**med'i·cal·ly** *adv.*

**medical jurisprudence** the application of medical knowledge to questions of law

**Med·i·care** (med′i ker′) *n.* ⟦MEDI(CAL) + CARE⟧ [*also* m-] a federal health program for paying certain medical expenses of the aged and the needy

**med'i·cate'** (-kāt′) *vt.* -cat·ed, -cat·ing ⟦< L *medicari*, heal⟧ to treat with medicine —**med'i·ca'tion** *n.*

**me·dic·i·nal** (mə dis′ən əl) *adj.* of, or having the properties of, medicine

**med·i·cine** (med′i sən) *n.* ⟦< L *medicus*, physician⟧ **1** the science and art of treating and preventing disease **2** any substance, as a drug, used in treating disease, relieving pain, etc.

**medicine man** among North American Indians, etc., a man supposed to have supernatural powers for healing the sick, etc.

**me·di·e·val** (mē′dē ē′vəl, mi dē′vəl) *adj.* ⟦< L *medius*, middle + *aevum*, age⟧ of or characteristic of the Middle Ages

**me·di·o·cre** (mē′dē ō′kər) *adj.* ⟦< L *medius*, middle + *ocris*, peak⟧ **1** ordinary; average **2** inferior —**me'di·oc'ri·ty** (-äk′rə tē), *pl.* -ties, *n.*

**med·i·tate** (med′ə tāt′) *vt.* -tat·ed, -tat·ing ⟦< L *meditari*⟧ to plan —*vi.* to think deeply —**med'i·ta'tion** *n.* —**med'i·ta'tive** *adj.*

**Med·i·ter·ra·ne·an** (med′ə tə rā′nē ən) *adj.* **1** *a)* of the large sea (**Mediterranean Sea**) surrounded by Europe, Africa, & Asia *b)* of the regions near this sea **2** designating furniture made to simulate heavy, ornately carved Renaissance furniture —*n.* a Mediterranean person

**me·di·um** (mē′dē əm) *n., pl.* -di·ums *or* -di·a (-ə) ⟦L < *medius*, the middle⟧ **1** an intermediate thing or state **2** an intervening thing through which a force acts **3** *pl. usually* **me′dia** any means, agency, etc.; specif., a means of communication that reaches the general public: a singular form **media** (*pl.* **medias**) is now often used **4** any surrounding substance or environment **5** *pl.* **me′di·ums** one through whom messages are supposedly sent from the dead —*adj.* intermediate in size, quality, etc.

**med·ley** (med′lē) *n., pl.* -leys ⟦< L *miscere*, to mix⟧ **1** a mixture of dissimilar things **2** a musical piece made up of various tunes or passages

**me·dul·la** (mi dul′ə) *n., pl.* -las *or* -lae (-ē) ⟦L, marrow⟧ *Anat.* **1** a widening of the spinal cord

forming the lowest part of the brain: in full
**medulla ob·lon·ga·ta** (äb′läŋ gät′ə) 2 the inner
substance of an organ, as of the kidney

**meek** (mēk) *adj.* ⟦< ON *miukr*, gentle⟧ 1 patient
and mild 2 too submissive; spiritless —**meek′ly**
*adv.* —**meek′ness** *n.*

**meer·schaum** (mir′shəm, -shôm′) *n.* ⟦Ger, sea
foam⟧ 1 a white, claylike, heat-resistant mineral
used for tobacco pipes, etc. 2 a pipe made of this

**meet**[1] (mēt) *vt.* **met, meet′ing** ⟦OE *metan*⟧ 1 to
come upon; encounter 2 to be present at the
arrival of [to *meet* a bus] 3 to come into contact
with 4 to be introduced to 5 to contend with;
deal with 6 to experience [to *meet* disaster] 7 to
be perceived by (the eye, etc.) 8 *a*) to satisfy (a
demand, etc.) *b*) to pay (a bill, etc.) —*vi.* 1 to
come together 2 to come into contact, etc. 3 to be
introduced 4 to assemble —*n.* a meeting as for a
sporting competition —**meet with** 1 to experience 2 to receive

**meet**[2] (mēt) *adj.* ⟦OE (*ge*)*mæte*, fitting⟧ [Now
Rare] suitable; proper

**meet′ing** *n.* 1 a coming together 2 a gathering of
people 3 a junction

**mega-** ⟦Gr < *megas*, great⟧ *combining form* 1
large, great, powerful 2 one million Also **meg-**

**meg·a·byte** (meg′ə bīt′) *n.* [prec. + BYTE] a unit
of storage capacity in a computer system, equal to
$2^{20}$ bytes, or, loosely, one million bytes

**meg′a·hertz′** (-hurts′) *n.,* *pl.* **-hertz** ⟦MEGA- +
HERTZ⟧ one million hertz

**meg·a·lo·ma·ni·a** (meg′ə lō mā′nē ə) *n.* ⟦< Gr
*megas*, large + -MANIA⟧ a mental disorder characterized by delusions of grandeur, power, etc. —
**meg′a·lo·ma′ni·ac** *adj., n.*

**meg·a·lop·o·lis** (meg′ə läp′ə lis) *n.* ⟦Gr, great
city⟧ a vast, continuously urban area, including
any number of cities

**meg·a·phone** (meg′ə fōn′) *n.* ⟦MEGA- + -PHONE⟧ a
cone-shaped device for increasing the volume of
the voice

**meg′a·ton′** (-tun′) *n.* ⟦MEGA- + TON⟧ the explosive
force of a million tons of TNT

**Me·kong** (mā′käŋ′, -kôŋ′) river in SE Asia, flowing into the South China Sea

**mel·a·mine** (mel′ə mēn′) *n.* ⟦Ger *melamin*⟧ a
white, crystalline compound used in making synthetic resins

**mel·an·cho·li·a** (mel′ən kō′lē ə) *n.* a mental disorder, often psychotic, characterized by extreme
depression

**mel′an·chol′y** (-käl′ē) *n., pl.* **-ies** ⟦< Gr *melas*,
black + *cholē*, bile⟧ sadness and depression of
spirits —*adj.* 1 sad and depressed 2 causing sadness —**mel′an·chol′ic** *adj.*

**Mel·a·ne·sia** (mel′ə nē′zhə) group of islands in the
S Pacific —**Mel′a·ne′sian** *adj., n.*

**mé·lange** (mā lônzh′, -lônj′) *n.* ⟦Fr < *mêler*, to
mix⟧ a mixture; medley

**mel·a·nin** (mel′ə nin) *n.* ⟦< Gr *melas*, black⟧ a
blackish pigment found in skin, hair, etc.

**mel·a·no·ma** (-nō′mə) *n., pl.* **-mas** or **-ma·ta** (-mə
tə) ⟦< Gr *melas*, black + -*ōma*, mass⟧ a skin tumor
derived from cells capable of melanin formation

**Mel·ba toast** (mel′bə) ⟦after N. *Melba* (1861-
1931), Australian soprano⟧ [*also* **m- t-**] very crisp,
thinly sliced toast

**Mel·bourne** (mel′bərn) seaport in SE Australia:
pop. 2,833,000

**meld** (meld) *vt., vi.* ⟦< MELT + WELD⟧ to blend;
merge

**me·lee** or **mê·lée** (mā′lā′, mā lā′) *n.* ⟦Fr⟧ a confused fight or hand-to-hand struggle

**mel·io·rate** (mēl′yə rāt′) *vt., vi.* **-rat′ed, -rat′ing** ⟦<
L *melior*, better⟧ to make or become better

**mel·lif·lu·ous** (mə lif′lōō əs) *adj.* ⟦< L *mel*, honey
+ *fluere*, to flow⟧ sounding sweet and smooth: also
**mel·lif′lu·ent** —**mel·lif′lu·ence** *n.*

**mel·low** (mel′ō) *adj.* ⟦ME *melwe*, ripe⟧ 1 full-fla-

vored: said of wine, etc. 2 full, rich, soft, etc.; not
harsh: said of sound, light, etc. 3 made gentle,
understanding, etc. by age 4 [Inf.] genial, as
from drinking liquor —*vt., vi.* to make or become
mellow

**me·lo·di·ous** (mə lō′dē əs) *adj.* 1 producing
melody 2 pleasing to hear; tuneful —**me·lo′di·
ous·ly** *adv.*

**mel·o·dra·ma** (mel′ə drä′mə, -dram′ə) *n.* ⟦< Fr <
Gr *melos*, song + LL *drama*, drama⟧ a drama with
exaggerated conflicts and emotions, stereotyped
characters, etc. —**mel′o·dra·mat′ic** (-drə mat′ik)
*adj.*

**mel′o·dra·mat′ics** (-drə mat′iks) *pl.n.* melodramatic behavior

**mel·o·dy** (mel′ə dē) *n., pl.* **-dies** ⟦< Gr *melos*, song
+ *aeidein*, sing⟧ 1 pleasing sounds in sequence 2
*Music a*) a tune, song, etc. *b*) the leading part in
a harmonic composition —**me·lod·ic** (mə läd′ik)
*adj.* —**me·lod′i·cal·ly** *adv.*

**mel·on** (mel′ən) *n.* ⟦< Gr *mēlon*, apple⟧ the large,
juicy, thick-skinned, many-seeded fruit of certain
trailing plants, as the watermelon or cantaloupe

**melt** (melt) *vt., vi.* ⟦OE *m(i)eltan*⟧ 1 to change
from a solid to a liquid state, generally by heat 2
to dissolve 3 to disappear or cause to disappear
gradually 4 to soften; become gentle, tender, etc.

**melt′down′** *n.* a dangerous situation in which a
nuclear reactor begins to melt its fuel rods

**melting pot** a country, etc. in which people of
various nationalities and races are assimilated

**Mel·ville** (mel′vil), **Her·man** (hur′mən) 1819-91;
U.S. novelist

**mem·ber** (mem′bər) *n.* ⟦< L *membrum*⟧ 1 a limb
or other part of a person, animal, or plant 2 a
distinct part of a whole 3 a person belonging to
some group, society, etc.

**mem′ber·ship′** *n.* 1 the state of being a member:
with *in* 2 members collectively, as of a group 3
the number of members

**mem·brane** (mem′brān′) *n.* ⟦< L *membrum*,
member⟧ a thin, soft layer, esp. of animal or plant
tissue, that covers or lines an organ, part, etc. —
**mem′bra·nous** (-brə nəs) *adj.*

**me·men·to** (mə men′tō) *n., pl.* **-tos** or **-toes** ⟦< L
*meminisse*, remember⟧ a souvenir

**mem·o** (mem′ō) *n., pl.* **-os** *short for* MEMORANDUM

**mem·oirs** (mem′wärz′) *pl.n.* ⟦< L *memoria*,
memory⟧ 1 an autobiography 2 a record of
events based on the writer's personal knowledge

**mem·o·ra·bil·i·a** (mem′ə rə bil′ē ə, -bil′yə; -bēl′-)
*pl.n.* ⟦L⟧ things serving as a record or reminder

**mem·o·ra·ble** (mem′ə rə bəl) *adj.* worth remembering; notable; remarkable —**mem′o·ra·bly** *adv.*

**mem·o·ran·dum** (mem′ə ran′dəm) *n., pl.* **-dums**
or **-da** (-də) ⟦L⟧ 1 a short note written to remind
one of something 2 an informal written communication, as in an office 3 *Law* a short written
statement of the terms of an agreement, etc.

**me·mo·ri·al** (mə môr′ē əl) *adj.* ⟦< L *memoria*,
memory⟧ serving to help people remember —*n.*
anything meant to help people remember a person or event, as a monument or holiday —**me·
mo′ri·al·ize′** (-īz′), **-ized′, -iz′ing,** *vt.*

**Memorial Day** a legal holiday in the U.S. (the
last Monday in May in most States) in memory of
members of the armed forces killed in war

**mem·o·rize** (mem′ə rīz′) *vt.* **-rized′, -riz′ing** to
commit to memory —**mem′o·ri·za′tion** *n.*

**mem·o·ry** (mem′ə rē, mem′rē) *n., pl.* **-ries** ⟦< L
*memor,* mindful⟧ 1 the power or act of remembering 2 all that one remembers 3 something
remembered 4 the period of remembering
[within my *memory*] 5 commemoration 6 storage capacity, as of a computer or disk

**Mem·phis** (mem′fis) city in SW Tennessee: pop.
610,000

**men** (men) *n. pl. of* MAN

**men·ace** (men′əs) *n.* ⟦< L *minari*, threaten⟧ 1 a
threat 2 [Inf.] one who is a nuisance —*vt., vi.*
**-aced, -ac·ing** to threaten —**men′ac·ing·ly** *adv.*

**mé·nage** or **me·nage** (mā näzh′, mə-) *n.* ⟦Fr < L *mansio*, house⟧ a household

**me·nag·er·ie** (mə naj′ər ē, -nazh′-) *n.* ⟦see prec.⟧ a collection of wild animals kept in cages, etc. for exhibition

**mend** (mend) *vt.* ⟦< ME *amenden,* amend⟧ **1** to repair **2** to make better; reform —*vi.* **1** to improve, esp. in health **2** to heal, as a fracture — *n.* **1** a mending **2** a mended place —**on the mend** improving, esp. in health —**mend′er** *n.*

**men·da·cious** (men dā′shəs) *adj.* ⟦< L *mendax*⟧ not truthful; lying —**men·dac′i·ty** (-das′ə tē), *pl.* **-ties,** *n.*

**Men·del** (men′dəl), **Gre·gor** (grā′gôr) 1822-84; Austrian monk & geneticist

**Men·dels·sohn** (men′dəl sən, -sōn′), **Fe·lix** (fā′liks) 1809-47; Ger. composer

**men·di·cant** (men′di kənt) *adj.* ⟦< L *mendicus,* needy⟧ begging —*n.* **1** a beggar **2** a mendicant friar

**men′folk′** (-fōk′) *pl.n.* [Inf. or Dial.] men: also **men′folks′**

**men·ha·den** (men hād″n) *n., pl.* **-den** or **-dens** ⟦< AmInd⟧ a common fish of the W Atlantic, used for bait or for making oil and fertilizer

**me·ni·al** (mē′nē əl) *adj.* ⟦< L *mansio,* house⟧ **1** of or fit for servants **2** servile; low —*n.* **1** a domestic servant **2** a servile, low person —**me′ni·al·ly** *adv.*

**me·nin·ges** (mə nin′jēz′) *pl.n., sing.* **me·ninx** (mē′ninks′) ⟦< Gr *mēninx,* membrane⟧ the three membranes that envelop the brain and the spinal cord —**me·nin′ge·al** (-jē əl) *adj.*

**men·in·gi·tis** (men′in jīt′is) *n.* ⟦ModL: see prec. & -ITIS⟧ inflammation of the meninges

**me·nis·cus** (mə nis′kəs) *n., pl.* **-cus·es** or **-ci** (-ī′) ⟦< Gr dim. of *mēnē,* the moon⟧ **1** a crescent or crescent-shaped thing **2** the convex or concave upper surface of a column of liquid

**Men·non·ite** (men′ən īt′) *n.* ⟦after *Menno* Simons, 16th-c. Du reformer⟧ a member of an evangelical Christian sect that opposes military service and favors plain living and dress

**men·o·pause** (men′ə pôz′) *n.* ⟦< Gr *mēn,* month + *pauein,* to end⟧ the permanent cessation of menstruation

**me·no·rah** (mə nō′rə, -nôr′ə) *n.* ⟦Heb *menora,* lamp stand⟧ a candelabrum with seven (or nine) branches: a symbol of Judaism

**men·ses** (men′sēz′) *pl.n.* ⟦L, pl. of *mensis,* month⟧ the periodic flow, usually monthly, of blood from the uterus

**men·stru·ate** (men′stroo āt′) *vi.* **-at′ed, -at′ing** ⟦< L *mensis,* month⟧ to have a discharge of the menses —**men′strual** (-strəl) *adj.* —**men′stru·a′tion** *n.*

**men·su·ra·tion** (men′shə rā′shən) *n.* ⟦< L *mensura,* measure⟧ a measuring

**-ment** (mənt, mint) ⟦< L *-mentum*⟧ *suffix* **1** a result **2** a means of **3** an act **4** a state [*enchantment*]

**men·tal** (ment″l) *adj.* ⟦< L *mens,* the mind⟧ **1** of, for, by, or in the mind **2** of, having, or related to mental illness **3** for the mentally ill [a *mental* hospital] —**men′tal·ly** *adv.*

**men′tal·ist** *n.* MIND READER

**men·tal·i·ty** (men tal′i tē) *n., pl.* **-ties 1** mental capacity or power **2** mental attitude or outlook

**mental reservation** a qualification (of a statement) that one makes to oneself but does not express

**mental retardation** a condition, usually congenital, characterized by subnormal intelligence

**men·ta·tion** (men tā′shən) *n.* ⟦< L *mens,* mind + -ATION⟧ the act or process of using the mind

**men·thol** (men′thôl′) *n.* ⟦Ger < L *mentha,* MINT²⟧ a white, crystalline alcohol obtained from oil of peppermint and used in medicine, cosmetics, etc. —**men′tho·lat′ed** (-thə lāt′id) *adj.*

**men·tion** (men′shən) *n.* ⟦< L *mens,* the mind⟧ **1** a brief reference **2** a citing for honor —*vt.* to refer to briefly or incidentally —**make mention of** to

mention —**not to mention** without even mentioning

**men·tor** (men′tər, -tôr′) *n.* ⟦after *Mentor,* friend and advisor of Odysseus⟧ **1** a wise advisor **2** a teacher or coach

**men·u** (men′yōō) *n., pl.* **-us** ⟦Fr, small, detailed⟧ **1** a detailed list of the foods served at a meal or those available at a restaurant **2** a list, as on a computer screen, of the various choices available to the user

**me·ow** or **me·ou** (mē ou′) *n.* ⟦echoic⟧ the characteristic vocal sound made by a cat —*vi.* to make such a sound

**mer·can·tile** (mur′kən tīl′, -til) *adj.* ⟦Fr⟧ of or characteristic of merchants or trade

**mer·ce·nar·y** (mur′sə ner′ē) *adj.* ⟦< L *merces,* wages⟧ working or done for payment only —*n., pl.* **-ies** a soldier hired to serve in a foreign army

**mer′cer·ize′** (-īz′) *vt.* **-ized′, -iz′ing** ⟦after J. *Mercer* (1791-1866), Eng calico dealer⟧ to treat (cotton thread or fabric) with a sodium hydroxide solution to strengthen it, give it a silky luster, etc.

**mer·chan·dise** (mur′chən dīz′; *for n., also,* -dīs′) *n.* ⟦see fol.⟧ things bought and sold; goods; commodities —*vt., vi.* **-dised′, -dis′ing 1** to buy and sell **2** to promote the sale of (a product) Also, for v., **mer′chan·dize′** (-dīz′), **-dized′, -diz′ing** —**mer′chan·dis′er** or **mer′chan·diz′er** *n.*

**mer·chant** (mur′chənt) *n.* ⟦ult. < L *merx,* wares⟧ **1** one whose business is buying and selling goods **2** a retail dealer; storekeeper —*adj.* mercantile; commercial

**mer′chant·man** (-mən) *n., pl.* **-men** (-mən) a ship used in commerce

**merchant marine 1** all of a nation's commercial ships **2** their personnel

**mer·ci** (mer sē′) *interj.* ⟦Fr⟧ thank you

**mer·ci·ful** (mur′si fəl) *adj.* having or showing mercy; compassionate; lenient —**mer′ci·ful·ly** *adv.*

**mer′ci·less** *adj.* without mercy; pitiless —**mer′ci·less·ly** *adv.*

**mer·cu·ri·al** (mər kyoor′ē əl) *adj.* **1** of or containing mercury **2** quick, changeable, fickle, etc.

**Mer·cu·ry** (mur′kyoor ē) *n.* **1** *Rom. Myth.* the messenger of the gods **2** a small planet in the solar system: see PLANET **3** [m-] a heavy, silver-white metallic chemical element, liquid at ordinary temperatures, used in thermometers, etc. — **mer·cu·ric** (mər kyoor′ik) *adj.* —**mer·cu′rous** *adj.*

**mer·cy** (mur′sē) *n., pl.* **-cies** ⟦< L *merces,* payment⟧ **1** a refraining from harming offenders, enemies, etc. **2** imprisonment rather than death for a capital crime **3** a disposition to forgive or be kind **4** the power to forgive **5** kind or compassionate treatment **6** a lucky thing; blessing —**at the mercy of** completely in the power of

**mercy killing** EUTHANASIA

**mere** (mir) *adj. superl.* **mer′est** ⟦< L *merus,* pure⟧ nothing more or other than [a *mere* boy]

**mere′ly** *adv.* only; no more than

**mer·e·tri·cious** (mer′ə trish′əs) *adj.* ⟦< L *meretrix,* a prostitute⟧ **1** attractive in a flashy way **2** superficially plausible; specious

**mer·gan·ser** (mər gan′sər) *n.* ⟦< L *mergus,* diver (bird) + *anser,* goose⟧ a fish-eating, diving duck with a long bill

**merge** (murj) *vi., vt.* **merged, merg′ing** ⟦L *mergere,* to dip⟧ **1** to lose or cause to lose identity by being absorbed or combined **2** to unite; combine

**merg·er** (mur′jər) *n.* a merging; specif., a combining of two or more companies into one

**me·rid·i·an** (mə rid′ē ən) *n.* ⟦< L *meridies,* noon⟧ **1** the highest point of power, etc. **2** *a*) a circle on the earth's surface passing through the geographical poles and any given point *b*) any of the lines of longitude

**me·ringue** (mə raŋ′) *n.* ⟦Fr⟧ egg whites beaten with sugar until stiff: used as a pie covering, etc.

**me·ri·no** (mə rē′nō) *n., pl.* **-nos** ⟦Sp⟧ **1** any of a breed of hardy, white-faced sheep with long, fine wool **2** the wool **3** yarn or cloth made of it

**mer·it** (mer′it) *n.* ⟦< L *merere,* deserve⟧ **1** worth; value; excellence **2** something deserving reward, praise, etc. **3** [*pl.*] intrinsic rightness or wrongness —*vt.* to deserve

**mer·i·to·ri·ous** (mer′i tôr′ē əs) *adj.* having merit; deserving reward, praise, etc. —**mer′i·to′ri·ous·ly** *adv.*

**Mer·lin** (mur′lin) *n. Arthurian Legend* a magician and seer, helper of King Arthur

**mer·maid** (mur′mād′) *n.* ⟦< OE *mere,* sea + MAID⟧ an imaginary sea creature with the head and upper body of a woman and the tail of a fish — **mer′man′** (-man′), *pl.* -**men′** (-mən′), *masc.n.*

**mer·ri·ment** (mer′i mənt) *n.* a merrymaking; gaiety and fun; mirth

**mer·ry** (mer′ē) *adj.* **-ri·er, -ri·est** ⟦< OE *myrge,* pleasing⟧ **1** full of fun; lively **2** festive —**make merry** to be festive and have fun —**mer′ri·ly** *adv.* —**mer′ri·ness** *n.*

**mer′ry-go-round′** *n.* **1** a circular, revolving platform with forms of animals as seats on it, used at carnivals, etc. **2** a busy series of activities

**mer′ry·mak′ing** *n.* a having fun; festivity — **mer′ry·mak′er** *n.*

**me·sa** (mā′sə) *n.* ⟦Sp < L *mensa,* a table⟧ a small, high plateau with steep sides

**Me·sa** (mā′sə) city in SC Arizona: pop. 288,000

**mes·cal** (mes kal′) *n.* ⟦< Sp < AmInd(Mex)⟧ a small cactus of N Mexico and the SW U.S.

**mes·ca·line** (mes′kə lin) *n.* ⟦< AmInd(Mex) *mexcalli,* a spineless cactus⟧ a psychedelic drug obtained from the mescal

**mes·clun** (mes′klən) *n.* ⟦Fr⟧ a mixture of salad greens and herbs

**mes·dames** (mā däm′; *Fr,* -dám′) *n. pl. of* MADAME, MADAM (sense 1), or MRS.

**mes·de·moi·selles** (mād mwä zel′) *n. pl. of* MADEMOISELLE

**mesh** (mesh) *n.* ⟦prob. < MDu *mæsche*⟧ **1** any of the open spaces of a net, screen, etc. **2** a net or network **3** a netlike material, as for stockings **4** the engagement of the teeth of gears —*vt., vi.* **1** to entangle or become entangled **2** to engage or become engaged: said of gears **3** to interlock

**mes·mer·ize** (mez′mər īz′, mes′-) *vt.* **-ized′, -iz′ing** ⟦after F. A. *Mesmer* (1734-1815), Ger physician⟧ **1** to hypnotize **2** to spellbind —**mes′mer·ism′** *n.* —**mes′mer·ist** *n.*

**Mes·o·a·mer·i·ca** (mes′ō ə mer′i kə, mez′-) region including parts of modern Mexico and Central America, formerly inhabited by the Maya, the Aztecs, etc.

**mes·on** (mes′än′, mez′-) *n.* ⟦< Gr *mesos,* middle + (ELECTR)ON⟧ any of a group of unstable subatomic particles having a mass between those of an electron and a proton

**Mes·o·po·ta·mi·a** (mes′ə pə tā′mē ə) ancient country in SW Asia, between the upper Tigris & Euphrates rivers

**Mes·o·zo·ic** (mes′ə zō′ik, mez′-) *adj.* ⟦< Gr *mesos,* middle + ZO(O)- + -IC⟧ designating the geologic era (c. 240 to 66 million years ago) characterized by dinosaurs and by the appearance of flowering plants, mammals, birds, etc.

**mes·quite** or **mes·quit** (me skēt′) *n.* ⟦< AmInd(Mex) *mizquitl*⟧ a thorny tree or shrub of Mexico and the SW U.S.

**mess** (mes) *n.* ⟦< L *missus,* course (at a meal)⟧ **1** a portion of food for a meal **2** a group of people who regularly eat together, as in the army **3** the meal they eat **4** a jumble **5** a state of trouble, disorder, or confusion **6** [Inf.] a person in such a state **7** [Inf.] an untidy place —*vt.* **1** to make dirty or untidy **2** to muddle; botch Often with *up* —*vi.* **1** to eat as one of a mess **2** to make a mess **3** to putter or meddle (*in* or *with*) —**mess′y, -i·er, -i·est,** *adj.* —**mess′i·ly** *adv.* —**mess′i·ness** *n.*

**mes·sage** (mes′ij) *n.* ⟦< L *mittere,* send⟧ **1** a communication sent by speech, in writing, etc. **2** the chief idea that an artist, writer, etc. seeks to communicate in a work —**get the message** [Inf.] to understand a hint, etc.

**mes·sen·ger** (mes′ən jər) *n.* one who carries a message or goes on an errand

**messenger RNA** a single-stranded form of RNA, derived from DNA, that carries the genetic information needed to form proteins

**mess hall** a room or building where soldiers, etc. regularly have meals

**Mes·si·ah** (mə sī′ə) *n.* ⟦< Heb *māshīah,* anointed⟧ **1** *Judaism* the expected deliverer of the Jews **2** *Christianity* Jesus **3** [m-] any expected savior or liberator —**Mes′si·an′ic** or **me·si·an·ic** (mes′ē an′ik) *adj.*

**mes·sieurs** (mes′ərz; *Fr* mā syö′) *n. pl. of* MONSIEUR

**Messrs.** (mes′ərz) *abbrev.* messieurs: now used chiefly as the pl. of MR.

**mes·ti·zo** (me stē′zō) *n., pl.* **-zos** or **-zoes** ⟦Sp < L *miscere,* to mix⟧ a person of mixed parentage, esp. Spanish and American Indian

**met**[1] (met) *vt., vi. pt. & pp. of* MEET[1]

**met**[2] *abbrev.* metropolitan

**meta-** ⟦< Gr *meta,* after⟧ *prefix* **1** changed [*metathesis*] **2** after, beyond, higher [*metaphysics*]

**me·tab·o·lism** (mə tab′ə liz′əm) *n.* ⟦< Gr *meta,* beyond + *ballein,* throw⟧ the chemical and physical processes continuously going on in living organisms and cells, including the changing of food into living tissue and the changing of living tissue into waste products and energy —**met·a·bol·ic** (met′ə bäl′ik) *adj.* —**me·tab′o·lize′** (-līz′), **-lized′, -liz′ing,** *vt., vi.*

**met·a·car·pus** (met′ə kär′pəs) *n., pl.* **-pi′** (-pī′) ⟦< Gr *meta,* over + *karpos,* wrist⟧ the part of the hand between the wrist and the fingers —**met·a·car′pal** *adj., n.*

**met·al** (met′l) *n.* ⟦< Gr *metallon,* a mine⟧ **1** *a)* any of a class of chemical elements, as iron or gold, that have luster, can conduct heat and electricity, etc. *b)* an alloy of such elements, as brass **2** anything consisting of metal —**me·tal·lic** (mə tal′ik) *adj.*

**met·al·lur·gy** (met′ə lur′jē) *n.* ⟦< Gr *metallon,* metal + *ergon,* work⟧ the science of separating metals from their ores and preparing them for use, by smelting, refining, etc. —**met′al·lur′gi·cal** *adj.* —**met′al·lur′gist** *n.*

**met·a·mor·phose** (met′ə môr′fōz′, -fōs′) *vt., vi.* **-phosed′, -phos′ing** to change in form; transform

**met′a·mor·pho·sis** (-môr′fə sis) *n., pl.* **-ses′** (-sēz′) ⟦< Gr *meta,* over + *morphē,* form⟧ **1** a change of form, structure, substance, or function; specif., the physical change undergone by some animals during development, as of the tadpole to the frog **2** a marked change of character, appearance, condition, etc. —**met′a·mor′phic** *adj.*

**met·a·phor** (met′ə fôr′) *n.* ⟦< Gr *meta,* over + *pherein,* to bear⟧ a figure of speech in which one thing is spoken of as if it were another (Ex.: "all the world's a stage") —**met′a·phor′ic** or **met′a·phor′i·cal** *adj.*

**met·a·phys·i·cal** (met′ə fiz′i kəl) *adj.* **1** of, or having the nature of, metaphysics **2** very abstract or subtle **3** supernatural

**met′a·phys′ics** (-iks) *n.* ⟦< Gr *meta* (ta) *physika,* after (the) *Physics* (of Aristotle)⟧ **1** the branch of philosophy that seeks to explain the nature of being and reality **2** speculative philosophy in general

**me·tas·ta·sis** (mə tas′tə sis) *n., pl.* **-ses′** (-sēz′) ⟦< Gr *meta,* after + *histanai,* to place⟧ the spread of disease from one part of the body to another, esp. the spread of cancer cells by way of the bloodstream —**me·tas′ta·size′** (-sīz′), **-sized′, -siz′ing,** *vi.*

**met·a·tar·sus** (met′ə tär′səs) *n., pl.* **-si′** (-sī′) ⟦< Gr *meta,* over + *tarsos,* flat of the foot⟧ the part of the human foot between the ankle and the toes — **met′a·tar′sal** *adj., n.*

**me·tath·e·sis** (mə tath′ə sis) *n., pl.* **-ses′** (-sēz′) ⟦< Gr *meta*, over + *tithenai*, to place⟧ transposition, specif. of sounds in a word

**mete** (mēt) *vt.* **met′ed, met′ing** ⟦OE *metan*, to measure⟧ to allot; distribute: usually with *out*

**me·tem·psy·cho·sis** (mi tem′sī kō′sis) *n., pl.* **-ses′** (-sēz′) ⟦< Gr *meta*, over + *en*, in + *psychē*, soul⟧ transmigration of souls

**me·te·or** (mēt′ē ər, -ôr′) *n.* ⟦< Gr *meta*, beyond + *eōra*, a hovering⟧ **1** the streak of light, etc. observed when a meteoroid enters the earth's atmosphere; shooting star **2** loosely, a meteoroid or meteorite

**me′te·or′ic** (-ôr′ik) *adj.* **1** of a meteor **2** like a meteor; momentarily brilliant, swift, etc.

**me′te·or·ite′** (-ər īt′) *n.* that part of a meteoroid that survives passage through the atmosphere of a planet and falls to its surface

**me′te·or·oid′** (-ər oid′) *n.* a small, solid body traveling through outer space, seen as a meteor when in the earth's atmosphere

**me′te·or·ol·o·gy** (-ə räl′ə jē) *n.* ⟦see METEOR & -LOGY⟧ the science of the atmosphere and its phenomena; study of weather **—me′te·or·o·log′i·cal** (-ə läj′i kəl) *adj.* **—me′te·or·ol′o·gist** *n.*

**me·ter**[1] (mēt′ər) *n.* ⟦< Gr *metron*, a measure⟧ **1** rhythm in verse; measured arrangement of syllables according to stress **2** the basic pattern of beats in a piece of music **3** ⟦Fr *mètre*⟧ the basic metric unit of length, equal to 39.3701 inches

**me·ter**[2] (mēt′ər) *n.* ⟦METE + -ER⟧ **1** an apparatus for measuring and recording the quantity of gas, water, etc. passing through it **2** PARKING METER

**-me·ter** (mēt′ər, mi tər) ⟦< Gr *metron*, a measure⟧ *combining form* a device for measuring [*barometer*]

**meth·a·done** (meth′ə dōn′) *n.* ⟦< its chemical name⟧ a synthetic narcotic drug used in medicine to treat heroin and morphine addicts

**meth·ane** (meth′ān′) *n.* ⟦< METHYL⟧ a colorless, odorless, flammable gas formed by the decomposition of vegetable matter, as in marshes

**meth·a·nol** (meth′ə nôl′) *n.* ⟦< METHAN(E) + (ALCOH)OL⟧ a colorless, flammable, poisonous liquid used as a fuel, solvent, antifreeze, etc.

**me·thinks** (mē thiŋks′) *v.impersonal pt.* **-thought′** (-thôt′) ⟦OE *me*, to me + *thyncth*, it seems⟧ [Archaic] it seems to me

**meth·od** (meth′əd) *n.* ⟦< Fr < Gr *meta*, after + *hodos*, a way⟧ **1** a way of doing anything; procedure; process **2** orderliness in doing things or handling ideas

**me·thod·i·cal** (mə thäd′i kəl) *adj.* characterized by method; orderly; systematic **—me·thod′i·cal·ly** *adv.*

**Meth·od·ist** (meth′ə dist) *n.* a member of a Protestant Christian denomination that developed from the teachings of John Wesley **—Meth′od·ism′** *n.*

**meth·od·ol·o·gy** (meth′ə däl′ə jē) *n., pl.* **-gies** a system of methods, as in a science

**Me·thu·se·lah** (mə thōō′zə lə) *n. Bible* a patriarch who lived 969 years

**meth·yl** (meth′əl) *n.* ⟦< Gr *methy*, wine + *hylē*, wood⟧ a hydrocarbon radical found in methanol

**methyl alcohol** METHANOL

**me·tic·u·lous** (mə tik′yōō ləs, -yə-) *adj.* ⟦< L *metus*, fear⟧ extremely or excessively careful about details; scrupulous or finicky **—me·tic′u·lous·ly** *adv.*

**mé·tier** (mā tyā′) *n.* ⟦Fr, a trade⟧ work that one is particularly suited for

**me·tre** (mēt′ər) *n. Brit. sp.* of METER[1]

**met·ric** (me′trik) *adj.* **1** METRICAL **2** *a)* of the METER[1] (sense 3) *b)* of the metric system

**met·ri·cal** (me′tri kəl) *adj.* **1** of or composed in meter or verse **2** of or used in measurement **—met′ri·cal·ly** *adv.*

**met·ri·cate** (me′tri kāt′) *vt.* **-cat′ed, -cat′ing** to change over to the metric system **—met′ri·ca′tion** *n.*

**metric system** a decimal system of weights and measures in which the kilogram (2.2046 pounds), the meter (39.3701 inches), and the liter (1,000 cubic centimeters or 1.0567 quarts) are the basic units

**met·ro**[1] (me′trō) *adj. short for* METROPOLITAN

**met·ro**[2] (me′trō) *n., pl.* **-ros** ⟦ult. < *metro(politan)*⟧ [*often* M-] a subway

**met·ro·nome** (me′trə nōm′) *n.* ⟦< Gr *metron*, measure + *nomos*, law⟧ a device that beats time at a desired rate, as for piano practice

**me·trop·o·lis** (mə träp′ə lis) *n.* ⟦< Gr *mētēr*, mother + *polis*, city⟧ **1** the main city of a country, state, etc. **2** any large or important city **—me·tro·pol·i·tan** (me′trə päl′i tən) *adj.*

**met·tle** (met′'l) *n.* ⟦var. of METAL⟧ spirit; courage; ardor **—on one's mettle** prepared to do one's best

**met′tle·some** (-səm) *adj.* full of mettle; spirited; ardent, brave, etc.

**mew** (myōō) *n.* ⟦echoic⟧ the characteristic vocal sound made by a cat **—vi.** to make this sound

**mewl** (myōōl) *vi.* ⟦< prec.⟧ to cry weakly, like a baby; whimper

**mews** (myōōz) *pl.n.* ⟦< L *mutare*, to change⟧ [*usually with sing. v.*] [Chiefly Brit.] stables or carriage houses in a court or alley

**Mex** *abbrev.* **1** Mexican **2** Mexico

**Mex·i·ca·li** (mek′si kä′lē) city in NW Mexico, on the U.S. border: pop. 602,000

**Mex·i·co** (mek′si kō′) **1** country in North America, south of the U.S.: 759,529 sq. mi.; pop. 81,250,000 **2 Gulf of** arm of the Atlantic, east of Mexico **—Mex′i·can** *adj., n.*

**Mexico City** capital of Mexico: pop. 8,831,000 (met. area, 15,048,000)

**mez·za·nine** (mez′ə nēn′, mez′ə nēn′) *n.* ⟦< It *mezzano*, middle⟧ **1** a low-ceilinged story between two main stories, usually in the form of a balcony over the main floor **2** the first few rows of the balcony in some theaters

**mez·zo-so·pra·no** (met′sō sə pran′ō) *n., pl.* **-nos** or **-ni** (-ē) ⟦It < *mezzo*, medium + SOPRANO⟧ **1** the range of a female voice between soprano and contralto **2** a voice or singer with such a range

**MFA** or **M.F.A.** *abbrev.* Master of Fine Arts

**mfg** *abbrev.* manufacturing

**mfr** *abbrev.* **1** manufacture **2** manufacturer

**Mg** *Chem. symbol for* magnesium

**mg** *abbrev.* milligram(s)

**Mgr** or **mgr** *abbrev.* manager

**MHz** *abbrev.* megahertz

**mi** (mē) *n.* ⟦ML⟧ *Music* the third tone of the diatonic scale

**mi** *abbrev.* **1** mile(s) **2** mill(s)

**MI** *abbrev.* **1** Michigan **2** middle initial

**Mi·am·i** (mī am′ē) city on the SE coast of Florida: pop. 359,000 **—Mi·am′i·an** *n.*

**mi·as·ma** (mī az′mə, mē-) *n.* ⟦< Gr *miainein*, pollute⟧ **1** a vapor as from marshes, formerly supposed to poison the air **2** an unwholesome atmosphere or influence

**mi·ca** (mī′kə) *n.* ⟦L, a crumb⟧ a mineral that crystallizes in thin, flexible layers, resistant to heat and electricity

**mice** (mīs) *n. pl.* of MOUSE

**Mi·chel·an·ge·lo** (mī′kəl an′jə lō′, mik′əl-) 1475-1564; It. sculptor, painter, & architect

**Mich·i·gan** (mish′i gən) **1** Midwestern state of the U.S.: 58,110 sq. mi.; pop. 9,295,000; cap. Lansing: abbrev. *MI* **2 Lake** one of the Great Lakes, between Michigan & Wisconsin **—Mich′i·gan′der** (-gan′dər) *n.* **—Mich′i·ga′ni·an** (-gä′nē ən) or **Mich′i·gan·ite′** *adj., n.*

**Mick·ey Finn** (mik′ē fin′) ⟦< ?⟧ [*also* m- f-] [Slang] a drink of liquor to which a narcotic, etc. has been added, given to an unsuspecting person: often shortened to **Mick′ey** or **mick′ey** *n., pl.* **-eys**

**micro-** ⟦< Gr *mikros*, small⟧ *combining form* **1** little, small [*microcosm*] **2** enlarging [*microscope*]

3 involving microscopes [*microsurgery*] **4** one millionth [*microsecond*] Also **micr-**

**mi·crobe** (mī′krōb′) *n.* [< Gr *mikros,* small + *bios,* life] a microorganism, esp. one causing disease

**mi·cro·bi·ol·o·gy** (mī′krō bī äl′ə jē) *n.* the branch of biology dealing with microorganisms —**mi′cro·bi·ol′o·gist** *n.*

**mi′cro·brew′er·y** *n., pl.* **-er·ies** a small brewery producing high-quality beer for local consumption

**mi′cro·chip′** *n.* CHIP (*n.* 5)

**mi′cro·com·put′er** *n.* a small, inexpensive computer having a microprocessor and used in the home, etc.

**mi′cro·cosm** (-käz′əm) *n.* [see MICRO- & COSMOS] something regarded as a world in miniature

**mi′cro·dot′** *n.* a copy, as of written or printed matter, photographically reduced to pinhead size, used in espionage, etc.

**mi′cro·ec′o·nom′ics** *n.* a branch of economics dealing with certain specific factors affecting an economy, as the behavior of individual consumers

**mi′cro·fiche** (-fēsh′) *n., pl.* **-fich′es** or **-fiche′** [Fr < *micro-,* MICRO- + *fiche,* small card] a small sheet of microfilm containing a group of microfilmed pages

**mi′cro·film′** *n.* film on which documents, etc. are photographed in a reduced size for storage, etc. —*vt., vi.* to photograph on microfilm

**mi′cro·man′age** *vt.* **-aged, -ag·ing** to manage or control closely, often so closely as to be counterproductive

**mi·crom·e·ter** (mī kräm′ət ər) *n.* [< Fr: see MICRO- & -METER] a tool for measuring very small distances, angles, etc.

SCALE

MICROMETER

**mi·cron** (mī′krän′) *n.* [< Gr *mikros,* small] one millionth of a meter

**Mi·cro·ne·sia** (mī′krə nē′zhə) country on a group of islands in the Pacific east of the Philippines: 271 sq. mi.; pop. 108,000 —**Mi′cro·ne′sian** *adj., n.*

**mi·cro·or·gan·ism** (mī′krō ôr′gə niz′əm) *n.* a microscopic animal, plant, bacterium, virus, etc.

**mi′cro·phone** (mī′krə fōn′) *n.* [MICRO- + -PHONE] an instrument for converting sound waves into an electric signal

**mi′cro·proc·es·sor** (mī′krō prä′ses′ər) *n.* a chip that functions to control the operation of a microcomputer

**mi′cro·scope** (mī′krə skōp′) *n.* [see MICRO- & -SCOPE] an instrument consisting of a combination of lenses, for making very small objects, as microorganisms, look larger

**mi′cro·scop′ic** (-skäp′ik) *adj.* **1** so small as to be invisible or obscure except through a microscope; minute **2** of, with, or like a microscope —**mi′cro·scop′i·cal·ly** *adv.*

**mi′cro·sur·ger·y** (mī′krō sur′jər ē) *n.* surgery performed using a microscope and minute instruments or laser beams

**mi′cro·wave** *adj.* **1** designating equipment, etc. using microwaves for radar, communications, etc. **2** designating an oven that cooks quickly using microwaves —*vt.* **-waved′, -wav′ing** to cook in a microwave oven —*n.* **1** an electromagnetic wave with a frequency of about 300,000 megahertz to 300 megahertz **2** a microwave oven

**mid**[1] (mid) *adj.* [OE *midd-*] middle

**mid**[2] (mid) *prep.* [Old Poet.] amid: also **'mid**

**mid-** *combining form* middle, middle part of [*mid-*May]

**mid′air′** *n.* any point in space not in contact with the ground or any other surface

**Mi·das** (mī′dəs) *Gr. Myth.* a king granted the power to turn everything he touches into gold

**mid′course′** *adj.* happening in the middle of a flight, journey, or course of action

**mid·dle** (mid′'l) *adj.* [OE *middel*] **1** halfway between two given points, times, etc. **2** intermediate **3** [M-] designating a stage in language development intermediate between *Old* and *Modern* [*Middle* English] —*n.* **1** a middle point, part, time, etc. **2** something intermediate **3** the middle part of the body; waist

**middle age** the time between youth and old age —**mid′dle-aged′** *adj.*

**Middle Ages** the period of European history between ancient and modern times, A.D. 476-c. 1450

**Middle America** the American middle class, seen as being conventional or conservative

**mid′dle-brow′** (-brou′) *n.* [Inf.] one regarded as having conventional, middle-class tastes or opinions —*adj.* of or for a middlebrow

**middle class** the social class between the aristocracy or very wealthy and the lower working class —**mid′dle-class′** *adj.*

**middle ear** the part of the ear including the eardrum and the adjacent cavity containing three small bones

**Middle East** area from Afghanistan to Libya, including Arabia, Cyprus, & Asiatic Turkey —**Middle Eastern**

**Middle English** the English language between *c.* 1100 and *c.* 1500

**mid′dle·man′** (-man′) *n., pl.* **-men** (-men′) **1** a trader who buys from a producer and sells at wholesale or retail **2** a go-between

**mid′dle·most′** *adj.* MIDMOST

**mid′dle-of-the-road′** *adj.* avoiding extremes, esp. political extremes

**middle school** a school with three or four grades, variously including grades 5 through grade 8

**mid′dle·weight′** *n.* a boxer with a maximum weight of 160 pounds

**Middle West** MIDWEST —**Middle Western**

**mid·dling** (mid′liŋ) *adj.* of middle size, quality, etc.; medium —*adv.* [Inf.] fairly; moderately

**mid·dy** (mid′ē) *n., pl.* **-dies** [< MIDSHIPMAN] a loose blouse with a sailor collar, worn by women and children

**Mid·east′** MIDDLE EAST —**Mid·east′ern** *adj.*

**midge** (mij) *n.* [OE *mycg*] a small, gnatlike insect

**midg·et** (mij′it) *n.* **1** a very small person **2** anything very small of its kind —*adj.* very small of its kind

**mid·land** (mid′lənd) *n.* the middle region of a country; interior —*adj.* in or of the midland

**mid′most′** *adj.* exactly in the middle, or nearest the middle

**mid′night′** *n.* twelve o'clock at night —*adj.* **1** of or at midnight **2** like midnight; very dark

**mid′point′** *n.* a point at or close to the middle or center

**mid·riff** (mid′rif) *n.* [< OE *midd-,* MID[1] + *hrif,* belly] **1** DIAPHRAGM (sense 1) **2** the middle part of the torso, between the abdomen and the chest

**mid·ship·man** (mid′ship′mən) *n., pl.* **-men** (-mən) a student in training to be a naval officer

**mid-size** or **mid-size** (mid′sīz′) *adj.* of a size intermediate between large and small [a *mid-size* car]

**midst** (midst) *n.* the middle; central part —*prep.* [Old Poet.] in the midst of; amid —**in our** (or **your** or **their**) **midst** among us (or you or them) —**in the midst of 1** in the middle of **2** during

**mid·stream** (mid′strēm′) *n.* the middle of a stream

**mid′sum′mer** *n.* **1** the middle of summer **2** the time of the summer solstice, about June 21

**mid′term′** *adj.* in the middle of the term —*n.* [Inf.] a midterm examination, as at a college

**mid′town′** *adj.* of or in the central part of a city, esp. a large city —*n.* a midtown area

**mid′way′** *n.* that part of a fair where sideshows, etc. are located —*adj., adv.* in the middle of the way or distance; halfway

**Mid·west'** region of the NC U.S. between the Rocky Mountains & the E border of Ohio & the S borders of Kansas & Missouri —**Mid·west'ern** *adj.*

**mid·wife'** (-wīf') *n.*, *pl.* **-wives'** [< ME *mid,* with + *wif,* woman] a person who helps women in childbirth —**mid'wife'ry** (-wīf'rē) *n.*

**mid·win'ter** *n.* **1** the middle of winter **2** the time of the winter solstice, about Dec. 22

**mid'year'** *adj.* in the middle of the year —*n.* [Inf.] a midyear examination, as at a college

**mien** (mēn) *n.* [short for DEMEAN²] one's appearance, bearing, or manner

**miff** (mif) *vt.* [prob. orig. cry of disgust] [Inf.] to offend

**MIG** (mig) *n.* [after *Mi(koyan)* & *G(urevich),* its Soviet designers] a high-speed, high-altitude jet fighter plane: also **MiG**

**might¹** (mīt) *v.aux.* [OE *mihte*] **1** *pt.* of MAY **2** used as an auxiliary generally equivalent to MAY [it *might* rain]

**might²** (mīt) *n.* [OE *miht*] strength, power, or vigor

**might'y** *adj.* **-i·er, -i·est 1** powerful; strong **2** remarkably large, etc.; great —*adv.* [Inf.] very — **might'i·ly** *adv.* —**might'i·ness** *n.*

**mi·gnon·ette'** (min'yə net') *n.* [< Fr *mignon,* small] a plant with spikes of small greenish, whitish, or reddish flowers

**mi·graine** (mī'grān') *n.* [< Gr *hēmi-,* half + *kranion,* skull] an intense, periodic headache, usually limited to one side of the head

**mi·grant** (mī'grənt) *adj.* migrating —*n.* **1** one that migrates **2** a farm laborer who moves from place to place to harvest seasonal crops

**mi·grate** (mī'grāt') *vi.* **-grat'ed, -grat'ing** [< L *migrare*] **1** to settle in another country or region **2** to move to another region with the change in seasons, as many birds do —**mi·gra·to·ry** (mī'grə tôr'ē) *adj.*

**mi·gra·tion** (mī grā'shən) *n.* **1** a migrating **2** a group of people, birds, etc., migrating together

**mi·ka·do** (mi kä'dō) *n.*, *pl.* **-dos** [< Jpn *mi,* an honorific title + *kado,* gate] [often **M-**] the emperor of Japan: title no longer used

**mike** (mīk) [Inf.] *n.* a microphone —*vt.* **miked, mik'ing** to record, amplify, etc. with a microphone

**mil¹** (mil) *n.* [L *mille,* thousand] a unit of linear measure, equal to 1/1000 inch

**mil²** (mil) *n.* [Slang] *short for* million

**Mi·lan** (mi lan', -län') city in NW Italy: pop. 1,602,000

**milch** (milch) *adj.* [ME *milche*] kept for milking [*milch* cows]

**mild** (mīld) *adj.* [OE *milde*] **1** gentle or kind; not severe **2** having a soft, pleasant flavor [a *mild* cheese] —**mild'ly** *adv.* —**mild'ness** *n.*

**mil·dew** (mil'dōō') *n.* [OE *meledeaw,* honeydew] a fungus that attacks some plants or appears on damp cloth, etc. as a whitish coating —*vt., vi.* to affect or be affected with mildew

**mile** (mīl) *n.* [< L *milia (passuum),* thousand (paces)] a unit of linear measure equal to 5,280 feet

**mile'age** *n.* **1** an allowance per mile for traveling expenses **2** total miles traveled **3** the average number of miles that can be traveled, as per gallon of fuel

**mile'post'** *n.* a signpost showing the distance in miles to or from a place

**mil'er** *n.* one who competes in mile races

**mile'stone'** *n.* **1** a stone set up to show the distance in miles to or from a place **2** a significant event in history, in a career, etc.

**mi·lieu** (mēl yœ', -yoo', -yōō'; mil-) *n.*, *pl.* **-lieus'** [Fr < L *medius,* middle + *locus,* a place] environment; esp., social setting

**mil·i·tant** (mil'i tənt) *adj.* [< L *miles,* soldier] **1** fighting **2** ready to fight, esp. for some cause —*n.* a militant person —**mil'i·tan·cy** *n.* —**mil'i·tant·ly** *adv.*

**mil·i·ta·rism** (mil'ə tə riz'əm) *n.* **1** military spirit **2** a policy of aggressive military preparedness — **mil'i·ta·rist** *n.* —**mil'i·ta·ris'tic** *adj.*

**mil'i·ta·rize'** (-rīz') *vt.* **-rized', -riz'ing** to equip and prepare for war

**mil·i·tar·y** (mil'ə ter'ē) *adj.* [< L *miles,* soldier] **1** of, for, or done by soldiers **2** of, for, or fit for war **3** of the army —**the military** the armed forces

**military police** soldiers assigned to police duties in the army

**mil·i·tate** (mil'ə tāt') *vi.* **-tat'ed, -tat'ing** [< L *militare,* be a soldier] to operate or work (*against*)

**mi·li·tia** (mə lish'ə) *n.* [< L *miles,* soldier] **1** an army composed of citizens rather than professional soldiers, called up in time of emergency **2** a group of disaffected citizens organized like an army and opposing federal authority —**mi·li'tia·man** (-mən), *pl.* **-men** (-mən), *n.*

**milk** (milk) *n.* [OE *meolc*] **1** a white fluid secreted by the mammary glands of female mammals for suckling their young **2** cow's milk, etc., drunk by humans as a food or used to make butter, cheese, etc. **3** any liquid like this, as the liquid in coconuts —*vt.* **1** to squeeze milk from (a cow, goat, etc.) **2** to extract money, ideas, etc. from as if by milking —**milk'er** *n.*

**milk glass** a nearly opaque whitish glass

**milk'maid'** *n.* a girl or woman who milks cows or works in a dairy

**milk'man'** (-man') *n.*, *pl.* **-men'** (-mən') a man who sells or delivers milk for a dairy

**milk of magnesia** a milky-white suspension of magnesium hydroxide in water, used as a laxative and antacid

**milk'shake'** *n.* a drink made of milk, flavoring, and ice cream, mixed or shaken until frothy

**milk'sop'** (-säp') *n.* a man thought of as timid, ineffectual, effeminate, etc.

**milk tooth** any of the temporary, first teeth of a child or young animal

**milk'weed'** *n.* any of a group of plants with a milky juice

**milk'y** *adj.* **-i·er, -i·est 1** like milk; esp., white as milk **2** of or containing milk —**milk'i·ness** *n.*

**Milky Way** the galaxy containing our sun: seen as a broad, faintly luminous band of very distant stars and interstellar gas arching across the night sky

**mill¹** (mil) *n.* [< L *mola,* millstone] **1** a building with machinery for grinding grain into flour or meal **2** any of various machines for grinding, crushing, cutting, etc. **3** a factory [a textile *mill*] —*vt.* **1** to grind, form, etc. by or in a mill **2** to raise and ridge the edge of (a coin) —*vi.* to move (*around* or *about*) confusedly —**in the mill** in preparation —**through the mill** [Inf.] through a hard, painful, instructive experience, test, etc.

**mill²** (mil) *n.* [< L *mille,* thousand] 1/10 of a cent: unit used in calculating

**mill'age** *n.* taxation in mills per dollar of valuation

**mil·len·ni·um** (mi len'ē əm) *n.*, *pl.* **-ni·ums** or **-ni·a** (-ə) [< L *mille,* thousand + *annus,* year] **1** a thousand years **2** *Christian Theol.* the period of a thousand years during which Christ will reign on earth: with *the* **3** any period of great happiness, peace, etc.

**mill'er** *n.* one who owns or operates a mill, esp. a flour mill

**mil·let** (mil'it) *n.* [< L *milium*] **1** a cereal grass whose grain is used for food in Europe and Asia **2** any of several similar grasses

**milli-** [< L *mille,* thousand] *combining form* one thousandth part of [*millimeter*]

**mil·li·gram** (mil'i gram') *n.* one thousandth of a gram

**mil·li·li·ter** (-lēt'ər) *n.* one thousandth of a liter: Brit. sp. **mil'li·li·tre**

**mil·li·me·ter** (-mēt'ər) *n.* one thousandth of a meter: Brit. sp. **mil'li·me·tre**

**mil·li·ner** (mil′i nər) *n.* ⟦< *Milaner*, vendor of dress wares from Milan⟧ one who makes or sells women's hats

**mil·li·ner·y** (mil′i ner′ē) *n.* **1** women's hats, head-dresses, etc. **2** the work or business of a milliner

**mil·lion** (mil′yən) *n.* ⟦< L *mille,* thousand⟧ a thousand thousands; 1,000,000

**mil′lion·aire′** (-yə ner′) *n.* a person whose wealth comes to at least a million dollars, pounds, francs, etc.

**mil·li·pede** (mil′i pēd′) *n.* ⟦< L *mille,* thousand + *pes,* foot⟧ a many-legged arthropod with an elongated body

**mill′race′** *n.* the channel in which water runs to turn the wheel driving the machinery in a mill

**mill′stone′** *n.* **1** either of a pair of round, flat stones used for grinding grain, etc. **2** a heavy burden

**mill′stream′** *n.* the water flowing in a millrace

**mill′wright′** *n.* a worker who builds, installs, or repairs the machinery in a mill

**milt** (milt) *n.* ⟦prob. < Scand⟧ the sex glands or sperm of male fishes

**Mil·ton** (milt′′n), **John** 1608-74; Eng. poet

**Mil·wau·kee** (mil wô′kē) city & port in SE Wisconsin, on Lake Michigan; pop. 628,000

**mime** (mīm) *n.* ⟦< Gr *mimos,* imitator⟧ **1** the representation of an action, mood, etc. by gestures, not words **2** a mimic or pantomimist —*vt.* **mimed, mim′ing** to mimic or pantomime

**mim·e·o·graph** (mim′ē ə graf′) *n.* ⟦< Gr *mimeomai,* I imitate⟧ a machine for making copies of graphic matter by means of an inked stencil —*vt.* to make (such copies) of

**mi·met·ic** (mi met′ik, mī-) *adj.* ⟦< Gr *mimeisthai,* to imitate⟧ **1** imitative **2** characterized by mimicry

**mim·ic** (mim′ik) *adj.* ⟦< Gr *mimos,* actor⟧ imitative —*n.* an imitator; esp., an actor skilled in mimicry —*vt.* **-icked, -ick·ing 1** to imitate, often so as to ridicule **2** to copy or resemble closely

**mim·ic·ry** (mim′ik rē) *n., pl.* **-ries** the practice or art of, or a way of, mimicking

**mi·mo·sa** (mi mō′sə) *n.* ⟦see MIME⟧ a tree, shrub, or herb growing in warm regions and usually having spikes of white, yellow, or pink flowers

**min** *abbrev.* **1** minimum **2** minute(s)

**min·a·ret** (min′ə ret′) *n.* ⟦< Ar *manāra(t),* lighthouse⟧ a high, slender tower attached to a mosque

**min·a·to·ry** (min′ə tôr′ē) *adj.* ⟦< L *minari,* threaten⟧ menacing

**mince** (mins) *vt.* **minced, minc′ing** ⟦< L *minutus,* small⟧ **1** to cut up (meat, etc.) into small pieces **2** to lessen the force of [to *mince* no words] —*vi.* to speak, act, or walk with an affected daintiness —**minc′ing** *adj.*

**mince′meat′** *n.* a mixture of chopped apples, spices, suet, raisins, etc., and sometimes meat, used as a pie filling

**mind** (mīnd) *n.* ⟦< OE *(ge)mynd*⟧ **1** memory [to bring to *mind* a story] **2** opinion [speak your *mind*] **3** the seat of consciousness, in which thinking, feeling, etc. takes place **4** intellect **5**

MINARET

PSYCHE (*n.* 2) **6** reason; sanity —*vt.* **1** to pay attention to; heed **2** to obey **3** to take care of [*mind* the baby] **4** to be careful about [*mind* the stairs] **5** to care about; object to [they don't *mind* the noise] —*vi.* **1** to pay attention **2** to be obedient **3** to be careful **4** to care; object —**bear** (or **keep**) **in mind** to remember —**change one's mind** to change one's opinion, purpose, etc. —**have in mind** to intend —**never mind** don't be concerned —**on someone's mind 1** filling someone's thoughts **2** worrying someone —**out of one's mind 1** insane **2** frantic (*with* worry, etc.)

**mind′-blow′ing** *adj.* [Slang] **1** causing shock, etc.; overwhelming **2** hard to comprehend

**mind′-bog′gling** *adj.* [Slang] **1** hard to comprehend **2** surprising, overwhelming, etc.

**mind′ed** *adj.* having a (specified kind of) mind: used in compounds [high-*minded*]

**mind′ful** (-fəl) *adj.* having in mind; aware or careful (*of*) —**mind′ful·ly** *adv.* —**mind′ful·ness** *n.*

**mind′less** (-lis) *adj.* stupid or foolish

**mind reader** one who seems or professes to be able to perceive another's thoughts

**mind's eye** the imagination

**mine¹** (mīn) *pron.* ⟦OE *min*⟧ that or those belonging to me: poss. form of I² [this is *mine; mine* are better]

**mine²** (mīn) *n.* ⟦< Fr⟧ **1** a large excavation made in the earth, from which to extract ores, coal, etc. **2** a deposit of ore, coal, etc. **3** any great source of supply **4** *Mil. a)* a tunnel dug under an enemy's fort, etc., in which an explosive is placed *b)* an explosive charge hidden underground or in the sea, for destroying enemy vehicles, ships, etc. —*vt., vi.* **mined, min′ing 1** to dig (ores, etc.) from (the earth) **2** to dig or lay military mines in or under **3** to undermine

**min′er** *n.* one whose work is digging coal, ore, etc. in a mine

**min·er·al** (min′ər əl) *n.* ⟦< ML *minera,* ore⟧ **1** an inorganic substance found naturally in the earth, as metallic ore **2** any substance that is neither vegetable nor animal —*adj.* of or containing a mineral

**mineral jelly** PETROLATUM

**min·er·al·o·gy** (min′ər äl′ə jē) *n.* the scientific study of minerals —**min′er·al′o·gist** *n.*

**mineral oil** a colorless, tasteless oil derived from petroleum, used as a laxative

**mineral water** water impregnated with mineral salts or gases

**Mi·ner·va** (mi nur′və) *n.* Rom. Myth. the goddess of wisdom

**mi·ne·stro·ne** (min′ə strō′nē) *n.* ⟦It.: ult. < L *ministrare,* serve⟧ a thick vegetable soup in a meat broth

**min·gle** (miŋ′gəl) *vt.* **-gled, -gling** ⟦< OE *mengan,* to mix⟧ to mix together; blend —*vi.* **1** to become mixed or blended **2** to join or unite with others

**mini-** ⟦< MINI(ATURE)⟧ *combining form* miniature, very small, very short [*miniskirt*]

**min·i·a·ture** (min′ē ə chər, min′i chər) *n.* ⟦< L *miniare,* to paint red⟧ **1** a small painting, esp. a portrait **2** a copy or model on a very small scale —*adj.* done on a very small scale

**min′i·a·tur·ize′** (-īz′) *vt.* **-ized, -iz′ing** to make in a small and compact form —**min′i·a·tur′i·za′tion** *n.*

**min·i·bike** (min′ē bīk′) *n.* a compact motorcycle, usually used as an off-road vehicle

**min′i·cam′** (-kam′) *n.* a portable TV camera for telecasting or videotaping news events, etc.

**min′i·com·put′er** (-kəm pyōōt′ər) *n.* a computer intermediate in size, power, etc. between a mainframe and a microcomputer

**min·i·mal** (min′i məl) *adj.* **1** smallest or least possible **2** of minimalism —**min′i·mal·ly** *adv.*

**min′i·mal·ism′** *n.* a movement in art, music, etc. in which only the simplest design, forms, etc. are used, often repetitiously —**min′i·mal·ist** *adj., n.*

**min′i·mal·ize′** (-īz′) *vt.* **-ized, -iz′ing** to reduce to basic components

**min·i·mize** (min′i mīz′) *vt.* **-mized′, -miz′ing** to reduce to or estimate at a minimum

**min′i·mum** (-məm) *n., pl.* **-mums** or **-ma** (-mə) ⟦L, least⟧ **1** the smallest quantity, number, etc. possible or permissible **2** the lowest degree or point reached —*adj.* smallest possible, permissible, or reached

**min·ion** (min′yən) *n.* ⟦Fr *mignon*, darling⟧ **1** a favorite, esp. one who is a servile follower: term of contempt **2** a subordinate official

**min·is·cule** (min′i skyōōl′) *adj. disputed var. of* MINUSCULE

**min·i·se·ries** (min′ē sir′ēz) *n., pl.* **-ries** a TV drama broadcast serially in a limited number of episodes

**min·i·skirt** (min′ē skurt′) *n.* a very short skirt ending well above the knee

**min·is·ter** (min′is tər) *n.* ⟦L, a servant⟧ **1** a person appointed to head a governmental department **2** a diplomat representing his or her government in a foreign nation **3** one authorized to conduct religious services in a church —*vi.* **1** to serve as a minister in a church **2** to give help (*to*) —**min′is·te′ri·al** (-tir′ē əl) *adj.* —**min′is·trant** (-trənt) *adj., n.*

**min′is·tra′tion** (-trā′shən) *n.* the act of giving help or care; service

**min′is·try** (-is trē) *n., pl.* **-tries 1** the act of ministering, or serving **2** *a*) the office or function of a religious minister *b*) ministers of religion collectively; clergy **3** *a*) the department under a minister of government *b*) the minister's term of office *c*) the ministers of a government as a group

**min·i·van** (min′ē van′) *n.* a passenger vehicle like a van but smaller, usually with windows all around and removable rear seats: also **min′i·van**

**mink** (miŋk) *n.* ⟦< Scand⟧ **1** a slim, erminelike carnivore living in water part of the time **2** its valuable, white to brown fur

**Min·ne·ap·o·lis** (min′ē ap′ə lis) city in E Minnesota: pop. 368,000 (met. area, incl. St. Paul, 2,464,000)

**Min·ne·so·ta** (min′ə sōt′ə) Midwestern state of the U.S.: 79,617 sq. mi.; pop. 4,375,000; cap. St. Paul: abbrev. *MN* —**Min′ne·so′tan** *adj., n.*

**min·now** (min′ō) *n.* ⟦< OE *myne*⟧ any of various, usually small, freshwater fishes used commonly as bait

**Mi·no·an** (mi nō′ən) *adj.* ⟦after *Minos*, mythical king of Crete⟧ of an advanced prehistoric culture in Crete from *c.* 3000 to *c.* 1100 B.C.

**mi·nor** (mī′nər) *adj.* ⟦< L⟧ **1** lesser in size, amount, importance, etc. **2** *Music* lower than the corresponding major by a half tone —*vi. Educ.* to have a secondary field of study (*in*) —*n.* **1** a person under full legal age **2** *Educ.* a secondary field of study

**mi·nor·i·ty** (mī nôr′ə tē, mi-) *n., pl.* **-ties 1** the lesser part or smaller number **2** a racial, religious, or political group that differs from the larger, controlling group **3** the period or state of being under full legal age

**minor scale** an eight-tone musical scale with a semitone between the second and third tones

**Min·o·taur** (min′ə tôr′) *n. Gr. Myth.* a monster with the body of a man and the head of a bull

**min·ox·i·dil** (min äk′sə dil) *n.* a drug that dilates blood vessels, used in treating high blood pressure and baldness

**min·strel** (min′strəl) *n.* ⟦see MINISTER⟧ **1** a medieval traveling singer **2** a member of a comic variety show (**minstrel show**) in which the performers blacken their faces —**min′strel·sy** (-sē) *pl.* **-sies,** *n.*

**mint**[1] (mint) *n.* ⟦< L < *Moneta*, epithet for Juno, whose temple was the Roman mint⟧ **1** a place where a government coins money **2** a large amount —*adj.* new, as if freshly minted —*vt.* to coin (money) —**mint′age** (-ij) *n.*

**mint**[2] (mint) *n.* ⟦< Gr *mintha*⟧ **1** an aromatic plant whose leaves are used for flavoring **2** a candy flavored with mint

**mint julep** an iced drink of bourbon, sugar, and mint leaves

**min·u·end** (min′yōō end′) *n.* ⟦< L *minuere*, lessen⟧ the number from which another is to be subtracted

**min·u·et** (min′yōō et′) *n.* ⟦< Fr < OFr *menu*, small: from the small steps taken⟧ **1** a slow, stately dance **2** the music for this

**mi·nus** (mī′nəs) *prep.* ⟦< L *minor*, less⟧ **1** reduced by subtraction of; less *[four minus two]* **2** [Inf.] without *[minus a toe]* —*adj.* **1** involving subtraction *[a minus sign]* **2** negative **3** less than *[a grade of A minus]* —*n.* a sign ( − ), indicating subtraction or negative quantity: in full **minus sign**

**mi·nus·cule** (mi nus′kyool′, min′i skyool′) *adj.* ⟦L *minusculus*⟧ very small

**min·ute**[1] (min′it) *n.* ⟦see fol.⟧ **1** the sixtieth part of an hour, or of a degree of an arc **2** a moment **3** a specific point in time **4** [*pl.*] an official record of a meeting, etc. —**the minute** (**that**) just as soon as

**mi·nute**[2] (mī nōōt′, -nyōōt′) *adj.* ⟦< L *minor*, less⟧ **1** very small **2** of little importance **3** of or attentive to tiny details; precise —**mi·nute′ly** *adv.*

**minute hand** the longer hand of a clock, indicating the minutes

**min′ute·man′** (-man′) *n., pl.* **-men′** (-men′) [*also* M-] a member of the American citizen army at the time of the American Revolution

**minute steak** a small, thin steak that can be cooked quickly

**mi·nu·ti·ae** (mi nōō′shə, -nyōō′-) *pl.n., sing.* **-ti·a** (-shə) ⟦see MINUTE[2]⟧ small or unimportant details

**minx** (miŋks) *n.* ⟦< ?⟧ a pert, saucy girl

**mir·a·cle** (mir′ə kəl) *n.* ⟦< L *mirus*, wonderful⟧ **1** an event or action that apparently contradicts known scientific laws **2** a remarkable thing

**mi·rac·u·lous** (mi rak′yōō ləs, -yə-) *adj.* **1** having the nature of, or like, a miracle **2** able to work miracles —**mi·rac′u·lous·ly** *adv.* —**mi·rac′u·lous·ness** *n.*

**mi·rage** (mi räzh′) *n.* ⟦< VL *mirare*, look at⟧ an optical illusion, caused by the refraction of light, in which a distant object appears to be nearby, inverted, etc.

**mire** (mīr) *n.* ⟦< ON *myrr*⟧ **1** an area of wet, soggy ground **2** deep mud —*vt.* **mired, mir′ing 1** to cause to get stuck as in mire **2** to soil with mud, etc. —*vi.* to sink in mud —**mir′y, -i·er, -i·est,** *adj.*

**mir·ror** (mir′ər) *n.* ⟦< L *mirare*, look at⟧ **1** a smooth, reflecting surface; esp., a glass coated as with silver on the back **2** anything giving a true representation —*vt.* to reflect, as in a mirror

**mirth** (murth) *n.* ⟦< OE *myrig*, pleasant⟧ joyfulness or gaiety, esp. when shown by laughter —**mirth′ful** *adj.* —**mirth′less** *adj.*

**MIRV** (murv) *n., pl.* **MIRV's** ⟦*m(ultiple)* *i(ndependently targeted)* *r(eentry)* *v(ehicle)*⟧ an intercontinental ballistic missile whose several warheads can be launched individually

**mis-** ⟦< OE *mis-* or OFr *mes-*⟧ *prefix* **1** wrong(ly), bad(ly) **2** no, not

**mis·ad·ven·ture** (mis′əd ven′chər) *n.* a mishap; an instance of bad luck

**mis·an·thrope** (mis′ən thrōp′) *n.* ⟦Gr *misein*, to hate + *anthropos*, man⟧ a person who hates or distrusts all people: also **mis·an·thro·pist** (mi san′thrə pist) —**mis′an·throp′ic** (-thräp′ik) *adj.* —**mis·an′thro·py** *n.*

**mis′ap·ply′** *vt.* **-plied′, -ply′ing** to use badly, improperly, or wastefully

**mis′ap·pre·hend′** (-ap rē hend′) *vt.* to misunderstand —**mis′ap·pre·hen′sion** *n.*

**mis′ap·pro′pri·ate′** *vt.* **-at·ed, -at′ing** to appropriate to a wrong or dishonest use —**mis′ap·pro′pri·a′tion** *n.*

**mis′be·got′ten** *adj.* **1** wrongly or unlawfully begotten; illegitimate **2** badly conceived

**mis·be·have′** *vt., vi.* **-haved′, -hav′ing** to behave (oneself) wrongly —**mis·be·hav′ior** *n.*

**misc** *abbrev.* **1** miscellaneous **2** miscellany

**mis·cal′cu·late′** *vt., vi.* **-lat·ed, -lat′ing** to calculate incorrectly; miscount or misjudge —**mis′cal·cu·la′tion** *n.*

**mis·call′** *vt.* to call by a wrong name

**mis·car·ry** (mis kar′ē, mis′kar′ē) *vi.* -ried, -ry·ing **1** to go wrong; fail: said of a plan, etc. **2** to fail to arrive: said of mail, freight, etc. **3** to give birth to a fetus before it has developed enough to live — **mis·car′riage** *n.*

**mis·cast′** *vt.* -cast′, -cast′ing to cast (an actor or a play) unsuitably

**mis·ce·ge·na·tion** (mi sej′ə nā′shən) *n.* ⟦< L *miscere*, to mix + *genus*, race⟧ marriage or sexual relations between a man and woman of different races

**mis·cel·la·ne·ous** (mis′ə lā′nē əs) *adj.* ⟦< L *miscere*, to mix⟧ consisting of various kinds or qualities

**mis·cel·la·ny** (mis′ə lā′nē) *n., pl.* -nies a miscellaneous collection, esp. of literary works

**mis·chance′** *n.* bad luck

**mis·chief** (mis′chif) *n.* ⟦< OFr *mes-*, MIS- + *chief*, end⟧ **1** harm or damage **2** a cause of harm or annoyance **3** *a)* a prank *b)* playful teasing

**mis·chie·vous** (mis′chə vəs) *adj.* **1** causing mischief; specif., *a)* harmful *b)* prankish **2** inclined to annoy with playful tricks —**mis′chie·vous·ly** *adv.* —**mis′chie·vous·ness** *n.*

**mis·ci·ble** (mis′ə bəl) *adj.* ⟦< L *miscere*, to mix⟧ that can be mixed

**mis·con·ceive** (mis′kən sēv′) *vt., vi.* -ceived′, -ceiv′ing to misunderstand —**mis′con·cep′tion** (-sep′shən) *n.*

**mis·con′duct** *n.* **1** bad or dishonest management **2** willfully improper behavior

**mis·con·strue** (mis′kən strōō′) *vt.* -strued′, -stru′ing to misinterpret —**mis′con·struc′tion** (-struk′shən) *n.*

**mis·count** (mis kount′; *for n.* mis′kount′) *vt., vi.* to count incorrectly —*n.* an incorrect count

**mis·cre·ant** (mis′krē ənt) *adj.* ⟦< OFr *mes-*, MIS- + *croire*, believe⟧ villainous —*n.* a criminal; villain

**mis·deal** (mis dēl′; *for n.* mis′dēl′) *vt., vi.* -dealt′, -deal′ing to deal (playing cards) incorrectly —*n.* an incorrect deal

**mis·deed′** *n.* a wrong or wicked act; crime, sin, etc.

**mis·de·mean·or** (mis′də mēn′ər) *n. Law* any minor offense bringing a lesser punishment than a felony

**mis·di·rect′** *vt.* to direct wrongly or badly —**mis′di·rec′tion** *n.*

**mis·do′ing** *n.* wrongdoing

**mi·ser** (mī′zər) *n.* ⟦< L, wretched⟧ a greedy, stingy person who hoards money for its own sake — **mi′ser·ly** *adj.* —**mi′ser·li·ness** *n.*

**mis·er·a·ble** (miz′ər ə bəl, miz′rə bəl) *adj.* **1** in misery **2** causing misery, discomfort, etc. **3** bad; inadequate **4** pitiable —**mis′er·a·bly** *adv.*

**mis·er·y** (miz′ər ē) *n., pl.* -ies ⟦see MISER⟧ **1** a condition of great suffering; distress **2** a cause of such suffering; pain, poverty, etc.

**mis·file′** *vt.* -filed′, -fil′ing to file (papers, etc.) in the wrong place

**mis·fire′** *vi.* -fired′, -fir′ing **1** to fail to go off or ignite properly: said as of a firearm or engine **2** to fail to achieve a desired effect —*n.* a misfiring

**mis·fit** (mis fit′; *for n.* mis′fit′) *vt., vi.* -fit′ted, -fit′ting to fit badly —*n.* **1** an improper fit **2** a maladjusted person

**mis·for′tune** *n.* **1** ill fortune; trouble **2** a mishap, calamity, etc.

**mis·giv′ing** *n.* a disturbed feeling of fear, doubt, etc.: *usually used in pl.*

**mis·gov′ern** *vt.* to govern badly —**mis·gov′ern·ment** *n.*

**mis·guide′** (-gīd′) *vt.* -guid′ed, -guid′ing to lead into error or misconduct; mislead —**mis·guid′ance** *n.* —**mis·guid′ed·ly** *adv.*

**mis·han′dle** *vt.* -dled, -dling to handle badly or roughly; abuse or mismanage

**mis·hap** (mis′hap′) *n.* an unlucky or unfortunate accident

**mis·hear′** *vt., vi.* -heard′, -hear′ing to hear wrongly

**mish·mash** (mish′mash′) *n.* a jumble

**mis·in·form′** *vt.* to supply with false or misleading information —**mis′in·for·ma′tion** *n.*

**mis·in·ter′pret** *vt.* to interpret wrongly; understand or explain incorrectly —**mis′in·ter′pre·ta′tion** *n.*

**mis·judge′** *vt., vi.* -judged′, -judg′ing to judge wrongly or unfairly —**mis·judg′ment** *n.*

**mis·la′bel** *vt.* -beled or -belled, -bel·ing or -bel·ling to label incorrectly or improperly

**mis·lay′** (-lā′) *vt.* -laid′, -lay′ing to put in a place that is then forgotten

**mis·lead′** *vt.* -led′, -lead′ing **1** to lead in a wrong direction **2** to deceive **3** to lead into wrongdoing

**mis·man′age** *vt., vi.* -aged, -ag·ing to manage badly or dishonestly —**mis·man′age·ment** *n.*

**mis·match** (mis mach′; *for n.* mis′mach′) *vt.* to match badly or unsuitably —*n.* a bad match

**mis·name′** *vt.* -named′, -nam′ing to give an inappropriate name to

**mis·no·mer** (mis nō′mər) *n.* ⟦< OFr < *mes-*, MIS- + *nommer*, to name⟧ a wrong name

**mi·sog·y·ny** (mi säj′ə nē) *n.* ⟦< Gr *misein*, to hate + *gynē*, woman⟧ hatred of women —**mi·sog′y·nist** *n.*

**mis·place** (mis plās′) *vt.* -placed′, -plac′ing **1** to put in a wrong place **2** to bestow (one's trust, etc.) unwisely **3** MISLAY

**mis·play** (mis plā′; *for n.* mis′plā′) *vt., vi.* to play wrongly or badly, as in games or sports —*n.* a wrong or bad play

**mis·print** (mis print′; *for n.* mis′print′) *vt.* to print incorrectly —*n.* a printing error

**mis·pri·sion** (-prizh′ən) *n.* ⟦< OFr *mesprendre*, take wrongly⟧ misconduct or neglect of duty by a public official

**mis·pro·nounce′** *vt., vi.* -nounced′, -nounc′ing to pronounce differently from the accepted pronunciations —**mis′pro·nun′ci·a′tion** *n.*

**mis·quote′** *vt., vi.* -quot′ed, -quot′ing to quote incorrectly —**mis′quo·ta′tion** *n.*

**mis·read′** (-rēd′) *vt., vi.* -read′ (-red′), -read′ing (-rēd′iŋ) to read wrongly, esp. so as to misunderstand

**mis·rep·re·sent′** *vt.* to represent falsely; give an untrue idea of —**mis′rep·re·sen·ta′tion** *n.*

**mis·rule** (mis rōōl′) *vt.* -ruled′, -rul′ing to rule badly; misgovern —*n.* misgovernment

**miss¹** (mis) *vt.* ⟦OE *missan*⟧ **1** to fail to hit, meet, do, attend, see, hear, etc. **2** to let (a chance, etc.) go by **3** to avoid /he just *missed* being hit/ **4** to notice or feel the absence or loss of **5** to lack /this book is *missing* a page/ —*vi.* **1** to fail to hit something **2** to fail to be successful **3** to misfire: said as of an engine —*n.* a failure to hit, obtain, etc.

**miss²** (mis) *n., pl.* **miss′es** ⟦< MISTRESS⟧ **1** [M-] a title used before the name of an unmarried woman or a girl **2** a young unmarried woman or a girl

**mis·sal** (mis′əl) *n.* ⟦< LL *missa*, Mass⟧ [*often* M-] a book of prayers, readings, etc. authorized by the Roman Catholic Church for the celebration of Mass

**mis·shape′** *vt.* -shaped′, -shap′ing to shape badly; deform —**mis·shap′en** *adj.*

**mis·sile** (mis′əl) *n.* ⟦< L *mittere*, send⟧ an object, as a spear, bullet, or rocket, designed to be thrown, fired, or launched toward a target

**mis·sile·ry** or **mis′sil·ry** (-rē) *n.* **1** the science of building and launching guided missiles **2** such missiles

**miss·ing** (mis′iŋ) *adj.* absent; lost

**mis·sion** (mish′ən) *n.* ⟦< L *mittere*, send⟧ **1** a sending out or being sent out to perform a special service **2** *a)* a group of persons sent by a religious body to spread its religion, esp. in a foreign land *b*) its headquarters **3** a diplomatic delegation **4** a group of technicians, specialists, etc. sent to a foreign country **5** the special duty for which one is sent **6** a special task to which one devotes one's life; calling

**mis·sion·ar·y** (-er'ē) *adj.* of religious missions or missionaries —*n.*, *pl.* **-ies** a person sent on a religious mission

**Mis·sis·sip·pi** (mis'ə sip'ē) **1** river in the central U.S., flowing from NC Minnesota to the Gulf of Mexico **2** Southern state of the U.S.: 47,689 sq. mi.; pop. 2,573,000; cap. Jackson: abbrev. *MS* — **Mis'sis·sip'pi·an** *adj.*, *n.*

**mis·sive** (mis'iv) *n.* ⟦< L *mittere*, send⟧ a letter or written message

**Mis·sou·ri** (mi zoor'ē, -ə) **1** river in the central U.S., flowing from SW Montana into the Mississippi **2** Midwestern state of the U.S.: 68,898 sq. mi.; pop. 5,117,000; cap. Jefferson City: abbrev. *MO* —**Mis·sou'ri·an** *adj.*, *n.*

**mis·spell'** *vt.*, *vi.* **-spelled'** or **-spelt'**, **-spell'ing** to spell incorrectly

**mis·spend'** *vt.* **-spent'**, **-spend'ing** to spend improperly or wastefully

**mis·state'** *vt.* **-stat'ed**, **-stat'ing** to state incorrectly or falsely —**mis·state'ment** *n.*

**mis'step'** *n.* **1** a wrong or awkward step **2** a mistake in conduct

**mist** (mist) *n.* ⟦OE⟧ **1** a large mass of water vapor, less dense than a fog **2** anything that dims or obscures —*vt.*, *vi.* to make or become misty

**mis·take** (mi stāk') *vt.* **-took'**, **-tak'en**, **-tak'ing** ⟦< ON *mistaka*, take wrongly⟧ to understand or perceive wrongly —*n.* an idea, answer, act, etc. that is wrong; error or blunder —**mis·tak'a·ble** *adj.*

**mis·tak'en** *adj.* **1** wrong; having an incorrect understanding **2** incorrect: said of ideas, etc. — **mis·tak'en·ly** *adv.*

**mis·ter**[1] (mis'tər) *n.* ⟦< MASTER⟧ [M-] a title used before the name of a man or his office and usually written *Mr.*

**mist'er**[2] *n.* a bottle for directing a fine spray of water onto a houseplant, etc.

**mis·time** (mis tīm') *vt.* **-timed'**, **-tim'ing** to do or say at the wrong time

**mis·tle·toe** (mis'əl tō') *n.* ⟦< OE *mistel*, mistletoe + *tan*, a twig⟧ a parasitic evergreen plant with yellowish flowers and poisonous, white berries

**mis·took** (mis took') *vt.*, *vi. pt. of* MISTAKE

**mis·treat'** *vt.* to treat wrongly or badly —**mis·treat'ment** *n.*

**mis·tress** (mis'tris) *n.* ⟦< OFr, fem. of *maistre*, master⟧ **1** a woman who is head of a household or institution **2** a woman, nation, etc. that has control, power, etc. **3** a woman in a sexual relationship with, and typically supported by, a man without being married to him **4** [M-] [Obs.] a title used before the name of a woman: now replaced by *Mrs.*, *Miss*, or *Ms.*

**mis'tri·al** *n. Law* a trial made void, as by an error in the proceedings or by the inability of the jury to reach a verdict

**mis·trust'** *n.* lack of trust or confidence —*vt.*, *vi.* to have no trust in; doubt —**mis·trust'ful** *adj.*

**mist'y** *adj.* **-i·er**, **-i·est** of, like, or covered with mist **2** blurred, as by mist; vague —**mist'i·ly** *adv.* —**mist'i·ness** *n.*

**mis'un·der·stand'** *vt.* **-stood'**, **-stand'ing** to fail to understand correctly; misinterpret

**mis'un·der·stand'ing** *n.* **1** a failure to understand **2** a quarrel or disagreement

**mis·use** (mis yōoz'; *for n.*, -yōos') *vt.* **-used'**, **-us'ing** **1** to use improperly **2** to treat badly or harshly — *n.* incorrect or improper use

**mite** (mīt) *n.* ⟦OE⟧ **1** a tiny arachnid, often parasitic upon animals or plants **2** a very small sum of money **3** a very small creature or object

**mi·ter** (mīt'ər) *n.* ⟦< Gr *mitra*, headband⟧ **1** a tall, ornamented cap worn by bishops and abbots **2** *Carpentry* a joint formed by fitting together two

pieces beveled to form a corner: now usually **miter joint**

**mit·i·gate** (mit'ə gāt') *vt.*, *vi.* **-gat'ed**, **-gat'ing** ⟦< L *mitis*, soft⟧ **1** to make or become less severe, less painful, etc. **2** ⟦< confusion with MILITATE⟧ to operate or work (*against*): a loose usage —**mit'i·ga'tion** *n.*

**mi·to·sis** (mī tō'sis) *n.* ⟦< Gr *mitos*, thread⟧ the process by which a cell divides into two with the nucleus of each new cell having the full number of chromosomes —**mi·tot'ic** (-tät'ik) *adj.*

**mitt** (mit) *n.* ⟦< fol.⟧ **1** a woman's glove covering the hand and forearm, but only part of the fingers **2** [Slang] a hand **3** *a*) *Baseball* a padded glove, worn for protection *b*) a boxing glove

**mit·ten** (mit'n) *n.* ⟦< OFr *mitaine*⟧ a glove with a thumb but no separately divided fingers

**mix** (miks) *vt.* ⟦< L *miscere*⟧ **1** to blend together in a single mass **2** to make by blending ingredients [to *mix* a drink] **3** to combine [to *mix* work and play] **4** to blend electronically (recorded sounds, etc.) on (a tape, etc.) —*vi.* **1** to be mixed or blended **2** to get along together —*n.* **1** a mixture **2** a commercial mixture of ingredients [a cake *mix*] **3** MIXER (*n.* 4) **4** the blend of sounds in a recording, etc. —**mix up 1** to mix thoroughly **2** to confuse **3** to involve or implicate (*in*): usually used in the passive —**mix'a·ble** *adj.*

**mixed** (mikst) *adj.* **1** blended **2** made up of different parts, classes, races, etc., or of both sexes **3** confused; muddled

**mixed number** a number consisting of a whole number and a fraction, as $3\frac{2}{3}$

**mixed'-up'** *adj.* confused, troubled, etc.

**mix'er** *n.* **1** a person with reference to the ability to get along with others **2** a machine for mixing ingredients together **3** a social dance for helping people meet one another **4** a beverage for mixing with alcoholic beverages

**mix·ture** (miks'chər) *n.* **1** a mixing or being mixed **2** something made by mixing

**mix'-up'** *n.* a confusion; tangle

**miz·zen·mast** (miz'ən mast'; *naut.*, -məst) *n.* ⟦< L *medius*, middle⟧ the mast third from the bow in a ship

**mkt** *abbrev.* market

**ml** *abbrev.* milliliter(s)

**Mlle** *abbrev.* Mademoiselle

**mm** *abbrev.* millimeter(s)

**MM** *abbrev.* Messieurs

**Mme** *abbrev.* Madame

**Mmes** *abbrev.* mesdames

**Mn** *Chem. symbol for* manganese

**MN** Minnesota

**mne·mon·ic** (nē män'ik) *adj.* ⟦< Gr *mnēmōn*, mindful⟧ of or helping the memory

**mo** *abbrev.* month

**Mo** *Chem. symbol for* molybdenum

**MO** *abbrev.* **1** Missouri **2** ⟦L *modus operandi*⟧ mode of operation

**moan** (mōn) *n.* ⟦prob. < OE *mænan*, complain⟧ a low, mournful sound, as of sorrow or pain —*vi.*, *vt.* **1** to utter or say with a moan **2** to complain (about)

**moat** (mōt) *n.* ⟦< OFr *mote*, a mound⟧ a deep, broad ditch, often filled with water, around a fortress or castle

**mob** (mäb) *n.* ⟦< L *mobile* (*vulgus*), movable (crowd)⟧ **1** a disorderly, lawless crowd **2** any crowd **3** the masses: contemptuous term **4** [Inf.] a gang of criminals —*vt.* **mobbed**, **mob'bing 1** to crowd around and attack, annoy, etc. **2** to throng; crowd into

**mo·bile** (mō'bəl, -bīl'; *for n.*, -bēl') *adj.* ⟦< L *movere*, to move⟧ **1** moving or movable **2** movable by means of a motor vehicle [a *mobile* X-ray unit] **3** that can change rapidly or easily; adaptable **4** characterized by ease in change of social status —*n.* a piece of abstract sculpture that aims to depict movement, as by an arrangement of thin forms, rings, etc. suspended and set in motion by air currents —**mo·bil'i·ty** (-bil'ə tē) *n.*

**Mo·bile** (mō bēl') seaport in SW Alabama: pop. 196,000

**-mo·bile** (mō bēl') ⟦< (AUTO)MOBILE⟧ *combining form* motorized vehicle *[bookmobile]*

**mo·bile home** (mō'bəl) a movable dwelling set more or less permanently at a location: cf. MOTOR HOME

**mo'bi·lize'** (-bə līz') *vt., vi.* **-lized', -liz'ing** to make or become organized and ready, as for war — **mo'bi·li·za'tion** *n.*

**mob·ster** (mäb'stər) *n.* [Slang] a gangster

**moc·ca·sin** (mäk'ə sən) *n.* ⟦< AmInd⟧ **1** a heelless slipper of soft, flexible leather **2** any similar heeled slipper

**mo·cha** (mō'kə) *n.* a choice grade of coffee grown orig. in Arabia —*adj.* flavored with coffee or coffee and chocolate

**mock** (mäk) *vt.* ⟦< OFr *mocquer*⟧ **1** to ridicule **2** to mimic, as in fun or derision —*vi.* to express scorn, ridicule, etc. —*adj.* sham; imitation; pretended —*adv.* falsely or insincerely

**mock'er·y** (-ər ē) *n., pl.* **-ies 1** a mocking **2** a person or thing receiving or deserving ridicule **3** a false or derisive imitation

**mock'ing·bird'** *n.* a bird of the U.S. that imitates the calls of other birds

**mock'-up'** *n.* ⟦< Fr *maquette*⟧ a model built to scale, often full-sized, for teaching, testing, etc.

**mod** (mäd) *adj.* ⟦< MOD(ERN)⟧ up-to-date, fashionable, stylish, etc.

**mode** (mōd) *n.* ⟦< L *modus*⟧ **1** a manner or way of acting, doing, or being **2** customary usage or current fashion **3** *Gram.* MOOD²

**mod·el** (mäd''l) *n.* ⟦< L *modus*, a measure⟧ **1** a small representation of a planned or existing object **2** a hypothetical description, often based on an analogy, used in analyzing something **3** a person or thing regarded as a standard of excellence to be imitated **4** a style or design **5** *a)* one who poses for an artist or photographer *b)* one employed to display clothes by wearing them — *adj.* **1** serving as a model **2** representative of others of the same style, etc. *[a model home]* —*vt.* **-eled** or **-elled, -el·ing** or **-el·ling 1** *a)* to make a model of *b)* to plan or form after a model **2** to display (clothes) by wearing —*vi.* to serve as a MODEL (*n.* 5)

**mo·dem** (mō'dəm) *n.* ⟦MO(DULATOR) + DEM(ODU-LATION)⟧ a device that converts data for transmission, as by telephone, to data-processing equipment

**mod·er·ate** (mäd'ər it; *for v.*, -āt') *adj.* ⟦< L *moderare*, restrain⟧ **1** within reasonable limits; avoiding extremes **2** mild; calm **3** of medium quality, amount, etc. —*n.* one holding moderate opinions —*vt., vi.* **-at·ed, -at'ing 1** to make or become moderate **2** to preside over (a meeting, etc.) —**mod'er·ate·ly** *adv.*

**mod'er·a'tion** *n.* **1** a moderating **2** avoidance of extremes **3** calmness

**mod'er·a'tor** *n.* one who presides at an assembly, debate, etc.

**mod·ern** (mäd'ərn) *adj.* ⟦< L *modo*, just now⟧ **1** of the present or recent times; specif., up-to-date **2** [*often* M-] designating the most recent form of a language —*n.* a person living in modern times, having modern ideas, etc. —**mo·der·ni·ty** (mä dur'nə tē) *n.*

**Modern English** the English language since about the mid-15th c.

**mod'ern·ism'** *n.* (a) modern usage, practice, thought, etc. —**mod'ern·ist** *n., adj.* —**mod'ern·is'tic** *adj.*

**mod'ern·ize'** *vt., vi.* **-ized', -iz'ing** to make or become modern —**mod'ern·i·za'tion** *n.*

**mod·est** (mäd'ist) *adj.* ⟦< L *modus*, a measure⟧ **1**

not vain or boastful **2** shy or reserved **3** decorous; decent **4** unpretentious —**mod'est·ly** *adv.* —**mod'es·ty** *n.*

**mod·i·cum** (mäd'i kəm) *n.* ⟦< L, moderate⟧ a small amount; bit

**mod·i·fy** (mäd'ə fī') *vt.* **-fied', -fy'ing** ⟦< L *modificare*, to limit⟧ **1** to change partially in character, form, etc. **2** to limit slightly **3** *Gram.* to limit in meaning —**mod'i·fi·ca'tion** *n.* —**mod'i·fi'er** *n.*

**mod·ish** (mōd'ish) *adj.* fashionable; stylish — **mo'dish·ly** *adv.* —**mod'ish·ness** *n.*

**mod·u·lar** (mäj'ə lər) *adj.* of modules

**mod·u·late'** (-lāt') *vt.* **-lat'ed, -lat'ing** ⟦< L *modus*, a measure⟧ **1** to regulate or adjust **2** to vary the pitch, intensity, etc. of (the voice) **3** *Radio* to vary the frequency of (radio waves, etc.) —**mod'u·la'tion** *n.* —**mod'u·la'tor** *n.*

**mod·ule** (mäj'ōōl') *n.* ⟦Fr < L *modus*, a measure⟧ **1** a standard or unit of measurement, as of building materials **2** any of a set of units to be variously fitted together **3** a detachable unit with a specific function, as in a spacecraft

**mo·gul** (mō'gul') *n.* ⟦Pers *Mughul*, Mongol⟧ a powerful or important person

**mo·hair** (mō'her') *n.* ⟦< Ar *mukhayyar*, fine cloth⟧ **1** the hair of the Angora goat **2** yarn or fabric made of this

**Mo·ham·med** (mō ham'id) A.D. 570?-632; Arab prophet: founder of Islam

**Mo·ham'med·an** *adj.* of Mohammed or Islam — *n.* MUSLIM Term used, esp. formerly, by non-Muslims —**Mo·ham'med·an·ism'** *n.*

**moi·e·ty** (moi'ə tē) *n., pl.* **-ties** ⟦< L *medius*, middle⟧ **1** a half **2** an indefinite part

**moire** (mwär, môr) *n.* ⟦Fr⟧ a fabric, esp. silk, etc., having a wavy pattern: also **moi·ré** (mwä rā', mō-)

**moist** (moist) *adj.* ⟦< L *mucus*, mucus⟧ slightly wet; damp —**moist'ly** *adv.* —**moist'ness** *n.*

**mois·ten** (mois'ən) *vt., vi.* to make or become moist

**mois·ture** (-chər) *n.* water or other liquid causing a slight wetness

**mois'tur·ize'** (-īz') *vt., vi.* **-ized', -iz'ing** to make (the skin, air, etc.) moist —**mois'tur·iz'er** *n.*

**Mo·ja·ve Desert** (mō hä'vē) desert in SE California: also sp. **Mo·ha've Desert**

**mo·lar** (mō'lər) *adj.* ⟦< L *mola*, millstone⟧ designating a tooth or teeth adapted for grinding —*n.* a molar tooth

**mo·las·ses** (mə las'iz) *n.* ⟦< L *mel*, honey⟧ a thick, dark syrup produced during the refining of sugar

**mold¹** (mōld) *n.* ⟦< L *modus*, a measure⟧ **1** a hollow form for giving a certain shape to something plastic or molten **2** a frame on which something is modeled **3** a pattern; model **4** something that is formed in or on a mold **5** distinctive character —*vt.* **1** to make in or on a mold **2** to form; shape

MOLARS

**mold²** (mōld) *n.* ⟦ME *moul*⟧ **1** a fungus producing a furry growth on the surface of organic matter **2** this growth —*vi.* to become moldy

**mold³** (mōld) *n.* ⟦OE *molde*⟧ loose, soft soil rich in decayed organic matter

**mold·er** (mōl'dər) *vi.* ⟦< OE *molde*, dust⟧ to crumble into dust

**mold·ing** (mōl'diŋ) *n.* **1** the act of one that molds **2** something molded **3** a shaped strip of wood, etc., as around the upper walls of a room

**Mol·do·va** (mōl dō'və) country in E Europe: formerly a republic of the U.S.S.R.: 13,000 sq. mi.; pop. 4,339,000

**mold·y** *adj.* **-i·er, -i·est 1** covered or overgrown with mold **2** musty or stale —**mold'i·ness** *n.*

**mole¹** (mōl) *n.* ⟦OE *mal*⟧ a small, congenital spot

on the human skin, usually dark-colored and raised

**mole**[2] (mōl) *n.* ⟦ME *molle*⟧ **1** a small, burrowing mammal with soft fur **2** a spy in an enemy intelligence agency, etc. who infiltrates long before engaging in spying

**mole**[3] (mōl) *n.* ⟦< L *moles*, a dam⟧ a breakwater

**mol·e·cule** (mäl′i kyōōl′) *n.* ⟦< ModL dim. of L *moles*, a mass⟧ **1** the smallest particle of an element or compound that can exist in the free state and still retain the characteristics of the substance **2** a small particle —**mo·lec·u·lar** (mō lek′yōō lər) *adj.*

**mole′hill**′ *n.* a small ridge of earth, formed by a burrowing mole

**mole′skin**′ *n.* a napped cotton fabric

**mo·lest** (mə lest′) *vt.* ⟦< L *moles*, a burden⟧ **1** to annoy or meddle with so as to trouble or harm **2** to make improper sexual advances to **3** to assault or attack (esp. a child) sexually —**mo·les·ta·tion** (mō′les tā′shən) *n.* —**mo·lest′er** *n.*

**Mo·lière** (mōl yer′) 1622-73; Fr. dramatist

**mol·li·fy** (mäl′ə fī′) *vt.* **-fied′, -fy′ing** ⟦< L *mollis*, soft + *facere*, make⟧ **1** to soothe; appease **2** to make less severe or violent

**mol·lusk** (mäl′əsk) *n.* ⟦< L *mollis*, soft⟧ any of a group of invertebrates, as an oyster or snail, having a soft body, often in a shell

**mol·ly** (mäl′ē) *n.*, *pl.* **-lies** ⟦after F. N. *Mollien* (1758-1850), Fr statesman⟧ any of various brightly colored fishes often kept in aquariums: also **mol′lie**

**mol·ly·cod·dle** (mäl′ē käd′′l) *n.* ⟦< *Molly*, dim. of *Mary* + CODDLE⟧ a man or boy used to being coddled, protected, etc. —*vt.* **-dled, -dling** to pamper; coddle

**molt** (mōlt) *vi.* ⟦< L *mutare*, to change⟧ to shed hair, skin, horns, etc. prior to replacement by a new growth: said of reptiles, birds, etc.

**mol·ten** (mōlt′′n) *vt.*, *vi.* ⟦ME⟧ *archaic pp. of* MELT —*adj.* melted by heat

**mo·lyb·de·num** (mə lib′də nəm) *n.* ⟦ult. < Gr *molybdos*, lead⟧ a silvery metallic chemical element, used in alloys

**mom** (mäm) *n.* [Inf.] MOTHER

**mo·ment** (mō′mənt) *n.* ⟦< L *momentum*, movement⟧ **1** an indefinitely brief period of time; instant **2** a definite point in time **3** a brief time of importance **4** importance

**mo·men·tar·i·ly** (mō′mən ter′ə lē) *adv.* **1** for a short time **2** in an instant **3** at any moment

**mo·men·tar·y** (mō′mən ter′ē) *adj.* lasting for only a moment; passing

**mo·men·tous** (mō men′təs) *adj.* of great moment; very important —**mo·men′tous·ness** *n.*

**mo·men·tum** (mō men′təm) *n.*, *pl.* **-tums** or **-ta** (-tə) ⟦L: see MOMENT⟧ the impetus of a moving object, equal to the product of its mass and its velocity

**mom·my** (mäm′ē) *n.*, *pl.* **-mies** *child's term for* MOTHER

**Mon** *abbrev.* Monday

**Mon·a·co** (män′ə kō) country on the Mediterranean: an independent principality & an enclave in SE France: .75 sq. mi.; pop. 30,000

**mon·arch** (män′ərk, -ärk′) *n.* ⟦< Gr *monos*, alone + *archein*, to rule⟧ **1** a hereditary ruler; king, queen, etc. **2** a large butterfly of North America, having black-edged orange wings —**mo·nar·chi·cal** (mə när′ki kəl) *adj.*

**mon′ar·chist** (-ər kist) *n.* one who favors monarchical government

**mon′ar·chy** (-kē) *n.*, *pl.* **-chies** a government or state headed by a monarch

**mon·as·ter·y** (män′ə ster′ē) *n.*, *pl.* **-ies** ⟦< Gr *monos*, alone⟧ the residence of a group of monks, etc. who have withdrawn from the world for religious reasons

**mo·nas·tic** (mə nas′tik) *adj.* of or like that of a monastery, monk, nun, etc.: also **mo·nas′ti·cal** —**mo·nas′ti·cism**′ (-tə siz′əm) *n.*

**mon·au·ral** (män ôr′əl) *adj.* of sound reproduction in which only one source of sound is used

**Mon·day** (mun′dā) *n.* ⟦OE *monandæg*, moon's day⟧ the second day of the week: abbrev. *Mon*

**mon·e·tar·y** (män′ə ter′ē) *adj.* ⟦< L *moneta*, a MINT[1]⟧ **1** of the coinage or currency of a country **2** of money —**mon′e·tar′i·ly** *adv.*

**mon·ey** (mun′ē) *n.*, *pl.* **-eys** or **-ies** ⟦< L *moneta*, a MINT[1]⟧ **1** stamped pieces of metal, or any paper notes, authorized by a government as a medium of exchange **2** property; wealth —**in the money** [Slang] **1** among the winners in a race, etc. **2** wealthy —**make money** to gain profits; become wealthy —**put money into** to invest money in

**mon′ey·bag**′ *n.* **1** a bag for money **2** [*pl.*, *with sing. v.*] [Inf.] a rich person

**mon·eyed** (mun′ēd) *adj.* rich; wealthy

**mon′ey·mak′er** *n.* **1** one successful at acquiring money **2** something profitable —**mon′ey·mak′ing** *adj.*, *n.*

**money market** the short-term system for lending and borrowing funds, especially by governments and large corporations

**money market fund** a mutual fund that puts funds into short-term investments, as government treasury bills

**money order** an order for payment of a specified sum of money, issued for a fee at one post office, bank, etc. and payable at another

**mon·ger** (muŋ′gər) *n.* ⟦< OE *mangere*⟧ [Chiefly Brit.] a dealer or trader: usually in compounds

**Mon·gol** (män′gəl) *n.* a person born or living in Mongolia —*adj.* MONGOLIAN

**Mon·go·li·a** (män gō′lē ə) **1** region in EC Asia, consisting of the country of Mongolia and a region of China (*Inner Mongolia*) **2** country in EC Asia: 604,250 sq. mi.; pop. 2,096,000

**Mon·go·li·an** (män gō′lē ən) *n.* **1** MONGOL **2** a family of languages spoken in Mongolia —*adj.* **1** of Mongolia or its peoples, languages, etc. **2** [Obs.] affected with Down syndrome

**Mon·gol·ic** (män gäl′ik) *adj. var. of* MONGOLIAN

**Mon·gol·oid** (män′gəl oid′) *adj.* **1** *var. of* MONGOLIAN **2** designating or of one of the major geographical varieties of human beings, including most of the peoples of Asia **3** [*often* **m-**] [Old-fashioned] affected with Down syndrome —*n.* **1** a member of the Mongoloid population of human beings **2** [*often* **m-**] [Old-fashioned] one affected with Down syndrome

**mon·goose** (mäŋ′gōōs′) *n.*, *pl.* **-goos′es** ⟦< native name in India⟧ a civetlike Old World carnivore that kills snakes, rodents, etc.

**mon·grel** (muŋ′grəl) *n.* ⟦< OE *mengan*, to mix⟧ an animal or plant, esp. a dog, of mixed breed —*adj.* of mixed breed, origin, character, etc.

**mon·ied** (mun′ēd) *adj.* MONEYED

**mon·i·ker** (män′i kər) *n.* ⟦< ?⟧ [Slang] a person's name: also **mon′ick·er**

**mo·ni·tion** (mō nish′ən) *n.* ⟦< L *monere*, warn⟧ admonition; warning

**mon·i·tor** (män′i tər) *n.* ⟦< L *monere*, warn⟧ **1** a student chosen to help the teacher **2** any device for regulating the performance of a machine, an aircraft, etc. **3** *Comput.* a video screen for displaying data, images, etc. **4** *Radio, TV* a receiver for checking the quality of transmission —*vt.*, *vi.* to watch or check on (a person or thing)

**monk** (muŋk) *n.* ⟦< Gr *monos*, alone⟧ a man who is a member of an ascetic religious order

**mon·key** (muŋ′kē) *n.*, *pl.* **-keys** ⟦< ? Fr or Sp *mona*, ape + LowG *-ke*, -KIN⟧ **1** a primate having a flat, hairless face and a long tail **2** loosely, another, similar primate, as a chimpanzee —*vi.* [Inf.] to play, trifle, or meddle (*around* or *with*)

**monkey business** [Inf.] foolishness, mischief, or deceit

**mon′key·shines**′ (-shīnz′) *pl.n.* [Inf.] playful tricks or pranks

**monkey wrench** a wrench with an adjustable

jaw —**throw a monkey wrench into** [Inf.] to disrupt the orderly functioning of

**monk's cloth** a heavy cloth with a basket weave, used for drapes, etc.

**mon·o** (män'ō) *adj. short for* MONOPHONIC —*n. short for* MONONUCLEOSIS

**mono-** ⟦< Gr *monos,* single⟧ *prefix* one, alone, single

**mon·o·chrome** (män'ə krōm') *adj.* ⟦< MONO- + -CHROME⟧ in one color or shades of one color

**mon·o·cle** (män'ə kəl) *n.* ⟦ult. < Gr *monos,* single + L *oculus,* eye⟧ an eyeglass for one eye only

**mon·o·clon·al** (män'ō klōn'əl) *adj.* of cells derived or cloned from one cell

**mon·o·cot·y·le·don** (män'ō kät'ə lēd''n) *n. Bot.* a plant having an embryo with only one cotyledon, or seed leaf: also **mon'o·cot'**

**mo·nog·a·my** (mə näg'ə mē) *n.* ⟦ult. < Gr *monos,* single + *gamos,* marriage⟧ the practice or state of being married to only one person at a time —**mo·nog'a·mous** *adj.*

**mon·o·gram** (män'ə gram') *n.* ⟦< Gr *monos,* single + *gramma,* letter⟧ the initials of a name, combined in a single design —*vt.* **-grammed', -gram'ming** to put a monogram on

**mon'o·graph'** (-graf') *n.* ⟦MONO- + -GRAPH⟧ a book or long article, esp. a scholarly one, on a single subject

**mon·o·lin·gual** (män'ō liŋ'gwəl) *adj.* using or knowing only one language

**mon·o·lith** (män'ə lith') *n.* ⟦< Gr *monos,* single + *lithos,* stone⟧ **1** a single large block of stone, as one made into an obelisk **2** any massive, unyielding structure —**mon'o·lith'ic** *adj.*

**mon·o·logue** or **mon·o·log** (män'ə lôg') *n.* ⟦< Gr *monos,* single + *legein,* speak⟧ **1** a long speech **2** a soliloquy **3** a skit, etc. for one actor only

**mon·o·ma·ni·a** (män'ō mā'nē ə) *n.* an excessive interest in or enthusiasm for some one thing; craze —**mon'o·ma'ni·ac'** (-mā'nē ak') *n.* —**mon'o·ma·ni'a·cal** (-mə nī'ə kəl) *adj.*

**mon·o·nu·cle·o·sis** (män'ō nōō'klē ō'sis) *n.* ⟦MONO- + NUCLE(US) + -OSIS⟧ an acute disease, with fever, swollen lymph nodes, etc.

**mon'o·phon'ic** (-fän'ik) *adj.* of sound reproduction using a single channel to carry sounds

**mo·nop·o·list** (mə näp'ə list) *n.* one who has a monopoly or favors monopoly —**mo·nop'o·lis'tic** *adj.*

**mo·nop·o·lize** (-līz') *vt.* **-lized', -liz'ing** **1** to get, have, or exploit a monopoly of **2** to get full control of [he *monopolized* the conversation]

**mo·nop·o·ly** (-lē) *n., pl.* **-lies** ⟦< Gr *monos,* single + *pōlein,* sell⟧ **1** exclusive control of a commodity or service in a given market **2** such control granted by a government **3** something held as a monopoly **4** a company that has a monopoly

**mon·o·rail** (män'ə rāl') *n.* **1** a single rail that is a track for cars suspended from it or balanced on it **2** a railway with such a track

**mon·o·so·di·um glu·ta·mate** (män'ō sō'dē əm glōō'tə māt') a white powder made from vegetable protein, used to intensify flavor in foods

**mon·o·syl·la·ble** (män'ō sil'ə bəl) *n.* a word of one syllable —**mon'o·syl·lab'ic** (-si lab'ik) *adj.*

**mon'o·the·ism'** (-thē iz'əm) *n.* ⟦MONO- + THEISM⟧ the belief that there is only one God —**mon'o·the·ist'** *n.* —**mon'o·the·is'tic** *adj.*

**mon·o·tone** (män'ə tōn') *n.* ⟦see MONO- & TONE⟧ **1** utterance of successive words without change of pitch or key **2** tiresome sameness of style, color, etc. **3** a single, unchanging tone

**mo·not·o·nous** (mə nät''n əs) *adj.* **1** going on in the same tone **2** having no variety **3** tiresome because unvarying —**mo·not'o·ny** *n.*

**Mon·roe** (mən rō'), **James** (jāmz) 1758-1831; 5th president of the U.S. (1817-25)

**mon·sieur** (mə syʉr'; *Fr* mə sy͞o') *n., pl.* **mes·sieurs** (mes'ərz; *Fr* mā syö') ⟦Fr, lit., my lord⟧ **1** a

man; gentleman **2** [M-] French title, equivalent to *Mr.* or *Sir*

**Mon·si·gnor** (män sēn'yər) *n., pl.* **-gnors** ⟦It, lit., my lord⟧ *R.C.Ch.* a title of certain Roman Catholic prelates

**mon·soon** (män sōōn') *n.* ⟦< Ar *mausim,* a season⟧ **1** a seasonal wind of the Indian Ocean and S Asia **2** the rainy season during which this wind blows from the southwest

**mon·ster** (män'stər) *n.* ⟦< L *monere,* warn⟧ **1** any grotesque imaginary creature **2** a very wicked person **3** any huge animal or thing —*adj.* huge

**mon·strance** (män'strəns) *n.* ⟦ult. < L *monstrare,* to show⟧ *R.C.Ch.* a receptacle for displaying the consecrated Host

**mon·strous** (män'strəs) *adj.* **1** huge; enormous **2** greatly malformed **3** horrible; hideous **4** evil —**mon·stros'i·ty** (-sträs'ə tē), *pl.* **-ties,** *n.*

**mon·tage** (män täzh') *n.* ⟦Fr < *monter,* to mount⟧ **1** a composite picture **2** a rapid sequence of film scenes, often superimposed

**Mon·taigne** (män tān'), **Mi·chel de** (mē shel' də) 1533-92; Fr. essayist

**Mon·tan·a** (män tan'ə) Mountain State of the NW U.S.: 145,556 sq. mi.; pop. 799,000; cap. Helena: abbrev. *MT* —**Mon·tan'an** *adj., n.*

**Mon·te Car·lo** (mänt'ə kär'lō) town in Monaco: gambling resort: pop. 13,000

**Mon·tes·so·ri method** (mänt'ə sôr'ē) ⟦after M. *Montessori* (1870-1952), It educator⟧ a method of teaching young children, emphasizing training of the senses

**Mon·te·vi·de·o** (mänt'ə və dā'ō) capital & seaport of Uruguay: pop. 1,247,000

**Mont·gom·er·y** (munt gum'ər ē, -gum'rē) capital of Alabama: pop. 188,000

**month** (munth) *n.* ⟦OE *monath*⟧ **1** any of the twelve divisions of the calendar year **2** a period of four weeks or 30 days **3** one twelfth of the solar year

**month'ly** *adj.* done, happening, payable, etc. every month —*n., pl.* **-lies** a periodical published once a month —*adv.* once a month; every month

**Mon·ti·cel·lo** (män'tə sel'ō, -chel'ō) home & burial place of Thomas Jefferson, in central Virginia

**Mont·pel·ier** (mänt pēl'yər) capital of Vermont: pop. 8,200

**Mon·tre·al** (män'trē ôl') city & seaport in SW Quebec, Canada, on an island in the St. Lawrence River: pop. 1,016,000

**mon·u·ment** (män'yōō mənt) *n.* ⟦< L *monere,* remind⟧ **1** something set up to keep alive the memory of a person or event, as a tablet or statue **2** a work of enduring significance

**mon'u·men'tal** (-ment''l) *adj.* **1** of or serving as a monument **2** like a monument; massive, enduring, etc. **3** very great; colossal

**moo** (mōō) *n., pl.* **moos** ⟦echoic⟧ a cow's vocal sound —*vi.* **mooed, moo'ing** to make this sound

**mooch** (mōōch) *vi., vt.* ⟦ult. < OFr *muchier,* to hide⟧ [Slang] to get (food, money, etc.) by begging, imposition, etc. —**mooch'er** *n.*

**mood¹** (mōōd) *n.* ⟦< OE *mod,* mind⟧ **1** a particular state of mind or feeling **2** a predominant or pervading feeling or spirit

**mood²** (mōōd) *n.* ⟦< MODE⟧ a characteristic of verbs that indicates whether the action expressed is regarded as a fact, supposition, or command

**mood'y** *adj.* **-i·er, -i·est** **1** changing in mood **2** gloomy —**mood'i·ly** *adv.* —**mood'i·ness** *n.*

**moon** (mōōn) *n.* ⟦OE *mona*⟧ [*often* M-] **1** the celestial body that revolves around the earth once about every 29½ days **2** anything shaped like the moon (i.e., an orb or crescent) **3** any natural satellite of a planet —*vi.* to behave in an idle or abstracted way

**moon'beam'** *n.* a ray of moonlight

**moon'light'** *n.* the light of the moon —*vi.* to engage in moonlighting

**moon'light'ing** *n.* the holding of a second job along with one's main job

**moon·lit'** *adj.* lighted by the moon

**moon·scape'** (-skāp') *n.* [MOON + (LAND)SCAPE] the surface of the moon or a representation of it

**moon·shine'** *n.* 1 MOONLIGHT 2 [Inf.] whiskey unlawfully distilled —**moon'shin'er** *n.*

**moon·shot'** *n.* the launching of a spacecraft to the moon

**moon·stone'** *n.* a feldspar with a pearly luster, used as a gem

**moon·struck'** *adj.* 1 crazed; lunatic 2 romantically dreamy

**moon·walk'** *n.* a walking about by an astronaut on the surface of the moon

**moor**¹ (moor) *n.* [OE *mor*] [Brit.] open wasteland covered with heather and often marshy

**moor**² (moor) *vt.* [< ? MDu *maren,* to tie] 1 to hold (a ship, etc.) in place by cables attached as to a pier 2 to secure —*vi.* to moor a ship, etc.

**Moor** (moor) *n.* a member of a Muslim people of NW Africa —**Moor'ish** *adj.*

**moor·ing** *n.* 1 [*often pl.*] the cables, etc. by which a ship is moored 2 [*pl.*] a place where a ship is moored

**moose** (moos) *n., pl.* **moose** [< AmInd] a large deer of N regions, the male of which has broad, flat antlers

**moot** (moot) *adj.* [< OE *mot,* a meeting] 1 debatable 2 resolved and thus not worthy of discussion

**mop** (mäp) *n.* [earlier *mappe*] 1 a bundle of rags or yarns, a sponge, etc. fastened to the end of a stick, as for washing floors 2 anything suggesting this, as a thick head of hair —*vt.* **mopped, mop'ping** to wash or wipe with a mop — **mop up** [Inf.] 1 to finish 2 to clear remnants of beaten enemy forces from

**mope** (mōp) *vi.* **moped, mop'ing** [akin to MDu *mopen*] to be gloomy and apathetic —**mop'ey, mop'y,** or **mop'ish** *adj.*

**mop·pet** (mäp'it) *n.* [< ME *moppe,* rag doll] [Inf.] a little child

**mo·raine** (mə rān') *n.* [Fr] a mass of rocks, sand, etc. left by a glacier

**mor·al** (môr'əl, mär'-) *adj.* [< L *mos,* pl. *mores, morals*] 1 dealing with, or capable of distinguishing between, right and wrong 2 of, teaching, or in accordance with the principles of right and wrong 3 good in conduct or character; specif., sexually virtuous 4 involving sympathy without action [*moral* support] 5 virtually such because of effects on thoughts or attitudes [a *moral* victory] 6 based on probability [a *moral* certainty] —*n.* 1 a moral lesson taught by a fable, event, etc. 2 [*pl.*] principles or standards with respect to right or wrong in conduct — **mor'al·ly** *adv.*

**mo·rale** (mə ral') *n.* mental condition related to courage, confidence, enthusiasm, etc.

**mor·al·ist** (môr'əl ist) *n.* 1 a teacher of or writer on morals 2 one who seeks to impose personal morals on others —**mor'al·is'tic** *adj.*

**mo·ral·i·ty** (mō ral'i tē, mə-) *n., pl.* **-ties** 1 rightness or wrongness, as of an action 2 right or moral conduct 3 moral principles

**mor·al·ize** (môr'əl īz') *vi.* **-ized', -iz'ing** to think, write, etc. about moral questions, often in a self-righteous or tedious way

**mo·rass** (mə ras') *n.* [< OFr *maresc*] a bog; marsh; swamp: often used figuratively of a difficult or troublesome situation

**mor·a·to·ri·um** (môr'ə tôr'ē əm) *n., pl.* **-ri·ums** or **-ri·a** (-ə) [< L *mora,* a delay] 1 a legal authorization to delay payment of money due 2 any authorized delay of a specified activity

**mo·ray (eel)** (môr'ā) [< Gr *myraina*] a voracious, brilliantly colored eel

**mor·bid** (môr'bid) *adj.* [< L *morbus,* disease] 1 of or caused by disease; diseased 2 resulting as from a diseased state of mind 3 gruesome [*morbid* details] —**mor·bid'i·ty** *n.* —**mor'bid·ly** *adv.*

**mor·dant** (môr'dənt) *adj.* [< L *mordere,* to bite]

caustic; sarcastic —*n.* a substance that fixes colors in dyeing —**mor'dan·cy** *n.* —**mor'dant·ly** *adv.*

**more** (môr) *adj.* [OE *mara*] 1 greater in amount, degree, or number: comparative of MUCH or MANY 2 additional [take *more* tea] —*n.* 1 a greater amount or degree 2 [*with pl. v.*] a greater number (*of*) 3 something additional —*adv.* 1 in or to a greater degree or extent 2 in addition

**more·o·ver** *adv.* in addition to what has been said; besides

**mo·res** (môr'ēz', -āz') *pl.n.* [L, customs] ways of thinking, behaving, etc. that develop the force of law because most people follow them

**morgue** (môrg) *n.* [Fr] 1 a place where the bodies of unknown dead persons or those dead of unknown causes are temporarily kept 2 the file of back numbers, photographs, etc. kept as in a newspaper's office

**mor·i·bund** (môr'i bund') *adj.* [< L *mori,* to die] dying

**Mor·mon** (môr'mən) *n.* a member of the Church of Jesus Christ of Latter-day Saints, founded (1830) in the U.S. —**Mor'mon·ism'** *n.*

**morn** (môrn) *n.* [Old Poet.] morning

**morn·ing** (môr'niŋ) *n.* [OE *morgen*] the first or early part of the day, from midnight, or esp. dawn, to noon

**morning glory** a twining vine with trumpet-shaped flowers

**morning sickness** nausea, vomiting, etc. affecting many women early in pregnancy, occurring usually in the morning

**mo·roc·co** (mə rä'kō) *n.* [< fol.] a fine, soft leather

**Mo·roc·co** (mə rä'kō) kingdom on the NW coast of Africa: 274,461 sq. mi.; pop. 25,897,000 —**Mo·roc'can** *adj., n.*

**mo·ron** (môr'än') *n.* [< Gr *mōros,* foolish] 1 a retarded person mentally equal to a child between eight and twelve years old: an obsolescent term 2 a very foolish or stupid person —**mo·ron'ic** *adj.*

**mo·rose** (mə rōs') *adj.* [< L *mos,* manner] ill-tempered; gloomy, sullen, etc. —**mo·rose'ly** *adv.*

**morph** (môrf) *vt., vi.* to transform or be transformed as by morphing

**mor·pheme** (môr'fēm') *n.* [< Gr *morphē,* a form] the smallest meaningful unit in a language, as an affix or base

**mor·phine** (môr'fēn') *n.* [after *Morpheus,* Gr god of dreams] an alkaloid derived from opium and used in medicine to relieve pain

**morph·ing** *n.* [< (META)MORPH(OSIS) + *-ing*] a film or video process in which persons or objects seem to change form through a continuous series of images created by a computer

**mor·phol·o·gy** (môr fäl'ə jē) *n.* [Ger < Gr *morphē,* form + Ger *-logie, -*LOGY] the study of form and structure, as in biology or linguistics

**mor·row** (mär'ō, môr'-) *n.* [< OE *morgen,* morning] [Archaic] 1 morning 2 the next day

**Morse** (môrs) *adj.* [after S. *Morse,* 19th-c. U.S. inventor] [*often* **m-**] designating or of a code of dots and dashes used in telegraphy

**mor·sel** (môr'səl) *n.* [< L *morsum,* a bite] a small piece or amount, as of food

**mor·tal** (môrt''l) *adj.* [< L *mors,* death] 1 that must eventually die 2 of a human being seen as a being who must eventually die 3 of death 4 causing physical or spiritual death; deadly; fatal 5 very intense [*mortal* terror] —*n.* a human being —**mor'tal·ly** *adv.*

**mor·tal·i·ty** (môr tal'ə tē) *n.* 1 the mortal nature of human beings 2 death on a large scale, as from war 3 the ratio of deaths to population

**mor·tar** (môrt'ər) *n.* [< L *mortarium*] 1 a bowl in which substances are pulverized with a pestle 2 a short-barreled cannon which hurls shells in a high trajectory 3 a mixture of cement or lime with sand and water, used to bind bricks or stones

**mor'tar·board'** *n.* 1 a square board for holding mortar 2 an academic cap with a square, flat top

**mort·gage** (môr'gij) *n.* ⟦< OFr *mort*, dead + *gage*, pledge⟧ 1 the pledging of property to a creditor as security for the payment of a debt 2 the deed by which this is done —*vt.* **-gaged, -gag·ing** 1 to pledge (property) by a mortgage 2 to put an advance claim on [to *mortgage* one's future] —**mort'ga·gor** or **mort'gag·er** (-gi jər) *n.*

**mort·ga·gee'** (-gə jē') *n.* a person to whom property is mortgaged

**mor·ti·cian** (môr tish'ən) *n.* ⟦< L *mors*, death⟧ FUNERAL DIRECTOR

**mor·ti·fy** (môrt'ə fī') *vt.* **-fied', -fy'ing** ⟦< L *mors*, death + *facere*, make⟧ 1 to subdue (physical desires) by self-denial, fasting, etc. 2 to humiliate —**mor'ti·fi·ca'tion** *n.*

**mor·tise** (môrt'is) *n.* ⟦< Ar *murtazza*, joined⟧ a hole or recess cut, as in a piece of wood, to receive a projecting part (*tenon*) shaped to fit into it

**mor·tu·ar·y** (môr'chōō er'ē) *n.*, *pl.* **-ies** a place where dead bodies are kept before burial or cremation; morgue or funeral home

**mo·sa·ic** (mō zā'ik) *n.* ⟦< L *musivus*, artistic⟧ 1 the making of pictures or designs by inlaying small bits of colored stone, etc. in mortar 2 a picture or design so made

**Mo·sa·ic** (mō zā'ik) *adj.* of Moses or the laws, etc. attributed to him

**Mos·cow** (mäs'kō, -kou') capital of Russia, in the W part: pop. 8,769,000

**Mo·ses** (mō'zəz, -zəs) *n. Bible* the leader and lawgiver who brought the Israelites out of slavery in Egypt

**mo·sey** (mō'zē) *vi.* ⟦prob. < VAMOOSE⟧ [Slang] to stroll or amble along

**Mos·lem** (mäz'ləm) *n., adj.* MUSLIM

**mosque** (mäsk) *n.* ⟦< Ar *masjid*, temple⟧ a Muslim place of worship

**mos·qui·to** (mə skēt'ō) *n., pl.* **-toes** or **-tos** ⟦Sp & Port < L *musca*, a fly⟧ a two-winged insect, the female of which sucks blood from animals, including humans

**moss** (môs, mäs) *n.* ⟦OE *mos*, a swamp⟧ a very small, green plant that grows in velvety clusters on rocks, trees, etc. —**moss'y, -i·er, -i·est,** *adj.*

**moss'back'** *n.* [Inf.] an old-fashioned or very conservative person

**most** (mōst) *adj.* ⟦OE *mast*⟧ 1 greatest in amount, degree, or number: superlative of MUCH or MANY 2 in the greatest number of instances [*most* fame is fleeting] —*n.* 1 the greatest amount, quantity, or degree 2 [*with pl. v.*] the greatest number (*of*) —*adv.* in or to the greatest degree or extent

**most'ly** *adv.* 1 for the most part 2 chiefly; principally 3 usually

**mote** (mōt) *n.* ⟦OE *mot*⟧ a speck, as of dust

**mo·tel** (mō tel') *n.* ⟦< MO(TOR) + (HO)TEL⟧ a hotel for motorists

**moth** (môth) *n., pl.* **moths** (môthz, môths) ⟦OE *moththe*⟧ a four-winged, chiefly night-flying insect, similar to the butterfly: the larvae of one kind feed on wool, etc.

**moth'ball'** *n.* a small ball, as of naphthalene, the fumes of which repel moths from woolens, etc. —**in mothballs** put into storage or reserve

**moth·er** (muth'ər) *n.* ⟦OE *modor*⟧ 1 a female parent 2 the origin or source of something 3 [*often* M-] a woman who is the head (**mother superior**) of a religious establishment —*adj.* 1 of or like a mother 2 native [*mother* tongue] —*vt.* 1 to be

the mother of 2 to care for as a mother does —**moth'er·hood'** *n.* —**moth'er·less** *adj.*

**Mother Goose** the imaginary creator of a collection of nursery rhymes

**moth'er-in-law'** *n., pl.* **moth'ers-in-law'** the mother of one's husband or wife

**moth'er·land'** *n.* one's native land

**moth'er·ly** *adj.* of or like a mother; protective, nurturing, etc. —**moth'er·li·ness** *n.*

**moth'er-of-pearl'** *n.* the hard internal layer of the shell of the pearl oyster, etc., used to make buttons, etc.

**mother tongue** one's native language

**mo·tif** (mō tēf') *n.* ⟦Fr: see MOTIVE⟧ 1 *Art, Literature, Music* a main theme for development 2 a repeated figure in a design

**mo·tile** (mōt'l) *adj.* ⟦< L *movere*, to move⟧ *Biol.* capable of or exhibiting spontaneous motion —**mo·til'i·ty** *n.*

**mo·tion** (mō'shən) *n.* ⟦< L *movere*, to move⟧ 1 a moving from one place to another; movement 2 a moving of a part of the body; specif., a gesture 3 a proposal formally made in an assembly —*vi.* to make a meaningful movement of the hand, etc.; gesture —*vt.* to direct by a meaningful gesture — **go through the motions** to do something as from habit, without enthusiasm, enjoyment, etc. —**in motion** moving —**mo'tion·less** *adj.*

**motion picture** FILM (*n.* 4)

**motion sickness** nausea, vomiting, etc. caused by the motion of a car, boat, etc.

**mo·ti·vate** (mōt'ə vāt') *vt.* **-vat'ed, -vat'ing** to provide with, or affect as, a motive; incite —**mo'ti·va'tion** *n.* —**mo'ti·va'tion·al** *adj.*

**mo·tive** (mōt'iv) *n.* ⟦< L *movere*, to move⟧ 1 an inner drive, impulse, etc. that causes one to act; incentive 2 MOTIF (sense 1)

**-mo·tive** (mōt'iv) *combining form* moving, of motion [*automotive*]

**mot·ley** (mät'lē) *adj.* ⟦< ?⟧ 1 of many colors 2 of many different or clashing elements

**mo·to·cross** (mōt'ō krôs') *n.* ⟦Fr⟧ a cross-country race for lightweight motorcycles

**mo·tor** (mōt'ər) *n.* ⟦L < *movere*, to move⟧ 1 anything that produces motion 2 an engine; esp., an internal-combustion engine 3 a machine for converting electric energy into mechanical energy — *adj.* 1 producing motion 2 of or powered by a motor 3 of, by, or for motor vehicles 4 of or involving muscular movements [*motor* skills] — *vi.* to travel by automobile

**mo'tor·bike'** *n.* [Inf.] 1 a motor-driven bicycle 2 a light motorcycle

**mo'tor·boat'** *n.* a small motor-driven boat

**mo'tor·cade'** (-kād') *n.* ⟦MOTOR + -CADE⟧ an automobile procession

**mo'tor·car'** *n.* [Now Chiefly Brit.] an automobile

**mo'tor·cy'cle** (-sī'kəl) *n.* a two-wheeled vehicle propelled by an internal-combustion engine

**motor home** a motor vehicle with a truck chassis, outfitted as a traveling home

**mo'tor·ist** (mōt'ər ist) *n.* one who drives an automobile or travels by automobile

**mo'tor·ize'** (-īz') *vt.* **-ized', -iz'ing** to equip with a motor or with motor-driven vehicles

**motor vehicle** an automotive vehicle, esp. an automobile, truck, or bus

**mot·tle** (mät''l) *vt.* **-tled, -tling** ⟦< MOTLEY⟧ to mark with blotches, streaks, etc. of different colors

**mot·to** (mät'ō) *n., pl.* **-toes** or **-tos** ⟦It, a word⟧ a word or saying that expresses the goals, ideals, etc. of a nation, group, etc.

**mould** (mōld) *n., vt., vi.* chiefly *Brit. sp.* of MOLD¹, MOLD², MOLD³

**mould'ing** *n.* chiefly *Brit. sp.* of MOLDING

**mould'y** *adj.* chiefly *Brit. sp.* of MOLDY

**moult** (mōlt) *vi.* chiefly *Brit. sp.* of MOLT

**mound** (mound) *n.* ⟦< ? MDu *mond*, protection⟧ a heap or bank of earth, sand, etc. —*vt.* to heap up

**mount¹** (mount) *n.* ⟦< L *mons*⟧ a mountain

**mount²** (mount) *vi.* ⟦< L *mons*, mountain⟧ 1 to

climb; ascend **2** to climb up on something, as onto a horse **3** to increase in amount —*vt.* **1** to go up; ascend *[to mount* stairs*]* **2** to get up on (a horse, platform, etc.) **3** to provide with horses *[mounted* police*]* **4** to place or fix (a jewel, picture, etc.) on or in the proper support, backing, etc. **5** to arrange (a dead animal, etc.) for exhibition **6** to place (a gun) into proper position for use **7** to prepare for and undertake (an expedition, etc.) — *n.* **1** the act of mounting **2** a horse, etc. for riding **3** the support, setting, etc. on or in which a thing is mounted

**moun·tain** (mount′'n) *n.* ⟦ult. < L *mons*⟧ **1** a natural raised part of the earth, larger than a hill **2** a large pile, amount, etc. —*adj.* of or in the mountains

**mountain bike** a heavy-duty bicycle with wide tires for use on and off regular road surfaces

**moun′tain·eer′** (-ir′) *n.* **1** one who lives in a mountainous region **2** a mountain climber

**mountain goat** a long-haired, goatlike antelope of the Rocky Mountains

**mountain lion** COUGAR

**moun′tain·ous** *adj.* **1** full of mountains **2** huge

**mountain sickness** weakness, nausea, etc. caused by thin air at high altitudes

**Mountain State** any of the eight states of the W U.S. through which the Rocky Mountains pass; Montana, Idaho, Wyoming, Nevada, Utah, Colorado, Arizona, or New Mexico

**moun·te·bank** (mount′ə baŋk′) *n.* ⟦It *montambanco*, lit., mounted on a bench: orig. a person on a bench, or platform, selling quack medicines⟧ a charlatan or quack

**mount′ed** *adj.* **1** on horseback, a bicycle, etc. **2** on or in a mounting

**mount′ing** *n.* something serving as a backing, support, setting, etc.

**mourn** (môrn) *vi., vt.* ⟦OE *murnan*⟧ **1** to feel or express sorrow for (something regrettable) **2** to grieve for (someone who has died) —**mourn′er** *n.*

**mourn′ful** *adj.* **1** feeling or expressing grief or sorrow **2** causing sorrow

**mourn′ing** *n.* **1** the expression of grief, esp. at someone's death **2** black clothes, etc., worn as such an expression **3** the period during which one mourns

**mouse** (mous; *for v., also* mouz) *n., pl.* **mice** ⟦OE *mus*⟧ **1** any of many small rodents, esp. a species that commonly infests buildings **2** a timid person **3** [Slang] a black eye **4** a hand-held device for controlling the video display of a computer —*vi.* **moused, mous′ing** to hunt mice

**mousse** (mo͞os) *n.* ⟦Fr, foam⟧ **1** a light, chilled dessert made with egg white, whipped cream, etc. **2** an aerosol foam used to keep hair in place, etc. —*vt.* **moussed, mouss′ing** to style (hair) using mousse

**mous·tache** (mus′tash′, məs tash′) *n. alt. sp. of* MUSTACHE

**mous·y** (mous′ē, mouz′-) *adj.* **-i·er, -i·est** of or like a mouse; specif., quiet, timid, drab, etc.: also **mous′ey** —**mous′i·ness** *n.*

**mouth** (mouth; *for v.* mou_th_) *n., pl.* **mouths** (mou_th_z) ⟦OE *muth*⟧ **1** the opening in the head through which food is taken in and sounds are made **2** any opening regarded as like this *[the mouth of a jar, river, etc.]* —*vt.* **1** to say, esp. insincerely **2** to form (a word) with the mouth silently —**down in** (or **at**) **the mouth** [Inf.] unhappy —**mouth off** [Slang] to talk loudly, impudently, etc.

**mouth′ful′** *n., pl.* **-fuls′ 1** as much as the mouth can hold **2** as much as is usually taken into the mouth **3** [Slang] a pertinent remark: chiefly in **say a mouthful**

**mouth organ** HARMONICA

**mouth′piece′** *n.* **1** a part, as of a musical instrument, held in or to the mouth **2** a person, periodical, etc. which expresses the views as of a group

**mouth′wash′** *n.* a flavored, often antiseptic liquid for rinsing the mouth

**mouth′wa′ter·ing** *adj.* appetizing; tasty

**mouth′y** *adj.* **-i·er, -i·est** talkative, esp. in a bombastic or rude way —**mouth′i·ness** *n.*

**mou·ton** (mo͞o′tän′) *n.* ⟦Fr, sheep⟧ lambskin or sheepskin made to resemble beaver, seal, etc.

**mov·a·ble** (mo͞o′və bəl) *adj.* that can be moved from one place to another —*n.* **1** something movable **2** *Law* personal property, esp. furniture: *usually used in pl.* Also **move′a·ble**

**move** (mo͞ov) *vt.* **moved, mov′ing** ⟦< L *movere*⟧ **1** to change the place or position of **2** to set or keep in motion **3** to cause (*to do, say,* etc.) **4** to arouse the emotions, etc. of **5** to propose formally, as in a meeting —*vi.* **1** to change place or position **2** to change one's residence **3** to be active **4** to make progress **5** to take action **6** to be, or be set, in motion **7** to make a formal application (*for*) **8** to evacuate: said of the bowels **9** to be sold: said of goods —*n.* **1** act of moving **2** an action toward some goal **3** a change of residence **4** *Chess, Checkers, etc.* the act of moving a piece, or one's turn to move —**move up** to promote or be promoted —**on the move** [Inf.] moving about from place to place

**move′ment** *n.* **1** a moving or manner of moving **2** an evacuation (of the bowels) **3** a change in the location of troops, etc. **4** organized action by people working toward a goal **5** the moving parts of a mechanism, as of a clock **6** *Music a*) a principal division of a symphony, etc. *b*) rhythm

**mov·er** (mo͞o′vər) *n.* one that moves; specif., one whose work is moving furniture, etc. for those changing residence

**mov·ie** (-vē) *n.* ⟦< *moving picture*⟧ FILM (*n.* 4) — **the movies 1** the film industry **2** a showing of a film

**moving van** a large van for transporting belongings, as of a person moving to a new residence

**mow**[1] (mō) *vt., vi.* **mowed, mowed** or **mown** (mōn), **mow′ing** ⟦OE *mawan*⟧ to cut down (grass, etc.) from (a lawn, etc.) —**mow down 1** to cause to fall like cut grass **2** to overwhelm (an opponent) —**mow′er** *n.*

**mow**[2] (mou) *n.* ⟦OE *muga*⟧ a heap of hay, etc., esp. in a barn

**Mo·zam·bique** (mō′zəm bēk′) country in SE Africa: 308,642 sq. mi.; pop. 11,674,000

**Mo·zart** (mō′tsärt′), **Wolf·gang A·ma·de·us** (vôlf′gäŋk′ ä′mä dā′o͞os) 1756-91; Austrian composer

**MP** *abbrev.* **1** Member of Parliament **2** Military Police

**mpg** *abbrev.* miles per gallon

**mph** *abbrev.* miles per hour

**Mr.** or **Mr** (mis′tər) *abbrev.* mister: used before a man's name or title: pl. *Messrs*

**MRI** *n.* ⟦*m*(*agnetic*) *r*(*esonance*) *i*(*maging*)⟧ imaging by means of atomic nuclei in a strong magnetic field, used in medical diagnosis

**Mrs.** or **Mrs** (mis′iz) *abbrev.* mistress: now used before a married woman's name: pl. *Mmes*

**MS** *abbrev.* **1** manuscript: also **ms 2** Master of Science: also **M.S., MSc,** or **M.Sc. 3** Mississippi **4** multiple sclerosis

**Ms.** or **Ms** (miz) *abbrev.* a title, free of reference to marital status, used in place of *Miss* or *Mrs.*

**MSG** *abbrev.* monosodium glutamate

**Msgr** *abbrev.* Monsignor

**MST** *abbrev.* Mountain Standard Time

**MSW** or **M.S.W.** *abbrev.* Master of Social Work

**Mt** *abbrev.* **1** Mount **2** Mountain

**MT** *abbrev.* **1** Montana **2** megaton **3** Mountain Time

**mtg** *abbrev.* **1** meeting **2** mortgage: also **mtge**

**MTV** *trademark for* Music Television

**mu** (myo͞o, myo͞o) *n.* the 12th letter of the Greek alphabet (M, μ)

**much** (much) *adj.* **more, most** ⟦< OE *mycel*⟧ great in quantity, degree, etc. —*adv.* **more, most 1** to a great degree or extent *[much happier]* **2** nearly *[much* the same*] —n.* **1** a great amount **2** something great or outstanding *[not much* to look at*]*

**mu·ci·lage** (myōo′si lij′) *n.* ⟦< L *mucere,* be moldy⟧ **1** a thick, sticky substance in certain plants **2** any watery solution of gum, glue, etc. used as an adhesive

**muck** (muk) *n.* ⟦ME *muk*⟧ **1** moist manure **2** black earth with decaying matter, used as fertilizer **3** mud; dirt; filth —**muck′y,** **-i·er,** **-i·est,** *adj.*

**muck′rake′** *vi.* **-raked′,** **-rak′ing** ⟦see prec. & RAKE¹⟧ to search for and publicize real or alleged corruption in politics, etc. —**muck′rak′er** *n.*

**mu·cous** (myōo′kəs) *adj.* **1** of, containing, or secreting mucus **2** slimy

**mucous membrane** a mucus-secreting lining of certain body cavities

**mu·cus** (myōo′kəs) *n.* ⟦L⟧ the thick, slimy substance secreted by the mucous membranes for moistening and protection

**mud** (mud) *n.* ⟦ME⟧ **1** wet, soft, sticky earth **2** defamatory remarks

**mud·dle** (mud′'l) *vt.* **-dled,** **-dling** ⟦< prec.⟧ **1** to mix up; bungle **2** to confuse mentally; befuddle —*vi.* to act or think confusedly —*n.* **1** a mess, jumble, etc. **2** mental confusion

**mud′dle-head′ed** *adj.* confused

**mud′dy** *adj.* **-di·er,** **-di·est** **1** full of or spattered with mud **2** not clear; cloudy *[muddy* coffee*]* **3** confused, obscure, etc. *[muddy* thinking*] —vt., vi.* **-died,** **-dy·ing** to make or become muddy — **mud′di·ness** *n.*

**mud flat** low, muddy land that floods at high tide

**mud′sling′ing** *n.* the making of unscrupulous, malicious attacks, as against a political opponent —**mud′sling′er** *n.*

**mu·ez·zin** (myōo ez′in) *n.* ⟦< Ar *adhana,* proclaim⟧ a Muslim crier who calls the people to prayer

**muff** (muf) *n.* ⟦< Fr *moufle,* mitten⟧ **1** a cylindrical covering, as of fur, to warm the hands **2** any bungled action —*vt.* to bungle; specif., to miss (a catch, etc.)

**muf·fin** (muf′ən) *n.* ⟦< ?⟧ a quick bread baked in a cup-shaped mold

**muf·fle** (muf′əl) *vt.* **-fled,** **-fling** ⟦prob. < OFr *moufle,* mitten⟧ **1** to wrap or cover so as to keep warm, deaden sound, etc. **2** to deaden (a sound)

**muf′fler** (-lər) *n.* **1** a scarf worn around the throat, as for warmth **2** a device for deadening noise, esp. of a car's exhaust

**muf·ti** (muf′tē) *n., pl.* **-tis** ⟦< Ar⟧ ordinary clothes, esp. when worn by one usually wearing a uniform

**mug** (mug) *n.* ⟦prob. < Scand⟧ **1** a cup made of earthenware or metal, with a handle **2** as much as a mug will hold **3** [Slang] the face —*vt.* **mugged,** **mug′ging** to assault, usually with intent to rob —*vi.* [Slang] to grimace, esp. in overacting —**mug′ger** *n.*

**mug·gy** (mug′ē) *adj.* **-gi·er,** **-gi·est** ⟦< dial. *mug,* mist⟧ hot, damp, and close —**mug′gi·ness** *n.*

**mug shot** a police photograph of the face of a criminal or suspect

**Mu·ham·mad** (moo ham′əd) *var. of* MOHAMMED

**muk·luk** (muk′luk′) *n.* ⟦Esk *muklok,* a seal⟧ an Eskimo boot of sealskin or reindeer skin

**mu·lat·to** (mə lät′ō, -lat′ō) *n., pl.* **-toes** or **-tos** ⟦Sp & Port *mulato*⟧ a person who has one black parent and one white parent

**mul·ber·ry** (mul′ber′ē, -bər ē) *n., pl.* **-ries** ⟦< OE *morberie*⟧ **1** a tree with purplish-red, edible, berrylike fruit **2** the fruit

**mulch** (mulch) *n.* ⟦ME *molsh,* soft⟧ leaves, straw, etc., spread around plants to prevent freezing of roots, etc. —*vt.* to apply mulch to

**mulct** (mulkt) *vt.* ⟦< L *mul(c)ta,* a fine⟧ **1** to fine **2** to take (money, etc.) from (someone) by fraud — *n.* a fine

**mule¹** (myōol) *n.* ⟦< L *mulus*⟧ **1** the offspring of a jackass and a female horse **2** [Inf.] a stubborn person **3** [Slang] a drug smuggler

**mule²** (myōol) *n.* ⟦< L *mulleus,* red shoe⟧ a lounging slipper that does not cover the heel

**mu·le·teer** (myōo′lə tir′) *n.* ⟦OFr *muletier*⟧ a driver of mules: also [Inf.] **mule skin·ner** (skin′ər)

**mul′ish** *adj.* stubborn; obstinate

**mull¹** (mul) *vt., vi.* ⟦ME *mullen,* to grind⟧ to ponder *(over)*

**mull²** (mul) *vt.* ⟦< ?⟧ to heat, sweeten, and spice (wine, cider, etc.)

**mul·let** (mul′it) *n.* ⟦< L *mullus*⟧ an edible, spiny-finned fish of fresh and salt waters

**mul·li·gan stew** (mul′i gən) a stew made of bits of meat and vegetables, esp. as by hobos

**mul·li·ga·taw·ny** (mul′i gə tô′nē) *n.* ⟦Tamil *milagutaṇṇir,* lit., pepper water⟧ an East Indian soup of meat, etc., flavored with curry

**mul·lion** (mul′yən) *n.* ⟦prob. < OFr *moien,* median⟧ a vertical dividing bar, as between windowpanes

**multi-** ⟦L < *multus,* many⟧ *combining form* **1** having many **2** more than two **3** many times more than

**mul·ti·cul·tur·al·ism** (mul′tē kul′chər əl iz′əm) *n.* the practice of giving equal emphasis to the needs and contributions of all cultural groups, esp. traditionally underrepresented minority groups, in a society —**mul′ti·cul′tur·al** *adj.*

**mul′ti·fac′et·ed** (-fas′ət id) *adj.* having a variety of features, parts, etc. *[a multifaceted* career*]*

**mul·ti·far·i·ous** (mul′tə far′ē əs) *adj.* ⟦< L⟧ having many kinds of parts or elements; diverse

**mul·ti·lat·er·al** (mul′ti lat′ər əl) *adj.* involving more than two parties, nations, etc.

**mul′ti·lin′gual** *adj.* of, in, or capable of using several languages

**mul′ti·me′di·a** (-mē′dē ə) *adj.* combining or using several media, as film and live performance or TV, radio, and printed matter

**mul′ti·mil′lion·aire′** *n.* one whose wealth amounts to many millions of dollars, pounds, etc.

**mul′ti·na′tion·al** *adj.* **1** of many nations **2** having offices, etc. in many nations —*n.* a multinational corporation

**mul·ti·ple** (mul′tə pəl) *adj.* ⟦< L *multiplex*⟧ **1** having many parts, elements, etc. **2** shared by or involving many —*n.* a number which is a product of some specified number and another number

**mul′ti·ple-choice′** *adj.* listing several answers from which the correct one is to be chosen

**multiple sclerosis** a disease of the central nervous system, with loss of muscular coordination, etc.

**mul·ti·plex** (mul′tə pleks′) *adj.* ⟦L, multiple⟧ designating a system for sending two or more signals simultaneously over a common circuit, etc. —*n.* a film-theater complex with three or more screens —**mul′ti·plex′er** or **mul′ti·plex′or** *n.*

**mul′ti·pli·cand′** (-pli kand′) *n.* a number to be multiplied by another

**mul′ti·pli·ca′tion** (-pli kā′shən) *n.* a multiplying or being multiplied; specif., the process of finding the quantity obtained by repeated additions of a specified quantity a specified number of times

**mul′ti·plic′i·ty** (-plis′ə tē) *n.* a great number or variety *(of)*

**mul′ti·pli′er** (-plī′ər) *n.* the number by which another is to be multiplied

**mul′ti·ply′** (-plī′) *vt., vi.* **-plied′,** **-ply′ing** ⟦see MULTIPLE⟧ **1** to increase in number, degree, etc. **2** to find the product (of) by multiplication

**mul·ti·proc·es·sor** (mul′ti prä′ses′ər) *n.* a computer system capable of processing many programs at once

**mul′ti·stage′** *adj.* having more than one stage, as a missile, process, etc.

**mul·ti·tude** (mul′tə tōod′) *n.* ⟦< L *multus,* many⟧ a large number; host

**mul′ti·tu′di·nous** (-tōod′'n əs) *adj.* very numerous; many

**mum**[1] (mum) *n.* [Inf.] a chrysanthemum

**mum**[2] (mum) *adj.* ⟦ME *momme*⟧ silent; not speaking

**mum·ble** (mum'bəl) *vt., vi.* **-bled, -bling** ⟦ME *momelen*⟧ to speak or say indistinctly; mutter — *n.* a mumbled utterance —**mum'bler** *n.*

**mum·bo jum·bo** (mum'bō jum'bō) ⟦of Afr orig.⟧ meaningless ritual, talk, etc.

**mum·mer** (mum'ər) *n.* ⟦< OFr *momo*, grimace⟧ an actor, esp. one who wears a mask or costume

**mum·mi·fy** (mum'ə fī') *vt., vi.* **-fied', -fy'ing** to make into or become (like) a mummy

**mum·my** (mum'ē) *n., pl.* **-mies** ⟦ult. < Pers *mum*, wax⟧ a dead body preserved by embalming, as by the ancient Egyptians

**mumps** (mumps) *n.* ⟦< obs. *mump*, a grimace⟧ an acute communicable disease characterized by swelling of the salivary glands

**mun** *abbrev.* municipal

**munch** (munch) *vt., vi.* ⟦ME *monchen*⟧ to chew steadily, often with a crunching sound

**mun·dane** (mun'dān', mun dān') *adj.* ⟦< L *mundus*, world⟧ **1** of the world; worldly **2** commonplace, ordinary, etc. —**mun'dane·ly** *adv.*

**Mu·nich** (myoo'nik) city in SE Germany: pop. 1,256,000

**mu·nic·i·pal** (myoo nis'ə pəl) *adj.* ⟦< L *municeps*, inhabitant of a free town⟧ of or having to do with a city, town, etc. or its local government

**mu·nic'i·pal'i·ty** (-pal'ə tē) *n., pl.* **-ties** a city, town, etc. having its own incorporated government

**mu·nif·i·cent** (myoo nif'ə sənt) *adj.* ⟦< L *munus*, a gift + *facere*, make⟧ very generous; lavish —**mu·nif'i·cence** *n.*

**mu·ni·tions** (myoo nish'ənz) *pl.n.* ⟦< L *munire*, fortify⟧ weapons and ammunition for war

**mu·ral** (myoor'əl) *adj.* ⟦< L *murus*, wall⟧ of, on, or for a wall —*n.* a picture, esp. a large one, painted directly on a wall —**mu'ral·ist** *n.*

**mur·der** (mur'dər) *n.* ⟦OE *morthor*⟧ **1** the unlawful and malicious or premeditated killing of a person **2** [Inf.] something very hard, unsafe, etc. to do or deal with —*vt.* **1** to kill (a person) unlawfully and with malice **2** to spoil, mar, etc., as in performance [to *murder* a song] —**mur'der·er** *n.* —**mur'der·ess** *fem.n.*

**mur'der·ous** *adj.* **1** of or characteristic of murder; brutal **2** capable or guilty of, or intending, murder —**mur'der·ous·ly** *adv.*

**murk** (murk) *n.* ⟦< ON *myrkr*, dark⟧ darkness; gloom

**murk'y** *adj.* **-i·er, -i·est** dark or gloomy —**murk'i·ness** *n.*

**mur·mur** (mur'mər) *n.* ⟦< L⟧ **1** a low, steady sound **2** a mumbled complaint **3** *Med.* an abnormal sound in the body, esp. in the heart —*vi.* to make a murmur —*vt.* to say in a murmur

**mus·cat** (mus'kət) *n.* ⟦< LL *muscus*, musk⟧ a sweet European grape

**mus'ca·tel'** (-kə tel') *n.* a sweet wine made from the muscat

**mus·cle** (mus'əl) *n.* ⟦< L *musculus*, lit., little mouse⟧ **1** any body organ consisting of fibrous tissue that can be contracted and expanded to produce bodily movements **2** this tissue **3** muscular strength —*vi.* **-cled, -cling** [Inf.] to force one's way (*in*)

**mus'cle-bound'** *adj.* having some of the muscles enlarged and less elastic, as from too much exercise

**mus·cu·lar** (mus'kyoo lər, -kyə-) *adj.* **1** of, consisting of, or done by muscles **2** having well-developed muscles; strong —**mus'cu·lar'i·ty** (-lar'ə tē) *n.*

**muscular dys·tro·phy** (dis'trə fē) a chronic disease characterized by a progressive wasting of the muscles

**mus·cu·la·ture** (mus'kyoo lə chər, -kyə-) *n.* ⟦Fr⟧ the muscular system of a body, limb, etc.

**muse** (myooz) *vi.* **mused, mus'ing** ⟦< OFr *muser*, ponder⟧ to think deeply; meditate

**Muse** (myooz) *n.* ⟦< Gr *mousa*⟧ **1** *Gr. Myth.* any of the nine goddesses of literature and of the arts and sciences **2** [m-] the spirit thought to inspire a poet or other artist

**mu·sette** (**bag**) (myoo zet') ⟦< OFr, bagpipe⟧ a bag with a shoulder strap, carried as by soldiers

**mu·se·um** (myoo zē'əm) *n.* ⟦< Gr *mousa*, Muse⟧ a place for preserving and exhibiting artistic or historical objects

**mush**[1] (mush) *n.* ⟦prob. var. of MASH⟧ **1** a thick porridge of boiled meal **2** any thick, soft mass **3** [Inf.] maudlin sentimentality —**mush'y, -i·er, -i·est,** *adj.*

**mush**[2] (mush) *interj.* ⟦prob. < Fr *marchons*, let's go⟧ a shout to urge on sled dogs —*vi.* to travel on foot over snow with a dog sled

**mush'room'** *n.* ⟦< LL *mussirio*⟧ any of various fleshy fungi, typically with a stalk capped by an umbrellalike top; esp., any edible variety —*adj.* of or like a mushroom —*vi.* to grow or spread rapidly

**mu·sic** (myoo'zik) *n.* ⟦< Gr *mousikē* (*technē*), art of the Muses⟧ **1** the art of combining tones to form expressive compositions **2** such compositions **3** any rhythmic sequence of pleasing sounds —**face the music** [Inf.] to accept the consequences

**mu'si·cal** (-zi kəl) *adj.* **1** of or for music **2** melodious or harmonious **3** fond of or skilled in music **4** set to music —*n.* a play or film with a musical score featuring songs and dances —**mu'si·cal·ly** *adv.*

**mu·si·cale** (myoo'zi kal') *n.* ⟦Fr⟧ a social affair featuring a musical program

**mu·si·cian** (myoo zish'ən) *n.* one skilled in music; esp., a performer

**mu'si·col'o·gy** (-zi käl'ə jē) *n.* the study of the history, forms, etc. of music —**mu'si·col'o·gist** *n.*

**musk** (musk) *n.* ⟦< Sans *muṣka*, testicle⟧ a strong-smelling animal secretion, used in perfumes —**musk'y, -i·er, -i·est,** *adj.*

**mus·kel·lunge** (mus'kə lunj') *n.* ⟦< AmInd⟧ a very large, edible pike of North America: also **mus'kie** (-kē)

**mus·ket** (mus'kət) *n.* ⟦< L *musca*, a fly⟧ a former kind of firearm with a long barrel and smooth bore

**mus·ket·eer** (mus'kə tir') *n.* a soldier armed with a musket

**musk'mel'on** *n.* any of various sweet, juicy melons, as the cantaloupe

**musk ox** a hardy ox of arctic North America with a long, coarse coat and a musklike odor

**musk'rat'** *n.* **1** an American water rodent with webbed hind feet and a musklike odor **2** its fur

**Mus·lim** (muz'ləm, mooz'-, moos'-) *n.* ⟦Ar, true believer < *aslama*, to resign oneself (to God)⟧ an adherent of Islam —*adj.* of Islam or the Muslims

**mus·lin** (muz'lin) *n.* ⟦after *Mosul*, city in Iraq⟧ a strong, plain-woven cotton cloth

**muss** (mus) *n.* ⟦prob. var. of MESS⟧ [Inf.] a mess; disorder —*vt.* to make messy or disordered: often with *up* —**muss'y, -i·er, -i·est,** *adj.*

**mus·sel** (mus'əl) *n.* ⟦< OE *muscle*⟧ any of various bivalve mollusks; specif., an edible variety

**must** (must) *v.aux. pt.* **must** ⟦< OE *moste*⟧ used to express: **1** necessity [I *must* go] **2** probability [it *must* be Joe] **3** certainty [all men *must* die] —*n.* [Inf.] something that must be done, had, etc.

**mus·tache** (mus'tash', məs tash') *n.* ⟦ult. < Gr *mystax*⟧ hair growing on the upper lip; esp., the hair that a man has let grow

**mus·tang** (mus'taŋ) *n.* ⟦< L *mixtus*, a mingling⟧ a small wild horse of the SW plains

**mus·tard** (mus'tərd) *n.* ⟦< OFr⟧ **1** an herb with yellow flowers and round seeds in slender pods **2** a pungent seasoning made from the ground seeds

**mustard gas** ⟦< its mustardlike odor⟧ an oily liquid used in warfare for its blistering and disabling effects

**mus·ter** (mus'tər) *vt.* ⟦< L *monstrare*, to show⟧ **1**

to assemble (troops, etc.) **2** to collect; summon: often with *up* —*vi.* to assemble, as troops —*n.* **1** a gathering or assembling, as of troops for inspection **2** the persons or things assembled —**muster in** (or **out**) to enlist in (or discharge from) military service —**pass muster** to meet the required standards

**mus·ty** (mus′tē) *adj.* **-ti·er, -ti·est** ⟦< ? MOIST⟧ **1** having a stale, moldy smell or taste **2** stale or trite; antiquated —**mus′ti·ly** *adv.* —**mus′ti·ness** *n.*

**mu·ta·ble** (myōōt′ə bəl) *adj.* ⟦< L *mutare,* to change⟧ **1** that can be changed **2** inconstant; fickle —**mu′ta·bil′i·ty** *n.* —**mu′ta·bly** *adv.*

**mu·tant** (myōōt′′nt) *adj.* of mutation —*n.* an animal or plant with inheritable characteristics that differ from those of the parents; sport

**mu·ta·tion** (myōō tā′shən) *n.* **1** a change, as in form, nature, etc. **2** a sudden variation in some inheritable characteristic of an animal or plant — **mu′tate′, -tat′ed, -tat′ing,** *vi., vt.*

VIOLIN MUTE

TRUMPET MUTE

**mute** (myōōt) *adj.* ⟦< L *mutus*⟧ **1** not speaking; silent **2** unable to speak —*n.* **1** a deaf-mute **2** a device that softens the sound of a musical instrument —*vt.* **mut′ed, mut′ing** to soften the sound of

**mu·ti·late** (myōōt′′l āt′) *vt.* **-lat′ed, -lat′ing** ⟦< L *mutilus,* maimed⟧ to cut off, damage, or mar an important part of —**mu′ti·la′tion** *n.* —**mu′ti·la′tor** *n.*

**mu·ti·ny** (myōōt′′n ē) *n.,* pl. **-nies** ⟦< L *movere,* to move⟧ revolt against constituted authority; esp., rebellion of soldiers or sailors against their officers —*vi.* **-nied, -ny·ing** to take part in a mutiny —**mu′ti·neer′** *n.* —**mu′ti·nous** *adj.*

**mutt** (mut) *n.* [Slang] a mongrel dog

**mut·ter** (mut′ər) *vi., vt.* ⟦ME *moteren*⟧ **1** to speak or say in low, indistinct tones **2** to grumble —*n.* **1** a muttering **2** something muttered

**mut·ton** (mut′′n) *n.* ⟦< OFr, a ram⟧ the flesh of a sheep, esp. a grown sheep, used as food

**mu·tu·al** (myōō′chōō əl) *adj.* ⟦< L *mutare,* to exchange⟧ **1** *a)* done, felt, etc. by each of two or more for or toward the other or others *b)* of each other **2** in common [our *mutual* friend] —**mu′tu·al·ly** *adv.*

**mutual fund 1** a fund of securities owned jointly by investors who have purchased shares of it **2** a corporation which manages such a fund or funds

**muu·muu** (mōō′mōō′) *n.* ⟦< Haw⟧ a long, loose dress of Hawaiian style

**Mu·zak** (myōō′zak′) *trademark for* a system of transmitting recorded background music to stores, etc. —*n.* this music, variously regarded as unobtrusive, bland, etc.

**muz·zle** (muz′əl) *n.* ⟦< ML *musum*⟧ **1** the mouth, nose, and jaws of a dog, horse, etc. **2** a device put over the mouth of an animal to prevent its biting or eating **3** the front end of the barrel of a firearm —*vt.* **-zled, -zling 1** to put a muzzle on (an animal) **2** to prevent from talking

**MX missile** (em′eks′) ⟦< *m(issile),* (e)x(perimental)⟧ a U.S. ICBM armed with several nuclear warheads

**my** (mī) *poss. pronominal adj.* ⟦< OE *min*⟧ of, belonging to, or done by me

**Myan·mar** (myän′mär′) country in SE Asia: 261,228 sq. mi.; pop. 35,314,000

**my·col·o·gy** (mī käl′ə jē) *n.* the study of fungi — **my·col′o·gist** *n.*

**my·e·li·tis** (mī′ə līt′is) *n.* ⟦< Gr *myelos,* marrow + -ITIS⟧ inflammation of the spinal cord or the bone marrow

**My·lar** (mī′lär′) *trademark for* a strong, thin polyester used for recording tapes, fabrics, etc. —*n.* [*occas.* m-] this substance

**my·na** or **my·nah** (mī′nə) *n.* ⟦Hindi *mainā*⟧ any of various tropical birds of Southeast Asia: some can mimic speech

**my·o·pi·a** (mī ō′pē ə) *n.* ⟦< Gr *myein,* to close + *ōps,* eye⟧ nearsightedness —**my·op′ic** (-äp′ik) *adj.*

**myr·i·ad** (mir′ē əd) *n.* ⟦< Gr *myrios,* countless⟧ a great number —*adj.* countless; innumerable

**myr·mi·don** (mur′mə dän′, -dən) *n.* ⟦after name of a Gr tribe led by Achilles⟧ an unquestioning follower

**myrrh** (mur) *n.* ⟦< Ar *murr*⟧ a fragrant gum resin of Arabia and E Africa, used in incense, etc.

**myr·tle** (murt′′l) *n.* ⟦< Gr *myrtos*⟧ **1** an evergreen shrub with white or pink flowers and dark berries **2** any of various other plants, as the periwinkle

**my·self** (mī self′) *pron.* a form of I, used as an intensive [I went *myself*], as a reflexive [I hurt *myself*], or with the meaning "my true self" [I am not *myself* today]

**mys·te·ri·ous** (mis tir′ē əs) *adj.* of, containing, implying, or characterized by mystery —**mys·te′ri·ous·ly** *adv.* —**mys·te′ri·ous·ness** *n.*

**mys·ter·y** (mis′tə rē) *n.,* pl. **-ies** ⟦< Gr *mystērion,* secret rite⟧ **1** something unexplained or secret **2** a story involving unknown persons, facts, etc. [a murder *mystery*] **3** secrecy

**mys·tic** (mis′tik) *adj.* **1** of esoteric rites or doctrines **2** MYSTICAL **3** mysterious —*n.* a believer in mysticism

**mys·ti·cal** (-ti kəl) *adj.* **1** spiritually significant or symbolic **2** of mystics or mysticism **3** occult — **mys′ti·cal·ly** *adv.*

**mys·ti·cism** (mis′tə siz′əm) *n.* **1** belief in the possibility of attaining direct communion with God or knowledge of spiritual truths, as by meditation **2** obscure thinking or belief

**mys·ti·fy** (-fī′) *vt.* **-fied′, -fy′ing** to puzzle or perplex —**mys′ti·fi·ca′tion** *n.*

**mys·tique** (mis tēk′) *n.* [Fr, mystic] a complex of quasi-mystical attitudes and feelings surrounding some person, institution, etc.

**myth** (mith) *n.* ⟦< Gr *mythos*⟧ **1** a traditional story serving to explain some phenomenon, custom, etc. **2** mythology **3** any fictitious story, person, or thing —**myth′i·cal** *adj.*

**my·thol·o·gy** (mi thäl′ə jē) *n.,* pl. **-gies 1** the study of myths **2** myths collectively, as of a specific people —**myth·o·log·i·cal** (mith′ə läj′i kəl) *adj.*

# N

**n**¹ or **N** (en) *n., pl.* **n's, N's** the 14th letter of the
English alphabet

**n**² *abbrev.* **1** name **2** neuter **3** new **4** nominative
**5** noun **6** number

**N**¹ *abbrev.* **1** Navy **2** north **3** northern **4** November

**N**² *Chem. symbol for* nitrogen

**Na** ⟦L *natrium*⟧ *Chem. symbol for* sodium

**NA** *abbrev.* North America

**NAACP** *abbrev.* National Association for the
Advancement of Colored People

**nab** (nab) *vt.* **nabbed, nab′bing** ⟦prob. < dial. *nap*,
to snatch⟧ [Inf.] **1** to snatch or seize **2** to arrest
or catch (a felon or wrongdoer)

**na·bob** (nā′bäb′) *n.* ⟦< Ar *nā′ib*, deputy⟧ a very
rich or important man

**na·cre** (nā′kər) *n.* ⟦Fr < Ar *naqqārah*, small kettle-
drum⟧ MOTHER-OF-PEARL

**na·dir** (nā′dər, -dir) *n.* ⟦< Ar *nazīr*, opposite⟧ **1**
the point opposite the zenith and directly below
the observer **2** the lowest point

**nae** (nā) [Scot.] *adv.* no; not —*adj.* no

**nag**¹ (nag) *vt., vi.* **nagged, nag′ging** ⟦< ON *gnaga*⟧
**1** to annoy by continual scolding, urging, etc. **2** to
keep troubling [*nagged* by doubts] —*n.* one who
nags: also **nag′ger**

**nag**² (nag) *n.* ⟦ME *nagge*⟧ an old or inferior horse

**Na·ga·sa·ki** (nä′gə sä′kē) seaport in SW Japan:
U.S. atomic-bomb target (1945): pop. 438,000

**Na·go·ya** (nä′gô yä′) seaport in S Honshu, Japan:
pop. 2,088,000

**nai·ad** (nā′ad′, nī′-) *n.* ⟦< Gr *naein*, to flow⟧ [*also*
N-] *Gr. & Rom. Myth.* a nymph living in a spring,
river, etc.

**nail** (nāl) *n.* ⟦< OE *nægl*⟧ **1** the thin, horny growth
at the ends of fingers and toes **2** a tapered,
pointed piece of metal driven with a hammer, as
to join pieces of wood —*vt.* **1** to fasten, secure,
etc. with or as with nails **2** [Inf.] to catch, capture, etc. **3** [Inf.] to hit hard

**nail′-bit′er** (-bīt′ər) *n.* [Inf.] a suspenseful drama,
sports event, etc.

**Nai·ro·bi** (nī rō′bē) capital of Kenya: pop.
1,346,000

**na·ive** or **na·ïve** (nä ēv′) *adj.* ⟦Fr < L *nativus*,
natural⟧ **1** unaffectedly simple **2** credulous —
**na·ive′ly** or **na·ïve′ly** *adv.* —**na·ive·té′** or **na·ive·té′**
(-tā′) *n.*

**na·ked** (nā′kid) *adj.* ⟦OE *nacod*⟧ **1** completely
unclothed; nude **2** without covering **3** without
additions, disguises, etc.; plain [the *naked* truth]
—**na′ked·ly** *adv.* —**na′ked·ness** *n.*

**nam·by-pam·by** (nam′bē pam′bē) *adj.* ⟦18th-c.
play on name *Ambrose*⟧ weak, insipid, indecisive,
etc. —*n., pl.* **-bies** a namby-pamby person

**name** (nām) *n.* ⟦OE *nama*⟧ **1** a word or phrase by
which a person, thing, or class is known; title **2** a
word or words considered descriptive; epithet,
often an abusive one **3** reputation **4** appearance
only, not reality [chief in *name* only] —*adj.* well-
known —*vt.* **named, nam′ing 1** to give a name to
**2** to mention by name **3** to identify by the right
name [*name* the oceans] **4** to appoint to an office,
etc. **5** to specify (a date, price, etc.) —**in the name
of** by the authority of

**name′less** *adj.* **1** not having a name **2** left
unnamed **3** indescribable

**name′ly** *adv.* that is to say; to wit

**name′sake′** *n.* a person with the same name as
another, esp. if named after the other

**Na·mib·i·a** (nə mib′ē ə) country in S Africa:
318,251 sq. mi.; pop. 1,402,000 —**Na·mib′i·an** *adj.,
n.*

**Nan·jing** (nän′jiŋ′) city in E China, on the Chang:
pop. 2,091,000

**Nan·king** (nan′kiŋ′, nän′-) *a former transliteration of* NANJING

**nan·ny goat** (nan′ē) ⟦< fem. name *Nan*⟧ a female
goat

**na·no·sec·ond** (nan′ə sek′ənd) *n.* one billionth of
a second

**nap**¹ (nap) *vi.* **napped, nap′ping** ⟦OE *hnappian*⟧ to
sleep lightly for a short time —*n.* a brief, light
sleep

**nap**² (nap) *n.* ⟦ME *noppe*⟧ the downy or hairy surface of cloth or suede formed by short hairs or
fibers —**nap′less** *adj.*

**na·palm** (nā′päm′) *n.* ⟦*na*(*phthene*) + *palm*(*itate*)⟧
a jellylike substance used in flame throwers and
fire bombs —*vt.* to attack or burn with napalm

**nape** (nāp) *n.* ⟦ME⟧ the back of the neck

**naph·tha** (naf′thə, nap′-) *n.* ⟦< Pers *neft*, pitch⟧ a
flammable liquid distilled from petroleum, used
as a fuel, solvent, etc.

**naph·tha·lene′** (-lēn′) *n.* ⟦< prec.⟧ a white crystalline hydrocarbon distilled from coal tar, used in
moth repellents, dyes, etc.

**nap·kin** (nap′kin) *n.* ⟦< L *mappa*⟧ **1** a small piece
of cloth or paper used while eating to protect the
clothes and wipe the lips **2** any small cloth,
towel, etc.

**Na·ples** (nā′pəlz) seaport in S Italy: pop.
1,072,000

**Na·po·le·on** (nə pō′lē ən) *see* BONAPARTE, Napoleon

**narc** (närk) *n.* ⟦< NARC(OTIC)⟧ [Slang] a police
agent who enforces laws dealing with narcotics

**nar·cis·sism** (när′sə siz′əm) *n.* ⟦< fol.⟧ self-love;
specif., excessive interest in one's own appearance, comfort, etc. —**nar′cis·sist** *n., adj.* —**nar′cis·
sis′tic** *adj.*

**Nar·cis·sus** (när sis′əs) *n.* **1** *Gr. Myth.* a youth
who falls in love with his reflection in a pool and
changes into the narcissus **2** *pl.* **-cis′sus, -cis′sus·
es,** or **-cis′si** (-ī) [n-] any of various bulb plants
whose flowers have six parts and a cuplike or
tubelike center

**nar·co·sis** (när kō′sis) *n., pl.* **-ses′** (-sēz′) unconsciousness caused by a narcotic

**nar·cot·ic** (när kät′ik) *n.* ⟦< Gr *narkē*, numbness⟧
a drug, as morphine, used to relieve pain and
induce sleep: narcotics are often addictive —*adj.*
of or having to do with narcotics

**nar·co·tize** (när′kə tīz′) *vt.* **-tized′, -tiz′ing** to subject to a narcotic —**nar′co·ti·za′tion** *n.*

**nark** (närk) *n.* [Slang] *alt. sp. of* NARC

**nar·rate** (nar′āt′, na rāt′) *vt., vi.* **-rat′ed, -rat′ing**
⟦< L *narrare*, tell⟧ to tell (a story), relate (events),
etc.

**nar·ra·tion** (na rā′shən) *n.* **1** a narrating **2** a
narrative

**nar·ra·tive** (nar′ə tiv) *adj.* in story form —*n.* **1** a
story; account **2** the art or practice of narrating

**nar·row** (nar′ō) *adj.* ⟦OE *nearu*⟧ **1** small in
width; not wide **2** limited in meaning, size,
amount, etc. **3** limited in outlook; not liberal **4**
with limited margin [a *narrow* escape] —*vi., vt.* to
decrease or limit in width, extent, etc. —*n.* [*usually pl.*] a narrow passage; strait

**nar′row·cast′** (-kast′) *vt., vi.* **-cast′, -cast′ing** to
transmit by cable TV to a selected audience —*n.* a
narrowcasting

**nar′row-mind′ed** *adj.* limited in outlook; big-
oted; prejudiced —**nar′row-mind′ed·ness** *n.*

**nar·whal** (när′wəl) *n.* ⟦< ON *nahvalr*, lit., corpse
whale⟧ a small arctic whale: the male has a long,
spiral tusk

**nar·y** (ner′ē) *adj.* ⟦< *ne′er a*, never a⟧ [Dial.] not any; no: with *a* or *an* [nary a doubt]

**NASA** (nas′ə) *abbrev.* National Aeronautics and Space Administration

**na·sal** (nā′zəl) *adj.* ⟦< L *nasus*, nose⟧ **1** of the nose **2** uttered so that the breath passes through the nose

**na′sal·ize′** (-īz′) *vt., vi.* **-ized′, -iz′ing** to pronounce or speak with a nasal sound —**na′sal·i·za′tion** *n.*

**NASCAR** (nas′kär′) *trademark for* National Association for Stock Car Auto Racing

**nas·cent** (nas′ənt, nā′sənt) *adj.* ⟦< L *nasci*, be born⟧ **1** coming into being **2** beginning to form or develop: said of ideas, etc.

**Nash·ville** (nash′vil) capital of Tennessee: pop. 511,000

**nas·tur·tium** (nə stur′shəm) *n.* ⟦< L *nasus*, nose + *torquere*, to twist: from its pungent odor⟧ **1** a plant with trumpet-shaped, red, yellow, or orange flowers **2** its flower

**nas·ty** (nas′tē) *adj.* **-ti·er, -ti·est** ⟦< ?⟧ **1** filthy **2** morally offensive **3** very unpleasant **4** mean; malicious —**nas′ti·ly** *adv.* —**nas′ti·ness** *n.*

**na·tal** (nāt′'l) *adj.* ⟦< L *nasci*, be born⟧ of or relating to one's birth

**na·tion** (nā′shən) *n.* ⟦< L *natus*, born⟧ **1** a stable community of people with a territory, culture, and language in common **2** the people united under a single government; country

**na·tion·al** (nash′ə nəl) *adj.* of or affecting a nation as a whole —*n.* a citizen —**na′tion·al·ly** *adv.*

**National Guard** the organized militia forces of the individual U.S. states, part of the U.S. Army when called into active federal service

**na′tion·al·ism′** *n.* **1** devotion to one's nation; patriotism **2** the advocacy of national independence —**na′tion·al·ist** *n., adj.* —**na′tion·al·is′tic** *adj.*

**na·tion·al·i·ty** (-nal′ə tē) *n., pl.* **-ties** **1** the status of belonging to a nation by birth or naturalization **2** a national group, esp. of immigrants

**na′tion·al·ize′** (-nə līz′) *vt.* **-ized′, -iz′ing 1** to make national **2** to transfer ownership or control of (land, industries, etc.) to the government —**na′tion·al·i·za′tion** *n.*

**na′tion·wide′** *adj.* by or throughout the whole nation; national

**na·tive** (nāt′iv) *adj.* ⟦< L *natus*, born⟧ **1** inborn **2** belonging to a locality or country by birth, production, or growth **3** being, or connected with, the place of one's birth [one's *native* land or language] **4** as found in nature; natural **5** of or characteristic of the original inhabitants of a place —*n.* **1** a person born in the place indicated **2** an original inhabitant **3** an indigenous plant or animal

**Native American** AMERICAN INDIAN

**na′tive-born′** *adj.* of a specified place by birth

**na·tiv·i·ty** (nə tiv′ə tē) *n., pl.* **-ties** ⟦see NATIVE⟧ birth —**the Nativity** the birth of Jesus

**natl** *abbrev.* national

**NATO** (nā′tō) *n.* North Atlantic Treaty Organization

**nat·ty** (nat′ē) *adj.* **-ti·er, -ti·est** ⟦< ? NEAT⟧ trim and stylish —**nat′ti·ly** *adv.*

**nat·u·ral** (nach′ər əl) *adj.* ⟦< L *naturalis*, by birth⟧ **1** of or dealing with nature **2** produced or existing in nature; not artificial **3** innate; not acquired **4** true to nature; lifelike **5** normal [a *natural* result] **6** free from affectation; at ease **7** *Music* neither sharped nor flatted —*n.* [Inf.] a person or thing sure to be successful

**natural childbirth** childbirth without anesthesia but with prior training

**natural gas** a mixture of gaseous hydrocarbons, chiefly methane, occurring naturally in the earth and used as fuel

**natural history** the study of the animal, vegetable, and mineral world

**nat′u·ral·ism′** *n.* **1** action or thought based on natural desires **2** *Literature, Art, etc.* the realistic portrayal of persons or things

**nat′u·ral·ist** *n.* one who studies animals and plants

**nat′u·ral·ize′** (-īz′) *vt.* **-ized′, -iz′ing** to confer citizenship upon (an alien) —**nat′u·ral·i·za′tion** *n.*

**nat′u·ral·ly** *adv.* **1** in a natural manner **2** by nature; innately **3** of course

**natural number** any positive integer, as 1, 2, or 3

**natural resource** a form of wealth supplied by nature, as coal, oil, or water power

**natural science** the systematized knowledge of nature, including biology, chemistry, physics, etc.

**natural selection** the evolutionary process by which the most adaptable species survive

**na·ture** (nā′chər) *n.* ⟦< L *natus*, born⟧ **1** the essential quality of a thing; essence **2** inherent tendencies of a person **3** kind; type **4** *a)* the physical universe *b)* [sometimes N-] the power, force etc. that seems to regulate this **5** the primitive state of humans **6** natural scenery —**by nature** naturally; inherently

**Naug·a·hyde** (nôg′ə hīd′) ⟦arbitrary coinage⟧ *trademark for* an imitation leather, used for upholstery, luggage, etc. —*n.* [n-] this material

**naught** (nôt) *n.* ⟦OE *nawiht*⟧ **1** nothing **2** *alt. sp. of* NOUGHT

**naugh·ty** (nôt′ē) *adj.* **-ti·er, -ti·est** ⟦ME *naugti*⟧ **1** mischievous or disobedient **2** indelicate; improper —**naugh′ti·ly** *adv.* —**naugh′ti·ness** *n.*

**Na·u·ru** (nä ōō′rōō) country on an island in the W Pacific, south of the equator: 8 sq. mi.; pop. 8,000

**nau·sea** (nô′shə, -zhə; -sē ə, -zē ə) *n.* ⟦< Gr *nausia*, seasickness⟧ **1** a sick feeling in the stomach, with an impulse to vomit **2** disgust; loathing

**nau′se·ate′** (-shē āt′, -zhē-, -sē-, -zē-) *vt.* **-at′ed, -at′ing** to cause to feel nausea

**nau·seous** (nô′shəs, -zē əs, -sē-) *adj.* **1** causing nausea **2** feeling nausea; nauseated: usage objected to by some

**nau·ti·cal** (nôt′i kəl) *adj.* ⟦< Gr *naus*, ship⟧ of sailors, ships, or navigation —**nau′ti·cal·ly** *adv.*

**nautical mile** a unit of linear measure used in navigation, equal to 1.1508 miles or 1,852 meters

**nau·ti·lus** (nôt′'l əs) *n., pl.* **-lus·es** or **-li′** (-ī′) ⟦< Gr *naus*, a ship⟧ a tropical mollusk with a spiral shell divided into many chambers —**[N-]** *trademark for* a type of mechanical weight-lifting equipment

**Nav·a·jo** (nav′ə hō′) *n. pl.* **-jos′, -jo′,** or **-joes′** a member of a North American Indian people of the SW U.S.: also sp. **Nav′a·ho′**

**na·val** (nā′vəl) *adj.* ⟦< L *navis*, a ship⟧ of, having, characteristic of, or for a navy, its ships, etc.

**nave** (nāv) *n.* ⟦< L *navis*, a ship⟧ the main part of a church, from the chancel to the principal entrance

**na·vel** (nā′vəl) *n.* ⟦OE *nafela*⟧ the small scar in the abdomen marking the place where the umbilical cord was attached to the fetus

**navel orange** a seedless orange with a navel-like hollow at its apex

**nav·i·ga·ble** (nav′i gə bəl) *adj.* **1** wide or deep enough for the passage of ships **2** that can be steered —**nav′i·ga·bil′i·ty** *n.*

**nav·i·gate** (nav′ə gāt′) *vt., vi.* **-gat′ed, -gat′ing** ⟦< L *navis*, a ship + *agere*, to lead⟧ **1** to steer or direct (a ship or aircraft) **2** to travel through or over (water, air, etc.) in a ship or aircraft **3** [Inf.] to walk or make one's way (on or through)

**nav′i·ga′tion** (-gā′shən) *n.* **1** the science of locating the position and plotting the course of ships and aircraft **2** traffic by ship

**nav′i·ga′tor** *n.* one skilled or employed in the navigation of a ship or aircraft

**na·vy** (nā′vē) *n., pl.* **-vies** ⟦< L *navis*, a ship⟧ **1** all the warships of a nation **2** [often N-] a nation's entire military sea force, including ships, personnel, stores, etc. **3** NAVY BLUE

**navy bean** ⟦from use in U.S. *Navy*⟧ a small white variety of kidney bean

**navy blue** very dark, purplish blue

**nay** (nā) *adv.* [< ON *ne*, not + *ei*, ever] **1** no: now used only in voice votes **2** not that only, but also [I permit, *nay* encourage it] —*n.* **1** a denial **2** a negative vote or a person voting negatively

**nay·say·er** (nā'sā'ər) *n.* one who opposes, refuses, or denies, esp. habitually

**Na·zi** (nät'sē) *adj.* [Ger contr. of the party name] designating or of the German fascist political party which ruled Germany under Hitler (1933-45) —*n.* a member of this party

**NB** New Brunswick

**n.b.** *abbrev.* [L *nota bene*] note well: also **NB**

**NC** North Carolina

**NCO** *abbrev.* noncommissioned officer

**NC-17** *trademark for* a film rating indicating that no one under 17 may be admitted

**ND** North Dakota

**Ne** *Chem. symbol for* neon

**NE** *abbrev.* **1** Nebraska **2** northeast **3** northeastern

**Ne·an·der·thal** (nē an'dər thôl') *adj.* [after a Ger valley] **1** designating or of a widespread form of early human being of the Pleistocene Epoch **2** primitive or regressive —*n.* **1** a Neanderthal human being **2** one who is crude, primitive, etc.

**neap** (nēp) *adj.* [OE *nep*- in *nepflod*, neap tide] designating either of the two lowest high tides in the month —*n.* neap tide

**Ne·a·pol·i·tan** (nē'ə päl'ə tən) *adj.* of Naples —*n.* a person born or living in Naples

**Neapolitan ice cream** brick ice cream in layers of different flavors and colors

**near** (nir) *adv.* [OE compar. of *neah*, nigh] **1** at a short distance in space or time **2** closely; intimately —*adj.* **1** close in distance or time **2** close in relationship; akin **3** close in friendship **4** close in degree [a *near* escape] **5** short or direct [the *near* way] —*prep.* close to —*vt., vi.* to draw near (to); approach —**near'ness** *n.*

**near'by'** *adj., adv.* near; close at hand

**Near East** countries near the E end of the Mediterranean, including those of SW Asia, the Arabian Peninsula, & NE Africa

**near'ly** *adv.* almost; not quite

**near miss 1** a result that is nearly but not quite successful **2** a near escape

**near'sight'ed** *adj.* having better vision for near objects than for objects that are distant; myopic —**near'sight'ed·ness** *n.*

**neat** (nēt) *adj.* [< L *nitere*, to shine] **1** unmixed; undiluted [whiskey *neat*] **2** clean and tidy **3** skillful and precise **4** well-proportioned **5** cleverly said or done **6** [Slang] nice, pleasing, etc. —**neat'ly** *adv.* —**neat'ness** *n.*

**neat'en** *vt.* to make clean, tidy, orderly, etc.: often with *up*

**'neath** or **neath** (nēth) *prep.* [Old Poet.] *short for* BENEATH

**neb·bish** (neb'ish) *n.* [< Yiddish *nebekh*, pity] one who is pitifully inept, shy, dull, etc.

**Ne·bras·ka** (nə bras'kə) Midwestern state of the U.S.: 76,878 sq. mi.; pop. 1,578,000; cap. Lincoln: abbrev. *NE* —**Ne·bras'kan** *adj., n.*

**neb·u·la** (neb'yə lə) *n., pl.* **-lae'** (-lē') or **-las** [L, mist] a cloud of interstellar gas or dust, or, formerly, any hazy, distant celestial object, as a star cluster —**neb'u·lar** *adj.*

**neb'u·lous** (-ləs) *adj.* unclear; vague

**nec·es·sar·i·ly** (nes'ə ser'ə lē) *adv.* **1** because of necessity **2** as a necessary result

**nec'es·sar'y** (-ser'ē) *adj.* [< L *ne*-, not + *cedere*, give way] **1** essential; indispensable 2 inevitable **3** required —*n., pl.* **-sar'ies** something necessary

**ne·ces·si·tate** (nə ses'ə tāt') *vt.* **-tat'ed, -tat'ing** to make necessary or unavoidable

**ne·ces·si·ty** (-tē) *n., pl.* **-ties** [see NECESSARY] **1** natural causation; fate **2** great need **3** something that cannot be done without —**of necessity** necessarily

**neck** (nek) *n.* [OE *hnecca*] **1** that part of a human

or animal joining the head to the body **2** the part of a garment near the neck **3** a necklike part; specif., *a*) a narrow strip of land *b*) the narrowest part of a bottle, etc. *c*) a strait —*vt., vi.* [Slang] to hug, kiss, and caress passionately —**neck and neck** very close, as in a race

**neck·er·chief** (nek'ər chif, -chēf') *n.* [see prec. & KERCHIEF] a handkerchief or scarf worn around the neck

**neck'lace** (-lis) *n.* [NECK + LACE] an ornamental string of beads, chain of gold, etc., worn around the neck

**neck'tie'** *n.* a band worn around the neck under a collar and tied in front

**neck'wear'** *n.* articles worn about the neck, as neckties or scarves

**ne·crol·o·gy** (ne kräl'ə jē) *n., pl.* **-gies** [ult. < Gr *nekros*, corpse + -LOGY] a list of people who have died

**nec·ro·man·cy** (nek'rə man'sē) *n.* [< Gr *nekros*, corpse + *manteia*, divination] **1** divination by alleged communication with the dead **2** black magic; sorcery —**nec'ro·man'cer** *n.*

**ne·cro·sis** (ne krō'sis) *n., pl.* **-ses'** (-sēz') [< Gr *nekros*, corpse] the death or decay of tissue in a part of the body

**nec·tar** (nek'tər) *n.* [< Gr *nektar*] **1** *Gr. & Rom. Myth.* the drink of the gods **2** any very delicious beverage **3** the sweetish liquid in many flowers, used by bees to make honey

**nec·tar·ine** (nek'tə rēn', nek'tə rēn') *n.* [< prec.] a kind of smooth-skinned peach

**nee** or **née** (nā; *now often* nē) *adj.* [Fr] born [Mrs. Helen Jones, *nee* Smith]

**need** (nēd) *n.* [OE *nied*] **1** necessity **2** a lack of something useful, required, or desired [to have *need* of a rest] **3** something required or desired that is lacking [your daily *needs*] **4** *a*) a condition in which help is required [a friend in *need*] *b*) poverty —*vt.* **1** to have need of; require **2** to be obliged; must [she needs to be careful] —*vi.* to be in need —**have need to** to be required to —**if need be** if it is required

**need'ful** *adj.* necessary; required

**nee·dle** (nēd''l) *n.* [OE *nædl*] **1** a small, slender, pointed piece of steel with a hole for thread, used for sewing **2** a slender rod of steel, bone, etc. used for crocheting or knitting **3** STYLUS (sense 2b) **4** the pointer of a compass, gauge, etc. **5** the thin, short, pointed leaf of the pine, spruce, etc. **6** the sharp, slender metal tube at the end of a hypodermic syringe —*vt.* **-dled, -dling** [Inf.] **1** to goad; prod **2** to tease —**nee'dler** *n.*

**nee'dle·point'** *n.* **1** embroidery of woolen threads upon canvas **2** lace made on a paper pattern, with a needle: in full **needlepoint lace**

**need'less** *adj.* not needed; unnecessary [needless cruelty] —**need'less·ly** *adv.*

**nee'dle·work'** *n.* work done with a needle; embroidery, crocheting, sewing, etc.

**need·n't** (nēd'nt) *contr.* need not

**needs** (nēdz) *adv.* [OE *nedes*] of necessity: with *must* [he must *needs* obey]

**need'y** *adj.* **-i·er, -i·est** very poor —**need'i·ness** *n.*

**ne'er** (ner) *adv.* [Old Poet.] never

**ne'er'-do-well'** *n.* a shiftless, irresponsible person

**ne·far·i·ous** (nə fer'ē əs) *adj.* [< L *ne*-, not + *fas*, lawful] very wicked; villainous —**ne·far'i·ous·ly** *adv.* —**ne·far'i·ous·ness** *n.*

**ne·gate** (ni gāt') *vt.* **-gat'ed, -gat'ing** [< L *negare*, deny] **1** to deny **2** to make ineffective

**ne·ga·tion** (ni gā'shən) *n.* **1** the act or an instance of denying **2** the lack or opposite of something positive

**neg·a·tive** (neg'ə tiv) *adj.* **1** expressing denial or refusal; saying "no" **2** opposite to or lacking in that which is positive [a *negative* force] **3** *Math.* designating a quantity less than zero, or one to be subtracted **4** *Med.* not showing the presence of a condition, infection, etc. **5** *Photog.* reversing the relation of light and shade of the subject **6** *Elec.* a) of, generating, or charged with negative electricity b) having an excess of electrons —*n.* **1** a negative word, reply, etc. **2** the point of view that opposes the positive **3** the plate in a battery having an excess of electrons flowing out toward the positive **4** an exposed and developed photographic film or plate on which light and shadow are reversed —**in the negative** with a negative answer —**neg′a·tive·ly** *adv.* —**neg′a·tiv′i·ty** *n.*

**ne·glect** (ni glekt′) *vt.* ⟦< L *neg-*, not + *legere*, gather⟧ **1** to ignore or disregard **2** to fail to attend to properly **3** to leave undone —*n.* **1** a neglecting **2** lack of proper care **3** the state of being neglected —**ne·glect′ful** *adj.*

**neg·li·gee** (neg′lə zhā′) *n.* ⟦< Fr *négliger*, to neglect⟧ a woman's loosely fitting dressing gown

**neg·li·gent** (neg′lə jənt) *adj.* **1** habitually failing to do the required thing; neglectful **2** careless, inattentive, etc. —**neg′li·gence** *n.*

**neg′li·gi·ble** (-jə bəl) *adj.* that can be neglected or disregarded; trifling

**ne·go·ti·ate** (ni gō′shē āt′) *vi.* -**at′ed**, -**at′ing** ⟦< L *negotium*, business⟧ to discuss a matter with a view to reaching agreement —*vt.* **1** to settle (a business transaction, treaty, etc.) **2** to transfer or sell (bonds, stocks, etc.) **3** to succeed in crossing, passing, etc. —**ne·go′ti·a·ble** (-shē ə bəl, -shə bəl) *adj.* —**ne·go′ti·a′tion** *n.* —**ne·go′ti·a′tor** *n.*

**neg·ri·tude** (neg′rə tōōd′, nē′grə-) *n.* ⟦Fr *négritude*⟧ [*also* **N-**] an awareness and affirmation by black people of their distinctive cultural heritage

**Ne·gro** (nē′grō) *n.*, *pl.* -**groes** ⟦Sp & Port *negro*, black⟧ **1** a member of any of the indigenous dark-skinned peoples of Africa **2** a person having some African ancestors; a black person —*adj.* of or for Negroes

**Ne′groid′** (-groid′) *adj.* designating or of one of the major groups of human beings, including most of the peoples of Africa

**Neh·ru** (nā′rōō), **Ja·wa·har·lal** (jə wä′hər läl′) 1889-1964; prime minister of India (1947-64)

**neigh** (nā) *vi.* ⟦OE *hnægan*⟧ to utter the characteristic cry of a horse —*n.* this cry; a whinny

**neigh·bor** (nā′bər) *n.* ⟦OE *neah*, nigh + *gebur*, freeholder⟧ **1** one who lives or is situated near another **2** a fellow human being —*vt.*, *vi.* to live or be situated near (someone or something) Brit. sp. **neigh′bour** —**neigh′bor·ing** *adj.*

**neigh′bor·hood′** *n.* **1** a particular community, district, or area **2** the people living near one another —**in the neighborhood of** [Inf.] **1** near **2** about; approximately

**neigh′bor·ly** *adj.* like or appropriate to neighbors; friendly, helpful, etc. —**neigh′bor·li·ness** *n.*

**nei·ther** (nē′thər, nī′-) *adj.*, *pron.* ⟦OE *nahwæther*, lit., not whether⟧ not one or the other (of two); not either [*neither* boy went; *neither* of them was invited] —*conj.* not either [I could *neither* laugh nor cry]

**nem·a·tode** (nem′ə tōd′) *n.* ⟦ult. < Gr *nēma*, thread⟧ a long, cylindrical, unsegmented worm; roundworm

**nem·e·sis** (nem′ə sis) *n.*, *pl.* -**ses′** (-sēz′) ⟦< Gr *nemein*, deal out⟧ **1** a) just punishment b) one who imposes this **2** anyone or anything that seems inevitably to defeat or frustrate someone

**neo-** ⟦< Gr *neos*⟧ *combining form* [*often* **N-**] **1** new, recent **2** in a new or different way

**ne·o·clas·sic** (nē′ō klas′ik) *adj.* designating or of a revival of classic style and form in art, literature, etc.: also **ne′o·clas′si·cal** —**ne′o·clas′si·cism′** *n.*

**ne′o·co·lo′ni·al·ism′** *n.* exploitation by a foreign power of a region that has ostensibly achieved independence

**ne·ol·o·gism** (nē äl′ə jiz′əm) *n.* ⟦see NEO-, -LOGY, & -ISM⟧ a new word or a new meaning for an established word

**ne·on** (nē′än′) *n.* ⟦ult. < Gr *neos*, new⟧ a nonreac-

tive, gaseous chemical element found in small amounts in the earth's atmosphere

**ne·o·nate** (nē′ō nāt′) *n.* ⟦ModL < *neo-*, NEO- + L *natus*, born⟧ a newborn infant —**ne′o·na′tal** *adj.*

**neon lamp** a tube containing neon, which glows red when an electric current is sent through it

**ne·o·phyte** (nē′ō fīt′) *n.* ⟦< Gr *neos*, new + *phyein*, to produce⟧ **1** a new convert **2** a beginner; novice

**ne·o·plasm** (nē′ō plaz′əm) *n.* ⟦< NEO- + Gr *plassein*, to form⟧ an abnormal growth of tissue, as a tumor

**ne′o·prene′** (-prēn′) *n.* a synthetic rubber resistant to oil, heat, etc.

**Ne·pal** (nə pôl′, -päl′) country in the Himalayas: 56,827 sq. mi.; pop. 18,462,000 —**Nep·a·lese** (nep′ə lēz′) *adj.*, *n.*

**neph·ew** (nef′yōō) *n.* ⟦< L *nepos*⟧ the son of one's brother or sister, or of one's brother-in-law or sister-in-law

**ne·phri·tis** (nə frīt′əs) *n.* ⟦< Gr *nephros*, kidney + -ITIS⟧ a disease of the kidneys, characterized by inflammation

**ne·phro·sis** (nə frō′sis) *n.* ⟦< Gr *nephros*, kidney + -OSIS⟧ a degenerative disease of the kidneys, characterized by edema

**ne plus ul·tra** (nā plus ul′trə) ⟦L, no more beyond⟧ the ultimate

**nep·o·tism** (nep′ə tiz′əm) *n.* ⟦< L *nepos*, nephew⟧ favoritism shown to relatives, esp. in providing jobs —**nep′o·tis′tic** *adj.*

**Nep·tune** (nep′tōōn′) *n.* **1** the Roman god of the sea **2** the planet eighth in distance from the sun: see PLANET

**nep·tu·ni·um** (nep tōō′nē əm) *n.* ⟦after prec.⟧ a radioactive chemical element produced by irradiating uranium atoms

**nerd** (nurd) *n.* [Slang] a person regarded as dull, ineffective, etc. —**nerd′y** *adj.*

**Ne·ro** (nir′ō) A.D. 37-68; emperor of Rome (54-68)

**nerve** (nurv) *n.* ⟦< L *nervus*⟧ **1** any of the cordlike fibers carrying impulses between body organs and the central nervous system **2** coolness in danger; courage **3** [*pl.*] nervousness **4** [Inf.] impudent boldness —*vt.* **nerved**, **nerv′ing** to give strength or courage to —**get on someone's nerves** [Inf.] to make someone irritable or exasperated

**nerve center** a control center; headquarters

**nerve gas** a poisonous gas causing paralysis of the respiratory and nervous systems

**nerve′less** *adj.* **1** without strength, vigor, etc.; weak **2** not nervous; cool; controlled —**nerve′less·ly** *adv.*

**nerve′-rack′ing** or **nerve′-wrack′ing** (-rak′iŋ) *adj.* very trying to one's patience or equanimity

**nerv·ous** (nur′vəs) *adj.* **1** animated **2** of or made up of nerves **3** emotionally tense, restless, etc. **4** fearful —**nerv′ous·ly** *adv.* —**nerv′ous·ness** *n.*

**nervous system** all the nerve cells and nervous tissues in an organism, including, in the vertebrates, the brain, spinal cord, nerves, etc.

**nerv′y** *adj.* -**i·er**, -**i·est** **1** bold **2** [Inf.] brazen; impudent

**-ness** (nis, nəs) ⟦OE -*nes(s)*⟧ *suffix* state, quality, or instance of being [*togetherness*, *sadness*]

**nest** (nest) *n.* ⟦OE⟧ **1** the structure or place where a bird lays its eggs and shelters its young **2** the place used by insects, fish, etc. for spawning or breeding **3** a cozy place; retreat **4** a) a haunt or den b) the people who frequent such a place [a *nest* of thieves] **5** a set of things, each fitting within the one next larger —*vi.*, *vt.* **1** to build or settle in (a nest) **2** to fit (an object) closely within another

**nest egg** money, etc. put aside as a reserve or to establish a fund

**nes·tle** (nes′əl) *vi.* -**tled**, -**tling** ⟦OE *nestlian*⟧ **1** to settle down comfortably **2** to press close for comfort or in affection **3** to lie sheltered —*vt.* to cause to rest snugly

**nest·ling** (nest′liŋ) *n.* a young bird not yet ready to leave the nest

**net**¹ (net) *n.* ⟦OE *nett*⟧ **1** a loose fabric of woven or knotted string, etc., used to snare birds, fish, etc. **2** a trap; snare **3** a loose fabric of woven or knotted threads, etc., esp. one used to hold, protect, etc. [*a hairnet*] **4** [*usually* N-] [Inf.] *Comput. short for* INTERNET: with *the* —*vt.* **net'ted, net'ting** to snare or enclose, as with a net

**net**² (net) *adj.* ⟦Fr, clear⟧ remaining after deductions or allowances have been made —*n.* a net amount, profit, weight, price, etc. —*vt.* **net'ted, net'ting** to clear as profit, etc.

**neth·er** (neth'ər) *adj.* ⟦OE *neothera*⟧ lower or under [the *nether* world]

**Neth·er·lands** (neth'ər ləndz) country in W Europe: 16,033 sq. mi.; pop. 15,340,000: usually used with *the* —**Neth'er·land'er** (-land'ər, -lən dər) *n.*

**neth'er·most'** *adj.* lowest

**net'ting** *n.* NET¹ (*n.* 1 & 3)

**net·tle** (net''l) *n.* ⟦OE *netele*⟧ a weed with stinging hairs —*vt.* **-tled, -tling** to irritate; annoy; vex

**net'tle·some** (-səm) *adj.* that nettles, or irritates

**net'work'** *n.* **1** an arrangement of parallel wires, etc. crossed at intervals by others so as to leave open spaces **2** anything like this, as a system of interconnected roads, individuals, or computer terminals **3** *Radio, TV* a chain of transmitting stations —*adj.* broadcast over the stations of a network

**net'work'ing** *n.* **1** the developing of contacts or exchanging of information, as to further a career **2** the interconnection of computer systems

**neu·ral** (noor'əl) *adj.* ⟦NEUR(O)- + -AL⟧ of a nerve, nerves, or the nervous system

**neu·ral·gi·a** (noo ral'jə) *n.* ⟦see NEURO- & -ALGIA⟧ severe pain along a nerve —**neu·ral'gic** (-jik) *adj.*

**neu·ras·the·ni·a** (noor'əs thē'nē ə) *n.* ⟦< NEURO- + Gr *asthenia*, weakness⟧ a former category of mental disorder, characterized by fatigue, anxiety, etc. —**neu·ras·then'ic** (-then'ik) *adj., n.*

**neu·ri·tis** (noo rīt'əs) *n.* ⟦fol. + -ITIS⟧ inflammation of a nerve or nerves —**neu·rit'ic** (-rit'ik) *adj.*

**neuro-** ⟦< Gr *neuron*, nerve⟧ *combining form* of a nerve or the nervous system: also **neur-**

**neu·rol·o·gy** (noo räl'ə jē) *n.* ⟦prec. + -LOGY⟧ the branch of medicine dealing with the nervous system and its diseases —**neu·ro·log·i·cal** (noor'ə läj'i kəl) *adj.* —**neu·rol'o·gist** *n.*

**neu·ron** (noor'än') *n.* the nerve cell body and all its processes

**neu·ro·sis** (noo rō'sis) *n., pl.* **-ses'** (-sēz') ⟦NEUR(O)- + -OSIS⟧ any of various mental disorders characterized by anxiety, compulsions, phobias, etc.

**neu·ro·sur·ger·y** (noor'ō sur'jər ē) *n.* the branch of surgery involving the brain or spinal cord — **neu'ro·sur'geon** *n.*

**neu·rot·ic** (noo rät'ik) *adj.* of, characteristic of, or having a neurosis —*n.* a neurotic person —**neu·rot'i·cal·ly** *adv.*

**neu·ro·trans·mit·ter** (noor'ō trans'mit'ər) *n.* a biochemical substance that transmits or inhibits nerve impulses at a synapse

**neu·ter** (noot'ər) *adj.* ⟦< L *ne-*, not + *uter*, either⟧ **1** *Biol. a)* having no sexual organ *b)* having undeveloped sexual organs in the adult **2** *Gram.* designating or of the gender of words that are neither masculine nor feminine —*vt.* to castrate or spay (an animal)

**neu·tral** (noo'trəl) *adj.* ⟦see prec.⟧ **1** supporting neither side in a quarrel or war **2** of neither extreme in type, kind, etc.; indefinite **3** having little or no decided color; not vivid —*n.* **1** a neutral person or nation **2** a neutral color **3** *Mech.* a disengaged position of gears —**neu'tral·ly** *adv.*

**neu·tral·ism'** (-iz'əm) *n.* a policy of remaining neutral, esp. in international conflicts —**neu'tral·ist** *adj., n.*

**neu·tral·i·ty** (-tral'ə tē) *n.* **1** a being neutral **2** the status or policy of a neutral nation

**neu·tral·ize** (noo'trə līz') *vt.* **-ized', -iz'ing** to destroy or counteract the effectiveness, force, etc. of —**neu'tral·i·za'tion** *n.* —**neu'tral·iz'er** *n.*

**neutral spirits** ethyl alcohol of 190 proof or over, used in blended whiskeys, liqueurs, etc.

**neu·tri·no** (noo trē'nō) *n., pl.* **-nos** ⟦It, little neutron⟧ any of three leptons having almost no mass

**neu·tron** (noo'trän') *n.* ⟦< NEUTRAL⟧ an elementary particle in the nucleus of an atom, carrying no electrical charge

**neutron bomb** a small thermonuclear bomb that would release large numbers of neutrons intended to kill enemy soldiers without destroying buildings, etc.

**neutron star** a collapsed star of extremely high density composed almost entirely of neutrons

**Ne·vad·a** (nə vad'ə, -väd'ə) Mountain State of the W U.S.: 109,806 sq. mi.; pop. 1,202,000; cap. Carson City: abbrev. *NV* —**Ne·vad'an** *adj., n.*

**nev·er** (nev'ər) *adv.* ⟦< OE *ne*, not + *æfre*, ever⟧ **1** not ever; at no time **2** not at all; in no case

**nev'er·more'** *adv.* never again

**nev'er-nev'er land** an unreal or unrealistic place or situation

**nev'er·the·less'** (-thə les') *adv.* in spite of that; however

**Ne·vis** (nē'vis, nev'is) island of the West Indies: see ST. KITTS AND NEVIS

**ne·vus** (nē'vəs) *n., pl.* **ne'vi'** (-vī') ⟦< L *naevus*⟧ a birthmark or mole

**new** (noo) *adj.* ⟦OE *niwe*⟧ **1** appearing, thought of, developed, made, etc. for the first time **2** different from (the) one in the past [a *new* hairdo] **3** strange; unfamiliar **4** *a)* recently grown; fresh *b)* harvested early [*new* potatoes] **5** unused **6** modern; recent **7** more; additional **8** starting as a repetition of a cycle, series, etc. [the *new* moon] **9** having just reached a position, rank, etc. [a *new* arrival] —*adv.* **1** again **2** recently —**new'ness** *n.*

**New Age** [*often* n- a-] of or pertaining to a cultural movement variously combining belief in reincarnation, astrology, meditation, etc.

**New·ark** (noo'ərk) city in NE New Jersey: pop. 275,000

**new blood** new people as a potential source of new ideas, vigor, etc.

**new'born'** *adj.* **1** recently born **2** reborn —*n.* a newborn infant

**New Bruns·wick** (brunz'wik) province of SE Canada: 28,354 sq. mi.; pop. 738,000; cap. Fredericton: abbrev. *NB*

**new'com'er** (-kum'ər) *n.* a recent arrival

**New Deal** the principles and policies adopted by President F. D. Roosevelt in the 1930s to advance economic recovery and social welfare

**New Delhi** capital of India, adjacent to the old city of Delhi: pop. 301,000

**new·el** (noo'əl) *n.* ⟦ult. < L *nux*, nut⟧ **1** the pillar around which the steps of a winding staircase turn **2** the post that supports the handrail of a flight of stairs: also **newel post**

**New England** the six NE states of the U.S.: Maine, Vermont, New Hampshire, Massachusetts, Rhode Island, and Connecticut —**New Eng'land·er**

**new'fan'gled** (-faŋ'gəld) *adj.* ⟦ME *newe*, new + *-fangel* < OE *fon*, to take⟧ new; novel: a humorously derogatory term

**new'found'** (-found') *adj.* newly gained or acquired

**New·found·land** (noo'fənd lənd, -land') province of Canada, including an island off the E coast & Labrador: 143,501 sq. mi.; pop. 552,000; cap. St. John's: abbrev. *NF*

**New Guinea** large island in the East Indies, north of Australia

**New Hamp·shire** (hamp'shir) New England state of the U.S.: 8,993 sq. mi.; pop. 1,109,000; cap. Concord: abbrev. *NH* —**New Hamp'shir·ite'**

**New Ha·ven** (hā′vən) city in S Connecticut: pop. 130,000

**New Jer·sey** (jur′zē) state of the E U.S.: 7,417 sq. mi.; pop. 7,730,000; cap. Trenton: abbrev. *NJ* — **New Jer′sey·ite′**

**new′ly** *adv.* recently; lately

**new′ly·wed′** *n.* a recently married person

**New Mexico** Mountain State of the SW U.S.: 121,335 sq. mi.; pop. 1,515,000; cap. Santa Fe: abbrev. *NM* —**New Mexican**

**new moon** the moon when it is between the earth and the sun, with its dark side toward the earth: it is followed by a thin crescent phase

**New Or·le·ans** (ôr′lē ənz, -lənz; ôr lēnz′) city & port in SE Louisiana: pop. 497,000

**New·port News** (nōō′pôrt′) seaport in SE Virginia: pop. 171,000

**news** (nōōz) *n.* **1** new information; information previously unknown **2** *a*) recent happenings *b*) reports of these **3** *short for* NEWSCAST —**make news** to do something apt to be reported as news

**news′boy′** *n.* a boy who sells or delivers newspapers

**news′cast′** *n.* a radio or television news broadcast —**news′cast′er** *n.*

**news′deal′er** *n.* a retailer of newspapers, magazines, etc.

**news′let′ter** *n.* a bulletin issued regularly to subscribers, employees, club members, etc., containing news of upcoming events, etc.

**news′man′** (-man′, -mən) *n.*, *pl.* **-men′** (-men′, -mən) a newscaster or reporter, esp. a male

**news′pa′per** *n.* a regular publication, usually daily or weekly, containing news, opinions, advertising, etc.

**news′pa′per·man′** (-man′) *n.*, *pl.* **-men′** (-men′) **1** a person, esp. a man, who works for a newspaper as a reporter, editor, etc. **2** a newspaper owner or publisher —**news′pa′per·wom′an**, *pl.* **-wom′en**, *fem.n.*

**news′print′** *n.* a cheap, low-grade paper used chiefly for newspapers

**news′stand′** *n.* a stand at which newspapers, magazines, etc. are sold

**news′wom′an** *n.*, *pl.* **-wom′en** a female newscaster or reporter

**news′wor′thy** (-wur′*th*ē) *adj.* timely and important or interesting

**news′y** *adj.* **-i·er**, **-i·est** [Inf.] containing much news

**newt** (nōōt) *n.* [by merging of ME (a)n eute, a newt] any of various small, amphibious salamanders

**New Testament** the part of the Bible that contains the life and teachings of Jesus and his followers

**new·ton** (nōōt′'n) *n.* [after fol.] a unit of force

**New·ton** (nōōt′'n), Sir **Isaac** 1642-1727; Eng. mathematician & natural philosopher

**New World** the Western Hemisphere

**New Year's** (**Day**) Jan. 1

**New Year's Eve** the evening before New Year's Day

**New York** (yôrk) **1** state of the NE U.S.: 47,224 sq. mi.; pop. 17,990,000; cap. Albany: abbrev. *NY* **2** city & port in SE New York: pop. 7,323,000 (met. area, 8,547,000): often **New York City** — **New York′er**

**New Zea·land** (zē′lənd) country made up of two large islands in the S Pacific, southeast of Australia: 104,454 sq. mi.; pop. 3,435,000 —**New Zea′land·er**

**next** (nekst) *adj.* [OE neahst, superl. of neah, nigh] nearest; immediately preceding or following —*adv.* **1** in the nearest time, place, rank, etc. **2** on the first subsequent occasion

**next′-door′** *adj.* in or at the next house, building, etc.

**nex·us** (nek′səs) *n.*, *pl.* **nex′us·es** or **nex′us** [L] a connection, tie, or link

**NF** Newfoundland

**NH** New Hampshire

**Ni** *Chem. symbol for* nickel

**ni·a·cin** (nī′ə sin) *n.* [NI(COTINIC) AC(ID) + -*in*] NICOTINIC ACID

**Ni·ag·ara Falls** (nī ag′rə) large waterfall on a river (**Niagara**) flowing from Lake Erie into Lake Ontario

**nib** (nib) *n.* [< ME nebb, a bird's beak] a point, esp. a pen point

**nib·ble** (nib′əl) *vt.*, *vi.* **-bled**, **-bling** [ME nebyllen] **1** to eat (food) with quick, small bites **2** to bite (*at*) lightly and intermittently —*n.* a small bite — **nib′bler** *n.*

**nibs** (nibz) *n.* [< ?] [Inf.] a self-important person: preceded by *his* or *her*

**Nic·a·ra·gua** (nik′ə rä′gwə) country in Central America: 50,452 sq. mi.; pop. 4,395,000 —**Nic′a·ra′guan** *adj.*, *n.*

**nice** (nīs) *adj.* **nic′er**, **nic′est** [< L nescius, ignorant] **1** fastidious; refined **2** delicate; precise; subtle [a nice distinction] **3** calling for care, tact, etc. **4** pleasant, attractive, kind, good, etc.: a generalized term of approval —**nice′ly** *adv.* — **nice′ness** *n.*

**ni·ce·ty** (nī′sə tē) *n.*, *pl.* **-ties** **1** precision; accuracy **2** fastidiousness; refinement **3** a subtle or minute detail, distinction, etc.

**niche** (nich) *n.* [Fr < L nidus, a nest] **1** a recess in a wall, for a statue, vase, etc. **2** an especially suitable place or position **3** a specialized business market

**nicht wahr?** (niHt vär′) [Ger, not true?] isn't that so?

**nick** (nik) *n.* [ME nyke] a small cut, chip, etc. made on a surface —*vt.* **1** to make a nick or nicks in **2** to wound superficially —**in the nick of time** exactly when needed

NICHE

**nick·el** (nik′əl) *n.* [< Ger kupfernickel, copper devil: the copperlike ore contains no copper] **1** a hard, silver-white, metallic chemical element, much used in alloys **2** a U.S. or Canadian coin of nickel and copper, equal to five cents

**nick·el·o·de·on** (nik′əl ō′dē ən) *n.* [prec. + (mel)odeon, a small keyboard organ] a coin-operated player piano or early type of jukebox

**nick·er** (nik′ər) *vi.*, *n.* NEIGH

**nick·name** (nik′nām′) *n.* [by merging of ME (a)n ekename, a surname] **1** a substitute, often descriptive, name given in fun, etc., as "Shorty" **2** a familiar form of a proper name, as "Dick" for "Richard" —*vt.* **-named′**, **-nam′ing** to give a nickname to

**nic·o·tine** (nik′ə tēn′) *n.* [Fr, after J. Nicot, 16th-c. Fr diplomat who introduced tobacco into France] a toxic alkaloid found in tobacco leaves

**nic′o·tin′ic acid** (-tin′ik) a white, crystalline substance, a member of the vitamin B complex

**niece** (nēs) *n.* [< L neptis] the daughter of one's brother or sister or of one's brother-in-law or sister-in-law

**Nie·tzsche** (nē′chə), **Fried·rich** (frē′driH) 1844-1900; Ger. philosopher

**nif·ty** (nif′tē) *adj.* **-ti·er**, **-ti·est** [prob. < magnificent] [Slang] attractive, smart, stylish, etc.

**Ni·ger** (nī′jər) country in WC Africa, north of Nigeria: 489,191 sq. mi.; pop. 7,250,000

**Ni·ger·i·a** (nī jir′ē ə) country on the W coast of Africa: 356,669 sq. mi.; pop. 88,515,000 —**Ni·ger′i·an** *adj.*, *n.*

**nig·gard** (nig′ərd) *n.* ⟦prob. < Scand⟧ a stingy person; miser **—nig′gard·ly** *adj., adv.* **—nig′gard·li-ness** *n.*

**nig·gle** (nig′əl) *vi.* **-gled, -gling** ⟦prob. akin to Norw *niggla*⟧ to be finicky **—nig′gler** *n.* **—nig′gling** *adj., n.*

**nigh** (nī) *adv., adj., prep.* ⟦OE *neah*⟧ [Now Chiefly Dial.] NEAR

**night** (nīt) *n.* ⟦OE *niht*⟧ **1** the period of darkness from sunset to sunrise **2** any period or condition of darkness or gloom

**night blindness** imperfect vision in the dark or in dim light

**night′cap′** *n.* **1** a cap worn to bed, esp. formerly **2** [Inf.] an alcoholic drink taken just before going to bed

**night′clothes′** *n.* clothes to be worn in bed, as pajamas

**night′club′** *n.* a place of entertainment for eating, drinking, dancing, etc. at night

**night crawl′er** a large earthworm that comes to the surface at night

**night′fall′** *n.* the time in the evening when daylight is last visible; dusk

**night′gown′** *n.* a loose gown worn in bed by women or girls

**night′hawk′** *n.* **1** any of various usually nocturnal birds that feed on insects **2** NIGHT OWL

**night′ie** (-ē) *n.* [Inf.] NIGHTGOWN

**night·in·gale** (nīt′′n gāl′) *n.* ⟦< OE *niht*, night + *galan*, sing⟧ a small European thrush: the male sings melodiously, esp. at night

**Night·in·gale** (nīt′′n gāl′), **Florence** 1820-1910; Eng. nurse: regarded as the founder of modern nursing

**night life** pleasure-seeking activity at night, as in nightclubs

**night′ly** *adj.* done or occurring every night **—adv.** night after night; every night

**night′mare′** (-mer′) *n.* ⟦ME < *niht*, night + *mare*, demon⟧ **1** a frightening dream **2** any frightening experience **—night′mar′ish** *adj.*

**night owl** a person who works at night or otherwise stays up late

**night′shade′** *n.* **1** a chiefly tropical plant with five-lobed leaves and flowers of various colors **2** BELLADONNA

**night′shirt′** *n.* a loose garment like a long shirt, worn in bed

**night′spot′** *n. inf. var. of* NIGHTCLUB

**night stand** a small bedside table

**night′stick′** *n.* a policeman's club; billy

**night′time′** *n.* the time between dusk and dawn

**night′wear′** *n.* NIGHTCLOTHES

**NIH** *abbrev.* National Institutes of Health

**ni·hil·ism** (nī′ə liz′əm, nē′-) *n.* ⟦< L *nihil*, nothing⟧ the general rejection of customary beliefs in morality, religion, etc. **—ni′hil·ist** *n.* **—ni′hil·is′tic** *adj.*

**Ni·hon** (nē′hôn) *Jpn. name for* JAPAN

**nil** (nil) *n.* ⟦L, contr. of *nihil*⟧ nothing

**Nile** (nīl) river in NE Africa, flowing through Egypt into the Mediterranean

**nim·ble** (nim′bəl) *adj.* **-bler, -blest** ⟦< OE *niman*, to take⟧ **1** quick-witted; alert **2** moving quickly and lightly **—nim′bly** *adv.*

**nim·bus** (nim′bəs) *n., pl.* **-bi′** (-bī′) or **-bus·es** ⟦L⟧ **1** any rain-producing cloud **2** a halo around the head of a saint, etc., as in a painting

**Nim·rod** (nim′räd′) *n. Bible* a mighty hunter

**nin·com·poop** (nin′kəm pōōp′) *n.* ⟦< ?⟧ a stupid, silly person; fool

**nine** (nīn) *adj., n.* ⟦OE *nigon*⟧ one more than eight; 9; IX **—ninth** (nīnth) *adj., n.*

**nine′pins′** *n.* British version of the game of tenpins, played with nine pins

**nine′teen′** *adj., n.* nine more than ten; 19; XIX **— nine′teenth′** (-tēnth′) *adj., n.*

**nine·ty** (nīn′tē) *adj., n., pl.* **-ties** nine times ten; 90; XC (or LXXXX) **—the nineties** the numbers or

---

years, as of a century, from 90 through 99 — **nine′ti·eth** (-ith) *adj., n.*

**nin·ny** (nin′ē) *n., pl.* **-nies** ⟦< (*a*)*n inn*(*ocent*)⟧ a fool; dolt

**nip**[1] (nip) *vt.* **nipped, nip′ping** ⟦prob. < earlier LowG *nippen*⟧ **1** to pinch or bite **2** to sever (shoots, etc.) by clipping **3** to check the growth of **4** to have a painful or injurious effect on because of cold **—n.** **1** a nipping; pinch; bite **2** a stinging, as in cold air **3** stinging cold; frost **—nip and tuck** so close as to leave the outcome in doubt

**nip**[2] (nip) *n.* ⟦prob. < Du *nippen*, to sip⟧ a small drink of liquor **—vt., vi.** **nipped, nip′ping** to drink in nips

**nip·per** (nip′ər) *n.* **1** anything that nips **2** [*pl.*] pliers, pincers, etc. **3** the claw of a crab or lobster

**nip·ple** (nip′əl) *n.* ⟦prob. < earlier *neb*, a beak⟧ **1** the small protuberance on a breast or udder through which, in the female, the milk passes; teat **2** the teatlike part in the cap of a baby's bottle

**Nip·pon** (nip′än′, ni pän′) *var. of* NIHON

**Nip·pon·ese** (nip′ə nēz′) *adj., n., pl.* **-ese′** JAPANESE

**nip·py** (nip′ē) *adj.* **-pi·er, -pi·est** bitingly cold

**nir·va·na** (nir vä′nə) *n.* ⟦< Sans⟧ [*also* N-] **1** *Buddhism* the state of perfect blessedness **2** a place or condition of great bliss

**ni·sei** (nē′sā′) *n., pl.* **-sei′** or **-seis′** ⟦Jpn, second generation⟧ [*also* N-] a native U.S. or Canadian citizen born of immigrant Japanese parents

**nit** (nit) *n.* ⟦OE *hnitu*⟧ **1** the egg of a louse or similar insect **2** a young louse, etc.

**nite** (nīt) *n. inf. sp. of* NIGHT

**ni·ter** (nīt′ər) *n.* ⟦< Gr *nitron*⟧ potassium nitrate or sodium nitrate, used in making explosives, fertilizers, etc.; saltpeter: also [Chiefly Brit.] **ni′tre**

**nit-pick·ing** (nit′pik′iŋ) *adj., n.* stressing petty details; niggling **—nit′-pick′er** *n.*

**ni·trate** (nī′trāt′) *n.* a salt of nitric acid, as sodium nitrate **—vt.** **-trat·ed, -trat·ing** to combine with nitric acid or, esp., to make into a nitrate

**ni·tric acid** (nī′trik) a colorless, corrosive acid containing nitrogen

**ni·tro·cel·lu·lose** (nī′trō sel′yōō lōs′) *n.* a substance obtained by treating cellulose with nitric acid, used in making explosives, lacquers, etc.

**ni·tro·gen** (nī′trə jən) *n.* ⟦< Fr: see NITER & -GEN⟧ a colorless, odorless, gaseous chemical element forming nearly four fifths of the atmosphere **—ni·trog′e·nous** (-träj′ə nəs) *adj.*

**ni·tro·glyc·er·in** or **ni·tro·glyc·er·ine** (nī′trō glis′ər in) *n.* a thick, explosive oil prepared by treating glycerin with nitric and sulfuric acids: used in making dynamite

**ni·trous oxide** (nī′trəs) a colorless gas containing nitrogen, used as an anesthetic and in aerosols

**nit·ty-grit·ty** (nit′ē grit′ē) *n.* [Slang] the actual, basic facts, issues, etc.

**nit′wit′** *n.* ⟦? NIT + WIT[1]⟧ a stupid or silly person

**nix** (niks) [Slang] *adv.* **1** no **2** not at all **—interj.** **1** stop! **2** I forbid, disagree, etc. **—vt.** to disapprove of or put a stop to

**Nix·on** (nik′sən), **Richard M**(**ilhous**) 1913-94; 37th president of the U.S. (1969-74): resigned

**Nizh·ny Nov·go·rod** (nēzh′nē nôv′gə rət) city in central European Russia: pop. 1,438,000

**NJ** New Jersey

**NM** New Mexico

**no**[1] (nō) *adv.* ⟦< OE *ne a*, not ever⟧ **1** not at all [*no* worse] **2** nay; not so: used to deny, refuse, or disagree **—adj.** not any; not one [*no* errors] **—n.**, *pl.* **noes** or **nos** **1** a refusal or denial **2** a negative vote or voter

**no**[2] *abbrev.* ⟦L *numero*⟧ number

**No·ah** (nō′ə) *n. Bible* the patriarch commanded by God to build the ARK (sense 3)

**No·bel prizes** (nō bel′) ⟦after A. B. *Nobel*, 19th-c. Swed inventor who established them⟧ annual international prizes given for distinction in physics, chemistry, economics, medicine, and literature, and for promoting peace

**no·bil·i·ty** (nō bil′ə tē) *n.*, *pl.* **-ties** **1** a being noble **2** high rank in society **3** the class of people of noble rank

**no·ble** (nō′bəl) *adj.* **-bler, -blest** ⟦< L *nobilis*, well-known⟧ **1** having high moral qualities **2** excellent **3** grand; stately **4** of high hereditary rank —*n.* one having hereditary rank or title —**no′ble·ness** *n.* —**no·bly** (nō′blē) *adv.*

**no·ble·man** (-mən) *n.*, *pl.* **-men** (-mən) a member of the nobility; peer

**no·blesse o·blige** (nō bles′ ō blēzh′) ⟦Fr, nobility obliges⟧ the inferred obligation of people of high rank to behave nobly toward others

**no·bod·y** (nō′bäd′ē, -bud′ē, -bə dē) *pron.* not anybody; no one —*n.*, *pl.* **-ies** a person of no importance

**no-brain·er** (nō′brān′ər) *n.* something so obvious, simple, etc. as to require little thought

**noc·tur·nal** (näk tʉr′nəl) *adj.* ⟦< L *nox*, night⟧ **1** of the night **2** functioning, done, or active during the night —**noc·tur′nal·ly** *adv.*

**noc·turne** (näk′tʉrn′) *n.* ⟦Fr⟧ a romantic or dreamy musical composition thought appropriate to night

**nod** (näd) *vi.* **nod′ded, nod′ding** ⟦ME *nodden*⟧ **1** to bend the head forward quickly, as in agreement, greeting, etc. **2** to let the head fall forward because of drowsiness —*vt.* **1** to bend (the head) forward quickly **2** to signify (assent, etc.) by doing this —*n.* a nodding

**node** (nōd) *n.* ⟦L *nodus*⟧ **1** a knot; knob; swelling **2** that part of a stem from which a leaf starts to grow —**nod·al** (nōd″l) *adj.*

**nod·ule** (näj′o̅o̅l′) *n.* ⟦L *nodulus*⟧ a small knot or rounded lump

**No·el** or **No·ël** (nō el′) *n.* ⟦Fr < L *natalis*, natal⟧ CHRISTMAS

**no′-fault** *adj.* **1** designating a form of automobile insurance in which those injured collect damages without blame being fixed **2** designating a form of divorce granted without blame being charged

**nog·gin** (näg′in) *n.* ⟦prob. < Brit dial. *nog*, strong ale⟧ **1** a small cup or mug **2** [Inf.] the head

**no′-good′** *adj.* [Slang] contemptible

**noir** (nwär) *n.* ⟦Fr, black⟧ a film, novel, etc. pessimistic or cynical in mood and often dealing with urban crime —**noir′ish** *adj.*

**noise** (noiz) *n.* ⟦< OFr⟧ **1** din of voices; clamor **2** any sound; specif., a loud, disagreeable sound —*vt.* **noised, nois′ing** to spread (a report, rumor, etc.) *about, around,* etc.

**noise′less** *adj.* with little or no noise; very quiet —**noise′less·ly** *adv.*

**noi·some** (noi′səm) *adj.* ⟦see ANNOY & -SOME¹⟧ **1** injurious to health; harmful **2** foul-smelling

**nois·y** (noiz′ē) *adj.* **-i·er, -i·est** **1** making noise **2** full of noise —**nois′i·ly** *adv.* —**nois′i·ness** *n.*

**no-load** (nō′lōd′) *adj.* designating mutual funds charging no commissions on sales

**no·mad** (nō′mad′) *n.* ⟦< Gr *nemein*, to pasture⟧ **1** any of a people having no permanent home, but moving about constantly, as in search of pasture **2** a wanderer —**no·mad′ic** *adj.*

**no man's land** the unoccupied region separating opposing armies

**nom de plume** (näm′ də plo̅o̅m′) ⟦Fr⟧ a pen name

**Nome** (nōm) city in W Alaska: pop. 3,500

**no·men·cla·ture** (nō′mən klā′chər) *n.* ⟦< L *nomen*, a name + *calare*, to call⟧ the system of names used in a science, etc. or for the parts of a device

**-nom·ics** (näm′iks) *combining form* economics: also **-om′ics**

**nom·i·nal** (näm′ə nəl) *adj.* ⟦< L *nomen*, a name⟧

**1** in name only, not in fact [a *nominal* leader] **2** relatively very small —**nom′i·nal·ly** *adv.*

**nom′i·nate′** (-nāt′) *vt.* **-nat′ed, -nat′ing** ⟦< L *nomen*, a name⟧ **1** to appoint to an office or position **2** to name as a candidate for election —**nom′i·na′tion** *n.*

**nom′i·na·tive** (-nə tiv) *n. Gram.* the case of the subject of a verb

**nom′i·nee′** (-ə nē′) *n.* a person who is nominated

**non-** ⟦< L *non*, not⟧ *prefix* not: less emphatic than IN-² and UN-, which often give a word a strong opposite or reverse meaning: the terms in the following list will be understood if "not" is used before the meaning of the base word

| | |
|---|---|
| nonabrasive | nonfading |
| nonabsorbent | nonfat |
| nonactive | nonfatal |
| nonaddictive | nonfiction |
| nonadministrative | nonfictional |
| nonaggression | nonflammable |
| nonaggressive | nonflowering |
| nonalcoholic | nonfluctuating |
| nonallergenic | nonflying |
| nonallergic | nonfreezing |
| nonassignable | nonfunctional |
| nonathletic | nongovernmental |
| nonattendance | nongranular |
| nonautomotive | nonhazardous |
| nonavailability | nonhereditary |
| nonbasic | nonhuman |
| nonbeliever | nonidentical |
| nonbelligerent | noninclusive |
| nonbreakable | nonindependent |
| nonburnable | nonindustrial |
| non-Catholic | noninfected |
| nonchargeable | noninflammatory |
| nonclerical | noninflationary |
| nonclinical | nonintellectual |
| noncollectable | noninterference |
| noncombustible | nonintoxicating |
| noncommercial | nonirritating |
| noncommunicable | nonjudicial |
| non-Communist | nonlegal |
| noncompeting | nonliterary |
| noncompetitive | nonmagnetic |
| noncompliance | nonmalignant |
| noncomplying | nonmember |
| nonconducting | nonmigratory |
| nonconforming | nonmilitant |
| nonconsecutive | nonmilitary |
| nonconstructive | nonnarcotic |
| noncontagious | nonnegotiable |
| noncontributory | nonnumerical |
| noncontroversial | nonobjective |
| nonconvertible | nonobligatory |
| noncorroding | nonobservance |
| noncorrosive | nonobservant |
| noncriminal | nonoccupational |
| noncritical | nonoccurrence |
| noncrystalline | nonofficial |
| noncumulative | nonoperational |
| nondeductible | nonoperative |
| nondelivery | nonpaying |
| nondepartmental | nonpayment |
| nondepreciating | nonperishable |
| nondestructive | nonphysical |
| nondetachable | nonpoisonous |
| nondisciplinary | nonpolitical |
| nondiscrimination | nonporous |
| nondramatic | nonprejudicial |
| nondrinker | nonprescriptive |
| nondrying | nonproductive |
| noneducational | nonprofessional |
| noneffective | nonprofitable |
| nonenforceable | nonpunishable |
| non-English | nonracial |
| nonessential | nonreactive |
| nonexchangeable | nonreciprocal |
| nonexclusive | nonreciprocating |
| nonexempt | nonrecoverable |
| nonexistence | nonrecurring |
| nonexistent | nonredeemable |
| nonexplosive | nonrefillable |
| nonfactual | nonreligious |

nonrenewable
nonrepresentational
nonresidential
nonresidual
nonresistant
nonreturnable
nonrhythmic
nonrigid
nonsalaried
nonscientific
nonscoring
nonseasonal
nonsecular
nonsensitive
nonsmoker
nonsocial
nonspeaking
nonspecializing
nonspiritual
nonstaining
nonstandard
nonsticking
nonstrategic
nonstriking

nonstructural
nonsuccessive
nonsupporting
nonsustaining
nonsympathizer
nontaxable
nontechnical
nontheatrical
nonthinking
nontoxic
nontransferable
nontransparent
nontropical
nonuniform
nonuser
nonvenomous
nonverbal
nonvirulent
nonvocal
nonvocational
nonvoter
nonvoting
nonwhite
nonyielding

**non·age** (nän′ij, nō′nij) *n.* ⟦see prec. & AGE⟧ the state of being under full legal age.

**non·a·ge·nar·i·an** (nän′ə jə ner′ē ən) *n.* ⟦< L *nonaginta*, ninety⟧ a person between the ages of 90 and 100

**non′a·ligned′** (-ə līnd′) *adj.* not aligned with either side in a conflict —**non′a·lign′ment** *n.*

**no′-name′** *adj.* not famous or distinguished

**non′bind′ing** (-bīn′diŋ) *adj.* not holding one to an obligation, promise, etc.

**non′-book′** *n.* a book produced cheaply and quickly, often in response to a current fad, etc.

**nonce** (näns) *n.* ⟦by merging of ME (*for then*) *ones*, lit., (for the) once⟧ the present use, occasion, or time: chiefly in **for the nonce**

**nonce word** a word coined and used for a single occasion

**non·cha·lant** (nän′shə länt′) *adj.* ⟦Fr, ult. < L *non*, not + *calere*, be warm⟧ casually indifferent —**non′cha·lance′** (-läns′) *n.*

**non·com** (nän′käm′) *n.* [Inf.] *short for* NONCOMMISSIONED OFFICER

**non·com·bat·ant** (nän′käm·bat′′nt) *n.* **1** a member of the armed forces not engaged in actual combat **2** any civilian in wartime

**non′com·mis′sioned officer** (-kə mish′ənd) an enlisted person of any of various grades in the armed forces: in the U.S. Army, from corporal to sergeant major inclusive

**non′com·mit′tal** (-kə mit′l) *adj.* not committing one to a definite point of view or course of action

**non com·pos men·tis** (nän′ käm′pəs men′tis) ⟦L⟧ *Law* not of sound mind

**non·con·duc·tor** (-kən duk′tər) *n.* a substance that does not readily transmit sound, heat, or, esp., electricity

**non·con·form·ist** (-kən fôr′mist) *n.* **1** one who does not conform to prevailing beliefs and practices **2** [N-] a British Protestant who is not Anglican —**non′con·form′i·ty** *n.*

**non·cus·to·di·al** (-kəs tō′dē əl) *adj.* without custody, as of one's children after divorce

**non·dair·y** (nän′der′ē) *adj.* containing no milk or milk products

**non·de·script** (nän′di skript′) *adj.* ⟦< L *non*, not + *describere*, describe⟧ **1** belonging to no definite class or type; hard to classify or describe **2** not interesting; colorless

**none** (nun) *pron.* ⟦< OE *ne*, not + *an*, one⟧ **1** no one; not anyone **2** [*with pl. v.*] not any [there are *none* on the table] —*n.* not any (of); no part [I want *none* of it] —*adv.* not at all [*none* the worse for wear]

**non·en·ti·ty** (nän′en′tə tē) *n.*, *pl.* **-ties** a person or thing of little or no importance

**none·the·less** (nun′*th*ə les′) *adv.* nevertheless: also **none the less**

**non·e·vent** (nän′ē vent′) *n.* [Inf.] an event that is boring or deliberately staged, as for publicity

**non·fer·rous** (-fer′əs) *adj.* **1** not containing iron **2** designating or of metals other than iron

**non·in·ter·ven·tion** (-in′tər ven′shən) *n.* refusal to interfere; esp., a refusal by one nation to interfere in another's affairs

**non·in·va·sive** (-in vā′siv) *adj. Med.* not entering the skin or a body cavity

**non·judg·men·tal** (-juj ment′′l) *adj.* objective; tolerant

**non·met·al** (-met′′l) *n.* any chemical element, as oxygen, carbon, nitrogen, fluorine, etc., lacking the characteristics of a metal —**non′me·tal′lic** *adj.*

**no′-no′** *n.*, *pl.* **-nos′** [Slang] something forbidden or considered unwise to do, say, etc.

**no′-non′sense** *adj.* practical and serious

**non·pa·reil** (nän′pə rel′) *adj.* ⟦Fr < *non*, not + *pareil*, equal⟧ unequaled; unrivaled; peerless

**non·par′ti·san** (-pärt′ə zən) *adj.* not partisan; esp., not connected with any single political party

**non′per′son** (-pur′sən) *n.* a person officially ignored by the government

**non·plus** (nän plus′) *vt.* **-plused′** or **-plussed′**, **-plus′ing** or **-plus′sing** ⟦L *non*, not + *plus*, more⟧ to greatly perplex or bewilder

**non·prof′it** (-präf′it) *adj.* not established or done to earn a profit: said as of a charity

**non·res′i·dent** (-rez′ə dənt) *adj.* not residing in the locality where one works, attends school, etc. —*n.* a nonresident person

**non·re·stric′tive** (-ri strik′tiv) *adj. Gram.* designating a clause, phrase, or word felt as not essential to the sense, usually set off by commas (Ex.: John, *who is tall*, is Bill's brother)

**non·sched′uled** (-skej′oold) *adj.* licensed for commercial air flights as demand warrants rather than on a schedule

**non·sec·tar′i·an** (-sek ter′ē ən) *adj.* not confined to any specific religion

**non·sense** (nän′sens′) *n.* words, actions, etc. that are absurd or meaningless —*interj.* how absurd!: an exclamation —**non·sen′si·cal** (-sen′si kəl) *adj.*

**non se·qui·tur** (nän′ sek′wi tər) ⟦L, it does not follow⟧ **1** *Logic* a conclusion which does not follow from the premises **2** a remark having no bearing on what has just been said

**non′skid′** (-skid′) *adj.* having a surface made so as to reduce slipping or skidding

**non′-start′er** (-stärt′ər) *n.* [Slang] **1** an expected occurrence, project, etc. that fails to materialize **2** a worthless idea

**non′stop′** (-stäp′) *adj.*, *adv.* without a stop

**non′sup·port′** (-sə pôrt′) *n.* failure to provide for a legal dependent

**non·un′ion** (-yōōn′yən) *adj.* **1** not belonging to a labor union **2** not made or serviced by union workers

**non·vi′o·lence** (-vī′ə ləns) *n.* an abstaining from violence or the use of force, as in efforts to obtain civil rights —**non′vi′o·lent** *adj.*

**noo·dle**[1] (nōōd′′l) *n.* ⟦< ?⟧ [Slang] the head

**noo·dle**[2] (nōōd′′l) *n.* ⟦Ger *nudel*⟧ a flat, narrow strip of dry dough, usually made with egg and served in soup, etc.

**nook** (nook) *n.* ⟦ME *nok*⟧ **1** a corner or separate part of a room **2** a small, secluded spot

**noon** (nōōn) *n.* ⟦< L *nona* (*hora*), ninth (hour)⟧ twelve o'clock in the daytime; midday —*adj.* of or at noon Also **noon′time′** or **noon′day′**

**no one** not anyone; nobody

**noose** (nōōs) *n.* ⟦< L *nodus*, knot⟧ a loop in a rope, etc. formed by a slipknot so that the loop tightens as the rope is pulled

**nor** (nôr) *conj.* ⟦ME < *ne*-, not + *or*, other⟧ and not; and not either [I can neither go *nor* stay]

**Nor·dic** (nôr′dik) *adj.* ⟦OE *north*, north⟧ of a Caucasoid physical type exemplified by the tall, blond Scandinavians

**Nor·folk** (nôr′fək) seaport in SE Virginia: pop. 261,000

**norm** (nôrm) *n.* [L *norma*, rule] a standard or model for a group

**nor·mal** (nôr′məl) *adj.* 1 conforming with an accepted standard or norm; natural; usual 2 average in intelligence, etc. —*n.* 1 anything normal 2 the usual state, amount, etc. —**nor′mal·cy** (-sē) or **nor·mal′i·ty** (-mal′ə tē) *n.* —**nor′mal·ize′**, **-ized′**, **-iz′ing**, *vt.*, *vi.* —**nor′mal·i·za′tion** *n.*

**nor·mal·ly** *adv.* 1 in a normal manner 2 under normal circumstances

**Nor·man** (nôr′mən) *n.* [< OFr] 1 a member of the people of Normandy that conquered England in 1066 2 a person born or living in Normandy — *adj.* of Normandy or its people, etc.

**Nor·man·dy** (nôr′mən dē) historical region in NW France, on the English Channel

**norm·a·tive** (nôr′mə tiv) *adj.* of or establishing a norm

**Norse** (nôrs) *adj.*, *n.* [prob. < Du *noord*, north] 1 SCANDINAVIAN 2 (of) the Scandinavian group of languages

**Norse′man** (-mən) *n.*, *pl.* **-men** (-mən) a member of any of the medieval Scandinavian peoples

**north** (nôrth) *n.* [OE] 1 the direction to the right of one facing the sunset (0° or 360° on the compass) 2 a region in or toward this direction —*adj.* 1 in, of, toward, or facing the north 2 from the north [a *north* wind] —*adv.* in or toward the north —**the North** that part of the U.S. north of Maryland, the Ohio River, and Missouri

**North America** N continent in the Western Hemisphere: *c.* 9,400,000 sq. mi.; pop. *c.* 449,000,000 —**North American**

**North Car·o·li·na** (kar′ə lī′nə) state of the SE U.S.: 48,718 sq. mi.; pop. 6,629,000; cap. Raleigh: abbrev. *NC* —**North Car′o·lin′i·an** (-lin′ē ən)

**North Da·ko·ta** (də kōt′ə) Midwestern state of the U.S.: 68,994 sq. mi.; pop. 639,000; cap. Bismarck: abbrev. *ND* —**North Da·ko′tan**

**north′east′** *n.* 1 the direction halfway between north and east 2 a region in or toward this direction —*adj.* 1 in, of, or toward the northeast 2 from the northeast [a *northeast* wind] —*adv.* in or toward the northeast —**north′east′er·ly** *adj.*, *adv.* —**north′east′ern** *adj.* —**north′east′ward** *adj.*, *adv.* —**north′east′wards** *adv.*

**north·er·ly** (nôr*th*′ər lē) *adj.*, *adv.* 1 toward the north 2 from the north

**north·ern** (nôr′*th*ərn) *adj.* 1 in, of, or toward the north 2 from the north 3 [N-] of the North

**north′ern·er** *n.* a person born or living in the north

**Northern Hemisphere** the half of the earth north of the equator

**Northern Ireland** division of the United Kingdom, in the NE part of the island of Ireland: 5,467 sq. mi.; pop. 1,578,000

**northern lights** [*also* N- L-] the aurora borealis

**Northern Ma·ri·an·a Islands** (mer′ē an′ə) group of islands in the W Pacific: a commonwealth associated with the U.S.: land area *c.* 179 sq. mi.; pop. 43,000: also **Northern Marianas**

**North Pole** the northern end of the earth's axis

**North Sea** arm of the Atlantic, between Great Britain & the N European mainland

**North Star** POLARIS

**north′ward** *adv.*, *adj.* toward the north: also **north′wards** *adv.*

**north′west′** *n.* 1 the direction halfway between north and west 2 a region in or toward this direction —*adj.* 1 in, of, or toward the northwest 2 from the northwest [a *northwest* wind] —*adv.* in or toward the northwest —**north′west′er·ly** *adj.*, *adv.* —**north′west′ern** *adj.* —**north′west′ward** *adj.*, *adv.* —**north′west′wards** *adv.*

**Northwest Territories** division of N Canada: 552,909 sq. mi.; pop. 39,000; cap. Yellowknife: abbrev. *NT*

**North York** (yôrk) city in SE Ontario, Canada: part of metropolitan Toronto: pop. 590,000

**Norw** *abbrev.* 1 Norway 2 Norwegian

**Nor·way** (nôr′wā′) country in N Europe: 125,001 sq. mi.; pop. 4,248,000

**Nor·we·gian** (nôr wē′jən) *n.* 1 the language of Norway 2 a person born or living in Norway — *adj.* of Norway or its people, language, etc.

**nose** (nōz) *n.* [OE *nosu*] 1 the part of the face above the mouth, having two openings for breathing and smelling; in animals, the snout, muzzle, etc. 2 the sense of smell 3 anything like a nose in shape or position —*vt.* **nosed**, **nos′ing** 1 to nuzzle 2 to push (a way, etc.) with the front forward —*vi.* 1 to pry inquisitively 2 to move forward —**nose out** 1 to defeat by a very small margin 2 to discover, as by smelling —**on the nose** [Slang] precisely

**nose′bleed′** *n.* a bleeding from the nose

**nose cone** the cone-shaped foremost part of a rocket or missile

**nose dive** 1 a swift, steep downward plunge of an airplane, nose first 2 any sudden, sharp drop, as in profits —**nose′-dive′**, **-dived′**, **-div′ing**, *vi.*

**nose drops** medication administered through the nose with a dropper

**nose·gay** (nōz′gā′) *n.* [NOSE + GAY (obs. sense "bright object")] a small bouquet

**nose guard** *Football* the defensive lineman directly opposite the offensive center: also **nose tackle**

**nosh** (näsh) *vt.*, *vi.* [< Yiddish < Ger *nashchen*, to nibble] [Slang] to eat (a snack) —*n.* [Slang] a snack —**nosh′er** *n.*

**no′-show′** *n.* one who fails to claim or cancel a reservation

**nos·tal·gi·a** (nä stal′jə) *n.* [< Gr *nostos*, a return + -ALGIA] a longing for something far away or long ago —**nos·tal′gic** (-jik) *adj.*

**nos·tril** (näs′trəl) *n.* [< OE *nosu*, nose + *thyrel*, hole] either of the external openings of the nose

**nos·trum** (näs′trəm) *n.* [L, ours] 1 a quack medicine 2 a panacea

**nos·y** or **nos·ey** (nō′zē) *adj.* **-i·er**, **-i·est** [Inf.] prying; inquisitive

**not** (nät) *adv.* [< ME *nought*] in no manner, to no degree, etc.

**no·ta·ble** (nōt′ə bəl) *adj.* [< L *notare*, to note] worthy of notice; remarkable; outstanding —*n.* a person of distinction —**no′ta·bly** *adv.*

**no·ta·rize** (nōt′ə rīz′) *vt.* **-rized′**, **-riz′ing** to certify or attest (a document) as a notary public

**no′ta·ry** (-rē) *n.*, *pl.* **-ries** [< L *notare*, to note] an official authorized to certify or attest documents, take affidavits, etc.: in full **notary public**

**no·ta·tion** (nō tā′shən) *n.* 1 the use of signs or symbols to represent words, quantities, etc. 2 any such system of signs or symbols, as in mathematics or music 3 a brief note or noting

**notch** (näch) *n.* [prob. < ME (*a*)*n oche*, a notch] 1 a V-shaped cut in an edge or surface 2 a narrow pass with steep sides 3 [Inf.] a step; degree —*vt.* to cut a notch or notches in

**note** (nōt) *n.* [< L *nota*, a mark] 1 a distinguishing feature [a *note* of sadness] 2 importance, distinction, etc. [a person of *note*] 3 a brief writing to aid the memory; memorandum 4 a comment or explanation; annotation 5 notice; heed [worthy of *note*] 6 a short, informal letter 7 a written acknowledgment of a debt 8 *Music a*) a tone of definite pitch *b*) a symbol for a tone, indicating its duration and pitch —*vt.* **not′ed**, **not′ing** 1 to heed; observe 2 to set down in writing 3 to mention particularly —**compare notes** to exchange views

**note′book′** *n.* 1 a book in which notes, or memorandums, are kept 2 a small laptop computer

**not·ed** (nōt′id) *adj.* renowned; famous

**note′wor′thy** *adj.* worthy of note; outstanding; remarkable —**note′wor′thi·ness** *n.*

**noth·ing** (nuth′iŋ) *pron.* [OE *na thing*] 1 no

thing; not anything **2** a person or thing considered of little or no importance —*n.* **1** nothingness **2** a thing that does not exist **3** a person or thing considered of little or no importance **4** a zero; cipher —*adv.* not at all; in no way —**for nothing 1** free **2** in vain **3** without reason

**noth′ing·ness** *n.* **1** the condition of not existing **2** insignificance **3** unconsciousness or death

**no·tice** (nōt′is) *n.* [see NOTE] **1** announcement or warning **2** a brief article about a book, play, etc. **3** a sign giving some public information, warning, etc. **4** attention; heed **5** a formal warning of intention to end an agreement or contract at a certain time —*vt.* **-ticed, -tic·ing** to observe; pay attention to —**take notice** to pay attention

**no′tice·a·ble** *adj.* readily noticed; conspicuous —**no′tice·a·bly** *adv.*

**no·ti·fy** (nōt′ə fī′) *vt.* **-fied′, -fy′ing** [< L *notus*, known + *facere*, make] to give notice to; inform —**no′ti·fi·ca′tion** (-fi kā′shən) *n.*

**no·tion** (nō′shən) *n.* [see NOTE] **1** a general idea **2** a belief; opinion **3** an inclination; whim **4** [*pl.*] small, useful articles, as needles and thread, sold in a store —**no′tion·al** *adj.*

**no·to·ri·e·ty** (nōt′ə rī′ə tē) *n.* a being notorious

**no·to·ri·ous** (nō tôr′ē əs) *adj.* [see NOTE] widely known, esp. unfavorably —**no·to′ri·ous·ly** *adv.*

**not·with·stand·ing** (nät′with stan′diŋ, -with-) *prep.* in spite of —*adv.* nevertheless —*conj.* although

**nou·gat** (nōō′gət) *n.* [< Prov *noga*, nut] a confection of sugar paste with nuts

**nought** (nôt) *n.* [< OE *ne*, not + *awiht*, aught] *Arith.* the figure zero (0)

**noun** (noun) *n.* [< L *nomen*, a name] *Gram.* a word that names or denotes a person, thing, place, action, quality, etc.

**nour·ish** (nur′ish) *vt.* [< L *nutrire*] **1** to provide with substances necessary to life and growth **2** to foster; promote —**nour′ish·ing** *adj.*

**nour′ish·ment** (-mənt) *n.* **1** a nourishing or being nourished **2** food

**nou·veau riche** (nōō′vō rēsh′) *pl.* **nou·veaux riches** (nōō′vō rēsh′) [Fr] a newly rich person, esp. one lacking culture, taste, or social grace

**no·va** (nō′və) *n., pl.* **-vas** or **-vae** (-vē) [< L, new] a star that brightens intensely and then gradually dims

**No·va Sco·tia** (nō′və skō′shə) province of SE Canada: 21,425 sq. mi.; pop. 909,000; cap. Halifax: abbrev. *NS* —**No′va Sco′tian**

**nov·el** (näv′əl) *adj.* [< L dim. of *novus*, new] new and unusual —*n.* a relatively long fictional prose narrative

**nov′el·ette′** (-et′) *n.* a short novel

**nov′el·ist** *n.* one who writes novels

**nov′el·ize′** (-īz′) *vt.* **-ized′, -iz′ing** to make into or like a novel; specif., to use (a film script) as the basis of a novel

**nov′el·ty** *n., pl.* **-ties 1** the quality of being novel; newness **2** something new, fresh, or unusual **3** a small, often cheap, cleverly made article: *usually used in pl.*

**No·vem·ber** (nō vem′bər) *n.* [< L *novem*, nine: ninth month in Roman year] the 11th month of the year, having 30 days: abbrev. **Nov.**

**no·ve·na** (nō vē′nə) *n.* [< L *novem*, nine] *R.C.Ch.* the offering of special prayers and devotions for nine days

**nov·ice** (näv′is) *n.* [< L *novus*, new] **1** a person on probation in a religious order before taking final vows **2** a person new to something; beginner

**no·vi·ti·ate** (nō vish′it) *n.* the period or state of being a novice

**No·vo·cain** (nō′və kān′) [L *nov(us)*, new + (C)OCAIN(E)] *trademark for* PROCAINE

**now** (nou) *adv.* [OE *nu*] **1** *a*) at the present time *b*) at once **2** at that time; then **3** with things as they are [*now* we'll never know] —*conj.* since; seeing that —*n.* the present time [that's all for *now*]

—*adj.* of the present time —**just now** recently —**now and then** (or **again**) occasionally

**now′a·days′** (-ə dāz′) *adv.* at the present time

**no·way** (nō′wā′) *adv.* by no means; not at all: now often **no way**, used with the force of an interjection

**no′where′** *adv.* not in, at, or to any place —**nowhere near** not by a wide margin

**no-win** (nō′win′) *adj.* designating or of a situation, policy, etc. that cannot lead to success no matter what measures are taken

**no′wise′** (-wīz′) *adv.* in no manner; noway

**nox·ious** (näk′shəs) *adj.* [< L *nocere*, to hurt] harmful to health or morals; injurious or unwholesome —**nox′ious·ness** *n.*

**noz·zle** (näz′əl) *n.* [dim. of *nose*] the spout at the end of a hose, pipe, etc.

**Np** *Chem. symbol for* neptunium

**NR** *abbrev.* not rated: said of films

**NS** Nova Scotia

**NT** *abbrev.* **1** New Testament **2** Northwest Territories

**-n't** *suffix* not: used with certain verbs in contractions [aren't]

**nth** (enth) *adj.* of the indefinitely large or small quantity represented by *n*

**nt wt** *abbrev.* net weight

**nu** (nōō, nyōō) *n.* the 13th letter of the Greek alphabet (N, ν)

**NU** Nunavut

**nu·ance** (nōō′äns′) *n.* [Fr < *nuer*, to shade] a slight variation in tone, color, meaning, etc. —**nu′anced′** *adj.*

**nub** (nub) *n.* [var. of *knub*, knob] **1** a lump or small piece **2** [Inf.] the main point; gist

**nub·bin** (nub′in) *n.* [dim. of prec.] a small thing

**nub·by** (nub′ē) *adj.* **-bi·er, -bi·est** having a rough, knotted surface [a *nubby* fabric]

**nu·bile** (nōō′bəl, -bīl′) *adj.* [< L *nubere*, marry] **1** marriageable **2** sexually attractive Said of a young woman

**nu·cle·ar** (nōō′klē ər) *adj.* **1** of, like, or forming a nucleus **2** of or relating to atomic nuclei [*nuclear* energy] **3** of or operated by the use of nuclear energy [*nuclear* weapons] **4** of or involving nuclear weapons [*nuclear* warfare]

**nuclear energy** the energy released from an atom in nuclear reactions, esp. in nuclear fission or nuclear fusion

**nuclear family** a basic social unit consisting of parents and their children living in one household

**nuclear fission** the splitting of the nuclei of atoms, accompanied by conversion of part of their mass into energy, as in the atomic bomb

**nuclear fusion** the fusion of lightweight atomic nuclei into a nucleus of heavier mass with a resultant loss in the combined mass, which is converted into energy, as in the hydrogen bomb

**nuclear physics** the branch of physics dealing with the structure of atomic nuclei, nuclear forces, etc.

**nuclear reactor** a device for creating a controlled nuclear chain reaction using atomic fuel, as for the production of energy

**nuclear winter** a hypothetical condition following nuclear war in which sunlight is cut off by clouds of smoke and dust, resulting in very low temperatures, destruction of life forms, etc.

**nu·cle·ate** (nōō′klē it; *for v.*, -āt′) *adj.* having a nucleus —*vt., vi.* **-at′ed, -at′ing** to form into a nucleus —**nu′cle·a′tion** *n.*

**nu·cle·ic acid** (nōō klē′ik, -klā′-) any of a group of essential complex organic acids found in all living cells: the two types are DNA and RNA

**nucleo-** *combining form* **1** nucleus **2** nuclear **3** nucleic acid Also **nucle-**

**nu·cle·o·lus** (nōō klē′ə ləs) *n., pl.* **-li′** (-lī′) [< LL, dim. of L *nucleus*] a conspicuous, usually spherical, dense body in the nucleus of most cells, consisting of protein and RNA

**nu·cle·us** (nōō′klē əs) *n., pl.* **-cle·i′** (-ī′) or **-cle·us·es** ⟦< L, kernel⟧ **1** a central thing or part around which others are grouped; core **2** any center of growth or development **3** the central part of an atom **4** the central mass of protoplasm in a cell

**nude** (nōōd) *adj.* ⟦L *nudus*⟧ naked; bare —*n.* **1** a nude human figure, esp. in a work of art **2** the state of being nude *[in the nude]* —**nu′di·ty** *n.*

**nudge** (nuj) *vt.* **nudged, nudg′ing** ⟦< ?⟧ to push gently, esp. with the elbow, in order to get the attention of, hint slyly, etc. —*n.* a gentle push

**nud·ism** (nōō′diz′əm) *n.* the practice or cult of going nude for hygienic reasons —**nud′ist** *n., adj.*

**nu·ga·to·ry** (nōō′gə tôr′ē) *adj.* ⟦< L *nugari*, to trifle⟧ **1** trifling; worthless **2** not operative; invalid

**nug·get** (nug′ət) *n.* ⟦prob. < dial. *nug*, a lump⟧ a lump; esp., a lump of native gold

**nui·sance** (nōō′səns) *n.* ⟦< L *nocere*, annoy⟧ an act, thing, or person causing trouble, annoyance, etc.

**nuke** (nōōk) [Slang] *n.* ⟦< NUCLEAR⟧ a nuclear weapon —*vt.* **nuked, nuk′ing** to attack with nuclear weapons

**null** (nul) *adj.* ⟦< L *nullus*, none⟧ **1** without legal force; invalid: usually in the phrase **null and void 2** amounting to naught **3** of no value, effect, etc.

**nul·li·fy** (nul′ə fī′) *vt.* **-fied′, -fy′ing** ⟦< L *nullus*, none + *facere*, to make⟧ **1** to make legally null or valueless **2** to cancel out —**nul′li·fi·ca′tion** *n.*

**numb** (num) *adj.* ⟦< ME *nimen*, to take⟧ deadened; insensible —*vt.* to make numb —**numb′ly** *adv.* —**numb′ness** *n.*

**num·ber** (num′bər) *n.* ⟦< L *numerus*⟧ **1** a symbol or word showing how many or which one in a series (Ex.: 2, 35, four, ninth) **2** [*pl.*] ARITHMETIC **3** the sum of persons or things; total **4** *a*) [*often pl.*] many *b*) [*pl.*] numerical superiority **5** quantity **6** *a*) a single issue of a periodical *b*) a single song, dance, etc. in a program of entertainment **7** [Inf.] a person or thing singled out **8** *Gram.* the form of a word as indicating either singular or plural —*vt.* **1** to count; enumerate **2** to give a number to **3** to include as one of a group **4** to limit the number of **5** to have or comprise; total —*vi.* to be included —**a number of** several or many; some —**beyond** (or **without**) **number** too numerous to be counted —**the numbers** an illegal lottery based on certain numbers published in newspapers: also **numbers game** (or **racket**)

**num′ber·less** *adj.* countless

**Num·bers** (num′bərz) *n.* the fourth book of the Pentateuch in the Bible: abbrev. **Num.**

**nu·mer·al** (nōō′mər əl) *adj.* ⟦< L *numerus*, number⟧ of or denoting a number or numbers —*n.* a figure, a letter, or a group of figures or letters, expressing a number

**nu′mer·ate** (-it) *adj.* [Chiefly Brit.] able to understand basic mathematical concepts, etc.

**nu′mer·a′tor** (-āt′ər) *n.* the part of a fraction above the line

**nu·mer·i·cal** (nōō mer′i kəl) *adj.* **1** of, or having the nature of, number **2** in or by numbers **3** expressed by numbers, not letters —**nu·mer′i·cal·ly** *adv.*

**nu·mer·ol·o·gy** (nōō′mər äl′ə jē) *n.* divination by numbers, as with birth dates

**nu·mer·ous** (nōō′mər əs) *adj.* **1** consisting of many persons or things **2** very many

**nu·mi·nous** (nōō′mə nəs) *adj.* ⟦< L *numen*, deity⟧ having a deeply spiritual or mystical effect

**nu·mis·mat·ics** (nōō′miz mat′iks, -mis-) *n.* ⟦< L *numisma*, a coin⟧ the study or collection of coins, medals, paper money, etc. —**nu·mis′ma·tist** (-mə tist) *n.*

**num·skull** (num′skul′) *n.* ⟦NUM(B) + SKULL⟧ a dunce

**nun** (nun) *n.* ⟦< LL *nonna*⟧ a woman devoted to a

religious life, esp. one living in a convent under vows

**Nu·na·vut** (nōō′nə vōōt′) territory of N Canada: 770,000 sq. mi.; pop. 25,000; cap. Iqaluit: abbrev. *NU*

**nun·ci·o** (nun′shō′, -sē ō′) *n., pl.* **-ci·os′** ⟦< It < L *nuntius*, messenger⟧ a papal ambassador to a foreign state

**nun·ner·y** (nun′ər ē) *n., pl.* **-ies** *former term for* CONVENT

**nup·tial** (nup′shəl, -chəl) *adj.* ⟦< L *nubere*, marry⟧ of marriage or a wedding —*n.* [*pl.*] a wedding

**nurse** (nʉrs) *n.* ⟦< L *nutrire*, nourish⟧ **1** a woman hired to care for another's children **2** a person trained to care for the sick, assist surgeons, etc. —*vt.* **nursed, nurs′ing 1** to suckle (an infant) **2** to take care of (a child, invalid, etc.) **3** to nourish, foster, etc. **4** to try to cure *[to nurse a cold]* **5** to use or handle so as to protect or conserve —*vi.* **1** to feed at the breast; suckle **2** to serve as a nurse

**nurse′maid′** *n.* a woman hired to care for a child or children

**nurs·er·y** (nʉrs′ə rē) *n., pl.* **-ies 1** a room set aside for children **2** a place where parents may temporarily leave children to be cared for **3** a place where young trees or other plants are raised for transplanting, etc.

**nurs′er·y·man** (-mən) *n., pl.* **-men** (-mən) one who owns or works in a tree nursery

**nursery rhyme** a poem for children

**nursery school** PRESCHOOL

**nursing home** a residence providing care for the infirm, chronically ill, disabled, etc.

**nur·ture** (nʉr′chər) *n.* ⟦< L *nutrire*, nourish⟧ training; rearing —*vt.* **-tured, -tur·ing 1** to nourish **2** to train, educate, rear, etc. —**nur′tur·er** *n.*

**nut** (nut) *n.* ⟦OE *hnutu*⟧ **1** a dry, one-seeded fruit, consisting of a kernel, often edible, in a woody shell, as the walnut **2** the kernel itself **3** loosely, any hard-shell, relatively nonperishable fruit, as the peanut **4** a small metal block with a threaded hole for screwing onto a bolt, etc. **5** [Slang] *a*) a crazy or eccentric person *b*) a devotee; fan

NUTS

**nut case** [Slang] one who is eccentric or crazy: also **nut′case′** *n.*

**nut′crack′er** *n.* **1** an instrument for cracking nutshells **2** a crowlike bird that feeds on nuts

**nut′hatch′** *n.* a small nut-eating bird with a sharp beak

**nut′meat′** *n.* the kernel of a nut

**nut′meg′** (-meg′) *n.* ⟦< L *nux*, nut + LL *muscus*, musk⟧ the aromatic seed of an East Indian tree, grated and used as a spice

**nu·tri·a** (nōō′trē ə) *n.* ⟦Sp < L *lutra*, otter⟧ the soft, brown fur of a South American rodent

**nu·tri·ent** (nōō′trē ənt) *adj.* ⟦< L *nutrire*, nourish⟧ nourishing —*n.* anything nutritious

**nu′tri·ment** (-trə mənt) *n.* anything that nourishes; food

**nu·tri·tion** (nōō trish′ən) *n.* ⟦see NUTRIENT⟧ **1** the process by which an organism takes in and assimilates food **2** anything that nourishes; food **3** the study of diet and health —**nu·tri′tion·al** *adj.* —**nu·tri′tion·al·ly** *adv.* —**nu′tri·tive** (-trə tiv) *adj.*

**nu·tri′tious** (-trish′əs) *adj.* nourishing

**nuts** (nuts) [Slang] *adj.* crazy; foolish —*interj.* used to express disgust, scorn, refusal, etc.: often in the phrase **nuts to someone** (or **something**) — **be nuts about 1** to be greatly in love with **2** to be very enthusiastic about

**nuts and bolts** [Inf.] the basic elements or practical aspects of something —**nuts′-and-bolts′** *adj.*

**nut′shell′** *n.* the shell enclosing the kernel of a nut —**in a nutshell** in concise form; in a few words

**nut′ty** *adj.* **-ti·er, -ti·est 1** containing nuts **2** having a nutlike flavor **3** [Slang] *a)* very enthusiastic *b)* foolish, crazy, etc. —**nut′ti·ness** *n.*

**nuz·zle** (nuz′əl) *vt., vi.* **-zled, -zling** ⟦< ME *nose,* NOSE⟧ **1** to push (against) or rub with the nose, snout, etc. **2** to nestle; snuggle —**nuz′zler** *n.*

**NV** Nevada

**NW** *abbrev.* **1** northwest **2** northwestern

**NY** New York

**NYC** or **N.Y.C.** New York City

**ny·lon** (nī′län′) *n.* ⟦arbitrary coinage⟧ **1** an elastic, very strong synthetic material that is made into fiber, yarn, bristles, etc. **2** [*pl.*] stockings made of this

**nymph** (nimf) *n.* ⟦< Gr *nymphē*⟧ **1** *Gr. & Rom. Myth.* any of a group of minor nature goddesses, living in rivers, trees, etc. **2** a lovely young woman **3** the young of an insect with incomplete metamorphosis

**nym·pho·ma·ni·a** (nim′fō mā′nē ə) *n.* uncontrollable desire by a woman for sexual intercourse —**nym′pho·ma′ni·ac′** *adj., n.*

# O

**o** or **O** (ō) *n., pl.* **o′s, O′s** the 15th letter of the English alphabet

**O¹** (ō) *n., pl.* **O′s** **1** the numeral zero **2** a blood type

**O²** (ō) *interj.* **1** used in direct address *[O Lord!]* **2** OH

**O³** *abbrev.* **1** Ocean **2** *Physics* ohm **3** Old **4** *Baseball* out(s)

**O⁴** *Chem. symbol for* oxygen

**-o** (ō) *suffix* forming slangy words, as slang nouns from adjectives *[weirdo, sicko]*

**oaf** (ōf) *n.* ⟦< ON *alfr*, elf⟧ a stupid, clumsy fellow; lout —**oaf′ish** *adj.*

**O·a·hu** (ō ä′hōō) chief island of Hawaii

**oak** (ōk) *n.* ⟦OE *ac*⟧ **1** a large hardwood tree with nuts called *acorns* **2** its wood —*adj.* of oak — **oak′en** *adj.*

**Oak·land** (ōk′lənd) seaport in W California: pop. 372,000

**Oak Ridge** city in E Tennessee: center for atomic research: pop. 27,000

**oa·kum** (ō′kəm) *n.* ⟦< OE *a-*, out + *camb*, a comb⟧ stringy hemp fiber gotten by taking apart old ropes, used as a caulking material

**oar** (ôr) *n.* ⟦OE *ar*⟧ a long pole with a broad blade at one end, used in rowing —**oars·man** (ôrz′mən), *pl.* **-men**, *n.*

**oar′lock′** *n.* a device, often U-shaped, for holding an oar in place in rowing

**OAS** *abbrev.* Organization of American States

**o·a·sis** (ō ā′sis) *n., pl.* **-ses′** (-sēz′) ⟦< Gr, fertile spot⟧ a fertile place in a desert, resulting from the presence of water

**oat** (ōt) *n.* ⟦OE *ate*⟧ [*usually pl.*] **1** a hardy cereal grass **2** its edible grain —**oat′en** *adj.*

**oat′cake′** *n.* a thin, flat cake made of oatmeal

**oath** (ōth) *n., pl.* **oaths** (ō*th*z, ōths) ⟦OE *ath*⟧ **1** a declaration based on an appeal to God that one will speak the truth, keep a promise, etc. **2** a swearword; curse

**oat′meal′** *n.* **1** oats ground or rolled into meal or flakes **2** a porridge of this

**OB** *abbrev.* **1** obstetrician **2** obstetrics

**ob.** *abbrev.* ⟦L *obiit*⟧ he (or she) died

**ob-** ⟦< L *ob*⟧ *prefix* **1** to, toward, before *[obtrude]* **2** against *[obstinate]* **3** upon, over *[obscure]* **4** completely *[obdurate]*

**ob·bli·ga·to** (äb′li gät′ō) *n., pl.* **-tos** or **-ti** (-ē) ⟦see OBLIGE⟧ a musical accompaniment, usually by a solo instrument

**ob·du·rate** (äb′dŏŏr it) *adj.* ⟦< L *obduratus* < *ob-*, intens. + *durus*, hard⟧ **1** hardhearted **2** stubborn; obstinate —**ob′du·ra·cy** (-ə sē) *n.*

**o·be·di·ent** (ō bē′dē ənt) *adj.* obeying or willing to obey —**o·be′di·ence** *n.* —**o·be′di·ent·ly** *adv.*

**o·bei·sance** (ō bā′səns, -bē′-) *n.* ⟦< OFr *obeir*, obey⟧ **1** a gesture of respect, as a bow **2** homage; deference —**o·bei′sant** *adj.*

**ob·e·lisk** (äb′ə lisk, ō′bə-) *n.* ⟦< Gr *obelos*, needle⟧ a tall, four-sided stone pillar tapering to its pyramidal top

**o·bese** (ō bēs′) *adj.* ⟦< L *obesus* < *ob-* (see OB-) + *edere*, to eat⟧ very fat; stout —**o·be′si·ty** (-ə tē) *n.*

**o·bey** (ō bā′) *vt.* ⟦< L *obedire* < *ob-* (see OB-) + *audire*, hear⟧ **1** to carry out the orders of **2** to carry out (an order, etc.) **3** to be guided by *[to obey one's conscience]* —*vi.* to be obedient

**ob·fus·cate** (äb′fəs kāt′, äb fus′kāt) *vt.* **-cat·ed, -cat·ing** ⟦< L *obfuscatus* < *ob-* (see OB-) + *fuscus*, dark⟧ to obscure; confuse —**ob′fus·ca′tion** *n.*

**ob·i·ter dic·tum** (äb′i tər dik′təm, ō bi-) *pl.* **ob′i·ter dic′ta** (-tə) an incidental remark

**o·bit·u·ar·y** (ō bich′ōō er′ē) *n., pl.* **-ar·ies** ⟦< L *obire*, to die⟧ a notice of someone's death, usually with a brief biography: also **o·bit** (ō′bit)

**obj** *abbrev.* **1** object **2** objective

**ob·ject** (äb′jikt; *for v.* äb jekt′) *n.* ⟦< ML *objectum*, thing thrown in the way < L *objectus* < *ob-* (see OB-) + *jacere*, to throw⟧ **1** a thing that can be seen or touched **2** a person or thing to which action, feeling, etc. is directed **3** purpose; goal **4** *Gram.* a noun or other substantive receiving the action of a verb or governed by a preposition —*vt.* to state by way of objection —*vi.* to feel or express disapproval or opposition —**ob·jec′tor** *n.*

**ob·jec·tion** (əb jek′shən) *n.* **1** a feeling or expression of opposition or disapproval **2** a reason for objecting

**ob·jec′tion·a·ble** *adj.* **1** open to objection **2** disagreeable; offensive

**ob·jec·tive** (əb jek′tiv) *adj.* **1** existing as an object or fact, independent of the mind; real **2** determined by the realities of the thing dealt with rather than the thoughts of the writer or speaker **3** without bias or prejudice **4** *Gram.* designating or of the case of an object of a preposition or verb —*n.* something aimed at —**ob·jec′tive·ly** *adv.* — **ob·jec·tiv·i·ty** (äb′jek tiv′ə tē) or **ob·jec′tive·ness** *n.*

**object lesson** an actual or practical demonstration or exemplification of some principle

**ob·jet d'art** (äb′zhā där′) *pl.* **ob′jets d'art** (-zhā-) ⟦Fr⟧ a small object of artistic value, as a figurine

**ob·jur·gate** (äb′jər gāt′) *vt.* **-gat·ed, -gat·ing** ⟦< L *objurgatus* < *ob-* (see OB-) + *jurgare*, chide⟧ to upbraid sharply; rebuke

**ob·late** (äb′lāt′) *adj.* ⟦ModL *oblatus*, thrust forward⟧ *Geom.* flattened at the poles

**ob·la·tion** (äb lā′shən) *n.* ⟦< L *oblatus*, offered⟧ an offering or sacrifice to God or a god

**ob·li·gate** (äb′li gāt′) *vt.* **-gat·ed, -gat·ing** ⟦see OBLIGE⟧ to bind by a promise, sense of duty, etc.

**ob·li·ga′tion** (-gā′shən) *n.* **1** an obligating or

OBELISK

being obligated **2** a binding contract, promise, responsibility, etc. **3** the binding power of a contract, etc. **4** a being indebted for a favor, etc.

**ob·lig·a·to·ry** (ə blig′ə tôr′ē, äb′lə gə-) *adj.* legally or morally binding

**o·blige** (ə blīj′) *vt.* **o·bliged′, o·blig′ing** ‖< L *obligare* < *ob-* (see OB-) + *ligare,* to bind‖ **1** to compel by moral, legal, or physical force **2** to make indebted for a favor; do a favor for

**o·blig′ing** *adj.* helpful; accommodating —**o·blig′ing·ly** *adv.*

**ob·lique** (ō blēk′) *adj.* ‖< L *obliquus* < *ob-* (see OB-) + *liquis,* awry‖ **1** slanting **2** indirect or evasive —**ob·lique′ly** *adv.* —**ob·liq·ui·ty** (ə blik′wə tē) or **ob·lique′ness** *n.*

**ob·lit·er·ate** (ə blit′ər āt′) *vt.* **-at′ed, -at′ing** ‖< L *obliteratus* < *ob-* (see OB-) + *littera,* a letter‖ **1** to blot out; efface **2** to destroy —**ob·lit′er·a′tion** *n.*

**ob·liv·i·on** (ə bliv′ē ən) *n.* ‖< L *oblivisci,* to forget‖ **1** forgetfulness **2** the condition of being forgotten

**ob·liv′i·ous** (-əs) *adj.* forgetful or indifferent: usually with *to* or *of*

**ob·long** (äb′lôŋ′) *adj.* ‖< L *oblongus,* rather long < *ob-* (see OB-) + *longus,* long‖ longer than broad; specif., rectangular and longer in one direction —*n.* an oblong figure

**ob·lo·quy** (äb′lə kwē) *n., pl.* **-quies** ‖< L *obloqui* < *ob-* (see OB-) + *loqui,* speak‖ **1** widespread censure or abuse **2** disgrace resulting from this

**ob·nox·ious** (əb näk′shəs, äb-) *adj.* ‖< L *obnoxiosus* < *ob-* (see OB-) + *noxa,* harm‖ very unpleasant; offensive; repugnant —**ob·nox′ious·ly** *adv.* —**ob·nox′ious·ness** *n.*

**o·boe** (ō′bō) *n.* ‖< Fr *haut,* high (pitch) + *bois,* wood‖ a double-reed woodwind instrument having a high, penetrating tone —**o′bo·ist** *n.*

**obs** *abbrev.* obsolete

**ob·scene** (äb sēn′) *adj.* ‖< L *obscenus,* filthy‖ **1** offensive to modesty or decency; lewd **2** repulsive —**ob·scen′i·ty** (-sen′ə tē), *pl.* **-ties,** *n.*

**ob·scur·ant·ism** (äb′skyoor′ən tiz′əm) *n.* **1** opposition to human progress **2** a being deliberately obscure or vague

OBOE

**ob·scure** (əb skyoor′) *adj.* ‖< L *obscurus,* covered over‖ **1** dim; dark **2** not easily seen; faint **3** vague; ambiguous *[an obscure answer]* **4** inconspicuous or hidden **5** not well-known *[an obscure actor]* —*vt.* **-scured′, -scur′ing** to make obscure —**ob·scure′ly** *adv.* —**ob·scu′ri·ty** *n.*

**ob·se·quies** (äb′si kwēz′) *pl.n.* ‖< L *obsequium,* compliance, substituted for L *exsequiae,* funeral‖ funeral rites

**ob·se·qui·ous** (əb sē′kwē əs) *adj.* ‖< L *obsequi,* to comply with‖ servile or fawning

**ob·serv·ance** (əb zurv′əns) *n.* **1** the observing of a law, custom, etc. **2** a customary act, rite, etc.

**ob·serv′ant** (-ənt) *adj.* **1** strict in observing a law, custom, etc. **2** paying careful attention **3** perceptive or alert

**ob·ser·va·tion** (äb′zər vā′shən) *n.* **1** *a)* the act or power of noticing *b)* something noticed **2** a being seen **3** a noting and recording of facts, as for research **4** a comment or remark

**ob·serv·a·to·ry** (əb zurv′ə tôr′ē) *n., pl.* **-ries** a building equipped for astronomical research, esp. one with a large telescope

**ob·serve** (əb zurv′) *vt.* **-served′, -serv′ing** ‖< L *observare* < *ob-* (see OB-) + *servare,* to keep‖ **1** to adhere to (a law, custom, etc.) **2** to celebrate (a

holiday, etc.) **3** *a)* to notice (something) *b)* to pay special attention to **4** to say; remark **5** to examine scientifically —**ob·serv′a·ble** *adj.* —**ob·serv′er** *n.*

**ob·sess** (əb ses′) *vt.* ‖< L *obsessus* < *ob-* (see OB-) + *sedere,* sit‖ to haunt or trouble in mind; preoccupy —*vi.* to be obsessed or preoccupied: usually with *about, over,* or *on* —**ob·ses′sive** *adj.* —**ob·ses′sive·ly** *adv.*

**ob·ses′sion** (-sesh′ən) *n.* **1** a being obsessed **2** an idea, desire, etc. that obsesses one

**ob·sid·i·an** (əb sid′ē ən) *n.* ‖ModL *obsidianus,* ult. after *Obsius,* finder of a similar stone in ancient times‖ a hard, dark, volcanic glass

**ob·so·les·cent** (äb′sə les′ənt) *adj.* becoming obsolete —**ob′so·les′cence** *n.*

**ob·so·lete** (äb′sə lēt′) *adj.* ‖< L *obsoletus* < *ob-* (see OB-) + *exolescere,* to grow out of use‖ **1** no longer in use **2** out-of-date

**ob·sta·cle** (äb′stə kəl) *n.* ‖< L *obstaculum* < *ob-* (see OB-) + *stare,* to stand‖ anything that stands in the way; obstruction

**ob·stet·rics** (əb stet′riks) *n.* ‖< L *obstetrix,* midwife‖ the branch of medicine concerned with the care and treatment of women during pregnancy and childbirth —**ob·stet′ric** or **ob·stet′ri·cal** *adj.* —**ob·ste·tri·cian** (äb′stə trish′ən) *n.*

**ob·sti·nate** (äb′stə nət) *adj.* ‖< L *obstinare,* to resolve on‖ **1** determined to have one's own way; stubborn **2** hard to treat or cure *[an obstinate fever]* —**ob′sti·na·cy** (-nə sē) *n.* —**ob′sti·nate·ly** *adv.*

**ob·strep·er·ous** (əb strep′ər əs) *adj.* ‖< L *obstreperus* < *ob-* (see OB-) + *strepere,* to roar‖ noisy or unruly, esp. in resisting —**ob·strep′er·ous·ly** *adv.* —**ob·strep′er·ous·ness** *n.*

**ob·struct** (əb strukt′) *vt.* ‖< L *obstructus* < *ob-* (see OB-) + *struere,* to pile up‖ **1** to block or stop up (a passage) **2** to hinder (progress, etc.) **3** to cut off from view —**ob·struc′tive** *adj.* —**ob·struc′tive·ly** *adv.* —**ob·struc′tive·ness** *n.*

**ob·struc′tion** (-struk′shən) *n.* **1** an obstructing **2** anything that obstructs; hindrance

**ob·struc′tion·ist** *n.* one who obstructs progress —*adj.* that obstructs progress

**ob·tain** (əb tān′) *vt.* ‖< L *obtinere* < *ob-* (see OB-) + *tenere,* to hold‖ to get possession of by trying; procure —*vi.* to prevail or be in effect —**ob·tain′a·ble** *adj.* —**ob·tain′ment** *n.*

**ob·trude** (əb trōōd′, äb-) *vt.* **-trud′ed, -trud′ing** ‖< L *obtrudere* < *ob-* (see OB-) + *trudere,* to thrust‖ to force (oneself, one's opinions, etc.) upon others unasked or unwanted —*vi.* to obtrude oneself (*on* or *upon*) —**ob·tru′sion** *n.* —**ob·tru′sive** *adj.* —**ob·tru′sive·ly** *adv.* —**ob·tru′sive·ness** *n.*

**ob·tuse** (əb tōōs′, äb-) *adj.* ‖< L *obtundere,* to strike upon, blunt‖ **1** blunt **2** greater than 90° and less than 180° *[an obtuse angle]* **3** slow to understand —**ob·tuse′ly** *adv.* —**ob·tuse′ness** *n.*

**ob·verse** (äb vurs′; *also, and for n. always,* äb′vurs′) *adj.* ‖< L *obversus* < *ob-* (see OB-) + *vertere,* to turn‖ **1** turned toward the observer **2** forming a counterpart —*n.* **1** the side, as of a coin or medal, bearing the main design **2** a counterpart

**ob·vi·ate** (äb′vē āt′) *vt.* **-at′ed, -at′ing** ‖see fol.‖ to do away with or prevent by effective measures; make unnecessary —**ob′vi·a′tion** *n.*

**ob·vi·ous** (äb′vē əs) *adj.* ‖L *obvius,* in the way‖ easy to see or understand; evident —**ob′vi·ous·ly** *adv.* —**ob′vi·ous·ness** *n.*

**oc-** *prefix* OB-: used before *c [occur]*

**oc·a·ri·na** (äk′ə rē′nə) *n.* ‖It < LL *auca,* goose: from its shape‖ a small wind instrument with finger holes and a mouthpiece

**occas** *abbrev.* occasional(ly)

**oc·ca·sion** (ə kā′zhən, ō-) *n.* ‖< L *occasio* < *ob-* (see OB-) + *cadere,* to fall‖ **1** a favorable time; opportunity **2** an event, etc. that makes something else possible **3** *a)* a happening *b)* a particular time **4** a special time or event **5** need arising from circumstances —*vt.* to cause —**on occasion** sometimes

**oc·ca'sion·al** *adj.* **1** of or for special occasions **2** happening now and then; infrequent —**oc·ca'sion·al·ly** *adv.*

**oc·ci·dent** (äk'sə dənt, -dent') *n.* [< L *occidere,* to fall: with reference to the setting sun] [Old Poet.] the west —**the Occident** Europe and the Americas —**oc'ci·den'tal** or **Oc'ci·den'tal** *adj., n.*

**oc·clude** (ə klōōd') *vt.* -clud'ed, -clud'ing [< L *occludere* < *ob-* (see OB-) + *claudere,* to shut] **1** to close or block (a passage) **2** to shut in or out —*vi. Dentistry* to meet with the cusps fitting closely —**oc·clu'sion** (-klōō'zhən) *n.* —**oc·clu·sive** (ə klōō'siv) *adj.*

**oc·cult** (ə kult') *adj.* [< L *occulere,* to conceal] **1** hidden **2** secret **3** mysterious **4** of mystic arts, such as magic, astrology, etc.

**oc·cu·pan·cy** (äk'yōō pən sē) *n., pl.* **-cies** an occupying; a taking or keeping in possession

**oc'cu·pant** (-pənt) *n.* one who occupies

**oc·cu·pa·tion** (äk'yōō pā'shən) *n.* **1** an occupying or being occupied **2** that which occupies one's time; work; profession —**oc'cu·pa'tion·al** *adj.*

**oc·cu·py** (äk'yōō pī') *vt.* -pied', -py'ing [< L *occupare* < *ob-* (see OB-) + *capere,* seize] **1** to take possession of by settlement or seizure **2** to hold possession of; specif., *a*) to dwell in *b*) to hold (a position or office) **3** to take up (space, time, etc.) **4** to employ (oneself, one's mind, etc.)

**oc·cur** (ə kur') *vi.* -curred', -cur'ring [< L *occurrere* < *ob-* (see OB-) + *currere,* to run] **1** to be found; exist **2** to come to mind [an idea *occurred* to me] **3** to take place; happen

**oc·cur'rence** (-əns) *n.* **1** the act or fact of occurring **2** an event; incident

**o·cean** (ō'shən) *n.* [< Gr *Ōkeanos*] **1** the body of salt water that covers about 71% of the earth's surface **2** any of its four principal divisions: the Atlantic, Pacific, Indian, or Arctic Ocean **3** a great quantity —**o·ce·an·ic** (ō'shē an'ik) *adj.*

**o'cean·go'ing** (-gō'iŋ) *adj.* of, or made for, travel on the ocean

**O·ce·a·ni·a** (ō'shē an'ē ə) islands in the Pacific, including Melanesia, Micronesia, & Polynesia —**O'ce·an'i·an** *adj., n.*

**o·cean·og·ra·phy** (ō'shə näg'rə fē) *n.* the study of the environment in the ocean, its plants and animals, etc. —**o'cean·o·graph'ic** (-nō'graf'ik) *adj.* —**o'cean·og'ra·pher** *n.*

**o·cean·ol·o·gy** (-näl'ə jē) *n.* the study of the sea in all its aspects, including oceanography, undersea exploration, etc.

**o·ce·lot** (äs'ə lät, -lät') *n.* [Fr < AmInd] a spotted wildcat of North and South America

**o·cher** or **o·chre** (ō'kər) *n.* [< Gr *ōchros,* pale-yellow] **1** a yellow or reddish-brown clay containing iron, used as a pigment **2** its color

**o'clock** (ə kläk', ō-) *adv.* of or according to the clock [nine *o'clock* at night]

**octa-** [< Gr *oktō,* eight] *combining form* eight [*octagon*]

**oc·ta·gon** (äk'tə gän') *n.* [< Gr: see prec. & -GON] a plane figure with eight angles and eight sides —**oc·tag'o·nal** (-tag'ə nəl) *adj.*

**octane number** (or **rating**) (äk'tān') a number representing the antiknock properties of a gasoline, etc.

**oc·tave** (äk'tiv, -tāv') *n.* [< L *octavus,* eighth] **1** any group of eight **2** *Music a*) the eighth tone of a diatonic scale, or a tone seven degrees above or below a given tone *b*) the interval of seven degrees between a tone and either of its octaves *c*) the series of tones within this interval, or the keys of an instrument producing such a series

**oc·ta·vo** (äk tā'vō, -tä'-) *n., pl.* **-vos** [< L (*in*) *octavo,* (in) eight] **1** the page size (usually 6 by 9 in.) of a book made up of printer's sheets folded into eight leaves **2** a book of such pages

**oc·tet** or **oc·tette** (äk tet') *n.* [OCT(A)- + (DU)ET] **1** a composition for eight voices or instruments **2** the eight performers of this

**Oc·to·ber** (äk tō'bər) *n.* [< L *octo,* eight: eighth

month in Roman calendar] the tenth month of the year, having 31 days: abbrev. **Oct.**

**oc·to·ge·nar·i·an** (äk'tə ji ner'ē ən) *n.* [< L *octoginta,* eighty] a person between the ages of 80 and 90

**oc·to·pus** (äk'tə pəs) *n., pl.* **-pus·es** or **-pi** (-pī') [< Gr *oktō,* eight + *pous,* foot] a mollusk with a soft body and eight arms covered with suckers

**oc·u·lar** (äk'yōō lər) *adj.* [< L *oculus,* eye] **1** of, for, or like the eye **2** by eyesight

**oc'u·list** (-list) *n.* former term for OPHTHALMOLOGIST

OCTOPUS

**OD**[1] (ō'dē') [Slang] *n., pl.* **ODs** or **OD's** an overdose, esp. of a narcotic —*vi.* **OD'd** or **ODed**, **OD'ing** or **ODing** to take an overdose, esp. a fatal overdose of a narcotic

**OD**[2] or **O.D.** *abbrev.* [L] Doctor of Optometry

**o·da·lisque** or **o·da·lisk** (ō'də lisk') *n.* [Fr < Turk *ōdalik,* chambermaid] a female slave or concubine in a harem

**odd** (äd) *adj.* [< ON *oddi*] **1** remaining or separated from a pair, set, etc. **2** having a remainder of one when divided by two **3** with a few more: usually in hyphenated compounds [sixty-*odd* years ago] **4** occasional [*odd* jobs] **5** peculiar or eccentric —**odd'ly** *adv.* —**odd'ness** *n.*

**odd'ball'** *adj., n.* [Slang] strange or eccentric (person)

**odd'i·ty** (-ə tē) *n.* **1** strangeness **2** *pl.* **-ties** an odd person or thing

**odds** (ädz) *pl.n.* **1** difference in favor of one side over the other; advantage **2** an equalizing advantage in betting, based on a bettor's assumed chance of winning and expressed as a ratio [*odds* of 3 to 1] —**at odds** quarreling

**odds and ends** scraps; remnants

**odds'mak'er** *n.* an expert who estimates the odds in betting, etc.

**odds'-on'** *adj.* having a good chance of winning [an *odds-on* favorite]

**ode** (ōd) *n.* [< Gr *ōidē,* song] a lyric poem characterized by lofty feeling, elaborate form, and dignified style

**-ode** (ōd) [< Gr *hodos*] *suffix* way, path [*electrode*]

**O·des·sa** (ō des'ə) seaport in S Ukraine, on the Black Sea: pop. 1,101,000

**O·din** (ō'din) *n. Norse Myth.* the chief deity, god of art, war, and the dead

**o·di·ous** (ō'dē əs) *adj.* [< L *odium,* hatred] disgusting; offensive —**o'di·ous·ly** *adv.* —**o'di·ous·ness** *n.*

**o·di·um** (ō'dē əm) *n.* [< L *odi,* I hate] **1** hatred **2** the disgrace brought on by hateful action

**o·dom·e·ter** (ō däm'ət ər) *n.* [< Gr *hodometros* < *hodos,* way + *metron,* a measure] an instrument for measuring the distance traveled by a vehicle

**o·dor** (ō'dər) *n.* [L] a smell; scent; aroma Brit. sp. **o'dour** —**o'dor·less** *adj.* —**o'dor·ous** *adj.*

**o·dor·if·er·ous** (ō'dər if'ər əs) *adj.* [< L *odor,* odor + *ferre,* to bear] giving off an odor, now often, specif., a strong or offensive one

**O·dys·se·us** (ō dis'ē əs, ō dis'yōōs') *n.* [Gr] the hero of the *Odyssey,* one of the Greek leaders in the Trojan War

**Od·ys·sey** (äd'i sē) *n.* **1** an ancient Greek epic poem, ascribed to Homer, about the wanderings of Odysseus after the fall of Troy **2** *pl.* **-seys** [o-] any extended journey

**OE** *abbrev.* Old English

**Oed·i·pal** (ed'i pəl, ē'di-) *adj.* [also **o-**] of or relating to the Oedipus complex

**Oed·i·pus** (ed′i pəs, ē′di-) *n. Gr. Myth.* a king who unwittingly kills his father and marries his mother

**Oedipus complex** *Psychoanalysis* the unconscious tendency of a child to be attached to the parent of the opposite sex

**oe·nol·o·gy** (ē näl′ə jē) *n.* ⟦< Gr *oinos,* wine + -LOGY⟧ the science or study of wines and winemaking —**oe·nol′o·gist** *n.*

**oe·no·phile** (ē′nə fīl′) *n.* a connoisseur of wine

**o'er** (ō′ər, ôr) *prep., adv.* [Old Poet.] OVER

**oeu·vre** (ē′vr′) *n., pl.* **-vres** (-vr′) ⟦Fr⟧ all the works of a writer, artist, or composer

**of** (uv) *prep.* ⟦OE⟧ **1** from; specif., *a)* coming from [men *of* Ohio] *b)* resulting from [to die *of* fever] *c)* at a distance from [east *of* the city] *d)* by [the poems *of* Poe] *e)* separated from [robbed *of* his money] *f)* from the whole constituting [one *of* her hats] *g)* made from [a sheet *of* paper] **2** belonging to [the pages *of* a book] **3** *a)* possessing [a man *of* wealth] *b)* containing [a bag *of* nuts] **4** specified as [a height *of* six feet] **5** characterized by [a man *of* honor] **6** concerning; about [think *of* me] **7** during [*of* recent years]

**of-** *prefix* OB-: used before *f* [*offer*]

**off** (ôf) *adv.* ⟦ME var. of *of*⟧ **1** so as to be away, at a distance, etc. **2** so as to be no longer on, attached, etc. [take *off* your hat] **3** (a specified distance) away in space or time [20 yards *off*] **4** so as to be no longer in operation, etc. [turn the motor *off*] **5** so as to be less, etc. [5% *off* for cash] **6** away from one's work [take a week *off*] —*prep.* **1** (so as to be) no longer (or not) on, attached, etc. [*off* the road] **2** from the substance of [live *off* the land] **3** away from [a mile *off* shore] **4** branching out from [an alley *off* Main Street] **5** relieved from [*off* duty] **6** not up to the usual standard, etc. of [*off* one's game] —*adj.* **1** not on or attached **2** not in operation **3** on the way [*off* to bed] **4** away from work [we are *off* today] **5** not up to the usual standard, etc. **6** more remote [on the *off* chance] **7** in (specified) circumstances [to be well *off*] **8** wrong [his figures are *off*] —*vt.* [Slang] to kill; murder —*interj.* go away! —**off and on** now and then

**-off** (ôf, äf) *combining form* a contest of skill in a (specified) activity or field [a chili cook-*off*]

**of·fal** (ôf′əl) *n.* ⟦ME *ofall,* lit., off-fall⟧ **1** [*with sing. or pl. v.*] the entrails, etc. of a butchered animal **2** refuse; garbage

**off'beat'** *n. Music* a beat having a weak accent —*adj.* [Inf.] unconventional, unusual, strange, etc.

**off'-col'or** *adj.* **1** varying from the standard color **2** improper; risqué

**of·fend** (ə fend′) *vi.* ⟦< L *offendere,* to strike against < *ob-* (see OB-) + *fendere,* to hit⟧ **1** to commit a sin or crime **2** to create resentment, anger, etc. —*vt.* **1** to hurt the feelings of; insult **2** to be displeasing to (the taste, sense, etc.) —**of·fend′er** *n.*

**of·fense** (ə fens′, ô′fens′) *n.* **1** a sin or crime **2** a creating of resentment, displeasure, etc. **3** a feeling hurt, angry, etc. **4** something that causes anger, etc. **5** the act of attacking **6** the side that is attacking or seeking to score in any contest Brit. sp. **of·fence′** —**take offense** to become offended

**of·fen'sive** *adj.* **1** attacking or for attack **2** unpleasant; disgusting **3** insulting —*n.* **1** attitude or position of attack: often with *the* **2** an attack —**of·fen'sive·ly** *adv.* —**of·fen'sive·ness** *n.*

**of·fer** (ôf′ər, äf′-) *vt.* ⟦< L *offerre* < *ob-* (see OB-) + *ferre,* to bear⟧ **1** to present in worship [to *offer* prayers] **2** to present for acceptance [to *offer* help] **3** to suggest; propose **4** to show or give signs of [to *offer* resistance] **5** to bid (a price, etc.) —*n.* the act of offering or thing offered

**of'fer·ing** *n.* **1** the act of making an offer **2** something offered; specif., *a)* a gift *b)* presentation in worship

**of'fer·to'ry** (-tôr′ē) *n., pl.* **-ries** [*often* O-] **1** *a)* the

part of a Eucharistic service in which the bread and wine are offered to God *b)* the prayers said, or music used, then **2** *a)* the part of a church service during which money offerings are collected *b)* the collection itself

**off'hand'** *adv.* without preparation; extemporaneously —*adj.* **1** said or done offhand **2** casual, curt, etc. Also **off'hand'ed**

**off'-hour'** *adj.* not for or during rush hour or other busy periods

**of·fice** (ôf′is, äf′-) *n.* ⟦< L *officium*⟧ **1** a service done for another **2** a duty, esp. as a part of one's work **3** a position of authority or trust, as in government **4** *a)* the place where the affairs of a business, etc. are carried on *b)* the people working there **5** [*often* O-] a religious service or set of prayers

**off'ice·hold'er** *n.* a government official

**of·fi·cer** (ôf′i sər, äf′-) *n.* **1** anyone holding an office, or position of authority, in a government, business, club, etc. **2** a police officer **3** one holding a position of authority, esp. by commission, in the armed forces

**of·fi·cial** (ə fish′əl) *adj.* **1** of or holding an office, or position of authority **2** authorized or authoritative **3** formal —*n.* a person holding office —**of·fi'cial·dom** (-dəm) *n.* —**of·fi'cial·ly** *adv.*

**of·fi·ci·ate** (ə fish′ē āt′) *vi.* **-at'ed, -at'ing 1** to perform the duties of an office **2** to perform the functions of a priest, minister, rabbi, etc. at a religious ceremony

**of·fi·cious** (ə fish′əs) *adj.* ⟦see OFFICE⟧ offering unwanted advice or services; meddlesome, esp. overbearingly so —**of·fi'cious·ly** *adv.* —**of·fi'cious·ness** *n.*

**off·ing** (ôf′iŋ) *n.* ⟦< OFF⟧ used chiefly in **in the offing,** at some indefinite future time

**off'-key'** *adj.* **1** *Music* flat or sharp **2** not harmonious

**off'-lim'its** *adj.* ruled to be a place that cannot be entered, etc. by a specified group

**off'-line'** *adj.* designating or of equipment not directly connected to and controlled by the central processing unit of a computer

**off'load'** *vt., vi.* UNLOAD (1*a,* 2*b,* 4)

**off'-put'ting** *adj.* [Chiefly Brit.] distracting, annoying, etc.

**off'-road'** *adj.* designating or of a vehicle for use off regular highways, streets, etc.

**off'-sea'son** *n.* a time of the year when the usual activity is reduced or not carried on

**off·set** (ôf set′; *for n.* ôf′set′) *vt.* **-set', -set'ting** to balance, compensate for, etc. —*n.* **1** a thing that offsets another **2** OFFSET PRINTING

**offset printing** a printing process in which the inked impression is first made on a rubber-covered roller, then transferred to paper

**off'shoot'** *n.* anything that derives from a main source; specif., a shoot growing from the main stem of a plant

**off'shore'** *adj.* **1** moving away from the shore **2** at some distance from the shore **3** engaged in outside the U.S. as by U.S. banks or manufacturers [*offshore* investments] —*adv.* **1** away from the shore **2** outside the U.S. [to borrow *offshore*]

**off'side'** *adj. Sports* not in the proper position for play: also **off'sides'**

**off'spring'** *n., pl.* **-spring'** *or* **-springs'** a child or children; progeny; young

**off'stage'** *n.* the part of the stage not seen by the audience —*adj.* in or from this —*adv.* to the off-stage

**off'-the-wall'** *adj.* [Slang] very unusual, unconventional, eccentric, etc.

**off'-track'** *adj.* designating or of legalized betting on horse races, carried on away from the racetrack

**off'-white'** *adj.* grayish-white or yellowish-white

**off year 1** a year in which a major election does not take place **2** a year of little production

**oft** (ôft) *adv.* ⟦OE⟧ *literary var. of* OFTEN

**of·ten** (ôf′ən, -tən) *adv.* ⟦ME var. of prec.⟧ many times; frequently: also **of′ten·times′**

**o·gle** (ō′gəl) *vi., vt.* **o′gled, o′gling** ⟦prob. < LowG *oog,* an eye⟧ to keep looking (at) flirtatiously —*n.* an ogling look —**o′gler** *n.*

**o·gre** (ō′gər) *n.* ⟦Fr⟧ **1** in fairy tales and folklore, a man-eating giant **2** a hideous, cruel man

**oh** (ō) *interj., n., pl.* **oh′s** or **ohs** an exclamation of surprise, fear, pain, etc.

**O·hi·o** (ō hī′ō) **1** river flowing from W Pennsylvania into the Mississippi **2** Midwestern state of the U.S.: 40,952 sq. mi.; pop. 10,847,000; cap. Columbus: abbrev. **OH** —**O·hi′o·an** *adj., n.*

**ohm** (ōm) *n.* ⟦after G. S. *Ohm* (1789-1854), Ger physicist⟧ unit of electrical resistance

**ohm′me·ter** *n.* an instrument for measuring electrical resistance in ohms

**o·ho** (ō hō′) *interj.* used to express surprise or triumph

**-o·hol·ic** (ə häl′ik) *combining form* -AHOLIC

**-oid** (oid) ⟦< Gr *eidos,* a form⟧ *suffix* like or resembling [*crystalloid*]

**oil** (oil) *n.* ⟦< L *oleum*⟧ **1** any of various greasy, combustible, liquid substances obtained from animal, vegetable, and mineral matter **2** PETROLEUM **3** *a*) OIL COLOR *b*) OIL PAINTING —*vt.* to lubricate or supply with oil —*adj.* of, from, or like oil

**oil′cloth′** *n.* cloth made waterproof by being treated with oil or paint

**oil color** paint made by grinding a pigment in oil: also **oil paint**

**oil′man** (-mən) *n., pl.* **-men** (-mən) an entrepreneur or executive in the petroleum industry

**oil painting 1** a picture painted in oil colors **2** the art of painting in oil colors

**oil shale** shale from which oil can be extracted by distillation

**oil′skin′** *n.* **1** cloth made waterproof by treatment with oil **2** [*often pl.*] a garment or outfit made of this

**oil well** a well that supplies petroleum

**oil·y** (oil′ē) *adj.* **-i·er, -i·est 1** of, like, or containing oil **2** greasy **3** too suave or smooth; unctuous —**oil′i·ness** *n.*

**oink** (oiŋk) *n.* ⟦echoic⟧ the grunt of a pig —*vi.* to make this sound

**oint·ment** (oint′mənt) *n.* ⟦< L *unguentum,* a salve⟧ a fatty substance used on the skin for healing or cosmetic purposes; salve

**OK** or **O.K.** (ō kā′) [Inf.] *adj., adv., interj.* ⟦< "oll korrect," facetious misspelling of *all correct*⟧ all right; correct —*n., pl.* **OK′s** or **O.K.′s** approval —*vt.* **OK′d** or **O.K.′d, OK′ing** or **O.K.′ing** to approve or endorse Also **o′kay′**

**O·kla·ho·ma** (ō′klə hō′mə) state of the SC U.S.: 68,679 sq. mi.; pop. 3,146,000; cap. Oklahoma City: abbrev. **OK** —**O′kla·ho′man** *adj., n.*

**Oklahoma City** capital of Oklahoma: pop. 445,000

**o·kra** (ō′krə) *n.* ⟦< WAfr name⟧ **1** a plant with sticky green pods **2** the pods, used in soups, stews, etc.

**Ok·to·ber·fest** (äk tō′bər fest′) *n.* ⟦Ger⟧ a beer-drinking festival held in Germany and elsewhere in the fall

**old** (ōld) *adj.* **old′er** or **eld′er, old′est** or **eld′est** ⟦OE *ald*⟧ **1** having lived or existed for a long time **2** of aged people **3** of a specified age [*two years old*] **4** not new **5** worn out by age or use **6** former **7** experienced [*an old hand*] **8** ancient **9** [*often* O-] designating the earliest form of a language [*Old* English] **10** designating the earlier or earliest of two or more [*the Old* World] —*n.* **1** time long past [*days of old*] **2** something old: with *the* —**old′ness** *n.*

**Old Church Sla·von·ic** (slə vän′ik) the South Slavic language now used only as a liturgical language by Orthodox Slavs: also called **Old Church Slavic** or **Old Bulgarian**

**old country** the country, esp. in Europe, from which an immigrant came

**old·en** (ōl′dən) *adj.* [Old Poet.] (of) old

**Old English** the Germanic language of the Anglo-Saxons, spoken in England from *c.* A.D. 400 to *c.* 1100

**old′-fash′ioned** *adj.* suited to or favoring the styles, ideas, etc. of past times —*n.* [*also* **Old-Fashioned**] a cocktail made with whiskey, bitters, and bits of fruit

**old fogy** or **old fogey** *see* FOGY

**Old French** the French language from *c.* A.D. 800 to *c.* 1550

**Old Glory** *name for* the flag of the United States

**old′-growth′** *adj.* designating or of a forest having very large, very old trees

**old guard** ⟦transl. < Fr⟧ [*sometimes* **O- G-**] the conservative element of a group, party, etc.

**old hat** [Slang] old-fashioned or stale

**Old High German** the High German language before the 12th c.

**old·ie** or **old·y** (ōl′dē) *n., pl.* **-ies** [Inf.] an old joke, saying, song, movie, etc.

**old lady** [Slang] **1** one's mother **2** one's wife

**old′-line′** *adj.* long-established, traditional, conservative, etc.

**Old Low German** the Low German language before the 12th c.

**old maid 1** a woman, esp. an older woman, who has never married: mildly disparaging **2** a prim, prudish, fussy person

**old man** [Slang] **1** one's father **2** one's husband **3** [*usually* **O- M-**] any man in authority: with *the*

**old master 1** any of the great European painters before the 18th c. **2** a painting by any of these

**Old Norse** the Germanic language of the Scandinavians before the 14th c.

**Old Saxon** the Low German dialect of the Saxons before the 10th c.

**old school** a group of people who cling to traditional or conservative ideas, methods, etc.

**old′ster** (-stər) *n.* [Inf.] an old or elderly person

**Old Testament** *Christian designation for* the Holy Scriptures of Judaism, the first of the two general divisions of the Christian Bible

**old′-time′** *adj.* **1** of past times **2** of long standing

**old′-tim′er** *n.* [Inf.] a long-time resident, employee, member, etc.

**old′-tim′ey** (-tīm′ē) *adj.* [Inf.] reminiscent of the past, usually in a positive way

**old′-world′** *adj.* of or from the Eastern Hemisphere, esp. Europe

**o·lé** (ō lā′) *interj., n.* ⟦Sp⟧ used to express approval, triumph, joy, etc.

**o·le·ag·i·nous** (ō′lē aj′i nəs) *adj.* ⟦< L *olea,* olive tree⟧ oily; unctuous

**o·le·an·der** (ō′lē an′dər) *n.* ⟦ML⟧ a poisonous evergreen shrub with fragrant white, pink, or red flowers and narrow, leathery leaves

**o·le·o·mar·ga·rine** or **o·le·o·mar·ga·rin** (ō′lē ō mär′jə rin) *n.* ⟦< L *oleum,* oil + MARGARINE⟧ former term for MARGARINE: also **o′le·o′**

**ol·fac·to·ry** (äl fak′tə rē, ōl-) *adj.* ⟦< L *olere,* have a smell + *facere,* make⟧ of the sense of smell

**ol·i·gar·chy** (äl′i gär′kē) *n., pl.* **-chies** ⟦< Gr *oligos,* few + -ARCHY⟧ **1** government in which ruling power belongs to a few persons **2** a state governed in this way **3** the persons ruling such a state —**ol′i·gar′chic** *adj.*

**ol·ive** (äl′iv) *n.* ⟦< L *oliva*⟧ **1** *a*) an evergreen tree of S Europe and the Near East *b*) its small, oval fruit, eaten green or ripe as a relish or pressed, when ripe, to extract its oil (**olive oil**) **2** the yellowish-green color of the unripe fruit

**olive branch** the branch of the olive tree, a symbol of peace

**O·lym·pi·a** (ō lim′pē ə) capital of Washington: pop. 34,000

**O·lym·pic games** (ō lim′pik) ⟦< *Olympia,* plain in

Greece, site of ancient games] an international athletic competition now held every two years, alternating between summer games and winter games: also **O·lym'pics**

**O·lym·pus** (ō lim'pəs), **Mount** mountain in N Greece: in Greek mythology, the home of the gods —**O·lym'pi·an** (-pē ən) *adj., n.*

**om** (ōm) *n.* ⟦Sans⟧ *Hinduism* a word intoned as during meditation

**O·ma·ha** (ō'mə hô) city in E Nebraska: pop. 336,000

**O·man** (ō män') country on the SE coast of Arabia: 119,499 sq. mi.; pop. 2,070,000 —**O·man'i** (-ē) *adj., n.*

**om·buds·man** (äm'bədz mən) *n., pl.* **-men** (-mən) ⟦Swed < *ombud*, a deputy⟧ a public official appointed to investigate citizens' complaints

**o·me·ga** (ō mā'gə) *n.* ⟦Gr ō + *mega*, great, i.e., long o: see OMICRON⟧ the 24th & final letter of the Greek alphabet (Ω, ω)

**om·e·let** or **om·e·lette** (äm'lət) *n.* ⟦< L *lamella*, small plate⟧ eggs beaten and cooked flat in a pan

**o·men** (ō'mən) *n.* ⟦L⟧ a thing or happening supposed to foretell a future event, either good or evil

**om·i·cron** (äm'i krän', ō'mi-) *n.* ⟦Gr *o mikron*, small o: see OMEGA⟧ the 15th letter of the Greek alphabet (O, o)

**om·i·nous** (äm'ə nəs) *adj.* of or serving as an evil omen; threatening —**om'i·nous·ly** *adv.*

**o·mis·sion** (ō mish'ən) *n.* **1** an omitting **2** something omitted

**o·mit** (ō mit') *vt.* **o·mit'ted**, **o·mit'ting** ⟦< L *omittere* < *ob-* (see OB-) + *mittere*, send⟧ **1** to fail to include; leave out **2** to fail to do; neglect

**omni-** ⟦L < *omnis*, all⟧ *combining form* all, everywhere

**om·ni·bus** (äm'ni bəs) *n., pl.* **-bus·es** ⟦< L, for all⟧ **1** BUS **2** a collection of stories, articles, etc., as on one theme —*adj.* including many things

**om·nip·o·tent** (äm nip'ə tənt) *adj.* ⟦< L *omnis*, all + *potens*, able⟧ having unlimited power or authority; all-powerful —**the Omnipotent** God —**om·nip'o·tence** *n.*

**om·ni·pres·ent** (äm'ni prez'ənt) *adj.* present in all places at the same time —**om'ni·pres'ence** *n.*

**om·nis·cient** (äm nish'ənt) *adj.* ⟦< L *omnis*, all + *sciens*, knowing⟧ knowing all things —**the Omniscient** God —**om·nis'cience** *n.*

**om·niv·o·rous** (äm niv'ə rəs) *adj.* ⟦< L *omnis*, all + *vorare*, devour⟧ **1** eating any sort of food, esp. both animal and vegetable food **2** taking in everything indiscriminately —**om·niv'o·rous·ly** *adv.* —**om·niv'o·rous·ness** *n.*

**on** (än, ôn) *prep.* ⟦OE⟧ **1** in contact with, supported by, or covering **2** in the surface of ⟦scars *on* it⟧ **3** *a)* near to ⟦*on* my left⟧ *b)* having as its location ⟦a house *on* Main Street⟧ **4** at the time of ⟦*on* Monday⟧ **5** connected with ⟦*on* the team⟧ **6** engaged in ⟦*on* a trip⟧ **7** in a state of ⟦*on* parole⟧ **8** as a result of ⟦a profit *on* the sale⟧ **9** in the direction of ⟦light shone *on* us⟧ **10** through the use of ⟦live *on* bread⟧ **11** concerning ⟦an essay *on* war⟧ **12** onto **13** at the expense of ⟦a drink *on* the house⟧ **14** [Inf.] using; addicted to ⟦*on* drugs⟧ —*adv.* **1** in a situation of contacting, being supported by, or covering **2** in a direction toward ⟦he looked *on*⟧ **3** forward ⟦move *on*⟧ **4** without stopping ⟦she sang *on*⟧ **5** into action or operation ⟦turn *on* the light⟧ —*adj.* **1** in action or operation ⟦the TV is *on*⟧ **2** [Slang] performing very well ⟦she is really *on* today⟧ —**and so on** and more like the preceding —**on and off** intermittently —**on and on** for a long time; continuously —**on to** [Slang] aware of the real nature or meaning of

**ON** Ontario

**once** (wuns) *adv.* ⟦ME *ones*⟧ **1** one time only **2** at any time; ever **3** formerly ⟦a *once* famous woman⟧ **4** by one degree ⟦a cousin *once* removed⟧ —*conj.* as soon as ⟦*once* he is tired, he will quit⟧ —*n.* one time ⟦go this *once*⟧ —**at once 1** immedi-

ately **2** at the same time —**once** (and) **for all** conclusively —**once in a while** now and then

**once'-o'ver** *n.* [Inf.] a quick look

**on·co·gene** (äŋ'kə jēn') *n.* ⟦< Gr *onkos*, a mass + GENE⟧ a gene that, when activated as by a virus, may cause a normal cell to become cancerous

**on·col·o·gy** (än käl'ə jē, äŋ-) *n.* ⟦< Gr *onkos*, a mass + -LOGY⟧ the branch of medicine dealing with tumors —**on·col'o·gist** *n.*

**on·com·ing** (än'kum'iŋ) *adj.* coming nearer in position or time

**on·co·vi·rus** (äŋ'kə vī'rəs) *n.* a virus that causes cancer

**one** (wun) *adj.* ⟦OE *an*⟧ **1** being a single thing or unit **2** united ⟦with *one* accord⟧ **3** a certain but unnamed ⟦take *one* path or the other, *one* day last week⟧ **4** the same **5** unique; only ⟦the *one* solution⟧ —*n.* **1** the first and lowest cardinal number; 1; I **2** a single person or thing —*pron.* **1** a certain person or thing **2** any person or thing —**at one** in accord —**one another** each one the other or others; each other —**one by one** individually in succession

**one'-di·men'sion·al** *adj.* having one dominant aspect, quality, etc. and hence narrow, limited, etc.

**O'Neill** (ō nēl'), **Eu·gene** (yoo jēn') 1888-1953; U.S. playwright

**one'ness** *n.* **1** singleness; unity **2** unity of mind, feeling, etc.

**one'-on-one'** *adj., adv.* in direct personal confrontation

**on·er·ous** (än'ər əs) *adj.* ⟦< L *onus*, a load⟧ burdensome; oppressive

**one'self'** *pron.* a person's own self: also **one's self** —**be oneself 1** to function normally **2** to be natural —**by oneself** alone

**one'-sid'ed** *adj.* **1** on, having, or involving only one side **2** unfair **3** unequal ⟦a *one-sided* race⟧

**one'-stop'** *adj.* designating of a store, bank, etc. that offers a complete range of goods or services

**one'time'** *adj.* former: also **one'-time'**

**one'-track'** *adj.* [Inf.] limited in scope

**one'-up'** *adj.* [Inf.] having an advantage (over another)

**one-up'man·ship'** (-up'mən ship') *n.* [Inf.] skill in seizing an advantage over others

**one'-way'** *adj.* moving, or allowing movement, in one direction only

**on'go'ing** *adj.* going on; progressing

**on·ion** (un'yən) *n.* ⟦< L *unus*, one⟧ **1** a plant of the lily family with an edible bulb **2** this bulb, having a strong, sharp smell and taste

**on'ion·skin'** *n.* a tough, thin, translucent paper

**on'line'** *adj.* designating or of equipment directly connected to and controlled by the central processing unit of a computer: also **on'-line'**

**on'look'er** *n.* a spectator

**on·ly** (ōn'lē) *adj.* ⟦< OE *an*, one + *-lic*, -ly⟧ **1** alone of its or their kind; sole **2** alone in superiority; best —*adv.* **1** and no other; and no more; solely **2** (but) in the end ⟦to meet one crisis, *only* to face another⟧ **3** as recently as —*conj.* [Inf.] except that; but —**only too** very; exceedingly

**on·o·mat·o·poe·ia** (än'ō mat'ō pē'ə, -mät'-) *n.* ⟦< Gr *onoma*, a name + *poiein*, make⟧ the formation of words by imitating sounds (Ex.: *buzz*)

**on'rush'** *n.* a headlong dash forward

**on'set'** *n.* **1** an attack **2** a start

**on·slaught** (än'slôt') *n.* ⟦< Du *slagen*, to strike⟧ a violent attack

**on'stream'** or **on'-stream'** *adv.* into operation or production ⟦a new refinery coming *onstream*⟧

**On·tar·i·o** (än ter'ē ō) **1** province of SC Canada: 412,580 sq. mi.; pop. 10,754,000; cap. Toronto: abbrev. **ON 2 Lake** smallest of the Great Lakes, between New York & Ontario, Canada —**On·tar'i·an** *adj., n.*

**on·to** (än'tōō) *prep.* **1** to a position on **2** [Slang] aware of the real meaning or nature of

**on·tog·e·ny** (än täj'ə në) *n.* ⟦ult. < Gr *einai*, to be + *-genēs*, born⟧ the life cycle of a single organism

**o·nus** (ō'nəs) *n.* ⟦L⟧ **1** a burden, unpleasant duty, etc. **2** blame

**on'ward** *adv.* toward or at a position ahead; forward: also **on'wards** —*adj.* advancing

**on·yx** (än'iks) *n.* ⟦< Gr, fingernail⟧ a type of agate with alternate colored layers

**oo·dles** (ōōd'lz) *pl.n.* ⟦< ?⟧ [Inf.] a great amount; very many

**ooze**[1] (ōōz) *n.* ⟦OE *wos*, sap⟧ **1** an oozing **2** something that oozes —*vi.* **oozed**, **ooz'ing** to flow or leak out slowly —*vt.* to give forth (a fluid)

**ooze**[2] (ōōz) *n.* ⟦OE *wase*⟧ soft mud or slime, as at the bottom of a lake

**op-** *prefix* OB-: used before *p* [*oppress*]

**o·pal** (ō'pəl) *n.* ⟦< Sans *úpalah*, (precious) stone⟧ an iridescent mineral of various colors: some varieties are semiprecious —**o·pal·es·cent** (ō'pəl es'ənt) *adj.*

**o·paque** (ō pāk') *adj.* ⟦< L *opacus*, shady⟧ **1** not transparent **2** dull or dark **3** hard to understand —**o·pac·i·ty** (ō pas'ə tē) or **o·paque'ness** *n.* —**o·paque'ly** *adv.*

**op art** (äp) a style of abstract painting creating optical effects, as the illusion of movement

**op. cit.** *abbrev.* ⟦L *opere citato*⟧ in the work cited

**OPEC** (ō'pek') *n.* Organization of Petroleum Exporting Countries

**Op-Ed** (äp'ed') *adj.* ⟦*Op(posite) Ed(itorial page)*⟧ designating or on a page in a newspaper featuring a wide variety of columns, letters, etc.

**o·pen** (ō'pən) *adj.* ⟦OE⟧ **1** not closed, covered, clogged, or shut **2** not enclosed [*open* fields] **3** spread out; unfolded [an *open* book] **4** having gaps, holes, etc. **5** free to be entered, used, etc. [an *open* meeting] **6** not decided [an *open* question] **7** not closed to new ideas, etc. [an *open* mind] **8** generous **9** free from legal or discriminatory restrictions [*open* season, *open* housing] **10** not conventional [*open* marriage] **11** not already taken [the job is *open*] **12** not secret; public **13** frank; candid [an *open* manner] —*vt.*, *vi.* **1** to cause to be, or to become, open **2** to spread out; expand; unfold **3** to begin; start **4** to start operating —**open to 1** willing to receive, discuss, etc. **2** liable to **3** available to —**the open 1** the outdoors **2** public knowledge —**o'pen·er** *n.* —**o'pen·ly** *adv.* —**o'pen·ness** *n.*

**open air** the outdoors —**o'pen-air'** *adj.*

**o'pen-and-shut'** *adj.* easily decided

**o'pen-end'ed** (-en'did) *adj.* unlimited

**o'pen-eyed'** (-īd') *adj.* with the eyes wide open, as in surprise or watchfulness

**o'pen-faced'** *adj.* **1** having a frank, honest face **2** designating a sandwich without a top slice of bread Also **o'pen-face'**

**o'pen-hand'ed** *adj.* generous

**o'pen-heart'ed** *adj.* **1** not reserved; frank **2** kindly; generous

**o'pen-hearth'** *adj.* designating or using a furnace with a wide hearth and low roof, for making steel

**o'pen-heart' surgery** surgery on the heart during which the blood is diverted, circulated, and oxygenated by mechanical means

**open house 1** an informal reception at one's home **2** a time when an institution is open to visitors

**o'pen·ing** *n.* **1** an open place; hole; gap **2** a clearing **3** a beginning **4** start of operations **5** a favorable chance **6** an unfilled job

**o'pen-mind'ed** *adj.* having a mind open to new ideas; unprejudiced

**o'pen-work'** *n.* ornamental work, as in cloth, with openings in it

**op·er·a**[1] (äp'ə rə, äp'rə) *n.* ⟦< L, a work⟧ a play having its text set to music and sung to orchestral accompaniment —**op'er·at'ic** (-ə rat'ik) *adj.*

**o·pe·ra**[2] (ō'pə rə, äp'ə rə) *n. pl.* of OPUS

**op·er·a·ble** (äp'ər ə bəl) *adj.* ⟦see OPERATE &

---

-ABLE⟧ **1** able to function **2** that can be treated by surgery

**opera glasses** a small binocular telescope used in theaters, etc.

**op·er·ate** (äp'ə rāt') *vi.* **-at'ed**, **-at'ing** ⟦< L *operari*, to work⟧ **1** to be in action; act; work **2** to have an effect **3** to perform a surgical operation —*vt.* **1** to put or keep in action **2** to direct; manage

**op'er·a'tion** (-rā'shən) *n.* ⟦< L *operatio*⟧ **1** the act or method of operating **2** a being in action or at work **3** a process or action that is part of a series in some work **4** any surgical procedure to remedy a physical ailment

**op'er·a'tion·al** *adj.* **1** of or having to do with the operation of a device, system, process, etc. **2** *a*) that can be used or operated *b*) in use; operating

**op'er·a·tive'** (-rə tiv', -rāt'iv) *adj.* **1** in operation **2** effective **3** connected with physical work or mechanical action

**op'er·a'tor** (-rāt'ər) *n.* **1** one who operates a machine [a telephone *operator*] **2** one engaged in commercial or industrial operations **3** [Slang] a clever, persuasive person

**op·er·et·ta** (äp'ə ret'ə) *n.* ⟦It, dim. of *opera*, OPERA[1]⟧ an amusing opera with spoken dialogue

**oph·thal·mic** (äf thal'mik) *adj.* ⟦< Gr *ophthalmos*, the eye⟧ of or involving the eye

**oph·thal·mol·o·gy** (äf'thal mäl'ə jē, äp'thə-) *n.* ⟦< Gr *ophthalmos*, the eye + -LOGY⟧ the branch of medicine dealing with the eye and its diseases —**oph'thal·mol'o·gist** *n.*

**o·pi·ate** (ō'pē it) *n.* ⟦ML *opiatum*⟧ **1** a drug containing, or derived from, opium **2** anything that quiets, soothes, or deadens

**o·pine** (ō pīn') *vt.*, *vi.* **o·pined'**, **o·pin'ing** ⟦< L *opinari*, think⟧ to express (an opinion)

**o·pin·ion** (ə pin'yən) *n.* ⟦< L *opinari*, think⟧ **1** a belief based not on certainty but on what seems true or probable **2** an evaluation, estimation, etc. **3** formal expert judgment

**o·pin'ion·at'ed** (-āt'id) *adj.* holding obstinately to one's opinions

**o·pi·um** (ō'pē əm) *n.* ⟦< Gr *opos*, vegetable juice⟧ a narcotic drug prepared from the seed of a certain poppy

**o·pos·sum** (ə päs'əm) *n.* ⟦< AmInd, white beast⟧ a small, nocturnal, tree-dwelling American marsupial that becomes motionless when frightened

**op·po·nent** (ə pō'nənt) *n.* ⟦< L *ob-* (see OB-) + *ponere*, to place⟧ one who opposes, as in a game; adversary

**op·por·tune** (äp'ər tōōn') *adj.* ⟦< L *ob-* (see OB-) + *portus*, PORT[1]⟧ **1** suitable: said of time **2** well-timed

**op'por·tun'ism'** *n.* the adapting of one's actions, thoughts, etc. to circumstances, as in politics, without regard for principles —**op'por·tun'ist** *n.*, *adj.* —**op'por·tun·is'tic** (-tōō nis'tik) *adj.*

**op·por·tu·ni·ty** (äp'ər tōō'nə tē) *n.*, *pl.* **-ties 1** a combination of circumstances favorable for the purpose **2** a good chance, as to advance oneself

**op·pose** (ə pōz') *vt.* **-posed'**, **-pos'ing** ⟦< L *ob-* (see OB-) + *ponere*, to place⟧ **1** to place opposite **2** to contend with; resist —**op·pos'a·ble** *adj.*

**op·po·site** (äp'ə zit) *adj.* ⟦< L *ob-* (see OB-) + *ponere*, to place⟧ **1** set against; in a contrary direction: often with *to* **2** entirely different; exactly contrary —*n.* anything opposed —*prep.* across from —**op'po·site·ly** *adv.*

**opposite number** one whose position, rank, etc. parallels another's in a different place or organization

**op·po·si·tion** (-zish'ən) *n.* **1** an opposing **2** resistance, contrast, hostility, etc. **3** *a*) one that opposes *b*) [often O-] a political party opposing the party in power

**op·press** (ə pres') *vt.* ⟦< L *ob-* (see OB-) + *premere*, to press⟧ **1** to weigh heavily on the mind of; worry **2** to keep down by the cruel or unjust use of authority —**op·pres'sor** *n.*

**op·pres·sion** (ə presh′ən) *n.* **1** an oppressing or being oppressed **2** a thing that oppresses **3** physical or mental distress

**op·pres·sive** (ə pres′iv) *adj.* **1** causing discomfort **2** tyrannical **3** distressing —**op·pres′sive·ly** *adv.*

**op·pro·bri·ous** (ə prō′brē əs) *adj.* expressing opprobrium; abusive

**op·pro′bri·um** (-əm) *n.* ⟦< L *ob-* (see OB-) + *probrum,* a disgrace⟧ **1** the disgrace attached to shameful conduct **2** contempt for something regarded as inferior

**opt** (äpt) *vi.* ⟦< L *optare,* to wish⟧ to make a choice: often with *for* —**opt out** (**of**) to choose not to be or continue in (some activity, organization, etc.)

**op·tic** (äp′tik) *adj.* ⟦< Gr *ōps,* an eye⟧ of the eye or sense of sight

**op·ti·cal** (äp′ti kəl) *adj.* **1** of the sense of sight; visual **2** of optics **3** for aiding vision —**op′ti·cal·ly** *adv.*

**optical disc** (or **disk**) any disk on which data, as computer files or music, is stored in the form of microscopic pits to be read by a laser

**op·ti·cian** (äp tish′ən) *n.* one who makes or sells eyeglasses, etc.

**op·tics** (äp′tiks) *n.* the branch of physics dealing with light and vision

**op·ti·mism** (äp′tə miz′əm) *n.* ⟦< L *optimus,* best⟧ **1** the belief that good ultimately prevails over evil **2** the tendency to take the most hopeful view of matters —**op′ti·mist** *n.* —**op′ti·mis′tic** *adj.* —**op′ti·mis′ti·cal·ly** *adv.*

**op·ti·mum** (-məm) *n.,* pl. **-mums** or **-ma** (-mə) ⟦see prec.⟧ the best or most favorable degree, condition, etc. —*adj.* most favorable; best: also **op′ti·mal** (-məl)

**op·tion** (äp′shən) *n.* ⟦< L *optare,* to wish⟧ **1** a choosing; choice **2** the right of choosing **3** something that is or can be chosen **4** the right to buy, sell, or lease at a fixed price within a specified time —**op′tion·al** *adj.*

**op·tom·e·try** (äp täm′ə trē) *n.* ⟦< Gr *optikos,* optic + *metron,* a measure⟧ the profession of testing and examining the eyes and prescribing glasses to correct vision problems —**op·tom′e·trist** *n.*

**op·u·lent** (äp′yōō lənt, -yə-) *adj.* ⟦< L *ops,* riches⟧ **1** very wealthy **2** abundant —**op′u·lence** *n.*

**o·pus** (ō′pəs) *n.,* pl. **o·pe·ra** (ō′pə rə, äp′ə rə) or **o′pus·es** ⟦L, a work⟧ a work; composition; esp., any of the numbered musical works of a composer

**or** (ôr) *conj.* ⟦OE *oththe*⟧ a coordinating conjunction introducing: *a*) an alternative *[* red *or* blue*]* or the last in a series of choices *b*) a synonymous word or phrase *[*oral, *or* spoken*]*

**-or** (ər, ôr) ⟦< L⟧ *suffix* a person or thing that (does a specified thing) *[inventor]*

**OR** Oregon

**or·a·cle** (ôr′ə kəl) *n.* ⟦< L *orare,* pray⟧ **1** among the ancient Greeks and Romans, *a*) the place where, or medium by which, deities were consulted *b*) the revelation of a medium or priest **2** *a*) a person of great knowledge *b*) statements of such a person —**o·rac·u·lar** (ō rak′yoo lər) *adj.*

**o·ral** (ôr′əl) *adj.* ⟦< L *os,* the mouth⟧ **1** uttered; spoken **2** of or near the mouth —**o′ral·ly** *adv.*

**oral history 1** the gathering of personal recollections in tape recorded interviews **2** a historical account based on this

**or·ange** (ôr′inj, är′-) *n.* ⟦< Sans *naranga*⟧ **1** a round, edible, reddish-yellow citrus fruit, with a sweet, juicy pulp **2** the evergreen tree it grows on **3** reddish yellow

**or′ange·ade′** *n.* a drink made of orange juice, water, and sugar

**o·rang·u·tan** (ô raŋ′oo tan′) *n.* ⟦< Malay *oraṅ,* man + *utan,* forest⟧ an ape of Borneo and Sumatra with shaggy, reddish-brown hair and very long arms

**o·rate** (ō rāt′, ôr′āt′) *vi.* **-rat′ed, -rat′ing** to make an oration; speak in a pompous or bombastic way

**o·ra·tion** (ō rā′shən, ô-) *n.* ⟦< L *orare,* speak⟧ a formal speech, esp. one given at a ceremony

**or·a·tor** (ôr′ət ər, är′-) *n.* an eloquent public speaker

**or·a·to·ri·o** (ôr′ə tôr′ē ō′) *n.,* pl. **-os′** ⟦It, small chapel⟧ a long, dramatic musical work, usually on a religious theme, sung but not acted out

**or·a·to·ry** (ôr′ə tôr′ē, är′-) *n.,* pl. **-ries** ⟦< L *oratoria*⟧ skill in public speaking —**or′a·tor′i·cal** *adj.*

**orb** (ôrb) *n.* ⟦L *orbis,* a circle⟧ a sphere, esp. a celestial body, as the sun or moon

**or·bit** (ôr′bit) *n.* ⟦< L *orbis,* a circle⟧ **1** the path of a celestial body during its revolution around another **2** the path of an artificial satellite or spacecraft around a celestial body —*vt.,* *vi.* to move in, or put into, an orbit —**or′bit·al** *adj.*

**or·chard** (ôr′chərd) *n.* ⟦OE *ortgeard*⟧ **1** land for growing fruit trees **2** the trees

**or·ches·tra** (ôr′kis trə, -kes′-) *n.* ⟦< Gr *orcheisthai,* to dance⟧ **1** the space in front of a theater stage, where the musicians sit: in full **orchestra pit 2** the seats on the main floor of a theater **3** *a*) a group of musicians playing together *b*) their instruments —**or·ches′tral** (-kes′trəl) *adj.*

**or′ches·trate′** (-trāt′) *vt., vi.* **-trat′ed, -trat′ing 1** to arrange (music) for an orchestra **2** to coordinate or arrange (something) —**or′ches·tra′tion** *n.*

**or·chid** (ôr′kid) *n.* ⟦< Gr *orchis,* testicle: from the shape of the roots⟧ **1** a perennial plant having flowers with three petals, one of which is lip-shaped **2** this flower **3** pale purple

**or·dain** (ôr dān′) *vt.* ⟦< L *ordo,* an order⟧ **1** to decree; establish; enact **2** to invest with the office of minister, priest, or rabbi —**or·dain′ment** *n.*

**or·deal** (ôr dēl′) *n.* ⟦OE *ordal*⟧ any difficult or painful experience

**or·der** (ôr′dər) *n.* ⟦< L *ordo,* straight row⟧ **1** social position **2** a state of peace; orderly conduct **3** arrangement of things or events; series **4** a definite plan; system **5** a military, monastic, or social brotherhood **6** a condition in which everything is in its place and working properly **7** condition in general *[*in working *order]* **8** an authoritative command, instruction, etc. **9** a class; kind **10** an established method, as of conduct in meetings, etc. **11** *a*) a request to supply something *[*an *order* for books*]* *b*) the goods supplied **12** *[usually pl.]* the position of ordained minister, priest, etc. *[*to take holy *orders]* —*vt., vi.* **1** to put or keep (things) in order; arrange **2** to command **3** to request (something to be supplied) —**in** (or **out of**) **order 1** (or not in) proper position **2** in (or not in) good condition **3** in (or not in) accordance with the rules —**in order that** so that —**in order to** for the purpose of —**in short order** quickly —**on the order of** similar to —**to order** in accordance with the buyer's specifications

**or′der·ly** *adj.* **1** neat or tidy **2** well-behaved —*n.,* pl. **-lies 1** an enlisted person assigned to perform personal services for an officer **2** a male hospital attendant —**or′der·li·ness** *n.*

**or·di·nal** (ôrd′n əl) *adj.* ⟦< L *ordo,* order⟧ expressing order in a series —*n.* any number showing order in a series (e.g., first, tenth): in full **ordinal number**

**or·di·nance** (ôrd′n əns) *n.* ⟦< L *ordo,* an order⟧ a statute or regulation, esp. a municipal one

**or·di·nar·i·ly** (ôrd′n er′ə lē) *adv.* usually; as a rule

**or·di·nar·y** (ôrd′n er′ē) *adj.* ⟦< L *ordo,* an order⟧ **1** customary; usual **2** familiar; unexceptional; common —**out of the ordinary** unusual

**or·di·nate** (ôrd′n it, -āt′) *n.* ⟦< L *(linea) ordinate (applicata),* line applied in ordered manner⟧ *Math.* the vertical distance of a point from a horizontal axis

**or·di·na·tion** (ôrd′n ā′shən) *n.* an ordaining or being ordained to the clergy

**ord·nance** (ôrd′nəns) *n.* ⟦< ORDINANCE⟧ **1** artillery **2** all military weapons, ammunition, etc.

**or·dure** (ôr′jər) *n.* [< L *horridus,* horrid] dung; filth

**ore** (ôr) *n.* [OE *ar,* brass] a natural combination of minerals, esp. one from which a metal or metals can be profitably extracted

**o·reg·a·no** (ô reg′ə nō, ə-) *n.* [< Sp < Gr *origanon*] an herb of the mint family, with fragrant leaves used for seasoning

**Or·e·gon** (ôr′i gən, -gän′) NW coastal state of the U.S.: 97,060 sq. mi.; pop. 2,842,000; cap. Salem: abbrev. *OR* —**Or·e·go′ni·an** (-gō′nē ən) *adj., n.*

**or·gan** (ôr′gən) *n.* [< Gr *organon,* an implement] **1** a keyboard musical instrument with sets of graduated pipes through which compressed air is passed, causing sound by vibration **2** in animals and plants, a part adapted to perform a specific function **3** a means for performing some action **4** a means of communicating ideas, as a periodical

**or·gan·dy** or **or·gan·die** (ôr′gən dē) *n., pl.* **-dies** [Fr *organdi*] a very sheer, crisp cotton fabric

**or·gan·elle** (ôr′gə nel′) *n.* [< L *organum,* tool + dim. of *-ellus*] a discrete structure within a cell, as a chloroplast, having specialized functions, a distinctive chemical composition, etc.

**or·gan·ic** (ôr gan′ik) *adj.* **1** of or having to do with a bodily organ **2** inherent; inborn **3** systematically arranged **4** designating or of any chemical compound containing carbon **5** of, like, or derived from living organisms **6** grown with only natural fertilizers —**or·gan′i·cal·ly** *adv.*

**or·gan·ism** (ôr′gə niz′əm) *n.* any living thing

**or′gan·ist** *n.* an organ player

**or·gan·i·za·tion** (ôr′gə ni zā′shən) *n.* **1** an organizing or being organized **2** any organized group, as a club —**or·gan·i·za′tion·al** *adj.*

**or·gan·ize** (ôr′gə nīz′) *vt.* **-ized′, -iz′ing 1** to provide with an orderly structure or arrangement **2** to arrange for **3** to institute; establish **4** to persuade to join a cause, group, etc. —*vi.* to become organized —**or′gan·iz′er** *n.*

**or·gan·za** (ôr gan′zə) *n.* a thin, stiff fabric of rayon, silk, etc.

**or·gasm** (ôr′gaz′əm) *n.* [< Gr *organ,* to swell] the climax of a sexual act

**or·gy** (ôr′jē) *n., pl.* **-gies** [< Gr *orgia,* secret rites] **1** a wild party, esp. with sexual activity **2** unrestrained indulgence in any activity

**o·ri·el** (ôr′ē əl, ôr′-) *n.* [< ML *oriolum,* porch] a bay window resting on a bracket or a corbel

**o·ri·ent** (ôr′ē ənt; *for v.,* -ent′, -ənt) *n.* [< L *oriri,* arise: used of the rising sun] [Old Poet.] the east —*vt.* to adjust (oneself) to a particular situation, with regard to direction or position, etc. —**the Orient** the East, or Asia; esp. the Far East —**o′ri·en·ta′tion** *n.*

**O′ri·en′tal** (-ent′′l) *adj.* of the Far East or its people, etc. —*n.* a person born in the Far East or a member of a people of that region Now often regarded as a term of disparagement

**or·i·fice** (ôr′ə fis, är′-) *n.* [< L *os,* a mouth + *facere,* make] a mouth of a tube, cavity, etc.; opening

**orig** *abbrev.* **1** origin **2** original **3** originally

**o·ri·ga·mi** (ôr′ə gä′mē) *n.* [Jpn] the Japanese art of folding paper to form flowers, animals, etc.

**or·i·gin** (ôr′ə jin, är′-) *n.* [< L *oriri,* to rise] **1** a coming into existence or use; beginning **2** parentage; birth **3** source; root; cause

**o·rig·i·nal** (ə rij′i nəl) *adj.* **1** first; earliest **2** never having been before; new; novel **3** capable of creating something new **4** being that from which copies are made —*n.* **1** a primary type that has given rise to varieties **2** an original work, as of art or literature —**o·rig′i·nal′i·ty** (-nal′ə tē) *n.* — **o·rig′i·nal·ly** *adv.*

**o·rig′i·nate′** (-nāt′) *vt.* **-nat′ed, -nat′ing** to bring into being; esp., to invent —*vi.* to begin; start —**o·rig′i·na′tion** *n.* —**o·rig′i·na′tor** *n.*

**O-ring** (ō′riŋ′) *n.* a ring-shaped seal of rubber, plastic, etc., used to prevent leaks

**o·ri·ole** (ôr′ē ōl′) *n.* [< L *aurum,* gold] a bright-orange and black American bird that builds a hanging nest

**O·ri·on** (ō rī′ən) *n.* a very bright equatorial constellation

**Or·lon** (ôr′län′) *trademark for* a synthetic acrylic fiber similar to nylon, or a fabric made from this fiber

**or·mo·lu** (ôr′mə lōō′) *n.* [Fr *or moulu,* ground gold] a copper and tin alloy used to imitate gold

**or·na·ment** (ôr′nə mənt; *for v.,* -ment′) *n.* [< L *ornare,* adorn] **1** anything that adorns; decoration **2** one whose character or talent adds luster to the surroundings, etc. —*vt.* to decorate —**or′na·men′tal** *adj.* —**or′na·men·ta′tion** *n.*

**or·nate** (ôr nāt′) *adj.* [< L *ornare,* adorn] heavily ornamented; showy —**or·nate′ly** *adv.* —**or·nate′ness** *n.*

**or·ner·y** (ôr′nər ē) *adj.* [< ORDINARY] [Inf.] **1** mean; nasty **2** obstinate —**or′ner·i·ness** *n.*

**or·ni·thol·o·gy** (ôr′nə thäl′ə jē) *n.* [< Gr *ornis,* bird + -LOGY] the branch of zoology dealing with birds —**or′ni·thol′o·gist** *n.*

**o·ro·tund** (ôr′ə tund′) *adj.* [< L *os,* mouth + *rotundas,* round] **1** resonant: said of the voice **2** bombastic or pompous

**or·phan** (ôr′fən) *n.* [< Gr *orphanos*] a child whose parents are dead —*adj.* **1** being an orphan **2** of or for orphans —*vt.* to cause to become an orphan

**or′phan·age** (-ij) *n.* an institution that is a home for orphans

**Or·phe·us** (ôr′fē əs) *n. Gr. Myth.* a poet-musician with magic musical powers

**or·ris** (ôr′is, är′-) *n.* [< Gr *iris,* iris] a European iris, esp. one with a root (**or′ris·root′**) pulverized for perfumery, etc.

**ortho-** [< Gr *orthos,* straight] *combining form* **1** straight [orthodontics] **2** proper; correct [orthography] Also **orth-**

**or·tho·don·tics** (ôr′thə dän′tiks) *n.* [< ORTH(O)- + Gr *odōn,* tooth + -ICS] the branch of dentistry concerned with correcting tooth irregularities: also **or′tho·don′tia** (-dän′shə, -shē ə) —**or′tho·don′tist** *n.*

**or·tho·dox** (ôr′thə däks′) *adj.* [< Gr *orthos,* straight + *doxa,* opinion] conforming to the usual beliefs or established doctrines; approved or conventional —**or′tho·dox′y,** *pl.* **-ies,** *n.*

**or·thog·ra·phy** (ôr thäg′rə fē) *n., pl.* **-phies** [< Gr: see ORTHO- & -GRAPHY] **1** correct spelling **2** spelling as a subject for study —**or·tho·graph·ic** (ôr′thə graf′ik) *adj.*

**or·tho·pe·dics** or **or·tho·pae·dics** (ôr′thə pē′diks) *n.* [< Gr *orthos,* straight + *paideia,* training of children] the branch of medicine dealing with deformities, diseases, and injuries of the bones, joints, muscles, etc. —**or′tho·pe′dic** or **or′tho·pae′dic** *adj.* —**or′tho·pe′dist** or **or′tho·pae′dist** *n.*

**-o·ry** (ôr′ē, ər ē) [< L *-orius*] *suffix* **1** of, having the nature of [sensory] **2** a place or thing for [crematory]

**OS** *abbrev.* Old Saxon

**O·sa·ka** (ō′sä kə) seaport in S Honshu, Japan: pop. 2,648,000

**os·cil·late** (äs′ə lāt′) *vi.* **-lat′ed, -lat′ing** [< L *oscillum,* a swing] **1** to swing to and fro **2** to vacillate **3** *Physics* to vary regularly between high and low values: said as of an electric current —**os′cil·la′tion** *n.* —**os′cil·la′tor** *n.*

**os·cil·lo·scope** (ə sil′ə skōp′) *n.* [< L *oscillare,* to swing + -SCOPE] an instrument that visually displays an electrical wave on a fluorescent screen

**os·cu·late** (äs′kyōō lāt′, -kyə-) *vt., vi.* **-lat′ed, -lat′ing** [< L *osculum,* little mouth] to kiss: a facetious usage —**os′cu·la′tion** *n.*

**-ose**[1] (ōs) [Fr < (*gluc*)*ose*] *suffix* **1** a carbohydrate [sucrose] **2** the product of a protein hydrolysis

**-ose**[2] (ōs) [L *-osus*] *suffix* full of, like

**Osh·kosh** (äsh′käsh′) city in E Wisconsin: pop. 55,000

**o·sier** (ō′zhər) *n.* [< ML *auseria,* willow] a willow with branches used for baskets and furniture

**-o·sis** (ō′sis) [< Gr] *suffix* **1** condition, action [hyp-

*nosis]* **2** an abnormal or diseased condition *[psychosis]*

**Os·lo** (äz′lō, äs′-) seaport & capital of Norway: pop. 459,000

**os·mo·sis** (äs mō′sis, äz-) *n.* [< Gr *ōsmos,* impulse] **1** the tendency of fluids to pass through a membrane so as to equalize concentrations on both sides **2** the movement of fluids through a membrane **3** an apparently effortless absorption of ideas, feelings, etc. —**os·mot′ic** (-mät′ik) *adj.*

**os·prey** (äs′prē, -prā) *n., pl.* **-preys** [< L *os,* a bone + *frangere,* to break] a large diving bird that feeds mainly on fish

**os·si·fy** (äs′ə fī′) *vt., vi.* **-fied′, -fy′ing** [< L *os,* a bone + -FY] **1** to change into bone **2** to fix rigidly in a custom, practice, etc. —**os′si·fi·ca′tion** *n.*

**os·ten·si·ble** (ä sten′sə bəl) *adj.* [< L *ostendere,* to show] apparent; seeming —**os·ten′si·bly** *adv.*

**os·ten·ta·tion** (äs′tən tā′shən) *n.* [< L *ostendere,* to show] showy display; pretentiousness —**os′ten·ta′tious** *adj.*

**osteo-** [< Gr *osteon,* a bone] *combining form* bone or bones

**os·te·o·ar·thri·tis** (äs′tē ō′är thrīt′is) *n.* [prec. + ARTHRITIS] a common form of arthritis marked by cartilage degeneration and bone enlargement

**os·te·op·a·thy** (äs′tē äp′ə thē) *n.* [ModL: see OSTEO- & -PATHY] a school of medicine and surgery that emphasizes the interrelationship of muscles and bones to other body systems —**os·te·o·path** (äs′tē ə path′) *n.* —**os′te·o·path′ic** *adj.*

**os·te·o·po·ro·sis** (äs′tē ō′pə rō′sis) *n.* [OSTEO- + L *porus,* a pore + -OSIS] a bone disorder marked by porous, brittle bones

**os·to·my** (äs′tə mē) *n., pl.* **-mies** any surgery connecting a hollow organ to the outside of the body or to another hollow organ

**os·tra·cize** (äs′trə sīz′) *vt.* **-cized′, -ciz′ing** [< Gr *ostrakon,* a shell or potsherd (cast as a ballot)] to banish from a group, society, etc. —**os′tra·cism′** (-siz′əm) *n.*

**os·trich** (äs′trich, ôs′-) *n.* [< L *avis,* bird + *struthio,* ostrich] a large, swift-running bird of Africa and SW Asia

**OT** *abbrev.* **1** Old Testament **2** overtime

**O·thel·lo** (ō thel′ō) *n.* the title character of a tragedy by Shakespeare

**oth·er** (u*th*′ər) *adj.* [OE] **1** being the remaining one or ones *[Bill and the other boys]* **2** different or distinct from that or those referred to or implied *[use your other foot]* **3** additional *[he has no other coat]* —*pron.* **1** the other one **2** some other one *[do as others do]* —*adv.* otherwise *[he can't do other than go]* —**the other day** (or **night,** etc.) on a recent day (or night, etc.)

**oth·er·wise** (u*th*′ər wīz′) *adv.* **1** in another manner; differently *[she believes otherwise]* **2** in all other respects *[he is otherwise intelligent]* **3** in other circumstances **4** if not *[do it now; otherwise,* you'll forget it] —*adj.* different

**oth·er·world′ly** *adj.* being apart from earthly interests; spiritual

**o·ti·ose** (ō′shē ōs′) *adj.* [< L *otium,* leisure] **1** futile **2** useless

**Ot·ta·wa** (ät′ə wə, -wä′) capital of Canada, in SE Ontario: pop. 323,000

**ot·ter** (ät′ər) *n.* [OE *oter*] **1** a furry, carnivorous mammal with webbed feet **2** its fur

**ot·to·man** (ät′ə mən) *n.* [Fr *ottomane*] a low, cushioned seat or footstool

**ouch** (ouch) *interj.* used to express sudden pain

**ought** (ôt) *v.aux.* used with infinitives and meaning: **1** to be compelled by obligation, duty, or desirability *[you ought to eat more]* **2** to be expected *[it ought to be over soon]*

**oui** (wē) *adv., interj.* [Fr] yes

**Oui·ja** (wē′jə, -jē) [< prec. + Ger *ja,* yes] *trademark for* a board with the alphabet and various symbols on it and a sliding pointer: believed by some to convey messages from spirits

**ounce** (ouns) *n.* [< L *uncia,* a twelfth] **1** a unit of weight, $\frac{1}{16}$ pound avoirdupois or $\frac{1}{12}$ pound troy **2** fluid ounce, $\frac{1}{16}$ pint

**our** (our) *poss. pronominal adj.* [OE *ure*] of, belonging to, or done by us

**ours** (ourz) *pron.* that or those belonging to us: poss. form of WE *[that book is ours; ours are better]*

**our·selves** (our selvz′) *pron.* a form of WE, used as an intensive *[we went ourselves],* as a reflexive *[we saw ourselves in the mirror],* or with the meaning "our true selves" *[we are not ourselves when we are sick]*

**-ous** (əs) [< L *-osus*] *suffix* having, full of, characterized by *[beauteous]*

**oust** (oust) *vt.* [< L *ostare,* obstruct] to force out; expel; dispossess

**oust′er** *n.* an ousting or being ousted

**out** (out) *adv.* [OE *ut*] **1** away or removed from a place, position, etc. **2** into the open air **3** into existence or activity *[disease broke out]* **4** *a)* to a conclusion *[argue it out] b)* completely *[tired out]* **5** into sight or notice *[the moon came out]* **6** from existence or activity *[fade out]* **7** aloud *[sing out]* **8** beyond a regular surface, condition, etc. *[stand out]* **9** into disuse *[long skirts went out]* **10** from a group or stock *[pick out]* **11** [Slang] into unconsciousness **12** *Baseball* in a manner that results in an out *[to fly out]* —*adj.* **1** external: usually in combination *[outpost]* **2** beyond regular limits **3** away from work, etc. **4** in error *[out in one's estimates]* **5** not in use, operation, etc. **6** [Inf.] having suffered a financial loss *[out twenty dollars]* **7** [Inf.] outmoded **8** *Baseball* having failed to get on base —*prep.* **1** out of **2** along, and away from a central location —*n.* **1** something that is out **2** [Slang] a way out; excuse **3** *Baseball* the failure of a player to reach base safely —*vi.* to become known *[the truth will out]* —*vt.* [Inf.] to identify (a person) publicly as a homosexual —**on the outs** [Inf.] on unfriendly terms —**out for** trying to get or do —**out of 1** from inside of **2** beyond **3** from (material, etc.) *[made out of stone]* **4** because of *[out of spite]* **5** having no *[out of gas]* **6** so as to deprive —**out to** trying to

**out-** *combining form* **1** at or from a point away, outside, etc. *[outpatient]* **2** going away or forth, outward *[outbound]* **3** better or more than *[outdo]*

**out′age** *n.* an interruption of operation, as of electric power

**out′-and-out′** *adj.* thorough

**out′back′** *n.* any remote, sparsely settled region viewed as uncivilized

**out′bid′** *vt.* **-bid′, -bid′ding** to bid or offer more than (someone else)

**out′board′** *adj.* outside the hull of a ship or boat *[an outboard motor]*

**out′bound′** *adj.* outward bound

**out′break′** *n.* a breaking out; sudden occurrence, as of disease or rioting

**out′build′ing** *n.* a structure, as a shed, separate from the main building

**out′burst′** *n.* a sudden release, as of feeling or energy

**out′cast′** *adj.* driven out; rejected —*n.* a person rejected, as by society

**out′class′** *vt.* to surpass

**out′come′** *n.* result; consequence

**out′crop′** *n.* **1** the emergence of a mineral at the earth's surface **2** the mineral that so emerges

**out′cry′** *n., pl.* **-cries′ 1** a crying out **2** a strong objection

**out′dat′ed** *adj.* no longer current

**out′dis′tance** *vt.* **-tanced, -tanc·ing** to get ahead of, as in a race

**out′do′** *vt.* **-did′, -done′, -do′ing** to exceed or surpass —**outdo oneself** to do better than one expected to do

**out′door′** *adj.* **1** being or taking place outdoors **2** of or fond of the outdoors

**out'doors'** *adv.* in or into the open; outside —*n.* any area outside a building

**out'er** *adj.* farther out or away

**out'er·most'** *adj.* farthest out

**outer space** space beyond the earth's atmosphere or beyond the solar system

**out'er·wear'** *n.* garments, as overcoats, worn over the usual clothing

**out'field'** *n. Baseball* **1** the playing area beyond the infield **2** the players (**out'field'ers**) positioned there

**out'fit'** *n.* **1** the equipment used in an activity **2** clothing worn together; ensemble **3** a group associated in an activity —*vt.* **-fit'ted, -fit'ting** to furnish as with an outfit —**out'fit'ter** *n.*

**out'flank'** *vt.* to go around and beyond the flank of (enemy troops)

**out'fox'** *vt.* to outsmart

**out'go'** *n., pl.* **-goes'** that which is paid out; expenditure

**out'go'ing** *adj.* **1** *a*) leaving *b*) retiring from office **2** sociable, friendly, etc.

**out'grow'** *vt.* **-grew', -grown', -grow'ing** **1** to grow faster or larger than **2** to lose in becoming mature **3** to grow too large for

**out'growth'** *n.* **1** a growing out or that which grows out **2** a result or development

**out'guess'** *vt.* to outwit in anticipating

**out'house'** *n.* a small outdoor structure used as a toilet, having a seat with a hole over a deep pit

**out'ing** *n.* **1** a pleasure trip **2** an outdoor walk, ride, etc.

**out'land'ish** (-lan'dish) *adj.* very odd or strange; fantastic; bizarre

**out'last'** *vt.* to endure longer than

**out'law'** *n.* a habitual or notorious criminal —*vt.* to declare illegal

**out'lay'** *n.* **1** a spending (*of* money, etc.) **2** money, etc. spent

**out'let'** *n.* **1** a passage for letting something out **2** a means of expression [*an outlet* for anger] **3** a retail store selling defective or surplus goods at a discount: in full **outlet store** **4** a point in an electric circuit where a plug can be inserted to connect with a power supply

**out'line'** *n.* **1** a line bounding the limits of an object **2** a sketch showing only contours **3** [*also pl.*] a general plan **4** a systematic summary —*vt.* **-lined', -lin'ing** **1** to draw in outline **2** to give or write the main points of

**out'live'** *vt.* **-lived', -liv'ing** to live or endure longer than; outlast

**out'look'** *n.* **1** the view from a place **2** viewpoint **3** expectation or prospect

**out'ly'ing** *adj.* relatively far out from a certain point; remote

**out'ma·neu'ver** or **out'ma·noeu'vre** *vt.* **-vered** or **-vred, -ver·ing** or **-vring** to outwit by maneuvering

**out'match'** *vt.* to be superior to; outdo

**out'mod'ed** *adj.* no longer in fashion or accepted; obsolete

**out'num'ber** *vt.* to exceed in number

**out'-of-date'** *adj.* no longer in style or use; old-fashioned

**out'-of-doors'** *adj.* OUTDOOR —*adv., n.* OUTDOORS

**out'-of-the-way'** *adj.* **1** secluded **2** not common; unusual

**out'-of-town'er** *n.* a visitor from another town or city

**out'pa'tient** *n.* a patient treated at a hospital, etc. without becoming an inpatient

**out'place'ment** *n.* assistance in finding a new job, provided to an employee by the employer

**out'play'** *vt.* to play better than

**out'post'** *n.* **1** *Mil. a*) a small group stationed at a distance from the main force *b*) the station occupied by such a group *c*) a foreign base **2** a frontier settlement

**out'put'** *n.* **1** the work done or amount produced, esp. over a given period **2** information delivered by a computer **3** *Elec.* the useful voltage, current, or power delivered

**out'rage'** *n.* [ult. < L *ultra*, beyond] **1** an extremely vicious or violent act **2** a deep insult or offense **3** great anger, etc. aroused by this —*vt.* **-raged', -rag'ing** **1** to commit an outrage upon or against **2** to cause outrage in

**out·ra'geous** (-rā'jəs) *adj.* **1** involving or doing great injury or wrong **2** very offensive or shocking —**out·ra'geous·ly** *adv.* —**out·ra'geous·ness** *n.*

**out'rank'** *vt.* to exceed in rank

**ou·tré** (ōō trā') *adj.* [Fr] **1** exaggerated **2** eccentric; bizarre

**out·reach** (out'rēch'; *for v., also* out·rēch') *vt., vi.* to reach farther (than) —*n.* a reaching out —*adj.* designating or of a program extending assistance, services, etc. to people in the community

**out'rid'er** *n.* **1** a rider on horseback who accompanies a stagecoach, etc. **2** a cowboy riding a range, as to keep cattle from straying **3** a forerunner

**out'rig'ger** (-rig'ər) *n.* **1** a timber rigged out from the side of certain canoes to prevent tipping **2** a canoe of this type

**out·right** (out'rīt', out'rīt') *adj.* **1** without reservation **2** complete —*adv.* **1** entirely **2** openly **3** at once

CANOE WITH OUTRIGGER

**out'run'** *vt.* **-ran', -run', -run'ning** **1** to run faster than **2** to exceed

**out'sell'** *vt.* **-sold', -sell'ing** to sell in greater amounts than

**out'set'** *n.* a setting out; beginning

**out'shine'** *vt.* **-shone'** or **-shined', -shin'ing** **1** to shine brighter or longer than (another) **2** to surpass; excel

**out·side** (out'sīd', out'sīd') *n.* **1** the outer side or part; exterior **2** outward appearance **3** any area not inside —*adj.* **1** of or on the outside; outer **2** extreme [an *outside* estimate] **3** slight [an *outside* chance] —*adv.* **1** on or to the outside **2** outdoors —*prep.* **1** on or to the outer side of **2** beyond the limits of —**outside of 1** outside **2** [Inf.] other than

**out·sid·er** (out'sīd'ər, out'sīd'ər) *n.* one who is not included in a given group

**out'size'** *n.* an unusually large size —*adj.* unusually large

**out'skirts'** *pl.n.* districts remote from the center, as of a city

**out'smart'** *vt.* to overcome by cunning or cleverness; outwit —**outsmart oneself** to have one's efforts at cunning or cleverness result in one's own disadvantage

**out'source'** *vt.* **-sourced', -sourc'ing** to transfer (manufacturing tasks, etc.) to outside contractors, esp. in order to reduce operating costs

**out'spo'ken** *adj.* **1** unrestrained in speech **2** spoken boldly or candidly

**out'spread'** *adj.* spread out; extended

**out'stand'ing** *adj.* **1** prominent; distinguished **2** unpaid; uncollected **3** issued and sold: said of stocks and bonds

**out'sta'tion** *n.* a post or station in a remote or unsettled area

**out'stretch'** *vt.* to stretch out; extend

**out'strip'** *vt.* **-stripped', -strip'ping** **1** to go at a faster pace than **2** to excel; surpass

**out'take'** *n.* a filmed scene, defective recording, etc. not used as or in the final version

**out'vote'** *vt.* **-vot'ed, -vot'ing** to defeat in a vote

**out'ward** *adj.* **1** having to do with the outside; outer **2** clearly apparent **3** away from the interior —*adv.* toward the outside: also **out'wards** —**out'ward·ly** *adv.*

**out'wear'** *vt.* **-wore'**, **-worn'**, **-wear'ing** to outlast

**out'weigh'** *vt.* **1** to weigh more than **2** to be more important than

**out'wit'** *vt.* **-wit'ted**, **-wit'ting** to get the better of by cleverness

**o·va** (ō'və) *n. pl.* of OVUM

**o·val** (ō'vəl) *adj.* 〚< L *ovum,* egg〛 egg-shaped; elliptical —*n.* anything oval

**o·va·ry** (ō'və rē) *n., pl.* **-ries** 〚< L *ovum,* egg〛 **1** a female reproductive gland producing eggs **2** *Bot.* the enlarged, hollow part of the pistil, containing ovules —**o·var·i·an** (ō ver'ē ən) *adj.*

**o·vate** (ō'vāt') *adj.* egg-shaped; oval

**o·va·tion** (ō vā'shən) *n.* 〚< L *ovare,* celebrate a triumph〛 enthusiastic applause or an enthusiastic public welcome

**ov·en** (uv'ən) *n.* 〚OE *ofen*〛 a compartment or receptacle for baking, roasting, heating, etc.

**ov'en-proof'** *adj.* able to withstand the high temperatures of an oven without being damaged

**o·ver** (ō'vər) *prep.* 〚OE *ofer*〛 **1** *a)* in, at, or to a position above *b)* across and down from [to fall *over* a cliff] **2** so as to cover [shutters *over* the windows] **3** upon [to cast a spell *over* someone] **4** above in authority, power, etc. **5** on or to the other side of [fly *over* the lake] **6** throughout [*over* the whole city] **7** during [*over* the years] **8** more than [*over* ten cents] **9** in preference to **10** concerning —*adv.* **1** *a)* above or across *b)* across the brim or edge **2** more [three hours or *over*] **3** from start to finish [think it *over*] **4** *a)* from an upright position [to fall *over*] *b)* upside down [turn the cup *over*] **5** again [do it *over*] **6** at, on, to, or in a specified place [*over* in Spain] **7** from one belief, etc. to another [win him *over*] —*adj.* **1** upper, outer, superior, excessive, or extra [*overseer*] **2** finished; past **3** having reached the other side **4** [Inf.] as a surplus; extra

**over-** *combining form* **1** above in position, rank, etc. [*overlord*] **2** passing across or beyond [*overrun*] **3** excessively [*oversell*] The list below includes some common compounds formed with *over-* that can be understood if "too much" or "excessively" is added to the meaning of the base word:

| | |
|---|---|
| overabundance | overgenerous |
| overactive | overheat |
| overambitious | overindulge |
| overanxious | overindulgence |
| overbid | overload |
| overburden | overpay |
| overcautious | overpopulate |
| overconfident | overproduce |
| overcook | overproduction |
| overcritical | overrefined |
| overcrowd | overripe |
| overdevelop | oversell |
| overeager | oversensitive |
| overeat | overspecialize |
| overemphasize | overspend |
| overenthusiastic | overstimulate |
| overexercise | overstock |
| overexert | overstrict |
| overexpose | oversupply |
| overextend | overtire |

**o'ver·a·chieve'** *vi.* **-chieved'**, **-chiev'ing** **1** to do better, as in school, than expected **2** to drive oneself to reach unreasonable goals —**o'ver·a·chieve'ment** *n.* —**o'ver·a·chiev'er** *n.*

**o'ver·act'** *vt., vi.* to act (a dramatic role) with exaggeration

**o·ver·age'**[1] (ō'vər āj') *adj.* over the age fixed as a standard

**o·ver·age'**[2] (ō'vər ij) *n.* 〚OVER + -AGE〛 a surplus or excess

**o·ver·all** (ō'vər ôl', ō'vər ôl') *adj.* **1** from end to end **2** including everything; total —*adv.* **1** from end to end **2** in general

**o'ver·alls'** (-ôlz') *pl.n.* loose trousers extending up over the chest, worn, usually over other clothing, to protect against dirt

**o'ver·arch'ing** *adj.* including or linking all that is within its scope [an *overarching* theory]

**o'ver·awe'** *vt.* **-awed'**, **-aw'ing** to overcome or subdue by inspiring awe

**o'ver·bal'ance** *vt.* **-anced**, **-anc·ing** OUTWEIGH

**o'ver·bear'ing** *adj.* arrogant; domineering

**o'ver·bite'** *n.* a dental condition in which the upper incisors and canines project over the lower ones to an abnormal extent

**o'ver·blown'** (-blōn') *adj.* **1** overdone; excessive **2** pompous or bombastic

**o'ver·board'** *adv.* from a ship into the water —**go overboard** [Inf.] to go to extremes

**o'ver·book'** *vt., vi.* to issue more reservations for (a flight, hotel, etc.) than there are accommodations

**o'ver·cast'** *adj.* cloudy; dark: said of the sky

**o'ver·charge** (ō'vər chärj'; *also, and for n. always,* ō'vər chärj') *vt., vi.* **-charged'**, **-charg'ing** **1** to charge too high a price (to) **2** to overload —*n.* **1** an excessive charge **2** too full a load

**o'ver·cloud'** *vt., vi.* to make or become cloudy, gloomy, etc.

**o'ver·coat'** *n.* a heavy coat worn over the usual clothing for warmth

**o'ver·come'** *vt.* **-came'**, **-come'**, **-com'ing** **1** to get the better of in competition, etc. **2** to master, prevail over, or surmount —*vi.* to win

**o'ver·de·ter'mine** *vt.* **-mined**, **-min·ing** to bring about through many causes or factors

**o'ver·do'** *vt.* **-did'**, **-done'**, **-do'ing** **1** to do too much **2** to exaggerate **3** to overcook —*vi.* to exhaust oneself by doing too much

**o'ver·dose'** *n.* too large a dose —*vi.* to take too large an amount of a narcotic, etc.

**o'ver·draw'** *vt.* **-drew'**, **-drawn'**, **-draw'ing** to draw on in excess of the amount credited to the drawer —**o'ver·draft'** *n.*

**o'ver·dress'** *vt., vi.* to dress too warmly, too showily, or too formally

**o'ver·dub'** *n.* a recording of sounds, music, etc. superimposed on another recording —*vt., vi.* **-dubbed'**, **-dub'bing** to add (sounds, music, etc.) to (a recording)

**o'ver·due'** *adj.* past the time for payment, arrival, etc.

**o'ver·es'ti·mate'** *vt.* **-mat'ed**, **-mat'ing** to set too high an estimate on or for

**o'ver·flight'** *n.* the flight of an aircraft over a foreign territory, as in reconnaissance

**o·ver·flow** (ō'vər flō'; *also, and for n. always,* ō'vər flō') *vt.* **1** to flow across; flood **2** to flow over the brim of —*vi.* **1** to run over **2** to be superabundant —*n.* **1** an overflowing **2** the amount that overflows **3** an outlet for overflowing liquids

**o'ver·grow'** *vt.* **-grew'**, **-grown'**, **-grow'ing** to overspread with foliage so as to cover —*vi.* to grow too fast or beyond normal size —**o'ver·grown'** *adj.* —**o'ver·growth'** *n.*

**o'ver·hand'** *adj., adv.* with the hand raised above the elbow or the arm above the shoulder

**o·ver·hang** (ō'vər haŋ'; *also, and for n. always,* ō'vər haŋ') *vt., vi.* **-hung'**, **-hang'ing** to hang over or project beyond (something) —*n.* the projection of one thing over or beyond another

**o·ver·haul** (ō'vər hôl'; *also, and for n. always,* ō'vər hôl') *vt.* **1** *a)* to check thoroughly for needed repairs *b)* to restore (a motor, etc.) to good working order **2** to catch up with —*n.* an overhauling

**o·ver·head** (ō'vər hed'; *for adv.* ō'vər hed') *adj.* **1** above the head **2** in the sky **3** on a higher level, with reference to related objects —*n.* the general, continuing costs of a business, as of rent, maintenance, etc. —*adv.* above the head; aloft

**o'ver·hear'** *vt.* **-heard'**, **-hear'ing** to hear (something spoken or a speaker) without the speaker's knowledge or intention

**o'ver·joy'** *vt.* to give great joy to; delight —**o'ver·joyed'** *adj.*

**o·ver·kill′** *n.* much more of something than is necessary, appropriate, etc.

**o·ver·land′** (-land′, -lənd) *adv., adj.* by, on, or across land

**o·ver·lap** (ō′vər lap′; *also, and for n. always,* ō′vər lap′) *vt., vi.* **-lapped′, -lap′ping** to extend over a part of (something) so as to coincide with this part —*n.* an overlapping part or amount

**o·ver·lay′** *vt.* **-laid′, -lay′ing** **1** to lay or spread over **2** to cover, as with a decorative layer

**o·ver·lie′** *vt.* **-lay′, -lain′, -ly′ing** to lie on or over

**o·ver·look′** *vt.* **1** to look at from above **2** to give a view of from above **3** *a*) to fail to notice *b*) to ignore; neglect **4** to excuse

**o·ver·lord′** *n.* person having great authority over others

**o·ver·ly** *adv.* too or too much

**o·ver·mas′ter** *vt.* to overcome; subdue

**o·ver·much′** *adj., adv., n.* too much

**o·ver·night** (ō′vər nīt′, ō′vər nīt′) *adv.* **1** during the night **2** suddenly —*adj.* **1** done or going on during the night **2** staying through the night [an *overnight* guest] **3** of or for a brief trip [an *overnight* bag]

**o·ver·pass′** *n.* a bridge, etc. over a road, railway, etc.

**o·ver·play′** *vt.* to overact, overdo, or overemphasize

**o·ver·pow′er** *vt.* to get the better of; subdue or overwhelm —**o·ver·pow′er·ing** *adj.*

**o·ver·price′** *vt.* **-priced′, -pric′ing** to offer for sale at too high a price

**o·ver·pro·tect′** *vt.* to protect more than necessary; specif., to exercise excessive, damaging control over (one's child, etc.) in trying to shield from hurt, disappointment, etc.

**o·ver·qual′i·fied′** *adj.* having more knowledge, education, etc. than needed for a particular job

**o·ver·rate′** *vt.* **-rat′ed, -rat′ing** to rate or estimate too highly

**o·ver·reach′** *vt.* to reach beyond or above —**overreach oneself** to fail because of trying to do too much

**o·ver·re·act′** *vi.* to react in an overly emotional way

**o·ver·ride′** *vt.* **-rode′, -rid′den, -rid′ing** **1** to prevail over **2** to disregard or nullify

**o·ver·rule′** *vt.* **-ruled′, -rul′ing** **1** to set aside or decide against by virtue of higher authority; annul; reverse **2** to prevail over

**o·ver·run′** *vt.* **-ran′, -run′, -run′ning** **1** to spread out over so as to cover **2** to swarm over, as vermin do **3** to extend beyond (certain limits)

**o·ver·seas′** *adv.* over or beyond the sea —*adj.* **1** foreign **2** over or across the sea

**o·ver·see′** *vt.* **-saw′, -seen′, -see′ing** to supervise; superintend —**o·ver·se′er** (-sē′ər) *n.*

**o·ver·sexed′** (-sekst′) *adj.* having exceptional sexual drive or interest in sex

**o·ver·shad′ow** *vt.* **1** *a*) to cast a shadow over *b*) to darken **2** to be more important than by comparison

**o·ver·shoe′** *n.* a boot of rubber, etc. worn over the regular shoe to protect against cold or dampness

**o·ver·shoot′** *vt.* **-shot′, -shoot′ing** **1** to shoot or pass beyond (a target, mark, etc.) **2** to exceed

**o·ver·sight′** *n.* a careless mistake or omission

**o·ver·sim′pli·fy′** *vt., vi.* **-fied′, -fy′ing** to simplify to the point of distortion —**o·ver·sim′pli·fi·ca′tion** *n.*

**o·ver·size′** *adj.* **1** too large **2** larger than the usual Also **o·ver·sized′**

**o·ver·sleep′** *vi.* **-slept′, -sleep′ing** to sleep longer than intended

**o·ver·spread′** *vt.* **-spread′, -spread′ing** to spread or cover over

**o·ver·state′** *vt.* **-stat′ed, -stat′ing** to exaggerate —**o·ver·state′ment** *n.*

**o·ver·stay′** *vt.* to stay beyond the time or limit of

**o·ver·step′** *vt.* **-stepped′, -step′ping** to go beyond the limits of

**o·ver·strung′** *adj.* high-strung; tense

**o·ver·stuff′** *vt.* **1** to stuff with too much of something **2** to upholster with deep stuffing

**o·vert** (ō vurt′, ō′vurt) *adj.* [< L *aperire,* to open] not hidden; apparent; open —**o·vert′ly** *adv.*

**o·ver·take′** *vt.* **-took′, -tak′en, -tak′ing** **1** to catch up with **2** to come upon suddenly

**o·ver·tax′** *vt.* **1** to tax too heavily **2** to make excessive demands on

**o·ver-the-count′er** *adj.* **1** designating or of securities sold directly to buyers **2** sold legally without prescription: said of some drugs

**o·ver-the-top′** *adj.* outrageously or ridiculously excessive

**o·ver·throw** (ō′vər thrō′; *also & for n.* ō′vər thrō′) *vt.* **-threw′, -thrown′, -throw′ing** **1** to overcome; conquer **2** to throw beyond —*n.* **1** an overthrowing or being overthrown **2** destruction; end

**o·ver·time′** *n.* **1** time beyond the established limit, as of working hours **2** pay for work done in such time —*adj., adv.* of, for, or during overtime

**o·ver·tone′** *n.* **1** a faint, higher tone accompanying a fundamental tone produced by a musical instrument **2** an implication; nuance: *usually used in pl.*

**o·ver·ture** (ō′vər chər) *n.* [< L *apertura,* opening] **1** an introductory proposal or offer **2** a musical introduction to an opera, etc.

**o·ver·turn′** *vt.* **1** to turn over **2** to conquer —*vi.* to tip over; capsize

**o·ver·ween′ing** (-wēn′iŋ) *adj.* [< OE *ofer,* over + *wenan,* to think] **1** arrogant **2** excessive

**o·ver·weight** (ō′vər wāt′, ō′vər wāt′) *adj.* above the normal or allowed weight

**o·ver·whelm′** *vt.* **1** to pour down upon and bury beneath **2** to crush; overpower —**o·ver·whelm′ing** *adj.*

**o·ver·work** (ō′vər wurk′, ō′vər wurk′) *vt.* to work or use to excess —*vi.* to work too hard or too long —*n.* severe or burdensome work

**o·ver·wrought** (ō′vər rôt′) *adj.* **1** very nervous or excited **2** too elaborate

**Ov·id** (äv′id) 43 B.C.-A.D. 17?; Rom. poet

**o·vi·duct** (ō′vi dukt′, äv′i-) *n.* [< L *ovum,* egg + DUCT] a tube through which the ova pass from an ovary to the uterus

**o·vip·a·rous** (ō vip′ə rəs) *adj.* [< L *ovum,* egg + *parere,* to bear] producing eggs which hatch after leaving the female's body

**o·void** (ō′void′) *adj.* [< L *ovum,* egg + -OID] egg-shaped —*n.* anything ovoid

**ov·u·late** (äv′yə lāt′) *vi.* **-lat′ed, -lat′ing** [< L *ovum,* egg] to produce and discharge ova from the ovary —**ov′u·la′tion** *n.*

**ov·ule** (äv′yōōl, ō′vyōōl′) *n.* [< L *ovum,* egg] a small egg or seed, esp. one in an early stage of development —**ov′u·lar** *adj.*

**o·vum** (ō′vəm) *n., pl.* **o·va** (ō′və) [L, egg] a mature female germ cell

**ow** (ou) *interj.* a cry of pain

**owe** (ō) *vt.* **owed, ow′ing** [OE *agan,* to own] **1** to be indebted to the amount of **2** to have the need to do, give, etc., as because of gratitude **3** to be indebted to someone for the existence of

**ow·ing** (ō′iŋ) *adj.* [ME *owynge*] due; unpaid —**owing to** because of

**owl** (oul) *n.* [OE *ule*] **1** a predatory night bird having a large, flat face, large eyes, and a short, hooked beak **2** a person of nocturnal habits, solemn appearance, etc. —**owl′ish** *adj.*

**owl·et** (-it) *n.* a young or small owl

**own** (ōn) *adj.* [OE *agan,* possess] belonging or relating to oneself or itself [his *own* book] —*n.* that which belongs to oneself [that is her *own*] —*vt.* **1** to possess; have **2** to admit; acknowledge —*vi.* to confess (to) —**on one's own** [Inf.] by one's own efforts —**own′er** *n.* —**own′er·ship′** *n.*

**ox** (äks) *n., pl.* **ox′en** ⟦OE *oxa*⟧ any of certain cud-chewing, cattlelike mammals, esp. a castrated, domesticated bull used as a draft animal

**ox′blood′** *n.* a deep-red color

**ox′bow′** (-bō′) *n.* the U-shaped part of an ox yoke which passes under and around the animal's neck

**ox·ford** (äks′fərd) *n.* ⟦after *Oxford*, England⟧ [*sometimes* O-] **1** a low shoe laced over the instep: also **oxford shoe 2** a cotton or rayon fabric with a basketlike weave: also **oxford cloth**

**Ox·ford** (äks′fərd) city in SC England; site of Oxford University: county district pop. 110,000

**ox·i·dant** (äk′si dənt) *n.* an oxidizing agent

**ox·i·da·tion** (äk′si dā′shən) *n.* an oxidizing or being oxidized

**ox·ide** (äk′sīd′) *n.* ⟦Fr⟧ a compound of oxygen with another element or a radical

**ox·i·dize** (äk′si dīz′) *vt.* **-dized′, -diz′ing** to unite with oxygen, as in burning or rusting —*vi.* to become oxidized —**ox′i·diz′er** *n.*

**ox·y·a·cet·y·lene** (äk′sē ə set″l ēn′) *adj.* of or using a mixture of oxygen and acetylene, as for producing a hot flame used in welding

**ox·y·gen** (äk′si jən) *n.* ⟦Fr *oxygène*⟧ a colorless, odorless, gaseous chemical element: it is essential to life processes and to combustion

**ox′y·gen·ate** (-jə nāt′) *vt.* **-at′ed, -at′ing** to treat or combine with oxygen —**ox′y·gen·a′tion** *n.*

**oxygen tent** a transparent enclosure filled with oxygen, fitted around a bed patient to aid breathing

**ox·y·mo·ron** (äk′si môr′än′) *n., pl.* **-mo′ra** (-rə) ⟦< Gr *oxys*, sharp + *mōros*, foolish⟧ a figure of speech in which contradictory ideas or terms are combined (Ex.: thunderous silence)

**oys·ter** (ois′tər) *n.* ⟦< Gr *ostreon*⟧ an edible bivalve mollusk with an irregular shell

**oz** *symbol* ounce(s)

**o·zone** (ō′zōn′) *n.* ⟦Fr < Gr *ozein*, to smell⟧ **1** an unstable, pale-blue form of oxygen with a strong odor, formed by an electrical discharge in air and used as a bleaching agent, water purifier, etc. **2** [Slang] pure, fresh air

**ozone layer** the layer of ozone within the stratosphere that absorbs much ultraviolet radiation

# P

**p¹** or **P** (pē) *n., pl.* **p's, P's** the 16th letter of the English alphabet

**p²** *abbrev.* **1** page **2** participle **3** past **4** per **5** pint

**P¹** *abbrev.* petite

**P²** *Chem. symbol for* phosphorus

**pa** (pä) *n.* [Inf.] FATHER

**PA** *abbrev.* **1** Pennsylvania **2** public address (system)

**pab·lum** (pab′ləm) *n.* ⟦< *Pablum*, trademark for a soft, bland baby food⟧ simplistic or bland writing, ideas, etc.

**PAC** *n., pl.* **PAC's** political action committee

**pace** (pās) *n.* ⟦< L *passus*, a step⟧ **1** a step in walking, etc. **2** the length of a step or stride **3** the rate of speed in walking, etc. **4** rate of progress, etc. **5** a gait **6** the gait of a horse in which both legs on the same side are raised together —*vt.* **paced, pac′ing 1** to walk back and forth across **2** to measure by paces **3** to set the pace for (a runner, etc.) —*vi.* **1** to walk with regular steps **2** to move at a pace: said of a horse — **put through one's paces** to test one's ability, skills, etc. —**pac′er** *n.*

**pace′mak′er** *n.* **1** one that leads the way: also **pace′set′ter** (-set′ər) **2** an electronic device placed in the body to regulate the heartbeat

**pach·y·derm** (pak′ə dərm′) *n.* ⟦< Gr *pachys*, thick + *derma*, skin⟧ a large, thick-skinned, hoofed animal, as the elephant or rhinoceros

**pach·y·san·dra** (pak′ə san′drə) *n.* ⟦< ModL name of genus⟧ a low, hardy evergreen plant often used for a ground cover in the shade

**pa·cif·ic** (pə sif′ik) *adj.* ⟦see PACIFY⟧ **1** making peace **2** of a peaceful nature; tranquil; calm

**Pa·cif·ic** (pə sif′ik) largest of the earth's oceans, between Asia and the American continents

**pac·i·fi·er** (pas′ə fī′ər) *n.* **1** one that pacifies **2** a nipple or teething ring for babies

**pac′i·fism′** (-fiz′əm) *n.* opposition to the use of force under any circumstances; specif., refusal to participate in war —**pac′i·fist** *n., adj.*

**pac·i·fy** (pas′ə fī′) *vt.* **-fied′, -fy′ing** ⟦< L *pax*, peace + *facere*, make⟧ to make peaceful, calm, nonhostile, etc. —**pac′i·fi·ca′tion** *n.*

**pack¹** (pak) *n.* ⟦< MDu *pak*⟧ **1** a bundle of things tied up for carrying **2** a number of similar persons or things; specif., *a*) a group [a *pack* of lies] *b*) a package of a standard number [a *pack* of cigarettes] *c*) a number of wild animals living together —*vt.* **1** to make a pack of **2** *a*) to put together in a box, trunk, etc. *b*) to fill (a box, etc.) **3** to crowd; cram [the hall was *packed*] **4** to fill in tightly, as for prevention of leaks **5** to carry in a pack **6** to send (*off*) [to *pack* him off to school] **7** [Slang] to carry (a gun, etc.) **8** [Slang] to be able to deliver (a punch, etc.) with force —*vi.* **1** to make up packs **2** to put one's clothes, etc. into luggage for a trip **3** to crowd together **4** to settle into a compact mass —*adj.* used for carrying packs, loads, etc. [a *pack* animal] —**send packing** to dismiss abruptly

**pack²** (pak) *vt.* to choose (a jury, etc.) so as to get desired results

**pack·age** (pak′ij) *n.* **1** a wrapped or boxed thing or group of things; parcel **2** a number of items, plans, etc. offered as a unit —*vt.* **-aged, -ag·ing 1** to make a package of **2** to offer or present in an enticing way —**pack′ag·er** *n.*

**package store** a store where alcoholic beverages are sold by the bottle

**pack′et** (-it) *n.* **1** a small package **2** a boat that travels a regular route carrying passengers, freight, and mail: in full **packet boat**

**pack′ing** *n.* **1** the act or process of a person or thing that packs **2** any material used to pack

**pack′ing·house′** *n.* a plant where meats, etc. are processed and packed for sale

**pack rat 1** a North American rat that often hides small articles in its nest **2** [Inf.] one who hoards miscellaneous items

**pack′sad′dle** *n.* a saddle with fastenings to secure the load carried by a pack animal

**pact** (pakt) *n.* ⟦< L *pax*, peace⟧ an agreement; compact

**pad¹** (pad) *n.* ⟦echoic⟧ the dull sound of a footstep —*vi.* **pad′ded, pad′ding** to walk, esp. with a soft step

**pad²** (pad) *n.* ⟦? var. of POD⟧ **1** anything soft to protect against friction, pressure, etc.; cushion **2** the cushionlike sole of an animal's paw **3** the floating leaf of a water plant, as the waterlily **4** a number of sheets of paper glued along one edge; tablet **5** [Slang] the place where one lives —*vt.* **pad′ded, pad′ding 1** to stuff or cover with soft material **2** to lengthen (a speech, etc.) with unnecessary material **3** to fill (an expense account, etc.) with invented or inflated entries

**pad′ding** *n.* anything used to pad

**pad·dle¹** (pad′'l) *n.* ⟦ME *padell*, small spade⟧ **1** a short pole with a wide blade at one or both ends, used to propel a canoe, kayak, etc. **2** an implement shaped like this, used to hit a ball, beat something, etc. —*vt.*, *vi.* **-dled, -dling 1** to propel (a canoe, etc.) with a paddle **2** to beat as with a paddle; spank —**pad′dler** *n.*

**pad·dle**[2] (pad′'l) *vi.* **-dled, -dling** ⟦prob. < PAD[1]⟧ to move the hands or feet about in the water, as in playing —**pad′dler** *n.*

**paddle ball** a game like handball played with a short-handled paddle

**paddle wheel** a wheel with boards around it for propelling a steamboat

**pad·dock** (pad′ək) *n.* ⟦OE *pearruc*, enclosure⟧ **1** a small enclosure near a stable, in which horses are exercised **2** an enclosure at a racetrack, where horses are saddled

**pad·dy** (pad′ē) *n.*, *pl.* **-dies** ⟦Malay *padi*, rice in the husk⟧ a rice field

**pad·lock** (pad′läk′) *n.* a removable lock with a hinged link to be passed through a staple, chain, or eye —*vt.* to fasten or close up as with a padlock

PADLOCK

**pa·dre** (pä′drā′) *n.* ⟦< L *pater*⟧ **1** father: the title of a priest in Italy, Spain, etc. **2** [Inf.] a priest or chaplain

**pae·an** (pē′ən) *n.* ⟦< Gr *paian*, hymn⟧ a song of joy, triumph, etc.

**pa·gan** (pā′gən) *n.* ⟦< L *paganus*, peasant⟧ **1** a heathen **2** one who has no religion —*adj.* of pagans —**pa′gan·ism′** *n.*

**page**[1] (pāj) *n.* ⟦< L *pangere*, fasten⟧ **1** *a*) one side of a leaf of a book, etc. *b*) an entire leaf in a book, etc. **2** [*often pl.*] a record of events **3** WEB PAGE —*vi.* **paged, pag′ing** to look (*through*) by turning the pages

**page**[2] (pāj) *n.* ⟦OFr⟧ a boy attendant —*vt.* **paged, pag′ing 1** to try to find by calling out the name of **2** to contact with a pager

**pag·eant** (paj′ənt) *n.* ⟦ME *pagent*, stage scene⟧ **1** a spectacular exhibition, parade, etc. **2** an elaborate outdoor drama celebrating a historical event

**pag′eant·ry** (-ən trē) *n.*, *pl.* **-ries 1** grand spectacle; gorgeous display **2** empty show or display

**pag·er** (pā′jər) *n.* a portable electronic device used to contact people for messages

**pag·i·na·tion** (paj′ə nā′shən) *n.* **1** the numbering of pages **2** the arrangement and number of pages

**pa·go·da** (pə gō′də) *n.* ⟦prob. < Pers *but*, idol + *kadah*, house⟧ in India and the Far East, a temple in the form of a pyramidal tower of several stories

JAPANESE PAGODA

**paid** (pād) *vt.*, *vi.* *pt.* & *pp.* of PAY —*adj.* **1** settled by payment **2** with pay [a *paid* vacation]

**pail** (pāl) *n.* ⟦< OE *pægel*, wine vessel⟧ **1** a container, usually with a handle, for holding liquids, etc.; bucket **2** the amount held by a pail: also **pail′ful′**, *pl.* **-fuls′**

**pain** (pān) *n.* ⟦< Gr *poinē*, penalty⟧ **1** physical or mental suffering caused by injury, disease, grief, anxiety, etc. **2** [*pl.*] great care [take *pains* with one's work] —*vt.* to cause pain to; hurt —**on** (or **under**) **pain of** at the risk of a penalty —**pain′ful** *adj.* —**pain′ful·ly** *adv.* —**pain′less** *adj.*

**Paine** (pān), **Thom·as** (täm′əs) 1737-1809; Am. Revolutionary patriot & writer

**pain′kill′er** *n.* [Inf.] a medicine that relieves pain

**pains·tak·ing** (pānz′tā′kiŋ) *adj.* requiring or showing great care; very careful

**paint** (pānt) *vt.* ⟦< L *pingere*⟧ **1** *a*) to make (a picture, etc.) in colors applied to a surface *b*) to depict with paints **2** to describe vividly **3** to cover or decorate with paint —*vi.* to paint pictures —*n.* **1** a mixture of a pigment with oil, water, etc., used as a covering or coloring **2** a dried coat of paint

**paint′er** *n.* **1** an artist who paints pictures **2** one whose work is covering walls, etc. with paint

**paint′ing** *n.* a painted picture

**pair** (per) *n.*, *pl.* **pairs** or **pair** ⟦< L *par*, equal⟧ **1** two corresponding things associated or used together [a *pair* of shoes] **2** a single unit of two corresponding parts [a *pair* of pants] **3** any two persons or animals regarded as a unit —*vi.*, *vt.* **1** to form a pair (of) **2** to mate

**pais·ley** (pāz′lē) *adj.* ⟦after *Paisley*, Scotland⟧ [*also* P-] having an intricate, multicolored pattern of swirls, etc.

PAISLEY PATTERN

**pa·ja·mas** (pə jä′məz, -jam′əz) *pl.n.* ⟦< Pers *pāi*, a leg + *jāma*, garment⟧ a loosely fitting sleeping or lounging suit consisting of jacket (or blouse) and trousers

**Pa·ki·stan** (pak′i stan′, pä′ki stän′) country in S Asia, west of India: 307,293 sq. mi.; pop. 131,500,000 —**Pak′i·stan′i** (-ē) *adj.*, *n.*

**pal** (pal) *n.* ⟦Romany, brother, ult. < Sans⟧ [Inf.] a close friend

**pal·ace** (pal′əs) *n.* ⟦< L *Palatium*, one of the Seven Hills of Rome⟧ **1** the official residence of a king, etc. **2** any large, magnificent building

**pal·at·a·ble** (pal′it ə bəl) *adj.* pleasant or acceptable to the taste or mind

**pal·ate** (pal′it) *n.* ⟦< L *palatum*⟧ **1** the roof of the mouth **2** sense of taste —**pal′a·tal** (-it′l) *adj.*

**pa·la·tial** (pə lā′shəl) *adj.* ⟦see PALACE⟧ **1** of, suitable for, or like a palace **2** magnificent; stately

**pal·a·tine** (pal′ə tīn′, -tin) *adj.* ⟦see PALACE⟧ designating or of a count or earl who ruled in his own territory

**Pa·lau** (pä lou′) country on a group of islands in the W Pacific: 630 sq. mi.; pop. 15,000

**pa·lav·er** (pə lav′ər) *n.* ⟦Port *palavra*, a word⟧ talk, esp. idle talk —*vi.* to talk idly

**pale**[1] (pāl) *adj.* **pal′er, pal′est** ⟦< L *pallidus*⟧ **1** of a whitish or colorless complexion **2** faint; dim **3** feeble; weak —*vi.* **paled, pal′ing** to become pale —**pale′ly** *adv.* —**pale′ness** *n.*

**pale**[2] (pāl) *n.* ⟦< L *palus*, a stake⟧ **1** a pointed stake used in fences **2** a boundary; restriction: now chiefly figurative

**pale′face′** *n.* a white person: a term allegedly first used by North American Indians

**pa·le·on·tol·o·gy** (pā′lē ən täl′ə jē) *n.* ⟦< Fr⟧ the branch of geology studying prehistoric life by means of fossils —**pa′le·on·tol′o·gist** *n.*

**Pa′le·o·zo′ic** (-ə zō′ik) *adj.* ⟦< Gr *palaios*, ancient + ZO(O)- + -IC⟧ designating the geologic era (c. 570-240 million years ago) characterized by the first fishes, reptiles, and land plants

**Pal·es·tine** (pal′əs tīn′) historical region in SW Asia at the E end of the Mediterranean, including modern Israel & Jordan

**Pal·es·tin′i·an** (-tin′ē ən) *n.* a person, esp. an Arab, born or living in Palestine —*adj.* of Palestine or the Palestinians

**pal·ette** (pal′it) *n.* ⟦Fr < L *pala*, a shovel⟧ **1** a thin board on which an artist arranges and mixes paints **2** the colors used as for a painting

**pal·frey** (pôl′frē) *n.*, *pl.* **-freys** ⟦ult. < Gr *para*, beside + L *veredus*, post horse⟧ [Archaic] a saddle horse, esp. a gentle one for a woman

**pal·i·mo·ny** (pal′ə mō′nē) *n.* ⟦PAL + (AL)IMONY⟧ an allowance or a property settlement claimed by or granted to one member of an unmarried couple who separate after having lived together

**pal·imp·sest** (pal′imp sest′) *n.* ⟦< Gr *palimpsēstos*, lit., rubbed again⟧ a parchment previously written upon that bears traces of the erased texts

**pal·in·drome** (pal′in drōm′) *n.* ⟦< Gr *palindromos*, running back⟧ a word, phrase, or sentence that reads the same backward or forward (Ex.: madam)

**pal·ing** (pāl′iŋ) *n.* a fence made of pales

**pal·i·sade** (pal′ə sād′) *n.* ⟦< Fr < L *palus*, a stake⟧ **1** any of a row of large, pointed stakes forming a fence as for fortification **2** such a fence **3** [*pl.*] a line of steep cliffs

**pall¹** (pôl) *vi.* **palled, pall′ing** ⟦ME *pallen*, appall⟧ **1** to become cloying, insipid, boring, etc. **2** to become satiated

**pall²** (pôl) *n.* ⟦< L *pallium*, a cover⟧ **1** a cloth covering for a coffin **2** a dark or gloomy covering

**pall·bear·er** (pôl′ber′ər) *n.* ⟦prec. + BEARER⟧ one of the persons who attend or carry the coffin at a funeral

**pal·let¹** (pal′it) *n.* ⟦see PALETTE⟧ a low, portable platform used for stacking materials, as in a warehouse

**pal·let²** (pal′it) *n.* ⟦< L *palea*, chaff⟧ a small bed or a pad filled as with straw and used on the floor

**pal·li·ate** (pal′ē āt′) *vt.* **-at′ed, -at′ing** ⟦< L *pallium*, a cloak⟧ **1** to lessen the severity of without curing; alleviate **2** to make (an offense) appear less serious; excuse —**pal′li·a′tion** *n.* —**pal′li·a′tive** (-āt′iv, -ə tiv) *adj.*, *n.*

**pal·lid** (pal′id) *adj.* ⟦L *pallidus*, pale⟧ faint in color; pale —**pal′lid·ly** *adv.*

**pal·lor** (pal′ər) *n.* ⟦< L *pallere*, be pale⟧ unnatural paleness

**palm¹** (päm) *n.* ⟦< L *palma*: from its handlike leaf⟧ **1** any of a large group of tropical or subtropical trees or shrubs with a branchless trunk and a bunch of large leaves at the top **2** a leaf of such a tree carried as a symbol of victory, etc.

**palm²** (päm) *n.* ⟦< L *palma*⟧ the inner surface of the hand between the fingers and wrist —*vt.* to hide (something) in the palm, as in a sleight-of-hand trick —**palm off** [Inf.] to pass off by fraud

**palm·met·to** (pal met′ō) *n.*, *pl.* **-tos** or **-toes** any of certain palms with fan-shaped leaves

**palm·is·try** (päm′is trē) *n.* ⟦prob. < ME *paume*, PALM² + *maistrie*, mastery⟧ fortunetelling by interpreting the lines, etc. on the palm of a person's hand —**palm′ist** *n.*

**Palm Springs** resort city in SW California: pop. 40,000

**Palm Sunday** the Sunday before Easter, commemorating Jesus' entry into Jerusalem, when palm branches were strewn before him

**palm′top′** *n.* a small, portable computer for storing personal information, sending e-mail, etc.

**palm·y** (päm′ē) *adj.* **-i·er, -i·est** **1** of, like, or full of palm trees **2** prosperous [*palmy days*]

**pal·o·mi·no** (pal′ə mē′nō) *n.*, *pl.* **-nos** ⟦AmSp < Sp, dove-colored⟧ a golden or cream-colored horse with a white tail

**pal·pa·ble** (pal′pə bəl) *adj.* ⟦< L *palpare*, to touch⟧ **1** that can be touched, felt, etc. **2** easily perceived by the senses; perceptible **3** obvious; plain — **pal′pa·bly** *adv.*

**pal·pi·tate** (pal′pə tāt′) *vi.* **-tat′ed, -tat′ing** ⟦< L *palpare*, to feel⟧ **1** to beat rapidly, as the heart **2** to throb —**pal′pi·ta′tion** *n.*

**pal·sy** (pôl′zē) *n.*, *pl.* **-sies** ⟦ult. < L *paralysis*, paralysis⟧ paralysis of a muscle, sometimes with involuntary tremors —*vt.* **-sied, -sy·ing** to affect with or as with palsy

**pal·try** (pôl′trē) *adj.* **-tri·er, -tri·est** ⟦prob. < LowG

*palte*, rag⟧ almost worthless; trifling —**pal′tri·ness** *n.*

**pam·pa** (pam′pə, päm′-) *n.* ⟦AmSp < AmInd *pampa*, plain, field⟧ an extensive, treeless plain of Argentina

**pam·per** (pam′pər) *vt.* ⟦ME *pampren*, to feed too much < LowG⟧ to be overindulgent with; coddle

**pam·phlet** (pam′flit) *n.* ⟦< OFr *Pamphilet*, shortened name of a ML poem⟧ a thin, unbound booklet, often on some topic of current interest — **pam′phlet·eer′** (-flə tir′) *n.*

**pan¹** (pan) *n.* ⟦OE *panne*⟧ **1** any broad, shallow container used in cooking, etc. **2** a pan-shaped part or object —*vt.* **panned, pan′ning 1** [Inf.] to criticize unfavorably **2** *Mining* to wash (gravel) in a pan, as to separate (gold) —*vi.* *Mining* to wash gravel in a pan, searching for gold —**pan out** [Inf.] to turn up; esp., to succeed

**pan²** (pan) *Film, TV, etc.* *vt.*, *vi.* **panned, pan′ning** ⟦< PAN(ORAMA)⟧ to move (a camera) so as to get a panoramic effect —*n.* the act of panning

**Pan** (pan) *n.* *Gr. Myth.* a god of fields, forests, flocks, and shepherds, represented as having the legs of a goat

**pan-** ⟦< Gr *pan*, all, every⟧ *combining form* **1** all [*pantheism*] **2** [P-] of, comprising, or uniting every [*Pan-American*]

**pan·a·ce·a** (pan′ə sē′ə) *n.* ⟦< Gr *pan*, all + *akos*, healing, medicine⟧ a supposed remedy for all ills

**pa·nache** (pə nash′, -näsh′) *n.* ⟦Fr, ult. < L *pinna*, feather⟧ dashing elegance of manner or style

**Pan·a·ma** (pan′ə mä′, -mô′) country in Central America, a strip of land connecting Central & South America: 29,761 sq. mi.; pop. 2,329,000 — **Pan′a·ma′ni·an** (-mä′nē ən) *adj.*, *n.*

**Panama Canal** ship canal across Panama, connecting the Atlantic & Pacific

**Panama** (**hat**) [*also* p-] a hand-woven hat made with strawlike strips of the leaves of a tropical plant

**Pan′-A·mer′i·can** *adj.* of North, South, and Central America, collectively

**pan·cake** (pan′kāk′) *n.* a flat cake of batter fried on a griddle or in a pan

**pan·chro·mat·ic** (pan′krō mat′ik) *adj.* sensitive to light of all colors [*panchromatic film*]

**pan·cre·as** (pan′krē əs, pan′-) *n.* ⟦< Gr *pan*, all + *kreas*, flesh⟧ a large gland that secretes a digestive juice into the small intestine and produces insulin —**pan′cre·at′ic** (-at′ik) *adj.*

**pan·da** (pan′də) *n.* ⟦< native name in Nepal⟧ **1** a black-and-white, bearlike mammal of China: in full **giant panda 2** a reddish, raccoonlike mammal of the Himalayas: in full **lesser panda**

**pan·dem·ic** (pan dem′ik) *adj.* ⟦< Gr *pan*, all + *dēmos*, the people⟧ epidemic over a large region

**pan·de·mo·ni·um** (pan′də mō′nē əm) *n.* ⟦< name of demons' abode in Milton's *Paradise Lost* < Gr *pan*, all + *daimōn*, evil spirit⟧ wild disorder or noise

**pan·der** (pan′dər) *n.* ⟦< L *Pandarus*, lovers' go-between in Chaucer, etc.⟧ **1** a procurer; pimp **2** one who helps others to satisfy their vices, etc. Also **pan·der·er** —*vi.* to act as a pander (*to*)

**P & H** *abbrev.* postage and handling

**Pan·do·ra** (pan dôr′ə) *n.* ⟦< Gr *pan*, all + *dōron*, gift⟧ *Gr. Myth.* the first mortal woman: she opens a box, letting all human ills into the world

**pane** (pān) *n.* ⟦< L *pannus*, piece of cloth⟧ a sheet of glass in a frame of a window, etc.

**pan·e·gyr·ic** (pan′ə jir′ik) *n.* ⟦< Gr *panēgyris*, public meeting⟧ **1** a formal speech or piece of writing praising a person or event **2** high praise

**pan·el** (pan′əl) *n.* ⟦see PANE⟧ **1** *a*) a section or division, usually rectangular, forming a part of a wall, door, etc. *b*) a board for instruments or controls **2** a lengthwise strip in a skirt, etc. **3** a list of persons summoned for jury duty **4** a group of persons selected for judging, discussing, etc. —*vt.* **-eled** or **-elled, -el·ing** or **-el·ling** to provide with panels

**pan·el·ing** or **pan·el·ling** *n.* **1** panels collectively **2** sheets of plastic, wood, etc. from which to cut panels

**pan·el·ist** *n.* a member of a PANEL (*n.* 4)

**panel truck** an enclosed pickup truck

**pang** (paŋ) *n.* ⟦< ?⟧ a sudden, sharp pain, physical or emotional

**pan·han·dle**[1] (pan′han΄dəl) *n.* a strip of land projecting like the handle of a pan

**pan·han·dle**[2] (pan′han΄dəl) *vi.* **-dled, -dling** [Inf.] to beg on the streets —**pan′han΄dler** *n.*

**pan·ic** (pan′ik) *n.* ⟦< Gr *panikos*, of Pan, as inspirer of sudden fear⟧ a sudden, unreasoning fear, often spreading quickly —*vt.* **-icked, -ick·ing** to affect with panic —*vi.* to show panic —**pan′ick·y** *adj.*

**pan′ic-strick′en** *adj.* badly frightened: also **pan′ic-struck′**

**pan·nier** or **pan·ier** (pan′yər, -ē ər) *n.* ⟦< L *panis*, bread⟧ a large basket for carrying loads on the back

**pa·no·cha** (pə nō′chə) *n.* ⟦AmSp, ult. < L *panis*, bread⟧ **1** a coarse Mexican sugar **2** *var. of* PENUCHE

**pan·o·ply** (pan′ə plē) *n., pl.* **-plies** ⟦< Gr *pan*, all + *hopla*, arms⟧ **1** a complete suit of armor **2** any complete or magnificent covering or array

**pan·o·ram·a** (pan′ə ram′ə) *n.* ⟦< PAN- + Gr *horama*, a view⟧ **1** a wide view in all directions **2** a constantly changing scene —**pan′o·ram′ic** *adj.*

**pan·sy** (pan′zē) *n., pl.* **-sies** ⟦< Fr *penser*, think⟧ a small plant of the violet family, with velvety petals

**pant** (pant) *vi.* ⟦ult. < L *phantasia*, nightmare⟧ **1** to breathe rapidly and heavily, as from running fast **2** to yearn eagerly: with *for* or *after* —*vt.* to gasp out —*n.* any of a series of rapid, heavy breaths; gasp

**pan·ta·loons** (pan′tə lo͞onz′) *pl.n.* ⟦< It: ult. after St. *Pantalone*⟧ [Historical] trousers

**pan·the·ism** (pan′thē iz′əm) *n.* ⟦< Gr *pan*, all + *theos*, a god + -ISM⟧ **1** the doctrine that all forces, manifestations, etc. of the universe are God **2** the worship of all gods —**pan′the·ist** *n.*

**pan·the·on** (pan′thē än′) *n.* ⟦< Gr *pan*, all + *theos*, a god⟧ **1** all the gods of a people **2** [*often* P-] a building in which famous dead persons of a nation are entombed or commemorated

**pan·ther** (pan′thər) *n.* ⟦< Gr *panthēr*⟧ **1** a leopard, specif. one that is black **2** COUGAR

**pant·ies** (pan′tēz) *pl.n.* women's or children's short underpants: also **pant′ie** or **pant′y** *n.*

**pan·to·mime** (pan′tə mīm′) *n.* ⟦ult. < Gr *pan*, all + *mimos*, a mimic⟧ **1** a drama played without words, using only action and gestures **2** action or gestures without words —*vt., vi.* **-mimed′, -mim′ing** to express or act in pantomime —**pan′to·mim′ist** (-mīm′ist) *n.*

**pan·to·then·ic acid** (pan′tō then′ik) ⟦< Gr *pantothen*, from every side⟧ a viscous oil, part of the vitamin B complex, occurring widely in animal and plant tissues and thought essential for cell growth

**pan·try** (pan′trē) *n., pl.* **-tries** ⟦< L *panis*, bread⟧ a small room off the kitchen, where cooking ingredients and utensils, china, etc. are kept

**pants** (pants) *pl.n.* ⟦< PANTALOONS⟧ **1** trousers **2** drawers or panties

**pant′suit′** *n.* matched pants and jacket for women: also **pants suit**

**pant·y·hose** (pan′tē hōz′) *n.* women's hose that extend to the waist, forming a one-piece garment

**pant′y·waist** (-wāst′) *n.* [Slang] a sissy

**pap** (pap) *n.* ⟦ME⟧ **1** any soft food for babies or invalids **2** any oversimplified or tasteless writing, ideas, etc.

**pa·pa** (pä′pə, pə pä′) *n.* ⟦< baby talk⟧ *child's term for* FATHER

**pa·pa·cy** (pā′pə sē) *n., pl.* **-cies** ⟦LL *papa*, pope⟧ **1** the rank of pope **2** the term of office of a pope **3**

the governing of the Roman Catholic Church by the pope, its head

**pa·pal** (pā′pəl) *adj.* of or relating to a pope or the papacy

**pa·pa·raz·zi** (pä′pä rät′tsē) *pl.n.* photographers who take candid shots of celebrities

**pa·paw** (pə pô′, pô′pô′) *n.* ⟦< fol.⟧ **1** PAPAYA **2** *a*) a tree of central and S U.S. with an oblong, yellowish, edible fruit *b*) its fruit

**pa·pa·ya** (pə pī′ə) *n.* ⟦Sp < WInd name⟧ **1** a tropical American tree with a large, oblong, yellowish-orange fruit **2** its fruit

**pa·per** (pā′pər) *n.* ⟦ult. < Gr *papyros*, papyrus⟧ **1** a thin, flexible material in sheets, made from rags, wood, etc. and used for writing or printing on, for packaging, etc. **2** a single sheet of this **3** an official document **4** an essay, dissertation, etc. **5** a newspaper **6** wallpaper **7** [*pl.*] credentials —*adj.* **1** of, or made of, paper **2** like paper; thin —*vt.* to cover with wallpaper —**pa′per·y** *adj.*

**pa′per·back′** *n.* a book bound in paper covers

**pa′per·boy′** *n.* a boy who sells or delivers newspapers —**pa′per·girl′** *fem.n.*

**paper clip** a flexible clasp for holding loose sheets of paper together

**pa′per·hang′er** *n.* a person whose work is covering walls with wallpaper

**paper tiger** a person, nation, etc. that seems to pose a threat but is really powerless

**paper trail** written records that serve as evidence of a person's actions

**pa′per·weight′** *n.* any small, heavy object set on papers to keep them from being scattered

**pa′per·work′** *n.* the keeping of records, etc. incidental to some task

**pa·pier-mâ·ché** (pā′pər mə shā′) *n.* ⟦Fr < *papier*, paper + *mâcher*, to chew⟧ a material made of paper pulp mixed with size, glue, etc., and molded into various objects when moist

**pa·pil·la** (pə pil′ə) *n., pl.* **-lae** (-ē) ⟦L < *papula*, pimple⟧ any small nipplelike projection of tissue, as on the surface of the tongue —**pap·il·lar·y** (pap′ə ler′ē) *adj.*

**pa·poose** (pa po͞os′, pä-) *n.* ⟦< AmInd⟧ a North American Indian baby

**pa·pri·ka** (pə prē′kə) *n.* ⟦Hung, ult. < Gr *peperi*, pepper⟧ a mild or hot, red, powdered condiment ground from the fruit of certain pepper plants

**Pap test** (pap) ⟦after G. *Papanicolaou*, 20th-c. U.S. anatomist⟧ a test for uterine cancer

**Pap·u·a New Guinea** (pap′yo͞o ə) country occupying the E half of the island of New Guinea & nearby islands: 178,703 sq. mi.; pop. 3,689,000

**pa·py·rus** (pə pī′rəs) *n., pl.* **-ri** (-rī) or **-rus·es** ⟦< Gr *papyros*⟧ **1** a tall water plant of Egypt **2** a writing material made from the pith of this plant by the ancients

**par** (pär) *n.* ⟦L, an equal⟧ **1** the established value of a currency in terms of the money of another country **2** an equal status, level, etc.: usually in **on a par (with) 3** the average state, condition, etc. [work that is above *par*] **4** the face value of stocks, etc. **5** *Golf* the number of strokes established as a skillful score for a hole or course —*adj.* **1** of or at par **2** average

**par** *abbrev.* **1** paragraph **2** parish

**para-** *prefix* **1** beside, beyond [*parapsychology*] **2** helping, accessory [*paramedical*]

**par·a·ble** (par′ə bəl) *n.* ⟦< Gr *parabolē*, analogy < *para-*, beside + *ballein*, to throw⟧ a short, simple story teaching a moral lesson

**pa·rab·o·la** (pə rab′ə lə) *n.* ⟦see prec.⟧ *Geom.* a curve formed by the intersection of a cone with a plane parallel to its side —**par·a·bol·ic** (par′ə bäl′ik) *adj.*

**par·a·chute** (par′ə sho͞ot′) *n.* ⟦Fr < *para-*, protecting + *chute*, a fall⟧ a cloth contrivance usually shaped like an umbrella when expanded, and used to retard the speed of one dropping from an airplane, etc. —*vt., vi.* **-chut′ed, -chut′ing** to drop by parachute —**par′a·chut′ist** *n.*

**pa·rade** (pə rād′) *n.* [< L *parare*, prepare] **1** ostentatious display **2** a review of marching troops **3** any organized procession or march, as for display —*vt.* **-rad′ed, -rad′ing** **1** to march or walk through, as for display **2** to show off [*to parade* one's knowledge] —*vi.* **1** to march in a parade **2** to walk about ostentatiously

**par·a·digm** (par′ə dīm′) *n.* [< Gr *para-*, beside + *deigma*, example] **1** an example or model **2** a generally accepted concept that explains a complex idea, set of data, etc. **3** *Gram.* an example of a declension or conjugation, giving all the inflections of a word

**Par·a·dise** (par′ə dīs′) *n.* [< Gr *paradeisos*, garden] **1** the garden of Eden **2** heaven **3** [p-] any place or state of great happiness

**par·a·dox** (par′ə däks′) *n.* [< Gr *para-*, beyond + *doxa*, opinion] **1** a statement that seems contradictory, etc. but may be true in fact **2** a statement that is self-contradictory and, hence, false —**par′a·dox′i·cal** *adj.* —**par′a·dox′i·cal·ly** *adv.*

**par·af·fin** (par′ə fin) *n.* [Ger < L *parum*, too little + *affinis*, akin: from its inertness] a white, waxy substance obtained from petroleum and used for making candles, sealing jars, etc.

**par·a·gon** (par′ə gän′) *n.* [< It *paragone*, touchstone] a model of perfection or excellence

**par·a·graph** (par′ə graf′) *n.* [< Gr *para-*, beside + *graphein*, write] **1** a distinct section of a piece of writing, begun on a new line and often indented **2** a brief item in a newspaper, etc. —*vt.* to arrange in paragraphs

**Par·a·guay** (par′ə gwä′, -gwī′) inland country in SC South America: 157,042 sq. mi.; pop. 4,120,000 —**Par′a·guay′an** *adj., n.*

**par·a·keet** (par′ə kēt′) *n.* [prob. < MFr *perrot*, parrot] a small, slender parrot with a long tail

**par·a·le·gal** (par′ə lē′gəl) *adj.* designating or of persons trained to aid lawyers but not licensed to practice law —*n.* such a person

**par·al·lax** (par′ə laks′) *n.* [< Gr *para-*, beyond + *allassein*, to change] the apparent change in the position of an object resulting from a change in the viewer's position

**par·al·lel** (par′ə lel′) *adj.* [< Gr *para-*, side by side + *allēlos*, one another] **1** extending in the same direction and at the same distance apart, so as never to meet **2** similar or corresponding —*n.* **1** a parallel line, surface, etc. **2** any person or thing similar to another; counterpart **3** any comparison showing likeness **4** any of the imaginary lines parallel to the equator and representing degrees of latitude: in full **parallel of latitude** — *vt.* **-leled′** or **-lelled′, -lel′ing** or **-lel′ling** **1** to be parallel with **2** to match; equal —**par′al·lel·ism′** *n.*

**par′al·lel′o·gram′** (-ə gram′) *n.* a four-sided plane figure having the opposite sides parallel and equal

**parallel parking** the parking of vehicles close to and parallel to the curb

**pa·ral·y·sis** (pə ral′ə sis) *n., pl.* **-ses′** (-sēz′) [< Gr *paralyein*, to loosen or weaken at the side] **1** partial or complete loss of voluntary motion or of sensation in part or all of the body **2** any condition of helpless inactivity —**par·a·lyt·ic** (par′ə lit′ik) *adj., n.*

**par·a·lyze** (par′ə līz′) *vt.* **-lyzed′, -lyz′ing** **1** to cause paralysis in **2** to make ineffective or powerless

**par·a·me·ci·um** (par′ə mē′sē əm, -shē əm) *n., pl.* **-ci·a** (-ə) [< Gr *paramēkēs*, oval] an elongated protozoan that moves by means of cilia

**par·a·med·ic** (par′ə med′ik) *n.* a person in paramedical work

**par′a·med′i·cal** (-med′i kəl) *adj.* [PARA- + MEDI-CAL] of auxiliary medical personnel, as midwives and nurses' aides

**pa·ram·e·ter** (pə ram′ət ər) *n.* [< Gr *para-*, beside + *metron*, a measure] **1** any of a set of interdependent variables **2** *a)* a boundary or limit *b)* a characteristic (*usually used in pl.*)

**par·a·mil·i·tar·y** (par′ə mil′ə ter′ē) *adj.* [PARA- + MILITARY] of forces working along with, or in place of, a regular military organization

**par·a·mount** (par′ə mount′) *adj.* [< OFr *par*, by + *amont*, uphill] ranking higher than any other; chief

**par·a·mour** (par′ə moor′) *n.* [< OFr *par amour*, with love] a lover or mistress; esp., the illicit sexual partner of a married man or woman

**par·a·noi·a** (par′ə noi′ə) *n.* [< Gr *para-*, beside + *nous*, the mind] a mental disorder characterized by delusions, as of grandeur or, esp., persecution —**par′a·noid′** *adj., n.*

**par·a·pet** (par′ə pet′, -pət) *n.* [< It *parare*, to guard + *petto*, breast] **1** a wall or bank for screening troops from enemy fire **2** a low wall or railing

**par·a·pher·na·li·a** (par′ə fər nāl′yə, -nā′lē ə) *pl.n.* [< Gr *para-*, beyond + *phernē*, dowry] [*often with sing. v.*] **1** personal belongings **2** equipment

**par·a·phrase** (par′ə frāz′) *n.* [< Gr *para-*, beside + *phrazein*, say] a rewording of the meaning of something spoken or written —*vt., vi.* **-phrased′, -phras′ing** to express (something) in a paraphrase

**par·a·ple·gi·a** (par′ə plē′jē ə, -jə) *n.* [< Gr *para-*, beside + *plēgē*, a stroke] paralysis of the lower half of the body —**par′a·ple′gic** (-plē′jik) *adj., n.*

**par′a·pro·fes′sion·al** *n.* [see PARA-] a trained assistant to licensed professionals, as in medicine

**par′a·psy·chol′o·gy** *n.* [see PARA-] psychology that investigates psychic phenomena, such as telepathy

**par·a·sail′** *n.* [< PARACHUTE] a kind of parachute worn by a person who is pulled by a boat, car, etc. fast enough to glide in the air —**par′a·sail′ing** *n.*

**par·a·site** (par′ə sīt′) *n.* [< Gr *para-*, beside + *sitos*, food] **1** one who lives at others' expense without making any useful return **2** a plant or animal that lives on or in another organism, usually with harmful effects —**par′a·sit′ic** (-sit′ik) *adj.*

**par·a·sol** (par′ə sôl′) *n.* [< It *parare*, ward off + *sole*, sun] a lightweight umbrella used for protection from the sun's rays

**par·a·sym·pa·thet·ic** (par′ə sim′pə thet′ik) *adj.* [PARA- + SYMPATHETIC] *Physiology* designating the part of the autonomic nervous system whose functions include constricting the pupils of the eyes, slowing the heartbeat, and stimulating some digestive glands

**par·a·thi·on** (par′ə thī′än′) *n.* [PARA- + Gr *theion*, sulfur] a highly poisonous insecticide

**par·a·thy·roid′** (-thī′roid′) *adj.* [PARA- + THYROID] designating or of the small glands near the thyroid that regulate calcium and phosphorus metabolism

**par·a·troops** (par′ə trōōps′) *pl.n.* [< PARA(CHUTE) + TROOP] troops trained and equipped to parachute into a combat area —**par′a·troop′er** *n.*

**par·boil** (pär′boil′) *vt.* [< L *per*, through + *bullire*, to boil: infl. by *part*] to boil until partly cooked

**par·cel** (pär′səl) *n.* [ult. < L *pars*, part] **1** a small, wrapped bundle; package **2** a piece (of land) —*vt.* **-celed** or **-celled, -cel·ing** or **-cel·ling** to separate into parts and distribute: with *out*

**parcel post** a mail service for parcels not over a specified weight and size

**parch** (pärch) *vt.* [< ?] **1** to make hot and dry **2** to make very thirsty —*vi.* to become very dry, hot, thirsty, etc.

**parch·ment** (pärch′mənt) *n.* [< L (*charta*) *Pergamena*, (paper) of Pergamum, city in Asia Minor] **1** the skin of a sheep, goat, etc. prepared as a surface for writing **2** paper like parchment **3** a manuscript on parchment

**par·don** (pärd′n) *vt.* [< L *per-*, through + *donare*, give] **1** to release from further punishment **2** to forgive (an offense) **3** to excuse (a person) for a fault, etc. —*n.* **1** forgiveness **2** an official document granting a pardon —**par′don·a·ble** *adj.*

**pare** (per) *vt.* **pared, par'ing** [[< L *parare,* prepare]] **1** to cut or trim away (the rind, skin, etc.) of; peel **2** to reduce gradually: often with *down*

**par·e·gor·ic** (par'ə gôr'ik) *n.* [[< Gr *paregoros,* soothing]] a tincture of opium, used to relieve diarrhea

**par·ent** (per'ənt) *n.* [[< L *parere,* beget]] **1** a person in relation to his or her offspring; a mother or father **2** any organism in relation to its offspring **3** a source; origin —*adj.* of a corporation in relation to a subsidiary that it owns —**pa·ren·tal** (pə rent'l) *adj.* —**par'ent·hood'** *n.*

**par'ent·age** *n.* descent from parents or ancestors; lineage

**pa·ren·the·sis** (pə ren'thə sis) *n., pl.* **-ses'** (-sēz') [[< Gr *para-,* beside + *entithenai,* to insert]] **1** a word, clause, etc. added as an explanation or comment within a sentence **2** either or both of the curved lines, ( ), used to set this off —**par·en·thet·i·cal** (par'ən thet'i kəl) or **par'en·thet'ic** *adj.*

**par'ent·ing** *n.* the work or skill of a parent in raising a child or children

**pa·re·sis** (pə rē'sis) *n., pl.* **-ses'** (-sēz') [[Gr < *parienai,* relax]] **1** partial paralysis **2** a brain disease caused by syphilis of the central nervous system

**par ex·cel·lence** (ek'sə läns) [[< Fr]] in the greatest degree of excellence

**par·fait** (pär fā') *n.* [[Fr, lit., perfect]] a frozen dessert of cream, eggs, etc., or of layers of ice cream, crushed fruit, etc. in a tall glass

**pa·ri·ah** (pə rī'ə) *n.* [[< Tamil *paraiyan,* drummer]] **1** a member of one of the lowest social castes in India **2** any outcast

**par·i·mu·tu·el** (par'ə myoo'chōo əl) *n.* [[Fr, lit., a mutual bet]] a system of betting on races in which the winning bettors share the net of each pool in proportion to their wagers

**par·ing** (per'iŋ) *n.* a piece pared off

**Par·is**[1] (par'is) *n.* Gr. Legend a prince of Troy: see HELEN OF TROY

**Par·is**[2] (par'is; *Fr* pä'rē') capital of France: pop. 2,166,000 —**Pa·ri·sian** (pə rizh'ən, -rē'zhən) *adj., n.*

**par·ish** (par'ish) *n.* [[< Gr *paroikia,* diocese]] **1** a part of a diocese, under the charge of a priest or minister **2** the congregation of a church **3** a civil division in Louisiana, like a county

**pa·rish·ion·er** (pə rish'ə nər) *n.* a member of a parish

**par·i·ty** (par'ə tē) *n.* [[< L *par,* equal]] **1** equality in power, value, etc. **2** equality of value at a given ratio between different kinds of money, etc.

**park** (pärk) *n.* [[< ML *parricus*]] **1** wooded land held as part of an estate or preserve **2** an area of public land, with walks, playgrounds, etc., for recreation **3** the system in an automatic transmission that locks the drive wheels of a motor vehicle —*vt., vi.* **1** to leave (a vehicle) in a place temporarily **2** to maneuver (a vehicle) into a space where it can be left temporarily

**par·ka** (pär'kə) *n.* [[< Russ, fur coat]] a heavy jacket with a hood

**parking meter** a timing device installed near a parking space: drivers pay to park there for a certain length of time by inserting coins in it

PARKA

**Par·kin·son's disease** (pär'kin sənz) [[after J. *Parkinson* (1755-1824), Eng physician]] a degenerative disease of later life, causing a rhythmic tremor and muscular rigidity

**park'way'** *n.* a broad roadway landscaped with trees, bushes, etc.

**par·lance** (pär'ləns) *n.* [[< OFr *parler,* speak]] language or idiom

**par·lay** (pär'lā) *vt., vi.* [[< It *paro,* a pair]] to bet (an original wager plus its winnings) on another race, etc. —*n.* a parlayed bet

**par·ley** (pär'lē) *vi.* [[< Fr *parler,* speak]] to confer, esp. with an enemy —*n., pl.* **-leys** a conference, as to settle a dispute or discuss terms

**par·lia·ment** (pär'lə mənt) *n.* [[< OFr *parler,* speak]] **1** an official government council **2** [P-] the national legislative body of certain countries, esp. Great Britain

**par·lia·men·tar·i·an** (-men ter'ē ən) *n.* one skilled in parliamentary rules or debate

**par·lia·men·ta·ry** (-ment'ə rē, -men'trē) *adj.* **1** of or by a parliament **2** conforming to the rules of a parliament

**par·lor** (pär'lər) *n.* [[< OFr *parler,* speak]] **1** [Old-fashioned] any living room **2** any of certain kinds of business establishment [a beauty *parlor*]

**Parmesan (cheese)** (pär'mə zän', -zhän') [[after *Parma,* It city]] a very hard, dry cheese orig. of Italy

**par·mi·gia·na** (pär'mə zhä'nə, pär'mə zhän') *adj.* prepared with Parmesan cheese

**pa·ro·chi·al** (pə rō'kē əl) *adj.* [[see PARISH]] **1** of or in a parish or parishes **2** narrow in scope; provincial

**parochial school** a school supported and run by a church

**par·o·dy** (par'ə dē) *n., pl.* **-dies** [[< Gr *para-,* beside + *ōidē,* song]] a humorous imitation of a literary or musical work or style —*vt.* **-died, -dy·ing** to make a parody of

**pa·role** (pə rōl') *n.* [[< LL *parabola,* a speech]] the release of a prisoner whose sentence has not expired, on condition of future good behavior —*vt.* **-roled', -rol'ing** to release on parole

**par·ox·ysm** (par'ək siz'əm) *n.* [[< Gr *para-,* beyond + *oxynein,* sharpen]] **1** a sudden attack of a disease **2** a sudden outburst as of laughter

**par·quet** (pär kā') *n.* [[Fr, < MFr *parchet,* dim. of *parc,* park]] **1** the main floor of a theater: usually called *orchestra* **2** a flooring of parquetry —*vt.* **-queted'** (-kād'), **-quet'ing** (-kā'iŋ) to make of parquetry

**parquet circle** the part of a theater beneath the balcony on the main floor

PARQUET

**par·quet·ry** (pär'kə trē) *n.* inlaid wooden flooring in geometric forms

**par·ri·cide** (par'ə sīd') *n.* [[< L *paricida:* see -CIDE]] **1** the act of murdering one's parent, close relative, etc. **2** one who does this

**par·rot** (par'ət) *n.* [[Fr dial. *perrot*]] **1** a tropical bird with a hooked bill and brightly colored feathers: some parrots can learn to imitate human speech **2** one who parrots what others say —*vt.* to repeat without understanding

**par·ry** (par'ē) *vt.* **-ried, -ry·ing** [[prob. ult. < L *parare,* prepare]] **1** to ward off (a blow, etc.) **2** to evade (a question, etc.) —*n., pl.* **-ries** a parrying

**parse** (pärs) *vt., vi.* **parsed, pars'ing** [[< L *pars* (*orationis*), part (of speech)]] to separate (a sentence) into its parts, giving the form and function of each part

**par·si·mo·ny** (pär'sə mō'nē) *n.* [[< L *parcere,* to spare]] stinginess; extreme frugality —**par'si·mo'ni·ous** *adj.*

**pars·ley** (pärs'lē) *n.* [[< Gr *petros,* stone + *selinon,* celery]] a plant with aromatic, often curled leaves used to flavor or garnish some foods

**pars·nip** (pärs'nip') *n.* [[< L *pastinare,* dig up]] **1** a plant with a long white root used as a vegetable **2** its root

**par·son** (pär'sən) *n.* [[see PERSON]] **1** an Anglican minister having a parish **2** [Inf.] any minister

**par'son·age** *n.* the dwelling provided by a church for its minister

**part** (pärt) *n.* [[< L *pars*]] **1** a portion, division, etc.

of a whole *[a part of a book]* **2** an essential, separable element *[automobile parts]* **3** a portion or share; specif., *a*) a share of work *[to do one's part]* *b*) *[usually pl.]* talent; ability *[a man of parts]* *c*) a role in a play *d*) any of the voices or instruments in a musical ensemble, or the score for this **4** *[usually pl.]* a portion of a country **5** a dividing line formed in combing the hair —*vt.* **1** to break or divide into parts **2** to comb (the hair) so as to leave a part **3** to break or hold apart —*vi.* **1** to break or divide into parts **2** to separate and go different ways **3** to cease associating **4** to go away; leave: with *from* —*adj.* partial —**for one's part** as far as one is concerned —**for the most part** mostly —**in part** partly —**part with** to relinquish —**take part** to participate —**take someone's part** to side with someone

**par·take** (pär tāk′) *vi.* **-took′, -tak′en, -tak′ing** [< *part taker*] **1** to participate (*in* an activity) **2** to eat or drink something, esp. with others: usually with *of* —**par·tak′er** *n.*

**part·ed** (pärt′id) *adj.* separated; divided

**par·terre** (pär ter′) *n.* [Fr < *par*, on + *terre*, earth] **1** a garden with the flower beds and path in a pattern **2** PARQUET CIRCLE

**par·the·no·gen·e·sis** (pär′thə nō′jen′ə sis) *n.* [see fol. & GENESIS] reproduction from an unfertilized ovum, seed, or spore

**Par·the·non** (-nän′) *n.* [< Gr *parthenos*, a virgin (i.e., Athena)] the Doric temple of Athena on the Acropolis

**par·tial** (pär′shəl) *adj.* [< L *pars*, a part] **1** favoring one person, faction, etc. more than another; biased **2** not complete —**partial to** fond of — **par·ti·al′i·ty** (-shē al′ə tē) *n.* —**par′tial·ly** *adv.*

**par·tic·i·pate** (pär tis′ə pāt′) *vi.* **-pat′ed, -pat′ing** [< L *pars*, a part + *capere*, to take] to have or take a share with others (*in* some activity) —**par·tic′i·pant** *adj., n.* —**par·tic′i·pa′tion** *n.* —**par·tic′i·pa′tor** *n.* —**par·tic′i·pa·to′ry** (-pə tôr′ē) *adj.*

**par·ti·ci·ple** (pärt′i sip′əl) *n.* [see prec.] a verbal form having characteristics of both verb and adjective —**par′ti·cip′i·al** (-sip′ē əl) *adj.*

**par·ti·cle** (pärt′i kəl) *n.* [< L *pars*, a part] **1** a tiny fragment or trace **2** a short, usually invariable part of speech, as an article or preposition **3** *Physics* a subatomic particle that cannot be divided

**par·ti·col·ored** (pär′ti kul′ərd) *adj.* [< Fr *parti*, divided + COLORED] having different colors in different parts

**par·tic·u·lar** (pär tik′yə lər) *adj.* [< L *particula*, particle] **1** of or belonging to a single person, group, or thing **2** regarded separately; specific **3** unusual **4** exacting; fastidious —*n.* a distinct fact, item, detail, etc. —**in particular** especially — **par·tic′u·lar′i·ty** (-lar′ə tē) *n., pl.* **-ties,** *n.*

**par·tic′u·lar·ize′** (-lər īz′) *vt., vi.* **-ized′, -iz′ing** to give particulars or details (of) —**par·tic′u·lar·i·za′tion** *n.*

**par·tic′u·lar·ly** *adv.* **1** in detail **2** especially **3** specifically

**par·tic′u·late** (-lit, -lāt′) *adj.* of or formed of separate tiny particles

**part′ing** *adj.* **1** dividing; separating **2** departing **3** given, spoken, etc. at parting —*n.* **1** a breaking or separating **2** a departure

**par·ti·san** (pärt′ə zən) *n.* [< L *pars*, a part] **1** a strong supporter of a faction, party, etc. **2** a guerrilla fighter —*adj.* of or like a partisan Also sp. **par′ti·zan** —**par′ti·san·ship′** *n.*

**par·ti·tion** (pär tish′ən) *n.* [< L *partitio*] **1** division into parts **2** something that divides, as a wall separating rooms —*vt.* **1** to divide into parts; apportion **2** to divide by a partition

**part′ly** *adv.* not fully or completely

**part·ner** (pärt′nər) *n.* [< ME] **1** one who joins in an activity with another or others; specif., one of two or more persons jointly owning a business **2** a spouse **3** either of two persons not married to

each other but in an intimate, spouse-like relationship **4** either of two persons dancing together **5** either of two players on the same side or team —**part′ner·ship′** *n.*

**part of speech** any of the classes to which a word can be assigned as by form, function, or meaning; noun, verb, adverb, etc.

**par·took** (pär took′) *vi. pt. of* PARTAKE

**par·tridge** (pär′trij) *n.* [< Gr *perdix*] any of several short-tailed game birds, esp. one with an orange-brown head and grayish neck

**part song** a song for several voices, usually without accompaniment

**part′-time′** *adj.* designating, of, or engaged in work, study, etc. taking less time than a regular or full schedule

**part′-tim′er** *n.* a part-time employee, student, etc.

**par·tu·ri·tion** (pär′too rish′ən) *n.* [< L *parere*, bring forth] childbirth

**part′way′** *adv.* to some degree, but not fully

**par·ty** (pär′tē) *n., pl.* **-ties** [< L *pars*, a part] **1** a group of people working to promote a political platform or group of candidates, a cause, etc. **2** a group acting together to accomplish a task **3** a gathering for social entertainment **4** one concerned in an action, plan, lawsuit, etc. *[a party to the action]* **5** [Inf.] a person —*vi.* **-tied, -ty·ing** to attend or hold social parties

**par′ty·go′er** (-gō′ər) *n.* a person who attends a party or many parties

**party line 1** a single circuit connecting two or more telephone users with the exchange **2** the policies of a political party

**par·ve·nu** (pär′və nōō′) *n.* [< L *pervenire*, arrive] a newly rich person who is considered an upstart

**Pas·a·de·na** (pas′ə dē′nə) city in SW California: pop. 132,000

**pas·chal** (pas′kəl) *adj.* [< LL < Gr < Heb *pesach*, Passover] **1** of Passover **2** of Easter

**pa·sha** (pə shä′, pä′shə) *n.* [Turk] [Historical] in Turkey, a title of rank or honor placed after the name

**pass** (pas) *vi.* [< L *passus*, a step] **1** to go or move forward, through, etc. **2** to go or be conveyed from one place, form, condition, etc. to another **3** *a*) to cease *b*) to depart **4** to die: usually with *away* or *on* **5** to go by **6** to elapse *[an hour passed]* **7** to make a way: with *through* or *by* **8** to be accepted without question **9** to be approved, as by a legislature **10** to go through a test, course, etc. successfully **11** to give a judgment, sentence, etc.: with *on* or *upon* **12** *Card Games* to decline a chance to bid —*vt.* **1** to go by, beyond, over, or through; specif., *a*) to leave behind *b*) to go through (a test, course, etc.) successfully **2** to cause or allow to go, move, or proceed; specif., *a*) to ratify; enact *b*) to spend (time) *c*) to excrete **3** to cause to move from place to place; circulate **4** to give (an opinion or judgment) —*n.* **1** an act of passing; passage **2** a condition; situation *[a strange pass]* **3** *a*) a ticket, etc. giving permission to come or go freely or without charge *b*) *Mil.* a brief leave of absence **4** a motion of the hand, as in card tricks or hypnotism, or as if to strike **5** a tentative attempt **6** a narrow passage, etc., esp. between mountains **7** [Inf.] an overly familiar attempt to embrace or kiss **8** *Sports* a transfer of a ball, etc. to another player during play —**come (or bring) to pass** to (cause to) happen —**pass for** to be accepted as —**pass off** to cause to be accepted through deceit —**pass out 1** to distribute **2** to faint —**pass over** to disregard; ignore — **pass up** [Inf.] to refuse or let go by —**pass′er** *n.*

**pass′a·ble** *adj.* **1** that can be passed, traveled over, etc. **2** adequate; fair —**pass′a·bly** *adv.*

**pas·sage** (pas′ij) *n.* **1** a passing; specif., *a*) migration *b*) transition *c*) the enactment of a law **2** permission or right to pass **3** a voyage **4** a means of passing; road, passageway, etc. **5** an exchange, as of blows or words **6** a portion of a book, musical composition, etc.

**pas'sage·way'** *n.* a narrow way for passage, as a hall or alley

**pass'book'** *n.* BANKBOOK

**pas·sé** (pa sā', pä-) *adj.* ⟦Fr, past⟧ out-of-date; old-fashioned

**pas·sel** (pas'əl) *n.* ⟦< PARCEL⟧ [Inf. or Dial.] a group, esp. a fairly large one

**pas·sen·ger** (pas'ən jər) *n.* ⟦< OFr *passage*, passage⟧ a person traveling in a train, boat, car, etc.

**pass'er·by'** *n., pl.* **pass'ers·by'** one who passes by: also **pass'er-by'**, *pl.* **pass'ers-by'**

**pass'-fail'** *adj. Educ.* designating a grading system recording "pass" or "fail" instead of a letter or number grade

**pass'ing** *adj.* **1** going by, beyond, etc. **2** fleeting **3** casual *[a passing remark]* **4** satisfying given requirements *[a passing grade]* —*n.* the act of one that passes; specif., death —**in passing** incidentally

**pas·sion** (pash'ən) *n.* ⟦< L *pati*, endure⟧ **1** any emotion, as hate, love, or fear **2** intense emotional excitement, as rage, enthusiasm, or lust **3** the object of any strong desire **4** [P-] the sufferings of Jesus, beginning after the Last Supper and continuing to his death on the Cross

**pas'sion·ate** (-ə nit) *adj.* **1** having or showing strong feelings **2** hot-tempered **3** ardent; intense **4** sensual —**pas'sion·ate·ly** *adv.*

**pas·sive** (pas'iv) *adj.* ⟦see PASSION⟧ **1** inactive, but acted upon **2** offering no resistance; submissive **3** *Gram.* denoting the voice of a verb whose subject is the recipient (object) of the action —**pas'sive·ly** *adv.* —**pas·siv·i·ty** (pa siv'ə tē) *n.*

**pas·sive-ag·gres'sive** *adj. Psychol.* showing disguised resistance to others' expectations, as by procrastination or inefficiency

**passive resistance** opposition to a government, etc. by refusal to comply or by nonviolent acts such as fasting

**pass'key'** *n.* **1** *a)* MASTER KEY *b)* SKELETON KEY **2** any private key

**Pass·o·ver** (pas'ō'vər) *n.* a Jewish holiday commemorating deliverance of the ancient Hebrews from slavery in Egypt

**pass'port'** *n.* a government document carried by a citizen traveling abroad, certifying identity and citizenship

**pass'word'** *n.* **1** a secret term used for identification, as in passing a guard **2** any means of gaining entrance

**past** (past) *vi., vt. rare pp. of* PASS —*adj.* **1** gone by; ended **2** of a former time **3** immediately preceding **4** *Gram.* indicating an action completed, or a condition in existence, at a former time *[the past tense]* —*n.* **1** time gone by **2** the history of a person, group, etc. **3** a personal background that is hidden or questionable —*prep.* beyond in time, space, etc. —*adv.* to and beyond some point

**pas·ta** (päs'tə) *n.* ⟦It⟧ **1** a flour paste or dough of which spaghetti, etc. is made **2** any food made of this

**paste** (pāst) *n.* ⟦< Gr *pastē*, porridge⟧ **1** dough for making pastry, etc. **2** any soft, moist, smooth preparation *[toothpaste]* **3** a mixture of flour, water, etc. used as an adhesive **4** the hard, brilliant glass of artificial gems —*vt.* **past'ed**, **past'ing 1** to make adhere with paste **2** [Slang] to hit

**paste'board'** *n.* a stiff material made as of layers of paper pasted together

**pas·tel** (pas tel') *n.* ⟦< LL *pasta*, paste⟧ **1** a crayon of ground coloring matter **2** a picture drawn with such crayons **3** a soft, pale shade of a color —*adj.* soft and pale: said of colors

**pas·tern** (pas'tərn) *n.* ⟦< L *pastor*, shepherd⟧ the part of the foot of a horse, dog, etc. just above the hoof or toes

**Pas·teur** (pas tʉr'), **Louis** 1822-95; Fr. chemist & bacteriologist

**pas·teur·ize** (pas'chər īz', -tər-) *vt.* **-ized'**, **-iz'ing** ⟦after prec.⟧ to destroy bacteria in (milk, etc.) by

---

heating to a prescribed temperature for a specified time —**pas'teur·i·za'tion** *n.*

**pas·tiche** (pas tēsh') *n.* ⟦Fr⟧ an artistic composition made up of bits from various sources

**pas·time** (pas'tīm') *n.* a way of spending spare time; diversion

**past master** ⟦for *passed master*⟧ a person of long experience in an occupation, art, etc.; expert

**pas·tor** (pas'tər) *n.* ⟦L, a shepherd⟧ a priest or minister in charge of a congregation —**pas'tor·ate** (-it) *n.*

**pas'to·ral** (-tə rəl) *adj.* **1** of or relating to a pastor **2** of shepherds **3** of rustic life **4** peaceful; simple

**past participle** *Gram.* a participle used *a)* to express completed action (Ex.: *gone* in "he has gone") *b)* to form the passive voice (Ex.: *done* in "the deed was done") *c)* as an adjective (Ex.: *fried* in "fried fish")

**pas·tra·mi** (pə strä'mē) *n.* ⟦E Yiddish, ult. < Turk *basdyrma*, dried meat⟧ highly spiced smoked beef

**pas·try** (pās'trē) *n., pl.* **-tries** ⟦see PASTE & -ERY⟧ **1** pies, tarts, etc. with crusts baked from flour dough made with shortening **2** broadly, all fancy baked goods

**pas·tur·age** (pas'chər ij) *n.* PASTURE

**pas·ture** (pas'chər) *n.* ⟦< L *pascere*, to feed⟧ **1** grass, etc. used as food by grazing animals **2** ground suitable for grazing —*vt.* **-tured**, **-tur·ing** to put (cattle, etc.) out to graze in a pasture

**past·y** (pās'tē) *adj.* **-i·er**, **-i·est** of or like paste in color or texture

**pat**[1] (pat) *n.* ⟦prob. echoic⟧ **1** a gentle tap or stroke with the hand or a flat object **2** the sound made by this **3** a small lump, as of butter —*vt.* **pat'ted**, **pat'ting 1** to tap or stroke gently, esp. with the hand **2** to shape or apply by patting —*adj.* **1** exactly suitable **2** so glibly plausible as to seem contrived —**pat on the back** a compliment **2** to praise —**stand pat** to refuse to change an opinion, etc.

**pat**[2] *abbrev.* **1** patent **2** patented

**patch** (pach) *n.* ⟦ME *pacche*⟧ **1** a piece of material applied to mend a hole or strengthen a weak spot **2** a bandage **3** an area or spot *[patches* of blue sky*]* **4** a small plot of land **5** a scrap; bit **6** an adhesive pad containing a drug or hormone that is absorbed through the skin —*vt.* **1** to put a patch on **2** to produce crudely or hurriedly —**patch up** to settle (differences, a quarrel, etc.)

**patch test** *Med.* a test for allergy, made by attaching a sample of a substance to the skin and observing the reaction

**patch'work'** *n.* needlework, as a quilt, made of patches of cloth sewn together at their edges

**patch'y** *adj.* **-i·er**, **-i·est 1** made up of patches **2** not consistent or uniform; irregular — **patch'i·ness** *n.*

**pate** (pāt) *n.* ⟦< ?⟧ the head, esp. the top of the head: a humorous term

**pâ·té** (pä tā') *n.* ⟦Fr⟧ a meat paste or pie

**pa·tel·la** (pə tel'ə) *n., pl.* **-las** or **-lae** (-ē) ⟦< L *patina*, a pan⟧ a movable bone at the front of the human knee

PATCHWORK QUILT

**pat·ent** (pat'nt; *also for adj. 1 & 2*, pāt'-) *adj.* ⟦< L *patere*, be open⟧ **1** obvious; plain **2** of or having to do with patents —*n.* **1** a document granting the exclusive right to produce or sell an invention, etc. for a specified time **2** *a)* the right so granted *b)* the thing protected by such a right —*vt.* to secure a patent for

**patent leather** (pat'nt) leather with a hard, glossy finish: formerly patented

**patent medicine** (pat'nt) a trademarked medical preparation

**pa·ter·nal** (pə tur'nəl) *adj.* ⟦< L *pater*, father⟧ **1** of, like, or from a father **2** related through the father's side of the family —**pa·ter'nal·ly** *adv.*

**pa·ter'nal·ism'** *n.* the governing or controlling of a country, employees, etc. in a manner suggesting a father's relationship with his children —**pa·ter'nal·is'tic** *adj.*

**pa·ter'ni·ty** (-nə tē) *n.* **1** the state of being a father **2** male parentage.

**pa·ter·nos·ter** (pät'ər näs'tər) *n.* ⟦L, our father⟧ the Lord's Prayer, esp. in Latin: often **Pater Noster**

**path** (path) *n.* ⟦OE *pæth*⟧ **1** a way worn by footsteps **2** a walk for the use of people on foot **3** a line of movement **4** a course of conduct, thought, etc. —**path'less** *adj.*

**pa·thet·ic** (pə thet'ik) *adj.* ⟦see PATHOS⟧ **1** arousing pity, sorrow, etc.; pitiful **2** pitifully unsuccessful, etc. —**pa·thet'i·cal·ly** *adv.*

**pathetic fallacy** in literature, the attribution of human feelings and characteristics to inanimate things (Ex.: the angry sea)

**patho-** ⟦< Gr: see PATHOS⟧ *combining form* suffering, disease, feeling: also **path-**

**path·o·gen** (path'ə jən) *n.* ⟦prec. + -GEN⟧ a microorganism, etc. capable of causing disease —**path·o·gen'ic** (-jen'ik) *adj.*

**pa·thol·o·gy** (pə thäl'ə jē) *n., pl.* **-gies** ⟦< Gr *pathologia*: see fol. & -LOGY⟧ **1** the branch of medicine that deals with the nature of disease, esp. with structural and functional effects **2** any abnormal variation from a sound condition —**path·o·log·i·cal** (path'ə läj'i kəl) *adj.* —**pa·thol'o·gist** *n.*

**pa·thos** (pā'thäs') *n.* ⟦Gr, suffering, disease, feeling⟧ the quality in something which arouses pity, sorrow, sympathy, etc.

**path'way'** *n.* PATH

**-pa·thy** (pə thē) ⟦< Gr: see PATHOS⟧ *combining form* **1** feeling *[telepathy]* **2** (treatment of) disease *[osteopathy]*

**pa·tience** (pā'shəns) *n.* a being patient; calm endurance

**pa'tient** (-shənt) *adj.* ⟦< L *pati*, endure⟧ **1** enduring pain, trouble, etc. without complaining **2** calmly tolerating delay, confusion, etc. **3** diligent; persevering —*n.* one receiving medical care —**pa'tient·ly** *adv.*

**pat·i·na** (pat''n ə, pə tē'nə) *n.* ⟦Fr < It⟧ a fine greenish crust on bronze or copper, formed by oxidation

**pa·ti·o** (pat'ē ō', pät'-) *n., pl.* **-os'** ⟦Sp⟧ **1** a courtyard open to the sky **2** a paved area adjoining a house, for outdoor lounging, dining, etc.

**pa·tois** (pa'twä') *n., pl.* **-tois'** (-twäz') ⟦Fr⟧ a provincial or local dialect

**pat pend** *abbrev.* patent pending

**patri-** ⟦< Gr *patēr*⟧ *combining form* father: also **patr-**

**pa·tri·arch** (pā'trē ärk') *n.* ⟦< Gr *patēr*, father + *archein*, to rule⟧ **1** the father and head of a family or tribe, as Abraham, Isaac, or Jacob in the Bible **2** a man of great age and dignity **3** [often P-] a high-ranking bishop, as in the Eastern Orthodox Church —**pa'tri·ar'chal** *adj.*

**pa'tri·arch'y** (-är'kē) *n., pl.* **-ies** **1** a form of social organization in which the father is head of the family, descent being traced through the male line **2** rule or domination by men

**pa·tri·cian** (pə trish'ən) *n.* ⟦< L *pater*, father⟧ an aristocrat

**pat·ri·cide** (pa'trə sīd') *n.* **1** the murdering of one's father **2** a person who does this —**pat'ri·ci'dal** *adj.*

**pat'ri·mo'ny** (-mō'nē) *n., pl.* **-nies** ⟦< L *pater*, father⟧ property inherited from one's father or ancestors —**pat'ri·mo'ni·al** *adj.*

**pa·tri·ot** (pā'trē ət) *n.* ⟦< Gr *patris*, fatherland⟧ one who loves and zealously supports one's own country —**pa'tri·ot'ic** (-ät'ik) *adj.* —**pa'tri·ot'i·cal·ly** *adv.* —**pa'tri·ot·ism'** *n.*

**pa·trol** (pə trōl') *vt., vi.* **-trolled', -trol'ling** ⟦Fr *patrouiller*⟧ to make a regular, repeated circuit (of) in guarding —*n.* **1** a patrolling **2** a person or group patrolling

**patrol car** a police car used to patrol an area

**pa·trol'man** (-mən) *n., pl.* **-men** (-mən) a police officer who patrols a certain area

**patrol wagon** an enclosed truck used by police to carry prisoners

**pa·tron** (pā'trən) *n.* ⟦< L *pater*, father⟧ **1** a protector; benefactor **2** a person, usually wealthy, who sponsors and supports some person, activity, etc. **3** a regular customer —**pa'tron·ess** *fem.n.*

**pa·tron·age** (pā'trə nij, pa'-) *n.* **1** support, encouragement, etc. given by a patron **2** *a)* clientele *b)* business; trade **3** *a)* the power to grant political favors *b)* such favors

**pa·tron·ize** (pā'trə nīz', pa'-) *vt.* **-ized', -iz'ing 1** to sponsor; support **2** to be kind or helpful to, but in a haughty or snobbish way **3** to be a regular customer of

**patron saint** a saint looked upon as a special guardian

**pat·ro·nym·ic** (pa'trə nim'ik) *n.* ⟦< Gr *patēr*, father + *onyma*, name⟧ a name showing descent from a given person (Ex.: *Johnson*, son of John)

**pat·sy** (pat'sē) *n., pl.* **-sies** [Slang] a person easily imposed upon or victimized

**pat·ter¹** (pat'ər) *vi.* ⟦< PAT¹⟧ to make, or move so as to make, a patter —*n.* a series of quick, light taps *[the patter of rain]*

**pat·ter²** (pat'ər) *vi.* ⟦< PATERNOSTER⟧ to speak rapidly or glibly —*n.* **1** glib, rapid speech, as of salespeople or comedians **2** idle chatter

**pat·tern** (pat'ərn) *n.* ⟦< OFr *patrun*, patron⟧ **1** a person or thing worthy of imitation **2** a model or plan used in making things **3** a design **4** a regular way of acting or doing **5** a predictable route, movement, etc. —*vt.* to make or do in imitation of a pattern

**pat·ty** (pat'ē) *n., pl.* **-ties** ⟦Fr *pâté*, pie⟧ **1** a small pie **2** a small, flat cake of ground meat, fish, etc.

**patty shell** a small pastry case for a single portion of creamed fish, etc.

**pau·ci·ty** (pô'sə tē) *n.* ⟦< L *paucus*, few⟧ **1** smallness of number or amount **2** scarcity

**Paul** (pôl) (original name *Saul*) (died A.D. 67?); the Apostle of Christianity to the Gentiles: author of several Letters in the New Testament: also **Saint Paul**

**Paul Bun·yan** (bun'yən) *American Folklore* a giant lumberjack who performs superhuman feats

**paunch** (pônch) *n.* ⟦< L *pantex*, belly⟧ a potbelly —**paunch'y** *adj.*

**pau·per** (pô'pər) *n.* ⟦L⟧ an extremely poor person, esp. one who lives on charity —**pau'per·ize', -ized', -iz'ing,** *vt.*

**pause** (pôz) *n.* ⟦< Gr *pauein*, to bring to an end⟧ a temporary stop or rest —*vi.* **paused, paus'ing** to make a pause; stop

**pave** (pāv) *vt.* **paved, pav'ing** ⟦< L *pavire*, to beat⟧ to cover the surface of (a road, etc.), as with concrete —**pave the way (for)** to prepare the way (for)

**pave'ment** *n.* a paved surface, as of concrete; specif., a paved road, etc.

**pa·vil·ion** (pə vil'yən) *n.* ⟦< L *papilio*, tent⟧ **1** a large tent **2** a building, often partly open, for exhibits, etc., as at a fair or park **3** any of a group of related buildings, as of a hospital

**Pav·lov** (pav'lôv'), **I·van** (i vän') 1849-1936; Russ. physiologist

**paw** (pô) *n.* ⟦< OFr *poue*⟧ **1** the foot of a fourfooted animal having claws **2** [Inf.] a hand —*vt., vi.* **1** to touch, dig, hit, etc. with paws or feet **2** to handle clumsily or roughly

**pawl** (pôl) *n.* ⟦< ?⟧ a device, as a hinged tongue

which engages cogs in a wheel, allowing rotation in only one direction

**pawn**[1] (pôn) *n.* ⟦< L *pannus,* cloth⟧ **1** anything given as security, as for a debt **2** the state of being pledged [a ring in *pawn*] —*vt.* **1** to give as security **2** to wager or risk

**pawn**[2] (pôn) *n.* ⟦< ML *pedo,* foot soldier⟧ **1** a chess piece of the lowest value **2** a person used to advance another's purposes

**pawn'bro'ker** *n.* a person licensed to lend money at interest on personal property left as security

**pawn'shop'** *n.* a pawnbroker's shop

**paw·paw** (pô'pô') *n. var. of* PAPAW

**pay** (pā) *vt.* **paid** or [Obs.] (except in PAY OUT) **payed, pay'ing** ⟦< L *pacare,* pacify⟧ **1** to give to (a person) what is due, as for goods or services **2** to give (what is due) in return, as for goods or services **3** to settle (a debt, etc.) **4** *a)* to give (a compliment, etc.) *b)* to make (a visit, etc.) **5** to be profitable to —*vi.* **1** to give due compensation **2** to be profitable —*n.* money paid; esp., wages or salary —*adj.* **1** operated by the insertion of coins [a *pay* phone] **2** designating a service, etc. paid for by fees [*pay* TV] —**in the pay of** employed and paid by —**pay back 1** to repay **2** to retaliate upon —**pay down** to pay (part of the price) at purchase as an installment —**pay for** to suffer or atone for (a wrong) —**pay off 1** to pay all that is owed on or to **2** to yield full recompense **3** [Inf.] to succeed —**pay out** to let out (a rope, cable, etc.) —**pay up** to pay in full or on time —**pay'er** *n.*

**pay'a·ble** *adj.* **1** that can be paid **2** due to be paid (*on* a specified date)

**pay'check'** *n.* a check in payment of wages or salary

**pay'day'** *n.* the day on which salary or wages are paid

**pay dirt** soil, ore, etc. rich in minerals —**hit (or strike) pay dirt** [Inf.] to discover a source of wealth, success, etc.

**pay·ee** (pā ē') *n.* one to whom a payment is made or owed

**pay'load'** *n.* **1** a cargo **2** a load, as a warhead or satellite, carried by an aircraft, rocket, etc. but not essential to its flight operations

**pay'mas'ter** *n.* the official in charge of paying employees

**pay'ment** *n.* **1** a paying or being paid **2** something that is paid

**pay'off'** *n.* **1** a settlement, reckoning, or payment **2** [Inf.] a bribe **3** [Inf.] a climax or culmination

**pay·o·la** (pā ō'lə) *n.* [Slang] a bribe, as to a disc jockey for unfairly promoting a certain record

**pay'out'** *n.* **1** a paying out; disbursement **2** an amount paid out; dividend

**pay'-per-view'** *adj. TV* of a system for paying for single showings of films or programs, as by cable or satellite —*n.* such a system

**pay phone** (or **station**) a public telephone, usually coin-operated

**pay'roll'** *n.* **1** a list of employees to be paid, with the amount due to each **2** the total amount needed for this

**Pb** ⟦L *plumbum*⟧ *Chem. symbol for* lead

**PBX** *n.* ⟦*p(rivate) b(ranch) (e)x(change)*⟧ a telephone system within an organization, having outside lines

**PC**[1] *n., pl.* **PCs** or **PC's** PERSONAL COMPUTER

**PC**[2] *abbrev.* politically correct or political correctness

**pct** *abbrev.* percent

**PCV valve** ⟦*p(ositive) c(rankcase) v(entilation)*⟧ a valve regulating the pollution control system of a motor vehicle

**pd** *abbrev.* paid

**Pd** *Chem. symbol for* palladium

**PE** *abbrev.* **1** physical education **2** Prince Edward Island

**pea** (pē) *n., pl.* **peas** ⟦< ME *pese,* a pea, taken as pl.; ult. < Gr *pison*⟧ **1** a climbing plant with green pods **2** its small round seed, used as a vegetable

---

**peace** (pēs) *n.* ⟦< L *pax*⟧ **1** freedom from war **2** an agreement to end war **3** law and order **4** harmony; concord **5** serenity or quiet —**hold** (or **keep**) **one's peace** to be silent —**peace'a·ble** *adj.*

**peace'ful** *adj.* **1** not quarrelsome **2** free from disturbance; calm **3** of or in a time of peace —**peace'ful·ly** *adv.*

**peace'mak'er** *n.* a person who makes peace, as by settling quarrels —**peace'mak'ing** *n., adj.*

**peace officer** an officer entrusted with maintaining law and order, as a sheriff

**peace pipe** a ceremonial pipe smoked by American Indians as part of a peace conference

**peace'time'** *n.* a time of freedom from war —*adj.* of such a time

**peach** (pēch) *n.* ⟦< L *Persicum* (*malum*), Persian (apple)⟧ **1** a tree with round, juicy, orange-yellow fruit having a fuzzy skin and a rough pit **2** its fruit **3** the color of this fruit **4** [Slang] a well-liked person or thing

**pea·cock** (pē'käk') *n.* ⟦< L *pavo,* peacock⟧ the male of a pheasantlike bird (**pea'fowl'**), with a long, showy tail that can be spread out like a fan —**pea'hen'** *fem.n.*

**pea jacket** (pē) ⟦< Du *pijjekker*⟧ a hip-length, double-breasted coat of heavy woolen cloth, worn orig. by seamen

**peak** (pēk) *n.* ⟦var. of Brit dial. *pike,* prob. < ON *pic*⟧ **1** a pointed end or top, as of a cap or roof **2** *a)* the summit of a hill or mountain ending in a point *b)* a mountain with such a summit **3** the highest or utmost point of anything —*adj.* maximum —*vi.* to come to a peak

**peak·ed** (pē'kid) *adj.* ⟦< ?⟧ thin and drawn, or weak and pale, as from illness

**peal** (pēl) *n.* ⟦ME *apele,* appeal⟧ **1** the loud ringing of a bell or bells **2** a set of tuned bells **3** a loud, prolonged sound, as of thunder or laughter —*vi., vt.* to sound in a peal; ring

**pea'nut'** *n.* **1** a vine related to the pea, with underground pods containing edible seeds **2** the pod or any of its seeds **3** [*pl.*] [Slang] a trifling sum of money

**peanut butter** a food paste or spread made by grinding roasted peanuts

**pear** (per) *n.* ⟦< L *pirum*⟧ **1** a tree with greenish-yellow, brown, or reddish fruit **2** the juicy fruit, round at the base and narrowing toward the stem

**pearl** (purl) *n.* ⟦< L *perna,* sea mussel⟧ **1** a smooth, hard, usually white or bluish-gray object, a roundish growth formed within the shell of some oysters and other mollusks: used as a gem **2** MOTHER-OF-PEARL **3** any person or thing like a pearl in beauty, value, etc. **4** bluish-gray —**pearl'y, -i·er, -iest,** *adj.*

**Pearl Harbor** inlet on the S coast of Oahu, Hawaii: site of a U.S. naval base bombed by Japan on Dec. 7, 1941

**peas·ant** (pez'ənt) *n.* ⟦< LL *pagus,* district⟧ **1** a small farmer or farm laborer, as in Europe or Asia **2** a person regarded as boorish, ignorant, etc. —**peas'ant·ry** *n.*

**peat** (pēt) *n.* ⟦< ML *peta,* piece of turf⟧ partly decayed plant matter from ancient swamps, used for fuel

**peat moss** peat composed of residues of mosses, used as mulch

**peb·ble** (peb'əl) *n.* ⟦< OE *papol-*(*stan*), pebble (stone), prob. echoic⟧ a small stone worn smooth and round, as by running water —**peb'bly, -bli·er, -bli·est,** *adj.*

**pe·can** (pi kän', -kan'; pi-; pē'kän', -kan') *n.* ⟦< AmInd⟧ **1** an edible nut with a thin, smooth shell **2** the tree it grows on

**pec·ca·dil·lo** (pek'ə dil'ō) *n., pl.* **-loes** or **-los** ⟦< Sp < L *peccare,* to sin⟧ a small fault or offense

**pec·ca·ry** (pek'ə rē) *n., pl.* **-ries** ⟦< native name⟧ a piglike animal of North and South America, with sharp tusks

**peck**[1] (pek) *vt.* ⟦ME *picken,* to pick⟧ **1** to strike, as with a beak **2** to make by doing this *[to peck a hole]* **3** to pick up with the beak —*vi.* to make strokes as with a pointed object —*n.* **1** a stroke so made **2** [Inf.] a quick, casual kiss —**peck at** [Inf.] **1** to eat very little of **2** to criticize constantly

**peck**[2] (pek) *n.* ⟦< OFr *pek*⟧ a unit of dry measure, ¼ bushel or eight quarts

**pecking order** a hierarchy of members of a group, based on status, relative power, etc.

**pec·tin** (pek'tin) *n.* ⟦< Gr *pēktos*, congealed⟧ a carbohydrate, obtained from certain fruits, which yields a gel that is the basis of jellies and jams

**pec·to·ral** (pek'tə rəl) *adj.* ⟦< L *pectus*, breast⟧ of or located in or on the chest or breast

**pec·u·la·tion** (pek'yōō lā'shən) *n.* ⟦ult. < L *peculium*, private property⟧ embezzlement

**pe·cu·liar** (pi kyōōl'yər) *adj.* ⟦< L *peculium*: see prec.⟧ **1** of only one person, thing, etc.; exclusive **2** special **3** odd; strange —**pe·cu'liar·ly** *adv.*

**pe·cu·li·ar·i·ty** (pi kyōō'lē er'ə tē) *n.* a being peculiar **2** *pl.* **-ties** something that is peculiar, as a trait

**pe·cu·ni·ar·y** (pi kyōō'nē er'ē) *adj.* ⟦< L *pecunia*, money⟧ of or involving money

**ped·a·gogue** or **ped·a·gog** (ped'ə gäg') *n.* ⟦< Gr *paidagōgos* < *pais*, child + *agein*, to lead⟧ a teacher, esp. a pedantic one

**ped'a·gog'y** (-gäj'ē, -gō'jē) *n.* the art or science of teaching; esp., instruction in teaching methods —**ped'a·gog'ic** or **ped'a·gog'i·cal** *adj.*

**ped·al** (ped'l) *adj.* ⟦< L *pes*, FOOT⟧ of the foot or feet —*n.* a lever operated by the foot, as on a bicycle or organ —*vt.*, *vi.* **-aled** or **-alled**, **-al·ing** or **-al·ling** to operate by pedals; use the pedals of

**ped·ant** (ped'nt) *n.* ⟦ult. < Gr *paidagōgos*: see PEDAGOGUE⟧ **1** one who emphasizes trivial points of learning **2** a narrow-minded teacher who insists on exact adherence to rules —**pe·dan'tic** *adj.* —**ped'ant·ry** *n.*

**ped·dle** (ped'l) *vt.*, *vi.* **-dled**, **-dling** ⟦< ? ME *ped*, basket⟧ to go from place to place selling (small articles) —**ped'dler** *n.*

**-pede** (pēd) ⟦< L *pes*⟧ *combining form* foot or feet *[centipede]*

**ped·er·as·ty** (ped'ər as'tē) *n.* ⟦< Gr *paiderastēs*, lover of boys⟧ sodomy between males, esp. between a man and a boy —**ped'er·ast'** *n.*

**ped·es·tal** (ped'əs təl) *n.* ⟦< It *piè*, foot + *di*, of + *stal*, a rest⟧ a bottom support of a pillar, statue, etc.

**pe·des·tri·an** (pi des'trē ən) *adj.* ⟦< L *pes*, foot⟧ **1** going or done on foot **2** of or for pedestrians **3** ordinary and dull; prosaic —*n.* one who goes on foot; walker

**pe·di·at·rics** (pē'dē a'triks) *n.* ⟦< Gr *pais*, child + *iatros*, physician⟧ the branch of medicine dealing with the care of infants and children —**pe'di·a·tri'cian** (-ə trish'ən) *n.* —**pe'di·at'ric** *adj.*

**ped·i·cab** (ped'i kab') *n.* ⟦< L *pes*, foot + CAB⟧ a three-wheeled carriage, esp. formerly in SE Asia, pedaled like a bicycle by the driver

**ped·i·cure** (ped'i kyoor') *n.* ⟦< L *pes*, FOOT + *cura*, care⟧ a trimming, polishing, etc. of the toenails

**ped·i·gree** (ped'i grē') *n.* ⟦< MFr *pié de grue*, lit., crane's foot: from lines in genealogical tree⟧ **1** a list of ancestors **2** descent; lineage **3** a known line of descent, esp. of a purebred animal —**ped'i·greed'** *adj.*

**ped·i·ment** (ped'i mənt) *n.* ⟦< earlier *periment*, prob. < PYRAMID⟧ an ornamental gable or triangular piece on the front of a building, over a doorway, etc.: see PORTICO, illus.

**pe·dom·e·ter** (pē däm'ət ər, pi-) *n.* ⟦< L *pes*, foot + Gr *metron*, a measure⟧ an instrument carried to measure the distance walked

**ped·o·phil·i·a** (ped'ə fil'ē ə) *n.* ⟦< Gr *pais*, child + *philos*, loving⟧ an abnormal condition in which an adult has a sexual desire for children —**pe'do·phile'** *n.*

**pe·dun·cle** (pē dun'kəl, pē'dun'-) *n.* ⟦< L *pes*, foot⟧ a stalklike part in some plants, animals, etc.

**peek** (pēk) *vi.* ⟦ME *piken*⟧ to look quickly and furtively —*n.* such a look

**peel** (pēl) *vt.* ⟦< L *pilare*, make bald⟧ to cut away (the rind, skin, etc.) of —*vi.* **1** to shed skin, etc. **2** to come off in layers or flakes —*n.* the rind or skin of fruit —**peel'er** *n.*

**peel'ing** *n.* a peeled-off strip

**peen** (pēn) *n.* ⟦prob. < Scand⟧ the end of a hammerhead opposite the flat striking surface, usually ball-shaped or wedge-shaped

**peep**[1] (pēp) *vi.* ⟦echoic⟧ to make the short, high-pitched cry of a young bird —*n.* a peeping sound

**peep**[2] (pēp) *vi.* ⟦ME *pepen*⟧ **1** to look through a small opening or from a place of hiding **2** to appear gradually or partially —*n.* a brief look; furtive glimpse —**peep'er** *n.*

**peep'hole'** *n.* a hole to peep through

**peeping Tom** ⟦after legendary tailor who peeped at Lady GODIVA⟧ one who gets sexual pleasure from furtively watching others

**peer**[1] (pir) *n.* ⟦< L *par*, an equal⟧ **1** a person or thing of the same rank, ability, etc.; an equal **2** a British noble —**peer'age** (-ij) *n.* —**peer'ess** *fem.n.*

**peer**[2] (pir) *vi.* ⟦< ? APPEAR⟧ **1** to look closely, as in trying to see more clearly **2** to appear partially

**peer'less** *adj.* without equal

**peeve** (pēv) [Inf.] *vt.* **peeved**, **peev'ing** to make peevish; annoy —*n.* an annoyance

**pee·vish** (pē'vish) *adj.* ⟦ME *pevische*⟧ irritable; fretful; cross —**pee'vish·ly** *adv.* —**pee'vish·ness** *n.*

**pee·wee** (pē'wē') *n.* ⟦< ?⟧ [Inf.] an unusually small person or thing

**peg** (peg) *n.* ⟦ME *pegge*⟧ **1** a short piece of wood, metal, etc. used to hold parts together, hang things on, etc. **2** a step or degree **3** [Inf.] a throw —*vt.* **pegged**, **peg'ging 1** to fasten, fix, secure, mark, etc. with pegs **2** [Inf.] to throw —**peg away (at)** to work steadily (at)

**Peg·a·sus** (peg'ə səs) *n. Gr. Myth.* a winged horse

**peg'board'** *n.* a piece of boardlike material with rows of holes for hooks or pegs to hold displays, tools, etc.

**peign·oir** (pān wär', pen-) *n.* ⟦Fr⟧ a woman's full, loose dressing gown

**Pei·ping** (bā'piŋ') *a former transliteration of* BEIJING

**pe·jo·ra·tive** (pi jôr'ə tiv) *adj.* ⟦< L *pejor*, worse⟧ disparaging or derogatory —**pe·jo'ra·tive·ly** *adv.*

**Pe·king** (pē'kiŋ') *a former transliteration of* BEIJING

**Pe·king·ese** (pē'kə nēz') *n., pl.* **-ese'** a small dog with a long, straight coat, short legs, and a short, wrinkled muzzle: also **Pe'kin·ese'** (-kə nēz')

**pe·koe** (pē'kō) *n.* ⟦< Chin dial. *pek-ho*, white down (on the leaves used)⟧ a black tea of Sri Lanka and India

**pe·lag·ic** (pi laj'ik) *adj.* ⟦< Gr *pelagos*, sea⟧ of the open sea or ocean

**pelf** (pelf) *n.* ⟦< ? MFr *pelfre*, booty⟧ money or wealth regarded with contempt

**pel·i·can** (pel'i kən) *n.* ⟦< Gr *pelekan*⟧ a large, web-footed water bird with an expandable pouch in the lower bill for scooping up fish

**pel·la·gra** (pə lā'grə, -lag'rə) *n.* ⟦It ult. < L *pellis*, skin + Gr *agra*, seizure⟧ a chronic disease caused by a lack of nicotinic acid in the diet, characterized by skin eruptions and mental disorders

**pel·let** (pel'it) *n.* ⟦< L *pila*, a ball⟧ **1** a little ball, as of clay or medicine **2** a bullet, piece of lead shot, etc.

**pell-mell** (pel'mel') *adv.*, *adj.* ⟦< OFr *mesler*, to mix⟧ **1** in a jumble **2** in wild, disorderly haste; headlong Also **pell'mell'**

**pel·lu·cid** (pə lōō'sid) *adj.* ⟦< L *per*, through + *lucere*, to shine⟧ **1** transparent; clear **2** easy to understand

**pelt**[1] (pelt) *vt.* ⟦ME *pelten*⟧ **1** to throw things at **2**

to beat repeatedly —*vi.* to strike heavily or steadily: said as of hard rain

**pelt**[2] (pelt) *n.* ⟦prob. < OFr *pel*, a skin⟧ the skin of a fur-bearing animal, esp. when stripped from the carcass

**pel·vis** (pel′vis) *n., pl.* **-vis·es** or **-ves′** (-vēz′) ⟦L, basin⟧ **1** the basinlike cavity in the posterior part of the trunk in many vertebrates: in humans, it supports the spinal column and rests on the legs **2** the bones forming this cavity —**pel′vic** *adj.*

**pem·mi·can** (pem′i kən) *n.* ⟦< AmInd⟧ a concentrated food made of dried beef, suet, dried fruit, etc.

**pen**[1] (pen) *n.* ⟦OE *penn*⟧ **1** a small enclosure for domestic animals **2** any small enclosure —*vt.* **penned** or **pen′ning** to enclose as in a pen

**pen**[2] (pen) *n.* ⟦< L *penna*, a feather⟧ a device used in writing, etc. with ink; specif., *a*) a device with a metal point split into two nibs *b*) BALLPOINT (PEN) *c*) FOUNTAIN PEN —*vt.* **penned, pen′ning** to write with or as with a pen

**pen**[3] (pen) *n.* [Slang] a penitentiary

**Pen** or **pen** *abbrev.* peninsula

**pe·nal** (pē′nəl) *adj.* ⟦< Gr *poinē*, penalty⟧ of, for, constituting, or making a person liable to punishment

**pe·nal·ize** (pē′nə līz′, pen′ə-) *vt.* **-ized′, -iz′ing** to impose a penalty on; punish —**pe′nal·i·za′tion** *n.*

**pen·al·ty** (pen′əl tē) *n., pl.* **-ties 1** a punishment **2** the handicap, etc. imposed on an offender, as a fine

**pen·ance** (pen′əns) *n.* ⟦see PENITENT⟧ voluntary self-punishment to show repentance for wrongdoing, sins, etc.

**pence** (pens) *n.* [Brit.] *pl.* of PENNY

**pen·chant** (pen′chənt) *n.* ⟦Fr < *pencher*, to incline⟧ a strong liking

**pen·cil** (pen′səl) *n.* ⟦< L *penis*, a tail⟧ a rod-shaped instrument with a core of graphite, crayon, etc. that is sharpened to a point for writing, drawing, etc. —*vt.* **-ciled** or **-cilled, -cil·ing** or **-cil·ling** to write, etc. with a pencil

**pend** (pend) *vi.* ⟦< L *pendere*, hang⟧ to await judgment or decision

**pend·ant** (pen′dənt) *n.* ⟦see prec.⟧ a hanging ornamental object, as one on a necklace or earring

**pend·ent** (pen′dənt) *adj.* ⟦see PEND⟧ **1** suspended **2** overhanging **3** undecided; pending

**pend′ing** *adj.* ⟦prp. of PEND, infl. by Fr *pendant*, L *pendens*⟧ **1** not decided **2** impending —*prep.* until

**pen·du·lous** (pen′dyōō ləs, -jōō-) *adj.* ⟦see PEND⟧ hanging freely; drooping

**pen·du·lum** (pen′dyōō ləm, -jōō-) *n.* ⟦see PEND⟧ a weight hung so as to swing freely to and fro: used to regulate clock movements

**pen·e·trate** (pen′i trāt′) *vt., vi.* **-trat′ed, -trat′ing** ⟦< L *penitus*, inward⟧ **1** to enter by or as by piercing **2** to have an effect throughout **3** to affect deeply **4** to understand —**pen′e·tra·ble** (-trə bəl) *adj.* —**pen′e·tra′tion** *n.*

**pen·e·trat·ing** (pen′i trāt′iŋ) *adj.* **1** that penetrates **2** sharp; piercing **3** acute; discerning Also **pen′e·tra′tive** (-trāt′iv)

**pen·guin** (peŋ′gwin, pen′-) *n.* ⟦prob. < Welsh⟧ a flightless bird of the Southern Hemisphere with webbed feet and flippers for swimming

**pen·i·cil·lin** (pen′i sil′in) *n.* ⟦< L *penicillus*, brush⟧ an antibiotic obtained from certain molds or produced synthetically

**pen·in·su·la** (pə nin′sə lə) *n.* ⟦< L *paene*, almost + *insula*, isle⟧ a land area almost surrounded by water —**pen·in′su·lar** *adj.*

**pe·nis** (pē′nis) *n., pl.* **-nis·es** or **-nes′** (-nēz′) ⟦L⟧ the male organ of sexual intercourse —**pe′nile** (-nīl′) *adj.*

**pen·i·tent** (pen′i tənt) *adj.* ⟦< L *paenitere*, repent⟧ sorry for having done wrong and willing to atone —*n.* a penitent person —**pen′i·tence** *n.* —**pen′i·ten′tial** (-ten′shəl) *adj.* —**pen′i·tent·ly** *adv.*

**pen·i·ten·tia·ry** (pen′i ten′shə rē) *n., pl.* **-ries** a

state or federal prison for persons convicted of serious crimes

**pen′knife′** *n., pl.* **-knives′** (-nīvz′) a small pocket-knife

**pen′light′** or **pen′lite′** *n.* a flashlight about the size of a fountain pen

**pen′man** (-mən) *n., pl.* **-men** (-mən) one skilled in penmanship

**pen′man·ship′** *n.* handwriting as an art or skill

**Penn** (pen), **William** 1644-1718; Eng. Quaker: founder of Pennsylvania

**pen name** a pseudonym

**pen·nant** (pen′ənt) *n.* ⟦< PENNON⟧ **1** any long, narrow flag **2** such a flag symbolizing a championship, esp. in baseball

**pen·ne** (pen′ā′) *n.* pasta in the form of tubes, cut diagonally on the ends

**pen·ni·less** (pen′ə lis) *adj.* without even a penny; extremely poor

**pen·non** (pen′ən) *n.* ⟦< L *penna*, a feather⟧ a flag or pennant

**Penn·syl·va·ni·a** (pen′səl vān′yə) state of the NE U.S.: 44,820 sq. mi.; pop. 11,882,000; cap. Harrisburg: abbrev. *PA* —**Penn′syl·va′ni·an** *adj., n.*

**pen·ny** (pen′ē) *n., pl.* **-nies** or **pence** (pens) ⟦< OE *penig*⟧ **1** in the United Kingdom, $\frac{1}{100}$ of a pound **2** a U.S. or Canadian cent

**penny arcade** a building, as at an amusement park, with coin-operated games, etc.

**penny pincher** a miserly person —**pen′ny-pinch′ing** *n., adj.*

**pen′ny·weight′** *n.* a unit of weight, equal to $\frac{1}{20}$ ounce troy weight

**pen′ny-wise′** *adj.* thrifty in small matters — **penny-wise and pound-foolish** thrifty in small matters but wasteful in major ones

**pe·nol·o·gy** (pē näl′ə jē) *n.* ⟦< Gr *poinē*, punishment + -LOGY⟧ the study of prison management and prison reform

**pen pal** a person, esp. a stranger in another country, with whom one exchanges letters

**pen·sion** (pen′shən) *n.* ⟦< L *pensio*, a paying⟧ a regular payment, not wages, as to one who is retired or disabled —*vt.* to grant a pension to

**pen′sion·er** *n.* one who receives a pension

**pen·sive** (pen′siv) *adj.* ⟦< L *pensare*, consider⟧ thoughtful or reflective, often in a melancholy way —**pen′sive·ly** *adv.* —**pen′sive·ness** *n.*

**pent** (pent) *vt. alt. pt. & pp.* of PEN[1] —*adj.* held or kept in; penned: often with *up*

**penta-** ⟦< Gr *pente*, FIVE⟧ *combining form* five

**pen·ta·gon** (pen′tə gän′) *n.* ⟦< Gr *penta-*, five + *gōnia*, an angle⟧ a plane figure with five angles and five sides —**the Pentagon** the pentagonal office building of the Defense Department, near Washington, DC —**pen·tag′o·nal** (-tag′ə nəl) *adj.*

**pen·tam·e·ter** (pen tam′ət ər) *n.* ⟦see PENTA- & METER[1]⟧ a line of verse containing five metrical feet; esp., English iambic pentameter (Ex.: "Hĕ jĕsts| ăt scărs| whŏ nĕv′ ĕr fĕlt| ă woúnd")

PENTAGON

**Pen·ta·teuch** (pen′tə tōōk′) *n.* ⟦< Gr *penta-*, five + *teuchos*, book⟧ the first five books of the Bible

**pen·tath·lon** (pen tath′län′) *n.* ⟦< Gr *penta-*, five + *athlon*, a contest⟧ an athletic contest in which each contestant takes part in five events —**pen·tath′lete′** (-lēt′) *n.*

**Pen·te·cost** (pen′tə kôst′) *n.* ⟦< Gr *pentēkostē (hēmera)*, the fiftieth (day)⟧ a Christian festival on the seventh Sunday after Easter

**Pen·te·cos·tal** (pen′tə kôs′təl) *adj.* **1** of Pentecost **2** designating or of any of various Protestant fundamentalist sects often stressing direct inspiration by the Holy Spirit —**Pen′te·cos′tal·ism′** *n.*

**pent·house** (pent′hous′) *n.* ⟦ult. < L *appendere*, append⟧ an apartment on the roof or on the top floor of a building

**pent-up** (pent′up′) *adj.* held in check; curbed [*pent-up* emotion]

**pe·nu·che** or **pe·nu·chi** (pə nōō′chē) *n.* ⟦var. of PANOCHA⟧ a candy similar to fudge

**pe·nul·ti·mate** (pē nul′tə mət) *adj.* ⟦< L *paene*, almost + ULTIMATE⟧ next to the last

**pe·nu·ri·ous** (pe nyoor′ē əs, -noor′-) *adj.* ⟦see fol.⟧ miserly; stingy —**pe·nu′ri·ous·ly** *adv.* —**pe·nu′ri·ous·ness** *n.*

**pen·u·ry** (pen′yōō rē, -yə-) *n.* ⟦< L *penuria*, want⟧ extreme poverty

**pe·on** (pē′än) *n.* ⟦< ML *pedo*, foot soldier⟧ **1** in Spanish America, a member of the laboring class **2** in the SW U.S., a person forced into servitude to work off a debt —**pe′on·age** (-ə nij) *n.*

**pe·o·ny** (pē′ə nē) *n., pl.* **-nies** ⟦< Gr *Paiōn*, Apollo as god of medicine: from its former medicinal use⟧ **1** a plant with large, showy, pink, white, red, or yellow flowers **2** the flower

**peo·ple** (pē′pəl) *n., pl.* **-ples** ⟦< L *populus*, nation, crowd⟧ all the persons of a racial or ethnic group; nation; race, etc. —*pl.n.* **1** *pl.* of PERSON (sense 1) **2** the persons of a certain place, group, or class **3** one's family; relatives **4** the populace **5** persons considered indefinitely [*what will people say?*] **6** human beings —*vt.* **-pled, -pling** to populate

**Pe·or·i·a** (pē ôr′ē ə) city in central Illinois: pop. 114,000

**pep** (pep) [Inf.] *n.* ⟦< fol.⟧ energy; vigor —*vt.* **pepped, pep′ping** to fill with pep; invigorate: with *up* —**pep′py, -pi·er, -pi·est,** *adj.*

**pep·per** (pep′ər) *n.* ⟦< Gr *peperi*⟧ **1** *a*) a pungent condiment ground from the dried fruits of an East Indian vine *b*) this vine **2** a plant with red or green, sweet or hot pods —*vt.* **1** to season with ground pepper **2** to pelt with small objects

**pep′per·corn′** *n.* the dried berry of the pepper

**pepper mill** a hand mill used to grind pepper-corns

**pep′per·mint′** *n.* **1** a plant of the mint family that yields a pungent oil used for flavoring **2** the oil **3** a candy flavored with this oil

**pep·per·o·ni** (pep′ər ō′nē) *n., pl.* **-nis** or **-ni** ⟦< It *peperoni*⟧ a hard, highly spiced Italian sausage

**pepper shaker** a container for ground pepper, with a perforated top

**pep′per·y** *adj.* **1** of, like, or highly seasoned with pepper **2** sharp or fiery, as words **3** hot-tempered

**pep·sin** (pep′sin) *n.* ⟦< Gr *peptein*, to digest⟧ a stomach enzyme, aiding in the digestion of proteins

**pep talk** a talk, as to an athletic team by its coach, to instill enthusiasm, determination, etc.

**pep·tic** (pep′tik) *adj.* ⟦see PEPSIN⟧ **1** of or aiding digestion **2** caused by digestive secretions [*a peptic ulcer*]

**per** (pur) *prep.* ⟦L⟧ **1** through; by; by means of **2** for each [*fifty cents per yard*] **3** [Inf.] according to

**per-** ⟦< prec.⟧ *prefix* **1** through, throughout **2** thoroughly

**per·ad·ven·ture** (pur′əd ven′chər) *adv.* ⟦< OFr *par*, by + *aventure*, chance⟧ [Archaic] possibly

**per·am·bu·late** (pər am′byōō lāt′) *vt., vi.* **-lat·ed, -lat·ing** ⟦< L *per*, through + *ambulare*, to walk⟧ to walk (through, over, etc.)

**per·am′bu·la′tor** (-lāt′ər) *n.* [Chiefly Brit.] a baby carriage

**per an·num** (pər an′əm) ⟦L⟧ yearly

**per·cale** (pər kāl′) *n.* ⟦Fr < Pers *pargāla*, scrap⟧ fine, closely woven cotton cloth, used for sheets, etc.

**per cap·i·ta** (pər kap′i tə) ⟦ML, lit., by heads⟧ for each person

**per·ceive** (pər sēv′) *vt., vi.* **-ceived′, -ceiv′ing** ⟦< L *per*, through + *capere*, take⟧ **1** to understand **2** to become aware (of) through the senses

**per·cent** (pər sent′) *adv., adj.* ⟦< L *per centum*⟧ in,

to, or for every hundred: symbol, %: also **per cent** —*n.* [Inf.] percentage

**per·cent·age** *n.* **1** a given part in every hundred **2** part; portion **3** [Inf.] advantage; profit

**per·cen·tile** (pər sen′tīl′, -sent′'l) *n. Statistics* any of 100 divisions of a series, each of equal frequency

**per·cep·ti·ble** (pər sep′tə bəl) *adj.* that can be perceived —**per·cep′ti·bly** *adv.*

**per·cep·tion** (-shən) *n.* ⟦< L *percipere*, perceive⟧ **1** the mental grasp of objects, etc. through the senses **2** insight or intuition **3** the knowledge, etc. gotten by perceiving —**per·cep′tion·al** *adj.*

**per·cep·tive** (-tiv) *adj.* **1** of perception **2** able to perceive quickly —**per·cep′tive·ly** *adv.* —**per·cep′tive·ness** *n.*

**per·cep·tu·al** (-chōō əl) *adj.* of or involving perception

**perch¹** (purch) *n., pl.* **-es** ⟦< Gr *perkē*⟧ **1** a small, spiny-finned, freshwater food fish **2** any of various other spiny-finned fishes

**perch²** (purch) *n.* ⟦< L *pertica*, pole⟧ **1** a horizontal pole, etc. serving as a roost for birds **2** any high resting place —*vi., vt.* to rest or place on or as on a perch

**per·chance** (pər chans′) *adv.* ⟦< OFr *par*, by + *chance*, chance⟧ [Archaic] **1** by chance **2** perhaps

**per·co·late** (pur′kə lāt′) *vt.* **-lat·ed, -lat·ing** ⟦< L *per*, through + *colare*, to strain⟧ to filter (a liquid) through a porous substance —*vi.* to ooze through a porous substance

**per′co·la′tor** (-lāt′ər) *n.* a coffeepot in which the boiling water bubbles up through a tube and filters back down through the ground coffee

**per·cus·sion** (pər kush′ən) *n.* ⟦< L *per-*, thoroughly + *quatere*, shake⟧ **1** the hitting of one body against another, as the hammer of a firearm against a powder cap (**percussion cap**) **2** the shock, vibration, etc. from this —*adj.* of a musical instrument producing a tone when struck, as a drum, cymbal, etc.

**per·cus′sion·ist** *n.* a musician who plays percussion instruments

**per di·em** (pər dē′əm) ⟦L⟧ daily

**per·di·tion** (pər dish′ən) *n.* ⟦< L *perdere*, to lose⟧ *Theol.* **1** the loss of the soul **2** HELL

**per·dure** (pər door′) *vi.* **-dured′, -dur′ing** ⟦< L *perdurare*, to endure⟧ to remain in existence; last

**per·e·gri·nate** (per′ə gri nāt′) *vt., vi.* **-nat·ed, -nat·ing** ⟦see PILGRIM⟧ to travel (along, over, or through) —**per′e·gri·na′tion** *n.*

**per·e·grine (falcon)** (per′ə grin) a swift falcon much used in falconry

**per·emp·to·ry** (pər emp′tə rē) *adj.* ⟦< L *perimere*, destroy⟧ **1** *Law* barring further action; final **2** that cannot be denied, delayed, etc., as a command **3** dogmatic; imperious

**per·en·ni·al** (pə ren′ē əl) *adj.* ⟦< L *per-*, through + *annus*, year⟧ **1** continuing for a long time **2** becoming active again and again **3** living more than two years: said of plants —*n.* a perennial plant

**per·fect** (pur′fikt; *for v.* pər fekt′) *adj.* ⟦< L *per-*, through + *facere*, do⟧ **1** complete in all respects; flawless **2** excellent, as in skill or quality **3** completely accurate **4** utter; absolute [*a perfect fool*] **5** *Gram.* expressing a state or action completed at the time of speaking —*vt.* **1** to complete **2** to make perfect or nearly perfect —**per′fect·ly** *adv.*

**per·fec·ta** (pər fek′tə) *n.* ⟦Sp, perfect⟧ a bet in which one wins if one correctly picks the first and second place finishers in a race

**per·fect·i·ble** (pər fek′tə bəl) *adj.* that can become, or be made, perfect

**per·fec·tion** (pər fek′shən) *n.* **1** the act of perfecting **2** a being perfect **3** a person or thing that is the perfect embodiment of some quality

**per·fec′tion·ism′** *n.* obsessive striving for perfection —**per·fec′tion·ist** *n., adj.*

**per·fi·dy** (pur′fə dē) *n., pl.* **-dies** ⟦< L *per*, through

+ *fides,* faith‖ betrayal of trust; treachery —**per·fid·i·ous** (pər fid′ē əs) *adj.*

**per·fo·rate** (pur′fə rāt′) *vt., vi.* -**rat·ed, -rat·ing** ‖< L *per,* through + *forare,* to bore‖ **1** to make a hole or holes through (something), as by boring **2** to pierce with holes in a row —**per′fo·ra′tion** *n.*

**per·force** (pər fôrs′) *adv.* ‖< OFr: see PER & FORCE‖ necessarily

**per·form** (pər fôrm′) *vt.* ‖< OFr *parfournir*‖ **1** to do (a task, etc.) **2** to fulfill (a promise, etc.) **3** to render or enact (a piece of music, dramatic role, etc.) —*vi.* to execute an action or process, esp. in a PERFORMANCE (sense 4) —**per·form′er** *n.*

**per·form′ance** *n.* **1** the act of performing **2** functional effectiveness **3** deed or feat **4** *a)* a formal exhibition or presentation, as a play *b)* one's part in this

**performance art** an art form combining elements of several art forms, as dance, film, etc., in a presentation of juxtaposed images on various themes

**performing arts** arts, such as drama, for performance before an audience

**per·fume** (pər fyo͞om′; *for n. usually* pur′fyo͞om′) *vt.* -**fumed′, -fum′ing** ‖< L *per-,* intens. + *fumare,* to smoke‖ **1** to scent **2** to put perfume on —*n.* a pleasing odor, or a substance producing this, as a volatile oil extracted from flowers

**per·fum′er·y** (-fyo͞o′mə rē) *n., pl.* -**ies** perfumes collectively

**per·func·to·ry** (pər funk′tə rē) *adj.* ‖< L *per-,* intens. + *fungi,* perform‖ **1** done without care or interest; superficial **2** indifferent; unconcerned —**per·func′to·ri·ly** *adv.*

**per·go·la** (pur′gə lə) *n.* ‖< L *pergula*‖ an arbor with a latticework roof

**per·haps** (pər haps′) *adv.* ‖PER + pl. of *hap,* chance‖ possibly; maybe

**peri-** ‖Gr‖ *prefix* **1** around; about **2** near

**per·i·car·di·um** (per′ə kär′dē əm) *n., pl.* -**di·a** (-ə) ‖< Gr *peri-,* around + *kardia,* heart‖ in vertebrates, the thin, closed sac surrounding the heart —**per′i·car′di·al** *adj.*

**Per·i·cles** (per′ə klēz′) 495?-429 B.C.; Athenian statesman & general

**per·i·gee** (per′ə jē′) *n.* ‖< Gr *peri-,* near + *gē,* earth‖ the point nearest to the earth in the orbit of the moon or of a man-made satellite

**per·i·he·li·on** (per′ə hē′lē ən) *n., pl.* -**li·ons** or -**li·a** (-ə) ‖< Gr *peri-,* around + *hēlios,* sun‖ the point nearest the sun in the orbit of a planet, comet, or man-made satellite

**per·il** (per′əl) *n.* ‖< L *periculum,* danger‖ **1** exposure to harm or injury **2** something that may cause harm

**per·il·ous** (-ə ləs) *adj.* involving peril or risk; dangerous —**per′il·ous·ly** *adv.*

**pe·rim·e·ter** (pə rim′ə tər) *n.* ‖< Gr *peri-,* around + *metron,* measure‖ **1** the outer boundary of a figure or area **2** the total length of this

**per·i·ne·um** (per′ə nē′əm) *n., pl.* -**ne·a** (-ə) ‖< Gr *perineon*‖ the small area between the anus and the genitals

**pe·ri·od** (pir′ē əd) *n.* ‖< Gr *periodos,* a cycle‖ **1** the interval between successive occurrences of an event **2** a portion of time characterized by certain processes, etc. *[a period of change]* **3** any of the portions of time into which a game, school day, etc. is divided **4** the menses **5** an end, conclusion **6** *a)* the pause in speaking or a mark of punctuation (.) used at the end of a sentence *b)* the dot (.) following many abbreviations —*interj.* an exclamation used for emphasis

**pe·ri·od·ic** (pir′ē äd′ik) *adj.* **1** appearing or recurring at regular intervals **2** intermittent

**pe′ri·od′i·cal** *adj.* **1** PERIODIC **2** published at regular intervals, as weekly, etc. **3** of a periodical —*n.* a periodical publication —**pe′ri·od′i·cal·ly** *adv.*

**periodic table** an arrangement of the chemical elements according to their atomic numbers

**pe·ri·od·i·za·tion** (pir′ē ə də zā′shən) *n.* the dividing, as of history, into chronological periods

**per·i·o·don·tal** (per′ē ə dänt′'l) *adj.* ‖< PERI- + Gr *odōn,* tooth‖ occurring around a tooth or affecting the gums

**per·i·pa·tet·ic** (per′i pə tet′ik) *adj.* ‖< Gr *peri-,* around + *patein,* walk‖ walking or moving about; itinerant

**pe·riph·er·al** (pə rif′ər əl) *adj.* **1** of or forming a periphery **2** outer; external —*n.* a piece of equipment used with a computer to increase its range or efficiency, as a disk, etc.

**pe·riph·er·y** (pə rif′ər ē) *n., pl.* -**ies** ‖< Gr *peri-,* around + *pherein,* to bear‖ **1** an outer boundary, esp. of a rounded object **2** surrounding space

**pe·riph·ra·sis** (pə rif′rə sis) *n., pl.* -**ses′** (-sēz′) ‖< Gr *peri-,* around + *phrazein,* to speak‖ the use of many words where a few would do —**per·i·phras·tic** (per′ə fras′tik) *adj.*

**per·i·scope** (per′ə skōp′) *n.* ‖PERI- + -SCOPE‖ an optical instrument which allows one to see around or over an obstacle: used on submarines, etc.

**per·ish** (per′ish) *vi.* ‖< L *per-,* through + *ire,* go‖ **1** to be destroyed or ruined **2** to die, esp. violently

**per·ish·a·ble** (per′ish ə bəl) *adj.* that may perish; esp., liable to spoil, as some foods —*n.* something, esp. a food, liable to spoil

**per·i·stal·sis** (per′ə stal′sis, -stôl′-) *n., pl.* -**ses′** (-sēz′) ‖< Gr *peri-,* around + *stellein,* to place‖ the contractions and

PERISCOPE

dilations of the alimentary canal, moving the contents onward —**per·i·stal′tic** *adj.*

**per·i·to·ne·um** (per′ə tə nē′əm) *n., pl.* -**ne′a** (-ə) or -**ne′ums** ‖< Gr *peri-,* around + *teinein,* to stretch‖ the serous membrane lining the abdominal cavity

**per′i·to·ni′tis** (-nīt′is) *n.* inflammation of the peritoneum

**per·i·wig** (per′ə wig′) *n.* ‖altered < Fr *perruque*‖ a wig of a type formerly worn by men

**per·i·win·kle**[1] (per′ə wiŋ′kəl) *n.* ‖< L *pervincire,* entwine‖ a creeping plant with blue, white, or pink flowers

**per·i·win·kle**[2] (per′ə wiŋ′kəl) *n.* ‖OE *pinewincle*‖ a small saltwater snail with a spherical shell

**per·jure** (pur′jər) *vt.* -**jured, -jur·ing** ‖< L *per,* through + *jurare,* swear‖ to make (oneself) guilty of perjury —**per′jur·er** *n.*

**per·ju·ry** (pur′jə rē) *n., pl.* -**ries** ‖< L *perjurus,* false‖ the willful telling of a lie while under oath

**perk**[1] (purk) *vt.* ‖ME *perken*‖ **1** to raise (the head, ears, etc.) briskly **2** to give a smart, fresh, or vivacious look to: Often with *up* —*vi.* to become lively: with *up* —**perk′y, -i·er, -i·est,** *adj.*

**perk**[2] (purk) *vt., vi.* [Inf.] *short for* PERCOLATE

**perk**[3] (purk) *n.* [Inf.] *short for* PERQUISITE

**perm** (purm) [Inf.] *n. short for* PERMANENT —*vt.* to give a permanent to

**per·ma·frost** (pur′mə frôst′) *n.* permanently frozen subsoil

**per·ma·nent** (pur′mə nənt) *adj.* ‖< L *per,* through + *manere,* remain‖ lasting or intended to last indefinitely or for a long time —*n.* a long-lasting hair wave produced by use of chemicals or heat

**per·me·a·ble** (pur′mē ə bəl) *adj.* that can be permeated, as by fluids —**per′me·a·bil′i·ty** *n.*

**per′me·ate′** (-āt′) *vt., vi.* -**at·ed, -at·ing** ‖< L *per,* through + *meare,* to glide] to spread or diffuse; penetrate (*through* or *among*)

**per·mis·si·ble** (pər mis′ə bəl) *adj.* that can be permitted; allowable

**per·mis·sion** (pər mish′ən) *n.* the act of permitting; esp., formal consent

**per·mis·sive** (-mis′iv) *adj.* **1** that permits **2** allowing freedom; lenient —**per·mis′sive·ly** *adv.* —**per·mis′sive·ness** *n.*

**per·mit** (pər mit′; *for n.* pʉr′mit′, pər mit′) *vt.* **-mit′ted, -mit′ting** [< L *per,* through + *mittere,* send] **1** to allow; consent to **2** to authorize —*vi.* to give opportunity [if time *permits*] —*n.* a license

**per·mu·ta·tion** (pʉr′myoo tā′shən) *n.* [< L *per-,* intens. + *mutare,* change] **1** any radical alteration **2** any of the total number of groupings possible within a group

**per·ni·cious** (pər nish′əs) *adj.* [< L < *per,* thoroughly + *necare,* kill] very harmful or destructive —**per·ni′cious·ly** *adv.*

**per·o·ra·tion** (per′ə rā′shən) *n.* [< L *per,* through + *orare,* speak] the concluding part of a speech

**per·ox·ide** (pər äk′sīd) *n.* [< L *per,* through + OXIDE] any oxide containing the oxygen group linked by a single bond; specif., hydrogen peroxide —*vt.* **-id′ed, -id′ing** to bleach (hair, etc.) with hydrogen peroxide

**per·pen·dic·u·lar** (pʉr′pən dik′yoo lər, -yə-) *adj.* [< L *perpendiculum,* plumb line] **1** at right angles to a given plane or line **2** exactly upright; vertical —*n.* a line or plane at right angles to another line or plane

**per·pe·trate** (pʉr′pə trāt′) *vt.* **-trat′ed, -trat′ing** [< L *per,* thoroughly + *patrare,* to effect] **1** to do (something evil, criminal, etc.) **2** to commit (a blunder, etc.) —**per′pe·tra′tion** *n.* —**per′pe·tra′tor** *n.*

**per·pet·u·al** (pər pech′oo əl) *adj.* [< L *perpetuus,* constant] **1** lasting forever or for a long time **2** continuing without interruption; constant —**per·pet′u·al·ly** *adv.*

**per·pet·u·ate** (-āt′) *vt.* **-at′ed, -at′ing** to make perpetual; cause to continue or be remembered —**per·pet′u·a′tion** *n.*

**per·pe·tu·i·ty** (pʉr′pə too′ə tē) *n., pl.* **-ties** unlimited time; eternity —**in perpetuity** forever

**per·plex** (pər pleks′) *vt.* [< L *per,* through + *plectere,* twist] to make (a person) uncertain, doubtful, etc.; confuse —**per·plex′ing** *adj.* —**per·plex′i·ty,** *pl.* **-ties,** *n.*

**per·qui·site** (pʉr′kwi zit) *n.* [< L *per-,* intens. + *quaerere,* seek] something in addition to regular pay for one's work, as a tip

**per se** (pʉr′ sā′, -sē′) [L] by (or in) itself; intrinsically

**per·se·cute** (pʉr′si kyoot′) *vt.* **-cut′ed, -cut′ing** [< L *per,* through + *sequi,* follow] to afflict constantly so as to injure or distress, as for reasons of religion, race, etc. —**per′se·cu′tion** *n.* —**per′se·cu′tor** *n.*

**per·se·vere** (pʉr′sə vir′) *vi.* **-vered′, -ver′ing** [< L *per-,* intens. + *severus,* severe] to continue a course of action, etc. in spite of difficulty, opposition, etc. —**per′se·ver′ance** *n.*

**Per·sia** (pʉr′zhə) *former name for* IRAN

**Per·sian** (pʉr′zhən, -shən) *adj.* of Persia or its people, language, etc. —*n.* **1** person born or living in Persia **2** the language of Iran **3** a variety of domestic cat with a long, thick, glossy coat

**Persian Gulf** arm of the Indian Ocean, between Iran & Arabia

**Persian lamb** the pelt of karakul lambs

**per·si·flage** (pʉr′sə fläzh′) *n.* [Fr < L *per,* through + *sifilare,* to hiss] frivolous talk or writing

**per·sim·mon** (pər sim′ən) *n.* [< AmInd] **1** a hardwood tree with plumlike fruit **2** the fruit

**per·sist** (pər sist′, -zist′) *vi.* [< L *per,* through + *sistere,* cause to stand] **1** to refuse to give up, esp. when faced with opposition **2** to continue insistently **3** to endure; remain

**per·sist′ent** *adj.* **1** continuing, esp. in the face of opposition, etc. **2** continuing to exist or endure **3** constantly repeated —**per·sist′ence** *n.*

**per·snick·e·ty** (pər snik′ə tē) *adj.* [< Scot dial.] [Inf.] too particular or precise; fussy

**per·son** (pʉr′sən) *n.* [< L *persona*] **1** a human being: now usually pluralized as *people* **2** the human body **3** personality; self **4** *Gram.* any of the three sets of pronouns and corresponding verb forms: see FIRST PERSON, SECOND PERSON, THIRD PERSON **5** *Law* any individual or incorporated group having certain legal rights and responsibilities —**in person** actually present

**-per·son** (pʉr′sən) *combining form* person in a (specified) activity: used to avoid the masculine implication of *-man* [*chairperson*]

**per·son·a·ble** *adj.* [ME *personabilis*] having a pleasing appearance and personality

**per·son·age** *n.* a person; esp., an important person; notable

**per·son·al** (-nəl) *adj.* **1** private; individual **2** done in person **3** involving human beings [*personal* relationships] **4** of the body or physical appearance **5** *a*) having to do with the character, conduct, etc. of a person [a *personal* remark] *b*) tending to make personal, esp. derogatory, remarks **6** *Gram.* indicating PERSON (sense 4) **7** *Law* of property (**personal property**) that is movable

**personal computer** MICROCOMPUTER

**personal effects** personal belongings, esp. those worn or carried

**per·son·al·i·ty** (pʉr′sə nal′ə tē) *n., pl.* **-ties** **1** distinctive individual qualities of a person, considered collectively **2** such qualities seen as being attractive to others **3** a notable person **4** [*pl.*] offensive remarks aimed at a person

**per·son·al·ize** (pʉr′sə nə līz′) *vt.* **-ized′, -iz′ing** **1** to apply to a particular person, esp. to oneself **2** to have marked with one's name, etc.

**per·son·al·ly** *adv.* **1** in person **2** as a person [I dislike him *personally*] **3** in one's own opinion **4** as though directed at oneself

**per·so·na non gra·ta** (pər sō′nə nōn grät′ə) [L] an unwelcome person

**per·son·i·fy** (pər sän′ə fī′) *vt.* **-fied′, -fy′ing** **1** to think of or represent (a thing) as a person **2** to typify; embody —**per·son′i·fi·ca′tion** *n.*

**per·son·nel** (pʉr′sə nel′) *n.* [Fr] **1** persons employed in any work, enterprise, service, etc. **2** a personnel department or office —*adj.* of or relating to the division within a business, etc. responsible for hiring and training employees, etc.

**per·spec·tive** (pər spek′tiv) *n.* [< L *per,* through + *specere,* look] **1** the art of picturing objects so as to show relative distance or depth **2** the appearance of objects as determined by their relative distance and positions **3** sense of proportion **4** *a*) a specific point of view in understanding things or events *b*) the ability to see things in a true relationship

**per·spi·ca·cious** (pʉr′spi kā′shəs) *adj.* [see prec.] having keen judgment; discerning —**per′spi·ca′cious·ly** *adv.* —**per′spi·cac′i·ty** (-kas′ə tē) *n.*

**per·spic·u·ous** (pər spik′yoo əs) *adj.* [see PERSPECTIVE] easily understood; lucid —**per·spi·cu·i·ty** (pʉr′spi kyoo′ə tē) *n.*

**per·spi·ra·tion** (pʉr′spə rā′shən) *n.* **1** the action of perspiring **2** sweat

**per·spire** (pər spīr′) *vt., vi.* **-spired′, -spir′ing** [< L *per-,* through + *spirare,* breathe] to sweat

**per·suade** (pər swād′) *vt.* **-suad′ed, -suad′ing** [< L *per-,* intens. + *suadere,* to urge] to cause to do or believe something by reasoning, urging, etc.; induce or convince —**per·suad′er** *n.*

**per·sua·sion** (pər swā′zhən) *n.* **1** a persuading or being persuaded **2** power of persuading **3** a strong belief **4** a particular religious belief

**per·sua·sive** *adj.* having the power, or tending, to persuade —**per·sua′sive·ly** *adv.*

**pert** (pʉrt) *adj.* [< L *apertus,* open] **1** impudent; saucy **2** chic and jaunty —**pert′ly** *adv.*

**per·tain** (pər tān') *vi.* ⟦< L *per-*, intens. + *tenere*, hold⟧ **1** to belong; be connected or associated **2** to be appropriate **3** to have reference

**per·ti·na·cious** (purt''n ā'shəs) *adj.* ⟦< L *per-*, intens. + *tenax*, holding fast⟧ **1** holding firmly to some purpose, belief, etc. **2** hard to get rid of — **per'ti·nac'i·ty** (-as'ə tē) *n.*

**per·ti·nent** (purt''n ənt) *adj.* ⟦see PERTAIN⟧ having some connection with the matter at hand — **per'ti·nence** *n.*

**per·turb** (pər turb') *vt.* ⟦< L *per-*, intens. + *turbare*, disturb⟧ to cause to be alarmed, agitated, or upset —**per·tur·ba·tion** (purˈtər bāˈshən) *n.*

**Pe·ru** (pə rōō') country in W South America, on the Pacific: 480,041 sq. mi.; pop. 22,048,000 —**Pe·ru'vi·an** (-vē ən) *adj., n.*

**pe·ruke** (pə rōōk') *n.* ⟦Fr *perruque*⟧ PERIWIG

**pe·ruse** (pə rōōz') *vt.* **-rused', -rus'ing** ⟦prob. < *per-*, intens. + ME *usen*, to use⟧ **1** to read carefully; study **2** to read in a leisurely way —**pe·rus'al** *n.*

**per·vade** (pər vād') *vt.* **-vad'ed, -vad'ing** ⟦< L *per*, through + *vadere*, go⟧ to spread or be prevalent throughout —**per·va'sive** (-vā'siv) *adj.*

**per·verse** (pər vurs') *adj.* ⟦see PERVERT⟧ **1** deviating from what is considered right or good **2** stubbornly contrary **3** obstinately disobedient — **per·verse'ly** *adv.* —**per·verse'ness** or **per·ver'si·ty** *n.*

**per·ver·sion** (pər vur'zhən) *n.* **1** a perverting or being perverted **2** something perverted **3** any sexual act or practice considered abnormal

**per·vert** (pər vurt'; *for n.* pur'vurt) *vt.* ⟦< L *per-*, intens. + *vertere*, turn⟧ **1** to lead astray; corrupt **2** to misuse **3** to distort —*n.* one practicing sexual perversion

**pe·se·ta** (pə sāt'ə) *n.* ⟦Sp, dim. of *peso*, peso⟧ the monetary unit of Spain

**pes·ky** (pes'kē) *adj.* **-ki·er, -ki·est** ⟦prob. var. of *pesty*⟧ [Inf.] annoying; troublesome —**pes'ki·ness** *n.*

**pe·so** (pā'sō) *n., pl.* **-sos** ⟦Sp < L *pensum*, something weighed⟧ the monetary unit of various countries, including Mexico, Colombia, Chile, etc.

**pes·si·mism** (pes'ə miz'əm) *n.* ⟦< L *pejor*, worse⟧ **1** the belief that the evil in life outweighs the good **2** the tendency to expect the worst —**pes'si·mist** *n.* —**pes'si·mis'tic** *adj.* —**pes'si·mis'ti·cal·ly** *adv.*

**pest** (pest) *n.* ⟦< L *pestis*, plague⟧ a person or thing that is troublesome, destructive, etc.; specif., a rat, fly, weed, etc.

**pes·ter** (pes'tər) *vt.* ⟦< OFr *empestrer*, entangle⟧ to annoy; vex

**pest'hole'** *n.* a place infested with an epidemic disease

**pes·ti·cide** (pes'tə sīd') *n.* any chemical for killing insects, weeds, etc.

**pes·tif·er·ous** (pes tif'ər əs) *adj.* ⟦< L *pestis*, plague + *ferre*, to bear⟧ **1** noxious **2** [Inf.] annoying

**pes·ti·lence** (pes'tə ləns) *n.* **1** a deadly epidemic disease; plague **2** anything regarded as harmful

**pes·ti·lent** (pes'tə lənt) *adj.* ⟦< L *pestis*, plague⟧ **1** likely to cause death **2** dangerous to society /the *pestilent* threat of war/ **3** annoying

**pes·tle** (pes'əl) *n.* ⟦< L *pinsere*, to pound⟧ a tool used to pound or grind substances, esp. in a mortar

**pes·to** (pes'tō) *n.* ⟦see prec.⟧ a sauce for pasta, of ground basil and garlic mixed with olive oil

**pet**[1] (pet) *n.* ⟦orig. Scot dial.⟧ **1** an animal that is domesticated and kept as a companion **2** a person treated with particular indulgence —*adj.* **1** kept or treated as a pet **2** especially liked **3** particular /a pet peeve/ **4** showing fondness /a pet name/ —*vt.* **pet'ted, pet'ting** to stroke or pat gently; caress —*vi.* [Inf.] to kiss, embrace, etc. as lovers do

**pet**[2] (pet) *n.* ⟦< ?⟧ a sulky mood

**pet·al** (pet''l) *n.* ⟦< Gr *petalos*, outspread⟧ any of the leaflike parts of a blossom

**pe·tard** (pi tärd') *n.* ⟦< Fr⟧ used chiefly in **hoist with (or by) one's own petard**, destroyed by the very thing with which one meant to destroy others

**pet·cock** (pet'käk') *n.* ⟦< L *pedere*, break wind + *cock*, valve⟧ a small valve for draining pipes, etc.

**pe·ter** (pēt'ər) *vi.* ⟦< ?⟧ [Inf.] to become gradually smaller, weaker, etc. and then disappear: with *out*

**Pe·ter** (pēt'ər) *n.* Bible (original name *Simon*) (died A.D. 64?); one of the twelve Apostles, a fisherman: reputed author of two Letters: also **Saint Peter**

**Peter I** 1672-1725; czar of Russia (1682-1725): called *Peter the Great*

**pet·i·ole** (pet'ē ōl') *n.* ⟦< L *pes*, FOOT⟧ LEAFSTALK

**pe·tite** (pə tēt') *adj.* ⟦Fr⟧ small and trim in figure: said of a woman

**pe·tit four** (pet'ē fôr') *pl.* **pe·tits fours** or **pe·tit fours** (pet'ē fôrz') ⟦Fr, lit., small oven⟧ a tiny, frosted cake

**pe·ti·tion** (pə tish'ən) *n.* ⟦< L *petere*, seek⟧ **1** a solemn, earnest request; entreaty **2** a formal document embodying such a request, often signed by many people **3** *Law* a written formal request asking for a specific court action —*vt.* to address a petition to —*vi.* to make a petition —**pe·ti'tion·er** *n.*

**pe·tit jury** (pet'ē) a group of citizens picked to decide the issues of a trial in court

**pet·rel** (pe'trəl) *n.* ⟦< ?⟧ a small sea bird with long wings

**pet·ri·fy** (pe'tri fī') *vt.* **-fied', -fy'ing** ⟦< L *petra*, rock + *facere*, make⟧ **1** to turn into stone **2** to harden or deaden **3** to paralyze, as with fear

**petro-** ⟦< Gr *petra*, rock⟧ *combining form* **1** rock or stone **2** petroleum **3** of or relating to the petroleum business

**pet·ro·chem·i·cal** (pe'trō kem'i kəl) *n.* a chemical with a petroleum base

**pet'ro·dol'lars** *pl.n.* revenue from the sale of petroleum

**pet·rol** (pe'trəl) *n.* ⟦see PETROLEUM⟧ *Brit.* term for GASOLINE

**pet·ro·la·tum** (pe'trə lāt'əm) *n.* ⟦< fol.⟧ a greasy, jellylike substance derived from petroleum and used in ointments, etc.: also **petroleum jelly**

**pe·tro·le·um** (pə trō'lē əm) *n.* ⟦< L *petra*, rock + *oleum*, oil⟧ an oily, liquid solution of hydrocarbons, occurring naturally in certain rock strata: it yields kerosene, gasoline, etc.

**PET (scan)** (pet) ⟦*p(ositron) e(mission) t(omography)*, an X-ray technique⟧ a type of X-raying that shows metabolic activity, used to detect abnormalities, esp. of the brain: also **PETT scan**

**pet·ti·coat** (pet'ē kōt', pet'i-) *n.* ⟦< PETTY + COAT⟧ a woman's underskirt

**pet·ti·fog·ger** (pet'i fäg'ər, -fôg'-; pet'ē-) *n.* ⟦< PETTY + *fogger* < ?⟧ **1** a lawyer who handles petty cases, esp. unethically **2** one who quibbles — **pet'ti·fog', -fogged', -fog'ging,** *vt.*

**pet·tish** (pet'ish) *adj.* ⟦< PET[2]⟧ peevish; petulant —**pet'tish·ly** *adv.*

**pet·ty** (pet'ē) *adj.* **-ti·er, -ti·est** ⟦< OFr *petit*⟧ **1** relatively unimportant **2** small-minded; mean **3** relatively low in rank —**pet'ti·ness** *n.*

**petty cash** a cash fund for incidentals

**petty officer** *U.S. Navy* a naval enlisted person who is a noncommissioned officer

**pet·u·lant** (pech'ə lənt) *adj.* ⟦< L *petere*, to rush at⟧ impatient or irritable, esp. over a petty annoyance —**pet'u·lance** *n.* —**pet'u·lant·ly** *adv.*

**pe·tu·ni·a** (pə tōōn'yə) *n.* ⟦ult. < AmInd (Brazil)⟧ a plant with showy, funnel-shaped flowers

**pew** (pyōō) *n.* ⟦ult. < Gr *pous*, foot⟧ any of the

benches with a back that are fixed in rows in a
church

**pe·wee** (pē′wē′) *n.* [echoic of its call] a small fly-catcher

**pew·ter** (pyōōt′ər) *n.* [OFr *peautre*] **1** an alloy of tin with antimony, copper, lead, etc. **2** articles made of this

**pe·yo·te** (pā ōt′ē) *n.* [AmSp < AmInd (Mexico) *peyotl*, caterpillar] MESCAL: see also MESCALINE

**pf** or **pfd** *abbrev.* preferred

**PFC** or **Pfc** *abbrev.* Private First Class

**pg** *abbrev.* page

**PG** *trademark for* a film rating indicating parents may find some content unsuitable for children under 17

**PG-13** *trademark for* a film rating indicating parents may find some content especially unsuitable for children under 13

**pH** (pē′āch′) *n.* [< Fr *p(ouvoir) h(ydrogène)*, lit., hydrogen power] the degree of acidity or alkalinity of a solution

**pha·e·ton** or **pha·ë·ton** (fā′ə tən) *n.* [after *Phaetōn*, son of Helios, Gr sun god] **1** a light, four-wheeled carriage **2** an early type of open automobile

**phag·o·cyte** (fag′ə sīt′) *n.* [< Gr *phagein*, to eat + *kytos*, hollow] any cell, esp. a leukocyte, that destroys foreign matter in the blood and tissues

**pha·lan·ger** (fə lan′jər) *n.* [< Gr *phalanx*, bone between fingers or toes] a small, tree-dwelling Australian marsupial

**pha·lanx** (fā′laŋks′) *n.*, *pl.* **-lanx·es**; also, and for 3 always, **pha·lan·ges** (fə lan′jēz′) [Gr, line of battle] **1** an ancient close-ranked infantry formation **2** any massed group **3** any of the bones forming the fingers or toes

**phal·lo·cen·tric** (fal′ō sen′trik) *adj.* dominated by attitudes regarded as typically masculine

**phal·lus** (fal′əs) *n.*, *pl.* **-li′** (-ī′) or **-lus·es** [Gr *phallos*] an image of the penis —**phal′lic** *adj.*

**phan·tasm** (fan′taz′əm) *n.* [< Gr *phantazein*, to show] **1** a figment of the mind **2** a deceptive likeness

**phan·tas·ma·go·ri·a** (fan taz′mə gôr′ē ə) *n.* [< Gr *phantasma*, phantasm + *ageirein*, assemble] a rapid sequence of images, as in a dream

**phan·tom** (fan′təm) *n.* [see PHANTASM] **1** an apparition; specter **2** an illusion —*adj.* of or like a phantom; illusory

**Phar·aoh** (far′ō, fā′rō′) *n.* [*sometimes* **p-**] the title of the kings of ancient Egypt

**Phar·i·see** (far′ə sē′) *n.* **1** a member of an ancient Jewish group that observed both the written and the oral law **2** [< characterization in NT] [**p-**] a self-righteous, hypocritical person —**phar′i·sa′ic** (-sā′ik) *adj.*

**phar·ma·ceu·ti·cal** (fär′mə sōōt′i kəl) *adj.* [< Gr *pharmakon*, a drug] of pharmacy or drugs: also **phar′ma·ceu′tic** —*n.* a drug or medicine

**phar′ma·ceu′tics** (-iks) *n.* PHARMACY (sense 1)

**phar·ma·cist** (fär′mə sist) *n.* one licensed to practice pharmacy; druggist

**phar·ma·col·o·gy** (-käl′ə jē) *n.* [< Gr *pharmakon*, a drug] the science dealing with the effect of drugs on living organisms

**phar′ma·co·pe′ia** or **phar′ma·co·poe′ia** (-kō pē′ə) *n.* [< Gr *pharmakon*, a drug + *poiein*, to make] an official book listing drugs and medicines

**phar·ma·cy** (fär′mə sē) *n.*, *pl.* **-cies** [< Gr *pharmakon*, a drug] **1** the art or profession of preparing drugs and medicines **2** a drugstore

**phar·yn·gi·tis** (far′in jīt′is) *n.* inflammation of the pharynx; sore throat

**phar·ynx** (far′iŋks) *n.*, *pl.* **pha·ryn·ges** (fə rin′jēz′) or **phar′ynx·es** [Gr *pharynx*, throat] the cavity leading from the mouth and nasal passages to the larynx and esophagus —**pha·ryn·ge·al** (fə rin′jē əl) *adj.*

**phase** (fāz) *n.* [< Gr *phainesthai*, appear] **1** any stage in a series or cycle of changes, as in the moon's illumination **2** an aspect or side, as of a problem —*vt.* **phased, phas′ing** to introduce or carry out in stages: often with *in* or *into* —**in** (or **out of**) **phase** in (or not in) synchronization —**phase out** to bring or come to an end by stages

**phase′out′** *n.* a phasing out; gradual termination or withdrawal

**PhD** or **Ph.D.** *abbrev.* [L *Philosophiae Doctor*] Doctor of Philosophy

**pheas·ant** (fez′ənt) *n.* [< Gr *phasianos*, (bird) of *Phasis*, river in Asia] a large game bird with a long, sweeping tail and brilliant feathers

**phe·nac·e·tin** (fē nas′ə tin) *n.* a white, crystalline powder used to reduce fever, relieve headaches, etc.

**phe·no·bar·bi·tal** (fē′nə bär′bi tôl′) *n.* an odorless, white, crystalline powder used as a sedative

**phe·nol** (fē′nōl′, -nôl′, -näl′) *n.* a white, crystalline compound, corrosive and poisonous, used to make synthetic resins, etc. and, in dilute solution (*carbolic acid*) as an antiseptic

**phe·nol·phthal·ein** (fē′nōl thal′ēn′, -ē in) *n.* a white to pale-yellow, crystalline powder used as a laxative, as an acid-base indicator in chemical analysis, etc.

**phe·nom** (fē′näm) *n.* [< fol.] [Slang] one who is very talented or skilled; specif., a young, very gifted athlete

**phe·nom·e·non** (fə näm′ə nən, -nän′) *n.*, *pl.* **-na** (-nə); also, esp. for 2 and usually for 3, **-nons′** [< Gr *phainesthai*, appear] **1** any observable fact or event that can be scientifically described **2** anything very unusual **3** [Inf.] an extraordinary person; prodigy —**phe·nom′e·nal** *adj.*

**pher·o·mone** (fer′ə mōn′) *n.* [< Gr *pherein*, carry + (HOR)MONE] a chemical substance secreted by certain animals, as ants, that conveys information to others of the same species

**phi** (fī, fē) *n.* the 21st letter of the Greek alphabet (Φ, φ)

**phi·al** (fī′əl) *n.* [< Gr *phialē*, shallow bowl] a small glass bottle; vial

**Phil·a·del·phi·a** (fil′ə del′fē ə) city & port in SE Pennsylvania: pop. 1,586,000

**Philadelphia lawyer** [Inf.] a shrewd or tricky lawyer

**phi·lan·der** (fi lan′dər, fə-) *vi.* [ult. < Gr *philos*, loving + *anēr*, a man] to engage lightly in love affairs: said of a man —**phi·lan′der·er** *n.*

**phi·lan·thro·py** (fə lan′thrə pē) *n.* [< Gr *philein*, to love + *anthrōpos*, human being] **1** a desire to help mankind, esp. as shown by gifts to institutions, etc. **2** *pl.* **-pies** a philanthropic gift, institution, etc. —**phil·an·throp·ic** (fil′ən thräp′ik) *adj.* —**phi·lan′thro·pist** *n.*

**phi·lat·e·ly** (fə lat′'l ē) *n.* [< Fr < Gr *philos*, loving + *ateleia*, exemption from (further) tax (meaning "postage prepaid")] the collection and study of postage stamps, postmarks, etc. —**phi·lat′e·list** *n.*

**-phile** (fīl, fil) [< Gr *philos*, loving] *combining form* one that loves or is attracted to

**Phil·har·mon·ic** (fil′här män′ik) *adj.* [ult. < Gr *philos*, loving + *harmonia*, harmony] designating a group formed to sponsor a symphony orchestra —*n.* an orchestra so sponsored

**phi·lip·pic** (fi lip′ik) *n.* [< Gr *Philippos*, Philip, Macedonian king denounced by Demosthenes] a bitter verbal attack

**Phil·ip·pines** (fil′ə pēnz′) country consisting of *c.* 7,100 islands (**Philippine Islands**) in the SW Pacific off the SE coast of Asia: 115,830 sq. mi.; pop. 60,559,000 —**Phil′ip·pine** (-pēn′) *adj.*

**Phil·is·tine** (fil′ə stēn′) *n.* **1** a member of a non-Semitic people of SW Palestine in biblical times **2** [< a Ger slang word] [*often* **p-**] a person regarded as smugly conventional, lacking culture, etc.

**Phil·lips** (fil′ips) [after H. F. *Phillips* (?-1958), its U.S. developer] *trademark for* a screwdriver (**Phillips screwdriver**) with a cross-shaped, pointed tip

**philo-** [< Gr *philos*, loving] *combining form* loving, liking

**phil·o·den·dron** (fil'ə den'drən) *n.* [< Gr *philos*, loving + *dendron*, tree] a tropical American vine used as a houseplant

**phi·lol·o·gy** (fi läl'ə jē) *n.* [< Gr *philein*, to love + *logos*, word] *former term for* LINGUISTICS —**phil·o·log·i·cal** (fil'ə läj'i kəl) *adj.* —**phi·lol'o·gist** *n.*

**phi·los·o·pher** (fə läs'ə fər) *n.* [< Gr *philos*, loving + *sophos*, wise] **1** one who is an expert in philosophy **2** one who expounds a system of philosophy **3** one who meets difficulties calmly

**phil·o·soph·ic** (fil'ə säf'ik) *adj.* **1** of philosophy or philosophers **2** sensibly composed or calm Also **phil'o·soph'i·cal**

**phi·los·o·phize** (fə läs'ə fīz') *vi.* **-phized', -phiz'ing 1** to think or reason like a philosopher **2** to moralize, express truisms, etc.

**phi·los·o·phy** (fə läs'ə fē) *n.* [see PHILOSOPHER] **1** the study of the principles underlying conduct, thought, and the nature of the universe **2** the general principles of a field of knowledge **3** *pl.* **-phies** a particular system of principles for the conduct of life

**phil·ter** (fil'tər) *n.* [< Gr *philein*, to love] a magic potion, esp. one thought to arouse sexual love: also [Chiefly Brit.] **phil'tre** (-tər)

**phle·bi·tis** (flə bīt'is) *n.* [< Gr *phleps*, vein + -ITIS] inflammation of a vein

**phle·bot·o·my** (flə bät'ə mē) *n.* [< Gr *pheps*, vein + *temnein*, to cut] the practice of taking blood from the body for therapeutic purposes

**phlegm** (flem) *n.* [< Gr *phlegma*, inflammation] **1** thick mucus discharged from the throat, as during a cold **2** sluggishness or apathy

**phleg·mat·ic** (fleg mat'ik) *adj.* [see prec.] sluggish or unexcited —**phleg·mat'i·cal·ly** *adv.*

**phlo·em** (flō'em') *n.* [< Gr *phloos*, bark] the vascular tissue through which food is distributed in a plant

**phlox** (fläks) *n.* [Gr, lit., a flame] a North American plant with clusters of white, pink, or bluish flowers

**-phobe** (fōb) [< Gr *phobos*, fear] *combining form* one who fears or hates

**pho·bi·a** (fō'bē ə) *n.* [see prec.] an irrational, excessive, and persistent fear of some thing or situation —**pho'bic** *adj.*

**-pho·bi·a** (fō'bē ə) [Gr *-phobia* < *phobos*, fear] *combining form* fear, dread, hatred

**phoe·be** (fē'bē) *n.* [echoic, with sp. after *Phoebe*, Gr goddess of the moon] an American bird with a grayish or brown back, that catches insects in flight

**Phoe·ni·cia** (fə nish'ə, -nē'shə) ancient region at the E end of the Mediterranean —**Phoe·ni'cian** *adj.*, *n.*

**phoe·nix** (fē'niks) [< Gr *phoinix*] *Egypt. Myth.* a bird that lives for 500 years and then sets itself on fire, rising renewed from the ashes

**Phoe·nix** (fē'niks) capital of Arizona: pop. 983,000

**phone** (fōn) *n.*, *vt.*, *vi.* **phoned, phon'ing** *short for* TELEPHONE

**-phone** (fōn) [< Gr *phōnē*, a sound] *combining form* **1** a device producing or transmitting sound **2** a telephone

**phone card** CALLING CARD (sense 2)

**pho·neme** (fō'nēm') *n.* [Fr < Gr *phōnē*, voice] *Linguistics* a set of related speech sounds with slight variations, that are heard as the same sound by native speakers —**pho·ne·mic** (fō nē'mik, fə-) *adj.*

**pho·net·ics** (fō net'iks, fə-) *n.* [< Gr *phōnē*, a sound] the study of the production of speech sounds and their representation in written symbols —**pho·net'ic** *adj.* —**pho·ne·ti·cian** (fō'nə tish'ən) *n.*

**phon·ics** (fän'iks) *n.* [< Gr *phōnē*, a sound] a phonetic method of teaching reading —**phon'ic** *adj.*

**phono-** [< Gr *phōnē*, a sound] *combining form* sound, tone, speech [*phonology*]

**pho·no·graph** (fō'nə graf') *n.* [prec. + -GRAPH] a device for reproducing sound recorded in a spiral groove on a revolving disk —**pho'no·graph'ic** *adj.*

**pho·nol·o·gy** (fō näl'ə jē, fə-) *n.* [PHONO- + -LOGY] **1** the study of speech sounds **2** a description of the sounds of a given language —**pho'no·log'i·cal** (-nō läj'i kəl, -nə-) *adj.* —**pho·nol'o·gist** *n.*

**pho·ny** (fō'nē) [Inf.] *adj.* **-ni·er, -ni·est** [< Brit thieves' argot *fawney*, gilt ring] not genuine; false —*n.*, *pl.* **-nies** something or someone not genuine; fraud; fake Also sp. **pho'ney** —**pho'ni·ness** *n.*

**phoo·ey** (foo'ē) *interj.* [echoic] used to express scorn, disgust, etc.

**phos·phate** (fäs'fāt') *n.* [Fr] **1** a salt or ester of phosphoric acid **2** a fertilizer containing phosphates

**phos·phor** (fäs'fər, -fôr') *n.* [see PHOSPHORUS] a phosphorescent or fluorescent substance

**phos·pho·res·cence** (fäs'fə res'əns) *n.* **1** the property of giving off a lingering emission of light after exposure to radiant energy such as light **2** a continuing luminescence without noticeable heat —**phos'pho·res'cent** *adj.*

**phos·phor·ic acid** (fäs fôr'ik) any of several oxygen acids of phosphorus

**phos·pho·rus** (fäs'fə rəs) *n.* [< Gr *phōs*, a light + *pherein*, to bear] a nonmetallic chemical element, a waxy solid that ignites spontaneously at room temperature

**pho·to** (fōt'ō) *n.*, *pl.* **-tos** *short for* PHOTOGRAPH

**photo-** *combining form* **1** [< Gr *phōs*, a light] of or produced by light **2** [< PHOTOGRAPH] photograph, photography

**pho·to·cop·y** (fōt'ō käp'ē) *n.*, *pl.* **-ies** a photographic reproduction, as of a book page, made by a special device (**pho'to·cop'i·er**)

**pho'to·e·lec'tric cell** any device in which light controls an electric circuit that operates a mechanical device, as for opening doors

**pho·to·en·grav·ing** *n.* **1** a process by which photographs are reproduced on relief printing plates **2** such a plate, or a print made from it —**pho'to·en·grave'**, **-graved'**, **-grav'ing**, *vt.* —**pho'to·en·grav'er** *n.*

**photo finish** a race finish so close that the winner can be determined only from a photograph of the finish

**pho'to·fin'ish·ing** *n.* the process of developing photographic film, making prints, etc.

**pho'to·flash'** *adj.* designating a flashbulb, etc. electrically synchronized with the camera shutter

**pho·to·gen·ic** (fōt'ə jen'ik) *adj.* [PHOTO- + -genic, suitable for] likely to look attractive in photographs

**pho·to·graph** (fōt'ə graf') *n.* a picture made by photography —*vt.* to take a photograph of —*vi.* to appear (as specified) in photographs —**pho·tog·ra·pher** (fə täg'rə fər) *n.*

**pho·tog·ra·phy** (fə täg'rə fē) *n.* [PHOTO- + -GRAPHY] the art or process of producing pictorial images on a surface sensitive to light or other radiant energy, as on film in a camera —**pho·to·graph·ic** (fōt'ə graf'ik) *adj.*

**pho·ton** (fō'tän') *n.* [PHOT(O)- + (ELECTR)ON] a subatomic particle that is a quantum of electromagnetic energy, including light

**pho'to·off'set'** *n.* offset printing in which the text or pictures are photographically transferred to a metal plate from which inked impressions are made on the roller

**pho·to·stat** (fōt'ə stat') *n.* [< former trademark] **1** a device for making photocopies on special paper **2** a copy so made —*vt.* **-stat'ed** or **-stat'ted**, **-stat'ing** to make a photostat of

**pho·to·syn·the·sis** (fōt'ō sin'thə sis) *n.* the production of organic substances, esp. sugars, from carbon dioxide and water by the action of light on the chlorophyll in green plant cells

**pho'to·syn'the·size'** (-sīz') *vi.*, *vt.* **-sized'**, **-siz'ing** to carry on, or produce by, photosynthesis

**phrase** (frāz) *n.* ⟦< Gr *phrazein,* speak⟧ **1** a short, colorful expression **2** a group of words, not a full sentence or clause, conveying a single thought **3** a short, distinct musical passage —*vt.*, *vi.* **phrased, phras′ing** to express in words —**phras·al** (frā′zəl) *adj.*

**phra·se·ol·o·gy** (frā′zē äl′ə jē) *n., pl.* **-gies** choice and pattern of words

**phre·net·ic** (fri net′ik) *adj.* ⟦< Gr *phrenētikos,* mad⟧ *archaic sp. of* FRENETIC

**phre·nol·o·gy** (fri näl′ə jē, frə-) *n.* ⟦< Gr *phrēn,* mind + -LOGY⟧ a system, popular esp. in the 19th c., based on the assumption that character can be analyzed based on the shape of the skull

**phy·lac·ter·y** (fi lak′tər ē) *n., pl.* **-ies** ⟦< Gr *phylaktērion,* safeguard⟧ TEFILLIN

**phyl·lo** (fē′lō, fī′-) *n.* ⟦< Gr *phyllon,* leaf⟧ dough in very thin sheets that becomes very flaky when baked

**phy·log·e·ny** (fī läj′ə nē) *n., pl.* **-nies** ⟦< Gr *phylon,* tribe + -*geneia,* origin⟧ the origin and evolution of a group or race of animals or plants

**phy·lum** (fī′ləm) *n., pl.* **-la** (-lə) ⟦< Gr *phylon,* tribe⟧ a major category in the classification of organisms, esp. animals

**phys** *abbrev.* **1** physical **2** physician **3** physics

**phys·ic** (fiz′ik) *n.* ⟦< Gr *physis,* nature⟧ a medicine, esp. a laxative

**phys·i·cal** (fiz′i kəl) *adj.* **1** of nature and all matter; material **2** of or according to the laws of nature **3** of, or produced by the forces of, physics **4** of the body as opposed to the mind —*n.* a general medical examination —**phys′i·cal·ly** *adv.*

**physical anthropology** a major division of anthropology that deals with the physical characteristics and evolution of humans

**physical education** instruction in physical exercise and in the care of the body, including sports, calisthenics, and hygiene

**physical science** any science dealing with nonliving matter or energy, as physics, chemistry, geology, or astronomy

**physical therapy** the treatment of disease, injury, etc. by physical means, as by exercise or massage

**phy·si·cian** (fi zish′ən) *n.* ⟦see PHYSIC⟧ a doctor of medicine

**phys·ics** (fiz′iks) *n.* ⟦see PHYSIC⟧ the science dealing with the properties, changes, interactions, etc. of matter and energy —**phys′i·cist** (-ə sist) *n.*

**phys·i·og·no·my** (fiz′ē äg′nə mē) *n.* ⟦< Gr *physis,* nature + *gnōmōn,* one who knows⟧ facial features and expression

**phys′i·ol′o·gy** (-äl′ə jē) *n.* ⟦< Gr *physis,* nature + -LOGY⟧ the science dealing with the functions and vital processes of living organisms —**phys′i·o·log′i·cal** (-ə läj′i kəl) *adj.* —**phys′i·ol′o·gist** *n.*

**phys·i·o·ther·a·py** (fiz′ē ō′ther′ə pē) *n.* PHYSICAL THERAPY —**phys′i·o·ther′a·pist** *n.*

**phy·sique** (fi zēk′) *n.* ⟦Fr⟧ the structure or form of the body; build

**pi** (pī) *n.* **1** the 16th letter of the Greek alphabet (Π, π) **2** the symbol (π) designating the ratio of the circumference of a circle to its diameter, about 3.1416

**pi·a·nis·si·mo** (pē′ə nis′i mō′) *adj., adv.* ⟦It⟧ *Music* very soft(ly)

**pi·an·ist** (pē′ə nist, pē an′ist) *n.* one who plays the piano

**pi·a·no**[1] (pē ä′nō) *adj., adv.* ⟦It⟧ *Music* soft(ly)

**pi·an·o**[2] (pē an′ō) *n., pl.* **-os** ⟦< fol.⟧ a large, stringed keyboard instrument: each key operates a felt-covered hammer that strikes a corresponding wire or wires

**pi·an·o·for·te** (pē an′ō fôrt′, pē an′ō fôr′tā) *n.* ⟦It < *piano,* soft + *forte,* loud⟧ PIANO[2]

**pi·as·ter** (pē as′tər) *n.* ⟦ult. < L *emplastrum,* plaster⟧ a 100th part of a pound in Egypt, Lebanon, and Syria

**pi·az·za** (pē ät′sə; *for 2* pē az′ə) *n.* **1** in Italy, a public square **2** [Dial.] a large, covered porch

**pi·broch** (pē′bräk′) *n.* ⟦< Gael *piob,* bagpipe⟧ music for the bagpipe, usually of a martial kind

**pi·ca** (pī′kə) *n.* ⟦< ? ML, a directory⟧ a size of printing type, 12 point

**pi·can·te** (pē kän′tā) *adj.* ⟦Sp⟧ designating, prepared with, or served with a hot, spicy sauce

**pic·a·resque** (pik′ə resk′) *adj.* ⟦< Sp *pícaro,* rascal⟧ dealing with sharp-witted vagabonds or rogues and their adventures [a *picaresque* novel]

**Pi·cas·so** (pi kä′sō), **Pa·blo** (pä′blō) 1881-1973; Sp. painter & sculptor in France

**pic·a·yune** (pik′ə yōōn′, pik′ə yōōn′) *adj.* ⟦< Fr *picaillon,* small coin⟧ trivial or petty

**pic·ca·lil·li** (pik′ə lil′ē) *n.* ⟦prob. < PICKLE⟧ a relish of chopped vegetables, mustard, vinegar, and hot spices

**pic·co·lo** (pik′ə lō′) *n., pl.* **-los′** ⟦It, small⟧ a small flute, pitched an octave above the ordinary flute

**pick**[1] (pik) *n.* ⟦OE *pic,* PIKE[2]⟧ **1** any of several pointed tools or instruments for picking, esp. a heavy one used in breaking up soil, rock, etc. **2** PLECTRUM

**pick**[2] (pik) *vt.* ⟦ME *picken*⟧ **1** to probe, scratch at, etc. so as to remove or clear something from **2** to gather (flowers, berries, etc.) **3** to prepare (a fowl) by removing the feathers **4** to choose; select **5** to provoke (a quarrel or fight) **6** to pluck (the strings) of (a guitar, etc.) **7** to open (a lock) with a wire, etc. instead of a key **8** to steal from (another's pocket, etc.) —*vi.* **1** to use a pick **2** to select, esp. in a fussy way —*n.* **1** the act of choosing or the choice made —**pick at** to eat small amounts of, esp. fussily —**pick off 1** to remove by picking **2** to hit with a carefully aimed shot —**pick on** [Inf.] to single out for criticism or abuse; annoy; tease —**pick out** to choose —**pick up 1** to grasp and lift **2** to get, find, or learn, esp. by chance **3** to stop for and take along **4** to gain (speed) **5** to improve **6** [Inf.] to become acquainted with casually, esp. for sexual activity —**pick′er** *n.*

**pick·ax** or **pick·axe** (pik′aks′) *n.* ⟦< OFr *picquois*⟧ a pick with a point at one end of the head and a chisel-like edge at the other

**pick·er·el** (pik′ər əl) *n., pl.* **-el** or **-els** ⟦ME < *pik,* PIKE[3]⟧ any of various small North American freshwater fishes

**pick·et** (pik′it) *n.* ⟦< Fr *pic,* PIKE[2]⟧ **1** a pointed stake used in a fence, as a hitching post, etc. **2** a soldier or soldiers stationed to guard against surprise attack **3** a person, as a member of a striking labor union, stationed outside a factory, store, etc. to demonstrate opposition, keep workers out, etc. —*vt.* **1** to hitch (an animal) to a picket **2** to post as a military picket **3** to place pickets, or serve as a picket, at (a factory, etc.)

**picket line** a line or cordon of people serving as pickets

**pick′ings** *pl.n.* [*occas. sing.*] something picked; specif., *a*) scraps; remains *b*) something gotten by effort, often dishonestly

**pick·le** (pik′əl) *n.* ⟦< MDu *pekel*⟧ **1** any brine, vinegar, etc. used to preserve or marinate food **2** a vegetable, specif. a cucumber, preserved in this **3** [Inf.] an awkward situation —*vt.* **-led, -ling** to treat or preserve in a pickle solution

**pick′pock′et** *n.* a thief who steals from pockets, as in a crowd

**pick′up′** *n.* **1** a picking up **2** the process or power of increasing in speed **3** a small, open delivery truck **4** [Inf.] a casual acquaintance, esp. one formed for sexual purposes **5** [Inf.] improvement **6** *a*) a device for producing electric currents from the vibrations of a phonograph needle *b*) the pivoted arm holding this device —*adj.* [Inf.] assembled informally for a single occasion

**pick′y** *adj.* **-i·er, -i·est** [Inf.] overly fastidious; fussy

**pic·nic** (pik′nik) *n.* ⟦< Fr⟧ a pleasure outing at which a meal is eaten outdoors —*vi.* **-nicked, -nick·ing** to have a picnic —**pic′nick·er** *n.*

**pi·cot** (pē′kō) *n., pl.* **-cots** ⟦< Fr *pic,* a point⟧ any of the small loops forming a fancy edge, as on lace

**pic·to·graph** (pik′tə graf′) *n.* **1** a picture or picturelike symbol used in a system of writing **2** a graph using pictures to convey data

**pic·to·ri·al** (pik tôr′ē əl) *adj.* **1** of, containing, or expressed in pictures **2** suggesting a mental image; vivid —**pic·to′ri·al·ly** *adv.*

**pic·ture** (pik′chər) *n.* ⟦< L *pingere,* to paint⟧ **1** a likeness of a person, scene, etc. produced by drawing, painting, photography, etc. **2** a perfect likeness or image *[the picture of health]* **3** anything suggestive of a beautiful painting, drawing, etc. **4** a vivid description **5** FILM (*n.* 4) **6** the image on a TV screen —*vt.* **-tured, -tur·ing 1** to make a picture of **2** to show visibly **3** to describe **4** to imagine —**in** (or **out of**) **the picture** considered (or not considered) as being involved in a situation

**pic′ture-per′fect** *adj.* perfect or flawless

**pic′tur·esque′** (-chər esk′) *adj.* like or suggesting a picture; beautiful, vivid, quaint, etc.

**picture tube** a cathode-ray tube in a TV receiver, monitor, etc., that produces visual images on its screen

**picture window** a large window that seems to frame the outside view

**pid·dle** (pid′'l) *vi., vt.* **-dled, -dling** ⟦< ?⟧ to dawdle; trifle

**pid·dling** (pid′liŋ) *adj.* insignificant; trifling

**pid·dly** (pid′lē) *adj.* PIDDLING

**pidg·in** (pij′in) *n.* ⟦supposed Chin pronunciation of *business*⟧ a mixed language for trade purposes, using words from one language and simplified grammar from another: **pidgin English** uses English words and Chinese or Melanesian syntax

**pie** (pī) *n.* ⟦ME⟧ a baked dish as of fruit or of meat, with an under crust or upper crust, or both —**(as) easy as pie** [Inf.] extremely easy

**pie·bald** (pī′bôld′) *adj.* ⟦< *pie,* magpie + BALD⟧ covered with patches of two colors —*n.* a piebald horse, etc.

**piece** (pēs) *n.* ⟦OFr *pece*⟧ **1** a part broken or separated from the whole **2** a section of a whole regarded as complete in itself **3** any single thing, specimen, example, etc. *[a piece of music]* **4** a quantity, as of cloth, manufactured as a unit —*vt.* **pieced, piec′ing 1** to add pieces to, as in repairing **2** to join (*together*) the pieces of —**go to pieces 1** to fall apart **2** to lose self-control

**pièce de ré·sis·tance** (pyes də rä zēs täns′) ⟦Fr, piece of resistance⟧ **1** the principal dish of a meal **2** the main item in a series

**piece goods** YARD GOODS

**piece′meal′** *adv.* ⟦< ME *pece,* a piece + *-mele,* part⟧ piece by piece —*adj.* made or done piecemeal

**piece′work′** *n.* work paid for at a fixed rate (**piece rate**) per piece of work done

**pie chart** a graph in the form of a circle divided into sectors in which relative quantities are indicated by the sizes of the sectors

**pied** (pīd) *adj.* ⟦< *pie,* magpie⟧ spotted with various colors

**pied-à-terre** (pyä tá ter′) *n., pl.* **pied-à-terre** ⟦Fr, foot on the ground⟧ a residence, esp. one used only part of the time or temporarily

**pie′-eyed′** *adj.* [Slang] intoxicated

**pier** (pir) *n.* ⟦< ML *pera*⟧ **1** a structure supporting the spans of a bridge **2** a structure built out over the water and supported by pillars: used as a landing place, pavilion, etc. **3** *Archit.* a heavy column used to support weight

**pierce** (pirs) *vt.* **pierced, pierc′ing** ⟦< OFr *percer*⟧ **1** to pass into or through as a pointed instrument does; stab **2** to make a hole in **3** to force a way into; break through **4** to sound sharply through **5** to penetrate with the sight or mind —*vi.* to penetrate

**Pierce** (pirs), **Franklin** 1804-69; 14th president of the U.S. (1853-57)

**Pierre** (pir) capital of South Dakota: pop. 13,000

**pi·e·ty** (pī′ə tē) *n., pl.* **-ties** ⟦< L *pius,* pious⟧ **1** devotion to religious duties, etc. **2** devotion to parents, family, etc. **3** a pious act

**pif·fle** (pif′əl) *n.* [Inf.] anything regarded as insignificant or nonsensical —**pif·fling** (pif′liŋ) *adj.*

**pig** (pig) *n.* ⟦ME *pigge*⟧ **1** any swine, esp. the unweaned young of the thick-bodied domesticated species; hog **2** a greedy or filthy person

**pi·geon** (pij′ən) *n.* ⟦< L *pipire,* to chirp⟧ any of various related birds with a small head, a plump body, and short legs

**pi′geon·hole′** *n.* a small, open compartment, as in a desk, for filing papers —*vt.* **-holed′, -hol′ing 1** to put in the pigeonhole of a desk, etc. **2** to put aside indefinitely **3** to classify

**pi′geon-toed′** (-tōd′) *adj.* having the toes or feet turned in

**pig·gish** (pig′ish) *adj.* like a pig; gluttonous or filthy —**pig′gish·ness** *n.*

**pig·gy** (pig′ē) *n., pl.* **-gies** a little pig: also sp. **pig′gie** —*adj.* **-gi·er, -gi·est** PIGGISH

**pig′gy·back′** *adv., adj.* **1** on the shoulders or back **2** by or of a transportation system in which truck trailers are carried on flatcars **3** carried by or connected with something else as an adjunct —*vt.* **1** to carry piggyback **2** to place on something in piggyback fashion

**pig′head′ed** *adj.* stubborn

**pig iron** crude iron, as it comes from the blast furnace

**pig·ment** (pig′mənt) *n.* ⟦< L *pingere,* to paint⟧ **1** coloring matter used to make paints **2** any coloring matter in the tissues of plants or animals

**pig·men·ta·tion** (pig′mən tā′shən) *n.* coloration in plants or animals due to pigment in the tissue

**Pig·my** (pig′mē) *n., pl.* **-mies,** *adj.* PYGMY

**pig′pen′** *n.* a pen where pigs are kept: also **pig′sty′** (-stī′), *pl.* **-sties′**

**pig′skin′** *n.* **1** leather made from the skin of a pig **2** [Inf.] a football

**pig′tail′** (-tāl′) *n.* a long braid of hair hanging at the back of the head

**pike**[1] (pīk) *n.* a highway: now chiefly in [Inf.] **come down the pike,** to happen or appear

**pike**[2] (pīk) *n.* ⟦Fr *pique*⟧ a weapon, formerly for foot soldiers, consisting of a metal spearhead on a long wooden shaft (**pike′staff′**)

**pike**[3] (pīk) *n., pl.* **pike** or **pikes** ⟦ME *pik*⟧ a slender, freshwater bony fish with a narrow, pointed head

**pik·er** (pīk′ər) *n.* ⟦< ? *Pike* County, Missouri⟧ [Slang] a person who does things in a petty or stingy way

**pi·laf** or **pi·laff** (pē′läf′) *n.* ⟦Pers *pilāv*⟧ a dish made of rice boiled in a seasoned liquid

**pi·las·ter** (pi las′tər) *n.* ⟦< L *pila,* a pile⟧ a supporting column projecting partially from a wall

**Pi·late** (pī′lət), **Pon·tius** (pun′chəs) 1st c. A.D.; Rom. procurator of Judea (26?-36?) who condemned Jesus to be crucified

**pil·chard** (pil′chərd) *n.* ⟦< ?⟧ **1** a small, oily marine fish, the commercial sardine of W Europe **2** any of several related fishes

**pile**[1] (pīl) *n.* ⟦< L *pila,* pillar⟧ **1** a mass of things heaped together **2** a heap of wood, etc. on which a corpse or sacrifice is burned **3** a large building **4** [Inf.] a large amount —*vt.* **piled, pil′ing 1** to heap up **2** to load **3** to accumulate Often with *up* —*vi.* **1** to form a pile **2** to move in a mass: with *in, into, out, on, off,* etc.

**pile**[2] (pīl) *n.* ⟦< L *pilus,* hair⟧ a soft, velvety, raised surface of yarn loops, often sheared, as on a rug

**pile**[3] (pīl) *n.* ⟦OE *pil*⟧ a long, heavy beam driven into the ground to support a bridge, dock, etc.

**pile driver** (or **engine**) a machine for driving piles by raising and dropping a heavy weight on them

**piles** (pīlz) *pl.n.* ⟦< L *pila,* a ball⟧ hemorrhoids

**pile′up′** *n.* **1** an accumulation of tasks, etc. **2** [Inf.] a collision involving several vehicles

**pil·fer** (pil′fər) *vt.*, *vi.* ⟦< MFr *pelfre*, booty⟧ to steal (esp. small sums, etc.) —**pil′fer·age** (-ij) *n.* — **pil′fer·er** *n.*

**pil·grim** (pil′grəm) *n.* ⟦< L *peregrinus*, foreigner⟧ 1 a wanderer 2 one who travels to a shrine or holy place as a religious act 3 [P-] any of the band of English Puritans who founded Plymouth Colony in 1620

**pil′grim·age** *n.* 1 a journey made by a pilgrim, esp. to a shrine or holy place 2 any long journey

**pill** (pil) *n.* ⟦< L *pila*, a ball⟧ a small ball, tablet, etc. of medicine to be swallowed whole —**the pill** (or **Pill**) [Inf.] any contraceptive drug for women, in the form of a pill

**pil·lage** (pil′ij) *n.* ⟦< MFr *piller*, to rob⟧ 1 a plundering 2 goods stolen or taken by force —*vt.*, *vi.* -laged, -lag·ing to plunder

**pil·lar** (pil′ər) *n.* ⟦< L *pila*, column⟧ 1 a slender, vertical structure used as a support or monument; column 2 a main support of something

**pill′box′** *n.* 1 a small box for holding pills 2 an enclosed gun emplacement of concrete and steel

**pil·lion** (pil′yən) *n.* ⟦< L *pellis*, a skin⟧ an extra seat behind the saddle on a horse or motorcycle

**pil·lo·ry** (pil′ə rē) *n.*, *pl.* -ries ⟦< OFr *pilori*⟧ a device consisting of a board with holes for the head and hands, in which petty offenders were formerly locked and exposed to public scorn —*vt.* -ried, -ry·ing 1 to punish by placing in a pillory 2 to subject to public scorn or ridicule

**pil·low** (pil′ō) *n.* ⟦OE *pyle*⟧ a cloth case filled with down, foam rubber, etc., used as a support, as for the head in sleeping —*vt.* to rest as on a pillow

**pil′low·case′** *n.* a removable covering for a pillow: also **pil′low·slip′**

**pi·lot** (pī′lət) *n.* ⟦< Gr *pēdon*, oar⟧ 1 *a*) [Archaic] HELMSMAN *b*) a person licensed to direct ships into or out of a harbor or through difficult waters 2 a qualified operator of aircraft or spacecraft 3 a guide; leader 4 *a*) pilot light *b*) pilot film (or tape) —*vt.* 1 to act as a pilot of, on, etc. 2 to guide —*adj.* serving as a trial unit in testing

**pilot film** (or **tape**) a film (or videotape) of a single segment of a projected series of TV shows

**pi′lot·house′** *n.* an enclosure for the helmsman on the upper deck of a ship

**pilot light** a small gas burner that is kept burning for use in lighting a main burner

**Pil·sen·er** or **Pil·sner** (pilz′nər) *n.* [*often* p-] a light lager beer

**pi·men·to** (pi men′tō) *n.*, *pl.* -tos ⟦< Sp < L *pigmentum*, pigment⟧ a variety of sweet red pepper: also **pi·mien′to** (-myen′-, -men′-)

**pimp** (pimp) *n.* ⟦< ?⟧ a prostitute's agent —*vi.* to act as a pimp

**pim·ple** (pim′pəl) *n.* ⟦< OE *piplian*, to break out in pimples⟧ a small, usually inflamed swelling of the skin —**pim′ply**, -pli·er, -pli·est, *adj.*

**pin** (pin) *n.* ⟦OE *pinn*⟧ 1 a peg, as of wood, or a pointed piece of stiff wire, for fastening things together, etc. 2 anything like a pin 3 an ornament or badge with a pin or clasp for fastening to clothing 4 *Bowling* one of the bottle-shaped wooden objects at which the ball is rolled —*vt.* pinned, pin′ning 1 to fasten as with a pin 2 to hold firmly in one position —**pin down** 1 to get (someone) to make a commitment, etc. 2 to determine (a fact, etc.) —**pin something on someone** [Inf.] to lay the blame for something on someone

**PIN** (pin) *n.* ⟦p(ersonal) i(dentification) n(umber)⟧ an identification number, as for use at an ATM

**pin·a·fore** (pin′ə fôr′) *n.* ⟦PIN + archaic *afore*, before⟧ a sleeveless garment worn over a dress

**pi·ña·ta** (pē nyä′tä) *n.* ⟦Sp, ult. < L *pinus*, pine tree⟧ in Mexico, a papier-mâché container hung from the ceiling in a game in which blindfolded children take turns trying to break it open and release the toys, candy, etc. inside

**pin′ball′ machine** a game machine consisting of an inclined board and a rolling ball that hits objects, etc. on it to score points

**pince-nez** (pans′nā′) *n.* ⟦Fr, nose-pincher⟧ *pl.* **pince′-nez′** (-nāz′; -nā′) eyeglasses kept in place by a spring gripping the bridge of the nose

**pin·cers** (pin′sərz) *pl.n.* ⟦< OFr *pincier*, to pinch⟧ 1 a tool formed of two pivoted parts, used in gripping things 2 a grasping claw, as of a crab

PINCERS

**pinch** (pinch) *vt.* ⟦ME *pinchen* < OFr *pincier*⟧ 1 to squeeze between a finger and the thumb or between two edges, surfaces, etc. 2 to press painfully upon (some part of the body) 3 to make cramped, thin, etc., as by hunger or cold 4 [Slang] *a*) to steal *b*) to arrest —*vi.* 1 to squeeze painfully 2 to be stingy or frugal —*n.* 1 a squeeze or nip 2 *a*) an amount grasped between finger and thumb *b*) a small amount 3 distress or difficulty 4 an emergency: usually in **in a pinch** —*adj.* *Baseball* substitute

**pinch′-hit′** *vi.* -hit′, -hit′ting 1 *Baseball* to bat in place of the batter whose turn it is 2 to substitute in an emergency (*for*) —**pinch hitter**

**pin curl** a strand of hair kept curled with a bobby pin while it sets

**pin·cush′ion** *n.* a small cushion to stick pins in to keep them handy

**pine¹** (pīn) *n.* ⟦< L *pinus*⟧ 1 an evergreen tree with cones and needle-shaped leaves 2 its wood

**pine²** (pīn) *vi.* pined, pin′ing ⟦< L *poena*, a pain⟧ 1 to waste (*away*) through grief, etc. 2 to yearn

**pin·e·al body** (pin′ē əl) ⟦< L *pinea*, pine cone⟧ a small, cone-shaped body in the brain that produces a hormone

**pine·ap·ple** (pīn′ap′əl) *n.* ⟦ME *pinappel*, pine cone⟧ 1 a juicy, edible tropical fruit somewhat resembling a pine cone 2 the plant it grows on

**pine tar** a thick, dark liquid obtained from pine wood, used in disinfectants, paints, etc.

**pin′feath′er** *n.* an undeveloped, emerging feather

**ping** (piŋ) *n.* ⟦echoic⟧ the sound made as by a bullet striking something sharply —*vi.*, *vt.* to make or cause to make this sound

**Ping-Pong** (piŋ′pôŋ′) ⟦echoic⟧ *trademark for* table-tennis equipment —*n.* [*often* **ping-pong**] TABLE TENNIS

**pin′head′** *n.* 1 the head of a pin 2 a person regarded as stupid or silly

**pin′hole′** *n.* 1 a tiny hole as from a pin 2 a hole to stick a pin into

**pin·ion** (pin′yən) *n.* ⟦< L *pinna*, feather⟧ 1 a small cogwheel that meshes with a larger gear or with a RACK¹ (*n.* 2) 2 a wing; specif., the outer part of a bird's wing —*vt.* 1 to bind the wings or arms of 2 to shackle

**pink¹** (piŋk) *n.* ⟦< ?⟧ 1 any of certain plants with white, pink, or red flowers 2 the flower 3 pale red 4 the highest degree, finest example, etc. — *adj.* 1 pale-red 2 [Inf.] somewhat leftist: a derogatory term —**in the pink** [Inf.] healthy; fit

**pink²** (piŋk) *vt.* ⟦ME *pynken*⟧ 1 to cut a saw-toothed edge on (cloth, etc.) 2 to prick or stab

**pink′eye′** *n.* a contagious eye infection in which the eyeball and the lining of the eyelid are red and inflamed

**pink·ie** or **pink·y** (piŋ′kē) *n.*, *pl.* -ies the smallest finger

**pink′ing shears** (piŋ′kiŋ) shears with notched blades, for pinking edges of cloth

**pink slip** [Inf.] notice to an employee that he or she is fired

**pin money** a small sum of money, as for incidental minor expenses

**pin·na·cle** (pin′ə kəl) *n.* ⟦< L *pinna,* feather⟧ **1** a small turret or spire **2** a slender, pointed formation, as a mountain peak **3** the highest point

**pin·nate** (pin′āt′, -it) *adj.* ⟦< L *pinna,* feather⟧ *Bot.* with leaflets on each side of a common stem

**pi·noch·le** or **pi·noc·le** (pē′nuk′əl) *n.* ⟦< Fr *binocle,* pince-nez⟧ a card game played with a 48-card deck (two of every card above the eight)

**pi·not noir** (pē′nō nwär′, pē nō′-) [*also* P- N-] **1** the main red-wine grape of the Burgundy region **2** a dry red wine made from this grape

**pin′point′** *vt.* to locate precisely —*adj.* precise

**pin′prick′** *n.* **1** a tiny puncture as by a pin **2** a minor annoyance

**pins and needles** a tingling feeling as in a numb limb —**on pins and needles** in anxious suspense

**pin′set′ter** *n.* a person or automatic device that sets up bowling pins on the alley: also **pin′spot′ter**

**pin′stripe′** *n.* a pattern of very narrow stripes in suit fabrics, etc.

**pint** (pīnt) *n.* ⟦< ML⟧ a unit of measure equal to ½ quart

**pin·to** (pin′tō) *adj.* ⟦< obs. Sp, spotted⟧ having patches of white and some other color —*n., pl.* **-tos** a pinto horse

**pinto bean** a kind of mottled kidney bean grown in the SW U.S.

**pin′up′** *adj.* **1** that is or can be fastened to a wall **2** [Inf.] designating a sexually attractive person whose picture is often pinned up on walls

**pin′wheel′** *n.* **1** a small wheel with vanes of paper, etc., pinned to a stick so as to revolve in the wind **2** a revolving fireworks device

**Pin·yin** (pin yin′) *n.* ⟦Chin *pinyin,* lit., phonetic sound⟧ [*also* **p-**] system for transliterating Chinese ideograms into the Latin alphabet

**pi·o·neer** (pī′ə nir′) *n.* ⟦< OFr *peonier,* foot soldier⟧ one who goes before, preparing the way for others, as an early settler —*vi.* to be a pioneer —*vt.* to be a pioneer in or of

**pi·ous** (pī′əs) *adj.* ⟦< L *pius*⟧ **1** having or showing religious devotion **2** only seemingly virtuous **3** sacred —**pi′ous·ly** *adv.*

**pip**¹ (pip) *n.* ⟦< PIPPIN⟧ a small seed, as of an apple

**pip**² (pip) *n.* ⟦< ?⟧ any of the figures or spots on playing cards, dice, or dominoes

**pip**³ (pip) *n.* ⟦< L *pituita,* phlegm⟧ a contagious disease of fowl

**pipe** (pīp) *n.* ⟦< L *pipare,* chirp⟧ **1** a tube of wood, metal, etc. for making musical sounds **2** [*pl.*] the bagpipe **3** a long tube for conveying water, gas, etc. **4** a tube with a small bowl at one end in which tobacco is smoked **5** any tubular part, organ of the body, etc. —*vi.* **piped, pip′ing 1** to play on a pipe **2** to utter shrill sounds —*vt.* **1** to play (a tune) on a pipe **2** to utter in a shrill voice **3** to bring, call, etc. by piping **4** to convey (water, gas, etc.) by pipes —**pipe down** [Slang] to stop shouting, talking, etc. —**pip′er** *n.*

**pipe dream** [Inf.] a fantastic idea, vain hope or plan, etc.

**pipe fitter** a mechanic who installs and maintains plumbing pipes, etc.

**pipe′line′** *n.* **1** a line of pipes for conveying water, gas, oil, etc. **2** any means whereby something is passed on

**pipe organ** ORGAN (sense 1)

**pi·pette** or **pi·pet** (pi pet′, pī-) *n.* a slender tube for taking up and measuring small amounts of a liquid

**pip·ing** (pīp′iŋ) *n.* **1** music made by pipes **2** a shrill sound **3** a pipelike fold of material for trimming seams, etc. —**piping hot** very hot

**pip·it** (pip′it) *n.* ⟦echoic⟧ a small bird with a slender bill, streaked breast, and the habit of walking rather than hopping

**pip·pin** (pip′in) *n.* ⟦< OFr *pepin,* seed⟧ any of several varieties of apple

**pip·squeak** (pip′skwēk′) *n.* [Inf.] anyone or anything regarded as small or insignificant

**pi·quant** (pē′kənt) *adj.* ⟦Fr < *piquer,* to prick⟧ **1** agreeably pungent to the taste **2** exciting interest; stimulating —**pi′quan·cy** (-kən sē) *n.*

**pique** (pēk) *n.* ⟦see prec.⟧ resentment at being slighted —*vt.* **piqued, piqu′ing 1** to arouse such resentment in **2** to stir up; excite

**pi·qué** or **pi·que** (pē kā′) *n.* ⟦see PIQUANT⟧ a cotton fabric with ribbed or corded wales

**pi·ra·cy** (pī′rə sē) *n., pl.* **-cies 1** robbery of ships on the high seas **2** the unauthorized use of copyrighted or patented work

**pi·ra·nha** (pi rä′nə) *n.* ⟦< Brazilian Port < AmInd (Brazil) *pirá,* fish + *sainha,* tooth⟧ any of various small, freshwater South American fishes: they hunt in schools, attacking any animals

**pi·rate** (pī′rət) *n.* ⟦< Gr *peirān,* to attack⟧ one who practices piracy —*vt., vi.* **-rat·ed, -rat·ing 1** to take (something) by piracy **2** to publish, reproduce, etc. (a book, recording, etc.) in violation of a copyright —**pi·rat′i·cal** (-rat′ i kəl) *adj.*

**pi·ro·gi** (pi rō′gē) *n., pl.* **-gi** or **-gies** ⟦Russ⟧ a small pastry turnover filled with meat, cheese, etc.

**pir·ou·ette** (pir′ōō et′) *n.* ⟦Fr, spinning top⟧ a whirling on one foot or the point of the toe —*vi.* **-et′ted, -et′ting** to do a pirouette

**pis·ca·to·ri·al** (pis′kə tôr′ē əl) *adj.* ⟦< L *piscator,* fisherman⟧ of fishes or fishing

**Pis·ces** (pī′sēz′) *n.* ⟦ L, pl. of *piscis,* fish⟧ the 12th sign of the zodiac

**pis·mire** (pis′mīr′, piz′-) *n.* ⟦< ME *pisse,* urine + *mire,* ant⟧ [Archaic] an ant

**piss·ant** (pis′ant′) *adj., n.* [Slang] insignificant and contemptible (person)

**pis·tach·i·o** (pi stash′ē ō) *n., pl.* **-os′** ⟦< OPers *pistah*⟧ **1** a small tree of the cashew family **2** its edible, greenish seed (**pistachio nut**)

**pis·til** (pis′təl) *n.* ⟦< L *pistillum,* pestle⟧ the seed-bearing organ of a flower —**pis′til·late′** *adj.*

**pis·tol** (pis′təl) *n.* ⟦< Czech *pišt′al*⟧ a small firearm operated with one hand

**pis′tol-whip′** *vt.* **-whipped′, -whip′ping** to beat with a pistol, esp. about the head

**pis·ton** (pis′tən) *n.* ⟦ult. < L *pinsere,* to pound⟧ the snug-fitting engine part that is forced back and forth within a cylinder by the pressure of combustion, steam, etc. and a reciprocating connecting rod (**piston rod**)

**piston ring** a split ring fitted into a groove around a piston to seal the cylinder, transfer heat, etc.

**pit**¹ (pit) *n.* ⟦< MDu *pitte*⟧ the hard stone, as of the plum, peach, or cherry, containing the seed —*vt.* **pit′ted, pit′ting** to remove the pit from

**pit**² (pit) *n.* ⟦< L *puteus,* a well⟧ **1** a hole in the ground **2** an abyss **3** hell: used with *the* **4** a pitfall **5** an enclosed area in which animals are kept or made to fight **6** a small hollow in a surface, as a scar left by smallpox **7** the section for the orchestra in front of the stage **8** a work area for mechanics beside an auto-racing track —*vt.* **pit′ted, pit′ting 1** to make pits or scars in **2** to set in competition (*against*)

**pi·ta** (pēt′ə) *n.* ⟦< Heb < Modern Greek⟧ a round, flat bread of the Middle East: also **pita bread**

**pit·a·pat** (pit′ə pat′) *adv.* with rapid beating —*n.* a rapid series of beats or taps

**pit bull** a short, heavy dog with powerful jaws

**pitch**¹ (pich) *n.* ⟦< L *pix*⟧ a black, sticky substance formed from coal tar, etc. and used for roofing, etc.

**pitch**² (pich) *vt.* ⟦ME *picchen*⟧ **1** to set up [*pitch a tent*] **2** *a*) to throw or toss *b*) to throw away **3** to fix at a certain point, degree, key, etc. **4** *Baseball a*) to throw (the ball) to the batter *b*) to act as pitcher for (a game, etc.) —*vi.* **1** to pitch a ball, etc. **2** to plunge forward or dip downward **3** to rise and fall, as a ship in rough water —*n.* **1** a throw or toss **2** anything pitched **3** a point or degree **4** the degree of slope **5** [Inf.] a line of talk for persuading **6** *Music, etc.* the highness or low-ness of a sound due to vibrations of sound waves —**pitch in** [Inf.] **1** to begin working hard **2** to make a contribution —**pitch into** [Inf.] to attack

**pitch′-black′** *adj.* very black

**pitch′blende′** (-blend′) *n.* [< Ger *pech*, PITCH¹ + *blenden*, to blind] a dark mineral, a major source of uranium

**pitch′-dark′** *adj.* very dark

**pitched battle** **1** a battle in which troop place-ment is relatively fixed beforehand **2** a hard-fought battle

**pitch′er¹** *n.* [< OFr *pichier*] a container, usually with a handle and lip, for holding and pouring liquids

**pitch′er²** *n.* [PITCH² + -ER] the baseball player who pitches the ball to the batters

**pitcher plant** a plant with pitcherlike leaves that trap and digest insects

**pitch′fork′** *n.* a large, long-handled fork for lifting and tossing hay, etc.

**pitch′man** (-mən) *n., pl.* -**men** (-mən) **1** a hawker of novelties, as at a carnival **2** [Inf.] any high-pressure salesman

**pitch pipe** a small pipe that produces a fixed tone used as a standard in tuning instruments, etc.

**pit·e·ous** (pit′ē əs) *adj.* arousing or deserving pity —**pit′e·ous·ly** *adv.*

**pit′fall′** *n.* [< PIT² + OE *fealle*, a trap] **1** a lightly covered pit for trapping animals **2** an unsus-pected danger, etc.

**pith** (pith) *n.* [OE *pitha*] **1** the soft, spongy tissue in the center of certain plant stems **2** the essen-tial part; gist

**pith′y** *adj.* -**i·er**, -**i·est** **1** of, like, or full of pith **2** terse and full of meaning —**pith′i·ly** *adv.*

**pit·i·ful** (pit′i fəl) *adj.* **1** arousing or deserving pity **2** contemptible Also **pit·i·a·ble** (pit′ē ə bəl) —**pit′i·ful·ly** *adv.*

**pit′i·less** (-lis) *adj.* without pity

**pi·ton** (pē′tän′) *n.* [Fr < MFr, a spike] a metal spike with an eye for a rope, driven into rock or ice for support in mountain climbing

**pit stop** **1** a temporary stop in the PIT² (*n.* 8) by a racing car **2** [Slang] *a*) a pause for food, etc. dur-ing a journey *b*) a visit to a restroom

**pit·tance** (pit′'ns) *n.* [< OFr *pitance*, food allowed a monk] **1** a meager allowance of money **2** any small amount or share

**pit·ter-pat·ter** (pit′ər pat′ər) *n.* [echoic] a rapid succession of light tapping sounds

**Pitts·burgh** (pits′burg′) city in SW Pennsylvania: pop. 370,000

**pi·tu·i·tar·y** (pi tōō′ə ter′ē) *adj.* [< L *pituita*, phlegm] of a small, oval endocrine gland (**pitui-tary gland**) attached to the brain: it secretes hor-mones affecting growth, etc.

**pit viper** any of several poisonous vipers with a heat-sensitive pit on each side of the head

**pit·y** (pit′ē) *n., pl.* -**ies** [< L *pietas*, piety] **1** sorrow for another's suffering or misfortune **2** a cause for sorrow or regret —*vt., vi.* -**ied**, -**y·ing** to feel pity (for)

**piv·ot** (piv′ət) *n.* [Fr] **1** a point, shaft, etc. on which something turns **2** a person or thing on which something depends, etc. **3** a pivoting movement —*vt.* to provide with a pivot —*vi.* to turn as on a pivot —**piv′ot·al** *adj.*

**pix·el** (pik′səl) *n.* [< *pic*(*ture*) + *el*(*ement*)] any of the dots that make up an image on a video screen

**pix·ie** or **pix·y** (pik′sē) *n., pl.* -**ies** [< Brit dial.] a fairy, elf, etc.

**pi·zazz** or **piz·zazz** (pi zaz′) *n.* [Inf.] **1** vigor **2** style, flair, etc.

**piz·za** (pēt′sə) *n.* [It] an Italian dish made by bak-ing thin dough covered with tomatoes, cheese, etc.

**piz·ze·ri·a** (pēt′sə rē′ə) *n.* [It] a place where piz-zas are made and sold

**piz·zi·ca·to** (pit′si kät′ō) *adj.* [It] *Music* plucked: a note to pluck the strings with the finger instead of bowing: also written **piz′zi·ca′to**

**pj's** (pē′jāz′) *pl.n. inf. var.* of PAJAMAS

**pk** *abbrev.* **1** pack **2** park **3** peck

**pkg** *abbrev.* package(s)

**Pkwy** or **Pky** *abbrev.* Parkway

**pl** *abbrev.* **1** place: also **Pl** **2** plural

**plac·ard** (plak′ärd; -ərd) *n.* [< MDu *placke*, a piece] a notice for display in a public place —*vt.* to place placards on or in

**pla·cate** (plā′kāt′) *vt.* -**cat′ed**, -**cat′ing** [< L *pla-care*] to appease; pacify —**pla·ca′tion** *n.*

**place** (plās) *n.* [< Gr *plateia*, a street] **1** a court or short street in a city **2** space; room **3** a region **4** *a*) the part of space occupied by a person or thing *b*) situation **5** a city, town, etc. **6** a residence **7** a building or space devoted to a special purpose [a *place* of amusement] **8** a particular point, part, position, etc. [a sore *place* on the leg, a *place* in history] **9** a step or point in a sequence **10** the proper position, time, etc. **11** a space, seat, etc. reserved or occupied by a person **12** a job or posi-tion **13** the duties of any position **14** the second position at the finish of a race —*vt.* **placed**, **plac′ing** **1** *a*) to put in a particular place, condi-tion, or relation *b*) to recognize or identify **2** to find employment for **3** to repose (trust) *in* a per-son or thing **4** to finish in (a specified position) in a race —*vi.* to finish second or among the first three in a race —**take place** to occur

**pla·ce·bo** (plə sē′bō) *n., pl.* -**bos** or -**boes** [< L, I shall please] a harmless, unmedicated prepara-tion given as a medicine, as to humor a patient

**place mat** a small mat serving as an individual table cover for a person at a meal

**place′ment** *n.* **1** a placing or being placed **2** loca-tion or arrangement

**pla·cen·ta** (plə sen′tə) *n., pl.* -**tas** or -**tae** (-tē) [ult. < Gr *plax*, a flat object] the structure in the uterus through which the fetus is nourished: cf. AFTERBIRTH —**pla·cen′tal** *adj.*

**plac·er** (plas′ər) *n.* [< Sp *placel*] a deposit of gravel or sand containing particles of gold, etc. that can be washed out

**place setting** the dish, utensils, etc. used for set-ting one place at a table for a meal

**plac·id** (plas′id) *adj.* [L *placidus*] calm; quiet —**pla·cid·i·ty** (plə sid′ə tē) *n.* —**plac′id·ly** *adv.*

**plack·et** (plak′it) *n.* [< ?] a slit at the waist of a skirt or collar of a shirt, to make it easy to put on and take off

**pla·gia·rize** (plā′jə rīz′) *vt., vi.* -**rized′**, -**riz′ing** [< L *plagiarius*, kidnapper] to take (ideas, writings, etc.) from (another) and pass them off as one's own —**pla′gia·rism′** (-riz′əm) *n.* —**pla′gia·rist** *n.*

**plague** (plāg) *n.* [< Gr *plēgē*, a misfortune] **1** any affliction or calamity **2** any deadly epidemic dis-ease —*vt.* **plagued**, **plagu′ing** **1** to afflict with a plague **2** to vex; torment

**plaice** (plās) *n., pl.* **plaice** or **plaices** any of various American and European flounders

**plaid** (plad) *n.* [Gael *plaide*, a blanket] **1** cloth with a crossbarred pattern **2** any pattern of this kind —*adj.* having such a pattern

**plain** (plān) *adj.* [< L *planus*, flat] **1** open; clear [in *plain* view] **2** clearly understood; obvious **3** outspoken; straightforward **4** not luxurious or ornate **5** not complicated; simple **6** homely **7** pure; unmixed **8** common; ordinary [a *plain* man] —*n.* an extent of level country —*adv.* clearly —**plain′ly** *adv.* —**plain′ness** *n.*

**plain′clothes′ man** a detective or police officer who wears civilian clothes while on duty: also **plain′clothes′man**, *pl.* -**men**

**plain′song′** *n.* a very old, plain kind of church music chanted in unison

**plaint** (plānt) *n.* [< L *plangere*, to lament] a com-plaint or lament

**plain·tiff** (plān′tif) *n.* [see prec.] one who brings a suit into a court of law

**plain'tive** (-tiv) *adj.* ⟦see PLAINT⟧ expressing sorrow or melancholy; mournful; sad

**plait** (plāt) *n.* ⟦< L *plicare,* to fold⟧ a braid of hair, etc. —*vt.* to braid

**plan** (plan) *n.* ⟦Fr, plan, foundation⟧ **1** a diagram showing the arrangement of a structure, piece of ground, etc. **2** a scheme for making, doing, or arranging something **3** any outline or sketch —*vt.* **planned, plan'ning 1** to make a plan of (a structure, etc.) **2** to devise a scheme for doing, etc. **3** to have in mind as a project or purpose —*vi.* to make plans —**plan'ner** *n.*

**plane**[1] (plān) *adj.* ⟦L *planus*⟧ **1** flat; level **2** of or having to do with flat surfaces or points, lines, etc. on them *[plane geometry]* —*n.* **1** a flat, level surface **2** a level of achievement, etc. **3** *short for* AIRPLANE

**plane**[2] (plān) *n.* ⟦< L *planus,* level⟧ a carpenter's tool for shaving a wood surface to make it smooth or level —*vt.* **planed, plan'ing** to smooth or level with a plane

PLANE

**plan·et** (plan'it) *n.* ⟦< Gr *planan,* wander⟧ any celestial body that revolves about a star; esp., one of the sun's nine major planets: Mercury, Venus, Earth, Mars, Jupiter, Saturn, Uranus, Neptune, and Pluto —**plan'e·tar'y** (-ə ter'ē) *adj.*

**plan·e·tar·i·um** (plan'ə ter'ē əm) *n., pl.* **-i·ums** or **-i·a** (-ə) **1** a revolving projector used to simulate the past, present, or future motions or positions of the sun, planets, etc. on the inside of a large dome **2** the room or building containing this

**plane tree** any of various trees with ball-shaped fruits and bark that sheds in large patches; sycamore

**plan·gent** (plan'jənt) *adj.* ⟦< L *plangere,* to beat⟧ loud or resonant, and, often, mournful-sounding

**plank** (plaŋk) *n.* ⟦< LL *planca*⟧ **1** a long, broad, thick board **2** an item in the platform of a political party —*vt.* **1** to cover with planks **2** to broil and serve (steak, fish, etc.) on a board **3** [Inf.] to set (*down*) with force

**plank'ing** *n.* **1** planks in quantity **2** the planks of a structure

**plank·ton** (plaŋk'tən) *n.* ⟦< Gr *plazesthai,* wander⟧ the microscopic animal and plant life found floating in bodies of water

**plant** (plant) *n.* ⟦< L *planta,* a sprout⟧ **1** any of a group of living organisms, excluding animals, bacteria, and certain other simple organisms, typically having leaves, stems, and roots and the ability to carry on photosynthesis **2** an herb, as distinguished from a tree or shrub **3** the machinery, buildings, etc. of a factory, etc. —*vt.* **1** to put into the ground to grow **2** to set firmly in position **3** to settle; establish **4** [Slang] to place (a person or thing) in such a way as to trick, trap, etc.

**plan·tain**[1] (plan'tin) *n.* ⟦< L *plantago*⟧ a plant with basal leaves and spikes of tiny, greenish flowers

**plan·tain**[2] (plan'tin) *n.* ⟦< Sp *plátano,* banana tree⟧ a hybrid banana plant yielding a fruit that is usually cooked while green

**plan·tar** (plant'ər) *adj.* ⟦< L *planta,* sole⟧ of or on the sole of the foot

**plan·ta·tion** (plan tā'shən) *n.* ⟦< L *plantare,* to plant⟧ **1** an estate, as in a warm climate, cultivated by workers living on it **2** a large, cultivated planting of trees

**plant·er** (plant'ər) *n.* **1** the owner of a plantation **2** one that plants **3** a decorative container for plants

**plant'ing** *n.* **1** the act of putting seeds, etc. into soil **2** something planted

**plant louse** APHID

**plaque** (plak) *n.* ⟦Fr < MDu *placke,* disk⟧ **1** a flat,

inscribed piece of wood or metal, used to commemorate an event, etc. **2** a thin film of matter on uncleaned teeth

**plash** (plash) *vt., vi., n.* ⟦echoic⟧ SPLASH

**plas·ma** (plaz'mə) *n.* ⟦Ger < Gr, something molded⟧ **1** the fluid part of blood, lymph, or milk **2** a high-temperature, ionized gas that is electrically neutral

**plasma membrane** a very thin living membrane surrounding a plant or animal cell

**plas·ter** (plas'tər) *n.* ⟦< Gr *emplassein,* to daub over⟧ **1** a pasty mixture, as of lime, sand, and water, that hardens when it dries, for coating walls, etc. **2** PLASTER OF PARIS **3** a pasty, medicinal preparation spread on cloth and applied to the body —*vt.* **1** to cover as with plaster **2** to apply like a plaster *[to plaster posters on walls]* **3** to make lie smooth and flat —**plas'ter·er** *n.*

**plas'ter·board'** *n.* thin board consisting of plaster of Paris covered with heavy paper, used in wide sheets for walls, etc.

**plaster of Paris** ⟦from use of gypsum from *Paris,* France⟧ a thick paste of gypsum and water that sets quickly: used for casts, statuary, etc.

**plas·tic** (plas'tik) *adj.* ⟦< Gr *plassein,* to form⟧ **1** molding or shaping matter; formative **2** that can be molded or shaped **3** made of plastic —*n.* **1** any of various nonmetallic compounds, synthetically produced, which can be molded and hardened for commercial use **2** [Inf.] a credit card or credit cards, or credit based on their use —**plas·tic'i·ty** (-tis'ə tē) *n.*

**plas'ti·cize'** (-tə sīz') *vt., vi.* **-cized', -ciz'ing** to make or become plastic

**plastic surgery** surgery dealing with the repair of deformed or destroyed parts of the body, as by transferring skin, bone, etc. from other parts —**plastic surgeon**

**plat** (plat) *n.* ⟦var. of PLOT⟧ **1** a small piece of ground **2** a map or plan, as of a subdivision —*vt.* **plat'ted, plat'ting** to make a map or plan of

**plate** (plāt) *n.* ⟦< Gr *platys,* broad⟧ **1** a smooth, flat, thin piece of metal, etc., specif. one on which an engraving is cut **2** an impression taken from an engraved surface **3** dishes, utensils, etc. of, or plated with, silver or gold **4** a shallow dish **5** the food in a dish; a course **6** a denture, specif. that part of it which fits to the mouth **7** *Baseball short for* HOME PLATE **8** *Photog.* a sheet of glass, metal, etc. coated with a film sensitive to light **9** *Printing* a cast to be printed from —*vt.* **plat'ed, plat'ing 1** to coat with gold, silver, etc. **2** to cover with metal plates

**pla·teau** (pla tō') *n.* ⟦Fr: see prec.⟧ **1** an elevated tract of level land **2** a period of relative stability or little change

**plate glass** polished, clear glass in thick sheets, for windows, mirrors, etc.

**plate·let** (plāt'lit) *n.* a small blood cell involved in clotting

**plat·en** (plat'n) *n.* ⟦< OFr *plat,* flat⟧ **1** in a printing press, a flat metal plate which presses the paper against the type **2** a typewriter roller on which the keys strike

**plate tec·ton·ics** (tek tän'iks) *Geol.* the theory that the earth's surface consists of plates whose constant motion explains continental drift, etc.

**plat·form** (plat'fôrm') *n.* ⟦Fr *plate-forme,* lit., flat form⟧ **1** a raised horizontal surface, as a stage for speakers, etc. **2** a statement of policy, esp. of a political party

**plat·i·num** (plat'n əm) *n.* ⟦< Sp *plata,* silver⟧ a silvery, metallic chemical element, resistant to corrosion: used for jewelry, etc.

**plat·i·tude** (plat'ə tōōd') *n.* ⟦Fr < *plat,* flat, after *latitude,* etc.⟧ a commonplace or trite remark

**Pla·to** (plāt'ō) 427?-347? B.C.; Gr. philosopher

**Pla·ton·ic** (plə tän'ik) *adj.* **1** of Plato or his philosophy **2** *[usually* p-] not sexual but purely spiritual: said of a relationship, etc.

**pla·toon** (plə tōōn′) *n.* ⟦Fr *peloton*, a ball, group⟧ **1** a military unit composed of two or more squads **2** *Sports* any of the specialized squads making up a team —*vt. Sports* to alternate (players) at a position

**plat·ter** (plat′ər) *n.* ⟦< OFr *plat*, flat⟧ a large, shallow dish, usually oval, for serving food

**plat·y** (plat′ē) *n., pl.* **plat′y, plat′ys,** or **plat′ies** ⟦clipped < ModL *Platypoecilus*, genus name⟧ a brightly colored, freshwater fish of Central America: used in aquariums

**plat·y·pus** (plat′ə pəs) *n., pl.* **-pus·es** or **-pi′** (-pī′) ⟦< Gr *platys*, flat + *pous*, foot⟧ a small, egg-laying water mammal of Australia, with webbed feet and a ducklike bill; duckbill

**plau·dit** (plô′dit) *n.* ⟦< L *plaudere*, applaud⟧ [*usually pl.*] applause

**plau·si·ble** (plô′zə bəl) *adj.* ⟦< L *plaudere*, applaud⟧ seemingly true, trustworthy, honest, etc. —**plau′si·bil′i·ty** *n.*

**play** (plā) *vi.* ⟦OE *plegan*⟧ **1** to move lightly, rapidly, etc. [sunlight *played* on the water] **2** to engage in recreation **3** to take part in a game or sport **4** to trifle (*with* a thing or person) **5** to perform on a musical instrument **6** to give out sounds **7** to act in a specified way [to *play* dumb] **8** to act in a drama **9** to impose unscrupulously (*on* another's feelings) —*vt.* **1** to take part in (a game or sport) **2** to oppose (a person, team, etc.) in a game **3** to do, as in fun [to *play* tricks] **4** to bet on **5** to cause to move, etc.; wield **6** to cause [to *play* havoc] **7** to perform (music, a drama, etc.) **8** to perform on (an instrument) **9** to act the part of [to *play* Hamlet] —*n.* **1** motion or activity, esp. when free or rapid **2** freedom for motion or action **3** recreation; sport **4** fun; joking **5** the playing of a game **6** a move or act in a game **7** a dramatic composition or performance; drama —**in** (or **out of**) **play** *Sports* in (or not in) the condition for continuing play: said of a ball, etc. —**play down** to attach little importance to —**played out** exhausted —**play up** [Inf.] to give prominence to —**play up to** [Inf.] to try to please by flattery

**play′act′** *vi.* **1** to pretend **2** to behave in an affected or dramatic manner —**play′act′ing** *n.*

**play′back′** *n.* **1** reproduction of sounds, images, etc. from a recorded disc, tape, etc. **2** the control or device for such reproduction

**play′bill′** *n.* **1** a poster advertising a play **2** a program of a play, listing the cast, etc.

**play′boy′** *n.* a man of means who is given to pleasure-seeking

**play′er** *n.* **1** one who plays a specified game, instrument, etc. **2** an actor

**play′ful** *adj.* **1** fond of play or fun **2** jocular —**play′ful·ly** *adv.* —**play′ful·ness** *n.*

**play′go′er** (-gō′ər) *n.* one who goes to the theater frequently or regularly

**play′ground′** *n.* a place, often near a school, for outdoor recreation

**play′house′** *n.* **1** a theater for live dramatic productions **2** a small house for children to play in

**playing cards** cards used in playing various games, arranged in four suits

**play′mate′** *n.* a companion in games and recreation

**play′off′** *n.* a contest to break a tie or to decide a championship

**play on words** a pun or punning

**play′pen′** *n.* a portable enclosure for an infant to play or crawl in safely

**play′thing′** *n.* a toy

**play′wright′** (-rīt′) *n.* one who writes plays

**pla·za** (plä′zə, plaz′ə) *n.* ⟦Sp < L *platea*, street⟧ **1** a public square in a city or town **2** a shopping center **3** a service area along a superhighway

**plea** (plē) *n.* ⟦< L *placere*, to please⟧ **1** a statement in defense; excuse **2** a request; appeal **3** *Law* the response of a defendant to criminal charges

**plea′-bar′gain** *vi.* to engage in plea bargaining

**plea bargaining** pretrial negotiations in which the defendant agrees to plead guilty to a lesser charge if more serious charges are dropped

**plead** (plēd) *vi.* **plead′ed** or **pled** or **plead** (pled), **plead′ing** ⟦see PLEA⟧ **1** to present a plea in a law court **2** to make an appeal; beg —*vt.* **1** to argue (a law case) **2** to answer (guilty or not guilty) to a charge **3** to offer as an excuse —**plead′er** *n.*

**pleas·ant** (plez′ənt) *adj.* ⟦< Fr *plaisir*, to please⟧ **1** agreeable to the mind or senses; pleasing **2** having an agreeable manner, look, etc.; amiable —**pleas′ant·ly** *adv.* —**pleas′ant·ness** *n.*

**pleas′ant·ry** (-ən trē) *n., pl.* **-ries** **1** a humorous remark **2** a polite social remark [to exchange *pleasantries*]

**please** (plēz) *vt.* **pleased, pleas′ing** ⟦< L *placere*⟧ **1** to be agreeable to; satisfy **2** to be the wish of [it *pleased* him to go] —*vi.* **1** to be agreeable; satisfy **2** to have the wish; like [to do as one *pleases*] *Please* is also used in polite requests [*please* sit down]

**pleas′ing** *adj.* giving pleasure —**pleas′ing·ly** *adv.*

**pleas·ur·a·ble** (plezh′ər ə bəl) *adj.* pleasant; enjoyable

**pleas·ure** (plezh′ər) *n.* **1** a pleased feeling; delight **2** one's wish, will, or choice **3** a thing that gives delight or satisfaction —**pleas′ure·ful** *adj.*

**pleat** (plēt) *n.* ⟦ME *pleten*⟧ a flat double fold in cloth, etc. pressed or stitched in place —*vt.* to lay and press (cloth) in a pleat or pleats

**ple·be·ian** (pli bē′ən) *n.* ⟦< L *plebs*, the common people⟧ **1** one of the common people **2** a vulgar, coarse person —*adj.* vulgar or common

**pleb·i·scite** (pleb′ə sīt′) *n.* ⟦< L *plebs*, the common people + *scitum*, a decree⟧ a direct vote of the people on a political issue, such as independent nationhood or annexation

**plec·trum** (plek′trəm) *n., pl.* **-trums** or **-tra** (-trə) ⟦L < Gr *plēssein*, to strike⟧ a thin piece of metal, plastic, etc., for plucking the strings of a guitar, etc.; pick

**pled** (pled) *vi., vt. pt. & pp. of* PLEAD

**pledge** (plej) *n.* ⟦prob < OS *plegan*, to warrant⟧ **1** the condition of being given or held as security for a contract, payment, etc. **2** a person or thing given or held thus as security **3** a promise or agreement **4** something promised —*vt.* **pledged, pledg′ing 1** to give as security **2** to bind by a promise **3** to promise to give

**Pleis·to·cene** (plīs′tə sēn′) *adj.* ⟦< Gr *pleistos*, most + *kainos*, recent⟧ designating an epoch in the Cenozoic Era, characterized by the appearance of modern humans

**ple·na·ry** (plē′nə rē, plen′ə-) *adj.* ⟦< L *plenus*, full⟧ **1** full; complete **2** for attendance by all members [a *plenary* session]

**plen·i·po·ten·ti·ar·y** (plen′i pō ten′shē er′ē) *adj.* ⟦< L *plenus*, full + *potens*, powerful⟧ having or conferring full authority —*n., pl.* **-ar′ies** a diplomat given full authority

**plen·i·tude** (plen′i tōōd′) *n.* ⟦< L *plenus*, full⟧ **1** fullness; completeness **2** abundance; plenty

**plen·te·ous** (plen′tē əs) *adj.* plentiful

**plen·ti·ful** (plen′ti fəl) *adj.* **1** having or yielding plenty **2** abundant —**plen′ti·ful·ly** *adv.*

**plen·ty** (plen′tē) *n., pl.* **-ties** ⟦< L *plenus*, full⟧ **1** prosperity; opulence **2** a sufficient supply **3** a large number —*adv.* [Inf.] fully; quite

**pleth·o·ra** (pleth′ə rə) *n.* ⟦< Gr *plēthein*, to be full⟧ an overabundance

**pleu·ra** (ploor′ə) *n., pl.* **-rae** (-ē) ⟦< Gr, rib, side⟧ the thin membrane that covers a lung and lines the chest cavity in mammals

**pleu·ri·sy** (ploor′ə sē) *n.* ⟦< Gr *pleura*, rib, side⟧ inflammation of the pleura, characterized by painful breathing

**Plex·i·glas** (plek′si glas′) *trademark for* a lightweight, transparent thermoplastic substance —*n.* this material

**plex·i·glass** (plek′si glas′) *n.* a material like Plexiglas

**plex·us** (plek′səs) *n.*, *pl.* **-us·es** or **-us** ⟦< L *plectere*, to twine⟧ a network of blood vessels, nerves, etc.

**pli·a·ble** (plī′ə bəl) *adj.* ⟦< L *plicare*, to fold⟧ **1** easily bent; flexible **2** easily influenced or persuaded **3** adaptable —**pli′a·bil′i·ty** *n.*

**pli·ant** (plī′ənt) *adj.* **1** easily bent; pliable **2** compliant —**pli′an·cy** *n.*

**pli·ers** (plī′ərz) *pl.n.* ⟦< PLY¹⟧ small pincers for gripping small objects, bending wire, etc.: often **pair of pliers**

**plight**¹ (plīt) *n.* ⟦< OFr *pleit*, a fold⟧ a distressing situation

**plight**² (plīt) *vt.* ⟦< OE *pliht*, pledge, danger⟧ to pledge, or bind by a pledge

PLIERS

**plinth** (plinth) *n.* ⟦< Gr *plinthos*, a brick⟧ the block at the base of a column, pedestal, etc.

**PLO** *abbrev.* Palestine Liberation Organization

**plod** (pläd) *vi.* **plod′ded, plod′ding** ⟦of echoic orig.⟧ **1** to move heavily and laboriously; trudge **2** to work steadily; drudge —**plod′der** *n.*

**plop** (pläp) *vt.*, *vi.* **plopped, plop′ping** ⟦echoic⟧ to drop with a sound like that of something flat falling into water —*n.* such a sound

**plot** (plät) *n.* ⟦OE⟧ **1** a small area of ground **2** a secret, usually evil, scheme **3** the plan of action of a play, novel, etc.: also **plot′line′** —*vt.* **plot′ted, plot′ting 1** to mark or trace on a chart or map **2** to make secret plans for —*vi.* to scheme —**plot·ter** *n.*

**plov·er** (pluv′ər, plō′vər) *n.* ⟦< L *pluvia*, rain⟧ a bird living near the shore, having a short tail and long, pointed wings

**plow** (plou) *n.* ⟦OE *ploh*⟧ **1** a farm implement used to cut and turn up the soil **2** any implement like this, as a snowplow —*vt.* **1** to cut and turn up (soil) with a plow **2** to make (one's way) through by or as if by plowing —*vi.* **1** to use a plow **2** to move (*through, into,* etc.) with force **3** to plod **4** to begin work vigorously: with *into* Also, chiefly Brit., **plough** —**plow′man** (-mən), *pl.* **-men,** *n.*

**plow′share′** *n.* the cutting blade of a plow

**ploy** (ploi) *n.* ⟦? < (EM)PLOY⟧ an action intended to outwit someone

**pluck** (pluk) *vt.* ⟦OE *pluccian*⟧ **1** to pull off or out; pick **2** to snatch **3** to pull feathers or hair from **4** to pull at (a guitar string, etc.) and release quickly —*vi.* to pull: often with *at* —*n.* **1** a pulling; tug **2** courage

**pluck′y** *adj.* **-i·er, -i·est** brave; spirited —**pluck′i·ness** *n.*

**plug** (plug) *n.* ⟦MDu *plugge*⟧ **1** an object used to stop up a hole, etc. **2** a cake of pressed tobacco **3** an electrical device, as with prongs, for making contact or closing a circuit **4** a kind of fishing lure **5** [Inf.] a free boost, advertisement, etc. **6** [Slang] an old, worn-out horse —*vt.* **plugged, plug′ging 1** to fill (a hole, etc.) with a plug **2** to insert a plug of **3** [Inf.] to advertise with a plug **4** [Slang] to shoot a bullet into —*vi.* [Inf.] to work doggedly —**plug in** to connect (an electrical device) by inserting a plug into a jack, socket, etc.

**plum** (plum) *n.* ⟦OE *plume*⟧ **1** *a*) a tree bearing a smooth-skinned fruit with a flattened stone *b*) the fruit **2** a raisin [*plum* pudding] **3** the bluish-red color of some plums **4** something desirable

**plum·age** (plō̄′mij) *n.* ⟦Fr < *plume*, a feather⟧ a bird's feathers

**plumb** (plum) *n.* ⟦< L *plumbum*, LEAD²⟧ a lead weight (**plumb bob**) hung at the end of a line (**plumb line**), used to determine how deep water is or whether a wall, etc. is vertical —*adj.* perfectly vertical —*adv.* **1** straight down **2** [Inf.] entirely —*vt.* **1** to test or sound with a plumb **2** to probe

or fathom —**out of** (or **off**) **plumb** not vertical

**plumb·er** (plum′ər) *n.* ⟦see prec.⟧ a skilled worker who installs and repairs pipes, fixtures, etc., as of water systems

**plumber's helper** [Inf.] PLUNGER (sense 2): also **plumber's friend**

**plumb·ing** (plum′iŋ) *n.* **1** the work of a plumber **2** the pipes and fixtures with which a plumber works

**plume** (plō̄m) *n.* ⟦< L *pluma*⟧ **1** a feather, esp. a large, showy one **2** a group of these —*vt.* **plumed, plum′ing 1** to adorn with plumes **2** to preen —**plum′y, -i·er, -i·est,** *adj.*

**plum·met** (plum′it) *n.* ⟦see PLUMB⟧ **1** a plumb **2** a thing that weighs heavily —*vi.* to fall straight downward

**plump**¹ (plump) *adj.* ⟦< MDu *plomp*, bulky⟧ full and rounded in form; chubby —**plump′ness** *n.*

**plump**² (plump) *vi.*, *vt.* ⟦echoic⟧ to drop or bump suddenly or heavily —*n.* **1** a falling, bumping, etc. **2** the sound of this —*adv.* **1** suddenly; heavily **2** straight down

**plun·der** (plun′dər) *vt.*, *vi.* ⟦< Ger *plunder*, baggage⟧ **1** to rob or pillage **2** to take (property) by force or fraud —*n.* **1** a plundering **2** things taken by force or fraud

**plunge** (plunj) *vt.* **plunged, plung′ing** ⟦see PLUMB⟧ to thrust or throw suddenly (*into* a liquid, condition, etc.) —*vi.* **1** to dive or rush **2** to move violently and rapidly downward or forward **3** [Inf.] to gamble heavily —*n.* **1** a dive or fall **2** [Inf.] a gamble

**plung′er** *n.* **1** one who plunges **2** a large rubber suction cup used to free clogged drains **3** any cylindrical device that operates with a plunging motion, as a piston

**plunk** (pluŋk) *vt.* ⟦echoic⟧ **1** to strum (a banjo, etc.) **2** to throw or put down heavily —*vi.* **1** to give out a twanging sound **2** to fall heavily —*n.* the sound made by plunking —**plunk down** [Inf.] to give in payment

**plu·ral** (ploor′əl) *adj.* ⟦< L *plus*, more⟧ more than one —*n.* *Gram.* the form of a word designating more than one (Ex.: *hands, men*)

**plu′ral·ism′** *n.* various ethnic, religious, etc. groups existing together in a nation or society — **plu′ral·ist** *n., adj.* —**plu′ral·is′tic** *adj.*

**plu·ral·i·ty** (ploo ral′ə tē) *n., pl.* **-ties 1** a being plural or numerous **2** *a*) the excess of votes in an election that the leading candidate has over the nearest rival *b*) a majority

**plu·ral·ize** (ploor′ə līz′) *vt., vi.* **-ized′, -iz′ing** to make plural

**plus** (plus) *prep.* ⟦L, more⟧ **1** added to [2 *plus* 2] **2** in addition to —*adj.* **1** indicating addition **2** positive [a *plus* quantity] **3** somewhat higher than [a grade of B *plus*] **4** involving extra gain [a *plus* factor] **5** [Inf.] and more [personality *plus*] —*n., pl.* **plus′es** or **plus′ses 1** a sign (**plus sign**, +) indicating addition or positive quantity **2** something added **3** an advantage; benefit

**plush** (plush) *n.* ⟦< L *pilus*, hair⟧ a fabric with a soft, thick pile —*adj.* [Inf.] luxurious: also **plush′y, -i·er, -i·est**

**Plu·tarch** (plō̄′tärk′) A.D. 46?-120?; Gr. biographer & historian

**Plu·to** (plō̄′tō) **1** Gr. & Rom. Myth. the god of the lower world **2** the outermost planet: see PLANET

**plu·toc·ra·cy** (plō̄ täk′rə sē) *n., pl.* **-cies** ⟦< Gr *ploutos*, wealth + *kratein*, to rule⟧ **1** government by the wealthy **2** a group of wealthy people who control a government

**plu·to·crat** (plō̄t′ə krat′) *n.* **1** a member of a plutocracy **2** one whose wealth is the source of control or influence —**plu′to·crat′ic** *adj.*

PLUMB

**plu·to·ni·um** (plōō tō′nē əm) *n.* ⟦after PLUTO (planet)⟧ a radioactive metallic chemical element

**plu·vi·al** (plōō′vē əl) *adj.* ⟦< L *pluvia*, rain⟧ of, or having much, rain

**ply**[1] (plī) *vt.* **plied, ply′ing** ⟦< L *plicare*, to fold⟧ [Now Rare] to twist, fold, etc. —*n., pl.* **plies** 1 a thickness or layer, as of cloth or plywood 2 one of the twisted strands in rope, yarn, etc.

**ply**[2] (plī) *vt.* **plied, ply′ing** ⟦contr. < APPLY⟧ 1 to use (a tool, faculty, etc.), esp. with energy 2 to work at (a trade) 3 to keep supplying, assailing, etc. (*with*) 4 to sail back and forth across —*vi.* 1 to keep busy (*at*) 2 to travel regularly (*between* places)

**Ply·mouth** (plim′əth) town in SE Massachusetts: settled by the Pilgrims (1620): pop. 46,000

**ply′wood**′ *n.* ⟦PLY[1] + WOOD⟧ a construction material made of thin layers of wood glued together

**PM** *abbrev.* 1 ⟦L *post meridiem*⟧ after noon: used for the time from noon to midnight: also **P.M.** or **p.m.** or **pm** 2 Postmaster 3 Prime Minister

**PMS** *abbrev.* ⟦*p(re)m(enstrual) s(yndrome)*⟧ the physical and emotional symptoms that may precede menstruation

**pneu·mat·ic** (nōō mat′ik) *adj.* ⟦< Gr *pneuma*, breath⟧ 1 of or containing wind, air, or gases 2 filled with or worked by compressed air

**pneu·mo·ni·a** (nōō mōn′yə) *n.* ⟦< Gr *pneumōn*, lung < *pnein*, breathe⟧ inflammation of the lungs caused as by bacteria or viruses

**Po** (pō) river in N Italy, flowing from the Alps into the Adriatic

**PO** *abbrev.* 1 Post Office 2 post office box

**poach**[1] (pōch) *vt.* ⟦< MFr *poche*, pocket: the yolk is "pocketed" in the white⟧ to cook (fish, an egg without its shell, etc.) in or over boiling water

**poach**[2] (pōch) *vt., vi.* ⟦< MHG *puchen*, to plunder⟧ 1 to trespass on (private property), esp. to hunt or fish 2 to hunt or catch (game or fish) illegally — **poach′er** *n.*

**pock** (päk) *n.* ⟦OE *pocc*⟧ 1 a pustule caused by smallpox, etc. 2 POCKMARK —**pocked** *adj.*

**pock·et** (päk′it) *n.* ⟦< Fr *poque*, a pouch⟧ 1 a little bag or pouch, esp. one sewn into clothing, for carrying small articles 2 a pouchlike cavity or hollow 3 a small area or group *[a pocket of poverty]* —*adj.* 1 that can be carried in a pocket 2 small —*vt.* 1 to put into a pocket 2 to envelop; enclose 3 to take (money, etc.) dishonestly 4 to suppress *[to pocket one's pride]* —**pock′et·ful**′, *pl.* **-fuls**′, *n.*

**pock′et·book**′ *n.* 1 a woman's purse or handbag 2 monetary resources

**pock′et·knife**′ *n., pl.* **-knives**′ a knife with a blade or blades that fold into the handle

**pock′mark**′ *n.* a scar left by a pustule, as of smallpox

**pod** (päd) *n.* ⟦< ?⟧ a dry fruit or seed vessel, as of peas or beans

**-pod** (päd) ⟦< Gr *pous*, foot⟧ *combining form* 1 foot 2 (one) having (a specified number or kind of) feet Also **-pode** (pōd)

**po·di·a·try** (pō dī′ə trē) *n.* ⟦< Gr *pous*, foot + -IATRY⟧ the profession dealing with the care and treatment of the feet —**po·di′a·trist** *n.*

**po·di·um** (pō′dē əm) *n.* ⟦L < Gr *pous*, foot⟧ 1 a small platform, as for an orchestra conductor 2 LECTERN

**Poe** (pō), **Ed·gar Al·lan** (ed′gər al′ən) 1809-49; U.S. poet & short-story writer

**po·em** (pō′əm) *n.* ⟦< Gr *poiein*, to make⟧ an arrangement of words, esp. a rhythmical composition, sometimes rhymed, in a style more imaginative than ordinary speech or prose

**po·e·sy** (pō′ə sē′) *n. old-fashioned var. of* POETRY

**po·et** (pō′ət) *n.* 1 one who writes poems or verses 2 one who displays imaginative power and beauty of thought, language, etc. —**po′et·ess** *fem.n.*

**po·et·as·ter** (pō′ə tas′tər) *n.* ⟦< prec. + L *-aster*, dim. suffix⟧ a writer of mediocre verse

**po·et·ic** (pō et′ik) *adj.* 1 of or for poets or poetry 2 displaying the beauty, imaginative qualities, etc. found in good poetry Also **po·et′i·cal** *adj.* —**po·et′i·cal·ly** *adv.*

**poetic justice** justice, as in stories, applied in an especially fitting way

**poetic license** deviation from strict fact or rules, for artistic effect

**poet laureate** the official poet of a nation, appointed to write poems celebrating national events, etc.

**po·et·ry** (pō′ə trē) *n.* 1 the art, theory, or structure of poems 2 poems 3 poetic qualities

**po·grom** (pō′grəm, -gräm′) *n.* ⟦< Russ, earlier, riot, storm⟧ an organized massacre, as of Jews in czarist Russia

**poi** (poi) *n.* ⟦Haw⟧ a Hawaiian food that is a paste of taro root

**poign·ant** (poin′yənt) *adj.* ⟦< L *pungere*, to prick⟧ 1 pungent 2 *a)* sharply painful to the feelings *b)* emotionally moving 3 sharp, biting, pointed, etc. —**poign′an·cy** *n.*

**poin·ci·an·a** (poin′sē an′ə) *n.* ⟦after M. de *Poinci*, early governor of the Fr West Indies⟧ a small tropical tree or shrub with showy red, orange, or yellow flowers

**poin·set·ti·a** (poin set′ə, -set′ē ə) *n.* ⟦after J. R. *Poinsett*, 19th-c. U.S. ambassador to Mexico⟧ a tropical shrub with yellow flowers and petal-like red leaves

**point** (point) *n.* ⟦< L *pungere*, to prick⟧ 1 a dot in writing, etc. *[a decimal point]* 2 a position or location 3 the exact moment 4 a condition reached *[boiling point]* 5 a detail; item *[point by point]* 6 a distinguishing feature 7 a unit, as of value or game scores 8 a sharp end 9 a projecting piece of land; cape 10 the essential fact or idea *[the point of a joke]* 11 a purpose; object 12 a convincing idea or fact 13 a helpful hint 14 a mark showing direction on a compass 15 *Finance a)* a $1 change in the price of a stock *b)* a unit or amount equal to one percent 16 *Printing* a measuring unit for type, about $\frac{1}{72}$ of an inch —*vt.* 1 to sharpen to a point 2 to give (a story, etc.) emphasis: usually with *up* 3 to show: usually with *out* *[point out the way]* 4 to aim —*vi.* 1 to direct one's finger (*at* or *to*) 2 to call attention (*to*) 3 to be directed (*to* or *toward*) —**at the point of** very close to —**beside the point** irrelevant —**to the point** pertinent; apt

**point′-blank**′ *adj., adv.* ⟦prec. + *blank* (white center of a target)⟧ 1 (aimed) straight at a mark 2 direct(ly); blunt(ly)

**point′ed** *adj.* 1 having a sharp end 2 sharp; incisive 3 aimed at someone: said as of a remark 4 very evident —**point′ed·ly** *adv.*

**poin·telle** (poin tel′) *n.* a lacy, loosely formed fabric, often of acrylic, used for blouses, sweaters, etc.

**point′er** *n.* 1 a long, tapered rod for pointing to things 2 an indicator on a meter, etc. 3 a large, muscular hunting dog with a smooth coat 4 [Inf.] a helpful hint or suggestion

**poin·til·lism** (pwan′tə liz′əm) *n.* ⟦Fr⟧ a style of painting using dots of color that blend together when seen from a distance —**poin′til·list** *n., adj.*

**point′less** *adj.* 1 without a point 2 without meaning or force; senseless

**point man** 1 the soldier in the front position in a patrol 2 anyone in the forefront a movement of attacking or supporting a political program, etc.

**point of view** 1 the way in which something is viewed 2 a mental attitude or opinion

**point′y** *adj.* **-i·er, -i·est** 1 coming to a sharp point 2 many-pointed

**poise** (poiz) *n.* ⟦< L *pendere*, weigh⟧ 1 balance; stability 2 ease and dignity of manner 3 carriage, as of the body —*vt., vi.* **poised, pois′ing** to balance or be balanced

**poised** *adj.* 1 calm; self-assured 2 readied

**poi·son** (poi′zən) *n.* ⟦< L *potio*, potion⟧ a substance that can cause illness or death when ingested even in small quantities —*vt.* 1 to harm or kill with poison **2** to put poison into **3** to influence wrongfully —*adj.* poisonous

**poison ivy** a plant having leaves of three leaflets and ivory-colored berries: it can cause a severe rash if touched

**poi·son·ous** *adj.* that can injure or kill by or as by poison —**poi'son·ous·ly** *adv.*

**poison pill** any defensive measure which makes the takeover of a corporation prohibitively expensive

POISON IVY

**poke**[1] (pōk) *vt.* **poked, pok'ing** ⟦< MDu *poken*⟧ **1** *a*) to prod, as with a stick *b*) [Slang] to hit **2** to make (a hole, etc.) by poking —*vi.* **1** to jab (*at*) **2** to pry or search (*about* or *around*) **3** to move slowly (*along*) —*n.* **1** a jab; thrust **2** [Slang] a blow with the fist —**poke fun at** to ridicule

**poke**[2] (pōk) *n.* ⟦OFr⟧ [Dial.] a sack

**pok·er**[1] (pōk'ər) *n.* ⟦< ? Ger *pochspiel*, lit., game of defiance⟧ a card game in which the players bet on the value of their hands

**pok·er**[2] (pō'kər) *n.* a rod, usually of iron, for stirring a fire

**poker face** an expressionless face, as of a poker player trying to conceal the nature of his or her hand

**pok·y** (pō'kē) *adj.* **-i·er, -i·est** ⟦POKE[1] + -Y[2]⟧ **1** slow, dull, etc. **2** small and uncomfortable [a *poky* room] Also **pok'ey**

**pol** (päl) *n.* [Slang] a politician

**Pol** *abbrev.* **1** Poland **2** Polish

**Po·land** (pō'lənd) country in EC Europe, on the Baltic Sea: 120,628 sq. mi.; pop. 38,309,000

**po·lar** (pō'lər) *adj.* **1** of or near the North or South pole **2** of a pole or poles

**polar bear** a large white bear of coastal arctic regions

**Po·la·ris** (pō lar'is) *n.* the bright star almost directly above the North Pole

**po·lar·i·ty** (pō lar'ə tē) *n.*, *pl.* **-ties 1** the tendency of bodies having opposite magnetic poles to have their ends point to the earth's magnetic poles **2** the tendency to turn, grow, think, etc. in contrary directions, as if because of magnetic repulsion

**po·lar·i·za·tion** (pō'lə ri zā'shən) *n.* **1** a polarizing or being polarized **2** *Optics* the condition of electromagnetic waves in which the motion of the wave is confined to one plane or one direction

**po·lar·ize** (pō'lə rīz') *vt.* **-ized', -iz'ing** to give polarity to —*vi.* to acquire polarity; specif., to separate into opposed or antagonistic groups, viewpoints, etc.

**Po·lar·oid** (pō'lə roid') *trademark for:* **1** a transparent material capable of polarizing light **2** ⟦< *Polaroid* (Land Camera)⟧ *a*) a camera that produces a print within seconds *b*) such a print

**pole**[1] (pōl) *n.* ⟦< L *palus*, a stake⟧ a long, slender piece of wood, metal, etc. —*vt.* **poled, pol'ing** to push along with a pole

**pole**[2] (pōl) *n.* ⟦< Gr *polos*⟧ **1** either end of any axis, as of the earth's axis **2** either of two opposed forces, parts, etc., as the ends of a magnet or the terminals of a battery

**Pole** (pōl) *n.* a person born or living in Poland

**pole·cat** (pōl'kat') *n.* ⟦prob. < OFr *poule*, hen + CAT⟧ **1** a small Old World weasel **2** SKUNK

**po·lem·ic** (pō lem'ik) *adj.* ⟦< Gr *polemos*, war⟧ of or involving dispute: also **po·lem'i·cal** —*n.* a controversy

**po·lem·ics** *n.* [*sometimes with pl. v.*] the art or practice of disputation —**po·lem'i·cist** (-i sist) *n.*

**pole·star'** Polaris, the North Star: usually **Pole Star** —*n.* a guiding principle

**pole vault** a leap for height by jumping over a bar

---

with the aid of a long pole —**pole'-vault'** *vi.* —**pole'-vault'er** *n.*

**po·lice** (pə lēs') *n.* ⟦Fr: ult. < Gr *polis*, city⟧ **1** the governmental department (of a city, state, etc.) for keeping order, detecting crime, etc. **2** [*with pl. v.*] the members of such a department —*vt.* **-liced', -lic'ing 1** to control, protect, etc. with police or a similar force **2** to keep (a military camp, etc.) clean and orderly

**po·lice'man** (-mən) *n.*, *pl.* **-men** (-mən) a member of a police force —**po·lice'wom'an**, *pl.* **-wom'en**, *fem.n.*

**police officer** a member of a police force

**police state** a government that seeks to suppress political opposition by means of police

**pol·i·cy**[1] (päl'ə sē) *n.*, *pl.* **-cies** ⟦see POLICE⟧ **1** wise management **2** a principle, plan, etc., as of a government

**pol·i·cy**[2] (päl'ə sē) *n.*, *pl.* **-cies** ⟦< Gr *apodeixis*, proof⟧ a written insurance contract: in full **insurance policy**

**pol'i·cy·hold'er** *n.* a person to whom an insurance policy is issued

**po·li·o·my·e·li·tis** (pō'lē ō mī'ə līt'is) *n.* ⟦< Gr *polios*, gray + MYELITIS⟧ an acute infectious disease caused by viral inflammation of the gray matter of the spinal cord, often resulting in muscular paralysis: also **po'li·o'**

**pol·ish** (päl'ish) *vt.* ⟦< L *polire*⟧ **1** to smooth and brighten, as by rubbing **2** to refine (manners, style, etc.) —*vi.* to take a polish —*n.* **1** a surface gloss **2** elegance, refinement, etc. **3** a substance used to polish —**polish off** [Inf.] to finish (a meal, job, etc.) completely

**Pol·ish** (pōl'ish) *adj.* of Poland or its people, language, etc. —*n.* the Slavic language of Poland

**po·lite** (pə līt') *adj.* ⟦< L *polire*, to polish⟧ **1** cultured; refined **2** courteous; mannerly —**po·lite'ly** *adv.* —**po·lite'ness** *n.*

**pol·i·tesse** (päl'i tes') *n.* ⟦Fr⟧ politeness

**pol·i·tic** (päl'ə tik') *adj.* ⟦see POLICE⟧ **1** having practical wisdom; prudent **2** expedient: said as of a plan —*vi.* **-ticked', -tick'ing** to campaign in politics

**po·lit·i·cal** (pə lit'i kəl) *adj.* **1** of, concerned with, or engaged in government, politics, etc. **2** of or characteristic of political parties or politicians —**po·lit'i·cal·ly** *adv.*

**politically correct** holding orthodox liberal political views: usually used disparagingly to connote dogmatism, etc. —**political correctness**

**political science** the science of the principles, organization, and methods of government —**political scientist**

**pol·i·ti·cian** (päl'ə tish'ən) *n.* one actively engaged in politics: often used with implications of seeking personal or partisan gain, scheming, etc.

**po·lit·i·cize** (pə lit'ə sīz') *vt.* **-cized', -ciz'ing** to make political in tone, character, etc.

**po·lit·i·co** (pə lit'ə kō') *n.*, *pl.* **-cos'** ⟦< Sp or It⟧ POLITICIAN

**pol·i·tics** (päl'ə tiks) *pl.n.* [*with sing. or pl. v.*] **1** the science and art of government **2** political affairs **3** political methods, tactics, etc. **4** political opinions, etc. **5** factional scheming for power

**pol'i·ty** (-ə tē) *n.*, *pl.* **-ties** ⟦see POLICE⟧ **1** governmental organization **2** a society with a government; state

**Polk** (pōk), **James K.** 1795-1849; 11th president of the U.S. (1845-49)

**pol·ka** (pōl'kə) *n.* ⟦Czech, Polish dance⟧ **1** a fast dance for couples **2** music for this

**pol·ka dot** (pō'kə, pōl'kə) any of a regular pattern of small, round dots on cloth

**poll** (pōl) *n.* ⟦ME *pol*⟧ **1** the head **2** a counting, listing, etc. of persons, esp. of voters **3** the number of votes recorded **4** [*pl.*] a place where votes are cast **5** a canvassing of people's opinions on some question —*vt.* **1** to register the votes of **2** to require each member of (a jury, etc.) to declare individual votes **3** to receive (a specified number of votes) **4** to cast (a vote) **5** to canvass in a POLL (sense 5)

**pol·len** (päl′ən) *n.* ⟦L, dust⟧ the fine, dustlike mass of grains in the anthers of seed plants

**pollen count** the number of grains of pollen, esp. of ragweed, in a given volume of air at a specified time and place

**pol·li·nate** (päl′ə nāt′) *vt.* **-nat′ed, -nat′ing** to transfer pollen to the pistil of (a flower) —**pol′li·na′tion** *n.* —**pol′li·na′tor** *n.*

**pol·li·wog** (päl′ē wäg′, -wôg′) *n.* ⟦< ME: see POLL + WIGGLE⟧ TADPOLE: also **pol′ly·wog′**

**poll·ster** (pōl′stər) *n.* one whose work is taking public-opinion polls

**pol·lute** (pə lōōt′) *vt.* **-lut′ed, -lut′ing** ⟦< L *polluere*⟧ to make unclean or impure —**pol·lu′tant** *n.* —**pol·lu′tion** *n.*

**Pol·ly·an·na** (päl′ē an′ə) *n.* ⟦after the young heroine of a novel (1913) by E. H. Porter⟧ an excessively optimistic person

**po·lo** (pō′lō) *n.* ⟦ult. < Tibetan *pulu*, ball⟧ a game played on horseback by two teams, using a wooden ball and long-handled mallets

**Po·lo** (pō′lō), **Mar·co** (mär′kō) 1254-1324; Venetian traveler in E Asia

**pol·o·naise** (päl′ə nāz′) *n.* ⟦Fr (fem.), Polish⟧ a stately Polish dance

**pol·ter·geist** (pōl′tər gīst′) *n.* ⟦Ger < *poltern*, to rumble + *geist*, ghost⟧ a ghost supposed to be responsible for mysterious noisy disturbances

**pol·troon** (päl trōōn′) *n.* ⟦< It *poltrone*⟧ a thorough coward

**poly-** ⟦< Gr⟧ *combining form* much, many

**pol·y·clin·ic** (päl′i klin′ik) *n.* ⟦POLY- + CLINIC⟧ a clinic or hospital for the treatment of various kinds of diseases

**pol·y·es·ter** (päl′ē es′tər) *n.* ⟦POLY(MER) + ESTER⟧ a polymeric resin used in making plastics, fibers, etc.

**pol·y·eth·yl·ene** (päl′ē eth′ə lēn′) *n.* ⟦POLY(MER) + ETHYLENE⟧ a thermoplastic resin used in making plastics, films, etc.

**po·lyg·a·my** (pə lig′ə mē) *n.* ⟦< Gr *poly-*, many + *gamos*, marriage⟧ the practice of having two or more spouses at the same time —**po·lyg′a·mist** *n.* —**po·lyg′a·mous** *adj.*

**pol·y·glot** (päl′i glät′) *adj.* ⟦< Gr *poly-*, many + *glōtta*, tongue⟧ **1** knowing several languages **2** written in several languages —*n.* a polyglot person

**pol′y·gon′** (-gän′) *n.* ⟦< Gr: see POLY- & -GON⟧ a closed plane figure consisting of straight lines —**po·lyg·o·nal** (pə lig′ə nəl) *adj.*

**pol′y·graph′** (-graf′) *n.* ⟦see POLY- & -GRAPH⟧ a device measuring changes in respiration, pulse rate, etc.: see LIE DETECTOR

**pol′y·he′dron** (-hē′drən) *n.* ⟦< Gr: see POLY- & -HEDRON⟧ a solid figure with usually more than six plane surfaces

**pol′y·math′** (-ə math′) *n.* ⟦< Gr *poly-*, much + *manthanein*, learn⟧ a person of great and varied learning

**pol′y·mer** (-mər) *n.* ⟦Ger < Gr *poly-*, many + *meros*, part⟧ a substance consisting of giant molecules formed from polymerization —**pol′y·mer′ic** (-mer′ik) *adj.*

**po·lym·er·i·za·tion** (pō lim′ər ə zā′shən) *n.* a chaining together of many simple molecules to form a more complex molecule with different properties —**po·lym′er·ize′** (-īz′), **-ized′, -iz′ing,** *vt.,* *vi.*

**Pol·y·ne·sia** (päl′i nē′zhə) group of Pacific islands, east of Micronesia, including Hawaii, etc. —**Pol′y·ne′sian** *adj., n.*

**pol·y·no·mi·al** (päl′i nō′mē əl) *n.* ⟦POLY- + (BI)NOMIAL⟧ a mathematical expression containing three or more terms (Ex: $x^3 + 3x + 2$)

**pol·yp** (päl′ip) *n.* ⟦< Gr *poly-*, many + *pous*, foot⟧ **1** a cnidarian with many small tentacles at the

top of a tubelike body **2** a growth of mucous membrane in the bladder, rectum, etc.

**po·lyph·o·ny** (pə lif′ə nē) *n.* ⟦< Gr *poly-*, many + *phōnē*, a sound⟧ *Music* a combining of independent, harmonizing melodies, as in a fugue; counterpoint —**pol·y·phon·ic** (päl′i fän′ik) *adj.* —**pol′y·phon′i·cal·ly** *adv.*

**pol·y·rhythm** (päl′i rith′əm) *n.* *Music* **1** the simultaneous use of strongly contrasting rhythms **2** such a rhythm: *usually used in pl.* —**pol′y·rhyth′mic** *adj.*

**pol′y·sty′rene** (-stī′rēn′) *n.* ⟦POLY(MER) + *styrene*, an organic compound⟧ a clear polymer used to make containers, etc.

**pol·y·syl·lab·ic** (päl′i si lab′ik) *adj.* **1** having four or more syllables **2** characterized by polysyllabic words —**pol′y·syl′la·ble** (-sil′ə bəl) *n.*

**pol′y·tech′nic** (-tek′nik) *n., adj.* ⟦< Gr *poly-*, many + *technē*, art⟧ (school) providing instruction in many scientific and technical subjects

**pol′y·the·ism′** (-thē iz′əm) *n.* ⟦< Gr *poly*, many + *theos*, god⟧ belief in more than one god —**pol′y·the·ist** *adj., n.* —**pol′y·the·is′tic** *adj.*

**pol·y·un·sat·u·rat·ed** (päl′ē un sach′ə rāt′id) *adj.* designating any of certain vegetable and animal fats and oils with a low cholesterol content

**pol′y·u·re·thane′** (-yoor′ə thän′) *n.* ⟦POLY- + URE-THANE⟧ any of various synthetic polymers, used in cushions, coatings, etc.

**pol·y·vi·nyl** (päl′i vī′nəl) *adj.* designating or of any of a group of polymerized vinyl compounds

**po·made** (päm ād′, pō-) *n.* ⟦< It *pomo*, apple (orig. an ingredient)⟧ a perfumed ointment, as for the hair

**pome·gran·ate** (päm′gran′it, päm′ə-) *n.* ⟦ult. < L *pomum*, fruit + *granum*, seed⟧ **1** a round, red fruit with a hard rind and many seeds **2** the bush or tree it grows on

**pom·mel** (päm′əl; *for v.* pum′əl) *n.* ⟦< L *pomum*, fruit⟧ **1** the knob on the end of the hilt of some swords and daggers **2** the rounded, upward-projecting part at the front of a saddle —*vt.* **-meled** or **-melled, -mel·ing** or **-mel·ling** PUMMEL

**pomp** (pämp) *n.* ⟦< Gr *pompē*, solemn procession⟧ **1** stately display **2** ostentatious show or display

**pom·pa·dour** (päm′pə dôr′) *n.* ⟦after Mme. *Pompadour*, mistress of Louis XV⟧ a hairdo in which the hair is brushed up high from the forehead

**pom·pa·no** (päm′pə nō′) *n., pl.* **-no** or **-nos′** ⟦< Sp⟧ a food fish of North America and the West Indies

**pom·pom** (päm′päm′) *n.* ⟦see POMP⟧ an ornamental tuft of silk, etc., used on clothing, etc. or waved as by a cheerleader: also **pom′pon′** (-pän′)

**pom·pous** (päm′pəs) *adj.* pretentious; self-important —**pom·pos′i·ty** (-päs′ə tē) *n.*

**pon·cho** (pän′chō) *n., pl.* **-chos** ⟦AmSp < AmInd, woolen cloth⟧ a cloak like a blanket with a hole in the middle for the head, esp. a waterproof one worn as a raincoat

**pond** (pänd) *n.* ⟦< ME *pounde*, enclosure⟧ a body of water smaller than a lake

**pon·der** (pän′dər) *vt., vi.* ⟦< L *ponderare*, weigh⟧ to think deeply (about); consider carefully

**pon·der·o·sa** (**pine**) (pän′dər ō′sə) ⟦< L *ponderosus*, very heavy⟧ a yellow pine of W North America

**pon′der·ous** *adj.* **1** very heavy **2** unwieldy **3** labored and dull

**pone** (pōn) *n.* ⟦< AmInd⟧ [Chiefly South] corn bread in the form of small ovals

**pon·gee** (pän jē′, pun-) *n.* ⟦< Mandarin Chin dial. *pen-chi*, one's own loom⟧ a soft, thin silk cloth, usually left in its natural light-brown color

**pon·iard** (pän′yərd) *n.* ⟦ult. < L *pugnus*, fist⟧ a dagger

**pon·tiff** (pänt′if) *n.* ⟦< L *pontifex*, high priest⟧ **1** a bishop **2** [P-] the pope

**pon·tif·i·cal** (pän tif′i kəl) *adj.* ⟦see prec.⟧ **1** having to do with a bishop, the pope, etc. **2** pompous, dogmatic, etc.

**pon·tif′i·cate** (-i kit; *for v.,* -kāt′) *n.* the office or

term of a pontiff —*vi.* **-cat′ed, -cat′ing 1** to offici-
ate as a pontiff **2** to be pompous or dogmatic

**pon·toon** (pän tōōn′) *n.* ⟦< L *pons*, a bridge⟧ **1** a
flat-bottomed boat **2** any of a row of boats or
floating objects used to support a temporary
bridge **3** a float on an aircraft's landing gear

**po·ny** (pō′nē) *n., pl.* **-nies** ⟦prob. < L *pullus*, foal⟧
**1** a horse of any small breed **2** a small liqueur
glass **3** [Inf.] a literal translation of a foreign
work, used in doing schoolwork

**po′ny·tail′** *n.* a hair style in which the hair is tied
tightly at the back and hangs down

**pooch** (pōōch) *n.* ⟦< ?⟧ [Slang] a dog

**poo·dle** (pōōd′'l) *n.* ⟦Ger *pudel*⟧ a dog with a
thick, wiry coat of tight curls in a solid color

**pooh** (pōō) *interj.* used to express disdain, disbelief, or impatience

**pooh-pooh** (pōō′pōō′) *vt.* to treat disdainfully;
make light of

**pool**[1] (pōōl) *n.* ⟦OE *pol*⟧ **1** a small pond **2** a small
collection of liquid, as a puddle **3** a tank for
swimming

**pool**[2] (pōōl) *n.* ⟦< LL *pulla*, hen⟧ **1** a game related
to billiards, played on a table with six pockets **2** a
combination of resources, funds, supplies, etc. for
some common purpose **3** the parties forming
such a combination —*vt., vi.* to contribute to a
common fund

**poop**[1] (pōōp) *n.* ⟦< L *puppis*, stern of a ship⟧ a
raised deck at the stern of a sailing ship: also
**poop deck**

**poop**[2] (pōōp) *vt.* [Slang] to tire

**poop**[3] (pōōp) *n.* [Slang] current inside information

**poor** (poor) *adj.* ⟦< L *pauper*, poor⟧ **1** having little
or no means to support oneself; needy **2** lacking
in some quality; specif., *a)* inadequate *b)* inferior
or worthless *c)* contemptible **3** worthy of pity;
unfortunate —**the poor** poor, or needy, people —
**poor′ly** *adv.*

**poor′house′** *n.* [Historical] a publicly supported
institution for paupers

**poor′-mouth′** *vi.* [Inf.] to complain about one's
lack of money

**pop**[1] (päp) *n.* ⟦echoic⟧ **1** a sudden, light explosive
sound **2** any carbonated, nonalcoholic beverage
—*vi.* **popped, pop′ping 1** to make, or burst with,
a pop **2** to move, go, etc. suddenly **3** to open wide
or bulge: said of the eyes **4** *Baseball* to hit the
ball high into the infield —*vt.* **1** to cause to pop,
as corn by heating it **2** to put suddenly [to *pop*
one's head in] **3** [Slang] to swallow (a pill, etc.) —
**pop′per** *n.*

**pop**[2] (päp) *n.* ⟦< PAPA⟧ [Inf.] FATHER

**pop**[3] (päp) *adj.* **1** of music popular with the general public **2** intended for the popular taste, esp.
as exploited commercially [*pop* culture] **3** of a
realistic art style using techniques and subjects
adapted from commercial art, comic strips, posters, etc. —*n.* pop music, etc.

**pop** *abbrev.* **1** popular **2** popularly **3** population

**pop′corn′** *n.* **1** a variety of corn with hard grains
that pop open into a white, puffy mass when
heated **2** the popped grains

**pope** (pōp) *n.* ⟦< Gr *pappas*, father⟧ [*often* **P-**]
R.C.Ch. the bishop of Rome and head of the
Church

**Pope** (pōp), **Alexander** 1688-1744; Eng. poet

**pop′gun′** *n.* a toy gun that shoots a piece of cork,
etc. by air compression, with a pop

**pop·in·jay** (päp′in jā′) *n.* ⟦< Ar *babghā′*, a parrot⟧
a conceited person

**pop·lar** (päp′lər) *n.* ⟦< L *populus*⟧ **1** a tall tree of
the willow family having soft wood **2** its wood

**pop·lin** (päp′lin) *n.* ⟦prob. after *Poperinge*, city in
Flanders⟧ a sturdy ribbed fabric of cotton, silk,
etc.

**pop′o′ver** *n.* a very light, puffy, hollow muffin

**pop·py** (päp′ē) *n., pl.* **-pies** ⟦< L *papaver*⟧ **1** a
plant with a milky juice and variously colored
flowers **2** its flower

**pop′py·cock′** (-käk′) *n.* [Inf.] foolish talk; nonsense

**poppy seed** the small, dark seed of the poppy,
used in baking, etc.

**pops** (päps) *adj.* of a symphony orchestra that
plays light classical music or arrangements of
popular music —*n.* a pops orchestra, concert, etc.

**Pop·si·cle** (päp′si kəl) ⟦blend of POP[1] + I(CICLE)⟧
*trademark for* a flavored ice frozen around a stick
—*n. [also* **p-**] such a confection

**pop-top** (päp′täp′) *n.* a container with a tab or
ring pulled or pushed to make an opening in the
top

**pop·u·lace** (päp′yə lis) *n.* ⟦< L *populus*⟧ **1** the
common people; the masses **2** POPULATION (sense
1*a*)

**pop·u·lar** (päp′yə lər) *adj.* ⟦< L *populus*, the peo-
ple⟧ **1** of, carried on by, or intended for people
generally **2** not expensive [*popular* prices] **3**
commonly accepted; prevalent **4** liked by many
people —**pop′u·lar′i·ty** (-lar′ə tē) *n.* —**pop′u·lar·ly**
*adv.*

**pop·u·lar·ize** (päp′yə lə rīz′) *vt.* **-ized′, -iz′ing** to
make popular —**pop′u·lar·i·za′tion** *n.*

**pop·u·late** (päp′yə lāt′) *vt.* **-lat′ed, -lat′ing** ⟦< L
*populus*, the people⟧ **1** to inhabit **2** to supply
with inhabitants

**pop·u·la′tion** *n.* **1** *a)* all the people in a country,
region, etc. *b)* the number of these **2** a populat-
ing or being populated

**population explosion** the great and rapid
increase in human population in modern times

**pop·u·list** (päp′yə list) *n.* a politician, etc. who
claims to represent the common people: often
used to suggest demagogy —*adj.* of a populist —
**pop′u·lism′** *n.*

**pop·u·lous** (-ləs) *adj.* full of people; thickly populated

**por·ce·lain** (pôr′sə lin) *n.* ⟦< It *porcellana*⟧ a hard,
white, translucent variety of ceramic ware

**porch** (pôrch) *n.* ⟦< L *porta*, gate⟧ **1** a covered
entrance to a building **2** an open or enclosed gallery or room on the outside of a building

**por·cine** (pôr′sīn′, -sin) *adj.* ⟦< L *porcus*, hog⟧ of or
like pigs or hogs

**por·cu·pine** (pôr′kyə pīn′) *n.* ⟦< L *porcus*, pig +
*spina*, spine⟧ a rodent having coarse hair mixed
with long, stiff, sharp spines

**pore**[1] (pôr) *vi.* **pored, por′ing** ⟦ME *poren*⟧ **1** to
study carefully: with *over* **2** to ponder: with *over*

**pore**[2] (pôr) *n.* ⟦< Gr *poros*, passage⟧ a tiny opening, as in skin or plant leaves, for absorbing or
discharging fluids

**pork** (pôrk) *n.* ⟦< L *porcus*, pig⟧ the flesh of a pig,
used as food

**pork barrel** [Inf.] government appropriations for
political patronage

**pork′y** *adj.* **-i·er, -i·est 1** of or like pork **2** fat **3**
[Slang] saucy, cocky, etc.

**porn** (pôrn) *n., adj.* [Slang] *short for* PORNOGRA-
PHY, PORNOGRAPHIC: also **por·no** (pôr′nō)

**por·nog·ra·phy** (pôr näg′rə fē) *n.* ⟦< Gr *pornē*, a
prostitute + *graphein*, write⟧ writings, pictures,
etc. intended to arouse sexual desire —**por·
nog′ra·pher** *n.* —**por′no·graph′ic** (-nə graf′ik) *adj.*

**po·rous** (pôr′əs) *adj.* full of pores, through which
fluids, air, or light may pass —**po·ros·i·ty** (pō räs′
ə tē) *n.*

**por·phy·ry** (pôr′fə rē) *n., pl.* **-ries** ⟦< Gr *porphyros*,
purple⟧ any igneous rock with large, distinct crystals

**por·poise** (pôr′pəs) *n.* ⟦< L *porcus*, pig + *piscis*, a
fish⟧ **1** a small whale with a blunt snout **2** a
dolphin

**por·ridge** (pôr′ij) *n.* ⟦< POTTAGE by confusion with
VL *porrata*, leek broth⟧ [Chiefly Brit.] a soft food
of cereal or meal boiled in water or milk

**por·rin·ger** (-in jər) *n.* ⟦< Fr *potager*, soup dish:
infl. by prec.⟧ a small, shallow bowl

**port**[1] (pôrt) *n.* 〖< L *portus*, haven〗 1 a harbor 2 a city with a harbor where ships load and unload cargo

**port**[2] (pôrt) *n.* 〖after *Oporto*, city in Portugal〗 a sweet, dark-red wine

**port**[3] (pôrt) *vt.* 〖< L *portare*, carry〗 to hold (a rifle, etc.) diagonally in front of one, as for inspection

**port**[4] (pôrt) *n.* 〖< PORT[1]〗 the left side of a ship, etc. as one faces forward —*adj.* of or on this side

**port**[5] (pôrt) *n.* 〖< L *porta*, door〗 1 PORTHOLE 2 an opening, as in a valve face, for the passage of steam, etc. 3 *Comput.* the circuit, outlet, etc. which connects a computer and its peripheral

**Port** *abbrev.* 1 Portugal 2 Portuguese

**port·a·ble** (pôr′tə bəl) *adj.* 〖< L *portare*, carry〗 1 that can be carried 2 easily carried —*n.* something portable —**port′a·bil′i·ty** *n.*

**por·tage** (pôr′tij, pôr täzh′) *n.* 〖< L *portare*, carry〗 1 a carrying of boats and supplies overland between navigable lakes, rivers, etc. 2 any route over which this is done —*vt., vi.* **-taged, -tag·ing** to carry (boats, etc.) over a portage

**por·tal** (pôrt′'l) *n.* 〖< L *porta*, door〗 a doorway, gate, or entrance

**port·cul·lis** (pôrt kul′is) *n.* 〖< MFr *porte*, gate + *coleïce*, sliding〗 a heavy iron grating lowered to bar the gateway of a castle or fortified town

**por·tend** (pôr tend′) *vt.* 〖< L *por-*, forth + *tendere*, to stretch〗 1 to be an omen of; presage 2 to signify

**por·tent** (pôr′tent) *n.* 1 something that portends an event 2 significance

**por·ten·tous** (pôr ten′təs) *adj.* 1 portending evil; ominous 2 amazing 3 pompous; self-important —**por·ten′tous·ly** *adv.*

**por·ter**[1] (pôr′tər) *n.* 〖< L *porta*, gate〗 a doorman or gatekeeper

**por·ter**[2] (pôr′tər) *n.* 〖< L *portare*, carry〗 1 one who carries luggage, etc. for hire 2 an employee who sweeps, cleans, etc. in a bank, store, etc. 3 a railroad attendant for passengers as on a sleeper 4 a dark-brown beer

**por·ter·house′** *n.* 〖orig. a tavern: see PORTER[2], sense 4〗 a choice cut of beef next to the sirloin: in full **porterhouse steak**

**port·fo·li·o** (pôrt fō′lē ō′) *n., pl.* **-li·os′** 〖< L *portare*, carry + *folium*, leaf〗 1 a flat, portable case, for loose papers; briefcase 2 the office of a minister of state 3 a list of an investor's securities 4 a selection from an artist's, etc. work

**port·hole** (pôrt′hōl′) *n.* an opening in a ship's side to admit light and air

**por·ti·co** (pôr′ti kō′) *n., pl.* **-coes′** or **-cos′** 〖< L *porticus*, porch〗 a porch or covered walk, consisting of a roof supported by columns

PEDIMENT

PORTICO

**por·tiere** or **por·tière** (pôr tyer′) *n.* 〖Fr < *porte*, door〗 a curtain hung in a doorway

**por·tion** (-shən) *n.* 〖< L *portio*〗 1 a part, esp. that allotted to a person; share 2 one's fate 3 a helping of food —*vt.* to give out in portions

**Port·land** (pôrt′lənd) city & port in NW Oregon: pop. 439,000

**port·ly** (pôrt′lē) *adj.* **-li·er, -li·est** 1 large and stately 2 stout; corpulent —**port′li·ness** *n.*

**port·man·teau** (pôrt man′tō) *n., pl.* **-teaus** or **-teaux** (-tōz) 〖< Fr *porter*, carry + *manteau*, cloak〗 a stiff suitcase that opens into two compartments

**portmanteau word** a word that is a combination of two other words (Ex.: *smog*, from *smoke* and *fog*)

**por·to·bel·lo mushroom** (pôr′tə bel′ō) a dark,

flavorful mushroom with a broad cap: also **porto·bello** *n., pl.* **-los**

**port of entry** a place where customs officials check people and goods entering a country

**Por·to Ri·co** (pôr′tə rē′kō) *former var. of* PUERTO RICO —**Por′to Ri′can**

**por·trait** (pôr′trit, -trāt′) *n.* 〖see PORTRAY〗 1 a painting, photograph, etc. of a person, esp. of the face 2 a description, portrayal, etc.

**por·trai·ture** (-tri chər) *n.* the practice or art of portraying

**por·tray** (pôr trā′) *vt.* 〖< L *pro-*, forth + *trahere*, draw〗 1 to make a portrait of 2 to describe graphically 3 to play the part of as in a play or movie —**por·tray′al** *n.*

**Por·tu·gal** (pôr′chə gəl) country in SW Europe, on the Atlantic: 35,456 sq. mi.; pop. 9,863,000

**Por·tu·guese** (pôr′chə gēz′, -gēs′) *adj.* of Portugal or its people, language, etc. —*n.* 1 *pl.* **-guese′** a person born or living in Portugal 2 a Romance language of Portugal and Brazil

**por·tu·lac·a** (pôr′chə lak′ə) *n.* 〖< L *portula*, small door: from the opening in its seed capsule〗 a fleshy plant with yellow, pink, or purple flowers

**pose** (pōz) *vt.* **posed, pos′ing** 〖< L *pausare*, to stop〗 1 to propose (a question, etc.) 2 to put (a model, etc.) in a certain attitude —*vi.* 1 to assume a certain attitude, as in modeling for an artist 2 to strike attitudes for effect 3 set oneself up (*as*) [to *pose* as an officer] —*n.* 1 a bodily attitude, esp. one held for an artist, etc. 2 a way of behaving assumed for effect

**Po·sei·don** (pō sī′dən) *n.* the Greek god of the sea

**pos·er** (pō′zər) *n.* one who poses; esp., a poseur

**po·seur** (pō zur′) *n.* 〖Fr〗 one who assumes attitudes or manners merely for effect

**posh** (päsh) *adj.* 〖< ?〗 [Inf.] luxurious and fashionable

**pos·it** (päz′it) *vt.* 〖see fol.〗 to suppose to be a fact; postulate

**po·si·tion** (pə zish′ən) *n.* 〖< L *ponere*, to place〗 1 the way in which a person or thing is placed or arranged 2 one's attitude or opinion 3 the place where one is; location 4 the usual or proper place 5 rank, esp. high rank 6 a post of employment; job —*vt.* to put into a certain position

**pos·i·tive** (päz′ə tiv) *adj.* 〖see prec.〗 1 definitely set; explicit [*positive* instructions] 2 *a*) having the mind set; confident *b*) overconfident or dogmatic 3 showing agreement; affirmative 4 constructive [*positive* criticism] 5 regarded as having real existence [a *positive* good] 6 based on facts [*positive* proof] 7 *Elec. a*) of the kind of electricity predominating in a glass body after it has been rubbed with silk *b*) charged with positive electricity *c*) having a deficiency of electrons 8 *Gram.* of an adjective or adverb in its uncompared degree 9 *Math.* greater than zero 10 *Med.* showing the presence of a condition, infection, etc. 11 *Photog.* with the light and shade corresponding to those of the subject —*n.* 1 something positive, as a degree, quality, quantity, photographic print, etc. 2 the plate in a battery having an excess of electrons flowing out toward the negative —**pos′i·tive·ly** *adv.*

**pos′i·tron′** (-trän′) *n.* 〖POSI(TIVE) + (ELEC)TRON〗 the positive antiparticle of an electron, having the same mass and magnitude of charge

**poss** *abbrev.* 1 possessive 2 possibly

**pos·se** (päs′ē) *n.* 〖< L, be able〗 [Historical] a band of men, usually armed, summoned to assist the sheriff in keeping the peace, etc.

**pos·sess** (pə zes′) *vt.* 〖< L *possidere*〗 1 to have as belonging to one; own 2 to have as an attribute, quality, etc. 3 to gain control over [*possessed* by an idea] —**pos·ses′sor** *n.*

**pos·sessed′** *adj.* 1 owned 2 controlled, as if by a demon; crazed

**pos·ses·sion** (-zesh′ən) *n.* 1 a possessing or being possessed 2 anything possessed 3 [*pl.*] property 4 territory ruled by an outside country

**pos·ses·sive** (-zes′iv) *adj.* 1 of possession 2

showing or desiring possession, domination, control, influence, etc. **3** *Gram.* designating or of a case, form, or construction expressing possession (Ex: *my, Bill's*) —*n. Gram.* **1** the possessive case **2** a word or phrase in this case —**pos·ses'sive·ness** *n.*

**pos·si·ble** (päs'ə bəl) *adj.* [< L *posse*, be able] **1** that can be or exist **2** that may or may not happen **3** that can be done, selected, etc. **4** permissible —**pos'si·bil'i·ty** (-bil'ə tē), *pl.* **-ties,** *n.*

**pos'si·bly** (-blē) *adv.* **1** by any possible means **2** perhaps; maybe

**pos·sum** (päs'əm) *n.* [Inf.] OPOSSUM —**play possum** to pretend to be asleep, dead, ill, etc.

**post¹** (pōst) *n.* [< L *postis*] **1** a piece of wood, metal, etc. set upright to support a building, sign, etc. **2** the starting point of a horse race —*vt.* **1** to put up (a poster, etc.) on (a wall, etc.) **2** to announce by posting notices [to *post* a reward] **3** to warn against trespassing on by posted notices **4** to put (a name) on a posted or published list

**post²** (pōst) *n.* [< Fr < It *posto*] **1** the place where a soldier, guard, etc. is stationed **2** a place where troops are garrisoned **3** the place assigned to one **4** a job or duty —*vt.* **1** to assign to a post **2** to put up (a bond, etc.)

**post³** (pōst) *n.* [< Fr < It *posta*] [Chiefly Brit.] (the) mail —*vi.* to travel fast; hasten —*vt.* **1** [Chiefly Brit.] to mail **2** to inform [keep me *posted*]

**post-** [L < *post*, after] *prefix* **1** after in time, later (than) [*postnatal*] **2** after in space, behind

**post·age** (pōs'tij) *n.* the amount charged for mailing a letter, etc., esp. as represented by stamps

**post·al** (pōs'təl) *adj.* [Fr] of mail or post offices

**post-bel·lum** (pōst bel'əm) *adj.* [L] after the war; specif., after the American Civil War

**post'card'** *n.* a card, usually with a picture on one side, for sending short messages by mail

**post'date'** *vt.* **-dat'ed, -dat'ing 1** to assign a later date to than the actual date **2** to be subsequent to

**post·er** (pōs'tər) *n.* a large advertisement or notice posted publicly

**pos·te·ri·or** (päs tir'ē ər) *adj.* [L < *post*, after] **1** later; following **2** at the rear; behind —*n.* the buttocks

**pos·ter·i·ty** (päs ter'ə tē) *n.* [see prec.] **1** all of a person's descendants **2** all succeeding generations

**post'grad'u·ate** *adj.* of or taking a course of study after graduation, esp. after receipt of the bachelor's degree

**post'haste'** *adv.* with great haste

**post'hole'** *n.* a hole dug to hold the end of an upright post

**post·hu·mous** (päs'chŏo məs, -tyŏo-) *adj.* [< L *postumus,* last] **1** published after the author's death **2** arising or continuing after one's death —**post'hu·mous·ly** *adv.*

**post'hyp·not'ic** *adj.* in the time after a hypnotic trance [*posthypnotic* suggestion]

**pos·til·ion** or **pos·til·lion** (pōs til'yən, päs-) *n.* [Fr < It *posta,* a post] one who rides the leading left-hand horse of a team drawing a carriage

**post'in·dus'tri·al** *adj.* of a society in which the economy has shifted from heavy industry to service industries, technology, etc.

**Post'-it'** *trademark for* small sheets of adhesive-backed paper for attaching notes —*n.* a sheet of this

**post·lude** (pōst'lŏod') *n.* [POST- + (PRE)LUDE] a concluding musical piece

**post'man** (-mən) *n. pl.* **-men** (-mən) MAIL CARRIER

**post'mark'** *n.* a post-office mark stamped on mail, canceling the postage stamp and recording the date and place —*vt.* to stamp with a postmark

**post'mas'ter** *n.* the manager of a post office

**postmaster general** *pl.* **postmasters general** the head of a government's postal system

**post'me·rid'i·an** (-mə rid'ē ən) *adj.* [L] after noon

**post me·ri·di·em** (mə rid'ē əm) [L] after noon: abbrev. *P.M., p.m., PM,* or *pm*

**post'mod'ern·ism'** *n.* an eclectic cultural and artistic trend in art, etc. of the late 20th c. —**post'mod'ern** *adj.* —**post'mod'ern·ist** *adj., n.*

**post-mor·tem** (pōst'môr'təm) *adj.* [L] **1** after death **2** of a post-mortem —*n.* **1** AUTOPSY **2** an evaluation of some event just ended

**post'na·sal drip** (pōst'nā'zəl) a discharge of mucus from behind the nose onto the pharynx, due to a cold, allergy, etc.

**post'na'tal** (-nāt''l) *adj.* after birth

**post office 1** the governmental department in charge of the mail **2** a place where mail is sorted, postage stamps are sold, etc.

**post'op'er·a·tive** (-äp'ər ə tiv) *adj.* occurring after a surgical operation

**post'paid'** *adj.* with postage prepaid

**post'par'tum** (-pär'təm) *adj.* [L < *post-,* after + *parere,* to bear] of the time after childbirth

**post·pone** (pōst pōn') *vt.* **-poned', -pon'ing** [< L *post-,* after + *ponere,* put] to put off until later; delay —**post·pone'ment** *n.*

**post'script'** *n.* [< L *post-,* after + *scribere,* write] a note added below the signature in a letter

**post time** the scheduled starting time of a horse race

**pos·tu·late** (päs'chə lāt'; *for n.,* -lit) *vt.* **-lat'ed, -lat'ing** [< L *postulare,* to demand] to assume to be true, real, etc., esp. as a basis for argument —*n.* something postulated

**pos·ture** (päs'chər) *n.* [MFr < L *ponere,* to place] **1** the position or carriage of the body **2** a position assumed as in posing **3** an official stand or position [our national *posture*] —*vi.* to pose or assume an attitude merely for effect

**post'war'** *adj.* after the (or a) war

**po·sy** (pō'zē) *n., pl.* **-sies** [< POESY] [Old-fashioned] a flower or bouquet

**pot¹** (pät) *n.* [OE *pott*] **1** a round vessel for holding liquids, for cooking, etc. **2** a pot with its contents **3** [Inf.] all the money bet at a single time —*vt.* **pot'ted, pot'ting** to put into a pot —**go to pot** to go to ruin —**pot'ful',** *pl.* **-fuls',** *n.*

**pot²** (pät) *n.* [< AmSp *potiguaya*] [Slang] MARIJUANA

**po·ta·ble** (pōt'ə bəl) *adj.* [< L *potare,* to drink] drinkable —**po'ta·bil'i·ty** *n.*

**pot'ash'** *n.* [< Du *pot,* POT¹ + *asch,* ASH¹] any of various potassium compounds used in fertilizers, soaps, etc.

**po·tas·si·um** (pə tas'ē əm) *n.* [see prec.] a soft, silver-white, metallic chemical element

**po·ta·to** (pə tāt'ō) *n., pl.* **-toes** [< WInd] **1** the starchy tuber of a widely cultivated plant, eaten as a cooked vegetable **2** this plant

**potato chip** a very thin slice of potato fried crisp and then salted

**pot'bel'lied** *adj.* **1** having a potbelly **2** having bulging sides [a *potbellied* stove]

**pot'bel'ly** *n., pl.* **-lies** a protruding belly

**pot'boil'er** *n.* a piece of writing, etc., done quickly and for money only

**pot'-bound'** *adj.* having outgrown its container: said of a potted plant

**po·tent** (pōt'nt) *adj.* [< L *posse,* be able] **1** having authority or power **2** convincing; cogent **3** effective, as a drug **4** able to have sexual intercourse: said of a male —**po'ten·cy** *n.*

**po·ten·tate** (pōt'n tāt') *n.* a person having great power; ruler; monarch

**po·ten·tial** (pō ten'shəl) *adj.* [see POTENT] that can come into being; possible; latent —*n.* **1** something potential **2** the difference in voltage between two points in an electric circuit or field —**po·ten'ti·al'i·ty** (-shē al'ə tē), *pl.* **-ties,** *n.* —**po·ten'tial·ly** *adv.*

**pot'herb'** *n.* any herb whose leaves and stems are boiled and eaten or used as a flavoring

**pot'hold'er** *n.* a small pad, or piece of thick cloth, for handling hot pots, etc.

**pot'hole'** *n.* 1 a deep hole or pit 2 CHUCKHOLE

**pot'hook'** *n.* an S-shaped hook for hanging a pot over a fire

**po·tion** (pō'shən) *n.* ⟦< L *potare*, to drink⟧ a drink as of medicine, poison, or a supposedly magic substance

**pot'luck'** *n.* 1 whatever the family meal happens to be [to take *potluck*] 2 a dinner to which everyone brings a dish to share: in full **potluck dinner**

**Po·to·mac** (pə tō'mək) river in the E U.S., flowing into Chesapeake Bay

**pot'pie'** *n.* a meat pie made in a deep dish

**pot·pour·ri** (pō'poo rē', pät'poo rē') *n.* ⟦Fr < *pot*, a pot + *pourrir*, to rot⟧ 1 a mixture of dried flowers, spices, etc., kept for its fragrance 2 a medley or miscellany; mixture

**pot roast** a large cut of beef cooked in one piece by braising

**pot·sherd** (pät'shurd') *n.* ⟦see POT¹ & SHARD⟧ a piece of broken pottery

**pot'shot'** *n.* 1 an easy or random shot 2 a haphazard try 3 a random attack

**pot·tage** (pät'ij) *n.* ⟦< earlier Fr *pot*, a pot⟧ a kind of thick soup or stew

**pot'ter** *n.* one who makes earthenware pots, dishes, etc.

**potter's field** a burial ground for paupers or unknown persons

**potter's wheel** a rotating disk upon which clay is molded into bowls, etc.

**pot'ter·y** *n., pl.* **-ies** 1 a potter's workshop 2 the art of a potter; ceramics 3 pots, dishes, etc. made of clay hardened by heat

**pot·ty** (pät'ē) *n., pl.* **-ties** 1 a small pot used as a toilet for a child 2 a child's chair for toilet training with such a pot: in full **potty chair** 3 a toilet: a child's word

POTTER'S WHEEL

**pouch** (pouch) *n.* ⟦< earlier Fr *poche*⟧ 1 a small bag or sack [a tobacco *pouch*] 2 a mailbag 3 a saclike structure, as that on the abdomen of the kangaroo, etc. for carrying young —*vi.* to form a pouch

**poul·tice** (pōl'tis) *n.* ⟦< ML *pultes*, pap⟧ a hot, soft, moist mass applied to a sore part of the body —*vt.* **-ticed, -tic·ing** to apply a poultice to

**poul·try** (pōl'trē) *n.* ⟦< L *pullus*, chicken⟧ domestic fowls; chickens, ducks, etc.

**pounce** (pouns) *n.* ⟦ME *pownce*, talon⟧ a pouncing —*vi.* **pounced, pounc'ing** to swoop down or leap (*on, upon,* or *at*) in, or as in, seizing

**pound¹** (pound) *n., pl.* **pounds**; sometimes, after a number, **pound** ⟦< L *pondus*, weight⟧ 1 a unit of weight equal to 16 oz. avoirdupois or 12 oz. troy: abbrev. *lb.* 2 the monetary unit of the United Kingdom: symbol, £ 3 the monetary unit of various other countries, as Egypt and Syria

**pound²** (pound) *vt.* ⟦OE *punian*⟧ 1 to beat to a pulp, powder, etc. 2 to hit hard —*vi.* 1 to deliver repeated, heavy blows (*at* or *on*) 2 to move with heavy steps 3 to throb

**pound³** (pound) *n.* ⟦< OE *pund-*⟧ a municipal enclosure for stray animals [a dog *pound*]

**pound'cake'** *n.* a rich cake made (orig. with a pound each) of flour, butter, sugar, etc.

**pound sign** a symbol (#) on a button on a telephone keypad

**pour** (pôr) *vt.* ⟦ME *pouren*⟧ 1 to cause to flow in a continuous stream 2 to emit, utter, etc. profusely

or steadily —*vi.* 1 to flow freely, continuously, etc. 2 to rain heavily

**pout** (pout) *vi.* ⟦ME *pouten*⟧ 1 to thrust out the lips, as in sullenness 2 to sulk —*n.* the act of pouting —**pout'er** *n.*

**pov·er·ty** (päv'ər tē) *n.* ⟦< L *pauper*, poor⟧ 1 the condition or quality of being poor; need 2 deficiency; inadequacy 3 scarcity

**pov'er·ty-strick'en** *adj.* very poor

**POW** *n., pl.* **POW's** prisoner of war

**pow·der** (pou'dər) *n.* ⟦< L *pulvis*, dust⟧ 1 any dry substance in the form of fine, dustlike particles, produced by crushing, grinding, etc. 2 a specific kind of powder [bath *powder*] —*vt.* 1 to sprinkle, etc. with powder 2 to make into powder —**pow'der·y** *adj.*

**powder keg** 1 a keg for gunpowder 2 a potential source of violence, war, etc.

**powder room** a lavatory for women

**pow·er** (pou'ər) *n.* ⟦ult. < L *posse*, be able⟧ 1 ability to do or act 2 vigor; force; strength 3 *a*) authority; influence *b*) legal authority 4 physical force or energy [electric *power*] 5 a person or thing having great influence, force, or authority 6 a nation with influence over other nations 7 the product of the multiplication of a quantity by itself 8 the degree of magnification of a lens —*vt.* to supply with a source of power —*adj.* 1 operated by electricity, a fuel engine, etc. [*power* tools] 2 served by an auxiliary system that reduces effort [*power* steering] 3 carrying electricity

**pow'er·ful** *adj.* strong, mighty, influential, etc. —**pow'er·ful·ly** *adv.*

**pow'er·house'** *n.* 1 a building where electric power is generated 2 [Inf.] a powerful person, team, etc.

**pow·er·less** (pou'ər lis) *adj.* without power; weak, unable, etc. —**pow'er·less·ly** *adv.*

**power of attorney** written legal authority for one person to act for another

**pow'er·train'** *n.* DRIVETRAIN

**pow·wow** (pou'wou') *n.* ⟦< AmInd⟧ 1 a conference of or with North American Indians 2 [Inf.] any conference

**pox** (päks) *n.* ⟦for *pocks*: see POCK⟧ 1 a disease characterized by skin eruptions, as smallpox 2 syphilis: with *the*

**pp** *abbrev.* 1 pages 2 parcel post 3 past participle 4 postpaid 5 prepaid Also, for 4 & 5, **ppd**

**PP** *abbrev.* parcel post

**PPO** *n., pl.* **PPO's** ⟦*p(referred) p(rovider) o(rganization)*⟧ a healthcare system having certain hospitals, doctors, etc. under contract at a reduced cost

**ppr** *abbrev.* present participle

**P.P.S., p.p.s., PPS,** or **pps** *abbrev.* ⟦L *post postscriptum*⟧ an additional postscript

**pr** *abbrev.* 1 pair(s) 2 price

**Pr** *abbrev.* Provençal

**PR** or **P.R.** *abbrev.* 1 public relations 2 Puerto Rico

**prac·ti·ca·ble** (prak'ti kə bəl) *adj.* 1 that can be put into practice; feasible 2 that can be used; useful —**prac'ti·ca·bil'i·ty** *n.* —**prac'ti·ca·bly** *adv.*

**prac·ti·cal** (prak'ti kəl) *adj.* 1 of or obtained through practice or action 2 useful 3 concerned with the application of knowledge to useful ends [*practical* science] 4 dealing realistically and sensibly with everyday matters 5 that is so in practice, if not in theory, law, etc. —**prac'ti·cal'i·ty** (-kal'ə tē), *pl.* **-ties,** *n.*

**practical joke** a trick played on someone in fun —**practical joker**

**prac·ti·cal·ly** (prak'tik lē, -tik ə lē) *adv.* 1 in a practical manner 2 from a practical viewpoint 3 in effect; virtually 4 [Inf.] nearly

**practical nurse** a nurse with less training than a registered nurse, often one licensed by a U.S. state (**licensed practical nurse**) for specified duties

**prac·tice** (prak'tis) *vt.* **-ticed, -tic·ing** ⟦< Gr *prassein*, do⟧ 1 to do or engage in frequently; make a habit of 2 to do repeatedly so as to become proficient **3** to work at, esp. as a profession —*vi.* to do something repeatedly so as to become proficient; drill Chiefly Brit. sp. **prac′tise** —*n.* **1** a practicing; habit, custom, etc. **2** *a)* repeated action to acquire proficiency *b)* proficiency so acquired **3** the actual doing of something **4** *a)* the exercise of a profession *b)* a business based on this

**prac′ticed** *adj.* experienced; skilled

**prac·ti·cum** (prak′ti kəm) *n.* [see PRACTICE] a course involving activities emphasizing the practical application of theory, as on-the-job experience in a field of study

**prac·ti·tion·er** (prak tish′ə nər) *n.* one who practices a profession

**Prae·to·ri·an** (prē tôr′ē ən) *adj.* [< L *praetor,* magistrate] of or belonging to the bodyguard (**Praetorian Guard**) of a Roman emperor

**prag·mat·ic** (prag mat′ik) *adj.* [< Gr *pragma,* thing done] **1** practical **2** testing the validity of all concepts by their practical results —**prag·mat′i·cal·ly** *adv.* —**prag′ma·tism′** (-mə tiz′əm) *n.* —**prag′ma·tist** *n.*

**Prague** (präg) capital of the Czech Republic: pop. 1,217,000

**prai·rie** (prer′ē) *n.* [Fr < L *pratum,* meadow] a large area of level or rolling, grassy land

**prairie dog** a small, burrowing rodent of North America

**prairie schooner** a box-shaped covered wagon

**praise** (prāz) *vt.* **praised, prais′ing** [< L *pretium,* worth, price] **1** to express approval or admiration of **2** to glorify (God, etc.), as in song —*n.* a praising or being praised; commendation

**praise′wor′thy** *adj.* worthy of praise — **praise′wor′thi·ly** *adv.* —**praise′wor′thi·ness** *n.*

**pra·line** (prā′lēn′, prä′-) *n.* [Fr] any of various soft or crisp candies made of nuts, sugar, etc.

**prance** (prans) *vi.* **pranced, pranc′ing** [< ?] **1** to rise up, or move along, on the hind legs, as a horse does **2** to caper or strut —*n.* a prancing — **pranc′er** *n.* —**pranc′ing·ly** *adv.*

**prank** (praŋk) *n.* [< ?] a mischievous trick — **prank′ster** *n.*

**prate** (prāt) *vi., vt.* **prat′ed, prat′ing** [< MDu *praten*] to talk much and foolishly; chatter

**prat·tle** (prat′'l) *vi., vt.* **-tled, -tling** [LowG *pratelen*] to prate or babble —*n.* chatter or babble

**prawn** (prôn) *n.* [< ?] a large shrimp or other similar crustacean

**pray** (prā) *vt.* [< L *prex,* prayer] **1** to implore /(I) *pray* (you) tell me/ **2** to ask for by prayer —*vi.* to say prayers, as to God

**prayer**[1] (prer) *n.* **1** the act of praying **2** an entreaty; supplication **3** *a)* a humble request, as to God *b)* any set formula for this **4** [*often pl.*] a devotional service chiefly of prayers **5** something prayed for —**prayer′ful** *adj.* —**prayer′ful·ly** *adv.*

**pray·er**[2] (prā′ər) *n.* one who prays

**praying mantis** MANTIS

**pre-** [< L *prae,* before] *prefix* before in time, place, rank, etc.

**preach** (prēch) *vi.* [< L *prae-,* before + *dicare,* proclaim] **1** to give a religious sermon **2** to give moral advice, esp. in a tiresome manner —*vt.* **1** to urge as by preaching **2** to deliver (a sermon) — **preach′ment** *n.*

**preach′er** *n.* one who preaches; esp., a member of the Protestant clergy

**preach′y** *adj.* **-i·er, -i·est** [Inf.] given to or marked by preaching, or moralizing

**pre·am·ble** (prē′am′bəl) *n.* [< L *prae-,* before + *ambulare,* go] an introduction, esp. one to a constitution, statute, etc., stating its purpose

**pre′ap·prove′** (-ə prōōv′) *vt.* **-proved′, -prov′ing** to authorize before an application is submitted

**pre′ar·range′** (-ə rānj′) *vt.* **-ranged′, -rang′ing** to arrange beforehand

**pre·can·cer·ous** (prē kan′sər əs) *adj.* likely to become cancerous

**pre·car·i·ous** (prē ker′ē əs) *adj.* [see PRAY] dependent upon circumstances or chance; uncertain; risky —**pre·car′i·ous·ly** *adv.*

**pre·cau·tion** (pri kô′shən) *n.* [< L *prae-,* before + *cavere,* take care] care taken beforehand, as against danger or failure —**pre·cau′tion·ar′y** *adj.*

**pre·cede** (prē sēd′) *vt., vi.* **-ced′ed, -ced′ing** [< L *prae-,* before + *cedere,* to go] to be, come, or go before in time, place, rank, etc.

**prec·e·dence** (pres′ə dəns; prē sēd′′ns) *n.* the act, right, or fact of preceding in time, order, rank, etc.

**prec·e·dent** (pres′ə dənt) *n.* an act, statement, etc. that may serve as an example or justification for a later one

**pre·ced′ing** *adj.* that precedes

**pre·cept** (prē′sept′) *n.* [< L *prae-,* before + *capere,* take] a rule of moral conduct; maxim

**pre·cep·tor** (prē sep′tər) *n.* a teacher

**pre·cinct** (prē′siŋkt′) *n.* [< L *prae-,* before + *cingere,* surround] **1** [*usually pl.*] an enclosure between buildings, walls, etc. **2** [*pl.*] environs **3** *a)* police district *b)* a subdivision of a voting ward **4** a limited area

**pre·ci·os·i·ty** (presh′ē äs′ə tē, pres′-) *n., pl.* **-ties** [see fol.] affectation, esp. in language

**pre·cious** (presh′əs) *adj.* [< L *pretium,* a price] **1** of great price or value; costly **2** beloved; dear **3** very fastidious, affected, etc. —**pre′cious·ly** *adv.*

**precious stone** a rare and costly gem: applied to the diamond, emerald, ruby, and sapphire

**prec·i·pice** (pres′i pis) *n.* [< L *prae-,* before + *caput,* a head] a vertical or overhanging rock face

**pre·cip·i·tant** (prē sip′i tənt) *adj.* [see prec.] PRECIPITATE

**pre·cip·i·tate** (prē sip′ə tāt′; *for adj. & n.,* -tit, -tāt′) *vt.* **-tat′ed, -tat′ing** [see PRECIPICE] **1** to hurl downward **2** to cause to happen before expected, needed, etc. **3** *Chem.* to separate (a soluble substance) out of a solution —*vi.* **1** *Chem.* to be precipitated **2** *Meteorol.* to condense and fall as rain, snow, etc. —*adj.* **1** acting or done hastily or rashly **2** very sudden or abrupt —*n.* a substance precipitated out of a solution

**pre·cip·i·ta·tion** (-tā′shən) *n.* **1** a headlong fall or rush **2** rash haste; impetuosity **3** a bringing on suddenly **4** *Chem.* a precipitating or being precipitated from a solution **5** *Meteorol.* *a)* rain, snow, etc. *b)* the amount of this

**pre·cip′i·tous** (-təs) *adj.* **1** steep like a precipice **2** rash; impetuous

**pré·cis** (prā sē′) *n., pl.* **-cis′** (-sēz′) [Fr: see fol.] a concise abridgment; summary

**pre·cise** (prē sīs′) *adj.* [< L *prae-,* before + *caedere,* to cut] **1** accurately stated; definite **2** minutely exact **3** strict; scrupulous; fastidious —**pre·cise′ly** *adv.* —**pre·cise′ness** *n.*

**pre·ci·sion** (prē sizh′ən) *n.* the quality of being precise; exactness —*adj.* requiring exactness /*precision* work/

**pre·clude** (prē klōōd′) *vt.* **-clud′ed, -clud′ing** [< L *prae-,* before + *claudere,* to close] to make impossible, esp. in advance; prevent —**pre·clu′sion** (-klōō′zhən) *n.*

**pre·co·cious** (prē kō′shəs) *adj.* [< L *prae-,* before + *coquere,* to cook] matured earlier than usual /a *precocious* child/ —**pre·coc′i·ty** (-käs′ə tē) *n.*

**pre·cog·ni·tion** (prē′käg nish′ən) *n.* [see PRE- & COGNITION] *Parapsychology* the perception of an event, etc. before it occurs, esp. by extrasensory means —**pre·cog′ni·tive** (-nə tiv) *adj.*

**pre-Co·lum·bi·an** (prē′kə lum′bē ən) *adj.* of any period in the Americas before Columbus's voyages

**pre·con·ceive** (prē′kən sēv′) *vt.* **-ceived′, -ceiv′ing** to form (an opinion) in advance —**pre′con·cep′tion** (-sep′shən) *n.*

**pre′con·di′tion** (-dish′ən) *vt.* to prepare (someone) to behave, react, etc. in a certain way under certain conditions —*n.* a condition required beforehand if something else is to occur

**pre·cur·sor** (prē kur′sər, prē′kur′-) *n.* ⟦< L *praecurrere*, run ahead⟧ **1** a forerunner **2** a predecessor —**pre·cur′so·ry** *adj.*

**pred·a·to·ry** (pred′ə tôr′ē) *adj.* ⟦< L *praeda*, a prey⟧ **1** of or living by plundering or robbing **2** preying on other animals —**pred′a·tor** (-tər) *n.*

**pre·de·cease** (prē′dē sēs′) *vt.* -ceased′, -ceas′ing to die before (someone else)

**pred·e·ces·sor** (pred′ə ses′ər) *n.* ⟦< L *prae-*, before + *decedere*, go away⟧ a person preceding another, as in office

**pre·des·ti·na·tion** (prē des′tə nā′shən) *n.* **1** *Theol.* the doctrine that *a)* God foreordained everything that would happen *b)* God predestines souls to salvation or to damnation **2** one's destiny

**pre·des′tine** (-des′tin) *vt.* -tined, -tin·ing to destine beforehand; foreordain

**pre′de·ter′mine** (-dē tur′min) *vt.* -mined, -min·ing to determine beforehand

**pre·dic·a·ment** (prē dik′ə mənt) *n.* ⟦see PREACH⟧ an unpleasant or embarrassing situation

**pred·i·cate** (pred′i kāt′; *for n. & adj.,* -kit) *vt.* -cat′ed, -cat′ing ⟦see PREACH⟧ **1** to affirm as a quality or attribute **2** to base (something) on or *upon* facts, conditions, etc. —*n. Gram.* the word or words that make a statement about the subject —*adj. Gram.* of a predicate —**pred′i·ca′tion** *n.*

**pre·dict** (prē dikt′) *vt., vi.* ⟦< L *prae-*, before + *dicere*, tell⟧ to say in advance (what one believes will happen); foretell —**pre·dict′a·ble** *adj.* —**pre·dic′tion** *n.* —**pre·dic′tor** *n.*

**pre·di·gest** (prē′di jest′, -dī-) *vt.* to treat (food) as with enzymes for easier digestion when eaten

**pred·i·lec·tion** (pred′ə lek′shən, prē′də-) *n.* ⟦< L *prae-*, before + *diligere*, prefer⟧ a partiality or preference (*for*)

**pre·dis·pose** (prē′di spōz′) *vt.* -posed′, -pos′ing to make receptive or susceptible (*to*); incline —**pre′dis·po·si′tion** (-dis pə zish′ən) *n.*

**pre·dom·i·nant** (prē däm′ə nənt) *adj.* **1** having authority or influence over others; superior **2** most frequent; prevailing —**pre·dom′i·nance** *n.* —**pre·dom′i·nant·ly** *adv.*

**pre·dom·i·nate** (prē däm′ə nāt′) *vi.* -nat·ed, -nat·ing **1** to have authority or influence (*over* others) **2** to be dominant in amount, number, etc.; prevail

**pre·em·i·nent** (prē em′ə nənt) *adj.* eminent above others; surpassing —**pre·em′i·nence** *n.* —**pre·em′i·nent·ly** *adv.*

**pre·empt** or **pre-empt′** (prē empt′) *vt.* ⟦ult. < L *prae-*, before + *emere*, buy⟧ **1** to gain the right to buy (public land) by settling on it **2** to seize before anyone else can **3** *Radio, TV* to replace (a scheduled program)

**pre·emp′tion** (-emp′shən) *n.* **1** a preempting **2** action taken to check other action beforehand —**pre·emp′tive** *adj.*

**preen** (prēn) *vt.* ⟦< ME *proinen*, to dress up⟧ **1** to clean and trim (the feathers) with the beak **2** to dress up or adorn (oneself)

**pre·ex·ist** (prē′eg zist′) *vt., vi.* to exist previously or before (another person or thing) —**pre′ex·ist′ence** *n.*

**pref** *abbrev.* **1** preface **2** preferred **3** prefix

**pre·fab** (prē′fab′) *n.* [Inf.] a prefabricated building

**pre·fab·ri·cate** (prē fab′ri kāt′) *vt.* -cat′ed, -cat′ing to build (a house, etc.) in standardized sections for shipment and quick assembly

**pref·ace** (pref′is) *n.* ⟦< L *prae-*, before + *fari*, speak⟧ an introduction to a book, speech, etc. —*vt.* -aced, -ac·ing **1** to furnish with a preface **2** to introduce —**pref′a·to·ry** (-ə tôr′ē) *adj.*

**pre·fect** (prē′fekt′) *n.* ⟦< L *praeficere*, to set over⟧ any of various administrators —**pre′fec′ture** (-fek′chər) *n.*

**pre·fer** (prē fur′, pri-) *vt.* -ferred′, -fer′ring ⟦< L *prae-*, before + *ferre*, to bear⟧ **1** to put before a court, etc. for consideration **2** to like better

**pref·er·a·ble** (pref′ər ə bəl) *adj.* more desirable —**pref′er·a·bly** *adv.*

**pref·er·ence** (-əns) *n.* **1** a preferring or being preferred **2** something preferred **3** advantage given to one person, country, etc. over others —**pref′er·en′tial** (-ər en′shəl) *adj.*

**pre·fer·ment** (prē fur′mənt) *n.* an advancement in rank, etc.; promotion

**pre·fig·ure** (prē fig′yər) *vt.* -ured, -ur·ing to suggest beforehand; foreshadow

**pre·fix** (prē′fiks′; *for v., also* prē fiks′) *vt.* ⟦< L *prae-*, before + *figere*, fix⟧ to fix to the beginning of a word, etc.; esp., to add as a prefix —*n.* a syllable, group of syllables, or word joined to the beginning of another word or a base to alter its meaning

**preg·nant** (preg′nənt) *adj.* ⟦< L *pregnans*⟧ **1** having (an) offspring developing in the uterus; with child **2** mentally fertile; inventive **3** full of meaning, etc. [*a pregnant* silence] **4** filled (*with*); abounding —**preg′nan·cy,** *pl.* -cies, *n.*

**pre·hen·sile** (prē hen′səl) *adj.* ⟦< L *prehendere*, take⟧ adapted for seizing or grasping, esp. by wrapping around something: said as of a monkey's tail

**pre·his·tor·ic** (prē′his tôr′ik) *adj.* of the period before recorded history

**pre·ig·ni·tion** (prē′ig nish′ən) *n.* in an internal-combustion engine, ignition occurring before the intake valve is closed or before the spark plug fires

**pre·judge** (prē juj′) *vt.* -judged′, -judg′ing to judge beforehand or without all the evidence —**pre·judg′ment** *n.*

**prej·u·dice** (prej′ə dis) *n.* ⟦< L *prae-*, before + *judicium*, judgment⟧ **1** a preconceived, usually unfavorable idea **2** an opinion held in disregard of facts that contradict it; bias **3** intolerance or hatred of other races, etc. **4** injury or harm as from some judgment —*vt.* -diced, -dic·ing **1** to injure or harm, as by some judgment **2** to cause to have prejudice; bias —**prej′u·di′cial** (-dish′əl) *adj.*

**prel·ate** (prel′it) *n.* ⟦< L *praelatus*, placed before⟧ a high-ranking member of the clergy, as a bishop —**prel′a·cy,** *pl.* -cies, *n.*

**pre·lim·i·nar·y** (prē lim′ə ner′ē, pri-) *adj.* ⟦< L *prae-*, before + *limen*, threshold⟧ leading up to the main action, discussion, etc.; introductory —*n.*, *pl.* -ies [*often pl.*] a preliminary step, procedure, etc.

**pre·lit·er·ate** (prē lit′ər it) *adj.* of a society not having a written language

**prel·ude** (prel′yōōd′, prā′lōōd′) *n.* ⟦< Fr < L *prae-*, before + *ludere*, to play⟧ **1** a preliminary part **2** *Music a)* an introductory instrumental composition, as the overture to an opera *b)* a short, romantic composition

**pre·mar·i·tal** (prē mar′ət′l) *adj.* occurring before marriage

**pre·ma·ture** (prē′mə toor′, -choor′) *adj.* ⟦< L *prae-*, before + *maturus*, ripe⟧ happening, done, arriving, etc. before the proper or usual time; too early —**pre′ma·ture′ly** *adv.*

**pre·med′i·tate′** (-med′ə tāt′) *vt., vi.* -tat·ed, -tat·ing to think (out) or plan beforehand —**pre·med′i·ta′tion** *n.*

**pre·men·stru·al** (prē men′strəl) *adj.* occurring before a menstrual period

**pre·mier** (pri mir′, -myir′) *adj.* ⟦Fr < L *primus*, first⟧ first in importance; foremost —*n.* a chief official; specif., a prime minister —**pre·mier′ship** *n.*

**pre·mière** or **pre·miere** (pri mir′, -myer′) *n.* ⟦Fr: see prec.⟧ a first performance of a play, movie, etc.

**prem·ise** (prem′is) *n.* ⟦< L *prae-*, before + *mittere*, send⟧ **1** a previous statement serving as a basis for an argument **2** [*pl.*] a piece of real estate —*vt.* -ised, -is·ing to state as a premise

**pre·mi·um** (prē′mē əm) *n.,* *pl.* -ums ⟦< L *prae-*, before + *emere*, get, buy⟧ **1** a reward or prize, esp. as an inducement to buy **2** an additional amount paid or charged **3** a payment, as for an insurance policy **4** very high value *[to put a premium on wit]* —**at a premium** very valuable because of scarcity

**prem·o·ni·tion** (prĕm′ə nish′ən, prē′mə-) *n.* ⟦< L *prae-*, before + *monere*, warn⟧ **1** a forewarning **2** a foreboding —**pre·mon·i·to·ry** (prē män′i tôr′ē) *adj.*

**pre·na·tal** (prē nāt′'l) *adj.* before birth

**pre·nup·tial** (prē nup′shəl) *adj.* before a marriage or wedding

**pre·oc·cu·pied**′ *adj.* completely absorbed in one's thoughts; engrossed

**pre·oc·cu·py** (prē äk′yoo pī′) *vt.* **-pied**′, **-py′ing** ⟦< L *prae-*, before + *occupare*, seize⟧ to wholly occupy the thoughts of; engross —**pre·oc′cu·pa′tion** (-pā′shən) *n.*

**pre·or·dain** (prē′ôr dān′) *vt.* to ordain or decree beforehand

**pre·owned**′ *adj.* previously owned; used

**prep**[1] (prep) *adj. short for* PREPARATORY *[a prep school]* —*vt.* **prepped, prep′ping** to prepare (a patient) for surgery, etc.

**prep**[2] *abbrev.* **1** preparatory **2** preposition

**pre·pack·age** (prē pak′ij) *vt.* **-aged, -ag·ing** to package (foods, etc.) in standard units before selling

**pre·paid** (prē pād′) *vt. pt. & pp. of* PREPAY

**prep·a·ra·tion** (prep′ə rā′shən) *n.* **1** a preparing or being prepared **2** a preparatory measure **3** something prepared, as a medicine or cosmetic

**pre·par·a·to·ry** (prē par′ə tôr′ē, prep′ə rə-) *adj.* serving to prepare; introductory

**preparatory school** a private secondary school that prepares students for college

**pre·pare** (prē par′, pri-) *vt.* **-pared′, -par′ing** ⟦< L *prae-*, before + *parare*, get ready⟧ **1** to make ready **2** to equip or furnish **3** to put together *[to prepare dinner]* —*vi.* **1** to make things ready **2** to make oneself ready

**pre·par′ed·ness** (-par′id nəs) *n.* the state of being prepared, esp. for waging war

**pre·pay**′ *vt.* **-paid′, -pay′ing** to pay or pay for in advance —**pre·pay′ment** *n.*

**pre·pon·der·ate** (prē pän′dər āt′, pri-) *vi.* **-at·ed, -at′ing** ⟦< L *prae-*, before + *ponderare*, weigh⟧ to be superior in amount, power, etc. —**pre·pon′der·ance** *n.* —**pre·pon′der·ant** *adj.*

**prep·o·si·tion** (prep′ə zish′ən) *n.* ⟦< L *prae-*, before + *ponere*, to place⟧ a word, as *in*, *by*, or *to*, that connects a noun or pronoun to another element of a sentence —**prep′o·si′tion·al** *adj.*

**pre·pos·sess** (prē′pə zes′) *vt.* to bias, esp. favorably

**pre·pos·sess′ing** *adj.* that impresses favorably

**pre·pos·ter·ous** (prē päs′tər əs, pri-) *adj.* ⟦< L *prae-*, before + *posterus*, following⟧ absurd; ridiculous; laughable

**prep·py** or **prep·pie** (prep′ē) *n., pl.* **-pies** a student at or graduate of a preparatory school —*adj.* **-pi·er, -pi·est** of or like the clothes worn by such students

**pre·puce** (prē′pyoos′) *n.* ⟦< L *praeputium*⟧ FORE-SKIN

**pre·re·cord** (prē′ri kôrd′) *vt. Film, Radio, TV* to record (music, a program, etc.) for later use

**pre′re·cord′ed** *adj.* designating or of a magnetic tape, as in a cassette, on which sound, etc. has been recorded before its sale

**pre·req·ui·site** (prē rek′wə zit, pri-) *adj.* required beforehand as a necessary condition —*n.* something prerequisite

**pre·rog·a·tive** (prē räg′ə tiv, pri-) *n.* ⟦< L *prae-*, before + *rogare*, ask⟧ an exclusive right or privilege

**pres** *abbrev.* present

**Pres** *abbrev.* President

**pres·age** (pres′ij; *for v., usually* prē sāj′, pri-) *n.* ⟦< L *prae-*, before + *sagire*, perceive⟧ **1** an omen; portent **2** a foreboding —*vt.* **-aged′, -ag′ing** to give warning of

**pres·by·ter** (prez′bi tər) *n.* ⟦see PRIEST⟧ **1** in the Presbyterian Church, an elder **2** in the Episcopal Church, a priest

**Pres′by·te′ri·an** (-tir′ē ən) *adj.* designating or of a church of a traditionally Calvinistic Protestant denomination governed by presbyters —*n.* a member of a Presbyterian church

**pre·school**′ *adj.* of or for a child between infancy and school age —*n.* a school for very young children, usually those three to five years of age —**pre·school′er** *n.*

**pres·cience** (prē′shəns, -shē əns) *n.* ⟦< L *prae-*, before + *scire*, know⟧ foreknowledge; foresight —**pres′cient** *adj.*

**pre·scribe** (prē skrīb′, pri-) *vt.* **-scribed′, -scrib′ing** ⟦< L *prae-*, before + *scribere*, write⟧ **1** to order; direct **2** to order as a medicine or treatment: said as of physicians

**pre·script** (prē′skript′) *n.* a prescribed rule —**pre·scrip′tive** *adj.*

**pre·scrip·tion** (prē skrip′shən, pri-) *n.* **1** something prescribed **2** *a)* a written direction for the preparation and use of medicine *b)* such a medicine

**pres·ence** (prez′əns) *n.* **1** the fact or state of being present **2** immediate surroundings *[in his presence]* **3** *a)* a person's bearing or appearance *b)* impressive bearing, personality, etc.

**presence of mind** ability to think and act quickly in an emergency

**pres·ent** (prez′ənt; *for v.* prē zent′, pri-) *adj.* ⟦< L *prae-*, before + *esse*, be⟧ **1** being at the specified place **2** existing or happening now **3** *Gram.* indicating action or state occurring now or action that is always the same *[present tense]* —*n.* **1** the present time **2** the present tense **3** a gift —*vt.* **pre·sent**′ **1** to introduce (a person) **2** to exhibit; show **3** to offer for consideration **4** to give (a gift, etc.) to a person, etc. —**present arms** to hold a rifle vertically in front of the body

**pre·sent·a·ble** (prē zent′ə bəl, pri-) *adj.* **1** suitable for presentation **2** suitably groomed for meeting people

**pres·en·ta·tion** (prez′ən tā′shən, prē′zən-) *n.* **1** a presenting or being presented **2** something presented

**pres′ent-day**′ *adj.* of the present time

**pre·sen·ti·ment** (prē sen′tə mənt, pri-) *n.* ⟦see PRE- & SENTIMENT⟧ a feeling that something, esp. of an unfortunate nature, is about to take place

**pres′ent·ly** *adv.* **1** soon; shortly **2** at present; now: a usage objected to by some

**pre·sent·ment** (prē zent′mənt, pri-) *n.* presentation

**present participle** a participle used *a)* to express present or continuing action or existence (Ex.: he is *growing*) *b)* as an adjective (Ex.: a *growing* boy)

**pres·er·va·tion·ist** (prez′ər vā′shən ist) *n.* one who advocates positive measures to preserve historic buildings, wilderness lands, etc.

**pre·serv·a·tive** (prē zurv′ə tiv, pri-) *adj.* preserving —*n.* anything that preserves *[a preservative added to foods]*

**pre·serve** (prē zurv′, pri-) *vt.* **-served′, -serv′ing** ⟦< L *prae-*, before + *servare*, keep⟧ **1** to protect from harm, damage, etc. **2** to keep from spoiling **3** to prepare (food), as by canning, for future use **4** to carry on; maintain —*n.* **1** *[usually pl.]* fruit preserved by cooking with sugar **2** a place where game, fish, etc. are maintained —**pres·er·va·tion** (prez′ər vā′shən) *n.* —**pre·serv′er** *n.*

**pre·set** (prē set′) *vt.* **-set′, -set′ting** to set (automatic controls) beforehand

**pre·shrink** (prē shriŋk′) *vt.* **-shrank′** or **-shrunk′, -shrunk′** or **-shrunk′en, -shrink′ing** to shrink by a special process in manufacture, to minimize further shrinkage in laundering —**pre·shrunk**′ *adj.*

**pre·side** (prē zīd′, pri-) *vi.* **-sid′ed, -sid′ing** ⟦< L *prae*-, before + *sedere*, sit⟧ **1** to serve as chairman **2** to have control or authority (*over*)

**pres·i·dent** (prez'ə dənt) *n.* ⟦see prec.⟧ **1** the highest executive officer of a company, club, etc. **2** [*often* P-] the chief executive (as in the U.S.), or the nominal head (as in Italy), of a republic — **pres'i·den·cy**, *pl.* **-cies**, *n.* —**pres'i·den'tial** (-den'shəl) *adj.*

**press**[1] (pres) *vt.* ⟦< L *premere*⟧ **1** *a*) to act on with steady force or weight; push against, squeeze, compress, etc. *b*) to push against (a button, key, etc.) as in using an elevator, keyboard, etc. **2** to squeeze (juice, etc.) from **3** to iron (clothes, etc.) **4** to embrace closely **5** to urge persistently; entreat **6** to try to force **7** to emphasize **8** to distress or trouble [I'm *pressed* for time] **9** to urge on —*vi.* **1** to exert pressure; apply weight **2** to go forward with determination **3** to crowd —*n.* **1** pressure, urgency, etc. **2** a crowd **3** a machine for crushing, stamping, etc. **4** *a*) *short for* PRINTING PRESS *b*) a printing establishment *c*) newspapers, magazines, etc., or the persons who write for them *d*) publicity, etc. in newspapers, etc. **5** a closet for storing clothes, etc. —**press'er** *n.*

**press**[2] (pres) *vt.* ⟦< L *praes*, surety + *stare*, to stand⟧ to force into service, esp. military or naval service

**press agent** one whose work is to get publicity for a client

**press box** a place for reporters at sports events, etc.

**press conference** a group interview granted to media personnel as by a celebrity

**press'ing** *adj.* calling for immediate attention; urgent

**press'man** (-mən) *n., pl.* **-men** (-mən) an operator of a printing press

**press secretary** one whose job is to deal with the news media on behalf of a prominent person

**pres·sure** (presh'ər) *n.* **1** a pressing or being pressed **2** a state of distress **3** a compelling influence [social *pressure*] **4** urgent demands; urgency **5** *Physics* force per unit of area exerted upon a surface, etc. —*vt.* **-sured, -sur·ing** to exert pressure on

**pressure cooker** a container for quick cooking by steam under pressure

**pressure group** a group trying to influence government through lobbying, propaganda, etc.

**pres·sur·ize'** (-īz') *vt.* **-ized', -iz'ing** to keep nearly normal atmosphere pressure inside (an airplane, etc.), as at high altitudes —**pres'sur·i·za'tion** *n.*

**pres·ti·dig·i·ta·tion** (pres'tə dij'i tā'shən) *n.* ⟦Fr < *preste*, quick + L *digitus*, finger⟧ sleight of hand

**pres·tige** (pres tēzh', -tēj') *n.* ⟦< L *praestrigiae*, deceptions⟧ **1** the power to impress or influence **2** reputation based on high achievement, character, etc.

**pres·ti'gious** (-tij'əs, -tē'jəs) *adj.* having or imparting prestige or distinction

**pres·to** (pres'tō) *adv., adj.* ⟦It, quick⟧ **1** fast or at once **2** *Music* in fast tempo Also written **pres'to**

**pre·stressed concrete** (prē'strest') concrete containing tensed steel cables for strength

**pre·sume** (prē zōōm', pri-) *v.* **-sumed', -sum'ing** ⟦< L *prae*-, before + *sumere*, take⟧ **1** to dare (to say or do something); venture **2** to take for granted; suppose —*vi.* to act presumptuously; take liberties —**pre·sum'a·ble** *adj.* —**pre·sum'a·bly** *adv.*

**pre·sump·tion** (prē zump'shən, pri-) *n.* **1** a presuming; specif., *a*) an overstepping of proper bounds *b*) a taking of something for granted **2** the thing presumed **3** a reason for presuming —**pre·sump'tive** *adj.*

**pre·sump'tu·ous** (-chōō əs) *adj.* too bold or forward

**pre·sup·pose** (prē'sə pōz') *vt.* **-posed', -pos'ing** **1** to suppose or assume beforehand **2** to require or imply as a preceding condition —**pre'sup·po·si'tion** (-sup ə zish'ən) *n.*

**pre·teen** (prē'tēn') *n.* a child nearly a teenager

**pre·tend** (prē tend', pri-) *vt.* ⟦< L *prae*-, before + *tendere*, to stretch⟧ **1** to profess [to *pretend* ignorance] **2** to feign; simulate [to *pretend* anger] **3** to make believe [to *pretend* to be astronauts] —*vi.* to lay claim (*to*) —**pre·tend'er** *n.*

**pre·tense** (prē tens', pri-; prē'tens') *n.* **1** a claim; pretension **2** a false claim **3** a false show of something **4** a pretending, as at play Brit. sp. **pre·tence'**

**pre·ten·sion** (prē ten'shən, pri-) *n.* **1** a pretext **2** a claim **3** assertion of a claim **4** pretentiousness

**pre·ten·tious** (-shəs) *adj.* **1** making claims to some distinction, importance, etc. **2** affectedly grand; ostentatious —**pre·ten'tious·ly** *adv.* —**pre·ten'tious·ness** *n.*

**pret·er·it** or **pret·er·ite** (pret'ər it) *adj.* ⟦< L *praeter*-, beyond + *ire*, go⟧ *Gram.* expressing past action or state —*n.* the past tense

**pre·term** (prē'tʉrm') *adj.* of premature birth

**pre·ter·nat·u·ral** (prēt'ər nach'ər əl) *adj.* ⟦ML *praeternaturalis*⟧ **1** differing from or beyond what is natural; abnormal **2** SUPERNATURAL

**pre·test** (prē test') *vt., vi.* to test in advance

**pre·text** (prē'tekst') *n.* ⟦< L *prae*-, before + *texere*, weave⟧ a false reason put forth to hide the real one

**Pre·to·ri·a** (prē tôr'ē ə) administrative capital of South Africa: pop. 526,000

**pret·ti·fy** (prit'i fī') *vt.* **-fied', -fy'ing** to make pretty

**pret·ty** (prit'ē) *adj.* **-ti·er, -ti·est** ⟦OE *prættig*, crafty⟧ attractive in a dainty, graceful way —*adv.* fairly; somewhat —*vt.* **-tied, -ty·ing** to make pretty: usually with *up* —**pret'ti·ly** *adv.* —**pret'ti·ness** *n.*

**pret·zel** (pret'səl) *n.* ⟦< L *brachium*, an arm⟧ a hard, brittle, salted biscuit, often formed in a loose knot

**pre·vail** (prē vāl', pri-) *vi.* ⟦< L *prae*-, before + *valere*, be strong⟧ **1** to be victorious; triumph: often with *over* or *against* **2** to succeed **3** to be or become more widespread **4** to be prevalent —**pre·vail on** (or **upon** or **with**) to persuade

**pre·vail'ing** *adj.* **1** superior in strength or influence **2** prevalent

**prev·a·lent** (prev'ə lənt) *adj.* ⟦see PREVAIL⟧ widely existing; generally accepted, used, etc. —**prev'a·lence** *n.*

**pre·var·i·cate** (pri var'i kāt') *vi.* **-cat'ed, -cat'ing** ⟦< L *prae*-, before + *varicare*, straddle⟧ **1** to evade the truth **2** to lie —**pre·var'i·ca'tion** *n.* —**pre·var'i·ca'tor** *n.*

**pre·vent** (prē vent', pri-) *vt.* ⟦< L *prae*-, before + *venire*, come⟧ to stop or keep from doing or happening; hinder —**pre·vent'a·ble** or **pre·vent'i·ble** *adj.* —**pre·ven'tion** *n.*

**pre·ven'tive** (-vent'iv) *adj.* preventing or serving to prevent —*n.* anything that prevents Also **pre·vent'a·tive** (-vent'ə tiv)

**pre·view** (prē'vyōō') *n.* **1** an advance, restricted showing, as of a movie **2** a showing of scenes from a movie, etc. to advertise it Also sp. **pre'vue'**

**pre·vi·ous** (prē'vē əs) *adj.* ⟦< L *prae*-, before + *via*, a way⟧ occurring before; prior —**previous to** before —**pre'vi·ous·ly** *adv.*

**pre·war** (prē'wôr') *adj.* before a (or the) war

**prex·y** (prek'sē) *n., pl.* **-ies** [Slang] the president, esp. of a college, etc.

**prey** (prā) *n.* ⟦< L *prehendere*, seize⟧ **1** an animal hunted for food by another animal **2** a victim **3** the mode of living by preying on other animals [a bird of *prey*] —*vi.* **1** to plunder **2** to hunt other animals for food **3** to weigh as an obsession Generally used with *on* or *upon*

**pri·ap·ic** (prī ap'ik) *adj.* ⟦after *Priapos*, Gr god of procreation⟧ overly concerned with masculinity

**price** (prīs) *n.* ⟦< L *pretium*⟧ **1** the amount of money, etc. asked or paid for something; cost **2** value or worth **3** the cost, as in life, labor, etc., of obtaining some benefit —*vt.* **priced, pric'ing 1** to fix the price of **2** [Inf.] to find out the price of

**price'less** *adj.* of inestimable value; invaluable

**price'y** *adj.* [Inf.] expensive: also sp. **pri'cy**

**prick** (prik) *n.* ⟦OE *prica*, a point⟧ **1** a tiny puncture made by a sharp point **2** a sharp pain caused as by being pricked —*vt.* **1** to make (a hole) in (something) with a sharp point **2** to pain sharply —**prick up one's ears 1** to raise the ears erect **2** to listen closely

**prick·le** (prik'əl) *n.* ⟦OE *prica*, a point⟧ **1** a small, sharply pointed growth, as a thorn: also **prick'er 2** a tingling sensation —*vt.*, *vi.* **-led, -ling** to tingle —**prick'ly, -li·er, -li·est,** *adj.*

**prickly heat** a skin eruption caused by inflammation of the sweat glands

**pride** (prīd) *n.* ⟦< OE *prut*, proud⟧ **1** *a*) an unduly high opinion of oneself *b*) haughtiness; arrogance **2** dignity and self-respect **3** satisfaction in something done, owned, etc. **4** a person or thing in which pride is taken —**pride oneself on** to be proud of —**pride'ful** *adj.* —**pride'ful·ly** *adv.*

**pri·er** (prī'ər) *n.* one who pries

**priest** (prēst) *n.* ⟦< Gr *presbys*, old⟧ **1** a person of special rank who performs religious rites in a temple of God or a god **2** *R.C.Ch.* a clergyman ranking next below a bishop —**priest'hood'** *n.* —**priest'ly, -li·er, -li·est,** *adj.*

**priest·ess** (prēs'tis) *n.* a pagan female priest

**prig** (prig) *n.* ⟦< 16th-c. cant⟧ one who smugly affects great propriety or morality —**prig'gish** *adj.*

**prim** (prim) *adj.* **prim'mer, prim'mest** ⟦< ?⟧ stiffly formal, precise, or moral —**prim'ly** *adv.*

**pri·ma·cy** (prī'mə sē) *n.*, *pl.* **-cies** ⟦< L *primus*, first⟧ **1** a being first in time, rank, etc.; supremacy **2** the rank or office of a primate

**pri·ma don·na** (prē'mə dän'ə, prim'ə) *pl.* **pri'ma don'nas** ⟦It, lit., first lady⟧ the principal woman singer in an opera

**pri·ma fa·ci·e** (prī'mə fā'shē) ⟦L, lit., at first sight⟧ **1** self-evident **2** *Law* designating evidence that establishes a fact unless refuted

**pri·mal** (prī'məl) *adj.* ⟦< L *primus*, first⟧ **1** first in time; original **2** first in importance; chief **3** fundamental; basic *[primal* instincts*]*

**pri·mar·i·ly** (prī mer'ə lē) *adv.* **1** at first; originally **2** mainly; principally

**pri·mar·y** (prī'mer'ē) *adj.* ⟦< L *primus*, first⟧ **1** first in time or order; original **2** from which others are derived; fundamental *[primary* colors*]* **3** first in importance; chief —*n.*, *pl.* **-ries 1** something first in order, importance, etc. **2** a preliminary election at which candidates are chosen for the final election

**primary school 1** ELEMENTARY SCHOOL **2** a school including the first three elementary grades and, sometimes, kindergarten

**primary stress** (or **accent**) the heaviest stress (ˊ) in pronouncing a word

**pri·mate** (prī'mit; *for* 2, -māt') *n.* ⟦< L *primus*, first⟧ **1** an archbishop, or the highest-ranking bishop in a province, etc. **2** any of the order of mammals that includes humans, the apes, etc.

**prime** (prīm) *adj.* ⟦< L *primus*, first⟧ **1** first in time; original **2** first in rank or importance; chief; principal **3** first in quality **4** fundamental **5** *Math.* that can be evenly divided by no other whole number than itself and 1 —*n.* **1** the first or earliest part **2** the best or most vigorous period **3** the best part —*vt.* **primed, prim'ing 1** to make ready; prepare **2** to get (a pump) into operation by pouring water into it **3** to undercoat, size, etc. before painting **4** to provide with facts, answers, etc. beforehand

**prime meridian** the meridian at Greenwich, England, from which longitude is measured east and west

**prime minister** in some countries, the chief executive of the government

**prim·er**[1] (prim'ər) *n.* ⟦< L *primus*, first⟧ **1** a simple book for teaching reading **2** any elementary textbook

**prim·er**[2] (prī'mər) *n.* a thing that primes; specif., *a*) an explosive cap, etc. used to set off a main charge *b*) a preliminary coat of paint, etc.

**prime rate** the most favorable interest rate charged on bank loans to large corporations: also **prime interest rate** or **prime lending rate**

**prime time** *Radio, TV* the hours when the largest audience is available

**pri·me·val** (prī mē'vəl) *adj.* ⟦< L *primus*, first + *aevum*, an age⟧ of the earliest times or ages; primordial

**prim·i·tive** (prim'i tiv) *adj.* ⟦< L *primus*, first⟧ **1** of the earliest times; original **2** crude; simple **3** primary; basic —*n.* a primitive person or thing

**pri·mo·gen·i·ture** (prī'mə jen'i chər) *n.* ⟦< L *primus*, first + *genitura*, a begetting⟧ the exclusive right of inheritance of the eldest son

**pri·mor·di·al** (prī môr'dē əl) *adj.* ⟦< L *primus*, first + *ordiri*, begin⟧ primitive; fundamental

**primp** (primp) *vt.*, *vi.* ⟦prob. < PRIM⟧ to groom or dress up in a fussy way

**prim·rose** (prim'rōz') *n.* ⟦altered (after *rose*) < ML *primula*⟧ a plant with tubelike, often yellow flowers

**primrose path 1** the path of pleasure, self-indulgence, etc. **2** a course of action that seems easy but that can lead to disaster

**prince** (prins) *n.* ⟦< L *princeps*, chief⟧ **1** a ruler ranking below a king; head of a principality **2** a son of a sovereign **3** any preeminent person

**prince consort** the husband of a reigning queen

**Prince Edward Island** island province of SE Canada: 2,185 sq. mi.; pop. 135,000; cap. Charlottetown: abbrev. *PE*

**prince'ly** *adj.* **-li·er, -li·est 1** of a prince **2** magnificent; generous —**prince'li·ness** *n.*

**prin·cess** (prin'sis, -ses') *n.* **1** a daughter of a sovereign **2** the wife of a prince

**prin·ci·pal** (prin'sə pəl) *adj.* ⟦see PRINCE⟧ first in rank, importance, etc. —*n.* **1** a principal person or thing **2** the head of a school **3** the amount of a loan, on which interest is computed —**prin'ci·pal·ly** *adv.*

**prin·ci·pal·i·ty** (-pal'ə tē) *n.*, *pl.* **-ties** the territory ruled by a prince

**principal parts** the principal inflected forms of a verb: in English, the infinitive, past tense, and past participle (Ex: *drink, drank, drunk*)

**prin·ci·ple** (prin'sə pəl) *n.* ⟦see PRINCE⟧ **1** a fundamental truth, law, etc. upon which others are based **2** *a*) a rule of conduct *b*) adherence to such rules; integrity **3** a basic part **4** *a*) the scientific law explaining a natural action *b*) the method of a thing's operation

**prin'ci·pled** *adj.* having principles, as of conduct

**print** (print) *n.* ⟦< L *premere*, to press⟧ **1** a mark made on a surface by pressing or stamping **2** cloth printed with a design **3** the impression of letters, designs, etc. made by inked type or from a plate, block, etc. **4** a photograph, esp. one made from a negative —*vt.*, *vi.* **1** to stamp (a mark, letter, etc.) on a surface **2** to produce on (paper, etc.) the impression of inked type, etc. **3** to produce (a book, etc.) **4** to write in letters resembling printed ones **5** to make (a photographic print) —**in** (or **out of**) **print** still (or no longer) being sold by the publisher: said of books, etc. —**print'er** *n.*

**printed circuit** an electrical circuit of conductive material, as in fine lines, applied to an insulating sheet

**print'ing** *n.* **1** the act of one that prints **2** something printed **3** all the copies printed at one time

**printing press** a machine for printing from inked type, plates, or rolls

**print'out'** *n.* the printed or typewritten output of a computer

**pri·or** (prī'ər) *adj.* ⟦L⟧ **1** earlier; previous **2** preceding in order or importance —*n.* the head of a priory —**prior to** before in time

**pri·or·ess** (-is) *n.* a woman who heads a priory of nuns

**pri·or·i·tize** (prī ôr′ə tīz′) *vt.* **-tized′, -tiz′ing** to arrange (items) in order of importance

**pri·or·i·ty** (prī ôr′ə tē) *n., pl.* **-ties** **1** a being prior; precedence **2** a prior right to get, buy, or do something **3** something to be given prior attention

**pri·o·ry** (prī′ə rē) *n., pl.* **-ries** a monastery governed by a prior, or a convent governed by a prioress

**prism** (priz′əm) *n.* ⟦< Gr *prizein*, to saw⟧ **1** *Geom.* a solid figure whose ends are parallel and equal in size and shape, and whose sides are parallelograms **2** a transparent, triangular prism used to disperse light into the spectrum — **pris·mat·ic** (priz mat′ik) *adj.*

TRIANGULAR
HEXAGONAL

PRISMS

**pris·on** (priz′ən) *n.* ⟦< L *prehendere*, take⟧ a place of confinement for convicted criminals or persons who are awaiting trial

**prison camp** **1** a camp with minimum security for holding reliable prisoners **2** a camp for confining prisoners of war

**pris·on·er** *n.* one held captive or confined, esp. in prison

**pris·sy** (pris′ē) *adj.* **-si·er, -si·est** ⟦prob. PR(IM) + (S)ISSY⟧ [Inf.] very prim or prudish — **pris′si·ness** *n.*

**pris·tine** (pris′tēn′, pris tēn′) *adj.* ⟦L *pristinus*, former⟧ **1** characteristic of the earliest period **2** unspoiled

**prith·ee** (pri*th*′ē) *interj.* ⟦< pray thee⟧ [Archaic] I pray thee; please

**pri·va·cy** (prī′və sē) *n., pl.* **-cies** **1** a being private; seclusion **2** secrecy **3** one's private life

**pri·vate** (prī′vət) *adj.* ⟦< L *privus*, separate⟧ **1** of or concerning a particular person or group **2** not open to or controlled by the public *[a private school]* **3** for an individual person *[a private room]* **4** not holding public office *[a private citizen]* **5** secret *[a private matter]* —*n.* **1** *[pl.]* the genitals: also **private parts 2** the lowest-ranking enlisted man of either the U.S. Army or Marine Corps —**go private** to restore private corporate ownership by buying back publicly held stock —**in private** not publicly —**pri′vate·ly** *adv.*

**pri·va·teer** (prī′və tir′) *n.* **1** a privately owned ship commissioned in war to capture enemy ships **2** a commander or crew member of a privateer

**private eye** [Slang] a private detective

**pri·va·tion** (prī vā′shən) *n.* the lack of ordinary necessities or comforts

**pri·va·tize** (prī′və tīz′) *vt.* **-tized′, -tiz′ing** to turn over (a public property, etc.) to private interests —**pri′va·ti·za′tion** *n.*

**priv·et** (priv′it) *n.* ⟦< ?⟧ an evergreen shrub used for hedges

**priv·i·lege** (priv′ə lij, priv′lij) *n.* ⟦< L *privus*, separate + *lex*, law⟧ a special right, favor, etc. granted to some person or group —*vt.* **-leged, -leg·ing** to grant a privilege to

**priv·y** (priv′ē) *adj.* private: now only in such phrases as **privy council,** a body of confidential advisers named by a ruler —*n., pl.* **priv′ies** an outhouse —**privy to** privately informed about

**prize**[1] (prīz) *vt.* **prized, priz′ing** ⟦see PRICE⟧ to value highly; esteem —*n.* **1** something given to the winner of a contest, etc. **2** anything worth striving for —*adj.* **1** that has won or is worthy of a prize **2** given as a prize

**prize**[2] (prīz) *n.* ⟦< L *prehendere*, to take⟧ something taken by force, esp. a captured ship —*vt.* **prized, priz′ing** to pry, as with a lever

**prize′fight′** *n.* a professional boxing match — **prize′fight′er** *n.*

**pro**[1] (prō) *adv.* ⟦L, for⟧ favorably —*adj.* favorable

—*n., pl.* **pros 1** a person or vote on the affirmative side **2** an argument in favor of something

**pro**[2] (prō) *adj., n., pl.* **pros** *short for* PROFESSIONAL

**pro-**[1] ⟦Gr < *pro*, before⟧ *prefix* before in place or time

**pro-**[2] ⟦L < *pro*, forward⟧ *prefix* **1** moving forward or ahead of *[proclivity]* **2** forth *[produce]* **3** substituting for *[pronoun]* **4** defending, supporting *[prolabor]*

**pro-am** (prō′am′) *n.* a sports competition for both amateurs and professionals

**prob** *abbrev.* **1** probably **2** problem

**prob·a·bil·i·ty** (präb′ə bil′ə tē) *n., pl.* **-ties 1** a being probable; likelihood **2** something probable

**prob·a·ble** (präb′ə bəl) *adj.* ⟦< L *probare*, prove⟧ **1** likely to occur or be **2** reasonably so, but not proved —**prob′a·bly** *adv.*

**pro·bate** (prō′bāt′) *n.* ⟦see PROBE⟧ the act or process of probating —*adj.* having to do with probating *[probate court]* —*vt.* **-bat′ed, -bat′ing** to establish officially that (a document, esp. a will) is genuine

**pro·ba·tion** (prō bā′shən) *n.* ⟦see PROBE⟧ **1** a testing, as of one's character, ability, etc. **2** the conditional suspension of a convicted person's sentence —**pro·ba′tion·ar′y** *adj.*

**pro·ba′tion·er** *n.* a person on probation

**probation officer** an officer who watches over persons on probation

**probe** (prōb) *n.* ⟦< L *probare*, to test⟧ **1** a surgical instrument for exploring a wound, etc. **2** a searching examination **3** a device, as a spacecraft with instruments, used to get information about an environment —*vt.* **probed, prob′ing 1** to explore (a wound, etc.) with a probe **2** to investigate thoroughly —*vi.* to search

**pro·bi·ty** (prō′bə tē, präb′ə-) *n.* ⟦< L *probus*, good⟧ honesty; integrity

**prob·lem** (präb′ləm) *n.* ⟦< Gr *problēma*⟧ **1** a question proposed for solution **2** a perplexing or difficult matter, person, etc.

**prob·lem·at·ic** (präb′lə mat′ik) *adj.* **1** hard to solve **2** uncertain Also **prob′lem·at′i·cal**

**pro·bos·cis** (prō bäs′is) *n., pl.* **-cis·es** ⟦< Gr *pro-,* before + *boskein,* to feed⟧ an elephant's trunk, or any similar long, flexible snout

**pro·caine** (prō′kān′) *n.* ⟦PRO-[2] + (CO)CAINE⟧ a synthetic compound used as a local anesthetic

**pro·ce·dure** (prō sē′jər, prə-) *n.* the act or method of proceeding in an action —**pro·ce′dur·al** *adj.*

**pro·ceed** (prō sēd′, prə-) *vi.* ⟦< L *pro-,* forward + *cedere,* go⟧ **1** to go on, esp. after stopping **2** to carry on some action **3** to take legal action (*against*) **4** to come forth or issue (*from*)

**pro·ceed′ing** *n.* **1** a going on with what one has been doing **2** a course of action **3** *[pl.]* a record of the business carried on, as by a learned society **4** *[pl.]* legal action

**pro·ceeds** (prō′sēdz′) *pl.n.* the sum derived from a sale, business venture, etc.

**proc·ess** (prä′ses′) *n.* ⟦see PROCEED⟧ **1** the course of being done: chiefly in **in process 2** course (*of* time, etc.) **3** a continuing development involving many changes *[the process of digestion]* **4** a method of doing something, with all the steps involved **5** *Biol.* a projecting part **6** *Law* a court summons —*vt.* to prepare by or subject to a special process —**proc′ess·or** *n.*

**pro·ces·sion** (prō sesh′ən, prə-) *n.* ⟦see PROCEED⟧ a number of persons or things moving forward, as in a parade

**pro·ces·sion·al** *n.* a hymn sung at the beginning of a church service during the entrance of the clergy

**pro′-choice′** *adj.* advocating the legal right to obtain an abortion —**pro′-choic′er** *n.*

**pro·claim** (prō klām′) *vt.* ⟦< L *pro-,* before + *clamare,* cry out⟧ to announce officially; announce to be

**proc·la·ma·tion** (präk′lə mā′shən) *n.* **1** a proclaiming **2** something that is proclaimed

**pro·cliv·i·ty** (prō kliv′ə tē) *n., pl.* **-ties** ⟦< L *pro*-, before + *clivus*, a slope⟧ a tendency or inclination

**pro·cras·ti·nate** (prō kras′tə nāt′) *vi., vt.* **-nat′ed, -nat′ing** ⟦< L *pro*-, forward + *cras*, tomorrow⟧ to put off doing (something) until later; delay —**pro·cras′ti·na′tion** *n.* —**pro·cras′ti·na′tor** *n.*

**pro·cre·ate** (prō′krē āt′) *vt., vi.* **-at′ed, -at′ing** ⟦< L *pro*-, before + *creare*, create⟧ to produce (young); beget (offspring) —**pro′cre·a′tion** *n.*

**proc·tor** (präk′tər) *n.* ⟦see PROCURE⟧ one who supervises students, as at an examination —*vt.* to supervise (an academic examination)

**proc·u·ra·tor** (präk′yoo rāt′ər) *n.* ⟦see fol.⟧ in the Roman Empire, the governor of a lesser province

**pro·cure** (prō kyoor′) *vt.* **-cured′, -cur′ing** ⟦< L *pro*-, before + *curare*, attend to⟧ to obtain; get —**pro·cur′a·ble** *adj.* —**pro·cure′ment** *n.*

**pro·cur′er** *n.* a pimp

**prod** (präd) *vt.* **prod′ded, prod′ding** ⟦< ?⟧ **1** to jab as with a pointed stick **2** to goad into action —*n.* **1** a jab or thrust **2** something that prods

**prod·i·gal** (präd′i gəl) *adj.* ⟦< L *pro*-, forth + *agere*, to drive⟧ **1** exceedingly or recklessly wasteful **2** extremely abundant —*n.* a spendthrift —**prod′i·gal′i·ty** (-gal′ə tē), *pl.* **-ties,** *n.*

**pro·di·gious** (prō dij′əs, prə-) *adj.* ⟦see fol.⟧ **1** wonderful; amazing **2** enormous; huge —**pro·di′gious·ly** *adv.*

**prod·i·gy** (präd′ə jē) *n., pl.* **-gies** ⟦< L *prodigium*, omen⟧ an extraordinary person, thing, or act; specif., a child of genius

**pro·duce** (prə doōs′; *for n.* prō′doōs′) *vt.* **-duced′, -duc′ing** ⟦< L *pro*-, forward + *ducere*, to lead⟧ **1** to bring to view; show /to *produce* identification/ **2** to bring forth; bear **3** to make or manufacture **4** to cause **5** to get (a play, etc.) ready for presentation —*vi.* to yield something —*n.* something produced; esp., fruit and vegetables —**pro·duc′er** *n.*

**prod·uct** (präd′əkt) *n.* **1** something produced by nature, industry, or art **2** result; outgrowth **3** *Math.* the quantity obtained by multiplying two or more quantities together

**pro·duc·tion** (prə duk′shən) *n.* a producing or something produced

**pro·duc′tive** *adj.* **1** fertile **2** marked by abundant production **3** bringing as a result (with *of*) /war is *productive* of misery/ —**pro·duc′tive·ly** *adv.* —**pro·duc·tiv·i·ty** (prō′dək tiv′ə tē) or **pro·duc′tive·ness** *n.*

**prof** (präf) *n.* [Inf.] *short for* PROFESSOR

**Prof** *abbrev.* Professor

**pro·fane** (prō fān′) *adj.* ⟦< L *pro*-, before + *fanum*, temple⟧ **1** not connected with religion; secular **2** showing disrespect or contempt for sacred things —*vt.* **-faned′, -fan′ing** **1** to treat (sacred things) with irreverence or contempt **2** to debase; defile —**prof·a·na·tion** (präf′ə nā′shən) *n.* —**pro·fane′ly** *adv.* —**pro·fane′ness** *n.*

**pro·fan·i·ty** (-fan′ə tē) *n.* **1** a being profane **2** *pl.* **-ties** profane language; swearing

**pro·fess** (prō fes′, prə-) *vt.* ⟦< L *pro*-, before + *fateri*, avow⟧ **1** to declare openly; affirm **2** to claim to have (some feeling, etc.): often insincerely **3** to declare one's belief in —**pro·fessed′** *adj.*

**pro·fes·sion** (prō fesh′ən, prə-) *n.* **1** a professing, or declaring; avowal **2** an occupation requiring advanced academic training, as medicine, law, etc. **3** all the persons in such an occupation

**pro·fes′sion·al** *adj.* **1** of or engaged in a profession **2** engaged in some sport or in a specified occupation for pay —*n.* a person who is professional —**pro·fes′sion·al·ly** *adv.*

**pro·fes·sor** (prō fes′ər, prə-) *n.* a college or university teacher, esp. one of the highest rank —**pro·fes·so·ri·al** (prō′fə sôr′ē əl, prä′-) *adj.* —**pro·fes′sor·ship′** *n.*

**prof·fer** (präf′ər) *vt.* ⟦< OFr: see PRO-² & OFFER⟧ to offer (usually something intangible) /to *proffer* friendship/ —*n.* an offer

**pro·fi·cient** (prō fish′ənt, prə-) *adj.* ⟦< L *pro*-, for-

ward + *facere*, make⟧ highly competent; skilled —**pro·fi′cien·cy** *n.* —**pro·fi′cient·ly** *adv.*

**pro·file** (prō′fīl′) *n.* ⟦< It *profilare*, to outline⟧ **1** a side view of the face **2** a drawing of this **3** an outline **4** a short, vivid biography **5** a degree of public exposure /keeping a low *profile*/ —*vt.* **1** to draw or write a profile **2** to identify by profiling

**pro′fil·ing** *n.* the use of a set of characteristics to identify those likely to belong to a certain group, as in detaining suspected criminals

**prof·it** (präf′it) *n.* ⟦see PROFICIENT⟧ **1** advantage; gain **2** [*often pl.*] financial gain; esp. the sum remaining after deducting costs —*vt.* **1** to be of advantage (to) **2** to benefit —**prof′it·a·bil′i·ty** *n.* —**prof′it·a·ble** *adj.* —**prof′it·a·bly** *adv.* —**prof′it·less** *adj.*

**prof·it·eer** (präf′i tir′) *n.* one who makes excessive profits by charging exorbitant prices —*vi.* to be a profiteer

**pro·fi·te·role** (prə fit′ə rōl′) *n.* a small cream puff

**prof·li·gate** (präf′li git) *adj.* ⟦< L *pro*-, forward + *fligere*, to drive⟧ **1** dissolute **2** recklessly wasteful —**prof′li·ga·cy** (-gə sē) *n.*

**pro for·ma** (prō fôr′mə) ⟦L⟧ for (the sake of) form; as a matter of form

**pro·found** (prō found′, prə-) *adj.* ⟦< L *pro*-, forward + *fundus*, bottom⟧ **1** marked by intellectual depth **2** deeply felt [*profound* grief] **3** thoroughgoing [*profound* changes] —**pro·found′ly** *adv.* —**pro·fun·di·ty** (-fun′də tē), *pl.* **-ties,** *n.*

**pro·fuse** (prō fyoōs′, prə-) *adj.* ⟦< L *pro*-, forth + *fundere*, pour⟧ giving or given freely and abundantly —**pro·fuse′ly** *adv.* —**pro·fu′sion** (-fyoō′zhən) *n.*

**pro·gen·i·tor** (prō jen′ə tər) *n.* ⟦< L *pro*-, forth + *gignere*, beget⟧ **1** an ancestor in direct line **2** a precursor

**prog·e·ny** (präj′ə nē) *n., pl.* **-nies** ⟦see prec.⟧ children; offspring

**pro·ges·ter·one** (prō jes′tər ōn′) *n.* a female hormone secreted by the ovary or made synthetically

**prog·na·thous** (präg′nə thəs) *adj.* [PRO-¹ + Gr *gnathos*, jaw⟧ having the jaws projecting beyond the upper face

**prog·no·sis** (präg nō′sis) *n., pl.* **-no′ses** (-sēz′) ⟦< Gr *pro*-, before + *gignōskein*, know⟧ a prediction, esp. of the course of a disease

**prog·nos′tic** (-näs′tik) *adj.* ⟦see prec.⟧ **1** foretelling **2** of a medical prognosis

**prog·nos·ti·cate′** (-näs′ti kāt′) *vt.* **-cat′ed, -cat′ing** ⟦see PROGNOSIS⟧ to foretell —**prog·nos′ti·ca′tion** *n.* —**prog·nos′ti·ca′tor** *n.*

**pro·gram** (prō′gram′, -grəm) *n.* ⟦< Gr *pro*-, before + *graphein*, write⟧ **1** a list of the acts, speeches, musical pieces, etc. as of an entertainment **2** a plan or procedure **3** a scheduled radio or TV broadcast **4** a logical sequence of coded instructions specifying the operations to be performed by a computer **5** a series of operations used to control an electronic device —*vt.* **-grammed′** or **-gramed′, -gram′ming** or **-gram′ing** **1** to schedule in a program **2** to prepare (a textbook, etc.) for use in programmed instruction **3** to plan a computer program for **4** to furnish (a computer) with a program Also [Chiefly Brit.] **pro′gramme′** —**pro·gram·ma·ble** (prō′gram′ə bəl, prō gram′-) *adj.,* *n.* —**pro′gram′mer** or **pro′gram′er** *n.*

**pro·gram·mat·ic** (prō′grə mat′ik) *adj.* of or like a program; often, specif., predictable, mechanical, uninspired, etc.

**programmed instruction** instruction in which individual students answer questions about a unit of study at their own rate, checking their own answers and advancing only after answering correctly

**prog·ress** (präg′res; *for v.* prō gres′, prə-) *n.* ⟦< L *pro*-, before + *gradi*, to step⟧ **1** a moving forward or onward **2** development **3** improvement —*vi.* **1** to move forward or onward **2** to move forward toward completion **3** to improve

**pro·gres·sion** (prō gresh′ən, prə-) *n.* **1** a moving forward **2** a succession, as of events **3** *Math.* a series of numbers, each of which is obtained from its predecessor by the same rule

**pro·gres′sive** (-gres′iv, prə-) *adj.* **1** moving forward **2** continuing by successive steps **3** of or favoring progress, reform, etc. **4** *Gram.* indicating continuing action or state, as certain verb forms —*n.* one who is progressive —**pro·gres′sive·ly** *adv.*

**pro·hib·it** (prō hib′it, prə-) *vt.* [< L *pro-*, before + *habere*, have] **1** to forbid by law or an order **2** to prevent; hinder —**pro·hib′i·tive** *adj.*

**pro·hi·bi·tion** (prō′i bish′ən) *n.* **1** a prohibiting **2** the forbidding by law of the manufacture or sale of alcoholic beverages —**pro′hi·bi′tion·ist** *n.*

**proj·ect** (prä′jekt′; *for v.* prō jekt′, prə-) *n.* [< L *pro-*, before + *jacere*, to throw] **1** a proposal; scheme **2** an organized undertaking —*vt.* **pro·ject′** **1** to propose (a plan) **2** to throw forward **3** to cause to jut out **4** to cause (a shadow, image, etc.) to fall upon a surface —*vi.* to jut out —**pro·jec′tion** *n.*

**pro·jec·tile** (prō jek′təl, prə-) *n.* **1** an object designed to be shot forward, as a bullet **2** anything thrown or hurled forward

**projection booth** a small chamber, as in a theater, from which images on film, slides, etc. are projected

**pro·jec′tion·ist** *n.* the operator of a film or slide projector

**pro·jec′tor** *n.* a machine for projecting images onto a screen

**pro·lapse** (prō laps′, prō′laps′) *n.* [L *pro-*, forward + *labi*, to fall] *Med.* the slipping out of place of an internal organ: said as of the uterus

**pro·le·tar·i·at** (prō′lə ter′ē ət) *n.* [< L *proletarius*, a citizen of the lowest class] the working class; esp., the industrial working class —**pro′le·tar′i·an** *adj., n.*

**pro′-life′** *adj.* opposing the legal right to abortion —**pro′-lif′er** *n.*

**pro·lif·er·ate** (prō lif′ər āt′, prə-) *vi.* -**at′ed**, -**at′ing** [ult. < L *proles*, offspring + *ferre*, to bear] to increase rapidly —**pro·lif·er·a′tion** *n.*

**pro·lif·ic** (prō lif′ik, prə-) *adj.* [< L *proles*, offspring + *facere*, make] **1** producing many young or much fruit **2** turning out many products of the mind —**pro·lif′i·cal·ly** *adv.*

**pro·lix** (prō liks′, prō′liks′) *adj.* [< L *prolixus*, extended] wordy or long-winded —**pro·lix′i·ty** *n.*

**pro·logue** (prō′lôg′) *n.* [< Gr *pro-*, before + *logos*, discourse] **1** an introduction to a poem, play, etc. **2** any preliminary act, event, etc.

**pro·long** (prō lôŋ′, prə-) *vt.* [< L *pro-*, forth + *longus*, long] to lengthen in time or space: also **pro·lon′gate** (-gāt′, -gat′ed, -gat′ing) —**pro·lon·ga·tion** (prō′lôŋ gā′shən) *n.*

**prom** (präm) *n.* [< fol.] a dance, as of a particular class in a school

**prom·e·nade** (präm′ə nād′, -näd′) *n.* [Fr < L *pro-*, forth + *minare*, to herd] **1** a leisurely walk taken for pleasure, display, etc. **2** a public place for walking —*vi., vt.* -**nad′ed**, -**nad′ing** to take a promenade (along or through)

**Pro·me·the·us** (prō mē′thē əs) *n.* Gr. Myth. a Titan who steals fire from heaven for the benefit of human beings

**prom·i·nent** (präm′ə nənt) *adj.* [< L *prominere*, to project] **1** sticking out; projecting **2** noticeable; conspicuous **3** widely and favorably known — **prom′i·nence** *n.* —**prom′i·nent·ly** *adv.*

**pro·mis·cu·ous** (prō mis′kyōo əs, prə-) *adj.* [< L *pro-*, forth + *miscere*, to mix] **1** consisting of different elements indiscriminately mingled **2** characterized by a lack of discrimination, esp. in sexual liaisons —**prom·is·cu·i·ty** (präm′is kyōō′ə tē), *pl.* -**ties**, *n.* —**pro·mis′cu·ous·ly** *adv.*

**prom·ise** (präm′is) *n.* [< L *pro-*, forth + *mittere*, send] **1** an agreement to do or not to do some-

thing **2** indication, as of a successful future **3** something promised —*vi., vt.* -**ised**, -**is·ing** **1** to make a promise of (something) **2** to give a basis for expecting (something)

**Promised Land** *Bible* Canaan, promised by God to Abraham and his descendants: Genesis 17:8

**prom·is·so·ry** (präm′i sôr′ē) *adj.* containing a promise

**pro·mo** (prō′mō) [Inf.] *adj.* of or engaged in the promotion or advertising of a product, etc. —*n., pl.* -**mos** a recorded announcement, radio or TV commercial, etc. used in advertising, etc.

**prom·on·to·ry** (präm′ən tôr′ē) *n., pl.* -**ries** [prob. < L *prominere*, to project] a peak of high land that juts out into a body of water; headland

**pro·mote** (prə ōt′) *vt.* -**mot′ed**, -**mot′ing** [< L *pro-*, forward + *movere*, to move] **1** to raise to a higher position or rank **2** to further the growth, establishment, sales, etc. of —**pro·mo′tion** *n.* —**pro·mo′tion·al** *adj.*

**pro·mot′er** *n.* one who begins, organizes, and furthers an undertaking

**prompt** (prämpt) *adj.* [< L *pro-*, forth + *emere*, take] **1** ready, punctual, etc. **2** done, spoken, etc. without delay —*vt.* **1** to urge into action **2** to remind (a person) of something he or she has forgotten; specif., to help (an actor, etc.) with a cue **3** to inspire —**prompt′er** *n.* —**prompt′ly** *adv.* —**prompt′ness** or **promp′ti·tude′** *n.*

**prom·ul·gate** (präm′əl gāt′, prō mul′gāt′) *vt.* -**gat′ed**, -**gat′ing** [< L *promulgare*, publish] **1** to make known officially **2** to make widespread —**prom′ul·ga′tion** *n.*

**pron** *abbrev.* **1** pronoun **2** pronunciation

**prone** (prōn) *adj.* [< L *pronus*] **1** lying face downward or prostrate **2** disposed or inclined (*to*) [*prone* to error]

**prong** (prôŋ) *n.* [ME *pronge*] **1** any of the pointed ends of a fork; tine **2** any projecting part — **pronged** *adj.*

**prong′horn′** *n.* an animal of the W U.S. having curved horns and resembling both the deer and the antelope

**pro·noun** (prō′noun′) *n.* [< L *pro*, for + *nomen*, noun] *Gram.* a word used in place of a noun (Ex.: *I, he, them, ours, which, yourself, anyone*) —**pro·nom′i·nal** (-näm′i nəl) *adj.*

**pro·nounce** (prə nouns′, prō-) *vt.* -**nounced′**, -**nounc′ing** [< L *pro-*, before + *nuntiare*, announce] **1** to declare officially, solemnly, etc. **2** to utter or articulate (a sound or word) —**pro·nounce′a·ble** *adj.*

**pro·nounced′** *adj.* clearly marked; decided [a *pronounced* change]

**pro·nounce′ment** *n.* a formal statement, as of an opinion

**pron·to** (prän′tō) *adv.* [Sp: see PROMPT] [Slang] at once; quickly

**pro·nun·ci·a·tion** (prə nun′sē ā′shən, prō-) *n.* **1** the act or manner of pronouncing words **2** an accepted way of pronouncing a word; also, a rendering of this in symbols

**proof** (prōof) *n.* [see PROBE] **1** a proving or testing of something **2** evidence that establishes the truth of something **3** the relative strength of an alcoholic liquor **4** *Photog.* a trial print of a negative **5** a sheet printed from set type, for checking errors, etc. —*adj.* of tested strength in resisting: with *against*

**-proof** (prōof) [< prec.] *combining form* **1** impervious to [*waterproof*] **2** protected from [*rustproof*] **3** resistant to [*fireproof*]

**proof′read′** (-rēd′) *vt., vi.* to read and mark corrections on (printers' proofs, etc.) —**proof′read′er** *n.*

**prop**[1] (präp) *n.* [< MDu *proppe*] a support, as a pole, placed under or against something: often used figuratively —*vt.* **propped**, **prop′ping** **1** to support with or as with a prop: often with *up* **2** to lean (something) *against* a support

**prop**[2] (präp) *n.* PROPERTY (sense 4)

**prop**[3] (präp) *n.* short for PROPELLER

**prop**[4] *abbrev.* **1** proper(ly) **2** property **3** proposition **4** proprietor

**prop·a·gan·da** (präp'ə gan'də) *n.* ⟦ModL: see fol.⟧ **1** any widespread promotion of particular ideas, doctrines, etc. **2** ideas, etc. so spread —**prop'a·gan'dist** *n.*, *adj.* —**prop'a·gan'dize'** (-dīz'), **-dized'**, **-diz'ing**, *vt.*, *vi.*

**prop·a·gate** (präp'ə gāt') *vt.* **-gat'ed**, **-gat'ing** ⟦< L *propago*, slip (of a plant)⟧ **1** to cause (a plant or animal) to reproduce itself **2** to reproduce (itself): said of a plant or animal **3** to spread (ideas, customs, etc.) —*vi.* to reproduce: said of plants or animals —**prop'a·ga'tion** *n.*

**pro·pane** (prō'pān') *n.* a gaseous hydrocarbon obtained from petroleum, used as a fuel

**pro·pel** (prə pel', prō-) *vt.* **-pelled'**, **-pel'ling** ⟦< L *pro-*, forward + *pellere*, to drive⟧ to drive onward or forward

**pro·pel'lant** or **pro·pel'lent** *n.* one that propels; specif., the fuel for a rocket

**pro·pel'ler** *n.* a device having two or more blades in a revolving hub, for propelling a ship or aircraft

**pro·pen·si·ty** (prə pen'sə tē) *n.*, *pl.* **-ties** ⟦< L *propendere*, hang forward⟧ a natural inclination or tendency

**prop·er** (präp'ər) *adj.* ⟦< L *proprius*, one's own⟧ **1** specially suitable; appropriate; fitting **2** naturally belonging (*to*) **3** conforming to a standard; correct **4** decent; decorous **5** in the most restricted sense [Chicago *proper* (i.e., apart from its suburbs)] **6** designating a noun that names a specific individual, place, etc. (Ex.: *Bill, Paris*) — **prop'er·ly** *adv.*

**prop·er·ty** (präp'ər tē) *n.*, *pl.* **-ties** ⟦see prec.⟧ **1** ownership **2** something owned, esp. real estate **3** a characteristic or attribute **4** any of the movable articles used in a stage setting —**prop'er·tied** (-tēd) *adj.*

**proph·e·cy** (präf'ə sē) *n.*, *pl.* **-cies** ⟦see PROPHET⟧ **1** prediction of the future, as by divine guidance **2** something predicted

**proph'e·sy'** (-sī') *vt.*, *vi.* **-sied'**, **-sy'ing** **1** to predict as by divine guidance **2** to predict in any way

**proph·et** (präf'it) *n.* ⟦< Gr *pro-*, before + *phanai*, speak⟧ **1** a religious leader regarded as, or claiming to be, divinely inspired **2** one who predicts the future —**proph'et·ess** *fem.n.*

**pro·phet·ic** (prə fet'ik, prō-) *adj.* **1** of or like a prophet **2** like or containing a prophecy —**pro·phet'i·cal·ly** *adv.*

**pro·phy·lac·tic** (prō'fə lak'tik) *adj.* ⟦< Gr *pro-*, before + *phylassein*, to guard⟧ preventive or protective; esp., preventing disease —*n.* **1** a prophylactic medicine, device, etc. **2** a condom

**pro'phy·lax'is** (-lak'sis) *n.*, *pl.* **-lax'es'** (-sēz') **1** prophylactic treatment **2** *Dentistry* a cleaning of the teeth to remove plaque and tartar

**pro·pin·qui·ty** (prō piŋ'kwə tē) *n.* ⟦< L *propinquus*, near⟧ nearness

**pro·pi·ti·ate** (prō pish'ē āt', prə-) *vt.* **-at'ed**, **-at'ing** ⟦see fol.⟧ to win the good will of; appease —**pro·pi'ti·a'tion** *n.* —**pro·pi'ti·a·to'ry** (-ē ə tôr'ē) *adj.*

**pro·pi·tious** (prō pish'əs, prə-) *adj.* ⟦< L *pro-*, before + *petere*, seek⟧ **1** favorably inclined **2** favorable; auspicious

**prop'jet'** *n.* TURBOPROP

**pro·po·nent** (prə pō'nənt, prō-) *n.* ⟦see PROPOSE⟧ one who espouses or supports a cause, etc.

**pro·por·tion** (prə pôr'shən, prō-) *n.* ⟦< L *pro*, for + *portio*, a part⟧ **1** the comparative relation in size, amount, etc. between things; ratio **2** a part, share, etc. in its relation to the whole **3** balance or symmetry **4** [*pl.*] dimensions —*vt.* **1** to put in proper relation with something else **2** to arrange the parts of (a whole) so as to be harmonious — **pro·por'tion·al** or **pro·por'tion·ate** (-shə nit) *adj.*

**pro·pos·al** (prə pōz'əl) *n.* **1** a proposing **2** a proposed plan, etc. **3** an offer of marriage

**pro·pose** (prə pōz') *vt.* **-posed'**, **-pos'ing** ⟦< L *pro-*, forth + *ponere*, to place⟧ **1** to put forth for consid-

---

eration, approval, etc. **2** to plan or intend —*vi.* to offer marriage

**prop·o·si·tion** (präp'ə zish'ən) *n.* **1** something proposed; plan **2** [Inf.] a proposed deal, as in business **3** [Inf.] an undertaking, etc. to be dealt with **4** a subject to be discussed **5** *Math.* a problem to be solved

**pro·pound** (prə pound', prō-) *vt.* ⟦see PROPOSE⟧ to put forward for consideration

**pro·pri·e·tar·y** (prə prī'ə tər ē, prō-) *adj.* ⟦see PROPERTY⟧ belonging to a proprietor, as under a patent, trademark, or copyright

**pro·pri'e·tor** *n.* an owner —**pro·pri'e·tor·ship'** *n.* —**pro·pri'e·tress** (-tris) *fem.n.*

**pro·pri·e·ty** (-tē) *n.*, *pl.* **-ties** ⟦see PROPER⟧ **1** the quality of being proper, fitting, etc. **2** conformity with accepted standards of behavior

**pro·pul·sion** (prə pul'shən) *n.* ⟦see PROPEL⟧ **1** a propelling or being propelled **2** something that propels —**pro·pul'sive** *adj.*

**pro·rate** (prō rāt', prō'rāt') *vt.*, *vi.* **-rat'ed**, **-rat'ing** ⟦< L *pro rata*, in proportion⟧ to divide or assess proportionally

**pro·sa·ic** (prō zā'ik) *adj.* ⟦< L *prosa*, prose⟧ commonplace; dull

**pro·sce·ni·um** (prō sē'nē əm) *n.*, *pl.* **-ni·ums** or **-ni·a** (-ə) ⟦< Gr *pro-*, before + *skēnē*, tent⟧ in a theater, the plane separating the stage proper from the audience and including the arch (**proscenium arch**) and the curtain within it

**pro·scribe** (prō skrīb') *vt.* **-scribed'**, **-scrib'ing** ⟦< L < *pro-*, before + *scribere*, write⟧ **1** to outlaw **2** to banish; exile **3** to denounce or forbid the use, etc. of —**pro·scrip'tion** (-skrip'shən) *n.*

**prose** (prōz) *n.* ⟦< L *prorsus*, straight on⟧ ordinary language; writing that is not poetry

**pros·e·cute** (präs'ə kyōōt') *vt.* **-cut'ed**, **-cut'ing** ⟦< L *pro-*, before + *sequi*, follow⟧ **1** to carry on **2** to conduct legal action against —**pros'e·cu'tion** *n.* — **pros'e·cu'tor** *n.* —**pros'e·cu·to'ri·al** *adj.*

**pros·e·lyte** (präs'ə līt') *n.* ⟦< Gr *prosēlytos*, a stranger⟧ one who has been converted from one religion, sect, etc. to another

**pros·e·lyt·ize** (präs'ə li tīz') *vi.*, *vt.* **-ized'**, **-iz'ing** **1** to try to convert (a person), esp. to one's religion **2** to persuade to do or join something —**pros'e·lyt·ism'** (-li tiz'əm) *n.* —**pros'e·lyt·iz'er** *n.*

**pro·sim·i·an** (prō sim'ē ən) *n.* any of various small, arboreal primates

**pros·o·dy** (präs'ə dē) *n.* ⟦< Gr *prosōidia*, accent⟧ versification; study of meter, rhyme, etc.

**pros·pect** (präs'pekt') *n.* ⟦< L *pro-*, forward + *specere*, to look⟧ **1** a broad view; scene **2** a viewpoint; outlook **3** anticipation **4** *a*) something expected *b*) [*usually pl.*] apparent chance for success **5** a likely customer, candidate, etc. —*vi.* to explore or search (*for*) —**pros'pec·tor** *n.*

**pro·spec·tive** (prə spek'tiv, prä-, prō-) *adj.* expected; likely

**pro·spec'tus** (-spek'təs) *n.* ⟦L: see PROSPECT⟧ a statement of the features of a new work, enterprise, etc.

**pros·per** (präs'pər) *vi.* ⟦< L *prospere*, fortunately⟧ to succeed; thrive

**pros·per·i·ty** (präs per'ə tē) *n.*, *pl.* **-ties** prosperous condition; wealth

**pros·per·ous** (präs'pər əs) *adj.* **1** prospering; successful **2** wealthy —**pros'per·ous·ly** *adv.*

**pros·tate** (präs'tāt') *adj.* ⟦< Gr *prostatēs*, one standing before⟧ of or designating a gland surrounding the male urethra at the base of the bladder —*n.* this gland: in full **prostate gland**

**pros·the·sis** (präs thē'sis) *n.*, *pl.* **-ses'** (-sēz') *Med.* **1** the replacement of a missing part of the body, as a limb, by an artificial substitute **2** such a substitute —**pros·thet'ic** (-thet'ik) *adj.*

**pros·ti·tute** (präs'tə tōōt') *n.* ⟦< L *pro-*, before + *statuere*, cause to stand⟧ one who engages in promiscuous sexual activity for pay —*vt.* **-tut'ed**, **-tut'ing** **1** to offer (oneself) as a prostitute **2** to sell (oneself, one's talents, etc.) for base purposes —**pros'ti·tu'tion** *n.*

**pros·trate** (präs'trāt') *adj.* [< L *pro-*, before + *sternere*, stretch out] **1** lying face downward **2** lying prone or supine **3** laid low; overcome —*vt.* **-trat'ed, -trat'ing 1** to lay flat on the ground **2** to lay low; subjugate —**pros·tra'tion** *n.*

**pros·y** (prō'zē) *adj.* **-i·er, -i·est** prosaic; commonplace, dull, etc.

**pro·tag·o·nist** (prō tag'ə nist) *n.* [< Gr *prōtos*, first + *agōnistēs*, actor] the main character in a drama, novel, etc.

**pro·te·an** (prōt'ē ən, prō tē'ən) *adj.* [after *Proteus*, Gr god who changes his form] readily taking on different forms

**pro·tect** (prə tekt', prō-) *vt.* [< L *pro-*, before + *tegere*, to cover] to shield from injury, danger, etc.; defend —**pro·tec'tor** *n.*

**pro·tec'tion** *n.* **1** a protecting or being protected **2** a person or thing that protects

**pro·tec'tive** *adj.* **1** protecting **2** *Economics* intended to protect domestic industry from foreign competition [a *protective* tariff] —**pro·tec'tive·ly** *adv.* —**pro·tec'tive·ness** *n.*

**pro·tec'tor·ate** (-tər it) *n.* a weak state under the protection and control of a strong state

**pro·té·gé** (prōt'ə zhā') *n.* [Fr: see PROTECT] a person guided and helped in his or her career by another person

**pro·tein** (prō'tēn', prō'tē in) *n.* [< Gr *prōtos*, first] any of numerous nitrogenous substances occurring in all living matter and essential to diet

**pro tem·po·re** (prō tem'pə rē') [L] for the time (being); temporarily: shortened to **pro tem**

**pro·test** (prō test'; *also, and for n. always* prō'test') *vt.* [< L *pro-*, forth + *testari*, affirm] **1** to state positively **2** to speak strongly against —*vi.* to express disapproval; object —*n.* **1** an objection **2** a formal statement of objection —**prot·es·ta·tion** (prät'es tā'shən) *n.* —**pro'test'er** *n.*

**Prot·es·tant** (prät'əs tənt) *n.* [see prec.] any Christian not belonging to the Roman Catholic Church or the Eastern Orthodox Church — **Prot'es·tant·ism'** *n.*

**proto-** [< Gr *prōtos*, first] *combining form* **1** first in time, original **2** first in importance, chief

**pro·to·col** (prōt'ə kôl') *n.* [< Gr *prōtokollon*, contents page] **1** an original draft of a document, etc. **2** the code of ceremonial forms accepted as correct in official dealings, as between heads of state or diplomatic officials

**pro·ton** (prō'tän') *n.* [< Gr *prōtos*, first] an elementary particle in the nucleus of all atoms, carrying a unit positive charge of electricity

**pro·to·plasm** (prōt'ə plaz'əm) *n.* [see PROTO- & PLASMA] a semifluid, viscous colloid, the essential living matter of all animal and plant cells — **pro'to·plas'mic** (-plaz'mik) *adj.*

**pro·to·type** (prōt'ə tīp') *n.* the first thing or being of its kind; model

**pro·to·zo·an** (prōt'ə zō'ən) *n., pl.* **-zo'a** (-ə) [< Gr *prōtos*, first + *zōion*, an animal] any of various microscopic, single-celled animals: also **pro'to·zo'on'** (-än'), *pl.* **-zo'a** (-ə)

**pro·tract** (prō trakt', prə-) *vt.* [< L *pro-*, forward + *trahere*, draw] to draw out; prolong —**pro·trac'tion** *n.*

**pro·trac·tor** (prō'trak'tər) *n.* a graduated semicircular instrument for plotting and measuring angles

**pro·trude** (prō trōōd', prə-) *vt., vi.* **-trud'ed, -trud'ing** [< L *pro-*, forth + *trudere*, to thrust] to jut out; project —**pro·tru'sion** (-trōō'zhən) *n.*

**pro·tu·ber·ance** (prō tōō'bər əns, prə-) *n.* a part or thing that protrudes; bulge —**pro·tu'ber·ant** *adj.*

**proud** (proud) *adj.* [< LL *prode*, beneficial] **1** having a proper pride in oneself **2** arrogant; haughty **3** feeling or causing great pride or joy **4** caused by pride **5** stately; splendid [a *proud* fleet] — **proud of** highly pleased with —**proud'ly** *adv.*

**proud flesh** [from the notion of swelling up] an abnormal growth of flesh around a healing wound

**Proust** (prōost), **Mar·cel** (mär sel') 1871-1922; Fr. novelist

**prove** (prōov) *vt.* **proved, proved** or **prov'en, prov'ing** [< L *probare*, to test] **1** to test by experiment, a standard, etc. **2** to establish as true —*vi.* to be found by experience or trial — **prov'a·bil'i·ty** *n.* —**prov'a·ble** *adj.*

**prov·e·nance** (präv'ə nəns) *n.* [< L *provenire*, come forth] origin; source

**Pro·ven·çal** (prō'vən säl') *n.* **1** the vernacular of S France, a Romance language **2** the medieval literary language of S France

**prov·en·der** (präv'ən dər) *n.* [< L *praebere*, give] **1** dry food for livestock **2** [Inf.] food

**prov·erb** (präv'ərb) *n.* [< L *pro-*, PRO-² + *verbum*, word] a short, traditional saying expressing an obvious truth —**pro·ver·bi·al** (prō vur'bē əl) *adj.*

**Prov'erbs** *n.* a book of the Bible containing maxims

**pro·vide** (prə vīd', prō-) *vt.* **-vid'ed, -vid'ing** [< L *pro-*, PRO-² + *videre*, see] **1** to make available; supply **2** to furnish (someone) *with* something **3** to stipulate —*vi.* **1** to prepare (*for* or *against* a possible situation, etc.) **2** to furnish support (*for*) —**pro·vid'er** *n.*

**pro·vid'ed** or **pro·vid'ing** *conj.* on the condition or understanding (*that*)

**prov·i·dence** (präv'ə dəns) *n.* **1** provident management **2** the benevolent guidance of God or nature **3** [P-] God

**Prov·i·dence** (präv'ə dəns) capital of Rhode Island: pop. 161,000

**prov'i·dent** (-dənt) *adj.* [see PROVIDE] **1** providing for the future **2** prudent or economical — **prov'i·dent·ly** *adv.*

**prov'i·den'tial** (-den'shəl) *adj.* of, by, or as if decreed by divine providence

**prov·ince** (präv'ins) *n.* [< L *provincia*] **1** an administrative division of a country; specif., of Canada **2** *a*) a district; territory *b*) [*pl.*] the parts of a country removed from the major cities **3** range of duties or work; sphere

**pro·vin·cial** (prə vin'shəl, prō-) *adj.* **1** of a province **2** having the ways, speech, etc. of a certain province **3** countrylike; rustic **4** narrow; limited —**pro·vin'cial·ism'** *n.*

**proving ground** a place for testing new equipment, new theories, etc.

**pro·vi·sion** (prə vizh'ən, prō-) *n.* **1** a providing or preparing **2** something provided for the future **3** [*pl.*] a stock of food **4** a stipulation; proviso —*vt.* to supply with provisions

**pro·vi'sion·al** *adj.* temporary —**pro·vi'sion·al·ly** *adv.*

**pro·vi·so** (prə vī'zō', prō-) *n., pl.* **-sos'** or **-soes'** [see PROVIDE] a condition or stipulation, or a clause making one

**prov·o·ca·tion** (präv'ə kā'shən) *n.* **1** a provoking **2** something that provokes; incitement

**pro·voc·a·tive** (prə väk'ə tiv, prō-) *adj.* provoking or tending to provoke, as to action, thought, or feeling —**pro·voc'a·tive·ly** *adv.*

**pro·voke** (prə vōk', prō-) *vt.* **-voked', -vok'ing** [< L *pro-*, forth + *vocare*, to call] **1** to excite to some action or feeling **2** to anger or irritate **3** to stir up (action or feeling) **4** to evoke —**pro·vok'er** *n.* —**pro·vok'ing** *adj.*

**pro·vost** (prō'vōst') *n.* [< L *praepositus*, chief] a high executive official, as in some colleges

**pro·vost guard** (prō'vō') a detail of military police under the command of an officer (**provost marshal**)

**prow** (prou) *n.* [< Gr *prōira*] the forward part of a ship, etc.

**prow·ess** (prou'is) *n.* [< OFr *prouesse*] **1** bravery; valor **2** superior ability, skill, etc.

**prowl** (proul) *vi., vt.* [< ?] to roam about furtively

(in), as in search of prey or loot —*n.* a prowling — **prowl′er** *n.*

**prowl car** PATROL CAR

**prox·im·i·ty** (präk sim′ə tē) *n.* ⟦< L *prope*, near⟧ nearness

**prox·y** (präk′sē) *n.*, *pl.* **-ies** ⟦< ME *procuracie*, function of a procurator⟧ **1** the authority to act for another, as in voting **2** one given such authority

**Pro·zac** (prō′zak′) *trademark for* a drug used in treating depression, eating disorders, etc.

**prude** (prōōd) *n.* ⟦Fr < *prudefemme*, excellent woman⟧ one who is overly modest or proper in behavior, dress, etc. —**prud′er·y** *n.* —**prud′ish** *adj.* —**prud′ish·ness** *n.*

**pru·dent** (prōō′dənt) *adj.* ⟦< L *providens*, providing⟧ **1** exercising sound judgment in practical matters **2** cautious in conduct; not rash **3** managing carefully —**pru′dence** *n.* —**pru·den·tial** (prōō den′shəl) *adj.*

**prune**[1] (prōōn) *n.* ⟦< Gr *proumnon*, plum⟧ a dried plum

**prune**[2] (prōōn) *vt.* **pruned**, **prun′ing** ⟦< OFr *prooignier*⟧ **1** to trim dead or living parts from (a plant) **2** to cut out (unnecessary parts, etc.)

**pru·ri·ent** (proor′ē ənt) *adj.* ⟦< L *prurire*, to itch⟧ tending to excite lust; lewd —**pru′ri·ence** *n.*

**Prus·sia** (prush′ə) former kingdom in N Europe & later the dominant state of the German Empire (1871-1919) —**Prus′sian** *adj.*, *n.*

**pry**[1] (prī) *n.*, *pl.* **pries** ⟦< PRIZE[2]⟧ a lever or crowbar —*vt.* **pried**, **pry′ing** **1** to raise or move with a pry **2** to obtain with difficulty

**pry**[2] (prī) *vi.* **pried**, **pry′ing** ⟦< ?⟧ to look closely and inquisitively; snoop

**pry′er** *n.* PRIER

**PS** *abbrev.* Public School

**P.S.**, **p.s.**, or **PS** *abbrev.* postscript

**psalm** (säm) *n.* ⟦< Gr *psallein*, to pluck (a harp)⟧ **1** a sacred song or poem **2** [*usually* P-] any of the songs in praise of God constituting the Book of Psalms —**psalm′ist** *n.*

**Psalms** (sämz) *n.* a book of the Bible consisting of 150 psalms

**Psal·ter** (sôl′tər) *n.* ⟦< Gr *psaltērion*, a harp⟧ **1** PSALMS **2** [*also* p-] a version of the Book of Psalms for use in religious services

**pseu·do** (sōō′dō) *adj.* ⟦ME: see fol.⟧ sham; false; spurious

**pseudo-** ⟦< Gr *pseudein*, deceive⟧ *combining form* sham, counterfeit

**pseu·do·nym** (sōō′də nim′) *n.* ⟦< Gr *pseudēs*, false + *onyma*, a name⟧ a fictitious name, esp. one assumed by an author; pen name

**pshaw** (shô) *n.*, *interj.* (an exclamation) used to express impatience, disgust, etc.

**psi**[1] (sī, psē) *n.* the 23d letter of the Greek alphabet (Ψ, ψ)

**psi**[2] *abbrev.* pounds per square inch

**psit·ta·co·sis** (sit′ə kō′sis) *n.* ⟦< Gr *psittakos*, parrot + -OSIS⟧ a disease of birds, esp. parrots, often transmitted to humans

**pso·ri·a·sis** (sə rī′ə sis) *n.* ⟦ult. < Gr *psōra*, an itch⟧ a chronic skin disease characterized by scaly, reddish patches

**psst** (pst) *interj.* [Inf.] used to attract someone's attention quietly

**PST** *abbrev.* Pacific Standard Time

**psych**[1] (sīk) *vt.* **psyched**, **psych′ing** ⟦< PSYCHOANALYZE⟧ [Slang] **1** to outwit, overcome, etc. by psychological means: often with *out* **2** to prepare (oneself) psychologically: often with *up*

**psych**[2] *abbrev.* psychology

**psych-** *combining form* PSYCHO-

**psy·che** (sī′kē) *n.* ⟦Gr *psychē*⟧ **1** the soul **2** the mind regarded as an entity based ultimately upon physical processes but with its own complex processes **3** [P-] *Rom. Folklore* the wife of Cupid

**psy·che·del·ic** (sī′kə del′ik) *adj.* ⟦< prec. + Gr *dēloun*, make manifest⟧ **1** of or causing extreme

changes in the conscious mind, as hallucinations **2** of or associated with psychedelic drugs

**psy·chi·a·try** (sī kī′ə trē) *n.* ⟦see PSYCHO- & -IATRY⟧ the branch of medicine dealing with disorders of the mind, including psychoses and neuroses —**psy·chi·at·ric** (sī′kē a′trik) *adj.* —**psy′chi′a·trist** *n.*

**psy·chic** (sī′kik) *adj.* ⟦see PSYCHE⟧ **1** of the psyche, or mind **2** beyond known physical processes **3** apparently sensitive to forces beyond the physical world Also **psy′chi·cal** —*n.* **1** a person apparently sensitive to nonphysical forces **2** a MEDIUM (*n.* 5) —**psy′chi·cal·ly** *adv.*

**psy·cho** (sī′kō) *adj.*, *n.* [Inf.] *short for* PSYCHOTIC, PSYCHOPATHIC, and PSYCHOPATH

**psycho-** ⟦see PSYCHE⟧ *combining form* the mind or mental processes

**psy·cho·a·nal·y·sis** (sī′kō ə nal′ə sis) *n.* a method of treating some mental disorders by analyzing repressed feelings, emotional conflicts, etc. through the use of free association, dream analysis, etc. —**psy′cho·an′a·lyst** (-an′ə list) *n.* — **psy′cho·an′a·lyze** (-līz′), **-lyzed′**, **-lyz′ing**, *vt.*

**psy′cho·bab′ble** (-bab′əl) *n.* [Inf.] talk or writing that uses psychological terms and concepts in a trite or superficial way

**psy′cho·gen′ic** (-jen′ik) *adj.* ⟦see PSYCHO- & GENESIS⟧ originating in the mind or caused by mental conflicts

**psy·chol·o·gy** (sī käl′ə jē) *n.*, *pl.* **-gies** ⟦see PSYCHO- & -LOGY⟧ **1** the science dealing with the mind and with mental and emotional processes **2** the science of human and animal behavior — **psy′cho·log′i·cal** (-kə läj′i kəl) *adj.* —**psy·chol′o·gist** *n.*

**psy·cho·neu·ro·sis** (sī′kō nōō rō′sis) *n.*, *pl.* **-ses′** (-sēz′) NEUROSIS

**psy′cho·path′** (-path′) *n.* ⟦see PSYCHO- & -PATHY⟧ one who has a severe mental disorder and whose behavior is asocial —**psy′cho·path′ic** *adj.*

**psy·cho·sis** (sī kō′sis) *n.*, *pl.* **-ses′** (-sēz′) ⟦see PSYCHO- & -OSIS⟧ a mental disorder in which the personality is seriously disorganized and contact with reality is usually impaired —**psy·chot′ic** (-kät′ik) *adj.*

**psy′cho·so·mat′ic** (-sō mat′ik) *adj.* ⟦PSYCHO- + SOMATIC⟧ designating or of a physical disorder brought on, or made worse, by one's emotional state

**psy′cho·ther′a·py** (-ther′ə pē) *n.* ⟦PSYCHO- + THERAPY⟧ treatment of mental disorders by counseling, psychoanalysis, etc. —**psy′cho·ther′a·pist** *n.*

**pt** *abbrev.* **1** part **2** pint(s) **3** point

**Pt**[1] *abbrev.* **1** Point **2** Port

**Pt**[2] *Chem. symbol for* platinum

**PT** *abbrev.* Pacific Time

**PTA** *abbrev.* Parent-Teacher Association

**ptar·mi·gan** (tär′mi gən) *n.* ⟦< Scot *tarmachan*⟧ a grouse of northern regions

**ptero-** ⟦< Gr *pteron*, wing⟧ *combining form* feather, wing

**pter·o·dac·tyl** (ter′ə dak′təl) *n.* ⟦see prec. & DACTYL⟧ an extinct flying reptile with wings of skin stretched from the hind limbs to the long digits of each forelimb

**Ptol·e·my** (täl′ə mē) 2d c. A.D.; Greco-Egyptian astronomer & mathematician

**pto·maine** (tō′mān′) *n.* ⟦< Gr *ptōma*, corpse⟧ an alkaloid substance, often poisonous, formed in decaying matter

**Pu** *Chem. symbol for* plutonium

**pub** (pub) *n.* ⟦< *pub(lic house)*⟧ [Inf.] a bar or tavern

**pu·ber·ty** (pyōō′bər tē) *n.* ⟦< L *puber*, adult⟧ the stage of physical development when sexual reproduction first becomes possible —**pu′ber·tal** *adj.*

**pu·bes·cent** (pyōō bes′ənt) *adj.* ⟦see prec.⟧ reaching or having reached puberty —**pu·bes′cence** *n.*

**pu'bic** (-bik) *adj.* of or in the region of the genitals

**pub·lic** (pub′lik) *adj.* ⟦ult. < L *populus*, the people⟧ 1 of the people as a whole 2 for the use or benefit of all /a *public* park/ 3 acting officially for the people /a *public* prosecutor/ 4 known by, open to, or available to most or all people /to make *public*, a *public* company/ —*n.* 1 the people as a whole 2 a specific part of the people /the reading *public*/ —**in public** openly —**pub′lic·ly** *adv.*

**pub·li·can** (pub′li kən) *n.* 1 in ancient Rome, a tax collector 2 [Brit.] a saloon proprietor

**pub·li·ca·tion** (pub′li kā′shən) *n.* ⟦see PUBLISH⟧ 1 public notification 2 the printing and distribution of books, magazines, etc. 3 something published, as a periodical or book

**public defender** an attorney employed at public expense to defend indigent people who are accused of crimes

**public domain** the condition of being free from copyright or patent

**pub·li·cist** (pub′lə sist) *n.* a person whose business is publicity

**pub·lic·i·ty** (pub lis′ə tē) *n.* 1 *a*) any information or action that brings a person, cause, etc. to public notice *b*) work concerned with such promotional matters 2 notice by the public

**pub·li·cize** (pub′lə sīz′) *vt.* **-cized′, -ciz′ing** to give publicity to

**public relations** relations of an organization, etc. with the general public as through publicity

**public school** 1 in the U.S., an elementary or secondary school maintained by public taxes, free to students, and supervised locally 2 in England, a private boarding school

**public servant** a government official or a civil-service employee

**pub′lic-spir′it·ed** *adj.* having or showing zeal for the public welfare

**public utility** an organization supplying water, electricity, transportation, etc. to the public

**pub·lish** (pub′lish) *vt.* ⟦< L *publicare*⟧ 1 to make publicly known; announce 2 to issue (a printed work) for sale —*vi.* 1 to issue books, newspapers, printed music, etc. to the public 2 to write books, etc. that are published —**pub′lish·er** *n.*

**Puc·ci·ni** (poo chē′nē), **Gia·co·mo** (jä′kō mō′) 1858-1924; It. operatic composer

**puck** (puk) *n.* ⟦< dial. *puck*, to strike⟧ the hard rubber disk used in ice hockey

**puck·er** (puk′ər) *vt., vi.* ⟦< POKE²⟧ to gather into wrinkles or small folds —*n.* a wrinkle or small fold made by puckering

**puck·ish** (puk′ish) *adj.* ⟦after *Puck*, elf in a Shakespeare play⟧ mischievous

**pud·ding** (pood′iŋ) *n.* ⟦ME *puddyng*, a sausage⟧ a soft, sweet food made of eggs, milk, fruit, etc.

**pud·dle** (pud′′l) *n.* ⟦dim. < L *pudd*, a ditch⟧ a small pool of water, esp. stagnant, spilled, or muddy water

**pud′dling** (-liŋ) *n.* the making of wrought iron from pig iron melted and stirred in an oxidizing atmosphere

**pudg·y** (puj′ē) *adj.* **-i·er, -i·est** ⟦< Scot *pud*, belly⟧ short and fat

**pueb·lo** (pweb′lō) *n., pl.* **-los** (-lōz) ⟦Sp < L *populus*, people⟧ an Amerindian communal village, as in the SW U.S., of terraced adobe dwellings

**pu·er·ile** (pyoo′ər əl, pyoor′il′) *adj.* ⟦< L *puer*, boy⟧ childish; silly —**pu′er·il′i·ty** *n.*

**Puer·to Ri·co** (pwer′tə rē′kō, pôr′-) island in the West Indies: a commonwealth associated with the U.S.: 3,427 sq. mi.; pop. 3,522,000; cap. San Juan —**Puer′to Ri′can** (-kən)

**puff** (puf) *n.* ⟦OE *pyff*⟧ 1 a short, sudden gust or expulsion of air, breath, smoke, etc. 2 a draw at a cigarette, etc. 3 a light pastry filled with whipped cream, etc. 4 a soft pad /a powder *puff*/ 5 a book review, etc. giving undue praise —*vi.* 1 to blow in puffs 2 to breathe rapidly 3 to fill or swell (*out* or *up*) 4 to take puffs at a cigarette, etc. —*vt.* 1 to

blow, smoke, etc. in or with puffs 2 to swell; inflate 3 to praise unduly —**puff′y, -i·er, -i·est,** *adj.* —**puff′i·ness** *n.*

**puff′ball′** *n.* a fungus that bursts at the touch and discharges a brown powder

**puff′er** *n.* a small saltwater fish that can expand its body by swallowing water or air

**puf·fin** (puf′in) *n.* ⟦ME *poffin*⟧ a northern sea bird with a brightly colored, triangular beak

**puff pastry** rich, flaky pastry made of many thin layers of dough

**pug** (pug) *n.* ⟦< ? *Puck*: see PUCK⟧ any of a breed of small, short-haired, snub-nosed dog

**pu·gil·ism** (pyoo′jə iz′əm) *n.* ⟦L *pugil*, boxer⟧ the sport of boxing —**pu′gil·ist** *n.* —**pu′gil·is′tic** *adj.*

**pug·na·cious** (pug nā′shəs) *adj.* ⟦< L *pugnare*, to fight⟧ eager and ready to fight; quarrelsome —**pug·na′cious·ly** *adv.* —**pug·nac′i·ty** (-nas′ə tē) *n.*

**pug nose** a short, thick, turned-up nose —**pug′-nosed′** *adj.*

**puke** (pyook) *n., vt., vi.* **puked, puk′ing** ⟦< ?⟧ [Inf.] VOMIT

**puk·ka** (puk′ə) *adj.* ⟦Hindi *pakka*, ripe⟧ 1 [Anglo-Ind.] first-rate 2 genuine; real

**pul·chri·tude** (pul′krə tood′) *n.* ⟦< L *pulcher*, beautiful⟧ physical beauty

**pule** (pyool) *vi.* **puled, pul′ing** ⟦echoic⟧ to whimper or whine, as a sick or fretful child does

**pull** (pool) *vt.* ⟦< OE *pullian*, to pluck⟧ 1 to exert force on so as to move toward the source of the force 2 to pluck out /to *pull* a tooth/ 3 to rip; tear 4 to strain (a muscle) 5 [Inf.] to carry out; perform /to *pull* a raid/ 6 [Inf.] to restrain /to *pull* one's punches/ 7 [Inf.] to draw out (a gun, etc.) —*vi.* 1 to exert force in dragging, tugging, or attracting something 2 to be capable of being pulled 3 to move (*away, ahead,* etc.) —*n.* 1 the act, force, or result of pulling; a tugging, attracting, etc. 2 a difficult, continuous effort 3 something to be pulled, as a handle 4 [Inf.] *a*) influence *b*) drawing power —**pull for** [Inf.] to cheer on —**pull off** [Inf.] to accomplish —**pull oneself together** to regain one's poise, etc. —**pull out** to depart or withdraw —**pull through** [Inf.] to get over (an illness, etc.) —**pull up** 1 to bring or come to a stop 2 to move ahead —**pull′er** *n.*

**pull′back′** *n.* a pulling back; esp., a planned military withdrawal

**pul·let** (pool′it) *n.* ⟦ult. < L *pullus*, chicken⟧ a young hen

**pul·ley** (pool′ē) *n., pl.* **-leys** ⟦< medieval Gr *polos*, pivot⟧ a small wheel with a grooved rim in which a rope, belt, etc. runs, as to raise weights or transmit power

**Pull·man** (pool′mən) *n.* ⟦after G. M. *Pullman* (1831-97), U.S. inventor⟧ a railroad car with convertible berths for sleeping: also **Pullman car**

**pull′out′** *n.* 1 a pulling out; esp. removal, withdrawal, etc. 2 something to be pulled out, as a magazine insert

**pull′o′ver** *adj.* that is put on by being pulled over the head —*n.* a pullover sweater, shirt, etc.

**pull′-up′** or **pull′up′** *n.* the act of chinning oneself

**pul·mo·nar·y** (pul′mə ner′ē) *adj.* ⟦< L *pulmo*, lung⟧ of the lungs

**pul·mo·tor** (pool′mō′tər) *n.* ⟦< L *pulmo*, lung + MOTOR⟧ an apparatus for applying artificial respiration

**pulp** (pulp) *n.* ⟦< L *pulpa*, flesh⟧ 1 a soft, moist, sticky mass 2 the soft, juicy part of a fruit or the pith inside a plant stem 3 the soft, sensitive tissue in the center of a tooth 4 ground-up, moistened fibers of wood, rags, etc., used to make paper —**pulp′y, -i·er, -i·est,** *adj.*

**pul·pit** (pool′pit) *n.* ⟦< L *pulpitum*, a stage⟧ 1 a raised platform from which a member of the clergy preaches in a church 2 preachers collectively

**pul·sar** (pul′sär) *n.* ⟦< PULSE⟧ any of several celestial objects that emit radio waves at short, regular intervals

**pul·sate** (pul′sāt′) *vi.* -sat′ed, -sat′ing ⟦< L *pulsare*, to beat⟧ **1** to beat or throb rhythmically **2** to vibrate; quiver —**pul·sa′tion** *n.*
**pulse** (puls) *n.* ⟦< L *pulsus*, a beating⟧ **1** the regular beating in the arteries, caused by the contractions of the heart **2** any regular beat **3** a brief, abnormal burst or surge, as of electric current — *vi.* **pulsed, puls′ing** to pulsate; throb
**pul·ver·ize** (pul′vər īz′) *vt., vi.* -ized′, -iz′ing ⟦< L *pulvis*, powder⟧ to grind or be ground into powder
**pu·ma** (pyoo′mə) *n.* ⟦AmSp⟧ COUGAR
**pum·ice** (pum′is) *n.* ⟦< L *pumex*⟧ a light, porous volcanic rock used for scouring, polishing, etc.
**pum·mel** (pum′əl) *vt.* -meled or -melled, -mel·ing or -mel·ling ⟦< POMMEL⟧ to hit with repeated blows, esp. with the fist
**pump**[1] (pump) *n.* ⟦< Sp *bomba*⟧ a machine that forces a liquid or gas into, or draws it out of, something —*vt.* **1** to move (fluids) with a pump **2** to remove water, etc. from **3** to drive air into with a pump **4** to draw out, move up and down, pour forth, etc. as a pump does **5** [Inf.] to question persistently, or to elicit (information) by this — **pump′er** *n.*

WATER PUMP

**pump**[2] (pump) *n.* ⟦prob. < Fr *pompe*, boot⟧ a low-cut shoe without straps or ties
**pumped** *adj.* [Slang] full of confidence, enthusiasm, etc.
**pum·per·nick·el** (pum′pər nik′əl) *n.* ⟦Ger⟧ a coarse, dark rye bread
**pump·kin** (pump′kin) *n.* ⟦< Gr *pepōn*, ripe⟧ a large, round, orange-yellow, edible gourdlike fruit that grows on a vine
**pun** (pun) *n.* ⟦< ? It *puntiglio*, fine point⟧ the humorous use of a word, or of different words sounded alike, so as to play on the various meanings —*vi.* **punned, pun′ning** to make puns
**punch**[1] (punch) *n.* ⟦ult. < L *pungere*, to prick⟧ a tool driven against a surface that is to be stamped, pierced, etc. —*vt.* **1** to pierce, stamp, etc. with a punch **2** to make (a hole) with or as with a punch
**punch**[2] (punch) *vt.* ⟦ME *punchen*⟧ **1** to prod with a stick **2** to herd (cattle) as by prodding **3** to strike with the fist —*n.* **1** a thrusting blow with the fist **2** [Inf.] effective force —**punch in** (or **out**) to record with a time clock one's arrival (or departure)
**punch**[3] (punch) *n.* ⟦Hindi *pañca*, five⟧ a sweet drink made with fruit juices, sherbet, etc., often mixed with wine or liquor
**punch′-drunk′** *adj.* confused, unsteady, etc., as from many blows to the head in boxing
**punch line** the surprise line carrying the point of a joke
**punch′y** *adj.* -i·er, -i·est [Inf.] **1** forceful; vigorous **2** PUNCH-DRUNK
**punc·til·i·ous** (puŋk til′ē əs) *adj.* ⟦see fol.⟧ **1** very careful about fine points of behavior **2** very exact; scrupulous
**punc·tu·al** (puŋk′choo əl) *adj.* ⟦< L *punctus*, a point⟧ on time; prompt —**punc·tu·al′i·ty** (-al′ə tē) *n.* —**punc′tu·al·ly** *adv.*
**punc′tu·ate′** (-āt′) *vt.* -at′ed, -at′ing ⟦see prec.⟧ **1** to use standardized marks (**punctuation marks**), as the period and comma, in (written matter) to clarify meaning **2** to interrupt [a speech *punctuated* with applause] **3** to emphasize —**punc′tu·a′tion** *n.*
**punc·ture** (puŋk′chər) *n.* ⟦< L *pungere*, pierce⟧ **1** a piercing **2** a hole made by a sharp point —*vt., vi.* -tured, -tur·ing to pierce or be pierced with or as with a sharp point
**pun·dit** (pun′dit) *n.* ⟦< Sans *paṇḍita*⟧ a person of great learning

**pun·gent** (pun′jənt) *adj.* ⟦< L *pungere*, pierce⟧ **1** producing a sharp sensation of taste and smell **2** sharp, biting, or stimulating [*pungent* wit] — **pun′gen·cy** *n.* —**pun′gent·ly** *adv.*
**pun·ish** (pun′ish) *vt.* ⟦< L *punire*⟧ **1** to cause to undergo pain, loss, etc., as for a crime **2** to impose a penalty for (an offense) —**pun′ish·a·ble** *adj.*
**pun′ish·ment** *n.* **1** a punishing or being punished **2** the penalty imposed **3** harsh treatment
**pu·ni·tive** (pyoo′ni tiv) *adj.* inflicting, or concerned with, punishment —**pu′ni·tive·ly** *adv.*
**punk**[1] (puŋk) *n.* ⟦prob. < SPUNK⟧ **1** decayed wood used as tinder **2** a fungous substance that smolders when ignited, used to light fireworks, etc.
**punk**[2] (puŋk) *n.* ⟦< ?⟧ **1** [Slang] *a*) a young hoodlum *b*) a young person regarded as inexperienced, insignificant, etc. **2** PUNK ROCK —*adj.* **1** [Slang] poor; inferior **2** of punk rock
**punk rock** a loud, fast, and deliberately offensive style of rock music
**pun·ster** (pun′stər) *n.* one who is fond of making puns
**punt**[1] (punt) *n.* ⟦< ? dial. *bunt*, to kick⟧ *Football* a kick in which the ball is dropped and kicked before it hits the ground —*vt., vi.* to kick (a football) in this way
**punt**[2] (punt) *n.* ⟦< L *ponto*⟧ a flat-bottomed boat with square ends —*vt., vi.* to propel (a punt) with a long pole
**pu·ny** (pyoo′nē) *adj.* -ni·er, -ni·est ⟦< OFr *puis*, after + *né*, born⟧ of inferior size, strength, or importance —**pu′ni·ness** *n.*
**pup** (pup) *n.* **1** a young dog; puppy **2** a young fox, seal, etc.
**pu·pa** (pyoo′pə) *n., pl.* -pae (-pē) or -pas ⟦< L, a doll⟧ an insect in the stage between the last larval form and the adult form
**pu·pil**[1] (pyoo′pəl) *n.* ⟦< L *pupillus*, a ward⟧ a person taught under the supervision of a teacher or tutor
**pu·pil**[2] (pyoo′pəl) *n.* ⟦< L *pupilla*, figure reflected in the eye⟧ the contractile circular opening, apparently black, in the center of the iris of the eye
**pup·pet** (pup′ət) *n.* ⟦< L *pupa*, a doll⟧ **1** a small figure, as of a person, moved by strings or the hands, as in a performance (**puppet show**) **2** one whose actions, ideas, etc. are controlled by another —**pup′pet·ry** *n.*
**pup′pet·eer′** (-ə tir′) *n.* one who operates, designs, etc. puppets
**pup·py** (pup′ē) *n., pl.* -pies ⟦< medieval Fr *popee*, a doll⟧ a young dog
**pup tent** a small, portable tent
**pur·blind** (pur′blīnd′) *adj.* ⟦ME *pur blind*, quite blind⟧ **1** partly blind **2** slow in understanding
**pur·chase** (pur′chəs) *vt.* -chased, -chas·ing ⟦< OFr *pour*, for + *chacier*, to chase⟧ to buy —*n.* **1** anything bought **2** the act of buying **3** a firm hold applied to move something heavy or to keep from slipping —**pur′chas·a·ble** *adj.* —**pur′chas·er** *n.*
**pure** (pyoor) *adj.* pur′er, pur′est ⟦< L *purus*⟧ **1** free from anything that adulterates, taints, etc.; unmixed **2** simple; mere **3** utter; absolute **4** faultless **5** blameless **6** virgin or chaste **7** abstract or theoretical [*pure* physics] —**pure′ly** *adv.* —**pure′ness** *n.*
**pure′bred′** *adj.* belonging to a recognized breed with genetic attributes maintained through generations of unmixed descent —*n.* a purebred animal or plant
**pu·rée** or **pu·ree** (pyoo rā′) *n.* ⟦Fr: see PURE⟧ **1** cooked food pressed through a sieve or whipped in a blender to a soft, smooth consistency **2** a thick soup made with this —*vt.* -réed′ or -reed′, -rée′ing or -ree′ing to make a purée of
**pur·ga·tive** (pur′gə tiv) *adj.* purging —*n.* a purging substance; cathartic
**pur·ga·to·ry** (pur′gə tôr′ē) *n., pl.* -ries ⟦see fol.⟧

[*often* P-] *Theol.* a state or place after death, in some Christian doctrine, for expiating sins by suffering —**pur′ga·to′ri·al** *adj.*

**purge** (purj) *vt.* **purged, purg′ing** 〖< L *purus,* clean + *agere,* do〗 **1** to cleanse of impurities, etc. **2** to cleanse of sin **3** to rid (a nation, party, etc.) of (individuals held to be disloyal) **4** to empty (the bowels) —*n.* **1** a purging **2** that which purges; esp., a cathartic —**purg′er** *n.*

**pu·ri·fy** (pyoor′ə fī′) *vt.* **-fied′, -fy′ing** 〖see PURE & -FY〗 **1** to rid of impurities, etc. **2** to free from guilt, sin, etc. —*vi.* to become purified —**pu′ri·fi·ca′tion** *n.*

**Pu·rim** (poor′im) *n.* 〖Heb〗 a Jewish holiday commemorating Esther's deliverance of the Jews from a massacre

**pu·rine** (pyoor′ēn, -in) *n.* 〖Ger *purin*〗 **1** a colorless, crystalline organic compound, from which is derived a group of compounds including uric acid and caffeine **2** a purine derivative, as adenine

**pur·ism** (pyoor′iz′əm) *n.* strict or excessive observance of precise usage or formal rules in language, style, etc. —**pur′ist** *n.*

**Pu·ri·tan** (pyoor′i tən) *n.* 〖see fol.〗 **1** a member of a group in 16th-17th-c. England and America that wanted to make the Church of England simpler in its forms and stricter about morality **2** [p-] a person regarded as excessively strict in morals and religion —**pu′ri·tan′i·cal** (-tan′i kəl) *adj.* —**Pu′ri·tan·ism′** or **pu′ri·tan·ism′** *n.*

**pu·ri·ty** (-tē) *n.* 〖< LL *puritas*〗 a being pure; specif., *a*) freedom from adulterating matter *b*) cleanness *c*) freedom from sin; chastity

**purl**[1] (purl) *vi.* 〖< ? Scand〗 to move in ripples or with a murmur —*n.* the sound of purling water

**purl**[2] (purl) *vt., vi.* 〖earlier *pirl,* prob. ult. < It〗 to invert (stitches) in knitting

**pur·lieu** (purl′yoo) *n.* 〖< OFr *pur-,* through + *aler,* go〗 **1** [*pl.*] environs **2** an outlying part

**pur·loin** (pər loin′, pur′loin′) *vt., vi.* 〖< OFr *pur-,* for + *loin,* far〗 to steal

**pur·ple** (pur′pəl) *n.* 〖ult. < Gr *porphyra,* shellfish yielding a dye〗 **1** a dark bluish red **2** crimson cloth or clothing, esp. as a former emblem of royalty —*adj.* **1** bluish-red **2** imperial **3** ornate [*purple* prose] **4** profane or obscene

**pur·port** (pur pôrt′; *for n.* pur′pôrt′) *vt.* 〖< OFr *por-,* forth + *porter,* to bear〗 **1** to profess or claim as its meaning **2** to give the appearance, often falsely, of being, intending, etc. —*n.* **1** meaning; sense **2** intention —**pur·port′ed** *adj.* —**pur·port′ed·ly** *adv.*

**pur·pose** (pur′pəs) *vt., vi.* **-posed, -pos·ing** 〖see PROPOSE〗 to intend or plan —*n.* **1** something one intends to get or do; aim **2** determination **3** the object for which something exists or is done —**on purpose** by design; intentionally —**pur′pose·ful** *adj.* —**pur′pose·less** *adj.*

**pur′pose·ly** *adv.* with a definite purpose; intentionally; deliberately

**pur′pos·ive** *adj.* serving or having a purpose

**purr** (pur) *n.* 〖echoic〗 a low, vibratory sound made by a cat at ease —*vi., vt.* to make, or express by, such a sound

**purse** (purs) *n.* 〖< Gr *byrsa,* a hide〗 **1** a small bag for carrying money **2** finances; money **3** a sum of money for a present or prize **4** a woman's handbag —*vt.* **pursed, purs′ing** to draw (the lips) tightly, as in disapproval

**purs·er** (pur′sər) *n.* 〖ME, purse-bearer〗 a ship's officer in charge of accounts, tickets, etc.

**pur·su·ance** (pər soo′əns) *n.* a pursuing of a project, plan, etc.

**pur·su′ant** *adj.* [Now Rare] pursuing —**pursuant to** in accordance with

**pur·sue** (pər soo′) *vt.* **-sued′, -su′ing** 〖< L *pro-,* forth + *sequi,* follow〗 **1** to follow in order to overtake or capture; chase **2** to follow (a specified course, action, etc.) **3** to strive for **4** to continue to annoy —**pur·su′er** *n.*

**pur·suit** (-soot′) *n.* **1** a pursuing **2** an occupation, interest, etc.

**pu·ru·lent** (pyoor′ə lənt) *adj.* 〖< L *pus, pus*〗 of, like, or discharging pus —**pu′ru·lence** *n.*

**pur·vey** (pər vā′) *vt.* 〖see PROVIDE〗 to supply (esp. food) —**pur·vey′or** *n.*

**pur·view** (pur′vyoo′) *n.* 〖< OFr *pourveü,* provided〗 scope or extent, as of control or activity

**pus** (pus) *n.* 〖L〗 the yellowish-white liquid matter produced by an infection

**push** (poosh) *vt.* 〖< L *pulsare,* to beat〗 **1** to press against so as to move **2** to press or urge on **3** to urge the use, sale, etc. of —*n.* **1** a pushing **2** a vigorous effort **3** an advance against opposition **4** [Inf.] aggressiveness; drive

**push button** a small knob pushed to operate something, as with electricity

**push′er** *n.* **1** one that pushes **2** [Slang] one who sells drugs, esp. narcotics, illegally

**push′o·ver** *n.* [Slang] **1** anything very easy to do **2** one easily persuaded, defeated, etc.

**push′-up′** or **push′up′** *n.* an exercise in which a prone person, with hands under shoulders, raises the body by pushing down on the palms

**push′y** *adj.* **-i·er, -i·est** [Inf.] annoyingly aggressive and persistent —**push′i·ness** *n.*

**pu·sil·lan·i·mous** (pyoo′si lan′ə məs) *adj.* 〖< L *pusillus,* tiny + *animus,* the mind〗 timid; cowardly —**pu·sil·la·nim′i·ty** (-si lə nim′ə tē) *n.*

**puss** (poos) *n.* 〖< ?〗 a cat: also **puss′y·cat′** or **puss′y,** *pl.* **-ies**

**puss′y·foot′** *vi.* [Inf.] **1** to move with stealth or caution, like a cat **2** to avoid committing oneself

**pussy willow** a willow bearing silvery, velvetlike catkins

**pus·tule** (pus′chool′) *n.* 〖L *pustula*〗 a pus-filled blister or pimple

**put** (poot) *vt.* **put, put′ting** 〖< or akin to OE *potian,* to push〗 **1** *a*) to thrust; drive *b*) to propel with an overhand thrust [to *put* the shot] **2** to cause to be in a certain place, condition, relation, etc.; place; set **3** to impose (a tax, etc.) **4** to attribute; ascribe **5** to express [*put* it plainly] **6** to present for decision [*put* the question] **7** to bet (money) on — *Finance* an option to sell a stock, etc. — *adj.* [Inf.] fixed [stay *put*] —**put across** [Inf.] to cause to be understood or accepted —**put aside** (or **by**) to reserve for later use —**put down** **1** to crush; repress **2** to write down **3** [Slang] to belittle or humiliate —**put in for** to apply for —**put it** (or **something**) **over on** [Inf.] to deceive; trick — **put off** **1** to postpone; delay **2** to evade; divert — **put on** **1** to clothe oneself with **2** to pretend **3** to stage (a play) **4** [Slang] to fool; hoax —**put out** **1** to expel; dismiss **2** to extinguish (a fire or light) **3** to inconvenience **4** *Baseball* to retire (a batter or runner) —**put through** **1** to carry out **2** to cause to do or undergo —**put up** **1** to offer **2** to preserve (fruits, etc.) **3** to build **4** to provide lodgings for **5** to provide (money) **6** to arrange (the hair) with curlers, etc. **7** [Inf.] to incite to some action —**put up with** to tolerate

**pu·ta·tive** (pyoot′ə tiv) *adj.* 〖< L *putare,* suppose〗 generally considered or deemed such; reputed

**put′-down′** *n.* [Slang] a belittling remark or crushing retort

**Pu·tin** (poo′tən), **Vlad·i·mir** (vlad′ə mir) 1952- ; president of Russia (2000-  )

**put′-on′** *n.* [Slang] a hoax

**pu·tre·fy** (pyoo′trə fī′) *vt., vi.* **-fied′, -fy′ing** 〖see PUTRID & -FY〗 to make or become putrid; rot —**pu′tre·fac′tion** (-fak′shən) *n.*

**pu·tres·cent** (pyoo tres′ənt) *adj.* putrefying; rotting —**pu·tres′cence** *n.*

**pu·trid** (pyoo′trid) *adj.* 〖< L *putrere,* to rot〗 rotten and foul-smelling

**putt** (put) *n.* 〖< PUT, v.〗 *Golf* a shot which attempts to roll the ball into the hole —*vt., vi.* to hit (the ball) in making a putt

**putt·er**[1] (put′ər) *n.* *Golf* a short, straight-faced club used in putting

**put·ter**[2] (put′ər) *vi.* [< OE *potian*, to push] to busy oneself in an ineffective or aimless way (with *along, around*, etc.) —*vt.* to fritter (*away*)

**put·ty** (put′ē) *n.* [Fr *potée*, lit., potful] a soft, plastic mixture of powdered chalk and linseed oil, used to fill small cracks, etc. —*vt.* **-tied, -ty·ing** to cement or fill with putty

**put′-up′** *adj.* [Inf.] planned secretly beforehand

**puz·zle** (puz′əl) *vt.* **-zled, -zling** [< ?] to perplex; bewilder —*vi.* **1** to be perplexed **2** to exercise one's mind, as over a problem —*n.* **1** something that puzzles **2** a toy or problem for testing skill or ingenuity —**puzzle out** to solve by deep study —**puz′zle·ment** *n.* —**puz′zler** *n.*

**PVC** *n.* [*p(oly)v(inyl) c(hloride)*] a type of polymer used in packaging materials, plumbing, etc.

**Pvt** *abbrev. Mil.* Private

**PX** *service mark for* a general store at an army base

**Pyg·my** (pig′mē) *n., pl.* **-mies** [< Gr *pygmaios*, of a forearm's length] **1** a member of any of several groups of African or Asian peoples of small stature **2** [p-] a dwarf —*adj.* **1** of the Pygmies **2** [p-] very small

**py·ja·mas** (pə jä′məz, -jam′əz) *pl.n. Brit. sp. of* PAJAMAS

**py·lon** (pī′län′) *n.* [Gr *pylōn*, gateway] **1** a gateway, as of an Egyptian temple **2** a towerlike structure supporting electric lines, marking a flight course, etc.

**py·lo·rus** (pī lôr′əs) *n., pl.* **-ri** (-rī) [< Gr *pylōros*, gatekeeper] the opening from the stomach into the duodenum —**py·lor′ic** *adj.*

**py·or·rhe·a** (pī′ə rē′ə) *n.* [< Gr *pyon*, pus + *rheein*, to flow] a periodontal infection with formation of pus and loosening of teeth —**py′or·rhe′al** *adj.*

**pyr·a·mid** (pir′ə mid) *n.* [< Gr *pyramis*] **1** a huge

structure with a square base and four triangular sides meeting at the top, as a royal tomb of ancient Egypt **2** *Geom.* a solid figure with a polygonal base, the sides of which form the bases of triangular surfaces meeting at a common vertex —**py·ram·i·dal** (pi ram′i dəl) *adj.*

**pyre** (pīr) *n.* [< Gr *pyr*, fire] a pile of wood on which a dead body is burned in funeral rites

**Pyr·e·nees** (pir′ə nēz′) mountain range between France & Spain

**py·ret·ic** (pī ret′ik) *adj.* [< Gr *pyretos*, fever] of, causing, or characterized by fever

**Py·rex** (pī′reks′) [arbitrary coinage < *pie*] *trademark for* a heat-resistant glassware used for cooking, lab work, etc.

**py·rite** (pī′rīt′) *n., pl.* **py·ri·tes** (pi rīt′ēz′, pī′rīts′) [< Gr *pyritēs*, flint] iron sulfide, a lustrous yellow mineral used as a source of sulfur

**pyro-** [< Gr *pyr*, fire] *combining form* fire, heat

**py·ro·ma·ni·a** (pī′rə mā′nē ə) *n.* [ModL: see prec. & -MANIA] a compulsion to start destructive fires —**py′ro·ma′ni·ac′** *n., adj.*

**py·ro·tech·nics** (pī′rə tek′niks) *pl.n.* [< Gr *pyr*, fire + *technē*, art] **1** a display of fireworks **2** a dazzling display, as of wit

**Pyr·rhic victory** (pir′ik) [after *Pyrrhus*, Gr king who won such victories over the Romans, 280 and 279 B.C.] a too costly victory

**Py·thag·o·ras** (pi thag′ə rəs) 6th c. B.C.; Gr. philosopher & mathematician —**Py·thag′o·re′an** (-ə rē′ən) *adj., n.*

**py·thon** (pī′thän′, -thən) *n.* [< Gr *Pythōn*, a serpent slain by Apollo] a large, nonpoisonous snake of Asia, Africa, and Australia, that squeezes its prey to death

# Q

**q** or **Q** (kyōō) *n., pl.* **q's, Q's** the 17th letter of the English alphabet

**q** *abbrev.* **1** quart **2** question

**Qa·tar** (kä tär′) country on a peninsula of E Arabia, on the Persian Gulf: 4,416,000 sq. mi.; pop. 369,000

**QC** Quebec

**Q.E.D.** or **q.e.d.** *abbrev.* ⟦L *quod erat demonstrandum*⟧ which was to be demonstrated or proved

**qt** *abbrev.* quart(s)

**q.t.** *n.* ⟦< *q(uie)t*⟧ [Inf.] quiet: chiefly in **on the q.t.,** secretly: also **Q.T.**

**qua** (kwā, kwä) *prep.* ⟦L < *qui,* who⟧ in the function or character of; as ⟦the President *qua* Commander in Chief⟧

**quack**¹ (kwak) *vi.* ⟦echoic⟧ to utter the sound or cry of a duck —*n.* this sound

**quack**² (kwak) *n.* ⟦ult. < MDu *quacken,* to brag⟧ **1** a person who practices medicine fraudulently **2** one who falsely pretends to have knowledge or a skill —*adj.* fraudulent —**quack′er·y** *n.*

**quad**¹ (kwäd) *n. short for:* **1** QUADRANGLE **2** QUADRUPLET

**quad**² *abbrev.* **1** quadrangle **2** quadrant **3** quadruplice

**quad·ran·gle** (kwä′draŋ′gəl) *n.* ⟦see QUADRI- & ANGLE¹⟧ **1** *Geom.* a plane figure with four angles and four sides **2** an area surrounded on its four sides by buildings —**quad·ran′gu·lar** *adj.*

**quad·rant** (kwä′drənt) *n.* ⟦< L *quadrans,* fourth part⟧ **1** an arc of 90° **2** a quarter section of a circle **3** an instrument formerly used in measuring angular elevation and altitude in navigation, etc.

**quad·rat·ic** (kwä drat′ik) *adj. Algebra* involving a quantity or quantities that are squared but none that are raised to a higher power

QUADRANT

**quad·ren·ni·al** (kwä dren′ē əl) *adj.* ⟦< L *quadri-* (see fol.) + *annus,* year⟧ **1** happening every four years **2** lasting four years

**quadri-** ⟦L < *quattuor,* four⟧ *combining form* four, four times

**quad·ri·ceps** (kwä′dri seps′) *n.* ⟦< prec. + L *caput,* the head⟧ a muscle with four points of origin; esp., the large muscle at the front of the thigh

**quad·ri·lat·er·al** (kwä′dri lat′ər əl) *adj.* ⟦see QUADRI- & LATERAL⟧ four-sided —*n. Geom.* a plane figure having four sides and four angles

**qua·drille** (kwə dril′, kwä-) *n.* ⟦Fr: ult. < L *quadra,* a square⟧ a square dance performed by four couples

**quad·ri·ple·gi·a** (kwä′dri plē′jē ə, -jə) *n.* ⟦ModL < QUADRI- + Gr *plēgē,* a stroke⟧ total paralysis of the body from the neck down —**quad′ri·ple′gic** (-plē′jik) *adj., n.*

**quad·ru·ped** (kwä′drōō ped′) *n.* ⟦< L *quadru-,* four + *pes, foot*⟧ an animal, esp. a mammal, with four feet

**quad·ru·ple** (kwä drōō′pəl) *adj.* ⟦< L *quadru-,*

RECTANGLES

SQUARE    OBLONG

PARALLELOGRAMS

RHOMBUS    RHOMBOID

TRAPEZOID    TRAPEZIUM

QUADRILATERALS

four + *-plus, -fold*⟧ **1** consisting of four **2** four times as much or as many —*n.* an amount four times as much or as many —*vt., vi.* **-pled, -pling** to make or become four times as much or as many

**quad·ru·plet** (kwä drōō′plit, -drup′lit) *n.* **1** any of four offspring from the same pregnancy **2** a collection or group of four, usually of one kind

**quad·ru·pli·cate** (kwä drōō′pli kāt′; *for adj. & n.,* -kit, -kāt′) *vt.* **-cat′ed, -cat′ing** to make four identical copies of —*adj.* **1** fourfold **2** being the last of four identical copies —*n.* any one of such copies —**in quadruplicate** in four such copies —**quad·ru′pli·ca′tion** *n.*

**quaff** (kwäf, kwaf) *vt., vi.* ⟦prob. < LowG *quassen,* overindulge⟧ to drink deeply and heartily —*n.* a quaffing

**quag·mire** (kwag′mīr′) *n.* ⟦*quag,* a bog + MIRE⟧ wet, boggy ground

**qua·hog** or **qua·haug** (kō′häg′) *n.* ⟦AmInd⟧ an edible clam of the E coast of North America

**quail**¹ (kwāl) *vi.* ⟦prob. < L *coagulare,* coagulate⟧ to recoil in fear

**quail**² (kwāl) *n.* ⟦< OFr *quaille*⟧ a small, short-tailed bird resembling a partridge

**quaint** (kwānt) *adj.* ⟦< OFr *cointe* < L *cognitus,* known⟧ **1** pleasingly odd or old-fashioned **2** unusual; curious **3** fanciful; whimsical —**quaint′ly** *adv.* —**quaint′ness** *n.*

**quake** (kwāk) *vi.* **quaked, quak′ing** ⟦< OE *cwacian*⟧ **1** to tremble or shake **2** to shiver, as from fear or cold —*n.* **1** a shaking or tremor **2** an earthquake —**quak′y, -i·er, -i·est,** *adj.*

**Quak·er** (kwā′kər, *n.* ⟦< founder's admonition to "quake" at the word of the Lord⟧ *name for* a member of the SOCIETY OF FRIENDS

**qual·i·fi·ca·tion** (kwôl′ə fi kā′shən) *n.* **1** a qualifying or being qualified **2** a restriction; limiting condition **3** any skill, etc. that fits one for a job, office, etc.

**qual·i·fied** (kwôl′ə fīd′) *adj.* **1** fit; competent **2** limited; modified

**qual′i·fi′er** (-fī′ər) *n.* **1** one that qualifies **2** an adjective or adverb

**qual′i·fy′** (-fī′) *vt.* **-fied′, -fy′ing** ⟦< L *qualis,* of what kind + *facere,* make⟧ **1** to make fit for a job, etc. **2** to make legally capable **3** to modify; restrict **4** to moderate; soften —*vi.* to be or become qualified

**qual·i·ta·tive** (-tāt′iv) *adj.* having to do with quality or qualities —**qual′i·ta′tive·ly** *adv.*

**qual·i·ty** (-tē) *n., pl.* **-ties** ⟦< L *qualis,* of what kind⟧ **1** a characteristic element or attribute **2** basic nature; kind **3** the degree of excellence of a thing **4** excellence —*adj.* of high quality

**qualm** (kwäm) *n.* ⟦OE *cwealm,* disaster⟧ **1** a sudden, brief feeling of sickness, faintness, etc. **2** a doubt; misgiving **3** a twinge of conscience

**quan·da·ry** (kwän′də rē, -drē) *n., pl.* **-ries** ⟦prob. < L⟧ a state of uncertainty; dilemma

**quan·ti·fy** (kwänt′ə fī′) *vt.* **-fied′, -fy′ing** ⟦< L *quantus,* how much + *facere,* make⟧ **1** to determine or express the quantity of **2** to express as a quantity or number —**quan′ti·fi′er** *n.*

**quan′ti·ta·tive** (-tāt′iv) *adj.* having to do with quantity

**quan′ti·ty** (-tē) *n., pl.* **-ties** ⟦< L *quantus,* how great⟧ **1** an amount; portion **2** any indeterminate bulk or number **3** [*also pl.*] a great amount **4** that property by which a thing can be measured **5** a number or symbol expressing this property

**quan·tum** (kwän′təm) *n., pl.* **-ta** (-tə) ⟦L, how much⟧ *Physics* a fixed, elemental unit of energy: the **quantum theory** states that energy is radiated discontinuously in quanta

**quantum jump** (or **leap**) a sudden, extensive change

**quar·an·tine** (kwôr′ən tēn) *n.* [< L *quadraginta,* forty] **1** the period, orig. 40 days, during which a vessel suspected of carrying contagious disease is detained in port **2** any isolation imposed to keep contagious diseases, etc. from spreading —*vt.* **-tined′, -tin′ing** to place under quarantine

**quark** (kwôrk) *n.* [arbitrary coinage] any of a set of elementary particles that bind together to form protons, neutrons, mesons, etc.

**quar·rel** (kwôr′əl) *n.* [< L *queri,* complain] **1** a cause for dispute **2** a dispute, esp. an angry one —*vi.* **-reled** or **-relled, -rel·ing** or **-rel·ling 1** to find fault **2** to dispute heatedly **3** to have a breach in friendship —**quar′rel·er** or **quar′rel·ler** *n.* — **quar′rel·some** *adj.*

**quar·ry**[1] (kwôr′ē) *n., pl.* **-ries** [< OFr *cuiree,* parts of prey fed to dogs] an animal, etc. being hunted

**quar·ry**[2] (kwôr′ē) *n., pl.* **-ries** [< L *quadrare,* to square] a place where stone, slate, etc. is excavated —*vt.* **-ried, -ry·ing** to excavate from a quarry

**quart** (kwôrt) *n.* [< L *quartus,* fourth] **1** ¼ gallon in liquid measure **2** ⅛ peck in dry measure

**quar·ter** (-ər) *n.* [< L *quartus,* fourth] **1** a fourth of something **2** *a)* one fourth of a year *b)* any of the three terms of about eleven weeks each in an academic year **3** one fourth of an hour **4** one fourth of a dollar; 25 cents, or a coin of this value **5** any leg of a four-legged animal, with the adjoining parts **6** a particular district or section **7** [*pl.*] lodgings **8** mercy granted to a surrendering foe **9** a particular source [news from high *quarters*] — *vt.* **1** to divide into four equal parts **2** to provide lodgings for —*adj.* constituting a quarter —**at close quarters** close together

**quar′ter·back′** *n. Football* the offensive back who calls the play, passes the ball, etc.

**quar′ter·deck′** *n.* the after part of the upper deck of a ship, usually for officers

**quar′ter·fi′nal** *adj.* coming just before the semifinals —*n.* a quarterfinal match, etc.

**quarter horse** [< its speed in a *quarter*-mile sprint] any of a breed of muscular, solid-colored horse

**quar′ter·ly** *adj.* occurring regularly four times a year —*adv.* once every quarter of the year —*n., pl.* **-lies** a publication issued every three months

**quar′ter·mas′ter** *n.* **1** *Mil.* an officer who provides troops with quarters, clothing, equipment, etc. **2** *Naut.* a petty officer or mate involved in steering and navigating a ship

**quarter note** *Music* a note having one fourth the duration of a whole note

**quar·tet** (kwôr tet′) *n.* [ult. < L *quartus,* fourth] **1** a group of four **2** *Music a)* a composition for four voices or instruments *b)* the four performers of this

**quar·to** (kwôr′tō) *n., pl.* **-tos** [< L (*in*) *quarto,* (in) a fourth] **1** the page size (about 9 by 12 in.) of a book made up of sheets each of which is folded twice to form four leaves, or eight pages **2** a book with pages of this size

**quartz** (kwôrts) *n.* [Ger *quarz*] a crystalline mineral, a form of silica, usually colorless and transparent

**quartz crystal** *Electronics* a piece of quartz cut and ground so as to vibrate at a particular frequency

**qua·sar** (kwā′zär) *n.* [< *quas(i-stell)ar* (*radio source*)] a distant celestial object that emits immense quantities of light and radio waves

**quash**[1] (kwäsh) *vt.* [< L *cassus,* empty] *Law* to set aside (an indictment)

**quash**[2] (kwäsh) *vt.* [< L *quatere,* to break] to quell (an uprising)

**qua·si** (kwā′zī, kwä′zē′) *adv.* [L] as if; seemingly; in part —*adj.* seeming Often hyphenated as a prefix [*quasi*-legal]

**quat·rain** (kwä′trān′) *n.* [< L *quattuor,* four] a stanza of four lines

**qua·ver** (kwā′vər) *vi.* [ME *cwafien*] **1** to shake or tremble **2** to be tremulous: said of the voice —*n.* a tremulous quality in a voice or tone

**quay** (kē) *n.* [ult. < Celt] a wharf, usually of concrete or stone

**quea·sy** (kwē′zē) *adj.* **-si·er, -si·est** [ME *qwesye* < Gmc] **1** affected with nausea **2** squeamish; easily nauseated

**Que·bec** (kwi bek′) **1** province of E Canada: 594,860 sq. mi.; pop. 7,139,000: abbrev. *QC* **2** its capital, on the St. Lawrence River: pop. 167,000

**queen** (kwēn) *n.* [< OE *cwen*] **1** the wife of a king **2** a female monarch in her own right **3** a woman noted for her beauty or accomplishments **4** the fully developed, reproductive female in a colony of bees, ants, etc. **5** a playing card with a picture of a queen on it **6** *Chess* the most powerful piece —**queen′ly, -li·er, -li·est,** *adj.*

**Queens** (kwēnz) borough of New York City, on W Long Island: pop. 1,952,000

**queen′-size′** *adj.* larger than usual, but smaller than king-size [a *queen-size* bed is 60 by 80 in.]

**queer** (kwir) *adj.* [< ? Ger *quer,* crosswise] **1** different from the usual; strange **2** [Inf.] eccentric —*vt.* [Slang] to spoil the success of

**quell** (kwel) *vt.* [OE *cwellan,* kill] **1** to subdue **2** to quiet; allay

**quench** (kwench) *vt.* [OE *cwencan*] **1** to extinguish [to *quench* a fire with water] **2** to satisfy [to *quench* one's thirst] **3** to cool (hot steel, etc.) suddenly by plunging into water, etc. —**quench′less** *adj.*

**quer·u·lous** (kwer′yōō ləs, -ə-) *adj.* [< L *queri,* complain] **1** inclined to find fault **2** full of complaint; peevish —**quer′u·lous·ly** *adv.*

**que·ry** (kwir′ē) *n., pl.* **-ries** [< L *quaerere,* ask] a question; inquiry —*vt., vi.* **-ried, -ry·ing** to question

**quest** (kwest) *n.* [see prec.] **1** a seeking **2** a journey in pursuit of a lofty goal —*vi.* to go in pursuit

**ques·tion** (kwes′chən) *n.* [see QUERY] **1** an asking; inquiry **2** something asked **3** doubt; uncertainty **4** a matter open to discussion **5** a difficult matter [it's not a *question* of money] **6** a point being debated before an assembly —*vt.* **1** to ask questions of **2** to express doubt about **3** to dispute; challenge —*vi.* to ask questions —**out of the question** impossible

**ques′tion·a·ble** *adj.* **1** that can be questioned or doubted **2** suspected of being immoral, dishonest, etc. **3** uncertain

**question mark** a mark of punctuation (?) put after a sentence, word, etc. to indicate a direct question or to express doubt, etc.

**ques′tion·naire′** (-chə ner′) *n.* a written or printed set of questions used in gathering information from people

**queue** (kyōō) *n.* [< L *cauda,* tail] **1** a pigtail **2** [Chiefly Brit.] a line, as of persons waiting to be served **3** stored computer data or programs waiting to be processed —*vi.* **queued, queu′ing** [Chiefly Brit.] to line up in a queue: often with *up*

**quib·ble** (kwib′əl) *n.* [< L *qui,* who] a petty evasion or criticism —*vi.* **-bled, -bling** to evade the truth of a point under discussion by caviling

**quiche** (kēsh) *n.* a dish consisting of custard baked in a pastry shell with various ingredients, as bacon, cheese, or spinach

**quick** (kwik) *adj.* [< OE *cwicu,* living] **1** *a)* rapid; swift [a *quick* walk] *b)* prompt [a *quick* reply] **2** prompt to understand or learn [a *quick* mind] **3** easily stirred [a *quick* temper] —*adv.* quickly; rapidly —*n.* **1** the living: esp. in **the quick and the dead 2** the sensitive flesh under the nails **3** the deepest feelings [hurt to the *quick*] —**quick′ly** *adv.* —**quick′ness** *n.*

**quick bread** any bread leavened with baking powder, soda, etc. and baked as soon as the batter is mixed

**quick′en** *vt.* **1** to animate; enliven; revive **2** to cause to move more rapidly —*vi.* **1** to become enlivened; revive **2** to begin to show signs of life, as a fetus **3** to become more rapid

**quick'-freeze'** *vt.* -**froze'**, -**fro'zen**, -**freez'ing** to subject (food) to sudden freezing for long storage

**quick'ie** *n.* [Inf.] anything done or made quickly and, often, cheaply

**quick'lime'** *n.* unslaked lime

**quick'sand'** *n.* [< ME: see QUICK & SAND] a loose, deep sand deposit, engulfing heavy objects easily

**quick'sil'ver** *n.* mercury

**quick'-tem'pered** *adj.* easily angered

**quick'-wit'ted** *adj.* mentally nimble

**quid** (kwid) *n.* [var. of CUD] a piece, as of tobacco, to be chewed

**quid pro quo** (kwid' prō kwō') [L] one thing in return for another

**qui·es·cent** (kwī es'ənt) *adj.* [< L *quiescere*, become quiet] still; inactive —**qui·es'cence** *n.*

**qui·et** (kwī'ət) *adj.* [< L *quies*, rest] **1** still; motionless **2** *a*) not noisy; hushed *b*) not speaking; silent **3** not easily excited **4** not showy **5** not forward; unobtrusive **6** peaceful and relaxing —*n.* **1** calmness, stillness, etc. **2** a quiet or peaceful quality —*vt.* to make quiet —*vi.* to become quiet: usually with *down* —**qui'et·ly** *adv.*

**qui·e·tude** (kwī'ə tōōd') *n.* a state of being quiet; calmness

**qui·e·tus** (kwī ēt'əs) *n.* [< ML *quietus* (*est*), (he is) quit] **1** discharge from debt, etc. **2** death

**quill** (kwil) *n.* [prob. < LowG or MDu] **1** a large, stiff feather **2** *a*) the hollow stem of a feather *b*) anything made from this, as a pen **3** a spine of a porcupine or hedgehog

**quilt** (kwilt) *n.* [< L *culcita*, bed] a bedcover filled with down, cotton, etc. and stitched together in lines or patterns —*vt.* to stitch like a quilt —*vi.* to make a quilt —**quilt'er** *n.*

QUILL

**quince** (kwins) *n.* [< Gr *kydōnion*] **1** a yellowish, apple-shaped fruit, used in preserves **2** the tree it grows on

**qui·nel·la** (kwi nel'ə, kē-) *n.* [< AmSp < L *quinque*, five] a form of betting in horse-racing, in which the bettor, to win, must pick the first two finishers, in whichever order they finish: also **qui·nie·la** (kē nye'lə)

**qui·nine** (kwī'nīn') *n.* [< *quina*, cinchona bark] a bitter, crystalline alkaloid extracted from cinchona bark, used for treating malaria

**quin·tes·sence** (kwin tes'əns) *n.* [< ML *quinta essentia*] the pure essence or perfect type

**quin·tet** or **quin·tette** (kwin tet') *n.* [ult. < L *quintus*, a fifth] **1** a group of five **2** *Music a*) a composition for five voices or instruments *b*) the five performers of this

**quin·tu·ple** (kwin tōō'pəl) *adj.* [< L *quintus*, a fifth + *-plex*, -fold] **1** consisting of five **2** five times as much or as many —*vt.*, *vi.* -**pled**, -**pling** to make or become five times as much or as many

**quin·tu·plet** (kwin tup'lit, -tōō'plit) *n.* **1** any of five offspring from the same pregnancy **2** a group of five, usually of one kind

**quip** (kwip) *n.* [< L *quippe*, indeed] a witty or sarcastic remark or reply —*vi.* **quipped**, **quip'ping** to utter quips —**quip'ster** *n.*

**quire** (kwīr) *n.* [< L *quaterni*, four each] a set of 24 or 25 sheets of paper of the same size and stock

**quirk** (kwʉrk) *n.* [< ?] **1** a sudden twist or turn **2**

a peculiarity —**quirk'i·ness** *n.* —**quirk'y**, -**i·er**, -**i·est**, *adj.*

**quirt** (kwʉrt) *n.* [AmSp *cuarta*] a riding whip with a braided leather lash and a short handle

**quis·ling** (kwiz'liŋ) *n.* [after V. *Quisling*, Norw collaborator with the Nazis] a traitor

**quit** (kwit) *vt.* **quit**, **quit'ting** [< ML *quittus*, free] **1** to free (oneself) *of* **2** to stop having, using, or doing **3** to depart from **4** to resign from —*vi.* **1** to stop doing something **2** to give up one's job

**quit'claim'** *n.* a deed relinquishing a claim, as to property

**quite** (kwīt) *adv.* [see QUIT] **1** completely **2** really; positively **3** very or fairly [*quite* warm] —**quite a few** (or **bit**, etc.) [Inf.] more than a few (or bit, etc.)

**Qui·to** (kē'tō) capital of Ecuador: pop. 1,101,000

**quits** (kwits) *adj.* [< ML *quittus*, free] on even terms, as by discharge of a debt, retaliation, etc. —**call it quits** [Inf.] **1** to stop working, etc. **2** to end an association

**quit·tance** (kwit''ns) *n.* [see QUIT] **1** discharge from a debt **2** recompense

**quit'ter** *n.* [Inf.] one who quits or gives up easily, without trying hard

**quiv·er¹** (kwiv'ər) *vi.* [< OE *curifer-*, eager] to shake tremulously; tremble —*n.* a quivering; tremor

**quiv·er²** (kwiv'ər) *n.* [< OFr *coivre*] a case for holding arrows

**quix·ot·ic** (kwik sät'ik) *adj.* [after DON QUIXOTE] extravagantly chivalrous or foolishly idealistic

**quiz** (kwiz) *n.*, *pl.* **quiz'zes** [prob. < L *quis,* what] a questioning; esp., a short examination to test knowledge —*vt.* **quizzed**, **quiz'zing** to ask questions, or test the knowledge, of —**quiz'zer** *n.*

**quiz'zi·cal** (-i kəl) *adj.* **1** teasing **2** perplexed — **quiz'zi·cal·ly** *adv.*

**quoin** (koin, kwoin) *n.* [var. of COIN] **1** the external corner of a building; esp., any of the large stones at such a corner **2** a wedge-shaped block

**quoit** (kwoit) *n.* [prob. < OFr *coite*, a cushion] **1** a ring thrown in quoits **2** [*pl.*, *with sing. v.*] a game somewhat like horseshoes, in which rings are thrown at a peg

**quon·dam** (kwän'dəm) *adj.* [L] former

QUOINS

**Quon·set hut** (kwän'sit) [< *Quonset*, a trademark] a prefabricated, metal shelter like a half cylinder on its flat side

**quo·rum** (kwôr'əm) *n.* [< L *qui*, who] the minimum number of members required to be present before an assembly can transact business

**quot** *abbrev.* quotation

**quo·ta** (kwōt'ə) *n.* [< L *quota pars*, how large a part] a share or proportion assigned to each of a number

**quotation mark** either of a pair of punctuation marks (" . . . ") used to enclose a direct quotation

**quote** (kwōt) *vt.* **quot'ed**, **quot'ing** [< L *quotus*, of what number] **1** to repeat a passage from or statement of **2** to repeat (a passage, statement, etc.) **3** to state the price of (something) —*n.* [Inf.] **1** something quoted **2** QUOTATION MARK —**quot'a·ble** *adj.* —**quo·ta·tion** (kwō tā'shən) *n.*

**quoth** (kwōth) *vt.* [< OE *cwethan*, speak] [Archaic] said

**quo·tid·i·an** (kwō tid'ē ən) *adj.* [< L *quotidie*] **1** daily **2** ordinary

**quo·tient** (kwō'shənt) *n.* [< L *quot*, how many] *Math.* the result obtained when one number is divided by another

**Qu·ran** or **Qu·r'an** (koo rän') *n.* var. of KORAN

**q.v.** *abbrev.* [L *quod vide*] which see

# R

**r**[1] or **R** (är) *n., pl.* **r's, R's** the 18th letter of the English alphabet

**r**[2] *abbrev.* radius

**R**[1] *trademark for* a film rating indicating that no one under 17 may be admitted unless accompanied by a parent or guardian

**R**[2] *abbrev.* **1** ⟦L *Rex*⟧ king **2** ⟦L *Regina*⟧ queen **3** Republican **4** right **5** River **6** Road **7** route **8** *Baseball* run(s): also **r**

**Ra**[1] (rä) *n. Egypt. Myth.* the sun god and chief deity

**Ra**[2] *Chem. symbol for* radium

**rab·bet** (rab′it) *n.* ⟦< OFr *rabattre*, beat down⟧ a cut made in a board so that another may be fitted into it —*vt., vi.* to cut, or be joined by, a rabbet

**rab·bi** (rab′ī) *n., pl.* **-bis** ⟦< Heb *rabi*, my master⟧ an ordained teacher of the Jewish law

**rab·bin·ate** (rab′i nit, -nāt′) *n.* **1** the position of a rabbi **2** rabbis collectively —**rab·bi·ni·cal** (rə bin′i kəl) *adj.*

**rab·bit** (rab′it) *n.* ⟦ME *rabette*⟧ a swift, burrowing mammal with soft fur and long ears

**rabbit punch** *Boxing* a short, sharp blow to the back of the neck

**rab·ble** (rab′əl) *n.* ⟦< ?⟧ a mob

**rab·ble-rous·er** (-rou′zər) *n.* one who tries to arouse people to violent action by appeals to emotions, prejudices, etc.

**Ra·be·lais** (rab′ə lā′), **Fran·çois** (frän swä′) 1494?-1553; Fr. satirist & humorist

**Ra·be·lai·si·an** (rab′ə lā′zhən, -zē ən) *adj.* ⟦after prec.⟧ broadly and coarsely humorous or satirical

**rab·id** (rab′id) *adj.* ⟦< L *rabere*, to rage⟧ **1** violent; raging **2** fanatic **3** of or having rabies

**ra·bies** (rā′bēz) *n.* ⟦L, madness⟧ an infectious disease characterized by convulsions, etc., transmitted to people by the bite of an infected animal

**rac·coon** (ra kōōn′) *n.* ⟦< AmInd *aroughcun*⟧ **1** a small, tree-climbing, American mammal, with yellowish-gray fur and a black-ringed tail **2** its fur

**race**[1] (rās) *n.* ⟦< ON *rās*, a running⟧ **1** a competition of speed in running, etc. **2** any similar contest *[the race for mayor]* **3** a swift current of water, or its channel —*vi.* **raced, rac′ing 1** to take part in a race **2** to go or move swiftly —*vt.* **1** to compete with in a race **2** to enter or run (a horse, etc.) in a race **3** to cause to go swiftly —**rac′er** *n.*

**race**[2] (rās) *n.* ⟦Fr < It *razza*⟧ **1** any of the different varieties of human beings distinguished by physical traits, blood types, etc. **2** loosely, any geographical population sharing the same habits, ideas, etc. **3** any distinct group of people

**race′horse′** *n.* a horse bred and trained for racing

**ra·ceme** (rā sēm′, rə-) *n.* ⟦L *racemus*, cluster of grapes⟧ a flower cluster having a central stem along which individual flowers grow on small stalks

**race′track′** *n.* a course prepared for racing, esp. an oval track for horse races

**race′way′** *n.* **1** a narrow channel for water **2** a racetrack for harness racing, drag racing, etc.

**ra·cial** (rā′shəl) *adj.* **1** of or characteristic of a RACE[2] **2** between races —**ra′cial·ly** *adv.*

**rac·i·ness** (rā′sē nis) *n.* racy quality

**racing form** a chart, etc. of information about the horse races at a track or tracks

**rac·ism** (rā′siz′əm) *n.* the practice of racial discrimination, segregation, etc. —**rac′ist** *n., adj.*

**rack**[1] (rak) *n.* ⟦< LowG *rack*⟧ **1** a framework, etc. for holding or displaying various things *[dish rack]* **2** a toothed bar into which a pinion, etc. meshes **3** an instrument of torture which stretches the victim's limbs —*vt.* **1** to arrange in or on a rack **2** to torture on a rack **3** to torment

**—rack one's brains** to try hard to think of something —**rack up** [Slang] to score or achieve

**rack**[2] (rak) *n.* ⟦var. of WRACK⟧ used only in **go to rack and ruin,** to become ruined

**rack**[3] (rak) *n.* ⟦< ? RACK[1]⟧ the rib section of mutton: in full **rack of lamb**

**rack·et**[1] (rak′it) *n.* ⟦prob. echoic⟧ **1** a noisy confusion **2** *a)* a method or scheme for obtaining money illegally *b)* [Inf.] any dishonest practice

**rack·et**[2] (rak′it) *n.* ⟦< Ar *rāha(t)*, palm of the hand⟧ a light bat for tennis, etc., with a network, as of catgut or nylon, in an oval frame attached to a handle: also **rac′quet**

**rack·et·eer** (rak′ə tir′) *n.* one who obtains money illegally, as by fraud, extortion, etc. —**rack′et·eer′ing** *n.*

**rac·on·teur** (rak′än tur′) *n.* ⟦Fr < *raconter*, to recount⟧ one skilled at telling stories or anecdotes

**rac·quet·ball** (rak′it bôl′) *n.* a game like handball, but played with a short racket

**rac·y** (rā′sē) *adj.* **-i·er, -i·est** ⟦RACE[2] + -Y[2]⟧ **1** having the taste or quality of the genuine type *[racy fruit]* **2** lively; spirited **3** pungent **4** risqué

**rad** (rad) *n.* ⟦< RAD(IATION)⟧ a dosage of absorbed radiation

**ra·dar** (rā′där) *n.* ⟦*ra(dio) d(etecting) a(nd) r(anging)*⟧ an apparatus that transmits radio waves to a reflecting object, as an aircraft, to determine its location, speed, etc. by the reflected waves

**ra′dar·scope′** *n.* an oscilloscope that displays reflected radar wave signals

**ra·di·al** (rā′dē əl) *adj.* ⟦< L *radius*, ray⟧ **1** of or like a ray or rays; branching out from a center **2** of a radius

**radial (ply) tire** an automobile tire with plies of rubberized cords at right angles to the center line of the tread

**ra·di·ant** (rā′dē ənt) *adj.* ⟦< L *radius*, ray⟧ **1** shining brightly **2** showing pleasure, etc.; beaming **3** issuing (from a source) in or as in rays —**ra′di·ance** *n.* —**ra′di·ant·ly** *adv.*

**ra·di·ate** (rā′dē āt′) *vi.* **-at·ed, -at·ing** ⟦< L *radius*, ray⟧ **1** to send out rays of heat, light, etc. **2** to branch out in lines from a center —*vt.* **1** to send out (heat, light, etc.) in rays **2** to give forth or spread (happiness, love, etc.)

**ra′di·a′tion** *n.* **1** a radiating **2** the rays sent out **3** energy emitted as nuclear particles, etc.

**radiation sickness** sickness produced by overexposure to X-rays, radioactive matter, etc.

**ra′di·a′tor** *n.* **1** an apparatus for radiating heat, as into a room **2** a device for circulating coolant, etc., as for a car engine

**rad·i·cal** (rad′i kəl) *adj.* ⟦< L *radix*, root⟧ **1** fundamental; basic **2** favoring basic change, as in the social or economic structure —*n.* **1** a person holding radical views **2** *Chem.* a group of two or more atoms acting as a single atom **3** *Math.* the sign (√) used with a quantity to show that its root is to be extracted —**rad′i·cal·ism′** *n.* —**rad′i·cal·ly** *adv.*

**ra·dic·chio** (rə dē′kyō) *n., pl.* **-chios** ⟦It⟧ a variety of chicory used in salads

**ra·di·i** (rā′dē ī′) *n. alt. pl. of* RADIUS

**ra·di·o** (rā′dē ō′) *n.* ⟦< *radio(telegraphy)*⟧ **1** the transmission of sounds or signals by electromagnetic waves directly through space to a receiving set **2** *pl.* **-os′** such a set **3** broadcasting by radio as an industry, entertainment, etc. —*adj.* **1** of, using, used in, or sent by radio **2** of electromagnetic wave frequencies between *c.* 10 kilohertz and *c.* 300,000 megahertz —*vt., vi.* **-oed′, -o′ing** to transmit, or communicate with, by radio

**radio-** ⟦< L *radius*, ray⟧ *combining form* **1** ray,

raylike 2 by radio 3 using radiant energy 4 radioactive [*radiotherapy*]

**ra·di·o·ac·tive** *adj.* giving off radiant energy in the form of particles or rays by the disintegration of atomic nuclei —**ra·di·o·ac·tiv'i·ty** *n.*

**radio astronomy** astronomy dealing with radio waves in space in order to obtain information about the universe

**ra'di·o·gram'** *n.* a message sent by radio

**ra'di·o·i'so·tope'** *n.* a radioactive isotope of a chemical element

**ra·di·ol·o·gy** (rā'dē äl'ə jē) *n.* the use of radiant energy, as X-rays, in medical diagnosis and therapy —**ra'di·ol'o·gist** *n.*

**ra'di·o·paque'** (-ō pāk') *adj.* [RADIO- + (O)PAQUE] not allowing the passage of X-rays, etc.

**radio telescope** a radio antenna for receiving and measuring radio waves from stars, spacecraft, etc.

**ra'di·o·ther'a·py** *n.* the treatment of disease by the use of X-rays or rays from a radioactive substance

**rad·ish** (rad'ish) *n.* [< L *radix*, root] 1 an annual plant with an edible root 2 the pungent root, eaten raw

**ra·di·um** (rā'dē əm) *n.* [< L *radius*, ray] a radioactive, metallic chemical element found in some uranium, which undergoes spontaneous atomic disintegration

**ra·di·us** (rā'dē əs) *n., pl.* **-di·i'** (-ī') or **-us·es** [L, ray] 1 any straight line from the center to the periphery of a circle or sphere 2 the circular area limited by the sweep of such a line [*within a radius of two miles*] 3 the shorter, thicker bone of the forearm

**ra·don** (rā'dän') *n.* [< RADIUM] a radioactive chemical element, a nonreactive gas, formed in the atomic disintegration of radium

**RAF** *abbrev.* Royal Air Force

**raf·fi·a** (raf'ē ə) *n.* [< native name] 1 a palm tree of Madagascar, with large leaves 2 fiber from its leaves, used as string or for weaving

**raff·ish** (raf'ish) *adj.* [(RIFF)RAFF + -ISH] 1 carelessly unconventional 2 vulgar; low

**raf·fle** (raf'əl) *n.* [ME *rafle*] a lottery in which each participant buys a chance to win a prize — *vt.* **-fled, -fling** to offer as a prize in a raffle: often with *off*

**raft**[1] (raft) *n.* [< ON *raptr*, a log] 1 a flat, buoyant structure of logs, etc. fastened together 2 a flat-bottomed, inflatable boat —*vi.* to travel on a raft

**raft**[2] (raft) *n.* [< Brit dial. *raff*, rubbish] [Inf.] a large quantity

**raf·ter** (raf'tər) *n.* [OE *ræfter*] any of the beams that slope from the ridge of a roof to the eaves

**rag**[1] (rag) *n.* [< ON *rögg*, tuft of hair] 1 a waste piece of cloth, esp. one old or torn 2 a small piece of cloth for dusting, etc. 3 [*pl.*] old, worn clothes

**rag**[2] (rag) *vt.* **ragged, rag'ging** [< ?] [Slang] to tease or scold: often with *on*

**rag**[3] (rag) *n.* a tune in ragtime

**ra·ga** (rä'gə) *n.* [Sans *rāga*, color] any of various melody patterns improvised on by Hindu musicians

**rag·a·muf·fin** (rag'ə muf'in) *n.* [ME *Ragamoffyn*, name of a demon] a poor, ragged child

**rag'bag'** *n.* 1 a bag for rags 2 a collection of odds and ends

**rage** (rāj) *n.* [< LL *rabia*, madness] 1 a furious, uncontrolled anger 2 a great force, violence, etc. —*vi.* **raged, rag'ing** 1 to show violent anger in action or speech 2 to be forceful, violent, etc. 3 to spread unchecked, as a disease —**(all) the rage** a fad

**ragg** (rag) *adj.* designating or made of sturdy yarn having a speckled pattern

**rag·ged** (rag'id) *adj.* 1 shabby or torn from wear 2 wearing shabby or torn clothes 3 uneven;

imperfect 4 shaggy [*ragged* hair] —**run ragged** to tire out; exhaust —**rag'ged·ness** *n.*

**rag'ged·y** *adj.* tattered

**rag·lan** (rag'lən) *n.* [after Lord *Raglan*, 19th-c. Brit general] a loose coat with sleeves that continue in one piece to the collar —*adj.* designating or having such a sleeve

**ra·gout** (ra gōō') *n.* [< Fr *ragoûter*, revive the appetite of] a highly seasoned stew of meat and vegetables

**rag'time'** *n.* [prob. < *ragged time*] 1 a type of American music (*c.* 1890-1920), with strong syncopation in even time 2 its rhythm

RAGLAN SLEEVES

**rag'weed'** *n.* [< its ragged-looking leaves] a weed whose pollen is a common cause of hay fever

**rah** (rä) *interj.* hurrah: used as by cheerleaders

**raid** (rād) *n.* [dial. var. of ROAD] 1 a sudden, hostile attack, esp. by troops or bandits 2 a sudden invasion of a place by police, for discovering violations of the law —*vt., vi.* to make a raid (on) — **raid'er** *n.*

**rail**[1] (rāl) *n.* [< L *regula*, a rule] 1 a bar of wood, metal, etc. placed between posts as a barrier or support 2 any of the parallel metal bars forming a track for a railroad, etc. 3 railroad or railway —*vt.* to supply with rails or a railing —*adj.* of a railway or railroad

**rail**[2] (rāl) *vi.* [< LL *ragere*, to bellow] to speak bitterly; complain violently

**rail**[3] (rāl) *n.* [< Fr *raaler*, to screech] a marsh bird with a harsh cry

**rail'ing** *n.* 1 materials for rails 2 a fence, etc. made of rails and posts

**rail·ler·y** (rā'lər ē) *n., pl.* **-ies** [see RAIL[2]] light, good-natured ridicule

**rail'road'** *n.* 1 a track of parallel steel rails for a train 2 a complete system of such tracks, trains, etc. —*vt.* 1 to transport by railroad 2 [Inf.] to rush through quickly, so as to prevent careful consideration —*vi.* to work on a railroad — **rail'road'er** *n.* —**rail'road'ing** *n.*

**rail'way'** *n.* 1 any track with rails for guiding wheels 2 RAILROAD

**rai·ment** (rā'mənt) *n.* [see ARRAY & -MENT] [Archaic] clothing; attire

**rain** (rān) *n.* [OE *regn*] 1 water falling in drops condensed from the atmosphere 2 the falling of such drops 3 a rapid falling of many small objects —*vi.* 1 to fall: said of rain 2 to fall like rain —*vt.* 1 to pour down 2 to give in large quantities —**rain out** to cause (an event) to be postponed because of rain —**rain'y, -i·er, -i·est,** *adj.*

**rain'bow'** (-bō') *n.* [OE *regnboga*] an arc containing the colors of the spectrum, formed in the sky by the refraction, reflection, and dispersion of light in rain or fog

**rain check** a ticket stub to a ballgame, etc. allowing future admission if the event is rained out

**rain'coat'** *n.* a water-repellent coat

**rain'drop'** *n.* a single drop of rain

**rain'fall'** *n.* 1 a falling of rain 2 the amount of rain over a given area during a given time

**rain forest** a dense, evergreen forest in a rainy tropical region

**rain'storm'** *n.* a storm with heavy rain

**rain'wa'ter** *n.* water that is falling or has fallen as rain

**raise** (rāz) *vt.* **raised, rais'ing** [< ON *reisa*] 1 to cause to rise; lift 2 to construct; build 3 to increase in size, intensity, amount, degree, etc. [*raise* prices, *raise* one's voice] 4 to provoke; inspire 5 to present for consideration [*raise* a question] 6 to collect (an army, money, etc.) 7 to end [*raise* a siege] **8** *a*) to cause to grow *b*) to rear (children) —*n.* **1** a raising **2** an increase in salary or in a bet —**raise Cain** (or **hell,** etc.) [Slang] to create a disturbance

**rai·sin** (rā′zən) *n.* [< L *racemus,* cluster of grapes] a dried sweet grape

**rai·son d'être** (rā′zōn det′, det′rə) [Fr] reason for being; justification for existence

**raj** (räj) *n.* [Hindi: see fol.] in India, rule; government —**the Raj** the British government in, or its dominion over, India

**ra·jah** or **ra·ja** (rä′jə) *n.* [< Sans *rāj,* to rule] a prince in India

**rake**[1] (rāk) *n.* [OE *raca*] a long-handled tool with teeth at one end, for gathering loose hay, leaves, etc. —*vt.* **raked, rak′ing 1** to gather or smooth with a rake **2** to search through minutely **3** to direct gunfire along (a line of troops, etc.) —**rake in** to gather a great amount of rapidly —**rake up** to uncover facts or gossip about (the past, etc.)

**rake**[2] (rāk) *n.* [contr. of *rake-hell*] a dissolute, debauched man

**rake**[3] (rāk) *vi., vt.* **raked, rak′ing** [< ?] to slant —*n.* a slanting

**rake′-off** *n.* [Slang] a commission or rebate, esp. when illegitimate

**rak·ish** (rāk′ish) *adj.* [< RAKE[3] + -ISH] **1** having a trim appearance suggesting speed: said of a ship **2** dashing; jaunty —**rak′ish·ly** *adv.*

RAKES

**Ra·legh** or **Ra·leigh** (rô′lē, rä′lē), Sir **Wal·ter** (wôl′tər) 1552?-1618; Eng. explorer & poet

**Ra·leigh** (rô′lē, rä′lē) capital of North Carolina: pop. 212,000

**ral·ly**[1] (ral′ē) *vt., vi.* **-lied, -ly·ing** [< OFr *re-,* again + *alier,* join] **1** to bring back together in, or come back to, a state of order: said as of troops **2** to bring or come together for a common purpose **3** to recover; revive —*n., pl.* **-lies 1** a rallying or being rallied; esp., a gathering of people for some purpose **2** an organized automobile run designed to test driving skills

**ral·ly**[2] (ral′ē) *vt., vi.* **-lied, -ly·ing** [see RAIL[2]] to tease or ridicule

**ram** (ram) *n.* [OE *ramm*] **1** a male sheep **2** BATTERING RAM —*vt.* **rammed, ram′ming 1** to strike against with great force **2** to force into place; press down

**RAM** (ram) *n.* random-access memory

**ram·ble** (ram′bəl) *vi.* **-bled, -bling** [< ME *romen*] **1** to roam about; esp., to stroll about idly **2** to talk or write aimlessly **3** to spread in all directions, as a vine does —*n.* a stroll

**ram′bler** (-blər) *n.* a person or thing that rambles; esp., a climbing rose

**ram·bunc·tious** (ram bunk′shəs) *adj.* [altered, (after RAM) < earlier *rambustious*] disorderly, boisterous, unruly, etc. —**ram·bunc′tious·ness** *n.*

**ram·e·kin** or **ram·e·quin** (ram′ə kin) *n.* [< Fr < MDu] a small individual baking dish

**ra·men** (rä′mən) *pl.n.* [*sometimes with sing. v.*] Japanese wheat noodles

**ram·i·fy** (ram′ə fī′) *vt., vi.* **-fied′, -fy′ing** [< L *ramus,* a branch + *facere,* make] to divide or spread out into branches or branchlike divisions —**ram′i·fi·ca′tion** *n.*

**ramp** (ramp) *n.* [< OFr *ramper,* to climb] **1** a sloping surface, walk, etc. joining different levels **2** a means for boarding a plane, as a movable staircase **3** a sloping runway, as for launching boats

**ram·page** (ram′pāj′) *vi.* **-paged′, -pag′ing** to rush about wildly; rage —*n.* an outbreak of violent, raging behavior: chiefly in **on the** (or **a**) **rampage**

**ramp·ant** (ram′pənt) *adj.* [< OFr *ramper,* to climb] growing unchecked; widespread

**ram·part** (ram′pärt′, -pərt) *n.* [< Fr *re-,* again +

*emparer,* fortify] an embankment of earth surmounted by a parapet for defending a fort, etc.

**ram′rod′** *n.* a rod for ramming down the charge in a muzzle-loading gun

**ram·shack·le** (ram′shak′əl) *adj.* [< RANSACK] loose and rickety; likely to fall to pieces

**ran** (ran) *vi., vt. pt. of* RUN

**ranch** (ranch) *n.* [< Sp *rancho,* small farm] **1** a large farm, esp. in the W U.S., for raising cattle, horses, or sheep **2** a style of house with all the rooms on one floor: in full **ranch house** —*vi.* to work on or manage a ranch —**ranch′er** *n.*

**ranch dressing** creamy buttermilk salad dressing

**ran·cid** (ran′sid) *adj.* [< L *rancere,* to be rank] smelling or tasting of stale fats or oils; spoiled

**ran·cor** (ran′kər) *n.* [< L *rancere,* to be rank] a continuing and bitter hate or ill will: Brit. sp. **ran′cour** —**ran′cor·ous** *adj.* —**ran′cor·ous·ly** *adv.*

**rand** (rand) *n., pl.* **rand** the monetary unit of South Africa

**R & B** or **r & b** *abbrev.* rhythm and blues

**R & D** *abbrev.* research and development

**ran·dom** (ran′dəm) *adj.* [< OFr *randir,* run violently] purposeless; haphazard —**at random** haphazardly —**ran′dom·ly** *adv.*

**ran′dom-ac′cess** *adj. Comput.* of a kind of memory that allows data to be directly accessible

**ran′dom·ize** (-īz′) *vt.* **-ized′, -iz′ing** to select or choose (items of a group) in a random order

**ran·dy** (ran′dē) *adj.* **-di·er, -di·est** [Chiefly Scot.] amorous; lustful

**rang** (raŋ) *vi., vt. pt. of* RING[1]

**range** (rānj) *vt.* **ranged, rang′ing** [< OFr *renc,* a ring] **1** to arrange in order; set in a row or rows **2** to place (esp. oneself) with others in a cause, etc. **3** to roam through —*vi.* **1** to extend in a given direction **2** to roam **3** to vary between stated limits —*n.* **1** a row, line, or series **2** a series of connected mountains **3** the distance that a weapon can fire its projectile **4** *a*) a place for shooting practice *b*) a place for testing rockets in flight **5** extent; scope **6** a large, open area for grazing livestock **7** the limits of possible variations of amount, degree, pitch, etc. [a wide *range* of prices] **8** a cooking stove

**rang·er** (rān′jər) *n.* **1** *a*) a mounted trooper who patrols a region *b*) [*often* R-] a soldier trained for raiding and close combat **2** a warden who patrols parks and forests

**Ran·goon** (ran gōōn′) *former name for* YANGON

**rang·y** (rān′jē) *adj.* **-i·er, -i·est** long-limbed and slender —**rang′i·ness** *n.*

**rank**[1] (raŋk) *n.* [< OFr *ranc*] **1** a row, line, or series **2** a social class **3** a high position in society **4** an official grade [the *rank* of major] **5** a relative position in a scale [a poet of the first *rank*] **6** *a*) a row of soldiers, etc. placed side by side *b*) [*pl.*] the army; esp., enlisted soldiers —*vt.* **1** to place in a rank **2** to assign a position to **3** to outrank —*vi.* to hold a certain position —**rank and file 1** enlisted soldiers **2** the common people, as distinguished from leaders

**rank**[2] (raŋk) *adj.* [OE *ranc,* strong] **1** growing vigorously and coarsely [*rank* grass] **2** strong and offensive in smell or taste **3** in bad taste **4** complete; utter [*rank* deceit]

**rank′ing** *adj.* **1** of the highest rank **2** prominent or outstanding

**ran·kle** (raŋ′kəl) *vi., vt.* **-kled, -kling** [ult. < L dim. of *draco,* dragon] **1** [Obs.] to fester **2** to cause, or cause to have, long-lasting anger, rancor, etc.

**ran·sack** (ran′sak′) *vt.* [< ON *rann,* house + *sœkja,* seek] **1** to search thoroughly **2** to plunder

**ran·som** (ran′səm) *n.* [see REDEEM] **1** the redeeming of a captive by paying money or complying with demands **2** the price thus paid or demanded —*vt.* to obtain the release of (a captive, etc.) by paying the demanded price

**rant** (rant) *vi., vt.* [< obs. Du *ranten*] to talk or say in a loud, wild, extravagant way —*n.* loud, wild speech

**rap** (rap) *vt.* **rapped, rap′ping** ⟦prob. echoic⟧ **1** to strike quickly and sharply; tap **2** [Slang] to criticize sharply —*vi.* **1** to knock sharply **2** [Slang] to talk —*n.* **1** a quick, sharp knock **2** [Slang] blame or punishment **3** [Slang] a chat or serious discussion **4** a kind of popular music in which rhymed verses are chanted over repetitive rhythms

**ra·pa·cious** (rə pā′shəs) *adj.* ⟦< L *rapere,* seize⟧ **1** greedy; voracious **2** predatory —**ra·pa′cious·ly** *adv.* —**ra·pac′i·ty** (-pas′ə tē) *n.*

**rape¹** (rāp) *n.* ⟦prob. < L *rapere,* seize⟧ **1** the crime of having sexual intercourse with a person forcibly and without consent **2** the plundering (*of* a city, etc.), as in warfare —*vt.* **raped, rap′ing 1** to commit rape on; violate **2** to plunder or destroy —*vi.* to commit rape —**rap′ist** *n.*

**rape²** (rāp) *n.* ⟦< L *rapa,* turnip⟧ an annual plant whose leaves are used for fodder

**Raph·a·el** (rä′fā el′, -fī-) 1483-1520; It. painter & architect

**rap·id** (rap′id) *adj.* ⟦< L *rapere,* to rush⟧ moving or occurring with speed; swift; quick —*n.* [*usually pl.*] a part of a river where the current is swift —**ra·pid·i·ty** (rə pid′ə tē) *n.* —**rap′id·ly** *adv.*

**rapid transit** a system of public transportation in an urban area, using electric trains along an unimpeded right of way

**ra·pi·er** (rā′pē ər) *n.* ⟦Fr *rapière*⟧ a light, sharp-pointed sword used only for thrusting

**rap·ine** (rap′in) *n.* ⟦< L *rapere,* seize⟧ plunder; pillage

**rap·pel** (ra pel′) *n.* ⟦Fr, lit., a recall⟧ a descent by a mountain climber, using a double rope around the body to control the slide downward —*vi.* **-pelled′, -pel′ling** to make such a descent

**rap′per** *n.* a performer of rap music

**rap·port** (ra pôr′) *n.* ⟦Fr⟧ close relationship; harmony

**rap·proche·ment** (ra′prōsh män′) *n.* ⟦Fr⟧ an establishing of friendly relations

**rap·scal·lion** (rap skal′yən) *n.* ⟦< RASCAL⟧ ROGUE

**rap sheet** [Slang] one's police record of arrests and convictions

**rapt** (rapt) *adj.* ⟦< L *rapere,* seize⟧ **1** carried away with joy, love, etc. **2** completely engrossed (*in* meditation, study, etc.)

**rap·tor** (rap′tər, -tôr′) *n.* ⟦< L *rapere,* to snatch⟧ a bird, as a hawk, that preys on other animals

**rap·ture** (rap′chər) *n.* the state of being carried away with joy, love, etc.; ecstasy —**rap′tur·ous** *adj.* —**rap′tur·ous·ly** *adv.*

**ra·ra a·vis** (rer′ə ā′vis) *pl.* **ra·rae a·ves** (rer′ē ā′vēz) ⟦L, lit., strange bird⟧ an extraordinary person or thing

**rare¹** (rer) *adj.* **rar′er, rar′est** ⟦< L *rarus*⟧ **1** not frequently encountered; scarce; unusual **2** unusually good; excellent **3** not dense [*rare* atmosphere] —**rare′ness** *n.*

**rare²** (rer) *adj.* **rar′er, rar′est** ⟦OE *hrere*⟧ not completely cooked; partly raw: said esp. of meat —**rare′ness** *n.*

**rare³** (rer) *vi.* **rared, rar′ing** [Inf.] to be eager: used in prp. [*raring* to go]

**rare·bit** (rer′bit) *n.* WELSH RABBIT

**rar·e·fy** (rer′ə fī′) *vt., vi.* **-fied′, -fy′ing** ⟦< L *rarus,* RARE¹ + *facere,* make⟧ to make or become less dense —**rar′e·fac′tion** (-fak′shən) *n.*

**rare·ly** (rer′lē) *adv.* **1** infrequently; seldom **2** uncommonly

**rar·i·ty** (rer′ə tē) *n.* **1** a being rare; specif., *a*) scarcity *b*) lack of density **2** *pl.* **-ties** something remarkable or valuable because rare

**ras·cal** (ras′kəl) *n.* ⟦< OFr *rascaille,* rabble⟧ **1** a rogue **2** a mischievous child —**ras·cal′i·ty** (-kal′ə tē) *n.* —**ras′cal·ly** *adj., adv.*

**rash¹** (rash) *adj.* ⟦ME *rasch*⟧ too hasty in acting or speaking; reckless —**rash′ly** *adv.* —**rash′ness** *n.*

**rash²** (rash) *n.* ⟦< OFr *rascaille,* rabble⟧ **1** an eruption of spots on the skin **2** a sudden appearance of a large number of instances

**rash′er** *n.* ⟦< L *radere,* to scrape⟧ a thin slice of bacon, etc., or a serving of several such slices

**rasp** (rasp) *vt.* ⟦< OHG *raspon,* to scrape together⟧ **1** to scrape as with a file **2** to grate upon; irritate —*vi.* **1** to grate **2** to make a rough, grating sound —*n.* **1** a type of rough file **2** a rough, grating sound —**rasp′y, -i·er, -i·est,** *adj.*

**rasp·ber·ry** (raz′ber′ē, -bər-) *n., pl.* **-ries** ⟦< earlier *raspis*⟧ **1** a small, juicy, edible reddish fruit of a plant related to the rose **2** this plant **3** [Slang] a sound of derision

**rat** (rat) *n.* ⟦OE *ræt*⟧ **1** a long-tailed rodent, resembling, but larger than, the mouse **2** [Slang] a sneaky, contemptible person; esp., an informer —*vi.* **rat′ted, rat′ting** [Slang] to inform (*on*) — **smell a rat** to suspect a trick, plot, etc.

**ratch·et** (rach′it) *n.* ⟦< It *rocca,* distaff⟧ **1** a toothed wheel (in full **ratchet wheel**) or bar whose sloping teeth catch a pawl, preventing backward motion **2** such a pawl

**rate¹** (rāt) *n.* ⟦< L *reri,* reckon⟧ **1** the amount, degree, etc. of anything in relation to units of something else [*rate* of pay] **2** price, esp. per unit —*vt.* **rat′ed, rat′ing 1** to appraise **2** to consider **3** [Inf.] to deserve —*vi.* to have value, status, etc. —**at any rate 1** in any event **2** anyway

**rate²** (rāt) *vt., vi.* **rat′ed, rat′ing** ⟦< L *reputare,* to count⟧ to scold; chide

**rath·er** (rath′ər) *adv.* ⟦OE *hræthe,* quickly⟧ **1** more willingly; preferably **2** with more justice, reason, etc. [*I, rather* than you, should pay] **3** more accurately [*my son, or rather,* stepson] **4** on the contrary **5** somewhat [*rather* hungry] — **rather than** instead of

**rat′hole′** *n.* a great waste of money, etc.

**raths·kel·ler** (rath′skel′ər) *n.* ⟦Ger < *rat,* council, town hall + *keller,* cellar⟧ a restaurant, usually below the street level, where beer is served

**rat·i·fy** (rat′ə fī′) *vt.* **-fied′, -fy′ing** ⟦< L *ratus,* reckoned + *facere,* make⟧ to approve; esp., to give official sanction to —**rat′i·fi·ca′tion** *n.*

**rat·ing** (rāt′iŋ) *n.* **1** a rank or grade, as of military personnel **2** a placement in a certain rank or class **3** an evaluation; appraisal **4** *Film* a classification, based on content, restricting the age of those who may attend **5** *Radio, TV* the relative popularity of a program according to sample polls

**ra·tio** (rā′shō, -shē ō′) *n., pl.* **-tios** ⟦L, a reckoning⟧ a fixed relation in degree, number, etc. between two similar things; proportion

**ra·ti·oc·i·nate** (rash′ē äs′ə nāt′) *vi.* **-nat′ed, -nat′ing** ⟦see prec.⟧ to think or argue logically; reason —**ra′ti·oc′i·na′tion** *n.*

**ra·tion** (rash′ən, rā′shən) *n.* ⟦see RATIO⟧ **1** a fixed portion; share **2** a fixed allowance of food, as a daily allowance for a soldier **3** [*pl.*] food supply — *vt.* **1** to supply with rations **2** to distribute (food, clothing, etc.) in rations, as in times of scarcity

**ra·tion·al** (rash′ən əl) *adj.* ⟦see RATIO⟧ **1** of or based on reasoning **2** able to reason; reasoning **3** sensible or sane —**ra′tion·al′i·ty** (-ə nal′ə tē) *n.* — **ra′tion·al·ly** *adv.*

**ra·tion·ale** (rash′ə nal′) *n.* ⟦< L *rationalis,* rational⟧ **1** the reasons or rational basis for something **2** an explanation of principles

**ra′tion·al·ism′** *n.* the practice of accepting reason as the only authority in determining one's opinions or course of action —**ra′tion·al·ist** *n., adj.* — **ra′tion·al·is′tic** *adj.*

**ra′tion·al·ize′** *vt., vi.* **-ized′, -iz′ing 1** to make or be rational or reasonable **2** to devise plausible explanations for (one's acts, beliefs, etc.), usually in self-deception —**ra′tion·al·i·za′tion** *n.*

**rat·line** (rat′lin) *n.* ⟦< ?⟧ any of the horizontal ropes which join the shrouds of a ship and serve as a ladder: also sp. **rat′lin**

**rat race** [Slang] a mad scramble or intense struggle, as in the business world

**rat·tan** (ra tan′) *n.* ⟦Malay *rotan*⟧ **1** a tall palm tree with long, slender, tough stems **2** its stem, used in making furniture, etc.

**rat·tle** (rat''l) *vi.* **-tled, -tling** ⟦prob. echoic⟧ **1** to make a series of sharp, short sounds **2** to chatter: often with *on* —*vt.* **1** to cause to rattle **2** to confuse or upset —*n.* **1** a series of sharp, short sounds **2** a series of horny rings at the end of a rattlesnake's tail **3** a baby's toy, a percussion instrument, etc. made to rattle when shaken

**rat·tle·brain'** *n.* a frivolous, talkative person — **rat'tle-brained'** *adj.*

**rat'tler** *n.* a rattlesnake

**rat'tle·snake'** *n.* a poisonous American snake with horny rings at the end of the tail that rattle when shaken

**rat'tle·trap'** *n.* a rickety old car

**rat'tling** (-liŋ) *adj.* **1** that rattles **2** [Inf.] very fast, good, etc. —*adv.* [Inf.] very *[a rattling good time]*

**rat'trap'** *n.* **1** a trap for rats **2** [Inf.] a dirty, run-down building

**rat·ty** (rat'ē) *adj.* **-ti·er, -ti·est** [Slang] shabby or run-down

**rau·cous** (rô'kəs) *adj.* ⟦L *raucus*⟧ **1** hoarse **2** loud and rowdy —**rau'cous·ly** *adv.* —**rau'cous·ness** *n.*

**raun·chy** (rôn'chē) *adj.* **-chi·er, -chi·est** ⟦< ?⟧ [Slang] **1** dirty, sloppy, etc. **2** risqué, lustful, etc.

**rav·age** (rav'ij) *n.* ⟦see RAVISH⟧ destruction; ruin —*vt.* **-aged, -ag·ing** to destroy violently; ruin

**rave** (rāv) *vi.* **raved, rav'ing** ⟦< OFr *raver*, roam⟧ **1** to talk incoherently or wildly **2** to talk with great enthusiasm (*about*) —*n.* [Inf.] a very enthusiastic commendation

**rav·el** (rav'əl) *vt., vi.* **-eled** or **-elled, -el·ing** or **-el·ling** ⟦< MDu *ravelen*⟧ to separate into its parts, esp. threads; fray —*n.* a raveled part in a fabric

**ra·ven** (rā'vən) *n.* ⟦OE *hræfn*⟧ the largest crow, with a straight, sharp beak —*adj.* black and lustrous

**rav·en·ing** (rav'ə niŋ) *adj.* ⟦ult. < L *rapere*, seize⟧ greedily searching for prey *[ravening wolves]*

**rav·e·nous** (rav'ə nəs) *adj.* ⟦< L *rapere*, seize⟧ **1** greedily hungry **2** rapacious —**rav'e·nous·ly** *adv.*

**ra·vine** (rə vēn') *n.* ⟦Fr, flood⟧ a long, deep hollow in the earth, esp. one worn by a stream; gorge

**rav'ing** *adj.* **1** that raves; frenzied **2** [Inf.] exciting enthusiastic admiration *[a raving beauty]* —*adv.* so as to cause raving *[raving mad]*

**ra·vi·o·li** (rav'ē ō'lē) *n., pl.* **-li** or **-lis** ⟦It⟧ small casings of dough filled with meat, cheese, etc.

**rav·ish** (rav'ish) *vt.* ⟦< L *rapere*, seize⟧ **1** to seize and carry away forcibly **2** to rape (a woman) **3** to transport with joy or delight —**rav'ish·ment** *n.*

**rav'ish·ing** *adj.* causing great joy

**raw** (rô) *adj.* ⟦OE *hreaw*⟧ **1** not cooked **2** in its natural condition; not processed *[raw silk]* **3** inexperienced *[a raw recruit]* **4** abraded and sore **5** uncomfortably cold and damp *[a raw wind]* **6** brutal, coarse, indecent, etc. **7** [Inf.] harsh or unfair *[a raw deal]* —**in the raw 1** in the natural state **2** naked —**raw'ness** *n.*

**raw bar** a place serving uncooked shellfish

**raw'boned'** (-bōnd') *adj.* lean; gaunt

**raw'hide'** *n.* **1** an untanned cattle hide **2** a whip made of this

**ray¹** (rā) *n.* ⟦< L *radius*⟧ **1** any of the thin lines, or beams, of light that appear to come from a bright source **2** any of several lines radiating from a center **3** a tiny amount *[a ray of hope]* **4** a beam of radiant energy, radioactive particles, etc.

**ray²** (rā) *n.* ⟦< L *raia*⟧ a cartilaginous fish with a broad, flat body, widely expanded fins on both sides, and a whiplike tail

**ray·on** (rā'än) *n.* ⟦< RAY¹⟧ **1** a textile fiber made from a cellulose solution **2** a fabric of such fibers

**raze** (rāz) *vt.* **razed, raz'ing** ⟦< L *radere*, to scrape⟧ to tear down completely; demolish

**ra·zor** (rā'zər) *n.* ⟦see prec.⟧ **1** a sharp-edged cutting instrument for shaving, cutting hair, etc. **2** SHAVER (sense 2)

**razor wire** sharp-edged wire, as for fences

**razz** (raz) *vt.* ⟦< RASPBERRY⟧ [Slang] to tease, ridicule, etc.

**raz·zle-daz·zle** (raz'əl daz'əl) *n.* [Slang] a flashy, deceptive display

**razz·ma·tazz** (raz'mə taz') *n.* ⟦prob. < prec.⟧ [Slang] **1** lively spirit **2** flashy display

**RBI** or **rbi** *n., pl.* **RBIs** or **RBI, rbi's** or **rbi** *Baseball* run batted in

**RC** *abbrev.* Roman Catholic

**rd** *abbrev.* **1** rod **2** round

**Rd** *abbrev.* Road

**RD** *abbrev.* Rural Delivery

**RDA** *abbrev.* Recommended Daily (or Dietary) Allowance: the amount of protein, vitamins, etc. suggested for various age groups

**re¹** (rā) *n.* ⟦It⟧ *Music* the second tone of the diatonic scale

**re²** (rē, rā) *prep.* ⟦L < *res*, thing⟧ in the matter of; as regards

**re-** ⟦< Fr or L⟧ *prefix* **1** back **2** again; anew It is sometimes hyphenated, as before a word beginning with *e* or to distinguish between such forms as *re-cover* (to cover again) and RECOVER The words in the following list can be understood if "again" or "anew" is added to the meaning of the base word:

| | |
|---|---|
| reacquaint | reformulate |
| reacquire | refuel |
| readjust | refurnish |
| readmit | rehear |
| reaffirm | reheat |
| realign | rehire |
| reappear | reimpose |
| reapply | reinfect |
| reappoint | reinsert |
| reappraise | reinspect |
| rearm | reinvest |
| reassemble | reissue |
| reassert | rekindle |
| reassess | relearn |
| reassign | reload |
| reawaken | remake |
| reborn | remarry |
| rebroadcast | rematch |
| rebuild | remix |
| recharge | rename |
| recheck | renegotiate |
| reclassify | renominate |
| recommence | renumber |
| reconquer | reoccupy |
| reconsign | reoccur |
| reconvene | reopen |
| reconvert | reorder |
| recopy | repack |
| re-cover | repackage |
| redecorate | repaint |
| rededicate | repave |
| redesign | rephrase |
| redetermine | replant |
| redirect | replay |
| rediscover | re-press |
| redistribution | reprint |
| redivide | republish |
| redraw | reread |
| reedit | rerelease |
| reeducate | reroute |
| reelect | reschedule |
| reembark | resell |
| reemerge | reset |
| reemphasize | resettle |
| reenact | reshuffle |
| reengage | respell |
| reenlist | restate |
| reenter | restring |
| reestablish | restudy |
| reevaluate | restyle |
| reexamine | resubscribe |
| reexplain | resupply |
| refashion | retell |
| refasten | retest |
| refinance | rethink |

| | |
|---|---|
| retrain | revitalize |
| retrial | reweigh |
| reunite | rework |
| reupholster | rezone |
| reuse | |

**reach** (rēch) *vt.* ⟦OE *ræcan*⟧ **1** to thrust out (the hand, etc.) **2** to extend to by thrusting out, etc. **3** to obtain and hand over *[reach* me the salt*]* **4** to go as far as; attain **5** to influence; affect **6** to get in touch with, as by telephone —*vi.* **1** to thrust out the hand, etc. **2** to extend in influence, space, amount, etc. **3** to carry: said of sight, sound, etc. **4** to try to get something —*n.* **1** a stretching or thrusting out **2** the power of, or the extent covered in, stretching, obtaining, etc. **3** a continuous extent, esp. of water

**re·act** (rē akt′) *vi.* **1** to act in return or reciprocally **2** to act in opposition **3** to act in a reverse way; go back to a former condition, stage, etc. **4** to respond to a stimulus **5** *Chem.* to act with another substance in a chemical change

**re·act·ant** (rē ak′tənt) *n.* any substance involved in a chemical reaction

**re·ac·tion** (rē ak′shən) *n.* **1** a return or opposing action, etc. **2** a response, as to a stimulus or influence **3** a movement back to a former or less advanced condition; extreme conservatism **4** a chemical change

**re·ac·tion·ar·y** (-shə ner′ē) *adj.* of, characterized by, or advocating reaction, esp. in politics —*n., pl.* -ies an advocate of reaction, esp. in politics

**re·ac·ti·vate** (rē ak′tə vāt′) *vt., vi.* -vat′ed, -vat′ing to make or be made active again; specif., to return (a military unit, ship, etc.) to active status —re·ac′ti·va′tion *n.*

**re·ac·tive** (-tiv) *adj.* **1** tending to react **2** of, from, or showing reaction —re′ac·tiv′i·ty *n.*

**re·ac·tor** (-tər) *n.* NUCLEAR REACTOR

**read**[1] (rēd) *vt.* read (red), read·ing (rēd′iŋ) ⟦< OE *rædan*, to counsel⟧ **1** to get the meaning of (writing) by interpreting the characters **2** to utter aloud (written matter) **3** to understand or interpret **4** to foretell (the future) **5** [Brit.] to study *[to read* law*]* **6** to register: said as of a gauge **7** [Slang] to hear and understand *[I read* you*]* **8** *Comput.* to access (data) from (a disk, tape, etc.) —*vi.* **1** to read something written **2** to learn by reading: with *about* or *of* **3** to contain certain words —**read into** to attribute (a particular meaning) to —**read out of** to expel from (a group) — read′a·bil′i·ty *n.* —read′a·ble *adj.* —read′er *n.*

**read**[2] (red) *vt., vi. pt. & pp. of* READ[1] —*adj.* informed by reading *[well-read]*

**read·er·ship** (rēd′ər ship′) *n.* the people who read a certain publication, author, etc.

**read·i·ly** (red′ə lē) *adv.* **1** willingly **2** easily

**read·ing** (rēd′iŋ) *n.* **1** the act of one who reads **2** material to be read **3** the amount measured by a barometer, thermometer, etc. **4** a particular interpretation or performance

**read·out** (rēd′out′) *n.* **1** the retrieving of information from a computer **2** information from a computer, thermostat, etc. displayed visually or recorded, as on tape

**read·y** (red′ē) *adj.* -i·er, -i·est ⟦OE *ræde*⟧ **1** prepared to act or be used immediately **2** willing **3** likely or liable; apt *[ready* to cry*]* **4** dexterous **5** prompt *[a ready* reply*]* **6** available at once *[ready* cash*]* —*vt.* -ied, -y·ing to prepare —**at the ready** prepared for immediate use —read′i·ness *n.*

**read·y-made′** *adj.* made so as to be ready for use or sale at once: also, as applied to clothing, ready′-to-wear′

**Rea·gan** (rā′gən), **Ron·ald** (**Wilson**) (rän′əld) 1911- ; 40th president of the U.S. (1981-89)

**re·a·gent** (rē ā′jənt) *n. Chem.* a substance used to detect, measure, or react with another substance

**re·al** (rē′əl, rēl) *adj.* ⟦< L *res*, thing⟧ **1** existing as or in fact; actual; true **2** authentic; genuine **3** *Law* of or relating to permanent, immovable

things *[real* property*]* —*adv.* [Inf.] very —**for real** [Slang] real or really

**real estate 1** land, including the buildings, etc. on it **2** the buying and selling of this

**re·al·ism** (rē′ə liz′əm) *n.* **1** a tendency to face facts and be practical **2** the picturing in art and literature of people and things as they really appear to be —re′al·ist *n.* —re′al·is′tic *adj.* —re′al·is′ti·cal·ly *adv.*

**re·al·i·ty** (rē al′ə tē) *n., pl.* -ties **1** the quality or fact of being real **2** a person or thing that is real; fact —**in reality** in fact; actually

**re·al·ize** (rē′ə līz′) *vt.* -ized′, -iz′ing **1** to make real; achieve **2** to understand fully **3** to convert (assets, rights, etc.) into money **4** to gain; obtain *[to realize* a profit*]* **5** to be sold for (a specified sum) —re′al·i·za′tion *n.*

**re′al-life′** *adj.* actual; not imaginary

**re′al·ly** *adv.* **1** in reality **2** truly —*interj.* indeed: used to express surprise, doubt, etc.

**realm** (relm) *n.* ⟦see REGAL⟧ **1** a kingdom **2** a region; sphere

**Re·al·tor** (rē′əl tər, -tôr′) *trademark for* a real estate broker or appraiser who is a member of the National Association of Realtors —*n.* [r-] a real estate agent

**re·al·ty** (rē′əl tē) *n.* REAL ESTATE

**ream**[1] (rēm) *n.* ⟦< Ar *rizma*, a bale⟧ **1** a quantity of paper varying from 480 to 516 sheets **2** *[pl.]* [Inf.] a great amount

**ream**[2] (rēm) *vt.* ⟦OE *reman*⟧ to enlarge (a hole) as with a reamer

**ream′er** *n.* **1** a sharp-edged tool for enlarging or tapering holes **2** a juicer

**re·an·i·mate** (rē an′ə māt′) *vt.* -mat′ed, -mat′ing to give new life, power, or vigor to —re·an′i·ma′tion *n.*

**reap** (rēp) *vt., vi.* ⟦OE *ripan*⟧ **1** to cut (grain) with a scythe, reaper, etc. **2** to gather (a harvest) **3** to obtain as the reward of action, etc.

**reap′er** *n.* **1** one who reaps **2** a machine for reaping grain

**re·ap·por·tion** (rē′ə pôr′shən) *vt.* to apportion again; specif., to change the distribution of (a legislature) so that members represent constituents equally —re′ap·por′tion·ment *n.*

**rear**[1] (rir) *n.* ⟦see ARREARS⟧ **1** the back part **2** the position behind or at the back **3** the part of an army, etc. farthest from the enemy **4** [Slang] the buttocks —*adj.* of, at, on, or in the rear —**bring up the rear** to come at the end

**rear**[2] (rir) *vt.* ⟦OE *ræran*⟧ **1** to put upright; elevate **2** to build; erect **3** to grow or breed **4** to educate, train, etc. *[to rear* a child*]* —*vi.* **1** to rise on the hind legs, as a horse does **2** to rise (*up*), in anger, etc. **3** to rise high

**rear admiral** a naval officer ranking above a captain

**rear-end′** *vt.* to crash into, or cause one's vehicle to crash into, the back end of (another vehicle)

**rear′most′** *adj.* farthest in the rear

**re·ar·range** (rē′ə rānj′) *vt.* -ranged′, -rang′ing to arrange again or in a different way

**rear′ward** *adj.* at, in, or toward the rear —*adv.* toward the rear: also **rear′wards**

**rea·son** (rē′zən) *n.* ⟦< L *ratio*, a reckoning⟧ **1** an explanation of an act, idea, etc. **2** a cause or motive **3** the ability to think, draw conclusions, etc. **4** good sense **5** sanity —*vi., vt.* **1** to think logically (about); analyze **2** to argue or infer —**stand to reason** to be logical —rea′son·ing *n.*

**rea·son·a·ble** *adj.* **1** able to reason **2** fair; just **3** sensible **4** not excessive —rea′son·a·bly *adv.*

**re·as·sure** (rē′ə shoor′) *vt.* -sured′, -sur′ing to restore to confidence —re′as·sur′ance *n.*

**re·bate** (rē′bāt′) *vt.* -bat′ed, -bat′ing ⟦< OFr *re-*, RE- + *abattre*, beat down⟧ to give back (part of a payment) —*n.* a return of part of a payment

**Re·bek·ah** (ri bek′ə) *n. Bible* the wife of Isaac: also sp. **Re·bec′ca**

**reb·el** (reb′əl; *for v.* ri bel′) *n.* ⟦< L *re-*, again +

*bellare*, wage war⟧ one who resists authority —
**adj. 1** rebellious **2** of rebels —**vi. re·bel', -belled',
-bel'ling 1** to resist authority **2** to feel or show
strong aversion

**re·bel·lion** (ri bel'yən) **n. 1** armed resistance to
one's government **2** a defiance of any authority

**re·bel·lious** (-yəs) **adj. 1** resisting authority **2**
opposing control; defiant

**re·birth** (rē burth') **n. 1** a new or second birth **2** a
reawakening; revival

**re·boot** (rē bōōt') **vi., vt.** *Comput.* to boot again, as
to restore normal operation

**re·bound** (ri bound'; *for n.* rē'bound') **vi.** to spring
back, as upon impact —**n.** a rebounding, or a ball,
etc. that rebounds —**on the rebound 1** after it
bounces back **2** just after being jilted

**re·buff** (ri buf') **n.** ⟦< It *rabbuffare*, disarrange⟧ **1**
an abrupt refusal of offered advice, help, etc. **2**
any repulse —**vt. 1** to snub **2** to check or repulse

**re·buke** (ri byōōk') **vt. -buked', -buk'ing** ⟦< OFr
*re-*, back + *buchier*, to beat⟧ to scold in a sharp
way; reprimand —**n.** a reprimand

**re·bus** (rē'bəs) **n.** ⟦L, lit., by things⟧ a puzzle consisting of pictures, etc. combined to suggest words
or phrases

**re·but** (ri but') **vt. -but'ted, -but'ting** ⟦< OFr *re-*,
back + *buter*, to thrust⟧ to contradict or oppose,
esp. in a formal manner by argument, proof, etc.
—**re·but'tal** (-'l) **n.**

**rec** (rek) **n.** *short for* RECREATION: used in compounds, as **rec room**

**re·cal·ci·trant** (ri kal'si trənt) **adj.** ⟦< L *re-*, back +
*calcitrare*, to kick⟧ **1** refusing to obey authority,
etc. **2** hard to handle —**re·cal'ci·trance n.**

**re·call** (ri kôl'; *for n.* rē'kôl') **vt. 1** to call back **2** to
remember **3** to take back; revoke —**n. 1** a recal-
ling **2** memory **3** the removal of, or right to
remove, an official from office by popular vote

**re·cant** (ri kant') **vt., vi.** ⟦< L *re-*, back + *canere*,
sing⟧ to renounce formally (one's beliefs,
remarks, etc.) —**re·can·ta·tion** (rē'kan tā'shən) **n.**

**re·cap**[1] (rē kap'; *also, and for n. always,* rē'kap')
**vt. -capped', -cap'ping** to put a new tread on (a
worn tire) —**n.** such a tire

**re·cap**[2] (rē'kap') **n.** a recapitulation, or summary
—**vt., vi. -capped', -cap'ping** to recapitulate

**re·ca·pit·u·late** (rē'kə pich'ə lāt') **vi., vt. -lat'ed,
-lat'ing** ⟦see RE- & CAPITULATE⟧ to repeat briefly;
summarize —**re'ca·pit·u·la'tion n.**

**re·cap·ture** (rē kap'chər) **vt. -tured, -tur·ing 1** to
capture again; retake **2** to remember —**n.** a
recapturing

**recd** or **rec'd** *abbrev.* received

**re·cede** (ri sēd') **vi. -ced'ed, -ced'ing** ⟦see RE- &
CEDE⟧ **1** to go, move, or slope backward **2** to
diminish

**re·ceipt** (ri sēt') **n.** ⟦see RECEIVE⟧ **1** *old-fashioned
var. of* RECIPE **2** a receiving or being received **3** a
written acknowledgment that something has
been received **4** [*pl.*] the amount, as of money,
received —**vt.** to write a receipt for (goods, etc.)

**re·ceiv·a·ble** (ri sē'və bəl) **adj. 1** that can be
received **2** due —**n.** [*pl.*] outstanding bills, loans,
etc.

**re·ceive** (ri sēv') **vt. -ceived', -ceiv'ing** ⟦< L *re-*,
back + *capere*, take⟧ **1** to take or get (something
given, thrown, sent, etc.) **2** to experience;
undergo [*to receive* acclaim] **3** to bear or hold **4**
to react to in a specified way **5** to learn [*to receive*
news] **6** to let enter **7** to greet (visitors, etc.)

**re·ceived'** **adj.** accepted; considered as standard

**re·ceiv'er** **n.** one that receives; specif., *a*) a device
that converts electrical waves or signals into
audible or visual signals *b*) a football player designated to receive a forward pass *c*) one
appointed by a court to administer or hold in
trust property in bankruptcy or in a lawsuit —**re·
ceiv'er·ship' n.**

**re·cen·sion** (ri sen'shən) **n.** ⟦< L *recensere*, revise⟧
a revision of a text based on a critical study of
sources

**re·cent** (rē'sənt) **adj.** ⟦< L *recens*⟧ **1** done, made,
etc. just before the present; new **2** of a time just
before the present —**re'cent·ly adv.**

**re·cep·ta·cle** (ri sep'tə kəl) **n.** ⟦see RECEIVE⟧ a
container

**re·cep·tion** (ri sep'shən) **n. 1** *a*) a receiving or
being received *b*) the manner of this **2** a social
function for the receiving of guests **3** *Radio, TV*
the receiving of signals, with reference to the
quality of reproduction

**re·cep'tion·ist n.** an office employee who receives
callers, etc.

**re·cep'tive adj.** able or ready to accept new ideas,
suggestions, etc.

**re·cep'tor n.** a nerve ending or group of nerve
endings specialized for receiving stimuli

**re·cess** (rē'ses; *also, & for v. usually,* ri ses') **n.** ⟦<
L *recedere*, recede⟧ **1** a hollow place, as in a wall
**2** a hidden or inner place **3** a temporary halting
as of work, a session, etc. —**vt. 1** to place in a
recess **2** to halt temporarily —**vi.** to take a recess

**re·ces·sion** (ri sesh'ən) **n. 1** a going back; withdrawal **2** a temporary falling off of business
activity

**re·ces'sion·al n.** a piece of music at the end of a
church service played when the clergy, etc. march
out

**re·ces·sive** (ri ses'iv) **adj. 1** tending to recede **2**
*Genetics* designating or of that one of any pair of
hereditary factors which remains latent —**n.**
*Genetics* a recessive character or characters

**re·cher·ché** (rə sher'shā, -sher'shā') **adj.** ⟦Fr⟧ **1**
rare; choice **2** refined; esp., too refined

**re·cid·i·vism** (ri sid'ə viz'əm) **n.** ⟦< L *re-*, back +
*cadere*, to fall⟧ habitual or chronic relapse, esp.
into crime

**rec·i·pe** (res'ə pē') **n.** ⟦L < *recipere*, receive⟧ **1** a
list of materials and directions for preparing a
dish or drink **2** a way to achieve something

**re·cip·i·ent** (ri sip'ē ənt) **n.** ⟦see RECEIVE⟧ one that
receives

**re·cip·ro·cal** (ri sip'rə kəl) **adj.** ⟦< L *reciprocus*,
returning⟧ **1** done, given, etc. in return **2**
mutual [*reciprocal* love] **3** corresponding but
reversed **4** corresponding or complementary —**n.**
**1** a complement, counterpart, etc. **2** *Math.* the
quantity resulting from the division of 1 by the
given quantity [the *reciprocal* of 7 is ⅐]

**re·cip'ro·cate'** (-kāt') **vt., vi. -cat'ed, -cat'ing 1** to
give and get reciprocally **2** to do, feel, etc. in
return **3** to move alternately back and forth —**re·
cip'ro·ca'tion n.**

**rec·i·proc·i·ty** (res'ə präs'ə tē) **n., pl. -ties 1** reciprocal state **2** mutual exchange; esp., exchange of
special privileges between two countries

**re·cit·al** (ri sīt''l) **n. 1** a reciting **2** the account,
story, etc. told **3** a musical or dance program

**rec·i·ta·tion** (res'ə tā'shən) **n. 1** a reciting, as of
facts, events, etc. **2** *a*) a saying aloud in public of
something memorized *b*) a piece so presented **3**
a reciting by pupils of answers to questions on a
prepared lesson

**rec'i·ta·tive'** (-tə tēv') **n.** ⟦< It: see fol.⟧ a type of
declamation, as for operatic dialogue, with the
rhythms of speech, but in musical tones

**re·cite** (ri sīt') **vt., vi. -cit'ed, -cit'ing** ⟦see RE- &
CITE⟧ **1** to say aloud from memory, as a poem,
lesson, etc. **2** to tell in detail; relate

**reck·less** (rek'lis) **adj.** ⟦OE *recceleas*⟧ careless;
heedless —**reck'less·ly adv.** —**reck'less·ness n.**

**reck·on** (rek'ən) **vt.** ⟦OE *-recenian*⟧ **1** to count;
compute **2** to estimate **3** [Inf. or Dial.] to suppose —**vi. 1** to count up **2** [Inf.] to rely (*on*) —
**reckon with** to take into consideration

**reck'on·ing n. 1** count or computation **2** the settlement of an account

**re·claim** (ri klām') **vt.** ⟦see RE- & CLAIM⟧ **1** to
bring back (a person) from error, vice, etc. **2** to
make (wasteland, etc.) usable **3** to recover (use-

ful materials) from waste products —**rec·la·ma·tion** (rek'lə mā'shən) *n.*

**re·cline** (ri klīn') *vt., vi.* **-clined', -clin'ing** ⟦< L *re-*, back + *clinare,* lean⟧ to lie or cause to lie down

**re·clin'er** *n.* an upholstered armchair with an adjustable back and seat for reclining: also **reclining chair**

**rec·luse** (rek'lōos, ri klōos') *n.* ⟦< L *re-*, back + *claudere,* shut⟧ one who lives a secluded, solitary life

**rec·og·ni·tion** (rek'əg nish'ən) *n.* **1** a recognizing or being recognized **2** identification of a person or thing as having been known before

**re·cog·ni·zance** (ri käg'ni zəns, -kän'i-) *n.* ⟦< L *re-,* again + *cognoscere,* know⟧ *Law* a bond binding one to some act, as to appear in court

**rec·og·nize** (rek'əg nīz') *vt.* **-nized', -niz'ing** ⟦see prec.⟧ **1** to be aware of as someone or something known before **2** to know by some detail, as of appearance **3** to perceive **4** to accept as a fact [to *recognize* defeat] **5** to acknowledge as worthy of approval **6** to acknowledge the status of (a government, etc.) **7** to grant the right to speak in a meeting —**rec'og·niz'a·ble** *adj.*

**re·coil** (ri koil'; *also for n.* rē'koil') *vi.* ⟦< L *re-,* back + *culus,* buttocks⟧ **1** to draw back, as in fear, etc. **2** to spring or kick back, as a gun when fired —*n.* a recoiling

**rec·ol·lect** (rek'ə lekt') *vt., vi.* ⟦see RE- & COLLECT⟧ to remember, esp. with some effort —**rec'ol·lec'tion** *n.*

**re·com·bi·nant DNA** (rē käm'bə nənt) DNA formed in the laboratory by splicing together pieces of DNA from different species, as to create new life forms

**rec·om·mend** (rek'ə mend') *vt.* ⟦see RE- & COMMEND⟧ **1** to entrust **2** to suggest favorably as suited for some position, etc. **3** to make acceptable **4** to advise; counsel —**rec'om·men·da'tion** *n.*

**re·com·mit** (rē'kə mit') *vt.* **-mit'ted, -mit'ting 1** to commit again **2** to refer (a question, bill, etc.) back to a committee

**rec·om·pense** (rek'əm pens') *vt.* **-pensed', -pens'ing** ⟦see RE- & COMPENSATE⟧ **1** to repay or reward **2** to compensate (a loss, etc.) —*n.* **1** requital; reward **2** compensation

**rec·on·cile** (rek'ən sīl') *vt.* **-ciled', -cil'ing** ⟦see RE- & CONCILIATE⟧ **1** to make friendly again **2** to settle (a quarrel, etc.) **3** to make (ideas, accounts, etc.) consistent **4** to make acquiescent (*to*) —**rec'on·cil'a·ble** *adj.* —**rec'on·cil'i·a'tion** (-sil'ē ā'shən) *n.*

**rec·on·dite** (rek'ən dīt') *adj.* ⟦< L *re-,* back + *condere,* to hide⟧ beyond ordinary understanding; abstruse

**re·con·di·tion** (rē'kən dish'ən) *vt.* to put back in good condition, as by repairing

**re·con·nais·sance** (ri kän'ə səns) *n.* ⟦Fr: see RECOGNIZANCE⟧ a survey of a region, as in seeking out information about enemy positions

**rec·on·noi·ter** (rek'ə noit'ər, rē'kə-) *vt., vi.* to make a reconnaissance (of): also [Chiefly Brit.] **rec'on·noi'tre, -tred, -tring**

**re·con·sid·er** (rē'kən sid'ər) *vt., vi.* to think over again, esp. with a view to changing a decision

**re·con·sti·tute** (rē kän'stə tōot') *vt.* **-tut'ed, -tut'ing** to constitute again; specif., to restore (a dried or condensed substance) to its full liquid form by adding water

**re·con·struct** (rē'kən strukt') *vt.* **1** to construct again; rebuild **2** to build up, as from remains, an image of the original

**re·con·struc'tion** *n.* **1** a reconstructing **2** [R-] the process or period, after the Civil War, of reestablishing the Southern States in the Union

**re·cord** (ri kôrd'; *for n. & adj.* rek'ərd) *vt.* ⟦< L *recordari,* remember⟧ **1** to write down for future use **2** to register, as on a graph **3** to register (sound or visual images) on a disc, tape, etc. for later reproduction —*n.* **rec'ord 1** the condition of

being recorded **2** anything written down and preserved; account of events **3** *a*) the known facts about anyone or anything *b*) the recorded offenses or crimes of a person **4** a grooved disc for playing on a phonograph **5** the best official performance achieved —*adj.* **rec'ord** being the best, largest, etc. —**on** (or **off the**) **record** publicly (or confidentially) declared

**re·cord'er** *n.* **1** an official who keeps records **2** a machine or device that records; esp., a TAPE RECORDER **3** an early wind instrument

**re·cord'ing** *n.* **1** what is recorded, as on a disc or tape **2** a record, disc, etc.

RECORDER

**re·count**[1] (ri kount') *vt.* ⟦see RE- & COUNT[1]⟧ to tell in detail; narrate

**re·count**[2] (rē'kount'; *for n.* rē'kount') *vt.* to count again —*n.* a recounting, as of votes

**re·coup** (ri kōop') *vt.* ⟦< Fr *re-,* again + *couper,* to cut⟧ to make up for or regain [to *recoup* a loss]

**re·course** (rē'kôrs, ri kôrs') *n.* ⟦see RE- & COURSE⟧ **1** a turning for aid, safety, etc. **2** that to which one turns seeking aid, safety, etc.

**re·cov·er** (ri kuv'ər) *vt.* ⟦< L *recuperare*⟧ **1** to get back (something lost, etc.) **2** to regain (health, etc.) **3** to make up for [to *recover* losses] **4** to save (oneself) from a fall, etc. **5** to reclaim (land from the sea, etc.) **6** *Sports* to get control of (a fumbled ball, etc.) —*vi.* **1** to regain health, balance, or control **2** *Sports* to regain control of a fumbled ball, etc.

**re·cov'er·y** *n., pl.* **-ies** a recovering; specif., *a*) a regaining of something lost *b*) a return to health *c*) a retrieval of a capsule, etc. after a spaceflight

**recovery room** a hospital room where postoperative patients are kept for close observation and care

**rec·re·ant** (rek'rē ənt) [Archaic] *adj.* ⟦< OFr *recreire,* surrender allegiance⟧ **1** cowardly **2** disloyal —*n.* **1** a coward **2** a traitor

**rec·re·a·tion** (rek'rē ā'shən) *n.* ⟦< L *recreare,* refresh⟧ any form of play, amusement, etc. used to relax or refresh the body or mind —**rec're·ate', -at'ed, -at'ing, vi., vt.** —**rec're·a'tion·al** *adj.*

**re·crim·i·nate** (ri krim'ə nāt') *vi.* **-nat'ed, -nat'ing** ⟦< L *re-,* back + *crimen,* offense⟧ to answer an accuser by accusing that person in return —**re·crim'i·na'tion** *n.*

**re·cru·desce** (rē'krōo des') *vi.* **-desced', -desc'ing** ⟦< L *re-,* again + *crudus,* raw⟧ to break out again after being inactive —**re'cru·des'cence** *n.* —**re'cru·des'cent** *adj.*

**re·cruit** (ri krōot') *vt., vi.* ⟦< L *re-,* again + *crescere,* grow⟧ **1** to enlist (personnel) into an army or navy **2** to enlist (new members) for an organization —*n.* **1** a newly enlisted or drafted soldier, etc. **2** a new member of any group —**re·cruit'er** *n.*

**rec·tal** (rek'təl) *adj.* of, for, or near the rectum

**rec·tan·gle** (rek'taŋ'gəl) *n.* ⟦< L *rectus,* straight + *angulus,* a corner⟧ a four-sided plane figure with four right angles —**rec·tan'gu·lar** (-gyə lər) *adj.*

**rec·ti·fy** (rek'tə fī') *vt.* **-fied', -fy'ing** ⟦< L *rectus,* straight + *facere,* make⟧ **1** to put right; correct **2** *Elec.* to convert (alternating current) to direct current —**rec'ti·fi·ca'tion** *n.* —**rec'ti·fi'er** *n.*

**rec·ti·lin·e·ar** (rek'tə lin'ē ər) *adj.* bounded or formed by straight lines

**rec·ti·tude** (rek'tə tōod') *n.* ⟦< L *rectus,* right⟧ strict honesty; uprightness of character

**rec·tor** (rek'tər) *n.* ⟦< L *regere,* to rule⟧ **1** in some churches, a clergyman in charge of a parish **2** the head of certain schools, colleges, etc.

**rec·to·ry** (rek'tər ē) *n., pl.* **-ries** the house of a minister or priest

**rec·tum** (rek'təm) *n., pl.* **-tums** or **-ta** (-tə) ⟦< L *rectum* (*intestinum*), straight (intestine)] the lowest, or last, segment of the large intestine

**re·cum·bent** (ri kum′bənt) *adj.* [< L *re-*, back + *-cumbere*, lie down] lying down; reclining

**re·cu·per·ate** (ri kōō′pə rāt′) *vt., vi.* **-at·ed, -at·ing** [< L *recuperare*, recover] **1** to get well again **2** to recover (losses, etc.) —**re·cu′per·a′tion** *n.* —**re·cu′per·a′tive** (-pə rāt′iv, -pə rə tiv) *adj.*

**re·cur** (ri kʉr′) *vi.* **-curred′, -cur′ring** [< L *re-*, back + *currere*, run] **1** to return in thought, talk, etc. **2** to occur again or at intervals —**re·cur′rence** *n.* —**re·cur′rent** *adj.*

**re·cy·cle** (rē sī′kəl) *vt.* **-cled, -cling** **1** to pass through a cycle again **2** to use again and again, as the same water **3** *a*) to process in order to use again (*to recycle paper*) *b*) to gather up and turn in (newspapers, etc.) for such processing

**red** (red) *n.* [OE *read*] **1** the color of blood **2** any red pigment **3** [*often* R-] [Inf.] a communist —*adj.* **red′der, red′dest 1** of the color red **2** [*often* R-] communist —**in the red** losing money —**see red** [Inf.] to become angry —**red′dish** *adj.* —**red′ness** *n.*

**re·dact** (ri dakt′) *vt.* [< L *redigere*, get in order] to prepare for publication; edit —**re·dac′tion** *n.* —**re·dac′tor** *n.*

**red blood cell** (or **corpuscle**) ERYTHROCYTE

**red′-blood′ed** *adj.* high-spirited and strong-willed; vigorous

**red′cap′** *n.* a baggage porter, as in a railroad station

**red carpet** a very grand or impressive welcome and entertainment: with *the* —**red′-car′pet** *adj.*

**red′coat′** *n.* a British soldier in a uniform with a red coat, as during the American Revolution

**Red Cross** an international society for the relief of suffering in time of war or disaster

**redd** (red) *vt., vi.* **redd** or **redd′ed, redd′ing** [< OE *hreddan*, take away] [Inf. or Dial.] to put in order; tidy: usually with *up*

**red deer** a deer of Europe and Asia

**red·den** (red′n) *vt.* to make red —*vi.* to become red; esp., to blush

**re·deem** (ri dēm′) *vt.* [< L *re(d)-*, back + *emere*, get] **1** to buy or get back; recover **2** to pay off (a mortgage, etc.) **3** to turn in (a coupon, etc.) for a discount, premium, etc. **4** to ransom **5** to deliver from sin **6** to fulfill (a promise) **7** *a*) to make amends or atone for *b*) to restore (oneself) to favor —**re·deem′a·ble** *adj.* —**re·deem′er** *n.* —**re·demp·tion** (ri demp′shən) *n.*

**re·de·ploy** (rē′di ploi′) *vt., vi.* to move (troops, etc.) from one front or area to another —**re′de·ploy′ment** *n.*

**re·de·vel·op** (rē′di vel′əp) *vt.* **1** to develop again **2** to rebuild or restore —**re′de·vel′op·ment** *n.*

**red′-flag′** *vt.* **-flagged′, -flag′ging** to mark or otherwise indicate as being risky, etc.

**red′-hand′ed** *adv.* in the very commission of crime or wrongdoing

**red′head′** *n.* a person with red hair

**red herring** [< herring drawn across the trace in hunting to divert the hounds] something used to divert attention from the basic issue

**red′-hot′** *adj.* **1** hot enough to glow **2** very excited, angry, etc. **3** very new

**re·dis′trict** *vt.* to divide anew into districts

**red′-let′ter** *adj.* designating a memorable or joyous day or event

**red′lin′ing** (-līn′iŋ) *n.* [from outlining such areas in red on a map] the refusal by some banks or companies to issue loans or insurance on property in certain neighborhoods

**re·do** (rē dōō′) *vt.* **-did′, -done′, -do′ing** **1** to do again **2** to redecorate

**red·o·lent** (red′l ənt) *adj.* [< L *re(d)-*, intens. + *olere*, to smell] **1** sweet-smelling **2** smelling (*of*) **3** suggestive (*of*) —**red′o·lence** *n.*

**re·dou·ble** (rē dub′əl) *vt., vi.* **-bled, -bling** to make or become twice as much or twice as great

---

**405** ◀ **referee**

**re·doubt** (ri dout′) *n.* [see REDUCE] **1** a breastwork **2** any stronghold

**re·doubt′a·ble** *adj.* [< L *re-*, intens. + *dubitare*, to doubt] formidable —**re·doubt′a·bly** *adv.*

**re·dound** (ri dound′) *vi.* [< L *re(d)-*, intens. + *undare*, to surge] **1** to have a result (*to the credit or discredit of*) **2** to come back; react (*upon*)

**re·dress** (ri dres′; *for n., usually* rē′dres′) *vt.* [see RE- & DRESS] to compensate for (a wrong, etc.) —*n.* **1** compensation **2** a redressing

**Red Sea** sea between NE Africa & W Arabia

**red snapper** a reddish, edible, deep-water fish

**red tape** [< tape for tying official papers] rules and details that waste time and effort

**red tide** sea water discolored by red algae poisonous to marine life

**re·duce** (ri dōōs′) *vt.* **-duced′, -duc′ing** [< L *re-*, back + *ducere*, to lead] **1** to lessen, as in size, price, etc. **2** to put into a different form **3** to lower, as in rank or condition —*vi.* to lose weight, as by dieting

**re·duc·tion** (ri duk′shən) *n.* **1** a reducing or being reduced **2** anything made by reducing **3** the amount by which anything is reduced

**re·dun·dant** (ri dun′dənt) *adj.* [see REDOUND] **1** excess; superfluous **2** wordy **3** unnecessary to the meaning: said of words and affixes —**re·dun′dan·cy** *n.*

**red′wood′** *n.* **1** a giant evergreen of the Pacific coast **2** its reddish wood

**re·ech·o** or **re-ech·o** (rē ek′ō) *vt., vi.* **-oed, -o·ing** to echo back or again —*n., pl.* **-oes** the echo of an echo

**reed** (rēd) *n.* [OE *hreod*] **1** a tall, slender grass **2** a rustic musical instrument made from a hollow stem **3** *Music* a thin strip of wood, plastic, etc. placed against the mouthpiece, as of a clarinet, and vibrated by the breath to produce a tone —**reed′y, -i·er, -i·est,** *adj.*

**reef**[1] (rēf) *n.* [prob. < ON *rif*, a rib] a ridge of rock, coral, or sand at or near the surface of the water

**reef**[2] (rēf) *n.* [ME *riff*] a part of a sail which can be folded or rolled up and made fast to reduce the area exposed to the wind —*vt., vi.* to reduce the size of (a sail) by taking in part of it

**reef′er** *n.* [Slang] a marijuana cigarette

**reek** (rēk) *n.* [OE *rec*] a strong, unpleasant smell —*vi.* to have a strong, offensive smell

**reel**[1] (rēl) *n.* [OE *hreol*] **1** a spool on which wire, film, fishing line, etc. is wound **2** the quantity of wire, film, etc. usually wound on one reel —*vt.* to wind on a reel —*vi.* **1** to sway, stagger, etc. as from drunkenness or dizziness **2** to spin; whirl —**reel in 1** to wind on a reel **2** to pull in (a fish) by using a reel —**reel off** to tell, write, etc. easily and quickly —**reel out** to unwind from a reel

**reel**[2] (rēl) *n.* [prob. < prec.] a lively dance

**re·en·try** or **re-en·try** (rē en′trē) *n., pl.* **-tries** a coming back, as of a space vehicle, into the earth's atmosphere

**ref**[1] (ref) *n., vt., vi.* [Inf.] *short for* REFEREE

**ref**[2] *abbrev.* **1** referee **2** reference **3** reformed **4** refund

**re·face** (rē fās′) *vt.* **-faced′, -fac′ing** to put a new facing or covering on

**re·fec·tion** (ri fek′shən) *n.* [< L *re-*, again + *facere*, make] a light meal; lunch

**re·fec·to·ry** (ri fek′tə rē) *n., pl.* **-ries** a dining hall, as in a monastery

**re·fer** (ri fʉr′) *vt.* **-ferred′, -fer′ring** [< L *re-*, back + *ferre*, to bear] **1** to submit (a quarrel, etc.) for settlement **2** to direct *to* someone or something for aid, information, etc. —*vi.* **1** to relate or apply (*to*) **2** to direct attention (*to*) **3** to turn (*to*) for information, aid, etc. —**re·fer′rer** *n.*

**ref·er·ee** (ref′ə rē′) *n.* **1** one to whom something is referred for decision **2** an official who enforces the rules in certain sports contests —*vt., vi.* **-eed′, -ee′ing** to act as referee (in)

**ref·er·ence** (ref′ər əns, ref′rəns) *n.* **1** a referring or being referred **2** relation [in *reference* to his letter] **3** *a*) the directing of attention to a person or thing *b*) a mention **4** *a*) an indication, as in a book, of some other source of information *b*) such a source **5** *a*) one who can offer information or recommendation *b*) a statement of character, ability, etc. by such a person

**ref·er·en·dum** (ref′ə ren′dəm) *n.*, *pl.* **-dums** or **-da** (-də) [L: see REFER] **1** the submission of a law to a direct vote of the people **2** the vote itself

**ref·er·ent** (ref′ər ənt) *n.* the thing referred to, esp. by a word or expression

**re·fer·ral** (ri fʉr′əl) *n.* **1** a referring or being referred **2** a person who is referred to another

**re·fill** (rē fil′; *for n.* rē′fil′) *vt.*, *vi.* to fill again —*n.* **1** a unit to refill a special container **2** a refilling of a medical prescription —**re·fill′a·ble** *adj.*

**re·fine** (ri fīn′) *vt.* **-fined′**, **-fin′ing** [RE- + *fine*, make *fine*] **1** to free from impurities, etc. **2** to make more polished or elegant

**re·fined′** *adj.* **1** made free from impurities; purified **2** cultivated, elegant, etc. **3** subtle, precise, etc.

**re·fine′ment** *n.* **1** *a*) a refining or being refined *b*) the result of this **2** delicacy or elegance of manners, etc. **3** an improvement **4** a fine distinction; subtlety

**re·fin′er·y** *n.*, *pl.* **-er·ies** a plant for purifying materials, as oil, sugar, etc.

**re·fin·ish** (rē fin′ish) *vt.* to change or restore the finish of (furniture, etc.) —**re·fin′ish·er** *n.*

**re·fit** (rē fit′) *vt.*, *vi.* **-fit′ted**, **-fit′ting** to make or be made fit for use again by repairing, reequipping, etc.

**re·flect** (ri flekt′) *vt.* [< L *re-*, back + *flectere*, to bend] **1** to throw back (light, heat, or sound) **2** to give back an image of **3** to bring as a result [to *reflect* honor on the city] —*vi.* **1** to throw back light, heat, etc. **2** to give back an image **3** to think seriously (*on* or *upon*) **4** to cast blame or discredit (*on* or *upon*) —**re·flec′tive** *adj.*

**re·flec′tion** *n.* **1** a reflecting or being reflected **2** anything reflected **3** contemplation **4** a thoughtful idea or remark **5** blame; discredit

**re·flec′tor** *n.* a surface, object, etc. that reflects light, sound, heat, etc.

**re·flex** (rē′fleks′) *adj.* [see REFLECT] designating or of an involuntary action, as a sneeze, resulting from the direct transmission of a stimulus to a muscle or gland —*n.* a reflex action

**re·flex·ive** (ri flek′siv) *adj.* **1** designating a grammatical relation in which a verb's subject and object refer to the same person or thing (Ex.: I wash myself) **2** designating a verb, pronoun, etc. in such a relation —**re·flex′ive·ly** *adv.*

**re·for·est** (rē fôr′ist) *vt.*, *vi.* to plant new trees on (land once forested) —**re′for·est·a′tion** *n.*

**re·form** (ri fôrm′) *vt.* [see RE- & FORM] **1** to make better as by stopping abuses **2** to cause (a person) to behave better —*vi.* to become better in behavior —*n.* a reforming

**re-form** (rē fôrm′) *vt.*, *vi.* to form again

**ref·or·ma·tion** (ref′ər mā′shən) *n.* a reforming or being reformed —**the Reformation** the 16th-c. religious movement that resulted in establishing the Protestant churches

**re·form·a·to·ry** (ri fôr′mə tôr′ē) *n.*, *pl.* **-ries** an institution to which young offenders are sent to be reformed

**re·form′er** *n.* one who seeks to bring about political or social reform

**re·fract** (ri frakt′) *vt.* [< L *refractus*, turned aside < *re-*, back + *frangere*, to break] to cause (a ray of light, etc.) to undergo refraction

**re·frac′tion** *n.* the bending of a ray or wave of

light, heat, or sound as it passes from one medium into another

**re·frac·to·ry** (ri frak′tər ē) *adj.* [see REFRACT] hard to manage; stubborn

**re·frain**[1] (ri frān′) *vi.* [< L *re-*, back + *frenare*, to curb] to hold back; keep oneself (*from* doing something)

**re·frain**[2] (ri frān′) *n.* [see REFRACT] a phrase or verse repeated at intervals in a song or poem

**re·fresh** (ri fresh′) *vt.* **1** to make fresh by cooling, wetting, etc. **2** to make (a person) feel cooler, stronger, etc., as by food, sleep, etc. **3** to replenish **4** to stimulate (the memory, etc.)

ILLUSION CAUSED BY REFRACTION

**re·fresh′ing** *adj.* **1** that refreshes **2** pleasingly new or different

**re·fresh′ment** *n.* **1** a refreshing or being refreshed **2** something that refreshes **3** [*pl.*] food or drink or both

**re·frig·er·ant** (rē frij′ə rənt) *n.* a substance used in refrigeration

**re·frig·er·ate** (ri frij′ə rāt′) *vt.* **-at·ed**, **-at·ing** [< L *re-*, intens. + *frigus*, cold] to make or keep cool or cold, as for preserving —**re·frig·er·a′tion** *n.*

**re·frig·er·a′tor** *n.* a box or room in which food, drink, etc. are kept cool

**ref·uge** (ref′yōōj) *n.* [< L *re-*, back + *fugere*, flee] (a) shelter or protection from danger, difficulty, etc.

**ref·u·gee** (ref′yōō jē′, ref′yōō jē′) *n.* one who flees from home or country to seek refuge elsewhere

**re·ful·gent** (ri ful′jənt) *adj.* [< L *re-*, back + *fulgere*, shine] shining; radiant; glowing —**re·ful′gence** *n.*

**re·fund** (ri fund′; *for n.* rē′fund′) *vt.*, *vi.* [< L *re-*, back + *fundere*, pour] to give back (money, etc.); repay —*n.* a refunding or the amount refunded

**re·fur·bish** (ri fʉr′bish) *vt.* [RE- + FURBISH] to renovate —**re·fur′bish·ment** *n.*

**re·fuse**[1] (ri fyōōz′) *vt.*, *vi.* **-fused′**, **-fus′ing** [< L *re-*, back + *fundere*, pour] **1** to decline to accept **2** to decline (to do something), to grant the request of (someone), etc. —**re·fus′al** *n.*

**ref·use**[2] (ref′yōōs, -yōōz) *n.* [see prec.] waste; trash; rubbish

**re·fute** (ri fyōōt′) *vt.* **-fut′ed**, **-fut′ing** [L *refutare*, repel] to prove to be false or wrong —**re·fut′a·ble** *adj.* —**ref·u·ta·tion** (ref′yə tā′shən) *n.*

**reg** *abbrev.* **1** registered **2** regular **3** regulation

**re·gain** (ri gān′) *vt.* **1** to get back; recover **2** to get back to

**re·gal** (rē′gəl) *adj.* [< L *rex*, king] of, like, or fit for a monarch

**re·gale** (ri gāl′) *vt.* **-galed′**, **-gal′ing** [< Fr *ré-* (see RE-) + OFr *gale*, joy] to amuse or delight as with a story

**re·ga·li·a** (ri gāl′yə) *pl.n.* [see REGAL] **1** royal insignia **2** the insignia as of a rank or society **3** finery

**re·gard** (ri gärd′) *n.* [see RE- & GUARD] **1** a steady look; gaze **2** consideration; concern **3** respect and affection **4** reference; relation [in *regard* to your plan] **5** [*pl.*] good wishes —*vi.* **1** to look at attentively **2** to consider **3** to hold in affection and respect **4** to concern or involve —**as regards** concerning

**re·gard′ing** *prep.* concerning; about

**re·gard′less** *adv.* [Inf.] without regard for objections, etc.; anyway —**regardless of** in spite of

**re·gat·ta** (ri gät′ə) *n.* [< It] **1** a boat race **2** a series of boat races

**re·gen·er·ate** (ri jen′ə rit; *for v.*, -rāt′) *adj.* [see RE- & GENERATE] **1** spiritually reborn **2** renewed or restored —*vt.* **-at·ed**, **-at·ing** **1** to cause to be spiritually reborn **2** to cause to be completely reformed **3** to bring into existence again —*vi.* to form again, or be made anew —**re·gen′er·a′tion** *n.* —**re·gen′er·a′tive** *adj.*

**re·gent** (rē′jənt) *n.* ⟦< L *regere*, to rule⟧ **1** a person appointed to rule when a monarch is absent, too young, etc. **2** a member of a governing board, as of a university —**re′gen·cy** *n.*

**reg·gae** (reg′ā) *n.* ⟦< ?⟧ a form of strongly syncopated popular Jamaican music

**reg·i·cide** (rej′ə sīd′) *n.* ⟦< L *regis*, of a king + *-cida* (see -CIDE)⟧ **1** one who kills a monarch **2** the killing of a monarch

**re·gime** or **ré·gime** (rə zhēm′, rā-) *n.* ⟦see fol.⟧ **1** a political system **2** an administration

**reg·i·men** (rej′ə mən) *n.* ⟦< L *regere*, to rule⟧ a system of diet, exercise, etc. to improve health

**reg·i·ment** (rej′ə mənt; *for v.*, -ment′) *n.* ⟦< L *regere*, to rule⟧ a military unit, smaller than a division —*vt.* **1** to organize systematically **2** to subject to strict discipline and control —**reg′i·men′tal** *adj.* —**reg′i·men·ta′tion** *n.*

**Re·gi·na** (ri jī′nə) capital of Saskatchewan, Canada: pop. 180,000

**re·gion** (rē′jən) *n.* ⟦< L *regere*, to rule⟧ **1** a large, indefinite part of the earth's surface **2** a division or part, as of an organism —**re′gion·al** *adj.*

**re′gion·al·ism′** *n.* **1** regional quality or character in life or literature **2** a word, etc. peculiar to some region

**reg·is·ter** (rej′is tər) *n.* ⟦< L *regerere*, to record⟧ **1** *a)* a list of names, items, etc. *b)* a book in which this is kept **2** a device for recording [a cash *register*] **3** an opening into a room by which the amount of warm or cold air passing through can be controlled **4** *Music* a part of the range of a voice or instrument —*vt.* **1** to enter in a list **2** to indicate on or as on a scale **3** to show, as by facial expression [to *register* surprise] **4** to protect (mail) by paying a fee to have it handled by a special postal service —*vi.* **1** to enter one's name in a list, as of voters **2** to enroll in a school **3** to make an impression —**reg′is·trant** (-trənt) *n.*

**registered nurse** a trained nurse who has passed a state examination

**reg·is·trar** (rej′i strär′) *n.* one who keeps records, as in a college

**reg·is·tra·tion** (rej′i strā′shən) *n.* **1** a registering or being registered **2** an entry in a register **3** the number of persons registered

**reg·is·try** (-is trē) *n., pl.* **-tries** **1** a registering **2** an office where registers are kept **3** an official record or list

**reg·nant** (reg′nənt) *adj.* **1** ruling **2** predominant **3** prevalent

**re·gress** (rē′gres; *for v.* ri gres′) *n.* ⟦< L *re-*, back + *gradi*, go⟧ backward movement —*vi.* to go back —**re·gres′sion** *n.* —**re·gres′sive** *adj.*

**re·gret** (ri gret′) *vt.* **-gret′ted, -gret′ting** ⟦< OFr *regreter*, mourn⟧ to feel sorry about (an event, one's acts, etc.) —*n.* remorse, esp. over one's acts or omissions —(one's) **regrets** a polite declining of an invitation —**re·gret′ful** *adj.* —**re·gret′ta·ble** *adj.*

**re·group′** *vt., vi.* **1** to reassemble or reorganize **2** to collect oneself, as after a setback

**reg·u·lar** (reg′yə lər) *adj.* ⟦< L *regula*, a rule⟧ **1** conforming to a rule, type, etc.; orderly; symmetrical **2** conforming to a fixed principle or procedure **3** customary or established **4** consistent [a *regular* customer] **5** functioning in a normal way [a *regular* pulse] **6** properly qualified [a *regular* doctor] **7** designating or of the standing army of a country [Inf.] *a)* thorough; complete [a *regular* nuisance] *b)* pleasant, friendly, etc. —*n.* **1** a regular soldier or a player who is not a substitute **2** [Inf.] one who is regular in attendance **3** *Politics* a loyal party member —**reg′u·lar′i·ty** (-lar′ə tē), *pl.* **-ties**, *n.* —**reg′u·lar·ize′**, **-ized′, -iz′ing**, *vt.* —**reg′u·lar·ly** *adv.*

**reg·u·late** (reg′yə lāt′) *vt.* **-lat′ed, -lat′ing** ⟦< L *regula*, a rule⟧ **1** to control or direct according to a rule, principle, etc. **2** to adjust to a standard,

rate, etc. **3** to adjust for accurate operation —**reg′u·la·tor** *n.* —**reg′u·la·to′ry** (-lə tôr′ē) *adj.*

**reg′u·la′tion** *n.* **1** a regulating or being regulated **2** a rule or law regulating conduct —*adj.* usual; regular

**re·gur·gi·tate** (ri gur′jə tāt′) *vi., vt.* **-tat′ed, -tat′ing** ⟦< ML *re-*, back + LL *gurgitare*, to flood⟧ to bring (partly digested food) back up to the mouth —**re·gur′gi·ta′tion** *n.*

**re·hab** (rē′hab′) *n. short for* REHABILITATION —*vt.* **-habbed′, -hab′bing** *short for* REHABILITATE

**re·ha·bil·i·tate** (rē′hə bil′ə tāt′) *vt.* **-tat′ed, -tat′ing** ⟦< L *re-*, back + *habere*, have⟧ **1** to restore to rank, reputation, etc. which one has lost **2** to put back in good condition **3** to bring or restore to a state of health, constructive activity, etc. —**re′ha·bil′i·ta′tion** *n.* —**re′ha·bil′i·ta′tive** *adj.*

**re·hash** (rē′hash′; *for v.*, *also* rē hash′) *vt.* ⟦RE- + HASH⟧ to work up again or go over again —*n.* a rehashing

**re·hearse** (ri hurs′) *vt., vi.* **-hearsed′, -hears′ing** ⟦< OFr *re-*, again + *hercer*, to harrow⟧ to practice (a play, etc.) for public performance —**re·hears′al** *n.*

**reign** (rān) *n.* ⟦< L *regere*, to rule⟧ **1** royal power **2** dominance or sway **3** the period of rule, dominance, etc. —*vi.* **1** to rule as a sovereign **2** to prevail [peace *reigns*]

**re·im·burse** (rē′im burs′) *vt.* **-bursed′, -burs′ing** ⟦RE- + archaic *imburse*, to pay⟧ to pay back —**re′im·burse′ment** *n.*

**rein** (rān) *n.* ⟦see RETAIN⟧ **1** a narrow strap of leather attached in pairs to a horse's bit and manipulated to control the animal: *usually used in pl.* **2** [*pl.*] a means of controlling, etc. —**give (free) rein to** to allow to act without restraint

**re·in·car·na·tion** (rē′in kär′nā′shən) *n.* ⟦see RE- & INCARNATE⟧ rebirth of the soul in another body —**re′in·car′nate′, -nat′ed, -nat′ing,** *vt.*

**rein·deer** (rān′dir′) *n., pl.* **-deer′** ⟦< ON *hreinn*, reindeer + *dȳr*, animal⟧ a large deer found in northern regions and domesticated there as a beast of burden

REINDEER

**re·in·force** (rē′in fôrs′) *vt.* **-forced′, -forc′ing** ⟦RE- + var. of ENFORCE⟧ **1** to strengthen (a military force) with more troops, ships, etc. **2** to strengthen, as by patching, propping, or adding new material —**re′in·force′ment** *n.*

**re·in·state** (rē′in stāt′) *vt.* **-stat′ed, -stat′ing** to restore to a former state, position, etc. —**re′in·state′ment** *n.*

**re·it·er·ate** (rē it′ə rāt′) *vt.* **-at′ed, -at′ing** ⟦< L *re-*, back + *iterare*, repeat⟧ to say or do again or repeatedly —**re·it′er·a′tion** *n.* —**re·it′er·a′tive** (-ə rāt′iv, -ər ə tiv) *adj.*

**re·ject** (ri jekt′; *for n.* rē′jekt) *vt.* ⟦< L *re-*, back + *jacere*, to throw⟧ **1** to refuse to take, agree to, use, believe, etc. **2** to discard —*n.* a rejected thing or person —**re·jec′tion** *n.*

**re·jig·ger** (rē jig′ər) *vt.* to adjust or alter the structure, terms, etc. of

**re·joice** (ri jois′) *vi., vt.* **-joiced′, -joic′ing** ⟦< OFr *re-*, again + *joïr*, be glad⟧ to be glad or happy

**re·join** (rē join′) *vt., vi.* **1** to join again; reunite **2** to answer

**re·join·der** (ri join′dər) *n.* ⟦see RE- & JOIN⟧ an answer, esp. to a reply

**re·ju·ve·nate** (ri jōō′və nāt′) *vt.* **-nat′ed, -nat′ing** ⟦< RE- + L *juvenis*, young⟧ to make feel or seem young again —**re·ju′ve·na′tion** *n.*

**rel** *abbrev.* **1** relative(ly) **2** religion

**re·lapse** (ri laps′; *for n., usually* rē′laps) *vi.* **-lapsed′, -laps′ing** ⟦see RE- & LAPSE⟧ to slip back into a former state, esp. into illness after apparent recovery —*n.* a relapsing

**re·late** (ri lāt′) *vt.* -lat′ed, -lat′ing 〖< L *relatus,* brought back〗 1 to tell the story of; narrate 2 to connect, as in thought or meaning —*vi.* to have some connection or relation (*to*)

**re·lat′ed** *adj.* connected by kinship, origin, marriage, etc.

**re·la′tion** *n.* 1 a narrating 2 a narrative; account 3 connection, as in thought or meaning 4 connection by blood or marriage 5 a relative 6 [*pl.*] the connections between or among persons, nations, etc. —**in** (or **with**) **relation to** concerning; regarding —**re·la′tion·ship′** *n.*

**rel·a·tive** (rel′ə tiv) *adj.* 1 related each to the other 2 pertinent; relevant 3 comparative [living in *relative* comfort] 4 meaningful only in relationship [“cold” is a *relative* term] 5 *Gram.* that refers to an antecedent [a *relative* pronoun] —*n.* one related by blood or marriage —**rel′a·tive·ly** *adv.*

**relative humidity** the ratio of the amount of moisture in the air to the maximum amount possible at the given temperature

**rel·a·tiv·i·ty** (rel′ə tiv′ə tē) *n.* 1 a being relative 2 *Physics* the theory of the relative, rather than absolute, character of motion, velocity, mass, etc., and the interdependence of matter, time, and space

**re·lax** (ri laks′) *vt., vi.* 〖< L *re-,* back + *laxare,* loosen〗 1 to make or become less firm, tense, severe, etc. 2 to rest, as from work —**re·lax′er** *n.*

**re·lax′ant** *adj.* causing relaxation, esp. of muscles —*n.* a relaxant drug

**re·lax·a·tion** (rē′lak sā′shən) *n.* 1 a relaxing or being relaxed 2 *a*) rest from work or effort *b*) recreation

**re·lay** (rē′lā′; *for v., also* ri lā′) *n.* 〖< Fr *re-,* back + *laier,* to leave〗 1 a fresh supply of horses, etc., as for a stage of a journey 2 a relief crew of workers 3 a race (in full **relay race**) between teams, each member of which goes a part of the distance —*vt.* -layed′, -lay′ing to get and pass on

**re·lease** (ri lēs′) *vt.* -leased′, -leas′ing 〖see RELAX〗 1 to set free from confinement, work, pain, etc. 2 to let go [to *release* an arrow] 3 to permit to be issued, published, etc. —*n.* 1 a releasing, as from prison 2 a film, news story, etc. released to the public 3 a written surrender of a claim, etc.

**rel·e·gate** (rel′ə gāt′) *vt.* -gat′ed, -gat′ing 〖< L *re-,* away + *legare,* send〗 1 to exile or banish (*to*) 2 to consign or assign, esp. to an inferior position 3 to refer or hand over for decision —**rel′e·ga′tion** *n.*

**re·lent** (ri lent′) *vi.* 〖< L *re-,* again + *lentus,* pliant〗 to become less severe, stern, or stubborn; soften

**re·lent′less** *adj.* 1 harsh; pitiless 2 not letting up; persistent —**re·lent′less·ly** *adv.* —**re·lent′less·ness** *n.*

**rel·e·vant** (rel′ə vənt) *adj.* 〖see RELIEVE〗 relating to the matter under consideration; pertinent —**rel′e·vance** or **rel′e·van·cy** *n.*

**re·li·a·ble** (ri lī′ə bəl) *adj.* that can be relied on; dependable —**re·li′a·bil′i·ty** *n.* —**re·li′a·bly** *adv.*

**re·li′ance** (-əns) *n.* 1 a relying 2 trust, dependence, or confidence 3 a thing relied on —**re·li′ant** *adj.*

**rel·ic** (rel′ik) *n.* 〖see RELINQUISH〗 1 an object, custom, etc. surviving from the past 2 a souvenir 3 [*pl.*] ruins 4 the venerated remains, etc. of a saint

**re·lief** (ri lēf′) *n.* 1 a relieving of pain, anxiety, a burden, etc. 2 anything that lessens tension, or offers a pleasing change 3 aid, esp. by a public agency to the needy 4 release from work or duty, or those bringing it 5 the projection of sculptured forms from a flat surface 6 the differences in height, collectively, of land forms shown as by lines on a map (**relief map**) —*adj. Baseball* designating a pitcher who replaces another during a game —**in relief** carved so as to project from a surface

**re·lieve** (ri lēv′) *vt.* -lieved′, -liev′ing 〖< L *re-,* again + *levare,* to raise〗 1 to ease (pain, anxiety, etc.) 2 to free from pain, anxiety, a burden, etc. 3 to give or bring aid to 4 to set free from duty or work by replacing 5 to make less tedious, etc. by providing a pleasing change —**relieve oneself** to urinate or defecate

**re·li·gion** (ri lij′ən) *n.* 〖< L *religio,* holiness〗 1 belief in and worship of God or gods 2 a specific system of belief, worship, etc., often involving a code of ethics

**re·li·gi·os·i·ty** (-ē äs′ə tē) *n.* a being religious, esp. excessively or sentimentally religious

**re·li·gious** (-əs) *adj.* 1 devout; pious 2 of or concerned with religion 3 conscientiously exact; scrupulous —*n., pl.* -**gious** a monk or nun —**re·li′gious·ly** *adv.*

**re·lin·quish** (ri liŋ′kwish) *vt.* 〖< L *re-,* from + *linquere,* to leave〗 1 to give up (a plan, etc.) or let go (one's grasp, etc.) 2 to renounce or surrender (property, a right, etc.) —**re·lin′quish·ment** *n.*

**rel·ish** (rel′ish) *n.* 〖< OFr *relais,* something remaining〗 1 an appetizing flavor 2 enjoyment; zest [to listen with *relish*] 3 a food, as pickles or raw vegetables, served with a meal to add flavor 4 a condiment of chopped pickles, spices, etc. for use as on hot dogs —*vt.* to enjoy; like

**re·live** (rē liv′) *vt.* -lived′, -liv′ing to experience again (a past event) as in the imagination

**re·lo·cate** (rē lō′kāt′) *vt., vi.* -cat′ed, -cat′ing to move to a new location —**re′lo·ca′tion** *n.*

**re·luc·tant** (ri luk′tənt) *adj.* 〖< L *re-,* against + *luctari,* to struggle〗 1 unwilling; disinclined 2 marked by unwillingness [a *reluctant* answer] —**re·luc′tance** *n.* —**re·luc′tant·ly** *adv.*

**re·ly** (ri lī′) *vi.* -lied′, -ly′ing 〖< L *re-,* back + *ligare,* bind〗 to trust or depend: used with *on* or *upon*

**rem** (rem) *n., pl.* **rem** 〖*r(oentgen) e(quivalent), m(an)*〗 a dose of ionizing radiation with a biological effect equal to one roentgen of X-ray

**REM** (rem) *n., pl.* **REMs** 〖*r(apid) e(ye) m(ovement)*〗 the rapid, jerky movement of the eyeballs during stages of sleep associated with dreaming

**re·main** (ri mān′) *vi.* 〖< L *re-,* back + *manere,* to stay〗 1 to be left over when the rest has been taken away, etc. 2 to stay 3 to continue [to *remain* a cynic] 4 to be left to be done, said, etc.

**re·main′der** *n.* 1 those remaining 2 what is left when a part is taken away 3 what is left when a smaller number is subtracted from a larger 4 what is left undivided when a number is divided by another that is not one of its factors

**re·mains** (-mānz′) *pl.n.* 1 what is left after use, destruction, etc. 2 a dead body

**re·mand** (ri mand′) *vt.* 〖< L *re-,* back + *mandare,* to order〗 to send back (a prisoner, etc.) into custody

**re·mark** (ri märk′) *vt.* 〖< Fr *re-,* again + *marquer,* to mark〗 1 to notice or observe 2 to say or write as a comment —*vi.* to make a comment: with *on* or *upon* —*n.* a brief comment

**re·mark′a·ble** *adj.* worthy of notice; extraordinary —**re·mark′a·bly** *adv.*

**Rem·brandt** (rem′brant′) 1606-69; Du. painter & etcher

**re·me·di·al** (ri mē′dē əl) *adj.* 1 providing a remedy 2 for correcting deficiencies: said as of some courses of study

**re·me′di·ate** (-āt′) *vt.* -at′ed, -at′ing to provide a remedy for

**rem·e·dy** (rem′ə dē) *n., pl.* -**dies** 〖< L *re-,* again + *mederi,* heal〗 1 any medicine or treatment for a disease 2 something to correct a wrong —*vt.* -**died, -dy·ing** to cure, correct, etc.

**re·mem·ber** (ri mem′bər) *vt.* 〖< L *re-,* again + *memorare,* bring to mind〗 1 to think of again 2 to bring back to mind by an effort; recall 3 to be careful not to forget 4 to mention (a person) to another as sending greetings —*vi.* to bear something in mind or call something back to mind

**re·mem'brance** (-brəns) *n.* **1** a remembering or being remembered **2** the power to remember **3** a souvenir

**re·mind** (ri mīnd') *vt., vi.* to put (a person) in mind (*of* something); make remember —**re·mind'er** *n.*

**rem·i·nisce** (rem'ə nis') *vi.* **-nisced', -nisc'ing** [< fol.] to think, talk, or write about remembered events

**rem'i·nis'cence** (-əns) *n.* [Fr < L *re-*, again + *memini*, remember] **1** a remembering **2** a memory **3** [*pl.*] an account of remembered experiences —**rem'i·nis'cent** *adj.*

**re·miss** (ri mis') *adj.* [see REMIT] careless; negligent —**re·miss'ness** *n.*

**re·mis·sion** (ri mish'ən) *n.* [see fol.] **1** forgiveness; pardon **2** release from a debt, tax, etc. **3** an abating of pain, a disease, etc.

**re·mit** (ri mit') *vt.* **-mit'ted, -mit'ting** [< L *re-*, back + *mittere*, send] **1** to forgive or pardon **2** to refrain from exacting (a payment), inflicting (punishment), etc. **3** to slacken; decrease **4** to send (money) in payment —**re·mit'tance** *n.*

**rem·nant** (rem'nənt) *n.* [see REMAIN] what is left over, as a piece of cloth at the end of a bolt

**re·mod·el** (rē mäd''l) *vt.* **-eled** or **-elled, -el·ing** or **-el·ling** to make over; rebuild

**re·mon·strate** (ri män'strāt') *vt.* **-strat'ed, -strat'ing** [< L *re-*, again + *monstrare*, to show] to say in protest, objection, etc. —*vi.* to protest; object —**re·mon'strance** (-strəns) *n.*

**re·morse** (ri môrs') *n.* [< L *re-*, again + *mordere*, to bite] a torturing sense of guilt for one's actions —**re·morse'ful** *adj.* —**re·morse'less** *adj.*

**re·mote** (ri mōt') *adj.* **-mot'er, -mot'est** [< L *remotus*, removed] **1** distant in space or time **2** distant in connection, relation, etc. **3** distantly related **4** aloof **5** slight [a *remote* chance] —**re·mote'ly** *adv.*

**remote control 1** control of aircraft, etc. from a distance, as by radio waves **2** a device to control a TV set, recorder, etc. from a distance

**re·move** (ri mōōv') *vt.* **-moved', -mov'ing** [see RE- & MOVE] **1** to move (something) from where it is; take away or off **2** to dismiss, as from office **3** to get rid of —*vi.* to move away, as to another residence —*n.* a step or degree away —**re·mov'a·ble** *adj.* —**re·mov'al** *n.* —**re·mov'er** *n.*

**re·mu·ner·ate** (ri myōō'nə rāt') *vt.* **-at'ed, -at'ing** [< L *re-*, again + *munus*, gift] to pay (a person) for (work, a loss, etc.) —**re·mu·ner·a'tion** *n.* —**re·mu'ner·a'tive** *adj.*

**ren·ais·sance** (ren'ə säns') *n.* [Fr] a rebirth; renascence —**the Renaissance** the great revival of art and learning in Europe in the 14th, 15th, and 16th centuries

**Renaissance man** (or **woman**) one skilled and knowledgeable in many fields

**re·nal** (rē'nəl) *adj.* [< L *renes*, kidneys] of or near the kidneys

**re·nas·cence** (ri nas'əns, -nās'-) *n.* [< L *renasci*, be born again] [*also* R-] RENAISSANCE

**rend** (rend) *vt.* **rent, rend'ing** [OE *rendan*] to tear or split with violence —*vi.* to tear; split apart

**ren·der** (ren'dər) *vt.* [ult. < L *re(d)-*, back + *dare*, give] **1** to submit, as for approval or payment **2** to give in return or pay as due [*render* thanks] **3** to cause to be **4** to give (aid) or do (a service) **5** to depict, as by drawing **6** to play (music), act (a role), etc. **7** to translate **8** to melt down (fat) **9** to pronounce (a verdict)

**ren·dez·vous** (rän'dā vōō') *n., pl.* **-vous** (-vōōz') [< Fr *rendez-vous*, present yourself] **1** a meeting place **2** an agreement to meet **3** the meeting itself —*vi., vt.* **-voused'** (-vōōd'), **-vous'ing** (-vōō'iŋ) to meet or assemble at a certain time or place

**ren·di·tion** (ren dish'ən) *n.* a rendering; performance, translation, etc.

**ren·e·gade** (ren'ə gād') *n.* [< L *re-*, again + *negare*, deny] one who abandons a party, movement, etc. to join the opposition; turncoat

**re·nege** (ri nig') *vi.* **-neged', -neg'ing** [see prec.] to go back on a promise

---

**re·new** (ri nōō') *vt.* **1** to make new or fresh again **2** to reestablish; revive **3** to resume **4** to put in a fresh supply of **5** to give or get an extension of [*renew* a lease] —**re·new'a·ble** *adj.* —**re·new'al** *n.*

**ren·net** (ren'it) *n.* [< ME *rennen*, coagulate] an extract from the stomach of calves, etc. used to curdle milk

**Re·no** (rē'nō) city in W Nevada: pop. 134,000

**Re·noir** (rən wär', ren'wär'), **Pierre Au·guste** (pyer ô güst') 1841-1919; Fr. painter

**re·nounce** (ri nouns') *vt.* **-nounced', -nounc'ing** [< L *re-*, back + *nuntiare*, tell] **1** to give up formally (a claim, etc.) **2** to give up (a habit, etc.) **3** to disown —**re·nounce'ment** *n.*

**ren·o·vate** (ren'ə vāt') *vt.* **-vat'ed, -vat'ing** [< L *re-*, again + *novus*, new] to make as good as new; restore —**ren'o·va'tion** *n.* —**ren'o·va'tor** *n.*

**re·nown** (ri noun') *n.* [< OFr *re-*, again + *nom(m)er*, to name < L *nominare*] great fame or reputation —**re·nowned'** *adj.*

**rent**[1] (rent) *n.* [< L *reddita*, paid] a stated payment at fixed intervals for the use of a house, land, etc. —*vt.* to get or give use of in return for rent —*vi.* to be let for rent —**for rent** available to be rented —**rent'er** *n.*

**rent**[2] (rent) *vt., vi. pt. & pp. of* REND —*n.* a hole or gap made by tearing

**rent·al** (rent''l) *n.* **1** an amount paid or received as rent **2** a house, car, etc. offered for rent **3** a renting —*adj.* of or for rent

**re·nun·ci·a·tion** (ri nun'sē ā'shən) *n.* a renouncing, as of a right

**re·or·gan·ize** (rē ôr'gə nīz') *vt., vi.* **-ized', -iz'ing** to organize (a business, etc.) anew —**re·or'gan·i·za'tion** *n.*

**rep**[1] (rep) *n.* [Fr *reps* < Eng *ribs*] a ribbed fabric

**rep**[2] (rep) *n.* a representative

**rep**[3] *abbrev.* **1** repeat **2** report(ed) **3** reporter

**Rep** *abbrev.* **1** Representative **2** Republican

**re·paid** (ri pād') *vt., vi. pt. & pp. of* REPAY

**re·pair**[1] (ri per') *vt.* [< L *re-*, again + *parare*, prepare] **1** to put back in good condition; fix; renew **2** to make amends for —*n.* **1** a repairing **2** [*usually pl.*] work done in repairing **3** the state of being repaired [kept in *repair*] —**re·pair'a·ble** *adj.*

**re·pair**[2] (ri per') *vi.* [< L *re-*, back + *patria*, native land] to go (*to* a place)

**re·pair·man** (-mən, -man') *n., pl.* **-men** (-mən, -men') one whose work is repairing things

**rep·a·ra·tion** (rep'ə rā'shən) *n.* [see REPAIR[1]] **1** a making of amends **2** [*usually pl.*] compensation, as for war damage

**rep·ar·tee** (rep'är tē', -tā') *n.* [< Fr *repartir*, to return a blow quickly] a series of quick, witty retorts; banter

**re·past** (ri past') *n.* [< OFr *re-*, RE- + *past*, food] food and drink; a meal

**re·pa·tri·ate** (rē pā'trē āt') *vt., vi.* **-at'ed, -at'ing** [see REPAIR[2]] to return to the country of birth, citizenship, etc. —**re·pa'tri·a'tion** *n.*

**re·pay** (ri pā') *vt.* **-paid', -pay'ing** **1** to pay back **2** to make return to for (a favor, etc.) —**re·pay'ment** *n.*

**re·peal** (ri pēl') *vt.* [see RE- & APPEAL] to revoke; cancel; annul —*n.* revocation; abrogation

**re·peat** (ri pēt') *vt.* [< L *re-*, again + *petere*, to demand] **1** to say again **2** to recite (a poem, etc.) **3** to say (something) as said by someone else **4** to tell to someone else [to *repeat* a secret] **5** to do or make again —*vi.* to say or do again —*n.* **1** a repeating **2** anything said or done again, as a rebroadcast of a television program **3** *Music a)* a passage to be repeated *b)* a symbol for this —**re·peat'er** *n.*

**re·peat'ed** *adj.* said, made, or done again, or often —**re·peat'ed·ly** *adv.*

**re·pel** (ri pel') *vt.* **-pelled', -pel'ling** [< L *re-*, back + *pellere*, to drive] **1** to drive or force back **2** to reject **3** to cause dislike in; disgust **4** to be resistant to (water, dirt, etc.) —**re·pel'lent** *adj., n.*

**re·pent** (ri pent') *vi., vt.* ⟦< L *re-*, again + *poenitere*, repent⟧ **1** to feel sorry for (an error, sin, etc.) **2** to feel such regret over (an action, intention, etc.) as to change one's mind (about) — **re·pent'ance** *n.* —**re·pent'ant** *adj.*

**re·per·cus·sion** (rē'pər kush'ən) *n.* ⟦see RE- & PERCUSSION⟧ **1** reverberation **2** a far-reaching, often indirect reaction to some event

**rep·er·toire** (rep'ər twär') *n.* ⟦< Fr < L *reperire*, discover⟧ the stock of plays, songs, etc. that a company, singer, etc. is prepared to perform

**rep·er·to·ry** (-tôr'ē) *n., pl.* **-ries 1** REPERTOIRE **2** the system of alternating several plays throughout a season with a permanent group of actors

**rep·e·ti·tion** (rep'ə tish'ən) *n.* ⟦< L *repetitio*⟧ **1** a repeating **2** something repeated —**rep'e·ti'tious** *adj.* —**re·pet·i·tive** (ri pet'ə tiv) *adj.*

**re·pine** (ri pīn') *vi.* **-pined', -pin'ing** ⟦RE- + PINE[2]⟧ to feel or express unhappiness or discontent

**re·place** (ri plās') *vt.* **-placed', -plac'ing 1** to put back in a former or the proper place **2** to take the place of **3** to provide an equivalent for —**re·place'a·ble** *adj.* —**re·place'ment** *n.*

**re·plen·ish** (ri plen'ish) *vt.* ⟦< L *re-*, again + *plenus*, full⟧ **1** to make full or complete again **2** to supply again —**re·plen'ish·ment** *n.*

**re·plete** (ri plēt') *adj.* ⟦< L *re-*, again + *plere*, to fill⟧ **1** plentifully supplied **2** stuffed; gorged —**re·ple'tion** *n.*

**rep·li·ca** (rep'li kə) *n.* ⟦see REPLY⟧ a reproduction or close copy, as of a work of art

**rep·li·cate** (rep'li kāt') *vt.* **-cat'ed, -cat'ing** ⟦see REPLY⟧ to repeat or duplicate

**rep·li·ca'tion** *n.* **1** a replicating **2** a reply; answer **3** a copy; reproduction

**re·ply** (ri plī') *vi.* **-plied', -ply'ing** ⟦< L *re-*, back + *plicare*, to fold⟧ to answer or respond —*n., pl.* **-plies'** an answer or response

**re·port** (ri pôrt') *vt.* ⟦< L *re-*, back + *portare*, carry⟧ **1** to give an account of, as for publication **2** to carry and repeat (a message, etc.) **3** to announce formally **4** to make a charge about (something) or against (someone) to one in authority —*vi.* **1** to make a report **2** to present oneself, as for work —*n.* **1** rumor **2** a statement or account **3** a formal presentation of facts **4** the noise of an explosion —**re·port'ed·ly** *adv.*

**re·port·age** (ri pôrt'ij, rep'ər täzh') *n.* **1** the reporting of the news **2** journalistic writings

**report card** a periodic written report on a student's progress: often used figuratively

**re·port·er** *n.* one who reports; specif., one who gathers and reports news for a newspaper, etc. — **rep·or·to·ri·al** (rep'ər tôr'ē əl) *adj.*

**re·pose[1]** (ri pōz') *vt.* **-posed', -pos'ing** ⟦< L *re-*, again + *pausare*, to rest⟧ to lay or place for rest — *vi.* **1** to lie at rest **2** to rest from work, etc. **3** to lie dead —*n.* **1** *a*) rest *b*) sleep **2** composure **3** calm; peace —**re·pose'ful** *adj.*

**re·pose[2]** (ri pōz') *vt.* **-posed', -pos'ing** ⟦see fol.⟧ **1** to place (trust, etc.) *in* someone **2** to place (power, etc.) *in* the control of some person or group

**re·pos·i·to·ry** (ri päz'ə tôr'ē) *n., pl.* **-ries** ⟦< L *re-*, back + *ponere*, to place⟧ a box, room, etc. in which things may be placed for safekeeping

**re·pos·sess** (rē'pə zes') *vt.* to take back, as from a buyer who missed payments —**re'pos·ses'sion** *n.*

**rep·re·hend** (rep'ri hend') *vt.* ⟦< L *re-*, back + *prehendere*, to take⟧ to rebuke, blame, or censure

**rep·re·hen·si·ble** (-hen'sə bəl) *adj.* deserving to be reprehended —**rep're·hen'si·bly** *adv.*

**rep·re·sent** (rep'ri zent') *vt.* ⟦< L *re-*, again + *praesentare*, to present⟧ **1** to present to the mind **2** to present a likeness of **3** to describe **4** to stand for; symbolize **5** to be the equivalent of **6** to act (a role) **7** to act in place of, esp. by conferred authority **8** to serve as an example of

**rep·re·sen·ta·tion** *n.* **1** a representing or being represented, as in a legislative assembly **2** legislative representatives, collectively **3** a likeness, image, picture, etc. **4** [*often pl.*] a statement of facts, arguments, etc. meant to influence action, make protest, etc. —**rep're·sen·ta'tion·al** *adj.*

**rep·re·sent·a·tive** *adj.* **1** representing **2** of or based on representation of the people by elected delegates **3** typical —*n.* **1** an example or type **2** one authorized to act for others; delegate, agent, salesman, etc. **3** [R-] a member of the lower house of Congress or of a state legislature

**re·press** (ri pres') *vt.* ⟦see RE- & PRESS[1]⟧ **1** to hold back; restrain **2** to put down; subdue **3** *Psychiatry* to force (painful ideas, etc.) into the unconscious —**re·pres'sion** *n.* —**re·pres'sive** *adj.*

**re·prieve** (ri prēv') *vt.* **-prieved', -priev'ing** ⟦< Fr *reprendre*, take back⟧ **1** to postpone the punishment of, esp. the execution of **2** to give temporary relief to —*n.* a reprieving or being reprieved

**rep·ri·mand** (rep'rə mand') *n.* ⟦< L *reprimere*, repress⟧ a severe or formal rebuke —*vt.* to rebuke severely or formally

**re·pris·al** (ri prī'zəl) *n.* ⟦see REPREHEND⟧ injury done in return for injury received

**re·proach** (ri prōch') *vt.* ⟦< L *re-*, back + *prope*, near⟧ to accuse of a fault; rebuke —*n.* **1** shame, disgrace, etc. or a cause of this **2** rebuke or censure —**re·proach'ful** *adj.*

**rep·ro·bate** (rep'rə bāt') *adj.* ⟦LL *reprobare*, reprove⟧ unprincipled or depraved —*n.* a reprobate person

**re·proc·ess** (rē prä'ses) *vt.* to process again so as to reuse; esp., to recover plutonium, etc. from

**re·pro·duce** (rē'prə dōōs') *vt.* **-duced', -duc'ing** to produce again; specif., *a*) to produce by propagation *b*) to make a copy of —*vi.* to produce offspring —**re'pro·duc'i·ble** *adj.*

**re·pro·duc·tion** (-duk'shən) *n.* **1** a reproducing **2** a copy, imitation, etc. **3** the process by which animals and plants produce new individuals — **re'pro·duc'tive** *adj.*

**re·proof** (ri prōōf') *n.* a reproving; rebuke: also **re·prov·al** (-prōō'vəl)

**re·prove** (ri prōōv') *vt.* **-proved', -prov'ing** ⟦see RE- & PROVE⟧ **1** to rebuke **2** to express disapproval of (something done or said)

**rep·tile** (rep'til') *n.* ⟦< L *repere*, to creep⟧ a cold-blooded vertebrate covered as with scales, as a snake, lizard, turtle, or dinosaur —**rep·til·i·an** (rep til'ē ən) *adj.*

**re·pub·lic** (ri pub'lik) *n.* ⟦< L *res*, thing + *publica*, public (adj.)⟧ a state or government, specif. one headed by a president, in which the power is exercised by officials elected by the voters

**re·pub·li·can** (-li kən) *adj.* **1** of or like a republic **2** [R-] of or belonging to the Republican Party —*n.* **1** one who favors a republican form of government **2** [R-] a member of the Republican Party

**Republican Party** one of the two major political parties in the U.S.

**re·pu·di·ate** (ri pyōō'dē āt') *vt.* **-at'ed, -at'ing** ⟦< L *repudium*, separation⟧ **1** to refuse to have anything to do with **2** to refuse to accept or support (a belief, treaty, etc.) —**re·pu'di·a'tion** *n.*

**re·pug·nant** (ri pug'nənt) *adj.* ⟦< L *re-*, back + *pugnare*, fight⟧ **1** contradictory **2** distasteful; offensive —**re·pug'nance** *n.*

**re·pulse** (ri puls') *vt.* **-pulsed', -puls'ing** ⟦see REPEL⟧ **1** to drive back (an attack, etc.) **2** to refuse or reject with discourtesy, etc.; rebuff —*n.* a repelling or being repelled

**re·pul·sion** (ri pul'shən) *n.* **1** a repelling or being repelled **2** strong dislike **3** *Physics* the mutual action by which bodies tend to repel each other

**re·pul·sive** (-siv) *adj.* causing strong dislike or aversion; disgusting —**re·pul'sive·ly** *adv.* —**re·pul'sive·ness** *n.*

**rep·u·ta·ble** (rep'yə tə bəl) *adj.* having a good reputation —**rep'u·ta·bil'i·ty** *n.* —**rep'u·ta·bly** *adv.*

**rep·u·ta·tion** (rep'yōō tā'shən) *n.* ⟦see fol.⟧ **1** esti-

**re·pute** (ri pyōōt′) *vt.* **-put′ed, -put′ing** [< L *re-*, again + *putare*, think] to consider or regard [*reputed* to be rich] —*n.* REPUTATION (senses 1 & 3)

**re·put′ed** *adj.* generally supposed to be such [the *reputed* owner] —**re·put′ed·ly** *adv.*

**re·quest** (ri kwest′) *n.* [see REQUIRE] **1** an asking for something **2** something asked for **3** the state of being asked for; demand —*vt.* **1** to ask for **2** to ask (a person) to do something

**Re·qui·em** (rek′wē əm, rā′kwē-) *n.* [< L, rest] [*also* r-] **1** *R.C.Ch.* a Mass for a dead person or persons **2** a musical setting for this

**re·quire** (ri kwīr′) *vt.* **-quired′, -quir′ing** [< L *re-*, again + *quaerere*, ask] **1** to insist upon; demand **2** to order **3** to need —**re·quire′ment** *n.*

**req·ui·site** (rek′wə zit) *adj.* [see prec.] required; necessary; indispensable —*n.* something requisite

**req·ui·si·tion** (rek′wə zish′ən) *n.* **1** a requiring; formal demand **2** a formal written order, as for equipment —*vt.* **1** to demand or take, as by authority **2** to submit a written request for

**re·quite** (ri kwīt′) *vt.* **-quit′ed, -quit′ing** [RE- + *quite,* obs. var. of QUIT] to repay (someone) for (a benefit, service, etc. or an injury, wrong, etc.) —**re·quit′al** *n.*

**re·run** (rē′run′) *n.* the showing of a film or TV program after the first run or showing

**re·sale′** *n.* a selling of something bought to a third party

**re·scind** (ri sind′) *vt.* [< L *re-*, back + *scindere,* to cut] to revoke or cancel (a law, etc.) —**re·scis′sion** (-sizh′ən) *n.*

**res·cue** (res′kyōō) *vt.* **-cued, -cu·ing** [ult. < L *re-*, again + *ex-*, off + *quatere,* to shake] to free or save from danger, imprisonment, evil, etc. —*n.* a rescuing; deliverance —**res′cu·er** *n.*

**re·search** (rē′sʉrch′, ri sʉrch′) *n.* [see RE- & SEARCH] careful, systematic study and investigation in some field of knowledge —*vi., vt.* to do research (on or in) —**re′search′er** *n.*

**re·sec·tion** (ri sek′shən) *n.* [< L *re-,* back + *secare,* to cut] *Surgery* the removal of part of an organ, bone, etc.

**re·sem·blance** (ri zem′bləns) *n.* a similarity of appearance; likeness

**re·sem′ble** (-bəl) *vt.* **-bled, -bling** [ult. < L *re-*, again + *simulare,* feign] to be like or similar to

**re·sent** (ri zent′) *vt.* [ult. < L *re-*, again + *sentire,* to feel] to feel or show displeasure and hurt or indignation over or toward —**re·sent′ful** *adj.* —**re·sent′ful·ly** *adv.* —**re·sent′ment** *n.*

**re·ser·pine** (ri sʉr′pin, -pēn) *n.* [Ger] a crystalline alkaloid used in treating hypertension, mental illness, etc.

**res·er·va·tion** (rez′ər vā′shən) *n.* **1** a reserving or that which is reserved; specif., *a)* a withholding *b)* public land set aside for a special use, as for American Indians *c)* holding of a hotel room, etc. until called for **2** a limiting condition

**re·serve** (ri zʉrv′) *vt.* **-served′, -serv′ing** [< L *re-,* back + *servare,* to keep] **1** to keep back or set apart for later or special use **2** to keep back for oneself —*n.* **1** something kept back or stored up, as for later use **2** the keeping one's thoughts, feelings, etc. to oneself **3** reticence; silence **4** [*pl.*] troops, players, etc. kept out of action for use as replacements **5** land set apart for a special purpose **6** cash, etc. held back to meet future demands —**in reserve** reserved for later use —**without reserve** subject to no limitation

**re·served′** *adj.* **1** kept in reserve; set apart **2** self-restrained; reticent

**re·serv′ist** *n.* a member of a country's military reserves

**res·er·voir** (rez′ər vwär′, -vwôr′) *n.* [< Fr: see RESERVE] **1** a place where water is collected and stored for use **2** a receptacle for holding a fluid **3** a large supply

**re·side** (ri zīd′) *vi.* **-sid′ed, -sid′ing** [< L *re-*, back +

*sedere,* sit] **1** to dwell for a long time; live (*in* or *at*) **2** to be present or inherent (*in*): said of qualities, etc.

**res·i·dence** (rez′i dəns) *n.* **1** a residing **2** the place where one resides —**res′i·den′tial** (-den′shəl) *adj.*

**res′i·den·cy** (-dən sē) *n., pl.* **-cies 1** RESIDENCE (sense 1) **2** a period of advanced, specialized medical or surgical training at a hospital

**res′i·dent** (-dənt) *adj.* residing; esp., living in a place while working, etc. —*n.* **1** one who lives in a place, not just a visitor **2** a doctor who is serving a residency

**re·sid·u·al** (ri zij′ōō əl) *adj.* of or being a residue; remaining —*n.* **1** something remaining **2** [*often pl.*] the fee paid for reruns on television, etc.

**res·i·due** (rez′ə dōō) *n.* [< L *residuus,* remaining] that which is left after part is taken away; remainder

**re·sid·u·um** (ri zij′ōō əm) *n., pl.* **-u·a** (-ə) RESIDUE

**re·sign** (ri zīn′) *vt., vi.* [< L *re-,* back + *signare,* to sign] to give up (a claim, position, etc.) —**resign oneself** (**to**) to become reconciled (to)

**res·ig·na·tion** (rez′ig nā′shən) *n.* **1** *a)* the act of resigning *b)* formal notice of this **2** patient submission

**re·signed** (ri zīnd′) *adj.* feeling or showing resignation; submissive —**re·sign′ed·ly** (-zīn′id lē) *adv.*

**re·sil·ient** (ri zil′yənt) *adj.* [< L *re-,* back + *salire,* to jump] **1** springing back into shape, etc. **2** recovering strength, spirits, etc. quickly —**re·sil′ience** *or* **re·sil′ien·cy** *n.*

**res·in** (rez′ən) *n.* [< L *resina*] **1** a substance exuded from various plants and trees and used in varnishes, plastics, etc. **2** ROSIN —**res′in·ous** *adj.*

**re·sist** (ri zist′) *vt.* [< L *re-,* back + *sistere,* to set] **1** to withstand; fend off **2** to oppose actively; fight against —*vi.* to oppose or withstand something —**re·sist′er** *n.* —**re·sist′i·ble** *adj.*

**re·sist′ance** *n.* **1** a resisting **2** power to resist, as to ward off disease **3** opposition of some force, thing, etc. to another, as to the flow of an electric current —**re·sist′ant** *adj.*

**re·sist′less** *adj.* **1** irresistible **2** unable to resist

**re·sis′tor** *n.* a device used in an electrical circuit to provide resistance

**re·sole** (rē sōl′) *vt.* **-soled′, -sol′ing** to put a new sole on (a shoe, etc.)

**res·o·lute** (rez′ə lōōt′) *adj.* [see RE- & SOLVE] fixed and firm in purpose; determined —**res′o·lute′ly** *adv.*

**res·o·lu′tion** *n.* **1** the act or result of resolving something **2** a thing determined upon; decision as to future action **3** a resolute quality of mind **4** a formal statement of opinion or determination by an assembly, etc.

**re·solve** (ri zälv′, -zôlv′) *vt.* **-solved′, -solv′ing** [see RE- & SOLVE] **1** to break up into separate parts **2** to change: used reflexively **3** to reach as a decision; determine [to *resolve* to go] **4** to solve (a problem) **5** to decide by vote —*n.* **1** firm determination **2** a formal resolution —**re·solv′a·ble** *adj.*

**re·solved′** *adj.* determined; resolute

**res·o·nant** (rez′ə nənt) *adj.* [< L *resonare,* resound] **1** resounding **2** intensifying sound [*resonant* walls] **3** sonorous; vibrant [a *resonant* voice] —**res′o·nance** *n.* —**res′o·nate′** (-nāt′), **-nat′ed, -nat′ing, vi., vt.**

**res′o·na′tor** *n.* a device that produces, or increases sound by, resonance

**re·sort** (ri zôrt′) *vi.* [< OFr *re-,* again + *sortir,* go out] to have recourse; turn (*to*) for help, etc. [to *resort* to lies] —*n.* **1** a place to which people go often or generally, as on vacation **2** a source of help, support, etc.; recourse —**as a last resort** as the last available means

**re·sound** (ri zound′) *vi.* [< L *resonare*] **1** to reverberate **2** to make a loud, echoing sound —**re·sound′ing** *adj.* —**re·sound′ing·ly** *adv.*

**re·source** (rē′sôrs′, ri sôrs′) *n.* [< OFr *re-,* again +

*sourdre,* spring up] **1** something that lies ready for use or can be drawn upon for aid **2** [*pl.*] wealth; assets **3** resourcefulness

**re·source'ful** *adj.* able to deal effectively with problems, etc. —**re·source'ful·ness** *n.*

**re·spect** (ri spekt') *vt.* [< L *re-,* back + *specere,* look at] **1** to feel or show honor or esteem for **2** to show consideration for —*n.* **1** honor or esteem **2** consideration or regard **3** [*pl.*] expressions of regard **4** a particular detail **5** reference; relation [with *respect* to the problem] —**re·spect'ful** *adj.* —**re·spect'ful·ly** *adv.*

**re·spect'a·ble** *adj.* **1** worthy of respect or esteem **2** proper; correct **3** fairly good in quality or size **4** presentable —**re·spect'a·bil'i·ty** *n.*

**re·spect'ing** *prep.* concerning; about

**re·spec'tive** *adj.* as relates individually to each one

**re·spec'tive·ly** *adv.* in regard to each, in the order named

**res·pi·ra·tion** (res'pə rā'shən) *n.* [< L *re-,* back + *spirare,* breathe] act or process of breathing — **res·pi·ra·to·ry** (res'pər ə tôr'ē, ri spī'rə-) *adj.*

**res'pi·ra'tor** *n.* **1** a mask, as of gauze, to prevent the inhaling of harmful substances **2** an apparatus to maintain breathing by artificial means

**res·pite** (res'pit) *n.* [see RESPECT] **1** a delay or postponement **2** temporary relief, as from pain or work; lull

**re·splend·ent** (ri splen'dənt) *adj.* [< L *re-,* again + *splendere,* to shine] shining brightly; dazzling —**re·splend'ence** *n.* —**re·splend'ent·ly** *adv.*

**re·spond** (ri spänd') *vi.* [< L *re-,* back + *spondere,* to pledge] **1** to answer; reply **2** to react **3** to have a favorable reaction

**re·spond'ent** *adj.* responding —*n. Law* a defendant

**re·sponse** (ri späns') *n.* [see RESPOND] **1** something said or done in answer; reply **2** words sung or spoken by the congregation or choir replying to the clergyman **3** any reaction to a stimulus

**re·spon·si·bil·i·ty** (ri spän'sə bil'ə tē) *n., pl.* **-ties** **1** a being responsible; obligation **2** a thing or person that one is responsible for

**re·spon'si·ble** (-bəl) *adj.* **1** expected or obliged to account (*for*); answerable (*to*) **2** involving obligation or duties **3** that is the cause of something **4** able to distinguish between right and wrong **5** dependable; reliable —**re·spon'si·bly** *adv.*

**re·spon'sive** *adj.* reacting readily, as to suggestion or appeal —**re·spon'sive·ness** *n.*

**rest**[1] (rest) *n.* [OE] **1** sleep or repose **2** ease or inactivity after exertion **3** relief from anything distressing, tiring, etc. **4** absence of motion **5** a resting place **6** a supporting device **7** *Music* a measured interval of silence between tones, or a symbol for this —*vi.* **1** to get ease and refreshment by sleeping or by ceasing from work **2** to be at ease **3** to be or become still **4** to lie, sit, or lean **5** to be placed or based (*in,* on, etc.) **6** to be found [the fault *rests* with him] **7** to rely; depend —*vt.* **1** to give rest to **2** to put for ease, support, etc. [*rest* your head here] **3** *Law* to stop introducing evidence in (a case) —**lay to rest** to bury

**rest**[2] (rest) *n.* [< L *restare,* remain] **1** what is left **2** [with pl. v.] the others —*vi.* to go on being [*rest* assured]

**res·tau·rant** (res'tə ränt', res'tränt') *n.* [Fr: see RESTORE] a place where meals can be bought and eaten

**res·tau·ra·teur** (res'tə rə tur', -toor') *n.* [Fr] one who owns or operates a restaurant: also **res·tau·ran·teur** (res'tə rän'tur', -toor')

**rest·ful** (rest'fəl) *adj.* **1** full of or giving rest **2** quiet; peaceful

**rest home** a residence that provides care for aged persons or convalescents

**res·ti·tu·tion** (res'tə tōō'shən) *n.* [< L *re-,* again + *statuere,* set up] **1** a giving back of something

that has been lost or taken away; restoration **2** reimbursement, as for loss

**res·tive** (res'tiv) *adj.* [< OFr *rester,* remain] **1** unruly or balky **2** nervous under restraint; restless —**res'tive·ly** *adv.* —**res'tive·ness** *n.*

**rest'less** *adj.* **1** unable to relax; uneasy **2** giving no rest; disturbed [*restless* sleep] **3** rarely quiet or still; active **4** discontented —**rest'less·ly** *adv.* —**rest'less·ness** *n.*

**res·to·ra·tion** (res'tə rā'shən) *n.* **1** a restoring or being restored **2** something restored, as by rebuilding

**re·stor·a·tive** (ri stôr'ə tiv) *adj.* able to restore health, consciousness, etc. —*n.* something that is restorative

**re·store** (ri stôr') *vt.* **-stored', -stor'ing** [< L *re-,* again + *-staurare,* to erect] **1** to give back (something taken, lost, etc.) **2** to return to a former or normal state, or to a position, rank, use, etc. **3** to bring back to health, strength, etc.

**re·strain** (ri strān') *vt.* [< L *re-,* back + *stringere,* draw tight] **1** to hold back from action; check; suppress **2** to limit; restrict

**re·straint** (ri strānt') *n.* **1** a restraining or being restrained **2** a means or instrument of restraining **3** confinement **4** control of emotions, impulses, etc.; reserve

**re·strict** (ri strikt') *vt.* [see RESTRAIN] to keep within limits; confine —**re·strict'ed** *adj.* —**re·stric'tion** *n.*

**re·stric'tive** *adj.* **1** restricting **2** *Gram.* designating a modifier, as a subordinate clause or phrase, that limits the reference of the word it modifies and is not set off by punctuation

**rest'room'** *n.* a room in a public building, equipped with toilets, washbowls, etc.: also **rest room**

**re·struc·ture** (rē struk'chər) *vt.* **-tured, -tur·ing** **1** to plan or provide a new structure or organization for **2** to change the terms of (a loan, etc.)

**re·sult** (ri zult') *vi.* [< L *resultare,* to rebound] **1** to happen as an effect **2** to end as a consequence (*in* something) —*n.* **1** *a*) anything that comes about as an effect *b*) [*pl.*] the desired effect **2** the number, etc. obtained by mathematical calculation —**re·sult'ant** *adj., n.*

**re·sume** (ri zōōm') *vt.* **-sumed', -sum'ing** [< L *re-,* again + *sumere,* take] **1** to take or occupy again **2** to continue after interruption —*vi.* to proceed after interruption —**re·sump'tion** (-zump'shən) *n.*

**ré·su·mé** (rez'ə mā') *n.* [Fr: see prec.] a summary, esp. of employment experience: also written **resume** or **resumé**

**re·sur·face** (rē sur'fis) *vt.* **-faced, -fac·ing** to put a new surface on —*vi.* to come to the surface again

**re·sur·gent** (ri sur'jənt) *adj.* [see fol.] rising or tending to rise again —**re·sur'gence** *n.*

**res·ur·rec·tion** (rez'ə rek'shən) *n.* [< L *resurgere,* rise again] **1** a rising from the dead **2** a coming back into notice, use, etc.; revival —**the Resurrection** *Theol.* the rising of Jesus from the dead —**res·ur·rect'** *vt.*

**re·sus·ci·tate** (ri sus'ə tāt') *vt., vi.* **-tat'ed, -tat'ing** [< L *re-,* again + *suscitare,* revive] to revive when apparently dead or in a faint, etc. —**re·sus·ci·ta'tion** *n.* —**re·sus·ci·ta'tor** *n.*

**ret** *abbrev.* **1** retired **2** return(ed)

**re·tail** (rē'tāl') *n.* [< OFr *re-,* again + *tailler,* to cut] the sale of goods in small quantities directly to the consumer —*adj.* of or engaged in such sale — *adv.* at a retail price —*vt., vi.* to sell or be sold directly to the consumer —**re'tail'er** *n.*

**re·tain** (ri tān') *vt.* [< L *re-,* back + *tenere,* to hold] **1** to keep in possession, use, etc. **2** to hold in **3** to keep in mind **4** to hire by paying a retainer

**re·tain'er** *n.* **1** something that retains **2** a servant, attendant, etc. **3** a fee paid in advance to engage the services of a lawyer, etc.

**retaining wall** a wall for keeping earth from sliding or water from flooding

**re·take** (rē tāk'; *for n.* rē'tāk') *vt.* **-took', -tak'en,**

**-tak′ing 1** to take again; recapture **2** to photograph again —*n.* a scene, etc. rephotographed

**re·tal·i·ate** (ri tal′ē āt′) *vi.* **-at′ed, -at′ing** ⟦< L *re-*, back + *talio,* punishment in kind⟧ to return like for like, esp. injury for injury —**re·tal′i·a′tion** *n.* —**re·tal′i·a·to′ry** *adj.*

**re·tard** (ri tärd′) *vt.* ⟦< L *re-*, back + *tardare,* make slow⟧ to hinder, delay, or slow the progress of — **re·tar·da·tion** (rē′tär dā′shən) *n.*

**re·tard′ant** *n.* something that retards; esp., a substance that delays a chemical reaction —*adj.* that retards

**re·tard′ed** *adj.* slowed or delayed in development, esp. mentally

**retch** (rech) *vi.* ⟦OE *hræcan,* clear the throat⟧ to strain to vomit, esp. without bringing anything up

**re·ten·tion** (ri ten′shən) *n.* **1** a retaining or being retained **2** capacity for retaining **3** a remembering; memory —**re·ten′tive** *adj.*

**ret·i·cent** (ret′ə sənt) *adj.* ⟦< L *re-*, again + *tacere,* be silent⟧ disinclined to speak; taciturn —**ret′i·cence** *n.*

**ret·i·na** (ret′'n ə) *n., pl.* **-nas** or **-nae** (-ē′) ⟦prob. < L *rete,* a net⟧ the innermost coat lining the eyeball, containing light-sensitive cells that are directly connected to the brain

**ret·i·nue** (ret′'n ōō′) *n.* ⟦< OFr, ult. < L: see RETAIN⟧ a group of persons attending a person of rank or importance

**re·tire** (ri tīr′) *vi.* **-tired′, -tir′ing** ⟦< Fr *re-*, back + *tirer,* draw⟧ **1** to withdraw to a secluded place **2** to go to bed **3** to retreat, as in battle **4** to give up one's work, business, etc., esp. because of age — *vt.* **1** to pay off (bonds, etc.) **2** to cause to retire from a position, office, etc. **3** to withdraw from use **4** *Baseball* to put out (a batter, side, etc.) — **re·tire′ment** *n.*

**re·tired′** *adj.* **1** secluded **2** *a*) no longer working, etc. as because of age *b*) of or for such retired persons

**re·tir′ing** *adj.* reserved; modest; shy

**re·tool** (rē tōōl′) *vt., vi.* **1** to adapt (factory machinery) for a different product **2** to reorganize to meet new or different needs or conditions

**re·tort**[1] (ri tôrt′) *vt.* ⟦< L *re-*, back + *torquere,* to twist⟧ to say in reply —*vi.* to make a sharp, witty reply —*n.* a sharp, witty reply

**re·tort**[2] (ri tôrt′) *n.* ⟦< ML *retorta:* see prec.⟧ a glass container with a long tube, in which substances are distilled

**re·touch** (rē tuch′) *vt.* to touch up details in (a painting, essay, etc.) so as to improve or change it

**re·trace** (rē trās′) *vt.* **-traced′, -trac′ing** ⟦see RE- & TRACE[1]⟧ to go back over again [to *retrace* one's steps]

RETORT

**re·tract** (ri trakt′) *vt., vi.* ⟦< L *re-*, back + *trahere,* draw⟧ **1** to draw back or in **2** to withdraw (a statement, charge, etc.) —**re·tract′a·ble** or **re·trac′tile** (-trak′təl, -tīl′) *adj.* —**re·trac′tion** *n.*

**re·tread** (rē tred′; *for n.* rē′tred′) *vt., n.* RECAP[1]

**re·treat** (ri trēt′) *n.* ⟦< L *retrahere:* see RETRACT⟧ **1** a withdrawal, as from danger **2** a safe, quiet place **3** a period of seclusion, esp. for spiritual renewal **4** *a*) the forced withdrawal of troops under attack *b*) a signal for this *c*) a signal, as by bugle, or a ceremony at sunset for lowering the national flag —*vi.* to withdraw; go back

**re·trench** (rē trench′) *vi.* ⟦< Fr: see RE- & TRENCH⟧ to cut down expenses; economize —**re·trench′ment** *n.*

**ret·ri·bu·tion** (re′trə byōō′shən) *n.* ⟦< L *re-*, back + *tribuere,* to pay⟧ punishment for evil done —**re·trib·u·tive** (ri trib′yoo tiv) *adj.*

**re·trieve** (ri trēv′) *vt.* **-trieved′, -triev′ing** ⟦< OFr *re-*, again + *trouver,* find⟧ **1** to get back; recover **2** to restore **3** to make good (a loss, error, etc.) **4**

to access (data) stored in a computer **5** to find and bring back (killed or wounded game): said of dogs —*vi.* to retrieve game —**re·triev′al** *n.*

**re·triev′er** *n.* a dog trained to retrieve game

**retro-** ⟦< L⟧ *combining form* backward, back, behind

**ret·ro·ac·tive** (re′trō ak′tiv) *adj.* having an effect on things that are already past —**ret′ro·ac′tive·ly** *adv.*

**ret′ro·fire** (re′trə fīr′) *vt.* **-fired′, -fir′ing** to ignite (a retrorocket)

**ret′ro·fit′** (-fit′) *n.* a change in design or equipment, as of an aircraft already in operation, so as to incorporate later improvements —*vt., vi.* **-fit′ted, -fit′ting** to modify with a retrofit

**ret′ro·grade′** (-grād′) *adj.* ⟦< L: see RETRO- & GRADE⟧ **1** moving backward **2** going back to a worse condition

**ret′ro·gress′** (-gres′) *vi.* ⟦< L: see prec.⟧ to move backward, esp. into a worse condition; degenerate —**ret′ro·gres′sion** *n.* —**ret′ro·gres′sive** *adj.*

**ret·ro·rock·et** or **ret·ro-rock·et** (re′trō räk′it) *n.* a small rocket, as on a spacecraft, producing thrust opposite to the direction of flight to reduce speed, as for maneuvering

**ret′ro·spect** (re′trə spekt′) *n.* ⟦< L *retro-*, back + *specere,* to look⟧ contemplation of the past — **ret′ro·spec′tion** *n.*

**ret′ro·spec′tive** *adj.* looking back on the past —*n.* a representative show of an artist's lifetime work

**ret·si·na** (ret sē′nə) *n.* ⟦ModGr, prob. < It *resina,* resin⟧ a Greek wine flavored with pine resin

**re·turn** (ri turn′) *vi.* ⟦< OFr: see RE- & TURN⟧ **1** to go or come back **2** to answer; reply —*vt.* **1** to bring, send, or put back **2** to do in reciprocation [to *return* a visit] **3** to yield (a profit, etc.) **4** to report officially **5** to elect or reelect —*n.* **1** a coming or going back **2** a bringing, sending, or putting back **3** something returned **4** a recurrence **5** repayment; requital **6** [*often pl.*] yield or profit, as from investments **7** an answer; reply **8** *a*) an official report [election *returns*] *b*) a form for computing income tax —*adj.* **1** of or for a return [*return* postage] **2** given, done, etc. in return —**in return** as a return; as an equivalent, response, etc. —**re·turn′a·ble** *adj.*

**re·turn′ee′** *n.* one who returns, as home from military service

**Reu·ben (sandwich)** (rōō′bən) a sandwich of rye bread, corned beef, sauerkraut, Swiss cheese, etc. served hot

**re·u·ni·fy** (rē yōō′nə fī′) *vt., vi.* **-fied′, -fy′ing** to unify again after being divided —**re·u′ni·fi·ca′tion** *n.*

**re·un·ion** (rē yōōn′yən) *n.* a coming together again, as after separation

**re-up** (rē up′) *vi.* **-upped′, -up′ping** ⟦RE- + (*sign*) *up*⟧ [Mil. Slang] to reenlist

**rev**[1] (rev) *vt.* **revved, rev′ving** ⟦< REV(OLUTION)⟧ [Inf.] **1** to increase the speed of (an engine) **2** to accelerate, intensify, etc. Usually with *up*

**rev**[2] *abbrev.* **1** revenue **2** revise(d) **3** revolution

**Rev** *abbrev.* **1** *Bible* Revelation **2** Reverend

**re·vamp** (rē vamp′) *vt.* to renovate; redo

**re·veal** (ri vēl′) *vt.* ⟦< L *re-*, back + *velum,* veil⟧ **1** to make known (something hidden or secret) **2** to show; exhibit; display

**rev·eil·le** (rev′ə lē) *n.* ⟦< Fr < L *re-*, again + *vigilare,* to watch⟧ a signal on a bugle, drum, etc. in the morning to waken soldiers, etc.

**rev·el** (rev′əl) *vi.* **-eled** or **-elled, -el·ing** or **-el·ling** ⟦< MFr < L *rebellare,* to rebel: see REBEL⟧ **1** to be festive; make merry **2** to take much pleasure (*in*) —*n.* merrymaking —**rev′el·er** or **rev′el·ler** *n.* — **rev′el·ry,** *pl.* **-ries,** *n.*

**rev·e·la·tion** (rev′ə lā′shən) *n.* **1** a revealing **2** a striking disclosure **3** *Theol.* God's disclosure to humanity of divine truth, etc. —[R-] the last book of the New Testament

**re·venge** (ri venj′) *vt.* **-venged′, -veng′ing** ⟦< OFr:

see RE- & VENGEANCE] to inflict harm in return for (an injury, etc.) —*n.* **1** the act or result of revenging **2** desire to take vengeance —**re·venge′ful** *adj.*

**rev·e·nue** (rev′ə nōō′) *n.* [< MFr, returned] **1** return, as from investment; income **2** the income from taxes, licenses, etc., as of a city or nation

**re·ver·ber·ate** (ri vʉr′bə rāt′) *vi.*, *vt.* -at′ed, -at′ing [< L *re-*, again + *verberare*, to beat] to reecho or cause to reecho —**re·ver·ber·a′tion** *n.*

**re·vere** (ri vir′) *vt.* -vered′, -ver′ing [< L *re-*, again + *vereri*, to fear] to regard with deep respect, love, etc.

**Re·vere** (ri vir′), **Paul** 1735-1818; Am. silversmith & patriot

**rev·er·ence** (rev′ə rəns) *n.* a feeling of deep respect, love, and awe —*vt.* -enced, -enc·ing to treat or regard with reverence; venerate —**rev′er·ent** or **rev′er·en′tial** (-ə ren′shəl) *adj.* —**rev′er·ent·ly** *adv.*

**rev·er·end** (rev′ə rənd) *adj.* worthy of reverence: used with *the* as a title of respect for a member of the clergy [the *Reverend* A. B. Smith]

**rev·er·ie** (rev′ə rē) *n.* [< Fr] daydreaming or a daydream

**re·vers** (ri vir′, -ver′) *n.*, *pl.* **-vers′** (-virz′, -verz′) [Fr: see REVERT] a part (of a garment) turned back to show the reverse side, as a lapel: also **re·vere′** (-vir′)

**re·verse** (ri vʉrs′) *adj.* [see fol.] **1** turned backward; opposite or contrary **2** causing movement in the opposite direction —*n.* **1** the opposite or contrary **2** the back of a coin, medal, etc. **3** a change from good fortune to bad **4** a mechanism for reversing, as a gear on a machine —*vt.* -versed′, -vers′ing **1** to turn backward, in an opposite position or direction, upside down, or inside out **2** to change to the opposite **3** *Law* to revoke or annul (a decision, etc.) —*vi.* to go or turn in the opposite direction —**re·ver′sal** (-vʉr′səl) *n.* —**re·vers′i·ble** *adj.* —**re·vers′i·bly** *adv.*

**re·vert** (ri vʉrt′) *vi.* [< L *re-*, back + *vertere*, to turn] **1** to go back, as to a former practice, state, subject, etc. **2** *Biol.* to return to a former or primitive type **3** *Law* to go back to a former owner or his or her heirs —**re·ver′sion** (-vʉr′zhən) *n.* —**re·vert′i·ble** *adj.*

**re·vet·ment** (ri vet′mənt) *n.* [< Fr] **1** a facing of stone, cement, etc., as to protect an embankment **2** RETAINING WALL

**re·view** (ri vyōō′) *n.* [< L *re-*, again + *videre*, see] **1** a looking at or looking over again **2** a general survey or report **3** a looking back on (past events, etc.) **4** reexamination, as of the decision of a lower court **5** a critical evaluation of a book, play, etc. **6** a formal inspection, as of troops on parade —*vt.* **1** to look back on **2** to survey in thought, speech, etc. **3** to inspect (troops, etc.) formally **4** to give a critical evaluation of (a book, etc.) **5** to study again —**re·view′er** *n.*

**re·vile** (ri vīl′) *vt.* -viled′, -vil′ing [< OFr: see RE- & VILE] to use abusive language to or about —**re·vile′ment** *n.* —**re·vil′er** *n.*

**re·vise** (ri vīz′) *vt.* -vised′, -vis′ing [< L *re-*, back + *visere*, to survey] **1** to read over carefully and correct, improve, or update **2** to change or amend —**re·vi′sion** (-vizh′ən) *n.*

**Revised Standard Version** a 20th-c. version of the Bible

**re·vi′sion·ist** *n.* a person who revises, or favors the revision of, some accepted theory, doctrine, etc. —*adj.* of revisionists or their policy or practice —**re·vi′sion·ism′** *n.*

**re·vis·it** (rē viz′it) *vt.* **1** to visit again **2** to reconsider or reevaluate

**re·viv·al** (ri vī′vəl) *n.* **1** a reviving or being revived **2** a bringing or coming back into use, being, etc. **3** a new presentation of an earlier play, etc. **4** restoration to vigor or activity **5** a meeting led by an evangelist to stir up religious feeling —**re·viv′al·ist** *n.*

**re·vive** (ri vīv′) *vi.*, *vt.* -vived′, -viv′ing [< L *re-*, again + *vivere*, to live] **1** to return to life or consciousness **2** to return to health or vigor **3** to come or bring back into use, attention, popularity, etc.

**re·viv·i·fy** (ri viv′ə fī′) *vt.* -fied′, -fy′ing to put new life or vigor into —*vi.* to revive —**re·viv′i·fi·ca′tion** *n.*

**re·voke** (ri vōk′) *vt.* -voked′, -vok′ing [< L *re-*, back + *vocare*, to call] to withdraw, repeal, or cancel (a law, etc.) —**rev·o·ca·ble** (rev′ə kə bəl, ri vō′kə-) *adj.* —**rev′o·ca′tion** (-kā′shən) *n.*

**re·volt** (ri vōlt′) *n.* [< Fr: see REVOLVE] a rebelling against the government or any authority —*vi.* to rebel against authority —*vt.* to disgust —**re·volt′ing** *adj.* —**re·volt′ing·ly** *adv.*

**rev·o·lu·tion** (rev′ə lōō′shən) *n.* [see REVOLVE] **1** the movement of a body in an orbit **2** a turning around an axis; rotation **3** a complete cycle of events **4** a complete change **5** overthrow of a government, social system, etc. —**rev′o·lu′tion·ar′y,** *pl.* **-ies,** *n.*, *adj.* —**rev′o·lu′tion·ist** *n.*

**Revolutionary War** *see* AMERICAN REVOLUTION

**rev′o·lu′tion·ize′** (-shə nīz′) *vt.* -ized′, -iz′ing to make a fundamental change in

**re·volve** (ri välv′, -vôlv′) *vt.* -volved′, -volv′ing [< L *re-*, back + *volvere*, to roll] to turn over in the mind —*vi.* **1** to move in a circle or orbit **2** to rotate —**re·volv′a·ble** *adj.*

**re·volv′er** *n.* a handgun with a revolving cylinder containing cartridges

**re·vue** (ri vyōō′) *n.* [Fr, review] a musical show with skits, dances, etc., often parodying recent events

**re·vul·sion** (ri vul′shən) *n.* [< L *re-*, back + *vellere,* to pull] extreme disgust; loathing

**re·ward** (ri wôrd′) *n.* [< OFr *regarde:* see REGARD] **1** something given in return for something done **2** money offered, as for capturing a criminal —*vt.* to give a reward to (someone) for (service, etc.)

**re·ward′ing** *adj.* giving a sense of reward or worthwhile return

**re·wind** (rē wīnd′) *vt.* -wound′, -wind′ing to wind again; specif., to wind (film or tape) back on the original reel

**re·word′** *vt.* to change the wording of

**re·write′** *vt.*, *vi.* -wrote′, -writ′ten, -writ′ing **1** to write again **2** to revise (something written) **3** to write (news turned in) in a form suitable for publication

**Rey·kja·vik** (rā′kyə vēk′, -vik′) seaport & capital of Iceland: pop. 103,000

**RFD** *abbrev.* Rural Free Delivery

**rhap·so·dize** (rap′sə dīz′) *vi.*, *vt.* -dized′, -diz′ing to speak or write in a rhapsodic manner

**rhap′so·dy** (-sə dē) *n.*, *pl.* **-dies** [< Gr *rhaptein,* stitch together + *ōidē,* song] **1** any ecstatic or enthusiastic speech or writing **2** a musical composition of free, irregular form, suggesting improvisation —**rhap·sod′ic** (-säd′ik) or **rhap·sod′i·cal** *adj.*

**rhe·a** (rē′ə) *n.* [< Gr] a large, flightless South American bird, like an ostrich but smaller

**rhe·o·stat** (rē′ə stat′) *n.* [< Gr *rheos,* current + -STAT] a device for varying the resistance of an electric circuit, used as for dimming or brightening electric lights

**rhesus (monkey)** (rē′səs) [< Gr proper name] a brownish-yellow monkey of India: used in medical research

**rhet·o·ric** (ret′ə rik) *n.* [< Gr *rhētōr,* orator] **1** the art of using words effectively; esp., the art of prose composition **2** showy, elaborate language that is empty or insincere —**rhe·tor·i·cal** (ri tôr′i kəl) *adj.* —**rhet′o·ri′cian** (-ə rish′ən) *n.*

**rhetorical question** a question asked only for rhetorical effect, no answer being expected

**rheum** (rōōm) *n.* [< Gr *rheuma,* a flow] watery discharge from the eyes, nose, etc., as in a cold

**rheumatic fever** an acute or chronic disease,

usually of children, with fever, swelling of the joints, inflammation of the heart, etc.

**rheu·ma·tism** (rōō′mə tiz′əm) *n.* ⟦see RHEUM⟧ *nontechnical term for* a painful condition of the joints and muscles —**rheu·mat′ic** (-mat′ik) *adj., n.* —**rheu′ma·toid′** (-mə toid′) *adj.*

**rheumatoid arthritis** a chronic disease with painful swelling of joints, often leading to deformity

**Rh factor** (är′āch′) ⟦first discovered in RH(ESUS) monkeys⟧ a group of antigens, usually present in human blood: people who have this factor are **Rh positive**; those who do not are **Rh negative**

**Rhine** (rīn) river in W Europe, flowing from E Switzerland through Germany & the Netherlands into the North Sea

**rhine·stone** (rīn′stōn′) *n.* a bright, colorless artificial gem of hard glass, often cut like a diamond

**Rhine wine** a light white wine, esp. one produced in the valley of the Rhine

**rhi·ni·tis** (rī nīt′is) *n.* ⟦< Gr *rhis*, nose + -ITIS⟧ inflammation of the nasal mucous membrane

**rhi·no** (rī′nō) *n., pl.* **-nos** or **-no** *short for* RHINOCEROS

**rhi·noc·er·os** (rī näs′ər əs) *n.* ⟦< Gr *rhis*, nose + *keras*, horn⟧ a large, thick-skinned, plant-eating mammal of Africa and Asia, with one or two upright horns on the snout

**rhi·zome** (rī′zōm′) *n.* ⟦< Gr *rhiza*, a root⟧ a horizontal stem on or under soil, bearing leaves near its tips and roots from its undersurface

**rho** (rō) *n.* the 17th letter of the Greek alphabet (Ρ, ρ)

**Rhode Island** (rōd) New England state of the U.S.: 1,045 sq. mi.; pop. 1,003,000; cap. Providence: abbrev. *RI* —**Rhode Islander**

**Rhodes** (rōdz) large Greek island in the Aegean

**rho·do·den·dron** (rō′də den′drən) *n.* ⟦< Gr *rhodon*, rose + *dendron*, tree⟧ any of various trees or shrubs, mainly evergreen, with showy flowers

**rhom·boid** (räm′boid′) *n.* ⟦< Fr: see fol. & -OID⟧ a parallelogram with oblique angles and only the opposite sides equal

**rhom·bus** (räm′bəs) *n., pl.* **-bus·es** or **-bi′** (-bī′) ⟦L < Gr *rhombos*, turnable object⟧ an equilateral parallelogram, esp. one with oblique angles

**Rhone** or **Rhône** (rōn) river flowing through SW Switzerland & France into the Mediterranean

**rhu·barb** (rōō′bärb′) *n.* ⟦< Gr *rheon*, rhubarb + *barbaron*, foreign⟧ 1 a plant with long, thick stalks that are cooked into a sauce, etc. 2 [Slang] a heated argument

**rhyme** (rīm) *n.* ⟦< OFr⟧ 1 a poem or verse with like recurring sounds, esp. at ends of lines 2 such verse, poetry, or likeness of sounds 3 a word like another in end sound —*vi.* **rhymed, rhym′ing** 1 to make (rhyming) verse 2 to form a rhyme ⟦"more" *rhymes* with "door"⟧ —*vt.* 1 to put into rhyme 2 to use as a rhyme

**rhym′er** *n.* a maker of rhymes, esp. a rhymester

**rhyme′ster** *n.* a maker of trivial rhyme

**rhythm** (rith′əm) *n.* ⟦< Gr *rhythmos*, measure⟧ 1 movement, flow, etc. characterized by regular recurrence of beat, accent, etc. 2 the pattern of this in music, verse, etc. —**rhyth′mic** (-mik) or **rhyth′mi·cal** *adj.* —**rhyth′mi·cal·ly** *adv.*

**rhythm and blues** the form of American popular music from which rock-and-roll derives

**rhythm method** a method of seeking birth control by abstaining from intercourse during the woman's probable ovulation period

**RI** Rhode Island

**rib** (rib) *n.* ⟦OE⟧ 1 any of the arched bones attached to the spine and enclosing the chest cavity 2 anything like a rib in appearance or function —*vt.* **ribbed, rib′bing** 1 to strengthen or form with ribs 2 [Slang] to make fun of; kid

**rib·ald** (rib′əld) *adj.* ⟦< OHG *riban*, to rub⟧ coarse or vulgar in joking, speaking, etc. —**rib′ald·ry** *n.*

**rib·bon** (rib′ən) *n.* ⟦< MFr *ruban*⟧ 1 a narrow strip of silk, rayon, etc. used for decoration, tying,

etc. 2 [*pl.*] torn shreds 3 an inked strip for printing, as in a typewriter, etc.

**rib′bon-cut′ting** *n.* a ceremony to officially open a new building, construction site, etc.

**rib′-eye′** (**steak**) boneless beefsteak from the rib section

**ri·bo·fla·vin** (rī′bə flā′vin) *n.* ⟦< *ribose*, a sugar + L *flavus*, yellow⟧ a B vitamin found in milk, eggs, fruits, etc.: see VITAMIN B (COMPLEX)

**rice** (rīs) *n.* ⟦< Gr *oryza*⟧ 1 an aquatic cereal grass grown widely in warm climates, esp. in East Asia 2 the starchy grains of this grass, used as food —*vt.* **riced, ric′ing** to make ricelike granules from (cooked potatoes, etc.) using a utensil with small holes (**ric′er**)

**rich** (rich) *adj.* ⟦< OE⟧ 1 owning much money or property; wealthy 2 well-supplied (*with*); abounding (*in*) 3 valuable or costly 4 full of choice ingredients, as butter, sugar, etc. *[rich* pastries*]* 5 *a)* full and mellow (said of sounds) *b)* deep; vivid (said of colors) *c)* very fragrant 6 abundant 7 yielding in abundance, as soil 8 [Inf.] very amusing —**the rich** wealthy people collectively —**rich′ly** *adv.* —**rich′ness** *n.*

**Rich·ard I** (rich′ərd) 1157-99; king of England (1189-99): called **Richard Coeur de Li·on** (kʉr′ də lē′ən) or **Richard the Li′on-Heart′ed**

**rich·es** (rich′iz) *pl.n.* ⟦< OFr *richesse*⟧ wealth

**Rich·mond** (rich′mənd) capital of Virginia: pop. 203,000

**Rich·ter scale** (rik′tər) ⟦devised by C. *Richter* (1900-85), U.S. geologist⟧ a scale for measuring the magnitude of earthquakes

**rick** (rik) *n.* ⟦OE *hreac*⟧ a stack of hay, straw, etc.

**rick·ets** (rik′its) *n.* ⟦< ? Gr *rhachis*, spine⟧ a disease, chiefly of children, characterized by a softening and, often, bending of the bones

**rick·et·y** (rik′it ē) *adj.* feeble; weak; shaky

**rick·shaw** or **rick·sha** (rik′shô′) *n.* JINRIKISHA

**ric·o·chet** (rik′ə shā′) *n.* ⟦Fr⟧ the oblique rebound of a bullet, etc. after striking a surface at an angle —*vi.* **-cheted′** (-shād′), **-chet′ing** (-shā′iŋ) to make a ricochet

**ri·cot·ta** (ri kät′ə) *n.* ⟦It < L *recocta*, recooked⟧ a soft cheese made from whey, whole milk, or both

**rid** (rid) *vt.* **rid** or **rid′ded, rid′ding** ⟦< ON *rythja*, to clear (land)⟧ to free or relieve, as of something undesirable —**get rid of** to give or throw away or to destroy

**rid·dance** (rid′′ns) *n.* a ridding or being rid — **good riddance** an expression of satisfaction at being rid of something

**rid·den** (rid′′n) *vi., vt. pp. of* RIDE —*adj.* dominated: used in compounds *[fear-ridden]*

**rid·dle**[1] (rid′′l) *n.* ⟦OE *rædels*⟧ 1 a puzzling question, etc. requiring some ingenuity to answer 2 any puzzling person or thing

**rid·dle**[2] (rid′′l) *vt.* **-dled, -dling** ⟦< OE *hriddel*, a sieve⟧ 1 to make many holes in 2 to affect every part of *[riddled* with errors*]*

**ride** (rīd) *vi.* **rode, rid′den, rid′ing** ⟦OE *ridan*⟧ 1 to be carried along by a horse, in a vehicle, etc. 2 to be supported in motion (*on* or *upon*) *[tanks ride* on treads*]* 3 to admit of being ridden *[the car rides* smoothly*]* 4 to move or float on water 5 [Inf.] to continue undisturbed *[let the matter ride]* —*vt.* 1 to sit on or in and control so as to move along 2 to move over, along, or through (a road, area, etc.) by horse, car, etc. 3 to control, dominate, etc. *[ridden* by doubts*]* 4 [Inf.] to tease with ridicule, etc. —*n.* 1 a riding 2 a thing to ride at an amusement park

**rid′er** *n.* 1 one who rides 2 an addition or amendment to a document

**rid′er·ship′** *n.* the passengers of a particular transportation system

**ridge** (rij) *n.* ⟦< OE *hrycg*, animal's spine⟧ 1 the long, narrow crest of something 2 a long, narrow elevation of land 3 any raised narrow strip 4 the horizontal line formed by the meeting of two sloping surfaces —*vt., vi.* **ridged, ridg'ing** to mark or be marked with, or form into, ridges

**ridge'pole'** *n.* the horizontal beam at the ridge of a roof, to which the rafters are attached

**rid·i·cule** (rid'i kyōōl') *n.* [< L *ridere,* to laugh] **1** the act of making someone the object of scornful laughter **2** words or actions intended to produce such laughter —*vt.* **-culed', -cul'ing** to make fun of; deride; mock

**ri·dic·u·lous** (ri dik'yə ləs) *adj.* deserving ridicule —**ri·dic'u·lous·ly** *adv.* —**ri·dic'u·lous·ness** *n.*

**rife** (rīf) *adj.* [OE *ryfe*] **1** widespread **2** abounding *[rife* with error]

**riff** (rif) *n.* [prob. altered < REFRAIN²] *Jazz* a constantly repeated musical phrase —*vi. Jazz* to perform a riff

**rif·fle** (rif'əl) *n.* [< ?] **1** a ripple in a stream, produced by a reef, etc. **2** a certain way of shuffling cards —*vt., vi.* **-fled, -fling** to shuffle (playing cards) by letting a divided deck fall together as the corners are slipped through one's thumbs

**riff·raff** (rif'raf') *n.* [< OFr] those people regarded as worthless, disreputable, etc.

**ri·fle¹** (rī'fəl) *vt.* **-fled, -fling** [Fr *rifler,* to scrape] to cut spiral grooves within (a gun barrel, etc.) — *n.* a gun, fired from the shoulder, with a rifled barrel to spin the bullet for greater accuracy

**ri·fle²** (rī'fəl) *vt.* **-fled, -fling** [< OFr *rifler*] to ransack and rob —**ri'fler** *n.*

**ri·fle·man** (-mən) *n., pl.* **-men** (-mən) a soldier armed with a rifle

**ri·fling** (rī'fliŋ) *n.* spiral grooves cut within a gun barrel to make the projectile spin

**rift** (rift) *n.* [< Dan, fissure] an opening caused by splitting; cleft —*vt., vi.* to burst open; split

**rig** (rig) *vt.* **rigged, rig'ging** [< Scand] **1** to fit (a ship, mast, etc.) with (sails, shrouds, etc.) **2** to assemble **3** to equip **4** to arrange dishonestly **5** [Inf.] to dress: with *out* —*n.* **1** the way sails, etc. are rigged **2** equipment; gear **3** oil-drilling equipment **4** a tractor-trailer

**rig·a·ma·role** (rig'ə mə rōl') *n. var. of* RIGMAROLE

**rig'ging** *n.* the ropes, chains, etc. for a vessel's masts, sails, etc.

**right** (rīt) *adj.* [< OE *riht,* straight] **1** with a straight line or plane perpendicular to a base *[a right* angle] **2** upright; virtuous **3** correct **4** fitting; suitable **5** designating the side or surface meant to be seen **6** mentally or physically sound **7** *a)* designating or of that side of the body toward the east when one faces north *b)* designating or of the corresponding side of anything *c)* closer to the right side of one who is facing the thing mentioned —*n.* **1** what is right, just, etc. **2** power, privilege, etc. belonging to one by law, nature, etc. **3** the right side **4** the right hand **5** *[often* R-] *Politics* a conservative or reactionary position, party, etc.: often with *the* —*adv.* **1** straight; directly *[go right* home] **2** properly; fittingly **3** completely **4** exactly *[right* here] **5** according to law, justice, etc. **6** correctly **7** on or toward the right side **8** very: in certain titles *[the right* reverend] —*interj.* agreed! OK! —*vt.* **1** to put upright **2** to correct **3** to put in order —**right away** (or **off**) at once —**right on!** [Slang] that's right! —**right'ly** *adv.* —**right'ness** *n.*

**right'a·bout'-face'** *n.* ABOUT-FACE

**right angle** an angle of 90 degrees

**right·eous** (rī'chəs) *adj.* **1** acting in a just, upright manner; virtuous **2** morally right or justifiable —**right'eous·ly** *adv.* —**right'eous·ness** *n.*

**right'ful** *adj.* **1** fair and just; right **2** having a lawful claim —**right'ful·ly** *adv.* —**right'ful·ness** *n.*

**right'-hand'** *adj.* **1** on or toward the right **2** of, for, or with the right hand **3** most helpful or reliable *[a right-hand* man]

**right'-hand'ed** *adj.* **1** using the right hand more skillfully than the left **2** done with or made for use with the right hand —*adv.* **1** with the right

hand **2** in such a way that the bat, club, etc. swings leftward —**right'-hand'ed·ness** *n.*

**right'ist** *n., adj.* conservative or reactionary

**right'-mind'ed** *adj.* having sound principles

**right of way 1** the right to move first at intersections **2** land over which a road, power line, etc. passes **3** right of passage, as over another's property Also **right'-of-way'**

**right'-to-life'** *adj.* designating any movement, party, etc. opposed to abortion —**right'-to-lif'er** *n.*

**right triangle** a triangle with a right angle

**right wing** the more conservative or reactionary section of a political party or group —**right'-wing'** *adj.* —**right'-wing'er** *n.*

**rig·id** (rij'id) *adj.* [< L *rigere,* be stiff] **1** not bending or flexible; stiff **2** not moving; fixed **3** severe; strict **4** having a rigid framework: said of a dirigible —**ri·gid·i·ty** (ri jid'ə tē) or **rig'id·ness** *n.* — **rig'id·ly** *adv.*

**rig·ma·role** (rig'mə rōl') *n.* [< ME *rageman rolle,* long list] **1** nonsense **2** a foolishly complicated procedure

**rig·or** (rig'ər) *n.* [< L *rigere:* see RIGID] **1** severity; strictness **2** hardship Brit. sp. **rig'our** —**rig'or·ous** *adj.* —**rig'or·ous·ly** *adv.*

**rigor mor·tis** (môr'tis) [L, stiffness of death] the stiffening of the muscles after death

**rile** (rīl) *vt.* **riled, ril'ing** [var. of ROIL] [Inf. or Dial.] to anger; irritate

**rill** (ril) *n.* [< Du *ril*] a rivulet

**rim** (rim) *n.* [OE *rima*] **1** an edge, border, or margin, esp. of something circular **2** the outer part of a wheel —*vt.* **rimmed, rim'ming** to put a rim or rims on or around —**rim'less** *adj.*

**rime¹** (rīm) *n., vi., vt.* **rimed, rim'ing** RHYME

**rime²** (rīm) *n.* [OE *hrim*] FROST (sense 2)

**rind** (rīnd) *n.* [OE] a hard outer layer or covering

**ring¹** (riŋ) *vi.* **rang** or [Now Chiefly Dial.] **rung, rung, ring'ing** [OE *hringan*] **1** to give forth a resonant sound, as a bell **2** to seem *[to ring* true] **3** to sound a bell, esp. as a summons **4** to resound *[to ring* with laughter] **5** to have a ringing sensation, as the ears —*vt.* **1** to cause (a bell, etc.) to ring **2** to signal, announce, etc., as by ringing **3** to call by telephone —*n.* **1** the sound of a bell **2** a characteristic quality *[the ring* of truth] **3** the act of ringing a bell **4** a telephone call —**ring a bell** to stir up a memory

**ring²** (riŋ) *n.* [OE *hring*] **1** an ornamental circular band worn on a finger **2** any similar band *[a key ring]* **3** a circular line, mark, figure, or course **4** a group of people or things in a circle **5** a group working to advance its own interests, esp. by dishonest means **6** an enclosed area for contests, exhibitions, etc. *[a circus ring]* **7** prizefighting: with *the* —*vt.* **ringed, ring'ing 1** to encircle **2** to form into a ring —**run rings around 1** to run much faster than **2** to do much better than

**ring'er¹** *n.* a horseshoe, etc. thrown so that it encircles the peg

**ring'er²** *n.* **1** one that rings a bell, etc. **2** [Slang] *a)* a person or thing closely resembling another *b)* a fraudulent substitute in a competition

**ring'lead'er** *n.* one who leads others, esp. in unlawful acts, etc.

**ring'let** (-lit) *n.* a long curl of hair

**ring'mas'ter** *n.* a person who directs the performances in a circus ring

**ring'side'** *n.* **1** the place just outside a boxing or circus ring **2** any place providing a close view

**ring'worm'** *n.* a contagious skin disease caused by a fungus

**rink** (riŋk) *n.* [< OFr *renc,* a rank] **1** an expanse of ice for skating **2** a smooth floor for roller-skating

**rinse** (rins) *vt.* **rinsed, rins'ing** [ult. < L *recens,* fresh] **1** to wash or flush lightly **2** to remove soap, etc. from with clear water —*n.* **1** a rinsing or the liquid used **2** a solution used to rinse or tint hair

**Ri·o de Ja·nei·ro** (rē'ō dā' zhə ner'ō) city & seaport in SE Brazil: pop. 5,093,000

**Ri·o Gran·de** (rē′ō grand′, -gran′dē) river flowing from S Colorado into the Gulf of Mexico: the S border of Texas

**ri·ot** (rī′ət) *n.* [< OFr *riote*, dispute] **1** wild or violent disorder, confusion, etc.; esp., a violent public disturbance **2** a brilliant display **3** [Inf.] something very funny —*vi.* to take part in a riot —**read the riot act** to command to stop by threatening punishment —**run riot 1** to act wildly **2** to grow wild in abundance —**ri′ot·er** *n.* —**ri′ot·ous** *adj.*

**rip** (rip) *vt.* **ripped, rip′ping** [ME *rippen*] **1** *a*) to cut or tear apart roughly *b*) to remove in this way (with *off, out,* etc.) *c*) to sever the threads of (a seam) **2** to saw (wood) along the grain —*vi.* **1** to become ripped **2** [Inf.] to rush; speed —*n.* a ripped place —**rip into** [Inf.] to attack, esp. verbally —**rip off** [Slang] **1** to steal **2** to cheat or exploit —**rip′per** *n.*

**R.I.P.** or **RIP** *abbrev.* may he (she) rest in peace

**rip cord** a cord, etc. pulled to open a parachute during descent

**ripe** (rīp) *adj.* [OE] **1** ready to be harvested, as grain or fruit **2** of sufficient age, etc. to be used [*ripe* cheese] **3** fully developed; mature **4** fully prepared; ready [*ripe* for action] —**ripe′ly** *adv.* —**ripe′ness** *n.*

**rip·en** (rī′pən) *vi., vt.* to become or make ripe; mature, age, etc.

**rip′-off′** *n.* [Slang] the act or an instance of stealing, cheating, etc.

**ri·poste** or **ri·post** (ri pōst′) *n.* [Fr < L *respondere,* to answer] a sharp, swift response; retort

**rip·ple** (rip′əl) *vi., vt.* **-pled, -pling** [prob. < RIP] to have or form little waves on the surface (of) —*n.* **1** a small wave **2** a rippling

**ripple effect** the spreading effects caused by a single event

**rip′-roar′ing** (-rôr′iŋ) *adj.* [Slang] boisterous; uproarious

**rip′saw′** *n.* a saw with coarse teeth, for cutting wood along the grain

**rip′tide′** *n.* a current opposing other currents, esp. along a seashore: also **rip tide**

**rise** (rīz) *vi.* **rose, ris·en** (riz′ən), **ris′ing** [< OE *risan*] **1** to stand or sit up after sitting, kneeling, or lying **2** to rebel; revolt **3** to go up; ascend **4** to appear above the horizon, as the sun **5** to attain a higher level, rank, etc. **6** to extend, slant, or move upward **7** to increase in amount, degree, etc. **8** to expand and swell, as dough with yeast **9** to originate; begin **10** *Theol.* to return to life —*n.* **1** upward movement; ascent **2** an advance in status, rank, etc. **3** a slope upward **4** an increase in degree, amount, etc. **5** beginning; origin —**give rise to** to bring about

**ris′er** *n.* **1** one that rises **2** a vertical piece between the steps in a stairway

**ris·i·ble** (riz′ə bəl) *adj.* [< L *ridere,* to laugh] causing laughter; funny —**ris′i·bil′i·ty,** *pl.* **-ties,** *n.*

**ris′ing** *n.* an uprising; revolt

**risk** (risk) *n.* [< Fr < It *risco*] the chance of injury, damage, or loss —*vt.* **1** to expose to risk [to *risk* one's life] **2** to incur the risk of [to *risk* a war] —**risk′y, -i·er, -i·est,** *adj.*

**ris·qué** (ris kā′) *adj.* [Fr < *risquer,* to risk] very close to being improper or indecent; suggestive

**Rit·a·lin** (rit′′l in) *trademark for* a stimulant drug used to treat depression, hyperactivity, etc.

**rite** (rīt) *n.* [L *ritus*] a ceremonial, solemn act, as in religious use

**rite of passage** a significant event, ceremony, etc. in a person's life

**rit·u·al** (rich′ōō əl) *adj.* of, like, or done as a rite —*n.* a set form or system of rites, religious or otherwise —**rit′u·al·ism′** *n.* —**rit′u·al·ly** *adv.*

**ri·val** (rī′vəl) *n.* [< L *rivalis*] one who tries to get or do the same thing as another, or to equal or surpass another; competitor —*adj.* acting as a rival; competing —*vt.* **-valed** or **-valled, -val·ing** or **-val·ling 1** to try to equal or surpass **2** to equal in some way —**ri′val·rous** *adj.* —**ri′val·ry,** *pl.* **-ries,** *n.*

**riv·en** (riv′ən) *adj.* torn apart or split

**riv·er** (riv′ər) *n.* [< L *ripa,* a bank] a natural stream of water flowing into an ocean, a lake, etc.

**river basin** the area drained by a river and its tributaries

**riv′er·side′** *n.* the bank of a river

**Riv·er·side** (riv′ər sīd′) city in S California: pop. 227,000

**riv·et** (riv′it) *n.* [Fr < *river,* to clinch] a metal bolt with a head and a plain end that is flattened after the bolt is passed through parts to be held together — *vt.* to fasten with or as with rivets —**riv′et·er** *n.*

**Riv·i·er·a** (riv′ē er′ə) strip of the Mediterranean coast of SE France & NW Italy: a resort area

**riv·u·let** (riv′yōō lit) *n.* [< L *rivus,* brook] a little stream

**rm** *abbrev.* **1** ream **2** room

**Rn** *Chem. symbol for* radon

**RN** *abbrev.* Registered Nurse

**RNA** *n.* [r(ibo)n(ucleic) a(cid)] an essential component of all living matter: one form carries genetic information

**roach**[1] (rōch) *n. short for* COCKROACH

**roach**[2] (rōch) *n., pl.* **roach** or **roach′es** [< OFr *roche*] a freshwater fish of the carp family

**road** (rōd) *n.* [OE *rad,* a ride] **1** a way made for traveling; highway **2** a way; course [the *road* to fortune] **3** [often *pl.*] a place near shore where ships can ride at anchor —**on the road** traveling, as by a salesman or a touring troupe of actors

**road′bed′** *n.* the foundation laid for railroad tracks, a highway, etc.

**road′block′** *n.* **1** a blockade set up in a road as to prevent movement of vehicles **2** any hindrance

**road′kill′** *n.* [Slang] the body of an animal killed by a passing vehicle

**road rage** angry or violent behavior by motorists, as caused by stress in traffic

**road′run′ner** *n.* a long-tailed, swift-running desert bird of the SW U.S. and N Mexico: also **road runner**

**road′show′** *n.* a touring theatrical show

**road′side′** *n.* the side of a road —*adj.* on or at the side of a road

**road′way′** *n.* a road; specif., the part of a road used by vehicles

**road′work′** *n.* distance running or jogging as an exercise, esp. by a boxer

**roam** (rōm) *vi., vt.* [ME *romen*] to wander aimlessly (over or through) —**roam′er** *n.*

**roan** (rōn) *adj.* [< OSp *roano*] bay, black, etc. thickly sprinkled with white —*n.* a roan horse

**roar** (rôr) *vi.* [OE *rarian*] **1** to make a loud, deep, rumbling sound **2** to laugh boisterously —*vt.* to say loudly —*n.* a loud, deep, rumbling sound

**roast** (rōst) *vt.* [< OFr *rostir*] **1** to cook (meat, etc.) with little or no moisture, as in an oven or over an open fire **2** to process (coffee, etc.) by exposure to heat **3** to expose to great heat **4** [Inf.] to criticize severely —*vi.* **1** to undergo roasting **2** to be or become very hot —*n.* **1** roasted meat **2** a cut of meat for roasting **3** a picnic at which food is roasted —*adj.* roasted [*roast* pork] —**roast′er** *n.*

**rob** (räb) *vt.* **robbed, rob′bing** [< OFr *rober*] **1** to take money, etc. from unlawfully by force; steal from **2** to deprive of something unjustly or injuriously —*vi.* to be one who robs —**rob′ber** *n.* —**rob′ber·y,** *pl.* **-ies,** *n.*

**robe** (rōb) *n.* [< OFr] **1** a long, loose outer garment **2** such a garment worn to show rank or office, as by a judge **3** a bathrobe or dressing gown **4** a covering or wrap [a lap *robe*] —*vt., vi.* **robed, rob′ing** to dress in a robe

RIVET    RIVET HOLDING
STEEL BEAMS
TOGETHER

**rob·in** (räʹbən) *n.* [< OFr dim. of *Robert*] a North American thrush with a dull-red breast

**Robin Hood** *Eng. Legend* the leader of a band of outlaws who robs the rich to help the poor

**Ro·bin·son Cru·soe** (räʹbən sən krōōʹsō) the title hero of Defoe's novel (1719) about a shipwrecked sailor

**ro·bot** (rōʹbät) *n.* [< Czech < OSlav *rabu*, servant] **1** a mechanical device operating automatically, in a seemingly human way **2** a person acting like a robot

**ro·bot·ics** *n.* the science or technology of robots, their design, use, etc.

**ro·bust** (rō bustʹ, rōʹbust) *adj.* [< L *robur*, oak] strong and healthy —**ro·bustʹly** *adv.* —**ro·bustʹness** *n.*

**Roch·es·ter** (rächʹəs tər) city in W New York: pop. 230,000

**rock**¹ (räk) *n.* [< ML *rocca*] **1** a large mass of stone **2** broken pieces of stone **3** mineral matter formed in masses in the earth's crust **4** anything like a rock; esp., a firm support —**on the rocks** [Inf.] **1** in trouble or near ruin **2** served over ice cubes: said of liquor, etc.

**rock**² (räk) *vt., vi.* [OE *roccian*] **1** to move back and forth or from side to side **2** to sway strongly; shake —*n.* **1** a rocking motion **2** ROCK-AND-ROLL

**rock·a·bil·ly** (-ə bilʹē) *n.* [ROCK(-AND-ROLL) + -*a*- + (HILL)BILLY] an early form of rock-and-roll with a strong country music influence

**rock·and-roll** *n.* a form of popular music that evolved from rhythm and blues, characterized by a strong rhythm with an accent on the offbeat

**rock bottom** the lowest level

**rockʹbound** *adj.* surrounded or covered by rocks

**rock candy** large, hard, clear crystals of sugar formed on a string

**rockʹer** *n.* **1** either of the curved pieces on which a cradle, etc. rocks **2** a chair mounted on such pieces: also **rocking chair**

**rocker panel** any panel section below the doors of an automotive vehicle

**rock·et** (räkʹit) *n.* [It *rocchetta*, spool] any device driven forward by gases escaping through a rear vent, as a firework, a projectile weapon, or the propulsion mechanism of a spacecraft —*vi.* to move in or like a rocket; soar

**rock·et·ry** (-ə trē) *n.* the science of building and launching rockets

**rock garden** a garden of flowers, etc. in ground studded with rocks

**rocking horse** a toy horse on rockers or springs, for a child to ride

**rock lobster** SPINY LOBSTER

**rockʹ-ribbed** *adj.* **1** having rocky ridges **2** firm; unyielding

**rock salt** common salt in rocklike masses

**rock wool** a fibrous material made from molten rock, used for insulation

**rock·y**¹ (räkʹē) *adj.* -i·er, -i·est **1** full of rocks **2** consisting of rock **3** like a rock; firm, hard, etc. —**rockʹi·ness** *n.*

**rock·y**² (räkʹē) *adj.* -i·er, -i·est inclined to rock; unsteady —**rockʹi·ness** *n.*

**Rocky Mountains** mountain system in W North America, extending from New Mexico to N Alaska: also **Rockʹies**

**Rocky Mountain sheep** BIGHORN

**ro·co·co** (rə kōʹkō) *n.* [Fr < *rocaille*, shell work] [*occas.* R-] a style of architecture, art, music, etc. marked by profuse and delicate ornamentation, etc. —*adj.* **1** of or in rococo **2** too elaborate

**rod** (räd) *n.* [< OE *rodd*, straight shoot or stem] **1** a straight stick or bar **2** a stick for beating as punishment **3** a staff carried as a symbol of office; scepter **4** a pole for fishing **5** a measure of length equal to 5½ yards **6** [Slang] a pistol

**rode** (rōd) *vi., vt. pt. & archaic pp.* of RIDE

**ro·dent** (rōdʹ'nt) *n.* [< L *rodere*, gnaw] any of an order of gnawing mammals, as rats or mice

**ro·de·o** (rōʹdē ō′) *n., pl.* -os′ [Sp < L *rotare*, to turn] a public exhibition of the skills of cowboys, with contests in bull riding, lassoing, etc.

**Ro·din** (rô dan′), (François) Au·guste (René) (ô güst′) 1840-1917; Fr. sculptor

**roe**¹ (rō) *n.* [ME *rowe*] fish eggs

**roe**² (rō) *n., pl.* roe or roes [< OE *ra*] a small, agile deer of Europe and Asia

**roeʹbuck** *n.* the male roe deer

**roent·gen** (rentʹgən) *n.* [after W. K. *Roentgen* (1845-1923), Ger physicist] the unit for measuring the radiation of X-rays or gamma rays

**Rog·er** (räʹjər) *interj.* [< name of signal flag for *R*] [*also* r-] **1** received **2** [Inf.] right! OK!

**rogue** (rōg) *n.* [< ?] **1** a scoundrel **2** a mischievous person —**ro·guer·y** (rōʹgər ē), *pl.* -ies, *n.* —**ro·guish** (rōʹgish) *adj.*

**rogues' gallery** a police collection of photographs of criminals

**roil** (roil) *vt.* [< L *robigo*, rust] **1** to make (a liquid) cloudy, muddy, etc. by stirring up sediment **2** to vex

**roist·er** (roisʹtər) *vi.* [see RUSTIC] to revel noisily —**roistʹer·er** *n.*

**role** (rōl) *n.* [Fr] **1** the part played by an actor **2** a function assumed by someone [an advisory *role*] Often **rôle**

**role model** a person so effective or inspiring as to be a model for others

**roleʹ-play·ing** *n. Psychol.* a technique in which participants assume and act out roles so as to practice appropriate behavior, etc.

**roll** (rōl) *vi.* [< L *rota*, a wheel] **1** to move by turning around or over and over **2** to move on wheels **3** to pass [the years *roll* by] **4** to extend in gentle swells **5** to make a loud rising and falling sound [thunder *rolls*] **6** to rock from side to side —*vt.* **1** to make move by turning around or over and over **2** to make move on wheels **3** to utter with full, flowing sound **4** to pronounce with a trill [to *roll* one's r's] **5** to give a swaying motion to **6** to move around or from side to side [to *roll* one's eyes] **7** to make into a ball or cylinder [*roll* up the rug] **8** to flatten or spread with a roller, etc. —*n.* **1** a rolling **2** a scroll **3** a list of names **4** something rolled into a cylinder **5** a small portion of bread, etc. **6** a swaying motion **7** a loud, reverberating sound, as of thunder **8** a slight swell on a surface —**on a roll** [Slang] at a high point —**roll back** to reduce (prices) to a previous level —**strike off** (or **from**) **the rolls** to expel from membership

**rollʹback** *n.* a rolling back, esp. of prices to a previous level

**roll call** the reading aloud of a roll to find out who is absent

**roll·er** (rōlʹər) *n.* **1** one that rolls **2** a cylinder of metal, wood, etc. on which something is rolled, or one used to crush, smooth, or spread something

**roller bearing** a bearing in which the shaft turns with rollers in a circular track

**Rollʹer·blade′** *trademark for* a kind of IN-LINE SKATE —*n.* [r-] any IN-LINE SKATE —**rollʹer·blad′ing** *n.*

**roller coaster** an amusement ride in which small open cars move on tracks that dip and curve sharply

**roller skate** SKATE¹ (sense 2) —**rollʹer-skate′, -skat′ed, -skat′ing,** *vi.* —**roller skater**

**rol·lick** (rälʹik) *vi.* [< ? FROLIC] to play or behave in a lively, carefree way —**rolʹlick·ing** *adj.*

**rolling pin** a smooth, heavy cylinder of wood, etc. used to roll out dough

**rollʹ-top** *adj.* having a sliding, flexible top of parallel slats [a *roll-top* desk]

**Ro·lo·dex** (rōʹlə deks′) *trademark for* a kind of desktop file holding cards containing names and addresses for ready reference

**ro·ly-po·ly** (rō'lē pō'lē) *adj.* [< ROLL] short and plump; pudgy

**ROM** (räm) *n.* [r(ead-)o(nly) m(emory)] computer memory whose contents can be read but not altered; also, a memory chip like this

**Rom** *abbrev.* Roman

**ro·maine** (rō mān') *n.* [Fr., ult. < L *Romanus*, Roman] a type of lettuce with long leaves forming a slender head

**Ro·man** (rō'mən) *adj.* **1** of or characteristic of ancient or modern Rome or its people, etc. **2** of the Roman Catholic Church **3** [*usually* **r-**] designating or of the usual upright style of printing types; not italic —*n.* **1** a person born or living in ancient or modern Rome **2** [*usually* **r-**] roman type or characters

**Roman candle** a firework consisting of a tube that sends out balls of fire, etc.

**Roman Catholic 1** of the Christian church (**Roman Catholic Church**) headed by the pope **2** a member of this church

**ro·mance** (rō mans', rō'mans') *adj.* [ult. < L *Romanicus*, Roman] [R-] designating or of any of the languages derived from Vulgar Latin, as Italian, Spanish, or French —*n.* **1** a long poem or tale, orig. written in a Romance dialect, about the adventures of knights **2** a novel of love, adventure, etc. **3** excitement, love, etc. of the kind found in such literature **4** a love affair —*vt.* **-manced', -manc'ing** to make love to; woo

**Roman Empire** empire of the ancient Romans (27 B.C.-A.D. 395), including W & S Europe, N Africa, & SW Asia

**Ro·ma·ni·a** (rō mā'nē ə) country in SE Europe: 91,699 sq. mi.; pop. 22,760,000 —**Ro·ma'ni·an** *adj., n.*

**Roman numerals** Roman letters used as numerals: I = 1, V = 5, X = 10, L = 50, C = 100, D = 500, and M = 1,000

**ro·man·tic** (rō man'tik) *adj.* **1** of, like, or characterized by romance **2** fanciful or fictitious **3** not practical; visionary **4** full of thoughts, feelings, etc. of romance **5** suited for romance **6** [*often* **R-**] of a 19th-c. cultural movement characterized by freedom of form and spirit, emphasis on feeling and originality, etc. —*n.* a romantic person —**ro·man'ti·cal·ly** *adv.* —**ro·man'ti·cism'** (-tə siz'əm) *n.*

**ro·man'ti·cize'** (-tə sīz') *vt.* **-cized', -ciz'ing** to treat or regard romantically —*vi.* to have romantic ideas, etc.

**Rom·a·ny** (räm'ə nē, rō'mə-) *n.* the language of the Gypsies

**Rome** (rōm) capital of Italy &, formerly, of the Roman Empire: pop. 2,605,000

**Ro·me·o** (rō'mē ō') *n.* the hero of Shakespeare's *Romeo and Juliet* (c. 1595)

**romp** (rämp) *n.* [prob. < OFr *ramper*, to climb] boisterous, lively play —*vi.* to play in a boisterous, lively way

**romp'er** *n.* **1** one who romps **2** [*pl.*] a loose, one-piece outer garment with pants like bloomers, for a small child

**Rom·u·lus** (räm'yoo ləs) *n. Rom. Myth.* founder and first king of Rome: he and his twin brother Remus are suckled by a female wolf

**rood** (rood) *n.* [OE *rod*] **1** a crucifix **2** [Brit.] an old unit of area equal to ¼ acre

**roof** (roof, roof) *n., pl.* **roofs** [OE *hrof*] **1** the outside top covering of a building **2** anything like this in position or use [the *roof* of the mouth] —*vt.* to cover with or as with a roof —**roof'less** *adj.*

**roof'er** *n.* a roof maker or repairer

**roof'ing** *n.* material for roofs

**roof'top'** *n.* the roof of a building

**rook**[1] (rook) *n.* [OE *hroc*] a European crow —*vt., vi.* to swindle; cheat

**rook**[2] (rook) *n.* [< Pers *rukh*] a chess piece that can move horizontally or vertically

**rook'er·y** *n., pl.* **-ies** a breeding place of rooks, or of seals, penguins, etc.

**rook·ie** (rook'ē) *n.* [Slang] **1** an inexperienced army recruit **2** [Inf.] any beginner

**room** (room, room) *n.* [OE *rum*] **1** space to contain something **2** suitable scope [*room* for doubt] **3** an interior space enclosed or set apart by walls **4** [*pl.*] living quarters **5** the people in a room —*vi., vt.* to have or provide with lodgings —**room'ful'** *n.* —**room'y, -i·er, -i·est,** *adj.* —**room'i·ness** *n.*

**room and board** lodging and meals

**room'er** *n.* one who rents a room or rooms to live in; lodger

**room·ette** (room met') *n.* a small room in a railroad sleeping car

**rooming house** a house with furnished rooms for rent

**room'mate'** *n.* a person with whom one shares a room or rooms

**Roo·se·velt** (rō'zə velt') **1 Franklin Del·a·no** (del'ə nō') 1882-1945; 32d president of the U.S. (1933-45) **2 Theodore** 1858-1919; 26th president of the U.S. (1901-09)

**roost** (roost) *n.* [OE *hrost*] **1** a perch on which birds, esp. domestic fowls, can rest **2** a place with perches for birds **3** a place for resting, sleeping, etc. —*vi.* **1** to perch on a roost **2** to stay or settle down, as for the night

**roost'er** *n.* a male chicken

**root**[1] (root, root) *n.* [< ON *rot*] **1** the part of a plant, usually underground, that anchors the plant, draws water from the soil, etc. **2** the embedded part of a tooth, a hair, etc. **3** a source or cause **4** a supporting or essential part **5** a quantity that, multiplied by itself a specified number of times, produces a given quantity **6** the basic element of a word or form, without affixes or phonetic changes —*vi.* to take root —*vt.* **1** to fix the roots of in the ground **2** to establish; settle —**root up** (or **out**) to pull up by the roots; destroy completely —**take root 1** to begin growing by putting out roots **2** to become fixed, settled, etc.

**root**[2] (root, root) *vt.* [< OE *wrot*, snout] to dig (*up* or *out*) with or as with the snout —*vi.* **1** to search about; rummage **2** [Inf.] to encourage a team, etc.: usually with *for*

**root beer** a carbonated drink made or flavored with certain plant root extracts

**root canal 1** a tubular channel in a tooth's root **2** a treatment involving opening, cleaning, filling, etc. such a channel

**root'let** (-lit) *n.* a little root

**rope** (rōp) *n.* [OE *rap*] **1** a thick, strong cord made of strands of fiber, etc. twisted together **2** a ropelike string, as of pearls —*vt.* **roped, rop'ing 1** to fasten or tie with a rope **2** to mark off or enclose with a rope **3** to catch with a lasso —**know the ropes** [Inf.] to be well acquainted with a procedure, etc. —**rope in** [Slang] to entice or trick into doing something

**Roque·fort** (rōk'fərt) [after *Roquefort,* France, where made] *trademark for* a strong French cheese with a bluish mold

**Ror·schach test** (rôr'shäk') [after H. *Rorschach* (1884-1922), Swiss psychiatrist] *Psychol.* a personality test in which the subject's interpretations of standard inkblot designs are analyzed

**ro·sa·ry** (rō'zər ē) *n., pl.* **-ries** [ML *rosarium*] *R.C.Ch.* a string of groups of beads, used to keep count in saying prayers

**rose**[1] (rōz) *n.* [< L *rosa* < Gr *rhodon*] **1** a shrub with prickly stems and with flowers of red, pink, white, yellow, etc. **2** its flower **3** pinkish red or purplish red —*adj.* of this color

**rose**[2] (rōz) *vi. pt. of* RISE

**ro·sé** (rō zā') *n.* [Fr, pink] a pink wine, tinted by the grape skins early in fermentation

**ro·se·ate** (rō'zē it) *adj.* rose-colored

**rose'bud'** *n.* the bud of a rose

**rose'bush'** *n.* a shrub that bears roses

**rose'-col'ored** *adj.* **1** pinkish-red or purplish-red

**2** optimistic —**through rose-colored glasses** with optimism, esp. undue optimism

**rose·mar·y** (rōz′mer′ē) *n.* ⟦< L *ros marinus*, sea dew⟧ an evergreen herb of the mint family, with fragrant leaves used in perfumes, in cooking, etc.

**ro·sette** (rō zet′) *n.* an ornament or arrangement, as of ribbons, resembling a rose

**rose water** a preparation of water and attar of roses, used as a perfume

**rose window** a circular window with a roselike pattern of tracery

**rose′wood′** *n.* ⟦< its odor⟧ **1** a hard, reddish wood, used in furniture, etc. **2** a tropical tree yielding this wood

**Rosh Ha·sha·na** (rōsh′ hə shô′nə, -shä′-) the Jewish New Year

ROSE WINDOW

**ros·in** (räz′ən) *n.* ⟦see RESIN⟧ the hard resin left after the distillation of turpentine: it is rubbed on violin bows, used in making varnish, etc.

**ros·ter** (räs′tər) *n.* ⟦< Du *rooster*⟧ a list or roll, as of military personnel

**ros·trum** (räs′trəm) *n., pl.* **-trums** or **-tra** (-trə) ⟦L, beak⟧ a platform for public speaking

**ros·y** (rō′zē) *adj.* **-i·er, -i·est** ⟦ME⟧ **1** rose in color **2** bright, promising, etc. —**ros′i·ly** *adv.* —**ros′i·ness** *n.*

**rot** (rät) *vi., vt.* **rot′ted, rot′ting** ⟦OE *rotian*⟧ to decompose; decay —*n.* **1** a rotting or something rotten **2** a disease characterized by decay **3** [Slang] nonsense

**ro·ta·ry** (rōt′ər ē) *adj.* ⟦< L *rota*, wheel⟧ **1** turning around a central axis, as a wheel does **2** having rotating parts [a *rotary* press] —*n., pl.* **-ries 1** a rotary machine **2** TRAFFIC CIRCLE

**ro·tate** (rō′tāt′) *vi., vt.* **-tat·ed, -tat′ing** ⟦< L *rota*, wheel⟧ **1** to turn around an axis **2** to change or cause to change in regular succession —**ro·ta′tion** *n.* —**ro′ta′tor** *n.*

**ROTC** *abbrev.* Reserve Officers' Training Corps

**rote** (rōt) *n.* ⟦ME⟧ a fixed, mechanical way of doing something —**by rote** by memory alone, without thought

**rot·gut** (rät′gut′) *n.* [Slang] raw, low-grade whiskey or other liquor

**ro·tis·ser·ie** (rō tis′ər ē) *n.* ⟦Fr < earlier Fr *rostir*, to roast⟧ a grill with an electrically turned spit

**ro·to·gra·vure** (rōt′ə grə vyoor′) *n.* ⟦< L *rota*, wheel + Fr *gravure*, engraving⟧ a printing process using a rotary press with cylinders etched from photographic plates

**ro·tor** (rōt′ər) *n.* **1** the rotating part of a motor, etc. **2** a system of rotating airfoils, as on a helicopter

**ro·to·till·er** (rōt′ə til′ər) *n.* a motorized machine with rotary blades, for loosening the earth around growing plants —**ro′to·till′** *vt.*

**rot·ten** (rät′'n) *adj.* ⟦< ON *rotinn*⟧ **1** decayed; spoiled **2** foul-smelling **3** morally corrupt **4** unsound, as if decayed within **5** [Slang] very bad, unpleasant, etc. —**rot′ten·ness** *n.*

**Rot·ter·dam** (rät′ər dam′) seaport in SW Netherlands: pop. 599,000

**ro·tund** (rō tund′) *adj.* ⟦L *rotundus*⟧ plump or stout —**ro·tun′di·ty** or **ro·tund′ness** *n.*

**ro·tun·da** (rō tun′də) *n.* ⟦see prec.⟧ a round building, hall, or room, esp. one with a dome

**rou·é** (roo ā′) *n.* ⟦Fr < L *rota*, wheel⟧ a dissipated man; rake

**rouge** (roozh) *n.* ⟦Fr, red⟧ **1** a reddish cosmetic powder or paste for adding color to the cheeks **2** a reddish powder for polishing jewelry, etc. —*vt.* **rouged, roug′ing** to use cosmetic rouge on

**rough** (ruf) *adj.* ⟦OE *ruh*⟧ **1** not smooth or level; uneven **2** shaggy [a *rough* coat] **3** stormy [rough

weather] **4** disorderly [rough play] **5** harsh or coarse **6** lacking comforts and conveniences **7** not polished or finished; crude **8** approximate [a rough guess] **9** [Inf.] difficult [a rough time] —*n.* **1** rough ground, material, condition, etc. **2** Golf any part of the course with grass, etc. left uncut —*adv.* in a rough way —*vt.* **1** to roughen: often with *up* **2** to treat roughly: usually with *up* **3** to sketch, shape, etc. roughly: usually with *in* or *out* —**rough it** to live without customary comforts, etc. —**rough′ly** *adv.* —**rough′ness** *n.*

**rough′age** *n.* rough or coarse food or fodder

**rough′en** *vt., vi.* to make or become rough

**rough′-hew′** *vt.* **-hewed′** or **-hewn′, -hew′ing 1** to hew (timber, stone, etc.) roughly, or without smoothing **2** to form roughly Also **rough′hew′**

**rough′house′** [Inf.] *n.* rough, boisterous play, fighting, etc. —*vt., vi.* **-housed′, -hous′ing** to treat or act roughly or boisterously

**rough′neck′** *n.* **1** [Inf.] a rowdy **2** a worker on an oil rig —*vi.* to work as a roughneck

**rough′shod′** *adj.* shod with horseshoes having metal points —**ride roughshod over** to treat harshly and arrogantly

**rou·lette** (roo let′) *n.* ⟦Fr < L *rota*, wheel⟧ a gambling game played by tossing a small ball into a whirling shallow bowl (**roulette wheel**) with numbered, red or black compartments

**round** (round) *adj.* ⟦< L *rotundus*, rotund⟧ **1** shaped like a ball, circle, or cylinder **2** plump **3** full; complete [a *round* dozen] **4** expressed by a whole number or in tens, hundreds, etc. —*n.* **1** something round, as the rung of a ladder **2** the part of a beef animal between the rump and the leg **3** a series or succession [a *round* of parties] **4** [often pl.] a regular, customary circuit, as by a watchman **5** a single shot from a gun, or from several guns together; also, the ammunition for this **6** a single outburst, as of applause **7** a single period of action, as in boxing **8** a short song which one group begins singing when another reaches the second phrase, etc. —*vt.* **1** to make round **2** to express as a round number: with *off* **3** to finish: with *out* or *off* **4** to go around —*vi.* **1** to turn; reverse direction **2** to become plump: often with *out* —*adv.* **1** AROUND **2** through a recurring period of time [to work the year *round*] **3** for each of several **4** in a roundabout way — *prep.* AROUND —**in the round 1** in an arena theater **2** in full, rounded form: said of sculpture **3** in full detail —**round about** in or to the opposite direction —**round up** to collect in a herd, group, etc. —**round′ness** *n.*

**round′a·bout′** *adj.* indirect; circuitous

**roun·de·lay** (roun′də lā′) *n.* ⟦< OFr *rondel*, a short lyrical poem⟧ a simple song in which some phrase, line, etc. is continually repeated

**round′house′** *n.* a circular building for storing and repairing locomotives

**round′ly** *adv.* **1** in a round form **2** vigorously **3** fully; completely and thoroughly

**round′-shoul′dered** *adj.* having the shoulders bent forward

**round steak** a steak cut from a round of beef

**Round Table 1** in legend, the circular table around which King Arthur and his knights sit **2** [r- t-] a group gathered for an informal discussion

**round′-the-clock′** *adj., adv.* throughout the day and night; continuous(ly)

**round trip** a trip to a place and back again — **round′-trip′** *adj.*

**round′-trip′per** *n.* [Slang] *Baseball* a home run

**round′up′** *n.* **1** a driving together of cattle, etc. on the range, as for branding **2** any similar collecting **3** a summary, as of news

**round′worm′** *n.* NEMATODE

**rouse** (rouz) *vt., vi.* **roused, rous′ing** ⟦prob. < earlier Fr⟧ **1** to excite or become excited **2** to wake

**Rous·seau** (roo sō′), **Jean Jacques** (zhän zhäk′) 1712-78; Fr. philosopher & writer, born in Switzerland

**roust·a·bout** (rous′tə bout′) *n.* ⟦< ROUSE + ABOUT⟧ an unskilled or transient laborer, as on a wharf or in an oil field

**rout**[1] (rout) *n.* ⟦< L *rupta,* broken⟧ **1** a disorderly flight **2** an overwhelming defeat —*vt.* **1** to put to flight **2** to defeat overwhelmingly

**rout**[2] (rout) *vt.* ⟦< ROOT[2]⟧ to force out —**rout out 1** to gouge out **2** to make (a person) get out

**route** (rōōt, rout) *n.* ⟦< L *rupta (via),* (path) broken through⟧ a road or course for traveling; often, a regular course, as in delivering mail —*vt.* **rout′ed, rout′ing 1** to send by a certain route **2** to arrange the route for

**rou·tine** (rōō tēn′) *n.* ⟦see prec.⟧ a regular procedure, customary or prescribed —*adj.* like or using routine —**rou·tine′ly** *adv.*

**rou·tin′ize** (-tē′nīz) *vt.* **-ized, -iz·ing** to make routine; reduce to a routine —**rou·tin·i·za′tion** *n.*

**rove** (rōv) *vi., vt.* **roved, rov′ing** ⟦ME *roven*⟧ to roam —**rov′er** *n.*

**row**[1] (rō) *n.* ⟦OE *ræw*⟧ **1** a number of people or things in a line **2** a line of seats in a theater, etc. —**in a row** in succession; consecutively

**row**[2] (rō) *vt., vi.* ⟦OE *rowan*⟧ **1** to propel (a boat) with oars **2** to carry in a rowboat —*n.* a trip by rowboat

**row**[3] (rou) *n., vi.* ⟦< ? ROUSE⟧ quarrel or brawl

**row·boat** (rō′bōt′) *n.* a small boat made for rowing

**row·dy** (rou′dē) *n., pl.* **-dies** ⟦< ? ROW[3]⟧ a rough, quarrelsome, and disorderly person —*adj.* **-di·er, -di·est** rough, quarrelsome, etc. —**row′di·ness** *n.* —**row′dy·ism′** *n.*

**row·el** (rou′əl) *n.* ⟦ult. < L *rota,* wheel⟧ a small wheel with sharp points, at the end of a spur

**row house** (rō) any of a line of identical houses joined by common walls

**roy·al** (roi′əl) *adj.* ⟦< L *regalis*⟧ **1** of a king or queen **2** like, or fit for, a king or queen; magnificent, majestic, etc. **3** of a kingdom, its government, etc. —**roy′al·ly** *adv.*

**roy′al·ist** *n.* one who supports a monarch or a monarchy

**roy′al·ty** *n., pl.* **-ties 1** the rank or power of a king or queen **2** a royal person or persons **3** royal quality **4** a share of the proceeds from a patent, book, etc. paid to the owner, author, etc.

**rpm** *abbrev.* revolutions per minute

**rps** *abbrev.* revolutions per second

**RR 1** railroad **2** Rural Route: also **R.R.**

**RSV** *abbrev.* Revised Standard Version (of the Bible)

**R.S.V.P.** or **r.s.v.p.** *abbrev.* ⟦Fr, for *répondez s'il vous plaît*⟧ please reply: also **RSVP** or **rsvp**

**rte** *abbrev.* route

**rub** (rub) *vt.* **rubbed, rub′bing** ⟦ME *rubben*⟧ **1** to move (one's hand, a cloth, etc.) over (something) with pressure and friction **2** to apply (polish, etc.) in this way **3** to move (things) over each other with pressure and friction **4** to make sore by rubbing **5** to remove by rubbing (*out, off,* etc.) —*vi.* **1** to move with pressure and friction (*on,* etc.) **2** to rub something —*n.* **1** a rubbing **2** an obstacle, difficulty, or source of irritation —**rub down 1** to massage **2** to smooth, polish, etc. by rubbing — **rub elbows with** to associate or mingle with: also **rub shoulders with** —**rub it in** [Slang] to keep reminding someone of his or her mistake —**rub the wrong way** to annoy

**ru·ba·to** (rōō bät′ō) *adj., adv.* ⟦It, stolen⟧ *Music* intentionally and temporarily not in strict tempo

**rub·ber** (rub′ər) *n.* **1** one that rubs **2** ⟦< orig. use as an eraser⟧ an elastic substance made from the milky sap of various tropical plants or made synthetically **3** something made of this substance;

421                                                  ◄ **ruff**

specif., *a*) a low-cut overshoe *b*) [Slang] a condom —*adj.* made of rubber —**rub′ber·y** *adj.*

**rubber band** a narrow, continuous band of rubber as for holding small objects together

**rubber cement** an adhesive of unvulcanized rubber in a solvent that quickly evaporates when exposed to air

**rubber check** ⟦from the notion that it "bounces": see BOUNCE (*vi.* 3)⟧ [Slang] a check that is worthless because of insufficient funds in the writer's account

**rubber game** (rub′ər) ⟦< ?⟧ the deciding game in a series

**rub′ber·ize** (-īz′) *vt.* **-ized, -iz′ing** to coat or impregnate with rubber

**rub′ber·neck** *vi.* to look at things or gaze about in curiosity by stretching the neck or turning the head, as a sightseer might do

**rubber plant 1** any plant yielding latex **2** a house plant with large, glossy leaves

**rubber stamp 1** a stamp of rubber, inked for printing dates, signatures, etc. **2** [Inf.] *a*) a person, bureau, etc. that gives routine or automatic approval *b*) such approval —**rub′ber-stamp′** *vt.*

**rub·bish** (rub′ish) *n.* ⟦ME *robous*⟧ **1** any material thrown away as worthless; trash **2** nonsense

**rub·ble** (rub′əl) *n.* ⟦ME *robel*⟧ rough, broken pieces of stone, brick, etc.

**rub′down′** *n.* a brisk rubbing of the body, as in massage

**rube** (rōōb) *n.* ⟦< name *Reuben*⟧ [Slang] an unsophisticated rustic

**ru·bel·la** (rōō bel′ə) *n.* ⟦< L *ruber,* red⟧ an infectious disease causing small red spots on the skin; German measles

**Ru·bens** (rōō′bənz), **Peter Paul** 1577-1640; Fl. painter

**ru·bi·cund** (rōō′bə kund′) *adj.* ⟦< L *ruber,* red⟧ reddish; ruddy

**ru·ble** (rōō′bəl) *n.* ⟦Russ *rubl*⟧ the monetary unit of Russia, Belarus, & Tajikistan

**ru·bric** (rōō′brik) *n.* ⟦< L *ruber,* red⟧ **1** in early books, a section heading, letter, etc., often printed in red **2** any rule, explanatory comment, etc.

**ru·by** (rōō′bē) *n., pl.* **-bies** ⟦ult. < L *rubeus,* reddish⟧ **1** a clear, deep-red precious stone: a variety of corundum **2** deep red —*adj.* deep-red

**ruck·sack** (ruk′sak′, rōōk′-) *n.* ⟦Ger, back sack⟧ a kind of knapsack

**ruck·us** (ruk′əs) *n.* ⟦prob. merging of RUMPUS & *ruction,* uproar⟧ [Inf.] noisy confusion; disturbance

**rud·der** (rud′ər) *n.* ⟦OE *rother*⟧ a broad, flat, movable piece hinged to the rear of a ship or aircraft, used for steering —**rud′der·less** *adj.*

**rud·dy** (rud′ē) *adj.* **-di·er, -di·est** ⟦OE *rudig*⟧ **1** having a healthy red color **2** reddish —**rud′di·ness** *n.*

**rude** (rōōd) *adj.* **rud′er, rud′est** ⟦< L *rudis*⟧ **1** crude; rough **2** uncouth **3** discourteous **4** unskillful —**rude′ly** *adv.* —**rude′ness** *n.*

**ru·di·ment** (rōō′də mənt) *n.* ⟦see RUDE⟧ [*usually pl.*] **1** a first principle as of a subject to be learned **2** a first slight beginning of something —**ru·di·men′ta·ry** (-men′tər ē) *adj.*

**rue**[1] (rōō) *vt., vi.* **rued, ru′ing** ⟦OE *hreowan*⟧ **1** to feel remorse for (a sin, fault, etc.) **2** to regret (an act, etc.) —*n.* [Archaic] sorrow —**rue′ful** *adj.* — **rue′ful·ly** *adv.*

**rue**[2] (rōō) *n.* ⟦< Gr *rhytē*⟧ a strong-scented shrub with bitter leaves

**ruff** (ruf) *n.* ⟦< RUFFLE⟧ **1** a high, frilled starched collar of the 16th and 17th c. **2** a band of colored or protruding feathers or fur about an animal's neck

**ruf·fi·an** (ruf'ē ən) *n.* 〖< It *ruffiano,* a pimp〗 a rowdy or hoodlum

**ruf·fle** (ruf'əl) *vt.* **-fled, -fling** 〖< ON or LowG〗 **1** to disturb the smoothness of **2** to make (feathers, etc.) stand up **3** to disturb or annoy —*vi.* to become uneven —*n.* a strip of cloth, lace, etc.

RUFF

gathered along one edge, used as a trimming

**rug** (rug) *n.* 〖< Scand〗 a piece of thick fabric used as a floor covering

**rug·by** (rug'bē) *n.* 〖first played at *Rugby* School in England〗 a game from which American football developed

**rug·ged** (rug'id) *adj.* 〖ME〗 **1** uneven; rough **2** severe; harsh **3** not refined **4** strong; robust — **rug'ged·ly** *adv.* —**rug'ged·ness** *n.*

**Ruhr** (roor) **1** river in WC Germany, flowing into the Rhine **2** major coal-mining & industrial region along this river: also called **Ruhr Basin**

**ru·in** (rōo'ən) *n.* 〖< L *ruere,* to fall〗 **1** [*pl.*] the remains of something destroyed, decayed, etc. **2** anything destroyed, etc. **3** downfall, destruction, etc. **4** anything causing this —*vt.* to bring to ruin; destroy, spoil, bankrupt, etc. —**ru'in·a'tion** *n.* —**ru'in·ous** *adj.*

**rule** (rōol) *n.* 〖< L *regere,* to rule〗 **1** an established regulation or guide for conduct, procedure, usage, etc. **2** custom **3** the customary course **4** government; reign **5** RULER (sense 2) —*vt., vi.* **ruled, rul'ing 1** to have an influence (over); guide **2** to govern **3** to determine officially **4** to mark lines (on) as with a ruler —**as a rule** usually —**rule out** to exclude

**rule of thumb** a practical, though imprecise or unscientific, method

**rul'er** *n.* **1** one who governs **2** a strip of wood, etc. with a straight edge, used in drawing lines, measuring length, etc.

**rul'ing** *adj.* that rules —*n.* an official decision, as of a court

**rum** (rum) *n.* 〖< ?〗 **1** an alcoholic liquor distilled from fermented sugar cane, etc. **2** any alcoholic liquor

**Ru·ma·ni·a** (rōo mā'nē ə) *var. of* ROMANIA —**Ru·ma'ni·an** *adj., n.*

**rum·ba** (room'bə, rum'-) *n.* 〖AmSp〗 a dance of Cuban origin, or music for it —*vi.* to dance the rumba

**rum·ble** (rum'bəl) *vi., vt.* **-bled, -bling** 〖ME *romblen*〗 **1** to make or cause to make a continuous deep, rolling sound **2** to move with such a sound —*n.* **1** a rumbling sound **2** [Slang] a fight between teenage gangs

**ru·mi·nant** (rōo'mə nənt) *adj.* 〖see RUMINATE〗 **1** of or belonging to the group of cud-chewing animals **2** meditative —*n.* any of a group of cud-chewing mammals, as cattle, deer, or camels, having a stomach with three or four chambers

**ru'mi·nate'** (-nāt') *vi.* **-nat'ed, -nat'ing** 〖< L *ruminare*〗 **1** to chew a cud **2** to meditate — **ru'mi·na'tion** *n.*

**rum·mage** (rum'ij) *n.* 〖< Fr *rum,* ship's hold〗 **1** odds and ends **2** a rummaging —*vt., vi.* **-maged, -mag·ing** to search through (a place, etc.) thoroughly

**rummage sale** a sale of contributed miscellaneous articles, as for charity

**rum·my** (rum'ē) *n.* 〖< ?〗 a card game in which the object is to match cards into sets and sequences

**ru·mor** (rōo'mər) *n.* 〖L, noise〗 **1** general talk not based on definite knowledge **2** an unconfirmed report, story, etc. in general circulation —*vt.* to tell or spread by rumor Brit. sp. **ru'mour**

**rump** (rump) *n.* 〖< ON *rumpr*〗 **1** the hind part of an animal, where the legs and back join **2** the buttocks

**rum·ple** (rum'pəl) *n.* 〖< MDu *rompe*〗 an uneven crease; wrinkle —*vt., vi.* **-pled, -pling** to wrinkle; muss

**rum·pus** (rum'pəs) *n.* 〖< ?〗 [Inf.] an uproar or commotion

**run** (run) *vi.* **ran, run, run'ning** 〖< ON & OE〗 **1** to go by moving the legs faster than in walking **2** to go, move, etc. easily and freely **3** to flee **4** to make a quick trip (*up to, down to,* etc.) **5** to compete in a race, election, etc. **6** to ply between two points: said as of a train **7** to climb or creep, as a vine does **8** to ravel: said as of a stocking **9** to operate: said of a machine **10** to flow **11** to spread over cloth, etc. when moistened, as colors do **12** to discharge pus, etc. **13** to extend in time or space; continue **14** to pass into a specified condition, etc. [*to run* into trouble] **15** to be written, etc. in a specified way **16** to be at a specified size, price, etc. [eggs *run* high] —*vt.* **1** to follow (a specified course) **2** to perform as by running [*to run* a race] **3** to incur (a risk) **4** to get past [*to run* a blockade] **5** to cause to run, move, compete, etc. **6** to drive into a specified condition, place, etc. **7** to drive (an object) into or against something **8** to make flow in a specified way, place, etc. **9** to manage (a business, etc.) **10** to undergo (a fever, etc.) **11** to publish (a story, etc.) in a newspaper —*n.* **1** an act or period of running **2** the distance covered in running **3** a trip; journey **4** a route [a delivery *run*] **5** *a)* movement onward, progression, or trend [the *run* of events] *b)* a continuous period [a *run* of good luck] **6** a continuous course of performances, etc., as of a play **7** a continued series of demands, as on a bank **8** a brook **9** a kind or class; esp., the average kind **10** the output during a period of operation **11** an enclosed area for domestic animals **12** freedom to move about at will [the *run* of the house] **13** a large number of fish migrating together **14** a ravel, as in a stocking **15** *Baseball* a scoring point, made by a successful circuit of the bases — **in the long run** in the final outcome —**on the run** running or running away —**run across** to encounter by chance: also **run into** —**run down 1** to stop operating **2** to run against so as to knock down **3** to pursue and capture or kill **4** to speak of disparagingly —**run out** to come to an end; expire — **run out of** to use up —**run over 1** to ride over **2** to overflow **3** to examine, rehearse, etc. rapidly —**run through 1** to use up quickly or recklessly **2** to pierce —**run up 1** to raise, rise, or accumulate rapidly **2** to sew rapidly

**run'a·round'** *n.* [Inf.] a series of evasions

**run'a·way'** *n.* **1** a fugitive **2** a horse, etc. that runs away —*adj.* **1** escaping, fleeing, etc. **2** easily won: said as of a race **3** rising rapidly: said as of prices

**run'down'** *n.* a concise summary

**run'-down'** *adj.* **1** not wound and therefore not running, as a watch **2** in poor physical condition, as from overwork **3** fallen into disrepair

**rune** (rōon) *n.* 〖OE *run*〗 **1** any of the characters of an ancient Germanic alphabet **2** [*often pl.*] writing in these characters

**rung**[1] (run) *n.* 〖OE *hrung,* staff〗 a rod or bar forming a step of a ladder, a crosspiece on a chair, etc.

**rung**[2] (run) *vi., vt. pp. of* RING[1]

**run'-in'** *n.* [Inf.] a quarrel, fight, etc.

**run·nel** (run'əl) *n.* 〖OE *rynel*〗 a small stream

**run'ner** *n.* **1** *a)* one that runs, as a racer *b)* a messenger, etc. *c)* a smuggler **2** a long, narrow cloth or rug **3** a ravel, as in hosiery **4** a long, trailing stem, as of a strawberry **5** either of the long, narrow pieces on which a sled, etc. slides

**run'ner-up'** *n., pl.* **-ners-up'** a person or team that finishes second, etc. in a contest

**run'ning** *n.* the act of one that runs; racing, managing, etc. —*adj.* **1** that runs (in various senses)

**2** measured in a straight line **3** continuous *[a running* commentary*]* **4** current or concurrent —*adv.* in succession *[for five days running]* —**in** (or **out of**) **the running** having a (or no) chance to win

**running back** *Football* an offensive back, responsible primarily for rushing the ball

**running lights** the lights that a ship or aircraft must display at night

**running mate** the candidate for the lesser of two closely associated offices, as for the vice-presidency

**run'ny** *adj.* -ni·er, -ni·est **1** flowing, esp. too freely **2** discharging mucus *[a runny* nose*]*

**run'off'** *n.* **1** something that runs off, as rain that is not absorbed into the ground **2** a deciding, final contest

**run'-of-the-mill'** *adj.* ordinary; average

**runt** (runt) *n.* ⟦< ?⟧ **1** a stunted animal, plant, or (contemptuously) person **2** the smallest animal of a litter —**runt'y**, -i·er, -i·est, *adj.*

**run'-through'** *n.* a complete rehearsal, from beginning to end

**run'way'** *n.* a channel, track, etc. in, on, or along which something moves; esp., *a)* a strip of leveled ground for use by airplanes in taking off and landing *b)* a narrow platform extending from a stage into the audience

**ru·pee** (rōo′pē, rōo pē′) *n.* ⟦< Sans *rūpyah*, wrought silver⟧ the monetary unit of India, Nepal, Pakistan, Sri Lanka, etc.

**rup·ture** (rup′chər) *n.* ⟦< L *rumpere*, to break⟧ **1** a breaking apart or being broken apart; breach **2** a hernia —*vt.*, *vi.* -tured, -tur·ing to cause or suffer a rupture

**ru·ral** (roor′əl) *adj.* ⟦< L *rus*, the country⟧ of, like, or living in the country; rustic —**ru'ral·ism'** *n.*

**ruse** (rōoz) *n.* ⟦< OFr *reuser*, deceive⟧ a stratagem, trick, or artifice

**rush**[1] (rush) *vi.*, *vt.* ⟦< Fr *ruser*, repel⟧ **1** to move, push, drive, etc. swiftly or impetuously **2** to make a sudden attack (*on*) **3** to pass, go, send, act, do, etc. with unusual haste; hurry **4** *Football* to run with (the ball) on a running play —*n.* **1** a rushing **2** an eager movement of many people to get to a place **3** busyness; haste *[the rush* of modern life*]* **4** a press, as of business, necessitating unusual haste **5** [Slang] a sudden thrill, etc.

**rush**[2] (rush) *n.* ⟦OE *risc*⟧ a grasslike marsh plant with round stems used in making mats, etc.

**rush hour** a time of the day when business, traffic, etc. is heavy

**rusk** (rusk) *n.* ⟦Sp *rosca*, twisted bread roll⟧ **1** sweet, raised bread or cake toasted until browned and crisp **2** a piece of this

**Russ** *abbrev.* **1** Russia **2** Russian

**rus·set** (rus′it) *n.* ⟦< L *russus*, reddish⟧ **1** yellowish brown or reddish brown **2** a winter apple with a mottled skin

**Rus·sia** (rush′ə) **1** former empire (1547-1917) in E Europe & N Asia: in full **Russian Empire 2**

loosely, the UNION OF SOVIET SOCIALIST REPUBLICS **3** country in E Europe and N Asia, stretching from the Baltic Sea to the Pacific: formerly a republic of the U.S.S.R.: 6,592,844 sq. mi.; pop. 148,022,000

**Rus·sian** (rush′ən) *adj.* of Russia or its people, language, etc. —*n.* **1** a person born or living in Russia **2** the East Slavic language of the Russians

**rust** (rust) *n.* ⟦OE⟧ **1** the reddish-brown coating on iron or steel caused by oxidation during exposure to air and moisture **2** any stain resembling this **3** a reddish brown **4** a plant disease causing spotted stems and leaves —*vi.*, *vt.* **1** to form rust (on) **2** to deteriorate, as through disuse

**rus·tic** (rus′tik) *adj.* ⟦< L *rus*, the country⟧ **1** rural **2** simple or artless **3** rough or uncouth —*n.* a country person —**rus'ti·cal·ly** *adv.*

**rus·ti·cate** (rus′tə kāt′) *vi.*, *vt.* -cat′ed, -cat′ing **1** to go or send to live in the country **2** to become or make rustic —**rus'ti·ca'tion** *n.*

**rus·tle**[1] (rus′əl) *vi.*, *vt.* -tled, -tling ⟦ult. echoic⟧ to make or cause to make soft sounds, as of moving leaves, etc. —*n.* a series of such sounds

**rus·tle**[2] (rus′əl) [Inf.] *vi.*, *vt.* -tled, -tling ⟦< ?⟧ to steal (cattle, etc.) —**rustle up** to gather together —**rus'tler** *n.*

**rust'proof'** *vt.*, *adj.* (make) resistant to rust

**rust·y** (rus′tē) *adj.* -i·er, -i·est **1** coated with rust, as a metal **2** *a)* impaired by disuse, neglect, etc. *b)* having lost facility through lack of practice —**rust'i·ly** *adv.* —**rust'i·ness** *n.*

**rut**[1] (rut) *n.* ⟦< ? Fr *route*, route⟧ **1** a groove, track, etc., as made by wheels **2** a fixed, routine course of action, thought, etc. —*vt.* rut′ted, rut′ting to make ruts in —**rut'ty**, -ti·er, -ti·est, *adj.*

**rut**[2] (rut) *n.* ⟦< L *rugire*, to roar⟧ the periodic sexual excitement of certain male mammals —*vi.* rut′ted, rut′ting to be in rut —**rut'tish** *adj.*

**ru·ta·ba·ga** (rōot′ə bā′gə) *n.* ⟦Swed dial. *rotabagge*⟧ **1** a turniplike plant with a large, yellow root **2** this root

**Ruth**[1] (rōoth) *n.* *Bible* a woman devoted to her mother-in-law, for whom she left her own people

**Ruth**[2] (rōoth), **Babe** (bāb) (born *George Herman Ruth*) 1895-1948; U.S. baseball player

**ruth'less** (-lis) *adj.* ⟦OE *hreowan*, to rue⟧ without pity or compassion —**ruth'less·ly** *adv.* —**ruth'less·ness** *n.*

**RV** *n.*, *pl.* **RVs** ⟦*R(ecreational) V(ehicle)*⟧ a camper, trailer, motor home, etc. outfitted for living in

**Rwan·da** (rōo än′də) country in EC Africa, east of Democratic Republic of the Congo: 10,169 sq. mi.; pop. 7,165,000

**Rwy** or **Ry** *abbrev.* Railway

**Rx** *symbol* PRESCRIPTION (sense 2)

**-ry** (rē) *suffix* -ERY *[foundry]*

**rye** (rī) *n.* ⟦OE *ryge*⟧ **1** a hardy cereal grass **2** its grain or seeds, used for making flour, etc. **3** whiskey distilled from this grain

# S

**s**[1] or **S** (es) *n.*, *pl.* **s's**, **S's** the 19th letter of the English alphabet —*adj.* shaped like S

**s**[2] *abbrev.* **1** second(s) **2** shilling(s)

**S**[1] *abbrev.* **1** Saturday **2** small **3** south **4** southern **5** Sunday

**S**[2] *Chem. symbol for* sulfur

**-s** ⟦alt. of -ES⟧ *suffix* **1** forming the plural of most nouns *[hips]* **2** forming the 3d pers. sing., pres. indic., of certain verbs *[shouts]*

**-'s**[1] ⟦OE⟧ *suffix* forming the possessive singular of nouns and some pronouns, and the possessive plural of nouns not ending in s *[boy's, men's]*

**-'s**[2] *suffix* **1** is *[he's a sailor]* **2** has *[she's asked*

them both*]* **3** [Inf.] does *[what's it matter?]* **4** us *[let's go]*

**SA** South America

**Saar** (sär, zär) rich coal-mining region in a river valley of SW Germany: also called **Saar Basin**

**Sab·bath** (sab′əth) *n.* ⟦< Heb *shabat*, to rest⟧ **1** the seventh day of the week (Saturday), set aside in Jewish scripture for rest and worship **2** Sunday as the usual Christian day of rest and worship

**Sab·bat·i·cal** (sə bat′i kəl) *adj.* **1** of the Sabbath **2** [s-] bringing a period of rest —*n.* [s-] SABBATICAL LEAVE

**sabbatical leave** [orig. given every seven years] a period of absence with pay, for study, travel, etc., given as to teachers: also **sabbatical year**

**sa·ber** (sā′bər) *n.* [< Hung *szablya*] a heavy cavalry sword with a slightly curved blade: also **sa′bre**

**Sa·bin vaccine** (sā′bin) [after Dr. A. B. *Sabin* (1906-93), its U.S. developer] a polio vaccine taken orally

**sa·ble** (sā′bəl) *n.* [< Russ *sobol*] **1** any marten **2** its costly fur pelt —*adj.* black or dark brown

**sa·bot** (sa bō′, sab′ō) *n.* [Fr, ult. < Ar *sabbāt*, sandal] a shoe shaped from a single piece of wood

**sab·o·tage** (sab′ə täzh′) *n.* [Fr < *sabot*, wooden shoe + -AGE: from damage done to machinery by sabots] deliberate destruction or obstruction, as of railroads, bridges, etc. by enemy agents —*vt.*, *vi.* -taged′, -tag′ing to commit sabotage (on) — **sab′o·teur′** (-tur′) *n.*

**sa·bra** (sä′brə) *n.* [Heb *sabra*, a native cactus fruit] [*sometimes* S-] a native-born Israeli

**sabre saw** a portable electric saw with a narrow, oscillating blade

**sac** (sak) *n.* [see SACK¹] a pouchlike part in a plant or animal

**sac·cha·rin** (sak′ə rin′) *n.* [< Gr *sakcharon*] a white, crystalline coal-tar compound used as a sugar substitute

**sac′cha·rine′** (-rin′) *adj.* **1** of or like sugar **2** too sweet *[a saccharine voice]*

**sac·er·do·tal** (sas′ər dōt′′l; *occas.* sak′-) *adj.* [< L *sacerdos*, priest] of priests or the office of priest

**sa·chem** (sā′chəm) *n.* [AmInd] among some North American Indian tribes, the chief

**sa·chet** (sa shā′) *n.* [Fr] a small perfumed packet used to scent clothes

**sack¹** (sak) *n.* [ult. < Heb *saq*] **1** a bag, esp. a large one of coarse cloth **2** [Slang] dismissal from a job: with *the* **3** *Football* a sacking of a quarterback —*vt.* **1** to put into sacks **2** [Slang] to fire (a person) **3** *Football* to tackle (a quarterback) behind the line of scrimmage —**hit the sack** [Slang] to go to bed: also **sack out**

**sack²** (sak) *n.* [see prec.] the plundering of a city, etc. —*vt.* to plunder

**sack³** (sak) *n.* [< Fr (*vin*)*sec*, dry (wine) < L] a dry, white Spanish wine popular in England during the 16th and 17th c.

**sack′cloth′** *n.* **1** SACKING **2** [Historical] coarse cloth worn as a symbol of mourning

**sack′ing** *n.* a cheap, coarse cloth used for sacks

**sac·ra·ment** (sak′rə mənt) *n.* [< L *sacer*, holy] any of certain Christian rites, as baptism, the Eucharist, etc. —**sac′ra·men′tal** (-ment′′l) *adj.*

**Sac·ra·men·to** (sak′rə men′tō) capital of California: pop. 369,000

**sa·cred** (sā′krid) *adj.* [< L *sacer*, holy] **1** consecrated to a god or God; holy **2** having to do with religion **3** venerated; hallowed **4** inviolate — **sa′cred·ly** *adv.* —**sa′cred·ness** *n.*

**sac·ri·fice** (sak′rə fīs′) *n.* [< L *sacrificium* < *sacer*, sacred + *facere*, make] **1** an offering, as of a life or object, to a deity **2** a giving up of one thing for the sake of another —*vt.*, *vi.* -ficed′, -fic′ing **1** to offer as a sacrifice to a deity **2** to give up one thing for the sake of another **3** to sell at less than the supposed value —**sac′ri·fi′cial** (-fish′əl) *adj.*

**sac·ri·lege** (sak′rə lij) *n.* [< L *sacer*, sacred + *legere*, take away] desecration of what is sacred —**sac′ri·le′gious** (-lij′əs, -lē′jəs) *adj.*

**sac·ris·tan** (sak′ris tən) *n.* a person in charge of a sacristy

**sac′ris·ty** (-tē) *n., pl.* -ties [ult. < L *sacer*, sacred] a room in a church for sacred vessels, etc.

**sac·ro·il·i·ac** (sak′rō il′ē ak′, sā′krō-) *n.* [ModL, ult. < L *sacrum*, bone at bottom of spine + *ileum*, flank, groin] the joint between the top part of the hipbone and the fused bottom vertebrae

**sac·ro·sanct** (sak′rō saŋkt′) *adj.* [< L *sacer*, sacred + *sanctus*, holy] very sacred, holy, or inviolable

**sad** (sad) *adj.* **sad′der, sad′dest** [OE *sæd*, sated] **1** having or expressing low spirits; unhappy; sorrowful **2** causing dejection, sorrow, etc. **3** [Inf.] very bad; deplorable —**sad′ly** *adv.* —**sad′ness** *n.*

**sad′den** *vt., vi.* to make or become sad

**sad·dle** (sad′′l) *n.* [OE *sadol*] **1** a seat for a rider on a horse, bicycle, etc., usually padded and of leather **2** a cut of lamb, etc., including part of the backbone and the two loins —*vt.* -dled, -dling **1** to put a saddle upon **2** to encumber or burden — **in the saddle** in control

**sad′dle·bag′** *n.* **1** a bag hung behind the saddle of a horse, etc. **2** a bag carried on a bicycle, etc.

**saddle horse** a horse for riding

**saddle shoes** white oxford shoes with a contrasting band across the instep

**Sad·du·cee** (saj′oo sē′) *n.* a member of an ancient Jewish party that accepted only the written law

**sad·ism** (sā′diz əm, sad′iz əm) *n.* [after Marquis de *Sade* (1740-1814), Fr writer] the getting of pleasure from mistreating others —**sad′ist** *n.* — **sa·dis′tic** *adj.* —**sa·dis′ti·cal·ly** *adv.*

**sad·o·mas·o·chism** (sā′dō mas′ə kiz′əm, sad′ō-) *n.* the getting of sexual pleasure from sadism or masochism, or both —**sad′o·mas′o·chist** *n.* — **sad′o·mas′o·chis′tic** *adj.*

**sa·fa·ri** (sə fär′ē) *n., pl.* -ris [< Ar *safar*, to journey] a journey or hunting expedition, esp. in Africa

**safe** (sāf) *adj.* **saf′er, saf′est** [< L *salvus*] **1** *a*) free from damage, danger, etc.; secure *b*) having escaped injury; unharmed **2** *a*) giving protection *b*) trustworthy —*n.* a locking metal container for valuables —**safe′ly** *adv.* —**safe′ness** *n.*

**safe′-con′duct** *n.* permission to travel safely through enemy regions

**safe′-de·pos′it** *adj.* designating or of a box or vault, as in a bank, for storing valuables: also **safe′ty-de·pos′it**

**safe′guard′** *n.* a protection; precaution —*vt.* to protect or guard

**safe house** a house, etc. used as a refuge or hiding place, as by an underground organization

**safe′keep′ing** *n.* protection or custody

**safe sex** sexual activity incorporating practices, as condom use, that reduce the risk of spreading sexually transmitted diseases

**safe·ty** (sāf′tē) *n., pl.* -ties **1** a being safe; security **2** any device for preventing an accident **3** *Football a*) a grounding of the ball by the offense behind its own goal line, that scores two points for the defense *b*) a defensive back responsible for covering pass receivers in the middle of the field —*adj.* giving safety

**safety glass** shatterproof glass

**safety match** a match that lights when struck on a prepared surface

**safety net 1** a net suspended as beneath aerialists **2** any protection against failure or loss

**safety pin** a pin bent back on itself and having the point held in a guard

**safety razor** a razor with a detachable blade held between guards

**safety valve 1** an automatic valve that releases steam if the pressure in a boiler, etc. becomes excessive **2** any outlet for the release of strong emotion, etc.

**saf·flow·er** (saf′lou′ər) *n.* [ult. < Ar *asfar*, yellow] a thistlelike, annual plant with large, orange flowers and seeds yielding an edible oil

**saf·fron** (saf′rən) *n.* [< Ar *za'farān*] **1** a plant having orange stigmas **2** the dried stigmas, used as a dye and flavoring **3** orange yellow

**sag** (sag) *vi.* **sagged, sag′ging** [prob. < Scand] **1** to sink, esp. in the middle, from weight or pressure **2** to hang down unevenly **3** to weaken through weariness, age, etc. —*n.* **1** a sagging **2** a sagging place —**sag′gy, -gi·er, -gi·est,** *adj.*

**sa·ga** (sä′gə) *n.* [ON, a tale] **1** a medieval Scandinavian story relating the legendary history of a family **2** any long story of heroic deeds

**sa·ga·cious** (sə gā′shəs) *adj.* ⟦< L *sagax*, wise⟧ very wise; shrewd —**sa·gac′i·ty** (-gas′ə tē) *n.*

**sage**[1] (sāj) *adj.* **sag′er, sag′est** ⟦ult. < L *sapere*, know⟧ **1** wise, discerning, etc. **2** showing wisdom —*n.* a very wise man

**sage**[2] (sāj) *n.* ⟦< L *salvus*, safe: from its reputed healing powers⟧ **1** a plant of the mint family with leaves used for seasoning meats, etc. **2** SAGEBRUSH

**sage′brush′** *n.* a plant with aromatic leaves, in the dry areas of the W U.S.

**Sag·it·tar·i·us** (saj′ə ter′ē əs) *n.* ⟦L, archer⟧ the ninth sign of the zodiac

**sa·go** (sā′gō) *n., pl.* **-gos** an edible starch from a Malayan palm tree, etc.

**sa·gua·ro** (sə gwär′ō) *n., pl.* **-ros** ⟦< native name⟧ a giant cactus of the SW U.S. and N Mexico

**Sa·ha·ra** (sə har′ə) vast desert region extending across N Africa

**sa·hib** (sä′ib′) *n.* ⟦Hindi < Ar⟧ sir; master: title used in colonial India when speaking to or of a European

**said** (sed) *vt., vi. pt. & pp. of* SAY —*adj.* aforesaid

**Sai·gon** (sī gän′) *former name for* HO CHI MINH CITY

**sail** (sāl) *n.* ⟦OE *segl*⟧ **1** a sheet, as of canvas, spread to catch the wind, so as to drive a vessel forward **2** sails collectively **3** a trip in a ship or boat **4** anything like a sail —*vi.* **1** to be moved forward by means of sails **2** to travel on water **3** to begin a trip by water **4** to manage a sailboat **5** to glide or move smoothly **6** [Inf.] to move quickly —*vt.* **1** to move upon (a body of water) in a vessel **2** to manage or navigate (a vessel) —**set** (or **make**) **sail** to begin a trip by water —**under sail** sailing

**sail′board′** *n.* a board used in windsurfing

**sail′boat′** *n.* a boat propelled by a sail or sails

**sail′cloth′** *n.* canvas or other cloth for making sails, tents, etc.

**sail′fish′** *n., pl.* **-fish′** or (for different species) **-fish′es** a large marine fish with a sail-like dorsal fin

**sail′or** *n.* **1** a person whose work is sailing **2** an enlisted person in the navy

**sail′plane′** *n.* a light glider

**saint** (sānt) *n.* ⟦< L *sanctus*, holy⟧ **1** a holy person **2** a person who is exceptionally charitable, patient, etc. **3** in certain Christian churches, a person officially recognized for having attained heaven after an exceptionally holy life —**saint′li·ness** *n.* —**saint′ly, -li·er, -li·est,** *adj.*

SAILFISH

**Saint Ber·nard** (bər närd′) a large dog of a breed once used to rescue travelers lost in the snow

**Saint Nich·o·las** (nik′ə ləs) SANTA CLAUS: also **Saint Nick**

**Saint Pat·rick's Day** (pa′triks) March 17, observed by the Irish in honor of the patron saint of Ireland

**Saint Valentine's Day** Feb. 14, observed in honor of a martyr of the 3d c. and as a day for sending valentines

**saith** (seth) *vt., vi.* [Archaic] says

**sake**[1] (sāk) *n.* ⟦OE *sacu*, suit at law⟧ **1** motive; cause [for the *sake* of money] **2** behalf [for my *sake*]

**sa·ke**[2] (sä′kē) *n.* ⟦Jpn⟧ a Japanese alcoholic beverage made from rice: also sp. **sa′ki**

**sa·laam** (sə läm′) *n.* ⟦Ar *salām*, peace⟧ in India and the Near East, a greeting, etc. made by bowing low in respect or obeisance

**sal·a·ble** (sāl′ə bəl) *adj.* that can be sold; marketable: also **sale′a·ble**

**sa·la·cious** (sə lā′shəs) *adj.* ⟦< L *salire*, to leap⟧ **1** lustful **2** obscene —**sa·la′cious·ly** *adv.* —**sa·la′cious·ness** *n.*

**sal·ad** (sal′əd) *n.* ⟦< L *sal*, salt⟧ a dish, usually cold, of fruits, vegetables (esp. lettuce), meat, eggs, etc. usually mixed with salad dressing

**salad bar** a buffet in a restaurant, at which diners make their own salads

**salad dressing** oil, vinegar, spices, etc. put on a salad

**sa·lade niçoise** (sal′əd nē swäz′) a salad of tuna, tomatoes, etc. with a garlic vinaigrette

**sal·a·man·der** (sal′ə man′dər) *n.* ⟦< Gr *salamandra*⟧ **1** a mythological reptile said to live in fire **2** an amphibian with a tail and soft, moist skin

**sa·la·mi** (sə lä′mē) *n.* ⟦It < L *sal*, salt⟧ a spiced, salted sausage

**sal·a·ry** (sal′ə rē) *n., pl.* **-ries** ⟦< L *salarium*, orig. part of a soldier's pay for buying salt < *sal*, salt⟧ a fixed payment at regular intervals for work —**sal′a·ried** (-rēd) *adj.*

**sale** (sāl) *n.* ⟦< ON *sala*⟧ **1** a selling **2** opportunity to sell; market **3** an auction **4** a special offering of goods at reduced prices **5** [*pl.*] receipts in business **6** [*pl.*] the work of, or a department involved in, selling [a job in *sales*] —**for sale** to be sold —**on sale** for sale, esp. at a reduced price

**Sa·lem** (sā′ləm) capital of Oregon, in the NW part: pop. 108,000

**sales·clerk** (sālz′klurk′) *n.* a person employed to sell goods in a store

**sales′girl′** *n.* a girl or woman salesclerk

**sales′la·dy** *n., pl.* **-dies** [Inf.] a woman employed as a salesclerk

**sales′man** (-mən) *n., pl.* **-men** (-mən) **1** a man employed as a salesclerk **2** SALES REPRESENTATIVE

**sales′man·ship′** *n.* the skill of selling

**sales′per·son** *n., pl.* **-peo′ple** a person employed to sell goods or services

**sales representative** a salesperson, esp. one employed as a traveling agent for a manufacturer, etc.

**sales slip** a receipt or bill of sale

**sales tax** a tax on sales

**sales′wom·an** *n., pl.* **-wom′en** a woman salesclerk or sales representative

**sal·i·cyl·ic acid** (sal′ə sil′ik) ⟦< L *salix*, willow⟧ a crystalline compound used to make aspirin, etc.

**sa·lient** (sāl′yənt) *adj.* ⟦< L *salire*, to leap⟧ **1** pointing outward; jutting **2** conspicuous; prominent —*n.* a salient angle, part, etc. —**sa′lience** *n.*

**sa·line** (sā′lēn′, -līn′) *adj.* ⟦< L *sal*, salt⟧ of, like, or containing salt —*n.* a saline solution used in medicine, etc. —**sa·lin·i·ty** (sə lin′ə tē) *n.*

**sa·li·va** (sə lī′və) *n.* ⟦L⟧ the watery fluid secreted by glands in the mouth: it aids in digestion —**sal·i·var·y** (sal′ə ver′ē) *adj.*

**sal·i·vate** (sal′ə vāt′) *vi.* **-vat′ed, -vat′ing** ⟦< L *salivare*⟧ to secrete saliva —**sal′i·va′tion** *n.*

**sal·low** (sal′ō) *adj.* ⟦ME *salou*⟧ of a sickly, pale-yellowish complexion

**sal·ly** (sal′ē) *n., pl.* **-lies** ⟦< L *salire*, to leap⟧ **1** a sudden rushing forth, as to attack **2** a witty remark; quip **3** an excursion —*vi.* **-lied, -ly·ing** to rush or set (*forth* or *out*) on a sally

**salm·on** (sam′ən) *n., pl.* **-on** or **-ons** ⟦< L *salmo*⟧ **1** a game and food fish with yellowish pink flesh, that lives in salt water and spawns in fresh water **2** yellowish pink: also **salmon pink**

**sal·mo·nel·la** (sal′mə nel′ə) *n., pl.* **-nel′lae** (-ē) **-nel′la,** or **-nel′las** ⟦after D. E. *Salmon* (1850-1914), U.S. doctor⟧ any of a genus of bacilli that cause typhoid fever, food poisoning, etc.

**sa·lon** (sə län′) *n.* ⟦Fr: see fol.⟧ **1** a large reception hall or drawing room **2** a regular gathering of distinguished guests **3** a shop furnished to provide some personal service [beauty *salon*]

**sa·loon** (sə loōn′) *n.* [< Fr < It *sala*] **1** any large room or hall for receptions, etc. **2** [Old-fashioned] a place where alcoholic drinks are sold; bar

**sal·sa** (säl′sə) *n.* [AmSp, sauce < L, salted food] **1** a kind of Latin American dance music usually played at fast tempos **2** a hot sauce made with chilies, tomatoes, etc.

**salt** (sôlt) *n.* [OE *sealt*] **1** a white, crystalline substance, sodium chloride, found in natural beds, in sea water, etc., and used for seasoning food, etc. **2** a chemical compound derived from an acid by replacing hydrogen with a metal **3** piquancy; esp., pungent wit **4** [*pl.*] mineral salts used as a cathartic or restorative **5** [Inf.] a sailor —*adj.* containing, preserved with, or tasting of salt —*vt.* to sprinkle, season, or preserve with salt —**salt away** [Inf.] to store or save (money, etc.) —**salt of the earth** any person or persons regarded as the finest, etc. —**with a grain of salt** with allowance for exaggeration, etc.; skeptically —**salt′ed** *adj.*

**salt′cel′lar** (-sel′ər) *n.* [< prec. + Fr *salière*, salt-cellar] **1** a small dish for holding salt **2** a salt-shaker

**salt·ine** (sôl tēn′) *n.* [SALT + -INE³] a flat, crisp, salted cracker

**Salt Lake City** capital of Utah: pop. 160,000

**salt lick** a natural deposit or a block of rock salt which animals lick

**salt′pe′ter** (-pēt′ər) *n.* [< L *sal*, salt + *petra*, rock] NITER

**salt pork** pork cured in salt

**salt′shak′er** *n.* a container for salt, with a perforated top

**salt′wa′ter** *adj.* of salt water or the sea

**salt′y** *adj.* -i·er, -i·est **1** of or having salt **2** suggesting the sea **3** *a*) sharp; witty *b*) coarse *c*) cross or caustic

**sa·lu·bri·ous** (sə loō′brē əs) *adj.* [< L *salus*, health] healthful; wholesome

**sal·u·tar·y** (sal′yoō ter′ē) *adj.* [see prec.] **1** healthful **2** beneficial

**sal·u·ta·tion** (sal′yoō tā′shən) *n.* [see fol.] **1** the act of greeting, addressing, etc. **2** a form of greeting, as the "Dear Sir" of a letter

**sa·lute** (sə loōt′) *vt., vi.* -lut·ed, -lut′ing [< L *salus*, health] **1** to greet with friendly words or ceremonial gesture **2** to honor by performing a prescribed act, such as raising the right hand to the head, in military and naval practice **3** to praise; commend —*n.* an act or remark made in saluting

**sal·vage** (sal′vij) *n.* [see SAVE¹] **1** *a*) the rescue of a ship and cargo from shipwreck, etc. *b*) compensation paid for such rescue **2** *a*) the rescue of any property from destruction or waste *b*) the property saved —*vt.* -vaged, -vag·ing to save or rescue from shipwreck, fire, etc.

**sal·va·tion** (sal vā′shən) *n.* [< L *salvare*, save] **1** a saving or being saved **2** a person or thing that saves **3** *Theol.* deliverance from sin and from the penalties of sin; redemption

**salve** (sav) *n.* [OE *sealf*] **1** any soothing or healing ointment for wounds, burns, etc. **2** anything that soothes —*vt.* salved, salv′ing to soothe

**sal·ver** (sal′vər) *n.* [ult. < L *salvare*, save] a tray

**sal·vo** (sal′vō) *n., pl.* -vos or -voes [< It < L *salve*, hail!] a discharge of a number of guns, in salute or at a target

**SAM** (sam) *n.* surface-to-air missile

**sam·ba** (sam′bə, säm′-) *n.* [Port] a Brazilian dance of African origin, or music for it

**same** (sām) *adj.* [< ON *samr*] **1** being the very one; identical **2** alike in kind, quality, amount, etc. **3** unchanged [to keep the *same* look] **4** before-mentioned Usually used with *the* —*pron.* the same person or thing —*adv.* in like manner: usually with *the* —**same′ness** *n.*

**sam·iz·dat** (säm′iz dät′) *n.* [Russ, self-published]

in the U.S.S.R., a system by which writings officially disapproved of were circulated secretly

**Sa·mo·a** (sə mō′ə) country in the SW Pacific, consisting of two large islands & several small ones: 1,093 sq. mi.; pop. 160,000 —**Sa·mo′an** *adj., n.*

**sam·o·var** (sam′ə vär′) *n.* a Russian metal urn with a spigot, for heating water in making tea

**sam·pan** (sam′pan′) *n.* [< Chin dial.] a small boat used in China and Japan, rowed with a scull from the stern

**sam·ple** (sam′pəl) *n.* [see EXAMPLE] **1** a part or item taken as representative of a whole thing, group, etc.; specimen **2** an example —*vt.* -pled, -pling to take (and test) a sample of

**sam′pler** (-plər) *n.* **1** one who samples **2** a collection of representative selections **3** a cloth embroidered with designs, mottoes, etc. in different stitches

**Sam·son** (sam′sən) *n. Bible* an Israelite noted for his great strength

**Sam·u·el** (sam′yoō əl) *n. Bible* a Hebrew leader and prophet

**sam·u·rai** (sam′ə rī′) *n., pl.* -rai′ [Jpn] a member of a military class in feudal Japan

**San An·to·ni·o** (san′ an tō′nē ō′) city in SC Texas: site of the Alamo: pop. 935,000

**san·a·to·ri·um** (san′ə tôr′ē əm) *n., pl.* -ri·ums or -ri·a (-ə) *chiefly Brit. var. of* SANITARIUM

**San Ber·nar·di·no** (bʉr′nər dē′nō, -nə-) city in S California: pop. 164,000

**sanc·ti·fy** (saŋk′tə fī′) *vt.* -fied′, -fy′ing [see SAINT & -FY] **1** to set apart as holy; consecrate **2** to make free from sin —**sanc′ti·fi·ca′tion** *n.*

**sanc·ti·mo·ni·ous** (saŋk′tə mō′nē əs) *adj.* pretending to be pious —**sanc′ti·mo′ni·ous·ly** *adv.*

**sanc·ti·mo·ny** *n.* [< L *sanctus*, holy] pretended piety

**sanc·tion** (saŋk′shən) *n.* [see SAINT] **1** authorization **2** support; approval **3** a coercive measure, as an official trade boycott against a nation defying international law: *often used in pl.* —*vt.* **1** to confirm; ratify **2** to authorize; permit

**sanc·ti·ty** (saŋk′tə tē) *n., pl.* -ties [< L *sanctus*, holy] **1** holiness **2** sacredness

**sanc·tu·ar·y** (saŋk′choō er′ē) *n., pl.* -ies [< L *sanctus*, sacred] **1** a holy place; specif., *a*) a church, temple, etc. *b*) a particularly holy place within a church or temple **2** a place of refuge or protection

**sanc·tum** (saŋk′təm) *n.* [L] **1** a sacred place **2** a private room where one is not to be disturbed

**sand** (sand) *n.* [OE] **1** loose, gritty grains of eroded rock, as on beaches, in deserts, etc. **2** [*usually pl.*] a tract of sand —*vt.* **1** to sprinkle with sand **2** to smooth or polish, as with sandpaper —**sand′er** *n.*

**san·dal** (san′dəl) *n.* [< Gr *sandalon*] **1** a shoe made of a sole fastened to the foot by straps **2** any of various low slippers or shoes

**san′dal·wood′** *n.* [ult. < Sans] **1** the hard, sweet-smelling wood at the core of certain Asiatic trees **2** such a tree

**sand′bag′** *n.* a bag filled with sand, used for ballast, protecting levees, etc. —*vt.* -bagged′, -bag′ging **1** to put sandbags in or around **2** [Inf.] to force into doing something

**sand′bar′** *n.* a ridge of sand, as one formed in a river or along a shore: also **sand bar** or **sand′bank′**

SANDALS

**sand′blast′** *vt.* to clean with a current of air or steam carrying sand at a high velocity,

**sand′box′** *n.* a box containing sand for children to play in

**sand dollar** any of various flat, round, disklike echinoderms that live on sandy ocean beds

**S & H** *abbrev.* shipping and handling

**sand'hog'** *n.* a laborer in underground or underwater construction

**San Di·e·go** (san' dē ā'gō) seaport in S California: pop. 1,111,000

**S & L** *abbrev.* savings and loan (association)

**sand'lot'** *adj.* of or having to do with baseball played by amateurs, orig. on a sandy lot

**sand'man'** *n.* a mythical person supposed to make children sleepy by dusting sand in their eyes

**sand'pa'per** *n.* paper coated on one side with sand, used for smoothing and polishing —*vt.* to smooth or polish with sandpaper

**sand'pip'er** (-pī'pər) *n.* a small shorebird with a long, soft-tipped bill

**sand'stone'** *n.* a sedimentary rock composed of sand grains cemented together, as by silica

**sand'storm'** *n.* a windstorm in which large quantities of sand are blown about in the air

**sand trap** a hollow filled with sand, serving as a hazard on a golf course

**sand·wich** (sand'wich') *n.* ⟦after 4th Earl of *Sandwich* (1718-92)⟧ slices of bread with meat, cheese, etc. between them —*vt.* to place or squeeze between other persons, things, etc.

**sand·y** (san'dē) *adj.* **-i·er, -i·est** **1** of or like sand **2** pale reddish-yellow

**sane** (sān) *adj.* ⟦L *sanus,* healthy⟧ **1** mentally healthy; rational **2** sound; sensible —**sane'ly** *adv.*

**San Fran·cis·co** (san' frən sis'kō) seaport on the coast of central California: pop. 724,000

**San Francisco Bay** an inlet of the Pacific in WC California: the harbor of San Francisco

**sang** (saŋ) *vi., vt. alt. pt. of* SING[1]

**sang-froid** (sän frwä') *n.* ⟦Fr, lit., cold blood⟧ cool self-possession or composure

**san·gri·a** (san grē'ə, saŋ-) *n.* ⟦Sp < *sangre,* blood⟧ an iced punch made with red wine, fruit juice, pieces of fruit, etc.

**san·gui·nar·y** (saŋ'gwi ner'ē) *adj.* ⟦see fol.⟧ **1** accompanied by much bloodshed **2** bloodthirsty

**san·guine** (saŋ'gwin) *adj.* ⟦< L *sanguis,* blood⟧ **1** of the color of blood; ruddy **2** cheerful; confident

**san·i·tar·i·um** (san'ə ter'ē əm) *n., pl.* **-i·ums** or **-i·a** (-ə) ⟦ModL < L *sanitas,* health⟧ **1** a resort where people go to regain health **2** an institution for the care of invalids or convalescents

**san·i·tar·y** (san'ə ter'ē) *adj.* ⟦< L *sanitas,* health⟧ **1** of or bringing about health and healthful conditions **2** in a clean, healthy condition

**sanitary napkin** an absorbent pad worn by women during menstruation

**san·i·ta·tion** (san'ə tā'shən) *n.* **1** the science and practice of effecting hygienic conditions **2** drainage and disposal of sewage

**san·i·tize** (san'ə tīz') *vt.* **-tized', -tiz'ing** **1** to make sanitary **2** to free from anything considered undesirable, damaging, etc.

**san·i·ty** (san'ə tē) *n.* **1** the state of being sane **2** soundness of judgment

**San Jo·se** (san' hō zā') city in WC California: pop. 782,000

**San Juan** (san' hwän') seaport & capital of Puerto Rico: pop. 438,000

**sank** (saŋk) *vi., vt. alt. pt. of* SINK

**San Ma·ri·no** (san' mə rē'nō) independent country within E Italy: 24 sq. mi.; pop. 24,000

**sans** (sanz; *Fr* sän) *prep.* ⟦Fr < L *sine*⟧ without

**San·skrit** (san'skrit) *n.* the classical literary language of ancient India: also **San'scrit**

**San·ta An·a**[1] (san'tə an'ə) hot desert wind from the east or northeast in S California

**San·ta An·a**[2] (san'tə an'ə) city in SW California: pop. 294,000

**San·ta Claus** (san'tə klôz') ⟦< Du *Sant Nikolaas,* St. Nicholas⟧ *Folklore* a fat, white-bearded, jolly old man in a red suit, who distributes gifts at Christmas

**San·ta Fe** (san'tə fā') capital of New Mexico: pop. 56,000

**San·ti·a·go** (sän'tē ä'gō, san'-) capital of Chile: pop. 4,100,000

**São Pau·lo** (soun pou'loo) city in SE Brazil: pop. 8,491,000

**São To·mé and Prín·ci·pe** (tô me' and prin'sə pē') country off the W coast of Africa, comprising two islands (**São Tomé** and **Príncipe**): 387 sq. mi.; pop. 120,000

**sap**[1] (sap) *n.* ⟦OE *sæp*⟧ **1** the juice that circulates through a plant, bearing water, food, etc. **2** vigor; energy **3** [Slang] a fool —**sap'less** *adj.*

**sap**[2] (sap) *vt.* **sapped, sap'ping** ⟦< Fr *sappe,* a hoe⟧ **1** to dig beneath; undermine **2** to weaken

**sa·pi·ent** (sā'pē ənt) *adj.* ⟦< L *sapere,* to taste, know⟧ wise —**sa'pi·ence** *n.*

**sap·ling** (sap'liŋ) *n.* a young tree

**sap·phire** (saf'īr) *n.* ⟦< Sans *śanipriya*⟧ a precious stone of a clear, deep-blue corundum

**sap·py** (sap'ē) *adj.* **-pi·er, -pi·est** **1** full of sap; juicy **2** [Slang] foolish; silly —**sap'pi·ness** *n.*

**sap·ro·phyte** (sap'rə fīt') *n.* ⟦< Gr *sapros,* rotten + *phyton,* a plant⟧ any plant that lives on dead or decaying organic matter, as some fungi —**sap'ro·phyt'ic** (-fit'ik) *adj.*

**sap'suck'er** *n.* an American woodpecker that often drills holes in trees for the sap

**Sar·a·cen** (sar'ə sən) *n.* any Arab or any Muslim, esp. at the time of the Crusades

**Sar·ah** (ser'ə) *n. Bible* the wife of Abraham and mother of Isaac

**Sa·ra·je·vo** (sar'ə yā'vō) capital of Bosnia and Herzegovina: pop. 416,000

**sa·ran** (sə ran') *n.* ⟦arbitrary coinage⟧ a thermoplastic substance used in various fabrics, wrapping material, etc.

**sar·casm** (sär'kaz'əm) *n.* ⟦< Gr *sarkazein,* to tear flesh⟧ **1** a taunting or caustic remark, generally ironic **2** the making of such remarks

**sar·cas·tic** (sär kas'tik) *adj.* **1** of, like, or full of sarcasm **2** using sarcasm —**sar·cas'ti·cal·ly** *adv.*

**sar·co·ma** (sär kō'mə) *n., pl.* **-mas** or **-ma·ta** (-mə tə) ⟦< Gr *sarx,* flesh⟧ a malignant tumor in connective tissue

**sar·coph·a·gus** (sär käf'ə gəs) *n., pl.* **-gi** (-jī') or **-gus·es** ⟦< Gr *sarx,* flesh + *phagein,* to eat: limestone coffins hastened disintegration⟧ a stone coffin, esp. one exposed to view, as in a tomb

**sar·dine** (sär dēn') *n.* ⟦< L *sarda,* a fish⟧ any of various small ocean fishes preserved in tightly packed cans for eating

**sar·don·ic** (sär dän'ik) *adj.* ⟦< Gr *sardonios*⟧ scornfully or bitterly sarcastic —**sar·don'i·cal·ly** *adv.*

**sa·ri** (sä'rē) *n.* ⟦< Sans⟧ the outer garment of a woman of India, Pakistan, etc., consisting of a long cloth wrapped around the body

**sa·rong** (sə rôŋ', -räŋ') *n.* ⟦Malay *sarung*⟧ a garment of men and women in the East Indies, etc., consisting of a cloth worn like a skirt

**sar·sa·pa·ril·la** (sas'pə ril'ə) *n.* ⟦< Sp *zarza,* bramble + *parra,* vine⟧ **1** a tropical American vine with fragrant roots **2** a carbonated drink flavored with or as with the dried roots

**sar·to·ri·al** (sär tôr'ē əl) *adj.* ⟦< LL *sartor,* tailor⟧ **1** of tailors or their work **2** of men's dress

**SASE** *abbrev.* self-addressed, stamped envelope

**sash**[1] (sash) *n.* ⟦Ar *shāsh,* muslin⟧ an ornamental band, ribbon, etc. worn over the shoulder or around the waist

SARI

**sash²** (sash) *n.* [< Fr *châssis*, a frame] a frame for holding the glass pane of a window or door, esp. a sliding frame

**sa·shay** (sa shā′) *vi.* [< Fr *chassé*, a dance step] [Inf.] 1 to walk or go, esp. casually 2 to move, walk, etc. so as to attract attention

**Sas·katch·e·wan** (sas kach′ə wän′) province of SC Canada: 251,700 sq. mi.; pop. 990,000; cap. Regina: abbrev. *SK*

**sass** (sas) [Inf.] *n.* [var. of SAUCE] impudent talk —*vt.* to talk impudently to

**sas·sa·fras** (sas′ə fras′) *n.* [Sp *sasafras*] 1 a small tree having small, bluish fruits 2 its dried root bark, used for flavoring

**sass·y** (sas′ē) *adj.* -i·er, -i·est [var. of SAUCY] [Inf.] impudent; saucy

**sat** (sat) *vi., vt. pt. & pp. of* SIT

**Sat** *abbrev.* Saturday

**SAT** *trademark for* Scholastic Assessment Tests

**Sa·tan** (sāt′n) *n.* [< Heb *satan*, adversary] the Devil

**sa·tan·ic** (sā tan′ik, sə-) *adj.* like Satan; wicked — **sa·tan′i·cal·ly** *adv.*

**satch·el** (sach′əl) *n.* [< L *saccus*, a bag] a small bag for carrying clothes, books, etc.

**sate** (sāt) *vt.* sat′ed, sat′ing [prob. < L *satiare*, fill full] 1 to satisfy (an appetite, etc.) completely 2 to satiate

**sa·teen** (sa tēn′) *n.* [< SATIN] a cotton cloth made to imitate satin

**sat·el·lite** (sat′'l īt′) *n.* [< L *satelles*, an attendant] 1 *a)* a celestial body revolving around a larger celestial body *b)* a man-made object rocketed into orbit around the earth, moon, etc. 2 a small state dependent on a larger one

**sa·ti·ate** (sā′shē āt′) *vt.* -at′ed, -at′ing [< L *satis*, enough] to provide with more than enough, so as to weary or disgust; glut

**sa·ti·e·ty** (sə tī′ə tē) *n.* a being satiated

**sat·in** (sat′n) *n.* [< Ar *zaitūnī*, of *Zaitūn*, former name of a Chinese seaport] a fabric of silk, nylon, rayon, etc. with a smooth, glossy finish on one side —**sat′in·y** *adj.*

**sat·in·wood′** *n.* 1 a smooth wood used in fine furniture 2 any of the trees yielding such a wood

**sat·ire** (sa′tīr′) *n.* [< L *satira*] 1 a literary work in which vices, follies, etc. are held up to ridicule and contempt 2 the use of ridicule, sarcasm, etc. to attack vices, follies, etc. —**sa·tir·i·cal** (sə tir′i kəl) *adj.* —**sat·i·rist** (sat′ə rist) *n.*

**sat·i·rize** (sat′ə rīz′) *vt.* -rized′, -riz′ing to attack with satire

**sat·is·fac·tion** (sat′is fak′shən) *n.* 1 a satisfying or being satisfied 2 something that satisfies; specif., *a)* anything that brings pleasure or contentment *b)* settlement of debt

**sat·is·fac′to·ry** (-tə rē) *adj.* good enough to fulfill a need, wish, etc.; satisfying or adequate —**sat′is·fac′to·ri·ly** *adv.*

**sat·is·fy** (sat′is fī′) *vt.* -fied′, -fy′ing [< L *satis*, enough + *facere*, make] 1 to fulfill the needs or desires of; content 2 to fulfill the requirements of 3 to free from doubt; convince 4 *a)* to give what is due to *b)* to discharge (a debt, etc.)

**sa·to·ri** (sä tôr′ē) *n.* [Jpn] spiritual enlightenment: term in Zen Buddhism

**sa·trap** (sā′trap′, sa′-) *n.* [< Pers] a petty tyrant

**sat·u·rate** (sach′ə rāt′) *vt.* -rat′ed, -rat′ing [< L *satur*, full] 1 to make thoroughly soaked 2 to cause to be filled, charged, etc. with the most it can absorb —**sat′u·ra′tion** *n.*

**Sat·ur·day** (sat′ər dā′) *n.* [< OE *Sæterdæg*, Saturn's day] the seventh and last day of the week

**Saturday night special** [from their use in weekend crimes] [Slang] any small, cheap handgun

**Sat·urn** (sat′ərn) *n.* 1 the Roman god of agriculture 2 the second largest planet of the solar system, with thin, icy rings of particles around its equator: see PLANET

**sat·ur·nine** (sat′ər nīn′) *adj.* [< supposed influence of planet Saturn] sluggish, gloomy, grave, etc.

**sat·yr** (sāt′ər, sat′-) *n.* [< Gr *satyros*] 1 *Gr. Myth.* a lecherous woodland deity represented as a man with a goat's legs, pointed ears, and short horns 2 a lecherous man

**sat·y·ri·a·sis** (sāt′ə rī′ə sis, sat′-) *n.* [< Gr: see prec.] uncontrollable desire by a man for sexual intercourse

**sauce** (sôs) *n.* [< L *sal*, salt] 1 a liquid or soft mixture served with food to add flavor 2 stewed or preserved fruit 3 [Inf.] impudence 4 [Slang] alcoholic liquor: with *the*

**sauce′pan′** *n.* a small pot with a projecting handle, used for cooking

**sau·cer** (sô′sər) *n.* [see SAUCE] 1 a small, round, shallow dish, esp. one designed to hold a cup 2 anything shaped like a saucer

**sau·cy** (sô′sē) *adj.* -ci·er, -ci·est [SAUC(E) + -Y²] 1 rude; impudent 2 pert; sprightly —**sau′ci·ly** *adv.* —**sau′ci·ness** *n.*

**Sa·u·di Arabia** (sou′dē, sô′-) kingdom occupying most of Arabia: 849,400 sq. mi.; pop. 16,900,000

**sau·er·bra·ten** (sou′ər brät′'n, zou′ər-) *n.* [Ger *sauer*, sour + *braten*, roast] beef marinated in vinegar with onions, spices, etc. before cooking

**sau·er·kraut** (sou′ər krout′) *n.* [Ger *sauer*, sour + *kraut*, cabbage] chopped cabbage fermented in brine

**Saul** (sôl) *n. Bible* first king of Israel

**sau·na** (sô′nə, sä′-) *n.* [Finnish] a bath involving exposure to hot, dry air

**saun·ter** (sôn′tər) *vi.* [ME *santren*, to muse] to walk about idly; stroll —*n.* a leisurely walk; stroll

**sau·ri·an** (sôr′ē ən) *adj.* [< Gr *sauros*, lizard] of or like lizards

**sau·ro·pod** (sôr′ə päd′) *n.* [< Gr *sauros*, lizard + -POD] a gigantic dinosaur with a long neck and tail and a small head, as an apatosaurus

**sau·sage** (sô′sij) *n.* [see SAUCE] pork or other meat, chopped fine, seasoned, and often stuffed into a casing

**sau·té** (sô tā′, sō-) *vt.* -téed′, -té′ing [Fr < *sauter*, to leap] to fry quickly with a little fat

**Sau·ternes** (sō turn′) *n.* [after *Sauternes*, town in France] [*often* s-] any of various white wines, of varying sweetness: also sp. **Sau·terne′**

**sav·age** (sav′ij) *adj.* [< L *silva*, a wood] 1 fierce; untamed [a savage tiger] 2 primitive; barbarous 3 cruel; pitiless —*n.* 1 [Now Rare] a member of a preliterate, often tribal, culture 2 a brutal or crude person —**sav′age·ly** *adv.* —**sav′age·ry** *n.*

**sa·van·na** or **sa·van·nah** (sə van′ə) *n.* [Sp *sabana*] a treeless plain or a grassland with scattered trees

**Sa·van·nah** (sə van′ə) seaport in SE Georgia: pop. 138,000

**sa·vant** (sə vänt′, -vant′; sav′ənt) *n.* [Fr < *savoir*, know] a learned person

**save¹** (sāv) *vt.* saved, sav′ing [< L *salvus*, safe] 1 to rescue or preserve from harm or danger 2 to preserve for future use 3 to prevent loss or waste of [to save time] 4 to prevent or lessen [to save expense] 5 *Theol.* to deliver from sin —*vi.* 1 to avoid expense, waste, etc. 2 to store (*up*) money or goods —*n. Sports* an action that keeps an opponent from scoring or winning —**sav′er** *n.*

**save²** (sāv) *prep., conj.* [< OFr *sauf*, safe] except; but

**sav·ing** (sā′viŋ) *adj.* that saves; specif., *a)* economizing or economical *b)* redeeming —*n.* 1 [*often pl., with sing. v.*] any reduction in expense, time, etc. 2 [*pl.*] sums of money saved

**sav·ior** or **sav·iour** (sāv′yər) *n.* [< L *salvare*, to save] 1 one who saves 2 [S-] Jesus Christ

**sa·voir-faire** (sav′wär fer′) *n.* [Fr, to know (how) to do] ready knowledge of what to do or say in any situation

**sa·vor** (sā'vər) *n.* ⟦< L *sapor*⟧ **1** a particular taste or smell **2** distinctive quality —*vi.* to have the distinctive taste, smell, or quality (*of*) —*vt.* to taste with delight Brit. sp. **sa'vour**

**sa·vor·y** (sā'vər ē) *adj.* -i·er, -i·est **1** pleasing to the taste or smell **2** pleasant, agreeable, etc. Brit. sp. **sa'vour·y**

**sav·vy** (sav'ē) *n.* ⟦< Port *saber*, to know⟧ [Slang] shrewdness or understanding

**saw**[1] (sô) *n.* ⟦OE *sagu*⟧ a cutting tool consisting of a thin metal blade or disk with sharp teeth —*vt.* to cut or shape with a saw —*vi.* **1** to cut with or as with a saw **2** to be cut with a saw

**saw**[2] (sô) *n.* ⟦OE *sagu*⟧ a maxim; proverb

**saw**[3] (sô) *vt.*, *vi.* *pt. of* SEE[1]

**saw'dust'** *n.* fine particles of wood formed in sawing wood

**sawed'-off'** *adj.* short or shortened

**saw'horse'** *n.* a rack on which wood is placed while being sawed

**saw'mill'** *n.* a factory where logs are sawed into boards

**saw'-toothed'** *adj.* having notches along the edge like the teeth of a saw: also **saw'tooth'**

**saw·yer** (sô'yər) *n.* one whose work is sawing wood

**sax** (saks) *n.* [Inf.] *short for* SAXOPHONE

**Sax·on** (sak'sən) *n.* **1** a member of an ancient Germanic people, some of whom settled in England **2** an Anglo-Saxon **3** any dialect of the Saxons

**sax·o·phone** (sak'sə fōn') *n.* ⟦Fr, after A. J. *Sax*, 19th-c. Belgian inventor + -PHONE⟧ a single-reed, keyed woodwind instrument with a metal body — **sax'o·phon'ist** (-fōn'ist) *n.*

**say** (sā) *vt.* **said**, **say'ing** ⟦OE *secgan*⟧ **1** to utter or speak **2** to express in words; state **3** to state positively or as an opinion **4** to indicate or show /the clock *says* one/ **5** to recite /to *say* one's prayers/ **6** to estimate; assume /he is, I'd *say*, forty/ —*n.* **1** a chance to speak /I had my *say*/ **2** authority, as to make a final decision: often with *the* —**that is to say** in other words

**say'ing** *n.* an adage, proverb, or maxim

**say'-so'** *n.* [Inf.] **1** one's word, assurance, etc. **2** right of decision

**Sb** ⟦L *stibium*⟧ *Chem. symbol for* antimony

**sc** *abbrev. Printing* small capitals

**SC** South Carolina

**scab** (skab) *n.* ⟦< ON *skabb*⟧ **1** a crust forming over a sore during healing **2** a worker who replaces a striking worker —*vi.* **scabbed**, **scab'bing** to become covered with a scab — **scab'by**, **-bi·er**, **-bi·est**, *adj.* —**scab'bi·ness** *n.*

**scab·bard** (skab'ərd) *n.* ⟦< ? OHG *scar*, sword⟧ a sheath for the blade of a sword, dagger, etc.

**sca·bies** (skā'bēz) *n.* ⟦L, the itch⟧ a contagious, itching skin disease caused by a mite

**scab·rous** (skab'rəs, skā'brəs) *adj.* ⟦< L *scabere*, to scratch⟧ **1** scaly or scabby **2** indecent, shocking, etc.

**scads** (skadz) *pl.n.* ⟦< ?⟧ [Inf.] a very large number or amount

**scaf·fold** (skaf'əld) *n.* ⟦< OFr *escafalt*⟧ **1** a temporary framework for supporting workers during the repairing, painting, etc. of a building, etc. **2** a raised platform on which criminals are executed

**scaf'fold·ing** *n.* **1** the materials forming a scaffold **2** a scaffold

**scal·a·wag** (skal'ə wag') *n.* ⟦< ?⟧ [Inf.] a scamp; rascal

**scald** (skôld) *vt.* ⟦< L *ex-*, intens. + *calidus*, hot⟧ **1** to burn with hot liquid or steam **2** to heat almost to the boiling point **3** to use boiling liquid on —*n.* a burn caused by scalding

**scale**[1] (skāl) *n.* ⟦< L *scala*, ladder⟧ **1** *a)* a series of marks along a line used in measuring /the *scale* of a thermometer/ *b)* any instrument so marked **2** the proportion that a map, etc. bears to the thing it represents /a *scale* of one inch to a mile/ **3** *a)* a series of degrees classified by size, amount, etc. /a

wage *scale*] *b)* any degree in such a series **4** *Music* a series of tones, rising or falling in pitch, according to a system of intervals —*vt.* **scaled**, **scal'ing 1** to climb up or over **2** to make according to a scale —**scale back** SCALE DOWN (see phrase below) —**scale down** (or **up**) to reduce (or increase) according to a fixed ratio

**scale**[2] (skāl) *n.* ⟦< OFr *escale*, shell⟧ **1** any of the thin, flat horny plates covering many fishes, reptiles, etc. **2** any thin, platelike layer or piece —*vt.* **scaled**, **scal'ing** to scrape scales from —*vi.* to flake or peel off in scales —**scal'y**, **-i·er**, **-i·est**, *adj.*

**scale**[3] (skāl) *n.* ⟦< ON *skāl*, bowl⟧ **1** either pan of a balance **2** [*often pl.*] *a)* BALANCE (sense 1) *b)* any weighing machine —*vt.* **scaled**, **scal'ing** to weigh —**turn the scales** to decide or settle

**scale insect** any of various small insects destructive to plants: the females secrete a waxy scale

**sca·lene** (skā'lēn, skā lēn') *adj.* ⟦< Gr *skalēnos*, uneven⟧ having unequal sides /a *scalene* triangle/

**scal·lion** (skal'yən) *n.* ⟦< L (*caepa*) *Ascalonia*, (onion of) Ascalon (Philistine city)⟧ any of various onions or onionlike plants, as the shallot, green onion, or leek

**scal·lop** (skäl'əp, skal'-) *n.* ⟦< OFr *escalope*⟧ **1** *a)* any of various edible mollusks with two curved, hinged shells *b)* one of the shells **2** any of a series of curves, etc. forming an ornamental edge — *vt.* **1** to cut the edge of in scallops **2** to bake until brown, usually with a creamy sauce and bread crumbs

SHELL OF SCALLOP

**scalp** (skalp) *n.* ⟦< Scand⟧ the skin on the top and back of the head, usually covered with hair —*vt.* **1** to cut or tear the scalp from **2** [Inf.] to buy (theater tickets, etc.) and resell them at higher prices —**scalp'er** *n.*

SCALLOPED BORDER

**scal·pel** (skal'pəl) *n.* ⟦< L *scalprum*, a knife⟧ a small, sharp, straight knife used in surgery, etc.

**scam** (skam) *n.* ⟦prob. < *scheme*⟧ [Slang] a swindle or fraud, esp. a CONFIDENCE GAME —*vt.* **scammed**, **scam'ming** [Slang] to cheat or swindle, as in a confidence game

**scamp** (skamp) *n.* ⟦< It *scampare*, to flee⟧ a mischievous fellow; rascal

**scam·per** (skam'pər) *vi.* ⟦see prec.⟧ to run or go quickly —*n.* a scampering

**scam·pi** (skam'pē) *n.*, *pl.* **-pi** or **-pies** ⟦It⟧ a large, edible shrimp

**scan** (skan) *vt.* **scanned**, **scan'ning** ⟦< L *scandere*, to climb⟧ **1** to analyze (verse) by marking the metrical feet **2** to look at closely **3** to glance at quickly **4** to examine the structure or condition of (an internal body organ) with ultrasound, etc. **5** to pass radar beams over (an area) —*vi.* to conform to metrical principles: said of poetry —*n.* the act or an instance of scanning

**Scan** or **Scand** *abbrev.* Scandinavia(n)

**scan·dal** (skan'dəl) *n.* ⟦< Gr *skandalon*, a snare⟧ **1** anything that offends moral feelings and leads to disgrace **2** shame, outrage, etc. caused by this **3** disgrace **4** malicious gossip

**scan'dal·ize'** (-də līz') *vt.* **-ized'**, **-iz'ing** to outrage the moral feelings of by improper conduct

**scan'dal·mon'ger** (-dəl muŋ'gər, -mäŋ'-) *n.* one who spreads scandal or gossip

**scan'dal·ous** (-də ləs) *adj.* **1** causing scandal; shameful **2** spreading slander —**scan'dal·ous·ly** *adv.*

**Scan·di·na·vi·a** (skan'də nā'vē ə) region in N Europe, including Norway, Sweden, & Denmark and, sometimes, Iceland

**Scan·di·na·vi·an** (skan'də nā'vē ən) *adj.* of Scandinavia or its peoples, languages, etc. —*n.* **1** a person born or living in Scandinavia **2** the sub-branch of the Germanic languages spoken by Scandinavians

**scan·sion** (skan'shən) *n.* ⟦Fr < L *scansio*⟧ the act of scanning, or analyzing, poetry

**scant** (skant) *adj.* ⟦< ON *skammr*, short⟧ **1** inadequate; meager **2** not quite up to full measure

**scant'y** *adj.* -**i·er**, -**i·est 1** barely sufficient **2** insufficient; not enough —**scant'i·ly** *adv.* —**scant'i·ness** *n.*

**scape·goat** (skāp'gōt') *n.* ⟦< ESCAPE + GOAT; see Lev. 16:7-26⟧ one who bears the blame for the mistakes of others —*vt.* to make a scapegoat of

**scape·grace** (skāp'grās') *n.* ⟦< ESCAPE + GRACE⟧ a rogue; scamp

**scap·u·la** (skap'yə lə) *n.*, *pl.* -**lae'** (-lē') or -**las** ⟦< L⟧ either of the two flat bones in the upper back; shoulder blade

**scar** (skär) *n.* ⟦< Gr *eschara*, orig., fireplace⟧ **1** a mark left after a wound, burn, etc. has healed **2** the lasting mental or emotional effects of suffering —*vt.* **scarred, scar'ring** to mark as with a scar —*vi.* to form a scar in healing

**scar·ab** (skar'əb) *n.* ⟦< L *scarabaeus*⟧ **1** a large, black beetle **2** a carved image of such a beetle

**scarce** (skers) *adj.* ⟦ult. < L *excerpere*, pick out⟧ **1** not common; rarely seen **2** not plentiful; hard to get —**make oneself scarce** [Inf.] to go or stay away —**scarce'ness** *n.*

**scarce'ly** *adv.* **1** hardly; only just **2** probably not or certainly not

**scar·ci·ty** (sker'sə tē) *n.*, *pl.* -**ties 1** an inadequate supply; dearth **2** rarity; uncommonness

**scare** (sker) *vt.* **scared, scar'ing** ⟦< ON *skjarr*, timid⟧ to fill with sudden fear —*vi.* to become frightened —*n.* a sudden fear —**scare away** (or **off**) to drive away (or off) by frightening —**scare up** [Inf.] to produce or gather quickly

**scare·crow** (sker'krō') *n.* a human figure made with sticks, old clothes, etc., put in a field to scare birds away from crops

**scarf** (skärf) *n.*, *pl.* **scarves** (skärvz) or sometimes **scarfs** ⟦< OFr *escharpe*, purse hung from the neck⟧ **1** a piece of cloth worn about the neck, head, etc. **2** a long, narrow covering for a table, etc.

**scar·i·fy** (skar'ə fī') *vt.* -**fied'**, -**fy'ing** ⟦< L *scarifare*⟧ to make small cuts in (the skin, etc.) —**scar'i·fi·ca'tion** *n.*

**scar·let** (skär'lit) *n.* ⟦< ML *scarlatum*⟧ very bright red —*adj.* **1** of this color **2** sinful; specif., whorish

**scarlet fever** an acute contagious disease characterized by sore throat, fever, and a scarlet rash

**scar·y** (sker'ē) *adj.* -**i·er**, -**i·est** [Inf.] frightening —**scar'i·ness** *n.*

**scat**[1] (skat) *vi.* **scat'ted, scat'ting** ⟦? short for SCATTER⟧ [Inf.] to go away: usually in the imperative

**scat**[2] (skat) *adj.* ⟦< ?⟧ *Jazz* using improvised, meaningless syllables in singing —*n.* such singing —*vi.* **scat'ted, scat'ting** to sing scat

**scath·ing** (skā'thiŋ) *adj.* ⟦< ON *skathi*, harm⟧ harsh or caustic *[scathing* remarks*]* —**scath'ing·ly** *adv.*

**sca·tol·o·gy** (skə täl'ə jē) *n.* ⟦< Gr *skōr*, excrement⟧ obsession with excrement or excretion in literature —**scat·o·log·i·cal** (skat'ə läj'i kəl) *adj.*

**scat·ter** (skat'ər) *vt.* ⟦ME *skateren*⟧ **1** to throw here and there; sprinkle **2** to separate and drive in many directions; disperse —*vi.* to separate and go off in several directions

**scat'ter·brain'** *n.* one who is incapable of concentrated thinking

**scatter rug** a small rug

**scav·eng·er** (skav'in jər) *n.* ⟦< NormFr *escauwer*, to inspect⟧ **1** one who gathers things discarded by others **2** any animal that eats refuse and decaying matter —**scav'enge** (-inj), -**enged**, -**eng·ing**, *vt.*, *vi.*

**sce·nar·i·o** (sə ner'ē ō'; -när'-) *n.*, *pl.* -**os'** ⟦see fol.⟧

**1** *a*) an outline of a play, etc. *b*) the script of a film **2** an outline for any planned series of events, real or imagined —**sce·nar'ist** *n.*

**scene** (sēn) *n.* ⟦< Gr *skēnē*, stage⟧ **1** the place where an event occurs **2** the setting of a play, story, etc. **3** a division of a play, usually part of an act **4** a unit of action in a play, film, etc. **5** SCENERY (sense 1) **6** a display of strong feeling *[*to make a *scene]* **7** [Inf.] the locale for a specified activity

**sce·ner·y** (sēn'ə rē) *n.*, *pl.* -**ies 1** painted screens, backdrops, etc., used on the stage to represent places, as in a play, etc. **2** the features of a landscape

**sce·nic** (sē'nik) *adj.* **1** of stage scenery **2** *a*) of natural scenery *b*) having beautiful scenery

**scent** (sent) *vt.* ⟦ult. < L *sentire*, to feel⟧ **1** to smell **2** to get a hint of **3** to fill with an odor; perfume —*n.* **1** an odor **2** the sense of smell **3** a perfume **4** an odor left by an animal, by which it is tracked —**scent'ed** *adj.*

**scep·ter** (sep'tər) *n.* ⟦< Gr *skēptron*, staff⟧ a staff held by a ruler as a symbol of sovereignty: chiefly Brit. sp. **scep'tre**

**scep·tic** (skep'tik) *n.*, *adj. chiefly Brit. sp.* of SKEPTIC —**scep'ti·cal** *adj.* —**scep'ti·cism'** *n.*

**sched·ule** (ske'jool; *Brit & often Cdn* shej'ool) *n.* ⟦< L *scheda*, a strip of papyrus⟧ **1** a list of details **2** a list of times of recurring events, projected operations, etc.; timetable **3** a timed plan for a project —*vt.* -**uled**, -**ul·ing 1** to place in a schedule **2** to plan for a certain time

**sche·mat·ic** (skē mat'ik) *adj.* of or like a scheme, diagram, etc.

**scheme** (skēm) *n.* ⟦< Gr *schēma*, a form⟧ **1** *a*) a systematic program for attaining some end *b*) a secret plan; plot **2** an orderly combination of things on a definite plan **3** a diagram —*vt.*, *vi.* **schemed, schem'ing** to devise or plot —**schem'er** *n.*

**scher·zo** (sker'tsō) *n.*, *pl.* -**zos** or -**zi** (-tsē) ⟦It, jest⟧ *Music* a lively composition, usually in 3/4 time, as the third movement of a symphony, etc.

**schism** (siz'əm, skiz'-) *n.* ⟦< Gr *schizein*, to cleave⟧ a split, as in a church, because of difference of opinion, doctrine, etc. —**schis·mat'ic** (-mat'ik) *adj.*

**schist** (shist) *n.* ⟦< Gr *schistos*, easily cleft⟧ a crystalline rock easily split into layers

**schiz·o·phre·ni·a** (skit'sə frē'nē ə) *n.* ⟦< Gr *schizein*, cleave + *phrēn*, the mind⟧ a mental disorder characterized by separation between thought and emotions, by delusions, bizarre behavior, etc. —**schiz'oid** (-soid) or **schiz'o·phren'ic** (-ə fren'ik) *adj.*, *n.*

**schle·miel** (shlə mēl') *n.* ⟦Yiddish⟧ [Slang] a bungling person who habitually fails or is easily victimized

**schlep** or **schlepp** (shlep) [Slang] *vt.* **schlepped, schlep'ping** ⟦via Yiddish < LowG *slepen*, to drag⟧ to carry, haul, etc. —*vi.* to go or move with effort —*n.* an ineffectual person

**schlock** (shläk) [Slang] *n.* ⟦< ? Ger *schlacke*, dregs⟧ anything cheap or inferior; trash —*adj.* cheap; inferior: also **schlock'y**, -**i·er**, -**i·est**

**schmaltz** (shmälts, shmôlts) *n.* ⟦? via Yiddish < Ger *schmaltz*, rendered fat⟧ [Slang] highly sentimental music, literature, etc.

**schnapps** (shnäps) *n.*, *pl.* **schnapps** ⟦Ger, a nip < Du *snaps*, a gulp⟧ a strong alcoholic liquor: also sp. **schnaps**

**schnau·zer** (shnou'zər) *n.* ⟦Ger < *schnauzen*, to snarl⟧ a sturdily built dog with a wiry coat and bushy eyebrows

**schol·ar** (skäl'ər) *n.* ⟦< L *schola*, a school⟧ **1** a learned person **2** a student or pupil —**schol'ar·ly** *adj.*

**schol'ar·ship'** *n.* **1** the quality of knowledge a student shows **2** the systematized knowledge of a scholar **3** a gift of money, etc. as by a foundation, to help a student

**scho·las·tic** (skə las'tik) *adj.* ⟦see fol.⟧ of schools, colleges, students, etc.; educational; academic

**school**¹ (skōōl) *n.* ⟦< Gr *scholē*, leisure⟧ **1** a place or institution, with its buildings, etc., for teaching and learning **2** all of its students and teachers **3** a regular session of teaching **4** formal education; schooling **5** a particular division of a university **6** a group following the same beliefs, methods, etc. —*vt.* **1** to train; teach **2** to discipline or control —*adj.* of a school or schools

**school**² (skōōl) *n.* ⟦Du, a crowd⟧ a group of fish, etc. swimming together

**school board** an elected or appointed group of people in charge of public or private schools

**school'book'** *n.* a textbook

**school'boy'** *n.* a boy attending school

**school'girl'** *n.* a girl attending school

**school'house'** *n.* a building used as a school

**school'ing** *n.* training or education; esp., formal instruction at school

**school'marm'** (-märm', -mäm') *n.* **1** [Old-fashioned] a woman schoolteacher **2** [Inf.] any person who tends to be prudish, pedantic, etc.

**school'mas'ter** *n.* [Old-fashioned] a man who teaches in a school

**school'mate'** *n.* a companion or acquaintance at school

**school'mis'tress** *n.* [Old-fashioned] a woman who teaches in a school

**school'room'** *n.* a room in which pupils are taught, as in a school

**school'teach'er** *n.* one who teaches in a school

**school'work'** *n.* lessons worked on in classes or done as homework

**school'yard'** *n.* the ground around a school, used as a playground, etc.

**school year** the part of a year when school is in session, usually September to June

**schoon·er** (skōōn'ər) *n.* ⟦< ?⟧ **1** a ship with two or more masts, rigged fore and aft **2** a large beer glass

**Schu·bert** (shōō'bərt), **Franz** (fränts) 1797-1828; Austrian composer

**schuss** (shoos) *n.* ⟦Ger, lit., shot⟧ a straight run down a hill in skiing —*vi.* to do a schuss

**schwa** (shwä) *n.* ⟦Ger < Heb *sheva*⟧ **1** the neutral vowel sound of most unstressed syllables in English, as of *e* in *agent* **2** the symbol (ə) for this

**sci·at·ic** (sī at'ik) *adj.* ⟦see fol.⟧ of or in the hip or its nerves

**sci·at·i·ca** (sī at'i kə) *n.* ⟦< Gr *ischion*, the hip⟧ any painful condition in the hip or thigh; esp., neuritis of the long nerve (**sciatic nerve**) passing down the back of the thigh

**sci·ence** (sī'əns) *n.* ⟦< L *scire*, know⟧ **1** systematized knowledge derived from observation, study, etc. **2** a branch of knowledge, esp. one that systematizes facts, principles, and methods, as NATURAL SCIENCE **3** skill or technique

**science fiction** highly imaginative fiction typically involving some actual or projected scientific phenomenon

**sci·en·tif·ic** (sī'ən tif'ik) *adj.* **1** of or dealing with science **2** based on, or using, the principles and methods of science; systematic and exact —**sci·en·tif'i·cal·ly** *adv.*

**sci·en·tist** *n.* a specialist in science, as in biology, chemistry, or physics

**sci-fi** (sī'fī') *n.* [Inf.] *short for* SCIENCE FICTION

**scim·i·tar** (sim'ə tər) *n.* ⟦It *scimitarra*⟧ a short, curved sword used chiefly by Turks and Arabs

**scin·til·la** (sin til'ə) *n.* ⟦L⟧ **1** a spark **2** a particle; the least trace: figurative only

**scin·til·late** (sint''l āt') *vi.* **-lat·ed, -lat·ing** ⟦< L *scintilla*, a spark⟧ **1** to sparkle or twinkle **2** to be brilliant and witty —**scin·til·la'tion** *n.*

**sci·on** (sī'ən) *n.* ⟦< OFr *cion*⟧ **1** a shoot or bud of a plant, esp. one for grafting **2** a descendant; heir

**scis·sor** (siz'ər) *vt.* ⟦< fol.⟧ to cut, cut off, or cut out with scissors —*n.* SCISSORS, esp. in adjectival use

**scis·sors** (siz'ərz) *n.* ⟦< LL *cisorium*, cutting tool⟧

[*also with pl. v.*] a cutting instrument with two opposing blades pivoted together so that they can work against each other as the instrument is closed on paper, etc.: also called **pair of scissors**

**scle·ra** (sklir'ə) *n., pl.* **-ras** or **-rae** (-ē) ⟦< Gr *sklēros*, hard⟧ the tough, white membrane covering all of the eyeball except the area covered by the cornea

**scle·ro·sis** (skli rō'sis) *n., pl.* **-ses** (-sēz') ⟦< Gr *sklēros*, hard⟧ an abnormal hardening of body tissues —**scle·rot'ic** (-rät'ik) *adj.*

**scoff** (skäf, skôf) *n.* an expression of scorn or derision —*vt., vi.* to mock or jeer (at) —**scoff'er** *n.*

**scoff'law'** *n.* [Inf.] one who flouts traffic laws, liquor laws, etc.

**scold** (skōld) *n.* ⟦< ON *skald*, poet (prob. of satirical verses)⟧ a person, esp. a woman, who habitually uses abusive language —*vt., vi.* to find fault (with) angrily; to rebuke —**scold'ing** *adj., n.*

**sco·li·o·sis** (skō'lē ō'sis) *n.* ⟦< Gr *skolios*, crooked⟧ lateral curvature of the spine

**sconce** (skäns) *n.* ⟦ult. < L *abscondere*, to hide⟧ a wall bracket for candles

**scone** (skōn, skän) *n.* ⟦Scot⟧ a light cake resembling a biscuit and often quadrant-shaped

**scooch** (skōōch) *vi.* **1** [Inf.] to scrunch (*down, through*, etc.) **2** to slide jerkily

**scoop** (skōōp) *n.* ⟦< MDu *schope*, bailing vessel, *schoppe*, a shovel⟧ **1** any of various small, shovel-like utensils, as for taking up flour or ice cream **2** the deep shovel of a dredge, etc. **3** the act or motion of scooping **4** the amount scooped up at one time **5** [Inf.] *a*) the publication or broadcast of a news item before a competitor *b*) such a news item —*vt.* **1** to take up or out with or as with a scoop **2** to hollow (*out*) **3** [Inf.] to publish news before (a competitor)

**scoot** (skōōt) *vi., vt.* ⟦prob. < ON *skjōta*, to shoot⟧ [Inf.] to go or move quickly; hurry (off)

**scootch** (skōōch) *vi.* [Inf.] *alt. sp. of* SCOOCH

**scoot'er** *n.* ⟦< SCOOT⟧ **1** a child's two-wheeled vehicle moved by pushing one foot against the ground **2** a similar, motor-driven vehicle with a seat: in full **motor scooter**

**scope** (skōp) *n.* ⟦< Gr *skopos*, watcher⟧ **1** the extent of the mind's grasp **2** the range or extent of action, inclusion, inquiry, etc. **3** room or opportunity for freedom of action or thought

**-scope** (skōp) ⟦< Gr *skopein*, see⟧ *combining form* an instrument, etc. for seeing or observing [*telescope, kaleidoscope*]

**scorch** (skôrch) *vt.* ⟦< ? Scand⟧ **1** to burn slightly or superficially **2** to parch by intense heat —*vi.* to become scorched —*n.* a superficial burn

**score** (skôr) *n.* ⟦< ON *skor*⟧ **1** a scratch, mark, notch, incised line, etc. **2** an account or debt **3** a grievance one seeks to settle **4** a reason or motive **5** the number of points made, as in a game **6** a grade, as on a test **7** *a*) twenty people or things *b*) [*pl.*] very many **8** a copy of a musical composition showing all parts for the instruments or voices **9** [Inf.] the basic facts [*to know the score*] —*vt.* **scored, scor'ing 1** to mark with notches, cuts, lines, etc. **2** *a*) to make (runs, points, etc.) in a game *b*) to record the score of **3** to achieve [*score a success*] **4** to evaluate, as in testing **5** *Music* to arrange in a score —*vi.* **1** to make points, as in a game **2** to keep the score of a game **3** to gain an advantage, a success, etc. —**scor'er** *n.*

**score'board'** *n.* a large board for posting scores, etc., as in a stadium

**score'less** *adj.* with no points scored

**scorn** (skôrn) *n.* ⟦< OFr *escharnir*, to scorn⟧ extreme, often indignant, contempt —*vt.* **1** to regard with scorn **2** to refuse or reject with scorn —**scorn'ful** *adj.* —**scorn'ful·ly** *adv.*

**Scor·pi·o** (skôr'pē ō') *n.* ⟦L, scorpion⟧ the eighth sign of the zodiac

**scor'pi·on** (-ən) *n.* ⟦< Gr *skorpios*⟧ an arachnid

with a long tail ending in
a poisonous sting

**Scot** (skät) *n.* a person
born or living in Scotland

**Scot** *abbrev.* **1** Scotland
**2** Scottish

**scotch** (skäch) *vt.* [prob. <
OFr *coche,* a nick] **1** to
maim **2** to put an end to;
stifle *[to scotch a rumor]*

**Scotch** (skäch) *adj.* of
Scotland: cf. SCOTTISH —
*n.* **1** SCOTTISH **2** *[often* **s-**] whiskey distilled in
Scotland from malted barley: in full **Scotch
whisky**

SCORPION

**Scotch′man** (-mən) *n., pl.* **-men** (-mən) *var. of*
SCOTSMAN

**Scotch tape** [< *Scotch,* a trademark] a thin,
transparent adhesive tape

**scot-free** (skät′frē′) *adv., adj.* [< earlier *scot,* a
tax] without being punished or hurt

**Scot·land** (skät′lənd) division of the United Kingdom: the N half of Great Britain: 29,794 sq. mi.;
pop. 4,962,000

**Scotland Yard** the London police headquarters,
esp. its detective bureau

**Scots** (skäts) *adj., n.* SCOTTISH

**Scots′man** (-mən) *n., pl.* **-men** (-mən) a person
born or living in Scotland, esp. a man: *Scotsman*
or *Scot* is preferred to *Scotchman* in Scotland —
**Scots′wom′an,** *pl.* **-wom′en, fem.n.**

**Scot·tie** or **Scot·ty** (skät′ē) *n., pl.* **-ties** SCOTTISH
TERRIER

**Scot·tish** (skät′ish) *adj.* of Scotland or its people,
variety of English, etc.: *Scottish* is formal usage,
but with some words, *Scotch* is used (e.g., tweed,
whisky), with others, *Scots* (e.g., law) —*n.* the
variety of English spoken in Scotland —**the Scottish** the Scottish people

**Scottish terrier** a short-legged terrier with a wiry
coat

**scoun·drel** (skoun′drəl) *n.* [prob. ult. < L *ab(s)-,*
from + *condere,* to hide] a mean, immoral, or
wicked person

**scour**[1] (skour) *vt., vi.* [< ? L *ex-,* intens. + *cura,*
care] **1** to clean by rubbing hard, as with abra-
sives **2** to clean or clear out as by a flow of water

**scour**[2] (skour) *vt.* [< L *ex-,* out + *currere,* to run] to
pass over quickly, or range over, as in searching
*[to scour a library for a book]*

**scourge** (skurj) *n.* [< L *ex,* off + *corrigia,* a whip]
**1** a whip **2** any cause of serious affliction —*vt.*
**scourged, scourg′ing 1** to whip or flog **2** to punish or afflict severely

**scout** (skout) *n.* [< L *auscultare,* to listen] **1** a
soldier, plane, etc. sent to spy out the enemy's
strength, actions, etc. **2** a person sent out to survey a competitor, find new talent, etc. **3** [S-] a
Boy Scout or Girl Scout —*vt., vi.* **1** to reconnoiter
**2** to go in search of (something)

**scout′ing** *n.* **1** the act of one who scouts **2** *[often*
**S-]** the activities of the Boy Scouts or Girl Scouts

**scout′mas′ter** *n.* the adult leader of a troop of
Boy Scouts

**scow** (skou) *n.* [Du *schouw*] a large, flat-bottomed
boat used for carrying loads, often towed by a
tugboat

**scowl** (skoul) *vi.* [prob. < Scand] to look angry,
sullen, etc., as by contracting the eyebrows —*n.* a
scowling look —**scowl′er** *n.*

**scrab·ble** (skrab′əl) *vi.* **-bled, -bling** [< Du *schrab-
ben,* to scrape] **1** to scratch, scrape, etc. as
though looking for something **2** to struggle

**scrag·gly** (skrag′lē) *adj.* **-gli·er, -gli·est** [prob. <
ON] uneven, ragged, etc. in growth or form

**scram** (skram) *vi.* **scrammed, scram′ming** [< fol.]
[Slang] to get out, esp. in a hurry

**scram·ble** (skram′bəl) *vi.* **-bled, -bling** [< ?] **1** to
climb, crawl, etc. hurriedly **2** to scuffle or struggle for something —*vt.* **1** to mix haphazardly **2**

to stir and cook (slightly beaten eggs) **3** to make
(transmitted signals) unintelligible without special receiving equipment —*n.* **1** a hard climb or
advance **2** a disorderly struggle, as for something
prized

**scrap**[1] (skrap) *n.* [ult. < ON *skrapa,* to scrape] **1** a
small piece; fragment **2** discarded material **3**
*[pl.]* bits of food —*adj.* **1** in the form of pieces,
leftovers, etc. **2** used and discarded —*vt.*
**scrapped, scrap′ping 1** to make into scrap **2** to
discard; junk —**scrap′per** *n.*

**scrap**[2] (skrap) *n., vi.* **scrapped, scrap′ping** [< ?
SCRAPE] [Inf.] fight or quarrel —**scrap′per** *n.* —
**scrap′py, -pi·er, -pi·est, adv.**

**scrap′book′** *n.* a book in which to mount clip-
pings, pictures, etc.

**scrape** (skrāp) *vt.* **scraped, scrap′ing** [< ON
*skrapa*] **1** to make smooth or clean by rubbing
with a tool or abrasive **2** to remove in this way:
with *off, out,* etc. **3** to scratch or abrade **4** to
gather slowly and with difficulty *[scrape* up some
cash*]* —*vi.* **1** to rub against something harshly;
grate **2** to manage to get by: with *through, along,
by* —*n.* **1** a scraping **2** a scraped place **3** a grating sound **4** a predicament —**scrap′er** *n.*

**scrap′heap′** (-hēp′) *n.* a pile of discarded material,
as of scrap iron —**throw** (or **toss, cast,** etc.) **on the
scrapheap** to get rid of as useless

**scratch** (skrach) *vt.* [ME *scracchen*] **1** to mark,
break, or cut the surface of slightly **2** to tear or
dig with the nails or claws **3** to scrape lightly to
relieve itching **4** to scrape with a grating noise **5**
to write hurriedly or carelessly **6** to strike out
(writing, etc.) **7** *Sports* to withdraw (a contestant,
etc.) —*vi.* **1** to use nails or claws in digging,
wounding, etc. **2** to scrape —*n.* **1** a scratching **2**
a mark, tear, etc. made by scratching **3** a grating
or scraping sound —*adj.* used for hasty notes,
figuring etc. *[scratch* paper*]* —**from scratch** from
nothing; without resources, etc. —**up to scratch**
[Inf.] up to standard —**scratch′y, -i·er, -i·est, adj.**
—**scratch′i·ly** *adv.* —**scratch′i·ness** *n.*

**scratch′pad′** *n.* a pad of paper for jotting notes

**scrawl** (skrôl) *vt., vi.* [< ?] to write or draw
hastily, carelessly, etc. —*n.* sprawling, often illegible handwriting

**scraw·ny** (skrô′nē) *adj.* **-ni·er, -ni·est** [prob. <
Scand] very thin; skinny —**scraw′ni·ness** *n.*

**scream** (skrēm) *vi.* [ME *screamen*] **1** to utter a
shrill, piercing cry in fright, pain, etc. **2** to shout,
laugh, etc. wildly —*vt.* to utter with or as with a
scream —*n.* **1** a sharp, piercing cry or sound **2**
[Inf.] a very funny person or thing

**screech** (skrēch) *vi., vt.* [< ON *skraekja*] to utter
(with) a shrill, high-pitched sound —*n.* such a
sound —**screech′y, -i·er, -i·est, adj.**

**screen** (skrēn) *n.* [< OFr *escren*] **1** a partition,
curtain, etc. used to separate, conceal, etc. **2** anything that shields, conceals, etc. **3** a coarse mesh
of wire, etc., used as a sieve **4** a frame covered
with a mesh *[a window screen]* **5** *a)* a surface on
which films, slides, etc. are projected *b)* the film
industry *c)* the surface of a TV set, computer,
etc. on which images are formed —*vt.* **1** to conceal or protect, as with a screen **2** to sift through
a screen **3** to separate according to skills, etc. **4**
to show (a film, etc.) to critics, the public, etc.

**screen′play′** *n.* the script from which a film is
produced

**screen′writ′er** *n.* the writer of a script for a film
—**screen′writ′ing** *n.*

**screw** (skrōō) *n.* [< Fr *escroue,* hole in which the
screw turns] **1** a cylindrical or conical piece of
metal threaded in an advancing spiral, for fastening things: it penetrates when turned **2** any spiral thing like this **3** anything operating or
threaded like a screw —*vt.* **1** to twist; turn **2** to
fasten, tighten, etc. as with a screw **3** to contort
—*vi.* **1** to go together or come apart by being
turned like a screw *[the lid screws on]* **2** to twist
or turn —**put the screws on** (or **to**) [Inf.] to subject to great pressure; coerce —**screw up** [Inf.] to
bungle

**screw·ball'** *n.* [Slang] an erratic, irrational or unconventional person

**screw·driv·er** *n.* a tool used for turning screws

**screw·worm'** *n.* the larva of an American blowfly that infests wounds, and the nostrils, navel, etc. of animals

**screw·y** (skrōō′ē) *adj.* **-i·er, -i·est** [Slang] **1** crazy **2** peculiar, eccentric

**scrib·ble** (skrib′əl) *vt., vi.* **-bled, -bling** ⟦< L *scribere*, write⟧ **1** to write carelessly, hastily, etc. **2** to make meaningless or illegible marks (on) —*n.* scribbled writing —**scrib′bler** *n.*

**scribe** (skrīb) *n.* ⟦< L *scribere*, write⟧ **1** a person who copied manuscripts before the invention of printing **2** a writer

**scrim** (skrim) *n.* ⟦< ?⟧ **1** a light, sheer, loosely woven cotton or linen cloth **2** such a cloth used as a stage backdrop or semitransparent curtain

**scrim·mage** (skrim′ij) *n.* ⟦< SKIRMISH⟧ **1** *Football* play that follows the snap from center **2** a practice game —*vi.* **-maged, -mag·ing** to take part in a scrimmage

**scrimp** (skrimp) *vt., vi.* ⟦< ? Scand⟧ to be sparing or frugal (with)

**scrim′shaw'** (-shô′) *n.* an intricate carving of bone, ivory, etc. done esp. by sailors

**scrip** (skrip) *n.* ⟦< fol.⟧ a certificate of a right to receive something, as money or goods

**script** (skript) *n.* ⟦< L *scribere*, to write⟧ **1** handwriting **2** a copy of the text of a play, film etc.

**scrip·ture** (skrip′chər) *n.* ⟦see prec.⟧ **1** any sacred writing **2** [S-] [*often pl.*] the sacred writings of the Jews; Old Testament **3** [S-] [*often pl.*] the Christian Bible; Old and New Testaments —**scrip′tur·al** *adj.*

**script′writ·er** *n.* one who writes scripts for films, TV, etc.

**scrod** (skräd) *n.* ⟦prob. < MDu *schrode*, piece cut off⟧ a young codfish or haddock, esp. one prepared for cooking

**scrof·u·la** (skräf′yə lə) *n.* ⟦< L *scrofa*, a sow⟧ tuberculosis of the lymphatic glands, esp. of the neck —**scrof′u·lous** *adj.*

**scroll** (skrōl) *n.* ⟦< ME *scrowle*⟧ **1** a roll of parchment, paper, etc., usually with writing on it **2** an ornamental design in coiled or spiral form —*vi.* to move lines of text, etc. vertically on a video screen

**scro·tum** (skrōt′əm) *n., pl.* **-ta** (-ə) or **-tums** ⟦L⟧ the pouch of skin holding the testicles

**scrounge** (skrounj) *vt.* **scrounged, scroung′ing** ⟦< ?⟧ [Inf.] **1** to get by begging or sponging; mooch **2** to pilfer —*vi.* [Inf.] to seek (*around*) for something —**scroung′er** *n.*

**scroung′y** *adj.* **-i·er, -i·est** [Slang] shabby, dirty, unkempt, etc. —**scroung′i·ness** *n.*

**scrub**[1] (skrub) *n.* ⟦ME, var. of *shrubbe*, shrub⟧ **1** a thick growth of stunted trees or bushes **2** any person or thing smaller than the usual, or inferior **3** *Sports* a substitute player —*adj.* small, stunted, inferior, etc. —**scrub′by, -bi·er, -bi·est,** *adj.*

**scrub**[2] (skrub) *vt., vi.* **scrubbed, scrub′bing** ⟦prob. < Scand⟧ **1** to clean or wash by rubbing hard **2** to rub hard —*n.* a scrubbing —**scrub′ber** *n.*

**scrub′wom·an** *n., pl.* **-wom·en** CHARWOMAN

**scruff** (skruf) *n.* ⟦< ON *skrufr*, a tuft of hair⟧ the nape of the neck

**scruff·y** (skruf′ē) *adj.* **-i·er, -i·est** ⟦< SCURF + -Y[2]⟧ shabby; unkempt

**scrump·tious** (skrump′shəs) *adj.* ⟦< SUMPTUOUS⟧ [Inf.] very pleasing, etc., esp. to the taste

**scrunch** (skrunch) *vt., vi.* ⟦< CRUNCH⟧ **1** to crunch, crush, etc. **2** to huddle, squeeze, etc. —*n.* a crunching or crumpling sound

**scru·ple** (skrōō′pəl) *n.* ⟦< L *scrupulus*, small stone⟧ **1** a very small quantity **2** doubt arising from difficulty in deciding what is right —*vt., vi.* **-pled, -pling** to hesitate (at) from doubt

**scru·pu·lous** (-pyə ləs) *adj.* **1** having or showing scruples; conscientiously honest **2** careful of details; precise —**scru′pu·los′i·ty** (-läs′ət ē) *pl.* **-ties,** *n.* —**scru′pu·lous·ly** *adv.*

**scru·ti·nize** (skrōōt′'n īz′) *vt.* **-nized′, -niz′ing** to examine closely

**scru·ti·ny** (skrōōt′'n ē) *n., pl.* **-nies** ⟦< L *scrutari*, examine⟧ **1** a close examination or watch **2** a lengthy, searching look

**scu·ba** (skōō′bə) *n.* ⟦*s(elf-)c(ontained) u(nderwater) b(reathing) a(pparatus)*⟧ a diver's equipment with compressed-air tanks for breathing underwater

**scud** (skud) *vi.* **scud′ded, scud′ding** ⟦prob. < ON⟧ to move swiftly —*n.* a scudding

**scuff** (skuf) *vt., vi.* ⟦prob. < ON *skufa*, to shove⟧ **1** to wear or get a rough place on the surface (of) **2** to drag (the feet) —*n.* **1** a worn or rough spot **2** a flat-heeled house slipper with no back upper part

**scuf·fle** (skuf′əl) *vi.* **-fled, -fling** ⟦< prec.⟧ **1** to struggle or fight in rough confusion **2** to drag the feet —*n.* **1** a confused fight **2** a shuffling of feet

**scull** (skul) *n.* ⟦ME *skulle*⟧ **1** an oar worked from side to side over the stern of a boat **2** a light rowboat for racing —*vt., vi.* to propel with a scull

**scul·ler·y** (skul′ər ē) *n., pl.* **-ies** ⟦< L *scutella*, tray⟧ [Now Rare] a room near the kitchen, where pots, pans, etc. are cleaned and stored

**scul·lion** (skul′yən) *n.* ⟦ult. < L *scopa*, a broom⟧ [Archaic] a servant doing the rough kitchen work

**sculpt** (skulpt) *vt., vi.* SCULPTURE

**sculp·tor** (skulp′tər) *n.* an artist who creates works of sculpture

**sculp·ture** (skulp′chər) *n.* ⟦< L *sculpere*, to carve⟧ **1** the art of shaping stone, clay, wood, metal, etc. into statues, figures, etc. **2** a work or works of sculpture —*vt., vi.* **-tured, -tur·ing** **1** to cut, carve, chisel, etc. (statues, figures, etc.) **2** to make or form like sculpture —**sculp′tur·al** *adj.*

**scum** (skum) *n.* ⟦< MDu *schum*⟧ **1** a thin layer of impurities on the top of a liquid **2** refuse **3** [Inf.] a despicable person or persons —*vi.* to become covered with scum —**scum′my, -mi·er, -mi·est,** *adj.*

**scup·per** (skup′ər) *n.* ⟦< OFr *escopir*, to spit⟧ an opening in a ship's side to allow water to run off the deck

**scurf** (skurf) *n.* ⟦< ON⟧ **1** little, dry scales shed by the skin, as dandruff **2** any scaly coating —**scurf′y, -i·er, -i·est,** *adj.*

**scur·ri·lous** (skur′ə ləs) *adj.* ⟦< L *scurra*, buffoon⟧ vulgarly abusive —**scur·ril·i·ty** (skə ril′ə tē) *pl.* **-ties,** *n.* —**scur′ri·lous·ly** *adv.*

**scur·ry** (skur′ē) *vi.* **-ried, -ry·ing** ⟦< ?⟧ to run hastily; scamper —*n.* a scurrying

**scur·vy** (skur′vē) *adj.* **-vi·er, -vi·est** ⟦< SCURF⟧ low; mean —*n.* a disease resulting from a deficiency of vitamin C, characterized by weakness, anemia, spongy gums, etc. —**scur′vi·ly** *adv.*

**scut·tle**[1] (skut′'l) *n.* ⟦< L *scutella*, tray⟧ a bucket for carrying coal

**scut·tle**[2] (skut′'l) *vi.* **-tled, -tling** ⟦ME *scutlen*⟧ to scamper —*n.* a scamper

**scut·tle**[3] (skut′'l) *n.* ⟦< Sp *escotilla*, an indentation⟧ an opening fitted with a cover, as in the hull or deck of a ship —*vt.* **-tled, -tling** to cut holes through the lower hull of (a ship, etc.) to sink it

**scut·tle·butt** (skut′'l but′) *n.* ⟦< *scuttled butt*, lidded cask⟧ [Inf.] rumor or gossip

**scuz·zy** (skuz′ē) *adj.* **-zi·er, -zi·est** ⟦< ?⟧ [Slang] dirty, shabby, etc.

**scythe** (sīth) *n.* ⟦OE *sithe*⟧ a tool with a long, single-edged blade on a long, curved handle, for cutting grass, grain, etc.

**SD** South Dakota

**Se** *Chem. symbol for* selenium

**SE** *abbrev.* **1** southeast **2** southeastern

**sea** (sē) *n.* ⟦OE *sæ*⟧ **1** the ocean **2** any of various smaller bodies of salt water [the Red *Sea*] **3** a large body of fresh water [*Sea* of Galilee] **4** the condition of the surface of the ocean [a calm *sea*] **5** a heavy wave **6** a very great amount [a *sea* of debt] —**at sea 1** on the open sea **2** uncertain; bewildered

**sea anemone** a sea polyp with a gelatinous body and petal-like tentacles

**sea bass** (bas) a saltwater food fish

**sea'bed'** *n.* the mineral-rich ocean floor

**sea'board'** *n.* ⟦SEA + BOARD⟧ land bordering on the sea —*adj.* bordering on the sea

**sea'coast'** *n.* land bordering on the sea

**sea cow** a large sea mammal with a cigar-shaped body and a blunt snout, as the manatee

**sea'far'er** (-fer'ər) *n.* a sea traveler; esp., a sailor —**sea'far'ing** *adj., n.*

**sea'floor'** *n.* the ground along the ocean bottom

**sea'food'** *n.* food prepared from or consisting of saltwater fish or shellfish

**sea'go'ing** *adj.* 1 made for use on the open sea 2 SEAFARING

**sea gull** GULL[1]

**sea horse** a small semitropical fish with a head somewhat like that of a horse

**seal**[1] (sēl) *n.* ⟦< L *sigillum*⟧ 1 *a*) a design or initial impressed, often into wax, on a letter or document as a mark of authenticity *b*) a stamp or ring for making such an impression 2 a piece of paper, etc. bearing an impressed design recognized as official 3 something that seals or closes tightly 4 anything that guarantees; pledge 5 an ornamental paper stamp —*vt.* 1 to mark with a seal, as to authenticate or certify 2 to close or shut tight as with a seal 3 to confirm the genuineness of (a promise, etc.) 4 to decide finally

**seal**[2] (sēl) *n.* ⟦OE *seolh*⟧ 1 a sea mammal with a torpedo-shaped body and four flippers 2 the fur of some seals —*vi.* to hunt seals —**seal'er** *n.*

**seal·ant** (sēl'ənt) *n.* a substance, as a wax or plastic, used for sealing

**sea legs** the ability to walk without loss of balance on board a ship at sea

**sea level** the mean level of the sea's surface: used in measuring heights

**sea lion** a seal of the N Pacific

**seal'skin'** *n.* 1 the skin of the seal 2 a garment made of this

**seam** (sēm) *n.* ⟦OE⟧ 1 a line formed where two pieces of material are sewn together 2 a line that marks adjoining edges 3 a mark like this, as a scar or wrinkle 4 a layer of ore, coal, etc. —*vt.* 1 to join together so as to form a seam 2 to mark with a seamlike line, etc. —**seam'less** *adj.*

**sea·man** (sē'mən) *n., pl.* **-men** (-mən) 1 a sailor 2 *U.S. Navy* an enlisted person ranking below a petty officer —**sea'man·ship'** *n.*

**seam·stress** (sēm'stris) *n.* a woman whose occupation is sewing

**seam'y** *adj.* **-i·er, -i·est** unpleasant or sordid [the *seamy* side of life]

**sé·ance** (sā'äns) *n.* ⟦Fr < L *sedere*, to sit⟧ a meeting at which a medium seeks to communicate with the spirits of the dead

**sea'plane'** *n.* an airplane designed to land on and take off from water

**sea'port'** *n.* a port or harbor used by ocean ships

**sear** (sir) *vt.* ⟦< OE *sear*, dry (adj.)⟧ 1 to wither 2 to burn the surface of 3 to brand

**search** (surch) *vt.* ⟦< LL *circare*, go about⟧ 1 to look through in order to find something 2 to examine (a person) for something concealed 3 to examine carefully; probe —*vi.* to make a search —*n.* a searching —**in search of** making a search for —**search'er** *n.*

**search engine** software for locating documents, websites, etc. on a specified topic, etc.

**search'ing** *adj.* 1 examining thoroughly 2 piercing; penetrating

**search'light'** *n.* 1 an apparatus on a swivel that projects a strong beam of light 2 such a beam

**search warrant** a legal document authorizing a police search

**sea'scape'** (-skăp') *n.* ⟦SEA + (LAND)SCAPE⟧ 1 a view of the sea 2 a drawing, painting, etc. of such a scene

**sea'shell'** *n.* a saltwater mollusk shell

**sea'shore'** *n.* land along the sea

**sea'sick'ness** *n.* nausea, dizziness, etc. caused by the rolling of a ship or boat —**sea'sick'** *adj.*

**sea'side'** *n.* SEASHORE

**sea·son** (sē'zən) *n.* ⟦< VL *satio*, season for sowing⟧ 1 any of the four divisions of the year; spring, summer, fall, or winter 2 the time when something takes place, is popular, is permitted, etc. 3 the suitable time —*vt.* 1 to make (food) more tasty by adding salt, spices, etc. 2 to add zest to 3 to make more usable, as by aging 4 to make used to; accustom —*vi.* to become seasoned

**sea'son·a·ble** *adj.* 1 suitable to the season 2 opportune; timely

**sea'son·al** *adj.* of or depending on the season —**sea'son·al·ly** *adv.*

**sea'son·ing** *n.* anything that adds zest; esp., salt, spices, etc. added to food

**season ticket** a ticket or set of tickets for a series of concerts or baseball games

**seat** (sēt) *n.* ⟦ON *sæti*⟧ 1 *a*) a place to sit *b*) a thing to sit on; chair, etc. 2 *a*) the buttocks *b*) the part of a chair, garment, etc. that one sits on 3 the right to sit as a member [a *seat* on the council] 4 the center or the chief location [the *seat* of government] —*vt.* 1 to set in or on a seat 2 to have seats for [the car *seats* six] 3 to put or fix in a place, position, etc. —**be seated** to sit down: also **take a seat**

**seat belt** straps across the hips, to protect a seated passenger: also **seat'belt'** *n.*

**Se·at·tle** (sē at''l) seaport in WC Washington: pop. 516,000

**sea urchin** a small sea animal with a round body in a shell covered with sharp spines

**sea'ward** *adj., adv.* toward the sea: also **sea'wards** *adv.*

**sea'way'** *n.* an inland waterway to the sea for ocean ships

**sea'weed'** *n.* a sea plant, esp. an alga

**sea'wor'thy** (-wur'thē) *adj.* fit to travel on the sea: said of a ship

**se·ba·ceous** (sə bā'shəs) *adj.* ⟦< L *sebum*, tallow⟧ of, like, or secreting fat or a fatty substance [*sebaceous* glands]

**seb·or·rhe·a** or **seb·or·rhoe·a** (seb'ə rē'ə) *n.* ⟦ult. < L *sebum*, tallow + Gr *rhein*, flow⟧ an excessive discharge from the sebaceous glands, causing abnormally oily skin

**sec** *abbrev.* 1 second(s) 2 secondary 3 secretary 4 section(s)

**SEC** *abbrev.* Securities and Exchange Commission

**se·cede** (si sēd') *vi.* **-ced'ed, -ced'ing** ⟦< L *se-*, apart + *cedere*, to go⟧ to withdraw formally from a group, organization, etc.

**se·ces·sion** (si sesh'ən) *n.* 1 a seceding 2 [often S-] the withdrawal of the Southern states from the federal Union at the start of the Civil War —**se·ces'sion·ist** *n.*

**se·clude** (si klōōd') *vt.* **-clud'ed, -clud'ing** ⟦< L *se-*, apart + *claudere*, to close⟧ to shut off from others; isolate

**se·clu·sion** (si klōō'zhən) *n.* a secluding or being secluded; retirement; isolation

**sec·ond**[1] (sek'ənd) *adj.* ⟦< L *sequi*, follow⟧ 1 coming next after the first; 2d or 2nd 2 another of the same kind; other [a *second* chance] 3 next below the first in rank, value, etc. —*n.* 1 one that is second 2 an article of merchandise not of first quality 3 an aide or assistant, as to a duelist or boxer 4 the gear next after first gear 5 [*pl.*] a second helping of food —*vt.* 1 to assist 2 to indicate formal support of (a motion) before discussion or a vote —*adv.* in the second place, group, etc.

**sec·ond**[2] (sek'ənd) *n.* ⟦< ML (*pars minuta*) *secunda*, second (small part): from being a further division‖ **1** the sixtieth part of a minute of time or of angular measure **2** a moment; instant

**sec·ond·ar·y** (sek′ən der′ē) *adj.* **1** second in order, rank, importance, place, etc.; subordinate; minor **2** derived, not primary; derivative —*n., pl.* **-ar·ies 1** a secondary person or thing **2** *Football* the defensive backfield —**sec′ond·ar′i·ly** *adv.*

**secondary school** a school, esp. a high school, coming after elementary school

**secondary stress** (or **accent**) a weaker stress (′) than the primary stress of a word

**sec′ond-class′** *adj.* **1** of the class, rank, etc. next below the highest, best, etc. **2** of a cheaper mail class, as for periodicals **3** inferior, inadequate, etc. or treated as such —*adv.* by second-class mail or travel accommodations

**sec′ond-guess′** *vt., vi.* [Inf.] to use hindsight in criticizing (someone), remaking (a decision), etc.

**sec′ond-hand′** *adj.* **1** not from the original source **2** used before; not new **3** of or dealing in used merchandise

**second lieutenant** *Mil.* a commissioned officer of the lowest rank

**sec′ond·ly** *adv.* in the second place

**second nature** an acquired habit, etc. deeply fixed in one's nature

**second person** the form of a pronoun or verb that refers to the person(s) spoken to

**sec′ond-rate′** *adj.* **1** second in quality, rank, etc. **2** inferior

**sec′ond-string′** *adj.* [Inf.] *Sports* that is a substitute player at a specified position —**sec′ond-string′er** *n.*

**second thought** a change in thought after reconsidering —**on second thought** after reconsideration

**second wind 1** the return of easy breathing after initial exhaustion, as while running **2** any fresh ability to continue

**se·cre·cy** (sē′krə sē) *n., pl.* **-cies 1** a being secret **2** a tendency to keep things secret

**se·cret** (sē′krit) *adj.* ‖< L *se-*, apart + *cernere*, sift‖ **1** kept from the knowledge of others **2** beyond general understanding; mysterious **3** concealed from sight; hidden —*n.* a secret fact, cause, process, etc. —**in secret** secretly —**se′cret·ly** *adv.*

**sec·re·tar·i·at** (sek′rə ter′ē ət) *n.* a staff headed by a secretary; specif., an administrative staff, as in a government

**sec·re·tar·y** (sek′rə ter′ē) *n., pl.* **-tar·ies** ‖< ML *secretarius*, one entrusted with secrets‖ **1** one who keeps records, handles correspondence, etc. for an organization or person **2** [*often* **S-**] the head of a government department **3** a writing desk —**sec′re·tar′i·al** *adj.*

**se·crete** (si krēt′) *vt.* **-cret′ed, -cret′ing** ‖see SECRET‖ **1** to hide; conceal **2** to form and release (a substance) as a gland, etc. does

**se·cre·tion** (si krē′shən) *n.* **1** a secreting **2** a substance secreted by an animal or plant

**se·cre·tive** (sē′krə tiv) *adj.* concealing one's thoughts, etc.; not frank or open —**se′cre·tive·ly** *adv.* —**se′cre·tive·ness** *n.*

**se·cre·to·ry** (si krēt′ər ē) *adj.* having the function of secreting, as a gland

**Secret Service** a division of the U.S. Treasury Department for uncovering counterfeiters, guarding the President, etc.

**sect¹** (sekt) *n.* ‖< L *sequi*, follow‖ **1** a religious denomination **2** any group of people having a common philosophy, set of beliefs, etc.

**sect²** *abbrev.* section

**sec·tar·i·an** (sek ter′ē ən) *adj.* **1** of or devoted to some sect **2** narrow-minded —*n.* a sectarian person —**sec·tar′i·an·ism′** *n.*

**sec·tion** (sek′shən) *n.* ‖< L *secare*, to cut‖ **1** a cutting or cutting apart **2** a part cut off; portion **3** any distinct part, group, district, etc. **4** a drawing, etc. of a thing as it would appear if cut straight through —*vt.* to divide into sections

**sec′tion·al** *adj.* **1** of or characteristic of a given

section or district **2** made up of sections — **sec′tion·al·ism′** *n.*

**sec·tor** (sek′tər) *n.* ‖< L *secare*, to cut‖ **1** part of a circle bounded by any two radii and the included arc **2** any of the districts into which an area is divided for military operations **3** a distinct part of society or of an economy, group, etc.

**sec·u·lar** (sek′yə lər) *adj.* ‖< LL *saecularis*, worldly‖ not religious; not connected with a church —**sec′u·lar·ism′** *n.*

**sec′u·lar·ize′** (-lə rīz′) *vt.* **-ized′, -iz′ing** to change from religious to civil use, control, influence, etc. —**sec′u·lar·i·za′tion** *n.*

**se·cure** (si kyoor′) *adj.* ‖< L *se-*, free from + *cura*, care‖ **1** free from fear, care, etc. **2** free from danger, risk, etc.; safe **3** firm, stable, etc. [make the knot *secure*] —*vt.* **-cured′, -cur′ing 1** to make secure; protect **2** to make certain, as with a pledge **3** to make firm, fast, etc. **4** to obtain or bring about —**se·cure′ly** *adv.*

**se·cu·ri·ty** (si kyoor′ə tē) *n., pl.* **-ties 1** a feeling secure; freedom from fear, doubt, etc. **2** protection; safeguard **3** something given as a pledge of repayment, etc. **4** [*pl.*] bonds, stocks, etc. **5** a private police force

**secy** or **sec′y** *abbrev.* secretary

**se·dan** (si dan′) *n.* ‖< ? L *sedere*, to sit‖ an automobile with two or four doors, a permanent rigid top, and a full-sized rear seat

**se·date¹** (si dāt′) *adj.* ‖< L *sedare*, to settle‖ calm or composed; esp., serious and unemotional —**se·date′ly** *adv.*

**se·date²** (si dāt′) *vt.* **-dat′ed, -dat′ing** to dose with a sedative —**se·da′tion** *n.*

**sed·a·tive** (sed′ə tiv) *adj.* ‖see SEDATE¹‖ tending to soothe or quiet; lessening excitement, irritation, nervousness, etc. —*n.* a sedative medicine

**sed·en·tar·y** (sed′'n ter′ē) *adj.* ‖< L *sedere*, to sit‖ marked by much sitting

**Se·der** (sā′dər) *n., pl.* **Se·dar·im** (sə där′im) or **Se′ders** ‖Heb lit., arrangement‖ [*also* **s-**] *Judaism* the feast of Passover as observed in the home on the eve of the first (by some also of the second) day of the holiday

**sedge** (sej) *n.* ‖OE *secg*‖ a coarse, grasslike plant growing in wet ground

**sed·i·ment** (sed′ə mənt) *n.* ‖< L *sedere*, sit‖ **1** matter that settles to the bottom of a liquid **2** *Geol.* matter deposited by water or wind

**sed′i·men′ta·ry** (-men′tər ē) *adj.* **1** of or containing sediment **2** formed by the deposit of sediment, as certain rocks

**sed′i·men·ta′tion** (-men tā′shən, -mən-) *n.* the depositing of sediment

**se·di·tion** (si dish′ən) *n.* ‖< L *sed-*, apart + *itio*, a going‖ a stirring up of rebellion against the government —**se·di′tion·ist** *n.* —**se·di′tious** *adj.*

**se·duce** (si dōōs′) *vt.* **-duced′, -duc′ing** ‖< L *se-*, apart + *ducere*, to lead‖ **1** to tempt to wrongdoing **2** to entice into having, esp. for the first time, illicit sexual intercourse —**se·duc′er** *n.* —**se·duc′tion** (-duk′shən) *n.* —**se·duc′tive** *adj.* —**se·duc′tress** (-tris) *fem.n.*

**sed·u·lous** (sej′oo ləs) *adj.* ‖L *sedulus*‖ diligent

**se·dum** (sē′dəm) *n.* ‖< L‖ a perennial plant found on rocks or walls, with white, yellow, or pink flowers

**see¹** (sē) *vt.* **saw, seen, see′ing** ‖OE *seon*‖ **1** to get knowledge of through the eyes; look at **2** to understand **3** to learn; find out **4** to experience **5** to make sure [*see* that he goes] **6** to escort [*see* her to her door] **7** to encounter **8** to call on; consult **9** to receive [too ill to *see* anyone] —*vi.* **1** to have the power of sight **2** to understand **3** to think [let me *see*, who's next?] —**see off** to accompany (someone) to the place from which that person is to depart, as on a journey —**see through 1** to perceive the true nature of **2** to finish **3** to help through difficulty —**see to** to attend to

**see**[2] (sē) *n.* ⟦< L *sedes*, a seat⟧ the official seat or jurisdiction of a bishop

**seed** (sēd) *n., pl.* **seeds** or **seed** ⟦OE *sæd*⟧ **1** *a*) the part of a plant, containing the embryo, from which a new plant can grow *b*) such seeds collectively **2** the source of anything **3** [Archaic] descendants; posterity **4** sperm or semen **5** a seeded contestant —*vt.* **1** to plant with seeds **2** to remove the seeds from **3** to distribute (contestants in a tournament) so that the best teams or players are not matched in early rounds —*vi.* to produce seeds —**go** (or **run**) **to seed 1** to shed seeds after flowering **2** to deteriorate, weaken, etc. —**seed′less** *adj.*

**seed′ling** (-liŋ) *n.* **1** a plant grown from a seed **2** a young tree

**seed money** money to begin a long-term project

**seed vessel** any dry, hollow fruit containing seeds: also **seed′case′** *n.*

**seed′y** *adj.* **-i·er, -i·est 1** full of seed **2** gone to seed **3** shabby, rundown, etc. —**seed′i·ness** *n.*

**seek** (sēk) *vt.* **sought, seek′ing** ⟦OE *secan*⟧ **1** to try to find; search for **2** to try to get **3** to aim at **4** to try; attempt [to *seek* to please] —**seek′er** *n.*

**seem** (sēm) *vi.* ⟦prob. < ON *sœma*, conform to⟧ **1** to appear to be [to *seem* happy] **2** to give the impression: usually with an infinitive [she *seems* to know]

**seem′ing** *adj.* that seems real, true, etc. without necessarily being so; apparent —**seem′ing·ly** *adv.*

**seem′ly** *adj.* **-li·er, -li·est** suitable, proper, etc. — **seem′li·ness** *n.*

**seen** (sēn) *vt., vi. pp. of* SEE[1]

**seep** (sēp) *vi.* ⟦OE *sipian*, to soak⟧ to leak through small openings; ooze —**seep′age** *n.*

**seer** (sir) *n.* one who supposedly foretells the future —**seer′ess** *fem.n.*

**seer·suck·er** (sir′suk′ər) *n.* ⟦< Pers *shir u shakar*, lit., milk and sugar⟧ a crinkled fabric of linen, cotton, etc.

**see·saw** (sē′sô′) *n.* ⟦< SAW[1]⟧ **1** a plank balanced at the middle on which children at play, riding the ends, rise and fall alternately **2** any up-and-down or back-and-forth motion or change —*vt., vi.* to move up and down or back and forth

**seethe** (sēth) *vi.* **seethed, seeth′ing 1** to boil, surge, or bubble **2** to be violently agitated

**seg·ment** (seg′mənt; *for v.,* -ment) *n.* ⟦< L *secare*, to cut⟧ any of the parts into which something is or can be separated; section —*vt., vi.* to divide into segments —**seg′men·ta′tion** *n.*

**seg·re·gate** (seg′rə gāt′) *vt.* **-gat·ed, -gat·ing** ⟦< L *se-*, apart + *grex*, a flock⟧ to set apart from others; specif., to impose racial segregation on

**seg′re·ga′tion** *n.* the policy of compelling racial groups to live apart and use separate schools, facilities, etc. —**seg′re·ga′tion·ist** *n.*

**se·gue** (seg′wā, sā′gwā) *vi.* **-gued, -gue·ing** ⟦It, (it follows) < L *sequi*, to follow⟧ to continue without break (*to* or *into* the next part) —*n.* an immediate transition to the next part

**sei·gnior** (sān′yər, sān yôr′) *n.* ⟦< OFr *seignor* < L *senior*⟧ a feudal lord

**seine** (sān) *n.* ⟦< Gr *sagēnē*⟧ a large fishing net weighted along the bottom —*vt., vi.* **seined, sein′ing** to fish with a seine —**sein′er** *n.*

**Seine** (sān; *Fr* sen) river in N France, flowing through Paris

**seis·mic** (sīz′mik) *adj.* ⟦< Gr *seismos*, earthquake⟧ of or caused by an earthquake —**seis′mi·cal·ly** *adv.*

**seis′mo·graph′** (-mə graf′) *n.* ⟦see prec. & -GRAPH⟧ an instrument that records the intensity and duration of earthquakes

**seis·mol·o·gy** (sīz mäl′ə jē, sīs-) *n.* ⟦see SEISMIC & -LOGY⟧ the science dealing with earthquakes — **seis′mo·log′ic** (-mə läj′ik) or **seis′mo·log′i·cal** *adj.* —**seis·mol′o·gist** *n.*

**seize** (sēz) *vt.* **seized, seiz′ing** ⟦< ML *sacire*⟧ **1** *a*) to take legal possession of *b*) to capture; arrest **2**

to take forcibly and quickly **3** to grasp suddenly **4** to attack or afflict suddenly [*seized* with pain] — *vi.* to stick or jam: said of a machine: often with *up*

**sei·zure** (sē′zhər) *n.* **1** a seizing or being seized **2** a sudden attack, as of epilepsy

**sel·dom** (sel′dəm) *adv.* ⟦OE *seldan*, strange⟧ rarely; infrequently

**se·lect** (sə lekt′) *adj.* ⟦< L *se-*, apart + *legere*, to choose⟧ **1** chosen in preference to others **2** choice; excellent **3** exclusive —*vt., vi.* to choose or pick out —**se·lec′tor** *n.*

**se·lec′tion** (-lek′shən) *n.* **1** a selecting or being selected **2** that or those selected

**se·lec′tive** *adj.* **1** of selection **2** careful in choosing; discriminating —**se·lec′tiv′i·ty** *n.*

**selective service** compulsory military service set by age, fitness, etc.

**se·lect′man** (-mən) *n., pl.* **-men** (-mən) one of a board of governing officers in most New England towns

**se·le·ni·um** (sə lē′nē əm) *n.* ⟦ModL < Gr *selēnē*, the moon⟧ a nonmetallic chemical element, used in photoelectric devices

**self** (self) *n., pl.* **selves** ⟦OE⟧ **1** the identity, character, etc. of any person or thing **2** one's own person as distinct from all others **3** one's own welfare or interest —*adj.* of the same kind, color, material, etc. [drapes with a *self* lining]

**self-** *prefix* of, by, in, to, or with oneself or itself The following list includes some common compounds formed with *self-* that do not have special meanings:

| | |
|---|---|
| self-abasement | self-induced |
| self-advancement | self-indulgence |
| self-appointed | self-indulgent |
| self-complacent | self-inflicted |
| self-criticism | self-knowledge |
| self-deception | self-love |
| self-defeating | self-perpetuating |
| self-delusion | self-pity |
| self-destructive | self-pollination |
| self-discipline | self-preservation |
| self-employed | self-protection |
| self-examination | self-reproach |
| self-help | self-sealing |
| self-imposed | self-support |
| self-improvement | self-supporting |
| self-incrimination | self-sustaining |

**self′-ad·dressed′** *adj.* addressed to oneself [a *self-addressed* envelope]

**self′-ad·he′sive** *adj.* made to stick without moistening

**self′-as·ser′tion** *n.* a demanding to be acknowledged or an insisting upon one's rights, etc.

**self′-as·sur′ance** *n.* confidence in oneself —**self′-as·sured′** *adj.*

**self′-cen′tered** *adj.* **1** egocentric **2** selfish

**self′-con′fi·dence** *n.* confidence in one's own abilities, etc. —**self′-con′fi·dent** *adj.*

**self′-con′scious** *adj.* unduly conscious of oneself as an object of notice; specif., ill at ease —**self′-con′scious·ly** *adv.* —**self′-con′scious·ness** *n.*

**self′-con·tained′** *adj.* **1** keeping one's affairs to oneself **2** showing self-control **3** complete within itself

**self′-con·tra·dic′tion** *n.* **1** contradiction of oneself or itself **2** any statement containing elements that contradict each other —**self′-con′tra·dic′to·ry** *adj.*

**self′-con·trol′** *n.* control of one's own emotions, desires, actions, etc. —**self′-con·trolled′** *adj.*

**self′-de·fense′** *n.* defense of oneself or of one's rights, beliefs, actions, etc.

**self′-de·ni′al** *n.* denial or sacrifice of one's own desires or pleasures

**self′-de·scribed′** *adj.* described so by the person himself or herself [a *self-described* expert]

**self′-de·struct′** *vi.* **1** to destroy itself automatically **2** to greatly harm oneself as the result of inherent flaws

**self′-de·ter·mi·na′tion** *n.* **1** a making up one's

own mind **2** the right of a people to choose its own form of government —**self'-de·ter'mined** *adj.*

**self'-dis·cov'er·y** *n.* a becoming aware of one's true potential, character, motives, etc.

**self'-ed'u·cat'ed** *adj.* educated by oneself, with little formal schooling

**self'-ef·fac'ing** *adj.* modest; retiring —**self'-ef·face'ment** *n.*

**self'-es·teem'** *n.* **1** self-respect **2** undue pride in oneself; conceit

**self'-ev'i·dent** *adj.* evident without need of proof

**self'-ex·plan'a·to'ry** *adj.* explaining itself; obvious

**self'-ex·pres'sion** *n.* expression of one's own personality or emotions, esp. in the arts

**self'-ful·fill'ing** *adj.* **1** bringing about one's personal goals **2** brought about chiefly as an effect of having been expected or predicted

**self'-gov'ern·ment** *n.* government of a group by its own members —**self'-gov'ern·ing** *adj.*

**self'-im'age** *n.* one's conception of oneself and of one's own abilities, worth, etc.

**self'-im·por'tant** *adj.* having an exaggerated opinion of one's own importance —**self'-im·por'tance** *n.*

**self'-in'ter·est** *n.* **1** one's own interest or advantage **2** an exaggerated regard for this

**self'ish** *adj.* having or showing too much concern for one's own interests, etc., with little concern for others —**self'ish·ly** *adv.* —**self'ish·ness** *n.*

**self'less** *adj.* having or showing devotion to others' welfare; unselfish —**self'less·ly** *adv.* —**self'less·ness** *n.*

**self'-made'** *adj.* **1** made by oneself or itself **2** successful through one's own efforts

**self'-por'trait** *n.* a portrait of oneself, done by oneself

**self'-pos·ses'sion** *n.* full control of one's feelings, actions, etc. —**self'-pos·sessed'** *adj.*

**self'-pro·pelled'** *adj.* propelled by its own motor or power

**self'-re·crim'i·na'tion** *n.* a blaming of oneself

**self'-reg'u·lat'ing** *adj.* regulating oneself or itself, so as to function automatically or without outside control

**self'-re·li'ance** *n.* reliance on one's own judgment, abilities, etc. —**self'-re·li'ant** *adj.*

**self'-re·spect'** *n.* proper respect for oneself —**self'-re·spect'ing** *adj.*

**self'-re·straint'** *n.* restraint imposed on oneself by oneself; self-control

**self'-right'eous** *adj.* regarding oneself as being morally superior to others; smugly virtuous —**self'-right'eous·ly** *adv.* —**self'-right'eous·ness** *n.*

**self'-sac'ri·fice'** *n.* sacrifice of oneself or one's own interests for the benefit of others —**self'-sac'ri·fic'ing** *adj.*

**self'same'** *adj.* identical

**self'-sat'is·fied'** *adj.* feeling or showing an often smug satisfaction with oneself —**self'-sat'is·fac'tion** *n.*

**self'-seek'er** *n.* one who seeks mainly to further his or her own interests —**self'-seek'ing** *n.*, *adj.*

**self'-serve'** *adj. short for* SELF-SERVICE

**self'-serv'ice** *adj.* of or being a store, cafeteria, etc. set up so that customers pay a cashier and serve themselves

**self'-serv'ing** *adj.* serving one's own selfish interests

**self'-styled'** *adj.* so called only by oneself

**self'-suf·fi'cient** *adj.* able to get along without help; independent —**self'-suf·fi'cien·cy** *n.*

**self'-taught'** *adj.* having taught oneself through one's own efforts

**self'-willed'** *adj.* stubborn; obstinate

**self'-wind'ing** (-wīn'diŋ) *adj.* wound automatically, as some wristwatches

**sell** (sel) *vt.* **sold**, **sell'ing** ⟦OE *sellan*, to give⟧ **1** to exchange (goods, services, etc.) for money, etc. **2** to offer for sale **3** to promote the sale of —*vi.* **1**

to engage in selling **2** to be sold (*for* or *at*) **3** to attract buyers —**sell out 1** to get rid of completely by selling **2** [Inf.] to betray —**sell'er** *n.*

**sell'out'** *n.* [Inf.] **1** a selling out; betrayal **2** a show, game, etc. for which all seats have been sold

**selt·zer** (selt'sər) *n.* ⟦< *Niederselters*, Germany⟧ **1** [*often* **S-**] natural, effervescent mineral water **2** any carbonated water, often flavored

**sel·vage** or **sel·vedge** (sel'vij) *n.* ⟦< SELF + EDGE⟧ a specially woven edge that prevents cloth from raveling

**selves** (selvz) *n. pl. of* SELF

**se·man·tics** (sə man'tiks) *pl.n.* ⟦< Gr *sēmainein*, to show⟧ the study of the meanings of words —**se·man'tic** *adj.*

**sem·a·phore** (sem'ə fôr') *n.* ⟦< Gr *sēma*, sign + *pherein*, to bear⟧ any apparatus or system for signaling, as by lights, flags, etc.

**sem·blance** (sem'bləns) *n.* ⟦< L *similis*, like⟧ **1** outward appearance **2** a likeness or copy

**se·men** (sē'mən) *n.* ⟦L, seed⟧ the fluid secreted by the male reproductive organs

**se·mes·ter** (sə mes'tər) *n.* ⟦< L *sex*, six + *mensis*, month⟧ either of the two terms usually making up a school year

**sem·i** (sem'ī') *n.* [Inf.] a semitrailer and its attached TRACTOR (sense 2)

**semi-** ⟦L⟧ *prefix* **1** half **2** partly, not fully **3** twice in a (specified period)

**sem·i·an·nu·al** (sem'ē an'yo͞o əl) *adj.* happening, coming, etc. every half year

**sem'i·au'to·mat'ic** *adj.* designating an automatic weapon requiring a trigger pull for each round fired —*n.* a semiautomatic firearm

**sem·i·cir·cle** (sem'i sur'kəl) *n.* a half circle —**sem'i·cir'cu·lar** (-kyə lər) *adj.*

**sem'i·co'lon** *n.* a mark of punctuation (;) indicating a degree of separation greater than that marked by the comma

**sem'i·con·duc'tor** *n.* a substance, as germanium, used as in transistors

**sem'i·con'scious** *adj.* not fully conscious or awake

**sem·i·fi·nal** (sem'i fīn'əl; *for n.*, sem'i fīn'əl) *adj.* coming just before the final match, as of a tournament —*n.* a semifinal match, etc.

**sem'i·month'ly** (sem'i munth'lē) *adj.* done, happening, etc. twice a month —*adv.* twice monthly

**sem·i·nal** (sem'ə nəl) *adj.* ⟦see SEMEN⟧ **1** of seed or semen **2** that is a source **3** of essential importance; specif., *a*) basic; central *b*) crucial

**sem·i·nar** (sem'ə när') *n.* ⟦see fol.⟧ **1** a group of supervised students doing research **2** a course for such a group

**sem·i·nar·y** (sem'ə ner'ē) *n.*, *pl.* **-nar'ies** ⟦< L *seminarium*, nursery⟧ a school where ministers, priests, or rabbis are trained —**sem'i·nar'i·an** *n.*

**Sem·i·nole** (sem'ə nōl') *n.*, *pl.* **-noles'** or **-nole'** a member of a North American Indian people of S Florida & Oklahoma

**se·mi·ot·ics** (sē'mē ät'iks) *n.* ⟦< Gr *sēmeion*, sign⟧ *Philos.* a general theory of signs and symbols; esp., the analysis of signs in language

**sem·i·pre·cious** (sem'i presh'əs) *adj.* designating gems, as the garnet, turquoise, etc., of lower value than precious stones

**sem'i·pri'vate** *adj.* of a hospital room with two, three, or sometimes four beds

**sem'i·pro·fes'sion·al** *n.* one who engages in a sport for pay but not as a regular occupation: also **sem'i·pro'**

**sem'i·skilled'** *adj.* of or doing manual work requiring only limited training

**Sem·ite** (sem'īt') *n.* ⟦< Heb *Shem*, son of Noah⟧ a member of any of the peoples speaking a Semitic language

**Se·mit·ic** (sə mit'ik) *n.* a major group of African and Asian languages, including Hebrew, Arabic, etc. —*adj.* designating or of the Semites or their languages, etc.

**sem·i·tone** (sem'i tōn') *n. Music* the difference in pitch between any two immediately adjacent keys on the piano

**sem'i·trail'er** *n.* a detachable trailer designed to be attached to a coupling at the rear of a TRACTOR (sense 2)

**sem'i·trop'i·cal** *adj.* partly tropical

**sem'i·week'ly** *adj.* done, happening, etc. twice a week —*adv.* twice weekly

**sem·o·li·na** (sem'ə lē'nə) *n.* [It] coarse flour from hard wheat

**Sen** *abbrev.* **1** Senate **2** Senator **3** [*also* **s-**] senior

**sen·ate** (sen'it) *n.* [< L *senex*, old] **1** a legislative assembly **2** [**S-**] the upper house of the U.S. Congress or of most of the U.S. state legislatures

**sen·a·tor** (sen'ət ər) *n.* a member of a senate — **sen·a·to·ri·al** (sen'ə tôr'ē əl) *adj.*

**send** (send) *vt.* sent, send'ing [OE *sendan*] **1** to cause to go or be transmitted; dispatch; transmit **2** to cause (a person) to go **3** to impel; drive **4** to cause to happen, come, etc. —**send for 1** to summon **2** to place an order for —**send'er** *n.*

**send'-off'** *n.* [Inf.] **1** a farewell demonstration for someone starting out on a trip, career, etc. **2** a start given to someone or something

**Sen·e·gal** (sen'i gôl') country on the W coast of Africa: 76,124 sq. mi.; pop. 6,982,000

**se·nile** (sē'nīl') *adj.* [< L *senex*, old] **1** of or resulting from old age **2** showing the deterioration accompanying old age, esp. confusion, memory loss, etc. —**se·nil·i·ty** (si nil'ə tē) *n.*

**sen·ior** (sēn'yər) *adj.* [< L *senex*, old] **1** older: written *Sr.* after a father's name if his son's name is the same **2** of higher rank or longer service **3** of or for seniors —*n.* **1** one who is older, of higher rank, etc. **2** a student in the last year of high school or college **3** *short for* SENIOR CITIZEN

**senior citizen** an elderly person, esp. one who is retired

**senior high school** high school, usually grades 10, 11, and 12

**sen·ior·i·ty** (sēn yôr'ə tē) *n., pl.* **-ties 1** a being senior **2** status, priority, etc. achieved by length of service in a given job

**sen·na** (sen'ə) *n.* [< Ar *sanā*, cassia plant] the dried leaflets of a tropical cassia plant used, esp. formerly, as a laxative

***se·ñor*** (se nyôr') *n., pl.* ***se·ño·res*** (-nyô'res) [Sp] a man; gentleman: as a title, equivalent to *Mr.* or *Sir*

***se·ño·ra*** (se nyô'rä) *n.* [Sp] a married woman: as a title, equivalent to *Mrs.* or *Madam*

***se·ño·ri·ta*** (se'nyô rē'tä) *n.* [Sp] an unmarried woman or girl: as a title, equivalent to *Miss*

**sen·sa·tion** (sen sā'shən) *n.* [< L *sensus*, sense] **1** the receiving of sense impressions through hearing, seeing, etc. **2** a conscious sense impression **3** a generalized feeling [a *sensation* of joy] **4** *a*) a feeling of general excitement *b*) the cause of such a feeling

**sen·sa'tion·al** *adj.* **1** arousing intense interest **2** intended to shock, thrill, etc. —**sen·sa'tion·al·ism'** *n.*

**sense** (sens) *n.* [< L *sentire*, to feel] **1** any faculty of receiving impressions through body organs; sight, touch, taste, smell, or hearing **2** *a*) feeling, perception, etc. through the senses *b*) a generalized feeling or awareness **3** an ability to understand some quality [a *sense* of humor] **4** sound judgment **5** [*pl.*] normal ability to reason [to come to one's *senses*] **6** meaning, as of a word — *vt.* sensed, sens'ing **1** to perceive **2** to detect as by sensors —**in a sense** to a limited degree — **make sense** to be intelligible or logical

**sense'less** *adj.* **1** unconscious **2** stupid; foolish **3** meaningless

**sen·si·bil·i·ty** (sen'sə bil'ə tē) *n., pl.* **-ties 1** the

ability to respond to stimuli **2** [*often pl.*] (sensitive) awareness or responsiveness

**sen·si·ble** (-bəl) *adj.* **1** that can cause physical sensation **2** easily perceived **3** aware **4** having or showing good sense; wise —**sen'si·bly** *adv.*

**sen·si·tive** (-tiv) *adj.* **1** keenly susceptible to stimuli **2** tender; raw **3** highly perceptive or responsive **4** easily offended; touchy **5** detecting or reacting to slight changes [*sensitive* instruments] **6** of delicate or secret matters —**sen'si·tiv'i·ty** *n.*

**sen·si·tize** (-tīz') *vt.* **-tized', -tiz'ing** to make sensitive

**sen·sor** (sen'sər) *n.* a device to detect, measure, or record physical phenomena, as radiation, heat, etc.

**sen·so·ry** (sen'sər ē) *adj.* of the senses or sensation

**sen·su·al** (sen'shōō əl) *adj.* [< L *sensus*, sense] **1** of the body and the senses as distinguished from the intellect or spirit **2** connected or preoccupied with sexual pleasure —**sen'su·al'i·ty** (-al'ə tē) *n.* —**sen'su·al·ly** *adv.*

**sen·su·ous** (sen'shōō əs) *adj.* **1** of, derived from, or perceived by the senses **2** enjoying sensation

**sent** (sent) *vt., vi. pt. & pp. of* SEND

**sen·tence** (sen'təns) *n.* [< L *sententia*, opinion] **1** *a*) a decision as of a court; esp., the determination by a court of a punishment *b*) the punishment **2** a word or group of words, usually containing a subject and predicate, that states, asks, etc. —*vt.* **-tenced, -tenc·ing** to pronounce punishment upon (a convicted person)

**sen·ten·tious** (sen ten'shəs) *adj.* characterized by pompous moralizing

**sen·tient** (sen'shənt) *adj.* [see SENSE] of or capable of perception; conscious

**sen·ti·ment** (sen'tə mənt) *n.* [see SENSE] **1** a complex combination of feelings and opinions **2** an opinion, etc., often, one colored by emotion: *often used in pl.* **3** tender feelings **4** appeal to the emotions in literature, etc. **5** maudlin emotion

**sen·ti·men·tal** (sen'tə ment''l) *adj.* **1** having or showing tender or delicate feelings **2** maudlin; mawkish **3** of or resulting from sentiment — **sen'ti·men'tal·ism'** *n.* —**sen'ti·men'tal·ist** *n.* — **sen'ti·men·tal'i·ty** (-tal'ə tē) *n.* —**sen'ti·men'tal·ly** *adv.*

**sen'ti·men'tal·ize** (-īz') *vi., vt.* **-ized', -iz'ing** to be sentimental or treat in a sentimental way

**sen·ti·nel** (sent''n əl) *n.* [< L *sentire*, to sense] a guard or sentry

**sen·try** (sen'trē) *n., pl.* **-tries** [< ? obs. *centrinell*, var. of *prec.*] a sentinel; esp., a soldier posted to guard against danger

**Seoul** (sōl) capital of South Korea: pop. 8,367,000

**se·pal** (sē'pəl) *n.* [< Gr *skepē*, a covering + *petalon*, petal] any of the leaflike parts of the calyx

**sep·a·ra·ble** (sep'ə rə bəl) *adj.* that can be separated —**sep'a·ra·bly** *adv.*

**sep·a·rate** (sep'ə rāt'; *for adj.* sep'ə rit, sep'rit) *vt.* **-rat·ed, -rat·ing** [< L *se-*, apart + *parare*, arrange] **1** to set apart into sections, groups, etc.; divide **2** to keep apart by being between —*vi.* **1** to withdraw **2** to part, become disconnected, etc. **3** to go in different directions **4** to stop living together without a divorce —*adj.* **1** not joined, united, etc.; severed **2** distinct; individual **3** not shared — **sep'a·rate·ly** *adv.* —**sep'a·ra'tor** *n.*

**sep·a·ra·tion** (sep'ə rā'shən) *n.* **1** a separating or being separated **2** the place this occurs; break; division **3** something that separates

**sep'a·ra·tism'** (-rə tiz'əm) *n.* advocacy of political, religious, or racial separation —**sep'a·ra·tist** *n.*

**se·pi·a** (sē'pē ə) *n., adj.* [< Gr *sēpia*, cuttlefish secreting inky fluid] (of) a dark reddish-brown color

**sep·sis** (sep'sis) *n.* [see SEPTIC] a poisoning caused by the absorption of pathogenic microorganisms into the blood

**Sep·tem·ber** (sep tem'bər) *n.* [< L *septem*, seven:

seventh month in Roman calendar] the ninth month of the year, having 30 days: abbrev. **Sept.**

**sep·tet** or **sep·tette** (sep tet') *n.* [< L *septem,* seven] *Music* **1** a composition for seven voices or instruments **2** the seven performers of this

**sep·tic** (sep'tik) *adj.* [< Gr *sēpein,* to make putrid] causing, or resulting from, sepsis or putrefaction

**sep·ti·ce·mi·a** (sep'tə sē'mē ə) *n.* [see prec.] a disease caused by infectious microorganisms in the blood

**septic tank** an underground tank in which waste matter is putrefied and decomposed by bacteria

**sep·tu·a·ge·nar·i·an** (sep'tōō ə jə ner'ē ən) *n.* [< L *septuaginta,* seventy] a person between the ages of 70 and 80

**Sep·tu·a·gint** (sep'tōō ə jint') *n.* [< L *septuaginta,* seventy: in tradition, done in 70 days] a translation into Greek of the Hebrew Scriptures

**sep·tum** (sep'təm) *n., pl.* **-tums** or **-ta** (-tə) [< L *saepire,* enclose, fence] *Biol.* a wall or part that separates, as in the nose or in a fruit

**sep·ul·cher** (sep'əl kər) *n.* [< L *sepelire,* bury] a vault for burial; tomb

**se·pul·chral** (sə pul'krəl) *adj.* **1** of sepulchers, burial, etc. **2** suggestive of the grave or burial; gloomy **3** deep and melancholy: said of sound

**seq.** *abbrev.* [L *sequentes*] the following

**se·quel** (sē'kwəl) *n.* [< L *sequi,* follow] **1** something that follows; continuation **2** a result; consequence **3** any literary work, film, etc. continuing a story begun in an earlier one

**se·quence** (sē'kwəns) *n.* [< L *sequi,* follow] **1** *a*) the coming of one thing after another; succession *b*) the order in which this occurs **2** a series **3** a resulting event **4** *Film* a succession of scenes forming a single episode

**se·quen·tial** (si kwen'shəl) *adj.* of or occurring in a sequence —**se·quen'tial·ly** *adv.*

**se·ques·ter** (si kwes'tər) *vt.* [< L *sequester,* trustee] **1** to set off or apart **2** to withdraw; isolate —**se·ques·tra·tion** (sē'kwə strā'shən) *n.*

**se·quin** (sē'kwin) *n.* [Fr; ult. < Ar *sikka,* a stamp, die] a spangle, esp. one of many sewn on fabric for decoration —**se'quined** or **se'quinned** *adj.*

**se·quoi·a** (si kwoi'ə) *n.* [after *Sequoyah* (1760?-1843), Indian inventor of Cherokee writing system] REDWOOD (sense 1)

**se·ra** (sir'ə) *n. alt. pl. of* SERUM

**se·ra·glio** (si ral'yō) *n., pl.* **-glios** [< L *sera,* a lock] HAREM (sense 1)

**se·ra·pe** (sə rä'pē) *n.* [MexSp] a bright-colored wool blanket used as a garment by men in Mexico, etc.

**ser·aph** (ser'əf) *n., pl.* **-aphs** or **-a·phim'** (-ə fim') [< Heb *serafim,* pl.] *Theol.* a heavenly being, or any of the highest order of angels —**se·raph·ic** (sə raf' ik) *adj.* —**se·raph'i·cal·ly** *adv.*

**Serb** (surb) *n.* a person born or living in Serbia; esp., a member of a Slavic people of Serbia and adjacent areas —*adj.* SERBIAN

**Ser·bi·a** (sur'bē ə) the major constituent republic of Yugoslavia —**Ser'bi·an** *adj., n.*

**Ser·bo-Cro·a·tian** (sur'bō krō ā'shən) *n.* the major Slavic language of Yugoslavia, Bosnia and Herzegovina, and Croatia

**ser·e·nade** (ser'ə nād') *n.* [ult. < L *serenus,* clear] **1** music played or sung at night, esp. by a lover **2** a piece of music like this —*vt., vi.* **-nad'ed, -nad'ing** to play or sing a serenade (to)

**ser·en·dip·i·ty** (ser'ən dip'ə tē) *n.* [after Pers tale *The Three Princes of Serendip* (Sri Lanka)] a seeming gift for finding good things accidentally —**ser'en·dip'i·tous** *adj.*

**se·rene** (sə rēn') *adj.* [L *serenus*] **1** clear; unclouded **2** undisturbed; calm —**se·rene'ly** *adv.* —**se·ren'i·ty** (-ren'ə tē) or **se·rene'ness** *n.*

**serf** (surf) *n.* [< L *servus,* a slave] a person in feudal servitude, bound to a master's land and transferred with it to a new owner —**serf'dom** *n.*

**serge** (surj) *n.* [< L *sericus,* silken] a strong twilled fabric

**ser·geant** (sär'jənt) *n.* [< L *servire,* serve] **1** a noncommissioned officer ranking above a corporal **2** a police officer ranking next below a captain or a lieutenant

**ser'geant-at-arms'** *n., pl.* **ser'geants-at-arms'** an officer appointed to keep order, as in a court

**sergeant major** *pl.* **sergeants major** the highest ranking noncommissioned officer

**se·ri·al** (sir'ē əl) *adj.* [< L *series,* a row, order] appearing in a series of continuous parts at regular intervals —*n.* a story, etc. presented in serial form —**se'ri·al·i·za'tion** *n.* —**se'ri·al·ize', -ized', -iz'ing,** *vt.*

**serial number** one of a series of numbers given for identification

**se·ries** (sir'ēz) *n., pl.* **-ries** [L < *serere,* join together] a number of similar things or persons arranged in a row or coming one after another

**se·ri·ous** (sir'ē əs) *adj.* [< L *serius*] **1** earnest, grave, sober, etc. **2** not joking; sincere **3** requiring careful consideration **4** weighty **5** dangerous —**se'ri·ous·ly** *adv.* —**se'ri·ous·ness** *n.*

**ser·mon** (sur'mən) *n.* [< L *sermo,* a discourse] **1** a speech on religion or morals, esp. by a member of the clergy **2** any serious talk on behavior, duty, etc., esp. a tedious one —**ser'mon·ize', -ized', -iz'ing,** *vi.*

**se·rous** (sir'əs) *adj.* **1** of or containing serum **2** thin and watery

**ser·pent** (sur'pənt) *n.* [< L *serpere,* to creep] a snake

**ser'pen·tine'** (-pən tēn', -tīn') *adj.* of or like a serpent; esp., *a*) cunning; treacherous *b*) coiled; winding

**ser·rate** (ser'āt') *adj.* [< L *serra,* a saw] having sawlike notches along the edge: said of some leaves: also **ser'rat'ed** —**ser·ra'tion** *n.*

**ser·ried** (ser'ēd) *adj.* [< LL *serare,* to lock] placed close together

**se·rum** (sir'əm) *n., pl.* **-rums** or **-ra** (-ə) [L, whey] **1** a clear, watery animal fluid, as the yellowish fluid (**blood serum**) separating from a blood clot after coagulation **2** blood serum used as an antitoxin, taken from an animal inoculated for a specific disease

**serv·ant** (sur'vənt) *n.* [ult. < L *servire,* serve] **1** a person employed by another, esp. to do household duties **2** a person devoted to another or to a cause, creed, etc.

**serve** (surv) *vt.* **served, serv'ing** [< L *servus,* slave] **1** to work for as a servant **2** to do services for; aid; help **3** to do military or naval service for **4** to spend (a term of imprisonment, etc.) [to *serve* ten years] **5** to provide (customers, etc.) with goods or services **6** to set food, etc. before (a person) **7** to meet the needs of **8** to be used by [this hospital *serves* the whole city] **9** to function for [if memory *serves* me well] **10** to deliver (a summons, etc.) to (someone) **11** to hit (a tennis ball, etc.) in order to start play —*vi.* **1** to work as a servant **2** to do service [to *serve* in the navy] **3** to carry out the duties of an office **4** to be of service **5** to meet needs **6** to provide guests with food or drink **7** to be favorable: said of weather, etc. —*n.* a serving of the ball in tennis, etc. —**serve someone right** to be what someone deserves, for doing something wrong

**serv'er** *n.* **1** one who serves **2** a thing for serving, as a tray **3** *Comput.* the central computer in a network, on which shared files, etc. are stored

**serv·ice** (sur'vis) *n.* [< L *servus,* slave] **1** the occupation of a servant **2** *a*) public employment [diplomatic *service*] *b*) a branch of this; specif., the armed forces **3** work done for others [repair *service*] **4** any religious ceremony **5** *a*) benefit; advantage *b*) [*pl.*] friendly help; also, professional aid **6** the act or manner of serving food **7** a set of articles used in serving [a tea *service*] **8** a system of providing people with some utility, as water or gas **9** the act or manner of serving the ball in tennis, etc. —*vt.* **-iced, -ic·ing 1** to furnish with a service **2** to make fit for service, as by repairing —**at someone's service 1** ready to serve someone **2** ready for someone's use —**in service** functioning —**of service** helpful

**serv·ice·a·ble** *adj.* **1** that can be of service; useful **2** that will give good service; durable

**serv·ice·man'** (-man', -mən) *n., pl.* **-men'** (-men', -mən) **1** a member of the armed forces **2** a person whose work is repairing something [a TV *serviceman*]: also **service man**

**service mark** a word, etc. used like a trademark by a supplier of a service

**service station** a place selling gasoline, oil, etc., for motor vehicles

**ser·vile** (sur'vəl, -vīl') *adj.* [< L *servus*, slave] **1** of slaves **2** like that of slaves or servants **3** humbly submissive —**ser·vil·i·ty** (sər vil'ə tē) *n.*

**ser·vi·tude** (sur'və tood') *n.* [see SERF] **1** slavery or bondage **2** work imposed to punish a crime

**ser·vo** (sur'vō) *n., pl.* **-vos** *short for:* **1** SERVO-MECHANISM **2** SERVOMOTOR

**ser·vo·mech'a·nism** *n.* an automatic control system of low power, used to exercise remote but accurate mechanical control

**ser·vo·mo'tor** *n.* a device, as an electric motor, for changing a small force into a large force, as in a servomechanism

**ses·a·me** (ses'ə mē') *n.* [of Semitic origin] **1** a plant whose edible seeds yield an oil **2** its seeds

**ses·qui·cen·ten·ni·al** (ses'kwi sen ten'ē əl) *adj.* [< L *sesqui-*, more by a half + CENTENNIAL] of a period of 150 years —*n.* a 150th anniversary

**ses·sion** (sesh'ən) *n.* [< L *sedere*, sit] **1** *a*) the meeting of a court, legislature, etc. *b*) a series of such meetings *c*) the period of these **2** a school term **3** a period of activity of any kind

**set** (set) *vt.* **set, set'ting** [OE *settan*] **1** to cause to sit; seat **2** to put in a specified place, condition, etc. [to *set* books on a shelf, *set* slaves free] **3** to put in a proper condition; fix (a trap for animals), adjust (a clock or dial), arrange (a table for a meal), fix (hair) in a desired style, etc., put (a broken bone, etc.) into normal position, etc. **4** to make settled, rigid, or fixed [pectin *sets* jelly] **5** to mount (gems) **6** to direct; point **7** to appoint; establish; fix (boundaries, the time for an event, a rule, a quota, etc.) **8** to furnish (an example) for others **9** to fit (words *to* music or music *to* words) **10** to arrange (type) for printing —*vi.* **1** to sit on eggs: said of a fowl **2** to become firm, hard, or fixed [this cement *sets* quickly] **3** to begin to move (*out, forth, off*, etc.) **4** to sink below the horizon [the sun *sets*] —*adj.* **1** fixed; established [a *set* time] **2** intentional **3** fixed; rigid; firm **4** obstinate **5** ready [get *set*] —*n.* **1** a setting or being set **2** the way or position in which a thing is set [the *set* of his jaw] **3** direction; tendency **4** the scenery for a play, etc. **5** a group of persons or things classed or belonging together **6** assembled equipment for radio or TV reception, etc. **7** *Tennis* a group of six or more games won by a margin of at least two —**set about** (or **in** or **to**) to begin —**set down 1** to put in writing **2** to establish (rules, etc.) —**set forth 1** to publish **2** to state —**set off 1** to make prominent or enhance by contrast **2** to make explode —**set on** (or **upon**) to attack —**set up 1** to erect **2** to establish; found

**set'back'** *n.* a reversal in progress

**set'screw'** *n.* a screw used in regulating the tension of a spring, etc.

**set·tee** (se tē') *n.* **1** a seat or bench with a back **2** a small sofa

**set'ter** *n.* a long-haired dog trained to hunt

**set'ting** *n.* **1** the act of one that sets **2** the position of a dial, etc. that has been set **3** a mounting, as of a gem **4** the time, place, etc., as of a story **5** actual physical surroundings

**set·tle** (set''l) *vt.* **-tled, -tling** [< OE *setl*, a seat] **1** to put in order; arrange [to *settle* one's affairs] **2** to set in place firmly or comfortably **3** to colonize

**4** to cause to sink and become more compact **5** to free (the nerves, etc.) from disturbance **6** to decide (doubt) **7** to end (a dispute) **8** to pay (a debt, etc.) —*vi.* **1** to stop moving and stay in one place **2** to descend, as fog does over a landscape, or gloom over a person **3** to become localized: said as of pain **4** to take up permanent residence **5** to sink [the house *settled*] **6** to become more dense by sinking, as sediment does **7** to become more stable **8** to reach an agreement or decision (*with* or *on*) —**set'tler** *n.*

**set'tle·ment** *n.* **1** a settling or being settled **2** a new colony **3** a village **4** an agreement

**set'-to'** *n., pl.* **-tos'** [Inf.] **1** a fight **2** an argument

**set'up'** *n.* **1** *a*) the plan, makeup, or arrangement of equipment, an organization, etc. *b*) the details of a situation, plan, etc. **2** [Inf.] a contest, etc. arranged to result in an easy victory

**sev·en** (sev'ən) *adj., n.* [OE *seofon*] one more than six; 7; VII —**sev'enth** *adj., n.*

**sev'en·teen'** (-tēn') *adj., n.* seven more than ten; 17; XVII —**sev'en·teenth'** (-tēnth') *adj., n.*

**seventeen-year locust** a cicada which lives underground for 13-17 years before emerging as an adult

**seventh heaven** perfect happiness

**sev·en·ty** (sev'ən tē) *adj., n., pl.* **-ties** seven times ten; 70; LXX —**the seventies** the years, from 70 through 79, as of a century —**sev'en·ti·eth** (-ith) *adj., n.*

**sev·er** (sev'ər) *vt., vi.* [ult. < L *separare*] to separate, divide, or divide off —**sev'er·ance** *n.*

**sev·er·al** (sev'ər əl) *adj.* [ult. < L *separ*] **1** separate; distinct **2** different; respective **3** more than two but not many; few —*pl.n.* a small number (*of*) —*pron.* [*with pl. v.*] a few —**sev'er·al·ly** *adv.*

**se·vere** (sə vir') *adj.* **-ver'er, -ver'est** [< L *severus*] **1** harsh or strict, as in treatment **2** serious or grave, as in expression **3** rigidly accurate or demanding **4** extremely plain [a dress with *severe* lines] **5** intense [*severe* pain] **6** rigorous; trying —**se·vere'ly** *adv.* —**se·vere'ness** or **se·ver'i·ty** (-ver'ə tē) *n.*

**Se·ville** (sə vil') city in SW Spain: pop. 720,000

**Sè·vres** (sev'rə; *Fr* se'vr') *n.* [after *Sèvres*, SW suburb of Paris, where made] a type of fine French porcelain

**sew** (sō) *vt., vi.* **sewed, sewn** (sōn) or **sewed, sew'ing** [OE *siwian*] **1** to fasten with stitches made with needle and thread **2** to make, mend, etc. by sewing —**sew up 1** [Inf.] to get full control of **2** to make sure of success in —**sew'er** *n.*

**sew·age** (soo'ij) *n.* the waste matter carried off by sewers or drains

**sew·er** (soo'ər) *n.* [ult. < L *ex*, out + *aqua*, water] a pipe or drain, usually underground, used to carry off water and waste matter

**sew'er·age** *n.* **1** a system of sewers **2** SEWAGE

**sew'ing** *n.* **1** the act of one who sews **2** something to be sewn

**sewing machine** a machine with a mechanically driven needle used for sewing

**sex** (seks) *n.* [< L *sexus*] **1** either of two divisions, male or female, into which persons, animals, or plants are divided **2** the character of being male or female **3** the attraction between the sexes **4** sexual intercourse —*adj.* SEXUAL

**sex-** [< L *sex*, six] *combining form* six

**sex·a·ge·nar·i·an** (sek'sə ji ner'ē ən) *n.* [< L] a person between the ages of 60 and 70

**sex appeal** the physical charm that attracts members of the opposite sex

**sex chromosome** a sex-determining chromosome in the germ cells: eggs carry an X chromosome and spermatozoa either an X or a Y chromosome, with a female resulting from an XX pairing and a male from an XY

**sex'ism'** *n.* discrimination against people, esp. women, on the basis of sex —**sex'ist** *adj., n.*

**sex·tant** (seks'tənt) *n.* [< L *sextans*, a sixth part (of a circle)] an instrument for measuring the angular distance of the sun, a star, etc. from the horizon, as to determine position at sea

**sex·tet** or **sex·tette** (seks tet′) *n.* ⟦ult. < L *sex*, six⟧ 1 a group of six 2 *Music* a composition for six voices or instruments, or its six performers

**sex·ton** (seks′tən) *n.* ⟦ult. < L *sacer*, sacred⟧ a church official who maintains church property

**sex·u·al** (sek′shŏŏ əl) *adj.* of or involving sex, the sexes, the sex organs, etc. —**sex′u·al·ly** *adv.* — **sex′u·al′i·ty** (-ə′ tē) *n.*

SEXTANT

**sexual harassment** inappropriate, unwelcome behavior by an employer or colleague that is sexual in nature

**sexual intercourse** a joining of the sexual organs of a male and a female human being

**sex′y** *adj.* **-i·er, -i·est** 1 [Inf.] exciting or intended to excite sexual desire 2 [Slang] exciting, glamorous, etc. —**sex′i·ly** *adv.* —**sex′i·ness** *n.*

**Sey·chelles** (sā shel′, -shelz′) country on a group of islands in the Indian Ocean, northeast of Madagascar: 175 sq. mi.; pop. 67,000

**sf** or **SF** *abbrev.* science fiction

**Sgt** *abbrev.* Sergeant

**sh** (sh) *interj.* used to ask for silence

**shab·by** (shab′ē) *adj.* **-bi·er, -bi·est** ⟦OE *sceabb*, scab⟧ 1 rundown; dilapidated 2 *a*) ragged; worn *b*) wearing worn clothing 3 mean; shameful *[shabby* treatment*]* —**shab′bi·ly** *adv.* —**shab′bi·ness** *n.*

**shack** (shak) *n.* ⟦< ?⟧ a small, crudely built house or cabin; shanty

**shack·le** (shak′əl) *n.* ⟦OE *sceacel*⟧ 1 a metal fastening, usually in pairs, for the wrist or ankle of a prisoner; fetter 2 anything that restrains freedom, as of expression 3 a device for fastening or coupling —*vt.* **-led, -ling** 1 to put shackles on 2 to restrain in freedom of expression or action

**shad** (shad) *n., pl.* **shad** or **shads** ⟦OE *sceadd*⟧ an American coastal food fish

**shade** (shād) *n.* ⟦OE *sceadu*⟧ 1 comparative darkness caused by an object cutting off rays of light 2 an area with less light than its surroundings 3 degree of darkness of a color *[shades* of blue*]* 4 *a*) a small difference *[shades* of opinion*] b*) a slight amount or degree 5 [Chiefly Literary] a ghost 6 a device used to screen from light *[a window shade]* 7 [pl.] [Slang] sunglasses —*vt.* **shad′ed, shad′ing** 1 to screen from light 2 to darken; dim 3 to represent shade in (a painting, etc.) —*vi.* to change slightly or by degrees —**shades of** *exclamation used to refer to* a reminder of the past

**shad′ing** *n.* 1 a shielding against light 2 shade in a picture 3 a small variation

**shad·ow** (shad′ō) *n.* ⟦< OE *sceadu*, shade⟧ 1 (a) shade cast by a body intercepting light rays 2 gloom or that which causes gloom 3 a shaded area in a picture 4 a ghost 5 a remnant; trace — *vt.* 1 to throw a shadow upon 2 to follow closely, esp. in secret —**shad′ow·y** *adj.*

**shad′ow·box′** *vi. Boxing* to spar with an imaginary opponent in training

**shad·y** (shā′dē) *adj.* **-i·er, -i·est** 1 giving shade 2 shaded; full of shade 3 [Inf.] of questionable character —**on the shady side of** beyond (a given age) —**shad′i·ness** *n.*

**shaft** (shaft) *n.* ⟦OE *sceaft*⟧ 1 an arrow or spear, or its stem 2 anything hurled like a missile *[shafts* of wit*]* 3 a long, slender part or object, as a pillar, a bar transmitting motion to a mechanical part, or either of the poles between which an animal is harnessed to a vehicle 4 a long, narrow passage sunk into the earth 5 a vertical opening

passing through a building, as for an elevator — *vt.* [Slang] to cheat, trick, exploit, etc.

**shag**[1] (shag) *n.* ⟦< OE *sceacga*, rough hair⟧ a rough, heavy nap, as on some cloth

**shag**[2] (shag) *vt.* **shagged, shag′ging** to chase after and retrieve (baseballs hit in batting practice)

**shag′gy** *adj.* **-gi·er, -gi·est** 1 covered with long, coarse hair or wool 2 unkempt, straggly, etc. 3 having a rough nap

**shah** (shä) *n.* ⟦Pers *šāh*⟧ the title of any of the former rulers of Iran

**shake** (shāk) *vt., vi.* **shook, shak′en, shak′ing** ⟦OE *sceacan*⟧ 1 to move quickly up and down, back and forth, etc. 2 to bring, force, mix, etc. by brisk movements 3 to tremble or cause to tremble 4 *a*) to become or cause to become unsteady *b*) to unnerve or become unnerved 5 to clasp (another's hand), as in greeting —*n.* 1 an act of shaking 2 a wood shingle 3 *short for* MILKSHAKE 4 [pl.] a convulsive trembling: usually with *the* —**no great shakes** [Inf.] not outstanding — **shake down** 1 to cause to fall by shaking 2 [Slang] to extort money from —**shake off** to get rid of

**shake′down′** *n.* 1 [Slang] an extortion of money, as by blackmail 2 a thorough search —*adj.* for testing new equipment, etc. *[a shakedown* cruise*]*

**shake′out′** *n.* a drop in economic activity that eliminates unprofitable businesses, etc.

**shak′er** *n.* 1 one that shakes 2 a device used in shaking 3 [S-] a member of a religious sect that lived in celibate communities in the U.S.

**Shake·speare** (shāk′spir), **William** 1564-1616; Eng. poet & dramatist —**Shake·spear′e·an** or **Shake·spear′i·an** *adj., n.*

**shake′-up′** *n.* a shaking up; specif., an extensive reorganization

**shak′y** *adj.* **-i·er, -i·est** 1 not firm; weak or unsteady 2 *a*) trembling *b*) nervous 3 not reliable; questionable —**shak′i·ness** *n.*

**shale** (shāl) *n.* ⟦< OE *scealu*, shell⟧ a rock formed of hard clay: it splits easily into thin layers

**shale oil** oil distilled from a hard shale containing veins of a greasy organic solid

**shall** (shal) *v.aux. pt.* **should** ⟦OE *sceal*⟧ 1 used in the first person to indicate simple future time 2 used in the second or third person, esp. in formal speech or writing, to express determination, compulsion, obligation, or necessity See usage note at WILL[2]

**shal·lot** (shə lät′, shal′ət) *n.* ⟦< OFr *eschaloigne*, scallion⟧ 1 a small onion whose clustered bulbs are used for flavoring 2 GREEN ONION

**shal·low** (shal′ō) *adj.* ⟦ME *shalow*⟧ 1 not deep 2 lacking depth of character, intellect, etc. —*n.* *[usually pl., often with sing. v.]* SHOAL[2] (sense 1)

**shalt** (shalt) *v.aux.* archaic 2d pers. sing., pres. indic., of SHALL: used with *thou*

**sham** (sham) *n.* ⟦< ? shame⟧ something false or fake; person or thing that is a fraud —*adj.* false or fake —*vt., vi.* **shammed, sham′ming** to pretend; feign

**sham·ble** (sham′bəl) *vi.* **-bled, -bling** ⟦< obs. use in *shamble legs*, bench legs⟧ to walk clumsily; shuffle —*n.* a shambling walk

**sham′bles** *n.* ⟦ME *schamel*, butcher's bench; ult. < L⟧ 1 a slaughterhouse 2 a scene of great slaughter, destruction, or disorder

**shame** (shām) *n.* ⟦OE *scamu*⟧ 1 a painful feeling of guilt for improper behavior, etc. 2 dishonor or disgrace 3 something regrettable or outrageous —*vt.* **shamed, sham′ing** 1 to cause to feel shame 2 to dishonor or disgrace 3 to force by a sense of shame —**put to shame** 1 to cause to feel shame 2 to surpass; outdo —**shame′ful** *adj.* —**shame′ful·ly** *adv.* —**shame′ful·ness** *n.*

**shame′faced′** *adj.* showing shame; ashamed

**shame′less** *adj.* having or showing no shame, modesty, or decency; brazen —**shame′less·ly** *adv.*

**sham·poo** (sham pŏŏ′) *vt.* **-pooed′, -poo′ing**

〖Hindi *chāmpnā*, to press〗 **1** to wash (the hair) **2** to wash (a rug, sofa, etc.) —*n.* **1** a shampooing **2** a liquid soap, etc. used for this

**sham·rock** (sham′räk) *n.* 〖Ir *seamar*, clover〗 a plant, esp. a clover, with leaflets in groups of three: the emblem of Ireland

**shang·hai** (shaŋ′hī′) *vt.* 〖< such kidnapping for crews on the China run〗 to kidnap, usually by drugging, for service aboard ship

**Shang·hai** (shaŋ′hī′) seaport in E China: pop. 6,293,000

**shank** (shaŋk) *n.* 〖OE *scanca*〗 **1** the part of the leg between the knee and ankle in humans, or a corresponding part in animals **2** the whole leg **3** the part between the handle and the working part of a tool, etc. —**shank of the evening** early evening

**shan't** (shant) *contr.* shall not

**Shan·tung** (shan′tuŋ′) *n.* 〖< Chin province〗 [*sometimes* **s-**] a silk or silky fabric with an uneven surface

**shan·ty** (shan′tē) *n., pl.* **-ties** 〖< CdnFr *chantier*, workshop〗 a small, shabby dwelling; shack; hut

**shape** (shāp) *n.* 〖< OE *(ge)scap*, a form〗 **1** that quality of a thing which depends on the relative position of all the points on its surface; physical form **2** the contour of the body **3** definite or regular form [to begin to take *shape*] **4** good physical condition —*vt.* **shaped, shap′ing 1** to give definite shape to **2** to arrange, express, etc. (a plan, etc.) in definite form **3** to adapt [*shaped* to our needs] —**shape up** [Inf.] **1** to develop to a definite form, satisfactorily, etc. **2** to behave as required —**take shape** to begin to have definite form —**shape′less** *adj.* —**shape′less·ness** *n.*

**shape′ly** *adj.* **-li·er, -li·est** having a pleasing figure: used esp. of a woman

**shard** (shärd) *n.* 〖OE *sceard*〗 a broken piece, esp. of pottery

**share**[1] (sher) *n.* 〖OE *scearu*〗 **1** a portion that belongs to an individual **2** any of the equal parts of capital stock of a corporation —*vt.* **shared, shar′ing 1** to distribute in shares **2** to receive, use, etc. in common with others —*vi.* to have a share (*in*)

**share**[2] (sher) *n.* 〖OE *scear*〗 a plowshare

**share′crop′** *vi., vt.* **-cropped′, -crop′ping** to work (land) for a share of the crop, esp. as a tenant farmer —**share′crop′per** *n.*

**share′hold′er** *n.* a person who owns shares of stock in a corporation

**shark**[1] (shärk) *n.* 〖prob. < Ger *schurke*, scoundrel〗 **1** a swindler **2** [Slang] an expert in an activity

**shark**[2] (shärk) *n.* 〖< ?〗 a large, predatory sea fish with a tough, gray skin

**shark′skin′** *n.* a smooth, silky cloth of cotton, wool, rayon, etc.

**sharp** (shärp) *adj.* 〖OE *scearp*〗 **1** having a fine edge or point for cutting or piercing **2** having a point or

WHITE SHARK

edge; not rounded **3** not gradual; abrupt **4** clearly defined; distinct [a *sharp* contrast] **5** quick in perception; clever **6** attentive; vigilant **7** crafty; underhanded **8** harsh; severe [a *sharp* temper] **9** violent [a *sharp* attack] **10** brisk; active **11** intense [a *sharp* pain] **12** pungent **13** nippy [a *sharp* wind] **14** [Slang] stylishly dressed **15** *Music* above the true pitch —*adv.* **1** in a sharp manner; specif., *a*) abruptly or briskly *b*) attentively or alertly *c*) *Music* above the true pitch **2** precisely [one o'clock *sharp*] —*n.* **1** [Inf.] an expert or adept **2** *Music a*) a tone one half step above another *b*) the symbol (♯) for such a note —*vt., vi. Music* to make, sing, or play sharp —**sharp′ly** *adv.* —**sharp′ness** *n.*

**sharp′en** *vt., vi.* to make or become sharp or sharper —**sharp′en·er** *n.*

**sharp′er** *n.* a swindler or cheat

**sharp′-eyed′** *adj.* having keen sight or perception: also **sharp′-sight′ed** *adj.*

**sharp·ie** (shär′pē) *n.* [Inf.] a shrewd, cunning person, esp. a sharper

**sharp′shoot′er** *n.* a good marksman

**sharp′-tongued′** *adj.* using sharp or harshly critical language

**sharp′-wit′ted** (-wit′id) *adj.* thinking quickly and effectively

**shat·ter** (shat′ər) *vt.* 〖ME *scateren*, scatter〗 **1** to break or burst into pieces suddenly, as with a blow **2** to damage or be damaged severely

**shat′ter·proof′** *adj.* that will resist shattering

**shave** (shāv) *vt.* **shaved, shaved** *or* **shav′en, shav′ing** 〖OE *sceafan*〗 **1** to cut away thin slices or sections from **2** *a*) to cut off (hair) at the surface of the skin *b*) to cut the hair to the surface of (the face, etc.) *c*) to cut the beard of (a person) **3** to barely touch in passing; graze —*vi.* to cut off a beard with a razor, etc. —*n.* the act or an instance of shaving

**shav′er** *n.* **1** a person who shaves **2** an instrument used in shaving, esp. one with electrically operated cutters **3** [Inf.] a boy; lad

**shav′ing** *n.* **1** the act of one who shaves **2** a thin piece of wood, metal, etc. shaved off

**Shaw** (shô), **George Ber·nard** (bər närd′, bʉr′nərd) 1856-1950; Brit. dramatist & critic, born in Ireland —**Sha·vi·an** (shā′vē ən) *adj., n.*

**shawl** (shôl) *n.* 〖prob. < Pers *shāl*〗 a cloth worn as a covering for the head or shoulders

**shay** (shā) *n.* 〖< CHAISE, assumed as pl.〗 [Dial.] a light carriage; chaise

**she** (shē) *pron., pl. see* THEY 〖< OE *seo*〗 the woman, girl, or female animal previously mentioned —*n., pl.* **shes** a female

**sheaf** (shēf) *n., pl.* **sheaves** 〖OE *sceaf*〗 **1** a bundle of cut stalks of grain, etc. **2** a collection, as of papers, bound in a bundle

**shear** (shir) *vt.* **sheared, sheared** *or* **shorn, shear′ing** 〖OE *scieran*〗 **1** to cut with or as with shears **2** to clip (hair) from (the head), (wool) from (sheep), etc. **3** to divest (someone) of (a power, etc.) —*n.* a shearing —**shear′er** *n.*

**shears** *pl.n.* **1** a large pair of scissors **2** a large cutting tool or machine with two opposed blades

**sheath** (shēth) *n., pl.* **sheaths** (shēthz, shēths) 〖OE *sceath*〗 **1** a case for the blade of a knife, sword, etc. **2** a covering resembling this, as the membrane around a muscle **3** a woman's closefitting dress

**sheathe** (shēth) *vt.* **sheathed, sheath′ing 1** to put into a sheath **2** to enclose in a case or covering

SHEATH

**sheath·ing** (shē′thiŋ) *n.* something that sheathes, as boards, etc. forming the base for roofing or siding

**she·bang** (shə baŋ′) *n.* [Inf.] an affair, business, contrivance, etc.: chiefly in **the whole shebang**

**shed**[1] (shed) *n.* 〖OE *scead*〗 a small structure for shelter or storage

**shed**[2] (shed) *vt.* **shed, shed′ding** 〖< OE *sceadan*, to separate〗 **1** to pour out; emit **2** to cause to flow [to *shed* tears] **3** to cause to flow off [oilskin *sheds* water] **4** to cast off or lose (a natural growth, as hair, etc.) **5** to get rid of (something unwanted) [to *shed* a few pounds] —*vi.* to shed hair, etc. —**shed blood** to kill violently

**sheen** (shēn) *n.* 〖< OE *sciene*, beautiful〗 brightness; luster

**sheep** (shēp) *n., pl.* **sheep** 〖< OE *sceap*〗 **1** a cud-chewing mammal with heavy wool and edible flesh called *mutton*, closely related to goats, antelope, etc. **2** one who is meek, timid, etc.

**sheep'dog'** *n.* a dog trained to herd sheep

**sheep'fold'** *n.* a pen or enclosure for sheep: also, chiefly Brit., **sheep'cote'** (-kōt') *n.*

**sheep'ish** *adj.* **1** embarrassed or chagrined **2** shy or bashful —**sheep'ish·ly** *adv.* —**sheep'ish·ness** *n.*

**sheep'skin'** *n.* **1** the skin of a sheep **2** parchment or leather made from it **3** [Inf.] a diploma

**sheer**[1] (shir) *vi., vt.* ⟦var. of SHEAR⟧ to turn aside or cause to turn aside from a course; swerve

**sheer**[2] (shir) *adj.* ⟦< ON *skærr*, bright⟧ **1** very thin; transparent: said of textiles **2** absolute; utter [*sheer* folly] **3** extremely steep **4** not mixed with anything; pure [*sheer* ice] —*adv.* very steeply

**sheet**[1] (shēt) *n.* ⟦OE *sceat*⟧ **1** a large piece of cotton, linen, etc., used on a bed **2** *a*) a single piece of paper *b*) [Inf.] a newspaper **3** a broad, continuous surface or expanse, as of flame or ice **4** a broad, thin piece of any material, as glass, plywood, or metal

**sheet**[2] (shēt) *n.* ⟦short for OE *sceatline*⟧ a rope for controlling the set of a sail

**sheet'ing** *n.* **1** cotton or linen material used for making sheets **2** material used to cover or line a surface [copper *sheeting*]

**sheet metal** metal rolled thin in the form of a sheet

**sheet music** music printed on unbound sheets of paper

**sheik** or **sheikh** (shēk, shāk) *n.* ⟦Ar *shaikh*, lit., old man⟧ the chief of an Arab family, tribe, or village

**shek·el** (shek'əl) *n.* ⟦Heb < *shakal*, weigh⟧ **1** a gold or silver coin of the ancient Hebrews **2** the monetary unit of Israel **3** [*pl.*] [Slang] money

**shelf** (shelf) *n., pl.* **shelves** ⟦prob. < MLowG *schelf*⟧ **1** a thin, flat board fixed horizontally to a wall, used for holding things **2** something like a shelf; specif., *a*) a ledge *b*) a sandy reef —**on the shelf** out of use, activity, etc.

**shelf life** the length of time a packaged food, etc. can be stored without deteriorating

**shell** (shel) *n.* ⟦OE *sciell*⟧ **1** a hard outer covering, as of a turtle, egg, nut, etc. **2** something like a shell in being hollow, empty, a covering, etc. **3** a light, narrow racing boat rowed by a team **4** an explosive artillery projectile **5** a small-arms cartridge —*vt.* **1** to remove the shell or covering from [to *shell* peas] **2** to bombard with shells from a large gun —**shell out** [Inf.] to pay out (money)

**shel·lac** or **shel·lack** (shə lak') *n.* ⟦< SHELL & LAC⟧ **2** a thin varnish containing lac and alcohol —*vt.* **-lacked', -lack'ing 1** to apply shellac to **2** [Slang] *a*) to beat *b*) to defeat decisively

**-shelled** (sheld) *combining form* having a (specified kind of) shell

**Shel·ley** (shel'ē) **1** Mary Woll·stone·craft (wool'stən kraft') 1797-1851; Eng. novelist: second wife of Percy **2** Per·cy Bysshe (pur'sē bish) 1792-1822; Eng. poet

**shell'fire'** *n.* the firing of artillery shells

**shell'fish'** *n., pl.* **-fish'** or (for different species) **-fish·es** any aquatic animal with a shell, esp. an edible one, as the clam or lobster

**shel·ter** (shel'tər) *n.* ⟦< ? OE *scield*, shield + *truma*, a troop⟧ **1** something that protects, as from the elements, danger, etc. **2** a being covered, protected, etc.; protection **3** a place that provides food and lodging on a temporary basis —*vt.* to provide shelter for; protect —*vi.* to find shelter

**shelve** (shelv) *vt.* **shelved, shelv'ing 1** to equip with shelves **2** to put on a shelf **3** to put aside; defer

**shelves** (shelvz) *n. pl. of* SHELF

**shelv·ing** (shel'viŋ) *n.* **1** material for shelves **2** shelves collectively

**she·nan·i·gan** (shi nan'i gən) *n.* ⟦altered < ? Ir *sionnachuighim*, I play the fox⟧ [Inf.] a deceitful or mischievous trick: *usually used in pl.*

**shep·herd** (shep'ərd) *n.* ⟦see SHEEP & HERD⟧ **1** one who herds sheep **2** a religious leader **3** GERMAN SHEPHERD —*vt.* to herd, lead, etc. as a shepherd —**shep'herd·ess** *fem.n.*

**sher·bet** (shur'bət) *n.* ⟦< Ar *sharba(t)*, a drink⟧ a frozen dessert like an ice but with gelatin and, often, milk added: also, erroneously, **sher'bert** (-bərt)

**sher·iff** (sher'if) *n.* ⟦< OE *scir*, shire + *gerefa*, chief officer⟧ the chief law-enforcement officer of a county

**Sher·pa** (shur'pə, sher'-) *n. pl.* **-pas** or **-pa** a member of a Tibetan people of Nepal, famous as mountain climbers

**sher·ry** (sher'ē) *n., pl.* **-ries** ⟦after *Jerez*, Spain⟧ **1** a yellow or brown Spanish fortified wine **2** any similar wine

**shib·bo·leth** (shib'ə leth', -ləth) *n.* ⟦< Heb *shibolet*, a stream⟧ **1** *Bible* the test word used to distinguish the enemy: Judg. 12:4-6 **2** any phrase, custom, etc. peculiar to a certain party, class, etc.

**shied** (shīd) *vi., vt. pt. & pp. of* SHY[1], SHY[2]

**shield** (shēld) *n.* ⟦OE *scield*⟧ **1** a flat piece of metal, etc. worn on the forearm to ward off blows, etc. **2** one that guards, protects, etc. **3** anything shaped like a triangular shield with curved sides —*vt., vi.* to defend; protect

SHIELD

**shift** (shift) *vt.* ⟦OE *sciftan*, divide⟧ **1** to move from one person or place to another **2** to replace by another or others **3** to change the arrangement of (gears) —*vi.* **1** to change position, direction, etc. **2** to get along; manage [to *shift* for oneself] —*n.* **1** a shifting; transfer **2** a plan of conduct, esp. for an emergency **3** an evasion; trick **4** a gearshift **5** *a*) a group of people working in relay with another *b*) their regular work period

**shift'less** *adj.* incapable, inefficient, lazy, etc. —**shift'less·ness** *n.*

**shift'y** *adj.* **-i·er, -i·est** of a tricky or deceitful nature; evasive —**shift'i·ly** *adv.* —**shift'i·ness** *n.*

**Shih Tzu** (shēd'zōō', shēt'sōō') *pl.* **Shih Tzus** or **Shih Tzu** ⟦Mandarin *shihtzu*, lion⟧ a small dog with long, silky hair and short legs

**shii·ta·ke** (shē tä'kē) *n.* ⟦Jpn⟧ an edible Japanese mushroom

**shill** (shil) [Slang] *n.* a confederate of a gambler, auctioneer, etc. who pretends to bet, bid, etc. so as to lure others —*vi.* to act as a shill

**shil·le·lagh** or **shil·la·lah** (shil lā'lē, -lə) *n.* ⟦after *Shillelagh*, Ir village⟧ a club or cudgel: used chiefly of or by the Irish

**shil·ling** (shil'iŋ) *n.* ⟦OE *scylling*⟧ **1** a former British monetary unit and coin, equal to $\frac{1}{20}$ of a pound **2** the basic monetary unit of various countries

**shil·ly-shal·ly** (shil'ē shal'ē) *vi.* **-lied, -ly·ing** ⟦< *shall I*?⟧ to vacillate, esp. over trifles

**shim** (shim) *n.* ⟦< ?⟧ a thin wedge of wood, metal, etc. used as for filling space

**shim·mer** (shim'ər) *vi.* ⟦OE *scymrian*⟧ to shine with an unsteady light; glimmer —*n.* a shimmering light

**shim·my** (shim'ē) *n.* ⟦< a jazz dance < CHEMISE⟧ a marked vibration or wobble, as in a car's front wheels —*vi.* **-mied, -my·ing** to vibrate or wobble

**shin** (shin) *n.* ⟦OE *scinu*⟧ the front part of the leg between the knee and the ankle —*vi.* **shinned, shin'ning** to climb a pole, etc. by gripping with hands and legs: also **shin'ny**: with *up* or *down*

**shin'bone'** *n.* TIBIA

**shin·dig** (shin'dig') *n.* ⟦< old informal *shindy*, com-

**motion**‖ [Inf.] a dance, party, or other informal gathering

**shine** (shīn) *vi.* **shone** or, esp. for *vt.* 2, **shined**, **shin'ing** ‖OE *scinan*‖ **1** to emit or reflect light **2** to stand out; excel **3** to exhibit itself clearly /love *shining* from her face/ —*vt.* **1** to direct the light of **2** to make shiny by polishing /to *shine* shoes/ —*n.* **1** brightness **2** luster; gloss **3** *short for* SHOESHINE

**shin·er** (shī'nər) *n.* [Slang] BLACK EYE

**shin·gle** (shiŋ'gəl) *n.* ‖OE *scindel*‖ **1** a thin, wedge-shaped piece of wood, slate, etc. laid with others in overlapping rows, as in covering roofs **2** a small signboard, as that of a doctor —*vt.* **-gled**, **-gling** to cover (a roof, etc.) with shingles

SHINGLES

**shin·gles** (shiŋ'gəlz) *n.* ‖< L *cingere*, to gird‖ *nontechnical name for* HERPES ZOSTER

**shin·guard** (shin'gärd') *n.* a padded guard worn to protect the shins in some sports

**shin'splints'** *pl.n.* ‖< SHIN & *splint*, growth on bone of a horse's leg‖ [*with sing. or pl. v.*] painful strain of muscles of the lower leg

**Shin·to** (shin'tō) *n.* ‖Jpn < Chin *shen*, god + *tō, dō*, way‖ a religion of Japan, emphasizing ancestor worship —**Shin'to·ism'** *n.*

**shin·y** (shī'nē) *adj.* **-i·er**, **-i·est** **1** bright; shining **2** highly polished —**shin'i·ness** *n.*

**ship** (ship) *n.* ‖OE *scip*‖ **1** any large vessel for traveling on deep water **2** an aircraft —*vt.* **shipped**, **ship'ping 1** to put or take on board a ship **2** to send or transport by any carrier /to *ship* coal by rail/ **3** to take in (water) over the side, as in a stormy sea **4** to put (an object) in place on a vessel **5** [Inf.] to send (*away, out,* etc.); get rid of —*vi.* to go aboard, or travel by, ship —**ship'per** *n.*

**-ship** (ship) ‖OE *-scipe*‖ *suffix* **1** the quality or state of being [*friendship*] **2** *a*) the rank or office of [*professorship*] *b*) one having the rank of [*lordship*] **3** skill as [*leadership*] **4** all persons (of a specified group) collectively [*readership*]

**ship'board'** *n.* used chiefly in **on shipboard**, aboard a ship

**ship'build'er** *n.* one whose business is building ships —**ship'build'ing** *n.*

**ship'mate'** *n.* a fellow sailor on the same ship

**ship'ment** *n.* **1** the shipping of goods **2** goods shipped

**ship'ping** *n.* **1** the act or business of transporting goods **2** ships collectively, as of a nation or port

**shipping clerk** an employee who prepares goods for shipment, and keeps records of shipments made

**ship'shape'** *adj.* having everything neatly in place; trim

**ship'wreck'** *n.* **1** the remains of a wrecked ship **2** the loss of a ship through storm, etc. **3** ruin; failure —*vt.* to cause to undergo shipwreck

**ship'yard'** *n.* a place where ships are built and repaired

**shire** (shīr) *n.* ‖OE *scir*, office‖ in England, a county

**shirk** (shurk) *vt., vi.* ‖< ?‖ to neglect or evade (a duty, etc.) —**shirk'er** *n.*

**shirr** (shur) *vt.* ‖< ?‖ **1** to make shirring in (cloth) **2** to bake (eggs) in buttered dishes

**shirr'ing** *n.* a gathering made in cloth by drawing the material up on parallel rows of short stitches

**shirt** (shurt) *n.* ‖OE *scyrte*‖ **1** a garment worn on the upper part of the body, usually with a collar and a buttoned front **2** an undershirt —**keep one's shirt on** [Slang] to remain patient or calm

**shirt'tail'** *n.* the part of a shirt extending below the waist

**shirt'waist'** *n.* **1** [Archaic] a woman's blouse tailored like a shirt **2** a dress with a bodice like this: in full **shirtwaist dress**

**shish ke·bab** (shish' kə bäb') ‖< Ar *shīsh*, skewer + *kabāb*, kebab‖ a dish of kebabs, esp. lamb, stuck on a skewer, often with vegetables, and broiled

**shiv** (shiv) *n.* ‖prob. < Romany *chiv*, blade‖ [Slang] a knife

**shiv·er**[1] (shiv'ər) *n.* ‖ME *schievere*‖ a fragment — *vt., vi.* to break into fragments; shatter

**shiv·er**[2] (shiv'ər) *vi.* ‖< ? OE *ceafl*, jaw‖ to shake or tremble, as from fear or cold —*n.* a shaking, trembling, etc. —**shiv'er·y** *adj.*

**shlep** or **shlepp** (shlep) *n., vt., vi.* **shlepped**, **shlep'ping** [Slang] *alt. sp. of* SCHLEP

**shmaltz** (shmôlts, shmälts) *n.* [Slang] *alt. sp. of* SCHMALTZ

**shoal**[1] (shōl) *n.* ‖OE *scolu*‖ a school of fish

**shoal**[2] (shōl) *n.* ‖< OE *sceald*, shallow‖ **1** a shallow place in a river, sea, etc. **2** a sandbar forming a shallow place

**shoat** (shōt) *n.* ‖ME *schote*‖ a young, weaned pig

**shock**[1] (shäk) *n.* ‖< MFr *choquer*, to collide‖ **1** a sudden, powerful blow, shake, etc. **2** *a*) a sudden emotional disturbance *b*) the cause of this **3** an extreme stimulation of the nerves by the passage of electric current through the body **4** [Inf.] *short for* SHOCK ABSORBER **5** a disorder of the blood circulation produced by hemorrhage, disturbance of heart function, etc. —*vt.* **1** to astonish, horrify, etc. **2** to produce electrical shock in —**shock'er** *n.*

**shock**[2] (shäk) *n.* ‖ME *schokke*‖ a number of grain sheaves stacked together

**shock**[3] (shäk) *n.* ‖< ? prec.‖ a thick, bushy mass of hair

**shock absorber** a device, as on a motor vehicle, that absorbs the force of bumps and jarring

SHOCKS OF CORN

**shock'ing** *adj.* **1** causing great surprise and distress **2** disgusting — **shock'ing·ly** *adv.*

**shock'proof'** *adj.* able to absorb shock without being damaged

**shock therapy** the treatment of certain mental disorders by using electricity or drugs to produce convulsions or coma

**shock troops** troops trained to lead an attack

**shod** (shäd) *vt. alt. pt.* & *pp. of* SHOE

**shod·dy** (shäd'ē) *n., pl.* **-dies** ‖< ?‖ an inferior woolen cloth made from used fabrics —*adj.* **-di·er**, **-di·est 1** made of inferior material **2** poorly done or made **3** contemptible; low —**shod'di·ly** *adv.* — **shod'di·ness** *n.*

**shoe** (shōō) *n.* ‖OE *sceoh*‖ **1** an outer covering for the foot **2** *short for* HORSESHOE **3** the part of a brake that presses against a wheel —*vt.* **shod** or **shoed**, **shoe'ing** to furnish with shoes —**fill someone's shoes** to take someone's place

**shoe'horn'** *n.* an implement used to help slip the heel of a foot into a shoe —*vt.* to force or squeeze into a narrow space

**shoe'lace'** *n.* a length of cord, etc. used for lacing and fastening a shoe

**shoe'mak'er** *n.* one whose business is making or repairing shoes

**shoe'shine'** *n.* the cleaning and polishing of a pair of shoes

**shoe'string'** *n.* **1** a shoelace **2** a small amount of capital /a business started on a *shoestring*/ —*adj.* **1** like a shoestring; long and narrow **2** of or characterized by a small amount of money **3** at or near the ankles /a *shoestring* catch/

**shoe tree** a form made of wood, etc. inserted in a shoe to stretch it or preserve its shape

**sho·gun** (shō′gun′) *n.* ⟦< Chin *chiang-chun*⟧ any of the hereditary governors of Japan who, until 1867, were absolute rulers —**sho′gun·ate** (-gə nit) *n.*

**shone** (shōn) *vi., vt. alt. pt. & pp. of* SHINE

**shoo** (sho͞o) *interj.* go away! get out! —*vt.* **shooed**, **shoo′ing** to drive away, as by crying "shoo"

**shoo′-in′** *n.* [Inf.] one expected to win easily in a race, etc.

**shook** (shook) *vt., vi. pt. and dial. pp. of* SHAKE —**shook up** [Inf.] upset; agitated

**shoot** (sho͞ot) *vt.* **shot**, **shoot′ing** ⟦OE *sceotan*⟧ **1** to move swiftly over, by, etc. [to *shoot* the rapids] **2** to streak or vary (*with* another color, etc.) **3** to thrust or put forth **4** to discharge or fire (a bullet, arrow, etc.) **5** to send forth swiftly or with force **6** to hit, wound, etc. with a bullet, arrow, etc. **7** to photograph **8** *Sports a)* to throw or drive (a ball, etc.) toward the objective *b)* to score (a goal, points, etc.) —*vi.* **1** to move swiftly **2** to be felt suddenly, as pain **3** to grow rapidly **4** to jut out **5** to send forth a missile; discharge bullets, etc. **6** to use guns, etc. as in hunting —*n.* **1** a shooting trip, contest, etc. **2** a new growth; sprout —**shoot at** (or **for**) [Inf.] to strive for —**shoot′er** *n.*

**shooting star** METEOR (sense 1)

**shoot′out′** or **shoot′-out′** *n.* **1** a battle with handguns, etc., as between police and criminals **2** *Sports* a procedure used to break a tie at the end of a game, esp. in soccer

**shop** (shäp) *n.* ⟦OE *sceoppa*, booth⟧ **1** a place where certain things are offered for sale; esp., a small store **2** a place where a particular kind of work is done —*vi.* **shopped**, **shop′ping** to visit shops to examine or buy goods —**talk shop** to discuss one's work

**shop′keep′er** *n.* one who owns or operates a shop, or small store

**shop′lift′** *vt., vi.* to steal (articles) from a store during shopping hours —**shop′lift′er** *n.*

**shoppe** (shäp) *n. alt. sp. of* SHOP (*n.* 1): now used only in shop names

**shop′per** *n.* **1** one who shops **2** one hired by a store to shop for others **3** one hired by a store to compare competitors' prices, etc.

**shopping center** a complex of stores, restaurants, etc. with a common parking area

**shop′talk′** *n.* **1** the specialized words and idioms of those in the same work **2** talk about work, esp. after hours

**shop′worn′** *adj.* soiled, faded, etc. from having been displayed in a shop

**shore**[1] (shôr) *n.* ⟦ME *schore*⟧ land at the edge of a body of water

**shore**[2] (shôr) *n.* ⟦ME *schore*⟧ a prop, beam, etc. used for support, etc. —*vt.* **shored**, **shor′ing** to support as with shores; prop (*up*)

**shore′bird′** *n.* a bird that lives or feeds near the shore

**shore′line′** *n.* the edge of a body of water

**shore patrol** a detail of the U.S. Navy, Coast Guard, or Marine Corps acting as military police on shore

**shorn** (shôrn) *vt., vi. alt. pp. of* SHEAR

**short** (shôrt) *adj.* ⟦OE *scort*⟧ **1** not measuring much from end to end in space or time **2** not great in range or scope **3** not tall **4** brief; concise **5** not retentive [a *short* memory] **6** curt; abrupt **7** less than a sufficient or correct amount **8** crisp or flaky, as pastry rich in shortening **9** designating a sale of securities, etc. which the seller does not yet own but expects to buy later at a lower price —*n.* **1** something short **2** [*pl.*] *a)* short trousers *b)* a man's undergarment like these **3** *short for a)* SHORTSTOP *b)* SHORT CIRCUIT —*adv.* **1** abruptly; suddenly **2** briefly; concisely **3** so as to be short in length **4** by surprise [caught *short*] —*vt., vi.* **1** to give less than what is needed or usual **2** *short for a)* SHORTCHANGE *b)* SHORT-CIRCUIT —**in short** briefly —**run short** to have less than

enough —**short of 1** less than or lacking **2** without actually resorting to —**short′ness** *n.*

**short′age** *n.* a deficiency in the amount needed or expected; deficit

**short′bread′** *n.* a rich, crumbly cake or cookie made with much shortening

**short′cake′** *n.* a light biscuit or a sweet cake served with fruit, etc.

**short′change′** *vt., vi.* **-changed′**, **-chang′ing** [Inf.] **1** to give less money than is due in change **2** to cheat by depriving of something due

**short circuit 1** a usually accidental connection between two points in an electric circuit, resulting in excessive current flow that causes damage **2** popularly, a disrupted electric circuit caused by this —**short′-cir′cuit** *vt., vi.*

**short′com′ing** *n.* a defect or deficiency

**short′cut′** *n.* **1** a shorter route **2** any way of saving time, effort, etc.

**short′en** *vt., vi.* to make or become short or shorter

**short·en·ing** (shôrt′'n iŋ, shôrt′niŋ) *n.* edible fat used to make pastry, etc. crisp or flaky

**short′fall′** *n.* a falling short, or the amount of the shortage

**short′hand′** *n.* any system of speed writing using symbols for words

**short′-hand′ed** *adj.* short of workers

**short′-lived′** (-līvd′, -livd′) *adj.* having a short life span or existence

**short′ly** *adv.* **1** briefly **2** soon **3** abruptly and rudely; curtly

**short order** any food that can be cooked or served quickly when ordered

**short′-range′** *adj.* reaching over a short distance or period of time

**short ribs** the rib ends from the front half of a side of beef

**short shrift** very little care or attention —**make short shrift of** to dispose of quickly and impatiently

**short′sight′ed** *adj.* **1** NEARSIGHTED **2** lacking in foresight —**short′sight′ed·ly** *adv.* —**short′sight′ed·ness** *n.*

**short′-spo′ken** *adj.* using few words, esp. to the point of rudeness; curt

**short′stop′** *n. Baseball* the infielder usually positioned to the left of second base

**short story** a piece of prose fiction shorter than a short novel

**short subject** a short film, as that shown with a film feature

**short′-tem′pered** *adj.* easily or quickly angered

**short′-term′** *adj.* for or extending over a short time

**short ton** 2,000 pounds: see TON

**short′-waist′ed** (-wās′tid) *adj.* unusually short between shoulders and waistline

**short′wave′** *n.* **1** a radio wave 60 meters or less in length: shorter than the waves used in commercial broadcasting **2** a radio or radio band for broadcasting or receiving shortwaves: in full **shortwave radio**

**short′-wind′ed** (-win′did) *adj.* easily put out of breath by exertion

**shot**[1] (shät) *n.* ⟦OE *sceot*⟧ **1** the act of shooting **2** range; scope **3** an attempt or try **4** a pointed, critical remark **5** the path of an object thrown, etc. **6** *a)* a projectile for a gun *b)* projectiles collectively **7** small pellets of lead or steel for a shotgun **8** the heavy metal ball used in the shot put **9** a marksman **10** a photograph or a film sequence **11** a hypodermic injection **12** a drink of liquor —**call the shots** [Inf.] to direct or control what is done

**shot**[2] (shät) *vt., vi. pt. & pp. of* SHOOT —*adj.* [Inf.] ruined or worn out

**shot′gun′** *n.* **1** a gun for firing a charge of shot at short range **2** *Football* a formation in which the quarterback stands several yards behind the line of scrimmage to receive the ball

**shot put** a contest in which a heavy metal ball is propelled with an overhand thrust from the shoulder —**shot′-put′ter** *n.* —**shot′-put′ting** *n.*

**should** (shood) *v.aux.* [OE *sceolde*] **1** *pt. of* SHALL **2** used to express: *a)* obligation, duty, etc. [*you should* help] *b)* expectation or probability [he *should* be here soon] *c)* a future condition [if I *should* die tomorrow]

**shoul·der** (shōl′dər) *n.* [OE *sculdor*] **1** *a)* the joint connecting the arm or forelimb with the body *b)* the part of the body including this joint **2** [*pl.*] the two shoulders and the part of the back between them **3** a shoulderlike projection **4** the land along the edge of a paved road —*vt.* **1** to push along or through, as with the shoulder **2** to carry upon the shoulder **3** to assume the burden of —**straight from the shoulder** without reserve; frankly — **turn** (or **give**) **a cold shoulder to** to snub or shun

**shoulder blade** SCAPULA

**shoulder harness** an anchored strap passing across the chest, used with a seat belt, as in a car: also called **shoulder belt**

**shout** (shout) *n.* [ME *schoute*] a loud cry or call —*vt., vi.* to utter or cry out in a shout —**shout′er** *n.*

**shove** (shuv) *vt., vi.* shoved, shov′ing [OE *scufan*] **1** to push, as along a surface **2** to push roughly —*n.* a push —**shove off 1** to push (a boat) away from shore **2** [Inf.] to leave

**shov·el** (shuv′əl) *n.* [OE *scofl*] a tool with a broad scoop or blade and a long handle, for lifting and moving loose material —*vt.* -eled or -elled, -el·ing or -el·ling **1** to move with a shovel **2** to dig out with a shovel

**shov·el·ful′** *n., pl.* -fuls′ as much as a shovel will hold

**show** (shō) *vt.* showed, shown or showed, show′ing [< OE *sceawian*] **1** to bring or put in sight **2** to guide; conduct **3** to point out **4** to reveal, as by behavior **5** to prove; demonstrate **6** to bestow (favor, mercy, etc.) —*vi.* **1** to be or become seen; appear **2** to be noticeable **3** to finish third or better in a horse race —*n.* **1** a showing or demonstration **2** pompous display **3** pretense [sorrow that was mere *show*] **4** a public display or exhibition **5** a presentation of entertainment —**show off 1** to make a display of **2** to attract attention to oneself —**show up 1** to expose **2** to be seen **3** to arrive

**show′biz′** (-biz′) *n.* [Inf.] SHOW BUSINESS

**show′boat′** *n.* **1** a boat with a theater and actors who play river towns **2** [Slang] a showoff —*vi.* [Slang] to show off

**show business** the theater, films, TV, etc. as a business or industry

**show′case′** *n.* a glass-enclosed case for displaying things, as in a store —*vt.* -cased′, -cas′ing to display to good advantage

**show′down′** *n.* [Inf.] an action that brings matters to a climax or settles them

**show·er** (shou′ər) *n.* [OE *scur*] **1** a brief fall of rain, etc. **2** a sudden, abundant fall or flow, as of sparks **3** a party at which gifts are presented to the guest of honor **4** a bath in which the body is sprayed from overhead with fine streams of water —*vt.* **1** to spray with water, etc. **2** to pour forth as in a shower —*vi.* **1** to fall or come as a shower **2** to bathe under a shower —**show′er·y** *adj.*

**show·ing** (shō′iŋ) *n.* **1** a bringing to view or notice; exhibition **2** a performance, appearance, etc. [a good *showing* in the contest]

**show·man** (shō′mən) *n., pl.* -men (-mən) **1** one whose business is producing shows **2** a person skilled at presenting anything in a striking manner —**show′man·ship′** *n.*

**shown** (shōn) *vt., vi. alt. pp. of* SHOW

**show′off′** *n.* one who shows off

**show of hands** a raising of hands, as in voting or volunteering

**show′piece′** *n.* **1** something displayed or exhibited **2** something that is a fine example of its kind

**show′place′** *n.* **1** a place displayed to the public for its beauty, etc. **2** any beautiful place

**show′room′** *n.* a room where merchandise is displayed for advertising or sale

**show′time′** *n.* the time when a show begins

**show window** a store window in which merchandise is displayed

**show′y** *adj.* -i·er, -i·est **1** of striking appearance **2** attracting attention in a gaudy way —**show′i·ness** *n.*

**shpt** *abbrev.* shipment

**shrank** (shraŋk) *vt., vi. alt. pt. of* SHRINK

**shrap·nel** (shrap′nəl) *n.* [after Gen. H. *Shrapnel* (1761-1842), its Brit inventor] **1** an artillery shell filled with an explosive charge and small metal balls **2** these balls **3** any fragments scattered by an exploding shell, bomb, etc.

**shred** (shred) *n.* [OE *screade*] **1** a narrow strip cut, torn off, etc. **2** a fragment —*vt.* **shred′ded** or **shred, shred′ding** to cut or tear into shreds — **shred′da·ble** *adj.* —**shred′der** *n.*

**Shreve·port** (shrēv′pôrt′) city in NW Louisiana: pop. 199,000

**shrew** (shrōō) *n.* [< OE *screawa*] **1** a small, mouselike mammal with a long snout **2** a nagging, bad-tempered woman —**shrew′ish** *adj.*

**shrewd** (shrōōd) *adj.* [see prec.] clever or sharp in practical affairs; astute —**shrewd′ly** *adv.* — **shrewd′ness** *n.*

**shriek** (shrēk) *vi., vt.* [ME *schriken*] to make or utter with a loud, piercing cry —*n.* such a cry

**shrift** (shrift) *n.* [ult. < L *scribere*, write] [Archaic] confession to and absolution by a priest: see also SHORT SHRIFT

**shrike** (shrīk) *n.* [OE *scric*] a shrill-voiced, predatory songbird with a hooked beak

**shrill** (shril) *adj.* [echoic] producing a high, thin, piercing sound —*vi., vt.* to utter (with) a shrill sound —**shril′ly** *adv.* —**shrill′ness** *n.*

**shrimp** (shrimp) *n.* [OE *scrimman*, to shrink] **1** a small, long-tailed crustacean, valued as food **2** [Inf.] a small or insignificant person

**shrine** (shrīn) *n.* [< L *scrinium*, box] **1** a container holding sacred relics **2** a saint's tomb **3** a place of worship **4** any hallowed place

**shrink** (shriŋk) *vi.* **shrank** or **shrunk, shrunk** or **shrunk′en, shrink′ing** [OE *scrincan*] **1** to contract, as from heat, cold, moisture, etc. **2** to lessen, as in amount **3** to draw back; flinch —*vt.* to make shrink —**shrink′a·ble** *adj.*

**shrink′age** *n.* **1** a shrinking **2** the amount of shrinking

**shrinking violet** a very shy person

**shrink′-wrap′** *vt.* -wrapped′, -wrap′ping to wrap in a plastic material that is then shrunk by heating to fit tightly —*n.* a wrapping of such material

**shrive** (shrīv) *vt.* shrived or shrove, shriv·en (shriv′ən) or shrived, shriv′ing [OE *scrifan*] [Archaic] to hear the confession of and absolve

**shriv·el** (shriv′əl) *vt., vi.* -eled or -elled, -el·ing or -el·ling [prob. < Scand] to shrink and wrinkle or wither

**shroud** (shroud) *n.* [OE *scrud*] **1** a cloth used to wrap a corpse for burial **2** something that covers, veils, etc. **3** any of the ropes from a ship's side to a masthead —*vt.* to hide; cover

**Shrove Tuesday** [see SHRIVE] the last day before Lent

**shrub** (shrub) *n.* [OE *scrybb*, brushwood] a low, woody plant with several stems; bush —**shrub′by** *adj.*

**shrub·ber·y** (-ər ē) *n.* shrubs collectively

**shrug** (shrug) *vt., vi.* shrugged, shrug′ging [ME *schruggen*] to draw up (the shoulders), as in indifference, doubt, etc. —*n.* the gesture so made

—**shrug off** to dismiss or disregard in a carefree way

**shrunk** (shruŋk) *vi.*, *vt. alt. pt. & pp. of* SHRINK

**shrunk′en** *vi.*, *vt. alt. pp. of* SHRINK —*adj.* contracted in size; shriveled

**shtick** (shtik) *n.* 〚Yiddish〛 **1** a comic scene or gimmick **2** an attention-getting device

**shuck** (shuk) *n.* 〚< ?〛 a shell, pod, or husk —*vt.* to remove shucks from

**shucks** (shuks) *interj.* used to express mild disappointment, embarrassment, etc.

**shud·der** (shud′ər) *vi.* 〚ME *schoderen*〛 to shake or tremble, as in horror —*n.* a shuddering

**shuf·fle** (shuf′əl) *vt.*, *vi.* **-fled**, **-fling** 〚prob. < LowG *schuffeln*〛 **1** to move (the feet) with a dragging gait **2** to mix (playing cards) **3** to mix together in a jumble —*n.* a shuffling —**shuf′fler** *n.*

**shuf′fle·board′** *n.* 〚< earlier *shovel board*〛 a game in which disks are pushed with a cue toward numbered squares on a diagram

**shun** (shun) *vt.* **shunned**, **shun′ning** 〚OE *scunian*〛 to keep away from; avoid scrupulously

**shunt** (shunt) *vt.*, *vi.* 〚ME *schunten*〛 **1** to move or turn to one side **2** to switch from one track to another: said as of a train —*n.* **1** a shunting **2** a railroad switch **3** a surgically created channel allowing flow from one organ, etc. to another

**shush** (shush) *interj.* 〚echoic〛 hush! be quiet! —*vt.* to say "shush" to

**shut** (shut) *vt.* **shut**, **shut′ting** 〚OE *scyttan*〛 **1** to move (a door, lid, etc.) so as to close (an opening, container, etc.) **2** *a*) to prevent entrance to or exit from *b*) to confine *in* a room, etc. **3** to bring together the parts of (a book, the eyes, etc.) —*vi.* to be or become shut —*adj.* closed, fastened, etc. —**shut down** to cease operating —**shut off** to prevent passage of or through —**shut out 1** to deny entrance to **2** to prevent from scoring —**shut up 1** to confine **2** [Inf.] to stop or cause to stop talking

**shut′down′** *n.* a stoppage of work or activity, as in a factory

**shut′-eye′** *n.* [Slang] sleep

**shut′-in′** *adj.* confined indoors by illness —*n.* an invalid who is shut-in

**shut′out′** *n.* a game in which a team is kept from scoring

**shut·ter** (shut′ər) *n.* **1** a person or thing that shuts **2** a movable cover for a window **3** a device for opening and closing the aperture of a camera lens —*vt.* to close or furnish with a shutter

**shut·tle** (shut′'l) *n.* 〚< OE *scytel*, missile〛 **1** a device that carries thread back and forth, as in weaving **2** *a*) a traveling back and forth over a short route *b*) an airplane, bus, etc. used in a shuttle —*vt.*, *vi.* **-tled**, **-tling** to move back and forth rapidly

**shut′tle·cock′** (-käk′) *n.* in badminton, a rounded piece of cork having a flat end stuck with feathers, or a similar plastic device

**shy**[1] (shī) *adj.* **shy′er** or **shi′er**, **shy′est** or **shi′est** 〚OE *sceoh*〛 **1** easily frightened; timid **2** not at ease with others; bashful **3** distrustful; wary **4** [Slang] lacking —*vi.* **shied**, **shy′ing 1** to move suddenly as when startled **2** to be or become cautious, etc. —**shy′ly** *adv.* —**shy′ness** *n.*

**shy**[2] (shī) *vt.*, *vi.* **shied**, **shy′ing** 〚< ?〛 to fling, esp. sideways

**shy·ster** (shī′stər) *n.* 〚prob. < Ger *scheisser*, one who defecates〛 [Slang] a lawyer who uses unethical or tricky methods

**Si** *Chem. symbol for* silicon

**Si·am** (sī am′) *former name for* THAILAND

**Si·a·mese** (sī′ə mēz′) *n.*, *pl.* **-mese′ 1** *former name for* THAI **2** a domestic cat with blue eyes and a light-colored coat —*adj. former term for* THAI

**Siamese twins** 〚after such a pair born in *Siam*〛 any pair of twins born with bodies joined together

**Si·ber·i·a** (sī bir′ē ə) region in N Asia, between the Urals & the Pacific: Asian section of Russia —**Si·ber′i·an** *adj.*, *n.*

**sib·i·lant** (sib′ə lənt) *adj.* 〚< L *sibilare*, to hiss〛 having or making a hissing sound —*n.* a sibilant consonant, as (s) or (z)

**sib·ling** (sib′liŋ) *n.* 〚< OE *sib*, kinsman + -LING〛 a brother or sister

**sib·yl** (sib′əl) *n.* 〚< Gr *sibylla*〛 ancient Greek or Roman prophetess —**sib′yl·line′** (-īn′, -ēn′) *adj.*

**sic** (sik) *vt.* **sicced** or **sicked**, **sic′cing** or **sick′ing** 〚< SEEK〛 to incite (a dog) to attack

*sic* (sik, sēk) *adv.* 〚L〛 thus; so: used within brackets, [*sic*], to show that a quoted passage, esp. one containing an error, is reproduced accurately

**Sic·i·ly** (sis′ə lē) island of Italy, off its S tip —**Si·cil·i·an** (si sil′yən) *adj.*, *n.*

**sick**[1] (sik) *adj.* 〚OE *seoc*〛 **1** suffering from disease; ill **2** having nausea **3** of or for sick people [*sick* leave] **4** deeply disturbed, as by grief **5** disgusted by an excess [*sick* of excuses] **6** [Inf.] sadistic, morbid, etc. [a *sick* joke] —**the sick** sick people —**sick′ish** *adj.*

**sick**[2] (sik) *vt. alt. sp. of* SIC (incite)

**sick bay** a hospital and dispensary on a ship

**sick′bed′** *n.* the bed of a sick person

**sick′en** *vt.*, *vi.* to make or become ill, disgusted, etc. —**sick′en·ing** *adj.*

**sick′ie** (-ē) *n.* [Slang] a sick person, esp. one who is emotionally disturbed, sadistic, etc.

**sick·le** (sik′əl) *n.* 〚ult. < L *secare*, to cut〛 a tool having a crescent-shaped blade on a short handle, for cutting tall grasses and weeds

**sickle cell anemia** an inherited chronic anemia found chiefly among black people, in which defective hemoglobin causes sickle-shaped red blood cells

**sick′ly** *adj.* **-li·er**, **-li·est 1** in poor health **2** produced by sickness [a *sickly* pallor] **3** faint **4** weak

**sick′ness** *n.* **1** a being sick or diseased **2** a malady **3** nausea

**sick′out′** *n.* a staying out of work on the claim of illness, as by a group of employees trying to win demands but forbidden to strike

**sick′room′** *n.* the room of a sick person

**side** (sīd) *n.* 〚OE〛 **1** the right or left half, as of the body **2** a position beside one **3** *a*) either of the lines or surfaces that bound something *b*) either of the two bounding surfaces of an object that are not the front, back, top, or bottom **4** either of the two surfaces of paper, cloth, etc. **5** an aspect [his cruel *side*] **6** any location, etc. with reference to a central point **7** the position or attitude of one person or faction opposing another **8** one of the parties in a contest, conflict, etc. **9** a line of descent —*adj.* **1** of, at, or on a side **2** to or from one side [a *side* glance] **3** secondary [a *side* issue] —*vi.* to align oneself (*with* a faction, etc.) —**side by side** together —**take sides** to support a faction

**side′arm′** *adj.*, *adv.* with a forward arm motion at or below shoulder level

**side arm** a weapon worn at the side or waist, as a sword or pistol: *often used in pl.*

**side′bar′** *n.* a short article about a sidelight of a major news story and printed alongside it

**side′board′** *n.* a piece of furniture for holding linen, china, silverware, etc.

**side′burns′** *pl.n.* 〚< *burnsides*, side whiskers worn by A. E. *Burnside*, Civil War general〛 the hair growing on the sides of a man's face, just in front of the ears

**side′car′** *n.* a small car attached to the side of a motorcycle

**side dish** any food served along with the main course, usually in a separate dish

**side effect** an incidental effect, as an unrelated symptom produced by a drug

**side′kick′** *n.* [Slang] **1** a close friend **2** a partner; confederate

**side′light′** *n.* a bit of incidental knowledge or information

**side·line′** *n.* **1** either of two lines marking the side limits of a playing area, as in football **2** a secondary line of merchandise, work, etc.

**side′long′** *adv.* toward the side —*adj.* directed to the side: said as of a glance

**side′man′** (-man′) *n.*, *pl.* **-men′** (-men′) a band member other than the leader or soloist

**side′piece′** *n.* a piece on the side of something

**si·de·re·al** (sī dir′ē əl) *adj.* ⟦< L *sidus*, star⟧ with reference to the stars

**side′sad′dle** *n.* a saddle designed for a rider sitting with both legs on the same side of the animal —*adv.* on or as if on a sidesaddle

**side′show′** *n.* a small show in connection with the main show, as of a circus

**side′slip′** *vi.* **-slipped′**, **-slip′ping** to slip or skid sideways —*vt.* to cause to sideslip —*n.* a slip or skid to the side

**side′split′ting** *adj.* **1** very hearty: said of laughter **2** very funny

**side′step′** *vt.*, *vi.* **-stepped′**, **-step′ping** to dodge as by stepping aside

**side′swipe′** *vt.* **-swiped′**, **-swip′ing** to hit along the side in passing —*n.* such a glancing blow

**side′track′** *vt.*, *vi.* **1** to switch (a train) to a siding **2** to turn away from the main issue

**side′walk′** *n.* a path for pedestrians, usually paved, along the side of a street

**side′wall′** *n.* the side of a tire between the tread and the wheel rim

**side′ways′** (-wāz′) *adv.*, *adj.* **1** toward or from one side **2** with one side forward Also **side′wise′** (-wīz′)

**sid·ing** (sīd′iŋ) *n.* **1** a covering, as of overlapping boards, for the outside of a frame building **2** a short railroad track connected with a main track by a switch and used for unloading, etc.

**si·dle** (sīd′'l) *vi.* **-dled**, **-dling** ⟦< *sideling*, sideways⟧ to move sideways, esp. shyly or stealthily

**SIDS** (sidz) *abbrev.* SUDDEN INFANT DEATH SYNDROME

**siege** (sēj) *n.* ⟦ult. < L *sedere*, sit⟧ **1** the encirclement of a fortified place by an enemy intending to take it **2** any persistent attempt to gain control, etc. —**lay siege to** to subject to a siege

**si·en·na** (sē en′ə) *n.* ⟦It⟧ yellowish brown or reddish brown

**si·er·ra** (sē er′ə) *n.* ⟦Sp < L *serra*, a saw⟧ a range of hills or mountains with a saw-toothed appearance

**Si·er·ra Le·one** (sē er′ə lē ōn′) country in W Africa, on the Atlantic: 27,925 sq. mi.; pop. 3,518,000

**si·es·ta** (sē es′tə) *n.* ⟦Sp < L *sexta* (*hora*), sixth (hour), noon⟧ a brief nap or rest after the noon meal

**sieve** (siv) *n.* ⟦OE *sife*⟧ a utensil with many small holes for straining liquids, etc.; strainer

**sift** (sift) *vt.* ⟦OE *siftan*⟧ **1** to pass (flour, etc.) through a sieve **2** to examine (evidence, etc.) with care **3** to separate [to sift fact from fable] —*vi.* to pass as through a sieve —**sift′er** *n.*

**sigh** (sī) *vi.* ⟦< OE *sican*⟧ **1** to take in and let out a long, deep, audible breath, as in sorrow, relief, or longing **2** to feel longing or grief (*for*) —*n.* the act or sound of sighing

**sight** (sīt) *n.* ⟦< OE *seon*, to see⟧ **1** something seen or worth seeing **2** the act of seeing **3** a device to aid the eyes in aiming a gun, etc. **4** aim or an observation taken, as on a sextant **5** the power or range of seeing; eyesight **6** [Inf.] anything that looks unpleasant, odd, etc. —*vt.* **1** to observe **2** to glimpse; see **3** to aim at **4** to adjust the sights of —*vi.* to look carefully [*sight* along the line] —**at** (or **on**) **sight** as soon as seen —**by sight** by appearance —**not by a long sight 1** not nearly **2** not at all —**out of sight 1** not in sight **2** far off **3** [Inf.] beyond reach **4** [Slang] excellent; wonderful

**sight′ed** *adj.* **1** having sight; not blind **2** having (a specified kind of) sight [*farsighted*]

**sight′ing** *n.* an observation, as of something rare

**sight′less** *adj.* blind

**sight′ly** *adj.* **-li·er**, **-li·est** pleasant to the sight —**sight′li·ness** *n.*

**sight reading** the skill of performing written music on first sight —**sight′-read′** *vt.*, *vi.*

**sight′see′ing** *n.* the visiting of places of interest —**sight′seer** (-sē′ər) *n.*

**sig·ma** (sig′mə) *n.* the eighteenth letter of the Greek alphabet (Σ, σ, ς)

**sign** (sīn) *n.* ⟦< L *signum*⟧ **1** something that indicates a fact, quality, etc.; token **2** a gesture that conveys information, etc. **3** a mark or symbol having a specific meaning [a dollar *sign* ($)] **4** a placard, etc. bearing information, advertising, etc. **5** any trace or indication —*vt.* **1** to write (one's name) on (a letter, check, contract, etc.) **2** to engage by written contract —*vi.* to write one's signature —**sign in** (or **out**) to sign a register on arrival (or departure) —**sign off** to stop broadcasting, as for the day —**sign off on** to approve

**sign′age** *n.* public signs collectively, often, specif., when graphically coordinated

**sig·nal** (sig′nəl) *n.* ⟦< L *signum*, a sign⟧ **1** a sign or event that initiates action [a bugle *signal* to attack] **2** a gesture, device, etc. that conveys command, warning, etc. **3** in radio, etc., the electrical impulses transmitted or received —*adj.* **1** remarkable; notable **2** used as a signal —*vt.*, *vi.* **-naled** or **-nalled**, **-nal·ing** or **-nal·ling 1** to make a signal or signals (to) **2** to communicate by signals

**sig′nal·ize′** (-nə līz′) *vt.* **-ized′**, **-iz′ing** to make known or draw attention to

**sig′nal·ly** *adv.* in a signal way; notably

**sig·na·to·ry** (sig′nə tôr′ē) *adj.* having joined in signing something —*n.*, *pl.* **-ries** a signatory person, nation, etc.

**sig·na·ture** (sig′nə chər) *n.* ⟦< L *signare*, to sign⟧ **1** a person's name written by that person **2** *Music* a staff sign showing key or time

**sign·board** (sīn′bôrd′) *n.* a board bearing a sign or advertisement

**sig·net** (sig′nit) *n.* ⟦< Fr *signe*, a sign⟧ a seal, as on a ring, used in marking documents as official, etc.

**sig·nif·i·cance** (sig nif′ə kəns) *n.* **1** that which is signified; meaning **2** the quality of being significant; expressiveness **3** importance

**sig·nif′i·cant** (-kənt) *adj.* ⟦< L *significare*, signify⟧ **1** having or expressing a meaning, esp. a special or hidden one **2** full of meaning **3** important —**sig·nif′i·cant·ly** *adv.*

**sig·ni·fy** (sig′nə fī′) *vt.* **-fied′**, **-fy′ing** ⟦< L *signum*, a sign + *facere*, make⟧ **1** to be an indication of; mean **2** to make known by a sign, words, etc. —*vi.* to be important —**sig′ni·fi·ca′tion** *n.*

**sign language** hand signals and gestures used, as by the deaf, as a language

**sign of the cross** an outline of a CROSS (sense 2) made symbolically by moving the hand or fingers

**sign of the zodiac** any of the twelve divisions of the zodiac, each represented by a symbol

**si·gnor** (sē nyôr′) *n.*, *pl.* **-gno′ri** (-nyô′rē) ⟦It⟧ **1** [S-] Mr.: Italian title **2** a man; gentleman

**si·gno·ra** (sē nyô′rä) *n.*, *pl.* **-gno′re** (-rē) ⟦It⟧ **1** [S-] Mrs.; Madam: Italian title **2** a married woman

**si·gno·ri·na** (sē′nyô rē′nä) *n.*, *pl.* **-ri′ne** (-ne) ⟦It⟧ **1** [S-] Miss: Italian title **2** an unmarried woman or a girl

**sign′post′** *n.* **1** a post bearing a sign **2** an obvious clue, symptom, etc.

**Sikh** (sēk, sik) *n.* ⟦Hindi, disciple⟧ a member of a monotheistic religion founded in N India

**si·lage** (sī′lij) *n.* green fodder preserved in a silo

**si·lence** (sī′ləns) *n.* **1** a keeping silent **2** absence of sound **3** an omission of mention —*vt.* **-lenced**, **-lenc·ing 1** to make silent **2** to put down; repress —*interj.* be silent!

**si′lenc·er** *n.* **1** one that silences **2** a device to muffle the sound of a gun

**si·lent** (sī′lənt) *adj.* ⟦< L *silere*, be silent⟧ **1** making no vocal sound; mute **2** not talkative **3** still;

noiseless **4** not expressed; tacit **5** not active [a *silent* partner] —**si′lent·ly** *adv.*

**sil·hou·ette** (sil′ə wet′) *n.* [Fr, after E. de *Silhouette*, 18th-c. Fr statesman] **1** a solid, usually black, outline drawing, esp. a profile **2** any dark shape seen against a light background —*vt.* **-et′ted, -et′ting** to show in silhouette

**sil·i·ca** (sil′i kə) *n.* [< L *silex*, flint] a hard, glassy mineral found in a variety of forms, as in quartz, opal, or sand —**si·li·ceous** (sə lish′əs) *adj.*

**sil′i·cate** (-kit, -kāt′) *n.* a salt or ester derived from silica

**sil′i·con** (-kän′, -kən) *n.* [ult. < L *silex*, flint] a nonmetallic chemical element found always in combination

SILHOUETTE

**sil′i·cone** (-kōn′) *n.* an organic silicon compound highly resistant to heat, water, etc.

**Silicon Valley** [after the material used for electronic chips] *name for* an area near San Francisco: a center of high-technology activities

**sil′i·co′sis** (-kō′sis) *n.* [see SILICON & -OSIS] a chronic lung disease from inhaling silica dust

**silk** (silk) *n.* [ult. < ? L *sericus*, (fabric) of the *Seres*, prob. the Chinese] **1** *a*) the fine, soft fiber produced by silkworms *b*) thread or fabric made from this **2** any silklike filament or substance —**silk′en** *adj.* —**silk·y** (sil′kē), **-i·er, -i·est,** *adj.* —**silk′i·ness** *n.*

**silk-screen process** a stencil method of printing a color design through a piece of silk or other fine cloth on which parts of the design not to be printed have been blocked out —**silk′-screen′** *vt.*

**silk′worm′** *n.* any of certain moth caterpillars that produce cocoons of silk fiber

**sill** (sil) *n.* **1** a heavy horizontal timber or line of masonry supporting a house wall, etc. **2** a horizontal piece forming the bottom frame of a window or door opening

**sil·ly** (sil′ē) *adj.* **-li·er, -li·est** [< OE *sælig*, happy] having or showing little sense, judgment, or sobriety; foolish, absurd, etc. —**sil′li·ness** *n.*

**si·lo** (sī′lō) *n., pl.* **-los** [< Gr *siros*] **1** an airtight pit or tower in which green fodder is preserved **2** an underground facility for a long-range ballistic missile

**silt** (silt) *n.* [prob. < Scand] a fine-grained, sandy sediment carried or deposited by water —*vt., vi.* to fill or choke up with silt

**sil·ver** (sil′vər) *n.* [< OE *seolfor*] **1** a white metallic chemical element that is very ductile and malleable: a precious metal **2** *a*) silver coin *b*) money; riches **3** silverware **4** a lustrous, grayish white —*adj.* **1** of, containing, or plated with silver **2** silvery **3** marking a 25th anniversary —*vt.* to cover with or as with silver

**sil′ver·fish′** *n., pl.* **-fish′** a wingless insect with silvery scales and long feelers, found in damp places

**silver lining** some basis for hope or comfort in the midst of despair

**silver nitrate** a colorless crystalline salt, used in photography, as an antiseptic, etc.

**sil′ver·smith′** *n.* an artisan who makes and repairs silver articles

**sil′ver·tongued′** (-tuŋd′) *adj.* eloquent

**sil′ver·ware′** *n.* **1** articles, esp. tableware, made of or plated with silver **2** any metal tableware

**sil′ver·y** *adj.* **1** of, like, or containing silver **2** soft and clear in tone

**sim·i·an** (sim′ē ən) *adj., n.* [< L *simia*, an ape] (of or like) an ape or monkey

**sim·i·lar** (sim′ə lər) *adj.* [< L *similis*] nearly but not exactly the same or alike —**sim′i·lar′i·ty** (-ler′ə tē), *pl.* **-ties,** *n.* —**sim′i·lar·ly** *adv.*

**sim·i·le** (sim′ə lē′) *n.* [< L, a likeness] a figure of speech likening one thing to another by the use of *like, as,* etc. (Ex.: tears flowed like wine)

**si·mil·i·tude** (sə mil′ə tood′) *n.* [< L *similitudo*] likeness; resemblance

**sim·mer** (sim′ər) *vi.* [echoic] **1** to remain at or just below the boiling point **2** to be about to break out, as in anger or revolt —*vt.* to keep at or just below the boiling point —*n.* a simmering

**si·mon-pure** (sī′mən pyoor′) *adj.* [after *Simon Pure*, a character in an 18th-c. play] genuine; authentic

**si·mo·ny** (sī′mə nē, sim′ə-) *n.* [after *Simon Magus*: Acts 8:9-24] the buying or selling of sacraments or benefices

**sim·pa·ti·co** (sim pät′i kō, -pat′-) *adj.* [< It or Sp] compatible or congenial

**sim·per** (sim′pər) *vi.* [early Modern Eng] to smile in a silly or affected way —*n.* such a smile

**sim·ple** (sim′pəl) *adj.* **-pler, -plest** [< L *simplus*] **1** having only one or a few parts; uncomplicated **2** easy to do or understand **3** without additions [the *simple* facts] **4** not ornate or luxurious; plain **5** without guile or deceit **6** without ostentation; natural **7** of low rank or position **8** stupid or foolish —**sim′ple·ness** *n.*

**simple interest** interest computed on principal alone, and not on principal plus interest

**sim′ple-mind′ed** *adj.* **1** artless; unsophisticated **2** foolish **3** mentally retarded

**sim′ple·ton** (-tən) *n.* a fool

**sim·plic·i·ty** (sim plis′ə tē) *n., pl.* **-ties 1** a simple state or quality; freedom from complexity **2** absence of elegance, luxury, etc.; plainness

**sim·pli·fy** (sim′plə fī′) *vt.* **-fied′, -fy′ing** to make simpler or less complex —**sim′pli·fi·ca′tion** *n.*

**sim·plis·tic** (sim plis′tik) *adj.* making complex problems unrealistically simple —**sim·plis′ti·cal·ly** *adv.*

**sim·ply** (sim′plē) *adv.* **1** in a simple way **2** merely [simply trying] **3** completely [simply furious]

**sim·u·late** (sim′yoo lāt′) *vt.* **-lat′ed, -lat′ing** [< L *simulare*] **1** to give a false appearance of; feign **2** to look or act like —**sim′u·la′tion** *n.* —**sim′u·la′tor** *n.*

**si·mul·cast** (sī′məl kast′) *vt.* **-cast′** or **-cast′ed, -cast′ing** to broadcast (a program) simultaneously by radio and television —*n.* a program so broadcast

**si·mul·ta·ne·ous** (sī′məl tā′nē əs) *adj.* [< L *simul*, together] occurring, done, etc. at the same time —**si′mul·ta·ne′i·ty** (-tə nē′ə tē, -nā′-) *n.* —**si′mul·ta′ne·ous·ly** *adv.*

**sin** (sin) *n.* [OE *synne*] **1** the willful breaking of religious or moral law **2** any offense or fault —*vi.* **sinned, sin′ning** to commit a sin

**Si·nai** (sī′nī′), **Mount** *Bible* the mountain where Moses received the law from God: Exodus 19

**since** (sins) *adv.* [ult. < OE *sith*, after + *thæt*, that] **1** from then until now [I've been here ever *since*] **2** at some time between then and now [he has *since* recovered] **3** before now; ago [long *since* gone] —*prep.* **1** continuously from (then) until now [since noon] **2** during the period between (then) and now [twice *since* May] —*conj.* **1** after the time that [two years *since* they met] **2** continuously from the time when [lonely ever *since* she left] **3** because [since you're done, let's go]

**sin·cere** (sin sir′) *adj.* **-cer′er, -cer′est** [< L *sincerus*, pure] **1** truthful; honest **2** genuine [sincere grief] —**sin·cere′ly** *adv.* —**sin·cer′i·ty** (-ser′ə tē) *n.*

**si·ne·cure** (sī′nə kyoor′, sin′ə-) *n.* [< L *sine*, without + *cura*, care] any position providing an income but requiring little or no work

**si·ne di·e** (sī′nē dī′ē) [LL, without a day] for an indefinite period

**si·ne qua non** (sī′nē kwä nän′, sin′ā kwä nōn′) [L, without which not] an indispensable condition or thing

**sin·ew** (sin′yoo) *n.* [OE *seonwe*] **1** a tendon **2** muscular power; strength —**sin′ew·y** *adj.*

**sin'ful** *adj.* wicked; immoral —**sin'ful·ly** *adv.*

**sing**[1] (sing) *vi.* **sang, sung, sing'ing** [[OE *singan*]] 1 to produce musical sounds with the voice 2 to use song or verse in praise, etc. [of thee I *sing*] 3 to make musical sounds, as a songbird does 4 to hum, buzz, etc., as a bee does —*vt.* 1 to render (a song, etc.) by singing 2 to extol, etc. in song 3 to bring or put by singing [to *sing* a baby to sleep] —*n.* [Inf.] group singing —**sing'er** *n.*

**sing**[2] *abbrev.* singular

**sing'a·long'** *n.* an informal gathering of people to sing songs

**Sin·ga·pore** (sin'ə pôr') 1 island country off the S tip of the Malay Peninsula: 248 sq. mi.; pop. 2,930,000 2 its capital, a seaport on the S coast: pop. 2,756,000

**singe** (sinj) *vt.* **singed, singe'ing** [[OE *sengan*]] 1 to burn superficially 2 to expose (an animal carcass) to flame in removing feathers, etc. —*n.* 1 a singeing 2 a superficial burn

**sin·gle** (sin'gəl) *adj.* [[< L *singulus*]] 1 *a*) one only *b*) separate and distinct [every *single* time] 2 solitary 3 of or for one person or family 4 between two persons only [*single* combat] 5 unmarried 6 having only one part; not multiple, etc. 7 whole; unbroken [a *single* front] —*vt.* **-gled, -gling** to select from others: usually with *out* —*vi. Baseball* to hit a single —*n.* 1 a single person or thing 2 *Baseball* a hit on which the batter reaches first base 3 [*pl.*] *Racket Sports* a match with only one player on each side —**sin'gle·ness** *n.*

**sin'gle-breast'ed** (-bres'tid) *adj.* overlapping in front enough to fasten [a *single-breasted* coat]

**single file** 1 a single line of people or things, one behind another 2 in such a line

**sin'gle-hand'ed** *adj., adv.* 1 using only one hand 2 without help —**sin'gle-hand'ed·ly** *adv.*

**sin'gle-mind'ed** *adj.* with only one aim or purpose —**sin'gle-mind'ed·ly** *adv.*

**sin'gle·ton** (-tən) *n.* 1 a playing card that is the only one of its suit held by a player 2 a single person or thing

**sin'gle-track'** *adj.* ONE-TRACK

**sin'gle·tree'** (-trē') *n.* [[< ME *swingle*, rod + *tre*, tree]] the crossbar on the hitch of a wagon, etc. to which the traces of a horse's harness are hooked

**sin·gly** (sin'glē) *adv.* 1 alone 2 one by one 3 unaided

**sing'song'** *n.* a monotonous rise and fall of tone, as in speaking

**sin·gu·lar** (sin'gyə lər) *adj.* [[< L *singulus*, single]] 1 unique 2 extraordinary; remarkable 3 peculiar; odd 4 *Gram.* designating only one —*n. Gram.* the singular form of a word —**sin'gu·lar'i·ty** (-ler'ə tē) *n.* —**sin'gu·lar·ly** *adv.*

**Sin·ha·lese** (sin'hə lēz', -lēs') *adj.* of Sri Lanka (island country of S Asia) or its principal people, language, etc. —*n.* 1 *pl.* **-lese'** a member of the Sinhalese people 2 the language of this people

**sin·is·ter** (sin'is tər) *adj.* [[< L *sinister*, left-hand (side)]] 1 [Archaic] on or to the left-hand side 2 threatening harm, evil, etc. 3 wicked; evil

**sink** (sink) *vi.* **sank** or **sunk, sunk, sink'ing** [[OE *sincan*]] 1 to go beneath the surface of water, etc. 2 to go down slowly 3 to appear to descend, as the sun does 4 to become lower, as in level, value, or rank 5 to subside: said as of wind or sound 6 to become hollow: said as of the cheeks 7 to pass gradually (*into* sleep, etc.) 8 to approach death —*vt.* 1 to cause to sink 2 to make (a mine, engraving, etc.) by digging, cutting, etc. 3 to invest 4 to defeat; undo —*n.* 1 a cesspool or sewer 2 a basin, as in a kitchen, with a drainpipe 3 an area of sunken land —**sink in** [Inf.] to be understood in full —**sink'a·ble** *adj.*

**sink'er** *n.* 1 one that sinks 2 a lead weight used in fishing

**sink'hole'** *n.* a surface depression resulting when ground collapses

**sinking fund** a fund built up over time to pay off a future debt, as of a corporation

**sin'ner** *n.* a person who sins

**Sino-** [[< Gr *Sinai*]] *combining form* Chinese and

**sin tax** a tax on something seen as sinful or harmful, as on liquor, tobacco, or gambling

**sin·u·ous** (sin'yōō əs) *adj.* [[< L *sinus*, a bend]] bending or winding in and out; wavy —**sin'u·os'i·ty** (-äs'ə tē) *n.* —**sin'u·ous·ly** *adv.*

**si·nus** (sī'nəs) *n.* [[L, a bend]] a cavity, hollow, etc.; specif., any of the air cavities in the skull opening into the nasal cavities

**si'nus·i'tis** (-īt'is) *n.* inflammation of the sinuses, esp. those of the skull

**Sioux** (sōō) *n., pl.* **Sioux** (sōō, sōōz) a member of a group of Indian tribes of the N U.S. and S Canada —*adj.* of these tribes

**sip** (sip) *vt., vi.* **sipped, sip'ping** [[ME *sippen*]] to drink a little at a time —*n.* 1 the act of sipping 2 a quantity sipped —**sip'per** *n.*

**si·phon** (sī'fən) *n.* [[< Gr *siphōn*, tube]] a bent tube for carrying liquid out over the edge of a container to a lower level —*vt.* to draw off through or as through a siphon

SIPHON

**sir** (sur) *n.* [[ME < *sire*, SIRE]] 1 [*sometimes* S-] a respectful term of address used to a man: not followed by the name 2 [S-] the title used before the name of a knight or baronet

**sire** (sīr) *n.* [[< OFr < L *senior*, compar. of *senex*, old]] 1 [S-] a title of respect used in addressing a king 2 [Old Poet.] a father or forefather 3 the male parent of a four-legged mammal —*vt.* **sired, sir'ing** to beget: said esp. of animals

**si·ren** (sī'rən) *n.* [[< Gr *Seirēn*]] 1 *Gr. & Rom. Myth.* any of several sea nymphs whose singing lures sailors to their death on rocky coasts 2 a woman considered seductive 3 a warning device producing a loud, wailing sound

**sir·loin** (sur'loin') *n.* [[< OFr *sur*, over + *loigne*, loin]] a choice cut of beef from the loin end in front of the rump

**si·roc·co** (sə räk'ō) *n., pl.* **-cos** [[It < Ar *sharq*, the east]] a hot, oppressive wind blowing from the deserts of N Africa into S Europe

**sir·ree** or **sir·ee** (sə rē') *interj.* [[< SIR]] used to provide emphasis after *yes* or *no*

**sir·up** (sur'əp, sir'-) *n. alt. sp. of* SYRUP

**sis** (sis) *n.* [Inf.] *short for* SISTER (senses 1-3)

**si·sal** (sī'səl, sis'əl) *n.* [[after *Sisal*, in SE Mexico]] a strong fiber obtained from the leaves of an agave

**sis·sy** (sis'ē) *n., pl.* **-sies** [[dim. of SIS]] [Inf.] 1 an effeminate boy or man 2 a timid person —**sis'si·fied'** (-ə fīd') *adj.*

**sis·ter** (sis'tər) *n.* [[< ON *systir*]] 1 a woman or girl as she is related to the other children of her parents 2 a half sister or stepsister 3 a female friend who is like a sister 4 a female fellow member of the same race, organization, etc. 5 [*often* S-] a nun 6 something of the same kind, model, etc. —**sis'ter·hood'** *n.* —**sis'ter·ly** *adj.*

**sis'ter-in-law'** *n., pl.* **sis'ters-in-law'** 1 the sister of one's spouse 2 the wife of one's brother 3 the wife of the brother of one's spouse

**Sis·y·phus** (sis'ə fəs) *Gr. Myth.* a greedy king doomed in Hades to roll uphill a stone which always rolls down again

**sit** (sit) *vi.* **sat, sit'ting** [[OE *sittan*]] 1 *a*) to rest oneself upon the buttocks, as on a chair *b*) to rest on the haunches with the forelegs braced (said of a dog, etc.) *c*) to perch (said of a bird) 2 to cover and warm eggs for hatching; brood 3 *a*) to occupy a seat as a judge, legislator, etc. *b*) to be in session (said as of court) 4 to pose, as for a portrait 5 to be located 6 to rest or lie as specified [cares *sit* lightly on him*]* **7** BABY-SIT —*vt.* **1** to cause to sit; seat **2** to keep one's seat on (a horse, etc.) — **sit down** to take a seat —**sit in** to attend: often with *on* —**sit out** to take no part in (a dance, etc.) —**sit up 1** to sit erect **2** to postpone going to bed **3** [Inf.] to become suddenly alert —**sit'ter** *n.*

**si·tar** (si tär′, si′tär*)* *n.* ⟦Hindi *sitār*⟧ a lutelike instrument of India with a long, fretted neck

**sit·com** (sit′käm′) *n.* [Inf.] *short for* SITUATION COMEDY

**sit′-down′** (**strike**) a strike in which the strikers refuse to leave the premises

**site** (sīt) *n.* ⟦< L *situs*, position⟧ a location or scene

**sit′-in′** *n.* a method of protest in which demonstrators sit in, and refuse to leave, a public place

SITAR

**sit′ting** *n.* **1** the act or position of one that sits **2** a session, as of a court **3** a period of being seated

**sitting duck** [Inf.] a person or thing especially vulnerable to attack; easy target

**sit·u·ate** (sich′oo āt′) *vt.* **-at′ed, -at′ing** ⟦see SITE⟧ to put in a certain place or position; place; locate

**sit′u·a′tion** *n.* **1** location; position **2** condition with regard to circumstances **3** state of affairs **4** a position of employment

**situation comedy** a comic TV series made up of episodes involving the same group of characters

**sit′-up′** or **sit′up′** *n.* an exercise in which a person lying supine rises to a sitting position without using the hands

**sitz bath** (sits, zits) ⟦< Ger⟧ a therapeutic bath in which only the hips and buttocks are immersed

**Si·va** (sē′və, shē′-) *n.* Hindu god of destruction and reproduction

**six** (siks) *adj., n.* ⟦OE *sex*⟧ one more than five; 6; VI —**sixth** *adj., n.*

**six′-pack′** *n.* a package of six units, as one with six cans of beer

**six′-shoot′er** *n.* [Inf.] a revolver having a cylinder that holds six cartridges: also **six′-gun′**

**six′teen′** (-tēn′) *adj.* ⟦OE *syxtene*⟧ six more than ten; 16; XVI —**six′teenth′** *adj., n.*

**sixth sense** intuitive power

**six·ty** (siks′tē) *adj., n., pl.* **-ties** ⟦OE *sixtig*⟧ six times ten; 60; LX —**the sixties** the numbers or years, as of a century, from 60 through 69 —**six′ti·eth** (-ith) *adj., n.*

**siz·a·ble** (sī′zə bəl) *adj.* quite large or bulky: also sp. **size′a·ble**

**size¹** (sīz) *n.* ⟦ult. < L *sedere*, sit⟧ **1** that quality of a thing which determines how much space it occupies; dimensions or magnitude **2** any of a series of graded classifications of measure into which merchandise is divided —*vt.* **sized, siz′ing** to make or grade according to size —**size up** [Inf.] **1** to make an estimate or judgment of **2** to meet requirements

**size²** (sīz) *n.* ⟦ME *syse*⟧ a pasty substance used as a glaze or filler on plaster, paper, cloth, etc. —*vt.* **sized, siz′ing** to fill, stiffen, or glaze with size

**-sized** (sīzd) *combining form* having a (specified) size *[medium-sized]*: also **-size**

**siz′ing** *n.* **1** SIZE² **2** the act of applying SIZE²

**siz·zle** (siz′əl) *vi.* **-zled, -zling** ⟦echoic⟧ **1** to make a hissing sound when in contact with heat **2** to be extremely hot —*n.* a sizzling sound

**S.J.** *abbrev.* Society of Jesus

**SK** Saskatchewan

**skate¹** (skāt) *n.* ⟦< OFr *eschace*, stilt⟧ **1** a metal runner in a frame, fastened to a shoe for gliding on ice **2** a similar frame or shoe with wheels, for

gliding on a floor, sidewalk, etc. —*vi.* **skat′ed, skat′ing** to glide or roll on or as on skates — **skat′er** *n.*

**skate²** (skāt) *n.* ⟦< ON *skata*⟧ any ray fish

**skate′board′** *n.* a short, oblong board with two wheels at each end, ridden standing up, as down an incline —*vi.* to ride on a skateboard

**ske·dad·dle** (ski dad′'l) *vi.* **-dled, -dling** ⟦< ?⟧ [Inf.] to run away

**skeet** (skēt) *n.* ⟦< ON *skeyti*, projectile⟧ trapshooting in which the shooter fires from different angles

**skein** (skān) *n.* ⟦< MFr *escaigne*⟧ a quantity of thread or yarn in a coil

**skel·e·ton** (skel′ə tən) *n.* ⟦< Gr *skeletos*, dried up⟧ **1** the hard framework of bones of an animal body **2** a supporting framework **3** an outline, as of a book —*adj.* greatly reduced *[a skeleton crew]* — **skel′e·tal** *adj.*

**skeleton key** a key that can open many simple locks

**skep·tic** (skep′tik) *n.* ⟦L < Gr *skeptikos*, inquiring⟧ **1** an adherent of skepticism **2** one who habitually questions matters generally accepted **3** one who doubts religious doctrines

**skep′ti·cal** (-ti kəl) *adj.* doubting; questioning — **skep′ti·cal·ly** *adv.*

**skep′ti·cism′** (-tə siz′əm) *n.* **1** the doctrine that the truth of all knowledge must always be in question **2** skeptical attitude **3** doubt about religious doctrines

**sketch** (skech) *n.* ⟦ult. < Gr *schedios*, extempore⟧ **1** a rough drawing or design, done rapidly **2** a brief outline **3** a short, light story, play, etc. — *vt., vi.* make a sketch or sketches (of) —**sketch′y, -i·er, -i·est,** *adj.*

**skew** (skyoo) *vi., vt.* ⟦< OFr *eschiver*, shun < OHG⟧ **1** to slant or set at a slant **2** to distort — *adj.* slanting —*n.* a slant or twist

**skew·er** (skyoo′ər) *n.* ⟦< ON *skifa*, a slice⟧ a long pin used to hold meat together while cooking —*vt.* to fasten or pierce with or as with skewers

**ski** (skē) *n., pl.* **skis** ⟦Norw < ON *skith*, snowshoe⟧ either of a pair of long runners of wood, etc. fastened to shoes for gliding over snow —*vi.* **skied, ski′ing** to glide on skis —**ski′er** *n.*

**skid** (skid) *n.* ⟦prob. < ON *skith*, snowshoe⟧ **1** a plank, log, etc., often used as a track upon which to slide a heavy object **2** a low, wooden platform for holding loads **3** a runner on aircraft landing gear **4** a sliding wedge used to brake a wheel **5** the act of skidding —*vt., vi.* **skid′ded, skid′ding** to slide or slip, as a vehicle on ice —**be on** (or **hit**) **the skids** [Slang] to be on the decline, or to fail

**skid row** ⟦altered < *skid road*, trail to skid logs along⟧ a section of a city frequented by vagrants, derelicts, etc.

**skiff** (skif) *n.* ⟦< It *schifo*⟧ any light, open boat propelled by oars, motor, or sail

**ski lift** an endless cable with seats, for carrying skiers up a slope

**skill** (skil) *n.* ⟦< ON *skil*, distinction⟧ **1** great ability or proficiency **2** *a*) an art, craft, etc., esp. one involving the hands or body *b*) ability in such an art, etc. —**skilled** *adj.* —**skill′ful** or **skil′ful** *adj.*

**skil·let** (skil′it) *n.* ⟦< ? L *scutra*, dish⟧ a pan for frying

**skim** (skim) *vt., vi.* **skimmed, skim′ming** ⟦ME *skimen*⟧ **1** to remove (floating matter) from (a liquid) **2** to glance through (a book, etc.) without reading word for word **3** to glide lightly (over)

**skim milk** milk with the cream removed: also **skimmed milk**

**skimp** (skimp) *vi., vt.* SCRIMP

**skimp′y** *adj.* **-i·er, -i·est** [Inf.] barely enough; scanty

**skin** (skin) *n.* ⟦< ON *skinn*⟧ **1** the outer covering of the animal body **2** a pelt **3** something like skin, as fruit rind, etc. —*vt.* **skinned, skin′ning 1**

to remove skin from **2** to injure by scraping (one's knee, etc.) **3** [Inf.] to swindle

**skin diving** underwater swimming with such gear as a face mask, flippers, scuba equipment, etc. —**skin′-dive′**, **-dived′**, **-div′ing**, *vi.* —**skin diver**

**skin′flick′** *n.* [Slang] a film emphasizing nudity or explicit sexual activity

**skin′flint′** *n.* [lit., one who would skin a flint for economy] a miser

**-skinned** *combining form* having (a specified kind of) skin *[dark-skinned]*

**skin′ny** *adj.* **-ni·er**, **-ni·est** without much flesh; very thin —**skin′ni·ness** *n.*

**skin′ny-dip′** *vi.* **-dipped′**, **-dip′ping** [Inf.] to swim nude —*n.* [Inf.] a swim in the nude

**skin′tight′** *adj.* tightfitting *[skintight jeans]*

**skip** (skip) *vi.*, *vt.* **skipped**, **skip′ping** [ME *skippen*] **1** to move along by hopping on first one foot and then the other **2** to ricochet or bounce **3** to pass from one point to another, omitting or ignoring (what lies between) **4** [Inf.] to leave (town, etc.) hurriedly —*n.* a skipping —**skip it!** [Inf.] it doesn't matter

**skip·per** (skip′ər) *n.* [< MDu *schip*, a ship] the captain of a ship

**skir·mish** (skur′mish) *n.* [< It *schermire* < Gmc] **1** a brief fight between small groups, as in a battle **2** any slight, unimportant conflict —*vi.* to take part in a skirmish

**skirt** (skurt) *n.* [< ON *skyrt*, shirt] **1** that part of a dress, coat, etc. that hangs below the waist **2** a woman's garment that hangs from the waist **3** something like a skirt —*vt.*, *vi.* to be on, or move along, the edge (of)

**ski run** a slope or course for skiing

**skit** (skit) *n.* [prob. ult. < ON *skjōta*, to shoot] a short, humorous sketch, as in the theater

**ski tow** a kind of ski lift for pulling skiers up a slope on their skis

**skit·ter** (skit′ər) *vi.* [< Scand] to move along quickly and lightly

**skit·tish** (skit′ish) *adj.* [see SKIT & -ISH] **1** lively; playful **2** easily frightened; jumpy **3** fickle

**skiv·vy** (skiv′ē) *n.*, *pl.* **-vies** [< ?] [Slang] **1** a man's, esp. a sailor's, short-sleeved undershirt: usually **skivvy shirt 2** [*pl.*] men's underwear

**skoal** (skōl) *interj.* [< ON *skål*, a bowl] to your health!: used as a toast

**skul·dug·ger·y** or **skull·dug·ger·y** (skul dug′ər ē) *n.* [< obs. Scot] [Inf.] sneaky, dishonest behavior; trickery

**skulk** (skulk) *vi.* [ME *sculken*] to move in a stealthy manner; slink

**skull** (skul) *n.* [< Scand] **1** the bony framework of the head, enclosing the brain **2** the head; mind

**skull′cap′** *n.* a light, closefitting, brimless cap, usually worn indoors

**skunk** (skuŋk) *n.* [< AmInd] **1** a small, bushy-tailed mammal having black fur with white stripes down the back: it ejects a foul-smelling liquid when disturbed or frightened **2** its fur **3** [Inf.] a despicable person

**sky** (skī) *n.*, *pl.* **skies** [< ON, a cloud] **1** [*often pl.*] the upper atmosphere *[blue skies, a cloudy sky]* **2** the firmament **3** heaven

**sky′box′** *n.* a private section of seats, often luxurious and usually elevated, in a stadium, etc.

**sky′cap′** *n.* a porter at an airport terminal

**sky diving** parachute jumping involving free-fall maneuvers

**sky′-high′** *adj.* very high —*adv.* **1** very high **2** in or to pieces

**sky′jack′** *vt.* to hijack (an aircraft) —**sky′jack′er** *n.*

**sky′lark′** *n.* a Eurasian lark famous for the song it utters as it soars —*vi.* to romp or frolic

**sky′light′** *n.* a window in a roof or ceiling

**sky′line′** *n.* **1** the visible horizon **2** the outline, as of a city, seen against the sky

**sky′rock′et** *n.* a fireworks rocket that explodes aloft —*vi.*, *vt.* to rise or cause to rise rapidly

**sky′scrap′er** *n.* a very tall building

**sky′ward** *adv.*, *adj.* toward the sky: also **sky′wards** *adv.*

**sky′way′** *n.* **1** AIR LANE **2** an elevated highway or walkway

**sky′writ′ing** *n.* the tracing of words, etc. in the sky by trailing smoke from an airplane — **sky′writ′er** *n.*

**slab** (slab) *n.* [ME *sclabbe*] a flat, broad, and fairly thick piece

**slack**[1] (slak) *adj.* [< OE *slæc*] **1** slow; sluggish **2** not busy; dull *[a slack period]* **3** loose; not tight **4** careless *[a slack worker]* —*vt.*, *vi.* to slacken —*n.* **1** a part that hangs loose **2** a lack of tension **3** a dull period; lull —**cut someone some slack** [Slang] to demand less of someone —**slack off** to slacken —**slack′ness** *n.*

**slack**[2] (slak) *n.* [ME *sleck*] a mixture of small pieces of coal, coal dust, etc. left from screening coal

**slack·en** (slak′ən) *vt.*, *vi.* **1** to make or become less active, brisk, etc. **2** to loosen or relax, as rope

**slack′er** *n.* one who shirks

**slacks** (slaks) *pl.n.* trousers for men or women

**slag** (slag) *n.* [< earlier LowG *slagge*] the fused refuse separated from metal in smelting

**slain** (slān) *vt. pp.* of SLAY

**slake** (slāk) *vt.* **slaked**, **slak′ing** [< OE *slæc*, SLACK[1]] **1** to satisfy (thirst, etc.) **2** to produce a chemical change in (lime) by mixing with water

**sla·lom** (slä′ləm) *n.* [Norw] a downhill ski race over a zigzag course —*vi.* to take part in a slalom

**slam** (slam) *vt.* **slammed**, **slam′ming** [prob. < Scand] **1** to shut, hit, throw, or put with force and noise **2** [Inf.] to criticize severely —*n.* **1** a slamming **2** [Inf.] a severe criticism

**slam′-bang′** [Inf.] *adv.* **1** swiftly or abruptly and recklessly **2** noisily —*adj.* lively, noisy, etc.

**slam′-dunk′** *n. Basketball* a forceful shot from directly above the basket

**slam·mer** (slam′ər) *n.* [Slang] a prison or jail

**slan·der** (slan′dər) *n.* [see SCANDAL] **1** the utterance of a falsehood that damages another's reputation **2** such a spoken statement —*vt.* to utter a slander about —**slan′der·er** *n.* —**slan′der·ous** *adj.*

**slang** (slaŋ) *n.* [< ?] highly informal speech that is outside standard usage and consists both of coined words and phrases and of new meanings given to established terms —**slang′y**, **-i·er**, **-i·est**, *adj.*

**slant** (slant) *vt.*, *vi.* [< Scand] **1** to incline; slope **2** to tell so as to express a particular bias —*n.* **1** an oblique surface, line, etc. **2** a point of view or attitude —*adj.* sloping

**slap** (slap) *n.* [echoic] **1** a blow with something flat, as the palm of the hand **2** an insult or rebuff —*vt.* **slapped**, **slap′ping 1** to strike with something flat **2** to put, hit, etc. with force

**slap′dash′** *adj.*, *adv.* hurried(ly), careless(ly), haphazard(ly), etc.

**slap′-hap′py** *adj.* [Slang] **1** dazed, as by blows **2** silly or giddy

**slap′stick′** *n.* crude comedy full of horseplay — *adj.* characterized by such comedy

**slash** (slash) *vt.* [< ? OFr *esclachier*, to break] **1** to cut with sweeping strokes, as of a knife **2** to cut slits in **3** to reduce drastically *[slash prices]* —*vi.* to make a sweeping stroke as with a knife —*n.* **1** a slashing **2** a cut made by slashing **3** a virgule —**slash′er** *n.*

**slash′-and-burn′** *adj.* **1** of a method of clearing fields by cutting down and burning vegetation **2** indiscriminately destructive

**slash pocket** a pocket (in a garment) with a finished diagonal opening

**slat** (slat) *n.* [< OFr *esclat*, fragment] a narrow strip of wood, metal, etc.

**slate** (slāt) *n.* [see prec.] **1** a hard, fine-grained rock that cleaves into thin, smooth layers **2** a thin piece of slate or slatelike material, as a roofing tile or writing tablet **3** the bluish-gray color of most slate: also **slate blue** —*vt.* **slat′ed, slat′ing 1** to cover with slate **2** to designate, as for candidacy —**a clean slate** a record showing no marks of discredit, dishonor, etc.

**slath·er** (slath′ər) *vt.* [< ?] [Inf. or Dial.] to cover or spread on thickly

**slat·tern** (slat′ərn) *n.* [< dial. *slatter*, to slop] a slovenly or sluttish woman —**slat′tern·ly** *adj.*

**slaugh·ter** (slôt′ər) *n.* [< ON *slātr*, lit., slain flesh] **1** the killing of animals for food; butchering **2** the brutal killing of a person **3** the killing of many people, as in battle —*vt.* **1** to kill (animals) for food; butcher **2** to kill (people) brutally or in large numbers —**slaugh′ter·er** *n.*

**slaugh′ter·house′** *n.* a place where animals are butchered for food

**Slav** (släv, slav) *n.* a member of a group of peoples of E and SE Europe, including Russians, Serbs, Czechs, Poles, etc. —*adj. var. of* SLAVIC

**slave** (slāv) *n.* [< Gr *Sklabos*, ult. < OSlav *Slověne*, first used of captive Slavs] **1** a human being who is owned as property by another **2** one dominated by some influence, etc. **3** one who slaves —*vi.* **slaved, slav′ing** to work like a slave; drudge

**slave driver 1** one who oversees slaves **2** any merciless taskmaster

**slav·er** (slav′ər) *vi.* [< Scand] to drool

**slav·er·y** (slā′vər ē) *n.* **1** the owning of slaves as a practice **2** the condition of a slave; bondage **3** drudgery; toil

**Slav·ic** (släv′ik, slav′-) *adj.* of the Slavs, their languages, etc. —*n.* a family of languages, including Russian, Polish, Czech, Bulgarian, etc.

**slav·ish** (slā′vish) *adj.* **1** of or like slaves; servile **2** blindly dependent or imitative —**slav′ish·ly** *adv.*

**slaw** (slô) *n.* [Du *sla* < Fr *salade*, salad] *short for* COLESLAW

**slay** (slā) *vt.* **slew, slain, slay′ing** [OE *slean*] to kill in a violent way —**slay′er** *n.*

**sleaze** (slēz) *n.* [< SLEAZY] [Slang] **1** sleaziness **2** someone or something sleazy

**slea·zoid** (slē′zoid′) [Slang] *adj.* SLEAZY (sense 2) —*n.* a coarse or immoral person

**slea·zy** (slē′zē) *adj.* **-zi·er, -zi·est** [< *silesia*, orig. cloth made in central Europe] **1** flimsy or thin in substance **2** shoddy, shabby, immoral, etc. —**slea′zi·ly** *adv.* —**slea′zi·ness** *n.*

**sled** (sled) *n.* [ME *sledde*] a vehicle on runners for moving over snow, ice, etc. —*vt., vi.* **sled′ded, sled′ding** to carry or ride on a sled —**sled′der** *n.*

**sledge¹** (slej) *n.* [OE *slecge*] SLEDGEHAMMER

**sledge²** (slej) *n.* [MDu *sleedse*] a sled or sleigh

**sledge′ham′mer** *n.* [see SLEDGE¹] a long, heavy hammer, usually held with both hands

**sleek** (slēk) *adj.* [var. of SLICK] **1** smooth and shiny; glossy **2** of well-fed or well-groomed appearance **3** suave, elegant, etc. —*vt.* to make sleek —**sleek′ly** *adv.* —**sleek′ness** *n.*

**sleep** (slēp) *n.* [OE *slæp*] **1** the natural, regularly recurring rest for the body, during which there is little or no conscious thought **2** any state like this —*vi.* **slept, sleep′ing** to be in a state of or like sleep —**sleep off** to rid oneself of by sleeping —**sleep′less** *adj.* —**sleep′less·ness** *n.*

**sleep′er** *n.* **1** one who sleeps **2** a railroad car with berths for sleeping: also **sleeping car 3** a beam laid flat to support something **4** something that achieves an unexpected success

**sleeping bag** a warmly lined, zippered bag for sleeping in outdoors

**sleeping sickness** an infectious disease, esp. of Africa, transmitted by the tsetse fly and characterized by lethargy, prolonged coma, etc.

**sleep′o′ver** *n.* a spending the night at another's home, as by a group of young people for fun

**sleep′walk′ing** *n.* the act of walking while asleep —**sleep′walk′er** *n.*

**sleep′wear′** *n.* NIGHTCLOTHES

**sleep′y** *adj.* **-i·er, -i·est 1** ready or inclined to sleep; drowsy **2** dull; idle [a *sleepy* town] —**sleep′i·ly** *adv.* —**sleep′i·ness** *n.*

**sleet** (slēt) *n.* [ME *slete*] **1** partly frozen rain **2** the icy coating formed when rain freezes on trees, etc. —*vi.* to fall as sleet —**sleet′y** *adj.*

**sleeve** (slēv) *n.* [OE *sliefe*] **1** that part of a garment that covers the arm **2** a tubelike part fitting over or around another part —**up one's sleeve** hidden but ready at hand —**sleeve′less** *adj.*

**sleigh** (slā) *n.* [Du *slee*] a vehicle on runners, usually horse-drawn, for moving over snow, ice, etc.

**sleight of hand** (slīt) [< ON *slœgr*, crafty] **1** skill with the hands, esp. in deceiving onlookers, as in magic **2** a trick thus performed

**slen·der** (slen′dər) *adj.* [ME *s(c)lendre* < ?] **1** long and thin **2** slim of figure **3** small in amount, size, force, etc. —**slen′der·ness** *n.*

**slen′der·ize′** *vt., vi.* **-ized′, -iz′ing** to make or become slender

**slept** (slept) *vi., vt. pt. & pp. of* SLEEP

**sleuth** (slooth) *n.* [< ON *slóth*, a trail] [Inf.] a detective

**slew¹** (sloo) *n.* [Ir *sluagh*, a host] [Inf.] a large number or amount

**slew²** (sloo) *vt. pt. of* SLAY

**slice** (slīs) *n.* [< OFr *esclicier*] **1** a relatively thin, broad piece cut from something **2** a part or share —*vt.* **sliced, slic′ing 1** to cut into slices **2** to cut off as in a slice or slices: often with *off, from, away*, etc. **3** to hit (a ball) so that it curves to the right if right-handed or the left if left-handed —**slic′er** *n.*

**slick** (slik) *vt.* [OE *slician*] **1** to make smooth **2** [Inf.] to make smart, neat, etc.: usually with *up* —*adj.* **1** sleek; smooth **2** slippery **3** adept; clever **4** [Inf.] smooth but superficial, tricky, etc. —*n.* **1** a smooth area on the water, as from a layer of oil **2** a slippery, oily area on the surface of a road —**slick′ly** *adv.* —**slick′ness** *n.*

**slick′er** *n.* **1** a loose, waterproof coat **2** [Inf.] a tricky person

**slide** (slīd) *vi.* **slid** (slid), **slid′ing** [OE *slidan*] **1** to move along in constant contact with a smooth surface, as on ice **2** to glide **3** to slip [it *slid* from his hand] —*vt.* **1** to cause to slide **2** to place quietly or deftly (*in* or *into*) —*n.* **1** a sliding **2** a smooth, often inclined surface for sliding down **3** something that works by sliding **4** a photographic transparency for use with a viewer or projector **5** a small glass plate on which objects are mounted for microscopic study **6** the fall of a mass of rock, snow, etc. down a slope —**let slide** to fail to attend to properly

**slide fastener** a zipper or a zipperlike device with two grooved plastic edges joined or separated by a sliding tab

**slid′er** *n.* **1** one that slides **2** *Baseball* a fast pitch that curves

**sliding scale** a schedule, as of fees, wages, etc., that varies with given conditions, as cost of living, etc.

**slight** (slīt) *adj.* [OE *sliht*] **1** *a)* light in build; slender *b)* frail; fragile **2** lacking strength, importance, etc. **3** small in amount or extent —*vt.* **1** to neglect **2** to treat with disrespect **3** to treat as unimportant —*n.* a slighting or being slighted —**slight′ly** *adv.* —**slight′ness** *n.*

**slim** (slim) *adj.* **slim′mer, slim′mest** [< Du, bad] **1** small in girth; slender **2** small in amount, degree, etc. —*vt., vi.* **slimmed, slim′ming** to make or become slim —**slim′ness** *n.*

**slime** (slīm) *n.* [OE *slim*] any soft, moist, slippery, often sticky matter —**slim′y, -i·er, -i·est,** *adj.*

**sling** (sliŋ) *n.* [prob. < ON *slyngua*, to throw] **1** a primitive instrument whirled by hand for throwing stones **2** a cast; throw; fling **3** *a)* a supporting band, etc. as for raising a heavy object *b)* a cloth looped from the neck under an injured arm for support —*vt.* **slung**, **sling'ing 1** to throw as with a sling **2** to suspend

**sling'shot'** *n.* a Y-shaped piece of wood, etc. with an elastic band attached to it for shooting stones, etc.

**slink** (sliŋk) *vi.* **slunk**, **slink'ing** [[OE *slincan*, to creep]] to move in a furtive or sneaking way

**slink'y** *adj.* **-i·er**, **-i·est 1** furtive; sneaking **2** [Slang] sinuous in movement or line

**slip**[1] (slip) *vi.* **slipped**, **slip'ping** [[ME *slippen*, ult. < Ger]] **1** to go quietly or secretly [to *slip* out of a room] **2** to pass smoothly or easily **3** to escape from one's memory, grasp, etc. **4** to slide, lose footing, etc. **5** to make a mistake; err **6** to become worse —*vt.* **1** to cause to slip **2** to put, pass, etc. deftly or stealthily **3** to escape from (the memory) —*n.* **1** a space between piers for docking ships **2** a woman's undergarment the length of a skirt **3** a pillow case **4** a slipping or falling down **5** an error or mistake —**let slip** to say without intending to —**slip up** to make a mistake

**slip**[2] (slip) *n.* [[< MDu *slippen*, to cut]] **1** a stem, root, etc. of a plant, used for planting or grafting **2** a young, slim person **3** a small piece of paper

**slip'case'** *n.* a boxlike container for a book or books, open at one end

**slip'cov'er** *n.* a removable, fitted cloth cover for a chair, sofa, etc.

**slip'knot'** *n.* a knot that will slip along the rope around which it is tied

**slip·page** (slip'ij) *n.* a slipping, as of one gear past another

**slipped disk** a ruptured cartilaginous disk between vertebrae

**slip·per** (slip'ər) *n.* a light, low shoe easily slipped on the foot, esp. one for indoor wear —**slip'pered** *adj.*

**slip·per·y** (slip'ər ē, slip'rē) *adj.* **-i·er**, **-i·est 1** liable to cause slipping, as a wet surface **2** tending to slip away, as from a grasp **3** unreliable; deceitful

**slip'shod'** (-shäd') *adj.* [[< obs. *slip-shoe*, a slipper]] careless, as in workmanship

**slip'-up'** *n.* [Inf.] an error: also **slip'up'**

**slit** (slit) *vt.* **slit**, **slit'ting** [[ME *slitten*]] **1** to cut or split open, esp. lengthwise **2** to cut into strips — *n.* a straight, narrow cut, opening, etc.

**slith·er** (sli*th*'ər) *vi.* [[< OE *slidan*, to slide]] to slip, slide, or glide along —**slith'er·y** *adj.*

**sliv·er** (sliv'ər) *n.* [[< OE *slifan*, to split]] a thin, sharp piece cut or split off; splinter —*vt., vi.* to cut or break into slivers

**slob** (släb) *n.* [[Ir *slab*, mud]] [Inf.] a sloppy or coarse person

**slob·ber** (släb'ər) *vi.* [[prob. < LowG *slubberen*, to swig]] to drool

**sloe** (slō) *n.* [[OE *sla*]] **1** the blackthorn **2** its small, plumlike fruit

**sloe'-eyed'** *adj.* **1** having large, dark eyes **2** having almond-shaped eyes

**sloe gin** a liqueur of gin flavored with sloes

**slog** (släg) *vt., vi.* **slogged**, **slog'ging** [[ME *sluggen*, go slowly]] **1** to make (one's way) with great effort; plod **2** to toil (at) —*n.* an arduous trip, task, etc. —**slog'ger** *n.*

**slo·gan** (slō'gən) *n.* [[< Gael *sluagh*, a host + *gairm*, a call: orig., a battle cry]] **1** a motto associated with a political party, etc. **2** a catchy phrase used in advertising

**sloop** (slo͞op) *n.* [[< LowG *slupen*, to glide]] a sailing vessel having a single mast with a mainsail and a jib

**slop** (släp) *n.* [[OE *sloppe*]] **1** watery snow or mud; slush **2** a puddle of spilled liquid **3** unappetizing, watery food **4** [often *pl.*] liquid waste —*vi., vt.* **slopped**, **slop'ping** to spill or splash

**slope** (slōp) *n.* [[< OE *slupan*, to glide]] **1** rising or falling ground **2** any inclined line, surface, etc.; slant **3** the amount or degree of deviation from

the horizontal or vertical —*vi.* **sloped**, **slop'ing** to have an upward or downward inclination; incline; slant —*vt.* to cause to slope

**slop·py** (släp'ē) *adj.* **-pi·er**, **-pi·est 1** splashy; slushy **2** *a)* slovenly *b)* slipshod **3** [Inf.] gushingly sentimental —**slop'pi·ness** *n.*

**sloppy Joe** (jō) ground meat cooked with tomato sauce, spices, etc. and served on a bun

**slosh** (släsh) *vi.* [var. of SLUSH] **1** to splash through water, mud, etc. **2** to splash about: said of a liquid —*n.* the sound of sloshing liquid — **slosh'y** *adj.*

**slot** (slät) *n.* [[< OFr *esclot*, hollow between the breasts]] **1** a narrow opening, as for a coin in a vending machine **2** [Inf.] a position in a group, etc. —*vt.* **slot'ted**, **slot'ting 1** to make a slot in **2** [Inf.] to place in a series or sequence

**sloth** (slôth, släth; *also* slōth) *n.* [[< OE *slaw*, slow]] **1** laziness; idleness **2** a slow-moving, tree-dwelling mammal of tropical America that hangs, back down, from branches —**sloth'ful** *adj.* —**sloth'ful·ness** *n.*

**slot machine** a machine, specif. a gambling device, activated by the insertion of a coin in a slot

**slouch** (slouch) *n.* [[< ON *slōka*, to droop]] **1** a lazy or incompetent person **2** a drooping or slovenly posture —*vi.* to sit, stand, walk, etc. in a slouch — **slouch'y**, **-i·er**, **-i·est**, *adj.*

THREE-TOED SLOTH

**slough**[1] (sluf) *n.* [[ME *slouh*, a skin]] a castoff layer or covering, as the skin of a snake —*vt.* to throw off; discard

**slough**[2] (slou) *n.* [[OE *sloh*]] **1** a place full of soft, deep mud **2** deep, hopeless dejection

**Slo·vak** (slō'väk', -vak') *n.* **1** a member of a Slavic people living chiefly in Slovakia **2** the language of this people —*adj.* of the Slovaks

**Slo·va·ki·a** (slō vä'kē ə) country in central Europe: formerly the E republic of Czechoslovakia: 18,933 sq. mi.; pop. 5,297,000

**slov·en** (sluv'ən) *n.* [[prob. < MDu *slof*, lax]] a careless, untidy person —**slov'en·ly**, **-li·er**, **-li·est**, *adj.*

**Slo·ve·ni·a** (slō vē'nē ə) country in SE Europe: 7,819 sq. mi.; pop. 1,966,000 —**Slo·ve'ni·an** or **Slo'vene'** *adj., n.*

**slow** (slō) *adj.* [[OE *slaw*]] **1** not quick in understanding **2** taking a longer time than is usual **3** marked by low speed, etc.; not fast **4** behind the correct time, as a clock **5** passing tediously; dull —*vt., vi.* to make or become slow or slower: often with *up* or *down* —*adv.* in a slow manner — **slow'ly** *adv.* —**slow'ness** *n.*

**slow'down'** *n.* a slowing down, as of production

**slow'-mo'tion** *adj.* **1** moving slowly **2** designating a film or taped TV sequence showing the action slowed down

**slow'poke'** (-pōk') *n.* [Slang] a person who acts or moves slowly

**slow'-wit'ted** *adj.* mentally slow; dull

**SLR** *n.* [[*s(ingle) l(ens) r(eflex)*]] a camera allowing the photographer to see the subject through the same lens that brings the image to the film

**slub** (slub) *n.* [[< ?]] a soft, thick lump or irregularity in yarn or fabric

**sludge** (sluj) *n.* [var. of *slutch*, mud]] any heavy, slimy deposit, sediment, etc.

**slue** (slo͞o) *vt., vi.* **slued**, **slu'ing** [[< ?]] to turn or swing around, as on a pivot

**slug**[1] (slug) *n.* [[ME *slugge*, clumsy one]] a small mollusk like a shell-less snail

**slug**[2] (slug) *n.* [[prob. < prec.]] a small piece of metal; specif., a bullet or counterfeit coin

**slug**³ (slug) *n.* 〚prob. < Dan *sluge*, to gulp〛 [Slang] a drink of liquor

**slug**⁴ (slug) [Inf.] *vt.* **slugged, slug′ging** 〚< ON *slag*〛 to hit hard, esp. with the fist or a bat —*n.* a hard blow or hit —**slug′ger** *n.*

**slug·gard** (slug′ərd) *n.* 〚< ME *sluggen*, be lazy〛 a lazy person

**slug′gish** (-ish) *adj.* 〚< SLUG¹〛 **1** lacking energy or alertness **2** slow or slow-moving **3** not functioning with normal vigor —**slug′gish·ness** *n.*

**sluice** (slo͞os) *n.* 〚< L *excludere*, to shut out〛 **1** an artificial channel for water, with a gate to regulate the flow **2** such a gate: also **sluice gate 3** any channel for excess water **4** a sloping trough, as for washing gold ore —*vt.* **sluiced, sluic′ing 1** to draw off through a sluice **2** to wash with water from a sluice

**slum** (slum) *n.* 〚< ?〛 a populous area characterized by poverty, poor housing, etc. —*vi.* **slummed, slum′ming** to visit a slum, etc. for reasons held to be condescending —**slum′my, -mi·er, -mi·est,** *adj.*

**slum·ber** (slum′bər) *vi.* 〚OE *sluma*〛 **1** to sleep **2** to be inactive —*n.* **1** sleep **2** an inactive state

**slum′lord′** *n.* [Slang] an absentee landlord who exploits slum property

**slump** (slump) *vi.* 〚prob. < Ger〛 **1** to fall or sink suddenly **2** to slouch —*n.* a decline in activity, prices, performance, etc.

**slung** (sluŋ) *vt. pt. & pp. of* SLING

**slunk** (sluŋk) *vi. pt. & pp. of* SLINK

**slur** (slur) *vt.* **slurred, slur′ring** 〚prob. < MDu *sleuren*, to drag〛 **1** to pass over lightly: often with *over* **2** to pronounce indistinctly **3** to disparage **4** *Music* to produce (successive notes) by gliding without a break —*n.* **1** a slurring **2** an aspersion **3** *Music* a curved line connecting notes to be slurred

**slurp** (slurp) [Slang] *vt., vi.* 〚Du *slurpen*, to sip〛 to drink or eat noisily —*n.* a loud sipping or sucking sound

**slur·ry** (slur′ē) *n., pl.* **-ries** 〚< MDu *slore*, thin mud〛 a thin, watery mixture of clay, cement, etc.

**slush** (slush) *n.* 〚prob. < Scand〛 **1** partly melted snow or ice **2** soft mud **3** sentimentality; drivel —**slush′y, -i·er, -i·est,** *adj.*

**slush fund** money used for bribery, political pressure, etc.

**slut** (slut) *n.* 〚ME *slutte*〛 **1** a dirty, slovenly woman **2** a sexually promiscuous woman: a derogatory term —**slut′tish** *adj.*

**sly** (slī) *adj.* **sli′er** or **sly′er, sli′est** or **sly′est** 〚< ON *slœgr*〛 **1** skillful at trickery; crafty **2** cunningly underhanded **3** playfully mischievous —**on the sly** secretly —**sly′ly** or **sli′ly** *adv.* —**sly′ness** *n.*

**smack**¹ (smak) *n.* 〚OE *smæc*〛 **1** a slight taste or flavor **2** a small amount; trace —*vi.* to have a smack (*of*)

**smack**² (smak) *n.* 〚< ?〛 **1** a sharp noise made by parting the lips suddenly **2** a loud kiss **3** a slap —*vt.* **1** to part (the lips) with a smack **2** to slap loudly —*adv.* **1** with a smack **2** directly

**smack**³ (smak) *n.* 〚prob. < Du *smak*〛 a fishing boat with a well for keeping fish alive

**smack**⁴ (smak) *n.* 〚< ?〛 [Slang] heroin

**smack′er** *n.* [Old Slang] a dollar

**small** (smôl) *adj.* 〚OE *smæl*〛 **1** comparatively little in size; not big **2** little in quantity, extent, duration, etc. **3** of little importance; trivial **4** young [*small* children] **5** mean; petty **6** lowercase —*n.* the small part [the *small* of the back]

**small arms** firearms of small caliber, as pistols, rifles, etc.

**small fry** [see FRY²] **1** children **2** persons considered insignificant

**small intestine** the narrow section of the intestines, extending from the stomach to the large intestine

**small′-mind′ed** *adj.* mean, narrow-minded, or selfish

**small′pox′** *n.* an acute, contagious viral disease characterized by fever and pustules

**small talk** light conversation about common, everyday things; chitchat

**small′-time′** *adj.* [Inf.] minor or petty

**smarm·y** (smär′mē) *adj.* **-i·er, -i·est** 〚< *smarm*, to smear〛 [Inf., Chiefly Brit.] flattering in an insincere way

**smart** (smärt) *vi.* 〚OE *smeortan*〛 **1** *a)* to cause sharp, stinging pain, as a slap does *b)* to feel such pain **2** to feel mental distress or irritation —*n.* **1** a stinging sensation **2** [*pl.*] [Slang] intelligence —*adj.* **1** causing sharp pain **2** sharp, as pain **3** brisk; lively [a *smart* pace] **4** intelligent **5** neat; trim **6** stylish **7** [Inf.] insolent **8** *Comput. a)* working by means of a computer or microchip *b)* programmed in advance —**smart′ly** *adv.* —**smart′ness** *n.*

**smart al·eck** or **smart al·ec** (al′ik) 〚prec. + *Aleck*, dim. of *Alexander*〛 [Inf.] an offensively conceited person

**smart bomb** [Mil. Slang] a guided missile directed to its target by electronic means

**smart′en** *vt., vi.* to make or become smart or smarter: usually with *up*

**smash** (smash) *vt., vi.* 〚prob. < MASH〛 **1** to break into pieces with noise or violence **2** to hit, collide, or move with force **3** to destroy or be destroyed —*n.* **1** a hard, heavy hit **2** a violent, noisy breaking **3** a violent collision **4** a popular success

**smash′ing** *adj.* [Inf.] extraordinary

**smash′up′** *n.* **1** a violent wreck or collision **2** total failure; ruin

**smat·ter·ing** (smat′ər iŋ) *n.* 〚ME *smateren*, to chatter〛 **1** a slight knowledge **2** a small number or limited amount

**smear** (smir) *vt.* 〚< OE *smerian*, to anoint〛 **1** to cover or soil with something greasy, sticky, etc. **2** to apply (something greasy, etc.) **3** to streak by rubbing **4** to slander —*vi.* to be or become smeared —*n.* **1** a mark made by smearing **2** slander —**smear′y, -i·er, -i·est,** *adj.*

**smell** (smel) *vt.* **smelled** or (*Chiefly Brit.*) **smelt, smell′ing** 〚ME *smellen*〛 **1** to be aware of through the nose; detect the odor of **2** to sense the presence of [to *smell* trouble] —*vi.* **1** to use the sense of smell; sniff **2** to have an odor **3** to stink —*n.* **1** the sense by which odors are perceived **2** odor; scent **3** a smelling

**smelling salts** an ammonia compound sniffed to relieve faintness

**smell′y** *adj.* **-i·er, -i·est** having an unpleasant smell

**smelt**¹ (smelt) *n.* 〚OE〛 a small, silvery food fish found esp. in northern seas

**smelt**² (smelt) *vt.* 〚< MDu *smelten*〛 **1** to melt (ore, etc.) so as to extract the pure metal **2** to refine (metal) in this way

**smelt**³ (smelt) *vt., vi. chiefly Brit. pt. & pp. of* SMELL

**smelt′er** *n.* **1** one whose work is smelting **2** a place for smelting

**smidg·en** (smij′ən) *n.* 〚prob. < dial. *smidge*, particle〛 [Inf.] a small amount; bit: also **smidg′in** or **smidge**

**smile** (smīl) *vi.* **smiled, smil′ing** 〚ME *smilen*〛 to show pleasure, amusement, affection, etc. by an upward curving of the mouth —*vt.* to express with a smile —*n.* the act or expression of smiling —**smil′ing·ly** *adv.*

**smirch** (smurch) *vt.* 〚prob. < OFr *esmorcher*, to hurt〛 **1** to soil or stain **2** to dishonor —*n.* **1** a smudge; smear **2** a stain on reputation, etc.

**smirk** (smurk) *vi.* 〚< OE *smearcian*, to smile〛 to smile in a conceited or complacent way —*n.* such a smile

**smite** (smīt) *vt.* **smote, smit′ten** or **smote, smit′ing** 〚OE *smitan*〛 **1** to strike with powerful effect **2** to affect or impress strongly

**smith** (smith) *n.* **1** one who makes or repairs metal objects **2** *short for* BLACKSMITH

**Smith** (smith), Captain **John** 1580?-1631; Eng. colonist in America

**smith·er·eens** (smi*th*'ər ēnz') **pl.n.** ⟦Ir *smidirīn*⟧ [Inf.] fragments; bits

**smith·y** (smith'ē) **n.**, *pl.* **-ies** the workshop of a smith, esp. a blacksmith

**smock** (smäk) **n.** ⟦OE *smoc*⟧ a loose, shirtlike outer garment worn to protect the clothes

**smock'ing n.** decorative stitching used to gather cloth and make it hang in folds

**smog** (smäg, smôg) **n.** ⟦SM(OKE) + (F)OG⟧ a low-lying, perceptible layer of polluted air **—smog'gy, -gi·er, -gi·est, adj.**

**smoke** (smōk) **n.** ⟦OE *smoca*⟧ **1** the vaporous matter arising from something burning **2** any vapor, etc. like this **3** an act of smoking tobacco, etc. **4** a cigarette, cigar, etc. **—vi. smoked, smok'ing 1** to give off smoke **2** *a*) to draw in and exhale the smoke of tobacco, etc. *b*) to be a habitual user of cigarettes, etc. **—vt. 1** to cure (meat, etc.) with smoke **2** to use (a pipe, cigarette, etc.) in smoking **3** to drive out as with smoke **—smoke out** to force out of hiding **— smoke'less adj. —smok'er n.**

**smoke detector** a warning device that sets off a loud signal when excessive smoke or heat is detected

**smoke'house' n.** a building where meats, fish, etc. are cured with smoke

**smoke screen 1** a cloud of smoke for hiding troop movements, etc. **2** anything said or done to conceal or mislead

**smoke'stack' n.** a pipe for discharging smoke from a factory, etc.

**smok·y** (smō'kē) **adj. -i·er, -i·est 1** giving off smoke **2** of or like smoke **3** filled with smoke **— smok'i·ness n.**

**smol·der** (smōl'dər) **vi.** ⟦ME *smoldren*⟧ **1** to burn and smoke without flame **2** to exist in a suppressed state **—n.** a smoldering

**smooch** (smōōch) **n., vt., vi.** [Slang] kiss

**smoosh** (smōōsh) **vt.** [Inf.] *alt. sp. of* SMUSH

**smooth** (smōō*th*) **adj.** ⟦OE *smoth*⟧ **1** having an even surface, with no roughness **2** without lumps **3** even or gentle in movement [a *smooth* voyage] **4** free from interruptions, obstacles, etc. **5** pleasing to the taste; not harsh or bitter **6** having an easy, flowing rhythm or sound **7** polished or ingratiating, esp. in an insincere way **—vt. 1** to make level or even **2** to remove lumps or wrinkles from **3** to free from difficulties, etc.; make easy **4** to make calm; soothe **5** to polish or refine **—adv.** in a smooth manner **—smooth'ly adv. — smooth'ness n.**

**smooth muscle** involuntary muscle tissue occurring in the uterus, stomach, blood vessels, etc.

**smooth'-spo'ken adj.** speaking in a pleasing, persuasive, or polished manner

**smor·gas·bord** or **smör·gås·bord** (smôr'gəs bôrd', smur'-) **n.** ⟦Swed⟧ a wide variety of appetizers, cheeses, meats, etc., served buffet style

**smote** (smōt) **vt., vi.** *pt.* & *alt. pp. of* SMITE

**smoth·er** (smu*th*'ər) **vt.** ⟦< ME *smorther*, dense smoke⟧ **1** to keep from getting air; suffocate **2** to cover over thickly **3** to stifle [to *smother* a yawn] **—vi.** to be suffocated

**smoul·der** (smōl'dər) **vi., n.** *Brit. sp. of* SMOLDER

**smudge** (smuj) **vt., vi. smudged, smudg'ing** ⟦ME *smogen*⟧ to make or become dirty; smear **—n. 1** a dirty spot **2** a fire made to produce dense smoke **—smudg'y, -i·er, -i·est, adj.**

**smug** (smug) **adj. smug'ger, smug'gest** ⟦prob. < LowG *smuk*, trim, neat⟧ annoyingly self-satisfied; complacent **—smug'ly adv. —smug'ness n.**

**smug·gle** (smug'əl) **vt. -gled, -gling** ⟦< LowG *smuggeln*⟧ **1** to bring into or take out of a country secretly or illegally **2** to bring, take, etc. secretly **—vi.** to practice smuggling **—smug'gler n.**

**smush** (smoosh) **vt.** [Inf.] to smash, squeeze, etc.

**smut** (smut) **n.** ⟦< LowG *smutt*⟧ **1** a particle of soot **3** indecent talk, writing, etc. **4** a fungal disease of plants **—smut'ty, -ti·er, -ti·est, adj.**

**Sn** ⟦L *stannum*⟧ *Chem.* symbol *for* tin

**snack** (snak) **n.** ⟦< ME *snaken*, to bite⟧ a light meal between regular meals **—vi.** to eat a snack

**snack bar** a counter for serving snacks

**snag** (snag) **n.** ⟦< Scand⟧ **1** a sharp point or projection **2** an underwater tree stump or branch **3** a tear, as in cloth, made by a snag, etc. **4** an unexpected or hidden difficulty, etc. **—vt. snagged, snag'ging 1** to catch, tear, etc. on a snag **2** to impede with a snag

**snail** (snāl) **n.** ⟦OE *snægl*⟧ a slow-moving mollusk having a wormlike body and a spiral protective shell

**snake** (snāk) **n.** ⟦OE *snaca*⟧ **1** a long, scaly, limbless reptile with a tapering tail **2** a treacherous or deceitful person **3** a plumber's tool for clearing pipes **—vi. snaked, snak'ing** to move, twist, etc. like a snake **—snake'like' adj.**

**snak·y** (snā'kē) **adj. -i·er, -i·est 1** of or like a snake or snakes **2** winding; twisting **3** cunningly treacherous or evil

**snap** (snap) **vi., vt. snapped, snap'ping** ⟦< MDu *snappen*⟧ **1** to bite or grasp suddenly: with *at* **2** to speak or utter sharply: often with *at* **3** to break suddenly **4** to make or cause to make a sudden, cracking sound **5** to close, fasten, etc. with this sound **6** to move or cause to move suddenly and smartly [to *snap* to attention] **7** to take a snapshot (of) **—n. 1** a sudden bite, grasp, etc. **2** a sharp cracking sound [the *snap* of a whip] **3** a short, angry way of speaking **4** a brief period of cold weather **5** a fastening that closes with a click **6** a hard, thin cookie **7** *short for* SNAPSHOT **8** [Inf.] alertness or vigor **9** [Slang] an easy job, problem, etc. **—adj. 1** made or done quickly [a *snap* decision] **2** that fastens with a snap **3** [Slang] easy **—snap back** to recover quickly **— snap out of it** to improve or recover quickly **— snap'per n.**

**snap bean** a green bean or wax bean

**snap'drag'on n.** ⟦SNAP + DRAGON: from the mouth-shaped flowers⟧ a plant with saclike, two-lipped flowers

**snap'pish adj. 1** likely to bite **2** irritable

**snap'py adj. -pi·er, -pi·est 1** cross; irritable **2** that snaps **3** [Inf.] *a*) brisk or lively *b*) sharply chilly **4** [Inf.] stylish

**snap'shot' n.** an informal photograph taken with a hand camera

**snare** (sner) **n.** ⟦< ON *snara*⟧ **1** a trap for small animals **2** anything dangerous, etc. that tempts or attracts **3** a length of wire or gut across the bottom of a drum **—vt. snared, snar'ing** to catch as in a snare; trap

**snarl¹** (snärl) **vi.** ⟦< earlier *snar*, to growl⟧ **1** to growl, baring the teeth, as a dog does **2** to speak sharply, as in anger **—vt.** to utter with a snarl **—** *n.* a fierce growl **—snarl'ing·ly adv.**

**snarl²** (snärl) **n., vt., vi.** ⟦< SNARE⟧ tangle **— snarl'y, -i·er, -i·est, adj.**

**snatch** (snach) **vt.** ⟦ME *snacchen*⟧ to take suddenly, specif. without right or warning **—vi. 1** to try to seize; grab (*at*) **2** to take advantage of a chance, etc. eagerly: with *at* **—n. 1** a snatching **2** a brief period **3** a fragment; bit

**sneak** (snēk) **vt., vi. sneaked** or [Inf.] **snuck, sneak'ing** ⟦prob. < OE *snican*, to crawl⟧ to move, act, give, put, take, etc. secretly or stealthily **—n. 1** one who sneaks **2** a sneaking **—adj.** without warning [a *sneak* attack] **—sneak'y, -i·er, -i·est, adj.**

**sneak'er n.** a shoe with a canvas upper and a soft rubber sole

**sneak preview** an advance showing of a film, as for evaluating audience reaction

**sneer** (snir) **vi.** ⟦ME *sneren*⟧ **1** to show scorn as by curling the upper lip **2** to express derision, etc. in speech or writing **—n.** a sneering

**sneeze** (snēz) **vi. sneezed, sneez'ing** ⟦ME *snesen*⟧

to exhale breath from the nose and mouth in an involuntary, explosive action —*n.* a sneezing

**snick·er** (snik′ər) *vi.* ⟦echoic⟧ to laugh in a sly, partly stifled way —*n.* a snickering

**snide** (snīd) *adj.* ⟦prob. < Du dial.⟧ slyly malicious or derisive

**sniff** (snif) *vi., vt.* ⟦ME *sniffen*⟧ **1** to draw in (air) forcibly through the nose **2** to express (disdain, etc.) by sniffing **3** to smell by sniffing —*n.* **1** an act or sound of sniffing **2** something sniffed

**snif·fle** (snif′əl) *vi.* -fled, -fling to sniff repeatedly, as in checking mucus running from the nose —*n.* an act or sound of sniffling —**the sniffles** [Inf.] a head cold

**snif·ter** (snif′tər) *n.* ⟦< *snift*, var. of SNIFF⟧ a goblet tapering to a small opening to concentrate the aroma, as of brandy

**snig·ger** (snig′ər) *vi., n.* ⟦echoic⟧ SNICKER

**snip** (snip) *vt., vi.* snipped, snip′ping ⟦Du *snippen*⟧ to cut or cut off in a short, quick stroke, as with scissors —*n.* **1** a small piece cut off **2** [Inf.] a young or insignificant person

**snipe** (snīp) *n.* ⟦< ON *snipa*⟧ a long-billed wading bird —*vi.* sniped, snip′ing to shoot from a hidden position, as at individuals —**snip′er** *n.*

**snip·pet** (snip′it) *n.* ⟦dim. of SNIP⟧ a small piece or scrap, specif. of information

**snip′py** *adj.* -pi·er, -pi·est [Inf.] insolently curt, sharp, etc.

**snit** (snit) *n.* ⟦< ? prec. + (F)IT²⟧ a fit of anger, resentment, etc.: usually **in** (or **into**) **a snit**

**snitch** (snich) [Slang] *vt.* to steal; pilfer —*vi.* to tattle (*on*) —*n.* an informer

**sniv·el** (sniv′əl) *vi.* -eled or -elled, -el·ing or -el·ling ⟦ME *snivelen*⟧ **1** to cry and sniffle **2** to complain and whine **3** to make a tearful, often false display of grief, etc. —**sniv′el·er** *n.*

**snob** (snäb) *n.* ⟦< ?⟧ one who disdains supposed inferiors —**snob′bish** *adj.* —**snob′bish·ness** or **snob′ber·y** *n.*

**snood** (snōōd) *n.* ⟦OE *snod*⟧ a baglike net worn at the back of a woman's head to hold the hair

**snook·er** (snook′ər) *n.* a variety of the game of pool —*vt.* [Slang] to deceive

**snoop** (snōōp) [Inf.] *vi.* ⟦Du *snoepen*, eat on the sly⟧ to pry about in a sneaking way —*n.* one who snoops: also **snoop′er** —**snoop′y**, -i·er, -i·est, *adj.*

**snoot** (snōōt) *n.* ⟦see SNOUT⟧ [Inf.] the nose

**snoot′y** *adj.* -i·er, -i·est [Inf.] haughty; snobbish — **snoot′i·ness** *n.*

**snooze** (snōōz) *n., vi.* ⟦< LowG *snusen*, to snore⟧ snoozed, snooz′ing [Inf.] nap; doze —**snooz′er** *n.*

**snore** (snôr) *vi.* snored, snor′ing ⟦see SNARL¹⟧ to breathe, while asleep, with harsh sounds —*n.* the act or sound of snoring —**snor′er** *n.*

**snor·kel** (snôr′kəl) *n.* ⟦Ger *schnorchel*, inlet⟧ a breathing tube extending above the water, used in swimming just below the surface —*vi.* -keled, -kel·ing to swim underwater using a snorkel —**snor′kel·er** *n.*

SNORKEL

**snort** (snôrt) *vi.* **1** to force breath audibly through the nostrils **2** to express contempt, etc. by a snort —*vt.* **1** to express with a snort **2** [Slang] to inhale (a drug) through the nose —*n.* **1** a snorting **2** [Slang] a quick drink of liquor

**snot** (snät) *n.* ⟦OE (*ge*)*snot*, mucus⟧ [Slang] **1** nasal mucus: considered mildly vulgar **2** an impudent young person —**snot′ty**, -ti·er, -ti·est, *adj.*

**snout** (snout) *n.* ⟦prob. < MDu *snute*⟧ the projecting nose and jaws of an animal

**snow** (snō) *n.* ⟦OE *snaw*⟧ **1** frozen particles of water vapor that fall to earth as soft, white flakes **2** a falling of snow —*vi.* to fall or like snow —

*vt.* **1** to cover or obstruct with snow: with *in, up, under,* etc. **2** [Slang] to deceive or mislead — **snow under 1** to overwhelm with work, etc. **2** to defeat decisively —**snow′y**, -i·er, -i·est, *adj.*

**snow′ball′** *n.* a mass of snow packed into a ball — *vi.* to grow rapidly like a ball of snow rolling downhill

**snow′bank′** *n.* a large mass of snow

**Snow′belt′** the NE and Midwestern U.S., characterized by cold, snowy winters: also **Snow Belt**

**snow′board′** *n.* a board somewhat like a small surfboard, for sliding down snowy hills for sport —*vi.* to use a snowboard —**snow′board′er** *n.*

**snow′bound′** *adj.* shut in or blocked off by snow

**snow′cone′** *n.* crushed ice mixed with a flavored syrup, served in a paper cone

**snow′drift′** *n.* a heap of snow piled up by the wind

**snow′drop′** *n.* a small plant with small, bell-shaped, white flowers

**snow′fall′** *n.* a fall of snow or the amount of this in a given area or time

**snow fence** a light fence of lath and wire to control the drifting of snow

**snow′flake′** *n.* a single snow crystal

**snow′man′** (-man′) *n., pl.* -men′ (-men′) a crude human figure made of snow packed together

**snow′mo·bile′** *n.* a motor vehicle with steerable runners at the front and tractor treads at the rear —*vi.* -biled′, -bil′ing to travel by snowmobile

**snow′plow′** *n.* a plowlike machine used to clear snow off a road, etc.

**snow′shoe′** *n.* one of a pair of racket-shaped wooden frames crisscrossed with leather strips, etc., worn on the feet to prevent sinking in deep snow

**snow′storm′** *n.* a storm with a heavy snowfall

**snow′suit′** *n.* a child's heavily lined, hooded garment, for cold weather

**snow tire** a tire with a deep tread for added traction on snow or ice

**snub** (snub) *vt.* snubbed, snub′bing ⟦< ON *snubba*, chide⟧ **1** to treat with scorn, disdain, etc. **2** to check suddenly the movement of (a rope, etc.) —*n.* scornful treatment —*adj.* short and turned up: said of a nose

**snub′-nosed′** *adj.* **1** having a snub nose **2** having a short barrel: said of a handgun

**snuck** (snuk) *vi., vt.* [Inf.] *alt. pt. & pp. of* SNEAK

**snuff¹** (snuf) *vt.* ⟦ME⟧ **1** to trim off the charred end of (a wick) **2** to put out (a candle) —**snuff out 1** to extinguish **2** to destroy —**snuff′er** *n.*

**snuff²** (snuf) *vt., vi.* ⟦< MDu *snuffen*⟧ to sniff or smell —*n.* **1** a sniff **2** powdered tobacco taken up into the nose or put on the gums —**up to snuff** [Inf.] up to the usual standard

**snuff′box′** *n.* a small box for snuff

**snuf·fle** (snuf′əl) *n., vi.* -fled, -fling ⟦< SNUFF²⟧ SNIFFLE

**snug** (snug) *adj.* snug′ger, snug′gest ⟦prob. < Scand⟧ **1** warm and cozy **2** neat; trim [a snug cottage] **3** tight in fit —**snug′ly** *adv.*

**snug′gle** (-əl) *vi., vt.* -gled, -gling ⟦< prec.⟧ to nestle; cuddle

**so** (sō) *adv.* ⟦OE *swa*⟧ **1** as shown or described [hold the bat just so] **2** to such an extent [why are you so late?] b) very [they are so happy] c) [Inf.] very much [she so wants to go] **3** therefore [they were tired, and so left] **4** more or less [fifty dollars or so] **5** also; likewise [I am going, and so are you] **6** then [and so to bed] —*conj.* **1** in order (that) **2** with the result that —*pron.* that which has been specified or named [he is a friend and will remain so] —*interj.* used to express surprise, triumph, etc. —*adj.* true [that's so] —**and so on** (or **forth**) and the rest; et cetera —**so as to** with the purpose or result —**so what?** [Inf.] even if so, what then?

**soak** (sōk) *vt.* ⟦OE *socian*⟧ **1** to make thoroughly

wet **2** to take in; absorb: usually with *up* **3** [Inf.] to overcharge —*vi.* **1** to stay in a liquid for wetting, softening, etc. **2** to penetrate —*n.* **1** a soaking or being soaked **2** [Slang] a drunkard

**so'-and-so'** *n., pl.* **so'-and-sos'** [Inf.] an unspecified person or thing: often used euphemistically

**soap** (sōp) *n.* [OE *sape*] **1** a substance, usually a salt derived from fatty acids, used with water to produce suds for washing **2** [Slang] SOAP OPERA —*vt.* to lather, etc. with soap —**no soap** [Slang] (it is) not acceptable —**soap'y, -i·er, -i·est,** *adj.*

**soap'box'** *n.* any improvised platform used in speaking to a street audience

**soap opera** [Inf.] a radio or television serial melodrama

**soap'stone'** *n.* a soft, impure talc in rock form, used as an insulator, etc.

**soap'suds'** *pl.n.* foamy, soapy water

**soar** (sôr) *vi.* [ult. < L *ex-*, out + *aura*, air] **1** to rise or fly high into the air **2** to glide along high in the air **3** to rise above the usual level

**So·a·ve** (sə wä'vā, swä'vā) *n.* [It] an Italian dry white wine

**sob** (säb) *vi.* **sobbed, sob'bing** [ME *sobben*] to weep aloud with short, gasping breaths —*vt.* to utter with sobs —*n.* the act or sound of sobbing

**so·ber** (sō'bər) *adj.* [< L *sobrius*] **1** temperate, esp. in the use of liquor **2** not drunk **3** serious, reasonable, sedate, etc. **4** not flashy; plain —*vt., vi.* to make or become sober: often with *up* — **so'ber·ly** *adv.* —**so'ber·ness** *n.*

**so·bri·e·ty** (sə brī'ə tē) *n.* a being sober; specif., *a*) temperance, esp. in the use of liquor *b*) seriousness

**so·bri·quet** (sō'brə kā', -ket') *n.* [Fr] **1** a nickname **2** an assumed name

**soc** *abbrev.* **1** social **2** socialist **3** society

**so'-called'** *adj.* **1** known by this term **2** inaccurately or questionably designated as such [a so-called liberal]

**soc·cer** (säk'ər) *n.* [alt. < (as)soc(*iation football*)] a team game played by kicking a round ball

**so·cia·ble** (sō'shə bəl) *adj.* [see fol.] **1** friendly; gregarious **2** characterized by informal conversation and companionship —**so'cia·bil'i·ty** *n.* — **so'cia·bly** *adv.*

**so·cial** (sō'shəl) *adj.* [< L *socius*, companion] **1** of or having to do with human beings, etc. in their living together **2** living with others; gregarious [man as a *social* being] **3** of or having to do with society, esp. fashionable society **4** sociable **5** of or for companionship **6** of or doing welfare work —*n.* an informal gathering —**so'cial·ly** *adv.*

**social disease** any venereal disease

**so'cial·ism'** *n.* **1** a theory or system of ownership of the means of production and distribution by society rather than by individuals **2** [*often* S-] a political movement for establishing such a system —**so'cial·ist** *n., adj.* —**so'cial·is'tic** *adj.*

**so·cial·ite** (sō'shə līt') *n.* a person prominent in fashionable society

**so'cial·ize'** (-shə līz') *vt.* **-ized', -iz'ing 1** to make fit for living in a group **2** to subject to governmental ownership or control —*vi.* to take part in social activity —**so'cial·i·za'tion** *n.*

**socialized medicine** a system supplying complete medical and hospital care to all through public funds

**social science** a field of study, as economics or anthropology, dealing with the structure, etc. of society —**social scientist**

**Social Security** [*sometimes* s- s-] a federal system of old-age, unemployment, or disability insurance

**social studies** a course of study including history, geography, etc.

**social work** any service or activity promoting the welfare of the community and the individual, as through counseling services, etc. —**social worker**

**so·ci·e·ty** (sə sī'ə tē) *n., pl.* **-ties** [< L *socius*, companion] **1** a group of persons, etc. forming a sin-

gle community **2** the system of living together in such a group **3** all people, collectively **4** companionship **5** an organized group with some interest in common **6** the wealthy, dominant class —**so·ci'e·tal** (-təl) *adj.*

**Society of Friends** a Christian denomination that believes in plain worship, pacifism, etc.: see also QUAKER

**so·ci·o·e·co·nom·ic** (sō'sē ō ē'kə näm'ik, -shē-; -ek'ə-) *adj.* of or involving both social and economic factors

**so·ci·ol·o·gy** (sō'sē äl'ə jē, -shē-) *n.* [see SOCIAL & -LOGY] the science of social relations, organization, and change —**so'ci·o·log'i·cal** (-ə lä'ji kəl) *adj.* —**so'ci·ol'o·gist** *n.*

**so·ci·o·path** (sō'sē ə path', -shē-) *n.* an aggressively antisocial psychopath

**sock**[1] (säk) *n., pl.* **socks** or **sox** [< L *soccus*, type of light shoe] a short stocking —**sock away** [Inf.] to set aside (money) as savings

**sock**[2] (säk) [Slang] *vt.* to hit with force —*n.* a blow

**sock·et** (säk'it) *n.* [< OFr *soc*, plowshare] a hollow part into which something fits [an eye *socket*]

**sock·eye salmon** (säk'ī') a red-fleshed salmon of the N Pacific

**Soc·ra·tes** (säk'rə tēz') 470?-399 B.C.; Athenian philosopher & teacher —**So·crat·ic** (sə krat'ik) *adj., n.*

**sod** (säd) *n.* [prob. < MDu *sode*] **1** a surface layer of earth containing grass with its roots; turf **2** a piece of this —*vt.* **sod'ded, sod'ding** to cover with sod

**so·da** (sō'də) *n.* [ML] **1** *a*) SODIUM BICARBONATE *b*) SODA WATER *c*) SODA POP **2** a confection of soda water mixed with syrup and having ice cream in it

**soda cracker** a light, crisp cracker made from flour, water, and leavening, orig. baking soda

**soda fountain** a counter for making and serving soft drinks, sodas, etc.

**soda pop** a flavored, carbonated soft drink

**soda water 1** water charged under pressure with carbon dioxide gas **2** SODA POP

**sod·den** (säd''n) *adj.* **1** soaked through **2** soggy from improper cooking **3** dull or stupefied, as from liquor —**sod'den·ly** *adv.*

**so·di·um** (sō'dē əm) *n.* [< *soda*] an alkaline, metallic chemical element

**sodium bicarbonate** a white powder, used in baking powder, as an antacid, etc.

**sodium chloride** common salt

**sodium hydroxide** a caustic base used in oil refining, etc.

**sodium nitrate** a clear, crystalline salt used in explosives, fertilizers, etc.

**sodium pen·to·thal** (pen'tə thôl') a yellowish powder injected in solution as a general anesthetic

**Sod·om and Go·mor·rah** (säd'əm and gə môr'ə) *Bible* two sinful cities destroyed by fire

**sod·om·y** (säd'ə mē) *n.* [after *Sodom*] any sexual intercourse held to be abnormal —**sod'om·ite'** (-mīt') *n.*

**so·fa** (sō'fə) *n.* [< Ar *şuffa*, a platform] an upholstered couch with fixed back and arms

**sofa bed** a sofa that can be opened into a bed

**So·fi·a** (sō'fē ə, sō fē'ə) capital of Bulgaria: pop. 1,116,000

**soft** (sôft) *adj.* [OE *softe*, gentle] **1** giving way easily under pressure **2** easily cut, marked, shaped, etc. [a *soft* metal] **3** not as hard as is normal, desirable, etc. [*soft* butter] **4** smooth to the touch **5** easy to digest: said of a diet **6** nonalcoholic: said of drinks **7** having few of the mineral salts that keep soap from lathering **8** mild, as a breeze **9** weak; not vigorous **10** easy [a *soft* job] **11** kind or gentle **12** not bright: said of color or light **13** gentle; low: said of sound —*adv.* gently; quietly —**soft'ly** *adv.* —**soft'ness** *n.*

**soft'ball'** *n.* **1** a kind of baseball played with a larger ball **2** this ball

**soft′-boiled′** *adj.* boiled a short time to keep the yolk soft: said of an egg

**soft coal** BITUMINOUS COAL

**soft drink** a nonalcoholic drink, esp. one that is carbonated

**soft·en** (sôf′ən) *vt., vi.* to make or become soft or softer —**soft′en·er** *n.*

**soft′heart′ed** *adj.* **1** full of compassion **2** not strict or severe; lenient

**soft landing** a landing of a spacecraft without damage to the craft or its contents

**soft money** money donated to a political party but not for a particular candidate

**soft palate** the soft, fleshy part at the rear of the roof of the mouth; velum

**soft′-ped′al** *vt.* **-aled** or **-alled, -al·ing** or **-al·ling** [[from pedal to soften an instrument's tone]] [Inf.] to make less emphatic; tone down; play down

**soft sell** selling that relies on subtle inducement or suggestion

**soft soap** [Inf.] flattery or smooth talk —**soft′-soap′** *vt.*

**soft′ware′** *n.* the programs, routines, etc. for a computer

**soft′wood′** *n.* **1** any light, easily cut wood **2** the wood of any tree bearing cones, as the pine

**soft′y** *n., pl.* **soft′ies** [Inf.] one who is too sentimental or trusting

**sog·gy** (säg′ē, sôg′ē) *adj.* **-gi·er, -gi·est** [[prob. < ON *sea*, a sucking]] soaked; moist and heavy —**sog′gi·ness** *n.*

**soil**[1] (soil) *n.* [[< L *solum*]] **1** the surface layer of earth, supporting plant life **2** land; country [native *soil*] **3** ground or earth [barren *soil*]

**soil**[2] (soil) *vt.* [[ult. < L *sus*, pig]] **1** to make dirty; stain **2** to disgrace —*vi.* to become soiled or dirty —*n.* a soiled spot; stain

**soi·ree** or **soi·rée** (swä rā′) *n.* [[< Fr *soir*, evening]] an evening party

**so·journ** (sō′jurn; *also, for v.,* sō jurn′) *vi.* [[< L *sub-*, under + *diurnus*, of a day]] to live somewhere temporarily —*n.* a brief stay; visit

**sol** (sōl) *n.* [[< ML]] *Music* the fifth tone of the diatonic scale

**Sol** (säl) *n.* [[L]] **1** *Rom. Myth.* the sun god **2** the sun personified

**sol·ace** (säl′is) *n.* [[< L *solacium*]] **1** an easing of grief, loneliness, etc. **2** a comfort or consolation —*vt.* **-aced, -ac·ing** to comfort; console

**so·lar** (sō′lər) *adj.* [[< L *sol*, the sun]] **1** of or having to do with the sun **2** produced by or coming from the sun

**solar battery** an assembly of cells (**solar cells**) used to convert solar energy into electric power

**so·lar·i·um** (sō ler′ē əm) *n., pl.* **-i·a** (-ē ə) [[< L *sol*, sun]] a glassed-in porch, etc. to sun oneself

**solar plexus** a network of nerves in the abdomen behind the stomach

**solar system** that portion of our galaxy subject to the sun's gravity; esp., the sun and its planets

**sold** (sōld) *vt., vi. pt. & pp. of* SELL

**sol·der** (säd′ər) *n.* [[ult. < L *solidus*, solid]] a metal alloy heated and used to join or patch metal parts, etc. —*vt., vi.* to join with solder

**sol·dier** (sōl′jər) *n.* [[< LL *solidus*, a coin]] **1** a member of an army **2** an enlisted person, as distinguished from an officer **3** one who works for a specified cause —*vi.* **1** to serve as a soldier **2** to proceed stubbornly (*on*) —**sol′dier·ly** *adj.*

**soldier of fortune** a mercenary or any adventurer

**sole**[1] (sōl) *n.* [[< L *solum*, a base]] **1** the bottom surface of the foot **2** the part of a shoe, etc. corresponding to this —*vt.* **soled, sol′ing** to furnish a shoe, etc.) with a sole

**sole**[2] (sōl) *adj.* [[< L *solus*]] without another; single; one and only

**sole**[3] (sōl) *n., pl.* **sole** or **soles** [[< L *solea*, SOLE[1]: from its shape]] a sea flatfish valued as food

**sol·e·cism** (säl′ə siz′əm) *n.* [[< Gr *soloikos*, speak-

ing incorrectly]] a violation of the conventional usage, grammar, etc. of a language

**sole·ly** (sōl′lē) *adv.* **1** alone **2** only, exclusively, or merely

**sol·emn** (säl′əm) *adj.* [[< L *sollemnis*, annual, hence religious: said of festivals]] **1** sacred **2** formal **3** serious; grave; earnest —**sol′emn·ly** *adv.*

**so·lem·ni·ty** (sə lem′nə tē) *n., pl.* **-ties 1** solemn ceremony, ritual, etc. **2** seriousness; gravity

**sol·em·nize** (säl′əm nīz′) *vt.* **-nized′, -niz′ing 1** to celebrate formally or according to ritual **2** to perform the ceremony of (marriage, etc.)

**so·le·noid** (sō′lə noid′, säl′-) *n.* [[< Gr *sōlēn*, channel + *eidos*, a form]] a coil of wire with a movable iron core, used as an electromagnetic switch

**so·lic·it** (sə lis′it) *vt., vi.* [[see SOLICITOUS]] **1** to appeal to (persons) for (aid, donations, etc.) **2** to entice or lure —**so·lic′i·ta′tion** *n.*

**so·lic·i·tor** *n.* **1** one who solicits trade, contributions, etc. **2** in England, a lawyer other than a barrister **3** the law officer for a city, etc.

**so·lic·i·tous** (sə lis′ə təs) *adj.* [[< L *sollus*, whole + *ciere*, set in motion]] **1** showing care or concern [solicitous for her welfare] **2** desirous; eager

**so·lic′i·tude′** (-tōod′) *n.* a being solicitous; care, concern, etc.

**sol·id** (säl′id) *adj.* [[< L *solidus*]] **1** relatively firm or compact; neither liquid nor gaseous **2** not hollow **3** having three dimensions **4** firm; strong; substantial **5** having no breaks or divisions **6** of one color, material, etc. throughout **7** showing unity; unanimous **8** reliable or dependable —*n.* **1** a solid substance, not a liquid or gas **2** an object having length, breadth, and thickness —**sol′id·ly** *adv.* —**sol′id·ness** *n.*

**sol·i·dar·i·ty** (säl′ə dar′ə tē) *n.* complete unity, as of opinion or feeling

**so·lid·i·fy** (sə lid′ə fī′) *vt., vi.* **-fied′, -fy′ing** to make or become solid, hard, etc. —**so·lid′i·fi·ca′tion** *n.*

**so·lid·i·ty** (-tē) *n.* a being solid

**sol′id-state′** *adj.* **1** of the branch of physics dealing with the structure, properties, etc. of solids **2** equipped with transistors, etc.

**so·lil·o·quy** (sə lil′ə kwē) *n., pl.* **-quies** [[< L *solus*, alone + *loqui*, speak]] **1** a talking to oneself **2** lines in a drama spoken by a character as if to himself or herself —**so·lil′o·quize′** (-kwīz′), **-quized′, -quiz′ing,** *vi., vt.*

**sol·i·taire** (säl′ə ter′) *n.* [[Fr: see fol.]] **1** a diamond or other gem set by itself **2** a card game for one player

**sol′i·tar′y** (-ter′ē) *adj.* [[< L *solus*, alone]] **1** living or being alone **2** single; only [a *solitary* example] **3** lonely; remote **4** done in solitude

**sol′i·tude′** (-tōod′) *n.* [[see prec.]] **1** a being solitary, or alone; seclusion **2** a secluded place

**so·lo** (sō′lō) *n., pl.* **-los** or **-li** (-lē) [[It < L *solus*, alone]] **1** a musical piece or passage to be performed by one person **2** any performance by one person alone —*adj.* for or by a single person —*adv.* alone —*vi.* **-loed, -lo·ing** to perform a solo —**so′lo·ist** *n.*

**Sol·o·mon** (säl′ə mən) *n.* *Bible* king of Israel noted for his wisdom

**Solomon Islands** country on a group of islands in the SW Pacific, east of New Guinea: 10,954 sq. mi.; pop. 286,000

**So·lon** (sō′lən, -län′) 640?-559? B.C.; Athenian statesman & lawgiver

**so long** [Inf.] GOODBYE

**sol·stice** (säl′stis, sōl′-) *n.* [[< L *sol*, sun + *sistere*, to stand]] the time of the year when the sun reaches the point farthest north (about June 21) or farthest south (about Dec. 21) of the equator: in the Northern Hemisphere, the **summer solstice** and **winter solstice**, respectively

**sol·u·ble** (säl′yə bəl) *adj.* [[see SOLVE]] **1** that can be dissolved **2** capable of being solved

**sol·ute** (säl′yōot′) *n.* the substance dissolved in a solution

**so·lu·tion** (sə lōō′shən) *n.* ⟦see fol.⟧ **1** the solving of a problem **2** an answer, explanation, etc. **3** the dispersion of one substance in another, usually a liquid, so as to form a homogeneous mixture **4** the mixture so produced

**solve** (sälv, sôlv) *vt.* **solved, solv′ing** ⟦< L *se-*, apart + *luere*, let go⟧ to find the answer to (a problem, etc.) —**solv′a·ble** *adj.* —**solv′er** *n.*

**sol·vent** (säl′vənt, sôl′-) *adj.* ⟦see prec.⟧ **1** able to pay all one's debts **2** that can dissolve another substance —*n.* a substance that can dissolve another substance —**sol′ven·cy** *n.*

**So·ma·li·a** (sō mä′lē ə) country of E Africa, on the Indian Ocean: 246,201 sq. mi.; pop. 9,200,000

**so·mat·ic** (sō mat′ik) *adj.* ⟦< Gr *sōma*, body⟧ of the body; physical

**somatic cell** any of the cells that form the tissues and organs of the body: opposed to GERM CELL

**som·ber** (säm′bər) *adj.* ⟦< L *sub*, under + *umbra*, shade⟧ **1** dark and gloomy **2** melancholy **3** solemn Also [Chiefly Brit.] **som′bre** —**som′ber·ly** *adv.*

**som·bre·ro** (säm brer′ō) *n., pl.* **-ros** ⟦Sp < *sombra*, shade: see prec.⟧ a broad-brimmed, tall-crowned hat worn in Mexico, the Southwest, etc.

**some** (sum) *adj.* ⟦OE *sum*⟧ **1** certain but not specified or known [some *some* evenings] **2** of a certain unspecified quantity, degree, etc. [have *some* candy] **3** about [some ten of them] **4** [Inf.] remarkable, striking, etc. [it was *some* fight] —*pron.* a certain unspecified number, quantity, etc. [some of them agree] —*adv.* **1** approximately [some ten men] **2** [Inf.] to some extent; somewhat [slept *some*] **3** [Inf.] to a great extent or at a great rate [must run *some* to catch up] —**and then some** [Inf.] and more than that

**-some**[1] (səm) ⟦OE *-sum*⟧ *suffix* tending to (be) [tiresome]

**-some**[2] (sōm) ⟦< Gr *sōma*, body⟧ *combining form* body [chromosome]

**some·bod·y** (sum′bäd′ē, -bud′ē) *pron.* a person unknown or not named; some person; someone —*n., pl.* **-bod′ies** a person of importance

**some′day′** *adv.* at some future day or time

**some′how′** *adv.* in a way or by a method not known or stated: often in **somehow or other**

**some′one′** *pron.* SOMEBODY

**som·er·sault** (sum′ər sôlt′) *n.* ⟦< L *supra*, over + *saltus*, a leap⟧ an acrobatic stunt performed by turning the body one full revolution, heels over head —*vi.* to perform a somersault

**some′thing** *pron.* **1** a thing not definitely known, understood, etc. [something went wrong] **2** a definite but unspecified thing [have *something* to eat] **3** a bit; a little —*n.* [Inf.] an important or remarkable person or thing —*adv.* **1** somewhat [looks *something* like me] **2** [Inf.] really; quite [sounds *something* awful] —**something else** [Slang] one that is quite remarkable

**some′time′** *adv.* at some unspecified or future time —*adj.* **1** former **2** occasional

**some′times′** *adv.* occasionally

**some′way′** *adv.* in some way: also **some′ways′**

**some′what′** *pron.* some degree, amount, part, etc. —*adv.* to some extent or degree; a little

**some′where′** *adv.* **1** in, to, or at some place not known or specified **2** at some time, degree, age, etc. (with *about, around, near, in, between,* etc.)

**som·nam·bu·lism** (säm nam′byōō liz′əm) *n.* ⟦< L *somnus*, sleep + *ambulare*, to walk⟧ sleepwalking —**som·nam′bu·list** *n.*

**som·no·lent** (säm′nə lənt) *adj.* ⟦< L *somnus*, sleep⟧ **1** sleepy **2** inducing drowsiness —**som′no·lence** *n.*

**son** (sun) *n.* ⟦OE *sunu*⟧ **1** a boy or man as he is related to his parents **2** a male descendant —**the Son** Jesus Christ

**so·nar** (sō′när′) *n.* ⟦*so*(*und*) *n*(*avigation*) *a*(*nd*) *r*(*anging*)⟧ an apparatus that transmits sound waves in water, used to find depths, etc.

**so·na·ta** (sə nät′ə) *n.* ⟦It < L *sonare*, to sound⟧ a musical composition for one or two instruments, usually consisting of several movements

**song** (sôŋ) *n.* ⟦OE *sang*⟧ **1** the act or art of singing **2** a piece of music for singing **3** *a*) [Old Poet.] poetry *b*) a lyric set to music **4** a sound like singing —**for a song** [Inf.] for a small sum; cheap

**song′bird′** *n.* a bird that makes vocal sounds that are like music

**song′fest′** *n.* ⟦SONG + -FEST⟧ an informal gathering of people for singing, esp. folk songs

**song′ster** (-stər) *n.* a singer —**song′stress** (-stris) *fem.n.*

**son·ic** (sän′ik) *adj.* ⟦< L *sonus*, a sound⟧ of or having to do with sound or the speed of sound

**sonic boom** the explosive sound of a supersonic jet passing overhead

**son′-in-law′** *n., pl.* **sons′-in-law′** the husband of one's daughter

**son·net** (sän′it) *n.* ⟦ult. < L *sonus*, a sound⟧ a poem normally of fourteen lines in any of several rhyme schemes

**son·ny** (sun′ē) *n., pl.* **-nies** little son: used as a familiar term of address to a young boy

**So·no·ra** (sô nô′rä) state of NW Mexico: 71,403 sq. mi.; pop. 1,824,000

**so·no·rous** (sə nôr′əs, sän′ər əs) *adj.* ⟦< L *sonor*, a sound⟧ **1** producing sound; resonant **2** full, deep, or rich in sound —**so·nor′i·ty** (-ə tē), *pl.* **-ties,** *n.*

**soon** (sōōn) *adv.* ⟦OE *sona*, at once⟧ **1** in a short time [will soon be there] **2** promptly; quickly [as soon as possible] **3** ahead of time; early [we left too soon] **4** readily; willingly [as soon go as stay] —**sooner or later** inevitably; eventually

**soot** (soot) *n.* ⟦OE *sot*⟧ a black substance consisting chiefly of carbon particles, in the smoke of burning matter —**soot′y, -i·er, -i·est,** *adj.*

**sooth** (sōōth) *n.* ⟦OE *soth*⟧ [Archaic] truth

**soothe** (sōōth) *vt.* **soothed, sooth′ing** ⟦OE *sothian*, prove true⟧ **1** to make calm or composed, as by gentleness or flattery **2** to relieve (pain, etc.) —**sooth′er** *n.* —**sooth′ing** *adj.*

**sooth·say·er** (sōōth′sā′ər) *n.* ⟦ME *sothseyere*, one who speaks the truth⟧ [Historical] a person who professes to predict the future —**sooth′say′ing** *n.*

**sop** (säp) *n.* ⟦OE *sopp*⟧ **1** a piece of food, as bread, soaked in milk, etc. **2** *a*) something given to appease *b*) a bribe —*vt.* **sopped, sop′ping 1** to soak, steep, etc. **2** to take up (liquid) by absorption: usually with *up*

**SOP** *abbrev.* standard operating procedure

**soph·ism** (säf′iz′əm) *n.* ⟦< Gr *sophos*, clever⟧ a clever and plausible but fallacious argument

**soph′ist** *n.* one who uses clever, specious reasoning —**so·phis·ti·cal** (sə fis′ti kəl) *adj.*

**so·phis·ti·cate** (sə fis′tə kāt′; *for n., usually,* -kit) *vt.* **-cat′ed, -cat′ing** ⟦ult. < Gr *sophistēs*, wise man⟧ to change from a natural or simple state; make worldly-wise —*n.* a sophisticated person

**so·phis′ti·cat′ed** *adj.* **1** not simple, naive, etc.; worldly-wise or knowledgeable, subtle, etc. **2** for sophisticated people **3** highly complex or developed —**so·phis′ti·ca′tion** *n.*

**soph·ist·ry** (säf′is trē) *n.* misleading but clever reasoning

**Soph·o·cles** (säf′ə klēz′) 496?-406 B.C.; Gr. writer of tragic dramas

**soph·o·more** (säf′môr′, säf′ə môr′) *n.* ⟦< obs. *sophumer*, sophism⟧ a student in the second year of college or the tenth grade in high school —*adj.* of or for sophomores

**soph′o·mor′ic** *adj.* of or like sophomores; seen as opinionated, immature, etc.

**-so·phy** (sə fē) ⟦< Gr *sophia*, wisdom⟧ *combining form* knowledge

**sop·o·rif·ic** (säp′ə rif′ik, sō′pə-) *adj.* ⟦< L *sopor*, sleep + -FIC⟧ causing sleep —*n.* a soporific drug, etc.

**sop·py** (säp′ē) *adj.* **-pi·er, -pi·est 1** very wet: also **sop′ping 2** [Inf.] sentimental

**so·pra·no** (sə pran′ō, -prä′nō) *n., pl.* **-nos** or **-ni** ⟦It

< *sopra,* above]] **1** the range of the highest voice of women or boys **2** a voice, singer, or instrument with such a range **3** a part for a soprano —*adj.* of or for a soprano

**sor·bet** (sôr bāʹ, sôrʹbət) *n.* [[Fr < Ar *sharba(t),* a drink]] a tart ice, as of fruit juice

**sor·cer·y** (sôrʹsər ē) *n., pl.* **-ies** [[< L *sors,* lot, chance]] **1** in the belief of some, the use of an evil supernatural power over people **2** charm, influence, etc. —**sorʹcer·er** *n.* —**sorʹcer·ess** *fem.n.*

**sor·did** (sôrʹdid) *adj.* [[< L *sordes,* filth]] **1** dirty; filthy **2** squalid; wretched **3** base; ignoble; mean —**sorʹdid·ly** *adv.* —**sorʹdid·ness** *n.*

**sore** (sôr) *adj.* **sorʹer, sorʹest** [[OE *sar*]] **1** giving or feeling pain; painful **2** filled with grief **3** causing irritation [a sore point] **4** [Inf.] angry; offended — *n.* a sore, usually infected spot on the body —*adv.* [Archaic] greatly —**soreʹness** *n.*

**soreʹhead** *n.* [Inf.] a person easily angered, made resentful, etc.

**soreʹly** *adv.* **1** grievously; painfully **2** urgently [sorely needed]

**sor·ghum** (sôrʹgəm) *n.* [[< It *sorgo*]] **1** a cereal grass grown for grain, syrup, fodder, etc. **2** syrup made from its juices

**so·ror·i·ty** (sə rôrʹə tē) *n., pl.* **-ties** [[< L *soror,* sister]] a group of women or girls joined together for fellowship, etc., as in some colleges

**sor·rel**[1] (sôrʹəl, särʹ-) *n.* [[< OFr *surele*]] any of various plants with edible sour leaves

**sor·rel**[2] (sôrʹəl, särʹ-) *n.* [[< OFr *sor,* light brown]] **1** light reddish brown **2** a horse, etc. of this color

**sor·row** (särʹō, sôrʹō) *n.* [[OE *sorg*]] **1** mental suffering caused by loss, disappointment, etc.; grief **2** that which causes such suffering —*vi.* to grieve —**sorʹrow·ful** *adj.* —**sorʹrow·ful·ly** *adv.*

**sor·ry** (särʹē, sôrʹē) *adj.* **-ri·er, -ri·est** [[< OE *sar,* sore]] **1** full of sorrow, pity, or regret **2** inferior; poor **3** wretched —**sorʹri·ly** *adv.* —**sorʹri·ness** *n.*

**sort** (sôrt) *n.* [[< L *sors,* lot, chance]] **1** any group of related things; kind; class **2** quality or type —*vt.* to arrange according to class or kind —**of sorts** or **of a sort** also **out of sorts** [Inf.] not in good humor or health —**sort of** [Inf.] somewhat

**sor·tie** (sôrtʹē) *n.* [[Fr < *sortir,* go out]] **1** a quick raid by forces from a besieged place **2** one mission by a single military plane

**SOS** (esʹōʹesʹ) *n.* a signal of distress, as in wireless telegraphy

**soʹ-soʹ** *adv., adj.* just passably or passable; fair

**sot** (sät) *n.* [[< ML *sottus,* a fool]] a drunkard — **sotʹtish** *adj.*

**sot·to vo·ce** (sätʹō vōʹchē) [[It, under the voice]] in a low voice, so as not to be overheard

**souf·flé** (sōō flāʹ) *n.* [[Fr < L *sufflare,* puff out]] a baked food made light and puffy by beaten egg whites added before baking

**sough** (sou, suf) *n.* [[OE *swogan,* to sound]] a soft sighing or rustling sound —*vi.* to make a sough

**sought** (sôt) *vt., vi. pt. & pp. of* SEEK

**soul** (sōl) *n.* [[OE *sawol*]] **1** an entity without material reality, regarded as the spiritual part of a person **2** the moral or emotional nature of a person **3** spiritual or emotional warmth, force, etc. **4** vital or essential part, quality, etc. **5** a person [I didn't see a *soul*] **6** the deep spiritual and emotional quality of black American culture; also, the expression of this, as in music —*adj.* of, for, or like black Americans

**soul food** [Inf.] food items, as chitterlings, popular orig. in the South, esp. among blacks

**soulʹful** *adj.* full of deep feeling —**soulʹful·ly** *adv.* —**soulʹful·ness** *n.*

**soul mate** [Inf.] a person, esp. of the opposite sex, with whom one has a deeply personal relationship

**sound**[1] (sound) *n.* [[< L *sonus*]] **1** that which is heard, resulting from stimulation of auditory nerves by vibrations (**sound waves**) in the air; also the vibrations **2** the distance within which a sound may be heard; earshot **3** the mental

impression produced [the *sound* of his report] — *vi.* **1** to make a sound **2** to seem upon being heard [to *sound* troubled] —*vt.* **1** to cause to sound **2** to signal, express, etc. **3** to utter distinctly [to *sound* one's r's] —**soundʹless** *adj.*

**sound**[2] (sound) *adj.* [[OE *(ge)sund*]] **1** free from defect, damage, or decay **2** healthy [a sound body] **3** safe; stable [a sound bank] **4** based on valid reasoning; sensible **5** thorough; forceful [a sound defeat] **6** deep and undisturbed: said of sleep **7** honest, loyal, etc. —*adv.* deeply [sound asleep] —**soundʹly** *adv.* —**soundʹness** *n.*

**sound**[3] (sound) *n.* [[< OE & ON *sund*]] **1** a wide channel linking two large bodies of water or separating an island from the mainland **2** a long inlet or arm of the sea

**sound**[4] (sound) *vt., vi.* [[< L *sub,* under + *unda,* a wave]] **1** to measure the depth of (water), esp. with a weighted line **2** to try to find out the opinions of (a person), usually subtly: often with *out* —**soundʹing** *n.*

**sound barrier** the large increase of air resistance of some aircraft flying near the speed of sound

**sound bite** a brief, quotable remark, as by a politician, suitable for use in radio or TV news

**sounding board 1** something to increase resonance or reflect sound: often **soundʹboard** *n.* **2** a person on whom one tests one's ideas, etc.

**soundʹproof** *adj.* that keeps sound from coming through —*vt.* to make soundproof

**soundʹstage** *n.* an enclosed soundproof area for producing films or TV shows

**soundʹtrack** *n.* the sound portion of a film

**soup** (sōōp) *n.* [[Fr *soupe*]] a liquid food made by cooking meat, vegetables, etc. in water, milk, etc. —**soup up** [Slang] to increase the capacity for speed of (an engine, etc.)

**soup·çon** (sōōp sônʹ) *n.* [[Fr < L *suspicio,* suspicion]] **1** a slight trace, as of a flavor **2** a tiny bit

**soup·y** (sōōʹpē) *adj.* **-i·er, -i·est 1** watery like soup **2** [Inf.] foggy

**sour** (sour) *adj.* [[OE *sur*]] **1** having the sharp, acid taste of vinegar, etc. **2** made acid or rank by fermentation **3** cross; bad-tempered **4** distasteful or unpleasant —*vt., vi.* to make or become sour — **sourʹly** *adv.* —**sourʹness** *n.*

**source** (sôrs) *n.* [[< L *surgere,* to rise]] **1** a spring, etc. from which a stream arises **2** a place or thing from which something originates or develops **3** a person, book, etc. that provides information

**sour cream** thickened and soured cream

**sour·dough** (sourʹdōʹ) *n.* **1** bread made from fermented dough **2** a lone prospector for gold, etc., as in the W U.S.

**sour grapes** a scorning of something only because it cannot be had or done

**sourʹpuss** (-poosʹ) *n.* [Slang] a gloomy or disagreeable person

**souse** (sous) *n.* [[< OHG *sulza,* brine]] **1** a pickled food, as pigs' feet **2** liquid for pickling; brine **3** a plunging into a liquid **4** [Slang] a drunkard —*vt., vi.* **soused, sousʹing 1** to pickle **2** to plunge into a liquid **3** to make or become soaking wet

**soused** *adj.* [Slang] drunk

**south** (south) *n.* [[OE *suth*]] **1** the direction to the left of one facing the sunset (180° on the compass) **2** a region in or toward this direction —*adj.* **1** in, of, or toward the south **2** from the south —*adv.* in or toward the south —**go south** [Inf.] to decline, deteriorate, fail, etc. —**the South** that part of the U.S. south of Pennsylvania and the Ohio River, and generally east of the Mississippi; specif., the states that formed the Confederacy

**South Africa** country in southernmost Africa: 472,855 sq. mi.; pop. 37,714,000

**South America** S continent in the Western Hemisphere: *c.* 6,900,000 sq. mi.; pop. *c.* 318,000,000 —**South American**

**South Bend** city in N Indiana: pop. 106,000

**South Car·o·li·na** (karʹə līʹnə) state of the SE

U.S.: 30,111 sq. mi.; pop. 3,487,000; cap. Columbia: abbrev. *SC* —**South Car·o·lin'i·an** (-lin'ē ən)

**South China Sea** arm of the W Pacific, between SE Asia & the Philippines

**South Da·ko·ta** (də kōt'ə) Midwestern state of the U.S.: 75,898 sq. mi.; pop. 696,000; cap. Pierre: abbrev. *SD* —**South Da·ko'tan**

**south·east'** *n.* **1** the direction halfway between south and east **2** a region in or toward this direction —*adj.* **1** in, of, or toward the southeast **2** from the southeast —*adv.* in or toward the southeast —**south'east'er·ly** *adj., adv.* —**south'east'ern** *adj.* —**south'east'ward** *adv., adj.* — **south'east'wards** *adv.*

**south·er·ly** (suth'ər lē) *adj., adv.* **1** toward the south **2** from the south

**south·ern** (suth'ərn) *adj.* **1** in, of, or toward the south **2** from the south **3** of the south

**south'ern·er** *n.* a person born or living in the south

**Southern Hemisphere** that half of the earth south of the equator

**southern lights** [*also* S- L-] aurora australis

**south·paw** (south'pô') *n.* [Slang] a left-handed person; esp., a left-handed baseball pitcher

**South Pole** the southern end of the earth's axis

**South Sea Islands** the islands in the S Pacific

**south'ward** *adv., adj.* toward the south: also **south'wards** *adv.*

**south'west'** *n.* **1** the direction halfway between south and west **2** a region in or toward this direction —*adj.* **1** in, of, or toward the southwest **2** from the southwest —*adv.* in or toward the southwest —**south'west'er·ly** *adj., adv.* — **south'west'ern** *adj.* —**south'west'ward** *adv., adj.* —**south'west'wards** *adv.*

**sou·ve·nir** (sōō'və nir') *n.* [< Fr < L *subvenire*, come to mind] something kept as a reminder

**sov·er·eign** (säv'rən, -ər in) *adj.* [< L *super*, above] **1** above all others; chief; supreme **2** supreme in power, rank, etc. **3** independent of all others [a *sovereign* state] —*n.* **1** a monarch or ruler **2** a British gold coin worth one pound: no longer minted

**sov'er·eign·ty** *n.* **1** the status, rule, etc. of a sovereign **2** supreme and independent political authority

**so·vi·et** (sō'vē et') *n.* [Russ *sovyet*, council] **1** in Russia, Uzbekistan, and, formerly, the Soviet Union, any of the various elected governing councils, local, intermediate, and national **2** any similar council in a socialist governing system —*adj.* [S-] of or connected with the Soviet Union

**Soviet Union** UNION OF SOVIET SOCIALIST REPUBLICS

**sow**[1] (sou) *n.* [OE *sugu*] an adult female pig

**sow**[2] (sō) *vt.* **sowed, sown** (sōn) or **sowed, sow'ing** [OE *sawan*] **1** to scatter (seed) for growing **2** to plant seed in (a field, etc.) **3** to spread or scatter —*vi.* to sow seed —**sow'er** *n.*

**sox** (säks) *n. alt. pl. of* SOCK[1]

**soy** (soi) *n.* [Jpn] **1** a dark, salty sauce made from fermented soybeans: in full **soy sauce 2** the soybean plant or its seeds Also [Chiefly Brit.] **soy·a** (soi'ə)

**soy'bean'** *n.* **1** a plant widely grown for its seeds, which contain much protein and oil **2** its seed

**sp** *abbrev.* **1** special **2** spelling

**Sp** *abbrev.* **1** Spain **2** Spanish

**spa** (spä) *n.* [after *Spa*, resort in Belgium] **1** a health resort having a mineral spring **2** a commercial establishment with exercise rooms, sauna baths, etc.

**space** (spās) *n.* [< L *spatium*] **1** *a*) the continuous, three-dimensional expanse in which all things are contained *b*) OUTER SPACE **2** *a*) the distance, area, etc. between or within things *b*) room for something [a parking *space*] **3** an interval of time —*vt.* **spaced, spac'ing** to arrange with space or spaces between

**space'craft'** *n., pl.* **-craft'** any vehicle or satellite for orbiting the earth, space travel, etc.

**spaced'-out'** *adj.* [Slang] under or as if under the influence of a drug: also **spaced**

**space'flight'** *n.* flight in a spacecraft

**space heater** a small heating unit for a room or other confined area

**space'man'** (-man', -mən) *n., pl.* **-men'** (-men', -mən) an astronaut or any of the crew of a spaceship

**space'port'** *n.* a center for assembling, testing, and launching spacecraft

**space'ship'** *n.* a spacecraft, esp. if manned

**space shuttle** an airplanelike spacecraft designed to carry personnel and equipment between earth and a space station

**space station** (or **platform**) a spacecraft in long-term orbit serving as a launch pad, research center, etc.

**space'suit'** *n.* a garment pressurized for use by astronauts

**space'walk'** *n.* the act of an astronaut in moving about in space outside a spacecraft

**space·y** or **spac·y** (spā'sē) *adj.* **-i·er, -i·est** [Slang] **1** SPACED-OUT **2** *a*) eccentric or unconventional *b*) flighty, irresponsible, neurotic, etc. —**spac'i·ness** *n.*

**spa·cious** (spā'shəs) *adj.* having more than enough space; vast —**spa'cious·ly** *adv.* — **spa'cious·ness** *n.*

**Spack·le** (spak'əl) [prob. < Ger *spachtel*, spatula] *trademark for* a powder mixed with water to form a paste that dries hard, used to fill holes, cracks, etc. in wallboard, wood, etc. —*n.* [s-] this substance —*vt.* **-led, -ling** [s-] to fill or cover with spackle

**spade**[1] (spād) *n.* [OE *spadu*] a flat-bladed, long-handled digging tool, like a shovel —*vt., vi.* **spad'ed, spad'ing** to dig with or as with a spade —**spade'ful** *n.*

**spade**[2] (spād) *n.* [ult. < Gr *spathē*, flat blade] **1** any of a suit of playing cards marked with black figures like this ♠ **2** [*pl.*] this suit

**spade'work'** *n.* preparatory work for some main project, esp. when tiresome

**spa·dix** (spā'diks) *n., pl.* **-dix·es** or **-di·ces'** (-də sēz') [ult. < Gr] a spike of tiny flowers, usually enclosed in a spathe

SPATHE    SPADIX

**spa·ghet·ti** (spə get'ē) *n.* [It < *spago*, small cord] pasta in long, thin strings, boiled or steamed

**Spain** (spān) country in SW Europe: 190,191 sq. mi.; pop. 38,872,000

**spake** (spāk) *vi., vt. archaic pt. of* SPEAK

**span** (span) *n.* [OE *sponn*] **1** *a*) the distance (about 9 in.) between the tips of the thumb and little finger **2** *a*) the full extent between any two limits *b*) the distance between ends or supports [the *span* of an arch] *c*) the full duration (*of*) [*span* of attention] **3** a part between two supports —*vt.* **spanned, span'ning 1** to measure, esp. by the span of the hand **2** to extend over

**Span** *abbrev.* Spanish

**span·dex** (span'deks') *n.* [< EXPAND] an elastic synthetic fiber used in girdles, etc.

**span·gle** (span'gəl) *n.* [< OE *spang*, a clasp] a small piece of bright metal sewn on fabric for decoration —*vt.* **-gled, -gling** to decorate as with spangles

**Span·iard** (span'yərd) *n.* a person born or living in Spain

**span·iel** (span'yəl) *n.* [< MFr *espagnol*, lit., Spanish] any of several breeds of dog with large, drooping ears and a dense, wavy coat

**Span·ish** (span'ish) *adj.* of Spain or its people,

language, etc. —*n.* the language of Spain and Spanish America —**the Spanish** the people of Spain

**Spanish America** those countries south of the U.S. in which Spanish is the chief language — **Span'ish-A·mer'i·can** *adj., n.*

**Spanish moss** a rootless plant that grows in long, graceful strands from tree branches in the SE U.S.

**spank** (spaŋk) *vt.* ⟦echoic⟧ to strike with the open hand, etc., esp. on the buttocks, as in punishment —*n.* a smack given in spanking

**spank'ing** *adj.* **1** swiftly moving **2** brisk: said of a breeze —*adv.* [Inf.] completely [*spanking* new]

**spar**¹ (spär) *n.* ⟦< ON *sparri* or MDu *sparre*⟧ any pole, as a mast or yard, supporting a sail of a ship

**spar**² (spär) *vi.* **sparred, spar'ring** ⟦prob. < It *parare,* to parry⟧ **1** to box with feinting movements, landing few heavy blows **2** to wrangle

**spare** (sper) *vt.* **spared, spar'ing** ⟦OE *sparian*⟧ **1** to refrain from killing, hurting, etc. **2** to save or free (a person) from something **3** to avoid using or use frugally **4** to part with or give up conveniently [can you *spare* a dime?] —*adj.* **1** not in regular use; extra **2** free [spare time] **3** meager; scanty **4** lean; thin —*n.* **1** a spare, or extra, thing **2** *Bowling* a knocking down of all the pins with two rolls of the ball —**spare'ly** *adv.*

**spare'ribs'** *pl.n.* a cut of meat, esp. pork, consisting of the thin end of the ribs

**spar'ing** *adj.* careful; frugal —**spar'ing·ly** *adv.*

**spark** (spärk) *n.* ⟦OE *spearca*⟧ **1** a glowing bit of matter, esp. one thrown off by a fire **2** any flash or sparkle **3** a particle or trace **4** a brief flash of light accompanying an electric discharge as through air —*vi.* to make sparks —*vt.* to stir up; activate

**spar·kle** (spär'kəl) *vi.* **-kled, -kling** **1** to throw off sparks **2** to glitter **3** to effervesce or bubble **4** to be brilliant and lively —*n.* **1** a sparkling **2** brilliance; liveliness —**spar'kler** (-klər) *n.*

**spark plug** an electrical device fitted into a cylinder of an engine to ignite the fuel mixture by making sparks

**spar·row** (spar'ō) *n.* ⟦OE *spearwa*⟧ any of numerous small, perching songbirds

**sparse** (spärs) *adj.* ⟦< L *spargere,* scatter⟧ thinly spread; not dense —**sparse'ly** *adv.* —**sparse'ness** or **spar'si·ty** (-sə tē) *n.*

**Spar·ta** (spärt'ə) ancient city in S Greece: a military power

SPARK PLUG

**Spar·tan** (spärt''n) *adj.* **1** of ancient Sparta or its people or culture **2** like the Spartans; warlike, hardy, disciplined, etc. —*n.* a Spartan person

**spasm** (spaz'əm) *n.* ⟦< Gr *spasmos*⟧ **1** a sudden, involuntary muscular contraction **2** any sudden, violent, temporary activity, feeling, etc. —*vi.* to undergo a spasm

**spas·mod·ic** (spaz mäd'ik) *adj.* ⟦see prec. & -OID⟧ of or like spasms; fitful —**spas·mod'i·cal·ly** *adv.*

**spas·tic** (spas'tik) *adj.* of or characterized by muscular spasms —*n.* one having spastic paralysis

**spat**¹ (spat) [Inf.] *n.* ⟦prob. echoic⟧ a brief, petty quarrel —*vi.* **spat'ted, spat'ting** to engage in a spat

**spat**² (spat) *n.* ⟦< *spatterdash,* a legging⟧ a gaiterlike covering for the instep and ankle

**spat**³ (spat) *vt., vi.* alt. pt. & pp. of SPIT²

**spate** (spāt) *n.* ⟦< ?⟧ an unusually large flow, as of words

**spathe** (spā*th*) *n.* ⟦< L *spatha,* a flat blade⟧ a large, leaflike part enclosing a flower cluster

**spa·tial** (spā'shəl) *adj.* ⟦< L *spatium,* space⟧ of, or existing in, space

**spat·ter** (spat'ər) *vt., vi.* ⟦< ?⟧ **1** to scatter or spurt out in drops **2** to splash —*n.* **1** a spattering **2** a mark caused by spattering

**spat·u·la** (spach'ə lə) *n.* ⟦L < Gr *spathē,* flat blade⟧ an implement with a broad, flat, flexible blade for spreading or blending foods, paints, etc.

**spat'u·late'** (-lāt') *adj.* shaped like a spatula

**spav·in** (spav'in) *n.* ⟦< MFr *esparvain*⟧ a disease that lames horses in the hock joint —**spav'ined** *adj.*

**spawn** (spôn) *vt., vi.* ⟦< L *expandere:* see EXPAND⟧ **1** to produce or deposit (eggs, sperm, or young) **2** to bring forth or produce prolifically —*n.* **1** the mass of eggs or young produced by fish, mollusks, etc. **2** something produced, esp. in great quantity, as offspring

**spay** (spā) *vt.* ⟦< Gr *spathē,* flat blade⟧ to sterilize (a female animal) by removing the ovaries

**speak** (spēk) *vi.* **spoke, spo'ken, speak'ing** ⟦OE *sp(r)ecan*⟧ **1** to utter words; talk **2** to communicate as by talking **3** to make a request (*for*) **4** to make a speech —*vt.* **1** to make known as by speaking **2** to use (a given language) in speaking **3** to utter (words) —**so to speak** that is to say — **speak out** (or **up**) to speak clearly or freely — **speak to** to respond to, deal with, etc. —**speak well for** to say or indicate something favorable about

**speak'-eas'y** (-ē'zē) *n., pl.* **-ies** [Old Slang] a place where alcoholic drinks are sold illegally

**speak'er** *n.* **1** one who speaks; esp., *a*) an orator *b*) the presiding officer of various lawmaking bodies *c*) [S-] the presiding officer of the U.S. House of Representatives **2** a device for converting electrical signals to audible sound waves

**spear** (spir) *n.* ⟦OE *spere*⟧ **1** a weapon with a long shaft and a sharp point, for thrusting or throwing **2** [var. of SPIRE] a long blade or shoot, as of grass —*vt.* **1** to pierce or stab with or as with a spear **2** [Inf.] to reach out and catch (a baseball, etc.)

**spear'fish'** *n., pl.* **-fish'** or (for different species) **-fish'es** any of a group of large food and game fishes of the open seas —*vi.* to fish with a spear, etc.

**spear'head'** *n.* **1** the pointed head of a spear **2** the leading person or group, as in an attack —*vt.* to take the lead in (an attack, etc.)

**spear'mint'** *n.* ⟦prob. from the shape of its flowers⟧ a fragrant plant of the mint family, used for flavoring

**spec**¹ (spek) [Inf.] *n. short for:* **1** SPECIFICATION (sense 1) **2** SPECULATION —**on spec 1** according to specification(s) **2** as a speculation or gamble

**spec**² *abbrev.* **1** special **2** specifically

**spe·cial** (spesh'əl) *adj.* ⟦< L *species,* kind⟧ **1** distinctive or unique **2** exceptional; unusual **3** highly valued **4** of or for a particular purpose, etc. **5** not general; specific —*n.* a special thing, as, specif., a sale item —**spe'cial·ly** *adv.*

**special delivery** mail delivery by a special messenger, for a special fee

**spe'cial·ist** *n.* one who specializes in a particular field of study, work, etc.

**spe'cial·ize'** *vi.* **-ized', -iz'ing** to concentrate on a particular branch of study, work, etc. —**spe'cial·i·za'tion** *n.*

**spe'cial·ty** *n., pl.* **-ties** **1** a special quality, feature, etc. **2** a special interest, study, etc.

**spe·cie** (spē'shē, -sē) *n.* ⟦< L *species,* kind⟧ coin, rather than paper money

**spe·cies** (spē'shēz, -sēz) *n., pl.* **-cies** ⟦L, appearance, kind⟧ **1** a distinct kind; sort **2** any of the groups of related plants or animals that usually breed only among themselves: similar species form a genus

**specif** *abbrev.* specifically

**spe·cif·ic** (spə sif'ik) *adj.* ⟦< L *species,* kind + *-ficus,* -FIC⟧ **1** definite; explicit **2** peculiar to or characteristic of something **3** of a particular kind **4** specially indicated as a cure for some disease — *n.* **1** a specific cure **2** a distinct item or detail; particular —**spe·cif'i·cal·ly** *adv.*

**-spe·cif'ic** *combining form* limited or specific to

**spec·i·fi·ca·tion** (spes′ə fi kā′shən) *n.* **1** [*usually pl.*] a statement or enumeration of particulars, as to size, quality, or terms **2** something specified

**specific gravity** the ratio of the weight or mass of a given volume of a substance to that of an equal volume of another substance (as water) used as a standard

**spec·i·fy** (spes′ə fī′) *vt.* **-fied′, -fy′ing** ⟦< LL *specificus,* specific⟧ **1** to state definitely **2** to include in a set of specifications

**spec·i·men** (spes′ə mən) *n.* ⟦L < *specere,* see⟧ **1** a part or individual used as a sample of a whole or group **2** *Med.* a sample, as of urine, for analysis

**spe·cious** (spē′shəs) *adj.* ⟦< L *species,* appearance⟧ seeming to be good, sound, correct, etc. without really being so —**spe′cious·ly** *adv.*

**speck** (spek) *n.* ⟦OE *specca*⟧ **1** a small spot, mark, etc. **2** a very small bit —*vt.* to mark with specks

**speck·le** (spek′əl) *n.* a small speck —*vt.* **-led, -ling** to mark with speckles

**specs** (speks) *pl.n.* [Inf.] **1** spectacles; eyeglasses **2** specifications

**spec·ta·cle** (spek′tə kəl) *n.* ⟦< L *specere,* see⟧ **1** a remarkable sight **2** a large public show **3** [*pl.*] [Old-fashioned] a pair of eyeglasses

**spec·tac·u·lar** (spek tak′yə lər) *adj.* unusual to a striking degree —*n.* an elaborate show or display —**spec·tac′u·lar·ly** *adv.*

**spec·ta·tor** (spek′tāt′ər) *n.* ⟦L < *spectare,* behold⟧ one who watches without taking an active part

**spec·ter** (spek′tər) *n.* ⟦< L *spectare,* behold⟧ a ghost; apparition: Brit. sp. **spec′tre**

**spec′tral** (-trəl) *adj.* **1** of or like a specter **2** of a spectrum

**spec·tro·scope** (spek′trə skōp′) *n.* ⟦< Ger., ult. < L *spectare,* behold⟧ an optical instrument used for forming spectra for study —**spec′tro·scop′ic** (-skäp′ik) *adj.* —**spec·tros′co·py** (-träs′kə pē) *n.*

**spec·trum** (spek′trəm) *n., pl.* **-tra** (-trə) or **-trums** ⟦< L: see SPECTER⟧ **1** the series of colored bands separated and arranged in order of their respective wavelengths by the passage of white light through a prism, etc. **2** a continuous range or entire extent

**spec·u·late** (spek′yə lāt′) *vi.* **-lat′ed, -lat′ing** ⟦< L *specere,* see⟧ **1** to ponder; esp., to conjecture **2** to take part in any risky venture (as buying or selling certain stocks, etc.) on the chance of making huge profits —**spec′u·la′tion** *n.* —**spec′u·la′tive** (-lāt′iv, -lə tiv) *adj.* —**spec′u·la′tor** *n.*

**speech** (spēch) *n.* ⟦< OE *sprecan,* speak⟧ **1** the act of speaking **2** the power to speak **3** that which is spoken; utterance, remark, etc. **4** a talk given to an audience **5** the language of a certain people

**speech′less** *adj.* **1** incapable of speech **2** silent, as from shock

**speed** (spēd) *n.* ⟦OE *spæd,* success⟧ **1** swiftness; quick motion **2** rate of movement; velocity **3** an arrangement of gears, as for the drive of an engine **4** [Inf.] one's kind of taste, capability, etc. **5** [Slang] any of various amphetamine compounds —*vi.* **sped** (sped) or **speed′ed, speed′ing** to move rapidly, esp. too rapidly —*vt.* **1** to help to succeed; aid **2** to cause to speed —**speed up** to increase in speed —**up to speed** **1** working, etc. at full speed **2** [Inf.] fully informed —**speed′er** *n.*

**speed′boat′** *n.* a fast motorboat

**speed·om·e·ter** (spi däm′ət ər) *n.* a device attached to a motor vehicle, etc. to indicate speed

**speed·ster** (spēd′stər) *n.* a very fast driver, runner, etc.

**speed′way′** *n.* a track for racing automobiles or motorcycles

**speed′y** *adj.* **-i·er, -i·est** **1** rapid; fast; swift **2** without delay; prompt —**speed′i·ly** *adv.*

**spe·le·ol·o·gy** (spē′lē äl′ə jē) *n.* ⟦< Gr *spēlaion,* a cave⟧ the scientific study and exploration of caves —**spe′le·ol′o·gist** *n.*

**spell¹** (spel) *n.* ⟦OE, a saying⟧ **1** a word or formula thought to have some magic power **2** irresistible influence; charm; fascination

**spell²** (spel) *vt.* **spelled** or **spelt, spell′ing** ⟦< OFr *espeller,* explain⟧ **1** to name, write, etc. in order the letters of (a word) **2** to make up (a word, etc.): said of specified letters **3** to mean [*red* spells danger] —*vi.* to spell words —**spell out** to explain in detail

**spell³** (spel) *vt.* **spelled, spell′ing** ⟦OE *spelian*⟧ [Inf.] to work in place of (another) for an interval; relieve —*n.* **1** a period of work, duty, etc. **2** a period of anything [a *spell* of brooding] **3** [Inf.] a fit of illness

**spell′bind′** *vt.* **-bound′, -bind′ing** to cause to be spellbound; fascinate —**spell′bind′er** *n.*

**spell′bound′** *adj.* held by or as by a spell; fascinated

**spell′-check′er** *n.* a word-processing program used to check the spelling of words in a document

**spell′down′** *n.* SPELLING BEE

**spell′er** *n.* **1** one who spells words **2** a textbook for teaching spelling

**spell′ing** *n.* **1** the act of one who spells words **2** the way a word is spelled; orthography

**spelling bee** a spelling contest, esp. one in which a contestant is eliminated after misspelling a word

**spe·lunk·er** (spi luŋ′kər) *n.* ⟦< Gr *spēlynx,* a cave⟧ a cave explorer —**spe·lunk′ing** *n.*

**spend** (spend) *vt.* **spent, spend′ing** ⟦< L *expendere:* see EXPEND⟧ **1** to use up, exhaust, etc. [his fury was *spent*] **2** to pay out (money) **3** to devote (time, labor, etc.) to something **4** to pass (time) —*vi.* to pay out or use up money, etc. —**spend′a·ble** *adj.* —**spend′er** *n.*

**spend′thrift′** *n.* one who wastes money —*adj.* wasteful

**spent** (spent) *vt., vi. pt. & pp. of* SPEND —*adj.* **1** tired out; exhausted **2** used up; worn out

**sperm** (spurm) *n.* ⟦< Gr *sperma,* seed⟧ **1** the male generative fluid; semen **2** *pl.* **sperm** or **sperms** a male germ cell, esp. a spermatozoon

**sper·ma·to·zo·on** (spur′mə tə zō′än′, -ən) *n., pl.* **-zo′a** (-zō′ə) ⟦< Gr *sperma,* seed + *zōion,* animal⟧ the male germ cell, found in semen, which penetrates the egg of the female to fertilize it

**sperm·i·cide** (spur′mə sīd′) *n.* ⟦SPERM + -*i*- + -CIDE⟧ an agent that kills spermatozoa —**sperm′i·cid′al** *adj.*

**sperm whale** a large toothed whale found in warm seas: its head contains a valuable lubricating oil (**sperm oil**)

**spew** (spyōō) *vt., vi.* ⟦OE *spiwan*⟧ **1** to throw up (something) from or as from the stomach; vomit **2** to flow or cause to flow or gush forth —*n.* something spewed

**sp gr** *abbrev.* specific gravity

**sphere** (sfir) *n.* ⟦< Gr *sphaira*⟧ **1** any round body having the surface equally distant from the center at all points; globe; ball **2** the place, range, or extent of action, existence, knowledge, experience, etc. —**spher·i·cal** (sfer′i kəl, sfir′-) *adj.*

**sphe·roid** (sfir′oid) *n.* a body that is almost but not quite a sphere —**sphe·roi′dal** *adj.*

**sphinc·ter** (sfiŋk′tər) *n.* ⟦< Gr *sphingein,* to draw close⟧ a ring-shaped muscle at a body orifice

**sphinx** (sfiŋks) *n.* ⟦< Gr, strangler⟧ **1** *Gr. Myth.* a winged monster with a lion's body and a woman's head **2** [S-] a statue with a lion's body and a man's head, near Cairo, Egypt **3** one who is difficult to know or understand

**spice** (spīs) *n.* ⟦< L *species,* kind⟧ **1** an aromatic vegetable substance, as nutmeg or pepper, used to season food **2** that which adds zest or interest —*vt.* **spiced, spic′ing** **1** to season with spice **2** to add zest to —**spic′y,** *-i·er, -i·est adj.*

**spick-and-span** (spik′′n span′) *adj.* ⟦< *spike,* nail + ON *spānn,* a chip⟧ **1** new or fresh **2** neat and clean

**spic·ule** (spik′yōōl′) *n.* ⟦< L *spica,* a point⟧ a hard, needlelike part

**spi·der** (spī'dər) *n.* ⟦< OE *spinnan,* to spin⟧ any of various arachnids that spin webs

**spi'der·y** *adj.* like a spider

**spiel** (spēl) *n.* ⟦Ger, play⟧ [Slang] a talk or harangue, as in selling

**spiff·y** (spif'ē) *adj.* **-i·er, -i·est** ⟦< dial. *spiff,* well-dressed person⟧ [Slang] spruce, smart, or dapper

**spig·ot** (spig'ət) *n.* ⟦ME *spigote*⟧ **1** a plug to stop the vent in a barrel, etc. **2** a faucet

**spike**[1] (spīk) *n.* ⟦< ON *spīkr* or MDu *spīker*⟧ **1** a long, heavy nail **2** a sharp-pointed projection, as on the sole of a shoe to prevent slipping —*vt.* **spiked, spik'ing** **1** to fasten or fit as with spikes **2** to pierce with, or impale on, a spike **3** to thwart (a scheme, etc.) **4** [Slang] to add alcoholic liquor to (a drink) —*vi.* to rise suddenly and rapidly

**spike**[2] (spīk) *n.* ⟦L *spica*⟧ **1** an ear of grain **2** a long flower cluster

**spill** (spil) *vt.* **spilled** or **spilt** (spilt), **spill'ing** ⟦OE *spillan,* destroy⟧ **1** to allow or cause, esp. unintentionally, to run, scatter, or flow over from a container **2** to shed (blood) **3** to throw off (a rider, etc.) **4** [Inf.] to let (a secret) become known —*vi.* to be spilled; overflow —*n.* **1** a spilling **2** a fall or tumble —**spill'age** *n.*

**spill'way'** *n.* a channel to carry off excess water, as around a dam

**spin** (spin) *vt.* **spun, spin'ning** ⟦OE *spinnan*⟧ **1** *a*) to draw out and twist fibers of (wool, cotton, etc.) into thread *b*) to make (thread, etc.) thus **2** to make (a web, cocoon, etc.), as a spider does **3** to draw *out* (a story) to a great length **4** to rotate swiftly —*vi.* **1** to spin thread or yarn **2** to form a web, cocoon, etc. **3** to whirl **4** to seem to be spinning from dizziness **5** to move along swiftly and smoothly —*n.* **1** a spinning or rotating movement **2** a ride in a motor vehicle **3** a descent of an airplane, nose first along a spiral path **4** a particular emphasis or slant given to news, etc. — **spin off** to produce as an outgrowth or secondary development, etc. —**spin'ner** *n.*

**spi·na bi·fi·da** (spī'nə bif'i də) a congenital defect in which part of the spinal column is exposed, causing paralysis, etc.

**spin·ach** (spin'ich) *n.* ⟦ult. < Pers *aspanākh*⟧ **1** a plant with dark-green, juicy, edible leaves **2** these leaves

**spi·nal** (spī'nəl) *adj.* of or having to do with the spine or spinal cord —*n.* a spinal anesthetic

**spinal column** the series of joined vertebrae forming the axial support for the skeleton; spine; backbone

**spinal cord** the thick cord of nerve tissue in the spinal column

**spin·dle** (spin'dəl) *n.* ⟦< OE *spinnan,* to spin⟧ **1** a slender rod used in spinning for twisting, winding, or holding thread **2** a spindlelike thing **3** any rod or pin that revolves or serves as an axis for a revolving part

**spin·dly** (spind'lē) *adj.* **-dli·er, -dli·est** long or tall and very thin

**spin doctor** [Slang] a person employed as by a politician to use spin in presenting information in a favorable light

**spine** (spīn) *n.* ⟦< L *spina,* thorn⟧ **1** *a*) a sharp, stiff projection, as on a cactus *b*) anything like this **2** *a*) SPINAL COLUMN *b*) anything like this, as the back of a book —**spin'y, -i·er, -i·est,** *adj.*

SPINAL COLUMN

**spine'less** *adj.* **1** having no spine or spines **2** lacking courage or willpower

**spin·et** (spin'it) *n.* ⟦< It *spinetta*⟧ a small upright piano

**spine'-tin'gling** *adj.* very thrilling, terrifying, etc.

---

**spin·ner·et** (spin'ə ret') *n.* the organ in spiders, caterpillars, etc., that spins thread for webs or cocoons

**spinning wheel** a simple machine for spinning thread with a spindle driven by a large wheel spun as by a treadle

**spin·off** (spin'ôf') *n.* a secondary benefit, product, development, etc.

**spin·ster** (spin'stər) *n.* ⟦ME < *spinnen,* to spin⟧ an unmarried woman, esp. an elderly one — **spin'ster·hood'** *n.*

**spiny lobster** a type of lobster with a spiny shell and no pincers

**spi·ra·cle** (spir'ə kəl) *n.* ⟦< L < *spirare,* breathe⟧ an opening for breathing, as on the sides of an insect's body or on the top of a whale's head

**spi·ral** (spī'rəl) *adj.* ⟦< Gr *speira,* a coil⟧ circling around a point in constantly increasing (or decreasing) curves, or in constantly changing planes —*n.* **1** a spiral curve, coil, path, etc. **2** a continuous, widening decrease or increase *[an inflationary spiral]* —*vi., vt.* **-raled** or **-ralled, -ral·ing** or **-ral·ling** to move in or form a spiral

**spire** (spīr) *n.* ⟦OE *spir*⟧ **1** the top part of a pointed, tapering object **2** anything tapering to a point, as a steeple

**spi·re·a** (spī rē'ə) *n.* ⟦< Gr *speira,* a coil⟧ a plant of the rose family, with dense clusters of small, pink or white flowers: also sp. **spi·rae'a**

**spir·it** (spir'it) *n.* ⟦< L *spirare,* breathe⟧ **1** *a*) the life principle, esp. in human beings *b*) SOUL (sense 1) **2** [*also* S-] life, will, thought, etc., regarded as separate from matter **3** a supernatural being, as a ghost or angel **4** an individual *[a brave spirit]* **5** [*usually pl.*] disposition; mood *[high spirits]* **6** vivacity, courage, etc. **7** enthusiastic loyalty *[school spirit]* **8** real meaning *[the spirit of the law]* **9** a pervading animating principle or characteristic quality *[the spirit of the times]* **10** [*usually pl.*] distilled alcoholic liquor — *vt.* to carry (*away, off,* etc.) secretly and swiftly — **spir'it·less** *adj.*

**spir·it·ed** *adj.* lively; animated

**spir·it·u·al** (spir'i choo əl) *adj.* **1** of the spirit or the soul **2** of or consisting of spirit; not corporeal **3** of religion; sacred —*n.* a folk hymn, specif. one originating among S U.S. blacks —**spir'it·u·al'i·ty** (-al'ə tē) *n.* —**spir'it·u·al·ly** *adv.*

**spir·it·u·al·ism'** *n.* the belief that the dead survive as spirits that can communicate with the living —**spir'it·u·al·ist** *n.* —**spir'it·u·al·is'tic** *adj.*

**spir·it·u·ous** (spir'i choo əs) *adj.* of or containing distilled alcohol

**spi·ro·chete** (spī'rō kēt') *n.* ⟦< Gr *speira,* a coil + *chaitē,* hair⟧ any of various spiral-shaped bacteria

**spit**[1] (spit) *n.* ⟦OE *spitu*⟧ **1** a thin, pointed rod on which meat is roasted over a fire, etc. **2** a narrow point of land extending into the water —*vt.* **spit'ted, spit'ting** to fix as on a spit

**spit**[2] (spit) *vt.* **spit** or **spat, spit'ting** ⟦OE *spittan*⟧ **1** to eject from the mouth **2** to eject explosively — *vi.* to eject saliva from the mouth —*n.* **1** a spitting **2** saliva —**spit and image** [Inf.] perfect likeness: also **spitting image**

**spit'ball'** *n.* **1** paper chewed up into a wad for throwing **2** *Baseball* a pitch, now illegal, made to curve by wetting one side of the ball as with spit

**spite** (spīt) *n.* ⟦see DESPITE⟧ ill will; malice —*vt.* **spit'ed, spit'ing** to vent one's spite upon by hurting, frustrating, etc. —**in spite of** regardless of — **spite'ful** *adj.*

**spit'fire'** *n.* a woman or girl easily aroused to violent anger

**spit·tle** (spit''l) *n.* saliva; spit

**spit·toon** (spi toon') *n.* a container to spit into

**splash** (splash) *vt.* ⟦echoic⟧ **1** to cause (a liquid) to scatter **2** to dash a liquid, mud, etc. on, so as to wet or soil —*vi.* to move, strike, etc. with a splash

—*n.* **1** a splashing **2** a spot made by splashing — **make a splash** [Inf.] to attract great attention

**splash'down'** *n.* a spacecraft's soft landing on the sea

**splash'y** *adj.* **-i·er, -i·est 1** splashing or apt to splash; wet, muddy, etc. **2** [Inf.] spectacular — **splash'i·ly** *adv.* —**splash'i·ness** *n.*

**splat**[1] (splat) *n.* ⟦< SPLIT⟧ a thin slat of wood, as in a chair back

**splat**[2] (splat) *n., interj.* ⟦echoic⟧ (used to suggest) a splattering or wet, slapping sound —*vi.* **1** to make such a sound **2** to flatten on impact

**splat·ter** (splat'ər) *n., vt., vi.* spatter or splash

**splay** (splā) *vt., vi.* ⟦ME *splaien*⟧ to spread out or apart: often with *out* —*adj.* spreading outward

**splay'foot'** *n., pl.* **-feet'** a foot that is flat and turned outward —**splay'foot'ed** *adj.*

**spleen** (splēn) *n.* ⟦< Gr *splēn*⟧ **1** a large lymphatic organ in the upper left part of the abdomen: it modifies the blood structure **2** malice; spite

**splen·did** (splen'did) *adj.* ⟦< L *splendere*, to shine⟧ **1** shining; brilliant **2** magnificent; gorgeous **3** grand; illustrious **4** [Inf.] very good; fine —**splen'did·ly** *adv.*

**splen·dor** (splen'dər) *n.* ⟦see prec.⟧ **1** great luster; brilliance **2** pomp; grandeur Brit. sp. **splen'dour**

**sple·net·ic** (spli net'ik) *adj.* **1** of the spleen **2** bad-tempered; irritable

**splice** (splīs) *vt.* **spliced, splic'ing** ⟦MDu *splissen*⟧ **1** to join (ropes) by weaving together the end strands **2** to join the ends of (timbers) by overlapping **3** to fasten the ends of (wire, film, etc.) together, as by soldering or twisting —*n.* a joint made by splicing —**splic'er** *n.*

**splint** (splint) *n.* ⟦prob. < MDu *splinte*⟧ **1** a thin strip of wood, etc. woven with others to make baskets, etc. **2**

SHORT
SPLICE

EYE
SPLICE

a thin, rigid strip of wood, etc. used to hold a broken bone in place

**splin·ter** (splint'ər) *vt., vi.* ⟦see prec.⟧ to break or split into thin, sharp pieces —*n.* a thin, sharp piece, as of wood, made by splitting, etc.; sliver

**split** (split) *vt., vi.* **split, split'ting** ⟦MDu *splitten*⟧ **1** to separate lengthwise into two or more parts **2** to break or tear apart **3** to divide into shares **4** to disunite **5** *a*) to break (a molecule) into atoms *b*) to produce nuclear fission in (an atom) **6** *Finance* to divide (stock) by converting each share into two for more shares with the same overall value —*n.* **1** a splitting **2** a break; crack **3** a division in a group, etc. **4** [*often pl.*] the feat of spreading the legs apart on the floor until they lie flat —*adj.* divided; separated

**split'-lev'el** *adj.* having floor levels staggered about a half story apart

**split pea** a green or yellow pea shelled, dried, and split: used esp. for soup

**split'ting** *adj.* severe, as a headache

**splotch** (spläch) *n.* ⟦prob. < SPOT + BLOTCH⟧ an irregular spot, splash, or stain —*vt., vi.* to mark or be marked with splotches —**splotch'y, -i·er, -i·est,** *adj.*

**splurge** (splurj) [Inf.] *n.* ⟦echoic⟧ a spell of extravagant spending —*vi.* **splurged, splurg'ing** to spend money freely

**splut·ter** (splut'ər) *vi.* ⟦var. of SPUTTER⟧ **1** to make hissing or spitting sounds **2** to speak hurriedly and confusedly —*n.* a spluttering

**spoil** (spoil) *vt.* **spoiled** or [Brit.] **spoilt, spoil'ing** ⟦< L *spolium*, plunder⟧ **1** to damage so as to make useless, etc. **2** to impair the enjoyment, etc.

of **3** to cause to expect too much by overindulgence —*vi.* to become spoiled; decay, etc., as food does —*n.* [*usually pl.*] plunder; booty —**spoil'age** *n.* —**spoil'er** *n.*

**spoil'sport'** *n.* one whose actions ruin the pleasure of others

**spoils system** the treating of public offices as the booty of a successful political party

**Spo·kane** (spō kan') city in E Washington: pop. 177,000

**spoke**[1] (spōk) *n.* ⟦OE *spaca*⟧ any of the braces or bars extending from the hub to the rim of a wheel

**spoke**[2] (spōk) *vi., vt. pt. & archaic pp.* of SPEAK

**spo·ken** (spō'kən) *vi., vt. pp.* of SPEAK —*adj.* **1** uttered; oral **2** having a (specified) kind of voice [*soft-spoken*]

**spokes·man** (spōks'mən) *n., pl.* **-men** (-mən) one who speaks for another or for a group — **spokes'wom'an,** *pl.* **-wom'en,** *fem.n.*

**spokes'per'son** SPOKESMAN: used to avoid the masculine implication of *spokesman*

**spo·li·a·tion** (spō'lē ā'shən) *n.* ⟦< L *spoliatio*⟧ robbery; plundering

**sponge** (spunj) *n.* ⟦< Gr *spongia*⟧ **1** a stationary aquatic animal with a porous structure **2** the highly absorbent skeleton of such animals, used for washing surfaces, etc. **3** any substance like this, as a piece of light, porous rubber, etc. —*vt.* **sponged, spong'ing 1** to dampen, wipe, absorb, etc. as with a sponge **2** [Inf.] to get as by begging, imposition, etc. —*vi.* [Inf.] to live as a parasite upon other people —**spong'er** *n.* —**spon'gy, -gi·er, -gi·est,** *adj.*

**sponge bath** a bath taken by using a wet sponge or cloth without getting into water

**sponge'cake'** *n.* a light, spongy cake without shortening: also **sponge cake**

**spon·sor** (spän'sər) *n.* ⟦L < *spondere*, promise solemnly⟧ **1** one who assumes responsibility for something; proponent, underwriter, endorser, etc. **2** a godparent **3** a business firm, etc. that pays for a radio or TV program advertising its product —*vt.* to act as sponsor for —**spon'sor·ship'** *n.*

**spon·ta·ne·i·ty** (spän'tə nē'ə tē, -nā'-) *n.* **1** a being spontaneous **2** *pl.* **-ties** spontaneous behavior, action, etc.

**spon·ta·ne·ous** (spän tā'nē əs) *adj.* ⟦< L *sponte*, of free will⟧ **1** acting or resulting from a natural feeling or impulse, without constraint, effort, etc. **2** occurring through internal causes

**spontaneous combustion** the process of catching fire through heat generated by internal chemical action

**spoof** (spōof) *n.* **1** a hoax or joke **2** a light satire —*vt., vi.* **1** to fool; deceive **2** to satirize playfully

**spook** (spōok) [Inf.] *n.* ⟦Du⟧ a ghost —*vt., vi.* to frighten or become frightened

**spook'y** *adj.* **-i·er, -i·est** [Inf.] **1** weird; eerie **2** easily frightened; nervous, jumpy, etc.

**spool** (spōol) *n.* ⟦< MDu *spoele*⟧ **1** a cylinder on which thread, wire, etc. is wound **2** the material wound on a spool

**spoon** (spōon) *n.* ⟦< OE *spon*, a chip⟧ **1** a utensil consisting of a small, shallow bowl and a handle, used for eating, stirring, etc. **2** something shaped like a spoon, as a shiny, curved fishing lure —*vt.* to take up with a spoon —**spoon'ful',** *pl.* **-fuls',** *n.*

**spoon'bill'** *n.* a wading bird whose flat bill is spoon-shaped at the tip

**spoon·er·ism** (spōon'ər iz'əm) *n.* ⟦after Rev. W. A. *Spooner* (1844-1930), of England, who made such slips⟧ an unintentional interchange of the initial sounds of words (Ex.: "a well-boiled icicle" for "a well-oiled bicycle")

**spoon'-feed'** *vt.* **-fed', -feed'ing 1** to feed with a spoon **2** to pamper; coddle

**spoor** (spoor) *n.* ⟦Afrik⟧ the track or trail of a wild animal

**spo·rad·ic** (spə rad'ik) *adj.* ⟦< Gr *sporas*, scattered⟧ happening or appearing in isolated instances [*sporadic* storms] —**spo·rad'i·cal·ly** *adv.*

**spore** (spôr) *n.* ⟦< Gr *spora*, a seed⟧ a small reproductive body produced by algae, ferns, etc. and capable of giving rise to a new individual

**sport** (spôrt) *n.* ⟦< DISPORT⟧ **1** any recreational activity; specif., a game, competition, etc. requiring bodily exertion **2** fun or play **3** [Inf.] a sportsmanlike person **4** [Inf.] a showy, flashy fellow **5** *Biol.* a plant or animal markedly different from the normal type —*vt.* [Inf.] to display [to *sport* a loud tie] —*vi.* to play —*adj.* **1** of or for sports **2** suitable for casual wear [a *sport* coat] Also, for adj., **sports** —**in** (or **for**) **sport** in jest —**make sport of** to mock or ridicule

**sport'ing** *adj.* **1** of or interested in sports **2** sportsmanlike; fair **3** of games, races, etc. involving gambling or betting

**spor·tive** (spôrt'iv) *adj.* **1** full of sport or fun **2** done in fun —**spor'tive·ly** *adv.*

**sports car** a small car characterized by above-average speed and handling

**sports'cast'** *n.* a broadcast of sports news on radio or TV —**sports'cast·er** *n.*

**sports'man** (-mən) *n., pl.* **-men** (-mən) **1** a man who takes part in sports, esp. hunting, fishing, etc. **2** one who plays fair and can lose without complaint or win without gloating —**sports'man·like'** *adj.* —**sports'man·ship'** *n.*

**sport utility vehicle** a vehicle like a station wagon, but with a small-truck chassis and, usually, four-wheel drive

**sport'y** *adj.* **-i·er, -i·est** [Inf.] **1** sporting or sportsmanlike **2** flashy or showy —**sport'i·ness** *n.*

**spot** (spät) *n.* ⟦prob. < MDu *spotte*⟧ **1** *a*) a small area differing in color, etc. from the surrounding area *b*) a stain, speck, etc. **2** a flaw or defect **3** a locality; place —*vt.* **spot'ted, spot'ting 1** to mark with spots **2** to stain; blemish **3** to place; locate **4** to see; recognize **5** [Inf.] to allow as a handicap [to *spot* an opponent points] —*vi.* **1** to become marked with spots **2** to make a stain —*adj.* **1** ready [*spot* cash] **2** made at random [a *spot* survey] —**hit the spot** [Inf.] to satisfy a craving or need —**in a** (**bad**) **spot** [Slang] in trouble —**on the spot** [Slang] in a bad or demanding situation —**spot'less** *adj.* —**spot'less·ly** *adv.* —**spot'ted** *adj.*

**spot'-check'** *vt.* to check or examine at random or by sampling —*n.* such a checking

**spot'light'** *n.* **1** *a*) a strong beam of light focused on a particular person, thing, etc. *b*) a lamp used to project such a beam **2** public notice or prominence —*vt.* to light or draw attention to, by or as by a spotlight

**spot'ty** *adj.* **-ti·er, -ti·est 1** having, occurring in, or marked with spots **2** not uniform or consistent —**spot'ti·ly** *adv.*

**spouse** (spous) *n.* ⟦< L *sponsus*, betrothed⟧ (one's) husband or wife —**spous·al** (spou'zəl) *adj.*

**spout** (spout) *n.* ⟦< ME *spouten*, to spout⟧ **1** a lip, orifice, or projecting tube by which a liquid is poured or discharged **2** a stream, etc. as of liquid from a spout —*vt., vi.* **1** to shoot out (liquid, etc.) as from a spout **2** to speak or utter (words, etc.) in a loud, pompous manner

**sprain** (sprān) *vt.* ⟦< ? L *ex-*, out + *premere*, to press⟧ to wrench a ligament or muscle of (a joint) without dislocating the bones —*n.* an injury resulting from this

**sprang** (spraŋ) *vi., vt. alt. pt.* of SPRING

**sprat** (sprat) *n.* ⟦OE *sprott*⟧ a small European herring

**sprawl** (sprôl) *vi.* ⟦< OE *spreawlian*, move convulsively⟧ **1** to sit or lie with the limbs in a relaxed or awkward position **2** to spread out awkwardly or unevenly —*n.* **1** a sprawling movement or position **2** the uncontrolled spread of real-estate development into areas around a city

**spray**[1] (sprā) *n.* ⟦prob. < MDu *spraeien*⟧ **1** a mist of fine liquid particles **2** *a*) a jet of such particles, as from a spray gun *b*) a device for spraying something likened to a spray —*vt., vi.* **1** to direct a spray (on) **2** to shoot out in a spray —**spray'er** *n.*

---

**467**　　　　　　　　◄ **spritz**

**spray**[2] (sprā) *n.* ⟦ME⟧ a small branch of a tree or plant, with leaves, flowers, etc.

**spray can** a can from which gas under pressure sprays out the contents

**spray gun** a device that shoots out a spray of liquid, as paint or insecticide

**spread** (spred) *vt., vi.* **spread, spread'ing** ⟦OE *sprædan*⟧ **1** to open or stretch out; unfold **2** to move (the fingers, wings, etc.) apart **3** to distribute or be distributed over an area or surface **4** to extend in time **5** to make or be made widely known, felt, etc. **6** to set (a table) for a meal **7** to push or be pushed apart —*n.* **1** the act or extent of spreading **2** an expanse **3** a cloth cover for a table, bed, etc. **4** jam, butter, etc. used on bread **5** [Inf.] a meal with many different foods —**spread'er** *n.*

**spread'-ea'gle** *adj.* having the figure of an eagle with wings and legs spread —*vt.* **-gled, -gling** to stretch out in this form, as for a flogging

**spread'sheet'** *n.* a computer program that organizes numerical data into rows and columns on a video screen

**spree** (sprē) *n.* ⟦< earlier *spray*⟧ **1** a noisy frolic **2** a period of drunkenness **3** a period of uninhibited activity [a shopping *spree*]

**sprig** (sprig) *n.* ⟦ME *sprigge*⟧ a little twig or spray

**spright·ly** (sprīt'lē) *adj.* **-li·er, -li·est** ⟦< *spright*, var. of SPRITE⟧ full of energy and spirit; lively —*adv.* in a sprightly manner —**spright'li·ness** *n.*

**spring** (spriŋ) *vi.* **sprang** or **sprung, sprung, spring'ing** ⟦OE *springan*⟧ **1** to leap; bound **2** to come, appear, etc. suddenly **3** to bounce **4** to arise as from some source; grow or develop **5** to become warped, split, etc. Often followed by *up* —*vt.* **1** to cause (a trap, etc.) to snap shut **2** to cause to warp, split, etc. **3** to make known suddenly

SPRINGS

**4** [Slang] to get (someone) released from jail —*n.* **1** a leap, or the distance so covered **2** elasticity; resilience **3** a device, as a coil of wire, that returns to its original form after being forced out of shape **4** a flow of water from the ground **5** *a*) a source or origin **6** *a*) the season of the year following winter, when plants begin to grow *b*) any period of beginning —*adj.* **1** of, for, appearing in, or planted in the spring **2** having, or supported on, springs **3** coming from a spring [*spring* water] —**spring a leak** to begin unexpectedly to leak —**spring for** [Inf.] to bear the cost of for someone else

**spring'board'** *n.* a springy board used as a takeoff in leaping or diving

**spring fever** the laziness or restlessness that many people feel in the early days of spring

**Spring·field** (spriŋ'fēld') **1** city in SW Missouri: pop. 140,000 **2** capital of Illinois: pop. 105,000

**spring'time'** *n.* the season of spring

**spring'y** *adj.* **-i·er, -i·est** having spring; elastic, resilient, etc. —**spring'i·ness** *n.*

**sprin·kle** (spriŋ'kəl) *vt., vi.* **-kled, -kling** ⟦ME *sprinklen*⟧ **1** to scatter or fall in drops or particles **2** to scatter drops or particles (upon) **3** to rain lightly —*n.* **1** a sprinkling **2** a light rain —**sprin'kler** *n.*

**sprin'kling** (-kliŋ) *n.* a small number or amount, esp. when scattered thinly

**sprint** (sprint) *vi., n.* ⟦ME *sprenten*⟧ run or race at full speed for a short distance —**sprint'er** *n.*

**sprite** (sprīt) *n.* ⟦< L *spiritus*, spirit⟧ *Folklore* an imaginary being, as an elf

**spritz** (sprits, shprits) *vt., vi., n.* ⟦< Ger *spritzen* & Yiddish *shprits*⟧ squirt or spray

**spritz′er** *n.* a drink consisting of white wine and soda water

**sprock·et** (spräk′it) *n.* ⟦< ?⟧ **1** any of the teeth, as on the rim of a wheel, arranged to fit the links of a chain **2** a wheel fitted with such teeth: in full **sprocket wheel**

**sprout** (sprout) *vi.* ⟦OE *sprutan*⟧ to begin to grow; give off shoots —*vt.* to cause to sprout or grow — *n.* **1** a young growth on a plant; shoot **2** a new growth from a bud, etc. **3** a new growth from a seed of alfalfa, etc., used as in salads

**spruce**[1] (sprōōs) *n.* ⟦ME *Spruce*, Prussia⟧ **1** an evergreen tree with slender needles **2** its wood

**spruce**[2] (sprōōs) *adj.* spruc′er, spruc′est ⟦< *Spruce leather* (see prec.)⟧ neat and trim in a smart way —*vt.*, *vi.* spruced, spruc′ing to make (oneself) spruce: usually with *up*

**sprung** (spruŋ) *vi.*, *vt. pp.* & *alt. pt. of* SPRING

**spry** (sprī) *adj.* spri′er or spry′er, spri′est or spry′est ⟦< Scand⟧ full of life; active, esp. though elderly —spry′ly *adv.* —spry′ness *n.*

**spud** (spud) *n.* [Inf.] a potato

**spume** (spyōōm) *n.* ⟦< L *spuma*⟧ foam, froth, or scum —*vi.* spumed, spum′ing to foam; froth

**spu·mo·ni** (spə mō′nē) *n.* ⟦It < L *spuma*, foam⟧ Italian ice cream in variously flavored and colored layers

**spun** (spun) *vt.*, *vi. pt.* & *pp. of* SPIN

**spunk** (spuŋk) *n.* ⟦Ir *sponc*, tinder⟧ [Inf.] courage; spirit —spunk′y, -i·er, -i·est, *adj.*

**spur** (spur) *n.* ⟦OE *spura*⟧ **1** a pointed device worn on the heel by a rider, used to urge a horse forward **2** anything that urges; stimulus **3** any spurlike projection **4** a short railroad track connected with the main track —*vt.* spurred, spur′ring **1** to prick with spurs **2** to urge or incite —on the spur of the moment abruptly and impulsively

**spurge** (spurj) *n.* ⟦< earlier Fr *espurger*, to purge⟧ any of a group of plants with milky juice and tiny flowers

**spu·ri·ous** (spyoor′ē əs, spur′-) *adj.* ⟦L *spurius*, illegitimate⟧ not genuine; false —spu′ri·ous·ly *adv.* —spu′ri·ous·ness *n.*

**spurn** (spurn) *vt.* ⟦OE *spurnan*⟧ to reject with contempt; scorn

**spurt** (spurt) *vt.* ⟦prob. < OE *sprutan*, to sprout⟧ to expel in a stream or jet —*vi.* **1** to gush forth in a stream or jet **2** to show a sudden, brief burst of energy, etc. —*n.* **1** a sudden shooting forth; jet **2** a sudden, brief burst of energy, etc.

**sput·nik** (spoot′nik, sput′-) *n.* ⟦Russ., lit., co-traveler⟧ any of a series of man-made satellites launched by the U.S.S.R. starting in 1957

**sput·ter** (sput′ər) *vi.*, *vt.* ⟦< MDu *spotten*, to spit⟧ **1** to spit out (bits, drops, etc.) explosively, as when talking excitedly **2** to speak or utter in a confused, explosive way **3** to make sharp, sizzling sounds, as frying fat does —*n.* a sputtering

**spu·tum** (spyōōt′əm) *n.*, *pl.* -ta (-ə) ⟦< L *spuere*, to spit⟧ saliva, usually mixed with mucus, ejected from the mouth

**spy** (spī) *vt.* spied, spy′ing ⟦< OHG *spehōn*, examine⟧ **1** to watch closely and secretly: often with *out* **2** to catch sight of; see —*vi.* to watch closely and secretly; act as a spy —*n.*, *pl.* spies **1** one who keeps close and secret watch on others **2** one employed by a government to get secret information about another government

**spy′glass′** *n.* a small telescope

**sq** *abbrev.* **1** sequence **2** squadron **3** square

**sqq.** *abbrev.* ⟦L *sequentes; sequentia*⟧ the following ones; what follows

**squab** (skwäb) *n.* ⟦prob. < Scand⟧ a nestling pigeon

**squab·ble** (skwäb′əl) *vi.* -bled, -bling ⟦< Scand⟧ to quarrel noisily over a small matter; wrangle —*n.* a noisy, petty quarrel —squab′bler *n.*

**squad** (skwäd) *n.* ⟦< Sp *escuadra* or It *squadra*, a square⟧ **1** a small group of soldiers, often a sub-division of a platoon **2** any small group of people working together

**squad car** PATROL CAR

**squad′ron** (-rən) *n.* ⟦< It *squadra*, a square⟧ a unit of warships, military aircraft, etc.

**squal·id** (skwäl′id, skwôl′id) *adj.* ⟦< L *squalere*, be foul⟧ **1** foul or unclean **2** wretched

**squall**[1] (skwôl) *n.* ⟦< Scand⟧ a brief, violent windstorm, usually with rain or snow —squall′y, -i·er, -i·est, *adj.*

**squall**[2] (skwôl) *vi.*, *vt.* ⟦< ON *skvala*⟧ to cry or scream loudly and harshly —*n.* a harsh cry or loud scream

**squal·or** (skwäl′ər, skwôl′ər) *n.* a being squalid; filth and wretchedness

**squa·mous** (skwā′məs) *adj.* ⟦< L *squama*, a scale⟧ like, formed of, or covered with scales

**squan·der** (skwän′dər) *vt.* ⟦prob. < dial. *squander*, to scatter⟧ to spend or use wastefully or extravagantly

COMBINATION SQUARE

TRY SQUARE

CARPENTER'S SQUARE

**square** (skwer) *n.* ⟦< L *ex*, out + *quadrare*, to square⟧ **1** *a*) a plane figure having four equal sides and four right angles *b*) anything of or approximating this shape **2** an open area bounded by several streets, used as a park, etc. **3** an instrument for drawing or testing right angles **4** the product of a number multiplied by itself **5** [Slang] a person who is SQUARE (*adj.* 10) —*vt.* squared, squar′ing **1** to make square **2** to make straight, even, right-angled, etc. **3** to settle; adjust [to *square* accounts] **4** to make conform [to *square* a statement with the facts] **5** to multiply (a quantity) by itself —*vi.* to fit; agree; accord (*with*) —*adj.* squar′er, squar′est **1** having four equal sides and four right angles **2** forming a right angle **3** straight, level, even, etc. **4** leaving no balance; even **5** just; fair **6** direct; straightforward **7** designating a unit of surface measure in the form of a square [a *square* foot] **8** sturdy and somewhat rectangular [a *square* jaw] **9** [Inf.] substantial [a *square* meal] **10** [Slang] old-fashioned, unsophisticated, etc. —*adv.* in a square manner —square off to assume a posture of attack or self-defense —square oneself [Inf.] to make amends —square′ly *adv.* —square′ness *n.* —squar′ish *adj.*

**square dance** a dance with various steps, in which couples are grouped in a given form, as a square —square′-dance′, -danced′, -danc′ing, *vi.*

**square′-rigged′** *adj.* rigged with square sails as the principal sails

**square root** the number or quantity which when squared will produce a given number or quantity [3 is the *square root of 9*]

**squash**[1] (skwôsh, skwäsh) *vt.* ⟦< L *ex*-, intens. + *quatere*, to shake⟧ **1** to crush into a soft or flat mass; press **2** to suppress; quash —*vi.* **1** to be squashed **2** to make a sound of squashing —*n.* **1** the act or sound of squashing **2** a game played in a walled court with rackets and a rubber ball — squash′y, -i·er, -i·est, *adj.*

**squash**[2] (skwôsh, skwäsh) *n.* ⟦< AmInd⟧ the fleshy fruit of various plants of the gourd family, eaten as a vegetable

**squat** (skwät) *vi.* squat′ted, squat′ting ⟦ult. < L

*ex-*, intens. + *cogere*, to force]] **1** to crouch so as to sit on the heels with knees bent and weight resting on the balls of the feet **2** to crouch close to the ground **3** to settle on land without right or title **4** to settle on public land in order to get title to it —*adj.* **-ter, -test** short and heavy or thick: also **squat′ty, -ti·er, -ti·est** —*n.* the act or position of squatting —**squat′ness** *n.* —**squat′ter** *n.*

**squaw** (skwô) *n.* [[< AmInd]] [Now Rare] a North American Indian woman or wife: term now considered offensive

**squawk** (skwôk) *vi.* [echoic]] **1** to utter a loud, harsh cry **2** [Inf.] to complain loudly —*n.* **1** a loud, harsh cry **2** [Inf.] a loud complaint

**squeak** (skwēk) *vi.* [ME *squeken*]] to make or utter a sharp, high-pitched sound or cry —*vt.* to say in a squeak —*n.* a thin, sharp sound or cry —**narrow** (or **close**) **squeak** [Inf.] a narrow escape —**squeak through** (or **by**, etc.) [Inf.] to succeed, survive, etc. with difficulty —**squeak′y, -i·er, -i·est,** *adj.*

**squeak′er** *n.* [Inf.] a narrow escape, victory, etc.

**squeal** (skwēl) *vi.* [ME *squelen*]] **1** to utter or make a long, shrill cry or sound **2** [Slang] to act as an informer —*vt.* to utter in a squeal —*n.* a squealing —**squeal′er** *n.*

**squeam·ish** (skwē′mish) *adj.* [ME *squaimous*]] **1** easily nauseated **2** easily shocked **3** fastidious —**squeam′ish·ly** *adv.* —**squeam′ish·ness** *n.*

**squee·gee** (skwē′jē) *n.* [prob. < fol.]] a rubber-edged tool for scraping water from a flat surface

**squeeze** (skwēz) *vt.* **squeezed, squeez′ing** [[< OE *cwysan*]] **1** to press hard, esp. from two or more sides **2** to extract (juice, etc.) from (fruit, etc.) **3** to force (*into, out,* etc.) by pressing **4** to embrace closely; hug —*vi.* **1** to yield to pressure **2** to exert pressure **3** to force one's way by pushing (*in, out,* etc.) —*n.* **1** a squeezing or being squeezed **2** a close embrace; hug **3** the state of being closely pressed or packed; crush **4** a period of scarcity, hardship, etc.

SQUEEGEE

**squeeze bottle** a plastic bottle that is squeezed to eject its contents

**squelch** (skwelch) [Inf.] *n.* [prob. echoic]] a crushing retort, rebuke, etc. —*vt.* to suppress or silence completely

**squib** (skwib) *n.* [prob. echoic]] **1** a firecracker that burns with a hissing noise before exploding **2** a short, witty attack in words; lampoon **3** a short news item

SQUID

**squid** (skwid) *n.* [prob. < *squit,* dial. for SQUIRT]] a long, slender sea mollusk with eight arms and two long tentacles

**squig·gle** (skwig′əl) *n.* [SQU(IRM) + (W)IGGLE]] a short, wavy line or illegible scrawl —*vt., vi.* **-gled, -gling** to write as, or make, a squiggle or squiggles

**squint** (skwint) *vi.* [< (*a*)*squint,* with a squint < ME *on skwyn,* sideways]] **1** to peer with the eyes partly closed **2** to be cross-eyed —*n.* **1** a squinting **2** a being cross-eyed **3** [Inf.] a quick look

**squire** (skwīr) *n.* [see ESQUIRE]] **1** in England, the owner of a large, rural estate **2** a man escorting a woman —*vt.* **squired, squir′ing** to escort

**squirm** (skwurm) *vi.* [prob. echoic, infl. by WORM]] **1** to twist and turn the body; wriggle **2** to show or feel shame or embarrassment —*n.* a squirming —**squirm′y, -i·er, -i·est,** *adj.*

**squir·rel** (skwur′əl, skwurl) *n.* [[< Gr *skia,* shadow + *oura,* tail]] **1** a small, tree-dwelling rodent with heavy fur and a long, bushy tail **2** its fur

**squirt** (skwurt) *vt.* [prob. < LowG *swirtjen*]] **1** to shoot out (a liquid) in a jet; spurt **2** to wet with liquid so shot out —*n.* **1** a jet of liquid **2** [Inf.] a small or young person, esp. an impudent one

**squish** (skwish) *vi.* [echoic var. of SQUASH[1]]] to make a soft, splashing sound when squeezed, etc. —*vt.* [Inf.] to squash —*n.* **1** a squishing sound **2** [Inf.] a squashing —**squish′y, -i·er, -i·est,** *adj.*

**Sr**[1] *abbrev.* **1** Senior **2** Sister

**Sr**[2] *Chem.* symbol for strontium

**Sri Lan·ka** (srē läŋ′kə) country coextensive with an island off the SE tip of India: 25,332 sq. mi.; pop. 14,847,000 —**Sri Lan′kan**

**SRO** *abbrev.* **1** single room occupancy **2** standing room only

**SS** *abbrev.* **1** Social Security **2** steamship

**SST** *abbrev.* supersonic transport

**St** *abbrev.* **1** Saint **2** Strait **3** Street

**stab** (stab) *n.* [prob. < ME *stubbe,* stub]] **1** a wound made by stabbing **2** a thrust, as with a knife **3** a sudden, sharp pain —*vt., vi.* **stabbed, stab′bing 1** to pierce or wound as with a knife **2** to thrust (a knife, etc.) into something **3** to pain sharply —**make** (or **take**) **a stab at** [Inf.] to make an attempt at

**sta·bil·i·ty** (stə bil′ə tē) *n.* **1** a being stable; steadiness **2** firmness of character, purpose, etc. **3** permanence

**sta·bi·lize** (stā′bə līz′) *vt.* **-lized′, -liz′ing 1** to make stable **2** to keep from changing **3** to give stability to (a plane or ship) —*vi.* to become stabilized —**sta′bi·li·za′tion** *n.* —**sta′bi·liz′er** *n.*

**sta·ble**[1] (stā′bəl) *adj.* **-bler, -blest** [[< L *stare,* to stand]] **1** not likely to give way; firm; fixed **2** firm in character, purpose, etc.; steadfast **3** not likely to change; lasting

**sta·ble**[2] (stā′bəl) *n.* [see prec.]] **1** a building in which horses or cattle are sheltered and fed **2** all the racehorses belonging to one owner —*vt., vi.* **-bled, -bling** to lodge, keep, or be kept in or as in a stable

**stac·ca·to** (stə kät′ō) *adj., adv.* [It < *distaccare,* detach]] *Music* with distinct breaks between successive tones

**stack** (stak) *n.* [[< ON *stakkr*]] **1** a large, neatly arranged pile of straw, hay, etc. **2** any orderly pile **3** SMOKESTACK **4** [*pl.*] a series of bookshelves, as in a library —*vt.* **1** to arrange in a stack **2** to rig so as to predetermine the outcome —**stack up** to stand in comparison (*with* or *against*)

**stack′up′** *n.* an arrangement of circling aircraft at various altitudes awaiting their turn to land

**sta·di·um** (stā′dē əm) *n.* [[< Gr *stadion,* ancient unit of length, *c.* 607 feet]] a large structure as for sports events, with tiers of seats for spectators

**staff** (staf) *n., pl.* **staffs;** also, for 1 & 4, **staves** [[OE *stæf*]] **1** a stick or rod used as a support, a symbol of authority, etc. **2** a group of people assisting a leader **3** a specific group of workers [a teaching *staff]* **4** *Music* the horizontal lines on and between which notes are written —*vt.* to provide with a staff, as of workers

**staff′er** *n.* a member of a staff, as of a newspaper

**stag** (stag) *n.* [OE *stagga*]] a full-grown male deer —*adj.* for men only [a *stag* dinner]

**stage** (stāj) *n.* [[< L *stare,* to stand]] **1** a platform **2** *a)* an area or platform on which plays, etc. are presented *b)* the theater, or acting as a profession (with *the*) **3** the scene of an event **4** a stopping place, or the distance between stops, on a journey **5** *short for* STAGECOACH **6** a period or level in a process of development [the larval *stage]* **7** any of the propulsion units used in sequence to launch a missile, spacecraft, etc. —*vt.* **staged, stag′ing 1** to present as on a stage **2** to plan and carry out [to *stage* an attack]

**stage′coach′** *n.* a horse-drawn public coach that, formerly, traveled a regular route

**stage′hand′** *n.* one who sets up scenery, furniture, lights, etc. for a stage play

**stage′-struck′** *adj.* having an intense desire to become an actor or actress

**stag·ger** (stag′ər) *vi.* [< ON *stakra,* totter] to totter, reel, etc. as from a blow or fatigue —*vt.* **1** to cause to stagger, as with a blow **2** to affect strongly with astonishment, grief, etc. **3** to set or arrange alternately, as on either side of a line; make zigzag **4** to arrange so as to come at different times [to *stagger* employees' vacations] —*n.* **1** a staggering **2** [*pl., with sing. or pl. v.*] a nervous disease of horses, etc. causing this

**stag·nant** (stag′nənt) *adj.* [see fol.] **1** not flowing or moving **2** foul from lack of movement: said of water **3** dull; sluggish

**stag′nate′** (-nāt′) *vi.,* *vt.* -nat′ed, -nat′ing [< L *stagnare*] to become or make stagnant —**stag·na′tion** *n.*

**staid** (stād) *vi.,* *vt. archaic pt. & pp. of* STAY³ —*adj.* sober; sedate —**staid′ly** *adv.*

**stain** (stān) *vt.* [ult. < L *dis-,* from + *tingere,* to tinge] **1** to spoil by discoloring or spotting **2** to disgrace; dishonor **3** to color (wood, etc.) with a dye —*n.* **1** a color or spot resulting from staining **2** a moral blemish **3** a dye for staining wood, etc.

**stain′less steel** steel alloyed with chromium, etc., virtually immune to rust and corrosion

**stair** (ster) *n.* [OE *stæger*] **1** [*usually pl.*] a stairway **2** a single step, as of a stairway

**stair′case′** *n.* a stairway in a building, usually with a handrail

**stair′way′** *n.* a means of access, as from one level of a building to another, consisting of a series of stairs

**stair′well′** *n.* a vertical shaft (in a building) containing a staircase

**stake** (stāk) *n.* [OE *staca*] **1** a pointed length of wood or metal for driving into the ground **2** the post to which a person was tied for execution by burning **3** [*often pl.*] money risked, as in a wager or business venture **4** [*often pl.*] the winner's prize in a race, etc. —*vt.* **staked, stak′ing 1** to mark the boundaries of [to *stake* out a claim] **2** to fasten to a stake or stakes **3** to gamble **4** [Inf.] to furnish with money or resources —**at stake** being risked —**pull up stakes** [Inf.] to change one's residence, etc. —**stake out** to put under police surveillance

**stake′out′** *n.* **1** the putting of a suspect or a place under police surveillance **2** an area under such surveillance

**sta·lac·tite** (stə lak′tīt) *n.* [< Gr *stalaktos,* trickling] an icicle-shaped mineral deposit hanging from a cave roof

**sta·lag** (shtä′läk; *E* stä′läg) *n.* [Ger] a German prisoner-of-war camp, esp. in WWII

**sta·lag·mite** (stə lag′mīt′) *n.* [< Gr *stalagmos,* a dropping] a cone-shaped mineral deposit built up on a cave floor by dripping water

**stale** (stāl) *adj.* **stal′er, stal′est** [prob. < OFr *estale,* quiet] **1** no longer fresh; flat, dry, etc. **2** trite [a *stale* joke] **3** out of condition, bored, etc.

**stale′mate′** *n.* [< OFr *estal,* fixed location] **1** *Chess* any situation in which a player cannot move: it results in a draw **2** any deadlock —*vt.* -mat′ed, -mat′ing to bring into a stalemate

**Sta·lin** (stä′lin), **Joseph** 1879-1953; Soviet premier (1941-53) —**Sta′lin·ism′** *n.* —**Sta′lin·ist** *adj., n.*

**stalk¹** (stôk) *vi., vt.* [OE *stealcian*] **1** to walk (through) in a stiff, haughty manner **2** to advance grimly **3** *a)* to pursue (game, etc.) stealthily *b)* to pursue (a person) in a persistent, harassing, obsessive way —*n.* **1** a slow, stiff, haughty stride **2** a stalking

**stalk²** (stôk) *n.* [ME *stalke*] **1** any stem or stem-like part **2** the main stem of a plant

**stall¹** (stôl) *n.* [OE *steall*] **1** a section for one ani-

mal in a stable **2** *a)* a booth, etc. as at a market *b)* a pew in a church **3** the state of being in a stop or standstill, as a result of some malfunction —*vt., vi.* **1** to keep or be kept in a stall **2** to bring or be brought to a standstill, esp. unintentionally

**stall²** (stôl) *vi., vt.* [< *stall,* a decoy] to act evasively so as to deceive or delay —*n.* any action used in stalling

**stal·lion** (stal′yən) *n.* [< OFr *estalon*] an uncastrated male horse

**stal·wart** (stôl′wərt) *adj.* [< OE *stathol,* foundation + *wyrthe,* worth] **1** strong; sturdy **2** brave; valiant **3** resolute; firm —*n.* a stalwart person

**sta·men** (stā′mən) *n.* [< L, thread] the pollen-bearing organ in a flower

**Stam·ford** (stam′fərd) city in SW Connecticut: pop. 108,000

**stam·i·na** (stam′ə nə) *n.* [L, pl. of STAMEN] resistance to fatigue, illness, hardship, etc.; endurance

**stam·mer** (stam′ər) *vt., vi.* [OE *stamerian*] to speak or say with involuntary pauses and rapid repetitions of some sounds —*n.* a stammering —**stam′mer·er** *n.*

**stamp** (stamp) *vt.* [ME *stampen*] **1** to bring (the foot) down forcibly **2** to crush or pound with the foot **3** to imprint or cut out (a design, etc.) **4** to cut (*out*) by pressing with a die **5** to put a stamp on —*vi.* **1** to bring the foot down forcibly **2** to walk with loud, heavy steps, as in anger —*n.* **1** a stamping **2** *a)* a machine, tool, or die for stamping *b)* a mark or form made by stamping **3** any of various seals, gummed pieces of paper, etc. used to show that a fee, as for postage, has been paid **4** any similar stamp **5** class; kind —**stamp out 1** to crush by treading on forcibly **2** to suppress, or put down —**stamp′er** *n.*

**stam·pede** (stam pēd′) *n.* [< Sp *estampar,* to stamp] a sudden, headlong rush or flight, as of a herd of cattle —*vi.* **-ped′ed, -ped′ing** to move, or take part, in a stampede

**stamping ground** [Inf.] a regular or favorite gathering place: *also used in pl.*

**stance** (stans) *n.* [< L *stare,* to stand] **1** the way one stands, esp. the placement of the feet **2** the attitude taken in a given situation

**stanch** *vt., vi., adj. see* STAUNCH

**stan·chion** (stan′chən) *n.* [see STANCE] **1** an upright post or support **2** a device for confining a cow, fitted loosely around the neck

**stand** (stand) *vi.* **stood, stand′ing** [OE *standan*] **1** to be in, or assume, an upright position on the feet **2** to be supported on a base, pedestal, etc. **3** to take or be in a (specified) position, attitude, etc. **4** to have a (specified) height when standing **5** to be placed or situated **6** to gather and remain: said as of water **7** to remain unchanged **8** to make resistance **9** *a)* to halt *b)* to be stationary —*vt.* **1** to place upright **2** to endure **3** to withstand **4** to undergo [to *stand* trial] —*n.* **1** a standing; esp., a halt or stop **2** a position; station **3** a view, opinion, etc. **4** a structure to stand or sit on **5** a place of business, esp. a stall, etc. where goods are sold **6** a rack, small table, etc. for holding things **7** a growth of trees, etc. —**stand a chance** to have a chance (*of* winning, surviving, etc.) —**stand by 1** to be ready if needed **2** to aid —**stand for 1** to represent; mean **2** [Inf.] to tolerate —**stand on 1** to be founded on **2** to insist upon —**stand out 1** to project **2** to be distinct, prominent, etc. —**stand up 1** to rise to a standing position **2** to prove valid, durable, etc. **3** [Slang] to fail to keep a date with —**take the stand** to testify in court

**stand·ard** (stan′dərd) *n.* [< OFr *estendard*] **1** a flag or banner used as an emblem of a military unit, etc. **2** something established for use as a rule or basis of comparison in measuring quantity, quality, etc. **3** an upright support —*adj.* **1** used as, or conforming to, a standard, rule, model, etc. **2** generally accepted as reliable or authoritative **3** typical; ordinary

**stand′ard-bear′er** *n.* **1** one who carries the flag **2** the leader of a movement, political party, etc.

**stand'ard·ize'** *vt.* **-ized'**, **-iz'ing** to make standard or uniform —**stand'ard·i·za'tion** *n.*

**standard time** the time in any of the 24 time zones, each an hour apart, into which the earth is divided, based on distance east or west of Greenwich, England

**stand'by'** *n., pl.* **-bys'** a person or thing that is dependable or is a possible substitute

**stand·ee** (stan dē') *n.* one who stands, as in a theater or bus

**stand'-in'** *n.* a temporary substitute, as for an actor at rehearsals

**stand'ing** *n.* **1** status or reputation *[in good standing]* **2** duration *[a rule of long standing]* —*adj.* **1** upright or erect **2** from a standing position *[a standing jump]* **3** stagnant: said as of water **4** lasting; permanent *[a standing order]*

**stand'off'** *n.* a tie in a game or contest

**stand'off'ish** *adj.* reserved; aloof

**stand'out'** *n.* [Inf.] a person or thing outstanding in performance, quality, etc.

**stand'pipe'** *n.* a high vertical pipe or cylindrical tank, as in a town's water-supply system, for storing water at a desired pressure

**stand'point'** *n.* point of view

**stand'still'** *n.* a stop or halt

**stand'-up'** *adj.* **1** in a standing position **2** designating a comedian who delivers monologues, tells jokes, etc., as in a nightclub

**stank** (staŋk) *vi. alt. pt. of* STINK

**stan·za** (stan'zə) *n.* [It: ult. < L *stare*, to stand] a group of lines of verse forming a division of a poem or song

**staph** (staf) *n. short for* STAPHYLOCOCCUS

**staph·y·lo·coc·cus** (staf'ə lō kä'kəs) *n., pl.* **-coc'ci** (-käk'sī') [< Gr *staphylē*, bunch of grapes + *kokkos*, kernel] any of certain spherical bacteria, a common source of infection

**sta·ple¹** (stā'pəl) *n.* [< MDu *stapel*, mart] **1** a chief commodity made or grown in a particular place **2** a chief part or element in anything **3** a regularly stocked item of trade, as flour, salt, etc. **4** the fiber of cotton, wool, etc. —*adj.* **1** regularly stocked, produced, or used **2** most important; principal

**sta·ple²** (stā'pəl) *n.* [OE *stapol*, a post] a U-shaped piece of metal with sharp ends, driven into wood, etc. as to hold a hook, wire, etc., or through papers as a binding —*vt.* **-pled**, **-pling** to fasten or bind with a staple or staples —**sta'pler** *n.*

**star** (stär) *n.* [OE *steorra*] **1** any of the luminous celestial objects seen as points of light in the sky; esp., any far-off, self-luminous one **2** such an object regarded as influencing one's fate: *often used in pl.* **3** a conventionalized figure with five or six points, or anything like this **4** ASTERISK **5** one who excels, as in a sport **6** a leading actor or actress —*vt.* **starred**, **star'ring 1** to mark with stars as a decoration, etc. **2** to feature (an actor or actress) in a leading role —*vi.* **1** to perform brilliantly **2** to perform as a star, as in films —*adj.* **1** having great skill; outstanding **2** of a star

**star·board** (stär'bərd, -bôrd') *n.* [< OE *steoran*, to steer (rudder formerly on right side) + *bord*, side (of ship)] the right-hand side of a ship, etc. as one faces forward —*adj.* of or on this side

**starch** (stärch) *n.* [< OE *stearc*, stiff] **1** a white, tasteless, odorless food substance found in potatoes, cereals, etc. **2** a powdered form of this, used in laundering for stiffening cloth, etc. —*vt.* to stiffen as with starch —**starch'y**, **-i·er**, **-i·est**, *adj.*

**star'-crossed'** *adj.* [see STAR, *n.* 2] ill-fated

**star·dom** (stär'dəm) *n.* the status of a star, as of films

**stare** (ster) *vi.* **stared**, **star'ing** [OE *starian*] to gaze steadily and intently —*vt.* to look fixedly at —*n.* a steady, intent look —**star'er** *n.*

**star'fish'** *n., pl.* **-fish'** or (for different species)

---

**-fish'es** a small, star-shaped sea animal

**star'gaze'** *vi.* **-gazed'**, **-gaz'ing 1** to gaze at the stars **2** to indulge in dreamy thought — **star'gaz'er** *n.*

**stark** (stärk) *adj.* [OE *stearc*] **1** rigorous; severe **2** sharply outlined **3** bleak; desolate **4** sheer; downright —*adv.* utterly; wholly

**star'less** *adj.* with no stars visible

STARFISH

**star·let** (stär'lit) *n.* a young actress being promoted as a future star

**star'light'** *n.* light given by the stars —**star'lit'** *adj.*

**star·ling** (stär'liŋ) *n.* [OE *stær*] any of an Old World family of birds; esp., the **common starling** with iridescent plumage, introduced into the U.S.

**Star of David** a six-pointed star, Judaic symbol

**star'ry** *adj.* **-ri·er**, **-ri·est 1** shining; bright **2** lighted by or full of stars

**star'ry-eyed'** *adj.* **1** with sparkling eyes **2** overly optimistic

**Stars and Stripes** *name for* the U.S. flag

**star'-span'gled** *adj.* studded with stars

**Star-Spangled Banner** the U.S. national anthem

**star'-struck'** or **star'struck'** *adj.* fascinated by celebrities, esp. by stars of movies, etc.

**start** (stärt) *vi.* [OE *styrtan*] **1** to make a sudden or involuntary move **2** to go into action or motion; begin; commence **3** to spring into being, activity, etc. —*vt.* **1** to flush (game) **2** to displace, loosen, etc. *[to start a seam]* **3** *a)* to begin to play, do, etc. *b)* to set into motion, action, etc. **4** to cause to be an entrant in a race, etc. **5** to play in (a game) at the beginning —*n.* **1** a sudden, startled reaction or movement **2** a starting, or beginning **3** *a)* a place or time of beginning *b)* a lead or other advantage **4** an opportunity of beginning a career —**start out** (or **off**) to start a journey, project, etc. —**start'er** *n.*

**star·tle** (stärt''l) *vt.* **-tled**, **-tling** [< ME *sterten*, to start] to surprise, frighten, or alarm suddenly; esp., to cause to start —*vi.* to be startled

**start'-up'** *adj., n.* (of) a new business venture

**starve** (stärv) *vi.* **starved**, **starv'ing** [< OE *steorfan*, to die] **1** to die from lack of food **2** to suffer from hunger **3** to suffer great need: with *for* —*vt.* **1** to cause to starve **2** to force by starvation —**star·va·tion** (stär vā'shən) *n.*

**starve'ling** (-liŋ) *n.* a person or animal that is weak from lack of food

**Star Wars** [from a film title] [Inf.] a proposed defense system of space-based weapons for destroying missiles

**stash** (stash) [Inf.] *vt.* [< ?] to put or hide away (money, etc.) —*n.* **1** a place for hiding things **2** something hidden away

**-stat** (stat) *combining form* a device or agent that keeps something (specified) stable *[thermostat]*

**state** (stāt) *n.* [< L *stare*, to stand] **1** a set of circumstances, etc. characterizing a person or thing; condition **2** condition as regards structure, form, etc. **3** rich display; pomp **4** [sometimes S-] a body of people politically organized under one government; nation **5** [often S-] any of the political units forming a federal government, as in the U.S. **6** civil government *[church and state]* —*adj.* **1** formal; ceremonial **2** [sometimes S-] of the government or of a state —*vt.* **stat'ed**, **stat'ing 1** to establish by specifying **2** *a)* to set forth in words *b)* to express nonverbally —**in a state** [Inf.] in an excited condition —**lie in state** to be displayed formally before burial —**the States** the United States

**state'hood'** *n.* the condition of being a state

**state'house'** *n.* [often S-] the official legislative meeting place of each U.S. state

**state'less** *adj.* having no state or nationality

**state'ly** *adj.* **-li·er, -li·est 1** imposing; majestic **2** slow, dignified, etc. —**state'li·ness** *n.*

**state'ment** *n.* **1** *a*) a stating *b*) a declaration, assertion, etc. **2** *a*) a financial account *b*) a bill; invoice

**Stat·en Island** (stat''n) island borough of New York City: pop. 379,000

**state of the art** the current level of sophistication, as of technology —**state'-of-the-art'** *adj.*

**state'room'** *n.* a private room on a ship or train

**state'side'** [Inf.] *adj.* of or in the U.S. (as viewed from abroad) —*adv.* in or to the U.S.

**states·man** (stāts'mən) *n., pl.* **-men** (-mən) one who is wise or experienced in the business of government —**states'man·ship'** *n.*

**stat·ic** (stat'ik) *adj.* [< Gr *statikos,* causing to stand] **1** of masses, forces, etc. at rest or in equilibrium **2** at rest; inactive **3** of or producing stationary electrical charges, as from friction **4** of or having to do with static —*n.* **1** noise in radio or TV reception, caused by atmospheric electrical discharges **2** [Slang] adverse criticism —**stat'i·cal·ly** *adv.*

**sta·tion** (stā'shən) *n.* [< L *stare,* to stand] **1** the place where a person or thing stands or is located; esp., an assigned post **2** a building, etc. at which a service, etc. is provided [police *station*] **3** a regular stopping place, as on a railroad **4** social standing **5** *a*) a place equipped for radio or TV transmission *b*) its assigned frequency or channel —*vt.* to assign to a station

**sta·tion·ar·y** (stā'shə ner'ē) *adj.* **1** not moving; fixed **2** unchanging

**station break** a pause in radio or TV programs for station identification

**sta·tion·er** (stā'shə nər) *n.* [< ML *stationarius,* shopkeeper] a dealer in office supplies, etc.

**sta·tion·er·y** (-ner'ē) *n.* writing materials; specif., paper and envelopes

**station wagon** an automobile with extra space for cargo or seating and a rear door for loading

**sta·tis·tics** (stə tis'tiks) *pl.n.* [< L *status,* standing] numerical data assembled and classified so as to present significant information —*n.* the science of compiling such data —**sta·tis'ti·cal** *adj.* —**stat·is·ti·cian** (stat'is tish'ən) *n.*

**stats** (stats) *pl.n.* [Inf.] *short for* STATISTICS

**stat·u·ar·y** (stach'ōō er'ē) *n.* statues collectively

**stat·ue** (stach'ōō) *n.* [< L *statuere,* to set] a figure, as of a person, or an abstract form carved in stone, cast in bronze, etc.

**stat·u·esque'** (-esk') *adj.* tall and stately

**stat·u·ette'** (-et') *n.* a small statue

**stat·ure** (stach'ər) *n.* [< L *statura*] **1** standing height, esp. of a person **2** level of attainment [moral *stature*]

**sta·tus** (stat'əs, stāt'-) *n., pl.* **-tus·es** [L, standing] **1** legal condition [the *status* of a minor] **2** *a*) position; rank *b*) prestige **3** state, or state of affairs

**status quo** (kwō') [L, the state in which] the existing state of affairs

**status symbol** a possession regarded as a mark of high social status

**stat·ute** (stach'ōōt) *n.* [see STATUE] **1** an established rule **2** a law passed by a legislative body

**statute of limitations** a statute limiting the time for legal action

**stat·u·to·ry** (stach'ōō tôr'ē) *adj.* **1** fixed or authorized by statute **2** punishable by statute

**St. Au·gus·tine** (ô'gəs tēn') seaport in NE Florida: oldest city (founded 1565) in the U.S.: pop. 12,000

**staunch** (stônch, stänch) *vt.* [< L *stare,* to stand] to check the flow of (blood, etc.) from (a cut, etc.) —*vi.* to stop flowing —*adj.* **1** seaworthy **2** stead-

fast; loyal **3** strong; solid Also, esp. for v., **stanch** (stänch, stanch) —**staunch'ly** *adv.*

**stave** (stāv) *n.* [< *staves,* pl. of STAFF] **1** any of the shaped strips of wood forming the wall of a barrel, bucket, etc. **2** a stick or staff **3** a stanza —*vt.* **staved** or **stove, stav'ing** to smash or break (*in*) — **stave off** to hold off or put off

**staves** (stāvz) *n.* **1** *alt. pl.* of STAFF **2** *pl.* of STAVE

**stay**[1] (stā) *n.* [OE *stæg*] a heavy rope or cable, used as a brace or support

**stay**[2] (stā) *n.* [Fr *estaie*] **1** a support or prop **2** a strip of stiffening material used in a corset, shirt collar, etc. —*vt.* to support, or prop up

**stay**[3] (stā) *vi.* **stayed, stay'ing** [< L *stare,* to stand] **1** to continue in the place or condition specified; remain **2** to live; dwell **3** to stop; halt **4** to pause; delay **5** [Inf.] to continue; last —*vt.* **1** to stop or check **2** to hinder or detain **3** to postpone (legal action) **4** to satisfy (thirst, etc.) for a time **5** *a*) to remain to the end of *b*) to be able to last through —*n.* **1** *a*) a stopping or being stopped *b*) a halt or pause **2** a postponement in legal action **3** the action of remaining, or the time spent, in a place —**stay put** [Inf.] to remain in place or unchanged

**staying power** endurance

**St. Cath·ar·ines** (kath'ər inz) city in SE Ontario, Canada: pop. 131,000

**St. Chris·to·pher** (kris'tə fər) St. Kitts: see ST. KITTS AND NEVIS

**STD** *abbrev.* sexually transmitted disease

**Ste** [Fr *Sainte*] *abbrev.* **1** Saint (female) **2** Suite

**stead** (sted) *n.* [OE *stede*] the place of a person or thing as filled by a substitute —**stand someone in good stead** to give someone good service

**stead'fast'** *adj.* [OE *stedefæste*] **1** firm; fixed **2** constant —**stead'fast'ly** *adv.*

**stead'y** *adj.* **-i·er, -i·est** [STEAD + -Y[2]] **1** firm; stable; not shaky **2** constant, regular, or uniform [a *steady* gaze] **3** constant in behavior, loyalty, etc. **4** habitual or regular; by habit [a *steady* customer] **5** calm and controlled [steady nerves] **6** sober; reliable —*vt., vi.* **-ied, -y·ing** to make or become steady —*n.* [Inf.] a person one dates regularly —*adv.* in a steady manner —**go steady** [Inf.] to date someone (or each other) exclusively — **stead'i·ly** *adv.* —**stead'i·ness** *n.*

**steak** (stāk) *n.* [< ON *steikja,* to roast on a spit] a slice of beef, fish, etc. for broiling or frying

**steal** (stēl) *vt.* **stole, stol'en, steal'ing** [OE *stælan*] **1** to take (another's property, etc.) dishonestly or unlawfully, esp. in a secret manner **2** to take (a look, etc.) slyly **3** to gain insidiously or artfully [he *stole* her heart] **4** to move, put, etc. stealthily (*in, from,* etc.) **5** *Baseball* to gain (a base), as by running to it from another base while the pitch is being delivered —*vi.* **1** to be a thief **2** to move, etc. stealthily —*n.* [Inf.] an extraordinary bargain

**stealth** (stelth) *n.* [< ME *stelen,* to steal] secret or furtive action —*adj.* of or using technology that prevents detection by enemy radar —**stealth'y** *adj.* —**stealth'i·ly** *adv.*

**steam** (stēm) *n.* [OE] **1** water as converted into a vapor by being heated to the boiling point **2** the power of steam under pressure **3** condensed water vapor **4** [Inf.] vigor; energy —*adj.* using, conveying, or operated by, steam —*vi.* **1** to give off steam **2** to become covered or coated with condensed steam: usually with *up* **3** to move by steam power —*vt.* to cook, remove, etc. with steam —**steam'y, -i·er, -i·est,** *adj.*

**steam'boat'** *n.* a small steamship

**steam engine** an engine using steam under pressure to supply mechanical energy

**steam'er** *n.* **1** something operated by steam, as a steamship **2** a container for cooking, cleaning, etc. with steam

**steam'fit'ter** *n.* one whose work is installing boilers, pipes, etc. in steam-pressure systems

**steam'roll'er** *n.* a construction machine or vehicle with a heavy roller —*vt., vi.* to move, crush, override, etc. as (with) a steamroller: also **steam'roll'**

**steam'ship'** *n.* a ship driven by steam power

**steam shovel** a large, mechanically operated digger

**steed** (stēd) *n.* ⟦OE *steda*⟧ a horse for riding

**steel** (stēl) *n.* ⟦OE *stiele*⟧ **1** a hard, tough alloy of iron with carbon **2** a thing of steel **3** great strength or hardness —*adj.* of or like steel —*vt.* to make hard, tough, etc. —**steel'y, -i·er, -i·est,** *adj.*

**steel wool** long, thin shavings of steel in a pad, used for scouring, polishing, etc.

**steel'yard'** *n.* ⟦STEEL + obs. *yard*, rod⟧ a scale consisting of a metal arm suspended from above

**steep**[1] (stēp) *adj.* ⟦OE *steap*, lofty⟧ **1** having a sharp rise or slope; precipitous **2** [Inf.] excessive; extreme —**steep'ly** *adv.* —**steep'ness** *n.*

**steep**[2] (stēp) *vt.* ⟦ME *stepen*⟧ to soak, saturate, imbue, etc.

**stee·ple** (stē'pəl) *n.* ⟦OE *stepel*⟧ **1** a tower rising above the main structure, as of a church **2** a spire

**stee'ple·chase'** *n.* a horse race run over a course obstructed with ditches, hedges, etc.

**stee'ple·jack'** *n.* one who builds or repairs steeples, smokestacks, etc.

**steer**[1] (stir) *vt., vi.* ⟦OE *stieran*⟧ **1** to guide (a ship, etc.) with a rudder **2** to direct the course of (an automobile, etc.) **3** to follow (a course) — **steer clear of** to avoid —**steer'a·ble** *adj.*

**steer**[2] (stir) *n.* ⟦OE *steor*⟧ a castrated male ox, esp. one raised for beef

**steer·age** (stir'ij) *n.* **1** a steering **2** [Historical] a section in a ship for the passengers paying the lowest fare

**steg·o·sau·rus** (steg'ə sôr'əs) *n., pl.* **-ri** (-ī) ⟦< Gr *stegos*, roof + *sauros*, lizard⟧ a large dinosaur with pointed, bony plates along the backbone

**stein** (stīn) *n.* ⟦Ger⟧ a beer mug

**stein'bok'** (-bäk') *n.* ⟦Ger⟧ an African antelope

**stel·lar** (stel'ər) *adj.* ⟦< L *stella*, a star⟧ **1** of a star **2** excellent **3** leading; chief [a *stellar* role]

**stem**[1] (stem) *n.* ⟦OE *stemn*⟧ **1** the main stalk of a plant **2** any stalk or part supporting leaves, flowers, or fruit **3** a stemlike part, as of a pipe, goblet, etc. **4** the prow of a ship; bow **5** the part of a word to which inflectional endings are added —*vt.* **stemmed, stem'ming** to make headway against [to *stem* the tide] —*vi.* to derive

**stem**[2] (stem) *vt.* **stemmed, stem'ming** ⟦< ON *stemma*⟧ to stop or check by or as if by damming up

**stem'ware'** *n.* goblets, wineglasses, etc. having stems

**stench** (stench) *n.* ⟦< OE *stincan*, to stink⟧ an offensive smell; stink

**sten·cil** (sten'səl) *vt.* **-ciled** or **-cilled, -cil·ing** or **-cil·ling** ⟦ult. < L *scintilla*, a spark⟧ to make or mark with a stencil —*n.* **1** a thin sheet, as of paper, cut through so that when ink, etc. is applied, designs, letters, etc. form on the surface beneath **2** a design, etc. so made

**ste·nog·ra·phy** (stə näg'rə fē) *n.* shorthand writing, as of dictation, testimony, etc., for later transcription —**ste·nog'ra·pher** *n.* —**sten·o·graph·ic** (sten'ə graf'ik) *adj.*

**stent** (stent) *n.* ⟦after C.R. *Stent*, Brit dentist⟧ a surgical device used to hold tissue in place, as inside a blood vessel to keep the vessel open

**sten·to·ri·an** (sten tôr'ē ən) *adj.* ⟦after *Stentor*, Gr herald in the *Iliad*⟧ very loud

**step** (step) *n.* ⟦OE *stepe*⟧ **1** a single movement of the foot, as in walking **2** the distance covered by such a movement **3** a short distance **4** a manner of stepping **5** the sound of stepping **6** a rest for the foot in climbing, as a stair **7** a degree; level; stage **8** any of a series of acts, processes, etc. — *vi.* **stepped, step'ping 1** to move by executing a step **2** to walk a short distance **3** to move briskly (*along*) **4** to enter (*into* a situation, etc.) **5** to press the foot down (*on*) —*vt.* to measure by taking steps: with *off* —**in** (or **out of**) **step** conforming (or not conforming) to a rhythm, a regular

procedure, etc. —**step by step 1** gradually **2** by noting each stage in a process —**step down** to resign —**step up 1** to advance **2** to increase, as in rate —**take steps** to do the things needed — **step'per** *n.*

**step'broth'er** *n.* one's stepparent's son by a former marriage

**step'child'** *n., pl.* **-chil'dren** ⟦< OE *steop*-, orphaned + *cild*, child⟧ one's spouse's child (**step'daugh'ter** or **step'son'**) by a former marriage

**step'-down'** *n.* a decrease, as in amount, intensity, etc.

**step'lad'der** *n.* a four-legged ladder with broad, flat steps

**step'par'ent** *n.* the person (**step'fa'ther** or **step'moth'er**) who has married one's parent after the death of or divorce from the other parent

**steppe** (step) *n.* ⟦Russ *styep'*⟧ any of the great plains of SE Europe and Asia, having few trees

**step'ping-stone'** *n.* **1** a stone to step on, as in crossing a stream **2** a means of bettering oneself

**step'sis'ter** *n.* one's stepparent's daughter by a former marriage

**step'-up'** *n.* an increase, as in amount, intensity, etc.

**-ster** (stər) ⟦OE *-estre*⟧ *suffix* one who is, does, creates, or is associated with (something specified) [*trickster, gangster*]

**ster·e·o** (ster'ē ō') *n., pl.* **-os'** a stereophonic device, system, effect, etc. —*adj.* short for STEREOPHONIC

**stereo-** ⟦< Gr *stereos*, solid⟧ *combining form* solid, firm, three-dimensional [*stereoscope*]

**ster·e·o·phon·ic** (ster'ē ə fän'ik) *adj.* designating or of sound reproduction using two or more channels to carry a blend of sounds from separate sources through separate speakers

**ster'e·o·scop'ic** (-skäp'ik) *adj.* appearing three-dimensional

**ster'e·o·type'** (-tīp') *n.* ⟦see STEREO- & -TYPE⟧ **1** a printing plate cast from a mold, as a page of set type **2** a fixed or conventional notion or conception —*vt.* **-typed', -typ'ing** to make a stereotype of —**ster'e·o·typed'** *adj.*

**ster'e·o·typ'i·cal** (-tip'i kəl) *adj.* **1** stereotyped **2** hackneyed

**ster·ile** (ster'əl) *adj.* ⟦L *sterilis*⟧ **1** incapable of producing offspring, fruit, etc.; barren **2** free from living microorganisms —**ste·ril·i·ty** (stə ril'ə tē) *n.*

**ster'i·lize'** (-ə līz') *vt.* **-lized', -liz'ing** to make sterile; specif., *a*) to make incapable of reproduction *b*) to make free of germs, etc. —**ster'i·li·za'tion** *n.* —**ster'i·liz'er** *n.*

**ster·ling** (stur'liŋ) *n.* ⟦ME *sterlinge*, Norman coin⟧ **1** sterling silver **2** British money —*adj.* **1** of silver that is at least 92.5 percent pure **2** of British money **3** made of sterling silver **4** excellent [a *sterling* reputation]

**stern**[1] (sturn) *adj.* ⟦OE *styrne*⟧ **1** severe; strict [*stern* measures] **2** grim [a *stern* face] **3** relentless or firm —**stern'ly** *adv.* —**stern'ness** *n.*

**stern**[2] (sturn) *n.* ⟦< ON *styra*, to steer⟧ the rear end of a ship, etc.

**ster·num** (stur'nəm) *n., pl.* **-nums** or **-na** (-nə) ⟦< Gr *sternon*⟧ the flat, bony structure to which most of the ribs are attached in the front of the chest; breastbone

**ster·oid** (stir'oid', ster'-) *n.* ⟦< (CHOLE)STER(OL) + -OID⟧ any of a group of compounds including the bile acids, sex hormones, etc. —**ste·roi'dal** *adj.*

**stet** (stet) *v. imper.* ⟦L⟧ let it stand: printer's term indicating that matter marked for deletion or change is to remain —*vt.* **stet'ted, stet'ting** to mark with "stet"

**steth·o·scope** (steth'ə skōp') *n.* ⟦< Gr *stēthos*, chest + -SCOPE⟧ *Med.* an instrument used to examine the heart, lungs, etc. by listening to the sounds they make

**ste·ve·dore** (stē′və dôr′) *n.* ⟦ult. < L *stipare*, cram⟧ LONGSHOREMAN

**Ste·ven·son** (stē′vən sən), **Rob·ert Lou·is** (rä′bərt lōō′is) 1850-94; Scot. writer

**stew** (stōō) *vt., vi.* ⟦ult. < L *ex-*, out + Gr *typhos*, steam⟧ **1** to cook by simmering or boiling slowly **2** to worry —*n.* **1** a dish, esp. of meat and vegetables, cooked by stewing **2** a state of worry

**stew·ard** (stōō′ərd) *n.* ⟦< OE *stig*, hall + *weard*, keeper⟧ **1** a person put in charge of a large estate **2** an administrator, as of finances and property **3** one responsible for the food and drink, etc. in a club, etc. **4** an attendant, as on a ship or airplane **5** a union representative —**stew′ard·ship′** *n.*

**stew′ard·ess** (-ər dis) *n.* a woman flight attendant

**stick** (stik) *n.* ⟦OE *sticca*⟧ **1** a twig or small branch broken or cut off **2** a long, slender piece of wood, as a club, cane, etc. **3** any sticklike piece *[a stick of gum]* —*vt.* **stuck, stick′ing 1** to pierce, as with a pointed instrument **2** to pierce with (a knife, pin, etc.) **3** to thrust (*in, into, out,* etc.) **4** to attach as by gluing, pinning, etc. **5** to obstruct, detain, etc. *[the wheels were stuck]* **6** [Inf.] to place; put; set **7** [Inf.] to puzzle; baffle **8** [Slang] *a)* to impose a burden, etc. upon *b)* to defraud —*vi.* **1** to be fixed by a pointed end, as a nail **2** to adhere; cling; remain **3** to persevere *[to stick at a job]* **4** to remain firm and resolute *[he stuck with us]* **5** to become embedded, jammed, etc. **6** to become stopped or delayed **7** to hesitate; scruple *[he'll stick at nothing]* **8** to protrude or project (*out, up,* etc.) —**stick by** to remain loyal to —**stick up for** [Inf.] to uphold; defend —**the sticks** [Inf.] the rural districts

**stick′er** *n.* a person or thing that sticks; specif., a gummed label

**stick′-in-the-mud′** *n.* [Inf.] one who resists change, new ideas, etc.

**stick·le·back** (stik′əl bak′) *n.* a small, bony-plated fish with sharp dorsal spines: the male builds a nest for the female's eggs

**stick·ler** (stik′lər) *n.* ⟦prob. < ME *stightlen,* to order⟧ **1** one who insists on a certain way of doing things *[a stickler for discipline]* **2** [Inf.] something difficult to solve

**stick′pin′** *n.* an ornamental pin worn in a necktie, on a lapel, etc.

**stick shift** a gearshift, as on a car, operated manually

**stick′um** (-əm) *n.* ⟦STICK + *'em,* short for THEM⟧ [Inf.] any sticky, or adhesive, substance

**stick′up′** *n.* *slang term for* HOLDUP (sense 2)

**stick′y** *adj.* **-i·er, -i·est 1** that sticks; adhesive **2** [Inf.] hot and humid **3** [Inf.] troublesome — **stick′i·ness** *n.*

**stiff** (stif) *adj.* ⟦OE *stif*⟧ **1** hard to bend or move; rigid; firm **2** sore or limited in movement: said of joints and muscles **3** not fluid; thick **4** strong; powerful *[a stiff wind]* **5** harsh *[stiff punishment]* **6** difficult *[a stiff climb]* **7** very formal or awkward **8** [Inf.] excessive *[a stiff price]* —*vt.* **stiffed, stiff′ing** [Slang] to cheat —**stiff′ly** *adv.* — **stiff′ness** *n.*

**stiff′-arm′** *vt.* to push (someone) away with one's arm out straight

**stiff′en** *vt., vi.* to make or become stiff or stiffer — **stiff′en·er** *n.*

**stiff′-necked′** (-nekt′) *adj.* stubborn

**sti·fle** (stī′fəl) *vt.* **-fled, -fling** ⟦< Fr *estouffer*⟧ **1** to suffocate; smother **2** to suppress; hold back; stop *[to stifle a sob]* —*vi.* to die or suffer from lack of air —**sti′fling·ly** *adv.*

**stig·ma** (stig′mə) *n., pl.* **-mas** or **stig·ma′ta** (-mät′ə) ⟦< Gr, lit., a puncture made with a sharp instrument⟧ **1** a mark of disgrace or reproach **2** a spot on the skin, esp. one that bleeds **3** the upper tip of the pistil of a flower, on which pollen falls and develops —**stig·mat′ic** (-mat′ik) *adj.*

**stig′ma·tize′** (-tīz′) *vt.* **-tized′, -tiz′ing** to mark or characterize as disgraceful

**stile** (stīl) *n.* ⟦< OE *stigan,* to climb⟧ a set of steps for climbing over a fence or wall

**sti·let·to** (sti let′ō) *n., pl.* **-tos** or **-toes** ⟦It < L *stilus,* pointed tool⟧ a small dagger with a slender blade

**still**[1] (stil) *adj.* ⟦OE *stille*⟧ **1** noiseless; silent **2** stationary **3** tranquil; calm **4** designating or of a single photograph taken from a film —*n.* **1** silence; quiet **2** a still photograph —*adv.* **1** at or up to the time indicated **2** even; yet *[still colder]* **3** nevertheless; yet *[rich but still unhappy]* —*conj.* nevertheless; yet —*vt., vi.* to make or become still —**still′ness** *n.*

**still**[2] (stil) *n.* ⟦< obs. *still,* to distill⟧ an apparatus used for distilling liquids, esp. alcoholic liquors

**still′birth′** *n.* **1** the birth of a stillborn fetus **2** such a fetus

**still′born′** *adj.* **1** dead when delivered from the uterus **2** unsuccessful from the start

**still life** *pl.* **still lifes** a picture of inanimate objects, as fruit, flowers, etc.

**stilt** (stilt) *n.* ⟦ME *stilte*⟧ **1** either of a pair of poles, each with a footrest, used for walking high off the ground **2** any of a number of long posts used to hold a building, etc. above ground or out of water **3** a bird with a long, slender bill and long legs

**stilt·ed** (stil′tid) *adj.* pompous, affected, etc.

**stim·u·lant** (stim′yə lənt) *n.* anything, as a drug, that stimulates

**stim′u·late′** (-lāt′) *vt.* **-lat′ed, -lat′ing** ⟦see fol.⟧ to rouse or excite to activity or increased activity — **stim′u·la′tion** *n.*

**stim·u·lus** (-ləs) *n., pl.* **-li′** (-lī′) ⟦L, a goad⟧ **1** an incentive **2** any action or agent that causes an activity in an organism, organ, etc.

**sting** (stiŋ) *vt.* **stung, sting′ing** ⟦OE *stingan*⟧ **1** to prick or wound with a sting **2** to cause sudden, pricking pain to **3** to make unhappy **4** to stimulate suddenly and sharply **5** [Slang] to cheat —*vi.* to cause or feel sharp, smarting pain —*n.* **1** a stinging **2** a pain or wound resulting from stinging **3** a sharp-pointed organ, as in insects and plants, that pricks, wounds, etc. **4** [Slang] *a)* a swindling, as in a confidence game *b)* a scheme by police, etc. for entrapping lawbreakers

**sting′er** *n.* one that stings; specif., a STING (*n.* 3)

**sting′ray′** *n.* a large ray with one or more poisonous spines that can inflict painful wounds

**stin·gy** (stin′jē) *adj.* **-gi·er, -gi·est** ⟦< dial. form of STING⟧ **1** giving or spending grudgingly; miserly **2** less than needed; scanty —**stin′gi·ly** *adv.* — **stin′gi·ness** *n.*

**stink** (stiŋk) *vi.* **stank** or **stunk, stunk, stink′ing** ⟦OE *stincan*⟧ to give off a strong, unpleasant smell —*n.* a strong, unpleasant smell; stench — **stink′er** *n.* —**stink′y,** *-i·er, -i·est, adj.*

**stint** (stint) *vt.* ⟦< OE *styntan,* to blunt⟧ to restrict to a certain quantity, often small —*vi.* to be sparing in giving or using —*n.* **1** restriction; limit **2** an assigned task or period of work —**stint′er** *n.*

**sti·pend** (stī′pənd) *n.* ⟦< L *stips,* coin + *pendere,* to pay⟧ a regular or fixed payment, as a salary

**stip·ple** (stip′əl) *vt.* **-pled, -pling** ⟦< Du *stippel,* a speckle⟧ to paint, draw, or engrave in small dots

**stip·u·late** (stip′yə lāt′) *vt.* **-lat′ed, -lat′ing** ⟦< L *stipulari,* to bargain⟧ **1** to arrange definitely **2** to specify as an essential condition of an agreement —**stip′u·la′tion** *n.*

**stir**[1] (stʉr) *vt., vi.* **stirred, stir′ring** ⟦OE *styrian*⟧ **1** to move, esp. slightly **2** to make or be active **3** to mix (a liquid, etc.) as by agitating with a spoon **4** to excite the feelings (of) **5** to incite: often with *up* —*n.* **1** a stirring **2** movement; activity **3** excitement; tumult —**stir′rer** *n.*

**stir**[2] (stʉr) *n.* ⟦19th-c. thieves' slang⟧ [Slang] a prison

**stir′-cra·zy** *adj.* [Slang] anxious, tense, etc. from long, close confinement, specif. in prison

**stir′-fry′** *vt.* **-fried′, -fry′ing** to fry (diced or sliced vegetables, meat, etc.) quickly in a wok while stirring constantly

**stir′ring** *adj.* **1** active; busy **2** rousing; exciting

**stir·rup** (stur′əp) *n.* [OE *stigrap*] **1** a flat-bottomed ring hung from a saddle and used as a footrest **2** one of the three small bones in the middle ear

**stitch** (stich) *n.* [OE *stice,* a puncture] **1** *a*) a single complete in-and-out movement of a needle in sewing, etc. *b*) a suture **2** a loop, knot, etc. made by stitching **3** a particular kind of stitch or style of stitching **4** a sudden, sharp pain **5** a bit or piece —*vi., vt.* to make stitches (in); sew —**in stitches** in a state of uproarious laughter

**stitch′er·y** (-ər ē) *n.* ornamental needlework

**St. John′s** seaport & capital of Newfoundland: pop. 102,000

**St. Kitts and Nevis** (kits) country in the Leeward Islands, consisting of two islands, St. Kitts & Nevis: *c.* 101 sq. mi.; pop. 41,000

**St. Lawrence** river flowing from Lake Ontario into the Atlantic: the main section of an inland waterway (**St. Lawrence Seaway**) connecting the Great Lakes with the Atlantic

**St. Lou·is** (lōō′is, lōō′ē) city & port in E Missouri, on the Mississippi: pop. 397,000

**St. Lu·ci·a** (lōō′shē ə, lōō sē′ə) island country of the West Indies: 238 sq. mi.; pop. 133,000

**stoat** (stōt) *n.* [ME *stote*] a large European ermine, esp. in its brown summer coat

**stock** (stäk) *n.* [OE *stocc*] **1** the trunk of a tree **2** *a*) descent; lineage *b*) a strain, race, etc. of animals or plants **3** a supporting or main part of an implement, etc., as the wooden handle to which the barrel of a rifle is attached **4** [*pl.*] a wooden frame with holes for confining the ankles or wrists, formerly used for punishment **5** raw material **6** water in which meat, fish, etc. has been boiled, used in soups **7** livestock **8** a supply of goods on hand in a store, etc. **9** (a certificate for) a share or shares of corporate ownership **10** a stock company or its repertoire —*vt.* **1** to furnish (a farm, shop, etc.) with stock **2** to keep a supply of, as for sale or for future use —*vi.* to put in a stock, or supply: with *up* —*adj.* **1** kept in stock *[stock* sizes*]* **2** common or trite *[a stock* excuse*]* **3** that deals with stock **4** relating to a stock company —**in** (or **out of**) **stock** (not) available for sale or use —**take stock 1** to inventory the stock on hand **2** to make an appraisal —**take** (or **put**) **stock in** to have faith in

**stock·ade** (stä kād′) *n.* [< Prov *estaca,* a stake] **1** a barrier of stakes driven into the ground side by side, for defense **2** an enclosure, as a fort, made with such stakes **3** an enclosure for military prisoners

**stock′bro′ker** *n.* one who acts as an agent in buying and selling stocks, bonds, etc.

**stock car** a standard automobile, modified for racing

**stock company** a theatrical company presenting a repertoire of plays

**stock exchange 1** a place where stocks and bonds are bought and sold **2** an association of stockbrokers Also **stock market**

**stock′hold′er** *n.* one owning stock in a given company

**Stock·holm** (stäk′hōm′, -hōlm′) seaport & capital of Sweden: pop. 704,000

**stock′ing** *n.* [< obs. sense of *stock*] a closefitting covering, usually knitted, for the foot and leg

**stocking cap** a long, tapered knitted cap, often with a tassel at the end

**stock′pile′** *n.* a reserve supply of goods, raw material, etc. —*vt., vi.* -piled′, -pil′ing to accumulate a stockpile (of)

**stock′-still′** *adj.* motionless

**Stock·ton** (stäk′tən) city in central California: pop. 211,000

**stock′y** *adj.* -i·er, -i·est heavily built; short and thickset —**stock′i·ness** *n.*

---

**stock′yard′** *n.* an enclosure where cattle, hogs, etc. are kept before slaughtering

**stodg·y** (stä′jē) *adj.* -i·er, -i·est [< *stodge,* heavy food] **1** dull; uninteresting **2** old-fashioned; conventional —**stodg′i·ness** *n.*

**sto·gie** or **sto·gy** (stō′gē) *n., pl.* **-gies** [after *Conestoga* Valley, PA] a cigar, esp. one that is long, thin, and, usually, inexpensive

**Sto·ic** (stō′ik) *n.* [< Gr *stoa,* a colonnade: where first Stoics met] **1** a member of an ancient Greek school of philosophy **2** [s-] a stoical person —*adj.* [s-] STOICAL —**sto′i·cism′** (-i siz′əm) *n.*

**sto′i·cal** (-i kəl) *adj.* showing indifference to joy, grief, pleasure, or pain; impassive —**sto′i·cal·ly** *adv.*

**stoke** (stōk) *vt., vi.* stoked, stok′ing [< Du *stoken,* to poke] **1** to stir up and feed fuel to (a fire) **2** to tend (a furnace, boiler, etc.) —**stok′er** *n.*

**STOL** *abbrev.* short takeoff and landing

**stole**[1] (stōl) *n.* [< Gr *stolē,* garment] **1** a long strip of cloth worn about the neck by members of the clergy at various rites **2** a woman's long scarf of cloth or fur worn around the shoulders

**stole**[2] (stōl) *vt., vi. pt. of* STEAL

**stol·en** (stō′lən) *vt., vi. pp. of* STEAL

**stol·id** (stäl′id) *adj.* [L *stolidus,* slow] having or showing little or no emotion; unexcitable —**sto·lid·i·ty** (stə lid′ə tē) *n.* —**stol′id·ly** *adv.*

**sto·lon** (stō′län′) *n.* [< L *stolo,* a shoot] a creeping stem lying above the soil surface and bearing leaves, as in the strawberry

**stom·ach** (stum′ək) *n.* [ult. < Gr *stoma,* mouth] **1** the saclike digestive organ into which food passes from the esophagus **2** the abdomen, or belly **3** appetite for food **4** desire or inclination —*vt.* **1** to be able to eat or digest **2** to tolerate; bear

**stom′ach·ache′** *n.* pain in the stomach or abdomen

**stom′ach·er** *n.* an ornamented piece of cloth formerly worn over the chest and abdomen, esp. by women

**stomp** (stämp) *vt., vi. var. of* STAMP (*vt.* 1, 2; *vi.* 1, 2)

**stomping ground** [Inf.] STAMPING GROUND: *also used in pl.*

**stone** (stōn) *n.* [OE *stan*] **1** the hard, solid, nonmetallic mineral matter of which rock is composed **2** a piece of rock **3** the seed of certain fruits **4** *short for* PRECIOUS STONE **5** *pl.* stone [Brit.] 14 pounds avoirdupois **6** an abnormal stony mass formed in the kidney, gall bladder, etc. —*vt.* stoned, ston′ing **1** to pelt or kill with stones **2** to remove the stone from (a peach, etc.) —*adv.* completely

**stone-** [< prec.] *combining form* completely *[stone*-blind*]*

**Stone Age** the period in human culture when stone tools were used

**stoned** *adj.* [Slang] drunk or under the influence of a drug

**stone′s throw** a short distance

**stone′wall′** *vi.* [Inf.] to behave in an obstructive manner, as by withholding information, etc.

**stone′ware′** *n.* a dense, opaque, glazed or unglazed pottery

**ston′y** *adj.* -i·er, -i·est **1** full of stones **2** of or like stone; specif., unfeeling; pitiless —**ston′i·ness** *n.*

**stood** (stood) *vi., vt. pt. & pp. of* STAND

**stooge** (stōōj) *n.* [< ?] [Inf.] **1** an actor who serves as the victim of a comedian's jokes, pranks, etc. **2** anyone who acts as a foil or underling

**stool** (stōōl) *n.* [OE *stol*] **1** a single seat having no back or arms **2** feces

**stool pigeon** [Inf.] a spy or informer, esp. for the police

**stoop**[1] (stōōp) *vi.* [OE *stupian*] **1** to bend the body forward **2** to carry the head and shoulders habitually bent forward **3** to degrade oneself —*n.* the act or position of stooping

**stoop**[2] (sto͞op) *n.* ⟦Du *stoep*⟧ a small porch at the door of a house

**stop** (stäp) *vt.* **stopped, stop′ping** ⟦< L *stuppa,* a kind of stuffing material⟧ **1** to close by filling, shutting off, etc. **2** to cause to cease motion, activity, etc. **3** to block; intercept; prevent **4** to cease; desist from [*stop* talking] —*vi.* **1** to cease moving, etc.; halt **2** to leave off doing something **3** to cease operating **4** to become clogged **5** to tarry or stay —*n.* **1** a stopping or being stopped **2** a finish; end **3** a stay or sojourn **4** a place stopped at, as on a bus route **5** an obstruction, plug, etc. **6** a finger hole in a wind instrument, closed to produce a desired tone **7** a pull, lever, etc. for controlling a set of organ pipes —**stop off** to stop for a while en route to a place —**stop over** to visit for a while: also **stop in** (or **by**)

**stop′cock′** *n.* a cock or valve to stop or regulate the flow of a fluid

**stop′gap′** *n.* a person or thing serving as a temporary substitute

**stop′light′** *n.* a traffic light, esp. when red to signal vehicles to stop

**stop′o′ver** *n.* a brief stop or stay at a place in the course of a journey

**stop′page** *n.* **1** a stopping or being stopped **2** an obstructed condition; block

**stop′per** *n.* something inserted to close an opening; plug

**stop′watch′** *n.* a watch that can be started and stopped instantly, as for timing races

**stor·age** (stôr′ij) *n.* **1** a storing or being stored **2** a place for, or the cost of, storing goods **3** computer memory

**storage battery** a battery for producing electric current, with cells that can be recharged

**store** (stôr) *vt.* **stored, stor′ing** ⟦< L *instaurare,* restore⟧ **1** to put aside for use when needed **2** to furnish with a supply **3** to put, as in a warehouse, for safekeeping —*n.* **1** a supply (*of* something) for use when needed; stock **2** [*pl.*] supplies, esp. of food, clothing, etc. **3** a retail establishment where goods are offered for sale —**in store** set aside for the future; in reserve —**set** (or **put** or **lay**) **store by** to value

**store′front′** *n.* a front room on the ground floor of a building, designed for use as a retail store

**store′house′** *n.* a place where things are stored; esp., a warehouse

**store′keep′er** *n.* **1** a person in charge of military or naval stores **2** a retail merchant

**store′room′** *n.* a room where things are stored

**sto·rey** (stôr′ē) *n., pl.* **-reys** *Brit., etc. sp.* of STORY[2]

**sto·ried** (stôr′ēd) *adj.* famous in story or history

**stork** (stôrk) *n.* ⟦OE *storc*⟧ a large, long-legged wading bird with a long neck and bill

**storm** (stôrm) *n.* ⟦OE⟧ **1** a strong wind, with rain, snow, thunder, etc. **2** any heavy fall of snow, rain, etc. **3** a strong emotional outburst **4** any strong disturbance **5** a sudden, strong attack on a fortified place —*vi.* **1** to blow rain, snow, etc. violently **2** to rage; rant **3** to rush violently [to *storm* into a room] —*vt.* to attack vigorously

**storm door** (or **window**) a door (or window) placed outside the regular one as added protection

**storm′y** *adj.* **-i·er, -i·est 1** of or characterized by storms **2** violent, raging, etc. —**storm′i·ly** *adv.* — **storm′i·ness** *n.*

**sto·ry**[1] (stôr′ē) *n., pl.* **-ries** ⟦< Gr *historia,* narrative⟧ **1** the telling of an event or events; account; narration **2** a fictional prose narrative shorter than a novel **3** the plot of a novel, play, etc. **4** [Inf.] a falsehood **5** a news report

**sto·ry**[2] (stôr′ē) *n., pl.* **-ries** ⟦< prec.⟧ a horizontal division of a building, from a floor to the ceiling above it

**sto′ry·board′** *n.* a large board on which sketches,

etc. for shots or scenes of a film are arranged in sequence —*vt.* to make a storyboard of (a shot or scene) for (a film)

**sto′ry·book′** *n.* a book of stories, esp. one for children

**sto′ry·tell′er** *n.* one who narrates stories —**sto′ry·tell′ing** *n.*

**stoup** (sto͞op) *n.* ⟦< ON *staup,* cup⟧ a font for holy water

**stout** (stout) *adj.* ⟦< OFr *estout,* bold⟧ **1** courageous **2** strong; sturdy; firm **3** powerful; forceful **4** fat; thickset —*n.* a heavy, dark-brown beer — **stout′ly** *adv.* —**stout′ness** *n.*

**stout′heart′ed** *adj.* courageous; brave

**stove**[1] (stōv) *n.* ⟦< MDu, heated room⟧ an apparatus for heating, cooking, etc.

**stove**[2] (stōv) *vt., vi. alt. pt. & pp.* of STAVE

**stove′pipe′** *n.* a metal pipe used to carry off smoke from a stove

**stow** (stō) *vt.* ⟦< OE *stowe,* a place⟧ to pack in an orderly way —**stow away 1** to put or hide away **2** to be a stowaway —**stow′age** *n.*

**stow′a·way′** *n.* one who hides aboard a ship, airplane, etc. as to get free passage

**St. Paul** capital of Minnesota: pop. 272,000

**St. Pe·ters·burg** (pēt′ərz burg′) **1** seaport in NW Russia: pop. 4,456,000 **2** city in WC Florida: pop. 240,000

**strad·dle** (strad′'l) *vt.* **-dled, -dling** ⟦< STRIDE⟧ **1** to stand or sit astride of **2** to take or appear to take both sides of (an issue) —*n.* a straddling — **strad′dler** *n.*

**strafe** (strāf) *vt.* **strafed, straf′ing** ⟦< Ger *Gott strafe England* (God punish England)⟧ to attack with machine-gun fire from low-flying aircraft

**strag·gle** (strag′əl) *vi.* **-gled, -gling** ⟦prob. < ME *straken,* roam⟧ **1** to wander from the main group **2** to be scattered over a wide area; ramble **3** to hang in an unkempt way, as hair —**strag′gler** *n.* —**strag′gly** *adj.*

**straight** (strāt) *adj.* ⟦< ME *strecchen,* to stretch⟧ **1** having the same direction throughout its length; not crooked, bent, etc. **2** direct; undeviating, etc. **3** in order; properly arranged, etc. **4** honest; sincere **5** undiluted **6** [Slang] normal or conventional **7** [Slang] heterosexual —*adv.* **1** in a straight line **2** upright; erectly **3** without detour, delay, etc. —*n. Poker* a hand of five cards in sequence —**straight away** (or **off**) without delay —**straight′ness** *n.*

**straight arrow** [Inf.] one who is proper, righteous, conscientious, etc. and often regarded as stodgy, dull, etc. —**straight′-ar′row** *adj.*

**straight′a·way′** *n.* a straight section of a racetrack, highway, etc. —*adv.* without delay

**straight′edge′** *n.* a strip of wood, etc. having a perfectly straight edge, used in drawing straight lines, etc.

**straight′en** *vt., vi.* to make or become straight — **straighten out 1** to make or become less confused, easier to deal with, etc. **2** to reform — **straight′en·er** *n.*

**straight face** a facial expression showing no amusement or other emotion —**straight′-faced′** *adj.*

**straight′for′ward** *adj.* **1** moving or leading straight ahead; direct **2** honest; frank —*adv.* in a straightforward manner: also **straight′for′wards**

**straight man** an actor whose remarks a comedian answers with a quip

**straight shooter** [Inf.] a person who is honest, sincere, etc.

**straight ticket** a ballot cast for candidates of only one party

**straight time 1** the standard number of working hours, as per week **2** the rate of pay for these hours

**straight′way′** *adv.* [Now Chiefly Literary] at once

**strain**[1] (strān) *vt.* ⟦< L *stringere*⟧ **1** to stretch tight **2** to exert to the utmost **3** to injure by overexertion *[to strain a muscle]* **4** to stretch beyond normal limits **5** to pass through a screen, sieve, etc.; filter —*vi.* **1** to strive hard **2** to filter, ooze, etc. —*n.* **1** a straining or being strained **2** great effort, exertion, etc. **3** a bodily injury from over-exertion **4** stress or force **5** a great demand on one's emotions, resources, etc.

**strain²** (strān) *n.* ⟦< OE *strynan*, to produce⟧ **1** ancestry; lineage **2** race; stock; line **3** a line of individuals differentiated from its species or race **4** an inherited tendency **5** a musical tune

**strained** *adj.* not natural or relaxed

**strain'er** *n.* a device for straining, sifting, or filtering; sieve, filter, etc.

**strait** (strāt) *adj.* ⟦< L *stringere*, draw tight⟧ [Archaic] narrow or strict —*n.* **1** *[often pl.]* a narrow waterway connecting two large bodies of water **2** *[usually pl.]* difficulty; distress

**strait'en** *vt.* to bring into difficulties: usually in **in straitened circumstances**, lacking enough money

**strait'jack'et** *n.* a coatlike device for restraining violent persons

**strait'-laced'** *adj.* narrowly strict in behavior or moral views

**strand¹** (strand) *n.* ⟦OE⟧ shore, esp. ocean shore —*vt., vi.* **1** to run or drive aground, as a ship **2** to put or be put into a helpless position *[stranded abroad with no money]*

**strand²** (strand) *n.* ⟦ME *stronde*⟧ **1** any one of the threads, wires, etc. that are twisted together to form a string, cable, etc. **2** a ropelike length of anything *[a strand of pearls]*

**strange** (strānj) *adj.* strang'er, strang'est ⟦< L *extraneus*, foreign⟧ **1** not previously known, seen, etc.; unfamiliar **2** unusual; extraordinary **3** peculiar; odd —**strange'ly** *adv.* —**strange'ness** *n.*

**stran·ger** (strān'jər) *n.* **1** a newcomer **2** a person not known to one

**stran·gle** (straŋ'gəl) *vt., vi.* -gled, -gling ⟦< Gr *strangos*, twisted⟧ **1** to choke to death **2** to suppress, stifle, or repress —**stran'gler** *n.*

**stran'gle·hold'** *n.* **1** an illegal wrestling hold that chokes an opponent **2** a force or action that suppresses freedom

**stran·gu·late** (straŋ'gyə lāt') *vt.* -lat'ed, -lat'ing **1** STRANGLE **2** *Med.* to block (a tube, etc.) by constricting —**stran'gu·la'tion** *n.*

**strap** (strap) *n.* ⟦dial. form of STROP⟧ a narrow strip of leather, etc., as for securing things —*vt.* strapped, strap'ping to fasten with a strap

**strap'less** *adj.* having no shoulder straps

**strapped** *adj.* [Inf.] in great need of money

**strap'ping** *adj.* [Inf.] tall and well-built; robust

**stra·ta** (strāt'ə, strat'ə) *n. alt. pl. of* STRATUM

**strat·a·gem** (strat'ə jəm) *n.* ⟦< Gr *stratos*, army + *agein*, to lead⟧ **1** a trick, plan, etc. for deceiving an enemy in war **2** any tricky scheme

**strat·e·gy** (strat'ə jē) *n., pl.* -gies **1** the science of planning and directing military operations **2** skill in managing or planning **3** a stratagem, plan, etc. —**stra·te·gic** (strə tē'jik) *adj.* —**stra·te'gi·cal·ly** *adv.* —**strat'e·gist** *n.*

**strat·i·fy** (strat'ə fī') *vt., vi.* -fied', -fy'ing ⟦< L *stratum*, layer + *facere*, make⟧ to form in layers or strata —**strat'i·fi·ca'tion** *n.*

**strat'o·sphere'** (-ə sfir') *n.* ⟦< ModL *stratum*, stratum + Fr *sphère*, sphere⟧ **1** the atmospheric zone at an altitude of *c.* 20 to 50 km **2** an extremely high point, level, etc. —**strat'o·spher'ic** (-sfer'ik, -sfir'-) *adj.*

**stra·tum** (strāt'əm, strat'-) *n., pl.* -ta (-ə) or -tums ⟦ModL < L *stratus*, a spreading⟧ **1** a horizontal layer of matter, as of sedimentary rock **2** any of the socioeconomic groups of a society

**stra'tus** (-əs) *n., pl.* -ti (-ī) [see prec.] a uniform, low, gray cloud layer

**Strauss** (strous), **Jo·hann** (yō'hän') 1825-99; Austrian composer, esp. of waltzes

**Stra·vin·sky** (strə vin'skē), **I·gor** (ē'gôr) 1882-1971; Russ. composer & conductor, in the U.S. after 1940

**straw** (strô) *n.* ⟦OE *streaw*⟧ **1** hollow stalks of grain after threshing **2** a single one of these **3** a tube used for sucking beverages **4** a trifle —*adj.* **1** straw-colored; yellowish **2** made of straw

**straw'ber'ry** (-ber'ē, -bər ē) *n., pl.* -ries ⟦prob. from the strawlike particles on the fruit⟧ **1** the small, red, fleshy fruit of a vinelike plant of the rose family **2** this plant

**straw boss** [Inf.] one having subordinate authority

**straw vote** (or **poll**) an unofficial vote taken to determine general group opinion

**stray** (strā) *vi.* ⟦< LL *strata*, street⟧ **1** to wander from a given place, course, etc. **2** to deviate *(from what is right)* —*n.* one that strays; esp., a lost domestic animal —*adj.* **1** having strayed; lost **2** isolated or incidental *[a few stray words]*

**streak** (strēk) *n.* ⟦< OE *strica*⟧ **1** a long, thin mark or stripe **2** a layer, as of fat in meat **3** a tendency in behavior, etc. *[a nervous streak]* **4** a period, as of luck —*vt.* to make streaks on or in —*vi.* **1** to become streaked **2** to go fast **3** to dash naked in public as a prank —**streak'er** *n.* —**streak'y, -i·er, -i·est,** *adj.*

**stream** (strēm) *n.* ⟦OE⟧ **1** a current of water; specif., a small river **2** a steady flow, as of air, light, etc. **3** a continuous series *[a stream of cars]* —*vi.* **1** to flow as in a stream **2** to move swiftly

**stream'er** *n.* **1** a long, narrow flag **2** any long, narrow strip hanging loose at one end

**stream'line'** *vt.* -lined', -lin'ing to make streamlined —*adj.* STREAMLINED

**stream'lined'** *adj.* **1** having a contour designed to offer the least resistance in moving through air, water, etc. **2** efficient, trim, simplified, etc.

**street** (strēt) *n.* ⟦< L *strata (via)*, paved (road)⟧ **1** a public road in a town or city, esp. a paved one **2** such a road with its sidewalks, buildings, etc. **3** the people living, working, etc. along a given street

**street'car'** *n.* a car on rails for public transportation along certain streets

**street'light'** *n.* a lamp on a post for lighting a street: also **street'lamp'**

**street'-smart'** *adj.* [Inf.] STREETWISE

**street smarts** [Inf.] cunning or shrewdness needed to live in an urban environment characterized by poverty, crime, etc.

**street'walk'er** *n.* a prostitute

**street'wise'** *adj.* [Inf.] experienced in dealing with the people in urban poverty areas where vice and crime are common

**strength** (streŋkth) *n.* ⟦OE *strengthu*⟧ **1** the state or quality of being strong; force; power **2** toughness; durability **3** the power to resist attack **4** potency or concentration, as of drugs, etc. **5** intensity, as of sound, etc. **6** force of an army, etc., as measured in numbers —**on the strength of** based or relying on

**strength'en** *vt., vi.* to make or become stronger —**strength'en·er** *n.*

**stren·u·ous** (stren'yōō əs) *adj.* ⟦L *strenuus*⟧ requiring or characterized by great effort or energy —**stren'u·ous·ly** *adv.* —**stren'u·ous·ness** *n.*

**strep** (strep) *n. short for:* **1** STREPTOCOCCUS **2** STREP THROAT

**strep throat** (strep) a sore throat caused by a streptococcus, with inflammation and fever

**strep·to·coc·cus** (strep'tə käk'əs) *n., pl.* -coc'ci' (-käk'sī') ⟦< Gr *streptos*, twisted + COCCUS⟧ any of various spherical bacteria that occur in chains: some cause serious diseases

**strep'to·my'cin** (-mī'sin) *n.* ⟦< Gr *streptos*, bent + *mykēs*, fungus⟧ an antibiotic drug used in treating various diseases

**stress** (stres) *n.* ⟦< L *strictus*, strict⟧ **1** strain; specif., force that strains or deforms **2** emphasis; importance **3** *a)* mental or physical tension *b)* urgency, pressure, etc. causing this **4** the relative force of utterance given a syllable or word; accent

—**vt. 1** to put stress or pressure on **2** to accent **3** to emphasize

**stressed'-out'** *adj.* tired, nervous, etc. as from overwork, mental pressure, etc.

**stress fracture** a leg fracture caused by repetitive stress, as in marathon running

**stretch** (strech) *vt.* ⟦OE *streccan*⟧ **1** to reach out; extend **2** to draw out to full extent or to greater size **3** to cause to extend too far; strain **4** to strain in interpretation, scope, etc. —*vi.* **1** *a)* spread out to full extent or beyond normal limits *b)* to extend over a given distance or time **2** *a)* to extend the body or limbs to full length *b)* to lie down (usually with *out*) **3** to become stretched — *n.* **1** a stretching or being stretched **2** an unbroken period [a ten-day *stretch*] **3** an unbroken length, tract, etc. **4** *short for* HOMESTRETCH **5** an action that exceeds someone's normal powers — *adj.* **1** made of elasticized fabric so as to stretch easily **2** designating a vehicle built extra long to enlarge seating capacity [a *stretch* limousine] — **stretch'a·ble** *adj.* —**stretch'y, -i·er, -i·est, *adj.***

**stretch'er** *n.* **1** one that stretches **2** a canvas-covered frame for carrying the sick or injured

**strew** (strōō) *vt.* **strewed, strewed or strewn, strew'ing** ⟦OE *streawian*⟧ **1** to spread here and there; scatter **2** to cover as by scattering

**stri·at·ed** (strī'āt'id) *adj.* ⟦< L *striare*, to groove⟧ marked with parallel lines, bands, furrows, etc.

**strick·en** (strik'ən) *vt., vi. alt. pp. of* STRIKE —*adj.* **1** struck or wounded **2** afflicted, as by something painful

**strict** (strikt) *adj.* ⟦< L *stringere*, draw tight⟧ **1** exact or precise **2** *a)* enforcing rules carefully *b)* closely enforced —**strict'ly** *adv.* —**strict'ness** *n.*

**stric·ture** (strik'chər) *n.* ⟦see prec.⟧ **1** adverse criticism **2** a limiting; restriction **3** an abnormal narrowing of a passage in the body

**stride** (strīd) *vi.* **strode, strid'den, strid'ing** ⟦OE *stridan*⟧ **1** to walk with long steps **2** to take a single, long step (esp. *over* something) —*n.* **1** a long step **2** the distance covered by such a step **3** [usually pl.] progress [to make *strides*]

**stri·dent** (strīd'nt) *adj.* ⟦< L *stridere*, to rasp⟧ harsh-sounding; shrill; grating —**stri'dent·ly** *adv.*

**strife** (strīf) *n.* ⟦< OFr *estrif*⟧ **1** contention **2** fighting or quarreling; struggle

**strike** (strīk) *vt.* **struck, struck** or, esp. for *vt.* 7 & 10, **strick'en, strik'ing** ⟦OE *strican*, to go, advance⟧ **1** to hit with the hand, a tool, etc. **2** to make by stamping, etc. [to *strike* coins] **3** to announce (time), as with a bell: said of clocks, etc. **4** to ignite (a match) or produce (a light, etc.) by friction **5** to collide with or cause to collide [he *struck* his head on a beam] **6** to attack **7** to afflict, as with disease, pain, etc. **8** to come upon; notice, find, etc. **9** to affect as if by contact, etc.; occur to [an idea *struck* me] **10** to remove (*from* a list, record, etc.) **11** to make (a bargain, truce, etc.) **12** to lower (a sail, flag, etc.) **13** to assume (an attitude, pose, etc.) —*vi.* **1** to hit (*at*) **2** to attack **3** to make sounds as by being struck: said of a bell, clock, etc. **4** to collide; hit (*against, on,* or *upon*) **5** to seize bait: said of a fish **6** to come suddenly (*on* or *upon*) **7** to refuse to continue to work until certain demands are met **8** to proceed, esp. in a new direction —*n.* **1** the act of striking; specif., a military attack **2** a refusal by employees to go on working, in an attempt to gain better working conditions, etc. **3** the discovery of a rich deposit of oil, etc. **4** *Baseball* a pitched ball missed, or fouled off, by the batter or called a good pitch by the umpire **5** *Bowling* a knocking down of all the pins on the first roll —**strike out 1** to erase **2** to start out **3** *Baseball* to put out, or be put out, on three strikes —**strike up** to begin —**strik'er** *n.*

**strike'out'** *n. Baseball* an out made by a batter charged with three strikes

**strik'ing** *adj.* very impressive, attractive, etc.

**string** (strin) *n.* ⟦OE *streng*⟧ **1** a thin line of fiber, leather, etc. used for tying, pulling, etc. **2** a group of like things on a string [a *string* of pearls] **3** a row, series, etc. of like things [a *string* of houses] **4** *a)* a slender cord of wire, gut, etc. bowed, plucked, or struck to make a musical sound *b)* [pl.] all the stringed instruments of an orchestra **5** a fiber of a plant **6** [Inf.] a condition attached to a plan, offer, etc.: *usually used in pl.* —*vt.* **strung, string'ing 1** to provide with strings **2** to thread on a string **3** to tie, hang, etc. with a string **4** to remove the strings from (beans, etc.) **5** to arrange in a row **6** to extend [string a cable] — **pull strings** to get someone to use influence in one's behalf, often secretly —**string'y, -i·er, -i·est, *adj.***

**string bean** SNAP BEAN

**stringed instrument** (strind) an instrument with vibrating strings, as a violin or guitar

**strin·gent** (strin'jənt) *adj.* ⟦see STRICT⟧ strict; severe —**strin'gen·cy** *n.*

**string'er** *n.* **1** a long horizontal piece in a structure **2** a part-time, local correspondent for a newspaper, magazine, etc.

**strip**[1] (strip) *vt.* **stripped, strip'ping** ⟦OE *stripan*⟧ **1** to remove (the clothing, etc.) from (a person) **2** to dispossess of (honors, titles, etc.) **3** to plunder; rob **4** to take off (a covering, etc.) from (a person or thing) **5** to make bare by taking away removable parts, etc. **6** to break the thread of (a nut, bolt, etc.) or the teeth of (a gear) —*vi.* to take off all clothing

**strip**[2] (strip) *n.* ⟦< STRIPE⟧ **1** a long, narrow piece, as of land, tape, etc. **2** *short for* AIRSTRIP

**strip cropping** crop planting in alternate rows to lessen erosion, as on a hillside

**stripe** (strīp) *n.* ⟦< MDu *strip*⟧ **1** a long, narrow band differing from the surrounding area **2** a strip of cloth on a uniform to show rank, years served, etc. **3** kind; sort [a man of his *stripe*] —*vt.* **striped, strip'ing** to mark with stripes

**strip·ling** (strip'lin) *n.* a grown boy

**strip mall** a shopping center of connected storefronts with a parking area in front

**strip mining** mining, esp. for coal, by laying bare a mineral deposit near the surface of the earth

**stripped'-down'** *adj.* reduced to essentials

**strip'-search'** *vt.* to search (a person) by requiring removal of the clothes —*n.* such a search Also **strip search**

**strip'tease'** *n.* an entertainment in which the performer undresses slowly, usually to musical accompaniment

**strive** (strīv) *vi.* **strove or strived, striv·en** (striv'ən) or **strived, striv'ing** ⟦< OFr *estrif*, effort⟧ **1** to make great efforts; try very hard **2** to struggle

**strobe** (**light**) (strōb) ⟦< Gr *strobus*, a twisting around⟧ an electronic tube emitting rapid, brief, and brilliant flashes of light

**strode** (strōd) *vi., vt. pt. of* STRIDE

**stroke** (strōk) *n.* ⟦ME⟧ **1** a blow of an ax, whip, etc. **2** a sudden action or event [a *stroke* of luck] **3** an interruption of normal blood flow to the brain, as from a hemorrhage, blood clot, etc., causing paralysis, etc. **4** a single strong effort **5** the sound of striking, as of a clock **6** *a)* a single movement, as with a tool, racket, etc. *b)* any of a series of repeated motions made in rowing, swimming, etc. **7** a mark made by a pen, etc. —*vt.* **stroked, strok'ing** to draw one's hand, a tool, etc. gently over the surface of

**stroll** (strōl) *vi.* ⟦prob. < Ger *strolch*, vagabond⟧ **1** to walk about leisurely; saunter **2** to wander — *vt.* to stroll along or through —*n.* a leisurely walk

**stroll'er** *n.* **1** one who strolls **2** a light, chairlike baby carriage

**strong** (strôn) *adj.* ⟦OE *strang*⟧ **1** *a)* physically powerful *b)* healthy; hearty **2** morally or intellectually powerful [a *strong* will] **3** firm; durable **4** powerful in wealth, numbers, etc. **5** of a specified number [troops 6,000 *strong*] **6** having a powerful effect **7** intense in degree or quality **8** forceful; vigorous, etc. —**strong'ly** *adv.*

**strong'-arm'** [Inf.] *adj.* using physical force —*vt.* to use force upon

**strong'box'** *n.* a heavily made box or safe for storing valuables

**strong'hold'** *n.* a place having strong defenses; fortress

**strong'-mind'ed** *adj.* unyielding; determined: also **strong'-willed'**

**stron·ti·um** (strän'shəm, -shē əm; stränt'ē əm) *n.* ⟦ult. after *Strontian*, Scotland, where first found⟧ a metallic chemical element resembling calcium in properties

**strop** (sträp) *n.* ⟦OE⟧ a leather band for sharpening razors —*vt.* **stropped**, **strop'ping** to sharpen on a strop

**stro·phe** (strō'fē) *n.* ⟦Gr *strophē*, a turning⟧ a stanza of a poem

**strove** (strōv) *vi.* *alt. pt. of* STRIVE

**struck** (struk) *vt.*, *vi. pt. & pp. of* STRIKE

**struc·ture** (struk'chər) *n.* ⟦< L *struere*, arrange⟧ **1** something built or constructed, as a building or dam **2** the arrangement of all the parts of a whole **3** something composed of related parts — *vt.* **-tured**, **-tur·ing** to put together systematically —**struc'tur·al** *adj.*

**stru·del** (strōōd''l) *n.* ⟦Ger⟧ a pastry made of a thin sheet of dough filled with apples, etc., rolled up, and baked

**strug·gle** (strug'əl) *vi.* **-gled**, **-gling** ⟦ME *strogelen*⟧ **1** to fight violently with an opponent **2** to make great efforts; strive; labor —*n.* **1** great effort **2** conflict; strife

**strum** (strum) *vt.*, *vi.* **strummed**, **strum'ming** ⟦echoic⟧ to play (a guitar, etc.) with long strokes across the strings, often casually

**strum·pet** (strum'pit) *n.* ⟦ME⟧ a prostitute

**strung** (struŋ) *vt.*, *vi. pt. & alt. pp. of* STRING

**strut** (strut) *vi.* **strut'ted**, **strut'ting** ⟦OE *strutian*, stand rigid⟧ to walk in a swaggering manner —*n.* **1** a swaggering walk **2** a brace fitted into a framework to stabilize the structure

**strych·nine** (strik'nin, -nēn', -nīn') *n.* ⟦< Gr *strychnos*, nightshade⟧ a colorless, highly poisonous, crystalline alkaloid

**stub** (stub) *n.* ⟦OE *stybb*⟧ **1** a tree or plant stump **2** a short piece left over /a pencil *stub*/ **3** any short or blunt projection **4** the part of a ticket, bank check, etc. kept as a record —*vt.* **stubbed**, **stub'bing** **1** to strike (one's toe, etc.) against something **2** to put out (a cigarette, etc.) by pressing the end against a surface: often with *out*

**stub·ble** (stub'əl) *n.* ⟦< L *stipula*, a stalk⟧ **1** short stumps of grain, corn, etc., left after harvesting **2** any short, bristly growth, as of a beard

**stub·born** (stub'ərn) *adj.* ⟦ME *stoburn*⟧ **1** refusing to yield or comply; obstinate **2** done in an obstinate or persistent way **3** hard to handle or deal with —**stub'born·ly** *adv.* —**stub'born·ness** *n.*

**stub·by** (stub'ē) *adj.* **-bi·er**, **-bi·est** **1** covered with stubs or stubble **2** short and dense **3** short and thickset

**stuc·co** (stuk'ō) *n.*, *pl.* **-coes** or **-cos** ⟦It⟧ plaster or cement for surfacing walls, etc. —*vt.* **-coed**, **-co·ing** to cover with stucco

**stuck** (stuk) *vt.*, *vi. pt. & pp. of* STICK

**stuck'-up'** *adj.* [Inf.] snobbish; conceited

**stud**[1] (stud) *n.* ⟦OE *studu*, a post⟧ **1** any of a series of small knobs, etc. used to ornament a surface **2** a small, buttonlike device for fastening a shirt front, etc. **3** an upright piece in the wall of a building, to which panels, laths, etc. are nailed —*vt.* **stud'ded**, **stud'ding** **1** to set or decorate with studs, etc. **2** to be set thickly on /rocks *stud* the hill/

**stud**[2] (stud) *n.* ⟦OE⟧ a male animal, esp. a horse (**stud'horse'**), kept for breeding

**stud'book'** *n.* a register of purebred animals, esp. racehorses: also **stud book**

**stud'ding** *n.* studs, esp. for walls

**stu·dent** (stōōd''nt) *n.* ⟦< L *studere*, to study⟧ **1** one who studies, or investigates **2** one who is enrolled for study at a school, college, etc.

**stud·ied** (stud'ēd) *adj.* **1** prepared by careful study **2** deliberate

**stu·di·o** (stōō'dē ō') *n.*, *pl.* **-os'** ⟦It⟧ **1** a place where an artist, etc. works or where music or dancing lessons, etc. are given **2** a place where films, radio or TV programs, etc. are produced

**studio apartment** a one-room apartment with a kitchen area and a bathroom

**studio couch** a couch that can be opened into a full-sized bed

**stu·di·ous** (stōō'dē əs) *adj.* ⟦< L *studiosus*⟧ **1** fond of study **2** zealous or attentive

**stud·y** (stud'ē) *n.*, *pl.* **-ies** ⟦< L *studere*, to study⟧ **1** the acquiring of knowledge, as by reading or investigating **2** careful examination of a subject, event, etc. **3** a branch of learning **4** [*pl.*] formal education; schooling **5** an essay, thesis, etc. containing the results of an investigation **6** an earnest effort **7** deep thought **8** a room for study, etc. —*vt.* **-ied**, **-y·ing** **1** to try to learn or understand by reading, thinking, etc. **2** to investigate carefully **3** to read (a book, etc.) intently **4** to take a course in, as at a school —*vi.* **1** to study something **2** to be a student **3** to meditate

**stuff** (stuf) *n.* ⟦< OFr *estoffe*⟧ **1** the material out of which anything is made **2** essence; character **3** matter of an unspecified kind **4** cloth, esp. woolen cloth **5** objects; things **6** worthless objects; junk **7** [Inf.] ability, skill, etc. —*vt.* **1** to fill or pack; specif., *a)* to fill the skin of (a dead animal) in taxidermy *b)* to fill (a turkey, etc.) with seasoning, bread crumbs, etc. before roasting **2** to fill too full; cram **3** to plug; block —*vi.* to eat too much

**stuffed shirt** [Slang] a pompous, pretentious person

**stuff'ing** *n.* something used to stuff, as padding in cushions or a seasoned mixture for stuffing fowl

**stuff'y** *adj.* **-i·er**, **-i·est** **1** poorly ventilated; close **2** having the nasal passages stopped up, as from a cold **3** [Inf.] dull, conventional, or pompous — **stuff'i·ness** *n.*

**stul·ti·fy** (stul'tə fī') *vt.* **-fied'**, **-fy'ing** ⟦< L *stultus*, foolish + *facere*, make⟧ **1** to make seem foolish, stupid, etc. **2** to make worthless, etc.

**stum·ble** (stum'bəl) *vi.* **-bled**, **-bling** ⟦ME *stumblen*⟧ **1** to trip in walking, running, etc. **2** to walk unsteadily **3** to speak, act, etc. in a blundering way **4** to do wrong **5** to come by chance —*n.* a stumbling —**stum'bler** *n.*

**stumbling block** a difficulty or obstacle

**stump** (stump) *n.* ⟦ME *stumpfe*⟧ **1** the end of a tree or plant left in the ground after the upper part has been cut off **2** the part of a limb, tooth, etc. left after the rest has been removed **3** the place where a political speech is made —*vt.* **1** to travel over (a district), making political speeches **2** [Inf.] to puzzle or perplex —*vi.* **1** to walk with a heavy step **2** to travel about, making political speeches —**stump'y**, **-i·er**, **-i·est**, *adj.*

**stun** (stun) *vt.* **stunned**, **stun'ning** ⟦ult. < L *ex-*, intens. + *tonare*, to thunder⟧ **1** to make unconscious, as by a blow **2** to daze; shock

**stung** (stuŋ) *vt.*, *vi. pt. & pp. of* STING

**stunk** (stuŋk) *vi. pp. & alt. pt. of* STINK

**stun·ning** (stun'iŋ) *adj.* [Inf.] remarkably attractive, excellent, etc.

**stunt**[1] (stunt) *vt.* ⟦< OE, stupid⟧ **1** to check the growth or development of **2** to hinder (growth, etc.)

**stunt**[2] (stunt) *n.* ⟦< ?⟧ something done to show one's skill or daring, get attention, etc. —*vi.* to do a stunt

**stu·pe·fy** (stōō'pə fī') *vt.* ⟦< L *stupere*, be stunned + *facere*, make⟧ **1** to produce stupor in; stun **2** to astound; bewilder —**stu'pe·fac'tion** (-fak'shən) *n.*

**stu·pen·dous** (stōō pen'dəs) *adj.* ⟦< L *stupere*, be stunned⟧ **1** astonishing **2** astonishingly great

**stu·pid** (stōō′pid) *adj.* ⟦see prec.⟧ **1** lacking normal intelligence **2** foolish; silly /a *stupid* idea/ **3** dull and boring —**stu·pid′i·ty,** *pl.* **-ties,** *n.*

**stu·por** (stōō′pər) *n.* ⟦see STUPENDOUS⟧ a state in which the mind and senses are dulled; loss of sensibility

**stur·dy** (stur′dē) *adj.* **-di·er, -di·est** ⟦< OFr *estourdi,* hard to control⟧ **1** firm; resolute **2** strong; vigorous **3** strongly constructed —**stur′di·ly** *adv.* —**stur′di·ness** *n.*

**stur·geon** (stur′jən) *n.* ⟦< OFr *esturjon*⟧ a large food fish valuable as a source of caviar

**stut·ter** (stut′ər) *vt., vi., n.* ⟦< ME *stutten*⟧ STAMMER

**Stutt·gart** (stoot′gärt′; *Ger* shtoot′gärt′) city in SW Germany: pop. 592,000

**St. Vin·cent and the Gren·a·dines** (sānt vin′sənt and *th*ə gren′ə dēnz′) country consisting of the island of St. Vincent and the N Grenadines, in the West Indies: 150 sq. mi.; pop. 106,000

**sty**[1] (stī) *n., pl.* **sties** ⟦< OE *sti,* hall, enclosure⟧ **1** a pen for pigs **2** any foul place

**sty**[2] or **stye** (stī) *n., pl.* **sties** or **styes** ⟦ult. < OE *stigan,* to rise⟧ a small, inflamed swelling on the rim of an eyelid

**Styg·i·an** (stij′ē ən, stij′ən) *adj.* **1** of the Styx **2** [*also* **s-**] *a*) infernal *b*) dark or gloomy

**style** (stīl) *n.* ⟦< L *stilus,* pointed writing tool⟧ **1** a stylus **2** *a*) manner of expression in language *b*) characteristic manner of expression, design, etc. in any art, period, etc. *c*) excellence of artistic expression **3** *a*) fashion *b*) something stylish —*vt.* **styled, styl′ing 1** to name; call **2** to design the style of **3** to arrange (hair) by cutting, etc.

**styl·ish** (stī′lish) *adj.* conforming to current style, as in dress; fashionable

**styl′ist** (-list) *n.* **1** a writer, etc. whose work has style and distinction **2** a person who styles hair —**sty·lis′tic** *adj.* —**sty·lis′ti·cal·ly** *adv.*

**styl·ize′** (-līz′) *vt.* **-ized′, -iz′ing** to design or represent according to a style rather than nature

**sty·lus** (stī′ləs) *n., pl.* **-lus·es** or **-li** (-lī) ⟦L, for *stilus,* pointed instrument⟧ **1** a sharp, pointed marking device **2** *a*) a sharp, pointed device for cutting the grooves of a phonograph record *b*) the short, pointed piece moving in such grooves, that transmits vibrations

**sty·mie** (stī′mē) *n.* ⟦prob. < Scot, person partially blind⟧ *Golf* a situation in which a ball to be putted has another ball between it and the hole —*vt.* **-mied, -mie·ing** to block; impede

**sty′my** *n. pl.* **-mies,** *vt.* **-mied, -my·ing** *alt. sp. of* STYMIE

**styp·tic pencil** (stip′tik) a piece of astringent, used to stop minor bleeding

**Sty·ro·foam** (stī′rə fōm′) *trademark for* a rigid, lightweight, spongelike polystyrene —*n.* [*also* **s-**] this substance

**Styx** (stiks) *n. Gr. Myth.* the river crossed by dead souls entering Hades

**sua·sion** (swā′zhən) *n.* ⟦< L *suadere,* to persuade⟧ PERSUASION: now chiefly in **moral suasion,** a persuading by appealing to one's sense of morality

**suave** (swäv) *adj.* ⟦< L *suavis,* sweet⟧ smoothly gracious or polite; polished —**suave′ly** *adv.* —**suav′i·ty** *n.*

**sub**[1] (sub) *n. short for:* **1** SUBMARINE **2** SUBSTITUTE **3** SUBMARINE SANDWICH —*vi.* **subbed, sub′bing** [Inf.] to be a substitute (*for* someone)

**sub**[2] *abbrev.* **1** substitute(s) **2** suburb(an)

**sub-** ⟦< L *sub,* under⟧ *prefix* **1** under [*submarine*] **2** lower than; inferior to [*subhead*] **3** to a lesser degree than [*subhuman*]

**sub·a·tom·ic** (sub′ə täm′ik) *adj.* of the inner part of or a particle smaller than an atom

**sub′branch′** *n.* a division of a branch

**sub′com·mit·tee** *n.* a small committee chosen from a main committee

**sub·com·pact′** *n.* an automobile model smaller than a compact

**sub·con′scious** *adj.* occurring with little or no conscious perception on the part of the individual: said of mental processes and reactions —**the subconscious** subconscious mental activity —**sub·con′scious·ly** *adv.*

**sub·con′ti·nent** *n.* a large land mass smaller than a continent

**sub·con′tract′** *n.* a secondary contract undertaking some or all obligations of another contract —*vt., vi.* to make a subcontract (for) —**sub′con′trac′tor** *n.*

**sub′cul′ture** *n.* **1** a distinctive social group within a larger social group **2** its cultural patterns

**sub′cu·ta′ne·ous** *adj.* beneath the skin

**sub′dea′con** *n.* a cleric ranking below a deacon

**sub′dis′trict** *n.* a subdivision of a district

**sub·di·vide′** *vt., vi.* **-vid′ed, -vid′ing 1** to divide further **2** to divide (land) into small parcels —**sub′di·vi′sion** *n.*

**sub·due** (səb dōō′) *vt.* **-dued′, -du′ing** ⟦< L *subducere,* take away⟧ **1** to conquer **2** to overcome; control **3** to make less intense; diminish

**sub′fam′i·ly** *n., pl.* **-lies** a main subdivision of a family, as of plants or of languages

**sub′head′** *n.* a subordinate heading or title, as of a magazine article

**subj** *abbrev.* **1** subject **2** subjunctive

**sub·ject** (sub′jikt, -jekt′; *for v.* səb jekt′) *adj.* ⟦< L *sub-,* under + *jacere,* to throw⟧ **1** under the authority or control of another **2** having a tendency [*subject* to anger] **3** exposed [*subject* to censure] **4** contingent upon: with *to* [*subject* to approval] —*n.* **1** one under the authority or control of another **2** one made to undergo a treatment, experiment, etc. **3** something dealt with in discussion, study, etc.; theme **4** a course of study in a school or college **5** *Gram.* the noun, etc. in a sentence about which something is said —*vt.* **1** to bring under the authority or control of **2** to cause to undergo something [to *subject* someone to questioning] —**sub·jec′tion** *n.*

**sub·jec·tive** (səb jek′tiv) *adj.* of or resulting from the feelings of the person thinking; not objective; personal —**sub·jec·tiv·i·ty** (sub′jek tiv′ə tē) *n.*

**sub·join** (səb join′) *vt.* ⟦see SUB- & JOIN⟧ to append

**sub·ju·gate** (sub′jə gāt′) *vt.* **-gat′ed, -gat′ing** ⟦< L *sub-,* under + *jugum,* a yoke⟧ to bring under control; conquer —**sub′ju·ga′tion** *n.*

**sub·junc·tive** (səb juŋk′tiv) *adj.* ⟦< L *subjungere,* subjoin⟧ designating or of the mood of a verb that is used to express supposition, desire, possibility, etc., rather than to state an actual fact

**sub·lease** (sub′lēs′; *for v.* sub lēs′) *n.* a lease granted by a lessee —*vt.* **-leased′, -leas′ing** to grant or hold a sublease of

**sub·let** (sub let′) *vt.* **-let′, -let′ting 1** to let to another (property which one is renting) **2** to let out (work) to a subcontractor

**sub·li·mate** (sub′lə māt′) *vt.* **-mat·ed, -mat·ing 1** to change (a solid) to a gas, or (a gas) to a solid, without becoming a liquid **2** to express (unacceptable impulses) in acceptable forms, often unconsciously —**sub′li·ma′tion** *n.*

**sub·lime** (sə blīm′) *adj.* ⟦< L *sub-,* up to + *limen,* lintel⟧ **1** noble; exalted **2** inspiring awe or admiration —*vt.* **-limed′, -lim′ing** SUBLIMATE (*vt.* 1) —**sub·lim·i·ty** (sə blim′ə tē) *n.*

**sub·lim·i·nal** (sub lim′ə nəl) *adj.* ⟦< SUB- + L *limen,* threshold + -AL⟧ below the threshold of consciousness

**sub′ma·chine′ gun** a portable automatic firearm

**sub·mar·gin·al** (sub mär′jə nəl) *adj.* below minimum requirements or standards

**sub·ma·rine** (sub′mə rēn′, sub′mə rēn′) *adj.* being, living, etc. underwater —*n.* a ship, esp. a warship, that can operate under water

**submarine sandwich** HERO SANDWICH

**sub·merge** (səb murj′) *vt.*, *vi.* -merged′, -merg′ing ⟦< L *sub-*, under + *mergere*, to plunge⟧ to place or sink beneath the surface, as of water —**sub·mer′gence** (-mur′jəns) *n.*

**sub·merse′** (-murs′) *vt.* -mersed′, -mers′ing SUB-MERGE —**sub·mers′i·ble** *adj.* —**sub·mer′sion** *n.*

**sub·mis·sion** (səb mish′ən) *n.* **1** a submitting or surrendering **2** obedience; resignation **3** *a*) the submitting of something to another *b*) the thing submitted, as a manuscript —**sub·mis′sive** *adj.*

**sub·mit′** (-mit′) *vt.* -mit′ted, -mit′ting ⟦< L *sub-*, down + *mittere*, send⟧ **1** to present to others for consideration, etc. **2** to yield to the control or power of another **3** to offer as an opinion —*vi.* to yield; give in

**sub·nor·mal** (sub nôr′məl) *adj.* below normal, esp. in intelligence

**sub·or·bit·al** (-ôr′bit′l) *adj.* designating a flight in which a rocket, spacecraft, etc. follows a trajectory of less than one orbit

**sub·or·di·nate** (sə bôrd′'n it; *for v.,* -bôr′də nāt′) *adj.* ⟦< L *sub-*, under + *ordinare*, to order⟧ **1** below another in rank, importance, etc. **2** under the authority of another **3** *Gram.* having the function of a noun, adjective, or adverb within a sentence *[a subordinate clause]* —*n.* one that is subordinate —*vt.* -nat′ed, -nat′ing to place in a subordinate position —**sub·or′di·na′tion** *n.*

**subordinate clause** *Gram.* DEPENDENT CLAUSE

**sub·orn** (sə bôrn′) *vt.* ⟦< L *sub-*, under + *ornare*, furnish⟧ to induce (another) to commit perjury — **sub·or·na·tion** (sub′ôr nā′shən) *n.*

**sub′plot′** *n.* a secondary plot in a play, novel, etc.

**sub·poe·na** (sə pē′nə) *n.* ⟦< L *sub poena*, under penalty⟧ a written legal order directing a person to appear in court to testify, etc. —*vt.* -naed, -na·ing to summon with such an order Also **na·pe′na**

**sub ro·sa** (sub rō′zə) ⟦L, under the rose, ancient symbol of secrecy⟧ secretly; privately

**sub·scribe** (səb skrīb′) *vt.*, *vi.* -scribed′, -scrib′ing ⟦< L *sub-*, under + *scribere*, write⟧ **1** to sign (one's name) at the end of a document, etc. **2** to give support or consent (to) **3** to promise to contribute (money) **4** to agree to receive and pay for a periodical, service, etc. (with *to*) —**sub·scrib′er** *n.*

**sub·script** (sub′skript′) *n.* ⟦see prec.⟧ a figure, letter, or symbol written below and to the side of another

**sub·scrip·tion** (səb skrip′shən) *n.* **1** a subscribing **2** money subscribed **3** a formal agreement to receive and pay for a periodical, etc.

**sub·se·quent** (sub′si kwənt) *adj.* ⟦< L *sub-*, after + *sequi*, follow⟧ coming after; following —**sub′se·quent·ly** *adv.*

**sub·ser·vi·ent** (səb sur′vē ənt) *adj.* ⟦< L *sub-*, under + *servire*, to serve⟧ **1** that is of service, esp. in a subordinate capacity **2** submissive —**sub·ser′vi·ence** *n.*

**sub·set** (sub′set′) *n.* a mathematical set containing some or all of the elements of a given set

**sub·side** (səb sīd′) *vi.* -sid′ed, -sid′ing ⟦< L *sub-*, under + *sidere*, to settle⟧ **1** to sink to the bottom or to a lower level **2** to become less active, intense, etc. —**sub·sid′ence** *n.*

**sub·sid·i·ar·y** (səb sid′ē er′ē) *adj.* ⟦see SUBSIDY⟧ **1** giving aid, service, etc.; auxiliary **2** being in a subordinate relationship —*n.*, *pl.* -ies one that is subsidiary; specif., a company controlled by another company

**sub·si·dize** (sub′sə dīz′) *vt.* -dized′, -diz′ing to support with a subsidy —**sub′si·di·za′tion** *n.*

**sub·si·dy** (sub′sə dē) *n.*, *pl.* -dies ⟦< L *subsidium*, auxiliary forces⟧ a grant of money, as from a government to a private enterprise

**sub·sist** (səb sist′) *vi.* ⟦< L *sub-*, under + *sistere*, to stand⟧ **1** to continue to be or exist **2** to continue to live; remain alive (*on* or *by*)

**sub·sist′ence** *n.* **1** existence **2** the act of providing sustenance **3** means of support or livelihood, esp. the barest means

**sub·soil** (sub′soil′) *n.* the layer of soil beneath the topsoil

**sub·son·ic** (sub sän′ik) *adj.* designating, of, or moving at a speed less than that of sound

**sub·stance** (sub′stəns) *n.* ⟦< L *substare*, be present⟧ **1** the real or essential part of anything; essence **2** the physical matter of which a thing consists **3** *a*) solid or substantial quality *b*) consistency; body **4** the real meaning; gist **5** wealth **6** a drug: see CONTROLLED SUBSTANCE

**sub·stand′ard** *adj.* below standard

**sub·stan·tial** (səb stan′shəl) *adj.* **1** having substance **2** real; true **3** strong; solid **4** ample; large **5** important **6** wealthy **7** with regard to essential elements —**sub·stan′tial·ly** *adv.*

**sub·stan·ti·ate** (-shē āt′) *vt.* -at′ed, -at′ing ⟦see SUBSTANCE⟧ to show to be true or real by giving evidence —**sub·stan′ti·a′tion** *n.*

**sub·stan·tive** (sub′stən tiv) *adj.* ⟦see SUBSTANCE⟧ of or dealing with essentials —*n. Gram.* a noun or any other word or group of words used as a noun

**sub·sta·tion** *n.* a small post-office station, as in a store

**sub·sti·tute** (sub′stə tōōt′) *n.* ⟦< L *sub-*, under + *statuere*, put⟧ a person or thing serving or used in place of another —*vt.*, *vi.* -tut′ed, -tut′ing to put, use, or serve in place of (another) —**sub·sti·tu′tion** *n.*

**sub·stra·tum** (sub′strāt′əm, -strat′-) *n., pl.* -ta (-ə) or -tums a part, substance, etc. which lies beneath and supports another

**sub′struc′ture** *n.* a part or structure that is a support, base, etc.

**sub·sume** (sub sōōm′) *vt.* -sumed′, -sum′ing ⟦< L *sub-*, under + *sumere*, take⟧ to include within a larger class

**sub′teen′** *n.* a child nearly a teenager

**sub′ten′ant** *n.* a person who rents from a tenant —**sub·ten′an·cy** *n.*

**sub·ter·fuge** (sub′tər fyōōj′) *n.* ⟦< L *subter*, secretly + *fugere*, flee⟧ any plan or action used to hide or evade something

**sub·ter·ra·ne·an** (sub′tə rā′nē ən) *adj.* ⟦< L *sub-*, under + *terra*, earth⟧ **1** underground **2** secret; hidden

**sub·text** (sub′tekst′) *n.* an underlying meaning, theme, etc.

**sub′ti′tle** *n.* **1** a secondary or explanatory title **2** one or more lines of translated dialogue, etc. at the bottom of a film or video image —*vt.* -ti′tled, -ti′tling to add a subtitle or subtitles to

**sub·tle** (sut′'l) *adj.* -tler (-lər, -'l ər), -tlest ⟦< L *subtilis*, fine, thin⟧ **1** thin; not dense **2** mentally keen **3** delicately skillful **4** crafty **5** not obvious —**sub′tle·ty**, *pl.* -ties, *n.* —**sub′tly** *adv.*

**sub′to′tal** *n.* a total that is part of a complete total —*vt.*, *vi.* -taled or -talled, -tal·ing or -tal·ling to add up so as to form a subtotal

**sub·tract** (səb trakt′) *vt.*, *vi.* ⟦< L *sub-*, under + *trahere*, to draw⟧ to take away or deduct (one quantity from another) —**sub·trac′tion** *n.*

**sub·tra·hend** (sub′trə hend′) *n.* a quantity to be subtracted from another (the *minuend*)

**sub·trop·i·cal** (sub trä′pi kəl) *adj.* **1** of regions bordering on the tropics **2** characteristic of such regions Also **sub·trop′ic**

**sub·urb** (sub′ərb) *n.* ⟦< L *sub-*, near + *urbs*, town⟧ a district, town, etc. on the outskirts of a city — **sub·ur·ban** (sə bur′bən) *adj.*

**sub·ur·ban·ite** (sə bur′bən īt′) *n.* a person living in a suburb

**sub·ur′bi·a** (-bē ə) *n.* the suburbs or suburbanites collectively

**sub·ven·tion** (səb ven′shən) *n.* ⟦< LL *subventio*, aid⟧ a subsidy

**sub·ver·sive** (səb vur′siv) *adj.* tending to subvert —*n.* a person seen as being subversive

**sub·vert** (səb vurt′) *vt.* ⟦< L *sub-*, under + *vertere*, to turn⟧ **1** to overthrow or destroy (something established) **2** to corrupt, as in morals —**sub·ver′sion** (-vʉr′zhən) *n.*

**sub′way′** *n.* an underground, electric metropolitan railway

**suc-** *prefix* SUB-: used before *c [succumb]*

**suc·ceed** (sək sēd′) *vi.* ⟦< L *sub-*, under + *cedere*, go⟧ **1** to follow, as into office **2** to be successful —*vt.* to come after; follow

**suc·cess** (sək ses′) *n.* **1** a favorable result **2** the gaining of wealth, fame, etc. **3** a successful person or thing

**suc·cess′ful** *adj.* **1** turning out as was hoped for **2** having gained wealth, fame, etc. —**suc·cess′ful·ly** *adv.*

**suc·ces·sion** (sək sesh′ən) *n.* **1** *a*) the act of succeeding another, as to an office *b*) the right to do this **2** a number of persons or things coming one after another

**suc·ces′sive** (-ses′iv) *adj.* coming one after another —**suc·ces′sive·ly** *adv.*

**suc·ces′sor** *n.* one that succeeds another, as to an office

**suc·cinct** (sək siŋkt′) *adj.* ⟦< L *sub-*, under + *cingere*, gird⟧ clear and brief; terse —**suc·cinct′ly** *adv.* —**suc·cinct′ness** *n.*

**suc·cor** (suk′ər) *vt.* ⟦< L *sub-*, under + *currere*, to run⟧ to help in time of need or distress —*n.* aid; relief

**suc·co·tash** (suk′ə tash′) *n.* ⟦< AmInd⟧ a dish of lima beans and corn kernels cooked together

**suc·cu·lent** (suk′yōō lənt) *adj.* ⟦< L *sucus*, juice⟧ full of juice —**suc′cu·lence** or **suc′cu·len·cy** *n.*

**suc·cumb** (sə kum′) *vi.* ⟦< L *sub-*, under + *cumbere*, to lie⟧ **1** to give way (*to*); yield **2** to die

**such** (such) *adj.* ⟦OE *swilc*⟧ **1** *a*) of the kind mentioned *b*) of the same or a similar kind **2** whatever *[at such* time as you go*]* **3** so extreme, so much, etc. *[such* an honor*]* —*adv.* to so great a degree *[such* good news*]* —*pron.* **1** such a person or thing **2** the person or thing mentioned *[such* was her nature*]* —**as such 1** as being what is indicated **2** in itself —**such as** for example

**such and such** (being) something particular but not named or specified *[such and such* a place*]*

**such′like′** *adj.* of such a kind —*pron.* persons or things of such a kind

**suck** (suk) *vt.* ⟦< OE *sucan*⟧ **1** to draw (liquid) into the mouth **2** to take in by or as by sucking **3** to suck liquid from (fruit, etc.) **4** to hold (ice, etc.) in the mouth and lick so as to dissolve **5** to place (the thumb, etc.) in the mouth and draw on —*vi.* to suck something —*n.* the act of sucking

**suck′er** *n.* **1** one that sucks **2** a freshwater bony fish with a mouth adapted for sucking **3** a part used for sucking or for holding fast by suction **4** LOLLIPOP **5** [Slang] one easily cheated **6** *Bot.* a subordinate shoot on the root or stem of a plant

**suck·le** (suk′əl) *vt.* **-led, -ling** ⟦ME *sokelen*⟧ **1** to cause to suck at the breast or udder; nurse **2** to bring up; rear —*vi.* to suck at the breast or udder

**suck′ling** *n.* an unweaned child or young animal

**su·crose** (sōō′krōs′) *n.* ⟦< Fr *sucre*, sugar + -OSE[1]⟧ a sugar extracted from sugar cane or sugar beets

**suc·tion** (suk′shən) *n.* ⟦< L *sugere*, to suck⟧ **1** a sucking **2** the production of a vacuum in a cavity or over a surface so that external atmospheric pressure forces fluid in or causes something to adhere to the surface

**Su·dan** (sōō dan′) country in NE Africa: 967,500 sq. mi.; pop. 20,564,000: often preceded by *the* —**Su·da·nese** (sōō′də nēz′), *pl.* **-nese′, *adj., n.***

**sud·den** (sud′′n) *adj.* ⟦< L *sub-*, under + *ire*, go⟧ **1** *a*) happening or coming unexpectedly *b*) sharp or abrupt **2** quick or hasty —**all of a sudden** unexpectedly —**sud′den·ly** *adv.* —**sud′den·ness** *n.*

**sudden death** *Sports* an extra period added to a tied game: the game ends when one side scores

**sudden infant death syndrome** the sudden death of an apparently healthy infant, possibly caused by a breathing problem

**suds** (sudz) *pl.n.* ⟦prob. < MDu *sudse*, marsh water⟧ **1** soapy, frothy water **2** foam —**suds′y, -i·er, -i·est,** *adj.*

**sue** (sōō) *vt., vi.* **sued, su′ing** ⟦< L *sequi*, follow⟧ **1** to appeal (to); petition **2** to prosecute in a court in seeking justice, etc.

**suede** or **suède** (swād) *n.* ⟦< Fr *gants de Suède*, Swedish gloves⟧ **1** tanned leather with the flesh side buffed into a nap **2** a kind of cloth like this

**su·et** (sōō′it) *n.* ⟦ult. < L *sebum*, tallow⟧ the hard fat of cattle and sheep: used in cooking, etc.

**Su·ez Canal** (sōō ez′) ship canal joining the Mediterranean & Red seas

**suf** or **suff** *abbrev.* suffix

**suf-** *prefix* SUB-: used before *f*

**suf·fer** (suf′ər) *vt., vi.* ⟦< L *sub-*, under + *ferre*, to bear⟧ **1** to undergo (pain, injury, grief, etc.) **2** to experience (any process) **3** to permit; tolerate —**suf′fer·er** *n.*

**suf·fer·ance** (suf′ər əns, suf′rəns) *n.* **1** the capacity to endure pain, etc. **2** consent, permission, etc. implied by failure to prohibit

**suf′fer·ing** (-ər iŋ, -riŋ) *n.* **1** the bearing of pain, distress, etc. **2** something suffered

**suf·fice** (sə fīs′) *vi.* **-ficed′, -fic′ing** ⟦< L *sub-*, under + *facere*, make⟧ to be enough or adequate

**suf·fi·cient** (sə fish′ənt) *adj.* as much as is needed; enough —**suf·fi′cien·cy** *n.* —**suf·fi′cient·ly** *adv.*

**suf·fix** (suf′iks) *n.* ⟦< L *sub-*, under + *figere*, fix⟧ a syllable or syllables joined to the end of a word to alter its meaning, etc. (Ex.: *-ness* in *darkness*)

**suf·fo·cate** (suf′ə kāt′) *vt.* **-cat′ed, -cat′ing** ⟦< L *sub-*, under + *fauces*, throat⟧ **1** to kill by cutting off the supply of air for breathing **2** to smother, suppress, etc. —*vi.* **1** to die by being suffocated **2** to choke; stifle —**suf′fo·ca′tion** *n.*

**suf·frage** (suf′rij) *n.* ⟦< L *suffragium*, a ballot⟧ **1** a vote or voting **2** the right to vote; franchise

**suf·fra·gette** (suf′rə jet′) *n.* ⟦< prec. + -ETTE⟧ a woman who advocates female suffrage: term objected to by some, who prefer *suffragist*

**suf′fra·gist** *n.* one who believes in extending the right to vote, esp. to women

**suf·fuse** (sə fyōōz′) *vt.* **-fused′, -fus′ing** ⟦< L *sub-*, under + *fundere*, pour⟧ to overspread so as to fill with a glow, etc. —**suf·fu′sion** *n.*

**sug-** *prefix* SUB-: used before *g*

**sug·ar** (shoog′ər) *n.* ⟦< Sans *śárkarâ*⟧ any of a class of sweet, soluble carbohydrates, as sucrose or glucose; specif., sucrose used as a food and sweetening agent —*vt.* to sweeten, etc. with sugar —*vi.* to form sugar —**sug′ar·less** *adj.* —**sug′ar·y** *adj.*

**sugar beet** a beet having a white root with a high sugar content

**sugar cane** a very tall tropical grass cultivated as the main source of sugar

**sug′ar·coat′** *vt.* **1** to coat with sugar **2** to make (something disagreeable) seem more pleasant

**sug′ar·plum′** *n.* a round piece of sugary candy

**sug·gest** (səg jest′) *vt.* ⟦< L *sub-*, under + *gerere*, carry⟧ **1** to bring to the mind for consideration **2** to call to mind by association of ideas **3** to propose as a possibility **4** to show indirectly; imply

**sug·gest′i·ble** *adj.* readily influenced by suggestion —**sug·gest′i·bil′i·ty** *n.*

**sug·ges′tion** (-jes′chən) *n.* **1** a suggesting or being suggested **2** something suggested **3** a hint or trace

**sug·ges′tive** *adj.* **1** that tends to suggest ideas **2** tending to suggest something considered improper or indecent —**sug·ges′tive·ly** *adv.*

**su·i·cide** (sōō′ə sīd′) *n.* ⟦L *sui*, of oneself + -CIDE⟧ **1** the act of killing oneself intentionally **2** one who commits suicide —**su′i·ci′dal** *adj.*

**su·i ge·ne·ris** (sōō′ē jen′ər is) ⟦L, of his (or her or its) own kind⟧ without equal; unique

**suit** (sōōt) *n.* ⟦< L *sequi*, follow⟧ **1** a set of clothes; esp., a coat and trousers (or skirt) **2** any of the four sets of playing cards **3** action to secure justice in a court of law **4** an act of suing, pleading, etc. **5** courtship —*vt.* **1** to be appropriate to **2** to make right or appropriate; fit **3** to please; satisfy [nothing *suits* him] —**follow suit** to follow the example set —**suit oneself** to act according to one's own wishes —**suit up** to put on an athletic uniform, spacesuit, etc. in preparation for a particular activity

**suit'a·ble** *adj.* that suits a given purpose, etc.; appropriate —**suit'a·bil'i·ty** *n.* —**suit'a·bly** *adv.*

**suit'case'** *n.* a travel case for clothes, etc.

**suite** (swēt; *for 3, also* sōōt) *n.* [Fr: see SUIT] **1** a group of attendants; staff **2** a set of connected rooms, as an apartment **3** a set of matched furniture for a given room

**suit'ing** *n.* cloth for making suits

**suit'or** *n.* a man courting a woman

**su·ki·ya·ki** (sōō'kē yä'kē) *n.* [Jpn] a Japanese dish of thinly sliced meat and vegetables, cooked quickly with soy sauce, sake, etc.

**Suk·kot** or **Suk·koth** (sook'ōt, sook'ōs) *n.* [Heb, lit., tabernacles] a Jewish fall festival commemorating the wandering of the Hebrews during the Exodus

**sul·fa** (sul'fə) *adj.* of a family of drugs used in combating certain bacterial infections

**sul·fate** (sul'fāt') *n.* a salt or ester of sulfuric acid

**sul'fide'** (-fīd') *n.* a compound of sulfur with another element or a radical

**sul·fur** (sul'fər) *n.* [< L *sulphur*] a pale-yellow, nonmetallic chemical element: it burns with a blue flame and a stifling odor

**sul·fu·ric** (sul fyoor'ik) *adj.* of or containing sulfur

**sulfuric acid** an oily, colorless, corrosive liquid used in making dyes, explosives, fertilizers, etc.

**sul·fu·rous** (sul'fər əs, sul fyoor'əs) *adj.* **1** of or containing sulfur **2** like burning sulfur in odor, color, etc.

**sulk** (sulk) *vi.* [< fol.] to be sulky —*n.* a sulky mood: also **the sulks**

**sulk·y** (sul'kē) *adj.* -i·er, -i·est [prob. < OE *-seolcan*, become slack] showing resentment by petulant withdrawal —*n., pl.* -ies a light, two-wheeled carriage for one person —**sulk'i·ly** *adv.* —**sulk'i·ness** *n.*

**sul·len** (sul'ən) *adj.* [< L *solus*, alone] **1** showing resentment and ill humor by morose, unsociable withdrawal **2** gloomy; sad —**sul'len·ly** *adv.* —**sul'len·ness** *n.*

**sul·ly** (sul'ē) *vt.* -lied, -ly·ing [prob. < OFr *soillier*] to soil, tarnish, etc., esp. by disgracing

**sul·phur** (sul'fər) *n. chiefly Brit. sp.* of SULFUR

**sul·tan** (sult''n) *n.* [Fr < Ar *sulṭān*] a Muslim ruler

**sul·tan·a** (sul tan'ə) *n.* **1** a sultan's wife, mother, sister, or daughter **2** a small, white, seedless grape used for raisins

**sul·tan·ate** (sult'n it, -āt') *n.* a sultan's authority, office, or domain

**sul·try** (sul'trē) *adj.* -tri·er, -tri·est [< SWELTER] **1** oppressively hot and moist **2** suggesting or showing passion, lust, etc.

**sum** (sum) *n.* [< L *summus*, highest] **1** an amount of money **2** gist; summary **3** the result obtained by adding quantities; total —**sum up** to summarize

**su·mac** or **su·mach** (sōō'mak', shōō'-) *n.* [< Ar *summāq*] any of numerous poisonous and nonpoisonous trees and shrubs of the cashew family

**Su·ma·tra** (sōō mä'trə) large island of Indonesia

**sum·ma·rize** (sum'ə rīz') *vt.* -rized', -riz'ing to make or be a summary of

**sum'ma·ry** (-rē) *adj.* [< L *summa*, a sum] **1** summarizing; concise **2** prompt and without formality **3** hasty and arbitrary —*n., pl.* -ries a brief statement covering the main points; digest —**sum·mar·i·ly** (sə mer'ə lē) *adv.*

**sum·ma·tion** (sə mā'shən) *n.* a final summary of arguments, as in a trial

**sum·mer** (sum'ər) *n.* [< OE *sumor*] the warmest season of the year, following spring —*adj.* of or

typical of summer —*vi.* to pass the summer —**sum'mer·y** *adj.*

**sum'mer·house'** *n.* a small, open structure in a garden, park, etc.

**summer sausage** a type of hard, dried or smoked sausage

**sum'mer·time'** *n.* the summer season

**sum·mit** (sum'it) *n.* [< L *summus*, highest] the highest or utmost point; top; apex —*adj.* of the heads of state [a *summit* conference]

**sum·mit·ry** (sum'i trē) *n., pl.* -ries the use of conferences between heads of state to resolve problems of diplomacy

**sum·mon** (sum'ən) *vt.* [< L *sub-*, under + *monere*, warn] **1** to call together; order to meet **2** to call or send for with authority **3** to rouse [*summon* up one's strength] —**sum'mon·er** *n.*

**sum'mons** (-ənz) *n., pl.* -mons·es [see prec.] **1** an order or command to come, attend, etc. **2** *Law* an official order to appear in court

**su·mo (wrestling)** (sōō'mō) [Jpn *sumō*, compete] [*sometimes* S- w-] Japanese wrestling by large, extremely heavy men

**sump** (sump) *n.* [ME *sompe*, swamp] a pit, cistern, cesspool, etc. for draining, collecting, or storing liquids

**sump·tu·ous** (sump'chōō əs) *adj.* [< L *sumptus*, expense] **1** costly; lavish **2** magnificent

**sun** (sun) *n.* [OE *sunne*] **1** the gaseous, self-luminous central star of the solar system **2** the heat or light of the sun **3** any star that is the center of a planetary system —*vt., vi.* **sunned**, **sun'ning** to expose (oneself) to direct sunlight

**Sun** *abbrev.* Sunday

**sun'bathe'** *vi.* -bathed', -bath'ing to expose the body to direct sunlight —**sun bath** —**sun'bath'er** *n.*

**sun'beam'** *n.* a beam of sunlight

**Sun'belt'** in the U.S., the S and SW states having a sunny climate and an expanding economy: also **Sun Belt**

**sun'block'** *n.* SUNSCREEN

**sun'bon'net** *n.* a bonnet for shading the face and neck from the sun

**sun'burn'** *n.* an inflammation of the skin from exposure to the sun's rays or to a sunlamp —*vi., vt.* -burned' or -burnt', -burn'ing to get or cause to get a sunburn

**sun'burst'** *n.* **1** sudden sunlight **2** a decorative device representing the sun with spreading rays

**sun·dae** (sun'dā, -dē) *n.* [prob. < fol.] a serving of ice cream covered with a syrup, fruit, nuts, etc.

**Sun·day** (sun'dā) *n.* [OE *sunnandæg*, sun day] the first day of the week: it is the Sabbath for most Christians: abbrev. **Sun**

**sun·der** (sun'dər) *vt., vi.* [< OE *sundor*, asunder] to break apart; split

SUNDIAL

**sun'di'al** *n.* an instrument that shows time by the shadow of a pointer cast by the sun onto a dial

**sun'down'** *n.* SUNSET

**sun'dries** (-drēz) *pl.n.* sundry items

**sun′dry** (-drē) *adj.* ⟦< OE *sundor,* apart⟧ miscellaneous

**sun′fish′** *n., pl.* **-fish′** or (for different species) **-fish′es** **1** any of a family of North American freshwater fishes **2** a large, sluggish ocean fish

**sun′flow′er** *n.* a tall plant having large, yellow, daisylike flowers

**sung** (suŋ) *vi., vt. pp. & rare pt. of* SING¹

**sun′glass′es** *pl.n.* eyeglasses with tinted lenses to shade the eyes

**sunk** (suŋk) *vi., vt. pp. & alt. pt. of* SINK

**sunk′en** (-ən) *adj.* **1** submerged **2** below the general level *[a sunken patio]* **3** deeply set; hollow *[sunken cheeks]*

**sun′lamp′** *n.* an ultraviolet-ray lamp, used for tanning the body, etc.

**sun′light′** *n.* the light of the sun

**sun′lit′** *adj.* lighted by the sun

**sun′ny** (-ē) *adj.* **-ni·er, -ni·est** **1** full of sunshine **2** bright; cheerful —**sun′ni·ness** *n.*

**sunny side** **1** the sunlit side **2** the brighter aspect —**sunny side up** fried upturned and with unbroken yolk *[two eggs sunny side up]*

**sun′rise′** *n.* **1** the daily appearance of the sun above the E horizon **2** the varying time of this

**sun′roof′** *n.* a panel in a car roof, that opens to let in light and air: also **sun roof**

**sun′room′** *n.* a room with large windows to let in sunlight

**sun′screen′** *n.* a chemical used in lotions, creams, etc. to block certain ultraviolet rays of the sun and reduce the danger of sunburn

**sun′set′** *n.* **1** the daily disappearance of the sun below the W horizon **2** the varying time of this

**sun′shine′** *n.* **1** the shining of the sun **2** the light and heat from the sun **3** a sunny place **4** cheerfulness, happiness, etc. —**sun′shin′y** *adj.*

**sun′spot′** *n.* any of the temporarily cooler regions appearing cyclically as dark spots on the sun

**sun′stroke′** *n.* a form of heatstroke caused by excessive exposure to the sun

**sun′suit′** *n.* short pants with a bib and shoulder straps, worn by babies and young children

**sun′tan′** *n.* a darkened condition of the skin resulting from exposure to the sun

**sun′up′** *n.* SUNRISE

**sup** (sup) *vi.* **supped, sup′ping** ⟦< OFr *soupe,* soup⟧ to have supper

**sup-** *prefix* SUB-: used before *p*

**su·per** (sōō′pər) *n.* ⟦< fol.⟧ *short for:* **1** SUPERNUMERARY (sense 2) **2** SUPERINTENDENT (sense 2) —*adj.* **1** [Inf.] outstanding; exceptionally fine **2** great, extreme, or excessive

**super-** ⟦L < *super,* above⟧ *prefix* **1** over, above *[superstructure]* **2** *a)* surpassing *[superabundant] b)* greater than others of its kind *[supermarket]* **3** additional *[supertax]*

**su′per·a·bun′dant** *adj.* being more than enough —**su′per·a·bun′dance** *n.*

**su·per·an·nu·at·ed** (sōō′pər an′yōō āt′id) *adj.* ⟦< L *super,* above + *annus,* year⟧ **1** too old for service **2** retired, esp. with a pension, because of old age **3** obsolete; old-fashioned

**su·perb** (sə purb′, sōō-) *adj.* ⟦see SUPER-⟧ **1** noble or majestic **2** rich or magnificent **3** extremely fine; excellent —**su·perb′ly** *adv.*

**su′per·car′go** *n., pl.* **-goes** or **-gos** an officer on a merchant ship in charge of the cargo

**su′per·charge′** *vt.* **-charged′, -charg′ing** to increase the power of (an engine), as with a device (**su′per·charg′er**) that forces extra air and fuel into the cylinders

**su·per·cil·i·ous** (sōō′pər sil′ē əs) *adj.* ⟦< L *super,* above + *cilium,* eyelid, hence (in allusion to raised eyebrows) haughtiness⟧ disdainful or contemptuous; haughty

**su′per·con·duc·tiv′i·ty** *n. Physics* the lack of resistance to electrical current in certain metals, etc. when cooled to low temperatures

**su′per·con·duc′tor** *n.* any material that exhibits superconductivity

**su′per·e′go** *n., pl.* **-gos** *Psychoanalysis* that part of the psyche that enforces moral standards

**su′per·er′o·ga′tion** (-er′ə gā′shən) *n.* ⟦< L *super-,* above + *erogare,* pay out⟧ a doing more than is needed or expected —**su′per·e·rog′a·to′ry** (-i räg′ə tôr′ē) *adj.*

**su′per·fi′cial** (-fish′əl) *adj.* ⟦< L *super-,* above + *facies,* face⟧ **1** of or being on the surface **2** concerned with and understanding only the obvious; shallow **3** quick and cursory **4** seeming such only at first glance —**su′per·fi′ci·al′i·ty** (-fish′ē al′ə tē), *pl.* **-ties,** *n.* —**su′per·fi′cial·ly** *adv.*

**su·per·flu·ous** (sə pur′flōō əs, sōō-) *adj.* ⟦< L *super-,* above + *fluere,* to flow⟧ excessive or unnecessary —**su·per·flu·i·ty** (sōō′pər flōō′ə tē), *pl.* **-ties,** *n.*

**su′per·he′ro** *n., pl.* **-roes** a nearly invincible hero, as in comic books

**su′per·high′way′** *n.* EXPRESSWAY

**su′per·hu′man** *adj.* **1** having a nature above that of man; divine **2** greater than that of a normal human being

**su′per·im·pose′** *vt.* **-posed′, -pos′ing** to put, lay, or stack on top of something else

**su·per·in·tend** (sōō′pər in tend′) *vt.* to act as superintendent of; supervise —**su′per·in·tend′ence** or **su′per·in·tend′en·cy** *n.*

**su′per·in·tend′ent** (-ten′dənt) *n.* ⟦< LL *super-intendere,* superintend⟧ **1** a person in charge of a department, institution, etc.; director **2** a person responsible for the maintenance of a building

**su·pe·ri·or** (sə pir′ē ər) *adj.* ⟦see SUPER-⟧ **1** higher in space, order, rank, etc. **2** greater in quality or value than: with *to* **3** above average in quality; excellent **4** refusing to give in to or be affected by: with *to* **5** showing a feeling of being better than others; haughty —*n.* **1** a superior person or thing **2** the head of a religious community —**su·pe′ri·or′i·ty** (-ôr′ə tē) *n.*

**Su·pe·ri·or** (sə pir′ē ər), **Lake** largest of the Great Lakes, between Michigan & Ontario, Canada

**superl** *abbrev.* superlative

**su·per·la·tive** (sə pur′lə tiv, sōō-) *adj.* ⟦< L *super-,* above + *latus,* pp. of *ferre,* to bear, carry⟧ **1** superior to all others; supreme **2** *Gram.* designating the extreme degree of comparison of adjectives and adverbs —*n.* **1** the highest degree; peak **2** *Gram.* the superlative degree *["finest" is the superlative of "fine"]* —**su·per′la·tive·ly** *adv.*

**su′per·ma·jor′i·ty** *n.* the quantity of votes, above a mere majority, required to pass certain bills, etc.

**su′per·man′** (-man′) *n., pl.* **-men′** (-men′) an apparently superhuman man

**su′per·mar′ket** *n.* a large, self-service, retail food store or market

**su·per·nal** (sōō purn′əl) *adj.* ⟦< L *supernus,* upper⟧ celestial or divine

**su′per·nat′u·ral** *adj.* not explainable by the known forces or laws of nature; specif., of or involving God, ghosts, spirits, etc.

**su′per·no′va** *n., pl.* **-vas** or **-vae** (-vē) a rare, extremely bright nova

**su·per·nu·mer·a·ry** (sōō′pər nōō′mə rer′ē) *n., pl.* **-ies** ⟦< L *super,* above + *numerus,* number⟧ **1** an extra person or thing **2** *Theater* a person with a small, nonspeaking part

**su′per·pose′** *vt.* **-posed′, -pos′ing** ⟦see SUPER- & POSE⟧ to place on or above something else —**su′per·pos′a·ble** *adj.* —**su′per·po·si′tion** *n.*

**su′per·pow′er** *n.* an extremely powerful, influential nation

**su′per·sat′u·rate′** *vt.* **-rat′ed, -rat′ing** to make more highly concentrated than in normal saturation —**su′per·sat′u·ra′tion** *n.*

**su′per·script′** *n.* ⟦see SUPER- & SCRIPT⟧ a figure, letter, or symbol written above and to the side of another

**su·per·sede** (sōō′pər sēd′) *vt.* **-sed′ed, -sed′ing** ⟦< L *supersedere,* sit over⟧ to replace or succeed

**su′per·son′ic** *adj.* ⟦SUPER- + SONIC⟧ **1** designating, of, or moving at a speed greater than that of sound **2** ULTRASONIC

**su′per·star′** *n.* a star performer, as in sports or entertainment

**su·per·sti·tion** (sōō′pər stish′ən) *n.* ⟦< L *superstitio,* lit., a standing (in awe) over⟧ **1** any belief that is inconsistent with known facts or rational thought, esp. such a belief in omens, the supernatural, etc. **2** any action or practice based on such a belief —**su′per·sti′tious** *adj.*

**su′per·store′** *n.* a very large retail store with a wide variety of goods

**su′per·struc′ture** *n.* **1** a structure built on top of another **2** that part of a building above the foundation **3** that part of a ship above the main deck

**su′per·tank′er** *n.* an extremely large tanker, of 300,000 tons or more

**su·per·vene** (sōō′pər vēn′) *vi.* **-vened′, -ven′ing** ⟦< L *super-,* over + *venire,* come⟧ to come or happen as something extraneous or unexpected

**su·per·vise** (sōō′pər vīz′) *vt., vi.* **-vised′, -vis′ing** ⟦< L *super-,* over + *videre,* see⟧ to oversee or direct (work, workers, etc.) —**su′per·vi′sion** (-vizh′ən) *n.* —**su′per·vi′sor** *n.* —**su′per·vi′so·ry** *adj.*

**su·pine** (sōō pīn′) *adj.* ⟦L *supinus*⟧ **1** lying on the back, face upward **2** inactive; sluggish; listless

**supp** or **suppl** *abbrev.* **1** supplement **2** supplementary

**sup·per** (sup′ər) *n.* ⟦see SUP⟧ an evening meal

**supper club** an expensive nightclub

**sup·plant** (sə plant′) *vt.* ⟦< L *sub-,* under + *planta,* sole of the foot⟧ **1** to take the place of, esp. by force or plotting **2** to remove in order to replace with something else

**sup·ple** (sup′əl) *adj.* **-pler, -plest** ⟦< L *supplex,* submissive⟧ **1** easily bent; flexible **2** lithe; limber **3** adaptable

**sup·ple·ment** (sup′lə mənt; *for v.,* -ment′) *n.* ⟦see SUPPLY⟧ **1** something added, esp. to make up for a lack **2** a section of additional material in a book, newspaper, etc. —*vt.* to provide a supplement to —**sup′ple·men′tal** or **sup′ple·men′ta·ry** *adj.*

**sup·pli·ant** (sup′lē ənt) *n.* one who supplicates —*adj.* supplicating

**sup′pli·cant** (-lə kənt) *adj., n.* SUPPLIANT

**sup·pli·cate** (sup′lə kāt′) *vt., vi.* **-cat′ed, -cat′ing** ⟦< L *sub-,* under + *plicare,* to fold⟧ **1** to ask for (something) humbly **2** to make a humble request (of) —**sup′pli·ca′tion** *n.*

**sup·ply** (sə plī′) *vt.* **-plied′, -ply′ing** ⟦< L *sub-,* under + *plere,* fill⟧ **1** to furnish or provide (what is needed) to (someone) **2** to compensate for (a deficiency, etc.); make good —*n., pl.* **-plies′ 1** the amount available for use or sale; stock **2** [*pl.*] needed materials, provisions, etc. —**sup·pli′er** *n.*

**sup·ply′-side′** *adj.* designating or of an economic theory that an increase in money for investment, as supplied by lowering taxes, will stimulate economic growth

**sup·port** (sə pôrt′) *vt.* ⟦< L *sub-,* under + *portare,* carry⟧ **1** to carry the weight of; hold up **2** to encourage; help **3** to advocate; uphold **4** to maintain (a person, institution, etc.) with money or subsistence **5** to help prove, vindicate, etc. **6** to bear; endure **7** to keep up; maintain **8** to have a role subordinate to (a star) in a play —*n.* **1** a supporting or being supported **2** a person or thing that supports **3** a means of maintaining a livelihood —**sup·port′a·ble** *adj.* —**sup·port′er** *n.*

**sup·port′ive** *adj.* giving support or help

**sup·pose** (sə pōz′) *vt.* **-posed′, -pos′ing** ⟦< L *sub-,* under + *ponere,* put⟧ **1** to assume to be true, as for argument's sake **2** to believe, think, etc. **3** to consider as a possibility [*suppose* I go] **4** to expect [I'm *supposed* to sing] —*vi.* to conjecture —**sup·posed′** *adj.* —**sup·pos′ed·ly** *adv.*

**sup·po·si·tion** (sup′ə zish′ən) *n.* **1** a supposing **2** something supposed

**sup·pos·i·to·ry** (sə päz′ə tôr′ē) *n., pl.* **-ries** ⟦see SUPPOSE⟧ a small piece of medicated substance placed in the rectum or vagina, where it melts

**sup·press** (sə pres′) *vt.* ⟦< L *sub-,* under + *premere,* to press⟧ **1** to put down by force; quell **2** to keep from being known, published, etc. **3** to keep back; restrain —**sup·pres′sion** (-presh′ən) *n.*

**sup·pres′sant** (-ənt) *n.* a drug, etc. that tends to suppress an action, condition, etc.

**sup·pu·rate** (sup′yōō rāt′) *vi.* **-rat′ed, -rat′ing** ⟦< L *sub-,* under + *pus,* pus⟧ to form or discharge pus

**supra-** ⟦< L *supra,* above⟧ *prefix* above, over, beyond

**su·pra·na·tion·al** (sōō′prə nash′ə nəl) *adj.* of, for, or above all or a number of nations

**su·prem·a·cist** (sə prem′ə sist, sōō-) *n.* one who believes in the supremacy of a particular group

**su·prem′a·cy** (-sē) *n., pl.* **-cies** supreme condition or power

**su·preme′** (-prēm′) *adj.* ⟦< L *superus,* that is above⟧ **1** highest in rank, power, etc. **2** highest in quality, achievement, etc. **3** highest in degree **4** final; ultimate —**su·preme′ly** *adv.*

**Supreme Being** God

**Supreme Court 1** the highest U.S. federal court **2** the highest court in most U.S. states

**Supreme Soviet 1** a part of the legislature of Russia **2** formerly, the parliament of the U.S.S.R.

**Supt** *abbrev.* Superintendent

**sur-** ⟦< L *super,* over⟧ *prefix* over, upon, above, beyond

**sur·cease** (sʉr′sēs′) *n.* ⟦< L *supersedere,* refrain from⟧ an end, or cessation

**sur·charge** (sʉr′chärj′) *vt.* **-charged′, -charg′ing** ⟦see SUR- & CHARGE⟧ **1** to overcharge **2** to mark (a postage stamp) with a surcharge —*n.* **1** an additional charge **2** a new valuation printed over the original valuation on a postage stamp

**sur·cin·gle** (sʉr′siŋ′gəl) *n.* ⟦< OFr *sur-,* over + L *cingulum,* a belt⟧ a strap passed around a horse's body to bind on a saddle, pack, etc.

**sure** (shoor) *adj.* **sur′er, sur′est** ⟦< L *securus*⟧ **1** that will not fail [a *sure* method] **2** that cannot be doubted or questioned [*sure* of the facts] **4** that can be counted on to be or happen [a *sure* defeat] **5** certain (to do, be, etc.) [*sure* to lose] —*adv.* [Inf.] certainly; indeed —**for sure** certain(ly) —**sure enough** [Inf.] without doubt —**sure′ness** *n.*

**sure′fire′** or **sure′-fire′** *adj.* [Inf.] sure to be successful or as expected

**sure′-foot′ed** *adj.* not likely to stumble, slip, fall, or err —**sure′-foot′ed·ness** *n.*

**sure′ly** *adv.* **1** with confidence **2** without a doubt; certainly

**sur·e·ty** (shoor′ə tē, shoor′tē) *n., pl.* **-ties 1** something that gives assurance, as against loss, etc. **2** one who takes responsibility for another

**surf** (sʉrf) *n.* ⟦prob. var. of SOUGH⟧ the waves of the sea breaking on the shore or a reef —*vi.* to engage in surfing —*vt.* [Inf.] to browse a succession of (TV channels, websites, etc.) on (a TV, computer network, etc.) —**surf′er** *n.*

**sur·face** (sʉr′fis) *n.* ⟦< Fr *sur-,* over + *face,* a face⟧ **1** *a)* the exterior of an object *b)* any of the faces of a solid **2** superficial features or outward appearance —*adj.* **1** of, on, or at the surface **2** external; superficial —*vt.* **-faced, -fac·ing** to give a surface to, as in paving —*vi.* **1** to rise to the surface of the water **2** to become known

**surf′board′** *n.* a long, narrow board used in the sport of surfing

**surf′-cast′** *vi.* **-cast′, -cast′ing** to fish by casting into the surf from or near the shore

**sur·feit** (sʉr′fit) *n.* ⟦< OFr *sorfaire,* overdo⟧ **1** too great an amount **2** overindulgence, esp. in food or drink **3** disgust, nausea, etc. resulting from excess —*vt.* to feed or supply to excess

**surf·ing** (sur'fiŋ) *n.* the sport of riding in toward shore on the crest of a wave, esp. on a surfboard

**surge** (surj) *n.* [< L *surgere*, to rise] 1 a large wave of water, or its motion 2 a sudden, strong increase, as of power —*vi.* **surged, surg'ing** 1 to move in or as in a surge 2 to increase suddenly

**sur·geon** (sur'jən) *n.* a doctor who specializes in surgery

**sur·ger·y** (sur'jər ē) *n., pl.* **-ger·ies** [< Gr *cheir*, the hand + *ergein*, to work] 1 the treatment of disease, injury, etc. by manual or instrumental operations 2 a room used for this

**sur'gi·cal** (-ji kəl) *adj.* 1 of surgeons or surgery 2 very accurate, precisely targeted, etc. —**sur'gi·cal·ly** *adv.*

**sur·gi·cen·ter** (sur'jə sent'ər) *n.* [< *Surgicenter*, a service mark] a facility for performing minor surgery on outpatients

**Su·ri·name** (soor'i näm') country in NE South America: 63,251 sq. mi.; pop. 355,000: formerly **Su'ri·nam'**

**sur·ly** (sur'lē) *adj.* **-li·er, -li·est** [earlier *sirly*, imperious < *sir*, sir] bad-tempered; sullenly rude

**sur·mise** (sər mīz') *n.* [OFr *sur-*, upon + *mettre*, put] a conjecture —*vt., vi.* **-mised', -mis'ing** to guess

**sur·mount** (sər mount') *vt.* [SUR- & MOUNT²] 1 to overcome (a difficulty) 2 to be at the top of; rise above 3 to climb up and across (a height, etc.) —**sur·mount'a·ble** *adj.*

**sur·name** (sur'nām') *n.* [< OFr *sur-* (see SUR-) + *nom*, name] the family name, or last name

**sur·pass** (sər pas') *vt.* [< Fr *sur-* (see SUR-) + *passer*, to pass] 1 to excel or be superior to 2 to go beyond the limit, capacity, etc. of

**sur·plice** (sur'plis) *n.* [< L *super-*, above + *pelliceum*, fur robe] a loose, white outer ecclesiastical vestment

**sur·plus** (sur'plus) *n.* [< OFr *sur-*, above (see SUR-) + L *plus*, more] a quantity over and above what is needed or used —*adj.* excess; extra

SURPLICE

**sur·prise** (sər prīz') *vt.* **-prised', -pris'ing** [< OFr *sur-* (see SUR-) + *prendre*, to take] 1 to come upon suddenly or unexpectedly; take unawares 2 to amaze; astonish —*n.* 1 a being surprised 2 something that surprises

**sur·re·al** (sə rē'əl) *adj.* 1 of or like surrealism 2 bizarre; fantastic

**sur·re'al·ism'** *n.* [see SUR- & REAL] a modern movement in the arts in which the workings of the unconscious are depicted —**sur·re'al·is'tic** *adj.* —**sur·re'al·ist** *adj., n.*

**sur·ren·der** (sə ren'dər) *vt.* [< Fr *sur-*, up + *rendre*, render] 1 to give up possession of; yield to another on compulsion 2 to give up or abandon —*vi.* to give oneself up, esp. as a prisoner —*n.* the act of surrendering

**sur·rep·ti·tious** (sur'əp tish'əs) *adj.* [< L *sub-*, under + *rapere*, seize] done, gotten, acting, etc. in a stealthy way

**sur·rey** (sur'ē) *n., pl.* **-reys** [after *Surrey*, county in England] a light, four-wheeled carriage with two seats and a flat top

**sur·ro·gate** (sur'ə git, -gāt') *n.* [< L *sub-*, in place of + *rogare*, ask] 1 a deputy or substitute 2 in some U.S. states, a probate court judge 3 a woman who bears a child for another woman, who will raise it —**sur'ro·ga·cy**, *pl.* **-cies**, *n.*

**sur·round** (sə round') *vt.* [< L *super-*, over +

*undare*, to rise] to encircle on all or nearly all sides

**sur·round'ings** *pl.n.* the things, conditions, etc. around a person or thing

**sur·tax** (sur'taks') *n.* an extra tax on top of the regular tax

**sur·veil·lance** (sər vā'ləns) *n.* [Fr < *sur-* (see SUR-) + *veiller*, to watch] close watch kept over someone, esp. a suspect

**sur·vey** (sər vā'; *for n.* sur'vā') *vt.* [< OFr *sur-* (see SUR-) + *veoir*, see] 1 to examine or consider in detail or comprehensively 2 to determine the location, form, or boundaries of (a tract of land) —*n., pl.* **-veys** 1 a detailed study, as by gathering information and analyzing it 2 a general view 3 *a*) the process of surveying a tract of land *b*) a written description of this —**sur·vey'or** *n.*

**sur·vey'ing** *n.* the science or work of making land surveys

**sur·viv·al·ist** (sər vī'vəl ist) *n.* one who takes measures, as storing food and weapons, to ensure survival after an economic collapse, nuclear war, etc.

**sur·vive** (sər vīv') *vt.* **-vived', -viv'ing** [< L *super-*, above + *vivere*, to live] to remain alive or in existence after —*vi.* to continue living or existing —**sur·viv'al** *n.*

**sur·vi'vor** (-ər) *n.* 1 one that survives 2 someone regarded as capable of surviving changing conditions, misfortune, etc.

**sus·cep·ti·ble** (sə sep'tə bəl) *adj.* [< L *sus-*, under + *capere*, take] easily affected emotionally —**susceptible of** admitting; allowing [testimony *susceptible of* error] —**susceptible to** easily influenced or affected by —**sus·cep'ti·bil'i·ty** *n.*

**su·shi** (soo'shē) *n.* [Jpn] a dish consisting of small cakes of cold rice garnished with raw or cooked fish, vegetables, etc.

**sus·pect** (sə spekt'; *for adj. & n.* sus'pekt') *vt.* [< L *sus-*, under + *spicere*, to look] 1 to believe to be guilty on little or no evidence 2 to believe to be bad, wrong, etc.; distrust 3 to guess; surmise —*adj.* suspected —*n.* one suspected of a crime, etc.

**sus·pend** (sə spend') *vt.* [< L *sus-*, under + *pendere*, hang] 1 to exclude as a penalty from an office, school, etc., for a time 2 to stop temporarily 3 to hold back (judgment, etc.) 4 to hang by a support from above 5 to hold in place as though hanging [dust particles *suspended* in the air]

**suspended animation** a temporary cessation of the vital functions, resembling death

**sus·pend'ers** *pl.n.* a pair of straps passed over the shoulders to hold up trousers

**sus·pense** (sə spens') *n.* [< L *suspendere*, suspend] 1 a state of uncertainty 2 the growing excitement felt while awaiting a climax of a novel, play, etc. —**sus·pense'ful** *adj.*

**sus·pen·sion** (sə spen'shən) *n.* 1 a suspending or being suspended 2 the system of springs, etc. supporting a vehicle upon its undercarriage or axles 3 a substance whose particles are dispersed through a fluid but not dissolved in it

**suspension bridge** a bridge suspended from cables anchored at either end and supported by towers at intervals

**sus·pi·cion** (sə spish'ən) *n.* [< L *suspicere*, suspect] 1 a suspecting 2 the feeling or state of mind of one who suspects 3 a very small amount; trace —*vt.* [Inf. or Dial.] to suspect

**sus·pi'cious** *adj.* 1 arousing suspicion 2 showing or feeling suspicion —**sus·pi'cious·ly** *adv.*

**sus·tain** (sə stān') *vt.* [< L *sus-*, under + *tenere*, to hold] 1 to keep in existence; maintain or prolong 2 to provide sustenance for 3 to carry the weight of; support 4 to endure; withstand 5 to comfort or encourage 6 to suffer (an injury, loss, etc.) 7 to uphold the validity of 8 to confirm; corroborate

**sus·te·nance** (sus'tə nəns) *n.* 1 a sustaining 2 means of livelihood 3 nourishment; food

**sut·ler** (sut'lər) *n.* [< 16th-c. Du *soeteler*] [Historical] a person following an army to sell things to its soldiers

**su·ture** (sōō'chər) *n.* [< L *suere,* sew] **1** the line of junction of two parts, esp. of bones of the skull **2** *a)* the stitching together of the two edges of a wound or incision *b)* the thread, etc. used or any of the stitches so made

**SUV** *abbrev.* SPORT UTILITY VEHICLE

**su·ze·rain** (sōō'zə rin', -rān') *n.* [Fr < L *sursum,* above] **1** a feudal lord **2** a state in relation to another over which it has some political control

**svelte** (svelt) *adj.* [Fr] **1** slender; lithe **2** suave

**Sw** **1** Sweden **2** Swedish

**SW** *abbrev.* **1** southwest **2** southwestern

**swab** (swäb) *n.* [< Du *zwabben,* do dirty work] **1** a yarn mop **2** a small piece of cotton, etc. used to medicate or cleanse a bodily orifice or a wound — *vt.* **swabbed, swab'bing** to use a swab on

**swad·dle** (swäd''l) *vt.* **-dled, -dling** [prob. < OE *swathian,* swathe] to wrap (a newborn baby) in a blanket or, formerly, in long, narrow bands of cloth (**swaddling clothes**)

**swag** (swag) *vt.* **swagged, swag'ging** [see SWAG-GER] to hang in a swag —*n.* **1** a valance, garland, etc. hanging decoratively in a curve **2** [Slang] loot

**swage** (swāj) *n.* a tool for bending or shaping metal

**swag·ger** (swag'ər) *vi.* [prob. < Norw *svagga,* sway] **1** to walk with a bold, arrogant stride **2** to boast or brag loudly —*n.* swaggering walk or manner

**Swa·hi·li** (swä hē'lē) *n.* [< Ar *sawāḥil,* the coasts] a Bantu language of E Africa

**swain** (swān) *n.* [< ON *sveinn,* boy] [Archaic] **1** a country youth **2** a lover

**swal·low**[1] (swäl'ō) *n.* [OE *swealwe*] a small, swift-flying bird with long, pointed wings and a forked tail

**swal·low**[2] (swäl'ō) *vt.* [OE *swelgan*] **1** to pass (food, etc.) from the mouth into the stomach **2** to take in; absorb: often with *up* **3** to retract (words said) **4** to put up with [to *swallow* insults] **5** to suppress [to *swallow* one's pride] **6** [Inf.] to accept as true without question —*vi.* to perform the actions of swallowing something, esp. as a result of emotion —*n.* **1** a swallowing **2** the amount swallowed at one time

**swam** (swam) *vi., vt. pt. of* SWIM[1] & SWIM[2]

**swa·mi** (swä'mē) *n., pl.* **-mis** [< Sans *svāmin,* lord] **1** lord; master: title of respect for a Hindu religious teacher **2** a learned man; pundit

**swamp** (swämp, swômp) *n.* [prob. < LowG] a piece of wet, spongy land; marsh; bog —*vt.* **1** to plunge or sink in a swamp, water, etc. **2** to flood as with water **3** to overwhelm [*swamped* by debts] **4** to sink (a boat) by filling with water — **swamp'y, -i·er, -i·est,** *adj.*

**swan** (swän, swôn) *n.* [OE] a large waterfowl, usually white, with a long, graceful neck

**swank** (swank) [Inf.] *n.* [akin to OE *swancor,* pliant] ostentatious display —*adj.* ostentatiously stylish

**swank'y** *adj.* **-i·er, -i·est** [Inf.] ostentatiously stylish

**swan's'-down'** *n.* **1** the soft down of the swan, used for trimming clothes, etc. **2** a soft, thick flannel Also **swans'down'**

**swan song** [after the song sung, in ancient fable, by a dying swan] the last act, final creative work, etc. of a person

**swap** (swäp, swôp) [Inf.] *vt., vi.* **swapped, swap'ping,** *n.* [ME *swappen,* to strike] trade; barter

**sward** (swôrd) *n.* [< OE *sweard,* a skin] grass-covered soil; turf

**swarm** (swôrm) *n.* [OE *swearm*] **1** a large number of bees, led by a queen, leaving a hive to start a new colony **2** a colony of bees in a hive **3** a moving mass, crowd, or throng —*vi.* **1** to fly off in

a swarm: said of bees **2** to move, be present, etc. in large numbers **3** to be crowded

**swarth·y** (swôr'*th*ē, -thē) *adj.* **-i·er, -i·est** [< OE *sweart*] having a dark complexion

**swash'buck'ler** (-buk'lər) *n.* [< *swash,* to swagger + *buckler,* a shield] a blustering, swaggering fighting man —**swash'buck'ling** *n., adj.*

**swas·ti·ka** (swäs'ti kə) *n.* [< Sans *svasti,* well-being] **1** an ancient design and mystic symbol in the form of a cross with four equal arms, each bent in a right angle **2** this design with the arms bent clockwise, used as an emblem of Nazism and anti-Semitism

**swat** (swät) *vt.* **swat'ted, swat'ting** [echoic] to hit with a quick, sharp blow —*n.* a quick, sharp blow —**swat'ter** *n.*

**SWAT** (swät) *n.* [S(*pecial*) W(*eapons*) a(*nd*) T(*actics*)] a special police unit trained to deal with violence, riots, terrorism, etc.: in full **SWAT team**

**swatch** (swäch) *n.* [orig., a cloth tag or label] a sample piece of cloth, etc.

**swath** (swäth, swôth) *n.* [OE *swathu,* a track] **1** the width covered with one cut of a scythe or other mowing device **2** a strip, row, etc. that has been mowed

**swathe** (swä*th,* swā*th*) *vt.* **swathed, swath'ing** [OE *swathian*] **1** to wrap up in a long strip of cloth **2** to envelop; enclose

**sway** (swā) *vi.* [< ON *sveigja,* to turn, bend] **1** to swing or move from side to side or to and fro **2** to lean or go to one side —*vt.* **1** to cause to sway **2** to influence —*n.* **1** a swaying or being swayed **2** influence [the *sway* of passion] —**hold sway** to reign or prevail

**sway'backed'** (-bakt') *adj.* having a sagging spine: said as of some horses

**Swa·zi·land** (swä'zē land') country in SE Africa: 6,705 sq. mi.; pop. 681,000

**swear** (swer) *vi.* **swore, sworn, swear'ing** [OE *swerian*] **1** to make a solemn declaration with an appeal to God to confirm it **2** to make a solemn promise; vow **3** to use profane language; curse — *vt.* to declare, pledge, or vow on oath —**swear in** to administer an oath to (a person taking office, a witness, etc.) —**swear off** to renounce —**swear out** to obtain (a warrant for arrest) by making a charge under oath —**swear'er** *n.*

**swear'word'** *n.* a profane word or phrase

**sweat** (swet) *vi., vt.* **sweat** or **sweat'ed, sweat'ing** [< OE *swat,* sweat] **1** to give forth or cause to give forth a salty moisture through the pores of the skin; perspire **2** to give forth or condense (moisture) on its surface **3** to work hard enough to cause sweating —*n.* **1** the salty liquid given forth in perspiration **2** moisture collected in droplets on a surface **3** a sweating or being sweated **4** a condition of eagerness, anxiety, etc. **5** [*pl.*] clothes worn for exercising, etc.; specif., a sweat suit —**sweat out** [Inf.] **1** to get rid of by sweating [to *sweat out* a cold] **2** to wait anxiously for or through —**sweat'y, -i·er, -i·est,** *adj.*

**sweat'er** *n.* a knitted or crocheted outer garment for the upper body

**sweat shirt** a heavy, long-sleeved pullover of cotton jersey worn to absorb sweat during or after exercise, sometimes with matching loose trousers (**sweat pants**) in an ensemble (**sweat suit**)

**sweat'shop'** *n.* a shop where employees work long hours at low wages under poor conditions

**Swed** *abbrev.* **1** Sweden **2** Swedish

**Swede** (swēd) *n.* a person born or living in Sweden

**Swe·den** (swēd''n) country in N Europe: 173,732 sq. mi.; pop. 8,587,000

**Swed·ish** (swē'dish) *adj.* of Sweden or its people, language, etc. —*n.* the Germanic language of Sweden

**sweep** (swēp) *vt.* **swept, sweep'ing** [OE *swapan*] **1** to clean (a floor, etc.) as by brushing with a broom **2** to remove (dirt, etc.) as with a broom **3** to strip, carry away, or destroy with a forceful movement **4** to touch in moving across /hands *sweeping* the keyboard/ **5** to pass swiftly over or across **6** *a*) to win all the games of (a series, etc.) *b*) to win overwhelmingly —*vi.* **1** to clean a floor, etc. as with a broom **2** to move steadily with speed or grace **3** to extend in a long curve or line [a road *sweeping* up the hill/ —*n.* **1** the act of sweeping **2** a steady sweeping movement **3** range or scope **4** extent, as of land; stretch **5** a line, curve, etc. that seems to flow or move **6** one whose work is sweeping [a chimney *sweep*] — **sweep'er** *n.* —**sweep'ing** *adj.* —**sweep'ing·ly** *adv.*

**sweep'ings** *pl.n.* things swept up, as litter from a floor

**sweep'stakes'** *n., pl.* **-stakes'** a lottery in which each participant puts up money in a common fund that is given as the prize to the winner or winners, as determined by the result of a horse race or other contest: also **sweep'stake'**

**sweet** (swēt) *adj.* ⟦OE *swete*⟧ **1** having a taste of, or like that of, sugar **2** *a*) having an agreeable taste, smell, sound, etc. *b*) gratifying *c*) friendly, kind, etc. **3** *a*) not rancid or sour *b*) not salty or salted —*n.* [*pl.*] sweet foods —**sweet'ish** *adj.* — **sweet'ly** *adv.* —**sweet'ness** *n.*

**sweet'bread'** (-bred') *n.* the thymus or sometimes the pancreas of a calf, lamb, etc., when used as food: *usually used in pl.*

**sweet'bri·er** or **sweet'bri·ar** (-brī'ər) *n.* EGLANTINE

**sweet corn** a variety of Indian corn eaten unripe as a table vegetable

**sweet'en** *vt.* **1** to make sweet **2** to make pleasant or agreeable **3** [Inf.] to increase the value of (collateral, an offer, etc.)

**sweet'en·er** *n.* a sweetening agent, esp. a synthetic one, as saccharin

**sweet'heart'** *n.* a loved one; lover

**sweetheart contract** a contract arranged by collusion between union officials and an employer with terms disadvantageous to union members

**sweet'meat'** *n.* a candy

**sweet pea** a climbing plant with butterfly-shaped flowers

**sweet pepper 1** a red pepper plant producing a large, mild fruit **2** the fruit

**sweet potato 1** a tropical plant with a fleshy, brownish root used as a vegetable **2** its root

**sweet'-talk'** *vt., vi.* [Inf.] to talk in a flattering way (to)

**sweet tooth** [Inf.] a fondness or craving for sweets

**swell** (swel) *vi., vt.* **swelled, swelled** or **swol'len, swell'ing** ⟦OE *swellan*⟧ **1** to expand as a result of pressure from within **2** to curve out; bulge **3** to fill (*with* pride, etc.) **4** to increase in size, force, intensity, loudness, etc. —*n.* **1** a part that swells; specif., a large, rolling wave **2** an increase in size, amount, degree, etc. **3** a crescendo —*adj.* [Slang] excellent

**swell'head'** *n.* [Inf.] a conceited person — **swell'head'ed** *adj.*

**swell'ing** *n.* **1** an increase in size, volume, etc. **2** a swollen part

**swel·ter** (swel'tər) *vi.* ⟦< OE *sweltan,* to die, faint⟧ to feel uncomfortably hot; sweat, feel weak, etc. from great heat

**swel'ter·ing** *adj.* very hot; sultry

**swept** (swept) *vt., vi. pt. & pp. of* SWEEP

**swept'back'** *adj.* having a backward slant: said of the wings of an aircraft

**swerve** (swʉrv) *vi., vt.* **swerved, swerv'ing** ⟦< OE *sweorfan,* to scour⟧ to turn aside from a straight line, course, etc. —*n.* a swerving

**swift** (swift) *adj.* ⟦OE⟧ **1** moving with great speed; fast **2** coming, acting, etc. quickly —*n.* a swift-flying, swallowlike bird —**swift'ly** *adv.* — **swift'ness** *n.*

**Swift** (swift), **Jon·a·than** (jän'ə thən) 1667-1745; Eng. satirist, born in Ireland

**swig** (swig) [Inf.] *vt., vi.* **swigged, swig'ging** ⟦< ?⟧ to drink in gulps —*n.* a big gulp, as of liquor

**swill** (swil) *vt., vi.* ⟦OE *swilian*⟧ **1** to drink greedily **2** to feed swill to (pigs, etc.) —*n.* **1** liquid garbage fed to pigs **2** garbage

**swim**[1] (swim) *vi.* **swam, swum, swim'ming** ⟦OE *swimman*⟧ **1** to move through water by moving arms, legs, fins, etc. **2** to move along smoothly **3** to float on or in a liquid **4** to overflow /eyes *swimming* with tears/ —*vt.* to swim in or across —*n.* the act of swimming —*adj.* [Inf.] of or for swimming [*swim* trunks] —**in the swim** active in what is popular at the moment —**swim'mer** *n.*

**swim**[2] (swim) *n.* ⟦OE *swima*⟧ a dizzy spell —*vi.* **swam, swum, swim'ming 1** to be dizzy **2** to seem to whirl /the room *swam* before me/

**swimming hole** a deep place in a river, creek, etc. used for swimming

**swim'ming·ly** *adv.* easily and with success

**swim'suit'** *n.* a garment worn for swimming

**swin·dle** (swin'dəl) *vt., vi.* **-dled, -dling** ⟦< Ger *schwindeln*⟧ to defraud (another) of money or property; cheat —*n.* an act of swindling; trick; fraud —**swin'dler** *n.*

**swine** (swīn) *n., pl.* **swine** ⟦OE *swīn*⟧ **1** a pig or hog: usually used collectively **2** a vicious, contemptible person

**swing** (swiŋ) *vi.* **swung, swing'ing** ⟦OE *swingan*⟧ **1** to sway or move backward and forward **2** to walk, trot, etc. with relaxed movements **3** to strike (*at*) **4** to turn, as on a hinge **5** to move in a curve **6** to hang; be suspended **7** [Slang] *a*) to be ultra-fashionable, esp. in seeking pleasure *b*) to engage in casual sexual relations —*vt.* **1** to move, lift, etc. with a sweeping motion **2** to cause to move backward and forward **3** to cause to turn, as on a hinge **4** to cause to move in a curve [*swing* the car around/ **5** [Inf.] to cause to come about successfully [to *swing* an election/ —*n.* **1** a swinging **2** the arc through which something swings **3** the manner of swinging a golf club, etc. **4** a relaxed motion, as in walking **5** a sweeping blow **6** the course of some activity, etc. **7** rhythm, as of music **8** a seat hanging from ropes, etc. on which one can swing **9** a trip or tour **10** jazz (c. 1935-45) characterized by large bands and written arrangements —*adj.* having decisive power, as in determining an election [the *swing* vote/

**swing'er** *n.* [Slang] a sophisticated, uninhibited, pleasure-seeking person

**swing shift** [Inf.] the evening work shift, commonly from 4:00 P.M. to midnight

**swipe** (swip) *n.* ⟦prob. var. of SWEEP⟧ [Inf.] **1** a hard, sweeping blow **2** a sweeping motion —*vt.* **swiped, swip'ing 1** [Inf.] to hit with a swipe **2** [Inf.] to pass across or through with a sweeping motion **3** [Slang] to steal

**swirl** (swʉrl) *vi., vt.* ⟦ME (Scot) *swyrl*⟧ to move or cause to move with a whirling motion —*n.* **1** a whirl; eddy **2** a twist; curl —**swirl'y** *adj.*

**swish** (swish) *vi.* ⟦echoic⟧ **1** to move with a sharp, hissing sound: said as of a cane swung through the air **2** to move with a light, brushing sound: said as of skirts in walking —*vt.* **1** to cause to swish **2** to move (liquid), esp. in the mouth, with a hissing or gurgling sound —*n.* a swishing sound or movement

**Swiss** (swis) *adj.* of Switzerland or its people, etc. —*n., pl.* **Swiss** a person born or living in Switzerland

**Swiss chard** CHARD

**Swiss (cheese)** a hard, pale-yellow cheese with many large holes

**Swiss steak** a thick cut of round steak pounded with flour and braised with vegetables

**switch** (swich) *n.* ⟦Early Modern Eng *swits*⟧ **1** a thin, flexible stick used for whipping **2** a separate tress of hair, used as part of a coiffure **3** a device used to open, close, or divert an electric circuit **4** a device used to transfer a train from one track to another **5** a shift; change —*vt.* **1** to whip as with a switch **2** to jerk sharply *[the cow switched its tail]* **3** to shift; change **4** to turn (an electric light, etc.) *on* or *off* **5** to transfer (a train, etc.) to another track **6** [Inf.] to change or exchange —*vi.* to shift —**switch′er** *n.*

**switch′back′** *n.* a road or railroad following a zig-zag course up a steep grade

**switch′blade′** (**knife**) a large jackknife that snaps open when a release button is pressed

**switch′board′** *n.* a panel for controlling a system of electric circuits, as in a telephone exchange

**switch′-hit′ter** *n.* a baseball player who can bat right-handed and left-handed

**Swit·zer·land** (swit′sər lənd) country in WC Europe: 15,880 sq. mi.; pop. 6,366,000

**swiv·el** (swiv′əl) *n.* [< OE *swifan*, to revolve] a coupling device that allows free turning of the parts attached to it —*vi., vt.* **-eled** or **-elled**, **-el·ing** or **-el·ling** to turn or cause to turn on or as on a swivel or pivot

**swiz·zle stick** (swiz′əl) [< ?] a small rod for stir-ring mixed drinks

**swob** (swäb) *n., vt.* **swobbed**, **swob′bing** *alt. sp. of* SWAB

**swol·len** (swōl′ən) *vi., vt. alt. pp. of* SWELL —*adj.* blown up; distended; bulging

**swoon** (swōōn) *vi., n.* [< OE *geswogen*, uncon-scious] FAINT

**swoop** (swōōp) *vi.* [< OE *swapan*, sweep along] to pounce or sweep (*down* or *upon*), as a bird does in hunting —*n.* the act of swooping

**swop** (swäp) *vt., vi.* **swopped**, **swop′ping**, *n.* [Chiefly Brit.] *alt. sp. of* SWAP

**sword** (sôrd) *n.* [OE *sweord*] a hand weapon with a long, sharp-pointed blade set in a hilt —**at swords′ points** ready to quarrel or fight

**sword′fish′** *n., pl.* **-fish′** a large marine food fish with an upper jawbone extending in a swordlike point

**sword′play′** *n.* the act or skill of using a sword, as in fencing

**swords·man** (sôrdz′mən) *n., pl.* **-men** one skilled in using a sword

**swore** (swôr) *vi., vt. pt. of* SWEAR

SWORDFISH

**sworn** (swôrn) *vi., vt. pp. of* SWEAR —*adj.* bound, pledged, etc. by or as by an oath

**swum** (swum) *vi., vt. pp. of* SWIM¹ & SWIM²

**swung** (swuŋ) *vi., vt. pp. & pt. of* SWING

**syb·a·rite** (sib′ə rīt′) *n.* [after *Sybaris*, ancient Gr city in Italy] anyone very fond of luxury and pleasure —**syb′a·rit′ic** (-rit′ik) *adj.*

**syc·a·more** (sik′ə môr′) *n.* [< Gr *sykomoros*, a fig tree mentioned in the Bible] **1** a maple tree of Europe and Asia **2** an American tree with bark that sheds in patches

**syc·o·phant** (sik′ə fənt) *n.* [< Gr *sykophantēs*, informer] one who seeks favor by flattering peo-ple of wealth or influence —**syc′o·phan·cy** *n.*

**Syd·ney** (sid′nē) seaport in SE Australia: pop. 3,365,000

**syl·lab·i·cate** (si lab′i kāt′) *vt.* **-cat′ed**, **-cat′ing** SYLLABIFY —**syl·lab′i·ca′tion** *n.*

**syl·lab·i·fy** (si lab′ə fī′) *vt.* **-fied′**, **-fy′ing** [ult. < L *syllaba*, syllable + *facere*, make] to form or divide into syllables —**syl·lab′i·fi·ca′tion** *n.*

**syl·la·ble** (sil′ə bəl) *n.* [< Gr *syn-*, together + *lambanein*, to hold] **1** a word or part of a word pronounced with a single, uninterrupted sound-ing of the voice **2** one or more letters written to represent a spoken syllable —**syl·lab·ic** (si lab′ik) *adj.*

**syl·la·bus** (sil′ə bəs) *n., pl.* **-bus·es** or **-bi′** (-bī′) [ult. < Gr *sittybos*, strip of leather] a summary or out-line, esp. of a course of study

**syl·lo·gism** (sil′ə jiz′əm) *n.* [< Gr *syn-*, together + *logizesthai*, to reason] a form of reasoning in which two premises are made and a logical con-clusion is drawn from them

**sylph** (silf) *n.* [Mod L *sylphus*, a spirit] **1** an imaginary being supposed to inhabit the air **2** a slender, graceful woman or girl —**sylph′like′** *adj.*

**syl·van** (sil′vən) *adj.* [< L *silva*, forest] **1** of, char-acteristic of, or living in the woods or forest **2** covered with trees; wooded

**sym·bi·o·sis** (sim′bī ō′sis, -bē-) *n.* [< Gr *symbioun*, to live together] the living together of two kinds of organisms to their mutual advantage —**sym′bi·ot′ic** (-ät′ik) *adj.*

**sym·bol** (sim′bəl) *n.* [< Gr *syn-*, together + *ballein*, to throw] **1** an object used to represent some-thing abstract *[the dove is a peace symbol]* **2** a mark, letter, etc. standing for an object, quality, quantity, process, etc., as in music or chemistry —**sym·bol′ic** (-bäl′ik) or **sym·bol′i·cal** *adj.* —**sym·bol′i·cal·ly** *adv.*

**sym′bol·ism′** *n.* **1** representation by symbols **2** a system of symbols **3** symbolic meaning

**sym′bol·ize′** *vt.* **-ized′**, **-iz′ing** **1** to be a symbol of; stand for **2** to represent by a symbol or symbols

**sym·me·try** (sim′ə trē) *n., pl.* **-tries** [< Gr *syn-*, together + *metron*, a measure] **1** correspondence of opposite parts in size, shape, and position **2** balance or beauty of form resulting from this —**sym·met·ri·cal** (si me′tri kəl) *adj.* —**sym·met′ri·cal·ly** *adv.*

**sym·pa·thet·ic** (sim′pə thet′ik) *adj.* **1** of, feeling, or showing sympathy **2** in agreement with one's tastes, mood, etc. **3** *Physiology* designating the part of the autonomic nervous system involved esp. in communicating the involuntary response to alarm, as by speeding the heart rate —**sym·pa·thet′i·cal·ly** *adv.*

**sym′pa·thize′** (-thīz′) *vi.* **-thized′**, **-thiz′ing** **1** to share the feelings or ideas of another **2** to feel or express sympathy —**sym′pa·thiz′er** *n.*

**sym′pa·thy** (-thē) *n., pl.* **-thies** [< Gr *syn-*, together + *pathos*, feeling] **1** sameness of feeling **2** mutual liking or understanding **3** *a*) ability to share another's ideas, emotions, etc. *b*) pity or compassion for another's trouble or suffering

**sym·pho·ny** (sim′fə nē) *n., pl.* **-nies** [< Gr *syn-*, together + *phōnē*, a sound] **1** harmony of sounds, color, etc. **2** an extended musical composition in several movements, for full orchestra **3** SYM-PHONY ORCHESTRA **4** [Inf.] a concert by a sym-phony orchestra —**sym·phon′ic** (-fän′ik) *adj.*

**symphony orchestra** a large orchestra for play-ing symphonic works

**sym·po·si·um** (sim pō′zē əm) *n., pl.* **-si·ums** or **-si·a** (-ə) [< Gr *syn-*, together + *posis*, a drinking] **1** a conference to discuss a topic **2** a published group of opinions on a topic

**symp·tom** (simp′təm) *n.* [< Gr *syn-*, together + *piptein*, to fall] any circumstance or condition that indicates the existence of something, as a particular disease —**symp′to·mat′ic** (-tə mat′ik) *adj.*

**syn** *abbrev.* synonym

**syn-** [Gr] *prefix* with, together, at the same time

**syn·a·gogue** (sin′ə gäg′, -gôg′) *n.* [< Gr *syn-*, together + *agein*, do] **1** an assembly of Jews for worship and religious study **2** a building or place for such assembly —**syn′a·gog′al** *adj.*

**syn·apse** (sin′aps′) *n.* [< Gr *syn-*, together + *apsis*, a joining] the space between nerve cells through which nerve impulses are transmitted

**sync** or **synch** (siŋk) *vi., vt.* **synced** or **synched**, **sync′ing** or **synch′ing** *short for* SYNCHRONIZE —*n.* *short for* SYNCHRONIZATION —**in** (or **out of**) **sync** in (or out of) synchronization or harmony (*with*)

**syn·chro·nize** (siŋ′krə nīz′) *vi.* **-nized′**, **-niz′ing** [< Gr *syn-*, together + *chronos*, time] to move or occur at the same time or rate —*vt.* to cause to agree in time or rate of speed —**syn′chro·ni·za′tion** *n.*

**syn′chro·nous** *adj.* happening at the same time or at the same rate

**syn·co·pate** (siŋ′kə pāt′) *vt.* **-pat′ed, -pat′ing** ⟦< Gr *syn-*, together + *koptein*, to cut⟧ *Music* to begin a tone on an unaccented beat and continue it through the next accented beat —**syn′co·pa′tion** *n.*

**syn·di·cate** (sin′də kit; *for v.*, -kāt′) *n.* ⟦< Gr *syn-*, together + *dikē*, justice⟧ **1** an association of individuals or corporations formed to carry out a project requiring much capital **2** any group, as of criminals, organized for some undertaking **3** an organization selling articles or features to many newspapers, etc. —*vt.* **-cat′ed, -cat′ing 1** to manage as or form into a syndicate **2** *a*) to sell (an article, etc.) through a syndicate *b*) to sell (a program, etc.) to a number of radio or TV stations —*vi.* to form a syndicate —**syn′di·ca′tion** *n.*

**syn·drome** (sin′drōm′) *n.* ⟦< Gr *syn-*, with + *dramein*, to run⟧ a set of symptoms characterizing a disease or condition

**syn·er·gism** (sin′ər jiz′əm) *n.* ⟦< Gr *syn-*, together + *ergon*, work⟧ an interaction of several things that results in a greater effect than the sum of the things' individual effects: said esp. of drugs —**syn′er·gis′tic** *adj.*

**syn·fu·el** (sin′fyōō′əl) *n.* ⟦SYN(THETIC) + FUEL⟧ a fuel, as oil or gas made from coal, used as a substitute for petroleum or natural gas

**syn·od** (sin′əd) *n.* ⟦< Gr *syn-*, together + *hodos*, way⟧ **1** an ecclesiastical council **2** a high governing body in certain Christian churches

**syn·o·nym** (sin′ə nim) *n.* ⟦< Gr *syn-*, together + *onyma*, a name⟧ a word having the same or nearly the same meaning as another in the same language —**syn·on·y·mous** (si nän′ə məs) *adj.*

**syn·op·sis** (si näp′sis) *n., pl.* **-ses′** (-sēz′) ⟦< Gr *syn-*, together + *opsis*, a seeing⟧ a brief, general review or condensation; summary

**syn·tax** (sin′taks′) *n.* ⟦< Gr *syn-*, together + *tassein*, arrange⟧ the arrangement of and relationships among words, phrases, and clauses forming sentences —**syn·tac′tic** (-tak′tik) or **syn·tac′ti·cal** *adj.*

**syn·the·sis** (sin′thə sis) *n., pl.* **-ses′** (-sēz′) ⟦< Gr

---

*syn-*, together + *tithenai*, to place⟧ the combining of parts or elements so as to form a whole, a compound, etc. —**syn′the·size′** (-sīz′), **-sized′, -siz′ing,** *vt.*

**syn′the·siz′er** *n.* an electronic device producing sounds unobtainable from ordinary musical instruments or imitating instruments and voices

**syn·thet′ic** (-thet′ik) *adj.* **1** of or involving synthesis **2** produced by chemical synthesis, rather than of natural origin **3** not real; artificial —*n.* something synthetic —**syn·thet′i·cal·ly** *adv.*

**syph·i·lis** (sif′ə lis) *n.* ⟦after *Syphilus*, hero of a L poem (1530)⟧ a sexually transmitted disease caused by a spirochete —**syph′i·lit′ic** *adj., n.*

**Syr·i·a** (sir′ē ə) country in SW Asia, at the E end of the Mediterranean: 71,498 sq. mi.; pop. 9,046,000 —**Syr′i·an** *adj., n.*

**sy·ringe** (sə rinj′, sir′inj) *n.* ⟦< Gr *syrinx*, a pipe⟧ **1** a device consisting of a tube with a rubber bulb or piston at one end, for drawing in a liquid and then ejecting it in a stream: used to inject fluids into body cavities, etc. **2** HYPODERMIC SYRINGE —*vt.* **-ringed′, -ring′ing** to cleanse, inject, etc. by using a syringe

**syr·up** (sur′əp, sir′-) *n.* ⟦< OFr *sirop* < ML *sirupus* < Ar *sharāb*, a drink⟧ any thick, sweet liquid; specif., a solution of sugar and water boiled together —**syr′up·y** *adj.* **1** like syrup **2** overly sentimental

**sys·tem** (sis′təm) *n.* ⟦< Gr *syn-*, together + *histanai*, to set⟧ **1** a set or arrangement of things related so as to form a whole [a solar *system*, a school *system*] **2** a set of facts, rules, etc. arranged to show a logical plan linking them **3** a method or plan **4** an established, orderly way of doing something **5** the body, or a number of bodily organs, functioning as a unit

**sys·tem·at′ic** (-tə mat′ik) *adj.* **1** constituting or based on a system **2** according to a system; orderly —**sys′tem·at′i·cal·ly** *adv.*

**sys′tem·a·tize′** (′-tə mə tīz′) *vt.* **-tized′, -tiz′ing** to arrange according to a system; make systematic —**sys′tem·a·ti·za′tion** *n.*

**sys·tem·ic** (sis tem′ik) *adj.* of or affecting the body as a whole

**sys·to·le** (sis′tə lē′) *n.* ⟦< Gr *syn-*, together + *stellein*, to set up⟧ the usual rhythmic contraction of the heart —**sys·tol′ic** (-täl′ik) *adj.*

---

# T

**t¹** or **T** (tē) *n., pl.* **t's, T's** the 20th letter of the English alphabet —**to a T** to perfection; exactly

**t²** *abbrev.* **1** teaspoon(s) **2** temperature **3** tense **4** ton(s) **5** transitive

**T** *abbrev.* **1** tablespoon(s) **2** temperature **3** Thursday **4** Tuesday

**'t-** *prefix* it: used chiefly in poetry ['twas]

**tab¹** (tab) *n.* ⟦< ?⟧ **1** a small, flat loop or strap fastened to something **2** a projecting piece as of a file folder, used in filing

**tab²** (tab) *n.* ⟦prob. < TABULATION⟧ [Inf.] **1** a bill, as for expenses **2** total cost —**keep tabs** (or **a tab**) **on** [Inf.] to keep a check on

**Ta·bas·co** (tə bas′kō) *trademark for* a very hot sauce made from a tropical American hot red pepper

**tab·bou·leh** (tə bōō′lē, -le) *n.* ⟦Ar⟧ a salad of coarsely ground wheat with chopped parsley, tomatoes, scallions, etc.

**tab·by** (tab′ē) *n., pl.* **-bies** ⟦ult. < Ar⟧ a domestic cat, esp. a female

**tab·er·nac·le** (tab′ər nak′əl) *n.* ⟦< L *taberna*, hut⟧ **1** a large place of worship **2** [T-] the portable sanctuary carried by the Jews during the Exodus

**tab·la** (täb′lä) *n.* ⟦< Ar *ṭabla*, a drum⟧ a set of two

---

small drums whose pitch can be varied, used esp. in India and played with the hands

**ta·ble** (tā′bəl) *n.* ⟦< L *tabula*, a board⟧ **1** [Obs.] a thin slab of metal, stone, etc. **2** *a*) a piece of furniture having a flat top set on legs *b*) such a table set with food *c*) food served *d*) the people seated at a table **3** *a*) a systematic list of details, contents, etc. *b*) an orderly arrangement of facts, figures, etc. **4** any flat, horizontal surface, piece, etc. —*vt.* **-bled, -bling** to postpone indefinitely the consideration of (a legislative bill, etc.) —**at table** at a meal —**turn the tables** to reverse a situation

**tab·leau** (tab′lō′, ta blō′) *n., pl.* **-leaux′** (-lōz′) or **-leaus′** ⟦Fr < OFr, dim. of *table*⟧ a striking, dramatic scene or picture

**ta′ble·cloth′** *n.* a cloth for covering a table, esp. at meals

**ta·ble d'hôte** (tä′bəl dōt′) ⟦Fr, table of the host⟧ a complete meal served at a restaurant for a set price

**ta′ble-hop′** *vi.* **-hopped′, -hop′ping** to leave one's table, as at a restaurant, and visit at other tables

**ta′ble·land′** *n.* a plateau

**ta′ble·spoon′** *n.* **1** a large spoon for serving or for eating soup **2** a measuring spoon holding ½ fluid ounce —**ta′ble·spoon′ful,** *pl.* **-fuls,** *n.*

**tab·let** (tab′lit) *n.* ⟦see TABLE⟧ **1** a thin, flat piece of stone, metal, etc. with an inscription **2** a writing pad of paper sheets glued together at one edge **3** a small, flat piece of compressed material, as of medicine

**table tennis** a game somewhat like tennis, played on a table with a small, hollow celluloid ball

**ta′ble·ware′** (-wer′) *n.* dishes, glassware, silverware, etc. for use at a meal

**tab·loid** (tab′loid′) *n.* ⟦TABL(ET) + -OID⟧ a newspaper, usually half size, with many pictures and short, often sensational, news stories

**ta·boo** (tə bōō′, ta-) *n.* ⟦< a Polynesian language⟧ **1** among some Polynesian peoples, a sacred prohibition making certain people or things untouchable, etc. **2** any conventional social restriction — *adj.* prohibited by taboo — *vt.* **-booed′, -boo′ing 1** to put under taboo **2** to prohibit or forbid Also **ta·bu′**

**ta·bou·li** (tə bōō′lē) *n. var. of* TABBOULEH

**tab·u·lar** (tab′yə lər) *adj.* ⟦see TABLE⟧ **1** flat **2** of, arranged in, or computed from a table or list

**tab′u·late′** (-lāt′) *vt.* **-lat′ed, -lat′ing** to put (facts, statistics, etc.) in a table — **tab′u·la′tion** *n.* — **tab′u·la′tor** *n.*

**ta·chom·e·ter** (ta käm′ət ər) *n.* ⟦< Gr *tachos*, speed + -METER⟧ a device that measures the rate of rotation of a revolving shaft

**tach·y·car·di·a** (tak′i kär′dē ə) *n.* ⟦< Gr *tachys*, swift + *kardia*, heart⟧ an abnormally fast heartbeat

**tac·it** (tas′it) *adj.* ⟦< L *tacere*, be silent⟧ **1** unspoken **2** not expressed openly, but implied or understood — **tac′it·ly** *adv.* — **tac′it·ness** *n.*

**tac·i·turn** (tas′ə turn′) *adj.* ⟦see prec.⟧ almost always silent; not liking to talk — **tac·i·tur′ni·ty** *n.*

**tack** (tak) *n.* ⟦< MDu *tacke*, twig, point⟧ **1** a short nail or pin with a sharp point and a large, flat head **2** a temporary stitch **3** a course of action **4** *a)* the direction a ship goes in relation to the position of the sails *b)* a change of a ship's direction — *vt.* **1** to fasten with tacks **2** to attach or add **3** to change the course of (a ship) — *vi.* to change course suddenly

**tack·le** (tak′əl) *n.* ⟦< MDu *takel*⟧ **1** equipment; gear **2** a system of ropes and pulleys for moving weights **3** a tackling, as in football **4** *Football* a lineman next to the end — *vt.* **tack′led, tack′ling 1** to take hold of; seize **2** to try to do; undertake **3** *Football* to throw (the ball carrier) to the ground — **tack′ler** *n.*

**tack·y** (tak′ē) *adj.* **-i·er, -i·est 1** sticky: said as of drying varnish **2** dowdy or shabby **3** in poor taste — **tack′i·ness** *n.*

**ta·co** (tä′kō) *n., pl.* **-cos** ⟦Sp, light lunch⟧ a fried tortilla filled with chopped meat, lettuce, etc.

**Ta·co·ma** (tə kō′mə) seaport in W Washington: pop. 177,000

**tact** (takt) *n.* ⟦< L *tangere*, to touch⟧ delicate perception of the right thing to say or do without offending — **tact′ful** *adj.* — **tact′less** *adj.*

**tac·tics** (tak′tiks) *pl.n.* ⟦< Gr *tassein*, arrange⟧ **1** [*with sing. v.*] the science of maneuvering military and naval forces **2** any skillful methods to gain an end — **tac′ti·cal** *adj.* — **tac·ti′cian** (-tish′ən) *n.*

**tac·tile** (tak′təl) *adj.* ⟦< L *tangere*, to touch⟧ of, having, or perceived by the sense of touch

**tad** (tad) *n.* ⟦prob. < TADPOLE⟧ a small amount or degree: often used adverbially [a *tad* tired]

**tad·pole** (tad′pōl′) *n.* ⟦ME *tadde*, toad + *poll*, head⟧ the larva of a frog or toad, having gills and a tail and living in water

**taf·fe·ta** (taf′i tə) *n.* ⟦< Pers *tāftan*, to weave⟧ a fine, stiff fabric of silk, nylon, etc., with a sheen

**taff·rail** (taf′rāl′) *n.* ⟦< Du⟧ the rail around the stern of a ship

**taf·fy** (taf′ē) *n.* ⟦< ?⟧ a chewy candy made of sugar or molasses

**Taft** (taft), **Wil·liam How·ard** (wil′yəm hou′ərd)

---

◀ **take**

1857-1930; 27th president of the U.S. (1909-13): chief justice of the U.S. (1921-30)

**tag** (tag) *n.* ⟦prob. < Scand⟧ **1** a hanging end or part **2** a hard-tipped end on a cord or lace **3** a card, etc. attached as a label **4** an epithet **5** ending for a story, etc. **6** TAG LINE **7** a children's game in which one player chases the others with the object of touching one of them — *vt.* **tagged, tag′ging 1** to provide with a tag; label **2** to choose or select **3** to touch in playing tag **4** [Inf.] to strike or hit hard — *vi.* [Inf.] to follow closely: with *along, after*, etc. — **tag′ger** *n.*

**Ta·ga·log** (tä gä′lôg′) *n.* **1** *pl.* **-logs′** or **-log′** a member of the ethnic group native to the Manila region in the Philippines **2** the language of this group, an official language of the Republic of the Philippines

**tag line** the last line or lines of a speech, etc.

**Ta·hi·ti** (tə hēt′ē) French island in the S Pacific — **Ta·hi′ti·an** (-hēsh′ən) *adj., n.*

**Tai** (tī) *n.* **1** a group of languages spoken in central and SE Asia **2** a member of a group of peoples of SE Asia that speak these languages — *adj.* of these languages or peoples

**tai chi** (tī′ jē′, tī chē′) ⟦Mandarin⟧ a Chinese exercise system consisting of a series of slow, relaxed movements: in full **t'ai chi ch'uan** (chwän)

**tai·ga** (tī′gə) *n.* ⟦Russ⟧ a type of plant community in the far north, having scattered trees

**tail** (tāl) *n.* ⟦OE *tægel*⟧ **1** the rear end of an animal's body, esp. when a distinct appendage **2** anything like an animal's tail in form or position **3** the hind, bottom, last, or inferior part of anything **4** [*often pl.*] the reverse side of a coin **5** [*pl.*] full-dress attire for men **6** [Inf.] one that follows another, esp. in surveillance — *adj.* **1** at the rear or end **2** from the rear [a *tail* wind] — *vt.* [Slang] to follow stealthily — *vi.* [Inf.] to follow close behind

**tail′back′** *n. Football* the offensive back farthest from the line

**tail′gate′** *n.* the hinged or removable gate at the back of a wagon, truck, etc. — *vi., vt.* **-gat′ed, -gat′ing** to drive too closely behind (another vehicle) — **tail′gat′er** *n.*

**tail′ings** *pl.n.* waste or refuse left in various processes of milling, mining, etc.

**tail′light′** *n.* a light, usually red, at the rear of a vehicle to warn vehicles coming from behind

**tai·lor** (tā′lər) *n.* ⟦< VL *taliare*, to cut⟧ one who makes, repairs, or alters clothes — *vt.* **1** to make by tailor's work **2** to form, alter, etc. for a certain purpose

**tail′pipe′** *n.* the exhaust pipe coming from the muffler of a motor vehicle

**tail′spin′** *n.* SPIN (*n.* 3)

**taint** (tānt) *vt.* ⟦< ?⟧ **1** to affect with something injurious, unpleasant, etc.; infect, spoil, etc. **2** to make morally corrupt — *n.* a trace of contamination, corruption, etc.

**Tai·pei** (tī′pā′) capital of Taiwan: pop. 2,108,000

**Tai·wan** (tī′wän′) island province of China, off the SE coast: together with nearby islands it forms the *Republic of China*: 13,970 sq. mi.; pop. 21,000,000

**Ta·jik·i·stan** (tä jik′i stan′) country in WC Asia: formerly a republic of the U.S.S.R.: 55,240 sq. mi.; pop. 5,093,000

**take** (tāk) *vt.* **took, tak′en, tak′ing** ⟦< ON *taka*⟧ **1** to get possession of; capture, seize, etc. **2** to get hold of **3** to capture the fancy of; charm **4** to obtain, acquire, assume, etc. **5** to use, consume, etc. **6** to buy, rent, subscribe to, etc. **7** to join with (one side in a disagreement, etc.) **8** to choose; select **9** to travel by [to *take* a bus] **10** to deal with; consider **11** to occupy [take a chair] **12** to require; demand [it *takes* money] **13** to derive (a name, quality, etc.) from **14** to excerpt; extract **15** to study **16** to write down [take notes] **17** to make by photographing **18** to win (a prize, etc.)

**19** to undergo [take punishment] **20** to occupy oneself in; enjoy [take a nap] **21** to accept (an offer, bet, etc.) **22** to react to [take a joke in earnest] **23** to contract (a disease, etc.) **24** to understand **25** to suppose; presume **26** to feel [take pity] **27** to lead, escort, etc. **28** to carry **29** to remove, as by stealing **30** to subtract **31** [Slang] to cheat; trick **32** *Gram.* to be used with [the verb "hit" *takes* an object] —*vi.* **1** to take root: said of a plant **2** to catch [the fire *took*] **3** to gain favor, success, etc. **4** to be effective [the vaccination *took*] **5** [Inf. or Dial.] to become (sick) —*n.* **1** a taking **2** *a)* the amount taken *b)* [Slang] receipts or profit —**on the take** [Slang] taking bribes, etc. —**take after** to be, act, or look like —**take back** to retract (something said, etc.) —**take down** to put in writing; record —**take for 1** to regard as **2** to mistake for —**take in 1** to admit; receive **2** to make smaller **3** to understand **4** to cheat; trick —**take off 1** to leave the ground, etc. in flight **2** [Inf.] to start **3** [Inf.] to imitate in a burlesque manner: with *on* —**take on 1** to acquire; assume **2** to employ **3** to undertake (a task, etc.) —**take over** to assume control or possession of —**take to 1** to become fond of **2** to go to or withdraw to [to *take to* the hills] —**take up 1** to make tighter or shorter **2** to become interested in (an occupation, study, etc.) —**tak′er** *n.*

**take′off′** *n.* **1** the act or place of leaving the ground, as in jumping or flight **2** [Inf.] a mocking imitation; caricature

**take′out′** *n.* prepared food bought to be taken away —*adj.* designating or of such food

**take′o′ver** *n.* **1** the usurpation of power in a nation, organization, etc. **2** the assumption of management in acquiring a corporation

**tak·ing** (tāk′iŋ) *adj.* attractive; winning —*n.* **1** the act of one that takes **2** [*pl.*] earnings; profits

**talc** (talk) *n.* [< Ar *ṭalq*] a soft mineral used to make talcum powder, etc. **2** *short for* TALCUM (POWDER)

**tal·cum (powder)** (tal′kəm) a powder for the body made of purified talc

**tale** (tāl) *n.* [OE *talu*] **1** a story; narrative **2** idle or malicious gossip **3** a fiction; lie

**tale′bear′er** (-ber′ər) *n.* a gossip

**tal·ent** (tal′ənt) *n.* [< Gr *talanton*, a weight] **1** an ancient unit of weight or money **2** any natural ability or power **3** a superior ability in an art, etc. **4** people, or a person, with talent —**tal′ent·ed** *adj.*

**tal·is·man** (tal′is mən, -iz-) *n., pl.* **-mans** [< 5th-c. medieval Gr *telesma*, religious rite] **1** a ring, stone, etc. bearing engraved figures thought to bring good luck, avert evil, etc. **2** a charm

**talk** (tôk) *vi.* [prob. < OE *talian*, reckon] **1** to put ideas into words; speak **2** to express ideas by speech substitutes [talk by signs] **3** to chatter; gossip **4** to confer; consult **5** to confess or inform on someone —*vt.* **1** to use in speaking [to *talk* French] **2** to discuss **3** to put into a specified condition, etc. by talking —*n.* **1** the act of talking **2** conversation **3** a speech **4** a conference **5** gossip **6** the subject of conversation, gossip, etc. **7** speech; dialect —**talk back** to answer impertinently —**talk down to** to talk patronizingly to, as by simple speech —**talk up** to promote in discussion —**talk′er** *n.*

**talk′a′tive** (-ə tiv) *adj.* talking a great deal; loquacious

**talking book** a recording of a reading of a book, etc. for use esp. by the blind

**talk·ing-to** (tôk′iŋ tōō′) *n.* [Inf.] a scolding

**talk show** *Radio, TV* a program in which a host talks with guest celebrities, experts, etc.

**talk′y** *adj.* **-i·er, -i·est 1** talkative **2** containing too much talk, or dialogue

**tall** (tôl) *adj.* [< OE (ge)tæl, swift] **1** higher in stature than the average **2** having a specified height **3** [Inf.] exaggerated [a *tall* tale] **4** [Inf.] large [a *tall* drink] —*adv.* in an upright, dignified manner [to stand *tall*] —**tall′ness** *n.*

**Tal·la·has·see** (tal′ə has′ē) capital of Florida: pop. 125,000

**tal·low** (tal′ō) *n.* [prob. < LowG *talg*] the solid fat of cattle, sheep, etc., used in candles, soaps, etc.

**tal·ly** (tal′ē) *n., pl.* **-lies** [< L *talea*, a stick (notched to keep accounts)] **1** anything used as a record for an account or score **2** an account, score, etc. **3** a tag or label —*vt.* **-lied, -ly·ing 1** to put on or as on a tally **2** to add (up) —*vi.* **1** to score a point **2** to agree; correspond

**tal·ly·ho** (tal′ē hō′) *interj.* the cry of a hunter on sighting the fox

**Tal·mud** (täl′mood, tal′məd) *n.* [Heb, learning] the body of early Jewish civil and religious law

**tal·on** (tal′ən) *n.* [< L *talus*, an ankle] the claw of a bird of prey

**tam** (tam) *n. short for* TAM-O′-SHANTER

**ta·ma·le** (tə mä′lē) *n.* [< MexSp] spicy minced meat wrapped in a dough of corn meal

**tam·a·rack** (tam′ə rak′) *n.* [< AmInd] **1** an American larch tree usually found in swamps **2** its wood

**tam·a·rind** (tam′ə rind′) *n.* [< Ar *tamr hindī*, date of India] **1** a tropical tree with yellow flowers and brown pods **2** its sharp-tasting, edible fruit

**tam·bou·rine** (tam′bə rēn′) *n.* [prob. < Ar *ṭanbūr*, stringed instrument] a shallow, single-headed hand drum with jingling metal disks in the rim: played by shaking, hitting, etc.

**tame** (tām) *adj.* **tam′er, tam′est** [OE *tam*] **1** changed from a wild state and trained for human use **2** gentle; docile **3** without spirit or force; dull —*vt.* **tamed, tam′ing 1** to make tame **2** to make gentle; subdue —**tam′a·ble** or **tame′a·ble** *adj.* —**tame′ly** *adv.* —**tame′ness** *n.* —**tam′er** *n.*

**Tam·il** (tam′əl) *n.* the language of the Tamils, a people of S India and N Sri Lanka

**tam-o′-shan·ter** (tam′ə shan′tər) *n.* [< title character of Robert Burns′s poem] a Scottish cap with a round, flat top

**tamp** (tamp) *vt.* [< ? Fr *tampon*, a plug] to pack firmly or pound (*down*) by a series of blows or taps

**Tam·pa** (tam′pə) seaport in WC Florida, on the Gulf of Mexico: pop. 280,000

**tam·per** (tam′pər) *vi.* [< TEMPER] **1** to make secret, illegal arrangements (*with*) **2** to interfere (*with*) or meddle (*with*)

TAM-O′-SHANTER

**tam·pon** (tam′pän′) *n.* [Fr] a plug of cotton, etc. put into a body cavity, etc., as to stop bleeding

**tan** (tan) *n.* [< ML *tanum*, a bark used to tan hides] **1** a yellowish-brown color **2** a darkening of the skin as by exposure to the sun, etc. —*adj.* **tan′ner, tan′nest** yellowish-brown —*vt.* **tanned, tan′ning 1** to change (hide) into leather by soaking in tannin **2** to produce a suntan in **3** [Inf.] to whip severely —*vi.* to become tanned

**tan·a·ger** (tan′ə jər) *n.* [< AmInd (Brazil) *tangara*] any of various small, American songbirds: the males usually are brightly colored

**tan·bark** (tan′bark′) *n.* any bark containing tannin, used to tan hides, etc.

**tan·dem** (tan′dəm) *adv.* [< punning use of L *tandem*, at length] one behind another; in single file —*n.* teamwork between two persons, etc. [to work in *tandem*]

**tang** (taŋ) *n.* [< ON *tangi*, a sting] **1** a prong on a file, etc., that fits into the handle **2** a strong, penetrating taste or odor —**tang′y, -i·er, -i·est,** *adj.*

**tan·ge·lo** (tan′jə lō′) *n., pl.* **-los′** [TANG(ERINE) + (*pom*)*elo*, grapefruit] a fruit produced by crossing a tangerine with a grapefruit

**tan·gent** (tan′jənt) *adj.* [< L *tangere*, to touch] **1** touching **2** *Geom.* touching a curved surface at one point but not intersecting it —*n.* a tangent line, curve, or surface —**go off at (or on) a tan-**

**gent** to change suddenly to another line of action, etc. —**tan·gen'tial** (-jen'shəl) adj.

**tan·ge·rine** (tan'jə rēn') n. ⟦after *Tangier*, city in N Africa⟧ a small, loose-skinned, reddish-yellow orange with easily separated segments

**tan·gi·ble** (tan'jə bəl) adj. ⟦< L *tangere*, to touch⟧ 1 that can be touched or felt 2 definite; objective —n. [pl.] assets having real substance and able to be appraised for value —**tan'gi·bil'i·ty** n.

**tan·gle** (taŋ'gəl) vt. **-gled**, **-gling** ⟦< ? Swed⟧ 1 to catch as in a snare; trap 2 to make a snarl of; intertwine —vi. 1 to become tangled 2 [Inf.] to argue —n. 1 an intertwined, confused mass 2 a confused condition or state

**tan·go** (taŋ'gō) n., pl. **-gos** ⟦AmSp⟧ 1 a South American dance for couples with long gliding steps and dips 2 music for this dance in 2/4 or 4/4 time —vi. to dance the tango

**tank** (taŋk) n. ⟦in sense 1 < Sans⟧ 1 any large container for liquid or gas 2 an armored combat vehicle with tractor treads —vi. [Slang] to fail

**tank·ard** (taŋ'kərd) n. ⟦< OFr *tanquart*⟧ a large drinking cup with a handle

**tank·er** (taŋ'kər) n. 1 a ship equipped to transport oil or other liquids 2 a plane designed to carry liquids, as for refueling another plane in flight 3 a truck, etc. equipped to transport liquids or dry commodities in bulk

**tank top** ⟦orig. worn in swimming tanks⟧ a sleeveless casual shirt with shoulder straps

**tank truck** a motor truck built to transport gasoline, oil, etc.

**tan·ner** (tan'ər) n. a person whose work is making leather by tanning hides

**tan'ner·y** n., pl. **-ner·ies** a place where leather is made by tanning hides

**tan'nic acid** (tan'ik) a yellowish, astringent substance used in tanning hides, dyeing, etc.

**tan'nin** (-in) n. ⟦< *tan*, TAN + -*in*, -INE³⟧ any of a group of compounds, as tannic acid, that convert hide into leather

**tan·sy** (tan'zē) n., pl. **-sies** ⟦< LL *tanacetum*⟧ a plant with a strong smell and small, yellow flowers

**tan·ta·lize** (tan'tə līz') vt. **-lized'**, **-liz'ing** ⟦after *Tantalus*, in Gr myth, a king doomed in Hades to stand in water that always recedes when he wishes to drink and under fruit he cannot reach⟧ to promise or show something desirable and then withhold it; tease

**tan·ta·mount** (tant'ə mount') adj. ⟦< OFr *tant*, so much + *amont*, upward⟧ equal (*to*) in value, effect, etc.

**tan·tra** (tun'trə, tän'-) n. ⟦Sans⟧ [often **T-**] a form of yoga teaching attainment of ecstasy —**tan'tric** adj.

**tan·trum** (tan'trəm) n. ⟦< ?⟧ a violent, willful outburst of rage, etc.

**Tan·za·ni·a** (tan'zə nē'ə) country in E Africa: 364,881 sq. mi.; pop. 23,174,000 —**Tan'za·ni'an** adj., n.

**Tao·ism** (dou'iz'əm, tou'-) n. ⟦Chin *tao*, the way⟧ a Chinese religion and philosophy advocating simplicity, selflessness, etc. —**Tao'ist** n., adj.

**tap¹** (tap) vt., vi. **tapped**, **tap'ping** ⟦echoic⟧ 1 to strike lightly 2 to make or do by tapping [to *tap* a message] 3 to choose, as for membership in a club —n. a light, rapid blow

**tap²** (tap) n. ⟦OE *tæppa*⟧ 1 a faucet or spigot 2 a plug, cork, etc. for stopping a hole in a cask, etc. 3 a tool used to cut threads inside a nut, pipe, etc. 4 the act or an instance of wiretapping 5 *Elec.* a place in a circuit where a connection can be made —vt. **tapped**, **tap'ping** 1 to put a tap or spigot on 2 to make a hole in, or pull the plug from, for drawing off liquid 3 to draw off (liquid) 4 to make use of [to *tap* new resources] 5 to make a connection with (a pipe, circuit, etc.); specif., to wiretap

**tap dance** a dance done with sharp, loud taps of the foot, toe, or heel at each step —**tap'-dance'**, **-danced'**, **-danc'ing**, vi. —**tap'-danc'er** n.

**tape** (tāp) n. ⟦OE *tæppe*, a fillet⟧ 1 a strong, narrow strip of cloth, paper, etc. used for binding, tying, etc. 2 *short for* MAGNETIC TAPE 3 *short for* TAPE MEASURE —vt. **taped**, **tap'ing** 1 to bind, tie, etc. with tape 2 to record on magnetic tape

**tape deck** a component of an audio system, that records and plays back magnetic tapes

**tape measure** a tape with marks in inches, feet, etc. for measuring

**ta·per** (tā'pər) n. ⟦OE *tapur*⟧ 1 a slender candle 2 a gradual decrease in width or thickness —vt., vi. 1 to decrease gradually in width or thickness 2 to lessen; diminish Often with *off*

**tape recorder** a device for recording on magnetic tape and for playing back what has been recorded

**tap·es·try** (tap'əs trē) n., pl. **-tries** ⟦< Gr *tapes*, a carpet⟧ a heavy woven cloth with decorative designs and pictures, used as a wall hanging, etc.

**tape'worm'** n. a long, tapelike flatworm that lives as a parasite in the intestines

**tap·i·o·ca** (tap'ē ō'kə) n. ⟦< AmInd (Brazil)⟧ a starchy substance from cassava roots, used for puddings, etc.

**ta·pir** (tā'pər) n. ⟦< AmInd (Brazil)⟧ a large, hoglike mammal of tropical America and the Malay Peninsula

**tapped out** [Slang] 1 having no money; broke 2 exhausted or depleted

**tap'room'** n. BARROOM

**tap'root'** n. ⟦TAP² + ROOT¹⟧ a main root, growing downward, from which small branch roots spread out

**taps** (taps) n. ⟦< TAP¹, because orig. a drum signal⟧ [*with sing. or pl. v.*] a bugle call to put out lights in retiring for the night

**tar¹** (tär) n. ⟦OE *teru*⟧ a thick, sticky, black liquid formed when hot coal, wood, etc. decomposes in the absence of air —vt. **tarred**, **tar'ring** to cover or smear with tar —**tar'ry**, **-ri·er**, **-ri·est**, adj.

**tar²** (tär) n. ⟦< TAR(PAULIN)⟧ [Inf.] a sailor

**ta·ran·tu·la** (tə ran'choo lə) n. ⟦after *Taranto*, city in S Italy⟧ any of several large, hairy, somewhat poisonous spiders of S Europe and tropical America

**tar·dy** (tär'dē) adj. **-di·er**, **-di·est** ⟦< L *tardus*, slow⟧ 1 slow in moving, acting, etc. 2 late, delayed, etc. —**tar'di·ly** adv. —**tar'di·ness** n.

**tare¹** (ter) n. ⟦ME⟧ 1 any of various vetches 2 *Bible* an undesirable weed

HAIRY TARANTULA

**tare²** (ter) n. ⟦< Ar *taraḥa*, to reject⟧ the weight of a container, etc. deducted from the total weight to determine the weight of the contents or load

**tar·get** (tär'git) n. ⟦< medieval Fr *targe*, a shield⟧ 1 a board, etc. marked as with concentric circles, aimed at in archery, rifle practice, etc. 2 any object that is shot at 3 an objective; goal 4 an object of attack, criticism, etc. —vt. to establish as a target, goal, etc.

**tar·iff** (tar'if) n. ⟦< Ar *ta'rīf*, information⟧ 1 a list or system of taxes upon exports or, esp., imports 2 such a tax, or its rate 3 a list or scale of prices, charges, etc. 4 [Inf.] any bill, charge, etc.

**tar·mac** (tär'mak') n. ⟦ult. < TAR¹ + MAC(ADAM)⟧ [Chiefly Brit.] an airport runway or apron

**tar·nish** (tär'nish) vt. ⟦< Fr *ternir*, make dim⟧ 1 to dull the luster of 2 to sully or mar —vi. 1 to lose luster 2 to become sullied —n. 1 dullness 2 a stain —**tar'nish·a·ble** adj.

**ta·ro** (ter'ō, tär'ō) n., pl. **-ros** ⟦< a Polynesian language⟧ a tropical Asiatic plant with a starchy, edible root

**tar·ot** (tar'ō, -ət; ta rō') n. ⟦Fr < Ar *taraḥa*, to reject⟧ [often **T-**] any of a set of 22 cards with pictures, used in fortunetelling

**tarp** (tärp) *n.* [Inf.] short for TARPAULIN

**tar·pau·lin** (tär pô′lin, tär′pə-) *n.* [< TAR¹ + PALL², a covering] **1** canvas coated with a waterproofing compound **2** a sheet of this

**tar·pon** (tär′pən) *n.* [< ?] a large, silvery game fish of the W Atlantic

**tar·ra·gon** (tar′ə gän′) *n.* [< Sp < Ar < Gr *drakōn*, a dragon] an Old World plant with fragrant leaves used for seasoning

**tar·ry** (tar′ē) *vi.* **-ried, -ry·ing** [< OE *tergan*, to vex & prob. OFr *targer*, to delay] **1** to delay; linger **2** to stay for a time **3** to wait

**tart**¹ (tärt) *adj.* [OE *teart*] **1** sharp in taste; sour; acid **2** sharp in meaning; cutting [a *tart* answer] —**tart′ly** *adv.* —**tart′ness** *n.*

**tart**² (tärt) *n.* [< OFr *tarte*] a small pastry shell filled with jam, jelly, etc.

**tart**³ (tärt) *n.* [< prec., orig., slang term of endearment] [Inf.] a prostitute

**tar·tan** (tärt′'n) *n.* [prob. < medieval Fr *tiretaine*, a cloth of mixed fibers] a woolen cloth in any of various woven plaid patterns, worn esp. in the Scottish Highlands

**tar·tar** (tärt′ər) *n.* [< medieval Gr *tartaron*] **1** cream of tartar, esp. the crude form present in grape juice and forming a crustlike deposit in wine casks **2** a hard deposit on the teeth

**Tar·tar** (tärt′ər) *n.* TATAR

**tar·tar sauce** (tärt′ər) [Fr] a sauce of mayonnaise with chopped pickles, olives, capers, etc.: also **tar′tare sauce**

**task** (task) *n.* [ult. < L *taxare*, to rate] **1** a piece of work to be done **2** any difficult undertaking —*vt.* to burden; strain —**take to task** to scold

**task force** a group, esp. a military unit, assigned a specific task

**task′mas′ter** *n.* one who assigns tasks to others, esp. when severe

**Tas·ma·ni·a** (taz mā′nē ə) island of Australia, off its SE coast —**Tas·ma′ni·an** *adj., n.*

**tas·sel** (tas′əl) *n.* [OFr, knob] **1** an ornamental tuft of threads, etc. hanging loosely from a knob **2** something resembling this, as a tuft of corn silk

**taste** (tāst) *vt.* **tast′ed, tast′ing** [< OFr *taster*] **1** to test the flavor of by putting a little in one's mouth **2** to detect the flavor of by the sense of taste **3** to eat or drink a small amount of **4** to experience [to *taste* success] —*vi.* to have a specific flavor —*n.* **1** the sense by which flavor is perceived through the taste buds on the tongue **2** the quality so perceived; flavor **3** a small amount tasted as a sample **4** a bit; trace **5** the ability to appreciate what is beautiful, appropriate, etc. **6** a specific preference **7** a liking; inclination —**in bad (or good) taste** in a style showing a bad (or good) sense of beauty, fitness, etc. —**taste′less** *adj.* —**tast′er** *n.*

**taste bud** any of the cells, esp. in the tongue, that are the organs of taste

**taste′ful** *adj.* having or showing good TASTE (*n.* 5) —**taste′ful·ly** *adv.*

**tast·y** (tās′tē) *adj.* **-i·er, -i·est** that tastes good; flavorful —**tast′i·ness** *n.*

**tat** (tat) *vt.* **tat′ted, tat′ting** to make by tatting — *vi.* to do tatting

**ta·ta·mi** (tə tä′mē) *n., pl.* **-mi** or **-mis** [Jpn] a floor mat of rice straw, used traditionally in Japanese homes for sitting on

**Ta·tar** (tät′ər) *n.* **1** a member of any of the E Asian peoples that invaded W Asia and E Europe in the Middle Ages **2** a Turkic language

**tat·ter** (tat′ər) *n.* [< ON *töturr*, rags] **1** a torn and hanging piece, as of a garment **2** [*pl.*] torn, ragged clothes —*vt., vi.* to make or become ragged — **tat′tered** *adj.*

**tat′ter·de·mal′ion** (-di māl′yən) *n.* [< prec. + ?] a person in torn, ragged clothes

**tat·ting** (tat′iŋ) *n.* [prob. < Brit dial. *tat*, to tangle] **1** a fine lace made by looping and knotting thread **2** the act or process of making this

**tat·tle** (tat′'l) *vi.* **-tled, -tling** [prob. < MDu *tatelen*] **1** to talk idly **2** to reveal others' secrets —*vt.* to reveal (a secret) by gossiping —**tat′tler** *n.*

**tat′tle·tale′** *n.* an informer; a gossip

**tat·too**¹ (ta tōō′) *vt.* **-tooed′, -too′ing** [< a Polynesian language] to make (permanent designs) on (the skin) by puncturing and inserting indelible color —*n., pl.* **-toos′** a tattooed design

**tat·too**² (ta tōō′) *n., pl.* **-toos′** [< Du *tap toe*, tap to (shut): a signal for closing barrooms] **1** a signal on a drum or bugle, summoning military personnel to their quarters at night **2** a drumming, rapping, etc.

**tau** (tou, tô) *n.* the 19th letter of the Greek alphabet (T, τ)

**taught** (tôt) *vt., vi. pt. & pp.* of TEACH

**taunt** (tônt, tänt) *vt.* [< ? Fr *tant pour tant*, tit for tat] to reproach scornfully or sarcastically; mock —*n.* a scornful or jeering remark

**taupe** (tōp) *n.* [Fr < L *talpa*, mole] a dark, brownish gray

**Tau·rus** (tôr′əs) *n.* [L, a bull] the second sign of the zodiac

**taut** (tôt) *adj.* [ME *toght*, tight] **1** tightly stretched, as a rope **2** tense [a *taut* smile] **3** trim, tidy, etc. —**taut′ly** *adv.* —**taut′ness** *n.*

**tau·tol·o·gy** (tô täl′ə jē) *n., pl.* **-gies** [< Gr < *to auto*, the same + -LOGY] needless repetition of an idea in a different word, phrase, etc.; redundancy —**tau′to·log′i·cal** *adj.*

**tav·ern** (tav′ərn) *n.* [< L *taberna*] **1** a saloon; bar **2** an inn

**taw·dry** (tô′drē) *adj.* **-dri·er, -dri·est** [after St. *Audrey laces,* sold at St. Audrey's fair in Norwich, England] cheap and showy; gaudy

**taw·ny** (tô′nē) *adj.* **-ni·er, -ni·est** [< OFr *tanner*, to tan] brownish-yellow; tan —**taw′ni·ness** *n.*

**tax** (taks) *vt.* [< L *taxare*, appraise] **1** to require to pay a tax **2** to assess a tax on (income, purchases, etc.) **3** to put a strain on **4** to accuse; charge —*n.* **1** a compulsory payment of a percentage of income, property value, etc. for the support of a government **2** a heavy demand; burden —**tax′a·ble** *adj.* —**tax·a′tion** *n.*

**tax·i** (tak′sē) *n., pl.* **-is** short for TAXICAB —*vi.* **-ied, -i·ing** or **-y·ing** **1** to go in a taxicab **2** to move along the ground or on the water as after landing: said of an airplane

**tax′i·cab′** *n.* [< *taxi*(*meter*) *cab*] an automobile in which passengers are carried for a fare

**tax·i·der·my** (tak′si dur′mē) *n.* [< Gr *taxis*, arrangement + *derma*, skin] the art of preparing, stuffing, etc. the skins of animals to make them appear lifelike —**tax′i·der′mist** *n.*

**tax·i·me·ter** (tak′sē mēt′ər) *n.* [< Fr, ult. < ML *taxa*, tax + *-meter*, -METER] an automatic device in taxicabs that registers the fare due

**tax·on·o·my** (tak sän′ə mē) *n., pl.* **-mies** [< Gr *taxis*, arrangement + *nomos*, law] classification, esp. of animals and plants —**tax·on′o·mist** *n.*

**tax′pay′er** *n.* one who pays a tax

**tax shelter** an investment made to reduce one's income tax

**tax·us** (tak′səs) *n.* [ModL] YEW (*n.* 1)

**Tay·lor** (tā′lər), **Zach·a·ry** (zak′ə rē) 1784-1850; U.S. general: 12th president of the U.S. (1849-50)

**TB** abbrev. *n.* tuberculosis

**TBA, t.b.a.,** or **tba** abbrev. to be announced

**T-ball** (tē′bôl′) *n.* a baseball game for young children in which the ball is placed on and struck from a tall TEE (*n.* 1)

**T-bone steak** (tē′bōn′) a beefsteak with a T-shaped bone, containing some tenderloin

**tbs** or **tbsp** abbrev. **1** tablespoon(s) **2** tablespoonful(s)

**T cell** any of the lymphocytes affected by the thymus, that regulate immunity, reject foreign tissue, etc.: cf. B CELL

**Tchai·kov·sky** (chī kôf′skē), **Peter** 1840-93; Russ. composer

**TD** abbrev. touchdown: sometimes **td**

**tea** (tē) *n.* ⟦< Chin dial. *t'e*⟧ **1** an evergreen plant grown in Asia **2** its dried leaves, used to make a beverage **3** the beverage made by soaking such leaves in boiling water **4** a tealike beverage made from other plants or from a meat extract **5** [Chiefly Brit.] a meal in the late afternoon at which tea is the drink **6** an afternoon party at which tea, etc. is served

**tea·ber·ry** (tē′ber′ē) *n., pl.* **-ries 1** WINTERGREEN (sense 1) **2** the berry of the wintergreen

**teach** (tēch) *vt.* **taught, teach′ing** ⟦OE *tæcan*⟧ **1** to show or help (a person) to learn (*how*) to do something **2** to give lessons to (a student, etc.) **3** to give lessons in (a subject) **4** to provide with knowledge, insight, etc. —*vi.* to give lessons or instruction —**teach′a·ble** *adj.*

**teach′er** *n.* one who teaches, esp. as a profession

**teach′ing** *n.* **1** the profession of a teacher **2** something taught; precept, doctrine, etc.: *usually used in pl.*

**tea′cup′** *n.* a cup for drinking tea, etc. —**tea′cup·ful′,** *pl.* **-fuls′, n.**

**teak** (tēk) *n.* ⟦< Malayalam *tēkka*⟧ **1** a tall SE Asian tree with hard, yellowish-brown wood **2** its wood: also **teak′wood′**

**tea′ket′tle** *n.* a kettle with a spout, for boiling water to make tea, etc.

**teal** (tēl) *n.* ⟦ME *tele*⟧ **1** a small, short-necked, freshwater wild duck **2** a dark grayish or greenish blue: also **teal blue**

**team** (tēm) *n.* ⟦OE, offspring⟧ **1** two or more horses, oxen, etc. harnessed to the same plow, etc. **2** a group of people working or playing together —*vi.* to join in cooperative activity: often with *up* —*adj.* of or done by a team

**team′mate′** *n.* one on the same team

**team′ster** (-stər) *n.* one whose work is hauling loads with a team or truck

**team′work′** *n.* joint action by a group of people

**tea′pot′** *n.* a pot with a spout and handle, for brewing and pouring tea

**tear**[1] (ter) *vt.* **tore, torn, tear′ing** ⟦OE *teran,* rend⟧ **1** to pull apart into pieces by force; rip **2** to make by tearing /to *tear* a hole/ **3** to lacerate **4** to disrupt; split /ranks *torn* by dissensions/ **5** to divide with doubt, etc. **6** to pull with force: with *up, out, away, off,* etc. —*vi.* **1** to be torn **2** to move with force or speed —*n.* **1** a tearing **2** a torn place; rent —**tear down 1** to wreck **2** to dismantle

**tear**[2] (tir) *n.* ⟦OE *tēar*⟧ a drop of the salty fluid which flows from the eye, as in weeping —**in tears** crying; weeping —**tear′ful** *adj.* —**tear′ful·ly** *adv.* —**tear′y, -i·er, -i·est,** *adj.*

**tear·drop** (tir′dräp′) *n.* a tear

**tear gas** (tir) a liquid or gas that causes irritation of the eyes, used as by the police to disperse rioters —**tear′-gas′, -gassed′, -gas′sing,** *vt.*

**tear·jerk·er** (tir′jur′kər) *n.* [Slang] a sad, overly sentimental film, play, etc.

**tea′room′** *n.* a restaurant that serves tea, coffee, light lunches, etc.

**tease** (tēz) *vt.* **teased, teas′ing** ⟦OE *tæsan*⟧ **1** *a*) to card or comb (flax, wool, etc.) *b*) to fluff (the hair) by combing toward the scalp **2** to annoy by mocking, poking fun, etc. **3** to beg; importune **4** to tantalize —*vi.* to indulge in teasing —*n.* one who teases

**tea·sel** (tē′zəl) *n.* ⟦see prec.⟧ a bristly plant with prickly flowers

**teas·er** (tē′zər) *n.* **1** a person or thing that teases **2** a puzzling problem

**tea′spoon′** *n.* **1** a spoon for stirring tea, etc. **2** a spoon for measuring ⅓ tablespoon —**tea′spoon·ful′,** *pl.* **-fuls′, n.**

**teat** (tēt) *n.* ⟦< OFr *tete*⟧ the nipple on a breast or udder

**tech** *abbrev.* **1** technical(ly) **2** technology

**tech·ie** (tek′ē) *n.* [Inf.] an expert in computer technology

**tech·ni·cal** (tek′ni kəl) *adj.* ⟦< Gr *technē,* an art⟧ **1** dealing with the industrial or mechanical arts

or the applied sciences **2** of a specific science, art, craft, etc. **3** of, in or showing technique **4** concerned with minute details —**tech′ni·cal·ly** *adv.*

**tech′ni·cal′i·ty** (-kal′ə tē) *n., pl.* **-ties 1** the state or quality of being technical **2** a technical point, detail, etc. **3** a minute point, detail, etc. brought to bear upon a main issue

**tech·ni·cian** (tek nish′ən) *n.* one skilled in the technique of some art, craft, or science

**Tech·ni·col·or** (tek′ni kul′ər) *trademark for* a process of making color movies —*n.* [t-] this process

**tech·nique** (tek nēk′) *n.* ⟦Fr⟧ **1** the method of procedure in artistic work, scientific activity, etc. **2** the degree of expertness in following this

**tech·noc·ra·cy** (tek näk′rə sē) *n.* ⟦< Gr *technē,* an art + -CRACY⟧ government by scientists and engineers —**tech′no·crat′** (-nə krat′) *n.*

**tech·nol·o·gy** (tek näl′ə jē) *n.* ⟦Gr *technologia,* systematic treatment⟧ **1** the science of the practical or industrial arts **2** applied science —**tech′no·log′i·cal** (-nə läj′i kəl) *adj.*

**tech·no·phile** (tek′nə fīl′) *n.* one who is enthusiastic about advanced technology

**tech′no·pho′bi·a** *n.* dislike or fear of advanced technology —**tech′no·phobe′** *n.*

**ted·dy bear** (ted′ē) ⟦after *Teddy* (Theodore) Roosevelt⟧ a child's stuffed toy made to look like a bear cub

**te·di·ous** (tē′dē əs) *adj.* full of tedium; long and dull —**te′di·ous·ly** *adv.*

**te′di·um** (-əm) *n.* ⟦< L *taedet,* it offends⟧ the condition or quality of being tiresome, boring, etc.

**tee** (tē) *n.* ⟦prob. < Scot dial. *teaz*⟧ *Golf* **1** a small peg from which the ball is driven **2** the place from which a player makes the first stroke on each hole —*vt., vi.* **teed, tee′ing** to place (a ball) on a tee —**tee off 1** to play a golf ball from a tee **2** [Slang] to make angry or disgusted

**teem** (tēm) *vi.* ⟦< OE *team,* progeny⟧ to be prolific; abound; swarm

**teen** (tēn) *n.* ⟦OE *tien,* ten⟧ **1** [*pl.*] the years from 13 through 19, as of a person's age **2** TEENAGER

**teen·age** (tēn′āj′) *adj.* **1** in one's teens **2** of or for people in their teens —**teen′ag′er** *n.*

**tee·ny** (tē′nē) *adj.* **-ni·er, -ni·est** *inf. var. of* TINY: also **teen·sy** (tēn′zē, -sē), **-si·er, -si·est**

**tee·ny-wee·ny** (tē′nē wē′nē) *adj.* [Inf.] tiny: also **teen·sy-ween·sy** (tēn′zē wēn′zē, tēn′sē wēn′sē)

**tee·pee** (tē′pē) *n. alt. sp. of* TEPEE

**tee shirt** *var. of* T-SHIRT

**tee·ter** (tēt′ər) *vi.* ⟦< ON *titra,* to tremble⟧ to totter, wobble, etc.

**tee′ter-tot′ter** (-tôt′ər, -tät′-) *n., vi.* SEESAW

**teeth** (tēth) *n. pl. of* TOOTH —**in the teeth of 1** directly against **2** defying

**teethe** (tēth) *vi.* **teethed, teeth′ing** to grow teeth; cut one's teeth

**tee·to·tal·er** or **tee·to·tal·ler** (tē tōt′′lər) *n.* ⟦< doubling of initial *t* in *total*⟧ one who practices total abstinence from alcoholic liquor

**te·fil·lin** (tə fil′in) *n.* either of two small, leather cases holding Scripture texts, worn in prayer on the forehead and arm by orthodox Jewish men

**Tef·lon** (tef′län′) *trademark for* a tough polymer, used for nonsticking coatings as for cookware —*n.* [t-] this substance

**Teh·ran** (te rän′) capital of Iran: pop. 6,043,000: also **Te·he·ran′**

**tek·tite** (tek′tīt′) *n.* ⟦< Gr *tēktos,* molten⟧ a small, dark, glassy body thought to have originated as a meteorite: also sp. **tec′tite′**

**tel** *abbrev.* **1** telegram **2** telephone

**Tel A·viv** (tel′ ə vēv′) seaport in W Israel: pop. 356,000

**tele-** *combining form* **1** ⟦< Gr *tēle,* far off⟧ at, over, etc. a distance [*telegraph*] **2** ⟦< TELE(VISION)⟧ of, in, or by television [*telecast*]

**tel·e·cast** (tel′ə kast′) *vt., vi.* **-cast′** or **-cast′ed,**

**-cast'ing** to broadcast by television —*n.* a television broadcast —**tel'e·cast'er** *n.*

**tel'e·com·mu'ni·ca'tion** *n.* [*also pl., with sing. or pl. v.*] communication by electronic or electrical means, as through radio, TV, computers, etc.: also **tel'e·com'** (-käm´)

**tel'e·com·mute'** *vi.* to do office work at home using a computer

**tel'e·con'fer·ence** *n.* a conference of persons in different locations, as by telephone, TV, etc.

**tel'e·gram'** *n.* a message transmitted by telegraph

**tel'e·graph'** *n.* ⟦see TELE- & -GRAPH⟧ an apparatus or system that transmits messages by electrical impulses sent by wire or radio —*vt., vi.* to send (a message) to (a person) by telegraph — **tel'e·graph'ic** *adj.*

**te·leg·ra·phy** (tə leg'rə fē) *n.* the operation of telegraph apparatus —**te·leg'ra·pher** *n.*

**tel·e·ki·ne·sis** (tel'ə ki nē'sis) *n.* ⟦see TELE- & KINETIC⟧ *Parapsychology* the causing of an object to move by psychic, rather than physical, force

**tel'e·mar'ket·ing** *n.* the use of the telephone in selling, market research, promotion, etc. —**tel'e·mar'ket·er** *n.*

**tel·e·me·ter** (tel'ə mēt'ər, tə lem'ət ər) *n.* a device for measuring and transmitting data about radiation, temperature, etc. from a remote point —**te·lem'e·try** *n.*

**te·lep·a·thy** (tə lep'ə thē) *n.* ⟦TELE- + -PATHY⟧ *Parapsychology* extrasensory communication between minds —**tel·e·path·ic** (tel'ə path'ik) *adj.*

**tel·e·phone** (tel'ə fōn') *n.* ⟦TELE- + -PHONE⟧ an instrument or system for conveying speech or computerized information over distances, usually by converting sound into electrical impulses sent through a wire —*vt., vi.* **-phoned', -phon'ing** to convey (a message) to (a person) by telephone — **tel'e·phon'ic** (-fän'ik) *adj.*

**te·leph·o·ny** (tə lef'ə nē) *n.* the making or operation of telephones

**tel·e·pho·to** (tel'ə fōt'ō) *adj.* designating or of a camera lens that produces a large image of a distant object

**tel'e·proc'ess·ing** *n.* computerized data processing, over communication lines

**tel'e·promp'ter** (-prämp'tər) *n.* ⟦< *TelePrompTer,* a former trademark⟧ an electronic device that unrolls a speech, script, etc. line by line, as an aid to a speaker, etc. on TV

**tel·e·scope** (tel'ə skōp') *n.* ⟦see TELE- & -SCOPE⟧ an optical instrument for making distant objects appear nearer and larger —*vi., vt.* **-scoped', -scop'ing** to slide one into another like the tubes of a collapsible telescope — **tel'e·scop'ic** (-skäp'ik) *adj.*

REFRACTING TELESCOPE

**tel'e·thon'** (-thän') *n.* ⟦TELE(VISION) + (MARA)THON⟧ a campaign, as on a lengthy telecast, seeking donations

**Tel·e·type** (tel'ə tīp') *n. trademark for* a former kind of telegraphic apparatus for transmitting typed messages —**tel'e·type'writ'er** *n.*

**tel·e·vise** (tel'ə vīz') *vt., vi.* **-vised', -vis'ing** to transmit by television

**tel·e·vi·sion** (-vizh'ən) *n.* 1 the process of transmitting images by converting light rays into electrical signals: the receiver reconverts the signals to reproduce the images on a screen 2 television broadcasting 3 a television receiving set 4 a television program or programs

**tel·ex** (tel'eks) *n.* ⟦TEL(ETYPEWRITER) + EX(CHANGE)⟧ 1 a teletypewriter which sends

messages over telephone lines 2 a message sent in this way —*vt.* to send by telex

**tell** (tel) *vt.* **told, tell'ing** ⟦OE *tellan,* calculate⟧ 1 to count; reckon [to *tell* time] 2 to narrate; relate [to *tell* a story] 3 to express in words; say [to *tell* the truth] 4 to reveal; disclose 5 to recognize; distinguish [to *tell* twins apart] 6 to inform [tell me later] 7 to order [tell him to go] —*vi.* 1 to give an account or evidence (*of* something) 2 to be effective [each blow *told*] —**tell off** [Inf.] to rebuke severely —**tell on** 1 to have an adverse effect on 2 [Inf.] to inform against

**tell'er** *n.* 1 one who tells (a story, etc.) 2 a bank clerk who pays out or receives money

**tell'ing** *adj.* 1 forceful; striking 2 that reveals much —**tell'ing·ly** *adv.*

**tell'tale'** *adj.* revealing what is meant to be kept secret or hidden

**tel·ly** (tel'ē) *n., pl.* **-lies** *Brit. inf.* term for TELEVISION

**tem·blor** (tem'blôr', -blər) *n.* ⟦Sp < *temblar,* to tremble⟧ EARTHQUAKE

**te·mer·i·ty** (tə mer'ə tē) *n.* ⟦< L *temere,* rashly⟧ foolish or rash boldness

**temp**[1] (temp) *n.* [Inf.] one who works at a place on a temporary basis

**temp**[2] *abbrev.* 1 temperature 2 temporary

**tem·per** (tem'pər) *vt.* ⟦< L *temperare,* regulate⟧ 1 to moderate, as by mingling with something else [to *temper* blame with praise] 2 to bring to the proper condition by some treatment [to *temper* steel] 3 to toughen —*n.* 1 the degree of hardness and resiliency of a metal 2 frame of mind; disposition 3 calmness of mind: in lose (or keep) one's temper 4 a tendency to become angry 5 anger; rage

**tem·per·a** (tem'pər ə) *n.* ⟦It: see prec.⟧ a process of painting with pigments mixed with size, casein, or egg

**tem·per·a·ment** (tem'pər ə mənt, -prə mənt) *n.* ⟦see TEMPER⟧ 1 one's natural disposition; nature 2 a nature that is excitable, moody, etc. — **tem'per·a·men'tal** *adj.*

**tem·per·ance** (tem'pər əns, -prəns) *n.* 1 self-restraint in conduct, indulgence of the appetites, etc.; moderation 2 moderation in drinking alcoholic liquors or total abstinence from them

**tem·per·ate** (tem'pər it, -prit) *adj.* ⟦see TEMPER⟧ 1 moderate, as in one's appetites, behavior, etc. 2 neither very hot nor very cold: said of climate, etc.

**Temperate Zone** either of the two zones of the earth (**North Temperate Zone** and **South Temperate Zone**) between the tropics and the polar circles

**tem·per·a·ture** (tem'pər ə chər, -prə chər) *n.* ⟦< L *temperatus,* temperate⟧ 1 the degree of hotness or coldness of anything 2 an excess of body heat over the normal; fever

**tem·pered** (tem'pərd) *adj.* 1 having been given the desired TEMPER (*n.* 1) 2 having a (specified) TEMPER (*n.* 2)

**tem·pest** (tem'pist) *n.* ⟦< L *tempus,* time⟧ a violent storm with high winds, esp. one accompanied by rain, hail, etc.

**tem·pes·tu·ous** (tem pes'chōō əs) *adj.* of or like a tempest; violent

**tem·plate** (tem'plit) *n.* ⟦< L *templum,* small timber⟧ a pattern, as a thin metal plate, for making an exact copy

**tem·ple**[1] (tem'pəl) *n.* ⟦< L *templum*⟧ 1 a building for the worship of God or gods 2 a large building for some special purpose [a *temple* of art]

**tem·ple**[2] (tem'pəl) *n.* ⟦< L *tempus*⟧ 1 the flat surface alongside the forehead, in front of each ear 2 either of the sidepieces of a pair of glasses

**tem·po** (tem'pō) *n., pl.* **-pos** or **-pi** (-pē) ⟦It < *tempus,* time⟧ 1 the speed at which a musical composition is performed 2 rate of activity

**tem·po·ral**[1] (tem'pə rəl) *adj.* ⟦< L *tempus,* time⟧ 1 worldly; not spiritual 2 secular 3 of or limited by time

**tem·po·ral**[2] (tem'pə rəl) *adj.* of or near the temples (of the head)

**tem·po·rar·y** (-rer'ē) *adj.* [< L *tempus,* time] lasting only a while; not permanent —**tem'po·rar'i·ly** *adv.*

**tem·po·rize** (-rīz') *vi.* **-rized', -riz'ing** to give temporary compliance, evade decision, etc., so as to gain time or avoid argument

**tempt** (tempt) *vt.* [< L *temptare,* to test] **1** to induce or entice, as to something immoral **2** to be inviting to; attract **3** to provoke or risk provoking (fate, etc.) **4** to incline strongly [to be *tempted* to accept] —**temp·ta·tion** (temp tā'shən) *n.*

**tempt·ress** (temp'tris) *n.* a woman who tempts, esp. sexually

**tem·pu·ra** (tem'poo rä', tem poor'ə) *n.* [Jpn] a Japanese dish of deep-fried shrimp, fish, vegetables, etc.

**ten** (ten) *adj., n.* [OE] one more than nine; 10; X

**ten·a·ble** (ten'ə bəl) *adj.* [< L *tenere,* to hold] that can be defended or believed —**ten'a·bil'i·ty** *n.*

**te·na·cious** (tə nā'shəs) *adj.* [< L *tenere,* to hold] **1** holding firmly [a *tenacious* grip] **2** retentive [a *tenacious* memory] **3** strongly cohesive or adhesive **4** persistent; stubborn [*tenacious* courage] —**te·na'cious·ly** *adv.* —**te·nac·i·ty** (tə nas'ə tē) *n.*

**ten·ant** (ten'ənt) *n.* [see prec.] **1** one who pays rent to occupy land, a building, etc. **2** an occupant —*vt.* to hold as a tenant; occupy —**ten'an·cy,** *pl.* **-cies,** *n.*

**tenant farmer** one who farms land owned by another and pays rent

**Ten Commandments** *Bible* the ten laws of moral and religious conduct given to Moses by God: Exodus 20:2-17

**tend**[1] (tend) *vt.* [see ATTEND] **1** to take care of **2** to manage or operate

**tend**[2] (tend) *vi.* [< L *tendere,* to stretch] **1** to be inclined, disposed, etc. (*to*) **2** to be directed (*to* or *toward*)

**tend·en·cy** (ten'dən sē) *n., pl.* **-cies** [see prec.] **1** an inclination to move or act in a particular direction or way **2** a course toward some object

**ten·den·tious** (ten den'shəs) *adj.* [< Ger *tendenz,* TENDENCY] advancing a definite point of view [*tendentious* writings] —**ten·den'tious·ly** *adv.*

**ten·der**[1] (ten'dər) *adj.* [< L *tener,* soft] **1** soft and easily chewed, broken, cut, etc. **2** physically weak **3** immature **4** that requires careful handling **5** gentle or light **6** acutely sensitive, as to pain **7** sensitive to emotions, others' feelings, etc. —**ten'der·ly** *adv.* —**ten'der·ness** *n.*

**ten·der**[2] (ten'dər) *vt.* [see TEND[2]] to offer formally —*n.* **1** a formal offer **2** money, etc. offered in payment

**tend·er**[3] (ten'dər) *n.* **1** one who tends something **2** a small ship for supplying a larger one **3** a railroad car attached behind, and carrying fuel and water for, a steam locomotive

**ten'der·foot'** *n., pl.* **-foots'** or **-feet'** **1** a newcomer to ranching in the West, unused to hardships **2** any novice

**ten'der·heart'ed** *adj.* quick to feel pity or compassion

**ten·der·ize** (ten'dər īz') *vt.* **-ized', -iz'ing** to make (meat) tender

**ten'der·loin'** *n.* the tenderest part of a loin of beef, pork, etc.

**ten·di·ni·tis** (ten'də nīt'is) *n.* inflammation of a tendon

**ten·don** (ten'dən) *n.* [< Gr *teinein,* to stretch] any of the inelastic cords of tough, connective tissue by which muscles are attached to bones, etc.

**ten·dril** (ten'drəl) *n.* [prob. ult. < L *tener,* delicate] a threadlike, clinging part of a climbing plant

**ten·e·ment** (ten'ə mənt) *n.* [< L *tenere,* to hold] a building divided into tenements; now specif., one that is run-down, overcrowded, etc.: in full **tenement house**

**ten·et** (ten'it) *n.* [L, he holds] a principle, doctrine, or belief held as a truth, as by some group

**Ten·nes·see** (ten'ə sē') state of the EC U.S.: 41,220 sq. mi.; pop. 4,877,000; cap. Nashville: abbrev. *TN* —**Ten'nes·se'an** *adj., n.*

**ten·nis** (ten'is) *n.* [prob. < OFr *tener,* hold (imperative)] a game in which players in a marked area (**tennis court**) hit a ball back and forth with rackets over a net

**tennis elbow** inflammation of the elbow tendons, caused by strain

**tennis shoe** a sneaker

**Ten·ny·son** (ten'i sən), **Al·fred** (al'frəd) 1809-92; Eng. poet: called *Alfred, Lord Tennyson*

**ten·on** (ten'ən) *n.* [ult. < L *tenere,* to hold] a projecting part cut on the end of a piece of wood for insertion into a mortise to make a joint

**ten·or** (ten'ər) *n.* [< L *tenere,* to hold] **1** general tendency **2** general meaning; drift **3** *a*) the range of the highest regular adult male voice *b*) a voice, singer, or instrument with such a range *c*) a part for a tenor —*adj.* of or for a tenor

**ten'pins'** *n.* the game of bowling in which ten pins are used

**tense**[1] (tens) *adj.* **tens'er, tens'est** [< L *tendere,* to stretch] **1** stretched tight; taut **2** feeling or showing tension —*vt., vi.* **tensed, tens'ing** to make or become tense

**tense**[2] (tens) *n.* [< L *tempus,* time] any of the forms of a verb that show the time of its action or existence

**ten·sile** (ten'səl) *adj.* **1** of, undergoing, or exerting tension **2** capable of being stretched

**ten·sion** (ten'shən) *n.* **1** a tensing or being tensed **2** mental or nervous strain **3** a state of strained relations due to mutual hostility **4** VOLTAGE **5** stress on a material produced by the pull of forces causing extension

**tent** (tent) *n.* [< L *tendere,* to stretch] a portable shelter made of canvas, etc. stretched over poles —*vi., vt.* to lodge in a tent or tents

**ten·ta·cle** (ten'tə kəl) *n.* [< L *tentare,* to touch] a long, slender, flexible growth on the head of some invertebrates, used to grasp, feel, etc.

**ten·ta·tive** (ten'tə tiv) *adj.* [< L *tentare,* to try] **1** made, done, etc. provisionally; not final **2** indicating timidity or uncertainty —**ten'ta·tive·ly** *adv.*

**ten·ter·hook** (ten'tər hook') *n.* [< L *tendere,* to stretch + HOOK] a kind of hooked nail —**on tenterhooks** in anxious suspense

**tenth** (tenth) *adj.* [OE *teogotha*] preceded by nine others in a series; 10th —*n.* **1** the one following the ninth **2** any of the ten equal parts of something; ¹⁄₁₀

**ten·u·ous** (ten'yoo əs) *adj.* [< L *tenuis,* thin] **1** slender or fine, as a fiber **2** rare, as air at high altitudes **3** flimsy [*tenuous* evidence]

**ten·ure** (ten'yər) *n.* [< medieval Fr < *tenir,* to hold] **1** the act or right of holding property, an office, etc. **2** the length of time, or the conditions under which, something is held **3** the status of holding one's position on a permanent basis, granted to teachers, etc.

**te·pee** (tē'pē) *n.* [< AmInd *t*ʰ*ípi,* dwelling] a cone-shaped tent used by some North American Indians

**tep·id** (tep'id) *adj.* [< L *tepidus*] **1** lukewarm **2** lacking enthusiasm

**te·qui·la** (tə kē'lə) *n.* [< AmInd (Mexico) *Tui-quila,* region in Mexico] an alcoholic liquor of Mexico, distilled from an agave mash

**ter·cen·te·nar·y** (tur'sen ten'ər ē, tər sen'tə ner'ē) *adj., n., pl.* **-ies** [[L *ter,* three times + CENTENARY] TRICENTENNIAL

TEPEE

**term** (turm) *n.* [< L *terminus,* a limit] **1** a set

date, as for payment, etc. **2** a set period of time [*school term, term* of office] **3** [*pl.*] conditions of a contract, etc. **4** [*pl.*] mutual relationship between persons [on speaking *terms*] **5** a word or phrase, esp. as used in some science, art, etc. **6** [*pl.*] words; speech [*unkind terms*] **7** *Math. a*) either quantity of a fraction or a ratio *b*) each quantity in a series or algebraic expression —*vt.* to call by a term; name —**bring** (or **come**) **to terms** to force into (or arrive at) an agreement

**ter·ma·gant** (tur′mə gənt) *n.* [< OFr *Tervagant*, imaginary Muslim deity] a quarrelsome, scolding woman

**ter·mi·na·ble** (tur′mi nə bəl) *adj.* that can be, or is, terminated

**ter·mi·nal** (tur′mə nəl) *adj.* [L *terminalis*] **1** of, at, or forming the end or extremity **2** concluding; final **3** close to causing death [*terminal* cancer] **4** of or at the end of a transportation line —*n.* **1** an end; extremity **2** a connective point on an electric circuit **3** either end of a transportation line, or a main station on it **4** a device, usually with a keyboard and video display, for putting data in, or getting it from, a computer

**ter·mi·nate** (tur′mə nāt′) *vt.* -nat′ed, -nat′ing [< L *terminus,* a limit] **1** to form the end of **2** to put an end to; stop **3** to dismiss from employment; fire —*vi.* **1** to come to an end **2** to have its end (*in* something) —**ter′mi·na′tion** *n.*

**ter·mi·nol·o·gy** (tur′mə näl′ə jē) *n., pl.* -gies the terms used in a specific science, art, etc.

**term insurance** life insurance that expires after a specified period

**ter·mi·nus** (tur′mə nəs) *n., pl.* -ni′ (-nī′) or -nus·es [L, a limit] **1** a limit **2** an end; extremity or goal **3** [Chiefly Brit.] either end of a transportation line

**ter·mite** (tur′mīt′) *n.* [< L *tarmes,* wood-boring worm] a social insect that is very destructive to wooden structures

**tern** (turn) *n.* [< ON *therna*] a gull-like seabird with webbed feet and a straight bill

**ter·race** (ter′əs) *n.* [< L *terra,* earth] **1** a raised, flat mound of earth with sloping sides, esp. one in a series on a hillside **2** an unroofed, paved area, between a house and lawn **3** a row of houses on ground above street level **4** a small, usually roofed balcony, as outside an apartment —*vt.* -raced, -rac·ing to form into a terrace or terraces

**ter·ra cot·ta** (ter′ə kät′ə) [It, lit., baked earth] a hard, brown-red earthenware, or its color

**ter·ra fir·ma** (ter′ə fur′mə) [L] firm earth

**ter·rain** (tə rān′) *n.* [< L *terra,* earth] a tract of ground, as with regard to its features

**ter·ra·pin** (ter′ə pin) *n.* [< Algonquian] **1** any of various terrestrial, freshwater or tidewater turtles **2** its edible flesh

**ter·rar·i·um** (tə rer′ē əm) *n., pl.* -i·ums or -i·a (-ə) [< L *terra,* earth + -*arium,* as in *aquarium*] an enclosure, as of glass, in which small plants are grown or small land animals are kept

**ter·raz·zo** (tə raz′ō, tə rät′sō) *n.* [It] flooring of small chips of marble set in cement and polished

**ter·res·tri·al** (tə res′trē əl) *adj.* [< L *terra,* earth] **1** worldly; mundane **2** of the earth **3** consisting of land, not water **4** living on land

**ter·ri·ble** (ter′ə bəl) *adj.* [< L *terrere,* frighten] **1** causing terror; dreadful **2** extreme; intense **3** [Inf.] very unpleasant, etc. —**ter′ri·bly** *adv.*

**ter·ri·er** (ter′ē ər) *n.* [< medieval Fr (*chien*) *terrier,* hunting (dog)] any of several breeds of small and typically aggressive dog

**ter·rif·ic** (tə rif′ik) *adj.* [< L *terrere,* frighten] **1** causing great fear **2** [Inf.] *a*) very great, intense, etc. *b*) unusually fine, admirable, etc.

**ter·ri·fy** (ter′ə fī′) *vt.* -fied′, -fy′ing to fill with terror; frighten greatly

**ter·ri·to·ry** (ter′ə tôr′ē) *n., pl.* -ries [< L *terra,* earth] **1** an area under the jurisdiction of a nation, ruler, etc. **2** a part of a country or empire

that does not have full status **3** any large tract of land **4** an assigned area **5** a sphere of action, thought, etc. —**ter′ri·to′ri·al** *adj.*

**ter·ror** (ter′ər) *n.* [< L *terrere,* frighten] **1** intense fear **2** (*a*) one that causes intense fear *b*) the quality of causing such fear **3** [Inf.] one who is very annoying or unmanageable, esp. a child

**ter′ror·ism′** *n.* the use of force or threats to intimidate, etc., esp. as a political policy —**ter′ror·ist** *n., adj.*

**ter′ror·ize′** (-īz′) *vt.* -ized′, -iz′ing **1** to terrify **2** to coerce, make submit, etc. by filling with terror

**ter·ry** (ter′ē) *n.* [prob. < Fr *tirer,* to draw] cloth having a pile of uncut loops, esp. cotton cloth used for toweling: also **terry cloth**

**terse** (turs) *adj.* ters′er, ters′est [L *tersus,* wiped off] free of superfluous words; concise; succinct —**terse′ly** *adv.* —**terse′ness** *n.*

**ter·ti·ar·y** (tur′shē er′ē) *adj.* [< L *tertius,* third] third in order

**tes·sel·late** (tes′ə lāt′) *vt.* -lat′ed, -lat′ing [< L *tessella,* little square stone] to lay out in a mosaic pattern of small, square blocks

**test** (test) *n.* [< OFr, assaying cup] **1** *a*) an examination or trial, as of something's value *b*) the method or a criterion used in this **2** an event, etc. that tries one's qualities **3** a set of questions, etc. for determining one's knowledge, etc. **4** *Chem.* a trial or reaction for identifying a substance —*vt.* to subject to a test; try —*vi.* to be rated by a test

**tes·ta·ment** (tes′tə mənt) *n.* [< L *testis,* a witness] **1** [T-] either of the two parts of the Bible, the *Old Testament* and the *New Testament* **2** *a*) a testimonial *b*) an affirmation of beliefs **3** *Law* a will —**tes′ta·men′ta·ry** (-men′tə rē) *adj.*

**tes·tate** (tes′tāt′) *adj.* [< L *testari,* make a will] having left a legally valid will

**tes·ta·tor** (tes′tāt′ər, tes tāt′-) *n.* one who has made a will

**tes·ti·cle** (tes′ti kəl) *n.* [< L *testis*] either of two male sex glands

**tes·ti·fy** (tes′tə fī′) *vi.* -fied′, -fy′ing [< L *testis,* a witness + *facere,* to make] **1** to give evidence, esp. under oath in court **2** to serve as evidence —*vt.* to affirm; declare, esp. under oath in court

**tes·ti·mo·ni·al** (tes′tə mō′nē əl) *n.* **1** a statement recommending a person or thing **2** something given or done to show gratitude or appreciation

**tes·ti·mo·ny** (tes′tə mō′nē) *n., pl.* -nies [< L *testis,* a witness] **1** a statement made under oath to establish a fact **2** any declaration **3** any form of evidence; proof

**tes·tis** (tes′tis) *n., pl.* -tes′ (-tēz′) [L] TESTICLE

**tes·tos·ter·one** (tes täs′tər ōn′) *n.* [see TESTICLE] a male sex hormone

**test tube** a tube of thin, transparent glass closed at one end, used in chemical experiments, etc.

**tes·ty** (tes′tē) *adj.* -ti·er, -ti·est [< L *testa,* the head] irritable; touchy

**tet·a·nus** (tet′ ′n əs, tet′nəs) *n.* [< Gr *tetanos,* spasm] an acute infectious disease, often fatal, caused by a toxin and characterized by spasmodic contractions and rigidity of muscles

**tête-à-tête** (tāt′ə tāt′) *n.* [Fr, lit., head-to-head] a private conversation between two people

**teth·er** (teth′ər) *n.* [< ON *tjothr*] **1** a rope or chain fastened to an animal to keep it from roaming **2** the limit of one's abilities, resources, etc. —*vt.* to fasten with a tether

**tet·ra** (te′trə) *n.* [< ModL] a brightly colored, tropical American fish

**tetra-** [Gr < *tettares,* four] *combining form* four

**tet·ra·cy·cline** (te′trə sī′klin) *n.* a yellow, crystalline compound, used as an antibiotic

**tet·ra·he·dron** (te′trə hē′drən) *n., pl.* -drons or -dra (-drə) [see TETRA- & -HEDRON] a solid figure with four triangular faces

**te·tram·e·ter** (te tram′ət ər) *n.* [see TETRA- & METER[1]] **1** a line of verse containing four metrical feet **2** verse consisting of tetrameters

**Teu·ton·ic** (tōō tän′ik) *adj.* designating or of a

group of north European peoples, esp. the Germans —**Teu·ton** (tōōt′'n) *n.*

**Tex·as** (tek′səs) state of the SW U.S.: 261,914 sq. mi.; pop. 16,987,000; cap. Austin: abbrev. *TX* —**Tex'an** *adj., n.*

**text** (tekst) *n.* ⟦< L *texere,* to weave⟧ **1** the actual words of an author, as distinguished from notes, etc. **2** any form in which a written work exists **3** the principal matter on a printed page, as distinguished from notes, headings, etc. **4** *a*) a Biblical passage used as the topic of a sermon, etc. *b*) any topic or subject **5** *short for* TEXTBOOK —**tex·tu·al** (teks′chōō əl) *adj.*

**text'book′** *n.* a book giving instructions in a subject of study —*adj.* so typical as to be a classic example or model of its kind

**tex·tile** (teks′tīl′, -təl) *adj.* ⟦see TEXT⟧ **1** having to do with weaving **2** that has been or can be woven —*n.* **1** a woven or knitted fabric; cloth **2** raw material suitable for this

**tex·ture** (teks′chər) *n.* ⟦< L *texere,* to weave⟧ **1** the character of a fabric, determined by the arrangement, size, etc. of its threads **2** the arrangement of the constituent parts of anything —**tex′tur·al** *adj.*

**tex′tured** *adj.* having an uneven surface; not smooth [*textured* wallpaper]

**-th**[1] ⟦OE⟧ *suffix* **1** the act of ___ing [*growth*] **2** the state or quality of being or having [*wealth*]

**-th**[2] ⟦< OE⟧ *suffix* forming ordinal numerals [*fourth, ninth*]

**Th** *Chem. symbol for* thorium

**Thai** (tī) *n.* **1** *pl.* **Thais** or **Thai** a person born or living in Thailand **2** the language of Thailand **3** *alt. sp. of* TAI —*adj.* of Thailand or its people, culture, etc.

**Thai·land** (tī′land′) country in SE Asia: 198,114 sq. mi.; pop. 54,532,000

**thal·a·mus** (thal′ə məs) *n., pl.* **-mi′** (-mī′) ⟦< Gr *thalamos,* inner chamber⟧ a mass of gray matter at the base of the brain, involved in the transmission of certain sensations

**tha·lid·o·mide** (thə lid′ə mīd′) *n.* a drug formerly used as a sedative, but found to cause severe birth deformities when taken in pregnancy

**thal·lo·phyte** (thal′ə fīt′) *n.* ⟦< Gr *thallos,* young shoot + *phyton,* a plant⟧ any of a large group of plants lacking true roots, leaves, or stems, as the fungi, the lichens, and most algae

**Thames** (temz) river in S England, flowing through London into the North Sea

**than** (than) *conj.* ⟦OE *thenne*⟧ introducing the second element in a comparison [A is taller *than* B]

**thank** (thaŋk) *vt.* ⟦OE *thancian*⟧ **1** to express gratitude to, as by saying "thank you" **2** to blame: an ironic use —**thank you** *short for* I thank you

**thank'ful** *adj.* feeling or expressing thanks —**thank'ful·ly** *adv.*

**thank'less** *adj.* **1** not feeling or expressing thanks; ungrateful **2** unappreciated

**thanks** (thaŋks) *pl.n.* an expression of gratitude —*interj.* I thank you —**thanks to 1** let thanks be given to **2** on account of; because of

**thanks'giv'ing** *n.* **1** a formal public expression of thanks to God **2** [T-] an annual U.S. holiday observed on the fourth Thursday of November

**that** (that) *pron., pl.* **those** ⟦OE *thæt*⟧ **1** the person or thing mentioned [*that* is John] **2** the farther one or the other one [this is better than *that*] **3** who, whom, or which [the road *that* we took] **4** where [the place *that* I saw her] **5** when [the year *that* I was born] —*adj., pl.* **those 1** designating the one mentioned [*that* man is John] **2** designating the farther one or the other one [this house is larger than *that* one] —*conj.* subordinating conjunction used to introduce: *a*) a noun clause [*that* she's gone is obvious] *b*) an adverbial clause expressing purpose [they died *that* we might live], result [I ran so fast *that* I won], or cause [I'm glad *that* I won] *c*) an elliptical sentence expressing surprise, desire, etc. [oh, *that* she were here!] —

*adv.* to that extent [I can't see *that* far] —**at that** [Inf.] **1** at that point: also **with that 2** even so —**that is 1** to be specific **2** in other words

**thatch** (thach) *n.* ⟦OE *thæc*⟧ **1** a roof of straw, rushes, etc. **2** material for such a roof: also **thatch'ing 3** a layer of tangled, partly decayed leaves, stems, etc. lying on top of the soil —*vt.* to cover as with thatch

**thaw** (thô) *vi.* ⟦OE *thawian*⟧ **1** *a*) to melt (said of ice, snow, etc.) *b*) to pass to an unfrozen state (said of frozen foods) **2** to become warmer so that snow, etc. melts **3** to lose one's coldness of manner —*vt.* to cause to thaw —*n.* **1** a thawing **2** a spell of weather warm enough to allow thawing

**THC** *n.* ⟦*t(etra)h(ydro)c(annabinol)*⟧ the principal and most active chemical in marijuana

**ThD** or **Th.D.** *abbrev.* ⟦L *Theologiae Doctor*⟧ Doctor of Theology

**the** (thə; *before vowels* thē, thi) *adj., definite article* ⟦< OE *se* with *th-* from other forms⟧ *the* (as opposed to *a, an*) refers to: **1** a particular person, thing, or group [*the* story ended; *the* President] **2** a person or thing considered generically [*the* cow is a domestic animal; *the* poor] —*adv.* **1** that much [*the* better to see you with] **2** by how much . . . by that much [*the* sooner *the* better]

**the·a·ter** or **the·a·tre** (thē′ə tər) *n.* ⟦< Gr *theasthai,* to view⟧ **1** a place, esp. a building, where plays, operas, films, etc. are presented **2** any similar place with banked rows of seats **3** any place where events occur **4** *a*) the dramatic art *b*) the theatrical world

**the·at·ri·cal** (thē a′tri kəl) *adj.* **1** having to do with the theater **2** dramatic; esp. (in disparagement), melodramatic —**the·at′ri·cal·ly** *adv.*

**thee** (thē) *pron.* ⟦OE *the*⟧ [Archaic] *objective form of* THOU

**theft** (theft) *n.* ⟦OE *thiefth*⟧ the act or an instance of stealing; larceny

**their** (ther) *poss. pronominal adj.* ⟦< ON *theirra*⟧ of, belonging to, or done by them

**theirs** (therz) *pron.* that or those belonging to them: poss. form of THEY [that book is *theirs; theirs* are better]

**the·ism** (thē′iz′əm) *n.* ⟦< Gr *theos,* god⟧ **1** belief in a god or gods **2** MONOTHEISM —**the′ist** *n., adj.* —**the·is′tic** *adj.*

**them** (them) *pron.* ⟦< ON *theim*⟧ *objective form of* THEY

**theme** (thēm) *n.* ⟦< Gr *thema,* what is laid down⟧ **1** a topic, as of an essay **2** a short essay **3** a short melody used as the subject of a musical composition **4** a recurring or identifying song in a film, musical, radio or TV series, etc.: in full **theme song** —**the·mat·ic** (thē mat′ik) *adj.*

**them·selves** (them selvz′) *pron.* a form of THEY, used as an intensive [they went *themselves*], as a reflexive [they hurt *themselves*], or with the meaning "their true selves" [they are not *themselves* when they are sick]

**then** (then) *adv.* ⟦see THAN⟧ **1** at that time [he was young *then*] **2** next in time or order [he took his hat and *then* left] **3** in that case; accordingly [if she read it, *then* she knows] **4** besides; moreover [he likes to walk, and *then* it's good exercise] **5** at another time [now it's warm, *then* freezing] —*adj.* being such at that time [the *then* director] —*n.* that time [by *then*, they were gone]

**thence** (thens) *adv.* ⟦OE *thanan*⟧ **1** from that place **2** from that time; thenceforth

**thence'forth′** *adv.* from that time onward; thereafter: also **thence·for'ward**

**the·oc·ra·cy** (thē äk′rə sē) *n., pl.* **-cies** ⟦< Gr *theos,* god + *kratos,* rule, power⟧ **1** government by a person or persons claiming divine authority **2** a country with this form of government

**the·o·lo·gi·an** (thē′ə lō′jən) *n.* a student of or specialist in theology

**the·ol·o·gy** (thē äl′ə jē) *n.* ⟦< Gr *theos,* god + *logos,* word⟧ the study of God and of religious doctrines and matters of divinity —**the′o·log′i·cal** (-ə läj′i kəl) *adj.*

**the·o·rem** (thē′ə rəm, thir′əm) *n.* ⟦< Gr *theōrein,* to view⟧ **1** a proposition that can be proved from accepted premises; law or principle **2** *Math., Physics* a proposition embodying something to be proved

**the·o·ret·i·cal** (thē′ə ret′i kəl) *adj.* **1** limited to or based on theory; hypothetical **2** tending to theorize; speculative Also **the′o·ret′ic** —**the′o·ret′i·cal·ly** *adv.*

**the·o·rize** (thē′ə rīz′) *vi.* **-rized′, -riz′ing** to form a theory or theories; speculate —**the′o·re·ti′cian** (-rə tish′ən) or **the′o·rist** (-rist) *n.*

**the·o·ry** (thē′ə rē, thir′ē) *n., pl.* **-ries** ⟦< Gr *theōrein,* to view⟧ **1** a speculative plan **2** a formulation of underlying principles of certain observed phenomena that has been verified to some degree **3** the principles of an art or science, rather than its practice **4** a conjecture or guess

**the·os·o·phy** (thē äs′ə fē) *n.* ⟦< Gr *theos,* god + *sophia,* wisdom⟧ [*also* T-] a religious or semireligious set of occult beliefs rejecting Christian theology and held to be based on a special mystical insight —**the′o·soph′ic** (-ə säf′ik) or **the′o·soph′i·cal** *adj.* —**the·os′o·phist** *n.*

**ther·a·peu·tic** (ther′ə pyo͞ot′ik) *adj.* ⟦< Gr *therapeuein,* to nurse⟧ serving to cure or heal or to preserve health

**ther′a·peu′tics** *n.* the branch of medicine that deals with the treatment of diseases; therapy

**ther·a·py** (-pē) *n., pl.* **-pies** [see THERAPEUTIC] **1** the treatment of any physical or mental disorder by medical or physical means, usually excluding surgery **2** *short for* PSYCHOTHERAPY —**ther′a·pist** *n.*

**there** (ther) *adv.* ⟦OE *ther*⟧ **1** at, in, or to that place **2** at that point; then [*there* I paused] **3** in that respect [*there* you are wrong] *There* is also used in impersonal constructions in which the real subject follows the verb [*there* is little time] —*n.* that place —*interj.* used to express defiance, satisfaction, sympathy, etc. —(**not**) **all there** [Inf.] (not) mentally sound

**there′a·bouts′** (-ə bouts′) *adv.* **1** near that place **2** near that time, number, degree, etc. Also **there′a·bout′**

**there·af′ter** *adv.* from then on

**there·at′** *adv.* **1** at that place; there **2** at that time **3** for that reason

**there·by′** *adv.* **1** by that means **2** connected with that

**there·for′** *adv.* for this; for that; for it

**there′fore′** (-fôr′) *adv.* for this or that reason; hence

**there·in′** *adv.* **1** in or into that place **2** in that matter, detail, etc.

**there·of′** *adv.* **1** of that **2** from that as a cause, reason, etc.

**there·on′** *adv.* **1** on that or it **2** THEREUPON

**there·to′** *adv.* to that place, thing, etc.: also **there·un·to** (ther un′to͞o, *ther*un to͞o′)

**there′to·fore′** *adv.* until that time

**there′up·on′** *adv.* **1** immediately following that **2** as a consequence of that **3** on that subject, etc.

**there′with′** *adv.* **1** along with that **2** immediately thereafter

**ther·mal** (thur′məl) *adj.* ⟦< Gr *thermē,* heat⟧ **1** having to do with heat **2** designating a loosely knitted material with air spaces for insulation —*n. Meteorol.* a rising column of warm air

**thermal pollution** the harmful discharge of heated liquid or air into lakes, rivers, etc.

**thermo-** ⟦< Gr *thermē,* heat⟧ *combining form* heat

**ther·mo·dy·nam·ics** (thur′mō dī nam′iks) *n.* the branch of physics dealing with the transformation of heat to and from other forms of energy —**ther′mo·dy·nam′ic** *adj.*

**ther·mom·e·ter** (thər mäm′ət ər) *n.* ⟦see THERMO- & -METER⟧ an instrument for measuring temperatures, as a graduated glass tube in which mercury, etc. rises or falls as it expands or contracts with changes in temperature

**ther·mo·nu·cle·ar** (thur′mō no͞o′klē ər) *adj. Physics* **1** designating a reaction in which isotopes of a light element fuse, at extremely high heat, into heavier nuclei **2** of or using the heat energy released in nuclear fusion

**ther·mo·plas·tic** (thur′mə plas′tik) *adj.* soft and moldable when subjected to heat: said of certain plastics —*n.* a thermoplastic substance

**Ther·mos** (thur′məs) ⟦< Gr *thermos,* hot⟧ *trademark for* a vacuum-insulated container for keeping liquids at almost their original temperature —*n.* [*usually* t-] such a container

**ther·mo·stat** (thur′mə stat′) *n.* ⟦THERMO- + -STAT⟧ an apparatus for regulating temperature, esp. one that automatically controls a heating or cooling unit

**the·sau·rus** (thi sô′rəs) *n., pl.* **-ri′** (-rī′) or **-rus·es** ⟦< Gr *thēsauros,* a treasure⟧ a book of synonyms and antonyms

**these** (thēz) *pron., adj. pl. of* THIS

**The·seus** (thē′so͞os′, thē′sē əs) *n. Gr. Legend* the king of Athens who kills the Minotaur

**the·sis** (thē′sis) *n., pl.* **-ses′** (-sēz′) ⟦< Gr *tithenai,* to put⟧ **1** a proposition to be defended in argument **2** a long research paper, esp. one written by a candidate for a master's degree

**Thes·pi·an** (thes′pē ən) *adj.* ⟦after *Thespis,* ancient Gr poet⟧ [*often* t-] having to do with the drama; dramatic —*n.* [*often* t-] an actor or actress

**the·ta** (thāt′ə, thēt′-) *n.* the eighth letter of the Greek alphabet (Θ, θ, ϑ)

**thews** (thyo͞oz) *pl.n., sing.* **thew** ⟦< OE *theaw,* habit⟧ muscles or sinews

**they** (thā) *pron., sing.* **he, she,** or **it** ⟦< ON *thei-r*⟧ **1** the persons, animals, or things previously mentioned **2** people generally [*they* say it's so]

**thi·a·mine** (thī′ə min, -mēn′) *n.* ⟦ult. < Gr *theion,* brimstone + (VIT)AMIN⟧ a white, crystalline B vitamin, found in cereals, egg yolk, liver, etc.; vitamin B₁: also **thi′a·min** (-min)

**thick** (thik) *adj.* ⟦OE *thicce*⟧ **1** of relatively great extent from side to side **2** as measured between opposite surfaces [one inch *thick*] **3** close and abundant [*thick* hair] **4** viscous **5** dense [*thick* smoke] **6** husky; blurred [*thick* speech] **7** [Inf.] stupid **8** [Inf.] close in friendship —*n.* the thickest part —**thick′ly** *adv.* —**thick′ness** *n.*

**thick′en** *vt., vi.* **1** to make or become thick or thicker **2** to make or become more complex —**thick′en·ing** *n.*

**thick·et** (thik′it) *n.* ⟦see THICK⟧ a thick growth of shrubs or small trees

**thick′set′** *adj.* **1** planted thickly or closely **2** thick in body; stocky

**thick′-skinned′** *adj.* insensitive, as to insult

**thief** (thēf) *n., pl.* **thieves** (thēvz) ⟦OE *theof*⟧ one who steals

**thieve** (thēv) *vt., vi.* **thieved, thiev′ing** to steal —**thiev′ish** *adj.*

**thiev′er·y** (-ər ē) *n., pl.* **-ies** the act or an instance of stealing; theft

**thigh** (thī) *n.* ⟦OE *theoh*⟧ that part of the leg between the knee and the hip

**thigh′bone′** *n.* FEMUR

**thim·ble** (thim′bəl) *n.* ⟦< OE *thuma,* a thumb⟧ a small cap worn to protect the finger that pushes the needle in sewing —**thim′ble·ful′,** *pl.* **-fuls′,** *n.*

**thin** (thin) *adj.* **thin′ner, thin′nest** ⟦OE *thynne*⟧ **1** of relatively little extent from side to side **2** lean; slender **3** not dense or compact [*thin* hair] **4** very fluid or watery [*thin* soup] **5** high-pitched and weak [a *thin* voice] **6** sheer: said as of fabric **7** flimsy or unconvincing [a *thin* excuse] **8** lacking substance, depth, etc.; weak —*vt., vi.* **thinned, thin′ning** to make or become thin or thinner —**thin′ly** *adv.* —**thin′ness** *n.*

**thine** (thīn) [Archaic] *pron.* ⟦OE *thin*⟧ that or those belonging to thee: poss. form of THOU —

*poss. pronominal adj.* thy: used esp. before a vowel

**thing** (thiŋ) *n.* ⟦OE, council⟧ **1** any matter, affair, or concern **2** a happening, act, incident, event, etc. **3** *a*) a tangible object *b*) an inanimate object **4** an item, detail, etc. **5** *a*) [*pl.*] personal belongings *b*) a garment **6** [Inf.] a person [*poor thing*] **7** [Inf.] a point of contention; issue **8** [Inf.] an irrational liking, fear, etc. **9** [Inf.] what one wants to do or is adept at [to do one's own *thing*] —**see things** [Inf.] to have hallucinations

**think** (thiŋk) *vt.* **thought, think'ing** ⟦OE *thencan*⟧ **1** to form or have in the mind [*thinking* good thoughts] **2** to judge; consider [many *think* her charming] **3** to believe [I *think* I can come] —*vi.* **1** to use the mind; reason **2** to have an opinion, etc.: with *of* or *about* **3** to remember or consider: with *of* or *about* **4** to conceive (*of*) —**think up** to invent, plan, etc. by thinking —**think'er** *n.*

**think tank** a group or center organized to do intensive research and problem-solving

**thin·ner** (thin'ər) *n.* a substance added to paint, shellac, etc. to thin it

**thin'-skinned'** *adj.* sensitive, as to insult

**Thin·su·late** (thin'sə lāt') *trademark for* thermal insulation made of synthetic fibers, for lining clothing

**third** (thʉrd) *adj.* ⟦OE *thridda*⟧ preceded by two others in a series; 3d or 3rd —*adv.* in the third place, etc.: also **third'ly** —*n.* **1** the one following the second **2** any of the three equal parts of something; ⅓ **3** the third forward gear of a transmission, providing more speed than second

**third'-class'** *adj.* **1** of the class, rank, etc. next below the second **2** of a low-cost mail class, as for advertisements —*adv.* by third-class mail or travel accommodations

**third degree** [Inf.] cruel treatment and questioning to force a confession: with *the*

**third dimension 1** *a*) depth *b*) solidity **2** the quality of seeming real

**third person** the form of a pronoun or verb that refers to the person or thing spoken of

**third'-rate'** *adj.* **1** third in quality or other rating **2** inferior; very poor

**Third World** [*also* t- w-] the economically underdeveloped countries of the world

**thirst** (thʉrst) *n.* ⟦OE *thurst*⟧ **1** the discomfort caused by a need for water **2** a strong desire; craving —*vi.* **1** to feel thirst **2** to have a strong desire or craving —**thirst'y, -i·er, -i·est,** *adj.* —**thirst'i·ly** *adv.*

**thir·teen** (thʉr'tēn') *adj., n.* ⟦OE *threotyne*⟧ three more than ten; 13; XIII —**thir'teenth'** *adj., n.*

**thir·ty** (thʉr'tē) *adj., n., pl.* **-ties** ⟦OE *thritig*⟧ three times ten; 30; XXX —**the thirties** the numbers or years, as of a century, from 30 through 39 —**thir'ti·eth** (-ith) *adj., n.*

**this** (*th*is) *pron., pl.* **these** ⟦OE *thes*⟧ **1** the person or thing mentioned [*this* is John] **2** the nearer one or another one [*this* is older than that] **3** something about to be presented [listen to *this*] —*adj., pl.* **these 1** designating the person or thing mentioned [*this* man is John] **2** designating the nearer one or another one [*this* desk is older than that one] **3** designating something about to be presented [hear *this* news] —*adv.* to this extent [it was *this* big]

**this·tle** (this'əl) *n.* ⟦OE *thistel*⟧ a plant with prickly leaves and white, purple, etc. flowers

**this'tle·down'** *n.* the down growing from the flowers of a thistle

THISTLE

**thith·er** (thith'ər, thith'-) *adv.* ⟦OE *thider*⟧ to or toward that place; there

**tho** or **tho'** (*th*ō) *conj., adv. phonetic sp. of* THOUGH

**thole** (thōl) *n.* ⟦OE *thol*⟧ one of a pair of pins set as an oarlock into the gunwale of a boat: also **thole'pin'**

**-thon** (thän) *suffix* -ATHON: used after a vowel [*radiothon*]

**thong** (thôŋ) *n.* ⟦OE *thwang*⟧ a narrow strip of leather, etc. used as a lace, strap, etc.

**Thor** (thôr) *n. Norse Myth.* the god of thunder, war, and strength

**tho·rax** (thôr'aks') *n., pl.* **-rax'es** or **-ra·ces'** (-ə sēz') ⟦< Gr⟧ **1** the part of the body between the neck and the abdomen; chest **2** the middle segment of an insect's body —**tho·rac·ic** (thō ras'ik, thô-) *adj.*

**Tho·reau** (thôr'ō, thə rō'), **Henry David** 1817-62; U.S. writer

**tho·ri·um** (thôr'ē əm) *n.* ⟦< THOR⟧ a rare, grayish, radioactive, metallic chemical element, used as a nuclear fuel

**thorn** (thôrn) *n.* ⟦OE⟧ **1** *a*) a very short, hard, leafless stem with a sharp point *b*) any small tree or shrub bearing thorns **2** a source of constant trouble or irritation —**thorn'y, -i·er, -i·est,** *adj.*

**thor·ough** (thʉr'ō) *adj.* ⟦var. of THROUGH⟧ **1** omitting nothing; complete **2** absolute [a *thorough* rascal] **3** very exact, accurate, or painstaking —**thor'ough·ly** *adv.* —**thor'ough·ness** *n.*

**thor·ough·bred** (thʉr'ō bred', thʉr'ə-) *adj.* of pure stock; pedigreed —*n.* [T-] any of a breed of light horse developed primarily for racing

**thor'ough·fare'** (-fer') *n.* a public street open at both ends, esp. a main highway

**thor'ough·go'ing** *adj.* very thorough

**those** (thōz) *pron., adj. pl. of* THAT

**thou** (*th*ou) *pron., pl.* **you** or **ye** ⟦OE *thu*⟧ [Archaic] you: in poetic or religious use

**though** (*th*ō) *conj.* ⟦OE *theah*⟧ **1** in spite of the fact that [*though* it rained, he went] **2** and yet [they can win, *though* no one thinks so] **3** even if [*though* he may fail, he will have tried] —*adv.* however; nevertheless [she sings well, *though*]

**thought**[1] (thôt) *n.* ⟦OE *thoht*⟧ **1** the act or process of thinking **2** the power of reasoning **3** an idea, concept, etc. **4** attention; consideration **5** mental concentration [deep in *thought*]

**thought**[2] (thôt) *vt., vi. pt. & pp. of* THINK

**thought'ful** *adj.* **1** full of thought; meditative **2** considerate of others —**thought'ful·ly** *adv.* —**thought'ful·ness** *n.*

**thought'less** *adj.* **1** not stopping to think; careless **2** ill-considered; rash **3** inconsiderate —**thought'less·ly** *adv.* —**thought'less·ness** *n.*

**thou·sand** (thou'zənd) *n., adj.* ⟦OE *thusend*⟧ ten hundred; 1,000; M —**thou'sandth** (-zəndth) *adj., n.*

**thrall** (thrôl) *n.* ⟦< ON *thræll*⟧ **1** [Now Chiefly Literary] a slave **2** the condition of being dominated or enslaved, esp. psychologically: now used chiefly in **hold in thrall** —**thrall'dom** or **thral'dom** (-dəm) *n.*

**thrash** (thrash) *vt., vi.* ⟦OE *therscan*⟧ **1** THRESH **2** to beat; flog **3** to toss about violently **4** to defeat overwhelmingly —**thrash out** to settle by detailed discussion

**thrash'er** *n.* ⟦E dial. *thresher*⟧ a thrushlike American songbird

**thread** (thred) *n.* ⟦OE *thræd*⟧ **1** a fine, stringlike length of spun cotton, silk, nylon, etc. used in sewing **2** any thin line, vein, etc. **3** something like a thread in its length, sequence, etc. [the *thread* of a story] **4** the spiral ridge of a screw, nut, etc. —*vt.* **1** to put a thread through (a needle, etc.) **2** to make (one's way) by twisting, weaving, etc. **3** to fashion a THREAD (sense 4) on or in (a screw, pipe, etc.)

**thread'bare'** *adj.* **1** worn down so that the threads show [a *threadbare* rug] **2** wearing worn clothes; shabby **3** stale; trite

**threat** (thret) *n.* ⟦OE *threat*, pressure⟧ **1** an

expression of intention to hurt, destroy, punish, etc. **2** an indication of, or a source of, imminent danger, harm, etc.

**threat'en** *vt., vi.* **1** to make threats, as of injury (against) **2** to indicate the likely occurrence of (something dangerous, unpleasant, etc.) **3** to be a source of danger (to)

**three** (thrē) *adj., n.* ⟦OE *threo*⟧ one more than two; 3; III

**three'-deck'er** (-dek'ər) *n.* anything having three levels, layers, etc.

**three'-di·men'sion·al** *adj.* having or seeming to have depth or thickness

**three'fold'** *adj.* **1** having three parts **2** having three times as much or as many —*adv.* three times as much or as many

**three R's** reading, writing, and arithmetic, regarded as the fundamentals of an education: with *the*

**three·score** (thrē'skôr') *adj., n.* sixty

**thren·o·dy** (thren'ə dē) *n., pl.* **-dies** ⟦< Gr *thrēnos*, lamentation + *ōidē*, song⟧ a song of lamentation; dirge

**thresh** (thresh) *vt., vi.* ⟦ME *threschen*: see THRASH⟧ **1** to beat out (grain) from (husks), as with a flail **2** THRASH —**thresh'er** *n.*

**thresh·old** (thresh'ōld', -hōld') *n.* ⟦OE *therscwold*⟧ **1** a length of wood, stone, etc. along the bottom of a doorway **2** the beginning point

**threw** (thrōō) *vt., vi. pt. of* THROW

**thrice** (thrīs) *adv.* ⟦OE *thriwa*⟧ **1** three times **2** threefold

**thrift** (thrift) *n.* ⟦< ON *thrifa*, to grasp⟧ economy; frugality —**thrift'less** *adj.* —**thrift'y**, **-i·er**, **-i·est**, *adj.* —**thrift'i·ly** *adv.* —**thrift'i·ness** *n.*

**thrift shop** a store where castoff clothes, etc. are sold to raise money for charity

**thrill** (thril) *vi., vt.* ⟦< OE *thurh*, through⟧ **1** to feel or cause to feel emotional excitement **2** to quiver or cause to quiver —*n.* a thrilling or being thrilled —**thrill'er** *n.*

**thrive** (thrīv) *vi.* **thrived** or **throve**, **thrived** or **thriv·en** (thriv'ən), **thriv'ing** ⟦< ON *thrifa*, to grasp⟧ **1** to prosper or flourish; be successful **2** to grow vigorously or luxuriantly

**throat** (thrōt) *n.* ⟦OE *throte*⟧ **1** the front part of the neck **2** the upper part of the passage from the mouth and nose to the stomach and lungs **3** any narrow passage

**throat'y** *adj.* **-i·er**, **-i·est** **1** produced in the throat: said of some sounds **2** husky; hoarse

**throb** (thräb) *vi.* **throbbed**, **throb'bing** ⟦ME *throbben*⟧ **1** to beat, pulsate, vibrate, etc., esp. strongly or fast **2** to feel excitement —*n.* **1** a throbbing **2** a strong beat or pulsation

**throe** (thrō) *n.* ⟦prob. < OE *thrawu*, pain⟧ a spasm or pang of pain: *usually used in pl.* [the *throes* of childbirth, death *throes*] —**in the throes of** in the act of struggling with (a problem, task, etc.)

**throm·bose** (thräm'bōs', -bōz') *vt., vi.* **-bosed', -bos'ing** to clot or become clotted with a thrombus

**throm·bo·sis** (thräm bō'sis) *n.* ⟦< Gr *thrombos*, a clot⟧ coagulation of the blood in the heart or a blood vessel, forming a clot

**throm·bus** (thräm'bəs) *n.* **-bi'** (-bī') ⟦see prec.⟧ the clot attached at the site of thrombosis

**throne** (thrōn) *n.* ⟦< Gr *thronos*, a seat⟧ **1** the chair on which a king, cardinal, etc. sits on formal occasions **2** the power or rank of a king, etc.

**throng** (thrôŋ) *n.* ⟦OE *thringan*, to crowd⟧ **1** a crowd **2** any great number of things considered together —*vi.* to gather together in a throng —*vt.* to crowd into

**throt·tle** (thrät''l) *n.* ⟦prob. dim. of THROAT⟧ the valve, or its control lever or pedal, that regulates the amount of fuel vapor entering an engine —*vt.* **-tled**, **-tling 1** to choke; strangle **2** to censor or suppress **3** to slow by means of a throttle

**through** (thrōō) *prep.* ⟦OE *thurh*⟧ **1** in one side and out the other side of **2** in the midst of; among **3** by way of **4** around [touring *through* France] **5** *a*) from the beginning to the end of *b*) up to and including **6** by means of **7** as a result of [done *through* error] —*adv.* **1** in one side and out the other **2** from the beginning to the end **3** completely to the end [to see something *through*] **4** completely [soaked *through*]: also **through and through** —*adj.* **1** extending from one place to another [a *through* street] **2** traveling to the destination without stops [a *through* train] **3** finished [*through* with the job]

**through·out'** *prep.* all the way through —*adv.* in every part; everywhere

**through'way'** *n. alt. sp. of* THRUWAY: see EXPRESSWAY

**throve** (thrōv) *vi. alt. pt. of* THRIVE

**throw** (thrō) *vt.* **threw**, **thrown**, **throw'ing** ⟦OE *thrawan*, to twist⟧ **1** to send through the air by a rapid motion of the arm, etc. **2** to cause to fall; upset **3** to send rapidly [to *throw* troops into battle] **4** to put suddenly into a specified state, etc. [*throw* into confusion] **5** to move (a switch, etc.) so as to connect, disconnect, etc. **6** to direct, cast, etc. [*throw* a glance] **7** [Inf.] to lose (a game, etc.) deliberately **8** [Inf.] to give (a party, etc.) **9** [Inf.] to confuse or disconcert (the question *threw* him] **10** [Inf.] to have (a tantrum, etc.) —*vi.* to cast or hurl something —*n.* **1** the act of one who throws **2** the distance something is or can be thrown [a stone's *throw*] **3** a spread for a bed, etc. —**throw away 1** to discard **2** to waste —**throw in** to add on free or add to others —**throw off 1** to rid oneself of **2** to mislead or confuse **3** to expel, emit, etc. —**throw oneself at** to try very hard to win the love of —**throw out 1** to discard **2** to reject or remove —**throw over 1** to give up; abandon **2** to jilt —**throw together** to assemble hurriedly —**throw up** to vomit —**throw'er** *n.*

**throw'a·way'** *n.* a leaflet, handbill, etc. given out on the streets, from house to house, etc. —*adj.* for discarding after use

**throw'back'** *n.* (a) reversion to an earlier or more primitive type

**throw rug** SCATTER RUG

**thru** (thrōō) *prep., adv., adj. informal sp. of* THROUGH

**thrush** (thrush) *n.* ⟦OE *thrysce*⟧ any of a family of songbirds, including the robin

**thrust** (thrust) *vt., vi.* **thrust**, **thrust'ing** ⟦< ON *thrysta*⟧ **1** to push with sudden force **2** to stab **3** to force or impose —*n.* **1** a sudden, forceful push **2** a stab **3** continuous pressure, as of a rafter against a wall **4** *a*) the driving force of a propeller *b*) the forward force produced by a jet or rocket engine **5** forward movement **6** the basic meaning; point

**thru·way** (thrōō'wā') *n.* EXPRESSWAY

**Thu·cyd·i·des** (thōō sid'i dēz') 460?-400? B.C.; Athenian historian

**thud** (thud) *vi.* **thud'ded**, **thud'ding** ⟦prob. < OE *thyddan*, to strike⟧ to hit or fall with a dull sound —*n.* a dull sound, as of an object dropping on a soft surface

**thug** (thug) *n.* ⟦Hindi *thag*, swindler⟧ a brutal hoodlum, gangster, etc. —**thug'gish** *adj.*

**thumb** (thum) *n.* ⟦OE *thuma*⟧ the short, thick digit of the hand —*vt.* **1** to handle, soil, etc. as with the thumb **2** [Inf.] to solicit or get (a ride) in hitchhiking by signaling with the thumb —**all thumbs** clumsy —**under someone's thumb** under someone's influence

**thumb'nail'** *n.* the nail of the thumb —*adj.* very small, brief, or concise

**thumb'screw'** *n.* **1** a screw that can be turned by the thumb and forefinger **2** a former instrument of torture for squeezing the thumbs

**thumb'tack'** *n.* a tack with a wide, flat head that can be pressed into a board, etc. with the thumb

**thump** (thump) *n.* ⟦echoic⟧ **1** a blow with something heavy and blunt **2** the dull sound made by such a blow —*vt.* to strike with a thump —*vi.* **1**

to hit or fall with a thump **2** to make a dull, heavy sound

**thump′ing** *adj.* **1** that thumps **2** [Inf.] very large; whopping

**thun·der** (thun′dər) *n.* 〖OE *thunor*〗 **1** the sound following a flash of lightning **2** any similar sound —*vi.* to produce thunder or a sound like this —*vt.* to say very loudly —**thun′der·ous** *adj.*

**thun′der·bolt′** *n.* **1** a flash of lightning and the accompanying thunder **2** something sudden and shocking, as bad news

**thun′der·clap′** *n.* a clap, or loud crash, of thunder

**thun′der·cloud′** *n.* a storm cloud charged with electricity and producing lightning and thunder

**thun′der·head′** *n.* a round mass of cumulus clouds appearing before a thunderstorm

**thun′der·show′er** *n.* a shower accompanied by thunder and lightning

**thun′der·storm′** *n.* a storm accompanied by thunder and lightning

**thun′der·struck′** *adj.* struck with amazement, terror, etc.: also **thun′der·strick′en** (-strik′ən)

**Thurs·day** (thurz′dā) *n.* 〖< ON *Thorsdagr,* Thor's day〗 the fifth day of the week: abbrev. **Thur** or **Thurs**

**thus** (*th*us) *adv.* 〖OE〗 **1** in this or that manner **2** to this or that degree or extent **3** therefore **4** for example

**thwack** (thwak) *vt., n.* 〖prob. echoic〗 WHACK

**thwart** (thwôrt) *n.* 〖< ON *thvert,* transverse〗 a seat across a boat —*vt.* to obstruct, frustrate, or defeat (a person, plans, etc.)

**thy** (*th*ī) *poss. pronominal adj.* 〖< ME *thin*〗 *archaic or poet. var. of* YOUR

**thyme** (tīm) *n.* 〖< Gr *thymon*〗 an herb of the mint family, with leaves used for seasoning

**thy·mo·sin** (thī′mə sin) *n.* 〖< Gr *thymos,* thymus〗 a hormone secreted by the thymus that stimulates the immune system

**thy·mus** (thī′məs) *n.* 〖Gr *thymos*〗 an endocrine gland situated near the throat: also **thymus gland**

**thy·roid** (thī′roid′) *adj.* 〖< Gr *thyreos,* large shield〗 designating or of a large endocrine gland near the trachea, secreting a hormone that regulates growth —*n.* **1** the thyroid gland **2** an animal extract of this gland, used in treating goiter

**thy·self** (*th*ī self′) *pron.* [Archaic] *reflexive or intensive form of* THOU

**ti** (tē) *n.* *Music* the seventh tone of the diatonic scale

**Ti** *Chem. symbol for* titanium

**Ti·a Jua·na** (tē′ə wä′nə) *former name for* TIJUANA

**Tian·jin** (tyen′jin′) seaport in NE China: pop. 5,152,000

**ti·ar·a** (tē er′ə, -ar′-, -är′-) *n.* 〖< Gr〗 **1** the pope's triple crown **2** a woman's crownlike headdress

**Ti·ber** (tī′bər) river in central Italy, flowing through Rome

**Ti·bet** (ti bet′) plateau region of SW China, north of the Himalayas —**Ti·bet′an** *adj., n.*

**tib·i·a** (tib′ē ə) *n., pl.* **-i·ae′** (-ē ē′) or **-i·as** 〖L〗 the inner and thicker of the bones of the lower leg

**tic** (tik) *n.* 〖Fr < ?〗 an involuntary, regularly repeated, spasmodic contraction of a muscle

**tick**[1] (tik) *n.* 〖prob. echoic〗 **1** a light clicking sound, as of a clock **2** a mark made to check off items —*vi.* to make a tick or ticks —*vt.* to record, mark, or check by ticks —**tick off** [Slang] to make angry

**tick**[2] (tik) *n.* 〖OE *ticia*〗 a wingless, bloodsucking mite that infests humans, cattle, etc.

**tick**[3] (tik) *n.* 〖< ? L *theca,* a cover〗 the cloth case of a mattress or pillow

**ticked** (tikt) *adj.* 〖< TICK OFF〗 [Slang] angry

**tick′er** *n.* **1** one that ticks **2** a telegraphic device for recording stock market quotations, etc. on a paper tape (**ticker tape**) **3** [Slang] the heart

**tick·et** (tik′it) *n.* 〖< obs. Fr *etiquet,* etiquette〗 **1** a printed card, etc. that gives one a right, as to attend a theater **2** a license or certificate **3** a label on merchandise giving size, price, etc. **4** the

---

list of candidates nominated by a political party **5** [Inf.] a summons to court for a traffic violation —*vt.* **1** to label with a ticket **2** to give a ticket to

**tick′ing** *n.* strong cloth, often striped, used for casings of pillows, etc.

**tick·le** (tik′əl) *vt.* **-led, -ling** 〖ME *tikelen*〗 **1** to please, gratify, delight, etc. **2** to stroke lightly so as to cause involuntary twitching, laughter, etc. —*vi.* to have or cause an itching or tingling sensation —*n.* a sensation of being tickled

**tick·ler** (tik′lər) *n.* a pad, file, etc. for noting matters to be remembered

**tick′lish** (-lish) *adj.* **1** sensitive to tickling **2** needing careful handling; precarious; delicate

**tick-tack-toe** or **tic-tac-toe** (tik′tak tō′) *n.* a game for two, each marking X (or O) in turn in a nine-square block so as to complete any one row before the other can

**tick-tock** (tik′täk′) *n.* the sound made by a clock or watch

**tid·al** (tīd′l) *adj.* of, having, or caused by, a tide or tides

**tidal wave 1** *nontechnical term for* a tsunami or a similar huge wave caused by strong winds **2** any widespread movement, feeling, etc.

**tid·bit** (tid′bit′) *n.* 〖dial. *tid,* small object〗 a choice bit of food, gossip, etc.

**tid·dly·winks** (tid′lē wiŋks′) *n.* 〖< ?〗 a game in which little disks are snapped into a cup by pressing their edges with a larger disk

**tide** (tīd) *n.* 〖OE *tid,* time〗 **1** a period of time: now only in combination [*Eastertide*] **2** the alternate rise and fall, about twice a day, of the surface of oceans, seas, etc., caused by the attraction of the moon and sun **3** something that rises and falls like the tide **4** a stream, trend, etc. —*vi.* **tid′ed, tid′ing** to help along temporarily: with *over*

**tide′land′** *n.* **1** land uncovered at low tide **2** [*pl.*] loosely, land under the sea within territorial waters of a country

**tide′wa′ter** *n.* **1** water that is affected by the tide **2** land that is affected by the tide —*adj.* of or along a tidewater

**ti·dings** (tī′diŋz) *pl.n.* 〖OE *tidung*〗 news; information

**ti·dy** (tī′dē) *adj.* **-di·er, -di·est** 〖<OE *tid,* time〗 **1** neat in appearance, arrangement, etc.; orderly **2** [Inf.] rather large [*a tidy sum*] —*vt., vi.* **-died, -dy·ing** to make tidy: often with *up* —**ti′di·ness** *n.*

**tie** (tī) *vt.* **tied, ty′ing** or **tie′ing** 〖< OE *teag,* a rope〗 **1** to bind, as with string, rope, etc. **2** to knot the laces, etc. of **3** to make (a knot) in **4** to bind in any way **5** to equal the score of, as in a contest —*vi.* to make an equal score, as in a contest —*n.* **1** a string, cord, etc. used to tie things **2** something that connects, binds, etc. **3** a necktie **4** a beam, rod, etc. that holds parts together **5** any of the crossbeams to which the rails of a railroad are fastened **6** *a)* an equality of scores, etc. *b)* a contest in which this occurs —*adj.* that has been made equal [*a tie score*] —**tie down** to confine; restrict —**tie up 1** to wrap up and tie **2** to moor to a dock **3** to obstruct; hinder **4** to cause to be already in use, committed, etc.

**tie′back′** *n.* a band or ribbon used to tie curtains, etc. to one side

**tie′break′er** *n.* an additional game, period of play, etc. used to establish a winner from among those tied at the end of a contest

**tie clasp** a decorative clasp for fastening a necktie to the shirt: also **tie clip**

**tie′-dye′** *n.* a method of dyeing designs on cloth by tying bunches of it so that the dye affects only exposed parts —*vt.* **-dyed′, -dye′ing** to dye in this way

**tie′-in′** *n.* a connection or relationship

**Tien·tsin** (tyen′tsin′) *a former transliteration of* TIANJIN

**tier** (tir) *n.* 〖< OFr *tire,* order〗 any of a series of rows arranged one above or behind another

**tie rod** a rod connecting certain parts in the steering linkage of a motor vehicle

**tie tack** or **tie tac** a decorative pin fitted into a snap to fasten a necktie to a shirt

**tie-up** (tī′up′) *n.* **1** a temporary stoppage of production, traffic, etc. **2** connection or relation

**tiff** (tif) *n.* ⟦< ?⟧ a slight quarrel; spat

**Tif·fa·ny** (tif′ə nē) *adj.* ⟦after L. C. *Tiffany* (1848-1933), U.S. designer⟧ of a style in stained glass

**ti·ger** (tī′gər) *n.* ⟦< Gr *tigris*⟧ **1** a large, fierce Asian cat, having a tawny coat striped with black **2** one who is dynamic, fierce, etc.

TIGER

**tight** (tīt) *adj.* ⟦< OE *-thight*, strong⟧ **1** so compact in structure that water, air, etc. cannot pass through **2** drawn, packed, etc. closely together **3** fixed securely; firm **4** fully stretched; taut **5** fitting so closely as to be uncomfortable **6** difficult: esp. in **a tight corner** (or **squeeze**, etc.), a difficult situation **7** showing tension, etc. [a *tight* smile] **8** almost tied [a *tight* race] **9** sharp; abrupt [a *tight* turn in the road] **10** difficult to get; scarce **11** [Inf.] stingy **12** [Slang] drunk **13** [Slang] very familiar —*adv.* **1** securely **2** [Inf.] soundly [sleep *tight*] —**sit tight** to keep one's opinion or position and wait —**tight′ly** *adv.* —**tight′ness** *n.*

**tight·en** *vt., vi.* to make or become tight or tighter —**tight′en·er** *n.*

**tight′fist′ed** *adj.* stingy

**tight′fit′ting** *adj.* fitting very tight

**tight′-lipped′** *adj.* secretive

**tight′rope′** *n.* a tightly stretched rope on which acrobats perform

**tights** *pl.n.* a tightly fitting garment for the lower half of the body, as worn by acrobats or dancers

**tight ship** [Inf.] an organization as efficient as a well-run ship

**tight′wad′** *n.* ⟦TIGHT + *wad*, roll of money⟧ [Slang] a stingy person

**ti·gress** (tī′gris) *n.* a female tiger

**Ti·gris** (tī′gris) river flowing from EC Turkey to a juncture with the Euphrates in SE Iraq

**Ti·jua·na** (tē′ə wä′nə) city in Baja California, NW Mexico, on the U.S. border: official pop. 747,000; actual pop. between 1,000,000 and 2,000,000

**til·de** (til′də) *n.* ⟦Sp < L *titulus*, a sign⟧ a diacritical mark (~)

**tile** (tīl) *n.* ⟦< L *tegula*⟧ **1** a thin piece of stone, fired clay, etc. used for roofing, flooring, etc. **2** a similar piece of plastic, etc. **3** a drain of earthenware pipe —*vt.* **tiled, til′ing** to cover with tiles

**til′ing** *n.* tiles collectively

**till¹** (til) *prep., conj.* ⟦OE *til*⟧ UNTIL

**till²** (til) *vt., vi.* ⟦< OE *tilian*, lit., strive for⟧ to prepare (land) for raising crops, as by plowing

**till³** (til) *n.* ⟦< ? ME *tillen*, to draw⟧ a drawer for keeping money

**till′age** *n.* **1** the tilling of land **2** land that is tilled

**till·er** (til′ər) *n.* ⟦< ML *telarium*, weaver's beam⟧ a bar or handle for turning a boat's rudder

**tilt** (tilt) *vt.* ⟦ME *tilten*, totter⟧ to cause to slant; tip —*vi.* **1** to slope; incline **2** to charge (*at* an opponent) **3** to take part in a tilt —*n.* **1** a medieval contest in which two horsemen fight with lances **2** any spirited contest **3** a slope —(**at**) **full tilt** at full speed

**tilt′-top′** *adj.* of a table with a hinged top that can be tipped vertically

**tim·bale** (tim′bəl) *n.* ⟦Fr⟧ **1** chicken, lobster, etc. in a cream sauce, baked in a drum-shaped mold **2** a pastry shell, filled with a cooked food

**tim·ber** (tim′bər) *n.* ⟦OE⟧ **1** wood for building houses, ships, etc. **2** a wooden beam used in building **3** trees collectively —**tim′bered** *adj.*

**tim′ber·line′** *n.* the line above or beyond which trees do not grow, as on mountains

**tim·bre** (tam′bər, tim′-) *n.* ⟦< OFr, kind of drum⟧ the quality of sound that distinguishes one voice or musical instrument from another

**time** (tīm) *n.* ⟦OE *tima*⟧ **1** every moment there has ever been or ever will be **2** a system of measuring duration [standard *time*] **3** the period during which something exists, happens, etc. **4** [*often pl.*] a period of history; age, era, etc. **5** [*usually pl.*] prevailing conditions [*times* are good] **6** a set period or term, as of work, confinement, etc. **7** standard rate of pay **8** rate of speed in marching, driving, etc. **9** a precise or designated instant, moment, day, etc. **10** an occasion or repeated occasion [the fifth *time* it's been on TV] **11** *Music* a) rhythm as determined by the grouping of beats into measures b) tempo **12** *Sports* TIMEOUT —*vt.* **timed, tim′ing 1** to arrange the time of so as to be suitable, opportune, etc. **2** to adjust, set, etc. so as to coincide in time [*time* our watches] **3** to calculate the pace, speed, etc. of —*adj.* **1** having to do with time **2** set to explode, open, etc. at a given time [a *time* bomb] **3** having to do with paying in installments —**ahead of time** early —**at the same time** however —**at times** occasionally —**do time** [Inf.] to serve a prison term —**for the time being** temporarily —**from time to time** now and then —**in time 1** eventually **2** before it is too late **3** keeping the set tempo, pace, etc. —**make time** to travel, work, etc. rapidly —**on time 1** at the appointed time **2** for or by payment by installments —**time after time** again and again: also **time and again**

**time clock** a clock with a mechanism for recording the time an employee begins and ends a work period

**time exposure** a photograph taken by exposure of a film or plate for a relatively long period

**time frame** a given period of time

**time′-hon′ored** *adj.* honored because of long existence or usage

**time′keep′er** *n.* one who keeps account of hours worked by employees or of the elapsed time in races, games, etc.

**time′-lapse′** *adj.* of filming a slow process by exposing single frames at long intervals: the film is projected at regular speed, showing the process greatly speeded up

**time′less** *adj.* **1** eternal **2** always valid or true

**time′line′** *n.* a chronological chart or list of events, dates, plans, etc.

**time′ly** *adj.* **-li·er, -li·est** well-timed; opportune —**time′li·ness** *n.*

**time′out′** *n.* *Sports* any temporary suspension of play

**time′piece′** *n.* any device for measuring and recording time, as a clock or watch

**tim·er** (tīm′ər) *n.* a device for controlling the timing of some mechanism

**time′-re·lease′** *adj.* releasing active ingredients gradually

**times** (tīmz) *prep.* multiplied by

**time sharing 1** a system for simultaneous computer use at many remote sites **2** a system for sharing ownership of a vacation home, etc., with each joint purchaser occupying the unit at a specific time each year: also **time share**

**time sheet** a sheet on which are recorded the hours an employee works

**time′ta′ble** *n.* a schedule of the times of arrival and departure of airplanes, trains, buses, etc.

**time′-test′ed** *adj.* having value proved by long use or experience

**time warp** displacement from one point in time to another, as in science fiction

**time′worn′** *adj.* **1** worn out by long use **2** hackneyed; trite

**time zone** see STANDARD TIME

**tim·id** (tim′id) *adj.* ⟦< L *timere*, to fear⟧ lacking

self-confidence; shy; fearful; hesitant —**ti·mid·i·ty** (tə mid′ə tē) *n.* —**tim′id·ly** *adv.*

**tim·ing** (tīm′iŋ) *n.* the regulation of pace or speed as it affects performance

**tim·or·ous** (tim′ər es) *adj.* [< L *timor*, fear] full of fear; timid; afraid

**tim·o·thy** (tim′ə thē) *n.* [after a *Timothy* Hanson, *c.* 1720] a perennial grass with dense spikes, grown for hay

**tim·pa·ni** (tim′pə nē) *pl.n., sing.* -**no′** (-nō′) [It: see TYMPANUM] [*often with sing. v.*] kettledrums; esp., a set of them played by one performer — **tim′pa·nist** *n.*

**tin** (tin) *n.* [OE] 1 a soft, silver-white, metallic chemical element 2 TIN PLATE 3 *a*) a pan, box, etc. made of tin plate *b*) [Chiefly Brit.] CAN² (*n.* 2, 3) Variously used to connote cheapness, etc. of something —*vt.* **tinned, tin′ning** 1 to plate with tin 2 [Chiefly Brit.] CAN² (*vt.* 1)

**tin can** CAN² (*n.* 2)

**tinc·ture** (tiŋk′chər) *n.* [< L *tingere*, to dye] 1 a light color; tinge 2 a slight trace 3 a dilute solution of a medicinal substance in alcohol —*vt.* -**tured, -tur·ing** to tinge

**tin·der** (tin′dər) *n.* [OE *tynder*] any dry, easily flammable material

**tin′der·box′** *n.* 1 [Obs.] a box to hold tinder 2 a highly flammable building, etc. 3 a potential source of war, rebellion, etc.

**tine** (tīn) *n.* [OE *tind*] a slender, projecting point; prong [fork *tines*]

**tin′foil′** *n.* 1 tin in thin sheets 2 aluminum in thin sheets, used for wrapping food, etc.

**tinge** (tinj) *n.* [see TINT] 1 a slight coloring; tint 2 a slight trace, flavor, etc. —*vt.* **tinged, tinge′ing** or **ting′ing** to give a tinge to

**tin·gle** (tiŋ′gəl) *vi.* -**gled, -gling** [var. of TINKLE] to have a prickling or stinging feeling, as from cold, excitement, etc. —*n.* this feeling —**tin′gly** *adj.*

**tin·ker** (tiŋk′ər) *n.* [ME *tinkere*] 1 one who mends pots, pans, etc. 2 a bungler —*vi.* 1 to attempt clumsily to mend something 2 to putter

**tin·kle** (tiŋk′əl) *vi.* -**kled, -kling** [echoic] to make a series of light sounds as of a tiny bell —*vt.* to cause to tinkle —*n.* a tinkling sound

**tin·ny** (tin′ē) *adj.* -**ni·er, -ni·est** 1 of or like tin 2 not well-made 3 high-pitched and lacking resonance [*tinny* music] —**tin′ni·ness** *n.*

**tin plate** thin sheets of iron or steel plated with tin

**tin·sel** (tin′səl) *n.* [< L *scintilla*, a spark] 1 thin strips of tin, metal foil, etc., as for decoration 2 something of little worth that glitters

**tin′smith′** *n.* one who works in tin or tin plate

**tint** (tint) *n.* [< L *tingere*, to dye] 1 a pale color 2 a gradation of a color; shade 3 a hair dye —*vt.* to give a tint to

**tin·tin·nab·u·la·tion** (tin′ti nab′yoo lā′shən) *n.* [< L *tintinnabulum*, little bell] the ringing sound of bells

**tin·type** (tin′tīp′) *n.* an old kind of photograph taken directly as a positive print on a treated plate of tin or iron

**ti·ny** (tī′nē) *adj.* -**ni·er, -ni·est** [< ME *tine*, *n.*, a little] very small

**-tion** (shən) [< Fr < L] *suffix* 1 the act of ___ing 2 the state of being ___ed 3 the thing that is ___ed

**-tious** (shəs) *suffix* of, having, or characterized by

**tip¹** (tip) *n.* [ME *tippe*] 1 the point or end of something 2 something attached to the end, as a cap, etc. —*vt.* **tipped, tip′ping** 1 to form a tip on 2 to cover the tip of

**tip²** (tip) *vt.* **tipped, tip′ping** [< ?] 1 to strike lightly and sharply 2 to give a gratuity to (a waiter, etc.) 3 [Inf.] to give secret information to: often with *off* —*vi.* to give a tip or tips —*n.* 1 a light, sharp blow 2 a piece of confidential information 3 a hint, warning, etc. 4 a gratuity —**tip one's hand** [Slang] to reveal a secret, one's plans, etc., often without meaning to —**tip′per** *n.*

**tip³** (tip) *vt., vi.* **tipped, tip′ping** [ME *tipen*] 1 to

overturn or upset: often with *over* 2 to tilt or slant —*n.* a tilt; slant

**tip′-off′** *n.* a tip; confidential disclosure, hint, or warning

**tip·ple** (tip′əl) *vi., vt.* -**pled, -pling** [< ?] to drink (alcoholic liquor) habitually —**tip′pler** *n.*

**tip·ster** (tip′stər) *n.* [Inf.] one who sells tips, as on horse races or the stock market

**tip·sy** (tip′sē) *adj.* -**si·er, -si·est** 1 that tips easily; not steady 2 somewhat drunk —**tip′si·ly** *adv.*

**tip′toe′** *vi.* -**toed′, -toe′ing** to walk carefully, with the heels raised —**on tiptoe** 1 standing with the heels raised 2 excited, alert, etc. 3 silently and stealthily

**tip′top′** *n.* [TIP¹ + TOP¹] the highest point —*adj., adv.* 1 at the highest point 2 [Inf.] at the highest point of excellence, health, etc.

**ti·rade** (tī′rād′) *n.* [< It *tirare*, to fire] a long, vehement speech or denunciation; harangue

**tire¹** (tīr) *vt., vi.* **tired, tir′ing** [OE *tiorian*] to make or become weary, exhausted, bored, etc.

**tire²** (tīr) *n.* [ME *tyre*] 1 a hoop of iron or rubber around the wheel of a vehicle 2 an inflatable, vulcanized rubber or synthetic casing sealed to a wheel rim by air pressure

**tired** (tīrd) *adj.* 1 weary 2 hackneyed —**tired′ly** *adv.* —**tired′ness** *n.*

**tire iron** a crowbar with a built-in wrench, for changing automobile tires

**tire′less** *adj.* persistent, unwavering, etc. — **tire′less·ly** *adv.* —**tire′less·ness** *n.*

**tire′some** (-səm) *adj.* 1 tiring; boring 2 annoying —**tire′some·ly** *adv.* —**tire′some·ness** *n.*

**Ti·rol** (ti rōl′, -räl′) E Alpine region in W Austria & N Italy —**Ti·ro·le·an** (ti rō′lē ən, tī-) *adj., n.*

**'tis** (tiz) *contr.* [Old Poet.] it is

**tis·sue** (tish′oo) *n.* [< L *texere*, to weave] 1 light, thin cloth 2 an interwoven mass; mesh; web 3 a piece of soft, absorbent paper, used as a disposable handkerchief, etc. 4 TISSUE PAPER 5 the substance of an organic body, consisting of cells and intercellular material

**tissue paper** very thin wrapping paper

**tit¹** (tit) *n.* a titmouse

**tit²** (tit) *n.* [OE] 1 NIPPLE (sense 1) 2 a breast: in this sense now vulgar

**ti·tan** (tīt′n) *n.* [< Gr *Titan*, a giant deity] any person or thing of great size or power

**ti·tan·ic** (tī tan′ik) *adj.* of great size, strength, or power

**ti·ta·ni·um** (tī tā′nē əm) *n.* [see TITAN] a silvery or dark-gray, metallic chemical element used in manufacturing

**tit for tat** [var. of earlier *tip for tap*] this for that: phrase indicating retribution

**tithe** (tī_th_) *n.* [OE *teothe*, a tenth] a tenth of one's income paid to a church —*vi.* **tithed, tith′ing** to pay a tithe

**ti·tian** (tish′ən) *n.* [after *Titian* (1490?-1576), Venetian painter] reddish gold

**tit·il·late** (tit′'l āt′) *vt.* -**lat′ed, -lat′ing** [< L *titillare*, tickle] to excite pleasurably —**tit′il·la′tion** *n.*

**ti·tle** (tīt′l) *n.* [< L *titulus*] 1 the name of a book, poem, picture, etc. 2 an epithet 3 an appellation indicating one's rank, profession, etc. 4 a claim 5 *Film, TV* a subtitle, credit, etc. 6 *Law a*) a right to ownership, esp. of real estate *b*) a deed 7 *Sports, etc.* a championship —*vt.* -**tled, -tling** to give a title to

**ti′tled** *adj.* having a title, esp. of nobility

**ti′tle·hold′er** *n.* the holder of a title; specif., the champion in some sport

**title role** (or **character**) the character in a play, film, etc. whose name is used as or in its title

**ti·tlist** (tīt′'l ist) *n.* a champion in some sport

**tit·mouse** (tit′mous′) *n., pl.* -**mice′** (-mīs′) [ME *titemose*] a small bird with ashy-gray feathers

**tit·ter** (tit′ər) *vi.* [echoic] to laugh in a half-suppressed way; giggle —*n.* a tittering

**tit·tle** (tit′'l) *n.* ⟦ME *title*⟧ a very small particle; jot

**tit·u·lar** (tich′ə lər, tit′yə-) *adj.* [see TITLE] **1** of a title **2** having a title **3** in name only /a *titular* sovereign/

**tiz·zy** (tiz′ē) *n., pl.* **-zies** ⟦< ?⟧ [Inf.] a state of frenzied excitement

**tko** or **TKO** *n. Boxing* a technical knockout

**TLC** *abbrev.* tender, loving care

**TM** *abbrev.* trademark

**tn** *abbrev.* ton(s)

**TN** Tennessee

**TNT** *n.* ⟦*t(ri)n(itro)t(oluene)*⟧ a high explosive used for blasting, etc.

**to** (tōō, too, tə) *prep.* ⟦OE⟧ **1** toward /turn *to* the left/ **2** so as to reach /she went *to* Boston/ **3** as far as /wet *to* the skin/ **4** into a condition of /a rise *to* fame/ **5** *a)* on, onto, against, at, etc. /tied *to* a post/ *b)* in front of /face *to* face/ **6** *a)* until /from noon *to* night/ *b)* before /the time is ten *to* six/ **7** for the purpose of /come *to* dinner/ **8** in regard to /open *to* attack/ **9** with the result of producing /torn *to* bits/ **10** along with /add this *to* the rest/ **11** belonging with /a key *to* the house/ **12** as compared with /a score of 10 *to* 0/ **13** in agreement with /not *to* my taste/ **14** constituting /four quarts *to* a gallon/ **15** with (a specified person or thing) as the recipient of the action /give it *to* me/ **16** in honor of /a toast *to* you/ **17** by /known *to* me/ *To* is also a sign of the infinitive (Ex.: I want *to* stay) —*adv.* **1** forward /wrong side *to*/ **2** shut; closed /pull the door *to*/ **3** into a state of consciousness /the boxer came *to*/ **4** at hand /we were close *to* when it happened/ —**to and fro** first in one direction and then in the opposite

**toad** (tōd) *n.* ⟦OE *tadde*⟧ a froglike amphibian that lives on moist land

**toad′stool′** (-stōōl′) *n.* a mushroom; esp., any poisonous mushroom

**toad·y** (tō′dē) *n., pl.* **-ies** ⟦short for *toadeater*, quack doctor's assistant⟧ a servile flatterer —*vt., vi.* **-ied, -y·ing** to be a toady (to)

**toast**[1] (tōst) *vt.* ⟦< L *torrere*, parch⟧ **1** to brown the surface of (bread, etc.) by heating **2** to warm thoroughly —*vi.* to become toasted —*n.* sliced bread made brown and crisp by heat —**toast′er** *n.*

**toast**[2] (tōst) *n.* ⟦from the use of toasted spiced bread to flavor the wine⟧ **1** a drink, or a proposal to drink, in honor of some person, etc. **2** someone greatly admired or acclaimed /the *toast* of Broadway/ —*vt., vi.* to propose or drink a toast (to)

**toast′mas′ter** *n.* the person at a banquet who proposes toasts, introduces after-dinner speakers, etc.

**toast′y** *adj.* **-i·er, -i·est** warm and comfortable or cozy

**to·bac·co** (tə bak′ō) *n., pl.* **-cos** ⟦Sp *tabaco* < ?⟧ **1** a plant with large leaves that are prepared for smoking, chewing, etc. **2** cigars, cigarettes, etc.

**to·bac·co·nist** (tə bak′ə nist) *n.* [Chiefly Brit.] a dealer in tobacco

**to·bog·gan** (tə bäg′ən) *n.* ⟦< AmInd⟧ a long, flat sled without runners, for coasting downhill —*vi.* **1** to coast on a toboggan **2** to decline rapidly

**toc·sin** (täk′sin) *n.* ⟦Fr < Prov *toc*, a stroke + *senh*, a bell⟧ an alarm bell or its sound

**to·day** (tə dā′) *adv.* ⟦OE *to dæg*⟧ **1** on or during the present day **2** in the present time —*n.* **1** the present day **2** the present time

**tod·dle** (täd′'l) *vi.* **-dled, -dling** ⟦? < *totter*⟧ to walk with short, uncertain steps

**tod′dler** *n.* a very young child

**tod·dy** (täd′ē) *n., pl.* **-dies** ⟦< Hindi⟧ a drink of whiskey, etc. mixed with hot water, sugar, etc.: also **hot toddy**

**to-do** (tə dōō′) *n., pl.* **-dos′** [Inf.] a commotion; fuss

**toe** (tō) *n.* ⟦OE *ta*⟧ **1** *a)* any of the digits of the foot *b)* the forepart of the foot **2** anything like a toe in location, shape, or use —*vt.* **toed, toe′ing** to touch, kick, etc. with the toes —*vi.* to stand, walk,

etc. with the toes in a specified position /he *toes* in/ —**on one's toes** [Inf.] alert —**toe the line** (or **mark**) to follow orders, rules, etc. strictly

**toed** (tōd) *adj.* having (a specified kind or number of) toes: usually in compounds /two-*toed*/

**toe dance** a dance performed on the tips of the toes, as in ballet —**toe′-dance′, -danced′, -danc′ing,** *vi.* —**toe′-danc′er** *n.*

**toe′hold′** *n.* **1** a small space to support the toe in climbing, etc. **2** a slight footing or advantage

**toe′less** *adj.* having the toe open or uncovered /a *toeless* shoe/

**toe′nail′** *n.* the nail of a toe

**tof·fee** or **tof·fy** (tôf′ē, täf′ē) *n.* ⟦< TAFFY⟧ a hard, chewy candy, a kind of taffy

**to·fu** (tō′fōō) *n.* ⟦Jpn⟧ a cheeselike food made from soybeans

**to·ga** (tō′gə) *n., pl.* **-gas** or **-gae** (-jē, -gē) ⟦L < *tegere*, to cover⟧ in ancient Rome, a loose outer garment worn in public by citizens

**to·geth·er** (tə geth′ər) *adv.* ⟦< OE *to*, to + *gædre*, together⟧ **1** in or into one group, place, etc. /we ate *together*/ **2** in or into contact, union, etc. /the cars skidded *together*/ **3** considered collectively /he lost more than all of us *together*/ **4** at the same time /shots fired *together*/ **5** in succession /sulking for three whole days *together*/ **6** in or into agreement, cooperation, etc. /to get *together* on a deal/ —*adj.* **1** with one another; not apart **2** [Slang] having a harmoniously organized personality

ROMAN TOGA

**to·geth′er·ness** *n.* the spending of much time together, as by family members, resulting in a more unified relationship

**tog·gle switch** (täg′əl) a switch consisting of a lever moved back and forth to open or close an electric circuit

**To·go** (tō′gō) country on the W coast of Africa: 21,925 sq. mi.; pop. 2,701,000

**togs** (tägz, tôgz) *pl.n.* ⟦ult. < L *toga*, toga⟧ [Inf.] clothes

**toil** (toil) *vi.* ⟦< L *tudiculare*, to stir about⟧ **1** to work hard and continuously **2** to proceed laboriously —*n.* hard, tiring work —**toil′er** *n.*

**toi·let** (toi′lit) *n.* ⟦< OFr *toile*, cloth < L *tela*, a web⟧ **1** TOILETTE **2** (a room with) a bowl-shaped fixture for defecation or urination

**toilet paper** (or **tissue**) soft paper for cleaning oneself after evacuation

**toi′let·ry** (-lə trē) *n., pl.* **-ries** soap, lotion, etc. used in grooming oneself

**toi·lette** (twä let′, toi-) *n.* [Fr] **1** the process of grooming oneself **2** dress; attire

**toilet water** a lightly scented liquid containing alcohol, applied to the skin after bathing, etc.

**toils** (toilz) *pl.n.* ⟦< L *tela*, web⟧ any snare suggestive of a net

**toil′some** (toil′səm) *adj.* laborious

**toke** (tōk) [Slang] *n.* ⟦? < fol.⟧ a puff on a cigarette, esp. one of marijuana or hashish —*vi.* **toked, tok′ing** to take such a puff

**to·ken** (tō′kən) *n.* ⟦OE *tacn*⟧ **1** a sign, indication, symbol, etc. /a *token* of one's affection/ **2** a keepsake **3** a metal disk to be used in place of currency, as for transportation fares —*adj.* **1** symbolic **2** merely simulated; slight /token resistance/ —**by the same token** for the same reason

**to′ken·ism′** *n.* the making of small, often merely formal concessions to a demand, etc.; specif., token integration of blacks, as in jobs

**To·ky·o** (tō′kē ō′) capital of Japan, on S Honshu: pop. 8,352,000

**told** (tōld) *vt., vi. pt. & pp. of* TELL —**all told** all things considered

**tole** (tōl) *n.* 〖Fr *tôle*, sheet iron〗 a type of lacquered or enameled metalware, usually dark-green, ivory, or black, used for lamps, trays, etc.

**To·le·do** (tə lē′dō) city & port in NW Ohio: pop. 333,000

**tol·er·a·ble** (täl′ər ə bəl) *adj.* **1** endurable **2** fairly good; passable —**tol′er·a·bly** *adv.*

**tol′er·ance** (-əns) *n.* **1** a being tolerant of others' views, beliefs, practices, etc. **2** the amount of variation allowed from a standard **3** *Med.* the (developed) ability to resist the effects of a drug, etc.

**tol′er·ant** (-ənt) *adj.* having or showing tolerance of others' beliefs, etc.

**tol·er·ate** (-āt′) *vt.* **-at′ed, -at′ing** 〖< L *tolerare*, to bear〗 **1** to allow **2** to respect (others' beliefs, practices, etc.) without sharing them **3** to bear (someone or something disliked); put up with **4** *Med.* to have tolerance for —**tol′er·a′tion** *n.*

**toll**[1] (tōl) *n.* 〖ult. < Gr *telos*, tax〗 **1** a tax or charge for a privilege, as for the use of a turnpike **2** a charge for service, as for a long-distance telephone call **3** the number lost, etc. *[the tornado took a heavy toll of lives]*

**toll**[2] (tōl) *vt.* 〖ME *tollen*, to pull〗 **1** to ring (a church bell, etc.) with slow, regular strokes **2** to announce, summon, etc. by this —*vi.* to ring slowly: said of a bell —*n.* the sound of a bell tolling

**toll′booth′** *n.* a booth at which a toll is collected, as before entering a toll road

**toll′gate′** *n.* a gate for stopping travel at a point where a toll is collected

**toll road** a road on which a toll must be paid: also **toll′way′** (-wā′) *n.*

**Tol·stoy** or **Tol·stoi** (tōl′stoi′), Count **Le·o** (lē′ō) 1828-1910; Russ. novelist

**tol·u·ene** (täl′yōō ēn′) *n.* 〖Sp *tolu*, after *Tolú*, seaport in Colombia + (BENZ)ENE〗 a colorless, poisonous liquid obtained from coal tar or petroleum and used in making dyes, explosives, etc.

**tom** (täm) *adj.* 〖after the name *Tom*〗 male *[a tomcat, a tom turkey]*

**tom·a·hawk** (täm′ə hôk′) *n.* 〖< AmInd〗 a light ax used by North American Indians as a tool and a weapon

**to·ma·to** (tə māt′ō, -mät′ō) *n., pl.* **-toes** 〖< AmInd (Mexico)〗 **1** a red or yellowish fruit with a juicy pulp, used as a vegetable **2** the plant it grows on

**tomb** (tōōm) *n.* 〖< Gr *tymbos*〗 a vault or grave for the dead

**tom·boy** (täm′boi′) *n.* a girl who behaves like an active boy

**tomb·stone** (tōōm′stōn′) *n.* a stone or monument marking a tomb or grave

**tom·cat** (täm′kat′) *n.* a male cat

**tome** (tōm) *n.* 〖< Gr *tomos*, piece cut off〗 a book, esp. a large one

**tom·fool·er·y** (täm′fōōl′ər ē) *n., pl.* **-ies** foolish behavior; silliness

**tom·my gun** (täm′ē) *[sometimes* **T- g-***]* a submachine gun

**to·mog·ra·phy** (tə mäg′rə fē) *n.* 〖< Gr *temnein*, to cut + -GRAPHY〗 an X-ray process for producing an image of a single plane of an object, used in medical diagnosis

**to·mor·row** (tə mär′ō, -môr′-) *adv.* 〖OE *to morgen*〗 on the day after today —*n.* the day after today

**tom·tit** (täm tit′, täm′tit′) *n.* [Chiefly Brit.] a titmouse or other small bird

**tom-tom** (täm′täm′) *n.* 〖Hindi *ṭamṭam*〗 a simple kind of drum, usually beaten with the hands

**-to·my** (tə mē) 〖< Gr < *tomē*, a cutting〗 *combining form* a surgical operation

**ton** (tun) *n.* 〖var. of TUN〗 **1** a unit of weight equal to 2,000 pounds **2** in Great Britain, a unit of weight equal to 2,240 pounds

**ton·al** (tō′nəl) *adj.* of a tone —**ton′al·ly** *adv.*

**to·nal·i·ty** (tō nal′ə tē) *n., pl.* **-ties** *Music* **1** KEY[1] (*n.* 6) **2** tonal character, as determined by the relationship of the tones to the keynote

**tone** (tōn) *n.* 〖< Gr *teinein*, to stretch〗 **1** a vocal or musical sound, or its quality as to pitch, intensity, etc. **2** a manner of expression showing a certain attitude *[a friendly tone]* **3** style, character, spirit, etc. **4** elegance **5** a quality of color; shade **6** normal, healthy condition of a muscle, organ, etc. **7** *Music a)* a sound of distinct pitch *b)* any of the full intervals of a diatonic scale —*vt.* **toned, ton′ing** to give a tone to —**tone down** (or **up**) to give a less (or more) intense tone to —**tone′less** *adj.*

**tone′arm′** *n.* the pivoted arm beside a phonograph turntable, holding the stylus

**tone′-deaf′** *adj.* not able to distinguish differences in musical pitch

**ton·er** (tō′nər) *n.* **1** the black or colored powder used to form images in xerography **2** a facial cleanser

**tone row** (or **series**) see TWELVE-TONE

**tong** (tôŋ, täŋ) *n.* 〖Mandarin *t'ang*, meeting place〗 a Chinese association, society, etc.

**Ton·ga** (täŋ′gə) kingdom on a group of islands (**Tonga Islands**) in the SW Pacific, east of Fiji: 289 sq. mi.; pop. 95,000 —**Ton′gan** *n.*

**tongs** (tôŋz, täŋz) *pl.n.* 〖OE *tange*〗 *[sometimes with sing. v.]* a device for seizing or lifting objects, having two long arms pivoted or hinged together

**tongue** (tuŋ) *n.* 〖OE *tunge*〗 **1** the movable, muscular structure in the mouth, used in eating, tasting, and (in humans) speaking **2** talk; speech **3** the act, power, or manner of speaking **4** a language or dialect **5** something like a tongue in shape, position, use, etc., as the flap under the laces of a shoe —**hold one's tongue** to keep from speaking —**speak in tongues** to utter unintelligible sounds, as while in a religious trance —(**with**) **tongue in cheek** in a humorously ironic or insincere way —**tongue′less** *adj.*

**tongue′-and-groove′ joint** a kind of joint in which a projection on one board fits into a groove in another

**tongue′-lash′ing** *n.* [Inf.] a harsh scolding or reproving; reprimand

**tongue′-tied′** *adj.* speechless from amazement, embarrassment, etc.

**tongue twister** a phrase or sentence hard to say fast (Ex: six sick sheiks)

**ton·ic** (tän′ik) *adj.* 〖see TONE〗 **1** of or producing good muscular tone **2** *Music* designating or based on a keynote —*n.* **1** anything that invigorates, as a drug or medicine **2** a quinine-flavored beverage served with gin, vodka, etc. **3** *Music* a keynote

**to·night** (tə nīt′) *adv.* 〖OE *to niht*〗 on or during the present or coming night —*n.* the present or coming night

**ton·nage** (tun′ij) *n.* **1** the total amount of shipping of a country or port, calculated in tons **2** the carrying capacity of a ship, calculated in tons

**ton·sil** (tän′səl) *n.* 〖L *tonsillae*, pl.〗 either of a pair of oval masses of tissue at the back of the mouth

**ton·sil·lec·to·my** (tän′sə lek′tə mē) *n., pl.* **-mies** 〖prec. + -ECTOMY〗 the surgical removal of the tonsils

**ton′sil·li′tis** (-līt′is) *n.* 〖ModL < L *tonsillae*, tonsils + -ITIS〗 inflammation of the tonsils

**ton·so·ri·al** (tän sôr′ē əl) *adj.* 〖see fol.〗 of a barber or barbering: often humorous *[a tonsorial artist]*

**ton·sure** (tän′shər) *n.* 〖< L *tondere*, to clip〗 **1** a shaving off of part of the hair of the head, done as a sign of entrance into the clerical or monastic state **2** the head area so shaved

**to·nus** (tō′nəs) *n.* 〖ModL, ult. < Gr *teinein*, to stretch〗 the slight, continuous contraction characteristic of a normal relaxed muscle

**ton·y** (tō′nē) *adj.* **-i·er, -i·est** [Slang] very elegant

**too** (tōō) *adv.* 〖stressed form of TO〗 **1** in addition;

also **2** more than enough /the hat is *too* big/ **3** extremely; very /it was just *too* delicious!/

**took** (took) *vt., vi. pt. of* TAKE

**tool** (tōol) *n.* ⟦OE *tol*⟧ **1** any hand implement, instrument, etc. used for some work **2** any similar instrument that is the working part of a machine, as a drill **3** anything that serves as a means **4** a stooge —*vt.* to impress designs on (leather, etc.) with a tool —*vi.* to install the tools, equipment, etc. needed: often with *up*

**toot** (tōot) *vi., vt.* ⟦echoic⟧ to sound (a horn, whistle, etc.) in short blasts —*n.* a short blast of a horn, whistle, etc.

**tooth** (tōoth) *n., pl.* **teeth** (tēth) ⟦OE *toth*⟧ **1** any of the hard, bonelike structures in the jaws, used for biting, chewing, etc. **2** a toothlike part, as on a saw, comb, gearwheel, etc.; tine, prong, cog, etc. **3** [*pl.*] effective means of enforcement /a law with *teeth*/ —**tooth and nail** with all one's strength — **toothed** *adj.* —**tooth′less** *adj.*

**tooth′ache′** *n.* pain in a tooth

**tooth′brush′** *n.* a small brush for cleaning the teeth

**tooth′paste′** *n.* a paste used for brushing the teeth

**tooth′pick′** *n.* a very small, pointed stick for getting bits of food free from between the teeth

**tooth powder** a powder used like toothpaste

**tooth′some** (-səm) *adj.* tasty; savory

**tooth′y** *adj.* **-i·er, -i·est** having or exposing teeth that show prominently —**tooth′i·ly** *adv.*

**top**[1] (täp) *n.* ⟦OE⟧ **1** the head or crown **2** the highest point or surface of anything **3** the part of a plant above ground **4** the uppermost part or covering, as a lid, cap, etc. **5** the highest degree /at the *top* of his voice/ **6** the highest rank /the *top* of the class/ —*adj.* of, at, or being the top; highest or foremost —*vt.* **topped, top′ping 1** to take off the top of (a plant, etc.) **2** to provide with a top **3** to be a top for **4** to reach the top of **5** to exceed in amount, etc. **6** to surpass; outdo — **blow one's top** [Slang] to lose one's temper —**on top** successful —**on top of 1** resting upon **2** besides **3** controlling successfully —**top off** to complete by adding a finishing touch —**top′per** *n.*

**top**[2] (täp) *n.* ⟦OE⟧ a cone-shaped toy with a point upon which it is spun

**to·paz** (tō′paz′) *n.* ⟦< Gr *topazos*⟧ any of various yellow gems, esp. a variety of aluminum silicate

**top brass** [Slang] important officials

**top′coat′** *n.* a lightweight overcoat

**top′-drawer′** (-drôr′) *adj.* of first importance

**top′-dress′ing** *n.* material applied to a surface, as fertilizer on land

**To·pe·ka** (tə pē′kə) capital of Kansas: pop. 120,000

**top·er** (tō′pər) *n.* ⟦< archaic *tope*, to drink (much liquor)⟧ a drunkard

**top′-flight′** *adj.* [Inf.] first-rate

**top hat** a man's tall, black, cylindrical silk hat, worn in formal dress

**top′-heav′y** *adj.* too heavy at the top, so as to be unstable

**top·ic** (täp′ik) *n.* ⟦ult. < Gr *topos*, place⟧ the subject of an essay, speech, discussion, etc.

**top′i·cal** *adj.* dealing with topics of the day; of current or local interest

**top′knot′** *n.* a tuft of hair or feathers on the top of the head

**top′less** *adj.* without a top: said as of a costume exposing the breasts

**top·lev·el** (täp′lev′əl) *adj.* of or by persons of the highest office or rank

**top′mast′** *n.* the second mast above the deck of a sailing ship, supported by the lower mast

**top′most′** *adj.* at the very top

**top′-notch′** *adj.* [Inf.] first-rate; excellent

**to·pog·ra·phy** (tə päg′rə fē) *n., pl.* **-phies** ⟦see TOPIC & -GRAPHY⟧ **1** the science of representing

surface features of a region on maps and charts **2** these surface features —**top·o·graph·ic** (täp′ə graf′ik) or **top′o·graph′i·cal** *adj.*

**top·ping** (täp′iŋ) *n.* something put on top of something else, as a sauce on food

**top·ple** (täp′əl) *vi.* **-pled, -pling** ⟦< TOP[1]⟧ to fall top forward; fall (*over*) because top-heavy, etc. —*vt.* to cause to topple; overturn

**top·sail** (täp′sāl′; *naut.*, -səl) *n.* in a square-rigged vessel, the square sail next above the lowest sail on a mast

**top′-se′cret** *adj.* designating or of the most secret information

**top·side** (täp′sīd′) *adv.* on or to an upper deck or the main deck of a ship

**top′soil′** *n.* the upper layer of soil, usually richer than the subsoil

**top·sy-tur·vy** (täp′sē tur′vē) *adv., adj.* ⟦prob. < *top*, highest part + ME *terven*, to roll⟧ **1** upside down; in a reversed condition **2** in disorder

**toque** (tōk) *n.* ⟦Fr⟧ a woman's small, round, usually brimless hat

**To·rah** or **To·ra** (tō′rə, tôr′ə) [*occas.* **t-**] *n.* ⟦< Heb, law⟧ **1** the body of Jewish religious literature **2** the Pentateuch

**torch** (tôrch) *n.* ⟦see TORQUE⟧ **1** a portable flaming light **2** a device for producing a very hot flame, as in welding **3** [Brit.] a flashlight —*vt.* [Slang] to set fire to, as in arson

**torch′bear′er** *n.* **1** one who carries a torch **2** *a*) one who brings enlightenment, truth, etc. *b*) an inspirational leader, as in some movement

**torch′light′** *n.* the light of a torch or torches — *adj.* done by torchlight

**torch song** a sentimental song of unrequited love —**torch singer**

**tore** (tôr) *vt., vi. pt. of* TEAR[1]

**tor·e·a·dor** (tôr′ē ə dôr′) *n.* ⟦Sp < L *taurus*, a bull⟧ a bullfighter

**tor·ment** (tôr′ment′; *for v.* tôr ment′) *n.* ⟦OFr < L: see TORQUE⟧ **1** great pain or anguish **2** a source of pain, anxiety, etc. —*vt.* **1** to cause great physical pain or mental anguish in **2** to annoy; harass —**tor·ment′ing·ly** *adv.* —**tor·men′tor** or **tor·ment′er** *n.*

**torn** (tôrn) *vt., vi. pp. of* TEAR[1]

**tor·na·do** (tôr nā′dō) *n., pl.* **-does** or **-dos** ⟦< Sp < L *tonare*, to thunder⟧ a violently whirling column of air seen as a funnel-shaped cloud that usually destroys everything in its narrow path

**To·ron·to** (tə ränt′ō) capital of Ontario, Canada: pop. 654,000 (met. area, 4,264,000)

**tor·pe·do** (tôr pē′dō) *n., pl.* **-does** ⟦< L: see fol.⟧ **1** a large, cigar-shaped, self-propelled underwater projectile containing explosives **2** any of various explosive devices —*vt.* **-doed, -do·ing** to attack, destroy, etc. as with a torpedo

**tor·pid** (tôr′pid) *adj.* ⟦< L *torpere*, be numb⟧ **1** dormant or inactive **2** dull; sluggish

**tor·por** (-pər) *n.* ⟦L⟧ **1** a torpid state; sluggishness; stupor **2** dullness; apathy

**torque** (tôrk) *n.* ⟦< L *torquere*, to twist⟧ **1** *Physics* a measure of the tendency of a force to cause rotation **2** popularly, the force that acts to produce rotation, as in an automotive vehicle

**tor·rent** (tôr′ənt, tär′-) *n.* ⟦< L *torrens*, rushing⟧ **1** a swift, violent stream, esp. of water **2** a flood or rush of words, mail, etc. —**tor·ren·tial** (tô ren′shəl) *adj.*

**tor·rid** (tôr′id, tär′-) *adj.* ⟦< L *torrere*, to dry⟧ **1** subjected to intense heat, esp. of the sun; parched **2** very hot; scorching **3** passionate; ardent

**Torrid Zone** the area of the earth's surface between the Tropic of Cancer & the Tropic of Capricorn and divided by the equator

**tor·sion** (tôr′shən) *n.* ⟦see TORQUE⟧ **1** a twisting or being twisted **2** the stress produced in a rod, wire, etc. by twisting along a longitudinal axis

**tor·so** (tôr′sō) *n., pl.* **-sos** or **-si** (-sē) ⟦< Gr *thyrsos*, a stem⟧ the trunk of the human body

**tort** (tôrt) *n.* ⟦< L *torquere*, to twist⟧ *Law* a wrongful act or damage (not involving a breach of contract), for which a civil action can be brought

**torte** (tôrt; *Ger* tôr′tə) *n., pl.* **tortes** or Ger. **tor·ten** (tôr′tən) 〚Ger < It < LL *torta*, a twisted bread〛 a rich cake, as one made of eggs, finely chopped nuts, crumbs, etc.

**tor·tel·li·ni** (tôrt′ə lē′nē) *n.* 〚It〛 pasta in tiny ring-shaped pieces, filled with meat, etc.

**tor·til·la** (tôr tē′ə) *n.* 〚Sp, dim. of *torta*, a cake〛 a flat cake of unleavened cornmeal, or of flour

**tor·toise** (tôrt′əs) *n.* 〚< ? c. 4th-c. Gr *tartarouchos*, evil demon〛 a turtle, esp. one that lives on land

**tor·toise-shell′** *n.* **1** the hard, mottled, yellow-and-brown shell of some turtles **2** a synthetic substance resembling this

**tor·to·ni** (tôr tō′nē) *n.* 〚prob. alt. < It *tortone*, lit., big pastry tart〛 an ice cream made with heavy cream, maraschino cherries, almonds, etc.

**tor·tu·ous** (tôr′chōō əs) *adj.* 〚see TORQUE〛 **1** full of twists, turns, etc.; crooked **2** deceitful or tricky

**tor·ture** (tôr′chər) *n.* 〚see TORQUE〛 **1** the inflicting of severe pain, as to elicit information or force a confession **2** any severe physical or mental pain; agony —*vt.* **-tured, -tur·ing 1** to subject to torture **2** to twist or distort (meaning, etc.) — **tor′tur·er** *n.*

**To·ry** (tôr′ē) *n., pl.* **-ries** 〚Ir *tōruidhe*, robber〛 **1** after 1689, a member of the major conservative party of England **2** in the American Revolution, one loyal to Great Britain **3** [*often* t-] any extreme conservative

**toss** (tôs, täs) *vt.* 〚prob. < Scand〛 **1** to throw about 〚*waves tossed* the boat〛 **2** to throw lightly from the hand **3** to jerk upward 〚to *toss* one's head〛 — *vi.* **1** to be thrown about **2** to fling oneself about in sleep, etc. —*n.* a tossing or being tossed

**toss′up′** *n.* **1** the flipping of a coin to decide something **2** an even chance

**tot**[1] (tät) *n.* 〚prob. < ON〛 **1** a young child **2** [Chiefly Brit.] a small drink of alcoholic liquor

**tot**[2] (tät) *vt., vi.* **tot′ted, tot′ting** [Inf., Chiefly Brit.] to total: with *up*

**to·tal** (tōt′'l) *adj.* 〚< L *totus*, all〛 **1** constituting a whole **2** complete; utter 〚a *total* loss〛 —*n.* the whole amount; sum —*vt.* **-taled** or **-talled, -tal·ing** or **-tal·ling 1** to find the total of **2** to add up to **3** [Slang] to demolish —**to′tal·ly** *adv.*

**to·tal·i·tar·i·an** (tō tal′ə ter′ē ən) *adj.* 〚prec. + (AUTHOR)ITARIAN〛 designating or of a government in which one political group maintains complete control, esp. under a dictator —*n.* one who favors such a government —**to·tal′i·tar′i·an·ism′** *n.*

**to·tal·i·ty** (tō tal′ə tē) *n., pl.* **-ties** the total amount or sum

**to·tal·i·za·tor** (tōt′'l ī zāt′ər) *n.* a machine for registering bets and computing the odds and payoffs, as at a horse race: also **to′tal·iz′er** (-ī′zər) *n.*

**tote** (tōt) *vt.* **tot′ed, tot′ing** 〚< ?〛 [Inf.] to carry or haul —*n.* **1** a small piece of luggage **2** a large, open handbag: in full **tote bag**

**to·tem** (tōt′əm) *n.* 〚< Algonquian〛 **1** among some peoples, an animal or natural object taken as the symbol of a family or clan **2** an image of this

**totem pole** a pole carved and painted with totems by Indian tribes of NW North America

TOTEM POLE

**tot·ter** (tät′ər) *vi.* 〚prob. < Scand〛 **1** to rock as if about to fall **2** to be unsteady on one's feet; stagger

**tou·can** (tōō′kan′) *n.* 〚< AmInd (Brazil)〛 a brightly colored bird of tropical America, with a very large beak

**touch** (tuch) *vt.* 〚< OFr *tochier*〛 **1** to put the hand, etc. on, so as to feel **2** to bring (something),

---

509                                     ◄ **tousle**

or come, into contact with (something else) **3** to border on **4** to strike lightly **5** to give a light tint, aspect, etc. to 〚*touched* with pink〛 **6** to handle; use **7** to come up to; reach **8** to compare with; equal **9** to affect; concern **10** to arouse sympathy, gratitude, etc. in **11** [Slang] to seek a loan or gift of money from —*vi.* **1** to touch a person or thing **2** to be or come in contact **3** to verge (*on* or *upon*) **4** to pertain; bear (*on* or *upon*) **5** to treat in passing: with *on* or *upon* —*n.* **1** a touching or being touched; specif., a light tap **2** the sense by which physical objects are felt **3** a special quality or skill **4** a subtle change or addition in a painting, story, etc. **5** a trace, tinge, etc. **6** a slight attack 〚a *touch* of the flu〛 **7** contact or communication 〚keep in *touch*〛 **8** [Slang] the act of seeking or getting a loan or gift of money **9** *Music* the manner of striking the keys of a piano, etc. — **touch down** to land: said of an aircraft or spacecraft —**touch up** to improve by minor changes

**touch′-and-go′** *adj.* uncertain, risky, etc.

**touch′down′** *n.* **1** the moment at which an aircraft or spacecraft lands **2** *Football* a play, scoring six points, in which a player carries, catches, or recovers the ball past the opponent's goal line

**tou·ché** (tōō shā′) *interj.* 〚Fr〛 touched: said when one's opponent in fencing scores a point, or as to acknowledge a clever retort

**touched** (tucht) *adj.* **1** emotionally affected; moved **2** slightly demented

**touch′ing** *adj.* arousing tender emotions; moving

**touch′stone′** *n.* **1** a stone formerly used to test the purity of gold or silver **2** any test of genuineness

**touch′-type′** *vi.* **-typed′, -typ′ing** to type without looking at the keyboard by regularly touching a given key with a specific finger

**touch′y** *adj.* **-i·er, -i·est 1** easily offended; oversensitive; irritable **2** very risky or precarious

**touch′y-feel′y** (-fē′lē) *adj.* [Inf.] having or showing too much affection, compassion, etc.

**tough** (tuf) *adj.* 〚OE *toh*〛 **1** that will bend, etc. without tearing or breaking **2** not easily cut or chewed 〚*tough* steak〛 **3** strong; hardy **4** stubborn **5** brutal or rough **6** very difficult; laborious —*n.* a tough person; thug

**tough′en** *vt., vi.* to make or become tough or tougher —**tough′en·er** *n.*

**tou·pee** (tōō pā′) *n.* 〚< Fr < OFr *toup*, tuft of hair〛 a man's small wig

**tour** (tōor) *n.* 〚< OFr *tourner*, to turn〛 **1** a turn, period, etc., as of military duty **2** a long trip, as for sightseeing **3** any trip, as for inspection, for giving performances, etc. —*vt., vi.* to go on a tour (through)

**tour de force** (tōor′ də fôrs′) *pl.* **tours de force** (tōor′) 〚Fr〛 an unusually skillful or ingenious creation or performance, sometimes a merely clever one

**Tou·rette's syndrome** (tōo rets′) 〚after G. de la *Tourette*, 19th-c. Fr doctor〛 a nervous disorder characterized by involuntary movements, obscene utterances, etc.

**tour′ism′** *n.* tourist travel

**tour′ist** *n.* one who tours, esp. for pleasure —*adj.* of or for tourists

**tour·ma·line** (tōor′mə lin, -lēn′) *n.* 〚Fr〛 a crystal-line mineral used as a gemstone, etc.

**tour·na·ment** (tōor′nə mənt, tʉr′-) *n.* 〚< OFr *tourner*, to turn〛 **1** in the Middle Ages, a contest between knights on horseback who tried to unseat one another with lances **2** a series of contests in competition for a championship Also **tour′ney** (-nē) *n., pl.* **-neys**

**tour·ni·quet** (tōor′ni kit, tʉr′-) *n.* 〚Fr < L *tunica*, tunic〛 a device for compressing a blood vessel to stop bleeding, as a bandage twisted about a limb and released at intervals

**tou·sle** (tou′zəl) *vt.* **-sled, -sling** 〚< ME *tusen*, to pull〛 to disorder, dishevel, muss, etc.

**tout** (tout) [Inf.] *vi.*, *vt.* ⟦OE *totian*, to peep⟧ **1** to praise highly **2** to sell betting tips on (racehorses) —*n.* one who touts

**tow** (tō) *vt.* ⟦OE *togian*⟧ to pull, as by a rope or chain —*n.* **1** a towing or being towed **2** something towed **3** TOWLINE —**in tow 1** being towed **2** in one's company or charge

**toward** (tôrd, twôrd) *prep.* ⟦see TO & -WARD⟧ **1** in the direction of **2** facing **3** along a likely course to [steps *toward* peace] **4** concerning **5** just before [*toward* noon] **6** for [save *toward* a car] Also **towards**

**tow·el** (tou′əl) *n.* ⟦< OFr *toaille*⟧ a piece of cloth or paper for wiping or drying things —*vt.* **-eled** or **-elled, -el·ing** or **-el·ling** to wipe or dry with a towel —**throw (or toss, etc.) in the towel** [Inf.] to admit defeat

**tow·el·ing** or **tow·el·ling** *n.* material for making towels

**tow·er** (tou′ər) *n.* ⟦< L *turris*⟧ **1** a high structure, often part of a building **2** such a structure used as a fortress, etc. —*vi.* to rise high like a tower — **tow′er·ing** *adj.*

**tow·head** (tō′hed′) *n.* ⟦< *tow*, fibers of flax, etc.⟧ a person with pale-yellow hair —**tow′head′ed** *adj.*

**tow·hee** (tō′hē, -ē) *n.* ⟦echoic⟧ any of various small North American sparrows

**tow·line** (tō′līn′) *n.* a rope, etc. used for towing

**town** (toun) *n.* ⟦OE *tun*⟧ **1** a concentration of houses, etc. somewhat larger than a village **2** a city **3** a township **4** the business center of a city **5** the people of a town —**on the town** [Inf.] out for a good time

**town crier** one who, formerly, cried public announcements through the streets of a village or town

**town hall** a building in a town, housing the offices of officials, etc.

**town house** a two-story or three-story dwelling, a unit in a complex of such dwellings

**town meeting** a meeting of the voters of a town, as in New England

**town′ship** *n.* a division of a county, constituting a unit of local government

**towns′peo′ple** *pl.n.* the people of a town: also **towns′folk′**

**tow·path** (tō′path′) *n.* a path along a canal, used by men or animals towing freight-carrying boats

**tow′rope′** *n.* a rope used in towing

**tox·e·mi·a** (täk sē′mē ə) *n.* ⟦see fol. & -EMIA⟧ a condition in which the blood contains poisonous substances, esp. toxins produced by pathogenic bacteria

**tox·ic** (täk′sik) *adj.* ⟦< Gr *toxicon*, a poison⟧ **1** of, affected by, or caused by a toxin **2** poisonous

**tox·i·col·o·gy** (täk′si käl′ə jē) *n.* ⟦see prec. & -LOGY⟧ the science of poisons and their effects, antidotes, etc. —**tox′i·col′o·gist** *n.*

**tox·in** (täk′sin) *n.* ⟦< TOXIC⟧ **1** any of various poisons produced by microorganisms and causing certain diseases **2** any poison secreted by plants or animals

**toy** (toi) *n.* ⟦< ? MDu *toi*, finery⟧ **1** a trifle **2** a plaything for children —*adj.* **1** like a plaything in size, use, etc. **2** made as a toy —*vi.* to trifle (*with* a thing, an idea, etc.)

**tr** *abbrev.* **1** translated **2** translation **3** translator **4** transpose

**trace**[1] (trās) *n.* ⟦< L *trahere*, to draw⟧ **1** a mark, track, sign, etc. left by a person, animal, or thing **2** a barely perceptible amount —*vt.* **traced, trac′ing 1** to follow the trail to; track **2** *a*) to follow the development or history of *b*) to determine (a source, etc.) by this procedure **3** to draw, outline, etc. **4** to copy (a drawing, etc.) by following its lines on a superimposed transparent sheet — **trace′a·ble** *adj.* —**trac′er** *n.*

**trace**[2] (trās) *n.* ⟦see TRAIT⟧ either of two straps, etc. connecting a draft animal's harness to the vehicle drawn

**trace element** a chemical element, as copper, zinc, etc., essential in nutrition, but only in minute amounts

**trac·er·y** (trās′ər ē) *n.*, *pl.* **-ies** ⟦< TRACE[1] + -ERY⟧ ornamental work of interlacing or branching lines

**tra·che·a** (trā′kē ə) *n.*, *pl.* **-che·ae** (-ē′) or **-che·as** ⟦< Gr *tracheia* (*arteria*), rough (windpipe)⟧ the passage that conveys air from the larynx to the bronchi; windpipe —**tra′che·al** *adj.*

**tra·che·ot·o·my** (trā′kē ät′ə mē) *n.*, *pl.* **-mies** ⟦see prec. & -TOMY⟧ an incision of the trachea to aid breathing in an emergency

**trac·ing** (trās′iŋ) *n.* something traced; specif., *a*) a copy of a drawing, etc. *b*) a traced line made by a recording instrument

**track** (trak) *n.* ⟦< Fr *trac*⟧ **1** a mark left in passing, as a footprint, wheel rut, etc. **2** a path or trail **3** a sequence of ideas, events, etc. **4** a path or circuit laid out for racing, etc. **5** a pair of parallel metal rails on which trains, etc. run **6** *a*) sports performed on a track, as running, hurdling, etc. *b*) these sports along with other contests in jumping, throwing, etc. **7** *a*) a band on a phonograph record, compact disc, etc. *b*) any of the separate, parallel recording surfaces along a magnetic tape —*vt.* **1** to follow the track of **2** to trace by means of evidence, etc. **3** to plot the path of, as with radar **4** to leave tracks of (mud, etc.) on: often with *up* —**in one's tracks** where one is at the moment —**keep (or lose) track of** to stay (or fail to stay) informed about —**track′less** *adj.*

**track lighting** a method of lighting a room with spotlights inserted along a narrow, wired track

**track record** [Inf.] the record of the performance of a person, etc. as in some activity

**tract**[1] (trakt) *n.* ⟦< L *trahere*, to draw⟧ **1** a continuous expanse of land **2** a system of organs having some special function [the digestive *tract*]

**tract**[2] (trakt) *n.* ⟦< LL *tractatus*, treatise⟧ a propagandizing pamphlet

**trac·ta·ble** (trak′tə bəl) *adj.* ⟦< L *trahere*, to draw⟧ easily managed; docile; compliant

**tract house** a house built to a design that is used many times throughout a housing development

**trac·tion** (trak′shən) *n.* ⟦< L *trahere*, to draw⟧ **1** *a*) a pulling or drawing *b*) a being pulled or drawn *c*) the kind of power used for pulling [electric *traction*] **2** the power, as of tires on pavement, to hold to a surface without slipping

**trac·tor** (trak′tər) *n.* ⟦see prec.⟧ **1** a powerful, motor-driven vehicle for pulling farm machinery, etc. **2** a truck with a driver's cab and no body, for hauling large trailers

**trac′tor-trail′er** *n.* a TRACTOR (sense 2) combined with a trailer or semitrailer, used for transporting goods

**trade** (trād) *n.* ⟦< LowG, a track⟧ **1** occupation; esp., skilled work **2** all the persons in a particular business **3** buying and selling; commerce **4** customers **5** an exchange; swap —*vi.* **trad′ed, trad′ing 1** to carry on a business **2** to have business dealings (*with*) **3** to make an exchange (*with*) **4** [Inf.] to be a customer (*at* a certain store) —*vt.* to exchange; barter —**trade on (or upon)** to take advantage of

**trade′-in′** *n.* a thing given or taken as part payment for something else

**trade journal** (or **magazine**) a magazine devoted to a specific trade or industry

**trade′mark′** *n.* **1** a symbol, word, etc. used by a manufacturer or dealer to distinguish a product: usually protected by law **2** [Inf.] a distinctive, identifying feature or characteristic

**trade name 1** the name by which a commodity is commonly known by those who deal in it **2** a name used as a trademark **3** the business name of a company

**trade′-off′** *n.* an exchange in which one benefit is given up for another considered more desirable: also **trade′off′**

**trad′er** *n.* **1** one who trades; merchant **2** a ship used in trade

**trades·man** (trādz'mən) *n.*, *pl.* **-men** (-mən) [Chiefly Brit.] a storekeeper —**trades'wom'an,** *pl.* **-wom'en,** *fem.n.*

**trade union** LABOR UNION

**trade wind** a wind that blows toward the equator from either side of it

**trading post** a store in an outpost, settlement, etc., where trading is done

**tra·di·tion** (trə dish'ən) *n.* [< L *tradere,* deliver] 1 the handing down orally of beliefs, customs, etc. from generation to generation 2 a story, belief, custom, etc. handed down in this way

**tra·di·tion·al** *adj.* of, handed down by, or conforming to tradition

**tra·di·tion·al·ism'** *n.* adherence to tradition; sometimes, specif., excessive devotion to tradition —**tra·di'tion·al·ist** *n.*

**tra·duce** (trə dōōs', -dyōōs') *vt.* **-duced', -duc'ing** [< L *trans,* across + *ducere,* to lead] to slander

**traf·fic** (traf'ik) *n.* [< It *traffico* < L *trans,* across +It *ficcare,* bring] 1 buying and selling; trade 2 dealings (*with* someone) 3 the movement or number of automobiles, pedestrians, etc. along a street, etc. 4 the business done by a transportation company —*adj.* of or having to do with traffic —*vi.* **-ficked, -fick·ing** 1 to carry on traffic (*in* a commodity) 2 to have dealings (*with* someone)

**traffic circle** a circular road at the intersection of several streets: vehicles move on it in one direction only

**traffic light** (or **signal**) a set of signal lights at a street intersection for regulating traffic

**tra·ge·di·an** (trə jē'dē ən) *n.* 1 a writer of tragedy 2 an actor in tragedies

**trag·e·dy** (traj'ə dē) *n.*, *pl.* **-dies** [< Gr *tragos,* goat + *ōidē,* song] 1 a serious play with an unhappy ending 2 a very sad or tragic event; disaster

**trag·ic** (traj'ik) *adj.* 1 of or like a tragedy 2 disastrous, fatal, etc. —**trag'i·cal·ly** *adv.*

**trail** (trāl) *vt.* [< L *trahere,* to draw] 1 to drag or let drag behind one 2 to follow the tracks of; track 3 to hunt by tracking 4 to follow behind — *vi.* 1 to drag along on the ground, etc. 2 to grow along the ground, etc., as some plants do 3 to flow behind: said as of smoke 4 to follow or lag behind; straggle 5 to grow weaker, dimmer, etc.: with *off* or *away* —*n.* 1 something that trails behind 2 a mark, scent, etc. left by a person, animal, or thing that has passed 3 a beaten path

**trail bike** a small motorcycle for off-road riding

**trail'blaz'er** *n.* 1 one who blazes a trail 2 a pioneer in any field

**trail'er** *n.* 1 one that trails 2 *a*) a wagon, van, etc. designed to be pulled by an automobile, truck, etc. *b*) such a vehicle designed to be lived in

**trailer park** an area, usually with piped water, electricity, etc., for trailers, esp. mobile homes

**trail mix** GORP

**train** (trān) *n.* [< L *trahere,* to pull] 1 something that drags along behind, as a trailing skirt 2 a group of followers; retinue 3 a procession; caravan 4 any connected order; sequence [a *train* of thought] 5 a line of connected railroad cars pulled by a locomotive —*vt.* 1 to guide the growth of (a plant) 2 to guide the mental, moral, etc. development of; rear 3 to instruct so as to make proficient 4 to make fit for an athletic contest, etc. 5 to aim (a gun, etc.) —*vi.* to undergo training —**train·ee** (trān ē') *n.* —**train'er** *n.*

**traipse** (trāps) *vi.*, *vt.* **traipsed, traips'ing** [< ?] [Inf. or Dial.] to walk, wander, or tramp

**trait** (trāt) *n.* [< L *trahere,* to draw] a distinguishing quality or characteristic

**trai·tor** (trāt'ər) *n.* [< L *tradere,* betray] one who betrays one's country, cause, friends, etc. — **trai'tor·ous** *adj.*

**tra·jec·to·ry** (trə jek'tə rē) *n.*, *pl.* **-ries** [ult. < L *trans,* across + *jacere,* to throw] the curved path of something hurtling through space

**tram** (tram) *n.* [prob. < LowG *traam,* a beam] [Brit.] a streetcar

**tram·mel** (tram'əl) *n.* [< L *tres,* three + *macula,* a mesh] [*usually pl.*] something that confines or restrains —*vt.* **-meled** or **-melled, -mel·ing** or **-mel·ling** to confine, restrain, etc.

**tramp** (tramp) *vi.* [ME *trampen*] 1 to walk or step heavily 2 to travel about on foot —*vt.* 1 to step on heavily 2 to walk through —*n.* 1 a vagrant; hobo 2 the sound of heavy steps 3 a journey on foot; hike 4 a freight ship with no schedule, that picks up cargo, etc. as it goes along 5 [Slang] a sexually promiscuous woman

**tram·ple** (tram'pəl) *vi.* **-pled, -pling** [see prec.] to tread heavily —*vt.* to crush, destroy, etc. by or as by treading heavily on

**tram·po·line** (tram'pə lēn', -lin) *n.* [< It] a sheet of strong canvas stretched tightly on a frame with springs, used in acrobatic tumbling and jumping

**trance** (trans) *n.* [< L *transire,* go across, die] 1 a state of altered consciousness, resembling sleep, as in hypnosis 2 a daze; stupor 3 a state of great mental abstraction

**tran·quil** (traŋ'kwəl) *adj.* **-quil·er** or **-quil·ler, -quil·est** or **-quil·lest** [L *tranquillus*] calm, serene, placid, etc. —**tran·quil'i·ty** or **tran·quil'i·ty** (-kwil'ə tē) *n.* —**tran'quil·ly** *adv.*

**tran'quil·ize'** or **tran'quil·lize'** (-kwə līz') *vt.*, *vi.* **-ized'** or **-lized', -iz'ing** or **-liz'ing** to make or become tranquil

**tran'quil·iz'er** or **tran'quil·liz'er** *n.* a drug used as a calming agent in treating various emotional disturbances, etc.

**trans** *abbrev.* 1 translated 2 translation 3 translator 4 transportation

**trans-** [L < *trans,* across] *prefix* over, across, beyond, through

**trans·act** (tran zakt', -sakt') *vt.* [< L *trans-,* over + *agere,* to drive] to carry on or complete (business, etc.)

**trans·ac'tion** *n.* 1 a transacting 2 something transacted; specif., *a*) a business deal *b*) [*pl.*] a record of the proceedings of a society, etc.

**trans·at·lan·tic** (trans'at lan'tik, tranz'-) *adj.* 1 crossing the Atlantic 2 on the other side of the Atlantic

**trans·ceiv·er** (tran sē'vər) *n.* a radio transmitter and receiver in a single housing

**tran·scend** (tran send') *vt.* [< L *trans-,* over + *scandere,* climb] 1 to go beyond the limits of; exceed 2 to surpass; excel —**tran·scend'ent** *adj.*

**tran·scen·den·tal** (tran'sen dent''l) *adj.* 1 supernatural 2 abstract —**tran'scen·den'tal·ly** *adv.*

**tran'scen·den'tal·ism'** *n.* [often T-] a philosophy based on a search for reality through spiritual intuition

**trans·con·ti·nen·tal** (trans'kän tə nent''l, tranz'-) *adj.* 1 that crosses a continent 2 on the other side of a continent

**tran·scribe** (tran skrīb') *vt.* **-scribed', -scrib'ing** 1 to write out or type out in full (shorthand notes, etc.) 2 to represent (speech sounds) in symbols

**tran·script** (tran'skript') *n.* 1 a written, typewritten, or printed copy 2 a copy, esp. an official copy, as of a student's record

**tran·scrip'tion** (-skrip'shən) *n.* 1 a transcribing 2 a transcript; copy 3 an arrangement of a piece of music for an instrument or voice other than that for which it was written

**trans·duc·er** (trans dōōs'ər, tranz-) *n.* [< L *trans-,* over + *ducere,* to lead] a device that transmits energy from one system to another, sometimes converting the energy to a different form

**tran·sept** (tran'sept') *n.* [< L *trans-,* across + *septum,* enclosure] the part of a cross-shaped church at right angles to the nave, or either of its arms

**trans·fer** (trans'fər) *vt.* **-ferred', -fer'ring** [< L *trans-,* across + *ferre,* to bear] 1 to carry, send, etc. to another person or place 2 to make over (property, etc.) to another 3 to convey (a picture, etc.) from one surface to another —*vi.* 1 to transfer oneself or be transferred 2 to change as to another school or another bus —*n.* **1** a transferring or being transferred **2** one that is transferred **3** a ticket entitling the bearer to change to another bus, etc. —**trans·fer′ral** (-fʉr′-) *n.*

**trans·fer·ence** (trans′fər əns, trans fʉr′-) *n.* a transferring or being transferred

**trans·fig·ure** (trans fig′yər) *vt.* **-ured, -ur·ing** 〚< L *trans-*, across + *figura*, figure〛 **1** to change the form or appearance of **2** to transform so as to glorify —**trans·fig′u·ra′tion** *n.*

**trans·fix** (trans fiks′) *vt.* 〚< L *trans-*, through + *figere*, to fix〛 **1** to pierce through; impale **2** to make motionless, as if impaled

**trans·form** (trans fôrm′) *vt.* 〚< L *trans-*, over + *forma*, a form〛 **1** to change the form or appearance of **2** to change the condition, nature, or function of —**trans′for·ma′tion** *n.*

**trans·form′er** *n.* a device for changing electrical energy to a different voltage

**trans·fuse′** (-fyo͞oz′) *vt.* **-fused′, -fus′ing** 〚< L *trans-*, across + *fundere*, pour〛 **1** to instill; imbue **2** to transfer (blood, etc.) into a blood vessel —**trans·fu′sion** *n.*

**trans·gress** (trans gres′, tranz-) *vt., vi.* 〚< L *trans-*, over + *gradi*, to step〛 **1** to break (a law, command, etc.); sin (against) **2** to go beyond (a limit, etc.) —**trans·gres′sion** (-gresh′ən) *n.* —**trans·gres′sor** *n.*

**tran·sient** (tran′shənt, -zē ənt) *adj.* 〚< L *trans-*, over + *ire*, to go〛 **1** passing away with time; temporary **2** passing quickly; fleeting **3** staying only a short time —*n.* a transient person —**tran′sience** or **tran′sien·cy** *n.*

**tran·sis·tor** (tran zis′tər, -sis′-) *n.* 〚TRAN(SFER) + (RE)SISTOR〛 a compact electronic device, composed of semiconductor material, that controls current flow —**tran·sis′tor·ize′, -ized′, -iz′ing** *vt.*

**trans·it** (tran′sit, -zit) *n.* 〚< L *trans-*, over + *ire*, to go〛 **1** passage through or across **2** *a)* a carrying through or across; conveyance *b)* a system of urban public transportation **3** a surveying instrument for measuring horizontal angles

**tran·si·tion** (tran zish′ən) *n.* a passing from one condition, place, etc. to another —**tran·si′tion·al** *adj.*

**tran·si·tive** (tran′sə tiv, -zə-) *adj.* designating a verb that takes a direct object

**tran·si·to·ry** (tran′sə tôr′ē, -zə-) *adj.* not enduring; temporary; fleeting

**transl** *abbrev.* **1** translated **2** translation

**trans·late** (trans lāt′, tranz-) *vt.* **-lat′ed, -lat′ing** 〚< L *translatus*, transferred〛 **1** to move from one place or condition to another **2** to put into the words of a different language **3** to put into different words —**trans·la′tor** *n.*

**trans·la′tion** *n.* **1** a translating **2** writing or speech translated into another language

**trans·lit·er·ate** (trans lit′ər āt′, tranz-) *vt.* **-at′ed, -at′ing** 〚< TRANS- + L *litera*, letter〛 to write (words, etc.) in the characters of another alphabet —**trans·lit′er·a′tion** *n.*

**trans·lu′cent** (-lo͞o′sənt) *adj.* 〚< L *trans-*, through + *lucere*, to shine〛 letting light pass through, but not transparent

**trans·mi′grate′** (-mī′grāt′) *vi.* **-grat′ed, -grat′ing** 〚see TRANS- & MIGRATE〛 to pass into another body at death: said of the soul, as in Hindu religious belief —**trans′mi·gra′tion** *n.*

**trans·mis′sion** (-mish′ən) *n.* **1** a transmitting **2** something transmitted **3** the part of a motor vehicle that transmits power to the wheels

**trans·mit′** (-mit′) *vt.* **-mit′ted, -mit′ting** 〚< L *trans-*, over + *mittere*, send〛 **1** to cause to go to another person or place; transfer **2** to hand down by heredity, inheritance, etc. **3** *a)* to pass (light, heat, etc.) through some medium *b)* to conduct [water *transmits* sound] **4** to convey (force, movement, etc.) to **5** to send out (radio or television broadcasts) —**trans·mis′si·ble** (-mis′ə bəl) *adj.* —**trans·mit′ta·ble** *adj.* —**trans·mit′tal** *n.*

**trans·mit′ter** *n.* the apparatus that transmits signals in telephony, radio, etc.

**trans·mute′** (-myo͞ot′) *vt., vi.* **-mut′ed, -mut′ing** 〚< L *trans-*, over + *mutare*, to change〛 to change from one form, nature, substance, etc. into another; transform —**trans′mu·ta′tion** *n.*

**trans·na′tion·al** (-nash′ə nəl) *adj.* transcending the limits, interests, etc. of a single nation

**trans·o′ce·an′ic** (-ō′shē an′ik) *adj.* crossing the ocean

**tran·som** (tran′səm) *n.* 〚prob. < L *transtrum*, crossbeam〛 **1** a horizontal crossbar, as across the top of a door or window **2** a small window just above a door or window

**trans·pa·cif·ic** (trans′pə sif′ik) *adj.* **1** crossing the Pacific **2** on the other side of the Pacific

**trans·par·en·cy** (trans per′ən sē) *n., pl.* **-cies** a transparent film or slide having an image that can be projected on a screen

**trans·par′ent** *adj.* 〚< L *trans-*, through + *parere*, appear〛 **1** transmitting light rays so that objects on the other side can be seen clearly **2** so fine in texture as to be seen through **3** easily understood or detected; clear; obvious —**trans·par′ent·ly** *adv.*

**tran·spire** (tran spīr′) *vi.* **-spired′, -spir′ing** 〚< L *trans-*, through + *spirare*, breathe〛 **1** to give off vapor, moisture, etc., as through pores **2** to become known **3** to happen

**trans·plant** (trans plant′; *also, and for n. always,* trans′plant′) *vt.* **1** to remove from one place and plant, resettle, etc. in another **2** *Surgery* to transfer (tissue or an organ) from one to another; graft —*n.* a transplanting or something transplanted, as a body organ or a seedling —**trans′plan·ta′tion** (-plan tā′shən) *n.*

**tran·spon·der** (tran spän′dər) *n.* 〚< TRAN(SMITTER) & RESPOND〛 a transceiver that automatically transmits signals

**trans·port** (trans pôrt′; *for n.* trans′pôrt′) *vt.* 〚< L *trans-*, over + *portare*, carry〛 **1** to carry from one place to another **2** to carry away with emotion —*n.* **1** a transporting; transportation **2** strong emotion, esp. joy **3** a vehicle for transporting

**trans′por·ta′tion** (-pər tā′shən) *n.* **1** a transporting or being transported **2** a means of conveyance **3** fare or a ticket for being transported

**trans·pose** (trans pōz′) *vt., vi.* **-posed′, -pos′ing** 〚see TRANS- & POSE〛 **1** to change the usual order or position of; interchange **2** to rewrite or play (a musical composition) in a different key —**trans′po·si′tion** (-pə zish′ən) *n.*

**trans·sex·u·al** (trans sek′sho͞o əl) *n.* a person who identifies with the opposite sex, sometimes so strongly as to undergo sex-change surgery

**trans·ship** (trans ship′) *vt., vi.* **-shipped′, -ship′ping** to transfer from one ship, train, truck, etc. to another for further shipment —**trans·ship′ment** *n.*

**trans·verse** (trans vʉrs′, tranz-; *also, and for n. usually,* trans′vʉrs′, tranz′-) *adj.* 〚< L *trans-*, across + *vertere*, to turn〛 situated across; crosswise —*n.* a transverse part, etc.

**trans·ves·tite** (trans ves′tīt′, tranz-) *n.* 〚< TRANS- + L *vestire*, to dress〛 a person who gets sexual pleasure from dressing in the clothes of the opposite sex

**trap** (trap) *n.* 〚< OE *træppe*〛 **1** a device for catching animals, as one that snaps shut tightly when stepped on **2** any stratagem designed to catch or trick **3** a device, as in a drainpipe, for preventing the escape of gas, etc. —*vt.* **trapped, trap′ping** to catch in or as in a trap —*vi.* to trap animals, esp. for their furs —**trap′per** *n.*

**trap′door′** *n.* a hinged or sliding door in a roof, ceiling, or floor

**tra·peze** (tra pēz′) *n.* 〚see fol.〛 a short horizontal bar, hung high by two ropes, on which gymnasts, etc. swing

**tra·pe·zi·um** (trə pē′zē əm) *n., pl.* **-zi·ums** or **-zi·a** (-ə) 〚< Gr *trapeza*, table〛 a plane figure with four sides, no two of which are parallel

**trap·e·zoid** (trap′i zoid′) *n.* 〚see prec.〛 a plane

figure with four sides, only two of which are parallel —trap′e·zoi′dal adj.

trap′pings pl.n. [< OFr drap, cloth] 1 an ornamental covering for a horse 2 adornments

trap′shoot′ing n. the sport of shooting at clay disks sprung into the air from throwing devices

trash (trash) n. [prob. < Scand] 1 broken, discarded, or worthless things; rubbish 2 a person or people regarded as disreputable, etc. —vt. [Slang] 1 to destroy (property) as by vandalism 2 to criticize or insult (a person, etc.) sharply or maliciously —trash′y, -i·er, -i·est, adj.

trau·ma (trô′mə, trä′-) n., pl. -mas or -ma·ta (-mə tə) [Gr] 1 a bodily injury or shock 2 an emotional shock, often having a lasting psychic effect —trau·mat·ic (trô mat′ik) adj.

trau′ma·tize′ (-tīz′) vt. -tized′, -tiz′ing to subject to a physical or mental trauma

trav·ail (trə vāl′, trav′āl′) n. [< L tri-, three + palus, stake: referring to a torture device] 1 very hard work 2 intense pain; agony

trav·el (trav′əl) vi. -eled or -elled, -el·ing or -el·ling [var. of prec.] 1 to go from one place to another 2 to move, pass, or be transmitted —vt. to make a journey over or through —n. 1 a traveling 2 [pl.] trips, journeys, etc. —trav′el·er or trav′el·ler n.

traveler's check a check, issued by a bank, etc., sold to a traveler who signs it at issuance and again when cashing it

trav·e·logue or trav·e·log (trav′ə lôg′) n. 1 an illustrated lecture on travels 2 a short film about a place, esp. one that is foreign, unusual, etc.

tra·verse (trə vurs′; for n. & adj. trav′ərs) vt. -versed′, -vers′ing [< L trans-, across + vertere, to turn] to pass over, across, or through —n. trav′erse 1 something that traverses or crosses, as a crossbar 2 a traversing —adj. trav′erse 1 extending across 2 designating or of draperies drawn by pulling a cord at the side

trav·es·ty (trav′is tē) n., pl. -ties [< L trans-, over + vestire, to dress] 1 a farcical imitation in ridicule 2 a ridiculous representation [a travesty of justice] —vt. -tied, -ty·ing to make a travesty of

trawl (trôl) n. [< ? MDu traghel, dragnet] 1 a large dragnet for fishing 2 a long line supported by buoys, from which fishing lines are hung —vi., vt. to fish or catch with a trawl

trawl′er n. a boat used in trawling

tray (trā) n. [< OE treg, wooden board] a flat receptacle with raised edges, for holding or carrying things

treach·er·ous (trech′ər əs) adj. 1 characterized by treachery; disloyal 2 untrustworthy or insecure —treach′er·ous·ly adv.

treach·er·y (trech′ər ē) n., pl. -ies [< OFr trichier, to cheat] 1 betrayal of trust; disloyalty 2 treason

trea·cle (trē′kəl) n. [< Gr (antidotos) thēriakē, (remedy) for venom] [Brit.] 1 molasses 2 anything very sweet or cloying —trea′cly (-klē) adj.

tread (tred) vt. trod, trod′den or trod, tread′ing [OE tredan] 1 to walk on, in, along, etc. 2 to do or follow by walking, dancing, etc. 3 to press or beat with the feet —vi. 1 to walk 2 to set one's foot (on, across, etc.) 3 to trample (on or upon) —n. 1 the manner or sound of treading 2 something for treading or moving on, as a shoe sole or surface of a stair 3 the thick outer layer of an automotive tire —tread water pt. & pp. usually tread′ed to stay upright in swimming by moving the legs and arms back and forth

trea·dle (tred′'l) n. [< OE tredan, to tread] a lever moved by the foot as to turn a wheel

tread′mill′ n. 1 a mill wheel turned by an animal treading an endless belt 2 any monotonous work in which one seems to make no progress 3 an exercise machine with an endless belt on which one walks or runs

treas abbrev. 1 treasurer 2 treasury

trea·son (trē′zən) n. [< L trans-, over + dare,

give] betrayal of one's country to an enemy —trea′son·a·ble or trea′son·ous adj.

treas·ure (trezh′ər) n. [< Gr thēsauros] 1 accumulated wealth, as money or jewels 2 any person or thing considered valuable —vt. -ured, -ur·ing 1 to save up for future use 2 to value greatly

treas·ur·er (trezh′ər ər) n. one in charge of a treasury, as of a government or club

treas′ure-trove′ (-trōv′) n. [trove < OFr trover, find] 1 treasure found hidden, the original owner of which is unknown 2 a valuable source or collection

treas·ur·y (trezh′ər ē) n., pl. -ies 1 a place where treasure or funds are kept 2 the funds or revenues of a state, corporation, etc. 3 [T-] the department of government in charge of revenue, taxation, and public finances

treat (trēt) vi. [ult. < L trahere, to draw] 1 to discuss terms (with) 2 to speak or write (of) —vt. 1 to deal with (a subject) in writing, music, etc. in a specified manner 2 to act toward (someone or something) in a specified manner 3 to pay for the food, etc. of (another) 4 to subject to some process, chemical, etc. 5 to give medical care to —n. 1 a meal, drink, etc. paid for by another 2 anything that gives great pleasure

trea·tise (trēt′is) n. [see prec.] a formal article or book on some subject

treat·ment (trēt′mənt) n. 1 act, manner, method, etc. of treating 2 medical or surgical care

trea·ty (trēt′ē) n., pl. -ties [< L trahere, to draw] a formal agreement between two or more nations

tre·ble (treb′əl) adj. [< L triplus, triple] 1 threefold; triple 2 of, for, or performing the treble —n. 1 the highest part in musical harmony; soprano 2 a high-pitched voice or sound —vt., vi. -bled, -bling to make or become threefold

tree (trē) n. [OE trēow] 1 a large, woody perennial plant with one main trunk and many branches 2 a) anything resembling a tree b) FAMILY TREE —vt. treed, tree′ing to chase up a tree —tree′less adj. —tree′like′ adj.

tre·foil (trē′foil′) n. [< L tri-, three + folium, leaf] 1 a plant with leaves divided into three leaflets, as the clover 2 a design, etc. shaped like such a leaf

trek (trek) vi. trekked, trek′king [Afrik < Du trekken, to pull] 1 to travel slowly or laboriously 2 [Inf.] to go on foot —n. 1 a journey 2 a migration

trel·lis (trel′is) n. [< L trilix, triple-twilled] a lattice on which vines are trained

trem·a·tode (trem′ə tōd′, trē′mə-) n. [< Gr trēmatōdēs, perforated] a parasitic flatworm with muscular suckers; fluke

trem·ble (trem′bəl) vi. -bled, -bling [< L tremere] 1 to shake or shiver from cold, fear, etc. 2 to feel great anxiety 3 to quiver, vibrate, etc. —n. 1 a trembling 2 [sometimes pl.] a fit of trembling

tre·men·dous (tri men′dəs) adj. [< L tremere, to tremble] 1 very large; great 2 [Inf.] wonderful, amazing, etc. —tre·men′dous·ly adv.

trem·o·lo (trem′ə lō′) n., pl. -los′ [It] Music a tremulous effect produced by rapid reiteration of the same tone

trem·or (trem′ər) n. [< L tremere, to tremble] 1 a trembling, shaking, etc. 2 a trembling sensation

trem·u·lous (trem′yōō ləs) adj. [< L tremere, to tremble] 1 trembling; quivering 2 fearful; timid

trench (trench) vt. [< OFr trenchier, to cut] to dig a ditch or ditches in —n. 1 a deep furrow 2 a long, narrow ditch dug by soldiers for cover, with earth heaped up in front

trench·ant (tren′chənt) adj. [see prec.] 1 sharp; incisive [trenchant words] 2 forceful; effective [a trenchant argument] —trench′ant·ly adv.

trench coat a belted raincoat in a military style

trench′er n. [see TRENCH] [Archaic] a wooden platter for meat

trench′er·man (-mən) n., pl. -men (-mən) an eater; esp., one who eats much

**trench foot** a diseased condition of the feet from prolonged exposure to wet and cold

**trench mouth** an infectious disease of the mucous membranes of the mouth and throat

**trend** (trend) *vi.* ⟦OE *trendan*⟧ to have a general direction or tendency —*n.* 1 a general tendency or course; drift 2 a current style

**trend·y** (tren′dē) *adj.* -i·er, -i·est [Inf.] of or in the latest style, or trend

**Tren·ton** (trent′'n) capital of New Jersey: pop. 89,000

**trep·i·da·tion** (trep′ə dā′shən) *n.* ⟦< L *trepidus*, disturbed⟧ fearful uncertainty; anxiety

**tres·pass** (tres′pəs, -pas′) *vi.* ⟦< L *trans-*, across + *passus*, a step⟧ 1 to go beyond the limits of what is considered right; do wrong; transgress 2 to enter another's property without permission or right —*n.* a trespassing; specif., a moral offense —**tres′pass·er** *n.*

**tress** (tres) *n.* ⟦< OFr *tresse*, braid of hair⟧ 1 a lock of human hair 2 [*pl.*] a woman's or girl's hair, esp. when long

**tres·tle** (tres′əl) *n.* ⟦< L *transtrum*, a beam⟧ 1 a horizontal beam fastened to two pairs of spreading legs, used as a support 2 a framework of uprights and crosspieces, supporting a bridge, etc.

**trey** (trā) *n.* ⟦< L *tres*, three⟧ a playing card with three spots

**tri-** ⟦< Fr, L, or Gr⟧ *prefix* 1 having or involving three 2 three times, into three 3 every third

**tri·ad** (trī′ad′) *n.* ⟦< Gr *treis*, three⟧ a group of three

**tri·age** (trē äzh′, trē′äzh′) *n.* ⟦< Fr *trier*, sift⟧ a system of establishing the order in which acts are to be carried out in an emergency, esp. acts of medical assistance —*vt.* -**aged′**, -**ag′ing** to prioritize (patients, problems, etc.)

**tri·al** (trī′əl) *n.* [see TRY] 1 the act or process of trying, testing, etc.; test; probation 2 a hardship, suffering, etc. 3 a source of annoyance 4 a hearing and deciding of a case in a court of law 5 an attempt; effort —*adj.* 1 of a trial 2 for the purpose of trying, testing, etc. —**on trial** in the process of being tried

**trial and error** the process of making repeated trials, tests, and adjustments until the right result is found

**trial balloon** something said or done to test public opinion on an issue

**tri·an·gle** (trī′aŋ′gəl) *n.* [see TRI- & ANGLE¹] 1 a plane figure having three angles and three sides 2 anything with three sides or three corners 3 a situation involving three persons [a love *triangle*] —**tri·an′gu·lar** (-gyoo lər) *adj.*

**tri·an′gu·late′** (-gyə lāt′) *vt.* -**lat′ed**, -**lat′ing** to divide (an area) into triangles in order to determine distance or relative positions —**tri·an′gu·la′tion** *n.*

**tri·ath·lon** (trī ath′län′, -lən) *n.* [TRI- + Gr *athlon*, a contest] an endurance race combining events in swimming, bicycling, and running

**tribe** (trīb) *n.* ⟦< L *tribus*⟧ 1 a group of persons or clans descended from a common ancestor and living under a leader or chief 2 a natural group of related plants or animals —**trib′al** *adj.* —**trib′al·ly** *adv.* —**tribes′man** (-mən), *pl.* -**men**, *n.*

**trib·u·la·tion** (trib′yə lā′shən) *n.* ⟦< L *tribulare*, to press⟧ great misery or distress, or the cause of it

**tri·bu·nal** (trī byoo′nəl, tri-) *n.* [see fol.] 1 a seat for a judge in a court 2 a court of justice

**trib·une** (trib′yoon′; *for 2, often* tri byoon′) *n.* ⟦< L *tribus*, tribe⟧ 1 in ancient Rome, a magistrate appointed to protect the rights of plebeians 2 a champion of the people: often used in newspaper names

**trib·u·tar·y** (trib′yoo ter′ē) *adj.* 1 paying tribute 2 subject [a *tributary* nation] 3 flowing into a larger one [a *tributary* stream] —*n.*, *pl.* -**ies** 1 a tributary nation 2 a tributary river

**trib·ute** (trib′yoot) *n.* ⟦< L *tribuere*, allot⟧ 1

money paid regularly by one nation to another as acknowledgment of subjugation, for protection, etc. 2 any forced payment 3 something given, done, or said to show gratitude, honor, or praise

**trice** (trīs) *n.* ⟦< MDu *trisen*, to pull⟧ an instant; moment: now only in **in a trice**

**tri·cen·ten·ni·al** (trī′sen ten′ē əl) *adj.* happening once every 300 years —*n.* a 300th anniversary

**tri·ceps** (trī′seps′) *n.*, *pl.* -**ceps′** or -**ceps′es** ⟦L < *tri-*, three + *caput*, head⟧ a muscle with three points of origin, esp. the muscle on the back of the upper arm

**tri·cer·a·tops** (trī ser′ə täps′) *n.* ⟦< TRI- + Gr *keras*, horn + *ōps*, eye⟧ a plant-eating dinosaur with three horns

**tri·chi·na** (tri kī′nə) *n.*, *pl.* -**nae** (-nē) ⟦< Gr *trichinos*, hairy⟧ a very small worm that causes trichinosis

**trich·i·no·sis** (trik′i nō′sis) *n.* ⟦< Gr *trichinos*, hairy⟧ a disease caused by intestinal worms, and acquired by eating insufficiently cooked pork from an infested hog

**trick** (trik) *n.* ⟦< OFr *trichier*, to cheat⟧ 1 something designed to deceive, cheat, etc. 2 a practical joke; prank 3 a clever act intended to amuse 4 any feat requiring skill 5 a personal mannerism 6 a round of duty; shift 7 *Card Games* the cards won in a single round —*vt.* to deceive or swindle —*adj.* apt to malfunction [a *trick* knee] —**do** (or **turn**) **the trick** [Inf.] to produce the desired result —**trick′er·y**, *pl.* -**ies**, *n.*

**trick·le** (trik′əl) *vi.* -**led**, -**ling** ⟦ME *triklen* < ?⟧ 1 to flow slowly in a thin stream or fall in drops 2 to move slowly [the crowd *trickled* away] —*n.* a slow, small flow

**trick′le·down′** *adj.* of an economic theory holding that government aid to the largest businesses will ultimately benefit the poor

**trick′ster** (-stər) *n.* a person who tricks; cheat

**trick′y** *adj.* -i·er, -i·est 1 given to or characterized by trickery 2 like a trick in deceptiveness or intricacy

**tri·col·or** (trī′kul′ər) *n.* a flag having three colors in large areas; esp., the flag of France

**tri·cy·cle** (trī′sə kəl) *n.* ⟦Fr: see TRI- & CYCLE⟧ a child's three-wheeled vehicle operated by pedals

**tri·dent** (trīd′'nt) *n.* ⟦< L *tri-*, three + *dens*, tooth⟧ a three-pronged spear

**tried** (trīd) *vt.*, *vi. pt. & pp. of* TRY —*adj.* 1 tested; proved 2 trustworthy

**tri·en·ni·al** (trī en′ē əl) *adj.* ⟦< L *tri-*, three + *annus*, year⟧ 1 happening every three years 2 lasting three years —**tri·en′ni·al·ly** *adv.*

**Tri·este** (trē est′) seaport in NE Italy: pop. 228,000

**tri·fle** (trī′fəl) *n.* ⟦< OFr *truffe*, deception⟧ 1 something of little value or importance 2 a small amount of money —*vi.* -**fled**, -**fling** 1 to talk or act jokingly 2 to toy (*with*) —*vt.* to waste [to *trifle* the hours away] —**tri′fler** *n.*

**tri′fling** (-fliŋ) *adj.* 1 frivolous; shallow 2 of little importance; trivial

**tri·fo·cals** (trī′fō′kəlz) *pl.n.* eyeglasses like bifocals, but with a third area in the lens ground for viewing objects at an intermediate distance

**trig** (trig) *n. short for* TRIGONOMETRY

**trig·ger** (trig′ər) *n.* ⟦< Du *trekken*, to pull⟧ a lever pulled to release a catch, etc., esp. one pressed to activate the firing mechanism on a firearm —*vt.* to initiate (an action)

**trig′ger-hap′py** *adj.* 1 tending to resort to force rashly or irresponsibly 2 ready to start a war for the slightest cause

**tri·glyc·er·ide** (trī glis′ər īd′) *n.* [TRI- + Gr *glykeros*, sweet] an ester derived from glycerol: the chief component of fats and oils

**trig·o·nom·e·try** (trig′ə näm′ə trē) *n.* ⟦< Gr *trigōnon*, triangle + *-metria*, measurement⟧ the branch of mathematics analyzing, and making calculations from, relations between the sides of right triangles with reference to their angles —**trig′o·no·met′ric** (-nə me′trik) *adj.*

**trill** (tril) *n.* [ult. echoic] **1** a rapid alternation of a musical tone with a slightly higher tone **2** a warble **3** a rapid vibration of the tongue or uvula — *vt., vi.* to sound, speak, or play with a trill

**tril·lion** (tril'yən) *n.* **1** 1 followed by 12 zeros **2** [Brit.] 1 followed by 18 zeros —**tril'lionth** *adj., n.*

**tril·li·um** (tril'ē əm) *n.* [ModL < L *tri-*, three] a woodland plant having a single flower with three petals and three sepals

**tril·o·gy** (tril'ə jē) *n., pl.* **-gies** [see TRI- & -LOGY] a set of three related plays, novels, etc.

**trim** (trim) *vt.* **trimmed, trim'ming** [< OE *trymman*, make firm] **1** to put in proper order; make neat or tidy [to trim hair] **2** to clip, lop, cut, etc. **3** to decorate, as by adding ornaments, etc. **4** *a)* to balance (a ship) by ballasting, etc. *b)* to put (sails) in order for sailing **5** to balance (a flying aircraft) **6** [Inf.] to beat, punish, defeat, cheat, etc. —*vi.* to adjust according to expediency —*n.* **1** order; arrangement **2** good condition **3** a trimming, as by clipping **4** decorative parts or borders —*adj.* **trim'mer, trim'mest 1** orderly; neat **2** well-proportioned **3** in good condition — **trim'ly** *adv.* —**trim'mer** *n.* —**trim'ness** *n.*

**tri·ma·ran** (trī'mə ran') *n.* a boat like a catamaran, but with three parallel hulls

**tri·mes·ter** (trī mes'tər, trī'mes'-) *n.* [< L *tri-*, three + *mensis*, month] **1** a three-month period, as of pregnancy **2** in some colleges, any of the three periods of the academic year

**trim·ming** (trim'iŋ) *n.* **1** decoration; ornament **2** [*pl.*] *a)* the side dishes of a meal *b)* parts trimmed off **3** [Inf.] a beating, defeat, cheating, etc.

**Trin·i·dad and To·ba·go** (trin'i dad' and tə bā'gō) island country in the West Indies: 1,980 sq. mi.; pop. 1,260,000

**trin·i·ty** (trin'i tē) *n., pl.* **-ties** [< L *trinitas*] a set of three —**the Trinity** *Christian Theol.* the union of Father, Son, and Holy Spirit in one Godhead

**trin·ket** (triŋ'kit) *n.* [ME *trenket*] **1** a small, cheap ornament, piece of jewelry, etc. **2** a trifle or toy

**tri·o** (trē'ō) *n., pl.* **-os** [< L *tres*, three] **1** a group of three **2** *Music a)* a composition for three voices or three instruments *b)* the three performers of such a composition

**trip** (trip) *vi., vt.* **tripped, trip'ping** [< OFr *treper*] **1** to move or perform with light, rapid steps; skip **2** to stumble or cause to stumble **3** to make or cause to make a mistake **4** to run past or release (a spring, wheel, etc.) —*n.* **1** a light, quick tread **2** a journey, jaunt, etc. **3** a stumble or a causing to stumble **4** [Slang] *a)* an experience induced by a psychedelic drug, esp. LSD *b)* an experience that is pleasing, exciting, etc. —**trip up** to catch in a lie, error, etc. —**trip'per** *n.*

**tri·par·tite** (trī pär'tīt') *adj.* [< L *tri-*, three + *partire*, to part] **1** having three parts **2** made between three parties, as an agreement

**tripe** (trīp) *n.* [prob. ult. < Ar *tharb*, layer of fat lining the intestines] **1** part of the stomach of an ox, etc., used as food **2** [Slang] anything worthless, etc.; nonsense

**trip'ham'mer** *n.* a heavy, power-driven hammer, alternately raised and allowed to fall by a tripping device: also **trip hammer**

**tri·ple** (trip'əl) *adj.* [< L *triplus*] **1** consisting of three; threefold **2** three times as much or as many —*n.* **1** an amount three times as much or as many **2** *Baseball* a hit on which the batter reaches third base —*vt., vi.* **tri'pled, tri'pling 1** to make or become three times as much or as many **2** *Baseball* to hit a triple —**tri'ply** *adv.*

TRILLIUM

**tri·plet** (trip'lit) *n.* **1** a group of three, as three successive lines of poetry **2** any of three offspring from the same pregnancy

**trip·li·cate** (trip'li kit; *for v.,* -kāt') *adj.* [< L *triplex*] **1** threefold **2** being the last of three identical copies —*n.* any one of such copies —*vt.* **-cat'ed, -cat'ing** to make three identical copies of —**in triplicate** in three identical copies

**tri·pod** (trī'päd') *n.* [< Gr *tri-*, three + *pous*, foot] a three-legged caldron, stool, support, etc.

**trip·tych** (trip'tik) *n.* [< Gr *tri-*, three + *ptychē*, a fold] a set of three hinged panels with pictures, etc., commonly placed above and behind an altar

**tri·sect** (trī sekt', trī'sekt') *vt.* [< TRI- + L *secare*, to cut] to cut or divide into three equal parts

**trite** (trīt) *adj.* **trit'er, trit'est** [< L *terere*, wear out] worn out by constant use; stale —**trite'ness** *n.*

**trit·i·um** (trit'ē əm) *n.* a radioactive isotope of hydrogen having an atomic weight of 3

**tri·umph** (trī'əmf) *n.* [< L *triumphus*] **1** a victory; success **2** exultation or joy over a victory, etc. — *vi.* **1** to gain victory or success **2** to rejoice over victory, etc. —**tri·um'phal** (-um'fəl) *adj.*

**tri·um'phal·ism'** *n.* an arrogant confidence in a set of beliefs —**tri·um'phal·ist** *adj., n.*

**tri·um'phant** (-fənt) *adj.* **1** successful; victorious **2** rejoicing for victory —**tri·um'phant·ly** *adv.*

**tri·um·vir** (trī um'vir') *n., pl.* **-virs'** or **-vi·ri'** (-vi rī') [L: see fol.] in ancient Rome, any of three administrators sharing authority

**tri·um·vi·rate** (trī um'və rit) *n.* [< L *trium virum*, of three men] government by three persons or parties

**tri·va·lent** (trī vā'lənt) *adj. Chem.* having three valences or a valence of three

**triv·et** (triv'it) *n.* [< L *tripes*, tripod] **1** a three-legged stand for holding pots, etc. near a fire **2** a short-legged stand for hot dishes to rest on

**triv·i·a** (triv'ē ə) *pl.n.* [*usually with sing. v.*] unimportant matters

**triv·i·al** (triv'ē əl) *adj.* [< L *trivialis*, commonplace] unimportant; insignificant —**triv·i·al'i·ty** (-al'ə tē) *n.*

**triv'i·al·ize'** (-īz') *vt.* **-ized', -iz'ing** to regard or treat as trivial; make seem unimportant

**-trix** (triks) [L] *suffix* forming feminine nouns of agency

**tro·chee** (trō'kē) *n.* [< Gr *trechein*, to run] a metrical foot of one accented syllable followed by one unaccented syllable —**tro·cha·ic** (-kā'ik) *adj.*

**trod** (träd) *vt., vi. pt. & alt. pp. of* TREAD

**trod·den** (träd''n) *vt., vi. alt. pp. of* TREAD

**trog·lo·dyte** (träg'lə dīt') *n.* [< Gr *trōglē*, hole + *dyein*, enter] **1** any of the prehistoric people who lived in caves **2** a recluse

**troi·ka** (troi'kə) *n.* [Russ] **1** a vehicle drawn by three horses abreast **2** an association of three in authority

**Tro·jan** (trō'jən) *adj.* of ancient Troy or its people or culture —*n.* **1** a person born or living in ancient Troy **2** a strong, hard-working, determined person

**Trojan horse 1** *Gr. Legend* a huge, hollow wooden horse with Greek soldiers inside: it is brought into Troy, the soldiers creep out and open the gates, and the Greek army destroys the city **2** one that subverts a nation, etc. from within

**troll**[1] (trōl) *vt., vi.* [ME *trollen*, to roll] **1** to sing the parts of (a round, etc.) in succession **2** to sing in a full voice **3** to fish (in) with a baited line trailed behind a slowly moving boat —**troll'er** *n.*

**troll**[2] (trōl) *n.* [ON] *Scand. Folklore* a supernatural being, as a giant or dwarf, living in a cave

**trol·ley** (trä'lē) *n., pl.* **-leys** [< TROLL[1]] **1** a wheeled basket, etc. that runs suspended from an overhead track **2** a grooved wheel at the end of a pole, for transmitting electric current from an overhead wire to a streetcar, etc. **3** a trolley car

**trolley bus** an electric bus powered by trolleys

**trolley car** an electric streetcar that gets its power from a trolley

**trol·lop** (trä′ləp) *n.* 〖prob. < Ger *trolle,* wench〗 a prostitute

**trom·bone** (träm bōn′) *n.* 〖It < *tromba,* a trumpet〗 a large brass instrument, usually with a slide, or movable section —**trom·bon′ist** *n.*

**troop** (trōōp) *n.* 〖< ML *troppus,* flock〗 **1** a group of persons or animals **2** [*pl.*] soldiers **3** a subdivision of a cavalry regiment **4** a unit of Boy Scouts or Girl Scouts —*vi.* **1** to gather or go together in a group **2** to walk or go

**troop′er** *n.* 〖prec. + -ER〗 **1** a soldier in the mounted cavalry **2** a mounted police officer **3** in the U.S., a state police officer

TROMBONE

**trope** (trōp) *n.* 〖< Gr *tropos,* a turning〗 figurative language or a word used in a figurative sense

**tro·phy** (trō′fē) *n., pl.* **-phies** 〖< Gr *tropaion*〗 a memorial of victory in war, sports competition, etc.; prize

**trop·ic** (träp′ik) *n.* 〖< Gr *tropikos,* of a turn (of the sun at the solstices)〗 **1** either of two parallels of latitude, one, the **Tropic of Cancer,** *c.* 23° 26′ north, and the other, the **Tropic of Capricorn,** *c.* 23° 26′ south **2** [*also* T-] [*pl.*] the region between these latitudes —*adj.* of the tropics; tropical

**trop′i·cal** (-i kəl) *adj.* **1** of, in, characteristic of, or suitable for the tropics **2** very hot; sultry; torrid

**tro·pism** (trō′piz′əm) *n.* 〖< Gr *tropē,* a turn〗 the tendency of a plant or animal to grow or turn toward, or away from, a stimulus, as light

**tro·po·sphere** (trō′pə sfir′, träp′ə-) *n.* 〖Fr < Gr *tropos,* a turning + Fr *sphère,* sphere〗 the atmospheric zone characterized by water vapor, weather, and decreasing temperatures with increasing altitude

**trot** (trät) *vt., vi.* **trot′ted, trot′ting** 〖< OHG *trottōn,* to tread〗 **1** to move, ride, go, etc. at a trot **2** to hurry; run —*n.* **1** a gait, as of a horse, in which a front leg and the opposite hind leg are lifted at the same time **2** a jogging gait of a person —**trot′ter** *n.*

**troth** (trôth, trōth) *n.* 〖ME *trouthe*〗 [Archaic] **1** faithfulness; loyalty **2** truth **3** a promise, esp. to marry

**trou·ba·dour** (trōō′bə dôr′) *n.* 〖Fr < Prov *trobar,* compose〗 **1** any of a class of lyric poets and poet-musicians in S France and N Spain and Italy in the 11th to 13th c. **2** a minstrel or singer

**trou·ble** (trub′əl) *vt.* **-bled, -bling** 〖< L *turba,* crowd〗 **1** to disturb or agitate **2** to worry; harass **3** to cause inconvenience to [don't *trouble* yourself] —*vi.* to take pains; bother —*n.* **1** a state of mental distress; worry **2** a misfortune; calamity **3** a person, event, etc. causing annoyance, distress, etc. **4** public disturbance **5** effort; bother [take the *trouble* to listen]

**trou′ble·mak′er** *n.* one who incites others to quarrel, rebel, etc.

**trou′ble·shoot′er** *n.* one whose work is to locate and fix breakdowns, eliminate the source of trouble in work flow, etc. —**trou′ble·shoot′ing** *n.*

**trou′ble·some** (-səm) *adj.* characterized by or causing trouble

**trough** (trôf, träf) *n.* 〖OE *trog*〗 **1** a long, narrow, open container, esp. one to hold water or food for animals **2** a channel or gutter for carrying off rainwater **3** a long, narrow hollow, as between waves **4** a low in an economic cycle **5** a long, narrow area of low barometric pressure

**trounce** (trouns) *vt.* **trounced, trounc′ing** 〖< ?〗 **1** to beat; flog **2** [Inf.] to defeat —**trounc′er** *n.*

**troupe** (trōōp) *n.* 〖Fr〗 a group of actors, singers, etc. —*vi.* **trouped, troup′ing** to travel as a member of a troupe

**troup′er** *n.* **1** a troupe member **2** [Inf.] one who is steady, dependable, etc., during trying times

**trou·sers** (trou′zərz) *pl.n.* 〖< Gael *triubhas*〗 a two-legged outer garment, esp. for men and boys, extending from the waist to the ankles

**trous·seau** (trōō sō′, trōō′sō) *n., pl.* **-seaux** (-sōz′) *or* **-seaus′** 〖Fr < OFr *trousse,* a bundle〗 a bride's clothes, linens, etc.

**trout** (trout) *n., pl.* **trout** *or* **trouts** 〖< Gr *trōgein,* gnaw〗 a food and game fish, related to the salmon, found chiefly in fresh water

**trow** (trō, trou) *vi., vt.* 〖< OE *treow,* faith〗 [Archaic] to believe

**trow·el** (trou′əl) *n.* 〖< L *trua,* ladle〗 **1** a flat hand tool for smoothing plaster or applying mortar **2** a scooplike tool for loosening soil, etc. —*vt.* **-eled** *or* **-elled, -el·ing** *or* **-el·ling** to spread, smooth, dig, etc. with a trowel

**troy** (troi) *adj.* 〖after *Troyes,* city in France, where first used〗 of or by a system of weights (**troy weight**) for gold, silver, gems, etc.

**Troy** (troi) ancient city in NW Asia Minor

**tru·ant** (trōō′ənt) *n.* 〖< OFr, beggar〗 **1** a pupil who stays away from school without permission **2** one who neglects duties —*adj.* **1** that is a truant **2** errant; straying —**tru′an·cy,** *pl.* **-cies,** *n.*

**truce** (trōōs) *n.* 〖< OE *treow,* faith〗 **1** a temporary cessation of warfare by agreement between the belligerents **2** respite from conflict, trouble, etc.

**truck**[1] (truk) *n.* 〖< Gr *trochos,* wheel〗 **1** a two-wheeled barrow or low, wheeled frame for carrying heavy articles **2** an automotive vehicle for hauling loads **3** a swiveling, wheeled frame under each end of a railroad car, etc. —*vt.* to carry on a truck —*vi.* to drive a truck —**truck′er** *n.*

**truck**[2] (truk) *vt., vi.* 〖< Fr *troquer*〗 to exchange; barter —*n.* **1** small articles of little value **2** vegetables raised for market **3** [Inf.] dealings **4** [Inf.] trash; rubbish

**truck farm** a farm where vegetables are grown to be marketed

**truck·le** (truk′əl) *n.* 〖< Gr *trochos,* wheel〗 TRUNDLE BED: in full **truckle bed** —*vi.* **-led, -ling** to be servile; submit (*to*)

**truc·u·lent** (truk′yōō lənt, -yə-) *adj.* 〖< L *trux*〗 **1** fierce; cruel; savage **2** pugnacious —**truc′u·lence** *n.* —**truc′u·lent·ly** *adv.*

**trudge** (truj) *vi.* **trudged, trudg′ing** 〖< ?〗 to walk, esp. wearily or laboriously —*n.* a wearying walk

**true** (trōō) *adj.* **tru′er, tru′est** 〖OE *treowe*〗 **1** faithful; loyal **2** in accordance with fact; not false **3** conforming to standard, etc.; correct **4** rightful; lawful **5** accurately fitted, shaped, etc. **6** real; genuine —*adv.* **1** truly **2** *Biol.* without variation from type —*vt.* **trued, tru′ing** *or* **true′ing** to fit, place, or shape accurately: often with *up* —*n.* that which is true: with *the*

**true believer** a dedicated follower or disciple, esp. one who follows without doubts or questions

**true bill** a bill of indictment endorsed by a grand jury

**true′-blue′** *adj.* very loyal; staunch

**truf·fle** (truf′əl) *n.* 〖ult. < L *tuber,* knob〗 a fleshy, edible underground fungus

**tru·ism** (trōō′iz′əm) *n.* a statement the truth of which is obvious

**tru·ly** *adv.* **1** in a true manner; accurately, genuinely, etc. **2** really; indeed **3** sincerely

**Tru·man** (trōō′mən), **Har·ry S** (har′ē) 1884-1972; 33d president of the U.S. (1945-53)

**trump** (trump) *n.* 〖< TRIUMPH〗 **1** any playing card of a suit ranked higher than any other suit for a given hand **2** such a suit **3** any advantage held in reserve —*vt., vi.* to play a trump on (a trick, etc.) —**trump up** to devise fraudulently

**trump·er·y** (trump′ər ē) *n., pl.* **-ies** 〖< Fr *tromper,* deceive‖ **1** something showy but worthless **2** nonsense

**trum·pet** (trum'pit) *n.* ⟦< OFr *trompe*⟧ **1** a brass instrument consisting of a looped tube with a flared bell and three valves **2** a trumpetlike device for channeling sound, as an early kind of hearing aid **3** a sound like that of a trumpet —*vi.* to make the sound of a trumpet —*vt.* to proclaim loudly —**trum'pet·er** *n.*

**trun·cate** (trun'kāt') *vt.* -**cat'ed**, -**cat'ing** ⟦< L *truncus*, stem⟧ to cut off a part of —**trun·ca'tion** *n.*

**trun·cheon** (trun'chən) *n.* ⟦< L *truncus*, stem⟧ [Chiefly Brit.] a policeman's stick or billy

**trun·dle** (trun'dəl) *vt.*, *vi.* -**dled**, -**dling** ⟦< OE *trendan*, to roll⟧ to roll along —**trun'dler** *n.*

**trundle bed** a low bed on small wheels, that can be rolled under another bed when not in use

**trunk** (truŋk) *n.* ⟦< L *truncus*⟧ **1** the main stem of a tree **2** a human or animal body, not including the head and limbs **3** a long snout, as of an elephant **4** a large, reinforced box to hold clothes, etc. in travel **5** [*pl.*] shorts worn by men for athletics **6** a compartment in a car, usually in the rear, for luggage, etc.

**trunk line** a main line of a railroad, telephone system, etc.

**truss** (trus) *vt.* ⟦< OFr *trousser*⟧ **1** to tie, bind, or bundle: often with *up* **2** to support with a truss —*n.* **1** a bundle or pack **2** a framework for supporting a roof, bridge, etc. **3** a padded device for giving support in cases of rupture or hernia

**trust** (trust) *n.* ⟦< ON *traust*⟧ **1** *a*) firm belief in the honesty, reliability, etc. of another; faith *b*) the one trusted **2** confident expectation, hope, etc. **3** responsibility resulting from confidence placed in one **4** care; custody **5** something entrusted to one **6** faith in a buyer's ability to pay; credit **7** a combination of corporations to establish a monopoly **8** *Law a*) the fact of having nominal ownership of property to keep, use, or administer for another *b*) such property —*vi.* to be confident —*vt.* **1** to have confidence in **2** to commit (something) *to* a person's care **3** to allow to do something without misgivings **4** to believe **5** to hope; expect **6** to grant business credit to —*adj.* **1** relating to a trust **2** acting as trustee —**in trust** entrusted to another's care

**trust·ee** (trus tē') *n.* **1** one to whom another's property or its management is entrusted **2** a member of a board managing the affairs of a college, hospital, etc. —**trust·ee'ship** *n.*

**trust'ful** *adj.* full of trust; ready to confide; trusting —**trust'ful·ly** *adv.* —**trust'ful·ness** *n.*

**trust fund** money, securities, etc. held in trust

**trust'ing** *adj.* that trusts; trustful

**trust territory** a territory placed under the administrative authority of a country by the United Nations

**trust'wor'thy** *adj.* -**thi·er**, -**thi·est** worthy of trust; reliable —**trust'wor'thi·ness** *n.*

**trust'y** *adj.* -**i·er**, -**i·est** dependable; trustworthy —*n.*, *pl.* -**ies** a convict granted special privileges as a trustworthy person

**truth** (trōōth) *n.*, *pl.* **truths** (trōō*th*z, trōōths) ⟦OE *treowth*⟧ **1** a being true; specif., *a*) sincerity; honesty *b*) conformity with fact *c*) reality; actual existence *d*) correctness; accuracy **2** that which is true **3** an established fact —**in truth** truly

**truth'ful** *adj.* **1** telling the truth; honest **2** corresponding with fact or reality —**truth'ful·ly** *adv.* —**truth'ful·ness** *n.*

**try** (trī) *vt.* **tried**, **try'ing** ⟦< OFr *trier*⟧ **1** to melt out or render (fat, etc.) **2** to conduct the trial of in a law court **3** to put to the proof; test **4** to subject to trials, etc.; afflict **5** to experiment with [to *try* a recipe] **6** to attempt; endeavor —*vi.* to make an effort, attempt, etc. —*n.*, *pl.* **tries** an attempt; effort; trial —**try on** to test the fit of (something to wear) by putting it on —**try out** **1** to test by putting into use **2** to test one's fitness, as for a place on a team

**try'ing** *adj.* that tries one's patience; annoying; irksome —**try'ing·ly** *adv.*

**try'out'** *n.* [Inf.] a test to determine fitness, etc.

**tryst** (trist) *n.* ⟦< OFr *triste*, hunting station⟧ **1** an appointment to meet, esp. one made by lovers **2** an appointed meeting or meeting place

**tsar** (tsär, zär) *n. alt. sp. of* CZAR (sense 1) —**tsa·ri·na** (tsä rē'nə, zä-) *fem.n.*

**tset·se fly** (tset'sē, tsēt'-) ⟦< Bantu name⟧ a small fly of central and S Africa: one kind carries sleeping sickness

**T'-shirt** *n.* a collarless pullover knit shirt with short sleeves: also **t'-shirt'**

**tsp** *abbrev.* **1** teaspoon(s) **2** teaspoonful(s)

**T square** a T-shaped ruler for drawing parallel lines

**tsu·na·mi** (tsōō nä'mē) *n.*, *pl.* -**mis** or -**mi** ⟦Jpn < *tsu*, a harbor + *nami*, a wave⟧ a huge sea wave caused by an undersea earthquake, volcanic eruption, etc.

**tub** (tub) *n.* ⟦< MDu *tubbe*⟧ **1** a round, wooden container, usually with staves and hoops **2** any large, open container, as of metal **3** a bathtub

**tu·ba** (tōō'bə) *n.* ⟦L, trumpet⟧ a large, low-pitched brass musical instrument

**tub·al** (tōō'bəl) *adj.* of or in a tube, esp. a fallopian tube [a *tubal* pregnancy]

TUBA

**tub·by** (tub'ē) *adj.* -**bi·er**, -**bi·est** **1** shaped like a tub **2** fat and short

**tube** (tōōb) *n.* ⟦< L *tubus*, pipe⟧ **1** a slender pipe of metal, glass, etc. for conveying fluids **2** a tubelike part, organ, etc. **3** a pliable cylinder with a screw cap, for holding paste, etc. **4** *short for:* *a*) ELECTRON TUBE *b*) VACUUM TUBE **5** [Brit.] a subway —**the tube** [Inf.] television —**tube'less** *adj.*

**tu·ber** (tōō'bər) *n.* ⟦L, lit., a swelling⟧ a short, thick part of an underground stem, as a potato —**tu'ber·ous** *adj.*

**tu'ber·cle** (-kəl) *n.* ⟦see prec.⟧ **1** a small, rounded projection, as on a bone or a plant root **2** any abnormal hard nodule or swelling; specif., the typical lesion of tuberculosis

**tu·ber·cu·lin** (tōō bur'kyə lin) *n.* a solution injected into the skin as a test for tuberculosis

**tu·ber·cu·lo'sis** (-lō'sis) *n.* ⟦see TUBERCLE & -OSIS⟧ an infectious disease characterized by the formation of tubercles in body tissue; specif., tuberculosis of the lungs —**tu·ber'cu·lar** or **tu·ber'cu·lous** *adj.*

**tube sock** a stretchable sock in the form of a long tube with no shaped heel

**tube top** a tight-fitting, one-piece, sleeveless and strapless women's garment for the upper body

**tub·ing** (tōō'biŋ) *n.* **1** a series or system of tubes **2** material in the form of a tube **3** a piece of tube

**tu·bu·lar** (tōō'byə lər) *adj.* ⟦< L *tubus*, pipe⟧ **1** of or like a tube **2** made with a tube or tubes

**tu'bule'** (-byōōl') *n.* a small tube

**tuck** (tuk) *vt.* ⟦< MDu *tucken*⟧ **1** to pull or gather (*up*) in a fold or folds **2** to sew a fold or folds in (a garment) **3** to fold the edges of (a sheet, etc.) under or in, to make secure **4** to press snugly into a small space —*n.* **1** a sewed fold in a garment **2** [Inf.] cosmetic plastic surgery to remove fat

**tuck·er** (tuk'ər) *vt.* ⟦prob. < prec., in obs. sense "to punish, rebuke"⟧ [Inf.] to tire (*out*); weary

**Tuc·son** (tōō'sän') city in S Arizona: pop. 405,000

**-tude** (tōōd, tyōōd) ⟦< L *-tudo*⟧ *suffix* state, quality, or instance of being

**Tues·day** (tōōz'dā) *n.* ⟦OE *Tiwes dæg*, day of the god of war *Tiu*⟧ the third day of the week: abbrev. **Tue, Tues**

**tuft** (tuft) *n.* ⟦< OFr *tufe*⟧ **1** a bunch of hairs, grass, etc. growing closely together **2** any cluster, as the fluffy ball forming the end of a cluster of threads drawn through a mattress —*vt.* **1** to provide with tufts **2** to secure the padding of (a mattress, etc.) with tufts —**tuft′ed** *adj.* —**tuft′er** *n.*

**tug** (tug) *vi., vt.* **tugged**, **tug′ging** ⟦prob. < ON *toga*, to pull⟧ **1** to pull hard; drag; haul **2** to tow with a tugboat —*n.* **1** a hard pull **2** a tugboat

**tug·boat** (tug′bōt′) *n.* a sturdy, powerful boat for towing or pushing ships, barges, etc.

**tug of war 1** a contest in which two teams pull at opposite ends of a rope **2** a power struggle

**tu·i·tion** (tōō ish′ən) *n.* ⟦< L *tueri*, protect⟧ the charge for instruction, as at a college

**tu·la·re·mi·a** (tōō′lə rē′mē ə) *n.* ⟦after *Tulare* County, CA⟧ an infectious disease of rodents, esp. rabbits, transmissible to humans

**tu·lip** (tōō′lip) *n.* ⟦< Turk *tülbend*, turban: from its shape⟧ **1** a bulb plant with a large, cup-shaped flower **2** the flower

**tulle** (tōōl) *n.* ⟦after *Tulle*, city in France⟧ a fine netting of silk, rayon, nylon, etc., used as for veils and scarves

**Tul·sa** (tul′sə) city in NE Oklahoma: pop. 367,000

**tum·ble** (tum′bəl) *vi.* **-bled**, **-bling** ⟦< OE *tumbian*, to jump⟧ **1** to do somersaults or similar acrobatic feats **2** to fall suddenly or helplessly **3** to toss or roll about **4** to move in a hasty, disorderly manner —*vt.* **1** to cause to tumble **2** to put into disorder; disarrange —*n.* **1** a fall **2** disorder

**tum·ble·down′** *adj.* dilapidated

**tum·bler** (-blər) *n.* **1** an acrobat who does somersaults, etc. **2** a drinking glass **3** a part of a lock whose position must be changed by a key in order to release the bolt

**tum·ble·weed′** *n.* a plant that breaks off near the ground in autumn and is blown about by the wind

**tum·brel** or **tum·bril** (tum′brəl) *n.* ⟦< Fr *tomber*, to fall⟧ a cart that can be tilted for emptying

**tu·mes·cence** (tōō mes′əns) *n.* ⟦see fol.⟧ **1** a swelling; distention **2** a swollen or distended part —**tu·mes′cent** *adj.*

**tu·mid** (tōō′mid) *adj.* ⟦< L *tumere*, to swell⟧ **1** swollen; bulging **2** inflated or pompous —**tu·mid′i·ty** *n.*

**tum·my** (tum′ē) *n., pl.* **-mies** [Inf.] the stomach or abdomen

**tu·mor** (tōō′mər) *n.* ⟦L, a swelling⟧ an abnormal growth of new tissue, independent of its surrounding structures; neoplasm: Brit. sp. **tu′mour**

**tu·mult** (tōō′mult′) *n.* ⟦< L *tumere*, to swell⟧ **1** noisy commotion **2** confusion; disturbance

**tu·mul·tu·ous** (tōō mul′chōō əs) *adj.* full of tumult, uproar, etc.

**tun** (tun) *n.* ⟦OE *tunne*⟧ a large cask

**tu·na** (tōō′nə) *n., pl.* **-na** or **-nas** ⟦AmSp⟧ **1** a large, edible ocean fish, as the albacore **2** the flesh of the tuna, canned for food: also **tuna fish**

**tun·dra** (tun′drə) *n.* ⟦Russ⟧ a vast, treeless arctic plain

**tune** (tōōn) *n.* ⟦ME, var. of *tone*, tone⟧ **1** a rhythmic succession of musical tones; melody **2** *a)* correct musical pitch *b)* agreement; concord: now used chiefly in the phrases **in tune** and **out of tune** —*vt.* **tuned**, **tun′ing 1** to adjust (a musical instrument) to some standard of pitch **2** to adapt to some condition, mood, etc. **3** to adjust (a motor, circuit, etc.) for proper performance —**to the tune of** [Inf.] to the sum, price, or extent of —**tune in** to adjust a radio or TV receiver so as to receive (a station, etc.) —**tun′er** *n.*

**tune′ful** *adj.* full of music; melodious

**tune′less** *adj.* **1** not melodious **2** not producing music —**tune′less·ly** *adv.* —**tune′less·ness** *n.*

**tune′up′** or **tune′-up′** *n.* an adjusting, as of an engine, to the proper condition

**tung·sten** (tuŋ′stən) *n.* ⟦Swed < *tung*, heavy + *sten*, stone⟧ a hard, heavy metallic chemical element, used in steel, etc.

**tu·nic** (tōō′nik, tyōō′-) *n.* ⟦L *tunica*⟧ **1** a loose, gownlike garment worn by men and women in ancient Greece and Rome **2** a blouselike garment extending to the hips, often belted

**tuning fork** a two-pronged steel instrument which when struck sounds a certain fixed tone in perfect pitch

**Tu·nis** (tōō′nis) seaport & capital of Tunisia: pop. 674,000

**Tu·ni·si·a** (tōō nē′zhə) country in N Africa, on the Mediterranean: 63,378 sq. mi.; pop. 6,966,000 —**Tu·ni′si·an** *adj., n.*

**tun·nel** (tun′əl) *n.* ⟦< Fr *tonnelle*, a vault⟧ **1** an underground passageway, as for autos, etc. **2** any tunnel-like passage, as in a mine —*vt., vi.* **-neled** or **-nelled**, **-nel·ing** or **-nel·ling** to make a tunnel (through or under) —**tun′nel·er** or **tun′nel·ler** *n.*

**tunnel vision** a narrow outlook, as on a particular problem

**tun·ny** (tun′ē) *n., pl.* **-nies** TUNA (sense 1)

**tur·ban** (tur′bən) *n.* ⟦< Pers *dulbänd*⟧ **1** a headdress worn by men in parts of Asia, consisting of cloth wound in folds about the head **2** any similar headdress

**TURBAN**

**tur·bid** (tur′bid) *adj.* ⟦< L *turba*, a crowd⟧ **1** muddy or cloudy from stirring sediment **2** thick, dense, or dark, as clouds **3** confused

**tur·bine** (tur′bin, -bīn′) *n.* ⟦< L *turbo*, a whirl⟧ an engine driven as by the pressure of steam, water, or air against the curved vanes of a wheel

**tur·bo·charge** (tur′bō chärj′) *vt.* **-charged′**, **-charg′ing** to increase the power of (an engine) by the use of a type of compressor (**tur′bo·charg′er**) driven by a turbine powered by exhaust gases

**tur′bo·fan′** (-fan′) *n.* a turbojet engine developing extra thrust from air that bypasses the combustion chamber and is accelerated by a fan: in full **turbofan engine**

**tur′bo·jet′** (-jet′) *n.* **1** a jet engine in which the energy of the jet spins a turbine which drives the air compressor: in full **turbojet engine 2** an aircraft with such an engine

**tur′bo·prop′** (-präp′) *n.* **1** a turbojet engine whose turbine shaft drives a propeller: in full **turboprop engine 2** an aircraft with such an engine

**tur·bot** (tur′bət) *n., pl.* **-bot** or **-bots** ⟦< OFr *tourbout*⟧ any of various flounders highly regarded as food

**tur·bu·lent** (tur′byə lənt) *adj.* ⟦< L *turba*, a crowd⟧ **1** wild or disorderly **2** full of violent motion —**tur′bu·lence** *n.* —**tur′bu·lent·ly** *adv.*

**tu·reen** (too rēn′) *n.* ⟦< Fr *terrine*, earthen vessel⟧ a large, deep dish with a lid, for soups, etc.

**turf** (turf) *n.* ⟦OE⟧ **1** *a)* a top layer of earth containing grass with its roots; sod *b)* [Chiefly Brit.] a piece of this **2** peat **3** a track for horse racing; also, horse racing: usually with *the* **4** [Slang] *a)* an area seen by a street gang as its territory to be defended *b)* one's own territory —*vt.* to cover with turf —**turf′y** *adj.*

**tur·gid** (tur′jid) *adj.* ⟦< L *turgere*, to swell⟧ **1** swollen; distended **2** bombastic; pompous —**tur·gid′i·ty** or **tur′gid·ness** *n.* —**tur′gid·ly** *adv.*

**Tu·rin** (toor′in) city in NW Italy: pop. 953,000

**Turk**[1] (turk) *n.* a person born or living in Turkey

**Turk**[2] *abbrev.* **1** Turkey **2** Turkish

**tur·key** (tur′kē) *n.* ⟦< similarity to a fowl formerly imported through *Turkey*⟧ **1** a large North American bird with a spreading tail **2** its flesh, used as food

**Tur·key** (tur′kē) country occupying Asia Minor &

a SE part of the Balkan Peninsula: 300,947 sq. mi.; pop. 56,473,000

**turkey vulture** a dark-colored vulture of temperate and tropical America: also **turkey buzzard**

**Turk·ic** (tur′kik) *adj.* designating or of a family of languages including Turkish, Tatar, etc.

**Turk·ish** (tur′kish) *adj.* of Turkey or its people, language, etc. —*n.* the language of Turkey

**Turkish bath** a bathhouse with steam rooms, showers, massage, etc.

**Turk·men·i·stan** (tərk men′i stan′) country in central Asia: formerly a republic of the U.S.S.R.: 186,400 sq. mi.; pop. 3,523,000

**tur·mer·ic** (tur′mər ik) *n.* ⟦< ML *terra merita*, deserved earth⟧ an East Indian plant whose powdered root is used as a yellow dye or a seasoning

**tur·moil** (tur′moil) *n.* ⟦< ?⟧ tumult; commotion

**turn** (turn) *vt.* ⟦ult. < Gr *tornos*, a lathe⟧ **1** to rotate (a wheel, etc.) **2** to move around or partly around *[turn* the key*]* **3** to give form to, as in a lathe **4** to change the position or direction of **5** to reverse the position or sides of **6** to wrench *[turn* one's ankle*]* **7** to upset (the stomach) **8** to deflect; divert **9** to cause to change actions, beliefs, aims, etc. **10** to go around (a corner, etc.) **11** to reach or pass (a certain age, amount, etc.) **12** to drive, set, let go, etc. *[turn* the dog loose*]* **13** to direct, point, aim, etc. **14** to change *[to turn* cream into butter*]* **15** to make sour **16** to affect in some way —*vi.* **1** to rotate or revolve; pivot **2** to move around or partly around **3** to reel; whirl **4** to become upset: said of the stomach **5** to change or reverse course, direction, etc., or one's feelings, allegiance, etc. **6** to refer (*to*) **7** to apply (*to*) for help **8** to shift one's attention *[he turned* to music*]* **9** to make a sudden attack (*on*) **10** to be contingent or depend (*on* or *upon*) **11** to become *[to turn* cold*]* **12** to change to another form *[the* rain *turned* to snow*]* **13** to become rancid, sour, etc. —*n.* **1** a turning around; rotation; revolution **2** a single twist, winding, etc. **3** a change or reversal of course or direction **4** a short walk, ride, etc. **5** a bend; curve *[a turn* in the road*]* **6** a change in trend, events, etc. **7** a sudden shock or fright **8** an action or deed *[a good turn]* **9** the right, duty, or chance to do something in regular order *[my turn* to go*]* **10** a distinctive form, detail, etc. *[an odd turn* of speech*]* **11** natural inclination *[a curious turn* of mind*]* —**in** (or **out of**) **turn** (not) in proper sequence —**turn down** to reject (a request, etc.) —**turn in 1** to deliver; hand in **2** [Inf.] to go to bed —**turn off 1** to stop the flow of (water, gas, etc.) **2** to make (an electrical device) stop functioning **3** [Slang] to cause to be bored, depressed, etc. —**turn on 1** to start the flow of **2** to make (an electrical device) start functioning **3** [Slang] to make or become elated, enthusiastic, etc. —**turn out 1** to put out (a light, etc.) **2** to dismiss **3** to come out or assemble **4** to produce **5** to result **6** to prove to be **7** [Inf.] to get out of bed —**turn over 1** to ponder **2** to hand over; transfer —**turn up** to happen, appear, arrive, etc. —**turn′er** *n.*

**turn′a·bout′** *n.* a shift or reversal of position, allegiance, opinion, etc.

**turn′a·round′** *n.* **1** TURNABOUT **2** a wide area, as in a driveway, for turning a vehicle around

TURNBUCKLE

**turn′buck·le** (-buk′əl) *n.* an adjustable coupling for two rods, etc., consisting of a metal sleeve with opposite internal threads at each end

**turn′coat′** *n.* a renegade; traitor

**turn′ing** *n.* **1** the action of one that turns **2** a place where a road, etc. turns

**turning point** a point in time when a decisive change occurs

**tur·nip** (tur′nip) *n.* ⟦prob. < Fr *tour*, round + ME *nepe*, turnip⟧ **1** a plant related to cabbage and

broccoli, with a light-colored, roundish, edible root **2** the root

**turn′key** *n., pl.* **-keys** a jailer

**turn′off** *n.* **1** a turning off **2** a place to turn off, as a road ramp **3** [Slang] someone or something regarded as being boring, distasteful, etc.

**turn′-on** *n.* [Slang] someone or something regarded as being interesting, exciting, etc.

**turn′out** *n.* **1** a gathering of people, as for a meeting **2** a wider part of a narrow road, enabling vehicles to pass each other

**turn′o′ver** *n.* **1** a small pie with half the crust folded back over the other half **2** *a)* the number of times a stock of goods is sold and replaced in a given period *b)* the amount of business done during a given period **3** the rate of replacement of workers

**turn′pike′** (-pīk′) *n.* ⟦ME *turnpyke*, a spiked road barrier⟧ a toll road, esp. one that is an expressway

**turn′stile′** (-stīl′) *n.* a device, as a post with revolving horizontal bars, placed in an entrance to allow the passage of persons one at a time

**turn′ta′ble** *n.* a circular rotating platform, as for supporting a phonograph record being played

**tur·pen·tine** (tur′pən tīn′) *n.* ⟦< Gr *terebinthos*, tree yielding this substance⟧ a colorless, volatile oil distilled from a substance extracted from various coniferous trees: used in paints, etc.

**tur·pi·tude** (tur′pi tōōd′) *n.* ⟦< L *turpis*, vile⟧ baseness; vileness

**tur·quoise** (tur′koiz′, -kwoiz′) *n.* ⟦< OFr *turqueis*, Turkish⟧ **1** a greenish-blue semiprecious stone **2** its color

**tur·ret** (tur′it) *n.* ⟦see TOWER⟧ **1** a small tower projecting from a building, usually at a corner **2** a dome or revolving structure for guns, as on a warship, tank, or airplane **3** a rotating attachment for a lathe, etc. holding cutting tools

**tur·tle** (turt′l) *n.* ⟦< Fr *tortue*, tortoise⟧ any of various land or water reptiles having a soft body encased in a tough shell —**turn turtle** to turn upside down

**tur′tle·dove′** *n.* ⟦< L echoic *turtur*⟧ a wild dove with a plaintive call

**tur′tle·neck′** *n.* **1** a high, snug, turned-down collar, as on a pullover sweater **2** a sweater, etc. with such a collar

**tusk** (tusk) *n.* ⟦OE *tucs*⟧ a very long, large, pointed tooth projecting outside the mouth

**tus·sle** (tus′əl) *vi.* **-sled, -sling,** *n.* ⟦< ME *tusen*, to pull⟧ struggle; scuffle

**tus·sock** (tus′ək) *n.* ⟦< ?⟧ a thick tuft or clump of grass, sedge, etc.

**tu·te·lage** (tōōt′l ij) *n.* ⟦< L *tutela*, protection⟧ **1** guardianship; care, protection, etc. **2** instruction —**tu′te·lar′y** (-er′ē) *adj.*

TUTU

**tu·tor** (tōōt′ər) *n.* ⟦< L *tueri*, to guard⟧ a private teacher —*vt., vi.* to act as a tutor (to); teach —**tu·to·ri·al** (tōō tôr′ē əl, tyōō-) *adj., n.*

**tut·ti-frut·ti** (tōōt′ē frōōt′ē) *n.* ⟦It, all fruits⟧ ice cream, etc. made with mixed fruits

**tu·tu** (tōō′tōō′) *n.* ⟦Fr⟧ a very short, full, projecting skirt worn by ballerinas

**Tu·va·lu** (tōō′və lōō′) country on a group of islands in the WC Pacific, north of Fiji: 10 sq. mi.; pop. 10,000

**tux** (tuks) *n., pl.* **tux′es** *short for* TUXEDO

**tux·e·do** (tuk sē′dō) *n., pl.* **-dos** ⟦after a country club near *Tuxedo* Lake, NY⟧ a man's semiformal suit with a tailless jacket

**TV** *n.* **1** television **2** *pl.* **TVs** or **TV's** a television receiving set

**TVA** *abbrev.* Tennessee Valley Authority

**TV dinner** a frozen, precooked dinner packaged in a divided tray for heating and serving

**twad·dle** (twäd″'l) *n.* ⟦prob. var. of TATTLE⟧ foolish, empty talk or writing; nonsense

**twain** (twān) *adj., n.* ⟦OE *twegen,* two⟧ *archaic var. of* TWO

**Twain** (twān), **Mark** *pseud. for* Samuel Langhorne CLEMENS

**twang** (twaŋ) *n.* ⟦echoic⟧ **1** a sharp, vibrating sound, as of a plucked string **2** a sharply nasal way of speaking —*vi., vt.* to make or cause to make a twang —**twang′y, -i·er, -i·est,** *adj.*

**'twas** (twuz, twäz) *contr.* [Old Poet.] it was

**tweak** (twēk) *vt.* ⟦OE *twiccan,* to twitch⟧ **1** to give a twisting pinch to (someone's nose, ear, etc.) **2** to adjust slightly —*n.* such a pinch

**tweed** (twēd) *n.* ⟦< misreading of *tweel,* Scot form of TWILL⟧ **1** a rough wool fabric in a weave of two or more colors **2** [*pl.*] clothes in tweed

**tweed′y** *adj.* **-i·er, -i·est 1** of, like, or wearing tweeds **2** having an informal style, a fondness for the outdoors, etc.

**'tween** (twēn) *contr. prep.* ⟦ME *twene*⟧ [Old Poet.] between

**tweet** (twēt) *interj., n.* ⟦echoic⟧ (used to signify or imitate) the thin, chirping sound of a small bird —*vi.* to make this sound

**tweet′er** *n.* a small, high-fidelity speaker for reproducing high-frequency sounds

**tweez·ers** (twē′zərz) *pl.n.* ⟦< obs. *tweeze,* surgical set⟧ [*also with sing. v.*] a small tool having two arms joined at one end, for plucking out hairs, etc.

**twelfth** (twelfth) *adj.* ⟦OE *twelfta*⟧ preceded by eleven others; 12th —*n.* **1** the one following the eleventh **2** any of the twelve equal parts of something; $\frac{1}{12}$

**Twelfth Day** Epiphany, the twelfth day after Christmas: **Twelfth Night** is the evening before, or of, Epiphany

**twelve** (twelv) *adj., n.* ⟦OE *twelf*⟧ two more than ten; 12; XII

**12-step** or **twelve-step** (twelv′step′) *adj.* designating or of any rehabilitation program modeled on that of AA

**twelve′-tone′** *adj. Music* of composition in which the twelve tones of the chromatic scale are fixed in some arbitrary succession (*tone row*)

**twen·ty** (twent′ē) *adj., n., pl.* **-ties** ⟦OE *twegentig*⟧ two times ten; 20; XX —**the twenties** the numbers or years, as of a century, from 20 through 29 —**twen′ti·eth** (-ith) *adj., n.*

**twen′ty-one′** *n.* BLACKJACK (*n.* 2)

**twen′ty-twen′ty** (or **20/20**) **vision** normal visual ability, i.e., seeing clearly at 20 feet what the normal eye sees at 20 feet

**twerp** (twurp) *n.* ⟦ult. < ? Dan *tver,* perverse⟧ [Slang] a person regarded as insignificant, contemptible, etc.

**twice** (twīs) *adv.* ⟦OE *twiga*⟧ **1** two times **2** two times as much or as many

**twid·dle** (twid″'l) *vt., vi.* **-dled, -dling** ⟦prob. < TW(IST) + (*d*)*iddle,* move back and forth rapidly⟧ to twirl or play with (something) lightly or idly —**twiddle one's thumbs** to be idle

**twig** (twig) *n.* ⟦OE *twigge*⟧ a small branch of a tree or shrub

**twi·light** (twī′līt′) *n.* ⟦ME⟧ **1** the subdued light just after sunset **2** the period from sunset to dark **3** a gradual decline —*adj.* of twilight

**twill** (twil) *n.* ⟦OE *twilic,* woven of double thread⟧ a kind of cloth woven in parallel diagonal lines —**twilled** *adj.*

**twin** (twin) *adj.* ⟦OE *twinn,* double⟧ **1** consisting of, or being one of a pair of, two similar things **2** being a twin or twins —*n.* **1** either of two off-

spring from the same pregnancy **2** either of two persons or things that are very much alike

**twin bed** either of a pair of single beds

**twine** (twīn) *n.* ⟦OE *twin*⟧ strong thread, string, etc. of strands twisted together —*vt., vi.* twined, **twin′ing 1** to twist together **2** to wind (around)

**twinge** (twinj) *vt., vi.* twinged, twing′ing ⟦OE *twengan,* to squeeze⟧ to (cause to) have a sudden, sharp pain, qualm, etc. —*n.* such a pain, etc.

**twi-night** or **twi·night** (twī′nīt′) *adj.* ⟦TWI(LIGHT) + NIGHT⟧ *Baseball* designating a double-header starting in late afternoon and going into evening

**twin·kle** (twiŋ′kəl) *vi.* **-kled, -kling** ⟦OE *twinclian*⟧ **1** to shine with quick, intermittent gleams **2** to light up, as with amusement: said of the eyes **3** to move to and fro quickly: said as of a dancer's feet —*n.* **1** a glint in the eye **2** a gleam; sparkle

**twin′kling** *n.* an instant

**twin′-size′** *adj.* of or being the standard size of a twin bed: also **twin′-sized′**

**twirl** (twurl) *vt., vi.* ⟦prob. < Scand⟧ **1** to rotate rapidly; spin **2** to whirl in a circle —*n.* **1** a twirling **2** a twist, coil, etc. —**twirl′er** *n.*

**twist** (twist) *vt.* ⟦< OE *-twist,* a rope⟧ **1** to wind (strands, etc.) around one another **2** to wind (rope, etc.) around something **3** to give spiral shape to **4** *a*) to subject to torsion *b*) to wrench; sprain **5** to contort or distort **6** to confuse **7** to pervert the meaning of **8** to cause to rotate **9** to break (*off*) by turning the end —*vi.* **1** to undergo twisting **2** to spiral, twine, etc. (*around* or *about*) **3** to revolve or rotate **4** to wind, as a path does **5** to squirm; writhe —*n.* **1** something twisted **2** a twisting or being twisted **3** stress produced by twisting **4** a contortion **5** a wrench or sprain **6** a turn; bend **7** distortion, as of meaning **8** an unexpected or different direction, method, slant, etc.

**twist′er** *n.* **1** a person or thing that twists **2** [Inf.] a tornado or cyclone

**twist′-tie′** *n.* a short wire covered with paper or plastic, twisted to tie closed a plastic bag, etc.

**twit**[1] (twit) *vt.* twit′ted, twit′ting ⟦< OE *æt,* at + *witan,* accuse⟧ to reproach, taunt, etc.

**twit**[2] (twit) *n.* ⟦< ?⟧ [Inf.] a foolish, contemptible person

**twitch** (twich) *vt., vi.* ⟦< OE *twiccian,* to pluck⟧ to pull (at) or move with a quick, slight jerk —*n.* **1** a twitching **2** a sudden, quick motion, esp. a spasmodic one

**twitch′y** *adj.* **-i·er, -i·est** [Inf.] nervous; jittery

**twit·ter** (twit′ər) *vi.* ⟦ME *twiteren*⟧ **1** to chirp rapidly **2** *a*) to chatter *b*) to giggle **3** to tremble with excitement —*n.* **1** a twittering **2** a condition of trembling excitement

**'twixt** (twikst) *prep.* [Old Poet.] betwixt; between

**two** (tōō) *adj., n.* ⟦OE *twa*⟧ one more than one; 2; II —**in two** in two parts

**two′-bit′** *adj.* [Slang] cheap, inferior, etc.

**two bits** [Inf.] twenty-five cents

**two′-by-four′** *n.* a piece of lumber two inches thick and four inches wide when untrimmed ($1\frac{1}{2}$ by $3\frac{1}{2}$ inches trimmed)

**two′-edged′** *adj.* **1** having two cutting edges **2** that can be taken two ways [a *two-edged* remark]

**two′-faced′** *adj.* **1** having two faces, surfaces, etc. **2** deceitful; hypocritical

**two′-fer** (tōō′fər) *n.* ⟦altered < *two for*⟧ [Inf.] a pair, as of theater tickets, sold for the price of one

**two′-fist′ed** *adj.* [Inf.] **1** able to use both fists **2** vigorous; virile

**two′fold′** *adj.* **1** having two parts **2** having twice as much or as many —*adv.* twice as much or as many

**two′-hand′ed** *adj.* **1** requiring the use of both hands **2** operated, played, etc. by two persons

**two·pence** (tup′əns) *n.* two pence

**two′-ply′** *adj.* having two layers, strands, etc.

**two′some** (-səm) *n.* two people; a couple

**two'-time'** *vt.* -timed', -tim'ing [Slang] to be unfaithful to —**two'-tim'er** *n.*

**two'-way'** *adj.* **1** allowing passage in either direction **2** involving two or used in two ways

**Twp** *abbrev.* township

**TX** Texas

**-ty** (tē, ti) ⟦< L *-tas*⟧ *suffix* quality of, condition of

**ty·coon** (tī kōōn') *n.* ⟦< Jpn < Chin *tai*, great + *kuan*, official⟧ a wealthy, powerful industrialist, financier, etc.

**ty·ing** (tī'iŋ) *vt., vi. prp.* of TIE

**tyke** (tīk) *n.* ⟦< ON *tik*, a bitch⟧ [Inf.] a small child

**Ty·ler** (tī'lər) **John** 1790-1862; 10th president of the U.S. (1841-45)

**tym·pa·ni** (tim'pə nē) *pl.n., sing.* **-no'** (-nō') *alt. sp.* of TIMPANI —**tym'pa·nist** *n.*

**tym·pan·ic membrane** (tim pan'ik) a thin membrane inside the ear that vibrates when struck by sound waves

**tym·pa·num** (tim'pə nəm) *n., pl.* **-nums** or **-na** (-nə) ⟦L, a drum⟧ **1** MIDDLE EAR **2** TYMPANIC MEMBRANE

**type** (tīp) *n.* ⟦< Gr *typos*, a mark⟧ **1** the characteristic form, plan, style, etc. of a class or group **2** a class, group, etc. with characteristics in common **3** a person, animal, or thing representative of a class **4** a perfect example; model **5** *a*) a piece of metal or wood with a raised letter, etc. in reverse on its top, used in printing *b*) such pieces collectively *c*) a printed or photographically reproduced character or characters —*vt.* **typed, typ'ing** **1** to classify **2** to write using the keyboard of a typewriter or computer —*vi.* to use the keyboard of a typewriter or computer

**-type** (tīp) *combining form* **1** type, representative form, example *[stereotype]* **2** print, printing type

**type'cast'** *vt.* **-cast', -cast'ing** to cast (an actor) repeatedly in the same type of part

**type'script'** *n.* typewritten matter

**type'set'** *vt.* **-set', -set'ting** to set in type; compose

**type'set'ter** *n.* **1** a person who sets type **2** a machine for setting type

**type'write'** *vt., vi.* **-wrote', -writ'ten, -writ'ing** to write with a typewriter: now usually *type*

**type'writ'er** *n.* a writing machine with a keyboard, for reproducing letters resembling printed ones

**ty·phoid** (tī'foid') *n.* ⟦TYPH(US) + -OID⟧ an acute infectious disease caused by a bacillus and acquired by ingesting contaminated food or water: characterized by fever, intestinal disorders, etc.: in full **typhoid fever**

**ty·phoon** (tī fōōn') *n.* ⟦< Chin *tai-fung*, great

wind⟧ a violent tropical cyclone originating in the W Pacific

**ty·phus** (tī'fəs) *n.* ⟦< Gr *typhos*, fever⟧ an acute infectious disease caused by certain bacteria, transmitted by fleas, lice, etc., and characterized by fever, skin rash, etc.: in full **typhus fever**

**typ·i·cal** (tip'i kəl) *adj.* **1** serving as a type **2** having the distinguishing characteristics of a class, group, etc.; representative **3** belonging to a type; characteristic —**typ'i·cal·ly** *adv.*

**typ·i·fy** (tip'i fī') *vt.* **-fied', -fy'ing** to have the characteristics of; be typical of; exemplify —**typ'i·fi·ca'tion** *n.*

**typ·ist** (tīp'ist) *n.* a person who operates a typewriter

**ty·po** (tī'pō) *n., pl.* **-pos** [Inf.] an error made in setting type or in typing

**ty·pog·ra·phy** (tī päg'rə fē) *n.* ⟦see TYPE & -GRAPHY⟧ **1** setting, and printing with, type **2** the arrangement, style, etc. of matter printed from type —**ty·pog'ra·pher** *n.* —**ty'po·graph'i·cal** (-pə graf'i kəl) *adj.* —**ty'po·graph'i·cal·ly** *adv.*

**ty·ran·ni·cal** (tə ran'i kəl, tī-) *adj.* **1** of or suited to a tyrant **2** harsh, cruel, unjust, etc. Also **ty·ran'nic** —**ty·ran'ni·cal·ly** *adv.*

**tyr·an·nize** (tir'ə nīz') *vi.* **-nized', -niz'ing 1** to govern as a tyrant **2** to govern or use authority harshly or cruelly —*vt.* to treat tyrannically; oppress

**ty·ran·no·saur** (tə ran'ə sôr') *n.* ⟦< Gr *tyrannos*, tyrant + *sauros*, lizard⟧ a huge, two-footed, flesh-eating dinosaur: also **ty·ran'no·saur'us** (-əs)

**tyr·an·ny** (tir'ə nē) *n., pl.* **-nies 1** the authority, government, etc. of a tyrant **2** cruel and unjust use of power **3** a tyrannical act — **tyr'an·nous** *adj.*

**ty·rant** (tī'rənt) *n.* ⟦< Gr *tyrannos*⟧ **1** an absolute ruler **2** a cruel, oppressive ruler, master, etc.

TYRANNOSAUR

**ty·ro** (tī'rō) *n., pl.* **-ros** ⟦< L *tiro*, young soldier⟧ a beginner in learning something; novice

**Ty·rol** (ti rōl', -räl') *alt. sp.* of TIROL

**tzar** (tsär, zär) *n. var.* of CZAR —**tza·ri·na** (tsä rē'nə, zä-) *fem.n.*

# U

**u¹** or **U** (yōō) *n., pl.* **u's, U's** the 21st letter of the English alphabet

**u²** *abbrev.* unit(s)

**U¹** *abbrev.* **1** Union **2** United **3** University

**U²** *Chem. symbol for* uranium

**UAW** *abbrev.* United Automobile Workers (of America)

**u·biq·ui·tous** (yōō bik'wə təs) *adj.* ⟦< L *ubique*, everywhere⟧ (seemingly) present everywhere at the same time —**u·biq'ui·ty** *n.*

**U'-boat'** *n.* ⟦< Ger *Unterseeboot*, undersea boat⟧ a German submarine

**U bolt** a U-shaped bolt with threads and a nut at each end

**ud·der** (ud'ər) *n.* ⟦OE *udr*⟧ a baglike, milk-secreting organ with two or more teats, as in cows

**UFO** *n., pl.* **UFOs** or **UFO's** an unidentified flying object

**u·fol·o·gy** (yōō fäl'ə jē) *n.* the study of UFOs, esp. when regarded as spacecraft from another planet —**u·fol'o·gist** *n.*

**U·gan·da** (yōō gan'də, -gän'-) country in EC Africa: 93,065 sq. mi.; pop. 16,583,000 —**U·gan'dan** *adj., n.*

**ugh** (ookh, oo, ug, *etc.*) *interj.* used to express disgust, horror, etc.

**ug·ly** (ug'lē) *adj.* **-li·er, -li·est** ⟦< ON *uggr*, fear⟧ **1** unpleasing to look at **2** bad, disgusting, etc. *[an ugly lie]* **3** ominous *[ugly storm clouds]* **4** [Inf.] cross; quarrelsome *[an ugly mood]* —**ug'li·ness** *n.*

**uh** (u, un) *interj.* **1** HUH **2** used when hesitating in speaking

**UHF** or **uhf** *abbrev.* ultrahigh frequency

**UK** United Kingdom

**u·kase** (yōō'kās', -kāz') *n.* ⟦Russ *ukaz*, edict⟧ an official decree

**U·kraine** (yōō krān') country in SE Europe: formerly a republic of the U.S.S.R.: 231,990 sq. mi.; pop. 51,452,000 —**U·krain'i·an** *n., adj.*

**u·ku·le·le** (yōō'kə lā'lē) *n.* ⟦Haw, leaping flea⟧ a small, four-stringed, guitarlike musical instrument

**UL** *trademark for* Underwriters Laboratories

**ul·cer** (ul'sər) *n.* ⟦L *ulcus*⟧ **1** an open sore, often one discharging pus, on the skin or some mucous membrane **2** any corrupt condition —**ul'cer·ous** *adj.*

**ul'cer·ate'** (-āt') *vt., vi.* -at·ed, -at·ing to make or become ulcerous —**ul'cer·a'tion** *n.*

**ul·na** (ul'nə) *n., pl.* -nae (-nē) *or* -nas ⟦L, the elbow⟧ the larger of the two bones of the forearm —**ul'nar** *adj.*

**ul·ster** (ul'stər) *n.* ⟦after *Ulster*, in N Ireland⟧ a long, loose, heavy overcoat

**ult** *abbrev.* ultimate(ly)

**ul·te·ri·or** (ul tir'ē ər) *adj.* ⟦L: see ULTRA-⟧ **1** lying beyond or on the farther side **2** beyond what is expressed or implied; undisclosed

**ul·ti·mate** (ul'tə mit) *adj.* ⟦< L *ultimus*, last⟧ **1** beyond which it is impossible to go **2** final; conclusive **3** basic **4** greatest possible —*n.* a final point or result —**ul'ti·mate·ly** *adv.*

**ul·ti·ma·tum** (ul'tə māt'əm) *n., pl.* -tums *or* -ta (-ə) ⟦see prec.⟧ a final offer or demand, as in negotiations

**ul·tra** (ul'trə) *adj.* ⟦< fol.⟧ going beyond the usual limit; extreme

**ultra-** ⟦L < *ultra*, beyond⟧ *prefix* **1** beyond [*ultrasonic*] **2** extremely [*ultraconservative*]

**ul·tra·con·serv·a·tive** (ul'trə kən sur'və tiv) *adj.* extremely conservative

**ul·tra·high frequency** (ul'trə hī') any radio frequency between 300 and 3,000 megahertz

**ul'tra·ma·rine'** (-mə rēn') *adj.* deep-blue —*n.* deep blue

**ul'tra·son'ic** (-sän'ik) *adj.* above the range of sound audible to the human ear —**ul'tra·son'i·cal·ly** *adv.*

**ul'tra·sound'** (-sound') *n.* ultrasonic waves, used in medical diagnosis and therapy, etc.

**ul·tra·vi'o·let** (-vī'ə lit) *adj.* of or designating those rays that are just beyond the violet end of the visible spectrum

**ul·u·late** (yool'yoo lāt', ul'-) *vi.* -lat·ed, -lat·ing ⟦< L *ululare*, to howl⟧ to howl, hoot, or wail loudly —**ul'u·la'tion** *n.*

**U·lys·ses** (yoo lis'ēz') *n.* ⟦ML⟧ ODYSSEUS

**um·bel** (um'bəl) *n.* ⟦L *umbella*, parasol: see UMBRELLA⟧ a cluster of flowers with stalks of similar length springing from the same point

**um·ber** (um'bər) *n.* ⟦< It (*terra d'*)*ombra*, (earth of) shade⟧ **1** a kind of earth used as a yellowish-brown or reddish-brown pigment **2** a yellowish-brown or reddish-brown color

**um·bil·i·cal** (um bil'i kəl) *adj.* ⟦< L *umbilicus*, navel⟧ of a cordlike structure (**umbilical cord**) connecting a fetus's navel to the placenta, for conveying nourishment to, and removing waste from, the fetus

**um·bil·i·cus** (um bil'i kəs) *n., pl.* -ci' (-sī') ⟦L⟧ NAVEL

**um·bra** (um'brə) *n., pl.* -brae (-brē) *or* -bras ⟦L, a shade⟧ **1** shade or a shadow **2** the dark cone of shadow from a planet or satellite on the side opposite the sun

**um·brage** (um'brij) *n.* ⟦< L *umbra*, a shade⟧ **1** [Obs.] 2 offense or resentment

**um·brel·la** (um brel'ə) *n.* ⟦< L *umbra*, a shade⟧ **1** a screen, usually of cloth on a folding frame, carried for protection against rain or sun **2** any comprehensive, protective alliance, strategy, device, etc.

**u·mi·ak** (oo'mē ak') *n.* ⟦Esk⟧ a large, open boat made of skins on a wooden frame, used by Eskimos

**um·laut** (oom'lout) *n.* ⟦Ger < *um*, about + *laut*, a sound⟧ *Linguistics* **1** a vowel changed in sound by its assimilation to another vowel **2** the mark (¨) placed over such a vowel

**ump** (ump) *n., vt., vi. short for* UMPIRE

**um·pire** (um'pīr') *n.* ⟦< Fr *nomper*, uneven, hence a third person⟧ **1** a person chosen to judge a dispute **2** an official who administers the rules in certain sports —*vt., vi.* -pired', -pir'ing to act as umpire (in or of)

**ump·teen** (ump'tēn') *adj.* [Slang] very many — **ump'teenth'** *adj.*

**UN** *abbrev.* United Nations

**un-** *prefix* **1** ⟦OE⟧ not, lack of, the opposite of [*unconcern*] **2** ⟦OE *un-*, *on-*⟧ back: indicating a reversal of action [*unfold*] The following list includes some common compounds formed with *un-* (either sense) that do not have special meanings:

| | |
|---|---|
| unabashed | undiscovered |
| unable | undiscriminating |
| unabridged | undisguised |
| unaccented | undisputed |
| unacceptable | undistinguished |
| unaccompanied | undisturbed |
| unacquainted | undivided |
| unadorned | uneducated |
| unadulterated | unemotional |
| unafraid | unending |
| unaided | unenlightened |
| unaltered | unenviable |
| unambiguous | unethical |
| unannounced | uneventful |
| unanswered | unexpired |
| unashamed | unexplained |
| unasked | unexplored |
| unassailable | unexpressed |
| unassisted | unexpurgated |
| unattainable | unfair |
| unattractive | unfashionable |
| unauthorized | unfasten |
| unavailable | unfavorable |
| unavoidable | unfit |
| unbearable | unflattering |
| unbeaten | unfocused |
| unbiased | unforeseen |
| unbleached | unforgivable |
| unblemished | unforgotten |
| unbound | unfulfilled |
| unbreakable | unfurnished |
| unbroken | ungrammatical |
| unbuckle | ungrateful |
| unbutton | unhampered |
| uncap | unhandy |
| unceasing | unharmed |
| uncensored | unhealthful |
| unchallenged | unheeded |
| unchanged | unhesitating |
| unchanging | unhitch |
| unchecked | unhook |
| uncivilized | unhurried |
| unclassified | unhurt |
| unclean | unidentified |
| unclear | unimaginable |
| uncomplaining | unimaginative |
| uncompleted | unimpaired |
| uncomplimentary | unimportant |
| unconcealed | unimproved |
| unconfirmed | unincorporated |
| unconnected | uninformed |
| uncontaminated | uninhabited |
| uncontrollable | uninjured |
| uncontrolled | uninspired |
| uncontroversial | uninsured |
| unconventional | unintelligent |
| unconvinced | unintelligible |
| uncooked | unintentional |
| uncooperative | uninteresting |
| uncoordinated | uninterrupted |
| uncultivated | uninvited |
| undamaged | uninviting |
| undefeated | unjustifiable |
| undemocratic | unjustified |
| undependable | unknowing |
| undeserved | unlace |
| undesirable | unlatch |
| undeveloped | unleavened |
| undifferentiated | unlicensed |
| undiminished | unlined |
| undisciplined | unlisted |

unloved
unmanageable
unmannerly
unmarked
unmarried
unmatched
unmerited
unmoved
unnamed
unnoticed
unobserved
unobstructed
unobtainable
unobtrusive
unoccupied
unofficial
unopened
unopposed
unorthodox
unpaid
unpalatable
unpardonable
unpaved
unpin
unplanned
unpolished
unpolluted
unpredictable
unprejudiced
unpremeditated
unprepared
unpretentious
unprofitable
unpromising
unprotected
unproved
unproven
unprovoked
unpunished
unquenchable
unquestioned
unquestioning
unreadable
unrealistic
unrealized
unrecognizable
unrecognized
unrecorded
unrefined
unregulated
unrelated
unreliable
unrelieved
unrepentant

unresponsive
unrestricted
unsafe
unsanitary
unsatisfactory
unsatisfied
unsaturated
unscientific
unseasoned
unseeing
unseen
unsegmented
unselfish
unshackle
unshakable
unshaken
unshaven
unsociable
unsold
unsolicited
unsought
unspoiled
unspoken
unsportsmanlike
unsuccessful
unsuitable
unsullied
unsupervised
unsure
unsurpassed
unsuspecting
unsweetened
unsympathetic
untainted
untamed
untarnished
untasted
untenable
untiring
untouched
untrained
untried
untroubled
untrue
untrustworthy
unvarying
unverified
unwanted
unwarranted
unwavering
unwed
unworkable
unyielding
unzip

**un·ac·count·a·ble** (un′ə kount′ə bəl) *adj.* **1** that cannot be explained; strange **2** not responsible

**un·ac·cus′tomed** *adj.* **1** not accustomed (*to*) **2** not usual; strange

**un·ad·vised′** *adj.* **1** without counsel or advice **2** indiscreet; rash

**un·af·fect′ed** *adj.* **1** not affected or influenced **2** without affectation; simple; sincere

**un·-A·mer′i·can** *adj.* regarded as not properly American; esp., regarded as opposed to the U.S., its institutions, etc.

**u·nan·i·mous** (yoō nan′ə məs) *adj.* [[< L *unus*, one + *animus*, the mind]] agreeing completely; without dissent —**u·nan·im·i·ty** (yoō′nə nim′ə tē) *n.* — **u·nan′i·mous·ly** *adv.*

**un′ap·proach′a·ble** *adj.* **1** not to be approached; inaccessible; aloof **2** having no equal; unmatched

**un·armed′** *adj.* having no weapons

**un·as·sum′ing** *adj.* not forward; modest

**un·at·tached′** *adj.* **1** not attached **2** not engaged or married

**un·at·tend′ed** *adj.* **1** not waited on **2** not accompanied (*by*) **3** neglected

**un·a·vail′ing** (-ə vāl′iŋ) *adj.* futile; useless

**un·a·ware′** *adj.* not aware or conscious —*adv.* UNAWARES

**un·a·wares′** *adv.* **1** unintentionally **2** unexpectedly

**un·backed′** *adj.* not backed, supported, etc.

**un·bal′anced** *adj.* **1** not in balance **2** *a*) mentally deranged *b*) erratic or unstable

**un·bar′** *vt.* **-barred′, -bar′ring** to remove the bar or bars from; open

**un′be·com′ing** *adj.* not appropriate or suited to one's appearance, character, etc.; unattractive, indecorous, etc.

**un′be·known** (un′bē nōn′) *adj.* without one's knowledge; unknown: usually with *to*: also **un′be·knownst′** (-nōnst′)

**un′be·lief′** *n.* lack of belief, esp. in religion

**un′be·liev′a·ble** *adj.* beyond belief; astounding; incredible

**un′be·liev′er** *n.* **1** one who does not believe **2** one who does not accept any, or any particular, religious belief

**un·bend′** *vt., vi.* **-bent′** or **-bend′ed, -bend′ing 1** to relax, as from formality **2** to straighten

**un·bend′ing** *adj.* **1** rigid; stiff **2** firm; resolute **3** aloof; austere

**un·bid′den** *adj.* **1** not commanded **2** not invited

**un·blush′ing** *adj.* **1** not blushing **2** shameless — **un·blush′ing·ly** *adv.*

**un·bolt′** *vt., vi.* to withdraw the bolt or bolts of (a door, etc.); open

**un·born′** *adj.* **1** not born **2** still in the mother's uterus **3** yet to be

**un·bos′om** (-booz′əm) *vt., vi.* to tell or reveal (feelings, secrets, etc.) —**unbosom oneself** to reveal one's feelings, secrets, etc.

**un·bound′ed** *adj.* **1** without bounds or limits **2** not restrained

**un′bowed′** (-boud′) *adj.* not yielding or giving in

**un·bri′dled** *adj.* **1** having no bridle on: said of a horse, etc. **2** uncontrolled

**un·bur′den** *vt.* **1** to free from a burden **2** to relieve (oneself, one's mind, etc.) by disclosing (guilt, etc.)

**un′but′toned** *adj.* **1** with buttons unfastened **2** free and easy; casual

**un·called′-for′** *adj.* **1** not needed **2** unnecessary and out of place

**un·can·ny** (un kan′ē) *adj.* **1** mysterious and eerie; weird **2** so good, acute, etc. as to seem preternatural —**un·can′ni·ly** *adv.*

**un·cared′-for′** *adj.* not cared for or looked after; neglected

**un′cer·e·mo′ni·ous** *adj.* **1** not ceremonious; informal **2** curt; abrupt

**un·cer′tain** *adj.* **1** *a*) not surely or certainly known *b*) not sure or certain in knowledge; doubtful **2** vague **3** not dependable or reliable **4** varying —**un·cer′tain·ty,** *pl.* **-ties,** *n.*

**un·char′i·ta·ble** *adj.* harsh or severe, as in opinion —**un·char′i·ta·bly** *adv.*

**un·chart′ed** *adj.* not marked on a chart or map; unexplored or unknown

**un·chris′tian** *adj.* **1** not Christian **2** [Inf.] outrageous; dreadful

**un·ci·al** (un′shē əl, -shəl) *adj.* [[L *uncialis,* inchhigh]] designating or of the large, rounded letters of Greek and Latin manuscripts between A.D. 300 and 900 —*n.* uncial script or an uncial letter

**un·cir′cum·cised′** *adj.* **1** not circumcised; specif., not Jewish; gentile **2** [Archaic] heathen

**un·clasp′** *vt.* **1** to unfasten the clasp of **2** to release from a clasp or grasp

**un·cle** (uŋ′kəl) *n.* [[< L *avunculus*]] **1** the brother of one's father or mother **2** the husband of one's aunt

**Uncle Sam** [[< abbrev. *U.S.*]] [Inf.] the U.S. (government or people), personified as a tall man with whiskers, dressed in red, white, and blue

**Uncle Tom** [[after main character in novel *Uncle Tom's Cabin* (1852)]] [Inf.] a black person regarded as servile toward whites: a term of contempt

**un·cloak′** *vt.* to reveal; expose

**un·clothe'** *vt.* **-clothed'** or **-clad'**, **-cloth'ing** to undress, uncover, etc.

**un·coil'** *vt.*, *vi.* to unwind

**un·com'fort·a·ble** *adj.* **1** feeling discomfort **2** causing discomfort **3** ill at ease —**un·com'fort·a·bly** *adv.*

**un·com·mit'ted** *adj.* **1** not committed or pledged **2** not taking a stand

**un·com'mon** *adj.* **1** rare; not common or usual **2** strange; remarkable

**un·com·mu'ni·ca'tive** *adj.* not communicative; reserved; taciturn

**un·com'pro·mis'ing** *adj.* not yielding; firm; inflexible

**un·con·cern'** *n.* **1** apathy; indifference **2** lack of concern, or worry

**un·con·cerned'** *adj.* **1** indifferent **2** not solicitous or anxious —**un·con·cern'ed·ly** *adv.*

**un·con·di'tion·al** *adj.* without conditions or reservations; absolute

**un·con·scion·a·ble** (un kän'shən ə bəl) *adj.* **1** not guided or restrained by conscience **2** unreasonable or excessive **3** not fair or just —**un·con'scion·a·bly** *adv.*

**un·con'scious** *adj.* **1** deprived of consciousness **2** not aware (*of*) **3** not doing or done on purpose [an *unconscious* habit] —**the unconscious** *Psychoanalysis* the sum of all thoughts, impulses, etc. of which the individual is not conscious but which influence the emotions and behavior —**un·con'scious·ly** *adv.*

**un·con·sti·tu'tion·al** *adj.* not in accordance with a constitution, specif. the U.S. constitution

**un·cool'** *adj.* [Slang] **1** unsophisticated **2** unfashionable, unacceptable, etc.

**un·cork'** *vt.* to pull the cork out of

**un·count'ed** *adj.* **1** not counted **2** inconceivably numerous

**un·cou'ple** *vt.* **-pled**, **-pling** to unfasten (things coupled together)

**un·couth** (un kōōth') *adj.* [OE < *un-*, not + *cunnan*, know] **1** awkward; ungainly **2** not cultured; crude

**un·cov'er** *vt.* **1** to disclose **2** to remove the cover from **3** to remove the hat, etc. from (the head) — *vi.* to bare the head, as in respect

**unc·tion** (uŋk'shən) *n.* [< L *ungere*, anoint] **1** *a*) the act of anointing, as for medical or religious purposes *b*) the oil, ointment, etc. used for this **2** anything that soothes or comforts

**unc·tu·ous** (uŋk'chōō əs) *adj.* [see prec.] **1** oily or greasy **2** characterized by a smooth but insincere show of deep or earnest feeling

**un·cut'** *adj.* not cut; specif., *a*) not ground to shape (said of a gem) *b*) not abridged or shortened

**un·daunt'ed** *adj.* not daunted; not hesitating because of fear or discouragement

**un·de·ceive'** *vt.* **-ceived'**, **-ceiv'ing** to cause to be no longer deceived or misled

**un·de·cid'ed** *adj.* **1** not decided **2** not having come to a decision

**un·de·mon'stra·tive** *adj.* not demonstrative; not showing feelings openly; reserved

**un·de·ni'a·ble** *adj.* that cannot be denied; indisputable —**un·de·ni'a·bly** *adv.*

**un·der** (un'dər) *prep.* [OE] **1** in, at, or to a position down from; below **2** beneath the surface of **3** below and to the other side of [drive *under* the bridge] **4** covered by [a vest *under* his coat] **5** *a*) lower in rank, position, amount, etc. than *b*) lower than the required degree of [under age] **6** subject to the control, limitations, etc. of [under oath] **7** undergoing [under repair] **8** with the disguise of [under an alias] **9** in (the designated category) **10** during the rule of [under Elizabeth I] **11** being the subject of [under discussion] **12** because of (the circumstances) **13** authorized by —*adv.* **1** in or to a lower position or state **2** so as to be covered, concealed, etc. —*adj.* lower in position, authority, amount, etc.

**under-** *prefix* **1** in, on, to, or from a lower place; beneath [undertow] **2** in a subordinate position [undersecretary] **3** too little; insufficiently [underdeveloped]

**un·der·a·chieve** (un'dər ə chēv') *vi.* **-chieved'**, **-chiev'ing** to fail to do as well in school as might be expected from intelligence tests —**un'der·a·chiev'er** *n.*

**un'der·act'** *vt.*, *vi.* to act (a theatrical role) with insufficient emphasis or too great restraint

**un'der·age'** *adj.* below the age required by law

**un'der·arm'** *adj.* **1** of, for, in, or used on the area under the arm, or the armpit **2** UNDERHAND (sense 1) —*adv.* UNDERHAND

**un'der·bel'ly** *n.* **1** the lower, posterior part of an animal's belly **2** any vulnerable area, point, etc.

**un'der·bid'** *vt.*, *vi.* **-bid'**, **-bid'ding** **1** to bid lower than (another person) **2** to bid less than the worth of (a thing, as one's hand in bridge)

**un'der·brush'** *n.* small trees, shrubs, etc. growing in woods or forests

**un'der·car'riage** *n.* a supporting frame, as of an automobile

**un'der·charge'** *vt.*, *vi.* **-charged'**, **-charg'ing** **1** to charge too low a price (to) **2** to provide with too small or low a charge

**un'der·class'** *n.* the socioeconomic class with incomes below subsistence level, including esp. the underprivileged

**un'der·class'man** (-mən) *n.*, *pl.* **-men** (-mən) a freshman or sophomore in high school or college

**un'der·clothes'** *pl.n.* UNDERWEAR: also **un'der·cloth'ing** *sing.n.*

**un'der·coat'** *n.* **1** a tarlike coating applied to the underside of a motor vehicle to retard rust, etc. **2** a coat of paint, etc. applied before the final coat Also **un'der·coat'ing** —*vt.* to apply an undercoat to

**un'der·cov'er** *adj.* acting or carried out in secret

**un'der·cur'rent** *n.* **1** a current flowing beneath the surface **2** an underlying tendency, opinion, etc.

**un'der·cut'** *vt.* **-cut'**, **-cut'ting** **1** to make a cut below or under **2** to undersell or work for lower wages than **3** to weaken or undermine

**un'der·de·vel'oped** *adj.* inadequately developed, esp. economically and industrially

**un'der·dog'** *n.* **1** a person or team that is losing or expected to lose **2** a person at a disadvantage because of injustice, prejudice, etc.

**un'der·done'** *adj.* not cooked enough

**un'der·em·ployed'** *adj.* **1** working less than full time **2** working at low-skilled, poorly paid jobs when capable of doing more highly skilled work

**un'der·es'ti·mate'** *vt.* **-mat'ed**, **-mat'ing** to set too low an estimate on or for —**un'der·es'ti·ma'tion** *n.*

**un'der·ex·pose'** *vt.* **-posed'**, **-pos'ing** to expose (photographic film, etc.) to inadequate light or for too short a time

**un'der·foot'** *adv.*, *adj.* **1** under the foot or feet **2** in the way

**un'der·gar'ment** *n.* a piece of underwear

**un'der·go'** *vt.* **-went'**, **-gone'**, **-go'ing** to experience; go through

**un'der·grad'u·ate** *n.* a college student who has not yet earned a degree

**un'der·ground'** *adj.* **1** under the earth's surface **2** secret; hidden **3** of newspapers, movies, etc. that are unconventional, radical, etc. —*adv.* **1** under the earth's surface **2** in or into secrecy —*n.* **1** the region under the earth's surface **2** a secret movement in a country to oppose the government or enemy occupation forces **3** [Brit.] a subway

**un'der·growth'** *n.* UNDERBRUSH

**un'der·hand'** *adj.* **1** done with the hand below the level of the elbow or shoulder **2** UNDERHANDED —*adv.* with an underhand motion

**un'der·hand'ed** *adj.* sly, deceitful, etc. —**un'der·hand'ed·ly** *adv.*

**un'der·lie'** *vt.* **-lay'**, **-lain'**, **-ly'ing** **1** to lie beneath **2** to be the basis for; form the foundation of

**un·der·line'** *vt.* **-lined', -lin'ing 1** to draw a line beneath **2** to stress

**un·der·ling** (un'dər liŋ) *n.* ⟦OE: see UNDER- & -LING⟧ a person in a subordinate position; inferior: usually a contemptuous term

**un·der·ly'ing** *adj.* **1** lying under **2** fundamental; basic

**un·der·mine'** *vt.* **-mined', -min'ing 1** to dig beneath, so as to form a tunnel or mine **2** to wear away and weaken the supports of **3** to injure or weaken, esp. by subtle or insidious means

**un·der·most'** *adj., adv.* lowest in place, position, rank, etc.

**un·der·neath** (un'dər nēth') *adv., prep.* ⟦< OE *under*, UNDER + *neothan*, below⟧ under; below

**un·der·nour'ished** *adj.* not getting the food needed for health and growth

**un·der·pants'** *pl.n.* an undergarment, long or short, for the lower part of the body

**un·der·pass'** *n.* a passage under something; esp., a passageway under a railway

**un·der·per·form'** *vi.* to be less successful than expected or needed —*vt.* to produce a smaller return than: said of stocks, etc.

**un·der·pin'ning** (-pin'iŋ) *n.* **1** a support or prop **2** [*pl.*] [Inf.] the legs

**un·der·play'** *vt., vi.* **1** UNDERACT **2** to make seem less important

**un·der·priv'i·leged** *adj.* deprived of a decent standard of living and economic security through poverty, discrimination, etc.

**un·der·pro·duce'** *vt., vi.* **-duced', -duc'ing** to produce less than is needed or wanted

**un·der·rate'** *vt.* **-rat'ed, -rat'ing** to rate or estimate too low

**un·der·score'** *vt.* **-scored', -scor'ing** UNDERLINE

**un·der·sea'** *adj., adv.* beneath the surface of the sea: also **un'der·seas'** *adv.*

**un·der·sec're·tar'y** *n., pl.* **-ies** an assistant secretary

**un·der·sell'** *vt.* **-sold', -sell'ing 1** to sell at a lower price than **2** to publicize or promote in a restrained or inadequate manner

**un·der·shirt'** *n.* a collarless undergarment worn under an outer shirt

**un·der·shorts'** *pl.n.* short underpants worn by men and boys

**un·der·shot'** *adj.* **1** with the lower part extending past the upper [an *undershot* jaw] **2** driven by water flowing along the lower part [an *undershot* water wheel]

**un·der·side'** *n.* the side or surface that is underneath

**un·der·signed'** *adj.* whose name is signed at the end —**the undersigned** the person or persons having signed at the end

**un·der·skirt'** *n.* a skirt worn under another

**un·der·staffed'** *adj.* having fewer workers on the staff than is needed

**un·der·stand'** *vt.* **-stood', -stand'ing** ⟦< OE *understandan*, lit., to stand among⟧ **1** to perceive the meaning of **2** to assume from what is heard, etc.; infer **3** to take as meant; interpret **4** to take as a fact **5** to know the nature, character, etc. of **6** to have a sympathetic rapport with —*vi.* **1** to have understanding, comprehension, etc. **2** to be informed; believe —**un'der·stand'a·ble** *adj.* — **un'der·stand'a·bly** *adv.*

**un·der·stand'ing** *n.* **1** comprehension **2** the power to think and learn; intelligence **3** a specific interpretation **4** mutual agreement, esp. one that settles differences —*adj.* that understands; sympathetic

**un·der·state'** *vt.* **-stat'ed, -stat'ing 1** to state too weakly **2** to state in a restrained style —**un'der· state'ment** *n.*

**un·der·stud'y** *n., pl.* **-ies** an actor prepared to substitute for another —*vt., vi.* **-ied, -y·ing** to learn (a part) as an understudy (to)

**un·der·take'** *vt.* **-took', -tak'en, -tak'ing 1** to

take upon oneself (a task, etc.) **2** to promise; guarantee

**un·der·tak'er** *n.* FUNERAL DIRECTOR: a somewhat old-fashioned usage

**un·der·tak'ing** *n.* **1** something undertaken; task; enterprise **2** a promise; guarantee

**un·der·the-count'er** *adj.* [Inf.] done secretly in an unlawful way: also **un'der-the-ta'ble**

**un·der·things'** *pl.n.* women's or girls' underwear

**un·der·tone'** *n.* **1** a low tone of voice **2** a subdued color **3** an underlying quality, factor, etc.

**un·der·tow'** *n.* a current of water moving beneath the surface water and in a different direction

**un·der·wa'ter** *adj.* being, done, etc. beneath the surface of the water

**un·der·way'** *adj.* **1** moving; making progress **2** *Naut.* not anchored or moored or aground

**un·der·wear'** *n.* clothing worn under one's outer clothes, usually next to the skin, as undershirts

**un·der·weight** (un'dər wāt', un'dər wāt') *adj.* below the normal, desirable, or allowed weight

**un·der·world'** *n.* **1** the mythical world of the dead; Hades **2** criminals regarded as a group

**un·der·write'** *vt.* **-wrote', -writ'ten, -writ'ing 1** to agree to market (an issue of securities), guaranteeing to buy any part remaining unsubscribed **2** to agree to pay the cost of or cover the losses of (an undertaking, etc.) **3** to sign one's name to (an insurance policy), thus assuming liability — **un'der·writ'er** *n.*

**un·dies** (un'dēz') *pl.n.* [Inf.] women's or girls' underwear

**un·do'** *vt.* **-did', -done', -do'ing 1** to untie, open, etc. **2** to do away with; cancel **3** to bring to ruin

**un·doc'u·ment·ed** *adj.* not having a proper visa for U.S. residence [an *undocumented* alien]

**un·do'ing** *n.* **1** an annulling **2** a bringing to ruin **3** the cause of ruin

**un·done'** *adj.* **1** not done; not performed, accomplished, etc. **2** ruined **3** emotionally upset

**un·doubt'ed** *adj.* not doubted or disputed; certain —**un·doubt'ed·ly** *adv.*

**un·dreamed'** *adj.* not even dreamed (*of*) or imagined: also **un·dreamt'** (-dremt')

**un·dress'** *vt.* to take off the clothing of —*vi.* to take off one's clothes

**un·due'** *adj.* **1** not appropriate; improper **2** excessive; immoderate

**un·du·lant** (un'jə lənt, -dyə-) *adj.* undulating

**un·du·late'** (-lāt') *vi., vt.* ⟦< L *unda*, a wave⟧ **1** to move or cause to move in waves **2** to have or cause to have a wavy form or surface —**un'du· la'tion** *n.*

**un·du·ly** *adv.* **1** improperly **2** excessively

**un·dy'ing** *adj.* immortal or eternal

**un·earned'** *adj.* not earned by work or service; specif., obtained as a return on an investment [*unearned* income]

**un·earth'** *vt.* **1** to dig up from the earth **2** to bring to light; disclose

**un·earth'ly** *adj.* **1** supernatural **2** weird; mysterious **3** [Inf.] fantastic, outlandish, etc.

**un·eas'y** *adj.* **-i·er, -i·est 1** having, showing, or allowing no ease of body or mind; uncomfortable **2** awkward; constrained **3** anxious; apprehensive —**un·eas'i·ly** *adv.* —**un·eas'i·ness** *n.*

**un·em·ploy'a·ble** *adj.* not employable, specif. because of severe physical or mental handicaps, outmoded skills, etc.

**un·em·ployed'** *adj.* **1** not employed; without work **2** not being used —**un·em·ploy'ment** *n.*

**un·e'qual** *adj.* **1** not equal, as in size, strength, ability, or value **2** not balanced, even, regular, etc. **3** not adequate (*to*)

**un·e'qualed** or **un·e'qualled** *adj.* not equaled; unmatched; unrivaled

**un·e·quiv'o·cal** *adj.* not equivocal; plain; clear

**un·err·ing** (un ʉr′iŋ, -er′-) *adj.* **1** free from error **2** not missing or failing; sure; exact

**UNESCO** (yoō nes′kō) *n.* United Nations Educational, Scientific, and Cultural Organization

**un·e·ven** *adj.* **1** not even, level, smooth, regular, etc. **2** unequal **3** *Math.* odd —**un·e·ven·ly** *adv.*

**un·ex·am·pled** *adj.* having no parallel or precedent; unprecedented

**un·ex·cep·tion·a·ble** *adj.* not exceptionable; without fault; beyond criticism

**un·ex·cep·tion·al** *adj.* ordinary

**un·ex·pect·ed** *adj.* not expected; unforeseen —**un·ex·pect·ed·ly** *adv.*

**un·fail·ing** *adj.* **1** not failing **2** never ceasing or falling short; inexhaustible **3** always reliable

**un·faith·ful** *adj.* **1** lacking or breaking faith or loyalty **2** not true, accurate, etc. **3** adulterous —**un·faith·ful·ness** *n.*

**un·fa·mil·iar** *adj.* **1** not well-known; strange **2** not acquainted (*with*) —**un·fa·mil·i·ar·i·ty** *n.*

**un·feel·ing** *adj.* **1** incapable of feeling; insensible **2** hardhearted; cruel —**un·feel·ing·ly** *adv.*

**un·feigned** (un fānd′) *adj.* genuine

**un·fin·ished** *adj.* **1** not finished; incomplete **2** not painted, varnished, etc.

**un·flap·pa·ble** (-flap′ə bəl) *adj.* ⟦< UN- + FLAP, *n.* 3 + -ABLE⟧ [Inf.] not easily excited; imperturbable

**un·flinch·ing** *adj.* steadfast; firm

**un·fold** *vt.* **1** to open and spread out (something folded) **2** to lay open to view; reveal, explain, etc. —*vi.* **1** to become unfolded **2** to develop fully

**un·for·get·ta·ble** *adj.* so important, beautiful, shocking, etc. as never to be forgotten

**un·for·giv·ing** *adj.* not willing or not able to forgive

**un·for·tu·nate** *adj.* **1** having or bringing bad luck; unlucky **2** not suitable or successful —*n.* an unfortunate person —**un·for·tu·nate·ly** *adv.*

**un·found·ed** *adj.* not founded on fact or truth

**un·friend·ly** *adj.* -li·er, -li·est **1** not friendly or kind **2** not favorable —**un·friend·li·ness** *n.*

**un·frock** *vt.* to deprive of the rank of priest or minister

**un·furl** *vt., vi.* to open or spread out from a furled state

**un·gain·ly** (un gān′lē) *adj.* ⟦< ME *un-*, not + ON *gegn*, ready⟧ awkward; clumsy

**un·god·ly** *adj.* **1** not godly or religious **2** [Inf.] outrageous —**un·god·li·ness** *n.*

**un·gov·ern·a·ble** *adj.* that cannot be governed or controlled; unruly

**un·gra·cious** *adj.* **1** not gracious; rude **2** unpleasant; unattractive

**un·guard·ed** *adj.* **1** unprotected **2** without guile or cunning **3** careless; imprudent

**un·guent** (uŋ′gwənt) *n.* ⟦< L *unguere*, anoint⟧ a salve or ointment

**un·gu·late** (uŋ′gyoō lit, -lāt′) *adj.* ⟦< L *unguis*, a nail⟧ having hoofs —*n.* a mammal having hoofs

**un·hand** *vt.* to release from the hand or hands; let go of

**un·hap·py** *adj.* -pi·er, -pi·est **1** unfortunate **2** sad; wretched **3** not suitable —**un·hap·pi·ly** *adv.* —**un·hap·pi·ness** *n.*

**un·health·y** *adj.* -i·er, -i·est **1** sickly; not well **2** harmful to health **3** harmful to morals **4** dangerous or risky —**un·health·i·ness** *n.*

**un·heard** *adj.* **1** not perceived by the ear **2** not given a hearing

**un·heard′-of** *adj.* **1** not heard of before; unprecedented or unknown **2** unacceptable or outrageous

**un·hinge** *vt.* -hinged′, -hing′ing **1** to remove from the hinges **2** to unbalance (the mind) of (someone)

**un·ho·ly** *adj.* -li·er, -li·est **1** not sacred, hallowed, etc. **2** wicked; profane **3** [Inf.] outrageous

**un·horse** *vt.* -horsed′, -hors′ing to throw (a rider) from a horse

**uni-** ⟦L < *unus*, one⟧ *prefix* one; having only one

**u·ni·bod·y** (yoō′nə bäd′ē) *adj.* designating automobile construction in which roof, floor, panels, etc. are welded together into a single unit

**u·ni·cam·er·al** (-kam′ər əl) *adj.* ⟦< UNI- + L *camera*, chamber⟧ of or having a single legislative chamber

**UNICEF** (yoō′nə sef′) *n.* United Nations Children's Fund: formerly, *United Nations International Children's Emergency Fund*

**u·ni·corn** (yoō′nə kôrn′) *n.* ⟦< L *unus*, one + *cornu*, horn⟧ a mythical horse-like animal with a single horn growing from its forehead

**u·ni·cy·cle** (yoō′nə sī′kəl) *n.* ⟦UNI- + (BI)CYCLE⟧ a one-wheeled vehicle straddled by the rider who pushes its pedals —**u·ni·cy′clist** *n.*

UNICORN

**u·ni·form** (yoō′nə fôrm′) *adj.* ⟦< L *unus*, one + *-formis*, -FORM⟧ **1** not varying in form, rate, degree, etc. **2** like others of the same class —*n.* the distinctive clothes of a particular group, as of soldiers —*vt.* to supply with a uniform —**u·ni·form′i·ty** *n.* —**u·ni·form′ly** *adv.*

**u·ni·fy** (yoō′nə fī′) *vt., vi.* -fied′, -fy′ing ⟦see UNI- & -FY⟧ to become or make united —**u·ni·fi·ca′tion** *n.*

**u·ni·lat·er·al** (yoō′nə lat′ər əl) *adj.* **1** of, occurring on, or affecting one side only **2** involving only one of several parties; not reciprocal

**un·im·peach·a·ble** (un′im pēch′ə bəl) *adj.* that cannot be doubted or discredited; irreproachable

**un·in·hib·it·ed** *adj.* without inhibition; esp., free of the usual social or psychological restraints on one's behavior

**un·in·ter·est·ed** *adj.* not interested; indifferent

**un·ion** (yoōn′yən) *n.* ⟦< L *unus*, one⟧ **1** a uniting or being united; combination **2** a grouping together of nations, etc. for some specific purpose **3** marriage **4** something united **5** *short for* LABOR UNION **6** a design symbolizing political union, used as in a flag **7** a device for joining parts, as of a machine —**the Union** **1** the United States **2** the North in the Civil War

**un·ion·ize** (-īz′) *vt., vi.* -ized′, -iz′ing to organize into a labor union —**un·ion·i·za′tion** *n.*

**union jack** **1** a flag, esp. a national flag, consisting only of a UNION (sense 6) **2** [U- J-] the flag of the United Kingdom

**Union of Soviet Socialist Republics** former country in E Europe & N Asia: formed as a union of 15 constituent republics, it was disbanded in 1991

**u·nique** (yoō nēk′) *adj.* ⟦< L *unus*, one⟧ **1** one and only; sole **2** without like or equal **3** very unusual: a usage still objected to by some

**u·ni·sex** (yoō′nə seks′) *adj.* of or involving a fashion, as in haircuts, that is not differentiated for the sexes

**u·ni·son** (yoō′nə sən, -zən) *n.* ⟦< L *unus*, one + *sonus*, a sound⟧ **1** a musical interval consisting of two identical pitches **2** agreement —**in unison** with all the voices or instruments performing the same part

**u·nit** (yoō′nit) *n.* ⟦< UNITY⟧ **1** the smallest whole number; one **2** a standard basic quantity, measure, etc. **3** a single person or group, esp. as a part of a whole **4** a distinct part or object with a specific purpose

**U·ni·tar·i·an** (yoō′nə ter′ē ən) *n.* a member of a religious denomination accepting the moral teachings of Jesus, but holding that God is a single being

**u·ni·tar·y** (yoō′nə ter′ē) *adj.* **1** of a unit or units **2** of or based on unity

**u·nite** (yoō nīt′) *vt., vi.* -nit′ed, -nit′ing ⟦< L *unus*, one⟧ **1** to put or join together so as to make one;

**combine 2** to bring or come together in common cause, action, etc.

**United Arab E·mir·ates** (em′ər əts) country in E Arabia, on the Persian Gulf: 32,300 sq. mi.; pop. 1,622,000

**United Arab Republic** *former name for* Egypt (1961-71)

**United Kingdom** country in W Europe, consisting of Great Britain & Northern Ireland: 93,636 sq. mi.; pop. 55,734,000

**United Nations** an international organization of nations for world peace and security: formed in 1945 and having, in 2001, a membership of 189

**United States of America** country including 49 states in North America, & Hawaii: 3,787,318 sq. mi.; pop. 248,710,000; cap. Washington, DC: also called **United States**

**u·nit·ize** (yoo′nə tīz′) *vt.* **-ized**′, **-iz′ing** to make into a single unit

**unit pricing** a system of showing prices, as of foods, in terms of standard units

**u·ni·ty** (yoo′nə tē) *n.*, *pl.* **-ties** ⟦< L *unus*, one⟧ **1** a being united; oneness **2** a single, separate thing **3** harmony; agreement **4** a complex that is a union of related parts **5** a harmonious, unified arrangement of parts in an artistic work **6** continuity of purpose, action, etc. **7** *Math.* any quantity, etc. identified as a unit, or 1

**univ** *abbrev.* university

**u·ni·va·lent** (yoo′nə vā′lənt) *adj.* *Chem.* **1** having one valence **2** having a valence of one

**u·ni·valve** (yoo′nə valv′) *n.* a mollusk with a one-piece shell, as a snail

**u·ni·ver·sal** (yoo′nə vur′səl) *adj.* **1** of the universe; present everywhere **2** of, for, or including all or the whole **3** used, or intended to be used, for all kinds, sizes, etc. or by all people —**u′ni·ver·sal′i·ty** (-vər sal′ə tē) *n.*

**u′ni·ver·sal·ize′** *vt.* **-ized**′, **-iz′ing** to make universal

**universal joint** (or **coupling**) a joint or coupling that permits a swing of limited angle in any direction, esp. one for transmitting rotary motion from one shaft to another not in line with it

**u′ni·ver·sal·ly** *adv.* **1** in every instance **2** in every part or place

**Universal Product Code** a patterned series of vertical bars printed on consumer products: it can be read by computerized scanners for pricing, etc.

UNIVERSAL JOINT

**u·ni·verse** (yoo′nə vurs′) *n.* ⟦< L *unus*, one + *vertere*, to turn⟧ **1** the totality of all things that exist **2** the world

**u·ni·ver·si·ty** (yoo′nə vur′sə tē) *n.*, *pl.* **-ties** ⟦see prec.⟧ **1** an educational institution offering bachelor's and advanced degrees **2** the grounds, buildings, etc. of a university

**un·just** (un just′) *adj.* not just or right; unfair —**un·just′ly** *adv.*

**un·kempt′** (-kempt′) *adj.* ⟦UN- + *kempt* < dial. *kemben*, to comb⟧ **1** tangled, disheveled, etc. **2** not tidy; slovenly

**un·kind′** *adj.* not kind; specif., *a)* not considerate of others *b)* harsh, severe, cruel, etc. —**un·kind′ness** *n.*

**un·kind′ly** *adj.* UNKIND —*adv.* in an unkind way

**un·known′** *adj.* not known; specif., *a)* unfamiliar (*to*) *b)* not identified, etc. —*n.* an unknown person or thing

**un·law′ful** *adj.* **1** against the law; illegal **2** immoral —**un·law′ful·ly** *adv.* —**un·law′ful·ness** *n.*

**un·lead′ed** *adj.* not containing lead compounds: said of gasoline

**un·learn′** *vt.*, *vi.* to forget or try to forget (something learned)

**un·learn′ed** (-lur′nid; *for* 2, -lurnd′) *adj.* **1** not

having much learning; uneducated **2** not learned or memorized [*unlearned* lessons]

**un·leash′** *vt.* to release from or as from a leash

**un·less** (un les′) *conj.* ⟦< ME *on lesse that*, at less than⟧ except if; except that

**un·let′tered** *adj.* **1** ignorant; uneducated **2** illiterate

**un·like′** *adj.* not alike; different —*prep.* **1** not like; different from **2** not characteristic of

**un·like′ly** *adj.* **1** not likely; improbable **2** not likely to succeed —**un·like′li·hood′** *n.*

**un·lim′ber** *vt.*, *vi.* to get ready for use or action

**un·lim′it·ed** *adj.* **1** without limits or restrictions **2** vast; immeasurable

**un·load′** *vt.*, *vi.* **1** *a)* to remove (a load) *b)* to take a load from **2** *a)* to tell (one's troubles, etc.) without restraint *b)* to relieve of something that troubles **3** to remove the charge from (a gun) **4** to get rid of

**un·lock′** *vt.* **1** *a)* to open (a lock) *b)* to open the lock of (a door, etc.) **2** to let loose; release **3** to reveal

**un·looked′-for′** *adj.* not expected

**un·loose′** *vt.* **-loosed**′, **-loos′ing** to set loose; loosen, release, etc.: also **un·loos′en**

**un·luck′y** *adj.* **-i·er**, **-i·est** having or bringing bad luck; unfortunate

**un·make′** *vt.* **-made**′, **-mak′ing** **1** to cause to be as before; undo **2** to ruin; destroy **3** to depose from a position or rank

**un·man′** *vt.* **-manned**′, **-man′ning** to deprive of manly courage, nerve, etc.

**un·man′ly** *adj.* **-li·er**, **-li·est** not manly; specif., *a)* cowardly, weak, etc. *b)* effeminate; womanish

**un·manned′** *adj.* without people aboard and operating by remote control

**un·mask′** *vi.*, *vt.* **1** to remove a mask or disguise (from) **2** to disclose the true nature or character (of)

**un·mean′ing** *adj.* lacking in meaning or sense

**un·men′tion·a·ble** *adj.* not fit to be mentioned

**un·mer′ci·ful** *adj.* having or showing no mercy; cruel; pitiless

**un·mis·tak′a·ble** *adj.* that cannot be mistaken or misinterpreted; clear —**un·mis·tak′a·bly** *adv.*

**un·mit′i·gat·ed** *adj.* **1** not lessened or eased **2** out-and-out; absolute

**un·mor′al** *adj.* AMORAL

**un·nat′u·ral** *adj.* **1** contrary to nature; abnormal **2** artificial **3** very cruel —**un·nat′u·ral·ly** *adv.*

**un·nec′es·sar′y** *adj.* not necessary; needless —**un·nec′es·sar′i·ly** *adv.*

**un·nerve′** *vt.* **-nerved**′, **-nerv′ing** to cause to lose one's self-confidence, courage, etc.

**un·num′bered** *adj.* **1** not counted **2** innumerable **3** having no identifying number

**un·or′gan·ized′** *adj.* not organized; specif., not belonging to a labor union

**un·pack′** *vt.*, *vi.* **1** to remove (the contents of a trunk, suitcase, etc.) **2** to take things out of (a trunk, etc.)

**un·par′al·leled′** *adj.* that has no parallel, equal, or counterpart

**un·pleas′ant** *adj.* offensive; disagreeable —**un·pleas′ant·ly** *adv.* —**un·pleas′ant·ness** *n.*

**un·plumbed′** *adj.* not fully understood

**un·pop′u·lar** *adj.* not liked by the public or by the majority —**un′pop·u·lar′i·ty** (-lar′ə tē) *n.*

**un·prac′ticed** *adj.* **1** not habitually or repeatedly done, etc. **2** not skilled or experienced

**un·prec′e·dent·ed** *adj.* having no precedent or parallel; unheard-of

**un·prin′ci·pled** *adj.* lacking moral principles; unscrupulous

**un·print′a·ble** *adj.* not fit to be printed, as because of obscenity

**un′pro·fes′sion·al** *adj.* not professional; esp., violating the ethical code of a given profession

**un·qual'i·fied'** *adj.* **1** lacking the necessary qualifications **2** not limited; absolute

**un·ques'tion·a·ble** *adj.* not to be questioned, doubted, or disputed; certain —**un·ques'tion·a·bly** *adv.*

**un·quote'** *interj.* I end the quotation

**un·rav'el** *vt.* **-eled** or **-elled, -el·ing** or **-el·ling 1** to separate the threads of (something woven, tangled, etc.) **2** to make clear; solve —*vi.* to become unraveled

**un·read'** (-red') *adj.* **1** not read, as a book **2** having read little or nothing

**un·re'al** *adj.* not real or actual; imaginary, fanciful, false, etc.

**un·rea'son·a·ble** *adj.* **1** not reasonable or rational **2** excessive; immoderate —**un·rea'son·a·bly** *adv.*

**un·rea'son·ing** *adj.* not reasoning or reasoned; irrational

**un're·con·struct'ed** *adj.* holding to an earlier, outmoded practice or point of view

**un're·gen'er·ate** *adj.* stubbornly defiant

**un're·lent'ing** *adj.* **1** inflexible; relentless **2** without mercy; cruel **3** not relaxing in effort, speed, etc.

**un're·mit'ting** *adj.* not stopping, relaxing, etc.; incessant; persistent

**un're·quit'ed** *adj.* not reciprocated

**un're·served'** *adj.* not reserved; specif., *a)* frank or open in speech *b)* not restricted; unlimited —**un're·serv'ed·ly** *adv.*

**un·rest'** *n.* restlessness; disquiet; specif., angry discontent verging on revolt

**un·ripe'** *adj.* not ripe or mature; green

**un·ri'valed** or **un·ri'valled** *adj.* having no rival, equal, or competitor

**un·roll'** *vt.* **1** to open (something rolled up) **2** to display —*vi.* to become unrolled

**un·ruf'fled** *adj.* not ruffled or disturbed; calm; smooth; serene

**un·rul·y** (un rōō'lē) *adj.* **-i·er, -i·est** hard to control, restrain, or keep in order —**un·rul'i·ness** *n.*

**un·sad'dle** *vt.* **-dled, -dling** to take the saddle off (a horse, etc.)

**un·said'** *adj.* not expressed

**un·sa'vor·y** *adj.* **1** unpleasant to taste or smell **2** morally offensive

**un·scathed'** (-skāᵗʰd') *adj.* [< *un-* + ON *skathi*, harm] unharmed

**un·schooled'** *adj.* not educated or trained, esp. by formal schooling

**un·scram'ble** *vt.* **-bled, -bling** to cause to be no longer scrambled, mixed up, or unintelligible

**un·screw'** *vt.* to detach or loosen by removing screws, or by turning

**un·script'ed** *adj.* without or not in a prepared script

**un·scru'pu·lous** *adj.* not restrained by ideas of right and wrong; unprincipled

**un·seal'** *vt.* **1** to break the seal of **2** to open

**un·sea'son·a·ble** *adj.* **1** not usual for the season **2** at the wrong time

**un·seat'** *vt.* **1** to dislodge from a seat **2** to remove from office

**un·seem'ly** *adj.* not seemly; not decent or proper; unbecoming

**un·set'tle** *vt., vi.* **-tled, -tling** to make or become unstable; disturb or displace

**un·set'tled** *adj.* **1** not settled; not fixed, orderly, stable, calm, decided, etc. **2** not paid **3** having no settlers

**un·sheathe'** (-shēᵗʰ') *vt.* **-sheathed', -sheath'ing** to remove (a sword, etc.) from a sheath

**un·sight'ly** *adj.* not sightly or pleasant to look at; ugly —**un·sight'li·ness** *n.*

**un·skilled'** *adj.* having or requiring no special skill or training

**un·skill'ful** *adj.* having little or no skill; awkward

**un·snap'** *vt.* **-snapped', -snap'ping** to undo the snaps of, so as to loosen or detach

**un·snarl'** *vt.* to untangle

**un'so·phis'ti·cat'ed** *adj.* not sophisticated; simple, ingenuous, etc.

**un·sound'** *adj.* not sound; specif., *a)* not healthy, safe, firm, etc. *b)* not reliable, sensible, etc.

**un·spar'ing** *adj.* **1** not sparing; lavish **2** not merciful; severe

**un·speak'a·ble** *adj.* **1** that cannot be spoken **2** so bad, foul, evil, etc. as to defy description or be unfit for discussion [*unspeakable* depravity] —**un·speak'a·bly** *adv.*

**un·sta'ble** *adj.* not stable; specif., *a)* easily upset *b)* changeable *c)* unreliable *d)* emotionally or psychologically unsettled *e) Chem.* tending to decompose

**un·stead'y** *adj.* not steady; specif., *a)* not firm; shaky *b)* changeable; inconstant *c)* erratic in habits, purpose, etc.

**un·stop'** *vt.* **-stopped', -stop'ping 1** to remove the stopper from **2** to clear (a pipe, etc.) of an obstruction

**un·struc'tured** *adj.* not formally organized; loose, free, open, etc.

**un·strung'** *adj.* **1** nervous or upset **2** with the strings loosened or detached, as a bow or racket

**un·stuck'** *adj.* loosened or freed from being stuck

**un·stud'ied** *adj.* not gotten by study or conscious effort; spontaneous; natural

**un'sub·stan'tial** *adj.* **1** having no material substance **2** not solid; flimsy **3** unreal; visionary

**un·sung'** *adj.* not honored or celebrated, as in song or poetry

**un·tan'gle** *vt.* **-gled, -gling 1** to free from a snarl or tangle **2** to free from confusion; put in order

**un·taught'** *adj.* **1** not taught; uneducated **2** acquired without being taught

**un·think'a·ble** *adj.* **1** that cannot be imagined; inconceivable **2** so foul, etc. as to be unfit to be considered [*unthinkable* war crimes]

**un·think'ing** *adj.* **1** thoughtless; heedless **2** unable to think

**un·ti'dy** *adj.* **-di·er, -di·est** not neat; messy

**un·tie'** *vt.* **-tied', -ty'ing** or **-tie'ing 1** to unfasten (a thing tied or knotted) **2** to free, as from restraint

**un·til** (un til') *prep.* [ME *untill*] **1** up to the time of [*until* death] **2** before [not *until* tomorrow] —*conj.* **1** up to the time when or that [*until* you leave] **2** to the point, degree, etc. that [cook *until* it is done] **3** before [not *until* I die]

**un·time'ly** *adj., adv.* **1** before the proper time; premature(ly) **2** at the wrong time —**un·time'li·ness** *n.*

**un·to** (un'tŏō, -tœ) *prep.* [ME] *old poet. var. of:* **1** TO **2** UNTIL

**un·told'** *adj.* **1** not told or revealed **2** too many to be counted **3** indescribably great [*untold* misery]

**un·touch'a·ble** *adj.* that cannot or should not be touched —*n.* in India, a member of the lowest castes (now called *Scheduled castes*)

**un·to·ward** (un tō'ərd, -tôrd') *adj.* **1** improper, unseemly, etc. **2** not favorable; adverse

**un·trav'eled** or **un·trav'elled** *adj.* **1** not used or frequented by travelers **2** not having done much traveling

**un·truth'** *n.* **1** falsity **2** a falsehood; lie —**un·truth'ful** *adj.*

**un·tu'tored** *adj.* uneducated

**un·twist'** *vt., vi.* to loosen or separate, as something twisted together; unwind

**un·used'** *adj.* **1** not in use **2** never used before **3** unaccustomed (*to*)

**un·u'su·al** *adj.* not usual or common; rare —**un·u'su·al·ly** *adv.*

**un·ut'ter·a·ble** *adj.* inexpressible

**un·var'nished** *adj.* **1** not varnished **2** plain; simple; unadorned

**un·veil'** *vt.* to reveal as by removing a veil from —*vi.* to take off one's veil

**un·voiced′** *adj.* not expressed; not spoken

**un·war′y** *adj.* not wary or cautious

**un·wea′ried** (-wir′ēd) *adj.* [ME *unweried* (see UN- & WEARY)] never wearying; tireless; indefatigable

**un·well′** *adj.* not well; sick

**un·whole′some** *adj.* **1** harmful to body or mind **2** of unsound health or unhealthy appearance **3** morally harmful —**un·whole′some·ness** *n.*

**un·wield′y** *adj.* hard to wield, manage, etc., as because of large size

**un·will′ing** *adj.* **1** not willing; reluctant **2** done, said, etc. reluctantly —**un·will′ing·ly** *adv.*

**un·wind′** (-wīnd′) *vt.* **-wound′, -wind′ing 1** to wind off or undo (something wound) **2** to untangle (something involved) —*vi.* **1** to become unwound **2** to become relaxed

**un·wise′** *adj.* having or showing a lack of wisdom or sound judgment

**un·wit′ting** *adj.* **1** not knowing; unaware **2** unintentional

**un·wont′ed** *adj.* not common, usual, or habitual

**un·wor′thy** *adj.* **-thi·er, -thi·est 1** lacking merit or value; worthless **2** not deserving (*of*) **3** not fit or becoming: usually with *of* —**un·wor′thi·ness** *n.*

**un·wrap′** *vt.* **-wrapped′, -wrap′ping** to take off the wrapping of

**un·writ′ten** *adj.* **1** not in writing **2** operating only through custom or tradition [an *unwritten* rule]

**up**[1] (up) *adv.* [OE] **1** to, in, or on a higher place or level **2** to a later period **3** to or into a higher condition, amount, etc. **4** *a*) in or into a standing or upright position *b*) out of bed **5** in or into action, view, consideration, etc. **6** aside; away [lay *up* wealth] **7** so as to be even with in time, degree, etc. **8** completely; thoroughly [eat *up* the cake] **9** *Baseball* to one's turn at batting **10** used with verbs: *a*) to form idioms with meanings different from the simple verb [look *up* this word] *b*) as an intensive [dress *up*] —*prep.* up to, toward, along, through, into, or upon —*adj.* **1** directed toward a higher position **2** in a higher place or position **3** advanced in amount, degree, etc. [rents are *up*] **4** in a standing or upright position **5** in an active or excited state **6** at an end; over [time's *up*] **7** available for use, as a computer **8** [Inf.] going on [what's *up*] **9** *Baseball* at bat —*n.* **1** an upward slope **2** an upward movement, etc. —*vi.* **upped, up′ping** [Inf.] to get up; rise —*vt.* [Inf.] **1** to put up, lift up, etc. **2** to cause to rise [to *up* prices] —**on the up and up** [Slang] honest —**up against** [Inf.] confronted with —**up on** (or **in**) [Inf.] well-informed concerning —**ups and downs** good periods and bad periods —**up to 1** doing or scheming **2** capable of (doing, etc.) **3** as many as **4** as far as **5** dependent upon —**up with!** give or restore power, favor, etc. to!

**up**[2] (up) *adv.* [phonetic respelling of *ap(iece)*] apiece [a score of ten *up*]

**up-** *combining form* up

**up′-and-com′ing** *adj.* **1** enterprising, promising, etc. **2** gaining in prominence

**up′beat′** *n. Music* an unaccented beat, esp. when on the last note of a bar —*adj.* [Inf.] cheerful; optimistic

**up·braid′** (up brād′) *vt.* [< OE *up-*, up + *bregdan*, to pull] to rebuke severely; censure; scold

**up′bring′ing** *n.* the training and education received while growing up

**UPC** *abbrev.* Universal Product Code

**up′chuck′** *vi., vt., n.* [Slang] VOMIT

**up′com′ing** *adj.* coming soon

**up′coun′try** *adj., adv.* in or toward the interior of a country

**up·date** (up dāt′; *also, and for n. always,* up′dāt′) *vt.* **-dat′ed, -dat′ing** to make up-to-date; make conform to the most recent facts, methods, etc. —*n.* **1** an updating **2** an updated report, etc.

**up·end′** *vt., vi.* **1** to set, turn, or stand on end **2** to topple

**up′front′** [Inf.] *adj.* **1** forthright **2** in advance

[upfront money] —*adv.* in advance Also **up′-front′**

**up·grade** (up′grād′; *also, and for v. usually,* up grād′) *n.* **1** an upward slope **2** an improvement —*adj., adv.* uphill; upward —*vt., vi.* **-grad′ed, -grad′ing** to raise or improve in value, grade, rank, quality, etc.

**up·heav·al** (up hē′vəl) *n.* **1** a heaving up **2** a sudden, violent change

**up′hill′** *adv.* **1** toward the top of a hill; upward **2** with difficulty —*adj.* **1** going or sloping up **2** laborious; tiring

**up·hold′** *vt.* **-held′, -hold′ing 1** to hold up **2** to keep from falling; support **3** to confirm; sustain

**up·hol·ster** (up hōl′stər) *vt.* [ult. < ME *upholder*, tradesman] to fit out (furniture, etc.) with coverings, padding, springs, etc. —**up·hol′ster·er** *n.*

**up·hol·ster·y** *n., pl.* **-ies 1** the material used in upholstering **2** the work of an upholsterer

**up′keep′** *n.* **1** maintenance **2** state of repair **3** the cost of maintenance

**up′land** (-lənd, -land′) *n.* land elevated above other land —*adj.* of or situated in upland

**up·lift** (up lift′; *also, and for n. always,* up′lift′) *vt.* **1** to lift up **2** to raise to a higher moral, social, or cultural level —*n.* **1** a lifting up **2** a movement for moral, social, or cultural betterment

**up′load′** *vt., vi.* to transfer (information) as from a personal computer to a main computer

**up′-mar′ket** *adj.* UPSCALE

**up·on** (ə pän′, ə pôn′) *prep.* on, or up and on: used interchangeably with *on* —*adv.* on

**up·per** (up′ər) *adj.* **1** higher in place **2** higher in rank, etc. **3** farther north —*n.* **1** the part of a shoe above the sole **2** [Slang] any drug that is a stimulant —**on one's uppers** [Inf.] in need

**up·per·case** (up′ər kās′) *n.* capital-letter type used in printing, as distinguished from small letters —*adj.* of or in uppercase

**upper class** the rich or aristocratic social class —**up′per-class′** *adj.*

**up′per·class′man** (-mən) *n., pl.* **-men** (-mən) a junior or senior in high school or college

**up′per·cut′** *n. Boxing* a short, swinging blow directed upward

**upper hand** the position of advantage or control

**up′per·most′** *adj.* highest in place, authority, etc. —*adv.* in the highest place, rank, etc.

**Upper Vol·ta** (väl′tə) *former name for* BURKINA FASO

**up·pi·ty** (up′ə tē) *adj.* [Inf.] haughty, arrogant, snobbish, etc.: also [Brit. Inf.] **up′pish**

**up·raise′** *vt.* **-raised′, -rais′ing** to raise up; lift

**up·rear′** *vt.* to lift up —*vi.* to rise up

**up·right** (up′rīt′; *for adj. and adv., also* up rīt′) *adj.* **1** standing, pointing, etc. straight up; erect **2** honest and just —*adv.* in an upright position or direction —*n.* something in an upright position

**upright piano** a piano with a vertical, rectangular body

**up′ris′ing** *n.* a revolt

**up′riv′er** *adv., adj.* in the direction against the current of a river

**up·roar** (up′rôr′) *n.* [Du *oproer*, a stirring up] **1** violent disturbance; tumult **2** loud, confused noise

**up·roar·i·ous** (up rôr′ē əs) *adj.* **1** making an uproar **2** boisterous **3** causing loud laughter

**up′root′** *vt.* **1** to tear up by the roots **2** to destroy or remove utterly

**UPS** *service mark for* United Parcel Service

**up′scale′** *adj.* of or for people who are affluent, stylish, etc.

**up·set** (up set′; *for n.,* up′set′) *vt.* **-set′, -set′ting 1** *a*) to tip over; overturn *b*) to defeat unexpectedly **2** *a*) to disturb the functioning of [to *upset* a schedule] *b*) to disturb emotionally or physically —*vi.* to become overturned or upset —*n.* **1** an upsetting **2** an unexpected victory or defeat **3** a disturbance —*adj.* **1** tipped over **2** overthrown or defeated **3** disturbed or disordered

**up'shot'** *n.* [[orig., final shot in an archery match]] the conclusion; result

**up'side'**[1] *prep.* [Chiefly Dial.] on or against the side of [struck *upside* the head]

**up'side'**[2] *n.* **1** the upper side or part **2** appreciation or gain, as on an investment

**upside down 1** with the top side or part underneath or turned over; inverted **2** in disorder — **up'side'-down'** *adj.*

**up·si·lon** (ōōp'sə län', up'-) *n.* the twentieth letter of the Greek alphabet (Υ, υ)

**up·stage** (up'stāj'; *for v.*, up stāj') *adv., adj.* toward or at the rear of a stage —*vt.* **-staged', -stag'ing** to draw attention away from another, as by moving upstage

**up'stairs'** *adv.* **1** up the stairs **2** on or to an upper floor or higher level **3** [Inf.] in the mind — *adj.* on an upper floor —*n.* an upper floor

**up'stand'ing** *adj.* **1** erect **2** upright in character; honorable

**up'start'** *n.* one who has recently come into wealth, power, etc., esp. one who is presumptuous, aggressive, etc. —*adj.* of or like an upstart

**up'state'** *adj., adv.* in, to, or from the northerly part of a U.S. state

**up'stream'** *adv., adj.* in the direction against the current of a stream

**up'surge'** *n.* a surge upward

**up'swing'** *n.* a swing, trend, or movement upward

**up'take'** *n.* a taking up —**quick** (or **slow**) **on the uptake** [Inf.] quick (or slow) to comprehend

**up'tight'** *adj.* [Slang] very tense, nervous, etc.: also **up-tight**

**up'-to-date'** *adj.* **1** extending to the present time **2** keeping up with what is most recent

**up'town'** *adj., adv.* in or toward the residential part of a city —*n.* the uptown section of a city

**up·turn'** (-tɜrn'; *for n.*, up'tɜrn') *vt., vi.* to turn up or over —*n.* an upward turn or trend — **up'turned'** *adj.*

**up'ward** *adv., adj.* toward a higher place, position, etc.: also **up'wards** *adv.* —**upwards** (or **upward**) **of** more than —**up'ward·ly** *adv.*

**upward mobility** movement to a higher social and economic status

**up'wind'** *adv., adj.* in the direction from which the wind is blowing or usually blows

**Ur** (oor, ɜr) ancient city on the Euphrates River

**u·ra·cil** (yoor'ə sil') *n.* a colorless, crystalline base that is a constituent of RNA

**U·ral Mountains** (yoor'əl) mountain system in Russia, regarded as the boundary between Europe & Asia: also **Urals**

**u·ra·ni·um** (yoo rā'nē əm) *n.* [[after fol.]] a very hard, heavy, silver-colored, radioactive, metallic chemical element: used in work on atomic energy

**U·ra·nus** (yoor'ə nəs, yoo rā'nəs) *n.* [[< Gr *Ouranos*, heaven]] the planet seventh in distance from the sun: see PLANET

**ur·ban** (ɜr'bən) *adj.* [[< L *urbs*, city]] **1** of, in, or constituting a city **2** characteristic of cities

**ur·bane** (ɜr bān') *adj.* [[see prec.]] polite in a smooth, polished way; refined —**ur·ban'i·ty** (-ban'ə tē) *n.*

**ur·ban·ize** (ɜr'bə nīz') *vt.* **-ized', -iz'ing** to change from rural to urban —**ur'ban·i·za'tion** *n.*

**urban legend** (or **myth**) a widely circulating secondhand report of a purportedly true incident

**urban renewal** rehabilitation of deteriorated urban areas, as by slum clearance and housing construction

**urban sprawl** the spread of urban congestion into surrounding areas

**ur·chin** (ɜr'chin) *n.* [[< L *ericius*, hedgehog]] a small child; esp., a mischievous boy

**-ure** (ər) [[Fr < L *-ura*]] *suffix* **1** act, process, or result [*exposure*] **2** agent of **3** state of being

ed [*composure*] **4** office, rank, or collective body [*legislature*]

**u·re·a** (yoo rē'ə) *n.* [[< Gr *ouron*, urine]] a soluble, crystalline solid found in urine or made synthetically

**u·re·mi·a** (yoo rē'mē ə) *n.* [[< Gr *ouron*, urine + *haima*, blood]] a toxic condition caused by the presence in the blood of waste products normally eliminated in the urine —**u·re'mic** *adj.*

**u·re·ter** (yoo rēt'ər) *n.* [[< Gr *ourein*, urinate]] a tube carrying urine from a kidney to the bladder

**u·re·thane** (yoor'ə thān') *n.* [[< Fr]] a white, crystalline compound used as a hypnotic and sedative, a solvent, etc.

**u·re·thra** (yoo rē'thrə) *n., pl.* **-thrae** (-thrē') or **-thras** [[< Gr *ouron*, urine]] the duct through which urine is discharged from the bladder: in males, also the duct for semen

**urge** (ɜrj) *vt.* **urged, urg'ing** [[L *urgere*, press hard]] **1** *a*) to press upon the attention; advocate *b*) to plead with; ask earnestly **2** to incite; provoke **3** to drive or force onward —*n.* **1** an urging **2** an impulse

**ur·gent** (ɜr'jənt) *adj.* [[see prec.]] **1** calling for haste, immediate action, etc. **2** insistent — **ur'gen·cy**, *pl.* **-cies**, *n.* —**ur'gent·ly** *adv.*

**-ur·gy** (ɜr'jē) [[< Gr *ergon*, work]] *combining form* a working with or by means of (something specified) [*chemurgy*]

**u·ric** (yoor'ik) *adj.* of, in, or from urine

**u·ri·nal** (yoor'ə nəl) *n.* **1** a receptacle or fixture for urinating **2** a place for urinating

**u·ri·nal·y·sis** (yoor'ə nal'ə sis) *n., pl.* **-ses'** (-sēz') chemical or microscopic analysis of urine

**u·ri·nar·y** (yoor'ə ner'ē) *adj.* **1** of urine **2** of the organs that secrete and discharge urine

**u·ri·nate** (yoor'ə nāt') *vi.* **-nat'ed, -nat'ing** to discharge urine from the body —**u'ri·na'tion** *n.*

**u·rine** (yoor'in) *n.* [[< L *urina*]] the yellowish liquid, containing waste products, secreted by the kidneys and discharged through the urethra

**URL** *n.* [[*u*(niform) *r*(esource) *l*(ocator)]] an address on the World Wide Web

**urn** (ɜrn) *n.* [[< L *urna*]] **1** *a*) a vase with a pedestal *b*) such a vase used to hold ashes after cremation **2** a metal container with a faucet, for making or serving hot coffee, tea, etc.

URN

**u·ro·gen·i·tal** (yoor'ō jen'i təl) *adj.* of the urinary and genital organs

**u·rol·o·gy** (yoo räl'ə jē) *n.* [[< Gr *ouron*, urine + -LOGY]] the branch of medicine dealing with the urinary and genital organs and their diseases —**u·rol'o·gist** *n.*

**Ur·sa Major** (ɜr'sə) [[L, lit., Great Bear]] a prominent N constellation

**Ursa Minor** [[L, lit., Little Bear]] a N constellation, containing Polaris

**ur·sine** (ɜr'sīn', -sin) *adj.* [[< L *ursus*, a bear]] of or like a bear

**ur·ti·car·i·a** (ɜrt'i ker'ē ə) *n.* [[< L *urtica*, a nettle]] HIVES

**U·ru·guay** (yoor'ə gwā', oor'-; -gwī') country in SE South America: 68,037 sq. mi.; pop. 2,940,000 — **Ur'u·guay'an** *adj., n.*

**us** (us) *pron.* [[OE]] *objective form of* WE

**US** or **U.S.** United States

**USA** *abbrev.* **1** United States of America: also **U.S.A.** **2** United States Army

**us·a·ble** or **use·a·ble** (yōō'zə bəl) *adj.* that can be used; fit for use —**us'a·bil'i·ty** (-bil'ə tē) or **use'a·bil'i·ty** *n.*

**USAF** *abbrev.* United States Air Force

**us·age** (yōō'sij) *n.* **1** the act, way, or extent of using; treatment **2** established practice; custom; habit **3** the way in which a word, phrase, etc. is used to express a particular idea

**USCG** *abbrev.* United States Coast Guard

**USDA** *abbrev.* United States Department of Agriculture

**use** (yo͞oz; *for n.,* yo͞os) *vt.* **used, us′ing** ⟦< L *uti*⟧ **1** to put into action or service **2** to exercise *[use your judgment]* **3** to deal with; treat *[to use a friend badly]* **4** to consume, expend: often with *up* **5** to consume habitually *[to use drugs]* **6** to exploit (someone) —*n.* **1** a using or being used **2** the ability to use **3** the right to use **4** the need or opportunity to use **5** a way of using **6** usefulness **7** the purpose for which something is used **8** function —**used to** (yo͞os′tə, -to͞o) **1** did at one time *[I used to live here]* **2** accustomed to

**used** (yo͞ozd) *vt. pt. & pp. of* USE —*adj.* not new; secondhand

**use·ful** (yo͞os′fəl) *adj.* that can be used; serviceable; helpful —**use′ful·ly** *adv.* —**use′ful·ness** *n.*

**use′less** (-lis) *adj.* **1** having no use **2** to no purpose —**use′less·ly** *adv.* —**use′less·ness** *n.*

**us·er** (yo͞o′zər) *n.* one that uses something; specif., one who uses drugs habitually, a computer, etc.

**us′er-friend′ly** *adj.* easy to use or understand: said esp. of computer hardware, programs, etc.

**ush·er** (ush′ər) *n.* ⟦< L *ostiarius*, doorkeeper⟧ **1** one who shows people to their seats in a theater, church, etc. **2** a bridegroom's attendant —*vt.* **1** to escort (others) to seats, etc. **2** to be a forerunner of: often with *in*

**USMC** *abbrev.* United States Marine Corps

**USN** *abbrev.* United States Navy

**USO** *abbrev.* United Service Organizations

**USP** *abbrev.* United States Pharmacopoeia

**USPS** *abbrev.* United States Postal Service

**USS** *abbrev.* United States Ship

**USSR** or **U.S.S.R.** Union of Soviet Socialist Republics

**u·su·al** (yo͞o′zhə wəl) *adj.* [see USE] such as is most often seen, used, etc.; common; customary —**u′su·al·ly** *adv.*

**u·surp** (yo͞o surp′, -zurp′) *vt., vi.* ⟦< L *usus*, a use + *rapere*, to seize⟧ to take (power, a position, etc.) by force —**u·sur·pa·tion** (yo͞o′zər pā′shən, -sər-) *n.* —**u·surp′er** *n.*

**u·su·ry** (yo͞o′zhə rē) *n., pl.* **-ries** [see USE] **1** the lending of money at an excessive rate of interest **2** an excessive interest rate —**u′su·rer** *n.* —**u·su·ri·ous** (yo͞o zhoor′ē əs) *adj.*

**U·tah** (yo͞o′tô′, -tä′) Mountain State of the W U.S.: 82,168 sq. mi.; pop. 1,723,000; cap. Salt Lake City: abbrev. **UT** —**U′tah·an** or (local usage) **U·tahn** (yo͞o′tôn′, -tän′) *adj., n.*

**u·ten·sil** (yo͞o ten′səl) *n.* ⟦< L *uti*, to use⟧ an implement or container, esp. one for use in a kitchen

**u·ter·us** (yo͞o′tə rəs) *n., pl.* **-ter·i′** (-ī′) ⟦L⟧ a hollow organ of female mammals in which the embryo and fetus are developed; womb —**u′ter·ine** (-rin, -rīn′) *adj.*

**u·til·i·tar·i·an** (yo͞o til′ə ter′ē ən) *adj.* **1** of or having to do with utility **2** stressing usefulness over beauty or other considerations

**u·til′i·tar′i·an·ism′** *n.* **1** the doctrine that worth or value is determined solely by utility **2** the doctrine that the purpose of all action should be to bring about the greatest happiness of the greatest number

**u·til·i·ty** (yo͞o til′ə tē) *n., pl.* **-ties** ⟦< L *uti*, to use⟧ **1** usefulness **2** something useful, as the service to the public of gas, water, etc. **3** a company providing such a service

**utility room** a room containing laundry appliances, heating equipment, etc.

**u·ti·lize** (yo͞ot′'l īz′) *vt.* **-lized′, -liz′ing** to put to profitable use; make use of —**u′ti·li·za′tion** *n.*

**ut·most** (ut′mōst′) *adj.* ⟦< OE superl. of *ut*, out⟧ **1** farthest **2** of the greatest degree, amount, etc. —*n.* the most that is possible

**U·to·pi·a** (yo͞o tō′pē ə) *n.* ⟦< Gr *ou*, not + *topos*, a place⟧ **1** an imaginary island with a perfect political and social system, described in *Utopia* (1516) by Sir Thomas More, Eng. statesman **2** *[often* **u-***]* *a)* any idealized place of perfection *b)* any visionary scheme for a perfect society —**U·to′pi·an** or **u·to′pi·an** *adj., n.*

**ut·ter**[1] (ut′ər) *adj.* ⟦< OE compar. of *ut*, out⟧ **1** complete; total **2** unqualified; absolute; unconditional —**ut′ter·ly** *adv.*

**ut·ter**[2] (ut′ər) *vt.* ⟦< ME *utter*, outward⟧ to speak or express audibly (sounds, words, etc.)

**ut′ter·ance** *n.* **1** an uttering **2** the power or style of speaking **3** that which is uttered

**ut′ter·most′** *adj., n.* UTMOST

**U′-turn′** *n.* **1** a turn by a car made so as to head in the opposite direction **2** a reversal of opinion, strategy, etc.

**UV** or **uv** *abbrev.* ultraviolet

**u·vu·la** (yo͞o′vyə lə) *n., pl.* **-las** or **-lae′** (-lē′) ⟦< L *uva*, grape⟧ the small, fleshy part hanging down from the soft palate above the back of the tongue —**u′vu·lar** *adj.*

**ux·o·ri·ous** (uk sôr′ē əs, -zôr′-) *adj.* ⟦< L < *uxor*, wife⟧ dotingly fond of or submissive to one's wife

**Uz·bek·i·stan** (o͞oz bek′i stan′) country in central Asia: formerly a republic of the U.S.S.R.: 172,741 sq. mi.; pop. 19,810,000

**U·zi** (o͞o′zē) *trademark for* a small submachine gun

# V

**v**[1] or **V** (vē) *n., pl.* **v's, V's** the 22d letter of the English alphabet

**v**[2] *abbrev.* **1** ⟦L *vide*⟧ see **2** velocity **3** verb **4** versus **5** volt(s) **6** volume

**V**[1] (vē) *n.* a Roman numeral for 5

**V**[2] *abbrev.* **1** velocity **2** volt(s) **3** volume

**V**[3] *Chem. symbol for* vanadium

**VA** *abbrev.* **1** Veterans Administration **2** Virginia

**va·can·cy** (vā′kən sē) *n., pl.* **-cies** **1** a being vacant **2** empty or vacant space **3** an unoccupied position, office, quarters, etc.

**va·cant** (vā′kənt) *adj.* ⟦< L *vacare*, be empty⟧ **1** having nothing in it **2** not held, occupied, etc., as a seat or house **3** free from work; leisure *[vacant time]* **4** without thought, interest, etc.

**va′cate** (-kāt′) *vt.* **-cat′ed, -cat′ing** **1** to cause (an office, house, etc.) to be vacant **2** *Law* to make void; annul

**va·ca·tion** (vā kā′shən, və-) *n.* ⟦< L *vacatio*⟧ a period of rest from work, study, etc. —*vi.* to take one's vacation —**va·ca′tion·er** or **va·ca′tion·ist** *n.*

**vac·ci·nate** (vak′sə nāt′) *vt., vi.* **-nat′ed, -nat′ing** to inoculate with a vaccine to prevent disease —**vac′ci·na′tion** *n.*

**vac·cine** (vak sēn′) *n.* ⟦< L *vacca*, cow: from use of cowpox virus in smallpox vaccine⟧ any preparation introduced into the body to produce immunity to a specific disease

**vac·il·late** (vas′ə lāt′) *vi.* **-lat′ed, -lat′ing** ⟦< L *vacillare*⟧ **1** to sway to and fro; waver **2** to fluctuate **3** to show indecision —**vac′il·la′tion** *n.*

**va·cu·i·ty** (va kyo͞o′ə tē) *n., pl.* **-ties** ⟦< L *vacuus*, empty⟧ **1** emptiness **2** an empty space **3** emptiness of mind **4** something senseless or silly

**vac·u·ous** (vak′yo͞o əs) *adj.* ⟦L *vacuus*⟧ **1** empty **2** stupid; senseless —**vac′u·ous·ly** *adv.*

**vac·uum** (vak′yo͞om) *n., pl.* **-ums** or **-u·a** (-yo͞o ə) ⟦L⟧ **1** space with nothing at all in it **2** a space from which most of the air or gas has been taken **3** any void —*adj.* **1** of or used to make a vacuum

**2** having or working by a vacuum —*vt., vi.* to clean with a vacuum cleaner

**vacuum cleaner** a machine for cleaning carpets, floors, etc. by suction

**vac′uum-packed′** *adj.* packed in an airtight container to maintain freshness

**vacuum tube** an electron tube from which most of the air has been evacuated, containing one or more grids, used as an amplifier, etc.

**vag·a·bond** (vag′ə bänd′) *adj.* ⟦< L *vagari*, wander⟧ **1** wandering **2** living a drifting or irresponsible life; shiftless —*n.* **1** one who wanders from place to place **2** a wandering beggar **3** an idle or shiftless person —**vag′a·bond′age** *n.*

**va·gar·y** (vā′gə rē, və ger′ē) *n., pl.* -ies ⟦see prec.⟧ **1** an odd or eccentric action **2** a whimsical or freakish notion; caprice —**va·gar′i·ous** *adj.*

**va·gi·na** (və ji′nə) *n., pl.* -nas or -nae (-nē) ⟦L, sheath⟧ in female mammals, the canal from the vulva to the uterus —**vag·i·nal** (vaj′ə nəl) *adj.*

**va·grant** (vā′grənt) *n.* ⟦prob. < OFr *walcrer*, wander⟧ one who wanders from place to place supporting oneself by begging, etc. —*adj.* **1** nomadic **2** of or like a vagrant **3** wayward, erratic, etc. —**va′gran·cy,** *pl.* -cies, *n.*

**vague** (vāg) *adj.* **va′guer, va′guest** ⟦< L *vagus*, wandering⟧ **1** indefinite in shape or form **2** not sharp, certain, or precise in thought or expression —**vague′ly** *adv.* —**vague′ness** *n.*

**vain** (vān) *adj.* ⟦< L *vanus*, empty⟧ **1** having no real value; worthless [*vain* pomp] **2** without effect; futile [a *vain* endeavor] **3** having an excessively high regard for one's self, looks, etc.; conceited —**in vain 1** fruitlessly **2** profanely

**vain′glo′ry** (-glôr′ē) *n.* ⟦< L *vana gloria*, empty boasting⟧ excessive vanity —**vain′glo′ri·ous** *adj.*

**val** *abbrev.* **1** valuation **2** value

**val·ance** (val′əns, vā′ləns) *n.* ⟦ME < ?⟧ a short curtain forming a border, esp. across the top of a window

**vale** (vāl) *n.* [Old Poet.] VALLEY

**val·e·dic·to·ri·an** (val′ə dik tôr′ē ən) *n.* the student, usually the one with the highest grades, who delivers the valedictory at graduation

**val·e·dic′to·ry** (-tər ē) *n., pl.* -ries ⟦< L *vale*, farewell + *dicere*, to say⟧ a farewell speech, esp. at graduation

**va·lence** (vā′ləns) *n.* ⟦< L *valere*, be strong⟧ *Chem.* the combining capacity of an element or radical as measured by the number of hydrogen or chlorine atoms which one radical or atom of the element will combine with or replace: also **va′len·cy,** *pl.* -cies

**Va·len·ci·a** (və len′shē ə, -shə) seaport in E Spain: pop. 763,000

**val·en·tine** (val′ən tīn′) *n.* **1** a sweetheart chosen or greeted on Saint Valentine's Day **2** a greeting card or gift sent on this day

**val·et** (va lā′; *also, but now rarely* val′it) *n.* ⟦Fr, a groom⟧ **1** a personal manservant who takes care of a man's clothes, helps him dress, etc. **2** an employee, as of a hotel, who cleans or presses clothes, etc.

**val·e·tu·di·nar·i·an** (val′ə tōō′də ner′ē ən) *n.* ⟦< L *valetudo*, state of health, sickness⟧ **1** a person in poor health **2** one who worries about one's health

**Val·hal·la** (val hal′ə, väl häl′ə) *n. Norse Myth.* the great hall where Odin feasts the souls of heroes slain in battle

**val·iant** (val′yənt) *adj.* ⟦< L *valere*, be strong⟧ brave; courageous —**val′iance** *n.* —**val′iant·ly** *adv.*

**val·id** (val′id) *adj.* ⟦< L *valere*, be strong⟧ **1** having legal force **2** based on evidence or sound reasoning —**val′id·ly** *adv.* —**val′id·ness** *n.*

**val·i·date** (val′ə dāt′) *vt.* -dat′ed, -dat′ing **1** to make legally valid **2** to prove to be valid

**va·lid·i·ty** (və lid′ə tē) *n., pl.* -ties the quality or fact of being valid

**va·lise** (və lēs′) *n.* ⟦Fr < L *valesium* < ?⟧ [Old-fashioned] a piece of hand luggage

**Val·i·um** (val′ē əm) *trademark for* a tranquilizing drug

**Val·kyr·ie** (val kir′ē, val′ki rē) *n. Norse Myth.* any of the maidens of Odin who conduct the souls of heroes slain in battle to Valhalla

**val·ley** (val′ē) *n., pl.* -leys ⟦< L *vallis*⟧ **1** low land lying between hills or mountains **2** the land drained by a river system **3** any valleylike dip

**Valley Forge** village in SE Pennsylvania: scene of Washington's winter encampment (1777-78)

**val·or** (val′ər) *n.* ⟦< L *valere*, be strong⟧ courage or bravery: Brit. sp. **val′our** —**val′or·ous** *adj.*

**Val·pa·rai·so** (val′pə rā′zō, -rī′sō) seaport in central Chile: pop. 277,000

**val·u·a·ble** (val′yə bəl, -yōō ə bəl) *adj.* **1** having value, esp. great monetary value **2** highly important, esteemed, etc. —*n.* an article of value: *usually used in pl.*

**val·u·a·tion** (val′yōō ā′shən) *n.* **1** the determining of the value of anything **2** determined or estimated value

**val·ue** (val′yōō) *n.* ⟦< L *valere* be worth⟧ **1** the worth of a thing in money or goods **2** estimated worth **3** purchasing power **4** that quality of a thing which makes it more or less desirable, useful, etc. **5** a thing or quality having intrinsic worth **6** [*pl.*] beliefs or standards **7** relative duration, intensity, etc. —*vt.* **val′ued, val′u·ing 1** to estimate the value of; appraise **2** to place a certain estimate of worth on [to *value* health above wealth] **3** to think highly of —**val′ue·less** *adj.*

**val′ue-add′ed tax** a tax based and paid on products, etc. at each stage of production or distribution, and included in the cost to the consumer

**val′ued** *adj.* highly thought of

**value judgment** an estimate made of the worth, goodness, etc. of a person, action, etc., esp. when such a judgment is not called for or desired

**valve** (valv) *n.* ⟦< L *valva*, leaf of a folding door⟧ **1** *Anat.* a membranous structure which permits body fluids to flow in one direction only, or opens and closes a tube, etc. **2** any device in a pipe, etc. that regulates the flow by means of a flap, lid, etc. **3** *Music* a device, as in the trumpet, that changes the tube length so as to change the pitch **4** *Zoology* one of the parts making up the shell of a mollusk, clam, etc.

**va·moose** (va mōōs′) *vi., vt.* -moosed′, -moos′ing ⟦< Sp *vamos*, let us go⟧ [Old Slang] to leave quickly

**vamp** (vamp) *n.* ⟦< OFr *avant*, before + *pié*, foot⟧ **1** the part of a boot or shoe covering the instep **2** *Music* a simple, improvised introduction or interlude —*vi. Music* to play a vamp

**vam·pire** (vam′pīr′) *n.* ⟦< Slavic⟧ **1** in folklore, a reanimated corpse that sucks the blood of sleeping persons **2** one who preys ruthlessly on others

**vampire bat** a tropical American bat that lives on the blood of animals

**van**[1] (van) *n. short for* VANGUARD

**van**[2] (van) *n.* ⟦< CARAVAN⟧ a large, closed truck used as for moving, or a small one used for deliveries, fitted out as an RV, etc.

**va·na·di·um** (və nā′dē əm) *n.* ⟦< ON *Vanadis*, goddess of love⟧ a ductile, metallic chemical element used in steel alloys, etc.

**Van Al·len radiation belt** (van al′ən) ⟦after J. *Van Allen* (1914- ), U.S. physicist⟧ a broad belt of radiation encircling the earth at varying levels

**Van Bu·ren** (van byoor′ən), **Mar·tin** (märt′′n) 1782-1862; 8th president of the U.S. (1837-41)

**Van·cou·ver** (van kōō′vər) seaport in SW British Columbia, Canada: pop. 514,000

**Van·dal** (van′dəl) *n.* **1** a member of a Germanic people that sacked Rome (A.D. 455) **2** [v-] one who maliciously destroys property

**van·dal·ize** (van′də līz′) *vt.* -ized′, -iz′ing to destroy or damage (property) maliciously —**van′dal·ism′** *n.*

**Van·dyke** (**beard**) (van dīk′) a closely trimmed, pointed beard

**vane** (vān) *n.* ⟦< OE *fana*, a flag⟧ **1** a free-swinging piece of metal, etc. that shows which way the wind is blowing; weather vane **2** any of the flat pieces set around an axle and rotated about it by moving air, water, etc. or rotated to move the air or water

**van Gogh** (van gō′, -gôkh′), **Vin·cent** (vin′sənt) 1853-90; Du. painter

**van·guard** (van′gärd′) *n.* ⟦< OFr *avant*, before + *garde*, guard⟧ **1** the part of an army which goes ahead of the main body **2** the leading position or persons in a movement

**va·nil·la** (və nil′ə) *n.* ⟦< Sp *vaina*, pod⟧ **1** a climbing orchid with podlike capsules (**vanilla beans**) **2** a flavoring made from these capsules —*adj.* **1** of or flavored with vanilla **2** [in allusion to the commonness of *vanilla* ice cream] [Inf.] bland, plain, or basic

**van·ish** (van′ish) *vi.* ⟦see EVANESCENT⟧ **1** to pass suddenly from sight; disappear **2** to cease to exist

**van·i·ty** (van′ə tē) *n., pl.* **-ties** ⟦< L *vanus*, vain⟧ **1** anything vain or futile **2** worthlessness; futility **3** being vain, or too proud of oneself **4** a small table with a mirror for use while putting on cosmetics, etc. **5** a bathroom cabinet containing a washbowl

VANILLA PLANT WITH BEANS

**vanity case** a woman's small traveling case for carrying cosmetics, toilet articles, etc.

**van·quish** (van′kwish, van′-) *vt.* ⟦< L *vincere*⟧ to conquer or defeat

**van·tage** (van′tij) *n.* ⟦see ADVANTAGE⟧ **1** a favorable position **2** a position allowing a clear view, understanding, etc.: also **vantage point**

**Va·nua·tu** (van′wä tōō′) country on a group of islands in the SW Pacific, west of Fiji: 4,706 sq. mi.; pop. 143,000

**vap·id** (vap′id) *adj.* ⟦L *vapidus*⟧ tasteless; dull — **va·pid·i·ty** (va pid′ə tē) or **vap′id·ness** *n.*

**va·por** (vā′pər) *n.* ⟦L⟧ **1** *a)* visible particles of moisture floating in the air, as fog or steam *b)* smoke, fumes, etc. **2** the gaseous form of any substance normally a liquid or solid Brit. sp. **va′pour**

**va′por·ize′** (-pə rīz′) *vt., vi.* **-ized′, -iz′ing** to change into vapor —**va′por·i·za′tion** *n.* —**va′por·iz′er** *n.*

**va·por·ous** (vā′pər əs) *adj.* **1** forming or full of vapor; foggy; misty **2** like vapor

**vapor trail** CONTRAIL

**va·que·ro** (vä ker′ō) *n., pl.* **-ros** ⟦Sp < *vaca*, cow⟧ [Southwest] a man who herds cattle; cowboy

**var** *abbrev.* **1** variant(s) **2** various

**var·i·a·ble** (ver′ē ə bəl, var′-) *adj.* **1** apt to change or vary; changeable, inconstant, etc. **2** that can be changed or varied —*n.* anything changeable; a thing that varies —**var′i·a·bil′i·ty** *n.*

**var·i·ance** (-əns) *n.* **1** a varying or being variant **2** degree of change or difference; discrepancy **3** official permission to bypass regulations —**at variance** not in agreement or accord

**var·i·ant** (-ənt) *adj.* varying; different in some way from others of the same kind —*n.* anything variant, as a different spelling of the same word

**var·i·a′tion** (-ā′shən) *n.* **1** a varying; change in form, extent, etc. **2** the degree of such change **3** a thing somewhat different from another of the same kind **4** *Music* the repetition of a theme with changes in rhythm, key, etc.

**var·i·col·ored** (ver′i kul′ərd, var′-) *adj.* of several or many colors

**var·i·cose** (var′ə kōs′) *adj.* ⟦< L *varix*, enlarged vein⟧ abnormally and irregularly swollen [*varicose* veins]

**var·ied** (ver′ēd, var′-) *adj.* **1** of different kinds; various **2** changed; altered

**var·i·e·gat·ed** (ver′ē ə gāt′id, var′-) *adj.* ⟦< L *varius*, various⟧ **1** marked with different colors in spots, streaks, etc. **2** having variety; varied

**va·ri·e·tal** (və rī′ə təl) *adj.* **1** of or being a variety **2** designating a wine named after the kind of grape from which it is made —*n.* a varietal wine

**va·ri′e·ty** (-tē) *n., pl.* **-ties 1** a being various or varied **2** a different form of some thing, condition, etc.; kind **3** a collection of different things

**variety store** a retail store selling many small, inexpensive items

**var·i·ous** (ver′ē əs, var′-) *adj.* ⟦L *varius*, diverse⟧ **1** differing one from another; of several kinds **2** several or many —**var′i·ous·ly** *adv.*

**var·let** (vär′lit) *n.* ⟦OFr, a page⟧ [Archaic] a scoundrel; knave

**var·mint** or **var·ment** (vär′mənt) *n.* ⟦var. of VERMIN⟧ [Inf. or Dial.] a person or animal regarded as objectionable

**var·nish** (vär′nish) *n.* ⟦< ML *veronix*, resin⟧ **1** a preparation of resinous substances dissolved in oil, alcohol, etc., used to give a hard, glossy surface to wood, metal, etc. **2** this surface **3** a surface smoothness, as of manner —*vt.* **1** to cover with varnish **2** to make superficially attractive

**var·si·ty** (vär′sə tē) *n., pl.* **-ties** ⟦< UNIVERSITY⟧ the main team representing a university, school, etc., as in a sport

**var·y** (ver′ē, var′ē) *vt.* **var′ied, var′y·ing** ⟦< L *varius, various*⟧ **1** to change; alter **2** to make different from one another **3** to give variety to [to *vary* one's reading] —*vi.* **1** to undergo change **2** to be different **3** to deviate or depart (*from*)

**vas·cu·lar** (vas′kyə lər) *adj.* ⟦< L *vas*, vessel⟧ of or having vessels or ducts for conveying blood, sap, etc.

**vase** (vās, vāz) *n.* ⟦< L *vas*, vessel⟧ an open container used for decoration, displaying flowers, etc.

**vas·ec·to·my** (va sek′tə mē) *n., pl.* **-mies** ⟦< L *vas*, vessel + -ECTOMY⟧ the surgical removal or tying of the duct carrying sperm from the testicle

**Vas·e·line** (vas′ə lēn′) ⟦< Ger *was(ser)*, water + Gr *el(aion)*, oil⟧ *trademark for* petrolatum —*n.* [**v-**] petrolatum

**vas·o·mo·tor** (vas′ō mōt′ər, vā′zō-) *adj.* ⟦< L *vas*, vessel + MOTOR⟧ regulating the diameter of blood vessels: said of a nerve, drug, etc.

**vas·sal** (vas′əl) *n.* ⟦< ML *vassus*, servant⟧ **1** under feudalism, one who held land, owing fealty to an overlord **2** a subordinate, servant, slave, etc. — **vas′sal·age** (-ij) *n.*

**vast** (vast) *adj.* ⟦L *vastus*⟧ very great in size, degree, etc. —**vast′ly** *adv.* —**vast′ness** *n.*

**vat** (vat) *n.* ⟦< OE *fæt*, cask⟧ a large container for holding liquids

**VAT** (vē′ā′tē′, vat) *abbrev.* value-added tax

**Vat·i·can** (vat′i kən) *n.* **1** the papal palace in Vatican City **2** the papal government

**Vatican City** independent papal state, an enclave in Rome (Italy), including the Vatican: 108 acres or 0.17 sq. mi.; pop. *c.* 1,000

**vaude·ville** (vôd′vil) *n.* ⟦Fr, after *Vau-de-Vire*, a valley in Normandy, famous for convivial songs⟧ a stage show consisting of various acts

**vault¹** (vôlt) *n.* ⟦< L *volvere*, to roll⟧ **1** an arched roof or ceiling **2** an arched chamber or space **3** a cellar room used for storage **4** a burial chamber **5** a room for the safekeeping of valuables, as in a bank —*vt.* to cover with, or build as, a vault —*vi.* to curve like a vault

GROINED VAULT

**vault²** (vôlt) *vi., vt.* ⟦< earlier It *voltare*⟧ to jump over (a barrier), esp. with the hands supported on the barrier or holding a long pole —*n.* a vaulting —vault'er *n.*

**vault'ing** *adj.* **1** leaping **2** unduly confident [*vaulting* ambition] **3** used in vaulting

**vaunt** (vônt) *vi., n.* [< L *vanus,* vain] boast — vaunt'ed *adj.*

**VCR** *n.* VIDEOCASSETTE RECORDER

**VD** *abbrev.* venereal disease

**VDT** *n.* a video display terminal

**-'ve** (v, əv) *suffix* have: used in contractions [*we've* seen it]

**veal** (vēl) *n.* [< L *vitulus,* calf] the flesh of a young calf, used as food

**vec·tor** (vek'tər) *n.* [< L *vehere,* to carry] **1** an animal that transmits a disease-producing organism **2** *Math. a)* an expression that denotes magnitude and direction, as velocity *b)* a line segment representing such an expression **3** the compass heading of an aircraft, etc.

**Ve·da** (vā'də, vē'-) *n.* [Sans *veda,* knowledge] any of four ancient sacred books of Hinduism —**Ve'dic** *adj.*

**Veep** (vēp) *n.* [*sometimes* v-] [Inf.] a vice-president

**veer** (vir) *vi., vt.* [< Fr *virer,* turn around] to change in direction; shift; turn —*n.* a change of direction

**veg·e·ta·ble** (vej'tə bəl, vej'ə tə-) *adj.* [see VEGETATE] **1** of plants in general **2** of, from, or like edible vegetables —*n.* **1** any plant, as distinguished from animal or inorganic matter **2** a plant eaten whole or in part, raw or cooked **3** a person thought of as like a vegetable, as a person in a coma

**veg·e·tar·i·an** (vej'ə ter'ē ən) *n.* one who eats no meat —*adj.* **1** of vegetarians **2** consisting only of vegetables

**veg·e·tate** (vej'ə tāt') *vi.* -tat'ed, -tat'ing [< L *vegere,* quicken] **1** to grow as plants **2** to lead a dull, inactive life —**veg'e·ta'tive** *adj.*

**veg·e·ta'tion** (-tā'shən) *n.* **1** a vegetating **2** plant life in general

**veg·gie** (vej'ē) [Slang] *n.* **1** a vegetable **2** a vegetarian —*adj.* vegetarian Also **veg'ie**

**ve·he·ment** (vē'ə mənt) *adj.* [< L *vehere,* carry] **1** violent; impetuous **2** full of intense or strong passion —**ve'he·mence** or **ve'he·men·cy** *n.* —**ve'he·ment·ly** *adv.*

**ve·hi·cle** (vē'ə kəl) *n.* [< L *vehere,* to carry] **1** any device for carrying or conveying persons or objects **2** a means of expressing thoughts, etc. — **ve·hic'u·lar** (-hik'yo͞o lər) *adj.*

**veil** (vāl) *n.* [< L *velum,* cloth] **1** a piece of light fabric, as of net, worn, esp. by women, over the face or head **2** anything used to conceal, cover, separate, etc. [a *veil* of silence] **3** a part of a nun's headdress —*vt.* **1** to cover with a veil **2** to hide or disguise —**take the veil** to become a nun

**veiled** (vāld) *adj.* **1** wearing a veil **2** concealed, hidden, etc. **3** not openly expressed

**vein** (vān) *n.* [< L *vena*] **1** any blood vessel carrying blood to the heart **2** any of the ribs of an insect's wing or of a leaf blade **3** a body of minerals occupying a fissure in rock **4** a lode **5** a streak of a different color, etc., as in marble **6** a distinctive quality in one's character, speech, etc. **7** a mood —*vt.* to mark as with veins

**Vel·cro** (vel'krō) *trademark for* a nylon material for fastenings, made up of matching strips with tiny hooks and adhesive pile, that can be easily pressed together or pulled apart —*n.* [*occas.* v-] this material

**veld** or **veldt** (velt) *n.* [Afrik < MDu *veld,* field] in S & E Africa, open, grassy country, with few bushes or trees

**vel·lum** (vel'əm) *n.* [< L *vitulus,* calf] **1** a fine parchment prepared from calfskin, lambskin, etc. used for writing on or for binding books **2** a strong paper made to resemble this

**ve·loc·i·ty** (və läs'ə tē) *n., pl.* -ties [< L *velox,*

swift] **1** quickness of motion; swiftness **2** rate of change of position, in relation to time; speed

**ve·lour** or **ve·lours** (və lo͞or') *n., pl.* -lours' (-lo͞orz', -lo͞or') [Fr < L *villus,* shaggy hair] a fabric with a soft nap like velvet

**ve·lum** (vē'ləm) *n., pl.* -la (-lə) [L, a veil] SOFT PALATE

**vel·vet** (vel'vət) *n.* [< L *villus,* shaggy hair] **1** a rich fabric of silk, rayon, etc. with a soft, thick pile **2** anything like velvet in texture —*adj.* **1** made of velvet **2** like velvet —**vel'vet·y** *adj.*

**vel·vet·een** (-və tēn') *n.* a cotton cloth with a short, thick pile like velvet

**ve·nal** (vē'nəl) *adj.* [L *venalis,* for sale] open to, or characterized by, bribery or corruption —**ve·nal·i·ty** (vi nal'ə tē) *n.*

**vend** (vend) *vt., vi.* [< L *venum dare,* offer for sale] to sell (goods) —**ven'dor** or **vend'er** *n.*

**ven·det·ta** (ven det'ə) *n.* [It < L *vindicta,* vengeance] a bitter feud, as between families

**vending machine** a coin-operated machine for selling small articles, refreshments, etc.

**ve·neer** (və nir') *vt.* [< Fr *fournir,* furnish] to cover with a thin layer of more costly material; esp., to cover (wood) with wood of finer quality — *n.* **1** a thin surface layer, as of fine wood, laid over a base of common material **2** superficial appearance [a *veneer* of culture]

**ven·er·a·ble** (ven'ər ə bəl) *adj.* worthy of respect because of age, dignity, etc. —**ven'er·a·bil'i·ty** *n.*

**ven·er·ate** (ven'ər āt') *vt.* -at'ed, -at'ing [< L *venerari,* to worship] to look upon with feelings of deep respect; revere —**ven'er·a'tion** *n.*

**ve·ne·re·al** (və nir'ē əl) *adj.* [< L *venus,* love] **1** of sexual intercourse **2** transmitted by sexual intercourse [*venereal* disease]

**Ve·ne·tian** (və nē'shən) *adj.* of Venice or its people or culture —*n.* a person born or living in Venice

**Venetian blind** [*also* v- b-] a window blind of thin, horizontal slats that can be set at any angle

**Ven·e·zue·la** (ven'ə zwā'lə) country in N South America: 352,143 sq. mi.; pop. 19,405,000 — **Ven·e·zue'lan** *adj., n.*

**venge·ance** (ven'jəns) *n.* [< L *vindicare,* avenge] the return of an injury for an injury, as in retribution; revenge —**with a vengeance 1** with great force or fury **2** excessively

**venge·ful** (venj'fəl) *adj.* seeking vengeance; vindictive —**venge'ful·ly** *adv.*

**ve·ni·al** (vēn'yəl, vē'nē əl) *adj.* [< L *venia,* a grace] that may be forgiven; pardonable [a *venial* sin]

**Ven·ice** (ven'is) seaport in N Italy built on more than 100 small islands: pop. 306,000

**ve·ni·re·man** (və nī'rē mən) *n., pl.* -men (-mən) [< ML *venire facias,* cause to come] one of a group of people from among whom a jury will be selected

**ven·i·son** (ven'i sən, -zən) *n.* [< L *venari,* to hunt] the flesh of a deer, used as food

**ven·om** (ven'əm) *n.* [< L *venenum,* a poison] **1** the poison secreted by some snakes, spiders, etc. **2** malice

**ven'om·ous** *adj.* **1** full of venom; poisonous **2** spiteful; malicious

**ve·nous** (vē'nəs) *adj.* [L *venosus*] **1** of veins **2** designating blood carried in veins

**vent**[1] (vent) *n.* [< L *ventus,* wind] **1** expression; release [giving *vent* to emotion] **2** a small opening to permit passage or escape, as of a gas —*vt.* **1** to make a vent in or for **2** to express; let out

**vent**[2] (vent) *n.* [< L *findere,* to split] a vertical slit in a garment

**ven·ti·late** (vent''l āt') *vt.* -lat'ed, -lat'ing [< L *ventus,* wind] **1** to circulate fresh air in (a room, etc.) **2** to provide with an opening for the escape of air, gas, etc. —**ven'ti·la'tion** *n.*

**ven'ti·la'tor** *n.* an opening or a device used to bring in fresh air and drive out foul air

**ven·tral** (ven'trəl) *adj.* [< L *venter,* belly] of, near, or on the belly

**ven·tri·cle** (ven'tri kəl) *n.* [see prec.] either of the two lower chambers of the heart —**ven·tric'u·lar** (-trik'yə lər) *adj.*

**ven·tril·o·quism** (ven tril'ə kwiz'əm) *n.* [< L *venter*, belly + *loqui*, speak] the art of speaking so that the voice seems to come from a source other than the speaker —**ven·tril'o·quist** *n.*

**ven·ture** (ven'chər) *n.* [see ADVENTURE] 1 a risky undertaking, as in business 2 something on which a risk is taken —*vt.* **-tured, -tur·ing** 1 to expose to danger or chance of loss 2 to express at the risk of criticism [to *venture* an opinion] —*vi.* to do or go at some risk

**ven'ture·some** (-səm) *adj.* 1 inclined to venture; daring 2 risky; hazardous Also **ven'tur·ous** (-əs)

**ven·ue** (ven'yōō) *n.* [< L *venire*, come] 1 *Law a*) the locality in which a cause of action or a crime occurs *b*) the locality in which a jury is drawn and a case is tried 2 the scene of a large gathering for some event

**Ve·nus** (vē'nəs) *n.* 1 the Roman goddess of love and beauty 2 the brightest planet in the solar system: see PLANET

**Venus' fly·trap** (fli'trap') a swamp plant with hinged leaves that snap shut, trapping insects

VENUS' FLYTRAP

**Ve·nu·si·an** (vi nōō' shən) *adj.* of the planet Venus —*n.* an imaginary inhabitant of Venus

**ve·ra·cious** (və rā' shəs) *adj.* [< L *verus*, true] 1 habitually truthful; honest 2 true; accurate

**ve·rac·i·ty** (və ras'ə tē) *n.* 1 honesty 2 accuracy 3 truth

**Ver·a·cruz** (ver'ə krōōz') state of Mexico, on the E coast: 28,114 sq. mi; pop. 6,228,000

**ve·ran·da** or **ve·ran·dah** (və ran'də) *n.* [< Port *varanda*, balcony] an open porch or portico, usually roofed, along the outside of a building

**verb** (vurb) *n.* [L *verbum*, a word] a word expressing action, existence, or occurrence

**ver·bal** (vur'bəl) *adj.* 1 of, in, or by means of words 2 in speech; oral 3 of, like, or derived from a verb —**ver'bal·ly** *adv.*

**ver·bal·ize** *vi.* **-ized', -iz'ing** to use words for communication —*vt.* to express in words —**ver'ba·li·za'tion** *n.*

**verbal noun** *Gram.* a noun derived from a verb (Ex.: *swimming* is fun)

**ver·ba·tim** (vər bāt'əm) *adv., adj.* [< L *verbum*, a word] word for word

**ver·be·na** (vər bē'nə) *n.* [L, foliage] an ornamental plant with spikes or clusters of showy red, white, or purplish flowers

**ver·bi·age** (vur'bē ij') *n.* [Fr < L *verbum*, a word] an excess of words; wordiness

**ver·bose** (vər bōs') *adj.* [< L *verbum*, a word] using too many words; wordy —**ver·bos'i·ty** (-bäs'ə tē) *n.*

**ver·dant** (vur'dənt) *adj.* [prob. VERD(URE) + -ANT] 1 green 2 covered with green vegetation

**Ver·di** (ver'dē), **Giu·sep·pe** (jōō zep'pe) 1813-1901; It. operatic composer

**ver·dict** (vur'dikt) *n.* [< L *vere*, truly + *dictum*, a thing said] 1 the formal finding of a judge or jury 2 any decision or judgment

**ver·di·gris** (vur'di grēs', -gris) *n.* [< OFr *vert de Grece*, lit., green of Greece] a greenish coating that forms on brass, bronze, or copper

**ver·dure** (vur'jər) *n.* [< OFr *verd*, green] 1 the fresh-green color of growing things 2 green vegetation

**verge¹** (vurj) *n.* [< L *virga*, rod] the edge, brink, or margin (*of* something) —*vi.* **verged, verg'ing** to be on the verge: usually with *on* or *upon*

**verge²** (vurj) *vi.* **verged, verg'ing** [L *vergere*, to

bend, turn] 1 to tend or incline (*to* or *toward*) 2 to change or pass gradually (*into*)

**verg·er** (vur'jər) *n.* [ME, ult. < L *virga*, rod] a church caretaker or usher

**Ver·gil** (vur'jəl) *alt. sp.* of VIRGIL

**ver·i·fy** (ver'ə fī') *vt.* **-fied', -fy'ing** [< L *verus*, true + *-ficare*, -FY] 1 to prove to be true by demonstration, evidence, etc.; confirm 2 to test the accuracy of —**ver'i·fi'a·ble** *adj.* —**ver'i·fi·ca'tion** *n.*

**ver·i·ly** (ver'ə lē) *adv.* [Archaic] truly

**ver·i·si·mil·i·tude** (ver'ə si mil'ə tōōd') *n.* [< L *verus*, true + *similis*, like] the appearance of being true or real

**ver·i·ta·ble** (ver'i tə bəl) *adj.* [see fol.] true; actual

**ver·i·ty** (ver'ə tē) *n.* [< L *verus*, true] 1 truth; reality 2 *pl.* **-ties** a principle, belief, etc. taken to be fundamentally true; a truth

**ver·mi·cel·li** (vur'mə sel'ē, -chel'ē) *n.* [It < L *vermis*, a worm] pasta like thin spaghetti

**ver·mic·u·lite** (vər mik'yə līt') *n.* [< L *vermis*, a worm] a hydrous silicate mineral that expands when heated, used as in insulation

**ver·mi·form** (vur'mə fôrm') *adj.* [< L *vermis*, a worm + -FORM] shaped like a worm

**vermiform appendix** the appendix extending from the cecum of the large intestine

**ver·mil·ion** (vər mil'yən) *n.* [< L *vermis*, a worm] 1 a bright-red pigment 2 a bright red or scarlet

**ver·min** (vur'mən) *n., pl.* **-min** [< L *vermis*, a worm] 1 [*pl.*] various destructive insects or small animals regarded as pests, as rats 2 a vile person

**Ver·mont** (vər mänt') New England state of the U.S.: 9,249 sq. mi.; pop. 563,000; cap. Montpelier: abbrev. *VT* —**Ver·mont'er** *n.*

**ver·mouth** (vər mōōth') *n.* [< Ger *wermut*, wormwood] a white fortified wine flavored with herbs, used in cocktails and as an aperitif

**ver·nac·u·lar** (vər nak'yə lər) *adj.* [< L *vernaculus*, indigenous] 1 of, in, or using the native language of a place 2 native to a country —*n.* 1 the native language or dialect of a country or place 2 the common, everyday language of a people 3 the jargon of a profession or trade

**ver·nal** (vur'nəl) *adj.* [< L *ver*, spring] 1 of or in the spring 2 springlike 3 youthful

**ver·ni·er** (vur'nē ər) *n.* [after P. *Vernier*, 17th-c. Fr mathematician] a short graduated scale sliding along a longer graduated instrument to indicate parts of divisions: also **vernier scale**

**Ver·sailles** (vər sī') city in NC France, near Paris: site of a palace built by Louis XIV: pop. 88,000

**ver·sa·tile** (vur'sə təl) *adj.* [< L *vertere*, to turn] competent in many things —**ver'sa·til'i·ty** (-til'ə tē) *n.*

**verse** (vurs) *n.* [< L *vertere*, to turn] 1 a single line of poetry 2 poetry 3 a particular form of poetry 4 a poem 5 a stanza 6 *Bible* any of the short divisions of a chapter

**versed** (vurst) *adj.* [< L *versari*, be busy] skilled or learned (*in* a subject)

**ver·si·fy** (vur'sə fī') *vi.* **-fied', -fy'ing** [< L *versus*, a verse + *facere*, make] to compose verses —*vt.* 1 to tell about in verse 2 to put into verse form —**ver'si·fi·ca'tion** *n.* —**ver'si·fi'er** *n.*

**ver·sion** (vur'zhən) *n.* [see VERSE] 1 a translation, esp. of the Bible 2 an account showing one point of view 3 a particular form of something

**ver·sus** (vur'səs) *prep.* [ML < L, toward] 1 against 2 in contrast with

**ver·te·bra** (vur'tə brə) *n., pl.* **-brae** (-brē', -brā') or **-bras** [L < *vertere*, to turn] any of the single bones of the spinal column —**ver'te·bral** *adj.*

**ver·te·brate** (-brit, -brāt') *adj.* 1 having a backbone, or spinal column 2 of the vertebrates —*n.* any of a large division of animals having a spinal column, as mammals, birds, etc.

**ver·tex** (vur'teks') *n., pl.* **-tex'es** or **-ti·ces'** (-tə sēz') [L] 1 the highest point; top 2 *Geom.* the point of intersection of the two sides of an angle

**ver·ti·cal** (vur'ti kəl) *adj.* **1** of or at the vertex **2** upright, straight up or down, etc. —*n.* a vertical line, plane, etc. —**ver'ti·cal·ly** *adv.*

**ver·tig·i·nous** (vər tij'ə nəs) *adj.* of, having, or causing vertigo

**ver·ti·go** (vur'ti gō') *n.* ⟦L < *vertere,* to turn⟧ a sensation of dizziness

**verve** (vurv) *n.* ⟦Fr < OFr, manner of speech⟧ vigor; energy; enthusiasm

**ver·y** (ver'ē) *adj.* ⟦< L *verus,* true⟧ **1** complete; absolute [the *very* opposite] **2** same [the *very* hat I lost] **3** being just what is needed **4** actual [caught in the *very* act]: often an intensive [the *very* rafters shook] —*adv.* **1** extremely **2** truly; really [the *very* same man]

**very high frequency** any radio frequency between 30 and 300 megahertz

**very low frequency** any radio frequency between 10 and 30 kilohertz

**ves·i·cant** (ves'i kənt) *adj.* ⟦< L *vesica,* a blister⟧ causing blisters —*n.* a vesicant agent, as mustard gas used in warfare to blister skin and lungs

**ves'i·cle** (-kəl) *n.* ⟦< L *vesica,* bladder⟧ a small, membranous cavity, sac, or cyst —**ve·sic·u·lar** (və sik'yə lər) or **ve·sic'u·late** (-lit) *adj.*

**ves·pers** (ves'pərz) *n.* ⟦ult. < L *vespera,* evening⟧ [often **V-**] [usually with sing v.] an evening prayer or service

**Ves·puc·ci** (ves pōōt'chē), **A·me·ri·go** (ä'me rē'gō) (L. name *Americus Vespucius*) 1454-1512; It. navigator & explorer

**ves·sel** (ves'əl) *n.* ⟦< L *vas*⟧ **1** a utensil for holding something, as a bowl, kettle, etc. **2** a boat or ship **3** a tube or duct of the body, containing a fluid

**vest** (vest) *n.* ⟦< L *vestis,* garment⟧ a short, sleeveless garment, esp. one worn under a suit coat by men —*vt.* **1** to dress, as in clerical robes **2** to place (authority, etc.) in someone **3** to put (a person) in control of, as power, etc. —*vi.* to pass to a person; become vested (*in* a person), as property

**ves·tal** (ves'təl) *adj.* ⟦< L *Vesta,* goddess of the hearth⟧ chaste; pure —*n.* a virgin priestess of the Roman goddess Vesta: in full **vestal virgin**

VEST

**vest·ed** (ves'tid) *adj.* ⟦pp. of VEST⟧ *Law* fixed; settled; absolute [a *vested* right]

**vested interest 1** an established right, as to some future benefit **2** [pl.] groups pursuing selfish goals and exerting controlling influence

**ves·ti·bule** (ves'tə byōōl') *n.* ⟦L *vestibulum*⟧ a small entrance hall, as to a building

**ves·tige** (ves'tij) *n.* ⟦< L *vestigium,* footprint⟧ **1** a trace, mark, or sign, esp. of something that has passed away **2** *Biol.* a degenerate part, more fully developed in an earlier stage —**ves·tig'i·al** (-tij'ē əl, -tij'əl) *adj.*

**vest'ing** *n.* the retention by an employee of all or part of pension rights

**vest·ment** (vest'mənt) *n.* ⟦< L *vestire,* clothe⟧ a garment or robe, esp. one worn by a the clergy

**vest'-pock'et** *adj.* very small, or unusually small

**ves·try** (ves'trē) *n., pl.* **-tries** ⟦< L *vestis,* garment⟧ **1** a room in a church where vestments, etc. are kept **2** a room in a church, used as a chapel **3** a group of church members managing the temporal affairs of the church

**Ve·su·vi·us** (və sōō'vē əs) active volcano in S Italy, near Naples

**vet**[1] (vet) *vt.* to evaluate thoroughly or expertly

**vet**[2] *abbrev.* **1** veteran **2** veterinarian **3** veterinary

**vetch** (vech) *n.* ⟦< L *vicia*⟧ a leafy, climbing or trailing plant of the pea family, grown for fodder

**vet·er·an** (vet'ər ən, ve'trən) *adj.* ⟦< L *vetus,* old⟧ **1** old and experienced **2** of veterans —*n.* **1** one who has served in the armed forces **2** one who has served long in some position

**Veterans Day** a legal holiday in the U.S. honoring all veterans of the armed forces: observed on ARMISTICE DAY

**vet·er·i·nar·i·an** (vet'ər ə ner'ē ən) *n.* one who practices veterinary medicine or surgery

**vet·er·i·nar·y** (-ē) *adj.* ⟦< L *veterina,* beasts of burden⟧ designating or of the branch of medicine dealing with animals —*n., pl.* **-ies** VETERINARIAN

**ve·to** (vē'tō) *n., pl.* **-toes** ⟦L, I forbid⟧ **1** *a*) an order prohibiting some act *b*) the power to prohibit action **2** *a*) the power of one branch of government to reject bills passed by another *b*) the exercise of this power —*vt.* **-toed, -to·ing 1** to prevent (a bill) from becoming law by a veto **2** to forbid

**vex** (veks) *vt.* ⟦< L *vexare,* agitate⟧ **1** to disturb; annoy, esp. in a petty way **2** to distress; afflict

**vex·a·tion** (vek sā'shən) *n.* **1** a vexing or being vexed **2** something that vexes —**vex·a'tious** *adj.*

**VHF** or **vhf** *abbrev.* very high frequency

**VHS** ⟦*v*(*ideo*) *h*(*ome*) *s*(*ystem*)⟧ *trademark for* an electronic system for recording video and audio information on videocassettes

**vi** *abbrev.* intransitive verb

**VI** *abbrev.* Virgin Islands: also **V.I.**

**vi·a** (vī'ə, vē'ə) *prep.* ⟦L, way⟧ by way of

**vi·a·ble** (vī'ə bəl) *adj.* ⟦< L *vita,* life⟧ **1** sufficiently developed to be able to live outside the uterus **2** workable [*viable* ideas] —**vi'a·bil'i·ty** *n.*

**vi·a·duct** (vī'ə dukt') *n.* ⟦< VIA + (AQUE)DUCT⟧ a bridge consisting of a series of short spans, supported on piers or towers

**Vi·ag·ra** (vī ag'rə) *trademark for* a compound used to treat erectile dysfunction of the penis

**vi·al** (vī'əl) *n.* ⟦< OFr *fiole*⟧ a small vessel or bottle for liquids

**vi·and** (vī'ənd) *n.* ⟦< L *vivere,* to live⟧ an article of food

**vibes** (vībz) *pl.n.* **1** VIBRAPHONE **2** [Slang] qualities thought of as being like vibrations which produce an emotional reaction in others

**vi·brant** (vī'brənt) *adj.* **1** quivering or vibrating **2** produced by vibration **3** vigorous, vivacious, etc. —**vi'bran·cy** *n.* —**vi'brant·ly** *adv.*

**vi·bra·phone** (vī'brə fōn') *n.* a musical instrument like the marimba, with electrically operated resonators —**vi'bra·phon'ist** *n.*

**vi·brate** (vī'brāt') *vt.* **-brat·ed, -brat·ing** ⟦< L *vibrare*⟧ to set in to-and-fro motion —*vi.* **1** to swing back and forth; oscillate **2** to move rapidly back and forth; quiver **3** to resound **4** to be emotionally stirred —**vi·bra'tion** *n.* —**vi'bra·tor** *n.*

**vi·bra·to** (vi brät'ō) *n., pl.* **-tos** ⟦It⟧ a pulsating effect produced by rapid alternation of a given tone with a barely perceptible variation in pitch

**vi·bra·to·ry** (vī'brə tôr'ē) *adj.* **1** of, like, or causing vibration **2** vibrating or capable of vibrating

**vi·bur·num** (vī bur'nəm) *n.* ⟦L, wayfaring tree⟧ a shrub or small tree with white flowers

**vic·ar** (vik'ər) *n.* ⟦< L *vicis,* a change⟧ **1** *Anglican Ch.* a parish priest receiving a stipend **2** *R.C.Ch.* a church officer acting as a deputy of a bishop

**vic'ar·age** *n.* **1** the residence of a vicar **2** the position or duties of a vicar

**vi·car·i·ous** (vī ker'ē əs) *adj.* ⟦< L *vicarius,* substituted⟧ **1** endured or performed by one person in place of another **2** shared in by imagined participation in another's experience [a *vicarious* thrill] —**vi·car'i·ous·ly** *adv.*

**vice**[1] (vīs) *n.* ⟦< L *vitium*⟧ **1** *a*) an evil action or habit *b*) evil conduct *c*) prostitution **2** a trivial fault or failing

**vi·ce**[2] (vī'sē) *prep.* ⟦L < *vicis,* a change⟧ in the place of

**vice-** 〖see prec.〗 *prefix* a subordinate; deputy [*vice*-president]

**vice·ge·rent** (vīs'jir'ənt) *n.* 〖< VICE- + L *gerere,* to direct〗 a deputy

**vice'-pres'i·dent** *n.* an officer next in rank below a president, acting during the president's absence or incapacity: for the U.S. official, usually **Vice President** —**vice'-pres'i·den·cy** *n.*

**vice·roy** (vīs'roi') *n.* 〖MFr < *vice-* (see VICE-) + *roy,* king〗 a person ruling a region as the deputy of a sovereign

**vi·ce ver·sa** (vī'sə vur'sə, vīs' vur'sə) 〖L〗 the relation being reversed

**vi·chys·soise** (vē'shē swäz', vish'ē-) *n.* a thick, cold soup of potatoes, leeks, and cream

**vi·cin·i·ty** (və sin'ə tē) *n.,* pl. **-ties** 〖< L *vicus,* village〗 **1** nearness; proximity **2** the surrounding area

**vi·cious** (vish'əs) *adj.* 〖< L *vitium,* vice〗 **1** characterized by vice; evil or depraved **2** faulty; flawed **3** unruly [a *vicious* horse] **4** malicious; spiteful [a *vicious* rumor] **5** very intense, forceful, etc. [a *vicious* blow] —**vi'cious·ly** *adv.* —**vi'cious·ness** *n.*

**vicious circle** a situation in which the solution of one problem gives rise to another, eventually bringing back the first problem: also **vicious cycle**

**vi·cis·si·tudes** (vi sis'ə tōōdz') *pl.n.* 〖< L *vicis,* a turn〗 unpredictable changes in life; ups and downs

**Vicks·burg** (viks'burg') city in W Mississippi: besieged & captured by Grant in the Civil War (1863): pop. 21,000

**vic·tim** (vik'təm) *n.* 〖L *victima*〗 **1** someone or something killed, destroyed, sacrificed, etc. **2** one who suffers some loss, esp. by being swindled

**vic'tim·ize'** (-īz') *vt.* **-ized', -iz'ing** to make a victim of

**vic·tor** (vik'tər) *n.* 〖< L *vincere,* conquer〗 the winner in a battle, struggle, etc.

**Vic·to·ri·a**[1] (vik tôr'ē ə) 1819-1901; queen of Great Britain & Ireland (1837-1901)

**Vic·to·ri·a**[2] (vik tôr'ē ə) capital of British Columbia, Canada: pop. 74,000

**Vic·to'ri·an** *adj.* **1** of or characteristic of the period of the reign of Queen Victoria **2** showing the respectability, prudery, etc. attributed to the Victorians —*n.* a person of that time —**Vic·to'ri·an·ism'** *n.*

**vic·to·ri·ous** (vik tôr'ē əs) *adj.* **1** having won a victory; triumphant **2** of or bringing about victory

**vic·to·ry** (vik'tər ē, -trē) *n.,* pl. **-ries** 〖< L *vincere,* conquer〗 the winning of a battle, war, or any struggle

**vict·uals** (vit''lz) *pl.n.* 〖< L *victus,* food〗 [Inf. or Dial.] articles of food

**vi·cu·ña** (vi kyōō'nyə, -nə) *n.* 〖Sp〗 **1** a small llama of South America **2** its soft, shaggy wool

**vi·de** (vī'dē) *v.* 〖L〗 see; refer to (a certain page, etc.)

**vid·e·o** (vid'ē ō') *adj.* 〖L, I see〗 **1** of television **2** of the picture portion of a telecast **3** of data display on a computer —*n.,* pl. **-os'** **1** TELEVISION **2** *short for* VIDEOCASSETTE, VIDEOTAPE

**vid'e·o·cas·sette'** *n.* a cassette of videotape

**videocassette recorder** a device for recording on and playing back videocassettes: also **vid'e·o·re·cord'er** *n.*

**vid'e·o·con'fer·enc·ing** *n.* the holding of a conference at several locations by TV

**vid'e·o·disc'** *n.* a disc on which images and sounds can be recorded for reproduction on a TV set: also **vid'e·o·disk'**

**video game** any of various games involving images, controlled by players, on a TV screen, computer monitor, etc.

**vid'e·o·tape'** *n.* a magnetic tape on which images and sounds can be recorded for reproduction on TV —*vt.* **-taped', -tap'ing** to record on videotape

**vie** (vī) *vi.* **vied, vy'ing** 〖< L *invitare,* invite〗 to struggle for superiority (*with* someone); compete

**Vi·en·na** (vē en'ə) capital of Austria: pop. 1,516,000 —**Vi·en·nese** (vē'ə nēz'), pl. **-nese'**, *adj., n.*

**Vi·et·nam** (vē'et näm', -nam') country on the E coast of Indochina: partitioned into two republics (**North Vietnam** & **South Vietnam**) in 1954, and reunified in 1976 as **Socialist Republic of Vietnam**: 127,246 sq. mi.; pop. 64,412,000 —**Vi·et·nam·ese'** (-nə mēz'), pl. **-ese'**, *adj., n.*

**view** (vyōō) *n.* 〖< L *videre,* to see〗 **1** a seeing or looking, as in inspection **2** range of vision **3** mental survey [a correct *view* of a situation] **4** a scene or prospect [a room with a *view*] **5** manner of regarding something; opinion —*vt.* **1** to inspect; scrutinize **2** to see; behold **3** to survey mentally; consider —**in view 1** in sight **2** under consideration **3** as a goal or hope —**in view of** because of —**on view** displayed publicly —**with a view to** with the purpose or hope of

**view'er** *n.* **1** one who views something **2** an optical device for individual viewing of slides

**view'find'er** *n.* a camera device for viewing what will appear in the photograph

**view'point'** *n.* the mental position from which things are viewed and judged; point of view

**vig·il** (vij'əl) *n.* 〖< L, awake〗 **1** *a)* a watchful staying awake *b)* a watch kept **2** the eve of a church festival

**vig·i·lant** (vij'ə lənt) *adj.* 〖< L *vigil,* awake〗 staying watchful and alert to danger or trouble —**vig'i·lance** *n.*

**vig·i·lan·te** (vij'ə lan'tē) *n.* 〖Sp, watchman〗 one who acts outside the law to punish or avenge a crime —**vig'i·lan'tism'** *n.*

**vi·gnette** (vin yet') *n.* 〖Fr < *vigne,* vine〗 **1** an ornamental design used on a page of a book, etc. **2** a picture shading off gradually at the edges **3** a short literary sketch, scene in a film, etc.

**vig·or** (vig'ər) *n.* 〖< L *vigere,* be strong〗 active force or strength; vitality; energy: Brit. sp. **vig'our** —**vig'or·ous** *adj.* —**vig'or·ous·ly** *adv.*

**vik·ing** (vī'kiŋ) *n.* 〖ON *vikingr*〗 [*also* V-] any of the Scandinavian pirates of the 8th to the 10th c.

**vile** (vīl) *adj.* 〖< L *vilis,* cheap, base〗 **1** morally evil; wicked **2** disgusting **3** degrading; mean **4** very bad [*vile* weather] —**vile'ness** *n.*

**vil·i·fy** (vil'ə fī') *vt.* **-fied', -fy'ing** 〖see prec. & -FY〗 to use abusive language about or of; defame —**vil'i·fi·ca'tion** *n.*

**vil·la** (vil'ə) *n.* 〖It < L, a farm〗 a country house or estate, esp. a large one

**vil·lage** (vil'ij) *n.* 〖see prec.〗 **1** a community smaller than a town **2** the people of a village, collectively —**vil'lag·er** *n.*

**vil·lain** (vil'ən) *n.* 〖< VL *villanus,* a farm servant〗 a wicked or evil person, or such a character in a play, etc. —**vil'lain·ess** *fem.n.* —**vil'lain·ous** *adj.*

**vil'lain·y** *n.,* pl. **-ies** **1** wickedness; evil **2** a villainous act

**vil·lein** (vil'ən) *n.* 〖see VILLAIN〗 a feudal serf who had become a freeman, except to his lord

**vim** (vim) *n.* 〖prob. echoic〗 vigor

**vin** (van; *E* vin) *n.* 〖Fr〗 wine

**vin·ai·grette** (vin'ə gret') *n.* 〖Fr < *vinaigre,* vinegar〗 a salad dressing of vinegar, oil, etc.

**Vinci, Leonardo da** *see* DA VINCI, Leonardo

**vin·di·cate** (vin'də kāt') *vt.* **-cat'ed, -cat'ing** 〖< L *vis,* force + *dicere,* say〗 **1** to clear from criticism, blame, etc. **2** to defend against opposition **3** to justify —**vin'di·ca'tion** *n.* —**vin'di·ca'tor** *n.*

**vin·dic·tive** (vin dik'tiv) *adj.* 〖see prec.〗 **1** revengeful in spirit **2** said or done in revenge —**vin·dic'tive·ly** *adv.* —**vin·dic'tive·ness** *n.*

**vine** (vīn) *n.* 〖< L *vinum,* wine〗 **1** *a)* a plant with a long, thin stem that grows along the ground or climbs a support *b)* the stem of such a plant **2** a grapevine

**vin·e·gar** (vin'ə gər) *n.* 〖< medieval Fr *vin,* wine + *aigre,* sour〗 a sour liquid made by fermenting cider, wine, etc. and used as a condiment and preservative —**vin′e·gar·y** *adj.*

**vine·yard** (vin′yərd) *n.* land devoted to cultivating grapevines

**vi·no** (vē′nô) *n.* ⟦It & Sp⟧ wine

**vin ro·sé** (rô zā′; *E* rō zā′) ⟦Fr⟧ ROSÉ

**vin·tage** (vin′tij) *n.* ⟦< L *vinum,* wine + *demere,* remove⟧ **1** the grape crop of a single season **2** the wine of a particular region and year **3** the model of a particular period [*a car of prewar vintage*] —*adj.* **1** of a particular vintage: said of wine **2** representative of the best [*vintage* Hemingway] **3** of a past period [*vintage* clothes]

**vint·ner** (vint′nər) *n.* ⟦< ME < L *vinum,* wine⟧ one who sells or makes wine

**vi·nyl** (vī′nəl) *n.* ⟦< L *vinum,* wine⟧ any of various compounds polymerized to form resins and plastics (**vinyl plastics**)

**vi·ol** (vī′əl) *n.* ⟦< VL *vitula,* a fiddle⟧ any of an early family of stringed instruments, usually having six strings, frets, and a flat back

**vi·o·la** (vē ō′lə, vī-) *n.* ⟦It⟧ a stringed instrument of the violin family, slightly larger than a violin

**vi·o·la·ble** (vī′ə lə bəl) *adj.* that can be, or is likely to be, violated

**vi·o·late** (vī′ə lāt′) *vt.* **-lat′ed, -lat′ing** ⟦< L *violare,* use violence⟧ **1** to fail to obey or keep (a law, etc.) **2** to rape **3** to desecrate (something sacred) **4** to break in upon; disturb —**vi′o·la′tor** *n.*

**vi·o·la·tion** (-lā′shən) *n.* a violating or being violated; specif., *a)* infringement, as of a law *b)* rape *c)* desecration of something sacred *d)* disturbance

**vi·o·lence** (-ləns) *n.* ⟦< L *violentus,* violent⟧ **1** physical force used so as to injure **2** powerful force, as of a hurricane **3** harm done by violating rights, etc. **4** a violent act or deed

**vi·o·lent** *adj.* **1** acting with or having great physical force **2** caused by violence **3** furious [*violent* language] **4** extreme; intense [*a violent* storm] —**vi′o·lent·ly** *adv.*

**vi·o·let** (vī′ə lit) *n.* ⟦< L *viola*⟧ **1** a plant with white, blue, purple, or yellow flowers **2** a bluish-purple color —*adj.* bluish-purple

**vi·o·lin** (vī′ə lin′) *n.* ⟦< VIOLA⟧ any of the modern family of four-stringed musical instruments played with a bow; specif., the smallest and highest-pitched one of this family —**vi′o·lin′ist** *n.*

**vi·ol·ist** (vī′əl ist; *for 2* vē ō′list) *n.* **1** a viol player **2** a viola player

**vi·o·lon·cel·lo** (vē′ə län chel′ō, vī′ə lən-) *n., pl.* **-los** CELLO

**VIP** (vē′ī′pē′) *n.* ⟦*v(ery) i(mportant) p(erson)*⟧ a high-ranking official or important guest

**vi·per** (vī′pər) *n.* ⟦OFr < L *vipera*⟧ **1** a venomous snake **2** a malicious or treacherous person —**vi′per·ous** *adj.*

**vi·ra·go** (vi rä′gō, -rā′-) *n., pl.* **-goes** or **-gos** ⟦< L *vir,* a man⟧ a shrewish woman; scold

**vi·ral** (vī′rəl) *adj.* of or caused by a virus

**vir·e·o** (vir′ē ō′) *n., pl.* **-os′** ⟦L, a type of finch⟧ a small American songbird, with olive-green or gray feathers

**Vir·gil** (vur′jəl) 70-19 B.C.; Rom. poet: author of the *Aeneid*

**vir·gin** (vur′jən) *n.* ⟦< L *virgo,* a maiden⟧ one, esp. a young woman, who has never had sexual intercourse —*adj.* **1** being a virgin **2** chaste; modest **3** untouched, unused, pure, etc. [*virgin* land] — **the Virgin Mary,** the mother of Jesus

**vir′gin·al** *adj.* VIRGIN

**Vir·gin·ia** (vər jin′yə) state of the S U.S.: 39,598 sq. mi.; pop. 6,187,000; cap. Richmond: abbrev. *VA* —**Vir·gin′i·an** *adj., n.*

**Virginia Beach** city in SE Virginia, on the Atlantic: pop. 393,000

**Virginia creeper** WOODBINE (sense 2)

**Virginia reel** an American variety of reel danced by couples in two parallel rows

**Virgin Islands** group of islands in the West Indies, divided between those forming a British territory & those constituting a U.S. territory (**Virgin Islands of the United States**): U.S. part, 134 sq. mi., pop. 102,000

**vir·gin·i·ty** (vər jin′ə tē) *n.* a being a virgin

**Virgin Mary** Mary, the mother of Jesus

**Vir·go** (vur′gō′) *n.* ⟦L, virgin⟧ the sixth sign of the zodiac

**vir·gule** (vur′gyool′) *n.* ⟦< L *virgula,* small rod⟧ a diagonal line (/) used in dates or fractions (3/8) and also standing for "or," "per," etc.

**vir·ile** (vir′əl) *adj.* ⟦< L *vir,* a man⟧ **1** of or characteristic of a man; masculine **2** having manly strength or vigor **3** sexually potent —**vi·ril·i·ty** (və ril′ə tē) *n.*

**vi·rol·o·gy** (vī räl′ə jē) *n.* ⟦< VIR(US) + -o- + -LOGY⟧ the study of viruses and virus diseases —**vi·rol′o·gist** *n.*

**vir·tu·al** (vur′choo əl) *adj.* being so in effect, although not in actual fact or name —**vir′tu·al·ly** *adv.*

**virtual reality** computer simulation of three-dimensional images, with which one may seemingly interact using special electronic devices

**vir·tue** (vur′choo) *n.* ⟦< L *virtus,* worth⟧ **1** general moral excellence **2** a specific moral quality regarded as good **3** chastity **4** *a)* excellence in general *b)* a good quality **5** efficacy, as of a medicine —**by** (or **in**) **virtue of** because of

**vir·tu·o·so** (vur′choo ō′sō) *n., pl.* **-sos** or **-si** (-sē) ⟦It, skilled⟧ one with great skill in a fine art — **vir′tu·os′i·ty** (-äs′ə tē) *n.*

**vir·tu·ous** (vur′choo əs) *adj.* **1** having, or characterized by, moral virtue **2** chaste: said of a woman —**vir′tu·ous·ly** *adv.*

**vir·u·lent** (vir′yoo lənt, -oo-) *adj.* ⟦see fol.⟧ **1** *a)* extremely poisonous *b)* full of hate **2** *Med. a)* violent and rapid in its course *b)* highly infectious —**vir′u·lence** *n.*

**vi·rus** (vī′rəs) *n.* ⟦L, a poison⟧ **1** a microscopic infectious agent causing various diseases **2** any harmful influence **3** unauthorized, disruptive, spreadable computer program instructions

**vi·sa** (vē′zə, -sə) *n.* ⟦< L *videre,* see⟧ an endorsement on a passport, granting entry into a country

**vis·age** (viz′ij) *n.* ⟦see prec.⟧ **1** the face; countenance **2** aspect; look

**vis-à-vis** (vē′zə vē′) *adj., adv.* ⟦Fr⟧ face to face; opposite —*prep.* **1** opposite to **2** in relation to

**vis·cer·a** (vis′ər ə) *pl.n., sing.* **vis′cus** (-kəs) ⟦L⟧ the internal organs of the body, as the heart, lungs, intestines, etc.

**vis′cer·al** *adj.* **1** of the viscera **2** intuitive, emotional, etc. rather than intellectual

**vis·cid** (vis′id) *adj.* ⟦< LL *viscidus,* sticky⟧ thick, syrupy, and sticky

**vis·cose** (vis′kōs′) *n.* ⟦see VISCID⟧ a syruplike solution of cellulose, used in making rayon and cellophane

**vis·cos·i·ty** (vis käs′ə tē) *n., pl.* **-ties 1** a viscous quality **2** *Physics* the resistance of a fluid to flowing freely

**vis·count** (vī′kount′) *n.* ⟦see VICE- & COUNT²⟧ a nobleman next below an earl or count and above a baron —**vis′count·ess** *fem.n.*

**vis·cous** (vis′kəs) *adj.* ⟦see VISCID⟧ **1** syrupy; viscid **2** *Physics* having viscosity

**vise** (vīs) *n.* ⟦< L *vitis,* vine, lit., that which winds⟧ a device having two jaws closed by a screw, used for holding firmly an object being worked on

**VISE**

**Vish·nu** (vish'nōō) *n.* a Hindu god, often in human incarnation

**vis·i·bil·i·ty** (viz'ə bil'ə tē) *n., pl.* **-ties 1** a being visible **2** *a*) the relative possibility of being seen under the prevailing conditions of distance, light, etc. *[red has good visibility]* *b*) range of vision

**vis·i·ble** (viz'ə bəl) *adj.* 〖< L *videre,* to see〗 **1** that can be seen **2** apparent —**vis'i·bly** *adv.*

**vi·sion** (vizh'ən) *n.* 〖see prec.〗 **1** the power of seeing **2** something seen in a dream, trance, etc., or supernaturally revealed **3** a mental image **4** the ability to perceive or foresee something, as through mental acuteness **5** something or someone of great beauty

**vi·sion·ar'y** (-er'ē) *adj.* **1** seen in a vision **2** not realistic; impractical *[a visionary scheme]* —*n., pl.* **-ies 1** one who sees visions **2** one whose ideas, etc. are impractical

**vis·it** (viz'it) *vt.* 〖< L *videre,* to see〗 **1** to go or come to see **2** to stay with as a guest **3** to afflict or trouble —*vi.* **1** to make a social call **2** [Inf.] to chat —*n.* **1** a social call **2** a stay as a guest

**vis'it·ant** *n.* a visitor

**vis·it·a·tion** (viz'ə tā'shən) *n.* **1** an official visit, as to inspect **2** a reward or punishment, as sent by God **3** the legal right to visit one's children, as after divorce **4** the visiting of a family in mourning

**vis'i·tor** *n.* a person making a visit

**vi·sor** (vī'zər) *n.* 〖< OFr *vis,* a face〗 **1** a part of a helmet that protects the face, often one that can be raised and lowered **2** a projecting brim, as of a cap, for shading the eyes

**vis·ta** (vis'tə) *n.* 〖< L *videre,* to see〗 **1** a view, esp. one seen through a long passage **2** a mental view of events

**vis·u·al** (vizh'ōō əl) *adj.* 〖< L *videre,* to see〗 **1** of or used in seeing **2** based on the use of sight **3** that can be seen; visible

**vis'u·al·ize** *vt., vi.* **-ized', -iz'ing** to form a mental image of (something not present to the sight) —**vis'u·al·i·za'tion** *n.*

**vi·ta** (vīt'ə, vēt'ə) *n.* 〖< *curriculum vitae* < L, course of life〗 a summary of one's personal history and professional qualifications, as that submitted by a job applicant; résumé

**vi·tal** (vīt''l) *adj.* 〖< L *vita,* life〗 **1** of or concerned with life **2** essential to life *[vital organs]* **3** fatal *[a vital wound]* **4** *a*) essential; indispensable *b*) very important **5** full of life; energetic —*n.* [pl.] **1** the vital organs, as the heart, brain, etc. **2** any essential parts —**vi'tal·ly** *adv.*

**vi·tal·i·ty** (vī tal'ə tē) *n., pl.* **-ties 1** power to live **2** power to endure **3** mental or physical vigor

**vi·tal·ize** (vīt''l īz') *vt.* **-ized', -iz'ing** to make vital; give life or vigor to

**vital signs** the pulse, respiration, and body temperature

**vital statistics** data on births, deaths, marriages, etc.

**vi·ta·min** (vīt'ə min) *n.* 〖< L *vita,* life〗 any of certain complex substances found variously in foods and essential to good health

**vitamin A** a fat-soluble alcohol found in fish-liver oil, egg yolk, carrots, etc.: a deficiency of this results in imperfect vision in the dark

**vitamin B** (**complex**) a group of unrelated water-soluble substances including *a*) **vitamin B₁** (see THIAMINE) *b*) **vitamin B₂** (see RIBOFLAVIN) *c*) NICOTINIC ACID *d*) **vitamin B₁₂**, a vitamin containing cobalt, used in treating anemia

**vitamin C** a compound occurring in citrus fruits, tomatoes, etc.: a deficiency of this results in scurvy

**vitamin D** any of several fat-soluble vitamins

found in fish-liver oils, milk, etc.: a deficiency of this results in rickets

**vitamin E** a substance occurring in wheat germ, etc., vital to the reproductive processes in some animals

**vitamin K** a substance occurring in green vegetables, fish meal, etc., that clots blood

**vi·ti·ate** (vish'ē āt') *vt.* **-at'ed, -at'ing** 〖< L *vitium,* a vice〗 **1** to spoil; corrupt; pervert **2** to invalidate (a contract, etc.) —**vi'ti·a'tion** *n.*

**vit·re·ous** (vi'trē əs) *adj.* 〖< L *vitrum,* glass〗 **1** of or like glass **2** derived from or made of glass

**vitreous humor** (or **body**) the transparent, jellylike substance filling the eyeball between the retina and the lens

**vit·ri·fy** (vi'trə fī') *vt., vi.* **-fied', -fy'ing** 〖< L *vitrum,* glass + Fr *-fier,* -FY〗 to change into glass or a glasslike substance by heat

**vit·rine** (vi trēn', vi'trēn) *n.* 〖see VITREOUS〗 a glass-paneled cabinet or display case

**vit·ri·ol** (vi'trē ôl') *n.* 〖< L *vitreus,* glassy〗 **1** *a*) any of several sulfates of metals, as of copper (*blue vitriol*) or iron (*green vitriol*) *b*) SULFURIC ACID **2** caustic remarks —**vit'ri·ol'ic** (-äl'ik) *adj.*

**vi·tu·per·ate** (vī tōō'pər āt', vi-) *vt.* **-at'ed, -at'ing** 〖< L *vitium,* a fault, + *parare,* prepare〗 to speak abusively to or about —**vi·tu'per·a'tion** *n.* —**vi·tu'per·a'tive** *adj.*

**vi·va** (vē'vä) *v.impersonal* 〖It & Sp〗 long live (someone specified)!

**vi·va·ce** (vē vä'chä) *adj., adv.* 〖It〗 *Music* in a lively, spirited manner: also written *vivace*

**vi·va·cious** (vī vā'shəs, vi-) *adj.* 〖< L *vivere,* to live〗 full of animation; lively —**vi·va'cious·ly** *adv.* —**vi·vac'i·ty** (-vas'ə tē) or **vi·va'cious·ness** *n.*

**vive** (vēv) *v.impersonal* 〖Fr〗 long live (someone specified)!

**viv·id** (viv'id) *adj.* 〖< L *vivere,* to live〗 **1** full of life **2** intense: said as of colors **3** active; daring *[a vivid imagination]* —**viv'id·ly** *adv.* —**viv'id·ness** *n.*

**viv·i·fy** (viv'ə fī') *vt.* **-fied', -fy'ing** 〖< L *vivus,* alive + *facere,* make〗 to give life to

**vi·vip·a·rous** (vī vip'ər əs) *adj.* 〖< L *vivus,* alive + *parere,* produce〗 bearing living young, instead of laying eggs

**viv·i·sec·tion** (viv'ə sek'shən) *n.* 〖< L *vivus,* alive + SECTION〗 surgery performed on a living animal in medical research —**viv'i·sec'tion·ist** *n.*

**vix·en** (vik'sən) *n.* 〖OE *fyxe,* female fox〗 **1** a female fox **2** a shrewish or malicious woman

**Vi·yel·la** (vī yel'ə) 〖arbitrary coinage〗 *trademark for* a fabric like flannel, a blend of lamb's wool and cotton

**viz.** or **viz** *abbrev.* 〖< L *videlicet*〗 that is; namely

**vi·zier** (vi zir', viz'yər) *n.* 〖< Ar *wazara,* bear a burden〗 a high government official in the Turkish empire (c. 1300-1918): also sp. **vi·zir'**

**viz·or** (vī'zər) *n. alt. sp. of* VISOR

**VLF** or **vlf** *abbrev.* very low frequency

**vo·cab·u·lar·y** (vō kab'yə ler'ē) *n., pl.* **-ies** 〖ult. < L *vocare,* to call〗 **1** a list of words, etc. as in a dictionary or glossary **2** all the words used in a language or by a person, group, etc.

**vo·cal** (vō'kəl) *adj.* 〖< L *vox,* voice〗 **1** of or produced by the voice **2** sung **3** capable of making oral sounds **4** speaking freely —**vo'cal·ly** *adv.*

**vocal cords** membranous folds in the larynx that vibrate to produce voice sounds

**vo·cal·ic** (vō kal'ik) *adj.* of, like, or involving a vowel or vowels

**vo·cal·ist** (vō'kəl ist) *n.* a singer

**vo'cal·ize'** *vt., vi.* **-ized', -iz'ing** to speak or sing

**vo·ca·tion** (vō kā'shən) *n.* 〖< L *vocare,* to call〗 **1** the career to which one feels one is called **2** any trade or occupation

**vo·ca'tion·al** *adj.* **1** of a vocation **2** designating or of training, etc. for an occupation or trade

**voc·a·tive** (väk'ə tiv) *n.* 〖see VOCATION〗 *Gram.* a case indicating the person or thing addressed

**vo·cif·er·ate** (vō sif′ər āt′) *vt.*, *vi.* **-at′ed, -at′ing** 〖< L *vox,* voice + *ferre,* to bear〗 to shout loudly; clamor —**vo·cif′er·a′tion** *n.*

**vo·cif·er·ous** (vō sif′ər əs) *adj.* noisy; clamorous

**vod·ka** (väd′kə) *n.* 〖Russ < *voda,* water〗 a colorless alcoholic liquor distilled from rye, wheat, etc.

**vo·ed** (vō′ed′) *adj., n.* [Inf.] (of) vocational education

**vogue** (vōg) *n.* 〖Fr〗 **1** the current fashion **2** popularity —*adj.* in vogue: also **vogu·ish** (vō′gish)

**voice** (vois) *n.* 〖< L *vox*〗 **1** sound made through the mouth, esp. by human beings **2** the ability to make such sounds **3** anything regarded as like vocal utterance **4** an expressed wish, opinion, etc. **5** the right to express one's wish, etc.; vote **6** utterance or expression **7** a verb form showing the relation of the subject to the action: see ACTIVE (*adj.* 4), PASSIVE (*adj.* 3) **8** singing ability —*vt.* **voiced, voic′ing** to give utterance or expression to —**with one voice** unanimously —**voice′less** *adj.*

**voice box** LARYNX

**voice mail 1** an electronic system whereby voice messages can be recorded, stored, and then delivered **2** such messages

**voice′-o′ver** *n.* the voice of an unseen announcer or narrator, as on TV

**void** (void) *adj.* 〖< L *vacare,* be empty〗 **1** containing nothing **2** devoid (*of*) [*void* of common sense] **3** ineffective; useless **4** of no legal force —*n.* **1** an empty space **2** a feeling of emptiness —*vt.* **1** to empty **2** to make void; annul —**void′a·ble** *adj.*

**voi·là** (vwä lä′) *interj.* 〖Fr〗 behold; there it is

**voile** (voil) *n.* 〖Fr, a veil〗 a thin fabric, as of cotton

**vol** *abbrev.* volume

**vol·a·tile** (väl′ə təl) *adj.* 〖< L *volare,* to fly〗 **1** evaporating quickly **2** *a*) unstable; explosive *b*) fickle —**vol′a·til′i·ty** (-til′ə tē) *n.* —**vol′a·til·ize′** (-īz′), **-ized′, -iz′ing,** *vt., vi.*

**vol·can·ic** (väl kan′ik, vôl-) *adj.* **1** of or caused by a volcano **2** like a volcano; violently explosive

**vol·ca·no** (väl kā′nō, vôl-) *n., pl.* **-noes** or **-nos** 〖< L *Volcanus,* Vulcan〗 **1** a vent in the earth's crust through which molten rock, ashes, etc. are ejected **2** a cone-shaped mountain of this material built up around the vent

**vole** (vōl) *n.* 〖< earlier *vole mouse* < Scand, as in ON *vollr,* meadow〗 any of various small rodents with a stout body and short tail

**Vol·ga** (väl′gə, vōl′-) river in European Russia, flowing into the Caspian Sea

**vo·li·tion** (vō lish′ən) *n.* 〖ult. < L *velle,* be willing〗 the act or power of using the will —**vo·li′tion·al** *adj.*

**vol·ley** (väl′ē) *n., pl.* **-leys** 〖< L *volare,* to fly〗 **1** *a*) the simultaneous discharge of a number of weapons *b*) the bullets, etc., so discharged **2** a burst of words or acts **3** *Sports a*) a returning of a ball, etc. before it touches the ground *b*) an extended exchange of shots, as in tennis —*vt., vi.* **-leyed, -ley·ing 1** to discharge or be discharged as in a volley **2** *Sports* to return (the ball, etc.) as a volley

**vol′ley·ball′** *n.* **1** a team game played by hitting a large, light, inflated ball back and forth over a net with the hands **2** this ball

**volt** (vōlt) *n.* 〖after A. *Volta* (1745-1827), It physicist〗 the basic unit of electromotive force

**volt·age** (vōl′tij) *n.* electromotive force expressed in volts

**vol·ta·ic** (väl tā′ik) *adj.* of or by electricity produced by chemical action

**Vol·taire** (vōl ter′) 1694-1778; Fr. writer & philosopher

**volt′me′ter** *n.* an instrument for measuring voltage

**vol·u·ble** (väl′yə bəl) *adj.* 〖< L *volvere,* to roll〗 characterized by a great flow of words; talkative —**vol′u·bil′i·ty** *n.* —**vol′u·bly** *adv.*

**vol·ume** (väl′yōōm) *n.* 〖< L *volumen,* a scroll〗 **1** *a*) a book *b*) one of a set of books **2** the amount of space occupied in three dimensions **3** *a*) a quantity, bulk, or amount *b*) a large quantity **4** the loudness of sound

**vo·lu·mi·nous** (və lōōm′ə nəs) *adj.* **1** producing or consisting of enough to fill volumes **2** large; bulky; full —**vo·lu′mi·nous·ly** *adv.*

**vol·un·ta·rism** (väl′ən tər iz′əm) *n.* (system of) voluntary participation in a course of action

**vol·un·tar·y** (-ter′ē) *adj.* 〖< L *voluntas,* free will〗 **1** brought about by one's own free choice **2** acting of one's own accord **3** intentional **4** controlled by one's mind or will —**vol′un·tar′i·ly** *adv.*

**vol·un·teer** (väl′ən tir′) *n.* one who chooses freely to do something, as entering military service — *adj.* **1** serving as a volunteer **2** of a volunteer or volunteers —*vt.* to offer or give of one's own free will —*vi.* to offer to enter into any service of one's own free will

**vo·lup·tu·ar·y** (və lup′chōō er′ē) *n., pl.* **-ar′ies** 〖< L *voluptas,* pleasure〗 one devoted to sensual pleasures

**vo·lup′tu·ous** (-chōō əs) *adj.* full of, producing, or fond of sensual pleasures —**vo·lup′tu·ous·ness** *n.*

**vo·lute** (və lōōt′) *n.* 〖< L *volvere,* to roll〗 a spiral or whorl

**vom·it** (väm′it) *n.* 〖< L *vomere,* to vomit〗 matter ejected from the stomach through the mouth — *vt., vi.* **1** to eject (the contents of the stomach) through the mouth; throw up **2** to discharge or be discharged with force —**vom′i·tous** (-ə təs) *adj.*

**voo·doo** (vōō′dōō′) *n., pl.* **-doos′** 〖of WAfr orig.〗 a religion of the West Indies, based on a belief in magic, charms, etc. —*adj.* of or resembling voodoo

**vo·ra·cious** (vô rā′shəs) *adj.* 〖< L *vorare,* devour〗 **1** greedy in eating; ravenous **2** very eager [a *voracious* reader] —**vo·rac′i·ty** (-ras′ə tē) *n.*

**vor·tex** (vôr′teks′) *n., pl.* **-tex′es** or **-ti·ces′** (-tə sēz′) 〖< L *vertere,* to turn〗 **1** a whirlpool **2** a whirlwind **3** anything like a whirlwind, etc. in effect

**vo·ta·ry** (vōt′ə rē) *n., pl.* **-ries** 〖< L *vovere,* to vow〗 **1** one bound by a vow, esp. by religious vows, as a monk or nun **2** one devoted to a cause, study, etc.

**vote** (vōt) *n.* 〖< L *votum,* a vow〗 **1** a decision on a proposal, etc., or a choice between candidates for office **2** *a*) the expression of such a decision or choice *b*) the ballot, etc. by which it is expressed **3** the right to vote **4** votes collectively —*vi.* **vot′ed, vot′ing** to give or cast a vote —*vt.* to decide or enact by vote —**vot′er** *n.*

**vo·tive** (vōt′iv) *adj.* 〖see prec.〗 designed to fulfill a promise, express devotion, etc.

**vouch** (vouch) *vi.* 〖< L *vocare,* to call〗 to give, or serve as, assurance, a guarantee, etc. (*for*) [*vouch* for someone's honesty]

**vouch′er** *n.* **1** one who vouches **2** a paper serving as evidence or proof; specif., a receipt

**vouch·safe** (vouch sāf′) *vt.* **-safed′, -saf′ing** 〖< ME *vouchen safe,* vouch as safe〗 to be kind enough to give or grant

**vow** (vou) *n.* 〖< L *votum*〗 **1** a solemn promise, esp. one made to God **2** a promise of love and fidelity [marriage *vows*] —*vt.* to promise or declare solemnly —*vi.* to make a vow —**take vows** to enter a religious order

**vow·el** (vou′əl) *n.* 〖< L *vocalis,* vocal〗 **1** a speech sound in which the air passes in a continuous stream through the open mouth **2** a letter representing such a sound, as *a, e, i, o,* or *u*

**voy·age** (voi′ij) *n.* 〖< L *via,* way〗 a relatively long journey by ship or spacecraft —*vi.* **-aged, -ag·ing** to make a voyage —**voy′ag·er** *n.*

**voy·eur** (voi ɵr′, vwä yɵr′) *n.* 〖< L *videre,* see〗 one who has an exaggerated interest in viewing sexual objects or activities —**voy·eur′ism′** *n.* — **voy·eur·is′tic** *adj.*

**VP** *abbrev.* Vice-President

**vs.** or **vs** *abbrev.* versus

**vt** *abbrev.* transitive verb

**VT** Vermont

**Vul·can** (vul′kən) *n.* the Roman god of fire and of metalworking

**vul·can·ize** (vul′kən īz′) *vt.* **-ized′, -iz′ing** to treat (crude rubber) with sulfur under heat to make it stronger and more elastic —**vul′can·i·za′tion** *n.*

**Vulg** *abbrev.* Vulgate

**vul·gar** (vul′gər) *adj.* [< L *vulgus*, common people] **1** of people in general; popular **2** vernacular **3** lacking culture, taste, etc.; crude; boorish **4** indecent or obscene —**vul′gar·ly** *adv.*

**vul·gar′i·an** (-ger′ē ən) *n.* a rich person with coarse, showy tastes

**vul·gar·ism′** (-gər iz′əm) *n.* **1** a word, phrase, etc. used widely but regarded as nonstandard, coarse, or obscene **2** vulgarity

**vul·gar′i·ty** (-ger′ə tē) *n.* **1** a being vulgar **2** *pl.* **-ties** a vulgar act, habit, usage in speech, etc.

**vul·gar·ize** (-gər īz′) *vt.* **-ized′, -iz′ing 1** to popularize **2** to make vulgar, coarse, obscene, etc. —**vul′gar·i·za′tion** *n.*

**Vulgar Latin** the everyday Latin spoken by ancient Romans as distinguished from standard written Latin

**Vul·gate** (vul′gāt′) *n.* [ML *vulgata* (*editio*), popu-

lar (edition)] a Latin version of the Bible, used in the Roman Catholic Church

**vul·ner·a·ble** (vul′nər ə bəl) *adj.* [< L *vulnus*, a wound] **1** that can be wounded or injured **2** open to, or easily hurt by, criticism or attack **3** affected by a specified influence, temptation, etc. —**vul′ner·a·bil′i·ty** *n.* —**vul′ner·a·bly** *adv.*

**vul·pine** (vul′pīn) *adj.* [< L *vulpes,* a fox] of or like a fox; cunning

**vul·ture** (vul′chər) *n.* [< L, akin to *vellere,* to tear] **1** a large bird that lives chiefly on carrion **2** a greedy, ruthless person

TURKEY VULTURE

**vul·va** (vul′və) *n., pl.* **-vae** (-vē) or **-vas** [L, womb] the external genital organs of the female

**vy·ing** (vī′iŋ) *adj.* that vies; competing

# W

**w¹** or **W** (dub′əl yōō′) *n., pl.* **w's, W's** the 23d letter of the English alphabet

**w²** *abbrev.* **1** waist **2** watt(s) **3** week(s) **4** weight **5** west(ern) **6** wide **7** width **8** wife **9** with **10** win(s)

**W¹** *abbrev.* **1** watt(s) **2** Wednesday **3** west(ern) **4** win(s)

**W²** [*w*(olfram), alt. name of tungsten] *Chem. symbol for* tungsten

**WA** Washington (state)

**Wac** (wak) *n.* a member of the Women's Army Corps (**WAC**)

**wack·o** (wak′ō) [Slang] *adj. var. of* WACKY —*n., pl.* **-os** one who is wacko

**wack·y** (wak′ē) *adj.* **-i·er, -i·est** [< ?] [Slang] erratic, eccentric, or irrational —**wack′i·ness** *n.*

**wad** (wäd) *n.* [ML *wadda,* wadding] **1** a small, soft mass, as of cotton or paper **2** a lump or small, firm mass —*vt.* **wad′ded, wad′ding 1** to compress, or roll up, into a wad **2** to plug or stuff with a wad or wadding

**wad′ding** *n.* any soft material for use in padding, packing, etc.

**wad·dle** (wäd′əl) *vi.* **-dled, -dling** [< fol.] to walk with short steps, swaying from side to side, as a duck does —*n.* a waddling gait

**wade** (wād) *vi.* **wad′ed, wad′ing** [OE *waden,* go] **1** to walk through any resisting substance, as water, mud, etc. **2** to proceed with difficulty [*to wade* through a dull book] **3** [Inf.] to attack with vigor: with *in* or *into* —*vt.* to cross by wading

**wad′er** *n.* **1** one that wades **2** [*pl.*] *a*) high waterproof boots *b*) waterproof overalls with bootlike parts for the feet

**wa·di** (wä′dē) *n., pl.* **-dis** or **-dies** [Ar *wādī*] in Arabia, N Africa, etc., a ravine or watercourse that is usually dry

**wading bird** any long-legged bird that wades the shallows and marshes for food

**wa·fer** (wā′fər) *n.* [< MDu *wafel*] **1** a thin, flat, crisp cracker or cookie **2** any disklike thing resembling this

**waf·fle¹** (wä′fəl) *n.* [see prec.] a crisp batter cake baked in a waffle iron

**waf·fle²** (wä′fəl) *vi.* **-fled, -fling** [< echoic *waff,* to yelp] to speak or write in a wordy or vague way

**waffle iron** a utensil with two flat, studded plates pressed together to bake a waffle

**waft** (wäft, waft) *vt., vi.* [< Du *wachter,* watcher] to carry (sounds, odors, etc.) lightly through the

air or over water or to move in this way —*n.* **1** an odor, sound, etc. carried through the air **2** a gust of wind **3** a wafting movement

**wag¹** (wag) *vt., vi.* **wagged, wag′ging** [ME *waggen*] to move rapidly back and forth, up and down, etc. —*n.* a wagging

**wag²** (wag) *n.* [prob. < obs. *waghalter,* joker] a comical person; wit —**wag′ger·y,** *pl.* **-ies,** *n.*

**wage** (wāj) *vt.* **waged, wag′ing** [< OFr *gage,* a pledge] to engage in or carry on (a war, etc.) —*n.* **1** [*often pl.*] money paid for work done **2** [*usually pl.*] what is given in return

**wa·ger** (wā′jər) *n.* [see prec.] a bet —*vt., vi.* to bet

**wag·gish** (wag′ish) *adj.* **1** of or like a wag; roguishly merry **2** playful; jesting

**wag·gle** (wag′əl) *vt., vi.* **-gled, -gling** [< WAG¹] to wag, esp. with short, quick movements —*n.* a waggling —**wag′gly** *adj.*

**Wag·ner** (väg′nər), **Rich·ard** (riH′ärt) 1813-83; Ger. composer

**wag·on** (wag′ən) *n.* [Du *wagen*] **1** a four-wheeled vehicle, esp. one for hauling heavy loads **2** *short for* STATION WAGON —**on** (or **off**) **the wagon** [Slang] no longer (or once again) drinking alcohol

**waif** (wāf) *n.* [< NormFr] a homeless person, esp. a child

**wail** (wāl) *vi.* [< ON *væ,* woe] to make a long, loud, sad cry, as in grief or pain —*n.* such a cry

**wain** (wān) *n.* [OE *wægn*] [Old Poet.] a wagon

**wain·scot** (wān′skät′, -skət) *n.* [< MDu *wagenschot*] a wood paneling on the walls of a room, sometimes on the lower part only —*vt.* **-scot′ed** or **-scot′ted, -scot′ing** or **-scot′ting** to line (a wall) with wood, etc.

**wain′scot·ing** or **wain′scot′ting** *n.* **1** WAINSCOT **2** material used to wainscot

**wain·wright** (wān′rīt) *n.* [WAIN + WRIGHT] one who builds or repairs wagons

**waist** (wāst) *n.* [< OE *weaxan,* grow] **1** the part of the body between the ribs and the hips **2** the part of a garment that covers the body from the shoulders to the waistline **3** the narrow part of any object that is wider at the ends

**waist′band′** *n.* a band encircling the waist, as on slacks or a skirt

**waist·coat** (wes′kət, wāst′kōt′) *n.* [Brit.] a man's vest

**waist′line′** *n.* (the circumference of) the narrowest part of the waist

**wait** (wāt) *vi.* [< NormFr *waitier*] **1** to remain (until something expected happens) **2** to be ready **3** to remain undone [it can *wait*] **4** to serve food at a meal: with *at* or *on* —*vt.* **1** to await **2** [Inf.] to delay serving (a meal) —*n.* an act or period of waiting —**lie in wait (for)** to wait so as to catch after planning a trap *(for)* —**wait on** (or **upon**) **1** to act as a servant to **2** to serve (a customer) —**wait table** to serve food to people at a table —**wait up** to delay going to bed until someone arrives, etc.

**wait′er** *n.* one who waits; esp., a man who waits on tables, as in a restaurant

**wait′ing** *adj.* **1** that waits **2** of or for a wait —*n.* the act of one that waits —**in waiting** in attendance, as on a king

**waiting game** a scheme by which one wins out over another by delaying action until one has an advantage

**waiting list** a list of applicants, in the order of their application

**waiting room** a room in which people wait, as in a bus station or doctor's office

**wait′per′son** *n.* a waiter or waitress

**wait·ress** (wā′tris) *n.* a woman who waits on tables, as in a restaurant

**waive** (wāv) *vt.* **waived**, **waiv′ing** [< ON *veifa*, fluctuate] **1** to give up or forgo (a right, etc.) **2** to postpone; defer

**waiv·er** (wā′vər) *n. Law* a waiving of a right, claim, etc.

**wake**[1] (wāk) *vi.* **woke** or **waked**, **waked** or **wok′en**, **wak′ing** [< OE *wacian*, be awake & *wacan*, arise] **1** to come out of sleep; awake: often with *up* **2** to stay awake **3** to become active: often with *up* **4** to become alert (*to* a realization, etc.) —*vt.* **1** to cause to wake: often with *up* **2** to arouse (passions, etc.) —*n.* a time set aside for viewing a corpse before burial

**wake**[2] (wāk) *n.* [< ON *vök*, hole] **1** the track left in water by a moving ship **2** the track or course of anything —**in the wake of** following closely

**wake′ful** *adj.* **1** alert; watchful **2** unable to sleep —**wake′ful·ness** *n.*

**wak·en** (wā′kən) *vi., vt.* to awake

**Wal·dorf salad** (wôl′dôrf′) [after the old *Waldorf*-Astoria Hotel in New York City] a salad made of diced raw apples, celery, and walnuts, with mayonnaise

**wale** (wāl) *n.* [OE *walu*, weal] **1** a welt raised by a whip, etc. **2** a ridge on the surface of cloth, as corduroy

**Wales** (wālz) division of the United Kingdom: a peninsula of WC Great Britain: 8,018 sq. mi.; pop. 2,812,000

**walk** (wôk) *vi.* [OE *wealcan*, to roll] **1** to go on foot at a moderate pace **2** to follow a certain course [*walk* in the ways of peace] **3** *Baseball* to go to first base after the pitching of four balls (see BALL[1], *n.* 6) —*vt.* **1** to go over, along, etc. on foot **2** to cause (a dog, etc.) to walk, as for exercise **3** to accompany on a walk or stroll [to *walk* a friend home] **4** *Baseball* to advance (a batter) to first base by pitching four balls (see BALL[1], *n.* 6) —*n.* **1** the act of walking **2** a stroll or hike **3** a distance walked [an hour's *walk*] **4** a sphere of activity, occupation, etc. [people from all *walks* of life] **5** a path for walking **6** *Baseball* the walking of a batter —**walk** (**all**) **over** [Inf.] to domineer over —**walk away** (or **off**) **with 1** to steal **2** to win easily —**walk out** to go on strike —**walk out on** [Inf.] to desert; abandon

**walk′a·way′** *n.* an easily won victory

**walk′er** *n.* **1** one that walks **2** a tubular frame with wheels used by babies who are learning to walk **3** a framework used as a support in walking, as by the lame

**walk·ie-talk·ie** (wôk′ē tôk′ē) *n.* a compact, portable radio transmitter and receiver

**walking stick** a stick for carrying when walking; cane

**Walk·man** (wôk′mən, -man′) *trademark for* a portable, pocket-size radio or tape player with headphones

**walk′-on′** *n.* a minor role in which the actor has few or no lines

**walk′out′** *n.* a labor strike

**walk′-up′** *n.* **1** an upstairs apartment or office in a building without an elevator **2** the building

**walk′way′** *n.* a path, passage, etc. for pedestrians, esp. one that is sheltered

**wall** (wôl) *n.* [< L *vallus*, palisade] **1** an upright structure of wood, stone, etc., serving to enclose, divide, or protect **2** something like a wall in appearance or function —*vt.* **1** to enclose, divide, etc. with or as with a wall **2** to close up (an opening) with a wall: usually with *up* —**drive** (or **push**) **to the wall** to place in a desperate position —**off the wall** [Slang] **1** insane; crazy **2** very eccentric

**wal·la·by** (wä′lə bē) *n., pl.* **-bies** [< Australian native name *wolabā*] a marsupial of Australia, etc., like a small kangaroo

**wall·board** (wôl′bôrd′) *n.* fibrous material in thin slabs for making or covering walls and ceilings

**wall′cov′er·ing** *n.* decorative fabric or material, as wallpaper, for covering the walls of a room

**wal·let** (wô′lit) *n.* [ME *walet*] a flat case or folder, as of leather, for carrying money, cards, etc.

**wall′eye′** *n.* [< ON *vagl*, a beam + *eygr*, eye] **1** an eye that turns outward, showing much white **2** a fish with large, glossy eyes, esp. a North American freshwater perch: in full **wall′eyed′ pike**

**wall′flow′er** *n.* [Inf.] a person who merely looks on at a dance, etc. as from shyness

**Wal·loon** (wä loon′) *n.* [< OHG *walh*, foreigner] **1** a member of a chiefly Celtic people in S Belgium **2** the French dialect of this people

**wal·lop** (wä′ləp) [Inf.] *vt.* [< OFr *galoper*, to gallop] **1** to beat or defeat soundly **2** to strike hard —*n.* **1** a hard blow **2** a thrill

**wal·low** (wä′lō) *vi.* [OE *wealwian*, roll around] **1** to roll about, as in mud **2** to indulge oneself fully (*in* a specified thing) —*n.* **1** a wallowing **2** a muddy or dusty place

**wall′pa′per** *n.* decorative paper for covering the walls of a room —*vt.* to hang wallpaper on or in

**Wall Street 1** street in New York City; financial center of the U.S. **2** U.S. financiers and their power, policies, etc. **3** the U.S. securities market

**wall′-to-wall′** *adj.* **1** covering a floor completely **2** [Inf.] *a)* pervasive *b)* comprehensive

**wal·nut** (wôl′nut′) *n.* [< OE *wealh*, foreign + *hnutu*, nut] **1** a shade tree valued for its nuts and wood **2** its edible nut **3** its wood

WALRUS

**wal·rus** (wôl′rəs) *n.* [< Dan *hvalros*] a massive arctic sea mammal somewhat like a seal, having two tusks projecting from the upper jaw

**waltz** (wôlts) *n.* [< Ger *walzen*, dance about] **1** a ballroom dance for couples, in 3/4 time **2** music for this —*vi.* **1** to dance a waltz **2** to move lightly

**wam·pum** (wäm′pəm) *n.* [< AmInd] small beads made of shells and used by North American Indians as money, for ornament, etc.

**wan** (wän) *adj.* **wan′ner**, **wan′nest** [OE *wann*, dark] **1** sickly pale **2** feeble or weak [a *wan* smile]

**wand** (wänd) *n.* [< ON *vöndr*] **1** a staff symbolizing authority **2** a rod regarded as having magical powers **3** any of various rod-shaped devices, as one for reading bar codes

**wan·der** (wän′dər) *vi.* [OE *wandrian*] **1** to roam aimlessly; ramble **2** to stray (*from* a path, etc.) **3**

to go astray in mind or purpose **4** to meander, as a river —*vt.* to roam in or over —**wan′der·er** *n.*

**wan′der·lust′** *n.* ⟦Ger⟧ an urge to wander or travel

**wane** (wān) *vi.* **waned, wan′ing** ⟦OE *wanian,* to decrease⟧ **1** to grow gradually less in extent: said of the visible face of the moon **2** to grow dim **3** to decline in power, etc. **4** to approach the end —*n.* a waning

**wan·gle** (waŋ′gəl) [Inf.] *vt., vi.* **-gled, -gling** ⟦< ? WAGGLE⟧ to get or cause (something) by persuasion, tricks, etc.

**wan·na·be** (wä′nə bē′) *n.* [Slang] one who wants to be like someone else or attain some status: also **wan′na·be′**

**want** (wänt, wônt) *vt.* ⟦< ON *vanta*⟧ **1** to lack **2** to wish for; desire **3** to wish to see or apprehend [*wanted* by the police] **4** [Chiefly Brit.] to require —*vi.* to have a need or lack: usually with *for* —*n.* **1** a shortage; lack **2** poverty **3** a craving **4** something needed

**want ad** [Inf.] an advertisement for something wanted, as a job

**want′ing** *adj.* **1** lacking **2** not up to standard —*prep.* without or minus —**wanting in** deficient in

**wan·ton** (wänt′'n) *adj.* ⟦< OE *wan,* lacking + *teon,* educate⟧ **1** sexually unrestrained **2** [Old Poet.] playful **3** unprovoked or malicious **4** recklessly ignoring justice, decency, etc. —*n.* a wanton person; esp., a sexually unrestrained woman

**wap·i·ti** (wä′pə tē) *n.* ⟦< AmInd⟧ a large North American deer with widely branching antlers; elk

**war** (wôr) *n.* ⟦< NormFr *werre*⟧ **1** open armed conflict as between nations **2** any active hostility or struggle **3** military operations as a science —*adj.* of, in, or from war —*vi.* **warred, war′ring 1** to carry on war **2** to contend; strive —**at war** in a state of active armed conflict

**war·ble** (wôr′bəl) *vt., vi.* **-bled, -bling** ⟦< NormFr *werbler*⟧ to sing (a song, etc.) melodiously, with trills, quavers, etc., as a bird does —*n.* a warbling

**war·bler** (wôr′blər) *n.* **1** one that warbles **2** a small, often brightly colored songbird

**war crime** a violation of laws or norms of humane behavior, committed during war

**ward** (wôrd) *vt.* ⟦OE *weardian,* to guard⟧ to turn aside; fend (*off*) —*n.* **1** a being under guard **2** one under the care of a guardian or court **3** a division of a jail, hospital, etc. **4** a division of a city or town, for purposes of voting, etc.

**-ward** (wərd) ⟦OE *-weard*⟧ *suffix* in a (specified) direction [*inward*]: also **-wards** (wərdz)

**war·den** (wôrd′'n) *n.* ⟦< NormFr *wardein*⟧ **1** one who guards, or has charge of, something [game *warden*] **2** the chief official of a prison

**ward′er** *n.* a watchman

**ward heeler** a follower of a politician, who solicits votes, etc.: often used with mild contempt

**ward·robe** (wôr′drōb′) *n.* **1** a closet, cabinet, etc. for holding clothes **2** one's supply of clothes

**ward′room′** *n.* in a warship, a room used for eating, etc. by commissioned officers

**ware** (wer) *n.* ⟦OE *waru*⟧ **1** anything for sale: *usually used in pl.* **2** pottery

**ware′house′** *n.* a building where goods are stored —*vt.* **-housed′, -hous′ing** to store in a warehouse

**war·fare** (wôr′fer′) *n.* (armed) conflict

**war′head′** *n.* the front part of a torpedo, etc., containing the explosive

**war′horse′** *n.* [Inf.] one who has been through many struggles; veteran

**war·i·ly** (wer′ə lē) *adv.* cautiously —**war′i·ness** (-ē nis) *n.*

**war′like′** *adj.* **1** fond of or ready for war **2** of war **3** threatening war

**war·lock** (wôr′läk′) *n.* ⟦OE *wærloga,* liar⟧ a man who practices black magic

**war′lord′** *n.* **1** a high military officer in a warlike nation **2** a local ruler or bandit leader

**warm** (wôrm) *adj.* ⟦OE *wearm*⟧ **1** *a)* having or giving off a moderate degree of heat *b)* hot [a

warm night] **2** that keeps body heat in [a *warm* hat] **3** ardent; enthusiastic **4** lively, vigorous, etc. **5** quick to anger **6** *a)* genial; cordial [a *warm* welcome] *b)* sympathetic or loving **7** newly made; fresh, as a trail **8** [Inf.] close to discovering something —*vt., vi.* to make or become warm —**warm up** to practice or exercise, as before going into a game, contest, etc. —**warm′er** *n.* —**warm′ish** *adj.* —**warm′ly** *adv.*

**warm′blood′ed** *adj.* having a body temperature that is relatively constant and usually higher than that of the surroundings

**warmed′-o′ver** *adj.* **1** reheated **2** presented again, without significant change, as ideas

**warm front** the forward edge of a warm air mass advancing into a colder mass

**warm′heart′ed** *adj.* kind, sympathetic, friendly, loving, etc.

**war′mon′ger** (-muŋ′gər, -mäŋ′-) *n.* one who tries to cause war —**war′mon·ger·ing** *adj., n.*

**warmth** (wôrmth) *n.* **1** *a)* the state of having heat *b)* mild heat **2** *a)* enthusiasm, ardor, etc. *b)* affectionate feelings

**warm′-up′** *n.* the act of warming up

**warn** (wôrn) *vt., vi.* ⟦OE *wearnian*⟧ **1** to tell of a danger, coming evil, etc. **2** to caution about certain acts **3** to notify in advance; inform

**warn′ing** *n.* **1** the act of one that warns **2** something that serves to warn —*adj.* that warns

**warp** (wôrp) *n.* ⟦OE *weorpan,* to throw⟧ **1** *a)* a distortion, as a twist or bend, in wood *b)* any similar distortion **2** a mental quirk, bias, etc. **3** *Weaving* the threads running lengthwise in the loom —*vt.* **1** to bend or twist out of shape **2** to distort, pervert, etc.: said of the mind, character, etc. —*vi.* to become bent or twisted

**war′path′** *n.* the path taken by American Indians on a warlike expedition —**on the warpath 1** ready for war **2** actively angry; ready to fight

**warp speed** ⟦< (TIME) WARP + SPEED⟧ [Slang] in science fiction, a very high rate of speed

**war·rant** (wôr′ənt, wär′-) *n.* ⟦< NormFr *warant*⟧ **1** *a)* authorization, as by law *b)* justification for some act, belief, etc. **2** something serving as a guarantee of some event or result **3** *Law* a writ authorizing an arrest, search, etc. —*vt.* **1** to authorize **2** to serve as justification for (an act, belief, etc.) **3** to guarantee

**warrant officer** a military officer ranking above a noncommissioned officer but below a commissioned officer

**war·ran·ty** (wôr′ən tē, wär′-) *n., pl.* **-ties** an assurance by a seller that goods will be repaired or replaced if not as represented; guarantee

**war·ren** (wôr′ən, wär′-) *n.* ⟦< NormFr *warir,* to preserve⟧ **1** an area in which rabbits breed or are numerous **2** any crowded building or buildings

**war·rior** (wôr′yər, -ē ər) *n.* [see WAR] a person experienced in conflict, esp. war; soldier

**War·saw** (wôr′sô′) capital of Poland: pop. 1,651,000

**war′ship′** *n.* any combat ship, as a battleship

**wart** (wôrt) *n.* ⟦OE *wearte*⟧ **1** a small, usually hard, tumorous growth on the skin, caused by a virus **2** a small protuberance, as on a plant —**wart′y, -i·er, -i·est,** *adj.*

**wart hog** a wild African hog with large tusks, and warts below the eyes

**war·y** (wer′ē) *adj.* **-i·er, -i·est** ⟦OE *wær,* aware⟧ on one's guard; cautious —**wary of** careful of

**was** (wuz, wäz) *vi.* ⟦OE *wæs*⟧ *1st & 3d pers. sing., pt., of* BE

**wash** (wôsh, wäsh) *vt.* ⟦OE *wæscan*⟧ **1** to clean with water or other liquid **2** to purify **3** to wet or moisten **4** to flow over, past, or against: said of a sea, waves, etc. **5** to soak (*out*), flush (*off*), or carry (*away*) with water **6** to erode; wear (*out* or *away*) by flowing over [the flood *washed* out the road] —*vi.* **1** to wash oneself **2** to wash clothes **3** to undergo washing **4** to be removed by washing:

usually with *out* or *away* **5** to be worn or carried (*out* or *away*) by the action of water /the bridge had *washed* out/ **6** [Inf.] to withstand examination /that excuse won't *wash*/ —*n.* **1** a washing **2** a quantity of clothes, etc. washed, or to be washed **3** the rush or surge of water **4** the eddy of water or air caused by a propeller, etc. **5** silt, mud, etc. carried and dropped by running water **6** a liquid for cosmetic or medicinal use /*mouthwash*/ **7** in the W U.S., the dry bed of a stream **8** [Inf.] a situation in which contrasted elements offset each other —*adj.* that can be washed without damage; washable —**wash down** to follow (food, etc.) with a drink —**wash′a·ble** *adj.*, *n.*

**wash′-and-wear′** *adj.* of fabrics that need little or no ironing after washing

**wash′board′** *n.* a ridged board for scrubbing dirt out of clothes

**wash′bowl′** *n.* a bowl, esp. a bathroom fixture, for use in washing one's hands, etc.: also **wash′ba·sin**

**wash′cloth′** *n.* a small cloth used in washing the body: also **wash′rag′**

**washed′-out′** *adj.* **1** faded **2** [Inf.] tired; spiritless; pale and wan

**washed′-up′** *adj.* **1** [Inf.] tired; exhausted **2** [Slang] finished; done for; having failed

**wash′er** *n.* **1** one who washes **2** a flat ring of metal, rubber, etc., used with a nut, faucet valve, bolt, etc. **3** a machine for washing

**wash′er·wom′an** *n.*, *pl.* **-wom′en** a woman whose work is washing clothes

**wash′ing** *n.* clothes, etc. to be washed

**washing machine** a clothes WASHER (*n.* 3)

**Wash·ing·ton**[1] (wôsh′iŋ tən, wäsh′-), **George** 1732-99; 1st president of the U.S. (1789-97)

**Wash′ing·ton**[2] **1** NW coastal state of the U.S.: 66,582 sq. mi.; pop. 4,867,000; cap. Olympia: abbrev. *WA* **2** capital of the U.S., coextensive with the District of Columbia: pop. 607,000: also called **Washington, DC** —**Wash′ing·to′ni·an** (-tô′ nē ən) *adj.*, *n.*

**wash′out′** *n.* **1** the washing away of soil, etc. by water **2** [Slang] a failure

**wash′room′** *n.* **1** a room for washing **2** REST-ROOM

**wash′stand′** *n.* a table or plumbing fixture with a washbowl, etc.

**wash′tub′** *n.* a tub, often with faucets and a drain, for washing clothes, etc.

**wash′y** *adj.* **-i·er**, **-i·est** feeble; insipid

**wasp** (wäsp, wôsp) *n.* ⟦OE *wæsp*⟧ a winged insect with a slender body and, in the females and workers, a painful sting

**WASP** or **Wasp** (wäsp, wôsp) *n.* a white Anglo-Saxon Protestant

**wasp′ish** *adj.* bad-tempered; snappish

**was·sail** (wäs′əl, -āl′) *n.* ⟦< ON *ves heill*, be hearty⟧ **1** a toast formerly used to drink to the health of a person **2** the spiced ale, etc. with which such toasts were drunk **3** a drinking party —*vi.*, *vt.* to drink a wassail

**wast·age** (wās′tij) *n.* **1** loss by use, decay, etc. **2** anything wasted

**waste** (wāst) *vt.* **wast′ed**, **wast′ing** ⟦< L *vastare*⟧ **1** to devastate; ruin **2** to wear away **3** to make weak or emaciated /*wasted* by age/ **4** to use up needlessly; squander **5** to fail to take advantage of **6** [Slang] to kill —*vi.* **1** to lose strength, etc., as by disease **2** to be used up or worn down gradually —*adj.* **1** uncultivated or uninhabited; desolate **2** left over or superfluous **3** excreted from the body **4** used for waste —*n.* **1** uncultivated or uninhabited land **2** a devastated area **3** a wasting or being wasted **4** discarded material, as ashes **5** excretions from the body, as urine —

**go to waste** to be wasted —**lay waste (to)** to destroy —**wast′er** *n.*

**waste′bas′ket** *n.* a container for wastepaper, etc.: also **wastepaper basket**

**wast·ed** (wās′təd) *adj.* [Slang] **1** intoxicated by a drug **2** drunk

**waste′ful** *adj.* using more than is necessary —**waste′ful·ly** *adv.* —**waste′ful·ness** *n.*

**waste′land′** *n.* **1** barren land **2** an unproductive activity, endeavor, etc.

**waste′pa′per** *n.* paper thrown away after use: also **waste paper**

**waste′wa′ter** *n.* water discharged as sewage

**wast·rel** (wās′trəl) *n.* one who wastes; esp., a spendthrift

**watch** (wäch, wôch) *n.* ⟦OE *wæcce*⟧ **1** a keeping awake, esp. in order to guard **2** close observation for a time **3** a guard, or the period of duty of a guard **4** a small timepiece carried in the pocket or worn on the wrist **5** *a*) any of the periods of duty (usually four hours) on shipboard *b*) the crew on duty during such a period —*vi.* **1** to stay awake, esp. at night; keep vigil **2** to be on the alert **3** to look or observe **4** to be looking or waiting attentively: with *for* —*vt.* **1** to guard or tend **2** to observe carefully **3** to wait and look for —**watch oneself** to be careful —**watch out** to be alert or careful —**watch′er** *n.*

**watch′band′** *n.* a band of leather, metal, etc. to hold a watch on the wrist

**watch′dog′** *n.* **1** a dog kept to guard property **2** one that keeps watch in order to prevent waste, unethical practices, etc.

**watch′ful** *adj.* watching closely; vigilant; alert —**watch′ful·ly** *adv.* —**watch′ful·ness** *n.*

**watch′man** (-mən) *n.*, *pl.* **-men** (-mən) a person hired to guard property

**watch′tow′er** *n.* a high tower from which watch is kept, as for forest fires

**watch′word′** *n.* **1** a password **2** a slogan or cry

**wa·ter** (wôt′ər, wät′-) *n.* ⟦OE *wæter*⟧ **1** the colorless liquid of rivers, lakes, etc., which falls as rain **2** water with reference to its depth, surface, or level /*above water*/ **3** a body secretion, as urine **4** a wavy, lustrous finish given to linen, silk, metal, etc. —*vt.* **1** to give (animals) water to drink **2** to supply (crops, etc.) with water **3** to moisten, soak, or dilute with water **4** to give a wavy luster to (silk, etc.) —*vi.* **1** to fill with tears: said of the eyes **2** to secrete saliva /his mouth *watered*/ **3** to take on a supply of water **4** to drink water —*adj.* of, for, in, on, near, from, or by water —**hold water** to remain sound, logical, etc.

**water bed** a heavy vinyl bag filled with water and used as a bed or mattress: also **wa′ter·bed′** *n.*

**water buffalo** a slow, powerful buffalo of S Asia used as a draft animal

**water chestnut 1** a Chinese sedge with a nut-like tuber **2** this tuber

**water closet** TOILET (*n.* 2)

**wa′ter·col′or** *n.* **1** a pigment mixed with water for use as a paint **2** a painting done with such paints **3** the art of painting with watercolors

**wa′ter-cooled′** *adj.* cooled by water circulated around or through it

**wa′ter·course′** *n.* **1** a stream, river, etc. **2** a channel for water, as a canal

**wa′ter·craft′** *n.*, *pl.* **-craft′** a boat, ship, or other water vehicle

**wa′ter·cress′** *n.* a white-flowered water plant: its leaves are used in salads, etc.

**wa′ter·fall′** *n.* a steep fall of water, as of a stream, from a height

**wa′ter·fowl′** *n.* a water bird, esp. one that swims

**wa′ter·front′** *n.* land or docks at the edge of a stream, harbor, etc.

**water hole** a pond or pool

**wa·ter·lil′y** *n.*, *pl.* **-lil′ies 1** a water plant with large, flat, floating leaves and showy flowers **2** the flower

**wa·ter·line′** *n.* the line to which the surface of the water comes on the side of a ship or boat

**wa·ter·logged′** (-lôgd′) *adj.* soaked or filled with water so as to be heavy and sluggish

WATERLILY

**Wa·ter·loo¹** (wôt′ər lōō′, wät′-) *n.* ⟦after fol.⟧ any disastrous or decisive defeat

**Wa·ter·loo′²** town in central Belgium: scene of Napoleon's final defeat (1815)

**water main** a main pipe in a system of water pipes

**wa·ter·mark′** *n.* **1** a mark showing the limit to which water has risen **2** a mark in paper, produced by pressure of a design, as in the mold —*vt.* to mark (paper) with a watermark

**wa·ter·mel′on** *n.* a large, green melon with sweet, juicy, red pulp

**water moccasin** a large, poisonous water snake of the SE U.S.

**water pipe 1** a pipe for water **2** a smoking pipe using water, as a hookah

**water polo** a water game played with a ball by two teams of swimmers

**water power** the power of running or falling water, used to drive machinery, etc.: also **wa′ter·pow′er** *n.*

**wa·ter·proof′** *adj.* that keeps out water, as by being treated with rubber, etc. —*vt.* to make waterproof

**water rat** any of various rodents living on the banks of streams and ponds

**wa·ter·re·pel′lent** *adj.* that repels water but is not fully waterproof

**wa·ter·shed′** *n.* **1** a ridge dividing the areas drained by different river systems **2** the area drained by a river system

**wa·ter·side′** *n.* land at the edge of a body of water —*adj.* of, at, or on the waterside

**wa·ter·ski′** *vi.* -skied′, -ski′ing to be towed on skilike boards (**water skis**) by a line attached to a speedboat —**wa′ter·ski′er** *n.*

**wa·ter·spout′** *n.* **1** a pipe for spouting water **2** a whirling funnel-shaped column of air full of spray occurring over water in tropical areas

**water table** the level below which the ground is saturated with water

**wa·ter·tight′** *adj.* **1** so snugly put together that no water can get in or through **2** that cannot be misconstrued, nullified, etc.; flawless

**water tower** an elevated tank for water storage

**wa·ter·way′** *n.* **1** a channel through which water runs **2** any body of water suitable for boats, ships, etc., as a canal or river

**water wheel** a wheel turned by running water, as for power

**water wings** an inflated device to keep one afloat as while learning to swim

**wa·ter·works′** *pl.n.* [*often with sing. v.*] a system of reservoirs, pumps, etc. supplying water to a city

**wa·ter·y** *adj.* **1** of or like water **2** full of water **3** thin; diluted **4** tearful **5** weak —**wa′ter·i·ness** *n.*

**WATS** (wäts) *n.* ⟦*w*(ide) *a*(rea) *t*(elecommunications) *s*(ervice)⟧ a long-distance telephone service using a network at special rates

**watt** (wät) *n.* ⟦after James *Watt* (1736-1819), Scot inventor of steam engine⟧ a unit of electrical power, equal to the power developed in a circuit by a current of one ampere flowing through a potential difference of one volt; $\frac{1}{746}$ horsepower

**watt′age** *n.* amount of electrical power, expressed in watts

**wat·tle** (wät′'l) *n.* ⟦OE *watul*⟧ **1** a woven work of sticks intertwined with twigs or branches **2** a

fleshy flap of skin hanging from the throat of certain birds or lizards —*vt.* -tled, -tling **1** to intertwine (sticks, twigs, etc.) **2** to build of or with wattle

**wave** (wāv) *vi.* **waved**, **wav′ing** ⟦OE *wafian*⟧ **1** to move or sway to and fro **2** to signal by moving a hand, arm, etc. to and fro **3** to have the form of a series of curves —*vt.* **1** to cause to wave **2** to brandish (a weapon) **3** *a*) to move or swing (something) as a signal *b*) to signal (something) to (someone) by doing this **4** to give an undulating form to (hair, etc.) —*n.* **1** a ridge or swell moving along the surface of the ocean, etc. **2** an undulation or curve, as in the hair **3** a motion to and fro, as with the hand in signaling **4** a thing like a wave in action or effect; specif., an upsurge [a crime *wave*] **5** *Physics* a periodic motion or disturbance, as in the propagation of sound or light

**Wave** (wāv) *n.* ⟦< *W*(omen) *A*(ppointed for) *V*(oluntary) *E*(mergency) *S*(ervice)⟧ a member of the women's branch of the U.S. Navy (**WAVES**)

**wave′length′** *n.* **1** *Physics* the distance measured along a wave from any given point to the next similar point **2** [Inf.] chiefly in the phrase **on the same wavelength**, in accord

**wave′let** (-lit) *n.* a little wave

**wa·ver** (wā′vər) *vi.* ⟦< ME *waven*, to wave⟧ **1** to sway to and fro **2** to show indecision; vacillate **3** to falter, flicker, tremble, etc. —*n.* a wavering

**wav·y** (wā′vē) *adj.* -i·er, -i·est **1** having or like waves **2** moving in a wavelike motion —**wav′i·ness** *n.*

**wax¹** (waks) *n.* ⟦OE *weax*⟧ **1** a plastic, dull-yellow substance secreted by bees; beeswax **2** any plastic substance like this; specif., *a*) paraffin *b*) a substance exuded by the ears —*vt.* to rub, polish, cover, or treat with wax

**wax²** (waks) *vi.* **waxed**, **wax′ing** ⟦OE *weaxan*, grow⟧ **1** to increase in strength, size, etc. **2** to become gradually full: said of the moon **3** [Literary] to become; grow [to *wax* angry]

**wax bean** a variety of the common garden bean with long, edible, yellow pods

**wax·en** (wak′sən) *adj.* **1** made of wax **2** pale

**wax museum** an exhibition of wax figures, as of famous persons

**wax myrtle** an evergreen shrub with grayish-white, wax-coated berries

**wax paper** a paper made moisture-proof by a wax coating: also **waxed paper**

**wax′wing′** *n.* a fruit-eating bird with brown or gray silky plumage and scarlet waxlike tips on the wings

**wax′works′** *n.* an exhibition of wax figures

**wax′y** *adj.* -i·er, -i·est of, full of, or like wax —**wax′i·ness** *n.*

**way** (wā) *n.* ⟦ME < OE *weg*⟧ **1** a road, street, path, etc. **2** space for passing **3** a route or course **4** course of life or conduct [avoid evil *ways*] **5** a method of doing something **6** a manner of living, acting, etc. [the *way* of the world] **7** distance [a long *way* off] **8** direction of movement or action **9** movement forward **10** respect; specific point [right in some *ways*] **11** wish; will [get one's own *way*] **12** [Inf.] *a*) a condition [he's in a bad *way*] *b*) a locality [out our *way*] **13** [*pl.*] a timber framework on which a ship is built —*adv.* [Inf.] away; far [*way* behind] —**by the way** incidentally —**by way of 1** passing through **2** as a method, etc. of —**give way 1** to yield **2** to break down —**lead the way** to be a guide or example —**make way 1** to clear a passage **2** to make progress —**under way** moving; advancing

**way′far′er** (-fer′ər) *n.* a traveler, esp. on foot —**way′far′ing** *adj.*, *n.*

**way·lay** (wā′lā′) *vt.* -laid′, -lay′ing **1** to lie in wait for and attack **2** to wait for and accost (a person) on the way

**way′-out′** *adj.* [Inf.] very unusual or unconventional

**-ways** (wāz) ⟦ME < *way* (see WAY)⟧ *suffix* in a (specified) direction, position, or manner [*sideways*]

**ways and means** methods of raising money; specif., such methods, including legislation, in government

**way'side'** *n.* the edge of a road

**way'ward** *adj.* ⟦see AWAY & -WARD⟧ **1** headstrong, willful, disobedient, etc. **2** unpredictable; erratic —**way'ward·ly** *adv.* —**way'ward·ness** *n.*

**we** (wē) *pron., sing.* I ⟦OE⟧ **1** the persons speaking or writing **2** I: used by a monarch, editor, etc. when speaking for others

**weak** (wēk) *adj.* ⟦< ON *veikr*⟧ **1** lacking physical strength; feeble **2** lacking moral strength or willpower **3** lacking mental power **4** lacking power, authority, force, etc. **5** easily torn, broken, etc. [a *weak* railing] **6** lacking intensity, etc. [a *weak* voice] **7** diluted [*weak* tea] **8** unconvincing [a *weak* argument]

**weak'en** *vt., vi.* to make or become weak or weaker

**weak'-kneed'** (-nēd') *adj.* lacking in courage, determination, resistance, etc.

**weak'ling** *n.* one that is low in physical or moral strength

**weak'ly** *adj.* -li·er, -li·est sickly; feeble —*adv.* in a weak manner

**weak'ness** *n.* **1** state of being weak **2** a weak point **3** an immoderate fondness (*for* something)

**weal**[1] (wēl) *n.* ⟦< WALE⟧ a mark raised on the skin, as by a blow; welt

**weal**[2] (wēl) *n.* ⟦< OE *wela*, wealth, well-being⟧ well-being; welfare [the public *weal*]

**wealth** (welth) *n.* ⟦< prec.⟧ **1** much money or property; riches **2** a large amount [a *wealth* of ideas] **3** valuable products, contents, etc. **4** everything having value in money

**wealth·y** (wel'thē) *adj.* -i·er, -i·est having wealth; rich —**wealth'i·ness** *n.*

**wean** (wēn) *vt.* ⟦OE *wenian*, to accustom, train⟧ **1** to accustom (a child or young animal) to take food other than by suckling **2** to withdraw (a person) by degrees (*from* a habit, etc.)

**weap·on** (wep'ən) *n.* ⟦OE *wæpen*⟧ **1** any instrument used to injure or kill **2** any means of attack or defense —**weap'on·less** *adj.*

**weap'on·ry** *n.* weapons collectively

**wear** (wer) *vt.* wore, worn, wear'ing ⟦OE *werian*⟧ **1** to have (clothing, etc.) on the body **2** to show in one's appearance [to *wear* a smile] **3** to impair or diminish by use, friction, etc.: often with *away* **4** to make by rubbing, flowing, etc. [to *wear* a hole in the rug] **5** to tire or exhaust —*vi.* **1** to become impaired or diminished, as by use **2** to hold up in use [that suit *wears* well] **3** to have an irritating effect (*on*) —*n.* **1** a wearing or being worn **2** things worn; clothes [women's *wear*] **3** impairment or loss, as from use, friction, etc. —**wear off** to diminish by degrees —**wear'a·ble** *adj.* —**wear'er** *n.*

**wear and tear** loss and damage resulting from use

**wea·ri·some** (wir'i səm) *adj.* causing weariness; tiresome or tedious —**wea'ri·some·ly** *adv.*

**wea·ry** (wir'ē) *adj.* -ri·er, -ri·est ⟦OE *werig*⟧ **1** tired; worn out **2** without further patience, zeal, etc. **3** tiring —*vt., vi.* -ried, -ry·ing to make or become weary —**wea'ri·ly** *adv.* —**wea'ri·ness** *n.*

**wea·sel** (wē'zəl) *n.* ⟦OE *wesle*⟧ **1** an agile flesh-eating mammal with a long, slender body and short legs **2** a sly, cunning person —*vi.* [Inf.] to avoid a commitment: with *out* —**wea'sel·ly** *adj.*

**weath·er** (weth'ər) *n.* ⟦OE *weder*⟧ **1** the condition of the atmosphere with regard to temperature, moisture, etc. **2** storm, rain, etc. —*vt.* **1** to expose to the action of weather **2** to pass through safely [to *weather* a storm] **3** *Naut.* to pass to the windward of —*vi.* to become worn, etc. by exposure to the weather —**under the weather** [Inf.] ill

**weath'er-beat'en** *adj.* showing the effect of exposure to sun, rain, etc.

**weath'er·cock'** *n.* a weather vane in the shape of a rooster

**weath'er·ing** *n.* the effects of the forces of weather on rock surfaces

**weath'er·ize'** *vt.* -ized, -iz'ing to weatherstrip, insulate, etc. (a building) —**weath'er·i·za'tion** *n.*

**weath'er·man'** (-man') *n., pl.* -men' (-men') one whose work is forecasting the weather, or, esp., reporting it, as on TV

**weath'er·proof'** *adj.* that can be exposed to wind, snow, etc. without being damaged —*vt.* to make weatherproof

**weath'er·strip'** *n.* a thin strip of metal, felt, etc. covering the joint between a door or window and the casing, to keep out drafts, etc.: also **weath'er·strip'ping** —*vt.* -stripped', **weath'er·strip'ping** to provide with weatherstrips

**weather vane** a vane for showing which way the wind is blowing

**weave** (wēv) *vt.* **wove** or, chiefly for *vt.* 5 & *vi.* 2, **weaved**, **wo'ven** or **wove** or, chiefly for *vt.* 5 & *vi.* 2, **weaved**, **weav'ing** ⟦OE *wefan*⟧ **1** to make (a fabric, basket, etc.) by interlacing (threads, straw, etc.), as on a loom **2** to construct in the mind **3** to twist (something) into or through **4** to spin (a web), as spiders do **5** to make (one's way) by moving from side to side or in and out —*vi.* **1** to do weaving **2** to move from side to side or in and out —*n.* a method or pattern of weaving —**weav'er** *n.*

**web** (web) *n.* ⟦OE *webb*⟧ **1** any woven fabric **2** the network spun by a spider, etc. **3** a carefully woven trap **4** a network **5** a membrane joining the digits of various water birds, etc. **6** [*usually* W-] *Comput.* WORLD WIDE WEB: usually with *the* —*vt.* **webbed**, **web'bing** to join by, or cover as with, a web

**web'bing** *n.* a strong fabric woven in strips and used for belts, etc.

**web'foot'** *n., pl.* -feet' a foot with the toes webbed —**web'-foot'ed** *adj.*

**Web page** a single file on the World Wide Web, providing text, pictures, etc.

**web'site'** *n.* [*occas.* W-] a location on the World Wide Web, consisting of one or more Web pages: also **web** (or **Web**) **site**

**Web·ster** (web'stər), **No·ah** (nō'ə) 1758-1843; U.S. lexicographer

**wed** (wed) *vt., vi.* **wed'ded**, **wed'ded** or **wed**, **wed'ding** ⟦OE *weddian*⟧ **1** to marry **2** to unite or join

**Wed** *abbrev.* Wednesday

**wed·ded** (wed'id) *adj.* **1** married **2** of marriage **3** devoted [*wedded* to one's work] **4** joined

**wed'ding** *n.* **1** the marriage ceremony **2** a marriage anniversary **3** a joining together

**wedge** (wej) *n.* ⟦OE *wecg*⟧ **1** a piece of wood, metal, etc. tapering to a thin edge: used to split wood, lift a weight, etc. **2** anything shaped like a wedge **3** any act serving to open the way for change, etc. —*vt.* **wedged**, **wedg'ing 1** to force apart, or fix in place, with a wedge **2** to crowd together or pack (*in*) —*vi.* to push or be forced as or like a wedge

WEDGE

**wedg'ie** (-ē) *n.* a shoe having a wedge-shaped piece under the heel, which forms a solid, flat sole

**wed'lock'** *n.* ⟦OE *wedlac*⟧ the state of being married

**Wednes·day** (wenz'dā) *n.* ⟦< *Woden*, Germanic god⟧ the fourth day of the week

**wee** (wē) *adj.* **we'er**, **we'est** ⟦OE *wege*⟧ **1** very small; tiny **2** very early [*wee* hours of the morning]

**weed** (wēd) *n.* ⟦OE *weod*⟧ any undesired, uncultivated plant, esp. one that crowds out desired plants —*vt., vi.* **1** to remove weeds from (a garden, etc.) **2** to remove as useless, harmful, etc.: often with *out* —**weed′er** *n.* —**weed′less** *adj.*

**weeds** (wēdz) *pl.n.* [< OE *wæde*, garment] black mourning clothes, esp. those worn by a widow

**weed′y** *adj.* **-i·er, -i·est 1** full of weeds **2** of or like a weed

**week** (wēk) *n.* [OE *wicu*] **1** a period of seven days, esp. one from Sunday through Saturday **2** the hours or days of work in this period

**week′day′** *n.* any day of the week except Sunday and, often, Saturday

**week′end′** or **week′-end′** *n.* the period from Friday night or Saturday to Monday morning: also **week end** —*vi.* to spend the weekend

**week′ly** *adj.* **1** done, happening, etc. once every week **2** of a week, or of each week —*adv.* once a week; every week —*n., pl.* **-lies** a periodical published once a week

**ween** (wēn) *vi., vt.* [OE *wenan*] [Archaic] to think

**weep** (wēp) *vi., vt.* **wept, weep′ing** [OE *wepan*] **1** to shed (tears) **2** to mourn (*for*) **3** to drip or exude (water, etc.) —**weep′er** *n.*

**weep′ing** *n.* the act of one who weeps —*adj.* **1** that weeps **2** having graceful, drooping branches

**weeping willow** an ornamental willow tree with drooping branches

**weep′y** *adj.* **-i·er, -i·est** (inclined to) weeping

**wee·vil** (wē′vəl) *n.* [OE *wifel*] a beetle whose larvae feed on grain, cotton, etc.

**weft** (weft) *n.* [< OE *wefan*, to weave] *Weaving* the yarns carried back and forth across the warp

**weigh** (wā) *vt.* [OE *wegan*, carry] **1** to determine the weight of **2** to have (a specified) weight **3** to consider and choose carefully [*weigh* one's words] —*vi.* **1** to have significance, importance, etc. **2** to be a burden —**weigh anchor** to hoist a ship's anchor —**weigh down** to burden or bear down on

**weight** (wāt) *n.* [OE *wiht*] **1** a quantity weighing a definite amount **2** *a*) heaviness *b*) *Physics* the force of gravity acting on a body **3** amount of heaviness **4** *a*) any unit of heaviness *b*) any system of such units *c*) a piece having a specific amount of heaviness, placed on a balance or scale in weighing **5** any mass of material used for its heaviness [a *paperweight*] **6** a burden, as of sorrow **7** importance or consequence **8** influence; power —*vt.* **1** to add weight to **2** to burden

**weight′less** *adj.* having little or no apparent weight: said as of an astronaut floating freely in an orbiting space vehicle —**weight′less·ness** *n.*

**weight lifting** the athletic exercise or sport of lifting barbells —**weight lift′er**

**weight′y** *adj.* **-i·er, -i·est 1** very heavy **2** burdensome **3** significant; important —**weight′i·ness** *n.*

**weir** (wir) *n.* [OE *wer*] **1** a low dam built to back up water, as for a mill **2** a fence, as of brushwood, in a stream, etc., for catching fish

**weird** (wird) *adj.* [< OE *wyrd*, fate] **1** of or about ghosts, etc.; mysterious, eerie, etc. **2** strange; bizarre —**weird′ly** *adv.* —**weird′ness** *n.*

**weird·o** (wir′dō) *n., pl.* **-os** [Slang] one that is weird, bizarre, etc.: also **weird′ie** (-dē)

**wel·come** (wel′kəm) *adj.* [OE *wilcuma*, welcome guest] **1** gladly received [a *welcome* guest] **2** freely permitted [he is *welcome* to use my car] —*n.* a welcoming —*vt.* **-comed, -com·ing** to greet or receive with pleasure, etc. —**you're welcome** you're under no obligation

**weld** (weld) *vt.* [< obs. *well*] **1** to unite (pieces of metal, etc.) by heating until fused or until soft enough to hammer together **2** to unite closely —*vi.* to be welded —*n.* **1** a welding **2** a joint formed by welding —**weld′a·ble** *adj.* —**weld′er** *n.*

**wel·fare** (wel′fer′) *n.* [ME: see WELL[2] & FARE] **1** a condition of health, happiness, prosperity, etc.; well-being **2** *a*) the organized efforts of government agencies granting aid to the poor, the unemployed, etc. *b*) such aid —**on welfare** receiving government aid because of poverty, etc.

**wel·kin** (wel′kin) *n.* [< OE *wolcen*, a cloud] [Archaic] the vault of the sky

**well**[1] (wel) *n.* [OE *wella*] **1** a natural spring and pool **2** a hole sunk into the earth to get water, oil, etc. **3** a source of abundant supply **4** a shaft, etc. resembling a well **5** a container for a liquid, as an inkwell —*vi., vt.* to flow or gush from or as from a well

**well**[2] (wel) *adv.* **bet′ter, best** [OE *wel*] **1** in a satisfactory, proper, or excellent manner [treat her *well*; you sing *well*] **2** prosperously [to live *well*] **3** with good reason [one may *well* ask] **4** to a considerable degree [*well* advanced] **5** thoroughly [stir it *well*] **6** with certainty; definitely **7** familiarly [I know her *well*] —*adj.* **1** suitable, proper, etc. **2** in good health **3** favorable; comfortable —*interj.* used variously to express surprise, agreement, etc. —**as well 1** in addition **2** equally —**as well as** in addition to

**well′-ad·vised′** (wel′əd vīzd′) *adj.* showing or resulting from careful consideration or sound advice; prudent

**well′-ap·point′ed** *adj.* excellently furnished

**well′-bal′anced** *adj.* **1** precisely adjusted or regulated **2** sane, sensible, etc.

**well′-be·haved′** *adj.* displaying good manners

**well′-be·ing** *n.* the state of being well, happy, or prosperous; welfare

**well′-born′** *adj.* born into a family of high social position

**well′-bred′** *adj.* showing good breeding; courteous and considerate

**well′-dis·posed′** *adj.* friendly (*toward* a person) or receptive (*to* an idea, etc.)

**well′-done′** *adj.* **1** performed with skill **2** thoroughly cooked: said esp. of meat

**well′-fed′** *adj.* plump or fat

**well′-fixed′** *adj.* [Inf.] wealthy

**well′-found′ed** *adj.* based on facts, good evidence, or sound judgment

**well′-groomed′** *adj.* clean and neat

**well′-ground′ed** *adj.* having a thorough basic knowledge of a subject

**well′head′** *n.* **1** a source; fountainhead **2** the top of a well, as an oil or gas well

**well′-heeled′** *adj.* [Slang] rich; prosperous

**well′-in·formed′** *adj.* having considerable knowledge of a subject or of many subjects

**Wel·ling·ton** (wel′iŋ tən) capital of New Zealand: pop. 149,000

**well′-in·ten′tioned** *adj.* having or showing good or kindly intentions

**well′-knit′** *adj.* sturdy in body build

**well′-known′** *adj.* **1** widely known; famous **2** thoroughly known

**well′-made′** *adj.* skillfully and soundly put together

**well′-man′nered** *adj.* polite; courteous

**well′-mean′ing** *adj.* **1** having good intentions **2** said or done with good intentions, but often not wisely or effectually: also **well′-meant′**

**well′-nigh′** *adv.* very nearly; almost

**well′-off′** *adj.* **1** in a fortunate condition **2** prosperous

**well′-pre·served′** *adj.* in good condition or looking good, in spite of age

**well′-read′** (-red′) *adj.* having read much

**well′-round′ed** *adj.* **1** well-planned for proper balance **2** showing diverse talents **3** shapely

**well′-spo′ken** *adj.* **1** speaking easily, graciously, etc. **2** properly or aptly spoken

**well′spring′** *n.* **1** the source of a stream, etc. **2** a source of abundant supply

**well′-tak′en** *adj.* apt and sound or cogent

**well′-thought′-of′** *adj.* having a good reputation

**well′-timed′** *adj.* timely; opportune

**well′-to-do′** *adj.* prosperous; wealthy

**well′-turned′** *adj.* **1** gracefully shaped **2** expressed or worded well [a *well-turned* phrase]

**well'-wish'er** *n.* one who wishes well to another or to a cause, etc.

**well'-worn'** *adj.* much worn or used

**welsh** (welsh) *vi.* [Slang] to fail to pay a debt, fulfill an obligation, etc.: often with *on* —**welsh'er** *n.*

**Welsh** (welsh) *n.* ⟦OE *Wealh*, foreigner⟧ the Celtic language of Wales —*adj.* of Wales or its people, language, etc. —**the Welsh** the people of Wales — **Welsh'man** (-mən), *pl.* **-men**, *n.*

**Welsh rabbit** a dish of melted cheese served on crackers or toast: also **Welsh rarebit**

**welt** (welt) *n.* ⟦ME *welte*⟧ 1 a strip of leather in the seam between the sole and upper of a shoe 2 a ridge raised on the skin as by a blow

**wel·ter** (wel'tər) *vi.* ⟦< MDu *welteren*⟧ to roll about or wallow —*n.* a confusion; turmoil

**wel·ter·weight** (wel'tər wāt') *n.* ⟦prob. < *welt*, to beat⟧ a boxer with a maximum weight of 147 pounds

**wen** (wen) *n.* ⟦OE *wenn*⟧ a benign skin tumor

**wench** (wench) *n.* ⟦OE *wencel*, child⟧ a young woman: derogatory or jocular term

**wend** (wend) *vt.* **wend'ed**, **wend'ing** ⟦OE *wendan*, to turn⟧ to go on (one's way)

**went** (went) *vi.*, *vt. pt. of* GO

**wept** (wept) *vi.*, *vt. pt. & pp. of* WEEP

**were** (wur) *vi.* ⟦OE *wæron*⟧ *pl. & 2d pers. sing., past indic., and the past subjunctive, of* BE

**we're** (wir) *contr.* we are

**were·wolf** (wer'woolf', wir'-) *n., pl.* **-wolves'** ⟦OE *wer*, man + *wulf*, wolf⟧ *Folklore* a person changed into a wolf: also sp. **wer'wolf'**, *pl.* **-wolves**

**Wes·ley** (wes'lē, wez'-), **John** 1703-91; Eng. clergyman; founder of Methodism —**Wes'ley·an** *adj., n.*

**west** (west) *n.* ⟦OE⟧ 1 the direction in which sunset occurs (270° on the compass) 2 a region in or toward this direction —*adj.* 1 in, of, toward, or facing the west 2 from the west [a *west* wind] — *adv.* in or toward the west —**the West** 1 the western part of the U.S. 2 Europe and the Western Hemisphere

**West Berlin** *see* BERLIN

**west'er·ly** *adj., adv.* 1 toward the west 2 from the west

**west'ern** *adj.* ⟦OE *westerne*⟧ 1 in, of, or toward the west 2 from the west 3 [W-] of the West —*n.* a movie, book, etc. about life in the western U.S., esp. during the frontier period

**west'ern·er** *n.* a person born or living in the west

**Western Hemisphere** that half of the earth which includes North & South America

**west'ern·ize** *vt.* **-ized', -iz'ing** to make Western in habits, ideas, etc.

**Western Samoa** *former name for* SAMOA

**West Germany** *see* GERMANY

**West In·dies** (in'dēz') large group of islands in the Atlantic between North America & South America —**West Indian**

**West Point** military reservation in SE New York: site of the U.S. Military Academy

**West Virginia** state of the E U.S.: 24,232 sq. mi.; pop. 1,793,000; cap. Charleston: abbrev. *WV* — **West Virginian**

**west'ward** *adv., adj.* toward the west: also **west'wards** *adv.*

**wet** (wet) *adj.* **wet'ter**, **wet'test** ⟦OE *wæt*⟧ 1 covered or saturated with water or other liquid 2 rainy; misty 3 not yet dry [wet paint] —*n.* 1 water or other liquid; moisture 2 rain or rainy weather —*vt., vi.* **wet** or **wet'ted**, **wet'ting** to make or become wet —**all wet** [Slang] wrong

**wet'back'** *n.* [Inf.] a Mexican who illegally enters the U.S. to work: term of derision or contempt

**wet blanket** a person or thing whose presence or influence lessens the enthusiasm of others

**wet'land'** *n.* [usually pl.] 1 swamps or marshes 2 an area of swamps, etc. preserved for wildlife

**wet nurse** a woman hired to suckle another's child —**wet'-nurse'**, **-nursed'**, **-nurs'ing**, *vt.*

**wet suit** a closefitting suit of rubber worn by skin divers for warmth: also **wet'suit'** *n.*

**whack** (hwak) *vt., vi.* ⟦echoic⟧ to strike or slap with a sharp, resounding blow —*n.* 1 a sharp, resounding blow 2 the sound of this —**have (or take) a whack at** [Inf.] 1 to aim a blow at 2 to make an attempt at —**out of whack** [Inf.] not in proper working condition —**whack'er** *n.*

**whacked'-out'** *adj.* [Slang] 1 exhausted 2 STONED 3 wacky, bizarre, etc.

**whale¹** (hwāl) *n.* ⟦OE *hwæl*⟧ a large, warm-blooded sea mammal that breathes air —*vi.* **whaled**, **whal'ing** to hunt whales —**a whale of a** [Inf.] an exceptionally large, fine, etc. example of a (class or group)

**whale²** (hwāl) *vt.* **whaled**, **whal'ing** ⟦prob. < WALE⟧ [Inf.] to beat, whip, etc.

**whale'bone'** *n.* BALEEN

**whal'er** *n.* 1 a whaling ship 2 one whose work is whaling

**wham** (hwam) *interj.* used to suggest the sound of a heavy blow, explosion, etc. —*n.* a heavy blow, etc. —*vt., vi.* **whammed**, **wham'ming** to strike, explode, etc. loudly

**wham'my** *n., pl.* **-mies** [Slang] a jinx

**wharf** (hwôrf) *n., pl.* **wharves** or **wharfs** ⟦OE *hwerf*, a dam⟧ a structure on a shore, at which ships are loaded or unloaded; dock

**what** (hwut, hwät) *pron.* ⟦OE *hwæt*, neuter of *wha*, who⟧ 1 which thing, event, etc. [what is that object?] 2 that or those which [to know what one wants] —*adj.* 1 which or which kind of: used interrogatively or relatively 2 as much, or as many, as [take what men you need] 3 how great, surprising, etc. [what nonsense!] —*adv.* 1 in what way? how? [what does it matter?] 2 how greatly, etc. [what tragic news!] —*interj.* used to express surprise, anger, etc. —**what about** what do you think, feel, etc. concerning? —**what for?** why? —**what with** because of [what with the bad weather, we'll be late]

**what·ev'er** *pron.* what: an emphatic variant; specif., *a*) which thing, event, etc.? *b*) anything that [say whatever you like] *c*) no matter what [whatever you do, don't hurry] —*adj.* 1 of any kind [I have no plans whatever] 2 being who it may be [whatever man said that, it is not true]

**what'not'** *n.* a set of open shelves, as for bric-a-brac

**what's** (hwuts) *contr.* 1 what is 2 what has 3 [Inf.] what does [what's he want?]

**what·so·ev·er** (hwut'sō ev'ər) *pron., adj.* whatever: an emphatic form

**wheal¹** (hwēl) *n.* ⟦ME *whele*⟧ a small, itching elevation of the skin, as from an insect bite

**wheal²** (hwēl) *n.* WEAL¹

**wheat** (hwēt) *n.* ⟦OE *hwæte*⟧ a cereal grass having spikes containing grains used in making flour, cereals, etc.

**wheat germ** the highly nutritious embryo of the wheat kernel, milled out as a flake

**whee·dle** (hwēd''l) *vt., vi.* **-dled**, **-dling** ⟦< ?⟧ to influence or persuade (a person), or get (something), by flattery, coaxing, etc.

**wheel** (hwēl) *n.* ⟦OE *hweol*⟧ 1 a circular disk or frame turning on a central axis 2 anything like a wheel in shape, movement, etc. 3 the steering wheel of a motor vehicle 4 [pl.] [Slang] an automobile 5 [usually pl.] the moving forces [the wheels of progress] 6 a turning movement 7 [Slang] an important person —*vt., vi.* 1 to move on or in (a wheeled vehicle) 2 to turn, revolve, etc. 3 to turn so as to change direction —**at (or behind) the wheel** steering a motor vehicle, ship, etc.

**wheel'bar'row** *n.* a kind of cart for carrying small loads, having a wheel in front and two shafts with handles in back for raising the vehicle off its two back legs and moving it

**wheel'base'** *n.* the length of a motor vehicle between the centers of the front and rear wheels

**wheel'chair'** *n.* a chair mounted on large wheels, for persons unable to walk

**wheeled** (hwēld) *adj.* having wheels

**wheel·er-deal·er** (hwēl'ər dēl'ər) *n.* [Slang] one who is aggressive in a showy way, as in arranging business deals

**wheel'house'** *n.* PILOTHOUSE

**wheel'wright'** *n.* one who makes and repairs wheels and wheeled vehicles

**wheeze** (hwēz) *vi.* **wheezed, wheez'ing** 《< ON *hvæsa*, to hiss》 to breathe hard with a whistling, breathy sound, as in asthma — *n.* a wheezing — **wheez'y, -i·er, -i·est,** *adj.*

**whelk** (hwelk) *n.* 《OE *wioluc*》 a kind of large marine snail

WHELK

**whelm** (hwelm) *vt.* 《ME *welmen*》 **1** to submerge **2** to overpower or crush

**whelp** (hwelp) *n.* 《OE *hwelp*》 a young dog, etc. — *vt., vi.* to give birth to (young): said of some animals

**when** (hwen) *adv.* 《OE *hwænne*》 **1** at what time? *[when* did they leave?] **2** on what occasion? — *conj.* **1** at what time *[tell* me *when* to go] **2** at the time that *[when* we were young] **3** at which *[a* time when people must work] **4** as soon as *[we* will eat *when* he comes] **5** although **6** if —*pron.* what or which time —*n.* the time *(of* an event)

**whence** (hwens) *adv.* 《ME *whennes*》 from what place, cause, etc.? *[whence* do you come?]

**when·ev·er** *adv.* [Inf.] when: an emphatic form —*conj.* at whatever time *[go* whenever you can]

**where** (hwer) *adv.* 《OE *hwær*》 **1** in or at what place? *[where* is it?] **2** to or toward what place? *[where* did he go?] **3** in what respect? *[where* is he to blame?] **4** from what place or source? *[where* did he learn it?] —*conj.* at what place *[I* see *where* it is] **2** at which place *[I* went home, *where* I ate dinner] **3** wherever **4** to the place to which *[we* go *where* you go] —*pron.* **1** the place at which *[it's* a mile to *where* I live] **2** what place *[where* are you from?] —*n.* the place *(of* an event)

**where'a·bouts'** (-ə bouts') *adv.* near or at what place? —*n.* *[now usually with pl. v.]* the place where one is

**where·as'** *conj.* **1** in view of the fact that **2** while on the contrary *[I'm* slim, *whereas* he is fat]

**where·at'** *conj.* [Archaic] at which point

**where·by'** *conj.* by which

**where'fore'** (-fôr') *adv.* [Archaic] for what reason? why? —*conj.* [Archaic] **1** for which **2** because of which —*n.* the reason; cause

**where·in'** *conj.* in which

**where·of'** *adv., conj.* of what, which, or whom *[the* things *whereof* he spoke]

**where·on'** *conj.* [Archaic] on which

**where·up·on'** *conj.* at which

**wher·ev·er** (hwer ev'ər) *adv.* [Inf.] where: an emphatic form —*conj.* in, at, or to whatever place or situation *[go* wherever you like]

**where·with'** *conj.* [Archaic] with which

**where·with·al'** (-with ôl') *n.* the necessary means, esp. money: usually with *the*

**wher·ry** (hwer'ē) *n., pl.* **-ries** 《ME *whery*》 a light rowboat

**whet** (hwet) *vt.* **whet'ted, whet'ting** 《< OE *hwæt,* keen》 **1** to sharpen by rubbing or grinding (the edge of a knife or tool) **2** to stimulate

**wheth·er** (hweth'ər) *conj.* 《OE *hwæther*》 **1** if it be the case that *[ask* whether she sings] **2** in case; in either case that: introducing alternatives *[whether* it rains or snows]

**whet·stone** (hwet'stōn') *n.* an abrasive stone for sharpening knives, etc.

**whew** (hyōō) *interj.* 《echoic》 used to express relief, surprise, dismay, etc.

**whey** (hwā) *n.* 《OE *hwæg*》 the watery part of milk, that separates from the curds

**which** (hwich) *pron.* 《OE *hwylc*》 **1** what one (or ones) of several? *[which* do you want?] **2** the one (or ones) that *[he* knows *which* he wants] **3** that *[the* boat *which* sank] —*adj.* what one or ones *[which* man (or men) left?]

**which·ev·er** *pron., adj.* **1** any one *[take* whichever (desk) you like] **2** no matter which *[whichever* (desk) he chooses, they won't be pleased]

**whiff** (hwif) *n.* 《echoic》 **1** a light puff or gust of air, etc. **2** a slight odor

**whif·fle·tree** (hwif'əl trē') *n. var. of* WHIPPLETREE

**Whig** (hwig) *n.* 《< *whiggamore* (derisive term for Scot Presbyterians)》 **1** a member of a former English political party that championed reform **2** a supporter of the American Revolution **3** a member of a U.S. political party (c. 1834-56)

**while** (hwīl) *n.* 《OE *hwil*》 a period of time *[a* short while] —*conj.* **1** during the time that *[I* read *while* I eat] **2** although; whereas *[while* not poor, she's not rich] —*vt.* **whiled, whil'ing** to spend (time) in a pleasant way: often with *away*

**whi·lom** (hwī'ləm) *adj.* 《< OE》 former

**whilst** (hwīlst) *conj.* [Chiefly Brit.] WHILE

**whim** (hwim) *n.* a sudden, passing idea or desire

**whim·per** (hwim'pər) *vi., vt.* 《? akin to WHINE》 to cry or utter with low, whining, broken sounds — *n.* a whimpering sound or cry

**whim·si·cal** (hwim'zi kəl) *adj.* **1** full of whims or whimsy **2** oddly out of the ordinary —**whim'si·cal'i·ty** (-kal'ə tē) *n.* —**whim'si·cal·ly** *adv.*

**whim·sy** (hwim'zē) *n., pl.* **-sies** 《< ?》 **1** a sudden, odd notion **2** quaint or fanciful humor Also sp. **whim'sey,** *pl.* **-seys**

**whine** (hwīn) *vi.* **whined, whin'ing** 《OE *hwinan*》 **1** *a)* to utter a high-pitched, nasal sound, as in complaint *b)* to make a prolonged sound like this **2** to complain in a childish way —*n.* **1** a whining **2** a complaint uttered in a whining tone —**whin'y, -i·er, -i·est,** *adj.*

**whin·ny** (hwin'ē) *vi.* **-nied, -ny·ing** 《prob. echoic》 to neigh in a low, gentle way: said of a horse —*n., pl.* **-nies** a whinnying

**whip** (hwip) *vt.* **whipped** or **whipt, whip'ping** 《< MDu *wippen,* to swing》 **1** to move, pull, throw, etc. suddenly *[to* whip out a knife] **2** to strike, as with a strap; lash **3** to wind (cord, etc.) around (a rope, etc.) so as to prevent fraying **4** to beat into a froth *[to* whip cream] **5** [Inf.] to defeat —*vi.* **1** to move quickly and suddenly **2** to flap about —*n.* **1** a flexible instrument for striking or flogging **2** a blow, etc. as with a whip **3** an officer of a political party in a legislature who maintains discipline, etc. **4** a whipping motion —**whip up 1** to rouse (interest, etc.) **2** [Inf.] to prepare quickly

**whip'cord'** *n.* **1** a hard, twisted or braided cord **2** a strong, diagonally ribbed worsted cloth

**whip hand** control or advantage

**whip'lash'** *n.* **1** the lash of a whip **2** a sudden, severe jolting of the neck, as in an automobile accident

**whip'per·snap'per** *n.* an insignificant person who appears presumptuous

**whip·pet** (hwip'it) *n.* 《< WHIP》 a swift dog resembling a small greyhound, used in racing

**whip·ple·tree** (hwip'əl trē') *n.* 《< WHIP + TREE》 SINGLETREE

**whip·poor·will** (hwip'ər wil') *n.* 《echoic》 a dark-colored bird of E North America, active at night

**whip'py** *adj.* springy; flexible

**whir** or **whirr** (hwur) *vi., vt.* **whirred, whir'ring** 《ME *quirren*》 to fly, revolve, vibrate, etc. with a whizzing or buzzing sound —*n.* such a sound

**whirl** (hwurl) *vi.* 《< ON *hvirfla*》 **1** to move rapidly in a circle or orbit **2** to rotate or spin fast **3** to seem to spin /my head is *whirling*/ —*vt.* to cause to rotate, revolve, or spin rapidly —*n.* **1** a whirling motion **2** a confused or giddy condition —**give it a whirl** [Inf.] to make an attempt

**whirl·i·gig** (hwʉr′li gig′) *n.* a child's toy that whirls or spins, as a pinwheel

**whirl′pool′** *n.* **1** water in violent, whirling motion, tending to draw floating objects into its center **2** a bath in which an agitating device propels a current of warm water with a swirling motion: in full **whirlpool bath**

**whirl′wind′** *n.* **1** a forward-moving current of air whirling violently in a vertical spiral **2** anything like a whirlwind —*adj.* impetuous; speedy

**whisk** (hwisk) *n.* ⟦< ON *visk*, a brush⟧ **1** a brushing with a quick, light, sweeping motion **2** such a motion **3** a kitchen utensil of wire loops in a handle, for whipping cream, etc. —*vt.* to move, carry, brush (*away, off, out,* etc.) with a quick, sweeping motion —*vi.* to move quickly or nimbly

**whisk broom** a small, short-handled broom for brushing clothes, etc.

**whisk·er** (hwis′kər) *n.* **1** [*pl.*] the hair growing on a man's face, esp. on the cheeks **2** any of the long, bristly hairs on the upper lip of a cat, rat, etc. **3** a very small amount or margin

**whis·key** (hwis′kē) *n.*, *pl.* **-keys** or **-kies** ⟦< Ir *uisce*, water + *beathadh*, life⟧ a strong alcoholic liquor distilled from the fermented mash of grain: also sp. **whis·ky**, *pl.* **-kies**: in general, U.S. and Irish usage favors *whiskey*, and Brit. and Cdn. usage favors *whisky*

**whis·per** (hwis′pər) *vi.*, *vt.* ⟦< OE *hwisprian*⟧ **1** to speak or say very softly, esp. without vibrating the vocal cords **2** to talk or tell furtively, as in gossiping **3** to make a rustling sound —*n.* **1** a whispering **2** something whispered **3** a soft, rustling sound

**whist** (hwist) *n.* ⟦< earlier *whisk*⟧ a card game that is the forerunner of bridge

**whis·tle** (hwis′əl) *vi.* **-tled, -tling** ⟦OE *hwistlian*⟧ **1** to make a clear, shrill sound as by blowing through puckered lips **2** to move with a shrill sound, as the wind does **3** *a*) to blow a whistle *b*) to have its whistle blown /the train *whistled*/ —*vt.* **1** to produce (a tune, etc.) by whistling **2** to signal, etc. by whistling —*n.* **1** a device for making whistling sounds **2** a whistling —**whis′tler** *n.*

**whis′tle-blow′er** *n.* one who informs on a wrongdoer

**whis′tle-stop′** *n.* **1** a small town **2** a brief stop in a small town on a tour

**whit** (hwit) *n.* ⟦< OE *wiht*, wight⟧ the least bit; jot

**white** (hwīt) *adj.* **whit′er, whit′est** ⟦OE *hwit*⟧ **1** having the color of pure snow or milk; opposite to black **2** of a light or pale color **3** pale; wan **4** lacking color **5** pure; innocent **6** [*sometimes* **W-**] having a light-colored skin; Caucasoid —*n.* **1** *a*) white color *b*) a white pigment **2** a white or light-colored part, as the albumen of an egg or the white part of the eyeball **3** [*sometimes* **W-**] a person with a light-colored skin —**white′ness** *n.*

**white blood cell** (or **corpuscle**) LEUKOCYTE

**white′-bread′** *adj.* [Inf.] **1** of or like the white middle class, its values, etc. **2** bland, conventional, etc.

**white′cap′** *n.* a wave with its crest broken into white foam

**white′-col′lar** *adj.* designating or of office or professional workers

**white-collar crime** fraud, embezzlement, etc., committed by a person in business, government, or a profession

**white elephant 1** an albino elephant **2** something of little use, but expensive to maintain **3** any object no longer wanted by its owner, but possibly useful to another

**white′fish′** *n.*, *pl.* **-fish′** or (for different species) **-fish′es** a white or silvery, edible fish, found in cool lakes of the Northern Hemisphere

**white flag** a white banner or cloth hoisted as a signal of truce or surrender

**white gold** a gold alloy that looks like platinum

**white goods 1** household linens, as sheets and towels **2** large household appliances, as refrigerators and stoves

**white heat 1** a temperature at which material glows white **2** a state of intense emotion, excitement, etc. —**white′-hot′** *adj.*

**White′horse′** capital of the Yukon Territory, Canada: pop. 19,000

**White House, the 1** official residence of the President of the U.S. in Washington, DC **2** the executive branch of the U.S. government

**white lead** a poisonous, white powder, lead carbonate, used in paint

**white lie** a lie about a trivial matter, often told to spare someone's feelings

**white metal** any of various light-colored alloys, esp. one containing much lead or tin, as pewter

**whit·en** (hwīt′'n) *vt.*, *vi.* to make or become white or whiter —**whit′en·er** *n.* —**whit′en·ing** *n.*

**white′-out′** *n.* ⟦< *Wite-Out*, a trademark⟧ a quick-drying, white fluid that is brushed on to cover printed errors and allow for corrections

**white paper 1** an official government report **2** any in-depth, authoritative report

**white sale** a sale of household linens

**white slave** a woman forced into prostitution for the profit of others —**white slavery**

**white′wall′** *adj.* designating or of a tire with a circular white band on the side —*n.* such a tire

**white′wash′** *n.* **1** a mixture of lime, chalk, water, etc., as for whitening walls, etc. **2** a concealing of faults in order to exonerate —*vt.* **1** to cover with whitewash **2** to conceal the faults of **3** [Inf.] *Sports* to defeat (an opponent) soundly

**white′-wa′ter** *adj.* of or having to do with recreational kayaking, rafting, etc. on rivers with rapids, fast currents, etc. (**white water**)

**whith·er** (hwi*th*′ər) [Now Rare] *adv.* ⟦OE *hwider*⟧ to what place, condition, result, etc.? —*conj.* **1** to which place, result, etc. **2** wherever

**whit·ing**[1] (hwīt′iŋ) *n.* ⟦< MDu *wit*, white⟧ any of various unrelated food fishes of North America, Europe, etc.

**whit·ing**[2] (hwīt′iŋ) *n.* ⟦ME *hwiting*⟧ powdered chalk used in paints, etc.

**whit′ish** *adj.* somewhat white

**Whit·man** (hwit′mən), **Walt(er)** 1819-92; U.S. poet

**Whit·ney** (hwit′nē), **Mount** mountain in EC California: 14,495 ft.

**Whit·sun·day** (hwit′sun′dā) *n.* ⟦OE *Hwita Sunnandæg*, lit., white Sunday⟧ PENTECOST

**whit·tle** (hwit′'l) *vt.* **-tled, -tling** ⟦< OE *thwitan*, to cut⟧ **1** *a*) to cut thin shavings from (wood) with a knife *b*) to carve (an object) thus **2** to reduce gradually —*vi.* to whittle wood

**whiz** or **whizz** (hwiz) *vi.* **whizzed, whiz′zing** ⟦echoic⟧ **1** to move swiftly with a buzzing or hissing sound **2** to make this sound —*n.* **1** this sound **2** [Slang] an expert /a *whiz* at football/

**who** (hōō) *pron.* ⟦OE *hwa*⟧ **1** what or which person or persons /*who* is he? I asked *who* he was/ **2** the person or persons that, or a person that /a man *who* knows/

**WHO** *abbrev.* World Health Organization

**whoa** (hwō) *interj.* stop!: used esp. in directing a horse to stand still

**who·dun·it** (hōō dun′it) *n.* ⟦< WHO + DONE + IT⟧ [Inf.] a mystery novel, story, etc.

**who·ev·er** *pron.* **1** any person that **2** no matter who /*whoever* said it, it's not so/ **3** who?: an emphatic usage /*whoever* told you that?/

**whole** (hōl) *adj.* ⟦OE *hal*⟧ **1** healthy; not diseased or injured **2** not broken, damaged, etc.; intact **3** containing all the parts; complete **4** not divided up; in a single unit **5** not a fraction —*n.* **1** the entire amount **2** a thing complete in itself —**on the whole** in general —**whole′ness** *n.*

**whole′heart′ed** *adj.* with all one's energy, enthusiasm, etc.; sincere

**whole′-hog′** *adj., adv.* [Slang] without reservation; complete(ly)

**whole milk** milk from which no butterfat, etc. has been removed

**whole note** *Music* a note having four times the duration of a quarter note

**whole′sale′** *n.* the selling of goods in large quantities and at lower prices, esp. to retailers —*adj.* **1** of or having to do with such selling **2** extensive or indiscriminate [wholesale criticism] —*adv.* **1** at wholesale prices **2** extensively or indiscriminately —*vt., vi.* **-saled′, -sal′ing** to sell wholesale —**whole′sal′er** *n.*

**whole′some** *adj.* [ME *holsom*] **1** promoting good health or well-being; healthful **2** improving the mind or character **3** healthy; sound — **whole′some·ness** *n.*

**whole tone** *Music* an interval consisting of two adjacent semitones: also **whole step**

**whole′-wheat′** *adj.* ground from whole kernels of wheat or made of flour so ground

**whol·ly** (hōl′lē) *adv.* to the whole amount or extent; totally; entirely

**whom** (hōōm) *pron. objective case of* WHO

**whom·ev·er** (-ev′ər) *pron. objective case of* WHO-EVER

**whoop** (hwōōp, wōōp, hōōp) *n.* [< ? OFr *houper*, cry out] **1** a loud shout, cry, etc., as of joy **2** the convulsive intake of air following a fit of coughing in whooping cough —*vt., vi.* to utter (with) a whoop or whoops

**whoop·ing cough** (hōō′piŋ, hwōō′-) an acute infectious disease, esp. of children, with coughing fits that end in a whoop

**whop·per** (hwäp′ər, wäp′ər) *n.* [< inf. *whop*, to beat] [Inf.] **1** anything extraordinarily large **2** a great lie

**whop′ping** *adj.* [Inf.] extraordinarily large

**whore** (hôr) *n.* [OE *hore*] a prostitute —**whor′ish** *adj.*

**who′re** (hōō′ər) *contr.* who are

**whorl** (hwôrl, hwurl) *n.* [ME *whorwyl*] anything with a coiled or spiral appearance, as any of the circular ridges that form the patterns of a fingerprint —**whorled** *adj.*

**who′s** (hōōz) *contr.* **1** who is **2** who has

**whose** (hōōz) *pron.* [OE *hwæs*] that or those belonging to whom —*poss. pronominal adj.* of, belonging to, or done by whom or which

**who·so·ev·er** (hōō′sō ev′ər) *pron.* whoever

**why** (hwī, wī) *adv.* [OE *hwæt*, what] for what reason, cause, or purpose? [why eat?] —*conj.* **1** because of which [no reason why you shouldn't go] **2** the reason for which [that is why he went] —*n., pl.* **whys** the reason; cause —*interj.* an exclamation of surprise, impatience, etc.

**WI** Wisconsin

**Wich·i·ta** (wich′ə tô′) city in S Kansas: pop. 304,000

**wick** (wik) *n.* [OE *weoca*] a piece of cord, etc., as in a candle or oil lamp, that absorbs the fuel and, when lighted, burns

**wick·ed** (wik′id) *adj.* [ME < *wikke*, evil] **1** morally bad; evil **2** generally bad, unpleasant, etc. [a *wicked* storm] **3** mischievous **4** [Slang] showing great skill —**wick′ed·ly** *adv.* —**wick′ed·ness** *n.*

**wick·er** (wik′ər) *n.* [< Scand] **1** a thin, flexible twig **2** *a*) such twigs or long, woody strips woven together, as in making baskets *b*) WICKERWORK (sense 1) —*adj.* made of wicker

**wick′er·work′** *n.* **1** things made of wicker **2** WICKER (*n.* 2a)

**wick·et** (wik′it) *n.* [ME *wiket*] **1** a small door or gate, esp. one in or near a larger one **2** a small window, as in a box office **3** *Croquet* any of the small wire arches through which balls are hit

**wide** (wīd) *adj.* **wid′er, wid′est** [OE *wid*] **1** extending over a large area, esp. from side to side **2** of a specified extent from side to side **3** of great extent [a *wide* variety] **4** open fully [eyes *wide* with fear] **5** far from the point, etc. aimed at: usually with *of* [wide of the target] —*adv.* **1** over a relatively large area **2** to a large or full extent [wide open] **3** so as to miss the point, etc. aimed at; astray —**wide′ly** *adv.* —**wide′ness** *n.*

**-wide** (wid) *combining form* existing or extending throughout [statewide]

**wide′-an′gle** *adj.* designating or of a camera lens having a wider than ordinary angle of view

**wide′-a·wake′** *adj.* **1** completely awake **2** alert

**wide′-eyed′** *adj.* **1** with the eyes opened widely, as in surprise or fear **2** naive or unsophisticated

**wid·en** (wīd′'n) *vt., vi.* to make or become wider

**wide′-o′pen** *adj.* **1** opened wide **2** having no or few legal restrictions against prostitution, gambling, etc. [a *wide-open* city]

**wide′spread′** *adj.* occurring over a wide area

**widg·eon** (wij′ən) *n. alt. sp. of* WIGEON

**wid·ow** (wid′ō) *n.* [OE *widewe*] a woman whose husband has died and who has not remarried —*vt.* to cause to become a widow —**wid′ow·hood′** *n.*

**wid′ow·er** *n.* a man whose wife has died and who has not remarried

**width** (width) *n.* **1** distance from side to side **2** a piece of a certain width [two *widths* of cloth]

**wield** (wēld) *vt.* [OE *wealdan*] **1** to handle (a tool, etc.), esp. with skill **2** to exercise (power, influence, etc.)

**wie·ner** (wē′nər) *n.* [< Ger *Wiener wurst*, Vienna sausage] a smoked link sausage; frankfurter: also [Inf.] **wie′nie** (-nē)

**wife** (wīf) *n., pl.* **wives** [OE *wif*, woman] a married woman —**wife′less** *adj.* —**wife′ly** *adj.*

**wig** (wig) *n.* [< PERIWIG] a covering of real or synthetic hair worn as to hide baldness —*vt.* **wigged, wig′ging 1** to furnish with a wig **2** [Slang] *a*) to annoy, upset, etc. *b*) to make excited, crazy, etc. (often with *out*) —*vi.* [Slang] to be or become upset, excited, etc.: often with *out*

**wi·geon** (wij′ən) *n.* [prob. < L *vipio*, small crane] any of certain wild, freshwater ducks

**wig·gle** (wig′əl) *vt., vi.* **-gled, -gling** [ME *wigelen*] to move or cause to move with short, jerky motions from side to side —*n.* a wiggling — **wig′gler** *n.* —**wig′gly, -gli·er, -gli·est,** *adj.*

**wight** (wīt) *n.* [OE *wiht*] [Archaic] a human being

**wig·let** (wig′lit) *n.* a small wig

**wig·wag** (wig′wag′) *vt., vi.* **-wagged′, -wag′ging** [< obs. *wig*, to move + WAG[1]] **1** to move back and forth; wag **2** to send (a message) by a visible code —*n.* the sending of messages in this way

**wig·wam** (wig′wäm′) *n.* [< Algonquian] a North American Indian dwelling of a dome-shaped framework of poles covered with mats or bark

**wild** (wīld) *adj.* [OE *wilde*] **1** living or growing in its original, natural state **2** not lived in or cultivated; waste **3** not civilized; savage **4** not socially or morally controlled [a *wild* child] **5** lacking social or moral restraint; dissolute [a *wild* time] **6** turbulent; stormy **7** enthusiastic [wild about golf] **8** fantastically impractical; reckless **9** missing the target [a *wild* shot] **10** *Card Games* having any desired value: said of a card —*adv.* in a wild manner —*n.* [usually pl.] a wilderness or wasteland —**wild′ly** *adv.* —**wild′ness** *n.*

**wild′cat′** *n.* **1** any fierce, medium-sized, undomesticated cat, as the bobcat, ocelot, etc. **2** an oil well in a previously unproductive area —*adj.* **1** unsound or risky **2** illegal or unauthorized [a *wildcat* strike] —*vi.* **-cat′ted, -cat′ting** to drill for oil in a previously unproductive area

**wil·de·beest** (wil′də bēst′, vil′-) *n.* [Afrik] GNU

**wil·der·ness** (wil′dər nis) *n.* [< OE *wilde*, wild + *deor*, animal] an uncultivated region

**wild′-eyed′** *adj.* **1** staring in a wild or demented way **2** very foolish or impractical

**wild′fire′** *n.* a fire that spreads widely and rapidly

**wild'flow'er** *n.* **1** any flowering plant growing wild in fields, etc. **2** its flower Also **wild flower**

**wild'fowl'** *n., pl.* **-fowls'** or **-fowl'** a wild bird, esp. a game bird: also **wild fowl**

**wild'-goose' chase** a futile search or pursuit

**wild'life'** *n.* wild animals and birds

**wild oats** a wild grass common in the W U.S. — **sow one's wild oats** to be promiscuous or dissolute in one's youth

**wild rice 1** an aquatic grass of the U.S. and Canada **2** its edible grain

**Wild West** [*also* w- W-] the western U.S. in its early frontier period of lawlessness

**wile** (wīl) *n.* [< OE *wigle*, magic] **1** a sly trick; stratagem **2** a beguiling trick: *usually used in pl.* —*vt.* **wiled, wil'ing** to beguile; lure —**wile away** to while away (time, etc.)

**wil·ful** (wil'fəl) *adj. alt. sp. of* WILLFUL

**Wilkes-Bar·re** (wilks'bar'ē) city in NE Pennsylvania: pop. 48,000

**will**[1] (wil) *n.* [OE *willa*] **1** the power of making a reasoned choice or of controlling one's own actions **2** determination **3** attitude toward others [a man of good *will*] **4** *a*) a particular desire, choice, etc. of someone *b*) mandate [the *will* of the people] **5** a legal document directing the disposal of one's property after death —*vt.* **1** to desire; want [to *will* to live] **2** to control by the power of the will **3** to bequeath by a will —*vi.* to wish, desire, or choose —**at will** when one wishes

**will**[2] (wil) *v.aux. pt.* **would** [OE *willan*, to desire] **1** used to indicate simple future time [when *will* she arrive?] **2** used to express determination, obligation, etc. [you *will* listen to me] **3** used in polite questions [*will* you have some wine?] **4** used to express habit, expectation, etc. [they *will* talk for hours] **5** used to express possibility

*USAGE*—the distinction between WILL[2] (for second and third person subjects) and SHALL (for the first person) in expressing simple future time or determination, etc. is today virtually nonexistent in North American English; WILL[2] and SHALL and their respective past tenses WOULD and SHOULD are usually interchangeable, with WILL[2] (and WOULD) being the preferred form in all persons

**will'ful** (-fəl) *adj.* **1** said or done deliberately **2** doing as one pleases —**will'ful·ly** *adv.* —**will'ful·ness** *n.*

**Wil·liam I** (wil'yəm) 1027?-87; duke of Normandy who invaded England: king of England (1066-87): called *William the Conqueror*

**Wil·liams·burg** (wil'yəmz bʉrg') city in SE Virginia, restored to its 18th-c. look: pop. 12,000

**wil·lies** (wil'ēz) *pl.n.* [< ?] [Slang] a nervous feeling; jitters: with *the*

**will'ing** *adj.* **1** favorably disposed; consenting [*willing* to play] **2** acting, giving, etc. or done, given, etc. readily and cheerfully —**will'ing·ly** *adv.* —**will'ing·ness** *n.*

**wil·li·waw** or **wil'ly·waw'** (wil'i wô') *n.* **1** a violent, cold wind blowing from mountain passes toward the coast **2** confusion; turmoil

**will-o'-the-wisp** (wil'ə thə wisp') *n.* a delusive hope or goal

**wil·low** (wil'ō) *n.* [OE *welig*] **1** a tree with narrow leaves, and flexible twigs used in weaving baskets, etc. **2** its wood

**wil'low·y** *adj.* like a willow; slender, lithe, etc.

**will'pow'er** *n.* strength of will, mind, or determination; self-control

**wil·ly-nil·ly** (wil'ē nil'ē) *adv., adj.* [contr. < *will I, nill I: nill* < OE *nyllan*, be unwilling] **1** (happening) whether one wishes it or not **2** in a disordered way; helter-skelter

**Wil·son** (wil'sən), (Thomas) **Wood·row** (wood'rō) 1856-1924; 28th president of the U.S. (1913-21)

**wilt** (wilt) *vi.* [< obs. *welk*, to wither] **1** to become limp, as from heat or lack of water; droop: said of

plants **2** to become weak or faint; lose strength or courage —*vt.* to cause to wilt

**Wil·ton** (**carpet** or **rug**) (wilt''n) [after *Wilton*, England] a kind of carpet with a velvety pile of cut loops

**wil·y** (wī'lē) *adj.* **-i·er, -i·est** full of wiles; crafty; sly —**wil'i·ness** *n.*

**wimp** (wimp) *n.* [< ?] [Slang] a weak, ineffectual, or insipid person —**wimp'ish** *adj.* —**wimp'y, -i·er, -i·est,** *adj.*

**wim·ple** (wim'pəl) *n.* [OE *wimpel*] a nun's head covering that leaves only the face exposed

**win** (win) *vi.* **won, win'ning** [< OE *winnan*, to fight] **1** *a*) to gain a victory *b*) to finish first in a race, etc. **2** to succeed in reaching a specified condition or place; get [to *win* back to health] —*vt.* **1** to get by labor, struggle, etc. **2** to be victorious in (a contest, etc.) **3** to get to with effort [they *won* the camp by noon] **4** to prevail upon; persuade: often with *over* **5** to gain (the sympathy, favor, etc.) of (someone) **6** to persuade to marry one — *n.* a victory

**wince** (wins) *vi.* **winced, winc'ing** [< OFr *guenchir*] to shrink or draw back slightly, usually with a grimace, as in pain —*n.* a wincing

**winch** (winch) *n.* [OE *wince*] **1** a crank with a handle for transmitting motion **2** a machine for hoisting, etc. using a cylinder upon which is wound the rope, etc. attached to an object

**Win·ches·ter** (win'ches'tər) [after O. F. *Winchester* (1810-80), the manufacturer] *trademark for* a type of repeating rifle

**wind**[1] (wīnd) *vt.* **wound** or [Rare] **wind'ed, wind'ing** [OE *windan*] **1** to turn [to *wind* a crank] **2** to coil into a ball or around something else; twine **3** to cover by entwining **4** *a*) to make (one's way) in a twisting course *b*) to cause to move in a twisting course **5** to tighten the spring of (a clock, etc.) as by turning a stem: often with *up* —*vi.* **1** to move or go in a curving or sinuous manner **2** to take a devious course **3** to coil (*about* or *around* something) —*n.* a turn; twist —**wind up 1** to wind into a ball, etc. **2** to bring to an end; settle **3** to make very tense, excited, etc. **4** *Baseball* to perform a WINDUP (sense 2) — **wind'er** *n.*

**wind**[2] (wind) *n.* [OE] **1** air in motion **2** a strong current of air; gale **3** air bearing a scent, as in hunting **4** air regarded as bearing information, etc. [a rumor in the *wind*] **5** breath or the power of breathing **6** empty talk **7** [*pl.*] the wind instruments of an orchestra —*vt.* **1** to get the scent of **2** to put out of breath —**break wind** to expel gas from the bowels —**get wind of** to hear of —**in the wind** happening or about to happen

**wind·bag** (wind'bag') *n.* [Inf.] one who talks much but says little of importance

**wind'break'** *n.* a hedge, fence, etc. serving as a protection from wind

**Wind'break'er** *trademark for* a warm jacket with closefitting waistband and cuffs

**wind'burn'** *n.* a reddened, sore skin condition, caused by overexposure to the wind

**wind'chill' factor** an estimated measure of the cooling effect of air and wind on exposed skin

**wind chimes** (or **bells**) a cluster of small chimes or pendants hung so that they strike one another and tinkle when blown by the wind

**wind·ed** (win'did) *adj.* out of breath

**wind·fall** (wind'fôl') *n.* an unexpected gain, stroke of good luck, etc.

**wind farm** a network of modern, high-speed windmills for generating electricity

**wind·ing sheet** (wīn'diŋ) a shroud

**wind instrument** (wind) a musical instrument sounded by blowing air through it, as a flute

**wind·jam·mer** (wind'jam'ər) *n.* a large sailing ship or one of its crew

**wind·lass** (wind'ləs) *n.* [< ON *vinda*, to WIND[1] + *ass*, a beam] a winch, esp. one worked by a crank

**wind'mill'** *n.* **1** a mill operated by the wind's rotation of large vanes radiating from a shaft **2** a device like this, as one to harness wind power

WINDLASS

**win·dow** (win'dō) *n.* [< ON *vindr*, WIND² + *auga*, an eye] **1** an opening in a building, vehicle, etc. for letting in light, air, etc. usually having a pane of glass in a movable frame **2** a windowpane **3** an opening resembling a window **4** the interval during which something can be done

**window box** a long, narrow box on or outside a window ledge, for growing plants

**window dressing 1** the display of goods in a store window **2** that which is meant to make something seem better than it really is — **win'dow-dress'** *vt.* —**window dresser**

**win'dow-pane'** *n.* a pane of glass in a window

**win'dow-shop'** *vi.* -**shopped'**, -**shop'ping** to look at goods in store windows without entering to buy

**win'dow-sill'** *n.* the sill of a window

**wind'pipe'** (wind'pīp') *n.* TRACHEA

**wind'row'** (-rō') *n.* a row of hay, etc. raked together to dry

**wind shear** a sudden change in wind direction, esp., dangerous vertical wind shifts

**wind'shield'** *n.* in automobiles, etc., a glass screen, in front, to protect from wind, etc.

**wind'sock'** *n.* a long, cloth cone flown at an airfield to show wind direction: also **wind sleeve**

**Wind·sor** (win'zər) port in SE Ontario, Canada: pop. 198,000

**Windsor knot** a double slipknot in a four-in-hand necktie

**wind'storm'** *n.* a storm with a strong wind but little or no rain, hail, etc.

**wind'surf'** *vi.* to ride for sport on a kind of surfboard with a pivoting sail —**wind'surf'ing** *n.*

**wind tunnel** a tunnel-like chamber through which air is forced, for testing the effects of wind pressure on aircraft, motor vehicles, etc.

**wind·up** (wīnd'up') *n.* **1** a conclusion; end **2** *Baseball* the motion of the pitcher leading up to throwing the ball

**wind·ward** (wind'wərd) *n.* the direction from which the wind blows —*adv.* toward the wind — *adj.* **1** moving windward **2** on the side from which the wind blows

**Windward Islands** S group of islands in the West Indies, south of the Leeward Islands

**wind·y** (win'dē) *adj.* -**i·er**, -**i·est 1** with much wind [a *windy* city] **2** stormy, blustery, etc. **3** long-winded, pompous, etc. —**wind'i·ness** *n.*

**wine** (wīn) *n.* [< L *vinum*] the fermented juice of grapes, etc., used as an alcoholic beverage —*vt.*, *vi.* **wined**, **win'ing** usually in the phrase **wine and dine**, to entertain lavishly

**wine'-col'ored** *adj.* dark purplish-red

**win·er·y** (wīn'ər ē) *n.*, *pl.* -**ies** an establishment where wine is made

**wing** (win) *n.* [ON *vaengr*] **1** either of the paired organs of flight of a bird, bat, insect, etc. **2** something like a wing in use, position, etc., esp., *a*) a (or the) main lateral supporting surface of an airplane *b*) a subordinate, projecting part of a building *c*) either side of the stage out of sight of the audience **3** the section of an army, fleet, etc. to the right (or left) of the center **4** a section, as of a political party, with reference to its radicalism or conservatism **5** a unit in an air force —*vt.* **1** to provide with wings **2** *a*) to send swiftly as on wings *b*) to make (one's way) by flying *c*) to pass through or over, as by flying **3** to wound in the wing, arm, etc. —*vi.* to fly —**on the wing** (while) flying —**take wing** to fly away —**under one's wing** under one's protection, etc. —**wing it** [Inf.] to improvise in acting, etc. —**winged** (wind; *poet.* win'id) *adj.* —**wing'less** *adj.*

**wing'ding'** (-din') *n.* [< ?] [Slang] an event, party, etc. that is very festive, lively, etc.

**wing'span'** *n.* **1** the distance between the tips of an airplane's wings **2** WINGSPREAD (sense 1)

**wing'spread'** *n.* **1** the distance between the tips of fully spread wings **2** WINGSPAN

**wink** (wink) *vi.* [OE *wincian*] **1** to close the eyelids and open them again quickly **2** to close and open one eyelid quickly, as a signal, etc. **3** to twinkle —*vt.* to make (an eye) wink —*n.* **1** a winking **2** an instant **3** a signal given by winking **4** a twinkle —**wink at** to pretend not to see

**win·ner** (win'ər) *n.* one that wins

**win·ning** (win'in) *adj.* **1** victorious **2** attractive; charming —*n.* **1** a victory **2** [*pl.*] money won

**Win·ni·peg** (win'ə peg') capital of Manitoba, Canada: pop. 618,000

**win·now** (win'ō) *vt.*, *vi.* [< OE *wind*, WIND²] **1** to blow (chaff) from (grain) **2** to scatter **3** to sift out

**win·o** (wī'nō) *n.*, *pl.* -**os** [Slang] an alcoholic who drinks cheap wine

**win·some** (win'səm) *adj.* [OE *wynsum*, pleasant] sweetly attractive; charming —**win'some·ly** *adv.*

**Win·ston-Sa·lem** (win'stən sā'ləm) city in NC North Carolina: pop. 143,000

**win·ter** (win'tər) *n.* [OE] **1** the coldest season of the year, following autumn **2** a period of decline, distress, etc. —*adj.* of, during, or for winter —*vi.* to pass the winter —*vt.* to keep, feed, etc. during winter

**win'ter·green'** *n.* **1** an evergreen plant with white flowers and red berries **2** an aromatic oil (**oil of wintergreen**) made from its leaves and used as a flavoring **3** the flavor

**win'ter·ize'** *vt.* -**ized'**, -**iz'ing** to put into condition for winter

**win'ter·kill'** *vt.*, *vi.* to kill or die by exposure to winter cold or excessive snow and ice —*n.* the process or an instance of winterkilling

**win'ter·time'** *n.* the winter season

**win·try** (win'trē) *adj.* -**tri·er**, -**tri·est** of or like winter; cold, bleak, etc. [a *wintry* day]

**win'-win'** *adj.* designating or of a situation from which all possible outcomes are satisfactory

**win·y** (wī'nē) *adj.* -**i·er**, -**i·est** like wine in taste, smell, color, etc.

**wipe** (wīp) *vt.* **wiped**, **wip'ing** [OE *wipian*] **1** to clean or dry by rubbing with a cloth, etc. **2** to rub (a cloth, etc.) over something **3** to apply or remove by wiping —*n.* a wiping —**wipe out 1** to remove; erase **2** to kill off **3** to destroy —**wip'er** *n.*

**wiped'-out'** *adj.* [Slang] exhausted

**wire** (wīr) *n.* [OE *wir*] **1** metal drawn into a long thread **2** a length of this **3** a telegram **4** the finish line of a horse race —*adj.* made of wire —*vt.* **wired**, **wir'ing 1** to furnish, connect, etc. with wire **2** to telegraph —*vi.* to telegraph

**wired** (wīrd) *adj.* [Slang] **1** provided with concealed electronic listening or recording equipment **2** extremely excited, nervous, etc.

**wire'hair'** *n.* a fox terrier with a wiry coat: also called **wire'-haired' terrier**

**wire'less** (-lis) *adj.* operating by electromagnetic waves, not with conducting wire —*n.* **1** wireless telegraphy or telephony **2** [Chiefly Brit.] *old-fashioned term for* RADIO

**wire service** an agency sending news electronically to subscribing newspapers, etc.

**wire'tap'** *vi.*, *vt.* -**tapped'**, -**tap'ping** to tap (a telephone wire, etc.) to get information secretly —*n.* **1** a wiretapping **2** a device for wiretapping

**wir'ing** *n.* a system of wires, as to provide a house with electricity

**wir·y** (wīr'ē) *adj.* -**i·er**, -**i·est 1** of wire **2** like wire; stiff **3** lean and strong —**wir'i·ness** *n.*

**Wis·con·sin** (wis kän'sən) Midwestern state of the U.S.: 56,154 sq. mi.; pop. 4,892,000; cap. Madison: abbrev. *WI* —**Wis·con'sin·ite'** *n.*

**wis·dom** (wiz′dəm) *n.* ⟦OE: see WISE¹ & -DOM⟧ **1** the quality of being wise; good judgment **2** learning; knowledge

**wisdom tooth** the back tooth on each side of each jaw

**wise¹** (wīz) *adj.* **wis′er, wis′est** ⟦OE *wis*⟧ **1** having or showing good judgment **2** informed ⟦none the *wiser*⟧ **3** learned **4** shrewd; cunning **5** [Slang] conceited, impudent, fresh, etc. —**wise′ly** *adv.*

**wise²** (wīz) *n.* ⟦OE⟧ way; manner

**-wise** (wīz) ⟦< prec.⟧ *suffix* **1** in a (specified) direction, position, or manner ⟦*lengthwise*⟧ **2** in a manner characteristic of ⟦*clockwise*⟧ **3** with regard to ⟦*budgetwise*⟧

**wise·a·cre** (wīz′ā′kər) *n.* ⟦ult. < OHG *wizzago*, prophet⟧ one who makes annoyingly conceited claims to knowledge

**wise′crack′** [Slang] *n.* a flippant or facetious remark —*vi.* to make wisecracks

**wish** (wish) *vt.* ⟦OE *wyscan*⟧ **1** to have a longing for; want **2** to express a desire concerning ⟦I *wish* you well⟧ **3** to request ⟦I *wish* you to go⟧ —*vi.* **1** to long; yearn **2** to make a wish —*n.* **1** a wishing **2** something wished for **3** a polite request, almost an order **4** [*pl.*] expressed desire for a person's health, etc. ⟦best *wishes*⟧ —**wish′er** *n.*

**wish′bone′** *n.* the forked bone in front of a bird's breastbone

**wish′ful** (-fəl) *adj.* having or showing a wish; desirous —**wish′ful·ly** *adv.*

**wish·y-wash·y** (wish′ē wôsh′ē) *adj.* [Inf.] **1** weak; feeble **2** vacillating; indecisive

**wisp** (wisp) *n.* ⟦prob. < Scand⟧ **1** a small bundle, as of straw **2** a thin or filmy piece, strand, etc. ⟦a *wisp* of smoke⟧ **3** something delicate, frail, etc. — **wisp′y, -i·er, -i·est,** *adj.*

**wis·te·ri·a** (wis tir′ē ə) *n.* ⟦after C. *Wistar* (1761-1818), U.S. anatomist⟧ a twining vine with showy clusters of flowers: also **wis·tar′i·a** (-ter′-)

**wist·ful** (wist′fəl) *adj.* ⟦< earlier *wistly*, attentive⟧ showing or expressing vague yearnings — **wist′ful·ly** *adv.* —**wist′ful·ness** *n.*

**wit¹** (wit) *n.* ⟦OE⟧ **1** [*pl.*] powers of thinking; mental faculties **2** good sense **3** *a*) the ability to make clever remarks in a sharp, amusing way *b*) one characterized by wit

**wit²** (wit) *vt., vi.* **wist** (wist), **wit′ting** ⟦OE *witan*⟧ [Archaic] to know —**to wit** that is to say; namely

**witch** (wich) *n.* ⟦OE *wicce*⟧ **1** a woman thought to have supernatural power as by a compact with evil spirits **2** an ugly, old shrew **3** [Inf.] a fascinating woman or girl

**witch′craft′** *n.* the power or practices of witches

**witch doctor** in certain primitive societies, one thought able to cure sickness, ward off evil, etc. by using magic or incantations

**witch′er·y** (-ər ē) *n., pl.* **-ies** **1** witchcraft; sorcery **2** bewitching charm

**witch hazel** ⟦< OE *wice*⟧ **1** a shrub with yellow flowers **2** a lotion made from its leaves and bark, used on inflammations, etc.

**witch hunt** ⟦so named in allusion to persecutions of persons alleged to be witches⟧ a highly-publicized investigation carried out ostensibly to uncover disloyalty, etc., relying upon little evidence

**with** (with, with) *prep.* ⟦OE⟧ **1** in opposition to ⟦to argue *with* a friend⟧ **2** *a*) alongside of; near to *b*) in the company of *c*) into; among ⟦mix blue *with* yellow⟧ **3** as a member of ⟦to play *with* a string quartet⟧ **4** concerning ⟦happy *with* his lot⟧ **5** compared to **6** as well as ⟦she rides *with* the best⟧ **7** in the opinion of ⟦it's OK *with* me⟧ **8** as a result of ⟦faint *with* hunger⟧ **9** by means of **10** having received ⟦*with* your consent, I'll go⟧ **11** having as a possession, attribute, etc. **12** in the keeping, care, etc. of ⟦leave it *with* me⟧ **13** in spite of **14** at the same time as **15** in proportion to ⟦wages that vary *with* skill⟧ **16** to; onto ⟦join one end

*with* the other⟧ **17** from ⟦to part *with* one's gains⟧ —**with that** after, or as a consequence of, that

**with-** *combining form* **1** away, back ⟦*withdraw*⟧ **2** against, from ⟦*withhold*⟧

**with·al** (with ôl′, with-) *adv.* **1** besides **2** despite that

**with·draw′** *vt.* **-drew′, -drawn′, -draw′ing** **1** to take back; remove **2** to retract or recall (a statement, etc.) —*vi.* **1** to move back; go away; retreat **2** to remove oneself (*from* an organization, activity, etc.)

**with·draw′al** *n.* **1** the act of withdrawing **2** the process of giving up a narcotic drug, typically accompanied by distressing physical and mental effects (**withdrawal symptoms**)

**with·drawn′** *vt., vi. pp. of* WITHDRAW —*adj.* shy, reserved, etc.

**withe** (with, with) *n.* ⟦< OE *withthe*⟧ a tough, flexible twig of willow, osier, etc., used for binding

**with·er** (with′ər) *vi.* ⟦< ME *wederen*, to weather⟧ **1** to dry up; wilt, as plants **2** to become wasted or decayed **3** to weaken; languish —*vt.* **1** to cause to wither **2** to cause to feel abashed

**with·ers** (with′ərz) *pl.n.* ⟦< OE *wither*, against⟧ the part of a horse's back between the shoulder blades

**with·hold** (with hōld′, with-) *vt.* **-held′, -hold′ing** **1** *a*) to hold back; restrain *b*) to deduct (taxes, etc.) from wages **2** to refrain from granting

**withholding tax** the amount of income tax withheld, as payment in advance, from an employee's pay

**with·in** (with in′, with-) *adv.* ⟦OE *withinnan*⟧ **1** on or into the inside **2** indoors **3** inside the body, mind, etc. —*prep.* **1** in the inner part of **2** not beyond **3** inside the limits of —*n.* the inside

**with′-it** (-it) *adj.* [Slang] **1** sophisticated, up-to-date, etc. **2** fashionable; stylish

**with·out′** *adv.* ⟦OE *withutan*⟧ **1** on the outside **2** out-of-doors —*prep.* **1** [Now Rare] at, on, or to the outside of **2** lacking **3** free from **4** with avoidance of ⟦to pass by *without* speaking⟧

**with·stand′** (-stand′) *vt., vi.* **-stood′, -stand′ing** to oppose, resist, or endure, esp. successfully

**wit·less** (wit′lis) *adj.* lacking wit; foolish — **wit′less·ly** *adv.*

**wit·ness** (wit′nis) *n.* ⟦< OE *witan*, know⟧ **1** evidence; testimony **2** one who saw, or can give a firsthand account of, something **3** one who testifies in court **4** one who observes, and attests to, a signing, etc. —*vt.* **1** to testify to **2** to serve as evidence of **3** to act as witness of **4** to be present at —**bear witness** to testify

**wit·ti·cism** (wit′ə siz′əm) *n.* ⟦< WITTY⟧ a witty remark

**wit·ting** (wit′iŋ) *adj.* ⟦ME *wytting*⟧ intentional

**wit·ty** (wit′ē) *adj.* **-ti·er, -ti·est** ⟦OE *wittig*⟧ having or showing wit; cleverly amusing —**wit′ti·ly** *adv.* —**wit′ti·ness** *n.*

**wive** (wīv) *vi., vt.* **wived, wiv′ing** ⟦OE *wifian*⟧ [Archaic] to marry (a woman)

**wives** (wīvz) *n. pl. of* WIFE

**wiz·ard** (wiz′ərd) *n.* ⟦ME *wisard*⟧ **1** a magician; sorcerer **2** [Inf.] one very skilled at a specified activity

**wiz′ard·ry** *n.* magic; sorcery

**wiz·ened** (wiz′ənd) *adj.* ⟦< OE *wisnian*, wither⟧ dried up; withered

**wk** *abbrev.* **1** week **2** work

**wkly.** *abbrev.* weekly

**w/o** *abbrev.* without

**wob·ble** (wäb′əl) *vi.* **-bled, -bling** ⟦prob. < LowG *wabbeln*⟧ **1** to move unsteadily from side to side **2** to shake **3** to vacillate —*vt.* to cause to wobble —*n.* wobbling motion —**wob′bly, -bli·er, -bli·est, *adj.* —**wob′bli·ness** *n.*

**woe** (wō) *n.* ⟦OE *wa*⟧ **1** great sorrow; grief **2** trouble —*interj.* alas!

**woe′be·gone′** (-bē gôn′, -bi-) *adj.* of woeful appearance; looking sad or wretched

**woe'ful** (-fəl) *adj.* **1** full of woe; sad **2** causing woe **3** pitiful; wretched —**woe'ful·ly** *adv.*

**wok** (wäk, wôk) *n.* ⟦Chin⟧ a bowl-shaped cooking pan used for frying, steaming, etc.

**woke** (wōk) *vi., vt. alt. pt. of* WAKE¹

**wok·en** (wō'kən) *vi., vt. alt. pp. of* WAKE¹

**wolf** (wŏolf) *n., pl.* **wolves** (wŏolvz) ⟦OE *wulf*⟧ **1** a wild, flesh-eating, doglike mammal of the Northern Hemisphere **2** *a*) a cruel or greedy person *b*) [Slang] a man who flirts with many women —*vt.* to eat greedily: often with *down* —**cry wolf** to give a false alarm —**wolf'ish** *adj.*

**wolf'hound'** *n.* a breed of large dog, once used for hunting wolves

**wol·ver·ine** (wŏol'vər ēn') *n.* ⟦< WOLF⟧ a stocky, flesh-eating mammal of N North America and N Eurasia

**wolves** (wŏolvz) *n. pl. of* WOLF

**wom·an** (wŏom'ən) *n., pl.* **wom·en** (wim'ən) ⟦< OE *wif*, a female + *mann*, human being⟧ **1** *a*) an adult female human being *b*) women collectively **2** a female servant **3** womanly qualities

**-wom·an** (wŏom'ən) *combining form* woman of a (specified) kind, in a (specified) activity, etc.: sometimes used to avoid the masculine implications of -MAN

**wom'an·hood'** *n.* **1** the state of being a woman **2** womanly qualities **3** women collectively

**wom'an·ish** *adj.* like or characteristic of a woman

**wom'an·ize'** *vt.* -ized', -iz'ing to make effeminate —*vi.* to be sexually promiscuous with women — **wom'an·iz'er** *n.*

**wom'an·kind'** *n.* women in general

**wom'an·ly** *adj.* **1** womanish **2** characteristic of or fit for a woman —**wom'an·li·ness** *n.*

**womb** (wŏom) *n.* ⟦OE *wamb*⟧ UTERUS

**wom·bat** (wäm'bat') *n.* ⟦< native name⟧ a burrowing marsupial resembling a small bear, found in Australia, etc.

**wom·en** (wim'in) *n. pl. of* WOMAN

**wom'en·folk'** *pl.n.* [Inf. or Dial.] women or womankind: also **wom'en·folks'**

**won** (wun) *vi., vt. pt. & pp. of* WIN

**won·der** (wun'dər) *n.* ⟦OE *wundor*⟧ **1** a person, thing, or event causing astonishment and admiration; marvel **2** the feeling aroused by something strange, unexpected, etc. —*vi.* **1** to be filled with wonder; marvel **2** to have curiosity, sometimes mingled with doubt —*vt.* to have curiosity or doubt about /he *wondered* what happened/

**won'der·ful** *adj.* **1** that causes wonder; marvelous **2** excellent, fine, etc. —**won'der·ful·ly** *adv.*

**won'der·land'** *n.* any place, real or imaginary, full of wonders

**won'der·ment** *n.* amazement

**won·drous** (wun'drəs) *adj.* wonderful: now chiefly literary —*adv.* [Archaic] surprisingly

**wont** (wônt, wōnt) *adj.* ⟦< OE *wunian*, dwell⟧ accustomed /she was *wont* to rise early/ —*n.* usual practice; habit

**won't** (wōnt) *contr.* will not

**wont·ed** (wôn'tid, wōn'-) *adj.* customary

**won ton** (wän' tän') ⟦Cantonese⟧ Chinese dumplings of noodle dough filled with chopped meat, etc., often served in a soup (**won'-ton' soup**)

**woo** (wŏo) *vt.* ⟦OE *wogian*⟧ **1** to seek the love of, usually in order to propose marriage **2** to seek /to *woo* fame/ —*vi.* to woo a person —**woo'er** *n.*

**wood** (wŏod) *n.* ⟦OE *wudu*⟧ **1** [usually pl., with sing. or pl. v.] a thick growth of trees; forest **2** the hard, fibrous substance beneath the bark of trees and shrubs **3** lumber or timber **4** *Golf* any of certain clubs, originally with wooden heads — *adj.* **1** made of wood; wooden **2** growing or living in woods —**out of the woods** [Inf.] out of difficulty, danger, etc.

**wood alcohol** METHANOL

**wood'bine'** (-bīn') *n.* ⟦< OE *wudu*, wood + *binde*, to bind⟧ **1** a climbing honeysuckle **2** a climbing vine with dark-blue berries

**wood'carv'ing** *n.* **1** the art of carving wood by hand **2** an object so made —**wood'carv'er** *n.*

**wood'chuck'** *n.* ⟦< AmInd name⟧ a burrowing and hibernating marmot of North America

WOODCHUCK

**wood'cock'** *n.* a small game bird with short legs and a long bill

**wood'craft'** *n.* **1** matters relating to the woods, as camping, hunting, etc. **2** WOODWORKING

**wood'cut'** *n.* **1** a wooden block engraved with a design, etc. **2** a print from this

**wood'cut'ter** *n.* one who fells trees, cuts wood, etc. —**wood'cut'ting** *n.*

**wood'ed** *adj.* covered with trees

**wood'en** *adj.* **1** made of wood **2** stiff, lifeless, etc. **3** dull; insensitive —**wood'en·ly** *adv.*

**wood'land** (-lənd, -land') *n.* land covered with woods —*adj.* of the woods

**wood'lot'** *n.* a piece of land where trees are raised, as for firewood, lumber, etc.

**wood'peck'er** (-pek'ər) *n.* a climbing bird with a strong, pointed bill used to peck holes in bark to get insects

**wood'pile'** *n.* a pile of wood, esp. of firewood

**wood screw** a screw with a sharp point, for use in wood

**wood'shed'** *n.* a shed for storing firewood

**woods·man** (wŏodz'mən) *n., pl.* -men (-mən) **1** one who lives or works in the woods **2** one skilled in woodcraft

**wood'sy** (-zē) *adj.* -si·er, -si·est of or like the woods —**wood'si·ness** *n.*

**wood·wind** (wŏod'wind') *n.* any of a family of wind instruments made, esp. orig., of wood, as the flute, clarinet, or oboe

**wood'work'** *n.* **1** work done in wood **2** the wooden moldings, doors, etc. of a house

**wood'work'ing** *n.* the art or work of making things of wood

**wood'y** *adj.* -i·er, -i·est **1** covered with trees **2** consisting of or forming wood **3** like wood — **wood'i·ness** *n.*

**woof¹** (wŏof) *n.* ⟦ult. < OE *wefan*, to weave⟧ WEFT

**woof²** (wŏof) *n.* ⟦echoic⟧ the gruff barking sound of a dog —*vi.* to make this sound

**woof·er** (wŏof'ər) *n.* a large, high-fidelity speaker for reproducing low-frequency sounds

**wool** (wŏol) *n.* ⟦OE *wull*⟧ **1** the soft, curly hair of sheep or of some other animals, as the goat **2** woolen yarn, cloth, clothing, etc. **3** anything that looks or feels like wool

**wool'en** *adj.* **1** made of wool **2** relating to wool or woolen cloth —*n.* [*pl.*] woolen goods Also [Chiefly Brit.] **wool'len**

**Woolf** (wŏolf), **Virginia** 1882-1941; Eng. novelist & critic

**wool'gath'er·ing** (-gath'ər iŋ) *n.* aimless daydreaming or speculation

**wool·ly** (wŏol'ē) *adj.* -li·er, -li·est **1** of or like wool **2** bearing or covered with wool **3** rough and uncivilized: used chiefly in **wild and woolly 4** confused /*woolly* ideas/ Also sp. **wool'y**

**wooz·y** (wŏo'zē, wŏoz'ē) *adj.* -i·er, -i·est [Inf.] dizzy or befuddled, as from drink or a blow — **wooz'i·ness** *n.*

**word** (wʉrd) *n.* ⟦OE⟧ **1** *a*) a speech sound, or series of such sounds, having meaning as a unit of language *b*) the written or printed representation of this **2** a brief remark /a *word* of advice/ **3** a promise or assurance /he gave his *word*/ **4** news; information **5** *a*) a password *b*) a command, order, etc. **6** [*usually pl.*] *a*) speech *b*) lyrics **7** [*pl.*] a quarrel —*vt.* to put into words; phrase —**in a word** briefly —**in so many words**

exactly and plainly —**the Word** the Bible —**word for word** in precisely the same words

**word'age** *n.* 1 words 2 wordiness

**word'ing** *n.* choice of words; diction

**word of honor** solemn promise

**word of mouth** speech, as opposed to writing

**word'play'** *n.* 1 repartee 2 punning

**word processor** a computerized device consisting of a keyboard, video screen, printer, etc., used to generate, edit, store, or duplicate documents, as letters or reports —**word processing**

**Words·worth** (wurdz'wərth), **William** 1770-1850; Eng. poet

**word·y** (wur'dē) *adj.* -i·er, -i·est containing or using too many words; verbose —**word'i·ness** *n.*

**wore** (wôr) *vt., vi. pt. of* WEAR

**work** (wurk) *n.* ⟦OE *weorc*⟧ 1 effort exerted to do or make something; labor; toil 2 employment; occupation 3 something one is making or doing; task 4 something made or done; specif., *a*) an act; deed (*usually used in pl.*) [good *works*] *b*) [*pl.*] collected writings *c*) [*pl.*] engineering structures, as bridges, dams, etc. 5 [*pl., with sing. v.*] a place where work is done, as a factory 6 workmanship —*adj.* of, for, or used in work —*vi.* **worked** or **wrought, work'ing** 1 to do work; labor; toil 2 to be employed 3 to function or operate, esp. effectively 4 to ferment 5 to move, proceed, etc. slowly and with difficulty 6 to come or become, as by repeated movement [the door *worked* loose] —*vt.* 1 to cause; bring about [his idea *worked* wonders] 2 to mold; shape 3 to solve (a mathematical problem, etc.) 4 to manipulate; knead 5 to bring into a specified condition, as by moving back and forth [to *work* a nail loose] 6 to cultivate (soil) 7 to operate; use 8 to cause to work [to *work* a crew hard] 9 to make (one's way, etc.) by effort 10 to provoke; rouse [to *work* oneself into a rage] 11 [Slang] to proceed ingratiatingly through (a crowd, etc.) —**at work** working —**out of work** unemployed —**the works** 1 the working parts (*of* a watch, etc.) 2 [Inf.] everything: also **the whole works** —**work off** to get rid of —**work on** 1 to influence 2 to try to persuade —**work out** 1 to solve 2 to result 3 to develop 4 to have a workout —**work up** 1 to advance 2 to develop 3 to excite

**work·a·ble** (wur'kə bəl) *adj.* 1 that can be worked 2 practicable; feasible

**work'a·day'** (-dā') *adj.* 1 of workdays; everyday 2 ordinary

**work'a·hol'ic** (-hôl'ik) *n.* ⟦WORK + -AHOLIC⟧ a person having an irrational need to work

**work'bench'** *n.* a table at which work is done, as by a carpenter

**work'book'** *n.* a book of questions, exercises, etc. for use by students

**work'day'** *n.* 1 a day on which work is ordinarily done 2 the part of a day during which work is done

**work'er** *n.* 1 one who works for a living 2 one who works for a cause, etc. 3 a sterile ant, bee, etc. that does work for the colony

**work'fare'** (-fer') *n.* ⟦WORK + (WEL)FARE⟧ a government program requiring employable recipients of welfare to register for work, training, etc.

**work'horse'** *n.* 1 a horse used for working 2 a reliable worker with a heavy workload

**work'house'** *n.* a prison where petty offenders are confined and made to work

**work'ing** *adj.* 1 that works 2 of, for, or used in work 3 sufficient to get work done 4 on which further work may be based [a *working* hypothesis] —*n.* the act of one that works

**working class** the social class consisting of industrial and manual workers

**work'ing·man'** (-man') *n., pl.* -**men'** (-men') a worker, esp. an industrial worker

**work'load'** *n.* the amount of work assigned for completion within a given time period

**work'man** (-mən) *n., pl.* -**men** (-mən) 1 WORKINGMAN 2 a craftsman

**work'man·like'** *adj.* capable; competent

**work'man·ship'** *n.* skill of a workman or the quality of the work done

**work'out'** *n.* a session of physical exercises or any strenuous work

**work'place'** *n.* the office, factory, etc. where one works

**work sheet** a paper sheet with working notes, etc., or with problems, etc. to be worked on by students

**work'shop'** *n.* 1 a room or building where work is done 2 a seminar for specified intensive study, work, etc.

**work'sta'tion** *n.* 1 a person's work area, including furniture, etc. and, often, a microcomputer 2 a terminal or personal computer connected to a network

**work'ta'ble** *n.* a table at which work is done

**work'-up'** *n.* a complete medical study of a patient, including tests

**work'week'** *n.* the total number of hours or days worked in a week

**world** (wurld) *n.* ⟦OE *werold*⟧ 1 *a*) the earth *b*) the universe 2 *a*) mankind *b*) people generally; the public 3 *a*) [*also* W-] some part of the earth [the Old *World*] *b*) any sphere or domain [the animal *world*] 4 individual experience, outlook, etc. [her *world* is narrow] 5 secular life and interests, or people concerned with these 6 [*often pl.*] a large amount [a *world* of good] —**for all the world** exactly

**world'-class'** *adj.* of the highest class, as in international competition

**world'ly** *adj.* -li·er, -li·est 1 of this world; secular 2 devoted to the affairs, pleasures, etc. of this world 3 worldly-wise —**world'li·ness** *n.*

**world'ly-wise'** *adj.* wise in the ways or affairs of the world; sophisticated

**world'-shak'ing** *adj.* of great significance, effect, or influence; momentous

**world'view'** *n.* a comprehensive, esp. personal, philosophy of the world and of human life

**World War I** the war (1914-18) involving Great Britain, France, Russia, the U.S., etc. on one side and Germany, Austria-Hungary, etc. on the other

**World War II** the war (1939-45) involving Great Britain, France, the Soviet Union, the U.S., etc. on one side and Germany, Italy, Japan, etc. on the other

**world'-wea'ry** *adj.* bored with living

**world'wide'** *adj., adv.* (extending) throughout the world

**World Wide Web** a group of Internet sources giving access to text, images, sound, etc.

**worm** (wurm) *n.* ⟦< OE *wyrm*, serpent⟧ 1 a long, slender, soft-bodied animal 2 an abject or contemptible person 3 something spiral in shape, etc., as the thread of a screw 4 [*pl.*] any disease caused by parasitic worms in the intestines, etc. —*vi.* to proceed like a worm, in a winding or devious manner —*vt.* 1 to bring about, get, make, etc. in a winding or devious manner 2 to purge of intestinal worms —**worm'y**, -i·er, -i·est, *adj.*

**worm gear** a gear consisting of a rotating screw meshed with a toothed wheel

**worm'wood'** (-wood') *n.* ⟦< OE *wermod*⟧ a strong-smelling plant that yields a bitter-tasting oil formerly used in making absinthe

**worn** (wôrn) *vt., vi. pp. of* WEAR —*adj.* 1 damaged by use or wear 2 showing the effects of worry or anxiety

**worn'-out'** *adj.* 1 used until no longer effective, usable, etc. 2 exhausted; tired out

**wor·ri·ment** (wur'ē mənt) *n.* (a) worry

**wor'ri·some** (-səm) *adj.* causing worry

**wor·ry** (wur'ē) *vt.* -ried, -ry·ing ⟦< OE *wyrgan*, to strangle⟧ 1 to treat roughly, as with continual biting [a dog *worrying* a bone] 2 to annoy, bother, etc. 3 to make troubled or uneasy —*vi.* 1 to bite or tear (*at* an object) **2** to be anxious, troubled, etc. —*n.*, *pl.* **-ries 1** a troubled state of mind; anxiety **2** a cause of this —**wor'ri·er** *n.*

**wor'ry·wart'** (-wôrt') *n.* [[prec. + WART]] [Inf.] one who tends to worry, esp. over trivial matters

**worse** (wɵrs) *adj.* [[OE *wiersa*]] **1** *compar. of* BAD[1] & ILL **2** *a*) bad, evil, harmful, etc. in a greater degree *b*) of inferior quality **3** in poorer health; more ill **4** in a less satisfactory condition —*adv.* **1** *compar. of* BADLY & ILL **2** in a worse manner **3** to a worse extent —*n.* that which is worse —**worse off** in worse circumstances

**wor·sen** (wɵr'sən) *vt.*, *vi.* to make or become worse

**wor·ship** (wɵr'ship) *n.* [< OE *weorthscipe*]] **1** a service or rite showing reverence for a deity **2** intense love or admiration **3** [W-] [Chiefly Brit.] a title of honor: used in addressing magistrates, etc. —*vt.* **-shiped** or **-shipped**, **-ship·ing** or **-ship·ping 1** to show religious reverence for **2** to have intense love or admiration for —*vi.* to engage in worship —**wor'ship·er** or **wor'ship·per** *n.*

**wor'ship·ful** (-fəl) *adj.* feeling or offering great devotion or respect

**worst** (wɵrst) *adj.* [[OE *wyrsta*]] **1** *superl. of* BAD[1] & ILL **2** *a*) bad, evil, harmful, etc. in the highest degree *b*) of the lowest quality **3** in the least satisfactory condition —*adv.* **1** *superl. of* BADLY & ILL **2** in the worst manner **3** to the worst extent —*n.* that which is worst —*vt.* to defeat —**at worst** under the worst circumstances —**if (the) worst comes to (the) worst** if the worst possible thing happens —**(in) the worst way** [Slang] very much; greatly

**wor·sted** (woos'tid, wɵr'stid) *n.* [[after *Worstead*, England]] **1** a smooth, firmly twisted wool thread or yarn **2** fabric made from this

**wort** (wɵrt) *n.* [[OE *wyrt-*]] a liquid, produced from malt, that can be fermented to make beer, etc.

**worth** (wɵrth) *n.* [[OE *weorth*]] **1** material value, esp. as expressed in terms of money **2** importance, value, merit, etc. **3** the quantity to be had for a given sum [a dollar's *worth*] —*prep.* **1** deserving or worthy of **2** equal in value to **3** having wealth amounting to

**worth'less** *adj.* without worth or merit; useless —**worth'less·ness** *n.*

**worth'while'** *adj.* worth the time or effort spent

**wor·thy** (wɵr'thē) *adj.* **-thi·er**, **-thi·est 1** having worth, value, or merit **2** meriting —*n.*, *pl.* **-thies** a person of outstanding worth, etc. —**wor'thi·ly** *adv.* —**wor'thi·ness** *n.*

**would** (wood) *v.aux.* [[OE *wolde*]] **1** *pt. of* WILL[2] **2** used to express a supposition or condition [he *would* write if he knew you *would* answer] **3** used to make a polite request [*would* you please open the window?] —*vt.* [Old Poet.] I wish [*would* that she were here] See usage note at WILL[2]

**would'-be'** *adj.* **1** wishing or pretending to be **2** intended to be

**wound**[1] (woond) *n.* [[OE *wund*]] **1** an injury in which tissue is cut, torn, etc. **2** any hurt to the feelings, honor, etc. —*vt.*, *vi.* to inflict a wound (on or upon); injure

**wound**[2] (wound) *vt.*, *vi. pt. & pp. of* WIND[1]

**wove** (wōv) *vt.*, *vi. pt. & alt. pp. of* WEAVE

**wo·ven** (wō'vən) *vt.*, *vi. alt. pp. of* WEAVE

**wow** (wou) *interj.* used to express surprise, pleasure, etc. —*vt.* [Slang] to arouse enthusiasm in

**wpm** *abbrev.* words per minute

**wrack** (rak) *n.* [< MDu *wrak*, a wreck]] *alt. sp. of* RACK[2]

**wraith** (rāth) *n.* [[Scot]] a ghost

**wran·gle** (raŋ'gəl) *vi.* **-gled**, **-gling** [< OE *wrin-gan*, to press]] to argue; quarrel, esp. noisily —*n.* a noisy dispute —**wran'gler** *n.*

**wran'gler** (-glər) *n.* [< AmSp *caballerango*, a groom] a cowboy who herds livestock, esp. saddle horses —**wran'gle**, **-gled**, **-gling**, *vt.*

**wrap** (rap) *vt.* **wrapped**, **wrap'ping** [[ME *wrap-pen*]] **1** to wind or fold (a covering) around something **2** to enclose and fasten in paper, etc. —*vi.*

to twine, coil, etc.: usually with *over, around*, etc. —*n.* **1** an outer covering or garment **2** [*pl.*] secrecy; censorship [to keep plans under *wraps*] **3** *Film* the completion of the filming of a scene, etc. —**wrapped up in** engrossed in or involved in —**wrap up** [Inf.] to conclude; settle

**wrap'per** *n.* **1** one that wraps **2** that in which something is wrapped **3** a woman's dressing gown

**wrap'ping** *n.* [*often pl.*] the material in which something is wrapped

**wrap'-up'** *n.* [Inf.] a concluding, summarizing statement, report, etc.

**wrath** (rath) *n.* [[OE, angry]] intense anger; rage; fury —**wrath'ful** *adj.*

**wreak** (rēk) *vt.* [[OE *wrecan*, to revenge]] **1** to give vent to (one's anger, etc.) **2** to inflict (vengeance, etc.)

**wreath** (rēth) *n.*, *pl.* **wreaths** (rēthz, rēths) [[OE *writha*]] **1** a twisted ring of leaves, flowers, etc. **2** something like this in shape [*wreaths* of smoke]

**wreathe** (rēth) *vt.* **wreathed**, **wreath'ing 1** to form into a wreath **2** to coil or twist around; encircle **3** to decorate with wreaths

**wreck** (rek) *n.* [< ON *vrek*, driftwood]] **1** a ship-wreck **2** the remains of something destroyed **3** a run-down person **4** a wrecking or being wrecked —*vt.* **1** to destroy or damage badly **2** to tear down (a building, etc.) **3** to overthrow or thwart

**wreck'age** *n.* **1** a wrecking or being wrecked **2** the remains of something wrecked

**wreck'er** *n.* **1** one who wrecks **2** one that salvages or removes wrecks

**wren** (ren) *n.* [[OE *wrenna*]] a small songbird with a stubby, erect tail

**wrench** (rench) *n.* [[OE *wrenc*, a trick]] **1** a sudden, sharp twist or pull **2** an injury caused by a twist, as to the back **3** a sudden feeling of grief, etc. **4** a tool for turning nuts, bolts, pipes, etc. —*vt.* **1** to twist or jerk violently **2** to injure with a twist **3** to distort (a meaning, etc.)

**wrest** (rest) *vt.* [[OE *wræstan*]] **1** to pull or force away violently with a twisting motion **2** to take by force; usurp

**wres·tle** (res'əl; *often* ras'-) *vi.*, *vt.* **-tled**, **-tling** [see prec.]] **1** to struggle hand to hand with (an opponent) in an attempt to throw him or her **2** to contend (*with*) —*n.* a wrestling —**wres'tler** *n.*

WRENCHES

**wres'tling** *n.* a sport in which the opponents wrestle, or struggle hand to hand

**wretch** (rech) *n.* [[OE *wrecca*, an outcast]] **1** a miserable or unhappy person **2** a despised person

**wretch'ed** *adj.* **1** very unhappy; miserable **2** distressing; dismal **3** poor in quality **4** contemptible —**wretch'ed·ly** *adv.* —**wretch'ed·ness** *n.*

**wrig·gle** (rig'əl) *vi.* **-gled**, **-gling** [[medieval Low G *wriggeln*]] **1** to twist and turn; squirm **2** to move along with a twisting motion **3** to make one's way by shifty means —*n.* a wriggling —**wrig'gler** *n.* —**wrig'gly**, **-gli·er**, **-gli·est**, *adj.*

**wright** (rīt) *n.* [< OE *wyrcan*, to work]] one who makes or constructs: chiefly in compounds [*ship-wright*]

**wring** (riŋ) *vt.* **wrung**, **wring'ing** [[OE *wringan*]] **1** *a*) to squeeze, press, or twist *b*) to force out (water, etc.) by this means (usually with *out*) **2** to clasp and twist (the hands) in distress **3** to clasp (another's hand) forcefully in greeting **4** to extract by force, threats, etc. —*n.* a wringing

**wring'er** *n.* a machine with rollers to squeeze water from wet clothes

**wrin·kle**[1] (riŋ'kəl) *n.* [[ME *wrinkel*]] **1** a small furrow in a normally smooth surface **2** a crease in the skin —*vt.*, *vi.* **-kled**, **-kling** to form wrinkles (in); pucker; crease —**wrin'kly**, **-kli·er**, **-kli·est**, *adj.*

**wrin·kle**[2] (riŋ'kəl) *n.* 〖< OE *wrenc*, a trick〗 [Inf.] a clever trick, idea, or device

**wrist** (rist) *n.* 〖OE〗 the joint between the hand and forearm —**a slap** (or **tap**) **on the wrist** a token punishment

**wrist'band'** *n.* a band that goes around the wrist, as on a cuff

**wrist'watch'** *n.* a watch worn on a strap or band around the wrist

**writ** (rit) *n.* 〖OE < *writan*, write〗 a formal legal document ordering or prohibiting some action

**write** (rīt) *vt.* **wrote**, **writ'ten**, **writ'ing** 〖OE *writan*〗 **1** to form (words, letters, etc.) on a surface, as with a pen **2** to compose (literary or musical material) **3** to communicate (with) in writing *[she wrote (me) that she was ill]* **4** to cover with writing *[to write three pages]* **5** to fill in (a bank check, etc.) **6** to show clearly *[anger was written on his face]* **7** *Comput.* to record (information) on a disk, etc. —*vi.* to produce writing —**write off 1** to remove from accounts (bad debts, etc.) **2** to drop from consideration **3** to amortize —**write out 1** to put into writing **2** to write in full —**write up** to write an account of

**write'-in'** *n.* **1** a candidate whose name is not on the ballot, but is written in by a voter **2** a vote of this kind

**write'-off'** *n.* a cancelled debt, amortized expense, etc.

**writ'er** *n.* one who writes, esp. as an occupation; author

**write'-up'** *n.* [Inf.] a written report

**writhe** (rīth) *vi.* **writhed**, **writh'ing** 〖OE *writhan*, to twist〗 **1** to twist or turn; squirm *[to writhe in agony]* **2** to suffer great emotional distress

**writ·ing** (rīt'iŋ) *n.* **1** the act of one who writes **2** something written **3** written form **4** *short for* HANDWRITING

**writ·ten** (rit'ʼn) *vt.*, *vi. pp. of* WRITE

**wrong** (rôŋ) *adj.* 〖< ON *rangr*, twisted〗 **1** not in accordance with justice, law, morality, etc. **2** not suitable or appropriate **3** *a)* contrary to fact, etc.; incorrect *b)* mistaken **4** not functioning properly **5** not meant to be seen *[the wrong side of a fabric]* —*adv.* in a wrong manner, direction, etc. —*n.* an unjust, immoral, or illegal act —*vt.* to treat badly or unjustly —**in the wrong** not on the side supported by truth, justice, etc. —**wrong'ly** *adv.* — **wrong'ness** *n.*

**wrong'do'ing** *n.* any wrong act or behavior — **wrong'do'er** *n.*

**wrong'ful** *adj.* **1** unjust or injurious **2** unlawful —**wrong'ful·ly** *adv.*

**wrong'head'ed** *adj.* stubborn or perverse — **wrong'head'ed·ly** *adv.* —**wrong'head'ed·ness** *n.*

**wrote** (rōt) *vt.*, *vi. pt. of* WRITE

**wroth** (rôth) *adj.* 〖OE *wrath*〗 angry

**wrought** (rôt) *vi.*, *vt. alt. pt. & pp. of* WORK —*adj.* **1** formed; made **2** shaped by hammering, etc.: said of metals

**wrought iron** tough, ductile iron containing very little carbon —**wrought'-i'ron** *adj.*

**wrought'-up'** *adj.* very disturbed or excited

**wrung** (ruŋ) *vt. pt. & pp. of* WRING

**wry** (rī) *adj.* **wri'er** or **wry'er**, **wri'est** or **wry'est** 〖< OE *wrigian*, to turn〗 **1** distorted in a grimace *[a wry face]* **2** ironic, dry, etc. *[wry humor]* —**wry'ly** *adv.* —**wry'ness** *n.*

**wt** *abbrev.* weight

**Wu·han** (woo'hän') city in EC China: pop. 3,288,000

**wuss** (woos) *n.* [Slang] a person regarded as weak, ineffectual, etc.; wimp: also **wuss'y**, *pl.* **wuss'ies**

**WV** West Virginia

**WWI** *abbrev.* World War I

**WWII** *abbrev.* World War II

**WWW** or **www** *abbrev.* World Wide Web

**Wy·o·ming** (wī ō'miŋ) Mountain State of the W U.S.: 97,105 sq. mi.; pop. 454,000; cap. Cheyenne: abbrev. **WY** —**Wy·o'ming·ite'** *n.*

# X

**x**[1] or **X** (eks) *n.*, *pl.* **x's**, **X's** **1** the 24th letter of the English alphabet **2** *Math.* an unknown quantity

**x**[2] *abbrev.* extra: also **X**

**x**[3] (eks) *symbol* **1** by (in indicating dimensions) *[3 ft. x 4 ft.]* **2** *Optics* the power of magnification **3** *Math.* times *[2 x 3 = 6]*

**X** (eks) *n.* **1** the Roman numeral 10 **2** a film rating meaning that no one under seventeen is to be admitted

**X chromosome** *see* SEX CHROMOSOME

**Xe** *Chem. symbol for* xenon

**xe·non** (zē'nän') *n.* a colorless, nonreactive, gaseous chemical element

**xen·o·pho·bi·a** (zen'ə fō'bē ə) *n.* 〖< Gr *xenos*, foreign + -PHOBIA〗 fear or hatred of strangers or foreigners —**xen'o·phobe'** (-fōb') *n.* —**xen'o·pho'bic** (-fō'bik) *adj.*

**xe·rog·ra·phy** (zir äg'rə fē) *n.* 〖< Gr *xēros*, dry + -GRAPHY〗 a process for copying printed material, etc. by the action of light on an electrically charged surface

**Xe·rox** (zir'äks') *trademark for* a device for copying by xerography —*vt.*, *vi.* [*usually* x-] to reproduce by xerography —*n.* [*usually* x-] a copy so made

**Xer·xes I** (zurk'sēz') 519?-465 B.C.; king of Persia (486-465)

**xi** (zī, sī) *n.* the 14th letter of the Greek alphabet (Ξ, ξ)

**XL** *abbrev.* extra large

**X·mas** (eks'məs) *n. inf. var. of* CHRISTMAS

**X-rat·ed** (eks'rāt'əd) *adj.* designating or like a film with a rating of X; explicit, obscene, etc.

**X-ray** (eks'rā') *n.* **1** a type of electromagnetic wave of very short wavelength, that can penetrate solid substances: used to study internal body structures and treat various disorders **2** a photograph made by means of X-rays —*adj.* of or by X-rays —*vt.* to examine, treat, or photograph with X-rays Also **X ray**, **x-ray**, or **x ray**

**XS** *abbrev.* extra small

**xy·lem** (zī'ləm) *n.* 〖< Gr *xylon*, wood〗 the woody vascular tissue of a plant

**xy·lo·phone** (zī'lə fōn') *n.* 〖< Gr *xylon*, wood + -PHONE〗 a musical percussion instrument consisting of a series of graduated wooden bars that are struck with small, wooden mallets —**xy'lo·phon'ist** (-fō'nist, zī läf'ə nist) *n.*

# Y

**y** or **Y** (wī) *n., pl.* **y's, Y's** the 25th letter of the English alphabet

**Y** *Chem. symbol for* yttrium

**-y**[1] (ē, i) ⟦ME⟧ *suffix* little one, dear *[kitty, daddy]*

**-y**[2] (ē, i) ⟦OE *-ig*⟧ *suffix* **1** full of, like *[dirty]* **2** somewhat *[yellowy]* **3** tending to *[sticky]*

**-y**[3] (ē, i) ⟦< L *-ia*⟧ *suffix* **1** quality or condition *[jealousy]* **2** a (specified) kind of shop, goods, or group *[bakery]*

**-y**[4] (ē, i) ⟦< L *-ium*⟧ *suffix* action of *[inquiry]*

**yacht** (yät) *n.* ⟦Du *jacht*⟧ a small vessel for pleasure cruises, racing, etc.

**yacht′ing** (-iŋ) *n.* the sport of sailing a yacht —**yachts′man** (-mən), *pl.* **-men** (-mən), *n.*

**ya·hoo** (yä′ho͞o′) *n.* ⟦after a race of people in Swift's novel *Gulliver's Travels*⟧ a person regarded as vulgar, uneducated, etc.

**Yah·weh** or **Yah·we** (yä′we, -wä) *n.* ⟦< Heb⟧ God

**yak**[1] (yak) *n.* ⟦< Tibet *g-yag*⟧ a long-haired wild ox of Tibet and central Asia

**yak**[2] (yak) [Slang] *vi.* **yakked, yak′king** ⟦echoic⟧ to talk much or idly —*n.* a yakking

**yam** (yam) *n.* ⟦< WAfr native name⟧ **1** the edible, starchy, tuberous root of a tropical climbing plant **2** an orange-colored variety of sweet potato

**yam·mer** (yam′ər) *vi.* ⟦< OE *geomerian*, to lament⟧ **1** to shout, yell, etc. **2** to talk loudly or continuously —**yam′mer·er** *n.*

**yang** (yäŋ, yaŋ) *n.* ⟦Chin⟧ in Chinese philosophy, the masculine force or principle in the universe: cf. YIN

**Yan·gon** (yan gôn′) capital of Myanmar: pop. 2,513,000

**Yang·tze** (yaŋk′sē) *a former transliteration of* CHANG

**yank** (yaŋk) *n., vt., vi.* ⟦< ?⟧ [Inf.] jerk

**Yank** (yaŋk) *n.* [Slang] a Yankee; esp., a U.S. soldier in WWI and WWII

**Yan·kee** (yaŋ′kē) *n.* ⟦< ? Du *Jan Kees*, a disparaging nickname⟧ **1** a New Englander **2** a person born or living in the northern U.S. **3** a citizen of the U.S. —*adj.* of or like Yankees

**yap** (yap) *vi.* **yapped, yap′ping** ⟦echoic⟧ **1** to make a sharp, shrill bark **2** [Slang] to talk noisily and stupidly —*n.* **1** a sharp, shrill bark **2** [Slang] *a)* jabber *b)* the mouth

**yard**[1] (yärd) *n.* ⟦OE *gierd*, rod⟧ **1** a measure of length, 3 feet or 36 inches **2** *Naut.* a slender rod or spar fastened across a mast to support a sail

**yard**[2] (yärd) *n.* ⟦OE *geard*, enclosure⟧ **1** the ground around or next to a building **2** an enclosed place for a particular purpose *[shipyard]*

**yard′age** *n.* **1** measurement in yards **2** the extent so measured

**yard′arm′** *n. Naut.* either half of a yard supporting a square sail, etc.

**yard goods** textiles made in standard widths, usually sold by the yard

**yard·man** (yärd′man′, -mən) *n., pl.* **-men′** (-men′, -mən) a person who works in a yard

**yard′stick′** *n.* **1** a graduated measuring stick one yard long **2** any standard used in judging, etc.

**yar·mul·ke** (yär′məl kə, yä′-) *n.* ⟦Yiddish < Pol⟧ a skullcap traditionally worn by Jewish men, as at prayer: also **yar′mel·ke**

**yarn** (yärn) *n.* ⟦OE *gearn*⟧ **1** fibers of wool, cotton, etc. spun into strands for weaving, knitting, etc. **2** [Inf.] a tale or story

**yat·ter** (yat′ər) [Slang] *vi.* ⟦prob. < YA(K)[2] + (CHA)TTER⟧ to talk idly about trivial things —*n.* idle talk; chatter

**yaw** (yô) *vi.* ⟦ON *jaga*, to sway⟧ **1** to swing back and forth across its course, as a ship does when pushed by high waves **2** to rotate or oscillate about the vertical axis: said of a spacecraft, etc. —*n.* a yawing

**yawl** (yôl) *n.* ⟦< Du *jol*⟧ a small, two-masted sailboat rigged fore-and-aft

**yawn** (yôn) *vi.* ⟦ME *yanen*⟧ **1** to open the mouth wide involuntarily and inhale, as when one is sleepy or bored **2** to open wide —*n.* a yawning

**yaws** (yôz) *n.* ⟦of WInd origin⟧ an infectious skin disease of the tropics

**yay** (yā) *adv.* **1** YEA (*adv.* 1) **2** [Inf.] this; so: often with a gesture indicating size —*interj.* YEA

**Y chromosome** *see* SEX CHROMOSOME

**y·clept** or **y-clept** (ē klept′) *vt.* ⟦<OE *clipian*, to call⟧ [Archaic] called; named: also sp. **y·cleped′**

**yd** *abbrev.* yard(s): also, for the plural, **yds**

**ye**[1] (thə, thi, thē; *now often erroneously or facetiously* yē) *adj., definite article* archaic var. of THE

**ye**[2] (yē) *pron.* ⟦OE *ge*⟧ [Archaic] YOU

**yea** (yā) *adv.* ⟦OE *gea*⟧ **1** yes **2** indeed; truly —*n.* **1** an affirmative vote **2** a person voting in the affirmative —*interj.* [Inf.] hurrah: a shout used in cheering for a team

**yeah** (ya, ye) *adv.* [Inf.] yes

**year** (yir) *n.* ⟦OE *gear*⟧ **1** a period of 365 days (366 days in leap year), divided into 12 months beginning Jan. 1 **2** the period (365 days, 5 hours, 48 minutes, and 46 seconds) of one revolution of the earth around the sun: also **solar year 3** a period of 12 calendar months reckoned from any date **4** an annual period of less than 365 days *[a school year]* **5** *[pl.] a)* age *[old for his years] b)* a long time *[years* ago] —**year after year** every year

**year′book′** *n.* an annual book; specif., *a)* a book giving data of the preceding year *b)* a publication of the graduating class of a school or college

**year′ling** *n.* an animal in its second year

**year′ly** *adj.* **1** done, happening, appearing, etc. once a year, or every year *[a yearly event]* **2** of a year, or of each year —*adv.* every year

**yearn** (yurn) *vi.* ⟦< OE *georn*, eager⟧ to be filled with longing or desire —**yearn′ing** *n.*

**year′-round′** *adj.* open, in use, operating, etc. throughout the year

**yea′say′er** *n.* one having a positive attitude toward life

**yeast** (yēst) *n.* ⟦OE *gist*⟧ **1** a moist, yellowish mass of certain fungi that cause fermentation: used in making beer, etc., and as leavening in baking **2** yeast dried in flakes or granules or compressed into cakes **3** ferment; agitation

**yeast′y** *adj.* **-i·er, -i·est 1** of, like, or containing yeast **2** in a ferment; restless

**yegg** (yeg) *n.* ⟦< ?⟧ [Old Slang] a burglar, etc.

**yell** (yel) *vi., vt.* ⟦OE *giellan*⟧ to cry out loudly; scream —*n.* **1** a loud outcry **2** a rhythmic cheer in unison

**yel·low** (yel′ō) *adj.* ⟦OE *geolu*⟧ **1** of the color of ripe lemons **2** having a somewhat yellow skin **3** [Inf.] cowardly **4** sensational: said as of a newspaper —*n.* **1** a yellow color **2** an egg yolk —*vi.* to become yellow —**yel′low·ish** *adj.*

**yellow fever** an infectious tropical disease caused by a virus transmitted by the bite of a certain mosquito

**yellow jacket** a wasp or hornet having bright-yellow markings

**Yel′low·knife′** capital of Northwest Territories, Canada: pop. 17,000

**Yellow River** HUANG HE

**Yellow Sea** arm of the East China Sea, between China & Korea

**yelp** (yelp) *vi.* ⟦OE *gielpan*, to boast⟧ to utter a short, sharp cry or bark, as a dog does —*n.* a short, sharp cry or bark

**Yel·tsin** (yelt'sin), **Bor·is** (bôr'is) 1931- ; president of Russia (1990-99)

**Yem·en** (yem'ən) country in S Arabia, formed (1990) by the merger of the Yemen Arab Republic and a country directly east of it, the **People's Democratic Republic of Yemen**: 214,287 sq. mi.; pop. 13,000,000 —**Yem'en·ite'** or **Yem'e·ni** (-ə nē) *adj., n.*

**yen**[1] (yen) *n., pl.* **yen** 〚Jpn〛 the monetary unit of Japan

**yen**[2] (yen) *n.* 〚prob. < Chin *yan*, opium〛 [Inf.] a strong longing or desire

**yeo·man** (yō'mən) *n., pl.* **-men** (-mən) 〚ME *yeman*〛 **1** [Brit. Historical] a freeholder of a class below the gentry **2** *U.S. Navy* a petty officer assigned to clerical duty

**yeo'man·ry** *n.* yeomen collectively

**yes** (yes) *adv.* 〚OE *gese*〛 **1** aye; yea; it is so: expressing agreement, consent, etc. **2** not only that, but more [ready, yes, eager to help] —*n., pl.* **yes'es** an act of saying *yes*; an affirmative reply, vote, etc. —*vt., vi.* **yessed, yes'sing** to say *yes* (to)

**ye·shi·va** (yə shē'və; *Heb* ye shē vä') *n., pl.* **-vas** or Heb, **-vot'** (-vōt') 〚Heb, lit., act of sitting〛 a Jewish school combining religious and secular studies

**yes man** [Slang] one who is always approving what is said by a superior

**yes·ter·day** (yes'tər dā') *n.* 〚OE *geostran*, yesterday + *dæg*, day〛 **1** the day before today **2** a recent day or time —*adv.* **1** on the day before today **2** recently

**yes'ter·year'** (-yir') *n., adv.* **1** last year **2** (in) past years

**yet** (yet) *adv.* 〚OE *giet*〛 **1** up to now; thus far [he hasn't gone *yet*] **2** at the present time; now [we can't go just *yet*] **3** still [there is *yet* a chance] **4** in addition; even [he was *yet* more kind] **5** nevertheless [she's kind, *yet* shy] —*conj.* but [she seems well, *yet* she is ill] —**as yet** up to now

**yew** (yōō) *n.* 〚OE *iw*〛 **1** an evergreen tree with flattened needle leaves **2** its wood

**Yid·dish** (yid'ish) *n.* 〚< Ger *jüdisch*, < L *Judaeus*, Jew〛 a language derived from medieval High German, written in the Hebrew alphabet and spoken esp. by East European Jews

**yield** (yēld) *vt.* 〚OE *gieldan*, to pay〛 **1** to produce as a crop, result, profit, etc. **2** to surrender **3** to concede —*vi.* **1** to produce **2** to surrender **3** to give way to physical force **4** to lose precedence, etc.: often with *to* —*n.* the amount yielded

**yield'ing** *adj.* **1** flexible **2** submissive

**yin** (yin) *n.* 〚Chin〛 in Chinese philosophy, the feminine force or principle in the universe: cf. YANG

**yip** (yip) *n.* 〚echoic〛 [Inf.] a yelp, or bark —*vi.* **yipped, yip'ping** [Inf.] to yelp, or bark

**YMCA** *abbrev.* Young Men's Christian Association

**yo** (yō) *interj.* [Inf.] used as to gain attention, greet someone, emphasize a remark, etc.

**yo·del** (yōd''l) *vt., vi.* **-deled** or **-delled, -del·ing** or **-del·ling** 〚Ger *jodeln*〛 to sing with abrupt alternating changes to the falsetto —*n.* a yodeling

**yo·ga** (yō'gə) *n.* 〚Sans, union〛 a mystic and ascetic Hindu discipline for achieving union with the supreme spirit through meditation, prescribed postures, controlled breathing, etc.

**yo·gi** (yō'gē) *n., pl.* **-gis** one who practices yoga: also **yo'gin** (-gin)

**yo·gurt** (yō'gərt) *n.* 〚Turk *yoğurt*〛 a thick, somewhat solid food made from fermented milk: also **yo'ghurt**

**yoke** (yōk) *n.* 〚OE *geoc*〛 **1** a wooden frame for harnessing together a pair of oxen, etc. **2** such a pair harnessed together **3** bondage; servitude **4** anything like a yoke, as something that binds or unites, or a part of a garment fitted to the shoulders or hips as a support for the gathered parts below —*vt.* **yoked, yok'ing 1** to harness (an animal) to (a plow, etc.) **2** to join together

**yo·kel** (yō'kəl) *n.* a person living in a rural area; bumpkin: a contemptuous term

**Yo·ko·ha·ma** (yō'kə hä'mə) seaport in S Honshu, Japan: pop. 2,774,000

**yolk** (yōk) *n.* 〚OE *geolca*〛 the yellow, principal substance of an egg

**Yom Kip·pur** (yäm' ki poor') the Day of Atonement: a major Jewish holiday and a day of fasting

**yon** (yän) *adj., adv.* 〚OE *geon*〛 [Now Chiefly Dial.] yonder

**yon·der** (yän'dər) *adj., adv.* 〚ME〛 (being) at or in that (specified or relatively distant) place; over there

**Yon·kers** (yäŋ'kərz) city in SE New York: pop. 188,000

**yoo-hoo** (yōō'hōō') *interj., n.* (a shout or call) used to attract someone's attention

**yore** (yôr) *adv.* 〚OE *geara*〛 [Obs.] long ago —**of yore** formerly

**you** (yōō) *pron., pl.* **you** 〚OE *eow* < *ge*, YE[2]〛 **1** the person or persons spoken to **2** a person or people generally; one [*you* can never tell]

**young** (yuŋ) *adj.* **young'er** (-gər), **young'est** (-gəst) 〚OE *geong*〛 **1** being in an early period of life or growth **2** youthful; fresh; vigorous **3** in an early stage **4** inexperienced; immature —*n.* **1** young people: often with *the* **2** young offspring — **with young** pregnant —**young'ish** *adj.*

**young adult** an age group, from about 12 to about 18 years of age, used as a reader category as in libraries

**young blood 1** young people; youth **2** youthful strength, vigor, etc.

**young'ster** *n.* a child or youth

**your** (yoor; *often* yôr) *poss. pronominal adj.* 〚OE *eower*〛 of, belonging to, or done by you: also used before some titles [*Your* Honor]

**you're** (yoor, yōōr) *contr.* you are

**yours** (yoorz; *often* yōrz) *pron.* that or those belonging to you: possessive form of YOU [that book is *yours; yours* are better]

**your·self** (yoor self', yər-) *pron., pl.* **-selves'** (-selvz') a form of YOU, used as an intensive [you said so *yourself*], as a reflexive [you hurt *yourself*], or with the meaning "your true self" [you are not *yourself* today]

**yours truly 1** a phrase used in ending a letter **2** [Inf.] I or me

**youth** (yōōth) *n., pl.* **youths** (yōō*th*z, yōōths) 〚OE *geoguthe*〛 **1** the state or quality of being young **2** the period of adolescence **3** an early stage of growth or existence **4** young people collectively **5** a young person; esp., a young man

**youth'ful** *adj.* **1** young; not yet old or mature **2** of, like, or fit for youth **3** fresh; vigorous **4** new; early —**youth'ful·ly** *adv.* —**youth'ful·ness** *n.*

**yowl** (youl) *vi., n.* 〚< ON *gaula*〛 howl or wail

**yo-yo** (yō'yō') *n., pl.* **yo'-yos'** 〚< ?〛 **1** a spool-like toy reeled up and let down by a string **2** [Slang] a person regarded as stupid, inept, etc. —*vi.* [Inf.] to move up and down; fluctuate

**yr** *abbrev.* **1** year(s) **2** your

**yrs** *abbrev.* **1** years **2** yours

**YT** Yukon Territory

**yt·tri·um** (i'trē əm) *n.* a rare, silvery, metallic chemical element: used in color TV tubes, etc.

**Yu·ca·tán** or **Yu·ca·tan** (yōō'kə tan') state of Mexico, on a peninsula separating the Gulf of Mexico from the Caribbean: 15,189 sq. mi.; pop. 1,363,000

**yuc·ca** (yuk'ə) *n.* 〚< AmSp *yuca*〛 **1** a desert plant with stiff leaves and white flowers **2** its flower

**yuck**[1] (yuk) *n., vi. alt. sp.* of YUK

**yuck**[2] (yuk) [Slang] *n.* something unpleasant, disgusting, etc. —*interj.* used to express distaste, disgust, etc. —**yuck'y, -i·er, -i·est,** *adj.*

**Yu·go·slav·i·a** (yōō'gō slä'vē ə, -gə-) country in the NW Balkan Peninsula: four republics separated from it in 1991: 39,449 sq. mi.; pop. 10,394,000 —**Yu'go·slav'** or **Yu'go·sla'vi·an** *adj., n.*

**yuk** (yuk) *n.* ⟦echoic⟧ [Slang] a loud laugh of amusement, or something causing such a laugh —*vi.* **yukked, yuk′king** [Slang] to laugh loudly

**Yu·kon** (yo͞o′kän′) territory of NW Canada, east of Alaska: 186,661 sq. mi.; pop. 31,000; cap. Whitehorse: abbrev. **YT**: usually used with *the*: in full **Yukon Territory**

**yule** (yo͞ol) *n.* ⟦OE *geol*⟧ [*often* Y-] Christmas or the Christmas season

**yule′tide′** (-tīd′) *n.* [*often* Y-] the Christmas season

**yum·my** (yum′ē) *adj.* **-mi·er, -mi·est** [Inf.] very tasty; delectable

**yup** (yup) *adv.* [Slang] yes: an affirmative reply

**yup·pie** (yup′ē) *n.* ⟦< *y(oung) u(rban) p(rofessional)*⟧ [Inf.] a young professional regarded as affluent, ambitious, materialistic, etc.

**YWCA** *abbrev.* Young Women's Christian Association

# Z

**z** or **Z** (zē; *Brit* zed) *n., pl.* **z's, Z's** the 26th and last letter of the English alphabet

**zaf·tig** (zäf′tig) *adj.* ⟦< Yiddish *zaft*, juice⟧ [Slang] having a full, shapely figure: said of a woman

**Za·ire** or **Za·ïre** (zä ir′) **1** CONGO (River) **2** *former name for Democratic Republic of the Congo*: see CONGO

**Zam·bi·a** (zam′bē ə) country in S Africa: 290,586 sq. mi.; pop. 7,818,000

**za·ny** (zā′nē) *n., pl.* **-nies** ⟦< It dial. *zanni*, < *Giovanni*, John⟧ a silly or foolish person —*adj.* **-ni·er, -ni·est** foolish or crazy —**za′ni·ness** *n.*

**Zan·zi·bar** (zan′zə bär′) island off the E coast of Africa: part of Tanzania

**zap** (zap) *vt., vi.* **zapped, zap′ping** ⟦echoic⟧ [Slang] to move, strike, stun, kill, etc. suddenly and with great speed and force —*interj.* used to signify sudden, swift action or change

**zeal** (zēl) *n.* ⟦< Gr *zēlos*⟧ strong interest or devotion; intense enthusiasm; fervor

**zeal·ot** (zel′ət) *n.* one who shows zeal, esp. fanatic zeal

**zeal·ous** (zel′əs) *adj.* of or showing zeal; fervent — **zeal′ous·ly** *adv.* —**zeal′ous·ness** *n.*

**ze·bra** (zē′brə) *n.* ⟦Port⟧ an African mammal related to the horse and having dark stripes on a white or tawny body

**ze·bu** (zē′byo͞o′) *n.* ⟦Fr *zébu* < ?⟧ a domesticated ox of Asia and Africa

**zed** (zed) *n.* ⟦< Gr *zēta*⟧ [Brit.] the letter Z, z

**zeit·geist** (tsīt′gīst′) *n.* ⟦Ger, time spirit⟧ the trend of thought and feeling in a period

**Zen** (zen) *n.* ⟦Jpn ult. < Sans *dhyāna*, thinking⟧ a variety of Buddhism in which enlightenment is sought through introspection and intuition

**ze·nith** (zē′nith) *n.* ⟦ult. < L *semita*, path⟧ **1** the point in the sky directly overhead **2** the highest point

**zeph·yr** (zef′ər) *n.* ⟦< Gr *zephyros*⟧ a breeze

**zep·pe·lin** (zep′ə lin, zep′lin) *n.* ⟦after Count F. von *Zeppelin* (1838-1917), its Ger designer⟧ [*often* Z-] a type of rigid airship designed around 1900

**ze·ro** (zir′ō, zē′rō) *n., pl.* **-ros** or **-roes** ⟦< Ar *ṣifr*, cipher⟧ **1** the symbol 0, representing the absence of any quantity or magnitude; cipher; naught **2** the point, marked 0, from which quantities are reckoned on a graduated scale **3** nothing **4** the lowest point —*adj.* of or at zero —**zero in on** to concentrate attention on; focus on

**zero hour 1** the time set for beginning an attack, etc. **2** any crucial moment

**zero (population) growth** a condition of equilibrium in a given population, in which the birthrate equals the death rate

**ze′ro-sum′** (-sum′) *adj.* of or being a situation in which a gain for one must result in a loss for another or others

**zest** (zest) *n.* ⟦Fr *zeste*, orange peel⟧ **1** a thin piece of orange or lemon peel used as flavoring **2** stimulating quality **3** keen enjoyment [a *zest* for life] —**zest′ful** *adj.*

**ze·ta** (zāt′ə) *n.* the sixth letter of the Greek alphabet (Z, ζ)

**Zeus** (zo͞os, zyo͞os) *n. Gr. Myth.* the chief deity

**zig·gu·rat** (zig′o͞o rat′) *n.* ⟦< Assyrian *ziqqurratu*⟧ an ancient Assyrian or Babylonian temple tower in the form of a terraced pyramid

**zig·zag** (zig′zag′) *n.* ⟦Fr⟧ **1** a series of short, sharp angles in alternate directions **2** a design, path, etc. in this form —*adj.* having the form of a zigzag —*adv.* in a zigzag course —*vt., vi.* **-zagged′, -zag′ging** to form or move in a zigzag

**zilch** (zilch) *n.* ⟦nonsense syllable⟧ [Slang] nothing; zero

**zil·lion** (zil′yən) *n.* ⟦< MILLION⟧ [Inf.] a very large, indefinite number

**Zim·ba·bwe** (zim bäb′wā′) country in S Africa, north of South Africa: 150,872 sq. mi.; pop. 10,402,000

**zinc** (ziŋk) *n.* ⟦Ger *zink*⟧ a bluish-white, metallic chemical element, used in alloys, as a protective coating for iron, etc.

**zinc oxide** a white powder used in making rubber articles, cosmetics, ointments, etc.

**zin·fan·del** (zin′fən del′) *n.* ⟦< ?⟧ a dry red wine made chiefly in California

**zing** (ziŋ) *n.* ⟦echoic⟧ [Slang] **1** a shrill, high-pitched sound, as of something moving fast **2** zest, vigor, etc.

**zing′er** *n.* [Slang] **1** a clever, witty remark **2** a sharp, usually critical remark

**zin·ni·a** (zin′ē ə, zin′yə) *n.* ⟦after J. G. *Zinn* (1727-59), Ger botanist⟧ a plant having colorful composite flowers

**Zi·on**[1] (zī′ən) *n.* ⟦< fol.⟧ **1** the Jewish people **2** heaven

**Zi·on**[2] (zī′ən) **1** a hill in Jerusalem, site of Solomon's Temple **2** Jerusalem **3** Israel

**Zi′on·ism′** *n.* a movement formerly for reestablishing, now for supporting, the state of Israel — **Zi′on·ist** *n., adj.*

**zip** (zip) *n.* ⟦echoic⟧ **1** a short, sharp hissing or whizzing sound **2** [Inf.] energy; vigor —*vi.* **zipped, zip′ping 1** to make, or move with, a zip **2** [Inf.] to move with speed —*vt.* to fasten with a zipper

**ZIP Code** (zip) ⟦*Z(one) I(mprovement) P(lan)*⟧ *trademark* for a system of code numbers assigned by the postal service: each code designates a delivery area —[*usually* **zip c-**] such a code number, containing five or nine digits

**zip·per** (zip′ər) *n.* a device used to fasten and unfasten two edges of material, as on clothing: it consists of two rows of interlocking tabs worked by a sliding part

**zip′py** *adj.* **-pi·er, -pi·est** [Inf.] full of energy; brisk

**zir·con** (zur′kän′) *n.* ⟦ult. < Pers *zar*, gold⟧ a crystalline silicate mineral, used as a gem

**zir·co·ni·um** (zər kō′nē əm) *n.* a ductile, metallic chemical element used in alloys, ceramics, etc.

**zit** (zit) *n.* [Slang] a pimple, esp. one on the face

**zith·er** (zith′ər, zith′-) *n.* ⟦< Gr *kithara*, lute⟧ any of various musical instruments with strings stretched across a flat soundboard and plucked, bowed, struck with mallets, etc., as the dulcimer

**Zn** *Chem. symbol* for zinc

**zo·di·ac** (zō′dē ak′) *n.* ⟦< Gr *zōdiakos* (*kyklos*), (circle) of animals⟧ **1** an imaginary belt across the sky extending on either side of the apparent path of the sun and divided into twelve equal parts, or signs, named for constellations 2 a diagram representing this —**zo·di·a·cal** (-dī′ə kəl) *adj.*

**zom·bie** (zäm′bē) *n.* ⟦of Afr orig.⟧ 1 in folklore, an animated corpse 2 [Slang] a person who is listless, machine-like, etc. Also **zom′bi**

**zone** (zōn) *n.* ⟦Fr < Gr *zōnē*⟧ 1 an encircling band, stripe, etc. 2 any of the five great latitudinal divisions of the earth's surface: see TORRID ZONE, TEMPERATE ZONE, and FRIGID ZONE 3 any area with reference to a specified use or restriction [a canal *zone*, war *zone*] —*vt.* **zoned, zon′ing** to mark off into zones —**in the** (or **a**) **zone** [Inf.] in a state producing high achievement, seemingly beyond explanation —**zon′al** *adj.*

**zonked** (zôŋkt, zäŋkt) *adj.* [Slang] 1 highly intoxicated or under the influence of a drug 2 exhausted

**zoo** (zōō) *n.* ⟦< zoo(*logical garden*)⟧ 1 a place where wild animals are kept for public showing 2 [Slang] a place of confusion, disorder, etc.

**zoo-** ⟦< Gr *zōion*, animal⟧ *combining form* animal(s) [*zoology*]

**zo·ol·o·gy** (zō äl′ə jē) *n.* ⟦ModL *zoologia*: see prec. & -LOGY⟧ the science that deals with animals and animal life —**zo′o·log′i·cal** (-ə läj′i kəl) *adj.* —**zo·ol′o·gist** *n.*

**zoom** (zōōm) *vi.* ⟦echoic⟧ 1 to make a loud, low-pitched, buzzing sound 2 to climb in an airplane suddenly and sharply 3 to move speedily upward or forward 4 to focus with a zoom lens —*vt.* to cause to zoom —*n.* a zooming

**zoom lens** a system of lenses, as in a film or TV camera, that can be rapidly adjusted for close-up or distant shots while keeping the image in focus

**zo·o·phyte** (zō′ə fīt′) *n.* ⟦ult. < Gr *zōion*, an animal + *phyton*, a plant⟧ any animal, as a coral or sponge, that looks and grows somewhat like a plant —**zo·o·phyt′ic** (-fit′ik) *adj.*

**Zo·ro·as·ter** (zō′rō as′tər) *c.* 6th or 7th c. B.C.; Pers. founder of Zoroastrianism

**Zo·ro·as·tri·an·ism** (zō′rō as′trē ən iz′əm) *n.* the religion of the ancient Persians before Islam

**Zr** *Chem. symbol for* zirconium

**zuc·chi·ni** (zōō kē′nē) *n., pl.* **-ni** or **-nis** ⟦It⟧ a summer squash that looks like a cucumber

**Zu·lu** (zōō′lōō) *n.* 1 *pl.* **-lus** or **-lu** a member of a people living in South Africa 2 the language of this people —*adj.* of the Zulus or their language, etc.

**Zu·ni** (zōō′nē) *n.* 1 *pl.* **-nis** or **-ni** a member of a pueblo-dwelling North American Indian people of W New Mexico 2 the language of this people Also, formerly, **Zu·ñi** (zōō′nyē)

**Zur·ich** (zoor′ik) city in N Switzerland: pop. 353,000

**zwie·back** (swē′bak′, swī′-) *n.* ⟦Ger < *zwie-*, twice + *backen*, to bake⟧ a kind of biscuit that is sliced and toasted after baking

**zy·de·co** (zī′də kō′) *n.* ⟦< ?⟧ a heavily syncopated dance music of S Louisiana, containing elements of blues, white Cajun music, etc.

**zy·gote** (zī′gōt′) *n.* ⟦< Gr *zygon*, a yoke⟧ a cell formed by the union of male and female gametes

**zymo-** ⟦< Gr *zymē*, a leaven⟧ *combining form* fermentation: also **zym-**

**zy·mur·gy** (zī′mər jē) *n.* ⟦prec. + -URGY⟧ the chemistry of fermentation, as applied in brewing, etc.

# TABLE OF CONTENTS

Introduction . . . . . . . . . . . . . . . . . . . . . . . . . . . . . . . . . . . . . . . . . . . 564

Basics of English Grammar . . . . . . . . . . . . . . . . . . . . . . . . . . . . . . . . 564

   Parts of Speech . . . . . . . . . . . . . . . . . . . . . . . . . . . . . . . . . . . . . . 564

   Phrases and Clauses . . . . . . . . . . . . . . . . . . . . . . . . . . . . . . . . . . . 565

   The Sentence . . . . . . . . . . . . . . . . . . . . . . . . . . . . . . . . . . . . . . . . 566

      Types of Sentences — Classified by Structure . . . . . . . . . . . . . . . . . 566

      Types of Sentences — Classified by Function . . . . . . . . . . . . . . . . . 567

      Parts of a Sentence . . . . . . . . . . . . . . . . . . . . . . . . . . . . . . . . . . 567

      Sentence Fragments . . . . . . . . . . . . . . . . . . . . . . . . . . . . . . . . . . 572

Details of Writing . . . . . . . . . . . . . . . . . . . . . . . . . . . . . . . . . . . . . . . 573

   Nouns and Pronouns . . . . . . . . . . . . . . . . . . . . . . . . . . . . . . . . . . . 573

   Verbs . . . . . . . . . . . . . . . . . . . . . . . . . . . . . . . . . . . . . . . . . . . . . 583

   Principal Parts of Irregular and Troublesome Verbs . . . . . . . . . . . . . . 589

   Modifiers . . . . . . . . . . . . . . . . . . . . . . . . . . . . . . . . . . . . . . . . . . . 594

   Connectives . . . . . . . . . . . . . . . . . . . . . . . . . . . . . . . . . . . . . . . . . 602

   Agreement, Reference, and Parallelism . . . . . . . . . . . . . . . . . . . . . . 607

   Gender-Inclusive Writing . . . . . . . . . . . . . . . . . . . . . . . . . . . . . . . . 617

Mechanics . . . . . . . . . . . . . . . . . . . . . . . . . . . . . . . . . . . . . . . . . . . . 620

   Abbreviations . . . . . . . . . . . . . . . . . . . . . . . . . . . . . . . . . . . . . . . . 620

   Abbreviations for U.S. States and Canadian Provinces . . . . . . . . . . . . 623

   Capitalization . . . . . . . . . . . . . . . . . . . . . . . . . . . . . . . . . . . . . . . . 625

   Compound Words . . . . . . . . . . . . . . . . . . . . . . . . . . . . . . . . . . . . . 629

   Italics . . . . . . . . . . . . . . . . . . . . . . . . . . . . . . . . . . . . . . . . . . . . . 630

   Numbers . . . . . . . . . . . . . . . . . . . . . . . . . . . . . . . . . . . . . . . . . . . 631

   Plurals . . . . . . . . . . . . . . . . . . . . . . . . . . . . . . . . . . . . . . . . . . . . 635

   Punctuation . . . . . . . . . . . . . . . . . . . . . . . . . . . . . . . . . . . . . . . . . 637

   Spelling Rules . . . . . . . . . . . . . . . . . . . . . . . . . . . . . . . . . . . . . . . 651

Manuscript Form . . . . . . . . . . . . . . . . . . . . . . . . . . . . . . . . . . . . . . . 653

   Manuscript Preparation . . . . . . . . . . . . . . . . . . . . . . . . . . . . . . . . . 653

   Source Documentation . . . . . . . . . . . . . . . . . . . . . . . . . . . . . . . . . 653

Usage — Troublesome Words . . . . . . . . . . . . . . . . . . . . . . . . . . . . . . . 657

Checklist: Writing Problems to Avoid . . . . . . . . . . . . . . . . . . . . . . . . . . 676

# INTRODUCTION

While a dictionary's purpose is to record and provide information on prevailing usage in a given language, a style guide offers advice on writing the language clearly and effectively. The goal of good writing is the effective communication of ideas and feelings. Never allow a reader to be distracted from *what you say* by *the way you say it*. This Style Guide can help a writer to avoid many types of potential barriers to effective communication, whether actual errors in grammar or usage, or simply a lack of clarity or precision. The goal is not just to "be right," but to be read and understood.

# BASICS OF ENGLISH GRAMMAR

First, let's briefly review some basics of English grammar and its terminology.

## Parts of Speech

Traditional English grammar recognizes eight basic types of words, or **parts of speech**. Some words function as more than one part of speech.

### Noun

A noun is a word naming a person, place, thing, action, or quality.

> woman, Shakespeare, park, Paris, desk, running, truth

### Pronoun

A pronoun is a word used in place of a noun.

> I, us, who, that, these, each, himself, anybody, no one

### Verb

A verb is a word or group of words expressing action, existence, or occurrence. The verb is the main element in the predicate of a sentence.

> write, kicks, ran, can see, will be helped, is going, must, becomes

### Adjective

An adjective is a word that modifies the meaning of a noun or pronoun (1) by describing qualities of the person or thing named, (2) by stating limits or quantity, or (3) by distinguishing that person or thing from others.

> *healthy* children, *brighter* skies, *ten* days, *our* town, *Pacific* Ocean

### Adverb

An adverb is a word that modifies a verb, an adjective, or another adverb, by expressing time, place, manner, degree, or cause.

> come *soon*, go *there*, write *legibly*, *very* slow; *therefore*, I will succeed

## Preposition

A preposition is a word or group of words that is used to connect a noun or pronoun to some other word in the sentence.

>     at, in, by, from, toward, in front of

## Conjunction

A conjunction is a word or group of words that is used to join words, phrases, or clauses.

>     and, but, nor, since, although, while, as soon as

## Interjection

An interjection is a word, especially an exclamation, that is inserted into a sentence, conversation, or passage but is not connected to it grammatically.

>     Ah!
>     Yes,
>     Shh!
>     Meow!
>     Adios.

# Phrases and Clauses

Phrases and clauses are groups of grammatically related words functioning as a single unit in a sentence.

## Phrase

A phrase is a group of grammatically related words *without a subject or predicate*. A phrase can function as a *noun, adjective,* or *adverb*. Phrases (some shown in italics for clarity) are classified as

### Prepositional:

>     with best wishes, in the mail, out of the house, instead of you

### Participial:

>     the woman *making bread*
>     covered with dust

### Gerund:

>     *Singing in the choir* is satisfying.

### Infinitive:

>     to go, to have a good time, to be famous, to be done

## Clause

A clause is a group of grammatically related words *containing both a subject and a predicate.*

An **independent** (or **main**) **clause** makes a complete statement and is not introduced by any subordinating word. When it stands alone, it is a simple sentence.

> We will return the favor.

A **dependent** (or **subordinate**) **clause** cannot make a complete statement, usually because it is introduced by a subordinating word, and cannot stand alone as a simple sentence.

Based on how it functions in a sentence, a dependent clause is classified as an adjective clause (modifying a noun or pronoun), an adverb clause (modifying a verb, adjective, or adverb), or a noun clause.

## Adjective Clause:

> The man *who came to dinner* ate everything in sight.

## Adverb Clause:

> *While we lounged by the fire with our hot chocolate,* the snowstorm obliterated the road home.

## Noun Clause:

> *Whoever chairs the meeting* will be able to answer your questions.

# The Sentence

A book, article, essay, letter, or other piece of writing arrives before the reader's eyes in paragraphs, the most readily visible unit of prose. Clear, logical paragraph structure is crucial to clear communication, but is not something a writer can learn from a style guide. The unit that this Guide focuses on is the *sentence*, the building block of the paragraph.

## Types of Sentences — Classified by Structure

### Simple Sentence

A simple sentence contains only one independent clause. But this does not mean that it must be short. It may include many phrases, a compound subject or predicate, and/or a number of modifiers.

> The prisoner escaped.
> George and Sam went ahead with their own selfish plans and ruined everyone else's chances.

### Compound Sentence

A compound sentence contains two or more *independent* clauses, each of which could be written as a simple sentence. A coordinating conjunction or a semicolon connects the clauses.

> You may want to vacation in France, or you may prefer Italy instead.
> I came; I looked around; I took over.

### Complex Sentence

A complex sentence contains one independent clause and one or more dependent clauses.

> We looked for a different route because the freeway was jammed.

## Compound-Complex Sentence

A compound-complex sentence contains two or more independent clauses and one or more dependent clauses.

> By the time we arrived, they had eaten all the food on the table, and they left us to search through the fridge.

# Types of Sentences — Classified by Function

## Declarative Sentence

A declarative sentence makes a statement.

> I'm hungry.
> Yesterday, all my troubles seemed so far away.

## Interrogative Sentence

An interrogative sentence asks a question.

> Do you know of a good restaurant nearby?

## Imperative Sentence

An imperative sentence expresses a command or a polite request.

> (Please) open the door.
> Let's eat!

## Exclamatory Sentence

An exclamation expresses strong feeling.

> I couldn't care less!
> Let's eat!

# Parts of a Sentence

The basic parts of a sentence are the **subject** and the **predicate**. The subject is the word or group of words naming the entity about which the sentence makes a statement. The predicate contains the verb that is central to the statement made about the subject. Various other words and word groups function as **modifiers** and **connectives** within the subject, the predicate, or the sentence as a whole.

Because structure problems are a major cause of miscommunication, it is important to understand, and be able to identify, the parts of the sentence in order to make them fit together properly.

## Subject

The subject of a sentence is the word or group of words that names the person, place, thing, or idea about which the sentence makes a statement. The subject is most often a noun or a personal pronoun.

> The *director* called the meeting for 3:00. (noun)
> *She* wants everybody to attend. (personal pronoun)

The demonstrative, interrogative, and indefinite *pronouns* may also function as the subject.

> *That* is going to be a difficult task. (demonstrative)
> *Who* are you? (interrogative)
> *Everyone* wants you to succeed. (indefinite)

A *phrase* serving as a noun may be the subject.

> *Adopting that kitten* was the smartest thing he ever did.
> *To learn as many languages as possible* is his goal.

An entire *clause* may be used as the subject.

> *Whoever answers the telephone* will take the message for you.
> *What you don't know* can hurt you.

Two **verbals**, the **gerund** and the **infinitive**, may also be the subject of a sentence. (A *verbal* is a word formed from a verb but functioning as a noun, adjective, or adverb. See the fuller discussion of verbals under PREDICATE, below.)

> *Walking* is good exercise. (gerund)
> *To run* is more tiring than to walk. (infinitive)

The subject may be modified by adjectives, phrases, or clauses.

See the section on NOUNS AND PRONOUNS later in this Guide.

## Predicate

The predicate makes a statement about the subject of the sentence. It contains the **verb**, which is central to this statement, and all elements that modify the verb.

### Verbs

The verb indicates what the subject does (**active** verb):

> A lexicographer *edits* dictionaries.

what is done to the subject (**passive** verb):

> Dictionaries *are edited* by lexicographers.

or what else the subject is, or in what way the subject can be described (**linking** verb):

> A dictionary *is* a book of words and definitions.
> A dictionary *can be* helpful to both readers and writers.

### Properties of Verbs

The properties of a verb are **number, person, tense, mood**, and **voice**. To indicate these properties, the verb itself changes form, or other verb forms, called **auxiliary verbs**, are added to the main verb.

**Number** indicates whether the verb is **singular** or **plural**.

**Person** indicates whether the **first person** (*I, we*), **second person** (*you*), or **third person** (*he, she, it, they*) is performing the action expressed by the verb. In English, only the third person singular, present tense, of a verb changes form to indicate person.

A verb and its subject must **agree**, or match, in number and person. This basic matter of agreement, so essential to the writing of clear sentences, is discussed in detail in the section on AGREEMENT, REFERENCE, AND PARALLELISM.

See the section on VERBS later in this Guide for more detail on number and person and for a discussion of tense, mood, and voice.

## *Verbals*

One other topic involving verbs gets a brief mention here for reference in the sections that follow.

A **verbal** is a **nonfinite** verb (one that does not change form to show its function in the sentence) that can function — in either the subject or the predicate of a sentence — as a noun, an adjective, or an adverb, or can be used with another verb in the sentence. A nonfinite verb can never stand as the only verb in a sentence.

There are three types of verbals: the **infinitive**, the **participles** (present and past), and the **gerund**.

An **infinitive** is preceded by the word *to*. It may function as a noun, an adjective, or an adverb.

> I like *to swim.*
> A book *to take* to the beach is what she wants.
> He went *to play* golf.

A **participle** functions as a verb or an adjective. There are two kinds of participles.

The **present participle** always ends in *-ing.*

> *Running* on the wet sidewalk, Susie slipped and fell.
> Susie was *running,* and she slipped and fell.
> The reporter gave a *running* account of every mistake the Governor made on his goodwill tour.

The **past participle** may be **regular** in form:

> We suddenly realized that we had *talked* all night.

or **irregular**:

> I've *seen* this movie before; let's leave.
> The *spoken* word, in the form of a sermon, can be more convincing than a *written* essay.

A **gerund** always ends in *-ing.* It functions as a noun.

> Charlie enjoys *running.*
> *Dancing* is fun for people without two left feet.

## The Remainder of the Predicate

A verb may be modified by one or more adverbs or by a group of words functioning as an adverb.

But for most types of verbs, the predicate is incomplete without a specific following word or phrase. Verbs may be classified by the way they structure the predicate: whether or not another word or construction follows the verb, and what form such a construction takes.

A **transitive** verb takes a **direct object**:

> He *hit* the *ball.*

It may also have an **indirect object** or an **object complement.**

An **intransitive** verb takes *no* direct object:

> She *fell* down.

A **linking** verb takes either a **predicate nominative**:

> Jim *is captain.*

or a **predicate adjective**:

> Jim *seems strong*.

Here are some examples of these sentence elements.

(1) Direct object

> He ate the *enchiladas*. (noun)
> We are trying to launch *a probe to Jupiter*. (phrase)
> Give me *whatever information you have*. (clause)

(2) Indirect object

> He gave *her* the tickets. (The pronoun *her* is the indirect object; *tickets* is the direct object.)

This sentence is the equivalent of

> He gave the tickets *to her*.
> Give *whoever answers the door* the bouquet of flowers. (The clause is the indirect object.)

Note that the form of the pronoun *whoever* matches its function as subject of the inserted clause; it does not change to *whomever* just because it follows the verb.

> David did *Jerry* a big favor. (*Jerry* is the indirect object.)

This sentence is the equivalent of

> David did a favor *for Jerry*.

(3) Object Complement

Sometimes an additional word or phrase follows the direct object and describes it or gives it a new name.

> We thought him *insane* to take the risk.
> They don't call me *The Human Bulldozer* for nothing.

(4) Predicate nominative

The predicate nominative is also called the **predicate noun**. It follows a linking verb and renames the subject. It can be a noun, a pronoun, a verbal, a phrase, or a clause.

> He is *chair* of the committee.
> They thought the author was *you*.
> My favorite exercise is *swimming*.
> The purpose of this experiment is *to test the new engine*.
> The next president should be *whoever is best qualified*.

(5) Predicate adjective

A predicate adjective is an adjective (or phrase) that appears in the predicate and modifies the subject. A predicate adjective occurs only after a linking verb.

> The flower smells *sweet*.
> The meeting Tuesday will be on that *subject*.
> The new material was *over my head*.
> She seems *enthusiastic* about our idea.

## Modifiers

A modifier is a single word, a phrase, or a clause that is used to limit, define, or describe some element of the sentence, or the sentence as a whole. For more on modifiers and modification, see the section that follows.

An **adjective** describes or limits the meaning of a noun or pronoun.

> The *wily* raccoon was caught in the *baited* trap and taken to a veterinarian for *medical* tests.
> The statistics on *juvenile crime* are alarming. (phrase)
> The report *that the committee submitted* is being studied. (clause)

An **adverb** modifies a verb, verbal, adjective, or other adverb, or the sentence as a whole. Adverbs express the concepts *where, how* or *how much, when,* and *why.*

> We will hold the meeting *here.* (where)
> The car accelerated *rapidly.* (how)
> Spending *excessively*, he ran out of funds. (how much)
> Let's eat the lasagna *as soon as it has finished cooking.* (when)
> Pete went downtown *to buy a tie.* (why)

## Connectives

A connective joins one part of a sentence with another and shows the relationship between the parts it connects. **Conjunctions** and **prepositions** are the most important connectives.

(1)   Connectives joining elements of equal rank

**A coordinating conjunction** joins sentence elements of equal grammatical importance — words with words, phrases with phrases, independent clauses with independent clauses. The main coordinating conjunctions are

> and, but, or, nor, for, yet

**Correlative conjunctions** work in pairs to connect sentence elements of equal rank. Each member of a pair of correlative conjunctions must be followed by the same part of speech (for this purpose, nouns and pronouns form one category). The main correlative conjunctions are

> either/or, neither/nor, not only/but also, both/and

> *Either* Jane or *I* will take care of it.

A **conjunctive adverb** connects independent clauses and shows a relationship between them. Although the clause introduced by the conjunctive adverb is grammatically independent, it is *logically* dependent upon the preceding clause for its complete meaning. Some conjunctive adverbs are

> therefore, thus, however, consequently, accordingly, furthermore, moreover, nevertheless

> You have not paid your dues; *however*, you will continue to receive the newsletter for two more months.

For specific information on punctuating sentences containing conjunctive adverbs, see the section on CONNECTIVES later in this Guide.

(2)   Connectives joining elements of unequal rank

A **subordinating conjunction** introduces a dependent clause and joins it to an independent clause. Some subordinating conjunctions are

> before, since, after, as, because, if, unless, until, although, that

We did not know *until* it happened.
We did not know *that* it had happened.

A **relative pronoun** not only introduces a noun or adjective clause but also acts as a pronoun within its own clause. These pronouns include

that, which, who, whom, whatever, whichever, whoever

The salesperson *who* called for an appointment has just arrived.
Tell me the news *that* you just heard.

A small group of **adverbs** can be used to introduce subordinate clauses. They include

how, where, when, while

(3) Prepositions

A preposition shows the relationship between a word that follows it, called its object, and a word before it to which the object is related. Prepositions include

to, of, by, from, between, for, according to, instead of

## Sentence Fragments

A sentence fragment is a grammatically incomplete sentence that is left in a piece of writing, often by accident. Although fragments may lend a poetic or conversational tone, they are not welcome in formal or business writing.

Occasionally, for effect, a writer may leave an incomplete sentence in a piece of writing and not change it to a complete sentence. However, this device should be used very rarely. An essay or letter containing too many sentence fragments suggests to the reader that the writer does not know how to write.

Fragments are of two basic types:

(1) A word or phrase followed by a period:

The scent of lavender.
Going over the river and through the woods.

(2) A dependent clause without an independent clause:

Why he was afraid.
The party we all attended.
What a moose knows that we don't know.

Note that an imperative sentence or an interjection is not a fragment.

Go away.
Hurry up!
Thank you.
Yes.

To fix sentence fragments:

(1) Review the section containing the fragment and recall what you intended to express in that section.

(2) Incorporate the fragment into a complete sentence that contains the thought you originally intended to express and fulfills your intention.

*Not:* Whatever you want to do.
*But:* *We'll do* whatever you want to do.
*Or:* Whatever you want to do *is fine with me.*

In some cases, the full sentence is already there, but has not been put together.

>*Not:* Speaking in a low voice and with hesitation. He gave us the ugly facts.
>
>*But:* Speaking in a low voice and with hesitation, he gave us the ugly facts.

# DETAILS OF WRITING

## Nouns and Pronouns

### Nouns

A noun names a person, place, thing, action, quality, concept, etc. Nouns are classified in several ways.

### Common Nouns and Proper Nouns

A common noun names a member of a group or class of persons, places, or things.

>child, engineer, countryside, peach, dancing, beauty, idealism

A proper noun names a single, specific person, place, or thing. A proper noun is always capitalized. If the name contains more than one word, all of the major words are capitalized.

>Margaret, Mr. Snow, Atlanta, Congress, the Secretary of the Treasury, the Lincoln Memorial

### Concrete Nouns and Abstract Nouns

A concrete noun names a particular or specific member of a group or class.

>apple, *not* food; air, sleet, *not* weather

An abstract noun names a quality, state, or idea.

>beauty, health, fairness

### Count Nouns and Mass Nouns

A count noun names something that can be counted; it can form a plural and can be preceded by *a* or *an* or by a number.

>dog, tree, idea, snowflake

A mass noun names an abstract entity or something that cannot be counted; it is used in a singular grammatical construction but may be singular or plural in form.

>butter, news, molasses, snow

### Collective Nouns

A collective noun names a group or collection of individuals. It is singular in form. The problem of determining the number of the verb to use with a collective noun is discussed in detail in the section AGREEMENT, REFERENCE, AND PARALLELISM.

>committee, jury, task force, family

## Pronouns

A pronoun stands in place of a noun. There are several categories of pronouns; some pronouns have more than one function.

### Personal Pronouns

The personal pronoun shows the **person** (**first, second,** or **third**) of the noun that is referred to by the pronoun. Personal pronouns are troublesome because of their many forms; they change form to indicate **number** (singular or plural), **person**, and **case** (nominative, objective, or possessive).

| | |
|---|---|
| First Person: | I, me, mine  (singular) |
| | we, us, ours  (plural) |
| Second Person: | you, yours (singular and plural) |
| Third Person: | he, him, his (singular) |
| | she, her, hers    " |
| | it, its    " |
| | they, them, theirs (plural) |

Corresponding to these are the **possessive pronominal adjectives**:

> my, your, his, her, its, our, their

### Relative Pronouns

The relative pronoun serves two purposes:  (1) it takes the place of a noun in the clause it introduces, and (2) like a conjunction, it connects its clause with the rest of the sentence.

The relative pronouns are

> who, whom, which, that, what, whoever, whomever, whichever, whatever

The relative pronoun has the same number, person, and case as its antecedent.

### Interrogative Pronouns

The interrogative pronouns are the same in form as the relative pronouns, but different in function. The interrogative pronouns ask a question.

| | | | |
|---|---|---|---|
| who | refers to persons | | |
| whom | " | " | " |
| what | " | " | things |
| which | " | " | persons or things |

The forms *which* and *what* may be used as adjectives.

> which book?
> what time?

### Indefinite Pronouns

Here are some examples of indefinite pronouns. They are singular.

> another, anyone, each, either, everyone, no one, nothing

### Demonstrative Pronouns

The demonstrative pronouns (*this, that, these, those*) point out or refer to a substantive (usually a noun) that has been clearly expressed or just as clearly implied.

*These* are the letters he wants.

These forms may also be used as adjectives.

Bring me *those* letters.

## Reflexive Pronouns

The reflexive pronouns correspond to the personal pronouns.

> myself, ourselves
> yourself, yourselves
> himself, herself, itself, themselves

A reflexive pronoun often appears as the direct object of a verb; its antecedent is the subject of the verb. The subject and object refer to the same person or thing.

I taught *myself* to type.

It can also be the object of a preposition:

> He finished the job by *himself*.
> He was beside *himself* with joy.

the indirect object of a verb:

I bought *myself* a new suit yesterday.

or a predicate nominative (in which case it does not refer to a person's literal self, but to a person's "true or normal self"):

I'm just not *myself* today.

A reflexive pronoun can also function as an **intensifier**, to emphasize or intensify a meaning. It is not set off by commas.

> I *myself* will see that it is done.
> You will take it to her *yourself.*

**Although the reflexive pronoun is used as a predicate nominative, it should *never* be used as a subject.** People often use *myself* in particular in a compound subject — or sometimes a compound object — especially in conversation, perhaps to avoid possible errors involving *I* or *me*. But this misuse of the reflexive will sound almost as unpleasant to many people as, say, "Me and John are going there"; nothing is gained by the substitution. The best thing to do is to get the rules for personal pronouns firmly in mind and use them correctly at all times.

> *Not*: John and myself stayed late and finished the project.
> *But:* John and I stayed late and finished the project.
>
> *Not:* I sent the invitation to Phyllis and yourself last week.
> *But:* I sent the invitation to you and Phyllis last week.

Also avoid using the form *theirselves* for *themselves*.

## Reciprocal Pronouns

The reciprocal pronouns are phrases:

> each other, one another

indicating the relationship between items in a compound subject. Some writers use *each other* for two and *one another* for more than two, but this distinction is becoming blurred.

> We phone *each other* every day.
> The committee members gave *one another* bad advice.

# Case

Case is the property of a noun or pronoun that indicates the function of the word in a sentence, or the way it is related to other parts of the sentence. In *highly inflected* languages such as German and Latin, case is shown mainly through a change in the word's form.

English, however, is not highly inflected. Our language mainly uses word order and prepositions to indicate a word's function in the sentence. So the term case refers to a much narrower set of form changes, most noticeably in pronouns and for one particular function of nouns.

English has three cases: nominative, objective, and possessive.

All nouns and a few pronouns have the same form in the nominative and the objective cases. Their position in the sentence indicates their function. The only source of difficulty with nouns comes in the formation and use of the possessive case.

On the other hand, some pronouns are inflected (that is, they change form) in the nominative and objective cases, as well as in the possessive. Because of this, the case of pronouns can create more difficulties than the case of nouns does.

## Nominative Case

The nominative (or subjective) case is used mainly to name the subject of a verb or the predicate nominative after a linking verb (such as seem, appear, or be).

> *Not:* Either *you* or *me* will be there.
> *But:* Either *you* or *I* will be there.

This sentence is the equivalent of

> Either *you* will be ... or *I* will be ....

### Subject of a Verb in a Main Clause

A noun or pronoun serving as the subject of a verb is in the nominative case. Do not be confused by compound subjects or by opening or intervening words and phrases.

> I was late for work this morning.

Pronouns in compound subjects must be in the same case.

> *Not:* Neither I nor her heard it.
> *But:* Neither *she* nor *I* heard it.

Pronouns in appositives must be in the same case.

> *Not:* The culprits, her and I, were punished.
> *But:* The culprits, *she and I*, were punished.

### Subject of a Relative Clause

A relative pronoun (for example, *who, whoever, which, whichever*) used as the subject of a clause is in the nominative case.

> Give the letter to *whoever* answers the door.
> You'll want to decide *who* goes.

The clause itself may be a subject or an object; however, the case of the relative pronoun depends upon its use *within the clause*.

> *Whoever is selected* must decide immediately.

The pronoun *who* used as the subject of a verb is not affected by a parenthetical expression such as *I think*, *he believes*, or *they say* intervening between the subject and the verb.

> She is the person *who* I think *is best qualified*.
> We asked Susan, *who* we knew *had always been a good judge of character*.
> Ms. Mann is the attorney *who* we suppose *will prepare the brief*.

In each of the above sentences, *who* is the subject of the clause.

In these kinds of sentences, people sometimes have a tendency to identify the relative pronoun as the object of the verb that follows it. Remember to analyze the sentence carefully to understand how the relative clause fits into it.

### Subject of a Clause Introduced by than or as

If the word following *than* or *as* introduces a clause, even if part of the clause is understood, that word must be in the nominative case. But if the word following *than* or *as* does not introduce a clause, it must be in the objective case (see below). To test whether the word should be in the nominative or the objective case, complete the clause.

> He has been here longer than *she*. (than *she has*)
> Mary is a better mathematician than *I*. (than *I am*)
> They were as late as *we* in filing their tax returns. (as *we were*)
> We were seated as promptly as *they*. (as *they were*)

This usage may sound very formal to twenty-first-century ears. In informal conversation, a person would probably use a form in the objective case ("longer than *her*"). But in formal writing, so as not to distract the reader from what one is saying, it is best to use the correct form. To ease the sound of the sentence slightly, it may be simplest to go ahead and complete the sentence explicitly with the verb that is used in the test for function.

> He has been there longer than she *has*.
> They were as late as we *were* in filing their tax returns.

In the following examples, the word following *than* or *as* may be in either the nominative or the objective case, depending on the intended meaning. If there is any chance that the sentence may be misinterpreted because more than one meaning is possible, complete the clause.

> She likes that book better than *I*. (than *I like it*)
> She likes John better than *me*. (than *she likes me*)

> I have known John as long as *she*. (as *she has*)
> I have known John as long as *her*. (as *I have known her*)

### Noun or Pronoun Following a Form of be (the predicate nominative)

A noun or pronoun that follows a form of the verb *be* (except for the infinitive if it has its own subject) must be in the nominative case. (This word is called the **predicate nominative.**) The general rule for this construction is that the word following the verb *be* must be in the same case as the word before the verb. Imagine that the verb *be* has the same meaning as the equal sign (=) in mathematics.

> *Not:* They thought I was *him*.
> *But:* They thought I was *he*. (I = he)

Again, this is the correct pattern for formal writing. In conversation, the first example above would be acceptable to most people.

A reader or speaker may have trouble when one or both of the members of a compound subject or predicate nominative are pronouns. Try this simple test: decide which case would be appropriate if *one* pronoun were the simple subject or predicate nominative, and then use the same case for both.

> The new co-*chairs* are *Beth and I.*

To test, reverse the positions of the parts on either side of the verb:

> *Beth and I* are the new co-*chairs.*

The following example, while grammatically correct, sounds stilted; it probably should be recast to avoid the pronoun as predicate nominative.

> If any one of the free agents is chosen, *it* should be *he.*

To test, reverse positions:

> If any one of the free agents is chosen, *he* should be *it.*

So we know that we are grammatically correct, but, especially in this context, the stilted language may not be appropriate. Possible solutions:

> If any one of the free agents is chosen, it should be Noonan. (use the person's name)
>
> If any one of the free agents is chosen, he should be the one. (restructure the end of the sentence)

The following example would probably be too formal even for a literary gathering.

> The author was thought to be I.

The sentence probably has been structured in this way to place emphasis on the identity of the person involved, but other devices can be used. To indicate spoken emphasis, use italics for the emphasized portion.

> *I was* thought to be the author.

Or use the simple declarative form, with emphasis.

> They thought *I* was the author.

## Objective Case

The objective (or accusative) case is used mainly to name the receiver of the action of a verb — the **direct** or **indirect object** — or to name the **object of a preposition.**

When one part of a compound expression (joined by a coordinating conjunction) is in the objective case, all other parts of the same expression must also be in the objective case.

> When you reach the station, call either *him* or *me.*
> They gave *you* and *me* the job.
> The job was given to *you* and *me.*

When the antecedent of an appositive (the word that the appositive renames) is in the objective case, the appositive must also be in the objective case.

> The teacher has appointed *two people, you and me,* to the committee.
> He gave *us passengers* a copy of the schedule.

### Direct Object of a Verb

A noun or pronoun serving as the direct object of a verb is in the objective case. Do not be confused by compound forms, intervening words, or appositives.

> The driver returned *them* to their home.
> The police officer told *him* and *me* to get back into the car.

> They will invite *us fans* to the football game.
> *Whomever* you called on Monday night is certainly upset.

This last example may sound stilted, but, for demonstration purposes, it is grammatically correct. It may be recast in various ways.

> *Whoever* it was that you called ....
> *The person whom* you called ....

The remaining examples show direct objects of *verbals*, verb forms that perform special functions and do not change their form.

> I enjoyed meeting *him*.
> I didn't intend to ask *them* again.
> Having called *him* and told *him* the news, we left for the evening.
> We have a letter from her cousin thanking *us* for our courtesy.

## Indirect Object of a Verb

A word used as the indirect object of a verb or verbal is in the objective case. A sentence must have a direct object in order to have an indirect object, but not all sentences having direct objects have indirect objects.

> The ballplayer gave *me* his autograph.

To identify the indirect object, recast the sentence using a phrase beginning with the preposition *to* or *for*.

> The ballplayer gave his autograph *to me*.

Do not be confused by compound forms, intervening words, verbals, or appositives.

> The supervisor assigned *him* and *me* the task of cleaning up the boardroom.
> The boss showed *us employees* how to do it.
> The attorney is preparing a letter giving *him* authority to handle his mother's finances.

## Object of a Preposition

A pronoun serving as the object of a preposition is in the objective case.

> From *whom* did you receive the letter? (*Whom* is the object of the preposition *from*.)

A special troublemaker is the compound object *you and me* after a preposition, especially the preposition *between*.

> *Not:* between *you* and *I*
> *Not:* between *you* and *myself*
> *But:* between *you* and *me*

## Noun or Pronoun Preceding an Infinitive

The infinitive is the form of a verb beginning with *to*; it does not change for person or number. A noun or pronoun that precedes an infinitive (and is understood as its subject) is in the objective case.

> I want *him* to have this car.
> We expect *you and her* to finish that job.

## Noun or Pronoun Following the Infinitive *to be*

The verb *to be* takes the same case after it as before it. Since the subject of an infinitive is in the objective case, a word following the infinitive is also in the objective case.

> We believed the writer of the letter to be *him*.

To test, reverse the elements:

> We believed *him* to be the *writer of the letter*.

## Noun or Pronoun before a Present Participle or a Gerund

Both the present participle and the gerund end in *-ing*. They are *verbals,* words formed from verbs but performing other functions in a sentence. The present participle often functions as an *adjective*. The gerund functions as a *noun*.

The word that precedes a present participle (and is understood as the subject of the verb from which it was formed) must be in the *objective* case. The word that precedes a gerund (and is understood as the subject of the verb from which it was formed) must be a *possessive* form — either a possessive pronominal adjective or a noun in the possessive case. (See POSSESSIVE CASE below.) The problem lies in determining whether the *-ing* word is a participle or a gerund.

The question to ask is: what is the focus of this sentence? Is it the action expressed by the verb, or is it the person or thing performing that action? Consider the following pair of sentences:

> Imagine him flying to Paris.
> Imagine his flying to Paris.

If the focus is on the person performing the action, the *-ing* form is a participle modifying the subject noun or pronoun, which is in the objective case.

> Imagine *him* flying to Paris.

If the focus is on the act of flying (to Paris), the *-ing* form is a gerund and the subject pronoun is a possessive pronominal adjective.

> Imagine *his* flying to Paris.

Here is another pair of example sentences.

> *Harry's rushing* to catch the plane was in vain.
> Maria watched *Harry rushing* to catch the plane.

In the first sentence, the focus is on the action of the verb, so the *-ing* form is a gerund and the subject noun is in the possessive case.

> *His* rushing ... was in vain.

In the second sentence, the focus is on the person. So the *-ing* form is a participle modifying the subject noun, which is in the objective case (note that the objective form of a *noun* is the same as the nominative form).

> Maria watched *him* rushing ....

## Possessive Case (and its proper punctuation)

The possessive case is used to indicate possession, or ownership.

See the detailed discussion of the rules for forming the possessive of nouns and pronouns in the APOSTROPHE portion of the PUNCTUATION section later in this Guide.

Below are a few of the most common points to note in using possessives.

(1) The apostrophe signifies "belonging to the noun or phrase everything to the left of this mark."

>  the *lady's* coat     the *ladies'* coats

(2) When the word *else* is used with an indefinite pronoun, form the possessive by adding the apostrophe and *s* to *else*, rather than to the pronoun.

>  *somebody's* hat     *somebody else's* hat

(3) While the possessive of most proper names is formed with an apostrophe, the apostrophe is omitted in some geographical or organization names that contain a possessive concept. Follow the spelling listed in a reference book or used by the organization.

>  Harpers Ferry
>  Pikes Peak
>  Citizens National Bank
>  American Friends Service Committee

(4) Do *not* use an apostrophe to form any possessive pronoun that ends in *s*. The correct forms are

>  yours, his, hers, its, ours, theirs

Note also the **possessive pronominal adjectives** that end in *s*. Some of them have the same form as that of the possessive case of the pronoun; some are slightly different.

>  his,  its

Note the spellings of the following pairs of words with the same pronunciation; these are the ones causing the most confusion.

>  possessive: *its*
>  contraction: *it's (it is)*

>  possessive: *whose*
>  contraction: *who's (who is)*

>  possessive: *theirs*
>  contraction: *there's (there is)*

(5) Use the *of* **phrase** to form possessives in long or awkward phrases, so as to avoid the "piling up" of possessives.

In the following pairs of sentences, the first one in each pair is acceptable but has just about reached the limit of clarity, flow, and readability. The second of each pair is a rewrite using *of* plus one of the original possessives, so as to "unpack" the meaning. On the other hand, the informal nature of the second pair of sentences may make the rewrite seem a little too formal.

>  The *taxpayer's wife's income* must be reported.
>  The *income of the taxpayer's wife* must be reported.

>  Her *brother's friend's bicycle* is red.
>  The *bicycle of her brother's friend* is red.

Use the *of* phrase to form the possessive of official names that are made up of several words.

>  *Not:*  The local chapter of the National Association of Radio and Television Broadcasters' first meeting was held on Thursday.
>  *But:*  The first meeting of the local chapter of the National Association of Radio and Television Broadcasters was held on Thursday.

>*Not:* The Director of the Parks and Recreation Division's report ....
>*But:* The report of the Director of the Parks and Recreation Division ....

For a sentence in which a somewhat formal tone is desired, use the *of* phrase to avoid adding a possessive to a pronoun that is already possessive. Both sentences of the following pair are acceptable, but note the difference in tone.

>We are going to a *friend of mine's* house.
>We are going to the *house of a friend of mine.*

(6) Form the possessive on the last word of a compound word. For long or awkward phrases, especially those involving plurals, use the *of* phrase to avoid confusion.

>the Attorney General's decision

For long or awkward phrases, especially those involving plurals, use the *of* phrase to avoid confusion.

>the views of several recent Attorneys General

(7) If a possessive is followed by an appositive or an explanatory phrase, form the possessive on the last of the explanatory words.

>That was *Mr. Smith the auditor's* idea.
>I was acting on my *friend John's* advice.
>Have you read the *senator from Arizona's* speech?

(8) Possessives of abbreviations are formed in the same way as other possessives. Place the apostrophe after the final period of the abbreviation (if a period is used).

(9) Be sure that a word in a construction parallel with a possessive is also possessive in form.

>*Not:* *His* work, like an *accountant*, is exacting.
>*But:* *His* work, like an *accountant's,* is exacting.

>*Not:* The *agent's* job differs from the *auditor.*
>*But:* The *agent's* job differs from the *auditor's.*

In relatively formal writing, the phrase *that of* may be substituted to indicate a parallel possessive.

>*Not:* *His* task is no more difficult than his *colleague.*
>*But:* *His* task is no more difficult than *that of* his *colleague.*

(10) Use the possessive with a gerund.

>*Our* being late delayed the meeting.
>*Mr. Jones's* being late delayed the meeting.
>You can always depend on *his* being a good friend.
>*Jim's* rendering of the Beethoven sonata deserved a standing ovation.

Note that there are no possessive forms for the pronouns *that, this, these,* and *those.* When these words are used as subject of a gerund, they do not change form.

>*Not:* We cannot be sure of *that's* being true.
>*But*: We cannot be sure of *that* being true.

Or recast the sentence:

>We cannot be sure *that that is* true.

# Verbs

## Definitions

The predicate of a sentence makes a statement about the subject. The **verb** is the core of the predicate.

A verb is a word or word group

(1) expressing action, existence, or occurrence:

> A lexicographer *edits* dictionaries.
> Dictionaries *are edited* by lexicographers.

(2) used to connect the subject with another element:

> A dictionary *is* a book of words and definitions.
> A good dictionary *is* a basic resource.

(3) used as an auxiliary to another verb:

> A dictionary *can* be helpful to both readers and writers.

## Types of Verbs

In terms of sentence structure, there are three types of verbs. The **transitive verb** takes a **direct object.**

> He *hit* the ball.

The **intransitive** verb stands alone; it takes no direct object.

> She *fell* down.

The **linking** verb takes a **predicate nominative** or a **predicate adjective.**

> Jim *is* captain.
> Jim *seems* strong.

## Properties of Verbs

To indicate tense, number, and so forth, a verb changes its form, or other verbs (called **auxiliaries**) are added to the main verb.

**Number** indicates whether the verb is **singular** (one person, place, or thing) or **plural** (more than one). The number of the subject determines the number of the verb.

**Person** indicates whether the **first person** performs the action expressed by the verb:

> *I understand* the situation.
> *We took* action.

or whether it is the **second person**:

> You *arrived* late.
> All of *you are* here now.

or the **third person**:

> Either *he* or *she is* going to be there by noon.
> *It is* snowing.
> *They have made* other plans.

In English, only the third person singular changes form to indicate person.

A verb and its subject must **agree**, or match, in number and person. This basic matter of agreement, so important to the writing of clear sentences, is discussed in detail in the section on AGREEMENT, REFERENCE, AND PARALLELISM.

**Tense** indicates the time of an action — whether it happened in **past** time, is happening in **present** time, or will happen in **future** time. See the detailed discussion of **tense** that follows.

**Mood** indicates the manner of assertion — the **indicative mood** expresses a statement or question, the **imperative mood** expresses a command or polite request, and the **subjunctive mood** expresses a wish or condition. See the detailed discussion of **mood** that follows.

**Voice** indicates whether the subject is performing or receiving the action of the verb. A verb in the **active voice** tells what the subject is doing; a verb in the **passive voice** tells what is being done to the subject. See the detailed discussion of **voice** that follows.

## Tense

### Basic Information

Tense refers to *time*.

English has six tenses: three simple tenses (**present, past,** and **future**), in which an action may be considered as simply occurring; and three compound — or perfect — tenses, in which an action may be considered as completed.

| | |
|---|---|
| Present: | I walk, it rains |
| Present Perfect: | I have walked, it has rained |
| Past: | I walked, it rained |
| Past Perfect: | I had walked, it had rained |
| Future: | I shall walk, it will rain |
| Future Perfect: | I shall have walked, it will have rained |

Each of the six tenses has a companion form — the **progressive** form — that indicates that the action named by the verb is a continued, or progressive, action. The progressive consists of the present participle (the *-ing* form of the verb) plus the relevant form of the verb *to be*. The progressive forms of the simple tenses are as follows.

| | |
|---|---|
| Present Progressive: | I am walking, it is raining |
| Past Progressive: | I was walking, it was raining |
| Future Progressive: | I shall be walking, it will be raining |

The present and past tenses also have an **emphatic** form, which uses the verb *do* as an auxiliary verb.

| | |
|---|---|
| Present Emphatic: | I do understand, she does understand |
| Past Emphatic: | I did understand, she did understand |

We indicate tense by changing the form of the verb itself (**inflection**) or by combining certain forms of the verb with auxiliary verbs (**periphrasis**). The auxiliary verbs used to form tenses are *be, have, do, will,* and *shall*. The basic verb forms from which we derive the tenses are called principal parts. The **principal parts** of a verb are

| | |
|---|---|
| Present Tense/Infinitive: | talk, write |
| Past Tense: | talked, wrote |
| Past Participle: | talked, written |
| Present Participle: | talking, writing |

Verbs are classified as **regular** and **irregular**, according to the way they form their principal parts. Regular verbs form their past tense and past participle by the addition of *-ed* to the infinitive, as in the case of *talked* above.

Irregular verbs form their principal parts through changes in form, or spelling.

| | |
|---|---|
| Present Tense/Infinitive: | write, go |
| Past Tense: | wrote, went |
| Past Participle: | written, gone |
| Present Participle: | writing, going |

Some principal parts of irregular verbs can be confusing and can cause writing problems. When in doubt, look them up in the dictionary or in the table of PRINCIPAL PARTS OF IRREGULAR AND TROUBLESOME VERBS at the end of this section.

Note that a verb sometimes has more than one form in a given category, and sometimes the forms have two different meanings or uses. Consult the dictionary to avoid confusion.

> She *wove* fine cloth.
> He *weaved* in and out of traffic.

> We startled the bird and it *flew* off the branch.
> The slugger *flied* out to center field.

## Past Tense vs. Past Perfect Tense

The past perfect indicates that the action or condition described was completed earlier than some other action that also occurred in the past. Distinguish carefully between this tense and the simple or progressive past tense.

> When I *came* back from lunch, he *finished* typing the letter. (Both verbs are in the past tense; therefore, both actions happened at about the same time in the past.)
> When I *came* back from lunch, he *had finished* typing the letter. (Again, both actions occurred in the past; but the use of the past perfect *had finished* tells us that this action was completed before the other action.)
> *Or:* He had already finished typing the letter when I came back from lunch.

Here is a further example.

> We *discovered* that a detective *was following* us. (Both actions happened at the same time in the past.)
> We *discovered* that a detective *had been following* us. (He had been following us some time before we discovered it.)

## Past Tense vs. Present Perfect Tense

The present perfect indicates that the action or condition described (1) has ended as of the time of writing or speaking, but not at any definite time in the past; (2) has ended in the present; or (3) continues into the present.

> He *has written* a striking memoir.
> They *have finished* the job just now.
> I *have been* sad for a long time.

Use the present perfect in questions asking whether something has happened. The sentence

> *Have* you *bought* the house?

asks whether the action has taken place as of now. But

> *Did* you *buy* the house?

asks whether the action took place at some point in the past.

Questions using the present perfect tense also tend to sound more formal or learned. There is a slight distinction in tone between

> *Have* you *seen* the new film?

and

> *Did* you *see* the new film?

as simple requests for information from the perspective of the present time.

## Mood

The mood of a verb tells what kind of utterance is being made. An English verb may be **indicative, imperative,** or **subjunctive** in mood.

### Indicative Mood

We use the indicative mood — which makes a statement or asks a question — in almost all of our writing and speaking.

> The new planting truly *beautified* the garden.
> What *is* the correct form to use in this sentence?
> It *seems* likely to rain.

### Imperative Mood

The imperative mood expresses a command, a request, or a suggestion. The subject of an imperative sentence is ordinarily understood to be the pronoun *you*.

> *Lock* the safe before you leave the office.
> *Let* me give you directions to the interstate.
> Please *sign* the receipt before returning it to us. (Note that the word *please* has no effect on the use of the imperative, but often has a positive effect on the listener or reader.)

There is one other imperative construction; it includes the speaker or writer in the command or request.

> *Let* us *pray*.
> *Let's go!*

For conciseness, try using the imperative more frequently to state a request or command, especially with the word *please*. It is more emphatic and is understood more quickly and easily.

| | |
|---|---|
| Indicative: | I would appreciate it if you would open the envelope promptly. |
| Imperative: | Please open the envelope promptly. |

### Subjunctive Mood

The subjunctive indicates (1) a hypothetical situation, (2) a conditional situation, or (3) an indirect command. The subjunctive is going out of use in English, but it can still be seen in the following forms.

(1) The third person singular present (which ends in -s in the indicative but not in the subjunctive):

Indicative:                 The plane usually *arrives* on schedule.

Subjunctive:             *Should* the plane *arrive* on schedule, we will be able to make our connection.

Indicative:                 The detective *prepares* his reports as soon as he completes a case.

Subjunctive:             We suggested that the detective *prepare* his reports immediately.

(2) Forms of the verb *be*:

He requested that we *be* there.

If I *were* rich, I would buy a house.

Present:                   If he *were* able to do it, I am sure he would.

Past:                       If he *had been* able to do it, I am sure he would have.

Uses of the subjunctive include the following:

(1) For a wish that is not likely to be fulfilled or is impossible to fulfill.

I wish it *were* possible for us to approve the loan. (It is *not* possible.)

I wish she *were* here to hear your praise of her work. (She is *not* here.)

Would that I *were* able to take this burden from you. (I am *not* able to do so.)

(2) In a parliamentary motion.

I move that the meeting *be adjourned*.

Resolved, that a committee *be appointed* to study this matter.

(3) In a subordinate clause after a verb that expresses a command, request, or suggestion.

He asked that the flowers *be watered* in his absence.

It is recommended that this office *be* responsible for preparing the statements.

We suggest that he *be made* aware of the situation.

We ask that you *consider* the possibility of a reversal.

It is highly desirable that they *be given* the keys to the apartment as soon as possible.

(4) For a condition that is known or supposed to be contrary to fact.

If this *were* up to me, we wouldn't be going.

If I *were* you, I wouldn't wait in the car.

(5) After *as if* or *as though*. In formal writing and speech, *as if* and *as though* are followed by the subjunctive, since they introduce as a supposition something that is not factual.

He talked as if he *were* an expert on karate. (He's not.)

This drawing looks as though it *were* the work of a master.

## Shifts in Mood

Be consistent in point of view. Determine which mood best expresses the message, and use that mood throughout the sentence or paragraph. A shift in mood can confuse the listener or reader; it suggests that the speaker or writer has changed his or her way of looking at the situation.

*Not:* The hospital suggests that newborns *be* fed by their mothers and *should be* changed by their fathers. (*Be* is subjunctive; *should be*, indicative.)

*But:* The hospital suggests that newborns *be* fed by their mothers and (*be*) changed by their fathers.

## Voice

Voice indicates whether the subject of the verb is performing or receiving the action indicated by the verb. There are two voices: **active** and **passive.**

If the subject is performing the action, the verb is in the active voice.

> This article *summarizes* the problem.
> The hostess *asked* everyone to take a seat.
> *Did* your neighbor *fix* the roof?

If the subject is being acted upon, the verb is in the passive voice. (The passive form always consists of some form of *be* plus the past participle.)

> The problem is *summarized* by this article.
> *Was* the roof *fixed* by your neighbor?
> Everyone *was asked* by the hostess to take a seat.

In the three sentences above, the active sentence turns into the passive by (1) reversing the positions of the subject and object; (2) changing the verb form to the past participle and placing the auxiliary *be* before it; (3) placing the preposition *by* before the former subject, which is now referred to as the *agent.*

In some cases, the *by* phrase disappears, so that the identity of the agent is not explicit within the sentence. This places greater emphasis on the remaining information.

> Jane *was elected.*
> The problem *is summarized* on page 203.

### Active vs. Passive Voice

Note that *active* and *passive* are grammatical terms pertaining solely to the structure of the sentence; they do not characterize its content.

Use the active voice wherever possible: it is briefer, and its effect is simpler and more direct. But if you wish to emphasize the action itself or the object of the action and not the agent, use the passive.

> Smoking is prohibited. (emphasizing the object, smoking)
> Lori is employed by the college. (emphasizing Lori)

Avoid having a series of passive sentences in close proximity in a piece of writing, however; this tends to create a plodding pace.

### Shifts in Voice

Shifts in voice — often accompanied by shifts in subject — usually occur in compound or complex sentences. Although it is not necessary for all the clauses in a sentence to be the same in structure, unnecessary shifts can result in confusion. So unless there is a good reason for changing, use the same subject and voice in the second clause as in the first.

> *Not:* As *I searched* through my dresser drawers, the missing *sock was found.* (The first subject is *I* — its verb is active; the second subject is *sock* — its verb is passive.)

*But:* As *I searched* through my dresser drawers, *I found* the missing sock. (The subject is *I* in both clauses; both verbs are active.)

## Principal Parts of Irregular and Troublesome Verbs

| *Infinitive / Present* | *Past Tense* | *Past Participle* | *Present Participle* |
|---|---|---|---|
| abide | abode or abided | abode or abided | abiding |
| arise | arose | arisen | arising |
| awake | awoke or awaked | awaked or awoken | awaking |
| awaken | awakened | awakened | awakening |
| be/am, is, are | was, were | been | being |
| bear (carry) | bore | borne | bearing |
| bear (give birth to) | bore | borne | bearing |
| | | born (passive participle, used without *by* phrase) | |
| beat | beat | beaten | beating |
| become | became | become | becoming |
| befall | befell | befallen | befalling |
| begin | began | begun | beginning |
| behold | beheld | beheld | beholding |
| bend | bent | bent | bending |
| beseech | besought or beseeched | besought or beseeched | beseeching |
| beset | beset | beset | besetting |
| bet | bet or betted | bet or betted | betting |
| bid (ask, tell, express) | bade or bid | bidden or bid | bidding |
| bid (in auction or card game) | bid | bid | bidding |
| bide | bode or bided | bided | biding |
| bind | bound | bound | binding |
| bite | bit | bitten or bit | biting |
| bleed | bled | bled | bleeding |
| blow | blew | blown | blowing |
| break | broke | broken | breaking |
| breed | bred | bred | breeding |
| bring | brought | brought | bringing |
| broadcast | broadcast or broadcasted | broadcast or broadcasted | broadcasting |
| build | built | built | building |
| burn | burned or burnt | burned or burnt | burning |
| burst | burst | burst | bursting |
| bust | busted | busted | busting |
| buy | bought | bought | buying |
| cast | cast | cast | casting |

| Infinitive/Present | Past Tense | Past Participle | Present Participle |
|---|---|---|---|
| catch | caught | caught | catching |
| chide | chided or chid | chided or chid or chidden | chiding |
| choose | chose | chosen | choosing |
| cleave (adhere) | cleaved | cleaved | cleaving |
| cleave (split) | cleaved or cleft or clove | cleaved or cleft or cloven | cleaving |
| cling | clung | clung | clinging |
| come | came | come | coming |
| cost | cost | cost | costing |
| creep | crept | crept | creeping |
| cut | cut | cut | cutting |
| deal | dealt | dealt | dealing |
| dig | dug | dug | digging |
| dive | dived or dove | dived | diving |
| do | did | done | doing |
| draw | drew | drawn | drawing |
| dream | dreamed or dreamt | dreamed or dreamt | dreaming |
| drink | drank | drunk | drinking |
| drive | drove | driven | driving |
| drown | drowned | drowned | drowning |
| dwell | dwelt or dwelled | dwelt or dwelled | dwelling |
| eat | ate | eaten | eating |
| fall | fell | fallen | falling |
| feed | fed | fed | feeding |
| feel | felt | felt | feeling |
| fight | fought | fought | fighting |
| find | found | found | finding |
| flee | fled | fled | fleeing |
| fling | flung | flung | flinging |
| flow | flowed | flowed | flowing |
| fly (move in air) | flew | flown | flying |
| fly (hit a fly ball) | flied | flied | flying |
| forbear | forbore | forborne | forbearing |
| forbid | forbade or forbad | forbidden | forbidding |
| forecast | forecast or forecasted | forecast or forecasted | forecasting |
| foresee | foresaw | foreseen | foreseeing |
| foretell | foretold | foretold | foretelling |
| forget | forgot | forgotten | forgetting |
| forgive | forgave | forgiven | forgiving |
| forgo | forwent | forgone | forgoing |
| forsake | forsook | forsaken | forsaking |
| freeze | froze | frozen | freezing |
| get | got | gotten or got | getting |
| give | gave | given | giving |

| _Infinitive / Present_ | _Past Tense_ | _Past Participle_ | _Present Participle_ |
| --- | --- | --- | --- |
| go | went | gone | going |
| grind | ground | ground | grinding |
| grow | grew | grown | growing |
| hang (suspend) | hung | hung | hanging |
| hang (execute) | hanged | hanged | hanging |
| have | had | had | having |
| hear | heard | heard | hearing |
| heave | heaved or hove | heaved or hove | heaving |
| hew | hewed | hewed or hewn | hewing |
| hide | hid | hidden or hid | hiding |
| hit | hit | hit | hitting |
| hold | held | held | holding |
| hurt | hurt | hurt | hurting |
| input | input | input | inputting |
| keep | kept | kept | keeping |
| kneel | knelt or kneeled | knelt or kneeled | kneeling |
| knit | knitted or knit | knitted or knit | knitting |
| know | knew | known | knowing |
| lay (put down) | laid | laid | laying |
| lead | led | led | leading |
| lean | leaned or (Chiefly Brit.) leant | leaned or (Chiefly Brit.) leant | leaning |
| leap | leapt or lept or leaped | leapt or lept or leaped | leaping |
| leave | left | left | leaving |
| lend | lent | lent | lending |
| let | let | let | letting |
| lie (recline) | lay | lain | lying |
| lie (speak falsely) | lied | lied | lying |
| light | lighted or lit | lighted or lit | lighting |
| lose | lost | lost | losing |
| make | made | made | making |
| mean | meant | meant | meaning |
| meet | met | met | meeting |
| mislay | mislaid | mislaid | mislaying |
| misspell | misspelled or misspelt | misspelled or misspelt | misspelling |
| mistake | mistook | mistaken | mistaking |
| mow | mowed | mowed or mown | mowing |
| overcome | overcame | overcome | overcoming |
| overlay | overlaid | overlaid | overlaying |
| overrun | overran | overrun | overrunning |
| overtake | overtook | overtaken | overtaking |
| partake | partook | partaken | partaking |
| pay | paid | paid | paying |

| Infinitive/Present | Past Tense | Past Participle | Present Participle |
|---|---|---|---|
| plead | pleaded or pled or plead | pleaded or pled or plead | pleading |
| prove | proved | proved or proven | proving |
| put | put | put | putting |
| quit | quit or (occas.) quitted | quit or (occas.) quitted | quitting |
| raise | raised | raised | raising |
| read | read | read | reading |
| recast | recast | recast | recasting |
| redo | redid | redone | redoing |
| rend | rent | rent | rending |
| rid | rid or ridded | rid or ridded | ridding |
| ride | rode | ridden | riding |
| ring | rang | rung | ringing |
| rise | rose | risen | rising |
| run | run | run | running |
| saw | sawed | sawed or (Chiefly Brit.) sawn | sawing |
| say | said | said | saying |
| see | saw | seen | seeing |
| seek | sought | sought | seeking |
| sell | sold | sold | selling |
| send | sent | sent | sending |
| set | set | set | setting |
| sew | sewed | sewn or sewed | sewing |
| shake | shook | shaken | shaking |
| shear | sheared | sheared or shorn | shearing |
| shed | shed | shed | shedding |
| shine (give off light) | shone | shone | shining |
| shine (make shiny) | shined | shined | shining |
| shoe | shod or shoed | shod or shoed | shoeing |
| shoot | shot | shot | shooting |
| shrink | shrank or shrunk | shrunk or shrunken | shrinking |
| shut | shut | shut | shutting |
| sing | sang | sung | singing |
| sink | sank | sunk | sinking |
| sit | sat | sat | sitting |
| ski | skied | skied | skiing |
| slay (kill) | slew | slain | slaying |
| slay (impress forcefully) | slayed | slain | slaying |
| sleep | slept | slept | sleeping |
| slide | slid | slid | sliding |
| sling | slung | slung | slinging |

| _Infinitive/Present_ | _Past Tense_ | _Past Participle_ | _Present Participle_ |
|---|---|---|---|
| slink | slunk | slunk | slinking |
| slit | slit | slit | slitting |
| smite | smote | smitten or smote | smiting |
| sow | sowed | sown or sowed | sowing |
| speak | spoke | spoken | speaking |
| speed | sped or speeded | sped or speeded | speeding |
| spend | spent | spent | spending |
| spin | spun | spun | spinning |
| spit | spit or spat | spit or spat | spitting |
| split | split | split | splitting |
| spread | spread | spread | spreading |
| spring | sprang | sprung | springing |
| stand | stood | stood | standing |
| steal | stole | stolen | stealing |
| stick | stuck | stuck | sticking |
| sting | stung | stung | stinging |
| stink | stank or stunk | stunk | stinking |
| strew | strewed | strewed or strewn | strewing |
| stride | strode | stridden | striding |
| strike (hit, etc.) | struck | struck | striking |
| strike (afflict; delete) | struck | stricken or struck | striking |
| string | strung | strung | stringing |
| strive | strove or strived | striven or strived | striving |
| swear | swore | sworn | swearing |
| sweat | sweat or sweated | sweat or sweated | sweating |
| sweep | swept | swept | sweeping |
| swell | swelled | swelled or swollen | swelling |
| swim | swam | swum | swimming |
| swing | swung | swung | swinging |
| take | took | taken | taking |
| teach | taught | taught | teaching |
| tear | tore | torn | tearing |
| tell | told | told | telling |
| think | thought | thought | thinking |
| throw | threw | thrown | throwing |
| thrust | thrust | thrust | thrusting |
| tread (walk, trample) | trod | trodden or trod | treading |
| tread (water) | treaded | treaded | treading |
| understand | understood | understood | understanding |
| undo | undid | undone | undoing |
| upset | upset | upset | upsetting |
| wake | woke or waked | waked or woken | waking |
| waken | wakened | wakened | wakening |

| Infinitive / Present | Past Tense | Past Participle | Present Participle |
|---|---|---|---|
| waylay | waylaid | waylaid | waylaying |
| wear | wore | worn | wearing |
| weave (make cloth) | wove | woven or wove | weaving |
| weave (move sideways) | weaved | weaved | weaving |
| wed | wedded | wedded or wed | wedding |
| weep | wept | wept | weeping |
| wet | wet or wetted | wet or wetted | wetting |
| win | won | won | winning |
| wind | wound | wound | winding |
| wring | wrung | wrung | wringing |
| write | wrote | written | writing |

# Modifiers

A modifier is a word or group of words that describes, qualifies, or limits another word or group of words.

## Classification of Modifiers

### Adjectives and Adverbs

Modifiers fall generally into two categories: adjectives (and phrases or clauses used as adjectives) and adverbs (and phrases or clauses used as adverbs). Sometimes the form of the modifier clearly shows whether it is an adjective or an adverb; sometimes the form is the same for both.

An adjective describes, limits, or makes more exact the meaning of a noun or pronoun.

> He liked the *red* car.
> The dresser *that is made of oak* is my favorite.

An adverb describes, limits, or makes more exact the meaning of a verb, an adjective, or another adverb. Most adverbs end in *-ly*.

> The moose bellowed *hoarsely* in the forest.
> Run around the track *as quickly as you can*.
> He liked the *pale* red car.

### Articles

The articles are a small category of adjectives. The **indefinite articles** are *a* and *an;* the **definite article** is *the*. Use *a* before words beginning with a consonant sound, and *an* before those beginning with a vowel sound.

> *a* desk, *a* house
> *an* agent, *an* unusual occurrence, *an* honor (the *h* is not pronounced)

When an article is used before each in a series of related nouns or adjectives, the words refer to different people or things.

> We elected *a* secretary and *a* treasurer. (two persons)
> He drives *a* tan and green car. (one vehicle, two colors)

Avoid using *a* or *an* after *sort of, kind of, manner of, style of,* or *type of.*

> *Not:* What *kind of a* book do you want?
> *But:* What *kind of* book do you want?

Never use *the* before *both.*

> *Not:* We'll buy *the both* of them.
> *But:* We'll buy *both* of them.

## Modifiers Functioning As Two Parts of Speech

Here are a few examples of modifiers that function as both adjective and adverb, depending on their use in the sentence.

> Study the *above* information carefully.
> We heard other climbers shouting high *above* on the mountain.

> That is a *better* way.
> She thinks she can do everything *better* than we can.

> It's a very *cheap* jacket.
> He bought the motorcycle *cheap.*

## Adverbs with Two Forms

As in the last sentence above, some adverbs have a second form that does not end in *-ly.* The longer form is nearly always acceptable; use it in more formal writing.

The short form of such an adverb has a less formal sound; use it in less formal writing, especially in brief, forceful sentences. (Notice the impact of the road sign "Drive Slow.")

But always use the *-ly* form to modify an adjective, except in very informal speech or writing.

> *Formal:* I'm *really* glad you could come.
> *Informal:* I'm *real* glad you could come.

Here are some examples of adverbs having two forms.

> cheap/cheaply
> clear/clearly
> deep/deeply
> direct/directly
> loud/loudly
> quick/quickly
> sharp/sharply
> slow/slowly
> soft/softly

Sometimes the intended meaning determines which form is used. Notice that either *direct* or *directly* may be used when the meaning is "in a straight line," but only *directly* means "soon." When in doubt, consult the dictionary.

## Degrees of Comparison for Adjectives and Adverbs

To indicate a greater or lesser degree of the characteristic expressed, an adjective or adverb changes form (**inflection**) or combines with another word (**periphrasis**). There are three degrees of comparison.

## Positive Degree

The positive degree names the *quality* expressed by the adjective or adverb. It does not imply a comparison with, or a relation to, a similar quality in any other thing.

> *high* morale, a *dependable* worker
> work *fast,* prepared *carefully*

## Comparative Degree

The comparative degree indicates that the quality described by the modifier exists to a greater or lesser degree in one thing than in another. It is formed by adding *-er* to the positive degree or by inserting *more* or *less* before the positive form.

> Our club has *higher* morale now than ever before.
> Jan is a *less dependable* worker than Tim.
> She can work *faster* than I can.
> This meal was prepared *more carefully* than the one we had last night.

## Superlative Degree

The superlative degree denotes the greatest or least amount of the quality named. It is formed by adding *-est* to the positive degree of the adjective or adverb or by inserting *most* or *least* before the positive form.

> That club has the *highest* morale of any club.
> Jan is the *least dependable* worker in the office.
> She works *fastest* of all.
> This is the *most carefully* prepared meal I have ever eaten.

The comparative degree indicates *only two things*; the superlative degree indicates *more than two.*

> *Not:* Which of these two boats is the *longest?*
> *But:* This boat is the *longer* of the two.
> *Or:* This boat is the *longest* of the three.

## Using *-er* and *-est* vs. *more* and *most, less* and *least*

There is no difference in meaning between *-er* and *more* or between *-est* and *most.* Some modifiers can be compared in either way. However:

(1) Obviously, the suffixes and *more* and *most* indicate an increase in the quality. Since *less* and *least* indicate a decrease, the suffixes can be used instead of them only with modifiers that indicate a negative or a lessening.

(2) Most adjectives of three or more syllables take *more / most / less / least.*

(3) Almost all adverbs take *more / most / less / least.*

(4) For adjectives that can be compared in either way, choose based on emphasis: adding the suffixes places emphasis on the *quality,* and adding *more / most / less / least* emphasizes the *degree of comparison.*

(5) For the sake of consistency and flow, in many cases it may be best to use only one method of comparison for related modifiers in a sentence.

> *Not:* a *hotter* and *more muggy* climate
> *But:* a *hotter* and *muggier* climate
> *Or:* a *more hot* and *muggy* climate

Should I have been *kinder* or *harsher* in handling that caller?

That boat is the *longest* of the three.

Should I have been *more firm* or *less firm* in handling that caller?

Of all these blank forms, this one is the *most simple* and that one is the *least simple* to fill out.

## Irregular Comparison

A number of modifiers are compared by internal change in the word itself. Here are a few examples; note that some modifiers have two possible forms. Consult the dictionary when in doubt.

| *Positive* | *Comparative* | *Superlative* |
|---|---|---|
| good | better | best |
| well | better | best |
| bad/ill | worse | worst |
| badly/ill | worse | worst |
| far | farther/ further | farthest/ furthest |
| late | later/latter | latest/last |
| little | littler less/lesser | littlest least |
| many | more | most |
| much | more | most |

## Comparison Problems

### Words Not Usually Compared

Some adjectives and adverbs convey qualities that are not readily compared because they already represent an absolute or the highest degree. The words listed below are representative of the kinds of general categories involved. Writers' opinions may differ in specific cases.

| | | |
|---|---|---|
| complete(ly) | horizontal(ly) | round |
| correct(ly) | immortal(ly) | square(ly) |
| dead | infinite(ly) | total(ly) |
| deadly | perfect(ly) | unique(ly) |
| exact(ly) | perpendicular(ly) | universal(ly) |

However, there may be situations in which words like those above can be compared validly. If we use such a modifier in a relative or approximate sense, it may be compared. But proceed with care — moderate the comparison with a qualifying adverb such as *nearly*. Try to develop a sense of the difference between the constructions in the following pairs:

| | | |
|---|---|---|
| more nearly round | vs. | rounder |
| more nearly perfect | vs. | more perfect |
| more nearly exact | vs. | more exact |

### Use of *unique*

Note that *unique* means "one and only." Not everyone accepts its somewhat informal meaning, "unusual." For those who do not accept it, the phrase "more unique" is illogical. It is best to avoid this usage — along with "truly unique," "very unique," "so unique," and other such phrases containing adverbs of degree.

## Comparison with *other* and *else*

A sentence such as

> This car is better than any that I have seen.

implies that *this car* is part of the group with which it is being compared — that it is better than itself. Of course we all know what the speaker or writer means, and many people use this construction informally; but this logically flawed usage is not acceptable in careful writing. Separate the thing being compared from the group by adding the word *other*.

> This car is better than any *other* that I have seen.

> *Not:* Our house is cooler than any house on the block.
> *But:* Our house is cooler than any *other* house on the block.

With pronouns, use the word *else*.

> *Not:* He has won more games than anyone in our league.
> *But:* He has won more games than anyone *else* in our league.

## Incomplete Comparison — Omitted Information

Be sure that both terms of a comparison are clearly identified. Omission of one term places the burden on the listener or reader, who may not clearly understand which two items are being compared. Be sure the listener or reader knows exactly what you mean when you say:

> There have been more successful ad campaigns in our district this year.

Does this mean "more than in any other district" or "more than in any previous year"?

Whenever a comparison is not completed, the meaning of the sentence is obscured. This is one form of the incomplete comparison. Here are a few more.

(1) Incomplete comparison with possessive:

> *Obscure:* Joe's letter states the problem better than John.

We cannot tell whether it is *John* or *John's letter* that is stating the problem.

> *Improved:* Joe's letter states the problem better than *John's*.
> *Ambiguous:* John's proposal is less complicated than management.
> *Improved:* John's proposal is less complicated than *management's*.
> *Or:* John's proposal is less complicated than *the one made by management*.

(2) Incomplete comparison with conjunction:

> *Obscure:* This text is as good, if not better than that one.

Because of the omission of the second *as* after *good*, this sentence contains the illogical structure "is as good ... *than*."

> *Improved:* This text is as good *as*, if not better than, that one.
> *Or:* This text is as good as that one, if not better.

> *Obscure:* This book is shorter, but just as comprehensive as that one.
> *Improved:* This book is shorter *than*, but just as comprehensive as, that one.
> *Or:* This book is shorter than that one, but just as comprehensive.

(3)   Incomplete comparison with verb:

> *Ambiguous:* I enjoy this kind of work more than John.

Revise the sentence to avoid the unintended meaning "I enjoy this kind of work more than I enjoy *John*."

> *Improved:* I enjoy this kind of work more than John *does*.
> *Ambiguous:* I have known him longer than John.

Revise the sentence to express the intended meaning.

> *Either:* I have known him longer than John *has*.
> *Or:* I have known him longer than *I have known* John.

## Split Infinitives

Inserting an adverb between *to* and the rest of an infinitive creates a **split infinitive**.

> She was known to willingly take on extra responsibilities.

In the past, the unequivocal rule was: avoid the split infinitive by repositioning the adverb or recasting the entire sentence.

> She was known to take on extra responsibilities willingly.

More recently, even careful writers have paid less attention to this rule. So:

(1)   Use split infinitives sparingly, removing them where possible, especially if this helps the sentence to flow better.

(2)   Leave the split infinitive in place if changing it would change the sentence's emphasis.

(3)   Leave the split infinitive in place if changing it would result in a more awkward sentence.

(4)   In a piece of very formal writing, especially one addressed to readers with conservative linguistic habits, avoid split infinitives entirely.

> *Not:* He wanted to *completely* ignore the problem.
> *But:* He wanted to ignore the problem *completely*.

## Verbals and Verbal Phrases As Modifiers

**Verbals** are sometimes used as modifiers, either singly or in phrases.

> *To get the most out of the course*, you must study regularly. (infinitive phrase modifying *you)*
>
> *Rising,* the lion roared. (present participle modifying *lion)*
>
> The card, *signed by all of us*, went into the mail today. (past participle modifying *card*)
>
> The letter, *having been corrected*, was dropped into the mailbox. (perfect participle modifying *letter)*

### Dangling Verbal Phrases

A dangling phrase is one that cannot logically modify the noun or pronoun to which it refers.

A verbal phrase is understood to have the same subject as that of the independent clause that follows it:

> Driving through the beautiful countryside, we all began sneezing violently. (*we* were driving; *we* sneezed)

As one reads through a sentence with a dangling phrase:

> Driving through the beautiful countryside, the pollen made us all sneeze violently.

one anticipates that the first noun in the independent clause is also the subject of the full clause that is implied by the phrase (in this case: as *we* were driving through the beautiful countryside). When this is not the case, the reader stops, at least briefly, with a mild thud, and has to go back and reinterpret the phrase. Here, the expected subject of the clause would be *we*. However, what is implied by the sentence structure is: *pollen* was driving; *pollen* made us sneeze.

Reread the above explanation and study the following examples until the logical relationships involved are completely clear.

Correct a dangling verbal phrase either:

(1) by changing the subject of the main clause to one that the phrase can refer to, as in the original example sentence above; or

(2) by changing the phrase itself to a dependent clause so that it has a subject of its own (here, the verb form has been adjusted as needed):

> As *we* drove through the beautiful countryside, *we* all began sneezing violently.
>
> *Dangling: To get the most out of this course,* careful *study* is necessary. (*study* cannot be the subject of the implied clause)
> *Corrected: To get the most out of this course, you* must study carefully.
> *Or:* If *you* are to get the most out of this course, *you* must study carefully.

Passive sentences and clauses are often a source of problems with dangling elements.

> *Dangling: To apply for this job*, an *application* must be completed. (an *application* can't apply)
> *Corrected: To apply for this job,* the *applicant* must complete an application.
> *Or:* When *a person* applies for this job, *he or she* must complete an application.
>
> *Dangling: By summarizing the information,* a clear *picture* of the situation was presented. (a picture cannot perform the act of summarizing information; since *picture* is the result, it cannot also be the thing that presents the picture)
> *Corrected: By summarizing the information, we* were able to present a clear picture of the situation.
> *Or:* After *we* had summarized the information, *we* were able to present a clear picture of the situation.

An infinitive or a participial phrase that modifies the whole sentence — designating general action rather than action by a specific agent — can be used correctly without a direct relation to the subject of the main clause.

> *To summarize*, New Mexico has some spectacular scenery.
> *Generally speaking*, these plants grow better in sunlight.
> *Resolved,* that Parisians shall no longer walk their dogs on the sidewalks.

## Prepositional Phrases As Modifiers

A prepositional phrase can function as an adjective or an adverb.

> The letter was addressed to the office *of the registrar*. (adjective modifying *office*)
> They have gone *to the rally*. (adverb modifying *have gone*)

## Dependent Clauses As Modifiers

A dependent clause can function as an adjective or an adverb. See the examples in the section PLACEMENT OF MODIFIERS.

### Relative Pronouns Introducing Clauses

Be careful to select the correct relative pronoun to introduce the adjective clause. *Who* refers to persons; *what, that,* and *which* refer to things; *that* is sometimes used also to refer to persons.

> The trainer *who tamed this lion* has had extensive experience.
> The homework assignment, *which is due tomorrow,* will contain that information.
> The time card *that you have been submitting weekly* will be required once a month from now on.

## Placement of Modifiers

A modifier should be placed as close as possible to the words it modifies. This rule of thumb applies whether the modifier is a single word, a phrase, or a clause. In English, the placement of a modifier is often the reader's only clue to which word it modifies.

Many ambiguous (and unintentionally humorous) sentences result from the mis-placement of modifiers.

### Modifier between Subject and Verb

Wherever possible, avoid structural awkwardness by not placing the modifier between subject and verb or between verb and object.

> *Not:* The driver, *to save money on fuel*, switched to a smaller car.
> *But:* *To save money on fuel*, the driver switched to a smaller car.

### Placement of Adverbs of Degree

Some adverbs — *only, almost, nearly, also, quite, merely, actually* — are frequent troublemakers. Be sure to place them as close as possible to the words they modify.

> *Ambiguous:* The problem can *only* be defined by this committee.
> *It could mean:* *Only* this committee can define the problem.
> *Or:* This committee can *only define* the problem, not solve it.

### Adverbs of Degree with a Negative

Do not use *hardly, only, scarcely, barely* — so-called subtractive adverbs — together with a negative construction. Doing so creates a double negative.

> *Not:* They *haven't only* a single blanket.
> *But:* They *have only* a single blanket.

> *Not:* He *hasn't scarcely* done anything worthwhile.
> *But:* He *has scarcely* done anything worthwhile.

## Phrases and Clauses

Phrases and clauses, like single-word modifiers, should be placed as close as possible to the words they modify. This will prevent the reader from applying the modifier to the wrong sentence element.

> *Not:* We need someone to design buildings *with architectural experience.*
> *But:* We need someone *with architectural experience* to design buildings.

> *Not:* Mr. Dough has resigned from Congress after having served four years *to the regret of all the members.*
> *But:* *To the regret of all the members,* Mr. Dough has resigned from Congress after having served four years.

## Relative Clauses

Relative clauses should also be placed immediately after the word they modify, since they attach themselves, in terms of meaning, to the sentence element nearest them.

> *Not:* The man has an appointment *who is waiting in my office.*
> *But:* The man *who is waiting in my office* has an appointment.

> *Not:* She mentioned the number of cases closed by agents in her group *that are over a year old.*
> *But:* She mentioned the number of cases *over a year old* that have been closed by agents in her group.

## Squinting Constructions

Avoid the squinting construction — that is, a sentence or clause containing a modifier that is placed in such a way that the reader cannot tell whether it modifies the words immediately preceding it or those immediately following it. Recast the sentence to clarify the intended meaning.

> *Obscure:* He agreed *that morning* to marry her.
> *Could mean:* He agreed to marry her *that morning*.
> *Or: That morning*, he agreed to marry her.

There are other squinting constructions among the examples above.

# Connectives

Four kinds of words function as connectives: **prepositions, conjunctions, relative pronouns,** and a small group of **adverbs.** A connective not only connects two sentence elements but also shows the relationship between them.

## Prepositions

A preposition connects the word, phrase, or clause that follows it (its **object**) with some other element in the sentence and shows the relationship between them. A preposition can be a single word:

> to, with, by, for, on, off, in, into

or a phrase:

> according to, as well as, owing to, regardless of, on top of, because of

## Placement of Prepositions

In the past, there was a stringent rule against ending a sentence with a preposition. This rule has now been relaxed in general use. If the sentence sounds natural and flows well with the preposition at the end, leave it there. In very formal use, however, try to avoid doing this.

> What did you do that *for?*
> We had so many things to talk *about.*
> They liked the hotel that they stayed *in.*

## Superfluous Prepositions

Especially in formal writing, avoid using extra prepositions that are not necessary to the meaning. Some such constructions are natural in certain dialects or historical forms of English or in informal speech, but they can distract the reader from the remainder of the sentence.

> *Not:* She is standing near *to* the ledge.
> *But:* She is standing near the ledge.

> *Not:* When are you going to start *in* to write that letter?
> *But:* When are you going to start to write that letter?

## Faulty Omission of Prepositions

Especially in formal writing, it is useful to repeat the preposition before the second of two connected elements.

> *Acceptable:* He seemed interested *in* us and our problems.
> *Often better:* He seemed interested *in* us and *in* our problems.

In the so-called **split** (or **suspended**) **construction,** in which two words need different prepositions, be especially careful to use both prepositions — with or without clarifying commas.

> *Not:* He has an interest and an aptitude *for* his work.
> *But:* He has an interest *in* and an aptitude *for* his work.
> *Or:* He has an interest in, and an aptitude for, his work.

> *Not:* They were puzzled and concerned *about* her erratic behavior.
> *But:* They were puzzled *by* and concerned *about* her erratic behavior.

# Conjunctions

Conjunctions connect sentence elements in a greater variety of ways than prepositions do. There are three basic types of conjunctions.

## Types of Conjunctions

**Coordinating conjunctions** connect sentence elements that are equivalent in rank within the sentence structure. They are

> and, or, nor; but, yet, for, so

The first three conjunctions in the above list can connect single words, phrases, or clauses; the remaining four are used mainly to connect independent clauses in a compound sentence.

**Subordinating conjunctions** connect the independent and dependent clauses in a complex sentence. They include:

> because, since, if, although, where, when, that, as soon as, in case, even if

**Correlative conjunctions** occur in pairs. Like coordinating conjunctions, they can connect pairs of words, phrases, or clauses that are equivalent in rank. They include:

either/or, neither/nor, both/and, not only/but also

"Equivalent in rank" means that the two sentence parts belong to the same structural category and are also logically equivalent.

Determining the structural equivalence of sentence parts is relatively simple: word = word; phrase = phrase; dependent clause = dependent clause; independent clause = independent clause.

See the section on AGREEMENT, REFERENCE, AND PARALLELISM for examples of sentence-structure problems involving conjunctions.

## Notes on Specific Conjunctions

### • *and* vs. *also*

*Also*, an adverb and a weak connective, should not be used in place of *and* in sentences such as:

He writes poems, stories, *and* [not *also*] art reviews.

### • *and etc.*

The abbreviation *etc.* stands for the Latin *et cetera*, meaning *and so forth*. Thus, an additional *and* is not only unnecessary, but incorrect.

*Not:* He used all our paper, pencils, pens, *and etc.*
*But:* He used all our paper, pencils, pens, *etc.*

### • *and which, but who,* etc.

Avoid using *and which, and who, but which, but that,* etc., when there is no preceding *who, which,* or *that* in the sentence to complete the parallel construction.

*Not:* We are looking for a car more economical to operate *and which* will be easy to maintain.
*But:* We are looking for a car *which* will be more economical to operate *and which* will be easy to maintain.

### • too many *and's*

Avoid stringing together a group of sentence elements connected by *and*.

*Not:* The evaluation of the training program was planned *and* conducted *and* reported to the appropriate officials.
*But:* The evaluation of the training program was planned *and* conducted; then it was reported to the appropriate officials.

### • *and* vs. *but*

Use *and* to show addition; use *but* to show contrast.

*Not:* I was expecting the promotion, *and* they just went ahead and gave it to him.
*But:* I was expecting the promotion, *but* they just went ahead and gave it to him.

### • Using *and* or *but* to begin a sentence

In the past, some grammarians have frowned on the use of a coordinating conjunction to begin a sentence. But it is perfectly acceptable to do so. A coordinating conjunction or a conjunctive adverb at the beginning of a sentence is often a helpful signpost for the reader: it can indicate the continuation of a viewpoint, the negation of a preceding statement, an alternative direction, a conclusion, or a cause or reason.

• *as, since, because*

These conjunctions can be used interchangeably to introduce clauses of cause or reason.

> *Because* the book was due at the library, I returned it.
> *Since* the book was due at the library, I returned it.
> *As* the book was due at the library, I returned it.

However, both *since* and *as* have additional functions: *since* introduces clauses of sequence of time, and *as* introduces clauses of duration of time. Because of the double function of these two words, be careful to use them only in sentences in which they cannot be misunderstood.

• *as* vs. *that* or *whether*

Avoid using *as* in place of *that* or *whether* to introduce clauses following such verbs as *say, think,* and *know.*

> *Not:* I don't know *as* I believe you.
> *But:* I don't know *that* I believe you.
> *Or:* I don't know *whether* I believe you.

• *if* vs. *whether*

*If* is used to introduce clauses of condition or supposition.

> We will stay *if* the fish are biting.
> *If* you cannot answer the phone immediately, please ask Erin to do it.

*Whether* introduces clauses indicating an alternative. The alternative may be expressed or understood.

> It will not make any difference *whether* John agrees or disagrees with the outcome of the polling.
> Please let me know *whether* you received the check.

Today, many grammarians endorse the use of either *if* or *whether* in such constructions as

> Please let me know *if* (or *whether*) you received the check.
> I wonder *if* (or *whether*) he is qualified for that job.

If there is any danger that the reader may misunderstand, use *whether*.

• *whether* vs. *whether or not*

Either of these forms may be used. The longer form carries more emphasis.

> *Either:* Please let me know *whether* you received our letter.
> *Or:* Please let me know *whether or not* you received our letter.

• *that* introducing parallel clauses

When either *that* or *which* introduces one of a series of parallel clauses, use the same conjunction to introduce the other clauses in the series. Do not change conjunctions within the sentence.

*Not:* We considered vacation sites *that* we liked and *which* we could afford.

*But:* We considered vacation sites *that* we liked and *that* we could afford.

In formal writing, do not omit the second *that.*

*Formal:* He said *that* he had finished editing the manuscript and *that* his assistant would return it to me. (conjunction retained)

*Less Formal:* He said *that* he had finished editing the manuscript and his assistant would return it to me. (conjunction omitted)

### • Omission of *that*

*That* can be omitted in noun clauses (especially those following such verbs as *say, think, feel, believe, hope*) and in adjective clauses, if the meaning of the sentence is clear.

Noun clauses:

*Either:* He said *that* he would call me before noon.
*Or:* He said he would call me before noon.

*Either:* I hope *that* we can finish this painting today.
*Or:* I hope we can finish this painting today.

Adjective clauses:

*Either:* The book *that* I asked for is out on loan.
*Or:* The book I asked for is out on loan.

*Either:* The instructions *that* she gave were perfectly clear.
*Or:* The instructions she gave were perfectly clear.

### • *when*

Avoid using *when* to introduce a definition unless the definition pertains to time.

*Not:* Their first important step in improving the situation was *when* they decided to examine the real problems. (the step was not "when")

*But:* Their first important step in improving the situation was *the decision* to examine the real problems.

*Normal Usage:* Three o'clock is *when* the meeting will be held.

### • *where*

Avoid using *where* to introduce a definition unless the definition pertains to place or location.

*Not:* A sentence is *where* you have a subject and a verb. (a sentence is not "where")

*But:* A sentence is *a group of words* having a subject and a verb.

*Normal Usage:* The large conference room is *where* the meeting will be held.

Avoid substituting *where* for *that.*

*Not:* I read in the bulletin *where* the new law has been put into effect.
*But:* I read in the bulletin *that* the new law has been put into effect.

- **_while_ vs. _though_, _although_, _and_, or _but_**

*While* pertains mainly to time. Although it is now used to express contrast, some still object to its use in place of *though, although, whereas, and,* or *but.* Avoid this in formal writing, and in any situation that could create ambiguity.

> *Limited Use: While* I did not remember the woman's name, I thought I would recognize her face.
>
> *More Formal: Although* I did not remember the woman's name, I thought I would recognize her face.
>
> *Ambiguous Use:* I assembled the material for the manual *while* he wrote the outline.

This could mean either "during the time that he ..." or "whereas he ...."

> *Clarification:* I assembled the material for the manual, *but* he wrote the outline.

- **_as ... as_ vs. _so ... as_**

Use the correlative *as ... as* in either affirmative or negative sentences; use *so ... as* only in negatives. It once was not acceptable to use the former with negatives, but this rule is no longer in force, except perhaps in very formal writing.

> This melon is *as* sweet *as* that one.
> This melon is not *as* sweet *as* that one.
> This melon is not *so* sweet *as* that one.

## Agreement, Reference, and Parallelism

One source of communication problems is errors in **agreement,** or uniformity — in number, person, or gender — between one part of a sentence and another. When these errors occur, the sentence does not hold together and guide the reader to the writer's intended meaning.

The parts of a sentence must agree in the following ways:

(1)   The verb must agree with the subject in person and number. If the subject is singular, the verb form must also be singular; if the subject is in the third person — *she, he, it* — the verb must be in the third person.

The main task here is to identify the true subject of the sentence and determine whether it is singular or plural.

(2)   A pronoun must agree with its antecedent (the word to which it refers) in person, number, and gender.

The main task here is to identify the antecedent and determine its person, number, and gender. Of the three, gender causes the writer the least difficulty.

The subject of the verb is often also the antecedent of the pronoun. This would seem to simplify things, and to some extent it does; once you have determined that the subject/antecedent is singular, you know that both the verb and the pronoun must be singular. But a word of caution: be consistent. Don't shift, for example, from a singular verb (which agrees with its singular subject) to a plural pronoun later in the sentence.

## Subject Problems

The first step in making the parts of a sentence agree is to identify the subject. In this section, we discuss only those kinds of subjects that may present special problems.

## Collective Words — Singular or Plural?

A **collective** names a group of people or things. Although it is usually singular in form, it is treated as *either* singular or plural, according to the *sense* of the sentence —

Singular when members of the group act, or are thought of, as a *unit:*

> The Survey Committee *is visiting* the district this week.
> The National Office Evaluation Team *has* five trips scheduled for this quarter.

Plural when the members act, or are thought of, as *individuals:*

> The jury *are* unable to agree on a verdict.
> The evaluation team *pool* the data *they* gather and then *prepare their* report.

British usage generally follows only the second point above.

Common collectives include:

> assembly, association, audience, board, class, company, corporation, council, couple, family, firm, group, jury, majority, minority, number, pair, public, staff

Company names also qualify as a type of collective.

> Flowers, Inc., *mails its* advertisements in envelopes with floral decorations.

## Short collectives

The following short words — although seldom listed as collectives — are governed by the rule for collectives. They are singular or plural according to the intended meaning of the sentence.

> all, any, more, most, none, some, who, which

When a prepositional phrase follows any of these words, the number of the noun in the phrase controls the number of the verb. When no such phrase follows, the writer signals the intended meaning by the choice of the singular or the plural verb.

> Some of the *work has been done.*
> Some of the *returns have been filed.*

> Most of the *correspondence is* routine.
> Most of the *letters are* well written.

> *Is* there *any* left? (any portion — any money, any ice cream)
> *Are* there *any* left? (any individual items — any copies, any sandwiches)

> *Who is* it?
> *Who are* they?

> *Which is* to be posted? (which one?)
> *Which are* to be posted? (which ones?)

## The Pronoun *none*

Many writers treat *none* as singular in every case, since it means, literally, "not one." This usage is grammatically correct. But it is now equally acceptable to treat *none* as plural (meaning "not any") when it is followed by a prepositional phrase with a plural noun. To emphasize the singular meaning, some writers often substitute *not one* for *none*. So it is possible to have:

> *None* of the birds *is building* a nest.
> *None* of the birds *are building* a nest.
> *Not one* of the birds *is building* a nest.

## Units of Measure

When a number is used with a plural noun to indicate a unit of measure (money, time, fractions, portions, distance, weight, quantity, etc.), a singular verb is used. When the term is thought of in its individual parts, a plural verb is used.

> *Ten years seems* like a long time.
> *Ten years have gone* by since I last saw him.
>
> *Twenty-one pages is* our homework for each day.
> *Twenty-one pages are needed* to complete the job.

When a fraction or an expression such as *the rest of, the remainder of, a part of,* or *percent of* is followed by a prepositional phrase, the noun or pronoun in that phrase governs the number of the verb.

> *Four-fifths* of the job *was finished* on time.
> *Four-fifths* of the students *were finishing* on time.
>
> The *rest* (or *remainder*) of the work *is* due Friday.
> The *rest* (or *remainder*) of the cards *are* in the mail.
>
> What *percentage* of the information *is* available?
> What *percentage* of the items *were lost*?

## Confusing Singular and Plural Forms

It is sometimes hard to tell by a word's form whether it is singular or plural. Some words that end in *-s* may be singular, and some seemingly singular words may be plural.

The following words take a singular verb although they may appear to be plural.

> apparatus, news, summons
> The *news is* disturbing.

The following words can take either a singular or a plural verb, depending on their meaning.

> ethics, headquarters, mechanics, politics, statistics, tactics
>
> *Ethics is* the subject on which she will speak.
> His business *ethics are* above question.
>
> *Statistics is* the only course I failed in school.
> The *statistics prove* that I am right.

The following irregular plural forms may be confusing because they do not have the usual English *-s* plural marker. For these and many others, consult the dictionary.

> Some interesting *phenomena are* disclosed in this report. (*phenomena* is the plural of *phenomenon*)
> His conclusion seems sound, but his *criteria are* not valid. (*criteria* is the plural of *criterion*)

## Indefinite Pronouns

The indefinite pronouns below are singular. When one of these is used as a subject, it takes a singular verb; when it is used as an antecedent, it requires a singular pronoun.

> anybody, anyone, anything, each, either, everybody, everyone, everything, neither, nobody, no one, nothing, one, somebody, someone, something

These related constructions also are singular. They are used before a prepositional phrase.

> any one (any one of a group), every one, some one

Here are some examples of this usage.

> *Anyone is* welcome, as long as *he or she* accepts our ground rules.
> *Any one* of you *is* capable of doing it.
>
> *Each* of us *is obliged* to go.
>
> *Either* of the alternatives *will work.*
> *Neither* of the plans *is* workable.
>
> *Everyone has* to buy the book for the course.
> *Every one* of her relatives *wants* to sign the card.
>
> *Someone has* to finish this dessert.

Even when two indefinite pronouns are joined by *and,* they take a singular verb.

> *Anyone* and *everyone is* welcome.
> *Nothing* and *no one escapes* her attention.

When *each* or *every* is used to modify a compound subject (subjects joined by *and*), the subject is considered singular.

> *Every* good *girl and boy is waiting* for lots and lots of presents.

When *each* is inserted (as a parenthetical or explanatory element) between a plural or compound subject and its plural verb, this does not affect either the plural form of the verb or the plural form of the pronoun.

> *Region A, Region B, and Region C* each *expect* to increase *their* investments.
> *They* each *want* the same thing.
> *The customers* each *have requested* permission to change *their* method of payment.

*Many a* (unlike *many*) is singular in meaning and takes a singular verb and pronoun.

> *Many a* brilliant *idea fails* to blossom into a success.

*More than one,* although its meaning is plural, takes a singular verb.

> *More than one* vacation *plan was changed* last night.
> *More than one detail is* often *overlooked.*

These words are plural:

> both, few, many, several, others
> *Both* of us *have received* new assignments.
> *Few will be* able to finish *their* work on time.
> *Many plan* to leave in the morning.
> *Several writers have submitted their* stories.
> *Others have* not *finished theirs* yet.

## Relative Pronouns

The verb in a relative clause must agree in number and in person with the relative pronoun (*who, which, that, what*) serving as the subject of the clause. The relative pronoun, in turn, must agree with its antecedent. So before we can make the verb agree with the relative pronoun, we must find the antecedent and determine its person and number.

Have you talked with the man *who was* waiting to see you?

*Man* is the antecedent of the relative pronoun *who*, and the verb *was* must agree with this antecedent in person and number.

Where are the books *that were* left on the table?

The verb in the relative clause — *were* — must agree with the relative pronoun — *that* — which must agree with its antecedent — *books*.

We *who have* met him do not doubt his ability.

The antecedent of the relative pronoun is *we;* the relative pronoun is *who;* and the verb, *have,* is plural because *who* stands for a plural antecedent.

In sentences that contain the phrases *one of the* or *one of those/these,* the antecedent of the relative pronoun is not *one,* but the plural words that follow.

One of the tools *that were* on my table has disappeared.

I spoke with one of those men *who are moving* the piano.

One of the women *who are attending* the conference is wanted on the telephone.

*Who, that,* or *which* may be used to refer to a collective noun. When the members of the group act, or are thought of, as a unit, either *that* or *which* should be used — *that* is usually preferred if the group is made up of persons rather than things. *Who* is used when the persons who make up a group act, or are thought of, as individuals.

The editorial maintains that there *is a group* of citizens *that* is unhappy with the new law.

We have heard from an *association* of *homeowners who feel* strongly opposed to cutting down trees.

## Subjects Joined by *and*

When two or more subjects are joined by *and,* they form a compound subject, which is considered plural. This is true whether the individual subjects themselves are singular or plural.

The *date and* the *time* of the party *have been changed.*

The *host and* his *guests are offering* toasts.

The *coins, pencils, and papers are* on the table where you left *them.*

He and I *deliver our* newspapers in the morning.

Phrases or clauses serving as subjects follow the same rule. When two or more phrases or clauses serving as the subject of a sentence are joined by *and,* the resulting compound subject takes a plural verb.

*Rising early in the morning* and *taking a walk before breakfast make* a person feel good all day.

*That your work is usually done properly* and *that you are usually prompt are* the factors I have considered.

Exception: When the subjects joined by *and* refer to the same person or object, represent a single idea, or form a stock phrase, the whole subject is considered singular.

*Ham and eggs is* a traditional American breakfast.

The *growth and development* of our country *is* a complex topic to study.

Note the difference in meaning in the following pairs of sentences. Repeating an article or a possessive pronominal adjective before the second member of the compound subject (as in the second sentence in each pair below) indicates that two different entities are involved. Check for verb agreement.

*The* lead *actress and star* of the film *has arrived.* (one person)
*The* lead *actress* and *the star* of the film *have arrived.* (two people)

*My teacher and friend helps* me with my problems. (one person)
*My teacher* and *my friend help* me with my problems. (two people)

## Subjects Joined by *or* or *nor*

When singular subjects are joined by *or* or *nor*, the subject takes a singular verb.

Neither the *cat nor* the *mouse knows* that *it* is being watched.
*One or* the *other* of us *has* to go.
Neither *love nor patience is* sufficient to solve such a problem.
Neither *heat nor cold nor sun nor wind affects* this paint.

When one singular subject and one plural subject are joined by *or* or *nor*, the subject closer to the verb determines the number of the verb.

I believe that *she or* her *sisters have* the keys to the car.
I believe that her *sisters* or *she has* the keys to the car.

When one antecedent is singular and the other antecedent is plural, the pronoun agrees with the closer antecedent.

Is it the general or the rebels who *deserve* praise?
Is it the rebels or the general who *deserves* praise?

Because the reader may be distracted by the use of a singular verb with a subject containing a plural element, place the plural element nearer the verb whenever possible.

*Ask* him whether the *card or* the *letters have been signed.*
Neither the *equipment nor* the *drivers are* capable of maintaining that pace.

When the subjects joined by *or* or *nor* are of different persons, the subject nearer the verb determines its person.

I was told that *she or you were* to be responsible.
I was told that *you or she was* to be responsible.

## Shifts in Number or Person

Once you establish a word as either singular or plural, keep it the same throughout the sentence. Be sure that *all* verbs and *all* pronouns related to that word agree with it in number.

*Not:* Because this *country* bases *its* economy on compliance with *its* tax laws, we all must pay our share if *they are* to carry out the necessary functions of government.

*But:* Because this *country* bases *its* economy on compliance with *its* tax laws, we all must pay our share if *it is* to carry out the necessary functions of government.

*Not:* A *person needs* someone to turn to when *they are* in trouble.

*But:* A *person needs* someone to turn to when *he or she is* in trouble.

Regarding *they:* in informal situations, especially informal conversation, the use of *they* to refer to a singular word earlier in the sentence (as in the first of the pair directly above) is increasingly acceptable. However, it is still far from being fully accepted in formal writing. Know your audience, and write accordingly.

**Be consistent.** If you decide that a collective is singular, keep it singular throughout the sentence — use a singular verb to agree with it and a singular pronoun to refer to it. If you establish the collective as plural, keep both the verb and the pronoun plural.

> The committee *has* announced *its* decision.
> The committee *have* adjourned and gone to *their* homes.
> Our staff *is* always glad to offer *its* advice and assistance.

Most indefinite pronouns are singular and require singular verbs and pronouns.

> *Not:* Has *anyone* turned in *their* report?
> *But:* Has *anyone* turned in *his or her* report?

The indefinite pronoun *anyone* takes both a singular verb and a singular pronoun.

Do not apply a verb form from one part of the sentence to another (elliptically) unless the same form is grammatically correct in both parts.

> *Not:* The *numbers were* checked and the total verified.
> *But:* The *numbers were* checked and the *total was* verified.

Avoid shifting the person of pronouns referring to the same antecedent.

> *Not:* When *one* is happy, it often seems as if everyone around *you* is happy, too.
> *But:* When *one* is happy, it often seems as if everyone around *one* (or *him or her*) is happy, too.
> *Or:* When *you* are happy, it often seems as if everyone around *you* is happy, too. (less formal)

> *Not:* As *the ship* entered *her* berth, *its* huge gray shadow seemed to swallow us.
> *But:* As the *ship* entered *its* berth, *its* huge gray shadow seemed to swallow us.
> *Or:* As the *ship* entered *her* berth, *her* huge gray shadow seemed to swallow us.

## Structure Problems

It usually is easy for us to identify the subject or antecedent and determine its number and person. But occasionally a puzzling sentence comes along. The subject is there, but something in the sentence structure can make us believe that another word is the subject.

### Verb Precedes Subject

When the verb precedes the subject in a sentence, locate the true subject and make the verb agree with it.

> *Are* the *lamp* and the *bookcase* in that room?
> Walking down the hall *are* the *men* we were waiting for.
> Clearly visible in the sky *were* the *stars* of the Pleiades.
> From these books *come some* of our best *ideas.*
> To us *falls* the *task* of restoring the environment.
> Among those in attendance *were* two former *teachers*.

- *where, here, there*

*Where, here,* or *there* at the beginning of a sentence does not influence the number or person of the verb. In such sentences, find the real subject and make the verb agree with it.

> Where *are* the *classes held?*
> Where *is* the *class held?*

> Here *are* the old *songs* that we loved as children.
> Here *is* the old *song* that we loved as children.

> There *are* two *books* on the table.
> There *is* a *book* on the table.

- *what, who, which*

*What, who,* or *which* used as an interrogative pronoun at the beginning of a sentence does not affect the number of the verb. Find the subject of the sentence and make the verb agree with it.

> What *is* the *point* of your argument?
> What *are* your *recommendations* on this problem?

> Who *is* your favorite *writer?*
> Who *are* the team *members* that we should watch?

> Which *is* the *book* that she recommended?
> Which *are* the *standards* that we are to apply?

- *it, there*

*It* or *there* may introduce a sentence, coming before the verb and displacing the subject, which comes later in the clause. *It* takes a singular verb, even when the real subject is plural. Following *there*, the verb is singular or plural according to the subject that follows it.

> It *is solutions* we are looking for, not problems.
> It *is* a long *story* that I have to tell.

> There *are* many different *ways* to stuff a turkey.
> There *is* always *room* for one more.

## Words Intervene between Subject and Verb

If there are explanatory or parenthetical phrases, or other modifiers, between the subject and verb, they do not change the number or person of the subject. Locate the real subject of the sentence and make the verb agree with it.

> His sworn *statement*, together with statements from other witnesses, *was heard* in court.
> The *amount* shown, plus interest, *is* due within 30 days.
> The *letter* with its several enclosures *has* just *arrived*.
> Our *manners*, like our speech, *are* indicators of character.
> The *policeman*, not the detectives, *is going* to interview our neighbor.
> That *fact*, added to our already large file on the case, *means* that our assumptions were correct.
> *No one* but you and me *knows* the secret.

## Subject and Predicate Differ in Number

The predicate nominative, coming after forms of the verb *to be,* refers to the same person or thing as the subject. When the predicate nominative differs in number from the subject, the verb must agree with the element that *precedes* it (the subject).

> The electrician said that a serious *problem was* the old lines.
>
> The electrician said that the old *lines were* a serious problem.

## Special Problems of Pronoun Reference

A pronoun should be placed as close as possible to its antecedent (the preceding word to which it refers), in the most logical way possible.

### Ambiguous Antecedents

In order to avoid ambiguity, be sure that the pronoun and the clause it introduces are placed near the word that the pronoun refers to. In the first example below, *that* must be understood as referring to *table* — not the intended antecedent. Reposition the pronoun and clause near *letter,* the intended antecedent.

> *Not:* The letter is on the conference table *that* we received yesterday.
>
> *But:* The *letter that* we received yesterday is on the conference table.

> *Not:* The mashed potatoes were full of huge, hard lumps *that* we ate for dinner.
>
> *But:* The mashed potatoes *that* we ate for dinner were full of huge, hard lumps.

### Indefinite Antecedents

Be sure that the reference to an antecedent is absolutely clear.

> *Not:* The copies of the letters were not initialed by the writers, so we are sending *them* back. (What are we sending back — the copies, the letters, or the writers?)
>
> *But:* We are sending back the copies of the letters because *they* were not initialed by the writers.
>
> *Or:* We are sending back the copies of the letters because the authors did not initial *them.*

> *Not:* When you have finished the book and written your summary, please return *it* to the library. (What is going to be returned — the book or the summary?)
>
> *But:* When you have finished the book and written your summary, please return the book to the library.

### Implied Antecedents

As a general rule,

(1) Be sure that the antecedent of a pronoun appears in the sentence — that it is not merely implied.

(2) Be sure that the antecedent is a specific word, not an idea expressed in a phrase or clause.

*It, which, this,* and *that* are the pronouns that most often lead meaning astray. Any of these pronouns may refer to an idea expressed in a preceding passage, *if* the idea and the reference are *unmistakably* clear. But too often, the idea that is unmistakably clear to the speaker or writer is nowhere to be found when the listener or reader looks for it.

*Not:* Although the doctor operated at once, *it* was not a success and the patient died.

*But:* Although the doctor performed the *operation* at once, *it* was not a success and the patient died.

*Or:* Although the doctor operated at once, the *operation* was not a success and the patient died.

## Parallelism and Sentence Structure

In a sentence containing two or more elements of the same grammatical rank, be sure that each of the elements is expressed in the same way — with balance in the grammatical structures involved. This balance or symmetry, known as **parallelism,** is important especially in formal writing. But strive for it in all kinds of writing, because it contributes both clarity and smoothness to a sentence.

Parallelism is basically a matter of logic. Determining equal grammatical rank is relatively simple:

> word = word (within the same part of speech)
> phrase = phrase (when the phrases are of the same type)
> dependent clause = dependent clause
> independent clause = independent clause

Parallel sentence elements are most often connected by coordinating or correlative conjunctions.

If two *phrases* are of the same rank, be sure that they are in the same basic form.

> *Not:* I really enjoyed *his piano playing* and *you singing.*
> *But:* I really enjoyed *his piano playing* and *your singing.*
> *Or:* I really enjoyed hearing *him playing the piano* and *you singing.*
> *Or:* I really enjoyed *hearing him play the piano* and *hearing you sing.*

In each of the alternative sentences above, the structures on either side of the conjunction are equivalent.

Make sure that *verb* forms are parallel.

> *Not:* They didn't know whom *to call,* what *to do,* or how.
> *But:* They didn't know whom *to call,* what *to do,* or how *to do it.*

If a *preposition* applies to all of the nouns or phrases in a series, *either* use one preposition at the beginning of the series *or* place the preposition before *every* element of the series.

> *Not:* We added pinches of salt, of pepper, and *nutmeg* [or: pinches *of salt, pepper,* and *of nutmeg*].
> *But:* We added pinches *of salt, pepper,* and *nutmeg.*
> *Or:* We added pinches *of salt, of pepper,* and *of nutmeg.*

If, on the other hand, the same preposition does *not* apply to all of the elements, be sure to insert all of the prepositions that are needed.

> *Not:* She has a real *sensitivity, love,* and *aptitude for* language.
> *But:* She has a real *sensitivity to, love of,* and *aptitude for* language.

To edit for parallelism in *clauses,* analyze the structure of the first one and determine what parts must appear in the clause or clauses that follow.

> *Not:* Either *they will do it my way* or *not at all.*
> *But:* Either *they will do it my way,* or *they will not do it at all.*

In the revised version, the second element has the same clause structure as the first (*not* does not affect the parallelism), and the two parts are introduced by correlative conjunctions. However, it is also possible to create parallelism with less than a full clause — so long as the connectives connect equivalent structures. Here are three more alternative forms.

> *Or:* They either *will do it my way,* or *will not do it at all.*
> *Or:* They will either *do it my way,* or *not do it at all.*
> *Or:* They will do it either *my way* or *not at all.*

In the first of these three alternatives, the conjunctions have moved into parallel positions before the respective predicates. In the second, they have moved into place before the main verbs. In the third, they come before the adverbial phrases.

Develop a sense of parallelism by working through the above examples. Note how the conjunctions "slide" through equivalent sections of each clause to a new position, eliminating the parts of the second clause that are understood to be the same as those of the first clause.

Here are some further examples of parallelism problems.

> *Not:* *To sing* and *dancing* are not permitted here.
> *But:* *Singing* and *dancing* are not permitted here.

Use only one type of verbal at a time. In the following example, a noun and a participial phrase are linked awkwardly.

> *Not:* The children are learning the value of *courtesy* and *being kind.*
> *But:* The children are learning the value of *courtesy* and *kindness.*
> *Or:* The children are learning the value of *being courteous* and (*being*) *kind.*

## Gender-Inclusive Writing

### Background

Traditionally, words such as *he* and *man*, and the suffix *-man*, have been understood to refer generically in certain contexts to people of both sexes; *he* has been used whenever the gender of the antecedent was unknown. Some more conservative speakers and writers continue to use these forms. Over time, however, many people have come to believe that language use should more explicitly reflect the makeup of society; the presence of women and girls in professions, athletics, and other areas; and a conscious effort to reduce gender stereotyping in all contexts. Many of these concerns have been dealt with in textbooks and storybooks for children and young adults, in order to avoid the sexism and stereotyping formerly found in them.

As we know, language is changing all the time. Conscious efforts to make specific changes have often failed in the past, however. But the wide acceptance of the introduction of the form *Ms.* to stand for either *Mrs.* or *Miss* (parallel to *Mr.,* which does not reflect a man's marital status) suggests that there is room for change in other areas as well. Many specific linguistic items are still very much in flux, but it is possible to point to certain trends that a speaker or writer may wish to adopt — or probably has already adopted to some degree.

The basic rule applies: know your audience. Try not to distract the reader from what you are saying by the way you are saying it. And avoid awkward phrasing wherever possible. Some specific items are discussed below.

## Generic *he*

> As the reader progresses, *he* will notice a definite increase in wordiness.

There are at least three basic strategies for avoiding this form: use two pronouns, pluralize, or use the pronoun *one*. It may also be necessary to recast the sentence into a somewhat different form.

(1)  Use two pronouns:

> As the reader progresses, *he or she* will notice a definite increase in wordiness.

This method will work in many cases, but do not overuse it. Too many instances of the basic form, or of the objective, possessive, or reflexive form, especially in the same paragraph or passage, will create awkwardness:

> As the reader progresses, *he or she* will find *himself or herself* pondering the increasing wordiness of the book and possibly questioning *his or her* decision to read it.
>
> *Better:* As the story progresses, the reader will ponder its increasing wordiness and possibly question *his or her* decision to read it.

Some writers use *she or he* either exclusively or in addition to *he or she.* Some use *she* exclusively, but this would constitute a distraction for most readers.

In formal writing, avoid forms such as *he/she, she/he,* and *s/he.* Readers have not generally become comfortable with these.

(2)  Pluralize the antecedent and the pronoun (which becomes *they*):

> As *readers* progress, *they* will notice a definite increase in wordiness.

In this particular case, this method is less satisfactory, since the intended focus is on the individual reader's reaction to the author's style. Try recasting the sentence without a pronoun:

> A *careful reader* will notice a definite increase in wordiness as the story progresses.

When pluralizing, be sure to check for agreement in number.

(3)  Use the pronoun *one:*

> As *one* progresses through the book, *one* will notice a definite increase in wordiness.

*One* is an acceptable pronoun to use after the antecedent *one* — in very formal writing. Again, though, do not overuse this method.

Note that the pronoun *you* for the generic is fine in informal speech and even in informal writing, but *not* in formal writing.

## Generic Use of *man/men*

(1)  As a count noun:

In using the noun *man,* be sure you intend to refer only to persons of the masculine gender; if not, use, for example, *a man or woman/men or women/men and women* where possible. Or use the neutral *a person/people, one,* or *anyone/anybody, everyone/everybody,* or *someone/somebody* as the context permits.

(2)  As a mass noun:

In this case, *man* means "the human race." The titles of many great books contain this word used in this way — a formal or elevated usage. However, this may be much too formal in many contexts.

A number of alternatives are possible.

(a) Pluralize (and check for agreement):

> *Instead of:* Prehistoric *man* learned to use fire for many purposes.
> *Use:* Prehistoric *people/humans/human beings* learned to use fire for many purposes.

(b) When the meaning is "the human race generally," synonymous with "mankind," try using *human beings, humans, people, the human race, humanity,* or *humankind,* as appropriate. The last term is not acceptable to every reader, however.

## Generic Use of the Suffix *-man*

(1) In many cases, a simple change from *-man/-men* to the suffix *-person/-persons* will make a noun inclusive. Remember also that the suffix *-woman/-women* is available for referring to women alone. Some forms are used more commonly than others.

> spokesman → spokesperson; also spokeswoman
> chairman → chairperson or chair; also chairwoman
> congressman → congressperson; also congresswoman

(2) Many job titles have been changed to account for participation of both men and women in those fields. For example:

> policeman/policewoman → police officer
> mailman → letter carrier
> fireman → firefighter

## Using *girl* vs. *woman*

Many women find it demeaning to be referred to as a "girl." Be sure you intend to refer only to children when you use this term, especially in formal writing. Otherwise, use *woman.* In informal situations, and among people who know one another well, rules of this kind are often relaxed.

> *Not:* The *girl* running the copy machine was rude to me.
> *But:* The *woman* running the copy machine was rude to me.
> *Informal:* So it's *girls'* night out — I can't wait!

## The Suffixes *-ess* and *-ette*

Although *-ess* and *-ette* have been in common use, they are now seen as connoting smallness and weakness in many or most cases. It is advisable to avoid terms such as *poetess* for *poet* and *suffragette* for *suffragist.* The dictionary often provides information on the use of specific words of this type.

## Other Aspects of Gender-Inclusive Writing

In addition to noting the specific items of word choice covered above, try to avoid explicit or implicit stereotypes involving gender (as well as ethnicity, socioeconomic status, age, and so forth, of course).

Stereotyping can be as subtle as the use of the phrase *woman doctor* in a context in which the person's femaleness is not the focus; the implication is that the norm for doctors is maleness. While women are still in the minority, they do make up a significant proportion of the physicians in this country.

By keeping generally aware of this concern as you write and revise, you can avoid distracting (or annoying) the reader much of the time.

# MECHANICS

## Abbreviations

1. Established abbreviations are acceptable in all but the most formal writing. But commonly used words and phrases are not likely to be abbreviated in ordinary writing unless they are pronounced letter by letter, as written. For example, *BC* and *AM* almost always take the place of *before Christ* and *ante meridiem,* but *lb.* and *mt.* are ordinarily written as *pound* and *mountain.*

2. For ease in reading, use only well-known abbreviations. If an abbreviation may not be familiar to the reader, spell out the word or phrase in parentheses after the abbreviation the first time it appears; after that, use it without further explanation. Use a given abbreviation consistently throughout the text.

   It was a typical NIMBY (Not In My BackYard) situation.

   SEATO (Southeast Asia Treaty Organization)

3. In general, an abbreviation follows the capitalization and hyphenation of the original word or phrase. Some abbreviations customarily have a period following each separate letter or group of letters; some customarily do not. Some may be written in either way. The current trend is to omit periods in many cases.

   aka *or* a.k.a.

   Note that although many abbreviations in the dictionary that precedes this Style Guide are listed without periods, certain categories of abbreviations do customarily retain the period in the following specific cases:

   a. courtesy titles

      Mr. Sparks
      Dr. Watson

   b. elements of calendar dates

      Tues., Jan. 1, 2002

      For brevity in a date or time reference, use the following abbreviations for the names of the months when they are used with the day or year, or both. Do *not* abbreviate in dates within the heading or inside address of a letter, or in very formal writing.

| Jan. | Apr. | Oct. |
|------|------|------|
| Feb. | Aug. | Nov. |
| Mar. | Sept. | Dec. |

Abbreviations for *May, June,* and *July* do exist, but many writers avoid them — either because they are hard to recognize or because the months' names themselves are so brief.

Use the following abbreviations for the names of the days of the week, with the same restrictions as those given above for the names of the months.

Sun.                         Thur. *or* Thurs.
Mon.                         Fri.
Tue. *or* Tues.              Sat.
Wed.

c. elements of business names

Heartfelt Greeting Cards, Inc.

Be sure to write the abbreviations in the name of a company, agency, or organization exactly as they are shown on the letterhead. The following abbreviations are those most commonly used in such names.

Bros. — Brothers
Co. — Company
Corp. — Corporation
Inc. — Incorporated
Ltd. — Limited (Ltd — British usage)

Do not abbreviate *Company* and *Corporation* in names of federal government units.

Commodity Credit Corporation

Do not abbreviate *Company* if it follows *the.*

*Not:* The Jones Co.
*But:* The Jones Company

*Not:* The Cheery Bouquet Co.
*But:* The Cheery Bouquet Company

d. certain elements of addresses — see section 6.

e. Latin terms

Ibid.
op. cit.

f. the initials of personal names

P. J. Stevens

4. In an established English abbreviation that has internal periods, there is no space after the periods.

N.Dak.

5. The initials of persons are ordinarily spaced as if they were words.

A. B. Herrera
T. S. Eliot

This is not true in British usage, however.

T.S. Eliot

6. In an address, it is best to spell out all the words, except in very informal writing. Do *not* abbreviate words — except for courtesy titles — in the heading or

inside address of a letter. For brevity in more informal situations, use the following abbreviations. Although these may be written without periods in the dictionary that precedes this Style Guide, they do customarily retain the period in this case.

Apt. — Apartment
Ave. — Avenue
Bldg — Building
Blvd. — Boulevard
Ct. — Court
Dr. — Drive
Pl. — Place
Sq. — Square
St. — Street

Note that compass directions do *not* have periods.

NE — Northeast
NW — Northwest
SE — Southeast
SW — Southwest

Consult the table of ABBREVIATIONS FOR U.S. STATES AND CANADIAN PROVINCES AND TERRITORIES as needed.

7. Certain abbreviations of courtesy titles, etc., are used with personal names in specific ways.

 a. Before the name: *Mister* and *Doctor* are customarily written *Mr.* (plural *Messrs.*) and *Dr.*

  Mr. Forrest
  Dr. Sarah Birch

 Certain other abbreviations used as courtesy titles do not have full forms.

  Mrs. King
  Ms. Kate McGrath

 The title *Miss* is not an abbreviation and does not take a period.

 b. After the name: *Junior* and *Senior* are customarily written *Jr.* and *Sr.;* they are preceded by a comma. Use them only with the full name — and only when both persons' names are spelled *exactly* the same.

  Abraham White, Sr.

 The forms *2d, 3d, II,* and *III* are used similarly — but without a comma.

  Thomas J. Mann III

 The abbreviation *Esq.* for *Esquire* (for any man or for an attorney of either gender) follows the name and is preceded by a comma.

  Anthony B. Just, Esq.

 Do not combine titles such as *Mr., Mrs., Ms., Dr.,* or *Esq.* with another title or with the abbreviation for an academic degree.

  James Robeson, MA, PhD; *not* Mr. James Robeson, MA, PhD
  Grace Clement, MD; *not* Dr. Grace Clement, MD, *or* Ms. Grace Clement, MD

c. For an academic degree following a full name that is not preceded by a title, the abbreviation is customarily used.

> Ida Hughes, PhD; *not* Dr. Ida Hughes, PhD

With or without the periods, such abbreviations are written without spaces.

d. For the title of a religious order following a full name. In some cases, there may also be a title before the name.

> Sister Angelique Christopher, OSB

> Father Theodore Bright, SJ, *or* Fr. Theodore Bright, SJ, *or* Theodore Bright, SJ

8. In very formal writing, spell out *United States* when it is used as a noun or when it is used as an adjective with the names of other countries. It can be abbreviated when used as an adjective in most other situations.

> US monetary policy *or* U.S. monetary policy

9. To save space, scientific texts, tables, footnotes, bibliographies, etc., rely heavily on abbreviations. In general, periods are omitted from abbreviations of units of measure in these cases.

> km
> ft-lb
> $cm^3$
> g
> FM

10. In nontechnical writing, abbreviations for units of English measure (*foot, mile, pound, ton, quart, gallon,* etc.) can be written with or without periods. Use a period if leaving it out would confuse the reader.

## Abbreviations for Names of U.S. States and Canadian Provinces and Territories

Following are the abbreviations for the names of U.S. states and Canadian provinces and territories. The postal-code abbreviations are becoming more common in general types of writing; the postal services encourage their use in the addresses on envelopes.

### U.S. States

| Name | Traditional Abbreviation | Postal Abbreviation |
|---|---|---|
| Alabama | Ala or Ala. | AL |
| Alaska | Alas or Alas. | AK |
| Arizona | Ariz or Ariz. | AZ |
| Arkansas | Ark or Ark. | AR |
| California | Cal or Cal. Calif or Calif. | CA |
| Colorado | Colo or Colo. | CO |
| Connecticut | Conn or Conn. | CT |
| Delaware | Del or Del. | DE |
| [District of Columbia] | DC or D.C. | DC |
| Florida | Fla or Fla. | FL |

| Name | Traditional Abbreviation | Postal Abbreviation |
|------|--------------------------|---------------------|
| Georgia | Ga or Ga. | GA |
| Hawaii | Haw or Haw. | HI |
| Idaho | Id or Id.<br>Ida or Ida. | ID |
| Illinois | Ill or Ill. | IL |
| Indiana | In or In.<br>Ind or Ind. | IN |
| Iowa | Ia or Ia. | IA |
| Kansas | Kans or Kans. | KS |
| Kentucky | Ky or Ky. | KY |
| Louisiana | La or La. | LA |
| Maine | Me or Me. | ME |
| Maryland | Md or Md. | MD |
| Massachusetts | Mass or Mass. | MA |
| Michigan | Mich or Mich. | MI |
| Minnesota | Minn or Minn. | MN |
| Mississippi | Miss or Miss. | MS |
| Missouri | Mo or Mo. | MO |
| Montana | Mont or Mont. | MT |
| Nebraska | Neb or Neb.<br>Nebr or Nebr. | NE |
| Nevada | Nev or Nev. | NV |
| New Hampshire | NH or N.H. | NH |
| New Jersey | NJ or N.J. | NJ |
| New Mexico | NM or N.M.<br>N Mex or N.Mex. | NM |
| New York | NY or N.Y. | NY |
| North Carolina | NC or N.C. | NC |
| North Dakota | ND or N. D.<br>N Dak or N.Dak. | ND |
| Ohio | O or O. | OH |
| Oklahoma | Okla or Okla. | OK |
| Oregon | Ore or Ore.<br>Oreg or Oreg. | OR |
| Pennsylvania | Pa or Pa.<br>Penn or Penn.<br>Penna or Penna. | PA |
| Rhode Island | RI or R.I. | RI |
| South Carolina | SC or S.C. | SC |
| South Dakota | SD or S.D.<br>S Dak or S.Dak. | SD |
| Tennessee | Tenn or Tenn. | TN |
| Texas | Tex or Tex. | TX |
| Utah | Ut or Ut. | UT |
| Vermont | Vt or Vt. | VT |
| Virginia | Va or Va. | VA |

| Name | Traditional Abbreviation | Postal Abbreviation |
|------|--------------------------|---------------------|
| Washington | Wash or Wash. Wa or Wa. | WA |
| West Virginia | WVa or W.Va. | WV |
| Wisconsin | Wis or Wis. Wisc or Wisc. | WI |
| Wyoming | Wyo or Wyo. | WY |

## Canadian Provinces and Territories

| Name | Traditional Abbreviation | Postal Abbreviation |
|------|--------------------------|---------------------|
| Alberta | Alta or Alta. | AB |
| British Columbia | BC or B.C. | BC |
| Manitoba | Man or Man. | MB |
| New Brunswick | NB or N.B. | NB |
| Newfoundland | Nfld or Nfld. Newf or Newf. Nfd or Nfd. | NF |
| Northwest Territories | NWT or N.W.T. | NT |
| Nova Scotia | NS or N.S. | NS |
| Nunavut | — | NU |
| Ontario | Ont or Ont. | ON |
| Prince Edward Island | PEI or P.E.I. | PE |
| Quebec | Que or Que. | QC |
| Saskatchewan | Sask or Sask. | SK |
| Yukon Territory | YT or Y.T. | YT |

# Capitalization

In standard editing practice, capital letters are referred to as "uppercase"; "small," or non-capital, letters are referred to as "lowercase."

1. Capitalize the first word of a complete sentence.

    A huge moose with a giant rack of antlers stood in the path of our car.

2. Capitalize the first word of a quoted sentence.

    "It's a great big moose!" gasped my son. "What do we do now?"

    Do *not* capitalize the first word within quotation marks if it does not begin a complete sentence.

    "What we do," whispered my daughter, "is sit perfectly still and be quiet and wait for it to leave."

3. Capitalize the first word of a direct question within a sentence.

    The essay poses the ever-more-relevant question, What are full human rights?

4. Capitalize the letter *I* when it stands alone, signifying the personal pronoun.

5. Capitalize the interjection *O* (which is used without a comma).

> O Lord!

6. In the title of a book, play, film, magazine, article, etc.:

Capitalize the first and last words, *plus* all other words *except* articles (*a, an, the*), coordinating conjunctions (*and, or, but,* etc.), and most prepositions.

> "The Mystery of the Green Ghost"
> *A Night at the Opera*

If there is a subtitle preceded by a colon, capitalize the first word after the colon.

> *The Moose and How to Observe It: A Naturalist's Year in the Canadian Woods*

7. Capitalize a title when it is used with the name of a person or group.

> Representative Jane Wise is a leading figure in the Republican Party.

Do *not* capitalize the same type of title when it does not make a specific reference.

> The senator is a liberal; his opponent is a conservative.

When a title is used alone in direct address, *do* capitalize it.

> While I agree with you, Governor, I am well aware that most people do not.

8. Capitalize *President* and *Presidency* when they refer to the office of President of the United States.

> The President spoke before a joint session of Congress.
> *But:* She is president of the local bar association.

9. Capitalize the names of the days of the week, the months of the year, and holidays; do *not* capitalize the names of the seasons.

> Labor Day, the last holiday of the summer, falls on the first Monday in September.

10. Capitalize the designations for points of the compass only when they refer to a specific place or region.

> Many retired persons spend the winter in the South.

Do not capitalize them when they refer to a direction.

> The geese were flying south.

11. Capitalize the words in the title of a course taught in a school or college in the same way as for titles of books (see item 4 above).

> History of Latin America, Part I
> Chemistry 201
> Linguistic Analysis of Modern English

In general references to school *subjects,* as opposed to specific *courses,* it is not necessary to capitalize words that are not capitalized in their own right.

> Next year she will study French, English, biology, math, and history.

12. A noun that is not regularly capitalized should be capitalized when it is used as part of a proper name.

> Yesterday I visited Uncle David, my favorite uncle.

13. In a letter:

    Capitalize all titles in the address.

    > Ms. Amy Smith, President
    > Mr. Charles Andrews, Chairman of the Board

    Capitalize the first and last words, the titles, and the proper names in the salutation.

    > Dear Dr. Williams,
    > My dear Sir:

    Capitalize only the first word in the closing phrase.

    > Very truly yours,

14. Capitalize all proper names — including, but not limited to, those for:

    *people:* Amelia Earhart, Babe Ruth, Dagwood Bumstead, John Doe

    *places:* Michigan, Pittsburgh, France, Lake Michigan

    Traditionally, a noun with two or more place names has been lowercased.

    > lakes Michigan and Erie

    More recently, however, it has become acceptable to capitalize the noun.

    > Lakes Michigan and Erie

    *derivatives of place names:* Michigander, Pittsburgher, French

    *ethnic groups, linguistic groups, and languages:* Basques, the Welsh, Mandarin, Cornish

    *buildings:* the Jefferson Memorial, Waterside Apartments, Stonehenge

    *events:* Thanksgiving, the Olympics, World War I

    *eras:* the Golden Age, the Jurassic Period, the Roaring Twenties

    *organizations:* the United Fund, the Whig Party

    *governmental bodies:* Parliament, the Supreme Court

    *educational institutions:* Yale University

    *academic designations:* Master of Arts (*but:* a master's degree)

    *military titles:* Sergeant Thompson, General of the Army (*but:* a lieutenant)

    *noble and royal titles:* the Duke of York, Her Highness (*but:* a count, a countess)

    *religious titles:* Rabbi Susan Klein, Father Murphy, Reverend Campbell

    *religious denominations and sects:* Judaism, Catholicism, the Shakers

    *deities:* God, Allah, Diana, Vishnu

    *religious texts:* the Old Testament, the New Testament, the Koran/the Qur'an, the Book of the Dead, Isaiah, the Nicene Creed (*but:* biblical)

    *awards:* the Nobel Peace Prize, the Purple Heart

    *specific boats, ships, and aircraft* (in italics): HMS *Pinafore,* the *Titanic,* the *Spirit of St. Louis*

    *scientific designations for plants and animals at all levels down to genus* (above genus, they are in roman type; from genus down, in italic type): Arthropoda (arthropods), *Ocimum basilicum* (sweet basil) *constellations, stars, planets, and other objects seen in the sky:* Orion, the Little Dipper, Sirius, the Pleiades, Mars, the Milky Way (*but, usually:* the earth, the sun, the moon)

*trademarked goods*

15. Capitalize the name of an abstract or inanimate thing that is personified.

> When Justice speaks, woe betide those who close their ears.
> And Winter charged in early, blowing away all my hopes and plans.

## Small capitals

These are used, in print:

1. For the time-reference abbreviations A.D., B.C., C.E., B.C.E., A.M., P.M., etc., with numerals.

2. For acronyms, according to some style guides.

3. For the names of speakers in the script of a play.

## Words Derived from Proper Nouns

Some words derived from proper names have lost their proper-name meaning and have acquired an independent meaning in a different context. Many of these words are no longer capitalized. Below is a list of some lowercase derivatives of proper names.

| | |
|---|---|
| angstrom | klieg light |
| argyle socks | knickerbockers/knickers |
| artesian well | lambert |
| astrakhan (a type of fabric) | lynch law |
| bologna | lyonnaise potatoes |
| bourbon | macadamized road |
| bowie knife | madras (a type of cloth) |
| brazilwood | maraschino cherries |
| britannia metal | maxwell |
| cashmere sweater | mercerized fabric |
| chesterfield (a type of coat) | merino sheep |
| chinook salmon | morocco leather |
| coulomb | navy blue |
| curie | newton |
| delftware | oxford cloth |
| diesel engine | parkerhouse roll |
| dotted swiss | pasteurization |
| fedora | petri dish |
| frankfurter | philistinism |
| gargantuan | portland cement |
| gauss | quisling |
| gilbert | quixotic |
| graham cracker | roentgen |
| herculean task | simon-pure |
| italic type/italics | timothy |
| japan varnish | utopianism |
| jersey | venturi tube |
| joule | zeppelin |

For questions regarding capitalization of other such derivatives, consult the dictionary.

## Compound Words

A compound is a combination of two or more words, often a combination that conveys a special meaning that is not apparent from the meaning of the two words taken separately.

> rock candy

A compound can also consist of a word with one or more prefixes, suffixes, or combining forms attached, or of one or more combining forms plus prefixes and/or suffixes.

> hypersensitivity

A compound made up of two or more words may be written *open* (with a space between its parts):

> durable goods

*hyphenated*:

> forget-me-not

or *solid* or *closed* (without a space or hyphen):

> praiseworthy

Compounds containing only combining forms and affixes may be written solid or with a hyphen.

Since language changes over time, the usual way of writing a given compound can change. An open compound sometimes gains a hyphen, but eventually loses it and is written solid. Another compound may start out, and remain, hyphenated. Others remain open. Some are routinely spelled in more than one way.

Some sources attempt to offer rules or generalizations to aid in the spelling of various categories of compounds, but these are helpful only to the degree that the reader is willing to memorize rules and lists, and they are incomplete at best. Ultimately, there is no simple way to predict which way a given word combination is to be written. Except for the few specific points below, the best source of information on the form of a compound is the dictionary. Look up the compound and memorize its form as with the spelling of any other new word.

1. Use a hyphen before a capitalized element — a proper noun or its derivative.

   > non-American
   > Anglo-Saxon

2. Use a hyphen to join a single capital letter to a following word.

   > X-ray
   > I-beam
   > V-necked

3. In a series of hyphenated compounds all having the same second element, which is omitted in all but the last item, keep the hyphen at the end of each truncated unit to indicate that the items are all related.

   > long-, short-, and medium-term rates
   > two- and five-ton trucks

4. In a hyphenated phrase that comes before a noun and modifies it, be sure to link all related words in the phrase with hyphens for clarity.

> *Not:* She displayed a real take-it or leave-it attitude.
> *But:* She displayed a real take-it-or-leave-it attitude.

> *Not:* a sun-dried tomato sauce over homemade linguini
> *But:* a sun-dried-tomato sauce over homemade linguini

In the second pair of examples above, the first sentence implies that the *sauce* is both sun-dried and made of tomatoes. In the second sentence, the hyphen connecting "sun-dried" with "tomato" makes it clear that only the *tomatoes* are sundried, and the whole hyphenated phrase modifies "sauce."

For rules for forming the plurals of compounds, see the PLURALS section below.

## Italics

Use italic (slanted) letters:

1. To set off the title of:

   a. a book, play, long poem, or poetry collection

   > *War and Peace*
   > *Othello*
   > *Paradise Lost*

   b. a journal, magazine, newspaper, or pamphlet

   > *American Speech*
   > *Newsweek*
   > *The Washington Post*

   In a reference within a text, "The" in a newspaper title is not italicized.

   > In a recent piece in the *New York Times,* a columnist takes issue with the notion that . . . .

   c. a long musical work (opera, operetta, oratorio, etc., but *not* a symphony, sonata, etc., identified by number or key)

   > *The Magic Flute*
   > Handel's *Messiah*

   d. a painting, sculpture, etc.

   > Picasso's *Guernica*
   > Rodin's *The Thinker*

   e. a film

   > *The Maltese Falcon*
   > *M\*A\*S\*H\**

   f. a television series or long-running radio program (but not an individual episode)

   > *NOVA*
   > *All Things Considered*

2.  To name a ship, train, aircraft, or spacecraft.

> HMS *Pinafore*
> the *Titanic*
> the *Orient Express*
> *Skylab*

3.  To emphasize a word or phrase within a sentence.

> Before the exam, be sure you *really* know the periodic table of the elements.
> It's not how *much* you write that counts; it's how *well* you write.

4.  To set off words used as words, letters used as letters, etc. (Quotation marks may also be used in such cases.)

> Remember, the word *potato* does not have an *e* at the end.

5.  To indicate a word or phrase that was borrowed from another language but that has not yet become a fully English construction. Consult the dictionary for the current status of a borrowed word or phrase.

> His appointment as treasurer was a *fait accompli.*

In the following example, one borrowed compound has been accepted as English and the other has not.

> I ordered a café au lait; she ordered a *café con leche.* Both are basically coffee with hot milk.

Overuse of italics in a piece of writing lessens their effect; use them judiciously.

# Numbers

## General Rules

Two general rules apply to the writing of numbers. Follow one or the other consistently within a piece of writing.

1.  Spell out numbers from one through nine; use figures from 10 on.

> two books
> three times as large
> 14 recommendations

2.  Spell out numbers from one through ninety-nine; use figures from 100 on.

> twenty books
> thirty times in one year
> 140 pages

Hyphenate spelled-out numbers from twenty-one to twenty-nine, from thirty-one to thirty-nine, etc.

## Specific Rules

1.  Spell out any number that begins a sentence. If the spelled-out form would be unwieldy or awkward, recast the sentence so that it does not begin with a number.

> Nineteen eighty-three was the company's best year.
> Two hundred forty workers were hired.

He received 1,234,567 votes.

*Not:* One million, two hundred thirty-four thousand, five hundred sixty-seven votes were cast for him.

2. Spell out an isolated number if it is a multiple of one hundred, a round number, or an indefinite expression.

hundreds of people
forty-odd thieves
a thousand and one reasons
less than a million dollars

3. Spell out an isolated number if it is a reference to a century or a truncated reference to a decade.

the twenty-first century
the early seventies (*but:* the 1890s, mid-1964)

4. Spell out a fraction that is not part of a mixed number (for example, 3½), or one that is followed by *of a* or *of an.*

one-third of an acre
three-fourths of a pie

5. Hyphenate a fraction that has been spelled out.

one-half inch

6. Spell out most ordinal numbers.

the twentieth century
the Eighty-second Congress
the Fifth Fleet
Twelfth Avenue

7. Express in figures any number over one hundred within ordinary text.

Enrollment reached 16,847.
952 ballots
101 districts

8. Use figures for all numbers in tables.

9. Use figures for:

a. a date

January 2, 1997 (*or* 1/2/97 *or* 2 January 1997)
54 BC
AD 450
Note the difference in placement of the abbreviations for the two eras.

b. a time designation with AM or PM

12:05 PM (*or* PM *or* p.m.)

c. an address

12345 Corduroy Road

d. chapter and page numbers

Part 1, Chapter 5, page 124

10. Use figures for:

a. a measurement, especially in scientific or technical writing or with a symbol or abbreviation for a unit

> 9 pounds of sugar
> Drive 40 miles and exit the freeway.
> 20/20 vision
> 43 mm
> 13 lb 2 oz
> 32°F (*but:* 32 degrees *or* thirty-two degrees)
> 17½′

b. a decimal fraction or percentage

> 2.54 cm

> Well, 51% of the population can't be wrong *all* the time.

c. sums of money

> 99 cents apiece
> $400,000
> $12,345.67

11. Use figures, as a rule, for all numbers referring to the same category in a single passage if the largest is over 100. (Some writers prefer, however, to spell out those under 100.)

> Membership for the three years was 9, 52, and 101.

12. Use figures for fractions that would be awkward if spelled out.

> 8½-by-11-inch paper

13. Use figures for ordinal numbers on the same basis as for cardinal numbers in the GENERAL RULES above.

> The first baseman was walked in the second, fourth, sixth, and ninth innings.
> She finished 105th out of 300 runners.

14. Use figures for an ordinal number:

a. in informal contexts

> Cong. Greene Loses Senate Election 3rd Time

Either *2nd/3rd* or *2d/3d* is acceptable. Choose one set for use in a piece of writing, and be consistent.

b. after a name to indicate a descendant's generation

> James J. James 3rd *or* James J. James 3d

When using these after a person's name, be sure to follow that person's spelling preference.

15. Numbers that are part of a sequence, including those indicating a section of a book.

> pages 15–40 *or* pp. 15–40
> Vol. IV, No. 10
> 1900 Fifth Avenue

16. Large numbers, although usually expressed in figures, can be expressed by a combination of figures and words. Numbers from a million up that end in

four or more zeros may be treated in this way for ease of comprehension. Here are some examples.

| | | |
|---|---|---|
| $12,000,000 | → | $12 million *or* 12 million dollars |
| $1,000,000,000 | → | $1 billion *or* 1 billion dollars |
| 3,250,000 | → | 3.25 million *or* 3¼ million |
| 9,000,000–1,000,000,000 | → | 9 million to 1 billion |

A number such as *1,234,000* is expressed in figures only.

## British Terminology

Note the differences between American and British terminology for large numbers. American names for values increase through multiplication of a million by successive *thousands;* British names, through multiplication by successive *millions.* There seems to be a gradual movement in Britain toward American usage, but this may just add to the ambiguity in the short run. Always clarify what is meant if it is possible for the reader to misinterpret a number.

| | | |
|---|---|---|
| 1,000,000 | *American:* | one million |
| | *British:* | one million |
| 1,000,000,000 | *American:* | one billion |
| | *British:* | one thousand million *or* one milliard |
| 1,000,000,000,000 | *American:* | one trillion |
| | *British:* | one billion |
| 1,000,000,000,000,000 | *American:* | one quadrillion |
| | *British:* | one thousand billion |
| 1,000,000,000,000,000,000 | *American:* | one quintillion |
| | *British:* | one trillion |

## Roman Numerals

Use Arabic numbers wherever possible, for ease of comprehension. Today, a knowledge of Roman numerals is useful mainly for making outlines of subject matter and for reading old-style dates on buildings, in older books, etc.

### Basics of the system

*Values:*

I = 1
V = 5
X = 10
L = 50
C = 100
D = 500
M = 1,000

*Rules:*

Repeat a letter to *repeat* its value.
Place a letter *after* one of greater value to *add* to it.

Place a letter *before* one of greater value to *subtract* from it.

Place a line over a letter to *multiply* it by 1,000.

## Examples

| | | | | | |
|---|---|---|---|---|---|
| I | .........1 | XXV | ......25 | CD | .........400 |
| II | .........2 | XXIX | ......29 | D | .........500 |
| III | .........3 | XXX | .......30 | DC | .........600 |
| IV | .........4 | XL | ........40 | CM | .........900 |
| V | .........5 | L | .........50 | M | .........1,000 |
| VI | .........6 | LX | .........60 | MD | ......1,500 |
| VII | ........7 | LXX | .......70 | MM | ......2,000 |
| VIII | ........8 | LXXX | .....80 | MMMM *or* | |
| IX | .........9 | XC | .........90 | M$\overline{\text{V}}$ | .......4,000 |
| X | .........10 | XCIX | ......99 | $\overline{\text{V}}$ | .........5,000 |
| XV | ........15 | C | .........100 | $\overline{\text{M}}$ | .....1,000,000 |
| XIX | .......19 | CL | ........150 | | |
| XX | .........20 | CC | .......200 | | |

*Dates:*

| | | | | |
|---|---|---|---|---|
| MD | ........1500 | MCML | .....1950 |
| MDC | .......1600 | MCMLX | ....1960 |
| MCM *or* | | MCMXC | ....1990 |
| MDCCCC | ...1900 | MCMXCIX | ..1999 |
| MCMX | .....1910 | MM | ........2000 |
| MCMXL | ....1940 | MMII | ......2002 |

# Plurals

## Basic Rule

Most nouns in English form the plural by adding *-s* or *-es*. When a singular noun ends in a sound that allows the sound (s) or (z) to be added and pronounced without the formation of a new syllable, *-s* is used.

> book — books
> bug — bugs

When the singular noun ends in a sound such that (s) or (z) cannot be joined to it and pronounced without the formation of a new syllable, *-es* is used.

> kiss — kisses
> torch — torches

## Main Exceptions to the Basic Rule

1. Words that end in *o* usually form the plural by adding *-es*.

> hero — heroes

However, some words ending in *o* do form the plural by adding *-s*.

> solo — solos

There is no absolute rule for dealing with this group of words.

2. Some words that end in *f* form the plural by changing the *f* to *v* and adding *-es*.

> wolf — wolves

3. Words that end in *y* preceded by a consonant usually form the plural by changing the *y* to *i* and adding *-es*.

> lady — ladies
> puppy — puppies

Exceptions include some proper nouns and compounds made from them.

> Mary — Marys
> Bloody Mary — Bloody Marys
> Mr. Daly — the Dalys
> the Kandinsky [painting] — two Kandinskys
> July — the last three Julys
> Grammy — Grammys

Do *not* change the *y* to *i* and add *-es* or add an apostrophe in such cases; use the *-s* alone.

If the *y* is preceded by a vowel, the word forms the plural regularly, by adding *-s*.

> day — days
> toy — toys

4. Some words form the plural through a vowel change. Among the commonest examples are

> foot — feet
> man — men
> tooth — teeth
> woman — women

5. Some words have a special plural form to which none of the above general statements apply. Among them are words such as

> alumnus — alumni
> alumna — alumnae
> child — children
> phenomenon — phenomena
> radius — radii
> sheep — sheep
> moose — moose

6. Letters, words, and figures that are referred to as such usually form the plural with *-'s*.

> p's and q's
> figure 8's
> *hello*'s

Abbreviations and figures that are *not* referred to as such vary in the use of *-s* and *-'s*.

Proper names do *not* form the plural with *-'s*.

> *Not:* the Smith's, the Jones'; all the Bill's in the class
> *But:* the Smiths, the Joneses; all the Bills in the class

## Rules for Pluralizing Compounds

1. A hyphenated compound usually takes the plural suffix on its most important element.

   editors-in-chief, daughters-in-law

2. A solid compound always adds the plural suffix at its end.

   stepdaughters, spoonfuls, bookshelves

3. Open compounds, varying in their inner structure, are less predictable.

   attorneys general, jogging shoes, baby blues

Consult the dictionary for the plurals of confusing words.

## Punctuation

The purpose of punctuation is to clarify the meaning of written language. In general, punctuation marks should prevent misreading by clearly indicating the author's intended meaning.

## Apostrophe [ ' ]

Use an apostrophe:

1. To show the possessive case of nouns and certain pronouns.

   **MEMORY AID:** The apostrophe signifies "belonging to everything to the left of this mark."

   a. Nouns and indefinite pronouns not ending in *-s* take an apostrophe and *-s*.

      a child's drawing        children's books
      a man's shirt            men's shirts
      a year's delay
      everyone's favorite

   This includes references to college degrees.

      a bachelor's degree
      working on her master's

   b. Singular nouns ending in the sound (s) or (z) or (sh) take an apostrophe and *-s*.

      Keats's poems
      Marx's writings
      Mrs. Jones's house
      the fish's habitat

   There are a few traditional exceptions to this rule:

   The proper names *Jesus* and *Moses* usually take only an apostrophe.

      Jesus' parables
      Moses' laws

Greek and other proper names, and a few plural nouns, that end in the syllable pronounced (ēz) generally take only an apostrophe.

Socrates' wisdom
the drama series' success

Certain words traditionally take only an apostrophe.

for conscience' sake
for goodness' sake!

c. Plural nouns ending in the sound (s) or (z) take only an apostrophe.

four years' delay
ladies' shoes
the Joneses' house

d. In compound constructions, the apostrophe and -s are added to the element closest to the modified word.

the Queen of England's palace
anyone else's opinion but hers
my sister-in-law's car
Henry VIII's wives
the attorney general's opinion

e. For joint ownership or a similar relationship, only the last noun takes the possessive form.

Roz, Joe, and Tom's computer

f. For separate ownership or a similar relationship, each noun takes the possessive form.

Roz's, Joe's, and Tom's e-mail addresses

g. For the possessive of a long phrase, it is best to rewrite the construction using the preposition *of*.

the briefcase of the lawyer who had already left
the dictates of the attorneys general
the hopes and fears of all concerned

h. Possessive personal pronouns do *not* take an apostrophe.

**MEMORY AID:** The possessive personal pronouns (and two pronominal adjectives) that end in -s are the *exception* to the usual rule for forming possessives in English.

Pronouns: hers his its ours theirs yours
Pronominal adjectives: his its

Do not confuse the possessive *its* with the contraction *it's* (it is).

2. To show the omission of letters or figures in contractions.

we've can't it's won't where's
'twas '97 '01

Do not confuse the contraction *it's* (it is) with the possessive *its*.

*To type an initial apostrophe:*

An initial apostrophe should appear the same as the apostrophe in the middle or at the end of a word. The word-processing program may be set to produce either straight

How ya' gonna keep 'em down on the farm?

or "curly"

How ya' gonna keep 'em down on the farm?

apostrophes (and quotation marks). The curly apostrophe should resemble a tiny *9,* not a *6.* Be sure that autoformatting does not produce the wrong character.

3. To show certain special plurals.

   a. Letters, words, and figures referred to as such usually take an apostrophe and -*s.*

      Mind your p's and q's.
      Did you dot your *i*'s and cross your *t*'s?
      *a*'s, 7's, #'s
      Underline the *which*'s and *that*'s.

      Note that the "s" after the apostrophe is in roman, not italic, type even when it follows an italicized letter or word.

   b. Abbreviations written with both internal and final periods usually take an apostrophe and -*s;* those with no periods or only final periods take only an -*s.*

      PhDs *or* Ph.D.'s
      ICBMs
      mts.

   c. Figures usually take an -*s* alone but may take an apostrophe and -*s.*

      1990s *or* 1990's
      the '90s (*not:* the '90's)

   *With the exceptions noted above, do not use an apostrophe to form a plural.*

4. To show inflected forms of verbs made up of abbreviations

   OK'd   O.K.'d   OK'ing   O.K.'ing

# Brackets [ [ ] ]

Use brackets, in pairs:

1. To enclose editorial corrections, explanations, or comments within a quoted passage.

   "The bill had *not* been paid [emphasis added]."
   "She was born in 1805 [actually in 1802] near the town of ...."
   According to the reviewer, "It [her latest novel] reeked of the stale perfume of romance writing at its very worst."
   "Andrew Johnson never attended school and was scarcely able to read when he met Eliza McCardle, whom he married on May 5, 1927 [*sic*]."

   The Latin word *sic,* meaning "thus," indicates that a quoted passage, especially one containing an error or a questionable statement, is reproduced precisely.

2. To indicate parentheses within parentheses.

   (The result [see Figure 2] is not typical.)

For the use of brackets with other marks of punctuation, follow the rules given for using parentheses with other marks of punctuation in the section on PARENTHESES.

## Colon [ : ]

Use a colon:

1. To introduce a formal statement, a long quotation, or a speech in a play.

> The witness made the declaration: "I know of no attempt to defraud the public."
> The Commencement speaker intoned: "The time has come."
> Macbeth: So foul and fair a day I have not seen.

2. To introduce an illustrating or amplifying item or series of items.

> English usage is like table etiquette: it is conventional and its sanction is a social one.
> Certain imports rose sharply: steel, cars, and electronic equipment.

3. After the salutation of a business letter.

> Dear Dr. Lloyd:
> Dear Sir or Madam:

4. To separate the initials of the person dictating a letter from the initials of the typist. Do not space after the colon. (A slash may also be used for this purpose.)

> DBG:cs    DBG/cs

5. To separate hours from minutes in notations of time and to separate chapter from verse in biblical citations. Do not space after the colon.

> 10:36 AM
> Exodus 4:6

6. To indicate a proportion; use two colons to indicate a ratio. Space before and after the colon or colons.

> concrete mixed 5 : 3 : 1
> 1 : 2 :: 4 : 12

For use of the colon with other marks of punctuation, see the notes at PARENTHESES and QUOTATION MARKS.

## Comma [ , ]

Use a comma:

1. Before a coordinating conjunction such as *and, but, or, nor, for, yet,* or *so* when it joins the clauses of a compound sentence.

> We had never before eaten such delicious meals, and my mother was delighted with the service.
> She often talked about her years as a singer, but no one in the chorus seemed to remember her.

The comma is often omitted between short clauses, and sometimes between long ones when the meaning is clear.

> First he stopped at the bank and then he went to his office.

2. To separate an introductory phrase or dependent clause from the main clause.

> When he had tired of the mad pace of Los Angeles, he moved to Dubuque.
> In the beginning, she liked the work.

If, as in the above examples, there is no possibility of ambiguity, the comma is often omitted. In the following examples, however, the comma is needed to prevent misreading.

> When the meeting was over, our heads were swimming.
> More and more, Americans are waiting until the last minute to file their taxes.
> He saw the woman who had rejected him, and blushed.

3. To set off a word such as *yes* or *no;* a mild interjection; a word or words in direct address; a transitional word or phrase; or an absolute phrase. Within the sentence, use a pair of commas.

> Yes, I plan to go.
> Oh, I didn't really care much one way or the other.
> Thanks, Maria, for bringing your cassette player.
> The last speaker was, by the way, the most interesting.
> Winter having arrived early, we left for home.

Do *not* set off the interjection *O* (used, as in poetry or hymns, to address a deity or highly respected person) with a comma.

4. Traditionally, the abbreviation *etc.,* when used in lists, has been set off by a pair of commas within the sentence.

> We had eggs, ham, hash browns, etc., for breakfast.

Now, however, to some degree, it is acceptable to omit the second comma.

> We had eggs, ham, hash browns, etc. for breakfast.

5. To set off a question following a statement.

> You are coming along, aren't you?

6. To set off the main elements in an address. Within the sentence, use a pair of commas.

> We lived at 45 Sycamore Street, Novelty, Ohio.
> We lived at 45 Sycamore Street, Novelty, Ohio, for more years than I care to remember.

7. To set off a title following a person's name. Within the sentence, use a pair of commas.

> We received a letter from Dr. Jane Friend, Director of Admissions.
> Dr. Jane Friend, Director of Admissions, replied.

8. To set off the year in a date if the month, day, and year are given. Within the sentence, use a pair of commas.

> The letter was dated July 14, 1987.
> The letter was dated July 14, 1987, and was mailed from Paris.

If only the month (or the season) and the year are given, the comma is usually omitted.

> The letter was written in July 1987 and was mailed from Paris.
> Summer 1987 was probably the best time of my childhood.

If the day and month are reversed (as in European and military style), no comma is used.

> 14 July 1987

9.  To set off an appositive. Within the sentence, use a pair of commas.

> It was Annie, our favorite cousin.
> Annie, our favorite cousin, makes unbelievably delicious fudge.
> Our favorite cousin, Annie, makes unbelievably delicious fudge.
> Acrophobia, or fear of heights, can severely limit a person's activities.
> a cerulean, or azure, gem
> his wish to ameliorate, or improve, his situation

An appositive essential to the meaning of the sentence is not set off by commas.

> Our son Jim is in college; our son Bill is finishing high school.

10.  To set off contrasted sentence elements. Within the sentence, use a pair of commas.

> It was Jessie, not Frances.
> Jessie, not Frances, was the first to arrive.

11.  To indicate an omitted word in a parallel construction.

> Bert always brings his lunch; Susan, never.

12.  To indicate that a word or words have been omitted, such as *of* or *of the*.

> President, Big Green Spaces Intl.

13.  To set off sentence elements that are out of natural order.

> That they would accept the money, none of us seriously doubted.

14.  To separate words, phrases, or clauses in a series.

> The menu offered the usual choices of steak, chops, and chicken.
> Expect it tomorrow, next Monday, or a week from today.
> They studied hard, they concentrated on the details, and they took their time in order to pass the course.

Some writers omit the *series comma* (the one before the conjunction), but this comma is useful in preventing ambiguity.

15.  To separate coordinate adjectives modifying the same noun. Each coordinate adjective modifies the noun individually. Test: If *and* can be substituted for the comma, the adjectives are coordinate.

> The cat had bright, mischievous, laughing eyes.

If the previous adjectives are modifying the noun *plus* the adjective closest to it as a unit, the adjectives are *not* coordinate and no comma is used.

> The cat had bright, mischievous, laughing gray eyes.

16.  To set off a clause, phrase, or word that interrupts the main clause.

> He did not really say, as you seem to believe, that he wanted the job.
> The apples, though freshly picked, were spoiled in shipment.
> I'm not really sure, though, that you understand the problem.

17.  To set off a *nonrestrictive* phrase or clause from the rest of the sentence. A nonrestrictive phrase or clause is not essential to the meaning of the sentence.

> Such a device, known as a reader, senses the data and enters it into the computer.
> My prize fishing rod, which now hangs over the mantelpiece, hasn't been used for years.

A *restrictive* phrase or clause *is* essential to the meaning of the sentence; it is *not* set off by commas.

> The man who robbed the bank has been apprehended.
> The secret that you shared with me will go nowhere.

18. To set off a direct quotation from such expressions as *she said* and *he replied.*

> "I know you'll like oysters," she said, "if only you'll try them."
> He replied, "I'll never believe you again."

If the *she said* or other similar expression comes between two independent clauses, it is followed by a period or a semicolon, not by a comma.

> "I know you'll like oysters," she said; "just try them."

19. To provide a pause to clarify meaning when a word is repeated.

> Whatever happened, happened for the best.

20. Following (1) the salutation of a personal letter or (2) the closing phrase of either a personal or a business letter.

> Dear Tina,
> Sincerely,
> Very truly yours,

21. To separate the parts of an inverted name, phrase, and so forth, as in a bibliography, index, or catalog.

> Horner, Martha D.
> Persia, architecture of
> radios, portable

22. To separate figures of five or more digits. The comma is inserted after each group of three digits, counting from the right.

> That year the costs totaled $1,341,680.

The comma is omitted in years, street addresses, etc. It is often omitted in four-digit figures as well.

> 1341 days until retirement

23. To create a pause in the flow of a sentence if that pause would make the sentence clearer and easier to read. Let your ear tell you when such a comma is needed. This informal rule can be helpful when no other rule seems to fit the situation.

For use of the comma with other marks of punctuation, see the notes at PARENTHESES and QUOTATION MARKS.

## Dash

### Em dash [ — ]

Use an em dash:

1. To indicate an abrupt change in thought, a break in the sentence flow, or an interruption of the speaker's words.

> He is — how shall I say it? — a colossal bore.
> She said, "But what if — "

2. To set off an appositive or parenthetical expression, especially when commas are needed for minor divisions within the expression or when a complete sentence is interpolated within another.

The three R's — reading, writing, and arithmetic — are again being stressed.

Eventually — but who knows when? — we will know the whole story.

3. To introduce a phrase or clause that summarizes what has just been said.

Eating right, drinking enough water every day, and getting regular exercise — these are the simple things we all can do to stay healthy.

Unless the set-off expression begins or ends a sentence, dashes must be used in pairs.

*To type an em dash:*

Type two unspaced hyphens; do not space on either side. Some writers, however, prefer to space once on each side of the dash. Publishers and typesetters may render em dashes per house style.

## En dash [ – ]

The en dash is longer than a hyphen and shorter than an em dash. Use it:

1. Between numbers or words and numbers indicating (1) the beginning and ending dates of a historical period, a person's lifetime in a biographical listing, or some other period; or (2) the first and last pages of a section of a book, the first and last verses in a biblical reference, and so forth.

    1900–1999    1900–99

    August 1947–April 1950

    9:30 AM–6:00 PM

    pages 1–50 *or* pp. 1–50

    I Corinthians 13:1–3

If only the beginning date is established, the en dash indicates that the period is open-ended.

    Greene, David (1955–)

Never use a dash to replace the word *to* if the word *from* precedes the numbers; never use a dash to replace the word *and* if the word *between* precedes the numbers.

    *Not:* from 100–150
    *But:* from 100 to 150

    *Not:* between 5:00–7:00
    *But:* between 5:00 and 7:00

2. Between parts of a compound if elements of the compound are open-compound (spaced) names.

    a Buenos Aires–Mexico City connecting flight

*To type an en dash:*

Use a hyphen. In marking copy for typesetting, the author or editor marks the hyphens that should be set as en dashes.

## Ellipsis [ . . . *or* ... ]

Use an ellipsis, or three periods (also called *suspension points*):

1. To show that material has been omitted from a quotation. (Four periods are used when the omission comes at the end of a declarative sentence.)

5. Between the letters of a spelled-out word.

> In front of the children, she asked me if I had bought the c-a-n-d-y.

6. Between figures or groups of figures:

   a. To separate numbers that are in random order, as in account numbers, serial numbers, telephone numbers, and Social Security numbers.

   > 000-555-1212
   > 987-65-4321

   b. In typewritten copy, for all uses described for the en dash, such as numbers or words indicating the beginning and end of a historical period or other length of time, numbers indicating the first and last pages in a section of a book, or numbers for years of birth and death in a biographical listing.

Never use a hyphen or dash to replace the word *to* if the word *from* precedes the numbers; never use a hyphen or dash to replace the word *and* if the word *between* precedes the numbers.

> *Not:* from 100-150
> *But:* from 100 to 150
>
> *Not:* between 5-7
> *But:* between 5 and 7

See also the notes at DASH (EN DASH).

## Parentheses [ ( ) ]

Use parentheses, in pairs:

1. To enclose material that is explanatory, supplementary, or illustrative.

   > This book describes life in the Middle Ages (between AD 476 and about 1450) from a scribe's perspective.
   > The example given on page 306 (and a startling one it is!) draws upon exhaustive research.
   > The tabulated results (see fig. 6) speak for themselves.

2. To enclose figures and letters indicating enumeration within a text.

   > The maps show (1) rainfall, (2) population, and (3) physical features.
   > The maps show (a) rainfall, (b) population, and (c) physical features.

3. To enclose figures following a spelled-out number, especially in a formal document.

   > All twenty-five (25) computers were found to be defective.

*Using parentheses with other punctuation marks:*

1. When a complete sentence within parentheses stands alone (that is, not as part of another sentence), its **end punctuation** goes inside the closing parenthesis.

   > He said that knowledge is sometimes useful. (That must be the most inane and useless statement of the century.)
   > He said that knowledge is sometimes useful. (Can you imagine a more inane and worthless statement?)

2. When a complete declarative sentence within parentheses is part of another sentence, do not put a **period** inside the closing parenthesis *unless* the last

word is an abbreviation that takes a period. However, a parenthetical question or exclamation may end with a **question mark** or **exclamation mark.** (Do not capitalize the first word of a parenthetical sentence unless that word is regularly capitalized.)

> Self-government (recall that the Virginia legislature had already been formed) was clearly on the rise.
>
> Self-government (how many years had it been since the formation of the Virginia legislature?) was clearly on the rise.

3. When a word, phrase, or clause within parentheses is part of a sentence,

   a. Do *not* place a **comma, semicolon, colon,** or **period** inside the closing parenthesis.

   b. Place a **question mark** or **exclamation mark** inside the closing parenthesis if it applies to the parenthetical material.

   c. Place a **comma, semicolon, colon,** or **period** after the closing parenthesis only if the main sentence (without the parenthetical material) requires that punctuation mark at that point.

> St. Augustine (?–AD 604?) was sent to convert the English to Christianity.
>
> The Wars of the Roses, between the hoses of Lancaster and York (1455–1485), are said to have ended feudalism in England.
>
> The Wars of the Roses were fought between the houses of Lancaster and York (1455–1485); they are said to have ended feudalism in England.

## Period [ . ]

Use a period:

1. After a declarative sentence, an indirect question, and most imperative sentences.

> Summer will soon be here.
> We asked who the pianist was.
> Come home.
> Please help me with this.

2. After most polite requests phrased as questions.

> Would you please send me a copy of your catalog.

3. After many abbreviations. However, some writers and editors now favor a style that omits the periods after many abbreviations. Consult the dictionary for current spellings of common abbreviations.

> BC *or* B.C.
> AD *or* A.D.

Do *not* omit a period that follows an abbreviation before any other mark of punctuation *except for* the period at the end of a sentence.

4. After initials. The initials for a personal name are spaced in American usage, but not in British usage.

> Alfred R. Jones; A. R. Jones
> T. S. Eliot *or* T.S. Eliot

5. As a decimal point with numerals.

> 5.5% of the total
> $450.01

6. After figures or letters indicating enumeration in a list arranged vertically.

> a. Reduce.
> b. Reuse.
> c. Recycle.

In general, do *not* use a period at the end of a heading or title.

For use of the period with other punctuation marks, see the notes at PARENTHESES and QUOTATION MARKS.

## Question Mark [ ? ]

Use a question mark:

1. After a direct question.

> Do you have the money?
> "Do you have the money?" he asked.
> You do have the money?

2. After each query in an unnumbered or unlettered series.

> Have you heard the candidate's views on civil rights? on urban problems? on the economy?
> *But:* Have you heard the candidate's views on (a) civil rights, (b) urban problems, (c) the economy?

3. After an interrogative element within a sentence (but not after an indirect question).

> "How soon?" she wondered.
> *But:* She wondered how soon it would happen.

4. To express uncertainty regarding the accuracy of information.

> We once attended a concert presented by Marian Anderson (1897?–1993).

For use of the question mark with other punctuation marks, see the notes at PARENTHESES and QUOTATION MARKS.

## Quotation Marks

### Double Quotation Marks [ " " ]

Use double quotation marks, in pairs:

1. To enclose a direct quotation short enough to be run into the text (Quotations of more than three or four lines usually appear without quotation marks but are set off from the text by space, indention, and so forth.)

> "Come in," he called.
> "Are you," she asked, "the man who helped my son?"

2. To enclose the title of a poem, essay, short story, article, lecture, chapter of a book, song, or individual radio or TV program (as opposed to a series).

> The third chapter, "How I Entertained My New In-Laws," may be the scariest in the book.
> Have you read her new story, "The Moose That Came to the Door"?
> We memorized the poem "Dover Beach" in class.

3. To enclose words referred to as words, used in a special sense, or given particular emphasis. (Italics may also be used in such cases.)

> He uses words like "never" and "always" much too often.
> Don't "push the envelope" any farther than you can reach to take it back.
> Why is luck always "good luck" unless we say it's bad?

## Single Quotation Marks [ ' ' ]

Use single quotation marks, in pairs, to enclose a quotation or a title within another quotation.

All of the rules for double quotation marks apply.

> In a note to me, Sally effused, "The memory of the way you played 'Hearts and Flowers' at my wedding still brings tears to my eyes."

In usual British punctuation style, the use of single and double quotation marks is the reverse of the above.

*Using quotation marks with other punctuation marks:*

1. The **period** and the **comma** always go inside closing quotation marks.

> "I'm so sorry," he said, "but I don't believe you."

2. The **colon** and the **semicolon** go outside closing quotation marks.

> I had not read Emerson's essay "Experience"; in fact, I had never heard of it.

3. The **question mark** and **exclamation mark** go inside closing quotation marks if they apply to the quoted material. They go outside if they apply to the whole sentence.

> She asked, "Am I going, too?"
> Did she say, "I am going, too"?

In usual British punctuation style, all end punctuation is placed according to this last rule.

## Semicolon [ ; ]

Use a semicolon:

1. Between independent clauses not joined by a coordinating conjunction. The same two clauses may be written in any of these three ways:

> Summer's almost gone. Winter's coming on.
> Summer's almost gone, and winter's coming on.
> Summer's almost gone; winter's coming on.

2. Between independent clauses joined by a conjunctive adverb (*however, indeed, nevertheless,* and so forth). Place a comma after the adverb.

> Summer's almost gone; however, winter's coming on.

3. Between independent clauses of a compound sentence if the clauses are very long or are themselves subdivided by commas, or if a more definite break is desired than one marked by a comma.

> When all was said and done, we had done most of it; they, however, ignored the fact, as usual.

4. To replace the comma in separating elements of a series if the elements themselves contain commas.

> The tour of capital cities included Vaduz, Liechtenstein; Luxembourg, Luxembourg; San Marino, San Marino; and Andorra, Andorra.

For use of the semicolon with other punctuation marks, see the notes at PARENTHESES and QUOTATION MARKS.

## Slash, Virgule, or Solidus [ / ]

Use the slash:

1. Between two words to show that either is applicable.

> and/or
> he/she
> Mars/Ares
> John/Jane Doe

This use is somewhat informal.

2. To separate the parts of a fraction.

> 17/32

Many computer programs are set to change the most commonly used fractions to a more compact form using a slanting or horizontal dividing line.

> ½        ¼

3. In reference to a period extending through parts of two consecutive years (in place of an en dash).

> 1950/51

4. In certain abbreviations.

> c/o (in care of)
> N/A (not applicable)
> A/C (air conditioning)

5. To indicate the word *per*.

> calico for $5.25/yd
> apples at 2 lb./$1
> km/h (kilometers per hour)

6. Between lines of poetry (usually not more than two) quoted within a paragraph. Space on each side of the slash.

> An old song that I love begins: "The water is wide, / I cannot get o'er."

# Spelling Rules

There are a number of regularly occurring patterns in English spelling; for most people, they have become automatic. But it is useful to state them explicitly, for review purposes or for those times when a word's spelling "just doesn't look quite right."

1. A word that ends in a silent *e* usually drops the *e* when a suffix beginning with a vowel is added.

> file — filed, filing

However, before the suffixes *-able* and *-ous,* the e is usually retained if it follows a c with the sound (s) or a g with the sound (j).

> trace — traceable
> outrage — outrageous

The e is usually kept when a suffix beginning with a consonant is added.

> time — timely

2.  A word that ends in a single consonant preceded by a single vowel usually doubles that consonant when a suffix beginning with a vowel is added, if:

a. the word is a single syllable

> run — running

b. the word has more than one syllable but is stressed on the last syllable.

> refer — referred, referring

If the final consonant is not preceded by a single vowel, or, in American usage, if the last syllable is not stressed, the final consonant is usually not doubled.

> curl — curled, curling
> travel — traveled, traveling

3.  A word that ends in ee usually drops one e when the inflectional suffix *-er, -est,* or *-ed* is added.

> free + -est = freest

In other cases in which a triple letter would occur, a hyphen is usually inserted.

> bell + -like = bell-like

4.  A word that ends in y preceded by a consonant usually changes the y to i when a suffix that does not begin with i is added.

> fluffy — fluffier

If the y is preceded by a vowel, the y is usually retained.

> play — played, playing

5.  A word that ends in ie changes the ie to y when the suffix *-ing* is added.

> lie — lying

6.  A word that ends in c usually takes a k when a suffix beginning with i or e is added.

> picnic — picnicker

7.  Words that contain ie or ei can be confusing. So remember that in most words native to English, ie is used. Two main exceptions are

a. Following the letter c, ei is usually used.

> receive

b. When the sound (ā) is represented, ei is used.

> reign

8.  Words that contain the suffix *-ful* need not cause spelling problems. Just remember that the suffix, unlike the word *full,* which is related in meaning, ends in only one l.

> fearful, cupful

9. Verbs that end in *-ceed* and *-cede* can be confusing. But remember that only three common verbs end in *-ceed:*

   exceed, proceed, succeed

   Most others end in *-cede:*

   recede, secede, intercede

# MANUSCRIPT FORM

## Manuscript Preparation

A writer must follow certain basic conventions in preparing a manuscript for publication, as opposed to writing a business letter, an essay for a class, or a report for internal use within an organization. Here are a few basic points.

1. To indicate *italics,* underline the word or words with <u>a straight line</u>.

2. To indicate **boldface type,** underline the word or words with a <u>wavy line</u>.

3. To indicate SMALL CAPITAL LETTERS, underline the word or words with <u>two straight lines</u>.

4. PROOFREAD CAREFULLY, more than once. DO NOT rely entirely on the computer's spell-checking program. It cannot distinguish between pairs of words that sound the same but are spelled differently. It is best to proofread on paper, rather than on the computer screen.

It is easier (and usually less expensive) to make corrections at this stage rather than on a printed proof.

## Source Documentation

Many works of nonfiction list the sources of information that the writer has used in preparing the text — both those that are quoted and those that are paraphrased. The writer does this both to credit those sources and to allow the reader to evaluate the statements made. The sources are usually acknowledged in notes within the text itself and in a bibliography or reference list at the end of the piece.

The writer generally follows one of two reference systems within the text, depending on the nature of the piece, the writer's academic discipline, and the intended audience. Publications intended for the general public are likely to use **bibliographic notes**, which are set (1) at the foot of the page (**footnotes**), (2) at the end of the chapter (**endnotes** or **notes**), or (3) at the end of the book or article (**endnotes** or **notes**). Publications in the natural and social sciences are likely to use **parenthetical text references**; this system is now becoming more common in the humanities as well.

## Bibliographic Notes

1. Whether a bibliographic note appears at the foot of the page or elsewhere in a piece of general writing, it is identified in the text by a superscript (raised)

numeral placed immediately after the last word of the direct or indirect quotation. The note to which this text reference applies is preceded by the same superscript numeral. Footnote numbering may be consecutive throughout the piece, or, particularly in a longer work, it may begin again with each chapter or section.

2. If a bibliography is not included (and sometimes even if it is), the full facts of publication are given in the text the first time a work is cited. However, any bibliographic information that appears in the text need not be repeated in the footnote. For example, if the text says, "As T. S. Eliot noted in his book *Poetry and Drama*," and then goes on to quote the passage, the footnote would probably give only the page number.

> [3] p. 43.

3. The following is the usual style of first footnotes for books. Note the use of commas and other marks of punctuation.

> [1] John Berryman, *Berryman's Shakespeare* (New York: Farrar, Straus & Giroux, 1999), p. 24.
>
> [2] Russell A. Fraser, *Shakespeare, the Later Years* (New York: Columbia University Press, 1992), pp. 35–42.

The separate elements of footnotes for books are treated as follows, in this order:

a. Name(s) of author(s), editor(s), compiler(s)

> John Berryman,
> Jonathan Dollimore and Alan Sinfield, [two authors]
> Peter Hunt and others, [more than two authors]

b. Title (and subtitle) of book

> *Shakespeare: His Life, His English, His Theater*

(Titles are underlined in typescript and italicized in print.)

c. Edition statement

> rev. ed.,
> 2nd (*or* 2d) ed., rev. and enl.,

d. Place of publication, publisher, year of publication (If a bibliography is included, footnotes usually omit these facts of publication. Publishers' names may be given either in full, as they appear on the title page or the reverse of the title page, or in shortened form.)

> (New York: HarperCollins Publishers, Inc., 1999),
> (New York: HarperCollins, 1999),

e. Page reference

> p. 17.    pp. 30–34.

4. The following is the usual style of first footnotes for parts of larger works:

> [3] Sara Powers, "The Baker's Wife," in *New Stories From the South*, ed. Shannon Ravenel (Chapel Hill: Algonquin Books, 1998), pp. 92–97.

5. First footnotes for articles usually contain these elements: author(s), title of article, title of periodical, volume number (if any), date, and page reference.

> [8] John Lahr, "Speaking Shakespeare," *The New Yorker*, Sept. 7, 1998, pp. 78–83.
>
> [9] J. C. Furnas, "Extrapolating Shakespeare: Let Will Enough Alone," *American Scholar*, 67 (Summer 1998), 95.

(Arabic numerals are used for volume numbers, whether or not the volume is shown in Roman numerals in the periodical itself; the abbreviation "vol." is not ordinarily used. When both volume and page numbers are given, no "p." or "pp." precedes the page number.)

6. Second and subsequent references to a work are ordinarily given in shortened form.

a. If a footnote refers to the work cited in the immediately preceding footnote, the Latin abbreviation *ibid.* (meaning "in the same place" or, in effect, "the same work I have just cited") may be used. Although it is a Latin abbreviation, *ibid.* is not italicized (underlined in typescript). As the first word in a footnote, it is capitalized.

> [4] John Berryman, *Berryman's Shakespeare* (New York: Farrar, Straus & Giroux, 1999), p. 24.
> [5] Ibid., p. 28.
> [6] Ibid.

(In the last example above, no page reference is needed, because this footnote refers to the same book *and* page as the one preceding it.)

b. Instead of using *ibid.*, many writers prefer to use simply the author's last name and the page reference.

> [4] John Berryman, *Berryman's Shakespeare* (New York: Farrar, Straus & Giroux, 1999), p. 24.
> [5] Berryman, p. 28.
> [6] Berryman, p. 28.

c. When two or more works by the same author are cited, the footnotes give the author's name, title of the work, and page reference.

> [8] Berryman, *Collected Poems, 1937–1971*, p. 45.
> [9] Berryman, *Berryman's Shakespeare*, pp. 19–26.

## Parenthetical Text References

1. In publications in the social and natural sciences (and increasingly in the humanities as well), parenthetical text references acknowledge direct and indirect quotations and, at the same time, direct the reader to a reference list for full information about those sources.

2. According to the widely used name-and-year system, parenthetical references give the name(s) of the author(s) and the year the work was published. Page references are sometimes added (they are not preceded by "p." or "pp.").

> (Reynolds 1991)
> (Hunt and Butts 1995) *or* (Hunt & Butts 1995) [two authors]
> (Hollingsworth and others 1994) *or* (Hollingsworth et. al. 1994) [*more than* three authors]

Page references are sometimes added (they are not preceded by "p." or "pp.").

> (Reynolds 1991, 116)

Lowercase letters distinguish between works published in the same year.

> (Horton 1990a)
> (Horton 1990b)

3. Two or more combined references are separated by semicolons.

> (Horton 1990b, 87; Reynolds 1991)

4. Any information that appears in the text need not be repeated in the reference. For example, if the text says, "Kline undertook similar studies in Canada," only the year of the work would be shown in parentheses next to Kline's name.

## Bibliographies and Reference Lists

1. Whether cited in footnotes or in parenthetical text references, the works used in a piece of writing are ordinarily grouped together at the end. This section is likely to be called **Bibliography** in a piece of general writing, or **References** or **Works Cited** in a scholarly work in the social or natural sciences, and sometimes in the humanities. Editorial style varies somewhat from one discipline to another.

2. All information about a book (author, title, place of publication, publisher, year of publication) should, if possible, be taken from the title page and the reverse of the title page. All information about an article (author, title of article, title of periodical, volume, date) should be taken from the periodical in which the article appears.

3. Bibliographies and reference lists are arranged in alphabetical order, by author. If more than one work by an author is cited, the listing under the author is usually alphabetical by title in a bibliography, and by date in a reference list. In the second and subsequent references, the author's name is ordinarily replaced by a long dash (although some writers prefer to repeat the name).

4. Bibliographies differ in form from the footnotes for the works cited. Reference lists, of course, differ even more from their corresponding parenthetical text references. Some of these differences, as well as the differences between bibliographies and reference lists, can be seen below. Note the use of periods and other marks of punctuation.

## Sample Bibliography

Berryman, John. *Collected Poems, 1937–1971.* New York: FSG, 1989.

Berryman, John. *Berryman's Shakespeare.* New York: FSG, 1999.

Dollimore, Jonathan, and Alan Sinfield. *Political Shakespeare: Essays in Cultural Materialism.* Ithaca: Cornell University Press, 1994.

Fraser, Russell A. *Shakespeare: The Later Years.* New York: Columbia University Press, 1992.

Furnas, J. C. "Extrapolating Shakespeare: Let Will Enough Alone." *American Scholar*, 67 (Summer 1998), 95.

Lahr, John. "Speaking Shakespeare." *The New Yorker*, Sept. 7, 1998, pp. 78–83.

Powers, Sara. "The Baker's Wife." In *New Stories From the South,* ed. Shannon Ravenel. Chapel Hill: Algonquin Books, 1998.

Schoenbaum, Samuel. *Shakespeare: His Life, His English, His Theater.* New York: Signet Classic Book, 1990.

## Sample Reference List

Hollingsworth, S., and A. Cody. 1994. *Teacher research and urban literacy education: lessons and conversations in a feminist key.* New York: Teachers College Press.

Horton, M. 1990a. *The long haul: an autobiography*. New York: Doubleday.

————. 1990b. *We make the road by walking: conversations on education and social change*. Philadelphia: Temple University Press.

Hunt, P., and D. Butts. 1995. *Children's literature: an illustrated history*. New York: Oxford University Press.

Reynolds, P. 1991. *Practical Approaches to Teaching Shakespeare*. Oxford: Oxford University Press.

# USAGE — TROUBLESOME WORDS

This section is a guide to the correct use of words and phrases that are frequently misused or misspelled.

**accede** to agree
**concede** to yield, but not necessarily in agreement
**exceed** to be more than
> We accede to your request for more evidence.
> The candidate conceded the victory to his opponent.
> My expenses often exceed my income.

**accept** to take when offered
**except** (verb) to leave out
**except** (preposition) excluding
> I accept the proposition that all of us are created equal.
> The final report will except all data that doesn't conform to standards.
> All eighteen-year-olds except seniors will be called.

**in accord with** in agreement with (a person)
**in accordance with** in agreement with (a thing)
> I am in accord with you about this.
> The police officer acted in accordance with the law.

**acoustics** (used as a singular noun) the science of sound
**acoustics** (used as a plural noun) the qualities of sound
> Acoustics is a subdivision of physics.
> The acoustics of Carnegie Hall are incomparable.

**adapt** to adjust or change
**adopt** to take as one's own
> I adapted an old rubber washer to fit the new faucet.
> I liked her writing style so much that I adopted it as my own.

**adverse** unfavorable
**averse** disliking or reluctant
> He took the adverse decision in poor spirit.
> Many students are averse to criticism by their classmates.

**affect** (verb) to influence or to pretend
**effect** (noun) an influence or result
**effect** (verb) to bring about
>   Your education will affect your future.
>   He affected a great love for opera, though in fact it bored him.
>   The effect of the last war is still being felt.
>   A diploma effected a tremendous change in his attitude.

**affection** feeling
**affectation** pose or artificial behavior
>   Alumni often develop a strong affection for their former schools.
>   The affectation of a Harvard accent is no guarantee of success.

**affinity** an attraction to a person or thing
**infinity** an unlimited time, space, or quantity
>   She has an affinity for men with beards.
>   It is impossible to visualize infinity.

**aggravate** to make worse
**exasperate** to irritate or annoy greatly
>   Her cold was aggravated by faulty medication.
>   He was exasperated by his inability to make a quick recovery.

**aid** help or assistance
**aide** an assistant
>   The Red Cross provided aid to survivors.
>   The teacher had a student aide to help grade papers.

**aisle** a passageway between seats
**isle** a small island
>   Please keep the aisle clear for passengers boarding late.
>   My perfect vacation would be a week alone on some Caribbean isle.

**alibi** an explanation on the basis of being in another place
**excuse** an explanation on any basis
>   The alibi offered at the trial was that he was twenty miles away from the scene of the crime.
>   His excuse for failing on the test was that he was sick.

**alimentary** of the process of nutrition
**elementary** primary
>   The alimentary canal includes the stomach and the intestines.
>   Elementary education is the foundation of all human development.

**all ready** everybody or everything ready
**already** at or by the given time
>   They were all ready [each one of them] to write when the teacher arrived.
>   They had already begun writing when the teacher arrived.

**allude** to make an indirect reference
**elude** to escape from
>Only incidentally does Coleridge allude to Shakespeare's puns.
>It is almost impossible for one to elude tax collectors.

**allusion** an indirect reference
**illusion** a deception of the eye or mind
>The student made allusions to his teacher's favorite book.
>Illusions of the mind, unlike those of the eye, cannot be corrected with glasses.

**all ways** in every possible way
**always** at all times
>She was in all ways acceptable to the voters.
>Their reputation had always been spotless.

**alright** an unacceptable spelling for **all right**

**alumnus** a male graduate; *plural* **alumni**
**alumna** a female graduate; *plural* **alumnae**
*Note:* Use *alumni* when referring to both men and women.

**amend** to correct
**emend** to correct a literary work; to edit
>Our Constitution, as amended by the Bill of Rights, was finally ratified.
>Before publication, several chapters of the book were emended by an editor.

**amount** applies to quantities that cannot be counted one by one.
**number** applies to quantities that can be counted one by one.
>A large amount of grain was delivered to the store.
>A large number of bags were delivered.

**annual** yearly
**biannual** and **semiannual** twice a year
**biennial** once in two years; every two years
>The Saint Patrick's Day parade is an annual event here.
>Some schools have biannual promotion, in January and June.
>The biennial election of members of Congress is held in even-numbered years.

**ante-** (prefix) before
**anti-** (prefix) against
>The antechamber is the room just before the main room.
>An antifascist is one who is opposed to fascists.

**appraise** to set a value for
**apprise** to inform
>The jeweler appraised the diamond at a very high value.
>We were apprised of their arrival by the entry of the butler.

**apprehend** to catch the meaning of something; to take into custody
**comprehend** to understand a thing completely
>At first I didn't apprehend his true intent.
>The sheriff succeeded in apprehending the rustler.
>It is often difficult to comprehend the Euclidean postulates.

**artisan** a mechanic or craftsman
**artist** one who practices one of the fine arts
>Many artisans participated in the building of the Sistine Chapel.
>The basic design, however, was prepared by the artist Michelangelo.

**ascent** the act of rising
**assent** approval
>The ascent to the top of the mountain was perilous.
>Congress gave its assent to the President's emergency directive.

**assay** (verb) to try or experiment
**essay** (noun) a piece of writing
>We shall assay the ascent of the mountain tomorrow.
>We wrote essays on the life of President Taft.

**attend to** to take care of
**tend to** to be inclined to
>One of the clerks will attend to my mail in my absence.
>Lazy people tend to lack ambition.

**audience** a group of listeners
**spectators** a group of watchers
>Leonard Bernstein conducted a brilliant concert for the rapt audience.
>The slow baseball game bored the spectators.

*Note:* A group that both watches and listens is an *audience.*

**average** conforming to norms or standards
**ordinary** usual, customary, or without distinction
>A book of about 300 pages is of average length.
>The contents of the book were rather ordinary.

**bazaar** a marketplace or a fair
**bizarre** odd or strange
>We are going to the bazaar to buy things.
>He dresses in a bizarre manner.

**berth** a resting place
**birth** the beginning of life
>The captain moved the liner to a safer berth in the harbor.
>She was a fortunate woman from the day of her birth.

**bloc** an alliance
**block** a solid piece of material
>A bloc of eastern counties voted against the levy.
>The child played quietly with her building blocks.

**born** brought to life or being; past participle of *bear*
**borne** carried
> I was born on June 8.
> The heavy camping pack was easily borne by our guide.

**bouillon** a soup
**bullion** gold or silver in the form of bars
> This restaurant serves tasty bouillon.
> A mint makes coins out of bullion.

**breath** an intake of air
**breathe** to draw air in and let it out
**breadth** width
> Before you dive in, take a very deep breath.
> It is impossible to breathe under water.
> In a square, the breadth is equal to the length.

**bridal** (adjective) of a wedding
**bridle** (noun) a head harness for guiding a horse
**bridle** (verb) to hold back
> The bridal party was late to the church.
> In the parade the policeman's horse wore a brand-new saddle and bridle.
> You must learn to bridle your temper.

**bring** to carry toward the person who is speaking
**take** to carry away from the speaker
> Bring the books here.
> Take your raincoat with you when you go out.

**broach** to mention for the first time
**brooch** an ornament for clothing
> At the meeting, one of the speakers broached the question of salary increases.
> Grandma was wearing an expensive brooch.

**but** should not be used after the expression *cannot help.*
> *Acceptable:* One cannot help noticing the errors.
> *Unacceptable:* One cannot help but notice the errors.

**calendar** a system of time
**calender** a smoothing and glazing machine
**colander** a kind of sieve
> In this part of the world, most people use the Gregorian calendar.
> In ceramic work, the potting wheel and the calender are indispensable.
> Vegetables should be washed in a colander before cooking.

**Calvary** the name of the place of the Crucifixion
**cavalry** a military unit on horseback
> Calvary and Gethsemane are place names in the Bible.
> Most of our modern cavalry is now motorized.

**can** to be physically able
**may** to have permission
> I can lift this chair over my head.
> You may leave after you finish your work.

**cannon** a heavy artillery gun
**canon** a rule or law, usually of a church
> Don't stand near the cannon when it is being fired.
> Churchgoers are expected to observe the canons of their faith.

**canvas** a coarse, heavy, closely woven cloth
**canvass** to examine in detail
> The ship's sails are made of canvas.
> Police canvassed the area in a search for clues.

**capital** the city
**capitol** the building
> Paris is the capital of France.
> The Capitol in Washington is occupied by the Congress.
*Note: Capitol* is capitalized when it refers to the building in Washington, D.C.

**carat** a unit of weight for precious stones
**caret** an editing mark (∧)
**carrot** an orange root vegetable
**karat** one-twenty-fourth part of pure gold
> A five-carat diamond is quite large.
> Use a caret to show where text should be inserted.
> Rabbits like carrots.
> This bracelet is 24-karat gold.

**cease** to end
**seize** to take hold of
> Will you please cease making those sounds?
> Seize the cat as it rounds the corner.

**censor** to examine for the purpose of judging morality
**censure** to find fault with
> In some countries, the government censors films.
> She censured her husband for coming home late.

**center around** is unacceptable. Use **center in** or **center on.**
> The maximum power was centered in the nuclear reactor.
> All attention was centered on the launching pad.

**cession** a yielding
**session** a meeting
> The cession of a piece of territory could have averted the war.
> The legislative session lasted three months.

**childish** silly; immature
**childlike** innocent; unspoiled
        Pouting appears childish in an adult.
        His childlike appreciation of art gave him great pleasure.

**cite** to quote
**sight** the ability to see; what is seen
**site** a place for a building
        He was fond of citing the Scriptures.
        The sight of the wreck was appalling.
        The Board of Education is seeking a site for the new school.

**coarse** (adjective) vulgar or harsh
**course** (noun) a path; a subject of study
        He was shunned because of his coarse behavior.
        The ship took its usual course.
        Which course in English are you taking?

**comic** intentionally funny
**comical** unintentionally funny
        A clown is a comic figure.
        The peculiar hat she wore gave her a comical appearance.

**comma** a mark of punctuation
**coma** (rhymes with *aroma*) a period of prolonged unconsciousness
        A comma can never separate two complete sentences.
        The accident put him into a coma lasting three days.

**common** shared equally by two or more
**mutual** interchanged
        The citizens had a common interest in better schools.
        We can do business to our mutual profit and satisfaction.

**compare to** to liken to something that has a different form
**compare with** to examine in order to find likenesses or differences
**contrast with** to show the difference between two things
        A minister is sometimes compared to a shepherd.
        Shakespeare's plays are often compared with those of Marlowe.
        The writer contrasted the sensitivity of the dancer with the grossness of the pugilist.

**complement** a completing part
**compliment** an expression of admiration
        His wit was a complement to her beauty.
        He received many compliments on his speech.

**comprehensible** understandable
**comprehensive** including a great deal
        Explain the law in language comprehensible to the average person.
        Toynbee's comprehensive study of history covers many centuries.

**comprise** to include
**compose** to form the substance of
>   Toynbee's study of history comprises seven volumes.
>   Some modern novels are composed of as little as two chapters.

*Note:* Do not use *be comprised of* for *comprise.*

**concur in** must be followed by a noun of action.
**concur with** must be followed by a noun designating a person.
>   I shall concur in the decision reached by the majority.
>   I cannot concur with the chairman, no matter how much I respect his opinion.

**connote** to suggest or imply
**denote** to show explicitly
>   Colloquial language connotes an informal atmosphere in conversation.
>   The color red often denotes danger or a warning of danger.

**conscience** a sense of what is right
**conscientious** faithful
**conscious** aware
>   Our conscience prevents us from becoming completely selfish.
>   We value her because she is conscientious.
>   The injured man was completely conscious.

**consistently** in harmony
**constantly** regularly; steadily
>   If you choose to give advice, act consistently with that advice.
>   Doctors constantly warn against overexertion.

**consul** a government's representative
**council** an assembly which meets for deliberation
**counsel** advice
>   Americans abroad should keep in touch with their consul.
>   The City Council enacts local laws and regulations.
>   The defendant heeded the counsel of his friends.

**contemptible** worthy of contempt
**contemptuous** feeling contempt
>   His spying activities were contemptible.
>   It was plain to all that he was contemptuous of his co-workers.

**continual** happening again and again at short intervals
**continuous** without interruption
>   The teacher gave the class continual warnings.
>   Noah saw continuous rain for forty days.

**corespondent** a joint defendant in a divorce case
**correspondent** one who communicates or writes letters
>   The corespondent declared that he loved the other man's wife.
>   Max Frankel is a special correspondent for *The New York Times.*

**corporeal** bodily, as opposed to spiritual
**corporal** bodily, as it pertains to a person

    Many believe that our corporeal existence changes to a spiritual one after death.

    Corporal punishment is not recommended in modern schools.

**corps** (pronounced like *core*) an organized military body
**corpse** a dead body

    The corps consisted of three full-size armies.

    The corpse was quietly slipped overboard after a brief service.

**credible** believable
**creditable** worthy of receiving praise
**credulous** believing too easily

    The pupil gave a credible explanation for his lateness.

    Considering all the handicaps, he gave a creditable performance.

    Politicians might prefer to address credulous people.

**decent** (adjective) proper and fitting
**descent** (noun) downward motion
**dissent** (noun) disagreement

    The fallen hero was given a decent burial.

    The descent into the cave was treacherous.

    Two of the nine justices expressed strong dissent.

**deference** respect
**difference** unlikeness

    In deference to his memory, we did not play yesterday.

    The difference between the two boys is unmistakable.

**definite** clear; with set limits
**definitive** final; decisive

    We would prefer a definite answer to our definite question.

    The dictionary is the definitive authority for word meanings.

**deprecate** to disapprove
**depreciate** to lower the value

    His classmates deprecated his lack of good manners.

    The new service station nearby depreciated the sale price of our house.

**desert** (pronounced DEZ-ert) an arid area
**desert** (pronounced di-ZERT) (1) to abandon; (2) a reward or punishment (can be used in the plural)
**dessert** (pronounced di-ZERT) the final course of a meal

    The Sahara is the world's most famous desert.

    A husband must not desert his wife.

    The heavy fine was a just desert for his infraction. She got her just deserts.

    We had peach pie for dessert.

**desirable** worth having; wanted
**desirous of** desiring or wanting
>It was a most desirable position.
>She was desirous of obtaining it.

**despise** to look down upon
**detest** to hate
>Some wealthy persons despise the poor.
>I detest cold weather.

**differ from** is used when there is a difference between things.
**differ with** is used when there is a difference in opinion.
>A coat differs from a cape.
>You have the right to differ with me on public affairs.

**different than** is unacceptable. Use **different from.**
>*Unacceptable:* Florida's climate is different than New York's.
>*Acceptable:* Jack is very different from his brother.

**discover** to find something that is already in existence
**invent** to create something that never existed before
>Pasteur discovered germs.
>Whitney invented the cotton gin.

**discreet** cautious
**discrete** separate
>The employee was discreet in her comments about her employer.
>Since these two questions are discrete, you must provide two separate answers.

**disinterested** impartial; not biased
**uninterested** not interested
>The judge must always be a disinterested party in a trial.
>As an uninterested observer, he was inclined to yawn at times.

**dual** relating to two
**duel** a contest between two persons
>Dr. Jekyll had a dual personality.
>Alexander Hamilton was fatally injured in a duel with Aaron Burr.

**e.g.** for example
**i.e.** that is (to say)
>The report gave some reasons for canceling the project, e.g., cost overruns and delays.
>The manager noted that "several staff members were negatively impacted," i.e., they were fired.

*Note:* Commas are traditionally used before and after these abbreviations, which are rendered in roman, not italic, type.

**either ... or** refers to choices.
**neither ... nor** is its negative form.
> Either you or I will win the election.
> Neither Bill nor Ellen is expected to have a chance.

**elegy** a mournful or melancholy poem
**eulogy** a speech in praise of a deceased person
> Gray's "Elegy Written in a Country Churchyard" is a melancholy poem.
> The minister delivered the eulogy.

**emigrate** to leave one's country for another
**immigrate** to enter another country
> The Norwegians emigrated to America in mid-1860.
> Many of the Norwegians who immigrated settled in the Midwest.

**enormity** viciousness or great wickedness
**enormousness** vastness
> The enormity of his crime was appalling.
> The enormousness of the Sahara exceeds that of any other desert.

**enthused** should be avoided.
**enthusiastic** is preferred.
> *Acceptable:* We were enthusiastic over the performance.
> *Unacceptable:* I am truly enthused about coming.

**equally as good** is unacceptable.
**(just) as good** is acceptable.
> *Unacceptable:* Your marks are equally as good as mine.
> *Acceptable:* This book is (just) as good as that one.

**exceed** to go beyond the limit
**excel** to exhibit superior quality
> You have exceeded the time allotted to you.
> All-around athletes are expected to excel in many sports.

**except** is acceptable.
**excepting** is unacceptable.
> *Unacceptable:* All cities, excepting Washington, are located in a state.
> *Acceptable:* All of us except Joe are going.

**exceptional** extraordinary
**exceptionable** objectionable
> Exceptional children learn to read before the age of five.
> Such awful behavior is exceptionable.

**excessively** beyond acceptable limits
**exceedingly** to a very great degree
> In view of our recent feud, he was excessively friendly.
> The weather in July was exceedingly hot.

**factitious** unnatural or artificial
**fictitious** imaginary
> His factitious enthusiasm did not deceive us.
> Jim Hawkins is a fictitious character.

**faint** to lose consciousness
**feint** to make a pretended attack
> The lack of fresh air caused her to faint.
> First he feinted to the left; then he lobbed the ball over the net.

**farther** is used to describe concrete distance.
**further** is used to describe an extension of time or degree.
> Chicago is farther from New York than Cincinnati is.
> I'll explain further my point of view.

**faze** to disturb or disconcert
**phase** a stage in a cycle
> Nothing ever fazes her.
> Last year the project entered its final phase.

**feel bad** to feel ill or sorry
**feel badly** is unacceptable.
> *Unacceptable:* I felt badly when I saw her fall.
> *Acceptable:* I feel bad about the accident I saw.

**fewer** refers to persons or things that can be counted.
**less** refers to something considered as a mass.
> We have fewer customers this week than last week.
> I have less money in my pocket than you have.
> *Exception:* (idiom) one less thing to worry about

**fiancé** a man engaged to be married
**fiancée** a woman engaged to be married
> Bill is Cynthia's fiancé; she is his fiancée.

**flout** to show contempt for
**flaunt** to make a display of
> He flouted the authority of the principal.
> She flaunted her wealth.

**flowed** past participle of *flow*
**flown** past participle of *fly*
> The flood waters had flowed over the levee before nightfall.
> He had flown for 500 hours before he crashed.

**forbear** to refrain from doing something
**forebear** ancestor
> Forbear seeking vengeance.
> Most of the family's forebears came from Ghana.

**foreword** an introductory statement to a book
**forward** at or toward the front
> My former professor asked me to write the foreword to his new book.
> To go forward, put the transmission lever into "Drive."

**formally** in a formal way
**formerly** at an earlier time
> The letter of reference was formally phrased.
> He was formerly a delegate to the convention.

**former** the first of two
**latter** the second of two
> The former half of the book was prose.
> The latter half of the book was poetry.

**fort** a fortified place
**forte** (pronounced FORT) a strong point
**forte** (pronounced FOR tay) to be played loudly
> A small band was able to hold the fort.
> Correct spelling was never my forte.
> He played the passage forte, as marked.

*Note:* There is no accent on the *e* in either of the two words *forte*.

**forth** forward
**fourth** number four in a series or succession
> They went forth like warriors of old.
> The Fourth of July is our Independence Day.

**freeze** to turn to ice
**frieze** a decorated band in or on a building
> As the temperature dropped, the water began to freeze.
> The friezes on the Parthenon are wonders of art.

**gibe** and **jibe** (pronounced alike) to scoff
**jibe** to agree
> We are inclined to gibe at awkward speakers.
> The two stories are now beginning to jibe.

**gourmand** one who eats large quantities of food
**gourmet** one who knows about fine food; a connoisseur
> My husband, the gourmand, is chomping his way through our budget.
> The gourmet chooses the right wine for each course.

**grisly** (adjective) terrifying or horrible
**grizzly** (noun) a variety of brown bear
> The corpse was grisly evidence of a fearful crime.
> Stay clear of grizzlies, and never feed them.

**habit** an individual tendency to repeat a thing
**custom** a group habit
> He had a habit of breaking his glasses before each ball game.
> The custom of the country was to eat fish raw.

**hangar** a building or structure for housing airplanes
**hanger** a person or thing that hangs; a device for hanging something up
> The pilot eased the large jet toward the hangar.
> Please put your clean shirts on hangers.

**hanged** refers to persons.
**hung** refers to things.
> The prisoner was hanged at dawn.
> The stockings were hung by the chimney with care.

**healthy** having health
**healthful** giving health
> The man is healthy.
> Fruit is healthful.

**idle** unemployed or unoccupied
**idol** an image or object of worship
> Idle men, like idle machines, are inclined to lose their sharpness.
> Some dictators prefer to be looked upon as idols by the masses.

**immunity** resistance to a disease
**impunity** freedom from punishment
> The Salk vaccine helps develop an immunity to polio.
> Because he was an only child, he frequently misbehaved with impunity.

**imply** to suggest or hint at (The speaker implies.)
**infer** to deduce or conclude (The listener infers.)
> Are you implying that I have disobeyed orders?
> From your carefree attitude, what else are we to infer?

**ingenious** skillful; imaginative
**ingenuous** naive; frank; candid
> The ingenious boy created his own rocket.
> One must be ingenuous to accept a dictator's definition of freedom.

**irregardless** is unacceptable.
**regardless** is acceptable.
> *Unacceptable:* Irregardless of the weather, I am going to the game.
> *Acceptable:* Regardless of his ability, he is not likely to win.

**irresponsible** having no sense of responsibility
**not responsible for** not accountable for something
> Irresponsible people are frequently late for appointments.
> Since you came late, we are not responsible for your having missed the first act.

**its** belonging to it
**it's** it is
> The house lost its roof in the tornado.
> Now it's just a wreck.

**judicial** pertaining to courts or to the law
**judicious** wise
> The problem required the judicial consideration of an expert.
> We were certainly in no position to make a judicious decision.

**legible** able to be read
**readable** able to be read with pleasure
> Your reports have become increasingly legible.
> I find most of his novels extremely readable.

**levy** (rhymes with *heavy)* to impose a tax
**levee** an embankment
> It is the duty of Congress to levy taxes.
> The Mississippi River is contained by massive levees.

**liable** (adjective) legally responsible; subject to; likely to
**libel** (noun) a written and published statement injurious to a person's reputation
**slander** (noun) a spoken statement of the same sort
> She is liable for the damages. His medical history shows him liable to heart attacks.
> The unfavorable references to me in your book are libels.
> When you say these vicious things about me, you are committing slander.

**lightening** present participle of *lighten*
**lightning** flashes of light often accompanied by thunder
> Lightening the pack made it easier to carry.
> Summer thunderstorms produce startling lightning bolts.

**loan** (noun) money given by lending
**lend** (verb) to give money as a loan
> The bank was willing to grant him a loan of $500.
> The bank was willing to lend him $500.

**many** refers to things that can be counted.
**much** refers to a quantities in bulk.
> How many inches of rain fell last night?
> I don't know, but I would say much rain fell last night.

**Messrs** (rhymes with *guessers)* is the plural of *Mr.*
> Messrs Smith, Jones, Brown, and Swift
*Note:* No period is used.

**metal** a substance
**mettle** spirit
> Lead is one of the more familiar metals.
> One had to admire his mettle in the face of such a crisis.

**Mmes** (pronounced may-DAHM) is the abbreviation for *Mesdames,* the plural of *Madam.*

Mmes Jones, Smith, and Wilson

*Note:* No period is used.

**moral** (adjective) good or ethical; (noun) an ethical lesson to be drawn
**morale** (pronounced more-AL) spirit

A moral person commits no crimes.

The moral of the story is that it pays to be honest.

The morale of the troops rose after the general's inspiring speech.

**nauseous** causing queasiness
**nauseated** feeling sick

That odor is nauseous.

It makes me quite nauseated.

**observance** the act of complying
**observation** the act of noting

In observance of the new regulation, we shall omit further tests.

His scientific observations became the basis for a new theory.

**occupancy** the mere act of occupying, usually legally
**occupation** the forceful act of occupying

According to the lease, the tenant still had occupancy of the apartment for another month.

The occupation of the town by troops worried the townspeople.

**ordinance** a regulation
**ordnance** guns, cannon, etc.

The local ordinance restricted driving speeds to 35 miles an hour.

Some rockets and guided missiles are now included in military ordnance.

**outdoor** (adjective)
**outdoors** (adverb)

We spent most of the summer at an outdoor music camp.

Most of the time we played string quartets outdoors.

**part from** is used with a noun indicating a person or persons.
**part with** is used with a noun indicating one or more things.

It was difficult for her to part from her classmates.

It will be difficult for him to part with his car.

**pedal** a lever operated by foot
**peddle** to sell from door to door

It is impossible to operate a bicycle without moving the pedals.

The traveling salesman peddling brushes is a thing of the past.

**persecute** to make life miserable for
**prosecute** to conduct criminal proceedings against

They were among the groups persecuted by the regime.

An assistant district attorney is prosecuting the racketeers.

**personal** of a person
**personnel** an organized body of individuals
> The general took a personal interest in every one of his men.
> He believed that this was necessary in order to maintain the morale of the personnel in his division.

**practicable** usable or workable. It applies only to objects.
**practical** realistic; having to do with action. It applies to persons and things.
> There is as yet no practicable method for resisting atomic bomb attacks.
> Practical technicians, nevertheless, are attempting to translate the theories of the atomic scientists into some form of defense.

**precede** to come before
**proceed** to go ahead
> What are the circumstances that preceded the attack?
> We can then proceed with our plan for resisting a second attack.

**prescribe** to lay down a course of action or write an order for medicine
**proscribe** to outlaw or forbid
> The doctor prescribed plenty of rest and good food for him.
> Some communities may proscribe various social activities.

**principal** (adjective) chief or main; (noun) a leader
**principle** a fundamental truth or belief
> His principal supporters came from among the peasants.
> The principal of the school asked for cooperation from the staff.
> Humility was the guiding principle of the Buddha's life.

**prodigy** a person endowed with extraordinary gifts or powers
**protégé** someone under the care or instruction of another
> Mozart was a musical prodigy at the age of three.
> For a time, Schumann was the protégé of Johannes Brahms.

**prophecy** (rhymes with *sea*) (noun) a prediction
**prophesy** (rhymes with *sigh*) (verb) to predict
> The prophecy of the three witches eventually misled Macbeth.
> The witches had prophesied that Macbeth would become king.

**rain** water from the clouds
**reign** to rule
**rein** a strap for guiding a horse
> The rain in Spain falls mainly on the plain.
> A queen now reigns over England.
> When the reins were pulled too tightly, the horse reared.

**reconcile to** to resign to or adjust to
**reconcile with** to become friendly again with someone; also, to bring one set of facts into harmony with another
> I am now reconciled to this chronic ache in my back.
> George was reconciled with his parents after many years.
> How can one reconcile the mayor's shabby accomplishments with his noble promises?

**respectably** in a manner deserving respect
**respectfully** with respect and decency
**respectively** in regard to each, in the order given
> Public officials should conduct themselves respectably at all times.
> The students listened respectfully to the principal.
> John and Bill are the sons of Mr. Smith and Mr. Brown, respectively.

**reverend** worthy of reverence or respect
**reverent** feeling or showing respect
> Shakespeare, the reverend master of the drama, still inspires most readers.
> Sometimes a too-reverent attitude toward Shakespeare causes the reader to miss much of the fun in his plays.

**sociable** friendly
**social** relating to people as a group
> Sociable individuals prefer to have plenty of people around them.
> The President's social program was a hopeful beginning.

**specie** money in the form of coins (*Specie* has no plural form.)
**species** a group of related things (*Species* is both singular and plural.)
> He preferred to be paid in specie, rather than in bank notes.
> The human species is relatively young. (singular)
> Many animal species existed before human beings appeared. (plural)

**stationary** not moving
**stationery** writing materials
> In ancient times people thought the earth was stationary.
> We bought writing paper at the stationery store.

**statue** a piece of sculpture
**statute** a law
> The Statue of Liberty stands in New York Harbor.
> Compulsory education was established by statute.

**tasteful** showing good taste
**tasty** pleasing to the physical sense of taste
> The home of our host was decorated in a tasteful manner.
> Our host served us very tasty meals.

**tenants** occupants
**tenets** principles
> Several tenants occupied that apartment during the first month.
> His religious tenets led him to perform many good deeds.

**their** belonging to them
**there** in that place
**they're** they are
> We took their books home with us.
> You will find your books over there on the desk.
> They're not as young as we expected them to be.

**tortuous** twisting
**torturous** causing pain
>The wagon train followed a tortuous trail through the mountains.
>The torturous memory of his defeat kept him awake all night.

**track** a path or road
**tract** (1) a brief but serious piece of writing; (2) a piece of land
>The horses raced around the track.
>John Locke wrote a famous tract on education.
>The heavily wooded tract was sold to a lumber company.

**trooper** (1) a cavalry soldier; (2) a mounted police officer; (3) a state police officer
**trouper** a steady, dedicated, dependable person
>Two troopers gathered evidence after the automobile accident.
>She volunteered to finish the work on a Saturday; what a trouper!

**unique** being one of a kind. This adjective cannot be modified by such adverbs
>as *very, most,* or *extremely.*
>The First Folio edition of Shakespeare's works is unique.

**valuable** of great worth
**valued** held in high regard
**invaluable** priceless
>This is a valuable manuscript.
>The expert gave him highly valued advice.
>A good name is an invaluable possession.

**virtually** in effect
**actually** in fact
>A tie in the final game was virtually a defeat for us.
>We had actually won more games than they had.

**virtue** goodness
**virtuosity** high technical skill
>We should expect a considerable degree of virtue in our public officials.
>The young pianist played with virtuosity at her debut.

**wet** moistened
**whet** to stimulate or sharpen
>Driving can be dangerous when the roads are wet.
>Reading her latest book whetted my appetite for more of her writing.

**whose** of whom
**who's** who is
>This cell phone I found — whose is it?
>Who's in the next office?

# CHECKLIST: WRITING PROBLEMS TO AVOID

As you proofread any piece of writing, look for the following common types of errors and problems, and correct any that you find.

1. Spelling errors and other typographical errors. Do NOT rely entirely on the computer's spelling checker.

2. Mechanical errors: punctuation, italics, capitalization, etc.

3. Faulty word choice.

4. Incorrect form of an irregular verb.

5. Faulty comparison of adjectives or adverbs.

6. Unintended sentence fragments:

    *Not:* The place where we met.

7. Run-on sentences and comma splices:

    *Not:* The phone rang she answered it.
    *Not:* I had always wanted to see a moose, there he was!

8. Dangling modifiers:

    *Not:* While preparing the Thanksgiving feast, the dog got into the wastebasket.

9. Faulty parallelism — see AGREEMENT, REFERENCE, AND PARALLELISM.

    *Not:* You are responsible for researching, writing, and for proofreading the paper.

10. Lack of agreement: subject and verb — see AGREEMENT, REFERENCE, AND PARALLELISM.

    *Not:* Every one of my good dinner plates are chipped.

11. Lack of agreement: pronoun and antecedent — see AGREEMENT, REFERENCE, AND PARALLELISM.

    *Not:* Each of the candidates is on their best behavior.

    *Not:* All of the candidates are on his or her best behavior.

12. Too many passive sentences, with or without a *by* phrase:

    *Not:* This editorial was written by our clearest thinker.
    *Not:* The editorial was finished and turned in on time.

13. Sentences that are too long to be followed easily.

14. Too many short sentences close together.

15. Inappropriate tone:

    a. too informal for a piece of formal writing.

    b. overly "formal" in an attempt to sound scholarly.

16. Unidentified or unacknowledged information sources.

17. Anything else that will distract the reader from what you are saying.

# WEIGHTS AND MEASURES

## Linear

| | | |
|---|---|---|
| 12 inches | = | 1 foot |
| 3 feet | = | 1 yard |
| 5.5 yards | = | 1 rod |
| 40 rods | = | 1 furlong |
| 8 furlongs | = | 1 mile |

## Liquid

| | | |
|---|---|---|
| 16 ounces | = | 1 pint |
| 2 pints | = | 1 quart |
| 4 quarts | = | 1 gallon |
| 31.5 gallons | = | 1 barrel |
| 2 barrels | = | 1 hogshead |

### Metric Equivalents

| | | |
|---|---|---|
| 1 inch | = | 2.5400 centimeters |
| 1 foot | = | 0.3048 meter |
| 1 yard | = | 0.9144 meter |
| 1 mile | = | 1.6093 kilometers |
| 1 centimeter | = | 0.3937 inch |
| 1 meter | = | 39.3701 inches |
| 1 kilometer | = | 0.6214 mile |
| 1 quart (dry) | = | 1.1012 liters |
| 1 quart (liquid) | = | 0.9464 liter |
| 1 gallon | = | 3.7854 liters |
| 1 liter | = | 0.9081 dry quart |
| 1 liter | = | 1.0567 liquid quarts |

## Square

| | | |
|---|---|---|
| 144 sq. inches | = | 1 sq. foot |
| 9 sq. feet | = | 1 sq. yard |
| 30.25 sq. yards | = | 1 sq. rod |
| 160 sq. rods | = | 1 acre |
| 640 acres | = | 1 sq. mile |

## Circular

| | | |
|---|---|---|
| 60 seconds | = | 1 minute |
| 60 minutes | = | 1 degree |
| 360 degrees | = | 1 circle |

### Metric Equivalents

| | | |
|---|---|---|
| 1 sq. inch | = | 6.4516 sq. centimeters |
| 1 sq. foot | = | 929.0304 sq. centimeters |
| 1 sq. mile | = | 2.590 sq. kilometers |
| 1 sq. centimeter | = | 0.155 sq. inch |
| 1 sq. meter | = | 1.196 sq. yards |
| 1 sq. kilometer | = | 0.3861 sq. mile |

## Cubic

| | | |
|---|---|---|
| 1,728 cu. inches | = | 1 cu. foot |
| 27 cu. feet | = | 1 cu. yard |
| 128 cu. feet | = | 1 cord (wood) |

## Dry

| | | |
|---|---|---|
| 2 pints | = | 1 quart |
| 8 quarts | = | 1 peck |
| 4 pecks | = | 1 bushel |

### Metric Equivalents

| | | |
|---|---|---|
| 1 cu. inch | = | 16.3871 cu. centimeters |
| 1 cu. inch | = | 16.3871 milliliters |
| 1 cu. foot | = | 0.0283 cu. meter |
| 1 cu. foot | = | 28.3169 liters |
| 1 cu. meter | = | 35.3147 cu. feet |
| 1 ounce (avdp.) | = | 28.3495 grams |
| 1 pound | = | 0.4536 kilogram |
| 1 gram | = | 0.0353 ounce |
| 1 kilogram | = | 2.2046 pounds |
| 1 ton (2,000 pounds) | = | 907.1847 kilograms |

### Temperature Conversion Formulas

$$°F = 32 + (1.8 \times °C)$$

$$°C = \frac{°F - 32}{1.8}$$

# THE INTERNATIONAL SYSTEM OF UNITS (SI)

Any prefix can be combined with any unit; e.g. milli- + ampere = milliampere (m + A = mA); kilo- + gram = kilogram (k + g = kg); mega- + hertz = megahertz (M + Hz = MHz).

## SI base units and prefixes

| unit | symbol | quantity | prefix | symbol | multiplier* |
|------|--------|----------|--------|--------|-------------|
| ampere | A | electric current | yotta- | Y | $\times 10^{24}$ |
| candela | cd | luminous intensity | zetta- | Z | $\times 10^{21}$ |
| kelvin | K | thermodynamic | exa- | E | $\times 10^{18}$ |
| | | temperature | peta- | P | $\times 10^{15}$ |
| kilogram | kg | mass | tera- | T | $\times 10^{12}$ |
| meter | m | length | giga- | G | $\times 10^{9}$ |
| mole | mol | amount of substance | mega- | M | $\times 10^{6}$ |
| second | s | time | kilo- | k | $\times 10^{3}$ |
| | | | hecto- | h | $\times 10^{2}$ |
| | | | deka-; deca- | da | $\times 10$ |
| | | | deci- | d | $\times 10^{-1}$ |
| | | | centi- | c | $\times 10^{-2}$ |
| | | | milli- | m | $\times 10^{-3}$ |
| | | | micro- | $\mu$ | $\times 10^{-6}$ |
| | | | nano- | n | $\times 10^{-9}$ |
| | | | pico- | p | $\times 10^{-12}$ |
| | | | femto- | f | $\times 10^{-15}$ |
| | | | atto- | a | $\times 10^{-18}$ |
| | | | zepto- | z | $\times 10^{-21}$ |
| | | | yocto- | y | $\times 10^{-24}$ |

\* $10^2 = 10 \times 10 = 100$; $10^3 = 10 \times 10 \times 10 = 1,000$; $10^{-1} = 1/10^1 = 0.1$; $10^{-2} = 1/10^2 = 0.01$
So, 2 km = $2 \times 10^3$ meters = 2,000 meters; 2 mm = $2 \times 10^{-3}$ meter = 0.002 meter.

## Common SI derived units with special names

| name | symbol | quantity |
|------|--------|----------|
| coulomb | C | electric charge |
| degree Celsius | °C | temperature (0°C = 273.16 K) |
| hertz | Hz | frequency |
| joule | J | energy; work |
| newton | N | force |
| ohm | $\Omega$ | electric resistance |
| pascal | Pa | pressure; stress |
| volt | V | electric potential; EMF |
| watt | W | power |

## Other common units used with the SI

| name | symbol | quantity |
|------|--------|----------|
| hectare | ha | area (=10,000 $m^2$ or 2.471 acres) |
| knot | kn; kt | speed (navigation) (= 1 NM per hour or 1.1508 mph) |
| liter | l; L | volume; capacity (= 1,000 $cm^3$) |
| metric ton | t | mass (= 1,000 kg) |
| nautical mile (U.S.) | NM | distance (navigation) (= 1.1508 statute miles) |
| standard atmosphere | atm | atmospheric pressure (= 101,325 Pa) |

# ALPHABETICAL LIST OF THE CHEMICAL ELEMENTS

| Element | Symbol | Atomic Number | Atomic Weight* |
|---|---|---|---|
| actinium | Ac | 89 | (227) |
| aluminum | Al | 13 | 26.981538 |
| americium | Am | 95 | (243) |
| antimony | Sb | 51 | 121.760 |
| argon | Ar | 18 | 39.948 |
| arsenic | As | 33 | 74.92160 |
| astatine | At | 85 | (210) |
| barium | Ba | 56 | 137.327 |
| berkelium | Bk | 97 | (247) |
| beryllium | Be | 4 | 9.012182 |
| bismuth | Bi | 83 | 208.98038 |
| bohrium | Bh | 107 | (262) |
| boron | B | 5 | 10.811 |
| bromine | Br | 35 | 79.904 |
| cadmium | Cd | 48 | 112.411 |
| calcium | Ca | 20 | 40.078 |
| californium | Cf | 98 | (251) |
| carbon | C | 6 | 12.0107 |
| cerium | Ce | 58 | 140.116 |
| cesium | Cs | 55 | 132.90545 |
| chlorine | Cl | 17 | 35.4527 |
| chromium | Cr | 24 | 51.9961 |
| cobalt | Co | 27 | 58.933200 |
| copper | Cu | 29 | 63.546 |
| curium | Cm | 96 | (247) |
| dubnium | Db | 105 | (262) |
| dysprosium | Dy | 66 | 162.50 |
| einsteinium | Es | 99 | (252) |
| element 110 | Uun | 110 | (269) |
| element 111 | Uuu | 111 | (272) |
| element 112 | Uub | 112 | (277) |
| erbium | Er | 68 | 167.26 |
| europium | Eu | 63 | 151.964 |
| fermium | Fm | 100 | (257) |
| fluorine | F | 9 | 18.9984032 |
| francium | Fr | 87 | (223) |
| gadolinium | Gd | 64 | 157.25 |
| gallium | Ga | 31 | 69.723 |
| germanium | Ge | 32 | 72.61 |
| gold | Au | 79 | 196.96655 |
| hafnium | Hf | 72 | 178.49 |
| hassium | Hs | 108 | (265) |
| helium | He | 2 | 4.002602 |
| holmium | Ho | 67 | 164.93032 |
| hydrogen | H | 1 | 1.00794 |
| indium | In | 49 | 114.818 |
| iodine | I | 53 | 126.90447 |
| iridium | Ir | 77 | 192.217 |
| iron | Fe | 26 | 55.845 |
| krypton | Kr | 36 | 83.80 |
| lanthanum | La | 57 | 138.9055 |
| lawrencium | Lr | 103 | (262) |
| lead | Pb | 82 | 207.2 |
| lithium | Li | 3 | 6.941 |
| lutetium | Lu | 71 | 174.967 |
| magnesium | Mg | 12 | 24.3050 |
| manganese | Mn | 25 | 54.938049 |
| meitnerium | Mt | 109 | (266) |
| mendelevium | Md | 101 | (258) |
| mercury | Hg | 80 | 200.59 |
| molybdenum | Mo | 42 | 95.94 |
| neodymium | Nd | 60 | 144.24 |
| neon | Ne | 10 | 20.1797 |

| Element | Symbol | Atomic Number | Atomic Weight* |
|---|---|---|---|
| neptunium | Np | 93 | (237) |
| nickel | Ni | 28 | 58.6934 |
| niobium | Nb | 41 | 92.90638 |
| nitrogen | N | 7 | 14.00674 |
| nobelium | No | 102 | (259) |
| osmium | Os | 76 | 190.23 |
| oxygen | O | 8 | 15.9994 |
| palladium | Pd | 46 | 106.42 |
| phosphorus | P | 15 | 30.973761 |
| platinum | Pt | 78 | 195.078 |
| plutonium | Pu | 94 | (244) |
| polonium | Po | 84 | (209) |
| potassium | K | 19 | 39.0983 |
| praseodymium | Pr | 59 | 140.90765 |
| promethium | Pm | 61 | (145) |
| protactinium | Pa | 91 | 231.03588 |
| radium | Ra | 88 | (226) |
| radon | Rn | 86 | (222) |
| rhenium | Re | 75 | 186.207 |
| rhodium | Rh | 45 | 102.90550 |
| rubidium | Rb | 37 | 85.4678 |
| ruthenium | Ru | 44 | 101.07 |
| rutherfordium | Rf | 104 | (261) |
| samarium | Sm | 62 | 150.36 |
| scandium | Sc | 21 | 44.955910 |
| seaborgium | Sg | 106 | (263) |
| selenium | Se | 34 | 78.96 |
| silicon | Si | 14 | 28.0855 |
| silver | Ag | 47 | 107.8682 |
| sodium | Na | 11 | 22.989770 |
| strontium | Sr | 38 | 87.62 |
| sulfur | S | 16 | 32.066 |
| tantalum | Ta | 73 | 180.9479 |
| technetium | Tc | 43 | (98) |
| tellurium | Te | 52 | 127.60 |
| terbium | Tb | 65 | 158.92534 |
| thallium | Tl | 81 | 204.3833 |
| thorium | Th | 90 | 232.0381 |
| thulium | Tm | 69 | 168.93421 |
| tin | Sn | 50 | 118.710 |
| titanium | Ti | 22 | 47.867 |
| tungsten | W | 74 | 183.84 |
| uranium | U | 92 | 238.0289 |
| vanadium | V | 23 | 50.9415 |
| xenon | Xe | 54 | 131.29 |
| ytterbium | Yb | 70 | 173.04 |
| yttrium | Y | 39 | 88.90585 |
| zinc | Zn | 30 | 65.39 |
| zirconium | Zr | 40 | 91.224 |

* parentheses indicate that the atomic weight is for the isotope with the longest known half-life

# THE UNITED STATES

| State | Capital | Postal Abbreviation |
|---|---|---|
| Alabama | Montgomery | AL |
| Alaska | Juneau | AK |
| Arizona | Phoenix | AZ |
| Arkansas | Little Rock | AR |
| California | Sacramento | CA |
| Colorado | Denver | CO |
| Connecticut | Hartford | CT |
| Delaware | Dover | DE |
| [District of Columbia] | — | DC |
| Florida | Tallahassee | FL |
| Georgia | Atlanta | GA |
| Hawaii | Honolulu | HI |
| Idaho | Boise | ID |
| Illinois | Springfield | IL |
| Indiana | Indianapolis | IN |
| Iowa | Des Moines | IA |
| Kansas | Topeka | KS |
| Kentucky | Frankfort | KY |
| Louisiana | Baton Rouge | LA |
| Maine | Augusta | ME |
| Maryland | Annapolis | MD |
| Massachusetts | Boston | MA |
| Michigan | Lansing | MI |
| Minnesota | St. Paul | MN |
| Mississippi | Jackson | MS |
| Missouri | Jefferson City | MO |
| Montana | Helena | MT |
| Nebraska | Lincoln | NE |
| Nevada | Carson City | NV |
| New Hampshire | Concord | NH |
| New Jersey | Trenton | NJ |
| New Mexico | Santa Fe | NM |
| New York | Albany | NY |
| North Carolina | Raleigh | NC |
| North Dakota | Bismarck | ND |
| Ohio | Columbus | OH |
| Oklahoma | Oklahoma City | OK |
| Oregon | Salem | OR |
| Pennsylvania | Harrisburg | PA |
| Rhode Island | Providence | RI |
| South Carolina | Columbia | SC |
| South Dakota | Pierre | SD |
| Tennessee | Nashville | TN |
| Texas | Austin | TX |
| Utah | Salt Lake City | UT |
| Vermont | Montpelier | VT |
| Virginia | Richmond | VA |
| Washington | Olympia | WA |
| West Virginia | Charleston | WV |
| Wisconsin | Madison | WI |
| Wyoming | Cheyenne | WY |

# PRESIDENTS OF THE UNITED STATES

| Name | Term | Political Party |
|------|------|-----------------|
| George Washington | 1789–1797 | Federalist |
| John Adams | 1797–1801 | Federalist |
| Thomas Jefferson | 1801–1809 | Democratic-Republican |
| James Madison | 1809–1817 | Democratic-Republican |
| James Monroe | 1817–1825 | Democratic-Republican |
| John Quincy Adams | 1825–1829 | Democratic-Republican |
| Andrew Jackson | 1829–1837 | Democratic |
| Martin Van Buren | 1837–1841 | Democratic |
| William Henry Harrison | 1841 | Whig |
| John Tyler | 1841–1845 | Whig |
| James K. Polk | 1845–1849 | Democratic |
| Zachary Taylor | 1849–1850 | Whig |
| Millard Fillmore | 1850–1853 | Whig |
| Franklin Pierce | 1853–1857 | Democratic |
| James Buchanan | 1857–1861 | Democratic |
| Abraham Lincoln | 1861–1865 | Republican |
| Andrew Johnson | 1865–1869 | Republican |
| Ulysses S. Grant | 1869–1877 | Republican |
| Rutherford B. Hayes | 1877–1881 | Republican |
| James A. Garfield | 1881 | Republican |
| Chester A. Arthur | 1881–1885 | Republican |
| Grover Cleveland | 1885–1889 | Democratic |
| Benjamin Harrison | 1889–1893 | Republican |
| Grover Cleveland | 1893–1897 | Democratic |
| William McKinley | 1897–1901 | Republican |
| Theodore Roosevelt | 1901–1909 | Republican |
| William Howard Taft | 1909–1913 | Republican |
| Woodrow Wilson | 1913–1921 | Democratic |
| Warren G. Harding | 1921–1923 | Republican |
| Calvin Coolidge | 1923–1929 | Republican |
| Herbert Hoover | 1929–1933 | Republican |
| Franklin D. Roosevelt | 1933–1945 | Democratic |
| Harry S Truman | 1945–1953 | Democratic |
| Dwight D. Eisenhower | 1953–1961 | Republican |
| John F. Kennedy | 1961–1963 | Democratic |
| Lyndon B. Johnson | 1963–1969 | Democratic |
| Richard M. Nixon | 1969–1974 | Republican |
| Gerald R. Ford | 1974–1977 | Republican |
| Jimmy Carter | 1977–1981 | Democratic |
| Ronald Reagan | 1981–1989 | Republican |
| George Bush | 1989–1993 | Republican |
| Bill Clinton | 1993–2001 | Democratic |
| George W. Bush | 2001– | Republican |

# CANADA

| Province or Territory | Capital | Postal Abbreviation |
|---|---|---|
| Alberta | Edmonton | AB |
| British Columbia | Victoria | BC |
| Manitoba | Winnipeg | MB |
| New Brunswick | Fredericton | NB |
| Newfoundland | St. John's | NF |
| Northwest Territories | Yellowknife | NT |
| Nova Scotia | Halifax | NS |
| Nunavut | Iqaluit | NU |
| Ontario | Toronto | ON |
| Prince Edward Island | Charlottetown | PE |
| Quebec | Quebec | QC |
| Saskatchewan | Regina | SK |
| Yukon Territory | Whitehorse | YT |

# NATIONS OF THE WORLD

| Nation | Capital | Currency |
|---|---|---|
| Afghanistan | Kabul | afghani |
| Albania | Tirana | lek |
| Algeria | Algiers | dinar |
| Andorra | Andorra la Vella | *(Fr.)* franc; *(Sp.)* peseta |
| Angola | Luanda | kwanza |
| Antigua and Barbuda | St. John's | dollar[1] |
| Argentina | Buenos Aires | peso |
| Armenia | Yerevan | dram |
| Australia | Canberra | dollar |
| Austria | Vienna | schilling[3] |
| Azerbaijan | Baku | manat |
| Bahamas | Nassau | dollar |
| Bahrain | Manama | dinar |
| Bangladesh | Dhaka | taka |
| Barbados | Bridgetown | dollar |
| Belarus | Minsk | ruble |
| Belgium | Brussels | franc[3] |
| Belize | Belmopan | dollar |
| Benin | Porto Novo | franc[2] |
| Bhutan | Thimphu | ngultrum |
| Bolivia | La Paz; Sucre | boliviano |
| Bosnia and Herzegovina | Sarajevo | dinar |
| Botswana | Gaborone | pula |
| Brazil | Brasília | real |
| Brunei | Bandar Seri Begawan | dollar |
| Bulgaria | Sofia | lev |
| Burkina Faso | Ouagadougou | franc[2] |
| Burundi | Bujumbura | franc |
| Cambodia | Phnom Penh | riel |
| Cameroon | Yaoundé | franc[2] |
| Canada | Ottawa | dollar |
| Cape Verde | Praia | escudo |
| Central African Republic | Bangui | franc[2] |
| Chad | N'Djamena | franc[2] |
| Chile | Santiago | peso |
| China | Beijing | yuan |
| Colombia | Bogotá | peso |
| Comoros | Moroni | franc |
| Congo, Democratic Republic of the | Kinshasa | franc |
| Congo, Republic of the | Brazzaville | franc[2] |
| Costa Rica | San José | colón |
| Croatia | Zagreb | kuna |

| Nation | Capital | Currency |
|---|---|---|
| Cuba | Havana | peso |
| Cyprus | Nicosia | pound |
| Czech Republic | Prague | koruna |
| Denmark | Copenhagen | krone |
| Djibouti | Djibouti | franc |
| Dominica | Roseau | dollar[1] |
| Dominican Republic | Santo Domingo | peso |
| Ecuador | Quito | *(U.S.) dollar |
| Egypt | Cairo | pound |
| El Salvador | San Salvador | *(U.S.) dollar |
| Equatorial Guinea | Malabo | franc[2] |
| Eritrea | Asmara | nakfa |
| Estonia | Tallinn | kroon |
| Ethiopia | Addis Ababa | birr |
| Fiji | Suva | dollar |
| Finland | Helsinki | markka[3] |
| France | Paris | franc[3] |
| Gabon | Libreville | franc[2] |
| Gambia | Banjul | dalasi |
| Georgia | Tbilisi | lari |
| Germany | Berlin | deutsche mark[3] |
| Ghana | Accra | cedi |
| Greece | Athens | drachma[3] |
| Grenada | St. George's | dollar[1] |
| Guatemala | Guatemala City | quetzal |
| Guinea | Conakry | franc |
| Guinea-Bissau | Bissau | franc[2] |
| Guyana | Georgetown | dollar |
| Haiti | Port-au-Prince | gourde |
| Honduras | Tegucigalpa | lempira |
| Hungary | Budapest | forint |
| Iceland | Reykjavík | króna |
| India | New Delhi | rupee |
| Indonesia | Jakarta | rupiah |
| Iran | Tehran | rial |
| Iraq | Baghdad | dinar |
| Ireland | Dublin | punt[3] |
| Israel | Jerusalem | shekel |
| Italy | Rome | lira[3] |
| Ivory Coast | Yamoussoukro | franc[2] |
| Jamaica | Kingston | dollar |
| Japan | Tokyo | yen |
| Jordan | Amman | dinar |
| Kazakhstan | Astana | tenge |
| Kenya | Nairobi | shilling |
| Kiribati | Tarawa | *(Austral.) dollar |
| Korea, North | Pyongyang | won |
| Korea, South | Seoul | won |
| Kuwait | Kuwait | dinar |
| Kyrgyzstan | Bishkek | som |
| Laos | Vientiane | kip |
| Latvia | Riga | lats |
| Lebanon | Beirut | pound |
| Lesotho | Maseru | loti |
| Liberia | Monrovia | dollar |
| Libya | Tripoli | dinar |
| Liechtenstein | Vaduz | *(Swiss) franc |
| Lithuania | Vilnius | litas |
| Luxembourg | Luxembourg | franc[3] |
| Macedonia | Skopje | denar |
| Madagascar | Antananarivo | franc |
| Malawi | Lilongwe | kwacha |
| Malaysia | Kuala Lumpur | ringgit |
| Maldives | Malé | rufiyaa |
| Mali | Bamako | franc[2] |
| Malta | Valletta | lira |
| Marshall Islands | Dalap-Uliga-Darrit | *(U.S.) dollar |

| Nation | Capital | Currency |
|---|---|---|
| Mauritania | Nouakchott | ouguiya |
| Mauritius | Port Louis | rupee |
| Mexico | Mexico City | peso |
| Micronesia | Palikir | *U.S.)* dollar |
| Moldova | Chişinau | leu |
| Monaco | Monaco | *(Fr.)* franc |
| Mongolia | Ulan Bator | tugrik |
| Morocco | Rabat | dirham |
| Mozambique | Maputo | metical |
| Myanmar | Yangon | kyat |
| Namibia | Windhoek | dollar |
| Nauru | — | *(Austral.)* dollar |
| Nepal | Katmandu | rupee |
| Netherlands | Amsterdam | guilder[3] |
| New Zealand | Wellington | dollar |
| Nicaragua | Managua | córdoba |
| Niger | Niamey | franc[2] |
| Nigeria | Abuja | naira |
| Norway | Oslo | krone |
| Oman | Muscat | rial |
| Pakistan | Islamabad | rupee |
| Palau | Koror | *(U.S.)* dollar |
| Panama | Panama City | *(U.S.)* dollar |
| Papua New Guinea | Port Moresby | kina |
| Paraguay | Asunción | guaraní |
| Peru | Lima | sol |
| Philippines | Manila | peso |
| Poland | Warsaw | złoty |
| Portugal | Lisbon | escudo[3] |
| Qatar | Doha | riyal |
| Romania | Bucharest | leu |
| Russia | Moscow | ruble |
| Rwanda | Kigali | franc |
| Samoa | Apia | tala |
| San Marino | San Marino | *(It.)* lira |
| São Tomé and Príncipe | São Tomé | dobra |
| Saudi Arabia | Riyadh | riyal |
| Senegal | Dakar | franc[2] |
| Seychelles | Victoria | rupee |
| Sierra Leone | Freetown | leone |
| Singapore | Singapore | dollar |
| Slovakia | Bratislava | koruna |
| Slovenia | Ljubljana | tolar |
| Solomon Islands | Honiara | dollar |
| Somalia | Mogadishu | shilling |
| South Africa | Pretoria | rand |
| Spain | Madrid | peseta[3] |
| Sri Lanka | Colombo | rupee |
| St. Kitts and Nevis | Basseterre | dollar[1] |
| St. Lucia | Castries | dollar[1] |
| St. Vincent and the Grenadines | Kingstown | dollar[1] |
| Sudan | Khartoum | dinar |
| Suriname | Paramaribo | guilder |
| Swaziland | Mbabane | lilangeni |
| Sweden | Stockholm | krona |
| Switzerland | Bern | franc |
| Syria | Damascus | pound |
| Taiwan | Taipei | dollar |
| Tajikistan | Dushanbe | ruble |
| Tanzania | Dodoma | shilling |
| Thailand | Bangkok | baht |
| Togo | Lomé | franc[2] |
| Tonga | Nukualofa | pa'anga |
| Trinidad and Tobago | Port-of-Spain | dollar |
| Tunisia | Tunis | dinar |
| Turkey | Ankara | lira |
| Turkmenistan | Ashgabat | manat |

| Nation | Capital | Currency |
|---|---|---|
| Tuvalu | Fongafale | *(Austral.) dollar |
| Uganda | Kampala | shilling |
| Ukraine | Kiev | hryvnia |
| United Arab Emirates | Abu Dhabi | dirham |
| United Kingdom | London | pound |
| United States | Washington, D.C. | dollar |
| Uruguay | Montevideo | peso |
| Uzbekistan | Tashkent | som |
| Vanuatu | Vila | vatu |
| Vatican City | — | *(It.) lira |
| Venezuela | Caracas | bolívar |
| Vietnam | Hanoi | dong |
| Yemen | Sana | rial |
| Yugoslavia | Belgrade | dinar |
| Zambia | Lusaka | kwacha |
| Zimbabwe | Harare | dollar |

\*    Indicates the use of the currency of another country, as specified.

[1]    Indicates the use of the currency of the Organization of Eastern Caribbean States, an organization of nine Caribbean states.

[2]    Indicates the use of the currency of the African Financial Community, an organization of fourteen African countries.

[3]    Indicates ongoing phased conversion to the euro, the basic monetary unit of the European Union.

# PLANETS OF THE SOLAR SYSTEM

| Name | Average Distance from Sun (in millions) | | Period of Revolution | Period of Rotation | Diameter | | Number of Moons |
|---|---|---|---|---|---|---|---|
| | km | mi | | | km | mi | |
| Mercury | 57.9 | 36 | 87.97 earth days | 58.65 earth days | 4,880 | 3,030 | 0 |
| Venus | 108.2 | 67.2 | 224.7 earth days | 243.01 earth days (retrograde) | 12,100 | 7,520 | 0 |
| Earth | 149.6 | 93 | 1 earth year (365.26 days) | 24 hours (mean solar day) | 12,760 | 7,930 | 1 |
| Mars | 227.9 | 141.5 | 1.88 earth years | 24.62 hours | 6,790 | 4,220 | 2 |
| Jupiter | 778.3 | 483.3 | 11.86 earth years | 9.92 hours | 142,980 | 88,850 | 28 |
| Saturn | 1,429.4 | 888.2 | 29.46 earth years | 10.66 hours | 120,540 | 74,900 | 30 |
| Uranus | 2,871 | 1,784 | 84.01 earth years | 17.24 hours (retrograde) | 51,120 | 31,770 | 21 |
| Neptune | 4,504.3 | 2,799 | 164.79 earth years | 16.11 hours | 49,530 | 30,780 | 8 |
| Pluto | 5,913.5 | 3,674.7 | 248.59 earth years | 6.39 earth days (retrograde) | 2,270 | 1,410 | 1 |

# INDEX

This index includes entries for items found in the Style Guide, the Guide to the Use of This Dictionary, and the tables at the back of this book.

Abbreviations  620–25
    days of the week  621
    geographic terms  622, 623–25
    months  620–21
    names and titles  622–23
    possessive of  582, 639
    provinces and territories of
      Canada  625
    punctuation for  620–23, 648
    states, U.S.  623–25
Abbreviations Used in This
  Dictionary  xiii
Abstract nouns  573
Active voice  568, 584, 588
Adjectives  564, 571, 594
Adverbs  564, 571, 594, 601
Agreement, Reference, and
  Parallelism  607
Alphabetization of entries  viii
Alternative Spellings and Variant
  Forms  viii
Apostrophe  581, 637–39
Articles  594
Bibliography  653–56
Boldface type  653
Brackets  639
Canada
    postal abbreviations  625, 683
    provinces, territories, and
      capitals  625, 683
Capitalization  625–29
Capitalization of a headword  ix
Capitals, small  628, 653
Case  576
    nominative  576
    objective  578
    possessive  580
Checklist of writing problems  676
Chemical Elements  679
Clauses  565, 576, 601, 602, 616
Collective nouns  573, 608
Colon  640
Combining Forms  629, 646
Comma  640–43
Comma splice  676
Common nouns  573
Comparison of adjectives and
  adverbs  595–99
Comparative degree  596
Complex sentence  566
Compound-complex sentence  567
Compound sentence  566

Compound Words  582, 629–30
    plural of  637
    spelling of  629
Concrete nouns  573
Conjunctions  565, 571, 603
    coordinating  566, 571, 603
    correlative  571, 604
    subordinating  571, 603
Connectives  571, 602
Coordinating conjunctions  566, 571, 603
Correlative conjunctions  571, 604
Count nouns  573
Cross-references  viii
Currency  683
Dangling modifiers  599
Dash  643–44
Definitions  ix
Degrees of comparison  595–97
Demonstrative pronouns  574
Dependent clause  566
Derived entries  x
Direct object  569, 570, 578, 583
Division of words  viii
Documentation  653–57
Elements, chemical  681
Ellipsis  644–45
Em dash  643
En dash  644
Entries, alphabetization of  viii
Entries, run-in derived  x
Entry word  viii
*-ess*  619
*-ette*  619
Etymology  ix
Examples, illustrative  x
Exclamation mark  645
Footnotes  653–55
Foreign Sounds  xi
Foreign Terms  viii, 631
Fragments, sentence  572
Gender-Inclusive Writing  617
Gerund  565, 580
Grammar  564
Guide to Pronunciation  xi
Guide to the Use of This Dictionary  viii
Guide Words  viii
*he,* generic use  618
Homographs  viii
Hyphen  629–30, 645–47
Imperative mood  584, 586
Inclusive writing  617
Indefinite pronouns  610

Independent clause 566
Indicative mood 584, 586
Indirect object 569, 570, 579, 583
Infinitive 565
Infinitive, split 599
Inflected Forms ix, 584, 589–94, 596
Interjections 565, 645
International System of Units 678
Interrogative pronouns 574
Intransitive verbs 569, 583
Irregular verbs 585, 589–94
Italics 630–31, 653
Linking verbs 569, 583
Main clause 566
Main Entry Word viii
*man* 618
*-man* 619
Manuscript form 653–57
Manuscript preparation 653
Mass nouns 573
Measure, units of 677
Mechanics 620
    Abbreviations 620–25
    Capitalization 625–29
    Compound words 629–30
    Italics 630–31
    Numbers 631–35
    Plurals 635–37
    Punctuation 637–51
    Spelling Rules 651–53
Metric System 677, 678
Modifiers 571, 594, 599
Mood 584, 586
    imperative 584, 586
    indicative 584, 586
    subjunctive 584, 586
Nations of the World 683
    capitals 683
    currency 683
Nominative case 576
Nouns 564, 573
    abstract 573
    collective 573
    common 573
    concrete 573
    count 573
    mass 573
    proper 573
Number 568, 583, 612
Numbers 631–35
    British forms 634
    expressed in figures 631–34
    large 633–34
    Roman numerals 634–35
    spelled out 631–34
Numerals, Roman 634–35
Object 569, 570, 578, 579, 583
    direct 569, 570, 578, 583
    indirect 569, 570, 579, 583
    of preposition 579

Objective case 578
Objective complement 569, 570
*of* phrase 581
Parallelism 607, 616
Parentheses 647–48
Participles 569
    past 569, 589–94
    present 569, 580, 589–94
Parts of Speech viii, 564
Passive voice 568, 584, 588, 600, 676
Past participle 569
Past tense 568, 584, 585
Period 648–49
Person 563, 588, 612
Personal pronouns 574
Phrases 565, 616
Planets of the Solar System 686
Plural forms ix
Plurals 583, 635–37
Positive degree 596
Possessive case 580
Possessive pronominal adjectives
    574, 581
Postal abbreviations
    Canada 625, 683
    United States 623, 681
Predicate 567
Predicate adjective 570, 583
Predicate nominative 569, 570, 577, 583
Prefixes 629, 646
Prefixes, Suffixes, & Combining
    Forms viii
Preposition, object of 579
Prepositions 565, 571, 572, 601, 602
Present participle 569, 580
Presidents of the United States 682
Principal Parts of Irregular and
    Troublesome Verbs 589–94
Pronoun reference 607, 615
Pronouns 564, 574, 581
    demonstrative 574
    indefinite 574, 610
    intensifiers 575
    interrogative 574
    personal 574
    possessive pronominal adjectives
      574, 581
    reciprocal 575
    reflexive 575, 611
    relative 572, 574, 601
Pronunciation xi
    of foreign terms xi
    truncation xi
    variants xi
Pronunciation Key xi
Proper nouns 573, 581, 628–29
Provinces and territories, Canadian 683
    abbreviations for 625, 683

Punctuation 637–51
Question mark 649
Quotation marks 649
   double 649
   single 650
Reciprocal pronouns 575
Reflexive pronouns 575, 611
Relative clauses 576, 602
Relative pronouns 572, 601, 611
Roman numerals 634–35
Run-in Derived Forms x
Run-on sentence 676
Semicolon 650–51
Senses ix
   numbering and grouping of ix
   order of ix
Sentence, parts of 567
   connectives 571
   modifiers 571
   predicate 568
   subject 567, 601, 607, 611, 612
   verb 568
   verbals 568, 599
Sentence Fragments 572, 676
Sentences, types of 566, 567
Simple sentence 566
Slash 651
Small capitals 628, 653
Solar System 686
Solidus 651
Source Documentation 653–57
Spelling checker 676
Spelling rules 651–53
Spellings, Variant viii
Split infinitive 599
Squinting construction 602
States, U.S. 623
   abbreviations for 623
   capitals 623
   postal abbreviations 623
Stress Marks xii
Subject 567, 601, 607, 611, 612, 613, 614, 615

Subjunctive mood 584, 586
Subordinate clause 566
Subordinating conjunctions 571, 603
Suffixes 629, 646
Superlative degree 596
Superscripts viii
Syllabification viii
Symbols Used in This Dictionary xiv
Tense 568, 584
   future 568, 584
   past 568, 584, 585
   present 568, 584
   progressive forms 584
Transitive verbs 569, 583
*unique* 597
United States
   postal abbreviations 623, 681
   presidents 682
   states and capitals 623, 681
Usage 657–75
Usage Labels x
Variant pronunciations xi
Variant spellings and forms viii
Verbals 568, 569, 599
Verbs 564, 568, 583, 601
   intransitive 569, 583
   irregular 585, 589–94
   linking 569, 583
   principal parts of 584–85, 589–94
   properties of 568
   in sentences 601
   transitive 569, 583
Verbs and objects x
Verbs and prepositions x
Verbs, properties of 568
   mood 568, 584, 586
   number 568, 583, 612
   person 568, 583, 612
   tense 568, 584
   voice 568, 584, 588, 600
Virgule 651
Voice 584, 588, 600
Weights and Measures 677